The American Historical Association's

GUIDE TO
HISTORICAL LITERATURE

The American Historical Association's

GUIDE TO HISTORICAL LITERATURE

BOARD OF EDITORS

George Frederick Howe, Chairman

Gray Cowan Boyce, Thomas Robert Shannon Broughton
Howard Francis Cline, Sidney Bradshaw Fay
Michael Kraus, Earl Hampton Pritchard
Boyd Carlisle Shafer, ex officio

Assisted by Section Editors,
A Central Editor
and Others

New York   THE MACMILLAN COMPANY

© The Macmillan Company 1961

Successor to *A Guide to Historical Literature,* Copyright 1931 by The Macmillan Company.

All rights reserved. No part of this book may be reproduced or transmitted in any form or by any means, electronic or mechanical, including photocopying, recording or by any information storage and retrieval system, without permission in writing from the Publisher.

Seventh Printing 1967

The Macmillan Company, New York
Collier-Macmillan Canada Ltd., Toronto, Ontario

Printed in the United States of America

Library of Congress catalog card number: 61-7602

Introduction

The American Historical Association's Guide to Historical Literature has been produced under a strong conviction that History has much to contribute to a living generation. The book should be a valuable aid to students, teachers, librarians and others who seek the most satisfactory works for historical studies. The Guide is in a sense a bibliographic panorama as well as an inventory of the best historical literature extant at the time of compilation. Its purpose is to furnish directions to the best means of gaining a broader knowledge of History. Although it is not designed for the specialist, it may serve to help him establish a good foundation for his later, more concentrated, research. It is an instrument of education and general reference.

This Guide is primarily intended to serve those students or teachers who know English, the language of the annotations. The Board of Editors, however, recognizing that the best historical writings have been published in many languages, concluded that it would be unwise to ignore the best simply because, in any instance, it had been published in a language not now conventionally taught in the schools or colleges of the United States. Indeed, we have implicitly acknowledged the obligation of historians to learn to use the languages pertinent to particular fields of history. The works presented here show exactly why they should do so.

Certain sections relate to topics; the remaining sections apply to geographical areas and their peoples. That arrangement invites overlapping, which has been minimized but purposely not eliminated altogether. For geographical areas, general sections list works relating to regions or to more than one nation. National histories, which have been grouped for convenience, are treated in subsequent sections.

Items published in 1957–1960, as the editing proceeded, are not systematically covered but the late completion of some sections and the opportunity to insert additions in a few sections which were submitted on schedule have permitted considerable attention to works published in those years.

The standard pattern of organization within the sections has been closely approximated rather than rigidly imposed. It is as follows:

Bibliographies, libraries and special museum collections
Encyclopedias and works of reference
Geographies, gazetteers and atlases
Anthropologic, demographic and linguistic works
Printed collections of sources

Shorter and longer general histories
Histories of periods, areas and topics
Biographies
Government publications
Publications of academies, universities and learned societies
Periodicals

The entries in each section and large subsection are numbered in sequence, each figure being preceded by the letters of the section or subsection. The same symbols are used in the index and the cross-references.

The present *Guide* resembles an earlier *Guide to Historical Literature* which was published in 1931, but it is larger and differs in more significant ways. The organization and principles of inclusion and exclusion reflect a different world outlook. Students of the histories of African, American, Asian, Australasian and Oceanic peoples will find more assistance here. That result has been accomplished by curtailing the relative space allocated to the literature of European History. The reduction is much less, however, than it might have been if the proportion of excellent historical literature relating to European peoples were not so preponderant. The scale to which the European sections and subsections have been held has required good judgment and resourcefulness by the compilers. Each undertook to cover the principal aspects of his field of history to the extent that reliable literature permitted. In achieving full range they often had to sacrifice depth.

The American Historical Association, which has sponsored the production of this volume, promotes scholarship in America in many aspects of History. It aids individuals and groups to accomplish historical projects, as in this instance, without censoring the product. It does not attempt to establish historical orthodoxy. It relies on the thorough and impartial scholarship of its members.

The present *Guide,* like its predecessor of 1931, was planned by a committee of the American Historical Association and then completed by them, acting as the Board of Editors. Professor Sidney Bradshaw Fay of Harvard University served on both groups. Having agreed upon the way the contents of the book should be organized and on the space to be allocated to the parts, the committee invited the Section Editors to accept responsibility for their portions of the whole and to obtain assistance as they needed from fellow scholars.

Compilation of the sections has been the work of many specialists, most of whom are members of the American Historical Association, who have generously donated their efforts to the cause of historical scholarship without personal remuneration. Their contributions were verified and standardized in the copy for the printer by a single Central Editor, employed by the Board of Editors, and by his assistants. His zealous efforts to obtain the material from Section Editors on schedule, to insure detailed accuracy and consistency in style and pattern, in conformity with the decisions of the Board of Editors, and to complete a prolonged and complex operation in an efficient manner were a large and important contribution which he maintained until the manuscript had been delivered to the printers. He then left the project, which was completed by the chairman and Nathan A. Haverstock, Editorial Assistant.

The very substantial costs of preparing the manuscript for the printer were met by a generous grant to the American Historical Association from the Rockefeller Foundation. The Librarian of Congress and many members of his staff were hospitable and invariably helpful to the project. Advice and assistance were received from Professor René Wellek of Yale University, representing the Modern Language Association of America, and Mr. William S. Dix, acting in behalf of the American Library Association. A list of contributing scholars is printed after the Table of Contents.

The Board of Editors wishes to acknowledge here its particular indebtedness to Geoffrey Bruun, John W. Fairbank, Leo Gershoy and Arthur W. Hummel for critical counsel, to N. J. Anthony for preparing the index so dependably, to the Central Editor and his assistants—Gay Haran, Virginia Rapport, Carol Shafer, Richard Stites and Marvelle Toney—for detailed verification, to Nora Friedman and to Gay and Herbert Hammerman for their painstaking work as proofreaders, and to Ada Shearon of The Macmillan Company, for discerning and cooperative action in our common effort to meet exacting standards.

In the first section of this *Guide*, History's potentialities and requirements are the major topic of a brief essay and of the listed publications. History's indebtedness to other studies for important assistance in discovering, analyzing and interpreting historical evidence is there acknowledged. History has reciprocated in its own way. It has recorded the social context of many matters with which studies other than History are concerned. Persons who now wish to benefit from that manner of repayment by History will find that this *Guide* shows them the way and that the benefits are substantial.

George F. Howe, Chairman
Gray C. Boyce
T. Robert S. Broughton
Howard F. Cline
Sidney B. Fay
Michael Kraus
Earl H. Pritchard
Boyd C. Shafer, *ex officio*

Table of Contents

PART II.   HISTORICAL BEGINNINGS

PART III. THE MIDDLE PERIOD IN EURASIA AND NORTHERN AFRICA

SECTION P   JAPAN *Page 296*

Hugh Borton and John Whitney Hall

SECTION Q   SOUTHEAST ASIA *Page 319*

John M. Echols

PART V. MODERN EUROPE

SECTION X   RUSSIA AND THE SOVIET UNION (INCLUDING THE RUSSIAN EMPIRE IN ASIA) *Page 621*

PART VI. THE AMERICAS

PART VII.   AFRICA

PART VIII. AUSTRALASIA AND OCEANIA

SECTION AD   AUSTRALIA AND NEW ZEALAND (WITH ANTARCTICA)

Andrew Delbridge Osborn

SECTION AE   OCEANIA

Harold Whitman Bradley

PART IX. THE WORLD IN RECENT TIMES

SECTION AF   RECENT HISTORY

Walter C. Langsam and Reginald C. McGrane

SECTION AG THE WORLD WARS   *Page 805*

Basil H. Liddell Hart and Hugh M. Cole

SECTION AH INTERNATIONAL RELATIONS: POLITICAL

Page 816

Henry L. Roberts and Janis A. Kreslins

SECTION AI INTERNATIONAL RELATIONS: NON-POLITICAL

Page 843

Henry L. Roberts and Janis A. Kreslins

List of Contributors

René Albrecht-Carrié, Professor of History, Barnard College, Columbia University, New York.

Paul J. Alexander, Professor of History, University of Michigan, Ann Arbor.

Edgar Anderson, Professor of History, San Jose State College, California.

George G. Arnakis, Professor of History, Texas Christian University, Fort Worth.

Frederick B. Artz, Professor of History, Oberlin College, Ohio.

Thomas A. Bailey, Professor of History, Stanford University, California.

Elemer Bakô, Hungarian Reference Librarian, Slavic and Central European Division, Library of Congress, Washington, D.C.

Edwin Swift Balch,[*] Philadelphia, Pennsylvania.

Paul Walden Bamford, Associate Professor of History, University of Minnesota, Minneapolis.

George Bárány, Assistant Professor of History, University of Denver, Colorado.

Arthur H. Basye,[*] Dartmouth College, Hanover, New Hampshire.

Robert D. Baum, Lecturer in African Affairs, The School of Advanced International Studies, The Johns Hopkins University, Washington, D.C.

Paul H. Beik, Professor of History, Swarthmore College, Pennsylvania.

Bernard Bellush, Assistant Professor of History, The City College, New York.

Harry J. Benda, Assistant Professor of History, University of Rochester, New York.

Charles Julian Bishko, Professor of History, University of Virginia, Charlottesville.

Cyril E. Black, Professor of History, Princeton University, New Jersey.

Arthur E. R. Boak,[*] University of Michigan, Ann Arbor.

Stig Boberg, Stadsbiblioteket, Gothenberg, Sweden.

G. V. Bobrinskoy, Professor of Sanskrit, University of Chicago, Illinois.

Wilfred D. Borrie, Australian National University, Canberra, Australia.

Hugh Borton, President, Haverford College, Pennsylvania.

Gray C. Boyce, Professor of History, Northwestern University, Evanston, Illinois.

[*] Contributors to the original *Guide* whose estimates have been re-used.

Catherine E. Boyd, Professor of History, Carleton College, Northfield, Minnesota.

Richard M. Brace, Professor of History, Northwestern University, Evanston, Illinois.

Charles S. Braden, Professor-emeritus of the History and Philosophy of Religions, Northwestern University, Evanston, Illinois.

Harold Whitman Bradley, Professor of History, Vanderbilt University, Nashville, Tennessee.

David J. Brandenberg, Associate Professor of History, American University, Washington, D.C.

Charles Breunig, Assistant Professor of History, Lawrence College, Appleton, Wisconsin.

John Otis Brew, Director, Peabody Museum of Archaeology and Ethnology, Harvard University, Cambridge, Massachusetts.

Crane Brinton, Professor of History, Harvard University, Cambridge, Massachusetts.

John F. Brohm, Assistant Professor of Anthropology, Harpur College, Binghamton, New York.

T. Robert S. Broughton, Professor of History, Bryn Mawr College, Pennsylvania.

Louise F. Brown,* Vassar College, Poughkeepsie, New York.

Geoffrey Bruun, Ithaca, New York.

Sidney A. Burrell, Associate Professor of History, Barnard College, Columbia University, New York.

Alfred Leroy Burt, Professor-emeritus of History, University of Minnesota, Minneapolis.

David Lyman Buttolph, Instructor, Manhattan School of Music, New York.

John Frank Cady, Professor of History, Ohio University, Athens.

Rondo Emmett Cameron, Associate Professor of History, University of Wisconsin, Madison.

Schuyler Van Rensselaer Cammann, Professor of History, Chinese Studies, University of Pennsylvania, Philadelphia.

John C. Campbell, Director, Political Studies, The Council on Foreign Relations, New York.

Vincent Phillip Carosso, Associate Professor of History, New York University, New York.

Lynn Marshall Case, Professor of History, The College, University of Pennsylvania, Philadelphia.

Richard D. Challener, Associate Professor of History, Princeton University, New Jersey.

Wing-Tsit Chan, Professor of Chinese Philosophy and Culture, Dartmouth College, Hanover, New Hampshire.

James Franklin Clarke, Associate Professor of Eastern European History, University of Pittsburgh, Pennsylvania.

Howard F. Cline, Director, Hispanic Foundation, Library of Congress, Washington, D.C.

Shepard Bancroft Clough, Professor of History, Columbia University, New York.

Hugh Marshall Cole, Senior Analyst, Operations Research Office, The Johns Hopkins University, Washington, D.C.

Rosalie L. Colie, Assistant Professor of History, Barnard College, Columbia University, New York.

Helen F. Conover, Bibliographer, Africana Section, General Reference and Bibliography Division, Library of Congress, Washington, D.C.

Judith S. Cousins, The National Gallery of Art, Washington, D.C.

David Cowan, Lecturer in Arabic, School of Oriental and African Studies, University of London, England.

Robert I. Crane, Associate Professor of History, University of Michigan, Ann Arbor.

Wesley Frank Craven, Edwards Professor of American History, Princeton University, New Jersey.

Merle Eugene Curti, Turner Professor of American History, University of Wisconsin, Madison.

William Stearns Davis,* University of Minnesota, Minneapolis.

Roderic Hollet Davison, Professor of History, George Washington University, Washington, D.C.

Clarence Ernest Dawn, Associate Professor of History, University of Illinois, Urbana.

Albert Lowther Demaree, Professor of History, Dartmouth College, Hanover, New Hampshire.

William Diebold, Jr., Director of Economic Studies, Council on Foreign Relations, New York.

Sidney Ditzion, Assistant Professor of History, The City College, New York.

William Shepherd Dix, Librarian, Princeton University, New Jersey.

Walter Louis Dorn, Professor of History, Columbia University, New York.

David Lloyd Dowd, Associate Professor of History, University of Florida, Gainesville.

Glanville Downey, Professor of Byzantine Literature, Dumbarton Oaks Research Library, Washington, D.C.

Mark J. Dresden, Associate Professor of Iranian Studies, University of Pennsylvania, Philadelphia.

Arthur L. Dunham, Ivy, Virginia; Professor of History, Emeritus, University of Michigan.

George M. Dutcher,* Wesleyan University, Middletown, Connecticut.

William E. Echard, Instructor, Department of History, Miami University, Oxford, Ohio.

John Minor Echols, Director, Department of Far Eastern Studies, Cornell University, Ithaca, New York.

Albert Elsen, Associate Professor of Fine Arts, Indiana University, Bloomington.

Poul Enemark, Stadsbiblioteket, Arhus, Denmark.

Fritz Theodor Epstein, Slavic Division, Library of Congress, Washington, D.C.

John Edwin Fagg, Associate Professor of History, New York University, New York.

Bernard B. Fall, Associate Professor of History, Howard University, Washington, D.C.

Henry G. Fischer, Assistant Curator, Department of Egyptian Art, Metropolitan Museum of Art, New York.

Edward W. Fox, Associate Professor of Modern European History, Cornell University, Ithaca, New York.

Tenney Frank,* The Johns Hopkins University, Baltimore, Maryland.

John Hope Franklin, Professor of History, Brooklyn College, New York.

J. William Frederickson, Professor of Economics, North Park College and Theological Seminary, Chicago, Illinois.

Carl Joachim Friedrich, Harvard University, Cambridge, Massachusetts.

Holden Furber, Professor of History, University of Pennsylvania, Philadelphia.

John G. Gagliardo, Instructor in History, Amherst College, Massachusetts.

Charles Sidney Gardner, Cambridge, Massachusetts.

Zygmunt J. Gasiorowski, Research Fellow, Russian Research Institute, Harvard University, Cambridge, Massachusetts.

Peter J. Gay, Assistant Professor of History, Columbia University, New York.

Betty George, Specialist in African Affairs, Washington, D.C.

Uldis Germanis, Högre Allmänna Läroverk, Solna, Sweden.

Leo Gershoy, Professor of History, New York University, New York.

J. Frank Gilliam, Associate Professor of History and Classics, State University of Iowa, Iowa City.

Myron Piper Gilmore, Professor of History, Harvard University, Cambridge, Massachusetts.

Frank H. Golay, Professor of History, Cornell University, Ithaca, New York.

Leland N. Goodrich, Professor of International Organization and Administration, The School of International Affairs, Columbia University, New York.

William D. Gray,* Smith College, Northampton, Massachusetts.

Wood Gray, Professor of History, George Washington University, Washington, D.C.

Adolphus W. Greely,* Chief Signal Officer, U.S. Army, 1887–1906.

Hans Gustav Güterbock, The Oriental Institute, University of Chicago, Illinois.

Oscar Halecki, Professor of Eastern European History, Fordham University, New York.

John Whitney Hall, Director, Center for Japanese Studies, University of Michigan, Ann Arbor.

Clarence Herbert Hamilton, Professor of the History and Philosophy of Religion, Graduate School of Theology, Oberlin, Ohio.

Peter Hardy, Lecturer in the History of Muslim India, School of Oriental and African Studies, University of London, England.

Clarence Henry Haring, Professor-emeritus of History, Harvard University, Cambridge, Massachusetts.

Virginia D. Harrington, Associate Professor of History, Barnard College, Columbia University, New York.

Richard Herr, Associate Professor of History, University of California, Berkeley.

Frederick G. Heymann, Professor of History, University of Alberta, Calgary.

Martin J. Higgins, Rt. Rev., Professor of History, Catholic University, Washington, D.C.

Frank H. Hodder,* late Professor of American History, University of Kansas, Lawrence.

William Richey Hogg, Assistant Professor of World Christianity, Perkins School of Theology, Southern Methodist University, Dallas, Texas.

Hajo Holborn, Townsend Professor of History, Yale University, New Haven, Connecticut.

Daniel C. Holtom, Baptist Foreign Missionary Society, Yokohama, Japan (until 1941), and now, San Gabriel, California.

Michael E. Howard, King's College, University of London, England.

George Frederick Howe, Department of Defense, Washington, D.C.

Arthur W. Hummel, formerly Chief, Division of Orientalia, Library of Congress, Washington, D.C.

Erling M. Hunt, Professor of History, Teachers College, Columbia University, New York.

Jacob Coleman Hurewitz, Professor of Government, Middle and Near East Institute, Columbia University, New York.

Fred Israel, Instructor in History, The City College, New York.

Gabriel Jackson, Assistant Professor of History, Wellesley College, Massachusetts.

Arthur Jeffery, Professor of Semitic Languages, Columbia University, New York.

Charles Jelavich, Associate Professor of History, University of California, Berkeley.

John M. B. Jones, Lecturer in Arabic, School of Oriental and African Studies, University of London, England.

Alphonse G. Juilland, Associate Professor of Romance Languages, University of Pennsylvania, Philadelphia.

Zuhair Jwaideh, Chief, Near Eastern and North African Law Division, Law Library, Library of Congress, Washington, D.C.

George McT. Kahin, Professor of History, Cornell University, Ithaca, New York.

Firuz Kazemzadeh, Assistant Professor of History, Yale University, New Haven, Connecticut.

George O. Kent, Department of State, Washington, D.C.

Clinton W. Keyes,* Columbia University, New York.

Mathias Charles Kiemen, O.F.M., Academy of American Franciscan History, Bethesda, Maryland.

Lennart Kjellberg, Universitets Bibliotek, Uppsala, Sweden.

Frank Joseph Klingberg,* Emeritus Professor of History, University of California, Los Angeles.

Halvdan Koht, Oslo, Norway.

Arvi Korhonen, Helsinki, Finland.

Edward A. Kracke, Jr., Associate Professor of Middle Chinese Literature and Institutions, University of Chicago, Illinois.

Michael Kraus, Professor of History, The City College, New York.

Janis A. Kreslins, The Library, Council on Foreign Relations, New York.

Leonard Krieger, Associate Professor of History, Yale University, New Haven, Connecticut.

Ann K. S. Lambton, Professor of Persian, University of London, England.

David S. Landes, Professor of History, University of California, Berkeley.

Walter Consuelo Langsam, President, University of Cincinnati, Ohio.

Bernard Lewis, Professor of History, School of Oriental and African Studies, University of London, England.

Naphtali Lewis, Professor of Classics, Brooklyn College, New York.

William H. Lewis, Specialist on African Affairs, Washington, D.C.

Basil H. Liddell Hart, Military Historian and Consultant to the British War Office, London, England.

Folke Lindberg, Stockholm, Sweden.

Oliver James Lissitzyn, Associate Professor of Public Law, Columbia University, New York.

Clinton Herbert Loehlin, Professor, Mission Compound, Ferozepore, Punjab, India.

Bert James Loewenberg, Professor of American History, Sarah Lawrence College, Bronxville, New York.

Rayford Whittingham Logan, Professor of History, Howard University, Washington, D.C.

Val R. Lorwin, Professor of History, University of Oregon, Eugene.

Leo Albert Loubere, Assistant Professor of History, University of Buffalo, New York.

David Magie,* Princeton University, New Jersey.

Jacob Rader Marcus, Ochs Professor of Jewish History, Hebrew Union College, Cincinnati, Ohio.

Bradford G. Martin, Department of Persian Studies, University of Manchester, England.

Joseph James Mathews, Professor of History, Emory University, Atlanta, Georgia.

Garrett Mattingly, Professor of European History, Columbia University, New York.

Lyle N. McAlister, Professor of History, University of Florida, Gainesville.

Evelyn B. McCune, Diablo Valley College, Concord, California.

Reginald Charles McGrane, Professor-emeritus of History, University of Cincinnati, Ohio.

Donald Vernon McKay, Professor of African Studies, School of Advanced International Studies, The Johns Hopkins University, Washington, D.C.

Gaudens Megaro, late Professor of History, Queens College, New York.

Roger Bigelow Merriman,* Harvard University, Cambridge, Massachusetts.

Agnes Kirsopp Lake Michels, Professor of Latin, Bryn Mawr College, Pennsylvania.

Philip Ira Mitterling, Associate Professor of History and Academic Dean, Thiel College, Greenville, Pennsylvania.

Theodor E. Mommsen, Professor of History, Cornell University, Ithaca, New York.

James Neilson, Professor of History, State Teachers College, Mayville, North Dakota.

John Noon, Lecturer on African Affairs, School of Advanced International Studies, The Johns Hopkins University, Washington, D.C.

Charles Edward Nowell, Professor of American History, University of Illinois, Urbana.

Wilhelm Odelberg, Kunglig Biblioteket, Stockholm, Sweden.

Otakar Odložilík, Professor of History, University of Pennsylvania, Philadelphia.

Robert F. Ogden, Chief, Near Eastern Section, Division of Orientalia, Library of Congress, Washington, D.C.

William A. Oldfather,* University of Illinois, Urbana.

Nils William Olsson, Department of State, Washington, D.C.

Andrew Delbridge Osborn, Librarian, University of Sydney, Australia.

Jess Norman Parmer, Assistant Professor of History, University of Maryland, College Park.

Vernon J. Parry, Lecturer in Arabic, School of Oriental and African Studies, University of London, England.

David Henry Pinkney, Jr., Professor of History, University of Missouri, Columbia.

Frank W. Pitman,* Pomona College, California.

Horace Irvin Poleman, Chief, Division of Orientalia, Library of Congress, Washington, D.C.

Sidney Irving Pomerantz, Professor of History, The City College, New York.

Earl Hampton Pritchard, Associate Professor of History, University of Chicago, Illinois.

James Bennett Pritchard, Professor of Old Testament Literature, Church Divinity School of the Pacific, Berkeley, California.

Olaf Prufer, Curator of Anthropology, Cleveland Museum of Natural History, Ohio.

Howard A. Reed, American Friends Service Committee, Philadelphia, Pennsylvania.

Bodo L. O. Richter, Associate Professor of Romance Languages, University of Pennsylvania, Philadelphia.

Robert Edgar Riegel, Professor of History, Dartmouth College, Hanover, New Hampshire.

Helen Anne Rivlin, Assistant Professor of Middle Eastern and European History, University of Maryland, College Park.

Henry Lithgow Roberts, Professor of History and Director of The Russian Institute, Columbia University, New York.

Carl Angus Roebuck, Associate Professor of Classical Languages, Northwestern University, Evanston, Illinois.

Francis Millet Rogers, Professor of Romance Languages and Literatures, Harvard University, Cambridge, Massachusetts.

Robert Samuel Rogers, Professor of Latin and Roman Studies, Duke University, Durham, North Carolina.

Gunther E. Rothenberg, Assistant Professor of History, Illinois State Normal University, Normal.

Inez Scott Ryberg, Professor of Latin, Vassar College, Poughkeepsie, New York.

Arshag Ohannes Sarkissian, Analyst, Middle Eastern and European Affairs, Library of Congress, Washington, D.C.

Dean M. Schmitter, Assistant Professor of English, Columbia University, New York.

Herbert Franz Schurmann, Lecturer in Sociology and Near Eastern Languages, University of California, Berkeley.

Franklin Daniel Scott, Professor of History, Northwestern University, Evanston, Illinois.

Jens Arup Seip, Oslo, Norway.

Kenneth Meyer Setton, Lea Professor of Medieval History, University of Pennsylvania, Philadelphia.

Ihor Ševčenko, Assistant Professor of Slavic Languages and Literatures, Columbia University, New York.

Lauriston Sharp, Professor of History, Cornell University, Ithaca, New York.

Mary Lucille Shay, Assistant Professor of History, University of Illinois, Urbana

Augustus H. Shearer, * Librarian, Grosvenor Library, Buffalo, New York.

Josef Silverstein, Assistant Professor of History, Wesleyan University, Middletown, Connecticut.

Stavro Skendi, Assistant Professor of Albanian and Balkan Slavic, Columbia University, New York.

Leslie Francis Smith, Associate Professor of History, University of Oklahoma, Norman.

Jean Stengers, Professor of History, University of Brussels, Belgium.

Ferris J. Stephens, Associate Professor of Assyriology, Yale University, New Haven, Connecticut.

John Hall Stewart, Bourne Professor of History, Western Reserve University, Cleveland, Ohio.

Lily Ross Taylor, Emeritus Professor of Latin, Bryn Mawr College, Pennsylvania.

Samuel Harrison Thomson, Professor of History, University of Colorado, Boulder.

Mary E. Townsend, * Teachers College, Columbia University, New York.

T. H. Tsien, Far Eastern Library, University of Chicago, Illinois.

Harriet E. Tuell, * Somerville, Massachusetts.

Ralph Edmund Turner, Durfee Professor of History, Yale University, New Haven, Connecticut.

Glyndon Garlock Van Deusen, Professor of History, University of Rochester, New York.

Rudolf A. J. Van Lier, Landbouwhogeschool, Wageningen, The Netherlands.

Robert Van Niel, Assistant Professor of History, Russell Sage College, Troy, New York.

Milos M. Velimirovic, Instructor, History of Music, Yale University, New Haven, Connecticut.

Walter Francis Vella, Cleveland Public Library, Ohio.

Cornelius Clarkson Vermeule, III, Boston Museum of Fine Arts, Massachusetts.

Francis Wagner, East European Accession-Index Project, Library of Congress, Washington, D.C. ·

John M. Ward, University of Sydney, Australia.

Robert Kiefer Webb, Assistant Professor of History, Columbia University, New York.

Bernerd C. Weber, Associate Professor of History, University of Alabama, University.

René Wellek, Sterling Professor of Comparative Literature, Yale University, New Haven, Connecticut.

Allen B. West, * late Professor of Ancient History, University of Cincinnati, Ohio.

Constance M. Winchell, The Libraries, Columbia University, New York.

Frederick Victor Winnett, Professor of Oriental Languages, University of Toronto, Ontario.

Joseph Ezra Wisan, Professor of History, The City College, New York.

William Wiseley, formerly Department of Defense, Washington, D.C.

John Baptist Wolf, Professor of History, University of Minnesota, Minneapolis.

Gordon Wright, Professor of History, Stanford University, California.

Norman P. Zacour, Associate Professor of History, Franklin and Marshall College, Lancaster, Pennsylvania.

I. INTRODUCTION AND GENERAL HISTORY

SECTION A

History and Related Studies

*BERT JAMES LOEWENBERG * and ERLING M. HUNT*

Events of the last quarter century have altered the face of the world. While these have transformed the contours of life, they have likewise deflected the direction of thought. The course of history has begun to change the course of historical thinking. History as experience and history as theory are in flux. A global depression, a second global war, and an era of global belligerence have tinged the facts of life with new connotations and weighted the concept of experience with more complicated meanings.

Two pervasive characteristics account for the shift in historical attitudes. One is growth, the other is complexity. The map of historical objective is being redrawn to meet alterations in the scale of experience, the depth of insight, and the projection of knowledge. Experience, insight, and knowledge have propelled historians toward different judgments, fresh understandings, and novel methods.

The expansion of time, space, and learning has expanded the historian's outlook. Time has extended the span of history by its own inexorable movement, but the character of change has accelerated the impact of time on the human mind. Contemporary experience is more readily apprehended in measures of portent than in units of chronology.

Nowhere has time moved more swiftly than in the conquest of space. A revolution took place when geographical relations began to be expressed in air hours instead of terrestrial miles. Distant places have ceased to exist, and it is proximity rather than remoteness that speaks to the imagination. A society in which every center has an airport has no real periphery. Only outermost space retains the allure of distance, and distance has become the most relative of words in languages that have added startling meanings to atomic, jet, fission, and projectile.

Historians, concerned with temporal or spatial parts, cannot fail to be concerned with the whole. If it is still difficult to define the significant, it is becom-

* In addition to Professor Loewenberg (whose entries are unsigned), the following contributed items and comments indicated by their respective initials: Erling M. Hunt (EMH), Geoffrey Bruun (GB), Walter L. Dorn (WLD), Peter Gay (PG), John W. Hall (JWH), George F. Howe (GFH), Earl H. Pritchard (EHP), Ralph E. Turner (RET).

1

ing less difficult to discern the insignificant. That the light of significance may emerge wherever the student probes remains the historian's hope. But there is less faith that incandescence is likely to emerge from the acquisition of random data. The maxim that light follows research has been modified by the working principle that light follows research informed by sharply-posed hypotheses. The precious documents of the historian do not reveal the past unaided. They reveal the past only when they are reconstructed with insight, that is when they are imaginatively assessed and creatively analyzed.

Learning has widened the range of scholarly vision as historical events have narrowed the range of human isolation. New unities have been discovered among older diversities. The Atlantic and the Pacific were as broad in the days of Christopher Columbus and Sir Francis Drake as they are in the present era. But engines made by man have transmuted oceans and mountains; barriers have become links. It was discovered during the so-called period of normalcy that deserts, mountains, and oceans were no bar to the sweep of economic malaise. More recently it has been recognized that neither technology nor politics is simply local in consequences.

The circle that historians are required to draw around their subjects has constantly widened; but scholars, in part because of the widening circumference of relations, have tended to draw progressively smaller ones. To the accustomed divisions of historical inquiry, as political, constitutional, diplomatic, and economic, have been added such divisions as global, urban, business, entrepreneurial, and technological. Research areas have been divided and subdivided and then divided again.

The search for meaning is synonymous with recorded history itself, but the altering shape of the world has added new dimensions to the nature of the inquiry. Modern history and modern scholarship have communicated a special urgency to the perennial quest for meanings. Problems of the unexplored relations among the special disciplines have intensified the quest. Despite indisputable evidence of achievement, approbation of history has been far from universal. Leading historians have felt compelled to ask where their profession was tending and what the historians believed they were accomplishing. Scholars in other areas have raised searching queries about the method, meaning, and purpose of historical research. Critical barbs have rarely been aimed at methodological techniques as such. Old and tried historical methods are still accounted true; it is their adequacy that is suspect. Few are inclined to doubt the efficacy of numismatics, paleography, or epigraphy in instances where these techniques are applicable. No one is disposed to disparage the method of meticulous cross-examination of documents or whatever other legacies of the past remain to be interrogated. Disputed is the sufficiency of standard devices, not their continuing relevance. Disputed too is the often-held conviction that the raw evidence transmitted from the past tells its own story.

The ancient dilemmas of the historian have been aggravated by the broadening scope of learning in science, social science, and the humanities. Unlike the nineteenth century, when advances in knowledge enhanced the prestige of history, twentieth century learning has raised basic problems about historical method, historical relevance, and historical knowledge.

The revival of theoretical interests has invigorated historical study. Since all questions cannot be of equal import, scholars are compelled to appraise the criteria of importance. Their efforts to evaluate measures of meaning ultimately require analysis of the grounds of choice and selection. Once embarked on that course, studies in the theory of knowledge, the basis of values, and the definition of purpose are inescapable. Historians in pursuit of meanings are, in fact if not in name, involved in the philosophy of history. Such historians distinguish between the canons of method employed in recording history and the speculative analysis of the process of history itself, the difference between history as recorded experience and history as actuality. The distinction, valid methodologically, nevertheless makes it apparent that the connections between the two are intimate and vital and that the one cannot be comprehended without the other. The history of the human mind is a record of sustained human effort to define meanings of the cosmos, of nature, of man, and of society. Historians are deeply immersed in the attempt. The references that follow illustrate how they have participated and how they may be reinforced.

RECONSTRUCTING THE PAST

Manuals of Historical Method

A1. Langlois, Charles V., and Charles Seignobos. **Introduction to the study of history.** Reprint, N.Y., 1912. Tr. by G. B. Berry from *Introduction aux études historiques* (Paris, 1898). A widely-used, methodical treatment of historical criticism and synthesis along common-sense lines.

A2. Bernheim, Ernst. **Lehrbuch der historischen Methode und der Geschichtsphilosophie.** 6th ed., Leipzig, 1908. The classic work on historical method.

A3. Wolf, Gustav. **Einführung in das Studium der neueren Geschichte.** Berlin, 1910. Inclusive in range and indispensable for German history.

A4. Meyer, Eduard. **Kleine Schriften.** 2 v. Halle, 1910–24. Contains discussions of theory and method in ancient classical history.

A5. Feder, Alfred L. **Lehrbuch der geschichtlichen Methode.** 3rd rev. ed., Regensburg, 1924. An approach to historical method by a professor in a Catholic theological seminary.

A6. Fling, Fred M. **The writing of history.** New Haven, 1920. Concise treatment of historical materials, emphasizing critical analysis.

A7. Bauer, Wilhelm. **Einführung in das Studium der Geschichte.** 2nd ed., Tübingen, 1928.

A8. Gustavson, Carl G. **A preface to history.** N.Y., 1955.

A9. George, Hereford B. **Historical evidence.** Oxford, 1909. Admirable, brief, logical discussions of different types of evidence.

A10. **Guide for research students working on historical subjects.** N.Y., 1959. Introduction prepared for Cambridge University, but useful to students of British history elsewhere. [EMH]

A11. Renier, Gustaaf J. **History, its purpose and method.** Boston, 1950.

A12. Vincent, John M. **Historical research: an outline of theory and practice.** Reprint, N.Y., 1929. Practical manual for a beginner rather than a philosophical treatment for a historian.

A13. ———. **Aids to historical research.** N.Y., 1934. Twelve brief essays on aspects of external criticism: diplomatics, palaeography, chronology, etc., with a bibliography for each. [EMH]

A14. Hockett, Homer C. **The critical method in historical research and writing.** N.Y., 1955. Revised and expanded version of *Introduction to research in American history* (1931). Practical manual for graduate students, providing an exposition and examples of historical criticism, detailed advice on techniques, well-selected lists of bibliographies and guides, and a brief survey of United States historiography. [EMH]

A15. Barzun, Jacques, and Henry F. Graff. **The modern researcher.** N.Y., 1957. Readable exposition of research techniques and approaches to synthesis. Major attention to maturity in organization and presentation, and to good writing. Selective bibliography. [EMH]

A16. Parker, Donald D. **Local history: how to gather it, write it, and publish it.** Ed. by Bertha E. Josephson. N.Y., 1944. Surveys types of sources; offers practical advice on research, organization, and publication. Includes a bibliography. [EMH]

A17. Nevins, Allan. **The gateway to history.** Boston, 1938. Chapters, for "general readers," on the value of history; sources and critical method; libraries, archives, and historical societies; and the relation to history of geography, sociology, biography, and literature. [EMH]

A18. Gottschalk, Louis R. **Understanding history: a primer of historical method.** N.Y., 1950. Considers the objectives of historians, methods of historical research, and the theory of history. [EMH]

Persistent Problems

Causal Analysis

A19. Cassirer, Ernst. **Das Erkenntnisproblem in der Philosophie und Wissenschaft der neueren Zeit.** 4 v. Berlin, 1906–57. A classic and authoritative study. [WLD]

A20. ———. **The problem of knowledge: philosophy, science and history since Hegel.** New Haven, 1950.

A21. Deininger, Whitaker T. "Some reflections on epistemology and historical inquiry." **Journal of philosophy,** 53 (July 5, 1956): 429–42. Incisive treatment of the leading issues involved in a consideration of these topics. Particularly valuable for its exposition of the similarity of problems confronting investigators in other than the historical field.

A22. Mandelbaum, Maurice H. "Causal analysis in history." **Journal of the history of ideas,** 3 (Jan. 1942): 30–50. Part of a suggestive symposium on this topic.

A23. Cohen, Morris R. "Causation and its application to history." **Journal of the history of ideas,** 3 (Jan. 1942): 12–29.

A24. Goldenweiser, Alexander. "The concept of causality in the physical and social sciences." **American sociological review,** 3 (Oct. 1938): 624–36.

A25. MacIver, Robert M. **Social causation.** Boston, 1942. A full-length study representing the fruit of a long career of speculative thought.

A26. Teggart, Frederick J. "Causation in historical events." **Journal of the history of ideas,** 3 (Jan. 1942): 3–11. Difficulties inherent in the language of causation; suggestiveness of "custom" as against "law," "process" instead of "cause."

A27. Feuer, Lewis S. "Causality in the social sciences." **Journal of philosophy,** 51 (Nov. 1954): 681–95. General discussion with pertinent comments on human powers versus determinism.

A28. Hempel, Carl G. "The function of general laws in history." **Journal of philosophy,** 39 (Jan. 1942): 35–48.

Explanation

A29. Dray, William. **Laws and explanation in history.** London, 1957.

A30. Gardiner, Patrick. **The nature of historical explanation.** London, 1952. A tightly constructed philosophical investigation. Au-

thor begins with the statement that explanation is a "vague concept" which, after an exploration of its ramifications, he provides with content.

A31. White, Morton G. "Historical explanation." **Mind,** 52 (July 1943): 212–29. Distinguishes between attempts to explain facts by reference to other facts and attempts to find explanations by recourse to other social disciplines. The first is labeled "historicist"; the second, "cultural organicism."

A32. Oakeley, Hilda D., K. Cornforth, and Morris Ginsberg. "Explanation in history." **Aristotelian Society proceedings,** suppl. v. 14 (London, 1935): 113–53.

Continuity and Change

A33. Boas, George. "Aristotle's presuppositions about change." **American journal of philology,** 68 (Oct. 1947): 404–13.

A34. Einstein, Louis. **Historical change.** Cambridge, Eng., 1946. An attempt to assess the meaning of change as it affects history. Two chapters are particularly suggestive: 13, "Some explanations of change," and 15, "The meaning of history."

A35. Lamprecht, Sterling P. **Nature and history.** N.Y., 1950. Precise attempt to differentiate the processes of inquiry between history and physics.

A36. McKeon, Richard. "Aristotle's conception of the development and the nature of scientific method." **Journal of the history of ideas,** 8 (Jan. 1947): 3–44. A closely reasoned exposition and evaluation.

A37. Berlin, Isaiah. **Historical inevitability.** London, 1954. A lucid essay. To refrain from making moral judgments, the author insists, "is one of the great alibis, pleaded by those who cannot and do not wish to face the facts of human responsibility, the existence of a limited but nevertheless real area of human freedom. . . ."

Logic

A38. Cohen, Morris R., and Ernest Nagel, **An introduction to logic and scientific method.** N.Y., 1934. A standard treatment by two distinguished philosophers which contains material basic for historical analysis.

A39. Nagel, Ernest. "Some issues in the logic of historical analysis." **The scientific monthly,** 74 (March 1952): 162–69.

A40. Sabine, George H. "Logic and social studies." **Philosophical review,** 48 (March 1939): 155–76.

A41. Jørgensen, Jørgen **A treatise of formal logic.** 3 v. Copenhagen and London, 1931. One of the fundamental histories of the development of logic. V. 1 treats historical development; 2, systematic exposition; while v. 3 is a discussion and criticism.

Older Auxiliaries (and Their Histories)

Philology

A42. Vendryes, Joseph. **Language: a linguistic introduction to history.** London, 1925. Tr. by Paul Radin from *La langue: introduction linguistique à l'histoire* (Paris, 1921). Specifically oriented to historical problems by a master of the subject.

A43. Drexel, Albert, ed. **Atlas linguisticus.** Innsbruck, 1934. Contains a series of maps showing the spread of languages from antiquity to modern times, particularly in Europe and Asia. [RET]

A44. Bloomfield, Leonard. **Language.** N.Y., 1933. Revision of an earlier book accomplished after twenty years' further study. Authoritative. [RET]

A45. Meillet, Antoine, and Marcel Cohen, eds. **Les langues du monde.** New ed., Paris, 1952. Indispensable. [RET]

A46. Deroy, Louis. **L'emprunt linguistic.** Paris, 1956. Borrowings in the main languages of Europe and Asia. Full bibliography. [RET]

A47. Pedersen, Holger. **Linguistic science in the 19th century: methods and results.** Tr. by John W. Spargo. Cambridge, Mass., 1931.

A48. Wundt, Wilhelm M. **Völkerpsychologie: eine Untersuchung der Entwicklungsgesetze von Sprache, Mythus, und Sitte.** 10 v. in 13. Leipzig, 1900–26. By one of the great founders of modern psychology. Deals with the evolution of language and related aspects.

A49. Langer, Susanne K. "On Cassirer's theory of language and myth." **The philosophy of Ernst Cassirer** (Evanston, Ill., 1949), pp. 381–400. [Paul A. Schilpp, ed., The library of living philosophers, 6.] Cogent analysis of Cassirer's theories, by the translator of his basic linguistic study. The author is herself a philosopher.

A50. Cassirer, Ernst. **Language and myth.** N.Y., 1946. Tr. by Susanne K. Langer from *Sprache und Mythos* (Leipzig, 1925). Influential and thought-provoking study by a learned idealist. Ch. 1 discusses language and myth in the development of culture; ch. 3, language and conception

A51. ——. "Le langage et la construction du monde des objets." **Journal de psychologie,** 30 (1933): 18–44. Contains additional insights on problems vital to historical thinking and research.

A52. ——. "The influence of language upon the development of scientific thought." **Journal of philosophy,** 39 (June 1942): 309–27. Provocative discussion by an outstanding philosopher, whose own contributions to this field heighten its import.

A53. Whitney, William D. **Language and the study of language.** 5th ed., N.Y., 1892. Represents the older school of philological research, but remains valuable as one of the pioneer studies in the United States.

A54. Sapir, Edward. **Language: an introduction to the study of speech.** N.Y., 1921. A noted work in the history of anthropology that still stirs controversy and cannot be considered outmoded. Emphasizes the role of the individual and individual linguistic forms.

Archaeology

A55. Daniel, Glyn E. **A hundred years of archaeology.** London, 1950. A competent survey.

A56. Hogarth, David G., ed. **Authority and archaeology, sacred and profane: essays on the relation of monuments to Biblical and classical literature.** London and N.Y., 1899. Old but valuable. Essays by specialists in various fields with an especially rewarding introductory essay by the editor.

A57. Deonna, Waldemar. **L'archéologie: son domaine, son but.** Paris, 1922. Suggests the need for a more inclusive definition of the field without regard to specific times and places; a broadly based treatment.

A58. Petrie, Sir William M. F. **Methods and aims in archaeology.** London and N.Y., 1904. Practical handbook by a great Egyptologist. Contains a chapter on the nature of archaeological evidence.

Chronology

A59. Cavaignac, Eugène. **Chronologie de l'histoire mondiale.** 2nd ed., Paris, 1934.

A60. Below, Georg A. H. von. **Über historische Periodisierungen.** Berlin, 1925.

A61. Milham, Willis I. **Time and timekeepers.** N.Y., 1947.

A62. Callahan, John F. **Four views of time in ancient philosophy.** Cambridge, Mass., 1948. Conceptions of Plato, Aristotle, Plotinus, and Augustine are analyzed. [RET]

A63. Brandon, Samuel G. F. **Time and mankind: an historical and philosophical study of mankind's attitude to the phenomena of change.** London, 1951.

A64. Gent, Werner. **Das Problem der Zeit: eine historische und systematische Untersuchung.** Frankfurt-am-Main, 1934. Broad in scope and reflective in substance. [RET]

A65. Zawirski, Zygmunt. **L'évolution de la notion du temps.** Cracow, 1936.

A66. Pot, Johan H. J. van der. **De Periodisiering der geschiedenis.** The Hague, 1951. A survey of efforts at periodization in world history and proposals for future application. [RET]

A67. Irwin, Alfred M. B. **The Burmese and Arakanese calendars.** Rangoon, 1909. Tables for the concordance of dates in Burmese chronology with Christian chronology from 1739 to 2000 A.D. [RET]

A68. Havret, P., J. Chambeau, and Pierre Hoang. **Mélanges sur la chronologie chinoise.** Shanghai, 1920. [Variétés sinologiques, 52.] Exposition of Chinese calendar and dating system, with tables for conversion into Christian chronology. [RET]

A69. Libby, Willard F. **Radiocarbon dating.** See *E13*.

A70. Ginzel, Friedrich K. **Handbuch der mathematischen und technischen Chronologie: das Zeitrechnungswesen der Völker.** 3 v. Leipzig, 1906–14. Study of broad historical sweep from Egypt to modern times. While these volumes require adjustment in terms of contemporary scholarship and recent data is lacking, the work is still a model for thoroughness and scope.

A71. Breasted, James H. "The beginnings of time-measurement and the origin of our calendar." **The scientific monthly,** 41 (Oct. 1935): 289–304. Specialized discussion by a famous expert in the history of ancient times.

A72. Nilsson, Martin P. **Primitive time-reckoning: a study in the origins and first development of the art of counting time among the primitive and early culture peoples.** Lund, Swe., 1920. A thorough historical account.

A73. Zeuner, Friedrich E. **Dating the past: an introduction to geochronology.** 4th ed., rev. and enl., London, 1958. A modern study which takes the most recent findings of geology into chronological account.

Diplomatics; Printing and Publishing

A74. Mabillon, Jean. **De re diplomatica libri VI in quibus quidquid ad veterum instrumentorum antiquitatem, materiam, scripturam et stilium.** 3rd ed., 2 v., Naples, 1789. First systematic study of diplomatics, the study of critical methods of establishing authenticity of documents, by the great founder of the subject.

A75. ——. **Librorum de re diplomatica supplementum.** Paris, 1704. Supplement to *A74*.

A76. Hall, Hubert, ed. **A formula book of English official historical documents.** 2 v. Cambridge, Eng., 1908–09. V. 1 is devoted to English documents; v. 2, to judicial and ministerial records.

A77. ——. **Studies in English official historical documents.** Cambridge, Eng., 1908. Coverage restricted to England, but basic for the area. Noteworthy as marking a beginning in methodology.

A78. Harrison, Wilson R. **Suspect documents: their scientific examination.** N.Y., 1958.

A79. Lehmann, Paul J. **Zur Paläographie und Handschriftenkunde.** Munich, 1909. Discussion of Latin handwriting and paleography; notable for inclusion of a history of the latter.

A80. Mason, William A. **A history of the art of writing.** N.Y., 1920. Old but useful short, general treatment. [RET]

A81. Angelo, Pietro d'. **Storia della scrittura.** Rome, 1953. Brief. Concerned with both oriental and western systems of writing. [RET]

A82. Fevrier, James G. **Histoire de l'écriture.** Paris, 1948.

A83. Higounet, Charles. **L'écriture.** Paris, 1955.

A84. Sethe, Kurt H. **Vom Bilde zum Buchstaben.** Leipzig, 1939.

A85. Jensen, Hans. **Die Schrift.** Glückstadt, 1936.

A86. Chiera, Edward. **They wrote in clay: the Babylonian tablets speak today.** Cambridge, Eng., 1939.

A87. Blum, André. **On the origin of paper.** Tr. by Harry M. Lydenberg. N.Y., 1934. From ancient China to European beginnings of paper making.

A88. Hunter, Dard. **Paper making through eighteen centuries.** N.Y., 1930.

A89. Lehmann-Haupt, Hellmut. **One hundred books about book making: a guide to the study and appreciation of printing.** N.Y., 1949.

A90. Oswald, John C. **A history of printing: its development through five hundred years.** N.Y., 1928. Survey of printing in the West and its spread from Europe to North America.

A91. Dahl, Sven. **History of the book.** N.Y., 1958. Originally published in Danish; translated also into French and German. Authoritative.

A92. Bogeng, Gustav A. E., and others. **Geschichte der Buchdruckerkunst.** 2 v. Dresden, 1930–41.

A93. González Blanco, Edmundo. **Historia del periodismo desde sus comienzos hasta nuestra época.** Madrid, 1919.

A94. Salmon, Lucy M. **The newspaper and the historian.** N.Y., 1923. One of the first efforts to deal systematically with special problems of research and method arising in recent periods.

A95. Weill, Georges J. **Le journal: origines, évolution et rôle de la presse périodique.** Paris, 1934. Excellent general history of newspapers and periodicals—European, North American, Islamic, Chinese, and Japanese. Bibliographies.

A96. Münster, Hans A. **Die moderne Presse: das Zeitungs- und Zeitschriftenwesen im In- und Ausland.** 2 v. Bad Kreuznach, 1955.

Numismatics

A97. Friedensburg, Ferdinand. **Die Münze in der Kulturgeschichte.** 2nd ed., Berlin, 1926. Comprehensive account of the cultural significance of coins and coinage.

A98. Luschin von Ebengreuth, Arnold.

Allgemeine Münzkunde und Geldgeschichte des Mittelalters und der neueren Zeit. 2nd ed., Munich and Berlin, 1926. Exhaustive study of money—uses and economic roles.

A99. Lane-Poole, Stanley E., ed. **Coins and medals: their place in history and art.** 3rd ed., London, 1894. Remains an excellent introduction to the subject, with biographical and geneological materials.

Newer Aids (and Their Histories)

Political Science

A100. Contemporary political science. Paris, 1950. [UNESCO publication no. 426.] Invaluable for comparative appraisals.

A101. Leiserson, Avery. "Problems of methodology in political research." **Political science quarterly,** 68 (Dec. 1953): 558–84. Brief introduction to problems of research.

A102. Finer, Herman. **Theory and practice of modern government.** Rev. ed., N.Y., 1949. Contains as much theory as practice, meaningfully and explicitly related.

A103. Lasswell, Harold D., and Abraham Kaplan. **Power and society: a framework for political inquiry.** New Haven, 1950. Definition of a theoretical framework for political science research extending the conventional boundaries.

A104. Sabine, George H. "What is a political theory?" **The journal of politics,** 1 (Feb. 1939): 1–16. A life-long student of political philosophy raises some serious queries.

A105. Neumann, Franz L. "Approaches to the study of political power." **Political science quarterly,** 45 (June 1950): 161–80. Incisive suggestions by a sharply inquiring student.

A106. Oakeshott, Michael. "Rationalism in politics." **The Cambridge journal,** 1 (Nov. and Dec. 1947): 81–98, 145–57. A critique of rationalism as the ultimate method of social and political problems.

A107. Gouldner, Alvin W., ed. **Studies in leadership: leadership and democratic action.** N.Y., 1950. Directed to the issue of manipulation of the many by the few.

A108. Babbitt, Irving. **Democracy and leadership.** Boston, 1924. Reprint, 1952. Important attempt to consider a fundamental problem in philosophical rather than narrower terms. The introduction summarizes the author's general position. [GFH]

A109. Neumann, Franz L. **The democratic and the authoritarian state.** Glencoe, Ill., 1957. Contribution by a close student of both.

A110. Neumann, Sigmund, ed. **Modern political parties: approaches to comparative politics.** Chicago, 1956. A pioneer attempt to study modern political parties comparatively. Exhaustive and important bibliographies.

A111. Schattschneider, Elmer E. **Party government.** N.Y., 1942. Presentation of a theory of democratic politics in which the political party is viewed as the creative instrument.

A112. Simon, Herbert A. **Administrative behavior: a study of decision-making processes in administrative organization.** N.Y., 1947. Constructs a theory of administrative functions and a theoretical basis for research.

A113. Morstein Marx, Fritz, ed. **Elements of public administration.** N.Y., 1946. Observations of a perceptive student of the subject. As in most modern works in this area, rigid structural analyses of administrative functions are integrated with fluid relationships of informal groups and their effects on bureaucratic behavior.

A114. Levi, Werner. **Fundamentals of world organization.** Minneapolis, 1950. A blending of administration, politics, institutional analysis, and history.

A115. Morgenthau, Hans J. **Politics among nations: the struggle for power and peace.** N.Y., 1948. Excellent example of the merger of disciplines.

Economics

A116. Hutchison, Terence W. **The significance and basic postulates of economic theory.** London, 1938. A basic volume of theoretical analysis.

A117. Weber, Max. **General economic history.** Tr. by Frank H. Knight. Glencoe, Ill., 1950. A readily accessible translation of this fundamental work.

A118. Heilbroner, Robert L. **The worldly philosophers.** N.Y., 1953. General history of the development of economic theories.

A119. Samuelson, Paul A. **Foundations of economic analysis.** Cambridge, Mass., 1947. General survey of concepts and hypotheses employed by economists.

A120. Ellis, Howard S., ed. **A survey of contemporary economics.** V. 1. Philadelphia, 1948. This and the following volume contain prime documents for the historian and succinct surveys of economic concepts.

A121. Haley, Bernard F., ed. **A survey of contemporary economics.** V. 2. Homewood, Ill., 1952.

A122. Cole, Arthur H. "Committee on Research in Economic History." **The Journal of economic history,** 13 (winter 1953): 79–87. A substantive report.

A123. Dillard, Dudley D. **The economics of John Maynard Keynes.** N.Y., 1948. Sensible and readable account of the theories of one of the great thinkers of the modern era.

A124. Friedrich, Carl J. **Alfred Weber's theory of the location of industries.** Chicago, 1929. Clear account of the position of an important social theorist.

A125. Hoover, Edgar M. **The location of**

economic activity. N.Y., 1948. An exposition of location theory, adding dimensions to the phenomena of social movement.

A126. Miller, William, ed. **Men in business: essays in the history of entrepreneurship.** Cambridge, Mass., 1952. Illustrates the development of entrepreneurial research and the social science orientation of business history.

A127. Sombart, Werner. **Der Bourgeois.** Munich, 1913. Tr., *The quintessence of capitalism,* London, 1915. Searching investigation of the role of the business group and its social affiliates.

A128. Lauterbach, Albert T. **Man, motives, and money: psychological frontiers of economics.** Ithaca, 1954. Successful exploratory investigation of the relationships between economic and psychological factors.

A129. Katona, George. **Psychological analysis of economic behavior.** N.Y., 1951. Supplemented by *A128*.

A130. Dickinson, Zenas C. **Economic motives: a study in the psychological foundations of economic theory.** Cambridge, Mass., 1922.

A131. Myrdal, K. Gunnar. **The political element in the development of economic theory.** Cambridge, Mass., 1954. Perspicacious study by a renowned Scandinavian scholar.

A132. Clark, Colin. **The conditions of economic progress.** See *A120*.

Geography

A133. Ratzel, Friedrich. **Anthropogeographie.** 2 v. Stuttgart, 1882–91. [Bibliothek geographischer Handbücher.] As one of the pioneer studies of relationships between lands and peoples, this is a classic. Ratzel's work likewise carved out an area of specialism and became the forerunner of a school. The role of environment is accorded heavy causal stress.

A134. Semple, Ellen C. **Influences of geographic environment, on the basis of Ratzel's system of anthropo-geography.** N.Y., 1911. A standard account of geographic influences. Important for itself as well as for its influence in making Ratzel's work available in English.

A135. Febvre, Lucien, and Lionel Bataillon. **A geographical introduction to history.** Tr. by E. G. Mountford and J. H. Paxton. London and N.Y., 1925. Follows Vidal de La Blache in making qualifications in the pronouncements of Ratzel and his school.

A136. Hassinger, Hugo. **Geographische Grundlagen der Geschichte.** 2nd ed., Freiburg, 1953.

A137. Sorre, Maximilien. **Les fondements de la géographie humaine.** 3 v. in 4. Paris, 1943–52.

A138. Keltie, Sir John S., and Osbert J. R. Howarth. **History of geography.** N.Y. and

London, 1913. Comprehensive though brief account.

A139. Vidal de La Blache, Paul M. **Principles of human geography.** Tr. by Millicent T. Bingham. N.Y. and London, 1926. An important corrective to the Ratzel school of interpretation. While giving full scope to influence of environment, takes account of the creative role of man in bending the environment to his needs.

A140. Brunhes, Jean. **Human geography: an attempt at a positive classification, principles, and examples.** Tr. by T. C. LeCompte. 2nd rev. ed., Paris, 1912. Substantive as well as methodological. Surveys the field and exemplifies the scholarly technique which the author helped to develop.

A141. ———. **Étude de géographie humaine: l'irrigation, ses conditions géographiques, ses modes, et son organisation dans la péninsule ibérique et dans l'Afrique du nord.** Paris, 1902. A specialized study illustrating the application of method.

A142. George, Hereford B. **The relations of geography and history.** 5th rev. ed., Oxford, 1924. A good, standard description of the relationship between geographical conditions and political developments.

A143. Alisov, Boris P., and others. **Kurs klimatologii.** 3 pts. in 2 v. Leningrad, 1952–54. Pt. 1 is a general treatment of climatology; pt. 2 deals with certain historical developments in climate, including a refutation of Huntington's thesis that drought impelled the migrations from central Asia; pt. 3 discusses climate of the earth's lands. [RET]

A144. Aubert de la Rüe, Edgar. **Man and the winds.** Tr. by Madge E. Thompson. N.Y., 1955.

A145. Hassinger, Hugo. **Geographische Grundlagen der Geschichte.** 2nd ed., Freiburg, 1953. [Heinrich Finke, Hermann Junker, and Gustav Schaurer, Geschichte der führenden Völker, 2.]

A146. Brown, Lloyd A. **The story of maps.** See *U119*.

A147. Bagrow, Leo. **Die Geschichte der Kartographie.** See *U115*.

A148. Franz, Günther. **Historische Kartographie: Forschung und Bibliographie.** Bremen, 1955. Very useful bibliography in addition to a discussion of modern historical map-making.

A149. Peattie, Roderick. **Geography in human destiny.** N.Y., 1940. Popular but informative. [GB]

Demography

A150. Spengler, Joseph J., and Otis D. Duncan, eds. **Demographic analysis: selected readings.** Glencoe, Ill., 1956. Highly satisfactory introduction to a technical subject.

A151. ———, eds. **Population theory and policy: selected readings.** Glencoe, 1956. Supplies a theoretical framework and illustrations of its application.

A152. Hauser, Philip M., ed. **Population and world politics.** Glencoe, 1958. Explores the interrelations of demography and other social sciences in papers contributed by leading experts in the field.

A153. Lavedan, Pierre. **Histoire de l'urbanisme. V. 2, Renaissance et temps modernes.** Paris, 1941.

A154. Dickinson, Robert E. **The west European city: a geographical interpretation.** London, 1951.

Anthropology

A155. Ratzel, Friedrich. **The history of mankind.** 3 v. London and N.Y., 1896–98. Tr. by A. J. Butler from *Völkerkunde* (2nd rev. ed., 2 v., Leipzig, 1894–95). Of major historical importance. A synthesis of anthropological knowledge to its time.

A156. Durkheim, David E. **The elementary forms of the religious life: a study in religious sociology.** London and N.Y., 1915. Tr. by J. W. Swain from *Les formes élémentaires de la vie religieuse: Le système totémique en Australie* (Paris, 1912). By a prominent figure in social research who has influenced anthropology, psychology, and sociology alike. Particularly significant for theoretical development of functionalism.

A157. ——. **The division of labor in society.** Tr. by George Simpson. Glencoe, Ill., 1947.

A158. Penniman, Thomas K. **A hundred years of anthropology.** 2nd ed., London, 1952. A basic source brought up to date and revised.

A159. Kroeber, Alfred L. **Anthropology: race, language, culture, psychology, prehistory.** 2nd ed., N.Y., 1948. A schematic discussion by one of the foremost theorists in the subject.

A160. ——. **The nature of culture.** Chicago, 1952. A collection of earlier papers devoted to the idea of culture.

A161. Kroeber, Alfred L., and others. **Anthropology today: an encyclopedic inventory.** Chicago, 1953. Research report of field work and theoretical findings in every branch of the field. Full bibliographies.

A162. Tax, Sol, and others, eds. **An appraisal of anthropology today.** Chicago, 1953.

A163. Kroeber, Alfred L., and Clyde Kluckhohn. **Culture: a critical review of concepts and definitions.** Cambridge, Mass., 1952. [Papers of the Peabody Museum, 47.] A probing effort at clarity and redefinition.

A164. Myres, Sir John L. **The influence of anthropology on the course of political science.** Berkeley, 1916. Provocative study of intellectual relationships.

A165. Casson, Stanley. **The discovery of man: the story of the inquiry into human origins.** N.Y. and London, 1939. A prime historical source of the human mind indicating the concern of western man in the study of his origins.

A166. Herskovits, Melville J. **Man and his works: the science of cultural anthropology.** N.Y., 1948. A well reasoned exposition of the scope of the discipline.

A167. Benedict, Ruth. **Patterns of culture.** N.Y., 1934. Case study of three tribes. Historically significant for development of the concept of the culture pattern and its popularization.

A168. Barnett, Homer G. **Innovation: the basis of cultural change.** N.Y., 1953. One of the better analyses of culture change in which the author exploits modern psychology, anthropology, and sociology.

A169. Niedermann, Joseph. **Kultur: Werden und Wandlungen des Begriffs und seiner Ersatzbegriffe von Cicero bis Herder.** Florence, 1941. Provocative study of the intellectual vicissitudes of the concept of culture.

A170. Boas, Franz. **The mind of primitive man.** N.Y., 1911. A crucial document in the history of ideas that deals with relations of culture to the physical environment, racial traits, and characteristics of the primitive mind.

A171. Wissler, Clark. **Man and culture.** N.Y. and London, 1923. Still relevant for the study of culture patterns, traits, and stages.

A172. White, Leslie A. **The science of culture: a study of man and civilization.** N.Y., 1949. Paperback reprint, 1958. Thesis that culture is a determinant of man's life and history.

A173. ——. "Man's control over civilization: an anthropocentric illusion." **The scientific monthly,** 66 (Mar. 1948): 235–47.

A174. Kluckhohn, Clyde. **Mirror for man: the relation of anthropology to modern life.** N.Y., 1949. Non-technical exposition of the boundaries and purposes of anthropology.

A175. Gilfillan, S. Colum. **The sociology of invention.** Chicago, 1935. Lucid treatment of the role of invention and its influence as a fulcrum of culture change.

A176. Lowie, Robert H. **The history of ethnological theory.** N.Y., 1937. Pivotal study of the evolution of ideas in a critical branch of social research.

A177. Malinowski, Bronislaw K. **A scientific theory of culture, and other essays.** Chapel Hill, 1944. A sober approach to culture in terms of psychological behavior.

A178. Kardiner, Abram. **The individual and his society: the psychodynamics of primitive social organization.** N.Y., 1939. A pathbreaking effort to understand the relations of personality and culture in neo-Freudian terms. A case study of two primitive societies, introducing the concept of basic personality structure.

A179. Kardiner, Abram, and others. **The psychological frontiers of society.** N.Y., 1945. A further development of *A178,* with additional materials.

A180. Klineberg, Otto. **Tensions affecting international understanding.** N.Y., 1950. [Social Science Research Council bulletin, 62.] Besides its substance, this monograph presents a critical survey of the literature of national character and gives measured stress to problems of method.

A181. Bidney, David. **Theoretical anthropology.** N.Y., 1953. By a critic of cultural determinism and proponent of possibilities of human controls.

A182. ——. "Human nature and the cultural process." **American anthropologist,** 49 (July-Sep. 1947): 375–99.

A183. Stern, Curt. **Principles of human genetics.** San Francisco, 1949. Straightforward account by one of the foremost research analysts.

A184. Simpson, George G. **The meaning of evolution: a study of the history of life and of its significance for man.** New Haven, 1949. The best and most readable account of this vital aspect of human history.

A185. Loewenberg, Bert J., ed. **Charles Darwin: evolution and natural selection.** Boston, 1959. A selection of basic Darwinian materials to which Wallace and Huxley selections are added.

A186. Hogben, Lancelot T. **Genetic principles in medicine and social science.** N.Y. and London, 1931. A specific exemplification oriented to the needs of scholars in allied areas.

A187. Aubrey, Edwin E. "Social psychology as liaison between history and sociology." **Am. hist. rev.,** 33 (Jan. 1928): 257–77.

A188. Gillin, John P., ed. **For a science of social man: convergences in anthropology, psychology, and sociology.** N.Y., 1954. A group of suggestive essays by careful specialists in their respective fields.

Sociology

A189. Kaufmann, Felix. **Methodology of the social sciences.** N.Y., 1944. One of the best books on its subject, by a well-trained scholar equipped with philosophic knowledge.

A190. Weber, Max. **On the methodology of the social sciences.** Ed. by Edward A. Shils and Henry A. Finch. Glencoe, Ill., 1949. New edition of a classical presentation. In these discussions the founder of the *Archiv für Sozialwissenschaft* stresses his view that the concern of the social sciences is with the real possibilities of human life.

A191. Bock, Kenneth E. **The acceptance of histories: toward a perspective for social science.** Berkeley, 1956. Discusses difficulties involved in the analysis of social process

stemming from traditional views of social change.

A192. Parker, Harold T. "A tentative reflection on the interdisciplinary approach and the historian." **South Atlantic quarterly,** 56 (Jan. 1957): 105–11. Mature comments on the relations of social science approaches to history.

A193. Lazarsfeld, Paul F., and Morris Rosenberg, eds. **The language of social research: a reader in the methodology of social research.** Glencoe, Ill., 1955. A basic volume which supersedes most of the earlier ones covering aspects of the same field.

A194. Wootton, Barbara. **Testament for social science: an essay in the application of scientific method to human problems.** London, 1950. Lessons from the notebook of a celebrated scholar, renowned for the practice of scientific analysis in humanitarian terms and for humanitarian purposes.

A195. McLaughlin, Isabella C. "History and sociology: a comparison of their methods." **American journal of sociology,** 32 (Nov. 1926): 379–95. Possesses historical as well as methodological significance.

A196. Gurvitch, Georges, and Wilbert E. Moore, eds. **Twentieth century sociology.** N.Y., 1945. A symposium reflecting the state of sociology at the time.

A197. Merton, Robert K. **Social theory and social structure.** Rev. ed., Glencoe, Ill., 1957. Collected papers. Essays on influence of bureaucratic structure on personality, on sociology of science, and on the sociology of knowledge deserve close examination.

A198. Parsons, Talcott. **The structure of social action.** 2nd ed., Glencoe, 1949.

A199. Parsons, Talcott, Robert F. Bales, and Edward A. Shils. **Working papers in the theory of action.** Glencoe, 1953.

A200. Parsons, Talcott, and Edward A. Shils, eds. **Toward a general theory of action.** Cambridge, Mass., 1951. Significant analytical investigation which lies at the core of one phase of historical interpretation.

A201. Parsons, Talcott. **The social system.** Glencoe, 1951. A theoretical exploration with large implications for historical method.

A202. Weber, Max. **The theory of social and economic organization.** Tr. by Talcott Parsons. Rev. ed., N.Y., 1947. The work of a master analyst.

A203. Becker, Howard P. **Through values to social interpretation.** Durham, 1950. Especially valuable for development and particularization of the concept of secularization.

A204. Bernard, Luther L., and Jessie S. Bernard. **Origins of American sociology: the social science movement in the United States.** N.Y., 1943. An inescapable monograph in the history of ideas.

A205. Bendix, Reinhard, and Seymour M. Lipset, eds. **Class, status and power: a reader in social stratification.** Glencoe, Ill., 1953. A useful selection of theoretical papers containing among others one by Talcott Parsons, "A revised analytical approach to the theory of social stratification."

A206. Halbwachs, Maurice. **The psychology of social class.** Tr. by Claire Delavenay. Glencoe, 1958. Work of a distinguished French student of Durkheim in which he discusses the influence of class membership and identification.

A207. Potter, David M. **People of plenty.** Chicago, 1954. An exemplification of social science concepts by a historian dealing with United States history. First two chapters illuminate the pertinence of the so-called behavioral sciences.

A208. Barnes, Harry E., ed. **An introduction to the history of sociology.** Chicago, 1948.

Psychology, Psychiatry, and Psychoanalysis

A209. Woodworth, Robert S. **Contemporary schools of psychology.** Rev. ed., N.Y., 1948. A helpful survey; confined to the 20th century.

A210. Koffka, Kurt. **Principles of Gestalt psychology.** N.Y., 1935. A leader in development of this branch of the subject explains its principles and meanings.

A211. Newcomb, Theodore M. **Social psychology.** N.Y., 1950. An exemplary text.

A212. Murphy, Gardner. **Historical introduction to modern psychology.** Rev. ed., N.Y., 1949. Temperate and judicious.

A213. Jones, Alfred Ernest. **The life and work of Sigmund Freud.** 3 v. N.Y., 1953–57. Already the standard analytical biography, told with sympathy and learning.

A214. Hoselitz, Berthold F., and Walter A. Weisskopf, eds. "The psychological approach to the social sciences." **American journal of economics and sociology,** 12 (Oct. 1952): entire issue.

A215. Allport, Gordon W. **Personality: a psychological interpretation.** N.Y., 1937. Searching examination of personality theory, stressing the singularity of personality. A non-psychoanalytical approach.

A216. ——. **The use of personal documents in psychological science.** N.Y., 1942. Cogent methodological prescriptions of great value to historians.

A217. Asch, Solomon E. **Social psychology.** N.Y., 1952. Much more than the text it was designed to be. Assumptions of Gestalt psychology serve as the criteria for critiques of assumptions employed by psychologists. Also contains a critical review of cultural relativism.

A218. Blum, Gerald S. **Psychoanalytic theories of personality.** N.Y., 1953. Summary of conventional and deviant hypotheses; bibliographical references.

A219. Freud, Sigmund. **Civilization and its discontents.** London, 1930. Implications of motivation theory rooted in sex and aggression for society.

A220. ——. **The ego and the id.** Tr. by Joan Riviere. London, 1927.

A221. ——. **New introductory lectures on psychoanalysis.** Tr. by W. J. H. Sprott. N.Y. and London, 1933.

A222. ——. **The problem of anxiety.** Tr. by Henry A. Bunker. N.Y., 1936.

A223. Schoenwald, Richard L. "Historians and the challenge of Freud." **Western humanities review,** 10 (spring 1956): 99–108. A very pertinent article.

A224. Lasswell, Harold D. "Impact of psychoanalytic thinking on the social sciences." Leonard D. White, ed., **The state of the social sciences** (Chicago, 1956), pp. 84–115.

A225. Stoodley, Bartlett H. **The concepts of Freud.** Glencoe, Ill., 1958. Clearly points out the cleavage in Freud's thinking between a biological and an interpersonal frame of reference. Suggests a close intellectual kinship between Freud and Durkheim.

A226. Sargent, Stephen S., and Marian W. Smith, eds. **Culture and personality.** N.Y., 1949. Papers by psychologists, psychiatrists, and anthropologists.

A227. Sullivan, Harry S. **Conceptions of modern psychiatry.** 2nd ed., Washington, 1947. Presentation of a psychiatric theory based on interpersonal relations which has had wide influence.

A228. Thompson, Clara M. **Psychoanalysis: evolution and development.** N.Y., 1950. Historical account unmarred by author's own neo-Freudian affiliations.

A229. American Psychiatric Association. **One hundred years of American psychiatry.** N.Y., 1944. A collaborative work.

A230. Fromm, Erich. **Escape from freedom.** N.Y., 1941. Analysis of culture and personality along neo-Freudian lines. Nazi Germany is employed as a case study.

A231. Róheim, Géza, ed. **Psychoanalysis and the social sciences.** 3 v. N.Y., 1947–51. An indispensable source for ideas as well as reference.

A232. Brosin, Henry W. "A review of the influence of psychoanalysis on current thought." Franz G. Alexander and Helen Ross, eds., **Dynamic psychiatry** (Chicago, 1952), pp. 508–53. A rewarding survey filled with reflections helpful to students of society.

A233. Murphy, Gardner. **Personality: a biosocial approach to origins and structure.** N.Y., 1947. Excellent survey by one of the clearest developmental psychologists.

A234. Lewin, Kurt. **Field theory in social science.** N.Y., 1951.

A235. ——. **A dynamic theory of personality: selected papers.** Tr. by Donald K. Adams and Karl E. Zener. N.Y., 1935. Emphasizes the "private world" of the actors in social situations, counter to behavioral emphases.

A236. Kluckhohn, Clyde, Henry A. Murray, and David M. Schneider, eds. **Personality in nature, society, and culture.** 2nd ed. rev. and enl., N.Y., 1953. Instructive collection of materials prefaced by introductions which together offer a theoretical introduction.

A237. Linton, Ralph. **The cultural background of personality.** N.Y., 1945. Group of lectures by an outstanding anthropologist in which the concept of status personality is presented.

A238. ———. **The study of man.** N.Y., 1936. Anthropological text famed for development of the concepts of role and status.

Mathematics

A239. Kline, Morris. **Mathematics in western culture.** N.Y., 1953.

A240. Cajori, Florian. **A history of mathematics.** Rev. and enl. ed., N.Y., 1919.

A241. Smith, David E. **History of mathematics.** 2 v. Boston, 1923–25. Reliable source for the investigator in other disciplines.

A242. Whitehead, Alfred N. **An introduction to mathematics.** London and N.Y., 1911. Paperback reprint, 1958. Incomparable for its charm and lucidity as well as for its authority.

A243. Bell, Eric T. **The development of mathematics.** N.Y., 1940.

A244. ———. **Men of mathematics.** N.Y., 1937. Informative and well-written biographical accounts of leading mathematicians.

A245. Boyer, Carl B. **The concepts of the calculus: a critical and historical discussion of the derivative and the integral.** N.Y., 1949. The standard and most recent account.

A246. Lazarsfeld, Paul F., ed. **Mathematical thinking in the social sciences.** Glencoe, Ill., 1954. Basic.

Science

A247. Miller, Hugh. **History and science: a study of the relation of historical and theoretical knowledge.** Berkeley, 1939. Interesting and suggestive.

A248. Sarton, George A. L. **A guide to the history of science.** Waltham, Mass., 1952.

A249. ———. **Introduction to the history of science.** 3 v. in 5. Baltimore, 1927–48. More of an encyclopedia than a history; indispensable for period from classical times to beginning of the 14th century. Written by a pioneer historian of science, these volumes cover world culture and treat science in its widest context. Unsurpassed for biographical and bibliographical data.

A250. ———. **The life of science: essays in the history of civilization.** N.Y., 1948.

A251. Thorndike, Lynn. **A history of magic and experimental science.** 8 v. N.Y., 1923–58. Complete to end of the 17th century. Indispensable to the student of early modern science. [WLD]

A252. Dampier, William C. **A history of science and its relations with philosophy and religion.** 4th ed., Cambridge, Eng., 1948.

A253. Taton, René, ed. **Histoire générale des sciences.** Paris, 1957 ff. To be complete in 3 v.

A254. Moulton, Forest R., and Justus J. Schifferes, eds. **The autobiography of science.** N.Y., 1945. Covers 16th–20th centuries; one of the best compilations of this order.

A255. Toulmin, Stephen E. **The philosophy of science.** London, 1953.

A256. Guerlac, Henry. "Three eighteenth-century social philosophers: scientific influences on their thought." **Science and the modern mind,** ed. by Gerald Holton (Boston, 1958), pp. 1–16. A series of illuminating remarks concerning Montesquieu, Voltaire, and Baron d'Holbach, and an inquiry of the extent to which they were influenced by Newton.

A257. Butterfield, Herbert. **The origins of modern science, 1300–1800.** N.Y., 1951. An arresting, sweeping survey, the merit of which lies in considering the hurdles that had to be overcome before science could be placed on a solid foundation. [WLD]

A258. Hall, Alfred R. **The scientific revolution, 1500–1800: the formation of the modern scientific attitude.** London, 1954. Best introduction to the scientific revolution of this period. Excellent introductory chapter on background.

A259. Crew, Henry. **The rise of modern physics.** 2nd ed., Baltimore, 1935. A brief survey.

A260. Cajori, Florian. **A history of physics.** Rev. ed., N.Y., 1929. A standard work and ready tool for non-specialists.

A261. Einstein, Albert, and Leopold Infeld. **The evolution of physics.** N.Y., 1938. History of physical concepts of the late 19th and early 20th centuries, distinguished by its authorship and for the clarity with which difficult problems are presented.

A262. Chase, Carl T. **The evolution of modern physics.** N.Y., 1947.

A263. Doig, Peter. **A concise history of astronomy.** London, 1950.

A264. Grant, Robert. **History of physical astronomy, from the earliest ages to the middle of the 19th century.** London, 1852. Remains the best and most substantial general account. No more recent study has yet replaced it as a reference work for other specialists.

A265. Davidson, Martin. **The stars and the mind: a study of the impact of astronomical development on human thought.** 2nd ed., London, 1948.

A266. Partington, James R. **A short history of chemistry.** 2nd ed., London, 1948. Excellent introduction. [WLD]

A267. Stillman, John M. **The story of early chemistry.** N.Y., 1924. Covers to middle of the 18th century. The most comprehensive work for the period, especially valuable for its quotations from original sources.

A268. Leicester, Henry M. **The historical background of chemistry.** N.Y., 1956. The most recent overall study, notable for its sweep and inclusiveness.

A269. Clow, Archibald, and Nan L. Clow. **The chemical revolution.** London, 1952. On industrial chemistry. [WLD]

A270. Adams, Frank D. **Birth and development of the geological sciences.** Baltimore, 1938. Paperback ed., 1954. Excellent, readable survey.

A271. Needham, Joseph. **A history of embryology.** Cambridge, Eng., 1934. Clear and imaginative account which transcends the scope implied by the title.

A272. Singer, Charles J. **The evolution of anatomy.** London, 1925. Paperback ed., N.Y., 1957. Valuable survey by a recognized student. [WLD]

A273. ——. **A history of biology.** Rev. ed., N.Y., 1950. Useful for reference and particularly helpful for its surveys of general developments.

A274. Nordenskiöld, Erik. **The history of biology.** Tr. by Leonard B. Eyre. N.Y., 1928. Full narrative account as well as a compendium. Contains excellent bibliography of continental sources.

A275. Abetti, Giorgio. **The history of astronomy.** N.Y., 1952.

A276. Farber, Eduard. **The evolution of chemistry.** N.Y., 1952.

A277. Beringer, Carl C. **Geschichte der Geologie.** Stuttgart, 1954.

A278. Fierz-David, Hans E. **Die Entwicklungsgeschichte der Chemie.** 2nd ed., Basel, 1952.

A279. Graebe, Carl, and Paul Walden. **Geschichte der organischen Chemie.** 2 v. Berlin, 1920–41.

Medicine

A280. Garrison, Fielding H. **An introduction to the history of medicine.** Philadelphia, 1929.

A281. Mettler, Cecilia C. **History of medicine.** Philadelphia, 1947. This and the above are encyclopedic works of reference. [WLD]

A282. Stern, Bernhard J. **Society and medical progress.** Princeton, 1941.

A283. Diepgen, Paul. **Geschichte der Medizin: die historische Entwicklung der Heilkunde und des ärztlichen Lebens.** 2 v. in 3. Berlin, 1949–55.

A284. Brunn, Walter von. **Geschichte der Chirurgie.** Bonn, 1948.

A285. Castiglioni, Arturo. **A history of medicine.** Tr. and ed. by Edward B. Krumbhaar. N.Y., 1941. Comparable to Shryock in coverage and dependability.

A286. Guthrie, Douglas. **A history of medicine.** Philadelphia, 1946.

A287. Shryock, Richard H. **The development of modern medicine.** Philadelphia, 1936. 2nd ed., N.Y., 1947. Modern research of high caliber.

A288. Sigerist, Henry E. **Civilization and disease.** See *C218.*

A289. ——. **A history of medicine.** N.Y., 1951. Traverses the primitive periods of the history of medicine and illustrates the pervasive belief in "laws of magic" as constants in the operation of nature.

A290. Leonardo, Richard A. **History of medical thought.** N.Y., 1946.

Technology

A291. Hansen, Alvin H. "The technological interpretation of history." **Quarterly journal of economics,** 36 (Nov. 1921): 72–83. Reflections of a noted economist.

A292. Singer, Charles J., and others, eds. **A history of technology.** See *C177.*

A293. Wolf, Abraham. **A history of science, technology and philosophy in the 16th, 17th and 18th centuries.** 2 v. London, 1935–39. 2nd ed., 1950–52. Very helpful, especially for reference. Full illustrations enhance the value of these volumes.

A294. Dickinson, Henry W. **A short history of the steam engine.** Cambridge, Eng., [1938].

A295. Dugas, René. **Histoire de mécanique.** Neuchâtel, 1950.

A296. Brocklehurst, Harold J., and Arthur P. M. Fleming. **A history of engineering.** London, 1925.

A297. Gould, Rupert T. **The marine chronometer, its history and development.** London, 1923.

A298. Mach, Ernst. **The science of mechanics.** Tr. by T. J. McCormack. 4th ed., Chicago, 1919. Broad in scope.

THE CONTINUING QUEST FOR FUNDAMENTALS

The Meaning of Man's Past

A299. Harrison, Frederic. **The meaning of history, and other historical pieces.** London and N.Y., 1894. Four of these papers treat the uses and importance of the study of history.

A300. Teggart, Frederick J. **Theory and processes of history.** 2 v. in 1. Berkeley, 1941. Learning and clarity characterize these attempts to explain a theory of history and evolve a comprehensive historical hypothesis of social change.

A301. ——. **Rome and China: a study of correlations in historical events.** Berkeley, 1939. An effort to test hypotheses of the theory of history presented in the author's earlier works.

A302. Gardiner, Patrick, ed. **Theories of history.** Glencoe, Ill., 1959. An exceedingly useful selection containing an essay by Bertrand Russell on historical materialism, papers on the Toynbee debate, and a series on the nature of historical explanation. These follow a selection of classical theorists from Vico to Croce.

A303. Frankel, Charles. **The faith of reason: the idea of progress in the French enlightenment.** N.Y., 1948. Thoughtful volume by a philosopher which has significant words for historians.

A304. Walsh, William H. **An introduction to philosophy of history.** N.Y. and London, 1951. Deals with the underlying issues of history critically. Brief but lucid discussions of Kant, Herder, and Hegel. A sharp and pertinent distinction is made between "critical" and "speculative" philosophies of history.

A305. Hook, Sidney. **The hero in history.** Reprint, Boston, 1955.

A306. Muller, Herbert J. **The uses of the past.** N.Y., 1952.

A307. Rothacker, Erich. **Geschichtsphilosophie.** Munich and Berlin, 1934. Reprint 1947.

A308. Halévy, Daniel. **Essai sur l'accélération de l'histoire.** Paris, 1948.

A309. Roupnel, Gaston. **Histoire et destin.** Paris, 1943.

A310. Wetter, Gustavo A. **Der dialektische Materialismus: seine Geschichte und sein System in der Sowjetunion.** See *AH48*.

A311. Weber, Alfred. **Kulturgeschichte als Kultursoziologie.** 2nd ed., Munich, 1950.

A312. Seidenberg, Roderick. **Posthistoric man.** Chapel Hill, 1950. An attempt to philosophize from the evidence of history that mankind, by substituting intelligence for instinct, has entered a course of development ("historic determinism") in which social organization will eliminate individual freedom. [GFH]

A313. Hofer, Walther. **Geschichtsschreibung und Weltanschauung.** Munich, 1950. Although dealing primarily with the great historian Friedrich Meinecke, this is one of the most complete expositions of the historicist position.

A314. Nietzsche, Friedrich W. **The use and abuse of history.** Tr. by Adrian Collins. N.Y., 1949. 2nd ed., 1957. Stemming from a realization that historicism exercises a psychological restraint on action and hence on culture, Nietzsche upholds action, a higher integration between contemplation and doing.

A315. Wright, Willard H., ed. **The philosophy of Nietzsche.** N.Y., 1937. Includes the major works, but is not generally considered a good translation.

A316. Kluback, William. **Wilhelm Dilthey's philosophy of history.** N.Y., 1956. Brief analytical survey.

A317. Hodges, Herbert A. **Wilhelm Dilthey: an introduction.** London and N.Y., 1944. The standard introduction to Dilthey's thought, with an appendix of translated passages.

A318. Kroeber, Alfred L. **Configurations of culture growth.** Berkeley, 1944. An enterprise of exceptional interest, scope, and value; an attempt to establish by the verifiable data of history (not by theorizing) the patterns and peaks of all known civilizations. [GB]

A319. Lovejoy, Arthur O. "Present standpoints and past history." **The journal of philosophy,** 36 (Aug. 1939): 477–89. Appraisal of the influence of historical presents in grounding knowledge of historical pasts.

A320. Randall, John H., Jr. "On understanding the history of philosophy." **The journal of philosophy,** 36 (Aug. 1939): 460–74. A reasoned, fully developed statement illustrating the view of history as dealing with consequences of events whether in a "past present" or a contemporary "living present."

A321. Aron, Raymond. "The philosophy of history." Marvin Farber, ed., **Philosophic thought in France and the United States** (Buffalo, 1950), pp. 301–20. Survey of the issues in the whole field, concluding with the admonition that "the moment has come for the philosophy of history to free itself from the historical absolutism instilled into it by the Marxist tradition."

A322. White, Morton G. "Toward an analytic philosophy of history." **Philosophic thought in France and the United States,** pp. 705–25. Far-ranging discussion of the problems involved in attempts to define the meanings of history and its methods.

A323. Toynbee, Arnold J. **A study of history.** 10 v. N.Y. and London, 1934–54. Unquestionably the most extended, important, and controversial restatement of the idealist position in modern times. The writing of this monumental work was inspired by the urge to span the conceptual gap between the view of the "archivists" and the view of those who try to see history as a whole, as the unified life of man. It was also inspired by a conviction that the present age is a revolutionary one. Religion, though not necessarily the Judaic-Christian, is central to the author's theme.

A324. ——. **A study of history.** Abridgement by D. C. Somervell. 2 v. N.Y. and London, 1947–57.

A325. Sorokin, Pitirim A. "Arnold J. Toynbee's philosophy of history." **Journal of modern history,** 12 (Sep. 1940): 374–87.

A326. Crossman, Richard H. S. "The mystic world of Arnold Toynbee." **New republic,** 117 (July 14, 1947): 24–26.

A327. Ashley Montagu, Montague F., ed. **Toynbee and history: critical essays and**

reviews. Boston, 1956. A group of critically important essays, including ones by Pieter Geyl, G. J. Renier, Sir Ernest Barker, Geoffrey Barraclough, W. H. Walsh, Walter Kaufmann, and comment by Toynbee.

A328. Padover, Saul K. "Kautsky and the materialist interpretation of history." James L. Cate and Eugene N. Anderson, eds., **Medieval and historiographical essays in honor of James Westfall Thompson** (Chicago, 1938), pp. 439–64. Cogent analysis with suggestive comments on the development of dialectical materialism.

A329. Hook, Sidney. **From Hegel to Marx: studies in the intellectual development of Karl Marx.** N.Y., 1936. Full and clear treatment of this highly significant transition in intellectual history.

A330. Warth, Robert D. "Leon Trotsky, writer and historian." **Journal of modern history,** 20 (Mar. 1948): 27–41.

A331. Sabine, George H. **Marxism.** Ithaca, 1958. Series of lectures by a political philosopher, treating the Marxist philosophy in human rather than abstract terms.

A332. Bober, Mandell M. **Karl Marx's interpretation of history.** 2nd rev. ed., Cambridge, Mass., 1948. The standard treatment in English.

A333. Mathews, Shailer. **The spiritual interpretation of history.** Cambridge, Mass., 1916. A wise and tolerant statement of the influence of "spiritual forces" in historical development.

A334. Kennick, William E. "The language of religion." **The philosophical review,** 65 (Jan. 1956): 56–71. Since most discussions of the spiritual interpretation are intimately related to one or all of the major world religions, philosophical analysis of the language of religion becomes an essential part of the historian's equipment. This study is a rare example in a virtually barren field.

A335. Milburn, Robert L. P. **Early Christian interpretations of history.** London and N.Y., 1954. A basic discussion.

A336. McLaughlin, Robert W. **The spiritual element in history.** N.Y. and Cincinnati, 1926. An essentially Christian interpretation of history.

A337. Rosenstock-Huessy, Eugen F. M. **The Christian future: or, the modern mind outrun.** N.Y., 1946. Arresting statement by a historical scholar.

A338. Löwith, Karl. **Meaning in history: the theological implications of the philosophy of history.** Chicago, 1949. Among a series of discussions on various leaders in the development of historical thought are two suggestive essays, "Progress versus Providence" and "The Biblical view of history."

A339. Cassirer, Ernst. **An essay on man.** N.Y., 1953. Contends that history together with art and poetry "is an organon of our self-knowledge, an indispensable instrument for building up our human universe."

A340. Kuhn, Helmut. "Ernst Cassirer's philosophy of culture." **The philosophy of Ernst Cassirer** (Evanston, Ill., 1949), pp. 547–74. [Paul A. Schilpp, 6.] Cassirer's influence has been widespread, and this discussion contains pertinent comments for historians.

A341. Randall, John H., Jr., "Cassirer's theory of history as illustrated in his treatment of Renaissance thought." **The philosophy of Ernst Cassirer,** pp. 691–728.

A342. Cassirer, Ernst. **The philosophy of the Enlightenment.** Tr. by Fritz C. A. Koelln and James P. Pettegrove. 2nd ed., Boston, 1955. Highly important contributions on the development of history, its relations to romanticism, and its internal intellectual development.

A343. Geyl, Pieter. **Use and abuse of history.** New Haven, 1955. A distinguished Dutch historian points to the partisan abuses of history and cites the historically oriented perspective as one of its uses.

A344. Barraclough, Geoffrey. **History in a changing world.** Norman, Okla., 1956. Provocative discussion of the factors that have altered the intellectual attitudes of a leading British historian. Especially important for evaluations of the influence of World War II, the concept of western Europe, and the analysis of the doctrine of historical continuity.

A345. Collingwood, Robin G. **The idea of history.** Oxford, 1946. Influential philosophy of history. The author, a philosophical idealist, denies assertions of the scientific schools of history and holds with Hegel that "there is no history except the history of human life . . . as rational life, the life of thinking beings." One of the best introductions to the problems involved in the changing concepts of history is to be found in the handling of critical problems, pp. 205–334.

A346. Strauss, Leo. "On Collingwood's philosophy of history." **The review of metaphysics,** 5 (June 1952): 559–86. A sharply critical view of Collingwood's assumptions and their consequences.

A347. Harris, R. W. "Collingwood's idea of history." **History,** n.s. 37 (Feb. 1952): 1–7. Sympathetic account which suggests the appeal of Collingwood's metaphysics.

A348. Collingwood, Robin G. **The historical imagination: an inaugural lecture.** Oxford, 1935. While valuable for itself, this essay is essential for an understanding of the author's intellectual development.

A349. Kahler, Erich von. **Man, the measure: a new approach to history.** N.Y., 1943. Stimulating discussion adding new dimensions to the humanist tradition.

A350. Butterfield, Herbert. **Man on his past: the study of the history of historical scholarship.** Cambridge, Eng., 1955. Excellent account by a noted English scholar, with particular emphasis on beginnings of the German historical school. Leopold von Ranke and Lord Acton are accorded special attention.

A351. ——. **History and human relations.** London, 1951.

A352. Lovejoy, Arthur O. **The great chain of being.** Cambridge, Mass., 1936. Contains some suggestive chapters on the "chain of being" in modern European thought. [PG]

A353. ——. **Essays in the history of ideas.** Baltimore, 1948. Stimulating collection of Lovejoy's most significant essays. [PG]

A354. Joad, Cyril E. M. **Guide to philosophy.** N.Y., 1936.

A355. ——. **A guide to modern thought.** N.Y., 1933.

A356. Whittaker, Thomas. **Reason: a philosophical essay with historical illustrations (Comte and Mill, Schopenhauer, Vico, Spinoza).** Cambridge, Eng., 1934.

A357. Mellone, Sydney H. **The dawn of modern thought: Descartes, Spinoza, Leibniz.** London, 1930. A popular introduction. [WLD]

The Scope and Function of Historical Literature

A358. Lamprecht, Karl G. **What is history? Five lectures on the modern science of history.** N.Y. and London, 1905. Tr. by E. A. Andrews from *Moderne Geschichtswissenschaft* (Berlin, 1905). Expounds a theory of explanation which rests upon the demonstration within each period of a dominant quality of its inner life, but attributes that quality to processes of social evolution.

A359. Meinecke, Friedrich. **Die Entstehung des Historismus.** 2 v. Munich, 1936. One of the clearest presentations of the historicist's faith, by an outstanding exponent of historical idealism.

A360. ——. **Staat und Persönlichkeit.** Berlin, 1933. The historicist position exemplified in the connections between personality and the state.

A361. Anderson, Eugene N. "Meinecke's *Ideengeschichte* and the crisis in historical thinking." James L. Cate and Eugene N. Anderson, eds., **Medieval and historiographical essays in honor of James Westfall Thompson** (Chicago, 1938), pp. 361–96. Sympathetic appraisal of Meinecke and the German historians ideologically related to him.

A362. Engel-Jánosi, Friedrich. **The growth of German historicism.** Baltimore, 1944. Brief but helpful.

A363. Ashton, John. **Wilhelm Dilthey and his early critique of historical reason.** Chicago, 1951. Basic study of a leader in the development of historical theory.

A364. Troeltsch, Ernst D. **Der Historismus und seine Probleme.** Tübingen, 1922. In a class with Meinecke for fervent and clear analysis of this philosophical position; and, like him, Troeltsch centers historical interest on the problems of meaning and value.

A365. ——. **Christian thought, its history and application.** London, 1923. A basic exposition. Indicates the manner in which a relational standpoint develops into an idealistic position. Reveals some of the intellectual sources of Mannheim's faith.

A366. Mannheim, Karl. "Troeltsch, Ernst." **Encyclopaedia of the social sciences** (N.Y., 1935), v. 15, pp. 106–07. Significant, brief analysis in which the author, in expounding the philosophical position of a leading theorist, exemplifies his own.

A367. Heussi, Karl. **Die Krisis des Historismus.** Tübingen, 1932.

A368. Popper, Karl R. **The poverty of historicism.** London, 1957. A trenchant criticism of all hypotheses which suggest the possibility of prediction in history and assume "that this aim is attainable by discovering the 'rhythms' or the 'patterns,' the 'laws' or the 'trends' that underlie the evolution of history."

A369. White, Morton G. "The attack on the historical method." **The journal of philosophy**, 42 (June 1945): 314–31. Analysis of the historicist position.

A370. Croce, Benedetto. **History, its theory and practice.** Tr. by Douglas Ainslie. N.Y., 1921.

A371. ——. **History as the story of liberty.** Tr. by Sylvia Sprigge. N.Y., 1941. An elaboration of Croce's philosophy of history.

A372. Beard, Charles A. "That noble dream." **Am. hist. rev.**, 41 (Oct. 1935): 74–87. Pungent statement in development of the relativistic debate.

A373. Beard, Charles A., and Alfred Vagts. "Currents of thought in historiography." **Am. hist. rev.**, 42 (Apr. 1937): 460–83. An expository article; one of the vehicles by which relativism entered historical thought in America.

A374. Marks, Harry J. "Ground under our feet: Beard's relativism." **Journal of the history of ideas**, 14 (Oct. 1953): 628–33. A clear presentation of Beard's thesis.

A375. Mannheim, Karl. **Ideology and Utopia: an introduction to the sociology of knowledge.** Tr. by Louis Wirth and Edward Shils. N.Y., 1936. One of the most influential modern studies in this area. Although Mannheim did not consider himself a relativist, he directed concentrated attention to the issue of the possibility of historical knowledge, gave specific content to definitions of "ideology," and provided the concept of the "sociology of knowledge" with hypothetical precision.

A376. Hinshaw, Virgil G., Jr., "The epistemological relevance of Mannheim's sociology of knowledge." **The journal of philosophy,** 40 (Feb. 1943): 57–72. A cogent and critical exposition.

A377. Merton, Robert K. "The sociology of knowledge." Georges D. Gurvitch and Wilbert E. Moore, eds., **Twentieth century sociology** (N.Y., 1945), pp. 366–405. Able summary and critique of the entire field by a well-known social theorist.

A378. Mandelbaum, Maurice H. **The problem of historical knowledge: an answer to relativism.** N.Y., 1938. Most complete investigation of the relativist position. The first part treats Croce, Dilthey, and Mannheim, considered as relativists, paralleled by selected counter-relativists; the second part presents an analysis of historical knowledge and the philosophy of history.

A379. Oppenheim, Felix E. "In defense of relativism." **The western political quarterly,** 8 (Sep. 1955): 411–17. Spirited defense of the relativist position.

A380. Loewenberg, Bert J. "Some problems raised by historical relativism." **Journal of modern history,** 21 (Mar. 1949): 17–23. Penetrating and provocative. [GFH]

A381. Hook, Sidney. "A pragmatic critique of the historico-genetic method." **Essays in honor of John Dewey on the occasion of his seventieth birthday** (N.Y., 1929), pp. 156–74. Analysis of the "genetic fallacy" demonstrating that history cannot explain everything, particularly "origins."

A382. Becker, Carl L. **Everyman his own historian.** N.Y., 1935. Contains, among other provocative papers, the famous essay with this title, which is another important document in the development of the relativist argument.

A383. Zagorin, Perez. "Carl Becker on history: Professor Becker's two histories, a skeptical fallacy." **Am. hist. rev.,** 62 (Oct. 1956): 1–11.

A384. Gershoy, Leo. "Zagorin's interpretation of Becker: some observations." **Am. hist. rev.,** 62 (Oct. 1956): 12–17.

A385. Strout, Cushing. **The pragmatic revolt in American history: Carl Becker and Charles Beard.** New Haven, 1958. Examination of the theoretical position of Beard and Becker which concludes that the position espoused was not sufficiently grounded in philosophy.

A386. Nichols, Roy F. "Confusions in historical thinking." **Journal of social philosophy and jurisprudence,** 7 (July 1942): 334–43. Points to certain limitations in the historian's attitudes and equipment and stresses the need for greater conceptual breadth.

A387. Ware, Caroline F., ed. **The cultural approach to history.** N.Y., 1940. A revealing series of essays.

A388. Nowell, Charles E. "Has the past a place in history?" **Journal of modern history,** 24 (Dec. 1952): 331–40.

A389. Powicke, Sir Frederick M. **Modern historians and the study of history.** See *VA75.*

A390. Romein, Jan. "Theoretical history." **Journal of the history of ideas,** 9 (Jan. 1948): 53–64. A Dutch historian's interpretation of the meaning of the term and its implications.

A391. Mandelbaum, Maurice. "Concerning recent trends in the theory of historiography." **Journal of the history of ideas,** 16 (Oct. 1955): 506–17. Descriptive and analytical essay in which some form or variety of the relativist approach is ascribed to United States historians. Also contends that conclusions reached on the issues of historical knowledge depend upon the general theory of knowledge held by the analyst.

A392. Randall, John H., Jr. **Nature and historical experience: essays in naturalism and in the theory of history.** N.Y., 1958. Collection of previously published papers with additional materials, part of which deal with the evaluation of a theory of history.

A393. Aron, Raymond. **Introduction à la philosophie de l'histoire: essai sur les limites de l'objectivité historique.** Paris, 1938. A full-scale and probing effort to define what Dilthey called a "critique of historical reason."

A394. ———. **Essai sur la théorie de l'histoire dans l'Allemagne contemporaine: la philosophie critique de l'histoire.** Paris, 1938. Elaboration of the analysis presented in *A393.*

A395. Friedell, Egon. "Truth in history." **The living age,** 338 (Aug. 1930): 674–81. Critique of Ranke's methodology as understood by the author. Friedell insists that the historian's prime function is to endow the past with meaning.

A396. Droysen, Johann G. **Outline of the principles of history.** Boston, 1893. Tr. by E. B. Andrews from *Grundriss der Historik* (3rd ed., Leipzig, 1882). A publication of the famous historian's notes prepared for the use of his students. Significant for presentation of principles of interpretation which are critical both of determinism and pure objectivity.

A397. Santayana, George. "History." **Reason in science** (N.Y., 1906), ch. 2. [The life of reason, 5.] Clear statement of a philosophic mood.

A398. Strong, Edward W. "How is practice of history tied to theory?" **The journal of philosophy,** 46 (Sep. 1949): 637–44. This and the following are reflective articles rich in fruitful comments.

A399. ———. "Fact and understanding in

history." **Jour. of philos.**, 44 (Nov. 1947): 617–25.

A400. Rossi, Pietro. **Lo storicismo tedesco contemporaneo.** Turin, 1956. Able criticism of the continental idealists from the viewpoint of critical realism.

A401. Pierce, Donald J. **An introduction to the logic of the philosophy of history.** Toronto, 1939.

A402. Bloch, Marc L. **The historian's craft.** Tr. by Peter Putnam. N.Y., 1953. Examines the problem of the uses of history and the methods required to make history significant. Presents the view that human experience is a unified whole, that historical analysis is dynamic.

THE DOCTRINE AND PRACTICE OF HISTORIOGRAPHY

A403. Fitzsimons, Mathew A., Alfred G. Pundt, and Charles E. Nowell, eds. **The development of historiography.** Harrisburg, 1954. Collaborative summary of the whole development of historical writing. Encyclopedic; contains material not easily accessible in other works.

A404. Barnes, Harry E. **A history of historical writing.** Norman, 1937. Descriptive account from the origins of history to the *New history*.

A405. Toynbee, Arnold J. **Greek historical thought from Homer to the age of Heraclius.** London, 1924. The record of Greek criticising Greek, by a distinguished English classicist and historian.

A406. Bury, John B. **The ancient Greek historians.** N.Y., 1909. A companion to Toynbee which casts light on the problems of Greek thought.

A407. McKeon, Richard. "Plato and Aristotle as historians: a study of method in the history of ideas." **Ethics,** 51 (Oct. 1940): 66–101. Suggestive statement by a well-known philosopher devoted to classical studies.

A408. Shotwell, James T. **An introduction to the history of history.** N.Y., 1922. Helpful in understanding the issues involved in reconstructing the past, as illustrated by sources of ancient history.

A409. Frank Tenney. "Roman historiography before Caesar." **Am. hist. rev.,** 32 (Jan. 1927): 232–40. Presentation of fundamental data by an acknowledged expert.

A410. Thompson, James Westfall, and Bernard J. Holm. **A history of historical writing.** 2 v. N.Y., 1942. A compendium of historical writings. Especially valuable for estimates in the areas of Thompson's specialties in the Middle Ages; notable sections on Syrian, Armenian, and Persian historians.

A411. Cate, James L., and Eugene N. Anderson, eds. **Medieval and historiographical essays in honor of James Westfall**

Thompson. Chicago, 1938. Contains essays by former students of Professor Thompson on Meinecke, Möser, Kautsky, and Theodore Roosevelt.

A412. Sampson, Ronald V. **Progress in the Age of Reason: the seventeenth century to the present day.** Cambridge, Mass., 1956. Historical and critical development of philosophies of history treated under the following categories: theological or metaphysical monism, secular monism, sociological theories, relativistic theories.

A413. Stern, Fritz R., ed. **The varieties of history, from Voltaire to the present.** N.Y., 1956. Selections from United States and continental historians.

A414. Brailsford, Henry N. **Voltaire.** N.Y. and London, 1935. The author, seeking to establish Voltaire as an exponent of the doctrine of historical continuity, exemplifies it in the process.

A415. Zerffi, George G. "Voltaire in his relation to the study of general history, from a philosophical point of view." **Transactions of the Royal Historical Society,** 10 (1882), 344–70. Makes a case for Voltaire's pessimism and his lack of any theory of historical continuity.

A416. Neff, Emery E. **The poetry of history.** N.Y., 1947. A study of the great literary craftsmen of modern historical writing. Severely criticizes scientific history as conceived by the 19th century, and particularly Ranke, who is taken as its chief exponent.

A417. Black, John B. **The art of history: a study of four great historians of the eighteenth century.** London and N.Y., 1926. Significant treatment of Voltaire, Hume, Robertson, and Gibbon.

A418. Peardon, Thomas P. **The transition in English historical writing, 1760–1830.** N.Y. and London, 1933. Covers the era from Hume to Lingard and treats the development of rationalism, romanticism, and nationalism.

A419. Usher, Roland G. **A critical study of the historical method of Samuel Rawson Gardiner.** St. Louis, 1915. Searching examination of Gardiner's technique.

A420. Fueter, Eduard. **Geschichte der neueren Historiographie.** Munich and Berlin, 1911. French tr., by Émile Jeanmaire, *Histoire de l'historiographie moderne*, Paris, 1914. A detailed account beginning with the Renaissance and ending at 1870. Biographical notices of the major historians are fuller than the critical estimates of their works. The French translation really amounts to a second edition.

A421. Gooch, George P. **History and historians in the nineteenth century.** London and N.Y., 1913. Remains standard for the period covered; the best general account in English.

A422. Von Laue, Theodore H. **Leopold**

Ranke: the formative years. Princeton, 1950.

A423. Schmitt, Bernadotte E., ed. **Some historians of modern Europe.** Chicago, 1942.

A424. Ritter, Moriz. **Die Entwicklung der Geschichtswissenschaft.** Munich and Berlin, 1919.

A425. Guilland, Antoine. **Modern Germany and her historians.** London and N.Y., 1915. Informed and critical account by a Swiss scholar. Includes Niebuhr, Ranke, Mommsen, Sybel, and Treitschke.

A426. ———. "German historical publications, 1914–1920." **Am. hist. rev.**, 25 (July 1920): 640–59. Continues the discussion presented in *A425.*

A427. Acton, John E. E. D., baron. "German schools of history." **English historical review,** 1 (Jan. 1886): 7–42. Reprinted in his *Historical essays and studies* (London, 1907). Full survey enhanced by critical estimates.

A428. Below, Georg A. H. von. **Die deutsche Geschichtsschreibung von den Befreiungskriegen bis zu unsern Tagen.** 2nd rev. ed., Munich and Berlin, 1924. Begins with era since the French Revolution and presents, with sharp insight, the thesis that conservatism, particularly as developed by thinkers in the romatic era, should guide the historians.

A429. Kohn, Hans, ed. **German history: some new German views.** London and Boston, 1954. A compilation of essays not readily accessible elsewhere.

A430. Holborn, Hajo. "Greek and modern concepts of history." **Journal of the history of ideas,** 10 (Jan. 1949): 3–13. Brief but penetrating survey which makes suggestive comparisons.

A431. Engel-Jánosi, Friedrich. **Four studies in French romantic historical writing.** Baltimore, 1955. Deals with Chateaubriand, de Barante, Thierry, and de Tocqueville. [WLD]

A432. Geyl, Pieter. **Debates with historians.** Groningen and London, 1955.

A433. Mason, Mary G. **Western concepts of China and the Chinese, 1840–1876.** N.Y., 1939.

A434. Bodde, Derk. "Types of Chinese categorical thinking." **Journal of the American Oriental Society,** 59 (June 1939): 200–19. A rare type of analysis which might well serve as a model for similar treatments of other areas.

A435. Hummel, Arthur W. "What Chinese historians are doing in their own history." **Am. hist. rev.,** 34 (July 1929): 715–24.

A436. ———, ed. and tr. **The autobiography of a Chinese historian: being the preface [of Ku Chieh-kang] to a symposium on ancient Chinese history (Ku shih pien).** Leiden, 1931. Ku's preface and Hummel's introduction range over the whole field of Chinese

historiography and provide information and insights to be found nowhere else in western languages. The *Ku shih pien* [Symposium on ancient Chinese history] (2 v., Peiping, 1926–30) is a series of letters and comments on methodology and articles on early Chinese history by numerous scholars which reflect the thinking and scholarship of the new school of critical scholarship developing in China at the time. [EHP]

A437. Chin, Yü-fu. **Chung-kuo shih-hsüeh-shih. [A history of Chinese historiography.]** Shanghai, 1946. Best general history of Chinese historiography. Surveys works of the various periods, and generally discusses the official histories, private histories, and sources and historical methods. [EHP]

A438. Teng, S. Y. "Chinese historiography in the last fifty years." **Far eastern quarterly,** 8 (Feb. 1949): 131–56.

A439. Borton, Hugh. "A survey of Japanese historiography." **Am. hist. rev.,** 43 (Apr. 1938): 489–99. See *P107.*

A440. Butterfield, Herbert. **The Englishman and his history.** See *VA71.*

A441. Hovde, Brynjolf J. **The Scandinavian countries, 1720–1865.** See *VB66.*

A442. Westergaard, Waldemar. "Danish history and Danish historians." **Journal of modern history,** 24 (June 1952): 167–80.

A443. Gilbert, Felix. "German historiography during the Second World War." **Am. hist. rev.,** 53 (Oct. 1947): 50–58.

A444. Deleito y Peñuela, José. "Quelques données sur l'historiographie en Espagne de 1900 à 1930." **Revue de synthèse historique,** n.s. 24 (Dec. 1930): 29–49.

A445. Bourgin, Georges. "Histoire contemporaine d'Italie." **Revue historique,** 175 (Jan.-June, 1935): 316–97.

A446. Barbagallo, Corrado. "The conditions and tendencies of historical writing in Italy today." **Journal of modern history,** 1 (June 1929): 236–44.

A447. Fairbank, John K. "East Asian views of modern European history." **Am. hist. rev.,** 62 (Apr. 1957): 527–36. One of the few studies of this order available in English. [JWH]

A448. Vucinich, Wayne S. "Postwar Yugoslav historiography." **Journal of modern history,** 23 (Mar. 1951): 41–57.

A449. Mosely, Philip E. "The post-war historiography of modern Bulgaria." **Jour. mod. hist.,** 9 (Sep. 1937): 348–66. See *W945.*

A450. Rose, William J. "Polish historical writing." **Jour. mod. hist.,** 2 (Dec. 1930): 569–85.

A451. Odložilik, Otakar. "Modern Czechoslovak historiography." **The Slavonic and east European review,** 30 (June 1952): 376–92.

A452. Werstadt, Jaroslav. "The philosophy of Czech history." **The Slavonic review**

[The Slavonic and east European review], 3 (Mar. 1925): 533–46.

A453. Borsody, Stephen. "Modern Hungarian historiography." **The journal of modern history,** 24 (Dec. 1952): 398–405. See *W729.*

A454. Bauer, Raymond A. "The psychocultural approach to Soviet studies." **World politics,** 7 (1954): 119–32. Stimulating interpretation in a much culled field.

A455. Krieger, Leonard. "Marx and Engels as historians." **Journal of the history of ideas,** 14 (June 1953): 381–403.

A456. Mazour, Anatole G., and Herman E. Bateman. "Recent conflicts in Soviet historiography." **Journal of modern history,** 24 (Mar. 1952): 56–68.

A457. Carson, George B. "Changing perspective in Soviet historiography." **South Atlantic quarterly,** 47 (Apr. 1948): 186–95. Deals particularly with the 1930's.

A458. Tompkins, Stuart R. "Trends in Communist historical thought." **The Slavonic review,** 13 (Jan. 1935): 294–319. Emphasis on the earlier period.

A459. Mazour, Anatole G. "Modern Russian historiography." **Journal of modern history,** 9 (June 1937): 169–202.

A460. Kraus, Michael. **The writing of American history.** See *AB30.*

A461. Bellot, Hugh H. **American history and American historians.** See *AB32.*

A462. Carbonell, Diego. **Escuelas de historia en América.** See *Z218.*

A463. Gibson, Charles, and Benjamin Keen. "Trends of United States studies in Latin American history." **Am. hist. rev.,** 62 (July 1957): 855–77. See *Z220.*

A464. Behrens, C. B. A. "History and the universities." **The twentieth century,** 160 (Oct. 1956): 330–38.

A465. **Theory and practice in historical study: a report of the Committee on Historiography.** N.Y., 1946. [Social Science Research Council, Bulletin no. 54.] A probing analysis of the major issues of historiography undertaken by a group of historians with the assistance of colleagues in philosophy. Written largely from standpoint of objective relativism. Contains an excellent and exhaustive bibliography on historiography and the philosophy of history, as well as a set of propositions and a chapter on terminology in historical writing.

A466. **The social sciences in historical study: a report by the Committee on Historiography.** N.Y., 1954. [Social Science Research Council, Bulletin no. 64.] Second study, by a succeeding committee, emphasizing the social science approach to historical problems. Contains useful footnote citations.

A467. Gottschalk, Louis R. **The use of personal documents in history, anthropology, and sociology.** N.Y., 1945. [Social Science Research Council, Bulletin no. 53.]

TEACHING HISTORY
(Erling M. Hunt)

A468. Johnson, Henry. **Teaching of history in elementary and secondary schools, with applications to allied studies.** Rev. ed., N.Y., 1940. Outstanding in its analysis of aims, procedures, and resources in history teaching. Extensive bibliography includes European publications.

A469. Horn, Ernest. **Methods of instruction in the social studies.** N.Y., 1937. [Report of the Commission on the Social Studies of the American Historical Association, pt. 15.] Mature and systematic consideration of teaching methods and the learning process, with attention to the use of textbooks, collateral reading, visual aids, and firsthand experience in effective teaching of history and other social studies.

A470. Wesley, Edgar B., and Stanley P. Wronski. **Teaching social studies in high schools.** 4th ed., Boston, 1958. Comprehensive survey of professional thought and practice in the teaching of history and other social studies in the United States.

A471. Johnson, Henry. **An introduction to the history of the social sciences in schools.** N.Y., 1932. [Report of the Commission on the Social Studies of the American Historical Association, pt. 2.] Brief survey, chiefly of history teaching in Europe.

A472. Tryon, Rolla M. **The social sciences as school subjects.** N.Y., 1935. [Report of the Commission on the Social Studies of the American Historical Association, pt. 11.] Detailed but badly organized treatment of history and related subjects in United States schools.

A473. Committee on American History in Schools and Colleges. **American history in schools and colleges.** Directed by Edgar B. Wesley. N.Y., 1944. Values, status and nature of instruction, and recommendations.

A474. McGrath, Earl J., ed. **Social science in general education.** Dubuque, Ia., 1948. Incidental attention to history within the introductory social science courses in 21 U. S. colleges as of 1948.

A475. Perkins, Dexter. "We shall gladly teach." **Am. hist. rev.,** 62 (Jan. 1957): 291–309. Mature and thoughtful consideration of the role of historians as college teachers, of the relation of research to teaching and interpretation, and of the qualities of effective teaching.

A476. United Nations Educational, Scientific and Cultural Organization. **History, geography, and social studies: a summary of school programmes in fifty-three countries.** Rev. ed., Paris, 1953. Notes, in chart form, the titles of history, geography, and civics courses taught in successive grades of elementary and secondary schools.

A477. Great Britain. Ministry of Education. **Teaching history.** London, 1952. Changing purposes of school instruction; emphases, teaching procedures, and resources; and a note on teacher preparation.

A478. Incorporated Association of Assistant Masters in Secondary Schools. **The teaching of history.** Cambridge, Eng., 1950. A manual reflecting changing thought and practice since 1925.

A479. Josserand, L., ed. **L'enseignement de l'histoire.** Paris, 1951. Essays on the aims and methods of history teaching in schools. Lists resources for keeping abreast of changing scholarship.

A480. Weniger, Erich. **Die Grundlagen des Geschichtsunterrichts.** Leipzig, 1926. Development of history teaching in Germany prior to Hitler's regime; its purposes and problems; responsibilities and qualifications of teachers.

A481. ——. **Neue Wege im Geschichtsunterricht.** Frankfurt-am-Main, 1949. Proposed adjustments following World War II.

A482. Zinoviev, M. A. **Soviet methods of teaching history.** Tr. by A. Musin-Pushkin. Ann Arbor, 1952. Concerned with history teaching in secondary schools. Procedures and teacher preparation, both directed toward Communist indoctrination.

A483. Beard, Charles A. **The nature of the social sciences in relation to objectives of instruction.** N.Y., 1934. [Report of the Commission on the Social Studies of the American Historical Association, pt. 7.] Potentialities of history and some related social sciences for school instruction.

A484. Stern, Fritz R., ed. **The varieties of history, from Voltaire to the present.** See *A413*.

A484a. The Service Center [of the American Historical Association] for Teachers of History publishes useful pamphlets on major historical topics. Washington, 1957 ff.

Journals

A485. The social studies. Philadelphia, 1909 ff. (8 issues per year. Title varies.)

A486. Social education. Washington, 1937 ff. (8 issues per year.)

A487. American heritage. N.Y., 1949 ff. (Bimonthly.)

A488. History. London, 1912 ff. (Quarterly.)

A489. History today. London, 1951 ff. (Monthly.)

A490. L'information historique. Paris, 1938 ff. (5 issues per year.) For history teachers.

A491. Geschichte in Wissenschaft und Unterricht: Zeitschrift des Verbandes der Geschichtslehrer Deutschlands. Stuttgart, 1950 ff. (Monthly.)

A492. Internationales Jahrbuch für Geschichtsunterricht. Brunswick, 1951 ff. (Annual.) Programs and textbooks in many nations, with reciprocal evaluations by teachers and professors.

SECTION B

General Reference Resources

CONSTANCE M. WINCHELL and SHEPARD B. CLOUGH

This section lists international and general reference sources basic to all types of historical research. Materials concerned with special periods or particular countries are treated in the appropriate sections of this *Guide*.

Additional titles and more detailed annotations may be found in:

GUIDES

B1. Winchell, Constance M. **Guide to reference books.** 7th ed., Chicago, 1951. Supplement, 1950–52, Chicago, 1954. Second supplement, 1953–55, Chicago, 1956. A general guide to basic reference books in all fields and in various languages, with emphasis on English language materials.

B2. Malclès, Louise-N. **Les sources du travail bibliographique.** Geneva and Lille, 1950 ff. A French counterpart to *B1*, particularly strong in materials in the romance languages and for other European countries.

BIBLIOGRAPHIES OF BIBLIOGRAPHIES

B3. Besterman, Theodore. **A world bibliography of bibliographies and of bibliographical catalogues, calendars, abstracts, digests, indexes, and the like.** 3rd and final ed., rev. and enl., 4 v., Geneva, 1955–56. International bibliography of some 80,000 separately published bibliographies of books, manuscripts, and patents. Classified with alphabetical index.

B4. Totok, Wilhelm, and Rolf Weitzel. **Handbuch der bibliographischen Nachschlagewerke.** Frankfurt-am-Main, 1954. A selective bibliography of bibliographies designed primarily for student use. Emphasis on European and United States works. Latin America, Africa, and Australia are not included.

B5. Bibliographic index: a cumulative bibliography of bibliographies. N.Y., 1938 ff. An alphabetical subject index of bibliographies, both separately published and those included in books and periodicals. Although devoted primarily to the United States, there is selective coverage of non-English language materials. Published quarterly with annual and four-year cumulations.

LIBRARY CATALOGS

Printed catalogs of the world's large libraries are very important as universal bibliographies in that they contain books of all periods and in many languages. Among the most useful are:

B6. A catalog of books represented by Library of Congress printed cards issued to July 31, 1942. 167 v. Ann Arbor, Mich., 1942–46. **Supplement: cards issued August 1, 1942–December 31, 1947.** 42 v. Ann Arbor, 1948. The Library of Congress, **Author catalog: a cumulative list of works represented by Library of Congress printed cards.** 24 v. Ann Arbor, 1953. Continued by monthly, quarterly, and annual cumulations. Since 1956 entitled **The national union catalog.** Of primary importance. Authors and main entries only.

B7. Library of Congress catalog: a cumulative list of works represented by Library of Congress printed cards. Books: subjects, 1950–54. 20 v. Ann Arbor, 1955. Continued by quarterly and annual supplements.

22

B8. British Museum. **Catalogue of printed books.** 95 v. London, 1881–1900. Supplement, 1900–05. 15 v. London, 1900–05. Reprint, 68 v., Ann Arbor, 1946–1950. **General catalogue of printed books.** London, 1931 ff. (In progress.) This 19th century catalog of one of the world's largest libraries has long been indispensable. A new edition, published 1931–56, covers the letters "A-Dez." Publication of this series is now to be discontinued in favor of a photographic reprint of the official catalog of the British Museum, to start with the letter "G," continue in rapid succession through the alphabet, and then to return to the letter "A." The schedule calls for completion of this publication in six years; and while it will not have the careful editing of the earlier work, it will be up to date.

B9. ——. **Subject index of the modern works added to the library of the British Museum in the years 1881–1900.** Ed. by G. K. Fortescue. 3 v. London, 1902–03. Supplements, 1901–45. V. 1–11, London, 1906–53. (In progress.) Subject index is to modern works only.

B10. Paris. Bibliothèque Nationale. **Catalogue général des livres imprimés de la Bibliothèque Nationale: auteurs.** Paris, 1897 ff. This great catalog, started in 1897 and still incomplete, covered in 1955 to "Tendil." Personal authors only. Each volume includes titles acquired up to date of publication.

MICROFILMS

Many materials needed for research are now being reproduced photographically. Lists of such reproductions are becoming increasingly useful to the scholar. Catalogs of special projects dealing with particular countries or subjects will be found in the appropriate sections. A few of the more general lists are:

B11. Philadelphia Bibliographical Center and Union Library Catalogue. **Union list of microfilms.** Rev., enl., and cumulated ed., Ann Arbor, 1951. Supplement, 1949–52. Ann Arbor, 1953. A union list of microfilms held by more than 200 cooperating United States libraries. Indicates location of negative and positive copies. Basic volume includes newspapers, but supplement omits them as they are included in *B12.*

B12. U. S. Library of Congress. **Newspapers on microfilm.** 2nd ed., comp. under the direction of George A. Schwegmann, Jr., Washington, 1953. Records holdings in United States libraries of foreign and domestic newspapers. All other serials are listed in *B11.*

B13. ——. **British manuscripts project: a checklist of the microfilms prepared in England and Wales for the American Council of Learned Societies, 1941–1945.** Comp. by Lester K. Born. Washington, 1955. Lists microfilms of materials from medieval times to the 18th century, giving contents of the 2,652 reels included in the project.

NATIONAL BIBLIOGRAPHIES

Most countries with a long publishing history have produced bibliographies of works published within the country. These usually consist of a retrospective bibliography from the beginning of printing to the time of publication. In this section are listed national bibliographies of the United States, Great Britain, France, and Germany. Others may be found in appropriate sections. Comprehensive lists are contained in *B1, B2,* and the following:

B14. U. S. Library of Congress. **Current national bibliographies.** Comp. by Helen F. Conover. Washington, 1955. Lists the current national bibliographies of some 65 countries, and also notes periodical indexes, government publications, and directories of periodicals and newspapers.

B15. Pinto, Olga. **Le bibliografie nazionali.** 2nd ed., rev. and enl., Florence, 1951. [Biblioteca di bibliografia italiana, 20.] Lists the national bibliographies of more than 70 countries. Annotated.

B16. **Bibliographical services throughout the world.** Prepared in accordance with the recommendation of the International Advisory Committee on Bibliography. Paris, 1951 ff. (Annual.) These annual reports describe the bibliographical services of the various countries of the world, including national bibliographies, official publication lists, union catalogs, etc.

United States

B17. Evans, Charles. **American bibliography: a chronological dictionary of all books, pamphlets and periodical publications printed in the United States of America from the genesis of printing in 1639 down to and including the year 1820; with bibliographical and biographical notes.** 13 v. Chicago, 1903–55. Arranged chronologically, full bibliographical information with indexes of authors, publishers, and subjects in each volume. Final date changed to 1800. A projected 14th volume would include additions and a master index to all volumes.

B18. Shaw, Ralph R., and Richard H. Shoemaker. **American bibliography: a preliminary checklist.** 1801 ff. N.Y., 1958 ff. A preliminary attempt to fill the gap between Evans and Roorbach.

B19. Sabin, Joseph. **A dictionary of books relating to America, from its discovery to the present time.** 29 v. N.Y., 1868–1936. Arranged alphabetically; covers to mid-19th century. Both this and *B17* indicate location of copies.

B20. Roorbach, Orville A. **Bibliotheca americana, 1820–1861.** 4 v. N.Y., 1852–61. This and *B21* are booksellers' catalogs with very brief information.

B21. Kelly, James. **The American catalogue of books published in the United States from Jan., 1861 to Jan., 1871.** 2 v. N.Y., 1866–71. Reprint, 1938.

B22. **The American catalogue of books, 1876–1910.** 9 v. in 13. N.Y., 1876–1910. National bibliography, each volume covering a span of years. Arranged alphabetically by author and title with separate subject volumes. After 1900 authors, titles, and subjects are in one alphabet.

B23. **The United States catalog.** N.Y., 1900–28. See comment under *B24*.

B24. **The cumulative book index.** N.Y., 1898 ff. Comprehensive record of United States publications and, since 1928, of books published in the English language in other parts of the world. The quinquennial, biennial, semi-annual, and monthly cumulations supplement the four editions of *B23*. Authors, titles, and subjects in one alphabet.

B25. **The publishers' weekly: the American book trade journal.** N.Y., 1872 ff. Includes weekly lists of new publications.

B26. **The publishers' trade list annual.** 1873 ff. N.Y., 1873 ff. (Annual.) Publishers' catalogs arranged alphabetically.

B27. **Books in print: an author-title-series index to "The publishers' trade list annual."** 1948 ff. N.Y., 1948 ff. (Annual.) Serves as index with separate author and title indexes.

B28. Church, Elihu D. **A catalogue of books relating to the discovery and early history of North and South America, forming a part of the library of E. D. Church.** Comp. and annotated by George W. Cole. 5 v. N.Y., 1907. Reprint, 1951. Catalog of a rich private library, arranged chronologically with author and title index. Contains facsimiles of title pages, etc.

Great Britain

B29. Pollard, Alfred W., and Gilbert R. Redgrave. **A short-title catalogue of books printed in England, Scotland, and Ireland, and of English books printed abroad, 1475–1640.** London, 1926. Frequently cited as *S. T. C.* Alphabetically arranged. An indispensable record of early printed books with a few locations, primarily in British libraries.

B30. Bishop, William W. **A checklist of American copies of "Short-title catalogue" books.** 2nd ed., Ann Arbor, 1950. By *S. T. C.* code number, indicates locations of copies in United States libraries.

B31. Morrison, Paul G. **Index of printers, publishers and booksellers in A. W. Pollard and G. R. Redgrave, "A short-title cata-**

logue." Charlottesville, 1950. Provides indexes to *B29*.

B32. Wing, Donald G. **Short-title catalogue of books printed in England, Scotland, Ireland, Wales, and British America, and of English books printed in other countries, 1641–1700.** 3 v. N.Y., 1945–51. Brings the record started in *B29* down to 1700. Locates copies in United States and British libraries.

B33. Morrison, Paul G. **Index of printers, publishers and booksellers in Donald Wing's "Short-title catalogue.'** Charlottesville, 1955. Provides indexes to *B32*.

B34. **The English catalogue of books . . . issued . . . in Great Britain and Ireland.** 1801 ff. London, 1864 ff. (Irregular.) Current lists of books published in the United Kingdom, superseding the annual volumes of *B35*.

B35. **The English catalogue of books . . . issued in the United Kingdom, being a continuation of the "London" and "British" catalogues.** 1835 ff. London, 1837 ff. (Annual.)

B36. **The publishers' circular and booksellers' record.** London, 1837 ff. A weekly which includes new lists of current publications.

B37. **The British national bibliography.** 1950 ff. London, 1950 ff. A comparatively new national bibliography. Appears weekly, with periodic cumulations and annual volumes. Dewey Decimal classification with author indexes.

B38. **The British national bibliography: cumulated index, 1950–1954.** Ed. under the direction of A. J. Wells. London, 1955. Cumulated index to *B37*.

France

B39. Brunet, Jacques C. **Manuel du libraire et de l'amateur de livres.** 5th ed., 9 v., Paris, 1860–90. (V. 9, *Dictionnaire de géographie ancienne et moderne*, by P. Deschamps.) This bibliography of rare, important, or noteworthy books is especially strong in French materials and in works published before the 19th century. V. 9 is a very useful geographical dictionary of place names, giving their Latin or early forms.

B40. Grässe, Johann G. T. **Trésor de livres rares et précieux.** 7 v. Dresden, 1859–69. Covers much the same ground as *B39*, but is stronger in German titles.

B41. Quérard, Joseph M., ed. **La France littéraire, ou dictionnaire bibliographique des savants, historiens et gens de lettres de la France, ainsi que des littérateurs étrangers qui ont écrit en français, plus particulièrement pendant les XVIIIe et XIXe siècles.** 12 v. Paris, 1827–64. Arranged alphabetically by author, giving brief biographical and bibliographical information. Covers the 18th and early 19th century to about 1826.

B42. Quérard, Joseph M., and others, eds. **La littérature française contemporaine, 1827– 49; le tout accompagné de notes biographiques et littéraires.** 6 v. Paris, 1842–57. Continues *B41* to 1849.

B43. Lorenz, Otto, and others, eds. **Catalogue général de la librairie française, 1840– 1925.** V. 1–34. Paris, 1867–1945. Usually cited as *Lorenz*. The standard French list, published to cover periods ranging from three to 25 years. For each period there are author and subject volumes.

B44. **"Biblio": catalogue des ouvrages parus en langue française dans le monde entier.** Oct. 1933 ff. Paris, 1933 ff. (Monthly. Ten issues per year with annual cumulations.) The current trade bibliography. Dictionary arrangement.

B45. **Bibliographie de la France: journal général de l'imprimerie et de la librairie.** Paris, 1811 ff. The standard weekly list. Arrangement and parts issued vary. Annual indexes.

Germany

B46. Heinsius, Wilhelm, and others, eds. **Allgemeines Bücher-Lexikon.** 1700–1892. 19 v. Leipzig, 1812–94. With some overlapping this and *B47* cover German book production from 1700 to 1911.

B47. Kayser, Christian G., and others, eds. **Vollständiges Bücher-Lexikon.** 1750–1910. 36 v. Leipzig, 1834–1911.

B48. **Deutsches Bücherverzeichnis der Jahre 1911–40: eine Zusammenstellung der im deutschen Buchhandel erschienenen Bücher, Zeitschriften und Landkarten, mit einem Stich- und Schlagwortregister.** 22 v. Leipzig, 1915–43. Continues the record of *B47*, for the most part in five-year cumulations arranged by authors with subject indexes.

Since World War II the record of German national bibliography has been recorded both in East Germany (Leipzig) and West Germany (Frankfurt). Each claims to cover publications of both areas, but neither is complete, so that it is well to consult both. For complete record see *B14*. The more comprehensive of the current bibliographies are:

East Germany

B49. **Deutsches Bücherverzeichnis, 1941– 1950: Verzeichnis der Deutschland, Oesterreich, der Schweiz und im übrigen Ausland herausg. deutschsprachigen Verlagsschriften . . . sowie der wichtigsten Veröffentlichungen ausserhalb des Buchhandels.** Leipzig, 1952 ff. (In progress.) A continuation of *B48*, a cumulated record for the period 1941– 50. List by authors in four volumes, and subject index still in process.

B50. **Jahresverzeichnis des deutschen Schrifttums.** 1945/46 ff. Leipzig, 1948 ff. The annual continuation of *B49*, which is a cumulation of the record in *B51*.

B51. **Deutsche Nationalbibliographie.** Leipzig, 1931 ff. The current publication in two series: A, weekly classified list of books and pamphlets available from book dealers; B, semi-monthly, lists materials outside the book trade, e.g., theses, reprints, etc.

West Germany

B52. **Deutsche Bibliographie, 1945–50.** Frankfurt-am-Main, 1953 ff. (In progress.) The cumulated record for five years.

B53. **Bibliographie der deutschen Bibliothek.** Frankfurt-am-Main, 1951 ff. Continuation of *B52*. Cumulates the record in the weekly issues of *B54*.

B54. **Deutsche Bibliographie: wöchentliches Verzeichnis.** Frankfurt-am-Main, 1953 ff. (Weekly.) [Published 1947–52 as *Bibliographie der deutschen Bibliothek*.] Attempts to include a record of all books published in the German language in Germany and other countries.

HISTORICAL BIBLIOGRAPHIES

B55. **International bibliography of historical sciences.** Ed. for the International Committee of Historical Sciences. 1926 ff. [Paris], 1930 ff. (Annual.) A selected, classified list of historical publications (periodical articles as well as books) of various countries covering political, constitutional, religious, cultural, economic, and social aspects. Although later volumes have appeared, v. 15, to cover 1940–46, has not yet been published. Meanwhile it may be supplemented by *B56–57*.

B56. Palumbo, Pier F. **Bibliografia storica internazionale, 1940–1947: con una introduzione sullo stato degli studi storici durante e dopo la seconda guerra mondiale.** Rome, 1950. International in scope; lists books and periodical articles.

B57. Frewer, Louis B. **Bibliography of historical writings published in Great Britain and the empire, 1940–1945.** Oxford, 1947. Record of books and periodical articles.

B58. Franz, Günther, and others. **Bücherkunde zur Weltgeschichte, vom Untergang des römischen Weltreiches bis zur Gegenwart.** Munich, 1956. Selective bibliographies with brief annotations listing relatively recent historical literature on various countries.

B59. **Foreign affairs bibliography: a selected and annotated list of books on international relations. 1919–52.** 3 v. N.Y. and London, 1933–55. [Council on Foreign Relations.] Very useful bibliographies with critical annotations, based on bibliographies appearing quarterly in *Foreign affairs*, but revised and enlarged.

B60. **Historical abstracts, 1775–1945: a quarterly of abstracts of historical articles appearing currently in periodicals the world**

over. Ed. by Erich H. Boehm. March, 1955 ff. Vienna, 1955 ff. (Quarterly.) Abstracts of articles on political, diplomatic, economic, social, cultural, and intellectual history.

SOCIAL SCIENCE BIBLIOGRAPHIES

B61. Bibliographie der Staats- und Wirtschaftswissenschaften: internationale Monatshefte der Buch- und Zeitschriftenliteratur über Volk, Wirtschaft, Kultur und Politik. 1905–41. 37 v. Dresden and Berlin, 1906–41. (Monthly (irregular). Suspended publication.) Title varies: until 1936 was usually *Bibliographie der Sozialwissenschaften* with variant subtitles. A comprehensive, international bibliography; classified with annual author and subject indexes. Lists both book and periodical material in the social and political sciences.

B62. Bibliographie der Sozialwissenschaften: internationale Dokumentation der Buch- und Zeitschriftenliteratur des Gesamtgebiets der Sozialwissenschaften. Göttingen, 1950 ff. A somewhat abridged continuation of *B61*.

B63. A London bibliography of the social sciences. 4 v. London, 1931. Supplements, June 1929-May 1950, London, 1934–55. [London School of Economics and Political Science Studies: Bibliographies, 8.] Most extensive subject bibliography in the field. Basic set consists of three volumes arranged by subject and one-volume author index.

B64. Grandin, A. **Bibliographie générale des sciences juridiques, politiques, économiques et sociales de 1800 à 1925–1926.** 3 v. Paris, 1926. Supplements, v. 1–19, 1926–50, Paris, 1928–51. (In progress.) An important classified bibliography with indexes by authors and subjects. Lists books and dissertations published in French in France and other countries, particularly Belgium and Switzerland.

B65. Current sociology. La sociologie contemporaine. 1952 ff. Paris, 1952 ff. (Quarterly.) An international current bibliography published by UNESCO. Some issues are on specific subjects, giving current trends in important aspects of sociology.

B66. International bibliography of sociology. Bibliographie internationale de sociologie. 1952 ff. Paris, 1952 ff. (Annual.) Issued as numbers of *B65*. Lists books and articles from almost 500 periodicals of many countries.

B67. International political science abstracts. Documentation politique internationale. Paris and Oxford, 1951 ff. (Quarterly.) An international abstract journal sponsored by UNESCO.

B68. International bibliography of political science. Bibliographie internationale de

science politique. Paris, 1953 ff. (Annual.) This and *B69*, published by UNESCO, contain current records of books and periodical articles from many countries.

B69. International bibliography of economics. Bibliographie internationale de science économique. 1952 ff. Paris, 1955 ff. (Annual.)

PERIODICAL AND NEWSPAPER GUIDES

The finding of material in periodicals and newspapers is of primary importance in historical research; thus indexes become essential. Locating files of the journals wanted is also necessary, and from this need has evolved the union list which indicates the holdings of libraries. Below are listed the outstanding national union lists of periodicals and newspapers, and the general indexes to periodicals.

Periodical Lists

B70. Union list of serials in libraries of the United States and Canada. 2nd ed., ed. by Winifred Gregory, N.Y., 1943. Supplements, Jan. 1941-Dec. 1943, N.Y., 1945; Jan. 1944-Dec. 1949, N.Y., 1953. This monumental work lists alphabetically some 120,000 periodicals in many languages to be found in United States libraries, with indication of exact holdings. An indispensable aid to students.

B71. New serial titles: a union list of serials commencing publication after December 31, 1949. Washington, 1954 ff. [Joint Committee on the Union List of Serials.] (Monthly with annual cumulations.) Continues the record in *B70*. Lists holdings in so far as reported by libraries to the Committee.

B72. New serial titles: classed subject arrangement. Jan.-May, 1955 ff. Washington, 1955 ff. (Monthly, no cumulations.) Lists periodicals reported in *B71*, since 1955, by a subject arrangement.

B73. British union-catalogue of periodicals: a record of the periodicals of the world, from the 17th century to the present day, in British libraries. Ed. by James D. Stewart with Muriel E. Hannond and Erwin Saenger. V. 1–2. London and N.Y., 1955–56. (In progress.) The British counterpart of *B70*. To list more than 140,000 titles in some 440 libraries with indication of holdings. Arrangement varies from that used in *B70*, and thus gives a different approach to identifying titles.

B74. List of serial publications of foreign governments, 1815–1931. Ed. by Winifred Gregory for the American Council of Learned Societies, American Library Association, National Research Council. N.Y.,

1932. A union list indicating holdings in United States libraries.

B75. Ulrich's periodicals directory: a classified guide to a selected list of current periodicals, foreign and domestic. 8th ed., ed. by Eileen C. Graves and Carolyn F. Ulrich, N.Y., 1956. A selected, classified bibliography of current periodicals in various languages. Indicates the index in which a specific periodical is indexed. Published triennially.

Periodical Indexes

B76. Bibliographie der fremdsprachigen Zeitschriftenliteratur. Répertoire bibliographique international des revues. International index to periodicals. 1911–20, 1925 ff. Leipzig, 1911 ff. [Internationale Bibliographie der Zeitschriftenliteratur, B.] Important, comprehensive series which indexes some 1,400 periodicals in the principal non-German European languages. Subject arrangement with author indexes.

B77. International index to periodicals. N.Y., 1907 ff. Title and coverage vary. Until 1955 indexed a selected list of periodicals in the humanities and science including, before World War II, a number of foreign titles. Beginning with v. 43 (1955), indexes about 175 English language periodicals in the social sciences and the humanities.

B78. Poole's index to periodical literature. 1802–81. Rev. ed., 2 v., Boston, 1893. Supplements, Jan. 1882-Jan. 1, 1907, 5 v., Boston, 1887–1908. A 19th century subject index to 470 United States and English periodicals.

B79. Nineteenth century readers' guide to periodical literature, 1890–1899, with supplementary indexing, 1900–1922. Ed. by Helen Grant Cushing and Adah V. Morris. 2 v. N.Y., 1944. An author, subject, and illustrator index to 51 English language periodicals. In some cases the indexing continues beyond 1899 to the point when the periodical was added to the list of one of the Wilson indexes.

B80. Readers' guide to periodical literature. 1900 ff. N.Y., 1905 ff. Basic index by author, subject, and title to the contents of a selected list of general periodicals. Semi-monthly and monthly issues cumulating at intervals into annual and three-year volumes.

B81. Annual magazine subject index: a subject index to a selected list of American and English periodical and society publications. 1907–49. 43 v. Boston, 1908–52. A subject index to periodicals not indexed in other periodical indexes; particularly strong in local history periodicals. No more published.

B82. The subject index to periodicals. 1915 ff. London, 1919 ff. (Annual.) Originally a classed list, but now a subject index. Since

1947 British periodicals only, although previously indexed United States and some foreign periodicals.

B83. Historical abstracts: a quarterly covering the world's periodical literature, 1775–1945. N.Y., 1955 ff. March issue contains index. See *B60*.

B84. Bibliographie der deutschen Zeitschriftenliteratur, mit Einschluss von Sammelwerken. 1896 ff. Leipzig, 1897 ff. [Internationale Bibliographie der Zeitschriftenliteratur, A.] (Semiannual.) Extensive index to German periodicals. A companion set to *B76*.

B85. Italy. Camera dei Deputati. Biblioteca. **Catalogo metodico degli scritti contenuti nelle pubblicazioni periodiche italiane e straniere.** 10 v. Rome, 1885–1935. Important Italian index to Italian and foreign periodicals, 1883–1930. Material covered is limited to biographical and critical information about persons.

Newspaper Lists

B86. Brigham, Clarence S. **History and bibliography of American newspapers, 1690–1820.** 2 v. Worcester, 1947. Arranged alphabetically by states and towns; lists more than 2,100 newspapers with indication of locations of files.

B87. American newspapers, 1821–1936: a union list of files available in the United States and Canada. Ed. by Winifred Gregory. N.Y., 1937. [Bibliographical Society of America.] Continues *B86* in period covered. Gives exact holdings.

B88. U. S. Library of Congress. **Check-list of foreign newspapers in the Library.** Comp. under direction of H. S. Parsons. Washington, 1929. As there is no union list of foreign newspapers in United States libraries for this period, this checklist of files in the Library of Congress is helpful.

B89. ———. **Postwar foreign newspapers: a union list.** Washington, 1953. Reports holdings in 76 United States libraries. Includes Russian, but not Latin American, newspapers.

BOOK REVIEWS

B90. Bibliographie der Rezensionen. 1900–43. 77 v. Leipzig, 1901–44. [Internationale Bibliographie der Zeitschriftenliteratur, C.] (Annual. Ceased publication.) A comprehensive index to book reviews in German periodicals and, for the years 1911–15 and 1925–43, those in other languages. Includes scholarly and specialized books, and covers many English and United States periodicals not indexed in *B91*.

B91. The book review digest. 1905 ff. N.Y., 1905 ff. (Monthly with annual cumulations.) Indexes and digests of selected book reviews from some 75 United States and

English periodicals, principally general in character.

DISSERTATIONS

Lists of doctoral dissertations are important to those wishing to find material on a given topic or discover subjects which have already been treated. Some of the few general lists in various countries may be found below. In addition to these, many universities issue lists or abstracts of their own dissertations, which are not included here.

B92. U. S. Library of Congress. **List of American doctoral dissertations.** 26 v. Washington, 1913–40. Lists the printed dissertations (1912–38) of some 45 universities. The most extensive bibliography of this period; ceased publication after appearance of *B93.*

B93. Doctoral dissertations accepted by American universities. 1933/34–1954/55. Comp. for the Association of Research Libraries. 22 v. N.Y., 1934–55. (Annual.) The most comprehensive list for this period, arranged by subject field with author index. No cumulations. Ceased publication, the listings to be taken over by and issued in the index volume of *B94.*

B94. Dissertation abstracts: a guide to dissertations and monographs available in microfilm. Ann Arbor, 1952 ff. Formerly *Microfilm abstracts* (Ann Arbor, 1938–51). Abstracts of dissertations of more than seventy universities which have been microfilmed by University Microfilms Service. Title and frequency have varied. Now monthly with annual author and subject indexes.

B95. List of doctoral dissertations in history now in progress at universities in the United States. Washington, 1909 ff. A useful list previously published annually. Now issued by the American Historical Association somewhat irregularly, but approximately every three years. Arranged by field of history with author indexes.

B96. Canadian Bibliographic Centre. **Canadian graduate theses in the humanities and social sciences, 1921–1946.** Ottawa, 1951. Cumulated list of Canadian dissertations, arranged by subject with an author index and English and French subject indexes.

B97. Index to theses accepted for higher degrees in the universities of Great Britain and Ireland. 1950/51 ff. Ed. by P. D. Record. London, 1954 ff. (Annual.) The first of its kind for dissertations completed in British universities.

B98. University of London. **Historical research for university degrees in the United Kingdom.** 1931/32 ff. London, 1933 ff. [Bulletin of the Institute of Historical Research. Theses supplements.] Annual list of dissertations in history.

B99. Maire, Albert. **Répertoire alphabétique des thèses de doctorat ès lettres des**

universités françaises, 1810–1900. Paris, 1903. This and *B100* contain lists of French dissertations.

B100. France. Ministère de l'Education Nationale. **Catalogue des thèses et écrits académiques.** 1884/85 ff. Paris [etc.], 1885 ff.

B101. Mundt, Hermann. **Bio-bibliographisches Verzeichnis von Universitäts- u. Hochschuldrucken (Dissertationen) vom Ausgang des 16. bis Ende des 19. Jahrhunderts.** Leipzig, 1934 ff. German dissertation lists, covering all dissertations published to the end of the 19th century.

B102. Klausmann, Rudolf. **Systematisches Verzeichnis der Abhandlungen welche in den Schulschriften sämtlicher an dem Programmtausche teilnehmenden Lehranstalten . . . erschienen sind.** 1876–1910. 5 v. Leipzig, 1889–1916. Includes dissertations of later 19th and early 20th centuries.

B103. Jahresverzeichnis der Deutschen Hochschulschriften. 1885 ff. Berlin and Leipzig, 1887. (Annual.) Comprehensive and well indexed.

B104. Madrid. Universidad. **Catálogo de las tesis doctorales manuscritas existentes en la Universidad de Madrid.** Madrid, 1952. A cumulated catalog of Spanish dissertations.

ENCYCLOPEDIAS

General encyclopedias in various languages are useful for beginning research on many topics, both for the information contained therein and for the bibliographies usually appended to articles. There are many foreign encyclopedias which are universal in content but especially strong in material relating to the country of publication. Of these, only a few are listed below. Others may be found in sections devoted to particular countries. United States encyclopedias for the most part use the "continuous revision policy," which means that with each annual printing some changes are made, but that the whole encyclopedia is not completely revised. A systematic survey is continually under way, and articles are revised or rewritten in an organized plan according to need. In some years more is done than in others.

B105. The encyclopedia americana. 30 v. N.Y. and Chicago, 1957. For many years a standard encyclopedia using the continuous revision policy. The 1957 edition is in a new format and shows considerable revision. Particularly strong in information about United States cities, institutions, biography, etc., and in its articles on scientific and technical subjects.

B106. Encyclopaedia britannica: a new survey of universal knowledge. 24 v. Chicago, 1957. The most famous encyclopedia in English. Established in England in 1768 and through the 11th edition (1911) published there. Main feature of the early editions, particularly the 9th and 11th, was the fundamental plan of including long monographic articles written by outstanding scholars. Many of these still have value for historical research. The detailed analytical indexes are essential for tracing particular items. With the 14th edition (1929), the publishing was transferred to the United States and the general plan changed to include short articles on small subjects, although some long articles are retained. This was the last numbered edition, as since that time the continuous revision policy has been used.

B107. Chambers's encyclopaedia. New ed., 15 v., London and N.Y., 1955. Completely new edition of a long established British work, published in 1950, revised 1955. Intended for the "educated layman," this is an authoritative encyclopedia written from the British point of view.

B108. Encyclopédie, ou dictionnaire raisonné des sciences, des arts et des métiers, par une société de gens de lettres. Ed. by Denis Diderot and Jean L. d'Alembert. 36 v. Lausanne and Bern, Switz., 1780–82. Famous 18th century encyclopedia, founded and written by scholars of the time. Still useful for students interested in this period.

B109. La grande encyclopédie: inventaire raisonné des sciences, des lettres et des arts. Ed. by André Berthelot, Hartwig Derenbourg, and others. 31 v. Paris, 1886–1902. The most important French encyclopedia. An excellent authority in many fields, strong in medieval and Renaissance subjects, and for the biography, literature, history, etc., of continental Europe.

B110. Larousse, Pierre A. **Grand dictionnaire universel du XIXe siècle.** 17 v. Paris, 1866–90. This and *B111–113* are parts of a series of encyclopedias by the same publisher, each different and each filling a special need. All combine features of encyclopedia and dictionary, and include numerous short articles on small subjects. Strong in biography, even of minor names, individual works of literature, and historical topics.

B111. Nouveau Larousse illustré: dictionnaire universel encyclopédique. Ed. by Claude Augé. 8 v. Paris, 1898–1907.

B112. Larousse du XXe siècle. Ed. by Paul Augé. 6 v. Paris, 1928–33. Supplement, Paris, 1953.

B113. Larousse mensuel illustré: revue encyclopédique universelle. Ed. by Claude Augé and Paul Augé. 1907 ff. Paris, 1907 ff.

B114. Zedler, Johann H. **Grosses vollständiges Universal-Lexikon aller Wissenschaften und Künste.** 64 v. Halle, Ger., 1732–50. One of the world's great encyclopedias, still valuable for biography, bibliography, and history of the 16th and 17th centuries.

B115. Allgemeine Encyclopädie der Wissenschaften und Künste in alphabetischer

Folge von genannten Schriftstellern. Ed. by Johann S. Ersch and Johann G. Gruber. 167 v. Leipzig, 1818–50. Usually cited as Ersch and Gruber. Incomplete, but an excellent example of its type.

B116. Der grosse Brockhaus. 16th rev. ed., 12 v., Wiesbaden, 1952–57. The most recent edition of a standard German encyclopedia characterized by numerous short articles on small subjects.

B117. Meyers Konversations-Lexikon. **Meyers Lexikon.** 8th rev. ed., Leipzig, 1936 ff. (In progress.) Another standard German encyclopedia characterized by short articles on small subjects. Earlier editions up to the 6th had longer articles still occasionally useful.

B118. Enciclopedia italiana di scienze, lettere ed arti. See *VE17*.

B119. Enciclopedia universal ilustrada europeo-americana. 70 v. in 72. Barcelona, 1907–30. Appendix, 10 v., 1930–33. Annual supplements (irregular), 1934 ff. Often cited as *Espasa*. Includes both long and short articles, bibliographies, good illustrations, maps, etc. Especially useful for Spanish and Spanish American subjects, biography, geography, etc. A dictionary feature is the inclusion of equivalents in French, Italian, English, German, Portuguese, Catalan, and Esperanto.

B120. Bol'shaia sovetskaia entsiklopediia. V. 1–44. Moscow, 1949–56. (In progress.) New edition of the Soviet encyclopedia, showing considerable revision. Earlier edition was published in 65 v., 1927–47.

B121. The Americana annual: an encyclopedia of current events. 1923 ff. N.Y., 1923 ff. The English language encyclopedias are usually kept up to date by annual surveys issued as supplements, which over a period of years furnish a valuable record of contemporary events. Some of the outstanding annuals of this kind are the above and *B122–123*, each of which is useful for the current history of the year covered, including survey articles, necrology lists, biographies of outstanding personalities, statistics, etc.

B122. Britannica book of the year. 1938 ff. Chicago and London, 1938 ff.

B123. New international year book: a compendium of the world's progress. 1907 ff. N.Y., 1908 ff.

B124. Appleton's annual cyclopaedia and register of important events. 1861–1902. 42 v. N.Y., 1862–1903. Very useful 19th century annual encyclopedia, giving in each volume a survey of events of the year covered.

SPECIAL ENCYCLOPEDIAS

B125. Dictionnaire des sciences économiques. 2 vols. Paris, 1956–58. Alphabetical by subject. Many short articles, a few with bibliography. Includes some biography.

B126. Diplomaticheskii slovar'. [Diplomatic dictionary.] 2 v. Moscow, 1948–50. Historical dictionary of diplomacy and international relations covering materials from the 16th century to May 1947. International in scope with emphasis on Russia.

B127. Dizionario di economia politica. Ed. by Claudio Napoleoni. Milan, 1956. Long, signed monographs with bibliographies on large subjects. No biography.

B128. Dizionario di politica. Ed. by the Partito Nazionale Fascista. 4 v. Rome, 1940. International in scope. Prepared under the Fascist party, but covering all periods.

B129. Enciclopedia di scienze politiche, economiche e sociali. Bologna, 1956 ff. A new encyclopedia with long, signed articles, including bibliographies; some biography. First volume covers "A-Ben."

B130. Encyclopaedia of the social sciences. Ed. by E. R. A. Seligman and Alvin Johnson. 15 v. N.Y., 1930–35. First comprehensive encyclopedia of the social sciences in English, still important although now out of date. International in scope, but fuller for the English-speaking world and western Europe than for other regions. Long, signed articles with bibliographies and considerable biography.

B131. Handwörterbuch der Sozialwissenschaften. Stuttgart, 1952 ff. (In progress.) Successor to Conrad's *Handwörterbuch der Staatswissenschaften* (4th ed., 8 v., 1923–29.) Most comprehensive German work in its field. Long articles, signed by specialists, with bibliographies. Publication of new edition is proceeding concurrently in different parts of the alphabet.

B132. Staatslexikon: im Auftrag der Görres-Gesellschaft. Ed. by Hermann Sacher. 5th ed., 5 v., Freiburg im Breslau, 1926–32. A standard German work written from the Catholic point of view.

YEARBOOKS

There are various types of yearbooks, such as those giving governmental, political or statistical information, almanacs of miscellaneous data, annual surveys of events, educational directories, etc.

B133. The statesman's year-book: statistical and historical annual of the states of the world. 1864 ff. London and N.Y., 1864 ff. A long-established, reliable manual of descriptive and statistical information about the governments of various countries.

B134. United Nations. Demographic yearbook. Annuaire démographique. 1948 ff. N.Y., 1949 ff. An international statistical yearbook.

B135. ———. Statistical yearbook. N.Y., 1948 ff. International in scope.

B136. Europa: the encyclopaedia of Europe; a survey of world economic and social conditions, a directory of international administration, and of European political, industrial, financial, cultural and scientific organisations. London, 1946 ff. (Loose-leaf.) This and *B137–138* are published by Europa Publications. Each gives descriptive surveys of the countries and governments included.

B137. Orbis: the encyclopaedia of extra-European countries; a survey and directory of political, industrial, financial, cultural and scientific organisations in the continents of Africa, America, Asia and Australasia. London, 1938 ff. (Loose-leaf.)

B138. The Middle East. 1948 ff. London, 1948 ff. (Loose-leaf.)

B139. Political handbook of the world: parliaments, parties and press. Jan. 1, 1927 ff. N.Y., 1927 ff. (Annual.) Gives chief governmental officials, party programs, and the names of newspapers with political affiliation, editor, etc.

B140. Almanach de Gotha: annuaire généalogique, diplomatique et statistique. 1763 ff. Gotha, Ger., 1763 ff. (Annual. Suspended publication in 1941.) A standard handbook, particularly useful because of its long span of publication. Each volume is in two sections: pt. 1, genealogies of the royal and princely houses of Europe; pt. 2, descriptive information about the various countries, with lists of principal executive, legislative, and diplomatic officials of each.

B141. The international year book and statesmen's who's who. 1953 ff. London, 1953 ff. Issued by the publishers of Burke's *Peerage*, this includes (1) international organizations and reigning royal families; (2) the states of the world, giving constitution and government, area and population, statistics of education, commerce, religion, etc.; (3) biographical sketches of some 8,000 world leaders.

Almanacs such as those listed below are very useful compilations of miscellaneous information and statistics. Older volumes are excellent sources of contemporary events.

B142. The world almanac and book of facts. 1868 ff. N.Y., 1868 ff. (Annual.) Probably the best known and most widely used in the United States.

B143. Information please almanac. 1947 ff. Supervised by Dan Golenpaul Associates. N.Y., 1947 ff. (Annual.) A newer work, good coverage.

B144. Whitaker, Joseph. An almanack. 1869 ff. London, 1868 ff. (Annual.) The standard British almanac.

B145. Almanach Hachette: petite encyclopédie populaire. 1894 ff. Paris, 1894 ff. (Annual.) Standard French almanac.

More detailed records of current events are given in such annuals as the following.

B146. The annual register of world events. London and N.Y., 1758 ff. (Title varies.) Reviews the year's happenings and includes obituaries.

B147. American yearbook: a record of events and progress. 1910–19, 1925–50. N.Y., 1929–51. (No more published.) Survey articles, signed by specialists, on politics and government, economics and business, social conditions, science, humanities, etc. Includes bibliography.

International directories of institutions of higher education, academies, learned societies, libraries, etc., are frequently needed. The following are the most generally useful. They may be supplemented by national and local directories.

B148. Minerva: Jahrbuch der gelehrten Welt. 1891/92–1913/14, 1920 ff. Strasbourg, 1891–1914; Berlin, 1920 ff. Somewhat irregularly published, but for many years the most comprehensive of these directories. In some years divided into sections, giving societies and other organizations in one part and universities in the other. The latest edition, 1952–56, covers universities and is issued in two parts, Europa and Aussereuropa. Includes names of faculty members and an index to names.

B149. Index generalis: general yearbook of universities and of higher educational institutions, academies, archives, libraries, scientific institutes, botanical and zoological gardens, museums, observatories, learned societies. . . . Paris, 1919 ff. French counterpart to *B148*. Suspended publication 1940–51. Title varies, and some volumes have subtitles in English, some in French. Includes names of faculties, officers, etc., with alphabetical index.

B150. The world of learning. 1947 ff. London, 1947 ff. (Annual.) Continues the section on institutions of learning formerly published in *Europa* and *Orbis*. Lists learned societies, museums, libraries, universities, etc., with names of officers and faculties. No name index.

B151. The yearbook of the universities of the Commonwealth. 1914 ff. London, 1914 ff. Title varies. Detailed information about British Commonwealth universities.

B152. Universities of the world outside U. S. A. Ed. by Merritt M. Chambers. Washington, 1950. Treats more than 2,000 institutions of higher education in some 70 countries. A companion volume to *American universities and colleges.*

CURRENT SURVEYS

There are several loose-leaf services which give extracts from newspapers and current digests of world news which are useful as contemporary surveys.

B153. Facts on file: a weekly world news digest with cumulative index. N.Y., 1941 ff. (Loose-leaf.)

B154. Keesing's contemporary archives: weekly diary of important world events with index continually kept up to date. July 1, 1931 ff. London, 1931 ff. (Loose-leaf.) Also issued in German, with some changes and altered emphasis, as *Archiv der Gegenwart.*

B155. Les archives internationales "Pharos." Paris, 1944 ff. (Loose-leaf.)

B156. Survey of international affairs. Ed. by Arnold J. Toynbee and others. 1920/23 ff. London, 1925 ff. This and *B157* are annual surveys of world politics and history published under the auspices of the Royal Institute of International Affairs. Some years include extra volumes on special subjects. From 1920/23 to 1927 contained appendices of documents which are continued from 1928 by *B157. Consolidated index, 1920–1930, and supplementary volumes,* published in 1932, indexes *B156* from 1920 to 1930 and *B157* from 1928 to 1930.

B157. Documents on international affairs. 1928 ff. London, 1929 ff. (Annual.) See comment under *B156*.

B158. Schulthess' europäischer Geschichtskalender. 1861–1940. 81 v. Munich, 1861–1942. (Annual.) Annual survey of world history, arranged by country and then chronologically. No more published.

B159. L'année politique. 1874–1905. 1st series, ed. by André Daniel, 32 v., Paris, 1875–1906. (Annual.) This and *B160* give a chronological review of the principal political, diplomatic, economic, and social happenings of France and the Union Française.

B160. L'année politique. 1944/45 ff. 2nd series, ed. by André Siegfried, Édouard Bonnefous, and J. B. Duroselle, Paris, 1945 ff. (Annual.)

STATISTICAL SOURCES BIBLIOGRAPHIES

Statistical sources for individual countries will be found under country. The following are a few guides to statistics covering more than one country.

B161. U. S. Library of Congress. National censuses and vital statistics in Europe, 1918–1939: an annotated bibliography. Washington, 1948. Supplement, 1940–48. Washington, 1948. Very useful guide to the national censuses and official statistical publications of the various countries of Europe.

B162. ———. Statistical bulletins: an annotated bibliography of the general statistical bulletins of major political subdivisions of the world. Prepared by Phyllis G. Carter. Washington, 1954. Arranged by continent and then by country. Lists periodicals issued by an official agency more frequently than annually.

B163. ——. **Statistical yearbooks: an annotated bibliography of the general statistical yearbooks of major political subdivisions of the world.** Prepared by Phyllis G. Carter. Washington, 1953. Full bibliographical data, including dates of first and most recent issues, types of statistics covered, frequency, etc.

B164. ——. **General censuses and vital statistics in the Americas.** Prepared under the supervision of Irene B. Taeuber. Washington, 1943. An annotated bibliography of historical censuses and current vital statistics.

B165. U. S. Bureau of the Census. **Summaries of biostatistics: maps and charts, population, natality, and mortality statistics.** Prepared in cooperation with Office of the Coordinator of Inter-American Affairs. 17 v. Washington, 1944–45. Each volume covers a separate country: Argentina, Bolivia, Brazil, Colombia, Costa Rica, Cuba, Dominican Republic, Ecuador, El Salvador, Guatemala, Haiti, Nicaragua, Panama, Paraguay, Peru, Uruguay, Venezuela.

B166. Inter-American Statistical Institute. **Bibliography of selected statistical sources of the American nations. Bibliografía de fuentes estadísticas escogidas de las naciones Americanas.** Washington, 1945. A comprehensive guide giving detailed information about the statistical publications of the American nations, indicating censuses, yearbooks, current serials, etc.

BIOGRAPHICAL DICTIONARIES

Biographical dictionaries are useful in many kinds of research. In many countries there are two main types, the retrospective dictionary and the current record. The former is usually a scholarly work including sketches of persons no longer living, often with bibliographies of works by the person and of those about him. These may refer to manuscripts and source materials of great value to the history student. The current record is contained in various types of "Who's who" volumes, for the most part following an established pattern, giving very concise personal and career information. Biographical dictionaries of particular countries will be found under country. Here are listed indexes to collected biography and a few works of international scope, both general and current.

Indexes

B167. Arnim, Max. **Internationale Personalbibliographie, 1800–1943.** 2 v. Leipzig, 1944–52. Comprehensive index to personal bibliographies, often leading to biographical information, contained in books, periodicals, biographical dictionaries, Festschriften, etc. International, with emphasis on German.

B168. Biography index: a cumulative index to biographical material in books and magazines. N.Y., 1947 ff. (In progress.) Published quarterly, cumulating annually and triennially. Indexes biographical material appearing in books and periodicals in the English language during the period covered. Universal in scope. Includes indexes by trade or profession.

B169. Hyamson, Albert M. **A dictionary of universal biography of all ages and of all peoples.** 2nd ed., entirely rewritten, N.Y., 1951. Index to the names appearing in some 24 standard biographical dictionaries.

International Biographies

B170. Biographie universelle (Michaud) ancienne et moderne. New ed., rev. and enl., 45 v., Paris, 1854–65. Important universal biographical dictionary of the 19th century, with emphasis on the French. In most cases the articles are longer and more carefully edited than those in *B171.*

B171. Nouvelle biographie générale depuis les temps les plus reculés jusqu'à nos jours, avec les renseignements bibliographiques et l'indication des sources à consulter. Ed. by Jean C. F. Hoefer. 46 v. Paris, 1853–66. Covers much the same ground as *B170,* but includes more names, many of them minor, with shorter articles. When possible it is advisable to consult both.

B172. Jöcher, Christian Gottlieb. **Allgemeines Gelehrten-Lexicon.** 4 v. Leipzig, 1750–51. ——, **Fortsetzungen und Ergänzungen, A-Romuleus.** 7 v. Leipzig, 1784–1897.

B173. The new Century cyclopedia of names. Ed. by Clarence L. Barnhart and others. 3 v. N.Y., 1954. More than twice as large as the earlier *Century cyclopedia of names,* this edition contains entries for over 100,000 proper names, persons, places, characters, historical events, etc.

B174. Webster's biographical dictionary. Springfield, Mass., 1943. A useful one-volume work giving pronunciations and concise biographical sketches of more than 40,000 names.

B175. Oettinger, Eduard M. **Moniteur des dates: Biographisch-genealogisch-historisches Welt-Register enthaltend die Personal-Akten der Menschheit . . . von mehr als 100,000 geschichtlichen Persönlichkeiten aller Zeiten und Nationen von Erschaffung der Welt bis auf den heutigen Tag.** 9 v. Leipzig, 1869–82. Very comprehensive, including some names not easily found elsewhere. Sketches limited to three or four lines.

B176. Current biography: who's news and why. 1940 ff. N.Y., 1940 ff. (Monthly, except Aug., cumulating annually.) A current work with fairly long discursive sketches of an average of 400 biographies annually. Includes bibliographies.

B177. Who's who in America. The monthly supplement: a current biographical reference service. Dec. 1939 ff. Chicago, 1939 ff. (Monthly.) Supplement to *Who's who in America,* with cumulative indexes. International in scope, but covers primarily the United States. Ceased publication, 1959.

CHRONOLOGIES, TABLES

Handbooks of dates and historical tables are useful aids. A few of the more general and comprehensive are listed below.

B178. Keller, Helen R. The dictionary of dates. 2 v. N.Y., 1934. One of the most comprehensive lists, giving an outline of events from the earliest times to 1930. Arranged by country and then chronologically. No index. Pt. 1 is based on Joseph Haydn's *Dictionary of dates* (1911).

B179. Langer, William L., ed. An encyclopaedia of world history, ancient, medieval and modern, chronologically arranged. See *C7.*

B180. Putnam, George Palmer, and George Haven Putnam. **Dictionary of events: a handbook of universal history.** N.Y., 1936. This edition covers noteworthy events of history from the earliest times through 1935. In parallel columns.

B181. Delorme, Jean. **Chronologie des civilisations.** Paris, 1949. [Clio: Introduction aux études historiques.] Chronological tables from 3000 B.C. to A.D. 1945 with alphabetical index.

B182. Morison, M. **Time tables of modern history, A.D. 400–1870.** 2nd ed., Westminster, 1908. Parallel tables of the history of various countries, with genealogical tables, chronological lists of rulers, etc.

B183. Steinberg, Sigfrid H. **Historical tables, 58 B.C.–A.D. 1945.** With a foreword by G. P. Gooch. 3rd ed., London, 1949. Tabular chronology arranged in parallel columns by period. Includes scientific and cultural events as well as political and economic history.

B184. Mayer, Alfred. **Annals of European civilization, 1501–1900.** Foreword by G. P. Gooch. London, 1949. A chronological record of biographical and bibliographical information giving, year by year, the authors and titles of great books published, paintings, music, and other cultural events. Complements the outlines of political history.

B185. "Genealogical tables and lists." The **Cambridge modern history,** v. 13 (N.Y., 1911), pp. 1–205. Tables of rulers and royal houses, church rulers, elected officials, etc.

B186. Fry, Edward A. **Almanacks for students of English history.** London, 1915.

A useful arrangement of calendars showing every day upon which Easter can fall, old and new style calendars, etc.

B187. Harbottle, Thomas B. Dictionary of battles from the earliest date to the present time. N.Y. and London, 1904. Statistics of forces engaged, losses, etc.

B188. Bodart, Gaston. **Militär-historisches Kriegs-Lexikon (1618–1905).** Vienna, 1908. A dictionary of battles.

GEOGRAPHIES, GAZETTEERS, AND ATLASES

Geographical bibliographies, gazetteers, and atlases are essential for historical work. The Wright and Platt *Aids to geographical research* should be consulted for further information. Here are listed only a few of the most general titles.

Geographies

B189. Wright, John K., and Elizabeth T. Platt. Aids to geographical research: bibliographies, periodicals, atlases, gazetteers and other reference books. 2nd ed., compl. rev., N.Y., 1947. [American Geographical Society research series, 22.] An invaluable manual to research aids, including materials in many languages.

B190. Cox, Edward G. **A reference guide to the literature of travel, including voyages, geographical descriptions, adventures, shipwrecks and expeditions.** See *U2.*

B191. Engelmann, Wilhelm. **Bibliotheca geographica: Verzeichnis der Zeit der Mitte des vorigen Jahrhunderts biz zu Ende des Jahres 1856 in Deutschland erschienenen Werke über Geographie und Reisen, mit Einschluss der Landkarten, Pläne und Ansichten.** Leipzig, 1858. Arranged by geographical location with subject index.

Current Geographical Surveys

B192. Bibliographie géographique internationale. 1891 ff. Paris, 1894 ff. (Annual.) Probably the most important of the annual surveys. Classified with author index. Full, signed annotations.

B193. Bibliotheca geographica. 1891–1912. 19 v. Berlin, 1895–1917. Classified with author index. Lists more titles than *B192,* but without annotations. No more published.

B194. Geographisches Jahrbuch. 1866 ff. Gotha, 1866 ff. (Annual, irregular.) Comprehensive survey of published works in special geographical fields, the fields varying from year to year.

B195. Bibliographie cartographique internationale. 1936 ff. Paris, 1938 ff. (Annual, irregular.) Lists general, political, and topographical maps and atlases, road maps, maps of cities, etc.

Gazetteers

B196. Chambers's world gazetteer and geographical dictionary. Ed. by T. C. Collocott and J. O. Thorne. Edinburgh and London, 1954. Issued in the United States as *Macmillan world gazetteer and geographical dictionary* (1955). A small general gazetteer. Indicates pronunciation.

B197. The Columbia Lippincott gazetteer of the world. Ed. by Leon E. Seltzer with the geographical research staff of Columbia University Press and the cooperation of the American Geographical Society. N.Y., 1952. A successor to *Lippincott's new gazetteer* (1906). Lists some 130,000 geographical names, including both political subdivisions and geographic features, giving pronunciation, population, location, altitude, economic and cultural facts, etc. Of first importance. The older Lippincott is still useful for historical information.

B198. Vivien de Saint-Martin, Louis, and Louis Rousselet. **Nouveau dictionnaire de géographie universelle.** 7 v. Paris, 1879–95. An older work still of great importance for its detailed information. Contains longer articles than *B197*, and includes many minor European and Asiatic places as well as the names of tribes and races.

B199. Webster's geographical dictionary: a dictionary of names of places with geographical and historical information and pronunciations. Rev. ed., Springfield, Mass., 1955. Contains more than 40,000 geographical names, historical as well as current. Cross references for equivalent and alternative spellings of names that have been changed. Usual gazetteer information.

B200. Besnier, Maurice. **Lexique de géographie ancienne.** Paris, 1914. Very brief information about each place, but full references to the ancient writers in whose works the place is mentioned.

B201. Deschamps, Pierre C. E. **Dictionnaire de géographie ancienne et moderne.** Paris, 1870. Also issued as v. 9 of Brunet's *Manuel du libraire* (*B39*). Arranged alphabetically by the medieval name with index of modern names.

B202. Grässe, Johann G. T. **Orbis latinus: oder, Verzeichnis der wichtigsten lateinischen Orts- und Ländernamen.** Rev. ed. by Friedrich Benedict, Berlin and N.Y., 1909. Reprint, 1922. Very useful list of Latin names. Only first edition includes an index to modern names.

B203. Smith, Sir William. **A dictionary of Greek and Roman geography.** 2 v. London and Boston, 1873–78. An earlier work still useful for ancient geography.

Atlases

Large general atlases are essential for many types of historical research. Below are listed recent editions of some of the outstanding atlases published in various countries. In some historical work it is also necessary to use earlier atlases, as boundaries and political divisions change and new discoveries are recorded. Historical atlases are compiled especially to show the state of the world and of special areas at particular periods.

B204. Aguilar, José, Elisa García Aráez, and Antonio Villarroya. **Atlas universal Aguilar.** Madrid, 1954. This and *B205–211* are folio atlases, each universal in scope, with particular attention to maps dealing with the country in which the atlas was published. Most of them have political, economic, and physical maps with gazetteer indexes.

B205. Atlante internazionale della Consociazione Turistica Italiana. 5th ed., rev., Milan, 1957.

B206. Atlas international Larousse politique et économique. Ed. by Jean Chardonnet. Paris, 1950.

B207. Atlas mira. Ed. by A. N. Baranov and others. Moscow, 1954.

B208. Atlas Mira. **Ukazatel' geograficheskikh nazvaniĭ.** Moscow, 1954.

B209. Kremling, Ernst. **Grosser I R O Weltatlas: Jubiläumsausgabe; mit meist zehnfarbigen Landkartenseiten mit über 125,000 Namen, einem ausführlichen Länderlexikon, Bildern aus aller Welt, Flaggentafel und zwei Registern.** 10th ed., Munich, 1954.

B210. Rand McNally and Co. **Rand McNally commercial atlas.** N.Y., 1956. (Annual.)

B211. The Times atlas of the world. Midcentury ed., ed. by John Bartholomew, London, 1955 ff. (In progress.)

B212. Collier's world atlas and gazetteer: presenting the world in its geographical, physical and commercial aspects. N.Y., 1953. This and *B213–216* are slightly smaller but generally useful atlases including the same types of information as *B204–211*.

B213. Encyclopaedia Britannica. **Encyclopaedia Britannica world atlas: physical and political maps, geographical comparisons, a glossary of geographical terms, a gazetteer index, geographical summaries, world spheres of influence.** G. Donald Hudson, geographical ed., under direction of Walter Yust. Chicago, 1949.

B214. Goode, John P. **Goode's world atlas, physical, political and economic.** Ed. by Edward B. Espenshade, Jr. 9th ed., N.Y., 1953.

B215. Hammond's ambassador world atlas. Maplewood, N.J., 1954.

B216. Oxford University Press. **Oxford economic atlas of the world.** Prep. by the Economist Intelligence Unit and the Cartographic Department of the Clarendon Press. Oxford, 1954.

B217. Shepherd, William R. **Historical atlas.** 8th ed., Pikesville, Md., 1956. Long a basic atlas; out of print for many years. The 8th edition is an offset of the 7th revised and enlarged edition of 1929, with special supplement of nine pages of maps for the period since 1929. Maps are excellent and cover from ancient times to 1945. Standard in its field.

B218. Muir's atlas of ancient and classical history. 2nd ed., ed. by George Goodall and R. F. Treharne. London and N.Y., 1956. Another standard atlas. Published with varying titles, e.g., *Philip's historical atlas, Putnam's historical atlas.* In some cases both parts are published in one volume.

B219. Muir's historical atlas: medieval and modern. 8th ed., ed. by George Goodall and R. F. Treharne. London and N.Y., 1952. See comment under *B218.*

B220. Fox, Edward W. **Atlas of European history.** N.Y., 1957. A new atlas done on different principles. Most of the maps are physical rather than political, with a minimum of place names. Designed to be used with college textbooks.

GUIDEBOOKS

Guidebooks, both old and new, are frequently very helpful for historical and geographical information, for locations and descriptions of places and buildings, for help in identifying streets, churches or buildings which have changed name or ceased to exist, for maps and city plans at particular dates, etc. In some cases there are individual guides to particular places, but especially useful because of their scope and varied editions are the series of guidebooks covering various countries. The most famous is **(B221) Baedeker,** a name that has become almost synonymous with guidebooks. This German series was started in 1839 and covered many countries. Most volumes saw numerous editions and were published in German, English, and French. Baedeker enjoyed its greatest popularity before World War I, although some new editions were published between the world wars and a few since World War II. Material is skillfully organized, the information accurate and given in condensed but very usable form. Numerous excellent maps and city plans add to the geographical and historical value of the series. There are volumes for most of the countries of Europe, for the United States, Canada, and a few Asiatic countries such as Palestine and India.

Another series particularly useful for the 19th century is **(B222) Murray's handbooks,** published in London since 1836. There were numerous editions of each volume, and they covered many countries of Europe, northern Africa, and southern Asia.

In organization and general plan **(B223) Muirhead's blue guides (Les guides bleues)** are similar to Baedeker. Started in 1922, various volumes were issued in London by Benn and in Paris by Hachette, primarily for European countries. After World War II publication was revived in two series. *Muirhead's blue guides* are still published in English by Benn and a number of new editions have appeared. In addition, **(B224) Nagel's guidebooks** began publication in 1949 by arrangement with Hachette. Earlier volumes were called *Les guides bleues,* but later volumes have been issued as *Nagel's guidebooks.* There are series in several languages including English, French, German, Italian, and Spanish, which for the most part deal with the various countries of Europe.

(B225) Fodor's modern guides, published in New York by McKay since 1953, is a new series, modern in format and tone with illustrations and maps. Volumes have been issued for several European countries which are informative for the modern traveler, but not so useful for historical purposes.

PERIODICALS

B226. Agricultural history. Washington, 1927 ff. (Quarterly.)

B227. Agricultural history review. Reading, Eng., 1953 ff. (Irregular.)

B228. The American archivist. Cedar Rapids, Ia., 1938 ff. (Quarterly.)

B229. American Association for State and Local History. **Bulletins.** Washington, 1941 ff. (Irregular.)

B230. American Catholic Historical Society of Philadelphia. **Records.** Philadelphia, 1886 ff. (Quarterly.)

B231. American heritage. N.Y., 1949 ff. (Bimonthly.)

B232. The American historical review. N.Y., 1895 ff. (Quarterly.)

B233. Economia e storia: rivista italiana di storia economica e sociale. Rome, 1954 ff. (Quarterly.)

B234. The economic history review. London, 1927 ff. (3 nos. per year.)

B235. The English historical review. London, 1886 ff. (Quarterly.)

B236. Historische Zeitschrift. Munich, 1859 ff. (Quarterly, 1859–76; bimonthly, 1877 ff.)

B237. History. London, 1912 ff. (Quarterly.)

B238. History today. London, 1951 ff. (Monthly.)

B239. The journal of economic history. N.Y., 1941 ff. (Quarterly.)

B240. Journal of the history of ideas. N.Y., 1940 ff. (Quarterly.)

B241. The journal of modern history. Chicago, 1929 ff. (Quarterly.)

B242. Journal of southern history. Baton Rouge, etc., 1935 ff. (Quarterly.)

B243. Journal of world history. See *C84*.

B244. Przeglad historyczny [Historical review.] Warsaw, 1905 ff. (Irregular.)

B245. Revue d'histoire économique et sociale. Paris, 1908 ff. (Quarterly.)

B246. Revue d'histoire moderne et contemporaine. Paris, 1954 ff. (Quarterly.)

B247. Revue de synthèse. Paris, 1931 ff. (Irregular.)

B248. Revue historique. Paris, 1876 ff. (Frequency varies.)

B249. Rivista storica italiana. See *VE443*.

B250. Speculum: a journal of mediaeval studies. Cambridge, Mass., 1926 ff. (Quarterly.)

B251. Tijdschrift voor geschiedenis. Groningen, Neth., 1886 ff. (Four times a year.)

B252. Vierteljahrschrift für Sozial- und Wirtschaftsgeschichte. Leipzig and Stuttgart, 1903 ff. (Quarterly.)

B253. Voprosy istorii. Moscow, 1945 ff. (Monthly.)

SECTION C

World History and Universal Treatments

RALPH E. TURNER *

World history is more than the sum of its parts, and has a literature of its own. A student of this field finds himself obliged to depend upon secondary scholarship, particularly in historical literature. The primary sources of any major subject of world history are voluminous, scattered, recorded in diverse languages and systems of writing, and unmanageable by individual scholars. When a student turns to a secondary work of general history, he usually encounters an expression of some particular outlook on life of which he must be critically aware.

Much explanation of mankind's experience with typical problems is not historical but anthropological, geographic, or sociological. Underlying many of those publications is the assumption that certain peoples and cultures are "primitive" and that an analysis of their ways of living will yield a better comprehension of "origins" and a corresponding key to understanding the past.

In its present state, the literature of world history may be less able to furnish reliable historical information than to invite historical investigation and interpretation. Tomorrow's students of the world's past may be more fortunate than today's, but today's students are far from destitute of meritorious works.

While the entire *Guide* can serve a student of world history, this section contains works which are concerned directly with the history of mankind, in either a universal or an inter-regional treatment of important topics. Works relevant to world history will also be found in Section A, particularly on the subjects of chronology and periodization, philosophy of history, and certain auxiliary studies applicable to all fields of history. With few exceptions, bibliographies, encyclopedias, atlases, and gazetteers are listed among the works of general reference in Section B.

* This section has been derived from an incomplete though lengthy compilation by Professor Turner, whose work was interrupted before he made a final selection. Therefore, its structure and contents reflect in an abnormal degree the judgment of the editors. The following contributed items and comments indicated by their respective initials: Geoffrey Brunn (GB), Shepard Clough (SC), J. S. Cousins (JSC), Walter L. Dorn (WLD), George F. Howe (GFH), Bert J. Loewenberg (BJL).

AUXILIARY INSTRUMENTS

C1. Herre, Paul, ed. **Quellenkunde zur Weltgeschichte.** Leipzig, 1910. Old but excellent.

C2. **Die Weltliteratur: biographisches, literarhistorisches und bibliographisches Lexikon in Übersichten und Stichwörtern.** Ed. by Erich Frauwallner and others. 3 v. Vienna, 1951–54. Good bibliographies.

C3. Grandin, A. **Bibliographie générale des sciences juridiques, politiques, economiques et sociales.** See *B64.*

C4. **Index translationum.** 1st ser., Paris, 1932–40. (Quarterly.) 2nd ser., Paris, 1949 ff. (Annual.) The League of Nations' International Institute of Intellectual Cooperation issued the first series of this international bibliography of translations, UNESCO the second. Increasingly complete as to countries and bibliographical information included. Both series carry an index of authors. Employs Universal Decimal Classification system, with history, geography, and biography in category 9 for each country. [GB]

C5. Franz, Günther, and others. **Bücherkunde zur Weltgeschichte, vom Untergang des römischen Weltreiches bis zur Gegenwart.** See *B58.*

C6. **Critical bibliography of the history, philosophy and organization of science and the history of civilization.** Ed. by George Sarton and others. Brussels, 1913 ff. (Annual.)

C7. Langer, William L., ed. **An encyclopaedia of world history, ancient, medieval and modern, chronologically arranged: a revised and modernized version of Ploetz's "Epitome."** Boston, 1940. Rev. ed., 1952. The foremost relatively complete chronology of world history. Mainly concerned with political, military, and diplomatic events, partly because cultural history is not effectively presented by the method used.

C8. Ploetz, Karl J. **Epitome of ancient, mediaeval and modern history.** Rev. and enl. ed., Boston, 1933. This standard book of its kind was enlarged by sections on Asia and America and published as an epitome of universal history.

C9. ——. **Auszug aus der alten, mittleren, neueren und neuesten Geschichte.** 28th ed., Würzburg, 1957.

C10. Stein, Werner. **Kleiner Kulturfahrplan: die wichtigsten Daten der Kulturgeschichte.** 6 v. Berlin, 1946–51.

C11. United Nations. **World weights and measures.** N.Y., 1955. A statistical handbook of international and national weights, measures, currencies, etc.

C12. Misch, Georg. **Geschichte der Autobiographie.** Latest and most complete ed., 2 v. in 4, Bern, 1949–55.

C13. Vidal de La Blache, Paul M., and

Lucien L. Gallois, eds. **Géographie universelle.** 15 v. Paris, 1927–48.

C14. Brunhes, Jean, and Camille Vallaux. **La géographie de l'histoire.** See *VC59.*

C15. Ancel, Jacques. **Géographie des frontières.** Paris, 1938.

C16. Palmer, Robert R., ed. **Atlas of world history.** Chicago, 1957. Mainly concerned with political organization. Conventional view of the western tradition through the 19th century; separate approach to the 20th century. [GFH]

C17. **The Columbia Lippincott gazetteer of the world.** See *B197.*

C18. Leonhardt, Karl. **Atlas zum Weltgeschichte.** 5th ed., Offenburg, 1956.

C19. Bengston, Hermann, and others. **Grosser historischer Weltatlas.** 2nd ed., Munich, 1954 ff. Part 1, dealing with prehistory and antiquity, is probably unexcelled.

C20. Fischer, Alois. **Das neue Weltbild in geographischstatistischer Darstellung.** Vienna, 1949.

C21. ——. **Neue Weltstatistik: Zahlen, Daten, Karten.** 2nd ed., Vienna, 1952. Revision of *C20.* Extremely valuable, short statistical and geographical data. Includes data derived from national censuses and international compilations as late as 1951.

C22. Philip, George, and T. Swinborne Sheldrake, eds. **The chambers of commerce atlas.** London, 1925.

C23. Herrmann, Albert. **Katastrophen, Naturgewalten und Menschenschicksale.** Berlin, 1936.

C24. United Nations. **Statistical yearbook.** N.Y., 1948 ff.

C25. Woytinsky, Wladimir S. **Die Welt in Zahlen.** 7 v. Berlin, 1925–28. Although emphasizes modern Europe, includes other areas and a broad scope.

C26. Carr-Saunders, Alexander M. **World population: past growth and present trends.** See *A1214.*

C27. National Bureau of Economic Research. **International migrations.** Ed. by Walter F. Willcox. 2 v. N.Y., 1929–31. Valuable analysis of world population growth and movement since 1650. [GB]

C28. Davie, Maurice R. **World immigration.** N.Y., 1949. Modern centuries only and the Atlantic migration in particular. [GB]

C29. Woytinsky, Wladimir S., and Emma S. Woytinsky. **World commerce and governments: trends and outlook.** See *A142.*

C30. ——. **World population and production: trends and outlook.** N.Y., 1953. Also very valuable. [GB]

C31. Kirsten, Ernst, Ernst W. Buchholz, and Wolfgang Köllmann, eds. **Raum und Bevölkerung in der Weltgeschichte.** 2 v. Würzburg, 1955–56.

C32. George, Pierre. **Introduction à l'étude géographique de la population du monde.** Paris, 1951.

C33. Balandier, Georges, and J. F. M. Middleton, eds. **International index of social and cultural anthropology.** N.Y., 1958.

C34. Die Religion in Geschichte und Gegenwart. Ed. by Hermann Gunkel and Leopold Zscharnack. 3rd ed., 5 v., Tübingen, 1955.

C35. Whittaker, Edmund T. **From Euclid to Eddington: a study of conceptions of the external world.** Cambridge, Eng., 1949.

C36. Ginzel, Friedrich K. **Handbuch der mathematischen und technischen Chronologie: das Zeitrechnungswesen der Völker.** See *A70*.

C37. Arnold-Baker, Charles, and Anthony Dent. **Everyman's dictionary of dates.** London and N.Y., 1954.

C38. Carter, Thomas F. **The invention of printing in China and its spread westward.** 2nd ed., N.Y., 1931.

SELECTED WORLD HISTORIES

World history, in contrast with ethnocentric history like the Hellenic epics, Hebrew Old Testament, and Roman legends, was first produced during the last two centuries B.C. by Hellenized orientals. By synchronization and systems of periodization, they brought Greek, Roman, and oriental history into a single perspective. Christian historians reinterpreted that inheritance according to their belief that the Incarnation was the pivotal event of the human past. The concept of world history appeared in Islamic culture, but did not persist. In Asiatic countries it did not arise. In the western cultural tradition it has been a persistent element, but until modern times was based upon a restricted comprehension of the world. The rise of national states in Europe inspired the study of national histories, although not to the exclusion of all historiography of world scope. The Americas responded to the same influences. The world histories listed below are illustrative of the changes in the past fifteen centuries.

C39. Orosius, Paulus. **Seven books of history against the pagans.** Tr. by Irving W. Raymond. N.Y., 1936. An influential history of the world as seen by a 5th century Christian.

C40. Belleforest, François de. **L'histoire universelle du monde.** Paris, 1577. Compares customs and cultures by geographical areas, including Africa, Asia, Europe, and the Americas.

C41. Doglioni, Giovanni N. **Compendio historico universale.** Venice, 1601. A true world history and example of Renaissance interests.

C42. Clüver, Johannes. **Historiarum totius mundi epitome.** Leiden, 1637. A departure from traditional periodization, but not a rejection of the traditional Christian point of view.

C43. Raleigh, Sir Walter. **The history of the world.** London, 1614.

C44. Bossuet, Jacques B. **Discours sur l'histoire universelle.** Paris, 1681. Keeps universal history within Catholic Christian theology, but ends with the age of Charlemagne.

C45. Bruzen de la Martinière, Antoine A. **Introduction à l'histoire de l'Asie, de l'Afrique et de l'Amérique.** 2 v. Amsterdam, 1735. A companion volume to Pufendorff's on the principal states of Europe.

C46. Bower, Archibald, John Campbell, and others. **An universal history, from the earliest account of time to the present, compiled from original authors.** 65 v. London, 1736–68. Introduced practice of cooperative scholarship in multi-volume historical enterprises. Last great rendering of world history in exclusively Christian terms. Broadened significantly the scope of the subject matter, and has had important effects on historical thinking.

C47. Millot, Claude F. X. **Élémens d'histoire générale.** 9 v. Paris, 1772–73. English tr., 5 v., Worcester, Mass., 1789.

C48. Voltaire, François M. A. de. **Essai sur l'histoire générale et sur les moeurs et l'esprit des nations.** 7 v. in 8. Geneva, 1756.

C49. Oncken, Wilhelm, ed. **Allgemeine Geschichte.** 45 v. Berlin, 1879–93. A collective history universal in scope but national in treatment, with meager connections between volumes. Blends all available knowledge of intellectual, religious, economic, and political history, but treatment of the Far East is inadequate. Certain volumes are outstanding.

C50. Ranke, Leopold von. **Weltgeschichte.** 9 v. Leipzig, 1883–88.

C51. Lavisse, Ernest, and Alfred Rambaud, eds. **Histoire générale du IVᵉᵐᵉ siècle à nos jours.** 12 v. Paris, 1893–1901. The unity of this cooperative history surpasses that of the Oncken work and its scope is greater. The point of view is strongly European.

C52. Heeren, Arnold H., Friedrich A. Uckert, Wilhelm von Giesebrecht, Karl G. Lamprecht, and Hermann Oncken, eds. **Allgemeine Staatengeschichte.** 53 separate works. Gotha, Hamburg, and Stuttgart, 1829–1925.

C53. Lindner, Theodor. **Weltgeschichte seit der Völkerwanderung.** 9 v. Berlin, 1901–16. Both Asian and European expansion are treated. Intellectual and technological developments are given within a political-geographical framework.

C54. Andrews, Charles McL., John Fiske, and others. **A history of all nations from the earliest times, being a universal historical library.** 24 v. Philadelphia and N.Y., 1905. In the main a revised, condensed version of *C49*, giving more attention to the Americas.

C55. Petit, Edouard, ed. **Histoire universelle illustrée des pays et des peuples.** 8 v. Paris, 1913–24. Good accounts of social and economic developments at a sacrifice of universal to nationalistic history.

C56. Berr, Henri, ed. **L'évolution de l'humanité: synthèse collective.** Paris, 1920 ff. A substantial departure from earlier efforts to organize universal history by periods, areas, ethnic units, stages, and cycles. History is conceived to be that of mankind, society, inter-societal relations, in continuous evolution. Although undue weight is given to Europe and the West, it is the best organized and most complete treatment of world history. To be complete in 100 v.

C57. **The history of civilization.** Ed. by Charles K. Ogden and Harry E. Barnes. N.Y. and London, 1924 ff. An expansion of the Berr series in some respects, and a translation of some of its volumes.

C58. Petit, Maxime. **Histoire générale des peuples.** 3 v. Paris, 1925–26. Useful work with a broad point of view.

C59. **Histoire du monde.** Ed. by Eugène Cavaignac. Paris, 1922 ff. Organized on the principles of geography, population, and chronology, with the world divided into zones which are treated first individually and next in their contacts with each other. The volumes are individually excellent, with bibliographies and maps.

C60. **Histoire générale.** Ed. by Gustave Glotz and Robert Cohen. Paris, 1926 ff. Concerned with pre-history and history to 1453. Good integration of geography, technology, economics, art, and literature with other aspects of the past.

C61. **Peuples et civilisations: histoire générale.** Ed. by Louis Halphen and Philippe Sagnac. Paris, 1926 ff. A new and successful approach to universal history. Some volumes are unsurpassed.

C62. **Propyläen Weltgeschichte: der Werdegang der Menschheit in Gesellschaft und Staat, Wirtschaft und Geistesleben.** Ed. by Walter Goetz. 10 v. Berlin, 1930–33. Emphasizes the cultural development of mankind. Excellent.

C63. Barbagallo, Corrado. **Storia universale.** New, rev. and enl. ed., 5 v. in 10, Turin, 1950–54. Overwhelmingly political. Excellent bibliographies.

C64. Bley, Wulf, ed. **Revolutionen der Weltgeschichte.** Munich, 1933. A world history with western emphasis and centered on a concept of revolution.

C65. **Clio: introduction aux études historiques.** Paris, 1934 ff. The plan of this series of manuals is that of a universal history. Individual volumes are of highest quality. As an introduction to a study of universal history it has superior merit.

C66. Valentin, Veit. **Weltgeschichte: Völker, Männer, Ideen.** 2 v. Amsterdam, 1939. Conceives of world history as a struggle to give ever larger groups or societies the four great possessions, religion, knowledge, art, and power, under economic and moral conditions which are bearable, a process marked by recurrent crises and by military or cultural conflicts.

C67. Bowle, John, ed. **The concise encyclopedia of world history.** London, 1958. Not a reference work, but an attempt to survey world history in one volume.

C68. Turner, Ralph E. **The great cultural traditions.** 2 v. N.Y., 1941. From earliest times to the 4th century A.D. Based on findings and methods of analysis of studies auxiliary to historical interpretation.

C69. Pirenne, Jacques. **Les grands courants de l'histoire universelle.** 7 v. Neuchâtel, 1944–56. Broad and frequently illuminating survey of the great civilizations, sustaining the thesis that landbound societies remain rigid and authoritarian whereas those leavened by trade and maritime ventures tend to foster a spirit of liberty and individualism. [GB]

C70. Ruestow, Alexander. **Ortsbestimmung der Gegenwart: eine universalgeschichtliche Kulturkritik.** 3 v. Erlenbach and Zürich, 1950–57. Uses the tools of modern disciplines—anthropology, archaeology, sociology, and psychology—and reviews present state of western culture in light of the history of power and freedom.

C71. Laviosa Zambotti, Pia. **Origini e diffusione della civiltà.** Milan, 1947. Reprint, 1950. Good bibliographies round out this excellent study.

C72. Webb, Walter P. **The great frontier: an interpretation of world history since Columbus.** See *Y155*.

C73. **The University of Michigan history of the modern world.** Ed. by Allan Nevins and Howard M. Ehrmann. Ann Arbor, 1958 ff. Comprehensive history of the leading nations and regions of the world, with heavy emphasis on the last two centuries. Each volume is a discrete unit with its own bibliography. 15 v. projected. [GB]

C74. Durant, Will. **The story of civilization.** 6 v. N.Y., 1935–57. A colorful exposition of Old World history, emphasizing characters and events. Loose in structure, captivating rather than profound, and somewhat superficial. [GB]

C75. Crouzet, Maurice, ed. **Histoire générale des civilisations.** 7 v. Paris, 1953–59. Central theme is the contact and cumulative exchanges between civilizations from situations separated either geographically or chronologically. Argument leads toward critical choice of today's underdeveloped peoples between liberal and communist civilizations. Excellent bibliographies.

C76. Akademiia Nauk, SSSR. **Vsemirnaia istoriia.** Ed. by Eugenii M. Zhukov and others. Moscow, 1955 ff. An official Marxist interpretation, beginning with "primitive communistic societies" and slave-holding societies of ancient times. It is planned to treat in 10 volumes world history through World War II. All volumes will express historical materialism.

C77. Kroeber, Alfred L. **Configurations of culture growth.** See *A318.*

C78. Toynbee, Arnold J. **A study of history.** 10 v. N.Y. and London, 1934–54. 2 v. abridgement by D. C. Somervell, N.Y. and London, 1947–57. One historian's courageous effort to synthesize world history from the investigations by predecessors and contemporaries, in the course of which a theory of the development of civilizations is formulated and illustrated. If erroneous in details and intuitive rather than wholly empirical, the work has relevance and value of a high order. For further comment see *A323.* [GFH]

C79. Dawson, Christopher H. **The dynamics of world history.** N.Y., 1956. Stimulating compilation from Dawson's critical writings on sociology and culture, edited by John J. Mulloy. [GB]

C80. Northrop, Filmer S. C. **The meeting of East and West: an inquiry concerning world understanding.** N.Y., 1946. An attempt to interpret and compare civilizations of the Orient and Occident by analyzing their cultural ideals. [GB]

C81. Díez del Corral, Luis. **El rapto del Europa.** Madrid, 1954. English tr., by Horace V. Livermore, N.Y., 1959. The universalization of European culture and its implications for Europe and the world. [GB]

C82. Fueter, Eduard. **World history, 1815–1920.** N.Y., 1922. Despite its age, this work of a Swiss historian still remains one of the most intelligent surveys of the 19th century. [WLD]

C83. Salis, Jean R. de. **Weltgeschichte der neuesten Zeit.** 2 v. Zürich, 1951–55.

C84. Journal of world history. Paris, 1953 ff. (Quarterly.) A tri-lingual outlet by which examples of contents of the collaborative history in preparation by the International Commission for a History of the Scientific and Cultural Development of Mankind are made available prior to its publication in final form. Six volumes on the development of peoples and cultures have been planned.

RACES, PEOPLES, AND NATIONS

Any treatment of world history is concerned primarily with the peoples of the past. Three major subdivisions of mankind have been accepted as instruments of thought: race, people, and nation. Race, a unit founded upon shared physiologic traits, has its history. Racism and other, less emotional, ideas about race have been influential upon the course of history. A people traces its sense of unity to a certain degree of shared historical experience, while the more intense feeling of narrower unity among a nation rests on a sense of destiny as well as of history, and seeks political expression. The substance of world history is the interrelationships of races, peoples, and nations and the interplay of their activities in successive epochs. Besides the works listed below, additional references pertinent to races, peoples, and nations will be found in Section A.

C85. Boule, Marcellin, and Henri V. Vallois. **Les hommes fossiles: éléments de paléontologie humaine.** 4th ed., Paris, 1952.

C86. Brodrick, Alan H. **Early man: a survey of human origins.** London, 1948.

C87. Foster, Thomas S. **Travels and settlements of early man: a study of the origins of human progress.** London, 1929. Darwinian. Broad generalization about prehistoric migrations of man and guesses concerning the points, times, and places of human divergence.

C88. Goldenweiser, Alexander A. **Anthropology: an introduction to primitive culture.** N.Y., 1937.

C89. Kroeber, Alfred L. **Anthropology: race, language, culture, psychology, prehistory.** See *A159.*

C90. Herskovits, Melville J. **Man and his works: the science of cultural anthropology.** See *A166.*

C91. Ware, Caroline F., ed. **The cultural approach to history.** See *A387.*

C92. Queen, Stuart A., and John B. Adams. **The family in various cultures.** Philadelphia, 1952.

C93. Letourneau, Charles. **La condition de la femme dans les diverses races et civilisations.** Paris, 1903.

C94. Ainsworth-Davis, James R. **Cooking through the centuries.** N.Y. and London, 1931.

C95. Pittard, Eugene. **Les races et l'histoire.** Paris, 1924. Tr., by V. E. C. Collum, *Race and history: an ethnological introduction to history,* N.Y., 1926. A standard work with a substantial bibliography.

C96. Coon, Carleton S., Stanley M. Garn, and Joseph B. Birdsell. **Races: a study of the problem of race formation in man.** Springfield, Ill., 1950.

C97. Boyd, William C. **Genetics and the races of man.** Boston, 1950.

C98. Dobzhansky, Theodosius G. **Evolution, genetics and man.** N.Y., 1955.

C99. Count, Earl W., ed. **This is race: an anthology selected from the international literature on the races of man.** N.Y., 1950.

C100. Biasutti, Renato, and others. **Le**

razze e i popoli della terra. 3 v. Turin, 1941.

C101. Blumenbach, Johann F. **De generis humani varietate nativa.** Göttingen, 1775. 3rd ed., 1795. First to go beyond color to skull, texture of hair, and other traits in identifying races. Source of many 19th century ideas about the inequalities of races.

C102. Montagu, M. F. Ashley. **Statement on race.** N.Y., 1951.

C103. Frazier, Edward F. **Races and culture contacts in the modern world.** N.Y., 1957.

C104. United Nations Educational, Scientific and Cultural Organization. **The race question in modern science.** N.Y., 1956.

C105. Shodo, Shinmei. **Shi-teki minzoku riron.** [History of treatises on race theories.] Tokyo, 1948. Summarizes western theories rather than offering an Asian view.

C106. André, Pierre J. **L'Islam et les races.** 2 v. Paris, 1922.

C107. Linton, Ralph, ed. **Most of the world: the peoples of Africa, Latin America, and the East today.** N.Y., 1949.

C108. Die neue grosse Völkerkunde. Ed. by Hugo A. Bernatzik. 2nd ed., 3 v., Frankfurt-am-Main, 1954.

C109. Preuss, Konrad T. **Lehrbuch der Völkerkunde.** Stuttgart, 1939. Valuable as an introduction to the subject.

C110. Barenton, Hillaire de. **L'origine des langues, des religions, et des peuples.** 2 v. Paris, 1932–33.

C111. Montandon, George. **L'ologénèse culturelle: traité d'ethnologie.** Paris, 1934.

C112. Abel, Wilhelm. "Wachstumsschwankungen mittel europäischer Völker seit dem Mittelalter." **Jahrbücher für Nationalökonomie,** 142 (July 1935): 670–92.

C113. Schwidetzky, Ilse. **Das Problem des Völkertodes: eine Studie zur historischen Bevölkerungsbiologie.** Stuttgart, 1954.

C114. Landry, Adolphe, and others. **Traité de démographie.** Paris, 1945.

C115. Chevalier, Louis. **Démographie générale.** Paris, 1951.

C116. Reinhard, Marcel R. **Histoire de la population mondiale, 1700–1948.** Paris, 1949.

C117. Isaac, Julius. **Economics of migration.** N.Y., 1947. An economic and sociological study of the movement of free individuals for the years since 1815. [WLD]

C118. Lavedan, Pierre. **Histoire de l'urbanisme.** 3 v. Paris, 1926–52.

C119. Pinson, Koppel S. **A bibliographical introduction to nationalism.** N.Y., 1935.

C120. Shafer, Boyd C. **Nationalism: myth and reality.** N.Y., 1955.

C121. Hayes, Carlton J. H. **The historical evolution of modern nationalism.** N.Y., 1931. 5th printing, 1955. A sequel to his earlier *Essays on nationalism* (N.Y., 1926), in which he appraises the strength of nationalism as a force in history.

C122. Kohn, Hans. **The idea of nationalism: a study in its origin and background.** See *AH59*.

C123. ——. **Prophets and peoples: studies in nineteenth century nationalism.** N.Y., 1946.

C124. Earle, Edward M., ed. **Nationalism and internationalism.** N.Y., 1950.

C125. Meinecke, Friedrich. **Weltbürgertum und Nationalstaat.** See *VF109*.

C126. Barker, Ernest. **National character and the factors in its formation.** London, 1927.

C127. Johannet, Réné. **Le principe des nationalitiés.** Paris, 1923.

C128. Nationalism: a report by a study group of members of the Royal Institute of International Affairs. London, 1939.

C129. Gooch, George P. **Nationalism.** London, 1920. The course of nationalism in Europe and Asia from the French Revolution to 1919.

C130. Snyder, Louis L. **The meaning of nationalism.** New Brunswick, N.J., 1954.

C131. Sturzo, Luigi. **Nationalism and internationalism.** N.Y., 1946.

C132. Baron, Solo W. **Modern nationalism and religion.** N.Y., 1947.

C133. Cobban, Alfred. **National self-determination.** See *AH32*.

C134. Hertz, Friedrich O. **Nationality in history and politics.** London, 1944.

TOPICAL HISTORIES

Philosophy

C135. Brie, G. A. de. **Bibliographia philosophica, 1934–1945.** 2 v. Brussels, 1950–54.

C136. Bibliographie de la philosophie. Paris, 1937 ff. (Semiannual.)

C137. Radhakrishnan, Sarvepalli, and others. **History of philosophy, eastern and western.** 2 v. London, 1952–53.

C138. Gomperz, Theodor. **Greek thinkers: a history of ancient philosophy.** Tr. by Laurie Magnus and G. G. Berry. 4 v. London, 1901–12. A fundamental source for both Greek philosophy and the history of critical opinion and evaluation. [BJL]

C139. Boer, Tjitze J. de. **The history of philosophy in Islam.** Tr. by Edward R. Jones. London, 1903. Reprint, 1933. The best volume on this subject. [BJL]

C140. Whitehead, Alfred N. **Adventures of ideas.** N.Y., 1933.

· **C141.** Westermarck, Edward A. **The origin and development of the moral ideas.** 2 v. London, 1906–08.

C142. Lecky, William E. H. **History of European morals from Augustus to Charlemagne.** 3rd rev. ed., 2 v., N.Y., 1879.

C143. Brinton, Crane. **A history of western morals.** N.Y., 1959. A rapid review in which the results of Christian religious faith and alternative bases for morals are appraised.

Political Theory and Institutions

C144. Cassirer, Ernst. **The myth of the state.** New Haven, 1946.

C145. Gierke, Otto F. von. **The development of political theory.** N.Y., 1939.

C146. Dunning, William A. **A history of political theories.** 3 v. N.Y. and London, 1920–43.

C147. Wigmore, John H. **A panorama of the world's legal systems.** 3 v. St. Paul, 1928. Describes sixteen major systems.

C148. Seagle, William. **The history of law.** 2nd ed., N.Y., 1946. Comprehensive summary and interpretation. Chapter bibliographies.

C149. Maine, Sir Henry J. S. **Lectures on the early history of institutions.** N.Y., 1875.

C150. Rose, Arnold M., ed. **The institutions of advanced societies.** Minneapolis, 1958.

Mathematics and Science

C151. Newman, James R. **The world of mathematics.** 4 v. N.Y., 1956. Excerpts with introduction of mathematical writings, mostly modern and western. [GB]

C152. Struik, Dirk J. **Concise history of mathematics.** 2 v. N.Y., 1948.

C153. Smith, David E. **A history of mathematics.** See *A241.*

C154. Hogben, Lancelot. **Science for the citizen.** N.Y., 1938. Relates scientific advances to social progress. Difficult style. [GB]

C155. Becker, Carl L. **Progress and power.** Stanford, 1936. 2nd ed., N.Y., 1949. Brief, illuminating survey of the human epic. [GB]

C156. Neugebauer, Otto. **The exact sciences in antiquity.** See *F254.*

C157. Taton, René, ed. **Histoire générale des sciences.** Paris, 1957 ff. To be complete in 3 v.

C158. Dannemann, Friedrich. **Die Naturwissenschaften in ihrer Entwicklung und in ihrem Zusammenhange.** 2nd ed., 4 v., Leipzig, 1920–23.

C159. Kraus, Paul. **Jābir ibn Hayyān: contribution à l'histoire des idées scientifiques dans l'Islam.** 2 v. Cairo, 1942–43. [Mémoires de l'Institut d'Egypt, 44–45.]

C160. Mieli, Aldo. **La science arabe et son rôle dans l'évolution scientifique mondiale.** Leiden, 1938.

C161. Berriman, Algernon E. **Historical metrology.** N.Y. and London, 1953. Analyzes archaeological and prehistoric evidence concerning weights and measures.

C162. Sarton, George A. L. **Introduction to the history of science.** See *A249.*

For other works on the history of science see *A247–279.*

Agriculture

C163. Gras, Norman S. B. **A history of agriculture in Europe and America.** 2nd ed., N.Y., 1940.

C164. Jensen, Lloyd B. **Man's foods: nutrition and environments in food gathering and food producing times.** Champaign, Ill., 1953.

C165. Hehn, Victor. **Kulturpflanzen und Haustiere in ihrem Übergang aus Asien nach Griechenland und Italien sowie in das übrige Europa.** 7th ed., Berlin, 1902.

C166. Antonius, Otto. **Grundzüge einer Stammesgeschichte der Haustiere.** Jena, 1920. The author modified his conclusions somewhat in Zoologisch-Botanischen Gesellschaft, *Verhandlungen,* v. 90 (Vienna, 1944), pp. 294–303.

C167. Food and Agriculture Organization of the United Nations. **Agriculture in the world economy.** Rome, 1955.

C168. Gottschalk, Alfred. **Histoire de l'alimentation.** 2 v. Paris, 1948.

C169. Hintze, Kurt. **Geographie und Geschichte der Ernährung.** Leipzig, 1934.

C170. Curwen, Eliot C., and Gudmund Hatt. **Plough and pasture.** N.Y., 1953.

C171. Francis, Clarence. **A history of food and its preservation.** Princeton, 1937.

C172. Bennett, Richard, and John Elton. **History of corn milling.** 4 v. London, 1898–1904.

Technology

C173. Feldhaus, Franz M. **Die Technik der Antike und des Mittelalters.** Potsdam, 1931.

C174. Franchet, L. **Les premiers instruments de labour et leur évolution.** Lausanne, 1932.

C175. Forbes, Robert J. **Studies in ancient technology.** 6 v. Leiden, 1955–58.

C176. Schrecker, Paul. **Work and history: an essay on the structure of civilization.** Princeton, 1948.

C177. Singer, Charles J., and others, eds. **A history of technology.** 5 v. Oxford, 1954–58. A monumental collective effort, authoritative, well-planned, and well-illustrated. Covers from prehistoric times to 1900. Most chapters include source references and bibliographies. [GB]

C178. Poirier, René. **L'épopée des grands travaux de la Tour de Babel à la cité de l'atome.** 2 v. Paris, 1957.

C179. Rickard, Thomas A. **Man and metals: a history of mining in relation to the development of civilization.** 2 v. N.Y., 1932.

C180. Agricola, Georgius. **De re metallica.** English tr. by Herbert C. Hoover and Lou H. Hoover. London, 1912; N.Y., 1950. Rich annotations make this a general history of metallurgy. [GB]

C181. Johannsen, Otto. **Geschichte des Eisens.** 3rd rev. ed., Düsseldorf, 1953.

C182. Uccelli, Arturo, ed. **Storia della tecnica dal medio evo ai nostri giorni.** Milan, 1944. Collaborative product, magnificently illustrated, but lacking notes or bibliography.

C183. Usher, Abbott P. **A history of mechanical inventions.** Rev. ed., Cambridge, Mass., 1954.

C184. Kirby, Richard S., and others. **Engineering in history.** N.Y., 1956. Sweeping in scope. Useful bibliography.

C185. Royal Microscopic Society. **Origin and development of the microscope.** Ed. by Alfred N. Disney, Cyril F. Hill, and Wilfred E. W. Baker. London, 1928.

Economic History

C186. André, Louis. **Histoire économique depuis l'antiquité jusqu'à nos jours.** 6th ed., Paris, 1939.

C187. Cipolla, Carlo M. **Money, prices, and civilization in the Mediterranean world, fifth to seventeenth century.** Princeton, 1956. Excellent introduction to the history of money and banking. [SC]

C188. Clark, Colin. **National and per capita incomes.** N.Y., 1948.

C189. Stark, Werner. **The history of economics in its relation to social development.** London, 1945.

C190. Kaulla, Rudolf. **Beiträge zur Entstehungsgeschichte des Geldes.** Bern, 1945.

C191. Weber, Max. **Wirtschaft und Gesellschaft.** 4th ed., Tübingen, 1956.

C192. ——. **Gesammelte aufsätze zur sozial- und Wirtschaftsgeschichte.** Tübingen, 1924.

C193. Allen, George C. **Western enterprise in far eastern economic development.** N.Y., 1954.

C194. Ashworth, William. **A short history of the international economy, 1850–1950.** London and N.Y., 1952.

C195. Lorwin, Lewis L. **The international labor movement: history, policies, outlook.** N.Y., 1953.

C196. Heaton, Herbert. **A history of trade and commerce.** New and rev. ed., London, 1941.

C197. Lacour-Gayet, Jacques, ed. **Histoire de commerce.** 6 v. Paris, 1950–55.

C198. Lefranc, Georges. **Histoire du commerce.** 2nd ed., Paris, 1948.

C199. Luzzatto, Gino. **Storia del commercio.** Florence, 1914.

C200. Warmington, Eric H. **The commerce between the Roman empire and India.** See *1292.*

Transportation

C201. Fayle, Charles E. **A short history of the world's shipping industry.** London, 1933.

C202. McDowell, Carl E., and Helen M. Gibbs. **Ocean transportation.** N.Y., 1954.

C203. Zechlin, Egmont. **Maritime Weltgeschichte.** 2 v. Hamburg, 1948–49.

C204. Hornell, James. **Water transport: origins and early evolution.** Cambridge, Eng., 1946.

C205. Gibson, Charles E. **The story of the ship.** N.Y., 1948.

C206. Anderson, Romola, and Roger C. Anderson. **The sailing-ship: six thousand years of history.** London, 1947.

C207. Lefebvre des Noëttes, Richard. **De la marine antique à la marine moderne: la révolution du gouvernail.** Paris, 1935.

C208. ——. **La force motrice animale à travers les âges.** Paris, 1924.

C209. Dollfus, Charles, and Edgar de Geoffroy. **Histoire de la locomotion terrestre.** 2 v. Paris, 1935–36.

C210. Gregory, John W., and C. J. Gregory. **The story of the road.** 2nd ed., London, 1938.

C211. Steinman, David B., and Sara R. Watson. **Bridges and their builders.** N.Y., 1941.

C212. Black, Archibald. **The story of tunnels.** N.Y., 1937.

C213. Robins, Frederick W. **The story of water supply.** London, 1946.

C214. Buffet, Bernard, and René Evrard. **L'eau potable à travers les âges.** 2nd ed., Liège, 1951.

C215. Kiely, Edmond R. **Surveying instruments: their history and classroom use.** N.Y., 1947.

C216. Straub, Hans. **A history of civil engineering.** London, 1952.

C217. Forbes, Robert J. **Short history of the art of distillation.** Leiden, 1949.

Medicine

C218. Sigerist, Henry E. **Civilization and disease.** Ithaca, 1943. Twelve historical essays on social, religious, legal, etc., attitudes toward disease. [GB]

C219. Diepgen, Paul. **Geschichte der Medizin.** 2 v. in 3. Berlin, 1949–55.

C220. Stemplinger, Eduard. **Antike und moderne Volksmedizin.** Leipzig, 1925.

C221. Gordon, Benjamin L. **Medicine throughout antiquity.** Philadelphia, 1949. Medicine as developed by various peoples of early times. [GB]

C222. Shryock, Richard H. **The development of modern medicine.** See *A287.*

C223. Filliozat, Jean. **La doctrine classique de la médecine indienne et ses parallèles grecs.** Paris, 1949.

Art and Architecture

C224. Cheney, Sheldon. **A world history of art.** N.Y., 1937.

C225. Propyläen-Kunstgeschichte. 16 v. Berlin, 1923–29.

C226. The encyclopedia of world art. N.Y., 1959 ff. Magnificent illustrations and comment by leading historians of art. 15 v. planned. [JSC]

C227. Holt, Elizabeth B., ed. **A documentary history of art.** 2nd ed., 2 v., Garden City, N.Y., 1957–58. Reprint from *Literary sources of art history* (Princeton, 1947). Anthology of texts from Theophilus to Goethe. [JSC]

C228. Panofsky, Erwin. **Meaning in the visual arts.** Garden City, 1955. Stimulating essays on problems of iconography and iconology. Concluding chapter relates progress in history of art in the United States. [JSC]

C229. Thieme, Ulrich, and Felix Becker, eds. **Allgemeines Lexikon der bildenden Künstler von der Antike bis zur Gegenwart.** 37 v. Leipzig, 1907–50. Thorough factual compilation of biographical and other information.

C230. Michel, André, ed. **Histoire de l'art depuis les premiers temps chrétiens jusqu'à nos jours.** 8 v. Paris, 1905–29. Broad in scope, but correspondingly brief on individual styles or periods. Probably unsurpassed as a general cooperative history of art since early Christian period. Useful bibliographies.

C231. Martin, Henry, ed. **La grammaire des styles: collection de précis sur l'histoire de l'art.** 3rd ed., 15 v., Paris, 1927–30. A set of small volumes covering architecture, sculpture, painting, and design. Emphasizes occidental and particularly French art. [JSC]

C232. Histoire universelle des arts des temps primitifs jusqu'à nos jours. Ed. by Louis Réau and others. 4 v. Paris, 1930–39. [1, Georges Contenau and Victor Chapot, *L'art antique—Orient, Grèce, Rome;* 2, Louis Réau, *L'art primitif—l'art mediéval;* 3, Louis Réau, *La Renaissance—l'art moderne;* 4, Serge Élisséeff and others, *Arts musulmans— Extrême Orient (Inde, Indochine, Insulinde Chine, Japon, Asie centrale, Tibet).*] Approach is that of comparative history. Illustrations are adequate, bibliographies useful. V. 4 is among the best available on its subject.

C233. Springer, Anton H. **Handbuch der Kunstgeschichte.** 11th ed., 5 v., Stuttgart and Leipzig, 1920–21. Factual and unimaginative.

C234. Lavedan, Pierre. **Histoire de l'art.** 2 v. Paris, 1944–49.

C235. Carotti, Giulio. **A history of art.** 3 v. N.Y., 1908–23.

C236. Carriere, Moriz. **Die Kunst im Zusammenhang der Culturentwickelung und die Ideale bis zur Menschenheit.** 3rd ed., 5 v., Leipzig, 1877–86. An effort to show that fundamental laws of aesthetics govern art, and not individuality or nationality except as aspects of an intellectual environment.

C237. Faure, Élie. **Histoire de l'art.** 4 v. Paris, 1909–21. Tr. by W. Pach, 5 v., N.Y., 1921–30; reprint, 1937. Imaginative, interpretive, and not recommended for details. Abundant illustrations.

C238. Muther, Richard. **The history of modern painting.** Rev. ed., 4 v., N.Y., 1907. Tr. from *Geschichte der Malerei* (5 v., Leipzig, 1899–1902).

C239. Woermann, Karl. **Geschichte der Kunst aller Zeiten und Völker.** 3 v. Leipzig, 1900–11. 2nd ed., 6 v., 1915–22.

C240. Gardner, Helen. **Art through the ages.** 3rd ed., N.Y., 1948. An admirable survey. [JSC]

C241. Mégroz, Rudolphe L. **Profile art through the ages: a study of the use and significance of profile and silhouette from the Stone Age to puppet films.** N.Y., 1949.

C242. Stites, Raymond S. **The arts and man.** N.Y., 1940.

C243. Reichwein, Adolf. **China and Europe: intellectual and artistic contacts in the eighteenth century.** Tr. by J. C. Powell. N.Y., 1925.

C244. New York Museum of Modern Art. **Masters of modern art.** Ed. by Alfred H. Barr. N.Y., 1954.

C245. Vollmer, Hans. **Allgemeines Lexikon der bildenden Künstler des XX. Jahrhunderts.** 4 v. Leipzig, 1953–58. A continuation of Thieme and Becker's universal and comprehensive treatment.

C246. Haftmann, Werner. **The mind and work of Paul Klee.** N.Y., 1955.

C247. Grohmann, Will. **Paul Klee.** N.Y., 1955.

C248. Berckelaers, Ferdinand L. (pseud., Michel Seuphor). **Piet Mondrian, life and work.** Amsterdam, 1956.

C249. Fletcher, Banister F. **A history of architecture.** N.Y., 1943.

C250. Fletcher, Banister, and Banister F. Fletcher. **A history of architecture on the comparative method.** 7th rev. ed., London, 1924. Reference work with illustrations and plans.

C251. Mukerjee, Radhakamal. **Man and his habitation.** London, 1940.

C252. Giedion, Siegfried. **Mechanization takes command.** N.Y., 1948. The effects of mechanization on human beings. [GB]

C253. Joseph, David. **Geschichte der Baukunst vom Altertum bis zur Neuzeit.** 3 v. in 4. Berlin, 1902–09. Little on Far East or South America

C254. Choisy, Auguste. **Histoire de l'architecture.** 2 v. Paris, 1899.

C255. Kimball, Sidney F., and George H. Edgell. **A history of architecture.** London and N.Y., 1918. A reliable but very compact history.

C256. Gropius, Walter. **The new archi-**

tecture and the Bauhaus. Tr. by P. Morton Shand. N.Y., 1937.

C257. Johnson, Philip C. **Mies van der Rohe.** N.Y., 1953.

C258. Chase, George H., and Chandler R. Post. **A history of sculpture.** N.Y., 1924. A useful summary.

C259. Ritchie, Andrew C. **Sculpture of the twentieth century.** N.Y., 1952.

C260. Schaefer-Simmern, Henry. **Sculpture in Europe today.** Berkeley, 1955.

C261. Seymour, Charles, Jr. **Tradition and experiment in modern sculpture.** See *T591*.

C262. Sweeney, James J. **Henry Moore.** N.Y., 1946.

Music and the Performing Arts

C263. Grove, Sir George, ed. **Dictionary of music and musicians.** 3rd rev. ed., 6 v., N.Y., 1927–28. 5th ed., 9 v., 1955. In spite of disproportion and omissions, this has been the standard work in English for many years.

C264. Burney, Charles. **A general history of music.** Ed. by Frank Mercer. Reprint, 2 v., N.Y., 1958. After 175 years, this most informative and charmingly written 18th century work stands up as a great example of the history of music.

C265. Combarieu, Jules. **Histoire de la musique des origines au début du XXᵉ siècle.** New ed., 3 v., Paris, 1948–50. The most reliable work in this field in French.

C266. Dufourcq, Norbert, ed. **La musique des origines à nos jours.** Paris, 1946. Articles by specialists covering the world of music since the ancients, with extensive bibliographies.

C267. Einstein, Alfred. **A short history of music.** 3rd U.S. rev. ed., N.Y., 1947. Concise and popular.

C268. Harmon, Alec, and Wilfred H. Mellers. **Man and his music.** 4 v. Fair Lawn, N.J., 1957. General and non-technical.

C269. **The Oxford history of music.** Ed. by William H. Hadow. 6 v. Oxford, 1901–05. 2nd ed., ed. by P. C. Buck, 8 v., London, 1929–38. Authoritative.

C270. **New Oxford history of music.** N.Y. and London, 1954 ff. Projected 11 v. A comprehensive, detailed treatment of each phase of the development of music.

C271. Sachs, Curt. **The rise of music in the ancient world, East and West.** N.Y., 1943.

C272. ——. **The history of musical instruments.** N.Y., 1940. Authoritative.

C273. **History of music in sound** [Album of records.] Ed. by Gerald Abraham. [RCA Victor LM 6015, 6016, 6029, 6030, 6031, 6057, 6137.] From ancient and oriental music through the growth of instrumental music and the symphony, the opera, and other complex forms. Designed as a supplement in sound to the *New Oxford history of music* (*C270*).

C274. Myers, Kurtz. **Record ratings.** Ed. by Richard S. Hill. N.Y., 1956. Good critical estimates of musical recordings. Covers through 1955.

C275. **The guide to long-playing records.** 3 v. N.Y., 1955. [1, Irving Kolodin, *Orchestral music;* 2, Philip L. Miller, *Vocal music;* 3, Harold C. Schonberg, *Chamber and solo instrument music.*] Generally reliable; among the best of the critical guides.

C276. Hall, David. **The record book.** International ed., N.Y., 1948. Valuable despite the rapid progress of the recording art.

C277. Sachs, Curt. **Eine Weltgeschichte des Tanzes.** Berlin, 1933. A brief work containing bibliography with which to delve further into the subject.

C278. Leloir, Maurice. **Dictionnaire des costumes et de ses accessoires, des armes, et des étoffes, des origines à nos jours.** Paris, 1951. Authoritative; mainly western.

C279. Klein, Julius L. **Geschichte des Drama's.** 13 v. in 15. Leipzig, 1865–86.

C280. Bowers, Faubion. **Theatre in the East: a survey of Asian dance and drama.** N.Y. and Toronto, 1956.

C281. Bogeng, Gustav A. E. **Geschichte des Sports aller Völker und Zeiten.** 2 v. Leipzig, 1926.

Literature

C282. Prampolini, Giacomo. **Storia universale della letteratura.** 5 v. Turin, 1933–38.

C283. Queneau, Raymond, ed. **Histoire des littératures.** Bruges, 1955 ff. Inclusive. Bibliography assists pursuit of special branches of the world's literature.

C284. **Handbuch der Literaturwissenschaft.** Ed. by Oskar Walzel. 30 v. Potsdam, 1923–43.

C285. Shipley, Joseph T., ed. **Dictionary of world literature: criticism, forms, technique.** N.Y., 1943; London, 1945. New rev. ed., 1953. Extremely concise. Includes dramatic literature.

C286. **Algemene literatuur Geschiedenis.** Ed. by Franz de Backer and others. 6 v. Utrecht, 1943–55.

C287. Auerbach, Erich. **Mimesis.** Princeton, 1953.

Warfare

C288. Nef, John U. **War and human progress.** Cambridge, Mass., 1950. A classic liberal study on the question of whether war is a major determinant of economic and technological progress. [WLD]

C289. Delbrück, Hans, and others. **Geschichte der Kriegskunst.** See *T208*.

C290. Montross, Lynn. **War through the ages.** See *AH85*.

C291. Phillips, Thomas R., ed. **Roots of strategy.** Harrisburg, 1940. Translation of a selection of military classics.

C292. Clausewitz, Karl von. **On war.** Tr. by James J. Graham. New and rev. ed., 3 v., London, 1908.

C293. Rothfels, Hans. **Carl von Clausewitz: Politik und Krieg.** Berlin, 1920.

SECTION D

History of Religions

CHARLES SAMUEL BRADEN *

Writings of importance in the history of religions greatly exceed the dimensions of this section. A select list appears here. Bibliographies in the books which are individually mentioned will lead to almost everything published which has genuine significance in the general field. Other references in the regional and national sections should also be consulted.

GENERAL

BIBLIOGRAPHIES, LIBRARIES, AND MUSEUMS

D1. Barrow, John G. **A bibliography of bibliographies in religion.** Ann Arbor, 1955. Annotated list of bibliographies of books dealing with religion, including works in most of the major languages of the world. Heavily weighted on the side of the Bible and the Christian tradition, it does have a section on non-Christian religions. Under Christianity it covers the Catholic Church, the Reformation, the Protestant sects, and includes an extensive section on persons who have figured prominently in the field of religion. Well indexed.

D2. Besterman, Theodore. **A world bibliography of bibliographies and of bibliographical catalogues, calendars, abstracts, digests, indexes, and the like.** See *B3.* Refer to theology, religion, and other appropriate headings in the field.

D3. Malclès, Louise N. **Les sources du travail bibliographique.** V. 2 (Geneva, 1952), ch. 13, "Sciences religieuses." Excellent coverage of European sources in French, German, and Italian as well as Latin.

D4. Bibliographic index: a cumulative bibliography of bibliographies. See *B5.* Refer to such topics as religion, religions and their subdivisions, the various countries, and specific religions.

D5. Index bibliographicus: directory of current periodical abstracts and bibliographies. V. 2, comp. by Theodore Besterman. Paris, 1952. [UNESCO pub. no. 863.] See section on religion and theology, pp. 12–14. Lists the major magazines of Europe and the United States dealing with religion, including English, French, Swiss, Italian, Spanish, Finnish, Russian, Danish, Belgian, and Portuguese.

D6. Haydon, A. Eustace. "Twenty-five years of history of religions." **The journal of religion,** 6 (Jan. 1926): 17–40. Survey of literature in the history of religions from 1900 to 1925, with discussion of the chief books published during that period. Is divided into three parts: (1) outstanding gains of the period, (2) a survey of changes in

* Professor Braden gratefully acknowledges the assistance and counsel of the following scholars in preparation of bibliographies of the various faiths: on Buddhism, Clarence H. Hamilton; Chinese religions, Wing-Tsit Chan; Christianity, Richey Hogg; Hinduism, G. V. Bobrinskoi; Islam, Arthur Jeffery; Judaism, Jacob Marcus; Shinto, D. C. Holtom; the Sikhs, C. H. Loehlin.

method, and (3) clarification of the meaning of religion. Major works of the 19th century are mentioned in a preliminary sketch.

D7. Braden, Charles S. "Research in the history of religions." **Journal of Bible and religion.** Abstracts of articles appearing in 1946–47, 16 (Jan. 1948): 51–54; 1947–48, 17 (Apr. 1949): 120–23; 1948–49, 18 (Jan. 1950): 48–52; 1950–51, 19 (July 1951): 142–45; 1952–53, 21 (Oct. 1953): 262–67; 1954–55, 23 (July 1955): 213–18. A series of abstracts of articles on the history of religions published in major periodicals of the United States, Europe, and some oriental countries. The series will continue. Does not include articles on either Christianity or Judaism, but the *Journal* has published a comparable series on research in archaeology, the Old Testament, the New Testament, the psychology of religion, and the sociology of religion. See indices in annual volumes.

D8. ———. **The scriptures of mankind.** N.Y., 1952. Introduction to the scriptures of the world's living religions, with selected bibliographies of each.

D9. International bibliography of the history of religions. Leiden, 1952 ff. Annual.

D10. The mythology of all races. Ed. by L. H. Gray. 13 v. Boston, 1916–32. Rich in notes and bibliography.

D11. Pinard de la Boullaye, Henry. **L'étude comparée des religions: essai critique.** 2 v. Paris, 1922–25. The value of this work for the modern reader lies in its critique of the various approaches to the history and comparison of religions. Ample bibliographies with discussion of major works.

D12. Diehl, Katharine S. **Religions, mythologies, folklores: an annotated bibliography.** New Brunswick, 1956. Good but quite limited, especially in foreign language items. Organized in three sections: (1) universal religious knowledge, (2) religions exclusive of the Judeo-Christian tradition, and (3) the Judeo-Christian tradition.

Libraries and museums rarely cover the entire field of the history of religions, but tend to specialize in some particular areas. In the United States the libraries of Harvard, Yale, and the University of Chicago are outstanding. The Chicago Historical Museum (formerly the Field Museum), the Oriental Institute of the University of Chicago, the American Museum of Natural History in New York, and the Smithsonian Institution in Washington are rich in exhibits bearing on some phases of religion. The British Museum in London, both as museum and library, is notable.

ENCYCLOPEDIAS AND WORKS OF REFERENCE

D13. Die Religion in Geschichte und Gegenwart: Handwörterbuch für Theologie und Religionswissenschaft. 5 v. and register. Tübingen, 1927–32. 3rd ed., 1957 ff.

D14. Encyclopédie des sciences religieuses. Ed. by F. A. Lichtenberger. 13 v. Paris, 1877–82.

D15. Encyclopaedia of religion and ethics. Ed. by James Hastings and others. 13 v. N.Y., 1908–27. Most complete coverage in English of the entire field of religion. All articles by competent specialists, generally at high scholarly level. Index volume is invaluable for study of special topics. Comprehensive bibliographies.

D16. The new Schaff-Herzog encyclopedia of religious knowledge. Ed. by Samuel M. Jackson. 13 v. N.Y., 1908–14. Primarily concerned with Christianity and Judaism, but some attention is given to other religions. Has been supplemented and brought up to date by publication of *D17*.

D17. Twentieth century encyclopedia of religious knowledge. Ed. by Lefferts A. Loetscher. 2 v. Grand Rapids, 1955. Most articles are accompanied by select bibliographies.

D18. The sacred books of the East. Ed. by F. Max Müller. 50 v. Oxford, 1897–1910. Selected portions of many sacred texts, translated by scholars who have provided in addition copious historical and literary introductions and explanatory notes. Bibliographies.

D19. Finegan, Jack. **Archeology in world religions.** Princeton, 1952. Bibliography in footnotes.

LONGER GENERAL HISTORIES

D20. Histoire générale des religions. 5 v. Paris, 1944–51. Comprehensive coverage of the entire field, with separate sections written by competent European specialists. Much fuller treatment of Christianity than any other faith. Extensive bibliographies, especially valuable for French sources, both books and periodicals.

D21. Lehrbuch des Religionsgeschichte. 4th ed., ed. by Alfred Bertholet and Edward Lehmann, 2 v., Tübingen, 1924–25.

D22. Frazer, Sir James G. **The golden bough.** 3rd ed., 12 v., N.Y., 1935. Not properly a history of religion, but touches almost every important aspect of religion. More concerned with older religions and those of primitive societies, but makes frequent reference to the major ones. Lengthy bibliography covers practically all principal sources, including journals, to beginning of the 20th century.

D23. Moore, George F. **The history of religions.** 2 v. N.Y., 1919. 2nd rev. ed., 1924–25. V. 2 covers Judaism, Christianity, and Islam; v. 1, the other major religions. Good bibliographies. Noteworthy for careful, objective scholarship.

HISTORIES OF SPECIAL PERIODS

Modern tendencies in the world's religions are described in the following books.

D24. Braden, Charles S. **Modern tendencies in world religions.** N.Y., 1933.

D25. Haydon, A. Eustace. **Modern trends in world religions.** Chicago, 1934.

D26. Widgery, Alban G. **Living religions and modern thought.** N.Y., 1936.

D27. Braden, Charles S. **War, communism, and world religions.** N.Y., 1953.

PERIODICALS

D28. American Theological Library Association. **Index to religious periodical literature, 1949–1952.** Chicago, 1953. Indexes 31 periodicals not included in the general periodical indices. Designed as a continuing project, with further volumes planned.

D29. International index to periodicals. See *B77.* Indexes at least 35 periodicals which from time to time carry articles, mostly scholarly, on the history of religion. The other periodical indices are worth consulting also, though most of these articles are more superficial.

D30. American journal of archaeology. Cambridge, Mass., 1885 ff. (Quarterly.)

D31. Antiquity: a quarterly review of archaeology. Gloucester, Eng., 1927 ff. Ranges over the world, with religion only one of its varied interests.

D32. Archeology. Cambridge, Mass., 1948

ff. (Quarterly.) Written by experts for non-technically equipped readers.

D33. Archives de sociologie des religions. Paris, 1956 ff. (Semiannual.)

Frequent articles on the history of some phase of religion appear in periodicals on archaeology. For many others not listed here see *Ulrich's periodicals directory (B75).*

D34. Journal of Bible and religion. Brattleboro, Vt., 1932 ff. (Quarterly.)

D35. Journal of religion. Chicago, 1921 ff. (Quarterly.)

D36. Quellen der Religions-Geschichte. Göttingen, 1909 ff.

D37. Religionsgeschichtliche Bibliografie. 10 v. in 5. Leipzig, 1914–23.

D38. Religionsgeschichtliche. Giessen, 1903 ff.

D39. Review of religion. N.Y., 1936–58. (Quarterly to 1950; semiannual, 1950 ff.) Regular feature is a bibliographical section listing current articles concerning religion in a wide range of eastern and western periodicals. These are classified under general, primitive, ancient, oriental, and Judeo-Christian.

D40. Revue de l'histoire des religions. Paris, 1880 ff. (Quarterly.) Cumulative index, v. 1–44.

D41. Southwestern journal of anthropology. Albuquerque, 1945 ff. (Quarterly.) Not limited to archaeology of the Southwest or to primitive religions. Frequent articles from the Orient and elsewhere.

PRIMITIVE RELIGIONS

Much of the study of primitive religions has been done by anthropologists. Almost every book on anthropology has at least a chapter on religion, usually describing it at the primitive level. Many provide ample bibliographies.

D42. Taylor, Edward B. **Primitive culture: researches into the development of mythology, philosophy, religion, art, language, and custom.** 4th rev. ed., 2 v., London, 1903. A pioneer book usually listed in the bibliographies of those who write on primitive religion in general.

D43. Durkheim, Emile. **Les formes elementaires de la vie religieuse.** Paris, 1912.

D44. Schmidt, Wilhelm. **The origin and growth of religion: facts and theories.** Tr. by H. J. Rose. London, 1931. A manual founded upon the 12 v. *Ursprung des Gottesidee* (Münster, 1926–55), but containing additional material. Good résumé and critique of the development of the historic study of religions, with ample bibliographical notes, including chiefly works of continental scholars.

D45. Lowie, Robert H. **Primitive religion.** N.Y., 1924.

D46. Radin, Paul. **Primitive religion, its nature and origin.** N.Y., 1937. Extensive bibliography.

For specific primitive religions see (1) *Encyclopaedia of religion and ethics (D15),* articles on particular peoples; (2) bibliographies in titles here mentioned; (3) monographs on the religions of specific peoples, or chapters on religion in monographs on particular peoples; (4) indices in periodicals mentioned in this subsection and in the one on religion in general.

PERIODICALS

Frequent articles on primitive religions or aspects of them are found in anthropological and ethnological journals, as well as in publications of the universities and museums of the world. For a listing of these see *Ulrich's periodicals directory (B75)* under anthropology. See also the following.

D47. U. S. Library of Congress. **Biological sciences serial publications: a world list, 1950–1954.** Comp. by John H. Richter and Charles P. Daly. Philadelphia, 1955.

HINDUISM

Four of the eleven usually regarded as world religions were born in India—Hinduism, Jainism, Buddhism, and Sikhism. Due to its world-wide spread, Buddhism has come to be regarded generally as a separate religion and is usually so treated by historians. But Jainism and Sikhism, despite the fact that each has a scripture of its own and insists upon separate listing as a religion in the Indian national census, are frequently treated as merely sects of Hinduism. A number of the books cited here include them as such. However, each does have a history and literature of its own, and is dealt with separately in this section at the conclusion of the bibliography on Buddhism.

BIBLIOGRAPHIES, LIBRARIES, AND MUSEUMS

There is no general bibliography on Hinduism as a whole. Two of limited coverage are listed below.

D48. Dandekar, Ramchandra Narayan. **Vedic bibliography: an up-to-date, comprehensive, and analytically arranged register of all important work done since 1930 in the field of the Veda and allied antiquities, including the Indus Valley civilization.** Bombay, 1946. [New Indian antiquary, extra ser. 7.]

D49. Renou, Louis. **Bibliographie védique.** Paris, 1931. For detailed description see *D48*, p. 105.

Bibliographies may also be found in the works that follow.

D50. Farquhar, John N. **An outline of the religious literature of India.** London, 1920. Lists, describes, and indicates vernacular translations where such exist of most of the basic documents for a study of Hinduism. It is, therefore, an extensive bibliography on an important aspect of Hinduism.

D51. Harvard oriental series. Cambridge, Mass., 1891 ff. V. 2, 7, 8, 17, 19, 20, 24, 25, 31, 32, 38, and 39 contain translations and/or commentary on some of the Hindu sacred books, together with introduction and critical notes. Many furnish extensive bibliographies on their area of interest. For details see the Harvard University Press catalog in *The publishers' trade list annual.*

D52. Dasgupta, Surendra N. **A history of Indian philosophy.** 5 v. Cambridge, Eng., 1923–55. Most detailed history of the philosophy of India, by one of her greatest scholars. While philosophy is the primary concern, religious thought is set forth in every period. Little bibliographical material except in footnotes, mostly original sources from which the author worked.

D53. Macdonell, Arthur A. **A history of Sanskrit literature.** N.Y., 1900. See *D48*, p. 70.

D54. Winternitz, Moriz. **A history of Indian literature.** 2 v. Calcutta, 1927–33. Discusses at length the greater number of sacred texts of Hinduism, Buddhism, Jainism, and Sikhism—all parts of Indian literature. Rich in notes and bibliographical suggestions.

D55. Bloomfield, Maurice. **A Vedic concordance.** Cambridge, Mass., 1910. [Harvard oriental series, 10.] Useful for linguistic, literary, and liturgical study. Text in Sanskrit. For detailed description see Diehl, *Religions, mythologies, folklores (D12)*.

See also *The sacred books of the East (D18)*. V. 1, 2, 7, 8, 12, 14, 15, 22, 23, 25, 26, 30, 32–34, 38, 41–46, and 48 contain translations accompanied usually by introductions, bibliographies, and critical notes on some Hindu source material. For detailed content see index volume, p. xvi.

In the United States the chief centers of study of Indian culture, including its religions, are Harvard, Yale, the University of Pennsylvania, Johns Hopkins University, the University of Chicago, and the University of California. All of these have extensive library resources in the field. Among the museums, the Boston Museum of Fine Arts, where Ananda Coomaraswamy was curator, has valuable material, particularly on the ancient Harrapan civilization and Indian art.

LONGER GENERAL HISTORIES

There are comparatively few longer histories of the whole of Hinduism, and most of these are now old. The major writers, such as Barth, Hopkins, and Monier-Williams, will be found listed in bibliographies of most textbooks on the history of religion. More recent works are the following.

D56. Eliot, Sir Charles N. E. **Hinduism and Buddhism.** 3 v. London, 1921; reissue, N.Y., 1954. The greater portion deals with Buddhism.

D57. Pratt, James B. **India and its faiths.** Boston, 1915. A traveler's record.

D58. Glasenapp, Helmuth von. **Der Hinduismus Religion und Gesellschaft im heutigen Indien.** Munich, 1922.

D59. Morgan, Kenneth W., ed. **The religion of the Hindus.** N.Y., 1953. Written by distinguished Indian scholars, each covering a phase of Hinduism.

D60. Macnicol, Nicol. **The living religions of the Indian people.** London, 1934. Historical development of each religion, with limited bibliography.

See also Dasgupta, *A history of Indian philosophy (D52)*, which deals with the developing religious thought in successive periods of Indian history; Dasgupta, *Hindu mysticism* (*D94*), which treats the major periods of Hindu religious development; and Radhakrishnan, *Indian philosophy* (*D86*).

HISTORIES OF SPECIAL PERIODS

Later scholars have tended to write on more limited periods of Hinduism. Pre-Vedic religion is discussed in the following.

D61. Marshall, Sir John H. **Mohenjo-daro and the Indus civilization.** See *G53*.

D62. The Cambridge history of India. V. 1, **Ancient India.** See *R247*.

Vedic Hinduism has been much studied. See *D48–49* above, and the following.

D63. Griffith, Ralph T. H., tr. **The hymns of the Rigveda.** 3rd ed., 2 v., Benares, 1920–26. Translation and commentary.

D64. Griswold, Hervey D. **The religion of the Rigveda.** London, 1923. Well documented from original as well as secondary sources. Extensive bibliography.

D65. Shende, N. J. **The religion and philosophy of the Atharvaveda.** Poona, 1952. Includes bibliography listing other studies of the Vedas as a whole and individual Vedas.

D66. Deshmukh, Panjabrao S. **The origin and development of religion in Vedic literature.** London, 1933. Includes the Brahmanas. Extensive bibliography.

There have been many studies of the Upanishads and the philosophies growing out of them. Most of these are listed in bibliographies of the two following works.

D67. Hume, Robert E. **The thirteen principal Upanishads.** 2nd rev. ed., Madras, 1949. Translated from the Sanskrit, with outline of the philosophy of the Upanishads and an annotated bibliography. Included in the bibliography are translations of collected and single Upanishads, or selections, some with text, and the text editions of single and collected Upanishads, as well as treatises on them.

D68. Radhakrishnan, Sarvepalli. **The principal Upanishads.** London, 1953. Contains selected bibliography listing major translations of single and groups of Upanishads, as well as expository and critical works in English. The author is the ranking philosopher of India today.

The major sects of Hinduism are discussed in standard works on Hinduism, and their bibliographies mention some of the principal monographs.

D69. Bhandarkar, Sir Ramkrishna G. **Vaisnavism, Saivism and minor religious systems.** Strasbourg, 1913. An outstanding work. See also "Sects-Hindu" in *Encyclopaedia of religion and ethics* (*D15*); and "Vaisnavism," "Saivism," etc., in index volume.

D70. Gonda, Jan. **Early aspects of Vishnuism.** Utrecht, 1954. Detailed and scholarly

study of the Hindu god Vishnu, his origin and development, incarnation, etc. Elaborate notes and documentation, but no formal bibliography. List of abbreviations reveals the original Sanskrit sources employed.

Since much of devotional Hinduism centers about one or another of the great gods of the sects, especially Krishna and Rama, see also the following.

D71. Otto, Rudolf. **India's religion of grace.** N.Y., 1930.

D72. Cave, Sydney. **Redemption, Hindu and Christian.** London, 1919.

D73. The Bhagavad Gita. Tr. and interpreted by Franklin Edgerton. 2 v. Cambridge, Mass., 1946. [Harvard oriental series, 38–39.] Notes on the bibliography and exegesis of the Gita. Lists and evaluates several of the major translations.

D74. The Bhagavad Gita. Tr. by Sarvepalli Radhakrishnan. N.Y., 1948. Contains introductory essay, Sanskrit text, English translation and notes, and select bibliography.

Modern Period

D75. Farquhar, John N. **Modern religious movements in India.** N.Y., 1915.

D76. Sarma, Dittakavi S. **Studies in the renaissance of Hinduism in the 19th and 20th centuries.** Benares, 1944. Account of rise of the major modern movements within Hinduism, built around certain outstanding figures, including Ram Mohun Roy, Ranade, Swami Dyananda, Ramakrishna, Sri Aurobindo, Tagore, Gandhi, and S. Radhakrishnan. Rich in biographies of the modern period. Extensive bibliography.

D77. Elmore, Wilbur T. **Dravidian gods in modern Hinduism.** N.Y., 1915. Religion at the village level and its relation to historic religion.

D78. Whitehead, Henry. **The village gods of Southern India.** 2nd ed., Madras, 1921. Based on personal observations. Covers an area hardly touched in books on Hinduism in general.

D79. Kane, Pandurang V. **History of dharmasastra.** 4 v. Poona, 1930–53. Highly detailed history of and commentary on ancient and medieval religious and civil law. A fifth volume is in progress.

HISTORIES OF SPECIAL TOPICS

On the subject of Indian art, including religious art, the following should be consulted.

D80. Coomaraswamy, Ananda K. **Bibliographies of Indian art.** Boston, 1925. Covers the whole cultural environment in which the art of India has developed.

D81. ———. **History of Indian and Indonesian art.** London, 1927. Lists principal museums where Indian art is found. Extensive bibliography.

D82. Kramrisch, Stella. **The art of India: traditions of Indian sculpture and architecture.** N.Y., 1954.

D83. ——. **The Hindu temple.** 2 v. Calcutta, 1946. Superbly illustrated. Bibliography.

For Hindu liturgy see

D84. Stevenson, Margaret. **The rites of the twice-born.** London, 1920. Not so much what Hindus think and believe as what they do, their rituals, feasts, etc. Includes the life story of a typical Brahman, a section on times and seasons, and on temple worship.

Hindu literature is covered in Macdonell, *A history of Sanskrit literature (D53)* and Winternitz, *A history of Indian literature (D54)*.

On philosophy see Dasgupta, *A history of Indian philosophy (D52)*, and works of Deussen, Hiriyanna, Radhakrishnan, and others in bibliographies found in books mentioned above. See also the following.

D85. Bernard, Theos. **Hindu philosophy.** N.Y., 1947. Very brief sketch of the major schools, with a selected bibliography of general works on Hindu philosophy and these schools.

D86. Radhakrishnan, Sarvepalli, and Charles Moore, eds. **A source book in Indian philosophy.** Princeton, 1957.

Formal treatises on the ethics of Hinduism include the two following works.

D87. Hopkins, E. Washburn. **Ethics of India.** New Haven, 1924. An objective discussion of the ethics of successive historic periods of Hinduism. No formal bibliography, but contains documentation in footnotes, chiefly from original sources.

D88. Mackenzie, John. **Hindu ethics.** London, 1922. Less objective than Hopkins.

On Indian mysticism, including Yoga, there is a considerable popular literature. Paul Brunton has several books on Yoga practice. A fairly extensive list of works, eastern and western, dealing with it in its more serious aspects may be found in

D89. Bernard, Theos. **Hatha Yoga: the report of a personal experience.** N.Y., 1944. Bibliography, pp. 63–64.

See also the following.

D90. Behanan, Kovoor T. **Yoga, a scientific evaluation.** N.Y., 1937. An attempt to study it by western scientific methods.

D91. Coster, Geraldine. **Yoga and western psychology, a comparison.** 3rd ed., London, 1943. Approaches Yoga from the standpoint of western psychology.

D92. Otto, Rudolf. **Mysticism east and west: a comparative analysis of the nature of mysticism.** Tr. by Bertha L. Bracey and Richindra C. Payne. N.Y., 1932. Meister Eckhart is the chief western mystic studied.

D93. Ranade, Ramchandra D. **Indian mysticism: mysticism in Maharashtra.** Poona, 1933. [History of Indian philosophy, 7.] Traces briefly the development of Indian mysticism to the age of Jnanesvara in the 13th century. Also considers intellectual, democratic, synthetic, personalistic, and activistic mysticism. Considerable biographical material as well as discussion of the metaphysics and ethics of each period.

D94. Dasgupta, Surendra N. **Hindu mysticism.** Chicago, 1927. Historical account of development of mysticism in India. Includes sacrificial mysticism, that of the Upanishads, Yoga mysticism, Buddhistic mysticism, and devotional mysticism in its classical and popular forms.

BIOGRAPHY

For information concerning important figures in ancient and medieval India see general sources on Hinduism. Especially consult index, *Encyclopaedia of religion and ethics (D15)*. On more recent figures see bibliography in Sarma, *Studies in the renaissance of Hinduism (D76)*.

UNIVERSITY, ACADEMY, AND SOCIETY PUBLICATIONS

A fairly complete list will be found under anthropology and ethnology in "Science of man," *Biological sciences (D47)*.

PERIODICALS

For a lengthy list of Indian periodicals, many of which carry articles on religion from time to time, see *Ulrich's periodicals directory (B75)*. Among the most important are the following.

D95. **Calcutta review.** Calcutta, 1844 ff. [University of Calcutta.] (Monthly.) Deals only occasionally with religion, more often with philosophy.

D96. **The Indian antiquary: a journal of oriental research.** 62 v. Bombay, 1872–1933. Succeeded by *New Indian antiquary* (1938 ff.). (Monthly.) Particularly valuable for archaeological material bearing on religion.

The following are modern periodicals of popular rather than scholarly nature, but valuable as representative of the religion of the period.

D97. **The Aryan path.** Bombay, 1930 ff. (Monthly.)

D98. **Indian social reformer.** Bombay, 1894–1953. (Weekly.) In its later years published as an organ of the Prarthana Samaj, one of the modern reform groups of Hinduism.

D99. **Prabuddha bharata: or awakened India.** Calcutta, etc., 1898 ff. (Monthly.)

D100. **Vedanta kesari.** Madras, 1940 ff. (Monthly.)

BUDDHISM

BIBLIOGRAPHIES, LIBRARIES, AND MUSEUMS

D101. Farquhar, John N. **An outline of the religious literature of India.** London, 1920. Lists the major Buddhist original sources in Pali and Sanskrit, with indication of translations into European vernaculars.

An up-to-date listing of translations in the *Sacred books of the Buddhists* and the Pali Text Society *Translation series,* both edited in the beginning by T. W. Rhys Davids (the former in collaboration with his wife, C. A. F. Rhys Davids) and both now under the editorship of I. B. Horner, is included in the bibliography of *A source book in Indian philosophy* (*D86*). This work also lists most of the major scholarly studies of Buddhism by Indian, Japanese, and western scholars. In the notes and bibliographies in these volumes may be found almost all the really significant studies of Buddhism.

D102. Thomas, Edward J. **The life of Buddha as legend and history.** See *D167.*

D103. Nanjio, Bunyiu. **A catalogue of the Chinese translation of the Buddhist Tripit-aka.** Oxford, 1883. Rev. ed., Tokyo, 1929. Catalogs all books accepted in the Chinese Tripitaka and a complete set published in Japan. See also Steinilber-Oberlin, *The Buddhist sects of Japan* (*D146*), p. 297.

D104. Bibliographie bouddhique. 1928 ff. Paris, 1930 ff. (Annual.) Edited by various well-known French scholars. All significant Buddhist studies in any language, both in books and periodicals, are listed, usually with critical comment. Indispensable for period covered. For detail as to publishers, etc., and for other Buddhist bibliographies not noted here see Barrow, *A bibliography of bibliographies in religion* (*D1*), p. 104.

D105. Held, Hans L. **Deutsche Bibliographie des Buddhismus.** Munich, 1916.

D106. Gard, Richard A. **A select bibliography for the study of Buddhism in Burma in western languages.** Rangoon and Tokyo, 1958.

D107. ——. **A bibliography for the study of Buddhism in Thailand in western languages.** Bangkok, 1957.

D108. ——. **A bibliography for the study of Buddhism in Ceylon in western languages.** 2nd ed., Berkeley, 1957.

D109. Hamilton, Clarence H. **Buddhism in India, Ceylon, China and Japan: a reading guide.** Chicago, 1931. Includes the major sources for a systematic study of Buddhism.

D110. Humphreys, Christmas. **A Buddhist students' manual.** London, 1956. An analysis of the Mahayana scriptures may be found on pp. 249–60.

D111. March, Arthur C. **A Buddhist bibliography.** London, 1935.

D112. Pratt, Ida A. **Buddhism: a list of references in the New York Public Library.** N.Y., 1916.

Most of the larger university libraries contain the major translated source materials for the study of Buddhism. At Harvard, Yale, the University of Pennsylvania, University of Chicago, and University of California major Sanskrit and Pali sources may be found. The American Academy of Asiatic Studies in San Francisco has specialized in Buddhistic studies. Oxford has long been a center of Buddhist research, and the Oxford Press has published the *Sacred books of the Buddhists* series and translations of the Pali Text Society in English. Distinguished work has also been done in France and Germany. In Japan there are several societies for the study of Buddhism. See Steinilber-Oberlin, *The Buddhist sects of Japan* (*D146*), pp. 302–3. There is also some activity in Ceylon. Celebration of the 2600th anniversary of the Buddha in Burma has been the occasion of renewed interest in the study of Buddhism among eastern scholars, resulting in publication of a number of new translations and studies of Buddhist sources.

ENCYCLOPEDIAS AND WORKS OF REFERENCE

Scholarly articles and bibliographies on almost every phase of Buddhism may be found in *D13–19.* The Buddhist sects of Japan (*D146*), p. 301, lists seven dictionaries and encyclopedias on Buddhism, all in Japanese. See also

D113. Hôbôgirin: dictionnaire encyclopédique du bouddhisme d'après les sources chinoises et japonaises. Ed. by Paul Demiéville. 2 v. Tokyo, 1929–30.

SHORTER GENERAL HISTORIES

D114. Conze Edward, **Buddhism: its essence and development.** N.Y., 1954.

D115. Coomaraswamy, Ananda K. **Buddha and the gospel of Buddhism.** London, 1916. Reprint, 1928. Includes selected bibliography, mainly of secondary sources.

D116. Humphreys, Christmas. **Buddhism.** Harmondsworth, Eng., 1951. [Pelican series.] Popular work by a western Buddhist.

D117. Morgan, Kenneth W., ed. **The path of the Buddha.** N.Y., 1956. All the authors are distinguished Buddhists, each writing on some aspect of his faith or of Buddhism in his own country. Excellent selected bibliography and extensive glossary.

D118. Rhys Davids, Caroline A. F. **Outlines of Buddhism: a historical sketch.** London, 1934.

See other works by same author on various aspects of Buddhism and translations of original sources. Mrs. Rhys Davids was associated with her husband in editing many writings from the Pali.

LONGER GENERAL HISTORIES

D119. Rhys Davids, Thomas W. **Buddhism, its history and literature.** Rev. ed., N.Y., 1926. See also his *Buddhist India* (N.Y., 1902) and numerous translations of original source materials. Author was editor of the *Sacred books of the Buddhists* series (London, 1895 ff.), as well as the publications of the Pali Text Society.

D120. Eliot, Sir Charles N. E. **Hinduism and Buddhism.** 3 v. London, 1954.

D121. Glasenapp, Helmuth von. **Der Buddhismus in Indien und im Ferner Osten.** Berlin, 1936.

D122. Oldenberg, Hermann. **Buddha: sein Leben, sein Lehre, sein Gemeinde.** 6th ed., Stuttgart, 1914. English tr., by William Hoey, *Buddha: his life, his doctrine, his order,* London, 1882. A standard German work.

D123. Pratt, James B. **The pilgrimage of Buddhism and a Buddhist pilgrimage.** N.Y., 1928.

D124. Ward, Charles H. S. **Buddhism.** 2 v. London, 1947–52.

HISTORIES OF SPECIAL PERIODS

D125. Dutt, Nalinaksha. **Early monastic Buddhism.** 2 v. Calcutta, 1924.

D126. Saunders, Kenneth J. **Epochs in Buddhist history.** Chicago, 1924.

D127. Hsüan-tsang. **Si-yu-ki: Buddhist records of the western world.** Tr. by Samuel Beal. London, 1884. New ed., Calcutta, 1957 ff. A basic Chinese source, good for Buddhism in India in the T'ang dynasty period.

D128. On Yuan Chwang's travels in India, 629–645 A.D. Ed. by T. W. Rhys Davids and S. W. Bushell. 2 v. London, 1904–05.

D129. Fa-hsiën. **A record of Buddhist kingdoms: being an account by the Chinese monk Fa-Hien of his travels in India and Ceylon (A.D. 399–414).** Tr. by James Legge. Oxford, 1886.

D130. I-tsing. **Mémoire composé à l'époque de la grande dynastie T'ang sur les religieux éminents qui allèrent chercher la loi dans les pays d'Occident.** Tr. by Edouard Chavannes. Paris, 1894.

D131. ———. **A record of the Buddhist religion as practised in India and the Malay archipelago (A.D. 671–695).** Tr. by Junjiro Takakusu. Oxford, 1896.

HISTORIES OF SPECIAL AREAS

D132. Kern, Hendrik. **Histoire du Buddhisme dans l'Inde.** Tr. by Gedeon Huet. 2 v. Paris, 1901–03.

D133. Getty, Alice. **The gods of northern Buddhism.** London, 1914.

D134. McGovern, William M. **Introduction to Mahāyāna Buddhism.** London, 1922.

D135. Suzuki, Daisetz T. **Outlines of Mahāyāna Buddhism.** London, 1907.

D136. Landon, Kenneth P. **Southeast Asia, crossroad of religions.** Chicago, 1947. A perceptive and sympathetic study.

D137. Ray, Hiharranjan. **An introduction to the study of Theravada Buddhism in Burma.** Calcutta, 1946.

D138. Wells, Kenneth E. **Thai Buddhism, its rites and activities.** Bangkok, 1939.

D139. Huth, Georg, tr. and ed. **Geschichte des Buddhismus in der Mongolei, aus dem Tibetischen des Jigs-med nam-mk'a.** 2 v. Strasbourg, 1892–96.

D140. Grünwedel, Albert. **Mythologie du Buddhisme au Tibet et en Mongolie basée sur la collection lamaïque du Prince Oukhtomsky.** Paris, 1900.

For the principal works on religion in Tibet see subsection on Tibet in Section N.

D141. Hodous, Lewis. **Buddhists and Buddhism in China.** N.Y., 1924.

D142. Reichelt, Karl L. **Truth and tradition in Chinese Buddhism.** Shanghai, 1927.

D143. Beal, Samuel. **A catena of Buddhist scriptures from the Chinese.** London, 1871.

For other works on Buddhism in China see subsection on religion in Section O.

D144. Anesaki, Masaharu. **History of Japanese religion.** London, 1930. The major part of this work, by a ranking Japanese Buddhist scholar, is devoted to Buddhism.

D145. Eliot, Sir Charles N. E. **Japanese Buddhism.** London, 1935.

D146. Steinilber-Oberlin, Émile. **The Buddhist sects of Japan.** Tr. by Marc Logé. London, 1938. Contains valuable annotated bibliography of books, chiefly Japanese, concerning Japanese Buddhism in general and its various sects. Also lists the chief Buddhist periodicals and leading Japanese societies for the study of Buddhism.

D147. Suzuki, Daisetz T. **An introduction to Zen Buddhism.** N.Y., 1949. The outstanding Zen authority. See also his numerous other works.

D148. Dasgupta, Shashi B. **An introduction to Tantric Buddhism.** Calcutta, 1950.

HISTORIES OF SPECIAL TOPICS

Art

D149. Anesaki, Masaharu. **Buddhist art.** Boston, 1915.

D150. Coomaraswamy, Ananda K. **His-**

tory of Indian and Indonesian art. See *D81*.

D151. Foucher, Alfred C. A. **L'art greco-bouddhique en Gandhara.** Paris, 1905.

D152. Grünwedel, Albert. **Buddhist art in India.** Tr. by A. C. Gibson. Rev. and enl. ed., London, 1901.

D153. Fenollosa, Ernest F. **Epochs of Chinese and Japanese art.** Rev. ed., 2 v., N.Y., 1913.

D154. Vogel, Jean P. **Buddhist art in India, Ceylon and Java.** Tr. by A. J. Barnouw. Oxford, 1936.

D155. Gordon, Antoinette K. **Thibetan religious art.** N.Y., 1952.

Philosophy

D156. Bahm, Archie J. **Philosophy of the Buddha.** N.Y., 1959. A provocative interpretation.

D157. Conze, Edward, ed. **Buddhist texts through the ages.** N.Y., 1954. Fresh translations from Pali, Sanskrit, Tibetan, Chinese, and Japanese.

D158. La Vallée-Poussin, Louis de. **Le dogme et la philosophie du Bouddhisme.** Paris, 1930. One of the outstanding French scholars in the field. See also his other books on Buddhism and his translations of source materials.

D159. Takakusu, Junjiro. **The essentials of Buddhist philosophy.** Ed. by Wing-tsit Chan and Charles A. Moore. Honolulu, 1947.

D160. Hamilton, Clarence H. **Buddhism, a religion of infinite compassion.** N.Y., 1952. Pp. 126–32 and 148–55 illustrate Mahāyāna philosophies.

D161. Keith, Arthur B. **Buddhist philosophy in India and Ceylon.** Oxford, 1923.

D162. Murti, T. R. V. **The central philosophy of Buddhism: a study of the Madhyamika system.** London, 1955.

D163. Thomas, Edward J. **The history of Buddhist thought.** London, 1933. Well documented; good bibliography.

D164. La Vallée-Poussin, Louis de. **La morale bouddhique.** Paris, 1927.

D165. Tachibana, Shundo. **The ethics of Buddhism.** London, 1926. Systematic treatment by a Japanese Buddhist scholar.

D166. Anesaki, Masaharu. "Ethics and morality." **Encyclopaedia of religion and ethics** (*D15*), v. 5, pp. 447–55.

BIOGRAPHIES

There are numerous biographies of the Buddha in several European languages, most of them semi-popular or popular. The more valuable critical studies are those of T. W. Rhys Davids, C. A. F. Rhys Davids, Hermann F. Oldenberg, and

D167. Thomas, Edward J. **The life of Buddha as legend and history.** 3rd ed., N.Y., 1952. Critical and well documented. Good bibliography, especially of original source materials.

For other Buddhist personalities see the following.

D168. Hui Li. **The life of Hiuen Tsiang.** Tr. by Samuel Beal. London, 1911.

D169. Shunjo (Japanese priest). **Honen, the Buddhist saint.** Tr. by Harper H. Coates and Ryugaku Ishizuka. Kyoto, 1925.

D170. Anesaki, Masaharu. **Nichiren, the Buddhist prophet.** Cambridge, Mass., 1916.

UNIVERSITY, ACADEMY, AND SOCIETY PUBLICATIONS

The most notable series is that of the Pali Text Society, fully listed in the bibliography of *A source book in Indian philosophy* (*D86*).

D171. A number of volumes of the **Harvard oriental series** deal with Buddhism.

PERIODICALS

Most of the periodicals included in *D30–41* contain studies of aspects of Buddhism. Steinilber-Oberlin, *The Buddhist sects of Japan* (*D146*) lists some twenty periodicals in Japan dealing with Buddhism in general or some of the major sects, all but one of them in Japanese. Articles on Buddhism appear in journals relating to Asia cited in Section N. See also

D172. **Zeitschrift für Buddhismus.** Munich, 1914–31. (Annual.)

JAINISM

BIBLIOGRAPHIES, LIBRARIES, AND MUSEUMS

There are no centers of specialized study of Jainism in the West, but wherever Hinduism is studied the major materials on Jainism will be found.

D173. Guérinot, Armand A. **Essai de bibliographie jaina.** Paris, 1906. For detail see *D1*, p. 105, or *D2*, p. 70.

D174. ———. "Notes de bibliographie jaina." **Journal asiatique**, 10th ser., 14 (July-Aug. 1909): 48–148. For detail see *D2*.

D175. Klatt, Johannes. **Specimen of a literary-bibliographical Jaina-onomasticon.** Leipzig, 1892.

ENCYCLOPEDIAS AND WORKS OF REFERENCE

In addition to works listed below, see under "Hinduism."

D176. Gaina Sutras. Tr. from Prakrit by Hermann Jacobi. 2 pts. Oxford, 1884–95. [Sacred books of the East, 22 and 45.]

D177. The sacred books of the Jainas. Ed. by Sarat Chandra Ghoshal. Arrah and Lucknow, various dates. For detailed list see *A source book in Indian philosophy* (*D86*), p. 653.

See also Farquhar, *An outline of the religious literature of India* (*D50*); and Winternitz, *A history of Indian literature* (*D54*).

GENERAL HISTORIES

D178. Glasenapp, Helmuth von. **Der Jainismus.** Berlin, 1925.

D179. Guérinot, Armand A. **La religion djaina.** Paris, 1906.

D180. Jaini, Jagmandar. **Outlines of Jainism.** Ed. by F. W. Thomas. Cambridge, Eng., 1916. Reprint with corrections, 1940.

D181. Schubring, Walther. **Die Lehre der Jainas.** Berlin and Leipzig, 1935.

D182. Stevenson, Margaret. **The heart of Jainism.** London, 1915.

D183. ——. **Notes on modern Jainism.** Oxford, 1910.

HISTORIES OF SPECIAL PERIODS AND TOPICS

D184. Shah, Chimanlal J. **Jainism in north India, 800 B.C.–A.D. 526.** N.Y., 1932.

D185. Shah, Umakant P. **Studies in Jaina art.** Benares, 1955. A Jaina rather than objective study, but asserted by them to be a lucid, comprehensive, and critical review of Jaina art in northern India and symbol worship in Jainism.

On Jaina art see also under "Hinduism."

D186. Tatia, Nathmal. **Studies in Jaina philosophy.** Benares, 1951.

D187. Mehta, Mohan L. **Outlines of Jaina philosophy.** Bangalore, 1954.

ACADEMY PUBLICATIONS

The Jaina Academy publishes a lengthening list of Jain studies in English and German as well as in the Hindi, available to members of the World Jain Mission. These studies would hardly be classed as objective, but are valuable for the materials they present. A list of those available is included in *The voice of Ahimsa,* v. 7, nos. 3–4, p. 109.

PERIODICALS

D188. The voice of Ahimsa. Aliganj (Etah), U. P., India, 1951 ff. Especially stresses the cardinal Jain principle, *Ahimsa,* but carries occasional scholarly articles, usually by Jains, on aspects of Jainism. Reviews books in the field.

D189. The Jain antiquary. Arrah, Bihar, India, 1935 ff. (Irregular.)

See also subsection on "Hinduism."

SIKHISM

BIBLIOGRAPHIES, LIBRARIES, AND MUSEUMS

The Sikh religion is often treated as a sect of Hinduism, and materials on Sikhism will generally be found in centers of Hindu studies. Bibliographies on Hinduism usually carry references to the rise and development of the Sikh faith.

ENCYCLOPEDIAS AND WORKS OF REFERENCE

D190. Kahn Singh. **Encyclopedia of Sikh literature.** 4 v. Amritsar, 1930. A standard dictionary and encyclopedia of the two Granths, recognized as authentic by the Sikhs. In the Gurmukhi language.

D191. Risley, Sir Herbert H. **The people of India.** 2nd ed., ed. by W. Crooke, Calcutta and London, 1915.

D192. The Ādi Granth: or the holy scriptures of the Sikhs. Tr. by Ernest Trumpp. London, 1877. The introduction is valuable, but the translation leaves much to be desired.

D193. Blunt, Sir Edward A. H. **The caste system of northern India.** London, 1931.

D194. Hutton, John H. **Caste in India, its nature, function and origins.** 2nd ed., Bombay and N.Y., 1951.

SHORTER GENERAL HISTORIES

D195. Archer, John C. **The Sikhs in relation to Hindus, Moslems, Christians, and Ahmadiyyas: a study in comparative religion.** Princeton, 1946. A mine of information on the Sikhs.

D196. Cunningham, Joseph D. **A history of the Sikhs from the origin of the nation to the battles of the Sutlej.** Ed. by H. L. O. Garrett. New and rev. ed., London, 1918. Reliable and readable history from the British viewpoint. The 41 appendices are especially useful.

D197. Princep, Sir Henry T. **History of the Punjab and the rise, progress and present condition of the sect and nation of the Sikhs.** London, 1846.

D198. Rama Krishna, Lajwanti. **Les Sikhs.** Paris, 1933.

D199. Sardha Ram. **Sikhan de Raj di Vidya.** Lahore, 1892. An old classic, in the Gurmukhi language, on the history and customs of the Sikhs.

D200. Singh, Teja, and Ganda Singh. **A short history of the Sikhs.** V. 1 (1469–1765). Bombay, 1950. Excellent, concise history, using much source material in Urdu and Persian, and written from a fairly objective viewpoint.

LONGER GENERAL HISTORIES

D201. Gupta, Hari Ram. **History of the Sikhs.** 3 v. Calcutta, 1939–44.

D202. Macauliffe, Max A. **The Sikh religion, its gurus, sacred writings, and authors.** 6 v. Oxford, 1909. The standard work on the subject. Embodies the traditional views of leading *gyanis* of the time, so needs to be used with caution.

HISTORIES OF SPECIAL PERIODS

D203. Narang, Sir Gokul C. **Transformation of Sikhism.** 3rd ed., Lahore, 1946. By an Arya Samjist.

D204. Singh, Khushwant. **The Sikhs.** London, 1953. Useful for the more modern movements and recent history.

HISTORIES OF SPECIAL TOPICS

Political

D205. Banerjee, Indubhusan. **Evolution of the Khalsa.** Calcutta, 1936. Valuable survey of the rise of the Sikh state.

D206. Sinha, Narendra K. **Rise of the Sikh power.** 2nd ed., Calcutta, 1936. History of the struggle for independence before Ranjit Singh.

Cultural

D207. Singh, Sir Jogendra. **Sikh ceremonies.** Bombay, 1941.

D208. Loehlin, C. H. **The Sikhs and their book.** Lucknow, 1946.

D209. Singh, Mohan. **An introduction to Panjabi literature.** Amritsar, 1951.

D210. Shromani Gurdwara Parbandhak Committee. **Sikh Rahit Maryada.** Amritsar, 1950. The official book of worship and discipline.

D211. Singh, Sher. **The philosophy of Sikhism.** Lahore, 1944. Rather diffuse, but with some good insights.

D212. Singh, Jodh. **Gurmati Nirnai.** Lahore, 1945. Exposition of the Guru's teachings, in the Gurmukhi language.

BIOGRAPHIES

See Macauliffe above (*D202*).

D213. Singh, Ganda. **Life of Banda Singh Bahadur.** Amritsar, 1935. A scholarly work, written from much source material in Persian and Gurmukhi.

D214. Keay, Frank E. **Kabir and his followers.** London, 1931.

PERIODICALS

See under "Hinduism."

THE RELIGIONS OF CHINA

BIBLIOGRAPHIES, LIBRARIES, AND MUSEUMS

Most of the source materials that have been translated into English may be found in libraries of the larger universities of the United States. Many original texts also are in such libraries as those of Harvard, Yale, Columbia, Stanford, Cornell, University of Chicago, and University of California. Oxford University in England has been a center for Chinese studies, and important work has been done in Germany and France.

The greater number of books dealing with religion in China cover all of the so-called three religions of China—Confucianism, Taoism, and Buddhism. For more specialized works see subsection on early China in Section G and subsection on religion in Section O. The most extensive general bibliographies are found in Shryock, *The origin and development of the state cult of Confucius* (*D233*); Chan, *Religious trends in modern*

China (*D232*); Krause, *Ju-Tao-Fo* (*D227*); and the following.

D215. Creel, Herrlee G. **Confucius, the man and the myth.** N.Y., 1949.

D216. Fung, Yu-lan. **A history of Chinese philosophy.** 2 v. Princeton, 1953.

D217. Encyclopedia of books on China. London, 1927.

ENCYCLOPEDIAS AND WORKS OF REFERENCE

Articles on every aspect of China's religions, usually with bibliography, may be found in the standard encyclopedias included in *D13–19*. See also

D218. Chan, Wing-Tsit. "Chinese terminology." **Encyclopedia of religion,** ed. by Vergilius Ferm (N.Y., 1945).

GENERAL HISTORIES

Older single volume treatments of China's religion by Joseph Edkins, James Legge,

Herbert A. Giles, E. H. Parker, and others are listed in the above mentioned bibliographies of Creel, Fung Yu-lan, Shryock, and others. Listed below are more recent works.

D219. Hughes, Ernest R., and K. Hughes. **Religion in China.** London, 1950.

D220. Clennell, Walter J. **The historical development of religion in China.** 2nd ed., London, 1926.

D221. Maspero, Henri. **Les religions chinoises.** Paris, 1950. Authoritative discussion.

D222. Weber, Max. **The religion of China: Confucianism and Taoism.** Tr. and ed. by Hans H. Gerth. Glencoe, Ill., 1951.

D223. Wei, F. Cho-min. **The spirit of Chinese culture.** N.Y., 1947.

D224. Yang, Yung-ch'ing. **China's religious heritage.** N.Y., 1943. Popular and lacking in bibliography. Interesting as one of the few books in English on Chinese religions by a Chinese.

D225. Reichelt, Karl L. **Religion in Chinese garment.** N.Y., 1951.

D226. Soothill, William E. **The three religions of China.** 2nd ed., London, 1923.

D227. Krause, Friedrich E. A. **Ju-Tao-Fo: die religiösen und philosophischen Systeme Ostasiens.** Munich, 1924. Contains extensive bibliography of European works on the religions and philosophies of eastern Asia.

D228. Wieger, Léon. **A history of the religious beliefs and philosophical opinions in China from the beginning to the present time.** Tr. by Edward T. C. Werner. Hsien Hsien, 1927.

D229. Groot, Jan J. M. de. **The religious system of China.** 6 v. Leiden, 1892–1910.

D230. Doré, Henri. **Researches into Chinese superstitions.** Tr. by M. Kennelly. 10 v. Shanghai, 1914–33.

French writers on Chinese religion may be found in *Histoire générale de religions (D20)*, v. 4, pp. 539–40.

D231. Day, Clarence B. **Chinese peasant cults.** Shanghai, 1940. Extensive bibliography.

D232. Chan, Wing-Tsit. **Religious trends in modern China.** N.Y., 1953. Discussion limited to trends in Confucianism, Taoism, and Buddhism in China in the last half century; but the excellent, comprehensive bibliography includes the most important older sources, both western and Chinese, for a study of religion in China. Chinese titles appear in Chinese script as well as transliteration.

CONFUCIUS AND CONFUCIANISM

D233. Shryock, John K. **The origin and development of the state cult of Confucius.**

N.Y., 1932. Contains extensive bibliographies in Chinese, Japanese, and the various European languages.

D234. Johnston, Sir Reginald F. **Confucianism and modern China.** London, 1934.

D235. Wilhelm, Richard. **K'ungtse und der Konfuzianismus.** Berlin and Leipzig, 1928. English tr., *Confucius and Confucianism,* N.Y., 1931. Even this is not a critical life.

D236. Liu Wu-chi. **Confucius, his life and time.** N.Y., 1955.

D237. Crow, Carl. **Master Kung.** N.Y., 1938.

D238. Collis, Maurice. **The first holy one.** N.Y., 1948.

D239. Lin Yutang. **The wisdom of Confucius.** N.Y., 1938.

For the Confucian classics and other works on Confucius see subsection on early China in Section G, and for works on Confucian philosophy see subsection on thought in Section O.

TAOISM

D240. Marceron, Désiré J. B. **Bibliographie du Taoisme . . . suive d'une biographie des principaux sinologues, japonistes, et autres savants adonnés a l'étude de l'extrême Orient.** Paris, 1898.

D241. Wieger, Léon. **Taoisme.** 2 v. Hsien Hsien, 1911–13. V. 1 contains a list of the Taoist canon.

D242. Maspero, Henri. **Mélanges posthumes sur les religions et l'histoire de la Chine.** V. 2, Le Taoisme. Paris, 1950.

D243. ——. "Les procédés de 'Norrir le principe vital' dans le religion taoïste ancienne." **Journal asiatique,** 229 (1937): 177–252, 353–430.

D244. Welch, Holmes. **The parting of the way: Lao Tzu and the Taoist movement.** Boston, 1957. The latter part of the book, giving something of the history of Taoism, is the most useful.

D245. The wisdom of Lao Tzu. Tr. and ed. by Lin Yutang. N.Y., 1948.

See also subsection on religion in Section O.

PERIODICALS

Occasional articles on Chinese religions appear in periodicals included in *D28–41,* in the long list of periodicals relating to Asia in Section N, and in those relating to China at the end of Section O. See also

D246. Löwenthal, Rudolf. **The religious periodical press in China.** Peiping, 1940.

SHINTOISM

BIBLIOGRAPHIES, LIBRARIES, AND MUSEUMS

While a number of United States universities have concerned themselves with the study of Japanese culture in general, including political and economic aspects, none has given special attention to Shinto, her national religion. However, since there has been such a close relationship between this and the national government, especially in more recent times, most of the major sources concerning at least Shinto may be found in such places as Columbia University, University of Michigan, Northwestern University, and the University of California.

D247. Holzman, Donald. **Japanese religion and philosophy: a guide to Japanese reference and research materials.** Ann Arbor, 1959.

D248. Kato, Genchi, Karl Reitz, and William Schiffer. **A bibliography of Shinto in western languages from the oldest times till 1952.** Tokyo, 1953.

D249. Kato, Genchi. **Shinto shoseki mokuroku.** [A bibliography of Shinto.] 2 v. Tokyo, 1938–53. Complete listing of publications in the Japanese language.

See also general bibliographies on Japan.

ENCYCLOPEDIAS AND WORKS OF REFERENCE

D250. Shinto dai jiten. [The Shinto encyclopedia.] 3 v. Tokyo, 1937–40. A thesaurus of information for the study of Shinto in all its aspects.

D251. Nihongi: chronicles of Japan from the earliest times to A.D. 697. Tr. by William G. Aston. 2 v. London, 1896. 1 v. ed., 1924. Indispensable for study of Shinto tradition.

D252. Ko-ji-ki: or records of ancient matters. Tr. by Basil H. Chamberlain. New ed., with annotations by W. G. Aston, Kobe, 1932. From creation to 628 A.D. Equally indispensable with the *Nihongi* for a knowledge of early Shinto.

D253. Florenz, Karl. "Ancient Japanese rituals." **Transactions of the Asiatic Society of Japan,** ser. 1, 27 (1899): 1–112; reprint, ser. 2, 2 (1927): 99–164.

D254. Kogoshui: gleanings from ancient stories. Tr. by Genchi Kato and Hikoshirō Hoshino. 3rd ed., Tokyo, 1926. From early part of the 9th century.

D255. Satow, Sir Ernest M. "Ancient Japanese rituals." **Transactions of the Asiatic Society of Japan,** ser. 2, v. 2 (Tokyo, 1927). Translation of 9 of the 27 rituals (norito). Indispensable for a first-hand knowledge of early Shinto ceremonies and belief.

SHORTER GENERAL HISTORY

D256. Harada, Tasuka. **The faith of Japan.** N.Y., 1914.

LONGER GENERAL HISTORIES

D257. Anesaki, Masaharu. **History of Japanese religion.** London, 1930. Special reference to the social and moral life of the nation.

D258. ——. **Religious life of the Japanese people.** Tokyo, 1938. Excellent introduction to the religious systems of Japan prior to World War II.

D259. Gundert, Wilhelm. **Japanische Religionsgeschichte.** Tokyo and Stuttgart, 1935.

D260. Holtom, Daniel C. **The national faith of Japan: a study in modern Shinto.** N.Y., 1938.

D261. Kato, Genchi. **A study of Shinto, the religion of the Japanese nation.** Tokyo, 1926. Author was professor of Shinto in the Imperial University of Tokyo.

D262. ——. **Shinto no shukyo hattatsushiteki kenkyu.** [A historical study of the development of Shinto as a religion.] Tokyo, 1935. Authoritative and voluminous.

HISTORIES OF SPECIAL PERIODS

D263. Aston, William G. **Shinto: the way of the gods.** London, 1905. Deals mainly with early Shinto of the classical period.

D264. Schurhammer, Georg. **Shinto: the way of the gods in Japan, according to reports of Japanese and Jesuit missionaries in the 16th and 17th centuries.** Bonn and Leipzig, 1923. In German and English.

D265. Chamberlain, Basil H. **The invention of a new religion.** London, 1912. Criticism of efforts of the Japanese government of the Meiji era to resuscitate Shinto as the state religion.

D266. Holtom, Daniel C. **Modern Japan and Shinto nationalism: a study of present day trends in Japanese religions.** Rev. ed., Chicago, 1947.

D267. Supreme Commander for the Allied Powers. **Religions in Japan.** Tokyo, 1948. Includes various SCAP directives concerning religion during the occupation, as well as much information on present systems of Japan.

D268. Kishimoto, Hideo, ed. **Japanese religion in the Meiji era.** Tr. by John Howe. Tokyo, 1956. Shinto, Buddhism, and Christianity of the era are discussed, each by a leading authority.

D269. Satow, Sir Ernest M. "The revival of pure Shintau." **Transactions of the Asiatic Society of Japan,** ser. 2, v. 2 (Tokyo,

1927). Valuable for study of Shinto in late Tokugawa era.

HISTORIES OF SPECIAL TOPICS

Political

D270. Hall, Robert K., ed. **Kokutai no hongi: cardinal principles of the national entity of Japan.** Tr. by John O. Gauntlett. Cambridge, Mass., 1949. An important educational and political policy document of the Japanese government for war and prewar years, based on Shinto teachings.
D271. Ballou, Robert O. **Shinto, the unconquered enemy.** N.Y., 1945. Shinto in relation to Japanese nationalism.
D272. Hibino, Yutaka. **Nippon shindo ron: or the national ideals of the Japanese people.** Tr. by A. P. McKenzie. Cambridge, Eng., 1928.
D273. Honaga, S. **The national spirit of Japan.** London, 1916.
D274. Hozumi, Nobushige. **Ancestor-worship and Japanese law.** 2nd ed., Tokyo, 1912.

Cultural

D275. Akiyama, Aisaburo. **Shinto and its architecture.** Kyoto, 1936. Main types of Shinto architecture, with drawings and photographs.
D276. Japan. Bureau of Religions. **Handbook of the old shrines and temples and their treasures in Japan.** Tokyo, 1920.
D277. Kato, Genchi. **A study of the development of religious ideas among the Japanese people as illustrated by Japanese phallicism.** Tokyo, 1924. [Transactions of the Asiatic Society of Japan, ser. 2, v. 1 suppl.]
D278. Hall, Robert K. **Shushin: the ethics of a defeated nation.** N.Y., 1949. Includes annotated translation of the official textbooks on ethics used in elementary schools of Japan at the time of Pearl Harbor.

UNIVERSITY, ACADEMY, AND SOCIETY PUBLICATIONS

D279. Transactions of the Asiatic Society of Japan. Ser. 1, 50 v., Tokyo, 1872–1923; ser. 2, 1924–40; ser. 3, 1948 ff. Index to v. 1–50, *List of books published by the Asiatic Society of Japan,* Yokohama, 1923. Catalogue of the contents of all books of second series is included in an appendix of ser. 3, v. 1.
D280. Meiji Seitoku Kinen Gakkai kiyo. [Transactions of the Meiji Japan Society.] Tokyo, 1914 ff. Published since 1952 by the Meiji Shrine of Tokyo. In Japanese with short English summaries.
D281. Monumenta Nipponica: studies on Japanese culture, past and present. Tokyo, 1938 ff. (Semiannual.) Published by Sophia University. Contains important papers on Shinto. Articles are in English, French, and German.
D282. Transactions and proceedings of the Japan Society. London, 1893 ff.

PERIODICALS

D283. Jinja Shimpo. [Shinto Shrine news.] Tokyo, 1946 ff. Weekly newspaper of Shinto. A record of current Shinto activities, but includes critical and interpretative discussions.
D284. Shūkyō jiho. [Review of religions.] Tokyo, etc., 1947 ff. (Monthly.) Articles on all religions, including Shinto.
Most magazines dealing with Japanese culture have occasional articles on Shinto. See the various periodical indices.

ZOROASTRIANISM

BIBLIOGRAPHIES, LIBRARIES, AND MUSEUMS

Comparatively few scholars have worked intensively in the field of Zoroastrianism in recent years. Universities which have interested themselves in the Near and Middle East include Columbia, Chicago, and Michigan. Here adequate research materials may be found.
D285. Casartelli, Louis C. "The literary activity of the Parsis during the past ten years (1883–1893) in Avestan and Pehlevi studies." **Transactions of the 9th Congress of Orientalists,** 2 (London, 1893), 528–36.
D286. Dhalla, Maneckji N. **History of Zoroastrianism.** London, 1938. The author, a high-priest of the Parsis, offers, besides a comprehensive history of the rise and development of the faith, an extensive bibliography which includes most studies of consequence, both occidental and oriental, down to publication date.
D287. Saklatwalla, Jamshedji E. **A bibliography of religion (mainly Avestan and Vedic).** London and Bombay, 1922. Alphabetical list with a few notes.

ENCYCLOPEDIAS AND WORKS OF REFERENCE

D288. Olmstead, Albert T. **History of the Persian empire, Achaemenid period.** See *F172.*
D289. West, Edward W., ed. and tr. **Pahlavi texts.** 5 v. Oxford, 1880–97. [The sacred books of the East, 5, 18, 24, 37, 47.]

SHORTER GENERAL HISTORIES

D290. Dhalla, Maneckji N. **Zoroastrian civilization from the earliest times to the downfall of the last Zoroastrian empire, 651 A.D.** N.Y., 1922.

D291. ——. **History of Zoroastrianism.** (See *D296*.)

D292. Nyberg, Henrik S. **Die Religionen des alten Iran.** See *F202*.

LONGER GENERAL HISTORIES

D293. Herzfeld, Ernst E. **Zoroaster and his world.** 2 v. Princeton, 1947. Highly technical study of Zoroastrianism, largely linguistic, involving historical as well as textual criticism of the Avestan texts. Numerous bibliographical items in footnotes.

D294. Lommel, Herman. **Die Religion Zarathustras.** See *F208*.

HISTORIES OF SPECIAL PERIODS

D295. Bailey, Harold W. **Zoroastrian problems in ninth century books.** Oxford, 1943.

D296. Clemen, Carl C., ed. **Fontes historiae religionis persicae.** See *F136*.

D297. Duchesne-Guillemin, Jacques. **Zoroastre: étude critique avec une traduction commentée des Gâthâ.** See *F133*.

D298. Moulton, James H. **Early Zoroastrianism.** London, 1913. Bibliography in notes.

D299. ——. **The treasure of the Magi: a study of modern Zoroastrianism.** London, 1917.

HISTORIES OF SPECIAL AREAS

For histories of Mithraism, an outgrowth of Zoroastrianism, see Sections H and I.

D300. Vermaseren, Maarten J. **Corpus inscriptionum et monumentorum religionis mithriacae.** The Hague, 1956. Very extensive bibliography and indices.

D301. Zaehner, Robert C. **Zurvan, A Zoroastrian dilemma.** Oxford, 1955. Concerned primarily with the Sassanian period and in particular the Zervanite sect and its tenets. Almost half the book is devoted to texts other than Avestan which are relative to the god Zurvan. Extensive bibliography on Zoroastrianism.

HISTORIES OF SPECIAL TOPICS

D302. Dawson, Miles M. **The ethical religion of Zoroaster.** N.Y., 1931. Largely a book of quotations from the Zoroastrian scriptures bearing on ethical questions. Noncritical.

D303. Buch, Morganlal A. **Zoroastrian ethics.** Baroda, 1912.

D304. Dhalla, Maneckji N. **Zoroastrian theology.** N.Y., 1914.

D305. ——. **Our perfecting world.** London, 1930.

BIOGRAPHIES

D306. Jackson, Abraham V. W. **Zoroaster, the prophet of ancient Iran.** See *F205*.

D307. ——. **Zoroastrian studies.** N.Y., 1928.

D308. Henning, Walter B. H. **Zoroaster, politician or witch doctor?** See *F207*.

PERIODICALS

See periodicals suggested in *D28–41*, especially those dealing with the Near and Middle East.

JUDAISM

Since it is practically impossible to keep Judaism as a religion separate from general history of the Jewish people, many items in this bibliography are necessarily concerned with the latter. All these do treat Judaism as a very important feature of Jewish culture.

BIBLIOGRAPHIES, LIBRARIES, AND MUSEUMS

D309. Barrow, John G. **A bibliography of bibliographies in religion.** (See *D1*.) On pp. 105–22 are listed in chronological order scores of bibliographies in English, German, French, Italian, and Hebrew, some annotated and classified, others simply listing titles. Includes most, if not all, bibliographies published prior to 1950.

D310. Marcus, Jacob R. **A brief introduc-**

tion to the bibliography of modern Jewish history. Cincinnati, 1935.

D311. Pfeiffer, Robert H. **Introduction to the Old Testament.** See *F194*.

D312. Shunami, Shlomo. **Bibliography of Jewish bibliographies.** Jerusalem, 1936. Extensive but selected bibliography of the Old Testament as a whole and each part, Bible editions, commentaries, versions, introductions, history and religion of Israel, the Apocrypha, the Pseudepigrapha, etc.

Libraries of the major Christian theological seminaries provide wide coverage of ancient Judaism as related to the Old Testament. The Hebrew Union College in Cincinnati and the Jewish Theological Seminary of New York have the most extensive collections of both primary and secondary source materials covering pre-Christian and post-Christian periods. Other valuable collections are at Johns Hopkins, the University of Pennsylvania, and New York Public Library. Increasingly the Hebrew University in Jerusalem is becoming a center of research in this field.

ENCYCLOPEDIAS AND WORKS OF REFERENCE

D313. Encyclopedia Biblica. Jerusalem, 1950 ff. In Hebrew.

D314. Encyclopaedia judaica. 10 v. Berlin, 1928–34. The 10 v. go through the letter "L." Discontinued after Hitler purge of Jews in Germany.

D315. The Jewish Encyclopedia. Ed. by Cyrus A. I. Singer and others. New ed., 12 v., N.Y. and London, 1901–06. Reprint, 1916. Scholarly and complete.

D316. The universal Jewish encyclopedia. 10 v. N.Y., 1939–43. More popular than the above. Should be used with caution. Good for material on 20th century.
See also *D13–19.*

GEOGRAPHIES, GAZETTEERS, AND ATLASES

D317. Smith, George A. The historical geography of the Holy Land. See *F34.*

D318. ——. Atlas of the historical geography of the Holy Land. London, 1915.

D319. Wright, George E., and Floyd V. Filson, eds. The Westminster historical atlas to the Bible. See *F36.*

PRINTED COLLECTIONS OF SOURCES

D320. The Babylonian Talmud. Ed. by I. Epstein. 35 v. London, 1935–52.

D321. Corpus codicum hebraicorum medii aevi. Copenhagen, 1956 ff. Planned to continue through the years presenting Hebrew and Judeo-Arabic manuscripts found in various libraries, which are of particular value as literary sources or because they represent an especially important text. Each volume contains introduction and notes by a specialist in the field.

D322. Midrash Rabbah. Ed. by H. Friedman and Maurice Simon. 2nd ed., London, 1951. English translation with glossary, notes, and indices.

D323. The Yale Judaica series. Ed. by Julian Obermann. New Haven, 1948 ff.

D324. The Zohar. Tr. by Harry Sperling and Maurice Simon. 5 v. London, 1931–34.

SHORTER GENERAL HISTORY

D325. Margolis, Max L., and Alexander Marx. A history of the Jewish people. Philadelphia, 1927. Bibliographies.

LONGER GENERAL HISTORIES

D326. Baron, Salo W. A social and religious history of the Jews. 2nd ed., N.Y., 1952 ff.

D327. Dubnow, Simon. Weltgeschichte des Jüdischen Volkes von seinen Uranfängen bis zur Gegenwart. 10 v. Berlin, 1925–30.

D328. Finkelstein, Louis, ed. The Jews: their history, culture, and religion. 2 v. N.Y., 1949. Contains 35 chapters, each on a special period or topic, several on religion. Detailed notes and extensive bibliographies. Popular.

D329. Graetz, Heinrich H. Geschichte der Juden von den ältesten Zeiten bis auf die Gegenwart. 11 v. in 13. Leipzig, 1897–1911. English ed., 6 v., N.Y., 1927. The classic history, but antiquated in part.

D330. Montefiore, Claude G. The Old Testament and after. London, 1923. A history of the Jewish faith from the viewpoint of a leading liberal Jewish scholar.

HISTORIES OF SPECIAL PERIODS

D331. Oesterley, William O. E., and Theodore H. Robinson. Hebrew religion: its origin and development. 2nd ed., London, 1937.

D332. Smith, Henry Preserved. The religion of Israel. N.Y., 1914.
See Pfeiffer, *Introduction to the Old Testament* (*D311*) for numerous other titles.

D333. Pfeiffer, Robert H. History of New Testament times. N.Y., 1949. This and the following work deal with Hellenistic Judaism.

D334. Marcus, Ralph. "A selected bibliography (1920–1945) of the Jews in the Hellenistic Roman period." **Proceedings of the American Academy for Jewish Research,** 16 (1946–47): 97–181.

D335. Grayzel, Solomon. A history of the Jews from the Babylonian exile to the establishment of Israel. Philadelphia, 1950. Popular.

D336. Moore, George F. Judaism in the first centuries of the Christian era. 3 v. Cambridge, Mass., 1927–30. No bibliography, but indices to passages cited in the Old and New Testaments, the Apocrypha and Pseudepigrapha, the Greek and Latin authors, the Talmud and Midrash, and from authorities in the age of the Tannaim and Amoraim indicate the basic sources. V. 3 contains additional notes and numerous bibliographical notations.
On medieval Judaism see the three following works.

D337. Bernfeld, Simon, ed. Die Lehren des Judentums—nach den Quellen—herausgegeben vom Verband der deutschen Juden. 5 v. Berlin, 1920–29.

D338. Marcus, Jacob R. The Jew in the

medieval world: a source book, 315–1791. Cincinnati, 1938.

D339. Roth, Cecil. "The Jews in the Middle Ages." **Cambridge medieval history,** v. 7 (N.Y., 1932): 937–49.

On Judaism in the modern period see

D340. Philipson, David. **The reform movement in Judaism.** New and rev. ed., N.Y., 1931.

See also chapters on Jewish publications in the *American Jewish year book* and *The Jewish book annual;* and the frequent book articles in the *Year book of the Central Conference of American Rabbis* and those of other rabbinical groups. Also see the general periodical indices, and the various publications of academies, societies, etc., noted below.

HISTORIES OF SPECIAL AREAS

From the standpoint of religion there is little advantage in an approach by areas. Religion will be found discussed to some extent in the regional histories of Jews, of which there are many.

HISTORIES OF SPECIAL TOPICS
Political

Most important in the contemporary period is that of Zionism, which while not religious per se, has a religious aspect. There is an enormous bibliography on the subject. The modern period begins with the writings of Theodore Hertzl.

D341. Kiev, Mary N. "A bibliography of Zionism." **The Brandeis Avukah annual of 1932** (Boston, 1932), pp. 735–805.

D342. Palestine and Zionism: a cumulative author, title and subject index to books, pamphlets and periodicals. N.Y., 1946 ff.

See also articles in encyclopedias mentioned above, each with bibliography; *The Israel year book; Book review digest,* subject index; and various newspaper and magazine indices.

Cultural

Liturgy, Holidays, etc.

See articles in encyclopedias (*D313–316*).

Religious art

D343. "Judaism and art." **The Jews: their history, culture, and religion** (*D328*), ch. 24. Extensive bibliography.

D344. Idelsohn, Abraham Z. **Jewish music in its historical development.** N.Y., 1929. Music from earliest times.

Literature

D345. Waxman, Meyer. **History of Jewish literature from the close of the Bible to 1935.** 4 v. N.Y., 1930–41.

The Synagogue

D346. Friedlander, Moriz. **Synagoge und Kirche in ihre Anfängen.** Berlin, 1908.

D347. Krauss, Samuel. **Synagogale altertümer.** Berlin, 1922.

See also articles in encyclopedias (*D313–316*), each with bibliography.

Other Topics

D348. Scholem, Gerhard. **Major trends in Jewish mysticism.** Rev. ed., N.Y., 1946. Extensive notes and bibliography.

See also "Cabala" in *The Jewish encyclopedia* (*D315*).

For other special topics consult indices of items in *D350–365.*

BIOGRAPHIES

D349. Wininger, Salomon. **Grosse jüdische National-Biographie.** 7 v. Cernăuti, 1925–36.

See also "Biography," *Universal Jewish encyclopedia,* which lists general Jewish biographical compilations by languages, countries, and professional and personal interests; and "Biographische Literatur," *Encyclopaedia judaica,* for very extended bibliography, chiefly in German.

GOVERNMENT PUBLICATIONS

There are official publications of the Israeli government, but few deal with religious questions.

UNIVERSITY, ACADEMY, AND SOCIETY PUBLICATIONS

D350. American Jewish archives. Cincinnati, 1948 ff. (Semiannual.)

D351. American Jewish Historical Society. Publications. Baltimore, 1893 ff.

D352. American Jewish year book. N.Y., 1900 ff.

D353. Hebraica. Chicago, 1884–95. (Irregular.) Succeeded by *American journal of Semitic languages and literatures,* 1895–1942 (quarterly); *The Journal of Near Eastern studies,* 1942 ff. (quarterly).

D354. Hebrew Union College annual. Cincinnati, 1924 ff. Wide range of studies of Jewish history, culture, and religion in English, French, German, Hebrew, and Yiddish.

D355. Historia judaica. N.Y., 1938 ff. (Irregular.)

D356. Jewish book annual. N.Y., 1942 ff. Published by the Jewish Book Council of America. Annotated list of books by Jews and about Jewish subjects published in the United States. Also contains articles on literary topics. Only partly religious.

D357. Jewish quarterly review. Philadelphia, 1910 ff. Published by Dropsie College. Principally religious.

D358. Jewish social studies. N.Y., 1939 ff. (Quarterly.) Published by the Conference of Jewish Relations. Only occasional articles bearing on religion, but contains reviews of religious books.

D359. Judaism: a quarterly journal of Jewish life and thought. N.Y., 1952 ff. Published by the American Jewish Congress.

D360. Proceedings of the American Academy for Jewish Research. Philadelphia, 1928 ff. (Annual.)

PERIODICALS

D361. "Periodicals and press." **The universal Jewish encyclopedia** (*D316*). Brief history of the press in Europe by countries, with descriptive list of all periodicals which appeared for as much as twenty years. Same for the United States to 1942. Briefer coverage of other countries, but complete coverage of Palestine. Not limited to religion, but most Jewish periodicals concern themselves with the Jewish faith to some degree.

See also current *American Jewish year book* (*D352*) for periodicals.

Other periodicals which deal with the Old Testament and the Jewish faith in some of its periods, but not published by Jews, are the following.

D362. The journal of Bible and religion. Garden City, 1933 ff. [National Association of Biblical Instructors.] (Quarterly.)

D363. The Journal of Biblical literature. Philadelphia, 1881 ff. [Society of Biblical Literature and Exegesis.]

D364. The journal of Semitic studies. Manchester, Eng., 1956 ff. (Quarterly.)

D365. The journal of Jewish studies. Cambridge, Eng., 1948 ff. (Quarterly.)

CHRISTIANITY

BIBLIOGRAPHIES, LIBRARIES, AND MUSEUMS

The most complete bibliographical work concerning Christianity in all its phases is

D366. Barrow, John G. **A bibliography of bibliographies in religon** (*D1*). Here may be found practically every bibliography of religion published prior to 1950.

D367. Case, Shirley J., ed. **A bibliographical guide to the history of Christianity.** Chicago, 1931. A selected bibliography covering the entire range of Christian history up to 1931. Besides the general field, covers the church in the Roman empire, the West, the British Isles, eastern Christianity, the American church, and the newer fields. Well classified, indexed, and annotated.

D368. Allison, William H. "History of Christianity." **A guide to historical literature** (N.Y., 1931), pp. 233–75. A more highly selective bibliography than *D367*, and more fully annotated.

Because of the above excellent bibliographies, which should be available in most large libraries dealing with religion, many items are not repeated here. In addition to the major standard works which are repeated, the attempt here is to cover the period since 1931 in somewhat greater detail.

D369. Senaud, Auguste. **Christian unity: a bibliography.** Geneva, 1937. [World's Committee of YMCA.] Selected titles concerning international relations between the churches and international Christian movements. Covers period from about 1850 to 1937.

D370. Diehl, Katharine S. **Religions, mythologies, folklores: an annotated bibliography.** (See *D12*.) More than two-thirds of the book devoted to the Judeo-Christian tradition.

D371. Grant, Robert M. "The future of the ante-Nicene fathers." **Journal of religion,** 30 (Apr. 1950): 109–16. Discusses and evaluates major works dealing with the ante-Nicene fathers during the last century.

D372. Metzger, Bruce M. **Index of articles on the New Testament and early church published in the Festschriften.** Philadelphia, 1951. [Journal of Biblical literature, Monograph series, 5.] Classified with author index.

See also Malclès, *Les sources du travail bibliographique,* v. 2, ch. 13 (*D3*).

D373. Rouse, Ruth, and Stephen C. Neil. **A history of the ecumenical movement.** Philadelphia, 1954. Bibliography of every aspect of the ecumenical movement from 1517 to and including formation of the World Council of Churches in 1948. Through the use of bibliographies in many of the works listed, almost every book or document of importance to the field is included.

D374. Vollmar, Edward R. **The Catholic Church in America: an historical bibliography.** New Brunswick, 1956. Covers period 1850–1950. Since 1950 the author has published an annual bibliography of writings on church history in the May issue of the *Historical bulletin.* In both cases the bibliography is selective but extensive.

D375. The guide to Catholic literature. Ed. by Walter Romig. Detroit and Grosse Pointe, Mich., 1940 ff. (Quadrennial.) An author-subject-title index in one alphabet. Books and booklets in all languages, on all subjects, by Catholics or of particular Catholic interest, published or reprinted since Jan. 1, 1888, with descriptive and critical notes.

Other valuable material may be found by

reference to such items as bibliography, biography, church and state, Middle Ages, etc.

ENCYCLOPEDIAS AND WORKS OF REFERENCE

The standard encyclopedias and dictionaries listed below may be found in most research libraries.

D376. Hastings, James, and others, eds. **A dictionary of the Bible, dealing with its language, literature, and contents, including the Biblical theology.** 5 v. Edinburgh and N.Y., 1898–1904. Reprint, 1911–12.

D377. ———. **Dictionary of the Bible.** Edinburgh and N.Y., 1909.

D378. ———. **Dictionary of Christ and the gospels.** 2 v. Edinburgh and N.Y., 1906–08.

D379. ———. **Dictionary of the apostolic church.** 2 v. Edinburgh and N.Y., 1916–18.

D380. ———. **Encyclopaedia of religion and ethics.** (See *D15*.)

D381. Cheyne, Thomas K., and John S. Black, eds. **Encyclopaedia biblica.** 4 v. N.Y. and London, 1899–1903.

D382. **The Catholic encyclopedia.** Ed. by Charles G. Herbermann and others. 16 v. N.Y., 1907–14. Supplement, 1922.

D383. **The new Schaff-Herzog encyclopedia of religious knowledge.** (See *D16*.)

D384. Mathews, Shailer, and Gerald B. Smith, eds. **A dictionary of religion and ethics.** N.Y., 1921.

D385. Ferm, Vergilius, ed. **An encyclopedia of religion.** N.Y., 1945.

D386. Dwight, Henry O., Henry A. Tupper, Jr., and Edwin M. Bliss, eds. **The encyclopedia of missions.** 2nd rev. ed., N.Y. and London, 1904.

D387. Smith, Sir William, and Henry Wace, eds. **Dictionary of Christian biography.** 4 v. London, 1877–87.

D388. **The Jewish encyclopedia.** See *D315*.

For a long list of foreign language dictionaries and encyclopedias see *D367*, pp. 18–20.

GEOGRAPHIES, GAZETTEERS, AND ATLASES

D389. Baly, Denis. **The geography of the Bible.** N.Y., 1956.

D390. Grollenberg, Luc H. **Atlas of the Bible.** See *F35*.

D391. Kraeling, Emil G. **Rand McNally Bible atlas.** See *F37*.

D392. **World atlas of Christian missions.** Ed. by Harlan P. Beach and Charles H. Fahs. N.Y., 1911.

PRINTED COLLECTIONS OF SOURCES

Basic writings of the early church fathers have appeared in various editions in different languages, including the works listed below.

D393. Migne, Jacques P., ed. **Patrologiae cursus completus: series graeca.** See *L77*.

D394. ———, ed. **Patrologiae cursus completus: scriptores latini.** 221 v. Paris, 1844–64.

D395. Roberts, Alexander, and James Donaldson, trs. and eds. **The ante-Nicene fathers.** New ed., 10 v., N.Y., 1911–19.

D396. Schaff, Philip, tr. and ed. **Select library of the Nicene and post-Nicene fathers of the Christian church.** 14 v. N.Y., 1886–90

D397. Schaff, Philip, and Henry Wace, trs. and eds. **Select library of the Nicene and post-Nicene fathers of the Christian church.** 2nd series. 14 v. N.Y., 1890–1900.

D398. **Die griechischen christlichen Schriftsteller der ersten drei Jahrhunderte.** Leipzig, 1910 ff.

D399. **Corpus scriptorum ecclesiasticorum latinorum.** Vienna, 1866 ff.

Among newer multi-volume sets are the following.

D400. **Corpus christianorum: series latina.** Turnhout, Belg., 1953 ff. Scholarly introductions, critical notes and bibliographies.

D401. **Corpus scriptorum christianorum orientalium.** Ed. by I. B. Chabot and others. Paris and Leipzig, 1903 ff.

D402. **The fathers of the church: a new translation.** Ed. by Ludwig Schopp and others. N.Y., 1947 ff. To be complete in 72 v., including all outstanding patristic writings, some not hitherto translated. Each volume contains brief introduction, selected bibliography, and critical notes.

D403. **Enciclopedia cattolica.** 12 v. Vatican City, 1949–54. Most longer articles provide bibliographies.

SHORTER GENERAL HISTORIES

D404. Fisher, George P. **History of the Christian church.** N.Y., 1887. Later reprints.

D405. Newman, Albert H. **A manual of church history.** 2 v. Philadelphia, 1900–03.

D406. Schubert, Hans von. **Outlines of church history.** Tr. by Maurice A. Canney. London and N.Y., 1907.

D407. Walker, Williston. **A history of the Christian church.** N.Y., 1918. Reprint, 1934.

D408. Guignebert, Charles A. H. **Christianity, past and present.** N.Y., 1927. Tr. from *Le Christianisme antique* (Paris, 1921) and *Le Christianisme mediéval et moderne* (Paris, 1922).

D409. Nagler, Arthur W. **The church in history.** N.Y., 1929.

For evaluations of the above works see *D367–368*.

D410. Baker, Archibald G., ed. **A short history of Christianity.** Chicago, 1940. A digest of church history. Bibliography, mostly of items since 1930.

D411. Cairns, Earle E. **Christianity through**

the centuries. Grand Rapids, 1954. The interpretation is that of conservative Christianity permeated with a Christian philosophy of history.

D412. Dawson, Christopher H. **Religion and the rise of western culture.** N.Y., 1950. Through the 13th century.

D413. Gifford, William A. **The story of the faith: a survey of Christian history for the undogmatic.** N.Y., 1946.

D414. Hudson, Cyril E., and M. B. Reckitt. **The church and the world.** 3 v. London, 1938. V. 3 deals with the church in England since 1800.

D415. Hughes, Philip. **A history of the church.** Rev. ed., 3 v. N.Y., 1935–49.

D416. Latourette, Kenneth S. **A history of Christianity.** N.Y., 1953. Each chapter contains a selected and usually annotated bibliography.

D417. McNeill, John T. **Environmental factors in Christian history.** Chicago, 1939.

D418. McSorley, Joseph. **An outline history of the church by centuries (from St. Peter to Pius XII).** 5th ed., St. Louis and London, 1946. Excellent bibliography by periods, largely Catholic sources.

D419. Richardson, Cyril C. **The church through the centuries.** N.Y. and London, 1938.

D420. Rowe, Henry K. **History of the Christian people.** N.Y., 1931.

LONGER GENERAL HISTORIES

D421. Baur, Ferdinand C. **Geschichte der Christlichen Kirche.** 5 v. Tübingen, 1853–63.

D422. Gieseler, Johann K. L. **A text-book of church history.** Tr. by Samuel Davidson. 5 v. N.Y., 1857–80.

D423. Hagenbach, Karl R. **Kirchengeschichte von der ältesten Zeit bis zum 19. Jahrhundert.** 7 v. Leipzig, 1869–72.

D424. Schaff, Philip. **History of the Christian church.** New and rev. ed., 7 v., N.Y., 1882–1910.

D425. Ten epochs of church history. Ed. by John Fulton. 10 v. N.Y., 1896–1900.

D426. Paget, R. Harold, ed. **An outline of Christianity.** 5 v. N.Y., 1926.

D427. Chastel, Étienne L. **Histoire du Christianisme depuis son origine jusqu'à nos jours.** 5 v. Paris, 1881–83.

For commentary on many of the above and for additional older titles see *D367–368*.

D428. Boulenger, Auguste. **Histoire générale de l'église.** 9 v. in 10. Lyon, 1931–50.

D429. Fargues, Paul. **Histoire du Christianisme.** 6 v. Paris, 1934.

D430. Fliche, Augustin, and Victor Martin, eds. **Histoire de l'église depuis les origines jusqu'à nos jours.** Paris, 1945 ff. By various Roman Catholic authors. To be completed in 26 volumes. Some have already been translated into English. See Jules Lebreton, *The history of the primitive church* (4 v., London, 1942–47).

D431. Latourette, Kenneth S. **A history of the expansion of Christianity.** See *D530*.

D432. Llorca, Bernardino, and others. **Historia de la Iglesia católica.** 3 v. Madrid, 1950. By Catholic writers.

D433. Mourret, Fernand. **A history of the Catholic Church.** Tr. by Newton Thompson. V. 1–4. St. Louis, 1930–45.

D434. Poulet, Charles. **Histoire du Christianisme.** 4 v. Paris, 1933–49. A luminous exposition of the internal life of the church.

D435. Troeltsch, Ernst. **The social teaching of the Christian churches.** 2 v. N.Y., 1931. The outstanding book in its field.

HISTORIES OF SPECIAL PERIODS

Early Church

For books on the early church see *D367*, pp. 34–56, and *D368*, pp. 247–52, where most of the standard works prior to 1931 are listed.

D436. Barnes, Ernest W. **The rise of Christianity.** London, 1947.

D437. Bultmann, Rudolf. **Primitive Christianity in its contemporary setting.** London, 1956.

D438. Case, Shirley J. **The social triumph of the ancient church.** N.Y., 1933.

D439. Cerfaux, Lucien. **La communauté apostolique.** Paris, 1943. Many interesting observations.

D440. Cochrane, Charles N. **Christianity and classical culture: a study of thought and action from Augustus to Augustine.** See *1299*.

D441. Cullmann, Oscar. **The early church.** London, 1956. Discussion of various aspects of life and thought of the early church rather than a history of the church. Bibliographical footnotes. See other books by same author.

D442. Craig, Clarence T. **The beginning of Christianity.** Nashville, 1943.

D443. Daniel-Rops, Henry. **L'église des apôtres et des martyrs.** Paris, 1948.

D444. Enslin, Morton S. **Christian beginnings.** N.Y., 1938. Rather radical.

D445. Klausner, Joseph. **From Jesus to Paul.** N.Y., 1943. By a distinguished Jewish scholar.

D446. Goguel, Maurice. **The birth of Christianity.** London, 1953. Selected bibliography, including a number of the more recent books, and numerous bibliographical references in footnotes.

D447. Leitzmann, H. **A history of the early church.** Tr. by B. L. Wolf. 3 v. London, 1950.

D448. Mackinnon, James. **From Christ to Constantine.** London, 1936. Bibliographical notes included in footnotes.

D449. Manson, T. W. **The beginning of the Gospel.** London, 1950.

D450. Riddle, Donald W. **Early Christian life as reflected in its literature.** Chicago, 1936.

D451. Torrey, Charles C. **Documents of the primitive church.** N.Y., 1941.

D452. Weiss, Johannes. **The history of primitive Christianity.** Tr. by F. C. Grant and others. 2 v. N.Y., 1936–37. Contains many radical suggestions.

D453. Werner, Martin. **Die Enstehung des Christlichen Dogmas.** Bern, 1941.

Medieval Church

For numerous standard works on the Medieval church published before 1931 see *D367*, pp. 57–90, and *D368*, pp. 252–54.

D454. Addison, James T. **The medieval missionary: a study of the conversion of northern Europe, A.D. 500–1300.** N.Y., 1936. Careful and accurate account of missionary methods.

D455. Arquillière, Henri X. **L'église au Moyen Âge.** Paris, 1931. Excellent essays.

D456. Baldwin, Marshall W. **The medieval papacy in action.** N.Y., 1940.

D457. Browne, Laurence E. **The eclipse of Christianity in Asia from the time of Muhammad until the fourteenth century.** Cambridge, Eng., 1933. Based on extensive reading in original and secondary sources.

D458. Coulton, George G. **Five centuries of religion.** See *K283.*

D459. ———. **Inquisition and liberty.** London, 1938. Strongly anti-Catholic.

D460. Daniel-Rops, Henry. **La iglesia en los tiempos bárbaros.** Tr. from French. Barcelona, 1956. Excellent selected bibliography includes a number of the better recent studies of the period.

D461. Elliott-Binns, Leonard E. **The beginnings of western Christendom.** London, 1948.

D462. Spinka, Matthew. **A history of the Balkans: a study of the spread of Byzantine culture among the Slavs.** Chicago, 1933. Thorough and competent.

The Reformation

For special bibliographies on the Reformation see *D1*, pp. 259–65, which lists some fifty such works in various European languages.

D463. Fisher, George P. **The Reformation.** New and rev. ed., N.Y., 1906.

D464. Lindsay, Thomas M. **A history of the Reformation.** 2 v. N.Y., 1906–07.

D465. Smith, Preserved. **The age of the Reformation.** N.Y., 1920.

D466. Walker, Williston. **The Reformation.** N.Y., 1900.

D467. Below, Georg A. H. von. **Die Ursachen der Reformation.** Berlin, 1917. For additional information on the above works and for other titles see *D367*, pp. 95–106. On the Catholic Counter-Reformation see *D367*, pp. 106–08.

D468. Holl, Karl. **Gesammelte Aufsätze zur Kirchengeschichte.** 3 v. Tübingen, 1928–32.

D469. Mackinnon, James. **The origins of the Reformation.** N.Y., 1939. Useful summary by a competent specialist. Bibliography.

D470. Bainton, Roland H. **The Reformation of the sixteenth century.** Boston, 1952. Popular summary.

D471. ———. **Bibliography of the continental Reformation: materials available in English.** Chicago, 1935.

D472. ———. **Here I stand: a life of Martin Luther.** N.Y., 1951. Includes excellent bibliography, listing major books on Luther and sources for his life.

D473. Buchwald, George, comp. **D. Martin Luthers Leben und Lehre.** Gütersloh, 1947.

D474. Lortz, Joseph. **Die Reformation in Deutschland.** See *VF53.*

D475. Pascal, Roy. **The social basis of the German Reformation: Martin Luther and his times.** London, 1933.

D476. Schwiebert, Ernest G. **Luther and his times: the Reformation from a new perspective.** St. Louis, 1950. Comprehensive and competent; by a Lutheran. Extensive bibliography, particularly rich in German sources; elaborate notes.

D477. Thiel, Rudolf. **Luther.** Tr. by Gustav K. Weincke. Philadelphia, 1955.

D478. Carew Hunt, Robert N. **Calvin.** London, 1933. Bibliography includes extensive French sources.

D479. Mackinnon, James. **Calvin and the Reformation.** London, 1936.

D480. Farner, Oskar. **Huldrych Zwingli.** Zürich, 1946.

D481. Bender, Harold S. **Conrad Grebel, c.1498–1526, the founder of the Swiss Brethren sometimes called Anabaptists.** Goshen, Ind., 1950. Scholarly.

D482. **Menno Simons' life and writings.** Scottdale, Pa., 1936. Semi-popular.

D483. Russell, Elbert. **The history of Quakerism.** N.Y., 1942. Standard work, by a Quaker author.

D484. Wilbur, Earl M. **A history of Unitarianism.** 2 v. Cambridge, Mass., 1945–52. By a United States Unitarian. Based on extensive research.

D485. Spinka, Matthew. **John Hus and the Czech reform.** See *W333.*

D486. Constant, Gustave. **The Reformation in England.** Tr. by R. E. Scantlebury and E. I. Watkin. 2 v. N.Y., 1934–42. Roman Catholic, but fairly objective

D487. Hughes, Philip. **The Reformation in England.** See *VA504.*

D488. Janelle, Pierre. **The Catholic reformation.** Milwaukee, 1949. Summary by a Roman Catholic.

D489. Jedin, Hubert. **Geschichte des Konzils von Trient.** Freiburg, 1949.

D490. Kidd, Beresford J. **The Counter-Reformation, 1550–1600.** See *VF57*.

D491. Durant, Will. **The Reformation: a history of European civilization from Wyclif to Calvin, 1300–1564.** N.Y., 1957.

Modern Period

General

Few good general treatments of the church as a whole after the Reformation are in single volumes, except at the popular level, but may be found in multi-volume and shorter histories of the church included above (*D404–435*). See also listings in *D367* and bibliographies in the histories of Latourette, McSorley, Mourret, and others.

D492. Nichols, James H. **History of Christianity, 1650–1950.** N.Y., 1956. A recent scholarly survey of the period.

Roman Catholic, by Roman Catholic Historians

D493. MacCaffrey, James. **History of the Catholic Church from the Renaissance to the French Revolution.** 2 v. Dublin, 1915. Extensive bibliography.

D494. McSorley, Joseph. **An outline history of the church by centuries.** See *D418*. About half this work deals with the modern period.

D495. Mourret, Fernand. **A history of the Catholic Church.** Tr. by Newton Thompson. 7 v. St. Louis, 1930–55. V. 5 deals with the modern period. Ample bibliographies.

Protestantism

There are various books which state the basic nature of Protestantism, such as the two following and others, but the history of Protestantism becomes that of a multitude of denominations and sects. In so limited a bibliography it is impossible to include even one work about each.

D496. Nichols, James H. **Primer for Protestants.** N.Y., 1947.

D497. Anderson, William K., ed. **Protestantism: a symposium.** Nashville, 1944.

Basic older histories of Protestantism will be found in *D15–16* and the *Encyclopaedia britannica.* Since the greater number of Protestant sects are in America, the more significant books on each are listed in bibliographies of Sweet (*D523–525*), Clark (*D519*), Mayer (*D521*), and *Twentieth century encyclopedia of religious knowledge* (*D17*). For a number of minority groups see Braden (*D518*); and *A bibliographical guide to the history of Christianity* (*D367*), ch. 8. See also the following.

D498. Ferm, Virgilius. **The American church of the Protestant heritage.** N.Y., 1953.

D499. The year book of the churches. N.Y., 1957 ff. Provides a list of main depositories of church history material and sources covering the larger denominations.

Eastern Orthodox Churches

D500. Brandreth, Henry R. T. **An outline guide to the study of eastern Christendom.** London, 1951. Selected, annotated bibliography on the Eastern Orthodox Church in general and its various sections—Russian, Greek, Coptic, Armenian, etc.

D501. Attwater, Donald. **The Christian churches of the East.** Rev. ed., 2 v., Milwaukee, 1947–48. By a Roman Catholic. V. 1 deals with the eastern churches in communion with Rome.

D502. Zernov, Nicolas. **The church of the eastern Christians.** London, 1942. Bibliography.

D503. ——. **The Russians and their church.** London, 1945. Bibliography.

For older books see *D367*, pp. 145–69.

Ecumenical Movements

D504. Duff, Edward, Jr., **The social thought of the World Council of Churches.** N.Y., 1956. By a Roman Catholic. Excellent bibliography, including both primary and secondary sources.

D505. Rouse, Ruth, and Stephen C. Neil. **A history of the ecumenical movement.** See *D373*.

D506. Visser t'Hooft, William A., ed. **The first assembly of the World Council of Churches held at Amsterdam August 22nd to September 4th, 1948.** N.Y., 1949. Official report.

D507. The Evanston report: second assembly of the World Council of Churches, 1954. N.Y., 1956.

D508. Sundkler, Bengt. **Church of South India: the movement towards union, 1900–1947.** London, 1954.

HISTORIES OF SPECIAL AREAS

Eastern Churches

See *D367*, ch. 7, which lists the older significant histories; and *D377*, p. 257. For more recent books see above (*D500–503*).

Western Europe

See *D367*, ch. 4 for pre-Reformation period, and ch. 5 for later centuries.

D509. Hermelink, Heinrich. **Das Christentum in der Menscheitsgeschichte von der Französchen Revolution bis zur Gegenwart.** V. 1, 1789–1835. Stuttgart, 1951. General survey dealing chiefly with Germany and France.

D510. Herman, Stewart W. **It's your souls we want.** N.Y., 1943. Contemporary account of the impact of Adolf Hitler and Nazism on Christianity in Germany.

D511. Keller, Adolf, and George Stewart. **Protestant Europe: its crisis and outlook.** N.Y., 1927. Protestant Europe in the post-World War I, pre-Hitler period. Bibliography.

D512. Keller, Adolf. **Christian Europe today.** N.Y., 1942. Protestant Europe at the height of the Hitler regime. Bibliography.

D513. Tobias, Robert. **Communist-Christian encounter in east Europe.** Indianapolis, 1956. Extensive bibliography, including most of the significant books on the subject of Christianity and Communism.

See also McSorley (*D418*).

British Isles

For older books see *D367,* ch. 6.

D514. James, Edwin O. **A history of Christianity in England.** London, 1949. Brief, popular, but comprehensive. Contains selected bibliography listing significant books on various periods.

D515. Moorman, John R. H. **A history of the church in England.** London, 1953. Bibliographies.

Christianity in the Americas

For books published prior to 1931 see *D367,* ch. 8, where histories of most of the denominations may be found. For lack of space, only books on a few of the larger denominations are included below.

D516. Addison, James T. **The Episcopal Church in the United States, 1789–1931.** N.Y., 1951. Well written.

D517. Atkins, Gaius G., and Frederick L. Fagley. **History of American Congregationalism.** Boston, 1942. Sympathetic and comprehensive. Bibliography.

D518. Braden, Charles S. **These also believe.** N.Y., 1949. Brief account of the rise and development of thirteen minority religious groups, with briefer mention of many more. Objective but sympathetic. Well documented and with bibliographies on each group.

D519. Clark, Elmer T. **The small sects of America.** Rev. ed., N.Y., 1949. Brief description of some 200 groups. Bibliography.

D520. Garrison, Wilfred E., and Alfred T. DeGroot. **The Disciples of Christ, a history.** St. Louis, 1948. Extensive bibliography.

D521. Mayer, Frederick E. **The religious bodies of America.** 2nd ed., St. Louis, 1956. Brief history of each denominational group and selected bibliography.

D522. Maynard, Theodore. **The story of American Catholicism.** N.Y., 1941. Bibliography.

D523. Sweet, William W. **The story of religion in America.** 2nd ed., N.Y., 1950. Useful survey with extensive bibliography.

D524. ———. **Religion on the American frontier: a collection of source materials.** 3 v. N.Y. and Chicago, 1931–39. [1, *The Baptists;* 2, *The Presbyterians;* 3, *The Congregationalists.*]

D525. ———. **Methodism in American history.** Rev. ed., N.Y., 1953. Extensive bibliography.

D526. Torbet, Robert G. **A history of the Baptists.** Philadelphia, 1950. Extensive bibliography.

D527. Wentz, Abdel R. **The Lutheran Church in American history.** 2nd ed., Philadelphia, 1933. Authoritative survey. Bibliography.

D528. Wilbur, Earl M. **A history of Unitarianism.** See *D484.*

D529. Zenos, Andrew C. **Presbyterianism in America.** N.Y., 1937.

Missions and Younger Churches

For older works on the history of missions see *D367,* pp. 215–22.

D530. Latourette, Kenneth S. **A history of the expansion of Christianity.** 7 v. N.Y., 1937–45. The most complete history of missions. In the very extensive bibliographies may be found most of the significant books and articles on missions in general and on the various countries into which Christian missions have extended.

See also *D504–508.*

D531. Dewick, Edward C. **The Christian attitude to other religions.** Cambridge, Eng., 1953. A balanced statement.

D532. Kraemer, Hendrik. **Religion and the Christian faith.** London, 1953. Brings up to date the discussion begun in his well-known *The Christian message in a non-Christian world* (N.Y., 1947).

D533. Van Dusen, Henry P. **World Christianity—yesterday, today, tomorrow.** N.Y., 1947.

D534. World Christian handbook. London, 1957.

HISTORIES OF SPECIAL TOPICS

Political

D535. Ryan, John A., and Francis J. Boland. **Catholic principles of politics.** N.Y., 1941. Earlier edition appeared under title *Church and state* (N.Y., 1936).

D536. Sturzo, Luigi. **Church and state.** N.Y., 1939. Extensive bibliography.

D537. Pfeffer, Leo. **Church, state and freedom.** Boston, 1953. Deals chiefly with the United States. Extensive bibliography.

D538. Mecham, John Lloyd. **Church and state in Latin America.** See *Z574*.

D539. Stokes, Anson P. **Church and state in the United States.** See *AB485*.

D540. Sykes, Norman. **Church and state in England in the 18th century.** Cambridge, Eng., 1934. Thoroughly competent treatment.

The Papacy

Since the popes have played a leading role in the political arena, as well as the spiritual, works on history of the papacy are included here.

D541. Attwater, Donald, ed. **A dictionary of the popes from Peter to Pius XII.** London, 1939.

D542. Mann, Horace K. **The lives of the popes in the early Middle Ages.** 2nd ed., 18 v., London, 1925–32.

D543. Pastor, Ludwig von. **The history of the popes from the close of the Middle Ages.** See *T127*.

D544. Pichon, Charles. **Histoire du Vatican.** Paris, 1946.

D545. Schmudlin, J. **Papstgeschichte der neuesten Zeit.** 3 v. Munich, 1933–36. Continuation of Pastor's work, covering period 1800–1922. Based largely on the archives.

Cultural

Christian Art, Music, and Architecture

For bibliographies on Christian art, music, and architecture, as well as worship and liturgy, see *D1*, pp. 313–30. Numerous older books on these subjects are included in *D367*, pp. 26–29, 51–52, and 69.

D546. Duchesne, Louis M. O. **Christian worship, its origin and evolution.** 5th ed., London, 1949. Classic study of the Latin liturgy to the time of Charlemagne.

D547. Lowrie, Walter. **Art in the early church.** N.Y., 1947. Selected bibliography; 500 illustrations.

D548. Morey, Charles R. **Christian art.** N.Y., 1935.

D549. Dickinson, Edward. **Music in the history of the western church.** N.Y., 1902. Various reprints.

D550. Nommer, E. E. **Twenty centuries of Catholic music.** Milwaukee, 1948.

D551. Wellesz, Egon. **A history of Byzantine music and hymnography.** See *L386*.

Worship and Liturgy

D552. Altmann, Ulrich, ed. **Hilfsbuch zur Geschichte des Christlichen Kultus.** 3 v. Berlin, 1941–47.

D553. Beckmann, Joachim. **Quellen zur Geschichte der Christlichen Gottesdienste.** Gütersloh, 1956.

D554. Dix, Gregory. **The shape of the liturgy.** London, 1945. Elaborate, well-docu-

mented history of development of the liturgy of the Eucharist.

D555. Hislop, David H. **Our heritage in public worship.** N.Y., 1935. Major varieties of Christian worship and how they arose.

D556. Maxwell, William D. **An outline of Christian worship: its development and forms.** London, 1936.

D557. Shepherd, Massey H., Jr. **The Oxford American prayer book commentary.** N.Y., 1950. Selected bibliography.

D558. Righetti, Mario. **Historia de la liturgia.** Tr. from Italian. 2 v. Madrid, 1955. By a consultant to the Sacred Congregation of Rites of the Catholic Church. Extensive bibliographies.

Literature

For books relating to the Old Testament by Christian as well as Jewish scholars see under Judaism, especially Pfeiffer, *Introduction to the Old Testament (D311)*. See also for both Old and New Testaments.

D559. **The interpreter's Bible.** 12 v. N.Y., 1951–57. Liberal in approach. Most of the more significant books will be found listed in bibliographies of the several volumes.

Most important books concerning the New Testament will be found in the following.

D560. Chicago Society of Biblical Research. **The study of the Bible today and tomorrow.** Ed. by Harold R. Willoughby. Chicago, 1947. See especially chs. 3, 6, 12, 16, 18, 19, 20, and 24.

D561. Nash, Arnold S., ed. **Protestant thought in the twentieth century.** See *D590*.

D562. Parvis, Merrill, ed. **New Testament literature: a bibliography.** V. 1. Chicago, 1948.

D563. Scott, Ernest F. **The literature of the New Testament.** N.Y., 1932. Selected bibliography.

D564. Tenney, Merrill C. **The New Testament, an historical and analytic survey.** Grand Rapids, 1953. Includes a conservative introduction listing major books in the field and indicating those regarded as definitely conservative.

D565. Goodspeed, Edgar J. **A history of early Christian literature.** Chicago, 1942. Selected bibliography.

The two following works, in the selections they include and in biographical and bibliographical notes, furnish a fair index of the great Christian literature since Biblical times.

D566. Kepler, Thomas S., comp. **The fellowship of the saints: an anthology of Christian devotional literature.** N.Y., 1948. Covers all Christian history. Bibliography.

D567. Shuster, George N., ed. **The world's great Catholic literature.** N.Y., 1942. Anthology with selections from the whole range of Christian history. Valuable notes and bibliography.

Ethics

D568. Beach, Waldo, and H. Richard Niebuhr. **Christian ethics: sources of the living tradition.** N.Y., 1955. Presents basic ethical sources from the Bible to the present day, with selected bibliography of primary and secondary sources on each individual or period.

D569. Carter, Paul A. **The decline and revival of the social gospel.** Ithaca, 1956. Social and political liberalism in Protestant churches of the United States, 1920–40.

D570. Hall, Thomas C. **History of ethics within organized Christianity.** N.Y., 1910.

D571. Hopkins, Charles H. **The rise of the social gospel in American Protestantism, 1865–1915.** See *AB326.*

D572. Ramsey, Paul. **Basic Christian ethics.** N.Y., 1950. Includes bibliography listing most of the significant ancient and modern books in the field of Christian ethics.

D573. Widgery, Alban G. **Christian ethics in history and modern life.** N.Y., 1940. First four chapters constitute a history of developing Christian ethics from time of the gospels to the present. Bibliographical notes include major works in the field.

Christian Doctrine

D574. Harnack, Adolf von. **History of dogma.** Tr. by N. Buchanan and others. 7 v. London, 1896–99.

D575. Seeberg, Reinhold. **Lehrbuch der Dogmengeschichte.** Reprint, 3rd and 4th eds., 4 v. in 5, Gratz, 1953–54.

D576. Allen, Alexander V. G. **The continuity of Christian thought.** Boston, 1884. Various reprints.

D577. Fisher, George P. **History of Christian doctrine.** N.Y., 1903.

D578. Loofs, Friedrich. **Leitfaden zum Studium der Dogmengeschichte.** 5th ed., 2 v., Halle, 1951–53.

D579. Workman, Herbert B. **Christian thought to the Reformation.** London, 1911.

D580. McGiffert, Arthur C. **Protestant thought before Kant.** N.Y., 1911.

D581. ——. **Rise of modern religous ideas.** N.Y., 1915.

For descriptions of these and other earlier works see *D368,* pp. 264–67, and *D367,* pp. 29–30.

D582. ——. **A history of Christian thought.** 2 v. N.Y., 1932–33. Briefer, less technical than Harnack, with extensive references to sources.

D583. Hocedez, Edgar. **Histoire de la théologie au XIX siècle.** 3 v. Paris, 1947–48. Standard survey of 19th century Roman Catholic theology, by a Jesuit.

More recent movements in Protestant Christian thought, reflecting the rise of liberalism and, in reaction to it, the rise of fundamentalism, followed in turn by the rise of continental theology and neo-orthodoxy and their spread to Britain and America, may be traced in the following works (*D584–587*).

D584. Horton, Walter M. **Contemporary continental theology.** N.Y., 1938. Lists and evaluates major continental theologians, both Catholic and Protestant, as well as their chief writings prior to 1938.

D585. ——. **Contemporary English theology.** N.Y., 1936. Lists and discusses the works of leading English Catholic and Protestant theologians, liberal and orthodox, prior to 1936.

D586. Mackintosh, H. R. **Types of modern religious theology.** London, 1937. Standard survey from Schleiermacher to Barth.

D587. Williams, Daniel D. **What present-day theologians are thinking.** N.Y., 1952. The major continental, British, and American theologians and their chief works are listed, discussed, and evaluated in relation to the following topics: The Bible and Christian truth, Christian ethics and society, Jesus Christ and the church.

The importance of Sören Kierkegaard in modern theology may be seen in the translation of his works and the growing bibliography concerning him.

D588. Lowrie, Walter. **Kierkegaard.** London, 1938. Valuable synopsis of Kierkegaard's works and a selected bibliography concerning him and his influence on theologians of the 20th century.

D589. Bretall, Robert, ed. **A Kierkegaard anthology.** Princeton, 1946. Valuable. Bibliography lists books and periodicals, particularly in English, and selected works from other languages.

A valuable statement of the present state of thinking within Protestantism is

D590. Nash, Arnold S., ed. **Protestant thought in the twentieth century.** N.Y., 1951. Survey of what has happened in the whole range of thought with respect to the Old Testament, the New Testament, the philosophy of religion, systematic theology, Christian ethics, church history, etc. Each chapter is by a competent specialist. The most important books in each area are evaluated.

Monasticism

For bibliographies on monasticism in general and on the several orders see *D1,* pp. 236–56; *D367,* pp. 73–77, 125–26; *D368,* pp. 258–60; *D416,* pp. 234–35 and 444–46.

D591. Heimbucher, Max J. **Die Orden und Kongregationen de Katholischen Kirche.** 3rd ed., 2 v., Paderborn, 1933–34.

D592. Coulton, George G. **Five centuries of religion.** See *K283.*
D593. Wishart, Alfred W. **A short history of monks and monasteries.** Trenton, N.J., 1900. Bibliography.
D594. Workman, Herbert B. **The evolution of the monastic ideal.** London, 1913. Good bibliography of original sources.

Mysticism

For bibliographies on the mystics and mysticism see *D1,* p. 379; "Mystique," *Dictionnaire de théologie catholique;* and "Mysticism," *The Catholic encyclopedia.*
D595. Jones, Rufus M. **Studies in mystical religion.** N.Y., 1909.
D596. ——. **The flowering of mysticism: the Friends of God in the fourteenth century.** N.Y., 1939. Solidly based on original sources.
D597. Underhill, Evelyn. **Mysticism.** Rev. ed., N.Y., 1930. The classic work in this field. Contains extensive bibliography on the lives and works of the great mystics; general works on mysticism, philosophy, psychology, and theology of mysticism and the mystics; etc. Texts and translations of original writings of the great mystics, as well as biographies and monographs concerning them.

BIOGRAPHIES

D598. Dargan, Marion. **Guide to American biography.** See *AB16.* See subject index under religion.
D599. Current biography. N.Y., 1900 ff. Published monthly and cumulated in annual volumes, with cumulative index through each decade. Biographies are classified by profession in appendix, but not as to particular faith.
See also *D368,* pp. 268–74, for list of collective biographical works and individual biographies published before 1931.
D600. Diehl, Katharine S. **Religion, mythologies, folklores: an annotated bibliography.** New Brunswick, 1956. See pp. 178 ff. for a number of collective biographies of saints and martyrs.
For Catholic biographies there are several sources. See the following.
D601. Brown, Stephen J. M. **An index of Catholic biographies.** Dublin, 1930.
D602. Kerff, Heinrich, ed. **Biographia catholica.** St. Louis, 1927. Includes 7,300 individual biographies and 1,000 works of collective biography, all in German.
D603. Holweck, Frederick G. **A biographical dictionary of the saints.** St. Louis, 1924.
See also under biography in Romig, *The guide to Catholic literature* (*D375*).
There is no index to Protestant biography. See *D367,* pp. 182–88, for certain Protestant leaders in America. A number of collective biographies, most of them popular, but some with bibliographies, deal with Protestants as well as members of other faiths. Among these are the following (*D604–608*).
D604. Hutchinson, Paul. **Men who made the churches.** Nashville, 1930.
D605. Bach, Marcus. **The circle of faith.** N.Y., 1957.
D606. Attwater, Donald, ed. **Modern Christian revolutionaries.** N.Y., 1947.
D607. Finklestein, Louis, ed. **American spiritual autobiographies: fifteen self-portraits.** N.Y., 1947.
D608. Institute for Religious and Social Studies, Jewish Theological Seminary of America. **Thirteen Americans: their spiritual autobiographies.** N.Y., 1953.
Significant books continue to appear on the great reformers. See under Reformation, above.
D609. McConnell, Francis J. **John Wesley.** N.Y., 1939. By a Methodist bishop.
D610. Piette, Maximin. **John Wesley in the evolution of Protestantism.** Tr. by J. B. Howard. N.Y., 1937. By a French Catholic.
Among biographies of great modern Christian leaders who have been related to the worldwide outreach of Christianity are the following.
D611. Chaturvedi, Benarsidas, and Marjorie Sykes. **Charles Freer Andrews, a narrative.** N.Y., 1950. Great missionary to India and friend of Gandhi.
D612. Brown, William Adams. **A teacher and his times: a story of two worlds.** N.Y., 1940. Autobiography of a theologian and leader in ecumenical movement.
D613. Zabriskie, Alexander C. **Bishop Brent, a crusader for Christian unity.** Philadelphia, 1948.
D614. Fosdick, Harry Emerson. **The living of these days.** N.Y., 1956. A leading liberal minister tells the story of the fundamentalist-modernist conflict, in which he played a leading role.
D615. McConnell, Francis J. **By the way: an autobiography.** N.Y., 1952. Author has been leader in the social gospel movement, and onetime president of the Federal Council of Churches.
D616. Mathews, Basil J. **John R. Mott, world citizen.** N.Y., 1934.
D617. Fisher, Galen M. **John R. Mott, architect of co-operation and unity.** N.Y., 1952. World leader in Y.M.C.A. and missions.
D618. Wheeler, William R. **A man sent from God: a biography of Robert E. Speer.** Westwood, N.J., 1956. Outstanding missionary statesman.
D619. Schweitzer, Albert. **Out of my life and thought.** Tr. by C. T. Campion. London and N.Y., 1933. See also other numerous books about him.

UNIVERSITY, ACADEMY, AND SOCIETY PUBLICATIONS

There exists at present no index to the various societies, academies, and universities which publish either periodicals or monographs. A search through the *Union list of serials* and supplements will disclose most of those of the English-speaking world. Probably the best sources of information for both American and European organizations are in such magazines as *Revue d'histoire ecclésiastique* and *Revue des sciences philosophiques et théologiques*. Numerous Catholic societies throughout the world publish annual or occasional monographs, such as

D620. Catholic Record Society. **Publications.** London, 1904 ff.

The Jesuits, Franciscans, Dominicans, and others are active in publishing studies relating to their own histories. The Catholic University of America publishes several series, as well as the following:

D621. Catholic historical review. Washington, 1916 ff.

PERIODICALS

D622. American ecclesiastical review. Washington, 1889 ff. [Catholic University of America.] (Monthly.)

D623. Church history. Scottdale, Pa. and Berne, Ind., 1932 ff. [The American Society of Church History.] (Quarterly.)

D624. The journal of ecclesiastical history. London, 1950 ff. (Semiannual.)

D625. Revue d'histoire ecclésiastique. Louvain, 1900 ff. (Quarterly.)

D626. Theologische Literaturzeitung. Halle and Berlin, 1876 ff. (Monthly.)

All of the above carry extensive reviews of books in the field.

D627. Zeitschrift für Kirchengeschichte. Gotha and Stuttgart, 1876 ff. (3 nos. per year.)

Many of the periodicals listed in *D28–41* carry articles on phases of the history of Christianity. See also *D368,* pp. 274–75.

ISLAM

BIBLIOGRAPHIES, LIBRARIES, AND MUSEUMS

D628. Chauvin, Victor C. **Bibliographie des ouvrages arabes ou relatifs aux Arabes.** See *M14.*

D629. Gabrieli, Giuseppe. **Manuale di bibliografia musulmana.** See *M3.*

D630. Pareja Casañas, Félix M. **Islamologia.** See *M22.*

D631. Pfannmüller, Gustav. **Handbuch der Islam-literatur.** Berlin, 1923.

D632. Sauvaget, Jean. **Introduction à l'histoire de l'Orient musulman: éléments de bibliographie.** See *M1.*

Distinguished scholarly work in the field of Islam has been done in a number of universities in Germany, France, Holland, Scandinavia, Great Britain, and the United States. At the University of London, the Sorbonne, such universities as Harvard, Yale, Princeton, Columbia, and Chicago, and at Hartford Theological Seminary will be found the major research materials.

ENCYCLOPEDIAS AND WORKS OF REFERENCE

D633. The encyclopaedia of Islam. See *F31.*

D634. The shorter encyclopedia of Islam. Ed. by H. A. R. Gibb and J. H. Kramers. Ithaca, 1953.

D635. Hurgronje, Christiaan S. **Verspreide Geschriften.** 6 v. Bonn and Leipzig, 1923–27.

D636. Caetani, Leone. **Chronographia islamica.** See *M27.*

D637. Lane-Poole, Stanley. **The Mohammedan dynasties: chronological and genealogical tables with historical introductions.** See *M28.*

D638. Faris, Nabih A., ed. **The Arab heritage.** Princeton, 1944.

There are various translations of the Quran, among them

D639. Bell, Richard. **The Quran, with critical rearrangement of the Surahs.** 2 v. Edinburgh, 1937–39.

D640. Le Coran. Tr. and ed. by Régis Blachère. 2 v. Paris, 1947–51.

D641. Kramers, Johannes H. **De Koran, uit het arabisch vertaald.** Amsterdam, 1956.

D642. Rodwell, John M., tr. **The Koran.** 2nd ed., London, 1876. Reprint, London and N.Y., 1909. There are various other sectarian translations which circulate widely, but need to be used with caution.

Complete translations of the Traditions or the Hadith are not yet available. One collection, that of al Bukhari, has been translated.

D643. El-Bokhâri: les Traditions islamiques. Tr. by O. Houdas and W. Marcais. 4 v. Paris, 1903–14.

GEOGRAPHY

D644. Hazard, Harry W., and Hereward L. Cooke. **An atlas of Islamic history.** 3rd ed., Princeton, 1954.

SHORTER GENERAL HISTORIES

Books listed here and in the following subsection are limited as far as possible to those dealing chiefly with history of the Islamic faith, and not that of the Moslem world in its political and general cultural sense.

D645. Cragg, Kenneth. **The call of the minaret.** N.Y., 1956.

D646. Guidi, Michelangelo. **Storia della religione dell' Islam.** 2nd ed., Turin, 1949.

D647. Hurgronje, Christiaan S. **Moham-medanism.** See *M172*.

D648. Kellerhals, Emanuel. **Der Islam: seine Geschichte, seine Lehre, sein Wesen.** Basel, 1945.

D649. Morgan, Kenneth, ed. **Islam: the straight path.** N.Y., 1958. Brief account, by distinguished Muslim scholars, of the rise, development, and spread of Islam; its major beliefs and practices; and its contemporary expression in the major areas of the Islamic world.

LONGER GENERAL HISTORIES

D650. Brockelmann, Carl. **Geschichte der Islamischen Völker und Staaten.** Munich, 1939. English tr., by Joel Carmichael and Moshe Perlmann, *History of the Islamic peoples*, N.Y., 1947.

D651. Caetani, Leone. **Annali dell' Islam.** See *M26*.

D652. Dias, Eduardo. **Árabes e Muçulma-nos.** 3 v. Paris, 1922.

D653. Hitti, Philip K. **History of the Arabs.** 4th ed., London, 1949.

D654. Huart, Clément I. **Histoire des Arabes.** 2 v. Paris, 1912–13.

D655. Müller, Friedrich A. **Der Islam im Morgen und Abenland.** 2 v. Berlin, 1885–87.

HISTORIES OF SPECIAL PERIODS

D656. Margoliouth, David S. **The early development of Mohammedanism.** N.Y., 1914.

D657. Wellhausen, Julius. **Prolegomena zur ältesten Geschichte des Islams.** Berlin, 1899.

D658. Von Grunebaum, Gustave E. **Medieval Islam: a study in cultural orienta-tion.** See *M170*.

D659. Le Tourneau, Roger. **L'Islam con-temporain.** Paris, 1950.

D660. Gibb, Hamilton A. R. **Modern trends in Islam.** Chicago, 1947.

D661. Ghirelli, Angelo. **El renacimiento musulmán.** Barcelona, 1948.

HISTORIES OF SPECIAL AREAS

Expansion of Islam

D662. André, Pierre J. **L'Islam et les races.** 2 v. Paris, 1922.

D663. Arnold, Thomas W. **The preaching of Islam.** See *M177*.

Spanish Islam

D664. Dozy, Reinhart P. A. **Histoire des Musulmans d'Espagne.** See *VD60*.

D665. Lévi-Provençal, Évariste. **Histoire de l'Espagne musulmane.** See *VD59*.

D666. González Palencia, Angel. **Historia de la España musulmana.** See *M121*.

Sects of Islam

D667. al-Baghdādi, Abn-Mansūr. **Moslem schisms and sects: being the history of the various philosophic systems developed in Islam.** Pt. 1, tr. by Kate C. Seelye, N.Y., 1920; pt. 2, tr. by Abraham S. Halkin, Tel-Aviv, 1935. Pt. 1, badly translated; pt. 2, very well done.

D668. Donaldson, Dwight M. **The Shi'ite religion: a history of Islam in Persia and Irak.** London, 1933.

D669. Hollister, John N. **The Shi'a of India.** London, 1953.

D670. Nöldeke, Theodor. **Zur Ausbreitung des Schiitismus.** Leipzig, 1923.

D671. Arendonk, Cornelius van. **De op-komst van het Zaidietische imamaat in Yemen.** Leiden, 1919.

D672. Strothmann, Rudolf. **Das Staats-recht der Zaiditen.** Strasbourg, 1912.

D673. Ivanov, Vladimir A. **A brief survey of the evolution of Ismailism.** Leiden, 1952.

D674. Goldziher, Ignác. **Die Zâhriten, ihr Lehrsystem und ihre Geschichte.** Leipzig, 1884.

HISTORIES OF SPECIAL TOPICS

Political

D675. Arnold, Thomas W. **The caliphate.** Oxford, 1924.

D676. Bergsträsser, Gotthelf. **Grundzüge des islamischen Rechts.** Berlin, 1935.

D677. Khadduri, Majid, and Herbert Liebesny, Jr. **Law in the Middle East.** V. 1, **Origin and development of Islamic law.** Washington, 1955.

D678. Milliot, Louis. **Introduction à l'étude du droit musulman.** Paris, 1953.

D679. Muir, Sir William. **The caliphate, its rise, decline, and fall.** See *M66*.

D680. Sanhūrī, 'Abd al-Razzāk Ahmad. **Le califat: son évolution vers une société des nations orientales.** Paris, 1926.

D681. Tschudi, Rudolf. **Das Chalifat.** Tübingen, 1926.

D682. Tyan, Émile. **Les institutions du droit public musulmane.** 2 v. Paris, 1954.

Economic

D683. Aghnides, Nicolas P. **Mohammedan theories of finance.** See *M254*.

Cultural

Muslim Art

D684. Creswell, Keppel A. C. **Early Muslim architecture.** 2 v. Oxford, 1932–40.

D685. Dimand, M. S. **Handbook of Mohammedan art.** 2nd ed., N.Y., 1944. [Metropolitan Museum of Art.]

D686. Glück, Heinrich, and Ernest Diez. **Die Kunst des Islams.** 3rd ed., Berlin, 1939.

D687. Kramers, Johannes H. **Over de Kunst van de Islam.** Leiden, 1953.

D688. Marcais, Georges. **Manuel d'art musulman.** 4 v. Paris, 1926–27.

D689. Richmond, Ernest T. **Moslem architecture, 623 to 1516: some causes and consequences.** London, 1926.

D690. Ziauddin, M. **A monograph on Moslem calligraphy.** Calcutta, 1936.

Rites, Ceremonies, Worship

D691. Bousquet, Georges H. **Les grandes pratiques rituelles de l'Islam.** Paris, 1949.

D692. Calverley, Edwin E., tr. **Worship in Islam: being a translation, with commentary and introduction, of al-Ghazzáli's Book of the Ihyá' on the worship.** Madras, 1925.

Literature

D693. Brockelmann, Carl. **Geschichte der arabischen Litteratur.** See *M18.*

D694. Browne, Edward G. **A literary history of Persia.** See *M258.*

D695. Gibb, Hamilton A. R. **Arabic literature.** London, 1926.

D696. González Palencia, Angel. **Historia de la literatura arábigo-española.** 2nd ed., Barcelona, 1945.

D697. Schmidt, Bertha. **Übersicht der türkischen Literatur.** Heidelberg, 1916.

D698. Storey, Charles A. **Persian literature.** See *M19.*

The Koran

D699. Bell, Richard. **Introduction to the Qur'ān.** Edinburgh, 1953.

D700. Blachère, Régis. **Introduction au Coran.** Paris, 1947.

D701. Jeffrey, Arthur. **The Qur'ān as scripture.** N.Y., 1952.

D702. Nöldeke, Theodor, and others. **Geschichte des Qorāns.** 3 v. Leipzig, 1909–38.

The Traditions

D703. Guillaume, Alfred. **The traditions of Islam.** Oxford, 1924.

D704. Robson, James, tr. **An introduction to the science of tradition.** London, 1953.

Philosophy and Ethics

D705. Boer, Tjitze J. de. **A history of philosophy in Islam.** London, 1933.

D706. Donaldson, Dwight M. **Studies in Moslem ethics.** London, 1953.

D707. Gauthier, Léon. **Introduction à l'étude de la philosophie musulmane.** Paris, 1935.

D708. Horten, Max J. H. **Die Philosophie des Islam.** Munich, 1924.

D709. Menasce, Pierre J. de. **Arabische Philosophie.** Bern, 1948. [Bibliographische Einführungen in das Studium der Philosophie, 6.]

Theology

D710. Gardet, Louis, and M. Anawati. **Introduction à la théologie musulmane.** Paris, 1948.

D711. Macdonald, Duncan B. **Development of Muslim theology, jurisprudence, and constitutional theory.** N.Y., 1903.

D712. Wensinck, Arent J. **The Muslim creed.** See *M179.*

Moslem Mystics and Mysticism

D713. Arberry, Arthur J. **An introduction to the history of Sufism.** See *M178.*

D714. Massignon, Louis. **Essai sur les origines du lexique technique de la mystique musulmane.** 2nd ed., Paris, 1954.

D715. Nicholson, Reynold A. **Studies in Islamic mysticism.** Cambridge, Eng., 1921.

D716. ——. **The mystics of Islam.** London, 1914.

Social

D717. Levy, Reuben. **The social structure of Islam.** See *M194.*

BIOGRAPHIES

There are numerous biographies of Mohammed in the chief European languages, many of them popular or semi-popular. The better of these will be found in bibliographies of the few mentioned here.

D718. Blachère, Régis. **Le problème de Mahomet: essai de biographie critique du fondateur de l'Islam.** See *M286.*

D719. Buhl, Frants P. W. **Das Leben Muhammeds.** See *M279.*

D720. Watt, W. Montgomery. **Muhammad at Mecca.** See *M284.*

D721. ——. **Muhammad at Medina.** See *M285.*

UNIVERSITY, ACADEMY, AND SOCIETY PUBLICATIONS

D722. Bibliotheca islamica. Leipzig and Istanbul, 1929 ff.

D723. Studia islamica. Paris, 1953 ff. (Annual.)

PERIODICALS

D724. Al-Andalus. Madrid, 1933 ff. (Semiannual.)

D725. Der Islam. Berlin, 1910 ff. (Annual.)

D726. Die Welt des Islams. Berlin, 1913 ff. (Annual.)

D727. Islamic culture. Hyderabad, 1927 ff. (Quarterly.)

D728. Revue des études islamiques. Paris, 1927 ff. (Quarterly.) Replaces the following.

D729. Revue du monde musulman. Paris, 1906–26. (Quarterly.)

D730. The Muslim world. N.Y., 1911 ff. (Quarterly.)

Also consult periodical indices for articles bearing on Islam in contemporary journals dealing with the history of religions and with the Near and Middle East.

II. HISTORICAL BEGINNINGS

SECTION E

Regions, Peoples, and Cultures: General and Prehistoric

JOHN OTIS BREW and OLAF PRUFER

Compared with other learned disciplines, archaeology is new. For some centuries it existed as a source of inspiration for the Renaissance, as a factor in the Gothic revival, or simply as an antiquarian hobby. During the last quarter of the 19th century and the first half of the 20th, archaeology developed as a humanistic subject in universities and museums, applying scientific techniques borrowed from the natural and physical sciences and working increasingly closely with the social sciences, particularly with anthropology. The growth has been rapid and the scholarship in the field is still exceptionally dynamic. One of the results has been a serious problem for the bibliographer.

To understand the various fields of prehistory, it is necessary to know the field work in progress at any given time and the relatively few centers in the world where developments in archaeology are focused. For example, the continued study of the Palaeolithic in western Europe is brought to a head by annual conferences in the so-called "capital of the Palaeolithic," Les Eyzies, in the Dordogne district of France. Here in 1958 Professor Movius inaugurated the excavation of a previously untouched site in the main section where the entire Upper Palaeolithic will be unveiled for a fresh look during the next few years. In North America, centering around museums and universities in Flagstaff, Tucson, Albuquerque, Santa Fe, Denver, and Mexico City, scholars are tracing the history of man in the New World from the earliest hunting cultures to the high civilizations which made such a striking impression on invading Europeans. In Egypt, where archaeology has a history of its own, the new UNESCO Documentation Center is a milestone in the growth of the field to maturity. Even in the farther reaches of Buryat, Mongolia, which people from the West can now visit, Professor Okladnikov and his Russian colleagues are making new discoveries which are shrinking the prehistoric world and bringing the Old World and the New World together on the level of our early Lithic cultures. In several larger metropolitan centers there are great institutions of archaeology, such as the Musée de l'Homme in Paris; the Archaeological Institute in London; The Peabody Museum, with its unique anthropological library, in Cambridge, Massachusetts; and the National Museum, Tokyo.

The bibliography presented in this section includes titles of well-known standard works and recent publications of outstanding importance. It does not lay claim to completeness, but rather attempts to give leads to the important avenues of study. A large part of the literature of prehistoric archaeology is still in the form of articles in scientific journals. The leading journals which carry these can be identified from the selections given. Included also are certain works with extensive bibliographies. From these the interested reader can take up the thread if he wishes.

GENERAL

E1. Clark, John G. D. **Archaeology and society.** 3rd ed., Cambridge, Mass. and London, 1957. Deals with archaeology as a science. Includes sections on the nature of archaeological evidence, types of sites, chronology, economic and cultural reconstruction, and the role of prehistory in the life of contemporary man.

E2. Clark, Wilfred E. Le Gros. **History of the primates.** 4th ed., London, 1954. Excellent introduction to primate evolution, discussing theoretical concepts of evolution, fossil primates, and palaeontological evidence from Oligocene tree shrews to Upper Palaeolithic sapiens forms.

E3. ———. **The fossil evidence for human evolution.** Chicago, 1955. Presents in an abbreviated and critical form the principal evidence for human evolution that can be deduced from the fossil record. Includes sections dealing with morphological and phylogenetic problems, discussions of the fossil remains, and a chapter on the origin of the Hominidae.

E4. Ehrich, Robert W., ed. **Relative chronologies in Old World archaeology.** Chicago, 1954. The result of reevaluating the archaeological sequences of Egypt, Mesopotamia, Asia Minor, Iran, China, and the Aegean in the light of recent researches and dating methods. Provides a foundation for new chronologically interrelated studies of the area sequences in question.

E5. Gjessing, Gutorm. **Circumpolar Stone Age.** Copenhagen, 1944. Examines certain prehistoric manifestations of the Arctic lands which seem to have a circumpolar distribution. The author concludes that similarities are due to a common cultural foundation which must have had its roots in ancient Asiatic Stone Age culture.

E6. Grahmann, Rudolf. **Urgeschichte der Menschheit.** 2nd ed., Stuttgart, 1956. A good and readable history of the Old Stone Age, with special reference to Pleistocene geology and human palaeontology. The archaeological section presents the evidence under conventional headings of Lower, Middle, and Upper Palaeolithic. Also included are sections on the Mesolithic and Neolithic periods.

E7. Heizer, Robert F. "Long range dating in archaeology." **Anthropology today,** ed. by Alfred L. Kroeber, Chicago, 1953, pp. 3–42. Outlines a number of methods for the dating of archaeological remains. Of special interest to those who wish to know how and to what degree of accuracy archaeological remains can be dated.

E8. Hooton, Earnest A. **Up from the ape.** 5th ed., N.Y., 1954. The most comprehensive textbook on physical anthropology that has appeared to date. In addition to presenting the detailed fossil record of man's ancestry, there are sections dealing with man's primate relations, the primate life cycle, individual life cycle, heredity and race, and the anthropology of the individual.

E9. Keesing, Felix M. **Culture change: an analysis and bibliography of anthropological sources to 1952.** Stanford, 1953. Valuable bibliography.

E10. Kühn, Herbert. **Das Erwachen der Menschheit.** Frankfurt am Main and Hamburg, 1954. Sketches the Palaeolithic archaeology of the Old World, including much interesting information concerning the history of discovery and research. Also included are discussions on Stone Age art, a topic on which the author qualifies as a world renowned expert.

E11. ———. **Der Aufstieg der Menschheit.** Frankfurt am Main and Hamburg, 1955. A sequel to *E10.* Offers a lucid survey of the Old World Neolithic, including the beginnings of civilization in Mesopotamia and Egypt. Includes many interesting facts on the history of prehistoric investigations in the areas concerned.

E12. Leakey, Louis S. B. **Adam's ancestors.** London, 1953. Summary of the Old World Palaeolithic with a heavy slant toward Africa. Includes interesting discussions on flint working, the more interesting since the author himself is an adept at that art.

E13. Libby, Willard F. **Radiocarbon dating.** 2nd ed., Chicago, 1955. Describes the radiocarbon method of dating, in recent years of increasing importance in chronological ordering of prehistoric remains. Included is a section by F. Johnson on the specific use of this method to the archaeologist.

E14. Menghin, Oswald. **Weltgeschichte der Steinzeit.** Vienna, 1931. Though largely out of date, this is one of the fundamental studies of Old World prehistory. The author, a follower of the Viennese "Kulturkreis" school, presents his material within a theoretical framework no longer acceptable. The importance of this work lies in the sheer bulk of material dealt with and in the attempt at giving a world-wide culture classification by stages.

E15. Milojčič, Vladimir, and Hermann Bengtson. **Grosser Historischer Weltatlas.** 2nd ed., 2 v., Munich, 1954. The two volumes (atlas and text) of this cartographic study of prehistory are complementary, each map in the atlas volume having its descriptive counterpart in the text volume. Included are maps outlining the distribution of prehistoric cultures from the Palaeolithic to the 5th century A.D.; others showing prehistoric settlement types reconstructed from archaeological remains; and three detailed, world-wide synoptic charts of culture periods and their interrelationships. An indispensable work to all interested in Old World prehistory and archaeology.

E16. Movius, Hallam L., Jr. "The Old Stone Age." **Man, culture and society,** ed. by Harry L. Shapiro, N.Y., 1956, pp. 49–93.

E17. Oakley, Kenneth P. "Dating fossil human remains." **Anthropology today,** ed. by Alfred L. Kroeber, Chicago, 1953, pp. 43–57. Discusses two fundamental ways of dating fossil human remains—relative dating and absolute dating. The former method involves the study of the fossil remains in their natural context; the latter involves scientific methods such as radiocarbon dating, fluorine testing, etc.

E18. ——. **Man the tool-maker.** 3rd ed., London, 1956. A short, excellent, though very general, introduction to the Palaeolithic, including valuable and detailed discussions on tool-making technology. Also there are sections on culture sequences in relation to geology, evolution of Palaeolithic cultures, and implements associated with remains of fossil man.

E19. Permanent International Committee of Linguistics. **Linguistic bibliography for the year 1950 and supplement for previous years.** Utrecht and Antwerp, 1952. A continuing source of great importance.

E20. Wheeler, Sir Robert E. M. **Archaeology from the earth.** Oxford, 1954. Harmondsworth, Eng., 1956. A study of archaeological methods covering techniques of excavation and preservation of antiquities, archaeological photography, publication methods, etc. Provides an interesting insight into aspects of archaeological research.

EUROPE

E21. Breuil, Henri. **Four hundred centuries of cave art.** Tr. by Mary E. Boyle. Montignac, France, 1952. Superb study by the world's greatest living authority on prehistoric art. Lavishly illustrated. Restricted to wall art, i.e. paintings, engravings, and bas reliefs. Included are nine essays on the origins of art, geographical distribution of decorated caves, chronology and evolution of cave art, technology of production, and the fauna represented. Art history of the Upper Palaeolithic of western Europe is presented in terms of two cycles belonging to the Aurignacian-Périgordian and the Solutrean-Magdalenian respectively.

E22. Childe, Vere G. **The Bronze Age.** Cambridge, Eng. and N.Y., 1930. Excellent introduction to the European Bronze Age, containing sections on the three standard subdivisions of this period—Early, Middle, and Late. Includes a very useful chapter on Bronze Age typology, and theoretical sections on implications of the Bronze Age, and on metallurgy and trade.

E23. ——. **Prehistoric migrations in Europe.** Cambridge, Mass. and Oslo, 1950. Discusses the European prehistoric evidence from the Upper Palaeolithic to the Iron Age in terms of migrations and diffusion from the Aegean via the Balkans, via the Mediterranean route through Spain, and from Russia. Included is an interesting and informative section on archaeological postulates such as "race" and "culture," mechanisms of culture change, chronology, and parallel evolution. The author introduces the interesting concept of "crises" at the end of the Neolithic and Bronze Ages.

E24. ——. **The dawn of European civilization.** 5th ed., N.Y., 1951. In this classic work Childe outlines the development of prehistoric Europe from the beginning of the Neolithic to the Middle Bronze Age. A readable, essential synthesis of the European prehistoric evidence, attempting to trace the roots of civilization back to the Aegean and Hither Asia.

E25. Clark, John G. D. **The Mesolithic settlement of northern Europe.** Cambridge, Eng., 1936. An authoritative survey of the Mesolithic cultures of northern Europe. Includes interpretative sections on the Tanged Point cultures, the Lyngby culture, the Maglamose culture, and a variety of microlithic assemblages.

E26. ——. **Prehistoric Europe: the economic basis.** London, 1952. This fundamental study examines archaeological remains in the light of cultural, technological, economic, and environmental reconstruction. Evidence is taken from archaeological remains, early historical sources, and the folk-cultures surviving in certain marginal areas of Europe. Sections on diverse subsistence activities, houses and settlements, technology, trade, and transportation are included.

E27. ———. **Excavations at Star Carr.** Cambridge, Eng., 1954. Results of an important Mesolithic excavation in Yorkshire, Eng. Included are sections on the archaeological finds, lake stratigraphy, pollen analysis, vegetational history, and fauna. The fundamental importance of this work to the study of European prehistory lies in its emphasis on environmental and cultural reconstruction. Though somewhat specialized, it is an excellent example of the new reconstructional and interpretative approach evolved in recent years.

E28. Coon, Carleton S. **The races of Europe.** N.Y., 1939. A study of European physical anthropology. Discusses the racial populations of Europe in terms of skeletal materials from archaeological deposits ranging from the Old Stone Age to the Iron Age. Second part is devoted to contemporary populations of Europe. Though largely outdated today, this is a classic well worth studying, and still represents the most complete summary of the skeletal evidence derived from archaeological sites.

E29. Gaul, James H. **The Neolithic period in Bulgaria.** Cambridge, Mass., 1948. Examines the Neolithic archaeology of Bulgaria. Included are discussions of the West Bulgarian Painted culture, Boian-A culture, Bulgarian Mound culture, the evidence from Bulgarian caves, and chapters on anthropometric evidence and the Early Bronze Age. In view of recently revived interest in the earliest Neolithic of the southern Balkans, this study provides a particularly good background to those interested in the earliest European agricultural communities.

E30. Gimbutas, Marija. **The prehistory of eastern Europe.** Pt. 1, **Mesolithic, Neolithic and Copper Age cultures in Russia and the Baltic areas.** Cambridge, Mass., 1956. The definitive study in English of the prehistory of eastern Europe from the end of the Old Stone Age to the beginning of the Bronze Age. For the first time the entire evidence is drawn together in one volume. Especially valuable because much of the original literature is in Russian or Polish, languages not readily understood in western Europe and America.

E31. Golomshtok, Eugene A. "The Old Stone Age in European Russia." **Transactions of the American Philosophical Society,** 29 n.s., pt. 2 (Mar. 1938): 191–468. This monograph, though somewhat out of date,

is the only comprehensive summary in English of the Palaeolithic of European Russia. Included are sections on Pleistocene geology, fauna and flora, skeletal remains, and discussions of Lower and Upper Palaeolithic sites.

E32. Guyan, Walter U., ed. **Das Pfahlbauproblem.** Basel, 1955. This superb study, published in commemoration of the first centenary of lake dwelling research, discusses in several definitive papers the nature of the Swiss lake dwellings, with special reference to the much disputed question of whether they were built on piles in open water or on dry ground. The authors conclusively prove the latter hypothesis by means of detailed and meticulous archaeological examinations of the evidence and by extensive use of pollen diagrams from the sites.

E33. Hawkes, Charles, and Jacquetta Hawkes. **Prehistoric Britain.** London, 1948. 2nd ed., Harmondsworth, Eng., 1949. Survey of prehistoric Britain from the Palaeolithic to the Roman colonization of the islands. Readable and concise.

E34. Hencken, Hugh O'Neill. **Indo-European languages and archaeology.** Menasha, Wis., 1955. Attempts to delineate in space and time the spread of Indo-European speakers, and to correlate the distribution of archaeological assemblages with linguistic groups.

E35. Navarro, José M. de. "Prehistoric routes between northern Europe and Italy defined by the amber trade." **Geographical journal,** 66 (1925): 481–504. Outlines the great amber trade routes from the Baltic to Italy and the Aegean which played such a vital role in the development of prehistoric Europe.

E36. Pallottino, Massimo. **The Etruscans.** See *187*.

E37. Tackenberg, Kurt, ed. **Der Neanderthaler und seine Umwelt: Gedenkschrift zur Erinnerung an die Auffindung im Jahre 1856.** Bonn, 1956. The series of papers by various authors contained in this book discusses the Neanderthal problem in the light of physical anthropology, geology and environment, and archaeology. It provides a good summary of all the aspects connected with the question of Neanderthal man and, because of its conciseness, is well worth reading.

E38. Zotz, Lothar F. **Altsteinzeitkunde Mitteleuropas.** Stuttgart, 1951. Excellent summary of the Old Stone Age of central and east central Europe, discussing the internal and external relationships of the various Palaeolithic industries.

AFRICA

E39. Balout, Lionel. **Préhistoire de l'Afrique du Nord.** Paris, 1955. A monumental volume dealing with the prehistory of North Africa from the earliest Palaeolithic to the Neolithic. The first part is devoted to methodological questions and to problems of chronology, geology, climatology, palaeontology, etc. The second part deals with the Palaeolithic sequence, with special reference to the Aterian problem. The third part covers the terminal Palaeolithic industries of the Iberomaurusian and Caspian, and the Neolithic, with special reference to rock paintings and engravings.

E40. Baumgärtel, Elise J. **The cultures of prehistoric Egypt.** V. 1. Rev. ed., London, 1955. Detailed survey of the Pre-Dynastic, Neolithic cultures of Egypt.

E41. Breuil, Henri. "L'Afrique préhistorique." **Cahiers d'art** (Paris, 1931): 61–122. Though partially out of date, this is one of the best and most readable summaries of prehistoric Africa from the Lower Palaeolithic to the arrival of the first Europeans. Also includes a valuable section on prehistoric art in Africa.

E42. Briggs, Lloyd C. **The Stone Age races of northwest Africa.** Cambridge, Mass., 1955. Thus far the most comprehensive summary of human remains of the Stone Age of northwest Africa, between Lybia and the Atlantic on the one hand, and the Mediterranean and southern Sahara on the other. For those interested in the physical anthropology and prehistory of Africa, this study is indispensable.

E43. Caton-Thompson, Gertrude, and Elinor W. Gardner. **The desert Fayum.** 2 v. London, 1934. A detailed study covering the prehistoric sequence of the Fayum desert in lower Egypt from the Lower Palaeolithic to the Neolithic.

E44. Clark, John D. **The Stone Age cultures of northern Rhodesia.** Claremont, Cape, 1950. An outline of the Stone Age sequence of this region, with special sections devoted to its geology, and appendices on the fauna and human remains found in association with some of the archaeological materials. Good and concise summary of the Palaeolithic of central Africa.

E45. Cole, Sonia M. **The prehistory of east Africa.** Harmondsworth, Eng., 1954. Comprehensive summary, including discussions of the fossil evidence, Palaeolithic and Mesolithic industries, Neolithic complexes, and the abundant artistic manifestations such as rock paintings and engravings. There are also sections dealing with environmental background and with the early historic influences from Egypt, Ethiopia (Aksum), and Arabia.

E46. Frobenius, Leo. "L'art africain." **Cahiers d'art** (Paris, 1931): 7–55. This splendid and well illustrated paper summarizes the prehistoric art of Africa. Covers the entire

continent, including rock paintings and engravings as well as sculpture.

E47. Leakey, Louis S. B. **Stone Age Africa: an outline of prehistory in Africa.** London, 1936. Covers the entire Stone Age of Africa. Though somewhat out of date, is an excellent and useful introduction to the prehistory of the dark continent.

E48. ——. **Tentative study of the Pleistocene climatic changes and Stone-Age culture sequence in northeastern Angola.** Lisbon, 1949. This monograph covers the interrelated geological and Palaeolithic sequences of Angola. Of special interest is the discussion of the Sangoan culture. Also included are sections on terminology and method, and a chapter attempting to correlate the Angola sequence with those of other parts of Africa.

THE MIDDLE EAST

E49. Albright, William F. **The archaeology of Palestine.** Harmondsworth, Eng., 1949. Survey of ancient Palestine from the Old Stone Age to Graeco-Roman times. Included are sections relating the archaeology to discoveries at Jericho. Although somewhat outdated, this little book still represents the best summary of the prehistory and archaeology of the Bible lands.

E50. Andrae, Walter. **Das Wiedererstandene Assur.** Leipzig, 1938. Excellent summary of the Mesopotamian city of Assur. Of particular interest and value because the author presents lengthy reconstructions not only of the various architectural phases of the city, but also its political and social life as reflected in the archaeological record and epigraphic evidence.

E51. Braidwood, Robert. **The Near East and the foundations for civilization.** Eugene, Ore., 1952. Presents evidence for the earliest known agricultural village communities in the Near East. Includes sections discussing the theoretical, geographical, and ecological aspects of the problem. An indispensable study to all interested in the beginnings of civilization in the Old World.

E52. Childe, Vere G. **New light on the most ancient East.** 4th ed., N.Y., 1953. This classic work gives an outline of the rise of civilization in Egypt, Mesopotamia, and India, and attempts to show the interrelatedness of cultural phenomena involved.

E53. ——. **Man makes himself.** 4th ed., N.Y., 1954. Readable and clear account of the origins of higher civilization in Mesopotamia and Egypt. Contains an outline of Childe's theoretical concepts of culture development, his "revolutions," and valuable chapters on intellectual achievements and progress of man during the periods in question.

E54. Frankfort, Henri. **The birth of civili-**

zation in the Near East. Garden City, 1956. While presenting the archaeological evidence for the beginnings of civilization in the Near East and Egypt, the author suggests that each of the two great areas involved developed along lines based on their different fundamental "forms." Mesopotamia's development is rooted in the original formation of independent city states, while Egypt's rise depended on a fundamentally unified religious and political system under a single ruler.

E55. Ghirshman, Roman. **Iran.** Harmondsworth, 1954. This comprehensive and eminently readable study summarizes the history of Iran as recorded by archaeology from the Palaeolithic to the Sassanian period in the first millennium A.D.

E56. Gurney, Oliver R. **The Hittites.** 2nd ed., Harmondsworth, 1954. History of the Hittites described on the basis of excavated remains and Hittite written documents. Provides excellent reconstructions of the Hittite state, its social and political organization, law, and economy. There also are sections on language and race, religion, literature, and art.

E57. Kenyon, Kathleen. **Digging up Jericho.** London and N.Y., 1957. A lucid and fascinating account of ancient Jericho, with special reference to recent discoveries of extremely early Neolithic levels which antedate the invention of pottery.

E58. Lloyd, Seton. **Early Anatolia.** Harmondsworth, 1956. This readable book discusses the prehistory and archaeology of Anatolia from the beginning of the Neolithic to the Phrygian period of the Iron Age. Included are informative sections on methodology and the history of research. Emphasis is on pre-Hittite archaeology.

E59. McCown, Donald E. **The comparative stratigraphy of early Iran.** Chicago, 1942. Analysis of the ceramics of various early Iranian sites. These are correlated with the early wares (Halaf, Samarra, and Al Ubaid) of Mesopotamia, whence a chronology is derived for the Iranian sequence.

E60. Perkins, Ann L. **The comparative archeology of early Mesopotamia.** See *F224*.

E61. Schaeffer, Claude F. **Stratigraphie comparée et chronologie de l'Asie occidentale, IIIe et IIe millénaires.** London, 1948. In this lavishly illustrated, monumental study the author compares the archaeological evidence from a large number of sites, ranging from Iran to Cyprus, in an attempt to establish area-wide chronological links during the second and third millennia, B.C. Included is a section trying to demonstrate relationships between certain Iranian materials and China.

E62. Woolley, Sir Charles L. **Ur of the Chaldees.** Harmondsworth, 1938. Subsequent reprints. In describing his seven years of excavations at Ur in southern Mesopotamia, the author presents in popular form the history, as documented by archaeology, of this crucial site from the Al Ubaid phase to that of Ur in the days of Nebuchadnezzar (about 600 B.C.).

E63. ——. **A forgotten kingdom.** Harmondsworth, 1953. A lucid account of his excavations in northwestern Syria at the important sites of Archana Alalakh and al Mina. Chronologically this report covers the period from circa 3400 B.C. to 1286 A.D., the latter date marking the end of the crusader's port of St. Symeon. The book provides a good chronological cross-section through the culture sequence of this part of the Near East.

NORTHERN ASIA, SOUTHEAST ASIA, AND THE FAR EAST

E64. Andersson, Johan G. **Children of the yellow earth.** London, 1934. This popularized summary of the prehistory of northern China includes sections on the geology and palaeontology of the area. Principal discussions revolve around the Neolithic sequences of Honan and Kansu provinces. There also are sections on Peking man and the interpretations of the archaeological remains in terms of grave symbolism, the death cult, magic, etc.

E65. ——. **Researches into the prehistory of the Chinese.** Stockholm, 1943. Enlarged and revised version of the author's earlier views regarding the six prehistoric stages he had postulated for northwestern China. Gives much archaeological material on predynastic China. Worth studying even though its chronological considerations are not too well founded.

E66. Chang, Kwang-chih. "A brief survey of the archaeology of Formosa." **Southwestern journal of anthropology,** 12 (Winter 1956): 371–86. Excellent summary dealing with the prehistoric sequence from the Middle Neolithic to historic times. Bulk of prehistoric remains of the island appears related to Southeast Asian materials, which is also supported by evidence of physical anthropology. Very useful because it is the first summary of its kind to appear in English.

E67. Groot, Gerard J. **The prehistory of Japan.** Ed. by B. S. Kraus. N.Y., 1951. First comprehensive survey of the prehistory of Japan to appear in English. The extremely involved and complicated evidence, notably that of the Jomon culture, is presented in considerable detail and with great clarity. Being the only one of its kind, this book is indispensable to all who study the archaeology of the Far East.

E68. Jettmar, Karl. "The Karasuk culture and its south-eastern affinities." Museum of Far Eastern Antiquities, **Bulletin 22,** Stockholm, 1950, pp. 83–126. Summarizes the Metal Age archaeology of western Siberia. Also attempts to correlate the finds with extra-Siberian sequences, notably with China.

E69. Krishnaswamy, V. D. "Progress in prehistory." **Ancient India,** 9 (New Delhi, 1953): 53–79. An overall survey of the Stone Age history of India, including sections on the Lower and Upper Palaeolithic industries, the Mesolithic complex, and Neolithic remains of the Indian subcontinent. Author attempts to relate the Indian evidence to extra-Indian sequences.

E70. Lal, B. B. "Further copper hoards from the Gangetic basin and a review of the problem." **Ancient India,** 7 (1951): 20–39. This important paper examines the nature and distribution of a large number of isolated hoards of copper implements found in the Gangetic basin. The chronological position is not clear. Older views favored an identification with the post-Indus civilization "Aryan" invaders, but recent evidence seems to suggest that these hoards represent the remains of a hitherto unknown "pre-Aryan" population of northern and northeastern India.

E71. ——. "Proto-historic investigation." **Ancient India,** 9 (1953): 80–102. A comprehensive review of the proto-historic sequences of India, including the greater Indus valley sequence, the upper Gangetic basin sequence, and evidence from central, western, and south India. Includes some very valuable, as yet otherwise unpublished, materials obtained in the course of recent explorations in the Indian desert.

E72. Li, Chi. **The beginnings of Chinese civilization.** Seattle, 1957. The three lectures published in this book represent a most lucid and readable short summary of Chinese prehistory from the Palaeolithic to the Bronze Age. A good introduction to early China.

E73. Maringer, Johannes. "Einige Faustkeilartige Geräte von Gongenyama (Japan) und die Frage des Japanischen Paläolithikums." **Anthropos,** 51 (Fribourg, Switz., 1956): 175–93. An important paper presenting what may be the first evidence for a Palaeolithic occupation of Japan. The tools are hand-axe like, including chopper and chopping tools and flake tools. Author believes that this complex may be related to the Patjitanian industry of Java.

E74. Mode, Heinz A. **Indische Frühkulturen.** Basel, 1944. An interesting and stimulating study which attempts to link the enigmatic Indus valley civilization of India to the Middle East and the Aegean. Despite its interest, must be read with caution because much of it is unsubstantiated and speculative.

E75. Movius, Hallam L., Jr. "The Lower Palaeolithic cultures of southern and eastern Asia." **Transactions of the American Philosophical Society,** 38 n.s., pt. 4 (1948): 329–420. This fundamental and indispensable monograph outlines the Lower Palaeolithic culture sequences of India, Burma, Java, and North China, defining and describing the typical chopper/chopping tool assemblages of Asia. Includes sections on the Pleistocene geology of the regions concerned and an exhaustive bibliography.

E76. ——. "Palaeolithic and Mesolithic sites in Soviet central Asia." **Proceedings of the American Philosophical Society,** 97 (1953): 383–421. Summarizes the Palaeolithic and Mesolithic remains in terms of three areas. The earliest finds, from Samarkand, are related to the Tayacian. They are succeeded by several Mousterian sites such as Teshik Tash, which has also yielded remains of Neanderthal man. The full Upper Palaeolithic seems absent; the sequence is taken up again in the Late Upper Palaeolithic or early Mesolithic times and carried through to the Neolithic. This summary is useful because most of the original sources, being in Russian, are not readily accessible to western Europeans and Americans.

E77. ——. "Palaeolithic archaeology in southern and eastern Asia, exclusive of India." Pts. 1 and 2. **Journal of world history,** 2, nos. 2 and 3 (Paris, 1955): 257–82, 520–53. Covers much the same ground as the author's earlier monograph (1948), but the material is brought up to date and includes the Upper Palaeolithic evidence from southern and eastern Asia as well. Also from the standpoint of the general reader this paper is easier to absorb.

E78. Piggott, Stuart. **Prehistoric India.** Harmondsworth, Eng., 1950. Comprehensive survey of prehistoric India from the Old Stone Age to circa 1000 B.C. The main discussion centers around the Indus valley civilization and its enigmatic downfall. There also are sections on the Early Bronze Age peasant communities in the western Punjab, as well as the "Aryans" and the hymns of the Rigveda in relation to the collapse of the Indus valley civilization.

E79. Srinivasan, K. R., and N. R. Banerjee. "Survey of south Indian megaliths." **Ancient India,** 9 (1953): 103–15. The megalithic monuments of south India have always been an interesting problem. Mainly the question of chronology is a baffling one. Investigations of these structures lead the author to the conclusion that they represent a common cultural background. The discovery of Roman and other coins in some of the megaliths demonstrates that at least some of them were erected as late as the first century A.D. Some of the funeral pottery can also be cross-dated with Roman pottery levels at Arikamedu.

E80. Subbarao, Bendapudi. **The personality of India.** Baroda, India, 1956. Summarizes present knowledge on the archaeology and prehistory of India from the Old Stone Age to the beginning of the historical period. Includes a few interesting theoretical concepts, such as that classifying archaeological regions of India into areas of attraction and areas of relative isolation. Attempts to correlate the latter with contemporary tribal India.

E81. Terra, Hellmut de, and Hallam L. Movius, Jr. "Research on early man in Burma." **Transactions of the American Philosophical Society,** 32 n.s. (1943): 265–394. Presents evidence for the presence of Palaeolithic man in Burma. Several phases of the Lower Palaeolithic Anyathian industry have been distinguished. This industry forms part of the chopper/chopping tool complex of Palaeolithic tools. Many of the artifacts are fashioned of fossil wood. There also is a chapter on the Neolithic of Burma.

E82. Wheeler, Sir Robert E. M., A. Ghosh, and Arikamedu Krishnadeva. "An Indo Roman trading station on the east coast of India." **Ancient India,** 2 (1946): 17–124. This site near the former French colony of Pondicherry is crucial to the prehistory of south India since it provides a chronological fixed point for cross-dating with other sites. Furthermore, it contains interesting evidence for the extent of Roman trade connections in early imperial times. Roman trade materials here permit for the first time accurate dating of certain essentially prehistoric culture assemblages.

E83. Wu, Chin-ting (G. D. Wu). **Prehistoric pottery in China.** London, 1938. Discusses in considerable detail the various Neolithic ceramic complexes of northern China. Particularly useful to those interested in pottery relationships between China and the West.

THE NEW WORLD

E84. Amsden, Charles A. **Prehistoric southwesterners from Basketmaker to Pueblo.** Los Angeles, 1949. The most carefully prepared consideration of the Basketmaker II and Basketmaker III periods, foundation of the Pueblo cultures in southwestern United States. Exceptionally well written and well illustrated.

E85. Anthropological Society of Washington. **New interpretations of aboriginal American culture history.** Washington, 1955. A series of essays by prominent Americanists. It is somewhat uneven, but gives a reasonably good coverage of the main areas and trends in New World archaeology.

E86. Arroyo de Anda, Luis, Manuel Malonado-Koerdell, and Pablo Martínez del Río. **Cueva de la candelaria.** Mexico, D.F., 1956. First of two volumes on an early prehistoric culture found in caves on the Durango-Coahuila boundary in northern Mexico. The material resembles that of the Basketmaker cultures of southwestern United States. V. 2 to be published soon.

E87. Bennett, Wendell C., and Junius B. Bird. **Andean culture history.** N.Y., 1949. Excellent summary of prehistory of the Peruvian area from earliest pre-pottery cultures through the Inca civilization. The sections on geology and aboriginal technology are also good.

E88. Brainerd, George W. **The Maya civilization.** Los Angeles, 1954. This small book, less than 100 pages, is the handiest instrument for obtaining quickly a general idea of the Maya culture. Presents the formative and classic stages, and treats architecture, religion, calendar and mathematics, ceramics, graphic arts, dress, settlement plan, social organization, economy, and population. There are brief concluding statements about the post-classic and post-conquest stages of Maya culture.

E89. Brew, John O. **The archaeology of Alkali Ridge, southeastern Utah.** Cambridge, Mass., 1946. Detailed report on the excavation of a series of sites in southeastern Utah, with a review of the prehistory of the Mesa Verde division of the San Juan Basketmaker-Pueblo culture and some observations on archaeological systematics.

E90. Chamberlain, Robert S. **The conquest and colonization of Yucatan, 1517–1550.** (See *Z255*.)

E91. Covarrubias, Miguel. **Mexico south: the isthmus of Tehuantepec.** N.Y., 1946. Excellent description of the prehistoric and historic cultures south of the Valley of Mexico by an artist who was also an archaeologist and anthropologist. An attractive book, copiously illustrated with paintings and drawings by the author and many photographs.

E92. Ford, James A., and Gordon R. Willey. "An interpretation of the prehistory of the eastern United States." **American anthropologist,** 43 n.s. (1941): 325–63. The first effective, systematic treatment of the prehistoric cultures of our southeastern states. Provides the basic framework upon which archaeologists in that area operate.

E93. Griffin, James B., ed. **The archaeology of eastern United States.** Chicago, 1952. A large, well illustrated *festschrift* for Professor Fay-Cooper Cole, including 29 essays on aspects of the archaeology of the United States east of the Rocky Mountains and a thorough bibliography. Several of the papers deal with the difficult problem of relating historic tribes with prehistoric sites and cultures in this area.

E94. Haury, Emil W. **The stratigraphy and archaeology of Ventana Cave.** Tucson, 1950.

A report of the excavation, in a southern Arizona cave, of one of the longest and most complete stratigraphic sequences yet discovered in the New World. The levels extend from early Lithic cultures up to modern times.

E95. Kelemen, Pál. **Medieval American art.** 2 v. N.Y., 1943. Covers architecture, sculpture, pottery, weaving, metal working, semi-precious stones, murals, and manuscripts of all the prehistoric high cultures from the Pueblo Indians at Mesa Verde in Colorado to the Incas of the Andes. Besides 414 pages of text, there are 306 plates, some with as many as eight photographs each. There is also a good bibliography.

E96. Kidder, Alfred V. **An introduction to the study of southwestern archaeology.** New Haven, 1924. The first inclusive, systematic presentation of southwestern archaeology. Although outmoded in some respects, it is an extremely valuable basic book for the area. Includes a section on the surviving and extinct historic pueblos.

E97. Kluckhohn, Clyde, and Paul Reiter. **Preliminary report on the 1937 excavations.** Albuquerque, 1939. Description of certain excavations in the Chaco division of the San Juan area in southwestern United States. Especially important because of observations on archaeological systematics.

E98. Kroeber, Alfred L. **Cultural and natural areas of native North America.** Berkeley, 1939. Thorough survey of prehistoric and historic aboriginal North American cultures in their geographic and ecological settings.

E99. Lothrop, Samuel K., W. F. Foshag, and Joy Mahler. **Pre-Columbian art.** N.Y., 1957. The most superbly illustrated book on American Indian art ever published. It is actually the catalog of the Robert Woods Bliss collection, a large part of which is on exhibit in the National Gallery of Art in Washington. The collection includes a full typological representation of prehistoric work in gold and other metals. It also illustrates the outstanding accomplishments in sculpture in the round, textile, and pottery designs, as well as carvings in semi-precious stones. There are 167 magnificent pictures in color and approximately the same number in black and white.

E100. MacGowan, Kenneth. **Early man in the New World.** N.Y., 1950. Of books on the earliest archaeological manifestations in the New World, this is the easiest for the layman. It does not make any attempt at completeness or detail, and was written before radiocarbon dating was applied to the problem. It is, however, an excellent indication for those interested only in a few of the major artifact assemblages.

E101. Marquina, Ignacio. **Arquitectura prehispánica.** Mexico, 1951. The most complete single publication to date on the prehistoric architecture of Mexico for the Maya area, including also a considerable amount of information about pottery, metal working, and other minor arts and crafts. Exceptionally well illustrated.

E102. Martin, Paul S., George I. Quimby, and Donald Collier. **Indians before Columbus.** Chicago, 1947. Summary of North American archaeology, including a good introduction to the subject and well selected illustrations. The dating is outmoded, but the general presentation is efficient and inclusive.

E103. Montgomery, Ross G., Watson Smith, and John O. Brew. **Franciscan Awatovi.** Cambridge, Mass., 1949. The excavation and conjectural reconstruction of a 17th century Spanish mission establishment at a Hopi Indian town in northeastern Arizona. In this monograph architecture, history, archaeology, and anthropology are blended in the descriptions of early Spanish contacts with an Arizona Pueblo culture.

E104. Morley, Sylvanus G. **The ancient Maya.** 3rd ed., rev. by George W. Brainerd, Stanford, 1956. A standard classic, first published in 1946 by the director of field work at Chichén Itzá for the Carnegie Institution of Washington. Thoroughly revised ten years later by one of the more competent and imaginative Maya scholars. Lavishly illustrated.

E105. Phillips, Philip, James A. Ford, and James B. Griffin. **Archaeological survey in the lower Mississippi alluvial valley, 1940–1947.** Cambridge, Mass., 1951. Detailed report of one of the most ambitious archaeological surveys ever attempted in the New World. Includes correlation of sites to the sequentially dated shifting channels of the Mississippi river.

E106. Proskouriakoff, Tatiana. **An album of Maya architecture.** Washington, 1946. A series of rendered drawings with accompanying explanatory text of outstanding prehistoric Maya buildings and other architectural features, by the outstanding architect on the staff of the Carnegie Institution of Washington.

E107. Redfield, Robert. **The folk culture of Yucatan.** Chicago, 1941. Analysis of the present population of the Yucatán peninsula by a leading social anthropologist. Describes the two heritages, Spanish and Indian; and traces the history of the changes in specific traits from prehistoric to modern times.

E108. Roberts, Frank H. H., Jr. **Shabik'-eshchee village: a late Basketmaker site in the Chaco canyon, New Mexico.** Washington, 1929. Short monograph describing a classic Basketmaker III site in southwestern United States, with important general observations on subterranean and semi-subterranean houses in western North America and northeast Asia.

E109. Roys, Ralph L. **The Indian background of colonial Yucatan.** Washington, 1943. A monograph resulting from archaeological and historical researches of the Carnegie Institution of Washington. Presents in considerable detail Maya culture at the time of the conquest, and the immediate developments in social and economic realms under the cacique system established by the Spaniards.

E110. Sahagún, Bernardino de. **Florentine codex: general history of the things of New Spain.** Tr. by Arthur J. O. Anderson and Charles E. Dibble. In 13 pts. (8 published through 1957). Sante Fe, 1950 ff. A contemporary ethnography produced in the Valley of Mexico shortly after the Spanish conquest. The most valuable single document on the civilization which dominated Mexico at the time. Originally published in Spanish and Aztec. Latest ed. in Spanish is *Historia general de las cosas de Nueva España* (5 v., Mexico, 1938). Other editions exist in varying degrees of completeness in Spanish, French, and English.

E111. Sayles, Edwin B., and Ernest Antevs. **The Cochise culture.** Globe, Ariz., 1941. Careful definition of an important early southwestern culture. Ethnological materials and the sites are described by Sayles and the geological situation is ably presented by Antevs.

E112. Sellards, Elias H. **Early man in America.** Austin, 1952. Reasonably detailed discussion of Lithic cultures in the New World, with particular emphasis on the faunal associations and an extensive bibliography.

E113. Smith, Watson. **Kiva mural decorations at Awatovi and Kawaika-a, with a survey of other wall paintings in the Pueblo Southwest.** Cambridge, Mass., 1952. Fully illustrated description of a series of prehistoric and early historic ceremonial wall paintings uncovered in the ruins of Hopi Pueblo villages in northeastern Arizona. Detailed comparisons are made with other indigenous murals in the Southwest. This book records one of the most important manifestations of aboriginal American Indian art, not previously systematically presented.

E114. Spinden, Herbert J. **Ancient civilizations of Mexico and Central America.** 3rd ed., N.Y., 1928. Useful basic statement of the high civilizations of northern Central America and Mexico. Clearly written and well illustrated, but does not reflect researches of the second quarter of the 20th century.

E115. ——. **A study of Maya art.** Cambridge, Mass., 1913. A classic treatise, admirably illustrated with drawings and photographs.

E116. Stallings, William S., Jr. **Dating prehistoric ruins by tree-rings.** Santa Fe, 1939. Clearest concise statement of dendrochronology as applied to southwestern archaeology.

E117. Stephens, John L. **Incidents of travel in Central America, Chiapas, and Yucatan.** 2 v. N.Y., 1841. Several subsequent editions. One of the best of early scientific travel books, containing a large number of sketches and ground plans made by the author at prehistoric sites in the Maya region.

E118. Thompson, John Eric S. **The rise and fall of Maya civilization.** Norman, 1954. Well written and detailed description of one of the major American Indian cultures by the outstanding living scholar in the field. Prehistoric codices and many sculptures and paintings permit a more elaborate reconstruction of the Maya civilization than is possible with any other prehistoric American culture, although much along the same line can be done for the Aztecs and Incas.

E119. Tozzer, Alfred M. **Landa's "Relación de las cosas de Yucatán."** Cambridge, Mass., 1941. Translation of the most important early Spanish document describing Maya civilization as found by the European conquerors. The source material presented by Landa includes practically every phase of social anthropology of the ancient Mayas, together with the history of Spanish discovery, the conquest, and ecclesiastical and native history. It presented the first accurate knowledge of the hieroglyphic writing, and is especially complete on Maya religion and rituals. The editorial notes are, in themselves, a major contribution to American archaeology.

E120. Vaillant, George C. **Aztecs of Mexico: origin, rise and fall of the Aztec nation.** Garden City, 1941. An archaeological classic of the prehistoric high cultures of the Valley of Mexico. The first four chapters deal with predecessors of the Aztecs. The Aztec period is described with much more detail than is usually possible for prehistoric cultures because of the existence of prehistoric codices and early historic writings in the area. An outstanding example of the blending of archaeology with written history.

E121. Wauchope, Robert, ed. **Seminars in archaeology: 1955.** Salt Lake City, 1956. Report of four conferences, each with a number of papers dealing with culture contact situations between indigenous and European groups, cultural continuity and suitability, cultural isolation, and the function and development of communities as reflected in the findings of American archaeology. Many of the important current theories of American prehistory are presented in interesting, full discussion and in language which the non-specialist can easily follow.

E122. Willey, Gordon R., and Philip Phillips. **Method and theory in American archaeology.** Chicago, 1958. The best introduction available under one cover to the theoretical problems in American archaeology. The overall "historical-developmental" interpretation is presented in considerable detail, but broad outlines of the various stages are clear. It is the only treatment of this subject in book form to date, and has an excellent bibliography which will lead the reader into both details and theory of the subject as they appear in articles in the various professional journals.

E123. Wormington, Hannah M. **Ancient man in North America.** 4th ed., Denver, 1957. The outstanding book and most detailed treatment of early remains covering the so-called Lithic periods. These are described under Paleoeastern, Paleowestern, and Paleonorthern traditions and non-projectile point assemblages. Human skeletal remains are also discussed, and there is a chapter on the peopling of North America.

E124. ———. **Prehistoric Indians of the Southwest.** Denver, 1947. Most complete single statement available in published form on archaeology of the United States Southwest. Covers the Basketmaker-Pueblo culture, including early historic Pueblo, the Athabascans, Hohokam, Mogollon, Sinagua, and Patayan. All sides of the important moot points are fairly presented and handled with restraint. There is an appendix by Erik K. Reed describing modern pueblos, outstanding archaeological sites exhibited by federal, state or local agencies, and a list of museums in the area.

The Ancient Orient

JAMES B. PRITCHARD *

A little more than a quarter of a century ago A. T. Olmstead wrote in his introduction to the Near East section in the original *Guide,* "So rapidly, indeed, are new discoveries enlarging and defining knowledge of the ancient Near East that historical works concerning them become superannuated as speedily as do those on contemporary times." The truth of this observation is here demonstrated by the fact that only about a dozen titles listed in 1931 have been included in the following list, compiled by six specialists who have attempted to appraise the present historical resources for this same area.

The phenomenal growth of new historical documents from the ancient Near East has not only made the older works antiquated, but has made it difficult for scholars to produce a synthesis of the history of the entire area. The absence of recent general histories which can be recommended is conspicuous in the following list. Even such a basic subject as the chronology of the ancient Orient is still a matter for debate. New materials coming from excavations, as well as new interpretations of former data, are modifying considerably older conclusions and theories. Consequently the user of this bibliography should pay special attention to the concluding section on periodicals.

BIBLIOGRAPHIES

F1. Porter, Bertha, and Rosalind L. Moss. **Topographical bibliography of ancient Egyptian hieroglyphic texts, reliefs, and paintings.** 7 v. Oxford, 1927–51. 2nd ed., V. 1, 1960. A highly valuable work which presents the ancient Egyptian material belonging to a given site. Includes a number of maps and plans. Indexes of personal names, periods, etc. facilitate cross-reference. [HGF]

F2. Janssen, Jozef M. A. **Annual Egypto**logical bibliography. 1947–58. 11 v. Leiden, 1948–59. An admirably comprehensive list of current publications dealing with ancient Egypt, with abstracts of varying length depending on the scope and complexity of the work treated. Recent bibliographies prior to this one are described in pp. 9–11 of v. 1. [HGF]

F3. Pratt, Ida A. **Ancient Egypt: sources of information in the New York Public Library.** N.Y., 1925. Supplement, 1942. Contains the bulk of Egyptological literature

* The following contributed items and comments indicated by their respective initials: M. J. Dresden (MJD), Henry G. Fischer (HGF), Hans G. Güterbock (HGG), Ferris J. Stephens (FJS), and F. V. Winnett (FVW).

through 1940 (most foreign publications through 1938 or 1939). [HGF]

F4. Berghe, L. vanden, and B. A. van Proosdij, eds. **Bibliographie analytique de l'assyriologie et de l'archéologie du Proche-Orient.** Leiden, 1956 ff. Only v. 1 is in print, but sponsorship by the Rencontre Internationale Assyriologique guarantees that the complete work will be of first importance. [FJS]

F5. Pohl, Alfred. "Keilschriftbibliographie." **Orientalia: commentarii periodici pontificii instituti biblici,** v. 9 ff. (1940 ff.). Complete coverage of the field, including books, periodical articles, and book reviews; no evaluations. [FJS]

F6. Schwartz, Benjamin. **The Hittites: a list of references in the New York Public Library.** N.Y., 1939. Detailed and, up to date of publication, almost complete bibliography of books and articles in various fields of Hittite and related studies. [HGG]

See also Laroche, "Catalogue des textes hittites" (*F111*) for bibliography of Hittite texts.

F7. Thomsen, Peter. **Die Palästina-Literatur: eine internationale Bibliographie in systematischer Ordnung mit Autoren- und Sachregister.** 6 v. Leipzig and Berlin, 1911–56. Indispensable tool for locating the scattered historical writings on Palestine. Now complete for the years 1895–1939.

F8. Internationale Zeitschriftenschau für Bibelwissenschaft und Grenzgebiete. Stuttgart, 1952 ff. (Semiannual.) Analysis of literature which has appeared in 393 journals and periodicals. Brief description of contents in some cases.

F9. Weidner, Ernst, ed. **Archiv für Orientforschung.** Berlin and Graz, 1926 ff. (Bimonthly. Title varies.) Bibliographies in this periodical contain a selected list of most important works on Palestine and Syria.

F10. "Elenchus bibliographicus biblicus." **Biblica: commentarii editi cura pontificii instituti biblici.** Rome, 1920 ff. (Quarterly.) Bibliographies of books, articles, and reviews in western languages and in Hebrew of material in the Biblical field. The sections on "Historia biblica," "Archaeologia biblica," and "Geographia biblica" are particularly relevant. No appraisal of the quality or scope of the works listed is attempted.

F11. Répertoire d'épigraphie sémitique. V. 5 (Paris, 1928), pp. i–lxxxiii. A complete, chronologically arranged bibliography of pre-Islamic Arabia up to 1928. For later publications see the following (*F12–16*). [FVW]

F12. Moubarac, Y. "Éléments de bibliographie sud-sémitique." **Revue des études islamiques,** 23 (1955): 121–76.

F13. Moscati, Sabatino. "Bibliographie sémitique." **Orientalia,** 16 (1947): 103–29, 17 (1948): 91–102, 19 (1950): 445–78, 22 (1953): 1–24, 26 (1957): 73–115. Last page

cited contains index to articles on pre-Islamic Arabia.

F14. Field, Henry. **Bibliography on southwestern Asia.** 3 v. Coral Gables, Fla., 1953–56.

F15. U. S. Library of Congress. **The Arabian peninsula: a selected, annotated list of periodicals, books and articles in English.** See *S20*.

F16. Ettinghausen, Richard, ed. **A selected and annotated bibliography of books and periodicals in western languages dealing with the Near and Middle East, with special emphasis on mediaeval and modern times.** Washington, 1952. Supplement, 1954.

F17. Henning, Walter B. H. **Bibliography of important studies on old Iranian subjects.** Teheran, 1950. Does not aim at completeness, but constitutes a minimum bibliography for work on this subject. Omits works in Arabic and Persian. [MJD]

ENCYCLOPEDIAS AND WORKS OF REFERENCE

F18. Vandier, Jacques. **Manuel d'archéologie égyptienne.** 3 v. Paris, 1952–58. This compilation has detailed references and many, small illustrations. After covering prehistory and the first three dynasties in the first volume, the second deals with architecture and the third with statuary. Reviews, A. Arkell, *Bibliotheca orientalis,* 11 (1954): 47 and I. E. S. Edwards, *ibid.,* 12 (Mar. 1955): 59 and 14 (Jan. 1957): 23. [HGF]

F19. Bonnet, Hans. **Reallexikon der ägyptischen Religionsgeschichte.** Berlin, 1952. Sound and comprehensive encyclopedia of Egyptian religion; well documented. Many articles contain bibliography. Review, H. Frankfort, *Bibliotheca orientalis,* 10 (Nov. 1953): 220 [HGF]

F20. Wreszinski, Walter. **Atlas zur altaegyptischen Kulturgeschichte.** 3 pts. Leipzig, 1923–39. A very large collection of excellent and well reproduced photographs, mostly from tomb paintings and reliefs, illustrating the various aspects of Egyptian life. Each plate is accompanied by explanatory text and sometimes by supplementary photographs and drawings. Part 3 is devoted exclusively to the Old Kingdom. [HGF]

F21. Helck, H. Wolfgang, and Eberhard Otto. **Kleines Wörterbuch der Aegyptologie.** Wiesbaden, 1956. Useful and reliable handbook, though the selection of topics is not as well balanced as it might be and there are serious omissions in the references. [HGF]

F22. Ebeling, Erich, Bruno Meissner, and Ernst Weidner. **Reallexikon der Assyriologie.** Berlin, 1932 ff. A series of articles ranging in length from a few sentences to more than 60 pages; scope of the subjects is intended to cover virtually everything of interest to the Assyriologist. Over 1,000 pages and 63 plates of photographic reproductions are now in print, but these only reach to the letter F. There is considerable unevenness in value of the articles, but the work as a whole is indispensable. [FJS]

F23. Gunkel, Hermann, and Leopold Zscharnack, eds. **Die Religion in Geschichte und Gegenwart.** 2nd ed., 6 v., Tübingen, 1927–32. Represents the best of German scholarship for the period. Now being revised in a 3rd edition.

F24. Vigouroux, Fulcran G., ed. **Diction- naire de la Bible.** 5 v. Paris, 1895–1912. Supplements, 1926 ff. Roman Catholic dic- tionary which has been brought up to date with many supplements.

F25. 'Entsiqlōpêdiyeh Miqrā'ît (Encyclo- paedia biblica). Jerusalem, 1950 ff. Biblical encyclopedia in modern Hebrew, fully illus- trated and annotated.

F26. Hastings, James, and others, eds. **A dictionary of the Bible.** See *D376*.

F27. Galling, Kurt. **Biblisches Reallexikon.** Tübingen, 1937. [Otto Eissfeldt, ed., Hand- buch zum Alten Testament.] A handbook of the results of Palestinian archaeology, ar- ranged in brief articles on such topics as principal excavations, elements of material, and religious culture. Full documentation for the period up to early 1930's.

F28. Barrois, Augustin G. **Manuel d'arché- ologie biblique.** 2 v. Paris, 1939–53. Well illustrated and fully documented analysis of the results of archaeology in Biblical Pales- tine, according to cultural elements and institutions.

F29. Rowley, H. H., ed. **The Old Testa- ment and modern study: a generation of discovery and research.** Oxford, 1951. Very useful book which aims "to survey the sig- nificant work that has been done during the last thirty years in order to bring out the changes that have come about and the new trends that have appeared." Chapters by recognized scholars on archaeology, criticism on various sections of the Hebrew Bible, textual criticism, Semitic epigraphy and He- brew philology, Hebrew religion, and Old Testament theology.

F30. Willoughby, Harold R., ed. **The study of the Bible today and tomorrow.** Chicago, 1947. Symposium of 24 articles which take stock of the state of Biblical research to date of publication. Important for a per- spective in the various fields of the subject.

F31. The encyclopaedia of Islam. Ed. by M. Th. Houtsma and others. 4 v. Leiden and London, 1913–36. Supplement, 1938. Many of the articles dealing with pre-Islamic Arabia are out-dated. A new, revised edition is in process of publication under editorship of Johannes H. Kramers, Hamilton A. R. Gibb, Bernard Lewis, and others. [FVW]

GEOGRAPHIES AND ATLASES

F32. Hommel, Fritz. **Ethnologie und Geo- graphie des alten Orients.** Munich, 1926. Useful as a systematic and detailed treatment of the subject; but only the first half of the book is concerned with Mesopotamia, and it is considerably in need of revision in light of more recent research. [FJS]

F33. Lees, G. M., and N. L. Falcon. "The geographical history of the Mesopotamian plains." **The geographical journal,** 118 (Mar. 1952): 24–39. Contains important informa- tion concerning the ancient location of the head of the Persian Gulf; disagrees with belief of many archaeologists. [FJS]

F34. Smith, George A. **The historical geography of the Holy Land.** 25th ed., N.Y., 1932. Although some identifications have been superseded by subsequent excavations and research, this remains the standard work in the field of Palestinian geography. The maps are clear and useful.

F35. Grollenberg, Luc H. **Atlas of the Bible.** Tr. and ed. by Joyce M. H. Reid and H. H. Rowley. London and N.Y., 1956. A de- pendable atlas, beautifully illustrated and accompanied by full text.

F36. Wright, George E., and Floyd V. Filson, eds. **The Westminster historical atlas to the Bible.** Rev. ed., Philadelphia, 1956. Eighteen large plates of maps in color of Bible lands, including one of excavated sites in modern Palestine. Particularly useful are the index of Arabic names identified with Biblical places in Palestine and Syria, and a topographical concordance to the Bible.

F37. Kraeling, Emil G. **Rand McNally Bible atlas.** Chicago, 1956. In addition to 22 color maps of Bible lands, contains a study of the history of the land from patriarchal times down through the period of the early Christian church.

F38. Abel, Félix M. **Géographie de la Palestine.** Rev. ed., 2 v., Paris, 1933–38. Most complete study of the physical, his- torical, and political geography of Palestine. V. 2 contains an alphabetical listing of Biblical cities and other historical places with full discussions of the proposed identi- fications with modern places.

F39. Dussaud, René. **Topographie histori- que de la Syrie antique et médiévale.** Paris, 1927. Standard work for historical geography of Syria, containing 16 maps, a good bib- liography, and an index of place names. Arrangement is by districts.

F40. Wissmann, Hermann von, and Maria Höfner. **Beiträge zur historischen Geographie des vorislamischen Südarabien.** Mainz, 1953. Very important contribution to both the geography and ancient history of southern Arabia. Contains two maps and excellent bibliography. [FVW]

LINGUISTIC WORKS

F41. Gardiner, Alan H. **Egyptian grammar: being an introduction to the study of hieroglyphs.** 3rd ed., London, 1957. This authoritative work is both a series of lessons and a treatise on Middle Egyptian. For those not intending to study the language, it is of value chiefly for its highly informative introduction, but also a useful source of information on such subjects as "The titulary and other designations of the king," Egyptian numbers, weights and measures, "The divisions of time and method of dating," and "The transcription of Egyptian proper names." [HGF]

F42. Ranke, Hermann. **Die ägyptischen Personennamen.** 2 v. Glückstadt, 1935–52. As a reference work these two volumes are essential to the specialist. The discussions in v. 2 are of more general interest. Review, J. A. Wilson, *Journal of the American Oriental Society,* 73 (June 1953): 99. [HGF]

F43. Grapow, Hermann. **Die bildlichen Ausdrücke des Aegyptischen.** Leipzig, 1924. Similes, metaphors, and similar literary devices, compiled under subject headings and quoted in German translation. An authoritative presentation of material that is important for understanding the ancient Egyptian mind. [HGF]

F44. Erman, Adolf, and Hermann Grapow, eds. **Wörterbuch der aegyptischen Sprache.** 6 v. Leipzig, 1926–53. The standard dictionary of the ancient Egyptian language, consisting of five volumes, each with a corresponding volume of references, and a sixth volume of German into Egyptian. The last is particularly useful for non-specialists, though the coverage of German word lists is not always adequate. [HGF]

F45. Poebel, Arno. **Grundzüge der sumerischen Grammatik.** Rostock, 1923. Remains the fundamental grammar of Sumerian although there are a number of more recent publications. At some points needs to be supplemented and improved by later works such as the following (*F46*). [FJS]

F46. Falkenstein, Adam. **Grammatik der Sprache Gudeas von Lagaš.** 2 v. Rome, 1949–50.

F47. Christan, Victor. **Beiträge zur sumerischen Grammatik.** Vienna, 1957. Useful discussion of the many moot points of Sumerian grammar. [FJS]

F48. Soden, Wolfram von. **Grundris der akkadischen Grammatik.** Rome, 1952. [Analecta orientalia, 33.] Systematic treatment of the subject in great detail. Contains introduction of a historical nature, giving the place of Akkadian in the Semitic family of languages and the various historical periods in its development. While it is of primary importance for the specialist, the non-specialist may find the following work more useful as a handbook. [FJS]

F49. Ungnad, Arthur. **Grammatik des Akkadischen.** 3rd ed., Munich, 1949.

F50. Deimel, Anton. **Sumerisches Lexikon.** Pt. 2. 4 v. Rome, 1928–50. Undertakes to list all cuneiform signs and sign groups, arranged in the conventional order which has become standard among Assyriologists. Because of the rapid advance of research, such a work is incomplete as soon as printed. This one is now in need of extensive revision, but still very useful. [FJS]

F51. Gelb, Ignace J., and others, eds. **The Assyrian dictionary of the Oriental Institute of the University of Chicago.** Chicago, 1956 ff. This project has been in process several decades, and now begins to present results. A volume is planned for each letter of the Roman alphabet used in transcribing Akkadian words, listing every known word in the language and quoting representative texts from each period in which the word occurs. Pending completion of this work, the following should be used. [FJS]

F52. Bezold, Carl. **Babylonisch-assyrisches Glossar.** Heidelberg, 1926.

F53. Hrozný, Friedrich. **Die Sprache der Hethiter.** Leipzig, 1917. Of historical value only. First presentation of the decipherment of the Hittite language; now superseded by recent grammars. [HGG]

F54. Sturtevant, Edgar H., and E. Adelaide Hahn. **A comparative grammar of the Hittite language.** Rev. ed., New Haven, 1951 ff. Emphasis is on comparison with Indo-European. V. 1, by Sturtevant, treats phonology and morphology. V. 2 will be by Miss Hahn on syntax. Supersedes the first edition of 1933. [HGG]

F55. Sturtevant, Edgar H., and George Bechtel. **A Hittite chrestomathy.** Philadelphia, 1935. Primarily for self-study of Hittite. Contains sign list and selected texts in cuneiform copy, transliteration, and English translation with explanatory notes. [HGG]

F56. Sturtevant, Edgar H. **A Hittite glossary.** 2nd ed., Philadelphia, 1936. Supplement, 1939. The subtitle, "Words of known or conjectured meaning with Sumerian and Akkadian words occurring in Hittite texts," describes the character of the glossary, which, by definition, is not a full dictionary of the Hittite language. Superseded by *F58*, but still the only glossary of Hittite in English. [HGG]

F57. Friedrich, Johannes. **Hethitisches Elementarbuch.** 2 pts. Heidelberg, 1940–46. Pt. 1 is a short descriptive grammar; pt. 2 gives selected Hittite texts in transliteration, with references to pt. 1 in footnotes and with brief comments, and also contains a supplement to the grammar. Glossary to words contained in the texts is superseded by *F58*. [HGG]

F58. ———. **Hethitisches Wörterbuch:**

kurzgefasste kritische Sammlung der deutungen hethitischer Wörter. Heidelberg, 1952. Like Sturtevant's Hittite glossary, this is not a full dictionary, but only contains words whose meaning is either known or conjectured. Sumerian and Akkadian words occurring in Hittite are listed separately, as are also words of other Anatolian languages. [HGG]

F59. ———. **Entzifferungsgeschichte der hethitischen Hieroglyphenschrift.** Stuttgart, 1939. Brief account of decipherment of the Hittite hieroglyphs from beginnings to 1938. Written before discovery of the Karatepe bilinguals, and shows what was achieved without the latter. [HGG]

F60. ———. **Extinct languages.** N.Y., 1957. Account of the technique and history of decipherment of unknown scripts and languages for the general reader. Contains chapters on Hittite (written in cuneiform) and on Hittite hieroglyphs. [HGG]

F61. ———. **Kleinasiastische Sprachdenkmäler.** Berlin, 1932. [Hans Lietzmann, ed., Kleine Texte für Vorlesungen und Übungen, 163.] Representative collection of texts in the various languages of ancient Anatolia except Hittite. Contains selected Hattic, Hurrian, Luwian, and Urartaen texts and a complete (to date of publication) collection of inscriptions in Eteo-cypriote, Lycian, Carian, Lydian, and Phrygian, as well as some minor groups. [HGG]

F62. ———. **Einführung ins Urartäische.** Leipzig, 1933. Brief but reliable grammar of Urartaen; an introduction to the study of the language. Selected texts in transliteration and German translation, with full philological commentary. [HGG]

F63. Speiser, Ephraim A. **Introduction to Hurrian.** New Haven, 1941. [The annual of the American schools of oriental research, 20.] The standard work on this language. [HGG]

F64. Gordon, Cyrus H. **Ugaritic handbook: revised grammar, paradigms, texts in transliteration, comprehensive glossary.** 3 v. Rome, 1947. [Analecta orientalia, 25.] Rev. ed., *Ugaritic manual,* Rome, 1955. [Analecta orientalia, 35.] Standard work on the Canaanite texts found at Ras Shamra, but does not include a translation. The author's translations of the texts appear in *Ugaritic literature* (Rome, 1949).

F65. Höfner, Maria. **Altsüdarabische Grammatik.** Leipzig, 1943; reprint, 1949. [Porta linguarum orientalium, 24.] The only adequate grammar of South Arabic. [FVW]

F66. Rhodokanakis, Nikolaus. "Altsabäische Texte, I." **Sitzungsberichte der Akademie der Wissenschaften, philosophisch-historische Klasse,** 206, no. 2 (Vienna, 1927). Translation, with commentary, of some of the longest and most important Sabaean inscriptions. [FVW]

F67. ———. "Altsabäische Texte, II." **Wiener Zeitschrift für die Kunde des Morgenländes,** 39 (Vienna, 1932): 173–226.

F68. ———. "Studien zur Lexikographie und Grammatik des Altsüdarabischen, I–III." **Sitzungsberichte der Akademie der Wissenschaften philosophisch-historische Klasse,** 178, no. 4 (Vienna, 1915); 185, no. 3 (1917); 213, no. 3 (1931). Rhodokanakis has contributed more than any other scholar to the elucidation of South Arabic. His works are of fundamental importance. [FVW]

F69. Pirenne, Jacques. **Paléographie des inscriptions sud-arabes: contribution à la chronologie et à l'histoire de l'Arabie du sud antique.** V. 1. Brussels, 1956. A more detailed exposition of views enunciated in his earlier work, *La Grèce et Saba.* For a detailed criticism see Albert Jamme, *La paléographie sud-arabe de J. Pirenne* (Washington, 1957). [FVW]

F70. Ryckmans, Gonzague. "Langues et écritures sémitiques: II, Groupe du Sud." F. G. Vigouroux, ed., **Dictionnaire de la Bible,** supplement (Paris, 1952), cols. 318–34. Contains a table of alphabets and bibliography. [FVW]

F71. Kent, Roland G. **Old Persian: grammar, texts, lexicon.** New Haven, 1950. 2nd ed., 1954. Indispensable for study of inscriptions of the Achaemenian kings, which are given in transcription and accompanied by translation. For some criticisms see review by E. Benveniste, *Jour. Am. Oriental Soc.,* 75 (July-Sept. 1955): 195. [MJD]

PRINTED COLLECTIONS OF SOURCES

F72. Breasted, James H. **Ancient records of Egypt: historical documents from the earliest times to the Persian conquest, collected, edited, and translated with commentary.** 5 v. Chicago, 1906–07. Although this admirable series is now out of date, there is no recent work that is by any means comparable in scope. Newer translations of some of the texts, by John A. Wilson, will be found in Pritchard, *Ancient near eastern texts (F124).* [HGF]

F73. Lewis, Bernard, ed. **Land of enchanters: Egyptian short stories from the earliest times to the present day.** London, 1948. The larger part of this collection is from ancient Egyptian and Coptic literature, ably translated by Battiscombe Gunn, with some explanatory notes added. Review, B. van de Walle, *Bibliotheca orientalis,* 6 (May 1949): 99. [HGF]

F74. Lefebvre, Gustave, ed. and tr. **Romans et contes égyptiens de l'époque pharaonique.** Paris, 1949. Up-to-date translation, with commentary, of the major prose literary works; very useful bibliographies for each piece. Review, Z. Žába, *Bibliotheca orientalis,* 7 (Nov. 1950): 172. [HGF]

F75. Schott, Siegfried. **Altägyptischen Liebeslieder: mit Märchen und Leibesgeschichten.** Zürich, 1950. Accurate and deft translation of an important category of Egyptian poetry, and a study of the same in the context of other literature. [HGF]

F76. Wiseman, Donald J., ed. and tr. **Chronicles of Chaldaean kings (626–556 B.C.) in the British Museum.** London, 1956. Here are published for the first time important new parts of this type of Babylonian literature. Preface contains references to older publications, giving remainder of the known material of this type. [FJS]

F77. Weidner, Ernst. "Die assyrischen Eponymen." **Archiv für Orientforschung,** 13 (1941): 308–18. This treatment of the ancient lists of eponyms should be used in connection with the long article by Arthur Ungnad, "Eponymen," *Reallexikon der Assyriologie,* v. 2 (Berlin and Leipzig, 1938), pp. 412–17. [FJS]

F78. Gelb, Ignace J. "Two Assyrian king lists." **Journal of near eastern studies,** 13 (Oct. 1954): 209–30. Main purpose of this article is to give the complete text of the two ancient copies of the "List." It is presented in very legible photographs and in transliteration and translation. [FJS]

F79. Poebel, Arno. "The Assyrian king list from Knorsabad." **Journal of near eastern studies,** 1 (July 1942): 247–306, 1 (Oct. 1942): 460–92, 2 (Jan. 1943): 56–90. "The Assyrian king list," an ancient document now known in two original copies, undertook to give the names of all the Assyrian kings, fathers' names, and length of reigns down to and including Shalmaneser V (726–722 B.C.). This article is the first thorough study of the text, and amounts to a kind of chronological history of Assyria. [FJS]

F80. Jacobsen, Thorkild P. **The Sumerian king list.** Chicago, 1939. Critical edition and reconstruction of an ancient Sumerian composition which undertook to list the names of all rulers of the land of Sumer, arranged according to ruling dynasties, from earliest times to about the beginning of the second millennium B.C., together with the length of reign of each ruler. Although the absolute chronology adopted by the author has been revised by later scholars, the book remains the most definitive work in print on this primary Sumerian source. [FJS]

F81. Luckenbill, Daniel D. **Ancient records of Assyria and Babylonia.** 2 v. Chicago, 1926–27. Essential work for specimens of inscriptions of virtually all the Assyrian kings. Later translations of texts from several kings are mentioned elsewhere. [FJS]

F82. Vorderasiatische Bibliothek. 7 v. Leipzig, 1907–16. [1, François Thureau-Dangin, ed., *Die sumerischen und akka-*dischen Königsinschriften; 2, Maximilian Streck, ed., *Assurbanipal und die letzten assyrischen Könige bis zum Untergange Ninivehs;* 3, Franz H. Weissbach, ed., *Die Keilinschriften der Achämeniden;* 4, Stephen H. Langdon, ed., *Die neubabylonischen Königsinschriften;* 5, Moses Schorr, ed., *Urkunden des Altbabylonischen Zivil- und Prozessrechts;* 6, Jørgen A. Knudtzon, ed., *Die El-Amarna-tafeln;* 7, Arthur Ungnad, ed., *Babylonische Briefe aus der Zeit der Hammurapi-Dynastie.*] Translations of this work can now be improved at many points, but it remains the most comprehensive collection of printed sources in translation. [FJS]

F83. Neugebauer, Otto, and Abraham Sachs, eds. **Mathematical cuneiform texts.** New Haven, 1945. Documents in this volume are sufficiently extensive to offer a fair impression of the main types of Babylonian mathematical texts. The latter are translated and explained in detail. Extensive bibliography. [FJS]

F84. Eisser, Georg, and Julius Lewy. **Die Altassyrischen Rechtsurkunden vom Kültepe.** 2 v. Leipzig, 1930–35. [Mitteilungen der Vorderasiatisch-aegyptischen Gesellschaft, 33, 35.] Although the documents translated here originated in a region outside Mesopotamia proper, they have a direct bearing on the economic history of upper Mesopotamia at the beginning of the second millennium B.C. A considerable number of similar texts have been published since 1935, but this remains the most comprehensive and best study available on the subject. [FJS]

F85. Ungnad, Arthur, and Marian San Nicolò, eds. **Neubabylonische Rechts- und Verwaltungsurkunden.** Leipzig, 1929. Representative of a large number of such texts already published. Contains translations and critical notes on 902 texts, arranged in systematic fashion according to subjects. A glossary was published by Ungnad in 1937. [FJS]

F86. Waterman, Leroy, ed. and tr. **Royal correspondence of the Assyrian empire.** 4 v. Ann Arbor, 1930–36. First two volumes contain transliteration and translation of all the cuneiform texts (1,471 in number) published in Robert F. Harper, *Assyrian and Babylonian letters* (14 v., Chicago, 1892–1914). V. 3 contains a commentary on each letter; and v. 4 consists of several short studies of subjects suggested by the letters, a selected glossary, and numerous indexes. The translations could now be improved at many points, but the work remains a useful compendium of this type of literature. [FJS]

F87. Ebeling, Erich R. **Neubabylonische Briefe.** Munich, 1949. [Abhandlungen der Bayerischen Akademie der Wissenschaften, philosophisch-historische Klasse, n.s., 30.] The 327 letters translated in this work come from several different museum collections and represent such ancient cities as Sippar, Uruk, Nippur, and Ur as their places of origin. They may be regarded as representative of a fairly large body of such sources, to which references will be found in the notes. [FJS]

F88. Parrot, André, and Georges Dossin, eds. **Archives royales de Mari.** Paris, 1950 ff. The first six volumes contain transliteration and translation of the letters of this important archive; v. 7, economic texts; and v. 15 furnishes a grammar of Akkadian as used in the letters from Mari. [FJS]

F89. Dijk, Johannes J. A. van. **La sagesse suméro-accadienne.** Leiden, 1953. Attempts to classify into rational categories the various kinds of Sumerian "wisdom" literature. Includes description of each type and samples in transliteration and translation with critical commentary. [FJS]

F90. Falkenstein, Adam, and Wolfram von Soden, eds. and trs. **Sumerische und akkadische Hymnen und Gebete.** Zürich and Stuttgart, 1953. Gives a brief history of Sumero-Akkadian literature against the background of general cultural history, and discusses the poetical religious literature as to its structure, style, language, and content. Most of the book is devoted to translation only of 127 examples of the poetical religious literature. [FJS]

F91. Driver, Godfrey R., and Sir John C. Miles. **The Assyrian laws.** Oxford, 1935. Essential for history of Mesopotamian law. Legal commentary occupies more than two-thirds of the volume; the remainder is transliteration and translation of the texts with critical notes and glossary. [FJS]

F92. Driver, Godfrey R., and Sir John C. Miles, eds. and trs. **The Babylonian laws.** 2 v. Oxford, 1952–55. Other translations of the laws are equally good, but this work is important for its discussion of the meaning and significance of them. [FJS]

F93. Goetze, Albrecht. **The laws of Eshnunna.** New Haven, 1956. [The annual of the American schools of oriental research, 31.] Of available excerpts of ancient law codes now known to have preceded that of Hammurabi, the "Laws of Eshnunna" are the most extensive. This work offers what should be regarded for some time as a definitive treatment of the subject. The text is presented in photograph, hand copy, transliteration, translation, and critical notes. [FJS]

F94. Falkenstein, Adam. **Die neusumerischen Gerichtsurkunden.** 3 v. Munich, 1956–57. The 224 texts treated in these volumes were written in a period of about 50 years at the beginning of the second millennium B.C. They are records of litigation in the courts on matters of family relationships and many kinds of business transactions. This work is indispensable for the study of ancient law. [FJS]

F95. Borger, Riekele. **Die Inschriften Asarhaddons Koenigs von Assyrien.** Graz, 1956. [Archiv für Orientforschung, 9.] Transliteration, translation, and critical notes for more than twice the number of texts of King Esarhaddon than were included in the previous collection of his texts (1927). Contains many tablets and fragments hitherto unpublished. [FJS]

F96. Michel, Ernst. "Die Assur-Texte Salmanassars III (858–824)." **Die Welt des Orients,** 1 (1947–52): 5–20, 57–71, 205–22, 255–71, 385–96, 454–75; 2 (1954–57): 27–45, 137–57, 221–33. The most complete collection of this king's inscriptions. Gives transliteration, translation, and full critical notes. [FJS]

F97. Ebeling, Erich, Bruno Meissner, and Ernst Weidner. **Die Inschriften der altassyrischen Könige.** Leipzig, 1926. The 122 inscriptions translated here represent 21 different rulers of Assyria from about 2000 to 1250 B.C. They report mainly the activities of these rulers in building or restoring temples, but occasionally accounts of military campaigns are given. [FJS]

F98. Gadd, Cyril J., and Léon Legrain. **Ur excavations: texts.** V. 1, **Royal inscriptions.** London, 1928. Includes translations of inscriptions representing rulers of Babylonia from early Sumerian times to Cyrus, but principally from the earlier part of this period. [FJS]

F99. Pritchard, James B., ed. **Ancient near eastern texts.** (See *F124.*) The portion concerned directly with Mesopotamia consists of selections from different types of ancient sources, including myths, epics, and legends; legal codes and documents; historical and historiographic documents; rituals, hymns, and prayers; didactic and wisdom literature; lamentations; and letters. The presentation of similar material from other contemporary cultures provides a perspective of their relation to the whole. [FJS]

F100. Sommer, Ferdinand, ed. and tr. **Die Aḫḫijavā-Urkunden.** Munich, 1932. [Abhandlungen der Bayerischen Akademie der Wissenschaften, philosophisch-historische Abteilung, n.s., 6.] Presentation, in transliteration and German translation, of all Hittite texts known to 1932 dealing with the country of Aḫḫiyawa. The discussion of whether this country is Mycenean Greece may be over-critical, but the book is indispensable as collection and thorough interpretation of the sources. [HGG]

F101. Sommer, Ferdinand, and Adam Falkenstein. **Bilingue.** Munich, 1938. [Abhandlungen der Bayerischen Akademie der Wissenschaften, Philosophisch-historische Abteilung, n.s., 16.] Source book; transliteration and German translation of a decree of

King Hattusili I of the Old Kingdom, with full philological commentary. [HGG]

F102. Weidner, Ernst F. **Politische Dokumente.** Leipzig, 1923. [Boghazköi-Studien, 8–9.] Transliteration and German translation of the Akkadian treaties found before 1914 in the Hittite capital. Though parts have been retranslated, this book retains its value as the only collection. [HGG]

F103. Sommer, Ferdinand, and Hans Ehelolf. **Papanikri.** Leipzig, 1924. [Boghazköi-Studien, 10.] Transliteration and German translation of a Hittite ritual text, with philological commentary. Still a standard work. [HGG]

F104. Götze, Albrecht. **Ḫattušiliš.** Leipzig, 1925. [Mitteilungen der Vorderasiatisch-aegyptischen Gesellschaft, 29, no. 3: Hethitische Texte, no. 1.] For comment on this and the following see *F110.*

F105. ——. **Neue Bruchstücke.** Leipzig, 1930. [Mitteilungen der Vorderasiatisch-aegyptischen Gesellschaft, 34, no. 2: Hethitische Texte, no. 5.]

F106. ——. **Madduwattaš.** Leipzig, 1928. [Mitteilungen der Vorderasiatisch-aegyptischen Gesellschaft, 32, no. 1: Hethitische Texte, no. 3.]

F107. Götze, Albrecht, ed. and tr. **Die Annalen des Muršiliš.** Leipzig, 1933. [Mitteilungen der Vorderasiatisch-aegyptischen Gesellschaft, 38: Hethitische Texte, no. 6.]

F108. Friedrich, Johannes, ed. **Staatsverträge.** 2 v. Leipzig, 1926–30. [Mitteilungen der Vorderasiatisch-aegyptischen Gesellschaft, 31, no. 1; 34, no. 1: Hethitische Texte, nos. 2, 4.]

F109. Otten, Heinrich. **Die Überlieferungen des Telipinu-Mythus.** Leipzig, 1942. [Mitteilungen der Vorderasiatisch-aegyptischen Gesellschaft, 46, no. 1: Hethitische Texte, no. 7.]

F110. Brandenstein, Carl G. von. **Bildbeschreibungen.** Leipzig, 1943. [Mitteilungen der Vorderasiatisch-aegyptischen Gesellschaft, 46, no. 2: Hethitische Texte, no. 8.] The above eight volumes (*F104–110*) comprise the representative collection of Hittite texts in transliteration and German translation. Each is provided with critical apparatus in footnotes, a philological commentary, and indices of Hittite words, names of gods, persons, and places or countries. Only a few of the texts presented in this series are also available in English translation, but even for the latter the fully annotated presentation in this series maintains its value. [HGG]

F111. Laroche, Emanuel. "Catalogue des textes hittites." **Revue hittite et asianique,** 14 (1956): 33–38, 69–116; 15 (1957): 30–89. A list of all Hittite texts and of Boghazköy texts in other languages, with bibliography of transliterations and translations. To be completed in subsequent issues. [HGG]

F112. Güterbock, Hans G. "The deeds of Suppiluliuma." **Journal of cuneiform studies,** 10 (July–Dec. 1956): 41–68, 75–98, 107–30. Transliteration and translation of a primary source.

F113. ——. "Die historische Tradition und ihre literarische Gestaltung bei Babyloniern und Hethitern bis 1200." (See *F141.*) Contains some literary and Old Hittite historical texts in transliteration and German translation.

F114. Goetze, Albrecht. **Kizzuwatna.** New Haven, 1940. [Yale oriental series, Researches, 22.] Establishes the localization of the country of Kizzuwatna in Cilicia. Contains the pertinent sources, both Akkadian and Hittite, in transliteration and translation. [HGG]

F115. König, Friedrich W. **Handbuch der chaldischen Inschriften.** 2 pts. Graz, 1955–57. [Archiv für Orientforschung, 8.] Author uses the name "Chaldisch" for the language called Urartaen by others. Collection of the cuneiform inscriptions in cuneiform copy, transliteration, and German translation. Text restorations and translations are less certain than indicated. To be used with caution, but thus far the only complete collection. [HGG]

F116. Pritchard, James B., ed. **Ancient near eastern texts.** (See *F124.*) Contains translations of Hittite texts and bibliographical references. [HGG]

F117. Sturtevant, Edgar H., and George Bechtel. **A Hittite chrestomathy.** (See *F55.*) Contains translations of historical sources.

F118. **The Holy Bible: revised standard version.** N.Y., 1952. Most recent translation of the Bible by 32 scholars under Protestant auspices. Variant readings of the manuscripts occasionally indicated in footnotes.

F119. **The Holy Bible: translated from the original languages with critical use of all the ancient sources by members of the Catholic Biblical Association of America.** Paterson, N.J., 1952 ff. Roman Catholic translation with textual notes at end of each volume. Competent and useful.

F120. **La Sainte Bible: traduite en français sous la direction de l'École Biblique de Jérusalem.** Paris, 1956. Roman Catholic translation produced by a number of distinguished scholars, generously supplied with footnotes indicating variant readings and brief introductions to the individual books.

F121. Diringer, David. **Le iscrizioni antico-ebraiche palestinesi.** Florence, 1934. Fully annotated list of all Hebrew inscriptions found in Palestine to time of publication.

F122. Moscati, Sabatino. **L'epigrafia ebraica antica, 1935–1950.** Rome, 1951. Continuation of *F121,* containing material found subsequently.

F123. Gressmann, Hugo, ed. **Altorientalische Texte und Bilder zum Alten Testa-**

ment. 2nd ed., 2 v., Berlin, 1926–27. Best scholarly view of material available in the early 1920's. Translations of the most important texts from Egypt, Mesopotamia, Palestine-Syria, and south Arabia by Ranke, Ebeling, Gressmann, and Rhodokanakis appear in v. 1. V. 2 contains pictures of monuments and artifacts.

F124. Pritchard, James B., ed. **Ancient near eastern texts relating to the Old Testament.** 2nd ed., Princeton, 1955. Translations of Egyptian, Sumerian, Akkadian, Hittite, Aramaic, Phoenician, and South Arabic texts by thirteen competent scholars, with bibliographical and philological notes.

F125. Corpus inscriptionum semiticarum. Inscriptiones himyariticas et sabaeas continens. 3 v. Paris, 1889–1931. *Tabulae,* 3 v., 1889–1932. Only about a third (985) of the known South Arabic inscriptions have been published in the *Corpus.* A great majority of the others will be found in *F126* or in *Le Muséon.* The Dedanite, Lihyanite, Thamudic, and Safaitic inscriptions are being published in pt. 5 of the *Corpus.* [FVW]

F126. Répertoire d'épigraphie sémitique. V. 5–7, **Inscriptions sud-arabes.** Ed. by Gonzague Ryckmans. Paris, 1928–50. Contains all the South Arabian inscriptions published to about 1942, with the partial exception of those already published in the *Corpus.* V. 5 contains a complete, chronologically arranged bibliography of pre-Islamic Arabia to 1928. [FVW]

F127. Branden, Albertus van den. **Les inscriptions thamoudéennes.** Louvain, 1950. Only comprehensive treatment of the so-called "Thamudic" inscriptions (all those published to 1950). Many problems still await solution. [FVW]

F128. Ryckmans, Gonzague. "Inscriptions sud-arabes." *Le Muséon,* v. 40–69 (1927–56). Translation, with commentary, of the many inscriptions recovered in recent years. A regular feature in each issue of this publication. [FVW]

F129. Jamme, Albert. "South-Arabian inscriptions." Pritchard, **Ancient near eastern texts** (*F124*), pp. 506–13.

F130. Wolff, Fritz. **Avesta: die heiligen Bücher der Parsen übersetzt auf der Grundlage von Chr. Bartholomae's Altiranischem Wörterbuch.** [Leipzig], 1910. Reprint, 1924. Translation of all of the Avesta exclusively based on the Old Iranian dictionary by Chr. Bartholomae. [MJD]

F131. Taraporewala, Irach J., ed. **The divine songs of Zarathustra.** Bombay, 1951. One of the most recent and most expert products of Parsee scholarship on the Avestan Gāthā. Text, translation, and commentary; appendices, glossary, indices, and bibliography. [MJD]

F132. Lommel, Herman. **Die Yäšt's des Awesta.** Göttingen and Leipzig, 1927.

[Quellen der Religionsgeschichte, 15, group 6.] Translation of the Avestan Yašt, with introduction. [MJD]

F133. Duchesne-Guillemin, Jacques. **Zoroastre: étude critique avec une traduction commentée des Gâthâ.** Paris, 1948. Besides a translation of the Gāthās with commentary, contains chapters on Indo-Iranian religion, Iran before Zoroaster, and Zarathustra's work. [MJD]

F134. Darmesteter, James. **Le Zend-Avesta.** 3 v. Paris, 1892–93. [Annales du Musée Guimet, 21, 22, 24.] Thus far the only complete Avesta translation which makes full use of the Pahlavi commentary. The date of its appearance necessitates constant consultation of the more recent literature. [MJD]

F135. Barr, Kaj, ed. **Avesta.** Copenhagen, 1954. Danish translation of important parts of the Avestan Yasna, Yašt, and Vendīdād, with introduction and list containing explanations of Avestan terms and concepts. [MJD]

F136. Clemen, Carl C., ed. **Fontes historiae religionis persicae.** Bonn, 1920. Collection of extracts from the classical authors dealing with Persian religion. [MJD]

F137. Cameron, George G. **Persepolis treasury tablets.** Chicago, 1948. Study of the Persepolis treasury tablets in the Elamite language found by the Oriental Institute of Chicago Persepolis expedition. Transliteration and translation of a hundred odd tablets of importance for political and economic history, religion, and archaeology, dating from first half of the 5th century B.C. [MJD]

F138. Driver, Godfrey R., ed. and tr. **Aramaic documents of the fifth century B.C.** Oxford, 1954. Abr. and rev. ed., 1957. Documents from the chancery of the Persian satrap of Achaemenian Egypt containing instructions issued by this chancery to the subordinate administrative officers in Egypt. [MJD]

F139. Kraeling, Emil G., ed. **The Brooklyn Museum Aramaic papyri: new documents of the fifth century B.C. from the Jewish colony at Elephantine.** New Haven, 1953. Collection of documents in Aramaic of importance for Achaemenian history. [MJD]

HISTORIOGRAPHY

F140. Dentan, Robert C., ed. **The idea of history in the ancient Near East.** New Haven, 1955. Contains essays on historiography in Egypt, Mesopotamia, Iran, and Israel, written by specialists in each of these areas.

F141. Güterbock, Hans G. "Die historische Tradition und ihre literarische Gestaltung bei Babyloniern und Hethitern bis 1200." **Zeitschrift für Assyriologie und vorderasi-**

atische Archäologie, 42 (Aug. 1934): 1–91, 44 (Jan. 1938): 45–149. The author distinguishes between contemporary documents as historical sources and writings based on the memory of events by persons of later times. This work deals with the latter category. Second part of the article is important to the historian of Mesopotamia proper because the Hittites adopted and preserved portions of Babylonian historical tradition. [FJS]

GENERAL HISTORIES

F142. Meyer, Eduard. **Geschichte des Altertums.** See *H121.*

F143. The **Cambridge ancient history.** V. 1–4. Cambridge, Eng., and N.Y., 1928–31. See *H118.*

F144. Kern, Fritz, and others. **Historia Mundi: ein Handbuch der Weltgeschichte.** V. 2–3. Bern, 1953–54. V. 2 contains contributions by 13 well-known scholars in the field. The article of H. S. Nyberg, v. 3, pp. 56–115, is important for later Mesopotamian history after the downfall of the Assyrian and Neo-Babylonian empires.

F145. Schmökel, Hartmut. **Geschichte des alten Vorderasien.** Leiden, 1957. Useful condensed history, so arranged that one may obtain a complete story of historical events by reading only the first half of each chapter. Second half of each chapter is devoted to the corresponding cultural history. [FJS]

HISTORIES OF SPECIAL AREAS

Egypt

F146. Drioton, Etienne, and Jacques Vandier. **Les peuples de l'orient méditerranéen.** V. 2, **L'Égypte.** 3rd ed., Paris, 1952. The most up-to-date and comprehensive history of ancient Egypt. Review, T. Säve-Söderbergh, *Bibliotheca orientalis,* 13 (May-July 1956): 118–23. [HGF]

F147. Wilson, John A. **The burden of Egypt.** Chicago, 1951. Paperbound ed., *The culture of ancient Egypt,* 1956. Stimulating and authoritative treatment of Egyptian history, written from a somewhat controversial viewpoint, but offering an abundance of fact and sound observation. Useful footnote references. [HGF]

F148. Breasted, James H. **A history of Egypt from the earliest times to the Persian conquest.** 2nd ed., N.Y., 1909. A classic account of Egyptian history, the finished product of the author's *Ancient records of Egypt (F72).* Still well worth reading, although many new developments have appeared since the 1909 version. [HGF]

F149. Hayes, William C. **The scepter of Egypt: a background for the study of the Egyptian antiquities in the Metropolitan** Museum of Art. Pt. 1, **From the earliest times to the end of the middle kingdom.** Pt. 2, **The Hyksos period and the new kingdom.** N.Y., 1953, 1959. Accurate, well written description of a collection with a background equivalent to the whole history of each period. Well illustrated; superior bibliography. [HGF]

F150. Steindorff, George, and Keith C. Seele. **When Egypt ruled the East.** 2nd ed., Chicago, 1957. Concise and readable account of Egyptian culture and history which concentrates on the new kingdom. Extensive revision of the second edition includes new material not available in other histories mentioned here. [HGF]

F151. Säve-Söderbergh, Torgny. **Ägypten und Nubien: ein Beitrag zur Geschichte altägyptischer Aussenpolitik.** Lund, Swe., 1941. Reliable, full-scale treatment of Egypt's relations with Nubia. [HGF]

Mesopotamia

F152. Scharff, Alexander, and Anton Moortgat. **Ägypten und Vorderasien im Altertum.** Munich, 1950. Second part of this volume covers the history of Babylonia and Assyria from earliest times through the Persian period. Particularly valuable for its bibliography. [FJS]

F153. Smith, Sidney. **Early history of Assyria to 1000 B.C.** London, 1928. Since it is impossible to separate Assyria's fortunes from affairs of her neighbors, this book covers a somewhat wider scope than Assyria proper. The chronology must be compared with results of more recent study. [FJS]

F154. Olmstead, Albert T. **History of Assyria.** N.Y., 1923. Covers the whole subject, and based on original sources known and understood at the time. No similar work has been produced since. [FJS]

F155. Edzard, Dietz O. **Die "Zweite Zwischenzeit" Babyloniens.** Wiesbaden, 1957. Concerned with period from the fall of the third dynasty of Ur to reunification of the land under Hammurabi, an important era hitherto inadequately treated. Firmly based on original sources. [FJS]

F156. Kupper, Jean R. **Les nomades en Mésopotamie au temps des rois de Mari.** Paris, 1957. Impact of the nomad upon Mesopotamian life during the time of Hammurabi and his immediate predecessor. Evidence is drawn mainly from the documents from Mari. [FJS]

F157. Goossens, Godefroy. "L'Assyrie après l'empire." **Compte rendu de la troisième rencontre assyriologique internationale** (Leiden, 1954), pp. 84–100. After some attention to the causes of the empire's downfall, paints a gloomy picture of complete destruction of the high culture down to the

Sassanian time, except for a brief revival of urban economy under the Parthians. [FJS]

F158. Gelb, Ignace J. **Hurrians and Subarians.** Chicago, 1944. Contrary to prevailing previous views, the author regards these two names as representing two distinct ethnic groups, and undertakes to present their status within the framework of the ancient Near East. Covers virtually the entire historical period down to Neo-Babylonian times. [FJS]

Asia Minor

F159. Goetze, Albrecht. **Kleinasien.** 2nd ed., Munich, 1957. The standard work on civilization of pre-classical Anatolia. First published in 1933; the 1957 edition is fully revised and largely rewritten. Emphasis is on Hittite period, based on the Boghazköy texts; but prehistory, Assyrian merchant colonies of Cappadocia, the kingdom of Urartu, and western Anatolia are also treated. Bibliographies for individual sections. [HGG]

F160. Gurney, Oliver R. **The Hittites.** See *E56.*

F161. Bilabel, Friedrich. **Geschichte Vorderasiens und Ägyptens vom 16.–11. Jahrhundert v. Chr.** Heidelberg, 1927. Divided into a first part, which is a coherent account of Egyptian and Hittite history, and a second part containing detailed discussions of sources and problems. Outdated in places, but still useful. [HGG]

Palestine-Syria

F162. Noth, Martin. **Geschichte Israels.** 3rd ed., Göttingen, 1956. Concise and original history of Israel.

F163. Oesterley, William O. E., and Theodore H. Robinson. **A history of Israel.** 2 v. Oxford, 1932. Covers from the Exodus to the Bar-Kokhba revolt in 135 A.D. Even though in need of revision, considered a standard history from the traditional orthodoxy of literary criticism.

F164. Kittel, Rudolf. **Geschichte des Volkes Israel.** 5th-7th eds., 3 v., Gotha, 1921–29. Many other eds. Old but standard history from beginnings down to the Babylonian Exile.

F165. Olmstead, Albert T. **History of Palestine and Syria to the Macedonian conquest.** N.Y., 1931. Aims to bring the Biblical and archaeological sources available at the end of the 1920's into a synthesis. For method see author's essay, "Hebrew history and historical method," *Persecution and liberty* (N.Y., 1931), pp. 21–54.

South Arabia

F166. Levi della Vida, Giorgio. "Pre-islamic Arabia." Nabih A. Faris, ed., **The**

Arab heritage (Princeton, 1944), pp. 25–57. Excellent survey. [FVW]

F167. 'Ali, Jawād. **Ta'rīkh al-Arab qabl al-Islam.** [History of the Arabs before Islam.] 6 v. Bagdad, 1951–57. Scholarly and comprehensive, with full documentation. Arabic text. Review, G. Ryckmans, *Le Muséon,* 69 (1956): 204. [FVW]

F168. Albright, William F. "The chronology of the Minaean kings of Arabia." **Bulletin of the American schools of oriental research,** 129 (Feb. 1953): 19–24.

F169. ——. "Dedan." **Geschichte und Altes Testament** (Tübingen, 1953), pp. 1–12. [Beiträge zur historischen Theologie, 16.] Important contribution to the early history of northern Arabia, especially valuable for discussion of chronology of the kingdoms of Dedan and Liḥyān. [FVW]

F170. Caskel, Werner. **Lihyan und Lihyanisch.** Cologne, 1954. First comprehensive treatment of the Dedanite and Lihyanite inscriptions, but many of the translations proposed are questionable, as is the chronology. [FVW]

Iran

F171. Prášek, Justin V. **Geschichte der Meder und Perser bis zur makedonischen Eroberung.** 2 v. Gotha, 1906–10. Dated but still useful account of earlier history of Medes and Persians. [MJD]

F172. Olmstead, Albert T. **History of the Persian empire, Achaemenid period.** Ed. by George G. Cameron. Chicago, 1948. Collection of essays on Achaemenian history, culture, civilization, and religion, rather than a systematic survey. [MJD]

F173. Hančar, F. "Die Skythen als Forschungsproblem." **Reinecke Festschrift** (Mainz, 1950), pp. 67–83. Valuable review of Russian publications since 1930 on the Scythians. [MJD]

F174. Rostovtzeff, Mikhail I. **Skythien und der Bosporus.** V. 1, **Kritische Übersicht der schriftlichen und archäologischen Quellen.** Berlin, 1931. Critical review of the literary and archaeological documentation on the Scythians in southern Russia. See also *Iranians and Greeks in south Russia* (Oxford, 1922) by the same author. [MJD]

F175. Ghirshman, Roman. **L'Iran des origines à l'Islam.** Paris, 1951. English tr., *Iran from the earliest times to the Islamic conquest,* Harmondsworth, 1954. Rich, imaginative, and in most respects expert account. The lack of documentation (only the English translation includes a selected bibliography) makes utilization and appreciation of the book at times difficult. [MJD]

F176. Geiger, Wilhelm, and Ernst Kuhn, eds. **Grundriss der iranischen Philologie.** 2 v. Strasbourg, 1895–1904. Survey of the history, literature, languages, and geography of Iran, both pre-Islamic and Islamic. Still the only handbook and, therefore, indispensable in spite of its date. [MJD]

F177. D'iakonov, I. M. **Istoriia Midii.** [History of the Medes.] Moscow and Leningrad, 1956. Political, sociological, and cultural history of the Medes and the Median state, based on extensive source materials from which, in a number of cases, bold conclusions are drawn. [MJD]

F178. Christensen, Arthur E. **Les Kayanides.** Copenhagen, 1931. Critical study of the Avestan *kavis,* the later Kayanids, legendary Iranian dynasty, previous to the Achaemenians. [MJD]

F179. ———. **Die Iranier.** Munich, 1923. The only comprehensive treatment of ancient Iranian culture until the end of the Achaemenian period, based on Iranian and non-Iranian source materials. Includes a summary survey of Iranian history from Alexander the Great to end of the Sassanian period. [MJD]

F180. Cameron, George G. **History of early Iran.** Chicago, 1936. Political history of Elamites, Medes, and pre-Achaemenian Persians. [MJD]

HISTORIES OF SPECIAL TOPICS

General Culture

F181. Erman, Adolf, and Hermann Ranke. **Ägypten und aegyptisches Leben im Altertum.** Tübingen, 1923. Revision, by Ranke, of Erman's classic work of the same title. Remains the most comprehensive account of the various aspects of ancient Egyptian life. [HGF]

F182. Frankfort, Henriette A., and others. **The intellectual adventure of ancient man.** Chicago, 1946. An essay on speculative thought in the ancient Near East. [FJS]

F183. Meissner, Bruno. **Babylonien und Assyrien.** 2 v. Heidelberg, 1920–25. Long the standard history of culture and civilization of ancient Mesopotamia. Although it can be supplemented by many detailed studies which have appeared more recently, no other such comprehensive treatment of the subject is available. [FJS]

F184. ———. **Die babylonisch-assyrische Literatur.** Berlin, 1928. May be used to supplement the older work of Otto Weber, *Die Literatur der Babylonier und Assyrer* (Leipzig, 1907); but the serious student will need to search current periodical literature on the various categories of literature mentioned in these publications. [FJS]

F185. Braidwood, Robert J. **The Near East and the foundations for civilization.** See *E51.*

F186. Garstang, John. **The Hittite empire.** London, 1929. Valuable guide to early literature. Supersedes this author's book, *The*

land of the Hittites (London, 1910). Although the historical chapter is outdated and further excavations of old and new sites have increased the knowledge of Hittite archaeology, the treatment of sites in their natural setting retains its value. [HGG]

F187. Pedersen, Johannes. **Israel: its life and culture.** 2 v. London, 1926–40. Cultural history of Israel, by topics of major importance.

F188. Noth, Martin. **Die Welt des Alten Testaments.** 2nd ed., Berlin, 1953. While intended as an introduction to the background of the Bible, it is well documented with references to the most important literature on the subjects with which it deals.

F189. Nielsen, Ditlef, ed. **Handbuch der altarabischen Altertumskunde.** V. 1, **Die altarabische Kultur.** Copenhagen and Leipzig, 1927. Best introduction to South Arabian civilization; but Fritz Hommel's chapter on the history stands in need of considerable revision. [FVW]

Religion

F190. Černý, Jaroslav. **Ancient Egyptian religion.** London, 1952. Compendious treatment of Egyptian religion down through Roman times. Excellent, but usefulness impaired by lack of references. [HGF]

F191. Kees, Hermann. **Der Götterglaube im altern Ägypten.** 2nd ed., Berlin, 1956. Comprehensive, well-documented account of the Egyptian gods. Review, J. Vandier, *Bibliotheca orientalis,* 14 (Jan. 1957): 34. [HGF]

F192. Dhorme, Edouard. **Les religions de Babylonie et d'Assyrie.** 2nd ed., Paris, 1949. Includes discussion of the nature of religious thought among Babylonians and Assyrians; their mythology; and the temple, clergy, and their functions. Bibliographical notes. [FJS]

F193. Kramer, Samuel N. **Sumerian mythology.** Philadelphia, 1944. Discusses the scope and significance of Sumerian mythology, and sketches the content of a large selection of literary compositions, enhanced by translations of portions of the texts. An authoritative work. [FJS]

F194. Pfeiffer, Robert H. **Introduction to the Old Testament.** N.Y., 1941. Most comprehensive introduction in English to the literature of the Old Testament, arranged according to books of the Hebrew canon. Good bibliography and references to the great variety of views on questions of dates, composition, and interpretation.

F195. Eissfeldt, Otto. **Einleitung in das Alte Testament unter Einschluss der Apokryphen und Pseudepigraphen: Entstehungsgeschichte des Alten Testaments.** Tübingen, 1934. Standard German introduction.

F196. Lods, Adolphe. **Histoire de la littérature hébraïque et juive depuis les ori-**

gines jusqu'à la ruine de l'état juif (135 après J.C.). Paris, 1950. Introduction to the books of the Old Testament and the Apocrypha according to the canons of literary criticism.

F197. Bentzen, Aage. **Introduction to the Old Testament.** 2nd ed., 2 v., Copenhagen, 1952. Incorporates the newer views of the Scandinavian school of Biblical criticism.

F198. Albright, William F. **From the Stone Age to Christianity: monotheism and the historical process.** Baltimore, 1940. A philosophical and historical inquiry into the development of man's idea of God from prehistoric antiquity to the time of Christ.

F199. Ryckmans, Gonzague. "Les religions arabes préislamiques." **Histoire générale des religions,** ed. by Maxime Gorce and Raoul Mortier, v. 4 (Paris, 1947), pp. 307–32. Excellent survey with extensive bibliography. [FVW]

F200. Jamme, Albert. "La religion sudarabe préislamique." **Histoire des religions,** ed. by Maurice Brillant and René Aigrain, v. 4 (Paris, 1956), pp. 239–307. Contains, among other things, a critique of Ditlef Nielsen's theories on South Arabian religion. [FVW]

F201. Widengren, Geo. "Stand und Aufgaben der iranischen Religionsgeschichte." **Numen,** 1 (Leiden, 1954): 16–83, 2 (1955): 47–132. Documented survey of problems of the history of Iranian religion; full bibliographical references. [MJD]

F202. Nyberg, Henrik S. **Die Religionen des alten Iran.** Tr. from Swedish by H. H. Schaeder. Leipzig, 1938. Collection of imaginative, often brilliant, but sometimes controversial essays on Zarathuštra, his work (theology, eschatology, Zoroastrianism), ancient Iranian religion (the "Mithra community," the "Gāthā community"), and the Avestan canon. [MJD]

F203. Duchesne-Guillemin, Jacques. **Ormazd et Ahriman: l'aventure dualiste dans l'antiquité.** Paris, 1953. Collection of essays on Iranian religion dealing with such topics as Ahura Mazdāh, Ahra Manyu, the religion of the Avesta, Iran and Judaism, Iran and Greek thought, Hermetism and Gnosis, and Zervan and Mazdeism. [MJD]

F204. Herzfeld, Ernst E. **Zoroaster and his world.** See *D293.*

F205. Jackson, Abraham V. W. **Zoroaster, the prophet of ancient Iran.** N.Y. and London, 1899. In spite of its age, still a highly useful book on Zoroaster and his work. Detailed bibliography. [MJD]

F206. ——. **Zoroastrian studies: the Iranian religion and various monographs.** N.Y., 1928.

F207. Henning, Walter B. H. **Zoroaster, politician or witch doctor?** London, 1951. Critical discussion in lecture form of the results of investigations of H. S. Nyberg

and E. Herzfeld on Zoroaster and Zoroastrianism. The author's own conclusions are partly based on new materials. [MJD]

F208. Lommel, Herman. **Die Religion Zarathustras.** Tübingen, 1930. Discussion of Zoroastrian religion and theology, with a concluding chapter on the pre-history of this religion. [MJD]

F209. Zaehner, Robert C. **The teachings of the magi: a compendium of Zoroastrian beliefs.** London and N.Y., 1956. Account of the main doctrines of the Zoroastrians based on original (Pahlavī) texts, which are given in translation. [MJD]

F210. Christensen, Arthur E. **Études sur le zoroastrisme de la Perse antique.** Copenhagen, 1928. Critical remarks on analysis of the Avestan Yašts (hymns); remarks on the Vendīdād and on Zurvanism. [MJD]

F211. Clemen, Carl C. **Die griechischen und lateinischen Nachrichten über die persische Religion.** Giessen, 1920. Companion volume to his *Fontes historiae religionis Persicae (F136),* containing comments on the texts given in the latter. [MJD]

F212. Benveniste, Émile. **The Persian religion according to the chief Greek texts.** Paris, 1929. Critical evaluation of the data on Zoroaster and Persian religion contained in Herodotus, Strabo, Theopompus, and Plutarch, and comparison with the Iranian texts. [MJD]

F213. Bidez, Joseph, and Franz Cumont. **Les mages hellénisés: Zoroastre, Ostanès et Hystaspe d'après la tradition grecque.** 2 v. Paris, 1938. Collection of passages of Greek and Latin authors dealing with biographies, works, and doctrines of Zoroaster, Ostanes, and Hystaspes. [MJD]

Art

F214. Smith, William S. **A history of Egyptian sculpture and painting in the old kingdom.** 2nd ed., London, 1949. Penetrating and detailed study of the earlier phases of Egyptian art up to, and to some extent into, the middle kingdom. Well illustrated. [HGF]

F215. ——. **Ancient Egypt as represented in the Museum of Fine Arts.** 3rd ed., Boston, 1952. This description of the large Boston collections incorporates an excellent brief account of Egyptian history and the history of Egyptian art. Well illustrated. [HGF]

F216. Aldred, Cyril. **The development of ancient Egyptian art.** 3 v. London, 1949–51. Inspiring introduction to the subject, with a large and good selection of illustrations, each accompanied by full information. Covers the three major periods to end of the 18th dynasty. [HGF]

F217. Schäfer, Heinrich. **Von ägyptischer Kunst.** 3rd ed., Leipzig, 1930. A masterly exposition of the methods and conventions employed in Egyptian representational art. Well illustrated. [HGF]

F218. Vieyra, Maurice. **Hittite art, 2300–750 B.C.** London, 1955. Good presentation of Hittite art, with the term "Hittite" being used in a broad sense to include the early Bronze Age and the late period from downfall of the Hittite empire to the Assyrian conquest. Includes good reproductions, short bibliography, and detailed notes on individual works of art. [HGG]

F219. Bossert, Helmuth T. **Altanatolien.** Berlin, 1942. [Die Ältesten ·Kulturen des Mittelmeerkreises, 2.] The most comprehensive collection of pictures, the majority pertaining to the Hittites, but including other periods and regions of Anatolia down to such works of the Greco-Roman period as show elements of local tradition. [HGG]

F220. Akurgal, Ekrem. **Spaethethitische Bildkunst.** Ankara, 1949. Thorough analysis of the art of the so-called late Hittite period (ca. 1200–700 B.C.). Reproductions of good photographs; line drawings in text. [HGG]

F221. Pope, Arthur U., ed. **A survey of Persian art from prehistoric times to the present.** 6 v. London and N.Y., 1938–39. Discussions of unequal value, by a large group of scholars, of development of Iranian art from the Stone Age to the present. Illustrated with many figures and plates, some of which are excellent. [MJD]

F222. Minns, Ellis H. "The art of the northern nomads." **Proceedings of the British Academy,** 28 (1942): 47–99. An expert survey with good bibliographical references. [MJD]

Archaeology

F223. Parrot, André. **Archéologie mésopotamienne.** 2 v. Paris, 1946–53. V. 1 gives a full history of exploration and excavation in Mesopotamia in modern times. V. 2 is devoted to (1) techniques of modern archaeology, from the organization of the expedition to publication of the results; and (2) the problems of origins of Mesopotamian civilization and of chronology, both raised by archaeological work here and open to further investigation. [FJS]

F224. Perkins, Ann L. **The comparative archeology of early Mesopotamia.** Chicago, 1949. Synthesis of results of much archaeological work, giving descriptions of the material remains as well as comparative stratigraphy of the sites. Covers the prehistoric era from the Hassunah to Gaura and Ninevite periods. [FJS]

F225. Frankfort, Henri. **The art and architecture of the ancient Orient.** Baltimore, 1955. Traces the history of art in Mesopotamia from about 3500 B.C. to beginning of the Persian period, and shows influences of Mesopotamian art in the peripheral regions. Illustrated by special drawings and excellent photographs. [FJS]

F226. Gadd, Cyril J. **History and monuments of Ur.** N.Y., 1929. Because the city of Ur existed in virtually all periods of Babylonian and Assyrian history and because it has been excavated to its lowest levels, its history amounts to that of the whole country told from the point of view of a single city. [FJS]

F227. Bittel, Kurt. **Grundzüge der Vor- und Frühgeschichte Kleinasiens.** 2nd ed., Tübingen, 1950. Presentation of the archaeological material of Anatolia, excavations, sites, stratigraphy, etc., with discussion of its bearing on reconstruction of the preclassical history. Detailed bibliography. [HGG]

F228. Lloyd, Seton. **Early Anatolia.** See *E58.*

F229. Albright, William F. **The archaeology of Palestine.** Harmondsworth, 1949. Synthesis of results of Palestinian archaeology by the leader in the field. While it does not contain references, these often can be found in the author's *From the Stone Age to Christianity (F198)* and in *F230.*

F230. ——. **Archaeology and the religion of Israel.** Baltimore, 1942. Designed to complement the treatment of Israelite religion given in *F198.* Ample documentation.

F231. Pritchard, James B. **The ancient Near East in pictures relating to the Old Testament.** Princeton, 1954. Contains 769 illustrations of monuments, artifacts, and other objects which illustrate the culture and history of the ancient Near East. Bibliographical details for each illustration.

F232. Watzinger, Carl. **Denkmäler Palästinas.** 2 v. Leipzig, 1933–35. Well-illustrated and judicial presentation of results of Palestinian archaeology, now badly out of date.

F233. Langhe, Robert de. **Les textes de Ras Shamra-Ugarit et leurs rapports avec le milieu biblique de l'Ancien Testament.** 2 v. Gembloux, 1945. Most useful discussion of the rich cache of texts discovered in North Syria at Ras Shamra. Full documentation and bibliography.

F234. Rathjens, Carl. **Sabaeica: Bericht über die archäologischen Ergebnisse seiner zweiten, dritten und vierten Reise nach Südarabien.** 2 v. Hamburg, 1953–55. Based on the author's journeys in the Ṣanʻa area in 1931, 1934, and 1937–38. Illustrates and describes the monuments of the area: aqueducts, cisterns, terraces, sculpture, pottery, etc. A valuable source book. [FVW]

F235. Rathjens-v. Wissmannsche Südarabien-Reise. 3 v. Hamburg, 1931–34. [1, Johannes H. Mordtmann and Eugen Mittwoch, *Sabäische Inschriften;* 2, Carl Rathjens and Hermann von Wissmann, *Vorislamische Altertümer;* 3, C. Rathjens and H. von Wissmann, *Landeskundliche Ergebnisse.*] Report of the first archaeological expedition ever conducted in the Yemen. Includes excavation in 1927–28 of a temple of the goddess Dhāt-Ba'dān at Ḥuqqa, in the Ṣan'a area, and much material recorded at other neighboring sites. [FVW]

F236. Tawfik, Mohammed. **Āthār Ma'īn fī jauf al-Yaman.** [The monuments of Ma'īn in the Yemenite Jōf.] Cairo, 1951. In Arabic, with résumé in French. The author, an entomologist on the staff of Fuad I University, Cairo, while engaged in fighting locusts in the Yemen in 1944–45, took the opportunity of exploring the Jōf, the old Minaean homeland. [FVW]

F237. Jaussen, Antonin J., and Raphaël Savignac. **Mission archéologique en Arabie.** 3 v. Paris, 1909–22. The most important collection of epigraphical and archaeological material from north Arabia, the fruits of three expeditions made to Madā'in Ṣāliḥ (ancient el-Ḥegr), el-'Ula (ancient Dedan), and Teima in 1907, 1909, and 1910. [FVW]

F238. Bowen, Richard, and others. **The early Arabian necropolis of Ain Jawan, a pre-Islamic and early Islamic site on the Persian Gulf.** New Haven, 1950. Devotes considerable attention to the tumuli of el-Hasa and Bahrein as well. [FVW]

F239. Fakhry, Ahmed. **An archaeological journey to Yemen (March-May, 1947).** 3 v. Cairo, 1952. The fruits of a journey by an Egyptian scholar to Ṣirwāh, Mārib, and the Minaean Jōf. Important for its photographs and sketch-plans of the Mārib dam, temples, etc. [FVW]

F240. McCown, Donald E. **The comparative stratigraphy of early Iran.** See *E59.*

F241. Herzfeld, Ernst E. **Archaeological history of Iran.** London, 1935. See below.

F242. ———. **Iran in the ancient East: archaeological studies presented in the Lowell lectures at Boston.** London and N.Y., 1941. Archaeology of Iran from earliest prehistoric times to end of the Sassanian period, with illustrations. A developed version of *F241.* [MJD]

F243. Vanden Berghe, L. "Irān, de stand van de archaeologische onderzoekingen in Irān." **Jaarbericht no. 13 van het Vooraziatisch-Egyptisch Genootschap,** pp. 347–93. Area by area survey (in Dutch) of the status of archaeological investigations in Iran. Many bibliographical references. [MJD]

F244. Schmidt, Erich F. **Persepolis.** 2 v. Chicago, 1953–57. Account of the activities and results of excavations at Persepolis by Ernst E. Herzfeld (1931–34) and Schmidt (1935–39). Beautifully printed and magnificently illustrated. [MJD]

F245. Minns, Ellis H. **Scythians and Greeks: a survey of ancient history and archaeology on the north coast of the Euxine from the Danube to the Caucasus.** Cambridge, Eng., 1913. Still an outstanding contribution to the study of archaeological evidence from southern Russia. [MJD]

Chronology

F246. Smith, Sidney. **Alalakh and chronology.** London, 1940. This work appeared early in the recent controversy about Babylonian chronology, and now represents a moderate position between the traditional and the ultra low chronology which many cuneiformists are adopting. There is a tendency among some scholars to return toward Smith's position. [FJS]

F247. Landsberger, Benno. "Assyrische Königsliste und 'Dunkles Zeitalter.'" **Journal of cuneiform studies,** 8 (1954): 31–45, 47–73, 106–33. After an exhaustive study of both old and new sources, the author favors a higher chronology for the period before 1500 B.C. than most scholars who have investigated the subject in recent years. [FJS]

F248. Goetze, Albrecht. "On the chronology of the second millennium B.C." **Journal of cuneiform studies,** 11 (1957): 53–61, 63–73. Author adduces evidence from Hittite material in support of his view that the chronology should be based somewhat higher than that accepted by a number of Assyriologists. Bibliographical notes serve as guide to the controversy concerning chronology. [FJS]

F249. Beeston, Alfred F. L. "Problems of Sabaean chronology." **Bulletin of the School of Oriental and African Studies,** 16 (1954): 37–56. Dates the beginning of the Sabaean era *ca.* 110 B.C. and reduces the number of Sabaean *mkrb* to 15. [FVW]

F250. Ryckmans, Jacques. **L'institution monarchique en Arabie méridionale avant l'islam (Ma'īn et Saba.)** Louvain, 1951. Based on a study of titles employed by the Minaean and Sabaean rulers, the author is able to solve a great many chronological problems and present the most reliable arrangement of these monarchs yet proposed. Extensive bibliography. [FVW]

F251. McCown, Donald E. "The relative stratigraphy and chronology of Iran." Robert W. Ehrich, ed., **Relative chronologies in Old World archeology** (Chicago, 1954), pp. 56–68. The author's *The comparative stratigraphy of early Iran (F240)* is basis of this paper, which considers new evidence, criticisms, chronology of Baluchistan cultures, and that of Iranian sites. [MJD]

Miscellaneous

F252. Lucas, Alfred. **Ancient Egyptian materials and industries.** 3rd ed., London, 1948. Reliable and detailed treatment, containing much information essential to the total picture of Egyptian civilization. Final chapter contains a historical summary. [HGF]

F253. Clarke, Somers, and Reginald Engelbach. **Ancient Egyptian masonry: the building craft.** London, 1930. This lucid, original, and well-illustrated work covers all phases of the subject from quarrying stone to construction of the various architectural elements. Provides fundamental information to an understanding of Egyptian art and architecture. [HGF]

F254. Neugebauer, Otto. **The exact sciences in antiquity.** Princeton, 1951. Deals with mathematics and astronomy, compares Babylonian and Egyptian knowledge and treatment of them, and considers their relation to the origin and transmission of Hellenistic science. [FJS]

F255. Contenau, Georges. **La médicine en Assyrie et en Babylonie.** Paris, 1938. Synthesis of Babylonian and Assyrian ideas of human anatomy, disease, and treatment, drawn from numerous original texts and works of art. Discusses relation of medicine to magic. Includes extensive quotations from the texts and a lengthy bibliography. [FJS]

F256. Speiser, Ephraim A. "The Sumerian problem reviewed." **Hebrew Union College annual,** 23 (1950–51): 339–55. Weighs the evidence of Sumerian origins for two conflicting views: (1) the Sumerians were not the first inhabitants of the land of Sumer; (2) they were themselves the founders of the earliest prehistoric culture of lower Mesopotamia. [FJS]

F257. Leemans, W. F. **The old Babylonian merchant: his business and his social position.** Leiden, 1950. Valuable discussion of economic life of the period indicated. [FJS]

F258. Falkenstein, Adam. "La cité-temple sumérienne." **Cahiers d'histoire mondiale,** 1 (Apr. 1954): 784–814. Discusses the interplay of economic, political, and religious forces on early Babylonian society. Conclusions are based on documents mainly from the period before 2000 B.C. [FJS]

F259. Jacobsen, Thorkild. "Early political development in Mesopotamia." **Zeitschrift für Assyriologie und vorderasiatische Archäologie,** n.s. 18 (Aug. 1957): 91–140. Soundly based on author's thorough knowledge of the original sources. Covers period from the beginning to end of the first empire, with a brief indication of how lines of political development proceeded from this point. Copious footnotes furnish much information of a technical nature on subjects peripheral to the main theme. [FJS]

F260. Frankfort, Henri. **Cylinder seals: a documentary essay on the art and religion of the ancient Near East.** London, 1939. The standard handbook on Mesopotamian glyptique. Traces development of various styles and techniques from prehistoric to Persian period; ample illustrations. [FJS]

F261. Meek, Theophile J. **Hebrew origins.** Rev. ed., N.Y., 1950. Scholarly inquiry into origins of Hebrew people, law, God, priesthood, prophecy, and monotheism.

F262. Meyer, Eduard. **Die Israeliten und ihre Nachbarstämme.** Halle, 1906. Memorable contribution to the history of Israel. Obviously out of date, but contains much of permanent importance.

F263. Greneberg, Moshe. **The Ḫab/piru.** New Haven, 1955. [American oriental series, 39.] Fully documented statement of the problem of equating the Ḫab/piru with the Biblical Hebrews.

F264. Grohmann, Adolf. **Südarabien als Wirtschaftsgebiet.** 2 v. Vienna and Brünn, 1922–33. Thorough discussion of ancient and modern South Arabian economy, natural resources, agriculture, industry, and trade. [FVW]

F265. Weidner, Ernst. "Das Reich Sargons von Akkad." **Archiv für Orientforschung,** 16 (1953): 1–24. All references to the Arabian regions of Magan and Heluḫḫa are brought together and discussed. [FVW]

F266. Christensen, Arthur E. **Les gestes des rois dans les traditions de l'Iran antique.** Paris, 1936. Study of the royal glory, kings, and heroes in narrative literature of the Sassanian epoch, the model king and royal legends in the ancient Medo-Persian religion. [MJD]

F267. Taqizadeh, Hasan. **Old Iranian calendars.** London, 1938. Expert discussion of the many involved problems connected with ancient Iranian calendars. [MJD]

PERIODICALS

General

F268. **Journal of the American Oriental Society.** New Haven, 1843 ff. (Irregular quarterly.)

F269. **Journal of near eastern studies.** Chicago, 1942 ff. (Quarterly.)

F270. **The Journal of Semitic studies.** Manchester, 1956 ff. (Quarterly.)

F271. **Bulletin of the American schools of oriental research.** New Haven and Baltimore, 1919 ff. (Quarterly.)

F272. **Bibliotheca orientalis.** Leiden, 1943 ff. (Quarterly.)

F273. **Orientalia.** Rome, 1920–30; n.s., 1932 ff. (3 nos. per year, 1920–34; quarterly, 1935 ff.)

F274. **Wiener Zeitschrift für die Kunde des Morgenländes.** Vienna, 1887 ff. (Irregular.)

F275. **Orientalistische Literaturzeitung.** Berlin and Leipzig, 1898 ff. (Monthly.)

F276. **Archiv für Orientforschung.** Berlin and Graz, 1923 ff. (Irregular.)

F277. Zeitschrift der deutschen morgenländischen Gesellschaft. Leipzig, 1847 ff. (Irregular quarterly.)

F278. Mitteilungen der deutschen Orient-Gesellschaft zu Berlin. Berlin, 1899 ff. (Irregular.)

F279. Le Muséon. Louvain, 1882 ff. (Quarterly.)

Egypt

F280. Annales du service des antiquités de l'Égypte. Cairo, 1900 ff. (Annual.)

F281. The journal of Egyptian archaeology. London, 1914 ff. (Quarterly.)

F282. Ancient Egypt. London, 1915–35. (Irregular annual. Title varies.)

F283. Proceedings of the Society of Biblical Archaeology. London, 1878–1918. (Irregular.)

F284. Recueil de travaux relatifs à la philologie et à l'archéologie égyptiennes et assyriennes. Paris, 1870–1923. (Irregular.)

F285. Revue égyptologique. Paris, 1880–1924. (Irregular.)

F286. Revue de l'Égypte ancienne. Paris, 1925–31. (Irregular.)

F287. Revue d'égyptologie. Paris, 1933 ff. (Irregular.)

F288. Kêmi: revue de philologie et d'archéologie égyptiennes et coptes. Paris, 1928 ff. (Quarterly.)

F289. Bulletin de la Société Française d'Égyptologie. Paris, 1949 ff. (3 nos. per year.)

F290. Bulletin de l'Institut Français d'Archéologie Orientale. Cairo, 1901 ff. (Annual.)

F291. Chronique d'Égypte. Brussels, 1925 ff. (Irregular.)

F292. Zeitschrift für ägyptische Sprache und Altertumskunde. Berlin, 1863 ff. (Frequency varies.)

F293. Mitteilungen des Deutschen Archäologischen Instituts, Abteilung Kairo. Wiesbaden, 1930–43, 1956 ff. (Semiannual.)

Anatolia

F294. Kleinasiatische Forschungen. V. 1 only. Weimar, 1930.

F295. Revue hittite et asianique. Paris, 1930 ff. (Irregular.)

F296. Jahrbuch für kleinasiatische Forschung. Heidelberg and Istanbul, 1950 ff. (Semiannual.) Turkish title, **Anadolu araştirmalari.**

F297. Anatolian studies. London, 1951 ff. (Annual.)

Hittite Materials

F298. Wissenschaftliche Veröffentlichungen der Deutschen Orient-Gesellschaft. Leipzig, Stuttgart, and Berlin, 1900 ff.

F299. Keilschrifturkunden aus Boghazköi. Berlin, 1921 ff. (Irregular.)

Palestine and Syria

F300. Journal of Biblical literature. N.Y., 1881 ff. (Semiannual, 1881–1911; quarterly, 1912 ff. Title varies.)

F301. Zeitschrift für die alttestamentliche Wissenschaft. Giessen and Berlin, 1881–1942, 1949 ff.

F302. Revue biblique. Paris, 1881–1941, 1945 ff. (Quarterly. Title varies.)

F303. Palestine exploration quarterly. London, 1869 ff. (Title varies.)

F304. Zeitschrift des deutschen Palästina-Vereins. Leipzig, 1878 ff. (Irregular.)

F305. Syria: revue d'art oriental et d'archéologie. Paris, 1920 ff. (Quarterly.)

F306. Vetus Testamentum. Leiden, 1951 ff. (Quarterly.)

F307. Israel exploration journal. Jerusalem, 1950 ff. (Quarterly.)

F308. Hebrew Union College annual. See *D354.*

F309. Biblica. Rome, 1920 ff. (Quarterly.)

Miscellaneous

F310. Journal of cuneiform studies. New Haven, 1947 ff. (Quarterly.)

F311. Zeitschrift für Assyriologie und vorderasiatische Archäologie. Berlin, 1890 ff. (Irregular. Title varies.)

F312. Revue d'assyriologie et d'archéologie orientale. Paris, 1884 ff. (Quarterly.)

F313. Iraq. London, 1934–40, 1947 ff. Supplement, 1944. (Semiannual.)

F314. Sumer: a journal of archaeology in Iraq. Baghdad, 1945 ff. (Semiannual.)

SECTION G

Early History of Asiatic Peoples

EARL H. PRITCHARD,* HORACE I. POLEMAN,
T. H. TSIEN, and JOHN W. HALL

This section deals with the beginning of civilizations in southern and eastern Asia. Systematic archaeological work in this area, except for Japan, only began in the 20th century, and has been seriously interrupted by foreign and domestic wars. Nevertheless, important discoveries have been made, especially in India, China, and southeast Asia, which confirm the existence of highly developed civilizations in India and China by the 3rd and 2nd millenniums B.C. Future archaeological work will unquestionably greatly expand our knowledge about the development of early civilizations in the area.

General works and a few relating to Korea and southeast Asia are given in the first subsection, but major details about the pre-history and early history of these two regions will be found in Sections N and Q. The detailed treatment of India, China, and Japan in this section is supplemented in Sections R, O, and P, where general histories and various bibliographies, aids, and guides which relate to India, China, and Japan as a whole are listed. Periodicals which carry articles on the early history of these areas are also included in Sections N, O, P, and R.

GENERAL WORKS

G1. Beardsley, Richard K., and others. **Bibliographic materials in the Japanese language on far eastern archaeology and ethnology.** Ann Arbor, 1950. Thorough survey of works relating to Japan, continental eastern Asia, and Micronesia. Largest number of the 1,063 titles relate to Japan.
G2. Early man in the Far East. Ed. by W. W. Howells. Detroit, 1949. [American Association of Physical Anthropologists,

Studies in physical anthropology, 1.] Valuable articles by Helmut de Terra, Hallam L. Movius, G. H. R. von Koenigswald, Edwin A. Colbert, and Franz Weidenreich.
G3. Weidenreich, Franz. **Giant early man from Java and south China.** N.Y., 1945. [Anthropological papers of the American Museum of Natural History, 40.] Discussion of early man in eastern Asia. Review, W. W. Howells, *Am. jour. physical anthrop.*, n.s. 4 (Sep. 1946): 404.

* Professor Pritchard is responsible for general planning and compilation, and for the subsection on General Works; Poleman for India; Pritchard and Tsien for China, with some suggestions from Charles S. Gardner; and Pritchard and Hall for Japan.

G4. ——. **Apes, giants, and man.** Chicago, 1946.

G5. Van Es, L. J. C. **The age of pithecanthropus.** The Hague, 1931.

G6. Menghin, O. **Weltgeschichte der Steinzeit.** Vienna, 1931. A general theory about the spread of Stone Age culture in Asia.

G7. Heine-Geldern, Robert. "Urheimat und früheste Wanderungen der Austronesier." **Anthropos,** 27 (May-Aug. 1932): 543–619. Theory as to the spread of Stone Age cultures and peoples.

G8. ——. "China, die ostkaspische Kultur und die Herkunft der Schrift." **Paideuma,** 4 (1950): 51–92. A theory on the origin and spread of writing.

G9. ——. "Sudostasien." Georg H. Buschan, ed., **Illustrierte Völkerkunde,** pt. 3, v. 2 (2nd ed., Stuttgart, 1923).

G10. Bishop, Carl W. **Origin of the far eastern civilizations.** Washington, 1942. [Smithsonian publication 3681.] Brief booklet presenting clearly a dominantly diffusionist interpretation which emphasizes the near eastern origin of major cultural elements. Although out of date in many respects, it contains much basic data.

G11. Movius, Hallam L., Jr. "The lower palaeolithic culture of southern and eastern Asia." **Transactions of the American Philosophical Society,** n.s. 38 (pt. 4, 1948): 329–420.

G12. ——. "Palaeolithic archaeology." **Cahiers d'histoire mondiale,** 2 (1954–55): 257–82, 520–53.

G13. Beyer, H. Otley, ed. **Proceedings of the fourth far eastern prehistory and the anthropology division of the eighth Pacific science congresses combined. Pt. 1, Prehistory, archaeology and physical anthropology.** 2 v. Quezon City, P. I., 1956. Eight papers on China, four on Japan, five on Formosa, and two on the Philippines. V. 3 is to contain seven more on the Philippines and one on southeast Asia.

G14. Umehara, Sueji and Fujita Ryōsaku. **Chōsen ko-bunka sōkan.** [Survey of ancient Korean culture.] 3 v. Kyoto, 1948. Detailed study of Korean archaeology and history from earliest times to 313 A.D. Review, M. Loehr, *Far eastern quar.,* 14 (May 1955): 416.

G15. Umehara, Sueji and Hamada Kosaku. **Keishu kinkan-tsuka to sono iho.** [The gold crown tomb at Kyongju and its treasures.] Keijo (Seoul), 1924. This publication of the Japanese government-general of Korea contains a text and 156 plates relating to an early Silla tomb. A summary and plate titles are in English. See also the two following articles.

G16. Sansom, George B. "An outline of recent Japanese archaeological research in Korea, in its bearing upon early Japanese

history." **Transactions of the Asiatic Society of Japan,** 2nd ser., 6 (Dec. 1929): 5–19.

G17. Umehara, Sueji. "Deux grandes découvertes archéologiques en Corée." **Revue des arts asiatiques,** 3 (Mar. 1926): 24–33.

G18. Heekeren, H. R. van. **The Stone Age of Indonesia.** The Hague, 1957.

G19. ——. **The Bronze-iron Age of Indonesia.** The Hague, 1958.

G20. Heine-Geldern, Robert. **The archaeology and art of Sumatra.** Vienna, 1935.

G21. Wales, H. G. Quaritch. **Prehistory and religion in southeast Asia.** London, 1957. An effort to show the continuity between the religion of megalithic and Dongsonian cultures and that of later times.

G22. Beyer, H. Otley. **Philippine and east Asian archaeology and its relation to the origin of the Pacific islands populations.** Quezon City, 1948. [National Research Council of the Philippines, Bulletin 29.] Summary of Philippine archaeology and an attempt to relate it to Pacific migrations.

INDIA TO THE MAURYAN EMPIRE
(321 B.C.)

Bibliographies

G23. Das Gupta, H. C. "Bibliography of prehistoric Indian antiquities." **Journal of the Asiatic Society of Bengal,** n.s. 27 (1931): 5–96. Valuable list of articles and books on anthropological, geological, and archaeological discoveries in India, Ceylon, and Burma.

G24. Renou, Louis. **Bibliographie védique.** Paris, 1931. Complete survey of texts, commentaries, translations, and expositions of the Vedas published to 1930. Includes periodical articles.

G25. Dandekar, Ramchandra N. **Vedic bibliography.** Bombay, 1946. Continues Renou's bibliography to 1945.

Ethnology and Language

G26. Guha, Biraja S. **An outline of the racial ethnology of India.** Calcutta, 1937. Probably the most authentic study of the subject, by an eminent anthropologist.

G27. Law, Bimala C. **Tribes in ancient India.** Poona, 1943. Citations from Sanskrit and Pali literature on tribal groups: pre-Mauryan and post-Mauryan.

G28. Shafer, Robert. **Ethnography of ancient India.** Wiesbaden, 1954. Provocative study based on names occurring in the Mahabharata.

G29. Lévi, Sylvain, Jean Przyluski, and Jules Bloch. **Pre-Aryan and pre-Dravidian in India.** Tr. by Prabodh C. Bagchi. Calcutta, 1929. Valuable linguistic study. Does not include Harappa script.

Sources and Translations

G30. Die Hymnen des Rigveda. Ed. by Theodor Aufrecht. 3rd ed., Wiesbaden, 1955. The best edition of the Rigveda in transliteration; a recent reprint.

G31. Der Rig-Veda aus dem Sanskrit ins Deutsch übers. von Karl Friedrich Geldner. 3 v. Cambridge, Mass., 1951. [Harvard oriental series, 33–35.] Best scholarly translation.

G32. The hymns of the Rigveda. Tr. by Ralph T. H. Griffith. 3rd ed., 2 v., Benares, 1920–26. Only complete English translation, but leaves much to be desired. Because of its inaccuracies it should be used for research only with the Sanskrit text and commentaries. However, the student without a knowledge of Sanskrit can get a fair idea of Vedic ideas by reading this translation.

G33. Rigveda Brāhmaṇas. Tr. by Arthur B. Keith. Cambridge, Mass., 1920. [Harvard oriental series, 25.] A very literal and exact translation of these two important Brāhmaṇas.

G34. Hymns of the Atharva-Veda. Tr. by Maurice Bloomfield. Oxford, 1897. [Sacred books of the East, 42.] Very sound and readable translation.

G35. The hymns of the Sâmaveda. Tr. by Ralph T. H. Griffith. 2nd ed., Benares, 1907. Only English translation; faulty.

G36. The Veda of the Black Yajus school. Tr. by Arthur B. Keith. 2 v. Cambridge, Mass., 1914. [Harvard oriental series, 18–19.] Excellent translation of this most important Yajurvedic text.

G37. Pañcaviṃśa-brāhmana. Tr. by Willem Caland. Calcutta, 1931. Excellent translation of an important text.

G38. The Gṛihya-Sûtras. Tr. by Hermann Oldenberg. 2 v. Oxford, 1886–92. [Sacred books of the East, 29–30.] The best anthology of its kind.

G39. The thirteen principal Upanishads. Tr. by Robert E. Hume. 2nd ed., London and N.Y., 1931. There are more popular translations, but this still remains the best introduction to a study of the Upanishads.

G40. The Śatapatha-Brâhmaṇa. Tr. by Julius Eggeling. 5 v. Oxford, 1882–1900. [Sacred books of the East, 12, 26, 51, 53, 54.] Very good translation of this representative Brāhmaṇa text.

G41. The texts of the White Yajur-Veda. Tr. by Ralph T. H. Griffith. Benares, 1899. Only English translation of this text; faulty.

General Works

G42. The Vedic age. London, 1951. [The history and culture of the Indian people, ed. by Ramesh Chandra Majumdar and Achut D. Pusalker.] Includes the prehistoric period as well as Vedic; extensive bibliography.

G43. Subbarao, Bendapudi. **The personality of India.** Baroda, 1956. Traces development of Indian culture in the prehistoric and protohistoric periods with liberal use of maps and synoptic charts.

G44. Ancient India. Ed. by Edward J. Rapson. Cambridge, Eng., 1922. [The Cambridge history of India, 1.] Written before the discovery of Harappa culture. Begins with the Aryan invasions and concludes with the Mauryan period.

G45. La Vallée-Poussin, Louis de. **Indo-Européens et Indo-Iraniens: l'Inde jusque vers 300 av. J.-C.** Paris, 1924. [Histoire du monde, 3.] Origin of the Aryans and the history of Vedic India are discussed in many general histories. This account will serve as an introduction.

G46. Sarkar, Subimal C. **Some aspects of the earliest social history of India (pre-Buddhistic ages).** London, 1928. Treats architecture, housing, dress, sex relations, marriage, and position of women.

Prehistoric Indus Civilization

G47. Mackay, Ernest J. H. **The Indus civilization.** London, 1935. A popular account.

G48. Piggott, Stuart. **Prehistoric India to 1000 B.C.** Harmondsworth, Eng., 1950. Popular account with a wealth of information.

G49. Wheeler, Sir Robert E. M. **The Indus civilization.** Cambridge, Eng., 1953. [The Cambridge history of India, suppl. vol.] Compact information on the period, with a bibliographic guide to more detailed sources.

G50. Pañchānana Mitra. **Prehistoric India, its place in the world's cultures.** 2nd ed., Calcutta, 1927. Includes a brief treatment of finds at Mohenjo-daro; covers races and cultures, geology and geography, palaeolithic, mesolithic, and neolithic remains.

G51. Brown, W. Norman. "The beginnings of civilization in India." **Journal of the American Oriental Society,** 59 (Dec. 1939): supplement, 32–44. Discusses the Amri, Harappa, Jhukar, and Jhangar cultures, with emphasis on the Harappa and its possible relationship to Mesopotamian culture.

G52. Dikshit, Kashinath N. **Prehistoric civilization of the Indus Valley.** Madras, 1939. Brief estimate of the civilization by one associated with the preservation of the sites.

G53. Marshall, Sir John H. **Mohenjo-daro and the Indus civilization: being an official account of archaeological excavations at Mohenjo-daro carried out by the government of India betwen the years 1922 and 1927.** 3 v. London, 1931. Monumental work by the director of excavations.

G54. Mackay, Ernest J. H. **Further excavations at Mohenjo-daro: being an official account of archaeological excavations carried out by the government of India between the years 1927 and 1931.** 2 v. Delhi, 1938. A thorough study.

G55. ———. **Chanhu-daro excavations, 1935–36.** New Haven, 1943. Thorough description by director of the expedition.

G56. Sen, Dharani. "Prehistoric researches in India." **Man in India,** 33 (July-Sep. 1953): 185–94. Account of recent work.

G57. Krishnaswami, V. D. "Progress in prehistory." **Ancient India,** no. 9 (1953): 53–79. Detailed account of recent work.

G58. Hunter, Guy G. R. **The script of Harappa and Mohenjodaro and its connection with other scripts.** London, 1934. The Harappa script has not been deciphered. Problems and some of the hypotheses are included in this work.

G59. Frankfort, Henri. "The Indus civilization and the Near East." **Annual bibliography of Indian archaeology** (Leiden, 1932), 1–12. Detailed comparison of the findings in India with early near eastern civilizations.

Vedic India

G60. Apte, Vinayak M. **Social and religious life in the Gṛihya-sūtras, with brief surveys of social conditions in Vedic literature (from the Rigveda to the Śrauta-sūtras) and in early Avestan literature.** Ahmedabad, 1939. Indispensable for study of the late Vedic period.

G61. Bhargava, Purushottam L. "Pre-Mauryan history according to the Purāṇas." **The Indian historical quarterly,** 28 (Sep. 1952): 232–39. Brief contribution to a little explored field of research.

G62. Bloomfield, Maurice. **The religion of the Veda.** N.Y., 1908. Still the best account of the Vedic religious ideas.

G63. Foote, Robert B. **The Foote collection of Indian prehistoric and protohistoric antiquities. V. 2, Notes on their ages and distribution.** Madras, 1916. Valuable for its plates and descriptions of the items.

G64. Hillebrandt, Alfred. **Vedische Mythologie.** 3 v. Breslau, 1891–1902. The standard, comprehensive work on the subject, although author's interpretations are not always generally accepted.

G65. Hopkins, Edward W. **The great epic of India, its character and origin.** N.Y., 1901. Standard analysis of the Mahabharata, based on early editions. The Poona edition requires a reworking of this study.

G66. Kaegi, Adolf. **Life in ancient India: studies in Rig Vedic India.** Tr. by R. Arrowsmith. Calcutta, 1950. Reprint of an earlier work based on conjectural interpretation of hints in the Rigveda. Suggestive but not exhaustive.

G67. Keith, Arthur B. **The religion and philosophy of the Veda and Upanishads.** 2 v. Cambridge, Mass., 1925. [Harvard oriental series, 31–32.] Indispensable reference work for study of the Vedic period.

G68. Lal, B. B. "Protohistoric investigation." **Ancient India,** no. 9 (1953): 80–102. Covers the progress made in this field of Indic research.

G69. Macdonell, Arthur A. **Vedic mythology.** Strasbourg, 1897. [Grundriss der indoarischen Philologie und Altertumskunde, 3.] Not as exhaustive as Hillebrandt; presents different points of view.

G70. McCrindle, John W. **Ancient India as described by Ktêsias the Knidian: being a translation of the abridgement of his "Indika" by Photios, and of the fragments of that work preserved in other writers.** London, 1882. Ancient natural history of the Indus region.

G71. ———, tr. **The invasion of India by Alexander the Great as described by Arrian, Q. Curtius, Diodorus, Plutarch, and Justin.** 2nd ed., Westminster, 1896. Important source material.

G72. Monier-Williams, Monier. **Indian epic poetry . . . with a full analysis of the Rámáyaṇa and the Mahá-Bhárata.** London and Edinburgh, 1863. A study based on early editions. Will need revision with use of the Poona edition of the Mahabharata and the Baroda edition of the Ramayana.

G73. Stein, Sir Mark A. **Archaeological reconnaissances in north-western India and south-eastern Iran.** London, 1937. Thorough survey of ancient routes and sites.

G74. ———. **On Alexander's track to the Indus: personal narrative of explorations on the north-west frontier of India.** London, 1929. Ancient sites and routes.

CHINA TO THE UNIFICATION BY CH'IN (221 B.C.)

Bibliographies, Chronologies, and Guides

G75. Goodrich, L. Carrington. "Archaeology in China: the first decades." **The journal of Asian studies,** 17 (Nov. 1957): 5–16. Review of archaeological work in China from the 1920's to the present.

G76. ———. "Antiquity: to the fall of Shang (ca. 1028 B.C.)." Harley F. MacNair, ed., **China** (Berkeley, 1946), pp. 41–53. Earlier summary of Chinese pre-history.

G77. Kaizuka, Shigeki. **Chūgoku kodai shigaku no hatten.** [Development of the study of ancient Chinese history.] 3rd ed., Tokyo, 1946. Valuable survey of the status of studies on early Chinese history as of the end of World War II, although Kaizuka has failed to utilize the all-important work on the Shang period, Tung Tso-pin, *Yin li p'u* (See *G179*).

G78. Hu, Hou-hsüan. **Wu-shih-nien chia-ku-hsüeh lun chu mu.** [A bibliography of the study of shell and bone inscriptions, 1899–1949.] Shanghai, 1952. List of 148 books and 728 articles relating to the Shang period written by over 300 scholars since discovery of the remains.

G79. Jung, Yüan. **Chin-shih shu lu-mu.** [Bibliography of Chinese archaeology.] Nanking, 1936. Classified catalog of 977 works on archaeology: bronzes, coins, seals, stone, jade, oracle bones, pottery, bamboo and woden tablets, and works relating to particular localities.

G80. Bishop, Carl W. "The chronology of ancient China." **Journal of the American Oriental Society,** 52 (Sep. 1932): 232–47. Perhaps few of the conclusions reached by Bishop can now stand, but the article is illustrative of the problem of chronology in early China. For more recent details on the Shang period see Tung Tso-pin, *Yin li p'u,* mentioned below; and also the following.

G81. Dubs, Homer H. "The date of the Shang period." **T'oung pao,** 40 (1951): 322–35 and 42 (1954): 101–05.

Paleography and Language

G82. Couvreur, Séraphin. **Dictionnaire classique de la langue chinoise.** 3rd ed., Hsien-hsien, 1911. Especially valuable for its specific examples of classical usage. For other dictionaries see Section O.

G83. Dobson, W. A. C. H. **Late archaic Chinese.** Toronto, 1959. Deals with the language of such classical texts as the *Mo-tzu, Mencius, Chuang-tzu,* and *Tso-chuan.* Claims to have laid the foundation for a systematic and scientific study of the grammar of classical Chinese.

G84. Karlgren, Bernhard. **Philology and ancient China.** Oslo, 1926. An important work.

G85. ——. "On the script of the Chou dynasty." **Bulletin of the Museum of Far Eastern Antiquities,** 8 (1936): 157–81. For other important works on the Chinese language by Karlgren see Section O.

G86. T'ang, Lan. **Ku-wen-tzu-hsüeh tao-lun.** [An introduction to Chinese paleography.] 2 ts'e. Peiping, 1935. Discussion of the scope, history, and sources for study of ancient Chinese writing and' on the origin, principles of construction, and changes of styles of the Chinese script.

G87. Ting, Fu-pao. **Shuo-wen chieh-tzu ku-lin.** [Collected commentaries on the ancient etymological dictionary.] 66 ts'e. Shanghai, 1930–32. Supplement, 16 ts'e, 1935. Collection of all available commentaries on the *Shuo-wen,* compiled by Hsü Shen about 100 A.D., arranged in the order of the original dictionary. Ancient forms appearing in stone, bronze, and bone inscriptions are given and an index to all characters in the modern form is included.

G88. Sun, Hai-po. **Chia-ku-wen pien.** [List of characters found in shell-and-bone inscriptions.] 5 ts'e. Peiping, 1927. Vocabulary of 1,006 legible and 1,112 illegible characters found in the oracle-bone inscriptions of the Shang dynasty.

G89. Jung, Keng. **Chin-wen pien.** [List of characters found in bronze inscriptions.] Rev. ed., 5 ts'e, Shanghai, 1939. Vocabulary of 1,382 legible and 924 illegible characters with 8,001 variant forms found in bronze inscriptions of the Shang and Chou dynasties. A supplement, *Chin-wen hsü-pien* (2 ts'e, Shanghai, 1935), includes 951 legible with 6,084 variant forms for the Ch'in and Han periods. Both series include careful citations of sources and indexes to characters in the modern form.

Sources and Translations

G90. Legge, James. **The Chinese classics: with a translation, critical and exegetical notes, prolegomena, and copious indexes.** 2nd rev. ed., 5 v. in 8, Oxford, 1893–95. Reprint, Peiping, 1939. Translations in this series include the four books and part of the thirteen classics: 1, *Confucian analects* [*Lun yü*], *The great learning* [*Ta hsüeh*], and *The doctrine of the mean* [*Chung yung*]; 2, *The works of Mencius* [*Meng-tzu*]; 3, *The Shoo king* [*Shu ching*], or *The book of historical documents;* 4, *The She king* [*Shih ching*] (Book of poetry); 5, *The Ch'un ts'ew* [*Ch'un ch'iu*], with *The Tso chuen* [*Tso chuan*] (Spring and autumn annals, with Tso commentary), including specimens of the commentaries of Kung-yang and Ku-liang. Others of the classics translated by Legge, not included in this series, are *The Hsiao king* [*Hsiao ching*] (Book of filial piety) in the *Sacred books of the East,* v. 3 (1879); *The Yi king* [*I ching*] (Book of changes) in v. 16 (1882); and *The Li ki* [*Li chi*] (Ceremonial records) in v. 27–28 (1885) of the same series. The *I-li,* or *Book of etiquette and ceremonial,* is translated by John Steele (2 v., London, 1917); and the *Chou li* (Rituals of Chou) is translated into French by Edouard Biot, *Le Tcheou-li,* or *Rites des Tcheou* (3 v. in 2, Paris, 1851). The *Erh ya,* an early dictionary, the thirteenth classic, has not been translated.

A standard French translation of many of the classics is by Séraphin Couvreur (Ho-chien-fu and Hsien-hsien, 1895–1916, with various later reprints at Hsien-hsien and the most recent in Paris since 1950).

Other especially important translations include the following (*G91–96*).

G91. Waley, Arthur, tr. **The book of songs.** London and Boston, 1937.

G92. ——, tr. **The analects of Confucius.** London and N.Y., 1938.

G93. Soothill, William E., tr. **The analects of Confucius.** Yokohama, 1910.

G94. Karlgren, Bernhard, tr. **The book of documents** and **The book of odes.** Stockholm, 1950.

G95. Lyall, L. A., tr. **Mencius.** London, 1932.

G96. Wilhelm, Richard, tr. **Li Gi: das Buch der Sitte des älteren und jungeren Dai.** Jena, 1930.

The standard Chinese edition of the thirteen classics is the one with commentaries of Han and T'ang scholars and critical notes by Juan Yüan, published in Nan-chang in 1815 and reprinted in the *Ssu-pu pei-yao* (Shanghai, 1927–36). Concordances to the texts of the classics and to quotations in some of the commentaries are included in the Harvard-Yenching Institute Sinological index series.

G97. Shang shu [Shu ching]. [The classic of history.] With commentaries by K'ung An-kuo, Lu Te-ming, and K'ung Ying-ta, and critical notes by Juan Yüan. Nan-chang, 1815. Reprinted in 6 ts'e in the *Su-pu pei-yao*, Shanghai, 1927. Probably the most useful edition of the *Classic of history,* the oldest book of Chinese historical documents. The most recent critical translation is by Bernhard Karlgren, *The book of documents* (*G94*), reprinted from *Bulletin of the Museum of Far Eastern Antiquities,* 22 (1950): 1–81. See also v. 20 (1948): 39–315 and 21 (1949): 63–206 of this publication for valuable "Glosses on the Book of documents." Older translations by Legge in *The Chinese classics* (*G90*), v. 3, and by Couvreur (Ho-chien-fu, 1897 and Hsien-hsien, 1926) are available. A valuable concordance with punctuated text and index was prepared by Ku Chieh-kang, *Shang-shu t'ung-chien,* and published by the Harvard-Yenching Institute at Peiping, 1936. For a discussion of the work and the controversies about the authenticity of its various books see Herrlee G. Creel, *Studies in early Chinese culture* (Baltimore, 1937), pp. 21–96; and Paul Pelliot, "Le *Chou king* et le *Chang chou che wen,*" *Mémoires concernant l'Asie orientale,* v. 2 (Paris, 1916).

G98. Ch'un-ch'iu ching chuan yin-te. [Combined concordance to Ch'un-ch'iu, Kung-yang, Ku-liang and Tso-chuan.] Comp. by Hung Yeh and others. 4 v. Peiping, 1937. The most useful edition, with punctuated texts and complete index, of the *Ch'un-ch'iu* (Spring and autumn annals of the state of Lu), *Tso-chuan, Kung-yang chuan,* and *Ku-liang chuan* (the last three works traditionally considered as different commentaries on the *Ch'un-ch'iu*) covering the period 722–468 B.C. Texts of the *Ch'un-ch'iu* and *Tso-chuan* were translated by Legge in *The Chinese*

classics, v. 5, and by Séraphin Couvreur, *Tch'ouen ts'iou et Tso tchouan* (3 v., Ho-chien-fu, 1914; Paris, 1951). Their historical importance and authenticity are discussed in William Hung's "Prolegomena" (in Chinese) to this edition; Ssu-ho Ch'i, "Professor Hung on the Ch'un-ch'iu," *Yenching jour. soc. studies,* 1 (June 1938): 49–71; Bernhard Karlgren, "On the authenticity and nature of the Tso-chuan," *Götesborgs högskolas årsskrift,* 32 (1926): 3–65; and Henri Maspero, "La composition et la date du Tso-tchouan," *Mélanges chinois et bouddhiques,* 1 (1931–32): 137–215. See also Everard D. H. Fraser and J. H. S. Lockhart, *Index to the Tso-chuan* (London, 1930).

G99. Kuo yü [Discourses of the states]. With commentary by Wei Chao (197–278). *Ssu-pu pei-yao* ed., 6 ts'e, Shanghai, 1927. Collection of historical conversations arranged under eight feudal states, covering about the same period as the *Tso-chuan.* Partly, but inadequately, translated by Charles de Harlez as "Koue yü (Discours des royaumes)," pt. 1, in *Journal asiatique,* 9th ser., 2 (July-Aug. 1893): 373–419 and 3 (Jan.-Feb. 1894): 5–91; and pt. 2 as *Koue yü* (Louvain, 1895). An index was published by the Tōhō Bunka Kenkyusho (Kyoto, 1934).

G100. Chan-kuo ts'e. [Plots of the warring states.] Annotated by Kao Yu (ca. 168–212) with amended commentaries by Yao Hung (ca. 1100–1146) and others. *Ssu-pu pei-yao* ed., 6 ts'e, Shanghai, 1927. Collection of state documents, anecdotes, and writings of the diplomatic school covering the period from about 453 to 209 B.C. This edition is arranged under the various states, but another (*Ssu-pu ts'ung-k'an* ed., Shanghai, 1929) is arranged by chronological order of various passages. Partially translated in Franz Hübotter, *Aus den Plänen der kämpfenden Reiche . . . nebst den entsprechenden biographien . . . des Se-ma Ts'ien* (Berlin, 1912) and in "Tales of the warring kingdom," George Kao, ed., *Chinese wit and humor* (N.Y., 1946), pp. 47–57. The text is indexed in the *T'ung-ch'ien* series of the Centre d'Études Sinologiques de Pekin, Université de Paris (Peiping, 1948).

G101. Chu-shu chi-nien. [The annals of the bamboo books.] Tr. by James Legge in *The Chinese classics* (*G90*), v. 3; and by Edouard Biot in the *Journal asiatique,* 3rd ser., 12 (Dec. 1841): 537–78 and 13 (May 1842): 381–431. The *Bamboo annals* is an ancient chronicle covering the period from antiquity to 295 B.C. The translations are based on the current text, which is generally considered to be a forgery. The original text, written on bamboo tablets and discovered in 279 A.D. in an ancient tomb, has been lost, but fragments of it have been reconstructed by Wang Kuo-wei and are included in his

Hai-nin Wang Ching-an hsien-sheng i-shu (Shanghai, 1936), ts'e 3.

G102. Ssu-Ma, Ch'ien. **[Shih-chi.] Les mémoires historiques de Sema Ts'ien.** Tr. by Edouard Chavannes. 5 v. in 6. Paris, 1895–1905. Translation by a great French sinologist of the first 47 chapters of the first great comprehensive history of China, covering the period to about 99 B.C. Best edition in Chinese is the one with the collected commentaries of Pei Yin (5th century), Ssuma Cheng (8th century), and Chang Shou-chieh (8th century) and punctuated with critical notes by Takigawa Kametaro, under the title *Shih-chi hui-chu k'ao-cheng* (10 v., Tokyo, 1934).

G103. Erh-shih-erh tzu. [Twenty-two philosophers.] Ed. by Chang Yü. Hangchow, 1874–77. Reprinted in the *Ssu-pu pei-yao,* in Shanghai, under separate titles. A collection of writings of ancient Chinese philosophers. Philosophical works in translation, aside from those under the classics, include the following (*G104–120*).

G104. Waley, Arthur, tr. **The way and its power.** London, 1934. Both a study of Taoism and a translation of the *Tao te ching* [Lao Tzu].

G105. Duyvendak, Jan J. L., tr. and ed. **Tao tö king.** French ed. with revised Chinese text, Paris, 1953; English ed., London, 1954.

G106. Legge, James, tr. "The writings of Kwang-zze" Chuang Tzu. **Sacred books of the east,** v. 39–40. London, 1891.

G107. Giles, H. A., tr. **Chuang Tzu.** 2nd ed., Shanghai, 1926.

G108. Fung [Feng], Yu-lan, tr. and ed. **Chuang Tzu.** Shanghai, 1931.

G109. Giles, Lionel, tr. **Taoist teachings from the book of Lieh Tzu.** London, 1912.

G110. Forke, Anton, tr. **Yang Chu's garden of pleasure.** London, 1912.

G111. Morgan, Evan, tr. and ed. **Tao, the great luminant: essays from Huai-nan-tzu.** London, 1935.

G112. Mei, Yi-pao, tr. **The ethical and political works of Motse.** London, 1929.

G113. Forke, Alfred, tr. and ed. **Me Ti des Sozialethikers und seiner Schüler philosophische Werke.** Berlin, 1922.

G114. Dubs, Homer H., tr. **The works of Hsüntze.** London, 1928.

G115. Duyvendak, Jan J. L., tr. **The book of Lord Shang.** London, 1928.

G116. Liao, W. K., tr. and ed. **The complete works of Han Fei Tzu.** V. 1. London, 1939.

G117. Maverick, Lewis, ed. **T'an Po-fu and Wen Kung-wen, trs. Selections from the Kuan-tzu.** Carbondale, Ill., 1954.

G118. Giles, Lionel, tr. and ed. **Sun Tzu on the art of war.** London, 1910.

G119. Wilhelm, Richard, tr. **Fruhling und Herbst des Lü Bu We.** Jena, 1928.

G120. Forke, Anton. "The Chinese sophists." **Journal North China Branch of the Royal Asiatic Society,** 34 (1901–02): 1–100. Concordances, accompanying the text, to *Chuang Tzu, Mo Tzu,* and *Hsü Tzu* are included in the Harvard-Yenching Institute Sinological index series.

G121. Ch'u tz'u [Elegies of Ch'u] Annotated by Wang I (d. 158 A.D.) and Hung Hsingtsu (1090–1155). *Ssu-pu pei-yao* ed., 6 ts'e, Shanghai, 1927. Anthology of early poems, including the *Li sao,* attributed to Ch'ü Yüan (ca. 338–288 B.C.), and imitations of those poems by later writers. The *Li sao* was translated by James Legge, "The Li sao poem and its author," *Journal of the Royal Asiatic Society* (July 1895): 571–99; Lim Boon Keng, *The Li sao: an elegy on encountering sorrows* (Shanghai, 1929); and Yang Hsien-yi and Gladys Yang, *Li sao and other poems of Chu Yuan* (Peking, 1953). A complete translation is David Hawkes, **Ch'u tz'u: the songs of the south** (Oxford, 1959). See also *G208.*

G122. Shan-hai ching. [Classic of mountains and rivers.] With commentaries by Kuo P'o (276–324) and Hao I-hsing (1757–1825). *Ssu-pu pei-yao* ed., 4 ts'e, Shanghai, 1933. An early work of geography and mythology, probably produced in the Chou dynasty. There are several incomplete translations, including Otto Mänchen-Helfen's "The later books of the Shan-hai king," *Asia Major,* 1 (1924): 550–86. It is indexed in the *T'ung chien* series of Centre d'Études Sinologiques de Pekin, Université de Paris (Peiping, 1948).

General Works

G123. Creel, Herrlee G. **The birth of China.** London, 1936; N.Y., 1937. Although no longer up-to-date, this is by all odds the best general account of the beginning of Chinese civilization from the Stone Age through the Shang and early Chou periods to about 770 B.C.

G124. Lü, Ssu-mien. **Hsien-Ch'in shih.** [History of the pre-Ch'in period.] Shanghai, 1941. Covers the history of China to 221 B.C.

G125. Ku, Chieh-kang, and others, eds. **Ku shih pien.** [A symposium on ancient Chinese history.] 7 v. in 10. Peiping and Shanghai, 1927–41. Collection of critical studies by modern historians of ancient Chinese history and historical materials. The authenticity of ancient literatures is discussed and controversial opinions are represented. The preface to v. 1 by Ku Chieh-kang is translated by Arthur W. Hummel, *The autobiography of a Chinese historian* (Leiden, 1931). V. 7 includes a monograph, "An introduction to ancient Chinese history," by Yang K'uan.

G126. Consten, E. von Erdberg. **Das alte China.** Stuttgart, 1958. Recent summary account of early Chinese history.

G127. Maspero, Henri. **La Chine antique.** Paris, 1927. Rev. ed., 1955. As much sociological as historical, it is probably the most widely used general history and analysis of Chinese civilization to 221 B.C. Completed just before the great archaeological discoveries revolutionized knowledge of early China, its early parts are now completely out of date and many of its later conclusions and generalizations are either too precise or sweeping. Nevertheless, an indispensable book.

G128. ——. **Mélanges posthumes sur les religions et l'histoire de la Chine.** 3 v. Paris, 1950. [1, *Les religions chinoises;* 2, *Le Taoisme;* 3, *Études historiques.*] Valuable studies by a great French scholar. V. 2 should be read along with H. G. Creel, "What is Taoism?" *Jour. Am. Oriental Soc.,* 76 (July-Sep. 1956): 139–52.

G129. ——. "Légendes mythologiques dans le Chou king." **Journal asiatique,** 204 (Jan.-Mar. 1924): 1–100.

G130. Hirth, Friedrich. **The ancient history of China to the end of the Chou dynasty.** N.Y., 1908. Critical account of early Chinese history prior to the great archaeological studies. Now antiquated in many respects.

G131. Granet, Marcel. **La civilisation chinoise.** Paris, 1929. English tr., London and N.Y., 1930. This and the six following works present Granet's Durkheimian interpretations of Chinese history and society. His conclusions are often either too sweeping or too precise.

G132. ——. **La religion des Chinois.** Paris, 1922.

G133. ——. **La pensée chinoise.** Paris, 1934.

G134. ——. **Études sociologiques sur la Chine.** Paris, 1953.

G135. ——. **La féodalité chinoise.** Oslo, 1952.

G136. ——. **Fêtes et chansons anciennes de la Chine.** Paris, 1919. 2nd ed., 1929. English tr. by Evangeline D. Edwards, London and N.Y., 1932. Essentially a translation and interpretation of the *Book of poetry* [*Shih ching*]. This and the following work are pioneer sociological interpretations of early Chinese society based on early legends and songs which are often too sweeping and overdrawn, but nevertheless stimulating and suggestive.

G137. ——. **Danses et légendes de la Chine ancienne.** 2 v. Paris, 1926.

G138. Hsü, Ping-ch'ang. **Chung-kuo ku-shih ti ch'uan-shuo shih-tai.** [The legendary period of ancient Chinese history.] Shanghai, 1943. Attempts to interpret some of the legends in Chinese literary sources, such as the primitive national groups, deluge, eclipse of the Hsia, five emperors, and myths before the Yellow Emperor.

G139. Kuo, Mo-jo. **Chung-kuo ku-tai she-hui yen-chiu.** [A study of ancient Chinese society.] Rev. ed., Shanghai, 1947. First edition appeared in 1930 as the earliest attempt to interpret ancient Chinese society with Marxist theories. The author brings up many new points from both archaeological and literary sources, but sometimes makes hasty conclusions without sufficient evidence.

G140. Wittfogel, Karl A. "The society of prehistoric China." **Zeitschrift für Sozialforschung,** 8 (1939): 138–86. This and the three following works present particularized theories which are suggestive rather than definitive.

G141. ——. "The foundations and stages of Chinese economic history." **Zeitschrift für Sozialforschung,** 4 (1935): 26–60.

G142. ——. "Die theorie der orientalischen gesellschaft." **Zeitschrift für Sozialforschung,** 7 (1938): 90–122.

G143. ——. **Oriental despotism.** New Haven, 1957.

G144. Eberhard, Wolfram. **Lokalkulturen in alten China.** 2 v. Leiden and Peking, 1942–43. These two volumes expand his ideas on "Early Chinese cultures and their development, a working hypothesis," *Annual report of the Smithsonian Institution* (Washington, 1937). These works are suggestive, but go beyond available facts.

G145. Siren, Osvald. **A history of early Chinese art.** V. 1, **The prehistoric and pre-Han periods.** London, 1929. A standard work, well illustrated.

G146. Bodde, Derk. "Feudalism in China." Rushton Coulborn, ed., **Feudalism in history** (Princeton, 1956), pp. 49–92. Well-balanced discussion.

G147. Ch'en, Wen-t'ao. **Hsien-Ch'in tzu-jan-hsüeh kai-lun.** [Introduction to the study of the natural sciences in the pre-Ch'in period.] Shanghai, 1933. Survey of contributions to astronomy, mechanics, optics, acoustics, biology, physiology, engineering, agriculture, and natural study.

G148. Maspero, Henri. "L'astronomie chinoise avant les Han." **T'oung pao,** 26 (1928–29): 265–356. Good account of astronomy in early China. See also the following.

G149. Chatley, Herbert. "Ancient Chinese astronomy." **Royal Astronomical Society occasional notes,** 5 (1939): 65–74.

G150. Dubs, Homer H. "The beginnings of Chinese astronomy." **Journal of the American Oriental Society,** 78 (Oct.-Dec. 1958): 295–300.

G151. Eberhard, Wolfram. "Neuere chinesische und japanische Arbeiten zur altchinesischen Astronomie." **Asia Major, 9** (1933): 592–611.

Early Man and the Stone Age

G152. Pei, Wen-chung. **Chung-kuo shih-ch'ien shih-ch'i chih yen-chiu.** [A study of the prehistoric period of China.] Shanghai, 1948. Comprehensive study of the paleolithic and neolithic periods of China as generalized from discoveries and researches during the last twenty or thirty years.

G153. Teilhard de Chardin, Pierre. **Early man in China.** Peking, 1941. [Institut de Géo-biologie, Publications, 7.] Best general account as of 1941. Expanded, especially in regard to technical details, in his *Fossil men* (Peking, 1943).

G154. Teilhard de Chardin, Pierre, and Wen-chung Pei. **Le néolithique de la Chine.** Peking, 1944. [Institut de Géo-biologie, Publications, 10.] General survey of China's neolithic period as understood in the early 1940's.

G155. Andersson, Johan G. **Children of the yellow earth: studies in prehistoric China.** Tr. by E. Classen. London, 1934. Popular account of early archaeological discoveries in China by a Swedish geologist who was a prominent participant.

G156. ———. "Researches into the prehistory of the Chinese." **Bulletin of the Museum of Far Eastern Antiquities, 15** (1943): 1–304. A basic study on the neolithic culture of China. For continued studies by Andersson see the *Bulletin*, nos. 17 (1945) and 19 (1947). See also the review by W. C. Pei, *Quarterly bulletin of Chinese bibliography*, n.s. 7 (1947): 1.

G157. Wu, D. G. **Prehistoric pottery in China.** London, 1938. Important early study dealing with the black pottery discoveries among others.

G158. Academia Sinica, Institute of History and Philology. **Ch'eng-tzu-yai: the black pottery culture site of Lung-shan-chen in Li-ch'eng-hsien, Shantung province.** Tr. by Kenneth Starr. Ed. by Chi Li and others. New Haven, 1956. [Yale University publications in anthropology, 52.] First important account of a black pottery site. The original of this work appeared in Chinese with English summary in 1934. Notes, explanations, and a bibliography have been added by the translator.

G159. Liang, S. Y. "The Lungshan culture: a prehistoric phase of Chinese civilization." **Quarterly bulletin of Chinese bibliography, 1** (Sep. 1940): 251–62.

G160. Cheng, Te-k'un. **Archaeological studies in Szechwan.** Cambridge, Eng., 1957. Largest parts deal with prehistoric sites, stone implements, pottery, etc. Review, R. C.

Rudolph, *Jour. Asian studies,* 17 (Nov. 1957): 116.

The Bronze Age of Shang and Early Chou

G161. Li, Chi. **The beginnings of Chinese civilization.** Seattle, 1957. Brief but up-to-date account illustrated by material from An-yang (the Shang capital), by one of China's greatest archaeologists.

G162. Cheng, Te-k'un. "The origin and development of Shang culture." **Asia Major, 6** (July 1957): 80–98. Summary of latest studies on the Shang period, including those made in Communist China.

G163. Tung, Tso-pin. **An interpretation of the ancient Chinese civilization.** Taipei, 1952. Brief but substantial summary of the institutions, modes of life, religion, sciences, and arts of the Shang dynasty, translated from an article which appeared in the *Ta-lu tsa-chih* [Continent magazine], 3 (1951).

G164. Creel, Herrlee G. **Studies in early Chinese culture.** Baltimore, 1937. Basic and scholarly; deals with problem of the Hsia dynasty and various questions of the Shang period.

G165. Ferguson, John C. **Li-tai chu-lu chi-chin mu.** [Catalog of recorded bronzes of sucessive dynasties.] Ch'ang-sha, 1939. Classified catalog of bronze objects as recorded in some eighty different Chinese works on archaeology published before 1935, together with transcribed inscriptions and sources.

G166. Hsia, Nai, and others, eds. **Hui-hsien fa-chüeh pao-kao.** [Report on excavations at Hui-hsien, Honan.] Peking, 1956. Recent excavations of five sites relating to the periods of Shang, Chan-kuo, and Han, under auspices of the Institute of Archeology, Academia Sinica, Peking in 1950–52.

G167. Hu, Hou-hsüan. **Yin-hsü fa-chueh.** [Excavations of the Shang ruins.] Shanghai, 1955. Comprehensive account of the excavations at An-yang, Cheng-chou, and Wei-hui in Honan, and at other sites in Shantung and Hopei provinces, covering the fifteen expeditions of Academia Sinica and other undertakings after 1949.

G168. ———. **Chia ku hsüeh shang shih lun ts'ung.** [Collected studies of the bone inscriptions and the history of the Shang dynasty.] 1st–3rd series, 7 ts'e, Chengtu, 1944–45. Collection of essays on the family system, religion, climate, agriculture, and other subjects relating to the Shang dynasty, based on interpretation of the oracle-bone inscriptions. Includes bibliography of the study of bone inscriptions, which has been revised and republished in Shanghai, 1952. See *G78*.

G169. Jung, Keng. **Shang-chou i-ch'i t'ung-k'ao.** [The bronzes of Shang and Chou.] 2 v. Peiping, 1941. Comprehensive study of the types, dating, inscriptions, motifs, rubbing, etc. of Chinese bronzes, with discussions of the various kinds of vessels and musical instruments.

G170. Karlgren, Bernhard. "Yin and Chou in Chinese bronzes." **Bulletin of the Museum of Far Eastern Antiquities,** 8 (1936): 9–154. This and the following article are important on early Chinese bronzes.

G171. ——. "New studies on Chinese bronzes." **Bulletin of the Museum of Far Eastern Antiquities,** 9 (1937): 1–117.

G172. Yetts, Walter P. **The Cull collection of Chinese bronzes.** London, 1939.

G173. Wenley, Archibald, and others. **A descriptive and illustrative catalogue of Chinese bronzes.** Washington, 1946.

G174. Kuo, Mo-jo. **Liang-chou chin-wen-tz'u ta-hsi.** [Collection of bronze inscriptions of the western and eastern Chou dynasties.] 8 v. Tokyo, 1935. Contains 5 v. of illustrations and 3 v. of critical studies.

G175. Creel, Herrlee G. "Bronze inscriptions of the western Chou dynasty as historical documents." **Journal of the American Oriental Society,** 56 (Sep. 1936): 335–49.

G176. Li, Chi, and others, eds. **An-yang fa-chüeh pao-kao.** [Preliminary reports of excavations at An-yang.] 4 v. Peiping, 1929–35. Earliest detailed reports on excavations at this Shang capital.

G177. Loehr, Max. **Chinese Bronze Age weapons: the Werner Jannings collection in the Chinese National Palace Museum, Peking.** Ann Arbor, 1956. Catalog of Shang and Chou bronze weapons, with descriptions, illustrations, and plates. A long introduction discusses the various weapons and problems of their origin and dating.

G178. Menzies, J. M. **Oracle records from the waste of Yin.** Shanghai, 1917. Early account of the oracle bones, by one of the discoverers of the famous Shang site.

G179. Tung, Tso-pin. **Yin li p'u.** [The chronology of the Shang dynasty.] 4 ts'e. Li-chuang, 1945. Introduction to the Shang calendar, chronology, and institutions as generalized from many related fragments of bone inscriptions and other materials, by the leading authority on the subject.

G180. Tung, Tso-pin, and others. **Yin-hsü wen-tzu.** [Oracle bone inscriptions of the Shang.] 1st-2nd series, 4 v., Shanghai and Taipei, 1948–53. [Archaeologica sinica.] The first two series contain 21,034 oracle bone inscriptions excavated by Academia Sinica during fifteen expeditions between 1928 and 1936. A third series (pt. 1, Taipei, 1957), edited by Chang Ping-ch'üan, consisting of reconstructions from broken pieces, is being published.

G181. Umehara, Sueji. **Kanan anyo iho.** [Selected ancient treasures found at An-yang, Yin sites.] Kyoto, 1940. Collection of plates, with an introduction to the ancient relics of the Shang dynasty. The plates consist of objects preserved in foreign collections, and include oracle bones, weapons, tools, bronze vessels, moulds, pottery, marble, jade, and stone.

G182. White, William C. **Bronze culture of ancient China: an archaeological study of bronze objects from northern Honan, dating from about 1400 B.C.-771 B.C.** Toronto, 1956.

G183. ——. **Bone culture of ancient China.** Toronto, 1945.

G184. Wu, Tse. **Ku-tai shih: Yin-tai nu-li-chih she-hui shih.** [The history of antiquity: a history of the slave society of the Yin dynasty.] Shanghai, 1949. New ed., 1953. A leftist interpretation which assembles a mass of material without successfully demonstrating that the Shang period was dominantly a slave society. See review, H. S. Levy, *Jour. Asian studies,* 16 (Nov. 1956): 122.

Later Chou Period

G185. T'ung, Shu-i. **Ch'un-ch'iu shih.** [History of the spring and autumn period.] Shanghai, 1946. Covers the period 722–468 B.C

G186. Yang, K'uan. **Chan-kuo shih.** [History of the warring states.] Shanghai, 1955. General treatise on political, social, and economic history and institutions of the period (453–221 B.C.), with valuable chapters on industry, commerce, and land system, and detailed documentation.

G187. Walker, Richard L. **The multi-state system of ancient China.** Hamden, Conn., 1954. Relations between feudal states of the late Chou period.

G188. Soothill, William E. **The hall of light: a study of early Chinese kingship.** London, 1951. The ancient Chinese institution, the *ming-t'ang,* and the sacrificial rituals connected with it.

G189. Karlgren, Bernhard. "Legends and cults in ancient China." **Bulletin of the Museum of Far Eastern Antiquities,** 18 (1946): 199–365. Important study by a great Swedish Sinologist.

G190. Hsü, Chung-shu. "Ching-t'ien chih-tu t'an-yuan." [A study of the Ching-t'ien system.] **Chung-kuo wen-hua yen chiu hui-k'an.** [Bulletin of Chinese studies.] 4 (1944): 121–56. Valuable study of the ancient well-field system of agriculture.

G191. Read, Thomas T. "Chinese iron: a puzzle." **Harvard journal of Asiatic studies,** 2 (Dec. 1937): 398–407. Discusses the problem of when iron began to be used in China.

G192. White, William C. **Tombs of old Lo-yang.** Shanghai, 1934. Deals with materials, principally from the later Chou period, which generally were not scientifically excavated.

G193. ———. **Tomb tile pictures of ancient China.** Toronto, 1939.

G194. Umehara, Sueji. **Raku-yo kin-son kobo shuei.** [Selected relics from the ancient tombs of Chin-ts'un, Loyang, Honan.] Kyoto, 1937. Collection of plates with a study of the bronzes, lacquer, sculptures, mirrors, jewelry, jade, etc. dating from the late Chou period.

G195. Ch'ang-sha fa-chüeh pao-kao. [Report of the excavation in Ch'ang-sha.] Comp. by Institute of Archaeology, Academia Sinica. Peking, 1957. Field report on excavation of various sites at Ch'ang-sha in 1951, relating primarily to the Warring States and Han periods.

G196. Ch'ien, Mu. **Hsien-Ch'in chu-tzu hsi-nien.** [Chronological studies of the pre-Ch'in philosophers.] 2nd ed., 2 v., Hong Kong, 1957. Critical studies of the dates of various ancient Chinese philosophers.

G197. Creel, Herrlee G. **Confucius: the man and the myth.** N.Y., 1949; London, 1951. Thorough scholarship, but somewhat controversial in that it emphasizes Confucius as a precursor of democracy.

G198. ———. **Chinese thought: from Confucius to Mao Tse-tung.** Chicago, 1953; London, 1954. Larger part relates to the early period, and is the most readable and dependable short account of early Chinese thought available in a western language.

G199. Dubs, Homer H. **Hsüntze . . . the moulder of ancient Confucianism.** London, 1927. Deals with life and times of Hsün Tzu, the last of the great early Confucians.

G200. Forke, Alfred. **Geschichte der altern chinesischen Philosophie.** Hamburg, 1927. Standard German work on early Chinese thought.

G201. Fung [Feng], Yu-lan. **A history of Chinese philosophy.** V. 1. Tr. by Derk Bodde. 2nd ed., Princeton, 1952. Most thorough account of early Chinese thought available. This volume covers period to about 100 B.C. First appeared in Chinese under title *Chung-kuo che-hsüeh shih* (Shanghai, 1931).

G202. Hu, Shih. **Chung-kuo che-hsüeh shih ta-kang.** [An outline history of Chinese philosophy.] Shanghai, 1919. 15th ed., 1930. Somewhat older account than Fung's which differs considerably with him on various points of fact and interpretation. For a statement of some of its main ideas see Hu's Ph.D. dissertation at Columbia (1917), published under the title *The development of the logical method in ancient China* (Shanghai, 1922).

G203. Hughes, Ernest R., ed. and tr. **Chinese philosophy in classical times.** London and N.Y., 1942. Handy and generally sound account of early Chinese thought.

G204. Liang, Ch'i-ch'ao. **History of Chinese political thought during the early Tsin**

period. Tr. by L. T. Chen. London, 1930. Important early study, now somewhat antiquated so far as dating is concerned, which emphasizes the political aspects of early Chinese thought.

G205. Mei, Yi-pao. **Mo Tse . . . the neglected rival of Confucius.** London, 1934. The life and times of Mo Ti.

G206. Richards, Ivor A. **Mencius on the mind: experiments in multiple definitions.** London, 1932.

G207. Waley, Arthur. **Three ways of thought in ancient China.** London, 1939. An important work dealing with Chuang Tzu, Mencius, and the Legalists.

G208. ———. **The nine songs: a study of shamanism in ancient China.** N.Y., 1955. Translation and interpretation of nine songs from the *Elegies of Ch'u* (Ch'u tz'u) of about the 3rd century B.C.

JAPAN TO THE INTRODUCTION OF BUDDHISM (552 A.D.)

Bibliographies and Aids

G209. Beardsley, Richard K. "Japan before history: a survey of the archaeological record." **The far eastern quarterly,** 14 (May 1955): 317–46. Discussion of recent archaeological work in Japan which brings his more general bibliography (*G1*) up to date.

G210. Nakaya, Jiujirō. **Catalogue of works relating to the Stone Age in Japan (in foreign languages), 1868–1927.** Tokyo, n.d. Brief bibliography published by the Anthropological Institute of Tokyo Imperial University.

G211. Sieffert, René. "Études d'ethnographie japonaise." **Bulletin de la Maison Franco-Japonaise,** n.s. 2 (1952): 7–110. Selected bibliography of works in Japanese, well-chosen and with excellent descriptive annotations.

G212. Groot, Gerard. "Archaeological activities in Japan since August 15, 1945." **American anthropologist,** n.s. 50 (Jan.-Mar. 1948): 166–71.

G213. Batchelor, John. "Helps to the study of ancient place names in Japan." **Transactions of the Asiatic Society of Japan,** 2nd ser. 6 (1929): 52–102. Standard work by a pioneer student.

Ethnology and Language

G214. Matsumoto, Nobuhiro. **Le Japonais et les langues austroasiatiques: étude de vocabulaire comparé.** Paris, 1928. Contains useful summary of theories about Japanese affinities.

G215. Chamberlain, Basil H., and M. Ueda. "A vocabulary of the most ancient words of the Japanese language." **Transactions of the Asiatic Society of Japan,** 16 (1889): 225–85.

G216. Chamberlain, Basil H. "The language, mythology and geographical nomenclature of Japan viewed in the light of Aino studies." **Memoirs of the Literature College** (Tokyo Imperial University), 1 (1887): 1–75. Important monograph.

G217. Hasebe, Gonjin. **Nihon minzoku no seiritsu.** [The establishment of the Japanese people.] Tokyo, 1949.

G218. Kiyono, Kenji. **Kojinkotsu ni motozuku Nihonjin no jinshugaku teki Kenkyū.** [An ethnological study of the Japanese people based on ancient skeletal remains.] Tokyo, 1949. An account by the foremost advocate of the theory that the Japanese people evolved on the Japanese islands, such evolution being more important than influences from outside the islands.

G219. Matsumoto, H. "Notes on the Stone Age people of Japan." **American anthropologist,** n.s. 23 (Jan.-Mar. 1921): 50–76. Analysis of Stone Age skeletal remains.

G220. Nishioka, Hideo, and W. Egbert Schenck. "An outline of theories concerning the prehistoric people of Japan." **American anthropologist,** n.s. 39 (Jan.-Mar. 1937): 23–33.

G221. Origuchi, Shinobu. **Kodai kenkyū.** [Studies of antiquity.] 3 v. Tokyo, 1954. [Origuchi Nobuo zenshū, 31.] Studies of the mythological record from the ethnological point of view.

Sources and Translations

G222. Chamberlain, Basil H., tr. **Translation of "Ko-ji-ki"** . . . or **"Records of ancient matters."** 2nd ed., Kobe, 1932. Careful translation of a very important early historical text. First edition appeared in *Transactions of the Asiatic Society of Japan,* 10 (1882), supplement.

G223. Kinoshita, Iwao. **Koziki. Aelteste japanische Reichsgeschichte.** 2 v. Tokyo, 1940. V. 1 includes the original text and an index; v. 2, transliteration in Roman letters, and name and item glossary.

G224. Aston, William G., tr. **Nihongi: chronicles of Japan from the earliest times to A.D. 697.** 2 v. London, 1896. [Transactions and proceedings of the Japan Society, London, suppl. 1.] Careful translation with commentary of the first official history of Japan.

G225. Florenz, Karl. **Japanische Mythologie: Nihongi, "Zeitalter der Götter."** Tokyo, 1901. Contains annotated translation of first five chapters of this basic early historical text and sections of the *Kojiki, Kūjiki,* and *Fudoki.*

G226. ——. **Die historischen Quellen der Shinto-Religion aus dem Altjapanischen und Chinesischen.** Leipzig, 1919. Contains translations, with notes, of passages from the *Kojiki, Nihongi,* and *Kogoshūi.*

General Works

G227. Aston, William G. "Early Japanese history." **Transactions of the Asiatic Society of Japan,** 16 (1889): 39–75. Pioneer study on ancient chronology, now superseded by Gaspardone and by Groot.

G228. Bishop, Carl W. "The historical geography of early Japan." **Geographical review,** 13 (Jan. 1923): 40–63. Penetrating discussion of racial and cultural origins.

G229. Gaspardone, Emile. "La chronologie ancienne du Japon." **Journal asiatique,** 230 (Apr.-June 1938): 235–77. Critical study of the complex problem of early Japanese chronology.

G230. Groot, Gerard. "An essay on early Japanese history." **Transactions of the Asiatic Society of Japan,** 3rd ser. 1 (1948): 24–46. Deals with problem of chronology.

G231. Kobayashi, Yukio. **Nihon kōkogaku gaisetsu.** [Introduction to the archaeology of Japan.] Tokyo, 1951. Probably most convenient survey of the work of Japanese archaeologists. Presents detailed descriptions of the life of the Jōmon, Yayoi, and tomb periods. The author, a leading disciple of Hamada Kosaku, is cited as an example of the Hamada school.

G232. Shiratori, Kurakichi. **Shindai shi no shinkenkyū.** [New studies of the history of the Mythological Age.] Tokyo, 1954. Critical interpretations of the myths contained in the *Kojiki* and *Nihonshoki.* A collection of pioneering articles originally published before World War II.

G233. Tsuda, Sōkichi. **Nihon koten no kenkyū.** [Studies of ancient Japanese classics.] 2 v. Tokyo, 1948–50. Contains the majority of Tsuda's now famous critical studies of such works as the *Kojiki* and *Nihonshoki.*

G234. Umehara, Sueji. **Nihon kōkogaku ronkō.** [Essays on Japanese archaeology.] Tokyo, 1940. Collected articles by the leading figure in the Kyoto school. Especially good on bronze relics of the tomb period.

Neolithic Period

G235. Groot, Gerard J. **The prehistory of Japan.** Ed. by Bertram S. Kraus. N.Y., 1951. Best survey in a western language, by a scholar and practical fieldworker. Contains valuable bibliography of Japanese and western works.

G236. Haguenauer, Charles. **Origines de la civilisation japonaise: introduction à l'étude de préhistoire du Japon.** Paris, 1956. Devotes much attention to linguistic evidence. Additional volumes planned.

G237. ——. "Notions d'archéologie japonaise." **Bulletin Maison Franco-Japonaise,** 3 (1931): 1–74. Earlier survey of the neolithic period.

G238. Hitchcock, Romyn. "The ancient pit dwellers of Yezo, Japan." **Annual report of the Board of Regents of the Smithsonian Institution for the year ending June 30, 1890,** pp. 417–27.

G239. ———. "The Ainos of Yezo, Japan." **Annual report of the Board of Regents of the Smithsonian Institution for the year ending June 30, 1890,** pp. 429–500.

G240. Kidder, J. Edward, Jr. **The Jomon pottery of Japan.** Ascona, Switz., 1957. Latest and most complete study in a western language of the oldest neolithic pottery of Japan. Well illustrated. See also his *Japan before Buddhism* (London and New York, 1959).

G241. Morse, Edward S. **Shell mounts of Ōmori.** Tokyo, 1879. Account of the first excavation of a Japanese prehistoric site.

G242. Munro, Neil G. **Prehistoric Japan.** Yokohama, 1908. Now outdated, but still the most comprehensive study.

G243. Nakaya, Jiujirō. "Contribution à l'étude de la civilisation néolithique du Japon, touchant particulièrement les domaines de distribution et de civilisation." **Revue des arts asiatiques,** 6 (1929–30): 151–67.

G244. ———. "L'influence des civilisations continentales sur l'Âge de Pierre au Japon." **Revue des arts asiatiques,** 7 (1931–33): 141–55.

G245. ———. "Figurines néolithiques au Japon." **Documents: archéologie, beaux-arts, ethnographie, variétés,** 2 (1930): 25–32.

G246. Ohyama, Kashiwa. "Korekawa-Funde von Korekawa, eine characteristischen steinzeitlichen Station von Kame-ga-oka Typus der Nord-Ost Jōmon-Kultur." **Shizengaku Zasshi,** 2 (1930): E 11–41. Scholarly presentation with a general introduction on divisions of the Jōmon culture.

G247. ———. "Yayoi-Kultur: eine prähistorische Kultur der japanischen Inseln." Deutsche Gesellschaft für Natur- und Völkerkunde Ostasiens, **Jubiläums band,** v. 1 (Tokyo, 1933), pp. 127–34.

G248. Sansom, G. B. "An outline of recent Japanese archaeological research in Korea in its bearing on early Japanese history." **Transactions of the Asiatic Society of Japan,** 2nd ser. 6 (1929): 5–19. Short but important summary of Japanese theories.

G249. Schnell, Ivar. "Prehistoric finds from the island world of the Far East." **Bulletin of the Museum of far eastern antiquities,** 4 (1932): 15–104. Valuable as a summary, but not sufficiently based on contemporary Japanese studies.

G250. Sternberg, Leo. "The Ainu problem." **Anthropos,** 24 (Sep.-Dec. 1929): 755–99. A thought-provoking article on the possible relations of the Ainu with southern Pacific peoples, by a Russian political exile long resident among the Ainu.

G251. Torii, R. "Études archéologiques et ethnologiques: les Ainou des Iles Kouriles." Imperial University of Tokyo, **Journal of the College of Science,** 42 (1919): 1–337. Principal study of the Ainu of the Kuriles, by a distinguished pioneer Japanese anthropologist.

G252. Yawata, Ichirō. **Nihonshi no reimei.** [The dawn of Japanese history.] Tokyo, 1953. Careful study of the Jōmon and Yayoi cultures, the relationship between them, and the nature of continental influence.

Dawn of History: The Dolmen Age

G253. Conrady, A. "Zu der Frage nach Alter und Herkunft der sog. Japanischen Dolmen." **Ostasiatische Zeitschrift,** 4 (Jan.-Mar. 1916): 229–47.

G254. Daifuku, Hiroshi: "The early cultures of the island of Kyushu, Japan." **Southwestern journal of anthropology,** 5 (autumn 1949): 253–71.

G255. Gotō, Morikazu. **Nihon kodai bunka kenkyū.** [Studies of ancient Japanese culture.] Tokyo, 1937. Articles on the tomb culture of Japan from the point of view of the Tokyo school.

G256. Gowland, W. "The burial mounds and dolmens of the early emperors of Japan." **Journal of Royal Anthropological Institute of Great Britain and Ireland,** 37 (Jan.-June 1907): 10–46.

G257. ———. "The dolmens and burial mounds in Japan." **Archaeologie,** 5 (1897): 439–524.

G258. Hashimoto, Masukichi. **Tōyōshi jō yori mitaru Nihon jōkoshi kenkyū.** [Ancient Japan studied in the light of far eastern history.] Tokyo, 1956. Critical study of Chinese documents relating to ancient Japan. One of the best treatments of the "Yamadai problem."

G259. Morimoto, Rokuji. "L'Âge du Bronze au Japon et l'expansion de la civilisation des Han vers l'est." **Revue des arts asiatiques,** 8 (1934): 65–76.

G260. Saitō, Tadashi. **Nihon kōko gaku zukan.** [Japanese archaeological illustrations.] Tokyo, 1955.

G261. Suematsu, Yasukazu. "Japan's relations with the Asian continent and the Korean peninsula (before 950 A.D.)." **Journal of world history,** 4 (1958): 671–87. Valuable account representing the most recent scholarship on the subject.

G262. Takahashi, Kenji. "Bronze culture of ancient Japan." **Proceedings of 3rd Pan-Pacific Science Congress (Tokyo),** 2 (1926): 2499–2513.

G263. Wedemeyer, André. **Japanische Frühgeschichte: Untersuchungen zur Chronologie und territorial Verfassung von Altjapan bis zum 5. Jahrh. N. Chr.** Tokyo, 1930.

Institutions, Religion, and Mythology

G264. Anesaki, Masaharu. "Japanese mythology." **The mythology of all races, v. 8** (Boston, 1928), pp. 207 ff. Relates the traditional myths and legends of ancient Japan and contains a useful bibliography.

G265. Florenz, Karl A. "Die stattliche und gesellschaftliche Organization in alten Japan." **Mitteilungen der deutschen Gesellschaft für Natur- und Völkerkunde Ostasiens** (Tokyo), 5 (1890): 164–82. Good account of the clan (*uji*) period prior to 645.

G266. Inoue, Mitsusada. **Nihon kodaishi no shomondai.** [Problems of ancient Japanese history.] Tokyo, 1949. Studies of social and political life of the Japanese prior to 645 A.D.

G267. Katō, Genchi. **A study of Shintō, the religion of the Japanese nation.** Tokyo, 1926. Important work on early Shinto, but reflects the traditional point of view.

G268. Martin, Jean M. **Le Shintoïsme, religion nationale.** 2 v. Hong Kong, 1924–27. Detailed study of ancient and primitive Shinto, marred by author's own personal religious bias.

G269. Matsumoto, Nobuhiro. **Essai sur la mythologie japonaise.** Paris, 1928.

G270. Matsumura, Takeo. **Nihon shinwa no kenkyū.** [Studies of Japanese mythology.] 3 v. Tokyo, 1954–55. From the comparative mythological approach.

G271. Ōta, Akira. **Nihon jōdai shakai soshiki no kenkyū.** [A study of the social organization of ancient Japan.] Rev. ed., Tokyo, 1955. Detailed exposition of the *uji* (clan) and *be* (corporation) systems of social organization.

G272. Satow, Ernest M. "Ancient Japanese rituals." **Transactions of the Asiatic Society of Japan,** 7 (Mar. 1879): 95–126, 393–434; 9 (Aug. 1881): 183–211.

G273. Tōma, Seita. **Nihon kodai kokka.** [The ancient Japanese state.] Tokyo, 1946. Marxist treatment, emphasizing the communal aspects of life in ancient Japan and origins of the "emperor system."

G274. Wakamori, Tarō. **Nihon kodai shaki.** [The ancient society of Japan.] Tokyo, 1949. Written from an anthropological point of view; emphasizes the family system of organization.

SECTION H

Ancient Greece and the Hellenistic World

CARL A. ROEBUCK *

Selections listed here reflect the considerable amount of recent scholarship in the earlier periods of Greek history and in Greek colonial areas. Publications which are more strictly institutional or more interpretative than cultural have received greater attention because bibliographical guidance to the latter type is so readily available in standard history textbooks. Certain works which are useful for both Greek and Roman history, such as bibliographies, encyclopedias and works of reference, geographies, gazetteers and atlases, and the great series of literary sources are included in this section.

BIBLIOGRAPHIES

H1. Marouzeau, Jules, and Juliette Ernst, eds. **L'année philologique: bibliographie critique et analytique de l'antiquité greco-latine.** Paris, 1927 ff. (Annual.) The standard bibliography for classical studies, with sections for Greek and Roman history and institutions. Entries include both publication data and brief notices of subject matter. Comprehensive and detailed; primarily for specialist use.

H2. "Geschichte." **Bibliotheca philologica classica.** Leipzig, 1873–1943. [Bursians Jahresbericht über die Fortsschritte der klassischen Altertumswissenschaft.] (Annual.) Until 1943 the standard bibliography for classical studies, with sections for Greek and Roman history. Listed both current items and, at intervals, had state-of-the-subject syntheses. Now replaced by Marouzeau.

H3. The year's work in classical studies. Bristol, Eng., 1906–47. [English Classical Association.] (Annual.) Contains current items for Greek and Roman history with

brief critical comment. Useful for the nonspecialist.

H4. Broughton, T. Robert S. "Other recent publications—Ancient history." **The American historical review.** (Quarterly.) Current listing of books and articles on ancient history, mainly Greek and Roman.

H5. Nairn, John A. **Classical hand-list.** 3rd rev. ed., Oxford, 1953. Useful manual containing bibliographical lists for the fields and disciplines of classical studies in general. One section is assigned to history and civilization.

Epigraphy

H6. Tod, Marcus N. "Epigraphy, Greek." **Oxford classical dictionary.** Very good short bibliography.

H7. ——. "The progress of Greek epigraphy." **Journal of Hellenic studies,** 34 ff. (1914 ff.). Biennial survey containing useful comment on the current publication of inscriptions and on works making use of epigraphical evidence.

* The following contributed items and comments indicated by their respective initials: Charles S. Braden (CSB) and Naphtali Lewis (NL).

120

Papyrology

Bibliographies of papyrological publications appear in **(H8) Journal of Egyptian archaeology; (H9) Revue des études grecques; (H10) Journal of juristic papyrology;** and **(H11) Chronique d'Égypte.** In addition, a bibliography on file cards is issued to subscribers several times per year by the Fondation Égyptologique Reine Elisabeth, Brussels. [NL]

ENCYCLOPEDIAS AND WORKS OF REFERENCE

H12. Paulys Realencyclopädie der classischen Altertumswissenschaft. Rev. ed., ed. by Georg Wissowa, Wilhelm Kroll, and others. 1st ser. (A-P), 23 v.; 2nd ser. (R-Z), 8 v.; suppl., 8 v. Stuttgart, 1894 ff. (In progress.) The standard long encyclopedia for classical studies in general. Articles are authoritative, with ample bibliography, and the work is indispensable for reference use. Completion is planned with about four more volumes in several years. Supplement volumes have enabled it to keep generally up-to-date and amplify its topics.

H13. Daremberg, Charles V., and Edmond Saglio, eds. **Dictionnaire des antiquités grecques et romaines.** 5 v. in 9. Paris, 1877–1919. Old, but still useful for political and social institutions. Has ample references to source material.

H14. The Oxford classical dictionary. Ed. by Max Cary, Alfred Nock, and others. Oxford, 1949. A useful and sound dictionary for general classical reference. See the review by A. S. Pease and S. Dow, *Classical weekly,* 44 (Apr. 9, 1951): 225, for correction, criticism, and supplementary reference.

H15. Lübker, Friedrich H., ed. **Reallexikon des klassischen Altertums.** 8th rev. ed. by J. Geffcken, E. Ziebarth, and others, Leipzig, 1914. Medium-length encyclopedia, but with considerable citation of books and articles.

H16. Smith, Sir William. **Classical dictionary of biography, mythology, and geography.** 4th rev. ed. by George E. Marindin, London, 1894. 24th impression, 1932. Medium-length encyclopedia.

H17. ——. **Dictionary of Greek and Roman antiquities.** 3rd rev. ed. by S. W. Wayte and G. E. Marindin, 2 v., London, 1890–91. Reprint, 1914. Some articles still of value.

H18. Handbuch der Altertumswissenschaft. Ed. by Iwan von Müller, Robert von Pöhlmann, and Walter Otto. Rev. ed., approx. 90 v. published, in preparation, and planned, Munich, 1920 ff. Handbooks to the various disciplines and areas for the study of antiquity. It is planned in 12 parts with numerous volumes in each: introductory and ancillary disciplines; Greek and Latin grammar; history of the ancient Near East, Greece, and Rome; Greek and Roman public and private life; philosophy, science, and religion; archaeology of the Near East, Greece, and Rome; Greek literature; Latin literature; ancient and classical tradition in the medieval period; Byzantine history and literature; two further medieval areas. Volumes of use for Greek and Roman history are noted individually in this and Section I of this *Guide.*

H19. Bengtson, Hermann. **Einführung in die alte Geschichte.** See *13.* Excellent manual to introduce the student to the serious study of Greek and Roman history.

H20. Gercke, Alfred, and Eduard Norden, eds. **Einleitung in die Altertumswissenschaft.** 3rd rev. ed., 3 v., Leipzig, 1927–35. Informative introductions by various scholars to the separate fields of classical antiquity and scholarship.

H21. Whibley, Leonard, ed. **A companion to Greek studies.** 4th ed., Cambridge, Eng., 1931. Useful reference book for general information on Greek antiquity.

GEOGRAPHIES, GAZETTEERS, AND ATLASES

H22. Cary, Max. **The geographic background of Greek and Roman history.** Oxford, 1949. Succinctly and pointedly written survey of the geography of the classical world, both Mediterranean and outlying regions. It admirably correlates physical environment and historical development, not only general factors as climate and food supply, but also specific topographical features.

H23. Semple, Ellen C. **The geography of the Mediterranean region: its relation to ancient history.** N.Y., 1931. Descriptive treatment of the general geographic conditions of the Mediterranean, barrier-boundaries, vegetation, and the like. Vividly written with keen observation of the topographical features and ample reference to classical sources.

H24. Philippson, Alfred. **Das Klima Griechenlands.** Bonn, 1948. Technical treatment of Greek climate (no real changes from antiquity), with references to antiquity.

H25. Myres, Sir John L. **Geographical history in Greek lands.** Oxford, 1953. A collection of the author's lectures and articles published in various journals. All concern the relation of Greek history to its physical environment, but some deal with specific areas rather than general topics.

H26. Thomson, James O. **History of ancient geography.** Cambridge, Eng., 1948. Complete treatment of the history of ancient geography, with sections on actual knowledge and theory for each major period. Also an interesting section on the influence of classical geographical theory.

H27. Cary, Max, and Eric H. Warmington. **The ancient explorers.** N.Y., 1929. Studies of the voyages of exploration in the outlying areas of the ancient world.

H28. Meritt, Benjamin D., Henry T. Wade-Gery, and Malcolm F. McGregor. "The gazetteer." **The Athenian tribute lists,** v. 1 (Cambridge, Mass., 1939), pp. 461–566. See *H179*.

H29. Bengtson, Hermann, and Vladimir Milojčič. **Grosser historischer Weltatlas.** V. 1, **Vorgeschichte und Altertum.** 2nd ed., Munich, 1954. Up-to-date and useful atlas for general reference, with 100 maps. Covers ancient history up to the 5th century A.D. Accompanied by an explanatory text.

H30. Kiepert, Heinrich. **Atlas antiquus.** 12th rev. ed., Berlin, 1902. Twelve maps and index of names.

H31. Philippson, Alfred. "Topographische Karte des westlichen Kleinasien, 1/300,000." **Petermanns Mitteilungen Ergänzungsheft,** nos. 167 (1910–11), 177, 180 (1913–14), and 183 (1914–15). The most useful and easily accessible maps for detailed reference to western Asia Minor. Chief defect is the old-fashioned spelling of Turkish place-names, now officially modernized.

ANTHROPOLOGICAL WORKS

H32. Angel, J. Lawrence. "Skeletal material from Attica." **Hesperia,** 14 (1945): 279–363. Mainly technical, but with a useful introduction on physical anthropology and Greek material.

H33. Thomson, George D. **Studies in ancient Greek society.** V. 1, **The prehistoric Aegean.** London, 1949. Important for its approach and new viewpoints, but weak in archaeological data and somewhat cavalier in interpretation of Homeric evidence. The author analyzes early Greek society in terms of social anthropology with lengthy discussions of totemism, kinship, matriarchy, etc.

H34. ——. **Studies in ancient Greek society.** V. 2, **The first Greek philosophers.** London, 1955. Analysis of Greek society in the archaic period to elucidate the historical reasons for the movement from religion to philosophy. Explanation is found in the changing social structure on Marxist principles, but the theory finds a somewhat Procrustean bed in the evidence.

H35. Willetts, R. F. **Aristocratic society in ancient Crete.** London, 1955. Discusses social institutions in Dorian Crete.

H36. Jeanmaire, Henri. **Couroi et courètes: essai sur l'éducation spartiate et sur les rites d'adolescence dans l'antiquité hellénique.** Lille, 1939. A voluminous study based on the thesis of a primitive system of age classes

in Greek society, perceptible in vestigial survivals in the historical period. The warrior class is particularly treated and analogies drawn with African social systems.

H37. Rose, Herbert J. **Primitive culture in Greece.** London, 1925. Examines in nontechnical fashion the survivals and vestiges of primitive institutions in classical Greece. Concludes that most were simply vestiges, with no great significance for their own period.

H38. Halliday, William R. **Indo-European folk tales and Greek legend.** Cambridge, Eng., 1933. Useful group of studies in Greek myth and legend, valuable for the method of treatment as well as relating certain Greek material specifically to Indo-European folk stories.

DEMOGRAPHIC STUDIES

H39. Myres, Sir John L. **Who were the Greeks?** Berkeley, 1930. [Sather classical lectures, University of California, 6.] A voluminous study of the evidence of ethnology, language, religion, and tradition bearing on the origin of the Greeks. The archaeological material is somewhat out of date, but particularly valuable are the discussions of folk memory and the influence of geographical factors.

H40. Jardé, Auguste F. **The formation of the Greek people.** London, 1926. General study on the growth of the Greeks as a people with discussion of the prehistoric migrations, dialects, and the like; also a treatment of unity and particularism in historical Greece.

H41. Beloch, Karl J. **Die Bevölkerung der griechisch-römischen Welt.** Leipzig, 1886. Still the standard comprehensive treatment of this difficult subject for the Greek and Roman world, although revisions have been made for various areas and fields. In general, Beloch's figures for Greece are probably rather low, particularly for the archaic period of its history.

H42. Gomme, Arnold W. "Population." **Oxford classical dictionary,** pp. 717–18. Oxford, 1949. A succinct and useful discussion of the type of evidence for the difficult subject of population in ancient Greece, with estimates for some of the states.

H43. ——. **The population of Athens in the fifth and fourth centuries B.C.** Oxford, 1933. Thorough and cautious treatment of the evidence on population for Athens about which we are best informed. Gomme suggests approximately 175,000 citizens and 110,000 slaves in 431 B.C. The latter estimate is particularly sensible in contrast to the extravagant figures sometimes suggested. Discussed, *Revue des études anciennes,* 38 (Jan.-Mar. 1936): 61.

H44. Segré, Arturo. "Note sull' economia

di Atene nel IV secolo av. Cr." **Studi italiani di filologia classica,** 22 (1947): 133–163. Calculation of Athenian population from the amount of grain consumption.

H45. Sargent, Rachel L. **The size of the slave population at Athens during the fifth and fourth centuries before Christ.** Urbana, 1924. A sound and useful attempt to estimate the slave population in classical Athens: less than 100,000 in the 5th century and under two-thirds that in the 4th. See also Arnold W. Gomme, "The slave population of Athens," *Journal of Hellenic studies,* 66 (1946): 127–29.

LINGUISTIC WORKS

H46. Atkinson, Basil F. C. **The Greek language.** London, 1931. A non-technical, descriptive, and historical account of the ancient Greek language, written before the decipherment of Mycenaean Greek (1953).

H47. Ventris, Michael, and John Chadwick. **Documents in Mycenaean Greek.** Cambridge, Eng., 1956. In 1953 Ventris and Chadwick published an article describing the process of decipherment and included some translations of Mycenaean Greek in the Linear B script, thus pushing back the documentary horizon of Greek history 500 years to about 1200 B.C. This book gives a description of the language, an estimate of the historical information obtained, and publishes translations of 300 tablets and vocabulary. Indispensable for this new field of study in Greek history.

H48. Dow, Sterling. "Minoan writing." **American journal of archaeology,** 58 (Apr.-June 1954): 77–157. Valuable article for the problem of literacy in Late Bronze Age Greece and its cessation with the dissolution of Mycenaean civilization. Contains useful bibliography for this new field of study in Greek history.

PRINTED COLLECTIONS OF SOURCES

Literary

The chief series of texts in which the classical authors are published are: the Teubner series (*Bibliotheca scriptorum graecorum et romanorum Teubneriana*); the *Oxford classical texts* (*Scriptorum classicorum bibliotheca Oxoniensis*); the Budé series with French translation, introductions, and commentary (*Collection des universités de France, publiée sous le patronage de l'Association Guillaume Budé*); the Loeb series with English translation, introductions, and commentary (*The Loeb classical library*). Listed below are plain texts of historical writers from these series, historical commentaries useful for their interpretation, and translations. Primary sources for the study of individual periods of Greek history are conveniently collected in the bibliographies to the separate chapters of the *Cambridge ancient history* (*H118*).

H49. Herodotus. **Herodoti historiae.** Ed. by Karl Hude. 3rd ed., 2 v., Oxford, 1927. [Oxford classical texts.] Greek text of Herodotus.

H50. ———. **Herodotus.** Ed. by Heinrich Stein. 6th ed., 5 v., Berlin, 1901. Greek text with useful commentary for language and interpretation of the text.

H51. How, Walter W., and Joseph Wells. **A commentary on Herodotus.** 2 v. Oxford, 1936. Historical and geographical commentary.

H52. Herodotus. **History.** Tr. by George Rawlinson. 4th ed., 4 v., London, 1880.

H53. ———. **History.** Tr. by George C. Macaulay. 2 v. London, 1890. Reprint, 1914.

H54. Thucydides. **Thucydidis historiae.** Ed. by Henry S. Jones and Johannes E. Powell. 2nd ed., 2 v., Oxford, 1942. [Oxford classical texts.] Greek text of Thucydides.

H55. Gomme, Arnold W. **An historical commentary on Thucydides.** 4 v. Oxford, 1944. Excellent and thorough linguistic, historical, and interpretative commentary. See also Bernard W. Henderson, *The great war between Athens and Sparta* (London, 1927).

H56. Thucydides. **History.** Tr. by Benjamin Jowett. 2nd ed., Oxford, 1900.

H57. ———. **History.** Tr. by Richard Crawley. N.Y., 1950. [Everyman's library.]

H58. Xenophon. **Xenophontis historia graeca.** Ed. by Edgar C. Marchant. Oxford, 1901. [Oxford classical texts.] Greek text of Xenophon.

H59. ———. **Works.** Tr. by Henry G. Dakyns. 3 v. in 4. N.Y., 1890–97.

H60. Hellenica Oxyrhynchia cum Theopompi et Cratippi fragmentis. Ed. by Bernard P. Grenfell and Arthur S. Hunt. Oxford, 1909. [Oxford classical texts.] Greek text of the Oxyrhynchus historian. This papyrus fragment of unknown authorship reveals a sound historian whose fragments are valuable for the year 396-5 B.C. The question of authorship has long been debated, but is still unresolved. (See *H109.*)

H61. Demosthenes. **Demosthenis orationes.** Ed. by Samuel H. Butcher and W. Rennie. 2nd ed., 3 v., Oxford, 1903–31. [Oxford classical texts.] Greek text of Demosthenes.

H62. ———. **Public orations.** Tr. by James H. and Charles A. Vince. 3 v. London, 1926–35. [Loeb classical library.]

H63. Aristotle. **Aristoteles politica.** Ed. by Otto Immisch. 2nd ed., Leipzig, 1929. [Bibliotheca Teubneriana.] Greek text of Aristotle's *Politics*.

H64. ———. **The politics of Aristotle.** Tr. by Sir Ernest Barker. Oxford, 1946. Barker's introduction, appendices, and notes are very helpful in interpretation of the *Politics*. A good translation.

H65. ——. **De republica atheniensium.** Ed. by Frederick G. Kenyon. Oxford, 1920. [Oxford classical texts.] Greek text of Aristotle's *Constitution of Athens*.

H66. Polybius. **Polybius.** Ed. by. Theodor Buttner-Wöbst. 6 v. Leipzig, 1882–1904. [Bibliotheca Teubneriana.] The best complete Greek text of Polybius' *History*.

H67. Walbank, Frank W. **A historical commentary on Polybius.** V. 1. Oxford, 1957. First volume of a new, thorough commentary of Polybius.

H68. Polybius. **History.** Tr. by Evelyn S. Shuckburgh. 2 v. London, 1889.

H69. Godolphin, Francis R. B., ed. **The Greek historians.** N.Y., 1942. Translations of the major Greek historians.

H70. Plutarch. **Vitae.** Ed. by H. Lindskog and K. Ziegler. 4 v. in 8. Leipzig, 1914–35. [Bibliotheca Teubneriana.] Greek text of Plutarch's *Lives*.

H71. ——. **Lives.** Tr. by Bernadotte Perrin. 11 v. London, 1914–26. [Loeb classical library.]

H72. ——. **Lives.** Tr. by John Dryden. Rev. ed. by Arthur H. Clough, 3 v., N.Y., 1912–14.

H73. Jacoby, Felix, ed. **Die Fragmente der griechischen Historiker.** 3 v. in 7. Berlin, 1923–58. The standard collection of fragments of the Greek historians, with commentary. For those authors not yet included see *Fragmenta historicorum graecorum*, ed. by C. and T. Müller (5 v., Paris, 1841–70).

H74. Botsford, George W., and Ernest G. Sihler. **Hellenic civilization.** N.Y., 1915. Collection of source material in translation for teaching purposes; excellent selection.

Epigraphical

H75. Larfeld, Wilhelm. **Griechische Epigraphik.** 3rd ed., Munich, 1913. [Handbuch der Altertumswissenschaft, v. 1, pt. 5.] A handbook for the study of Greek epigraphy.

H76. Meritt, Benjamin D. **Epigraphica attica.** Cambridge, Mass., 1940. [Martin classical lectures (Oberlin College), 9.] Collection of four lectures on reading, reconstruction, lettering, and restoration of epigraphical texts; an introduction to the techniques of epigraphy.

H77. Inscriptiones graecae. Berlin, 1877 ff. The *corpus* of the Greek inscriptions of Europe. Material is arranged by geographical locality; texts of the documents and brief bibliography are given. With 14 v. to date, the publication is not yet complete (see *H6*), but inscriptions for Attica, Argolis, and Thessaly have been published in a second edition.

H78. Dittenberger, Wilhelm. **Sylloge inscriptionum graecorum.** 3rd ed., 4 v., Leipzig, 1915–24. Very useful selection of Greek inscriptions of historical significance, published with brief commentary and bibliography.

H79. Tod, Marcus N. **A selection of Greek historical inscriptions.** 2 v. Oxford, 1933–48. Good selection of significant inscriptions of the 6th, 5th, and 4th centuries B.C., published with adequate commentary.

H80. Hill, Sir George F. **Sources for Greek history.** 2nd ed., rev. by R. Meiggs and A. Andrews, Oxford, 1951. Collection of primary source material, literary and epigraphical, for the 5th century B.C.

H81. Welles, Charles Bradford. **Royal correspondence in the Hellenistic period: a study in Greek epigraphy.** New Haven, 1934. Comprehensive selection of the rescripts issued by the Hellenistic monarchs, with generous commentary.

H82. Supplementum epigraphicum graecum. Ed. by Jacobus J. Hondius. Leiden, 1923 ff. New documents and discussions. Inscriptions are published also in *H406* and *412*.

Papyrological

H83. Mitteis, Ludwig, and Ulrich Wilcken, eds. **Grundzüge und Chrestomathie der Papyruskunde.** 2 v. in 4. Leipzig and Berlin, 1912. This and *H84–87* discuss the discipline and technique of papyrology. [NL]

H84. Schubart, Wilhelm. **Einführung in die Papyruskunde.** Berlin, 1918.

H85. ——. **Griechische Palaeographie.** Munich, 1925. [Handbuch der Altertumswissenschaft, 1.]

H86. Hunt, Arthur S. "Papyrology." *Encyclopaedia britannica.* 14th ed., London, 1929. Also subsequent editions.

H87. Kenyon, Sir Frederic G. **Books and readers in ancient Greece and Rome.** 2nd ed., N.Y., 1951.

H88. David, Martin, and Bernhard van Groningen. **Papyrological primer.** 3rd ed., Leiden, 1952. This and *H89–90* contain selections of papyri. [NL]

H89. Hunt, Arthur S., and Campbell C. Edgar. **Select papyri.** 2 v. London, 1932–34. [Loeb classical library.] V. 1, private documents; v. 2, official documents.

H90. Page, D. L. **Greek literary papyri.** 2 v. London, 1942. [Loeb classical library.]

HISTORIOGRAPHY

H91. Bury, John B. **The ancient Greek historians.** N.Y., 1909. Separate studies of the historiography of the principal Greek historical writers.

H92. Stier, Hans E. **Grundlagen und Sinn der griechischen Geschichte.** Stuttgart, 1945. Attempt to formulate a new interpretation of Greek history, which is long, verbose, and sometimes unintelligible in its thought and language. Much of the comment, however, is provocative and stimulating. The author gives no consideration to social and economic conditions, and ultimately explains the meaning of Greek history as a mystique —a clash between a European idea of freedom and an Aryan idea of order.

H93. Momigliano, Arnaldo. **Contributo alla storia degli studi classici.** Rome, 1955. Collection of separate studies and reviews printed in various journals, dealing mainly with historiography. The author's inaugural address on George Grote at the University of London (pp. 213–31) is particularly significant.

H94. Sanctis, Gaetano de. **Studi di storia della storiografia greca.** Florence, 1951. [Il pensiero storico, 34.] Collection of the author's journal articles on historiographical problems connected with Hecataeus, Herodotus, Thucydides, and Xenophon, thus giving a short exposition of the Greek historians of the classical period. A useful bibliography of de Sanctis' work is added.

H95. Cary, Max. **The documentary sources of Greek history.** Oxford, 1927. Informally written and stimulating survey of the value of non-literary sources for Greek history— inscriptions, papyri, coins, and archaeological material.

H96. Milne, Joseph G. **Greek and Roman coins and the study of history.** London, 1939. A brief and useful little book which illustrates the value of numismatic evidence for Greek and Roman historical studies.

H97. Tod, Marcus N. **Sidelights on Greek history.** Oxford, 1932. Collection of three general studies: the use of epigraphical evidence, arbitration processes between Greek states, and political clubs in Greek cities.

H98. Pearson, Lionel. **Early Ionian historians.** Oxford, 1939. Brief account of the early Ionian logographers and individual treatments of Hecataeus, Xanthus, Charon of Lampsacus, and Hellanicus of Lesbos. Reconstructions of their work are attempted and important fragments discussed, but no general estimate of their historiographical significance offered.

H99. Pohlenz, Max. **Herodot, der erste Geschichtschreiber des Abendlandes.** Leipzig, 1937. Good general study of Herodotus and his claim to be the father of history, with a defense of his techniques and the unity of his work.

H100. Powell, J. Enoch. **The history of Herodotus.** Cambridge, Eng., 1939. [Cambridge classical studies, 4.] The composition of Herodotus' history from a detailed study of cross-references and the weak points in the general argument. Its bases for analysis are not fully established.

H101. Myres, Sir John L. **Herodotus, father of history.** Oxford, 1953. Primarily concerned with the problem of the composition of Herodotus' history—the first organization and coordination of facts. Myres compares the arrangement to the principle of composition used in the pediment of a Greek temple rather than to the artless narrative of his predecessors.

H102. Glover, Terrot R. **Herodotus.** Berkeley, 1924. [Sather classical lectures (University of California), 3.] A genially written and somewhat Herodotean study of the historian and various aspects of his history.

H103. Finley, John H., Jr. **Thucydides.** Cambridge, Mass., 1942. Good general account of Thucydides' *History,* with emphasis on the intellectual and stylistic influences which affected the conception and expression of his work.

H104. Romilly, Jacqueline de. **Thucydide et l'impérialisme athénien: la pensée de l'historien et la genèse de l'oeuvre.** Paris, 1951. Analysis of the thought of Thucydides and the unity of his *History,* using his conception of imperialism as a key. Subtly reasoned and organized, demanding a close knowledge of the history for use.

H105. Romilly, Jacqueline de. **Histoire et raison chez Thucydide.** Paris, 1956. Study of the thought and historiography of Thucydides in relation to its formal expression.

H106. Cochrane, Charles N. **Thucydides and the science of history.** Oxford, 1929. Examines the influence of Hippocratic medical science on Thucydides' thought.

H107. Grundy, George B. **Thucydides and the history of his age.** 2nd ed., 2 v., Oxford, 1948. Valuable chiefly for the historical background of Thucydides' work, rather than as an interpretation of Thucydides. V. 1 contains useful surveys of the economic background of 5th century Greece, the art of war, and a lengthy survey of the problems of composition of the history. V. 2 is a collection of separate essays on Thucydidean topics.

H108. Jacoby, Felix. **Atthis.** Oxford, 1949. Authoritative but very specialized treatment of the tradition of Athenian history as represented in the school of writers known as the Atthidographers.

H109. Bloch, Herbert. "Studies in historical literature of the fourth century B.C." **Harvard studies in classical philology,** sup. v. 1, pp 303–76. Cambridge, Mass., 1940. Excellent but specialized treatment of the problem of authorship of the *Hellenica* of Oxyrhynchus, the *Attic history* of Androtion, and the relationship between Theophrastus' *Laws* and Aristotle.

H110. Barber, Godfrey L. **The historian Ephorus.** Cambridge, Eng., 1934. A necessarily technical book reconstructing Ephorus' work and estimating the rhetorical influence of Isocrates on his style and historiography.

SHORTER GENERAL HISTORIES

H111. Bengtson, Hermann. **Griechische Geschichte von den Anfängen bis in die römische Kaiserzeit.** Munich, 1950. [Handbuch der Altertumswissenschaft, v. 3, pt. 4.] Excellent and up-to-date history of Greece, with adequate citation of bibliography and notice of points of controversy. Unorthodox in beginning the Hellenistic period in 360 with the accession of Philip II.

H112. Bury, John B. **History of Greece to the death of Alexander.** 3rd ed., rev. by R. Meiggs, London, 1951. A standard history of Greece to the time of Alexander, brought up-to-date by its careful revision. Has adequate detail and good emphasis (possibly too full on military campaigns) for the historical narrative. The notes have been almost completely rewritten, and contain careful comment and citation of sources and bibliography. A good introduction for the serious student of Greek history.

H113. Cohen, Robert. **La Grèce et l'hellénisation du monde antique.** 2nd ed., Paris, 1948. [Collection Clio, 2.] Short history of Greece to the Roman conquest, with good emphasis on cultural development and bibliographical discussion of the general problems arising in connection with each chapter. Designed as a book for students beginning the serious study of Greek history.

H114. Wilcken, Ulrich. **Griechische Geschichte im Rahmen der Altertumsgeschichte.** 8th ed., Munich, 1958. [Geschichte der Völker und Staaten.] A history of Greece vividly and straightforwardly written to give a rapid narrative. Non-dogmatic and pleads no special causes and theses.

H115. Botsford, George W., and Charles A. Robinson, Jr. **Hellenic history.** 4th ed., N.Y., 1956. An up-to-date general history, well illustrated. College text.

H116. Rostovtzeff, Michael I. **History of the ancient world.** V. 1. 2nd ed., Oxford, 1930. The first volume of Rostovtzeff's survey contains a short history of Greece with emphasis on its social and economic development; excellent illustrative material.

LONGER GENERAL HISTORIES

H117. Grote, George. **A history of Greece.** New ed., 10 v., London, 1888. The "classic" history of Greece in English, still valuable to the student for its treatment of Athenian democratic principles. (See *H93*.)

H118. The Cambridge ancient history. Ed. by J. B. Bury, S. A. Cook, F. E. Adcock, and M. P. Charlesworth. V. 1–8. Cambridge, Eng., and N.Y., 1923–39. The standard long history of the ancient world in English, of which v. 3–8 are indispensable for Greek history. The work is of multiple authorship.

Good bibliographies. Revision of earlier volumes is in process.

H119. Glotz, Gustave, R. Cohen, and others. **Histoire grecque.** 4 v. Paris, 1925–38. [Histoire générale.] The standard long history of Greece in French. Separate chapters carry an adequate amount of bibliography with notice of controversial points and some discussion. Like the *Cambridge ancient history,* the earlier material is somewhat dated.

H120. Beloch, Karl J. **Griechische Geschichte.** 2nd ed., 4 v., Berlin, 1912–27. One of the standard modern German histories of Greece, particularly valuable for chronological discussion and its unorthodox views of earlier Greek history before the Persian wars. Succinctly and clearly written with a clear thesis of evolution in the Greek historical process. Pt. 2 of each volume contains a series of appendices on various problems of the narrative presented in pt. 1.

H121. Meyer, Eduard. **Geschichte des Altertums.** Ed. by H. E. Stier. 2nd ed., 5 v., Stuttgart, 1928–56. One of the standard, long ancient histories in German; basic for its synthesis of Near Eastern and Greek history. Its later volumes, dealing mainly with Greek history, have been or are in the process of being revised.

H122. Sanctis, Gaetano de. **Storia dei Greci dalle origini alla fine del sec. V.** 2 v. Florence, 1939. General history of Greece to the end of the 5th century, with particular emphasis on cultural growth, which is skilfully interrelated with the narrative. Unorthodox in various views, *e.g.,* the Dorian invasion is rejected as historical fact and Nicias is made the instigator of the Athenian attacks on Melos and Sicily. The bibliography has been brought up to date by A. Momigliano, *Appendice bibliografia (1940–52) alla Storia dei Greci di G. de Sanctis* (Florence, 1954).

H123. Busolt, Georg. **Griechische Geschichte.** 3 v. in 4. Gotha, 1893–1904. Very detailed account of Greek history to the 5th century B.C. Still valuable for its detail and very full citation and discussion of the literary source material.

H124. Berve, Helmut. **Griechische Geschichte.** 2nd ed., 2 v., Freiburg, 1950–52. [1, *Von den Anfängen bis Perikles*; 2, *Von Perikles bis zur politischen Auflösung.*]

H125. Pöhlmann, Robert von. **Geschichte der sozialen Frage und des Sozialismus in der antiken Welt.** 3rd ed., 2 v., Munich, 1925.

HISTORIES OF SPECIAL PERIODS

Bronze Age

H126. Schachermeyr, Fritz. **Die ältesten Kulturen Griechenlands.** Stuttgart, 1955. Synthesis and interpretation of the earliest period of Greek history up to the Middle Bronze Age (*ca.* 2000 B.C.). It is to be followed by a similar treatment of the Middle and Late Bronze Age.

H127. Childe, V. Gordon. **The dawn of European civilization.** 4th ed., London, 1947. Contains (pp. 15–79) a survey of prehistoric Greek civilization, valuable for its synthesis with European and Anatolian prehistory.

H128. Glotz, Gustave. **La civilisation égéenne.** 2nd ed., Paris, 1952. Social and economic character of Aegean civilization. Out of date in much of its archaeological data, but a useful synthesis for the study of the institutions of prehistoric Greece.

H129. Hall, Harry R. **The civilization of Greece in the Bronze Age.** London, 1928. Account of the Minoan-Mycenaean civilization of the Aegean, very well illustrated and utilizing the archaeological data fully to the date of its publication. Useful for its correlation with Egypt and the Near East, but now faulty in its Minoan focus.

H130. Wace, Alan J. B. **Mycenae: an archaeological history and guide.** Princeton, 1949. Primarily concerned with the archaeological remains at Mycenae, but with a useful chapter on the character of its civilization. See also the introduction to *H47.*

H131. Nilsson, Martin P. **Homer and Mycenae.** London, 1933. Excellent treatment of the relationship between the "Homeric" institutions of the *Iliad* and the *Odyssey* and those of Mycenaean Greece. It perhaps finds too many parallels for modern scholarship, but the problem has not been restudied from this point of view. Probably the best introduction for the serious student to the history of this period.
See also *H47* on the new documentary evidence available for Mycenaean Greece.

Homeric Greece

H132. Daniel, John F., Oscar Broneer, and Henry T. Wade-Gery. "The Dorian invasion." **American journal of archaeology,** 52 (Jan.-Mar. 1948): 107–18.

H133. Hammond, N. G. L. "Prehistoric Epirus and the Dorian invasion." **Annual of the British School at Athens,** 32 (1931–32): 131–79. Examination of the tradition and route of the Dorian invasion.

H134. Finley, Moses I. **The world of Odysseus.** N.Y., 1954. Short and "popular" account of Homeric society, with a good but too inflexible interpretation of the institutions. See also *H131* and, for the literary tradition, *H364;* also Henry T. Wade-Gery, *The poet of the Iliad* (Cambridge, Eng., 1952).

H135. Lorimer, Hilda L. **Homer and the monuments.** London, 1950. Primarily for specialist use, but a necessary starting point for any study of the material background of

"Homeric" society. The author has thoroughly correlated the material elements described in Homer's poems—arms, dress, houses, etc.,—with the archaeological material of the Near East and Greece from 1600 to 700 B.C. One of the important books in the field of early Greek history.

H136. Burn, Andrew R. **The world of Hesiod: a study of the Greek middle ages, 900–700 B.C.** London, 1936. General account based on Hesiod's poems.

Archaic Greece

Listed below are only some of the recent treatments of special topics in this period. See also the local histories, political and economic history, and, for general accounts, the longer histories, particularly *H118–120.*

H137. Démargne, P. **La Crète dédalique: études sur les origines d'une renaissance.** Paris, 1947. [Bibliothèque des écoles françaises d'Athènes et de Rome, 164.] Crete is made the focus for a study of the intricate problem of connection between Mycenaean and historical Greece and between the Near East and Greece in the obscure period from the 10th to 8th centuries B.C. Clearly organized and with a moderate, sensible treatment of difficult problems.

H138. Cook, Robert M. "Ionia and Greece in the eighth and seventh centuries B.C." **Journal of Hellenic studies,** 66 (1946): 67–98. Excellent survey of the evidence bearing on the problem of Ionia's role in the development of archaic Greece, particularly in colonization and trade. Cook concludes that its role was secondary.

H139. Mazzarino, Santo. **Fra Oriente e Occidente: ricerche di storia greca arcaica.** Florence, 1947. [Il pensiero storico.] Study of the social and cultural relationship between the Ionian Greeks and the Near East. While conceived as a synthesis, in execution it breaks down into a series of separate studies of minutely detailed problems. Of more value to the specialist than the student; difficult to use because of its involved organization and lack of index. Review, C. Roebuck, *Classical philology,* 45 (July 1950): 194.

H140. Ehrenberg, Victor. "When did the Polis rise?" **Journal of Hellenic studies,** 57 (1937):147–59. The age of Pericles marks the beginning of decline of the Greek city state, when statesmen began to detach themselves from the state.

H141. Andrewes, Antony. **The Greek tyrants.** London, 1956. Discusses the major Greek tyrants and tyrannies of archaic Greek history. A short but good and balanced account.

H142. Ure, Percy N. **The origin of tyranny.** Cambridge, Eng., 1922. Study of the rise of the major tyrannies of the archaic period in Greece, connecting their origin very directly with the growth of a capitalistic and trading class in Greek society, of which the tyrants were the leaders. The evidence is rather slight for the thesis.

H143. McGregor, Malcolm F. "Cleisthenes of Sicyon and the Panhellenic festivals." **Transactions and proceedings of the American Philological Association,** 72 (1941): 266–87. Panhellenic festivals in the 6th century B.C.

H144. Burn, Andrew R. "Dates in early Greek history." **Journal of Hellenic studies,** 55 (1935): 130–46. Revision of the chronology of archaic Greek history, lowering the traditional dates and suggesting new synchronisms.

H145. Prakken, Donald W. **Studies in Greek genealogical chronology.** Lancaster, Pa., 1943. Review, M. McGregor, *American journal of philology,* 65 (July 1944): 290.

Classical Greece

Listed below are general treatments. See also local histories, particularly of Athens; political, economic, and cultural history; and, for general accounts, the longer histories, especially *H118–120.*

H146. Laistner, Max L. W. **A history of the Greek world from 479 to 323 B.C.** 3rd ed., London, 1957. [Methuen's history of the Greek and Roman world.] Good general account of the history of Greece in the classical period.

H147. Zimmern, Sir Alfred E. **The Greek commonwealth.** 5th ed., Oxford, 1931. A sound, popular account of the society and economic structure of 5th century Athens.

H148. Freeman, Kathleen. **Greek city states.** London, 1950. General account of individual Greek city states.

Hellenistic Period

H149. Cary, Max. **A history of the Greek world from 323 to 146 B.C.** 2nd rev. ed., London, 1951. [Methuen's history of the Greek and Roman world.] Compact and well organized general history.

H150. Tarn, William W. **Hellenistic civilization.** 3rd rev. ed., London, 1952. Series of general studies on the Hellenistic kingdoms and their institutions. Valuable introduction for the study of this period.

H151. Rostovtzeff, Michael I. **The social and economic history of the Hellenistic world.** 3 v. Oxford, 1941. Indispensable for the study of Hellenistic history. A very comprehensive interpretation with full discussion; bibliography in the notes (v. 3).

H152. Droysen, Johann G. **Geschichte des Hellenismus.** 2nd ed., Gotha, 1877. The "classical" history of the Hellenistic period which established it as a field of study in Greek history.

H153. Niese, Benedictus. **Geschichte der griechischen und makedonischen Staaten.** 3 v. Gotha, 1893–1903. Valuable for its comprehensive use and citation of the literary source material, although dated in its interpretations.

H154. Kaerst, Julius. **Geschichte des Hellenismus.** 2nd ed., Leipzig, 1927. Emphasizes the cultural diffusion of Hellenism.

H155. Jouguet, Pierre. **Macedonian imperialism and the Hellenization of the East.** London, 1928. Alexander's empire and Hellenistic monarchies, with focus of attention on Egypt.

H156. Berve, Helmut. **Das Alexanderreich auf prosopographischer Grundlage.** 2 v. in 1. Munich, 1926. Technical and detailed; valuable for reference.

H157. Ehrenberg, Victor. **Alexander and the Greeks.** Tr. by R. Fraenkel von Velsen. Oxford, 1938. Examination of the political relationship between Alexander and the Greeks of Asia Minor primarily.

H158. Wilcken, Ulrich. "Zur Entstehung des hellenistischen Königskultes." **Sitzungsberichte der Preussischen Akademie der Wissenschaften: philosophisch-historische Klasse,** 1938: 298 ff. Study of the organization of the ruler cult in the Hellenistic monarchies.

H159. Bengtson, Hermann. **Die Strategie in der hellenistischen Zeit: ein Beiträg zum antiken Staatsrecht.** 3 v. Munich, 1937–52. Discussed in A. Aymard, "Esprit militaire et administration hellénistique," *Revue des études anciennes,* 55 (1953): 132–45.

H160. Meyer, Ernst. **Die Grenzen der hellenistischen Staaten in Kleinasien.** Zurich and Leipzig, 1925. For the Wars of the Successors and the 3rd century B.C. (to the Peace of Apamea).

H161. Jones, Arnold H. M. **The Greek city from Alexander to Justinian.** See *I182.*

H162. Fine, John van A. "The background of the social war of 220–17 B.C." **American journal of philology,** 61 (Apr. 1940): 129–65.

H163. Holleaux, Maurice. **Rome, la Grèce, et les monarchies hellénistiques au IIIe siècle avant J. C.** Paris, 1921. Basic study of the diplomatic relations in the early phases of the Roman conquest of Greece.

H164. Aymard, André. **Les premiers rapports de Rome et de la confédération achaienne.** Bordeaux, 1938. Very detailed examination of the initial stages of the Roman conquest of Greece in its diplomatic and political aspects.

H165. Bickermann, Elias J. "Bellum Philippicum: some Greek and Roman views concerning the causes of the Second Macedonian War." **Classical philology,** 40 (July 1945): 139–48. Interesting study in the historiography of this period.

H166. Oost, Stewart I. **Roman policy in Epirus and Acarnania in the age of the**

Roman conquest of Greece. Dallas, 1954. [Arnold Foundation studies (Southern Methodist University), 4.]

H167. Accame, Silvio. **Il dominio romano in Grecia dalla guerra acaica ad Augusto.** Rome, 1946. Excellent study of relations of the Greek communities with Rome between 146 and 31 B.C.

See also under local histories (Hellenistic kingdoms), political, economic and cultural history, and biographies. *H118* is particularly useful for the narrative and for bibliography.

HISTORIES OF SPECIAL AREAS

Aegean Area

Athens

H168. Hignett, Charles. **A history of the Athenian constitution to the end of the fifth century B.C.** Oxford, 1952. Scholarly treatment of the development of the Athenian constitution, discussing its successive phases of growth from the early monarchy and aristocracy to the decline of the Athenian empire.

H169. Ferguson, William S. "The Salaminioi of Heptaphylai and Sounion." **Hesperia**, 7 (1938): 1–74. Useful for study of Athenian gentile organization.

H170. Guarducci, Margherita. "L'origine e le vicenale del genos attico dei Salaminii." **Rivista di filologia classica,** 76 (1948): 223–37.

H171. Cloché, Paul. **La démocratie athénienne.** Paris, 1951. Discusses the evolution of Athenian government from Solon to 322 B.C. and gives a general historical account. Well balanced and moderate treatment.

H172. Bonner, Robert J. **Aspects of Athenian democracy.** Berkeley, 1933. [Sather classical lectures (University of California), 11.] These published lectures cover the main facets of political life in Athens—the judiciary, freedom of speech, citizenship, etc. A clear and moderate presentation.

H173. Larsen, Jakob A. O. "Cleisthenes and the development of the theory of democracy at Athens." **Essays in political theory presented to George H. Sabine.** Ithaca, N.Y., 1948. Discussion of *isonomia* as characteristic of early democracy in Athens. See also *H289.*

H174. Carcopino, Jérome. **L'ostracisme athénien.** Paris, 1935. Account of the origin (Cleisthenean) and working of the institution of ostracism and a review of the cases of its practice. Will be replaced by a new study by E. Vanderpool and A. Raubitschek, using the *ostraka* found in the Athenian Agora.

H175. Headlam-Morley, Sir James W. **Election by lot in Athens.** 2nd ed., rev. by D. C. MacGregor, Cambridge, Eng., 1933.

H176. Kahrstedt, Ulrich. **Staatsgebiet und Staatsangehörige in Athen: Studien zum öffentlichen Recht Athens.** V. 1. Stuttgart, 1934. [Göttinger Forschung, 4.] Not an authoritative, systematic study, but lively, hypothetical, and open to considerable criticism; provocative, but with sound observation. See review cited in *H177.*

H177. ——. **Untersuchungen zur Magistratur in Athen.** Stuttgart, 1936. Review, W. S. Ferguson, *American journal of philology,* 59 (Apr. 1938): 229.

H178. Highby, Leo I. **The Erythrae decree: contributions to the early history of the Delian league and the Peloponnesian confederacy.** Leipzig, 1936. Technical study of an important document for the organization of the Delian league, with useful discussion of early alliances in Greece. See also *H194.*

H179. Meritt, Benjamin, Henry T. Wade-Gery, and Malcolm McGregor. **The Athenian tribute lists.** 4 v. Cambridge, Mass., 1939–53. Definitive publication of the tribute lists of the Athenian empire. The texts are published in v. 1 and 2, and historical interpretation in v. 3. Particularly valuable for the financial organization of the empire and an account of the Delian league. V. 4 contains the index.

H180. Meiggs, Russell. "The growth of Athenian imperialism." **Journal of Hellenic studies,** 63 (1943): 21–34. Development of the Athenian empire in the 5th century B.C.

H181. Burn, Andrew R. **Pericles and Athens.** London, 1948. A general account.

H182. Ehrenberg, Victor. "The foundation of Thurii." **American journal of philology,** 69 (Apr. 1948): 149–70. Pericles' conception of the colony was Panhellenistic, not narrowly Athenian.

H183. ——. "Pericles and his colleagues between 441 and 429 B.C." **American journal of philology,** 66 (Apr. 1945): 113–34.

H184. Fuks, Alexander. **The ancestral constitution: four studies in Athenian party politics at the end of the fifth century B.C.** London, 1953.

H185. Lang, Mabel. "The revolution of the 400." **American journal of philology,** 69 (July 1948): 272–89. Study of the oligarchic revolution in Athens in 411 B.C.

H186. Dorjahn, Alfred P. **Political forgiveness in old Athens: the amnesty of 403 B.C.** Evanston, Ill., 1946. [Northwestern University studies in the humanities, 13.]

H187. Cloché, Paul. **La politique étrangère d'Athènes de 404 à 338 av. J. C.** Paris, 1934. A reasonably objective and clear account of Athenian foreign policy in the 4th century B.C.; perhaps too eulogistic of Demosthenes and unfair to the conceptions of Philip of Macedon.

H188. Accame, Silvio. **La lega ateniese del secolo IV. a.c.** Rome, 1941. The organization and historical circumstances of the second Athenian empire.

H189. Ferguson, William S. **Hellenistic Athens.** London, 1911. Best general study of Athens in this period.

H190. ——. **Athenian tribal cycles in the Hellenistic age.** Cambridge, Mass., 1932. Technical chronological study.

H191. Dinsmoor, William B. **The archons of Athens in the Hellenistic age.** Cambridge, Mass., 1931. A technical chronological study. Revision in *The Athenian archon list in the light of recent discoveries* (N.Y., 1939).

H192. Dow, Sterling. **Prytaneis: a study of the inscriptions honoring the Athenian councillors.** Athens, 1937. [Hesperia supplement, 1.] A technical epigraphical study which collects and discusses the decrees passed in honor of the Prytaneis in Athens. Valuable for the chronological detail and study of the Athenian council in the Hellenistic period.

H193. Pritchett, William K., and Benjamin D. Meritt. **The chronology of Hellenistic Athens.** Cambridge, Mass., 1940. Technical chronological study. For revisions and further study see W. K. Pritchett and O. Neugebauer, *The calendars of Athens* (Cambridge, Mass., 1947).

H194. Athenian studies presented to William Scott Ferguson. Cambridge, Mass., 1940. [Harvard studies in classical philology, 51 and sup. v. 1.] Two volumes of studies in Greek history, of which those in sup. v. 1 are centered on various problems of Athenian history. See in particular J. A. O. Larsen, "The constitution and original purpose of the Delian League," pp. 175–213; and H. T. Wade-Gery, "The peace of Kallias," pp. 121–56.

H195. Judeich, Walther. **Topographie von Athen.** 2nd ed., Munich, 1931. [Handbuch der Altertumswissenschaft, 3.] A standard handbook. For the Agora see the excavation reports in *Hesperia*, 1931 ff.; and for a recent general account of Athens with good bibliography, Ida C. T. Hill, *The ancient city of Athens: its topography and monuments* (London, 1953).

Central Greece

H196. Cloché, Paul. **Thèbes de Béotie, des origines à conquête romaine.** Namur, Belg., 1952. A general narrative history of Thebes, rather weak for its early history and in constitutional problems, but excellent for the 4th century B.C.

H197. Bersanetti, G. M. "Pelopida." **Athenaeum,** 27 (1949): 43–101.

H198. Carrata, Thomas F. **Egemonia beotica e potenza maritima nella politica di Epaminonda.** Turin, 1952. [Univ. di Torino, Pubblicazione delle Facoltà di Lettere e Filosofia, 4.]

H199. Feyel, Michel. **Polybe et l'histoire de Béotie au IIIᵉ siècle avant notre ère.** Paris, 1942. For discussion of this and *H206* see A. Aymard, "La Grèce centrale au IIIᵉ siècle avant J. C.," *Revue historique,* 196 (July-Sep. 1946): 287–316.

H200. Hanell, Krister. **Megarische Studien.** Lund, Swe., 1934. Not a history of Megara, but an interesting treatment of its religious institutions to determine its prehistoric affiliations. Also compares them with those of its colonies, thus illuminating the relations between mother-city and colony in Greece.

H201. Westlake, Henry D. **Thessaly in the fourth century.** London, 1935. Narrative history of Thessaly, with good appreciation of the policies of Jason and Philip II for its consolidation against the anarchy of its aristocratic local governments.

H202. Wallace, William. "The demes of Eretria." **Hesperia,** 16 (Apr.-June 1947): 115–46. Study of the organization of Eretria based on epigraphical evidence.

H203. Lerat, Lucien. **Les Locriens de l'ouest.** 2 v. Paris, 1952. [1, *Topographie et ruines;* 2, *Histoire, institutions, prosopographie.*]

H204. Parke, Herbert W., and D. W. Wormell. **The Delphic oracle.** 2 v. Oxford, 1956. History of the oracle and (v. 2) a collection of the oracles.

H205. Poulsen, P. Frederik S. **Delphi.** London, 1920. General descriptive study of the oracle.

H206. Flacelière, Robert. **Les Aitoliens à Delphes: contributions à l'histoire de la Grèce centrale au IIIᵉ siècle av. J. C.** Paris, 1937.

H207. Daux, Georges. **Delphes au IIᵉ et au Iᵉʳ siècle.** Paris, 1936. Very detailed, technical study utilizing epigraphical sources. For the early history of the oracle see *H204*.

Peloponnesus

H208. Will, Edouard. **Korinthiaka: recherches sur l'histoire et la civilisation de Corinthe des origines aux guerres médiques.** Paris, 1955. Very thorough study of the early history of Corinth, noteworthy for its full use of the archaeological evidence necessary for Greek history in the archaic period, but attempting a full synthesis of all the sources of information. Valuable for early Greek economic history.

H209. Roussel, Pierre. **Sparte.** Paris, 1939. A short, balanced, and well-written study of early Sparta, correlating its internal institutions with the expansion of its influence in Greece.

H210. Chrimes, Kathleen M. T. **Ancient Sparta, a re-examination of the evidence.** Manchester, 1949. Rather technical investigation, but not a historical account, of Spartan institutions. Studies inscriptions of the Hellenistic and Roman periods for survivals of earlier custom, and attempts to trace them back to the early period of Spartan history.

H211. Michell, Humfrey. **Sparta.** Cambridge, Eng., 1952. Study of the institutions of Sparta, particularly sensible on the economic problems of land tenure, use of money, and the like; but perhaps too antiquarian on social and political aspects of Spartan life, and rather uncritical in its use of source material.

H212. Hammond, N. G. L. "The Lycurgan reforms at Sparta." **Journal of Hellenic studies,** 70 (1950): 42–64.

H213. Hampl, Franz. "Die lakedaimonische Perióken." **Hermes,** 72 (1937): 1–39.

H214. Kroymann, Jürgen. **Sparta und Messenien: Untersuchungen zur Ueberlieferung der messenischen Kriege.** Berlin, 1937. [Neue philologischer Untersuchungen, 11.] Tradition of the Messenian-Spartan wars in the archaic period.

H215. Roebuck, Carl A. **A history of Messenia from 369 to 146 B.C.** Chicago, 1941. Political history of the "new" state of Messenia and its struggle to preserve its identity in 4th century and Hellenistic Greece.

H216. Callmer, Christian. **Studien zur Geschichte Arkadiens bis zur Gründung des Arkadischen Bundes.** Lund, 1943.

H217. Gardiner, Edward N. **Olympia, its history and remains.** Oxford, 1925. A general, descriptive account of the sanctuary. For excellent illustrations see W. Hege and G. Rodenwaldt, *Olympia* (London, 1936).

Northern Greece

H218. Cross, Geoffrey N. **Epirus: a study in Greek constitutional development.** Cambridge, Eng., 1932. Survey of Epirote history which fits it into the general context of Greek history. Main emphasis is on the constitutional development with its curiously limited monarchy.

H219. Casson, Stanley. **Macedonia, Thrace and Illyria.** Oxford, 1926. Mainly topographical and geographical description of these areas, but with estimates of their economic bases and useful material for the regions before consolidation of the Macedonian kingdom under Philip and Alexander.

H220. Geyer, Fritz. **Makedonien bis zur Thronbesteigung Philipps II.** Munich and Berlin, 1930. [Historische Zeitschrift Beiheft, 19.] General treatment of Macedonian history up to the accession of Philip II. The narrative of Macedonia's struggle to maintain its independence of Athens is well worked out, but there is little discussion of the monarchy and popular assembly in arms, which are akin to Homeric institutions.

H221. Granier, Friedrich. **Die makedonische Heeresversammlung, ein Beiträg zum antiken Staatsrecht.** Munich, 1931. [Münchener Beiträge zur Papyrusforschung und antiken Rechtsgeschichte, 13.] Exhaustive examination of the iuridical character of the Macedonian army assemblies, with a detailed study of each recorded meeting.

H222. Callart, P. **Philippes, ville de Macedoine.** Paris, 1937.

The Islands

H223. Pendlebury, John D. S. **The archaeology of Crete.** London, 1939. Excellent survey of the development of Minoan civilization and of the archaeological sites and excavation on Crete. For Dorian (early) Crete see *H35.*

H224. Effenterre, Henri van. **La Crète et le monde grec de Platon à Polybe.** Paris, 1948. A study of Crete in the 4th century and Hellenistic period, with interesting sections on the connection between Plato's *Laws* and Cretan law, and studies of the political institutions of the Hellenistic period. Discussion of this and *H137* in Y. Béquignon, "De la Crète mycénienne à la Crète hellénistique," *Journal des savants,* 1949, 38–55.

H225. Larsen, Jakob A. O. "Perioeci in Crete." **Classical philology,** 33 (Jan. 1936): 11–22. See also M. Guarducci, "Intorno ai perieci di Creta," *Rivista di filologia e d'istruzione classica,* 66 (1936): 356–63.

H226. Laidlaw, William A. **A history of Delos.** Oxford, 1933. General history of the island from Panionic sanctuary to trading city of the late Hellenistic period. The emphasis is on the later phase of Delos' history when it was the center in the Aegean for the grain and slave trade.

H227. Kent, John H. "The temple estates of Delos, Rheneia, and Mykonos." **Hesperia,** 17 (Oct.-Dec. 1948): 243–338. Based on the epigraphical documents from Delos. See also *H316.*

H228. Pouilloux, Jean. **Recherches sur l'histoire et les cultes de Thasos. V. 1, De la fondation de la cité à 196 av. J. C.** Paris, 1954.

H229. Fraser, Peter M., and George E. Bean. **The Rhodian Peraea and islands.** Oxford, 1954. Epigraphical studies. For the history of the island see H. van Gelder, *Geschichte der alten Rhodier* (Leiden, 1900), out of date in many respects, but still useful.

Colonial Areas

Black Sea

H230. Minns, Ellis H. **Scythians and Greeks.** See *F245.*

H231. Rostovtzeff, Michael I **Iranians and Greeks in South Russia.** Oxford, 1922. Study of the separate development and eventual fusion of the Greek colonists and Scythians in the colonial area of the Black Sea. Some of its archaeological data is obsolete, particularly for the earlier period.

H232. ——. **Skythien und der Bosporus.**

V. 1, **Kritische Übersicht der schriftlichen und archäologischen Quellen.** See *F174*.

H233. Iessen, Aleksandr A. **Grecheskaĩa kolonizatsiĩa severnogo Prichernomorĩa.** Leningrad, 1947. Review, S. V. Kiselev, *Vestnik drevnei istorii,* 3 (1948): 117.

Sicily and Magna Graecia

H234. Beaumont, R. L. "Greek influence in the Adriatic Sea before the fourth century B.C." **Journal of Hellenic studies,** 56 (1936): 159–204. Early Greek colonization in this area.

H235. Bérard, Jean. **Bibliographie topographique des principales cités grecques de l'Italie méridionale et de la Sicile dans l'antiquité.** Paris, 1941. Bibliography of the Greek colonial region of Sicily and south Italy.

H236. ——. **La colonisation grecque de l'Italie méridionale et de la Sicile dans l'antiquité: l'histoire et la légende.** 2nd ed., Paris, 1957. Very thorough study of the colonization of Sicily and southern Italy, important for its synthesis of legend and historical evidence.

H237. Dunbabin, Thomas J. **The western Greeks.** Oxford, 1948. Comprehensive study of the Greek cities of the colonial area of Sicily and southern Italy, with full treatment of their political, social, and economic development. Fundamental for problems of colonization and commerce in early Greek history, as well as for the study of this particular area.

H238. Ciaceri, Emanuele. **Storia della Magna Graecia.** 3 v. Rome, 1927–32. Detailed general history of the foundation and development of the Greek colonies of southern Italy and Sicily, with emphasis on the process of Hellenization and relations with the native communities.

H239. Pace, Baigio. **Arte e civiltà della Sicilia antica.** 4 v. Rome and Milan, 1935–49.

H240. Wuilleumier, Pierre. **Tarente, des origines à la conquête romaine.** Paris, 1939. Detailed history of Tarentum, with full synthesis of the evidence.

The Western Mediterranean

H241. García y Bellido, Antonio. **Hispania graeca.** 2 v. Barcelona, 1948. An account of the foundation and growth of the Greek colonies in Spain, with a virtually complete collection and illustration of the archaeological remains. Fundamental for the study of this area of colonial activity.

H242. Clerc, Michel. **Massilia.** 2 v. Paris, 1929. History of Marseilles.

Africa

H243. Chamoux, François. **Cyrène sous la monarchie des Battiades.** Paris, 1953. Comprehensive history of the Greek colony of Cyrene in Libya in its early period, its institutions and relations with the natives. Includes a catalog of the sculpture found on the site, and accounts and plans of its principal buildings of this period.

H244. Roebuck, Carl A. "The organization of Naukratis." **Classical philology,** 46 (1951): 212–20. Internal organization of the Greek trading colony at Naukratis and its relation to the Egyptian government. See also *H313*.

Hellenistic Kingdoms

H245. Bell, Sir Harold I. **Egypt from Alexander the Great to the Arab conquest.** Oxford, 1948. Brief study of Hellenism in Egypt, with a useful chapter on papyrology and a bibliography. See also items listed for Roman Egypt in Section I.

H246. Rostovtzeff, Michael I. **A large estate in Egypt in the third century B.C.** Madison, Wis., 1922. Based on Zenon's archives. [NL]

H247. Préaux, Claire. **Les Grecs en Égypte, d'après les archives de Zénon.** Brussels, 1947.

H248. ——. **L'économie royale des Lagides.** Brussels, 1939. General account of Ptolemaic organization. [NL]

H249. Heichelheim, Fritz. "Monopole." **Real-Encyclopädie,** v. 16 (Stuttgart, 1935), pp. 147–99. Study of Ptolemaic economic organization.

H250. Welles, Charles B. "The Ptolemaic administration in Egypt." **The journal of juristic papyrology,** 3 (1949): 21–47.

H251. Bevan, Edwyn R. **A history of Egypt under the Ptolemaic dynasty.** London, 1927.

H252. Otto, Walter G. A. **Zur Geschichte der Zeit des 6 Ptolemäers: ein Beiträg zur Politik und zum Staatsrecht des Hellenismus.** Munich, 1934.

H253. ——, and Hermann Bengtson. **Zur Geschichte des Niederganges des Ptolemäerreiches: ein Beiträg zur Regierungszeit der 8 and 9 Ptolemäers.** Munich, 1938.

H254. Manni, Eugenio. "L'Egitto tolemaico nei suoi rapporti politici con Roma." **Rivista di filologia classica,** 77 (1949): 79–106.

H255. Bikerman, Elie. **Institutions des Séleucides.** Paris, 1938. General study of Seleucid organization. See also the appropriate chapters in *H118*, v. 6–8.

H256. Bouché-Leclercq, Auguste. **Histoire des Séleucides.** 2 v. Paris, 1913–14.

H257. Otto, Walter G. A. "Beiträge zur Seleukiden-geschichte des 3 Jahrh. vor Christ." **Abhandlungen der bayerischen Akademie der Wissenschaften,** new ser. 11 (1934).

H258. Jansen, Herman L. **Die politik Antiochus der IV.** Oslo, 1943.

H259. Swain, Joseph W. "Antiochus Epiphanes and Egypt." **Classical philology,** 39 (Jan. 1944): 73–94.

H260. Bellinger, Alfred R. "The end of the Seleucids." **Transactions of the Connecticut Academy of Arts and Science,** 38 (1949): 51–102.

H261. Marcus, Ralph. "A selected bibliography (1920–1945) of the Jews in the Hellenistic-Roman period." **Proceedings of the American Academy for Jewish Research,** 16 (1946–47): 97–181.

H262. Tarn, William W. **The Greeks in Bactria and India.** 2nd ed., Cambridge, Eng., 1951. Indispensable for the study of Hellenization in the Middle East. Skilful use of numismatic evidence in historical reconstruction.

H263. Hansen, Esther V. **The Attalids of Pergamon.** Ithaca, N.Y., 1947. Comprehensive study of the Pergamon kingdom.

HISTORIES OF SPECIAL TOPICS
Political Institutions and Theory

H264. Larsen, Jakob A. O. "Histoire des institutions—antiquité." **Rapports présentés au IXᵉ Congrès International des Sciences Historiques,** 1 (Paris, 1950): 385–416. An estimate (in English), with useful bibliography, of the state of scholarship for Greek political institutions at time of this publication.

H265. Busolt, George, and Heinrich Swoboda. **Griechische Staatskunde.** 2nd ed., 2 v., Munich, 1920–26. [Handbuch der Altertumswissenschaft, 4.] A handbook for the study of Greek political institutions, very systematically organized for reference. Pt. 1 treats the general organization of Greek communities (tribal and urban); pt. 2, Sparta, Crete, and Athens in considerable detail; pt. 3, international relations. Contains excellent bibliography, citation of source material, and notice of controversial points; also lengthy historical introduction as well as the institutional analyses.

City State Institutions

H266. Fustel de Coulanges, Numa D. **La cité antique: étude sur le culte, le droit, les institutions de la Grèce et de Rome.** 14th reprint, Paris, 1893. A "classic" study of the nature of the ancient city state, with a logical rather than historical interpretation.

H267. Glotz, Gustave. **The Greek city and its institutions.** Paris, 1929. Tr. by N. Mallinson from *La cité grecque* (Paris, 1928). General account of the character and working of Greek political institutions at successive stages in the evolution of the Greek city state from the Homeric city through the 4th century B.C. Review, V. Ehrenberg, *Gnomon,* 5 (Jan. 1929): 1.

H268. **The Greek political experience: studies in honor of William Kelly Prentice.** Princeton, 1941. Collection of short, general studies.

H269. McDonald, William A. **The political meeting places of the Greeks.** Baltimore, 1943. [Johns Hopkins University studies in archaeology, 34.] A study of the types of buildings the Greeks developed to house their various political bodies. Emphasis is primarily on architectural form of the buildings, but the material is correlated to the type of political body and its functional needs.

H270. Bonner, Robert, and Gertrude Smith. **The administration of justice from Homer to Aristotle.** 2 v. Chicago, 1930–38. A rather specialized treatment with considerable controversial argument. V. 1, after an initial discussion of the Heroic Age, early Attica, and the law givers, centers on a history of the courts in Athens. V. 2 covers practice and procedure in classical Athens, with useful material for the political aspects of Athenian justice.

H271. Forbes, Clarence A. **Neoi: a contribution to the study of Greek associations.** Middletown, Conn., 1933. [American Philological Association philological monographs, 2.] Study of the ephebate and age classes.

Federal Institutions

H272. Larsen, Jakob A. O. **Representative government in Greek and Roman history.** Berkeley, 1955. [Sather classical lectures (University of California), 28.] The use of representative institutions in the Greek city states, federal leagues, and Roman provincial assemblies. Based on the generation of study of which the separate products may be seen in a series of articles in *Classical philology* from 1925. See also *H286.*

H273. Aymard, André L. **Les assemblées de la confédération achaienne.** Bordeaux, 1938. Very detailed; important for the organization of Greek federations in the Hellenistic period.

International Relations

H274. Walbank, Frank W. "The problem of Greek nationality." **The phoenix,** 5 (1951): 41–60. A consciousness of belonging to the same people, if not a Greek nation.

H275. Phillipson, Coleman. **International law and custom of ancient Greece and Rome.** 2 v. London, 1911. An old study, but not yet superseded.

H276. Martin, Victor. **La vie internationale dans la Grèce des cités.** Paris, 1940. General treatment with broad scope of the forms and organization of international relations among the Greek city states. The political nature of the city, imperialism, peace treaties, arbitration, and other such topics are discussed. There is adequate citation of source material and bibliography.

H277. Hammond, Mason. "Ancient imperialism: contemporary justifications." **Harvard studies in classical philology,** 58–9 (1948): 105–61.

H278. Ferguson, William S. **Greek imperialism.** N.Y., 1913. Brief but illuminating general history of imperialism from that of the city states, Athens and Sparta, through Alexander and the Hellenistic monarchies to the Hellenistic leagues.

H279. Schaefer, Hans. **Staatsform und Politik: Untersuchungen zur griechischen Geschichte des 6. and 5. Jahrhunderts.** Leipzig, 1932. Examines Greek political terminology with reference to interstate relations for the 6th and 5th centuries. The author discovers an "agonal" character in them which was transformed in the late 5th century to a more formal and businesslike relationship.

H280. Hampl, Franz. **Die griechischen Staatsverträge des 4 Jahrhunderts v. Christi Geb.** Leipzig, 1938. Examination of the circumstances calling forth the interstate treaties in 4th century Greece, and discussion of their character.

H281. Momigliano, Arnaldo. "La koine eirene dal 386 al 338 a. C." **Rivista di filologia,** 62 (1934): 482–514. The movement towards a common peace among the Greek states in the 4th century B.C.

H282. Martin, Victor. "Sur une interprétation nouvelle de la 'Paix du roi.' " **Museum helveticum,** 5–6 (1948–49): 127–39.

H283. Roos, A. G. "The peace of Sparta of 374 B.C." **Mnemosyne,** 4th ser., 2 (1949): 265–85.

H284. Taeger, Fritz. **Der Friede von 362–361: ein Beiträg zur Geschichte der panhellenischen Bewegung im 4 Jahrhundert.** Stuttgart, 1930. [Tübinger Beiträge zur Altertumswissenschaft, 11.] The general peace made among the Greek states in 362–61 after the battle of Mantinea. Valuable for study of the Panhellenic movement towards a common peace in the 4th century.

H285. Aymard, André. "Philippe de Macédoine ôtage à Thèbes." **Revue des études anciennes,** 56 (1954): 15–36. Hostages in classical Greece, as well as study of the tradition of Philip's stay in Thebes.

H286. Larsen, Jakob A. O. "Representative government in the Panhellenic leagues." **Classical philology,** 20 (Oct. 1925): 313–29; 21 (Jan. 1926): 52–71. Study of the institutional form of the Panhellenic leagues established by Philip II of Macedon and his successors. For recent bibliography see Carl Roebuck, "The settlements of Philip II with the Greek states in 338 B.C.," *Classical philology,* 43 (Apr. 1948): 73–92.

Classical Political Theory

H287. Barker, Sir Ernest. **Greek political theory.** 4th ed., London, 1951. History of Greek political theory from its origins through Plato, with emphasis on Platonic theory. Excellent treatments of the *Republic* and *Laws,* analytic and explanatory with the insight of a statesman of practical experience. For Aristotelian theory see *H64.*

H288. Sinclair, Thomas A. **A history of Greek political thought.** London, 1952. A succinct and clearly written sketch of the development of Greek political thought.

H289. Vlastos, Gregory. "Isonomia." **American journal of philology,** 74 (Oct. 1953): 337–66. Examination of the term in its political context.

H290. Jones, John W. **The law and legal theory of the Greeks.** Oxford, 1956. Treats the function and character of law in the Greek city state.

Hellenistic Political Theory

H291. Fritz, Kurt von. **The theory of the mixed constitution in antiquity: a critical analysis of Polybius' political ideas.** N.Y., 1954. Very detailed and complete study of the genesis and development of the theory of the mixed constitution; related in particular to Roman historical development, but with discussion of the roots of the theory in Greek political philosophy. A survey of Polybius' background is given.

H292. Kaerst, Julius. **Studien zur Entwickelung und theoretischen Begründung der Monarchie im Altertum.** Leipzig, 1898.

H293. Goodenough, Erwin R. "The political philosophy of Hellenistic kingship." **Yale classical studies,** 1 (1928): 55–102. Criticism of Kaerst's discussion.

H294. Zancan, Paola. **Il monarcato ellenistico nei suoi elementi federativi.** Padua, 1934.

H295. Heuss, Alfred. **Stadt und Herrscher des Hellenismus in ihren staats- und völkerrechtlichen Beziehungen.** Leipzig, 1937.

H296. Hammond, Mason. **City state and world state in Greek and Roman political theory until Augustus.** Cambridge, Mass., 1951. General thesis is the failure of the Romans to transfer adequately the Greek theory of the best state to Roman theory and practice, hence the failure of the empire. It is written for the political theorist and scientist in general, and contains a sketch of the development of Greek political theory.

Economic History

H297. Walbank, Frank W. "Histoire sociale—antiquité." **Rapports présentés au IXe Congrès International des Sciences Historiques,** 1 (Paris, 1950): 261–79. Survey (in English) of the position and trends of interpretation in Greek and Roman social and economic history. Author discusses the opposite poles of approach: (1) that the economic forces of the ancient world were primitive and undeveloped in contrast to medieval and modern society, and (2) the "modernizing" interpretation which ascribes a special form of capitalistic development to Greek and Roman society.

H298. Heichelheim, Fritz. **Wirtschaftsgeschichte des Altertums vom Paläolithikum bis zur Völkerwanderung.** 2 v. Leiden, 1938. A massive study with complex bibliography. For a slighter and general account see J. Toutain, *The economic life of the ancient world,* tr. by M. R. Dobie (N.Y., 1951).

H299. Blümner, Hugo. **Technologie und Terminologie der Gewerbe und Künste bei den Griechen und Römern.** 4 v. in 3, Leipzig, 1875–87. 2nd rev. ed. of v. 1, Leipzig, 1912. Valuable for reference.

H300. Michell, Humfrey. **The economics of ancient Greece.** Rev. ed., Cambridge, Eng., 1956. General, mainly descriptive, account of the economy of Aegean Greece, with chapters on agriculture, mining, labor, etc. Useful introduction to the field with a synthesis of the information.

H301. Glotz, Gustave. **Ancient Greece at work: an economic history of Greece from the Homeric period to the Roman conquest.** Tr. by M. R. Dobie. London, 1926. A primarily descriptive account of the organization of economic activity in ancient Greece, written for the general reader. Its interpretation of the institutions is conceived along "modernizing" lines like that of Beloch and Meyer. See also *H297*.

H302. Seltman, Charles T. **Greek coins: a history of metallic currency and coinage down to the fall of the Hellenistic kingdoms.** 2nd ed., London, 1955. General introduction to the history of Greek coinage. Arranged on a combined geographical and chronological scheme, discussing the principal Greek issues and metrology; perhaps too "traditional" in its account of early Greek coinage. A convenient manual for consultation is Barclay V. Head, *Historia numorum* (2nd ed., London, 1911).

Finance

H303. Andreades, Andreas M. **A history of Greek public finance.** Tr. by C. N. Brown. Cambridge, Mass., 1933. General history of the public financing of Greek states, useful for its synthesis and collection of evidence, although now out of date with respect to Athens.

H304. Ferguson, William S. **The treasurers of Athens.** Cambridge, Mass., 1932. Financial history of the Athenian empire, particularly valuable for the last phase of the Peloponnesian War. For the earlier period see *H179*.

Agriculture

H305. Vickery, Kenton F. **Food in early Greece.** Urbana, 1936. [University of Illinois studies in the social sciences, 20.]

H306. Jardé, Auguste F. **Les céréales dans l'antiquité grecque.** Paris, 1925. Valuable and detailed study of the production of grain in ancient Greece—types grown, yield, system of farming, and the like.

H307. Finley, Moses I. **Studies in land and credit in ancient Athens, 500–200 B.C.: the Horos inscriptions.** New Brunswick, N.J., 1952. Technical study of the "mortgage" inscriptions of Attica, complementary to that of Fine (*H308*) in that the author's viewpoint is that of an economic historian; an investigation of real estate security as part of a study of Greek business practice.

H308. Fine, John van A. **Horoi: studies in mortgage, real security, and land tenure in ancient Athens.** Baltimore, 1951. Technical study from a legal approach of the "mortgage" inscriptions of Attica, valuable for the problem of land tenure and sale. Fine suggests that land was not alienable until the late 5th century in Athens.

H309. Hasebroek, Johannes. **Griechische Wirtschafts- und Gesellschaftsgeschichte bis zur Perserzeit.** Tübingen, Ger., 1931. Interpretation of Greek economic organization as primitive in its forms and essentially of the "household" type (see *H297*). Reviews, M. Cary, *Journal of Hellenic studies,* 49 (Jan.-June 1929): 108 and 52 (Jan.-June 1932): 147.

H310. ———. **Staat und Handel im alten Griechenland.** Tübingen, 1928. Tr. by L. Fraser and D. C. MacGregor as *Trade and politics in ancient Greece* (London, 1932). A criticism of the "modernizing" interpretation of Greek economic organization, and development of the thesis that economic considerations had no part in the political actions of the Greek state. Criticized for its misinterpretation or neglect of archaeological and numismatic evidence.

H311. Sutherland, Carol H. V. "Corn and coin: a note on Greek commercial monopolies." **American journal of philology,** 64 (Apr. 1943): 129–47. Use of silver in the grain trade. Criticism of Hasebroek's views (*H310*).

H312. Roebuck, Carl A. "The economic development of Ionia." **Classical philology,** 48 (Jan. 1953): 9–16. Population estimate and study of the trade developed to provide the food supply of Ionia in the archaic period. The rhythm of Ionian growth was similar to that of the rest of Greece, the significant transition in development occurring in the last quarter of the 7th century.

H313. ———. "The grain trade between Greece and Egypt." **Classical philology,** 45 (Oct. 1950): 236–47. Study of this trade in the archaic period, with an estimate of the respective roles of those Greek states which shared in the foundation of Naukratis.

H314. Ehrenberg, Victor. **The people of Aristophanes: a sociology of old Attic comedy.** 2nd ed., Oxford, 1951. The plays of Aristophanes (and Euripides) are used to reconstruct a picture of society and economic life in late 5th century Athens. Very readable, but the evidence is of such a nature that a proper perspective is difficult to obtain.

H315. Hopper, R. J. "The Attic silver mines in the fourth century B.C." **Annual of the British School at Athens,** 48 (1953): 200–54. Based mainly on the epigraphical evidence.

H316. Larsen, Jakob A. O. "Roman Greece." **An economic survey of ancient Rome,** v. 4 (Baltimore, 1938), pp. 334–435. Valuable for period of Roman conquest and Delos in particular. See also *H227.*

H317. Bolkestein, Hendrik. **Wohltätigkeit und Armenpflege im vorchristlichen Altertum.** Utrecht, 1934.

Military History

H318. Kromayer, Johannes, and Georg Veith. **Heerwesen und Kriegführung der Griechen und Römer.** Munich, 1928. [Handbuch der Altertumswissenschaft, 4.] The standard handbook for military science in the Greek and Roman world.

H319. Adcock, Frank E. **The Greek and Macedonian art of war.** Berkeley, 1957. [Sather classical lectures (University of California), 30.] History of battle tactics and strategy.

H320. Rodgers, William L. **Greek and Roman naval warfare: a study of strategy, tactics and ship design from Salamis (480 B.C.) to Actium (31 B.C.).** London, 1937.

H321. Grundy, George B. **The great Persian War and its preliminaries: a study of the evidence, literary and topographical.** London, 1901. Very thorough and detailed account of the strategy, tactics, and battles of this war, and critique of the Herodotean account from that point of view.

H322. Tarn, William W. **Hellenistic military and naval developments.** Cambridge, Eng., 1930.

H323. Launey, Marcel. **Recherches sur les armées hellénistiques.** Paris, 1949.

H324. Parke, Herbert W. **Greek mercenary soldiers from the earliest times to the battle of Ipsus.** Oxford, 1933. Study of the practice of mercenary service in the Greek armies for the archaic and classical periods. Particularly useful for the 4th century.

H325. Griffith, Guy T. **The mercenaries of the Hellenistic world.** Cambridge, Eng., 1935.

Cultural History

Civilization and Thought

H326. Croiset, Maurice. **La civilisation de la Grèce antique.** N.Y., 1925. Reprint, Paris, 1943.

H327. Livingstone, Richard W. **The legacy of Greece.** Oxford, 1921. Separate chapters on aspects of Greek civilization—science, mathematics, etc.

H328. Gardiner, Edward N. **Athletics of the ancient world.** Oxford, 1930. General treatment of ancient athletics, but with the main emphasis on Greek and Roman games and sports. Discussion of the festivals is secondary. Well illustrated.

H329. Sarton, George A. L. **A history of science: ancient science through the golden age of Greece.** Cambridge, Mass., 1952.

H330. Farrington, Benjamin. **Science and politics in the ancient world.** London, 1939.

H331. Jaeger, Werner W. **Paideia.** Tr. by Gilbert Highet. 3 v. Oxford, 1939–44. Greek intellectual and spiritual development. Interprets the thought and ideals expressed in the literature from Homer through Plato.

H332. Snell, Bruno K. **Die Entstehung des Geistes: Studien zur Entstehung des europäischen Denkens bei der Griechen.** 3rd ed., Hamburg, 1955. Tr. by T. G. Rosenmeyer as *The discovery of the mind: the Greek origins of European thought* (Cambridge, Eng., 1953). Collection of separate studies on Greek thought, arranged chronologically to give a synthesis of its growth. The emphasis is on those qualities which are traditional in European thought.

H333. Marrou, Henri I. **Histoire de l'éducation dans l'antiquité.** 2nd ed., Paris, 1950. Excellent history of the methods and aims of Greek and Roman education.

H334. Ueberweg, Frederick, Max Heinze, and Karl Praechter. **Grundriss der Geschichte der Philosophie.** Pt. 1, **Das Altertum.** 12th ed., Berlin, 1926.

H335. Burnet, John. **Early Greek philosophy.** 4th ed., N.Y., 1930. Discussion of pre-Socratic philosophy.

H336. Grube, Georges M. A. **Plato's thought.** London, 1935.

H337. Taylor, Alfred E. **Plato, the man and his work.** 6th ed., London, 1949.

H338. Jaeger, Werner W. **Aristotle.** Tr. by R. Robinson. Oxford, 1934.

H339. Ross, Sir William D. **Aristotle.** 3rd ed., London, 1937.

H340. DeWitt, Norman W. **Epicurus and his philosophy.** Minneapolis, 1954.

H341. Pohlenz, Max. **Die Stoa.** 2 v. Göttingen, 1948.

Religion

H342. Nilsson, Martin P. **Geschichte der griechischen Religion.** 2nd ed., 2 v., Munich, 1941–50. [Handbuch der Altertumswissenschaft, 5.] Standard handbook and history for the study of Greek religion. Well documented, with good bibliography, notice of controversial points, and interpretation of the main conceptions and practices of Greek religious life. [CSB]

H343. Roscher, Wilhelm H., ed. **Ausführliches Lexikon der griechischen und röm-**

ischen Mythologie. 6 v. in 9, and 3 sup. v. Leipzig, 1884–1937. Valuable for reference.

H344. Picard, Charles. **Les religions préhelléniques (Crète et Mycènes).** Paris, 1948. General treatment of pre-Hellenic religion, clearly and cautiously written as a compendium and introduction to the subject. Excellent bibliography.

H345. Nilsson, Martin P. **Minoan-Mycenaean religion and its survival in Greek religion.** 2nd rev. ed., Lund, Swe., 1950. Somewhat technical, but important as establishing the continuity of the great cycles of legend from Mycenaean to historical Greek times.

H346. Farnell, Lewis R. **The cults of the Greek states.** 5 v. Oxford, 1896–1908. Survey of the main deities, the origin and ritual of their cults in the various Greek states. Historical and descriptive rather than interpretative. [CSB]

H347. Cook, Arthur B. **Zeus.** 3 v. in 5. Cambridge, Eng., 1914–40. Highly detailed and scholarly study of the development of the principal Greek divinity. Numerous notes and bibliographical items cover almost every aspect of Greek cults. Valuable for reference. [CSB]

H348. Deubner, Ludwig A. **Attische Feste.** Berlin, 1932. Account of the origin and practice of the main religious festivals of the Athenian state, arranged under the various gods who were honored rather than as a calendar. Well illustrated from the scenes on Athenian pottery.

H349. Kern, Otto. **Die Religion der Griechen.** 3 v. Berlin, 1926–38. General history of Greek religion from Homer to the end of antiquity. [CSB]

H350. Harrison, Jane E. **Prolegomena to the study of Greek religion.** 3rd ed., Cambridge, Mass., 1922.

H351. Murray, Gilbert H. **Five stages of Greek religion.** 3rd ed., Boston, 1951. A short, general account. [CSB]

H352. Guthrie, William K. C. **The Greeks and their gods.** Boston, 1951.

H353. Moore, Clifford H. **The religious thought of the Greeks from Homer to the triumph of Christianity.** 2nd ed., Cambridge, Mass., 1925.

H354. Macchioro, Vittorio D. **From Orpheus to Paul: a history of Orphism.** N.Y., 1930.

H355. Festugière, André M. J. **Personal religion among the Greeks.** Berkeley, 1954. [Sather classical lectures (University of California), 26.]

H356. Nilsson, Martin P. **Cults, myths, oracles and politics in ancient Greece.** Lund, 1951. Account of the part played in political life by religious institutions; *e.g.* political influence in the removal and duplication of cults, and political use of mythological argument in diplomacy.

H357. ——. **Greek piety.** Tr. by H. J. Rose. Oxford, 1948. General statement of Greek religious attitude toward the world and life. Particularly valuable for the Hellenistic period.

H358. ——. **Greek popular religion.** N.Y., 1940.

Literature

For the Greek historians see Historiography.

H359. Schmid, Wilhelm, and Otto Stählin. **Geschichte der griechischen Literatur.** 2 pts. in 8 v. Munich, 1920–48. Pt. 1, classical Greek literature; 2, post-classical to 530 A.D.

H360. Sinclair, Thomas A. **A history of classical Greek literature from Homer to Aristotle.** London, 1934. Convenient short history of Greek literature with good emphasis and balance.

H361. Bowra, Sir Cecil M. **Ancient Greek literature.** Rev. ed., Oxford, 1952. [Home university library.] A short, well organized sketch of Greek literary development.

H362. Wright, Frederick A. **A history of later Greek literature.** London, 1932.

H363. Gomme, Arnold W. **The Greek attitude to poetry and history.** Berkeley, 1954. [Sather classical lectures (University of California), 27.] Contains *inter alia* a discussion of the literary techniques of narration used by Herodotus and Thucydides.

H364. Bowra, Sir Cecil M. **Tradition and design in the Iliad.** Oxford, 1930.

H365. ——. **Greek lyric poetry from Alcman to Simonides.** Oxford, 1936.

H366. Pohlenz, Max. **Die griechische Tragödie.** 2nd ed., 2 v., Göttingen, 1954. A massive and thorough discussion of Greek tragedy.

H367. Thomson, George D. **Aeschylus and Athens.** London, 1941. Primarily a study of the social origins of Greek drama, but pts. 1 and 2 deal with the social evolution of the Greek state from tribal to urban society. (See *H33*.)

H368. Murray, Gilbert H. **Aristophanes.** Oxford, 1933.

H369. Dobson, John F. **The Greek orators.** London, 1919. Short general study.

Art

H370. Beazley, Sir John D., and Bernard Ashmole. **Greek sculpture and painting to the end of the Hellenistic period.** Cambridge, Eng., 1932. Well illustrated publication of chapters in the *Cambridge ancient history*.

H371. Anderson, William J., Richard P. Spiers, and William B. Dinsmoor. **The architecture of ancient Greece.** 3rd ed., N.Y., 1950. Handbook of ancient Greek architecture with very generous citation of bibliography. It is descriptive and technical rather than interpretative of the forms and influence of Greek building.

H372. Fyfe, Theodore H. **Hellenistic architecture.** Cambridge, Eng., 1936.

H373. Gerkan, Armin von. **Griechische Städteanlagen.** Berlin, 1924. Types and physical growth of the Greek city state.

H374. Wycherley, Richard E. **How the Greeks built cities.** London, 1949. An excellent and non-technical survey of Greek architecture from a functional and descriptive point of view. Brief, but good bibliography and notes. See also *H269*.

H375. Lawrence, Arnold W. **Classical sculpture.** New ed., London, 1944. General account of the development of Greek and Roman sculpture.

H376. Richter, Gisela M. A. **The sculpture and sculptors of the Greeks.** Rev. ed., New Haven, 1950. History of Greek sculpture, including evolution of its main types, and the surviving monuments from the archaic through the Hellenistic period.

H377. Bieber, Margarete. **The sculpture of the Hellenistic age.** N.Y., 1955.

H378. Swindler, Mary H. **Ancient painting from the earliest times to the period of Christian art.** New Haven, 1929.

H379. Pfuhl, Ernst. **Malerei und Zeichnung der Griechen.** 3 v. Munich, 1923.

H380. Beazley, Sir John D. **The development of Attic black-figure.** Berkeley, 1951. [Sather classical lectures (University of California), 24.]

H381. Payne, Humfry. **Necrocorinthia: a study of Corinthian art in the archaic period.** Oxford, 1931.

BIOGRAPHIES

The fragmentary evidence for Greek history hardly allows biographical studies to be made save in a very broad manner. These "lives" should, for the most part, be considered as period studies focusing around individual careers.

H382. Woodhouse, William J. **Solon the liberator.** Oxford, 1938. Study of Solon and the Solonian reforms, with emphasis on their agrarian and social character. Valuable for study of early Greek land tenure (see *H307–308*). Solon's reform consisted in breaking the system of limited slavery which placed citizens in bond to private individuals since their land was inalienable.

H383. Berve, Helmut. **Miltiades: Studien zur Geschichte des Mannes und seiner Zeit.** Berlin, 1937. [Hermes Einzelschriften, 2.]

H384. Bengtson, Hermann. "Einzelpersönlichkeit und Athenischer Staat zur Zeit des Peisistratus und des Miltiades." **Sitzungsbericht der bayerischen Akademie der Wissenschaft,** 1 (1939). Study of the individual in relation to the state in the period of the Peisistratid tyranny. Takes issue with the point of view of Berve, above.

H385. Homo, Léon. **Périclès: une expérience de démocratie dirigée.** Paris, 1954.

H386. Hatzfeld, Jean. **Alcibiade: étude sur l'histoire d'Athènes à la fin du Vᵉ siècle.** Paris, 1940. Biography of Alcibiades is used as a study of the history of Athens at the end of the 5th century. A serious and careful treatment of the first "individual" in Greek history.

H387. Cloché, Paul. **Demosthènes et la fin de la démocratie athénienne.** Paris, 1937. Biography and interpretation of the career of Demosthenes, with an analysis of his principal public speeches.

H388. Jaeger, Werner W. **Demosthenes, the origin and growth of his policy.** Cambridge, Eng., 1938. Not essentially a biography nor historical reconstruction of the period, but an interpretation of the speeches as documents of Demosthenes' thought and action. Emphasis on the formative part of his career to 348.

H389. Momigliano, Arnaldo. **Filippo il Macedone.** Florence, 1934. Brief appraisal of the career and aims of Philip of Macedonia in his program of Greek unification. Emphasis is on his foreign policy and appreciation of Philhellenism as a political tool for use in Macedonia and Greece.

H390. Wüst, Fritz R. **Philipp II. von Makedonien.** Munich, 1938. Detailed and well documented study of Philip's career, with full discussion of points of controversy and considerable sympathy towards Philip and his ideas.

H391. Hampl, Franz. "Alexander der Grosse und die Beurteilung geschichtlicher Persönlichkeiten in der modernen Historiographie." **Nouvelle Clio,** 6 (Mar.-Apr. 1954): 91–136. Survey of historical judgments, ancient and modern, on Alexander's career and political ideas.

H392. Robinson, Charles A., Jr. **Alexander the Great: the meeting of East and West in world government and brotherhood.** N.Y., 1947. A somewhat idealistic and romantic account of Alexander.

H393. Schachermeyr, Fritz. **Alexander der Grosse: Ingenium und Macht.** Graz, Austria, 1949. Review, T. Brown, *American journal of philology,* 72 (Jan. 1951): 74.

H394. Tarn, William W. **Alexander the Great.** 2 v. Cambridge, Eng., 1948. V. 1 is a short narrative of Alexander's career; v. 2, discussion of the sources and various problems. The most generally useful account of Alexander for the serious student.

H395. Wilcken, Ulrich. **Alexander der Grosse.** Leipzig, 1931. Tr. by G. S. Richards, London, 1932. Excellent narrative account and appreciation of Alexander, emphasizing the apparent growth of his ideas. Also contains valuable discussion of Panhellenism in the 4th century.

H396. Manni, Eugenio. **Demetrio Polior-cete.** Rome, 1951.

H397. Berve, Helmut. "Die Herrschaft des Agathokles." **Sitzungsbericht der bayerischen Akademie der Wissenschaft,** 5 (1952).

H398. Tarn, William W. **Antigonos Gonatas.** Oxford, 1913. Biographical study of the "refounder" of the Macedonian monarchy in the 3rd century.

H399. Walbank, Frank W. **Aratos of Sicyon.** Cambridge, Eng., 1933. Useful for Greek history in the 3rd century B.C.

H400. Treves, Piero. "Studi su Antigono Dosono." **Athenaeum,** 13 (1935): 22–56.

H401. Walbank, Frank W. **Philip V of Macedon.** Cambridge, Eng., 1940. Review, P. Treves, *Journal of Hellenic studies,* 63 (1943): 117.

PERIODICALS

In addition to the periodicals listed below, there are a large number for general classical studies or special fields within that area which publish articles of use for Greek history. The original *Guide* contains a full list current at its time of publication. For a current list see *L'année philologique* (*H1*). Among American universities, Harvard, Yale, and California publish studies in classical philology containing historical articles.

H402. The American historical review. N.Y., 1895 ff. Publishes an occasional article of general interpretative nature in Greek history, and carries short reviews of important books and a listing of current publication of articles and books in ancient history.

H403. The American journal of philology. Baltimore, 1880 ff. Publishes articles of specialist nature in Greek history, full-length reviews, and lists of current publications—mainly philological.

H404. Classical philology. Chicago, 1906 ff. Articles of specialist nature in Greek history, reviews, and list of current publications—mainly philological.

H405. Gnomon. Munich, 1925 ff. A review journal for general classical publications, including history. Full-length reviews by competent authorities.

H406. Hesperia: journal of the American School of Classical Studies at Athens. Baltimore, 1931 ff. Publishes archaeological material from the excavations of the American School, and also some historical articles, mainly epigraphical.

H407. Historia. Wiesbaden, 1950 ff. Articles, reviews, and summaries of the more inaccessible material (in Russian) in Greek and Roman history. Editorial board and authorship are international.

H408. Journal of Hellenic studies. London, 1880 ff. The most important English publication for articles in Greek history and archaeology. Reviewing is comprehensive, detailed, and of high quality.

H409. Klio: Beiträge zur alten Geschichte und Beihefte. Leipzig, 1902–44. The most important German journal for articles in ancient history until its publication was terminated in 1944. It published also a series of monographs as *Beihefte.*

H410. Vestnik drevnei istorii. Moscow, 1936 ff. Chief Russian journal for publication of articles, reviews, and summaries of meetings.

H411. The Phoenix: the journal of the Classical Association of Canada. Toronto, 1947 ff. Some excellent general articles on Greek history. Non-technical.

H412. Bulletin de correspondance hellénique. Paris, 1876 ff. Mainly archaeological material, but also epigraphical studies and publication of inscriptions from French excavations.

H413. Revue des études anciennes. Bordeaux, 1899 ff. This and *H414–415* contain articles in ancient history and philology.

H414. Revue des études grecques. Paris, 1888 ff.

H415. Rivista di filologia e di istruzione classica. Turin, 1873 ff.

Rome: Republic and Empire

T. ROBERT S. BROUGHTON *

The space devoted to political, constitutional, and legal history in this section may seem disproportionately large, but it reflects fairly the nature of material available and the fields in which Roman contribution was greatest. Advances in social and economic history and the increasing importance of the study of Roman provinces are reflected in the greater space allotted to them here than in the original *Guide*. The subsections on general cultural history, literature, religion, and art and archaeology have been enlarged in view of excellent recent work in these fields and increasing scholarly interest in them. For many works on classical antiquity it will be necessary to refer to the sections on Near East and Greek history. On the other hand, writings dealing with the history of the Greek East during the Roman period have been included here. In general, apart from a few outstanding exceptions, references have been restricted to books, and those to articles in current journals, avoided. However, the journals where current discussions may be found are listed.

BIBLIOGRAPHIES, LIBRARIES, AND MUSEUMS

The current literature on Roman history is contained mainly in classical and historical periodicals, of which lists appear in Sections F and H as well as in this one. A brief bibliography of articles in ancient (including Roman) history published in periodicals appears quarterly in *The American historical review*.

The most important annual bibliography of books and articles is *L'année philologique* (*H1*). It succeeds *Dix années de biblio-*graphie classique: bibliographie critique et analytique de l'antiquité greco-latine pour la periode 1914–1924, ed. by Jules Marouzeau (2 v., Paris, 1927–28).

Earlier material was presented in two annual bulletins entitled "Revue des comptes rendus d'ouvrages relatifs à l'antiquité classique" and "Revue des revues: bibliographie analytique des articles de periodiques relatifs à l'antiquité classique" in *Revue de philologie* from 1876 to 1925.

Even more complete were the general annual lists and the surveys of the literature on separate topics in *Bursians Jahresbericht*

* The following contributed items and comments indicated by their respective initials: Arthur E. R. Boak (AERB), James F. Gilliam (JFG), Agnes K. Michels (AKM), Robert S. Rogers (RSR), Inez S. Ryberg (ISR), Lily R. Taylor (LRT), Cornelius C. Vermeule, III (CCV). Comments by the following, appearing in the original *Guide*, are also included: William S. Davis (WSD), Tenney Frank (TF), William D. Gray (WDG), Clinton W. Keyes (CWK), David Magie (DM), William A. Oldfather (WAO), Allen B. West (ABW).

über die Fortschritte der klassischen Altertumswissenschaft (Leipzig), which ceased publication in 1945. The first numbers of *Lustrum: internationale Forschungsberichte aus dem Bereich des klassischen Altertums,* ed. by H. J. Mette and A. Thierfelder (Göttingen, 1957 ff.), a journal planned along the same lines, have recently appeared. *The year's work in classical studies* (*H3*) contains brief annual bibliographies. [AERB, TRSB]

The libraries best equipped for the study of Roman history are those of the larger universities. Harvard, Columbia, Yale, Princeton, Cornell, Chicago, and the University of California at Berkeley have excellent collections. Chicago is strong in editions of ancient authors and in dissertations; Princeton in texts, inscriptions, and papyri; Michigan in papyri and inscriptions; while Yale has the Wheeler collection on Roman law.

The best collections of Greek and Roman art and antiquities on the North American continent are in the Metropolitan Museum of Art, New York; Museum of Fine Arts, Boston; and the Museum of the University of Pennsylvania. Other collections of considerable importance are in the Fogg Art Museum at Harvard; Museum of Industrial Arts, Providence; the Art Institute and the Field Museum, both in Chicago; Art Museum, St. Louis; Walters Art Gallery, Baltimore; Royal Museum of Art, Toronto; Yale, Cornell, Princeton, Washington, and Stanford Universities; and the Universities of Michigan, Cincinnati, Chicago, and California.

ENCYCLOPEDIAS AND WORKS OF REFERENCE

The general dictionaries and encyclopedias of classical studies listed in Section H are equally valuable for Roman history. See also the following:

I1. Jones, Henry Stuart. **Companion to Roman history.** Oxford, 1912. Deals mostly with matters that may be illustrated from material remains in architecture, war, religion, economic life, amusements, and art. Antiquated in details, but not superseded.

I2. Sandys, Sir John E., ed. **A companion to Latin studies.** 3rd ed., Cambridge, Eng., 1921. Reprint, 1925. Thirty-five sections by twenty-eight specialists cover informatively many fields of Roman history, law, the army, and private, public and cultural life. For list of authors and titles see the original *Guide,* p. 182.

I3. Bengtson, Hermann. **Einführung in die alte Geschichte.** 2nd ed., Munich, 1953. Now the best combined introduction, critique of sources, and bibliographical aid for both Roman history and allied disciplines; but

does not entirely supersede the full discussion and analysis of the ancient sources in *14,* below, and for the empire *I5.*

I4. Rosenberg, Arthur. **Einleitung und Quellenkunde zu römische Geschichte.** Berlin, 1921.

I5. Peter, Hermann W. G. **Die geschichtliche Literatur über die römische Kaiserzeit bis Theodosius I und ihre Quellen.** 2 v. Leipzig, 1897.

I6. Laistner, Max L. W. **The greater Roman historians.** Berkeley, 1947. [Sather classical lectures, 37.]

I7. Sandys, Sir John E. **Latin epigraphy.** 2nd rev. ed., by S. G. Campbell, Cambridge, Eng., 1927. Best guide in English to the study of Latin inscriptions.

I8. Cagnat, René. **Cours d'épigraphie latine.** 4th rev. ed., Paris, 1914. Excellent; the standard work in French.

I9. Dessau, Hermann. "Lateinische Epigraphik." Alfred Gercke and Eduard Norden, eds., **Einleitung in die Altertumswissenschaft,** v. 1 (3rd rev. ed., Leipzig, 1927). Valuable brief account by a master.

I10. Ruggiero, Ettore de. **Dizionario epigrafico di antichità romane.** Ed. by G. Cardinali and A. Ferrabino. Rome, 1895 ff. [Istituto Italiano per la Storia Antica.] Arranged alphabetically under appropriate titles with commentary and bibliography the historical information contained in inscriptions.

I11. Gordon, Arthur E., and Joyce S. Gordon. **Album of dated Latin inscriptions.** 2 v. Berkeley, 1958. (In progress.) New and indispensable aid to the scientific study of inscriptions. Excellent photographs.

I12. Mommsen, Theodor. **Die römische Chronologie bis auf Caesar.** 2nd rev. ed., Berlin, 1859. Pioneer modern work, still a sound introduction to the problems of Roman chronology.

I13. Leuze, Oskar. **Die römische Jahrzählung.** Tübingen, 1909. Important attempt to explain Roman chronology of the kings and the early republic. For careful chronological analyses see W. Unger, *Römische Chronologie* and B. Niese, *Grundriss der römischen Geschichte nebst Quellenkunde,* both in *Handbuch der Altertumswissenschaft* (*H18*).

I14. Clinton, Henry F. **Fasti romani: the civil and literary chronology of Rome and Constantinople from the death of Augustus to the death of Justin II.** 2 v. Oxford, 1845– 50. V. 1 contains detailed chronological tables from A.D. 15 to 578; v. 2, chronological and historical investigations. The author's *Fasti hellenici,* v. 3, which covers from B.C 280 to 14 A.D., is useful for Roman history. All volumes require revision in light of recent discoveries.

I15. Peter, Karl L. **Zeittafeln der römischen Geschichte zum Handgebrauch und als**

Grundlage des Vortrags in höheren Gymnasialklassen mit fortlaufenden Belegen und Auszügen aus den Quellen. 6th rev. ed., Halle, 1882. Covers from B.C. 753 to 476 A.D. Correct in outline, but antiquated in details.

I16. Goyau, Georges. **Chronologie de l'Empire Romain.** Paris, 1891. Covers period from B.C. 31 to 541 A.D. Useful, but also requires revision. Summary chronological tables may be found at the end of each volume of the *Cambridge ancient history.*

I17. Degrassi, Attilio. **Fasti consulares et triumphales.** 2 v. Rome, 1947. [Inscriptiones italiae, 13.] New edition of all the inscriptional fasti, which incorporates recent discoveries and supersedes the edition by Theodor Mommsen in v. 1 of the *Corpus inscriptionum latinarum.* Lists, with full citation of evidence, the consuls, dictators, censors, and triumphs from the regal period to 13 A.D. The same author has published an edition with commentary of *Inscriptiones latinae liberae rei publicae* (Florence, 1957), a useful work for ready reference.

I18. ———. **I fasti consolari dell' impero romano dal 30 avanti Christo al 613 dopo Christo.** Rome, 1952. The most complete list, superseding all previous ones. Extremely useful indexes. Review, R. Syme, *Jour. Rom. studies,* 43 (1953): 148.

I19. Broughton, T. Robert S. **The magistrates of the Roman republic.** 2 v. Lancaster, Pa., 1951–52. [Monographs of the American Philological Association, 15.] List, year by year, of all known Roman magistrates from 509 to 31 B.C., with statements on their activities, and citations of ancient sources and significant modern bibliography. Provides a survey of Roman family history. Handbook of a type never before attempted; indispensable for the student of Roman republican history. For additional material see Ronald Syme, *Classical philology,* 50 (1955): 127–38; *Historia,* 4 (1955): 52–71. [LRT]

I20. Prosopographia imperii romani saeculorum I, II, III, consilio et auctoritate Academiae Scientiarum Regiae Borussicae. Ed. by E. Klebs, H. Dessau, and P. Rohden. 3 v. Berlin, 1897–98. 2nd ed. rev. and enl., 1932 ff. Indispensable for period from the battle of Actium to the reign of Diocletian. Lists in alphabetical order, as far as possible according to gentile names, members of the senatorial and equestrian orders, many imperial freedmen, a number of client princes, and prominent provincials, with full citation of inscriptional, numismatic, and literary evidence.

GEOGRAPHIES, GAZETTEERS, AND ATLASES

I21. Mela, Pomponius. **De chorographia.** Ed. by Carlos Frick. Leipzig, 1880. A brief sketch in highly rhetorical style written in the first century after Christ.

I22. Plinius Secundus, Caius (the elder). **Naturalis historia.** Ed. by Karl F. T. Mayhoff. 5 v. Leipzig, 1875–1906. Tr. by Harris Rackham and W. H. S. Jones, London and Cambridge, Mass., 1949 ff. (in progress). Pliny the elder, who filled high civil and military offices, was considered the most learned Roman of his time. In 77 A.D. he published his *Natural history* in 37 books, a compendium of natural science derived from many sources. Books 2–6, dealing primarily with geography and ethnography, depend in part on Agrippa's survey, but add information from other sources and from Pliny's own time. [AERB, TRSB]

I23. Ptolemaeus, Claudius. **Geographia.** Ed. by Karl Müller and C. T. Fischer. 1 v. in 2 pts. Paris, 1883–1901. See below.

I24. ———. **Die Geographie des Ptolemaeus: Galliae, Germania, Raetia, Noricum, Pannoniae, Illyricum, Italia: Handschriften, Text, und Untersuchung.** Ed. by Otto Cuntz. Berlin, 1923. This and *123* together constitute a complete scholarly edition, with annotation and commentary, of the work written by the Alexandrian astronomer and mathematician about 150 A.D. to accompany his maps. With the aim of locating accurately, according to tables of latitude and longitude, all places between 10° south and 60° north from the western islands to Java, it sums up the geographical knowledge of antiquity and marks the close of ancient scientific geographical study. A richer source of ancient materials may be found in Strabo's *Geography.* [AERB, TRSB]

I25. Geographi graeci minores. Ed. by Karl Müller. 2 v. Paris, 1882. See below.

I26. Geographi latini minores. Ed. by Alexander Riese. Heilbronn, Ger., 1882. This and *125* are useful collections of brief treatises of varying importance. New editions needed.

I27. Itineraria romana. Ed. by Otto Cuntz and Joseph Schnetz. 2 v. Leipzig, 1929–40. [1, *Itineraria Antonini Augusti et burdigalense;* 2, *Ravennatis anonymi cosmographia et guidonis geographica.*] See below.

I28. Die Peutingersche Tafel. Ed. by Konrad Miller. Stuttgart, 1916. This and *127* are modern editions of ancient itineraries, of which the Antonine derives from a description of roads in the time of Caracalla. Important in the study of ancient communications.

The atlases listed in Section H are also useful for Roman history. Those of Kiepert (*H30*) and Bengtson and Milojčič (*H29*) deserve special mention.

I29. Tabula imperii romani. Map of the Roman empire based on the *Carte internationale du monde au millionième.* Twelve maps have been published at different times and places from Edinburgh, 1931, to Mogontiacum (Mainz), 1940.

I30. Edizione archeologica della Carta d'Italia al 100,000. Florence, 1928 ff. [Istituto Geografico Militare.] Now almost complete.

I31. Forma italiae. 6 fasc. Rome, 1926–48. [Unione Accademia Nazionale d'Italia.]

I32. Map of Italy. Ed. by Plinius Fraccaro and Mario Baratta. In **Grande Atlante geografico** (4th ed., Novara, 1938). Map of ancient Italy especially useful for historical purposes.

I33. Carte archéologique de la Gaule romaine. Ed. by Adrien Blanchet. 10 fasc. Paris, 1931–46. [Académie des Inscriptions et Belles-Lettres.] Based on the 1 to 200,000 maps of the Service Géographique de l'Armée. Plans call for 81 fascicles.

I34. Map of Roman Britain. Southampton, 1924. 3rd ed. rev., 1951. [Ordnance Survey.]

I35. Atlas archéologique de l'Algérie. Explanatory text by Stéphane Gsell. Algiers and Paris, 1902–11. [Gouvernement Général de l'Algérie.]

I36. Atlas archéologique de la Tunisie. Explanatory text by E. Babelon, R. Cagnat, and S. Reinach. 1st ser., Paris, 1892–1913; 2nd serv., 1914 ff.

I37. Carta arqueologica de España. 2 sheets. Madrid, 1941–45.

I38. Thomson, James O. **History of ancient geography.** Cambridge, Eng., 1948. See *H26*.

I39. Cary, Max, and Eric H. Warmington. **The ancient explorers.** N.Y., 1929. See *H27*. Also see Henry F. Tozer, *A history of ancient geography* (2nd ed. rev. by M. Cary, Cambridge, Eng., 1935).

I40. Jung, Julius. **Grundriss der Geographie von Italien un dem Orbis romanus.** 2nd rev. ed., Munich, 1897. Comprehensive work on the geography of the Roman world, dealing with physical and historical geography, ethnography, topography of cities, and Roman administration. Philippson, below, should also be used for physical geography, ethnography, and economic conditions of the Mediterranean lands. [AERB, TRSB]

I41. Philippson, Alfred. **Das Mittelmeergebiet, seine geographische und kulturelle Eigenart.** 4th ed., Leipzig, 1922.

I42. Cary, Max. **The geographic background of Greek and Roman history.** Oxford, 1949. See *H22*.

Students of the geography and topography of Rome, Italy, and the provinces may profitably consult modern guide books such as *Baedeker* (*B221*), *Les guides bleues* (*B223*), and (for Italy) the series issued by the Touring Club Italiano in Milan. Many sites in Italy are described in the series *Municipie e colonie,* published by the Istituto di Studi Romani in Rome. Many books on history of

the provinces, cited later in this section, contain valuable geographical material. Among these should be mentioned Gsell on Africa (*I172*), Jullian on Gaul (*I159*), and Collingwood on Britain (*I157*). See also the studies of German and Austrian limes (*I166*) and those in Syria (*I186–187*). In Syria, Africa, and now increasingly in Italy and Britain, excellent use is being made of the techniques of aerial photography. See

I43. Bradford, John. **Ancient landscapes: studies in field archaeology.** London, 1957.

I44. Nissen, Heinrich. **Italische Landeskunde.** 2 v. Berlin, 1883–1902. Still a fundamental reference work for its detailed information on the geographical regions of Italy (v. 1) and the political geography of the Roman regions (v. 2). Historical and descriptive accounts of the towns.

I45. Tomassetti, Giuseppe. **La campagna romana antica, medioevale e moderna.** 4 v. Rome, 1910–26. V. 1 covers economic, administrative, and cultural conditions from ancient to modern times; v. 2–4 contain topographical data following the Roman roads in alphabetical order to about 20 miles from the city. Review of v. 1–3, T. Ashby, *Jour. Rom. studies,* 2 (1912): 275; of v. 4, *Jour. Rom. studies,* 16 (1926): 268.

I46. Ashby, Thomas. **The Roman campagna in classical times.** London, 1927. Presents with careful observation and accurate description of the ancient remains the results of thirty years of exploration.

I47. Bagnani, Gilbert. **The Roman campagna and its treasures.** London, 1929. Convenient guide, with excellent comments and good illustrations, to ancient and more recent sites and monuments from the Tiber to Tarracina.

I48. Afzelius, Adam. **Die römische Eroberung Italiens.** Copenhagen, 1942. Historical geography of the Roman conquest of Italy, presenting a careful analysis of the area and population under Roman control at each stage.

I49. Thomsen, Rudi. **The Italic regions from Augustus to the Lombard invasion.** Copenhagen, 1947. A thorough geographical and administrative history of the Augustan regions.

I50. Beloch, Karl J. **Campanien: Geschichte und Topographie des antiken Neapel und seiner Umgebung.** 2nd rev. ed., Breslau, 1890. A still useful study of an important region.

I51. Ramsey, Sir William M. **Historical geography of Asia Minor.** London, 1890. [Royal Geographical Society, Supplementary papers, 4.] The fundamental pioneer work. Supplemented and corrected by material in *Monumenta Asiae Minoris antiqua* (v. 1–7, Manchester, 1928–56); Louis Robert, *Études anatoliennes* (Paris, 1937); L. Robert, *Villes d'Asie Mineure* (Paris, 1935); L. Robert,

La Carie (v. 2, Paris, 1956); A. H. M. Jones, *Cities of the eastern Roman provinces* (Oxford, 1939); and scattered observations in L. Robert, *Hellenica* (v. 1–10, Paris, 1940–55).

I52. Bussard, René. **Topographie historique de la Syrie antique et médiévale.** Paris, 1927. Essential for detailed study of the historical geography of Syria. See also *I187*.

DEMOGRAPHIC STUDIES

I53. Beloch, Karl J. **Die Bevölkerung der griechisch-römischen Welt.** Leipzig, 1886. See *H41*.

I54. Boak, Arthur E. R. **Manpower shortage and the fall of the Roman empire in the West.** Ann Arbor, 1955. An important contribution which presents evidence for lack of manpower in the late empire for production, administration, and military service. Review, A. H. M. Jones, *Econ. hist. rev.*, 9 (1956–57): 379.

PRINTED COLLECTIONS OF SOURCES

There is as yet in English no good introduction to the sources of Roman history. Some works in other languages are mentioned under Works of Reference, above, and valuable notes on a number of source problems may be found in volumes of the *Cambridge ancient history* (*I77*). The various types of sources may be described briefly here with indications where they may most conveniently be consulted.

The **literary sources** comprise both the historical works of Greek and Latin authors and their other writings which throw light upon various aspects of life in the Roman world. Editions, translations, and critical estimates of the most important writers on Roman history are given below (*I93–99, 123–131*), and works of other authors are listed in the section on Latin literature. Texts and translations of a large part of the literary sources are available in the collections as mentioned in Section H. Most important of such series are the *Oxford classical texts*, the *Bibliotheca Teubneriana*, the *Corpus Paravianum*, the *Loeb classical library* (for English translations), and the *Guillaume Budé* series (for French translations). Existing fragments of the lost works of ancient historians are in collections listed in Section H and in *I56–57*, below.

The **inscriptions** consist chiefly of laws, treaties, decrees, dedications, and honorary and funerary inscriptions. They contribute to knowledge of the Roman administrative system as well as the social and economic conditions. The principal collections of inscriptions for Roman history are listed below (*I58–70*).

Papyri, found in large numbers in Egypt,

comprise public records of all sorts as well as private archives and correspondence. For the history of Roman Egypt they are invaluable. Similar in character, but less important, are **ostraka,** or records on potsherds, coming mostly from the same country. The principal publications of *papyri* and *ostraka* and bibliographies of literature concerning them are referred to in Section H and below (*I192–197*).

The great importance of Roman **coins** for chronology, politics, economics, and history of art has been increasingly recognized. The chief works on Roman coins are listed below (*I374–392*). Current material will be found in *Numismatic literature*, other numismatic journals, and the section on numismatics in *L'année philologique*.

Under **archaeological material** may be included other material remains of Roman civilization which have survived to the present time and often illuminate more strictly historical material. The catalogues of museums containing public and private collections are the best guides to material of this kind. Some handbooks are listed below (*1347 ff.*). New discoveries and excavations are regularly reported in the *American journal of archaeology*, the *Bulletin de correspondance hellénique*, and the *Archäologischer Anzeiger*. Excellent bibliography appears in the annual volumes of *Fasti archaeologici*. [AERB, TRSB]

I55. Lewis, Naphtali, and Meyer Reinhold. **Roman civilization: selected readings, edited with introduction and notes.** 2 v. N.Y., 1951–55. Excellent selection of passages in translation from literary sources, inscriptions, and papyri. V. 1 covers the period of the republic and v. 2 the empire. Many documents are translated for the first time, and material on many aspects of Roman civilization is included. Select bibliography.

I56. Peter, Hermann W. G., ed. **Historicorum romanorum reliquiae.** 2 v. Leipzig, 1870–1905. Rev. ed. of v. 1, 1914. The standard collection of surviving fragments of the lost works of ancient Roman annalists and historians. [AERB]

I57. Malcovati, Henrica, ed. **Oratorum romanorum fragmenta liberae rei publicae.** 2nd rev. ed., Turin, 1955. The only good edition of fragments of orators of the republican period. Bibliography and commentary.

I58. Corpus inscriptionum latinarum. Ed. by many scholars for the Preussische Akademie der Wissenschaften. V. 1–16 in many parts and supplements. Berlin, 1863 ff. [1, *Inscriptiones antiquissimae;* 2, *Hispaniae;* 3, *Asiae, provinciarum Europae, Illyrici;* 4, *Parietariae Pompeianae, Herculanenses, Stabianae;* 5, *Galliae Cisalpinae;* 6, *Urbis Romae;* 7, *Britanniae;* 8, *Africae;* 9, *Calabriae, Apuliae, Samnii, Sabinorum, Piceni;* 10,

Bruttiorum, Lucaniae, Campaniae, Siciliae, Sardiniae; 11, *Aemiliae, Etruriae, Umbriae;* 12, *Galliae Narbonensis;* 13, *Trium Galliarum et Germaniarum instrumenti domestici;* 14, *Latii veteris;* 15, *Instrumentum domesticum urbis Romae;* 16, *Diplomata militaria.*] The great standard collection of Latin inscriptions.

159. Ephemeris epigraphica: corporis inscriptionum latinarum supplementum. Ed. by Istituti Archaeologici Romani. 9 v. in 8. Berlin, 1872–1913. Forms a supplement to *158.*

160. Inscriptiones Italiae. Ed. by Unione Accademia Nazionale. Rome, 1936 ff. (In progress.) A new series in which the inscriptions of Italy, both Greek and Latin, are to be reviewed and published. Includes those in the older collections and those more recently discovered.

161. Inscriptiones graecae ad res romanas pertinentes. Ed. by Académie des Inscriptions et Belles-Lettres. 3 v. Paris, 1902–28. Useful collection of Greek inscriptions important for Roman history. Still incomplete and not always well edited.

162. Inscriptions latines de l'Algérie. V. 1, Inscriptions de la proconsulaire. Ed. by Stéphane Gsell. Paris, 1922. Revision and supplement, with commentary, of the Latin inscriptions of the same region as *158,* v. 8; complete for its date. The first fascicles of v. 2, ed. by H. G. Pflaum, have recently appeared.

163. Cagnat, René, Alfred Merlin, and Louis Chatelain, eds. **Inscriptions latines de l'Afrique (Tripolitaine, Tunisie, Maroc).** Paris, 1923. This and *164–65* bring revisions and much supplementary material to previous collections of inscriptions for their respective regions. Brief commentary and bibliography.

164. Merlin, Alfred, ed. **Inscriptions latines de la Tunisie.** Paris, 1944.

165. Reynolds, Joyce M., and J. B. Ward Perkins, eds. **The inscriptions of Roman Tripolitania.** Rome and London, 1952.

166. Espérandieu, Émile, ed. **Inscriptions latines de Gaule (Narbonaise).** 2 v. Paris, 1929. Revisions and supplementary material for this region of Gaul.

167. Jalabert, Louis, and René Mouterde, eds. **Inscriptions grecques et latines de la Syrie.** 4 v. Paris, 1929–55. Especially valuable due to lack of recent general collection of Syrian inscriptions.

168. Dessau, Hermann, ed. **Inscriptiones latinae selectae.** 3 v. in 5. Berlin, 1892–1916. The most valuable selection of Latin inscriptions in a convenient form. Notes and indexes.

169. Ehrenberg, Victor, and Arnold H. M. Jones, eds. **Documents illustrating the reigns of Augustus and Tiberius.** 2nd ed., Oxford, 1955. This and *170* together present a convenient and well edited collection of epigraphical documents for these reigns, many of them otherwise difficult of access.

170. Charlesworth, Martin P. **Documents illustrating the reigns of Claudius and Nero.** Cambridge, Eng., 1939.

Many items of importance for Roman history are included in collections mentioned in Section H. Newly discovered or recently published Latin inscriptions are published annually in *Revue archéologique,* and printed separately in *Année epigraphique.*

SHORTER GENERAL HISTORIES

171. Boak, Arthur E. R. **A history of Rome to 565 A.D.** 4th ed., N.Y., 1955. A clear and concise survey, based on excellent knowledge of sources and modern discussions, and well adapted to both students and general readers. Select bibliography of works in English.

172. Frank, Tenney. **A history of Rome.** N.Y., 1923. A readable and scholarly narrative to the death of Constantine, with a short summary of the following century. Written particularly for general readers, it emphasizes relations with American democracy. Good on social and economic conditions, but now in need of some revision. Select bibliography.

173. Cary, Max. **A history of Rome down to the time of Constantine.** London, 1935. A sensible and well-proportioned general history, suitable for students and general readers.

174. Vogt, Josef, and Eduard Kornemann. **Römische Geschichte.** Berlin and Leipzig, 1933. A compact history, somewhat advanced for beginners. Includes the period down to the 7th century A.D. Most interesting for its fresh and challenging treatment of the empire. Good notes and bibliographies.

175. Niese, Benedictus. **Grundriss der römischen Geschichte nebst Quellenkunde.** 5th ed., Munich, 1923. [Handbuch der Altertumswissenschaft.] Excellent reference work, containing a concise and accurate narrative of political history, reliable estimates of sources, but little treatment of social, economic, or cultural history.

176. Aymard, André, and Jeannine Auboyer. **Rome et son empire.** Paris, 1954. [Histoire générale des civilisations, 2.] Lively and penetrating survey, with little historical narrative, of the evolution of civilization in the ancient world during the period from Roman expansion in Italy to the 4th century after Christ, with emphasis on the unity produced by the Roman empire. Mlle. Auboyer contributes chapters on eastern and southern Asia in the same period.

LONGER GENERAL HISTORIES

177. The Cambridge ancient history. V. 7–12. Cambridge, Eng. and N.Y., 1923–39.

These volumes, the works of many scholars under one editorial board, constitute, with their companion volumes of plates, the most ample and up-to-date treatment we possess of the development of Rome and the Roman world to the time of Constantine in its many political, social, economic, and cultural aspects. The narrative is direct and the treatment factual. Detailed bibliographies. (See *H118*.)

178. Pareti, Luigi. **Storia di Roma e del mondo romano.** 4 v. Turin, 1952–55. (In progress.) A large-scale history of Rome and Italy from 1000 B.C. Conceived on broad lines and marked by independence; profusely illustrated. With v. 4 the series reached 69 A.D.

HISTORIES OF SPECIAL PERIODS

Pre-Roman Italy

179. Kaschnitz-Weinberg, Guido. **Italien mit Sardinien, Sizilien und Malta.** Munich, 1950. [Handbuch der Altertumswissenschaft, 6.] Convenient summary covering the period up to *ca.* 1000 B.C. Detailed bibliographies with each section.

180. Montelius, Gustav O. **La civilisation primitive en Italie depuis l'introduction des métaux.** 2 v. Stockholm and Berlin, 1895–1910. Still important, especially because of the illustrations, for the study of remains of prehistoric civilization in Italy. [AERB, TRSB]

181. Duhn, Friedrich K. von. **Italische Gräberkunde.** 2 v. Heidelberg, 1924–39. The great work on interpretation of archaeological material found in early Italian cemeteries. V. 2 on the Veneti, the Picentes, and the Iapyges was completed and supplemented by Franz Messerschmidt. [AERB, TRSB]

182. Messerschmidt, Franz. **Bronzezeit und frühe Eisenzeit in Italien, Pfahlbau, Terramare, Villanova.** Berlin and Leipzig, 1935. Critical survey of evidence and interpretations, presenting clearly the position reached in the study of ethnology and development of prehistoric Italy. Good bibliography. Review, G. M. A. Hanfmann, *Am. jour. archaeol.,* 40 (1936): 394.

183. Säflund, L. Gösta. **Le terremare delle provincie di Modena, Reggio Emilia, Parma, Piacenza.** Lund, Swe., 1939. Detailed investigation of all terramara sites which, by showing that there is no necessary connection between the terramaricoli and the Villanovans or the Romans, has set the study of Bronze Age ethnology and archaeology in a new perspective. Review, C. F. C. Hawkes and E. Stiassny, *Jour. Rom. studies,* 30 (1940): 89.

184. Randall-MacIver, David. **Villanovans and early Etruscans: a study of the early Iron Age in Italy as it is seen near Bologna,** in Etruria and in Latium. Oxford, 1924. See below.

185. ——. **Iron Age in Italy: a study of those aspects in the early civilization which are neither Villanovan nor Etruscan.** Oxford, 1927. This and *184* are works of remarkable scholarship, well illustrated, which together present for their date a clear discussion of the archaeological evidence and give a comprehensive view of Iron Age Italy. *Italy before the Romans,* by the same author (Oxford, 1928), summarizes for general readers the results of the more technical studies. [AERB, TRSB]

186. Whatmough, Joshua. **The foundations of Roman Italy.** London, 1937. Valuable attempt to coordinate, region by region, the linguistic and archaeological evidence for the development of pre-Roman Italy. Review, F. N. Pryce, *Jour. Rom. studies,* 27 (1937): 260.

187. Pallottino, Massimo. **The Etruscans.** Tr. by J. Cremona. Harmondsworth, Eng., 1955. Convenient survey of the present state of questions relating to Etruscan origins, expansion, political organization, cultural development, and language. Good notes, select bibliography.

188. Ducati, Pericle. **Etruria antica.** 2nd ed., 2 v., Turin, 1927. Extensive and balanced survey of Etruscan history and culture, especially valuable on Etruscan art. Review of 1st ed., G. de Sanctis, *Rivista di filologia,* 55 (1927): 101.

189. ——. **Le problème étrusque.** Paris, 1938. Impartial presentation of the problem of Etruscan origins, the evidence and opposing theories. Summary history of Etruscan research and critical estimate of bibliography.

190. Dennis, George. **The cities and cemeteries of Etruria.** New ed. by W. M. Lindsay, 2 v., London, 1907. A still important work of reference for the topography, history, and archaeology of cities and sites in Etruria.

191. Heurgon, Jacques. **Recherches sur l'histoire, la religion et la civilisation de Capoue préromaine des origines à la deuxième guerre punique.** Paris, 1942. Study of early Campania, of Etruscan and Samnite Capua; a local history which illuminates a considerable region of early Italy as well as its relations with Rome.

192. Holland, Louise A. **The Faliscans in prehistoric times.** Rome, 1925. [Papers and monographs of the American Academy in Rome, 5.] Excellent study of the early history of the region, based on archaeological evidence.

Regal Period and Republic

Ancient Historians

193. Livius, Titus. **Ab urbe condita liber.** Ed. by Wilhelm Weissenborn. 6 v. Leipzig, 1850–56. Other editions and translations.

Livy of Patavium (B.C. 59–17 A.D.), though also a rhetorician and a philosopher, devoted himself to his history of Rome after 31 B.C. These 142 books covered the period from the landing of Aeneas to the death of Drusus (9 B.C.). Books 1–10 (to 293 B.C.), 21–45 (218–167 B.C.), and a fragment of 91 (on Sertorius) have been preserved. Of the remainder there exist epitomes, *periochae,* and a few excerpts. Livy was enthusiastic about Rome's distant past, where he found exemplars of true Roman virtue and morality, and the basis for a genuine patriotism. He was preeminently successful in creating a great literary masterpiece. Though he was not systematically critical of his sources, some of which were later annalists, his candor and love of truth, and his frequent use of good sources like Polybius, made him as good a guide as the Roman world possessed. See A. Klotz in *Realencyclopädie,* 13: 816–52 (*H12*). [WAO, TRSB]

194. Appianus. **Historia romana.** Ed. by Lovidicus Mendelssohn. 2 v. Leipzig, 1879–81. Other eds. Tr. by Horace White, J. D. Denniston, and E. I. Robson, 4 v., London and Cambridge, Mass., 1912–13. [Loeb classical library.] Appian, an Alexandrian Greek, held office in Alexandria. Upon receiving Roman citizenship, he became a knight and an imperial procurator. Under Antoninus Pius he wrote his history in 24 books, almost entirely military and arranged in geographical order, covering the period from the founding of Rome to Trajan. Books 6–7 (on the Spanish and Hannibalic wars) and 11–17 (on the Syrian, Mithridatic, and Civil wars) are complete, but the rest are fragmentary or lost. Appian was an admirer of Rome. Though often found lacking in learning and judgment, he is valuable, particularly in preserving material from earlier sources. Review, E. Schwartz, *Realencyclopädie,* 2: 216. See also E. Gabba, *Appiano e la storia delle guerre civili* (Florence, 1956). [WAO, TRSB]

195. Dionysius of Halicarnassus. **De antiquitatibus romanarum quae supersunt.** Ed. by C. Jacoby. 4 v. Leipzig, 1885–1905. Ed. and tr. Earnest Cary, on basis of version by Edward Spelman, 7 v., 1937–50. [Loeb classical library.] Dionysius, a rhetor and historian who resided in Rome after 30 B.C., published in or after 7 B.C. the twenty books of his history of Rome, covering the period from the origins to 265 B.C., the date at which Polybius' narrative begins. Only books 1–10, part of 11, and some fragments remain. His work was designed to present a favorable view, against current anti-Roman propaganda, of the origins and virtues of the Romans, and in this resembles Livy. His quotations of sources are valuable, but his narrative is vitiated by his endeavor to prove that the Romans were originally

Greek, by rhetorical elaboration, and by lack of historical sense. [AERB, TRSB]

196. Polybius. **Historiae.** Rev. ed. by T. Büttner-Wobst, 2 v., Leipzig, 1882–89. Text and tr. by W. R. Paton, 6 v., London and Cambridge, Mass., 1922–27. [Loeb classical library.] (See also *H68.*) Polybius (*ca.* 203–*ca.* 120 B.C.) of Megalopolis, began a political career in the Achaean League, but was deported to Rome in 167 B.C. and lived there in close association with Scipio Aemilianus and other leading Romans. Impressed by the strength of Roman institutions, he wrote his universal history of the period 220–145 B.C., with a preliminary survey beginning with 264, in order to explain to the Greeks the nature of "fortune's fairest work," the hegemony of Rome. Of forty books, the first five have survived in entirety, and there are considerable fragments of the rest, including descriptions of the Roman constitution and the Roman army in book 6. Polybius' accuracy, his usual impartiality, his experience in politics and war, and his sense of political realities, combine to make his "pragmatic" history, in spite of literary deficiencies, one of the most important histories of ancient times. See Bury (*H91*), pp. 191–223; Walbank (*H67*). [AERB, TRSB]

197. Caesar, Caius Julius. **Commentarii de bello gallico.** Ed. by T. Rice Holmes, London, 1914. Text and tr. by H. J. Edwards, London and Cambridge, Mass., 1914. [Loeb classical library.]

198. ——. **Commentarii de bello civili.** Ed. by A. Klotz, Leipzig, 1950. Text and tr. by A. G. Peskett, London and N.Y., 1914. [Loeb classical library.] Julius Caesar (100–44 B.C.), orator and man of letters, wrote, under the modest title of Commentarii, materials of history that served both as a partisan apology and the greatest of memoirs. The work on the Gallic war is in general fair and accurate as history and a fine example of plain style. Seven books were probably published in 51 to justify his military and political policy. Three books covering events of 49 and 48 are even more openly apologetic. Hirtius, his secretary in Gaul, added book 8 of the Gallic war, a narrative of 51 and 50 intended to connect the two works. Anonymous continuations on the Alexandrian, African, and Spanish wars are good historical accounts, but poor in style (ed. and tr. by A. G. Way, London and Cambridge, Mass., 1955). [WAO, TRSB]

199. Sallustius Crispus, Gaius. **C. Sallusti Crispi Catilina, Jugurtha, orationes et epistulae excerptae de historiis.** Ed. by A. W. Ahlberg, Leipzig, 1919. [Bibliotheca Teubneriana.] Ed. and tr. by A. Ernout, 2 v., Paris, 1941–46. [Budé series.] Tr. by J. C. Rolfe, London and Cambridge, Mass., 1921. [Loeb classical library.] Sallust (86–*ca.* 35

B.C.), a Caesarian who became proconsul of Africa Nova in 46 and is said to have been guilty of extortion, retired from public life by 44 to devote himself to historical writing. His monographs on the Catilinarian conspiracy and the war with Jugurtha remain; but of the five books of his histories, covering the years 78–67 B.C., only some speeches, letters, and a quantity of fragments survive (ed. by E. Maurenbrecher, Leipzig, 1891–93). His style is severe and his interpretations are colored by his popular background, but they do penetrate beneath the claims of all political factions and are based on more accurate investigation than might be expected. [AERB, TRSB]

Modern Historians

I100. Mommsen, Theodor. **History of Rome.** New ed., 4 v., London and N.Y., 1911. [Everyman's library.] Tr. by W. P. Dickson from *Römische Geschichte* (3 v., 1854–56; 12th–13th ed., 3 v., Berlin, 1920–23). Account of the growth of the Roman state from its origins to the death of Julius Caesar. Although there is little documentation or discussion of special problems, narrative and judgments reveal thorough mastery of the sources. Disillusionment with the 1848 revolution led the author to depreciate the Gracchi, Cicero's public career, and the senate of the late republic, and to exalt Caesar, who gave promise of founding a new era. Special chapters are devoted to Roman social, economic, intellectual, and religious development. Much of the work, especially in the earlier part, is now antiquated, but as a whole it remains one of the classics of historical literature. [AERB, TRSB]

I101. Sanctis, Gaetano de. **Storia dei Romani.** 4 v. Turin and Florence, 1907–53. A great history, the parts of which differ in scope, purpose, and usefulness, particularly due to the long interruption between pts. 1 and 2 of v. 4. V. 1–2, by their independent analysis of sources, recalled scholars from too great scepticism of Rome's early tradition, but now require revision. V. 3 is an outstandingly complete narrative of 260–200 B.C., but needs supplement on constitutional and economic questions. Pt. 1 of v. 4 carries the story through the period of expansion to 167 B.C.; and pt. 2 is a distinguished survey of art, architecture, and religion in Rome of the 2nd century B.C. [TF, TRSB]

I102. Pais, Ettore. **Histoire romaine: des origines à l'achèvement de la conquête (133 av. J.C.).** 2nd ed., Paris, 1940. Considerable revision and enlargement of 1st ed. Much of Pais' hypercritical analysis of early tradition and of his daring reconstruction has been corrected by Jean Bayet, who brought the book up to date.

I103. Bloch, Gustave, and Jérôme Carco-pino. **Histoire romaine: la république romaine de 133 à 44 avant J.C.** 1 v. in 2. Paris, 1935–36. [1, *Des Gracques à Sulla;* 2, *César.*] Almost entirely by Carcopino. Wide in scope, critical, vigorously written; an important work on an important period, which demands consideration even when dissent seems necessary.

I104. Scullard, Howard H. **A history of the Roman world from 753 to 146 B.C.** 2nd rev. ed., London, 1951. [Methuen's history of the Greek and Roman world.] The 1934 edition brought up to date. A judicious, sober, and readable history. Select bibliography.

I105. Marsh, Frank B. **A history of the Roman world from 146 to 30 B.C.** 2nd rev. ed. by H. H. Scullard, London, 1953. [Methuen's history of the Greek and Roman world.] By way of correction of the 1935 edition, Scullard has added valuable notes and appendices to this useful history, and revised the bibliography.

I106. Altheim, Franz. **Epochen der römischen Geschichte.** 2 v. Frankfurt-am-Main, 1934–35. [1, *Von den Anfängen bis zum Beginn der Weltherrschaft;* 2, *Weltherrschaft und Krise.*] A lively, original, and at times audacious, survey of periods and movements from early Rome to the late republic, with emphasis on religious developments.

I107. Piganiol, André. **La conquête romaine.** 4th ed., Paris, 1944. Clear and stimulating narrative of Roman history to the battle of Actium, particularly useful on the early period.

I108. Ryberg, Inez S. **An archaeological record of Rome from the seventh to the second century B.C.** London and Philadelphia, 1940. A standard discussion of the contribution of Roman archaeological discoveries to history of the kingship and the republic. See also author's earlier study, "Early Roman traditions in the light of archaeology," *Memoirs of the American Academy in Rome,* 7 (1929): 7–118. [LRT]

I109. Beloch, Karl J. **Römische Geschichte bis zum Beginn der punischen Kriege.** Berlin, 1926. Critical discussion of Roman conquest and colonization in Italy, characterized by great acumen and independence, but marred by capricious judgments.

I110. Frank, Tenney. **Roman imperialism.** N.Y., 1914. Analysis of the conditions and motives of Roman expansion leads to the conclusions that Rome was little inclined to aggression, that analogies to modern commercial imperialism were lacking until late in the 2nd century B.C., and that individual commanders, like Caesar, were more expansionistic. [ABW, TRSB]

I111. Scullard, Howard H. **Roman politics, 220–150 B.C.** Oxford, 1951. Detailed review of personal and party alignments in Roman political life during the period. Especially valuable for interpretations of Fabius Cunctator and Cato the censor. Review, L. T. Taylor, *Am. jour. of philology*, 73 (July 1952): 302.

I112. Drumann, Wilhelm K. A. **Geschichte Roms in seinem Übergange von der republikanischen zur monarchischen Verfassung: oder Pompeius, Caesar, Cicero, und ihre Zeitgenossen nach genealogischen Tabellen.** 2nd rev. ed., by P. Groebe, 6 v., Berlin, 1899–1929. Exhaustive study of the late republic in biographical form arranged in alphabetical order according to *gentes*. Indispensable reference work, especially valuable for full citations of sources. [AERB, TRSB]

I113. Carcopino, Jérôme. **Autour des Gracques: études critiques.** Paris, 1928. Ingenious essays on problems in the history of the Gracchi. Review, H. M. Last, *Jour. Rom. studies*, 18 (1928): 228.

I114. ———. **Sylla: ou, la monarchie manquée.** Paris, 1931. Valuable analysis of many points of detail; but the main thesis, that Sulla's position as dictator was a near monarchy for which the time was not yet ripe, remains unconvincing.

I115. Badian, Ernst. **Foreign clientelae (264–70 B.C.).** Oxford, 1958. Important, though perhaps too narrow, interpretation of Roman foreign policy in terms of the institution of clientship and related ideas, and the connections formed by Roman noble families.

I116. Holmes, Thomas R. **The Roman republic and the founder of the empire.** 3 v. Oxford and N.Y., 1923. Especially valuable for military history of the period from the dictatorship of Sulla to the assassination of Julius Caesar; not as good on social and political problems. Full documentation and discussion of problems in appendices.

I117. ———. **Caesar's conquest of Gaul.** 2nd rev. ed., Oxford, 1911. Remains indispensable for the study of Caesar's campaigns in Gaul.

I118. Meyer, Eduard. **Caesars Monarchie und das Principat des Pompeius: innere Geschichte Roms von 66 bis 44 v. Chr.** 3rd rev. ed., Stuttgart, 1922. Distinguished study of the period, broad in scholarship and keen in analysis. Emphasizes how Caesar's policies and honors pointed toward a divine monarchy, while Pompey's career provided major precedents for Augustus. At times misunderstands the institutions of the free republic.

I119. Taylor, Lily R. **Party politics in the age of Caesar.** Berkeley, 1949. [Sather classical lectures, 22.] Penetrating and lively analysis of the practical working of the Roman political system in the late republic, with descriptions of the manipulations by individuals and groups of the assemblies, the voting, religious restrictions, and the courts.

Stresses the roles and traditions of Caesar and the younger Cato.

I120. Syme, Ronald. **The Roman revolution.** Oxford, 1939. Brilliant survey and penetrating interpretation of movements, parties, and policies in Rome from 60 B.C. to the death of Augustus, based on a detailed study of the prosopography of the governing classes. Select bibliography. Review, A. Momigliano, *Jour. Rom. studies*, 30 (1940): 75.

I121. Marsh, Frank B. **The founding of the Roman empire.** 2nd rev. ed., Oxford, 1927. Covers in detail the period from the death of Sulla to the death of Augustus. Valuable primarily for a critical survey of constitutional problems and interpretations of the aims of the leading statesmen. [AERB, TRSB]

I122. Holmes, Thomas R. **The architect of the Roman empire.** 2 v. Oxford, 1928–31. V. 1 is a thorough review, with complete documentation and appendices on disputed questions, of the political and military history of the period from the assassination of Julius Caesar to 27 B.C. In v. 2 the same methods are applied with less unity and clarity to the principate of Augustus.

The Principate and the Autocracy

Ancient Writers

I123. Augustus. **Res gestae divi Augusti: ex monumentis Ancyrano et Apolloniensi.** Ed. by T. Mommsen. 2nd ed., Berlin, 1883. Composed by Augustus shortly before his death and set up as a public inscription in Rome and provincial cities, this major text placed before the Roman world his interpretation and report of his career. Mommsen's commentary remains fundamental. The fragments found in Antioch of Pisidia were published by William M. Ramsay and Anton von Premerstein, *Monumentum Antiochenum* (Leipzig, 1927). Jean Gagé, *Res gestae divi Augusti ex monumentis Ancyrano et Antiocheno latinis, Ancyrano et Apolloniensi graecis* (Paris, 1935) provides a convenient and up-to-date text and commentary, with a calendar of the most important dates drawn from the Fasti. [AERB, TRSB]

I124. Velleius Paterculus, Caius. **Ad M. Vinicium libri duo.** Ed. by A. Bolaffi. Turin, 1930. Ed. and tr. (with *Res gestae divi Augusti*) by Frederick W. Shipley, London and N.Y., 1924. [Loeb classical library.] Brief sketch of Roman history in two books (published in 30 A.D.), of which the first is only partially preserved. The second deals with period of the civil wars and the reigns of Augustus and Tiberius. Vellius is biased in favor of his old commander, Tiberius, and his minister, Sejanus, but provides a useful contrast to the Tacitean interpretation.

I125. Tacitus, Caius Cornelius. **Annales.**

Ed. by Charles D. Fisher. Oxford, 1906. [Oxford classical texts.] 7th rev. ed., by E. Koestermann, Leipzig, 1952. [Bibliotheca Teubneriana.] Tr. by George G. Ramsay, 2 v., London, 1904–09. Other eds. and trs.

I126. ——. Historiae. Ed. by C. D. Fisher. Oxford, 1910. [Oxford classical texts.] Ed. by C. Halm and G. Andresen, rev. by E. Koestermann, Leipzig, 1952. [Bibliotheca Teubneriana.] Tr. by G. G. Ramsay, London, 1915. Text and tr. by Clifford H. Moore, 2 v., London and N.Y., 1925–31. These two works constitute a history of Rome from the accession of Tiberius in 14 A.D. to the death of Domitian in 96. Of the *Annals* there are preserved the almost complete narrative of the reign of Tiberius (books 1–6), a portion of Claudius' and most of Nero's (books 11–16); and of the *Histories* the narratives of the civil wars after Nero's death, the revolt of Civilis, and the beginning of the siege of Jerusalem (books 1–5). Like a dramatist, Tacitus emphasizes persons, situations, character, and moral factors. His view of the principate was colored by his idealization of the free republic and his personal experience of despotism under Domitian. For him, therefore, the principate tended toward despotism and was characterized by a decline in virtue. His interest is primarily in the court and the senate and only secondarily in the provinces, and his omission of strategic detail makes him a poor military historian. Yet his brilliant and varied style, moral elevation, honest record of fact, and psychological insight make him a great writer and the indispensable historian of the early empire. See Bessie Walker, *The Annals of Tacitus* (Manchester, 1950); R. Syme, *Tacitus* (Oxford, 1958). [DM, TRSB]

I127. Suetonius Tranquillus, Caius. **De vita duodecim Caesarum.** Ed. by M. Ihm. Leipzig, 1907. Enl. ed., 1923. Ed. and tr. by John C. Rolfe, rev. ed., 2 v., London and N.Y., 1928–30. [Loeb classical library.] Suetonius (*ca.* 70–*ca.* 140) was an erudite biographer and collector of information who influenced greatly both biography and history. While secretary *ab epistulis* to Hadrian he wrote and dedicated to his patron, Septicius Clarus, the praetorian prefect, his lives of the Caesars from Julius to Domitian. In these he brought together under rubrics much evidence of great value from many sources, but also included on an equal basis much trivial gossip and partisan writing. See Friedrich Leo, *Die griechisch-römische Biographie* (Leipzig, 1901); Wolf Steidle, *Sueton und die entike Biographie* (Munich, 1951). [WAO, TRSB]

I128. Cassius Dio Cocceianus. **Historia romana.** Ed. by Ursulus P. Boissevain. 5 v. Berlin, 1895–1931. Ed. and tr. by Herbert B. Foster, 1905; rev. by E. Cary, 9 v., London and N.Y., 1914–28. [Loeb classical library.] Dio (*ca.* 155–*ca.* 235), of Nicaea of Bithynia, senator and twice consul, wrote a history of Rome in 80 books, covering the period from the founding of Rome to his second consulship with Alexander Severus in 229. Books 36–54 (68–10 B.C.) are preserved intact, while 55–60 (B.C. 9–46 A.D.) are abbreviated, and 17, 79–80 are extant only in part. Other parts can be reconstructed from the epitomes of Xiphilinus (for books 36 on) and Zonaras (for books 1–21, 44–80) and the *Excerpta Constantiniana.* He appears to have based his narrative of the early period on an annalistic tradition, from 68 to the Augustan age in part on Livy, the early empire on some imperial annalistic tradition, and his own period on his own observation. He fails to understand the free republic and reads later developments into early imperial institutions, but his interest in constitutional matters, laws, decrees of the senate, and his personal knowledge of the late period make it necessary to consider his statements of fact even when interpretations are disregarded. See E. Schwartz, *Realencyclopädie*, 3: 1648–1722. [WAO, TRSB]

I129. Scriptores historiae Augustae. Ed. by E. Hohl. 2 v. Leipzig, 1927. Text and tr. by David Magie, 3 v., London and N.Y., 1921–32. Collection of lives, composed on the model of Suetonius, of Roman emperors from Hadrian to Numerian (117–284 A.D.), including Caesars and usurpers. Lacking the preface, it remains unknown whether Nerva and Trajan were once included. The lives from Philip to the first part of Valerian (244–253) have been lost. The authorship, time of writing, and credibility of these lives are much disputed. Some, if not all, of the six authors named are a single person. The date, which purports to be that of Diocletian or Constantine, may be Julian or Theodosius I. Covert anti-Christian propaganda favors a setting in the late 4th century. The earlier lives up to Caracalla make use of Latin sources and are more reliable than the later ones, which make more use of Greek sources, but all must be treated with reserve. See N. H. Baynes, *The Historia Augusta, its date and purpose* (Oxford, 1926).

I130. Ammianus Marcellinus. **Rerum gestarum libri XXXI.** Ed. by C. U. Clark. 2 v. Berlin, 1910–15. Text and tr. by John C. Rolfe, rev. ed., 3 v., London and Cambridge, Mass., 1950. [Loeb classical library.] Ammianus Marcellinus (*ca.* 330–*ca.* 400), a Greek from Antioch, after distinguished service in the imperial army under Constantius and his successors resided in Rome and wrote in Latin 31 books. This work, a history covering the period 96–378 A.D., is a continuation of Tacitus. Only the part (books 14–31) on the years 353–378 has survived. His tolerance of other views, shrewd observation of character, sound judgment, and objectivity make him the most reliable source for the period and, in spite of a strained and rhetorical style, the last great historian of the ancient world. See E. A. Thompson, *The historical work of Ammianus Marcellinus* (Cambridge, Eng., 1947); Max L. Laistner, *The greater Roman historians* (Berkeley, 1947). [AERB, TRSB]

I131. Orosius, Paulus. **Historiae adversum paganos.** Ed. by K. Zangemeister. Leipzig, 1889. Tr. by I. W. Raymond, N.Y., 1936. A Spanish presbyter who, with encouragement from St. Augustine, wrote a universal history in seven books to refute the charge against the Christians that the evils of the time were due to the anger of the pagan gods. He used portions of the lost epitomes of Livy and the histories of Tacitus.

Modern Writers

I132. Gibbon, Edward. **The history of the decline and fall of the Roman empire.** Ed. by John B. Bury. 7 v. London and N.Y., 1896–1902. Later reprints. The classic work on the period from Marcus Aurelius to 1453. V. 1–3, covering to the mid-5th century, are characterized by unity of treatment and historical impartiality except in the account of the rise of the Christian church. The central theme is "the triumph of barbarism and religion," the outstanding development of these centuries. The style is brilliant and the work not yet superseded where treatment depends on literary sources. Bury's notes contain modern corrections and additions, and his introduction a good appreciation of the author. [AERB, TRSB]

I133. Charlesworth, Martin P. **The Roman empire.** Oxford, 1951. [Home university library.] Excellent brief account of the Roman empire from Augustus to Constantine, devoted less to narrative than to cogent comment on its more significant aspects.

I134. Albertini, Eugène. **L'empire romain.** 3rd ed., Paris, 1938. Brief yet comprehensive survey of the empire and its culture from Augustus to Theodosius, notable for good judgment and clear perspective.

I135. Salmon, Edward T. **A history of the Roman world from 30 B.C. to A.D. 138.** 3rd rev. ed., London, 1957. [Methuen's history of the Greek and Roman world.] A well-informed and critical survey of the period on the traditional plan. Select bibliography.

I136. Parker, Henry M. D. **A history of the Roman world from A.D. 138 to 337.** London, 1935. [Methuen's history of the Greek and Roman world.] Effective survey, excellent in selection and judgment of material and especially valuable on military matters. Select bibliography.

I137. Homo, Léon. **Histoire romaine: le haut empire.** Paris, 1933. Accurate, clear, and balanced account of the imperial system from Augustus to Commodus.

I138. Dessau, Hermann. **Geschichte der römischen Kaiserzeit.** 2 v. Berlin, 1924–30. Covers period from 44 B.C. to 69 A.D. V. 1 deals with the reign of Augustus; v. 2, pt. 1 with the Julio-Claudian emperors; and pt. 2 is a survey of the lands and peoples of the empire. A work of immense erudition and independent, at times questionable, interpretations, written in a difficult style.

I139. Gardthausen, Victor. **Augustus und seine Zeit.** 2 v. in 6. Leipzig, 1891–1904. Appendix, 1916. A monumental work, still the chief reference for evidence bearing on the life and administration of Augustus and various aspects of the world of his day. V. 1 contains the text; v. 2, the footnotes and references.

I140. Marsh, Frank B. **The reign of Tiberius.** London, 1931. Clear and impartial account of this principate, particularly important for careful analysis of the literary sources and relations between the emperor and the senate. Review, M. P. Charlesworth, *Class. rev.,* 46 (Dec. 1932): 264.

I141. Momigliano, Arnaldo. **Claudius, the emperor and his achievement.** Oxford, 1934. Tr. by W. D. Hogarth of *L'opera dell'imperatore Claudio* (Florence, 1932). A fresh analysis of selected aspects of the reign, especially valuable on Claudius' contribution to the imperial administration.

I142. Scramuzza, Vincent. **The emperor Claudius.** Cambridge, Mass., 1940. A more favorable estimate of the emperor's personality and policies, based on a fresh analysis of the sources.

I143. Henderson, Bernard. **Five Roman emperors: Vespasian, Titus, Domitian, Nerva, Trajan, A.D. 69–117.** Cambridge, Eng., 1927. Good general treatment of the reigns between Nero and Hadrian, especially of military and economic matters.

I144. ——. **The life and principate of the emperor Hadrian, A.D. 76–138.** London, 1923. Balanced account of Hadrian's career and policies.

I145. Hüttl, Willy. **Antoninus Pius.** 2 v. Prague, 1933–36. V. 1 contains the text, noteworthy for treatments of frontier defense and legal reform; v. 2, a useful prosopography of officials and a collection of inscriptions of the period. Review of v. 2, E. Groag, *Berlin. Philolog. Wochensch.,* 53 (1933): 1379.

I146. Seeck, Otto. **Geschichte des Untergangs der antiken Welt.** 6 v. in 8. Berlin and Stuttgart, 1897–1920. Subsequent revisions. Covers period from Diocletian to 476 A.D.— v. 1–3 on reigns of Diocletian to Constantine, v. 4–5 on dynasty of Constantine and its successors, and v. 6 on the 5th century with essays, illuminating and original but sometimes capricious, on the many causes of the decline of Rome. Especially valuable on administration and organization. [WSD, TRSB]

I147. Stein, Ernst. **Geschichte des spätrömischen Reiches.** 2 v. Vienna and Paris, 1928–49. V. 1 deals with period 284–476 A.D. V. 2 (476–565) was long delayed by political and military causes and published posthumously. The two constitute an outstanding history of the period, excellently documented. More useful for mastery of politics and administration than for cultural and religious history. Review of v. 1, N. H. Baynes, *Jour. Rom. studies*, 18 (1928): 217.

I148. Lot, Ferdinand. **La fin du monde antique et le début du Moyen Âge.** Paris, 1927. Tr. by Philip and Mariette Leon, London and N.Y., 1931. Admirable account of the decline of the Roman empire and the rise of the barbarian kingdoms. Treats the political and social development of the West with insight and independence. Review, N. H. Baynes, *Jour. Rom. studies*, 19 (1929): 224.

Other works on the history of the later Roman empire are listed in Sections K and L.

I149. Piganiol, André. **L'empire chrétien, 325–395.** Paris, 1947. [Histoire romaine, v. 4, pt. 2.] An effective synthesis, more useful for political, social, and economic history than for the religious and intellectual movements of the time. Review, K. Setton, *Am. Jour. philol.*, 69 (July 1948): 329.

I150. Alföldi, Andreas. "Die Ausgestaltung der monarchischen Zeremoniells am römischen Kaiserhofe." **Mitteilungen des deutschen archaeologischen Instituts, römische Abteilung,** 49 (1934): 1–118. See below.

I151. ———. "Insignien und Tracht der römischen Kaiser." **Mitteilungen des deutschen archaeologischen Instituts, römische Abteilung,** 50 (1935): 1–171. This and the above article together form a brilliant study of the ceremonial dress and insignia of the Roman emperors, especially as represented on coins, and document the evolution of the principate which produced the forms and ritual of the late empire.

I152. Burckhardt, Jakob C. **Die Zeit Constantins des Grossen.** Basel, 1853. 3rd ed., Leipzig, 1898. Tr. by M. Hadas, N.Y., 1949. A classic, now partly superseded by new evidence and by the rise of new concepts of the relation of emperor, church, and state.

I153. Jones, Arnold H. M. **Constantine and the conversion of Europe.** London, 1948. Brief but excellent account of the economic, social, and religious problems of the reign and times of Constantine.

I154. Vogt, Joseph. **Constantin der Grosse und sein Jahrhundert.** Munich, 1949. In part a survey of the development of the Roman empire in the century preceding Constantine,

and in part an account of his acts and policies. Useful critical bibliography.

I155. Baynes, Norman H. **Constantine the Great and the Christian church.** London, 1931. Remains a fundamental study.

HISTORIES OF SPECIAL AREAS

The Roman Provinces

I156. Mommsen, Theodor. **The provinces of the Roman empire from Caesar to Diocletian.** 2nd ed., by F. Haverfield, 2 v., London, 1908. Tr. by W. P. Dickson from *Geschichte der Provinzen von Cäsar bis Diocletian* (1885; 9th ed., Berlin, 1921). Mommsen wrote this as v. 5 of his *History of Rome* (I100). He used material then newly collected in the *Corpus inscriptionum latinarum* to give a masterly description of civilization in the various provinces under the principate. Thereby he seeks to show that the great achievement of the imperial government was the gift of three centuries of peace and prosperity to the provincials, and that the corrupt society of the court and capital did not constitute or even typify the Roman world of the time. Many corrections of detail are now required, but the work as a whole remains unsurpassed. [AERB, TRSB]

I157. Collingwood, Robin G., and John N. L. Myres. **Roman Britain and the English settlements.** 2nd ed., Oxford, 1936. [Oxford history of England, 1.] The fullest account of the development and institutions of the province. Continued past the Roman withdrawal by Professor Myres. Bibliography.

I158. Richmond, Ian A. **Roman Britain.** Harmondsworth, 1955. [Pelican history of England, 1.] Brief but outstanding synthesis by a leading British archaeologist. Excellent bibliography.

I159. Jullian, Camille L. **Histoire de la Gaule.** 8 v. Paris, 1908–29. The most authoritative history of Gaul from 600 B.C. to the end of Roman rule. Includes economic, social, and cultural aspects, and is especially valuable for the period when Roman emperors had their capital in Gaul.

I160. Brogan, Olwen. **Roman Gaul.** Cambridge, Mass. and London, 1953. Excellent brief survey of the history of Gaul and the material and cultural aspects of its civilization. Select bibliography.

I161. Cumont, Franz V. M. **Comment la Belgique fut romanisée.** 2nd rev. ed., Brussels, 1919. Excellent account of the Romanization and development of northern Gaul. For a useful summary of recent discoveries and results see S. J. De Laet, "La Gaule septentrionale à l'époque romaine à la lumière des fouilles, des recherches et des publications les plus récentes," *Bull. de l'Institut Historique Belge de Rome*, 26 (1950–51): 187–250. For detailed study of

Roman Gaul, Albert Grenier, *Manuel d'archéologie gallo-romaine* (2 v., Paris, 1931–34), is indispensable.

I162. Bosch y Gimpera, Pedro, and others. **España romana (218 a. de J. C.—414 de J. C.).** Madrid, 1935. [Ramón Menéndez Pidal, Historia de España, 2.] A fundamental work by eight specialists. Now requires supplement, especially on Roman colonization.

I163. Albertini, Eugène. **Les divisions administratives de l'Espagne romaine.** Paris, 1923. Important for the history of Roman administration in Spain.

I164. Sutherland, Carol H. V. **The Romans in Spain, 217 B.C.—A.D. 117.** London, 1939. Excellent introduction, valuable for the relation of geography to history and for the use of evidence from coins. Bibliographical notes.

I165. Thouvenot, Raymond. **Essai sur la province romaine de Bétique.** See *VD56*.

I166. Fabricius, Ernst, and others. **Der obergermanisch-rätische Limes des Römerreiches.** 14 v. Berlin and Leipzig, 1894–1937. The fundamental report of the occupation and fortification of this frontier, directed by Fabricius and described by many scholars. Pt. A is devoted to description of territories, pt. B to the forts. Consult also *Der römische Limes in Oesterreich* (17 v., Vienna, 1900–37) and the material on the development of frontiers everywhere in the empire in Fabricius' article, "Limes," *Realencyclopädie*, 13: 571–671.

I167. Stein, Ernst. **Die kaiserlichen Beamten und Truppenkörper im römischen Deutschland unter dem Prinzipat.** Vienna, 1932. [Beiträge zur Verwaltungs- und Heeresgeschichte von Gallien und Germanien, 1.] With Emil Ritterling, *Fasti des römischen Deutschland unter dem Prinzipat* (v. 2 of the series, Vienna, 1932), an indispensable foundation for study of the civil and military organization of these provinces.

I168. Koepp, Friedrich. **Die Römer in Deutschland.** 3rd rev. ed., Bielefeld and Leipzig, 1926. General treatment of civilization of the German provinces, based on literary, epigraphical, and archaeological material. Illustrations, bibliography.

I169. Stähelin, Felix. **Die Schweitz in römischer Zeit.** 3rd rev. ed., Basel, 1948. Valuable account of the history and civilization of Switzerland in Roman times.

Material on the Danubian provinces is scattered in many articles and monographs. It is recommended that students read the relevant chapters in the *Cambridge ancient history (I77)*, v. 10, ch. 12; v. 11, ch. 11 and 13; and bibliographies to these chapters. See also M. I. Rostovtzeff, *Social and economic history of the Roman empire (I284)*, ch. 6, notes 58 ff.

I170. Carcopino, Jérôme. **La loi de Hiéron et les Romains.** Paris, 1914. Important for

the study of Roman taxation in Sicily and other provinces. On the development of Sicily see V. Scramuzza in *Economic survey of ancient Rome (I282)*, 3: 225–377.

I171. Pais, Ettore. **Storia della Sardegna e della Corsica durante il dominio romano.** Rome, 1923. Good critical study.

I172. Gsell, Stéphane. **Histoire ancienne de l'Afrique du Nord.** 8 v. Paris, 1913–28. Indispensable work on the region from the Gulf of Syrtis to the Atlantic between the Mediterranean and the Sahara. V. 1–4 deal with the prehistoric and Carthaginian periods; 5–6, the native kingdoms; 7–8, the client kingdoms and the Roman province under the republic. Full bibliographical notes. [AERB, TRSB]

I173. Broughton, Thomas Robert S. **The Romanization of Africa Proconsularis.** Baltimore, 1929. Study of the Roman proconsular province from the fall of Carthage to the principate of Septimius Severus, chiefly from the standpoint of urbanization and municipal development.

I174. Warmington, Brian H. **The North African provinces from Diocletian to the Vandal conquest.** Cambridge, Eng., 1954. Deals with the relations of central and municipal governments and the cultural life of the North African cities in the later empire. Good account of the cities.

On the Roman provinces of Achaea, Macedonia, and Thrace see the excellent special bibliographies in *Cambridge ancient history (I77)*, v. 11, ch. 14, pp. 914 ff.; *Social and economic history of the Roman empire (I284)*, ch. 6; and the select bibliography in *Economic survey of ancient Rome (I282)*, 4: 497–98. Much new material of great importance for Greece is published in reports of the excavations in Athens, Sparta, Corinth, Delos, Delphi, and Olympia.

On the eastern provinces in general reference should be made to Rostovtzeff's *Social and economic history of the Hellenistic world (H151)*, ch. 7 and 8, and his *Social and economic history of the Roman empire*, ch. 7, both with full notes on sources and bibliography. In addition, see the following *(I175–178)*.

I175. Cumont, Franz V. M. "The frontier provinces of the East." **The Cambridge ancient history,** v. 11, ch. 15.

I176. Bell, H. Idris. "Egypt under the early principate." **The Cambridge ancient history,** v. 10, ch. 10.

I177. Bell, H. Idris, and P. Romanelli. "Egypt, Crete and Cyrenaica." **The Cambridge ancient history,** v. 11, ch. 16. This and *I175–176* have excellent selected bibliographies.

I178. Rostovtzeff, Michael I. "La Syrie romaine." **Rev. historique,** 175 (Jan.-Feb. 1935): 1–40.

I179. Accame, Silvio. **Il dominio romano**

in Grecia dalla guerra acaica ad Augusto. See *H167*.

I180. Day, John. **An economic history of Athens under Roman domination.** N.Y., 1942. Comprehensive use of available literary, epigraphical, and numismatic evidence. Bibliography. Other aspects of the history of Athens in this period are treated by Paul Graindor, *Athènes sous Auguste* (Cairo, 1927); *Athènes de Tibère à Trajan* (Cairo, 1931); *Athènes sous Hadrien* (Cairo, 1934); *Un milliardaire antique: Hérode Atticus et sa famille* (Cairo, 1930).

I181. Jones, Arnold H. M. **The cities of the eastern Roman provinces.** Oxford, 1937. See below.

I182. ———. **The Greek city from Alexander to Justinian.** Oxford, 1940. The first of these two books is a detailed regional description of the growth and organization of Greek city forms in the eastern Roman provinces from Thrace through Asia Minor, Syria, and Egypt around to Cyrenaica; the second is a general study of causes which promoted or retarded their growth, of their internal life, and their relations with the central government. Both are works of outstanding scholarship. Select bibliography.

I183. Magie, David. **Roman rule in Asia Minor.** 2 v. Princeton, 1950. A fundamental work, based on all available sources, which sums up a vast body of modern scholarship. Begins with the Hellenistic background and traces development under the empire of the provinces of Asia Minor. Full bibliographical notes and useful lists of officials.

I184. Chapot, Victor. **La frontière de l'Euphrate, de Pompée à la conquête arabe.** Paris, 1907. Useful study of Roman attempts to find a satisfactory eastern frontier and to organize its defense. To be supplemented now by *Cambridge ancient history*, v. 10, ch. 6, on the eastern frontier; and by A. Poidebard, *La trace de Rome dans le désert de Syrie* (*I187*).

I185. Gwatkin, William E. **Cappadocia as a Roman procuratorial province.** Columbia, Mo., 1930. Description of the organization, resources, and administration of Cappadocia in the early empire.

I186. Mouterde, René, and Antoine Poidebard. **Le limes de Chalcis: organisation de la steppe en haute Syrie romaine.** Paris, 1945. Essential for the detailed study of northern Syria.

I187. Poidebard, Antoine. **La trace de Rome dans le désert de Syrie: le limes de Trajan à la conquête arabe.** 2 v. Paris, 1934. Important for study of Roman occupation of Syria and Roman military history on the eastern frontier. Covers only the territory of the modern state of Syria.

I188. Rostovtzeff, Michael I. **Caravan cities.** Tr. from Russian by David and T. Talbot Rice. Oxford, 1932. Vivid and schol-arly account of the remains, life, and communications of Petra, Gerasa, Palmyra, and Dura. Should be supplemented by reports of later excavations.

I189. Josephus, Flavius. **Opera.** 1544. Ed. by B. Niese, 7 v., Berlin, 1887–95. Tr. by William Whiston, 1737; rev. ed. by A. R. Shilleto, 5 v., London, 1889–90. Tr. by Henry St. J. Thackery, contd. by R. Marcus, 7 v., London and Cambridge, Mass., 1926–43. [Loeb classical library.] The *Life*, *Contra Apion*, *Wars of the Jews*, and *Antiquities of the Jews* comprise a notable body of writings and a principal source for the history of the Jewish people. The later books of the *Antiquities* are invaluable on their relations with Rome; and the *Wars* is the chief contemporary source for narrative of the revolt of 66–70 A.D. [AERB, TRSB]

I190. Abel, Félix M. **Histoire de la Palestine depuis la conquête d'Alexandre jusqu'à l'invasion arabe.** 2 v. Paris, 1952. Comprehensive survey, at times uncritical, based on ancient sources, modern discussions, and a detailed knowledge of the land.

I191. Juster, Jean. **Les juifs dans l'empire romaine, leur condition juridique, économique, et sociale.** 2 v. Paris, 1914. Still important. Particularly valuable on relations of communities of Jews throughout the empire with the imperial and municipal authorities.

I192. Jones, Arnold H. M. **The Herods of Judaea.** Oxford, 1938. Well-informed and objective account which places the Herodian family in its setting in both Palestinian and Roman history.

I193. Mitteis, Ludwig, and Ulrich Wilcken, eds. **Grundzüge und Chrestomathie der Papyruskunde.** 2 v. in 4. Leipzig and Berlin, 1912. Original, but still indispensable, introduction to all major aspects of the government, legal system, economic, and social life of Egypt from 332 B.C. to 639 A.D. as revealed by papyrus documents, of which the *Chrestomathie* offers a rich selection with appropriate notes and comments. [AERB]

I194. Oertel, Friedrich. **Die Liturgie.** Leipzig, 1917. Meticulous study of all types of obligatory services imposed upon the population of Ptolemaic and more particularly Roman Egypt, and the part played by these liturgies in village, town, and home administration up to the end of the 4th century A.D. [AERB]

I195. Milne, John G. **A history of Egypt under Roman rule.** 3rd ed., London, 1924. [William M. F. Petrie, ed., A history of Egypt, 5.] The one significant narrative of Egypt from 30 B.C. to 642 A.D. Includes special chapters on government, taxation, the army, religion, urban and rural life. Review, H. I. Bell, *Jour. Egypt. arch.*, 12 (Oct. 1926): 317. [AERB]

I196. Johnson, Allan C. **Roman Egypt to**

the reign of **Diocletian**. Baltimore, 1936. [An economic survey of ancient Rome, 2.] Systematic description of the resources of Roman Egypt and the economic activities of its population, including a study of their fiscal obligations, copiously illustrated by documents in translation. Review, J. G. Milne, *Jour. Egypt. arch.*, 22 (June 1936): 113. [AERB]

I197. Wallace, Sherman L. **Taxation in Egypt from Augustus to Diocletian**. Princeton, 1938. [Princeton University studies in papyrology, 2.] Complete and coherent analysis of the tax structure and individual taxes in Roman Egypt. Although controversial in many of its interpretations and subject to correction in details, it remains the essential manual in its field. [AERB]

I198. Taubenschlag, Raphael. **The law of Greco-Roman Egypt in the light of the papyri, 332 B.C.—640 A.D.** 2nd ed., Warsaw, 1955. Comprehensive, scholarly, and dependable manual of the Egyptian, Greek, and Roman legal systems in force in Egypt under Ptolemaic and Roman rule. Supplements and in large part supersedes the earlier work of Mitteis. Review of 1st ed., A. Berger, *Aegyptus*, 25 (1944): 117.

HISTORIES OF SPECIAL TOPICS

Military History

I199. "Legio." **Paulys Realencyclopädie der classischen Altertumswissenschaft,** v. 12 (Stuttgart, 1925), cols. 1186–1237. The fundamental study, with full information for each legion from Augustus to Diocletian. [JFG]

I200. Kromayer, Johannes, and Georg Veith. **Heerwesen und Kriegführung der Griechen und Römer.** See *H318*.

I201. Domaszewski, Alfred von. **Die Rangordnung des römischen Heeres.** Bonn, 1908. The fundamental study of the commissioned and non-commissioned officers and internal organization of the Roman army from Augustus to Diocletian. Political and social policies of the emperors are kept in mind. Valuable appendix of inscriptions. [JFG]

I202. Marquardt, Karl J. **Römische Staatsverwaltung.** V. 2, pp. 319–621. 2nd ed., Leipzig, 1884. [Handbuch des römischen Alterthümer, 5.] Still useful as the only comprehensive account of the Roman army through the 3rd century A.D. that includes full references to sources. [JFG]

I203. Birley, Eric. **Roman Britain and the Roman army.** Kendal, 1953. A collection of papers, including important discussions of the origins of legionary centurions and of equestrian officers. [JFG]

I204. Parker, Henry M. D. **The Roman legions.** Oxford, 1928. Well-informed general survey covering the republic through the 2nd century A.D. [JFG]

I205. Forni, Giovanni. **Il reclutamento delle legioni da Augusto a Diocleziano.** Milan and Rome, 1953. Careful investigation of a topic of considerable importance for the general social history of the empire. [JFG]

I206. Durry, Marcel. **Les cohortes prétoriennes.** Paris, 1938. Comprehensive and thorough historical study of their role and function, with a full account of internal organization and activities. [JFG]

I207. Cheesman, George L. **The auxilia of the Roman imperial army.** Oxford, 1914. Lucid and judicious monograph dealing largely with the first two centuries. [JFG]

I208. Cichorius, Conrad. "Ala." **Paulys Realencyclopädie der classischen Altertumswissenschaft,** 1 (1894): 1224–70. This and *I209* are excellent surveys, largely arranged under individual units. Though out of date, still the only comprehensive collection of evidence for the order of battle of roughly half the Roman army. H. Nesselhauf's new edition of the military diplomas in *Corpus inscriptionum latinarum*, v. 16, in effect provides a valuable supplement. [JFG]

I209. ——. "Cohors." **Paulys Realencyclopädie der classischen Altertumswissenschaft,** 4 (1901): 231–356.

I210. Wagner, Walter. **Die Dislokation der römischen Auxiliarformationen in den Provinzen Noricum, Pannonien, Moesien und Dakien von Augustus bis Gallienus.** Berlin, 1938. Valuable, detailed study, arranged by units, with a brief general discussion. [JFG]

I211. Kraft, Konrad. **Zur Rekrutierung der Alen und Kohorten an Rhein und Donau.** Bern, 1951. Sound and illuminating monograph of general interest for Romanization and spread of Roman citizenship. [JFG]

I212. Thiel, Johannes H. **A history of Roman sea-power before the Second Punic War.** Amsterdam, 1954. A thorough work, combining enthusiasm and good sense. [JFG]

I213. ——. **Studies on the history of Roman sea-power in republican times.** Amsterdam, 1946. Another original and stimulating study of the strength and role of the navy, chiefly between 218 and 167 B.C. [JFG]

I214. Starr, Chester S., Jr. **The Roman imperial navy, 31 B.C.–A.D. 324.** Ithaca, 1941. [Cornell studies in classical philology, 26.] The authoritative study, comprehensive but treating organization and personnel most fully. [JFG]

I215. Cagnat, René. **L'armée romaine d'Afrique et l'occupation militaire de l'Afrique sous les empereurs.** 2nd ed., 2 v., Paris, 1912–13. Classic study of a provincial garrison based on abundant epigraphical and archaeological evidence. Covers the manifold activities of the troops in peace and war, and their influence on development of the area through the 4th century. [JFG]

I216. Lesquier, Jean. **L'armée romaine d'Égypte d'Auguste à Dioclétien.** Cairo, 1918. [Mémoires de l'Institut Français d'Archéologie Orientale du Caire, 41.] A masterly study of the Roman army. The rich materials, notably the papyri, permit a reconstruction of many aspects of military life and activities such as is hardly possible in other provinces. [JFG]

I217. Grosse, Robert. **Römische Militärgeschichte von Gallienus bis zum Beginn der byzantinischen Themenverfassung.** Berlin, 1920. As yet the best work on a subject needing much more investigation. [JFG]

I218. Couissin, Paul. **Les armes romaines: essai sur les origines et l'évolution des armes individuelles du légionnaire romain.** Paris, 1926. Illustrated account, arranged by periods, from the earliest times to the 6th century A.D. [JFG]

Constitutional and Legal History

I219. Abbott, Frank F. **History and description of Roman political institutions.** 3rd ed., Boston, 1911. Clearly and carefully written and well-arranged introduction, particularly helpful for its documentation. Appendices contain pertinent Latin selections from epigraphical and literary sources. Review, T. Nicklin, *Classical rev.,* 17 (July 1903): 324. [ABW, RSR]

I220. Greenidge, Abel H. J. **Roman public life.** London and N.Y., 1901. This standard and very useful handbook traces development of the Roman constitution from the earliest period to that of the principate, and describes its workings in Rome, Italy, and the provinces under the developed republic and principate. Well arranged and convenient for reference. Review, T. Nicklin, *Classical rev.,* 16 (Oct. 1902): 360; F. Cauer, *Berliner Philologische Wochenschrift,* 22 (Aug. 1902): 977. [CWK, RSR]

I221. Homo, Léon. **Les institutions politiques romaines de la cité à l'état.** Paris, 1927. 2nd ed., 1950. Constitutional history of Rome from the founding to the age of Constantine I. The first part is excellent; the latter, dealing with the later republic and empire, is much weaker and rather uncritical. Review, D. McFayden, *Am. hist. rev.,* 33 (Oct. 1927): 98. [ABW, RSR]

I222. Botsford, George W. **Roman assemblies from their origin to the end of the republic.** N.Y., 1909. Full description and history of the assemblies and their legislation. Still a standard, indispensable work; but there is much of significance in subsequent periodical literature. [RSR]

I223. Gelzer, Matthias. **Die Nobilität der römischen Republik.** Leipzig, 1912. Careful, interesting, and informative study of Roman

political life. Review, C. Bardt, *Berliner Philolog. Woch.,* 33 (Jan. 1913): 16. [AERB, RSR]

I224. Münzer, Friedrich. **Römische Adelsparteien und Adelsfamilien.** Stuttgart, 1920. Illuminating work bearing on the problem of traditional family politics in Rome. Shows a deep understanding of the structure of Roman society and the influence of the aristocracy in Roman history. Review, E. Hohl, *Berliner Philolog. Woch.,* 40 (Nov. 1920): 1091.

I225. Mommsen, Theodor. **Römisches Staatsrecht.** 3rd ed., 3 v. in 5, Leipzig, 1887–88. Reprint, 1952. This exposition of the Roman constitution as a well-knit system of offices and institutions based upon certain clearly grasped, fundamental, legal conceptions was a wholly original idea at the time of its publication. Its appearance put the study of Roman constitutional history upon a scientific basis; and it is still an indispensable work, the starting point of all investigation in this field, partly because of its complete citation of source materials on each topic. Deservedly this ranks as the greatest achievement of Mommsen's genius. [AERB, RSR]

I226. ——. **Abriss des römischen Staatsrechts.** 2nd ed., Leipzig, 1907. Stimulating survey of the constitutional growth of the Roman state, with more emphasis on the process of development than in *I225.* [AERB, RSR]

I227. ——. **Römisches Strafrecht.** Leipzig, 1899. Classic work on Roman criminal law. [AERB, RSR]

I228. ——. **Römische Forschungen.** 2 v. Berlin, 1864–79. Important contribution on problems of Roman history, chiefly in the republican period. [AERB, RSR]

I229. ——. **Gesammelte Schriften.** 8 v. Berlin, 1905–13. [1–3, *Juristische Schriften;* 4–6, *Historische Schriften;* 7, *Philologische Schriften;* 8, *Epigraphische und numismatische Schriften.*] General collection of Mommsen's contributions to periodical literature. [AERB, RSR]

I230. Marquardt, Karl J. **Römische Staatsverwaltung.** 2nd ed., 3 v., Leipzig, 1881–85. [1, *Organisation des römischen Reichs;* 2, *Finanz- und Militärwesen;* 3, *Das Sacralwesen.*] Work of primary importance. [AERB, RSR]

I231. Madvig, Johan N. **Die Verfassung und Verwaltung des römischen Staates.** 2 v. Leipzig, 1881–82. This and *I232* are also useful treatises. For much shorter but very suggestive discussion see K. J. Neumann, *Römische Staatsaltertümer,* in Gercke and Norden, *Einleitung in die Altertumswissenschaft (H20).* [AERB, RSR]

I232. Herzog, Ernst von. **Geschichte und System der römischen Staatsverfassung.** 3 v. in 2. Leipzig, 1884–91.

I233. Hardy, Ernest G. **Studies in Roman history.** 2 v. London, 1906–09. V. 1 contains an essay on "Christianity and the Roman government" and six shorter studies on constitutional questions of the principate. Review, P. J. Healy, *Am. hist. rev.*, 11 (July 1906): 931. V. 2 has essays on the armies and frontiers, and on the emperors of the year 68–69 A.D. [AERB, RSR]

I234. ——, ed. **Six Roman laws.** Oxford, 1911. Includes Lex Acilia and the Roman laws of the republic dealing with municipal administration; valuable commentary. [AERB, RSR]

I235. ——, ed. **Roman laws and charters.** Oxford, 1912. Republication of *1234* with addition of three municipal charters from Spain. [AERB, RSR]

I236. ——. **Some problems in Roman history: ten essays bearing on the administrative and legislative work of Julius Caesar.** Oxford, 1924. Collection of studies previously published in periodicals. [AERB, RSR]

I237. Schultz, Otto T. **Das Wesen des römischen Kaisertums der ersten zwei Jahrhunderte.** Paderborn, 1916. This and *1238* really form a single study whose principal thesis is that the right of appointment to the principate legally belonged to the senate alone, and that the army had no constitutional authority therein. [AERB, RSR]

I238. ——. **Vom Prinzipat zum Dominat: das Wesen des römischen Kaisertums des dritten Jahrhunderts.** Paderborn, 1919. Contains a useful collection of materials bearing on this problem. Review of this and *1237*, D. McFayden, *Classical philology*, 17 (July 1922): 274. [AERB, RSR]

I239. McFayden, Donald. **The history of the title Imperator under the Roman empire.** Chicago, 1920. Important restudy, correcting the conclusions of Mommsen. However, the subject must now be pursued in subsequent periodical literature. [AERB, RSR]

I240. Mattingly, Harold. **Imperial civil service of Rome.** Cambridge, Eng., 1910. [Cambridge historical essays, 17.] Outlines the general development of the service in the 1st and 2nd centuries; takes up in greater detail the *procuratores provinciarum*. Convenient summary: contains little or nothing original. Review, O. Hirschfeld, *Wochenschrift für klassische Philologie*, 28 (Feb. 1911): 243. [CWK, RSR]

I241. Stein, Arthur. **Der römische Ritterstand.** Munich, 1927. Authoritative study of the equestrian order from the time of its formation as a social and political class in the era of the Gracchi until its disappearance in the 4th century. Review, J. G. C. Anderson, *Jour. Rom. studies*, 16 (1926): 251. [CWK, RSR]

I242. Hirschfeld, Otto. **Die kaiserlichen Verwaltungsbeamten bis auf Diocletian.** 2nd ed., Berlin, 1905. Standard work on the officials employed in the administration of the Roman empire, their rank and duties, and the evolution of the offices. Deals with all important departments of administration. Concludes with a valuable general survey which brings out the growth of despotism and centralization, and the great importance of Hadrian and Septimius Severus in administrative history. An important supplement to older works. Review, H. Peter, *Wochenschrift für klassische Philologie*, 22 (Aug. 1905): 948; V. Chapot, *Revue de philologie*, 29 (July 1905): 274. [WDG, RSR]

I243. Pflaum, Hans G. **Les procurateurs équestres sous le haut-empire romain.** Paris, 1950. Partially corrects, partially supplements *1242* from the results of later studies. Review, J. H. Oliver, *Am. jour. of philology*, 72 (July 1951): 316. [RSR]

I244. Arnold, William T. **The Roman system of provincial administration to the accession of Constantine the Great.** 3rd rev. ed. by E. S. Bouchier, Oxford, 1914. Good general survey of Roman imperial government, including growth of the empire, subject territories and dependencies, general features of provincial government, and policy of particular emperors with respect to the provinces. Special chapters on the system of taxation and on the provincial municipalities. [AERB, RSR]

I245. ——. **Studies of Roman imperialism.** Ed. by E. Fiddes. Manchester, 1906. Posthumous publication of a series of essays which are fragments of a larger work on government of the Roman empire which Arnold had intended to write. Powers of the principate, relations of Augustus and the senate, and Augustus' domestic policy are discussed. Other chapters cover provincial organization in Gaul, Spain, Arabia, Egypt, Greece, and Asia Minor. Review of this and *1244*, H. S. Jones, *Eng. hist. rev.*, 22 (Apr. 1907): 325; 30 (Apr. 1915): 370. [AERB, RSR]

I246. Reid, James Smith. **The municipalities of the Roman empire.** Cambridge, Eng., 1913. Survey of the Roman empire as a vast federation of commonwealths, retaining many characteristics of the old city-state. Convenient synthesis of facts already familiar, but does not lack illuminating comments contributed by the author. No maps, notes, or bibliography. Review, G. W. Botsford, *Am. hist. rev.*, 19 (Jan. 1914): 335; H. S. Jones, *Eng. hist. rev.*, 28 (Oct. 1913): 758. [ABW, RSR]

I247. Abbott, Frank F., and Allan C. Johnson. **Municipal administration in the Roman empire.** Princeton, 1926. Very useful reference work in two parts, the first giving a general topical treatment, and the second a valuable collection of documents with commentary. Review, A. E. R. Boak, *Am. hist. rev.*, 33 (Jan. 1928): 375. [ABW, RSR]

I248. Liebenam, Wilhelm. **Städteverwaltung im römischen Kaiserreiche.** Leipzig, 1900. Studies the municipal budget, local administration, and relation of the municipality to the state. Valuable collection of material; suffers somewhat from neglect of chronological development. Review, J. Toutain, *Revue hist.*, 78 (Mar. 1902): 366. [AERB, RSR]

I249. Waltzing, Jean P. **Étude historique sur les corporations professionnelles chez les Romains depuis les origines jusqu'à la chute de l'empire d'occident.** 4 v. Louvain, 1895–1900. Complete history of the *collegia:* their origin as private institutions, repression in the late republic, permissive authorization in the principate, the progressively increasing imposition by the state of public duties, and the development in the 4th century into administrative institutions with compulsory and hereditary membership. Very scholarly monograph, based largely on inscriptions and legal literature; indispensable basis for any further investigation of the subject. [WDG, RSR]

I250. Bruns, Carl G., ed. **Fontes iuris romani antiqui.** 7th rev. ed. by Otto Gradenwitz, 4 v. in 2, Tübingen, 1909–12. Particularly valuable for inscriptions bearing on Roman law. The edition of Gradenwitz is based on the 5th and 6th eds. prepared by Mommsen. [AERB, RSR]

I251. Krueger, Paul, Theodor Mommsen, and Wilhelm F. A. Studemund, eds. **Collectio librorum iuris antejustiniani.** 3 v. Berlin, 1877–90. 7th rev. ed. of v. 1, 1923. Best edition of such writings of Gaius and other Roman jurisconsults as have been preserved outside of the *Corpus juris civilis* of Justinian. [AERB, RSR]

I252. Riccobono, Salvatore, and others, eds. **Fontes iuris romani antejustiniani.** 3 v. Florence, 1940–43. New standard edition replacing earlier Eduard Huschke, ed., *Jurisprudentiae antejustinianae que supersunt* (6th rev. ed., 2 v., Leipzig, 1908–11), and containing new material from the papyri. Review, F. Cramer, *Speculum*, 26 (Jan. 1951): 199. [RSR]

I253. Girard, Paul F., ed. **Textes de droit romain.** 6th rev. ed. by Felix Senn, Paris, 1937.

I254. Zulueta, Francis de, ed. **The Institutes of Gaius.** 2 v. Oxford, 1946–53. New standard edition of Gaius, replacing earlier one of Edward Poste (4th rev. ed., Oxford, 1904). Review, v. 1, F. Schultz, *Jour. Rom. studies*, 37 (1947): 208; v. 2, B. Nicholas, *Jour. Rom. studies*, 43 (1953): 178. [RSR]

I255. Muirhead, James, ed. and tr. **The Institutes of Gaius and Rules of Ulpian.** Rev. ed., Edinburgh, 1904. Another text, with good English translation and valuable notes. Gaius' work was composed as a textbook for the study of Roman law, by an otherwise almost unknown jurist, about the close of the principate of Antoninus Pius. [AERB, RSR]

I256. Godefroy (Gothofredus), Jacques, ed. **Codex Theodosianus cum perpetuis commentariis.** Rev. ed. by J. D. Ritter, 6 v., Leipzig, 1736–45. Old edition, but still valuable for its commentaries. [AERB, RSR]

I257. Mommsen, Theodor, and Paul M. Meyer, eds. **Theodosiani libri XVI cum Constitutionibus Sirmondianis et leges novellae ad Theodosianum pertinentes consilio et auctoritate Academiae Litterarum Regiae Borussicae.** 2 v. in 3. Berlin, 1905. 2nd ed. pt. 1 (bks. 1–6), by P. M. Meyer, 1923. Reprint, 1954. Standard edition of the Theodosian code, which is a collection of imperial constitutions issued after the accession of Constantine the Great, published in 438 A.D. by Theodosius II in the Eastern empire and by Valentinian III in the West. The novels included are those promulgated between 438 and 476. [AERB, RSR]

I258. Pharr, Clyde. **The Theodosian code and novels, and the Sirmondian constitutions.** Princeton, 1952. [Codex Theodosianus.] English translation, generally good, of the texts included in *1257*, together with useful commentary and glossary. [RSR]

I259. Krueger, Paul, and others, eds. **Corpus iuris civilis.** 3 v. Berlin, 1884–95. [1, *Institutiones*, ed. by P. Krueger, *Digesta*, ed. by T. Mommsen (15th ed., 1928); 2, *Codex*, ed. by P. Krueger (10th ed., 1929); 3, *Novellae*, ed. by R. Schoell and W. Kroll (5th ed., 1928).] Most complete and serviceable treatment of the subject. [AERB, RSR]

I260. Clark, Edwin C. **History of Roman private law.** 3 pts. in 4 v. Cambridge, Eng., 1906–19. [1, *Sources;* 2, *Jurisprudence;* 3, *Private law in the regal period.*] Most detailed and reliable account in English. Useful chronological sketch. Pt. 2, critical examination of ideas of Roman jurists from point of view of English jurisprudence; valuable as a work of reference. Pt. 3, full presentation of available materials, with wise emphasis on the conjectural character of the conclusions. [AERB, RSR]

I261. Roby, Henry J. **Roman private law in the times of Cicero and of the Antonines.** 2 v. Cambridge, Eng., 1902. Exhaustive treatment, elaborate and clear. Text and notes form an invaluable commentary on legal passages in the Roman authors of the period, dealing particularly with Cicero's private orations, to which four special studies are devoted. Review, S. G. Owen, *Classical rev.*, 18 (Apr. 1904): 174. [AERB, RSR]

I262. Buckland, William W. **Text-book of Roman law from Augustus to Justinian.** 2nd ed., Cambridge, Eng. and N.Y., 1932. Reprint, 1950. Exceptionally comprehensive and detailed account of pure Roman law, following the order of the *Institutes*. Review,

F. de Zulueta, *Classical rev.*, 36 (Aug. 1922): 134. [AERB, RSR]

I263. Girard, Paul F. Manuel élémentaire de droit romain. 8th rev. ed. by F. Senn, Paris, 1929. Brief preliminary survey of the constitutional and legal development of Rome, followed by an exposition of Roman civil law based on the arrangement of the *Institutes*. Companion to his edition of *Textes de droit romain*. [AERB, RSR]

I264. Czyhlarz, Karl, ritter von. Lehrbuch der Institutionen des römischen Rechts. 18th rev. ed. by M. San Nicolo, Vienna, 1924. Particularly clear and well-organized introduction to Roman law as it appears in the Justinian codification. Concerned with the study of pure Roman law as a key to law of the present day. [AERB, RSR]

I265. Sohm, Rudolf. The institutes: a textbook of the history and system of Roman private law. 3rd ed., Oxford and N.Y., 1907. Tr. by James S. Ledlie from *Institutionen: Geschichte und System des römischen Privatrechts* (17th rev. ed., Munich, 1923). Thorough treatment of the Roman private law of the *Corpus iuris civilis*. After brief survey of the sources of Roman law, traces its historical growth under the republic and empire, and its influence in Europe, particularly in Germany, in medieval and modern times. Then follows a systematic presentation of Roman law at the culmination of its development in Justinian's codification. [AERB, RSR]

I266. Krueger, Paul. Geschichte der Quellen und Literatur des römischen Rechts. 2nd ed., Munich, 1912. Most complete and serviceable treatment of the subject [AERB, RSR]

I267. Jolowicz, Herbert F. Historical introduction to the study of Roman law. 2nd ed., Cambridge, Eng., 1952. Excellent treatment of the subject in the three periods: the time of the twelve tables, the rest of the republic, and the empire. In the last the author discusses not the private law, but the constitution, machinery of government, law-making, and litigation. Review, P. W. Duff, *Classical rev.*, 47 (July 1933): 150. [RSR]

I268. Premerstein, Anton, ritter von. Vom Werden und Wesen des Prinzipats. Munich, 1937. Extremely valuable, if by no means always convincing, study of the bases of the principate: philosophic (native), sociological (*patrocinium*), and constitutional (*cura legum et morum, imperium*, and *tribunicia potestas*). Review, M. Hammond, *Amer. jour. of philol.*, 59 (Oct. 1938): 481. [RSR]

I269. Kornemann, Ernst. Doppelprinzipat und Reichsteilung im Imperium Romanum. Leipzig and Berlin, 1930. Highly informative, erudite, stimulating, and provocative study of the empire, although its principal thesis—that Augustus devised the collegiate system of M. Aurelius and Diocletian's east-west division of the empire—has found little acceptance. Review, M. P. Charlesworth, *Classical rev.*, 47 (July 1933): 143. [RSR]

I270. Cuq, Edouard. Manuel des institutions juridiques des Romains. Paris, 1917. Historical rather than doctrinal. Differs from *1271* in giving separate treatment of historical development of individual institutions from the earliest times to the late empire, instead of dividing the discussion into studies of various periods. [AERB, RSR]

I271. ——. Les institutions juridiques des Romains envisagées dans leurs rapports avec l'état social et avec les progrès de la jurisprudence. 2 v. and index. Paris, 1891–1908. 2nd rev. ed. v. 1, 1904.

I272. Costa, Emilio. Profilo storico del processo civile romano. Rome, 1918. Valuable, comprehensive historical survey of procedure in Roman private law. [AERB, RSR]

I273. Arangio-Ruiz, Vincenzo. Storia del diritto romano. 6th ed., Rome, 1950. Useful and valuable sketch of the historical development of Roman constitutional, criminal, and private law. Provides also a very suggestive history of Rome as reflected in the evolution of law, which is an unusual and illuminating approach to the history. [RSR]

I274. Mitteis, Ludwig. Reichsrecht und Volksrecht in den östlichen Provinzen des römischen Kaiserreichs, mit Beiträgen zur Kenntniss des griechischen Rechts und der spätrömischen Rechtsentwicklung. Leipzig, 1891. Treats the important problem of the conflict and coalescence of Roman and local legal principles and practices in the eastern Mediterranean world. Review, H. Lewy, *Berliner Philologische Wochenschrift*, 13 (Apr. 1893): 435. [AERB, RSR]

I275. ——. Römisches Privatrecht bis auf die Zeit Diokletians. V. 1. Leipzig, 1908. Reveals the Roman law of the principate freed from the contamination resulting from Justinian's codification; describes the reception of Roman law in Germany, and the principles of the Pandects. Review, A. Manigh, *Berliner Philol. Woch.*, 29 (Dec. 1909): 1630. [AERB, RSR]

I276. Meyer, Paul M. Juristische Papyri: Erklärung von Urkunden zur Einführung in die juristische Papyruskunde. Berlin, 1920. Extremely useful chrestomathy, accompanied by excellent discussions and annotations. Review, L. Mitteis, *Zeitschrift der Savigny-Stiftung für Rechtsgeschichte, Romanistische Abteilung*, 41 (1920): 309. [AERB, RSR]

I277. Strachan-Davidson, James L. Problems of the Roman criminal law. 2 v. Oxford, 1912. Written as a criticism and supplement to Mommsen, *Römisches Strafrecht*. Marked by strikingly independent views; mainly concerned with the Ciceronian period. Primarily an examination of the steps whereby a criminal in Rome was brought to trial, the theories on which the conduct of the trial was based, and the means whereby sentence was executed. [AERB, RSR]

I278. Buckland, William W. **The Roman law of slavery: the condition of the slave in private law from Augustus to Justinian.** Cambridge, Eng., 1908. Standard work on the subject. Review, F. de Zulueta, *Classical rev.*, 23 (June 1909): 116. [AERB, RSR]

I279. Sherman, Charles P. **Roman law in the modern world.** 2nd ed., 3 v., New Haven, 1922. V. 1 treats the history of Roman law; v. 2 is a manual of its legal principles; v. 3 contains a subject guide and very extensive bibliography. The work was prepared for the general reader, student, and teacher of law. [AERB, RSR]

I280. Sherwin-White, Adrian N. **The Roman citizenship.** Oxford, 1939. Important treatment of the process and methods of extension of Roman citizenship in the republic and in the principate to the *constitutio Antoniniana*, discussing the problem of how far and why Rome won the real loyalty of her world. Review, A. F. Giles, *Classical rev.*, 56 (Jan. 1942): 40. [RSR]

I281. Schulz, Fritz. "Bracton on kingship." **English historical review,** 60 (May 1945): 136–76. Important demonstration that the Roman emperors were bound by law until 536 A.D., contrary to prevalent conceptions. [RSR]

Social and Economic History

I282. Frank, Tenney, ed. **An economic survey of ancient Rome.** 5 v. Baltimore, 1933–40. A work of outstanding importance, indispensable to students of the economic history of the Roman world. The widely scattered and often fragmentary literary, inscriptional, numismatic, and papyrological evidence is assembled with interpretative comment and in great part translated. Select bibliographies. Review, v. 1, F. M. Heichelheim, *Jour. Rom. studies*, 24 (1934): 67; v. 4, M. I. Rostovtzeff, *Am. jour. philol.*, 60 (1939): 363.

I283. ——. **An economic history of Rome.** 2nd rev. ed., Baltimore, 1927. A pioneer work, enlarged in the 2nd ed. to include the empire up to the 4th century A.D. as well as a brief survey of the provinces. Indispensable for history of the republic and important for that of the empire.

I284. Rostovtzeff, Michael I. **The social and economic history of the Roman empire.** 2nd rev. ed., 2 v., Oxford, 1957. In spite of some questionable theories, a very important work for range, scholarship, and stimulating treatment. Copious notes on sources and good bibliography make this indispensable for reference. In ch. 6–8 of his *Social and economic history of the Hellenistic world* (*H151*), Rostovtzeff also contributes much

to the economic history of the eastern provinces under the Roman republic. Reference should be made to F. M. Heichelheim, *Wirtschaftsgeschichte des Altertums,* ch. 7–9, and to the discussion and bibliography in relevant chapters of *The Cambridge ancient history* (v. 10, ch. 13; v. 12, ch. 7).

I285. ——. **Studien zur Geschichte des römischen Kolonats.** Leipzig, 1910. Discussion of Hellenistic and Roman systems of tenant farming in Egypt, Asia Minor, Sicily, and Africa, based on thorough mastery of papyri and inscriptions. Despite criticism of the author's theory of development of the colonate (see T. Frank, *Jour. Rom. studies,* 17 (1927): 141–61), the work remains important. Bibliography.

I286. Westermann, William L. **The slave systems of Greek and Roman antiquity.** Philadelphia, 1955. The author's article on "Sklaverei" in *Realencyclopädie* (*H12*) revised and enlarged, especially on the later empire. Excellent scholarship, particularly valuable for use of papyri. Bibliography. Review, A. H. M. Jones, *Eng. hist. rev.*, 71 (1956): 272.

I287. Barrow, Reginald H. **Slavery in the Roman empire.** N.Y., 1928. Sensible treatment based on sound investigation of sources.

I288. Duff, Arnold M. **Freedmen in the early Roman empire.** Oxford, 1928. Useful study of the legal, political, social, and economic status of freedmen during the first two centuries of the empire.

I289. Loane, Helen J. **Industry and commerce of the city of Rome.** Baltimore, 1938. Systematic study, based on inscriptions and other evidence, of the industry and commercial life of the capital. On industry and trade in the Roman empire see *I282* and *284;* bibliographies and discussions in *Cambridge ancient history,* v. 10, ch. 13, and v. 12, ch. 7; and F. M. Heichelheim, *Wirtschaftsgeschichte des Altertums,* ch. 7–9.

I290. Charlesworth, Martin P. **Trade-routes and commerce of the Roman empire.** 2nd rev. ed., Cambridge, Eng., 1925. Interesting but incomplete presentation of the evidence for the network of land and sea routes and the products exchanged during the early empire. See also the author's article, "Roman trade with India: a resurvey," *Johnson studies* (Princeton, 1951).

I291. Hatzfeld, Jean. **Les trafiquants italiens dans l'Orient hellénique.** Paris, 1919. Valuable study of the diffusion, organization, activities, and influence of Italian businessmen in Greece and the Near East from the 3rd century B.C. to the 1st century A.D.

I292. Warmington, Eric H. **The commerce between the Roman empire and India.** Cambridge, Eng., 1928. Excellent account, based on archaeological and literary sources (including Chinese), of the trade routes and objects of trade in the early empire. To be revised in the light of discoveries at Dura and Arikamedu.

I293. Wheeler, Sir Mortimer. **Rome beyond the imperial frontiers.** London, 1954. Pelican ed., 1955. Lively account, based on author's excavations and research, of trade of the Roman empire with Germany, Africa, India, and China in the early empire.

I294. Gren, Erik. **Kleinasien und der Ostbalkan in der Wirtschaftlichen Entwicklung der römischen Kaiserzeit.** Uppsala, 1941. Useful study of the road and trade connections between Asia Minor and the eastern Balkans and of the role of the army in their economic development. Full bibliography.

I295. Rostovtzeff, Michael I. **Geschichte der Staatspacht in der römischen Kaiserzeit bis Diokletian.** Leipzig, 1904. Remains a most important discussion of the development of the public contract in both the Greek East and the Roman West, and of related historical problems.

I296. Laet, Siegfried J. de. **Portorium: étude sur l'organisation douanière chez les romains, surtout à l'époque du haut-empire.** Bruges, 1949. Full account of imperial and local customs at all periods of Roman history. Contribution to both economic and administrative history. On other indirect taxes see René Cagnat, *Étude historique sur les impôts indirects chez les romains* (Paris, 1882).

Cultural History

General

I297. Bailey, Cyril, ed. **The legacy of Rome.** Oxford, 1923. Essays by several scholars on different aspects of Roman civilization, with emphasis on its relation to later civilization. Designed for the general reader, but valuable for special students. (Full titles in original *Guide*, p. 219.) [AERB, TRSB]

I298. Grenier, Albert. **The Roman spirit in religion, thought, and art.** Tr. from French by M. R. Dobie. London and N.Y., 1926. Attractive survey, best on Etruscan period, but valuable to advanced students also for penetrating judgments on Roman life and thought.

I299. Cochrane, Charles N. **Christianity and classical culture: a study of thought and action from Augustus to Augustine.** 2nd rev. ed., N.Y., 1944. A fundamental, strongly philosophical study which reviews the intellectual background for events and development of the empire, and its opposition to and eventual reconcilement with Christianity.

I300. Moore, Frank G. **The Roman's world.** N.Y., 1936. Comprehensive and well-illustrated introduction to the many aspects of Roman life and culture, intended for both serious students and the general public.

I301. Fowler, William W. **Social life at Rome in the age of Cicero.** N.Y., 1909. Attractive general survey of the city of Rome and society of the late republic, based largely on Cicero's correspondence.

I302. Friedländer, Ludwig. **Darstellungen aus der Sittengeschichte Roms in der Zeit von August bis zum Ausgang der Antonine.** 9th and 10th ed., rev. by G. Wissowa, 4 v., Leipzig, 1921–23. Tr. by L. A. Magnus, J. H. Freese, and A. B. Gough as *Roman life and manners under the early empire* (4 v., London and N.Y., 1908–13). A basic reference work, scholarly, sound, well-documented up to its date, on the cultural history of Rome from 31 B.C. to 180 A.D.; important also for material on special topics. V. 4 contains still valuable notes and appendices.

I303. Carcopino, Jérôme. **Daily life in ancient Rome: the people and the city at the height of the empire.** Tr. from French by E. O. Lorimer. 3rd rev. ed., New Haven, 1946. Excellent treatise, especially good on the city of Rome and conditions of the lower classes. Select bibliography.

I304. Dill, Sir Samuel. **Roman society from Nero to Marcus Aurelius.** 2nd rev. ed., London and N.Y., 1905. Penetrating account of the period, based primarily on literary sources; philosophical in treatment. [WSD, TRSB]

I305. ———. **Roman society in the last century of the western empire.** 2nd rev. ed., London and N.Y., 1899. Represents the society of the time of great pagan senators, many of the great church fathers, and the Germanic invasions. Refers mostly to Italy and Gaul. [WSD, TRSB]

I306. Starr, Chester G. **Civilization and the Caesars: the intellectual revolution in the Roman empire.** Ithaca, N.Y., 1954. Attributes the decline of classical civilization to the absolutism inherent in the Augustan system. Valuable for range and information, despite an uncertain thesis. Bibliographical notes.

I307. Haarhoff, Theodore J. **The stranger at the gate: aspects of exclusiveness and co-operation in ancient Greece and Rome, with some reference to modern times.** 2nd rev. ed., Oxford, 1948. Study of effects of the meeting of cultures and peoples in Greece and in Rome of the republic and empire. Notes and bibliography.

Education, Thought, and Philosophy

For education, and the advancement of learning, science, and technology see relevant articles in encyclopedias cited above in this section and in Section H.

I308. Singer, Charles J., and others, eds. **A history of technology.** V. 2, **The Mediterranean civilizations and the Middle Ages.** Oxford, 1956. Includes Roman material of special value. Roman philosophy is treated in various works on ancient philosophy, especially those that deal with Epicureanism, Stoicism, and Neo-Platonism, and incidentally in treatises on Roman literature. See also relevant chapters in *Cambridge ancient history*, v. 9–12, and their bibliographies.

I309. Lucretius, Carus T. **De rerum natura.** Ed. and tr. by Cyril Bailey. 3 v. Oxford, 1947. Tr. by W. H. D. Rouse, London and Cambridge, Mass., 1924. [Loeb classical library.] An interpretation, by a great poet, of the universe from the point of view of Epicurean philosophy. See E. E. Sikes, *Lucretius, poet and philosopher* (Cambridge, Eng., 1936). [AERB, TRSB]

I310. Cicero, Marcus Tullius. **De finibus bonorum et malorum.** Ed. and tr. by H. Rackham. London and N.Y., 1914. [Loeb classical library.] In this and the following philosophical essays Cicero gave the Roman world the substance of the teachings of the Greek schools of philosophy, usually in Roman settings and with Roman examples. [AERB, TRSB]

I311. ——. **De natura deorum; Academica.** Ed. and tr. by H. Rackham. London, 1933.

I312. ——. **De officiis.** Ed. and tr. by Walter Miller. London and N.Y., 1913. [Loeb classical library.]

I313. ——. **De senectute; De amicitia; De divinatione.** Ed. and tr. by William A. Falconer. London and N.Y., 1923. [Loeb classical library.]

I314. ——. **De re publica; de legibus.** Ed. and tr. by C. W. Keyes. London and N.Y., 1928. [Loeb classical library.]

I315. ——. **Disputationes Tusculanae.** Ed. and tr. by J. E. King. London and N.Y., 1927. [Loeb classical library.]

I316. ——. **Scripta quae manserunt omnia.** Ed. by C. F. W. Müller. 10 v. Leipzig, 1889–1902.

I317. Seneca, Lucius Annaeus. **Opera quae supersunt.** Ed. by F. Haase. 3 v. Leipzig, 1852–53. In this and the following works Seneca, the philosopher, poet, and statesman of the age of Nero, presents discussions of moral and scientific questions, chiefly from the stoic point of view. [AERB, TRSB]

I318. ——. **Diologorum libri XII.** Ed. by E. Hermes. Leipzig, 1905.

I319. ——. **De beneficiis libri VII; De clementia libri II.** Ed. by C. Hosius. Leipzig, 1900.

I320. ——. **Naturalium quaestionum libri VIII.** Ed. by A. Gercke. Leipzig, 1907.

I321. ——. **Epistulae morales.** 2nd ed., by O. Hense, Leipzig, 1914. *Moral essays,* tr. by J. W. Basore, 3 v., London and N.Y., 1928–35.

I322. Aurelius Antoninus, Marcus. **Ta eis heauton** (To himself). Ed., text and commentary, *The meditations of the emperor Marcus Aurelius*, by A. S. L. Farquharson,

2 v., Oxford, 1944. Tr. by C. R. Haines, London and N.Y., 1926. [Loeb classical library.] The emperor's meditations on the ethical teachings of the Stoics, written in Greek in twelve books during the latter part of his reign.

I323. Arnold, Edward V. **Roman Stoicism.** Cambridge, Eng., 1911. Remains a standard treatise.

I324. Quintilianus, M. Fabius. **Institutionis oratoriae libri XII.** 5th ed. by C. Halm, Leipzig, 1913. Tr. by H. E. Butler, 4 v., London and N.Y., 1921–22. The course of education from elementary training through the advanced rhetorical school is set forth by the famous teacher whom Vespasian appointed to the first paid professorship of rhetoric in Rome.

I325. Gwynn, Aubrey. **Roman education from Cicero to Quintilian.** Oxford, 1926. Good analysis of the main principles and ideals of Roman education. Should now be supplemented by reference to the Roman section of Henri Irénée Marrou, *A history of education in antiquity* (tr. by G. Lamb, N.Y., 1956). [AERB, TRSB]

Literature

I326. Schanz, Martin von. **Geschichte der römischen Litteratur bis zum Gesetzgebungswerk des Kaisers Justinian.** 4 v. in 5. Munich, 1890–1935. Subsequent revisions. The fundamental work of reference for sources and critical scholarship on the biography, works, text, tradition, and criticism of Latin authors.

I327. Rostagni, Augusto. **Storia della letteratura latina.** 2 v. Turin, 1949–52. A full and abundantly illustrated history which discusses the authors in relation to their background and times. Bibliographies at ends of chapters.

I328. Duff, John W. **Literary history of Rome from the origins to the close of the golden age.** 3rd ed., London, 1953. Introductory history notable for good sense and fine appreciation of style. Excellent select bibliography by Arnold M. Duff.

I329. ——. **Literary history of Rome in the silver age from Tiberius to Hadrian.** 2nd impression, London, 1930. Excellent introductory history of the silver age.

I330. Frank, Tenney. **Life and literature in the Roman republic.** Berkeley, 1930. [Sather classical lectures.] The study which best describes in English how Roman conditions shaped the development of Roman literature.

I331. Büchner, Karl, and J. B. Hofmann. **Lateinische Literatur und Sprache in der Forschung seit 1937.** Bern, 1951. Valuable survey, with comment and criticism, of scholarly publications concerned with Latin language and literature and Roman culture.

I332. Sikes, Edward E. **Roman poetry.** London, 1923. Brief but penetrating treatment of the conception of poetry and the place of the poet as an interpreter of Roman life.

I333. D'Alton, John F. **Roman literary theory and criticism.** London and N.Y., 1931. Scholarly and appreciative summation of the material and its problems.

Religion

I334. Wissowa, Georg. **Religion und Kultus der Römer.** 2nd ed., Munich, 1912. [Handbuch der Altertumswissenschaft.] Short historical section, detailed analysis of individual cults and religious institutions. Legalistic approach and some interpretations no longer generally accepted, but still the one indispensable source book for the subject. A revision by K. Latte is forthcoming. [AKM]

I335. Marquardt, Karl J. **Römische Staatsverwaltung.** V. 3, **Das Sacralwesen.** 2nd ed., Leipzig, 1885. Excellent source book for details of religious organization and institutions. Useful for full quotation of source material. [AKM]

I336. Bailey, Cyril. **Phases in the religion of ancient Rome.** Berkeley, 1932. "An attempt to review the various elements which at different times went to compose" Roman religion. A pleasant, rather general treatment. More attention is given to the republic than the empire. [AKM]

I337. Turchi, Nicola. **La religione di Roma antica.** Bologna, 1939. Descriptive section and historical account; useful introduction to the subject. Presentation of debatable material is sometimes oversimplified. Good bibliography and guide to sources with selected quotations. [AKM]

I338. Bayet, Jean. **Histoire politique et psychologique de la religion romaine.** Paris, 1957. Imaginative, interesting interpretation, judicious recognition of difficulties in evidence, some synthesis of contributions from divergent schools of thought. Excellent topical bibliography; ancient sources sparingly cited. [AKM]

I339. Grenier, Albert. **Les religions étrusque et romaine.** Paris, 1948. Text is very brief, but notes contain useful statements of essential source material and modern bibliography, with indications of problems and controversy. Review, P. Boyancé, *Rev. ét. anc.,* 50 (1948): 380.

I340. Fowler, William W. **The Roman festivals of the period of the republic: an introduction to the study of the religion of the Romans.** London, 1899. Day-by-day study of the pre-Julian calendar. Later discoveries have made some sections obsolete, but still an invaluable handbook. References occasionally incorrect. [AKM]

I341. ——. **The religious experience of the Roman people from the earliest times to the age of Augustus.** London, 1911. Approach and interpretation in some ways out of date, but still an important book and good intro-

duction to the study of the period covered. [AKM]

I342. Sanctis, Gaetano de. **Storia dei Romani.** V. 4, **La fondazione dell' impero,** pt. 2, **Vita e pensiero nell'età delle grandi conquiste.** Florence, 1953. Contains a detailed analysis of the religion of the period in relation to earlier and later periods. Full references to ancient sources, modern bibliography limited. Conservative, brilliant, indispensable. [AKM]

I343. Boissier, Gaston. **La religion romaine d'Auguste aux Antonins.** 5th ed., 2 v., Paris, 1900. Unique in its coverage of the period and a classic work, but recent discoveries have made much of it obsolete. [AKM]

I344. Taylor, Lily R. **The divinity of the Roman emperor.** Middletown, Conn., 1931. Covers the origin and development of emperor cult through the Augustan period. Basic work, to be supplemented by later studies. [AKM]

I345. Beaujeu, Jean. **La religion romaine à l'apogée de l'empire.** V. 1, **La politique religieuse des Antonins (96–192).** Paris, 1955. Detailed analysis of policy of each emperor, preceded by general discussion of early empire and followed by general conclusions. First major work on the religion of the period in this century; admirably executed. To be followed by a second volume of a more general nature on the same period. [AKM]

I346. Cumont, Franz V. M. **Lux perpetua.** Paris, 1949. Deals with beliefs of the classical world as to death and after life. Fundamental, with full references to the author's earlier works in more specifically Roman areas: *The mysteries of Mithras* (2nd ed., Chicago, 1910); *Oriental religions in Roman paganism* (Chicago, 1911); *After life in Roman paganism* (New Haven, 1922); *Astrology and religion among the Greeks and Romans* (N.Y. and London, 1912); and others, all works of great importance. [AKM]

Art and Archaeology

Some excellent studies of Roman art and architecture are found in works listed in Section H.

I347. Helbig, Wolfgang. **Führer durch die öffentlichen Sammlungen klassischer Altertümer in Rom.** 3rd ed., by Walther Amelung, Emil Reisch, and Fritz Weege, 2 v., Leipzig, 1912–13. Indispensable as an introduction to works of art preserved in museums in Rome. Brief history and description of each object, supplemented by interpretation, resumé of scholarly work on which the interpretation is based, and bibliography. [ISR]

I348. Cagnat, René, and Victor Chapot, **Manuel d'archéologie romaine.** 2 v. Paris, 1916–20. Scholarly, systematic survey of almost every aspect of Roman civilization of which there are physical remains. Archaeological in purpose and method. Liberally illustrated descriptions of monuments throughout the Roman world, also sculptures, portraits, paintings, furniture, armor, and *instrumenta* of various kinds. [ISR]

I349. Koch, Herbert. **Römische Kunst.** 2nd ed., Weimar, 1949. Brief but authoritative introduction to Roman art, with emphasis on architecture and its relation to Greek and eastern art. [ISR]

I350. Platner, Samuel B. **The topography and monuments of ancient Rome.** 2nd ed. rev. and enl., Boston, 1911. Of fundamental usefulness as a topographical survey of ancient Rome, with description and illustrations of surviving monuments, and with compact citation of important ancient sources. Supplemented by *I351,* which adds material from subsequent excavations and more recent bibliography. [ISR]

I351. Platner, Samuel B., and Thomas Ashby. **A topographical dictionary of ancient Rome.** London, 1929. Based on *I350,* but arranged alphabetically rather than topographically. Includes description of the monuments, a resumé of ancient sources and of modern research, and important bibliography. A supplement to, rather than replacement of, the above. [ISR]

I352. Lugli, Giuseppe. **Monumenti antichi di Roma e suburbio.** V. 2–3. V. 1 replaced by **Roma antica, il centro monumentale.** Rome, 1934–46. *Roma antica* not only replaces v. 1 of the original, but is enlarged to include a more comprehensive survey of ancient sources. [ISR]

I353. Ducati, Pericle. **Storia dell'arte etrusca.** 2 v. Florence, 1927. Good comprehensive survey of Etruscan monuments and history of Etruscan art. The plates are of relatively poor quality and need to be supplemented by *I354.* [ISR]

I354. Giglioli, Giulio. **L'arte etrusca.** Milan, 1935. Primarily a collection of excellent illustrations of Etruscan art, arranged chronologically and provided with bibliography. [ISR]

I355. Poulsen, P. Frederik S. **Etruscan tomb paintings.** Tr. by Ingeborg Anderson. Oxford, 1922. Good, readable description of a representative selection of tomb paintings, with emphasis on their content as illustrative of Etruscan culture. [ISR]

I356. Mau, August. **Pompeii, its life and art.** Tr. by Francis W. Kelsey. 3rd rev. ed., N.Y. and London, 1907. Authoritative account of the topography, public buildings, and private houses of Pompeii; indispensable as introduction to Roman municipal architecture and town planning, domestic architecture, and wall decoration. Includes results of author's earlier work on wall decoration, which established the four Pompeian styles. Supplemented by *I357.* [ISR]

I357. Spinazzola, Vittorio. **Pompeii alla luce degli scavi nuovi.** 2 v. Rome, 1953. Description of new excavations, well illustrated by plans and photographs. More detailed that *I356,* with attention to construction of roofs, balconies, and second stories. Interpretation of both exterior and interior paintings, with comparative material from elsewhere in Pompeii and from other arts such as sculpture and coinage. [ISR]

I358. Curtius, Ludwig. **Die Wandmalerie Pompejis.** Leipzig, 1929. General introduction to Pompeian wall painting, with some attention to correlation of the paintings with the four styles of wall decoration. Description and numerous illustrations of the paintings, some in color. Supplemented by *I359– 360,* which include more penetrating artistic criticism and, together, carry the analysis of style through to the end of Roman painting. [ISR]

I359. Wirth, Fritz. "Der Stil der kampanischen Wandgemälde." **Mitteilungen des Deutschen Archäologischen Instituts, römischen Abteilung,** 42 (1927): 1–83.

I360. ——. **Römische Wandmalerei.** Berlin, 1934.

I361. Lehmann, Phyllis W. **Roman wall paintings from Boscoreale.** Cambridge, Mass., 1953. Detailed study of one important group of paintings, but so rich in comparative material and so penetrating in its discussion of older and more recent studies that it also serves as an excellent critical analysis of the second Pompeian style. Review, M. Bieber, *Am. jour. archae.,* 57 (1953): 237. [ISR]

I362. Strong, Eugénie. **La scultura romana da Augusto a Constantino.** 2 v. Florence, 1923–26. Best available survey of Roman sculpture, with emphasis on its essentially Roman character. [ISR]

I363. Vessberg, G. Olof. **Studien zur Kunstgeschichte der römische Republik.** Lund, 1941. Pt. 1 is a survey and analysis of ancient sources on Roman art to the Augustan age; pt. 2 is a history of Roman portraiture of the republican period as preserved in coinage and sculpture. [ISR]

I364. Rodenwaldt, Gerhart. **Kunst um Augustus.** Berlin, 1943. Excellent critical interpretation of Augustan art, with primary emphasis on sculpture, but with cursory consideration of its relations with painting and architecture. [ISR]

I365. Magi, Filippo. **I rilievi flavi del Palazzo della Cancelleria.** Rome, 1945. Scholarly study of two monumental reliefs, discovered in 1938, which have important bearing on the development of Roman relief. Important contribution to the study of Flavian relief. [ISR]

I366. Hamberg, Per Gustav. **Studies in Roman imperial art.** Tr. by Kathleen M. Pain. Uppsala, 1945. An original and penetrating study, based on the major reliefs of the 2nd century, of two divergent tendencies —one essentially Hellenistic, the other essentially Roman—which in varying proportions dominated the development of Roman monumental relief. [ISR]

I367. L'Orange, Hans P., and Armin von Gerkan. **Der spätantike Bildschmuck des Konstantinsbogens.** 2 v. Berlin, 1939. Authoritative work on the late sculptures of the Arch of Constantine, including comparison with other contemporary studies and general discussion of late antique styles. [ISR]

I368. Ryberg, Inez S. **Rites of the state religion in Roman art.** Rome, 1955. [Memoirs of the American Academy in Rome, 22.] Official religious ceremonies in Roman imperial art. Introductory sections on the Greek, Etruscan, and republican background. Valuable not only for the state religion, but for stylistic analysis and interpretation of the monuments and their historical setting. Review, O. Brendel, *Am. jour. philol.*, 78 (1957): 301. [LRT]

I369. West, Robert. **Römische Porträt-Plastik.** Munich, 1933. Competent history of the development of Roman portraiture through the reign of Hadrian, treated chronologically by a selected series of important portraits. [ISR]

I370. L'Orange, Hans P. **Studien zur Geschichte des spätantiken Porträts.** Oslo, 1933. Stylistic analysis and catalog of Roman portraits of the 3rd, 4th, and 5th centuries, illustrated by excellent plates. [ISR]

I371. Vitruvius Pollio. **De architectura libri decem.** Tr. by Morris H. Morgan. Cambridge, Mass., 1914. The only surviving ancient work on architecture, written by a practicing architect about 14 B.C. Chapters on important types of Roman buildings, temples of the three Greek orders, fora, basilicas, theaters, baths, dwelling houses, and their decoration. [ISR]

I372. Rivoira, Giovanni T. **Roman architecture and its principles of construction.** Tr. by G. M. Rushforth. Oxford, 1925. History of imperial architecture written with emphasis on the Roman origin of principles of construction important for European architecture. Since the material is arranged chronologically as illustrative of architectural development, the book needs to be used in conjunction with description of monuments supplied by *I350* or *352*. Wide range of material selected from various parts of the Roman world and well illustrated. [ISR]

I373. Boethius, C. Axel. **Roman architecture.** Göteborg, 1944. Brief but fundamentally important treatment of the development, within Roman architecture, of the unclassical elements which became predominant in the late antique period. [ISR]

Numismatics

I374. Mattingly, Harold. **Roman coins from the earliest times to the fall of the western empire.** London, 1928. The only full, general handbook of Roman coins. Sections on the republic need revision and the pages on the later empire need expansion. [CCV]

I375. Mommsen, Theodor. **Geschichte des römischen Münzwesens.** Berlin, 1860. French tr. by Duc de Blacas, ed. by J. de Witte, *Histoire de la monnaie romaine,* 4 v., Paris, 1865–75. Still important, especially for relationship of Roman coins to earlier Roman history. The French translation contains many emendations and additions by Mommsen himself. [CCV]

I376. Carson, Robert A. G. "A report on research in Roman numismatics, 1936–1952." **Congrès International de Numismatique.** V. 1, **Rapports** (Paris, 1953), pp. 31–54. A long, detailed evaluation of the Roman numismatic contributions in economic, epigraphic, historical, and other fields in the period when Roman numismatics emerged as a major factor in historical studies. [CCV]

I377. Carson, Robert A. G., and C. H. V. Sutherland, eds. **Essays in Roman coinage presented to Harold Mattingly.** Oxford, 1956. Fifteen British and other scholars written articles on all aspects of Roman coins from the early republic to the Middle Ages. A. H. M. Jones, "Numismatics and history" (pp. 13–33); A. R. Bellinger, "Greek mints under the Roman empire" (pp. 137–48); and J. P. C. Kent, "Gold coinage in the later Roman empire" (pp. 190–204) are particularly valuable. Review, C. C. Vermeule, *Am. jour. archae.,* 61 (1957): 117. [CCV]

I378. Hill, Sir George F. **Historical Roman coins from the earliest times to the reign of Augustus.** London, 1909. Although dated by more recent research on Roman republican numismatics, these essays relate coins and history in a readable, scientific manner. [CCV]

I379. Pink, Karl. **The triumviri monetales and the structure of the coinage of the Roman republic.** N.Y., 1952. A somewhat controversial, but nonetheless important, chronological arrangement of the gold and silver consular and later issues of the Roman republic according to the monetary offices or colleges. Review, A. Alföldi, *Gnomon,* 26 (1954): 381. [CCV]

I380. Sydenham, Edward A. **The coinage of the Roman republic.** Rev. by G. C. Haines, ed. by L. Forrer and C. A. Hersh, London, 1952. A full catalog of coin types, with chronologies of moneyers and types based on researches and coin hoards since the writings of Mommsen, E. Babelon, and Grueber. Concordances with older catalogs and other supplemental data are invaluable. [CCV]

I381. Bernhart, Max. **Handbuch zur Münzkunde der römischen Kaiserzeit.** 2 v. Halle, 1926. A guide or manual of problems in Roman imperial numismatics, rather than a handbook. The tables, indices, lists of mints, chronologies, and plates of v. 2 are most useful. A work for quick reference. [CCV]

I382. Grant, Michael. **Roman imperial money.** London, 1954. Six essays on historically noteworthy features of Roman imperial coinage, supplemented by a list of terms, full documentation, and forty plates. [CCV]

I383. Cohen, Henry. **Description historique des monnaies frappées sous l'Empire romain communément appellées médailles impériales.** 2nd rev. ed., 8 v., Paris, 1880–92. A widely used corpus of imperial coins (and medallions), though parts have been supplanted by Mattingly's catalogs. [CCV]

I384. Mattingly, Harold, and others, eds. **The Roman imperial coinage.** 6 v. London, 1923–51. Catalog of the principal types and varieties of Roman imperial coins, arranged by dates and places of issue, and with indices for rapid identification of coins. [CCV]

I385. Toynbee, Jocelyn M. C. **Roman medallions.** N.Y., 1944. Detailed survey of the history, chronologies, types, and purposes of Roman medallions. The plates show all the major medallions, and pieces not illustrated in Gnecchi's *Corpus.* Full bibliography. Review, H. Mattingly, *Numismatic chronicle,* 1944, p. 123. [CCV]

I386. Gnecchi, Francesco. **I medaglioni romani.** 3 v. Milan, 1912. Full catalog of most known Roman medallions and medallic coins in all metals from Augustus to Justinian. [CCV]

I387. Alföldi, Andreas. **Die Kontorniaten.** 2 v. Budapest, 1943. A critical, historical corpus of Roman 4th century jetons, pseudo-medallions, or tokens. They are usually large bronzes, and many bear references to Roman history, mythology, and literature. Principal varieties are illustrated. Review, J. M. C. Toynbee, *Jour. Rom. studies,* 35 (1945): 115. [CCV]

I388. Grueber, Herbert A. **Coins of the Roman republic in the British Museum.** 3 v. London, 1910. Catalog of all Roman republican coin types, both in the British Museum and other collections. Exhaustive historical and other documentation makes this an essential work in spite of later revisions in consular and moneyers' chronologies. [CCV]

I389. Mattingly, Harold. **Coins of the Roman empire in the British Museum.** 5 v. London, 1923–50. Catalogs and illustrates extensively not only the British Museum collection, but all varieties not in the museum. Introductions to each volume discuss the historical, economic, and related aspects of the coins. Bibliographies in each volume.

Review, J. M. C. Toynbee, *Numismatic chronicle,* 1940, p. 203. [CCV]

I390. Vogt, Joseph. **Die alexandrinischen Münzen: Grundlegung einer alexandrinischen Kaisergeschichte.** 2 v. in 1. Stuttgart, 1924. A detailed, illustrative survey of Roman Egypt and related areas, based on a re-study of the Graeco-Roman imperial issues of Alexandria and dependent mints. Older studies are utilized. Contains charts, tables of issues, and bibliography. [CCV]

I391. Milne, Joseph G. **Catalogue of Alexandrian coins.** Oxford, 1933. Most recent general catalog of Graeco-Roman imperial coins struck under emperors Augustus through Diocletian at the Alexandrian and related mints. [CCV]

I392. Sutherland, Carol H. V. **Coinage and currency in Roman Britain.** Oxford, 1937. A numismatic and historical survey, with detailed examples and illustrations, of the coinage in Roman Britain from *ca.* 50 B.C. to 400 A.D. Related issues and economic factors throughout the western Roman provinces are considered. [CCV]

BIOGRAPHIES

Besides the biographical works listed above, the following are among the most valuable biographies of Roman personages.

Ancient Collective Works

I393. Nepos, Cornelius. **Vitae.** Ed. by E. O. Winstedt. Oxford, 1904. Tr. by J. C. Rolfe, London and N.Y., 1929. [Loeb classical library.] Contains lives of Cato the Censor and of Atticus. See also Plutarch's *Lives* for Roman statesmen.

I394. Victor, Sextus Aurelius. **De Caesaribus.** Ed., together with *De viris illustribus* and *Epitome de Caesaribus,* by Franz Piehlmayr. Leipzig, 1911. These three works bring together brief lives of prominent Romans of the republic and of emperors from Augustus to Theodosius I.

Modern Collective Studies

The most important are *I112* and the articles in *Realencyclopädie (H12),* among which those on Crassus, Lucullus, and Cicero by M. Gelzer are outstanding.

I395. Birt, Theodor. **Römische Characterköpfe, ein Weltbild in Biographien.** Leipzig, 1913. Excellent sketches of prominent figures from the elder Scipio to Marcus Aurelius.

Republican Period

I396. Liddell Hart, B. H. **A greater than Napoleon: Scipio Africanus.** London and Boston, 1927.

I397. Scullard, Howard H. **Scipio Africanus in the Second Punic War.** Cambridge, Eng., 1930.

I398. Kienast, D. **Cato der Zensor: seine Personalichkeit und seine Zeit.** Heidelberg, 1954.

I399. Walbank, Frank W. **Philip V of Macedon.** Cambridge, Eng., 1940.

I400. Reinach, Theodore. **Mithridates Eupator, König von Pontus.** Tr. from the French by A. Goetz with revisions by author. Leipzig, 1896.

I401. Bennett, Harold. **Cinna and his times: a critical and interpretative study of Roman history during the period 87–84 B.C.** Menasha, Wis., 1923.

I402. Gelzer, Matthias. **Pompeius.** Munich, 1949.

I403. Boissier, Gaston. **Cicero and his friends: a study of Roman society in the time of Caesar.** Tr. from the French by A. D. Jones. London, 1897.

I404. Carcopino, Jérôme. **Cicero: the secrets of his correspondence.** Tr. from the French by E. O. Lorimer. 2 v. New Haven, 1951. A brilliant and well-informed but controversial interpretation.

I405. Sihler, Ernest G. **Annals of Caesar: a critical biography with a survey of the sources.** N.Y., 1911.

I406. Gelzer, Matthias. **Caesar, der Politiker und Staatsmann.** 3rd ed. rev. and enl., Munich, 1941.

Early Empire

I407. Reinhold, Meyer. **Marcus Agrippa, a biography.** Geneva, N.Y., 1933.

I408. Shuckburgh, Evelyn S. **Augustus, the life and times of the founder of the Roman empire, B.C. 63–A.D. 14.** London, 1903.

I409. Buchan, John. **Augustus.** Boston, 1937.

I410. Charlesworth, Martin P. **Five men: character studies from the Roman empire.** Cambridge, Mass., 1936. Lives of Agrippa, Musonius, Rufus, Josephus, and Agricola.

I411. Balsdon, John P. V. D. **The emperor Gaius.** Oxford, 1934.

I412. Levi, Mario A. **Nerone e i suoi tempi.** Milan, 1949.

I413. Waltz, René. **Vie de Sénèque.** Paris, 1909.

I414. Thackery, Henry St. J. **Josephus, the man and the historian.** N.Y., 1929.

I415. Burn, Andrew R. **Agricola and Roman Britain.** N.Y., 1953.

I416. Homo, Léon. **Vespasien, l'empereur du bon sens.** Paris, 1949.

Second Century

I417. Paribeni, Roberto. **Optimus princeps: saggio sulla storia e sui tempi dell'imperatore Trajano.** 2 v. Messina, 1927.

I418. Weber, Wilhelm. **Trajan und Hadrian.** Stuttgart, 1923.

I419. Sedgwick, Henry D. **Marcus Aurelius, a biography.** New Haven, 1921.

I420. Farquharson, A. S. L. **Marcus Aurelius, his life and his world.** Oxford, 1951.

Third Century

I421. Platnauer, Maurice. **The life and reign of the emperor Septimius Severus.** London and N.Y., 1918.

I422. Jardé, Auguste F. **Études critiques sur la vie et la règne de Sévère Alexandre.** Paris, 1925.

I423. Homo, Léon. **Essai sur le règne de l'empereur Aurélien.** Paris, 1904.

I424. Vitucci, Giovanni. **L'imperatore Probo.** Rome, 1952.

Fourth and Fifth Centuries

I425. Bidez, Joseph. **La vie de l'empereur Julien.** Paris, 1930.

I426. Thompson, E. A. **A history of Attila and the Huns.** Oxford, 1948.

I427. Homeyer, H. **Attila: der Hunnenkönig von seinen Zeitgenossen dargestellt.** Berlin, 1951.

ACADEMY, UNIVERSITY, AND SOCIETY PUBLICATIONS

Many articles relating to Roman history and allied subjects appear in the publications of national academies of European countries listed in other sections, and in the series of publications issued by American universities mentioned in Section H. The bulletins and reports of the various national schools established in Rome and those of the Italian government dealing with archaeological discoveries in Italy are devoted especially to Roman history.

I428. **Bibliothèque des Écoles Françaises d'Athènes et de Rome.** Paris, 1876 ff.

I429. **Mélanges d'archéologie et d'histoire de l'École Française de Rome.** Rome, 1885 ff.

I430. British School at Rome. **Papers.** London, 1902 ff.

I431. Deutsches Archaeologisches Institut, Rome. **Mitteilungen.** Rome, 1886 ff.

I432. American Academy in Rome. **Memoirs.** N.Y., 1917 ff.

I433. ———. **Papers and monographs.** N.Y., 1919.

I434. Accademia dei Lincei. **Notizie degli Scavi di Antichità.** Rome, 1876 ff. The *Memorie* and *Rendiconti* of this publication frequently contain important articles on Roman history.

I435. **Bulletino della Commissione Archeologia di Roma.** Rome, 1872 ff.

I436. Atti della Pontificia Accademia Romana di Archeologia. Rome, 1821 ff.

PERIODICALS

Some periodicals listed in Section F and nearly all those relating to philology, archaeology, and history in Section H contain articles in Roman history.

I437. Historia: a journal of ancient history. Wiesbaden, 1950 ff. (Quarterly.)

I438. Journal of Roman studies. London, 1911 ff. (Semiannual.)

I439. Revue des études latines. Paris, 1923 ff. (Quarterly.)

I440. Zeitschrift der Savigny-Stiftung für Rechtsgeschichte, Romanistische Abteilung. Weimar, 1880 ff. (Annual.)

I441. Journal of juristic papyrology. N.Y., 1946 ff. (Irregular.)

III. THE MIDDLE PERIOD IN EURASIA AND NORTHERN AFRICA

General: Eurasia and Northern Africa (ca. 476–1453 A.D.)

GRAY C. BOYCE

This brief section contains items which by title may seem to deal exclusively with European history, but on examination often will be found useful also for other areas of medieval studies. Books and articles of quality encompassing the whole or interrelated parts of the Eurasian and northern African medieval world are regrettably restricted in number. However, the insistence today on some attention to a global view of historical problems may be advantageous, and imaginative historians may be encouraged to broaden their horizons and write works that will challenge cherished preconceptions.

BIBLIOGRAPHIES, LIBRARIES, AND MUSEUMS

Bibliographies

J1. Paetow, Louis J. **A guide to the study of medieval history.** Ed. by Dana C. Munro and Gray C. Boyce. Rev. ed., N.Y., 1931. Comprehensive guide to the literature of medieval history, pertaining principally to western Europe, 500–1500. The important elements of political, economic, institutional, and cultural history of the period are accorded proper attention. A supplement for the years 1930–1960 is being prepared by Professor Boyce for the Mediaeval Academy of America.

J2. Vercauteren, Fernand. "Rapport général sur les travaux d'histoire du Moyen Âge de 1945 à 1954." **Relazioni del X congresso internazionale di scienze storiche.** V. 6, **Sintesi generali di orientamento** (Florence, 1955), pp. 41–165. Well-conceived essay; a

valuable critique by a highly competent medievalist. For reference to similar surveys for the period 1940–46 see Malclès, *Les sources du travail bibliographique* (*B2*), v. 2, p. 139.

J3. Franz, Günther, and others. **Bücherkunde zur Weltgeschichte, vom Untergang des römischen Weltreiches bis zur Gegenwart.** See *B58*.

J4. Frewer, Louis B. **Bibliography of historical writings published in Great Britain and the empire, 1940–1945.** See *B57*.

J5. Lancaster, Joan C. **Bibliography of historical works issued in the United Kingdom, 1946–1956.** See *VA10*.

J6. Ladner, Gerhart B. "Bibliographical survey: the history of ideas in the Christian Middle Ages from the fathers to Dante in American and Canadian publications of the years 1940–1952." **Traditio: studies in ancient and medieval history, thought, and religion,** 9 (1953): 439–514.

J7. Schleiffer, Hedwig, and Ruth Crandall.

Index to economic history essays in Festschriften, 1900–1950. Cambridge, Mass., 1953. For the Middle Ages see pp. 19–26 (nos. 152–504).

J8. Farrar, Clarissa P. and Austin P. Evans. **Bibliography of English translations from medieval sources.** N.Y., 1946. [Records of civilization: sources and studies, 39.] Although primarily listing literary sources, this is a rich, admirably conceived, and most useful aid. It may be supplemented for works appearing after its publication by the *International bibliography of historical sciences* (Paris, 1926 ff.); Alexander T. Milne, *Writings on British history* (London, 1937 ff.); and Lancaster (*J5*).

J9. Ricci, Seymour de, and William J. Wilson. **Census of medieval and Renaissance manuscripts in the United States and Canada.** 3 v. N.Y., 1935–40. The Bibliographical Society of America is to publish a *Supplement,* edited by W. H. Bond.

Libraries and Museums

In the United States the best collection of books on medieval history is undoubtedly that of the Harvard University Library, which includes the unrivalled Riant collection on the crusades and the Latin East, extensive collections for the Byzantine empire, the Normans, and medieval culture of the western, Byzantine, and Muslim worlds. The Princeton University Library has good collections on the crusades, and the library of the Princeton Department of Art and Archaeology is especially strong for medieval and Byzantine studies. The Index of Christian Art centered at Princeton is unique. Other universities with good libraries for medieval studies are Columbia, Cornell, Yale, Michigan, Chicago, Illinois, Wisconsin, and California (Berkeley). Syracuse University possesses the Ranke collection, which is rich in works on medieval Germany and Italy. The library of the Catholic University of America is important for history of medieval learning, philosophy, and canon law; while that of St. Louis University is the center for the important Vatican film collection. The Battle Abbey records are at the Huntington Library in San Marino, California. For Byzantine and patristic studies the Dumbarton Oaks Research Library and Collection is of increasing significance. The Pierpont Morgan Library in New York has works of inestimable value to scholars studying the Middle Ages and Renaissance. The Newberry Library of Chicago stresses the Renaissance period in adding to its holdings. Among museums the most dramatic display of medieval objects in the United States is undoubtedly that at The Cloisters, under direction of the Metropolitan Museum of Art of New York.

ENCYCLOPEDIAS AND WORKS OF REFERENCE

J10. Halphen, Louis. **Initiation aux études d'histoire du Moyen Âge.** 2nd ed., Paris, 1946. Serviceable manual recommended as an introduction to basic tools of research.

J11. The Catholic encyclopedia: an international work of reference on the constitution, doctrine, discipline, and history of the Catholic Church. 16 v. N.Y., 1907–14. Supplements, 2 v., 1922–54. A basic reference work for all medieval studies.

J12. Cabrol, Fernand, and others. **Dictionnaire d'archéologie chrétienne et de liturgie.** 15 v. Paris, 1907–53. Of special value to the medievalist.

J13. Baudrillart, Alfred. **Dictionnaire d'histoire et de géographie ecclésiastique.** Ed. by E. Baudrillart. Paris, 1912 ff. Although progress is slow on this monumental work, there is no rival of its kind, and it will long remain the basic work for ecclesiastical geography. V. 14, fasc. 80 appeared in 1958.

J14. Enciclopedia cattolica. Vatican City, 1948 ff. A work in progress that promises to be of major importance.

J15. Enciclopedia ecclesiastica. Milan and Turin, 1942 ff. V. 6, through Mignot, appeared in 1955.

J16. Cross, Frank L., ed. **The Oxford dictionary of the Christian church.** London and N.Y., 1957. Distinguished, noteworthy, indispensable. Review, H. Rosenberg, *Speculum,* 33 (July 1958): 387.

J17. Giry, Arthur. **Manuel de diplomatique.** Paris, 1894. Though now supplemented by *J18*, this well-known work is still an essential scholarly aid.

J18. Boüard, Alain de. **Manuel de diplomatique française et pontificale.** 2 v. Paris, 1929–51. Review, O. G. Darlington, *Am. hist. rev.,* 57 (Oct. 1951): 106. "The introduction (pp. 11–57) is perhaps the clearest and most brilliant short account in print of the history of diplomatics and should be required reading for all graduate students in history."

J19. Wattenbach, Wilhelm. **Deutschlands Geschichtsquellen im Mittelalter: deutsche Kaiserzeit.** Ed. by Robert Holtzmann. 2nd and 3rd eds., Tübingen, 1948 ff. Supplement, *Deutschlands Geschichtsquellen im Mittelalter: Vorzeit und Karolinger,* ed. by Wilhelm Levison, Heinz Löwe, and Rudolf Buchner, Weimar, 1952 ff. Very important introduction to the sources of German history. Reviews, M. L. W. Laistner, *Am. hist. rev.,* 63 (July 1958): 1033; Luitpold Wallach, *Speculum,* 29 (Jan. 1954): 131, 29 (Oct. 1954): 820, 30 (Jan. 1955): 92, 34 (Apr. 1959): 343.

J20. Bresslau, Harry. **Handbuch der Urkundenlehre für Deutschland und Italien.**

2nd and 3rd ed., 2 v., Berlin, 1958. The major work on German diplomatics.

J21. Bischoff, Bernhard. **Paläographie.** Bielefeld, Ger., 1950. [Deutsche Philologie im Aufriss, 1.] "An astonishingly concise 'syllabus' on *Schriftwesen* and the history of the various scripts used in western Europe up to the end of the Middle Ages." *Speculum,* 27 (July 1952): 363.

J22. Prou, Maurice. **Manuel de paléographie latine et française.** 4th ed. Paris, 1924. An indispensable introductory manual. See the important recommendations for other works given in Karl Strecker, *Introduction to medieval Latin* (Berlin, 1957), pp. 131–36.

J23. Reusens, Edmond H. J. **Éléments de paléographie.** Louvain, 1899. Old, but still very useful as an introduction to medieval palaeography.

J24. Lowe, Elias A. **Codices latini antiquiores: a palaeographical guide to Latin manuscripts prior to the ninth century.** Oxford, 1934 ff. (9 v. to date.) A major scholarly achievement by the dean of American palaeographers. The fine texts and well-reproduced plates of each volume now serve as the best basis for understanding the nature and problems of medieval Latin scripts for the period covered.

J25. Thomson, S. Harrison. **Progress of medieval and Renaissance studies in the United States and Canada.** Boulder, Colo., 1923 ff. Originally edited annually by James F. Willard, this useful bulletin now appears biennially, providing a list of active medieval and Renaissance scholars, their current writings, items of scholarly interest, and occasional special articles.

J26. Russell, Josiah C. **Dictionary of writers of thirteenth century England.** London, 1936. [Bulletin of the Institute of Historical Research, Special supplement 3.] For some necessary corrections see review by J. S. P. Tatlock, *Speculum,* 12 (July 1937): 413.

GEOGRAPHIES, GAZETTEERS, AND ATLASES

J27. Deschamps, Pierre C. E. **Dictionnaire de géographie ancienne et moderne.** See *B201.*

J28. Graesse, Johann G. T. **Orbis latinus: oder, Verzeichnis der wichtigsten lateinischen Orts- und Ländernamen.** Rev. ed., by Friedrich Benedict, Berlin and N.Y., 1909. Essential for medieval geographical terms, especially their Latin forms.

J29. Shepherd, William R. **Historical atlas.** See *B217.*

J30. Palmer, Robert R., ed. **Atlas of world history.** See *C16.*

J31. Calmette, Joseph L. A. **Atlas historique.** V. 2, **Le Moyen Âge.** 3rd ed., Paris, 1951. There is need for a historical atlas of

ample proportions devoted exclusively to the medieval scene. The 24 maps provided in this modest collection are useful, but made less so by lack of an index and by overcrowding of the plates with details.

J32. The Cambridge medieval history. (See *J43.*) There are eight portfolios of maps to accompany these volumes, which give illustrative details of a sort rarely found elsewhere.

DEMOGRAPHIC STUDIES

See Section K.

LINGUISTIC WORKS

See Section K.

PRINTED COLLECTIONS OF SOURCES

See Section K.

SHORTER GENERAL HISTORIES

J33. Previté-Orton, Charles W. **The shorter Cambridge medieval history.** 2 v. Cambridge, Eng., 1952. This condensation of the 8 volumes of *The Cambridge medieval history* (*J43*) presents a traditional interpretation of the age. Accent is on political and institutional developments, somewhat to the neglect of social, economic, and cultural history. There are numerous interesting and appropriate illustrations, but unfortunately no bibliographical aids.

J34. Thompson, James Westfall, and Edgar N. Johnson. **An introduction to medieval Europe, 300–1500.** N.Y., 1937. Sidney Painter refers to this as the best one volume history of the period. It is the result of a reworking by Johnson of a not-overly-successful two volume work by Thompson.

J35. Thorndike, Lynn. **The history of medieval Europe.** 3rd ed., Boston and N.Y., 1949.

J36. Barbagallo, Corrado. **Il medioevo, 476–1454.** 2 pts. Turin, 1950–54. [Storia universale, 3.] Excellent illustrations and plates; bibliographies provided for each chapter are rather full for printed sources, but not strictly up to date in listing modern works. Covers all of Europe.

J37. Strayer, Joseph R. **Western Europe in the Middle Ages: a short history.** N.Y., 1955. This compact volume presents a superb synthesis.

J38. Davis, Ralph H. C. **A history of medieval Europe from Constantine to Saint Louis.** London and N.Y., 1957. Lucid, well-written introductory survey. Each chapter has a list of carefully chosen but limited recommendations for further reading.

J39. Hoyt, Robert S. **Europe in the Middle Ages.** N.Y., 1957.

J40. Strayer, Joseph R., and Dana C. Munro. **The Middle Ages, 395–1500.** 4th ed., N.Y., 1959. [The Century historical series.] Well-written, interesting survey; a new book rather than mere revision of an old one. Illustrations are well chosen and the maps clear and helpful. The reading list offers an excellent selection of references for further study, and there are six convenient genealogical tables.

LONGER GENERAL HISTORIES

J41. Pirenne, Jacques. **Les grands courants de l'histoire universelle.** V. 1–2. Neuchâtel, 1944–45. [1, *Des origines à l'Islam;* 2, *De l'expansion musulmane aux traités de Westphalie.*] Review, *Am. hist. rev.,* 63 (Oct. 1957): 75. A remarkable achievement for a single author, who aims to sustain the thesis that maritime countries are liberal and individualistic whereas continental groups are " 'sociaux' et autoritaires."

J42. Gibbon, Edward. **The history of the decline and fall of the Roman empire.** See *I132.*

J43. **The Cambridge medieval history.** Ed. by Henry M. Gwatkin and others. Cambridge, Eng., and N.Y., 1911–36. A cooperative work fundamental for medieval studies. All volumes are not uniformly attractive or successful; but the work is boldly conceived, and executed with determination and skill. Important extensive bibliographies provided for each volume.

J44. Kern, Fritz, and others. **Historia mundi: ein Handbuch der Weltgeschichte.** Bern, 1952 ff. This ambitious work, to be complete in 10 v., contains chapters by distinguished authorities. V. 5 bears the subtitle *Frühes Mittelalter;* v. 6, *Höhes und Spätes Mittelalter,* includes sections on the Renaissance.

J45. Diehl, Charles, and Georges Marçais. **Le monde oriental de 395 à 1081.** See *M68.*

J46. Gaudefroy-Demombynes, Maurice, and Sergei F. Platonov. **Le monde musulman et byzantin jusqu'aux croisades.** Paris, 1931.

HISTORIES OF SPECIAL PERIODS

J47. Moss, Henry St. L. B. **The birth of the Middle Ages, 395–814.** Oxford, 1935. Serviceable for period of transition from antiquity to the medieval world. Author stresses the importance for the future of admission of the church under Constantine to a share in the government of the state. Work shows originality of insight.

J48. Bark, William C. **Origins of the medieval world.** Stanford, 1958. A challenging series of essays. The bibliography serves as an excellent introduction to significant literature for the ever-debated, complex problem of medieval origins. Review, L. White, Jr., *Am. hist. rev.,* 63 (July 1958): 942.

J49. Deanesly, Margaret. **A history of early medieval Europe, 476 to 911.** 2nd rev. ed., London and N.Y., 1960. In general excellent.

J50. Lot, Ferdinand. **The end of the ancient world and the beginnings of the Middle Ages.** Tr. by Philip and Mariette Leon. London and N.Y., 1931. Analysis of Mediterranean and Germanic civilizations from the 3rd to the 6th century. A noteworthy book.

J51. Adcock, Frank E., and others. **Römisches Weltreich und Christentum.** Bern, 1956. [Historia mundi, 4.] For Rome and the early Middle Ages.

J52. Altheim, Franz, and others. **Frühes Mittelalter.** Bern, 1956. [Historia mundi, 5.]

J53. Dawson, Christopher H. **The making of Europe: an introduction to the history of European unity.** London and N.Y., 1932. A work of considerable originality and recognized distinction.

J54. Halphen, Louis. **Les barbares, des grandes invasions aux conquêtes turques du XIe siècle.** 5th rev. ed., Paris, 1948. [Peuples et civilisations: histoire générale, 5.] Excellent introduction to the problem of European invasions prior to the crusades. Good bibliographies and maps.

J55. Latouche, Robert. **Les grandes invasions et la crise d'Occident au Ve siècle.** Paris, 1946.

J56. Stein, Ernst. **Histoire du bas-empire.** V. 2, De la disparition de l'empire d'Occident à la mort de Justinien (476–565). Paris, 1949. Political and institutional history.

J57. Perroy, Edouard, and others. **Le Moyen Âge: l'expansion de l'Orient et la naissance de la civilisation occidentale.** Paris, 1955. [Histoire générale des civilisations, 3.]

J58. Halphen, Louis. **L'essor de l'Europe (XIe–XIIIe siècles).** 3rd rev. ed., Paris, 1948. [Peuples et civilisations: histoire générale, 6.] Good synthesis for the high Middle Ages.

HISTORIES OF SPECIAL AREAS

J59. **European civilization: its origin and development.** Ed. by Edward J. Eyre. 7 v. N.Y., 1934–39. See V. 7, Douglas Woodruff, "The European frontier" [on Saracens, Mongols, Ottoman Turks, passing of frontier consciousness]; A. Hilliard Atteridge, "European contacts with Africa"; and his chapter on "European geographical discovery and expansion."

J60. Diehl, Charles. **Byzantium: greatness and decline.** Tr. by Naomi Walford. New Brunswick, N.J., 1957. Includes bibliography by Peter Charanis, containing many references to works dealing with interrelations of easterners, westerners, and Muslims.

J61. Vaughan, Dorothy M. **Europe and the Turk: a pattern of alliances, 1350–1700.** See *M141.*

J62. Gautier, Émile F. **Le passé de l'Afrique du nord: les siècles obscurs.** See *M111.*

J63. Julien, Charles A. **Histoire de l'Afrique du nord, Tunisie, Algérie, Maroc.** See *AC294.*

J64. Dvornik, Francis. **Les Slaves, Byzance et Rome au IXe siècle.** Paris, 1926. Important study of conversion of the Slavs to Christianity.

J65. Vasiliev, Alexander A. **Byzance et les Arabes.** See *M84.*

J66. Cheira, M. A. **La lutte entre Arabes et Byzantins.** See *M85.*

HISTORIES OF SPECIAL TOPICS

Political and Institutional

See Section K.

Economic; Geography and Travel

J67. **The Cambridge economic history.** V. 1, **The agrarian life of the Middle Ages,** ed. by John H. Clapham and Eileen E. Power; v. 2, **Trade and industry in the Middle Ages,** ed. by Michael M. Postan and Edwin E. Rich. Cambridge, Eng., 1941–52. Now the standard work for medieval economic history. The various chapters are the work of many authors.

J68. Lewis, Archibald R. **Naval power and trade in the Mediterranean, A.D. 500–1100.** Princeton, 1951. Review, *Am. hist. rev.,* 56 (July 1951): 858.

J69. Schaube, Adolf. **Handelsgeschichte der romanischen Völker des Mittelmeergebiets bis zum Ende der Kreuzzüge.** Munich and Berlin, 1906. A volume that commands attention and respect; a rich source of information.

J70. Heyd, Wilhelm von. **Histoire du commerce du Levant au Moyen Âge.** 2 v. Leipzig, 1885–86. Reprint, 1936. Basic study for European and Asiatic commercial relations.

J71. Pirenne, Henri. **Mahomet et Charlemagne.** 10th ed., Paris and Brussels, 1937. Tr. by Bernard Miall, *Mohammed and Charlemagne,* London and N.Y., 1939. Attributes the collapse of western civilization to the spread of Islam—a bold attempt to apply a questionable theory in a historical setting. This highly controversial book has been challenged in numerous fine essays.

J72. Havighurst, Alfred F., ed. **The Pirenne thesis: analysis, criticism, and revision.** Boston, 1958. See the critical comment of A. R. Lewis, *Speculum,* 34 (Apr. 1959): 279.

J73. Rüsing, Anne. "The fate of Henri Pirenne's thesis on the consequences of the Islamic expansion." **Classica et mediaevalia: revue danoise de philologie et d'histoire,** 13 (Copenhagen, 1952): 87–130.

J74. Cipolla, Carlo M. **Money, prices and civilization in the Mediterranean world, fifth to seventeenth century.** Princeton, 1956. Brief introduction to a complex, major historical problem. Useful bibliographies.

J75. Wright, John K. **The geographical lore of the time of the crusades: a study in the history of medieval science and tradition in western Europe.** N.Y., 1925. Contains excellent critical bibliography.

J76. Newton, Arthur P., ed. **Travel and travellers of the Middle Ages.** N.Y., 1926. Lectures delivered at the University of London by various speakers. Geographical knowledge of the Middle Ages, the Vikings, Arab travellers, and the opening of the trade routes to the Far East are among the topics discussed.

J77. **The travels of Leo of Rozmital through Germany, Flanders, England, France, Spain, Portugal and Italy, 1465–1467.** Tr. and ed. by Malcolm Letts. Cambridge, Eng., 1957. [Publications of the Hakluyt Society, 2nd ser., 108.]

J78. Goitein, Solomon D. "From the Mediterranean to India: documents on the trade to India, south Arabia, and east Africa from the eleventh and twelfth centuries." **Speculum,** 29 (Apr. 1954): 181–97.

J79. Olschki, Leonardo. **Marco Polo's precursors.** Baltimore, 1943. A short but good introduction to Europeans in Asia in the Middle Ages.

J80. Hart, Henry H. **Venetian adventurer: being an account of the life and times and of the book of Messer Marco Polo.** 3rd ed., Stanford, 1947.

J81. Polo, Marco. **The adventures of Marco Polo, as dictated in prison to a scribe in the year 1298.** Ed. by Richard J. Walsh. N.Y., 1948.

J82. ——. **The travels of Marco Polo.** Tr. by Ronald Latham. Harmondsworth, Eng., 1958.

Cultural

J83. Crump, Charles G., and Ernest F. Jacob, eds. **The legacy of the Middle Ages.** Oxford, 1926. Essays on various aspects of medieval life and culture.

Science and Technology

J84. Carmody, Francis J. "Ten years of American scholarship in medieval science." **Progress of medieval and Renaissance studies in the United States and Canada,** Bul. 18 (June 1944): 19–27.

J85. Thorndike, Lynn. **A history of magic and experimental science.** See *A251.* V. 1–4 cover the Middle Ages.

J86. Haskins, Charles H. **Studies in the history of mediaeval science.** 2nd ed., Cambridge, Mass., 1927. Reprint of strikingly original contributions to the history of medieval science.

J87. Sarton, George A. L. **Introduction to the history of science.** See *A249*.

J88. Crombie, Alistair C. **Augustine to Galileo: the history of science A.D. 400–1650.** London, 1952. 2nd ed., *Medieval and early modern science*, 2 v., Garden City, 1959. Commendable introduction to medieval science; but see Lynn Thorndike's criticism and reservations in *Speculum*, 29 (July 1954): 541.

J89. White, Lynn T., Jr. "Technology and invention in the Middle Ages." **Speculum**, 15 (Apr. 1940): 141–59. Still the best introduction to the problems of medieval technology; an imaginative, challenging essay.

J90. Singer, Charles J., and others, eds. **A history of technology. V. 2, The Mediterranean civilizations and the Middle Ages, c. 700 B.C. to A.D. 1500.** See *I308*.

J91. Forti, Umberto. **Storia della tecnica dal medioevo al Rinascimento.** Florence, 1957. Profusely illustrated, with chapters arranged to deal topically with technical developments in the Middle Ages and Renaissance.

Art of War

J92. Oman, Charles W. C. **The art of war in the Middle Ages, A.D. 378–1515.** Rev. and ed. by John H. Beeler. Ithaca, 1953. A classic.

J93. Lot, Ferdinand. **L'art militaire et les armées au Moyen Âge en Europe et dans le Proche-Orient.** 2 v. Paris, 1946. Excellent.

J94. Blair, Claude. **European armour, circa 1066–1700.** London, 1959. Useful, composite introduction to a subject whose basic literature is scattered in journals and costly volumes often not readily accessible. Good bibliography. Review, *The Times* (London) *literary supplement,* June 12, 1959, p. 358.

Castles

J95. Cusin, Fabio. "Per la storia del castello medioevale." **Rivista storica italiana,** ser. 5, 4 (Turin, Dec. 1939): 491–542.

J96. Brown, Reginald A. **English medieval castles.** London, 1954.

J97. Painter, Sidney. "English castles in the Middle Ages: their number, location, and legal position." **Speculum,** 10 (July 1935): 321–32.

J98. Beeler, John H. "Castles and strategy in Norman and early Angevin England." **Speculum,** 31 (Oct. 1956): 581–601.

BIOGRAPHIES

See Section K.

UNIVERSITY, ACADEMY, AND SOCIETY PUBLICATIONS

In addition to references in Paetow (*J1*), pp. 117–19, the organizations listed below lend strong support to medieval studies.

J99. Dumbarton Oaks Research Library and Collection, Washington. **Dumbarton Oaks papers.** Cambridge, Mass., 1941 ff.

J100. The Franciscan Institute, St. Bonaventure University. **Franciscan studies.** Monograph series, N.Y., 1924–40. Quarterly review, N.Y., 1941 ff.

J101. Institute of Historical Research, University of London. **Bulletin.** London, 1923 ff.

J102. Institut für Geschichtsforschung, Vienna. **Mitteilungen.** Graz, 1888–1944, 1948 ff.

J103. ——. **Ergänzungsbände.** Graz, 1885 ff.

The Mediaeval Academy of America, Cambridge, Mass., in addition to *Speculum* (*J125*), publishes the following (*J104–106*).

J104. Monographs. Cambridge, 1930 ff.

J105. Studies and documents. Cambridge, 1935 ff.

J106. Studies in Anglo-Papal relations during the Middle Ages. Cambridge, 1939 ff.

J107. Mediaeval studies. N.Y. and London, 1939 ff. [The Pontifical Institute of Mediaeval Studies, Toronto.]

J108. The Renaissance Society of America, New York. **Renaissance news.** Hanover, N.H., 1948–53; N.Y., 1954 ff.

J109. ——. **Studies in the Renaissance.** N.Y., 1954 ff.

J110. University of Notre Dame. **Publications in mediaeval studies.** Notre Dame, Ind., 1936 ff.

J111. The Mediaeval Institute, University of Notre Dame. **Texts and studies in the history of mediaeval education.** Notre Dame, 1953 ff.

J112. Warburg Institute, London. **Journal of the Warburg and Courtauld Institute.** London, 1937 ff.

J113. ——. **Mediaeval and Renaissance studies.** London, 1941 ff.

J114. Université Catholique de Louvain. **Spicilegium sacrum lovaniense.** Louvain, 1922 ff.

PERIODICALS

Journals and serial publications are of special importance for the history of the Middle Ages. In addition to the general historical periodicals which occasionally include items pertaining to medieval studies, the following contain material of particular interest for students of the Middle Ages and Renaissance.

J115. Annales: économies, sociétés, civilisations. Paris, 1946 ff. (Quarterly.) Published 1929–45 under varying titles.

J116. Archivio storico italiano. Florence, 1842 ff. (Frequency varies.)

J117. Archivum franciscanum historicum. Florence, 1908 ff. (Quarterly.)

J118. Archivum fratrum praedicatorum. Rome, 1930 ff. (Irregular.)

J119. Cahiers d'histoire mondiale. Journal of world history. Cuadernos de historia mundial. Paris, 1953 ff. (Quarterly.)

J120. Comparative studies in society and history. The Hague, 1958 ff. (Quarterly.)

J121. Le Moyen Âge. Paris and Brussels, 1888–1941, 1946 ff. (Monthly, 1888–96; bimonthly, 1896 ff.)

J122. Progress of medieval and Renais-sance **studies in the United States and Canada, bulletin.** Boulder, Colo., 1923 ff. (Irregular.)

J123. Rinascimento. Florence, 1950 ff. (Irregular.) Continuation of *La Rinascita* (Florence, 1938–44).

J124. Saeculum: Jahrbuch für Universalgeschichte. Freiburg im Breisgau, 1950 ff. (4 nos. per year.)

J125. Speculum: a journal of mediaeval studies. Cambridge, Mass., 1926 ff. (Quarterly.)

J126. Studi medievali. Turin, 1904–13. (Irregular.) New series, 1928 ff. (Semiannual.)

SECTION K

Medieval Europe

GRAY C. BOYCE

Although the history of medieval Europe has long attracted the attention of historians, it still offers continuing interest and challenge today. The study of medieval life, institutions, and culture is essential for a true understanding of contemporary western society, and is of perennial interest in its own right for the enduring inheritance left by its exuberant vitality and handed on to succeeding centuries. Only the uninformed now regard the medieval period as the "dark ages"; more judicious and balanced appraisals of its contributions permit a positive appreciation and evaluation of its richness and historical importance.

It is of more than casual significance to note how medieval studies command attention in America through institutes in Toronto, Montreal, and at the University of Notre Dame, as well as by the efforts of a host of devoted scholars in various other universities and libraries. The Mediaeval Academy of America, founded in 1925, is recognized in the world of scholarship for the important role it assumes in aiding and furthering medieval studies everywhere.

Those who study the history of the Middle Ages have readily available numerous well-known standard guides. Attention is directed to those below, but no attempt is made to duplicate, even in restricted fashion, the references they provide. Although important works bearing any date of publication are listed in this section, books and articles recently published are given preference. Most of these contain bibliographies of some sort. They and the standard guides serve adequately to direct inquirers to the literature of earlier decades.

In choosing titles for this section an attempt has been made to reflect through them the richness of medieval civilization and its infinite variety. Today we are interested not only in the medieval king, cathedral, and charter, but equally in the slave, hut, and business ledger of medieval times.

BIBLIOGRAPHIES

K1. Potthast, August. **Bibliotheca historica medii aevi: Wegweiser durch die Geschichtswerke des europäischen Mittelalters bis 1500.** 2nd rev. ed., 2 v., Berlin, 1896. Primarily a bibliography of medieval chronicles and biographies, including lives of saints, indicating in each instance the various editions and translations and the critical literature

Analyzes the great collections of sources and lists the chronicles chronologically by countries. A long-needed new edition is being prepared by an international committee of scholars.

K2. Chevalier, Ulysse. **Répertoire des sources historiques du Moyen Âge: bio-bibliographie.** 2nd rev. ed., 2 v., Paris, 1903–07. See below.

K3. ——. **Répertoire des sources historiques du Moyen Âge: topo-bibliographie.** 2 v. Paris, 1894–1903. These guides to a mass of special literature concerning persons and places are indispensable, although hopelessly incomplete and out of date.

K4. Gross, Charles. **The sources and literature of English history from the earliest times to about 1485.** 2nd rev. ed., London and N.Y., 1915. The basic bibliographical guide for medieval English history. A new edition is being prepared by Edgar B. Graves under auspices of The American Historical Association, The Mediaeval Academy of America, and The Royal Historical Society.

K5. Royal Historical Society. **Writings on British history.** Comp. by Alexander T. Milne. 1934 ff. London, 1937 ff. Annual compilations of a year's publications.

K6. Bonser, Wilfred. **An Anglo-Saxon and Celtic bibliography (450–1087).** 2 v. Berkeley, 1957. Supplements, but does not replace, the corresponding sections of Gross (*K4*). Review, E. B. Graves, *Am. hist. rev.*, 63 (Apr. 1958): 717.

K7. Ker, Neil R. **Catalogue of manuscripts containing Anglo-Saxon.** Oxford, 1957. "A book of fundamental importance for the study of Anglo-Saxon civilization." *The Times* (London) *literary supplement*, Dec. 19, 1958, p. 740.

K8. Kenney, James F. **The sources for the early history of Ireland: an introduction and guide.** V. 1. N.Y., 1929.

K9. Molinier, Auguste E. L. M. **Les sources de l'histoire de France des origines aux guerres d'Italie (1494).** 6 v. Paris, 1901–06. An old, but ever useful work that needs revision. The introduction in v. 5 serves as an excellent introduction to medieval French historiography.

K10. Pirenne, Henri, and others. **Bibliographie de l'histoire de Belgique: catalogue méthodique et chronologique des sources et des ouvrages principaux relatifs à l'histoire de tous les Pays-Bas jusqu'en 1598 et à l'histoire de Belgique jusqu'en 1914.** 3rd ed., Brussels, 1931. A model national bibliography by a master historian.

K11. Dahlmann, Friedrich C., and Georg Waitz. **Quellenkunde der deutschen Geschichte.** See *VF1*. Section B, pts. 1–4 of v. 1 cover German medieval times.

K12. Franz, Günther. **Bücherkunde zur deutschen Geschichte.** See *VF3*.

K13. Índice histórico español. See *VD2*.

K14. Strakhovsky, Leonid I., ed. **A handbook of Slavic studies.** Cambridge, Mass., 1949. Best introduction to medieval conditions in the Slavic states may be obtained by consulting the literature listed in various chapters of this publication. Each chapter is supplied with a good bibliography, sufficiently selective and restrictive to be useful for general purposes.

K15. Dean, Ruth J. "Latin palaeography, 1929–1943." **Progress of medieval and Renaissance studies**, 18 (June 1944): 6–18. See also S. Harrison Thomson, "Latin palaeography," *The year's work in classical studies*, 1935, pp. 79–86, for a similar review of the paleographic publications of the years 1928–35. These surveys draw attention to manuscript publications, critical problems, and controversies in this exacting, but highly significant, auxiliary discipline.

K16. Williams, Harry F. **An index of mediaeval studies published in Festschriften, 1865–1946, with special reference to Romanic material.** Berkeley, 1951.

WORKS OF REFERENCE

K17. Whiting, B. J. "Historical novels, 1948–1949." **Speculum**, 25 (Jan. 1950): 104–22. Excellent critical survey and evaluation of fourteen novels, most of which have medieval settings.

K18. ——. "Thirteen historical novels." **Speculum**, 32 (Jan. 1957): 118–42. Novels with medieval setting published during 1952–53.

GEOGRAPHIES, GAZETTEERS, AND ATLASES

K19. Hay, Denys. **Europe: the emergence of an idea.** Edinburgh, 1957. Analysis of growth of the idea of Europe, emerging from and replacing the concept of Christendom, its most characteristic medieval synonym.

K20. Mirot, Léon. **Manuel de géographie historique de la France.** 2nd ed., 2 v., Paris, 1947–50.

K21. **Westermanns Atlas zur Weltgeschichte.** Brunswick, 1956. Section on the Middle Ages may be purchased separately. It has excellent, clearly printed maps containing much useful detail not readily found elsewhere.

K22. Fox, Edward W. **Atlas of European history.** See *B220*.

K23. Meer, Frederik van der, and Christine Mohrmann. **Atlas of the early Christian world.** Tr. and ed. by Mary F. Hedlund and H. H. Rowley. London, 1958. Excellent for period 30–600 A.D.

K24. Roolvink, Roelof, and others. **Historical atlas of the Muslim peoples.** Amsterdam, 1957. Should be readily available to all students of the medieval world. A real contribution to medieval studies, providing in convenient form maps and information not easily found elsewhere.

DEMOGRAPHIC STUDIES

K25. Cipolla, Carlo M., and others. "La 'Pré-histoire démographique.' " Comité International des Sciences Historiques, **IXᵉ congrès international des sciences historiques** (Paris, 1950), v. 1, pp. 56–80. Important considerations and observations concerning medieval demographic problems.

K26. Lot, Ferdinand. **Recherches sur la population et la superficie des cités remontant à la période gallo-romaine.** 3 v. Paris, 1945–53.

K27. Beloch, Karl J. **Bevölkerungsgeschichte Italiens.** See *VE26*.

K28. Russell, Josiah C. **Late ancient and medieval population.** Philadelphia, 1958. [Transactions of the American Philosophical Society, new ser., v. 48, pt. 3.] A work of importance.

K29. ——. **British medieval population.** Albuquerque, 1948. Reviews, R. A. Newhall, *Am. hist. rev.*, 54 (July 1949): 866; and others.

K30. Thrupp, Sylvia L. "A survey of the alien population of England in 1440." **Speculum,** 32 (Apr. 1957): 262–73.

K31. Cooper, T. M. "The numbers and the distribution of the population of medieval Scotland." **The Scottish historical review,** 26 (Apr. 1947): 2–9.

K32. Mols, Roger. **Introduction à la démographie historique des villes d'Europe du XIVᵉ au XVIIIᵉ siècle.** 3 v. Gembloux, 1954–56. Review, W. D. Camp, *Am. hist. rev.,* 63 (July 1958): 950.

LINGUISTIC WORKS

K33. Du Cange, Charles Du Fresne. **Glossarium mediae et infimae latinitatis.** Best ed., 7 v., Paris, 1840–50; newest ed., 10 v., Niort, 1883–87. Indispensable for every student of the period. A new glossary of medieval Latin is being prepared under auspices of the Union Académique Internationale (see *K36*). Reference should be made to issues of *Bulletin Du Cange: archivum latinitatis medii aevi,* which contains numerous regional glossaries. For further guidance in reference to Du Cange and other dictionaries see Karl Strecker, *Introduction to medieval Latin* (Berlin, 1957), pp. 38–48.

K34. Maigne D'Arnis, W. H. **Lexicon manuale ad scriptores mediae et infimae latinitatis.** Paris, 1858. Reprint, 1890. An epitome of Du Cange and still conveniently useful.

K35. Niermeyer, Jan F. **Mediae latinitatis lexicon minus: lexique latin médiéval—français-anglais.** Leiden, 1954 ff.

K36. **Novum glossarium mediae latinitatis ab anno DCCC usque ad annum MCC.** Copenhagen, 1957 ff. Only v. 12 for the letter L has appeared. See also *Index scriptorum mediae latinitatis ab anno DCCC usque ad annum MCC qui afferuntur in Novo glossario ab Academiis Consociatis iuris publici facto* (Copenhagen, 1957).

K37. Souter, Alexander. **A glossary of later Latin to 600 A.D.** Oxford, 1949. See H. J. Rose, "Notes on Souter's Glossary of later Latin." *Bulletin Du Cange: archivum latinitatis medii aevi,* 21 (1949–50): 171–72; and J. H. Baxter, "Notes on Souter's Glossary," *Ibid.,* 23 (1953): 7–12, 25 (1955): 102–41.

K38. Baxter, James H., Charles Johnson, and others, eds. **Medieval Latin word-list from British and Irish sources.** London, 1934.

K39. Baxter, James H., Charles Johnson, and J. F. Willard. "An index of British and Irish Latin writers, 400–1520." **Bulletin Du Cange: archivum latinitatis medii aevi,** 7 (1932): 110–219.

K40. Mohrmann, Christine. **Liturgical Latin, its origins and character.** Washington, 1957.

K41. Strecker, Karl. **Introduction to medieval Latin.** Tr. and rev. by Robert B. Palmer. Berlin, 1957. Now unquestionably the most satisfactory introductory manual for students of medieval Latin. Contains copious bibliographical information, discusses grammatical, stylistic, and textural matters, and serves as well as the guide it was designed to be.

K42. Beeson, Charles H. **A primer of medieval Latin: an anthology of prose and poetry.** Chicago, 1925. Among the first attempts to provide a working tool for students interested in mastering medieval Latin, and still the most useful work of its type. The selections are well chosen, form a convenient *vade-mecum,* and reflect the influence of the German Traube on his American disciple.

PRINTED COLLECTIONS OF SOURCES

The source collections listed below are all excellent, though of varied types. They are convenient, well-selected, readily available, and useful for a proper understanding of the medieval and Renaissance worlds.

K43. Bettenson, Henry S., ed. **Documents of the Christian church.** London and N.Y., 1947. A most useful collection.

K44. **The library of Christian classics.** London and Philadelphia, 1953 ff. Volumes in this well-edited selection of sources pertaining to the Middle Ages are: 5, Stanley L. Greenslade, ed., *Early Latin theology* (1956); 6, John H. S. Burleigh, ed., *Augustine: earlier writings* (1953); 7, Albert

C. Outler, ed., *Augustine: Confessions and Enchiridion* (1955); 8, John Burnaby, ed., *Augustine: later works* (1955); 9, George E. McCracken, ed., *Early medieval theology* (1957); 10, Eugene R. Fairweather, ed., *A scholastic miscellany: Anselm to Ockham* (1956); 11, Alan M. Fairweather, ed., *Nature and grace: selections from the Summa theologica of Thomas Aquinas* (1954); 12, Owen Chadwick, ed., *Western asceticism* (1958); 13, Ray C. Petry, ed., *Late medieval mysticism* (1957); 14, Matthew Spinka, ed., *Advocates of reform: from Wyclif to Erasmus* (1953).

K45. Ross, James B., and Mary M. McLaughlin, eds. **The portable medieval reader.** N.Y., 1949. A rich garner from medieval sources.

K46. Records of civilization: sources and studies. Ed. by James T. Shotwell and others. N.Y., 1915 ff. Over fifty volumes have appeared in this fine series of translations of important medieval sources.

K47. University of Pennsylvania. **Translations and reprints from the original sources of history.** Philadelphia, 1894 ff. Most items in this series are for history of the Middle Ages.

K48. Downs, Norton, ed. **Basic documents in medieval history.** Princeton and N.Y., 1959. Convenient paper-back collection of representative medieval documents for handy reference. The selection is confined primarily to materials representative of western Europe.

K49. Calmette, Joseph, and Charles Higounet, eds. **Textes et documents d'histoire. V. 2, Moyen Âge.** New ed., Paris, 1953.

K50. Latouche, Robert, ed. **Textes d'histoire médiévale, Ve–XIe siècles.** Paris, 1951.

K51. Medieval texts. Ed. by V. H. Galbraith and R. A. B. Mynors. London and N.Y., 1949 ff. A merger and continuation of two earlier series: *Medieval classics* and *Medieval texts.*

K52. Sources of English constitutional history. Ed. and tr. by Carl Stephenson and Frederick G. Marcham. N.Y. and London, 1937. An excellent compilation. Sections 1–6 contain documents illustrative of English medieval history.

K53. English historical documents. Ed. by David C. Douglas. V. 1–4 (ca. 500–1485). London, 1953 ff. Fundamental for the student of English history. Each volume has good, though restricted, bibliography.

K54. Dickinson, William C., and others, eds. **A source book of Scottish history.** 3 v. London, 1952–54. V. 1, from earliest times to 1424, includes a limited selection of documents for the Middle Ages.

K55. Halphen, Louis, ed. **Les classiques de l'histoire de France au Moyen Âge.** Paris, 1923 ff. The most convenient collection of medieval sources for French history. Where the original text is in Latin, a translation into French is provided.

K56. Rau, Reinhold, ed. **Ausgewählte Quellen zur deutschen Geschichte des Mittelalters.** Berlin, 1956 ff. Convenient, well-edited selection of sources for medieval German history. Original texts are published along with German translation.

K57. Lopez, Robert S., and Irving W. Raymond, eds. and trs. **Medieval trade in the Mediterranean world.** N.Y., 1955. A rich compilation of documents in translation.

K58. Komroff, Manuel, ed. **Contemporaries of Marco Polo.** N.Y., 1928. Convenient introduction to European travelers in Asia.

K59. Jones, Charles W., ed. **Mediaeval literature in translation.** N.Y., 1950.

K60. Ross, James B., and Mary M. McLaughlin, eds. **The portable Renaissance reader.** N.Y., 1953.

K61. Vatican. Biblioteca Vaticana. **Studi e testi.** Vatican City, 1900 ff. A series of publications of remarkable richness and importance for medieval studies. Although all volumes are not actually printed texts, those that are not are usually based on careful examination of original sources and frequently represent exploitation of the Vatican manuscript collections.

SHORTER GENERAL HISTORIES

K62. Pirenne, Henri. **Histoire de l'Europe des invasions au XVIe siècle.** Paris and Brussels, 1936. English tr., by Bernard Miall, N.Y., 1939. A unique work, written while author was a prisoner of war in Germany during World War I. Attempts to draw with broad strokes the picture of European history of more than a thousand years. Unfortunately, both French and English texts were published without rigorous editing and are, therefore, not flawless. A paperbound edition is available in the Anchor series.

K63. Brooke, Zachary N. **A history of Europe from 911 to 1198.** 3rd ed., London, 1951.

K64. Previté-Orton, Charles W. **A history of Europe from 1198 to 1378.** 3rd ed., London, 1951.

K65. Waugh, William T. **A history of Europe, 1378 to 1494.** 3rd ed., London, 1949.

K66. Hashagen, Justus. **Europa im Mittelalter: alte Tatsachen und neue Geschichtspunkte.** Munich, 1951. Convenient survey of essentials of medieval history.

K67. Painter, Sidney. **A history of the Middle Ages, 284–1500.** N.Y., 1953.

LONGER GENERAL HISTORIES

K68. Lot, Ferdinand, and others. **Les destinées de l'empire en Occident de 395 à**

888. 2nd ed., 2 v., Paris, 1940–41. [Gustave Glotz, ed., Histoire générale: Histoire du Moyen Âge, 1.] Excellent factual, narrative history for a complex era.

K69. Fliche, Augustin. **L'Europe occidentale de 888 à 1125.** Paris, 1930. [Histoire générale: Histoire du Moyen Âge, 2.]

K70. Petit-Dutaillis, Charles, and Paul Guinard. **L'essor des états d'Occident (France, Angleterre, Péninsule ibérique).** New ed., Paris, 1944. [Histoire générale: Histoire du Moyen Âge, 4, pt. 2.]

K71. Calmette, Joseph, and Eugène Déprez. **L'Europe occidentale de la fin du XIVe siècle aux guerres d'Italie.** 2 v. Paris, 1937–39. [Histoire générale: Histoire du Moyen Âge, 7.]

K72. Pirenne, Henri, Gustave Cohen, and Henri Focillon. **La civilisation occidentale au Moyen Âge du XIe au milieu du XVe siècle.** Paris, 1933. 2nd ed., 1941. [Histoire générale: Histoire du Moyen Âge, 8.] Pirenne's section dealing with economic and social forces has become a classic; Focillon on medieval art is good; Cohen's contribution on intellectual, moral, and literary tendencies seems less satisfactory.

K73. Jordan, Edouard. **L'Allemagne et l'Italie au XIIe et XIIIe siècles.** Paris, 1939. [Histoire générale: Histoire du Moyen Âge 4, pt. 1.]

K74. Fawtier, Robert, and Alfred Coville. **L'Europe occidentale de 1270 à 1380.** 2 v. Paris, 1940–41. [Histoire générale: Histoire du Moyen Âge, 6, pts. 1 and 2.]

K75. Pirenne, Henri, and others. **La fin du Moyen Âge.** 2 v. Paris, 1931. [Peuples et civilisations: histoire générale, 7.] Review, E. J. Auweiler, *Catholic hist. rev.,* 19 (Oct. 1933): 344.

K76. Hampe, Karl. **Das Hochmittelalter: Geschichte des Abendlandes von 900 bis 1250.** 4th ed., Münster and Cologne, 1953.

K77. Falco, Giorgio. **La santa Romana repubblica: profilo storico del Medio Evo.** 2nd ed., Milan and Naples, 1954. An Italian writes about the Holy Roman Empire and its place in medieval times.

HISTORIES OF SPECIAL PERIODS

K78. Duckett, Eleanor S. **The gateway to the Middle Ages.** N.Y., 1938.

K79. Haller, Johannes. **Der Eintritt der Germanen in die Geschichte.** Berlin, 1939. Emphasizes the fusion of German with classical culture.

K80. Wahle, Ernst, and others. **Der Aufstieg des Germanentums und die Welt des Mittelalters.** Berlin, 1940. [Die neue Propyläen-Weltgeschichte, 2.]

K81. Sestan, Ernesto. **Stato e nazione nell'alto Medioevo: ricerche sulle origini nazionali in Francia, Italia, Germania.** Naples, 1952. "Brilliant, original, stimulat-

ing." Review, C. E. Boyd, *Am. hist. rev.,* 58 (July 1953): 889.

K82. Salin, Edouard. **La civilisation mérovingienne d'après les sépultures: les textes et la laboratoire.** 3 v. Paris, 1949–57. "Rich in information entirely new." Review, L. White, Jr., *Am. hist. rev.,* 64 (Apr. 1959): 616.

K83. Fichtenau, Heinrich. **The Carolingian empire.** Oxford, 1957. A forthright attempt to examine the disappointing aspects of Charlemagne's work, while also recognizing his positive contributions.

K84. Halphen, Louis. **Charlemagne et l'empire carolingien.** Paris, 1947.

K85. Calmette, Joseph. **Charlemagne, sa vie et son oeuvre.** Paris, 1945.

K86. Schramm, Percy E. "Die Anerkennung des Karl des Grossen als Kaiser: ein Kapital aus der Geschichte der mittelalterlichen 'Staatssymbolik.'" **Historische Zeitschrift,** 172 (Dec. 1951): 449–515.

K87. Sullivan, Richard E. **The coronation of Charlemagne: What did it signify?** Boston, 1959. [Ralph W. Greenlaw, ed., Problems in European civilization.] Collection of selections from contemporary and modern writers on the basis of which readers may attempt an answer to an almost eternally debatable problem of the Middle Ages.

K88. Folz, Robert. **Le souvenir et la légende de Charlemagne dans l'empire germanique médiéval.** Paris, 1950.

K89. Mor, Carlo G. **L'età feudale.** 2 v. Milan, 1952–53. Valuable for political, institutional, cultural, and economic history of Italy, 476–1268.

K90. Fasoli, Gina. **I re d'Italia, 888–962.** Florence, 1949. Coherent narrative history of the period for Italy.

K91. ———. **La incursioni ungare in Europa nel secolo X.** Florence, 1945. Account of the later invasions of the Hungarians.

K92. Kendrick, Thomas. **A history of the Vikings.** N.Y., 1930.

K93. Musset, Lucien. **Les peuples scandinaves au Moyen Âge.** Paris, 1951. Excellent survey.

K94. Turville-Petre, Gabriel. **The heroic age of Scandinavia.** London, 1951. Introduction to history of the Norsemen before 1030. Restricted in scope and heavy in style.

K95. Kulturhistorisk leksikon for nordisk Middelalder fra Vikingetid til Reformationstid. Ed. by Lis Jacobsen and others. Copenhagen, 1956 ff. To be completed in 10 v.

K96. Goetz, Walter W., and others, eds. **Das Mittelalter bis zum Ausgang der Staufer.** Berlin, 1932. [Propyläen Weltgeschichte, 3.] Contributions by various authors. Contains many fine illustrations.

K97. Southern, Richard W. **The making of the Middle Ages.** New Haven, 1953. Notable series of essays interpreting the formation of western Europe from the late 10th to early 13th century.

K98. Halphen, Louis. "La conquête de la Méditerranée par les européens au XIe et au XIIe siècles." **Mélanges d'histoire offerts à Henri Pirenne par ses anciens élèves et ses amis,** V. 1 (Brussels, 1926), pp. 175–80.

K99. Runciman, Steven. **The Sicilian vespers: a history of the Mediterranean world in the later thirteenth century.** Cambridge, Eng., and N.Y., 1958. Evaluation of an episode that shocked 13th century Europe. Review, Helene Wieruszowski, **Speculum,** 34 (Apr. 1959): 323.

K100. Perroy, Edouard. **La Guerre de Cent Ans.** Paris, 1945. English tr., by W. B. Wells, London, 1951. Best survey of major issues and problems of the Hundred Years' War.

K101. Cuttino, George P. "Historical revision: the causes of the Hundred Years War." **Speculum,** 31 (July 1956): 463–77.

K102. The trial of Jeanne d'Arc: a complete translation of the text of the original documents. Tr. by W. P. Barrett. London, 1931.

K103. The trial of Joan of Arc: being a verbatim report of the proceedings from the Orleans manuscript. Tr. by W. S. Scott. London, 1956.

K104. Pernoud, Régine. **The retrial of Joan of Arc: the evidence at the trial for her rehabilitation, 1450–1456.** Tr. by J. M. Cohen. N.Y., 1955.

K105. Cartellieri, Otto. **The court of Burgundy.** N.Y., 1929.

K106. Huizinga, Johan. **The waning of the Middle Ages: a study of the forms of life, thought and art in France and the Netherlands in the XIVth and XVth centuries.** London, 1924.

K107. Cheyney, Edward P. **The dawn of a new era, 1250–1453.** N.Y., 1936. Emphasizes social and economic developments.

K108. Goetz, Walter W., and others, eds. **Das Zeitalter der Gotik und Renaissance, 1250–1500.** Berlin, 1932. [Propyläen Weltgeschichte, 4.]

K109. Kohn, Hans. "The dawn of nationalism in Europe." **Am. hist. rev.,** 52 (Jan. 1947): 265–80. Kohn finds evidence of nationalism in the medieval communities.

K110. Näf, Werner. "Frühformen des 'Modernen Staates' im Spätmittelalter." **Historische Zeitschrift,** 171 (Mar. 1951): 225–43.

K111. Muralt, Leonhard von, and others. **Das Zeitalter der Entdeckungen, der Renaissance und der Glaubenskämpfe.** Berlin, 1941. [Die neue Propyläen-Weltgeschichte, 3.]

K112. Dannenfeldt, Karl H. **The Renaissance—medieval or modern?** Boston, 1959. [Problems in European civilization.] Selections from modern writers presenting some

of the many differing attitudes toward the nature and significance of the Renaissance.

HISTORIES OF SPECIAL AREAS

England, Scotland, and Ireland

K113. Stenton, Frank M. **Anglo-Saxon England.** 2nd ed., Oxford, 1947. [The Oxford history of England.]

K114. Poole, Austin L. **From Domesday book to Magna Carta, 1087–1216.** Oxford, 1951. 2nd ed., 1955. [The Oxford history of England, 3.]

K115. Powicke, Sir Frederick Maurice. **The thirteenth century, 1216–1307.** Oxford, 1953. [The Oxford history of England, 4.] The Oxford histories now serve as the best introduction to serious study of England in the periods they cover. Each volume contains a comprehensive critical bibliography of inestimable value. Reviews of each book in the series appear in major journals.

K116. Hunt, William, and Reginald L. Poole, eds. **Political history of England.** 12 v. London and N.Y., 1905–10. Now somewhat dated and in parts outmoded, but still useful, especially for periods not yet covered by the more recent *Oxford history of England.* V. 1–4 are on the Middle Ages.

K117. Oman, Charles W. C., ed. **A history of England.** 8 v. London and N.Y., 1905–55. In general more attractive, less political and detailed than *K116.* For the medieval period consult v. 1, Charles Oman, *England before the Norman conquest;* 2, H. W. C. Davis, *England under the Normans and Angevins;* 3, K. Vickers, *England in the later Middle Ages.*

K118. Hodgkin, Robert H. **A history of the Anglo-Saxons.** 3rd ed., 2 v., London, 1952. Covers period to the death of Alfred. Beautifully illustrated.

K119. Levison, Wilhelm. **England and the continent in the eighth century.** Oxford, 1946.

K120. Green, Vivian H. H. **The later Plantagenets: a survey of English history between 1307 and 1485.** London, 1955. Good analysis of English history in the 14th and 15th centuries.

K121. Myers, Alec R. **England in the late Middle Ages (1307–1536).** Harmondsworth, Eng. and Baltimore, 1952. "Presents in a truer and more attractive light an era once disparaged in contrast to the thirteenth or sixteenth century." F. Thompson in *Speculum,* 28 (July 1953): 599.

K122. Sayles, George O. **The medieval foundations of England.** London, 1948. Interpretative analysis of English social and institutional history from the 5th century to end of the reign of Henry III. Review, G. P. Cuttino, *Speculum,* 24 (Jan. 1949): 141.

K123. Medieval England: a new edition rewritten and revised. Ed. by Austin L. Poole. 2 v. Oxford, 1958. A complete rewriting, based on modern scholarship by different authors, of H. W. C. Davis' edition of Barnard's *Companion to English history*, published in 1924 under title *Mediaeval England*. This new edition contains essays on various aspects of English medieval civilization, and has many fine illustrations.

K124. Kelly, Amy. **Eleanor of Aquitaine and the four kings.** Cambridge, Mass., 1950. An imaginative work of literary distinction and sound scholarship.

K125. Painter, Sidney. **The reign of King John.** Baltimore, 1949. Review, R. A. Newhall, *Am. hist. rev.*, 55 (Apr. 1950): 581.

K126. Powicke, Sir Frederick Maurice. **King Henry III and the Lord Edward: the community of the realm in the thirteenth century.** 2 v. Oxford, 1947. A contribution of fundamental importance by a master medievalist. Review, W. E. Lunt, *Speculum*, 23 (Jan. 1948): 147.

K127. Mackenzie, Agnes M. **Foundations of Scotland.** New ed., Edinburgh, 1957.

K128. Ritchie, Robert L. G. **The Normans in Scotland.** Edinburgh, 1954. The Norman infiltration in Scotland began long before and was quite unlike the sudden conquest of England. This volume amplifies the picture of the Normans *outre mer* and their "empire" in the 11th and 12th centuries.

K129. De Paor, Máire, and Liam De Paor. **Early Christian Ireland.** London, 1958. Emphasis on cultural developments. Many handsome illustrations.

France

K130. Lavisse, Ernest, ed. **Histoire de France depuis les origines jusqu'à la Révolution.** See *VC138*. V. 2–4 are on the Middle Ages.

K131. Funck-Brentano, Frantz. **The earliest times.** N.Y., 1927. Introduction to early medieval French history.

K132. ——. **The Middle Ages.** N.Y., 1923. Good narrative history of medieval France.

K133. Fawtier, Robert. **Les Capétiens et la France: leur rôle dans sa construction.** Paris, 1942.

K134. Petit-Dutaillis, Charles. **La monarchie féodale en France et en Angleterre, Xe–XIIIe siècle.** Paris, 1933. English tr. by E. D. Hunt, London, 1936. The best comparative description of western feudal monarchies.

K135. Renouard, Yves. "Essai sur le rôle de l'empire angevin dans la formation de la France et dans la civilisation française aux XIIe et XIIIe siècles." **Revue historique**, 195 (Oct.-Dec. 1945): 289–304.

K136. Cartellieri, Alexander. **Philip II,** **August, König von Frankreich.** 4 v. in 5. Leipzig, 1899–1922. More than merely a biographical study; still the major work for the age of Philip II.

K137. Levron, Jacques. **Saint Louis ou l'apogée du Moyen Âge.** Paris, 1957.

K138. Joinville, Jean, sire de. **The history of St. Louis.** Tr. by Joan Evans. N.Y., 1938.

K139. Strayer, Joseph R. **The administration of Normandy under Saint Louis.** Cambridge, Mass., 1932. One of the best studies of a province in medieval France.

K140. ——. **The royal domain in the baillage of Rouen.** Princeton, 1936.

K141. ——. "Philip the Fair, a 'constitutional' king." **Am. hist. rev.,** 62 (Oct. 1956): 13–32. Good, remarkably compact essay for a modern evaluation of Philip IV; result of much original research.

K142. Digard, Georges A. L. **Philippe le Bel et le Saint Siège de 1285 à 1304.** 2 v. Paris, 1936.

K143. Lehugeur, Paul. **Philippe le Long, roi de France, 1316–1322: le mécanisme du gouvernement.** Paris, 1931.

K144. Peyronnet, Georges. "Les relations politiques entre la France et l'Italie, principalement au XIVe et dans la première moitié du XVe siècles." **Le Moyen Âge,** 55 (1949): 301–42 and 56 (1950): 85–113.

K145. Kirkland, Dorothy. "The growth of national sentiment in France before the fifteenth century." **History,** n.s. 23 (June 1938): 12–24.

K146. Haskins, Charles H. **The Normans in European history.** Boston and N.Y., 1915. Haskins, the master, at his best.

K147. ——. **Norman institutions.** Cambridge, Mass., 1918. A work of fine and enduring scholarship. The broad generalizations so brilliantly characteristic of *K146* arise from the solid study of the documents as represented by this volume.

K148. Stenton, Frank M., and others. **The Bayeux tapestry: a comprehensive survey.** N.Y., 1957. History of the tapestry and techniques employed by its makers. Excellent bibliography and plates (some in color) are provided in this beautiful book.

Italy

K149. Salvatorelli, Luigi. **L'Italia medioevale: dalle invasioni barbariche agli inizi del secolo XI.** Milan, 1938.

K150. ——. **L'Italia comunale: dal secolo XI alla metà del secolo XIV.** Milan, 1940.

K151. Mor, Carlo G. **L'età feudale.** See *K89*. Helpful for the little-known period 887–1024.

K152. Valeri, Nino. **L'Italia nell'età dei principati, dal 1343 al 1516.** See *VE42*.

K153. Simeoni, Luigi. **Le signorie.** See *VE43*.

K154. Van Cleve, Thomas C. **Markward of Anweiler and the Sicilian regency: a study of Hohenstaufen policy in Sicily during the minority of Frederick II.** Princeton, 1937. Review, L. T. White, *Am. hist. rev.*, 43 (Apr. 1938): 681.

K155. Jamison, Evelyn. **Admiral Eugenius of Sicily, his life and work, and the authorship of the "Epistola ad petrum" and the "Historia hugonis falcandi siculi."** London and N.Y., 1957. "A volume to be read, as well as consulted, by all who are concerned with the confused transition from Norman to Hohenstaufen rule." L. White, Jr. in *Am. hist. rev.*, 63 (Apr. 1958): 645.

K156. Runciman, Steven. **The Sicilian vespers: a history of the Mediterranean world in the later thirteenth century.** See *K99*.

K157. Labande, Edmond R. **L'Italie de la Renaissance: duecento, trecento, quattrocento; évolution d'une société.** See *VE44*.

K158. Brucker, Gene A. "The Medici in the fourteenth century." **Speculum,** 32 (Jan. 1957): 1–26.

K159. ——, ed. **Renaissance Italy.** N.Y., 1958. Documents in translation, with brief introductions, to illustrate the businessman, the statesman, the clergy, the humanists, and the artists.

Germany

K160. Gebhardt, Bruno. **Handbuch der deutschen Geschichte.** See *VF26*. V. 1 is *Frühzeit und Mittelalter*.

K161. Barraclough, Geoffrey, tr. and ed. **Mediaeval Germany, 911–1250: essays by German historians.** 2 v. Oxford, 1938. Excellent and important.

K162. ——. **The origins of modern Germany.** Oxford, 1946. Now the best English language introduction to medieval German problems.

K163. Thompson, James Westfall. **Feudal Germany.** Chicago, 1928. Often censured by critics, but pt. 2, dealing with the eastern frontier, can be commended.

K164. Haller, Johannes. **Von den Karolingern zu den Staufern: die altdeutsche Kaiserzeit (900–1250).** Berlin, 1934. Small, compact, admirably clear.

K165. Holtzmann, Robert. **Geschichte der sächsischen Kaiserzeit (900–1024).** 3rd ed., Berlin, 1955.

K166. Schramm, Percy E. **Kaiser, Rom und Renovatio: Studien und Texte zur Geschichte des römischen Erneuerungsgedankens vom Ende des karolingischen Reiches bis zum Investiturstreit.** 2 v. Leipzig and Berlin, 1929. Good study of the import of the revival of empire in the West, its implications in theory and practice. Discusses the setting and conditions in which the *Renovatio* occurred, age of the Ottos, importance of the city of Rome, the new empire and the popes, and effect of the new concept on Roman law and its political and cultural significance for the 12th century.

K167. Günter, Heinrich. **Das deutsche Mittelalter.** 2nd ed., 2 v., Freiburg im Breisgau, 1943.

K168. Hampe, Karl. **Deutsche Kaisergeschichte in der Zeit der Salier und Staufer.** 8th ed., Leipzig, 1943. Germany from Conrad II to the last Hohenstaufens.

K169. Kienast, Walther. **Deutschland und Frankreich in der Kaiserzeit (900 bis 1270).** Leipzig, 1943.

K170. Andreas, Willy. **Deutschland vor der Reformation: cine Zeitenwende.** 5th rev. ed., Stuttgart, 1948.

Spain

K171. Valdeavellano, Luis G. de. **Historia de España.** See *VD50*.

K172. Merriman, Roger B. **The rise of the Spanish empire in the Old World and in the New.** V. 1, **The Middle Ages.** See *VD71*.

K173. Lévi-Provençal, Évariste. **Histoire de l'Espagne musulmane.** See *VD59*.

K174. Menéndez Pidal, Ramón. **La España del Cid.** See *VD64*.

K175. Giunta, Francesco. **Aragonesi e Catalani nel Mediterraneo.** V. 1, **Dal regno al viceregno in Sicilia.** Palermo, 1953. Mediterranean politics following 1282, with attention focused on Sicily.

The Lowlands

K176. **Geschiedenis van Vlaanderen.** Ed. by Robert van Roosbroeck. 6 v. Brussels, 1936–49. See the following: V. 1, pt. 2, L. van der Essen and R. van Roosbroeck, *De middeleeuwen van het einde der IVe tot het begin der XIIIe eeuw;* v. 2, François L. Ganshof, *Der middeleeuwen: XIIIe en XIVe eeuw;* v. 3, F. Quicke, H. Joosen, and others, *Het Burgondisch tijdvak: XVe eeuw.* These handsome volumes, written by scholars of eminence, are a worthy monument of one of the most historically interesting and important counties in feudal and Renaissance Europe. There are copious illustrations and good bibliographies.

K177. Ganshof, François L. **La Belgique carolingienne.** Brussels, 1958. Brief, readable description of conditions and developments in "l'espace belge" between 751 and 888.

K178. Verberne, Louis G. J., ed. **Geschiedenis der Nederlanden.** 4 v. Nijmegen, 1948–55. See the following volumes: 1, P. C. Boeren, *Van Lotharingen naar Bourgondië;* 2, L. J. Rogier, *Eenheid en scheiding.*

K179. Quicke, Fritz. **Les Pays-Bas à la veille de la période bourguignonne, 1356–1384.** Brussels, 1947.

Russia and East Central Europe

K180. Halecki, Oskar. **Borderlands of western civilization: a history of east central Europe.** N.Y., 1952. The title of this book reflects the author's thesis that the western European orbit goes beyond the boundaries of Germany. Deals with areas between Germany and Russia and extending from Finland to Greece. Chs. 1–9 describe for the medieval period conditions in areas too long neglected by historians. The bibliographies are especially useful.

K181. Dvornik, Francis. **The making of central and eastern Europe.** London, 1949. Concentrates on 10th and 11th centuries.

K182. Vernadsky, George, and Michael Karpovich. **A history of Russia.** V. 1–3. New Haven, 1943–53. The first three volumes, all by Vernadsky, cover respectively ancient Russia, Kievan Russia, the Mongols and Russia.

K183. Vernadsky, George. **The origins of Russia.** Oxford, 1959. Examination of early background of the Russian people and formation of the Russian state, eastern expansion of the Vikings, and the Byzantine and oriental background of Russian civilization.

K184. Eck, Alexandre. **Le Moyen Âge russe.** Paris, 1933. Only survey treatment of the Russian Middle Ages in a western language. Social organization dominates the author's attention, and the work is criticized for being somewhat juridical in approach. Review, P. Pascal, *Revue historique,* 174 (July-Aug. 1934): 82.

K185. Florinsky, Michael T. **Russia: a history and an interpretation.** See *X136.* V. 1, pt. 1 serves as an introduction to the medieval period of Russian history.

K186. Nowak, Frank. **Medieval Slavdom and the rise of Russia.** N.Y., 1930.

K187. Pares, Sir Bernard. **A history of Russia.** Definitive ed., by Richard Pares, N.Y., 1953. Chs. 1–5 are a standard introduction to Russian history of the Middle Ages.

K188. Cross, Samuel H. "The Scandinavian infiltration into early Russia." *Speculum,* 21 (Oct. 1946): 505–14.

K189. The Cambridge history of Poland. Ed. by William F. Reddaway and others. 2 v. Cambridge, Eng., 1941–50. Now the standard introduction to Polish history. For the Middle Ages see v. 1, chs. 1–14.

K190. Gasiorowski, Zygmunt J. "The 'conquest' theory of the genesis of the Polish state." *Speculum,* 30 (Oct. 1955): 550–60.

HISTORIES OF SPECIAL TOPICS

Feudalism

K191. Ganshof, François L. **Feudalism.** London and N.Y., 1952. An excellent work,

with the best selective bibliography on the subject readily available.

K192. Stephenson, Carl. **Mediaeval feudalism.** Ithaca, 1942. Masterful condensation based on wide reading in the sources; the best brief introduction to a dangerously complex topic.

K193. Coulborn, Rushton, ed. **Feudalism in history.** Princeton, 1956. A serious, successful attempt at a comparative examination of feudal forms and practices.

K194. Lyon, Bryce D. **The Middle Ages in recent historical thought: selected topics.** Washington, 1959. [Service Center for Teachers of History, Publication no. 23.] A timely essay, with selected readings in English and bibliographical notes. Topics considered are: When did the Middle Ages begin?; The meaning of manorialism; The significance of feudalism; The value of Magna Carta; Representative institutions.

K195. Mitteis, Heinrich. **Lehnrecht und Staatsgewalt.** Weimar, 1933. François Ganshof calls this the best work on feudal institutions in western and central Europe, and refers readers to Walther Kienast, "Lehnrecht und Staatsgewalt im Mittelalter," *Historische Zeitschrift,* 158 (1938): 3–51.

K196. Calmette, Joseph L. A. **La société féodale.** 4th ed., Paris, 1938. This compact volume serves as a useful handbook, with chapters on feudal origins, feudal organization, the social classes, persons in relation to their holdings, feudal life, and the feudal world.

K197. Bloch, Marc. **La société féodale.** 2 v. Paris, 1939–40. A work of major importance—broadly conceived, and executed with the originality, skill, and remarkable learning found in all that Bloch wrote. V. 1 describes the setting in which feudal and seignorial institutions flourished after the later invasions, how men became bound one to another, vassalage and the fief, and conditions faced by the lower orders in the seignorial system. V. 2 considers the orders of medieval society, feudal government, and general characteristics.

K198. Stephenson, Carl. "The origin and significance of feudalism." *Am. hist. rev.,* 46 (July 1941): 788–812.

K199. Sánchez-Albornoz, Claudio. **En torno a los orígines del feudalismo.** See *VD137.*

K200. Recueils de la Société Jean Bodin pour l'histoire comparative des institutions. Brussels, 1936 ff. Although often sociological in approach, these volumes are rich in suggestions and offer a challenge to traditional concepts and interpretations.

K201. Odegaard, Charles E. **Vassi and fideles in the Carolingian empire.** Cambridge, Mass., 1945. Important contribution to the vexed question of feudal origins. "So far as the king was concerned," writes Odegaard, "vassals were a particular group of faithful servants entrusted with a certain function, not all persons who were in his commendation."

K202. Lyon, Bryce D. **From fief to indenture: the transition from feudal to nonfeudal contract in western Europe.** Cambridge, Mass., 1957. Minute analysis of how an annual income in money or kind granted by lord to vassal was gradually displaced by the indenture system and payment for services rendered. Somewhat technical in character, but an important contribution.

K203. Stenton, Frank M. **The first century of English feudalism, 1066–1166.** Oxford, 1932. "A book that is both original and important." A. B. White, *Am. hist. rev.,* 38 (Jan. 1933) : 360.

K204. Poole, Austin L. **Obligations of society in the XII and XIII centuries.** Oxford, 1946. A small book, rich in content; keen analysis of the social orders in a feudal society is presented with insight and skill.

K205. Keeney, Barnaby C. **Judgment by peers.** Cambridge, Mass., 1949. A study in social as well as legal and institutional history. Gives attention to the position and function of peers both in England and on the continent. Clause thirty-nine of Magna Carta is carefully analyzed.

K206. Painter, Sidney. **Studies in the history of the English feudal barony.** Baltimore, 1943.

K207. Gleason, Sarell E. **An ecclesiastical barony of the Middle Ages: the bishopric of Bayeux, 1066–1204.** Cambridge, Mass., 1936. Illuminating examination of the feudal aspects of an important episcopal holding in the Anglo-Norman state.

K208. Brunner, Otto. **Land und Herrschaft: Grundfragen der territorialen Verfassungsgeschichte Südostdeutschland im Mittelalter.** 3rd rev. ed., Vienna, 1943.

K209. Lewis, Archibald R. "Seigneurial administration in twelfth century Montpellier." **Speculum,** 22 (Oct. 1947) : 562–77.

Chivalry

K210. Painter, Sidney. **French chivalry: chivalric ideas and practices in mediaeval France.** Baltimore, 1940. Delightful reading, and still the sanest and most useful introduction to an elusive subject.

K211. Denholm-Young, Noël. "Feudal society in the thirteenth century: the knights." **History,** n.s. 29 (Sep. 1944) : 107–19.

K212. Ackerman, Robert W. "The knighting ceremonies in the middle English romances." **Speculum,** 19 (July 1944) : 285–313.

K213. Bühler, Johannes, comp. **Fürsten und Ritter, nach zeitgenössischen Quellen.** Leipzig, 1928. Collection of contemporary sources reflecting aspects of noble life in the Middle Ages.

K214. Kelly, Francis M., and Randolph Schwabe. **A short history of costume and armour, chiefly in England, 1066–1485.** London, 1931.

K215. Denholm-Young, Noël. "The tournament in the thirteenth century." **Studies in medieval history presented to Frederick Maurice Powicke** (Oxford, 1948), pp. 240–68.

K216. Wagner, Anthony R. **Heralds and heraldry in the Middle Ages: an inquiry into the growth of the armorial function of heralds.** 2nd ed., London, 1956.

Constitutional Developments

K217. Cam, Helen M., Antonic Marongiu, and Günther Stökl. "Recent work and present views on the origins and development of representative assemblies." **Relazioni del X congresso internazionale di scienze storiche** (Florence, 1955), v. 1, pp. 1–101.

K218. "Mediaeval representation in theory and practice: essays by American members of the International Commission for the History of Representative and Parliamentary Institutions." **Speculum,** 29 (Apr. 1954) : 347–476.

K219. Mitteis, Heinrich. **Der Staat des hohen Mittelalters: Grundlinien einer vergleichenden Verfassungsgeschichte des Lehnzeitalters.** 6th ed., Cologne, 1959. Good comparative study of the constitutional history of feudal Germany, France, Italy, and England.

K220. Stubbs, William. **Constitutional history of England in its origin and development.** 3 v. 5th ed. of v. 1, 3rd ed. of v. 2, 4th ed. of v. 3, Oxford, 1887–91. An original work still demanding respect.

K221. Jolliffe, John E. A. **The constitutional history of medieval England from the English settlement to 1485.** London, 1937. Important, but often controversial, presentation of English constitutional developments.

K222. Wilkinson, Bertie. **Constitutional history of medieval England, 1216–1399.** 3 v. London and N.Y., 1948–58. (Title varies.) Well-balanced, imaginative work of primary importance.

K223. Pollock, Sir Frederick, and Frederic W. Maitland. **The history of English law before the time of Edward I.** 2nd ed., 2 v., Cambridge, Eng., 1898. A work of learning and literary distinction rightly acclaimed a classic.

K224. Haskins, George L. "Executive justice and the rule of law: some reflections on thirteenth-century England." **Speculum,** 30 (Oct. 1955) : 529–38.

K225. Thompson, Faith. **A short history of Parliament, 1295–1642.** Minneapolis, 1953.

Readable introduction to the complexities of parliamentary history, written primarily for students. Pt. 1 covers the later Middle Ages.

K226. McIlwain, Charles H. **The high court of Parliament.** New Haven, 1910. This essay on the boundaries between legislation and adjudication has greatly influenced subsequent writers.

K227. Hoyt, Robert S. **The royal demesne in English constitutional history, 1066–1272.** Ithaca, 1950.

K228. Jolliffe, John E. A. **Angevin kingship.** London, 1955.

K229. Boussard, Jacques. **Le gouvernement d'Henri II Plantagenêt.** Paris, 1956. Study of the complexities of a feudal monarchy.

K230. Tout, Thomas F. **Chapters in medieval administrative history.** 6 v. Manchester, 1920–33. Studies that opened new vistas in English history.

K231. Wilkinson, Bertie. "English politics and politicians of the thirteenth and fourteenth centuries." **Speculum,** 30 (Jan. 1955): 37–48.

K232. Lot, Ferdinand, and Robert Fawtier, eds. **Histoire des institutions françaises au Moyen Âge.** Paris, 1957 ff. Analysis by various authors of the institutions of major feudal principalities of the realm and of the monarchy.

K233. Strayer, Joseph R., and Charles H. Taylor. **Studies in early French taxation.** Cambridge, Mass., 1939.

K234. Kern, Fritz. **Kingship and the law in the Middle Ages.** Tr. by S. B. Chrimes. Oxford, 1939.

K235. Folz, Robert. **L'idée d'empire en occident du Ve au XIVe siècle.** Paris, 1953. A work of high quality and excellence.

K236. Schramm, Percy E. **A history of the English coronation.** Tr. by Leopold G. Wickham Legg. Oxford, 1937. Schramm's long attention to comparative studies of medieval coronations gives authority to his work.

K237. ——. **Der König von Frankreich: das Wesen der Monarchie vom 9. zum 16. Jahrhundert.** 2 v. Weimar, 1939.

K238. Kantorowicz, Ernst H. **The king's two bodies: a study in mediaeval political theology.** Princeton, 1957. Scholarly, lucid examination of a basic concept in medieval political thought.

K239. Kisch, Guido. "A decade of American research in medieval legal history." **Progress of medieval and Renaissance studies,** 17 (Apr. 1942): 27–34.

Diplomacy and International Relations

K240. Ganshof, François L. **Histoire des relations internationales.** V. 1, **Le Moyen Âge.** Paris, 1953.

K241. Mattingly, Garrett. **Renaissance diplomacy.** Boston, 1955. This book has been accorded high critical appraisal which it truly merits. The opening chapters especially give valuable insights into the theory and practice of diplomacy in a medieval setting, and explain the changing modes and manners of diplomatic procedure that arose in Renaissance Italy and affected the political world everywhere.

K242. Ohnsorge, Werner. **Abendland und Byzanz: gesammelte Aufsätze zur Geschichte der byzantinisch-abendländischen Beziehungen und des Kaisertums.** Darmstadt, 1958.

K243. Cuttino, George P. **English diplomatic administration, 1259–1339.** London, 1940. Important for English and continental relationships.

K244. Ernst, Fritz. "Ueber Gesandschaftswesen und Diplomatie an der Wende vom Mittelalter zur Neuzeit." **Archiv für Kulturgeschichte,** 33 (1950): 64–95. Legations and diplomacy in the later Middle Ages.

The Crusades

K245. Erdmann, Carl. **Die Entstehung des Kreuzzugsdankens.** Stuttgart, 1935. Basic for understanding forces underlying the crusades.

K246. Grousset, René. **Histoire des croisades et du royaume franc de Jérusalem.** 3 v. Paris, 1934–36. "Combines wide learning with good writing"—Runciman. But see F. Duncalf, *Am. hist. rev.,* 41 (Oct. 1935): 124.

K247. Runciman, Steven. **A history of the crusades.** 3 v. Cambridge, Eng., 1951–54. Each volume provided with useful but uncritical bibliography. "The work deserves all the encomiums it has received in literary circles." A. C. Krey, *Am. hist. rev.,* 60 (Apr. 1955): 591. For an appreciative but reserved criticism see A. S. Atiya, *Speculum,* 31 (Apr. 1956): 403.

K248. Setton, Kenneth M., ed. **A history of the crusades.** Philadelphia, 1955 ff. A cooperative work planned to cover all aspects of crusade history in 5 volumes. Review of v. 1, R. N. Frye, *Speculum,* 30 (Oct. 1955): 684.

K249. Waas, Adolf. **Geschichte der Kreuzzüge.** 2 v. Freiburg, 1956. In spite of its deficiencies, is of some interest because of its not entirely convincing attempt to attribute the crusading movements to lay forces. Like Grousset and Runciman, Waas insists that the history of the crusades must be written by one author, rather than be presented in piece-meal fashion by a group of experts. Review, A. C. Krey, *Am. hist. rev.,* 63 (Jan. 1958): 383.

K250. Barker, Ernest. **The crusades.** London, 1923. Convenient reprint, with slight changes, of an article in the *Encyclopaedia britannica* (11th ed.). Barker's often-demonstrated abilities to synthesize a mass of material are evident here.

K251. Bréhier, Louis. **L'église et l'Orient au Moyen Âge: les croisades.** 6th ed., Paris, 1928. Although devoted mainly to the crusades, also treats earlier relations between East and West, especially Christian missions in the East and the theoretical propagandists.

K252. Newhall, Richard A. **The crusades.** N.Y., 1927. Clear, scholarly sketch, designed to furnish a week's reading in a college course of general European history.

K253. Munro, Dana Carleton. **The kingdom of the crusaders.** N.Y., 1935. The Lowell Lectures delivered in 1924 by the dean of American crusade historians. Although published posthumously, as printed they represent practically the final draft as planned by the author. From years of teaching and study Munro had come to know the sources for crusade history intimately and, when writing his lectures, had also the stimulus provided by first-hand observation of sites in the Levant so well known to the crusaders themselves.

K254. La Monte, John L. **Feudal monarchy in the Latin kingdom of Jerusalem, 1100 to 1291.** Cambridge, Mass., 1932. Stands high among important books concerning crusaders. Divided into three parts: constitutional development of the Latin kingdom of Jerusalem, its administrative machinery, and some political relationships of the kings of Jerusalem. There are also useful genealogical tables for the kings of Jerusalem and the House of Ibelin.

K255. The crusades and other historical essays presented to Dana C. Munro by his former students. Ed. by Louis J. Paetow. N.Y., 1928. "Eight of these twelve essays deal with the crusades and throw new light on the great German pilgrimage of 1064–65, the pope's plan for the first crusade, a neglected passage in the *Gesta*, Robert II of Flanders, Albert of Aachen, the Genoese colonies in Syria, Fulk of Neuilly, and John of Garland"—S. B. Fay, *A guide to historical literature* (1931 ed.), p. 311.

K256. Burr, George L. "The year 1000 and the antecedents of the crusades." **Am. hist. rev.,** 6 (Apr. 1901): 429–39. Burr disproves the validity of contentions that medieval eschatology put the world on nervous edge as the millennium was reached.

K257. Pognon, Edmond, ed. tr. **L'an mille: oeuvres de Liutprand, Raoul Glaber, Adémar de Chabannes, Adalbéron, Helgaud.** Paris, 1947.

K258. Munro, Dana C. "The speech of Pope Urban II at Clermont, 1095." **Am. hist. rev.,** 11 (Jan. 1906): 231–42. By a masterful examination of the sources, Munro reconstructs the speech of Urban, indicating what he doubtless said, what he probably said, and what is dubious in the various reports of his appeal.

K259. Krey, A. C. "Urban's crusade—success or failure?" **Am. hist. rev.,** 53 (Jan. 1948): 235–50. Argues that since Urban's hope for unification of Christendom failed, the crusade could not be considered successful.

K260. Munro, Dana C. "The children's crusade." **Am. hist. rev.,** 19 (Apr. 1914): 516–24. Munro combed the sources for tangible evidence of this always challenging and curious episode. It seems nothing more can be said than is found here.

K261. Throop, Palmer A. **Criticism of the crusade: a study of public and crusade propaganda.** Amsterdam, 1940. Important study of the methods used to sustain the crusading movement in a world of changing interests and outlook.

K262. Atiya, Aziz S. **The crusade in the later Middle Ages.** See *M89.*

K263. Fedden, Robin. **Crusader castles: a brief study in the military architecture of the crusades.** London, 1950. Brief, interesting introduction to problems of castle building. Contains many excellent illustrations and a useful bibliography.

K264. Smail, R. C. **Crusading warfare (1097–1193).** Cambridge, Eng., 1956.

Historical sources for a study of the crusades are readily available. The sources, in English translations, listed below serve well as introduction to a series of historical episodes perennially attracting wide attention.

K265. Krey, August C., ed. and tr. **The First Crusade: the accounts of eye-witnesses and participants.** Princeton, 1921.

K266. Odo de Deuil. **De profectione Ludovici VII in orientem.** Ed. with English tr. by Virginia G. Berry. N.Y., 1948.

K267. William, Archbishop of Tyre. **A history of deeds done beyond the sea.** Tr. and annotated by Emily A. Babcock and August C. Krey. 2 v. N.Y., 1943. "Probably the most significant translation of any source made in our generation." *Am. hist. rev.,* 49 (July 1944): 696.

K268. Marzials, Sir Frank, tr. **Villehardouin's Chronicle of the Fourth Crusade and the conquest of Constantinople, and Joinville's Chronicle of the crusade of St. Lewis.** London and N.Y., 1908.

K269. Robert de Clari. **The conquest of Constantinople.** Tr. by Edgar H. McNeal. N.Y., 1936.

K270. Ambroise. **The crusade of Richard Lion-Heart.** Tr. by Merton J. Hubert. N.Y., 1941.

Medieval Christianity and the Christian Church

K271. Latourette, Kenneth S. **A history of Christianity.** See *D416.* Chs. 10–19 cover the Middle Ages.

K272. ——. **A history of the expansion of Christianity.** See *D530.* V. 2, *The thousand* *years of uncertainty,* A.D. *500–*A.D. *1500,* covers the Middle Ages.

K273. Baldwin, Marshall W. **The medieval church.** Ithaca, 1953. The many aspects of church life and polity are succinctly described in this excellently balanced introduction. Good selective bibliography.

K274. Deansley, Margaret. **A history of the medieval church, 590–1500.** London, 1925. Written primarily to aid candidates for degrees in divinity schools; a useful manual.

K275. Hughes, Philip. **A history of the church.** N.Y., 1947 ff. V. 2–3 contain sections for the western European Middle Ages. Author writes as a Roman Catholic.

K276. Fliche, Augustin. **Histoire de l'église depuis les origines jusqu'à nos jours.** Paris, 1934 ff. V. 4–15 deal with the Middle Ages, from the death of Theodosius to 1517. This major work is fundamental for a study of the Christian church, its relations with other elements of the medieval world, and for medieval civilization in general.

K277. Flick, Alexander C. **The rise of the mediaeval church.** N.Y., 1909. An unpretentious, clear introduction to church history. Needs to be amplified and corrected by later studies.

K278. ——. **The decline of the medieval church.** 2 v. London, 1930.

K279. Caspar, Erich L. **Geschichte des Papsttums von der Anfangen bis zur Höhe der Weltherrschaft.** 2 v. Tübingen, 1930–33. Useful, highly respected work of a true scholar. Stress is on emergence and strengthening of the idea of the papacy rather than on individual popes. Latter are evaluated more for what they did for the new institution than for their personal lives.

K280. Haller, Johannes. **Das Papsttum: Idee und Wirklichkeit.** Rev. ed., 5 v., Basel, 1951–53. An authoritative standard work explaining the theories and realities of history of the papacy to 1316.

K281. Mercati, Angelo. "The new list of popes." **Mediaeval studies,** 9 (1947): 71–80.

K282. Mann, Horace K. **The lives of the popes in the Middle Ages, 590–1304.** 18 v. in 19. London, 1902–32. Written by the leading English Roman Catholic authority in the field, these volumes can always be consulted with profit. Mann's wide knowledge and use of the sources adds to their worth, but he has been criticized for failure to use all the German secondary literature.

K283. Coulton, George G. **Five centuries of religion.** 4 v. Cambridge, Eng., 1923–50. [1, *St. Bernard, his predecessors and successors, 1000–1200* A.D.; 2, *The friars and the dead weight of tradition;* 3, *Getting and spending;* 4, *The last days of medieval monachism.*] These rather weighty tomes contain a mass of material selected from wide reading in medieval monastic sources. They do not represent, however, judicious, systematic synthesis, and reflect, without any attempt at subterfuge, the anti-monastic attitude of the author. They are too rich in illustrations to be ignored.

K284. Fliche, Augustin. **La réforme grégorienne.** 3 v. Louvain, 1924–37. The fundamental work for study of Gregorian reforms and the investiture controversy. See the criticisms of E. Caspar, "Gregor VII in seinen Briefen," *Historische Zeitschrift,* 130 (1924): 1–30.

K285. Tellenbach, Gerd. **Church, state and Christian society at the time of the investiture contest.** Oxford, 1940.

K286. Belperron, Pierre. **La croisade contre les Albigeois et l'union du Languedoc à la France.** Paris, 1945.

K287. Daniel-Rops, Henry. **The church and the Dark Ages, 406–1050.** London, 1959.

K288. ——. **Cathedral and crusade: studies of the medieval church, 1050–1350.** Tr. by John Warrington. London and N.Y., 1957.

K289. Mollat, Guillaume. **Les papes d'Avignon (1305–1378).** 9th ed., Paris, 1950.

K290. Vischer, Melchior. **Jan Hus, Aufruhr wider Papst und Reich.** Frankfurt am Main, 1955.

K291. Jacob, Ernest F. **Essays in the conciliar epoch.** 2nd ed., Manchester, 1953. A variety of fine essays. Topics treated are: Conciliar thought; Dietrich of Niem; Englishmen and the general councils of the fifteenth century; English conciliar activity, 1395–1418; Ockham as a political thinker; Sir John Fortescue and the law of nature; The Brethren of the Common Life; The *De imitatione christi;* Cusanus the theologian; "Middle Ages" and "Renaissance"; Verborum florida venustas; English university clerks in the later Middle Ages.

K292. Tierney, Brian. **Foundations of the conciliar theory: the contribution of the medieval canonists from Gratian to the Great Schism.** Cambridge, Eng., 1955. Good exposition of the theory of church government.

K293. Chadwick, Nora K., and others. **Studies in the early British church.** Cambridge, Eng., 1958. Some special studies of the intellectual life of early Britain after departure of the Romans. Review, S. R. Packard, *Am. hist. rev.,* 64 (Apr. 1959): 688.

K294. Brooke, Zachary N. **The English church and the papacy from the conquest to the reign of John.** Cambridge, Eng., 1931.

K295. Gougaud, Louis. **Modern research, with special reference to early Irish ecclesiastical history: lectures delivered at University College, Dublin, April 1929.** Dublin, 1929.

K296. ——. **Christianity in Celtic lands: a history of the churches of the Celts, their origin, their development, influence and mutual relations.** Tr. by Maud Joynt. London, 1932.

K297. ——. **Les saints irlandais hors d'Irlande étudiés dans le culte et dans la dévotion traditionelle.** Louvain and Oxford, 1936.

K298. Grayzel, Solomon. **The church and the Jews in the XIIIth century.** Philadelphia, 1933.

K299. Boyd, Catherine E. **Tithes and parishes in medieval Italy: the historical roots of a modern problem.** Ithaca, 1952. Noteworthy contribution by a distinguished United States scholar who has made Italy her province. Although emphasis is on the period to 1300, importance of the tithe problem for Italian history of later ages has happily not been overlooked. The persistence of a medieval tradition into modern times demanded attention to post-medieval conditions. Review, M. R. P. McGuire, *Am. hist. rev.*, 60 (Jan. 1955): 345.

K300. Kantorowicz, Ernst H. **Laudes regiae: a study in liturgical acclamations and mediaeval ruler worship.** Berkeley, 1946. Author demonstrates in a series of learned essays the truth of his contention that the liturgy is today one of the most important auxiliaries to the study of medieval history and has too long been neglected. The book will interest readers concerned with numismatics, ecclesiastical studies, political theory, papal and princely claims, and the history of ideas.

Papal Government and Canon Law

K301. Ullmann, Walter. **The growth of papal government in the Middle Ages: a study in the ideological relation of clerical to lay power.** London and N.Y., 1955. ". . . the most learned study in English of the development of the papacy from the fourth to the twelfth century." G. Post, *Speculum*, 32 (Jan. 1957): 209.

K302. Lunt, William E. **Papal revenues in the Middle Ages.** 2 v. N.Y., 1934. Reflects research that instantly commands respect. Lunt sought every scrap of information about the origins and development of the papal *camera*, and, with the wealth of documentary material reproduced here, gives the picture of the papal treasury at work.

K303. Bertolini, Ottorino. "Il problema delle origini del potere temporale dei papi nei suoi presupposti teoretici iniziali: il concetto di 'Restitutio' nelle prime cessioni territoriali (756–757) alla chiesa di Roma." **Miscellanea Pio Paschini**, v. 1 (Rome, 1948), pp. 103–71.

K304. Mortimer, Robert C. **Western canon law.** Berkeley, 1953. Series of lectures giving a brief, clear introduction to the history of canon law. Selective bibliography.

K305. **Dictionnaire de droit canonique, contenant tous les termes du droit canonique, avec un sommaire de l'histoire et des insti-** tutions et de l'état actuel de la discipline. Ed. by R. Naz and others. Paris, 1935 ff. Now one of the best introductions to problems touching upon canon law.

K306. Plöchl, Willibald M. **Geschichte des Kirchenrechts.** 2 v. Vienna and Munich, 1953–55. [1, *Das Recht des ersten christlichen Jahrtausends, von der Urkirche bis zum grossen Schisma; 2, Das Kirchenrecht der abendländischen Christenheit 1055 bis 1517.*]

K307. Kemp, Eric W. **An introduction to canon law in the Church of England: being the Lichfield Cathedral divinity lectures for 1956.** London, 1957. Lecture 1 serves as an excellent elementary introduction to the nature and importance of medieval canon law.

K308. Tierney, Brian. **Medieval poor law: a sketch of canonical theory and its application in England.** Berkeley, 1959. While greatly extending the history of the social services, Tierney provides also a learned introduction to medieval canon law.

K309. Ullmann, Walter. **Medieval papalism: the political theories of the medieval canonists.** London, 1949. See the sympathetic critical comments of G. Post in *Speculum*, 26 (Jan. 1951): 227.

K310. Fournier, Paul E. L., and Gabriel Le Bras. **Histoire des collections canoniques en Occident depuis les Fausses décrétales jusqu'au Décret de Gratien.** 2 v. Paris, 1931–32. A work of major significance; indispensable for understanding of canon law and medieval ecclesiastical-political issues.

K311. Le Bras, Gabriel, ed. **Histoire du droit et des institutions de l'église en Occident.** V. 1, **Prolégomènes.** Paris, 1955.

K312. Ryan, John Joseph. **Saint Peter Damiani and canonical sources: a preliminary study in the antecedents of Gregorian reform.** Toronto, 1956. Excellent.

K313. Pacaut, Marcel. **Alexandre III: étude sur la conception du pouvoir pontifical dans sa pensée et dans son oeuvre.** Paris, 1956. A notable contribution.

K314. Kuttner, Stephan. "Methodological problems concerning the history of canon law." **Speculum**, 30 (Oct. 1955): 539–49.

Monasticism

K315. Lesne, Émile. **Histoire de la propriété ecclésiastique en France.** 6 v. in 8. Lille and Paris, 1910–43. Basic for French social, economic, ecclesiastical, and intellectual developments.

K316. Knowles, David. **The monastic order in England: a history of its development from the times of St. Dunstan to the Fourth Lateran Council, 943–1216.** Cambridge, Eng., 1940.

K317. ——. **The religious orders in England.** 2 v. Cambridge, Eng., 1950–55. A work of erudition bringing fresh points of view. Review, R. W. Emery, *Speculum*, 31 (Apr. 1956): 386.

K318. Knowles, David, and R. Neville Hadcock. **Medieval religious houses: England and Wales.** Rev. ed., London and N.Y., 1953. Review, R. W. Emery, *Speculum*, 29 (Apr. 1954): 290.

K319. Moorman, John R. H. **The Grey Friars in Cambridge, 1225–1538.** Cambridge, Eng., 1952.

K320. Hinnebusch, William A. **The early English Friars Preachers.** Rome, 1951. A model of scholarship; a classic for early Dominican history in England.

K321. Dickinson, John C. **The origins of the Austin canons.** London, 1950.

K322. Gougaud, Louis. **Gaelic pioneers of Christianity: the work and influence of Irish monks and saints in continental Europe (VIth–XIIth centuries).** Tr. by Victor Collins. Dublin, 1923.

K323. Schmitz, Philibert. **Histoire de l'Ordre de Saint Benoît.** 6 v. Maredsous, Belg., 1942–49. Now considered the fundamental work for history of one of the greatest monastic orders.

K324. Hallinger, Kassius. **Gorze-Kluny.** 2 v. Rome, 1950–51. Along with the above (*K323*), this is the best available work on Benedictine reform. Review, P. Volk, *Revue d'histoire ecclésiastique*, 47 (1952): 247.

K325. Williams, Watkin. **Monastic studies.** Manchester, 1938. Fourteen essays previously published elsewhere. These deal with Cluny, the Cistercians, and allied topics.

K326. Mahn, Jean B. **L'Ordre cistercien et son gouvernement des origines au milieu du XIIIᵉ siècle (1098–1265).** Paris, 1945.

K327. The letters of Bernard of Clairvaux. Tr. by Bruno Scott James. London, 1953.

K328. Boyd, Catherine E. **A Cistercian nunnery in mediaeval Italy: the story of Rifreddo in Saluzzo, 1220–1300.** Cambridge, Mass., 1943. Review, A. C. Krey, *Am. hist. rev.*, 49 (Oct. 1943): 88.

K329. White, Lynn T., Jr. **Latin monasticism in Norman Sicily.** Cambridge, Mass., 1938. Although it emphasizes monasticism, this now fundamental analysis is equally important for intercultural influences of Byzantines, Muslims, and Normans in Sicily.

K330. McDonnell, Ernest W. **The Beguines and Beghards in medieval culture, with special emphasis on the Belgian scene.** New Brunswick, N.J., 1954. Religious excitement in the Middle Ages was expressed in many ways. McDonnell has examined in exhaustive fashion the activities of two important brotherhoods and sisterhoods as a cultural force. Titles of the six parts indicate the breadth of treatment: "A case study in the *Vita apostolica*," "The extraregular in state and society," "Spiritual currents in Belgium and Rhineland," "Popular devotional litera-

ture," "Positive and negative evidence," "The extraregular and the Inquisition."

Heresies and Inquisition

K331. Lea, Henry C. **A history of the Inquisition of the Middle Ages.** 3 v. N.Y., 1888. One of the classics of United States scholarship.

K332. Turberville, Arthur S. **Mediaeval heresy and the Inquisition.** London, 1920. Good treatment of a highly controversial and complex subject.

K333. Vacandard, Elphège. **The Inquisition.** N.Y., 1908. Reflects a Roman Catholic point of view.

K334. Evans, Austin P. "Hunting subversion in the Middle Ages." **Speculum,** 33 (Jan. 1958): 1–22. Inquisitorial methods and procedures in southern France described by an author widely acquainted with French archival records and other sources that he has employed with meaning and skill.

K335. Obolensky, Dmitri. **The Bogomils: a study in Balkan neo-Manichaeism.** See *W1009.*

K336. Runciman, Steven. **The medieval Manichees: a study of the Christian dualist heresy.** Cambridge, Eng., 1955.

Economic and Social History

Economic History: General

K337. Cate, James L. "A decade of American publication on medieval economic history." **Progress of medieval and Renaissance studies,** 16 (1941): 8–26.

K338. Postan, Michael M. "Revisions in economic history: the fifteenth century." **Economic history review,** 9 (1939): 160–67.

K339. ———. "Studies in bibliography. Mediaeval capitalism." **Eco. hist. rev.,** 4 (1933): 212–27.

K340. Cave, Roy C., and Herbert H. Coulson, eds. **A source book for medieval economic history.** Milwaukee, 1936. Still very useful.

K341. Below, Georg A. H. von. **Probleme der Wirtschaftsgeschichte: eine Einführung in das Studium der Wirtschaftsgeschichte.** 2nd ed., Tübingen, 1926. Relates almost entirely to the Middle Ages.

K342. Pirenne, Henri. **Economic and social history of medieval Europe.** London, 1936. Fully merits the high praise it has been accorded. Still the best survey for medieval economic developments.

K343. ———. **Histoire économique de l'Occident médiéval.** Brussels, 1951. A priceless gathering in one volume of more than thirty of Pirenne's writings on medieval economic life, including original French text of his *Economic and social history*. The essays, reprinted from many different journals, fall readily into four major categories: the end of antiquity and early Middle Ages; end of the Middle Ages; Belgian economic history; commerce and industry.

K344. Thompson, James Westfall. **An economic and social history of the Middle Ages (300–1300).** N.Y., 1928. Somewhat dated and with obvious deficiencies, but still useful for the abundance of factual material.

K345. ——. **Economic and social history of Europe in the later Middle Ages (1300–1530).** N.Y., 1931. Considered superior to *K344*, but needs supplementing and revision.

K346. Boissonnade, Prosper. **Life and work in medieval Europe (fifth to fifteenth centuries).** London, 1927. Rich in detail and illustrative material.

K347. Lewis, Archibald R. "The closing of the mediaeval frontier, 1250–1350." **Speculum,** 33 (Oct. 1958): 475–83.

K348. Mollat, Michel, and others. "L'économie européenne aux deux derniers siècles du Moyen Âge." **Relazioni del X congresso internazionale di scienze storiche** (Florence, 1955), v. 3, pp. 655–811. A series of contributions of the first rank.

K349. Dopsch, Alfons. **The economic and social foundations of European civilization.** N.Y., 1937. Fundamental for early medieval civilization.

K350. Latouche, Robert. **Les origines de l'économie occidentale (IVe–XIe siècle).** Paris, 1956. Stresses France, Germany, and the Low Countries. "A book of the first order." B. D. Lyon, *Am. hist. rev.*, 62 (Jan. 1957): 373.

K351. Lestocquoy, Jean. "The tenth century." **Economic history review,** 17 (1947): 1–14. Analysis of the 10th century as an important link in the economic development and continuity of European economic activity.

K352. Sapori, Armando. **Studi di storia economica (secoli XIII, XIV, XV).** 3rd rev. ed., 2 v., Florence, 1955. Sapori is preeminent among economic historians, as is obvious from the quality of studies in these volumes. Among topics treated are: problems of usury and interest, the doctrine of the "just price," real estate values in medieval Florence, medieval "social security," culture of the Italian merchant class, medieval international commerce, and the evaluation of sources for medieval economic history. Review, G. A. Brucker, *Jour. eco. hist.* 17 (Mar. 1957): 139.

K353. Lipson, Ephraim. **The economic history of England.** 3 v. London, 1934–37. V. 1, for the Middle Ages (7th ed., 1937), is a standard and basic work.

K354. Bechtel, Heinrich. **Wirtschaftsgeschichte Deutschlands von der Vorzeit bis zum Ende des Mittelalters.** Frankfurt am Main, 1941.

K355. Luzzatto, Gino. **Storia economica d'Italia.** V. 1, **L'antichità e il Medioevo.**

Rome, 1949. "Well written, well organized, extraordinarily well informed." R. S. Lopez, *Speculum,* 28 (Apr. 1953): 403.

K356. Postan, Michael M. "Italy and the economic development of England in the Middle Ages." **Journal of economic history,** 11 (Fall 1951): 339–46.

K357. Fanfani, Amintore. "La préparation intellectuelle et professionnelle à l'activité économique, en Italie, du XIVe au XVIe siècle." **Le Moyen Âge,** 57 (1951): 327–46.

K358. Cipolla, Carlo M. "The trends in Italian economic history in the later Middle Ages." **Economic history review,** 2nd ser., 2 (1949): 181–84. Suggestive for further work.

K359. Gille, Bertrand. **Histoire économique et social de la Russie du Moyen Âge au XXe siècle.** Paris, 1949. Chs. 1–3 cover the origins, Kievan economy, and medieval economy.

K360. Lyashchenko, Peter. **History of the national economy of Russia to the 1917 revolution.** N.Y., 1949. See sections 4–9 (pp. 83–178).

Agrarian Economy

K361. Neilson, Nellie. **Medieval agrarian economy.** N.Y., 1936. Though designed for college class reading, the author's life-long work with the sources makes her essays especially important. There are chapters for the village framework, field systems, and forms of settlement; the people of the village; and the village in relation to king and church.

K362. Balon, Joseph. **Les fondements du régime foncier au Moyen Âge depuis la chute de l'empire romain en Occident: étude de dogmatique et d'histoire du droit.** Louvain, 1954.

K363. Grand, Roger, and Raymond Delatouche. **L'agriculture au Moyen Âge de la fin de l'empire romain au XVIe siècle.** Paris, 1950. [L'agriculture à travers les âges, 3.]

K364. Grand, Roger. "Les moyens de résoudre dans le haut Moyen Âge les problèmes ruraux." Centro Italiano di Studi sull'Alto Medioevo, **I problemi communi dell'Europa post-carolingia** (Spoleto, 1955), pp. 523–46.

K365. Kosminsky, E. A. **Studies in the agrarian history of England in the thirteenth century.** Ed. by R. H. Hilton, tr. by Ruth Kisch. Oxford, 1956. Marxist in point of view. Review, *The times* (London) *literary supplement,* Feb. 8, 1957, p. 78.

K366. Bennett, Henry S. **Life on the English manor: a study of peasant conditions, 1150–1400.** Cambridge, Eng. and N.Y., 1937. "A vivid and convincing picture of the lives of English peasants in a thoroughly readable book." B. H. Putnam, *Speculum,* 13 (July 1938): 351.

K367. Miller, Edward. **The abbey and bishopric of Ely: the social history of an ecclesiastical estate from the tenth century to the early fourteenth century.** Cambridge, Eng., 1951. Medieval social relationships of a feudal age were political, administrative, economic. This study shows that men like the abbots and bishops of Ely were often perplexed when forced to define precisely the nature of specific social types. Review, G. C. Boyce, *Annals of Am. Acad. of Pol. and Soc. Science*, 281 (May 1952): 236.

K368. Raftis, J. Ambrose. **The estates of Ramsey abbey: a study in economic growth and organization.** Toronto, 1957. ". . . the author goes far to explain to us the trends in the economic history of English agriculture for four hundred years." G. C. Homans, *Speculum*, 33 (Oct. 1958): 562. See also F. A. Cazel, Jr., *Am. hist. rev.*, 64 (Apr. 1959): 690, where the book is appraised as difficult to read and its organization regarded as unnecessarily complicated, although its merits are recognized.

K369. Hoyt, Robert S. "Farm of the manor and community of the vill in Domesday book." **Speculum**, 30 (Apr. 1955): 147–69.

K370. Bloch, Marc. **Les caractères originaux de l'histoire rurale française.** New ed., 2 v., Paris, 1952–56. V. 1, first published in Oslo, 1931, has long been recognized for its originality and importance. Robert Dauvergne has revised the work and supplemented it with materials from other of Bloch's writings.

K371. Déléage, André. **La vie rurale en Bourgogne jusqu'au début du onzième siècle.** 3 v. Mâcon, 1941. Also appears as thesis edition under title *La vie économique et sociale de la Bourgogne dans le haut Moyen Âge* (3 v., Mâcon, 1941). V. 3 is an atlas. ". . . a distinguished contribution to our knowledge of mediaeval society and institutions—one which every student of the subject must henceforth take into account." C. Stephenson, *Speculum*, 22 (Oct. 1947): 635. See also review, S. Painter, *Jour. eco. hist.*, 6 (Nov. 1946): 199.

K372. Saint Jacob, P. de. "Études sur l'ancienne communauté rurale en Bourgogne: le village." **Annales de Bourgogne.** 1, "Les conditions juridiques de l'habitat," 13 (1941): 169–202; 2, "La structure du manse," 15 (1943): 173–84; 3, "La banlieue du village," 18 (1946): 237–50.

K373. **Le Polyptyque illustré dit "Veil rentier" de Messire Jehan de Pamele-Audenarde (vers 1275): texte intégral et illustration de ce manuscrit.** Ed. by Léo Verriest. Gembloux, 1950. The manuscript has unique and striking medieval illustrations of objects referred to in the text, such as mechanical devices, etc. Review, L. M. J. Delaissé, *Scriptorium*, 6 (1952): 303.

K374. Dollinger, Philippe. **L'évolution des classes rurales en Bavière depuis la fin de l'époque carolingienne jusqu'au milieu du XIIIe siècle.** Paris, 1949. See critique of this important book by C. E. Perrin, *Revue historique*, 208 (July-Sep. 1952): 15–32.

K375. Abel, Wilhelm. **Die Wüstungen des ausgehenden Mittelalters.** 2nd rev. ed., Stuttgart, 1955. A significant work dealing with the decline of German agriculture and land settlement in the 14th and 15th centuries. Review, M. M. Postan, *Eco. hist. rev.*, 2nd ser., 3 (1950): 136.

K376. Luzzatto, Gino. "Per la storia dell'economia rurale in Italia nel secolo XIV." **Éventail de l'histoire vivante: hommage à Lucien Febvre,** v. 2 (Paris, 1933), pp. 105–13.

K377. Blum, Jerome. "The beginnings of large-scale private landownership in Russia." **Speculum,** 28 (Oct. 1953): 776–90.

Medieval Cities

K378. Mundy, John H., and Peter Riesenberg. **The medieval town.** Princeton, 1958. Good though brief introduction to medieval urban problems. Sixty selections from original sources support the text. Short but very well selected bibliography.

K379. Pirenne, Henri. **Medieval cities.** 2nd ed., Princeton, 1939.

K380. ——. **Les villes et les institutions urbaines.** 3rd ed., 2 v., Brussels, 1939.

K381. Lopez, Robert S. "Le città dell' Europa post-carolingia." **I problemi communi dell'Europa post-carolingia** (Spoleto, 1955), pp. 547–74.

K382. Institut für Geschichtliche Landesforschung des Bodenseegebietes. **Studien zu den Anfängen des europäischen Städtewesens: Reichenau-Vorträge, 1955–1956.** Constance and Lindau, 1958. "Though the serious scholar will find that these studies vary in value, in their totality they form a remarkable volume." A. R. Lewis, *Am. hist. rev.*, 64 (Jan. 1959): 347.

K383. Stephenson, Carl. **Borough and town: a study of urban origins in England.** Cambridge, Mass., 1933. Especially valuable for its consideration of English institutions with reference to continental developments. Ch. 1, "The mediaeval town in historical literature," provides an incisive evaluation and criticism of theories about town origins. Topics of other chapters include urban liberties on the continent, the Anglo-Saxon borough, the Domesday borough, the borough community, borough self-government, and the growth of the borough.

K384. Stenton, Frank M. **Norman London.** London, 1934.

K385. Gwynn, Aubrey. "Medieval Bristol and Dublin." **Irish historical studies,** 5 (Sep. 1947): 275–86.

K386. Hill, James W. F. **Medieval Lincoln.** Cambridge, Eng., 1948.

K387. Ganshof, François L. **Étude sur le développement des villes entre Loire et Rhin au Moyen Âge.** Paris and Brussels, 1943.

K388. Crozet, René. **Villes d'entre Loire et Gironde.** Paris, 1949.

K389. Petit-Dutaillis, Charles. "Les communes françaises au XIIe siècle: chartes de commune et chartes de franchises." **Revue historique de droit français et étranger,** 4th ser., 23 (July-Dec. 1944): 115–42, 24 (Jan.-Jun. 1945): 8–28.

K390. ——. **Les communes françaises: caractères et évolution, des origines au XVIIIe siècle.** Paris, 1947. Excellent. Review, F. Lot, *Revue hist.,* 201 (Jan.-Mar. 1949): 45.

K391. Grand, Roger. "La genèse du mouvement communal en France." **Revue historique de droit français et étranger,** 4th ser., 21 (July-Dec. 1942): 149–73.

K392. Chapin, Elizabeth. **Les villes de foires de Champagne.** Paris, 1937. [Bibliothèque de l'École des Hautes Études, Sciences historiques et philologiques, 268.] The four towns of the Champagne fairs, greatest marts of international trade prior to the 14th century, are here examined as demographic units.

K393. Lestocquoy, Jean. **Patriciens du Moyen-Âge: les dynasties bourgeoises d'Arras du XIe au XVe siècle.** Arras, 1945. Review, S. L. Thrupp, *Eco. hist. rev.,* 2nd ser., 2 (1949): 89.

K394. Ungureanu, Marie. **La bourgeoisie naissante: société et littérature bourgeoises d'Arras aux XIIe et XIIIe siècles.** Arras, 1955. [Mémoires de la Commission Departmentale des Monuments Historiques du Pas-de-Calais, 8.]

K395. Vaillant, Pierre. "Étude d'histoire urbaine: Grenoble et ses libertés (1226-1349)." **Annales de l'Université de Grenoble,** n.s. 12 (1935): 123–53, 14 (1937): 97–178.

K396. Müller, H. "Les origines de Grenoble: sa formation depuis l'époque gauloise jusqu'au VIIe siècle, d'après les documents extraits de son sous-sol." **Annales de l'Université de Grenoble,** n.s. 6 (1929): 237–75.

K397. Marquant, Robert. **La vie économique à Lille sous Philippe le Bon.** Paris, 1940.

K398. Lewis, Archibald R. "The development of town government in twelfth century Montpellier." **Speculum,** 22 (Jan. 1947): 51–67.

K399. Espinas, Georges. **Les origines de l'association.** V. 1, **Les origines du droit d'association dans les villes de l'Artois et de la Flandre française jusqu'au début du XVIe siècle.** Lille, 1941. Review, R. Grand, *Journal des savants,* Jan.-June 1947: 41–73.

K400. Lestocquoy, Jean. **Aux origines de la bourgeoisie: les villes de Flandre et d'Italie sous le gouvernement des patriciens, XIe-XVe siècles.** Paris, 1952.

K401. Coornaert, E. "L'état et les villes à la fin du Moyen Âge: la politique d'Anvers." **Revue historique,** 207 (Apr.-June 1952): 185–210.

K402. Bruxelles au XVme siècle. Brussels, 1953. A beautifully illustrated volume that owes its inspiration to an exposition held to illustrate Brussels life and interests in the 15th century.

K403. Lejeune, Jean. **Liège et son pays: naissance d'une patrie, XIIIe-XIVe siècles.** Liège, 1948. Review, E. Perroy, *Revue belge de philologie et d'histoire,* 28 (1950): 1261.

K404. Cuvelier, Joseph. **Les institutions de la ville de Louvain au Moyen Âge.** Brussels, 1935.

K405. ——. **La formation de la ville de Louvain des origines à la fin du XIVe siècle.** Brussels, 1935.

K406. Rörig, Fritz. **Magdeburgs Entstehung und die ältere Handelsgeschichte.** Berlin, 1952.

K407. Schneider, Jean. **La ville de Metz aux XIIIe et XIVe siècles.** Nancy, 1950. Review, C. E. Perrin, *Annales: économies, sociétés, civilisations,* 8 (Apr.-June 1953): 197–209.

K408. Soleder, Fridolin. **München im Mittelalter.** Munich, 1938.

K409. Vogel, Walther. "La Hanse, d'après des publications récentes." **Revue historique,** 179 (Jan.-Mar. 1937): 1–33.

K410. Rörig, Fritz. **Vom Werden und Wesen der Hanse.** Leipzig, 1940.

K411. Pagel, Karl. **Die Hanse.** Brunswick, 1952. "An informing and fascinating book." W. Westergaard, *Am. hist. rev.,* 59 (Oct. 1953): 90.

K412. Beuken, Josef H. A. **De Hanze in Vlaanderen.** Maastricht, Neth., 1950. Attractively written; well supplied with bibliographical data and references. Review, H. S. Lucas, *Speculum,* 28 (July 1953): 557.

K413. Bjork, David K. "Three Hansa towns and archives—Bruges, Lübeck, Tallinn." **The Pacific historical review,** 9 (Sep. 1940): 297–306.

K414. Chiappelli, Luigi. "La formazione storica del commune cittadino in Italia." **Archivo storico italiano,** 7th ser., 6 (1926): 3–59, 7 (1927): 177–229, 10 (1928): 3–89, 13 (1930): 3–59, 14 (1930): 3–56.

K415. Goetz, Walter W. **Die Entstehung der italienischen Kommunen im frühen Mittelalter.** Munich, 1944.

K416. Rubinstein, Nicolai. "Some ideas on municipal progress and decline in the Italy of the communes." Donald J. Gordon, ed., **Fritz Saxl, 1890–1948: a volume of memorial essays from his friends in England** (London, 1957), pp. 165–83.

K417. Wiel, Althea J. **The story of Bologna.** London, 1923.

K418. Schevill, Ferdinand. **History of Florence.** See *VE226.*

K419. Krey, August C. **A city that art built.** Minneapolis, 1936. Also published in his *History and the social web* (Minneapolis, 1955). An especially perceptive essay on the city of Florence. Handles complex material with sensitivity and taste.

K420. Bach, Erik. **La cité de Gênes au XIIᵉ siècle.** Copenhagen, 1955.

K421. Lopez, Robert S. **Studi sul'economia genovese nel Medio Evo.** Turin, 1936.

K422. **Storia di Milano.** V. 1–7. Milan, 1953–56. These volumes of this large work cover the Middle Ages. There are many illustrations.

K423. Violante, Cinzio. **La società milanese nell'età precommunale.** Bari, 1953. Milanese society in the 9th, 10th, and early 11th centuries. An important contribution to the economic and social history of northern Italy. Review, C. E. Boyd, *Am. hist. rev.,* 59 (July 1954): 908.

K424. Waley, Daniel. **Mediaeval Orvieto.** Cambridge, Eng., 1952.

K425. Herlihy, David. **Pisa in the early Renaissance: a study of urban growth.** New Haven, 1958. Problems of an Italian community in a critical period of Italian history are well explained in this pleasant volume, based on familiarity with the sources and the scene.

K426. Marinotti, Paolo, and others. **Storia di Venezia.** Venice, 1957 ff. To be complete in 16 v. V. 2–5 will cover the Middle Ages. Various chapters by different authors; many fine illustrations.

K427. Bacchelli, R., and others. **La civiltà veneziana del secolo di Marco Polo.** Florence, 1955. A series of essays.

K428. Bragadin, Marc'Antonio. **Histoire des républiques maritimes italiennes: Venise, Amalfi, Pise, Gênes.** Tr. from Italian by R. Juffé and R. Jouan. Paris, 1955.

Trade; Merchants

K429. Baldwin, Summerfield. **Business in the Middle Ages.** N.Y., 1937.

K430. Edler, Florence. **Glossary of mediaeval terms of business: Italian series, 1200–1600.** Cambridge, Mass., 1934.

K431. Pirenne, Henri. "L'instruction des marchands au Moyen Âge." **Annales d'histoire économique et sociale,** 1 (Jan. 1929): 13–28. Shows that commerce in the Middle Ages was not directed by illiterates.

K432. Sapori, Armando. "La cultura del mercante medievale italiano." **Rivista storica economica,** 2 (June 1937): 89–125. Sapori has republished this in his *Studi di storia economica medievale* (2nd ed., Florence, 1947), pp. 285–325.

K433. Carli, Filippo. "La riniscita del mercato nel secolo VIII." **Rivista di storia del diritto italiano,** 7 (Jan.-Apr. 1934): 5–32.

K434. Lopez, Robert S. "Il commercio dell' Europa post-carolingia." Centro Italiano di Studi sull'Alto Medioevo, **I problemi communi dell' Europa post-carolingia** (Spoleto, 1955), pp. 575–99.

K435. Dunning, G. C. "Trade relations between England and the continent in the late Anglo-Saxon period." E. B. Harden, ed., **Dark-age Britain: studies presented to E. T. Leeds** (London, 1956), pp. 218–33.

K436. Salzman, Louis F. **English trade in the Middle Ages.** Oxford, 1931. Useful and interesting consideration of medieval use of tools, money, weights and measures, centers of trade; the law merchant; and distribution (imports and exports).

K437. ——. **English industries of the Middle Ages.** New ed., Oxford, 1923.

K438. Power, Eileen. **The wool trade in English medieval history: being the Ford lectures for 1939.** N.Y. and London, 1941. The substance of many years of research by a gifted economic historian is presented without critical apparatus. Among topics discussed are sheep farming, wool production, development and organization of the wool trade, taxation of wool, and the staple system.

K439. Baker, Robert L. "The establishment of the English wool staple in 1313." **Speculum,** 31 (July 1956): 444–53.

K440. Carus-Wilson, Eleanor M. "Trends in export of English woollens in the fourteenth century." **Economic history review,** 2nd ser., 3 (1950): 162–79.

K441. ——. "The English cloth industry in the late twelfth and early thirteenth centuries." **Eco. hist. rev.,** 14 (1944): 32–50.

K442. Power, Eileen, and Michael M. Postan, eds. **Studies in English trade in the fifteenth century.** London, 1933.

K443. Thrupp, Sylvia L. **The merchant class of medieval London (1300–1500).** Chicago, 1948. Reference is made primarily to members of the greater companies in the city. See C. Stephenson, *Speculum,* 23 (Oct. 1948): 727, and C. P. Cuttino, *Am. hist. rev.,* 54 (Jan. 1949): 346, who question the author's procedure in selection and use of materials.

K444. Carus-Wilson, Eleanor M. **Medieval merchant venturers.** London, 1954.

K445. ——, ed. **The overseas trade of Bristol in the later Middle Ages.** Bristol, 1937.

K446. Kerling, Nelly J. M. **Commercial relations of Holland and Zeeland with England from the late 13th century to the close of the Middle Ages.** Leiden, 1954.

K447. Thrupp, Sylvia L. "Medieval gilds reconsidered." **Journal of economic history,** 2 (Nov. 1942): 164–73.

K448. Demaison, L. "Documents sur les drapiers de Reims au Moyen Âge." **Bibliothèque de l'École des chartes,** 89 (Jan.-June 1928): 5–39.

K449. Doehaerd, Renée. "Un paradoxe géographique: Laon, capitale du vin au XIIᵉ siècle." **Annales: économies, sociétés, civilisations,** 5 (Apr.-June 1950): 145–65. See J. de Sturler, "À propos de commerce du vin au Moyen Âge," *Le Moyen Âge,* 57 (1951): 93–128; Doehaerd's sharp reply to Sturler's criticism, 57 (1951): 359–71; and Sturler's rebuttal, 371–81.

K450. Mollat, Michel. **Le commerce maritime normand à la fin du Moyen Âge: étude d'histoire économique et sociale.** Paris, 1952.

K451. Wolff, Philippe. **Commerce et marchands de Toulouse (vers 1350-vers 1450).** Paris, 1955.

K452. Marseille. Chambre de Commerce. **Histoire du commerce de Marseille.** Ed. by Gaston Rambert. Paris, 1949 ff. A major contribution. V. 1–3 cover the Middle Ages.

K453. Dupont, André. **Les relations commerciales entre les cités maritimes de Languedoc et les cités méditerranéennes d'Espagne et d'Italie du Xᵉᵐᵉ au XIIIᵉᵐᵉ siècle.** Nîmes, 1942.

K454. Sapori, Armando. **Le marchand italien au Moyen Âge: conférences et bibliographie.** Paris, 1952. A work of exceptional quality with a remarkable bibliography.

K455. Jellema, Dirk. "Frisian trade in the dark ages." **Speculum,** 30 (Jan. 1955): 15–36.

K456. Lucas, Henry S. "Mediaeval economic relations between Flanders and Greenland." **Speculum,** 12 (Apr. 1937): 167–81.

K457. Lewis, Archibald R. **The northern seas: shipping and commerce in northern Europe, A.D. 300–1100.** Princeton, 1958. A lively, learned evaluation of the importance for medieval Europe of the Bay of Biscay, Irish Sea, English Channel, North Sea, Baltic, and their adjacent lands.

K458. Ruddock, Alwyn A. **Italian merchants and shipping in Southampton, 1270–1600.** Southampton, 1951.

K459. Renouard, Yves. **Les hommes d'affaires italiens du Moyen Âge.** Paris, 1949. An attractive, reliable, useful synthesis. Review, E. H. Byrne, *Speculum,* 26 (Apr. 1951): 404.

K460. Richards, Gertrude R. B., ed. **Florentine merchants of the age of the Medici.** Cambridge, Mass., 1932.

K461. Krueger, Hilmar C. "Genoese trade with northwest Africa in the twelfth century." **Speculum,** 8 (July 1933): 377–95.

K462. Reynolds, Robert L. "In search of a business class in thirteenth century Genoa." **The tasks of economic history,** 5 (Dec. 1945): 1–19.

K463. Lopez, Robert S. **Studi sull'economia genovese nel Medio Evo.** Turin, 1936.

K464. ——. "Majorcans and Genoese on the North Sea route in the thirteenth century." **Revue belge de philologie et d'histoire,** 29 (1951): 1163–79.

K465. Doehaerd, Renée. "Les galères génoises dans la Manche et la Mer du Nord à la fin du XIIIᵉ et du début du XIVᵉ s." **Bulletin de l'Institut Historique Belge de Rome,** 19 (1938): 5–76. This fine article makes necessary revisions in traditional theories concerning medieval commerce and trade.

K466. ——. **Les relations commerciales entre Gênes, la Belgique et l'Outremont, d'après les archives notariales génoises aux XIIIᵉ et XIVᵉ siècles.** 3 v. Brussels, 1941.

K467. Luzzatto, Gino. **Studi di storia economica veneziana.** Padua, 1954. Important collection of essays, published 1924–52, which serve to fill gaps in the economic history of Venice. Of the 16 selections 15 pertain to the Middle Ages.

K468. **Documenti del commercio veneziano nei secoli XI–XIII.** 2 v. Rome, 1940. [Antonino Lombardo and Raimondo Morozzo della Rocca, eds., Regesta chartarum italiae, 28–29.]

K469. **Nuovi documenti del commercio veneto dei secoli XI–XIII.** Venice, 1953. [Antonino Lombardo and Raimondo Morozzo della Rocca, eds., Monumenti storici pubblicati dalla deputazione di storia patria per le Venezie, n.s. 7.]

K470. Lane, Frederic C. **Venetian ships and shipbuilders of the Renaissance.** See *VE265.*

K471. ——. **Andrea Barbarigo, merchant of Venice, 1418–1449.** See *VE264.*

K472. Van Werveke, H. "Industrial growth in the Middle Ages: the cloth industry in Flanders." **Economic history review,** 2nd ser., 6 (1953–54): 237–45.

K473. Poerck, Guy de. **La draperie médiévale en Flandre et en Artois: technique et términologie.** 3 v. Bruges, 1951. Indispensable for all interested in the history of the woolen industry. Review, R. S. Lopez, *Speculum,* 27 (July 1952): 368.

K474. Espinas, Georges. **La draperie dans la Flandre français au Moyen Âge.** 2 v. Paris, 1923.

K475. ——. "Un grand commerce médiéval: les draps des Pays-Bas." **Annales d'histoire économique et sociale,** 9 (Jan. 1929): 58–74. A valuable review article.

K476. Gade, John A. **The Hanseatic control of Norwegian commerce during the late Middle Ages.** Leiden, 1951.

K477. Brutzukus, J. "Trade with eastern Europe, 800–1200." **Eco. hist. rev.,** 13 (1943): 31–41.

Money and Banking

K478. Le Goff, Jacques. **Marchands et banquiers du Moyen Âge.** Paris, 1956.

K479. Usher, Abbott P. **The early history of deposit banking in Mediterranean Europe.** Cambridge, Mass., 1943. Structure and functions of the early credit system; considerable attention to banking in Catalonia, 1240–1723.

Reviews, A. H. Stockder, *Jour. eco. hist.*, 5 (May 1945): 65; M. M. Postan, *Eco. hist. rev.*, 16 (1946): 63.

K480. De Roover, Raymond A. **L'évolution de la lettre de change, XIVᵉ–XVIIIᵉ siècles.** Paris, 1953.

K481. ——. **The Medici bank: its organization, management, operation and decline.** N.Y., 1948. "A masterly and probably definitive history of the business enterprises of the senior Medici." R. L. Reynolds, *Jour. eco. hist.*, 9 (May 1949): 68.

K482. ——. **Money, banking and credit in mediaeval Bruges; Italian merchant-bankers, lombards and money-changers: a study in the origins of banking.** Cambridge, Mass., 1948. Presents a vivid and lifelike picture. Reviews, B. N. Nelson, *Am. hist. rev.*, 56 (Apr. 1951): 539; B. W. Dempsey, *Jour. eco. hist.*, 9 (Nov. 1949): 257.

K483. Tourneur, Victor. "Le monnayage dans les villes de Flandre et de Brabant au XII siècle et au XIIIᵉ." Académie Royale de Belgique, **Bulletin de la classe des lettres et des sciences morales et politiques,** 5th ser., 26 (1940): 34–48.

K484. Laurent, Henri. **La loi de Gresham au Moyen Âge: essai sur le circulation monétaire entre la Flandre et le Brabant à la fin du XIVᵉ siècle.** Brussels, 1938.

K485. De Roover, Raymond. "The development of accounting prior to Luca Pacioli according to the account books of medieval merchants." **Studies in the history of accounting** (London, 1956), pp. 114–74.

K486. ——. "The concept of the just price: theory and economic policy." **Journal of economic history,** 18 (Dec. 1958): 418–34. Criticism and revision of traditional interpretations of the medieval attitude toward the just price.

K487. Nelson, Benjamin N. **The idea of usury.** Princeton, 1949. "The little book . . . is, indeed, a fine contribution. . . . Rather than a full-fledged history of usury it is an investigation of the psychologic background for the prohibition of interest." R. S. Lopez, *Speculum,* 26 (Apr. 1951): 401.

K488. Pirenne, Henri. **The stages in the social history of capitalism.** Stanford, 1953. Appears also in the original French version in *K343*, pp. 15–50.

K489. Sayous, André E., and Jean Combes. "Les commerçants et les capitalistes de Montpellier aux XIIIᵉ et XIVᵉ siècles." **Revue historique,** 188 (July-Dec. 1940): 341–77.

K490. Espinas, Georges. **Les origines du capitalisme.** 4 v. Lille, 1933–49. Special studies of the greatest significance.

K491. Postan, Michael M. "The rise of a money economy." **Economic history review,** 14 (1944): 123–34.

K492. Cipolla, Carlo M. **Money, prices and civilization in the Mediterranean world.** See *J74*.

K493. Le Gentilhomme, Pierre. "Le monnayage et la circulation monétaire dans les royaumes barbares en Occident (Vᵉ–VIIIᵉ siècle)." **Revue numismatique,** 5th ser., 7 (1943): 45–112.

K494. Lopez, Robert S. "An aristocracy of money in the early Middle Ages." **Speculum,** 28 (Jan. 1953): 1–43. Contends that moneyers held positions of wealth and prestige when money was scarce and declined during periods of economic expansion.

K495. Incarnati, Lamberto. **Moneta e scambio nell'antichità e nell'alto Medio Evo.** Rome, 1953.

K496. Lafaurie, Jean. **Les monnaies des rois de France.** 2 v. Paris, 1951–56.

K497. Bisson, Thomas N. "Coinages and royal monetary policy in Languedoc during the reign of Saint Louis." **Speculum,** 32 (July 1957): 443–69.

K498. Bautier, Robert H. "L'or et l'argent en Occident de la fin du XIIIᵉ siècle au début du XIVᵉ siècle." Académie des Inscriptions et Belles-Lettres, **Comptes rendus,** May 1951: 169–74.

K499. **The De moneta of Nicholas of Oresme.** Ed. and tr. by Charles Johnson. London, 1956.

K500. Suhle, Arthur. **Deutsche Münz- und Geldgeschichte von den Anfängen bis zum 15. Jahrhundert.** Berlin, 1955.

K501. Cipolla, Carlo M. **Studi di storia della moneta. V. 1, I movimenti dei cambi in Italia dal secolo XIII al XV.** Pavia, 1948. [Università di Pavia, Studi nelle scienze giuridiche e sociali, 101.]

K502. Hamilton, Earl J. **Money, prices and wages in Valencia, Aragon and Navarre, 1351–1500.** See *VD169*.

K503. Ives, Herbert E. **The Venetian gold ducat and its imitations.** Ed. by Philip Grierson. N.Y., 1954.

Social History

K504. Power, Eileen. "On medieval history as a social study." **Economica,** n.s. 1 (Feb. 1934): 13–29.

K505. Painter, Sidney. **Mediaeval society.** Ithaca, 1951. A pleasantly written, clear series of three essays describing the feudal system and feudal caste, the seignorial system, and the development of towns and commerce.

K506. Coulton, George G., ed. **Life in the Middle Ages.** 4 v. in 1. N.Y., 1930. A rich but miscellaneous collection of extracts from the sources.

K507. Power, Eileen. **Medieval people.** N.Y., 1935. The charm of these six lively essays has long held thousands of readers captive. Subjects are: 1, Bodo, a Frankish peasant in the time of Charlemagne; 2, Marco

Polo; 3, Madame Eglentyne, Chaucer's prioress; 4, The Ménagier's wife (Paris, 14th century); 5, Thomas Betson, a merchant of the staple in the 15th century; 6, Thomas Paycocke of Coggeshall, an Essex clothier in the days of Henry VII. This work is now available in a paperbound edition.

K508. Duby, Georges. **La société au XIe et XIIe siècles dans la région mâconnaise.** Paris, 1953. Review, E. C. Furber, *Speculum,* 30 (Apr. 1955): 272.

K509. Coulton, George G. **Social life in Britain from the Conquest to the Reformation.** N.Y., 1939.

K510. Stenton, Doris M. **English society in the early Middle Ages (1066–1307).** Harmondsworth, Eng., 1951.

K511. Holmes, Urban T. **Daily living in the twelfth century, based on observations of Alexander Neckham in London and Paris.** Madison, Wis., 1952. By following his medieval source carefully, the author manages to bring to the modern reader some of the excitement, wonder, and reality of daily living in the 12th century. Material of this type is an excellent antidote to royal charters, imperial edicts, and papal bulls.

K512. Homans, George C. **English villages of the thirteenth century.** Cambridge, Mass., 1941. An interesting, successful attempt of a sociologist to describe medieval conditions. Review, J. L. Cate, *Speculum,* 17 (July 1942): 420.

K513. Halphen, Louis, Roger Doucet, and others. **Histoire de la société française.** Paris, 1953. A popular survey containing beautiful illustrations.

K514. Evans, Joan. **Life in medieval France.** Rev. ed., N.Y., 1957. Text similar to 1925 edition except for omission of a chapter on medieval art. The new printing provides many exquisite illustrations, some in color.

K515. Faral, Edmond. **La vie quotidienne au temps de Saint Louis.** Paris, [1942].

K516. Strayer, Joseph R. "The laicization of French and English society in the thirteenth century." **Speculum,** 15 (Jan. 1940): 76–86. An explanation of how medieval governments in France and England asserted dominance in fields of major concern to them while willingly leaving other areas as provinces of the church.

K517. Siebert, Ferdinand. **Der Mensch um Dreizehnhundert im Spiegel deutscher Quellen.** Berlin, 1931. Deals chiefly with bourgeois class, emphasizing new beginnings and growing social forces.

K518. Pike, Joseph B., tr. **Frivolities of courtiers and footprints of philosophers, being a translation of the first, second and third books and selections from the seventh and eighth books of the Policraticus of John of Salisbury.** Minneapolis, 1938. The trans-

lator characterizes this section of the *Policraticus* as an encyclopedia of the culture of the age. Among topics here treated are hunting and its abuse, gaming, music, the actor and conjurer of various types, omens, astrology, and an outline of ancient philosophy.

K519. Blum, Jerome. "The rise of serfdom in eastern Europe." **Am. hist. rev.,** 62 (July 1957): 807–36. While declining in the West, serfdom rose in the East, where the nobility was able to establish economic and social control over the peasantry and to control the townsmen.

K520. Verlinden, Charles. **L'esclavage dans l'Europe médiévale.** Bruges, 1955 ff. This promises to be a major contribution for a problem that has long perplexed historians.

K521. Origo, Iris. "The domestic enemy: the eastern slaves in Tuscany in the fourteenth and fifteenth centuries." **Speculum,** 30 (July 1955): 321–66.

K522. Baron, Salo W. **A social and religious history of the Jews.** V. 3–8 (500–1200). 2nd rev. ed., N.Y., 1957–58. A work of major significance; broad in scope, with full bibliographical notes.

K523. Marcus, Jacob R. **The Jew in the medieval world: a source book, 315–1791.** Cincinnati, 1938.

K524. Kisch, Guido. **The Jews in medieval Germany: a study of their legal and social status.** Chicago, 1949. For contrasting opinions about this book see F. H. Cramer, *Speculum,* 25 (Apr. 1950): 274; G. C. Boyce, *Historia judaica,* 12 (Oct. 1950): 159; E. N. Johnson, *Am. hist. rev.,* 56 (Oct. 1950): 88; and Kisch's reply, *ibid.,* 56 (July 1951): 1040.

K525. ——. **Jewry-law in medieval Germany: laws and court decisions concerning Jews.** N.Y., 1949. Review, F. Rosenthal, *Am. hist. rev.,* 55 (July 1950): 962.

K526. ——. "The Jew's function in the mediaeval evolution of economic life." **Historia judaica,** 6 (Apr. 1944): 1–12.

K527. Roscher, Wilhelm. "The status of the Jews in the Middle Ages considered from the standpoint of commercial policy." **Historia judaica,** 6 (Apr. 1944): 13–26.

K528. Neuman, Abraham A. **The Jews in Spain.** See *VD156.*

K529. Emery, Richard W. **The Jews of Perpignan in the thirteenth century: an economic study based on notarial records.** N.Y., 1959. Covers period 1261–87, and devotes much attention to the economic role of the Jews in this area and period.

K530. Sheedy, Anna T. **Bartolus on social conditions in the fourteenth century.** N.Y., 1942.

K531. Jarrett, Bede. **Social theories of the Middle Ages, 1200–1500.** Westminster, Md., 1942.

Cultural History

General Works

K532. Artz, Frederick B. **The mind of the Middle Ages, A.D. 200–1500.** 2nd ed., N.Y., 1954. 3rd ed., 1958. The most recent attempt to survey in one volume medieval learning and cultural interests. The bibliographical notes are full and well presented.

K533. Taylor, Henry O. **The mediaeval mind.** 4th ed., 2 v., N.Y., 1925. Though in need of revision, still a valued survey of medieval intellectual interest.

K534. ——. **The emergence of Christian culture in the West: the classical heritage of the Middle Ages.** N.Y., 1958. Re-issue of a historical classic under a new title; possibly the best and most enduring of Taylor's many works. Contains excellent foreword by Kenneth M. Setton.

K535. Bühler, Johannes. **Die Kultur des Mittelalters.** 2nd ed., Leipzig, 1934. A compact volume containing essays that provide an introduction to the richness of medieval social and cultural history, especially for Germany.

K536. Cohn, Norman. **The pursuit of the millennium.** Fairlawn, N.J., 1957. Belief in the coming of the millennium held a fascination for medieval men and groups, though not always in ways too frequently inferred. This "first comprehensive study of the subject" for the period following 1000 A.D. should be consulted by all interested in medieval eschatology, social and religious history. Review, J. von Rohr, *Am. hist. rev.,* 63 (July 1958): 943.

K537. Rand, Edward K. **Founders of the Middle Ages.** Cambridge, Mass., 1928. Indispensable work of a master. Now available in a paperbound edition (N.Y., 1957).

K538. Laistner, Max L. W. **Thought and letters in western Europe, A.D. 500 to 900.** Rev. ed., London, 1957.

K539. ——. **The intellectual heritage of the early Middle Ages.** Ithaca, 1957.

K540. Dawson, Christopher H. **Medieval essays.** N.Y., 1954. Writing from the point of view of a Roman Catholic, Dawson interprets the Middle Ages with depth of insight and understanding of fundamental issues and presuppositions. From his *Medieval religion* (London, 1934), long out of print, he presents here, together with two previously unpublished ones, essays of much interest on medieval culture.

K541. Schnürer, Gustav. **Kirche und Kultur im Mittelalter.** 2nd ed., 3 v., Paderborn, 1927–29. English tr. of v. 1, Paterson, N.J., 1956. Useful and often stimulating discussion of the Christian contribution in development of medieval culture.

K542. Haskins, Charles H. **The renaissance of the twelfth century.** Cambridge, Mass., 1927. A book of wide and lasting appeal which has been the basis of, as well as a stimulus to, much subsequent scholarship.

K543. Holmes, Urban T. "The idea of a twelfth-century renaissance." **Speculum,** 26 (Oct. 1951): 643–51.

K544. Sanford, Eva M. "The twelfth century — renaissance or proto-renaissance?" **Speculum,** 26 (Oct. 1951): 635–42.

K545. Lopez, Robert S. "Still another renaissance?" **Am. hist. rev.,** 57 (Oct. 1951): 1–21. A plea in behalf of the often maligned tenth century.

K546. Heer, Friedrich. **Aufgang Europas: eine Studie zu den Zusammenhängen zwischen politischer Religiosität, Frömmigkeitsstil und dem Werden Europas im 12. Jahrhundert.** 2 v. Vienna and Zurich, 1949. An important and original work. Review, G. B. Ladner, *Speculum,* 27 (Oct. 1952): 555.

K547. Poole, Reginald L. **illustrations of the history of medieval thought and learning.** 2nd ed., London, 1920.

K548. Lagarde, Georges de. **La naissance de l'esprit laïque au déclin du Moyen Âge.** 6 v. Paris, 1942–48. 3rd rev. ed. of v. 1, Louvain, 1956; 2nd rev. ed. of v. 2, Louvain, 1958. A work of fundamental importance. For criticism of 3rd ed. of v. 1 see G. Post, *Am. hist. rev.,* 64 (Oct. 1958): 145.

K549. Haskins, Charles H. **Studies in mediaeval culture.** Oxford, 1929. 2nd ed., N.Y., 1958. Essays on medieval students, learning, and other topics that appeared previously in various learned journals.

Medieval Philosophy and Thought

K550. Gilson, Etienne. **History of Christian philosophy in the Middle Ages.** N.Y., 1955. Now a standard history. Brief indication of bibliographical sources, and notes on pp. 552–804 serve as a guide to pertinent literature.

K551. Leff, Gordon. **Medieval thought.** Harmondsworth, Eng., 1958. A fresh, well-balanced survey. Brief attention is given to pre-scholastic thought, and the contributions of Arabian and Jewish thinkers are accorded proper consideration. Augustine is well evaluated for his influence on the Middle Ages. The work ends with Ockham.

K552. Steenberghen, Fernand van. **The philosophical movement in the thirteenth century.** Edinburgh, 1955. A series of six succinct, helpful lectures, embodying much learning.

K553. ——. **Aristotle in the West: the origins of Latin Aristotelianism.** Tr. by Leonard Johnston. Louvain, 1955.

K554. Wulf, Maurice M. C. J. de. **Histoire de la philosophie médiévale.** 6th rev. ed., 3 v., Louvain, 1934–47. In its earlier editions had no serious competitors and in this definitive edition remains a work of significance. There are English translations of earlier editions, and the 6th is in process of translation.

K555. Cassidy, Frank P. **Molders of the medieval mind: the influence of the fathers of the church on the medieval schoolmen.** St. Louis, 1944. Brief introduction to the basis of medieval education.

K556. Grabmann, Martin. **Die Geschichte der scholastischen Methode, nach den gedruckten und ungedruckten Quellen.** 2 v. Munich, 1909–11. Reprint, Berlin, 1957. A basic treatise for medieval scholasticism.

K557. ——. **Mittelalterliches Geistesleben: Abhandlung zur Geschichte der Scholastik und Mystik.** 3 v. Munich, 1926–56. Special studies concerning the new Aristotle, translations of philosophical and theological sources, teaching, and the contributions of individuals in respect to scholastic learning.

K558. ——. **I papi del duecento e l'aristotelismo.** 2 v. in 1. Rome, 1941–46. First part examines the prohibitions against Aristotle under Innocent III and Gregory IX; second part deals with the Dominican translator, William of Moerbeke.

K559. Vajda, Georges. **Introduction à la pensée juive du Moyen Âge.** Paris, 1947.

Renaissance Thought and Culture

K560. Ferguson, Wallace K. **The Renaissance in historical thought.** See *T71.*

K561. Bouwsma, William J. **The interpretation of Renaissance humanism.** Washington, 1959. [Service Center for Teachers of History, Publication no. 18.] Well-informed, critical essay on the basic works essential for a study of the Renaissance.

K562. Baron, Hans. **Humanistic and political literature in Florence and Venice at the beginning of the quattrocento: studies in criticism and chronology.** Cambridge, Mass., 1955. Review, E. W. Nelson, *Am. hist. rev.,* 61 (Oct. 1955): 167.

K563. ——. **The crisis of the early Italian Renaissance: civic humanism and republican liberty in an age of classicism and tyranny.** 2 v. Princeton, 1955. See W. K. Ferguson, "The interpretation of Italian humanism: the contribution of Hans Baron," *Journal of the history of ideas,* 19 (Jan. 1958): 14–25. See also reviews, W. K. Ferguson, *Speculum,* 31 (Apr. 1956): 344; M. P. Gilmore, *Am. hist. rev.,* 61 (Apr. 1956): 622.

Political Thought

K564. McIlwain, Charles H. **The growth of political thought in the West: from the Greeks to the end of the Middle Ages.** N.Y., 1932. Best introduction to medieval political theory.

K565. Carlyle, Robert W., and Alexander J. Carlyle. **A history of mediaeval political theory in the West.** 6 v. Edinburgh and London, 1903–36. Indispensable for any serious study of medieval political thought.

K566. Morrall, John B. **Political thought in medieval times.** London, 1958. In spite of certain limitations, this book well meets the requirements for a brief introduction to political thought of the Middle Ages.

K567. Dickinson, John, tr. **The Statesman's book of John of Salisbury, being the fourth, fifth and sixth books and selections from the seventh and eighth books of the Policraticus.** N.Y., 1927. The *Policraticus* is the only important political treatise written before western thought again became familiar with the politics of Aristotle. Parts translated here refer to the prince and the law; the commonwealth, its members, and the administration of justice; the armed band; ambition; tyranny and tyrannicide.

K568. Gilby, Thomas. **The political thought of Thomas Aquinas.** Chicago, 1958.

Schools and Learning

K569. Boyce, Gray C. "American studies in medieval education." **Progress of medieval and Renaissance studies,** 19 (Sep. 1947): 6–30.

K570. Bolgar, R. R. **The classical heritage and its beneficiaries.** Cambridge, Eng., 1954. A history of thought and education; stimulating presentation of broad ideas.

K571. Delhaye, Philippe. "L'organisation scolaire au XIIe siècle." **Traditio,** 5 (1947): 211–68.

K572. Haskins, Charles H. **The rise of universities.** N.Y., 1923. A perennially popular volume. Now available also in a paperbound edition.

K573. Rashdall, Hastings. **The universities of Europe in the Middle Ages.** New ed., 3 v., Oxford, 1936. The standard work, one of enduring value and distinction, especially in this revision by F. M. Powicke and A. B. Emden.

K574. Kibre, Pearl. **The nations in the mediaeval universities.** Cambridge, Mass., 1948. In his review in *Speculum,* 24 (Apr. 1949): 271, Sir Maurice Powicke says this study "will long remain a standard work of reference to be kept beside the standard histories of mediaeval universities in every student's library." Provides information on the characteristics of the nations, their composition and development, their officers and functions.

K575. ——. "Scholarly privileges: their Roman origins and medieval expression." **Am. hist. rev.,** 59 (Apr. 1954): 543–67.

K576. Pegues, Frank. "Royal support of students in the thirteenth century." **Speculum,** 31 (July 1956): 454–62.

K577. ——. "Ecclesiastical provisions for the support of students in the thirteenth century." **Church history,** 26 (Dec. 1957): 307–18.

K578. Jacob, Ernest F. "English university clerks in the later Middle Ages: the problem of maintenance." **Bulletin of the John Rylands Library,** 29 (Feb. 1946): 304–25.

K579. Stelling-Michaud, Sven. **L'université de Bologne et la pénétration des droits romain et canonique en Suisse aux XIIIᵉ et XIVᵉ siècles.** Geneva, 1955. Review, S. Kuttner, *Renaissance news,* 9 (Autumn 1956): 154.

K580. Gabriel, Astrik L. **Student life in Ave Maria College, mediaeval Paris: history and chartulary of the college.** Notre Dame, 1955. Contains numerous documents and some interesting illustrations.

K581. Smith, Cyril E. **The University of Toulouse in the Middle Ages: its origins and growth to 1500 A.D.** Milwaukee, 1958. Well-documented study of a distinguished French university. Includes an important bibliographical essay.

K582. Calasso, Francesco. **Medio Evo del diritto.** Milan, 1954 ff. To be complete in 3 v. Useful for legal developments in medieval Italy. Contains important sections on law schools.

K583. Thompson, James Westfall. **The literacy of the laity in the Middle Ages.** Berkeley, 1939.

K584. Gailbraith, V. H. "The literacy of the medieval English kings." **Proceedings of the British Academy,** 21 (1935): 201–38.

K585. Smalley, Beryl. **The study of the Bible in the Middle Ages.** 2nd ed., Oxford, 1952. An original work of unquestioned value and distinction, based on thorough control of the sources. Contains much information about medieval learning.

K586. Blumenfield, Samuel M. **Master of Troyes: a study of Rashi the educator.** N.Y., 1946. The methods of a great Jewish teacher.

Literature

K587. Hélin, Maurice. **A history of medieval Latin literature.** Tr. by Jean C. Snow. Rev. ed., N.Y., 1949. See A. K. Ziegler, *Catholic historical review,* 38 (Oct. 1952): 346, who provides corrections and calls this "a masterpiece of condensation."

K588. Ghellinck, Joseph de. **Littérature latine au Moyen Âge.** 2 v. Paris, 1939. Covers only to the 12th century.

K589. ——. **L'essor de la littérature latine au XIIᵉ siècle.** 2 v. Brussels and Paris, 1946. Excellent.

K590. Manitius, Maximilianus. **Geschichte der lateinischen Literatur des Mittelalters.** 2 v. Munich, 1911–31. An indispensable reference work.

K591. Curtius, Ernst R. **Europäische Literatur und lateinisches Mittelalter.** Bern, 1948. English tr., by Willard R. Trask, N.Y., 1953. Recognized as a work of exceptional quality; a major contribution to medieval studies.

K592. Courcelle, Pierre. **Histoire littéraire**

des grands invasions germaniques. Paris, 1948.

K593. Raby, Frederic J. E. **A history of Christian Latin poetry.** 2nd ed., Oxford, 1953. The works of Raby are indispensable.

K594. ——. **A history of secular Latin poetry.** 2nd ed., 2 v., Oxford, 1957. The recognized standard work for topics covered. Second edition differs from the first primarily in bibliographical additions.

K595. The Oxford book of medieval Latin verse. Newly selected and ed. by F. J. E. Raby. Oxford, 1959. Although this edition contains more selections and is representative of more authors than the one of 1937, its terminal date is 1350 rather than 1500. Review, *The times literary supplement,* May 22, 1959: 302.

K596. Henshaw, Millett. "A survey of studies in medieval drama, 1933–1950." **Progress of medieval and Renaissance studies,** 21 (Aug. 1951): 7–35. Designed primarily for the student of literature, but contains many references and comments of interest to the cultural historian.

K597. Young, Karl. **The drama of the medieval church.** 2 v. Oxford, 1933. Although Young is descriptive in approach, these two volumes contain great riches for the student of medieval life and culture.

K598. Chambers, Edmund K. **The mediaeval stage.** 2 v. Oxford, 1903.

K599. Brittain, Fred. **The medieval Latin and romance lyric to A.D. 1300.** Cambridge, Eng., 1937.

K600. Allen, Philip S., and Howard Mumford Jones. **The Romanesque lyric: studies in its background and development from Petronius to The Cambridge songs, 50–1050.** Chapel Hill, 1928. A rich and rewarding book that provides insight into the world of the early Middle Ages through literature. Contains copious extracts from literary monuments in the original language and in translation.

K601. Holmes, Urban T. **A history of Old French literature, from the origins to 1300.** N.Y., 1937. Emphasis is on facts and dates rather than on critical study. Designed as an introduction to medieval French literature for English-speaking students.

K602. Ehrismann, Gustav. **Geschichte der deutschen Literatur bis zur Ausgang des Mittelalters.** 2 v. in 4. Munich, 1918–35. Excellent as introduction and reference for medieval German literature.

K603. Baur, Frank, and others, eds. **Geschiedenis van de letterkunde der Nederlanden.** Hertogenbosch, Neth., 1939 ff. [1, *De letterkunde van de middeleeuwen tot omstreeks 1300; 2, De middelnederlandsche letterkunde van omstreeks 1300 tot de Renaissance.*]

K604. Viscardi, Antonio. **Le origini.** Milan,

1939. [Storia letteraria d'Italia, 3rd ed., 1.] Supplements rather than supersedes corresponding volume of second edition of *Storia letteraria d'Italia* by Francesco Novati and Angelo Monteverdi (Milan, 1925).

K605. Valency, Maurice. **In praise of love: an introduction to the love-poetry of the Renaissance.** N.Y., 1958. Convenient, timely introduction to the complex manifestations of courtly love, from the Middle Ages through the time of Dante. Primarily important for the literary and social historian. Contains a useful, though uncritical, selective bibliography.

Art, Architecture, and Music

K606. Propyläen-Kunstgeschichte. 16 v. Berlin, 1923–29. V. 5–10 cover the Middle Ages and Renaissance.

K607. Morey, Charles R. **Mediaeval art.** N.Y., 1942. This beautiful book is the result of a lifetime of study, teaching, and reflection by a recognized peer among art historians.

K608. Mâle, Émile. **Art et artistes du Moyen Âge.** Paris, 1927.

K609. Kendrick, Thomas D. **Anglo-Saxon art to A.D. 900.** London, 1938.

K610. Rice, D. Talbot. **English art, 871–1100.** Oxford, 1952. [The Oxford history of English art, 2.]

K611. Boase, Thomas S. R. **English art, 1100–1216.** Oxford, 1953. [The Oxford history of English art, 3.]

K612. Brieger, P. **English art, 1216–1307.** Oxford, 1957. [The Oxford history of English art, 4.]

K613. Evans, Joan. **English art, 1307–1461.** Oxford, 1949. [The Oxford history of English art, 5.]

K614. Salzman, Louis F. **Building in England, down to 1540: a documentary history.** Oxford, 1952. Consideration is given to actual process of construction, masons and architects, organization of workers, wages, materials, and tools. An excellent selection of original documents is included.

K615. Mâle, Émile. **Religious art from the twelfth to the eighteenth century.** N.Y., 1949.

K616. ——. **Religious art in France, XIII century: a study in mediaeval iconography and its sources of inspiration.** Tr. by Dora Nussey. London, 1913. A work of remarkable richness.

K617. Evans, Joan. **Art in mediaeval France, 987–1498.** London and N.Y., 1948. Good, non-technical introduction to medieval French art. Contains well-chosen illustrations.

K618. Abbot Suger on the abbey church of St. Denis and its art treasures. Ed. and tr. by Erwin Panofsky. Princeton, 1946. Contains good introduction dealing with Suger and his place in the 12th century.

K619. Simson, Otto G. von. **The Gothic cathedral: the origins of Gothic architecture and the medieval concept of order.** London, 1956.

K620. Reese, Gustave. **Music in the Middle Ages.** N.Y., 1940.

K621. Harrison, Frank L. **Music in medieval Britain.** London, 1958.

BIOGRAPHIES

K622. McCann, Justin. **Saint Benedict.** London, 1937.

K623. Thompson, A. Hamilton, ed. **Bede, his life, times and writings: essays in commemoration of the twelfth centenary of his death.** Oxford, 1935. Essays on Bede, his writings, his library, and on Wearmouth and Jarrow.

K624. Duckett, Eleanor S. **Alcuin, friend of Charlemagne: his world and his work.** N.Y., 1951. Useful introduction.

K625. Kleinclausz, Arthur J. **Alcuin.** Paris, 1948. The best scholarly biography.

K626. ——. **Charlemagne.** Paris, 1934.

K627. ——. **Eginhard.** Paris, 1942.

K628. Stenton, Frank M. **William the Conqueror.** N.Y., 1908.

K629. Macdonald, Allan J. **Lanfranc: a study of his life, work and writing.** London, 1926.

K630. ——. **Hildebrand: a life of Gregory VII.** London, 1932.

K631. Yewdale, Ralph B. **Bohemond I, prince of Antioch.** Princeton, 1924.

K632. Andressohn, John C. **The ancestry and life of Godfrey of Bouillon.** Bloomington, Ind., 1947.

K633. Nicholson, Robert L. **Joscelyn I, prince of Edessa.** Urbana, Ill., 1954.

K634. ——. **Tancred: a study of his career and work in their relation to the First Crusade and the establishment of the Latin states in Syria and Palestine.** Chicago, 1940.

K635. Slaughter, Gertrude. **Saladin.** N.Y., 1955. "A true and just picture." H. A. R. Gibb. *Speculum,* 32 (July 1957): 614.

K636. Bland, C. C. Swinton, tr. **The autobiography of Guibert, abbot of Nogent-sous-Coucy.** London, [1926]. Living between 1053 and 1124, Guibert belongs to the great age of the crusades, monastic revival, and intellectual renaissance, as well as one of economic growth and expansion.

K637. Williams, Watkin. **St. Bernard of Clairvaux.** Manchester, 1935. A magnificent study not only of Bernard, but also of much of the 12th century before 1150.

K638. Commission de l'Histoire de l'Ordre de Cîteaux. **Bernard de Clairvaux.** Paris, 1953. Although written under Cistercians and thus an "official" biography, this large work has much to commend it.

K639. Calmette, Joseph, and Henri David. **Saint Bernard.** Paris, 1953.

K640. James, Bruno S. **Saint Bernard of Clairvaux.** N.Y., [1957].

K641. Aubert, Marcel. **Suger (1081–1151).** Rouen, 1950.

K642. Greenway, George W. **Arnold of Brescia.** Cambridge, Eng., 1931.

K643. Salzmann, Louis F. **Henry II.** Boston and N.Y., 1914.

K644. Walker, Curtis H. **Eleanor of Aquitaine.** Chapel Hill, 1950.

K645. Kendall, Paul M. **Richard the Third.** London, 1955.

K646. Henderson, Philip. **Richard Coeur de Lion.** London, 1958.

K647. Painter, Sidney. **William Marshal, knight-errant, baron and regent of England.** Baltimore, 1933.

K648. Scammell, Geoffrey V. **Hugh de Puiset, bishop of Durham.** Cambridge, Eng., 1956. Review, S. Painter, *Speculum,* 32 (Apr. 1957): 396.

K649. Poole, Austin L. **Henry the Lion.** Oxford, 1912.

K650. Appleby, John T. **John, king of England.** N.Y., 1959. A popular biography based primarily on readings in contemporary chronicles.

K651. Ellis, Clarence. **Hubert de Burgh: a study in constancy.** London, 1952.

K652. Douie, Decima L. **Archbishop Pecham.** Oxford, 1952.

K653. Bémont, Charles. **Simon de Montfort, earl of Leicester, 1208–1265.** Tr. by E. F. Jacob. New ed., Oxford, 1930.

K654. Vicaire, Marie H. **Histoire de Saint Dominique.** 2 v. Paris, 1957. [1, *Un homme évangélique;* 2, *Au coeur de l'église.*] "A full-length, critical biography . . . probably definitive." W. A. Hinnebusch, *Speculum,* 34 (Apr. 1959): 337.

K655. Elliott-Binns, Leonard. **Innocent III.** London, 1931. Brief but useful introduction.

K656. Jörgensen, Johannes. **Saint Francis of Assisi: a biography.** N.Y., 1912.

K657. Sabatier, Paul. **Vie de S. François d'Assise.** Definitive ed., Paris, 1931. Tr. by Louise S. Houghton, *Life of St. Francis of Assisi,* London, 1894. Many reprints.

K658. Mandonnet, Pierre. **Saint Dominique: l'idée, l'homme et l'oeuvre.** 2 v. Paris, 1938.

K659. Powicke, Sir Frederick M. **Stephen Langton.** Oxford, 1928.

K660. Bailly, Auguste. **Saint Louis.** Paris, 1949.

K661. Painter, Sidney. **The scourge of the clergy, Peter of Dreux, duke of Brittany.** Baltimore, 1937.

K662. Kantorowicz, Ernst. **Kaiser Friedrich der Zweite.** 4th ed., 2 v., Berlin, 1931–36. Authorized English version, by E. O. Lorimer, *Frederick the Second, 1194–1250,* N.Y., 1931; reprint, 1957. A classic. V. 2 of the German edition is important for supple-

mentary notes not included in the English version.

K663. Masson, Georgina. **Frederick II of Hohenstaufen.** London, 1957.

K664. Caggese, Romolo. **Roberto d'Angiò e i suoi tempi.** 2 v. Florence, 1922–30.

K665. Grabmann, Martin. **Thomas Aquinas, his personality and thought.** Tr. by Virgil Michel. N.Y., 1928.

K666. Boase, Thomas S. R. **Boniface VIII.** London, 1933.

K667. Vaughan, Richard. **Matthew Paris.** Cambridge, Eng., 1958. Critical study of one of the most renowned English historians (d. 1259), who knew the great of his day and wrote about them and also the seamier side of life.

K668. Denholm-Young, Noël. **Richard of Cornwall.** Oxford, 1947.

K669. Johnstone, Hilda. **Edward of Carnavon, 1284–1307.** Manchester, 1947.

K670. Mackenzie, Agnes M. **Robert Bruce, king of Scots.** London, 1934.

K671. Piur, Paul. **Cola di Rienzo.** See *VE52.*

K672. Origo, Iris. **The merchant of Prato: Francesco di Marco Datini, 1335–1410.** N.Y., 1957. Detailed, scholarly, readable biography of a self-made man of the later Middle Ages.

K673. Bellonci, Maria. **A prince of Mantua: the life and times of Vincenzo Gonzaga.** Tr. by Stuart Hood. N.Y., 1956.

K674. Brion, Marcel. **Laurent le Magnifique.** Paris, 1937.

K675. Bignami, Luigi. **Francesco Sforza.** Milan, 1937.

K676. Vischer, Melchior. **Jan Hus, sein Leben und seine Zeit.** 2 v. Frankfurt-am-Main, 1940.

K677. Lang, Andrew. **The maid of France.** 3rd ed., London, 1938.

K678. Hilliger, Benno. **Jeanne d'Arc: das Geheimnis ihrer Sendung.** 4th ed., Freiburg im Breisgau, 1949. A small, scholarly, beautifully written book in which the author occasionally assumes the privileges of the novelist.

K679. Fabre, Lucien. **Joan of Arc.** Tr. by Gerard Hopkins. N.Y., 1954.

K680. Stolpe, Sven. **The maid of Orleans.** Tr. by Eric Lewenhaupt. N.Y., 1956.

K681. Champion, Pierre. **Louis XI.** Rev. ed., 2 v., Paris, 1936.

K682. Man, Hendrik de. **Jacques Coeur: der königliche Kaufmann.** Bern, 1950.

K683. Kerr, Albert B. **Jacques Coeur, merchant prince of the Middle Ages.** N.Y., 1927.

K684. Kendall, Paul M. **Warwick the kingmaker.** London, 1957.

K685. Toudouze, G. G. **Anne de Bretagne, duchesse et reine.** New ed., Paris, 1950.

K686. Bennett, Henry S. **Six medieval men and women.** Cambridge, Eng., 1955.

Essays on Humphrey, duke of Gloucester; Sir John Fastolf; Thomas Hoccleve; Margaret Paston; Margery Kempe; and Richard Bradwater.

K687. Morison, Samuel E. **Admiral of the Ocean Sea: a life of Christopher Columbus.** See *U277*.

UNIVERSITY, ACADEMY, AND SOCIETY PUBLICATIONS

See Section J.

PERIODICALS

Periodical literature for the history of medieval Europe is rich and varied. In addition to publications listed below, reference should be made to those noted in Section J.

K688. Analecta bollandiana. Brussels, 1882 ff. (Irregular quarterly.)

K689. Antonianum. Rome, 1926 ff. (Quarterly.)

K690. Archiv für Kulturgeschichte. Berlin, etc., 1903 ff. (Quarterly.)

K691. Archives d'histoire doctrinale et littéraire du Moyen Âge. Paris, 1927 ff. (Annual.)

K692. Bulletin Du Cange: archivum latinitatis medii aevi. Paris, 1924 ff. (Quarterly.)

K693. Beiträge zur Geschichte der Philosophie und Theologie des Mittelalters: Texte und Untersuchungen. Münster, 1895–1942, 1952 ff. (Irregular.)

K694. Bibliothèque de l'École des Chartes. Paris, 1839 ff. (Irregular.)

K695. Cahiers de civilisation médiévale. Poitiers, 1958 ff. (Quarterly.)

K696. Classica et mediaevalia. Copenhagen, 1938 ff. (Semiannual.)

K697. Deutsches Archiv für Erforschung des Mittelalters. Marburg, 1937 ff. (Semiannual; title varies.)

K698. Franziskanische Studien. Münster, 1914–43, 1949 ff. (Quarterly.)

K699. Humanisme et renaissance. Paris, 1934–40. *Bibliothèque d'humanisme et renaissance,* 1941 ff. (Quarterly.)

K700. Latomus. Brussels, 1937 ff. (Quarterly.)

K701. Medievalia et humanistica. Boulder, Colo., 1943 ff. (Annual.)

K702. Medium Aevum. Oxford, 1932 ff. (3 nos. per year.)

K703. Recherches de théologie ancienne et médiévale. Louvain, 1929–40, 1946 ff. (Semiannual.)

K704. Revue belge de philologie et d'histoire. Brussels, 1922 ff. (Quarterly.)

K705. Revue bénédictine. Maredsous, 1884 ff. (Quarterly.)

K706. Revue d'histoire ecclésiastique. Louvain, 1900 ff. (Quarterly.)

K707. Revue du Moyen Âge latin. Lyons and Strasbourg, 1945 ff. (Quarterly.)

K708. Traditio. N.Y., 1943 ff. (Annual.)

K709. Zeitschrift der Savigny-Stiftung für Rechtsgeschichte. Weimar, 1880 ff. (Annual.)

K710. Zeitschrift für deutsches Altertum und deutsche Litteratur. Berlin, etc., 1841 ff. (Title and frequency vary.)

SECTION L

The Byzantine Empire

KENNETH M. SETTON *

The study of Byzantine history developed as a branch of Greek classical scholarship, being detached as a separate discipline largely through the perception and publications of Hieronymus Wolf (1516–80), the librarian of the Fuggers in Augsburg. Wolf's successors were Xylander (Holzmann), Hoeschel, and Leunclavius (Löwenklau) in Germany; Petavius (Petau) in France; Meursius (van Meurs) in Holland and Denmark; and the 17th century Greek librarians of the Vatican, N. Alamannus and L. Allatius, in Italy. Byzantine studies were much advanced by the historical and intellectual interests which Louis XIV and his minister, Colbert, promoted in France; and such outstanding scholars as Fabrot, Goar, Labbe, Poussines, Combéfis, and, above all, Du Cange contributed to the formation of the first great corpus of Byzantine writers, especially historians (Paris, 1645–1711). Their texts have been reprinted several times. For contents see **(L1)** August Potthast, **Wegweiser durch die Geschichtswerke des europäischen Mittelalters** (2 v., Berlin, 1896), v. 1, pp. xlvi–xlvii. For the individual writers see **(L2)** Karl Krumbacher, **Geschichte der byzantinischen Litteratur** (2nd ed., Munich, 1897); **(L3)** Gyula Moravcsik, **Byzantinoturcica: v. 1, Die byzantinischen Quellen der Geschichte der Türkvölker** (Budapest, 1942); and **(L4)** Maria E. Colonna, **Gli storici bizantini dal IV al XV secolo: v. 1, Storici profani** (Naples, 1956).

Charles DuCange made especially noteworthy contributions to Byzantine history, lexicography, and numismatics, as well as to the topography of Constantinople. His work was carried on by Mabillon in Byzantine diplomatics and de Montfaucon in palaeography. Although some valuable work was done in the 18th century, interest in Byzantine civilization suffered a severe decline in the era of the so-called Enlightenment, with Byzantium being held up to sustained opprobrium by Gibbon in his *Decline and fall*. Early in the 19th century, however, Barthold G. Niebuhr initiated the **(L5) Corpus scriptorum historiae byzantinae** (50 v., Bonn, 1828–97), which reprinted the texts of the Paris corpus, but supplied a fuller and more manageable collection. Then began also the long

* Subsections compiled by contributors other than Professor Setton are so indicated.

and varied series of works by Fallmerayer, Tafel, Miklosich, Müller, Thomas, Hopf, Zachariä von Lingenthal, and others. Particular mention should be made of George Finlay's popular **(L6) A history of Greece, from its conquest by the Romans to the present time**, ed. by Henry F. Tozer (7 v., Oxford, 1877). Later in the century Byzantine studies received the impetus which still maintains them from the works of Alfred Rambaud and Gustave Schlumberger in France, Vasilii G. Vasilievskii and Th. I. Uspenskii in Russia, Karl Krumbacher in Germany, and Spyridon P. Lampros in Greece. In more recent years there have been Charles Diehl in Paris, Louis Bréhier in Clermont-Ferrand, Nicolae Iorga in Bucharest, Cardinal Giovanni Mercati in Rome, Franz Dölger in Munich, Henri Grégoire in Brussels, Georg Ostrogorsky in Belgrade, and the Augustinians of the Assumption, now in Paris. The Russian scholar Alexander A. Vasiliev has been the Manuel Chrysoloras of Byzantine studies in the United States; and in the last generation a number of U. S. scholars have made contributions to the history of Byzantium and of Byzantine relations with Islam, the Crusades, and the Slavonic world.

BIBLIOGRAPHIES

L7. Cambridge medieval history. (See *J43*.) V. 4, pp. 779–898.

L8. Paetow, Louis J. **A guide to the study of medieval history.** See *J1*.

L9. Vasiliev, Alexander A. **History of the Byzantine empire, 324–1453.** 2nd ed., Madison, Wis., 1952. This and the following works contain valuable bibliographies.

L10. Ostrogorsky, George. **History of the Byzantine state.** Tr. by Joan Hussey. Oxford, 1956.

L11. Diehl, Charles. **Byzantium: greatness and decline.** Tr. by Naomi Walford. New Brunswick, N.J., 1957. See the bibliography by Peter Charanis, pp. 301–57.

L12. Association Internationale des Études Byzantines. **Dix années d'études byzantines: bibliographie internationale, 1939–1948.** Paris, 1949.

L13. Dölger, Franz, and Alfons M. Schneider. **Byzanz.** Bern, 1952. Best catalog of recent work on Byzantium.

L14. Byzantinische Zeitschrift. See *L397*. From its foundation in 1892 to the present this periodical has tried to list all significant works dealing with every aspect of Byzantine history and civilization.

LIBRARIES AND MUSEUMS
(Norman P. Zacour)

Among the chief libraries and museums are: Gennadeion, The American School of Classical Studies, Athens; Finlay Library of medieval and modern Greece in the Library of the British School at Athens, Athens and London; Library of the Greek Orthodox Patriarchate of Alexandria; Biblioteca Academiei Republicii Populare Romîne, Bucha-

rest; Library of the Ecumenical Patriarchate, Istanbul; Dumbarton Oaks Research Library and Collection, Washington; The Byzantine Museum, Athens; Benaki Museum, Athens; Coptic Museum, Cairo; Ayasofia (Santa Sophia) Museum, Istanbul; Museum of Classical Antiquities, Istanbul; Mozaik Müzesi, Istanbul; and Yedikule Müzesi, Istanbul.

WORKS OF REFERENCE
(Norman P. Zacour)

L15. Cabrol, Fernand, and others. **Dictionnaire d'archéologie chrétienne et de liturgie.** 15 v. Paris, 1903–53.

L16. Dictionnaire de droit canonique. Paris, 1924 ff.

L17. Dictionnaire de théologie catholique. 15 v. in 30. Paris, 1908–50.

L18. Dictionnaire d'histoire et de géographie ecclésiastiques. Paris, 1912 ff.

L19. Reallexikon für Antike und Christentum. Ed. by Theodor Klauser. Stuttgart, 1950 ff.

L20. Houtsma, M. T., and others. **The encyclopaedia of Islam.** 4 v. and supplement, Leiden and London, 1908–38. New ed., 1954 ff.

GEOGRAPHIES, GAZETTEERS, AND ATLASES
(Norman P. Zacour)

L21. Spruner-Menke Hand-Atlas für die Geschichte des Mittelalters und der neueren Zeit. See *T24*.

L22. Philippson, Alfred. **Das byzantinische Reich als geographische Erscheinung.** Leiden, 1939.

L23. Honigmann, Ernst. **Die Ostgrenze des byzantinischen Reiches von 363 bis 1071 nach**

griechischen, arabischen, syrischen und armenischen Quellen. Brussels, 1935.

L24. Janin, Raymond. **La géographie ecclésiastique de l'empire byzantin.** Pt. 1, Le siège de Constantinople et le patriarcat oecuménique. V. 3, Les églises et les monastères. Paris, 1953.

L25. ——. **Constantinople byzantine: développement urbain et répertoire topographique.** Paris, 1950.

ANTHROPOLOGICAL AND DEMOGRAPHIC STUDIES

(Ihor Ševčenko)

The following list contains works which provide bibliographical information, sometimes in preference to more fundamental studies.

L26. Dieterich, Karl. **Byzantinische Quellen zur Länder- und Völkerkunde (5.–15. Jhd.).** 2 v. Leipzig, 1912. Contains translated passages from Byzantine authors.

L27. Mayer, Robert. **Byzantion-Konstantinupolis-Istanbul: eine genetische Stadtgeographie.** Vienna, 1943. [Akademie der Wissenschaften, Vienna, Philosophisch-historische Klasse, Denkschriften, 71.] Contains rich bibliography.

L28. Schneider, Alfons M. "Die Bevölkerung Konstantinopels im XV. Jahrhundert." Nachrichten der Akademie der Wissenschaften in Göttingen, Philosophisch-historische Klasse, 9 (1949): 234–44.

L29. Barišič, Franjo, and others. **Vizantiski izvori za istoriju naroda Jugoslavije.** [Byzantine sources for the history of the south Slavs.] V. 1. Belgrade, 1955. An exemplary collection of texts (5th to 9th century), with comments, relating to Slavic invasions and settlements. Excellent bibliography.

L30. Vasmer, Max. **Die Slaven in Griechenland.** Berlin, 1941. Fundamental work on more than 1,200 Slavic place names in Greece.

L31. Lemerle, Paul. "Invasions et migrations dans les Balkans depuis la fin de l'époque romaine jusqu'au VIIIᵉ siècle." Revue historique, 121 (Apr.-June 1954): 265–308. Rich bibliography.

L32. Zakythinos, Denis (Dionysios) A. **Hoi Slaboi en Helladi.** [The Slavs in Greece.] Athens, 1945.

L33. Lipšic, E. E. **Byzanz und die Slaven: Beiträge zur byzantinischen Geschichte des 6.–9. Jahrhunderts.** Tr. from Russian. Weimar, 1951.

L34. Dölger, Franz. **Ein Fall slavischer Einsiedlung im Hinterland von Thessalonike im 10. Jahrhundert.** Munich, 1952. Contains recent bibliography.

L35. Kyriakidēs, Stilpon P. **The northern ethnological boundaries of Hellenism.** Thessaloníki, 1955.

L36. Pallas, D. I. "Ta archaiologika tek-

mēria tēs kathodou tōn barbarōn eis tēn Hellada." [The archaeological evidence of the descent of the barbarians on Greece.] Hellenika, 14 (1955): 87–105.

L37. Babinger, Franz C. **Beiträge zur Frühgeschichte der Türkenherrschaft in Rumelien (14.–15. Jahrhundert).** See *M140.*

L38. Cahen, Claude. "Le problème ethnique en Anatolie." Cahiers d'histoire mondiale, 2 (1954): 347–62.

L39. Wächter, Albert H. **Der Verfall des Griechentums in Kleinasien im XIV. Jahrhundert.** Leipzig, 1902.

L40. Starr, Joshua. **The Jews in the Byzantine empire, 641–1204.** Athens, 1939.

L41. ——. **Romania: the Jewries of the Levant after the fourth crusade.** Paris, 1949.

LINGUISTIC WORKS

(Ihor Ševčenko)

L42. Du Cange, Charles. **Glossarium ad scriptores mediae et infimae graecitatis.** 2 v. Reprint, Paris, 1943. Still indispensable.

L43. Sophocles, Evangelinus A. **Greek lexicon of the Roman and Byzantine periods (from B.C. 146 to A.D. 1100).** Boston, 1870. Reprint, 1957.

L44. Dēmētrakou, D. **Mega lexikon tēs hellēnikēs glōssēs.** [Great dictionary of the Greek language.] 9 v. Athens, 1933–51. Includes ancient Byzantine and modern lexical material derived from previous dictionaries.

L45. **Historikon lexikon tēs neas Hellēnikēs, tēs te koinēs homiloumenēs kai tōn idiōmatōn.** [Historical dictionary of modern Greek, as commonly spoken and its idioms.] Athens, 1933 ff. A monumental work now in progress.

L46. Jannaris, Anthony N. **An historical Greek grammar.** London, 1897.

L47. Hatzidakis, Geōrgios N. **Einleitung in die neugriechische Grammatik.** Leipzig, 1892.

L48. Schwyzer, Eduard. **Griechische Grammatik.** 3 v. Munich, 1939–53. Includes bibliographies and excellent index.

L49. Palmer, Leonard R. **A grammar of the post-Ptolemaic papyri.** V. 1, pt. 1. London, 1945. Unfortunately not continued.

L50. Tabachovitz, David. **Études sur le grec de la basse époque.** Uppsala, Swe., 1943.

L51. Triantaphyllidēs, Manolēs A. **Neoellēnikē grammatikē.** V. 1, Historikē eisagōgē. [Modern Greek grammar. Historical introduction.] Athens, 1938.

L52. Psaltes, Stamatios B. **Grammatik der byzantinischen Chroniken.** Göttingen, 1913.

L53. Linnér, Sture. **Syntaktische und lexikalische Studien zur Historia lausiaca des Palladios.** Uppsala, 1943.

L54. Böhlig, Gertrud R. **Untersuchungen zum rhetorischen Sprachgebrauch der Byzantiner, mit besonderer Berücksichtigung**

der Schriften des Michael Psellos. Berlin, 1956. Good grammar of "Attic" mannerisms applicable not only to Psellos, but also to earlier and later authors.

L55. Stepski Doliwa, Stephanie von. **Studien zur Syntax des byzantinischen Historikers Georgios Phrantzes.** Munich, 1935. A solid work useful for all late Byzantine historians.

Historical studies include the following (*L56–60*).

L56. Higgins, Martin J. "The renaissance of the first century and the origin of standard late Greek." **Traditio,** 3 (1945): 49–100.

L57. Costas, Procope S. **An outline of the history of the Greek language with particular emphasis on the Koine and the subsequent stages.** Chicago, 1936.

L58. Debrunner, Albert. **Geschichte der griechischen Sprache. V. 2, Grundfragen und Grundzüge des nachklassischen Griechisches.** Berlin, 1954.

L59. Zilliacus, Henrik. **Zum Kampf der Weltsprachen im oströmischen Reich.** Helsinki, 1935.

L60. Dieterich, Karl. **Untersuchungen zur Geschichte der griechischen Sprache von der hellenistischen Zeit bis zum 10. Jahrh. n. Chr.** Leipzig, 1898. Old, but not yet replaced.

PRINTED COLLECTIONS OF SOURCES
(*Glanville Downey*)

The sources for Byzantine history are widely scattered in periodicals and other works, but certain collections may be noted for their importance.

L61. Acta sanctorum. Ed. by Jean Bollandus and others. Antwerp and Brussels, 1643 ff. 3rd ed., Paris, 1863 ff. The indispensable collection of hagiographical texts.

L62. Analecta bollandiana. Brussels, 1882 ff. (Irregular quarterly.) Contains supplementary editions of *L61*.

L63. Brightman, Frank E., ed. **Liturgies eastern and western. V. 1, Eastern liturgies.** Oxford, 1896. Best single collection of Byzantine liturgical texts.

L64. Corpus scriptorum Christianorum orientalium. Louvain, Rome, etc., 1903 ff. Ecclesiastical documents in Arabic, Coptic, Ethiopic, and Syriac. Includes historical chronicles, etc. Translations in French, English, and Latin.

L65. Corpus scriptorum ecclesiasticorum latinorum. Vienna, 1866 ff. The "Vienna Corpus." Includes some Latin sources important for Byzantine history.

L66. Corpus scriptorum historiae byzantinae. See *L5*. The "Bonn Corpus." Still the most important single collection of sources, though some of the texts have been superseded by modern editions.

L67. Cramer, John A., ed. **Anecdota graeca e codd. manuscriptis bibliothecarum oxoniensium.** 4 v. Oxford, 1835–37.

L68. ——, ed. **Anecdota graeca e codd. manuscriptis bibliothecae regiae parisiensis.** 4 v. Oxford, 1839–41. This and *L67* contain valuable texts from collections in Oxford and Paris.

L69. Dölger, Franz, ed. **Corpus der griechischen Urkunden des Mittelalters und der neueren Zeit.** Pt. A, **Regesten der Kaiserurkunden des oströmischen Reiches von 565–1453.** 3 v. Munich and Berlin, 1924–32.

L70. Goar, Jacobus, ed. **Euchologion sive rituale graecorum complectens ritus et ordines divinae liturgiae, officiorum, sacramentorum.** Paris, 1647. Still the best collection of offices and prayers of the Byzantine church.

L71. Grumel, Venance, ed. **Les regestes des actes du patriarcat de Constantinople. V. 1, Les actes des patriarches.** Fasc. 1–2, **Les regestes de 381 à 1043.** Bucharest, 1932–36. Unfinished but valuable collection.

L72. Heimbach, Wilhelm E., ed. **Basilicorum libri LX.** 6 v. Leipzig, 1833–70. Still the basic text for Byzantine law, providing texts later modified and taken over into other collections. The name is that of the original collection, compiled under the emperors Basil I and Leo VI.

L73. Mai, Angelo, ed. **Scriptorum veterum nova collectio.** 10 v. Rome, 1825–38. This and *L74–75* are important publications of texts in the Vatican library.

L74. ——, ed. **Spicilegium romanum.** 10 v. Rome, 1839–44.

L75. ——, ed. **Novae patrum bibliothecae.** 8 v. Rome, 1852–71.

L76. Mansi, Johannes D., ed. **Sacrorum conciliorum nova et amplissima collectio.** 31 v. Florence and Venice, 1759–98. Reprint, Paris, 1901–06. Principal collection of the acts of the councils and related documents.

L77. Migne, Jacques P., ed. **Patrologiae cursus completus, series graeca.** 161 v. in 166. Paris, 1857–66. Largest single collection of Byzantine ecclesiastical material; texts often antiquated.

L78. Miklosich, Franz, and Josef Müller, eds. **Acta et diplomata graeca medii aevi sacra et profana.** 6 v. Vienna, 1860–90. Largest collection thus far published of material of this type; includes both official documents and private texts.

L79. Mommsen, Theodor, and others, eds. **Corpus iuris civilis.** 3 v. Berlin, 1872–95.

L80. Mommsen, Theodor, and Paul M. Meyer, eds. **Theodosiani libri XVI.** See *1257* and *258*.

L81. Müller, Karl, ed. **Fragmenta historicorum graecorum.** 5 v. Paris, 1841–83.

L82. Petit, Louis, and Vasilii E. Regel, eds. **Actes de l'Athos.** 7 v. St. Petersburg (Leningrad), 1903–15.

L83. Lemerle, Paul, ed. **Actes de Kutlumus.** 2 v. Paris, 1945–46. [Archives de l'Athos, 2.]

L84. Rouillard, Germaine, and others, eds. **Actes de Lavra.** 2 v. Paris, 1937. [Archives de l'Athos, 1.]

L85. Dölger, Franz. **Aus den Schatzkammern des heiligen Berges.** 2 v. Munich, 1948.

L86. Recueil des historiens des croisades. 14 v. Paris, 1841–1906. [Académie des Inscriptions et Belles-lettres.]

L87. Sathas, Kōnstantinos N., ed. **Mesaiōnikē bibliothēkē: bibliotheca graeca medii aevi.** 7 v. Venice and Paris, 1872–94. This and the following work contain valuable collections of previously unpublished texts bearing on various aspects of Byzantine history.

L88. ———, ed. **Mnēmeia hellēnikēs historias: documents inédits relatifs à l'histoire de la Grèce au Moyen-Âge.** See *W1123.*

L89. Schwartz, Eduard, ed. **Acta conciliorum oecumenicorum.** 4 v. in 12. Berlin, 1914–40. A modern edition of the councils of Ephesus and Chalcedon, superseding that of Mansi.

L90. Zachariä von Lingenthal, Karl E., ed. **Collectio librorum juris graeco-romani ineditorum.** Leipzig, 1852.

L91. Zachariä von Lingenthal, Karl E., ed. **Jus graeco-romanum.** 7 pts. Leipzig, 1856–84. Continuation of the above. One of the principal collections of Byzantine law.

L92. Regel, Vasilii E., ed. **Analecta byzantino-russica.** St. Petersburg (Leningrad), 1891. Relations between Byzantium and Russia, conversion of the Russians to Christianity, and early history of the church in Russia.

L93. Patrologia orientalis. Paris, 1907 ff. Collection of ecclesiastical documents and historical chronicles in various oriental languages, with translations in French, English, and Latin.

L94. Riant, Paul E. D., and Fernand de Mély, eds. **Exuviae sacrae Constantinopolitanae.** 3 v. Geneva, 1877–1904. Collection of documents concerning the sacred relics taken to Europe by members of the fourth crusade after the capture of Constantinople in 1204, and other texts bearing on the Latin empire of Constantinople.

L95. Matranga, Pietro, ed. **Anecdota graeca.** 2 v. Rome, 1850. Important collection of Byzantine documents.

L96. Boissevain, Ursul P., Carl G. de Boor, and Theodor Büttner-Wobst, eds. **Excerpta historica iussu imp. Constantini Porphyrogeniti confecta.** 4 v. Berlin, 1903–06. Important collection of excerpts from historical texts, all the more valuable since in many cases the originals are lost.

L97. Dölger, Franz, ed. **Sechs byzantinische Praktika des 14. Jahrhunderts für** das Athoskloster Iberon. Munich, 1949.

There does not yet exist any comprehensive collection of Byzantine inscriptions. Characteristic and important texts may be found in the following (*L98–101*).

L98. Corpus inscriptionum graecarum. V. 4. Berlin, 1877.

L99. Grégoire, Henri, ed. **Recueil des inscriptions grecques chrétiennes d'Asie Mineure.** Paris, 1922.

L100. Millet, Gabriel, Jean Pargoire, and Louis Petit, eds. **Recueil des inscriptions chrétiennes de l'Athos.** Paris, 1904.

L101. Lietzmann, Hans, Nikos A. Beēs, and G. Sotiriu, eds. **Corpus der griechisch-christlichen Inschriften von Hellas.** V. 1, pt. 1. Athens, 1941. Includes copious bibliography.

Several collections of translations which include Byzantine texts have been published. The two following are completed collections.

L102. The library of the Palestine Pilgrims' Text Society. 14 v. London, 1885–97.

L103. A select library of the Nicene and post-Nicene fathers. 2nd ser., 14 v., N.Y., 1890–1900. Reprint, 1952–56.

The following collections (*L104–108*) are in progress.

L104. Collection Guillaume Budé. Paris, 1926 ff.

L105. The Loeb classical library. Cambridge, Mass., and London, 1912 ff.

L106. The fathers of the church. N.Y., 1947 ff.

L107. Ancient Christian writers. Westminster, Md., 1946 ff.

L108. Sources chrétiennes. Paris, 1941 ff. See also the following work.

L109. Barker, Ernest, ed. and tr. **Social and political thought in Byzantium from Justinian I to the last Palaeologus.** Oxford, 1957. A brief anthology of selections; but the editor is not a Byzantine specialist, and the introduction embodies some beliefs which are no longer generally held.

Byzantine papyri are published in a number of collections which also include documents of earlier periods.

L110. Bataille, André. **Les papyrus.** Paris, 1955. [Traité d'études byzantines, 2.] Valuable handbook which lists publications of the important collections. Provides excellent material for study and teaching.

L111. Devresse, Robert. **Introduction à l'étude des manuscrits grecs.** Paris, 1954.

L112. Sigalas, Antōnios. **Historia tēs hellēnikēs graphēs.** [History of Greek writing.] Thessaloníki, 1934.

HISTORIOGRAPHY

(Paul J. Alexander)

L113. Hirsch, Ferdinand L. **Byzantinische Studien.** Leipzig, 1876.

L114. Gerland, Ernst. "Die Grundlagen

der byzantinischen Geschichtschreibung." **Byzantion**, 8 (1933): 93–105.

L115. ——. **Das Studium der byzantinischen Geschichte vom Humanismus bis zur Jetztzeit.** Athens, 1934. [Texte und Forschungen zur byzantinisch-neugriechischen Philologie, 12.]

L116. Beck, Hans G. "Byzanz: der Weg zu seinem geschichtlichen Verständnis." **Saeculum**, 5 (1954): 87–103.

L117. Seidler, Herbert. **Jakob Philipp Fallmerayers geistige Entwicklung.** Munich, 1947.

L118. Irmscher, Johannes, ed. **Aus der Sowjetbyzantinistik.** Berlin, 1956.

See also works by Karl Krumbacher, Heinrich Gelzer, Otto Bardenhewer, Wilhelm Schmid and Otto Stählin, Gyula Moravcsik, and Maria Colonna.

SHORTER GENERAL HISTORIES
(Paul J. Alexander)

L119. Diehl, Charles. **Byzance: grandeur et décadence.** Paris, 1919. Tr. by Naomi Walford, New Brunswick, N.J., 1957.

L120. ——. **History of the Byzantine empire.** Tr. by G. B. Ives. Princeton, 1925.

L121. ——. **Les grands problèmes de l'histoire byzantine.** Paris, 1943.

L122. Lemerle, Paul. **Histoire de Byzance.** Paris, 1943.

L123. Baynes, Norman H. **The Byzantine empire.** 2nd ed., London, 1946. Excellent.

L124. Baynes, Norman H., and Henry St. L. B. Moss, eds. **Byzantium: an introduction to east Roman civilization.** Oxford, 1948.

L125. Levchenko, Mitrofan V. **Byzance, des origines à 1453.** Paris, 1949. A Marxist interpretation.

L126. Baynes, Norman H. **Byzantine studies and other essays.** London, 1955.

L127. Hussey, Joan M. **The Byzantine world.** London, 1957.

LONGER GENERAL HISTORIES
(Paul J. Alexander)

L128. Gibbon, Edward. **The history of the decline and fall of the Roman empire.** See *I132*.

L129. The Cambridge medieval history. V. 4, **The eastern Roman empire (717–1453).** Cambridge, Eng., 1927. Rev. ed. in preparation.

L130. Uspenskii, Fedor I. **Istoriia Vizantiiskoi imperii.** [History of the Byzantine empire.] 3 v. St. Petersburg (Leningrad), 1913–48.

L131. Diehl, Charles, and Georges Marçais. **Le monde oriental de 395 à 1081.** Paris, 1936.

L132. Diehl, Charles, and others. **L'Europe orientale de 1081 à 1453.** Paris, 1945.

L133. Bréhier, Louis. **Le monde byzantin.** 3 v. Paris, 1947–50.

L134. Amantos, Kōnstantinos I. **Historia tou byzantinou kratous.** [History of the Byzantine empire.] 2 v. Athens, 1939–47.

L135. Vasiliev, Alexander A. **History of the Byzantine empire, 324–1453.** 2nd ed., Madison, 1952.

L136. Ostrogorsky, George. **History of the Byzantine state.** Tr. by Joan Hussey. Oxford, 1956.

HISTORIES OF SPECIAL PERIODS

L137. Seeck, Otto. **Geschichte des Untergangs der antiken Welt.** See *I146*.

L138. Lot, Ferdinand. **The end of the ancient world and the beginnings of the Middle Ages.** See *J50*.

L139. Piganiol, André. **L'empire chrétien, 325–395.** See *I149*.

L140. Stein, Ernst. **Geschichte des spätrömischen Reiches. V. 1, Vom römischen zum byzantinischen Staate (284–476 n. Chr.).** Vienna, 1928.

L141. ——. **Histoire du bas-empire, de la disparition de l'empire d'Occident à la mort de Justinien (476–565).** Tr. by Jean R. Palanque. Paris, 1949. [Geschichte des spätrömischen Reiches, 2.]

L142. Demougeot, E. **De l'unité à la division de l'empire romain, 395–410.** Paris, 1951.

L143. Goubert, Paul. **Byzance avant l'Islam.** 2 v. Paris, 1951–56.

L144. Bury, John B. **A history of the later Roman empire from Arcadius to Irene (395 A.D. to 800 A.D.).** 2 v. London, 1889.

L145. ——. **A history of the later Roman empire from the death of Theodosius I to the death of Justinian (A.D. 395 to A.D. 565).** 2 v. London, 1923.

L146. ——. **A history of the eastern Roman empire from the fall of Irene to the accession of Basil I (A.D. 802–867).** London, 1912.

L147. Vasiliev, Alexander A. **Byzance et les Arabes.** See *M84*.

L148. Schlumberger, Gustave L. **L'épopée byzantine à la fin du dixième siècle.** 3 v. Paris, 1896–1905.

L149. Gaudefroy-Demombynes, Maurice, and Sergei F. Platonov. **Le monde musulman et byzantin jusqu'aux croisades.** See *M69*.

L150. Neumann, Carl. **Die Weltstellung des byzantinischen Reiches vor den Kreuzzügen.** Leipzig, 1894.

L151. Cognasso, Francesco. **Partiti politici e lotte dinastiche in Bizanzio alla morte di Manuele Comneno.** Turin, 1912.

L152. Pears, Edwin. **The destruction of the Greek empire and the story of the capture of Constantinople by the Turks.** See *S102*.

L153. 1453–1953: le cinq-centième anniversaire de la prise de Constantinople. See *S301*.

HISTORIES OF SPECIAL AREAS

L154. Diehl, Charles. **L'Afrique byzantine: histoire de la domination byzantine en Afrique (533–709).** Paris, 1896.

L155. ——. **Études sur l'administration byzantine dans l'exarchat de Ravenne (568–751).** Paris, 1888.

L156. Hartmann, Ludo M. **Untersuchungen zur Geschichte der byzantinischen Verwaltung in Italien (540–750).** Leipzig, 1889.

L157. Gay, Jules. **L'Italie méridionale et l'empire byzantin depuis l'avènement de Basile Ier jusqu'à la prise de Bari par les Normands (867–1071).** Paris, 1904.

L158. Caspar, Erich L. **Roger II (1101–1154) und die Gründung der normannisch-sicilischen Monarchie.** Innsbruck, 1904.

L159. Chalandon, Ferdinand. **Histoire de la domination normande en Italie et en Sicile.** 2 v. Paris, 1907.

L160. Kretschmayr, Heinrich. **Geschichte von Venedig.** See *VE261*.

L161. Caro, Georg. **Genua und die Mächte am Mittelmeer, 1257–1311.** 2 v. Halle, 1895–99.

L162. Voinovitch, Louis de. **Histoire de Dalmatie.** 2 v. Paris, 1934.

L163. Rouillard, Germaine. **L'administration civile de l'Égypte byzantine.** 2nd ed., Paris, 1928.

L164. Gelzer, Matthias. **Studien zur byzantinischen Verwaltung Ägyptens.** Leipzig, 1909.

L165. Maspero, Jean. **Organisation militaire de l'Égypte byzantine.** Paris, 1912.

L166. Goubert, Paul. "Byzance et l'Espagne wisigothique." **Revue des études byzantines,** 2 (1944) : 5–78.

L167. ——. "L'Espagne byzantine." **Revue des études byzantines,** 3 (1945) : 127–42, 4 (1946) : 71–134.

L168. Cirac Estopañán, Sebastián. **Byzancio y España: la unión, Manuel II Paleólogo y sus recuerdos en España.** Barcelona, 1952.

L169. Bon, Antoine. **Le Péloponnèse byzantin jusqu'en 1204.** Paris, 1951.

L170. Tafrali, Oreste. **Thessalonique des origines au XIVe siècle.** Paris, 1919.

L171. ——. **Thessalonique au quatorzième siècle.** Paris, 1913.

L172. Lemerle, Paul. **Philippes et la Macédoine orientale à l'époque chrétienne et byzantine.** Paris, 1945. Excellent.

L173. Niederle, Lubor. **Manuel de l'antiquité slave.** 2 v. Paris, 1923–26. Abridgement of his larger work, *Slovanské Starožitnosti* (4 v., Prague, 1901–25).

L174. Stadtmüller, Georg. **Geschichte Südosteuropas.** Munich, 1950. Contains good bibliography of Byzantine and Balkan history.

L175. Spinka, Matthew. **A history of Christianity in the Balkans: a study in the** spread of Byzantine culture among the Slavs. Chicago, 1933.

L176. Dvornik, Francis. **Les Slaves, Byzance et Rome au IXe siècle.** Paris, 1926.

L177. ——. **Les légendes de Constantin et de Méthode, vues de Byzance.** Prague, 1933.

L178. Leib, Bernard. **Rome, Kiev et Byzance à la fin du XIe siècle.** Paris, 1924.

L179. Runciman, Steven. **A history of the first Bulgarian empire.** See *W960*.

L180. Wolff, Robert L. "The 'second Bulgarian empire': its origin and history to 1204." **Speculum,** 24 (Apr. 1949) : 167–206.

L181. Banescu, Nicolae. **Un problème d'histoire médiévale: création et caractère du second empire bulgare.** Bucharest, 1943.

L182. Jireček, Constantin. **Geschichte der Serben.** 2 v. Gotha, 1911–18.

L183. Šišić, Ferdinand. **Geschichte der Kroaten.** V. 1. Zagreb, 1917.

L184. Macartney, Carlile A. **The Magyars in the ninth century.** See *W807*.

L185. Der Nersessian, Sirarpie. **Armenia and the Byzantine empire.** Cambridge, Mass., 1945.

L186. Tournebize, Henri F. **Histoire politique et religieuse de l'Arménie depuis les origines des arméniens jusqu'à la mort de leur dernier roi (l'an 1393).** Paris, 1910.

L187. Grousset, René. **Histoire de l'Arménie des origines à 1071.** Paris, 1947.

L188. Laurent, Joseph. **L'Arménie entre Byzance et l'Islam depuis la conquête arabe jusqu'en 886.** See *M125*.

L189. ——. **Byzance et les Turcs seldjoucides dans l'Asie occidentale jusqu'en 1081.** Nancy and Paris, 1913.

L190. Wittek, Paul. **Das Fürstentum Mentesche.** See *M128*.

L191. Iorga, Nicolae. **Geschichte des osmanischen Reiches.** V. 1–2. Gotha, 1908–09.

L192. Babinger, Franz C. **Beiträge zur Frühgeschichte der Türkenherrschaft in Rumelien (14.–15. Jahrhundert).** See *M140*.

L193. ——. **Mehmed der Eroberer und seine Zeit: Weltenstürmer einer Zeitenwende.** Munich, 1953.

HISTORIES OF SPECIAL TOPICS
Religion

The history of the Byzantine church and other medieval eastern Orthodox churches should be studied in connection with that of the western Latin church. There are detailed general histories of the early church by Louis Duchesne and Beresford J. Kidd, and selections from the literary and documentary sources by Kidd in English translation and, in the original Greek and Latin, by Heinrich Denzinger (on doctrine) and C. Kirch (on history). The most extensive general history of the church in preparation today is

L194. Fliche, Augustin, and Victor Martin,

eds. **Histoire de l'église depuis les origines jusqu'à nos jours.** Paris, 1934 ff. From the Roman Catholic viewpoint. English translations of the early volumes.

From a voluminous literature the following may be cited.

L195. Grillmeier, Alois, and Heinrich Bacht, eds. **Das Konzil von Chalkedon: Geschichte und Gegenwart.** 3 v. Würzburg, 1951–54. Valuable articles by various scholars.

L196. Duchesne, Louis M. O. **L'église au VIe siècle.** Paris, 1925.

L197. Every, George. **The Byzantine patriarchate, 451–1204.** London, 1947.

L198. Adeney, Walter F. **The Greek and eastern churches.** N.Y., 1908.

L199. Fortescue, Adrian. **The orthodox eastern church.** London, 1929.

L200. ———. **The uniate eastern churches.** London, 1923.

L201. Honigmann, Ernst. **Évêques et évêchés monophysites d'Asie antérieure au VIe siècle.** Louvain, 1951.

L202. Schwarzlose, Karl. **Der Bilderstreit: ein Kampf der griechischen Kirche um ihre Eigenart und um ihre Freiheit.** Gotha, 1890.

L203. Ostrogorsky, Georg. **Studien zur Geschichte des byzantinischen Bilderstreites.** Breslau, 1929.

L204. Martin, Edward J. **A history of the Iconoclastic controversy.** London, 1930.

L205. Ladner, Gerhart B. "Origin and significance of the Byzantine Iconoclastic controversy." **Mediaeval studies,** 2 (1940): 127–49. See also articles by Ladner, Paul J. Alexander, Ernst Kitzinger, and Milton V. Anastos in *Dumbarton Oaks papers,* 7–8 (1953–54).

L206. Gardner, Alice. **Theodore of Studium: his life and times.** London, 1905.

L207. Alexander, Paul J. **The patriarch Nicephorus of Constantinople.** Oxford, 1958.

L208. Hergenröther, Joseph. **Photius, Patriarch von Constantinopel.** 3 v. Regensburg, 1867–69.

L209. Dvornik, Francis. **The Photian schism: history and legend.** Cambridge, Eng., 1948.

L210. Jugie, Martin. **Le schisme byzantin: aperçu historique et doctrinal.** Paris, 1941.

L211. Michel, Anton. **Humbert und Kerullarios.** 2 v. Paderborn, 1925–30.

L212. Lamma, Paolo. **Comneni e Staufer: ricerche sui rapporti fra Bisanzio e l'Occidente nel secolo XII.** 2 v. Rome, 1955–57.

L213. Norden, Walter. **Das Papsttum und Byzanz: die Trennung der beiden Mächte und das Problem ihrer Wiedervereinigung bis 1453.** Berlin, 1903.

L214. Geanakoplos, Deno J. "Michael VIII Palaeologus and the Union of Lyons." **Harvard theological review,** 46 (Apr. 1953): 79–89.

L215. Golubovich, Girolamo. **Biblioteca bio-bibliografica della Terra Santa e dell'Oriente francescano.** V. 1–5. Florence, 1906–27.

L216. Roncaglia, Martiniano. **Les Frères Mineurs et l'église grecque orthodoxe au XIIIe siècle, 1231–1274.** Cairo, 1954. [Biblioteca bio-bibliografica della Terra Santa e dell'Oriente francescano, ser. 4.]

L217. Altaner, Berthold. **Die Dominikanermissionen des 13. Jahrhunderts.** Habelschwerdt, 1924.

L218. Halecki, Oskar. **Un empereur de Byzance à Rome: vingt ans de travail pour l'union des églises et pour la défense de l'empire d'Orient, 1355–1375.** Warsaw, 1930. Excellent.

L219. Viller, M. "La question de l'union des églises entre grecs et latins depuis le concile de Lyon jusqu'à celui de Florence (1274–1438)." **Revue d'histoire ecclésiastique,** 17 (Apr. 1921): 260–305, 17 (Oct. 1921): 515–32, 18 (Jan. 1922): 20–60.

L220. Hofmann, Georg. "Die Konzilsarbeit in Ferrara." **Orientalia Christiana periodica,** 3 (1937): 110–40, 403–55.

L221. ———. "Die Konzilsarbeit in Florenz." **Orientalia Christiana periodica,** 4 (1938): 372–422.

L222. Chiaroni, Vincenzo. **Lo scisma greco e il concilio di Firence.** Florence, 1938.

Government

There are many recent studies of the Byzantine emperor and his authority, titles, court ceremonial, coronation, etc., by N. H. Baynes, H. Berkhof, L. Bréhier, P. Charanis, J. Deér, E. Demougeot, A. N. Diomedes, F. Dölger, H. Eger, W. Ensslin, R. Guilland, E. H. Kantorowicz, V. Laurent, A. Michel, G. Ostrogorsky, K. M. Setton, J. Straub, N. Svoronos, O. Treitinger, and others. For separate listing and penetrating discussion of these see

L223. Dölger, Franz, and Alfons M. Schneider. **Byzanz.** Bern, 1952. See especially pp. 93 ff.

For the now extensive literature on Byzantine governmental institutions and political theory see *ibid.*, pp. 101 ff.

L224. Bréhier, Louis. **Le monde byzantin.** V. 2, **Les institutions de l'empire byzantin.** Paris, 1949.

L225. Boak, Arthur E. R. **The master of the offices.** N.Y., 1924.

L226. Dunlap, James E. **The office of the grand chamberlain.** N.Y., 1924.

L227. Palanque, Jean R. **Essai sur la préfecture du prétoire du bas-empire.** Paris, 1933.

L228. Bury, John B. **The constitution of the later Roman empire.** Cambridge, Eng., 1910. Reprinted in Harold W. V. Temperley, ed., *Selected essays of J. B. Bury,* Cambridge, 1930.

L229. ——. **The imperial administrative system in the ninth century.** London, 1911.

L230. Brătianu, George I. **Privilèges et franchises municipales dans l'empire byzantin.** Paris and Bucharest, 1936.

L231. Beck, Hans G. "Der byzantinische 'Ministerpräsident.'" **Byzantinische Zeitschrift,** 48 (1955): 309–38.

L232. Dölger, Franz. **Byzanz und die europäische Staatenwelt.** Ettal, 1953. Fourteen learned studies with rich bibliographies.

L233. Stein, Ernst. "Untersuchungen zur spätbyzantinischen Verfassungs- und Wirtschaftsgeschichte." **Mitteilungen zur osmanischen Geschichte,** 2 (1923–26): 1–62. For individual emperors see the following.

L234. Schwartz, Eduard. **Kaiser Constantin und die christliche Kirche.** Leipzig, 1913.

L235. Baynes, Norman H. "Constantine the Great and the Christian church." **Proceedings of the British Academy,** 15 (1929): 341–442. See *1155.*

L236. Piganiol, André. **L'empereur Constantin.** Paris, 1932.

L237. Alföldi, András. **The conversion of Constantine and pagan Rome.** Tr. by H. Mattingly. Oxford, 1948.

L238. Vogt, Joseph. **Constantin der Grosse und sein Jahrhundert.** See *1154.*

L239. Kraft, Heinz. **Kaiser Konstantins religiöse Entwicklung.** Tübingen, 1955.

L240. Bidez, Joseph. **La vie de l'empereur Julien.** Paris, 1930.

L241. Vasiliev, Alexander A. **Justin the first: an introduction to the epoch of Justinian the Great.** Cambridge, Mass., 1950.

L242. Diehl, Charles. **Figures byzantines.** 2 v., Paris, 1925–27.

L243. Schubart, Wilhelm. **Justinian und Theodora.** Munich, 1943.

L244. Pernice, Angelo. **L'imperatore Eraclio.** Florence, 1905.

L245. Vogt, Albert. **Basile Iᵉʳ, empereur de Byzance (867–886) et la civilisation byzantine à la fin du IXᵉ siècle.** Paris, 1908.

L246. Adontz, Nikolai G. "L'âge et l'origine de l'empereur Basile I (867–886)." **Byzantion,** 8 (1933): 475–500, 9 (1934): 223–60.

L247. Runciman, Steven. **The emperor Romanus Lecapenus and his reign.** Cambridge, Eng., 1929.

L248. Rambaud, Alfred N. **L'empire grec au dixième siècle: Constantin Porphyrogénète.** Paris, 1870.

L249. Schlumberger, Gustave. **Un empereur byzantin au dixième siècle: Nicéphore Phocas.** Paris, 1890.

L250. Chalandon, Ferdinand. **Essai sur le règne d'Alexis Iᵉʳ Comnène (1081–1118).** Paris, 1900.

L251. ——. **Les Comnène: Jean II Comnène (1118–1143) et Manuel I Comnène (1143–1180).** Paris, 1912.

L252. Cognasso, Francesco. "Un imperatore bizantino della decadenza: Isacco II Angelo." **Bessarione,** ser. 4, 2 (Jan. 1915): 29–60.

L253. Dölger, Franz. "Johannes VI. Kantakuzenos als dynastischer Legitimist." **Annales de l'Institut Kondakov,** 10 (1938): 19–30.

L254. ——. "Johannes VII., Kaiser der Rhomaer, 1390–1408." **Byzantinische Zeitschrift,** 31 (1931): 21–36.

L255. Chapman, Conrad. **Michel Paléologue, restaurateur de l'empire byzantin.** Paris, 1926.

L256. Berger de Xivrey, Jules. "Mémoire sur la vie et les ouvrages de l'empereur Manuel Paléologue." **Mémoires de l'Institut de France, Académie des Inscriptions et Belles-lettres,** 19 (1853): 1–202.

Military History

On the military organization of the Byzantine provinces (the system of themes) there is a considerable literature and some controversy.

L257. Diehl, Charles. "L'origine du régime des thèmes dans l'empire byzantin." **Études d'histoire du Moyen-Âge dédiées à Gabriel Monod** (Paris, 1896), pp. 47–60. Reprinted in Diehl's *Études byzantines* (Paris, 1905), pp. 276–92.

L258. Gelzer, Heinrich. "Die Genesis der byzantinischen Themenverfassung." **Abhandlungen der Philologisch-historischen Classe der Königlich Sächsischen Gesellschaft der Wissenschaften,** 18 (Leipzig, 1899), 1–134.

L259. Kulakovskiĭ, Iulian A. **K voprosu o themakh vizantiĭskoi imperii.** [On the question of the themes in the Byzantine empire.] Kiev, 1904.

L260. Stein, Ernst. **Studien zur Geschichte des byzantinischen Reiches, vornehmlich unter den Kaisern Justinus II u. Tiberius Constantinus** (Stuttgart, 1919), pp. 117–40.

L261. ——. "Ein Kapitel vom persischen und vom byzantinischen Staate." **Byzantinisch-neugriechische Jahrbücher,** 1 (May 1920): 50–89.

L262. Kyriakides, Stilpon P. **Byzantinai meletai.** [Byzantine studies.] V. 2–5. Thessaloníki, 1939.

L263. Zakythinos, Dionysios A. "Meletai peri tēs dioikētikēs diaireseōs kai tēs eparchiakēs dioikēseos en tō Byzantinō kratei." [Studies of the administrative division and the provincial administration of the Byzantine empire.] **Epetēris Hetaireias Byzantinōn Spoudōn** [Yearbook of the Society for Byzantine Studies], 17 (1941): 208–74, 18 (1948): 42–62, 19 (1949): 3–25, 21 (1951): 179–209, 22 (1952): 159–82.

L264. Pertusi, A., ed. **Costantino Porfirogenito de thematibus: introduzione, testo critico, commento.** Vatican City, 1952. The most important work in this field.

Stein and Ostrogorsky believe the first four

themes were created in Asia Minor in the reign of Heraclius (see *L10,* pp. 86 ff.; and *Byzantion,* 23 (1954): 31–66). On the other hand, Baynes (*English historical review,* 67 (July 1952): 380–81) and Pertusi (see above and *Aevum,* 27 (Apr. 1954): 126–50) date the origin of the themes after Heraclius.

Byzantium and the Crusades

L265. Erdmann, Carl. **Die Entstehung des Kreuzzugsgedankens.** Stuttgart, 1935. Reprint, 1955.

L266. Röhricht, Reinhold. **Beiträge zur Geschichte der Kreuzzüge.** 2 v. Berlin, 1874–78.

L267. ——. **Geschichte des Königreichs Jerusalem (1100–1291).** Innsbruck, 1898. Famous for its accuracy and thoroughness.

L268. Grousset, René. **Histoire des croisades et du royaume franc de Jérusalem.** 3 v. Paris, 1934–36.

L269. Runciman, Steven. **A history of the crusades.** See *K247.*

L270. Waas, Adolf. **Geschichte der Kreuzzüge.** See *K249.*

L271. Longnon, Jean. **Les français d'outremer au Moyen-Âge.** Paris, 1929.

L272. Stevenson, William B. **The crusaders in the East.** See *M86.*

L273. Lamonte, John L. **Feudal monarchy in the Latin kingdom of Jerusalem.** Cambridge, Mass., 1932.

L274. Richard, Jean. **Le royaume latin de Jérusalem.** Paris, 1953.

L275. ——. **Le Comté de Tripoli sous la dynastie toulousaine (1102–1187).** Paris, 1945. [Bibliothèque archéologique et historique, 39.]

L276. Cahen, Claude. **La Syrie du nord à l'époque des croisades et la principauté franque d'Antioche.** Paris, 1940. Valuable.

L277. Setton, Kenneth M., ed. **A history of the crusades.** See *K248.*

Documents relating to the fourth crusade and the Latin states founded in Greece and the Aegean have been published by Jean A. C. Buchon, Gottlieb L. Tafel and Georg M. Thomas, Kōnstantinos N. Sathas, Vladimir Lamansky, Riccardo Predelli, Hippolyte Noiret, Nicolae Iorga, Antonio Rubió y Lluch, Spyridon P. Lampros, Ernst Gerland, Roberto Cessi, Jean Longnon, Giovanni Mercati, Morozzo della Rocca and A. Lombardo, Raymond J. Loenertz, and others. Of the secondary literature, mention may be made of the following (*L278–288*).

L278. Frolow, A. **Recherches sur la déviation de la IVᵉ croisade vers Constantinople.** Paris, 1955.

L279. Gerland, Ernst. **Geschichte des lateinischen Kaiserreiches von Konstantinopel.** Homberg v.d. Höhe, 1905.

L280. Longnon, Jean. **L'empire latin de Constantinople et la principauté de Morée.**

Paris, 1949. Concise and readable. See also Longnon's valuable articles in the *Journal des savants* for 1941, 1945, and 1946.

L281. ——. **Recherches sur la vie de Geoffroy de Villehardouin.** Paris, 1939.

L282. Heisenberg, August. "Neue Quellen zur Geschichte des lateinischen Kaisertums und der Kirchenunion." **Sitzungsberichte der bayerischen Akademie der Wissenschaften, Philosophisch-philologische und historische Klasse,** 1 (Munich, 1922): 1–75, 2 (1923): 1–56, 3 (1923): 1–96.

L283. Wolff, Robert L. "Politics in the Latin patriarchate of Constantinople, 1204–1261." **Dumbarton Oaks papers,** 8 (1954): 223–303.

L284. Mēliarakēs, Antōnios. **Istoria tou basileiou tēs Nikaias kai tou despotatou tēs Epeirou (1204–1261).** [History of the empire of Nicaea and the despotate of Epirus (1204–1261).] Athens, 1898.

L285. Nicol, Donald M. **The despotate of Epiros.** Oxford, 1957.

L286. Gardner, Alice. **The Lascarids of Nicaea.** London, 1912.

L287. Vasiliev, Alexander A. "The foundation of the empire of Trebizond." **Speculum,** 11 (Jan. 1936): 3–37.

L288. Miller, William. **Trebizond, the last Greek empire.** London, 1926.

L289. ——. **The Latins in the Levant: a history of Frankish Greece (1204–1566).** London, 1908. Brilliant, but now rather antiquated, with somewhat confused citation of sources.

L290. ——. **Essays on the Latin Orient.** Cambridge, Eng., 1921.

L291. Zakythinos, Denis (Dionysios) A. **Le despotat grec de Morée.** 2 v. Paris and Athens, 1932–53.

L292. Loenertz, Raymond J. "Pour l'histoire du Péloponèse au XIVᵉ siècle (1382–1404)." **Revue des études byzantines,** 1 (1943): 152–96.

L293. Gregorovius, Ferdinand. **Geschichte der Stadt Athen im Mittelalter.** 2 v. Stuttgart, 1889.

L294. Stadtmüller, Georg. "Michael Choniates, Metropolit von Athen (ca. 1138—ca. 1222)." **Orientalia Christiana,** 33 (Feb. 1934): 125–325. Very thorough.

L295. Giunta, Francesco. **Aragonesi e Catalani nel Mediterraneo.** V. 1, **Dal regno al viceregno in Sicilia.** Palermo, 1953.

L296. Setton, Kenneth M. **Catalan domination of Athens, 1311–1388.** Cambridge, Mass., 1948. Contains full summary and critical estimate of the works of the great Catalan historian Antonio Rubió y Lluch.

L297. Delaville Le Roulx, Joseph. **La France en Orient au XIVᵉ siècle.** 2 v. Paris, 1886.

L298. ——. **Les Hospitaliers en Terre Sainte et à Chypre (1100–1310).** Paris, 1904.

L299. ——. **Les Hospitaliers à Rhodes**

jusqu'à la mort de Philibert de Naillac, 1310–1421. Paris, 1913.

L300. Iorga, Nicolae. **Philippe de Mézières (1327–1405) et la croisade au XIVe siècle.** Paris, 1896.

L301. Smet, Joachim. **The life of Saint Peter Thomas by Philippe de Mézières.** Rome, 1954.

L302. Atiya, Aziz S. **The crusade in the later Middle Ages.** See *M89*.

L303. ———. **The crusade of Nicopolis.** See *M135*.

L304. Silberschmidt, Max. **Das orientalische Problem zur Zeit der Entstehung des türkischen Reiches nach venezianischen Quellen, 1381–1400.** Leipzig, 1923.

L305. Halecki, Oskar. **The crusade of Varna: a discussion of controversial problems.** N.Y., 1943.

L306. Mas Latrie, Louis de. **Histoire de l'île de Chypre sous le règne des princes de la maison de Lusignan.** 3 v. Paris, 1852–61.

L307. Hill, Sir George F. **A history of Cyprus.** V. 2–3. Cambridge, Eng., 1948.

Economic History

L308. Dölger, Franz. **Beiträge zur Geschichte der byzantinischen Finanzverwaltung besonders des 10. und 11. Jahrhunderts.** Leipzig, 1927.

L309. Andreades, Andreas M. "De la monnaie et de la puissance d'achat des métaux précieux dans l'empire byzantin." **Byzantion,** 1 (1924): 75–115.

L310. Ostrogorsky, Georg. "Löhne und Preise in Byzanz." **Byzantinische Zeitschrift,** 32 (1932): 293–333.

L311. ———. "Die ländliche Steuergemeinde des byzantinischen Reiches im X. Jahrhundert." **Vierteljahrschrift für Sozial- und Wirtschaftsgeschichte,** 20 (1927): 1–108.

L312. Brătianu, George I. **Études byzantines d'histoire économique et sociale.** Paris, 1938.

L313. Zakythinos, Denis (Dionysios) A. **Crise monétaire et crise économique à Byzance du XIIIe au XVe siècle.** Athens, 1948. Readable and stimulating.

L314. Runciman, Steven. "Byzantine trade and industry." **The Cambridge economic history of Europe,** v. 2 (Cambridge, Eng., 1952), pp. 86–118.

L315. Lopez, Roberto S. "The trade of medieval Europe: the South." **The Cambridge economic history of Europe,** v. 2, pp. 257–354.

L316. Heyd, Wilhelm von. **Histoire du commerce du Levant au Moyen-Âge.** See *J70*.

Agriculture

L317. Rouillard, Germaine. **La vie rurale dans l'empire byzantin.** Paris, 1953.

L318. Ostrogorsky, Georg. "Agrarian conditions in the Byzantine empire in the Middle Ages." **The Cambridge economic history of Europe,** v. 1 (Cambridge, Eng., 1941), pp. 194–223.

L319. Danstrup, John. "The state and landed property in Byzantium to c. 1250." **Classica et mediaevalia: revue danoise de philologie et d'histoire,** 8 (1947): 222–62.

L320. Charanis, Peter. "The monastic properties and the state in the Byzantine empire." **Dumbarton Oaks papers,** 4 (1948): 51–118.

L321. ———. "On the social structure and economic organization of the Byzantine empire in the thirteenth century and later." **Byzantinoslavica,** 12 (1951): 94–154.

L322. Ostrogorsky, Georg. **Quelques problèmes d'histoire de la paysannerie byzantine.** Brussels, 1956. [Corpus bruxellense historiae byzantinae, 2.]

L323. ———. **Pour l'histoire de la féodalité byzantine.** Brussels, 1954. [Corpus bruxellense historiae byzantinae, 1.]

Coins and Seals
(Glanville Downey)

L324. Sabatier, Justin. **Description générale des monnaies byzantines.** 2 v. Paris, 1862. Reprint, Graz, 1955.

L325. Goodacre, Hugh G. **A handbook of the coinage of the Byzantine empire.** London, 1957. Contains historical material not available in Wroth, but less detailed for description of individual coins.

L326. Wroth, Warwick W. **Catalogue of the imperial Byzantine coins in the British Museum.** 2 v. London, 1908.

L327. ———. **Catalogue of the coins of the empires of . . . Thessalonica, Nicaea, and Trebizond.** London, 1911.

L328. Schlumberger, Gustave L. **Sigillographie de l'empire byzantin.** Paris, 1884.

L329. Laurent, V. **Documents de sigillographie byzantine: la collection C. Orghidan.** Paris, 1952.

Circus Parties

For the circus parties in Byzantium and their apparent constitutional significance the following articles are valuable.

L330. Manojlović, G. "Carigradski narod." **Nastavni vjesnik,** 12 (Zagreb, 1904): 1–91. French tr., by Henri Grégoire, "Le peuple de Constantinople," **Byzantion,** 11 (1936): 617–716.

L331. Dvornik, Francis. "The circus parties in Byzantium: their evolution and their suppression." **Byzantina-Metabyzantina,** 1 (1946): 119–33.

L332. Maricq, A. "La durée du régime des partis populaires à Constantinople." Académie Royale de Belgique, **Bulletin de la** classe des lettres, 5th ser., 35 (1949): 63–74.

L333. ——. "Factions du cirque et partis populaires." Académie Royale de Belgique, **Bulletin de la classe des lettres,** 5th ser., 36 (1950): 396–421.

Literature, Education, Philosophy
(*Norman P. Zacour*)

L334. Krumbacher, Karl. **Geschichte der byzantinischen Litteratur.** 2nd ed., Munich, 1897.

L335. Moravcsik, Gyula. **Byzantinoturcica.** V. 1, **Die byzantinischen Quellen der Geschichte der Türkvölker.** Budapest, 1942.

L336. Montelatici, Giovanni. **Storia della letteratura bizantina (324–1453).** Milan, 1916.

L337. Courcelle, Pierre P. **Les lettres grecques en Occident.** Paris, 1943.

L338. Mavrogordato, John, ed. and tr. **Digenes Akrites.** Oxford, 1956. With English translation.

L339. Impellizzeri, Salvatore. **Il "Digenis Akritas": l'epopea di Bisanzio.** Florence, 1940. With Italian translation.

More detailed studies include the following.

L340. Gigante, Marcello. **Poeti italobizantini del secolo XIII.** Naples, 1953. [Collana di studi greci, 22.]

L341. Uspenskii, Fedor I. **Ocherki po istorii vizantiiskoi obrazovannosti.** [Sketches of the history of Byzantine education.] St. Petersburg (Leningrad), 1891.

L342. Fuchs, Friedrich. **Die höheren Schulen von Konstantinopel im Mittelalter.** Leipzig and Berlin, 1926.

L343. Hussey, Joan M. **Church and learning in the Byzantine empire, 867–1185.** London, 1937.

L344. Tatakis, Basile N. **La philosophie byzantine.** Paris, 1949.

L345. Stephanou, Pelodidas E. **Jean Italos, philosophe et humaniste.** Rome, 1949.

L346. Joannou, Perikles. **Christliche Metaphysik in Byzanz.** V. 1, **Die Illuminationslehre des Michael Psellos und Joannes Italos.** Ettal, 1956. [Studia patristica et byzantina, 3.]

L347. Guilland, Rodolphe J. **Essai sur Nicéphore Grégoras.** Paris, 1926.

L348. Beck, Hans G. **Theodoros Metochites: die Krise des byzantinischen Weltbildes im 14. Jahrhundert.** Munich, 1952.

L349. Mercati, Giovanni. **Notizie di Procoro e Demetrio Cidone.** Vatican City, 1931. [Studi e testi, 56.]

L350. Cammelli, Giuseppe. **I dotti bizantini e le origini dell'umanesimo.** 3 v. Florence, 1941–54.

L351. Masai, François. **Pléthon et le platonisme de Mistra.** Paris, 1956.

L352. Mohler, Ludwig. **Kardinal Bessarion als Theologie, Humanist und Staatsmann.** 3 v. Paderborn, 1923–42.

L353. Neumann, Carl. "Byzantinische Kultur und Renaissancekultur." **Historische Zeitschrift,** 91 (1903): 215–32.

L354. Heisenberg, August. "Das Problem der Renaissance in Byzanz." **Historische Zeitschrift,** 133 (1925–26): 393–412.

L355. Setton, Kenneth M. "The Byzantine background to the Italian Renaissance." **Proceedings of the American Philosophical Society,** 100 (Feb. 1956): 1–76. See *VE59*.

L356. Benz, Ernst. **Wittenberg und Byzanz: zur Begegnung und Auseinandersetzung der Reformation und der östlich-orthodoxen Kirche.** Marburg, 1949.

Art
(*Norman P. Zacour*)

Bibliographies of Byzantine art may be found in some of the general works on the subject, such as the following (*L357–360*).

L357. Diehl, Charles. **Manuel d'art byzantin.** 2nd ed., 2 v., Paris, 1925–26.

L358. Dalton, Ormonde M. **Byzantine art and archaeology.** Oxford, 1911.

L359. ——. **East Christian art.** Oxford, 1925.

L360. Wulff, Oskar K. **Altchristliche und byzantinische Kunst.** 2 v. Berlin, 1914–24.

L361. Diehl, Charles. "Civiltà bizantina." **Enciclopedia italiana,** 7 (1930): 165. Contains good selective bibliography.

L362. Morey, Charles R. **Early Christian art.** 2nd ed., Princeton, 1953.

L363. Grabar, André. **Byzantine painting.** Geneva, 1953.

L364. Felicetti-Liebenfels, Walter. **Geschichte der byzantinischen Ikonenmalerei.** Lausanne, 1956.

L365. Weitzmann, Kurt. **Die byzantinische Buchmalerei des 9. und 10. Jahrhunderts.** Berlin, 1935.

L366. ——. **Greek mythology in Byzantine art.** Princeton, 1951.

L367. **Atti del V Congresso Internazionale di Studi Bizantini.** V. 2. Rome, 1940. [Studi bizantini e neoellenici, 6.] Devoted almost entirely to studies in Byzantine art, architecture, liturgy, and music.

Recent works of more regional character include the following.

L368. Kondakov, Nikodim P. **The Russian icon.** Tr. by Ellis H. Minns. 4 v. in 3. Prague, 1928–33.

L369. Ainalov, Demetrius. **Geschichte der russischen Monumentalkunst der vormoskovitischen Zeit.** Berlin and Leipzig, 1933.

L370. Millet, Gabriel, and David Talbot Rice. **Byzantine painting at Trebizond.** London, 1936.

L371. Grabar, André. **La peinture religieuse en Bulgarie.** Paris, 1928.

L372. Weitzmann, Kurt. **Die armenische**

Buchmalerei des 10. und beginnenden 11. Jahrhunderts. Bamberg, 1933.
L373. Agnello, Giuseppe. **L'architettura bizantina in Sicilia.** Florence, 1952.

Theater

L374. Cottas, Vénétia. **Le théâtre à Byzance.** Paris, 1931.
L375. La Piana, George. "The Byzantine theater." **Speculum,** 11 (Apr. 1936): 171–211.

Music

(*Miloš M. Velimirović*)

L376. Monumenta musicae byzantinae. Copenhagen, 1935 ff. To date includes volumes of manuscript facsimiles in the main series; 9 v. of transcribed hymns in the *Transcripta* series; and in the series entitled *Subsidia* the following studies (*L377–380*).
L377. Tillyard, H. J. W. **Handbook of the middle Byzantine musical notation.** Copenhagen, 1935.
L378. Høeg, Carsten. **La notation ekphonétique.** Copenhagen, 1935.
L379. Wellesz, Egon. **Eastern elements in western chant.** Boston, 1947.
L380. Palikarova Verdeil, R. **La musique byzantine chez les bulgares et les russes.** Copenhagen, 1953.
L381. Angeli, Andrea d'. "La musica bizantina o neo-greca." **Studi bizantini e neoellenici,** 6 (1940): 481–88. Includes brief select bibliography on Byzantine music.
L382. Høeg, Carsten. "The oldest Slavonic tradition of Byzantine music." **Proceedings of the British Academy,** 39 (1953): 37–66.
L383. Strunk, Oliver. "Intonations and signatures of the Byzantine modes." **The musical quarterly,** 31 (1945): 339–55.
L384. ———. "The tonal system of Byzantine music." **The musical quarterly,** 28 (1942): 190–204.
L385. Wellesz, Egon, ed. **The Akathistos hymn.** Copenhagen, 1957. [Monumenta musicae byzantinae, Transcripta series, 9.] The first full transcription into modern notation of this hymn to the Virgin. Its availability may have far-reaching consequences for future studies in the relationship of eastern and western chants.
L386. ———. **A history of Byzantine music and hymnography.** Oxford, 1949. Indispensable handbook with valuable bibliography.

Byzantine Dating

(*Martin J. Higgins*)

L387. Ginzel, Friedrich K. **Handbuch der mathematischen und technischen Chronologie: das Zeitrechnungswesen der Völker.** 3 v. Leipzig, 1906–14. Indispensable work,

containing the essential elements of Byzantine dating.
L388. Degrassi, Attilio. **I fasti consolari dell' impero romano dal 30 avanti Christo al 613 dopo Christo.** See *118.* See also *L69.*
L389. Kase, Edmund H. **A papyrus roll in the Princeton collection.** N.Y., 1933. Contains information on the indiction, which began in 312.
L390. Grumel, Venance. "Indiction byzantine et neon etos." **Revue des études byzantines,** 12 (1954): 128–43.

Miscellaneous

L391. Grosse, Robert. **Römische Militärgeschichte von Gallienus bis zum Beginn der byzantinischen Themenverfassung.** See *1217.*
L392. Hadjinicolaou-Marava, Anne. **Recherches sur la vie des esclaves dans le monde byzantin.** Athens, 1950.
L393. Beylié, Léon M. E. de. **L'habitation byzantine.** Grenoble, 1902.
L394. Koukoules, Phaidōn. **Byzantinōn bios kai politismos.** [Byzantine life and civilization.] 6 v. in 7. Athens, 1948–57.
L395. Bréhier, Louis. **Le monde byzantin.** V. 3, **La civilisation byzantine.** Paris, 1950. Deals with social life.
L396. Iorga, Nicolae. **Histoire de la vie byzantine: empire et civilisation.** 3 v. Bucharest, 1934. Contains much political history.

PERIODICALS

(*George C. Soulis*)

L397. Byzantinische Zeitschrift. Leipzig, 1892 ff. (Irregular quarterly.) The first journal completely devoted to Byzantine studies. Contains rich, critically appraised bibliographical notices.
L398. Byzantinisches Archiv. Leipzig, 1898 ff. (Irregular.) A monographic series, supplement to *L397.*
L399. Vizantiiskii vremennik. [Annals of Byzantium.] St. Petersburg (Leningrad), 1894–1927; n.s., Moscow, 1947 ff. (Irregular.) The new series, published by the Soviet Academy of Sciences, represents the Soviet school, with great emphasis on the socio-economic problems of Byzantium and their Marxist interpretation.
L400. Byzantinisch-neugriechische Jahrbücher. Berlin and Athens, 1920 ff. (Irregular.)
L401. Texte und Forschungen zur byzantinisch-neugriechischen Philologie. Berlin, 1922 ff. (Irregular.) Monographic series, supplement to *L400.*
L402. Epetēris Hetaireias Byzantinōn Spoudōn. [Yearbook of the Society for Byzantine Studies.] Athens, 1924 ff. Great majority of articles in Greek, but extensive summaries of contents in French at end of each volume.

L403. Studi bizantini e neoellenici. Naples and Rome, 1924 ff. (Irregular. Title varies.) V. 5–8 (1939–53) are of special importance since they contain the proceedings of the fifth and eighth international congresses of Byzantine studies, held in Rome and Palermo.

L404. Byzantion. Paris, Boston, etc., 1924 ff. (Semiannual.) Contains many articles of broad nature, and numerous bibliographical essays on special topics.

L405. Annales de l'Institut Kondakov. Belgrade, 1927–40. (Annual. Title varies.) Contains articles in Russian and the main western languages, mostly by Russian emigré scholars, with special emphasis on art and archaeology.

L406. Byzantinoslavica. Prague, 1929 ff. (Irregular.) Began as a specialized periodical on Byzantino-Slavic relations, but now is considerably broader in scope. One volume of its *Supplementa* has appeared (1933).

L407. Revue des études byzantines. Bucharest, 1943 ff. (Annual. Title varies.) Published by the Institut Français des Études Byzantines of the order of Assumptionists, as a successor to their *Echos d'Orient* (Paris, 1897–1942).

L408. Dumbarton Oaks papers. Cambridge, Mass., 1941 ff. (Irregular.)

L409. Dumbarton Oaks studies. Cambridge, Mass., 1950 ff. (Irregular.) Monographs.

L410. Jahrbuch der österreichischen Byzantinischen Gesellschaft. Vienna, 1951 ff.

L411. Zbornik radova Vizantoloskog Instituta. [Collection of works of the Byzantine Institute.] Belgrade, 1952 ff. (Annual.) Published by the Byzantine Institute of the Serbian Academy of Sciences. Articles are principally by Yugoslav scholars in Serbo-Croatian, with summaries in main western languages.

L412. Posebna izdanja. [Special publications.] Belgrade, 1951 ff. (Irregular.) Monographic series, also issued by the Byzantine Institute.

SECTION M

The Muslim World

BERNARD LEWIS *

This section covers the history of Islam from its origins until the Ottoman capture of Constantinople in 1453—that is to say, the states and peoples that accepted the faith and law of Islam and professed to live by them. Beginning with the career of the prophet Mohammed in Arabia in the first half of the 7th century A.D., this period includes the religious and political unification of the peninsular Arabs, and the great movements of Islamic expansion, from Arabia into the Fertile Crescent then eastward across Persia to central Asia and India, westward across Egypt and north Africa to Sicily and Spain, and northward into Asia Minor and then Europe. Politically it is concerned with the first universal Islamic empire—that of the caliphs; with the smaller dynasties that arose out of it; with the invasions of the steppe peoples, Turks and later Mongols; and with the new empires and conquests that followed them. Culturally it embraces the rise and development of Islamic civilization and its three successive phases of efflorescence—Arabic, Persian, and Turkish.

The student of Islamic history enters a field where much—one might say almost all—still remains to be done. He will have at his disposal hardly any of the tools of research that are taken as a matter of course by his classicist or medievalist colleagues. Faced with the need to master several difficult oriental languages, he will find that there are no historical grammars or dictionaries for any of them, and that even the general dictionaries are few and inadequate. There are not many authorities worthy of the name on palaeography, epigraphy, sigillography, diplomatics, and the other ancillary sciences. The general works of reference even in such matters as biography, topography, and terminology are limited in number. The few comprehensive textbooks that do exist may help the reader grasp the main outlines, but most of them represent the findings and judgments of a time when the critical study of Islamic history was only beginning. Therefore, their evaluations and even their statements of fact will need to

* The following contributed items and comments indicated by their respective initials: David Cowan (DC), Peter Hardy (PH), John M. B. Jones (JMBJ), Leila Karmy (LK), Ann K. S. Lambton (AKSL), and Vernon J. Parry (VJP).

be strictly controlled by the results of research, published chiefly in specialist journals. The works listed below consist very largely of such specialist monographs.

BIBLIOGRAPHIES

M1. Sauvaget, Jean. **Introduction à l'histoire de l'Orient musulman: éléments de bibliographie.** Paris, 1946. Survey of problems and sources of Islamic history; an invaluable, practical handbook, a large part of which consists of a classified and annotated bibliography. Latter may be supplemented by *M2*.

M2. Spuler, Bertold, and Ludwig Forrer. **Der Vordere Orient in islamischer Zeit.** Bern, 1954. Includes more recent publications than the above, and is especially valuable for central Asia and the Volga basin.

M3. Gabrieli, Giuseppe. **Manuale di bibliografia musulmana.** Rome, 1916. Now somewhat out of date, but still valuable. Deals with technical questions of Islamic scholarship.

M4. Pfannmüller, Gustav. **Handbuch der Islam-Literatur.** Berlin and Leipzig, 1923. By a non-orientalist. Examines European literature on Islam.

M5. Ettinghausen, Richard, ed. **A selected and annotated bibliography of books and periodicals in western languages dealing with the Near and Middle East, with special emphasis on mediaeval and modern times.** Washington, 1952. Supplement, 1954. This and the following are invaluable classified bibliographies.

M6. Pearson, James D. **Index islamicus: a catalogue of articles on Islam published in periodicals and other collective works from 1906 to 1955.** Cambridge, Eng., 1958.

M7. Minorsky, Vladimir F. "Les études historiques et geographiques sur la Perse." **Acta orientalia,** 10 (1932): 278–93, 16 (1937): 49–58, 21 (1951): 108–23. Critical, classified survey of published works on Persian history and geography, by an acknowledged master.

M8. Rossi, Ettore. "Gli studi di storia ottomana in Europa ed in Turchia nell' ultimo venticinquennio (1900–1925)." **Oriente moderno,** 6 (Aug. 1926): 443–60. Bibliographical and critical survey of writings on Ottoman history, by one of the leading authorities on the subject.

M9. Gabrieli, Francesco. "Studi di storia musulmana, 1940–1950." **Rivista storica italiana,** 62 (1950): 99–111. Authoritative survey and evaluation of scholarly work.

M10. Mantran, Robert. "Les études historiques en Turquie de 1940 à 1945." **Journal asiatique,** 235 (1946–47): 89–111. This and the following (*M11–13*) are useful bibliographies of historical publications in Turkey and the Arab countries.

M11. Wittek, Paul. "Neuere wissenschaftliche Literatur in osmanisch-türkischer Sprache." **Orientalistische Literaturzeitung,** 31 (Mar. 1928): 172–76, 31 (July 1928): 556–62, 32 (Feb. 1929): 74–79, 32 (Mar. 1929): 244–50, 34 (May 1931): 411–20.

M12. el-Shayyal, Gamal el-Din. "A sketch of Arabic historical works published in Egypt and the Near East during the last five years (1940–1945)." Royal Society of Historical Studies, **Proceedings,** 1 (Cairo, 1951): 143–74.

M13. Rizzitano, Umberto. "Studi di storia islamica in Egitto (1940–1952)." **Oriente moderno,** 33 (Nov. 1953): 442–56.

M14. Chauvin, Victor C. **Bibliographie des ouvrages arabes ou relatifs aux Arabes publiés dans l'Europe chrétienne de 1810 à 1885.** 12 v. in 4. Liège, 1892–1922. Now largely superseded, but still of value.

M15. Wilson, Sir Arnold T. **A bibliography of Persia.** See *S11*.

M16. Mayer, Leo A. **Bibliography of Moslem numismatics, India excepted.** 2nd ed., London, 1954. The standard guide.

M17. Creswell, Keppel A. C. "A provisional bibliography of the Muhammadan architecture of India." **The Indian antiquary,** 51 (May 1922): 81–108.

M18. Brockelmann, Carl. **Geschichte der arabischen Litteratur.** 5 v. Weimar and Leiden, 1898–1942. The standard bio-bibliographical survey of Arabic literature; an indispensable reference.

M19. Storey, Charles A. **Persian literature: a bio-bibliographical survey.** 1 v. in 3. London, 1927–53. Comprehensive list of Persian mss. and printed works, with brief descriptions of them and their authors. [AKSL]

ENCYCLOPEDIAS AND WORKS OF REFERENCE

M20. **The encyclopaedia of Islam.** See *F31*.

M21. **Shorter encyclopaedia of Islam.** Ed. by Hamilton A. R. Gibb and Johannes H. Kramers. Leiden, 1953. A selection from first edition of the above, with some revisions. Limited mainly to articles on religious subjects.

M22. Pareja Casañas, Félix M. **Islamología.** Rome, 1951. Includes a survey of political and dynastic history, and useful bibliographies and indexes. Available in Spanish and Italian.

M23. Philips, Cyril H., ed. **Handbook of**

oriental history. London, 1951. Provides guidance on systems of transcription, names and titles, systems of dating, and technical terms. Also contains chronological and dynastic tables.

M24. Herbelot, Barthélemy d'. **Bibliothèque orientale: ou dictionnaire universel contenant tout ce qui fait connoître les peuples de l'Orient.** 4 v. The Hague, 1777–79. This and the following are two early works of reference, now for the most part superseded, but containing some useful material.

M25. Hughes, Thomas P. **A dictionary of Islam: being a cyclopaedia of the doctrines, rites, ceremonies, and customs, together with the technical and theological terms, of the Muhammadan religion.** 2nd ed., London, 1896.

M26. Caetani, Leone. **Annali dell' Islam.** 10 v. in 12. Milan, 1905–26. Detailed examination of events and problems, with translations of the chief sources, for the first forty years of the Hegira. An indispensable work of reference for this period.

M27. ——. **Chronographia islamica: ossia riassunto cronologico della storia di tutti i popoli musulmani dall'anno 1 all'anno 922 della higrah (622–1517 dell'èra volgare) corredato della bibliografia di tutte le principali fonti stampate e manoscritte.** Paris, 4 v. 1912–18. A list of events and sources, without citation or discussion, in chronological and topographical order. Completed only to beginning of the Abbasid period.

M28. Lane-Poole, Stanley. **The Mohammedan dynasties: chronological and genealogical tables with historical introductions.** Paris, 1925. Tables are accompanied by concise and usually reliable historical introductions. There are also Russian and Turkish versions.

M29. Zambaur, Eduard K. M. von. **Manuel de généalogie et de chronologie pour l'histoire de l'Islam.** Hanover, 1927. Includes vizirs and governors as well as sovereigns, and contains useful historical and bibliographical notes.

M30. Haig, Thomas W. **Comparative tables of Muhammadan and Christian dates, enabling one to find the exact equivalent of any day in any month from the beginning of the Muhammadan era.** London, 1932.

M31. Wüstenfeld, Heinrich F. **Wüstenfeld-Mahler'sche Vergleichungs-Tabellen der mohammedanischen und christlichen Zeitrechnung.** Leipzig, 1926.

M32. Hinz, Walther. **Islamische Masse und Gewichte: umgerechnet ins metrische System.** Leiden, 1955. Concise guide to the difficult problem of Muslim weights and measures.

M33. Mayer, Leo A. **Saracenic heraldry: a survey.** Oxford, 1933. The standard work on this subject.

GEOGRAPHIES, GAZETTEERS, AND ATLASES

M34. Le Strange, Guy. **Palestine under the Moslems.** Cambridge, Eng., 1930. This and the two following works, based on careful study of the Arabic and Persian sources, together form an indispensable guide to historical geography of the Middle East under the caliphate.

M35. ——. **The lands of the eastern caliphate: Mesopotamia, Persia and central Asia, from the Moslem conquest to the time of Timur.** Cambridge, Eng., 1930.

M36. ——. **Baghdad during the Abbasid caliphate, from contemporary Arabic and Persian sources.** London, 1924.

M37. Marmarji, A. Sebastianus, ed. and tr. **Textes géographiques arabes sur la Palestine.** Paris, 1951. Collection of translations of Arabic texts.

M38. Dussaud, René. **Topographie historique de la Syrie antique et médiévale.** See *F39.*

M39. Hazard, Harry W., and Hereward L. Cooke. **Atlas of Islamic history.** 3rd ed., Princeton, 1954. Mainly concerned with the borders between Islam and Christendom. This and the following are the only available general atlases of Islamic history.

M40. Roolvink, Roelof, and others. **Historical atlas of the Muslim peoples.** Amsterdam, 1957. Devotes more attention than the above to internal developments of the Muslim world.

LINGUISTIC WORKS

M41. Lane, Edward W. **An Arabic-English lexicon.** 8 pts. London and Edinburgh, 1863–93. Although unfortunately not completed, this is the standard dictionary of classical Arabic.

M42. Dozy, Reinhart P. A. **Supplément aux dictionnaires arabes.** 2nd ed., 2 v., Paris, 1927. The additions here and in the following work derive mainly from North African and Spanish Arabic texts.

M43. Fagnan, Edmond. **Additions aux dictionnaires arabes.** Algiers, 1923.

M44. Steingass, Francis J. **A comprehensive Persian-English dictionary . . . being Johnson and Richardson's Persian, Arabic, and English dictionary, revised, enlarged, and entirely reconstructed.** 2nd ed., London, 1930. Valuable for study of classical Persian and also Ottoman texts.

M45. Desmaisons, Jean J. P. **Dictionnaire persan-français.** 4 v. Rome, 1908–14. Useful for classical Persian.

M46. Fueck, Johann. **'Arabiya: recherches sur l'histoire de la langue et du style arabe.** Paris, 1955. Standard work on evolution of the Arab language; important for understanding and cultural and intellectual history.

M47. Redhouse, James W. **A Turkish and English lexicon, showing in English the significations of the Turkish terms.** Constantinople (Instanbul), 1890. The standard dictionary of Ottoman Turkish.

PRINTED COLLECTIONS OF SOURCES

M48. Berchem, Max van. **Matériaux pour un Corpus inscriptionum arabicarum.** 10 v. Paris, 1903–49. This and the following work are collections of Arabic inscriptions. *Matériaux* also includes many valuable notes and appendices on historical, topographical, and other problems.

M49. Combe, Étienne, J. Sauvaget, and G. Wiet. **Répertoire chronologique d'epigraphie arabe.** 14 v. Cairo, 1931–54.

M50. Wright, H. Nelson. **The coinage and metrology of the sultāns of Dehlī.** Oxford, 1936. Attempt at a comprehensive corpus. An indispensable sequel to E. Thomas, *The chronicles of the Pathān kings of Dehli* (London, 1871). [PH]

M51. Horovitz, Josef. "A list of the published Mohamedan inscriptions of India." **Epigraphia indo-moslemica,** 2 (1909–10): 30–144.

HISTORIOGRAPHY

M52. Margoliouth, David S. **Lectures on Arabic historians.** Calcutta, 1930. General survey of development, in chronological sequence. This and the following work are the best introductions to Arabic historiography.

M53. Rosenthal, Franz. **A history of Muslim historiography.** Leiden, 1952. Special attention to themes and methods; includes many translations. Both this and the above are limited to historians writing in classical Arabic.

M54. Gibb, Hamilton A. R. "Notes on the Arabic materials for the history of the early crusades." **Bulletin of the School of Oriental and African Studies,** 7 (1935): 739–54.

M55. Gabrieli, Francesco, ed. **Storici arabi delle crociate.** Turin, 1957. Collection of excerpts from the Arabic chronicles of the crusades, in Italian translation. Admirably selected, translated, and presented.

M56. Sauvaget, Jean, ed. **Historiens arabes: pages choisies.** Paris, 1946. This anthology of excerpts from Arabic historians, in French translation, forms a useful introduction to Arabic historiography.

M57. Babinger, Franz. **Die Geschichtsschreiber der Osmanen und ihre Werke.** See *S26.*

SHORTER GENERAL HISTORIES

M58. Spuler, Bertold. **Geschichte der islamischen Länder.** 2 v. Leiden and Cologne, 1952–53. Most up-to-date general outline of the whole period, by a competent scholar.

M59. Brockelmann, Carl. **Geschichte der islamischen Völker und Staaten.** Munich and Berlin, 1939. Tr., *History of the Islamic peoples,* London, 1949. Useful outline of Islamic history, compiled by an eminent oriental philologist. About half the book deals with the medieval period.

M60. Barthold, Vasilii V. **Mussulman culture.** Tr. by Shahid Suhrawardy. Calcutta, 1934. Interesting outline by an eminent Russian orientalist, first published in 1918.

M61. The Cambridge medieval history. See *J43.* This and the following work contain chapters on the Islamic world.

M62. Historia mundi. Ed. by Fritz Kern. Bern, 1952 ff.

M63. Le civiltà dell'Oriente. Ed. by Giuseppe Tucci. Rome, 1956. Contains outlines of Arab, Persian, and Turkish history. Excellent general introduction.

LONGER GENERAL HISTORIES

M64. Weil, Gustav. **Geschichte der Chalifen.** 5 v. Stuttgart, 1846–62. Only large-scale general history of the caliphate, based on original sources. Though in many ways out of date, still of value.

M65. Müller, F. August. **Der Islam im Morgen.** 2 v. Berlin, 1885–87. Still the only large-scale general history of the Islamic world. Worth consulting, though superseded in many parts.

HISTORIES OF SPECIAL PERIODS

M66. Muir, Sir William. **The caliphate, its rise, decline, and fall.** New and rev. ed. by T. H. Weir. Edinburgh, 1915. The most detailed general history of the caliphate available in English. Concerned chiefly with political and military events, it follows faithfully after the Arabic chronicles. The revised edition takes cognizance of the researches of De Goeje and Wellhausen on the period of Arab conquests.

M67. Kremer, Alfred. **Culturgeschichte des Orients unter den Chalifen.** 2 v. Vienna, 1875–77. Tr., *The Orient under the caliphs,* Calcutta, 1920. First major attempt at a cultural history of the caliphate. A few chapters of the original are available in the English translation. Though now outdated, it can still be of use to advanced students who are aware of its deficiencies.

M68. Diehl, Charles, and Georges Marçais. **Le monde oriental de 395 à 1081.** 2nd ed., Paris, 1944. [Histoire générale: histoire du

Moyen Âge, 3.] This and the following work are clear and reliable outlines of medieval Islamic history by qualified scholars.

M69. Gaudefroy-Demombynes, Maurice, and Sergei F. Platonov. **Le monde musulman et byzantin jusqu'aux croisades.** Paris, 1931. Particularly good on society and institutions.

M70. Guidi, Michelangelo. **Storia e cultura degli Arabi fino alla morte di Maometto.** Florence, 1951. Posthumous and incomplete work by a great Italian orientalist. A useful and reliable introduction to early Arab history, on which the author had some new ideas and interpretations.

M71. Wellhausen, Julius. **Skizzen und Vorarbeiten.** 6 v. Berlin, 1884–99. V. 4 and 6 include important studies on the prophet, the conquests, and the early caliphate.

M72. ——. **Das arabische Reich und sein Sturz.** Berlin, 1902. English tr., by Margaret G. Wier, Calcutta, 1927. A standard work on Arab history to the fall of the Umayyads (750 A.D.).

M73. Lammens, Henri. **Études sur le siècle des Omayyades.** Beirut, 1930. Father Lammens' studies have greatly enriched our knowledge of the Umayyad period. Some allowance must be made, however, for his strong religious loyalties, which color his judgments of Islam.

M74. ——. "Études sur le règne du Calife Omaiyade Mo'awia Ier." Université Saint-Joseph (Beirut), **Mélanges de la Faculté Orientale,** 1 (Paris, 1906): 1–108, 2 (1907): 1–172, 3 (1908): 145–312.

M75. ——. "Le Califat de Yazid Ier." See M74, 4 (1910): 233–312, 5 (1911–12): 79–267, 588–724, 6 (1913): 401–492.

M76. Gabrieli, Francesco. **Il califfato di Hishâm: studi di storia omayyade.** Alexandria, 1935. Important monograph by a distinguished scholar.

M77. Vloten, Gerlof van. **De opkomst der Abbasiden in Chorasan.** Leiden, 1890. A pioneer monograph, still the best comprehensive study of the fall of the Umayyads and accession of the Abbasids. Should be read in conjunction with more recent writings listed below.

M78. Moscati, Sabatino. "Studi su Abū Muslim." **Atti della Academia Nazionale dei Lincei anno CCCXLVI,** 4 (Rome, 1949): 323–35, 474–95; 5 (1950): 89–105.

M79. ——. "Studi storici sul califfato di al-Mahdī." **Orientalia,** n.s. 14 (Rome, 1945): 300–54. This and the following are two useful monographs on an important period of early Abbasid history.

M80. ——. "Le califat d'al-Hādī." **Studia orientalia,** 13 (Helsinki, 1946): 1–28.

M81. Hellige, Walther. **Die Regentschaft al-Muwaffaqs: ein Wendepunkt in der 'Abbâsidengeschichte.** Berlin, 1936. Only available monograph on this period.

M82. Minorsky, Vladimir F. **La domination des Dailmaites.** Paris, 1932. Brief but trustworthy outline of the period of Buyid rule, by an acknowledged authority.

M83. Mez, Adam. **Die Renaissance des Islâms.** Heidelberg, 1922. English tr. by Salahuddin Khuda Bukhsh and D. S. Margoliouth, London, 1937. Brilliant and penetrating survey of the civilization of Islam in the classical period, based on a profound knowledge of original sources. One of the two or three major works on medieval Islam.

M84. Vasiliev, Alexander A. **Byzance et les Arabes.** 3 v. Brussels, 1935–50. The standard work on Arab-Byzantine relations, including many translations of Arabic texts.

M85. Cheira, M. A. **La lutte entre Arabes et Byzantins: la conquête et l'organisation des frontières aux VIIe et VIIIe siècles.** Alexandria, 1947. Monograph based on Arabic sources.

M86. Stevenson, William B. **The crusaders in the East: a brief history of the wars of Islam with the Latins in Syria during the twelfth and thirteenth centuries.** Cambridge, Eng., 1907. This and the following work are still the only extensive studies of the crusades written by orientalists and based on Arabic as well as western sources. Both are indispensable for study of the crusades as part of the history of the Middle East.

M87. Cahen, Claude. **La Syrie du nord à l'époque des croisades et la principauté franque d'Antioche.** Paris, 1940.

M88. Runciman, Steven. **A history of the crusades.** See K247.

M89. Atiya, Aziz S. **The crusade in the later Middle Ages.** London, 1938. Important survey, based on wide reading in both the Arabic and western sources.

M90. Bouvat, Lucien. **L'empire mongol (2ème phase).** Paris, 1927. Deals with Timur and his successors in Persia, central Asia, and India. Still useful for the first two, though somewhat out of date.

HISTORIES OF SPECIAL AREAS

M91. Hitti, Philip K. **History of the Arabs from the earliest times to the present.** 6th ed., London, 1956. The most popular general narrative of events in the Arab world.

M92. Lewis, Bernard. **The Arabs in history.** 4th ed., London, 1958. Brief and general survey, especially concerned with the early development and full efflorescence of Muslim civilization. [VJP]

M93. Gabrieli, Francesco. **Gli Arabi.** Florence, 1957. Brilliant interpretation of Arab history.

M94. Levy, Reuben. **A Baghdad chronicle.** Cambridge, Eng., 1929. A chronicle of life and culture in the capital of the Abbasid caliphs.

M95. Goeje, Michel J. de. **Mémoire sur**

la conquête de la Syrie. 2nd ed., Leiden, 1900. Important monograph on the Arab conquest of Syria in the 7th century.

M96. Hitti, Philip K. **History of Syria, including Lebanon and Palestine.** London, 1951. This and the following are the only treatments covering medieval Syria. The different loyalties of the two authors make an instructive contrast.

M97. Lammens, Henri. **La Syrie, précis historique.** See *S177*.

M98. Gaudefroy-Demombynes, Maurice. **La Syrie à l'époque des Mamelouks.** Paris, 1923. French translation of an Arabic text on the geography and administration of Syria in the Mameluke period, together with a long and valuable introduction to the subject by the translator.

M99. Canard, Marius. **Histoire de la dynastie des Ḥamdanides de Jazîra et de Syrie.** Paris, 1953. Masterly monograph on Syria and Mesopotamia in the 10th century; especially good on Muslim-Byzantine relations.

M100. Hitti, Philip K. **Lebanon in history.** See *S178*.

M101. Lane-Poole, Stanley. **A history of Egypt in the Middle Ages.** 4th ed., London, 1925. Best outline of medieval Egyptian history available in English. Based on careful and extensive use of Arabic sources.

M102. Wiet, Gaston. **L'Égypte arabe de la conquête arabe à la conquête ottomane, 642–1517 de l'ère chrétienne.** Paris, 1937. Useful outline by an Arabist historian. Gives more attention than Lane-Poole to social and cultural factors.

M103. Butler, Alfred J. **The Arab conquest of Egypt and the last thirty years of the Roman dominion.** Oxford, 1902. Good monograph, though to some extent superseded by more recent material.

M104. Becker, Carl H. **Beiträge zur Geschichte Ägyptens unter dem Islam.** 2 v. Strasbourg, 1902–03. Important studies on Egypt in the Middle Ages, dealing with Fatimid history and historiography, and some social, economic, and fiscal problems of the first two centuries of Muslim rule.

M105. Hassan, Zaky Mohamed. **Les Tulunides: étude de l'Égypte musulmane à la fin du IXᵉ siècle, 868–905.** Paris, 1933. A monograph on this dynasty, devoting special attention to art and architecture.

M106. Lewis, Bernard. **The origins of Ismailism: a study of the historical background of the Fatimid caliphate.** Cambridge, Eng., 1940. This and the following provide two different accounts of the origin and accession of the Fatimid caliphs.

M107. Ivanov, Vladimir A. **Ismaili tradition concerning the rise of the Fatimids.** London, 1942.

M108. Canard, Marius. "L'impérialisme des Fatimides et leur propagande." **Annales**

de l'Institut d'Études Orientales d'Alger, 6 (1942–47): 156–93. Valuable monograph on an important aspect of Fatimid policy.

M109. O'Leary, De Lacy E. **A short history of the Fatimid khalifate.** London and N.Y., 1923. Only general history of the Fatimids in English.

M110. al-Maḳrīzī. **Histoire des sultans mamlouks de l'Égypte.** Ed. and tr. by Étienne M. Quatremère. 2 v. Paris, 1845. French translation of an Arabic chronicle, with introduction and notes. Despite its age, still very important for this period.

M111. Gautier, Émile F. **Le passé de l'Afrique du nord: les siècles obscurs.** Paris, 1937. Well-written, but at times uncritical, study of the process by which north Africa passed from Christianity to Islam. [DC]

M112. Marçais, Georges. **La Berbérie musulmane et l'Orient au Moyen Âge.** Paris, 1946. General, well-documented history of north Africa from the Islamic conquest to the decline of the Almohades. [DC]

M113. Brunschvig, Robert. **La Berbérie orientale sous les Ḥafṣides, des origines à la fin du XVᵉ siècle.** 2 v. Paris, 1940–47. Masterly use of at times insufficient sources to give a clear picture of the little-known Ḥafṣid dynasty which ruled eastern Barbary from 1228 to 1574. [DC]

M114. Marçais, Georges. **Les Arabes en Berbérie du XIᵉ au XIVᵉ siècle.** Paris, 1913. Thorough study of the great Bedouin invasions which led to the Berbers being driven back to their mountain fastnesses or assimilated. [DC]

M115. Terrasse, Henri. **Histoire du Maroc des origines à l'établissement du protectorat français.** See *AC305*.

M116. Lévi-Provençal, Évariste. **Islam d'Occident: études d'histoire médiévale.** Paris, 1948. Annotated edition of selected lectures and papers on various historical and cultural aspects of Islam in Spain and north Africa. [DC]

M117. ——. **La civilisation arabe en Espagne: vue générale.** Cairo, 1938. Short essay on Arab civilization in Spain and its contacts with and influence on western civilization. [DC]

M118. ——. **Histoire de l'Espagne musulmane.** See *VD59*.

M119. ——. **L'Espagne musulmane au Xᵉᵐᵉ siècle: institutions et vie sociale.** Paris, 1932. Thorough study of government and economic and social life at height of the Spanish Umayyad caliphate. Fully documented. [DC]

M120. Sánchez-Albornoz, Claudio. **La España musulmana según los autores islamitos y cristianos medievales.** 2 v. Buenos Aires, 1946. Excellent general history of Muslim Spain, based on a linking of well-selected extracts from medieval Arab and Spanish historians. [DC]

M121. González Palencia, Angel. **Historia de la España musulmana.** 4th ed., Barcelona, 1945. Concise and well-illustrated survey of the whole period for the general reader, dealing not only with political history, but also briefly with the cultural heritage of the Muslims of Spain. Full bibliography. [DC]

M122. Dozy, Reinhart P. A. **Spanish Islam: a history of the Moslems in Spain.** London, 1913. Tr. of *Histoire des Musulmans d'Espagne* (4 v., Leiden, 1861). The standard work of its time, now superseded by *M118.* [DC]

M123. Amari, Michele. **Storia dei Musulmani di Sicilia.** 2nd ed., 3 v., Catania, Sicily, 1933–39. Standard work on the period, fully documented and based on all known sources. [DC]

M124. Frye, Richard N., and Aydin M. Sayili. "Turks in the Middle East before the Saljugs." **Journal of the American Oriental Society,** 63 (July-Sep. 1943): 194–207.

M125. Laurent, Joseph. **L'Arménie entre Byzance et l'Islam depuis la conquête arabe jusqu'en 886.** Paris, 1919. Monographic treatment based chiefly on Greek sources.

M126. Cahen, Claude. "La première pénétration turque en Asie-Mineure." **Byzantion,** 18 (1946–48): 5–67. Scholarly examination of the Turkish invasion of Asia Minor in the 11th century, based on Islamic as well as Byzantine sources.

M127. Gordlevskii, Vladimir A. **Gosvdarstvo Sel'dzhukidov Maloi Azii.** [The Seljuk state in Asia Minor.] Moscow and Leningrad, 1941.

M128. Wittek, Paul. **Das Fürstentum Mentesche: Studie zur Geschichte Westkleinasiens im 13.–15. Jh.** Istanbul, 1934. This and the three following works, by the outstanding authority in the field, together form the best introduction to Turkish history in the 13th–15th centuries.

M129. ——. "Deux chapitres de l'histoire des Turcs de Roum." **Byzantion,** 11 (1936): 285–319.

M130. ——. **The rise of the Ottoman empire.** London, 1938.

M131. ——. "De la défaite d'Ankara à la prise de Constantinople." **Revue des études islamiques,** 12 (1938): 1–34.

M132. Gibbons, Herbert A. **The foundation of the Ottoman empire: a history of the Osmanlis up to the death of Bayezid I (1300–1403).** Oxford, 1916. Still very valuable, but should be consulted in conjunction with more recent studies on the same period, especially the following. [VJP]

M133. Köprülü, Mehmed F. **Les origines de l'empire ottoman.** Paris, 1935. Important on origins of the Ottoman empire. Largely a criticism of *M132.* [VJP]

M134. Langer, William L., and K. R. Blake. "The rise of the Ottoman Turks and its historical background." **Am. hist. rev.,** 37 (Apr. 1932): 468–505. Clear and concise account of factors which led to the emergence of the Ottoman state. [VJP]

M135. Atiya, Aziz S. **The crusade of Nicopolis.** London, 1934. Monographic treatment of Sultan Bayezid's victory over the crusade of 1396.

M136. Zinkeisen, Johann W. **Geschichte des osmanischen Reiches in Europa.** V. 1, **Urgeschichte und Wachsthum des Reiches bis zum Jahre 1453.** Hamburg, 1840. Admirable work, concerned mainly with relations between the Ottoman Turks and the states of Europe. Based largely on Venetian sources. [VJP]

M137. Iorga, Nicolae. **Geschichte des osmanischen Reiches.** V. 1. Gotha, 1908. Especially useful for events in the Balkans. [VJP]

M138. Hammer-Purgstall, Joseph von. **Geschichte des osmanischen Reiches.** V. 1, **Von der Gründung des osmanischen Reiches bis zur eroberung Constantinopels, 1300–1453.** Budapest, 1827. Still indispensable. Based largely on Turkish sources. [VJP]

M139. Babinger, Franz C. "Der Islam in Kleinasien: neue Wege der Islamforschung." **Zeitschrift der deutschen Morgenländischen Gesellschaft,** n.s. 1 (1922): 126–52. Survey of the main developments and local characteristics and forms that Islam assumed in Asia Minor. [VJP]

M140. ——. **Beiträge zur Frühgeschichte der Türkenherrschaft in Rumelien (14.–15. Jahrhundert).** Brünn, 1944. Valuable contribution to literature on early expansion of the Ottoman state in the Balkans. [VJP]

M141. Vaughan, Dorothy M. **Europe and the Turk: a pattern of alliances, 1350–1700.** Liverpool, 1954. Very useful account of the role of Turkey in European history, with some reference to Turkish internal affairs.

M142. Spuler, Bertold. **Iran in früh-islamischer Zeit: Politik, Kultur, Verwaltung und öffentliches Leben zwischen der arabischen und der seldschukischen Eroberung 633 bis 1055.** Wiesbaden, 1952. Brief account of the political history of Persia from the Islamic conquest to the rise of the Seljuqs, and description of religious, cultural, social, and economic conditions and administrative institutions. Based mainly on Arabic and Persian sources. Contains much useful information. [AKSL]

M143. ——. **Die Mongolen in Iran: Politik, Verwaltung und Kultur der Ilchanzeit, 1220–1350.** 2nd ed., Berlin, 1955. Valuable for the period of Mongol domination in Persia; based principally on Persian sources. [AKSL]

M144. Schwarz, Paul. **Iran im Mittelalter nach den arabischen Geographen.** 9 v. Leipzig and Stuttgart, 1910–36. Detailed description of Persia in the Middle Ages according to Arab geographers. A valuable reference book which includes considerable information on economic as well as geographical matters. [AKSL]

M145. Sadighi, Gholam H. **Les mouvements religieux iraniens au IIe et au IIIe siècle de l'hégire.** Paris, 1938. Information on religious movements and their social and political implications not easily accessible elsewhere. [AKSL]

M146. Barthold, Vasilii V. **Herāt unter Ḥusein Baiqara dem Timuriden.** German ed. by Walther Hinz. Leipzig, 1938. Useful account of Herat under the Timurids. [AKSL]

M147. Minorsky, Vladimir F. **Studies in Caucasian history.** London, 1953. History of Ganja in the 10th and 11th centuries, and of the effects of Kurdish intervention in Armenia. [AKSL]

M148. Howorth, Henry H. **History of the Mongols from the 9th to the 19th century.** 4 v. in 5. London, 1876–1927. Not entirely reliable on matters of detail. [AKSL]

M149. Grousset, René. **L'empire des steppes.** Paris, 1939. Important for political history of the Mongol empires in central Asia. [AKSL]

M150. Dunlop, D. M. **The history of the Jewish Khazars.** Princeton, 1954. Most recent survey of an obscure and difficult subject. A scholarly examination of sources and problems.

M151. Barthold, Vasilii V. **Histoire des Turcs d'Asie centrale.** Tr. by M. Donskis. Paris, 1945. Carefully documented history of the Turkish states and peoples of central Asia, including the states established by the Mongols and their successors. A standard work by a distinguished scholar. Based on a Turkish version; the Russian original has never been published.

M152. ——. **Turkestan down to the Mongol invasion.** Tr. and rev. by and with assistance of H. A. R. Gibb. 2nd ed., London, 1957. The standard work on the subject, and a classic of oriental scholarship.

M153. Gibb, Hamilton A. R. **The Arab conquests in central Asia.** London, 1923. Important monograph on establishment and first phase of Muslim rule in central Asia.

M154. Pritsak, Omeljan. "Karachanidische streitfragen 1–4." **Oriens,** 3 (Leiden, 1950): 209–28. Studies on an important topic of early Turkish-Islamic history.

M155. Spuler, Bertold. **Die Goldene Horde: die Mongolen in Russland, 1223–1502.** Leipzig, 1943. Standard account of the Muslim Mongol states in Russia, based on Islamic, Russian and European sources.

M156. Habibullah, A. B. M. **The foundation of Muslim rule in India.** Lahore, 1945. Best account of the Ghorid conquest of north India. Mainly political, but includes chapters on administration, society, and culture. [PH]

M157. Lal, Kishori S. **History of the Khaljis (1290–1320).** Allahabad, India, 1950.

Only monograph on the Khaljis. Painstaking and thorough in coverage of available evidence for political history; no account of religious and cultural life. [PH]

M158. Prasad, Ishwari. **History of medieval India from 647 A.D. to the Mughal conquest.** Allahabad, 1925. Good general account, with interesting chapter on cultural developments in Hindu society during the period. [PH]

M159. Sarkar, Jadunath, ed. **The history of Bengal. V. 2, The Muslim period.** Dacca, 1948. Deliberately a political account only. Follows closely the Muslim annals. Useful bibliography. [PH]

M160. The Cambridge history of India. V. 3, Turks and Afghans. Ed. by Thomas W. Haig. Cambridge, Eng., 1928. Political chronicle, not a rounded survey, of the history of peoples and civilizations of medieval India. [PH]

M161. Elliot, Henry M., and John Dowson. **The history of India as told by its own historians: the Muhammadan period. V. 1–4.** London, 1867–72. These volumes relate to the period ca. 700–1450. This study of medieval Muslim India is important as foundation for the modern era under European influence. The translations should be read in connection with *M166.* [PH]

M162. Sherwani, Haroon K. **The Bahmanis of the Deccan.** Hyderabad, Deccan, 1953. Brief political narrative of first important Muslim Deccan sultanate, founded upon a comprehensive survey of source materials. [PH]

M163. Commissariat, Mānekshāh S. **A history of Gujarat.** Bombay, 1938. General political history of Muslim Gujarat before the Mughal conquest, with valuable chapters on architecture and inscriptions. Profusely illustrated; excellent bibliography. [PH]

M164. Titus, Murray. **Indian Islam.** London, 1930. Useful compilation of data on the religious life of the Muslim community in south Asia. [PH]

M165. Moreland, William H. **The agrarian system of Moslem India.** Cambridge, Eng., 1929. The best account. Valuable glossary of revenue terms. [PH]

M166. Hodivala, Shahpurshah. **Studies in Indo-Muslim history.** Bombay, 1939. An essential companion to *M161,* on which it is a critical commentary, both textual and historical. [PH]

M167. Ashraf, Kunwar M. "Life and conditions of the People of Hindustan (1200–1550 A.D.)." **Journal of the Asiatic Society of Bengal,** ser. 3, 1 (1935): 103–359. Well-written pioneer account, from Muslim sources, of the social life of north India under the Delhi sultanate. Extensive bibliography. [PH]

M168. Qureshi, Ishtiaq H. **The administration of the sultanate of Delhi.** 2nd ed.,

Lahore, 1944. Most comprehensive account of pre-Mughal Indo-Muslim political institutions. Full bibliography, including works on political theory by Indo-Muslims. [PH]

M169. Chand, Tara. **Influence of Islam on Indian culture.** Allahabad, 1936. Concentrates on spheres of religion and art. Valuable on Ramananda, Kabir, and Guru Nanak. Extensive bibliography. [PH]

HISTORIES OF SPECIAL TOPICS

M170. Von Grunebaum, Gustave E. **Medieval Islam: a study in cultural orientation.** 2nd ed., Chicago, 1953. Brilliant and penetrating essay in interpretation, by an outstanding Arabic scholar. Predominantly literary and religious, but includes chapters on law and the state and on the social order.

M171. Goldziher, Ignác. **Le dogme et la loi de l'Islam: histoire du développement dogmatique et juridique de la religion musulmane.** Paris, 1920. 2nd ed., 1958. Written by one of the outstanding German orientalists of his time, this is still the best general introduction to the Islamic religion—law, dogma, mysticism, and sects. There are translations in French, Russian, Hungarian, Arabic, and Hebrew, but no satisfactory version in English.

M172. Hurgronje, Christiaan S. **Mohammedanism: lectures on its origin, its religious and political growth, and its present state.** N.Y. and London, 1916. Useful introduction by an eminent Dutch orientalist.

M173. Guidi, Michelangelo. **Storia della religione dell'Islam.** Turin, 1935. 2nd ed., 1949. This and the following are short accounts of historical development of the Islamic religion by two acknowledged masters of the subject.

M174. Gibb, Hamilton A. R. **Mohammedanism: an historical survey.** 2nd ed., London, 1953.

M175. Gaudefroy-Demombynes, Maurice. **Le pèlerinage à la Mekke: étude d'histoire religieuse.** Paris, 1923. [Annales du Musée Guimet: bibliothèque d'études, 33.] Historical study of one of the central rites of the Islamic religion—the pilgrimage to Mecca. A standard work.

M176. Birge, John K. **The Bektashi order of dervishes.** See *S91.*

M177. Arnold, Thomas W. **The preaching of Islam: a history of the propagation of the Muslim faith.** 3rd ed., London, 1935. The classic work on the subject, based on a profound and sympathetic knowledge of Islam, its history, and its literature. Mainly concerned with the Near and Middle East, but also includes chapters on Spain, tropical Africa, India, China, and Malaya.

M178. Arberry, Arthur J. **An introduction to the history of Sufism.** London and N.Y., 1943. Brief but authoritative introduction to the history of Muslim mysticism, by an outstanding scholar.

M179. Wensinck, Arent J. **The Muslim creed, its genesis and historical development.** Cambridge, Eng., 1932. The standard work on this subject.

M180. Macdonald, Duncan B. **Development of Muslim theology, jurisprudence and constitutional theory.** N.Y., 1903. This and the two following works by the same author, with their profound insight into the religious ideas and aspirations of Islam, form an excellent introduction to the study of any field of Islamic history.

M181. ——. **Aspects of Islam.** N.Y., 1911.

M182. ——. **The religious attitude and life in Islam.** Chicago, 1912.

M183. Vloten, Gerlof van. **Recherches sur la domination arabe: le chiitisme et les croyances messianiques sous le khalifat des Omayades.** Amsterdam, 1894. This and the following are two important monographs on the movements of religious opposition that helped to bring the Umayyad caliphate to an end.

M184. Wellhausen, Julius. **Die religiös-politischen Oppositionsparteien im alten Islam.** Berlin, 1901.

M185. Schacht, Joseph. **The origins of Muhammadan jurisprudence.** Oxford, 1950. A major work of orientalist scholarship, affecting many historical as well as legal questions.

M186. ——, ed. **G. Bergsträsser's Grundzüge des islamischen Rechts.** Berlin and Leipzig, 1935. This and the following (*M187–190*) are the best and most readily available textbooks of classical Islamic law.

M187. Santillana, David. **Istituzioni di diritto musulmano malichita, con riguardo anche al sistema sciafiita.** 2nd ed., 2 v., 1938. Includes a brilliant exposition of Islamic theories of the state and the sovereign.

M188. Sachau, Carl E. **Muhammedanisches Recht, nach Schafiitischer Lehre.** Stuttgart and Berlin, 1897.

M189. Juynboll, Theodor W. **Handbuch des islämischen Gesetzes nach der Lehre der schäfi'itischen Schule, nebst einer allgemeinen Einleitung.** Leiden and Leipzig, 1910.

M190. Fyzee, Asaf A. **Outlines of Muhammadan law.** 2nd ed., London, 1955.

M191. Tyan, Émile. **Histoire de l'organisation judiciaire en pays de l'Islam.** 2 v. Paris, 1938–43. The standard work on history of judicial institutions in Islamic countries, by an eminent Lebanese jurist.

M192. Gaudefroy-Demombynes, Maurice. "Notes sur l'histoire de l'organisation judiciaire en pays d'Islam." **Revue des études islamiques,** 13 (1939): 109–47. Provides some additions and corrections to the above.

M193. ——. **Muslim institutions.** London, 1950. Useful elementary introduction.

M194. Levy, Reuben. **The social structure**

of Islam: being the second edition of The sociology of Islam. Cambridge, Eng., 1957. Outline of Islamic government, society, customs, and ideas; relies largely on the normative statements of jurists and moralists.

M195. Abbott, Nabia. The Ḳurrah papyri from Aphrodito in the Oriental Institute. Chicago, 1938. An edition, translation, and evaluation of a group of Arabic papyri. Introduction includes study of Arab government in Egypt under the Umayyads.

M196. Husaini, Syed A. Arab administration. Madras, 1949. Survey of civil, military, fiscal, central, and provincial administration up to the early Abbasid period. Author brings out the better qualities of the institution he describes, but is not entirely uncritical.

M197. Duri, 'Abd al-'Aziz 'Abd al-Karim. Al-Nuzum al-islāmīya. [Islamic institutions.] Baghdad, 1950. Competent outline of classical Islamic institutions, by an Iraqi historian. Only the first volume has appeared, dealing with political, financial, and administrative institutions.

M198. Sauvaget, Jean. La poste aux chevaux dans l'empire des Mamelouks. Paris, 1941. Scholarly monograph on an important institution in medieval Egypt and Syria, by a good Arabist and historian.

M199. Strauss, Eli. "L'inquisition dans l'état mamelouk." Rivista degli studi orientali, 25 (1950): 11–26. Study of the apparatus of religious repression, based on Arabic sources.

M200. Tritton, Arthur S. The caliphs and their non-Muslim subjects: a critical study of the covenant of 'Umar. London, 1930. This and the two following are scholarly works on relations between the Muslim rulers and their Jewish and other non-Muslim subjects.

M201. Goitein, Solomon D. Jews and Arabs: their contacts through the ages. N.Y., 1955.

M202. Fischel, Walter J. Jews in the economic and political life of medieval Islam. London, 1937.

M203. Marçais, William. "Comment l'Afrique du nord a été arabisée. 1, L'arabisation des villes; 2, L'arabisation des campagnes." Annales de l'Institut d'Études Orientales, 4 (1938): 1–21, 14 (1956): 5–17.

M204. Poliak, Abraham N. "L'arabisation de l'Orient sémitique." Revue d'études islamiques, 12 (1938): 35–63.

M205. Cahen, Claude. "L'evolution de l'iqta' du IXe au XIIIe siècle: contributions à une histoire comparée des sociétés médiévales." Annales: économies, sociétés, civilisations, 8 (1953): 25–52. Masterly and well-documented study on military feudalism in medieval Islam.

M206. Köprülü, Memhet F. "Ortazaman Türk-Islâm feodalizmi." [Turkish-Islamic

feudalism in the Middle Ages.] Türk Tarih Kurumu, Belleten, 5 (1941): 319–34. Interpretation of medieval Turkish feudalism, by a brilliant Turkish historian.

M207. Poliak, Abraham N. Feudalism in Egypt, Syria, Palestine, and the Lebanon, 1250–1900. London, 1939. This and the two following are the most detailed studies available on this subject.

M208. ——. "Some notes on the feudal system of the Mamlūks." Journal of the Royal Asiatic Society of Great Britain and Ireland, 1937, pp. 97–107.

M209. ——. "La féodalité islamique." Revue des études islamiques, 10 (1936): 247–65.

M210. Løkkegaard, Frede. Islamic taxation in the classic period, with special reference to circumstances in Iraq. Copenhagen, 1950. This and the following work are scholarly and well-documented monographs on one of the central problems of early Islamic history. Indispensable for the economic historian.

M211. Dennett, Daniel C. Conversion and the poll tax in early Islam. Cambridge, Mass., 1950.

M212. Jahn, Karl. "Das iranische Papiergeld." Archiv orientální, 10 (Prague, June 1938): 308–40. Interesting study of the unsuccessful attempt by the Mongol Il-Khans to introduce paper money in Persia.

M213. Heyd, Wilhelm von. Histoire du commerce du Levant au Moyen-Âge. See J70.

M214. Hourani, George F. Arab seafaring in the Indian Ocean in ancient and early medieval times. Princeton, 1951. This and the two following are useful monographs on maritime and commercial relations with East and West.

M215. Lewis, Archibald R. Naval power and trade in the Mediterranean, A.D. 500–1100. See J68.

M216. Huzayyin, Suliman A. Arabia and the Far East: their commercial and cultural relations in Graeco-Roman and Irano-Arabian times. Cairo, 1942.

M217. Ayalon, David. L'esclavage de Mamelouk. Jerusalem, 1951. This and the following work are important monographs based on exhaustive study of Arabic sources.

M218. ——. Gunpowder and firearms in the Mamluk kingdom: a challenge to a mediaeval society. London, 1956.

M219. Torres Balbas, Leopoldo. "Les villes musulmanes d'Espagne et leur urbanisation." Annales de l'Institut d'Études Orientales d'Alger, 6 (1942–47): 5–30. A general restatement. Points out significance of the road system in Muslim towns. [LK]

M220. Abel, A. "Les marchés de Baghdad, essai historico-géographique: situation, voies d'accès, ressources." Bulletin de la Société Belge d'Études Géographiques, 9 (Dec.

1939): 148–64. Sound account, based on original and secondary sources. [LK]

M221. Massignon, Louis. "La 'Futuwwa' ou 'pacte d'honneur artisanal' entre les travailleurs musulmans au Moyen Âge." **La nouvelle Clio,** 4 (May 1952): 171–98. Outstanding on the economic and psychological environment of the Muslim artisan classes and their acceptance of "Futuwwa" ideals. Contains some novel suggestions which open large perspectives for further study. [LK]

M222. Marçais, Georges. "Les villes de la côte algérienne et la piraterie au Moyen Âge." **Annales de l'Institut d'Études Orientales d'Alger,** 13 (1955): 118–42. Deals with creation of towns on the North African coast and the Andalusian trading and piratical activities. [LK]

M223. Le Strange, Guy. **Baghdad during the Abbasid caliphate.** Oxford, 1900. Study of the topography of Baghdad in the Middle Ages, based on careful analysis of available evidence. Sound and painstaking, but should be supplemented by more recent studies. [LK]

M224. Pellat, Charles. **Le milieu baṣrien et la formation de Gāḥiẓ.** Paris, 1953. Contains much information about the development of Basra. [LK]

M225. Lewis, Bernard. "The Islamic guilds." **Economic history review,** 8 (1937): 20–37. A reassessment and revision of views dealing with the craft guilds and their organization and classification. Clear account of a complicated subject. [LK]

M226. Von Grunebaum, Gustave E. "Die islamische Stadt." **Saeculum,** 6 (1955): 138–53. General picture of Muslim urban life and institutions; particularly interesting in explaining the influence of the Muslim concept of authority on formation of urban administration. [LK]

M227. Ziadeh, Nicola A. **Urban life in Syria under the early Mamlūks.** Beirut, 1953. Brief sketch of urban problems and the Bahri administration. [LK]

M228. Reitemeyer, Else. **Die Städtegründungen der Araber im Islam nach den arabischen Historikern und Geographen.** Leipzig, 1912. List of towns founded by the Arabs, with a citation of available evidence. A sound treatise which has been superseded only by monographs on individual towns. [LK]

M229. Sauvaget, Jean. **Alep: essai sur le développement d'une grande ville syrienne, des origines au milieu du XIXe siècle.** See *S335.*

M230. Ashtor-Straus, E. "L'administration urbaine en Syrie médiévale." **Rivista degli studi orientali,** 31 (1956): 73–128. Deals with urban officials and especially with the "ra'is." Sound and well documented. [LK]

M231. Herzfeld, Ernst E. **Geschichte der Stadt Samarra.** Hamburg, 1948. The value of archaeological evidence for Islamic history is clearly shown in this beautifully presented book. Historical and geographic tracts have also been used to describe the erection and subsequent decay of a town, the basis of which was the royal court. [LK]

M232. Marçais, Georges. "Considérations sur les villes musulmanes et notamment sur le rôle du Mohtasib." **Recueils de la société Jean Bodin,** 6 (1954): 249–61. Conceives the Muslim town as a place of contact and exchange where the Muslim can most completely practice his faith. Written for non-orientalists. [LK]

M233. Cahen, Claude. "Mouvements et organisations populaires dans les villes de l'Asie musulmane au Moyen Âge: milices et associations de Foutouwwa." **Recueils de la Société Jean Bodin,** 7 (1955): 273–88. Refutation of the view that there was no civic spirit in Muslim towns, with a brief analysis of the part played by military and quasimilitary associations in the expression of local interests. [LK]

M234. Brunschvig, Robert. "Urbanisme médiéval et droit musulman." **Revue des études islamiques,** 15 (1947): 127–55. New approach to Muslim urbanism in which problems of public responsibility and obligations of vicinage are analyzed. [LK]

M235. Lévi-Provençal, Évariste. **Las ciudades y las instituciones urbanas del Occident musulmán en la Edad Media.** Tetuán, 1950. General account of urban institutions and their development in the Muslim West, emphasizing the importance of towns as centers of Muslim civilization. [LK]

M236. Torres Balbas, Leopoldo. "Extensión y demografía de las ciudades hispanomusulmanas." **Studia islamica,** 3 (1955): 35–59. Archaeological evidence is used to prove the rise in population of Spanish Muslim towns during the 10th, 11th, and 12th centuries and the subsequent decline. [LK]

M237. Lévi-Provençal, Évariste, ed. and tr. **Séville musulmane au début du XIIe siècle: le traité d'Ibn 'Abdun.** Paris, 1947. The introduction and notes appended to this translation of Ibn 'Abdun's treatise are well worth reading for an understanding of events in a Muslim town. [LK]

M238. Sauvaget, Jean. "Esquisse d'une histoire de la ville de Damas." **Revue des études islamiques,** 8 (1934): 421–80. A model for the writing of urban history. Describes the transformation of Damascus from a Greco-Roman city into a Muslim town and its subsequent history. [LK]

M239. Marçais, William. "L'Islamisme et la vie urbaine." Académie des Inscriptions et Belles-Lettres, **Comptes rendus des séances de l'année 1928** (Paris, 1928), pp. 86–100. Forceful refutation of the romantic view of Islam as a desert faith. Claims Islam belonged to a sedentary society and that

Muslim conquests encouraged urban groupings. [LK]

M240. Marçais, Georges. "L'urbanisme musulman." **Cinquième congrès de la Fédération des Sociétés Savantes de l'Afrique du Nord,** Tunis, 6–8 avril 1939 (Algiers, 1940), pp. 13–34. One of the best articles on Muslim urbanism and especially interesting to readers of North African history. [LK]

M241. Massignon, Louis. "Les corps de métiers et la cité islamique." **Revue internationale de sociologie,** 28 (Sep. 1920): 473–89. A brilliant article which pictures the Muslim town as the sociological development of the market. The conclusions must be regarded as tentative. [LK]

M242. Gardet, Louis. **La cité musulmane.** Paris, 1954. Examination of Muslim theory and practice, dealing with clash of universalism and particularism in the Muslim community.

M243. Siddiqi, Amir H. "Caliphate and kingship in mediaeval Persia." **Islamic culture,** 9 (Oct. 1935): 560–79, 10 (Jan. 1936): 97–126, 10 (Apr. 1936): 260–79, 10 (July 1936): 390–408, 11 (Jan. 1937): 37–59. Brief survey of development of the theory of the sultanate and its relations with the caliphate in eastern provinces of the Abbasid empire. [AKSL]

M244. Shirwani, Harun K. **Studies in Muslim political thought and administration.** 2nd ed., Lahore, 1945. Some aspects of the works of various writers compared with western theories. [AKSL].

M245. Rosenthal, Erwin I. T. "Some aspects of Islamic political thought." **Islamic culture,** 22 (Jan. 1948): 1–17. Useful article outlining the juristic, historico-political, and philosophical approach to the Muslim state. [AKSL]

M246. Pritsch, Emil. "Die islamische Staatsidee." **Zeitschrift für vergleichende Rechtswissenschaft,** 53 (1939): 33–72. Contains discussion of the theocratic nature of the Islamic state and the underlying assumptions on which it was based. Also traces the evolution of the Islamic doctrine of the state in the Ottoman empire. [AKSL]

M247. Laoust, Henri. **Essai sur les doctrines sociales et politiques de Takī-d-Dīn Ahmad b. Taīmiya, canoniste hanbalite, né à Harrān en 661/1262, mort à Damas en 728/1328.** Cairo, 1939. An important work. [AKSL]

M248. Khadduri, Majid. **War and peace in the law of Islam.** Baltimore, 1955. Brief and generally accurate. [AKSL]

M249. Hamidullah, Muhammad. **Muslim conduct of state.** Lahore, 1945. Brings together the theories of orthodox Muslim jurists on war and relations with other states. [AKSL]

M250. Gibb, Hamilton A. R. "Some considerations on the Sunni theory of the caliphate." **Archives d'histoire du droit orientale,** 3 (1947): 401–10. Valuable article on evolution of the doctrine of the caliphate. [AKSL]

M251. Becker, Carl H. "Barthold's Studien über Kalif und Sultan." **Der Islam,** 6 (1915–16): 350–412. Important account of evolution of the office of caliph under the Umayyads and Abbasids and the office of sultan. [AKSL]

M252. Arnold, Thomas W. **The caliphate.** Oxford, 1924. Outline of history of the doctrine of the caliphate. [AKSL]

M253. Tyan, Émile. **Institutions du droit public musulman.** 2 v. Paris, 1954–56. Comprehensive survey, by an eminent Lebanese jurist, of the central institutions of sovereignty in the medieval Islamic state.

M254. Aghnides, Nicolas P. **Mohammedan theories of finance.** N.Y. and London, 1916. Financial theories and practice of the early Muslim state. [AKSL]

M255. Gibb, Hamilton A. R. **Arabic literature: an introduction.** London, 1926. This and the two following works are the best general introductions to Arabic literature and literary history.

M256. Nicholson, Reynold A. **A literary history of the Arabs.** 2nd ed., Cambridge, Eng., 1930.

M257. Gabrieli, Francesco. **Storia della letteratura araba.** Milan, 1952.

M258. Browne, Edward G. **A literary history of Persia.** 4 v. Cambridge, Eng., 1951. Standard work on Persian literature in Islamic times. [AKSL]

M259. Levy, Reuben. **Persian literature: an introduction.** London, 1923. Brief account, in chronological order, of Persian writers and their works beginning with the 9th century A.D. [AKSL]

M260. Gibb, Elias J. W. **A history of Ottoman poetry.** See *S90.*

M261. Farmer, Henry G. **A history of Arabian music to the XIIIth century.** London, 1929. This and *M262–265* are standard works on aspects of scientific and cultural history.

M262. Creswell, Keppel A. C. **Early Muslim architecture.** 2 v. Oxford, 1932–40.

M263. Browne, Edward G. **Arabian medicine.** Cambridge, Eng., 1921.

M264. Sarton, George A. L. **Introduction to the history of science.** See *A249.*

M265. O'Leary, De Lacy E. **Arabic thought and its place in history.** 2nd ed., London, 1939. Outline of the influence, in Europe, of Islamic philosophy and science.

M266. Arberry, Arthur J. **The legacy of Persia.** Oxford, 1953. A series of essays on Persian culture and its influence on Persia's neighbors in pre-Islamic and Islamic times, written for the general reader. [AKSL]

M267. Nöldeke, Theodor. **Orientalische**

Skizzen. Berlin, 1892. Tr., *Sketches from eastern history,* Edinburgh, 1892. Important studies, including three on the Abbasid period.

M268. Khuda Bukhsh, Salahuddin. **Studies, Indian and Islamic.** London, 1927. Includes some translations from Van Kremer, as well as original essays on various topics.

M269. Von Grunebaum, Gustave E. **Islam: essays in the nature and growth of a cultural tradition.** Menasha, Wis., 1955. Collection of essays on aspects of Islamic cultural history, by an outstanding authority.

M270. Becker, Carl H. **Islamstudien.** 2 v. Leipzig, 1924–32. Essays and studies, mostly reprinted from learned journals. V. 1 contains important accounts of social and economic history of early medieval Islam. Both volumes are indispensable to the student of Islamic history.

M271. Arnold, Thomas W., and Alfred Guillaume, eds. **The legacy of Islam.** London, 1947. Collection of essays by various authors. Includes useful studies on geography and commerce (J. H. Kramers) and on law and society (D. de Santillana).

M272. Gabrieli, Francesco. **Storia e civiltà musulmana.** Naples, 1947. This and *M273–274* are collections of semi-popular essays written with great elegance by a distinguished Arabic scholar. They include several studies on Islamic history and culture in Sicily and Spain.

M273. ——. **Aspetti della civiltà arabo-islamica.** Turin, 1956.

M274. ——. **Dal mondo dell' Islàm: nuovi saggi di storia e civiltà musulmana.** Milan and Naples, 1954.

M275. Nallino, Carlo A. **Raccolta di scritti.** 6 v. Rome, 1939–48. Collected writings of one of the most outstanding Arabic scholars of his time. V. 3, dealing with history and institutions, includes a number of important studies.

M276. Kramers, Johannes H. **Analecta orientalia.** 2 v. Leiden, 1954–56. Collection of miscellaneous writings, including studies on Ottoman historiography and on Islamic geographical literature.

M277. Goldziher, Ignác. **Muhammedanische Studien.** 2 v. Halle, 1889–90. A fundamental work of scholarship, basic to an understanding of Islamic history and institutions. V. 1 deals extensively with problems of race, class, and nation in medieval Islam; v. 2, with development of legal and doctrinal traditions.

M278. Hurgronje, Christiaan S. **Selected works.** Ed. by G. H. Bousquet and J. Schacht. Leiden, 1957. Writings of one of the outstanding Islamic scholars of his time. Concerned mainly with history of Islamic law, but includes an important paper on the biography of Mohammed.

BIOGRAPHIES

M279. Buhl, Frants P. W. **Das Leben Muhammeds.** Tr. from the Danish by Hans H. Schaeder. Leipzig, 1930. In addition to career of Mohammed, deals with the civilization of pre-Islamic Arabia, and provides a very good introduction to the more specialized literature on both subjects. [JMBJ]

M280. ——. "Muhammad." **Encyclopaedia of Islam,** v. 3 (1936), pp. 641–57. Contains copious references to European works available to the author and to most Arabic sources. In conjunction with other articles in the *Encyclopaedia* referred to by Buhl, provides an unrivaled synoptic view of the subject. [JMBJ]

M281. Caetani, Leone. **La biografia di Maometto, profeta ed uomo di stato.** V. 1 and 3. Milan, 1911–14. V. 1 deals with prehistoric and pre-Islamic Arabia, and includes a useful section on Arabian armies and weapons. V. 3 contains a brilliant interpretive analysis of the career of Mohammed. [JMBJ]

M282. Andrae, Tor J. E. **Mohammed, sein Leben und sein Glaube.** Göttingen, 1932. Tr. *Mohammed, the man and his faith,* London, 1936. Most authoritative work to date on the psychological and philosophical aspects of Mohammed's call to prophecy. [JMBJ]

M283. Muir, William. **Life of Mohammad from original sources.** New ed., Edinburgh, 1923. In spite of the early date (1861) of the original edition and its somewhat uncritical and verbose presentation, contains much information of real value. [JMBJ]

M284. Watt, W. Montgomery. **Muhammad at Mecca.** Oxford, 1953. First of a 2 v. study of the life of Mohammed. Embodies an analysis of the social and moral background of Mohammed's teaching and its relevance to the contemporary situation. [JMBJ]

M285. ——. **Muhammad at Medina.** Oxford, 1956. Sequel to the above, but of considerably greater significance. The best-written and most thought-provoking treatment to appear thus far in English. Particularly worthy of note are those parts dealing with the tribal system in north and central Arabia and the social reforms instituted by Mohammed. [JMBJ]

M286. Blachère, Régis. **Le problème de Mahomet: essai de biographie critique du fondateur de l'Islam.** Paris, 1952. Critical reconsideration of the sources; a useful introduction to problems presented by the biography of the prophet.

M287. Gaudefroy-Demombynes, Maurice. **Mahomet.** Paris, 1957. First part is a conventional treatment of the life of Mohammed at Mecca and Medina. The second part uses Mohammed's message as basis for a series of discussions on belief and practice in early Islam. [JMBJ]

M288. Ibn Hisham, 'Abd al-Malik. **The life of Muhammad.** Tr. and ed. by Alfred Guillaume. London, 1956. Scholarly translation of one of the primary Arabic sources on the life of Mohammed, superseding Weil's earlier German version. [JMBJ]

M289. Andrae, Tor J. E. **Die Person Muhammeds in Lehre und Glauben seiner Gemeinde.** Stockholm, 1918. Illuminating treatment of growth of the Prophet legend in Islam. [JMBJ]

M290. Abbott, Nabia. **Aishah, the beloved of Mohammed.** Chicago, 1942. Semi-popular account of the most famous of Mohammed's wives. Based on Arabic sources.

M291. Gabrieli, Francesco. "L'eroe Omayyade Maslamah ibn 'Abd al-Malik." **Atti della Academia Nazionale dei Lincei: classe di science morali, storiche e filologiche,** 8th ser., 5 (1950): 22–39. Monograph on an important figure in early history of Islam—the Umayyad prince who led the Arab attack on Constantinople in 716–17.

M292. Palmer, Edward H. **Haroun Al-raschid, caliph of Bagdad.** London and Belfast, 1881. In the absence of monographic treatment of Caliph Harun, this and the following work may serve as popular introduction to his reign.

M293. Philby, Harry St. J. **Harun al Rashid.** London, 1933.

M294. Abbott, Nabia. **Two queens of Baghdad: mother and wife of Hārūn al-Rashīd.** Chicago, 1946. A popular account, but makes use of original sources. Describes some aspects of court life in Baghdad.

M295. Gabrieli, Francesco. **Al-Ma'mūn e gli 'Alidi.** Leipzig, 1929. Scholarly monograph on an important period and problem of early Abbasid history.

M296. Bowen, Harold. **The life and times of 'Alí ibn 'Isà, "the good vizier."** Cambridge, Eng., 1928. Detailed study of the Abbasid caliphate in the years 892–946, based on intimate knowledge of the period and sources.

M297. Massignon, Louis. **La passion d'al-Hosayn-ibn-Mansour al-Hallaj, martyr mystique de l'Islam, exécuté à Bagdad le 26 mars 922.** 2 v. Paris, 1922. Profound and sympathetic study of a key figure in the history of Islamic mysticism.

M298. Lane-Poole, Stanley. **Saladin and the fall of the kingdom of Jerusalem.** 2nd ed., N.Y. and London, 1926. Best available biography of Saladin, based directly on Arabic sources.

M299. Vladimirtsov, Boris Y. **The life of Chingis-Khan.** Tr. by D. S. Mirsky. London, 1930. By an acknowledged specialist in Mongol history and institutions.

M300. Ibn Khaldūn and Tamerlane, their historic meeting in Damascus, 1401 A.D.

(803 A.H.): **a study based on Arabic manuscripts of Ibn Khaldūn's "Autobiography."** Tr. and ed. by Walter J. Fischel. Berkeley, 1952. Account of the meeting between a great Arabic historian and a Turkish conqueror. Translation of an Arabic text, accompanied by many useful historical notes.

M301. Nāzim, Muḥammad. **The life and times of Sultàn Maḥmūd of Ghazna.** Cambridge, Eng., 1931. Monographic treatment of the Muslim conqueror of India.

M302. Habib, Mohammad. **Sultan Mahmud of Ghaznin.** Bombay, 1927. Lively and well written, presenting Mahmud as a hero of the 10th century Persian renaissance, a foreign conqueror in India, waging war for gold rather than religion. [PH]

M303. Ḥusain, Agha. **The rise and fall of Muḥammad Bin Tughluq.** London, 1938. Controverts many of the previously held views on the career of this sultan, who is here portrayed as a Muslim political hero. [PH]

M304. Barthold, Vasilii V. **Ulug Beg und seine Zeit.** Tr. by Walther Hinz. Leipzig, 1935. Valuable account of Timur's successors in Turkestan. [AKSL]

M305. Babinger, Franz C. **Mehmed der Eroberer und seine Zeit.** Munich, 1953. Contributes much valuable factual information about one of the most important Ottoman sultans. [VJP]

PERIODICALS

Most important of the journals devoted to Islamic studies are the following (*M306–311*).

M306. Der Islam. Strasbourg, Berlin, etc., 1910 ff. (Annual.)

M307. Revue des études islamiques. Paris, 1927 ff. (Quarterly.)

M308. Arabica. Leiden, 1954 ff. (3 nos. per year.)

M309. Studia islamica. Paris, 1953 ff. (Annual.)

M310. Islamic culture. Hyderabad, 1927 ff. (Quarterly.)

M311. Andalus. Madrid, 1933 ff. (Semi-annual.)

Important material will be found in the two following earlier journals, no longer published.

M312. Mïr islama. St. Petersburg (Leningrad), 1912–13.

M313. Islamica. Leipzig, 1924–35.

Material relating to Islamic history will also be found in general orientalist journals published by orientalist societies, institutions for oriental studies, etc. The most important of these are the following (*M314–324*).

M314. Journal of the Royal Asiatic Society of Great Britain and Ireland. London, 1834 ff. (Once irregular quarterly; now semi-annual.)

M315. Journal of the American Oriental Society. New Haven, 1843 ff. (Irregular quarterly.)

M316. Journal asiatique. Paris, 1822 ff. (Frequency varies.)

M317. Zeitschrift der deutschen morgenländischen Gesellschaft. Leipzig, 1847 ff. (Irregular quarterly.)

M318. Oriens. Leiden, 1948 ff. (Semiannual.)

M319. Acta orientalia. Leiden, 1922 ff. (4 nos. per year.)

M320. Bulletin of the School of Oriental and African Studies. London, 1917 ff.

M321. Rivista degli studi orientali. Rome, 1907 ff. (Irregular quarterly.)

M322. Mitteilungen des Seminars für orientalischen Sprachen. Berlin, 1898 ff. (Irregular annual.)

M323. Wiener Zeitschrift für die Kunde des Morgenländes. Vienna, 1887 ff. (Irregular.)

M324. Archiv orientální. Prague, 1929 ff. (Quarterly.)

Texts and studies also appear in journals published by historical learned societies and universities in the countries of the Islamic world.

For current bibliographical abstracts and reviews see the following.

M325. Bibliotheca orientalis. Leiden, 1943 ff. (Irregular quarterly.)

M326. Orientalistische Literaturzeitung. Berlin and Leipzig, 1898 ff. (Monthly.)

M327. The Middle East journal. Washington, 1947 ff. (Quarterly.) Contains quarterly bibliographical survey of periodical literature on the Middle East, including a short section on the medieval period, although more concerned with recent events.

IV. ASIA SINCE EARLY TIMES

SECTION N

Asia: General
(Ca. 200 B.C. to the Present)

EARL H. PRITCHARD,* EVELYN B. McCUNE,
H. F. SCHURMANN, and SCHUYLER van R. CAMMANN

This general section lists works dealing with two or more Asian countries or relating to Korea, Mongolia, central Asia, and Tibet, areas not covered in the detailed sections that follow. Each of the sections relating to Asian countries contains a considerable number of titles in Asian languages. This has been done for two reasons: (1) to acquaint western readers generally with the immense amount of historical material, both primary and interpretative, that exists in Asian languages, and to impress upon western historians that the key to understanding the history of Asian countries lies in a knowledge of their languages; and (2) because as far as a number of Asian countries are concerned, the only detailed critical studies of many aspects of their history have been done by native scholars. This latter is especially true of Japan, China, and India, although many of the studies by Indians are in English. The selections in Asian languages generally include some sources and classical works, examples of traditional historiography and scholarship, and modern general works and monographic studies on special subjects.

As to the material that follows in this section, the first part contains only general works that relate to a considerable segment of Asia. Detailed bibliographies of China and Japan, for example, will be found in Sections O and P. The same is true of journals and periodical publications. Journals specifically relating to central Asia, Mongolia, or Tibet will be found under Central Asia. It should also be noted that material on the beginnings of civilization in Asia is in Sections F and G, while works relating to the religions of Asian countries are included in Section D. Many works relating to western contacts with Asia, international affairs, and contemporary Asian history are in Section U and Part IX; those relating to Soviet Asia will be found in Section X.

* Professor Pritchard planned and edited this section and prepared the subsection on General Works; Korea was prepared by Mrs. McCune, assisted by P. K. Sohn; Mongolia and Central Asia by Professor Schurmann; and Tibet by Professor Cammann.

GENERAL WORKS

BIBLIOGRAPHIES, LIBRARIES, AND MUSEUMS

N1. Dobson, W. A. C. H., ed. **A select list of books on the civilizations of the Orient.** Oxford, 1955. Valuable selected bibliography by the Association of British Orientalists.

N2. Quan, Lau-king. **Introduction to Asia: a selective guide to background reading.** Washington, 1955. Useful selected bibliography issued by the Reference Department of the Library of Congress.

N3. Kerner, Robert J. **Northeastern Asia: a selected bibliography.** 2 v. Berkeley, 1939. Unusually valuable bibliography of nearly 14,000 titles in Chinese, Japanese, Korean, Russian, and other western languages relating to China, Manchuria, Mongolia, Tibet, central Asia, Japan, Korea, and Asiatic Russia. Titles of works in far eastern languages are romanized and provided with translated titles and characters.

N4. Bulletin of far eastern bibliography. Ed. by Earl H. Pritchard. 5 v. Washington, 1936–40. For the years 1941 through 1948 this bibliography was continued in the issues of the *Far eastern quarterly,* Gussie E. Gaskill becoming editor in 1946. For the years 1949–55 it was issued annually, sometimes (1949–52) in the August issue of the *Quarterly.* Since 1956 it has been continued as a separate annual volume entitled *Bibliography of Asian studies.* Provides the best general coverage of eastern Asia on a yearly basis since 1936.

N5. Gaskill, Gussie E., ed. **Far eastern bibliography.** 10 v. Ann Arbor, 1947–56. Annual volumes, 1946–55. Those for 1954 and 1955 were prepared by Howard P. Linton.

N6. Linton, Howard P., ed. **Bibliography of Asian studies.** 1956 ff. Ann Arbor, 1957 ff. (Annual.) Continuation of *N5,* with addition of works on south Asia (India, Ceylon, and Pakistan).

N7. Kyoto University. **Annual bibliography of oriental studies.** 1934 ff. Kyoto, 1936 ff. Very valuable classified catalog of new books and articles prepared by the Research Institute of Humanistic Sciences of Kyoto University. Includes works in Chinese and Japanese and in European languages, with author indexes. Several years were combined during and immediately after the war.

N8. Ōtsuka Shigakkai. **Hōbun rekishi-gaku kankei sho-zasshi Tōyō-shi ronbun yōmoku.** [List of articles on oriental history appearing in Japanese historical and related periodicals.] Tokyo, 1936. Valuable list of articles published in Japanese journals between 1865 and 1935, classified by area and subject, relating to Korea, China, Manchuria, Mongolia,

Tibet, central Asia, south Pacific, Turkey, Persia, India, and Formosa.

N9. Garde, P. K. **Directory of reference works published in Asia.** Paris, 1956. Valuable guide.

N10. Japanese National Commission for UNESCO. **Research in Japan in history of eastern and western cultural contacts: its development and present situation.** Tokyo, 1957. Important survey and summary, with much attention to central Asian studies.

Libraries

Aside from the great collections in various countries of Asia, a considerable number of European and American libraries and public repositories have large collections of books in western and Asiatic languages and documentary sources relating to various Asiatic countries. The most important libraries in the United States and Canada for such materials are the following: Library of Congress, Harvard, Columbia, Yale, Princeton, Pennsylvania, New York Public Library, Cornell, Cleveland Public Library, Michigan, Chicago, Newberry Library, Wisconsin, Minnesota, California at Berkeley and Los Angeles, Stanford, University of Washington, and University of Toronto.

Museums

Aside from European museums, the following in the United States and Canada have important collections of southern and east Asian, especially Chinese, art, archaeology, or natural history: Museum of Fine Arts, Boston; Fogg Museum, Harvard University; Metropolitan Museum of Art and the Museum of Natural History, New York; Freer Gallery of Art and the Smithsonian Institution, Washington; University of Pennsylvania Museum, Philadelphia; Chicago Art Institute, Oriental Institute of the University of Chicago, and Museum of Natural History, Chicago; William Rockhill Nelson Gallery, Kansas City; Minneapolis Art Institute; Cleveland Museum of Art; Museum of the University of Michigan, Ann Arbor; and Royal Ontario Museum of Archaeology, Toronto.

GENERAL REFERENCE WORKS

N11. Philips, Cyril H., ed. **Handbook of oriental history.** London, 1951. An invaluable handbook prepared by members of the Department of Oriental History of the London School of Oriental and African Studies. Deals with the Near and Middle East, India and Pakistan, southeast Asia, China, and Japan.

Each section discusses romanization, names and titles, place names, systems of dating, and provides a list of dynasties and rulers and a selected glossary.

N12. Hinton, Harold C., and Marius B. Jansen, eds. **Major topics on China and Japan: a handbook for teachers.** N.Y., 1957. Valuable discussion of major topics to be treated in an account of the history and culture of China and Japan, with bibliographical items.

N13. Tōyō rekishi dai-jiten. [Great dictionary of oriental history.] 9 v. Tokyo, 1937–39. Well-balanced historical dictionary covering China, Korea, India, and other Asian countries. Includes important events, institutions, persons, books, and places; arranged in *kana* order. V. 9 contains the indices.

N14. Tchang, Mathias. **Synchronismes chinois.** Shanghai, 1905. Chronology and concordance with Christian era dates of historical events in China, Japan, Korea, Annam, Mongolia, and other far eastern areas from 2357 B.C. to 1904 A.D. Although it is out of date and does not incorporate results of much recent critical scholarship, it is nevertheless quite valuable.

N15. Yule, Sir Henry, and Arthur C. Burnell. **Hobson-Jobson: a glossary of colloquial Anglo-Indian words and phrases, and of kindred terms, etymological, historical, geographical and discursive.** New ed., ed. by William Crooke, London, 1903. Invaluable guide to names and terms encountered in the literature relating to southern and eastern Asia.

N16. Balfour, Edward G. **Cyclopaedia of India and of eastern and southern Asia: commercial, industrial, and scientific.** 3rd ed., 3 v., London, 1885. Still useful since a more up-to-date work is not available. The various editions are of historical interest, especially for the ethnographical information given. Major emphasis is on India.

N17. Gellhorn, Eleanor C. **McKay's guide to the Far East and the Middle East.** Rev. ed., N.Y., 1956. Useful general guide designed especially for travelers.

N18. United Nations. **Economic survey of Asia and the Far East.** 1947 ff. Bangkok, 1948 ff. (Annual.) Valuable handbook of economic statistics and developments. The volume for 1957 is especially useful.

N19. Pan-Asian Newspaper Alliance. **The Asia who's who 1957.** Hong Kong, 1957. Contains over 2,000 brief biographies of prominent Asians from Burma, China (Free and Communist), Hong Kong, India, Indonesia, Japan, Pakistan, Philippines, Singapore, Thailand, Mongolia, Korea, and Vietnam.

N20. Morehouse, Ward, ed. **American institutions and organizations interested in Asia: a reference directory.** N.Y., 1957. Useful compilation prepared by the Conference on Asian Affairs.

N21. Asia Foundation. **Directory of cultural organizations in free Asia.** Taipei, 1956.

GEOGRAPHY, ANTHROPOLOGY, ETHNOLOGY, AND DEMOGRAPHY

N22. Linton, Ralph. **The tree of culture.** N.Y., 1955. A basic anthropological interpretation which devotes much space to Asia.

N23. Sellman, Roger R. **An outline atlas of eastern history.** London, 1954. Useful. Contains 51 pages of maps, mostly historical, dealing with India, southeast Asia, China, and Japan.

N24. Yanai, Wataru. **Tōyō tokushi chizu.** [Historical atlas of the Orient.] Tokyo, 1925. Rev. ed., 1941. Good atlas of Asia, with special emphasis on China.

N25. Buxton, L. H. Dudley. **The peoples of Asia.** London, 1925. A cautious book which recognizes the many racial and cultural elements involved. Now somewhat out of date, but the only acceptable general survey available.

N26. Thompson, Warren S. **Population and peace in the Pacific.** Chicago, 1946. Basic demographic study.

N27. Murray, Hugh. **Historical account of discoveries and travels in Asia.** 3 v. Edinburgh, 1820. Extensive general survey from earliest times to early 19th century.

N28. Sykes, Sir Percy M. **A history of exploration.** 3rd ed., London, 1950. A more recent general account.

N29. Polo, Marco. **The book of Ser Marco Polo, the Venetian, concerning the kingdoms and marvels of the East.** Tr. and ed. by Sir Henry Yule. 3rd ed., rev. by Henri Cordier, 2 v., London, 1903. Of the many editions and studies of Marco Polo, this is probably the best and most useful.

N30. Cordier, Henri. **Ser Marco Polo: notes and addenda to Sir Henry Yule's edition.** N.Y., 1920.

N31. Foster, Sir William. **England's quest of eastern trade.** London, 1933. Excellent general account of the development of England's connections with the East to about 1700.

N32. Cressey, George B. **Asia's lands and peoples.** Rev. ed., N.Y., 1951. The most complete descriptive, single volume reference geography on Asia.

N33. Spencer, Joseph E. **Asia, east by south.** N.Y., 1954. Dependable cultural geography which emphasizes southern and eastern Asia.

N34. East, W. Gordon, and Oskar H. K. Spate, eds. **The changing map of Asia.** 2nd ed., London, 1953. Especially valuable for its emphasis on historical background and discussion of changes in Asia's political and social geography.

N35. Ginsburg, Norton S., and others. eds. **The pattern of Asia.** N.Y., 1958. Up-to-date geography emphasizing the social science approach, as indicated by chapters on peoples and cultures, political organization, and the physical bases of life.

N36. Sion, Jules. **Asie des moussons.** 1 v. in 2. Paris, 1928–29. [Geographie universelle, 9.] Outstanding economic and geographical analysis of monsoon Asia.

N37. Gourou, Pierre. **L'Asie.** Paris, 1953. A first-class French geography.

N38. Stamp, L. Dudley. **Asia: a regional and economic geography.** 9th rev. ed., London and N.Y., 1957. A standard and well-known geography.

N39. Peterson, Alexander D. C. **The Far East.** 3rd ed., London, 1957. Recent, dependable social geography.

DOCUMENTS

N40. Maki, John M., comp. **Selected documents, far eastern international relations (1689–1951).** Seattle, 1951. Useful selection.

N41. Coedès, George, ed. and tr. **Textes d'auteurs grecs et latins relatifs à l'Extrême-Orient depuis le IVe siècle av. J.-C. jusqu'au XIVe siècle.** Paris, 1910.

N42. Isaacs, Harold, ed. **New cycle in Asia: selected documents on major international developments in the Far East, 1943–1947.** N.Y., 1947. Useful and convenient collection of documents on the war and postwar period.

N43. Moore, Harriet L. **Soviet far eastern policy, 1931–1945.** Princeton, 1945.

N44. Mandel, William, comp. **Soviet source materials on USSR relations with east Asia, 1945–1950.** N.Y., 1950. This work, issued by the Institute of Pacific Relations, continues *N43.* Documents are arranged by countries and emphasize China.

N45. Eudin, Xenia J., and Robert C. North. **Soviet Russia and the Far East, 1920–1927: a documentary survey.** Stanford, 1957.

N46. Tewksbury, Donald G., ed. **Source book on far eastern political ideologies.** Preliminary ed., 2 v., N.Y., 1949–50. Helpful collection of materials. V. 1 deals with modern China and Japan, v. 2 with Korea.

GENERAL HISTORIES

N47. Battistini, Lawrence H. **Introducing Asia.** N.Y., 1953. Layman's introduction to the history of Asia and its problems.

N48. Clyde, Paul H. **The Far East.** 3rd ed., Englewood Cliffs, N.J., 1958. Most up-to-date and in many respects the most usable general history of eastern and southeastern Asia during the 19th and 20th centuries.

N49. Vinacke, Harold M. **A history of the Far East in modern times.** N.Y., 1950. Similar to *N48,* but with more attention to internal developments.

N50. Durant, Will. **The story of civilization.** V. 1, **Our oriental heritage.** N.Y., 1935.

Well written, popular history of civilization of the Near East to the death of Alexander the Great, and of India, China, and Japan from the beginning to the 20th century.

N51. Eckel, Paul E. **The Far East since 1500.** N.Y., 1947. Best available account of the history of eastern and southeastern Asia from 1500 to the present.

N52. Peffer, Nathaniel. **The Far East: a modern history.** Ann Arbor, 1958. Interpretative.

N53. Grousset, René, Jeannine Auboyer, and Jean Buhot. **l'Asie orientale des origines au XVe siècle.** Paris, 1941. [Histoire du Moyen Âge, 10.] Concise general histories of India, southeast Asia, China, and Japan, by specialists on the areas concerned. For coverage of the Near and Middle East and more details on some of the areas, Grousset's earlier work, *Histoire de l'Asie* (3 v., Paris, 1921–22), should also be consulted.

N54. Michael, Franz H., and George E. Taylor. **The Far East in the modern world.** N.Y., 1956. Factual yet highly interpretative history of eastern and southeastern Asia, especially in the 19th and 20th centuries, with excellent account of the background, institutions, and civilization of these regions.

N55. Cameron, Meribeth E., Thomas A. B. Mahoney, and George E. McReynolds. **China, Japan and the powers.** N.Y., 1952. Similar to *N54* in background coverage of China and Japan.

N56. Steiger, G. Nye. **A history of the Far East.** Boston, 1936. Although not entirely up to date, this is still the best general survey in English of the whole history of southern, eastern, and central Asia.

N57. Latourette, Kenneth S. **A short history of the Far East.** 3rd ed., N.Y., 1957. A more up-to-date book of the same general type as *N56,* but with less factual details.

N58. Waldschmidt, Ernst, and others. **Geschichte Asiens.** Munich, 1950. Covers India, central Asia, China, Japan, and Korea.

N59. Krause, Friedrich E. A. **Geschichte Ostasiens.** 3 v. Göttingen, 1925. Of value for its concentration on China and the area influenced by it.

N60. Wittfogel, Karl A. **Oriental despotism: a comparative study of total power.** New Haven, 1957. A suggestive but highly controversial work on societies and civilizations, mostly Asiatic, that have depended heavily on the control and management of water resources and hence have developed despotic bureaucratic states. Review, S. N. Eisenstadt, *Jour. Asian studies,* 17 (May 1958): 435.

HISTORIES OF SPECIAL TOPICS

International Relations

N61. Dutcher, George M. **The political awakening of the East.** N.Y., 1925. Important early study of the rise of nationalism in Egypt, China, Japan, and the Philippines, and of the influence of western ideas and methods in these areas.

N62. Kohn, Hans. **A history of nationalism in the East.** N.Y., 1929. Deals extensively with India and the Middle East.

N63. Panikkar, Kavalam M. **Asia and western dominance: a survey of the Vasco da Gama epoch of Asian history, 1498–1945.** London, 1953. A somewhat partisan review of western contacts with Asia since the period of the great discoveries; especially kind to Russia.

N64. Datta, Surendra K. **Asiatic Asia.** London, 1932. Analysis of the forces and factors contributing to change in Asia, including a discussion of such things as industrial development, nationalism, and communism.

N65. Morse, Hosea B., and Harley F. MacNair. **Far eastern international relations.** Boston, 1931. Despite its age, still the most thorough and comprehensive single volume survey to 1930. Brought up to date in the following work.

N66. MacNair, Harley F., and Donald F. Lach. **Modern far eastern international relations.** 2nd ed., N.Y., 1955. Thorough survey of period since 1900, which places much emphasis on internal developments.

N67. Buss, Claude A. **The Far East.** N.Y., 1955. A generally less satisfactory book than the above, but with more details on developments since 1941.

N68. Quigley, Harold S., and George H. Blakeslee. **The Far East: an international survey.** Boston, 1938. Valuable detailed analysis of the far eastern situation as it existed before outbreak of the Sino-Japanese war in 1937.

N69. King-Hall, Stephen. **Western civilization and the Far East.** 2nd ed., London, 1925. Excellent survey of the internal and external developments of China and Japan under western impact.

N70. Pratt, Sir John T. **The expansion of Europe into the Far East.** London, 1947. Interpretative account, by the far eastern adviser to the British Foreign Office, which stresses Britain's role.

N71. Renouvin, Pierre. **La question d'Extrême-Orient, 1840–1940.** Paris, 1946. The European point of view on a century of far eastern diplomacy, by a distinguished historian. Places special emphasis on trade and World War I.

N72. Leger, François. **Les influences occidentales dans la révolution de l'Orient: Inde, Malaisie, Chine, 1850–1950.** 2 v. Paris, 1955.

N73. Shukow (Zhukov), Evgenii M. **Die internationalen Beziehungen in Fernen Osten (1870–1945).** Berlin, 1955. German translation of a Soviet Akademiia Nauk publication giving a Communist interpretation of far eastern diplomacy since 1870.

N74. Franke, Otto. **Die Grossmächte in Ostasiens von 1894 bis 1914.** Hamburg, 1923. German analysis and interpretation of a crucial period in far eastern international relations.

N75. Dennett, Tyler. **Americans in eastern Asia.** N.Y., 1922. Most thorough general account of U. S. relations with southern and eastern Asia to 1900. A classic.

N76. Griswold, A. Whitney. **The far eastern policy of the United States.** N.Y., 1938. Continuation of Dennett's work for the years 1898–1937, although its perspective is more narrowly diplomatic.

N77. Bisson, Thomas A. **America's far eastern policy.** N.Y., 1945. Reviews U. S. policy as a whole, but is primarily valuable for detailed survey of the years 1931–45.

N78. Hornbeck, Stanley K. **The United States and the Far East: certain fundamentals of policy.** Boston, 1942. A restatement of U. S. policy shortly after Pearl Harbor by the head of the Far Eastern Division of the State Department.

N79. Latourette, Kenneth S. **The American record in the Far East, 1945–1951.** N.Y., 1952. Unemotional evaluation of U. S. policies in the Far East since the end of World War II.

N80. Vinacke, Harold M. **The United States and the Far East, 1945–1951.** Stanford, 1952.

N81. Dallin, David J. **The rise of Russia in Asia.** New Haven, 1949. Most up-to-date general survey of Russian relations with Asia prior to 1930. Based primarily on Russian sources.

N82. ——. **Soviet Russia and the Far East.** New Haven, 1948. Brings his survey up to 1948. Very critical of Russian policy.

N83. Beloff, Max. **Soviet policy in the Far East, 1944–1951.** London and N.Y., 1953. Valuable survey based on western and Russian material.

N84. Yakhontoff, Victor A. **Russia and the Soviet Union in the Far East.** N.Y., 1931. Although out of date in many respects, still a valuable general survey. Continued to 1945 by Harriet L. Moore, *Soviet far eastern policy (N43)*, although her book intentionally reflects the Soviet point of view.

Political and Legal Institutions

N85. Kahin, George M., ed. **Major governments of Asia.** Ithaca, 1958. Most complete and up-to-date work on the governments of Asian countries.

N86. Linebarger, Paul, Djang Chu, and Ardath W. Burks. **Far eastern governments and politics: China and Japan.** 2nd ed., Princeton, 1956. Study in comparative government, historically applied; often too esoteric and erudite for the general reader.

N87. Washington Foreign Law Society.

Studies in the law of the Far East and southeast Asia. Washington, 1956. Seven lectures dealing with aspects of the law of China, Japan, Vietnam, Cambodia, Indonesia, and India.

Economic History

N88. Bain, Harry F. **Ores and industry in the Far East.** Rev., enl. ed., N.Y., 1933. Best general survey as of the early 1930's. Partially brought up to later date by the following.

N89. Field, Frederick V., ed. **An economic survey of the Pacific area.** 3 pts. N.Y., 1942. Valuable economic survey of the Far East as of 1942, prepared by the Institute of Pacific Relations. The statistical details on population and land utilization in pt. 1 are especially useful.

N90. United Nations. **Coal and iron resources of Asia and the Far East.** Bangkok, 1952.

N91. ———. **Agriculture in Asia and the Far East: development and outlook.** Rome, 1953. Useful survey of the agrarian situation and problems.

N92. Grist, Donald H. **Rice.** 2nd ed., London and N.Y., 1955. Thorough discussion of rice cultivation and production. More statistical details will be found in the following.

N93. Wickizer, Vernon D., and Merrill K. Bennett. **The rice economy of monsoon Asia.** Stanford, 1941.

N94. Hubbard, Gilbert E. **Eastern industrialization and its effect on the West.** 2nd ed., London, 1938. A trail-blazing study.

N95. Allen, George C., and Audrey G. Donnithorne. **Western enterprise in far eastern economic development: China and Japan.** London, 1954. Valuable study by careful scholars.

N96. Milburn, William. **Oriental commerce.** 2 v. London, 1813. Invaluable survey of history and status of the commerce of southern and eastern Asia as of the date of publication.

N97. Eldridge, Frank R. **Trading with Asia.** N.Y., 1921. Account of commercial relations and a convenient manual on the economies, products, industries, and markets of southern and eastern Asia as of date of publication.

N98. Ghate, Bhalchandra G. **Asia's trade: a study of the trade of Asian countries with each other and with the rest of the world.** New Delhi, 1948; N.Y., 1949. Useful survey published by the Indian Council of World Affairs. See also the following work.

N99. United Nations. **A study of trade between Asia and Europe.** Geneva, 1953.

N100. Ganguli, Birendranath. **India's economic relations with the far eastern and Pacific countries in the present century.** Bombay and Calcutta, 1956. Painstaking analysis of India's economic relations country-by-country, by a distinguished Indian economist.

Cultural History

N101. Grousset, René. **Les civilisations de l'Orient.** 4 v. Paris, 1929–30. Tr. by Catherine A. Philips, *The civilizations of the East,* 4 v., N.Y., 1931–34. Valuable introduction to the history of civilization and art of major Asian countries.

N102. Northrop, Filmer S. C. **The meeting of East and West: an inquiry concerning world understanding.** N.Y., 1946. A well-known but controversial book. Review, G. P. Conger, *Far eastern quar.,* 6 (Feb. 1947): 173.

N103. Grousset, René. **Histoire de la philosophie orientale: Inde-Chine-Japan.** Paris, 1923. Discussion of Hindu, Buddhist, Chinese, and Japanese thought.

N104. Radhakrishnan, Sarvepalli, ed. **History of philosophy, eastern and western.** 2 v. London, 1952–53. General account by specialists.

N105. Moore, Charles A., ed. **Philosophy —East and West.** Princeton, 1944. Various essays by specialists, dealing with philosophy of southern and eastern Asia.

N106. ———, ed. **Essays in East-West philosophy.** Honolulu, 1951. Supplements and extends the above.

N107. Ceadel, Eric B., ed. **Literatures of the East: an appreciation.** London, 1953. Excellent introduction to literatures of the ancient Hebrews, Arabs, Iranians, Persians, Indians, Chinese, and Japanese. Each chapter, contains a useful bibliography.

N108. Yohannan, John D., ed. **A treasury of Asian literature.** N.Y., 1956. Selection from the stories, dramas, poetry, and scriptures of Islam, India, China, and Japan.

N109. Gundert, Wilhelm, Annamarie Schimmel, and Walther Schubring, eds. **Lyrik des Ostens.** Munich, 1952. Well-selected collection.

N110. Horst, Franz, and G. L. Anderson, eds. **Indiana University conference on oriental-western literary relations.** Chapel Hill, N.C., 1955. Collection of papers of varying quality dealing with various aspects of literary relations between the East and West. Area covered extends from Spain through southern and eastern Asia to Japan.

N111. Bowers, Faubion. **Theatre in the East: a survey of Asian dance and drama.** N.Y., 1956. Very useful survey without much historical depth.

N112. Wellesz, Egon, ed. **Ancient and oriental music.** London, 1957. Best available general account of Asiatic music. Aside from ancient western music, specialists deal with music of Mesopotamia, Egypt, the Bible, post-Biblical Judaism, Islam, China, and other far eastern countries.

N113. Rowland, Benjamin, Jr. **Art in East and West: an introduction through comparisons.** Cambridge, Mass., 1954. Valuable introduction to eastern art, by a distinguished scholar.

N114. Binyon, Laurence. **The flight of the dragon.** London and N.Y., 1911. 8th printing, 1948. Brilliant introduction to and exposition of the general character of Chinese and Japanese art.

N115. ——. **Painting in the Far East.** 4th ed., London, 1934. A classic.

N116. Speiser, Werner. **Die Kunst Ostasiens.** New ed., Berlin, 1956. An up-to-date well-illustrated account.

N117. Christy, Arthur E., ed. **The Asian legacy and American life.** N.Y., 1945. Series of essays dealing with Asian influence on literature, art, music, and agriculture in the West, including one on the general subject of cultural contacts.

N118. Bagchi, Prabodh C. **India and China: a thousand years of cultural relations.** 2nd ed., N.Y., 1951. Careful work which brings together the author's studies over a long period. Emphasis is on the influence of Buddhism.

Contemporary Problems

N119. Ball, W. Macmahon. **Nationalism and communism in east Asia.** 2nd ed., N.Y. and London, 1956. Interpretative study of contemporary development in eastern Asia, by a well-known Australian diplomat and writer.

N120. Battistini, Lawrence H. **The United States and Asia.** N.Y., 1955. Popular account of U. S. relations with Asian countries.

N121. Charlesworth, James C., ed. **Asia and future world leadership.** Philadelphia, 1958. Up-to-date analysis and interpretation of developments in Asia.

N122. Jones, Francis C., Hugh Borton, and B. R. Pearn. **The Far East, 1942–1946.** London and N.Y., 1955. [Survey of international affairs: 1939–1946.] This publication of the Royal Institute of International Affairs is the most thorough and balanced survey of development in the Far East during and immediately after World War II.

N123. Keeton, George W. **China, the Far East, and the future.** New ed., London, 1949. Analysis of the far eastern situation by an English specialist in the area. A more recent British analysis dealing with the whole of Asia is the following.

N124. Low, Sir Francis. **Struggle for Asia.** London, 1955.

N125. Kennedy, Malcolm D. **A history of communism in east Asia.** N.Y., 1957. Best

available comprehensive survey of development of communism in southern and eastern Asia.

N126. Payne, Robert. **Red storm over Asia.** N.Y., 1951. Contains biographical notes on Asiatic Communists.

N127. Linton, Ralph, ed. **Most of the world: the peoples of Africa, Latin America and the East today.** N.Y., 1949. Valuable survey of peoples and problems, including resources, population trends, the Near East, India and Pakistan, southeast Asia and Indonesia, China, and Japan.

N128. Michener, James. **The voice of Asia.** N.Y., 1951. Paperback ed., 1952. One of the best journalistic efforts to present the Asians' point of view about affairs of their respective countries.

N129. Rosinger, Lawrence K., and others. **The state of Asia.** N.Y., 1951. Generally valuable survey of the situation in various Asian countries as of 1950, by specialists in each area. Deals with China, Mongolia, Sinkiang and Tibet, Korea, Japan, Indochina, Thailand, Burma, Malaya, Philippines, Indonesia, India, and Pakistan.

N130. Thayer, Philip W., ed. **Nationalism and progress in free Asia.** Baltimore, 1956. Useful and thought-provoking group of papers.

N131. Holland, William L., ed. **Asian nationalism and the West.** N.Y., 1953. Special attention to Indonesia, Indochina, and the Philippines.

N132. Thomson, Ian. **The rise of modern Asia.** London, 1957. General survey and interpretation of 20th century developments and trends.

N133. Vinacke, Harold M. **Far eastern politics in the postwar period.** N.Y., 1956. Best general survey of far eastern international relations since 1945, covering the Far East and southeast Asia.

N134. Zinkin, Maurice. **Asia and the West.** Rev. ed., London and N.Y., 1953. Interpretative analysis of social and economic problems of Asiatic countries and of their relations with the West, by a former British civil servant in India. Insufficient attention to Japan.

PERIODICALS AND SOCIETY PUBLICATIONS

The number of periodicals that relate in one way or another to Asia is enormous. Those listed below are a selection of the more scholarly publications devoted entirely to two or more Asian countries.

N135. Acta asiática. Buenos Aires, 1954 ff. (Quarterly.)

N136. Acta orientalia. Leiden, 1922 ff. (4 nos. per year.)

N137. Acta orientalia. Budapest, 1950 ff. (3 nos. per year.)

N138. **Ajia kenkyū.** [Asiatic studies.] Tokyo, 1954 ff.

N139. **Archiv orientální.** Prague, 1929 ff. (3 nos. per year.)

N140. **Ars orientalis.** Washington, 1954 ff. (Irregular.)

N141. **Artibus Asiae.** Ascona, Switz., 1925 ff. (Irregular annual.)

N142. **Arts asiatiques.** Paris, 1950 ff.

N143. **Asia: Asian quarterly of culture and synthesis.** Saigon, 1951 ff. (Quarterly.)

N144. **Asia major.** Leipzig and London, 1924 ff. (Irregular.)

N145. **Asian recorder.** New Delhi, 1955 ff. (Weekly.)

N146. **Asian affairs: quarterly journal of Asia kyokai.** Tokyo, 1956 ff. Its Japanese journal, *Ajia mondai,* has been published since 1953.

N147. **Asian review.** London, 1886 ff. (Irregular quarterly. Title varies.)

N148. **The Asiatic journal and monthly register.** London, 1816–45.

N149. **Asiatische Studien.** Bern, 1947 ff. (Quarterly.)

N150. **Bibliografiia vostoka.** [Bibliography of the East.] Leningrad and Moscow, 1932–39.

N151. **Bulletin de l'École Française d'Extrême-Orient.** Hanoi and Paris, 1901 ff. (Frequency varies.)

N152. **Bulletin of the Institute of Traditional Cultures.** Madras, 1957 ff.

N153. **Bulletin of the Museum of Far Eastern Antiquities.** Stockholm, 1929 ff. (Irregular.)

N154. **Bulletin of the School of Oriental and African Studies.** London, 1917 ff. (3 nos. per year.)

N155. **Economic bulletin for Asia and the Far East.** Bangkok, 1950 ff. (Quarterly.)

N156. **Far eastern review.** Shanghai, 1904–41. (Monthly.)

N157. **Far eastern survey.** N.Y., 1932 ff. (Biweekly.)

N158. **Harvard journal of Asiatic studies.** Cambridge, Mass., 1936 ff. (Quarterly.)

N159. **The Indo-Asian culture.** New Delhi, 1952 ff. (Quarterly.)

N160. **Journal of Asian studies.** Ann Arbor, 1941 ff. (Quarterly.) Formerly the *Far eastern quarterly.*

N161. **Journal asiatique.** Paris, 1822 ff. (Quarterly.)

N162. **Journal of the American Oriental Society.** New Haven, 1843 ff. (Frequency varies.)

N163. **Journal of east Asiatic studies.** Manila, 1951 ff. (Quarterly.)

N164. **Journal of oriental studies.** Hong Kong, 1954 ff. (Semiannual.)

N165. **Journal of the Royal Asiatic Society.** London, 1834 ff. (Irregular.)

N166. **Journal of economic and social history of the Orient.** Leiden, 1957 ff.

N167. **The kokka: illustrated journal of eastern art.** Tokyo, 1889 ff. (Monthly. Title varies.)

N168. **Kratkie soobshcheniia Instituta Vostokovedeniia.** [Brief reports of the Institute of Oriental Studies.] Moscow, 1951 ff. (Irregular.)

N169. **Mélanges asiatiques.** St. Petersburg (Leningrad), 1849–94, 1918–19. (Irregular.)

N170. **Mélanges chinois et bouddhiques.** Brussels, 1932 ff. (Annual.)

N171. **Memoirs of the Research Department of the Tōyō Bunko.** Tokyo, 1926 ff. (Irregular.)

N172. **Mitteilungen des Instituts für Orientforschung.** Berlin, 1953 ff. (3 nos. per year.)

N173. **Mitteilungen der Deutschen Gesellschaft für Natur- und Völkerkunde Ostasiens.** Tokyo and Berlin, 1873 ff. (Irregular.)

N174. **Mitteilungen des Seminars für Orientalische Sprachen.** Berlin, 1898 ff. (Irregular.)

N175. **Oriens.** Leiden, 1948 ff. (Semiannual.)

N176. **Oriens Extremus.** Wiesbaden, 1954 ff. (Semiannual.)

N177. **Oriental art.** London, 1948 ff. (Quarterly.)

N178. **Oriental economist.** Tokyo, 1934 ff. (Monthly.)

N179. **Ostasiatische Zeitschrift.** Berlin, 1912–43. (Quarterly.)

N180. **Pacific affairs.** N.Y., 1928 ff. (Frequency varies.)

N181. **Philosophy east and west.** Honolulu, 1951 ff. (Quarterly.)

N182. **Revoliutsionnyi Vostok.** [The revolutionary East.] Moscow, 1927–37. (Irregular.)

N183. **Revue des arts asiatiques.** Paris, 1924–42. (Irregular.)

N184. **Rivista degli studi orientali.** Rome, 1907 ff. (Irregular.)

N185. **Rocznik orientalistyczny.** [Yearbook on oriental studies.] Lwow and Warsaw, 1914 ff. (Irregular.)

N186. **Sovetskoe vostokovedenie.** [Annual of Soviet oriental studies.] Moscow, 1940 ff.

N187. **Sovremennyi Vostok.** [The contemporary East.] Moscow, 1957 ff.

N188. **Tikhii Okean.** [Pacific Ocean.] Moscow, 1934–38.

N189. **Tōhōgaku.** [Eastern studies.] Tokyo, 1951 ff. (Irregular.)

N190. **Tōhō gakuhō.** [Journal of eastern studies.] Kyoto, 1933 ff. (Irregular.)

N191. **T'oung pao.** Leiden, 1890 ff. (Irregular.)

N192. **Tōyō bunka.** [Oriental culture.] Tokyo, 1950 ff. (Semiannual.)

N193. **Tōyō Gakuhō.** [Reports of the Oriental Society.] Tokyo, 1913 ff. (Quarterly.)

N194. **Tung-fang tsa-chih.** [Eastern miscellany.] Shanghai, 1904–45. (Frequency varies.)
N195. **Wiener Beiträge zur Kunst- und Kulturgeschichte Asiens.** Vienna, 1926–37. (Annual.)
N196. **Wiener Zeitschrift für die Kunde des Morgenlandes.** Vienna, 1887 ff. (Quarterly.)
N197. **Zapiski Institut Vostokovedeniia**

Akademii Nauk S.S.S.R. [Memoirs of the Institute of Oriental Studies of the Academy of Sciences of the U.S.S.R.] Moscow and Leningrad, 1932 ff. (Annual.) Published under varying titles until 1950 when it became the *Uchenye zapiski* of the Institute (several nos. per year).
N198. **Zeitschrift der Deutschen Morgenländischen Gesellschaft.** Leipzig and Wiesbaden, 1847 ff. (Irregular.)

KOREA

BIBLIOGRAPHIES AND LIBRARIES

N199. **U. S. Library of Congress. Korea: an annotated bibliography of publications in western languages.** Washington, 1950. Compiled at beginning of Korean War. Contains 743 entries, largely post-1930 publications; strongest on history, government, and economics. Two companion volumes published same year list works in Russian and in far eastern languages.
N200. **University of California, Institute of East Asiatic Studies. Korean studies guide.** Berkeley, 1954. Selected and annotated bibliography covering works in the social sciences and humanities; emphasizes Japanese studies. Compiled by a group of students at the University of California, it is somewhat uneven in quality and to be used with caution. Appendices contain chronological list of kings and dynasties. **Russian Supplement to the Korean Studies Guide.** Berkeley, 1958. Contains 893 entries published in Russia from the mid-19th century to 1956.
N201. Underwood, Horace H. "A partial bibliography of occidental literature on Korea from early times to 1930." **Transactions of the Korea Branch of the Royal Asiatic Society,** 20 (1931): 117–185. Supplement, by E. and G. Gompertz, *ibid.*, 24 (1935): 23–48. Comprehensive bibliography, much of which is from periodical literature, classified under subjects.
N202. Courant, Maurice. **Bibliographie coréenne.** 3 v. Paris, 1894–96. Supplement, 1901. First and only comprehensive bibliography of Korean works in a western language. See also the following.
N203. Trollope, Mark. "Corean books and their authors." **Transactions of the Korea Branch of the Royal Asiatic Society,** 21 (1932): 1–104.
N204. **Chōsen sōtokufu ko-tosho mokuroku.** [Government-general catalog of old books.] 2 v. Seoul, 1921. Supplement, 1934. Better known as the *Kyujang-gak* or Royal Library bibliography, this is the most comprehensive list of Korean and Chinese titles in existence. Includes over 136,000 titles, of which 73,000 are of Korean works and over 62,000 Chinese. The library was the royal

collection of the Yi dynasty. Supplement contains titles of valuable archival material, diplomatic correspondence, land registration records, treasury records, etc. In Chinese without indices.
N205. **Chōsen tosho kaidai.** [Annotated bibliography of Korean books.] 3rd ed., Seoul, 1932. Compiled by the government-general of Korea in the Japanese language and arranged according to the classical Chinese classification. Included are author and title in *kana* order. The most complete selected and annotated bibliography available. Includes over 2,700 titles of works from the royal library.
N206. **Chōsen-shi no sho-mondai.** [Various problems of Korean history.] Tokyo, 1957. A special issue of the *Rekishi-gaku kenkyu* [Journal of historical studies] devoted to a list of Japanese articles on Korea appearing from 1927 to 1953.

Library Collections

The most important collection of manuscript documents relating to the history of Korea is in the Seoul National University Library. Some 45,000 photographic prints of the archives of the Japanese legation in Seoul, covering correspondence between the Tokyo foreign office and the legation between 1884 and 1909, are available in the library of the Korean National History Compilation Committee, Seoul, and in the Hoover Library, Stanford University. Some prints are missing from the Hoover collection. The original documents were destroyed in 1945. The Library of Congress, California (Berkeley), and Stanford have fair collections of printed books relating to Korea, as do the British Museum and the Bibliothèque Nationale. The great libraries of Tokyo, Kyoto and Tenri are especially important. The Library of Congress contains microfilms of some Japanese archives bearing upon Korean history.

ENCYCLOPEDIAS AND REFERENCE WORKS

N207. Allen, Horace N. **Korea, fact and fancy.** Seoul, 1904. Contains Korean folk tales and a valuable chronological index of the chief events in Korean-western relations. Events from 1876 to 1903 are based on first-hand knowledge and are detailed and accurate. Lists names of chief diplomatic and native officials of the period.

N208. O, Yun-jŏk. Tongsa yŏnp'yo. [Chronologies of Korean history.] Seoul, 1915. Best list of dates in Korean history, beginning with 2333 B.C. and ending with 1910. Concise, condensed information from original sources inserted under appropriate years. In Chinese.

N209. UNESCO Hanguk ch'ongnam. [UNESCO Korean survey.] Seoul, 1957. Very useful, up-to-date handbook on Korean education, sciences, and culture, prepared by prominent scholars.

N210. Taehan Yŏngam, Inmyŏng-nok. [Korean yearbook.] Seoul, 1957. Useful; contains a who's who of approximately 1,000 South Koreans.

N211. Pak, Yong-dae and others. Chŭngbo munhŏn pigo. [Enlarged and supplemented encyclopedia.] 51 v. Seoul, 1907. Convenient encyclopedia for Korean studies, tracing the history from earliest times to 1907. A revision of the *Tongguk munhŏn pigo* [Encyclopedia of Korea] of 1770. For a history of the encyclopedia see "A Korean cyclopaedia," *Korean review*, 4 (1906): 217–23.

N212. Chōsen jimmei jisho. [Biographical dictionary of Korea.] 2 v. Seoul, 1937. Convenient, but not always reliable. Includes some 13,000 biographies from early period to 1934, and lists 15,000 persons who passed civil service examinations from 1392 to 1894. Useful appendices and index. In Japanese. Concise data and indications of sources appear in **(N212a) Sohn, P. K. Biographical tables of the Koryŏ period.** Berkeley, 1958.

N213. O, Se-ch'ang. Kŭnyŏk Sŏhwa-ching. [Study of Korean painters and calligraphers.] Seoul, 1928. Extensive and comprehensive biographical dictionary from the Silla period to early 20th century, by a prominent calligrapher scholar.

GEOGRAPHY AND DEMOGRAPHY

N214. McCune, Shannon. Korea: a regional geography. Rutland, Vt., and Tokyo, 1956. Only recent geography of Korea in English. Very useful.

N215. Lautensach, Hermann. Korea, eine Landeskunde auf Grund eigener Reisen und der Literatur. Leipzig, 1945. Exhaustive and definitive work which describes and analyzes relationships of Korean physical and human geography, especially the dislocating effect upon Koreans of Japanese rule. Based on field studies and best sources in Japanese and western literature.

N216. Chōsen Government-General. Chōsen chishi shiryō. [Materials on Korean geography.] Seoul, 1919. Extensive geographical information. Because of changes in administrative areas, some of the figures are no longer correct, but most of the data is still useful.

N217. Sinjŭng tongguk yŏji sŭngnam. [Revised survey of Korean geography.] 6 v. Seoul, 1930–40. The most valuable guide book to historical geography of Korea. Originally compiled by Yang Song-ji and No Sa-sin (1481–86), it was revised in 1499 and 1530. This is a reprint of the 1530 edition. Gives administrative divisions and their changes. Invaluable for linguistic, historical, institutional, sociological, and geographic studies. In Sino-Korean.

N218. Chōsen no jinkō genshō. [Population analysis of Korea.] Seoul, 1927. Survey of population of Korea from the 15th century to 1925, based on the 1925 simplified census. Supplemented by *N219*.

N219. Chōsen ni okeru jinkō ni kansuru sho-tokei. [Statistics on the population of Korea.] Seoul, 1943.

ANTHROPOLOGY AND SOCIOLOGY

N220. Osgood, Cornelius. The Koreans and their culture. N.Y., 1951. Based on field study of a South Korean village in 1947. Best available anthropological work in English, but marred by an attempt to describe the artistic and literary culture of Korea from obsolete western sources.

N221. Son, Chin-t'ae. Chosŏn minjok munhwa-ŭi yŏngu. [Studies on the culture of the Korean people.] Seoul, 1948. Exhaustive ethnological studies on such items as dolmens, housing, heated floor, marriage, etc., documented by extensive source materials and field survey work. Comparisons are made with Chinese and Manchurian practices.

N222. Zenjō, Eisuke. Chōsen no shūraku. [Korean villages.] 3 v. Seoul, 1933–35. An over-all village study published by the government-general of Korea. Korean villages are treated in their historical, economic, administrative, and traditional aspects. Other exhaustive studies in the field can be found in case studies of special areas such as *Kyŏngju-gun, Kangnung-gun, Cheju-do,* and *P'yŏngyang-bu,* by the same author—all in Japanese.

N223. Kang, Younghill. The grass roof. London and N.Y., 1931. Valuable as first detailed presentation in English of life in Korea during first quarter of the 20th century. An intensely personal account.

N224. Kim, Tu-hŏn. Chosŏn kajok chedo yŏngu. [Study on the family system in Korea.] Seoul, 1949. Excellent study of the Korean family system in its historical and sociological aspects. Makes comparisons with the Chinese family system.

N225. Kim, Agnes D. **I married a Korean.** N.Y., 1953. Readable account of rural life in Korea, by an American.

LINGUISTICS

N226. McCune, George M., and E. O. Reischauer. "The Romanization of the Korean language based upon its phonetic structure." **Transactions of the Korea Branch of the Royal Asiatic Society,** 29 (1939): 1–55. Generally accepted in the United States as presenting the most accurate transliteration of Korean sounds. Closely follows Korean standard, reformed spelling.

N227. Yi, Sang-baek. **Hangŭl ŭi kiwŏn.** [Origin of the Korean alphabet, Hangŭl.] Seoul, 1957. Definitive study of the origin of the Korean alphabet, based on newly discovered original copy of *Hunmin chŏngŭm* [Correct sound for the instruction of the people]. Includes entire text in photostat plates of the "original copy."

N228. Ogura, Simpei. **Chōsen-go no keitō.** [Affinity of the Korean language.] Tokyo, 1935. Monograph on the philology of the Korean language, which concludes that it belongs to the Altaic family.

N229. Ramstedt, Gustaf J. **A Korean grammar.** Helsinki, 1939. Comprehensive and systematic, but cumbersome to use because it neglects the reformed Korean spelling system.

N230. Ch'oe, Hyŏn-bae. **Uri mal pon.** [Grammar of the Korean language.] Seoul, 1955. Best grammar in Korean. Covers phonetics, parts of speech, and syntax.

N231. Lee, Y. H., and J. W. Kwan. **Minjungsugwan's pocket English-Korean dictionary.** Seoul, 1954. Most comprehensive English-Korean dictionary. Even though pocket size, has complete standard coverage. Two new dictionaries—Korean-English and English-Korean—being completed by Y. H. Lee and Samuel Martin as part of the Yale dictionary project will soon be published and will render other like works obsolete.

N232. Chosŏn ŏhakhoe [Korean Language Research Society]. **Chosŏn-mal k'ŭn sajŏn.** [Great dictionary of the Korean language.] 6 v. Seoul, 1957. Most extensive and comprehensive dictionary of the Korean language. Gives the Chinese characters for Sino-Korean words. Arranged in Korean alphabetical order.

N233. Ch'oe, Namsŏn. **Sin chajŏn.** [New dictionary.] 3rd ed., Seoul, 1947. The most dependable Sino-Korean dictionary; necessary to Sino-Korean studies. Contains no compounds, but meanings are illustrated from the classics.

SOURCES, TRADITIONAL HISTORIES, AND DOCUMENTS

N234. **Chōsen-shi.** [Korean history.] 37 v. Seoul, 1932–40. Very useful collection of historical source materials in chronological order from the early period to 1894, including one index volume and one volume of tables. Pt. 1 (3 v.) contains extracts from the sources in their original form; the rest, in Japanese translation, is of less value because of some inadequate translation and poor selection.

N235. **Chōsen kinseki sōran.** [A complete guide to Korean epigraphy.] 2 v. Seoul, 1919. Supplement, 1923. Contains the texts of inscriptions on various epigraphic objects from 85 to 1910 collected by the government-general of Chosen. Arranged in chronological order.

N236. Kim, Pu-sik. **Samguk sagi.** [Annals of the Three Kingdoms.] Seoul, 1928. Oldest extant Korean history, finished in 1145. Begins with 57 B.C. and ends in 935 A.D. Contains annals of the Three Kingdoms; a chronology; monographs on festivals, music, clothing, geography, offices and ranks; and many biographies in the style of Chinese dynastic histories. Yi Pyŏng-do's edition (Seoul, 1947) is useful for its commentaries, Korean translation, and index.

N237. Iryŏn. **Samguk yusa.** [Remains of the Three Kingdoms.] Ed. by Ch'oe, Namsŏn. 2nd ed., Seoul, 1954. Very valuable source on the Three Kingdoms and early history, which contains much information not found in the *Samguk sagi.* Based on editions older than 1592. An annotated and translated edition by Yi, Pyŏng-do (Seoul, 1956) is very useful.

N238. Chŏng, In-ji. **Koryŏ sa.** [History of Koryŏ.] 3 v. Seoul, 1956. Basic source for the Koryŏ period (918–1392). Based on records of the Koryŏ kings, but reflects the biases of scholars of the Chosŏn dynasty who condemned the last kings of Koryŏ (Yi dynasty). This photolithograph edition by Yŏnhi University is the best as other reprints contain many errors.

N239. **Chosŏn wangjo sillok.** [Veritable records of Chosŏn dynasty.] 50 v. Seoul, 1955–58. Indispensable source both for the Chosŏn dynasty (1392–1864) and for general far eastern history. This edition, by the National History Compilation Committee, is a photolithographic copy. An index is planned.

N240. McCune, George M. "The Yi dynasty annals of Korea." **Transactions of the Korean Branch of the Royal Asiatic Society,** 29 (1939): 57–82.

N241. **T'ongmun-kwan chi.** [Records of the Office of Interpreters.] 2 v. Seoul, 1944. Important source for study of the foreign relations of Korea. This is a photolithographic reprint of the 1888 edition, covering mainly the years 1636–1888, but including an account of earlier periods.

N242. Hanguk saryo ch'ongsŏ. [Korean historical material series.] 4 v. Seoul, 1955–57. These pro-nationalistic historical materials, covering the period from 1864 to the time of Japanese domination, balance the Japanese sources, and contain valuable information on the Korean independence movement.

N243. Carnegie Endowment for International Peace. **Korea, treaties and agreements.** Washington, 1921. Copies and translations of 22 treaties and conventions between Korea and other powers, 1882–1910.

N244. McCune, George M., and John A. Harrison, eds. **Korean-American relations.** V. 1, **The initial period, 1883–1886.** Berkeley, 1951. Selected correspondence between the Department of State and the newly created legation in Korea.

GENERAL HISTORIES

N245. Longford, Joseph H. **The story of Korea.** N.Y., 1911. Best available short history of Korea in English, although out of date. Accurate, balanced, and critical; based on reliable though limited sources.

N246. Yi, In-yŏng. **Kuksa yoron.** [Essentials of national history.] Seoul, 1950. Best interpretative history. Provides a synthesis of previous studies, from ancient times to 1948.

N247. Yi, Pyŏng-do. **Sinsu Kuksa taegwan.** [Great view of Korean history.] Rev. ed., Seoul, 1959. A longer and more detailed history, with useful charts and tables.

N248. Hatata, Takashi. **Chōsen-shi.** [History of Korea.] Tokyo, 1951. Synthesis of previous Japanese studies on Korean history from ancient times to 1950. First interpretative, unbiased history by a Japanese scholar. Emphasis is on socio-economic development; gives rather frank account of Japanese exploitation of Korea. Contains bibliographies of Japanese works.

N249. Yi, Sun-bok, P. K. Sohn, and others. **Kuksa kaesŏl.** [Outline of Korean history.] 3rd ed., Seoul, 1952. A critical history by the Korean history studies group of Seoul National University. Emphasizes politico-economic trends and forces. Extensive and valuable bibliographies.

N250. Hulbert, Homer B. **The history of Korea.** 2 v. Seoul, 1905. Reprint, 1958. Covers Korean history from legendary times to 1905. Based on Korean sources except for period 1890–1905, which Hulbert, a friend of the Korean king and champion of the people, interprets in his own vivid and dynamic way from current experiences and sources. Although obsolete, it is still the only detailed history of Korea in a western language. A

condensed account is in Hulbert, *The passing of Korea* (N.Y., 1906), which also discusses literature, art, law, and political institutions.

N251. Chindan, Hakhoe. **Han'guk-sa** [History of Korea.] 5 v. Seoul, 1959 ff. (V. 1, 5 published to date.) Product of a symposium of authoritative Korean scholars. Based on extensive sources. Useful charts and plates.

N252. Hsü, Ching. **Hsuan-ho feng shih Kao-li t'u ching.** [An illustrated account of an embassy to Koryŏ.] Seoul, 1932. Very good account by a Sung envoy to Koryŏ in 1123. Provides a thoroughgoing contemporary picture of the geographical setting, palaces, offices, economic activities, social life, food, customs, utensils, and sea routes. Accompanying illustrations are lost, but the text itself is valuable because it is a unique view from an outside source. This edition by Imanishi Ryu compares two Chinese editions.

N253. Hamel, Hendrik. "An account of the shipwreck of a Dutch vessel on the coast of the Isle of Quelpaert, together with a description of the kingdom of Corea." **Transactions of the Korea Branch of the Royal Asiatic Society,** 9 (1918): 91–148. A unique western account of conditions in Korea in the 17th century by a shipwrecked Dutch sailor who lived there 14 years. See also a modern Korean study listing pertinent Japanese and Korean sources by Yi Pyŏng-do, *Hamel P'yoryu-gi* [Hamel's record of a castaway].

HISTORIES OF SPECIAL TOPICS

International Relations and Loss of Independence

N254. Nelson, M. Frederick. **Korea and the old orders in eastern Asia.** Baton Rouge, 1945. Presents Korea's international relations from three angles: the old Confucian system, the transition period, and the western state system. A useful and definitive study of a perplexing subject.

N255. Harrington, Fred H. **God, mammon, and the Japanese: Dr. Horace N. Allen and Korean-American relations, 1884–1905.** Madison, Wis., 1944. Based on papers of a medical missionary who later became a U. S. embassy official.

N256. Rockhill, William W. **China's intercourse with Korea from the XVth century to 1895.** London, 1905. Monograph describing Korea's relationship to China up to the Sino-Japanese War, from point of view of a U. S. diplomat wishing to assess the case for recognizing Korean independence. Based on Chinese official sources.

N257. Sands, William F. **Undiplomatic memories: the Far East, 1896–1904.** N.Y., 1930. Valuable eyewitness account of conditions in Korea in the crucial transition period, by a U. S. embassy official who entered the service of the Korean king as adviser.

N258. Scherzer, Fernand, tr. **Journal d'une mission en Corée par Koei Ling.** Paris, 1877. Valuable source book of conditions in Korea before its opening, from an oriental point of view.

N259. Tabohashi, Kiyoshi. **Kindai nissen kankei no kenkyū.** [Study of Japanese-Korean relations in modern times.] 2 v. Seoul, 1935. The most conscientious and exhaustive study on the subject, by a Japanese scholar. Well documented with Korean, Chinese, Japanese, and western sources.

Korea under the Japanese

N260. Chōsen Government-General. **Annual report on administration in Chōsen, 1907–1938.** Seoul and Keijo, 1908–38. Official Japanese reports in English on the administration of Korea during these years, with maps, charts, tables, and illustrations supporting the governmental point of view.

N261. ——. **Chōsen no genron to sesō.** [Social change in Korea.] Seoul, 1927. Official study in Japanese, describing social change in living conditions.

N262. Chosŏn yŏksa p'yonch'an iwŏn-hoe [Committee on Korean History Compilation]. **Chosŏn minjŏk haebang t'ujaeng-sa.** [History of the struggle for the liberation of the Korean people.] Pyongyang, 1949. Based on Marxist theory. Covers from latter half of the 19th century to establishment of the People's Republic of Korea. The treatment of Japanese imperialism is less biased; but the post-liberation period, by a Russian scholar, is more propaganda than fact.

N263. Chung, Henry. **The case of Korea.** N.Y., 1921. The author, a Korean patriot, claims that the Japanese objective in Korea was to use it as a bridge to the conquest of China. Deals with the passive resistance movement of 1919 in particular.

N264. Ireland, Alleyne. **The new Korea.** N.Y., 1926. Japanese reforms of the 1920's under Viscount Saito. Generally friendly to the Japanese. Appendix contains useful documents.

N265. Cynn, Hugh H. **The rebirth of Korea: the reawakening of the people, its causes and the outlook.** N.Y., and Cincinnati, 1920. Moderate statement of issues of the Korean independence demonstration of March, 1919, by a talented Christian leader. Attempts to be more pro-Korean than anti-Japanese. Appendices contain official statements of missionary bodies concerning their position on the Korean question.

N266. Kim, San (pseud.), and Nym Wales (Helen Foster Snow). **Song of Ariran: the life story of a Korean rebel.** N.Y., 1941. Biography of a young Korean, based on a series of personal interviews in China in 1937. Valuable for account of Communist and anti-Japanese movements in Siberia and China, 1919–36. Undocumented.

N267. Ladd, George T. **In Korea with Marquis Ito.** N.Y., 1908. Review of Japanese reforms in Korea by a paid spokesman for the Japanese government, with the object of proving that Japanese government was better for Koreans than their own.

N268. McKenzie, Frederick A. **Korea's fight for freedom.** N.Y., 1920. A contrasting interpretation which is generally accurate and judicious, although friendly to Korea and critical of the Japanese military. Good account of the independence movement to 1920.

N269. Pak, Ŭn-sik. **Han'guk tongnip ŏndongchi hyŏl-sa.** [The history of the bloody Korean independence movement.] Shanghai, 1922. 2nd ed., Seoul, 1946. By a Korean revolutionary who fled to Shanghai after the 1919 uprising. A valuable account from a Korean point of view. Bibliography contains titles of articles written by westerners involved in the movement. In Sino-Korean.

Political Institutions and Laws

N270. Wilkinson, William H. **The Corean government: constitutional changes, July 1894 to October 1895.** Shanghai, 1897. Only work in English which gives an accurate account of the old Korean legal and administrative system.

N271. Kyoju taejŏn hoet'ong. [Collated and annotated collections of fundamental statutes.] Seoul, 1939. Very convenient compendium of major law codes of the Chosŏn dynasty, with annotations (useful but sometimes incorrect) made by the last Korean officials who were familiar with the institutions. Original text is in Sino-Korean, and account of background of the book and the organization of the Korean government is in Japanese.

Economic History

N272. Ch'oe, Ho-jin. **Kŭndae Han'guk kyŏngje-sa yŏngu.** [Studies in recent Korean economic history.] Rev. ed. Seoul, 1960. Carefully documented study of economic potential at end of the Yi dynasty, with reference to economic characteristics, social structure, labor, and farming conditions.

N273. Grajdanzev, Andrew J. **Modern Korea, her economic and social development under the Japanese.** N.Y., 1944. Based on official reports of progress in Korea, 1907–38. Emphasizes economic aspects and concludes that retrogression rather than progress in Korean economy took place under Japan. Appendices contain statistics for population, economic data, and Korean place names.

N274. Hoshino, Tokuji, comp. **Economic history of Chosen.** Seoul, 1920. Account of first part (1907–20) of Japanese colonial administration in Korea from the official point of view. Illustrations devised to show great change for the better brought into Korean economic life by Japan.

N275. Lee, Hoon-koo. **Land utilization and rural economy in Korea.** Chicago and London, 1936. Survey of agricultural economic conditions in Korea, based on field studies in 1932, correlated with information about Korean rural society, education, literacy, etc. A unique study for its day.

N276. Paek, Nam-un. **Chōsen shakai keizai-shi.** [Socio-economic history of Korea.] 2 v. Tokyo, 1933–37. Economic interpretation of Korean history to end of Koryŏ, carefully documented from primary sources. Many of the conclusions reflect author's Marxist leanings.

Cultural History

N277. Yi, Sang-baek. **Chosŏn munhwa-sa yŏngu nongo.** [Study of the cultural history of Korea.] Seoul, 1947. Valuable studies of cultural, political, intellectual, and social problems, including the struggle between Confucianism and Buddhism, the social problem of concubines' sons, and the ban on remarriage of widows.

N278. Chōsen koseki zufu. [Album of Korean antiquities.] 15 v. Tokyo, 1915–35. Compiled by the Japanese government-general, this is the best known and most readily available of the many collections of reproductions of Korean artistic and historical remains dating from prehistoric times.

N279. Clark, Charles A. **Religions of old Korea.** N.Y., 1932. Introductory study not yet superseded by any in English, giving sketchy review of Korean religions—Confucianism, Buddhism, Ch'ŏndo-gyo, Shamanism, and other cults. The political aspects of Ch'ŏndo-gyo and Shamanism are neglected.

N280. Yi, Nŭng-hwa. **Chosŏn pulgyo t'ongsa.** [A comprehensive history of Korean Buddhism.] 2 v. Seoul, 1918. Very extensive and thorough collection of materials. Discusses other religions besides Buddhism. In Sino-Korean.

N281. Takahashi, Tōru. **Richō bukkyō.** Tokyo, 1929. [Buddhism during the Chosŏn dynasty.] Valuable Japanese work.

N282. Hyŏn, Sang-yun. **Chosŏn yuhak-sa.** [History of Confucian learning in Korea.] 2nd ed., Seoul, 1954. Emphasis is on individual scholars. Lacks interpretation of development of Confucian learning, but gives its merits and defects.

N283. Murayama, Chijun. **Chōsen no ruiji shūkyō.** [Pseudo-religions of Korea.] Seoul, 1935. Unique study of the popular religion of the common people since the rise of the secret religious society, the Tonghak, in 1860. Covers over 80 sects of this pseudo-religion which have flourished in modern Korea. Comprehensive but not necessarily accurate because of difficulty of access to secrets of religious societies. Prepared for the government-general of Chosen.

N284. Dallet, Charles. **Histoire de l'église de Corée précédé d'une introduction sur l'histoire, les institutions, la langue, les moeurs et coutumes coréennes.** 2 v. Paris, 1874. Account, based on official Catholic sources, of the history of Christianity in Korea from 1784 through the French punitive expedition of 1866. The introduction, based on first-hand accounts of French priests living in Korea in disguise, constitutes a source of unique value. It has been translated and published by Yale University under title *Traditional Korea.*

N285. Paik, L. George. **The history of Protestant missions in Korea, 1832–1910.** Pyongyang, 1929. Methodical and scholarly survey of entrance of Protestantism into Korea. Uses few oriental sources, but the bibliography in western languages was thoroughly explored. The date of 1832 is somewhat misleading, as Protestantism only entered Korea firmly in 1884.

N286. Cho, Yun-je. **Chosŏn siga sagang.** [Outline history of Korean poetry and songs.] 4th ed., Seoul, 1956. Good history from ancient times to 1910, arranged in eight periods according to dominant verse forms of each, with reference to social conditions.

N287. Yang, Chu-dong. **Koga yŏngu.** [Study of ancient songs.] 2nd ed. Seoul, 1954.

N288. Cho, Yŏn-hyŏn. **Hanguk hyŏndae munhak-sa.** [History of contemporary Korean literature.] Seoul, 1956. Carefully documented survey from 1894 to 1925. A second volume is planned to cover the later period. Should be used with the following.

N289. Paek, Ch'ŏl. **Sin munhak sajo-sa hyŏndae p'yŏn.** [History of new literary thought in Korea, current period.] Seoul, 1950.

N290. Kim, Won-yong. **Hanguk kohwaltcha kaeyo.** [Early movable type in Korea.] Seoul, 1954. Development of movable type in Korea from 13th to 19th century. There is an English summary. Review, P. K. Sohn and C. E. Hamilton, *Far eastern quarterly,* 15 (Nov. 1955): 155.

N291. McCune, Evelyn B. **Korean art.** Tokyo and Rutland Vt., 1960. Only chronological study of the subject in English, and based on authoritative sources.

Contemporary Problems

N292. McCune, George M., and Arthur L. Grey. **Korea today.** Cambridge, Mass., 1950. Excellent summary of conditions in Korea,

1945–50, preceded by concise statement of previous economic and political situation.

N293. Goodrich, Leland M. **Korea: a study of U. S. policy in the United Nations.** N.Y., 1956. Brief statement of the changing facets of the Korean problem, using it as a case study to illustrate how the U. S. has worked through the U. N. Objective, but lacking in analysis or assessment of motives behind the United Nations' actions in Korea.

N294. Meade, E. Grant. **American military government in Korea.** N.Y., 1951. Account of U. S. occupation of Korea, by a member of the military government, with a frank analysis of the problems. Emphasis is on local government. Accurate, honest, but lacking in first-hand knowledge of central over-all planning.

N295. Supreme Commander for the Allied Powers. "Summation of U. S. Army military government in Korea." [1946–47.] **Summation, non-military activities in Japan and Korea.** Tokyo, 1946–47. This and the following are monthly official reports of occupation activities in Korea.

N296. ——. "South Korean interim government activities." [1947–48.] **Summation, non-military activities in Japan and Korea.** Seoul, 1947–48.

N297. Hanguk chŏnjaeng ilnyŏn-ji, inyŏn-ji, samnyŏn-ji. [War history of Korea, 1st, 2nd, 3rd year.] 3 v. Seoul, 1953–56. Comprehensive history of the Korean War, compiled by the War History Compilation Committee. Contains a detailed diary of the war, accounts of the internal situation and external relations, and documents.

N298. Riley, John W., and Wilbur Schramm. **The Reds take a city: the Communist occupation of Seoul, with eye-witness accounts.** New Brunswick, N.J., 1951. Narratives of nine distinguished South Koreans translated into English by Hugh Cynn. The Korean accounts of their experiences during the North Korean invasion of 1950 are interspersed with analyses by Dr. Schramm, a communication specialist, and Professor Riley, a sociologist.

N299. Voorhees, Melvin B. **Korean tales.** N.Y., 1952. Collection of colorful short stories, by a former Eighth Army censor, dealing with U. S. generals, war correspondents, the ROK army, President Rhee, the refugee situation, etc. Though a controversial book, it is probably the best of Korean war fiction in short story form. For longer accounts see *N300–301.*

N300. Michener, James A. **The bridges at Toko-ri.** N.Y., 1953.

N301. Frank, Pat. **Hold back the night.** Philadelphia, 1952.

N302. United Nations. **Rehabilitation and development of agriculture, forestry, and fisheries in South Korea.** N.Y., 1954. Results of a study on Korean agriculture and fish-

eries by a team of international experts who worked with Korean specialists. Contains the only available up-to-date treatment of the subject in English. Not very thorough.

N303. Nathan (Robert R.) Associates. **An economic programme for Korean reconstruction.** N.Y., 1954. Detailed study of Korea's needs made for use of the United Nations Reconstruction Agency by a team who visited Korea in 1953. The flaws are those of specialists studying unfamiliar problems in too great a hurry.

OFFICIAL PUBLICATIONS

N304. **Taehan Min'guk Kukhoe sokkirok.** [Proceedings of the National Assembly, Republic of Korea.] Seoul, 1948 ff. This and the following, both issued by the secretariat of the National Assembly, are the two most important publications of the central government.

N305. **Kukchŏng kamsa pogo.** [Report of audits of the national administration.] Seoul, 1948 ff.

The following carefully prepared publications are issued by the Research Department of the Bank of Korea.

N306. **Kyŏngje yŏngam.** [Economic yearbook.] Seoul, 1948–49, 1955 ff.

N307. **Han'guk (Chosŏn) ŭnhaeng chosa wŏlbo.** [Monthly statistical review.] Seoul, 1947–50, 1952 ff.

N308. **Chosa charyo.** [Source materials of economic research.] 22 v. (mimeographed) to date.

N309. **Hanguk kyŏngje simnyŏn sa.** [Ten year history of Korean economics.] Seoul, 1957.

The National Museum of Korea (Seoul) also issues various series relating to the archaeology, ethnology, and cultural history of Korea.

PERIODICALS

The following scholarly periodicals relate almost exclusively to Korea.

N310. **Chindan hakpo.** [Journal of the Chintan Society.] Seoul, 1934 ff. (Quarterly.) Publication interrupted.

N311. **Yŏksa hakpo.** [Korean historical review.] Seoul, 1952 ff. [Korean Historical Association.] (Irregular.)

N312. **Yŏksa kwahak.** [Historical science.] Pyongyang, 1947 ff. [Historical Science Institute of the Academy of Science of North Korea.] (Semimonthly.)

N313. **Chōsen gakuhō.** [Journal of Academic Association of Koreanology of Japan.] Tenri City, 1951 ff. (Irregular.) Contains English résumés.

N314. **Journal of Asiatic studies.** Seoul, 1958 ff. [Asiatic Research Center, Korean University.] Partly in western languages.

N315. Asiatic research bulletin. Seoul, 1957 ff. [Asiatic Research Center, Korean University.] (Monthly.) In English.

N316. Transactions of the Korea Branch of the Royal Asiatic Society. Seoul, 1900 ff. (Irregular.)

N317. Seikyū gakusō and **Gakusō** [Green-hill journal.] 33 v. Seoul, 1930–44. [Keijo (Seoul) Imperial University.]

N318. The Korean repository (later **Korean review**). 11 v. Seoul, 1892–1906.

N319. Sahoe kwahak. Journal of social sciences. Seoul, 1957 ff. In Korean with English summaries and titles.

MONGOLIA

BIBLIOGRAPHIES

N320. Chang, Chih-yi. **A bibliography of books and articles on Mongolia.** London, 1950. Annotated bibliography of important works in Chinese, Japanese, and Russian, with emphasis on recent and modern history and politics.

N321. Iwamura, Shinobu, and Fujieda Akira, eds. **Mōkō kenkyū bunken mokuroku 1900–1950.** [Bibliography of Mongolia, 1900–1950.] Kyoto, 1953. Exhaustive list of Japanese contributions on Mongolia, arranged by author (which makes reference difficult). Though restricted to Japanese works, this is the most complete bibliography on Mongolia yet issued.

N322. Knoepfmacher, Hugo. **Outer Mongolia: a selection of references.** N.Y., 1944. A sketchy and now outdated bibliography.

N323. Iakovleva, Ekaterina N. **Bibliografiia Mongol'skoi Narodnoi Respubliki.** [Bibliography of the Mongolian People's Republic.] Moscow, 1935.

GEOGRAPHY AND ANTHROPOLOGY

N324. Maringer, John. **Contribution to the prehistory of Mongolia: a study of the prehistoric collections from Inner Mongolia.** Stockholm, 1950. Best account of all archaeological discoveries in Inner Mongolia relating to early prehistoric periods.

N325. Lattimore, Owen. **The Mongols of Manchuria.** N.Y., 1939. Account of their tribal divisions, geographical districts, historical relations with Manchus and Chinese, and recent political problems.

N326. Aberle, David F. **The kinship system of the Kalmuk Mongols.** Albuquerque, 1953. Highly analytical and systematic formulation of Kalmuk kinship structure based on extensive interviewing of refugee informants.

N327. Vreeland, Herbert H., III. **Mongol community and kinship structure.** New Haven, 1953. Though based on interviews of Mongols in the U. S. A., this is by far the best account of Mongol kinship and social structure in any language.

N328. Krader, Lawrence. "Buryat religion and society." **Southwestern journal of anthropology,** 10 (autumn 1954): 322–51. Analytical, conceptually sound treatment of the social structure of a north Mongolian ethnic group (the Buryats, most of whom are in the U.S.S.R.), based on critical use of Russian sources.

N329. Vladimirtsov, Boris I. **Obshchestvennyi stroi Mongolov: Mongol'skii kochevoi feodalizm.** [Social structure of the Mongols: Mongol nomadic feudalism.] Leningrad, 1934. French tr., by Michel Carsow, *Le régime social des Mongols,* Paris, 1948. Though some of the interpretations are questionable, this is the best social history of the Mongols. Author was one of Russia's greatest Mongolists.

N330. Riasanovsky, V. A. **Fundamental principles of Mongol law.** Tientsin, 1937. Thorough socio-historical survey of law among various Mongol tribes, based largely on Mongol legal compilations. Should be supplemented by the following.

N331. ——. **Customary law of the Mongol tribes.** Harbin, 1929.

N332. Pozdneev, Aleksei M. **Mongoliia i Mongoly.** [Mongolia and the Mongols.] 2 v. St. Petersburg (Leningrad), 1896–98. Perhaps the greatest account of travel in Mongolia ever written. Strong emphasis on society, culture, and economy.

N333. Kozlov, Petr K. **Mongoliia i Kam.** [Mongolia and Kham.] 2nd ed., Moscow, 1947. One of the great travel accounts of Russian scientific explorations in Mongolia and northern Tibet. First edition, 1905–06.

N334. ——. **Mongoliia i Amdo i mertvyi gorod Khara-Khoto.** [Mongolia and Amdo and the dead city of Khara-Khoto.] 6 v. St. Petersburg, 1905–08. 2nd, abr. ed., 1 v., Moscow, 1947. A companion volume to the above. Khara-Khoto was one of the pre-13th century steppe cities whose ruins Kozlov rediscovered. German tr. by Helmut Straübig, Leipzig, 1955.

N335. Potanin, G. N. **Ocherki sieverozapadnoi Mongolii.** [Sketches of northwestern Mongolia.] 4 v. St. Petersburg, 1881–83. Remains the best and most detailed ethnography of Outer Mongolia and Jungaria; an indispensable source for ethnology of the Mongols.

N336. ——. **Tangutsko-Tibetskaia okraina Kitaia i tsentral'naia Mongoliia.** [The Tangut-Tibetan march of China and central Mongolia.] 2 v. St. Petersburg, 1893. Detailed ethnology and ethnography of the peoples of central Mongolia and the Tibetan provinces of China (Amdo in particular).

N337. Murzaev, Ed M. **Mongol'skaia Narodnaia Respublika.** [The Mongolian People's Republic.] Moscow, 1948. Good description of the physical and human geography of Outer Mongolia. As do most Soviet works, this one devotes much attention to recent economic progress. German tr., Gotha, 1954.

N338. Obruchev, Vladimir A. **Vostochnaia Mongoliia.** [Eastern Mongolia.] Moscow and Leningrad, 1947 ff. The most detailed account yet published of the geography and geology of this region, by a scientist who participated in the expeditions at end of the 19th century.

N339. Ovdienko, Ivan K. **Vnutrenniaia Mongoliia.** [Inner Mongolia.] Moscow, 1954. A brief account.

LINGUISTICS

N340. Poppe, Nikolaus. **Khalkha-Mongolische Grammatik, mit Bibliographie, Sprachproben und Glossar.** Wiesbaden, 1951.

PRE-MODERN HISTORY

N341. Grousset, René. **L'empire des steppes.** Paris, 1939. Detailed account of the history of central Asia and Mongolia from earliest times through the main periods of Mongol and Turk conquests. Like most of Grousset's work, this book suffers from lack of analysis and ideas.

N342. ——. **L'empire mongol.** Paris, 1941. Description of the Mongol empire of the 13th and 14th centuries.

N343. Kiselev, Sergei V. **Drevniaia istoriia iuzhnoi Sibirii.** [The ancient history of southern Siberia.] 2nd ed., Moscow, 1951. Detailed history of those parts of southern Siberia bordering Mongolia and Jungaria from earliest known times (on basis of archaeological finds) to the 9th century.

N344. Egami, Namio. **Yurashia hoppō bunka no kenkyū.** [Studies in the culture of northern Eurasia.] Tokyo, 1950. Series of essays on culture problems of Eurasia in the ancient period.

N345. Lattimore, Owen. **Inner Asian frontiers of China.** N.Y., 1940. Analytical treatment of problems of Hunnic and Mongol nomad civilizations in their clash with sedentary societies (largely Chinese).

N346. Vladimirtsov, Boris I. **The life of Chingis-Khan.** Tr. by D. S. Mirsky. London, 1930. The classic account of the life of Genghis Khan, by one of Russia's greatest Mongolists.

N347. Ohsson, A. C. M. d'. **Histoire des Mongols.** 2nd ed., 4 v., Amsterdam, 1852. Author made the first scientific study of Muslim sources relating to the Mongol conquests, and compiled a history which remains

of primary importance since his sources are still largely untranslated.

N348. Howorth, Henry H. **History of the Mongols.** 4 v. London, 1876–1927. Detailed treatment of Mongol history. Based on secondary sources, especially d'Ohsson, but includes much more material than the latter. The classic descriptive work on Mongol history of the 13th and 14th centuries.

N349. Martin, Desmond H. **The rise of Chingis Khan and his conquest of north China.** Baltimore, 1950. Careful account with strong military emphasis on Genghis Kahn's campaigns.

N350. Juvaini, 'Ala-ad-Din 'Ata-Malik. **The history of the world-conqueror.** Tr. by John A. Boyle. 2 v. Cambridge, Mass., 1958. The most reliable contemporary history of the 13th century Mongols.

N351. Spuler, Bertold. **Die Goldene Horde.** See *M155.*

N352. ——. **Die Mongolen in Iran.** 2nd ed., Berlin, 1955. Exhaustive study of Mongol rule in Iran in the 13th and 14th centuries, based on primary sources.

N353. Grekov, Boris, and Aleksandr Iakoubovski. **La horde d'or.** Paris, 1939. Tr. from *Zolotaia Orda* (Leningrad, 1937). Somewhat slanted account of Mongol rule in Russia and western Siberia. Since the party line regarded the conquest as a catastrophe, the authors found it impossible to present new interpretations.

N354. Vernadsky, George. **The Mongols and Russia.** New Haven, 1953. Evaluation of the Mongol impact on Russia, by an eminent historian of Russia. Important supplement to *N351.*

N355. Aritaka, Iwao, and Aoki, Tomitaro. **Ugoku Moko.** [Moving Mongolia.] Tokyo, 1941. Short sketch of Mongol history and culture by two of Japan's older Mongolists. Emphasizes social and economic aspects.

N356. Korostovetz, Iwan J. **Von Cinggis Khan zur Sowjetrepublik: eine kurze Geschichte der Mongolei unter besonderer Berücksichtigung der neuesten Zeit.** Berlin, 1926. History of Mongolia, with emphasis on 19th century, by a man who helped make it.

N357. Pokotilov, Dmitri D. **History of the eastern Mongols during the Ming dynasty.** Tr. by R. Löwenthal. 2 v. Chengtu, 1947–49. The authoritative account of Mongol-Chinese relations during the period 1368–1644.

N358. Schmidt, Isaac J., ed. **Geschichte der Ost-Mongolen und ihres Fürstenhauses verfasst von Ssanang Ssetsen Chungtaidschi der Ordus.** St. Petersburg and Leipzig, 1829. Reprint, Peiping, 1938.

RECENT HISTORY

N359. Friters, Gerard M. **Outer Mongolia and its international position.** Baltimore,

1949. Thorough treatment of modern Mongol history with emphasis on relationships with outside powers.

N360. Grekov, Boris D., ed. **Istoriia Mongol'skoi Narodnoi Respubliki.** [History of the Mongolian People's Republic.] Moscow, 1954. Collection of articles on various subjects of recent Mongol history.

N361. Tsapkin, N. V. **Mongol'skaia Narodnaia Respublika.** [The Mongolian People's Republic.] Moscow, 1948. Brief account of facts and institutions; unfortunately marred by Communist party-line sloganism.

N362. Maslennikov, Vasilii A. **Mongol'-skaia Narodnaia Respublika.** [The Mongolian People's Republic.] Moscow, 1955. General, popular description of present-day Outer Mongolia. Follows official party line.

N363. Kallinikov, A. "Aratskoe revoliut-sionnoe dvizhenie v doavtonomnoi Mongolii." [The revolutionary movement of the Mongol masses in Mongolia's pre-autonomous period.] **Revoliutsionnyi Vostok,** 8 (1934): 137–56. Though a Communist interpretation, contains much data on social and economic changes.

N364. Shirendyb, B. **Narodnaia revoliutsiia v Mongolii i obrazovanie Mongol'skoi Narodnoi Respubliki, 1921–1924.** [National revolution in Mongolia and the formation of the Mongolian People's Republic, 1921–1924.] Moscow, 1956. Account of the formative period, by a Mongol.

N365. Shoizhelov, S. "Mongoliia i tsar'-skaia Rossiia." [Mongolia and Tsarist Russia.] **Novyii Vostok,** 13–14 (1926): 351–63. Though not very analytical, contains essential material on Tsarist-Mongol relations.

CENTRAL ASIA

BIBLIOGRAPHIES

N366. Loewenthal, Rudolf. **The Turkic languages and literatures of central Asia: a bibliography.** The Hague, 1957. Contains some 2,000 titles.

N367. ———. "Works on the Far East and Central Asia published in the USSR 1937–47." **Far eastern quarterly,** 8 (Feb. 1949): 172–83. Select bibliography of important contributions in Russian during the years indicated.

N368. Pierce, Richard A. **Russian central Asia, 1867–1917: a selected bibliography.** Berkeley, 1953. By far the best bibliography in English for period indicated. Works classified by subject.

N369. Vitkind, Nataliia I. **Bibliografiia po srednei Azii.** [A bibliography on central Asia.] Moscow, 1929. Best available bibliography of pre-revolutionary Russian material on this area.

N370. Akram, Mohammed. **Bibliographie analytique de l'Afghanistan.** Paris, 1947. Detailed and annotated bibliography of works in Russian and western languages.

GEOGRAPHY AND TRAVEL ACCOUNTS

N371. Schuyler, Eugene. **Turkistan: notes of a journey in Russian Turkistan, Khokand, Bukhara, and Kuldja.** 2 v. London, 1876; N.Y., 1877. Extensive study by a United States consular official.

N372. Machatschek, Fritz. **Landeskunde von Russisch-Turkestan.** Stuttgart, 1921. Good, detailed geography.

N373. Vámbéry, Armin. **Sketches of central Asia.** London, 1868. Account of travels in central Asia by one of the great scholars on this area; valuable for mid-19th century history.

N374. Stein, Sir Mark A. **Innermost Asia: detailed report of explorations in central Asia, Kan-su, and eastern Iran.** 4 v. Oxford, 1928. One of the great accounts of exploration in central Asia by one of its most famous explorers. Emphasizes archaeological and literary discoveries.

N375. ———. **Ancient Khotan.** 2 v. Oxford, 1907.

N376. ———. **Ruins of desert Cathay.** 2 v. London, 1912.

N377. ———. **Serindia.** 5 v. Oxford, 1921.

N378. Caspani, E., and E. Cagnacci. **Afghanistan, crocevia dell'Asia.** Milan, 1951. Though sketchy, a recent and usable general description.

N379. Coates, William P., and Zelda K. Coates. **Soviets in central Asia.** London, 1951. Detailed but uncritical account of conditions in the present Asiatic republics of the U.S.S.R.

N380. Hedin, Sven. **Through Asia.** 2 v. London, 1898; N.Y., 1899. A great Swedish explorer's expeditions in central Asia.

N381. ———. **Trans-Himalaya: discoveries and adventures.** 3 v. London and N.Y., 1909–13.

ANTHROPOLOGY AND SOCIOLOGY

N382. Schmidt, Wilhelm. **Die asiatischen Hirtenvölker: die primären Hirtenvölker der Alt-Türken, der Altai- und der Abakan-Tataren.** Fribourg, Switz., 1949. [Der Ursprung der Gottesidee, 9.] Analytical account of central Asiatic nomads and nomadism.

N383. Czaplicka, Marie A. **The Turks of central Asia.** Oxford, 1918.

N384. Jochelson, Waldemar. **Peoples of Asiatic Russia.** N.Y., 1928. Brief descriptive account, with main emphasis on primitive peoples.

N385. Hudson, Alfred E. **Kazak social structure.** New Haven, 1938. Anthropological study of Kazak social structure based on actual observation, with comments on Kazak social history.

N386. Tolstov, Sergei P., and T. A. Zhdanko, eds. **Arkeologicheskie i etnograficheskie raboty Khorezmskoi ekspeditsii, 1945–1948.** [Archaeological and ethnographical works of the Khorezm expedition of 1945–48.] Moscow, 1952. Divided into two sections, one giving an account of Tolstov's great archaeological discoveries, and the other some of the best ethnographic description and analysis of ethnic groups in central Asia which has yet appeared in the U.S.S.R.

N387. ———, eds. **Sredneaziatskii etnograficheskii sbornik.** [Central Asian ethnographical collection.] Moscow, 1954. Articles on various ethnographic problems of central Asia.

N388. Bernshtam, Aleksandr N. **Sotsial'no-ekonomicheskii stroi Orkhonoeniseiskikh Tiurok VI–VIII vekov.** [The social and economic structure of the Orkhon-Yenisei Turks from the 6th to 8th centuries.] Moscow and Leningrad, 1946. Careful study in ethnological history of the early Turks of southern Siberia, by one of Russia's foremost specialists on Turk peoples.

N389. Bruk, S. I. "Etnicheskii sostav stran perednei Azii." [The ethnic composition of non-Soviet southwest Asia.] Sovetskaia etnografiia, no. 2 (1955): 66–81. Probably best short ethnographic description of Afghanistan ever published.

GENERAL AND SPECIAL HISTORIES

N390. Vámbéry, Armin. **History of Bokhara from the earliest period down to the present.** 2nd ed., London, 1873. Still one of the best histories of central Asia. Compiled on basis of original sources.

N391. Sykes, Sir Percy M. **A history of Afghanistan.** 2 v. London, 1940. V. 1 goes to first Anglo-Afghan war (1838–42); v. 2 deals with Afghan-British-Russian relations during the 19th century.

N392. Fraser-Tytler, William K. **Afghanistan: a study of political developments in central Asia.** London, 1950. Although it contains a brief history of Afghanistan prior to the 19th century, most of the book deals with 19th and 20th century problems.

N393. Akademiia Nauk Uzbekskoi SSR. **Istoriia Uzbekskoi SSR.** [History of the Uzbek Soviet Socialist Republic.] 2 v. in 3. Tashkent, 1955–57. Despite party line views of

history, still a highly usable source. Especially valuable bibliography.

N394. Kary-Niiazov, Tashmukhamed N. **Ocherki istorii kul'tury Sovetskogo Uzbekistana.** [Sketches on the cultural history of Soviet Uzbekistan.] Moscow, 1955. Parts highly colored by the party line.

N395. Akademiia Nauk Kazakhskoi SSR. **Istoriia Kazakhskoi SSR.** [History of the Kazakh Soviet Socialist Republic.] 2nd ed., Alma Ata, 1957 ff. Only detailed history of the Kazakhs available. The first edition (1943) was severely criticized.

N396. Gafurov, B. G. **Istoriia tadzhikskogo naroda.** [History of the Tadjik people.] Moscow, 1949 ff. Brief, unanalytical history of central Asia to 1917, with particular emphasis on the Iranian peoples.

N397. Potapov, Leonid P. **Ocherki po istorii Altaitsev.** [Sketches on the history of the Altai peoples.] Moscow, 1953. Better than most histories on central Asia appearing in the U.S.S.R. (perhaps because these people are less controversial). Apart from introductory sketch, the book is divided into two parts: the Altai before and after the coming of the Russians.

N398. Reisner, I. M. **Razvitie feodalizma i obrazovanie gosudarstva u Afgantsev.** [The development of feudalism and the formation of the state in Afghanistan.] Moscow, 1954. Despite its title, a rather interesting and often sound study of social history of the Afghans.

ARCHAEOLOGY AND ANCIENT HISTORY

N399. Pumpelly, Raphael, ed. **Explorations in Turkestan: expedition of 1904.** 2 v. Washington, 1908. Detailed account by discoverer of Anau, the earliest known civilized site in central Asia.

N400. Tarn, William W. **The Greeks in Bactria and India.** Cambridge, Eng., 1938. The classic account of spread of Greek influence eastward and the rise of nomad-founded kingdoms in Bactria.

N401. McGovern, William M. **The early empires of central Asia.** Chapel Hill, 1939. Study of the Scythians and the Huns and their part in world history, with special reference to Chinese sources.

N402. Tolstov, Sergei P. **Po sledam drevnekhorezmiiskoi tsivilizatsii.** [On the tracks of ancient Khorezmian civilization.] Moscow, 1948. German tr., *Auf den Spuren der altchoresmischen Kultur,* Berlin, 1953. Excellent description of ancient civilizations of central Asia, based on evidence uncovered by the Tolstov expeditions.

N403. Hambis, Louis. **La Haute-Asie.** Paris, 1953. Brief account of Mongolia, Sinkiang, and central Asia from prehistoric times to the proto-Turk empires.

MEDIEVAL HISTORY

N404. Togan, A. Zeki Velidi. **Umumî Türk tarihine giris.** [Introduction to a general history of the Turks.] Istanbul, 1946. Detailed and analytical history of the Turks from prehistoric times to the early Ottoman period; best yet published.

N405. Barthold, Vasilii V. **Turkestan down to the Mongol invasion.** Tr. by V. M. Minorsky. 2nd ed., London, 1928. Basic work on medieval history of central Asia, by Russia's greatest scholar of this area.

N406. ——. **Histoire des Turcs d'Asie centrale.** Paris, 1945. Translation of twelve lectures delivered in Istanbul in 1926.

N407. ——. **Istoriko-geograficheskii obzor Irana.** [Historical and geographical survey of Iran.] St. Petersburg (Leningrad), 1903. Best work of its kind on medieval Iran and central Asia; an indispensable source.

N408. Pelliot, Paul. **Mission Pelliot en Asie centrale.** 6 v. Paris, 1914–24. Report with profuse illustrations of the famous Pelliot mission to Tun-huang (Sinkiang), which resulted in the acquisition of manuscripts of great importance for the medieval history of central Asia and China.

N409. ——. **La Haute-Asie.** Paris, 1931. Description of Mongolia, Chinese Turkestan, and Tibet by great French orientalist.

RECENT AND MODERN HISTORY

N410. Hayit, Baymirza. **Turkestan im XX. Jahrhundert.** Darmstadt, 1956. Detailed account of Turkestan before and after the Russian Revolution, with greatest emphasis on the Soviet period. Author is a refugee from the U.S.S.R.

N411. Hostler, Charles W. **Turkism and the Soviets.** London and N.Y., 1957. Thorough and detailed study of development of Turkic nationalism in Russia and the U.S.S.R.

N412. Caroe, Olaf. **Soviet empire: the Turks of central Asia and Stalinism.** London, 1953. General account of recent Turkestan, with emphasis on its role in Soviet society.

N413. Togan, A. Zeki Velidi. **Bügünkü Türkili (Türkistan) ve yakîn tarihi.** [Turkestan and its recent history.] Istanbul, 1942–47. Brief description of history and geography followed by detailed account of Turkestan under Russian and Soviet rule, by the leading authority on this region.

N414. Pipes, Richard. **The formation of the USSR: communism and nationalism, 1917–1923.** Cambridge, Eng., 1954. Thorough study of the nationality problem in the U.S.S.R., with emphasis on nationalist movements in the post-revolutionary years.

N415. ——. "Muslims of Soviet central Asia: trends and prospects." **Middle East journal,** 9 (spring 1955): 147–62, 9 (summer 1955): 295–308. Detailed account of social and cultural conditions of Soviet Muslims today, based on extensive studies of refugees.

N416. Kolarz, Walter. **Russia and her colonies.** London, 1952; N.Y., 1953. Brief description of Russia's ethnic minorities, last part of which deals with central Asia.

N417. Norins, Martin R. **Gateway to Asia: Sinkiang, frontier of the Chinese far west.** N.Y., 1944. Good source for recent history of Sinkiang, with emphasis on Sino-Soviet relations.

N418. Kazak, Fuad. **Ostturkistan zwischen den Grossmächten: ein Beitrag zur Wirtschaftskunde Ostturkistans.** Königsberg and Berlin, 1937. Description of Sinkiang's economic conditions, with some discussion of its history.

N419. Lattimore, Owen et al. **Pivot of Asia.** Boston, 1950. Articles on different aspects of Sinkiang and a brief summary of its modern history.

JOURNALS

Among the few journals that relate almost exclusively to central Asia, including Mongolia and Tibet, are the following.

N420. Journal of the Royal Central Asian Society. London, 1914 ff. (Quarterly.)

N421. Central Asian review. London, 1953 ff. (Quarterly.)

N422. Central Asiatic journal. The Hague and Wiesbaden, 1955 ff. (Quarterly.)

N423. Novyi Vostok. [New East.] Moscow, 1922–30. (Irregular.) This and the following Soviet journal carried articles relating to central Asia and Mongolia.

N424. Revoliutsionnyi Vostok. [The revolutionary East.] Moscow, 1927–37. (Irregular.)

Each of the Soviet central Asian republics also publishes periodicals, both within and without the framework of the Academy of Sciences, which relate to central Asia.

Between 1920 and 1945 several Japanese journals, such as *Mōkogaku, Mōko kenkyū, Mōkogaku kenkyū,* and *Mōko gakuhō* were devoted exclusively to Mongolia.

TIBET

BIBLIOGRAPHIES AND REFERENCE WORKS

N425. Miller, Beatrice D. "A selective survey of literature on Tibet." **The American political science review,** 47 (Dec. 1953): 1135–51. Thorough bibliographical study of books and articles, especially notable for its shrewd analysis of the general literature by European and Chinese travelers and civil servants.

N426. Fazy, Robert. "Essai d'une bibliographie raisonnée de l'exploration tibétaine." **Mitteilungen der schweizerischen Gesellschaft der Freunde ostasiatischen Kultur,** 2 (1940): 3–22. Lists most of the reports of travelers to central Tibet from earliest times to the present.

N427. Stein, Rolf A. "Récentes études tibétaines." **Journal asiatique,** 240 (1952): 79–106. Review of several recent books on Tibet, primarily literary and historical studies based on translations of Tibetan documents.

N428. Jackson, Ivy. **The religious art of Tibet: a bibliography.** Newark, 1936. A long, mimeographed bibliography distributed by the Newark Museum, listing books and articles dealing with Tibet in all its aspects. Contains many good and bad references, without comment, but very useful.

N429. Lalou, Marcelle. **Inventaire des manuscrits tibétains de Touen-houang conservés à la Bibliothèque Nationale (fonds Pelliot tibétain).** 2 v. Paris, 1939–50. Inventory of the Tibetan manuscripts recovered from Tun-huang by Paul Pelliot. Not a mere list of titles, but an analysis of various types of documents, including texts of great interest for historians and sociologists.

N430. Bibliographie bouddhique. Ed. by Gerard L. M. Clauson, A. J. Bernet Kempers, Nalinaksha Dutt, and others. 1928 ff. Paris, 1930 ff. (Annual.) Includes many articles on topics and aspects of Tibetan Buddhism, its iconography, hierarchy, etc.

N431. Liu, Li-ch'ien. **Hsü Tsang-shih chien. Tibetan history after Lañdarma.** Chengtu, 1947. [West China Frontier Research Institute monograph.] Chinese compilation from native Tibetan historical sources, consisting mostly of biographies and genealogical charts. Poorly printed with numerous errors, due to wartime conditions, but still useful.

N432. Das, Sarat Chandra. **A Tibetan-English dictionary.** Calcutta, 1902. In spite of many small inaccuracies, still the best general dictionary of the Tibetan language. Its very full definitions render it an encyclopedia of Tibetan life and the Lama religion.

GEOGRAPHY, DESCRIPTION AND TRAVEL

N433. Burrard, Sir Sidney G., and Henry H. Hayden. **A sketch of the geography and geology of the Himalaya Mountains and Tibet.** 2nd ed., Delhi, 1933. Revised edition of their basic study of Tibet and its southern borders. The earlier edition (Calcutta, 1907–08) also discussed the rivers of this region, and should be consulted for its greater detail.

N434. Chapman, F. Spencer. **Lhasa, the holy city.** London, 1938. Excellent descriptions of Tibet in the 1930's, discussing politics, religion, festivals and customs, geography, botany, etc. in a most readable and accurate fashion.

N435. Dutreuil de Rhins, Jules-Léon. **L'Asie centrale (Thibet et régions limitrophes).** Paris, 1889. Detailed geographical studies on Tibet and the neighboring regions by a noted French scientist and explorer.

N436. Jen, Nai-ch'iang. **Hsi-k'ang t'uching.** [Pictures from Sikang.] 2 v. Nanking, 1933. Large collection of photographs from eastern Tibet, dealing mostly with people of the various tribes of this region. Very useful for background material.

N437. Landon, Perceval. **The opening of Tibet.** N.Y., 1905. Account of the Younghusband expedition to Lhasa, with a description of the city and its inhabitants.

N438. Macdonald, David. **The land of the Lama.** Philadelphia, 1929. Very interesting book on all aspects of Tibetan life, by a British official who was half Tibetan and knew the language and people well.

N439. Sherring, Charles A. **Western Tibet and the British borderland.** London, 1906. Semi-popular but authoritative account of western Tibet, and Tibetan customs, trade, and religion and government in general.

ETHNOLOGY, ANTHROPOLOGY, AND SOCIOLOGY

N440. Bell, Sir Charles A. **The people of Tibet.** Oxford, 1928. Excellent presentation of the life and customs of the people of central and southern Tibet, from personal observation.

N441. Ekvall, Robert B. **Cultural relations on the Kansu-Tibetan border.** Chicago, 1939. Social and anthropological study of the Chinese, Mongol, and Tibetan tribesmen (both nomadic and sedentary) in the borderlands of northeastern Tibet, and the relations between them. Excellent background for understanding the history of the region.

N442. Li, An-che. "Dege: a study of a Tibetan population." **Southwestern journal**

of anthropology, 3 (winter 1947): 279–93. Brief history and demographic analysis of an important district of eastern Tibet (Sikang), noting particularly the peculiar composition of the Tibetan population.

N443. Rockhill, William W. "Notes on the ethnology of Tibet." **Report of the Smithsonian Institution (U. S. National Museum) for 1893,** Part II, pp. 669–747. Very valuable study, based on collections in the museum, with much information derived from personal experience acquired while exploring northeastern Tibet.

DOCUMENTS AND TRADITIONAL HISTORIES

N444. Roerich, George N., tr. **The blue annals, part I.** Calcutta, 1949. [Royal Asiatic Society of Bengal monograph series, 7.] Translation of chapters 1–7 of the *Deb-ther sñon-po,* a history of Tibet written in the 15th century, especially important for development of the various schools of Lamaism. For other native histories that heavily emphasize Buddhism see Bu-ston's *Chö-jung* [Treasury of the precious scriptures], completed about 1323; and the *Deb-ther dmar-po* [Red annals], written in the 14th century and revised about 1538.

N445. Marx, Karl. "Three documents relating to the history of Ladakh." **Journal of the Royal Asiatic Society of Bengal,** 60 (1891): 97–135. Typical Tibetan historical text with translation and notes, interesting as an example of native Tibetan historiography, which is exceedingly vague and uninforming by modern historical standards.

N446. Bacot, Jacques, Frederick W. Thomas, and Gustavec Toussaint, eds. and trs. **Documents de Touen-houang relatifs à l'histoire du Tibet.** Paris, 1946. [Annales du Musée Guimet, Bibliothèque d'études, 51.] Collection of translations of historical documents and epics found at Tun-huang; of great importance for the history, geography, linguistics, folklore, and literary studies of medieval Tibet.

N447. Meng-pao. **Hsi-tsang pei-wen.** [Tibetan memorial tablet inscriptions.] N.p., 1851. Reproductions of Chinese inscriptions on the memorial tablets in Lhasa, commemorating the principal events in Sino-Tibetan relations. Basic source material.

N448. Wang, Kuang-ch'i, ed. and tr. **Hsi-tsang wai-chiao wen-chien.** [Diplomatic documents on Tibet.] Shanghai, 1930. Primary source materials on Sino-Tibetan relations.

N449. Wu, Feng-p'ei. **Ch'ing-chi ch'ou-tsang tsou-tu.** [Memorials concerning Tibet in Ch'ing times.] 3 v. Changsha, 1938. Collection of official memorials concerning Tibetan affairs from the Ch'ing dynasty archives. Basic source material.

N450. ——. **Ch'ing-tai Hsi-tsang shih-liao ts-ung-k'an, ti-i.** [First collection of historical material on Tibet from the Ch'ing dynasty.] Shanghai, 1937. Valuable original data on Indo-Tibetan relations as well as Chinese relations with Tibet.

N451. Aitchison, Sir Charles U., comp. **A collection of treaties, engagements, and sanads relating to India and the neighbouring countries.** V. 14. Calcutta, 1929. Treaties, etc. relating to Tibet and her satellites. Basic source materials.

GENERAL HISTORIES

N452. Bell, Sir Charles A. **Tibet past and present.** Oxford, 1924. Extensive historical survey of Tibetan history and politics from point of view of a British official with much experience in Tibet.

N453. ——. **Portrait of the Dalai Lama.** London, 1946. Recapitulation of his previous books, with considerable new material on Tibetan history and politics in the early 20th century from author's own experience.

N454. Bushell, S. W. "The early history of Tibet from Chinese sources." **Journal of the Royal Asiatic Society,** n.s. 12 (1880): 435–541. Presents translations of the passages relating to Tibet in Chinese histories of the T'ang dynasty (618–907 A.D.).

N455. Cammann, Schuyler V. R. **Trade through the Himalayas.** Princeton, 1951. Discussion of early British attempts to open Tibet (1774–94), preceded by a historical sketch of Tibet from its founding as a nation to 1773. Based on Chinese historical records and reports of the British envoys, George Bogle and Samuel Turner.

N456. Desideri, Ippolito. **An account of Tibet.** Ed. by Filippo de Filippi. Rev. ed., London, 1937. Personal experiences of an Italian missionary in 18th century Tibet. Well edited.

N457. Francke, A. H. **A history of western Tibet.** London, 1907. Detailed history of Ladakh, an area of Tibetan culture that had hitherto been neglected, by a missionary who spent many years of residence and research in that region.

N458. Li, Tieh-tseng. **The historical status of Tibet.** N.Y., 1956. Discusses in detail the status of Tibet as a nation, from its first dealings with the T'ang dynasty in China (7th century) to the present; based chiefly on Chinese sources. By a former diplomat of wide experience and scholarly background. Though weak on religious aspects, this is a valuable history, especially for last two centuries.

N459. Rockhill, William W., ed. **Tibet: a geographical, ethnographical, and historical sketch, derived from Chinese sources.** Peking, 1939. First published in the *Journal of the Royal Asiatic Society* in 1891. Contains much useful information; but all statements should be carefully checked before quoting.

N460. Schulemann, Günther. **Die Geschichte der Dalailamas.** Heidelberg, 1911. [Religionswissenschaftliche Bibliothek, 3.] History of the religious rulers of Tibet in recent centuries. Since Tibet's history is intimately concerned with the development of its religion, this is an important book.

N461. Waddell, L. Austine. **Lhasa and its mysteries: with a record of the expedition of 1903–1904.** London, 1905. A rather popular account of the British invasion of Tibet, with much background material regarding Tibetan history, politics, and religion, and a detailed description of the capital.

N462. Wu, Ching-ao. **Hsi-ch'ui shih-ti yen-chiu.** [A study of the history and geography of the western regions.] Shanghai, 1948. Modern Chinese work on Tibet and the neighboring areas, based on older sources.

HISTORIES OF SPECIAL TOPICS

Archaeology

N463. Francke, A. H. **Antiquities of Indian Tibet.** 2 v. Calcutta, 1914–26. [Archaeological survey of India reports, 38 and 50.] Valuable archaeological material regarding Ladakh, with detailed plans and illustrations of ancient ruins, inscriptions, and other finds.

N464. Tucci, Giuseppe. **Indo-tibetica.** 4 v. in 7. Rome, 1932–41. Detailed archaeological study of Ladakh and the western regions of Tibet proper, describing ancient temples and their furnishings, inscriptions, and historical documents. Contains much basic historical material.

N465. ——. **The tombs of the Tibetan kings.** Rome, 1950. Describes tombs at Chongche Jong in the Yarlung valley, ascribed to the earliest kings of Tibet; translates inscriptions and numerous texts relating to these ancient remains.

Law and Institutions

N466. Li, Yü Shih-yü. "Tibetan folk-law." **Journal of the Royal Asiatic Society,** (1950): 127–48. Based on conditions in Amdo (northeastern Tibet), as observed during four years of field experience. Contains translation of the "Rules for punishment of Tibetans" from the Ch'ing dynasty imperial statutes, promulgated in 1733 and enforced until recently.

N467. Ma Chieh and Sheng Sheng-tsu. **Wei-Tsang t'u shih.** [Maps and information on eastern and western Tibet.] Peking, 1792. Geographical, ethnographical, historical, and administrative account of Tibet to the late 18th century, when the Manchu government attained its complete control. A basic Chinese source.

N468. Shen, Tsung-lien, and Liu Shen-chi. **Tibet and the Tibetans.** Stanford, 1953. Much useful information on the country, its history, geography, religion and government, social organization, etc., written from the authors' personal experiences as resident officials in Lhasa as well as from their broad scholarly backgrounds.

N469. Walsh, Ernst H. C. "The coinage of Tibet." **Memoirs of the Asiatic Society of Bengal,** 2 (1907): 11–23. Although containing numerous errors, is still useful on Tibetan economy and numismatics.

Foreign Relations

N470. Bell, Sir Charles A. "Tibet and its neighbors." **Pacific affairs,** 10 (Dec. 1937): 428–40. Short, simplified, yet penetrating study of Tibetan foreign relations to World War II, underlining the contrast between British and Chinese views regarding Tibet.

N471. Diskalkar, D. B. "The Tibeto-Nepalese War, 1788–1793." **Journal of the Bihar and Orissa Research Society,** 19 (Dec. 1933): 355–93. Contains valuable documents regarding this war, many of which are not otherwise available, but the author's conclusions drawn from them are often questionable.

N472. Hoffman, Helmut. "Tibets Eintritt in die Universalgeschichte." **Saeculum,** 1 (1950): 258–79. Brief but detailed survey of relations between Tibet and other Asian lands throughout her history, as well as the European relations in recent centuries.

N473. Lee, Wei-kuo. **Tibet in modern world politics (1774–1922).** N.Y., 1931. Although very useful for relations between China and England regarding Tibet, this book is generally unsatisfactory in its scholarship and especially weak in dealing with Anglo-Tibetan relations.

N474. Markham, Sir Clements. **Narratives of the mission of George Bogle in Tibet and of the journey of Thomas Manning to Lhasa.** 2nd ed., London, 1879. The primary source for study of the first British mission to Tibet in the 18th century, with a long introduction discussing Tibetan exploration to the time of writing. The full explanatory notes must be rechecked in light of more recent research.

N475. Petech, Luciano. **China and Tibet in the early 18th century: history of the establishment of the Chinese protectorate in Tibet.** Leiden, 1950. Very thorough study of a basic period in Manchu-Tibetan relations, based on original Chinese and Tibetan sources. Contains biographies of key Tibetan officials.

N476. Rockhill, William W. **The Dalai Lamas of Lhasa and their relations with the Manchu emperors of China, 1644–1908.** Leiden, 1910. Although derived from primary Chinese sources, this often-quoted work has many errors in dates, citations, and minor statements of fact; but the broad generalizations and the conclusions are mostly very sound, being based on the author's long experience in China and Tibet as a U. S. diplomat and explorer.

N477. Rouire, A. M. F. **La rivalité anglo-russe au XIXᵉ siècle en Asie.** Paris, 1908. Discusses British-Russian rivalry over Tibet, but the author's strong anti-British bias must be considered.

N478. Turner, Samuel. **An account of an embassy to the court of the Teshoo Lama in Tibet.** 2nd ed., London, 1806. The primary source regarding the second British mission to Tibet (1783–84) and its sequel.

N479. Younghusband, Sir Francis E. **India and Tibet.** London, 1910. Semi-popular book describing relations between India and Tibet from 1774 to 1910, with a special account of the author's military mission to Lhasa in 1904, to justify his own position. Useful for early 20th century.

Cultural History

N480. Bell, Sir Charles A. **The religion of Tibet.** Oxford, 1931. Rather rambling discussion of the Lama religion, with quotations from Tibetan texts in translation. The literary approach is emphasized, with little account of actual religious practices.

N481. Bleichsteiner, Robert. **Die gelbe Kirche.** Vienna, 1934. Discusses in great detail the Gelugs-pa, or Yellow Cap sect, which gained primacy over the other sects of Lamaism to become the rulers of Tibet in recent times.

N482. Clark, Walter E., ed. **Two Lamaistic pantheons.** 2 v. Cambridge, Mass., 1937. Provides good, illustrated analysis of Tibetan Buddhist deities, with their Tibetan, Sanskrit, and Chinese names. Indispensable for any study of the Lama religion or its iconography.

N483. Evans-Wentz, Walter Y., ed. **The Tibetan book of the dead: or, the after-death experiences on the Bardo plane, according to Lama Kazi Dawa-Samdup's English rendering.** 3rd ed., London, 1957. Translation by a Tibetan and an English scholar of an important Lamaist religious document, very helpful for insight into Tibetan thought and philosophy, and an understanding of the Tibetan people and their religion.

N484. Gruenwedel, Albert. **Mythologie des Buddhismus in Tibet und der Mongolei.** Leipzig, 1900. Discussion of Tibetan Buddhism and its practices, based on images and ethnological materials in the collection of Prince Uchtomsky and on the author's own broad knowledge of Lamaism. Still considered authoritative.

N485. Hoffman, Helmut. "Quellen zur Geschichte der tibetischen Bon-Religion." Aka-demie der Wissenschaften und der Literatur, Mainz, **Abhandlungen der Geistes- und Sozialwissenschaftlichen Klasse,** (1950): 129–443. Very thorough scholarly translation and analysis of basic Tibetan sources for the pre-Buddhist Bon religion, with good bibliography and helpful index.

N486. Koeppen, Carl F. **Die lamaische Hierarchie und Kirche.** Berlin, 1859. This detailed study of Tibetan Buddhism, with its important historical and political aspects, is still useful and often quoted, in spite of much later evidence from more modern research.

N487. Li, An-che. "Bon: the magico-religious belief of the Tibetan-speaking peoples." **Southwestern journal of anthropology,** 4 (spring 1948): 31–42. Brief but important history and analysis of the primitive religion of the Tibetans before introduction of Buddhism, and its continuance and development as a rival to Lamaism.

N488. ——. "Rñiṅ-ma-pa: the early form of Lamaism." **Journal of the Royal Asiatic Society,** (1948): 142–63. Authoritative discussion of the earliest form of the Lama religion, as founded by Padma Sambhava, with its institutions and practices.

N489. ——. "The Bkah-brgyud sect of Lamaism." **Journal of the American Oriental Society,** 69 (Apr.-June 1949): 51–59. A full discussion of the Kargyu-pa sect of Red Lamas, which played an important part in Tibetan history.

N490. ——. "The Sakya sect of Lamaism." **Journal of the West China Border Research Society,** 16 (1945): 72–87. Thorough discussion of the Sakya, which preceded the Gelugs-pa sect in furnishing the supreme rulers of Tibet.

N491. ——. "A lamasery in outline." **Journal of the West China Border Research Society,** 14 (1942): 35–68.

N492. Li, Yu-i. "Hsi-tsang-ti huo-fo." [The living Buddhas of Tibet.] **Yenching social sciences,** 1 (Nov. 1948): 117–31. Useful article on the Tibetan system of Lama reincarnations from the Dalai Lama down to minor local abbots, describing the methods of their finding, their education, and their roles in Tibetan life.

N493. Pallis, Marco. **Peaks and lamas.** Rev. ed., N.Y., 1949. While the places visited by the author were mostly in the borderlands south of Tibet proper, this book offers the clearest account yet written by a westerner of the Lama religion, its beliefs and practices, and its place in the lives of the Tibetan people.

N494. Petech, Luciano. **I missionari italiani nel Tibet e nel Nepal.** 1 v. in 7. Rome, 1952–56. A thorough, very scholarly study of the Capuchin mission and the life and work of Ippolito Desideri in 18th century Tibet.

N495. Schlagintweit, Emil. **Buddhism in Tibet.** Leipzig and London, 1863. Still an important book, often quoted.

N496. Tucci, Giuseppe. **Tibetan painted scrolls.** 2 v. and portfolio of plates. Rome, 1949. Excessively costly and sumptuous volumes, important for their extensive coverage of Tibetan art and cultural history. Weak with respect to Chinese influence and contributions.

N497. Stael-Holstein, A. von. "Notes on two Lama paintings." **Journal of the American Oriental Society,** 52 (Dec. 1932): 338–49. Very useful, scholarly biographical notes on the antecedents, real and legendary, of the earlier Dalai and Panchen Lamas, with their traditional portraits. Excellent for historical background.

N498. Waddell, L. Austine. **The Buddhism of Tibet, or Lamaism.** 2nd ed., reprint, Cambridge, Eng., 1939. Long considered the chief authority on Tibetan Buddhism, although based primarily on observations in Sikkim and southern Tibet. Contains illustrations and lengthy passages of text drawn from previous 19th century works; bibliography of books on Tibet to 1894.

Contemporary Tibet

N499. David-Neel, Alexandra. **Le vieux Tibet face à la Chine nouvelle.** Paris, 1953. Semi-popular analysis of the present situation of Tibet, after its conquest and occupation by Red China, with the impact of new ideas on old institutions.

N500. Maraini, Fosco. **Secret Tibet.** N.Y., 1952. Best modern account of Tibet and its people, by a European traveler. Excellent background material for understanding of the country, its people, their social structure and the national character.

SECTION O

*China**

CHARLES S. GARDNER and EARL H. PRITCHARD
WITH CONTRIBUTIONS BY
T. H. TSIEN and ARTHUR W. HUMMEL

Among all peoples on the globe, the Chinese are probably those most conscious of a recorded history, which stretches back over well nigh 3,000 years. The Chinese have made striking contributions to world culture. To cite only material things, we may list tea, silk, paper and porcelain. The leading art galleries of the western world compete avidly for Chinese bronze vessels cast under the Shang kings before 1000 B.C.; for Buddhist sculptures in stone carved by Chinese workmen in the 4th century; and for later water-color paintings on silk, which have never been surpassed. Even the illiterate laborer is conscious of the glories of his people, as exemplified by the monumental walls and gates which shelter every major city.

The quantity of historical material on China is so vast that the selection of books for a bibliography like this is especially difficult. In the pages that follow an effort has been made to strike a balance between traditional Chinese historical works (which had their own strict canons of scholarship), modern critical Chinese scholarship, and the works of western scholars. In general bibliographies, collections of biographies and documents, and legal, philosophical, religious, literary, and other works that relate to or were produced during a particular dynasty are placed in the appropriate special period. Thus most works relating to the T'ang dynasty or produced during it are listed under the T'ang period. However, the dynastic histories, famous traditional general histories, and compendia on institutions and culture have been listed together under "Printed Collections of Sources and Traditional Histories" in order to refer to them as units and because essentially they constitute a type of source material for the modern scholar.

Except for general reference works and histories, materials relating to China

* The Wade-Giles system of Chinese transliteration is used throughout this and other sections in which Chinese titles appear.

prior to the Ch'in dynasty (*ca.* 221 B.C.) will be found in the China subsection of Section G, while books and periodicals that deal with China but relate more generally to the Far East are in the first part of Section N. General works relating to the religions of China are in Section D, and others that touch on China are included in Part IX.

Traditional Chinese books were divided into *chüan* (chapters) and bound with string into convenient units (50 to 300 pages) with paper covers called *ts'e* (volumes). Several *ts'e* were assembled in cloth-covered boxes called *t'ao*. Unless the work was added to or changed, the number of *chüan* normally did not change, but the number of *ts'e* might vary from printing to printing or even within the same printing. Traditional bibliographers almost invariably gave the number of *chüan* in a work, but not necessarily the number of *ts'e*. Some recent books are bound in western style volumes, others in the traditional *ts'e*.

BIBLIOGRAPHIES

O1. Hucker, Charles O. **Chinese history: a bibliographical review.** Washington, 1958. Best short guide to works in western languages, especially English.

O2. Latourette, Kenneth S. **The Chinese, their history and culture.** 3rd ed., N.Y., 1946. Bibliographies at end of chapters are good guides.

O3. Maspero, Henri. "La Chine et l'Asie centrale." **Histoire et historiens depuis cinquante ans . . . 1876 à 1926,** v. 2 (Paris, 1928), pp. 517–59. Valuable survey of western historians dealing with China and their works.

O4. Franke, Herbert. **Sinologie.** Bern, 1953.

O5. Goodrich, L. Carrington, and Henry C. Fenn. **A syllabus of the history of Chinese civilization and culture.** 6th ed., N.Y., 1958. Topics with reading lists, maps, charts, and selected bibliography.

O6. Yang, Lien-sheng. **Topics in Chinese history.** Cambridge, Mass., 1950. These topics embrace political, social, and economic institutions, religions, literature, etc., each accompanied by a judicious choice among the best books in Chinese, Japanese, and western languages.

O7. Gardner, Charles S. **A union list of selected western books on China in American libraries.** 2nd ed., Washington, 1938. Cites principal reviews as well as holding libraries.

O8. ——. **Union list of selected Chinese books in American libraries.** Washington, 1932. Although not up-to-date, is the only thing of its kind readily available.

O9. Teng, Ssu-yü, and Knight Biggerstaff. **An annotated bibliography of selected Chinese reference works.** 2nd ed., Cambridge, Mass., 1950. Now a standard reference work. Includes bibliographies, encyclopedias, dic-

tionaries, geographical and biographical works, tables, yearbooks, and Sinological indexes.

O10. Liang, Tzu-han. **Chung-kuo li-tai shu-mu tsung-lu.** [A bibliography of Chinese bibliographies.] Taipei, 1953. Supersedes Shao Jui-p'eng, *Shu-mu ch'ang-pien* (2 v., Peiping, 1928).

O11. Chang, Chih-tung, and Miao Ch'üan-sun. **Shu-mu ta-wen pu-cheng.** [Answers to inquiries on bibliography.] Rev. and enl. by Fan Hsi-tseng. 2 ts'e, Nanking, 1931. Selected list of 2,266 works considered by a great scholar-official of the 19th century to be basic for students. Chang's preface is dated 1875 and Fan's revisions were made in the 1920's.

O12. Cordier, Henri. **Bibliotheca sinica.** 2nd ed., 4 v. and suppl., Paris, 1904–24. Reprint, 5 v., Peiping, 1938. The basic bibliography of books and articles in western languages on China, somewhat over-classified.

O13. Columbia University. **Author index to the Bibliotheca sinica of Henri Cordier.** N.Y., 1953. Valuable but somewhat imperfect author index to the above.

O14. Yüan, T'ung-li. **China in western literature: a continuation of Cordier's Bibliotheca sinica.** New Haven, 1958. Absolutely indispensable for books on China in English, French, and German (with some in Portuguese) published since Cordier's last volume.

O15. ——. **Economic and social development of modern China: a bibliographical guide.** New Haven, 1956.

O16. Fairbank, John K., and Liu Kwang-ching. **Modern China: a bibliographical guide to Chinese works, 1898–1937.** Cambridge, Mass., 1950. By far the best comprehensive guide for the period.

O17. Fairbank, John K., and Banno Masataka. **Japanese studies of modern China: a bibliographical guide to historical and social-**

science research on the 19th and 20th centuries. Rutland, Vt., 1955. Much basic work on China has been done by Japanese, and this is an indispensable guide to it.

O18. Sun, E-tu Zen, and John DeFrancis. **Bibliography on Chinese social history: a selected and critical list of Chinese periodical sources.** New Haven, 1952.

O19. U. S. Library of Congress. **China: a selected list of references on contemporary economic and industrial development, with special emphasis on post-war reconstruction.** Comp. by Helen F. Conover. Rev. ed., Washington, 1946.

O20. Nankai social and economic quarterly. Tientsin, 1935–41. Bibliographical sections are valuable guides to social and economic studies on China in Chinese during the 1930's.

O21. Skachkov, Petr E. **Bibliografiia Kitaia . . . 1730–1930.** Moscow, 1932. Systematic presentation of books and periodical articles on China in Russian, published by the Institute for Chinese Studies of the Communist Academy.

O22. Loewenthal, Rudolf. **Bibliography of Russian literature on China and adjacent countries, 1931–36.** Cambridge, Mass., 1949. This and the following article form a valuable supplement to Skachkov.

O23. ——. "Works on the Far East and central Asia published in the U.S.S.R., 1937–47." **Far eastern quarterly,** 8 (Feb., 1949): 172–83.

O24. Davidson, Martha, ed. **A list of published translations from Chinese into English, French, and German.** 2 v. Ann Arbor, 1952–57. For a more selective list of translations see Hightower, *Topics in Chinese literature* (*O1027*).

O25. Frankel, Hans H. **Catalogue of translations from the Chinese dynastic histories for the period 220–960.** Berkeley, 1957.

O26. Pa shih ching-chi-chih. [Collection of eight dynastic bibliographies.] First pub. in Japan, 1825; and by Chang Shou-jung in 16 ts'e, 1883. Contains the six bibliographical sections from the dynastic histories and four supplementary bibliographies compiled during the Ch'ing period.

O27. Chung-kuo li-tai i-wen-chih. [Essays on literature of the successive dynasties of China.] Shanghai, 1936. Reproduces ten historical bibliographies.

O28. Hung, William, and others. **I-wen-chih erh-shih-chung tsung-ko yin-te.** 4 v. Peiping, 1933. Indexes some twenty dynastic bibliographies, providing invaluable guide to literature of the successive dynasties from the Han onward.

O29. Chi, Yün, and others. **Ssu-k'u ch'üan-shu tsung-mu.** [Catalog of the library of the four treasuries.] 44 ts'e, Shanghai, 1930. Annotated catalog of 3,461 works in the Imperial Library of the Four Treasuries and

6,793 other works extant at the time of its compilation in 1773–82. This edition includes three supplements and an index.

O30. Wylie, Alexander. **Notes on Chinese literature . . . and a list of translations from the Chinese into various European languages.** Shanghai, 1867. Reprints, 1922; and Peiping, 1939. A standard work since 1867; still useful, although the system of transcription employed is completely outmoded. Based heavily on Chi Yün's *Ssu-k'u,* and, like it, is divided into four major parts: classics, histories (including geography and governmental matters), philosophers, and belles-lettres.

O31. Shih, T'ing-yung. **Ch'ing-hua ta-hsüeh ts'ung-shu tzu-mu shu ming so yin.** [A title index of Chinese collectanea in the Tsing Hua University library.] Peiping, 1936.

O32. Yang, Chia-lo. **Ts'ung-shu ta-tz'u-tien.** [Great dictionary of *ts'ung-shu.*] Nanking, 1936.

O33. Chang, Hsin-ch'eng. **Wei-shu t'ung-k'ao.** [A bibliography of forged books.] 2 v. Shanghai, 1939.

O34. Huang, Ch'u-ts'ang (P'ing-hsin). **Sheng-huo ch'üan-kuo tsung-shu-mu.** [A classified catalog of current Chinese books with complete index.] Shanghai, 1935. Covers the period 1911–34 and contains about 20,000 items.

O35. Kuo-hsüeh lun-wen so-yin. [Index to Sinological literature.] Comp. by National Library of Peiping. 4 v. Peiping, 1929–36.

O36. Chung-kuo shih-hsüeh lun-wen so-yin. [Index to periodical literature on Chinese history.] Comp. by the Chung-kuo K'o-hsüeh-yüan Li-shih Yen-chih-so and Pei-ching Ta-hsüeh Li-shih-hsi. 2 v. Peiping, 1957. Classified list of some 30,000 articles from 1,300 periodicals in Chinese published during the last 50 years.

O37. Chu, Shih-chia. **Chung-kuo ti-fang-chih tsung-lu.** [A union catalog of Chinese local histories.] 3 v. Shanghai, 1935. Contains some 5,832 titles arranged according to administrative units of the Ch'ing dynasty with indication of holdings in various libraries in China and abroad. A supplement by Chu appears in the *Shih-hsüeh nien-pao* [Historical annual], v. 2 (Peiping, 1938), pp. 401–34; and a further supplement by him on "Chinese local histories at Columbia University" is in the *Harvard journal of Asiatic studies,* 8 (Aug. 1944): 187–95.

O38. U. S. Library of Congress. **A catalog of Chinese local histories in the Library of Congress.** Comp. by Chu Shih-chia. Washington, 1942. Titles are in romanization and Chinese with most other data in Chinese.

O39. Kokuritsu Kokkai Toshokan [National Diet Library of Japan]. **Chūgoku chihoshi sōroku-ko.** [Draft union catalog of Chinese local histories.] Tokyo, 1950–53. An important complement to Chu's catalog.

Has been issued in small, paper-bound volumes, one for each province of China.

O40. Hervouet, Y. **Catalogue des monographies locales chinoises dans les bibliothèques d'Europe.** Paris, 1957.

O41. Wang, Chung-min. **A descriptive catalog of rare Chinese books in the Library of Congress.** Ed. by T. L. Yüan. 2 v. Washington, 1957. In Chinese with introduction in English.

O42. Ch'iu, Alfred K. **A classified catalogue of Chinese books in the Chinese-Japanese library of the Harvard-Yenching Institute at Harvard University.** 3 v. Cambridge, Mass., 1938–40. These 3 volumes contain classics, philosophy, religion and historical sciences; other subjects are available on microfilm. All titles and authors are cited in both Chinese and transcription.

O43. Paris. Bibliothèque Nationale. **Catalogue des livres chinois, coréens, japonais, etc.** Comp. by Maurice Courant. 3 v. Paris, 1902–12. Contains 9,080 items, mostly printed books, some of which are quite rare, including various works not found elsewhere.

O44. Pelliot, Paul. "Répertoire des collections Pelliot A et B du fonds chinois de la Bibliothèque Nationale." *T'oung pao,* 14 (Dec. 1913): 697–780.

O45. Douglas, R. K. **Catalogue of Chinese printed books, manuscripts . . . of the British Museum.** London, 1877. Supplement, 1903. Although not as valuable as *O43,* has some of the same merits.

O46. "Notes de bibliographie chinoise." **Bulletin de l'École Française d'Extrême-Orient,** 1901 ff. The notes of Paul Pelliot and other French scholars in these volumes are useful.

O47. Liu, I-cheng, and others. **Chiang-su sheng-li kuo-hsüeh t'u-shu-kuan t'u-shu tsung-mu.** [Catalog of the Kiangsu Provincial Sinological Library of Nanking.] 24 ts'e. Nanking, 1933–35. Supplement, 3 ts'e, 1937. Catalog of one of the finest libraries in China.

O48. Jüan, Yüan. **T'ien-i-ko shu-mu.** [Catalog of the T'ien-i Library.] 10 ts'e. Ningpo, 1808. This catalog of a famous private library in Ningpo may serve as an example of many others. The library was especially strong in history, local gazetteers, rare works, and manuscripts; but contains a much smaller collection now than the 4,094 items shown in 1808.

O49. Pei-ching Jen-wen k'o-hsüeh yen-chiu-so ts'ang shu mu-lu. [Catalog of the library of the Peking Humanistic Research Center.] 10 ts'e. Peiping, 1938–39. One of the more useful and up-to-date selective library catalogs. Especially strong in Ming editions, Ch'ing manuscripts, and local gazetteers.

O50. Tōhō bunka kenkyu sho kanseki bunri mokuroku. [Classified catalog of Chinese books in the Institute of Oriental Culture.] 2 v. Kyoto, 1943.

O51. Catalogue of the Asiatic library of Dr. G. E. Morrison. 2 v. Tokyo, 1924. The Morrison collection in the Tōyō Bunko, Tokyo, is probably the largest single collection of western books on China in the world and is especially valuable for its editions of early works.

O52. Quarterly bulletin of Chinese bibliography. Ed. by National Library of Peiping. Peiping, etc., 1934–48. The Chinese edition is somewhat more elaborate, but this one with translated titles and annotations is especially useful for westerners.

O53. Revue bibliographique de sinologie. Paris, 1957 ff.

O54. Woo, Kang [Wu, K'ang]. Histoire de la bibliographie chinoise. Paris, 1938.

See also Sections N and G. For bibliographies on special subjects and periods see the period and topical subsections that follow.

ENCYCLOPEDIAS AND WORKS OF REFERENCE

O55. Li, Shao-ch'ang. **The development of Chinese culture: a synoptic chart and bibliography.** Honolulu, 1926. 2nd rev. ed., East Lansing, 1952.

O56. Reischauer, Edwin O. **Chronological chart of far eastern history.** Cambridge, Mass., 1947.

O57. Mayers, William F. **The Chinese reader's manual: a handbook of biographical, historical, mythological, and general literary reference.** Shanghai, 1874; Peking, 1924. Inadequate, but a better manual has not appeared.

O58. Hsüeh, Chung-san, and Ouyang Yi [Ou-yang I]. **A Sino-western calendar for two thousand years: 1–2000 A.D.** Changsha, 1940. Best all-round manual for converting Chinese dates into western ones since 1 A.D. Its only limitation is that it does not give the cyclical sign for every day, but this can be determined.

O59. Chen, Yüan. **Chung Hsi Hui shih jih-li.** [Comparative daily calendar for Chinese, European and Islamic history.] 5 ts'e. Peking, 1926. Covers the years A.D. 1–1940.

O60. Cheng, Ho-sheng. **Chin-shih Chung-Hsi shih jih tui-chao-piao.** [Concordance of modern Sino-western historical dates.] Shanghai, 1936. Covers years 1516–1941 and contains the cyclical signs for each day so that any Chinese date can be converted immediately into a western one.

O61. Hoang, Pierre. **Concordance des chronologies néoméniques chinoise et européenne.** Shanghai, 1910. Superseded by *O58* for the Christian era, but still indispensable for earlier periods.

O62. Tchang, Mathias. **Synchronismes chinois.** See *N14*.

O63. Ch'en, Ch'ing-ch'i. **Chung-kuo ta-shih nien-pao.** [Chronological tables of important events in China.] Shanghai, 1934. Covers from earliest times to 1932.

O64. Moule, Arthur C. **The rulers of China, 221 B.C.–A.D. 1949.** London, 1957. Chronological table of all the rulers, including a section on the earlier dynasties.

O65. Hu, Cheng-chih. **Chung-kuo ti-hao piao-t'i i-lan.** [An index to the names of Chinese emperors.] Peiping, 1939. Personal and other names and reign titles of 373 emperors from Huang-ti to Yüan Shih-k'ai, including a chronological list of emperors with dates of their reigns.

O66. Giles, Herbert A. **A Chinese biographical dictionary.** Shanghai and London, 1898. Despite certain inaccuracies and defects, still the best biographical dictionary in a western language to cover the whole of Chinese history to end of 19th century. Contains 2,579 biographies.

O67. Tsang, Li-ho, Fang I, and others. **Chung-kuo jen-ming ta-tz'u-tien.** [Great dictionary of Chinese names.] 2nd ed., Shanghai, 1934. New ed., Taipei, 1958. This biographical dictionary of 40,000 persons, based chiefly on the standard histories, is the indispensable reference for all students of Chinese history.

O68. Gates, Jean. **A romanized index to the surnames in the Chinese biographical dictionary.** Washington, 1942.

O69. Chiang, Liang-fu. **Li-tai ming-jen nien-li pei chuan tsung-piao.** [Chronological tables of famous persons of successive dynasties.] Shanghai, 1937. Indispensable for birth and death dates of important people as well as sources. Largely supersedes Chang Wei-hsiang, ·*I-nien lu-hui pien* (8 ts'e, Wuching, Kiangsu, 1925).

O70. Ch'en, Te-yün. **Ku-chin jen-wu pieh-ming so-yin.** [Index to alternate names of ancient and modern times.] Canton, 1937. Dictionary of pen names and other alternate names; more useful than the following work.

O71. P'eng, Tso-chen. **Ku-chin tung hsing-ming ta-tz'u-tien.** [Dictionary of identical names in ancient and modern times.] Peiping, 1936.

O72. **Who's Who in China.** 6 issues and 3 supplements. Shanghai, 1918–50. Useful biographies of contemporary Chinese published by the *China weekly review.*

O73. Perleberg, Max. **Who's who in modern China.** Hong Kong, 1954. Biographies of over 2,000 persons from beginning of the republic to the end of 1953, including details on political parties and government organization, and a glossary of terms.

O74. Hashikawa, Tokio. **Chūgoku bunka-kai jimbutsu sōkan.** [A who's who of persons in Chinese cultural circles.] Peiping, 1940. Useful biographical dictionary of Chinese of the republican period, prepared by Japanese in north China during the war.

O75. **The China year book.** 20 v. London, etc., 1912–39. The annual issues contain, aside from statistical information, documents on current developments and a valuable "Who's who in China."

O76. **The Chinese year book.** 5 v. Shanghai, 1935–41. The first issue (for 1935–36) is the most detailed and the best of all Chinese yearbooks issued in English. Contains a useful who's who.

O77. Chang, Tzu-sheng, Chang Che-han, and others. **Shen-pao nien-chien.** [The Shen-pao yearbook.] Shanghai, 1933–44. Perhaps the most valuable of the yearbooks in Chinese. The 1944 issue covers the years 1936–42 and contains much material on the war period.

O78. **Chung-hua min-kuo t'ung-chi t'i-yao.** [Statistical abstract of the republic of China.] Nanking, 1936 and 1947; Taipei, 1955. Useful collection of data.

O79. **China handbook.** Chungking, N.Y., Taipei, 1943 ff. The Nationalist handbook on China currently issued every two years. Provides much of the same information as yearbooks.

O80. **Handbook on people's China.** Peiping, 1957. Deals with history, government, statistics, education, science, etc. of Communist China.

O81. **Jen-min shou-ts'e.** [People's handbook.] Shanghai, 1950 ff. (Annual.)

O82. Couling, Samuel. **The encyclopaedia sinica.** Shanghai, 1917. Valuable for western personalities and activities rather than those of the Chinese.

O83. Ball, J. Dyer. **Things Chinese.** 5th ed., rev. by Chalmers Werner, Shanghai, 1925.

O84. Huang, Shao-hsü, and others. **Jih-yung pai-k'o ch'üan-shu.** [Encyclopedia of materials of daily use.] 3 v. Shanghai, 1934. Collection of materials on a large variety of subjects, such as philosophy, literature, history, etc.

O85. [Ch'en, Meng-lei], Chiang T'ing-hsi and others. **Ku-chin t'u-shu chi-ch'eng.** [Imperial encyclopedia of ancient and modern matters.] Peking Palace edition, 5020 ts'e, 1725. Photolithographic ed., 808 ts'e, Shanghai, 1934. Items grouped into six major categories: heavenly phenomena, geography, human relations, arts and sciences, literature, and political economy.

O86. Giles, Lionel. **An alphabetical index to the Chinese encyclopaedia.** London, 1911.

O87. Li, Fang, and others. **T'ai-p'ing yü-lan.** [Classified encyclopedia of the T'ai-p'eng period of the Sung dynasty.] Completed in 983. Photolithographic reproduction, 136 ts'e,

Shanghai, 1935. Index by William Hung and others, Peiping, 1935 [Harvard-Yenching Institute Sinological index series, no. 23]. The most famous of early Chinese encyclopedias.

O88. Wang, Ying-lin. **Yü hai.** [The sea of jade.] 122 ts'e. Reprint, [n.p.], 1806 and 1883. Another early encyclopedia (13th century) of great merit.

O89. Chou, Mu-chai. **Chung-kuo li-shih hsiao-tz'u tien.** [Dictionary of Chinese historical terms.] Shanghai, 1934. Defines more than 600 historical terms.

See also Section N and the subsections on periods, topics, and sources and traditional histories.

GEOGRAPHIES, GAZETTEERS, AND ATLASES

O90. Cressey, George B. **Land of the 500 million: a geography of China.** N.Y. and London, 1955.

O91. ——. **China's geographic foundations.** N.Y., London, Shanghai, 1934. Best general geography of China in a western language.

O92. Shabad, Theodore. **China's changing map.** N.Y., 1956. Shows administrative changes in Communist China.

O93. Joüon, René. **Géographie de la Chine.** 3rd ed., Shanghai, 1932.

O94. ——. **Géographie commerciale de la Chine.** 4th ed., Shanghai, 1937.

O95. Furzholzer, Edmund. **China, Land und Volk.** Frankfurt-am-Main, 1954.

O96. Buxton, L. H. Dudley. **China, the land and the people: a human geography.** Oxford, 1929.

O97. Richard, Louis. **Géographie de l'empire de Chine.** Shanghai, 1905. English tr., *Comprehensive geography of the Chinese empire*, rev. and enl. by M. Kennelly, Shanghai, 1908. Best geographic manual of Manchu China in a western language. Gives characters for place names.

O98. Winfield, Gerald F. **China, the land and the people.** N.Y., 1948. Rev. ed., 1950.

O99. Shui-ching chu. [The water classic with commentaries.] By Li Tao-yüan. Imperial ed., 17 ts'e, 1753; Changsha, 1892. 1 v., Peiping, 1955. This work by a 6th century author discusses nearly 1,400 rivers and streams. There is an index and commentary to the Changsha edition, Cheng Te-k'un, *Shui-ching chu yin-te* (2 v., Peiping, 1934).

O100. Thorp, James. **Geography of the soils of China.** Peiping, 1939. Prepared for the Ministry of Industries.

O101. Shen, Tsung-han. **Agricultural resources of China.** Ithaca, 1951.

O102. Chang, Ch'i-yün. **The natural resources of China.** N.Y., 1945.

O103. "Mineral resources of China." U. S. Bureau of Mines, **Foreign minerals survey,** v. 2, no. 7 (Washington, 1948).

O104. Playfair, George M. H. **The cities and towns of China: a geographical dictionary.** 2nd ed., Shanghai, 1910.

O105. Couvreur, Séraphin. **Géographie ancienne et moderne de la Chine.** 3rd ed., Hsien-hsien, 1917.

O106. Tsang, Li-ho, and others. **Chung-kuo ku-chin ti-ming ta-tz'u-tien.** [A dictionary of ancient and modern place names.] Shanghai, 1930. An indispensable work.

O107. U. S. Office of Geography. **China: official standard names approved by the U. S. Board on Geographical Names.** 2 v. Washington, 1956.

O108. Chu, Fang, and Liu Chun-jen. **Chung-kuo ti-ming ta-tz'u-tien.** [Chinese gazetteer.] Peiping, 1930.

O109. Tsui-hsin Chung-hua min-kuo Manchou ti-kuo jen-ming ti-ming pien-lan. [A manual of Chinese and Manchurian personal and place names.] Tokyo, 1939. Personal names are arranged both according to a *kana* system and Wade-Giles romanization, with brief comments after each name. Place names are arranged according to a *kana* system and a romanization (more or less *Postal atlas*), and the province of each place is given.

O110. Ch'en, Fang-chi. **Li-tai ti-li yen-ko piao.** [Table of historical changes in place names.] Ed. by Huang T'ing-chien. 7 ts'e. Canton, 1836. [Kuang-ya ts'ung-shu, ts'e 176–82.] Author's preface is dated 1667 and the editor's introduction 1833.

O111. Herrmann, Albert. **Historical and commercial atlas of China.** Cambridge, Mass., 1935. Suffers from effort to show excessive detail on each plate. Special maps of 10 treaty ports. Bibliography.

O112. Yang, Shou-ching. **Li-tai yü-ti t'u.** [Historical atlas.] 42 ts'e. 1906–11. The best Chinese historical atlas of China.

O113. National Institute of Geography. **An atlas of the provinces of China.** Peking, 1926. Contains 28 double-page maps of individual provinces with interleaved text. Also includes a tabular comparison of rivers, and a concise review of treaties with foreign states and of Chinese ports open to foreign trade.

O114. Chinese Directorate-General of Posts. **Chung-hua yu-cheng yü-t'u.** [A postal atlas of China.] Shanghai, 1933. Its 30 maps are large but not accurately drawn and the number of places shown is limited. Its system of romanizing place names is widely used.

O115. Ting, Wen-chiang [V. K. Ting], and others. **Chung-hua min-kuo hsin ti-t'u.** [New atlas of the republic of China.] Shanghai, 1934. Best atlas of modern China. The postwar edition under title *Chung-kuo fen-sheng hsin-t'u* (Shanghai, 1948) is somewhat abbreviated.

See also Section N and the subsections on periods below.

ANTHROPOLOGY AND SOCIOLOGY

O116. Fried, Morton H. "Community studies in China." **Far eastern quarterly,** 14 (Nov. 1954): 11–36. Survey and analysis of studies on the subject.

O117. ——. **Fabric of Chinese society.** N.Y., 1953.

O118. Doolittle, Justus. **Social life of the Chinese.** 2 v. N.Y., 1865.

O119. Tcheng, Ki-tong. **The Chinese painted by themselves.** London, 1885.

O120. Tcheng, Ki-tong, and John H. Gray. **The Chinese empire, past and present.** N.Y., 1900.

O121. Smith, Arthur H. **Village life in China: a study in sociology.** N.Y., 1899.

O122. ——. **Chinese characteristics.** 2nd ed., N.Y., 1894.

O123. Leong, Y. K., and L. K. Tao. **Village and town life in China.** London, 1915.

O124. Gamble, Sidney D., and John S. Burgess. **Peking, a social survey.** N.Y., 1921.

O125. Burgess, John S. **The guilds of Peking.** N.Y., 1928.

O126. Kulp, Daniel H. **Country life in south China: the sociology of familism.** N.Y., 1925.

O127. Li, Ching-han [F. C. H. Lee]. **Ting-hsien she-hui kai-k'uang tiao-ch'a.** [General social survey of Ting-hsien.] Peiping, 1933.

O128. Gamble, Sidney D. **Ting Hsien, a north China rural community.** N.Y., 1954. Presents basic materials of the above.

O129. Chen, Ta. **Emigrant communities in south China.** N.Y., 1940.

O130. Fei, Hsiao-tung, and Chang Chih-i. **Earthbound China.** Chicago, 1945.

O131. Fei, Hsiao-tung. **Peasant life in China.** London and N.Y., 1939.

O132. ——. **China's gentry.** Chicago, 1953.

O133. Yang, Martin C. **A Chinese village: Taitou, Shantung province.** N.Y., 1945.

O134. Fitzgerald, Charles P. **The tower of five glories: a study of the Min Chia of Ta Li.** London, 1941.

O135. Hsü, Francis L. K. **Under the ancestors' shadow: Chinese culture and personality.** N.Y., 1948.

O136. ——. **Religion, science and human crises: a study of China in transition and its implications for the West.** London, 1952.

O137. ——. **Americans and Chinese: two ways of life.** N.Y., 1953; London, 1955.

O138. Lin, Yüeh-hwa [Lin, Yao-hua]. **The golden wing: a sociological study of Chinese familism.** London and N.Y., 1948.

O139. Lang, Olga. **Chinese family and society.** New Haven, 1946.

O140. Lin, Yu-t'ang. **My country and my people.** See *O261.*

O141. Hu, Hsien-chin. **The common descent group in China and its functions.** N.Y., 1948.

O142. Feng, Han-yi. "The Chinese kinship system." **Harvard journal of Asiatic studies,** 2 (July 1937): 141–276.

O143. Yang, Ching-kun. **The Chinese family in the Communist Revolution.** Cambridge, Mass., 1954.

O144. Bredon, Juliet, and Igor Mitrophanow. **The moon year: a record of Chinese customs and festivals.** Shanghai, 1927.

O145. Tun, Li-ch'en. **Annual customs and festivals in Peking as recorded in the Yen-ching Sui-shih-chi.** Tr. by Derk Bodde. Peiping, 1936.

O146. Li, Chi. **The formation of the Chinese people: an anthropological inquiry.** Cambridge, Mass., 1928.

O147. Shirokogoroff, Sergei M. **Anthropology of northern China.** Shanghai, 1923.

O148. ——. **Anthropology of eastern China and Kwangtung province.** Shanghai, 1925.

O149. ——. **Process of physical growth among the Chinese.** Shanghai, 1925.

DEMOGRAPHIC STUDIES

O150. Bielenstein, Hans. "The census of China during the period 2–742 A.D." **Bulletin of the Museum of Far Eastern Antiquities,** 19 (1947): 125–63. Supersedes all other works for the period covered.

O151. Giles, Lionel. "A census of Tun-huang." **T'oung pao,** 16 (1915): 468–88.

O152. Van der Sprenkel, Otto B. "Population statistics of Ming China." **Bulletin of the School of Oriental and African Studies,** 15 (1953): 289–326. Assembles population data for the period 1368–1644 from Chinese sources.

O153. Rockhill, William W. "Inquiry into the population of China." **Smithsonian miscellaneous collections,** 47 (1905): 303–21.

O154. ——. "The 1910 census of the population of China." **T'oung pao,** 13 (1912): 117–25.

O155. Willcox, Walter F. "A westerner's effort to estimate the population of China and its increase since 1650." **Journal of the American Statistical Association,** 25 (Sep. 1930): 255–68.

O156. ——. "The population of China in 1910." **Jour. Am. Stat. Assn.,** 23 (Mar. 1928): 18–30.

O157. Ho, Ping-ti. **Studies on the population of China, 1368–1953.** Cambridge, Mass., 1959.

O158. Ho, Ping-ti, and Irene B. Taeuber. **The growth of the total population of China, 1750–1830.** Cambridge, Mass., 1956.

O159. Wong, W. H. **The distribution of population and land utilization in China.** Shanghai, 1933.

O160. Liu, Nanming. **Contribution à l'étude de la population chinoise.** Geneva, 1935.

O161. Ch'en, Ta. **Population in modern China.** Chicago, 1946.

O162. ——. **Jen-k'ou wen-t'i.** [Population problem.] Shanghai, 1934. [Ta-hsüeh ts'ung-shu.]

O163. Cressey, George B. "The 1953 census of China." **Far eastern quarterly,** 14 (May 1955): 387–88.

O164. Orleans, Leo A. "The 1953 Chinese census in perspective." **Journal of Asian studies,** 16 (Aug. 1957): 565–73.

O165. ——. "The recent growth of China's urban population." **Geographical Review,** 49 (Jan. 1959): 43–57.

O166. Shabad, Theodore. "The population of China's cities." **Geographical review,** 49 (Jan. 1959): 32–42. *O163–O166* provide useful data on the Communist census.

For other demographic studies see Section N.

LINGUISTIC WORKS

O167. Karlgren, Bernhard. **The Chinese language: an essay on its nature and history.** N.Y., 1949. Excellent general survey.

O168. ——. **Sound and symbol in Chinese.** London, 1923.

O169. Chao, Yuen Ren [Yüan-jen]. **Mandarin primer.** Cambridge, Mass., 1957. A more technical linguistic description.

O170. Kennedy, George A. **ZH[Tz'u hai] guide: an introduction to Sinology.** New Haven, 1953. Guide to the use of Chinese dictionaries and other needs of the student of Chinese.

O171. ——. **Chinese reading for beginners.** New Haven, 1939. Introduction to Chinese grammar and characters.

O172. Creel, Herrlee G., and others, eds. **Literary Chinese by the inductive method.** 3 v. Chicago, 1938–52. [1, *The Hsiao ching;* 2, *Selections from the Lun yü;* 3, *The Mencius books 1–3.*] A valuable introductory text to literary Chinese. Introduction contains a discussion of the language, and each volume has text, vocabularies, and notes which also show and discuss the evolution of form of the characters.

O173. ——. **Chinese writing.** Washington, 1943.

O174. Creel, Herrlee G., and Teng Ssu-yü, eds. **Newspaper Chinese by the inductive method.** Chicago, 1943.

O175. Hirth, Friedrich. **Wen-chien tzu-chü Ju-men.** [Notes on the Chinese documentary style.] Shanghai, 1888. Helpful guide to the use of Chinese documents.

O176. Fairbank, John K. **Ch'ing documents: an introductory syllabus.** Cambridge, Mass., 1952. Texts, notes, and bibliography.

O177. Teng, Ssu-yü. **Conversational Chinese, with grammatical notes.** Chicago, 1947.

O178. Aldrich, Harry S. **Hua yü hsü chih: practical Chinese, including a topical dictionary of 5000 everyday terms.** 2nd ed., 2 v., Peiping, 1934. American rev. ed., New Haven, 1942. Manual of spoken Chinese as well as a textbook.

O179. Mullie, Joseph. **The structural principles of the Chinese language: an introduction to the spoken language.** 3 v. Peiping, 1932–37. Elaborate treatise on the north China (Mandarin) dialect.

O180. Wang, Li. **Chung-kuo yü-fa li-lun.** [A Chinese grammar.] 2 ts'e. Shanghai, 1945.

O181. Tai, T'ung. **The six scripts: or, the principles of Chinese writing.** Tr. by L. C. Hopkins. Cambridge, Eng., 1954.

O182. DeFrancis, John F. **Nationalism and language reform in China.** Princeton, 1950. Extended discussion of language reform and romanization problems.

O183. Hsia, Tao-t'ai. **China's language reforms.** New Haven, 1956. Discusses changes in Communist China.

O184. Gardner, Charles S. "The western transcription of Chinese." **Journal of the North China Branch of the Royal Asiatic Society,** 62 (1931): 137–47.

O185. Karlgren, Bernhard. **The romanization of Chinese.** London, 1928. [China Society papers.]

O186. ——. **Étude sur la phonologie chinoise.** 4 pts. Leiden, 1915–26. Tr. into Chinese by Chao Yüan-jên and others, Changsha, 1940.

O187. ——. **Grammata serica: script and phonetics in Chinese and Sino-Japanese.** Stockholm, 1940.

O188. ——. **Grammata serica.** Stockholm, 1957.

O189. ——. **Compendium of phonetics in ancient and archaic Chinese.** London, 1954.

O190. ——. **Analytic dictionary of Chinese and Sino-Japanese.** Paris, 1923.

O191. Fenn, Courtenay H. **The five thousand dictionary: a Chinese-English pocket dictionary.** 5th ed., Peiping, 1940. Rev. American ed., Cambridge, Mass., 1944. Most useful of small dictionaries of characters and compounds.

O192. Goodrich, Chauncey. **A pocket dictionary (Chinese-English).** Peking, 1891; Shanghai, 1933. Reprint, N.Y., 1944. Contains 10,587 characters, but not compounds.

O193. Soothill, William E. **The students' four thousand.** 20th ed., London, 1952. Characters plus compounds, arranged according to the phonetic element in the character.

O194. Mathews, Robert H. **A Chinese-English dictionary.** 2 v. Shanghai, 1931. Rev. American ed., Cambridge, Mass., 1943–44. Contains 7,785 characters with over 104,000 phrases and is the best medium-size dictionary. V. 2 is an English index to the Chinese-English text.

O195. Giles, Herbert A. **A Chinese-English dictionary.** 2nd ed., 3 v. (also in 1 or 2),

London and Shanghai, 1912. Despite defects, the largest and best Chinese-English dictionary.

O196. Couvreur, Séraphin. **Dictionnaire classique.** See *G82*. The standard Chinese-French dictionary, in some ways better than Giles.

O197. Huang, Shih-fu, and T'ieh Chiang, eds. **A comprehensive English-Chinese dictionary.** 2 v. Shanghai, 1928. Abr. ed., 1 v., 1937.

O198. Chao, Yuen Ren [Yüan-jên], and Lien-sheng Yang. **Concise dictionary of spoken Chinese.** Cambridge, Mass., 1947. This work, by one of China's great philologists, uses his own system of romanization with the Wade-Giles system in parentheses.

O199. Kuo-yü tz'u-tien. [Dictionary of the national language.] Comp. by the Chung-kuo tz'u-tien pien tsuan-ch'u. 8 v. Shanghai, 1943. A dictionary of words and phrases arranged according to the Chinese phonetic script, with special attention to proper pronunciation.

O200. Tz'u hai. [Sea of phrases.] Comp. by Shu Hsin-ch'eng and others. 2 v. Shanghai, 1937. 1 v. ed., 1948.

O201. Tz'u yüan. [Dictionary of phrases.] Comp. by Lu Erh-k'uei and others. 2 v. Shanghai, 1915. Rev. ed., 1 v., Taipei, 1957. This and the above are basic standard encyclopedic dictionaries of words and phrases, with numerous quotations from sources.

O202. K'ang-hsi tzu-tien. [K'ang-hsi dictionary.] Comp. by Chang Yü-shu and others. Palace ed., 40 ts'e, 1716. Photolithographic reprint, Shanghai, 1936. The standard Ch'ing dynasty dictionary of words.

O203. Chung-hua ta-tz'u-tien. [Grand dictionary of Chinese words.] Comp. by Hsu Yüan-kao and others. Shanghai, 1915. 4th ed., 4 v., 1935.

O204. P'ei-wen yün-fu. [Encyclopedic dictionary.] Comp. by Chang Yü-shu and others. 115 ts'e, 1711. Supplement, 1720. Photolithographic reprint, 7 v., Shanghai, 1937. The master Chinese dictionary of words, phrases, quotations, and allusions.

O205. Nash, Vernon. **Trindex: an index to three dictionaries.** Peiping, 1936. Index of *O195, 202,* and *204.*

O206. Hsüeh-hsi tz'u-tien. [Dictionary of new terms.] Comp. by the Peking Normal University and the Chung-kuo ta-tz'u-tien pien tsuan-ch'u. Peiping, 1951. Important for its new words and terms.

O207. Dai kanwa jiten. [Grand Chinese-Japanese dictionary.] Comp. by Morohashi Tetsuji. 13 v. Tokyo, 1955–59. A most comprehensive dictionary of Chinese characters, terms, and phrases with explanations in Japanese. Besides direct quotation from Chinese sources, pronunciation in Japanese *kana* or in Wade-Giles romanization is given.

For other linguistic works see topical sub-sections below and material relating to China in Section G.

PRINTED COLLECTIONS OF SOURCES

For collections relating to particular periods see the subsections on special periods and on international relations.

O208. Wieger, Léon. **Textes historiques: histoire politique de la Chine depuis l'origine jusqu'en 1929.** 3rd ed., 2 v., Hsien-hsien, 1929. Not an outstanding selection of sources in translation, but the only one covering the whole of Chinese history. Text and translation in parallel columns.

O209. Ch'ü, Hsüan-ying. **Chung-kuo she-hui shih-liao ts'ung ch'ao.** [A general repertory of historical materials on Chinese society.] Shanghai, 1937. Social history of various epochs; many items of widely diverse interests with sources.

O210. Yang, Shih-ch'i. **Li-tai ming-ch'en tsou-i.** [Memorials of the officials of successive generations.] Ed. of 1635, 64 ts'e. This work, completed in 1416, covers the period from antiquity to 1367. It was extended to the end of the Ming dynasty (1644) in *Ch'in-ting Ming-ch'en tsou-i* [Imperially published memorials of Ming officials], completed in 1781.

O211. **Erh-shih-ssu shih.** [Twenty-four dynastic histories.] T'ung-wen ed. (lithographic reprint of the Palace ed. of 1739 with valuable commentaries), 711 ts'e, 1884; Po-na ed. (photolithographic reprint of the finest and earliest eds. available), 820 ts'e, Shanghai, 1930–37; 932 ts'e, Taipei, 1956. In 1934–37 the K'ai-ming Book Co. of Shanghai published a reduced format ed. in 9 v. of text plus 6 v. of supplementary materials and commentaries which included a 25th history, the *Hsin Yüan shih* [New Yüan history]. To these must be added the *Ch'ing shih kao* [Draft history of the Ch'ing] (131 ts'e, Peking, 1927). These 26 standard or dynastic histories together with the dates they cover, the chief author or supervising editor, dates they were compiled, and the number of chüan (chapters) are as follows: *Shih chi* (Ant.–99 B.C.), Ssu-ma Ch'ien (104–87 B.C.), 130; *Han shu* (209 B.C.–25 A.D.), Pan Ku (58–76 A.D.), 120; *Hou-Han shu* (25–222), Fan Yeh (by 445), 120; *San-kuo chih* (220–80), Ch'en Shou (285–97), 65; *Chin shu* (265–419), Fang Hsüan-ling (644), 130; *Sung-shu* (420–79), Shen Yüeh (492–93), 100; *Nan-chi shu* (479–502), Hsiao Tzu-hsien (by 537), 59; *Liang shu* (502–56), Yao Ssu-lien (628–35), 56; *Ch'en-shu* (556–80), Yao Ssu-lien (622–29), 36; *Nan shih* (420–589), Li Yen-shou (630–50), 80; *Wei shu* (386–535), Wei Shou (551–54), 130; *Pei-ch'i shu* (550–77), Li Po-yao (627–36), 50; *Chou shu* (557–81), Ling-hu Te-fen (629), 50; *Pei shih* (386–581), Li Yen-shou

(630–50), 100; *Sui shu* (581–617), Wei Cheng (629–36), 85; *Chiu T'ang shu* (618–906), Liu Hsü (941–45), 200; *Hsin-T'ang shu* (618–906), Ou-yang Hsiu (1045–60), 225; *Wu-tai shih* (907–60), Hsüeh Chücheng (973–74), 150; *Hsin Wu-tai shih* (907–60), Ou-yang Hsiu (1044–60), 74; *Sung shih* (960–1279), T'o-t'o (1341–45), 496; *Liao shih* (916–1125), T'o-t'o and Öu-yäng (1343–45), 116; *Chin shih* (1115–1234), T'o-t'o and Öu-yäng (1343–45), 135; *Yüan shih* (1206–1367), Sung Lien (1369–70), 210; *Hsin-Yüan shih* (1206–1367), K'o Shao-min (1890–1920), 460; *Ming shih* (1368–1644), Chang T'ing-yü (1678–1739), 332; *Ch'ing shih kao* (1616–1911), K'o Shao-min (1914–27), 131.

O212. Ssu-ma, Kuang. **Tzu-chih t'ung-chien.** [Comprehensive mirror for aid in government.] Hu K'o-chia ed., 100 ts'e, 1814; 1887 ed., 120 ts'e. This work by an 11th century author is the greatest of the annalistic histories. It covers 403 B.C. to 959 A.D., and was supplemented, annotated, and amended by many works. The two most important supplements are Pi Yüan, *Hsü tzu-chih t'ung-chien* (1801 ed., 80 ts'e), covering the period 960–1367; and Hsia Hsieh, *Ming t'ung-chien,* for 1368–1644.

O213. Chu, Hsi, and Chao Shih-yüan. **Tzu-chih t'ung-chien kang-mu.** [Abridged view of the comprehensive mirror for aid in government.] First pub. 1172. Most famous and influential of the abridgements of Ssu-ma Kuang's work. It was also amended, supplemented, and corrected in many works, the most valuable being the imperial edition of 1746, *Yu-p'i tzu-chih t'ung-chien kang-mu,* which includes a supplement by Nan Hsien covering the period before 403, one by Shang Lu on the 960–1367 era, and one by Chang T'ing-yü concerning 1368–1644.

O214. Chiu-ch'ao chi-shih pen-mo. [Complete topical narratives of the nine periods.] 55 ts'e. Shanghai, 1902. Consists of nine works by eight authors, dealing with various periods of Chinese history under related topics. Oldest is the *T'ung-chien chi-shih pen-mo* by Yüan Shu (1131–1205), which rearranged the materials of *O212* covering 403 B.C.–959 A.D. Later works are on the earlier era of the *Tso chuan* (722–481 B.C.) and the later Sung, Yüan, and Ming periods, while five other works deal with the Hsi-hsia, Liao, Chin, and San-fan eras. All are essentially rearrangements of materials from the dynastic histories.

O215. Chiu t'ung. [The nine compendia on history and institutions.] Ch'ien-lung palace ed., 898 ts'e, 1747. *Chiu-t'ung ch'uan-shu* ed. by the Chekiang Shu-chü, 999 ts'e, 1882–96; 20 v., Shanghai, 1936. This collection consists of three original works and various supplements as follows: (1) *T'ung tien* by Tu Yü (735–812) covers the period down to 755 and is divided into major sections on economics, examinations, officials, rites, music, military, legal, political geography, and border affairs. The *Hsü t'ung-tien* covers the period 756–1644 and the *Huang-ch'ao t'ung-tien* the period 1644–1785. (2) The *T'ung chih* by Cheng Ch'iao (1104–62) is on the period to 907, with major headings of annals, chronological tables, biographies, and 20 monographs on subjects like those in the *T'ung tien* and other such as family and clan, philology, phonetics, political subdivisions, flora and insects, archaeology, and books. These monographs are the most valuable. The *Hsü t'ung-chih* covers the period 908–1644 and the *Huang-ch'ao t'ung-chih* the period 1644–1785. (3) The *Wen-hsien t'ung-k'ao* by Ma Tuan-lin (*ca* 1280) deals with the period to 1224 under 24 major topics, 19 being expansions of those in the *T'ung tien,* and the others on bibliography, imperial genealogies, feudal system, astronomy, and unusual phenomena added by Ma. The *Hsü* is on the period 1225–1644 and the *Huang-ch'ao* on 1644–1785. The 1936 (Commercial Press) edition (*Shih T'ung*) includes *Huang-chao hsü wen-hsien t'ung-k'ao* covering the period 1786–1911, and has an index of the whole collection.

O216. Yen, K'o-chün. **Ch'üan shang-ku san-tai Ch'in Han San-kuo Liu-ch'ao wen.** [A complete repertory of literature dating from the three epochs of high antiquity, the Ch'in, Han, Three Kingdoms and Six Dynasties.] 66 ts'e. Shanghai, 1930.

O217. Ssu-pu ts'ung-k'an. [A collectanea of Chinese literature.] Series 1–3, 3,100 ts'e, Shanghai, 1920–37. Annotated catalog, 1922. This work and the two following are the largest of the *ts'ung-shu,* a type of Chinese publication constituting a whole library of important works.

O218. Ssu-pu pei-yao. [A collectanea of Chinese literature.] 2,500 ts'e, Shanghai, 1927–37. Edition in western binding, 100 v., 1937. Annotated catalog, 1936.

O219. Ts'ung-shu chi-ch'eng. [A collection of 100 collectanea.] 4,100 ts'e. Shanghai, 1935–37.

HISTORIOGRAPHY

O220. Gardner, Charles S. **Chinese traditional historiography.** Cambridge, Mass., 1938.

O221. Han, Yu-shan. **Elements of Chinese historiography.** Hollywood, Calif., 1955.

O222. Chin, Yü-fu. **Chung-kuo-shih hsüeh-shih.** [A history of Chinese historiography.] 2nd ed., Shanghai, 1946. Best general history of the whole of Chinese historiography. Surveys works of the various periods and generally discusses the official histories, private histories, sources, and historical methods of each.

O223. Naitō, Torajirō. **Shina shigaku shi.** [History of Chinese historiography.] Tokyo, 1949. 2nd ed., 1950. Comprehensive and detailed survey, often quite critical.

O224. Ku, Chieh-kang. **The autobiography of a Chinese historian: being the preface to a symposium on ancient Chinese history.** Tr. by Arthur W. Hummel. Leiden, 1931. Ku's preface is an outstanding discussion of Chinese historical writing, past and present, relating to early Chinese history.

O225. ——. **Tang-tai chung-kuo shih-hsüeh.** [Chinese historiography of the recent past.] Nanking, 1947. One of the best accounts of Chinese historiography during the past century, but biased in favor of followers of the author.

O226. Teng, S. Y. "Chinese historiography in the last fifty years." **Far eastern quarterly,** 8 (Feb. 1949): 131–56. Discusses and uses Ku's work.

O227. Karlgren, Bernhard. "The authenticity of ancient Chinese texts." **Bulletin of The Museum of Far Eastern Antiquities,** 1 (1929): 165–83. Critical discussion of criteria traditionally used by Chinese to determine the authenticity of ancient texts.

O228. Watson, Burton D. **Ssu-ma Ch'ien, grand historian of China.** Ann Arbor, 1956; N.Y., 1958.

O229. Kierman, Frank A. **Ssu-ma Ch'ien's historiographical attitude as reflected in four late warring states biographies.** Ann Arbor, 1953.

O230. Chavannes, Edouard, tr. **Les mémoires historiques de Se-ma Ts'ien.** V. 1. Paris, 1895. Chavannes' introduction is of interest.

O231. Lo, Tchen-ying (Lo Chen-ying). **Une famille d'historiens et son oeuvre (les formes et les méthodes historiques en Chine).** Paris, 1931. Deals with Pan Piao, Pan Ku, and Pan Chao and the *Han shu.*

O232. Sargent, Clyde B. "Subsidized history: Pan Ku and the historical records of the former Han dynasty." **Far eastern quarterly,** 3 (Feb. 1944): 119–43.

O233. Dubs, Homer H. "The reliability of Chinese histories." **Far eastern quar.,** 6 (Nov. 1946): 23–43. A reply to the above rather critical evaluation.

O234. Liu, Chih-chi, and P'u Chi-lung. **Shih-t'ung t'ung-shih.** [Criticism of traditional history and historiography.] 2 ts'e. Shanghai, 1926. Expressed first by a critical scholar of the T'ang period, Liu Chih-chi (661–721), then amended by P'u Chi-lung (1679–1761).

O235. Wang, Gung-wu. "The *Chiu Wu-tai shih* and history-writing during the Five Dynasties." **Asia major,** V. 6 (1957), pt. 1.

O236. Franke, Otto. **Das Tse Tschi t'ung-kien und das T'ung kien kang mu, ihr Wesen, ihr verhältnis Zueinander und ihr Quellenwart.** Berlin, 1930.

O237. Wang, Ming-sheng. **Shih-ch'i-shih shang-ch'üeh.** [A critical study of the seventeen dynastic histories.] 1787. 24 ts'e, Canton, 1894. Important comments on these histories.

O238. Chao, I. **Nien-erh shih cha-chi.** [Critical notes on the twenty-two dynastic histories.] 16 ts'e. Canton, 1896.

O239. Ch'ien, Ta-hsin. **Nien-erh shih k'ao-i.** [Discrepancies in the twenty-two dynastic histories.] Canton, 1898. This and *O238* are critical studies on dynastic histories written in the late 18th century.

O240. Hsü, Hao. **Nien-wu shih lung-kang.** [Essentials of the twenty-five dynastic histories.] Shanghai, 1947. Discusses the form of Chinese histories, analyzes the 25 histories, and discusses objectives and schools of literature.

O241. Chang, Hsüeh-ch'eng. **Chang-shih i-shu.** [Complete works of Chang.] 50 chüan. 1922. Contains the historiographical works of the great 18th century historical thinker. The two most important of these are *Wen-shih t'ung-i* [Fundamental principles of cultural history], partly published in 1796 and reprinted in Shanghai, 1936; and *Chiao-ch'ou t'ung-i* [Fundamental principles of historical criticism], first published in 1833.

O242. Wright, Arthur F., ed. **Studies in Chinese thought** (Chicago, 1953), pp. 126–34. Contains account of Chang's thought.

O243. Nivison, David. **The literary and historical thought of Chang Hsüeh-ch'eng, 1738–1801: a study of his life and writing, with translations of six essays from the Wen-shih t'ung-i.** Cambridge, Mass., 1953. Detailed study.

O244. Chu, Shih-chia. **Chang Hsüeh-ch'eng, his contributions to Chinese local history.** Ann Arbor, 1950.

O245. Liang, Ch'i-ch'ao. **Chung-kuo li-shih yen-chiu-fa.** [Methods of research in Chinese history.] 2 v. Shanghai, 1933. Reprint, 1935. Has had great influence on modern (non-Communist) historical scholarship in China.

See also *O292, 298,* and *316.*

SHORTER GENERAL HISTORIES

O246. Goodrich, L. Carrington. **A short history of the Chinese people.** N.Y., 1943. Rev. ed., 1951. Best short history of China in terms of reliability, precision of statement, illustration, and bibliographic guidance.

O247. Callis, Helmut G. **China, Confucian and Communist.** N.Y., 1959. Balanced between a survey of traditional institutions, history prior to 1949, and Communist China. Has more material on the Communist regime than earlier general histories.

O248. Nourse, Mary A. **The four hundred million: a short history of the Chinese.** N.Y., 1935. 3rd ed., 1943.

O249. Latourette, Kenneth S. **The develop-**

ment of China. Boston, 1917. 6th ed., 1946.

O250. Wenley, Archibald G., and John A. Pope. **China.** Washington, 1944.

O251. Grousset, René. **Histoire de la Chine.** Paris, 1942. Tr., *The rise and splendour of the Chinese empire,* London, 1952; Berkeley, 1953. A rather episodic work which conveys the spirit of Chinese historical development.

O252. Eberhard, Wolfram. **Chinas Geschichte.** Bern, 1948. English tr., Berkeley and London, 1950. Marred by many careless errors and too sweeping generalizations, but full of suggestive ideas and interpretations.

O253. Miao, Feng-lin. **Chung-kuo t'ung-shih yao-lüeh.** [Essentials of a general history of China.] Chungking, 1944. An earlier version was published at Nanking, 1932.

O254. Fan, Wen-lan, and others. **Chung-kuo t'ung-shih chien-pien.** [A general history of China simplified.] Yenan, 1941. Rev. ed., Peiping, 1950, 1953. A Communist version.

O255. Fitzgerald, Charles P. **China: a short cultural history.** London, 1938. 4th ed., 1954. One of the better short histories, enlivened by excellent illustrations and helpful sketch maps.

O256. Wilhelm, Richard. **Geschichte der chinesischen Kultur.** Munich, 1928. Tr., *A short history of Chinese civilization,* London and N.Y., 1929. This and the following work are good general histories, but the pre-Chou parts of Wilhelm are completely antiquated.

O257. Ts'ui, Chi. **A short history of Chinese civilization.** London, 1942; N.Y., 1943. Contains a useful bibliography.

O258. Ch'ien, Mu. **Chung-kuo wen-hua-shih tao-lun.** [Introduction to the cultural history of China.] Shanghai, 1948.

O259. Kiang [Chiang], Kang-hu. **Chinese civilization: an introduction to Sinology.** Shanghai, 1935. An encyclopedic type of work which deals with Chinese history and geography, government and social institutions, religion and philosophy, literature and art, games, and science. Contains an immense amount of information, but requires some checking.

O260. Williams, Edward T. **China yesterday and to-day.** N.Y., 1923. 5th ed., 1932.

O261. Lin, Yu-t'ang. **My country and my people.** N.Y., 1935. Rev. ed., 1939. Excellent general analysis of Chinese civilization.

O262. MacNair, Harley F., and others. **China.** Berkeley, 1946. History, institutions, foreign relations, and culture of China.

O263. Coltman, Robert. **The Chinese, their present and future: medical, political, and social.** Philadelphia and London, 1891. Dr. Coltman describes vividly his introduction to itinerant medical practice in Shantung province, and the social as well as medical problems involved.

O264. Duyvendak, Jan J. L. **Wegen en gestalten der chineesche geschiedenis.** The Hague, 1935. 2nd ed., Amsterdam, 1948.

See also subsection on China in Section G.

LONGER GENERAL HISTORIES

O265. Latourette, Kenneth S. **The Chinese, their history and culture.** 2 v. N.Y., 1934. 3rd rev. ed., 2 v. in 1, 1946. The standard history of China in English. Especially valuable bibliographies.

O266. Franke, Otto. **Geschichte des chinesischen Reiches: eine Darstellung seiner Entstehung, seines Wesens und seiner Entwicklung bis zur neuesten Zeit.** 5 v. Berlin, 1930–52. Most valuable of the large histories in a western language despite fact that much of v. 1 is now completely out of date. Ends with the Yüan dynasty about 1280.

O267. Cordier, Henri. **Histoire générale de la Chine et de ses relations avec les pays étrangers depuis les temps les plus anciens jusqu'à la chute de la dynastie Mandchoue.** 4 v. Paris, 1920–21. Strongly biased to suggest French leadership in relations with China. Depends heavily on *O269.*

O268. Williams, Samuel W. **The middle kingdom.** See *O561.*

O269. Mailla, Joseph A. M. M. de, tr. **Histoire générale de la Chine.** 13 v. Paris, 1777–85. A free and not always accurate translation of Chu Hsi, *T'ung-chien kang-mu* and its supplements. Until recent times most western histories of China depended heavily upon it. Still the most detailed history of China in a western language.

O270. Boulger, Demetrius C. **History of China.** Rev. ed., 2 v., London, 1898. Longest general history in English dependent on *O269.*

O271. Lü, Ssu-mien. **Chung-kuo t'ung-shih.** [General history of China.] 2 v. Shanghai, 1940–47. Covers period from ancient times to 1926.

O272. Chou, Ku-ch'eng. **Chung-kuo t'ung-shih.** [General history of China.] 2 v. Shanghai, 1939. Rev. ed., 1955–56.

O273. Ch'ien, Mu. **Kuo-shih ta-kang.** [Main features of the nation's history.] 2 v. Chungking, 1944.

O274. Miao, Feng-lin. **Chung-kuo t'ung-shih.** [General history of China.] 3 v. Shanghai, 1945–48. From ancient times to the Ch'ing dynasty.

O275. Wang, T'ung-ling. **Chung-kuo shih.** [The history of China.] 4 v. Peiping, 1926–28. Histories of the various dynasties illustrated with charts and tables.

O276. Liu, I-cheng. **Chung-kuo wen-hua shih.** [A cultural history of China.] 2 v. Nanking, 1932–35. Huge body of rich material gathered by an erudite scholar of rather conservative views who has been continuously influential in central China.

O277. Chung-kuo wen-hua shih ts'ung-shu.

[Collected works on Chinese cultural history.] Series 1–2. Shanghai, 1936–38. Contains forty different works on almost all aspects of Chinese culture.

HISTORIES OF SPECIAL PERIODS

Ch'in and Han Dynasties
(221 B.C.–220 A.D.)

O278. Bodde, Derk. **China's first unifier: a study of the Ch'in dynasty as seen in the life of Li Ssu (280?–208 B.C.).** Leiden, 1938. A careful study.

O279. ——, tr. **Statesman, patriot, and general in ancient China: three Shih chi biographies of the Ch'in dynasty (255–206 B.C.).** New Haven, 1940.

O280. Chavannes, Edouard. "Les inscriptions des Ts'in." **Journal asiatique,** 9th ser., 1 (1893), 473–521.

O281. Lü, Ssu-mien. **Ch'in Han shih.** [History of the Ch'in and Han dynasties.] 2 v. Shanghai, 1947.

O282. Lao, Kan. **Ch'in Han shih.** [History of the Ch'in and Han dynasties.] 2 v. Chengtu, 1935. 1 v., Shanghai, 1946.

O283. ——. "Han-tai ping-chih chi Han-chien chung ti ping-chih." [The military system of the Han dynasty as recorded on wooden clips.] **Academia sinica: bulletin of the Institute of History and Philosophy,** 10 (1948): 23–55.

O284. Hsü, T'ien-lin. **Hsi-Han hui-yao.** [Collected essentials of the western Han dynasty.] Completed 1211. Edition in 10 ts'e, Kiangsu, 1884. Documentary materials from the **Han shu** arranged under 15 topics such as imperial genealogies, rites, music, schools, astronomy, officials, examinations, economics, military affairs, laws, foreign relations, etc.

O285. ——. **Tung-Han hui-yao.** [Collected essentials of the eastern Han dynasty.] 8 ts'e. Kiangsu, 1894. Includes material not in the Hou-Han shu.

O286. Dubs, Homer H., tr. **The History of the former Han dynasty by Pan Ku.** 3 v. Baltimore, 1938–55. Translation with extensive notes of the "Imperial annals" and Wang Mang biography sections of the **Han shu.** An indispensable work.

O287. Sargent, Clyde B., tr. and ed. **Wang Mang: a translation of the official account of his rise to power as given in the History of the former Han dynasty.** Shanghai, 1949.

O288. Dubs, Homer H. "Wang Mang and his economic reforms." **T'oung pao,** 35 (1940): 219–65. A critical view of Wang Mang.

O289. Hu, Shih. "Wang Mang, the socialist emperor of nineteen centuries ago." **Journal of the North China Branch of the Royal Asiatic Society,** 59 (1928): 218–30.

O290. Stange, Hans O. H. **Leben, Persön-**lichkeit und Werk Wang Mang's. Krahl, 1934.

O291. ——. **Die Monographie über Wang Mang.** Leipzig, 1939. A translation of the biography of Wang Mang from chüan 99 of the **Han shu.**

O292. Bielenstein, Hans. "The restoration of the Han dynasty." **Bulletin of the Museum of Far Eastern Antiquities,** 26 (1954): 5–165. Outstanding study with an observation on the historiography of the later Han history.

O293. Levy, Howard S. "Yellow Turban religion and rebellion at the end of Han." **Journal of the American Oriental Society,** 76 (Dec. 1956): 214–27. Study of a Taoist religious movement and rebellion that contributed to the fall of the later Han dynasty.

O294. Balázs, Etienne. "La crise sociale et la philosophie politique à la fin des Han." **T'oung pao,** 39 (1949): 83–131. Brilliant analysis of the end of the later Han dynasty.

O295. Wang, Yü-ch'üan. "An outline of the central government of the former Han dynasty." **Harvard journal of Asiatic studies,** 12 (June 1949): 134–87.

O296. Wilbur, C. Martin. **Slavery in China during the former Han dynasty, 206 B.C.– A.D. 25.** Chicago, 1943.

O297. Hulsewé, Anthony F. P. **Remnants of Han law.** Leiden, 1955. Introductory studies with annotated translations of chapters 22–23 of Pan Ku's **Han shu.**

O298. Swann, Nancy L., tr. **Food and money in ancient China.** Princeton, 1950. Annotated translation of chüan 24 of the **Han shu** and related texts dealing with economic matters.

O299. Blue, Rhea C. "The argumentation of the **Shih-huo chih** chapters of the Han, Wei and Sui dynastic histories." **Harvard journal of Asiatic studies,** 11 (1948), 1–118. Important study of economic monographs of the dynastic histories mentioned.

O300. Gale, Esson M., tr. **Discourses on salt and iron . . . a debate on state control of commerce and industry in ancient China translated from the Chinese of Huan K'uan.** Leiden, 1931. Annotated translation with introduction of the first 19 chapters of the **Yen-t'ieh lun.** Chs. 20–28 are translated by Gale in **Journal of the North China Branch of the Royal Asiatic Society,** 65 (1934): 73–110.

O301. Chang, Chün-ming. "The genesis and meaning of Huan K'uan's 'Discourses on salt and iron.'" **Chinese social and political science review,** Apr. 1934.

O302. Hirth, Friedrich. "The story of Chang K'ien, China's pioneer in western Asia." **Journal of the American Oriental Society,** 37 (1917): 89–152. Translation of chüan 123 of **Shih chi.** For other translations from the **Shih chi** and **Han shu** regarding the Huns and central Asia see the two following.

O303. Groot, Jan J. M. de. **Die Hunnen der Vorchristlichen Zeit.** Berlin, 1921.

O304. ——. **Die Westlande Chinas in der Vorchristlichen Zeit.** Berlin, 1926.

O305. Chavannes, Edouard. "Trois généraux chinois de la dynastie des Han Orientaux: Pan Tch'ao, son fils Pan Yong, Leang K'in." **T'oung pao,** 2nd ser., 7 (1906): 210–69.

O306. ——. "Les pays d'Occident d'après le Heou Han chou." **T'oung pao,** 2nd ser., 8 (1907): 149–234.

O307. ——. **Les documents chinois découverts par Aurel Stein dans les sables du Turkestan oriental.** Oxford, 1913.

O308. ——. **Documents sur les Tou-kiue (Turcs) occidentaux.** Paris, 1903. Valuable monograph on the conflict between China and the western Turks. Additional notes and errata appear in *T'oung pao,* 5 (1904): 1–110.

O309. Aurousseau, Léonard. "La première conquête chinoise des pays annamites." **Bulletin de l'École Française d'Extrême-Orient,** 23 (1923): 137–264.

O310. Maspero, Henri. "L'expédition de Ma Yüan." **Bulletin de l'École Française d'Extrême-Orient,** 18 (1918): 11–28.

O311. ——. "La vie privée en Chine à l'époque des Han." **Revue des arts asiatiques,** 7 (1931): 185–201.

O312. Eberhard, Alide, and Wolfram Eberhard. **Die mode der Han- und Chin-Zeit.** Antwerp, 1946. Deals with textiles and clothes.

O313. Franke, Otto. "Das Problem des *Tsch'un-ts'iu* und Tung Tschung-schu's *Tsch'un-ts'iu fan lu.*" **Mitteilungen des Seminars für orientalische Sprachen,** 21 (1918), pt. 1, pp. 1–80. Account of Tung Chung-shu and his Confucianism.

O314. Tjan Tjoe Som, tr. **Po Hu T'ung . . . the comprehensive discussions in the White Tiger Hall.** 2 v. Leiden, 1949–52.

O315. Forke, Alfred, tr. and ed. **Lun-Hëng.** 2 v. London and Berlin, 1907–11. [1, *Philosophical essays of Wang Ch'ung;* 2, *Miscellaneous essays of Wang Ch'ung.*]

O316. Swann, Nancy L. **Pan Chao, foremost woman scholar of China, first century A.D.** N.Y., 1932. This monograph should be of interest to all students of the Han dynasty.

O317. Han, Ying. **Han shih wai chuan. Han Ying's illustrations of the didactic application of the "classic of songs."** Tr. by James R. Hightower. Cambridge, Mass., 1952. Collection of 306 short anecdotes current during the Han period. See Hightower's article on the subject in *Harvard journal of Asiatic studies,* 11 (Dec. 1948): 241–310.

O318. Rudolph, Richard C., and Wen Yu. **Han tomb art of west China.** Berkeley, 1951.

O319. Chavannes, Edouard. **La sculpture sur pierre en Chine au temps des deux dynasties Han.** Leroux, 1893.

O320. Ségalen, Victor. **L'art funéraire à l'époque des Han.** Paris, 1935.

O321. Ségalen, Victor, and others. **Mission archéologique en Chine.** 3 v. Paris, 1923–35.

O322. Fairbank, Wilma. "The offering shrines of Wu Liang Tz'u." **Harvard journal of Asiatic studies,** 6 (Mar. 1941): 1–36.

O323. Fairbank, Wilma. "A structural key to Han mural art." **Harvard journal of Asiatic studies,** 7 (Apr. 1942): 52–88.

The Three Kingdoms and Six Dynasties (221–581)

O324. Lü, Ssu-mien. **Liang-Chin Nan-pei-chao shih.** [History of the two Chin and the northern and southern dynasties.] 2 v. Shanghai, 1948.

O325. Fang, Achilles, tr. **The Chronicle of the Three Kingdoms (220–265), chapters 69–78 from the Tzu chih t'ung chien . . . of Ssu-ma Kuang . . . (1019–1068).** V. 1. Cambridge, Mass., 1952.

O326. Hsü, Te-lin. **San-kuo shih chiang-hua.** [Lectures on the history of the Three Kingdoms.] Shanghai, 1955.

O327. Yang, Ch'en. **San-kuo hui-yao.** [Selected documents of the Three Kingdoms period.] 4 v. Kiangsu, 1936.

O328. Ts'ui, Hung. **Shih-Liu-kuo ch'un-ch'iu.** [Spring and autumn of the Sixteen Kingdoms.] 24 v. 1609. Chung Hua ed., 15 v., 1934.

O329. Wu, Shih-ch'ien, and Liu Ch'eng-kan. **Chin-shu chüeh-chu.** [Collation and commentary of Chin history.] 60 v. 1928.

O330. Eberhard, Wolfram. **Conquerors and rulers: social forces in medieval China.** Leiden, 1952. Much the same as his *Das Toba-Reich Nordchinas: eine soziologische Untersuchung* (Leiden, 1949). A study of the various T'o-pa or Wei dynasties of the Six Dynasties period.

O331. Schreiber, Gerhard. "The history of the former Yen dynasty." **Monumenta serica,** 14 (1949–55): 374–480, 15 (1956): 1–141.

O332. Chin shu. **Biography of Ku K'ai-chih.** Tr. by Chen Shih-hsiang. Berkeley, 1953.

O333. Carroll, Thomas D., tr. **Account of the T'u-yü-hun.** Berkeley, 1953. From the *Chin shu.*

O334. Rogers, Michael C., tr. **The rise of the former Ch'in state and its spread under Fu Chien through 370 A.D., based on Chin shu 113.** Berkeley, 1953.

O335. Chou shu. **Biography of Su Ch'o.** Tr. by Chauncey S. Goodrich. Berkeley, 1953.

O336. Chavannes, Edouard. "Les pays

d'Occident d'après le Wei 1io." **T'oung pao,** 2nd ser., 6 (1905): 519–71.

O337. Boodberg, Peter A. "Marginalia to the histories of the northern dynasties." **Harvard journal of Asiatic studies,** 3 (1938): 223–53, 4 (1939): 230–83.

O338. Wang, I-t'ung. "Slaves and other comparable social groups during the northern dynasties (386–618)." **Harvard journal of Asiatic studies,** 16 (Dec. 1953): 293–364.

O339. Yang, Lien-sheng. "Notes on the economic history of the Chin dynasty." **Harvard jour. of Asiatic studies,** 9 (June 1946): 107–85.

O340. Shryock, John K., tr. **The study of human abilities: the Jen wu chih of Liu Shao.** New Haven, 1937. Translation of a 3rd century treatise on psychology with an introduction on the period of the Three Kingdoms.

O341. Kramers, Robert P., tr. **Kung tzu chia yü** [The school sayings of Confucius.] Leiden, 1949.

O342. Feifel, E. "Po-p'u tzu." **Monumenta serica,** 6 (1941): 113–211, 9 (1944): 1–33, 11 (1946): 1–32. Deals with Taoism.

O343. Maspero, Henri. "Les procédés de 'Nourrir le principe vital' dans la religion taoïste ancienne." **Journal asiatique,** 229 (Apr.-June 1937): 177–252, 229 (July-Sep. 1937): 353–430.

O344. Ware, James R. "The *Wei-shu* and *Sui shu* on Taoism." **Journal of the American Oriental Society,** 53 (Sep. 1933): 215–50, 54 (Sep. 1934): 290–94.

O345. ——. "Notes on the history of the *Wei shu.*" **Jour. Am. Oriental Soc.,** 52 (1932): 33–45.

O346. ——. "Wei Shou on Buddhism." **T'oung pao,** 30 (1933): 100–81.

O347. Hu, Shih. "The development of Zen Buddhism in China." **Chinese social and political science review,** 15 (Jan. 1932): 475–505.

O348. Wright, Arthur F. "Fo-t'u Teng, a biography." **Harvard journal of Asiatic studies,** 11 (Dec. 1948): 321–71. Translation of the biography of a Buddhist monk.

O349. Liebenthal, Walter. "Chinese Buddhism during the 4th and 5th centuries." **Monumenta nipponica,** 11 (Apr. 1955): 44–83. Analysis of the reactions of various social classes to Buddhism.

O350. Acker, William R., tr. **T'ao the hermit: sixty poems by T'ao Ch'ien.** London, 1952. Study of the popular nature poet of the late 4th and early 5th centuries.

O351. Wong, Wen-po. **T'ao Yüan-ming.** Paris, 1934. On the greatest poet of the period.

O352. Liu, Hsieh. **The literary mind and the carving of dragons.** Tr. by Vincent Yu-chung Shih. N.Y., 1959. Translation of a classic work of Chinese literary criticism written about 500 A.D.

O353. Zach, Erwin von, tr. **Übersetzungen aus dem Wen-hsüan.** Batavia, 1937. Translation from a famous collection of literature compiled by Hsiao T'ung (*ca.* 501–31).

O354. Gulik, Robert H. van. **Hsi K'ang and his poetical essay on the lute.** Tokyo, 1941.

Sui and T'ang Periods (589–907)

O355. Ch'en, Yin-k'o. **T'ang-tai cheng-chih-shih shu-lun kao.** [Draft political history of the T'ang dynasty.] Chungking, 1943; Shanghai, 1947.

O356. Ch'en, Yin-k'o. **Sui T'ang chih-tu yüan yüan lüeh-lun kao.** [Draft history of Sui and T'ang institutions.] Chungking, 1945; Peiping, 1954.

O357. Wright, Arthur F. "The formation of Sui ideology, 581–604." **Chinese thought and institutions,** ed. by John K. Fairbank (Chicago, 1957), pp. 71–104.

O358. Gaubil, Antoine. "Abrégé de l'histoire chinoise de la grande dynastie T'ang." **Mémoires concernant . . . des Chinois** (*O560*), v. 14.

O359. Li, Chi-fu. **Yüan-ho chün-hsien chih.** [Topographical record of the Yüan-ho period.] Canton, 1899. [Wu-ying-tien ch'u-chen-pan ch'üan Shu.] A geography of the T'ang dynasty completed during Li's lifetime (758–814).

O360. Wang, P'u. **T'ang hui-yao.** [Selected documents of the T'ang.] 24 ts'e. Kiangsu, 1884. Classified account of state affairs by a Sung author; compiled in 961.

O361. Wen, Ta-ya. **Ta-T'ang ch'uang-yeh ch'i-chü-chu.** [Court journal of the founder of the Great T'ang.] Completed in 940. 3 ts'e. Shanghai, 1922. [Ching-tai pi-shu.] See Woodbridge Bingham, "Wen Ta-ya, the first recorder of T'ang history," *Jour. Am. Oriental Soc.,* 57 (Dec. 1937): 368–74.

O362. Bingham, Woodbridge. **The founding of the T'ang dynasty: the fall of Sui and rise of T'ang.** Baltimore, 1941.

O363. Fitzgerald, Charles P. **Son of Heaven: a biography of Li Shih-min, founder of the T'ang dynasty.** Cambridge, Eng., 1933.

O364. ——. **The Empress Wu.** Melbourne, 1955.

O365. Solomon, Bernard S., tr. and ed. **The veritable record of the T'ang emperor Shun-tsung (February 28, 805–August 31, 805): Han Yü's Shun-tsung shih-lu.** Cambridge, Mass., 1955.

O366. Pulleyblank, Edwin G. **The background of the rebellion of An Lu-shan.** London, 1955. Exhaustive study of the 8th century conditions that helped precipitate this rebellion which marked the beginning of the T'ang dynasty's decline.

O367. Levy, Howard S., tr. and ed. **Biography of Huang Ch'ao.** Berkeley, 1955. Account of a 9th century rebellion that contributed to the collapse of T'ang.

O368. Balázs, Etienne. **Le traité économique du "Souei-chou."** Leiden, 1953. This and the following study are of great importance for social, economic, and institutional developments during the previous Six Dynasties period.

O369. ——. **Le traité juridique du "Souei-chou."** Leiden, 1954.

O370. Balázs, Stefan. "Beiträge zur Wirtschaftsgeschichte der T'ang-Zeit (618–906)." **Mitteilungen des Seminars für orientalische Sprachen,** 34 (1931): 1–92, 35 (1932): 1–73, 36 (1933): 1–62.

O371. Gernet, Jacques. **Les aspects économiques du Bouddhisme dans la société chinoise du Vᵉ au Xᵉ siècle.** Saigon, 1956. Important study. See elaborating material in reviews by A. F. Wright, *Jour. Asian studies,* 16 (May 1957): 408–14; and D. C. Twitchett, *Bulletin Sch. of Oriental and African Studies,* 19 (1957): 526–49.

O372. Twitchett, D. C. "Monastic estates in T'ang China." **Asia major,** 2 (Nov. 1956): 123–46.

O373. T'ang Hsüan-tsung. **Ta-T'ang liu-tien.** [The six institutes of Hsüan-tsung of Great T'ang.] Ed. by Li Lin-fu (d. 1160). 6 ts'e. Kiangsu, 1800. Japanese ed., 8 ts'e, 1836. A principal source for study of T'ang government.

O374. Des Rotours, Robert, tr. **Traité des fonctionnaires et traité de l'armée, tr. de la Nouvelle histoire des T'ang (chap. XLVI–L).** 2 v. Brill and Leiden, 1947–48.

O375. ——. tr. **Le traité des examens, traduit de la Nouvelle histoire des T'ang (chap. XLIV–XLV).** Paris, 1932.

O376. Rideout, J. K. "The rise of the eunuchs during the T'ang dynasty." **Asia major,** 1 (1949): 53–74.

O377. Ch'ang-Sun, Wu-chi. **T'ang lü su-i.** [T'ang legal code with interpretations.] Shanghai, 1933. Completed in 654.

O378. Bünger, Karl. **Quellen zur Rechtsgeschichte der T'ang-zeit.** Peiping, 1946. Important work on T'ang laws and legal institutions.

O379. Kennedy, George A. **Die Rolle des Geständnisses im chinesischen Gesetz.** Berlin, 1939. Translates a small section of the T'ang code.

O380. Ou, Koei-hing. **La peine d'après le Code des T'ang: étude de droit pénal chinois ancien.** Shanghai, 1935.

O381. Niida, Noboru. **Toso horitsu bunsho no kenkyu.** [Critical study of legal documents of the T'ang and Sung dynasties.] Tokyo, 1937. An especially valuable study with English summary.

O382. Reischauer, Edwin O. **Ennin's travels in T'ang China.** N.Y., 1955. Scholarly and vivid reconstruction of life in 9th century China based on the life of Priest Ennin. This and the following are valuable for information on Buddhism in both China and Japan.

O383. ——, tr. **Ennin's diary: the record of a pilgrimage to China in search of the law.** N.Y., 1955. Carefully annotated translation.

O384. Waley, Arthur. **The real Tripitaka, and other pieces.** London, 1952. Account of Hsüan-tsang (Tripitaka) and his travels to India, of Ennin and Ensai and their travels from Japan to China, and of various short pieces of the T'ang period.

O385. Drake, F. S. "Foreign religions of the T'ang dynasty." **The Chinese recorder,** 71 (June 1940): 343–54, 71 (Oct. 1940): 643–49, 71 (Nov. 1940): 675–88.

O386. ——. "Mohammedanism in the T'ang dynasty." **Monumenta serica,** 8 (1943): 1–40.

O387. Chavannes, Edouard, tr. **Mémoire composé à l'époque de la grande dynastie T'ang sur les religieux éminents qui allèrent chercher la loi dans les pays d'Occident, par I-tsing.** Paris, 1894.

O388. Watters, Thomas, ed. **On Yuan Chwang's [Hsüan-Tsang] travels in India, 629–645 A.D.** 2 v. London, 1904–05.

O389. Ferrand, Gabriel, tr. and ed. **Voyage du marchand arabe Sulaymân en Inde et en Chine rédigé en 851 suivi de remarques par Abû Zayd Ḥasan (vers 916).** Paris, 1922.

O390. Sauvaget, Jean, tr. **Relation de la Chine et de l'Inde rédigée en 851.** Paris, 1948.

O391. Pelliot, Paul. "Deux itinéraires de Chine en Inde à fin du VIIIᵉ siècle." **Bulletin de l'École Française d'Extrême-Orient,** 4 (Jan.-June 1904): 131–413.

O392. Reischauer, Edwin O. "Notes on T'ang dynasty sea routes." **Harvard journal of Asiatic studies,** 5 (1940): 142–64.

O393. Maspero, Henri. "Le protectorat général d'Annam sous les T'ang." **Bulletin de l'École Française d'Extrême-Orient,** 10 (July-Sep. 1910): 539–84, 10 (Oct.-Dec. 1910): 665–82.

O394. Edwards, Evangeline D. **Chinese prose literature of the T'ang period, A.D. 618–906.** 2 v. London, 1937–38.

O395. Hung, William. **Tu Fu, China's greatest poet.** 2 v. Cambridge, Mass., 1952.

O396. Zach, Erwin von, tr. **Tu Fu's gedichte.** Ed. by James R. Hightower. 2 v. Cambridge, Mass., 1952.

O397. Obata, Shigeyoshi, tr. **The works of Li Po.** N.Y., 1922.

O398. Waley, Arthur. **The life and times of Po Chü-i, 772–846 A.D.** London, 1949.

O399. ——. **The poetry and career of Li Po, 701–762 A.D.** London, 1950.

O400. Acker, William R. B. **Some T'ang and pre-T'ang texts on Chinese painting, translated and annotated.** Leiden, 1954.

O401. Bynner, Witter, tr. **The jade mountain.** N.Y., 1929. Anthology of 300 poems from the T'ang period.

O402. **T'ang kien wen tse. Florilège de littérature des T'ang.** Tr. by Bruno Belpaire. Paris, 1957.

Five Dynasties and Sung Periods (907–1278)

O403. Ch'ao, Kung-wu. **Chün-chai tu-shu chih.** [A reading record from the commandery study.] 8 ts'e. Shanghai, 1933. Annotated catalog of private Sung collections of books originally compiled about 1151.

O404. Ch'en, Chen-sun. **Chih-chai shu-lu chieh-t'i.** [Catalog of Chih-chai collections.] 6 ts'e. Kiangsu, 1883. Originally compiled about 1235.

O405. Wang, P'u. **Wu-tai hui-yao.** [Selected documents of the Five Dynasties.] 6 ts'e. Kiangsu, 1886. Originally compiled in 961; a collection of basic documents.

O406. Schafer, Edward H. **The empire of Min.** Rutland, Vt., 1954. A study of one of the splinter states that arose in Fukien at the end of the T'ang period and existed between 833 and 943.

O407. ———. **The reign of Liu Ch'ang, first emperor of southern Han: a critical translation of the text of Wu-tai-shih.** Berkeley, 1947.

O408. Chavannes, Edouard. "Le royaume de Wou et de Yue." **T'oung pao,** 17 (1916): 129–264.

O409. Hamilton, James R. **Le Ouïghours à l'époque des cinq dynasties d'après les documents chinois.** Paris, 1955. Valuable study of the Uighurs of central Asia and their influence in China.

O410. Yueh, Shih. **T'ai-p'ing huan-yü chi.** [Geographical survey of the T'ai-p'ing period.] 36 ts'e. Nanking, 1882.

O411. Fang, Hao. **Sung shih.** [History of the Sung dynasty.] 2 v. Taipei, 1954. Good general survey by a Chinese Jesuit.

O412. Li, Tao. **Hsü tzu-chih t'ung-chien ch'ang-pien.** [Supplement to the comprehensive mirror for aid in government.] Peking Palace ed., 100 ts'e, 1819. Excellent work covering the northern Sung (960–1126), completed before 1183.

O413. Yang, Chung-liang. **Sung t'ung-chien ch'ang-pien chi-shih pen-mo.** [Comprehensive mirror of the Sung period from beginning to end.] Ed. of 1893, 150 chüan. Completed about 1253.

O414. Wang, Ch'eng. **Tung-tu shih-lüeh.** [Events of the eastern capital.] 8 ts'e. Kiangsu, 1883. Originally completed in 1175.

O415. Hsü, Sung. **Sung hui-yao chi-kao.** [Selected documents of the Sung dynasty.] 200 ts'e. Peiping, 1936. Completed in 1809, this is an indispensable collection of basic documents.

O416. Tou, I. **Hsing T'ung [Sung].** [Legal code of the Sung.] 6 ts'e. Wuhsing, 1921. Prepared in 960.

O417. Gulik, Robert H. van, tr. **T'ang-yin-pi-shih. Parallel cases from under the pear-tree: a thirteenth century manual of jurisprudence and detection.** Leiden, 1956.

O418. Kracke, Edward A. **Civil service in early Sung China, 960–1067.** Cambridge, Mass., 1953.

O419. ———. "Sung society." **Far eastern quarterly,** 14 (Aug. 1955): 479–88.

O420. Williamson, Henry R. **Wang An Shih . . . a Chinese statesman and educationalist of the Sung dynasty.** 2 v. London, 1935–37. Lucid exposition of the career and ideas of one of the leading statesmen and independent thinkers of the Sung period.

O421. Wimsatt, Genevieve B. **Apricot cheeks and almond eyes.** N.Y., 1939. A fictional biography of Empress Yang of the Sung.

O422. Lu, Hsin-Yüan. **Sung shih i.** [Supplement to the Sung history biographies.] 10 ts'e. 1906. Contains 800 biographies of Sung individuals omitted from standard histories.

O423. Ho, Ping-ti. "Early-ripening rice in Chinese history." **Economic history review,** n.s. 9 (Dec. 1956): 200–18. Extremely important contribution to Chinese economic history of the Sung period.

O424. Lo, Jung-Pang. "The emergence of China as a sea power during the late Sung and early Yüan periods." **Far eastern quarterly,** 14 (Aug. 1955): 489–503.

O425. Hirth, Friedrich, and William W. Rockhill, trs. **Chau Ju-kua [Chu fan chi]: his work on the Chinese and Arab trade in the twelfth and thirteenth centuries.** St. Petersburg (Leningrad), 1911. An important work on Chinese commercial relations with southeast Asia and the Indian Ocean area.

O426. Hsü, Meng-hsin. **San-ch'ao pei-meng hui-pien.** [Compilation of materials concerning the northern alliance during three reigns.] 40 ts'e. 1878 and 1909. Sung relations with Liao and Chin from 1101 to 1161. Originally compiled in the 13th century.

O427. Chang, Carsun. **The development of neo-Confucian thought.** N.Y., 1957.

O428. Chow, Yih-ching [Chou I-ch'ing]. **La philosophie morale dans le néo-Confucianisme.** Paris, 1954.

O429. Huang, Tsung-hsi. **Sung-Yüan hsüeh-an.** [A survey of schools of Confucianism of the Sung and Yüan dynasties.] 48 ts'e. Changsha, 1879.

O430. Chang, Po-hsing. **Cheng i-t'ang ch'uan-shu.** [Collection of works on Sung philosophy.] 160 ts'e. Foochow, 1866.

O431. **Ein Beitrag zur Kenntnis der chinesischen Philosophie . . . T'ung-su des**

Ceu-tsi [Chou Tun-i] mit Cu-Hi's [Chu Hsi's] Commentar. Tr. by Wilhelm Grube and Werner Eichhorn. Leipzig, 1932.

O432. Eichhorn, Werner. Chou Tun-i. Leipzig, 1936.

O433. ——. Die Westinschrift des Chang Tsai. Leipzig, 1937.

O434. Bruce, Joseph P. Chu Hsi and his masters: an introduction to Chu Hsi and the Sung school of Chinese philosophy. London, 1923.

O435. ——, tr. The philosophy of human nature by Chu Hsi. London, 1922.

O436. Chu, Hsi. Djin-si lu von Dschu Hsi: die sungkonfuzianische Summa mit dem Kommentar des Yä Tsai. Tr. and ed. by Olaf Graf. 3 v. in 4. Tokyo, 1953.

O437. Huang, Siu-chi. Lu Hsiang-shan, a twelfth century Chinese idealist philosopher. New Haven, 1944. Deals with the chief philosophical opponent of Chu Hsi.

O438. Lin, Yu-t'ang. The gay genius: the life and times of Su Tungpo. N.Y., 1947. Presents an anti-Wang An-shih view.

O439. Clark, Cyril D. L. G., tr. The prose poetry of Su Tung-p'o. Shanghai, 1935. Translations from the poetry of the greatest Sung poet.

O440. Candlin, Clara M. The herald wind. London, 1933.

O441. ——. The rapier of Lu, patriot poet of China. London, 1946.

Nomadic Regimes: Liao, Chin, Yüan (Mongol), etc. (907–1368)

O442. Shih, Kuo-ch'i. Chin-shih hsiang-chiao. [A detailed review of Chin history.] 12 ts'e. Canton, 1894.

O443. Yang, Lien-sheng. "Notes on the economic history of the Chin dynasty." Harvard journal of Asiatic studies, 9 (June 1946): 107–85.

O444. Chavannes, Edouard. "Voyageurs chinois chez les Khitan et les Joutchen." Journal asiatique, 9th ser., 9 (May-June 1897): 377–429, 11 (May-June 1898): 361–439.

O445. Minorsky, Vladimir F., tr. and ed. Marvozi on China, the Turks and India. London, 1942.

O446. Wittfogel, Karl A., and Feng Chia-sheng. History of Chinese society: Liao, 907–1125. Philadelphia, 1949. Exhaustive treatment of history and society of the Khitan dynasty, which instituted in China a pattern of conquest and rule that the Mongols later followed.

O447. ——. "Religion under the Liao dynasty (907–1125)." Review of religion, 12 (May 1948): 355–74.

O448. Wittfogel, Karl A. "Public office in the Liao dynasty and the Chinese examination system." Harvard journal of Asiatic studies, 10 (June 1947): 13–40.

O449. Li, E. Liao-shih shih-i. [Supplement to the Liao shih (History of the Liao).] 1743. 2nd ed., 8 ts'e, Kiangsu, 1875.

O450. Torii, Ryūzō. Sculptured stone tombs of the Liao dynasty. Peiping, 1942.

O451. Wang, Ching-ju. Hsi-hsia yen-chiu. [Tangut studies.] 3 v. Peiping, 1932–33.

O452. Chavannes, Edouard. "Documents historiques et géographiques relatifs à Li Kiang." T'oung pao, 13 (1912): 565–653.

O453. Waley, Arthur, tr. The travels of an alchemist: the journey of the Taoist Ch'ang-Ch'un from China to the Hindukush at the summons of Chingiz Khan recorded by his disciple Li Chih-ch'ang. London, 1931.

O454. Rockhill, William W., tr. and ed. The journey of William Rubruck to the eastern parts of the world, 1253–55 . . . with two accounts of the earlier journey of John Pian de Carpine. London, 1900.

O455. Olschki, Leonardo. Marco Polo's precursors. Baltimore, 1943.

O456. ——. Guillaume Boucher: a French artist at the court of the Khans. Baltimore, 1946.

O457. Polo, Marco. The book of Ser Marco Polo, the Venetian, concerning the kingdoms and marvels of the East. Tr. and ed. by Sir Henry Yule. 3rd ed., rev. by Henri Cordier, 2 v., London, 1903. Of the many editions and studies of Marco Polo this is probably the best and most useful.

O458. Yule, Sir Henry. Cathay and the way thither, being a collection of medieval notices of China. 2 v. London, 1866. 2nd rev. ed. by Henri Cordier, 4 v., London, 1913–16.

O459. Cordier, Henri. Ser Marco Polo: notes and addenda to Sir Henry Yule's edition. N.Y., 1920.

O460. Moule, Arthur C., and Paul Pelliot, trs. Marco Polo, the description of the world. 2 v. London, 1938. V. 2 is the Zelada Latin manuscript.

O461. Moule, Arthur C. Quinsai, with other notes on Marco Polo. Cambridge, Eng., 1957.

O462. Budge, E. A. Wallis, tr. The monks of Kublai Khan, emperor of China: or the history of the life and travels of Rabban Sâwmâ. London, 1928.

O463. Pelliot, Paul. Les Mongols et la Papauté. Paris, 1923.

O464. Charol, Michael (pseud. Michael Prawdin). The Mongol empire, its rise and legacy. Tr. by Eden and Cedar Paul. London, 1940.

O465. Haenisch, Erich. Die geheime Geschichte der Mongolon. Leipzig, 1948.

O466. Pelliot, Paul, tr. and ed. Histoire secrète des Mongols. Paris, 1949.

O467. Hung, William. "The transmission of the book known as The secret history of the Mongols." Harvard journal of Asiatic studies, 14 (Dec. 1951): 433–92.

O468. Blochet, Edgar. **Introduction à l'histoire des Mongols de Fadl Allah Rashideddin.** Leiden, 1910.

O469. Fuchs, Walter. **The "Mongol atlas" of China by Chu Ssu-pen and the Kuang-yü-t'u.** Peiping, 1946.

O470. Chavannes, Edouard. "Inscriptions et pièces de chancellerie chinoises de l'époque mongole." **T'oung pao,** 2nd ser., 5 (1904): 357–447, 6 (1905): 1–42, 9 (1908): 297–428.

O471. Cleaves, Francis W. "The Mongolian names and terms in the *History of the nation of the archers* by Grigor of Akanc'." **Harvard journal of Asiatic studies,** 12 (Dec. 1949): 400–43. Professor Cleaves has also published in this journal between 1949 and 1959 many articles dealing with Mongol inscriptions and related matters.

O472. Haenisch, Erich, tr. and ed. **Sino-mongolische Dokumente vom Ende des 14. Jahrhunderts.** Berlin, 1952.

O473. Hambis, Louis. **Le chapitre CVII du Yüan che: les généalogies impériales mongoles dans l'histoire chinoise officielle de la dynastie mongole.** Leiden, 1945.

O474. Ratchnevsky, Paul, tr. **Un code des Yuan.** Paris, 1937. Largely a translation of the *Yüan tien-chang* [Laws and regulations of the Yüan dynasty] (24 ts'e, Peking, 1908), a basic source of Sino-Mongol law of this dynasty. Despite its weak analysis, it is a valuable source.

O475. Iwamura, Shinobu. "Gen-ten-shō keibu no kenkyū." [Criminal procedure under the Yüan dynasty.] **Tōhō gakuhō,** 24 (Feb. 1954): 1–114. One of the best analyses of Sino-Mongol law that has appeared. Iwamura, one of Japan's leading Mongolists, approaches the problem from both the Mongol and Chinese sides.

O476. Schurmann, Herbert F., tr. and ed. **Economic structure of the Yüan dynasty: translation of chapters 93 and 94 of the Yüan shih.** Cambridge, Mass., 1956. Account of the principal economic institutions of the Yüan dynasty.

O477. Franke, Herbert. **Geld und Wirtschaft in China unter der Mongolenherrschaft.** Leipzig, 1949. The main monetary institutions of the Yüan or Mongol dynasty in China (13th and 14th centuries).

O478. Yang, Yü. **Beiträge zur Kulturgeschichte Chinas unter der Mongolenherrschaft: das Shan-kü sin-hua des Yang Yü.** Tr. by Herbert Franke. Wiesbaden, 1956.

O479. Crump, James I. "The elements of Yüan Opera." **Journal of Asian studies,** 17 (May 1958): 417–34.

O480. Hsiung, Shih-i, tr. **The romance of the western chamber.** London, 1935; N.Y., 1936. Translation of the drama *Hsi hsiang chi* of Kuang Han-ch'ing and Wang Shih-fu.

O481. ——, tr. **Lady precious stream.** 2nd ed., London, 1935. Written by Wang Pao-ch'uan.

See also subsection on the Mongols in Section N.

Ming Period (1368–1644)

O482. Franke, Wolfgang. **Preliminary notes on the important Chinese literary sources for the history of the Ming dynasty (1368–1644).** Chengtu, 1947. Published in the *Bulletin of Chinese studies,* 7 (Sep. 1947): 1–118. See also "Addenda and corrigenda," *Studia serica,* 9 (Sep. 1950): 33–41.

O483. Li, Hsien. **Ta-Ming ta-i-t'ung-chih.** [Great geography of the Ming period.] 51 ts'e. Peking, 1559.

O484. Delamarre, Louis C., tr. **Histoire de la dynastie des Ming.** Paris, 1865. Translation of an officially sponsored account of the period 1368–1505.

O485. Wang, Hung-hsü. **Ming shih kao.** [Draft history of the Ming dynasty.] 100 ts'e. 1723. Supplements the standard dynastic history.

O486. Ming shih lu. [Veritable records of the Ming dynasty.] 500 ts'e. Shanghai, 1940. The official history of each reign, prepared after its close and first published at Shanghai in 1940. The most important single source for the Ming period. For some account of this work see L. C. Goodrich and Han Shou-hsüan, "The Ming shih lu," *Far eastern quarterly,* 3 (Nov. 1943): 37–40.

O487. Lung, Wen-pin. **Ming hui-yao.** [Selected records of Ming.] 20 ts'e. Canton, 1887. Less valuable for the Ming than earlier dynasties because more extensive collections are available.

O488. Boxer, Charles R., tr. and ed. **South China in the sixteenth century.** London, 1953. New editions and translations of the early accounts of China by Galeote Pereira, Gaspar da Cruz, and Martín de Rada.

O489. Ricci, Matteo. **China in the sixteenth century: the journals of Matthew Ricci, 1583–1610.** Tr. from Nicholas Trigault's Latin version by L. J. Gallagher. N.Y., 1953.

O490. Gallagher, Louis J., tr. **The China that was: China as discovered by the Jesuits at the close of the sixteenth century.** Milwaukee, 1942. Earlier translation of first part of the above, dealing with Chinese institutions.

O491. Bernard, Henri. **Le Père Matthieu Ricci et la société chinoise de son temps (1552–1610).** 2 v. Tientsin, 1937.

O492. Elia, Pasquale M. d', tr. and ed. **Il mappamondo chinese del p. Matteo Ricci S. I. . . . commentato, tradotto e annotato.** Vatican City, 1938.

O493. Semedo, Alvarez. **The history of**

that great and renowned monarchy of China. London, 1655. Important early account of China by one of the Jesuits; a translation of the Spanish edition published in Madrid, 1642.

O494. Chan, David B. **The usurpation of the Prince of Yen, 1398–1402.** Berkeley, 1957.

O495. Duyvendak, Jan J. L. **Ma-huan re-examined.** Amsterdam, 1933. This and *O496-498* deal with the voyages of Cheng Ho.

O496. ——. "The true dates of the Chinese maritime expeditions in the early fifteenth century." **T'oung pao,** 34 (1939): 341–412.

O497. ——. **China's discovery of Africa.** London, 1949.

O498. Pelliot, Paul. "Les grands voyages maritimes Chinois au début de XVe siècle." **T'oung pao,** 30 (1933): 237–452, 31 (1935): 274–314, 32 (1936): 210–22.

O499. Chang, Yü-ch'üan. **Wang Shou-jen as a statesman.** Peiping, 1940. A study of Wang Yang-ming.

O500. Parsons, James B. "The culmination of a Chinese peasant rebellion: Chang Hsien-chung in Szechwan, 1644–46." **Journal of Asian studies,** 16 (May 1957): 387–400.

O501. Ta-Ming lü chi-chiai fu-li. [The Ming legal code with supplements.] 1610. 10 ts'e. Reprint, 1908.

O502. Hsu, P'u. Ta-Ming hui-t'ien. [Collected administrative regulations of the Ming.] 64 ts'e. Peking, 1587.

O503. Shen, Te-fu. Yeh huo p'ien. [Informal records of the Ming administration.] 24 ts'e. Canton, 1827.

O504. Wild, Norman. "Materials for the study of the Ssu-i-Kuan (Bureau of Translators)." **Bulletin of the School of Oriental and African Studies,** 11 (1945): 617–40.

O505. Wang, Yi-t'ung [I-t'ung]. **Official relations between China and Japan, 1368–1549.** Cambridge, Mass., 1953.

O506. Chang, Teh-ch'ang. "Maritime trade at Canton during the Ming dynasty." **Chinese social and political science review,** 17 (July 1933): 264–82.

O507. Lin, T. C. "Manchuria in the Ming empire." **Nankai social and economic quarterly,** 8 (1935): 1–43.

O508. ——. "Manchuria trade and tribute in the Ming." **Nankai social and economic quarterly,** 9 (1937): 855–92.

O509. Pokotilov, Dmitrii. **History of the eastern Mongols during the Ming dynasty from 1368 to 1631.** Tr. by Rudolph Löwenthal. 2 v. Chengtu, 1947–49.

O510. Pelliot, Paul. **Le Hoja et le Sayyid Hussain de l'histoire des Ming.** Leiden, 1948. Important study on the first Portuguese embassy to China in 1517.

O511. Chang, T'ien-tse. **Sino-Portuguese trade from 1514 to 1644: a synthesis of** Portuguese and Chinese sources. Leiden, 1934.

O512. Kammerer, Albert. **La découverte de la Chine par les Portugais au XVIeme siècle et la cartographie des Portulans.** Leiden, 1944.

O513. Ho, Ping-ti. "The introduction of American food plants into China." **American anthropologist,** 57 (Apr. 1955): 191–201.

O514. ——. "American food plants in China." **Plant science bulletin** (Jan. 1956).

O515. Huang, Tsung-hsi. Ming-ju hsüeh-an. [Philosophy during the Ming dynasty.] 32 ts'e. Nanchang, 1888. Unfavorable appraisal of Ming philosophy by a critical scholar of the 17th century.

O516. Liang, Ch'i-ch'ao. Chieh-pen Ming-ju hsüeh-an. [Abridged account of the philosophy of the Ming period.] 2 v. Shanghai, 1916.

O517. Henke, Frederick G., tr. **The philosophy of Wang Yang-ming.** Chicago, 1916. Deals with the idealistic philosophy of Wang Shou-jen (better known in the West as Wang Yang-ming), greatest thinker of the Ming dynasty.

O518. Wang, Tch'ang-tche [Ch'ang-chih]. **La philosophie morale de Wang Yang-ming.** Shanghai, 1936.

O519. Franke, Otto. **Li Tschi . . . ein Beitrag zur Geschichte der chinesischen Geisteskämpfe in 16. Jahrhundert.** Berlin, 1938.

O520. Busch, Heinrich. "The Tung-lin Academy and its political and philosophical significance." **Monumenta serica,** 14 (1949–55): 1–163.

O521. Hucker, C. O. "The Tung-lin movement in the late Ming period." **Chinese thought and institutions,** ed. by John K. Fairbank (Chicago, 1957), pp. 132–62.

O522. Lo, Kuan-chung. **San Kuo, or Romance of the Three Kingdoms.** Tr. by C. H. Brewitt-Taylor. 2 v. Shanghai, 1925.

O523. Shih, Nai-an, and Lo Kuan-chung. **Water margin.** Tr. by J. H. Jackson. 2 v. Shanghai, 1937. Translation of the famous novel *Shui-hu chuan*. See also the following translation.

O524. Buck, Pearl S., tr. **All men are brothers.** Rev. ed., 2 v., N.Y., 1957.

O525. Irwin, Richard G. **The evolution of a Chinese novel, Shui-hu-chuan.** Cambridge, Mass., 1953.

O526. Wu, Ch'eng-en. **Monkey.** Tr. by Arthur Waley. N.Y., 1943. Reprint, 1958. An adapted translation of the famous novel *Hsi yu chi,* dealing with a Buddhist pilgrimage to India.

O527. Edgerton, Clement, tr. **The golden lotus: a translation, from the Chinese original, of the novel Chin p'ing mei.** 4 v. London, 1939; N.Y., 1954.

O528. Chin p'ing mei: the adventurous history of Hsi Men and his six wives. Tr. by

Bernard Miall from the German translation of Franz Kuhn. London, 1939. An abridged version.

O529. Bishop, John L. **The colloquial short story in China: a study of the San-yen collections.** Cambridge, Mass., 1956.

O530. Soulié de Morant, George, tr. **Chinese love tales.** N.Y., 1935. This and the following work contain tales from the *Hsing-shih heng-yen.*

O531. Acton, Harold M., and Lee Yi-hsieh. **Glue and lacquer.** London, 1941.

O532. Howell, Edward B., tr. **The inconstancy of Madam Chuang.** London, 1924. This and the following volume are tales from the *Chin-ku ch'i-kuan.*

O533. ———, tr. **The restitution of the bride.** London, 1926.

O534. Hobson, Robert L. **The wares of the Ming dynasty.** London, 1923.

O535. Bouillard, G. **Les tombeaux impériaux des dynasties Ming et Ts'ing.** Peiping, 1931.

See also subsections on international contacts and on Christianity.

Ch'ing or Manchu Period (1644–1911)

O536. Hummel, Arthur W., ed. **Eminent Chinese of the Ch'ing period (1644–1912).** 2 v. Washington, 1943–44. Excellent example of scholarly collaboration. No student of modern Chinese history should be without it.

O537. Chih, Wei-ch'eng. **Ch'ing-tai p'u-hsüeh ta-shih lieh-chuan.** [Biographies of the masters of scholarship in the Ch'ing dynasty.] 2 v. Shanghai, 1925.

O538. Li, Huan. **Kuo-chao chi-hsien lei-cheng chu-pien, hsien-yüan chu-pien.** [Ch'ing biographies systematically arranged, indexed by rhymes.] 394 ts'e. Hsiang-yin, Hunan, 1884–90.

O539. Chiang, T'ing-hsi, and others. **Ta-Ch'ing i-t'ung chih.** [Great geography of the Ch'ing period.] Completed 1744. 3rd ed., 1842. Reprint, 210 ts'e, Shanghai, 1934. Deals with China as a whole and then with each of the political subdivisions of the Ch'ing period.

O540. Fuchs, Walter, ed. **Der Jesuiten-Atlas der Kanghsi-Zeit, seine Entstehungsgeschichte nebst Namensindices für die Karten der Mandjurei, Mongolei, Ostturkestan und Tibet mit Wiedergabe der Jesuiten-Karten in Originalgrösse.** Peiping, 1943.

O541. Anville, Jean B. B. d'. **Nouvel atlas de la Chine.** Paris and The Hague, 1737.

O542. Smith, George. **A narrative of an exploratory visit to each of the consular cities of China.** London, 1847; N.Y., 1857.

O543. Hirth, Friedrich. **Notes on the Chinese documentary style.** 2nd ed., Shanghai, 1909.

O544. Fairbank, John K., ed. **Ch'ing documents: an introductory syllabus.** 2 v. Cambridge, Mass., 1952.

O545. Fairbank, John K., and S. Y. Teng. "On the types and uses of Ch'ing documents." **Harvard journal of Asiatic studies,** 5 (Jan. 1940): 1–71.

O546. Ta-Ch'ing li-ch'ao shih-lu. [Veritable records of the Ch'ing dynasty.] 1220 ts'e. Changchun, 1937–38. Photographic reproduction of a manuscript copy of the official history of each reign of the Manchu dynasty. A basic source.

O547. Wang, Hsien-ch'ien, comp. **Tung-hua lu.** [Records of the Eastern Gate.] 188 ts'e. Peking, 1887. Records of important edicts and decrees covering the period 1616–1861. There are various other editions. See Knight Biggerstaff's comments on this and the *Shih lu* in *Harvard journal of Asiatic studies,* 4 (1939): 101–15.

O548. Shih-ch'ao sheng-hsün. [Sacred instructions of ten reigns.] 286 ts'e. Peking, 1880. Selected edicts of the various emperors.

O549. Ming-Ch'ing shih-liao. [Materials relating to the late Ming and early Ch'ing periods.] Series 1–6. Shanghai and Taipei, 1930–58. Large collection of documents selected from historical records in the hands of Academia Sinica. More detailed and complete than documents found in the *Shih lu.*

O550. Chang-ku ts'ung-pien. [Collected historical documents.] 10 v. Peiping, 1928–29. Continued as *Wen-hsien ts'ung-pien* [Collectanea from the historical records office], 46 v., Peiping, 1930–43. Various documents of the Ch'ing period published by the Palace Museum.

O551. Shih-liao hsün-k'an. [Historical materials.] 40 v. Peiping, 1930–31. Published by the Palace Museum.

O552. Lo, Chen-yü, comp. **Shih-liao ts'ung-k'an ch'u-pien.** [Miscellaneous historical materials, first series.] 10 v. Peking, 1924. Continued in his *Shih-liao ts'ung-pien,* 12 v., Peiping, 1933.

O553. Fairbank, John K., and others. "Documentary collections on modern Chinese history." **Journal of Asian studies,** 17 (Nov. 1957): 55–111. Reviews of eight collections of documents on aspects of 19th century history recently published in Communist China. The collections are: *Ya-p'ien chan-cheng* [The Opium War] (6 v., 1954); *T'ai-p'ing t'ien-kuo* [The heavenly kingdom of the great peace] (6 v., 1952); *Nien chün* [The Nien army] (6 v., 1953); *Hui-min ch'i-i* [The Moslem rebellions] (4 v., 1953); *Chung-Fa chan-cheng* [The Sino-French War] (7 v., 1955); *Chung-Jih chan-cheng* [The Sino-Japanese War] (7 v., 1956); *Wu-hsü pien-fa* [The reform movement of 1898] (4 v., 1953); *I-ho t'uan* [The Boxers] (4 v., 1951).

O554. Hsiao, I-shan. **Ch'ing-tai t'ung-shih.** [General history of the Ch'ing dynasty.] 4 v.

Shanghai, 1927–28. One of the earliest and best general works by modern Chinese historians.

O555. Haenisch, Erich. "Des Ts'ing-Shi-Kao und die sonstige chinesische Literatur zur Geschichte der letzten 300 Jahre." **Asia major,** 6 (1930): 403–44. Useful discussion of Ch'ing dynastic history.

O556. Cheng, Hao-sheng. **Chung-kuo chin-tai shih.** [China's modern history.] 2 v. Shanghai, 1944. Covers the period 1516–1795.

O557. Kuo, T'ing-i. **Chin-tai Chung-kuo shih.** [Modern history of China.] 3 v. Shanghai, 1940. Deals with 1516–1832.

O558. Li, Chien-nung. **The political history of China, 1840–1928.** Ed. and tr. by Ssu-yu Teng and Jeremy Ingalls. Princeton, 1956. Translation of *Chung-kuo chin-pai-nien cheng-chih shih* (Shanghai, 1948).

O559. Du Halde, Jean B. **Description géographique, historique, chronologique, politique, et physique de l'empire de la Chine.** 4 v. Paris, 1735. Best English tr. is by Edward Cave, *A description of the empire of China,* 2 v., London, 1738–41. Also English tr. by Richard Brookes, London, 1736. This work of the Jesuits is still of great value, especially for the Ch'ing dynasty.

O560. **Mémoires concernant l'histoire, les sciences, les arts, les moeurs, les usages, etc. des Chinois, par les missionaires de Pékin.** Ed. by Charles Batteux and others. 17 v. Paris, 1776–1814. Still an invaluable collection of Jesuit studies on various aspects of China.

O561. Williams, Samuel Wells. **The middle kingdom: a survey of the geography, government, literature, social life, arts, and history of the Chinese empire and its inhabitants.** 2 v. N.Y., and London, 1848. Rev. ed., 1883.

O562. Gray, John H. **China: a history of the laws, manners, and customs of the people.** 2 v. London, 1878.

O563. Backhouse, Edmund T., and John O. P. Bland. **Annals and memoirs of the court of Peking (from the 16th to the 20th century).** London and Boston, 1914. Most of the material is on the Ch'ing and the fall of the Ming.

O564. Michael, Franz. **The origin of Manchu rule in China: frontier and bureaucracy as interacting forces in the Chinese empire.** Baltimore, 1942. An up-to-date study based on Chinese sources.

O565. Hauer, Erich, tr. **Huang-ts'ing k'ai-kuo fang-lüeh: die Gründung des mandschurischen Kaiserreiches.** Berlin, 1926. A somewhat too rapid translation of the official account of founding of the dynasty, ordered by the emperor in 1773 and published in 1789.

O566. Ross, John. **The Manchus, or the reigning dynasty of China: their rise and progress.** Paisley, Scotland, 1880. Huge mass of material derived in large part from Chinese sources.

O567. Orléans, Pierre J. d'. **History of the two Tartar conquerors of China.** Tr. and ed. by the Earl of Ellesmere. London, 1854.

O568. Le Comte, Louis. **Nouveaux mémoires sur l'état présent de la Chine.** 2 v. Paris, 1696. Le Comte served in China, largely in Shansi, before composing this work, which is strongly tinged with propaganda for the extreme Jesuit position on the rites controversy. Eng. tr. London, 1697.

O569. Hibbert, Eloise T. **K'ang Hsi, emperor of China.** London, 1940. U. S. ed., *Jesuit adventure in China during the reign of K'ang Hsi,* N.Y., 1941.

O570. Bouvet, Joachim. **Portrait historique de l'empereur de la Chine, présenté au roy.** Paris, 1697. English tr., London, 1699.

O571. Goodrich, L. Carrington. **The literary inquisition of Ch'ien-Lung.** Baltimore, 1935. Careful, scholarly study.

O572. Malone, Carroll B. **History of the Peking summer palace under the Ch'ing dynasty.** Urbana, 1934.

O573. Grantham, Alexandra E. **A Manchu monarch: an interpretation of Chia Ch'ing.** London, 1934. Undocumented and often uncritical, but useful account of the period 1796–1820.

O574. Gutzlaff, Charles. **The life of Taou-Kwang, late emperor of China, with memoirs of the court of Peking.** London, 1852.

O575. Kuo, Pin-chia. **A critical study of the first Anglo-Chinese war, with documents.** Shanghai, 1935.

O576. Waley, Arthur. **The Opium War through Chinese eyes.** London, 1958. The views of Lin Tse-hsü are heavily featured.

O577. Overdijkink, Gerrit W. **Lin Tse-hsü: een biographische schets.** Leiden, 1938.

O578. Teng, Ssu-yü. **New light on the history of the Taiping rebellion.** Cambridge, Mass., 1950.

O579. Ch'eng, Yen-sheng. **T'ai-ping t'ien-kuo shih liao.** [Historical sources of the *T'ai-ping t'ien kuo.*] 3 v. Peking, 1926.

O580. Taylor, George E. "The Taiping rebellion: its economic background and social theory." **Chinese social and political science review,** 16 (1932–33): 545–614.

O581. Shih, Vincent Y. C. "The ideology of the Taiping t'ien kuo." **Sinologica,** 3 (1951): 1–15.

O582. Boardman, Eugene P., and Kwan-wai So. "Hung Jen-kan, Taiping prime minister, 1859–1864." **Harvard journal of Asiatic studies,** 20 (June 1957): 262–94.

O583. Boardman, Eugene P. **Christian influence upon the ideology of the Taiping rebellion, 1851–1864.** Madison, 1952.

O584. Hail, William J. **Tseng Kuo-fan and the Taiping rebellion.** New Haven, 1927.

O585. Meadows, Thomas T. **The Chinese**

and their rebellions, viewed in connection with their national philosophy, ethics, legislation, and administration. London, 1856; Stanford, 1953.

O586. Lin-le. [A. F. Lindley], **Ti-ping tien-kwoh: the history of the Ti-ping revolution.** 2 v. London, 1866.

O587. Chiang, Siang-tseh. **The Nien rebellion.** Seattle, 1954.

O588. Wright, Mary C. **The last stand of Chinese conservatism: the T'ung-chih restoration, 1862–1874.** Stanford, 1957. An outstanding study.

O589. Biggerstaff, Knight. "The secret correspondence of 1867–1868: views of leading Chinese statesmen regarding the further opening of China to western influence." **Journal of modern history,** 22 (June 1950): 122–36.

O590. Bales, William L. **Tso Tsung-t'ang.** Shanghai, 1937. Account of the reformer and soldier who regained Turkestan for China in the 19th century.

O591. Bland, John O. P. **Li Hung-Chang.** London, 1917.

O592. Wright, Stanley F. **Hart and the Chinese customs.** Belfast, 1950. Deals with the career of Sir Robert Hart in building the Chinese customs service.

O593. Fairbank, John K. "Creation of the foreign inspectorate of customs at Shanghai." **Chinese social and political science review,** 19 (Jan. 1936): 469–514, 20 (Apr. 1936): 42–100.

O594. Tan, Chester C. **The Boxer catastrophe.** N.Y., 1955.

O595. Steiger, George N. **China and the Occident: the origin and development of the Boxer movement.** New Haven, 1927.

O596. Smith, Arthur H. **China in convulsion.** 2 v. N.Y., 1901.

O597. Bland, John O. P., and Edmund Backhouse. **China under the Empress Dowager: being the history of the life and times of Tzu Hsi.** London, 1910. New ed., Peiping, 1939.

O598. Pruitt, Ida, tr. and ed. **The flight of an empress,** told by Wu Yung whose other name is Yü-ch'uan, transcribed by Liu K'un. New Haven, 1936.

O599. Cameron, Meribeth E. **The reform movement in China, 1898–1912.** Stanford, 1931.

O600. ——. "The public career of Chang Chih-tung, 1837–1909." **Pacific historical review,** 7 (Sep. 1938): 187–210.

O601. Reid, John G. **The Manchu abdication and the powers, 1908–1912, an episode in pre-war diplomacy: a study of the role of foreign diplomacy during the reign of Hsüan T'ung.** Berkeley, 1935.

O602. Dingle, Edwin J. **China's revolution, 1911–1912.** Shanghai, 1912.

O603. Kent, Percy H. **The passing of the Manchus.** London, 1912.

O604. Mayers, William F. **The Chinese government: a manual of Chinese titles.** 3rd ed., Shanghai, 1897. A basic work based on the *Hui-tien.*

O605. Hoang, Pierre. **Mélanges sur l'administration.** Shanghai, 1902.

O606. Brunnert, Ippolit S., and V. V. Haglestrom. **Present day political organization of China.** Tr. by A. Beltchenko and E. E. Moran. Shanghai, 1912. A more detailed account showing changes at end of the dynasty.

O607. Hsieh, Pao Chao. **The government of China (1644–1911).** Baltimore, 1925. Best available analysis of the Ch'ing government.

O608. Ta-Ch'ing hui-tien. [Collected administrative statutes of the Ch'ing dynasty.] 160 ts'e. Shanghai, 1908. Basic to the study of governmental organization and procedure. Five earlier *Hui-tien* exist. See also the *Ta-Ch'ing hui-tien shih-li* (150 ts'e, Shanghai, 1908) for supplementary material.

O609. Langlès, L., tr. **Rituel des Tatars-Mantchoux, rédigé par l'ordre de l'Empereur Kien-long, et précédé d'un discours préliminaire composé par ce souverain.** Paris, 1804.

O610. Morse, Hosea B. **The trade and administration of China.** London, 1908. 3rd ed., Shanghai, 1921. Still a basic work.

O611. Remer, Charles F. **The foreign trade of China.** Shanghai, 1926. Excellent study of period after 1860.

O612. Jernigan, Thomas R. **China in law and commerce.** N.Y. and London, 1905.

O613. Alabaster, Ernest. **Notes and commentaries on Chinese criminal law and cognate topics, with special relation to ruling cases.** London, 1899. For many years regarded as the principal manual for study of Chinese law and practice.

O614. Staunton, George T., tr. **Ta Tsing leu lee: being the fundamental laws, and a selection from the supplementary statutes, of the penal code of China.** London, 1810.

O615. Peake, Cyrus H. "Recent studies on Chinese law." **Political science quarterly,** 52 (Mar. 1937): 117–38.

O616. Li, Hsiung-fei. **Les censeurs sous la dynastie mandchoue (1616–1911) en Chine.** Paris, 1936.

O617. Li (Chou), Chung-cheng. **L'examen provincial en Chine . . . sous la dynastie des Ts'ing.** Paris, 1935.

O618. Zi, Etienne. **Pratique des examens littéraires en Chine.** Shanghai, 1894.

O619. ——. **Pratique des examens militaires en Chine.** Shanghai, 1896.

O620. Wade, Thomas F. "The army of the Chinese empire." **Chinese repository,** 20 (1851): 250–80, 300–40, 363–422.

O621. Powell, Ralph L. **The rise of Chinese military power, 1895–1912.** Princeton, 1955.

O622. Chen, Shao-kwan. **The system of**

taxation in China in the Tsing dynasty, 1644–1911. N.Y., 1914.

O623. Huang, Hanliang. **Land tax in China.** N.Y., 1918.

O624. Edkins, Joseph. **The revenue and taxation of the Chinese empire.** Shanghai, 1903.

O625. Lu, Lien-Tching. **Les greniers publics de prévoyance sous la dynastie des Ts'ing.** Paris, 1932.

O626. Chang, Chung-li. **The Chinese gentry: studies on their role in nineteenth-century Chinese society.** Seattle, 1955.

O627. Ward, John S. M., and William G. Stirling. **The Hung society, or the society of heaven and earth.** 3 v. London, 1925–26. A study of secret societies of the Ch'ing period.

O628. Ch'ien, Mu. **Chung-kuo chin-san-pai-nien hsüeh-shu-shih.** [A history of Chinese scholarship during the last three hundred years.] 1937. 2 v. Shanghai, 1945.

O629. Liang, Ch'i-ch'ao. **Intellectual trends in the Ch'ing period.** Tr. by Immanuel C. Y. Hsü. Cambridge, Mass., 1959. Excellent translation of the *Ch'ing-tai hsüeh-shu kai-lun* (Shanghai, 1921).

O630. Ku, Hung-ming. **Papers from a viceroy's yamen: a Chinese plea for the cause of good government and true civilization in China.** Shanghai, 1901.

O631. Waley, Arthur. **Yuan Mei, eighteenth century Chinese poet.** London, 1956; N.Y., 1958.

O632. Hung, Sheng. **Palace of eternal youth.** Tr. by Yang Hsien-yi and Gladys Yang. Peiping, 1956. Translation of the famous operatic drama written about 1688.

O633. P'u, Sung-ling. **Strange stories from a Chinese studio.** Tr. by H. A. Giles. 4th rev. ed., Shanghai, 1936. Translation of the short stories of *Liao-chai chih-i*.

O634. Tsao, Hsüeh-chin. **Dreams of the red chamber.** Tr. by Wang Chi-chen. N.Y., 1958. Translation of the novel *Hung-lou meng.* There is also an English version by Florence and Isabel McHugh (N.Y. and London, 1958) adapted from the German translation of Franz Kuhn.

O635. Wu, Ching-tzu. **The scholars.** Peiping, 1957. Translation of the novel *Ju-lin wai-shih.*

O636. Ho, Shih-chun, tr. **Jou lin wai che, le roman des lettrés.** Paris, 1933.

O637. Liu, T'ieh-yün (Liu, E.). **The travels of Lao Ts'an.** Tr. by Harold Shadick. Ithaca, 1952.

See also subsections on international contacts.

The Republic since 1911

O638. Latourette, Kenneth S. **A history of modern China.** London and Baltimore, 1954.

O639. Fitzgerald, Charles P. **Revolution in China.** London, 1953.

O640. Franke, Wolfgang. **Das Jahrhundert der chinesischen Revolution, 1851–1949.** Munich, 1958.

O641. Li, Chien-nung. **Tsui-chin san-shih-nien Chung-kuo cheng-chih shih.** [Political history of China during the last thirty years.] Shanghai, 1930.

O642. Chang, Ch'i-yün. **Chung-hua min-kuo shih kang.** [Outline history of the Republic of China.] Taipei, 1954 ff.

O643. Li, Ting-i, and others, comps. **Chung-kuo chin-tai-shih lun-ts'ung.** [A collection of articles on modern China.] 10 v. Taipei, 1956.

O644. Johnston, Sir Reginald F. **Twilight in the forbidden city.** London, 1934.

O645. La Fargue, Thomas E. **China and the World War.** Stanford, 1937.

O646. MacNair, Harley F. **China in revolution: an analysis of politics and militarism under the republic.** Chicago, 1931.

O647. Liu, Frederick F. **A military history of modern China, 1924–1949.** Princeton, 1956. Shows how Chiang built and dissipated the military power of the Nationalists.

O648. Sun, Yat-sen. **The triple demism of Sun Yat-sen.** Tr. by Paschal M. d'Elia. Wuchang, 1931.

O649. Price, Frank W., tr. **San Min Chu I: the three principles of the people.** Shanghai, 1927. This and the above are standard translations of Sun's basic work.

O650. Sun, Yat-sen, **his political and social ideals: a source book.** Comp., tr., and annotated by Leonard Shihlien Hsü. Los Angeles, 1933.

O651. Linebarger, Paul M. W. **Sun Yat-sen and the Chinese republic.** N.Y. and London, 1925. Account by a close associate of Sun.

O652. Linebarger, Paul M. A. **The political doctrines of Sun Yat-sen: an exposition of the San Min Chu I.** Baltimore, 1937.

O653. Sharman, Abbie M. (Lyon). **Sun Yat-sen, his life and its meaning: a critical biography.** N.Y., 1934. Probably the best biography of Sun.

O654. Jansen, Marius B. **The Japanese and Sun Yat-sen.** Cambridge, Mass., 1954. Analyzes the support Sun received from the Japanese.

O655. Holcombe, Arthur N. **The Chinese revolution, a phase in the regeneration of a world power.** Cambridge, Mass., 1930.

O656. T'ang, Leang-li. **The inner history of the Chinese revolution.** London, 1930.

O657. Isaacs, Harold R. **The tragedy of the Chinese revolution.** Rev. ed., Stanford, 1951. Deals with the Nationalist-Communist cooperation and split in the 1920's.

O658. Monroe, Paul. **China, a nation in evolution.** N.Y., 1928.

O659. Peffer, Nathaniel. **China, the collapse of a civilization.** N.Y., 1930.

O660. James, Henry F., ed. "China." **Annals of the American Academy of Political and Social Science,** Nov. 1930. Series of valuable articles on all phases of Chinese life as of 1930.

O661. Van Dorn, Harold A. **Twenty years of the Chinese republic.** London, 1932.

O662. Peake, Cyrus H. **Nationalism and education in modern China.** N.Y., 1932.

O663. Quigley, Harold S. **Far eastern war, 1937–1941.** Boston, 1942. Gives the background as well as progress of the war.

O664. Bisson, Thomas A. **Japan in China.** N.Y., 1938.

O665. Bates, Don. **Wang Ching-wei: puppet or patriot.** Chicago, 1941.

O666. Chiang, Kai-shek. **China's destiny.** Tr. by Wang Chung-hui. N.Y., 1947.

O667. ——. **China's destiny and Chinese economic theory.** Ed. by Philip Jaffe. N.Y., 1947.

O668. **The collected wartime messages of Generalissimo Chiang Kai-shek, 1937–45.** 2 v. N.Y., 1946.

O669. Tong, Hollington K. **Chiang Kai-shek, soldier and statesman: authorized biography.** 2 v. Shanghai, 1937. Rev. ed., Taipei, 1953.

O670. Hahn, Emily. **Chiang Kai-shek, an unauthorized biography.** N.Y., 1955. Well balanced and generally sympathetic.

O671. ——. **The Soong sisters.** London and N.Y., 1943.

O672. Freyn, Hubert. **Free China's new deal.** N.Y., 1943.

O673. Rosinger, Lawrence K. **China's crisis.** N.Y., 1945.

O674. Rowe, David N. **China among the powers.** N.Y., 1945.

O675. Lin, Yu-t'ang. **The vigil of a nation.** N.Y., 1944. Account of China at war.

O676. White, Theodore H., and Annalee Jacoby. **Thunder out of China.** N.Y., 1946. Critical appraisal of the Nationalists.

O677. Chiang, Monlin. **Tides from the West: a Chinese autobiography.** New Haven, 1947.

O678. Powell, John B. **My twenty-five years in China.** N.Y., 1945.

O679. Stuart, John L. **Fifty years in China: the memoirs of John Leighton Stuart, missionary and ambassador.** N.Y., 1954.

O680. Hou, Fu-wu (pseud. Houn, Franklin W.). **Central government of China, 1912–1928.** Madison, 1957.

O681. P'an, Wei-tung. **The Chinese constitution: a study of forty years of constitution-making in China.** Washington, 1946.

O682. Linebarger, Paul M. A. **The China of Chiang Kai-shek.** Boston, 1941.

O683. ——. **Government in republican China.** N.Y., 1938.

O684. Ch'ien, Tuan-sheng. **The government and politics of China.** Cambridge, Mass., 1950. Probably the best general survey in this field for period of the republic. Critical of the Nationalists.

O685. Meijer, Marinus J. **The introduction of modern criminal law in China.** Batavia, 1950.

O686. **The criminal code of the republic of China.** Tr. by S. L. Burdett and Lone Liang. Shanghai, 1928.

O687. **The civil code of the republic of China.** Tr. by Hsia Ching-lin and others. Shanghai, 1931.

O688. Valk, Marius H. van der. **An outline of modern Chinese family law.** Peiping, 1939.

O689. Condliffe, John B. **China to-day: economic.** Boston, 1932. Economic analysis as of 1930.

O690. Buck, John L. **Chinese farm economy.** Chicago, 1930.

O691. ——. **Land utilization in China.** 3 v. Chicago, 1937.

O692. Tamagna, Frank M. **Banking and finance in China.** N.Y., 1942. A basic study.

O693. T'ang, Liang-li, ed. **Reconstruction in China.** Shanghai, 1935. Account of developments, especially economic, under the Nationalists.

O694. Chang, Kia-ngau. **The inflationary spiral: the experience in China, 1939–50.** Cambridge, Mass., 1958. Emphasizes the importance of inflation in the fall of the Nationalists.

O695. ——. **China's struggle for railroad development.** N.Y., 1943.

O696. Levy, Marion J. **The family revolution in modern China.** Cambridge, Mass., 1949.

O697. Levenson, Joseph R. **Liang Ch'i-ch'ao and the mind of modern China.** Cambridge, Mass., 1953. Important study of the life, ideas, and time of Liang.

O698. Brière, O. **Fifty years of Chinese philosophy, 1898–1950.** Tr. by Laurence G. Thompson. London, 1956.

O699. De Francis, John F. **Nationalism and language reform in China.** See *O182.*

O700. Hu, Shih. **The Chinese renaissance.** Chicago, 1934.

O701. Forster, Lancelot. **The new culture in China.** London, 1936.

O702. Huang, Sung-k'ang. **Lu Hsün and the new culture movement of modern China.** Amsterdam, 1957. The literary and cultural upheaval from 1917 to 1930.

O703. Chou, Shu-jen (pseud. Lu Hsün). **Selected works.** 3 v. Peiping, 1956–59.

O704. Wang, Chi-chen, tr. **Ah q and others: selected stories of Lusin.** N.Y., 1941. Writings of Lu Hsün (Chou Shu-jen).

O705. ——, tr. **Contemporary Chinese stories.** N.Y., 1944.

O706. Snow, Edgar P., comp. **Living**

China: modern Chinese short stories. London and N.Y., 1936.

O707. Schyns, Joseph. **1500 modern Chinese novels and plays.** Peiping, 1948.

O708. Yüan, Chia-hua, and Robert Payne, tr. **Contemporary Chinese short stories.** London and N.Y., 1946.

The Communists

O709. Fan, Wen-lan. **Chung-kuo chin-tai shih.** [History of modern China.] Shanghai, 1947.

O710. North, Robert C. **Moscow and Chinese Communists.** Stanford, 1953. Probably the best over-all history of Chinese communism to date of publication.

O711. Hu, Ch'iao-mu. **Thirty years of the Communist party of China.** London, 1951; Peiping, 1952. A more or less official history of the party.

O712. Schwartz, Benjamin I. **Chinese communism and the rise of Mao.** Cambridge, Mass., 1951.

O713. Steiner, H. Arthur, ed. "Report on China." **Annals of the American Academy of Political and Social Science,** Sep. 1951. Series of articles by specialists, mostly on Communist China.

O714. Elegant, Robert S. **China's Red masters.** N.Y., 1951. Biographical sketches of Red China's leaders.

O715. ——. **The dragon's seed.** N.Y., 1959. Deals with Peiping's exploitation of the overseas Chinese.

O716. Mao, Tse-tung. **Selected works.** 5 v. N.Y. and London, 1954–57.

O717. Liu, Shao-ch'i. **On the party.** 3rd ed., Peiping, 1951.

O718. ——. **Internationalism and nationalism.** 4th ed., Peiping, 1954.

O719. ——. **How to be a good Communist.** 2nd ed., Peiping, 1952.

O720. Brandt, Conrad, Benjamin Schwartz, and John K. Fairbank. **A documentary history of Chinese communism.** Cambridge, Mass., 1952.

O721. Wilbur, C. Martin, and Julie Lien-ying How, eds. **Documents on communism, nationalism, and Soviet advisers in China, 1918–1927: papers seized in the 1927 Peking raid.** N.Y., 1956.

O722. Compton, Boyd, tr. and ed. **Mao's China: party reform documents, 1942–44.** Seattle, 1952.

O723. Yakhontoff, Victor A. **The Chinese Soviets.** N.Y., 1934. Contains basic documents of value, although there are factual errors.

O724. Snow, Edgar P. **Red star over China.** Rev. ed., N.Y., 1939.

O725. ——. **Random notes on Red China (1936–1945).** Cambridge, Mass., 1957.

O726. Stein, Guenther. **The challenge of Red China.** N.Y. and London, 1945. A friendly report based on a visit to China near the end of the war.

O727. Moraes, Francis R. **Report on Mao's China.** N.Y. and London, 1953.

O728. Rostow, Walt W., and others. **The prospects for Communist China.** Cambridge, Mass., 1954.

O729. ——. **An American policy in Asia.** Cambridge, Mass., 1955. A sequel to the above.

O730. Walker, Richard L. **China under communism: the first five years.** New Haven, 1955. Very adverse appraisal.

O731. Ch'en, Theodore Hsi-en. **The Chinese Communist regime: a documentary study.** 2 v. Los Angeles, 1956. Product of much careful work.

O732. Tang, Peter S. H. **Communist China today.** 2 v. N.Y., 1957–58. An encyclopedic work.

O733. Gluckstein, Ygael. **Mao's China: economic and political survey.** Boston, 1957. Careful compilation which shows pressure of the Communist program on the masses.

O734. Fitzgerald, Charles P. **Flood tide in China.** London, 1958. Interpretation of Communist China following a visit there in 1956.

O735. Migot, André. **Chine sans murailles.** Paris, 1958.

O736. Faure, Edgar. **The serpent and the tortoise.** N.Y., 1958. Problems of Red China.

O737. Wei, Henry. **China and Soviet Russia.** N.Y., 1956

O738. Brandt, Conrad. **Stalin's failure in China, 1924–1927.** Cambridge, Mass., 1958.

O739. Roy, Manabendra N. **Revolution and counter-revolution in China.** Calcutta, 1946. Account, by a participant, of the Communist movement in China in the 1920's.

O740. Chiang, Kai-shek. **Soviet Russia in China.** N.Y., 1957.

O741. McLane, Charles B. **Soviet policy and the Chinese Communists, 1931–1946.** N.Y., 1958.

O742. Boorman, Howard L., and others. **Moscow-Peking axis: strengths and strains.** N.Y., 1957.

O743. Leng, Shao-chüan. **Japan and Communist China.** N.Y., 1959.

O744. Thomas, S. B. **Government and administration in Communist China.** 2nd ed., N.Y., 1955.

O745. Chao, Kuo-chün. **Agrarian policies of mainland China, a documentary study (1949–1956).** Cambridge, Mass., 1957.

O746. Dumont, René. **Révolution dans les campagnes chinoises.** Paris, 1957.

O747. Wu, Yüan-li. **An economic survey of Communist China.** N.Y., 1956.

O748. Adler, Solomon. **The Chinese economy.** N.Y., 1957.

O749. Li, Choh-ming. **Economic development of Communist China: an appraisal of the five years of industrialization.** Berkeley, 1959. Thorough economic analysis.

O750. Cheng, Chu-yüan. **Income and standards of living in mainland China.** 2 v. Hong Kong, 1957–59.

O751. Kirby, E. Stuart, ed. **Contemporary China: economic and social studies.** 2 v. Hong Kong, 1956–58. Various studies on Communist China, presumably to be continued.

O752. Prüsek, Jaroslav. **The literatures of liberated China and its popular traditions.** Prague, 1953.
See also subsection on International Contacts since 1833.

HISTORIES OF SPECIAL AREAS

O753. U. S. Library of Congress. **Manchuria: an annotated bibliography.** Comp. by Peter A. Berton. Washington, 1951.

O754. Fuchs, Walter. **Beiträge zur mandjurischen Bibliographie und Literatur.** Tokyo, 1936. By one of a very small group of scholars fully competent to handle books and documents in Manchu.

O755. Gilbert, Lucien. **Dictionnaire historique et géographique de la Mandchourie.** Hong Kong, 1934.

O756. Shirokogoroff, Sergei M. **Social organization of the Manchus.** Shanghai, 1924.

O757. Jones, Francis C. **Manchuria since 1931.** London, 1949.

O758. Clyde, Paul H. **International rivalries in Manchuria, 1689–1922.** 2nd ed., Columbus, O., 1928. See also Owen Lattimore, **Manchuria, cradle of conflict.** New York, 1932.

O759. Young, C. Walter. **The international relations of Manchuria.** Chicago, 1929.

O760. Riggs, Fred W. **Formosa under Chinese Nationalist rule.** N.Y., 1952.

O761. Han, Lih-wu. **Taiwan today.** Rev. ed., Taipei, 1952.

O762. Lien, Heng. **T'ai-wan t'ung-shih.** [General history of Formosa.] 2 v. Shanghai, 1946.

O763. Ginsburg, Norton S. **The economic resources and development of Formosa.** N.Y., 1953.

O764. Barclay, George W. **Colonial development and population in Taiwan.** Princeton, 1954.

O765. Grad, Andrew J. **Formosa today.** N.Y., 1942.

O766. Braga, José M. "The western pioneers and their discovery of Macao." **Instituto Português de Hongkong, Boletim,** no. 2 (Sep. 1949): 7–214.

O767. Montalto de Jesus, Carlos A. **Historic Macao.** 2nd ed., rev. and enl., Macao, 1926.

O768. Endacott, George B. **A history of Hong Kong.** London, 1958.

O769. Davis, S. G. **Hong Kong in its geographical setting.** London, 1949.

O770. Lee, Edward Bing-Shuey (Li Pingjui). **Modern Canton.** Shanghai, 1936.

O771. Gray, John H. **Walks in the city of Canton.** Hong Kong, 1875.

O772. Murphey, W. Rhoads. **Shanghai, key to modern China.** Cambridge, Mass., 1953.

O773. Lanning, G., and Samuel Couling. **The history of Shanghai.** Shanghai, 1921. Probably the best history of this city.

O774. Pott, Francis L. H. **A short history of Shanghai.** Shanghai, 1928.

O775. Gaillard, Louis. **Nankin, d'alors et d'aujourd'hui: aperçu historique et géographique.** Shanghai, 1903. One of the series of valuable studies published by the French missionary fathers at Zikawei on outskirts of Shanghai.

O776. Arlington, Lewis C., and William Lewisohn. **In search of old Peking.** Peiping, 1935.

O777. Bredon, Juliet. **Peking, a historical and intimate description of its chief places of interest.** 3rd ed., Shanghai, 1931.

O778. Bretschneider, Emil. **Archaeological and historical researches in Peking and its environs.** Shanghai, 1876.

O779. Sirén, Osvald. **The imperial palaces of Peking.** Paris, 1926. Good survey.

O780. Siguret, J., tr. and ed. **Territoires et populations des confins du Yunnan.** 2 v. Peiping, 1937–40. Translation of *Yün-nan pien-ti wen-ti yen-chiu.* The work of a serious student.

O781. Sainson, Camille, tr. **Nan-tchao yeche . . . histoire particulière du Nan-tchao.** Paris, 1904.

O782. Vial, Paul. **Les Lolos: histoire, religion, moeurs, langue, écriture.** Shanghai, 1898.

O783. Young, Ching-chi (Yang Ch'ingchih). **L'écriture et les manuscrits Lolos.** Geneva, 1935.

O784. Savina, F. M. **Histoire des Miao.** Hong Kong, 1930.

O785. Lin, Yüeh-hwa. "The Miao-man peoples of Kweichow." **Harvard journal of Asiatic studies,** 5 (1941): 261–345.

O786. Rock, Joseph F. C. **The ancient Nakhi kingdom of southwest China.** 2 v. Cambridge, Mass., 1947. Deals with the Mosos.

HISTORIES OF SPECIAL TOPICS

International Contacts: Traditional to 1833

For contacts during particular periods see the appropriate special period and also Christianity in China.

O787. Hudson, Geoffrey F. **Europe and China: a survey of their relations from the earliest times to 1800.** London, 1931. An outstanding work.

O788. Fang, Hao. **Chung-hsi chiao-t'ungshih.** [History of Sino-western contacts.] 5 v.

Taipei, 1954. Elaborate study from early times by an outstanding scholar.

O789. Fairbank, John K. "Tributary trade and China's relations with the West." **Far eastern quarterly,** 1 (Feb. 1942): 129–49.

O790. Fairbank, John K., and S. Y. Teng. "On the Ch'ing tributary system." **Harvard journal of Asiatic studies,** 6 (June 1941): 135–246. This and *O789* are important studies on China's traditional approach to international relations.

O791. Pauthier, G. **Histoire des relations politiques de la Chine, avec les puissances occidentales depuis les temps les plus anciens jusquà nos jours.** Paris, 1859. Much of this material is translated from the *Ta-Ch'ing t'ung-li* and *Hui-tien.*

O792. Chang, Hsing-lang. **Chung-hsi chiao-t'ung shih-liao hui-pien.** [A collection of historical materials on the relations between China and the West.] 6 v. Peiping, 1930. Covers period from antiquity to end of the Ming dynasty and deals with neighboring Asiatic peoples as well as the western world.

O793. **Ch'ing-tai wai-chao shih-liao.** [Collection of documents on Chinese foreign relations.] 10 v. Peiping, 1932–33. For the period 1796 to about 1835.

O794. Kuwabara, Jitsuzō. "On P'u Shou-keng." **Memoirs of the research department of the Tōyō Bunko,** 2 (1928): 1–79, 7 (1935): 95–110. Important work on the trade of China with the southern regions during the T'ang, Sung, and Yüan periods.

O795. Ferrand, Gabriel, tr. **Relations de voyages et textes géographiques arabes, persans, et turks relatifs à l'Extrême-Orient du VIIIᵉ au XVIIIᵉ siècles.** 2 v. Paris, 1913–14.

O796. Ma, Tuan-lin. **Ethnographie des peuples étranger à la Chine.** Tr. by Hervey de Saint Denys. 2 v. Geneva, 1876–83. Translation of those parts of Ma's *Wen-hsien t'ung-k'ao* dealing with border peoples.

O797. Wiens, Herold J. **China's march toward the tropics.** Hamden, Conn., 1954. Deals with China's historic expansion southward.

O798. Groeneveldt, Willem P. **Notes on the Malay archipelago and Malacca, compiled from Chinese sources.** Batavia, 1876.

O799. Hinton, Harold C. **China's relations with Burma and Vietnam: a brief survey.** N.Y., 1958. Historical account pointed toward contemporary trends.

O800. Devéria, Gabriel. **Histoire des relations de la Chine avec l'Annam-Viêtnam du XVIᵉ au XIXᵉ siècle, d'après des documents chinois.** Paris, 1880.

O801. Hoontrakul, Likhit. **The historical records of the Siamese-Chinese relations commencing from ancient times up to . . . [the establishment] of Sukhotai as capital.** Bangkok, 1953.

O802. Kuno, Yoshi S. **Japanese expansion on the Asiatic continent.** See *P238.*

O803. Tsunoda, Ryūsaku, tr. **Japan in the Chinese dynastic histories: later Han through Ming dynasties.** Ed. by L. Carrington Goodrich. So. Pasadena, Calif., 1951. Important collection of sources.

O804. Rockhill, William W. **China's intercourse with Korea from the XVth century to 1895.** See *N256.*

O805. Hirth, Friedrich. **China and the Roman Orient: researches into their ancient and mediaeval relations as represented in old Chinese records.** Shanghai, 1885.

O806. Laufer, Berthold. **Sino-Iranica: Chinese contributions to the history of civilization in ancient Iran.** Chicago, 1919.

O807. Boxer, Charles R. **Fidalgos in the Far East, 1550–1770.** The Hague, 1948. Account of Macao and Portuguese relations with China.

O808. Baddeley, John F. **Russia, Mongolia, China: being some record of the relations between them from the beginning of the XVIIth century to the death of the Tsar Alexei Mikhailovich, A.D. 1602–1676.** 2 v. London, 1919. The central work in its field.

O809. Cahen, Gaston. **Histoire des relations de la Russe avec la Chine sous Pierre le Grand (1689–1730).** Paris, 1911. English tr. by W. Shelden Ridge, Shanghai, 1914.

O810. Pavlovsky, Michel N. **Chinese-Russian relations.** N.Y., 1949.

O811. Ravenstein, Ernest G. **The Russians on the Amur.** London, 1861.

O812. Madrolle, Claudius. **Les premiers voyages français à la Chine . . . 1698–1719.** Paris, 1901.

O813. Pritchard, Earl H. **The crucial years of early Anglo-Chinese relations, 1750–1800.** Pullman, Wash., 1936.

O814. ——. **Anglo-Chinese relations during the seventeenth and eighteenth centuries.** Urbana, Ill., 1929.

O815. Eames, James B. **The English in China: being an account of the intercourse and relations between England and China from the year 1600 to the year 1843 and a summary of later developments.** London, 1909.

O816. Greenberg, Michael. **British trade and the opening of China, 1800–42.** Cambridge, Eng., 1951.

O817. Morse, Hosea B. **The chronicles of the East India Company, trading to China 1635–1834.** 5 v. Oxford, 1926–29. Vast repository of facts and statistical data on trade and diplomacy.

O818. Staunton, George. **An authentic account of an embassy from the king of Great Britain to the emperor of China.** 2 v. London, 1797.

O819. Latourette, Kenneth S. **The history of early relations between the United States and China, 1784–1844.** New Haven, 1917.

International Contacts:
Modern since 1833

O820. Levi, Werner. **Modern China's foreign policy.** Minneapolis, 1953. Useful interpretative volume.

O821. Bau, Mingchien J. **The foreign relations of China: a history and a survey.** Rev. ed., N.Y. and Chicago, 1922. Based largely on western sources.

O822. Teng, Ssu-yü, and John K. Fairbank. **China's response to the West: a documentary survey, 1839–1923.** Cambridge, Mass., 1954.

O823. MacNair, Harley F., ed. **Modern Chinese history: selected readings.** Shanghai, 1923.

O824. Hughes, Ernest R. **The invasion of China by the western world.** N.Y., 1938. Deals with the cultural effects.

O825. Morse, Hosea B. **The international relations of the Chinese empire.** 3 v. London, 1910–19. Still the best general survey.

O826. Cordier, Henri. **Histoire des relations de la Chine avec les puissances occidentales, 1860–1900.** 3 v. Paris, 1901–02. Emphasizes the French documents.

O827. Pollard, Robert T. **China's foreign relations, 1917–1931.** N.Y., 1933.

O828. **Treaties, conventions, etc. between China and foreign states.** 2nd ed., 2 v., Shanghai, 1917. A basic collection.

O829. Mayers, William F., ed. **Treaties between the empire of China and foreign powers.** 4th ed., Shanghai, 1902.

O830. MacMurray, John V. A. **Treaties and agreements with and concerning China, 1894–1919.** 2 v. N.Y., 1921.

O831. Carnegie Endowment for International Peace. **Treaties and agreements with and concerning China, 1919–1929.** Washington, 1929.

O832. Chiang [Tsiang], T'ing-fu. **Chin-tai Chung-kuo wai-chiao-shih tzu-liao ch'i-yao.** [A collection of essential sources of Chinese modern diplomatic history.] 2 v. Shanghai, 1931–34.

O833. **Ch'ou-pan i-wu shih-mo.** [Complete account of our management of barbarian affairs.] 260 chüan. Peiping, 1930. Official collection covering the period 1836–74.

O834. Wang, Yen-wei, and Wang Liang, eds. **Ch'ing-chi wai-chiao shih-lao.** [Chinese diplomatic documents of the end of the Ch'ing dynasty.] 164 ts'e. Peiping, 1932–35. Entire collection covers the Kuang-hsü (1875–1908) and Hsüan-t'ung (1909–11) periods.

O835. Hai-fang tang. [Maritime defense files.] 9 v. Taipei, 1957. For the period 1860–1911.

O836. Ch'ing Kuang-hsu-ch'ao Chung-Jih chiao-she shih-liao. [Historical materials on Sino-Japanese relations during the Kuang-hsü reign.] 44 ts'e. Peiping, 1932. Covers 1875–1908. Three more ts'e (Peiping, 1933) are on the period 1909–11.

O837. Ch'ing Kuang-hsü-ch'ao Chung-Fa chiao-she shih-liao. [Historical materials relating to Sino-French relations during the Kuang-hsü reign.] 22 chüan. Peiping, 1933.

O838. Pratt, Sir John T. **War and politics in China.** London, 1943. By a career diplomat who was British adviser on far eastern affairs from 1925 to 1938.

O839. Pelcovits, Nathan A. **Old China hands and the Foreign Office.** N.Y., 1948. Deals with conflict between British diplomats and business interests over policy.

O840. Costin, William C. **Great Britain and China, 1833–60.** Oxford, 1937. Detailed study based on British documents.

O841. Fox, Grace E. **British admirals and Chinese pirates, 1836–1869.** London, 1940. Careful study of the destruction of piracy on the China coast.

O842. Fairbank, John K. **Trade and diplomacy on the China coast: the opening of the treaty ports, 1842–1854.** 2 v. Cambridge, Mass., 1953.

O843. Callery, Joseph M. **Correspondance diplomatique chinoise.** Paris, 1879. Account of the Lagrené mission to China in 1844, by the ambassador's interpreter.

O844. Grosse-Aschhoff, A. F. S. **The negotiations between Ch'i-ying and Lagrené, 1844–48.** St. Bonaventure, N.Y., 1950.

O845. Wang, Shen-tsu. **The Margary affair and the Chefoo agreement.** London and N.Y., 1940.

O846. Kiernan, E. V. G. **British diplomacy in China, 1880–1885.** Cambridge, Eng., 1939.

O847. Joseph, Philip. **Foreign diplomacy in China, 1894–1900: a study in political and economic relations with China.** London, 1928.

O848. Friedman, Irving S. **British relations with China, 1931–1939.** N.Y., 1940.

O849. Stoecker, Helmuth. **Deutschland und China im 19. Jahrhundert.** Berlin, 1958. Deals with German economic penetration of China from a Communist point of view. Filled with factual detail.

O850. Djang, F. D. **The diplomatic relations between China and Germany since 1898.** Shanghai, 1936.

O851. Fairbank, John K. **The United States and China.** Cambridge, Mass., 1948.

O852. Dulles, Foster R. **China and America: the story of their relations since 1784.** Princeton, 1946.

O853. Clyde, Paul H., ed. **United States policy toward China: diplomatic and public documents, 1839–1939.** Durham, 1940.

O854. Swisher, Earl, tr. and ed. **China's management of the American barbarians: a study of Sino-American relations, 1841–1861, with documents.** New Haven, 1953.

Translation of materials from the *Ch'ou-pan i-wu shih-mo.*

O855. U. S. Department of State. **United States relations with China, with special reference to the period 1944–1949.** Washington, 1949.

O856. Varg, Paul A. **Open door diplomat: the life of W. W. Rockhill.** Urbana, 1952.

O857. Stimson, Henry L. **The far eastern crisis: recollections and observations.** N.Y. and London, 1936. The Manchurian incident of 1931–32.

O858. Reinsch, Paul S. **An American diplomat in China.** N.Y. and Toronto, 1922. Memoir of the U. S. minister to China, 1913–19.

O859. Stilwell, Joseph W. **The Stilwell papers.** Ed. by Theodore H. White. N.Y., 1948. Diary of his conflict with Chiang.

O860. Feis, Herbert. **The China tangle.** Princeton, 1953. Best available study of U. S. policy toward China from Pearl Harbor to the Marshall mission.

O861. Tchen, Hoshien. **Les relations diplomatiques entre la Chine et le Japon de 1871 à nos jours.** Paris, 1921.

O862. Lévy, Roger B. **Relations de la Chine et du Japon.** Paris, 1938.

O863. Royal Institute of International Affairs. **China and Japan.** 3rd ed., London and N.Y., 1941.

O864. Akagi, Roy H. **Japan's foreign relations, 1542–1936.** Tokyo, 1936.

O865. Cheng, Tien-fong. **A history of Sino-Russian relations.** Washington, 1957.

O866. Wu, Aitchen K. **China and the Soviet Union.** London, 1950. Covers the period of Sino-Soviet relations.

O867. Weigh, Ken Shen. **Russo-Chinese diplomacy.** Shanghai, 1928. By an official of the Chinese foreign office.

O868. Malozemoff, Andrew. **Russian far eastern policy, 1881–1904.** Berkeley, 1958.

O869. Whiting, Allen S. **Soviet policies in China, 1917–1924.** N.Y., 1954.

O870. Tang, Peter S. H. **Russian and Soviet policy in Manchuria and Outer Mongolia, 1911–1931.** Durham, 1959.

O871. Willoughby, Westel W. **Foreign rights and interests in China.** 2nd ed., 2 v., Baltimore, 1927. Standard encyclopedic work.

O872. Keeton, George W. **The development of extraterritoriality in China.** 2 v. London and N.Y., 1928. A thorough, well-documented work.

O873. Fishel, Wesley R. **The end of extraterritoriality in China.** Berkeley, 1952.

O874. Wright, Stanley F. **China's struggle for tariff autonomy, 1843–1938.** Shanghai, 1938. Comprehensive, well-documented study.

O875. Remer, Charles F. **Foreign investments in China.** N.Y., 1933. An outstanding work.

O876. ——. **A study of Chinese boycotts.** Baltimore, 1933.

O877. MacNair, Harley F. **The Chinese abroad.** Shanghai, 1924.

O878. Purcell, Victor. **The Chinese in southeast Asia.** See *Q17.*

O879. Skinner, George W. **Leadership and power in the Chinese community of Thailand.** Ithaca, 1958.

See also subsections dealing with the Ch'ing period, the republic, the Communists, and with Christianity in China.

Influence of China on the West

O880. Bodde, Derk. **China's gift to the West.** Washington, 1942. [Asiatic studies in American education.]

O881. Chu, Ch'ien-chih. **Chung-kuo ssu-hsiang tui-yü Ou-chou wen-hua chih ying-hsiang.** [Influence of Chinese thought on European culture.] Shanghai, 1940.

O882. Pouzyna, I. V. **La Chine, l'Italie et les débuts de la Renaissance.** Paris, 1935. Carefully documented and illustrated; deals with 13th and 14th centuries.

O883. Reichwein, Adolf. **China und Europa.** Berlin, 1923. English ed., N.Y. and London, 1925. Study of intellectual and artistic contacts during the 18th century.

O884. Maverick, Lewis A. **China, a model for Europe.** San Antonio, Tex., 1946.

O885. Sirén, Osvald. **China and gardens of Europe of the eighteenth century.** N.Y., 1950.

O886. Von Erdberg, Eleanor. **Chinese influence on European garden structures.** Cambridge, Mass., 1936.

O887. Belevitch-Stankevitch, H. **Le goût chinois en France au temps de Louis XIV.** Paris, 1910.

O888. Pinot, Virgile. **La Chine et la formation de l'esprit philosophique en France.** Paris, 1932.

O889. ——. **Documents inédits relatifs à la connaissance de la Chine en France de 1685 à 1740.** Paris, 1932.

O890. Lach, Donald F. "China and the era of the enlightenment." **Journal of modern history,** 14 (June 1942): 209–23.

O891. ——. "Leibnitz and China." **Journal of the history of ideas,** 6 (Oct. 1945): 436–55.

O892. ——. "The Sinophilism of Christian Wolff (1679–1754)." **Jour. hist. of ideas,** 14 (Oct. 1953): 561–74.

O893. Tscharner, Eduard H. von. **China in der deutschen Dichtung.** Darmstadt, 1934.

O894. Selden, Elizabeth S. **China in German poetry from 1773 to 1883.** Berkeley, 1942.

O895. Ch'en, Shou-yi. "Sino-European cultural contacts since the discovery of the sea route." **Nankai social and economic quarterly,** 8 (Apr. 1935): 44–74.

O896. ——. "Daniel Defoe, China's severe critic." **Nankai soc. 'and eco. quar.,** 8 (Oct. 1935): 511–51.

O897. Appleton, William W. **A cycle of Cathay: the Chinese vogue in England during the seventeenth and eighteenth centuries.** N.Y., 1951. A careful work.

O898. Teng, Ssu-yü. "Chinese influence on the western examination system." **Harvard journal of Asiatic studies,** 7 (Sep. 1943): 267–312.

O899. Chang, Y. Z. "China and English civil service reforms." **Am. hist. rev.,** 47 (Apr. 1942): 539–44.

O900. Danton, George H. **The culture contacts of the United States and China . . . 1784–1844.** N.Y., 1931.

O901. Mason, Mary G. **Western concepts of China and the Chinese, 1840–76.** N.Y., 1939.

O902. Barthold, Vasilii V. **La découverte de l'Asie.** Tr. by B. Nikitine. Paris, 1947.

O903. Schwab, Raymond. **La renaissance orientale.** Paris, 1950. Effects of Asia on Europe, particularly in the 19th century.

O904. Lubac, Henri de. **La rencontre du Bouddhisme et de l'Occident.** Paris, 1952.

Law, Political Institutions, and Education

For laws and institutions of particular periods see the appropriate special period. See also subsection on China in Section G.

O905. U. S. Bureau of Foreign and Domestic Commerce. **"Finding list": bibliography of modern Chinese law in Library of Congress.** Washington, 1944. Contains items in Chinese and western languages.

O906. Sun, Tsu-chi. **Chung-kuo li-tai fa-chia chu-shu k'ao.** [Descriptive bibliography on Chinese law.] Shanghai, 1934.

O907. Cheng, Ching-i. **Fa-lü ta-tz'u shu.** [A dictionary of legal terms.] 3 v. Shanghai, 1936.

O908. Escarra, Jean. **Le droit chinois: conception et évolution, institutions législatives et judiciaires, science et enseignement.** Peiping, 1936.

O909. Cheng, F. T. "A sketch of the history, philosophy and reform of Chinese law." Foreign Law Society, **Studies of law in the Far East and southeast Asia** (Washington, 1956), pp. 29–45.

O910. Ch'eng, Shu-te. **Chiu-ch'ao lü-k'ao.** [A study of Chinese law from Han to Sui.] 2 v. Shanghai, 1927.

O911. Ch'en, Ku-yüan. **Chung-kuo fa-chih-shih.** [History of Chinese law and statutes.] Shanghai, 1935.

O912. Yang, Hung-lieh. **Chung-kuo fa-lü-fa-ta shih.** [History of the development of Chinese law, with a comparative table of codes in China.] 2 v. Shanghai, 1930.

O913. Chu, Tung-tsu. **Law and society in traditional China.** N.Y., 1959.

O914. Chi, Yün, and others. **Li-tai chih-kuan piao.** [Tables of official titles of the successive dynasties.] 8 v. Shanghai, 1936. The only comprehensive work which presents comparative data on the official titles during different dynasties. Compiled about 1780; has been reprinted several times.

O915. Wist, Hans. **Das chinesische Zensorat.** Hamburg, 1932.

O916. Walker, Richard L. "The control system of the Chinese government." **Far eastern quarterly,** 7 (Nov. 1947): 3–21.

O917. Kao, I-han. **Chung-kuo Yü-shih chih-tu ti yen-ko.** [Institutions of the censorate of China.] Shanghai, 1934.

O918. ——. **Chung-kuo nei-ko chih-tu ti yen-ko.** [The institutions of the grand secretariat.] Shanghai, 1933.

O919. Li, Chün. **Chung-kuo tsai-hsiang chih-tu.** [A history of the system of prime ministers in China.] Shanghai, 1947.

O920. Sheng, Lang-hsi. **Chung-kuo shu-yüan chih-tu.** [The institution of the Chinese academy.] Shanghai, 1934. Deals with academies from the Sung through Ming periods.

O921. Biot, Edouard. **Essai sur l'histoire de l'instruction publique en Chine et de la corporation des lettres.** 2 v. in 1. Paris, 1845–47.

O922. Kuo, Ping-wen. **The Chinese system of public education.** N.Y., 1915. Inadequate, but the only historical account in English.

Economic History and Conditions

O923. Kirby, E. Stuart. **Introduction to the economic history of China.** London, 1954. Based heavily on the views of Japanese writers.

O924. Chi, Ch'ao-ting. **Key economic areas in Chinese history, as revealed in the development of public works for water-control.** London, 1936.

O925. Wittfogel, Karl A. **Wirtschaft und Gesellschaft Chinas.** Leipzig, 1931.

O926. Sun, E-tu Zen, and John F. De Francis, trs. and eds. **Chinese social history.** Washington, 1956. Translation of 25 articles by modern Chinese scholars on various aspects of Chinese social and economic history.

O927. Ma, Ch'eng-feng. **Chung-kuo ching-chi shih.** [Economic history of China.] 2 v. Shanghai, 1937.

O928. Hou, Hou-p'ei. **Chung-kuo chin-tai ching-chi fa-chan-shih.** [History of the economic development of modern China.] Shanghai, 1932. A rather sketchy survey lacking documentary support.

O929. Chen, Huan-Chang. **The economic principles of Confucius and his school.** N.Y., 1911.

O930. Lee, Mabel Ping-hua. **The economic history of China, with special reference to agriculture.** N.Y., 1921.

O931. Yang, Lien-sheng. **Money and credit in China, a short history.** Cambridge, Mass., 1952.

O932. Vissering, Willem. **On Chinese currency: coin and paper money.** Leiden, 1877.

O933. Vissering, Gerard. **On Chinese currency.** 2 v. Amsterdam, 1912–14.

O934. Cheng, Yu-kwei. **Foreign trade and industrial development of China: an historical and integrated analysis through 1948.** Washington, 1956.

O935. Tawney, Richard H. **Land and labour in China.** London, 1932.

O936. Mallory, Walter H. **China: land of famine.** N.Y., 1926.

O937. King, Franklin H. **Farmers of forty centuries.** N.Y., 1926.

O938. Arnold, Julean H. **China: a commercial and industrial handbook.** Washington, 1926.

O939. Hommel, Rudolf P. **China at work.** N.Y., 1937.

See also subsections on geography, anthropology and sociology, demography, and the various special periods; and subsection on China in Section G.

Religion

O940. Chan, Wing-tsit. "Buddhist terminology." Vergilius T. A. Ferm, ed., **An encyclopedia of religion** (N.Y., 1945), pp. 91–110.

O941. ——. "Chinese terminology." **An encyclopedia of religion,** pp. 145–58.

O942. Hodous, Lewis. **Folkways in China.** London, 1929.

O943. Harvey, Edwin D. **The mind of China.** New Haven, 1933. Deals with animism and popular religious sects and practices.

O944. Chavannes, Edouard. **Le T'ai Chan: essai de monographie d'un culte chinois.** Paris, 1910. Remains the most comprehensive and adequate monograph on the Sacred Peak of the East, in Shantung province.

O945. Shryock, John K. **The temples of Anking and their cults: a study in modern Chinese religion.** Paris, 1931.

O946. Alexéiev, Basil M. **The Chinese god of wealth.** London, 1928.

O947. Groot, Jan J. M. de. **Sectarianism and religious persecution in China.** 2 v. Amsterdam, 1903–04. Well documented with translations from Chinese sources.

O948. Ch'en, Kenneth. "Anti-Buddhist propaganda during the Nan-ch'ao." **Harvard journal of Asiatic studies,** 15 (June 1952): 166–92.

O949. ——. "On some factors responsible for the anti-Buddhist persecutions under

the Pei-ch'ao." **Harvard jour. Asiatic stud.,** 17 (June 1954): 261–73.

O950. ——. "The economic background of the Hui-chang suppression of Buddhism." **Harvard jour. Asiatic stud.,** 19 (June 1956): 67–105.

O951. **Tao tsang.** [The Taoist canon.] Compiled ca. 1445; supplemented 1605. Reprint, 1120 ts'e, Shanghai, 1924–26.

O952. Mueller, Herbert. "Uber das taoistische Pantheon der Chinesen seine Grundlagen und seine historische Entwickelung." **Zeitschrift für Ethnologie,** 43 (1911): 393–428.

O953. Yetts, W. Perceval. "The eight immortals." **Journal of the Royal Asiatic Society,** (Oct. 1916): 773–807.

O954. ——. "More notes on the eight immortals." **Jour. Royal Asiatic Soc.,** (July 1922): 397–426.

O955. Imbault-Huart, Camille C. **La légende du premier pape des Taoistes et l'histoire de la famille pontificale des Tchang.** Paris, 1885.

O956. Ch'en, Hung-shun. "The Taoist press in China." Catholic Church in China, **Collectanea Commissionis Synodalis,** 11 (May 1938): 484–97.

O957. Wright, Arthur F. **Buddhism in Chinese history.** Stanford, 1959. Excellent survey.

O958. Johnston, Reginald F. **Buddhist China.** N.Y., 1913.

O959. Grousset, René. **In the footsteps of the Buddha.** London, 1932.

O960. Soothill, William E., and Lewis Hodous. **A dictionary of Chinese Buddhist terms, with Sanskrit and English equivalents and a Sanskrit-Pali index.** London, 1937.

O961. Eitel, Ernest J. **Hand-book of Chinese Buddhism: being a Sanskrit-Chinese dictionary with vocabularies of Buddhist terms in Pali, Singhalese, Siamese, Burmese, Tibetan, Mongolian and Japanese.** 2nd ed., Tokyo, 1904.

O962. Kao, Kuan-Ju, and others. **Fo hsüeh tz'u tien.** [Buddhist dictionary.] 2nd ed., 4 v., Shanghai, 1935.

O963. Ting, Fu-pao. **Fo-hsüeh ta-tz'u-tien.** [Dictionary of Buddhist terms.] 2nd ed., 16 ts'e, Shanghai, 1925.

O964. **Taishō shinshu daizōkyō. The tripitaka in Chinese.** Rev. by Takakusu Junjiro and Watanabe Kaigyoku. 85 v. Tokyo, 1924–34. This edition includes various supplementary works, and there is also a catalog of Buddhist literature, *Shōwa hobo sōmokuroku* (3 v.).

O965. Bagchi, Prabodh C. **Le canon bouddhique et Chine: les traducteurs et les traductions.** 2 v. Paris, 1927–38.

O966. Tao-shih. **Fa-yüan chu-lin.** [T'ang Buddhist encyclopedia.] 36 ts'e. Shanghai, 1929.

O967. Groot, Jan J. M. de. **Le code du Mahâyâna en Chine: son influence sur la vie monacale et sur le monde laïque.** Amsterdam, 1893.

O968. Chavannes, Edouard, tr. **Cinq cents contes et apologues extraits du Tripiṭaka chinois.** 4 v. Paris, 1910–34.

O969. Texts from the Buddhist canon, commonly known as Dhammapada. Tr. by S. Beal. London, 1878.

O970. The lotus of the wonderful law. Tr. by William E. Soothill. Oxford, 1930.

O971. Ashvaghosa's awakening of faith in the Mahayana doctrine. Tr. by Teitaro Suzuki, Chicago, 1900.

O972. The diamond sutra (Chin-kang-chin) or Prajna-paramita. Tr. by William Gemmel. London, 1912.

O973. Vasubandhu. **Wei-shih er-shih lun . . . or, the treatise in twenty stanzas on representation—only.** Tr. by Clarence H. Hamilton. New Haven, 1938.

O974. Le sutra des causes et des effets du bien et du mal, édité et traduit d'après les textes sogdien, chinois et tibétain. 3 fasc. Paris, 1920–28. [Mission Pelliot en Asie centrale, 2.]

O975. Pelliot, Paul. **Les grottes de Touen-houang: peintures et sculptures bouddhiques des époques des Wei, des T'ang et des Song.** 6 fasc. Paris, 1920–24. [Mission Pelliot en Asie centrale, 1.]

See also the various special periods in this section, subsections on Buddhism and Religions of China in Section D, and subsection on China in Section G.

Christianity and Other Western Religions in China

O976. Latourette, Kenneth S. **A history of Christian missions in China.** N.Y., 1929.

O977. Cary-Elwes, Columbia. **China and the cross: a survey of missionary history.** N.Y. and London, 1957.

O978. Elia, Pasquale M. d'. **The Catholic missions in China.** Shanghai, 1934. A short sketch from early times to the 1930's.

O979. Moule, Arthur C. **Christians in China before the year 1550.** London, 1930.

O980. Ghellinck, Joseph de. **Les Francis-cains en Chine au XIIIᵉ et XIVᵉ siècles.** 2 v. Louvain, 1927.

O981. Les voyages en Asie au XIVᵉ siècle du bienheureux frère Odoric de Pordenone, religieux de Saint-François. Ed. by Henri Cordier. Paris, 1891.

O982. Huc, Evariste R. **Le Christianisme en Chine, en Tartarie et au Thibet.** 4 v. Paris, 1857–58.

O983. Bernard, Henri. **Aux portes de la Chine: les missionnaires du seizième siècle, 1514–1588.** Tientsin, 1933.

O984. Rowbotham, Arnold H. **Missionary and Mandarin: the Jesuits at the court of China.** Berkeley, 1942. Despite some errors, probably the best general account of missions in China during the 17th and 18th centuries.

O985. Thomas, A. **Histoire de la mission de Pékin, depuis les origines jusqu'à l'arrivée des Lazaristes.** 2 v. Paris, 1923–25.

O986. Brou, Alexandre. **Cent ans de missions, 1815–1934.** Paris, 1935. Deals with last century of the Jesuit mission in China.

O987. Pfister, Louis. **Notices biographiques et bibliographiques sur les Jésuites de l'ancienne mission de Chine, 1552–1773.** 2 v. Shanghai, 1932–34.

O988. Cronin, Vincent. **The wise man from the West.** N.Y., 1955. Deals with Matteo Ricci.

O989. Väth, Alfons. **Johann Adam Schall von Bell, S.J., Missionar in China.** Cologne, 1933.

O990. Verbiest, Ferdinand. **Correspondance de Ferdinand Verbiest.** Ed. by Henri Josson and Leopold Willaert. Brussels, 1938.

O991. Wessels, Cornelius. **Early Jesuit travellers in central Asia, 1603–1721.** The Hague, 1924.

O992. Rosso, Antonio S. **Apostolic legations to China of the eighteenth century.** South Pasadena, Calif., 1948. Reviews history of Catholic missions prior to the embassies of the early 18th century.

O993. Jenkins, Robert C. **The Jesuits in China and the legation of Cardinal de Tournon.** London, 1894.

O994. Ripa, Matteo. **Memoirs of Father Ripa during thirteen years' residence at the court of Peking.** Tr. by Fortunato Prandi. London, 1844.

O995. Brandt, Joseph van den. **Les Lazaristes en Chine, 1697–1935.** Peiping, 1936. Biographical notes on some 964 Lazarist missionaries.

O996. Willeke, Bernward H. **Imperial government and Catholic missions in China during the years 1784–1785.** St. Bonaventure, N.Y., 1948.

O997. Varg, Paul A. **Missionaries, Chinese and diplomats: the American Protestant missionary movement in China, 1890–1952.** Princeton, 1958.

O998. Broomhall, Marshall. **Robert Morrison, a master-builder.** London, 1924.

O999. Taylor, F. Howard. **Hudson Taylor and the China Inland Mission.** London, 1918.

O1000. Soothill, William E. **Timothy Richard of China, seer, statesman, missionary and the most disinterested adviser the Chinese ever had.** London, 1924.

O1001. China Continuation Committee. **The Christian occupation of China: a general survey of the numerical strength and geographical distribution of the Christian forces in China.** Ed. by Milton T. Stauffer. Shanghai, 1922.

O1002. Lacy, Walter N. **A hundred years of Chinese Methodism.** Nashville, 1948.

O1003. Saeki, P. Y. **The Nestorian documents and relics in China.** Tokyo, 1937. Contains Chinese texts.

O1004. White, William C., comp. **Chinese Jews: a compilation of matters relating to the Jews of K'aifeng Fu.** 3 v. Toronto, 1942.

O1005. Chavannes, Edouard, and Paul Pelliot, trs. "Un traité manichéen retrouvé en Chine." *Journal asiatique*, 10th ser., 18 (Nov.-Dec. 1911): 499–617; 11th ser., 1 (Jan-Feb. 1913): 99–199; 11th ser., 1 (Mar.-Apr. 1913): 261–394.

O1006. Pickens, Claude L. **Annotated bibliography of literature on Islam in China.** Hankow, 1950.

O1007. Broomhall, Marshall. **Islam in China.** London, 1910.

O1008. Ollone, Henri M. G. d', and others. **Recherches sur les Musulmans chinois.** Paris, 1911.

O1009. Vissière, Arnold J. A. **Études sino-mahométanes.** 2 v. Paris, 1911–13.

O1010. **China mission year book.** Shanghai, 1910–39. From 1926 to 1939 this annual was known as *China Christian year book*.

Thought

For the thought and thinkers of particular periods see the appropriate special periods above; for early Chinese thought see subsection on China in Section G.

O1011. Chan, Wing-Tsit. **An outline and an annotated bibliography of Chinese philosophy.** New Haven, 1959.

O1012. Chan, Wing-Tsit. **Historical charts of Chinese philosophy.** New Haven, 1955.

O1013. Fung [Feng], Yu-lan. **A short history of Chinese philosophy.** Ed. by Derk Bodde. N.Y., 1948.

O1014. ——. **A history of Chinese philosophy.** Tr. by Derk Bodde. 2 v. Princeton, 1952–53.

O1015. ——. **The spirit of Chinese philosophy.** Tr. by E. R. Hughes. London, 1947.

O1016. Creel, Herrlee G. **Chinese thought.** See *G198*.

O1017. Forke, Alfred. **Geschichte der mittelalterlichen chinesischen Philosophie.** Hamburg, 1934.

O1018. ——. **Geschichte der neueren chinesischen Philosophie.** Hamburg, 1938.

O1019. Chung, T'ai. **Chung-kuo che-hsüeh-shih.** [History of Chinese philosophy.] Shanghai, 1929.

O1020. Lin, Mou-sheng. **Men and ideas: an informal history of Chinese political thought.** N.Y., 1942.

O1021. Hsiao, Kung-ch'üan. **Chung-kuo cheng-chih ssu-hsiang shih.** [History of Chinese political thought.] 5 v. Chungking, 1945.

O1022. Ts'ai, Yüan-p'ei. **Chung-kuo lun-li-hsüeh shih.** [A history of Chinese ethics.] Shanghai, 1921.

O1023. Levenson, Joseph R. **Confucian China and its modern fate: the problem of intellectual continuity.** Berkeley, 1958.

O1024. Wright, Arthur F., ed. **Studies in Chinese thought.** Chicago, 1953. Nine studies by various scholars.

O1025. Fairbank, John K., ed. **Chinese thought and institutions.** Chicago, 1957. Collection of articles by specialists.

O1026. Nivison, David S., and Arthur F. Wright, eds. **Confucianism in action.** Stanford, 1959. Articles dealing with effects of Confucian ideas on Chinese institutions at various periods.

Literature and Music

For the literature of particular periods see the appropriate special period above; for early literature see subsection on China in Section G.

O1027. Hightower, James R. **Topics in Chinese literature: outlines and bibliographies.** Rev. ed., Cambridge, Mass., 1953. Valuable guide to study of Chinese literature.

O1028. Giles, Herbert A. **A history of Chinese literature.** London and N.Y., 1901. Paperback reprint, 1958. Antiquated and inadequate, but the only general history in English except for *O1036*.

O1029. ——. **Gems of Chinese literature.** 2nd ed., 2 v., London, 1923.

O1030. Margouliès, Georges. **Histoire de la littérature chinoise.** 2 v. Paris, 1949–51.

O1031. ——. **Evolution de la prose artistique chinoise.** Munich, 1929.

O1032. ——. **Anthologie raisonnée de la littérature chinoise.** Paris, 1948.

O1033. Boven, Henri van. **Histoire de la littérature chinoise moderne.** Peiping, 1946.

O1034. Alexéiev, Basil M. **La littérature chinoise.** Paris, 1937.

O1035. Nagasawa, Kikuya. **Geschichte der chinesischen Literatur und ihrer gedanklichen Grundlage.** Tr. by Eugen Feifel. Peiping, 1945.

O1036. Feng, Yüan-chün. **A short history of classical Chinese literature.** Peiping, 1958. Traditional Chinese literature as viewed in Communist China.

O1037. Cheng, Chen-to. **Chung-kuo wen-hsüeh shih.** [Illustrated history of Chinese literature.] 4 v. Peiping, 1932.

O1038. Jung, Chao-tsu. **Chung-kuo wen-hsüeh-shih ta-kang.** [Outline history of Chinese literature.] Peiping, 1935.

O1039. Payne, P. S. Robert, comp. **The white pony: an anthology of Chinese poetry from the earliest times to the present day.** N.Y., 1947; London, 1949. Excellent anthology of translations done by modern Chinese in collaboration with Payne.

O1040. Hsü, Sung-nien, comp. and tr. **Anthologie de la littérature chinoise des origines à nos jours.** Paris, 1933.

O1041. Waley, Arthur, tr. **A hundred and seventy Chinese poems.** N.Y., 1919. Contains an introduction on Chinese poetry and its historical development.

O1042. ——, tr. **More translations from the Chinese.** N.Y., 1919.

O1043. ——, tr. **The temple and other poems.** N.Y., 1923.

O1044. ——, tr. **Translations from the Chinese.** N.Y., 1941.

O1045. Arlington, Lewis C. **The Chinese drama from the earliest times until to-day.** Shanghai, 1930.

O1046. Scott, Adolphe C. **The classical theatre of China.** N.Y., 1957.

O1047. Zung, Cecilia S. L. **Secrets of the Chinese drama.** Shanghai, 1937. A guide to action and symbols, and a synopsis of 50 popular plays with illustrations.

O1048. Chou, I-pai. **Chung-kuo hsi-chü shih.** [History of Chinese drama.] 3 v. Shanghai, 1953.

O1049. Hsü, Mu-yün. **Chung-kuo hsi-chü shih.** [History of Chinese drama.] Shanghai, 1938.

O1050. Arlington, Lewis C., and Harold Acton, trs. and eds. **Famous Chinese plays.** Peiping, 1937.

O1051. Ou, Itaï [Wu I-t'ai]. **Essai critique et bibliographique sur le roman chinois.** Paris, 1933.

O1052. Kuo, Chên-i. **Chung-kuo hsiao-shuo shih.** [History of Chinese fiction.] 2 v. Shanghai, 1939.

O1053. Lu, Hsün. **Chung-kuo hsiao-shuo shih-lüeh.** [A brief history of the Chinese novel.] Shanghai, 1942 Eng. tr. Peiping, 1959.

O1054. Eberhard, Wolfram. **Die chinesische Novelle des 17.–19. Jahrhunderts: eine soziologische Untersuchung.** Bern, 1948.

O1055. Wang, Chi-chen, tr. **Traditional Chinese tales.** N.Y., 1944. Selections from 6th to 16th century.

O1056. Lin, Yu-t'ang, tr. **Famous Chinese short stories.** N.Y., 1952.

O1057. Yang, Hsien-yi, and Gladys Yang, trs. **The courtesan's jewel box: Chinese stories of the Xth–XVIIth centuries.** Peiping, 1957. Twenty short stories, the largest group being from the Ming dynasty.

O1058. Courant, Maurice. **Essai historique sur la musique classique des Chinois, avec un appendice relatif à la musique coréenne.** Paris, 1912.

O1059. Liu, Ch'eng-fu. **Yin-yüeh tz'u-tien.** [A dictionary of musical terms.] Shanghai, 1935.

O1060. T'an, Cheng-pi. **Chung-kuo wen-hsüeh-chia ta-tz'u-tien.** [Biographies of nearly seven hundred literary figures.] Shanghai, 1934.

Art

For the art of particular periods see the appropriate special period above; for early art see subsection on China in Section G.

O1061. Guest, Grace D., and Archibald G. Wenley. **Annotated outlines of the history of Chinese arts.** Washington, 1949.

O1062. Hansford, S. Howard. **A glossary of Chinese art and archaeology.** London, 1954.

O1063. March, Benjamin F. **Some technical terms of Chinese painting.** Baltimore, 1935.

O1064. Carter, Dagny. **Four thousand years of China's art.** N.Y., 1948. Rev. print, 1951. A good popular history.

O1065. Silcock, Arnold. **Introduction to Chinese art and history.** London, 1947; N.Y., 1948.

O1066. Sickman, Laurence C. S., and Alexander Soper. **The art and architecture of China.** Baltimore, 1956. The best general survey.

O1067. Bachhofer, Ludwig. **A short history of Chinese art.** N.Y., 1946; London, 1947.

O1068. Encyclopaedia Britannica. **The romance of Chinese art.** N.Y., 1936. Well illustrated articles on all aspects of Chinese art by R. L. Hobson, Lawrence Binyon, Osvald Sirén, and others.

O1069. Ferguson, John C. **Survey of Chinese art.** Shanghai, 1939. Includes sections and illustrations on bronzes, stone monuments, calligraphy, painting, jades, ceramics, architecture, furniture, textiles, and miscellaneous.

O1070. Illustrated catalogue of Chinese government exhibits for the international exhibition of Chinese art in London. 4 v. Shanghai, 1936. Deals with bronzes, porcelains, painting and calligraphy, and miscellaneous.

O1071. Hobson, Robert L. **Chinese art: one hundred plates in colour reproducing pottery and porcelain of all periods, jades, lacquer, paintings, bronzes, furniture, etc.** London and N.Y., 1927. 2nd rev. ed., 1952.

O1072. Boerschmann, Ernst. **Chinesische Architektur.** 2 v. Berlin, 1925.

O1073. Itō, Chūta. **Architectural decoration in China.** Tr. by Jiro Harada. 3 v. Tokyo, 1941–42.

O1074. Li, Chieh. **Yin-tsao fa-shih.** [Methods of architectural construction.] 1103. Facsimile reproduction, 8 v., Shanghai, 1928. The most celebrated technical treatise on Chinese architecture. Review, P. Demiéville, *Bulletin de l'École Française d'Extrême-Orient,* 25 (Jan.-June 1925): 213.

O1075. Sirén, Osvald. **Gardens of China.** N.Y., 1949.

O1076. Ashton, Leigh. **An introduction to the study of Chinese sculpture.** London, 1924.

O1077. Fischer, Otto. **Chinesische Plastik.** Munich, 1948.

O1078. Sirén, Osvald. **Chinese sculpture from the fifth to the fourteenth century.** 4 v. London, 1925.

O1079. Waley, Arthur. **An introduction to the study of Chinese painting, 600 B.C. to the western Renaissance.** N.Y., 1923. Reprint, 1958.

O1080. Chiang, Yee. **The Chinese eye: an interpretation of Chinese painting.** 4th ed., London, 1956.

O1081. ——. **Chinese calligraphy.** London, 1938. 2nd ed., Cambridge, Mass., 1958.

O1082. Sirén, Osvald. **The history of early Chinese painting.** 2 v. London, 1933.

O1083. ——. **A history of later Chinese painting.** 2 v. London, 1938.

O1084. ——. **Chinese painting: leading masters and principles.** 3 v. N.Y. and London, 1956.

O1085. ——. **The Chinese on the art of printing: translations and comments.** Peiping, 1936.

O1086. Wang, Kai. **The tao of painting . . . with a translation of the Chieh-tzu-yüan hua-chüan, or Mustard seed garden manual of painting, 1679–1701.** Tr. by Sze Mai-mai. 2 v. N.Y., 1956.

O1087. Petrucci, Raphael, tr. and ed. **Kiai-tseu-yuan houa tchouan: . . . encyclopédie de la peinture chinoise.** Paris, 1918.

O1088. Ferguson, John C. **Li-tai chu lu hua mu.** [Catalog of paintings of the successive dynasties.] 6 v. Nanking, 1934. Catalogs of paintings by 1,700 artists as recorded in literature.

O1089. Cheng, Chen-to. **Chung-kuo pan-hua shih.** [A history of Chinese woodcuts.] 24 ts'e. Shanghai, 1940.

O1090. Yü, Shao-sung. **Shu-hua shu-lu chieh-t'i.** [Annotated bibliography of works on calligraphy and painting.] 6 v. Peiping, 1932. Deals with some 860 works.

O1091. Sun, Ta-kung. **Chung-kuo hua-chia jen-ing ta-tz'u-tien.** [Biographical dictionary of Chinese painters.] Shanghai, 1934.

O1092. P'eng, Yün-ts'an. **Li-tai hua-shih-hui chüan.** [Biographies of painters of all epochs.] 24 ts'e. Shanghai, 1882.

O1093. Jenyns, R. Soame. **Ming pottery and porcelain.** London, 1953.

O1094. ——. **Later Chinese porcelain: the Ch'ing dynasty, 1644–1912.** London, 1951.

O1095. Hobson, Robert L., and Arthur L. Hetherington. **The art of the Chinese potter from the Han dynasty to the end of the Ming.** London and N.Y., 1923.

O1096. Hobson, Robert L. **The later ceramic wares of China.** London, 1925.

O1097. ——. **Chinese pottery and porcelain.** 2 v. London, 1915.

O1098. Laufer, Berthold. **Jade: a study in Chinese archaeology and religion.** Chicago, 1912. 2nd ed., South Pasadena, 1946.

O1099. Nott, Stanley C. **Chinese jade throughout the ages.** London, 1936.

O1100. Priest, Alan, and Pauline Simmons. **Chinese textiles: an introduction to the study of their history, sources, technique, symbolism and use.** N.Y., 1934.

O1101. Kann, Eduard. **Illustrated catalog of Chinese coins.** Los Angeles, 1954.

Science, Medicine, and Technology

For early Chinese science see subsection on China in Section G.

O1102. Needham, Joseph, and Wang Ling. **Science and civilization in China.** Cambridge, Eng., 1954 ff. Three of the seven projected volumes of this monumental work have appeared. The last five are to concentrate on science in China, but total range of all volumes covers many aspects of Chinese history and ideas.

O1103. Mikami, Yoshio. **The development of mathematics in China and Japan.** Leipzig, 1913.

O1104. Saussure, Léopold de. **Les origines de l'astronomie chinoise.** Paris, 1930. Reproduction of earlier articles in *T'oung pao.*

O1105. Li, Ch'iao-p'ing. **The chemical arts of old China.** Easton, Pa., 1948.

O1106. Merrill, Elmer D., and Egbert H. Walker. **A bibliography of eastern Asiatic botany.** Jamaica Plain, Mass., 1938.

O1107. Bretschneider, Emil V. **Botanicon sinicum: notes on Chinese botany from native and western sources.** 3 v. Tokyo, 1937.

O1108. Young, T. I. (Yang Tsun-i). **Bibliography of Chinese geology up to 1934.** Peiping, 1935.

O1109. Huebotter, Franz. **A guide through the labyrinth of Chinese medical writers and medical writings: a bibliographical sketch.** Kumamoto, Japan, 1924.

O1110. Huard, Pierre A., and Ming Wong. **La médecine chinoise au cours des siècles.** Paris, 1959.

O1111. Hume, Edward H. **The Chinese way in medicine.** Baltimore, 1940.

O1112. Wong, K. Chimin, and Wu Lien-teh. **History of Chinese medicine: being a chronicle of medical happenings in China from ancient times to the present period.** 2nd ed., Shanghai, 1936.

O1113. Hsieh, Kuan. **Chung-kuo i-hsüeh ta-tz'u-tien.** [Encyclopedia of Chinese medicine.] Rev. ed., 2 v., Shanghai, 1933. A dictionary of over 70,000 medical terms with biographies of doctors and notes on medical books.

O1114. Ch'en, Ts'un-jen. **Chung-kuo yao-hsüeh ta-tz'u-tien.** [A pharmaceutical dictionary.] 3 v. Shanghai, 1935. Gives Latin, English, German, and Japanese equivalents.

O1115. Li, Shih-chen. **Pen-ts'ao kang-mu.** [Materia medica.] 1552–78. Reprint, 8 v., Shanghai, 1933.

O1116. Read, Bernard E. **Chinese materia medica.** 6 v. Peiping, 1931–41. Contains extensive translations from the above.
O1117. Sung, Ying-hsing. **T'ien-kung k'ai-wu.** [Illustration of industrial techniques.] 1637. Reprint, 3 v., Tientsin, 1927.
O1118. Goodrich, L. Carrington, and Feng Chia-sheng. "The early development of firearms in China." *Isis*, 36 (Jan. 1946): 114–23, 250–51.
O1119. Wang, Ling. "On the invention and use of gunpowder and firearms in China." *Isis*, 37 (July 1947): 160–78. Reviews basic Chinese source materials.
O1120. Pelliot, Paul. **Les débuts de l'imprimerie en Chine.** Paris, 1953.
O1121. Carter, Thomas F. **The invention of printing in China and its spread westward.** 2nd ed., rev. by L. C. Goodrich, N.Y., 1955.

BIOGRAPHIES

This subsection contains indexes to important collections of biography. The most important biographical dictionaries are listed under Encyclopedias and Works of Reference above; and significant biographies are included in subsections under Special Periods.
O1122. Erh-shih-wu-shih jen-ming so-yin. [Index to the biographies in the twenty-five dynastic histories.] Shanghai, 1935. Arranged according to the four-corner index system.
O1123. Liang, Ch'i-hsiung. **Nien-ssu-shih chuan-mu yin-te.** [Index of biographies in the twenty-four dynastic histories.] Shanghai, 1936. Contains lists of heroines, empresses, and imperial concubines, princes and princesses, foreigners, adventurers, etc.; a useful addition to the above.
O1124. Nieh, Ch'ung-ch'i. **Ssu-shih-ch'i-chung Sung-tai chuan-chi tsung-ho yin-te.** [Combined index to forty-seven collections of Sung dynasty biographies.] Peiping, 1939. [Harvard-Yenching Institute Sinological index series, 34.]
O1125. Hung, Yeh, and others. **Liao, Chin, Yüan chuan-chi san-shih-chung tsung-ho yin-te.** [Combined index to thirty collections of biographies of the Liao, Chin and Yüan dynasties.] Peiping, 1940. [Harvard-Yenching Institute Sinological index series, 35.]
O1126. T'ien, Chi-tsung. **Pa-shih-chiu-chung Ming-tai Chuan-chi tsung-ho yin-te.** [Combined index to eighty-nine collections of biographies of the Ming dynasty.] 3 v. Peiping, 1935. [Harvard-Yenching Institute Sinological index series, 24.]
O1127. Tu, Lien-che, and Fang Chao-ying. **San-shih-san-chung Ch'ing-tai chuan-chi tsung-ho yin-te.** [Combined index to thirty-three collections of biographies of the Ch'ing dynasty.] Peiping, 1932. [Harvard-Yenching Institute Sinological index series, 9.]
O1128. Yang, Li-ch'eng, and Chin Pu-ying. **Chung-kuo ts'ang-shu-chia k'ao-lüeh.** [Bio-graphical notes on book collectors.] Chekiang, 1929.

GOVERNMENT PUBLICATIONS

O1129. Cheng-fu kung-pao. [The government gazette.] Peking, 1912–28. Daily publication of government documents.
O1130. Kuo-min cheng-fu kung-pao. [Gazette of the national government.] Nanking and Chungking, 1927 ff. First issued three times per month; daily after Oct. 26, 1929. Contains proclamations, statutes, orders, etc.
O1131. Hsing-cheng-yüan kung-pao. [Gazette of the executive yüan.] Nanking and Chungking, 1928 ff. (Semiweekly.) Ordinances from the national government to the executive yüan and from the yüan to ministries, departments, and local authorities.
O1132. Chung-hua min-kuo nien-chien. [Yearbook of the Republic of China.] Taipei, 1951. Contains more information than the *China yearbook* in English (Taipei, 1957 ff.).
O1133. Chung-hua min-kuo fa-lüeh hui-pien. [Collection of laws and statutes of the Republic of China.] 3 v. Taipei, 1958.
O1134. Chung-hua jen-min kung-ho-kuo fa-kuei hui-pien. [Collection of laws and statutes of the People's Republic of China.] Peiping, 1956 ff. (Annual.)
O1135. Chung-hua jen-min kung-ho-kuo tui-wai-kuan-hsi wen-chien chi. [Collection of documents concerning foreign relations of the People's Republic of China.] 1949 ff. Peiping, 1957 ff. (Annual.)
O1136. Chung-hua jen-min kung-ho-kuo t'iao-yüeh chi. [Collection of treaties of the People's Republic of China.] 1949 ff. Peiping, 1957 ff.
O1137. Peking review. Peiping, 1958 ff. (Weekly.) This official publication in English was the fortnightly *People's China* from 1950 to 1957. Contains articles and documents on developments in Communist China.

PERIODICALS AND SERIALS

O1138. Walker, Richard L. **Western language periodicals on China (a selective list).** New Haven, 1949.
O1139. Hervouet, Y. **Catalogue des périodiques chinois dans les bibliothèques d'Europe.** Paris, 1958.
O1140. Britton, Roswell S. **The Chinese periodical press, 1800–1912.** Shanghai, 1933.
O1141. Lin, Mou-sheng. **A guide to leading Chinese periodicals.** N.Y., 1936.
For journals relating to Asia and the Far East see the list in Section N. The following relate almost exclusively to China.
O1142. Academia Sinica. **Annals.** Taipei, 1945 ff.
O1143. Bulletin de l'Université l'Aurore. Shanghai, 1909–50.

O1144. **Bulletin of the Catholic University of Peking.** Peiping, 1926–34.

O1145. **Chin-ling hsüeh-pao.** [Nanking journal.] Nanking, 1931–41. (Monthly.)

O1146. **China journal of science and arts.** Shanghai, 1923–41. (Irregular.)

O1147. **China law review.** Shanghai, 1922–40. (Quarterly.)

O1148. **China quarterly.** Shanghai, 1936–41.

O1149. **China reconstructs.** Peiping, 1952 ff. (Bimonthly.)

O1150. **China review.** Hong Kong, 1872–1901. (Bimonthly.)

O1151. **China society.** London, 1915–25. (Quarterly.)

O1152. **China weekly review.** Shanghai, 1917–50. (Title varies.)

O1153. **Chinese culture: a quarterly review.** Taipei, 1957 ff.

O1154. **Chinese economic journal.** Shanghai, 1927–37. (Monthly.)

O1155. **Chinese medical journal.** Shanghai, Chengtu, Taipei, 1887 ff. (Bimonthly.)

O1156. **Chinese recorder and missionary journal.** Shanghai, 1868–1941. (Monthly and bimonthly.)

O1157. **The Chinese repository.** Canton, 1832–51. (Monthly.)

O1158. **Chinese social and political science review.** Peking, 1916–41. (Quarterly.)

O1159. **Ch'ing-hua hsüeh-pao.** [Tsing Hua journal.] Peiping, 1924–48; Taipei, 1956 ff. (Annual.)

O1160. **Chugoku bungaku ho.** [Journal of Chinese literature.] Kyoto, 1954 ff. (Semiannual.)

O1161. **Chung-kuo wen-hua yen-chiu hui-kan.** [Bulletin of Chinese studies.] Chengtu, 1941–48.

O1162. **Chung-yang Yen-chiu Yüan li Shih-yü-Yen-yen Chiu-so chi-k'an.** [Bulletin of the Institute of History and Philosophy, Academia Sinica.] Nanking and Taipei, 1928 ff. (Annual.)

O1163. **Collectanea commissionis synodalis.** Peiping, 1928–47. (Irregular monthly.)

O1164. **Fu-jen hsüeh-pao.** [Journal of Fu-jen University.] Peiping, 1929–46. (Semiannual.)

O1165. **Hsüeh heng.** [Critical review.] Peiping, 1922–33. (Monthly.)

O1166. **Journal of the North China Branch of the Royal Asiatic Society.** Shanghai, 1858–1949. (Irregular.)

O1167. **Journal of the West China Border Research Society.** Chengtu, 1922 ff.

O1168. **Kuo-hsüeh chi-k'an.** [Journal of Sinological studies.] Peiping, 1923–50. (Quarterly.)

O1169. **Li-shih yen-chiu.** [The study of history.] Peiping, 1954 ff. (Monthly.)

O1170. **Ling-nan hsüeh-pao.** [Lingnan journal.] Canton, 1929–51. (Monthly.)

O1171. **Monumenta serica.** Peiping, 1935–48; Nagoya, 1949 ff. (Annual.) In English.

O1172. **Nankai social and economic quarterly.** Tientsin, 1928–41.

O1173. **The new China review.** Shanghai, 1919–22. (Bimonthly.)

O1174. **Philobiblon.** Nanking, 1946–48. (Irregular.)

O1175. **Shigaku zasshi.** [Historical journal of Japan.] Tokyo, 1889 ff. (Monthly.)

O1176. **Shih-hsüeh.** [History.] Peiping, 1953 ff.

O1177. **Shih-hsüeh nien-pao.** [Historical annual.] Peiping, 1929–40. (Annual.)

O1178. **Shinagaku.** [Sinology.] Kyoto, 1920–47. (Irregular.)

O1179. **Shirin.** [Journal of history.] Kyoto, 1916 ff. (Quarterly.)

O1180. **Sinica.** Frankfurt-am-Main, 1925–42. (Irregular.)

O1181. **Sinologische Arbeiten.** Peiping, 1943–45. (Annual.)

O1182. **Sinologica.** Basel, 1948 ff. (Quarterly.)

O1183. **Studia serica.** Chengtu and Peiping, 1940–50. (Irregular.)

O1184. **T'ien-hsia monthly.** Shanghai, 1935–41.

O1185. **T'u-shu chi-k'an.** [Quarterly bulletin of Chinese bibliography.] Peiping, 1934–48.

O1186. **Tōyōshi kenkyū.** [Journal of oriental research.] Kyoto, 1935 ff. (Bimonthly.)

O1187. **U. S. Consulate. Survey of China mainland press.** Hong Kong, 1950 ff. (Several issues per week.)

O1188. **Yen-ching hsüeh-pao.** [Yenching journal of Chinese studies.] Peiping, 1927–51. (Annual.)

O1189. **Yenching journal of social studies.** Peiping, 1938–50. (Semiannual.)

SECTION P

Japan

HUGH BORTON and JOHN WHITNEY HALL

Japan's rise as a first class world power during the 20th century stimulated the interest of western scholars in Japanese history, yet it was not until the 1930's in the United States that several major universities undertook to develop advanced study in this field. The outstanding prewar writers were chiefly British, such as Murdoch and Sansom. However, World War II and its aftermath changed this picture drastically; and a host of scholars, both English and American, with years of language experience and residence in Japan, entered the field. United States universities multiplied language and area programs on Japan. The capacity of the postwar western scholar to work with Japanese historical materials also greatly improved. The result is a sizable body of new monographs. Among western historians the subjects of overwhelming interest have been the Meiji restoration of 1868, the Pacific war, and the occupation which followed. While a few scholars took up the study of Tokugawa Japan (1603–1868), earlier periods have been almost totally neglected except in surveys. Western historical literature on Japan has been predominantly cultural and political in orientation. Social history is almost nonexistent, and economic history has only begun to find writers.

Meanwhile, Japanese historians have compiled an impressive record of historical scholarship based on a sound foundation of national libraries, universities, academic societies, and research institutions. The major western theories of history have all had their effect in Japan and have produced their particular brands of historical writing. There have been substantial publications of documentary collections and reference histories, of encyclopedias and special research tools. A number of scholarly historical journals have been in continuous publication since the turn of the 20th century, and Japanese bibliographers have been active. Since World War II interests of the Japanese and western historian have more nearly approached each other, though each is preoccupied by the different questions he asks of the past. Thus in looking over the last hundred years, the western historian is apt to inquire into the reason for Japan's rapid "modernization," while the Japanese asks why his country remained "backward" so long.

296

In comparing the two bodies of historical literature on Japan, one is impressed by the fact that vast areas of Japanese history and of Japanese writing on these areas have yet to be communicated to the West in any detail. On the whole, however, western writers of historical surveys have produced works of excellent scope and reliability.

BIBLIOGRAPHIES AND LIBRARIES

General Guides

The following works are useful as introductory guides to research in Japanese history. They provide a selective coverage of bibliography in various sub-fields, as well as orientation for scholars approaching Japanese history for the first time. Additional works of this kind will be found under Historiography.

P1. Kurita, Motoji. **Sōgō kokushi kenkyū.** [Synthetic guide to research in Japanese history.] 3 v. Tokyo, 1935. Though no longer adequate for contemporary research, this remains the best selective, annotated bibliography of historical sources and standard pre-World War II secondary works.

P2. Tōyama, Shigeki, and Satō Shin'ichi. **Nihonshi kenkyū nyūmon.** [Introduction to the study of Japanese history.] Tokyo, 1954. Useful introductory survey of historical research in Japan during the previous decade. Consists of series of bibliographical essays covering methodology and the major historical periods.

P3. Hall, John W. **Japanese history: a guide to Japanese reference and research materials.** Ann Arbor, 1954. Comprehensive, classified guide to research procedures and reference materials.

P4. Wenckstern, Friedrich von. **A bibliography of the Japanese empire.** 2 v. Leiden and Tokyo, 1895–1907. Covers period 1859–1906.

P5. Nachod, Oskar. **Bibliographie von Japan.** 7 v. in 9. Leipzig, 1928–44. Covers 1906–43.

P4 and *P5* constitute the standard bibliography of works in European languages on Japan. Earlier volumes list largely materials in English, French, and German; later ones also include Russian titles. Entries are arranged by subject, and each volume contains an index. They should be used in connection with *P6–7* for a coverage of European language works on Japan to the present.

P6. Bulletin of far eastern bibliography. See *N4*.

P7. Borton, Hugh, and others. **A selected list of books and articles on Japan in English, French and German.** Rev. and enl. ed., Cambridge, Mass., 1954. Concise, carefully selected and annotated list of nearly 2,000 items, arranged topically.

Selective Historical Bibliographies

The following works provide general access to contemporary historical literature on a selective and classified basis. They should be supplemented, when necessary, by the more specialized bibliographies which follow and by subject bibliographies in some of the historical works listed later in this section.

P8. Honjō, Eijirō. **Kaihan Nihon keizaishi bunken.** [Revised bibliography of Japanese economic history.] 4 v. Tokyo, 1933–54. The most useful bibliographical reference to books and articles in this field. Also covers nearly all other aspects of Japanese history.

P9. Shigakkai. **Nen no rekishi gakkai.** [Historical studies in Japan.] Tokyo, 1949 ff. [Annual special issue of Shigaku zasshi.] This series of bibliographical surveys was begun in 1916 in *Shirin,* journal of the Kyoto University Historical Society. Each issue covers Japanese, Chinese, and European history.

P10. ——. **Shigaku bunken mokuroku 1946–1950.** [Bibliography of historical studies, 1946–1950.] Tokyo, 1951. Selective, classified bibliography covering books and articles by Japanese scholars in the fields of Japanese, oriental, and occidental history. The section on Japan contains nearly 5,000 entries. A sequel appears in *Shigaku zasshi,* 1960 ff.

P11. Rekishigaku Kenkyūkai. **Rekishigaku nempō.** [Annual report of historical studies.] Tokyo, 1933–44. This and the following series are compiled by the so-called "progressive historians" of Japan, covering Japanese, oriental, and occidental history beginning with 1933.

P12. ——. **Rekishigaku no seika to kadai.** [Results and issues of historical science in Japan.] Tokyo, 1950 ff. (Annual.) The 1950 issue covers years 1944–49. Published as regular number of *Rekishigaku kenkyū* 1956–58.

P13. Ōtsuka Shigakkai Kōshi Bukai. **Sōgō kokushi rombun yōmoku.** [Combined catalog of selected articles on Japanese history.] Tokyo, 1939. Select but comprehensive catalog of articles from 169 scholarly journals and collections published during the years 1868–1938.

P14. Laures, John. **Kirishitan bunko: a manual of books and documents on the early Christian missions in Japan, with special reference to the principal libraries in Japan and more particularly to the collection

at Sophia University, Tokyo. Tokyo, 3rd combined ed., 1957 [*Monumenta Nipponica*, No. 5]. Invaluable for study of early Christianity in Japan.

P15. Robertson, James A. "Bibliography of early Spanish-Japanese relations, compiled from manuscripts and books in the Philippine Library, Manila." **Transactions of the Asiatic Society of Japan,** 43 (Feb. 1915): i–iv, 1–170.

Guides and Indices to Historical Sources

The following works offer guidance in the search for and identification of primary historical sources.

P16. Endō, Motoo, and Shimomura Fujio. **Kokushi bunken kaisetsu.** [Annotated bibliography of Japanese history.] Tokyo, 1957. Historical source materials and collections. While oriented to the pre-modern period, also lists important political and biographical materials for the recent period.

P17. Endō, Motoo, and others. **Kokushi Tōyōshi Seiyōshi shiseki kaidai.** [An annotated bibliography of source materials in Japanese, oriental and occidental history.] Tokyo, 1936. [Sekai rekishi taikei (Outline of world history), 25.] This and the following work provide comprehensive coverage of source materials for pre-modern history. Endō's bibliography is especially useful in location of primary sources in modern printed collections.

P18. Samura, Hachirō. **Zōtei kokusho kaidai.** [Annotated bibliography of Japanese books, revised and enlarged.] 2 v. Tokyo, 1926.

P19. Kokuritsu Kokkai Toshokan. **Zasshi kiji sakuin.** [Japanese periodicals index.] Tokyo, 1949 ff. (Monthly.) Cumulative, classified index to periodical articles appearing in journals received by the National Diet Library. Two series are issued concurrently, one dealing with natural sciences, the other with humanities and social sciences.

P20. Ōta, Tamesaburō. **Nihon zuihitsu sakuin.** [Index to Japanese miscellanies.] Rev. ed., 2 v., Tokyo, 1926–32. Excellent subject index to over 200 works, mostly written before the mid-19th century.

P21. Hirose, Bin. **Nihon sōsho sakuin.** [Index of Japanese series.] Enlarged ed., Tokyo, 1957. Comprehensive index to subject matter of all important Japanese series publications and collections.

Catalogs of Books and Periodicals

Prior to 1945 it was required by law that all published books and periodicals be submitted to the Ministry of Home Affairs for copyright and censorship purposes. After this date censorship was dropped. The National Diet Library, though lacking legal power to require all new publications to be deposited with it, has taken over the catalog functions of the Home Ministry. Although extremely cumbersome to use, the catalogs listed below are undoubtedly the most comprehensive sources of information on current bibliography.

P22. Kokuritsu Kokkai Toshokan. **Zen-Nihon shuppanbutsu sōmokuroku.** [General catalog of works published in Japan.] Tokyo, 1951 ff. (Annual.) The cumulative indices of all publications received by the National Diet Library. Only monthly indices were published from 1948 to 1951.

P23. Naimushō nōhon geppō. [Monthly list of books deposited with the Ministry of Home Affairs.] Tokyo, 1912–37. Classified lists of books and periodicals. For history of this series and its predecessors dating back to 1876 see John W. Hall, *Japanese history (P3)*.

Libraries and Library Catalogs

Library catalogs are useful for information on existence and availability of historical materials, especially manuscript collections. The catalogs cited here are but a few representative examples of the many works of this type. For more complete information see the appropriate section in Hall, *Japanese history (P3)*.

P24. Special Libraries Association. **Directory of research libraries.** Tokyo, 1956. A nearly bilingual compilation of information on Japanese libraries with research interests. Particularly useful is the information on special collections within each library and the various publications sponsored by the libraries.

P25. Tōkyō Daigaku Shiryō Hensanjo. **Tōkyō Daigaku Shiryō Hensanjo tosho mokuroku.** [Catalog of books held by the Tokyo University Historiographical Institute.] Tokyo, 1955 ff. Catalog of one of the best historical libraries in Japan, giving very complete coverage of materials published in Tokyo and elsewhere.

P26. Naikaku Kirokukyoku. **Naikaku bunko tosho mokuroku; washomon ruibetsu.** [Catalog of the Cabinet Library: classified index to Japanese works.] 3 v. Tokyo, 1889–90. This collection is especially distinguished for pre-modern and modern official documents. Subsequent accession lists have been published.

P27. Teikoku Toshokan. **Teikoku Toshokan wakan tosho bunrui mokuroku.** [Classified catalog of Japanese and Chinese books in the Imperial Library.] 9 v. Tokyo, 1900–07. Long the foremost official library in Japan, this was incorporated in the National Diet Library in 1949. Contains numerous special collections of historical materials, and became the repository of all books deposited with the Home Ministry for copyright purposes. This completely classified catalog covers holdings through 1899. Subsequent accession lists bring the catalog up to date.

ENCYCLOPEDIAS AND WORKS OF REFERENCE

Historical Dictionaries and Manuals

The following are modern in their conception and of general historical coverage. Many more specialized works of this variety are available.

P28. Kyōto Daigaku Bungakubu Kokushi Kenkyūshitsu. **Nihonshi jiten.** [Dictionary of Japanese history.] Tokyo and Osaka, 1955. Latest and most satisfactory of the one-volume dictionaries. First part is a subject dictionary covering historical personages, and political, social, economic, and cultural events. The second part contains various historical tables and charts.

P29. Nihon rekishi daijiten. [Encyclopedia of Japanese history.] 19 v., Tokyo, 1956–59. Arranged under small subject headings, this is the most comprehensive work of its kind. Extremely detailed coverage touching all fields broadly related to history.

P30. Sekai rekishi jiten. [Encyclopedia of world history.] 25 v. Tokyo, 1950–55. Most ambitious historical reference work to come out of Japan in recent years. Twenty volumes are devoted to world history, with about a third of the entries dealing with Japan. V. 21 is an index, and v. 22–25 are guides to historical sources in the fields of Japanese, Chinese, and western history.

P31. Nihon Keizaishi Kenkyūjo. **Nihon keizaishi jiten.** [Dictionary of Japanese economic history.] 3 v. Tokyo, 1940. The outstanding dictionary of Japanese economic history, especially valuable to the historian with a social science approach and with an interest in the Tokugawa period (1603–1868). Most articles include useful notes on primary and secondary reference material.

P32. Yashiro, Kuniharu, Hayakawa Junzaburō, and Inobe Shigeo. **Daizōtei kokushi daijiten.** [Further supplemented and revised dictionary of Japanese history.] Tokyo, 1936. Although originally compiled in 1903, this remains one of the most complete and useful dictionaries of Japanese history. Coverage of pre-modern political, institutional, and biographical history is extremely full. Most articles provide references to primary sources.

P33. Sekai rekishi jiten. V. 22, Shiryō hen, Nihon. [Encyclopedia of world history. V. 22, Sources, Japan.] Tokyo, 1955. Excellent introduction to primary sources covering the entire span of Japanese history; the most comprehensive and up-to-date guide available. Separately printed (1956) as *Nihon shiryō shūsei.*

P34. Jingūshichō. **Koji ruien.** [Encyclopedia of ancient matters.] Rev. popular ed., 60 v., Tokyo, 1936. Monumental work covering all phases of pre-modern Japanese history. Volumes of special interest include those on emperors, court ranks and practices, feudal institutions, land tax systems, law, currency, foreign affairs, military affairs, biography, and customs.

P35. Tōkyō Teikoku Daigaku Shiryō Hensanjo. **Tokushi biyō.** [Manual of Japanese history.] Tokyo, 1933. Extremely useful collection of historical data to 1932. Contains comparative chronological tables, tables of holders of offices in Japanese government, charts of Japanese administrative systems, genealogical tables, and important indexes to biographical literature on court nobles, military houses, and priests. Revised in 1942.

P36. Chihōshi Kenkyū Kyōgikai. **Chihōshi kenkyū hikkei.** [Manual for the study of local history.] Tokyo, 1952. Very important compendium of historical and bibliographical information for the student of Japanese local history. Arranged by periods, with subheadings on the major political, economic, social, and intellectual institutions.

Dictionaries and Related Fields

P37. Nihon Kokusei Jiten Kankōkai. **Nihon kokusei jiten.** [Dictionary of Japanese government.] Tokyo, 1953 ff. Each volume treats one or more of the Japanese cabinets, beginning with the first Itō cabinet of 1890. Includes data on the imperial household, political events, the administration, foreign affairs, military affairs, education, finance, commerce and trade, communications, and cultural activities. An important historical reference work.

P38. Ōtsuka Shigakkai. **Kyōdoshi jiten.** [Dictionary of local history.] Tokyo, 1955. Deals with the difficult terminology encountered by the student of Japanese local history, and provides an excellent supplement to the previously listed historical dictionaries which are concerned primarily with national affairs.

P39. Shintō daijiten. [Dictionary of Shinto.] 2nd ed., 3 v., Tokyo, 1937–40. The best and most modern dictionary of Japanese Shinto. Covers all aspects of the subject, including deities, shrines, ceremonies, religious terms, and biographies of priests.

P40. Mochizuki, Shinkō. **Bukkyō daijiten.** [Dictionary of Buddhism.] 6 v. Tokyo, 1931–36. Latest and most authoritative of the general Buddhist dictionaries, and the most satisfactory for those working in Buddhist history.

P41. Hôbôgirin: dictionnaire encyclopédique du bouddhisme d'après les sources

chinoises et japonaises. 4 v. Tokyo, 1929–37. Still incomplete, but detailed and authoritative.

P42. Hôbôgirin: dictionnaire . . . tables du Taishō Issaikyō. Ed. by J. Takakusu and K. Watanabe. New ed., Tokyo, 1931. This valuable index gives complete references to other Japanese editions of the *Tripitaka*. Includes short biographies of the monks who made the original Chinese translations.

P43. Fujimura, Saku. **Zōho kaitei Nihon bungaku daijiten.** [Dictionary of Japanese literature, revised and enlarged.] 8 v. Tokyo, 1950–52. Largest and most authoritative dictionary of Japanese literature, giving extensive coverage of all Japanese ancient and modern literary works and writers.

Chronologies and Concordances

Works of this type are quite numerous and are essential to the historian dealing with Japanese materials. Chronologies provide visual comparison between Japanese, Korean, Chinese, and western calendar systems, generally on a yearly basis. They also list under each year significant events in world history. Concordances make it possible to compute daily equivalents between eastern and western calendars.

P44. Nishioka, Toranosuke. **Shin Nihonshi nempyō.** [New chronology of Japanese history.] Tokyo, 1955. Latest and most comprehensive general chronology of Japanese and world history.

P45. Tsuji, Zennosuke. **Dai Nihon nempyō.** [Japanese chronological tables.] 5th rev. ed., Tokyo, 1943. Extremely useful chronology giving standard calendrical comparisons on a yearly basis. Also provides information for computing exact day to day equivalents between lunar and solar calendars.

P46. Gaimushō, ed. **Nihon gaikō nempyō narabini jūyō bunsho.** [Chronology of Japanese foreign relations with basic documents.] 2 v. Tokyo, 1955. Detailed chronology of events in Japan's foreign relations from 1840 to 1945. Includes basic documents such as treaties and other foreign agreements, and a table of personnel in foreign affairs posts.

P47. Tsuchihashi, P. Yachita. **Japanese chronological tables.** Tokyo, 1952. Latest and most accessible of the comparative tables of lunar and solar calendars. The most satisfactory tool available for calculating day to day concordances between the calendars.

Yearbooks

The Japanese produce a great number of yearbooks covering activities in a wide variety of fields. These are of primary value to historians working in recent and contemporary periods. Those listed below are illustrative of the most important yearbooks of general and specialized coverage.

P48. Jiji Tsūshinsha. **Jiji nenkan.** [Jiji yearbook.] Tokyo, 1918 ff. (Annual.) Undoubtedly the most detailed and best organized of the yearbooks, giving comprehensive coverage of events concerning the imperial house, politics, administrative and legal decisions, local government, national finances, labor, foreign relations, commerce and trade, shrines and temples, education, sports, and many other subjects.

P49. Asahi Shimbunsha. **Asahi nenkan.** [Asahi yearbook.] Tokyo and Osaka, 1919 ff. (Annual.) One of the most comprehensive general yearbooks, covering events and statistical information concerning politics, laws, local government, foreign relations, economics, labor relations, finance, and the like.

P50. Tōkyō Seiji Keizai Kenkyūjo. **1920–1930 seiji keizai nenkan.** [Political and economic yearbook, 1920–1930.] Tokyo, 1930. Arranged in yearbook style, this volume covers a decade of Japanese political and economic events and statistics. Succeeded by the annual series below.

P51. ——. **Nihon seiji keizai nenkan.** [Japanese political and economic yearbook.] Tokyo, 1931 ff. (Annual.) Excellent for coverage of political and economic affairs. Each volume contains descriptive essays on politics, administration, finance, military affairs, international relations, economic production, engineering, agriculture, commerce, etc. Essays are documented by tables and statistical summaries.

P52. Tōyō Keizai Shimpōsha. **Nihon keizai nempō.** [Japanese economic annual.] Tokyo, 1930 ff. (Quarterly.) Surveys the Japanese economic scene, providing statistics and interpretive articles.

P53. Ōhara Shakaimondai Kenkyūjo. **Nihon rōdō nenkan.** [Japanese labor yearbook.] Tokyo, 1920–41, 1949 ff. (Annual.) Highly regarded as the best yearbook in this field. Each issue provides information on labor conditions, movements, policy, and legislation, social conditions, and the like, and reviews the year's bibliography in the field.

GEOGRAPHIES, GAZETTEERS, AND ATLASES

P54. Nishioka, Toranosuke, and Hattori Shisō. **Nihon rekishi chizu.** [Historical atlas of Japan.] Tokyo, 1956. Best work of its kind. Includes maps on such subjects as archaeological finds, administrative divisions, city plans, major battles, communications, distribution of economic goods, etc.

P55. Yoshida, Tōgo. **Dai Nihon chimei jiten.** [Dictionary of Japanese place names.] Rev. ed., 6 v., Tokyo, 1922–23. The best of place name dictionaries, providing a wealth of historical data for the various places identified. Elaborate index facilitates use.

P56. Trewartha, Glenn T. **Japan, a physical, cultural and regional geography.** Madison, Wis., 1945. Excellent study on the various geographical characteristics of Japan, covering the physical equipment and resources and cultural features of the country as a whole and the six chief regional subdivisions. Extensively illustrated and supplied with charts and statistics.

P57. Papinot, Edmond. **Historical and geographical dictionary of Japan.** Ann Arbor, 1948. Short descriptions of leading events, persons, and places of importance in Japanese history. Originally published in French (Tokyo, 1906); this is a lithoprint of the English edition published in 1910.

P58. Teleki, Pál. **Atlas zur Geschichte der Kartographie der japanischen Inseln.** Leipzig, 1909. Carefully annotated study of the appearance of Japan on early European maps.

P59. Gerr, Stanley. **A gazetteer of Japanese place names in characters and in Rōmaji script giving latitudes and longitudes.** Cambridge, Mass., 1942. Useful reference for persons unable to use or find one of the standard Japanese gazetteers.

ANTHROPOLOGY

P60. Nihon Minzokugaku Kyōkai. **Nihon shakai minzoku jiten.** [Dictionary of Japanese sociology and ethnology.] 2 v. Tokyo, 1952–54. Very useful reference for the social historian. Articles, which tend to be lengthy, cover important aspects of Japanese social, political, economic, and religious affairs, and generally include notes on secondary references. A third volume will complete the series.

P61. Benedict, Ruth. **The chrysanthemum and the sword: patterns of Japanese culture.** Boston, 1946. Stimulating attempt, by a distinguished anthropologist, to interpret Japanese culture in terms of national character.

P62. Raper, Arthur F., and others. **The Japanese village in transition.** Tokyo, 1950. [Supreme Commander for the Allied Powers, Natural Resources Section, Report no. 136.] Survey of postwar social and economic changes in thirteen villages throughout Japan, by a competent group of sociologists and anthropologists.

P63. Batchelor, John. **The Ainu of Japan.** London, 1892. This and the following are the standard works on the Ainu, by a pioneer scholar who did not have the advantages of modern anthropological methods.

P64. ——. **Ainu life and lore, echoes of a departing race.** Tokyo, 1927.

DEMOGRAPHIC STUDIES

Most Japanese demographic studies are concerned with recent trends. Those listed below are included either because of their historical approach or for the special value of the statistics used and presented.

P65. Honjō, Eijirō. **Nihon jinkoshi.** [History of Japanese population.] Tokyo, 1941. Enlarged edition of earlier study dealing with population growth from earliest times to the mid-19th century, with special emphasis on problems in the Tokugawa period.

P66. Okazaki, Ayanori. **Nihon jinko no jisshoteki kenkyū.** [Factual study of Japanese population.] Tokyo, 1950. Valuable statistical study of the period 1899–1940, with summary of population changes since 1945.

P67. Japan. Bureau de la Statistique Générale. **Population du Japon depuis 1872.** Tokyo, 1930. Annual population data adjusted to allow for probable errors in the uncorrected registration figures during the period 1872–1919. Continued by *P68.*

P68. ——. **Résumé statistique du mouvement de la population de l'empire du Japon.** Tokyo, 1919 ff. (Annual.)

P69. Morita, Yūzō. **Jinkō zōka no bunseki.** [An analysis of population increase.] 2 v. Tokyo, 1944. By a well-known demographer. Summarizes modern views and theories of population and analyzes the factors affecting Japanese population growth in the 20th century. Contains valuable statistical data.

P70. Ishii, Ryōichi. **Population pressure and economic life in Japan.** London, 1937. A careful general survey based on Japanese sources.

PRINTED COLLECTIONS OF SOURCES

The Japanese have assiduously published collections of primary sources for documentation of their written history, only a few of which can be mentioned here. Fuller information on their contents and on the major historical series is available in Hall, *Japanese history (P3).* See also references in the subsection on Historiography.

General Collections Dealing Primarily with Pre-Restoration History

P71. Tōkyō Daigaku Shiryō Hensanjo, ed. **Dai Nihon shiryō.** [Japanese historical materials.] Tokyo, 1901 ff. Ambitious collection of primary materials from 887 to 1867, chronologically arranged. The Historiographical Institute of Tokyo University has been the most important agency for publication of Japanese historical records, issuing a wide variety of series of which this and the three following are major ones of general coverage.

P72. ——, ed. **Dai Nihon komonjo.** [Ancient documents of Japan.] Tokyo, 1901 ff. Groups of documents dealing with single institutions, famous families, or some important historical event.

P73. ——, ed. **Dai Nihon kinsei shiryō.** [Japanese historical materials of the early modern period.] Tokyo, 1955 ff. Groups of local historical documents from the Tokugawa period.

P74. ——, ed. **Dai Nihon kokiroku.** [Ancient records of Japan.] Tokyo, 1952 ff. Diaries and other semi-private materials covering the entire span of pre-modern Japanese history.

P75. Hanawa, Hokiichi, ed. **Gunsho ruijū.** [Classified collection of Japanese classics.] 19 v. Tokyo, 1897–1902. Second ser., 72 v., 1923–30. The work of a great 19th century bibliographer, revised and supplemented by his son. Contains over 3,500 historical documents arranged under subject headings. V. 1 of the 2nd series is index to both series. See also *P78*.

P76. Kuroita, Katsumi, ed. **Shintei zōho kokushi taikei.** [Revised and supplemented compendium of Japanese history.] Tokyo, 1929 ff. Important series of collated and annotated sources for Japanese pre-modern history. Contains most of the recognized historical writings beginning with the famous six national histories (*Rikkokushi*) down to the history of the Tokugawa house (*Tokugawa jikki*).

P77. Kokusho Kankōkai, ed. **Kokusho Kankōkai sōsho.** [Kokusho Kankōkai series.] 260 v. Tokyo, 1906–22. Contains many individual historical sources and collections produced by historians and bibliographers of the Tokugawa period. Access to this series must be through the standard indices such as *P78*.

P78. Hirose, Bin. **Nihon sōsho sakuin.** [Index of Japanese series.] Tokyo, 1939. Important reference guide to contents and subject matter of the series and collections of pre-modern historical documents published prior to 1930.

General Collections on the Meiji Restoration (1867–68) and Post-Restoration History

P79. Tōkyō Daigaku Shiryō Hensanjo, ed. **Dai Nihon Ishin shiryō.** [Historical materials relating to the Japanese Restoration.] Tokyo, 1938 ff. A gigantic repository of documents and other materials covering political history of the years 1846–71; still far from complete.

P80. Hashimoto, Hiroshi, ed. **Ishin nisshi.** [Restoration journals.] 20 v. Shizuoka, 1932–35. Official journals of the Restoration government from 1868 to 1876. Most important single item is the *Dajōkan nisshi*, which was the most authoritative and complete in its coverage of early Meiji governmental affairs.

P81. Yoshino, Sakuzō, ed. **Meiji bunka zenshū.** [Complete collection on Meiji culture.] 24 v. Tokyo, 1927–30. Comprehensive collection of documents and essays covering all aspects of Meiji Japanese culture. Brings together specialized articles by leading Japanese scholars; primary documents, newspapers, and magazine articles; and other sources. A reprint, begun in 1955, contains a number of significant additions.

P82. Nakayama, Yasumasa, ed. **Shimbun shūsei Meiji hennenshi.** [Chronological history of the Meiji era compiled from newspapers.] 15 v. Tokyo, 1935. Extremely valuable and comprehensive coverage of the history of Meiji Japan as seen through articles in contemporary newspapers.

P83. Taishō Shōwa Hennenshi Kai, ed. **Shimbun shūsei Shōwa hennenshi.** [Chronological history of the Showa era compiled from newspapers.] Tokyo, 1955 ff. This work, modeled after *P82*, will cover the years 1911 to the present, and when complete will be an invaluable source for modern Japanese history. Items are from a wide variety of newspapers, both national and local.

Collected Laws

P84. Kimura, Shōji, ed. **Kempō shiryō.** [Historical materials on administrative law.] Daigo Sha ed., 2 v., Tokyo, 1935. Originally published in 1877, this work has been translated into modern Japanese and reprinted for greater accessibility. Consists of a classified collection of legal materials covering Japanese administrative and legal practices from ancient times to the 17th century. The best available source on legal systems before 1600.

P85. Takayanagi, Shinzō, and Ishii Ryōsuke, eds. **Ofuregaki Kampō shūsei.** [Collected Tokugawa ordinances of the Kampō era.] Tokyo, 1934. First volume of a series of five modern reprintings of official collections of proclamations made by the Tokugawa government. Contains some 3,500 laws issued by the Hyōjōsho of the Shogunate from 1615 to 1743. Other volumes bring the coverage, with some large gaps, down to 1843. A major source for study of Tokugawa law and administrative practice.

P86. Shihōshō, ed. **Tokugawa kinreikō.** [Survey of Tokugawa regulations.] 12 v. Tokyo, 1931–32. Classified collection of Tokugawa regulations compiled for the Ministry of Justice and first published in 1894.

P87. Hall, John Carey. "Japanese feudal law: the Institutes of Judicature, being a translation of 'Go seibai shikimoku,' the magisterial code of the Hojo power-holders (A.D. 1232)." **Transactions of the Asiatic Society of Japan,** 34 (Aug. 1906): 1–44.

P88. ——. "Japanese feudal laws II: the Ashikaga code, 'Kemmu shikimoku'—A.D.

1336." **Transactions of the Asiatic Society of Japan,** 36 (1908): 3–23.

P89. ——. "Japanese feudal laws III: the Tokugawa legislation." **Transactions of the Asiatic Society of Japan,** 38 (1911): 269–331, 41 (1913): 683–804.

Foreign Relations

The following collections give a fair coverage of Japan's foreign relations beginning with the 17th century. It should be noted that a number of volumes of the *Dai Nihon shiryō* (*P71*) are complete for this period and include valuable material on early relations with the Portuguese and Dutch. The volume on foreign relations in *Koji ruien* (*P34*) is also a handy source of documents arranged chronologically for the pre-modern period.

P90. Tsunoda, Ryūsaku, tr. **Japan in the Chinese dynastic histories: later Han through Ming dynasties.** Ed. by L. Carrington Goodrich. South Pasadena, Calif., 1951. Annotated translations of accounts of Japan in the Chinese official histories from A.D. 25 to 1644.

P91. Hayashi, I [Fukusai], ed. **Tsūkō ichiran.** [Survey of foreign relations.] 8 v. Tokyo, 1913. A collection of documents dealing with Japan's relations with China, Korea, countries of southeast Asia, Portugal, Spain, Holland, and Russia, compiled at the official request of the Tokugawa Shogunate. Documents cover the period from early 1600's to the 1840's.

P92. Ishin Shigakukai, ed. **Bakumatsu ishin gaikō shiryō shūsei.** [Classified historical records on foreign relations.] 6 v. Tokyo, 1942–44. An incomplete collection of basic documents relating to Japan's foreign affairs, 1853–68. Twenty volumes were planned.

P93. Tōkyō Daigaku Shiryō Hensanjo, ed. **Dai Nihon Komonjo: bakumatsu gaikoku kankei monjo.** [Ancient documents of Japan: official documents of the later Tokugawa era concerning foreign relations.] Tokyo, 1910 ff. One of the major divisions under which the Historiographical Institute of Tokyo University is publishing official Japanese documents. Material is arranged chronologically and will cover the period 1853–67. The 26 volumes published to date extend to 1859.

P94. Beasley, William G., ed. and tr. **Select documents on Japanese foreign policy, 1853–1868.** N.Y., 1955. Scholarly and critical translation of some of the more important documents from *P93* dealing with foreign relations during these critical years. Includes helpful explanatory background material and interpretations.

P95. Gaimushō Jōyakukyoku, ed. **Jōyaku isan.** [Classified collection of treaties.] 9 v. Tokyo, 1926–29. Treaties current at time of compilation, classified according to country. For publication of the treaties in European languages see *P328*.

P96. Gaimushō, ed. **Dai Nihon gaikō bunsho.** [Documents on Japanese foreign relations.] Tokyo, 1936 ff. A series of chronologically arranged collections of Japanese documents on foreign relations released by the Ministry of Foreign Affairs. Each volume covers one year beginning with 1868.

Social and Economic History

Various Japanese government offices and schools of historical research have published collections of source materials in this field, most of which combine primary and secondary sources. Their coverage is most complete for the Tokugawa, Meiji, and Taishō periods (1603–1926). Those listed below should be supplemented by the voluminous collections of local histories and by various entries on special topics.

P97. Nihonshi. [History of Japan.] 3 v. Tokyo, 1935–36. [Sekai rekishi taikei (Survey of world history), 12, 13a, 13b.] Carefully organized and integrated multi-author survey of Japanese history from ancient to modern times. Especially valuable for contributions by the best social and economic historians of the prewar period.

P98. Honjō, Eijirō, ed. **Kinsei shakai keizai sōsho.** [Documentary series on modern society and economics.] 12 v. Tokyo, 1926–27. Collection of documents used by the Kyoto school of economic historians, headed by the editor. Contains numerous primary materials and social and economic treatises written by Tokugawa scholars.

P99. Takimoto, Seiichi, ed. **Nihon keizai taiten.** [Compendium of Japanese economics.] 54 v. Tokyo, 1928–30. Monumental collection of pre-modern works on economic and social affairs, mostly taken from the Tokugawa period (1603–1867).

P100. Ono, Takeo, ed. **Nihon nōmin shiryō shūsui.** [Collected materials on the history of the Japanese peasantry.] 7 v. Tokyo, 1941. Important collection of basic primary materials and secondary accounts and treatises concerning the peasantry of Tokugawa Japan.

P101. Takimoto, Seiichi, and Mukai Shikamatsu, eds. **Nihon sangyō shiryō taikei.** [Compendium of materials on Japanese agriculture and industry.] 13 v. Tokyo, 1926–27. Valuable collection of documents, reports, and statistics relating to the growth of modern industry in Japan.

P102. Ōkurashō, ed. **Nihon zaisei keizai shiryō.** [Source materials on Japanese financial and economic history.] 11 v. Tokyo, 1922–25. Significant documents drawn largely from the Tokugawa period and classified under finance, economy, civil engineering, transportation, population, island territories, and national inspection.

P103. Ōuchi, Hyōe, and Tsuchiya Takaō, eds. **Meiji zenki zaisei keizai shiryō shūsei.** [Collected historical materials relating to finance and economy during the early Meiji period.] 21 v. Tokyo, 1932–36. Important and comprehensive collection of basic materials on the development of national and private finance in Japan, 1868–1900.

HISTORIOGRAPHY

Japanese works on the theory and practice of historical research tend to be derivative or are of special interest only to Japanese historians. Those cited below deal mainly with the history of historical writing in Japan. Other useful works are *Nihonshi kenkyū nyūmon (P2)*, *Sōgō kokushi kenkyū (P1)*, and *Kokushi no kenkyū (P113)*. The English titles included in this subsection cover recent articles on the subject.

P104. Kiyohara, Sadao. **Nihon shigakushi.** [A history of Japanese historiography.] Rev. ed., Tokyo, 1944. A standard factual survey of historical writing in Japan from ancient times to the 1930's.

P105. Shigakkai. **Hompō shigakushi ronsō.** [Essays on the history of Japanese historiography.] 2 v. Tokyo, 1939. Essays on historiography and historical works by the best Japanese writers of pre-World War II era.

P106. Izu, Kimio. **Nihon shigakushi.** [A history of Japanese historiography.] Rev. ed., Tokyo, 1949. Critical review of historical writing in Japan evaluated from the Marxist point of view.

P107. Borton, Hugh. "A survey of Japanese historiography." **Am. hist. rev.,** 43 (Apr. 1938): 489–99. General survey of writing of their history by the Japanese from earliest to modern times, with mention of the most outstanding works.

P108. Hall, John W. "Historiography in Japan." Henry S. Hughes, ed., **Teachers of history: essays in honor of Laurence Bradford Packard** (Ithaca, 1954). Critical outline of Japanese historiography, using the most recent publications. A convenient guide to the author's bibliography *(P3)*.

P109. Yanaga, Chitoshi. "Source materials in Japanese history: the Kamakura period, 1192–1333." **Journal of the American Oriental Society,** 59 (1939): 38–55. Detailed, critical account of important source materials for study of the formation of the first military dictatorship established independently of the imperial court. Especially useful for study of feudalism.

P110. Rekishi Kyōiku Kenkyūkai, ed. **Meiji igo ni okeru rekishigaku no hattatsu.** [Development of historical studies since Meiji.] Tokyo, 1933. A detailed survey of historical writing in Japan, 1868–1925, re-

viewed under various sub-fields by outstanding contemporary historians.

P111. Ienaga, Saburō. **Gendai shigaku hihan.** [A critique of contemporary historiography.] Tokyo, 1953. Objective appraisal of contemporary historical research in Japan, especially valuable for its coverage of post-World War II historians and evaluation of the various schools of historical writing and their works.

P112. Brown, Delmer M. "Recent Japanese political and historical materials." **The American political science review,** 43 (Oct. 1949): 1010–17. Useful guide.

SHORTER GENERAL HISTORIES

The single volume interpretive history is a relative rarity in Japan, and these are generally written as textbooks. Consequently, only a limited number are listed below. The two English titles are the best known short histories. Many of the multi-volume series cited in the next subsection contain single volumes or introductory essays which give short surveys of Japan's history.

P113. Kuroita, Katsumi. **Kokushi no kenkyū.** [Study of Japanese history.] Rev. ed., 4 v., Tokyo, 1931–36. Probably the most influential modern work in Japanese history. V. 1 contains bibliographical chapters covering all aspects of Japanese history. The other volumes constitute a heavily documented political history.

P114. Sakamoto, Tarō. **Nihonshi gaisetsu.** [An introduction to Japanese history.] 2 v. Tokyo, 1950–51. Detailed and able survey from point of view of the postwar "academic" school, written by the senior historian of the Tokyo University Historiographical Institute.

P115. Kawakami, Tasuke. **Nihon rekishi gaisetsu.** [Introduction to Japanese history.] 2 v. Tokyo, 1937–40. One of the best standard political histories available; a product of the prewar "academic" school in Japan.

P116. Nishida, Naojirō. **Nihon bunkashi josetsu.** [An introduction to the history of Japanese culture.] Tokyo, 1932. One of the few truly interpretive cultural histories, which catches the spirit of each period through its literary, artistic, and intellectual achievements.

P117. Tōyama, Shigeki. **Sekai no rekishi: Nihon.** [History of the world: Japan.] Tokyo, 1949. Written for college level instruction, this is one of the most concise statements of the post-World War II "progressive" school of Japanese historians.

P118. Sansom, George B. **Japan, a short cultural history.** Rev. ed., N.Y., 1944. The best single volume history in English, utilizing modern Japanese historical studies. As title indicates, concentrates on cultural growth. Limited to pre-19th century.

P119. Reischauer, Edwin O. **Japan, past and present.** 2nd rev. and enl. ed., N.Y., 1953. Fast-moving survey of Japan's history from earliest times to the present. Excellent introduction to the subject.

LONGER GENERAL HISTORIES

Since the early 1920's Japanese historians, under stimulus from various publishing houses, have produced a remarkable stream of multi-volume, multi-author historical series. These are probably the best general repositories of historical writing on Japan, and are conveniently arranged to provide both survey and specialized coverage. Since World War II, however, there has been a tendency to display either Marxist or non-Marxist points of view. Some of the series listed below contain the best single volumes on individual periods or special subjects.

P120. Sōgō Nihonshi taikei. [Synthetic survey of Japanese history.] 8 v. Tokyo, 1926. [Naigai Shoseki Kabushiki Kaisha.] Written from political and cultural points of view. Still the most detailed and carefully annotated treatment of Japanese history.

P121. Iwanami kōza: Nihon rekishi. [Iwanami series: Japanese history.] 18 cases (132 pamphlets). Tokyo, 1933–35. [Iwanami Shoten.] First of the great pamphlet series on Japanese history. Provides both survey and specialized coverage to the 20th century. Each case contains from 5 to 10 pamphlets prepared by outstanding authorities.

P122. Nihon bunkashi taikei. [Survey of Japanese cultural history.] 12 v. Tokyo, 1937–42. [Seibundō Shinkōsha.] Probably the most useful general history of Japan, from early times to 1926. One or two volumes devoted to each major period, treating political, economic, social, religious, literary, artistic, and foreign affairs.

P123. Nihon rekishi zensho. [Complete series on Japanese history.] Tokyo, 1939 ff. [Mikasa Shobō.] Completed volumes cover several periods, including the modern era, and specialized subjects such as the *shōen* system, Japanese Confucianism, the arts, thought, technology, and foreign affairs.

P124. Taikan Nihon bunkashi sensho. [Survey of Japanese cultural history series.] 19 v. Tokyo, 1940. [Chijin Shokan.] Composed of short, authoritative volumes on Japan's cultural history and such subjects as Japanese thought, Confucianism, Christianity, agriculture, Bushido, and customs, with some of the best introductory surveys of the subjects covered.

P125. Nakamura, Kōya, ed. **Shinkō dai Nihonshi.** [New lectures on Japanese history.] 11 v. Tokyo, 1941–43. Contains excellent one-volume survey of Japanese cultural history by Tsuji Zennosuke. Other volumes are on the major historical periods and such subjects as foreign affairs, social and economic history, art, technology, science, and customs.

P126. Tsuji, Zennosuke. **Nihon bunkashi.** [Cultural history of Japan.] 11 v. Tokyo, 1948–53. An ambitious but somewhat loosely conceived work by a senior cultural historian of post-World War II Japan. First 7 volumes are a chronological cultural history arranged by periods; v. 7 contains an elaborate index; and the last 4 volumes deal with 33 representative historical figures.

P127. Shin-Nihonshi taikei. [New survey of Japanese history.] 7 v. Tokyo, 1952–57. [Asakura Shoten.] A multi-author, period-by-period survey by non-Marxist historians, important as a balance to other postwar multi-volume works. Each volume is divided into sections on political, social, economic, intellectual, and religious developments.

P128. Nishioka, Toranosuke, ed. **Shin-Nihonshi kōza.** [New series on Japanese history.] 69 pamphlets. Tokyo, 1947–53. Compiled in the tradition of the prewar Iwanami series, these pamphlets cover a wide range of general and specific subjects. The approach, though not uniform, is generally that of postwar "progressive" historians. Essays tend to be interpretive and are seldom annotated.

P129. Nihon rekishi kōza. [Japanese history series.] 8 v. Tokyo, 1951–53. [Kawade Shobō.] Compiled by leading "progressive" historians of the postwar period. Attempts to provide a more comprehensive coverage of general history than *P128*.

P130. Rekishigaku Kenkyūkai, Nihonshi Kenkyūkai. **Nihon rekishi kōza.** [Japanese history series.] 8 v. Tokyo, 1957. Very compact volumes of essays on Japanese history arranged by periods. Emphasis is on political history and political, social, and economic institutions. Last volume contains a history of Japanese historiography and a critique of modern Japanese historical scholarship. Contributors are mostly "progressive" historians.

P131. Zusetsu Nihon bunkashi taikei. [An illustrated survey of Japanese history.] 13 v. Tokyo, 1956–58. [Shogakkan.] This profusely illustrated cultural survey is similar to the prewar *Nihon bunkashi taikei* (*P122*), but text is somewhat more popular and does not supersede that of the previous work. Each volume contains an excellent bibliographical essay.

P132. Murdoch, James. **A history of Japan.** 3 v. Kobe and London, 1903–26. Though outmoded in several respects, still the standard and most detailed political history of Japan in English. V. 2–3 (1542–1868) have been largely superseded by more recent monographic studies. G. B. Sansom's projected *History of Japan* in 3 v. will, when completed, largely replace Murdoch as the standard multi-volume history in English.

P133. La Mazelière, Antoine Rous, marquis de. **Le Japon, histoire et civilisation.** 8 v. Paris, 1907–23. Detailed history, based mostly on western sources, with special emphasis on the Restoration period (1867–73).

P134. Sansom, George B. **A history of Japan to 1334.** Stanford, 1958. First volume of a 3 v. history of Japan to 1868, by the dean of English language writers on Japan.

HISTORIES OF SPECIAL PERIODS

Japanese historians of special periods have usually contributed to one or more volumes of a longer history. Therefore, a large portion of the items listed in this subsection, especially for earlier periods, are European. The reader should consult the series histories for many of the most important Japanese works. For special histories on the period prior to about 600 A.D. see Section G.

Period of Court Nobles (592–1167)

P135. Sakamoto, Taro. **Taika kaishin no kenkyū.** [Studies on the Taika reform of 645.] Tokyo, 1938. Standard study of the political, social, and economic history of the reform whereby the imperial system was thoroughly established.

P136. Asakawa, Kan'ichi. **The early institutional life of Japan: a study in the reform of 645 A.D.** Tokyo, 1903. Analysis of the social and economic forces which resulted in the imperial reform, by an outstanding scholar of Japanese feudalism.

P137. Aston, William G., tr. **Nihongi: chronicles of Japan from the earliest times to A.D. 697.** See *G224*.

P138. Chamberlain, Basil H., tr. **Translation of "Ko-ji-ki" . . . or "Records of ancient matters."** See *G222*.

P139. Snellen, J. B., tr. **"Shoku Nihongi: chronicles of Japan, continued from 697–791 A.D." Transactions of the Asiatic Society of Japan,** 2nd ser. 11 (Dec. 1934): 151–239, 14 (June 1937): 209–78. Careful translation, with notes, of part of the third of the six official histories of early Japan. Largely a record of events centering around the imperial court.

P140. Reischauer, Robert K. **Early Japanese history (c. 40 B.C.–A.D. 1167).** 2 v. Princeton, 1937. Detailed chronological register of early events, with a valuable introductory summary.

P141. Sansom, George B. **"Early Japanese law and administration." Transactions of the Asiatic Society of Japan,** 2nd ser. 9 (Dec. 1932): 67–109, 11 (Dec. 1934): 117–49. Detailed description of governmental structure of the Heian period (645–1185

A.D.), with partial translation of the Yōrō or "Taihō" code (718 A.D.).

P142. Reischauer, Edwin O., and Joseph K. Yamigawa, eds. and trs. **Translations from early Japanese literature.** Cambridge, Mass., 1951. Scholarly translation, with extensive and valuable introductions and notes, of four well-known texts of the 11th–13th centuries: the *Izayoi nikki, Tsutsumi chūnagon monogatari,* and parts of the *Ōkagami* and *Heiji monogatari.*

Medieval Period (1167–1603)

Many works on this period appear in the series previously listed.

P143. Shimmi, Kichiji. **Buke seiji no kenkyū.** [Studies on the government of the warrior class.] Tokyo, 1936. Contains three pioneer studies by one of the leading scholars of Japanese feudalism.

P144. Asakawa, Kan'ichi, ed. and tr. **The documents of Iriki, illustrative of the development of the feudal institutions of Japan.** New ed., Tokyo, 1955. Translation, with introduction, bibliography, notes, and Japanese text, of documents relating to the Iriki fief (southern Kyushu) from the 12th to 19th century.

P145. Joüon des Longrais, Frédéric. **Âge de Kamakura: sources (1150–1333), archives, chartes japonaises (monjo).** Paris and Tokyo, 1950. Detailed study of types of official documents issued by the government of the Kamakura period.

P146. Kitabatake, Chikafusa. **Jinnô Shôtôki: Buch von der wahren Gott-Kaiser-Herrschafts-Linie.** Tr. by Hermann Bohner. Tokyo, 1935. Important 14th century history, written in support of the legitimate court; widely used as a basic source by modern Japanese nationalists to justify the superior, unique characteristics of Japan's history.

P147. Sansom, George B., tr. **"The Tsuredzure gusa of Yoshida no kaneyoshi: being the meditations of a recluse in the 14th century." Transactions of the Asiatic Society of Japan,** 39 (1911): 1–146. Good translation of an important work.

P148. Wang, I-t'ung. **Official relations between China and Japan, 1368–1549.** Cambridge, Mass., 1953. Detailed study of relations between the Ashikaga shogunate and the Ming dynasty, based on Chinese and Japanese sources.

Tokugawa Period (1603–1867)

As in the case of other periods, the reader is referred to special volumes of the longer histories. See also Hall, *Japanese history* (*P3*) for works in Japanese on this period.

P149. Mikami, Sanji. **Edo jidai shi.** [A history of the Edo period.] 2 v. Tokyo,

1943. Analysis of origins of the power of the Tokugawa shoguns, and description of the rule of the most influential among them and the forces which led to their downfall.

P150. Frois, Luis. **Die Geschichte Japans (1549–1578).** Tr. by G. Schurhammer and E. A. Voretzsch. Leipzig, 1926. Valuable report by a Portuguese Jesuit, covering the years of his residence in Japan and the period when Christian influence was an important element in Japan's political development.

P151. Rundall, Thomas, ed. **Memorials of the empire of Japan in the XVI and XVII centuries.** London, 1850. Contains "A description of the empire" written during the time of Elizabeth I, taken from *The firste booke of relations of moderne states;* the letters of William Adams, 1611–17, with notes; and a summary of the residence of Don Rodrigo de Vivero y Velasco in Japan, 1608–10.

P152. Siebold, Philipp F. von. **Nippon: Archiv zur Beschreibung von Japan.** 3 v. Berlin, 1930–31. Outstanding European work of early 19th century, valuable as a contemporary account of late Tokugawa period. Originally published in 7 v. (Leiden, 1832–53). A 2nd ed. of 2 v. (Würtzburg and Leipzig, 1897) includes an index.

P153. Kaempfer, Engelbert. **The history of Japan, together with a description of the kingdom of Siam, 1690–92.** Tr. by J. G. Scheuchzer. 3 v. Glasgow, 1906. Still of interest as a contemporary record by a German physician employed by a Dutch factory in Japan. There are Latin, French, Dutch, and German editions.

P154. Boxer, Charles R. **The Christian century in Japan, 1549–1650.** Berkeley, 1951. Excellent study of early western contact with Japan, based on primary Japanese and western sources. Shows the value Japanese feudal barons placed on trade with the Portuguese and Spanish and how this influenced their interest in Christianity.

P155. Nachod, Oskar. **Die Beziehungen der Niederländischen Ostindischen Kompagnie zu Japan im siebzehnten Jahrhundert.** Leipzig, 1897. Detailed account based on archives of the Netherlands East India Company.

P156. Boxer, Charles R. **Jan Compagnie in Japan, 1600–1850: an essay on the cultural, artistic and scientific influence exercised by the Hollanders in Japan from the seventeenth to the nineteenth centuries.** 2nd rev. ed., The Hague, 1950. Despite the title, really ends with the late 18th century. Contains some valuable information relating to Isaac Titsingh, director of the Dutch factory between 1779 and 1784.

P157. Paske-Smith, Montague. **Western barbarians in Japan and Formosa in Tokugawa days, 1603–1868.** Kobe, 1930. Record of trade and residence in Japan by foreigners, especially English, based largely on British East India Company records and archives of the British consulate at Nagasaki and Osaka. Includes some documents.

P158. Keene, Donald. **The Japanese discovery of Europe: Honda Toshiaki and other discoverers, 1720–1798.** N.Y., 1954. Careful study of the writings of Honda Toshiaki (1744–1821), one of the early advocates of western learning, and of the rise of Dutch studies in the 18th and 19th centuries.

P159. Golovnin, Vasilii M. **Memoirs of a captivity in Japan during the years 1811, 1812 and 1813 with observations on the country and the people.** 2nd ed., 3 v., London, 1824. Valuable edition. V. 1 contains introduction on history of British trade with Japan; v. 2–3 give the author's impressions of 19th century Japan as a result of his arrest and detention for parts of three years.

P160. Perry, Matthew C. **Narrative of the expedition of an American squadron to the China seas and Japan performed in the years 1852, 1853, and 1854.** Comp. by Francis L. Hawks. 3 v. Washington, 1856. The official account of Commodore Perry's trip to Japan, compiled under his supervision from the original notes and journals. Last volume contains numerous charts and maps.

P161. Williams, Samuel Wells. "A journal of the Perry expedition to Japan (1853–1854)." Ed. by F. W. Williams. **Transactions of the Asiatic Society of Japan,** 37 (1910): i–ix, 1–259. Account of the expedition by a missionary-interpreter.

P162. Morrow, James. **A scientist with Perry in Japan.** Ed. by Allan B. Cole. Chapel Hill, 1947. One of several journals or reports written by persons who accompanied Perry.

P163. Walworth, Arthur. **Black ships off Japan: the story of Commodore Perry's expedition.** N.Y., 1946. Best single volume on the Perry expedition, based on extensive contemporary U. S. sources.

P164. Harris, Townsend. **The complete journal of Townsend Harris, first American consul general and minister to Japan.** Garden City, 1930. Covers 1855–58, depicting his difficulties in negotiating the first commercial treaty and establishing normal diplomatic relations.

P165. Gubbins, John H. **The progress of Japan, 1853–1871.** Oxford, 1911. Valuable analysis of the transition, with appendices of important treaties and memoranda from 1854 to 1869.

Recent History (1868–1919)

The recent period of Japanese history has so many ramifications that it cannot be left to the coverage provided in generalized series already cited. In fact, most of the latter are deficient in treatment of Japan after the Meiji restoration. Therefore, it is necessary to supplement them by such works as those listed below. Reference also should be made to political histories under Special Topics which pertain to this period, and to several of the listings under Government Publications.

P166. Tokutomi, Iichirō. **Kinsei Nihon kokuminshi.** [A history of the Japanese people in early modern times.] Tokyo, 1918 ff. Though the product of old-fashioned historical scholarship, this is an invaluable source of information on Tokugawa and Meiji history. The 77 volumes published to date cover Japanese political history from mid-16th century to the 1870's.

P167. Ishin Shiryō Hensan Jimukyoku, ed. **Gaikan Ishinshi.** [Introduction to the history of the Restoration.] Tokyo, 1940. The Meiji restoration has received much attention from modern Japanese historians, and interpretations of its causes and the nature of Japan's subsequent historical development are varied and hotly debated. The above is the work of a government-sponsored compilation committee and, therefore, represents the official view. It is a condensation of a much more extensive official history.

P168. Osatake, Takeshi. **Meiji ishin.** [The Meiji restoration.] 4 v. Tokyo, 1942–49. The work of an authoritative and respected political historian, providing one of the most detailed and unbiased accounts of political events of the restoration.

P169. Tōyama, Shigeki. **Meiji ishin.** [The Meiji restoration.] Tokyo, 1951. Perhaps the best known postwar history of the restoration, the work of a Marxist historian.

P170. Inoue, Kiyoshi. **Meiji ishin.** [The Meiji restoration.] Tokyo, 1951. Also the work of a "progressive" historian, but somewhat less Marxist in interpretation than *P169*.

P171. Kaikoku Hyakunen Kinen Bunka Jigyōkai. **Meiji bunka shi.** [Japanese culture in the Meiji era.] 14 v. Tokyo, 1953–57. Covers a wide range of subjects in history of Meiji Japan. V. 1 contains general articles on Meiji cultural history. Others treat education, thought, music, society, economics, life and customs, technology, art, drama, etc. This series is being translated into English.

P172. Gendai Nihon bummeishi. [History of contemporary Japanese civilization.] 18 v. Tokyo, 1940–44. [Tōyō Keizai Shimpōsha.] Probably the most generally useful series on recent Japanese history. V. 1 is a general survey of the last hundred years. Other volumes deal with foreign relations, national defense, law, farm life, emigration, economic development, science, religion, and manners and customs.

P173. Kindai Nihon rekishi kōza. [Series on recent Japanese history.] 11 v. Tokyo, 1939–49. [Hakuyōsha.] Covers Japan's political history from 1868 to the 1920's.

P174. Yanaihara, Tadao, ed. **Gendai Nihon shōshi.** [Short history of modern Japan.] 2 v. Tokyo, 1952. Short but well-balanced series of essays on Japan's recent history, edited by former president of Tokyo University.

P175. Oka, Yoshitake. **Kindai Nihon no keisei.** [The formation of modern Japan.] Tokyo, 1947. Brilliant analysis of the development of Japan's political, social, and economic institutions after the Restoration. One of the few attempts by non-Marxist Japanese historians to interpret this era.

P176. Inoue, Kiyoshi. **Nihon gendai shi.** [History of modern Japan.] 4 v. Tokyo, 1951–52. Interpretive history of Japan during the last hundred years, by a leading "progressive" historian.

P177. Borton, Hugh. **Japan's modern century.** N.Y., 1955. Detailed and interpretive account. Covers the opening of Japan, formation of a centralized monarchy (1868–90), establishment of the Japanese empire, its rise and decline, and the survival of defeat up to 1955. Contains valuable appendices, bibliography, tables, and maps.

P178. Norman, E. Herbert. **Japan's emergence as a modern state: political and economic problems of the Meiji period.** N.Y., 1940. Study of the Restoration (1868), and early industrial, agrarian, and political developments (1868–90). Some of the economic analysis is open to question.

P179. Ike, Nobutaka. **The beginnings of political democracy in Japan.** Baltimore, 1950. Account of the "democratic movement" from 1868 to promulgation of the Constitution of 1889. While containing much valuable material, tends to over-emphasize the importance of these early political movements.

P180. McLaren, Walter W. **A political history of Japan during the Meiji era, 1867–1912.** London, 1916. This account and the following collection of documents were long the standard works on Japan's Meiji restoration.

P181. ——, ed. **Japanese government documents.** London, 1914. Still a valuable primary source.

P182. Itō, Hirobumi. **Commentaries on the constitution of the Empire of Japan.** 3rd ed., Tokyo, 1931. Essential for understanding attitude of Japanese toward the Meiji constitution. Written by its chief author. See also *P317*.

P183. Beckmann, George. **The making of the Meiji constitution: the oligarchs and the constitutional development of Japan, 1868–1891.** Lawrence, Kan., 1957. Particularly valuable for translation of ten key documents which provide the material and structural pattern for author's historical analysis and interpretation. See also *P317*.

P184. Young, A. Morgan. **Japan in recent times, 1912–1926.** N.Y., 1929. Best general history of the period in English, by editor of the *Kobe chronicle;* written from point of view of a reporter of events rather than a historian.

Japan since 1919

As many works on recent history are concerned primarily with foreign relations or political developments, some of the items listed under Histories of Special Topics should also be consulted.

P185. Tōyama, Shigeki, Imai Seiichi, and Fujiwara Akira. **Shōwa shi.** [History of Shōwa Japan.] Tokyo, 1955. An interpretation of Japanese history since 1926, written from Marxist viewpoint. One of the few systematic works covering the Shōwa period.

P186. Hall, Robert K. **Shūshin: the ethics of a defeated nation.** N.Y., 1949. Annotated translation of the official ethics textbooks for primary schools; highly nationalistic. Supplementary to following work.

P187. Hall, Robert K., ed.; John O. Gauntlett, tr. **Kokutai no Hongi. Cardinal principles of the national entity of Japan.** Cambridge, Mass., 1949. Translation of an important text on Japanese "national polity" published by the Ministry of Education as a basis for Japanese nationalism. Valuable as indicating the type of propaganda taught and widely disseminated before World War II.

P188. Reischauer, Edwin O. **The United States and Japan.** Cambridge, Mass., 1950. Rev. ed., 1957. Basic problems facing the United States in its relations with Japan in the post-World War II period.

P189. Feis, Herbert. **The road to Pearl Harbor: the coming of the war between the United States and Japan.** See *AB426.*

P190. Jones, Francis C. **Japan's new order in east Asia: its rise and fall, 1937–45.** London, 1954. Though based on western sources, their exhaustive examination has resulted in a definitive study of Japanese relations in Asia before and during World War II.

P191. Rekishigaku Kenkyūkai. **Taiheiyō sensōshi.** [History of the Pacific War.] 3 v. Tokyo, 1953. Detailed history of Japan's military ventures from the conquest of Manchuria to the Pacific War, written by members of the "progressive" school. Contains collected documents and a bibliography.

P192. Hattori Takushirō. **Dai Tōa sensō shi.** [History of the Greater East Asia War.] 4 v. Tokyo, 1953. Factual history of Japan's participation in the Pacific War.

P193. Kurihara Takeshi ed. **Shūsen Shiroku.** [Documentary history of the end of World War II.] Tokyo, 1952. Invaluable, carefully edited collection of such Foreign Office documents as still existed after Japan's surrender, combined with a history of the war.

P194. Butow, Robert J. C. **Japan's decision to surrender.** Stanford, 1954. Carefully documented analysis of events leading to the Japanese surrender in August, 1945.

P195. Jones, Francis C., Hugh Borton, and B. R. Pearn. **The Far East, 1942–1946.** London, 1955. [Arnold Toynbee, ed., Survey of international affairs, 1939–1946.] Sections by Borton deal with Allied occupation of Japan and Korea, 1945–47, giving a detailed history of the formulation and implementation of occupational policy (which author helped formulate).

P196. Supreme Commander for the Allied Powers. **Political reorientation of Japan, September 1945 to September 1948.** 2 v. Washington, 1949. Though an official history of MacArthur's first three years of occupation of Japan, a surprisingly objective and valuable work.

P197. Tōgō, Shigenori. **The cause of Japan.** Tr. and ed. by Tōgō Fumihiko and Ben B. Blakeney. N.Y., 1956. One of the numerous accounts of Japan's war years by officials. Togo was minister of foreign affairs at the beginning and end of the war.

HISTORIES OF SPECIAL AREAS

Local histories, of varying degrees of scholarship and thoroughness, are popular in Japan. Most of the major cities have sponsored detailed histories; and large compilations of historical records, such as *Dai Nihon komonjo* (*P72*), have sections on the various feudal families and their domains.

P198. Kōshaku Maeda-ke Hensanbu, ed. **Kaga-han shiryō.** [Historical materials of the Kaga domain.] Tokyo, 1929 ff. This is the most ambitious private publication of documents relating to a single historical family. Materials are arranged in chronological order begnning with 1538. In 15 v. the series reached 1847; it is planned to continue it to 1871.

P199. Harrison, John A. **Japan's northern frontier.** Gainesville, Fla., 1953. Short study of Japanese expansion and colonization of Hokkaido, with special reference to relations of Japan and Russia in the 19th century.

P200. Ponsonby-Fane, Richard A. **Kyoto: its history and vicissitudes since its foundation in 792 to 1868.** Hong Kong, 1931. Development of the imperial capital during the zenith of its power, from cultural point of view.

P201. Montandon, George. **La civilisation aïnou et les cultures arctiques.** Paris, 1937. Important and stimulating work which attempts to relate the Ainu to cultures of northern Eurasia.

HISTORIES OF SPECIAL TOPICS

Political

Many histories of special periods are primarily political, and have been listed previously.

P202. Ōtsu, Jun'ichirō. **Dai Nihon kenseishi.** [Constitutional history of Japan.] 10 v. Tokyo, 1927–28. Authoritative and detailed chronological history of Japanese government and politics, 1867–1926; especially useful for quotations from primary sources and its statistical tables.

P203. Osatake, Takeshi. **Nihon kenseishi taikō.** [Outline of Japanese constitutional history.] 2 v. Tokyo, 1938. Authoritative political history of the Meiji period, especially valuable for detailed treatment of inner workings of the Japanese government.

P204. Shinobu, Seizaburō. **Taishō seijishi.** [Political history of the Taisho era.] 4 v. Tokyo, 1951–53. This detailed and profusely documented work by a leading Marxist historian covers the years 1912–26. Should be used with caution because of author's political prejudices.

P205. Royama, Masamichi. **Seiji shi.** [Political history.] Tokyo, 1940. A work by one of Japan's more conservative political scientists, concentrating on recent history.

P206. Reischauer, Robert K. **Japan, government-politics.** N.Y., 1939. Interpretive and provocative summary of personalities and forces behind the formation of a constitutional monarchy. Particularly valuable for period 1868–1919.

P207. Scalapino, Robert. **Democracy and the party movement in prewar Japan: the failure of the first attempt.** Berkeley, 1953. A basic study of Japanese politics to World War II. Particularly valuable for analysis of social origins of the early parties and the economic basis of their support.

P208. Ike, Nobutaka. **Japanese politics: an introductory survey.** N.Y., 1957. Analysis of Japanese politics through discussion of historical, social, ideological, and institutional settings and of such dominant political forces as business, labor, and agriculture. Especially valuable for its treatment of the bureaucracy, political parties, the electorate, and the ineffectual role of the intellectual in Japanese politics. Concentrates on modern times.

P209. Jansen, Marius B. **The Japanese and Sun Yat-sen.** Cambridge, Mass., 1954. Scholarly study of the Chinese patriot's relations with Japanese officials, nationalists, and politicians.

P210. Ballard, George A. **The influence of the sea on the political history of Japan.** London, 1921. An important study.

P211. Colbert, Evelyn S. **The left wing in Japanese politics.** N.Y., 1952. Leftist influences in Japan since formation of political parties in the 20th century, with special emphasis on postwar developments.

P212. Swearingen, Rodger, and Paul Langer. **Red flag in Japan: international communism in action, 1919–1951.** Cambridge, Mass., 1952. Careful and important analysis of operation of the Communist apparatus in Japan, greatly strengthened by the authors' use of Chinese, Japanese, and Russian sources.

Social, Economic, and Legal History

A great deal of specialized literature exists in these fields. The following selections are of a more general nature and will prove useful as supplements to the politically or culturally oriented histories in previous subsections. It should be remembered also that many of the larger series publications contain volumes which deal with Japanese social, economic, and legal institutions.

P213. Takigawa, Masajirō. **Nihon shakaishi.** [Social history of Japan.] Tokyo, 1929. Extremely detailed analysis of class structure of Japanese society during each of the major historical periods. Quotes extensively from laws and documents to establish the legal position of various strata of society and to describe the administrative and social structure of the times.

P214. Nakamura, Kichiji. **Nihon shakaishi gaisetsu.** [Outline history of Japanese society.] Tokyo, 1947. One of the best short surveys of Japanese socio-political history. Coverage is from ancient times to the 20th century.

P215. Nomura, Kanetarō. **Nihon shakai keizaishi.** [Social and economic history of Japan.] Tokyo, 1950 ff. Ambitious work by one of the leading conservative social and economic historians of Japan; to be complete in 12 v. Each volume covers a major historical period, and deals in broad interpretive fashion with its political, social, economic, and cultural development.

P216. Kimura Motoi, ed. **Nihon hōken shakai kenkyūshi.** [History of the study of Japanese feudalism.] Tokyo, 1956. Most comprehensive and generally satisfactory survey of the study of feudal institutions by Japanese historians. Major portion of volume is a detailed history of feudal institutions in Japan, with emphasis on problems, interpretations, and bibliography.

P217. Itō, Tasaburō. **Nihon hōken seidoshi.** [History of the feudal system in Japan.] Tokyo, 1950. Best single-volume survey of Japanese feudal institutions. Point of view is distinctly less Marxist than that of most writers in the field.

P218. Tsuchiya, Takao. **Nihon keizaishi gaiyō.** [An outline of Japanese economic history.] 2 v. Tokyo, 1934–39. Survey of Japanese history, with emphasis on economic institutions, from prehistoric times to the 1920's. While the author tends toward a Marxist interpretation, the work contains much valuable descriptive material. A short summary in English appears in *Transactions of the Asiatic Society of Japan*, 2nd ser. 15 (1937).

P219. Horie, Yasuzō. **Nihon keizaishi.** [Economic history of Japan.] Tokyo, 1949. Probably the best survey of Japanese economic institutions from early times to the present; a relatively unbiased account with emphasis on relationship of economic institutions to the political and social structure. Useful classified bibliography.

P220. Kajinishi, Mitsuhaya. **Nihon keizaishi.** [Economic history of Japan.] Tokyo, 1950. This and *P221*, by an outstanding economic historian of post-World War II Japan, provide an unbiased survey. Emphasis is more strictly economic than in previously cited works.

P221. ——. **Shōwa keizaishi.** [Economic history of the Shōwa era.] Tokyo, 1951.

P222. Tōyō Keizai Kenkyūjo. **Sakuin seiji keizai dai nempyō.** [Chronology of politics and economics with index.] 2 v. Tokyo, 1943. Invaluable to the student of post-Restoration history. V. 1 is a standard chronology of major events covering the period 1841–1943 in great detail. V. 2 is an exhaustive index to the chronology. Appendices provide tabular data on government officials, elections, and other political and economic matters.

P223. Nomura, Kanetarō. **Tokugawa jidai no keizai shisō.** [Economic thought of the Tokugawa period.] Tokyo, 1939. Brilliant analysis of economic thought of early modern Japan.

P224. Honjō, Eijirō. **The social and economic history of Japan.** Kyoto, 1935. Best single volume on the subject in English. As the chapters are translations of university lectures, there is some repetition of material and the volume appears to lack a central theme. Contains valuable glossary.

P225. ——. **Economic theory and history of Japan in the Tokugawa period.** Tokyo, 1943. Covers specific and more general aspects of economic history before 1868.

P226. Kada, Tetsuji. **Ishin igo no shakai keizai shisō gairon.** [Outline of post-Restoration social and economic thought.] Tokyo, 1934. Deals with the economic theory behind the Restoration (1868); economic policy of the Meiji government; and such intellectual movements as liberalism, socialism, and nationalism.

P227. Lockwood, William W. **The economic development of Japan: growth and structural change, 1868–1938.** Princeton, 1954. Careful and detailed account of Japan's economic growth in terms of gross national product, covering technology, capital, foreign trade, and structural changes.

P228. Allen, George C. **A short economic history of modern Japan, 1867–1937.** London, 1946. One of the best brief narratives of Japan's economic development prior to World War II. Contains valuable charts and tables.

P229. Smith, Thomas C. **Political change and industrial development in Japan: government enterprise, 1868–1880.** Stanford, 1955. Careful study of economic and political forces which led toward government ownership of some enterprises and sales of others.

P230. Kobayashi, Ushisaburō. **The basic industries and social history of Japan, 1914–1918.** New Haven, 1930. [Carnegie Endowment for International Peace, Japanese series.]

P231. Schumpeter, Elizabeth B., ed. **The industrialization of Japan and Manchukuo, 1930–1940.** N.Y., 1940. Authoritative surveys of developments in Japan's population, food, and raw material position; industrial organization; and balance of payments. Chapters covering 1936–40 are subject to revision in light of more recent information.

P232. Cohen, Jerome B. **Japan's economy in war and reconstruction.** Minneapolis, 1949. While written primarily as an economic study, is useful to the economic historian interested in the 1941–49 period.

P233. Nihon Keizaishi Kenkyūjo. **Nihon keizaishi nenkan.** [Yearbook of Japanese economic history.] Tokyo, 1932–44, 1955 ff. (Annual.) Prewar volumes appeared as special issues of the journal *Keizaishi kenkyū*, and provided annual bibliographical surveys of Japanese research on Japanese, oriental, and occidental economic history. Most of the bibliographical material from these issues has been included in references cited above. Postwar issues have adopted the format of the Honjō bibliographical series and serve as yearly supplements to this. They continue to list works on Chinese and European economic history. With the 1957 issue the title of this series was changed to *Keizaishi bunken* [Bibliography of economic history].

P234. Ishii, Ryōsuke. **Nihon hōseishi gaisetsu.** [An introduction to the history of Japanese jurisprudence.] Tokyo, 1948. This and the following contain considerable overlapping material. The above is an authoritative, broadly conceived treatment of Japanese legal institutions from earliest times through the Tokugawa period.

P235. ——. **Nihon hōseishiyō.** [Essentials of Japanese legal history.] Tokyo, 1949. Especially useful for its exhaustive classified bibliography of modern studies.

Foreign Relations

Many works on foreign relations are contained in the series and collections previously listed, and others will be found in the subsection on Special Periods. See also the Government Publications subsection for collections of treaties.

P236. Tsuji, Zennosuke. **Kaigai kotsū shiwa.** [Historical essays on foreign relations.] Rev. ed., Tokyo, 1935. Carefully annotated historical sketch of Japanese foreign relations from earliest times to 1853, with emphasis on cultural contacts, especially after the mid-16th century.

P237. Sansom, George B. **The western world and Japan: a study in the interaction of European and Asiatic cultures.** N.Y., 1950. Discusses cultural contacts of Europe and Asia to the mid-18th century, and the cultural history of Japan from the 17th century with special reference to western influences.

P238. Kuno, Yoshisaburo. **Japanese expansion on the Asiatic continent: a study in the history of Japan with special reference to her international relations with China, Korea, and Russia.** 2 v. Berkeley, 1937–40. Detailed but sometimes uncritical treatment of foreign relations from earliest times to 1868. Includes many valuable translations of documents.

P239. Nihon Kokusai Seiji Gakkai. **Nihon gaikōshi kenkyū, Meiji jidai.** [Studies in Japanese foreign relations, the Meiji period.] Tokyo, 1957. When joined by the promised companion issues on other periods, this work will stand as a valuable contribution to the scholarly study of Japanese foreign relations. Contains authoritative articles on important aspects of Meiji foreign relations, and a valuable bibliography of Japanese and western works.

P240. Kaikoku Hyakunen Kinen Bunka Jigyōkai. **Nichibei bunka kōshōshi.** [History of Japanese-American cultural relations.] 6 v. Tokyo, 1954–57. Voluminous, scholarly history of U. S. relations with Japan and their cultural effects, covering diplomatic, commercial, religious, educational, literary, and intellectual relations, and Japanese migration to the United States. Three volumes have been translated into English.

P241. Treat, Payson J. **Diplomatic relations between the United States and Japan, 1853–1895.** 2 v. Stanford, 1932. This and *P242* are selected excerpts from U. S. archives with commentary, covering chief problems of diplomacy.

P242. ——. **Diplomatic relations between the United States and Japan, 1895–1905.** Stanford, 1939.

P243. U. S. Department of State. **Papers relating to the foreign relations of the United States: Japan, 1931–1941.** 2 v. Washington, 1943. Basic documents on negotiations with Japan during the decade preceding Pearl Harbor.

P244. U. S. Congress. **Investigation of the Pearl Harbor attack: report of the Joint Committee on the Investigation of the Pearl Harbor Attack, 79th Congress.** Washington, 1946. [79th Cong., 2nd sess., Senate doc. 244.] This and *P245* contain testimony which throws considerable light on U. S.-Japanese negotiations before outbreak of the war.

P245. ——. **Pearl Harbor attack: hearings before the Joint Committee on the Investigation of the Pearl Harbor Attack.** 39 pts. Washington, 1946.

Religious and Intellectual History

Emphasis of the following works is on the pre-modern period. Modern religious and intellectual movements are less frequently treated by Japanese historians, whose attention is directed more toward political and social developments. While several large essay collections and series on thought and religion are in existence, they have been omitted because they are not exclusively historical in emphasis. However, some monographs of a similar nature have been included.

P246. Hiyane, Yasusada. **Nihon shūkyōshi.** [A history of religion in Japan.] Rev. ed., Tokyo, 1951. This monumental work is a vast repository of historical information on the various religious faiths of Japan.

P247. Saigusa, Hiroto, and Torii Hiroo. **Nihon shūkyō shisōshi.** [History of Japanese religion and thought.] Tokyo, 1948. Useful survey of religious sects and movements approached from the social historian's point of view.

P248. Kishimoto, Hideo, ed. **Japanese religion in the Meiji era.** Tr. by John F. Howes. Tokyo, 1956. One of a series on Japanese culture in the Meiji era, carefully edited and rearranged by the translator.

P249. Anesaki, Masaharu. **History of Japanese religion with special reference to the social and moral life of the nation.** London, 1930. Good summary by a recognized authority on Japanese religion.

P250. Muraoka, Maretsugu. **Nihon shisō-shi kenkyū.** [Studies in Japanese intellectual history.] 4 v. Tokyo, 1930–49. Collected essays of one of the outstanding intellectual historians of Japan, covering a wide range of subjects. Includes survey histories of Japanese thought, philosophy, and religion, and specialized studies of Shinto, "Japanese spirit," national learning, and various intellectual leaders.

P251. Tsuda, Sōkichi. **Bungaku ni arawaretaru waga kokumin shisō no kenkyū.** [A study of our national thought as manifested in literature.] 4 v. Tokyo, 1916–21.

Monumental study of great repute. Coverage is from early times to end of the Tokugawa period (1867).

P252. Watsuji, Tetsurō. **Nihon seishinshi kenkyū.** [Studies in the history of the Japanese spirit.] 2 v. Tokyo, 1926–35. Collected works of an outstanding non-conformist intellectual historian, containing essays on Japanese thought, esthetics, religion, and art.

P253. Brown, Delmer M. **Nationalism in Japan: an introductory historical analysis.** Berkeley, 1955. General survey from early times to the postwar period, with over half the volume devoted to modern nationalism. Contains copious translations from nationalist writers.

P254. Tsuji, Zennosuke. **Nihon Bukkyōshi.** [History of Japanese Buddhism.] 7 v. Tokyo, 1944–52. Largely cultural history with emphasis on the role of Buddhism in formation of Japanese culture. By an outstanding modern historian.

P255. Eliot, Sir Charles N. E. **Japanese Buddhism.** London, 1935. Standard work on the subject in English. Includes a chapter on Nichiren by Sir George Sansom.

P256. Visser, Marinus W. de. **Ancient Buddhism in Japan: sūtras and ceremonies in use in the seventh and eighth centuries A.D. and their history in later times.** 2 v. Leiden, 1935. A standard work showing extremely detailed and careful scholarship.

P257. Reischauer, Edwin O. **Ennin's travels in T'ang China.** See *O382*.

P258. ——, tr. **Ennin's diary: the record of a pilgrimage to China in search of the law.** See *O383*.

P259. Kiyohara, Sadao. **Shintōshi.** [A history of Shinto.] Tokyo, 1932. One of the most substantial historical surveys of Japanese Shinto.

P260. Tsuda, Sōkichi. **Nihon no Shintō.** [Japanese Shinto.] Tokyo, 1949. One of the first of the postwar essays on Shinto and Japanese thought, by a leading non-conformist.

P261. Holtom, Daniel C. **The national faith of Japan: a study in modern Shinto.** London, 1938. Careful, objective analysis.

P262. ——. **Modern Japan and Shinto nationalism: a study of present-day trends in Japanese religions.** Rev. ed., Chicago, 1947. Supplements *P261*.

P263. Inoue, Tetsujirō. **Teisei zōho Nihon shushi gakuha no tetsugaku.** [Revised and enlarged philosophy of Chu Hsi in Japan.] Tokyo, 1915. General account of Sung Confucianism as elaborated by one of Japan's leading philosophers.

P264. Fisher, Galen M., tr. "Dai gaku wakumon: a discussion of public questions in the light of the great learning by Kumazawa Banzan." **Transactions of the Asiatic Society of Japan,** 2nd ser. 16 (May 1938): 259–356. Translation of one of the chief

texts of a leading advocate of the Wang Yang Ming school of philosophy in Japan.

P265. Spae, Joseph J. **Itô Jinsai, a philosopher, educator and sinologist of the Tokugawa period.** Peiping, 1948. Careful study of a Tokugawa Confucianist of the classical school, emphasizing the Japanese traditional interpretation.

P266. Graf, Olaf. **Kaibara Ekiken . . . ein Beitrag zur japanischen Geistesgeschichte des 17. Jahrhunderts und zur chinesischen Sung-Philosophie.** Leiden, 1942. Important monograph. Contains, among other texts, translation of Kaibara's *Daigiraku.*

P267. Anesaki, Masaharu. **A concordance to the history of Kirishitan missions: Catholic missions in Japan in the sixteenth and seventeenth centuries.** Tokyo, 1930. [Proceedings of the Imperial Academy, suppl. to v. 6.] Basic study by the leading authority. Includes a map indicating where Christians existed or were persecuted.

P268. ——. **Kirishitan dendō no kōhai.** [History of Christian missionary work.] Tokyo, 1930. Detailed account of Christian activity in Japan.

P269. Cary, Otis. **A history of Christianity in Japan.** 2 v. N.Y. and London, 1909. Most comprehensive work in English. Though long out of date, still a valuable reference.

P270. Ototake, Iwazō. **Nihon kokumin kyōikushi.** [History of the education of the Japanese people.] Tokyo, 1944. Standard survey from earliest times to 1925, emphasizing the growth of popular education.

P271. Ōkubo, Toshiaki. **Nihon no daigaku.** [Japanese universities.] Tokyo, 1938. Chronological survey of development of educational centers beginning with the 8th century.

P272. Keenleyside, Hugh L., and A. F. Thomas. **History of Japanese education and present educational system.** Tokyo, 1937. One of the few studies in English prior to World War II.

Literature and Art

The following entries in Japanese are general surveys and will prove useful as introductions to the field of literary and art history. Some of the best translations of famous diaries, poetry, novels, and plays are also included as illustrations of available material.

P273. Sasaki, Nobutsuna, and others. **Nihon bungaku zenshi.** [Complete history of Japanese literature.] 13 v. Tokyo, 1935–43. The outstanding multi-volume historical survey, covering from Nara through Meiji period. Most volumes are well documented.

P274. Asō, Isoji. **Nihon bungakushi.** [History of Japanese literature.] Tokyo, 1949. Most satisfactory single-volume survey of Japanese literary history.

P275. Iwanami kōza: Nihon bungaku. [Iwanami series: Japanese literature.] 20 v. Tokyo, 1931–33. [Iwanami Shoten.] Many essays on all phases of Japanese literature, prepared by outstanding authorities of the 1930's.

P276. Nihon bungaku kōza. [Series on Japanese literature.] 8 v. Tokyo, 1951. Kawade Shobō. One of several postwar essay series modeled after the prewar Iwanami one. Modern in conception and primarily historical in approach. V. 8 is of special value for its treatment of methodology and its bibliographies.

P277. Keene, Donald L., ed. **Anthology of Japanese literature.** 2 v. N.Y., 1955–56. V. 1, from earliest era to mid-19th century, contains a brilliant, but necessarily brief, selection of representative writings with helpful annotations. V. 2, dealing with modern literature, is more extensive in coverage.

P278. The Manyōshū: one thousand poems selected and translated from the Japanese. Tokyo, 1940. [Nippon Gakujutsu Shinkōkai.] The best, though incomplete, translation of the oldest anthology.

P279. Waley, Arthur, tr. **The tale of Genji: a novel in six parts translated from the Japanese.** Boston, 1925–33. Excellent, complete translation of Japan's greatest early novel by Murasaki Shikibu (b. 978), giving a colorful, though perhaps idealized, account of life at the imperial court in the 11th century.

P280. ——, tr. **The pillow-book of Sei Shōnagon.** Boston, 1929. Selections from the *Makura no sōshi* by a court lady who was a contemporary of Murasaki Shikibu. Beautifully translated; scholarly introduction.

P281. Shively, Donald H., ed. and tr. **The love suicide at Amijima (Shinjū ten no Amijima).** Cambridge, Mass., 1953. Translation of famous play of Chikamatsu Monzaemon (1653–1725), with extensive notes on the theater of the Tokugawa period. Should be compared with the following.

P282. Keene, Donald L., ed. **The battle of Coxinga, Chikamatsu's puppet play, its background and importance.** London, 1951. Complete translation, with extended introduction, annotations, and bibliography regarding Japanese puppet theater, Chikamatsu Monzaemon, and the famous 17th century Sino-Japanese pirate, Coxinga.

P283. Tani, Shin'ichi. **Nihon bijutsushi gaisetsu.** [An introduction to the history of Japanese art.] Tokyo, 1948. Useful; best for its handling of the medieval period. This and *P284* are two of the most generally satisfactory surveys of Japanese art history prior to the 20th century.

P284. Kuno, Takeshi, ed. **Nihon bijutsushi.** [History of Japanese art.] 2 v. Tokyo, 1949–50. Attempts to relate developments in the field of art with social and political move-

ments for each of the major historical periods.

P285. Fujikake, Shizuya. **Nihon bijutsu zusetsu.** [A pictorial survey of Japanese art.] Tokyo, 1950. Latest of many illustrated histories of art. Draws upon the collaborative efforts of many specialists who have written introductory passages for each field of art.

P286. Fenollosa, Ernest F. **Epochs of Chinese and Japanese art: an outline history of Asiatic design.** New and rev. ed., 2 v., N.Y., 1921. A pioneer work, outstanding for interpretation of art as related to social conditions. Should be used only after consulting E. A. Grant, "A note on Fenollosa's attributions," *Bulletin of the Museum of Fine Arts, Boston,* 25 (Oct. 1927): 83–84.

P287. Warner, Langdon. **The enduring art of Japan.** Cambridge, Mass., 1952. Excellent short history of art, profusely illustrated. Centers around the early religious motivation for art, chief art periods from late 8th to mid-18th century, and the influence of Zen.

P288. Kimura, Shigeo. **Nihon kindai bijutsu shi.** [History of contemporary Japanese art.] Tokyo, 1956. Authoritative survey of period since 1868.

BIOGRAPHIES

Biographical Materials

Biographies of many Japanese who have been prominent since the mid-19th century are now available in printed collections. Most of these publications are devoted to individual figures. A few of the more prominent ones are listed below, together with some examples of biographical dictionaries.

P289. Shinsen daijimmei jiten. [Newly selected biographical dictionary.] 9 v. Tokyo, 1937–41. [Heibonsha.] Largest of the many biographical dictionaries of historical coverage. Contains lengthy biographies of famous men of modern and pre-modern times. Many of the articles cite bibliographical references.

P290. Nihon Chosakuken Kyōgikai. **Bunka jin meiroku.** [A who's who of persons in cultural activities.] Tokyo, 1951 ff. (Annual.) Valuable as a reference on contemporary scholars, this work gives essential biographical and career data on copyright holders in the fields of art, language, philosophy, economics, law, politics, criticism, history, geography, and others. Lists major publications for each individual. Contains tables of publishers, cultural organizations, newspapers, and journals.

P291. Nihon Shiseki Kyōkai, ed. **Nihon Shiseki Kyōkai kankōsho.** [Books published by Nihon Shiseki Kyōkai.] Tokyo, 1915 ff. One of the few major collections of biographical materials covering more than one individual. Volumes or groups of volumes are devoted to Japanese who distinguished themselves in the Meiji restoration. Materials include diaries, correspondence, and private papers.

P292. Dai Saigō Zenshū Kankōkai, ed. **Dai Saigō zenshū.** [Collected works of Saigō Takamori.] 3 v. Tokyo, 1926–27. One of several collections of correspondence and papers relating to Saigō Takamori, an outstanding leader of the Meiji restoration.

P293. Ōkubo-ke, ed. **Ōkubo Toshimichi monjo.** [Documents on Ōkubo Toshimichi.] 10 v. Tokyo, 1927–29. Chief collection of sources on another of the Meiji reformers.

P294. Ōkuma-ke, ed. **Ōkuma Shigenobu kankei monjo.** [Documents relating to Ōkuma Shigenobu.] 6 v. Tokyo, 1932–35. Part of the *Nihon Shiseki Kyōkai kankōsho* series *(P291)*. These documents cover the life of Ōkuma (statesman, educator, party leader, and opportunist) from 1868 to 1882.

P295. Shibusawa Sein Kinen Zaidan Ryumonsha, ed. **Shibusawa Eiichi denki shiryō.** [Biographical materials on Shibusawa Eiichi.] Tokyo, 1955 ff. Scheduled to run to 45 volumes, this vast repository on the life and times of Japan's pioneer modern industrialist will constitute a major source of information on the political and economic history of the Meiji and Taishō periods.

P296. Hara Keiichirō, ed. **Hara Kei nikki.** [Diary of Hara Kei.] 10 v. Tokyo, 1950–51. Diary of one of the foremost political figures of first two decades of the 20th century.

P297. Harada, Kumaō. **Saionji Kō to seikyoku.** [Prince Saionji and the political scene.] 9 v. Tokyo, 1950–55. Detailed diary account of the life and political activities of Prince Saionji from 1928 to 1940. Large portions of this were translated into the *Proceedings and exhibits of the International Military Tribunal for the Far East*.

Specific Biographies

The writing of personal biographies was not generally practiced in Japan prior to modern times. While a few modern biographies have been written for some of the great men of the past (such as *P298–299*), these generally leave much to be desired in completeness and interpretation. Since 1868, however, major figures in politics and other professional fields have received ample biographical attention. Several biographies in Japanese are listed to indicate the variety of materials available. Since most of these are the work of house biographers or compilation teams, they tend to be eulogistic and uninterpretive. This is compensated for by the frequency with which they quote documents and passages from writings of the individual. A few biographies in English are also listed to indicate the type of material available in that category.

P298. Shibata, Akimasa. **Tokugawa Ieyasu to sono shūi.** [Tokugawa Ieyasu and his environment.] 3 v. Okazaki, 1935. Life of the founder of the Tokugawa dictatorship.

P299. Shibusawa, Eiichi. **Tokugawa Keiki Kō den.** [Biography of Prince Tokugawa Yoshinobu.] 8 v. Tokyo, 1918. Life of the last Tokugawa shogun.

P300. Inoue Kowashi Kō Denki Hensankai. **Segai Inoue Kō den.** [The life of Prince Inoue.] 5 v. Tokyo, 1933–34.

P301. Shumpo Kō Tsuitōkai. **Itō Hirobumi den.** [The life of Itō Hirobumi.] 3 v. Tokyo, 1940. Leading figure in drafting Japan's constitution of 1889 and one of the most powerful of the Meiji reformers.

P302. Tokutomi, Iichirō. **Kōshaku Yamagata Aritomo den.** [The life of Prince Yamagata Aritomo.] 3 v. Tokyo, 1933. Outstanding military figure of the Meiji period.

P303. Itō, Masanori. **Katō Kōmei den.** [The life of Katō Takaaki.] 2 v. Tokyo, 1929.

P304. Tsurumi, Yūsuke. **Gotō Shimpei den.** [The life of Gotō Shimpei.] 11 v. Tokyo, 1943–47. A 4 v. biography by the same author appeared in 1937–38.

P305. Tokutomi, Iichirō. **Kōshaku Matsukata Masayoshi den.** [The life of Prince Matsukata Masayoshi.] 2 v. Tokyo, 1935. Japan's chief financier of the late 19th century.

P306. Bokudō Sensei Denki Kankōkai. **Inukai Bokudō den.** [The life of Inukai Tsuyoshi.] 3 v. Tokyo, 1938.

P307. Konoe Fumimaro Denki Hensan Kankōkai. **Konoe Fumimaro.** 2 v. Tokyo, 1952.

P308. Coates, Harper H., and Ishizuka Ryugaku, trs. and eds. **Hōnen, the Buddhist saint: his life and teaching.** 2nd ed., Kyoto, 1925. Translation of the official biography of Hōnen (1133–1212), founder of Jōdo Buddhism, one of Japan's leading sects. Copious footnotes make this a valuable dictionary of Japanese Buddhism. A 5 v. edition was published in Kyoto in 1949.

P309. Anesaki, Masaharu. **Nichiren, the Buddhist prophet.** Reprint, Cambridge, Mass., 1949. Short biography of the founder of an important sect.

P310. Hall, John W. **Tanuma Okitsugu, 1719–1788, forerunner of modern Japan.** Cambridge, Mass., 1955. Life and political career of a leading administrator of the Tokugawa period. Throws valuable light on the 18th century.

P311. Eckstein, Gustav. **Noguchi.** N.Y., 1931. Interesting biography of a heroic scientist (1876–1928).

P312. Falk, Edwin A. **Togo and the rise of Japanese sea power.** N.Y., 1936. Biography of Admiral Heihachirō Togō, the man chiefly responsible for defeat of the Russian navy in the Tsushima Strait in 1905.

P313. Fukuzawa, Yukichi. **The autobiography of Fukuzawa Yukichi.** Tr. by Kiyooka Eiichi. 3rd rev. ed., Tokyo, 1947. Contains valuable sidelights on Japanese life before and during the Meiji restoration by one of the leading educators of the 19th century.

GOVERNMENT PUBLICATIONS

The field of government records and publications is a vast one which only recently has begun to come under systematic organization by Japanese bibliographers. Availability of government documents will be found in the *Directory of research libraries* (*P24*). For information on government publications the two following works (*P314–315*) will prove useful.

P314. Naikaku Insatsukyoku. **Kanchō kankō tosho mokuroku.** [Catalog of government publications.] Tokyo, 1927–37. (Quarterly.) Catalog of all books, serial publications, pamphlets, and other materials published by government offices. Succeeded until 1943 by *Kanchō kankō tosho geppō* (monthly).

P315. Kokuritsu Kokkai Toshokan. **Kanchō kankōbutsu sōgōmokuroku.** [General catalog of government publications.] Tokyo, 1952 ff. (Annual.) First issue covers from Sep. 1945 to Dec. 1950, and subsequent issues one year each. There is generally a two year lag between catalog date and the material covered.

P316. Dai Nihon Teikoku Gikai Shi Kankōkai, ed. **Dai Nihon Teikoku Gikai shi.** [Records of the Imperial Japanese Diet.] 18 v. Tokyo, 1926–30. Combined collection of the stenographic records of the Japanese Diet from 1890 through 1928. Also contains information on the general elections and the lives of prominent Diet members. More convenient for these years than the officially published record of Diet proceedings contained in the *Kampō gōgai* (see *P319*).

P317. Itō, Hirobumi, ed. **Hisho ruisan.** [Classified collection of secret documents.] 25 v. Tokyo, 1933–36. Basic collection of documents drawn from the Meiji government files; an important primary source on the Japanese government from 1868 to 1900.

P318. Japan. Diet. **The official gazette extra.** Tokyo, 1946 ff. Proceedings of the Imperial Diet and of the National Diet from May 1946. For detailed information see the *Am. pol. sci. rev.*, 42 (June 1948): 642.

P319. Naikaku Insatsukyoku, ed. **Kampō.** Tokyo, 1883 ff. (Daily.) Official gazette of the Japanese government and the most authoritative source on governmental activities. Prints all laws, ordinances, regulations, official announcements, notices, schedules of promotion for the civil service, and informa-

tion on many other official matters. A supplement, *Kampō gōgai*, makes available stenographic records of proceedings of both houses of the Diet.

P320. ——, ed. **Hōrei zensho.** [Compendium of laws and ordinances.] Tokyo, 1885 ff. (Monthly.) The authoritative official collection of all laws, ordinances, and notices promulgated by the Japanese government in its *Kampō*. A separate issue covers the years from Oct. 1867 to the end of 1884.

P321. Teikoku Chihō Gyōsei Gakkai, ed. **Sankō jōbun sonyū kajo jizai genkō hōki zensho.** [Loose-leaf reference compendium of laws and regulations in force.] 25 v. Tokyo, 1930. One of several compilations of laws currently in effect. This series is published unofficially, but is perhaps the most complete and has the advantage of being brought up to date periodically by loose-leaf supplements.

P322. The **Commercial code of Japan.** 2 v. Tokyo, 1931–32. [International Association of Japan, Codes Translation Committee.] This and *P323* contain the Commercial code as first promulgated and amendments to 1938.

P323. The **Commercial code of Japan as amended in 1938.** 2 v. Tokyo, 1943–44. [International Association of Japan, Codes Translation Committee.]

P324. The **Criminal code of Japan, as amended in 1954, and the Minor offenses law of Japan.** Tr. by Thomas L. Blakemore. 2nd rev. ed., Rutland, Vt., and Tokyo, 1954. Full translation of the Criminal code with amendments resulting from World War II and the occupation.

P325. Supreme Commander for the Allied Powers. **Catalogue of SCAP directives to the Imperial Japanese government.** Tokyo, 1947 ff.

P326. ——. **Directives of the supreme commander for the Allied powers.** 5 v. Tokyo, 1946–48. Directives issued to the Japanese government from Sep. 1945 to 1948.

P327. Uyehara, Cecil H., comp. **Checklist of archives in the Japanese Ministry of Foreign Affairs, Tokyo, Japan, 1868–1945; microfilmed for the Library of Congress.** Washington, 1954.

P328. Japan. Foreign Office. **Treaties and conventions between the Empire of Japan and other powers.** 4 v. Tokyo, 1884–1925. Covers chief treaties from the Meiji restoration to the mid-1920's. See also *P95*.

P329. Sōrifu Tōkeikyoku, ed. **Nihon tōkei nenkan.** [Statistical yearbook of Japan.] Tokyo, 1882 ff. (Annual.) Originally issued by the Naikaku Tōkeikyoku, this series constitutes the basic official statistical publication of the Japanese government. Includes statistics on a wide variety of subjects.

SERIALS

As is evident from previous listings, a vast amount of historical material in Japanese appears in serial form, either published commercially or under the auspices of a university or official academy or society. Hence no attempt has been made to list any of these separately. However, a few of the more important serials published in western languages are included below.

P330. University of Michigan, Center for Japanese Studies. **Bibliographical series.** Ann Arbor, 1950 ff. Covers subjects such as history, political science, economics, archaeology, and ethnology. See Hall, *Japanese history (P3)*.

P331. Monumenta nipponica monographs. Tokyo, 1940 ff. [Sophia University.] To date 15 volumes have appeared, most of which deal with early Japanese-western relations or with sinological topics.

P332. Columbia University. **East Asian Institute studies.** N.Y., 1950 ff. Three volumes of this series concern Japanese history: 2, Shirato Ichirō, *Japanese sources on the history of the Chinese Communist movement: an annotated bibliography* (1953); 4, John E. Lane, ed., *Researches in the social sciences in Japan* (1957); 5, Kai Miwa, comp., *Political chronology of Japan, 1885–1957* (1957).

PERIODICALS

An exhaustive list of journals carrying articles on Japan of historical interest would run to well over 400 items. Most of the guides cited under Bibliographies contain convenient lists of periodicals of interest to the historian. Those in western languages devoted exclusively or largely to Japanese history are becoming increasingly numerous. The following items are limited to publications in Japanese within the professional historical field and those in European languages with important proportions devoted to Japanese history.

P333. Tōkyō (Teikoku) Daigaku Shigakkai. **Shigaku zasshi.** [Journal of historical science.] Tokyo, 1889 ff. (Monthly.) The senior historical journal of Japan, organ of the Institute of Historical Science of Tokyo University. Articles and reviews are few in number, but of highest scholarly quality.

P334. Kyōto (Teikoku) Daigaku Shigaku Kenkyūkai. **Shirin.** [Journal of history.] Kyoto, 1916 ff. (Quarterly.) Organ of the Historical Research Society, Kyoto University. Enjoys best reputation as a university journal after that of *P333*. Articles are scholarly and well documented and cover a variety of subject matter in Japanese and world history. Since 1950 has featured extensive bibliography.

P335. Nippon-rekishi. [Journal of Japanese history.] Tokyo, 1946 ff. (Monthly.) [Since 1955, Yoshikawa Kobunkan.] Somewhat popular journal with a conservative editorial policy. Short articles, often by outstanding members of major universities, dealing usually with specific historical incidents or individuals.

P336. Kyōto Daigaku Jimbun Kagaku Kenkyūjo. **Jimbun gakuhō.** [Journal of humanistic science.] Kyoto, 1950 ff. (Annual.) A scholarly journal published by the Japanese section of the Institute of Humanistic and Social Sciences at Kyoto University. Contains interpretive articles on Japanese history, especially the Meiji period.

P337. Rekishigaku Kenkyūkai. **Rekishigaku kenkyū.** [Journal of the Historical Science Society.] Tokyo, 1933 ff. (Frequency varies.) One of the leading historical journals in Japan, published by the independent Historical Science Association of Tokyo. Since World War II has largely been taken over by the Marxist-oriented so-called "progressive" historians, and consequently has definite political overtones.

P338. Waseda Daigaku Shigakkai. **Shikan.** [Historical review.] Tokyo, 1931 ff. (Irregular.) Organ of the Historical Society of Waseda University; good example of the product of a major private university of the Tokyo area.

P339. Nihonshi Kenkyūkai. **Nihonshi kenkyū.** [Journal of Japanese history.] Kyoto, 1946 ff. (Quarterly.) Organ of the Society for the Study of Japanese History; outlet for Marxist historians of the Kyoto area.

P340. Nihon Rekishi Chiri Gakkai. **Rekishi chiri.** [Historical geography.] Tokyo, 1899 ff. (Frequency varies.) One of the oldest historical publications, containing a high percentage of scholarly articles on Japanese history.

P341. Tōkyō Shakai Keizaishi Gakkai. **Shakai keizaishigaku.** [Journal of the Social and Economic History Society.] Tokyo, 1931 ff. (Monthly.) Foremost scholarly publication in the field of social and economic history.

P342. Nihon Keizaishi Kenkyūjo. **Keizaishi kenkyū.** [Studies in economic history.] Kyoto, 1929–44. (Monthly.) Organ of the Institute of Japanese Economic History at Kyoto University. Contains many valuable articles by outstanding figures in the field. Emphasis is on the Tokugawa period.

P343. Chihōshi Kenkyū Kyōgikai. **Chihōshi kenkyū.** [Local history.] Tokyo, 1951 ff. (3 nos. per year.) Organ of the Committee for the Study of Local History. Especially useful as a clearing house for information on latest developments in this field.

P344. Hiroshima Bunrika Daigaku Shigaku Kenkyūkai. **Shigaku kenkyū.** [Review of historical studies.] Hiroshima, 1929 ff. (Frequency varies.) Of interest for articles on local historical institutions.

P345. Rekishi Kyōiku Kenkyūkai. **Rekishi kyōiku.** [Historical education.] Tokyo, 1952 ff. (Monthly.) Postwar series of a journal published during the prewar era. A conservative historical periodical directed to secondary school and college teachers.

P346. Transactions of the Asiatic Society of Japan. Tokyo, 1872 ff. (Irregular.) Largest and most important collection of western language studies on all aspects of Japanese civilization, including many translations and monographs. In three series: 1st, 1872–1922; 2nd, 1924–40; 3rd, 1948 ff.

P347. Monumenta nipponica. Tokyo, 1938 ff. (Semiannual.) Important journal devoted almost exclusively to Japan, containing scholarly articles in English, French, and German, with critical bibliographies. Especially valuable for philosophical studies and early foreign relations.

P348. Nippon. Berlin, 1935–44. (Quarterly.) Contains articles of varying value and extensive German bibliographies.

P349. Transactions and proceedings of the Japan Society, London. London, 1892–1941. Exclusively on Japanese culture, with articles of varying scholarly value, but with several of special importance.

P350. Bulletin de la Maison Franco-Japonaise: série française. Tokyo, 1927 ff. (Irregular.) Many valuable articles on various topics, particularly bibliography; almost exclusively on Japan.

SECTION Q

Southeast Asia

JOHN M. ECHOLS *

The geographical term "Southeast Asia" has become well known only since World War II. It is generally, though not universally, understood to encompass the nations south of China and east of India—namely, Burma, Thailand, Laos, Cambodia, Vietnam (the last three formerly comprised French Indochina), and Malaya on the mainland, and two insular nations, Indonesia (formerly known as Dutch East Indies, Netherlands India, and Netherlands East Indies), and the Philippines. Some scholars do not include the latter country in their definition of Southeast Asia.

During the past twenty-five years a considerable body of scholarly and semi-popular publications has appeared on Southeast Asia. In the past the majority of works on Indonesia were written by Dutch scholars, those on Burma and Malaya by British, while the French dominated the writing on Indochina. A perusal of the titles listed in this section will reveal that the great majority of serious works on almost any aspect of Southeast Asia are the products of western scholars. There is some evidence, however, that indigenous scholars soon will produce significant studies which will make greater use of vernacular materials and tend to be much less Europe-centered in presentation. There are also a number of younger western scholars whose contributions are already beginning to render obsolete many long-time standard and definitive works.

GENERAL

BIBLIOGRAPHIES AND LIBRARIES

Q1. Embree, John F. **Books on Southeast Asia: a select bibliography.** 4th rev. ed., ed. by Bruno Lasker, N.Y., 1956.

Q2. U. S. Library of Congress. **Southeast Asia: an annotated bibliography of selected reference sources.** Comp. by Cecil C. Hobbs. Washington, 1952. Useful annotated listing of 345 books and articles on history, government, economics, social conditions, and cultural life.

* In addition to Professor Echols, the following contributed items and comments as indicated by their respective initials: Harry J. Benda (HJB), John F. Brohm (JFB), John F. Cady (JFC), Bernard B. Fall (BBF), Frank H. Golay (FHG), George McT. Kahin (GMK), J. Norman Parmer (JNP), Lauriston Sharp (LS), Josef Silverstein (JS), Robert Van Niel (RV), Walter F. Vella (WFV).

Q3. Embree, John F., and Lillian O. Dotson. **Bibliography of the peoples and cultures of mainland Southeast Asia.** New Haven, 1950. This large, essential bibliography covers Burma, Indochina, and Thailand, and their various tribal units. In addition to archaeology and ethnology, contains sections on cultural history and social organization and law. Includes both books and articles. Good critical list of bibliographies; occasional brief annotations. Review, J. F. Cady, *Far Eastern quarterly,* 10 (Aug. 1951): 407.

Q4. Cordier, Henri. **Biblioteca indosinica: dictionnaire bibliographique des ouvrages relatifs à la peninsule indochinoise.** 4 v. Paris, 1912–15. Index, 1932. Extensive and reliable coverage of books and articles on all of Southeast Asia up to 1913. Difficult to use.

Q5. Oey, Giok P. **Survey of Chinese language materials on Southeast Asia in the Hoover Institute and Library.** Ithaca, 1953. [Cornell Southeast Asia program data paper no. 8.] Useful, specialized listing.

Q6. Bulletin of Far Eastern bibliography. See *N4.*

Q7. Irikura, James K. **Southeast Asia: selected annotated bibliography of Japanese publications.** New Haven, 1956. Very well annotated bibliography, valuable to the specialist.

The following United States libraries contain important collections on Southeast Asia: Library of Congress; New York Public Library; Harvard; Yale (strong on Burma, Indochina, and Indonesia); Cornell (strong on Indonesia, Philippines, and Thailand); California (especially Indonesia and Philippines); Newberry Library, Chicago (Philippines); Hoover Research Institute (emphasizes Indonesia and Philippines); Michigan (Philippines); University of Chicago (Philippines); Stanford.

GEOGRAPHIES

Q8. Spencer, Joseph E. **Asia east by south: a cultural geography.** N.Y., 1954. Good treatment of Southeast Asia's historical geography.

Q9. Dobby, Ernest H. G. **Southeast Asia.** London, 1950. Detailed geographical account, country by country, by the professor of geography at the University of Malaya. Review, N. Ginsburg, *Far East. quar.,* 10 (Aug. 1951): 405.

ANTHROPOLOGICAL WORKS

Q10. Embree, John F., and William L. Thomas, eds. **Ethnic groups of northern Southeast Asia.** New Haven, 1950. An important reference work, intended to accompany a specially prepared ethno-linguistic map of the borderlands of Yunnan, Burma, Thailand, Laos, and northern Vietnam. Review, B. P. Groslier, *Bulletin de l'École Française d'Extrême Orient,** 46 (1954): 661.

Q11. Heine-Geldern, Robert. "Südostasien." **Illustrierte Völkerkunde,** ed. by Georg H. Buschan (Stuttgart, 1923), v. 2. In spite of much outdating, still the best single detailed account of the prehistoric and historic physical, linguistic, and cultural types of Southeast Asia broadly defined as an anthropological area. [LS]

GENERAL HISTORIES

Q12. Harrison, Brian. **South-east Asia: a short history.** N.Y., 1954. An attempt to depict in brief compass the diversity of this area. Well written, with little scholarly apparatus, it provides a good introduction.

Q13. Hall, Daniel G. E. **A history of South-east Asia.** N.Y., 1955. Most detailed history of Southeast Asia, by the professor of Southeast Asian history at the University of London. Good presentation of latest thinking and research on the pre-European period. Philippines not included. Excellent bibliography. Review, F. N. Trager, *Far East. quar.,* 15 (May 1956): 433.

HISTORIES OF SPECIAL PERIODS

Q14. Elsbree, Willard H. **Japan's role in Southeast Asian nationalist movements.** Cambridge, Mass., 1953. Comprehensive study, considering somewhat limited sources available to author; some parts are being superseded by more specialized works. [GMK] Emphasis largely on Indonesia, with extensive accounts of Burma and the Philippines. Review, J. F. Melby, *Pacific affairs,* 27 (Mar. 1954): 81.

Q15. Wales, Horace G. Quaritch. **Ancient South-east Asian warfare.** London, 1952.

HISTORIES OF SPECIAL TOPICS

Q16. Landon, Kenneth P. **Southeast Asia: crossroad of religions.** Chicago, 1949. Author spent a number of years as a missionary in Thailand; more recently with the U. S. Department of State. Treats primarily Indochina, Indonesia, and Thailand. Bibliography.

Q17. Purcell, Victor W. S. **The Chinese in Southeast Asia.** London, 1951. Comprehensive general historical and contemporary survey, the only one to date covering this area. Extensive bibliography. [LS]

Q18. Lasker, Bruno. **Human bondage in Southeast Asia.** Chapel Hill, 1950. A useful study; treats subject historically.

Q19. Thompson, Virginia M., and Richard Adloff. **The left wing in Southeast Asia.** N.Y., 1950. Summarizes left-wing revolutionary activities from 1930 on.

* Hereafter cited as BEFEO.

Q20. Wales, Horace G. Quaritch. **The making of greater India: a study in Southeast Asian culture change.** London, 1951. Brief, general study of the differential effects of early Indian artistic and religious influences in eastern and western zones of Southeast Asia. Review, L. A. Mills, *Far East. quar.*, 11 (May 1952): 407.

BURMA

BIBLIOGRAPHY

Q21. Trager, Frank N., ed. **Annotated bibliography of Burma.** New Haven, 1956. A layman's bibliography; weaker in its selection of journal articles than in choice of books. [JFB]

ANTHROPOLOGICAL WORKS

Q22. Leach, Edmund R. **Political systems of highland Burma: a study of Kachin social structure.** London, 1954. Useful, first-hand description of the Kachin (Jingpaw) peoples. [JFC]

Q23. Stevenson, Henry N. C. **The hill peoples of Burma.** London, 1944. Brief survey of the major hill groups.

Q24. Marshall, Harry I. **The Karen people of Burma.** Columbus, O., 1922. Author was president of the Karen Theological Seminary and foremost student of the Sgaw Karens.

DEMOGRAPHIC STUDIES

Q25. Burma (Union). Central Statistical and Economics Department, Census Division. **First stage census, 1953.** V. 1, **Population and housing.** Rangoon, 1957. Deals only with urban and semi-urban areas of Burma and is in no sense a comprehensive effort. Military conditions have thus far prohibited a more complete census taking in post-war Burma. [JFB]

Q26. India. Census Commissioner. **Census of India, 1931.** V. 11, **Burma.** Ed. by John J. Bennison. Rangoon, 1933. The latest census data on Burma; 1941 material disappeared during World War II.

Q27. Scott, James G., and John P. Hardiman. **Gazetteer of Upper Burma and the Shan states.** 5 v. Rangoon, 1900–01. Full of very useful information, rarely duplicated elsewhere. [JFC]

LINGUISTIC WORKS

Q28. Linguistic survey of Burma: preparatory stage of linguistic census. Rangoon, 1950. A civil servant's approach to linguistics. Not particularly useful to modern students since languages and dialects are not significantly distinguished from one another. [JFB]

Q29. Grierson, Sir George, ed. **Linguistic survey of India.** V. 1–3. Calcutta, 1903–27. These three volumes deal with Burma. A principal source in spite of certain limitations. Bibliography.

PRINTED COLLECTION OF SOURCES

Q30. Pe Maung Tin, U., and G. H. Luce, trs. **The glass palace chronicle of the kings of Burma.** London, 1923. [Text Publication Fund of the Burma Research Society.] A translation of portions of the *Hmannan Yazawin,* extending to 1287. Luce is an outstanding scholar of old Burmese.

SHORTER GENERAL HISTORIES

Q31. Hall, Daniel G. E. **Burma.** London, 1950. Brief account, valuable especially for the pre-British period. Review, *Pacific affairs,* 25 (1952): 102. [JFC]

Q32. Harvey, Godfrey E. **Outline of Burmese history.** Bombay, 1947. Abridged version of *Q33,* but extends his coverage to 1886.

LONGER GENERAL HISTORIES

Q33. Harvey, Godfrey E. **History of Burma from the earliest times to 10 March, 1824, the beginning of the English conquest.** London, 1925. Standard English account of old Burma, somewhat deprecating in tone; based largely on inscriptions and Burmese chronicles. Thorough analysis of historical events from the pagan kingdom to the Alaungpaya dynasty in early 19th century. Bibliography. Review, *Eng. hist. rev.,* 41 (July 1926): 476. [JFC]

Q34. Cady, John F. **A history of modern Burma.** Ithaca, 1958. Definitive, systematic study, covering the period since 1800, with emphasis on political developments since 1920.

HISTORIES OF SPECIAL PERIODS

Q35. Hall, Daniel G. E. **Europe and Burma: a study of European relations with Burma to the annexation of Thibaw's kingdom, 1886.** London, 1945.

Q36. ——. **Early English intercourse with Burma (1587–1743).** London, 1928. Hall's earliest book on Burma. A useful specialized study. Bibliography.

Q37. ——, ed. **Michael Symes: journal of his second embassy to the Court of Ava in 1802.** London, 1955. Excellent. Introduction is best account of Burma's history in the late 1700's. [JFC]

Q38. Mya Sein, Daw. **The administration of Burma: Sir Charles Crosthwaite and the**

consolidation of Burma. Rangoon, 1938. Valuable study of late 19th century Burmese history. [JFC]

Q39. Harvey, Godfrey E. **British rule in Burma, 1824–1942.** London, 1946. Brief and apologetic in tone. [JFC]

Q40. Furnivall, John S. **The fashioning of Leviathan: the beginnings of British rule in Burma.** Rangoon, 1939. Still the most important statement on development of British colonial policy in Tenasserim after the Anglo-Burmese War of 1824. [JS]

Q41. Desai, Walter S. **History of the British residency in Burma, 1826–1840.** Rangoon, 1939. Based on documentary research. [JFC]

Q42. Nu, U. **Burma under the Japanese: pictures and portraits.** Ed. and tr. by John S. Furnivall. N.Y., 1954. Important addition to the limited literature on Japanese occupation of Burma, by one who knew the principals and participated in important events. [JS]

Q43. Christian, John L. **Burma and the Japanese invader.** Bombay, 1945. A revised version of author's *Modern Burma* (Berkeley, 1942). Survey of political and economic developments except for appended chapters on the Japanese period. Pro-British and anti-Burmese in tone, with numerous mistakes. Bibliography. Review of *Modern Burma*, K. P. Landon, *Far East. quar.*, 2 (Nov. 1942): 90. [JFC]

Q44. Collis, Maurice. **Trials in Burma.** London, 1938. Valuable as a description of gathering tension between Burmese nationalists and British residents. [JFC]

Q45. ———. **Last and first in Burma (1941–1948).** London, 1956. Covers the governorship of Dorman-Smith and the rise of U Aung San. Author tries to be sympathetic to both. Review, J. Silverstein, *Jour. Asian stud.*, 16 (Nov. 1956): 158.

Q46. Tinker, Hugh. **The Union of Burma.** London, 1957. Very good account of the difficulties and shortcomings of independent Burma, but lacking in appreciation of historical background. [JFC]

HISTORIES OF SPECIAL TOPICS

Q47. Tinker, Hugh. **The foundations of local self-government in India, Pakistan, and Burma.** See *R6*.

Q48. Maung Maung, U. **Burma in the family of nations.** 2nd rev. ed., Amsterdam, 1957. Survey of Burma's history from standpoint of international law; reflects Burmese point of view. Author, a well-known publicist, wrote this as a dissertation at the University of Utrecht. Review, J. F. Cady, *Pac. aff.*, 30 (June 1957): 182. [JFC]

Q49. Furnivall, John S. **Colonial policy and practice: a comparative study of Burma and Netherlands India.** Cambridge, Eng., 1948; N.Y., 1956. Standard work by an outstanding authority and long-time resident of Burma. Reviews, R. Emerson, *Pac. aff.*, 21 (Dec. 1948): 428; F. N. Trager, *Jour. Asian stud.*, 16 (May 1957): 455. [JFC]

Q50. Andrus, James R. **Burmese economic life.** Stanford, 1948. Best description of the pre-war economy of Burma. Review, L. D. Stamp, *Pac. aff.*, 21 (Dec. 1948): 432. [JFC]

Q51. Bigandet, Paul A. **An outline of the history of the Catholic Burmese mission from the year 1720 to 1887.** Rangoon, 1887. Important study by a long-time French missionary in Burma.

Q52. Htin Aung, U. **Burmese drama: a study, with translations, of Burmese plays.** London, 1947. Historical survey of Burmese drama through the 19th century.

PERIODICAL

Q53. **The journal of the Burma Research Society.** Rangoon, 1911 ff. (Irregular.)

INDOCHINA (VIETNAM, CAMBODIA, LAOS)

BIBLIOGRAPHIES

Q54. U. S. Library of Congress. **Indo-China: a bibliography of the land and people.** Comp. by Cecil C. Hobbs and others. Washington, 1950. Selected bibliography of 1,850 titles, with occasional brief annotations. Lists titles in western European, Russian, and Vietnamese languages. [JFC]

Q55. Boudet, Paul, and Remi Bourgeois. **Bibliographie de l'Indochine française.** 4 v. Hanoi, 1929–43. Covers period 1913–35.

Q56. Brébion, Antoine. **Dictionnaire de bio-bibliographie générale, ancienne et moderne de l'Indochine française.** Paris, 1935.

GEOGRAPHY

Q57. Canada. Department of Mines and Technical Surveys. **Indo-China: a geographical appreciation.** Ottawa, 1953. Concise study of physical, demographic, and environmental factors of all three Indochinese states. Population statistics somewhat out of date. [BBF]

LINGUISTICS

Q58. Savina, François M. **Guide linguistique de l'Indochine française.** 2 v. Hongkong, 1939.

PRINTED COLLECTIONS OF SOURCES

Q59. Taboulet, Georges. **La geste française en Indochine: histoire par les textes de la France en Indochine des origines à 1914.** 2 v. Paris, 1955–56. The most comprehensive documentary history of French-Indochinese relations from 16th century to 1914. Uses documents from secret archives of the French foreign ministry, available to the public for the first time. [BBF]

Q60. Cole, Allan B. **Conflict in Indo-China and international repercussions: a documentary history, 1945–1955.** Ithaca, 1956. Only English-language collection of major documents relative to recent events in Indochina; a major tool for further research. Contains some small errors. Review, J. F. Cady, *Am. hist. rev.*, 62 (July 1957): 1002. [BBF]

SHORTER GENERAL HISTORIES

Q61. Masson, André. **Histoire de l'Indochine.** Paris, 1950. Comprehensive but somewhat superficial history of Cambodia, Laos, and Vietnam. *Q72* is preferable unless historical background of Laos and Cambodia is desired. [BBF]

Q62. Thompson, Virginia M. **French Indo-China.** London, 1937. Basic, but somewhat out-of-date. Provides an extensive survey of the history, economy, and culture.

LONGER GENERAL HISTORIES

Q63. Lévi, Sylvain. **Indochine.** 2 v. Paris, 1931. Dated, but contains a number of scholarly articles on all aspects of Indochina.

Q64. Maspéro, Georges, ed. **Un empire colonial français: l'Indochine.** 2 v. Paris, 1929–30. Comprehensive survey of many aspects of Indochina. Bibliography.

HISTORIES OF SPECIAL PERIODS

Q65. Coedès, Georges. **Les états hindouisés d'Indochine et d'Indonésie.** 2nd ed., Paris, 1948. [Histoire du monde, ed. by M. E. Cavaignac, v. 8, pt. 2.] Comprehensive and basic history of the Hinduization of these two areas; an authoritative study by the outstanding scholar on early history of Southeast Asia.

Q66. Hammer, Ellen J. **The struggle for Indochina.** Stanford, 1954. Most important U. S. attempt at interpreting post-war events in Indochina. Brief history of French colonial administration, with detailed account of Indochina's history since the Japanese occupation of 1940–41. In spite of some minor inaccuracies, an excellent tool for further research. [BBF]

Q67. ———. **The struggle for Indochina continues: Geneva to Bandung.** Stanford, 1955. A sequel to the above. Written at time of a particularly critical change in Viet-

namese history, it makes some predictions which failed to materialize. [BBF]

HISTORIES OF SPECIAL AREAS

Vietnam

Q68. Maybon, Charles B. **Histoire moderne du pays d'Annam (1592–1820): étude sur les premiers rapports des Européens et des Annamites et sur l'établissement de la dynastie.** Paris, 1919. Best book on the period covered. [JFC]

Q69. Buttinger, Joseph. **The smaller dragon: a political history of Vietnam.** N.Y., 1958. Documentary history of Vietnam during the past half century, with one chapter on recent events. The author, a former Austrian socialist, emphasizes the "class-struggle" aspects and holds some strong opinions on French colonial activities. Extensive bibliography. [BBF]

Q70. Lê-thánh-Khôi. **Le Viêt-Nam: histoire et civilisation, le milieu et l'histoire.** Paris, 1955. By far the most comprehensive study of Vietnamese history of the past two decades, by a competent Vietnamese scholar. Last chapters reflect impact of the Communist victory of 1954, and interpretation is extremely sympathetic to the Communist cause. Review, R. Jumper, *Jour. Asian stud.*, 16 (May 1957): 450. [BBF]

Q71. Huard, Pierre A., and Maurice Durand. **Connaissance du Viêt-Nam.** Paris, 1954. One of the more readable studies of various aspects of traditional Vietnamese culture, by two eminent scholars and long-time residents of Vietnam. Clearly shows cultural links between the latter and China; and comprehensive indexes include cross-references to Chinese origins and sources. Utilizes source materials in Vietnamese. [BBF]

Q72. Devillers, Philippe. **Histoire du Viet-Nam de 1940 à 1952.** Paris, 1952. Considered the best overall attempt to interpret post-war events in Indochina. Author, formerly a French officer in Indochina, had access to personalities directly involved in the events and to documents not easily available to outsiders. [BBF]

Q73. Chesneaux, Jean. **Contribution à l'histoire de la nation vietnamienne.** Paris, 1955. A thoroughly French Communist view of events in Vietnam. The author, a professor at the Sorbonne, uncritically accepts every propaganda argument of his party. Interesting only as an example of Communist thinking on the subject. [BBF]

Q74. Laniel, Joseph. **Le drame indochinois: de Dien Bien Phu au pari de Genève.** Paris, 1957. Author was premier of France at time of the defeat at Dien Bien Phu. This is a reply to the book by General Henri Navarre and attempts to show the latter's responsibility for the 1954 defeat. Also attacks Premier Mendès-France for having made the cease-fire agreement, alleging that better terms could have been obtained. Both this and *Q75* are valuable contributions to the history of the period. [BBF]

Q75. Navarre, Henri. **L'agonie de l'Indochine (1953–1954).** Paris, 1956. Written by the last war-time commander of French forces in Indochina. Seeks to explain the military defeat by the weakness and indecision among politicians in Paris. [BBF]

Q76. Fall, Bernard B. **The Viet-Minh regime: government and administration in the Democratic Republic of Vietnam.** Rev. and enl. ed., N.Y., 1956. The definitive work on the Communist government of North Vietnam, based on documentary and field research.

Q77. Blanchet, Marie-Thérèse. **La naissance de l'état associé du Viet-Nam.** Paris, 1954. Best book available on early development of the non-Communist Vietnamese government. [BBF]

Q78. Mus, Paul. **Viet-Nam: sociologie d'une guerre.** Paris, 1952. Seeks to show the influence of cultural factors in French-Vietnamese relations during the hostilities in Indochina. Rather difficult to read. Review, B. B. Fall, *Pac. aff.,* 27 (June 1954): 190. [BBF]

Cambodia

Q79. Human Relations Area Files. **Bibliography of Cambodia.** New Haven, 1956.

Q80. Leclère, Adhémard. **Histoire du Cambodge depuis le 1er siècle de notre ère, d'après les inscriptions lapidaires, les annales chinoises et annamites et les documents européens des six derniers siècles.** Paris, 1914. F. W. Williams' characterization of "scholarly, thoroughly documented, but very dull" is equally valid today. Has not been superseded.

Q81. Russier, Henri E. **Histoire sommaire du royaume de Cambodge des origines à 1929.** 5th ed., Hanoi, 1944. [Bibliothèque scolaire indochinoise.]

Q82. Herz, Martin. **A short history of Cambodia from the days of Angkor to the present.** N.Y., 1958.

Q83. Briggs, Lawrence P. **The ancient Khmer empire.** Philadelphia, 1951. Important scholarly study by a retired U. S. foreign service officer. Review, P. Mus, *Far East. quar.,* 11 (Feb. 1952): 259. [JFC]

Q84. Steinberg, David J. **Cambodia: its people, its society, its culture.** New Haven, 1957. Useful information concerning the new nation.

Laos

Q85. Le Boulanger, Paul. **Histoire du Laos français.** Paris, 1931. Though dated, still the best book on Laos' history. Bibliography. [BBF]

HISTORIES OF SPECIAL TOPICS

Q86. Pinto, Roger. **Aspects de l'évolution gouvernementale de l'Indochine française.** Paris, 1946. Shows development of French colonial administration in Indochina and impact of World War II upon it. Now somewhat obsolete, but interesting as illustration of French thinking on the subject in early post-war period. Review, L. Sharp, *Pac. aff.,* 20 (Sep. 1947): 345. [BBF]

Q87. Robequain, Charles. **The economic development of French Indo-China.** Tr. by Isabel A. Ward. London and N.Y., 1944. One of the most perceptive French books on French rule in Indochina. A supplementary chapter provides account of the principal economic developments since appearance of the 1939 French edition. Review, V. McKay, *Far East. quar.,* 4 (Aug. 1945): 340. [JFC]

Q88. Gourou, Pierre. **Land utilization in French Indochina.** N.Y., 1945. An extremely informative book. [JFC]

Q89. Launay, Adrien. **Histoire de la mission de Cochinchine, 1658–1823.** 3 v. Paris, 1923–25. Author is ablest of the French clerical historians. [JFC]

Q90. Janse, Olov R. T. **Archaeological research in Indochina.** 2 v. Cambridge, Mass., 1947–51. The definitive work on the subject. Author was associated for some years with the École Française d'Extrême-Orient at Hanoi. A third volume is in press.

Q91. Cordier, Georges. **Étude sur la littérature annamite.** 3 pts. Hanoi and Saigon, 1933–40. Comprehensive survey of Vietnamese literature before 1940.

PERIODICALS

Q92. Bulletin de l'École Française d'Extrême-Orient. Hanoi and Paris, 1901 ff. (Frequency varies.)

Q93. Bulletin de la Société des Études Indochinoises. Saigon, 1884 ff. (Quarterly.)

Q94. Bulletin des Amis de Laos. Hanoi, 1937 ff. (Irregular.)

Q95. Bulletin des Amis du Vieux Hué. Hanoi, 1914–41. [Association des Amis du Vieux Hué.] (Quarterly.)

Q96. Dân Viêt Nam. Le peuple vietnamien. Hanoi, 1948 ff. (Irregular.) In French and Vietnamese.

INDONESIA

BIBLIOGRAPHIES

Q97. Kennedy, Raymond. **Bibliography of Indonesian peoples and cultures.** Rev. ed., by T. W. Maretzki and H. T. Fischer, 2 v., New Haven, 1955. Extensive listing of books and articles, divided into items in Dutch and those in other languages. Uses anthropology in very broad sense. Indispensable for students of Indonesia. Contains good bibliography of bibliographies.

Q98. U. S. Library of Congress. **Netherlands East Indies: a bibliography of books published after 1930, and periodical articles after 1932, available in U. S. libraries.** Washington, 1945.

Q99. Hooykaas, J. C. **Repertorium op de koloniale litteratuur, of, systematische inhoudsopgaaf van hetgeen voorkomt over de koloniën . . . in mengelwerken en tijdschriften van 1595 tot 1865 uitgegeven in Nederland en zijne overzeesche bezittingen.** 2 v. Amsterdam, 1877–80.

Q100. **Repertorium op de litteratuur betreffende de Nederlandsche koloniën, voor zoover zij verspreid is in tijdschriften en mengelwerken.** Ed. by Alexander Hartmann. The Hague, 1895. 8 supplements, 1901–26. Continuation of *Q99.*

ENCYCLOPEDIA

Q101. **Encyclopaedie van Nederlandsch-Indië.** 2nd ed., 4 v. and 4 supp., The Hague, 1917–39. Standard reference work on the Dutch East Indies by thoroughly competent collaborators, covering all subjects relating to the islands. Addressed to the general reader, the articles are compact and comprehensive, without being popular in nature. Includes historical surveys for each of the larger territorial divisions, biographies of all persons prominent in history of the East Indies, and special articles on particular periods and institutions. Many articles include bibliographies.

GEOGRAPHIES AND ATLASES

Q102. **Atlas van tropisch Nederland.** The Hague and Batavia, 1938. Useful geographical, political, and historical atlas of Netherlands India. Should be kept close at hand for any historical work in the period before World War II. [RV]

Q103. Robequain, Charles. **Malaya, Indonesia, Borneo and the Philippines: a geographical, economic and political description.** London and N.Y., 1954. Translation of a work based on pre-World War II field investigation. In some respects outdated, but

still basic. Review, J. M. Echols, *Far East. quar.,* 15 (Nov. 1955): 139.

ANTHROPOLOGICAL WORKS

Q104. Cooper-Cole, Fay. **The peoples of Malaysia.** N.Y., 1945. Deals principally and in some detail with specific ethnic groups of Malaya proper, Philippines, and major islands of Indonesia. Useful as far as it goes. Good bibliography and ethnic maps. [JFB]

Q105. Duyvendak, Johan P. **Inleiding tot de ethnologie van de Indonesische Archipel.** 4th ed., Djakarta and Groningen, 1954. Useful but necessarily superficial survey of the ethnology of Indonesia.

Q106. Alkema, B., and T. J. Bezemer. **Beknopt handboek der volkenkunde van Nederlandsch-Indië.** Haarlem, 1927.

DEMOGRAPHY

Q107. Netherlands India. Departement van Economische Zaken. **Volkstelling 1930.** 8 v. Batavia, 1933–36. The last published census of Indonesia. Data collected for 1940 disappeared during the Japanese occupation. This series, though dated, still is important for research.

PRINTED COLLECTIONS OF SOURCES

Q108. Heeres, Jan E., and Frederik W. Stapel. **Corpus diplomaticum Neerlando-Indicum: verzameling van politieke contracten en verdere verdragen.** 6 v. The Hague, 1907–55. Essential collection of sources for any work on relations of the Dutch with peoples of the Indonesian archipelago. [RV]

Q109. Chijs, Jacobus A. van der. **Nederlandsch-Indisch plakaatboek.** 17 v. Batavia and The Hague, 1885–1900. [Bataviaasch Genootschap van Kunsten en Wetenschappen.] A publication of source materials containing all government publications on the East Indies from 1602 to 1811. Basic reference for any historical work on the period. [RV]

Q110. Jonge, Johan K. J. de, and Marinus L. van Deventer, eds. **De opkomst van het Nederlandsch gezag in Oost-Indië.** 13 v. The Hague, 1862–88. Supplement, 2 v., 1909. Major collection of source materials on the Dutch East India Company from 1595 to 1811. Supplement covers the time of Daendels (1808–11). Invaluable for any work on this period. [RV]

Q111. Tiele, Pieter A., and Jan E. Heeres, eds. **De opkomst van het Nederlandsch gezag in Oost-Indië. Bouwstoffen voor de geschiedenis der Nederlanders in den Maleischen Archipel.** 3 v. The Hague, 1886–95.

Really an extension of *Q110*. These volumes deal principally with the "outer islands," outside of Java. [RV]

Q112. Casparis, J. G. de. **Inscripties uit de Çailendra-tijd.** Bandung, 1950. [Prasasti Indonesia, 1.] Important study of certain Javanese inscriptions.

Q113. Raliby, Osman, ed. **Documenta historica: sedjarah dokumenter dari pertumbuhan dan perdjuangan Negara Republik Indonesia.** [A documentary history of the growth and struggle of the Indonesian people.] V. 1. Djakarta, 1953. Useful compilation of documents, speeches, acts, etc., from August 17, 1945 through December, 1946.

SHORTER GENERAL HISTORIES

Q114. Vandenbosch, Amry. **The Dutch East Indies: its government, problems and politics.** 3rd ed., Berkeley, 1942. Excellent for an understanding of the Dutch colonial system in the 20th century. Bibliography. [RV]

Q115. Vlekke, Bernard H. M. **Nusantara: a history of the East Indian archipelago.** Cambridge, Mass., 1943. Well-written presentation of enlightened, European view of the history of this region. Good introduction in spite of occasional dubious statements and generalizations. A new and revised edition is in preparation. [RV]

Q116. Klerck, Eduard S. de. **History of the Netherlands East Indies.** 2 v. Rotterdam, 1938. Comprehensive and detailed coverage; somewhat turgid. [GMK]

Q117. Graaf, Hermanus J. de. **Geschiedenis van Indonesië.** The Hague, 1949. Especially good on the 17th and 18th centuries; although principally Europe-centered, contains much insight into Indonesian society. [RV]

LONGER GENERAL HISTORY

Q118. Stapel, Frederik W., ed. **Geschiedenis van Nederlandsch Indië.** 5 v. Amsterdam, 1938–40. This large, unwieldy history is almost entirely concerned with activities of the Dutch in Indonesia. With this limitation, it has some excellent sections and is a storehouse of information. The various contributions are of unequal value. [RV]

HISTORIES OF SPECIAL PERIODS

Q119. Schnitger, Frederic M. **Forgotten kingdoms in Sumatra.** Leiden, 1939.

Q120. Krom, Nicolaas. **Hindoe-javaansche geschiedenis.** 2nd rev. ed., The Hague, 1931. Long regarded as the classic work on Java in the pre-European period, but has recently been challenged from several directions. See *Q65*. [RV]

Q121. Arx, Alexandre von. **L'évolution politique en Indonésie de 1900 à 1942.** Freiburg, 1949.

Q122. Pluvier, J. M. **Overzicht van de ontwikkeling der nationalistische beweging in Indonesië in de jaren 1930 tot 1942.** The Hague, 1953. A sequel to *Q123*. Fairly straightforward history of the Indonesian nationalist movement under Dutch colonial rule. Unlike Blumberger's work, it is biased in favor of Indonesian nationalism and, therefore, more or less anti-colonial. Gives rather detailed account of the various parties and movements, particularly political, religious, and economic, but lacks sociological depth. [HJB]

Q123. Blumberger, John Th. Petrus. **De nationalistische beweging in Nederlandsch-Indië.** Haarlem, 1931. This together with *Q122* gives a fairly adequate picture of the nationalist movement in Indonesia up to the time of World War II. Neither book presents a well-rounded picture, but tends to concentrate on one aspect of Indonesian history. [RV]

Q124. Kahin, George M. **Nationalism and revolution in Indonesia.** Ithaca, 1952. The definitive work on the subject. Author became well acquainted with the leaders during the revolution against the Dutch, and much is based on first-hand accounts. Especially strong on the 1945–49 period.

Q125. Wolf, Charles, Jr. **The Indonesian story.** N.Y., 1948. Account of the 1945–48 period, with excellent coverage of the Indonesian-Dutch negotiations which culminated in the Linggadjati agreement. [GMK]

Q126. Schiller, A. Arthur. **The formation of federal Indonesia, 1945–1949.** The Hague and Bandung, 1955. Scholarly study of the federal structure of Indonesia as it appeared in the books. [GMK]

HISTORIES OF SPECIAL TOPICS

Q127. Emerson, Rupert. **Malaysia: a study in direct and indirect rule.** See *Q168*. Classic analysis of colonial rule in Indonesia.

Q128. Allen, George C., and Audrey G. Donnithorne. **Western enterprise in Indonesia and Malaya: a study in economic development.** N.Y., 1957. Good historical survey, with emphasis on the 20th century and recent years. The authors compare development of western enterprise in Malaya and Indonesia with that of China and Japan, and praise western accomplishments while largely divorcing them from their economic, social, and political consequences on the Malayan and Indonesian peoples. [JNP]

Q129. Gonggrijp, George F. E. **Schets eener economische geschiedenis van Nederlandsch-Indië.** 3rd ed., Haarlem, 1949. A handy little introduction to Indonesian economy, especially its development during the colonial period. Not intended to be comprehensive. [RV]

Q130. Boeke, Julius H. **The evolution of the Netherlands Indies economy.** N.Y., 1946. Stresses the dual relationship between European and indigenous economic spheres. The author, long one of the outstanding authorities in tropical economics, here takes a more historical approach than in some of his other major writings. Review, C. Robequain, *Pac. aff.*, 20 (June 1947): 221. [RV]

Q131. Furnivall, John S. **Netherlands India: a study of plural economy.** Cambridge, Eng., 1939. A highly regarded history of Indonesia, with emphasis on the 19th and 20th centuries. Stresses the economic differences in various levels of the East Indian societies, and has been very influential in indoctrinating scholars in the dual economic idea. [RV]

Q132. Van Leur, Jacob C. **Indonesian trade and society: essays in Asian social and economic history.** The Hague, 1955. Interesting theses regarding Hindu and Moslem influences on Indonesia. Any research into Indonesian-centered history in general and commercial history in particular must take into account this work. Review, R. Van Niel, *Far East. quar.*, 15 (May 1956): 440. [RV]

Q133. Stutterheim, Willem F. **Cultuurgeschiedenis van Indonesië.** 3 v. Groningen, 1951–52. Mainly concerned with the plastic arts and humanities. For this purpose it is excellent, but falls short of the integrated, broad cultural approach of the anthropologist. [RV]

Q134. Brugmans, Izaak J. **Geschiedenis van het onderwijs in Nederlandsch-Indië.** Batavia and Groningen, 1938. Survey of education in the Netherlands Indies during the colonial period.

Q135. Wertheim, Willem F. **Indonesian society in transition.** The Hague, 1956. Account of Indonesia's transition from a colonial to non-colonial society, with useful introductory historical chapters. Sounder in analysis of pre-revolutionary than revolutionary and post-revolutionary periods, which are weakened by author's adherence to rather rigid semi-Weberian concepts not always well suited to the Indonesian milieu. Review, G. J. Pauker, *Jour. Asian stud.*, 17 (Feb. 1958): 318. [GMK]

Q136. Schrieke, Bertram J. O. **Indonesian sociological studies: selected writings.** 2 v. The Hague, 1955–57. Illustrative of sociological history at its best. Although some points of interpretation may be challenged in light of later research, the work in general remains excellent. Review of v. 1, R. F. Spencer, *Far East. quar.*, 15 (May 1956): 441. [RV]

Q137. Benda, Harry J. **The crescent and the rising sun: Indonesian Islam under the Japanese occupation, 1942–1945.** The Hague, 1958. Detailed treatment of a significant aspect of Indonesia during the Japanese occupation. Well-documented account of Dutch Islamic policy.

Q138. Mooij, Jakob, ed. **Bouwstoffen voor de geschiedenis der Protestantsche kerk in Nederlandsch-Indië.** 3 v. Batavia and Weltevreden, 1927–31.

BIOGRAPHIES

Q139. **Orang Indonesia jang terkemuka di Djawa.** [Prominent Indonesians in Java.] Djakarta, 1945. A *Who's who* compiled during the Japanese occupation. Contains 3,070 biographies of outstanding Indonesians then resident in Java.

Q140. Colenbrander, H. T., and W. P. Coolhaas, eds. **Jan Pietersz. Coen: bescheiden omtrent zijn bedrijf in Indië.** 8 v. The Hague, 1919–52. Very large collection of materials on an outstanding early governor general of the East India Company in Indonesia. Valuable for understanding conditions in early 17th century and company policies of that time. [RV]

OFFICIAL GOVERNMENT RECORDS

Q141. Staatsblad van Nederlandsch-Indië. Batavia, 1816 ff. (Irregular.)

Q142. Netherlands India. Departement voor Economische Zaken. **Javasche courant: officieel nieuwsblad.** Weltevreden, 1817 ff. (Irregular 1817–1941; not published 1942–45; semiweekly 1946 ff. Title varies.)

Q143. Netherlands India. Algemeene Secretarie. **Regeerings-almanak voor Nederlandsch-Indië.** Batavia, 1834–1942.

Q144. Netherlands. Departement van Koloniën. **Indisch verslag.** The Hague, 1931–39. (Annual.)

Q145. Indonesia (Republic). Kementerian Penerangan. **Ichtisar Parlemen.** [Parliamentary proceedings.] Djakarta, 1950 ff. (Monthly.)

Q146. Gerretson, Carel C., and others, eds. **Utrechtsche bijdragen tot de geschiedenis, het staatsrecht en de economie van Nederlandsch-Indië.** Utrecht, 1934 ff. A collection of dissertations of the School of Indology at Utrecht. Many show a definite bias, but they contain information and source materials not duplicated elsewhere in published form and cannot be ignored in any work on Indonesian history. [RV]

SOCIETY PUBLICATIONS

Q147. Instituut voor de Taal-, Land- en Volkenkunde van Nederlandsch-Indië. **Verhandelingen.** The Hague, 1938 ff. A monographic series.

Q148. Verhandelingen van het Bataviaasch Genootschap van Kunsten en Wetenschappen. Batavia. 1779–1949.

PERIODICALS

Q149. De Indische gids. Amsterdam, 1879–1941. (Monthly.)
Q150. Koloniaal tijdschrift. The Hague, 1912 ff. (Bimonthly.)

Q151. Koloniale studien. The Hague and Weltevreden, 1916–39. (Bimonthly.)
Q152. Bijdragen tot de taal-, land- en volkenkunde van Nederlandsch-Indië. The Hague, 1853 ff. (Irregular.)
Q153. Tijdschrift voor indische taal-, land- en volkenkunde. Batavia, 1853–1955. (Irregular quarterly.)
Q154. Indonesië: tweemaandelijks tijdschrift. The Hague, 1948 ff. (Bimonthly.)

MALAYA (INCLUDING BORNEO)

BIBLIOGRAPHIES

Q155. Pelzer, Karl J. **Selected bibliography on the geography of Southeast Asia.** Pt. 3, Malaya. New Haven, 1956. Best general bibliography on Malaya. Uses "geography" in broad sense; contains good section on history.
Q156. U. S. Library of Congress. **British Malaya and British North Borneo: a bibliographical list.** Comp. by Florence S. Hellman. Washington, 1943.

DEMOGRAPHIC STUDIES

Q157. Smith, T. E. **Population growth in Malaya: an analysis of recent trends.** London, 1952. Scholarly, somewhat statistical introduction to the plural society problem, by the superintendent of the 1957 census, who spent a number of years in the Malayan government. [JNP]
Q158. Tufo, Morobë V. del. **Malaya: a report on the 1947 census of population.** London, 1949. The most recent complete census for Malaya and principal source of demographic data.

GENERAL HISTORIES

Q159. Winstedt, Sir Richard O. **Malaya and its history.** 4th ed., London, 1957. [Hutchinson's university library, British empire history, 3.] A popular history of British Malaya. Review, L. A. Mills, *Am. hist. rev.,* 55 (July 1950): 988. [JNP]
Q160. ——. **A history of Malaya.** Singapore, 1935. [Journal of the Malayan branch of the Royal Asiatic Society, v. 13, pt. 1.] Concerned principally with prehistory and history prior to British rule. Treats the Hindu period, the Malacca and Johore Malay empires, the Portuguese and Dutch periods. [JNP]
Q161. Tregonning, K. G. **Under chartered company rule: North Borneo, 1881–1946.** Singapore, 1958.

HISTORIES OF SPECIAL PERIODS

Q162. Swettenham, Sir Frank. **British Malaya.** Rev. ed., London, 1948. Early

history of the Malay States under British rule, together with personal recollections of their best known British administrator. [JNP]
Q163. Mills, Lennox A. **British Malaya, 1824–1867.** Singapore, 1925. Also published as v. 3, pt. 2 of the *Journal of the Malayan branch of the Royal Asiatic Society* (1925). Only comprehensive history of the Straits Settlements in the 19th century. Based on original research. Contains chapters on Anglo-Dutch treaty of 1824, Anglo-Siamese relations 1824–67, East India Company policy, the Chinese and relations with the Malay States. [JNP]

HISTORIES OF SPECIAL TOPICS

Q164. Hanrahan, Gene Z. **The Communist struggle in Malaya.** N.Y., 1954. Study of Malayan communism, using information already known as well as some new material. Not a definitive work. [JNP]
Q165. Jones, Stanley W. **Public administration in Malaya.** London, 1953. A survey, largely historical, of British administration and constitutional development through World War II, by a prominent prewar British civil servant. Useful for prewar history, but not a definitive study. Review, U. A. Aziz, *Pac. aff.,* 26 (Dec. 1953): 361. [JNP]
Q166. Republic of India. Office of the Economic Adviser. **Indians in the Malayan economy.** By S. Nanjundan. New Delhi, 1950. Historical account of Indian labor in Malaya—immigration, wages and social conditions, and occupational distribution. Brief note on Indian investments and businesses there. Most information is prewar. [JNP]
Q167. Purcell, Victor W. S. **The Chinese in Malaya.** London, 1948. A largely historical survey of most aspects of the Chinese community in the Federation of Malaya and Singapore, based partly on uncited government documents and partly on hard-to-obtain secondary works. Bibliography; statistical data. [JNP]
Q168. Emerson, Rupert. **Malaysia: a study in direct and indirect rule.** N.Y., 1937. Probably the best one volume study of British rule in Malaya to about 1935. Comprehensive, provocative, critical, and contains

numerous keen observations and insights which still have relevancy to contemporary problems. Also describes colonial policies of the Dutch in Indonesia. [JNP]

Q169. International Bank for Reconstruction and Development. **The economic development of Malaya.** 2 v. Washington, 1955. Survey of Malayan economy with recommendations for utilization of resources for the period 1955–59. Review, C. Wolf, *Far East. quar.,* 15 (Aug. 1956): 608. [JNP]

Q170. Winstedt, Sir Richard O. **The Malays: a cultural history.** Rev. ed., N.Y., 1950. Treats briefly the archaeology of Southeast Asia and racial stocks of the Malay peninsula; and has useful chapters on social and political systems, economic life, and law. By an outstanding authority on Malaya.

Q171. ——. **History of Malay literature.** Singapore, 1940. *Journal of the Malayan Branch of the Royal Asiatic Society (1940).* Most important study of the subject.

Q172. Irwin, Graham. **Nineteenth-century Borneo: a study in diplomatic rivalry.** The Hague, 1955. [Verhandelingen van het koninklijk Instituut voor de Taal-, Land- en Volkenkunde, 15.] Covers 1809–88, with an interpretation of British and Dutch policies regarding Borneo. Makes extensive use of British and Dutch official records and archival material. Review, E. L. Erickson, *Am. hist. rev.,* 61 (Oct. 1955): 204.

BIOGRAPHIES

Q173. Sim, Victor. **Biographies of prominent Chinese in Singapore.** Singapore, 1950.

Q174. Wurtzburg, Charles E. **Raffles of the eastern isles.** London, 1954.

Q175. Coupland, Sir Reginald. **Raffles of Singapore.** 3rd ed., London, 1946. A scholarly biography, partly based on original sources and older biographies. [JNP]

PERIODICALS

Q176. Journal of the Malayan branch of the Royal Asiatic Society. Singapore, 1923 ff. (3 nos. per year.) Successor to *Journal of the Straits branch of the Royal Asiatic Society* (Singapore, 1878–1922).

Q177. Malayan historical journal. Kuala Lumpur, 1954 ff. (Semiannual.)

THE PHILIPPINES

BIBLIOGRAPHIES

Q178. University of Chicago. **Selected bibliography of the Philippines, topically arranged and annotated.** New Haven, 1956. Useful but uneven bibliography listing primarily those works consulted by the staff of the Philippines Studies Program, University of Chicago in preparing a handbook on the Philippines.

Q179. Pelzer, Karl J. **Selected bibliography on the geography of Southeast Asia.** Pt. 2, The Philippines. New Haven, 1950. Stresses geography, but uses the term in a very broad sense. Has a section on history.

Q180. Robertson, James A. **Bibliography of the Philippine Islands.** Cleveland, 1908. Valuable for historical research on the Philippines.

Q181. Retana, Wenceslao E. "Epitome de la bibliografía general de Filipinas." In v. 1–4 of Retana, **Archivo del bibliófilo filipino** (Madrid, 1895–98). Still a basic work.

Q182. Lietz, Paul S. **Calendar of Philippine documents in the Ayer Collection of the Newberry Library.** Chicago, 1956. Provides annotations for a list of 370 documents treating the Spanish period of Philippine history.

GEOGRAPHIES

Q183. Spencer, Joseph E. **Land and people in the Philippines.** Berkeley, 1952. Cultural and economic geography; a useful introduction to Philippine social and economic problems. [FHG]

Q184. Kolb, Albert. **Die Philippinen.** Leipzig, 1942. Best available geography of the Philippines. Review, J. E. Spencer, *Pac. aff.,* 22 (Sep. 1949): 314. [FHG]

ANTHROPOLOGICAL WORKS

Q185. Conklin, Harold C. **Outline gazetteer of native Philippine ethnic and linguistic groups.** New Haven, 1952. A thin but highly useful and reliable guide.

Q186. Kroeber, Alfred L. **Peoples of the Philippines.** 2nd rev. ed., N.Y., 1943. [American Museum of Natural History, Handbook series, 8.]

DEMOGRAPHY

Q187. Republic of the Philippines. Department of Commerce and Industry. **1948 census of the Philippines: population classified by province, by city, municipality and municipal district, and by barrio.** Manila, 1951. The latest census. Others appeared for 1903, 1918, and 1939. [FHG]

PRINTED COLLECTIONS OF SOURCES

Q188. Poblador, Filemon, ed. **Important documents illustrative of Philippine history.**

Manila, 1936. Contains a number of significant documents from 1898 to 1935.

Q189. Blair, Emma H., and James A. Robertson, eds. **Philippine Islands, 1493–1893.** 55 v. Cleveland, 1903–09. Collection of English translations of original sources on the discovery, exploration, pacification, and Christianization of the Philippines, and on the social, religious, political, and economic conditions to the end of Spanish sovereignty. The collection draws on many sources, particularly the Archivo General de Indias (Seville). [FHG]

GENERAL HISTORIES

Q190. Benítez, Conrado. **History of the Philippines.** Rev. ed., N.Y., 1954. High school textbook. Political and cultural history. [FHG]

Q191. Montero y Vidal, José. **Historia general de Filipinas desde el descubrimiento de dichas islas hasta nuestros días.** 3 v. Madrid, 1887–95. Good general history of the Philippines.

HISTORIES OF SPECIAL PERIODS

Q192. Elliott, Charles B. **The Philippines to the end of the military régime.** Indianapolis, 1916.

Q193. ——. **The Philippines to the end of the Commission government.** Indianapolis, 1917. Elliott's 2 v. history of the U. S. conquest and occupation from 1898 to 1916 is comprehensive and well documented. Author served for a time as associate justice of the Philippine Supreme Court and later as secretary of commerce and police. [FHG]

Q194. LeRoy, James A. **The Americans in the Philippines: a history of the conquest and first years of occupation.** 2 v. Boston, 1914. Unusually comprehensive and reliable account of campaigns of the U.S. occupation of the Philippines, 1898–99, and the transition from military to civil government. The author, a former foreign service officer with experience in the Far East, was private secretary to Secretary Worcester. [FHG]

Q195. Worcester, Dean C. **The Philippines past and present.** 2 v. N.Y., 1914. Rev. ed., ed. by Ralsten Hayden, 1 v., N.Y., 1930. History of U.S. occupation and government, 1898–1913. Worcester was a controversial administrator and biased in his account. [FHG]

Q196. Forbes, William C. **The Philippine Islands.** 2 v. Boston and N.Y., 1928. Rev., abr. ed., 1 v., Cambridge, Mass., 1945. Comprehensive survey of U. S. rule in the Philippines through 1927. Forbes was a member of the Philippine Commission from 1904 to 1913, serving as governor general 1910–13. [FHG]

Q197. Majul, Cesar A. **The political and** constitutional ideas of the Philippine Revolution. Quezon City, 1957.

Q198. Agoncillo, Teodoro A. **The revolt of the masses: the story of Bonifacio and the Katipunan.** Quezon City, 1956. Scholarly history of the Philippine revolution against Spain in 1896. [FHG]

Q199. Zaide, Gregorio F. **The Philippine Revolution.** Manila, 1954. A reliable, if somewhat stereotyped, history of the revolution of 1896. Complements *Q198,* but is hardly comparable as a work of scholarship. Primary sources are employed extensively and the documentation is useful. [FHG]

Q200. Hayden, Joseph R. **The Philippines: a study in national development.** N.Y., 1942. The standard study of Philippine development, based on primary and secondary historical sources and long experience of the author in the area. Review, G. Kirk, *Far East. quar.,* 2 (Nov. 1942): 88. [FHG]

Q201. Grunder, Garel A., and William E. Livezey. **The Philippines and the United States.** Norman, 1951. Concise, reliable summary of U. S.-Philippine relations from 1898 to 1947. Primarily concerned with evolution of United States policy and particularly valuable for the careful use of U. S. government documents. Good bibliography, especially on government documents. Review, I. B. Powell, *Pac. aff.,* 25 (Dec. 1952): 419. [FHG]

Q202. Malcolm, George A. **The Commonwealth of the Philippines.** N.Y., 1936. Cultural and social history. Author was dean, College of Law, University of the Philippines and Supreme Court justice before World War II. A later edition, *First Malayan republic: the story of the Philippines* (Boston, 1951), is inferior to the earlier work. [FHG]

Q203. Kirk, Grayson L. **Philippine independence: motives, problems and prospects.** N.Y., 1936. Survey of the independence movement. Particularly useful for analysis of development of the counterpart U. S. movement to grant Philippine independence. [FHG]

Q204. Harrison, Francis B. **The cornerstone of Philippine independence.** N.Y., 1922. Controversial survey of social, political, and economic developments 1913–21. Harrison was governor general during these years, and this is a defense of his administration. [FHG]

Q205. Bernstein, David. **The Philippine story.** N.Y., 1947. Useful survey of political, social, and economic developments during the liberation from Japanese occupation and transfer of sovereignty from the United States to the Philippines. Author served as adviser to President Osmeña during the period of government in exile and subsequent to Osmeña's return to the Philippines in 1944. Critical of U. S. policy. [FHG]

HISTORIES OF SPECIAL TOPICS

Q206. Zaide, Gregorio F. **Philippine political and cultural history.** 2 v. Manila, 1953. Describes the main historical events since 1762, ending with the Roxas administration. The outstanding collegiate history textbook. [FHG]

Q207. Liang, Dapen. **The development of Philippine political parties.** Hong Kong, 1939. Comprehensive, well-documented political history of the Philippines from 1899 to 1935, with a preliminary section describing the liberal movement and growth of Freemasonry in the 19th century. [FHG]

Q208. Kalaw, Maximo M. **The development of Philippine politics (1872–1920).** Manila, 1926. Useful survey of Philippine political history, by former dean, College of Liberal Arts, University of Philippines. [FHG]

Q209. Abelarde, Pedro E. **American tariff policy towards the Philippines, 1898–1946.** N.Y., 1947. Well documented and scholarly; particularly valuable for references to public documents. Good bibliography. [FHG]

Q210. Jenkins, Shirley. **American economic policy toward the Philippines.** Stanford, 1954. Surveys U.S.–Philippine economic relations following World War II. [FHG]

Q211. Hartendorp, A. V. H. **Short history of industry and trade of the Philippines from pre-Spanish times to the end of the Roxas administration.** Manila, 1953. Well-documented survey of economic and political developments 1940–48. Treatment of earlier periods is superficial. Author is long-time resident, and editor of the *American Chamber of Commerce journal* in Manila. [FHG]

Q212. Pelzer, Karl J. **Pioneer settlement in the Asiatic tropics: studies in land utilization and agricultural colonization in southeastern Asia.** N.Y., 1945. Part is a survey of land utilization and voluntary agricultural colonization in Southeast Asia; the larger portion surveys actions on the part of government in prewar Philippines and Indonesia to recruit, transport, and settle colonists in frontier areas. [FHG]

Q213. Luthringer, George F. **The gold-exchange standard in the Philippines.** Princeton, 1934. Financial history. [FHG]

Q214. Cannon, M. Hamlin. **The war in the Pacific. Leyte: the return to the Philippines.** Washington, 1954. [United States army in World War II.] Comprehensive, detailed, but pedestrian military history; narrowly focused on day-to-day field operations leading to the reoccupation of Leyte in 1944–45. [FHG]

Q215. Morton, Louis. **The war in the Pacific. The fall of the Philippines.** Washington, 1953. [United States army in World War II.]

Q216. Aruego, José M. **The framing of the Philippine constitution.** 2 v. Manila, 1936. Thorough, detailed analysis of work of the constitutional convention of 1934–35, by one of its members. Useful appendix of documents relevant to study of Philippine constitutional history. [FHG]

Q217. Romani, John H. **The Philippine presidency.** Manila, 1955. Political history of the Philippines, 1934–53. Surveys evolution of the office of president during the commonwealth and republic period. [FHG]

Q218. Coquia, Jorge R. **Legal status of the church in the Philippines.** Washington, 1950. History of the legal aspects of various religious groups, with emphasis on the Catholic Church.

Q219. Laubach, Frank C. **The people of the Philippines, their religious progress and preparation for spiritual leadership in the Far East.** N.Y., 1925. Religious history by a prominent Protestant educator, maintaining high level of scholarship and objectivity. Bibliography focused on religious development. Statistical appendix. [FHG]

Q220. Isidro, Antonio. **The Philippine educational system.** 2nd ed., Manila, 1949. The author, dean of the College of Education, University of the Philippines, covers thoroughly the organization and administration of the Philippine educational system. [FHG]

Q221. Panganiban, José V., and Consuelo T. Panganiban. **The literature of the Filipinos.** Manila, 1953. A textbook history, by two professors at the University of Santo Tomás. Weak on theoretical treatment.

BIOGRAPHIES

Q222. Manuel, E. Arsenio. **Dictionary of Philippine biography.** Quezon City, 1955 ff.

Q223. Retizos, Isidro, and D. H. Soriano. **Philippines who's who.** Quezon City, 1957.

Q224. Malcolm, George A. **American colonial careerist: half a century of official life and personal experience.** Boston, 1957.

Q225. Quezon, Manuel L. **The good fight.** N.Y., 1946.

Q226. Palma, Rafael. **The pride of the Malay race: a biography of José Rizal.** Tr. by Roman Ozaeta. N.Y., 1949. Definitive biography of Philippine author and nationalist leader who was martyred by the Spanish in 1896. Palma, a prominent leader of the Nacionalista party, served as senator and as president of the University of the Philippines. [FHG]

Q227. Taruc, Luis. **Born of the people.** N.Y., 1953. History of Hukbalahap movement during World War II by the leader until his surrender in 1953. Reliability sometimes questionable. Review, T. I. Moore, *Pac. aff.*, 26 (Dec. 1953): 359. [FHG]

OFFICIAL GOVERNMENT RECORDS

Q228. Philippines (Republic). **Official gazette.** Manila, 1902 ff. (Weekly, 1902–41; monthly, 1945 ff.) Contains acts, executive and administrative orders, and Supreme Court decisions.

Q229. Report of the Philippine Commission. 4 v. Washington, 1900–01. Report of the Advisory Commission sent by President McKinley to the Philippines in 1899 to ascertain conditions and make recommendations as to the government that should be established when pacification was completed. [FHG]

Q230. Journal of the Philippine Commission. 10 v. Washington, 1908–17.

Q231. Report of the Philippine Commission to the secretary of war. 32 v. Washington, 1901–16.

Q232. Report of the governor general of the Philippine Islands to the secretary of war. Washington, 1917–37. (Annual.)

Q233. Philippine Commission. **Public laws passed by the Philippine Commission.** 6 v. Manila, 1903–08. Includes acts nos. 1 to 1800.

Q234. Philippine Islands. **Public laws enacted by the Philippine Legislature.** 25 v. Manila, 1910–37. Acts nos. 1801 to 4275.

Q235. Philippines (Commonwealth). **Public laws of the commonwealth.** 6 v. Manila, 1938–47. Covers period 1935–46.

Q236. Report of the United States high commissioner to the Philippine Islands to the president and Congress of the United States. Washington, 1937–47. (Annual. Title varies.)

Q237. Joint Preparatory Committee on Philippine Affairs. **Report of May 20, 1938.** 3 v. in 4. Washington, 1938. [Department of State publications, Conference series 36.] Reports, public hearings, and briefs filed with the joint congressional committee created to consider changes in the transition to Philippine independence scheduled in the Tydings-McDuffie act of 1934. [FHG]

Q238. Report and recommendations of the Joint Philippine-American Finance Commission. Washington, 1947. [House document no. 390, 80th Congress, 1st session.] Includes "Interim report" of April 25, 1947 and "Philippine economic development technical memorandum." Contains far-reaching recommendations concerning monetary and fiscal policy, international economic policies, and economic development of the Philippines. [FHG]

Q239. U. S. Economic Survey Mission to the Philippines. **Report to the president of the United States.** Washington, 1950. Valuable survey of Philippine economic and social developments in the early period of the republic, by Daniel W. Bell, chief of mission, and others. [FHG]

Q240. U. S. Mutual Security Agency. Special Technical and Economic Mission to the Philippines. **Philippine land tenure reform: analysis and recommendations.** Manila, 1952. Known as the Hardie report, this attempted to deal with deep-seated agrarian problems which culminated in the Hukbalahap rebellion. [FHG]

PERIODICALS

Q241. Journal of history. Manila, 1941 ff. (3 nos. per year.) Formerly *Journal of the Philippine Historical Society.*

Q242. Philippine social sciences and humanities review. Manila and Quezon City, 1929 ff. (Quarterly. Title varies.)

Q243. Journal of east Asiatic studies. Manila, 1951 ff. (Quarterly.)

THAILAND

BIBLIOGRAPHY

Q244. Cornell University. **Bibliography of Thailand.** Ithaca, 1956. [Cornell Southeast Asia program data paper no. 20.] Selective bibliography of books and articles, annotated and topically arranged. Emphasis is on modern Thailand. [WFV]

GEOGRAPHY

Q245. Credner, Wilhelm. **Siam: das Land der Tai.** Stuttgart, 1935. This broad physical and cultural geography remains the best work of its kind on Thailand, even though the statistics are out of date. Review, E. Seidenfaden, *Journal of the Siam Society,* 31 (1939): 79. [WFV]

ANTHROPOLOGY

Q246. Le May, Reginald S. **An Asian Arcady: the land and peoples of northern Siam.** Cambridge, Eng., 1926. Informative, reliable, and engaging book on the history, customs, landscape, and lore of northern Thailand. Author was an economic adviser to the Thai government. Review, G. Coedès, *Jour. Siam Soc.,* 21 (1928): 219. [WFV]

PRINTED COLLECTIONS OF SOURCES

Q247. Coedès, Georges. **Recueil des inscriptions du Siam.** 2 pts. Bangkok, 1924–29. Fine collection of translations of stone inscriptions dating from the 6th to 16th centuries, with excellent notes by the author, **↑**

leading scholar of early Southeast Asian history and one-time director of the national library in Thailand. [WFV]

Q248. Notton, Camille, tr. **Annales du Siam.** 4 v. Paris and Bangkok, 1926–39. Translations of chronicles from various states in northern Siam. The chronicles and Notton's notes must both be used with caution. [WFV]

Q249. The Burney papers. 5 v. Bangkok, 1910–14. Valuable collection of official documents relating to British diplomatic contacts with Siam from 1822 to 1849. [WFV]

GENERAL HISTORIES

Q250. Thompson, Virginia M. **Thailand, the new Siam.** N.Y., 1941. Most recent general reference work on Thailand. Virtually all aspects of Thai culture are considered. Review, K. P. Landon, *Far East. quar.,* 1 (May 1942): 292. [WFV]

Q251. Wood, William A. R. **A history of Siam: from the earliest times to the year A.D. 1781, with a supplement dealing with more recent events.** 2nd rev. ed., Bangkok, 1933. The only really general history of Siam, this is primarily an outline of political events. Author was a British consular official in Siam for many years, and based his work on Thai sources. Review, G. Coedès, *Jour. Siam Soc.,* 21 (1927): 179. [WFV]

Q252. Graham, Walter A. **Siam.** 3rd ed., 2 v., London, 1924. Early handbook on Thailand—its history, educational system, government organization, arts, religion, etc. Is still useful, primarily for information about first decades of the 20th century. [WFV]

HISTORIES OF SPECIAL PERIODS

Q253. Hutchinson, E. W. **Adventurers in Siam in the seventeenth century.** London, 1940. Lively introduction to the first Portuguese, Dutch, English, and French contacts with Siam. The history centers on the remarkable career of the Greek adventurer, Constantine Phaulkon, who rose from cabin boy on a British ship to virtual prime minister of Siam. A Royal Asiatic Society prize publication volume. [WFV]

Q254. Vella, Walter F. **Siam under Rama III, 1824–1851.** Locust Valley, N.Y., 1957. Reliable history of Siam during reign of the last king of "Old Siam." Contains annotated bibliography of Thai and western language materials.

Q255. ——. **The impact of the West on government in Thailand.** Berkeley, 1955. Short and lucid history of the influences of western institutions and ideas on Thai political principles and practice. Based on Thai and western sources. Review, D. A. Wilson, *Far East. quar.,* 15 (Aug. 1956): 611.

HISTORIES OF SPECIAL TOPICS

Q256. Landon, Kenneth P. **Siam in transition: a brief survey of cultural trends in the five years since the revolution of 1932.** Shanghai, 1939. An early report, by a U.S. resident, of the political and cultural changes that followed the coup d'état of 1932. [WFV]

Q257. Wales, Horace G. Quaritch. **Ancient Siamese government and administration.** London, 1934. Excellent analysis of the organization of the Thai government before changes produced by western contacts. The author, a social anthropologist, based his work on Thai sources and on knowledge gained as adviser to the Thai Department of Court Pages. [WFV]

Q258. ——. **Siamese state ceremonies: their history and function.** London, 1931. Detailed description of the traditional rites performed at the Siamese court. [WFV]

Q259. Ingram, James C. **Economic change in Thailand since 1850.** Stanford, 1955. The first economic history of Thailand. A description of economic life in 1850 is followed by a highly informative discussion of development since then in the rice trade and other economic activities. Review, W. Henderson, *Far East. quar.,* 14 (Aug. 1955): 595. [WFV]

Q260. Skinner, G. William. **Chinese society in Thailand.** Ithaca, 1957. Detailed and penetrating analytical history of the Chinese minority in Thailand. Presentation is chronological; the chapters indicate significant periods in development of the Chinese community. Contains useful charts, maps, notes, exhaustive bibliography, and reference list of Chinese characters. [WFV]

Q261. Schweisguth, P. **Étude sur la littérature siamoise.** Paris, 1951. A pioneer historical survey of Thai literature, incorporating brief translations of important Thai works. Contains excellent bibliography of Thai sources. Review, G. Coedès, *BEFEO,* 46 (1954): 657. [WFV]

Q262. Wells, Kenneth E. **Thai Buddhism, its rites and activities.** Bangkok, 1939.

Q263. Le May, Reginald S. **A concise history of Buddhist art in Siam.** Cambridge, Eng., 1938. The only general history of sculpture and architecture in Siam. A clear exposition of the periods in and influences on art, it also provides many sidelights on Siamese history in general, beginning with the first century of the Christian era and ending at 1600. Numerous plates. Review, G. Coedès, *Jour. Siam. Soc.,* 31 (1939): 192. [WFV]

BIOGRAPHIES

Q264. Bhumiraj Bhakdi. [Who's who in Thailand.] Bangkok, 1954. Extremely limited coverage. In English and Thai.

Q265. Chandruang, Kumut. **My boyhood**

in Siam. N.Y., 1938. Popularly written autobiography by the son of a Thai provincial official. Depicts, as do the two following works, the traditional Siamese culture the author knew in his youth and the subsequent influence of western culture on both author and Thailand. [WFV]

Q266. Chula Chakrabongse, Prince. **Brought up in England.** London, 1943. Author is a grandson of King Mongkut. [WFV]

Q267. Rudivoravan, Princess. **The treasured one.** N.Y., 1957. Author is a granddaughter of King Mongkut. [WFV]

GOVERNMENT PUBLICATION

Q268. Royal Thai government gazette. Bangkok, 1946 ff. (Weekly. Title varies.) In English and Thai.

SOCIETY PUBLICATION

Q269. The Siam Society: fiftieth anniversary commemorative publication. Bangkok, 1954. Collection of some of the best short articles appearing in the *Journal of the Siam Society*. The articles, devoted to topics in Thai history, archaeology, philology, customs, art, etc., are individually highly informative; collectively they constitute a good general guide to traditional Thai culture. Review, K. E. Wells, *Far East. quar.,* 14 (May 1955): 426 [WFV]

PERIODICAL

Q270. Journal of the Siam Society. Bangkok, 1904 ff. (Irregular.)

SECTION R

South Asia

HORACE I. POLEMAN *

This section contains materials on Afghanistan, Ceylon, Pakistan, India, Nepal, Bhutan, and Sikkim covering the entire recorded period of history. Entries for the prehistoric and Vedic periods of the Indian sub-continent are included in Section G.

Since this area represents an underdeveloped academic field in the United States, the interests of college teacher and graduate student, as well as general reader and college student, were considered in the choice of entries. Although this cannot be considered a comprehensive, basic bibliography for research purposes and contains only a few hundred of the thousands of works which could have been included, it offers all that is needed for a fairly thorough study of any aspect of South Asian history. In addition to purely historical studies, an attempt has been made to provide a guide to essential related subjects.

GENERAL WORKS

R1. Brown, W. Norman. **The United States and India and Pakistan.** Cambridge, Mass., 1953. Brief but authoritative and perceptive account of historical background for the emergence of India and Pakistan as new nations. Emphasizes post-independence problems and progress. An excellent introduction to the subject. [RIC]

R2. Davis, Kingsley. **The population of India and Pakistan.** Princeton, 1951. First definitive demographic study of the sub-continent, well documented and conclusive.

R3. A handbook for travellers in India, Pakistan, Burma, and Ceylon. Ed. by Sir A. C. Lothian. 17th ed., London, 1955. Most complete and satisfying both as a guide book and ready reference.

R4. Spate, Oskar H. K. **India and Pakistan: a general and regional geography, with**
a chapter on Ceylon. London and N.Y., 1954. Definitive analysis.

R5. Spear, Thomas G. P. **India, Pakistan, and the West.** 2nd ed., London, 1952. Brief survey of Indian history, the British contribution, and the Indian response. Includes materials on post-independence period. [RIC]

R6. Tinker, Hugh. **The foundations of local self-government in India, Pakistan, and Burma.** London, 1954. Any study of the political structure of south Asia must consider the local aspects. This is an excellent guide.

R7. Wilson, Patrick G. **Government and politics of India and Pakistan, 1885–1955: a bibliography of works in western languages.** Berkeley, 1956. Most complete bibliography on the subject. Contains a special index of Command papers.

* The following contributed items and comments indicated by their respective initials: Robert I. Crane (RIC), Holden Furber (HF), and Robert F. Ogden (RFO).

AFGHANISTAN

R8. "Afghanistan." **The Middle East: a survey and directory of the Middle East** compiled by the publishers in collaboration with the intelligence unit of The economist (London, 1950), pp. 17–30. Encyclopedic. [RFO]

R9. Ahmad, Jamal-ud-Din. **Afghanistan: a brief survey.** London and N.Y., 1936. Survey section on history; good for brief summary. [RFO]

R10. Barthold, Vasiliĭ V. **Turkestan down to the Mongol invasion.** Tr. by V. M. Minorsky. 2nd ed., London, 1928. [E. J. W. Gibb memorial series, n.s. 5.] Valuable reference work. [RFO]

R11. De Croze, Joel. "Afghanistan today." **Journal of Indian Institute of International Affairs,** 3 (1947): 29–49. Survey of trend toward modernization. [RFO]

R12. Engert, Cornelius van H. **A report on Afghanistan.** Washington, 1924. [U. S. Department of State, Division of Publications, series C, no. 53, Afghanistan no. 1.] Estimate of Afghan situation at beginning of the modern period. Extensive bibliography. [RFO]

R13. Fraser-Tytler, William K. "Afghanistan: a brief description." **Journal of the Royal Central Asian Society,** 29 (July-Oct. 1942): 165–75. General survey article; topography, roads, and population elements. [RFO]

R14. ——. **Afghanistan: a study in po-** litical developments in central and southern Asia. 2nd ed., London and N.Y., 1953. Survey handbook with emphasis on foreign affairs and national political developments. [RFO]

R15. Habberton, William. **Anglo-Russian relations concerning Afghanistan, 1837–1907.** Urbana, Ill., 1937. Attempt to extract the material on Afghanistan from that on the larger question of international rivalry. [RFO]

R16. MacMunn, Sir George F. **Afghanistan, from Darius to Amanullah.** London, 1929. Detailed survey of Afghan history from earliest times through World War I. [RFO]

R17. Nazim, Muhammad. **The life and times of Sultan Mahmūd of Ghazna.** Cambridge, Eng., 1931. Detailed treatment of one period of Afghan history, based on primary sources. [RFO]

R18. Rishtiya, Sayyid K. **Afghanistan dar garn-i nuzdahum.** [Afghanistan in the 19th century.] Kabul, 1950. This work in Persian represents Afghan scholarship in the historical field. [RFO]

R19. Sykes, Sir Percy M. **A history of Afghanistan.** 2 v. London, 1940. The most extensive historical treatment of Afghanistan; best reference work. [RFO]

R20. Wilber, Donald N. **Annotated bibliography of Afghanistan.** New Haven, 1956. Best bibliography on Afghanistan.

CEYLON

R21. Bailey, Sydney D. **Ceylon.** N.Y., 1952. Brief, popular account from earliest times to 1948.

R22. Boltin, Lee. **Ceylon.** Garden City, N.Y., 1956. Brief, useful geography, prepared with the cooperation of the American Geographical Society.

R23. Ceylon. Archaeological Department. **Memoirs of the archaeological survey of Ceylon.** Colombo, 1924 ff. (Irregular.) A rich historical series.

R24. Ceylon. Government Archivist. **Report on the Dutch records in the government archives at Colombo.** By R. G. Anthonisz. Colombo, 1907. Useful as a companion volume to *R25.*

R25. ——. **Selections from the Dutch records of the Ceylon government.** Colombo, 1927 ff. Good selection of source materials.

R26. Ceylon. Superintendent of Census. **Census of Ceylon, 1881.** Comp. by Lionel Lee. Colombo, 1882. Valuable source of information on many subjects.

R27. ——. **Census of Ceylon, 1891.** Comp. by Lionel Lee. Colombo, 1892.

R28. ——. **The census of Ceylon, 1901.** Comp. by P. Arunachalam. 4 v. Colombo, 1902.

R29. ——. **Ceylon at the census of 1911.** By E. B. Denham. Colombo, 1912.

R30. ——. **Census of Ceylon, 1921.** By L. J. B. Turner. 4 v. in 5. Colombo, 1923–26.

R31. Ceylon. Department of Census and Statistics. **Census of Ceylon, 1931.** 2 v. Colombo, 1931.

R32. ——. **Census of Ceylon, 1946.** Colombo, 1950.

R33. ——. **Census of Ceylon, 1953.** Colombo, 1953.

R34. ——. **Demographic study of the city of Colombo.** Colombo, 1954. This study and *R75* offer a good approach to the understanding of rural and urban population problems.

R35. ——. **Statistical abstract of Ceylon.** Colombo, 1949 ff. An annual publication containing valuable information on a variety of subjects.

R36. The Ceylon historical journal. Dehiwela, 1952 ff. (Quarterly.) A new journal which shows great promise.

R37. The Ceylon year book: the official statistical annual of the social, economic and general conditions of the island. Colombo, 1948 ff. A new reference series, published by the government of Ceylon, covering a wide variety of subjects.

R38. Chitty, Simon C. **The Ceylon gazetteer.** Ceylon, 1834. This early account contains much material of historical value.

R39. Choudhary, Sukhbir. "Problem of citizenship rights for people of Indian origin in Ceylon—the background and the issues." **Foreign affairs reports,** 5 (Nov. 1956): 114–29. Good review of the problems and possible solutions.

R40. Codrington, Humphrey W. **Ceylon coins and currency.** Colombo, 1924.

R41. ——. **A short history of Ceylon.** London, 1929. A good introduction.

R42. Cook, Elsie K. **Ceylon: its geography, its resources and its people.** 2nd ed., rev. by K. Kularatnam, Madras, 1951. Best reference book on the subject.

R43. De Silva, Colvin R. **Ceylon under the British occupation, 1795–1833.** V. 1, **Its political and administrative development.** Colombo, 1953. A fair appraisal.

R44. D'Oyly, Sir John. **A sketch of the constitution of the Kandyan kingdom.** New ed., Colombo, 1929. Aside from its legal and administrative information, this is a valuable record of social values in 17th and 18th century Ceylon, the time of European occupation.

R45. Enríquez, Colin M. D. **Ceylon past and present.** London, 1927. Early history through the European occupations, with a brief account of governmental arrangements at time of writing. Contains also some ethnographic and descriptive material.

R46. Ferguson, Donald, tr. and ed. "The history of Ceylon from the earliest times to 1600 A.D. as related by João de Barros and Diogo do Couto." **Journal of the Ceylon Branch of the Royal Asiatic Society,** 20 (1909): 1–445. Principal source of information for this early period.

R47. Ferguson's Ceylon directory 1957. Colombo, 1957. Has been published since 1868 under various titles. Indispensable reference work on a variety of subjects, including government, trade, education, and communications.

R48. Geiger, Wilhelm. **A grammar of the Sinhalese language.** Colombo, 1938. Best work on this language.

R49. Godakumbura, C. E. **Sinhalese literature.** Colombo, 1955. Very readable account.

R50. Great Britain. Commission on Constitutional Reform in Ceylon. **Ceylon: report of the Commission on Constitutional Reform.** London, 1945.

R51. Jennings, Sir William I. **The consti-**tution of Ceylon. Bombay and N.Y., 1949. Authoritative analysis.

R52. ——. **The economy of Ceylon.** Madras and N.Y., 1948. Although somewhat out of date, most observations are still valid.

R53. ——. "Nationalism and political development in Ceylon: the background of self government." **Ceylon historical journal,** 3 (July 1953): 62–84, 3 (Jan.-Apr. 1953): 197–206.

R54. Journal of the Ceylon Branch of the Royal Asiatic Society. Colombo, 1845 ff. (Irregular.) Antiquarian journal on the history of Ceylon.

R55. Jurriaanse, Maria W. **Catalogue of the archives of the Dutch central government of coastal Ceylon, 1640–1796.** Colombo, 1943. Important collection of source material.

R56. Knox, Robert. **An historical relation of the island Ceylon in the East-Indies.** London, 1681. Reprint, ed. by James Ryan, Glasgow, 1911. Classic account of Knox's captivity in Ceylon. [HF]

R57. Law, Bimala C. **On the chronicles of Ceylon.** Calcutta, 1947. Critical appraisal of the ancient historical accounts of Ceylon in Singhalese and Pali.

R58. Mendis, Garrett C. **Ceylon today and yesterday: main currents of Ceylon history.** Colombo, 1957. Brief survey, useful as introductory study.

R59. ——. **Ceylon under the British.** 2nd rev. ed., Colombo, 1948. Brief, objective account packed with information.

R60. ——, ed. **The Colebrooke-Cameron papers: documents on British colonial policy in Ceylon, 1796–1833.** Bombay, 1956 ff. Compilation of valuable source material.

R61. ——. **The early history of Ceylon: or, the Indian period of Ceylon history.** 6th ed., Calcutta, 1948. Brief, popular account of the island from the 2nd century B.C. to 16th century A.D.

R62. Mills, Lennox A. **Britain and Ceylon.** London and N.Y., 1945. A brief account covering the principal events.

R63. ——. **Ceylon under British rule, 1795–1932: with an account of the East India Company's embassies to Kandy, 1762–1795.** London, 1933. Completeness of the text and the full bibliography make this indispensable for study of the period covered.

R64. Mitton, Geraldine E. **The lost cities of Ceylon.** London, 1916. Description of the ancient Hindu and Buddhist sites and the history surrounding them.

R65. Müller, Eduard. **Ancient inscriptions in Ceylon, collected and published for the government.** 2 v. London, 1883. Valuable compilation of sources.

R66. The new Lanka. Colombo, 1949 ff. (Quarterly.) A semi-popular periodical with occasional articles of substance.

R67. Parker, Henry. **Ancient Ceylon: an**

account of the aborigines and of part of the early civilization. London, 1909. Very complete description of the early cultures.

R68. Paulusz, J. H. O. "The outbreak of the Kandyan-Dutch war of 1761 and the great rebellion." **Journal of the Ceylon Branch of the Royal Asiatic Society,** n.s. 3 (June 1953): 29–52. Sound article on an important event.

R69. Pieris, Paulus E. **Ceylon and the Hollanders, 1658–1796.** 3rd ed., Colombo, 1947. The standard work in English on the Dutch period in Ceylon. [HF]

R70. ———. **Ceylon: the Portuguese era, being a history of the island for the period 1505–1658.** 2 v. Colombo, 1913–14. By the leading Ceylonese authority on Portuguese and Dutch periods of the island's history. [HF]

R71. Queyroz, Fernão de. **The temporal and spiritual conquest of Ceylon.** Tr. by S. G. Perera. 3 v. Colombo, 1930. This early 17th century account is a mine of information on the Portuguese in Ceylon and the life, habits, and beliefs of the Ceylonese.

R72. Rahula, Walpola. **History of Buddhism in Ceylon: the Anuradhapura period, 3rd century B.C.–10th century A.C.** Colombo, 1956. Covers an important period in the development of Hinayana Buddhism.

R73. Raven-Hart, Rowland, tr. and ed. **Germans in Dutch Ceylon by Von der Behr (1668), Herport (1669), Schweitzer (1682) and Fryke (1692).** Colombo, 1953. Another chapter in the early European expansion period in Ceylon, based on hitherto unexplored source material.

R74. Ryan, Bryce. **Caste in modern Ceylon: the Sinhalese system in transition.** New Brunswick, 1953. Excellent social study with historical background.

R75. Sarkar, N. K. **The demography of Ceylon.** Colombo, 1957. Only complete study of its kind. Contains historical chapter.

R76. Senaveratne, John M. **The story of the Sinhalese from the most ancient times.** 2 v. Colombo and London, 1923. Early history of Ceylon through the 3rd century A.D.

R77. Tambiah, Henry W. **The laws and customs of the Tamils of Ceylon.** [n.p.], 1954. Interesting and useful treatise on the people who comprise one-third of Ceylon's population.

R78. Tennent, Sir James. **Ceylon.** 3rd ed., 2 v., London, 1859. By the leading authority on Ceylon in the Victorian period. Still important for modern or early history. [HF]

R79. Toussaint, James R. **Annals of the Ceylon civil service.** Colombo, 1935. From its inception in 1798 into the 20th century.

R80. Weerawardana, I. D. S., and Marguerite I. Weerawardana. **Ceylon and her citizens.** Madras, 1956. Good analysis from the Indian point of view.

R81. Wijesekera, Nandadeva. **The people of Ceylon.** Colombo, 1949. A social and racial study.

PAKISTAN

R82. Abernethy, George L. **Pakistan: a selected, annotated bibliography.** N.Y., 1957. Intended for the general reader, but also useful to the student. Lists journal articles as well as books.

R83. Akhtar, Sardar M. **Economics of Pakistan.** 2nd ed., Lahore, 1951. Rather optimistic analysis, written when the situation appeared good.

R84. **Biographical encyclopedia of Pakistan.** Ed. by Khan Tahawar Ali. Lahore, 1955. Useful tool for historians and librarians.

R85. Bolitho, Hector. **Jinnah, creator of Pakistan.** London, 1954. Author was commissioned by the Pakistan government to write this biography. It is consequently based on official documentation.

R86. **Chronology of Pakistan, June 1947– June 1953.** Karachi, 1953. Very useful reference tool.

R87. **Crescent and green: a miscellany of writings on Pakistan.** London, 1955. Fairly good popular introduction to the study of Pakistan.

R88. Elahi, Khwaja Nur, A. Moid, and Akhtar H. Siddhiqui. **A guide to works of** reference published in Pakistan. Karachi, 1953. Useful bibliography.

R89. Franck, Dorothea S. "Pakhtunistan —disputed disposition of a tribal land." **Middle East journal,** 6 (winter 1952): 49–68. Fairly objective statement of the claims and problems of the Pathan tribal lands in Baluchistan, the former Northwest Frontier Province, and the so-called Tribal Territory.

R90. Ghani, A. R. **Pakistan: a select bibliography.** Lahore, 1951. Contains mostly material on the area of Pakistan, published while still a part of India.

R91. Ikram, Sheikh Mohamad, and Thomas G. P. Spear, eds. **The cultural heritage of Pakistan.** Karachi and N.Y., 1955. Series of articles on the various aspects of Pakistan's inherited culture.

R92. Jinnah, Mohamed Ali, ed. **India's problem of her future constitution: All-India Muslim League's Lahore resolution popularly known as "Pakistan."** Bombay, 1940. Interesting collection of source material, which may be called the beginning of Pakistan.

R93. **Journal of the Pakistan Historical Society.** Karachi, 1953 ff. (Quarterly.)

Shows promise of being a good, scholarly journal.

R94. Journal of the University of Peshawar. Peshawar, 1952 ff. (Irregular.) Sound and scholarly.

R95. Maron, Stanley, and others. **Annotated bibliography for Pakistan: sociology, economics, and politics.** Berkeley, 1956. Best bibliography yet to appear.

R96. Metz, William S. **Pakistan: government and politics.** Berkeley, 1956.

R97. North-west Frontier Province, Pakistan. Central Record Office. **A guide to the archives.** By S. M. Jaffar. Peshawar, 1948. Record of important source materials.

R98. Pakistan. Historical Records and Archives Commission. **Proceedings of the meeting.** Karachi, 1948 ff.

R99. Pakistan. Office of the Census Commissioner. **Census of Pakistan, 1951.** 8 v. Karachi, 1954–56.

R100. Pakistan. Stationery and Printing Dept. **Catalogue of the Government of Pakistan publications.** Karachi, 1952 ff. (Irregular.)

R101. Pakistan Historical Society. **Proceedings of the All Pakistan History Con-**ference. Karachi, 1951 ff. (Annual.) A guide to what may be expected from research in Pakistan.

R102. Pakistan quarterly. Karachi, 1949 ff. Popular magazine containing some articles on history; beautifully illustrated.

R103. Pakistan statistical yearbook. Karachi, 1952 ff. Volumes include comparative statistics for previous years.

R104. The Pakistan yearbook and who's who. Karachi, 1949 ff.

R105. Pithawalla, Manekji B. **An introduction to Pakistan: its resources and potentialities.** Karachi, 1948. Good material on geography and geology.

R106. Symonds, Richard. **The making of Pakistan.** 3rd ed., London, 1950. Soundest account of the factors leading to partition.

R107. Ten years of Pakistan, 1947–1957. Karachi, 1957. A government report on progress.

R108. Wheeler, Sir Robert E. M. **Five thousand years of Pakistan: an archaeological outline.** London, 1950. Starting with the Indus Valley civilization, contains mostly the story of Indian archaeology.

INDIA

BIBLIOGRAPHIES

R109. Cornell University. **Selected and annotated bibliography of the sociology of India.** New Haven, 1957. Very comprehensive; includes historical works.

R110. Dandekar, Ramachandra N., ed. **Progress of Indic studies, 1917–1942.** Poona, 1942. [Government oriental series, class B, no. 8.] Very complete evaluation of research published during the period. The lack of index, however, renders it almost useless as a handy reference.

R111. Hasan, Zafar. **Bibliography of Indo-Moslem history excluding provincial monarchies.** Calcutta, 1932. [Memoirs of the Archaeological survey of India, no. 45.] Excellent list. Nothing similar exists for post-1932 publications.

R112. India. National Library. **Catalogue of periodicals, newspapers and gazettes.** Calcutta, 1956. Very valuable addition to knowledge of 18th and 19th century serials; a rich collection.

R113. ——. **A tentative bibliography of basic publications on all aspects of Indian culture.** Sect. 1, **Indian anthropology.** Calcutta, 1951. A fairly comprehensive trial volume. Nothing additional has appeared.

R114. India. Parliament. **List of publications (periodical or ad hoc) issued by various ministries of the Government of India.** 2nd ed., New Delhi, 1952 ff. A new bibliographical series covering documents which may not appear in the ordinary lists of documents for sale.

R115. Mandelbaum, David G. **Materials for a bibliography of the ethnology of India.** Berkeley, 1949. Mimeographed and distributed by the author.

R116. Mitra, Haridas. **Contribution to a bibliography of Indian art and aesthetics.** Santiniketan, 1951. Excellent guide.

R117. Nifor guide to Indian periodicals. Poona, 1955 ff. The best listing to date, but not complete.

R118. Sharma, Sri R. **A bibliography of Mughal India (1526–1707 A.D.).** Bombay, 1938. Excellent guide to the sources.

R119. Singhal, C. R., comp. **Bibliography of Indian coins.** Ed. by A. S. Altekar. 2 pts. Bombay, 1950–52. Indispensable reference guide.

R120. U. S. Library of Congress. **Southern Asia accessions list.** Washington, 1952 ff. (Quarterly, 1952–56; monthly, 1957 ff.) Useful guide to current imprints.

R121. ——. **Working paper of the conference on American library resources on southern Asia.** No. 1–8. Washington, 1957. Paper no. 2 by Patrick Wilson is a bibliography of bibliographies, listing all bibliographies of government publications of any importance.

R122. Wilson, Patrick G., ed. **South Asia: a selected bibliography on India, Pakistan and Ceylon.** N.Y., 1957. Brief list intended for those needing an introduction to the area in their special fields.

REFERENCE WORKS

R123. Apte, Vinayak M. **Social and religious life in the Grihya-sūtras.** See *G60*.

R124. Barnett, Lionel D. **Antiquities of India: an account of the history and culture of ancient Hindustan.** London, 1913. A standard reference covering early history; chronology and eras; law and government; ritual; science; weights, measures, and coins; medicine; writing; architecture; sculpture and painting.

R125. Brown, C. J. **The coins of India.** London, 1922. [The heritage of India series.] Excellent brief introduction.

R126. Buckland, Charles E. **Dictionary of Indian biography.** London, 1906. Over 2,500 sketches of individuals since about 175 A.D.

R127. Bühler, Georg, tr. **The laws of Manu.** Oxford, 1886. [Sacred books of the East, 25.] Still the best translation of this work, which is the basis of Hindu law and Anglo-Indian law.

R128. Coomaraswamy, Ananda K. **Introduction to Indian art.** Madras, 1923. Any study of Indian art should begin with readings in the works of Coomaraswamy, this among the first.

R129. Cunningham, Alexander. **Book of Indian eras, with tables for calculating Indian dates.** Calcutta, 1883. Useful guide to a complicated subject.

R130. Dowson, John. **A classical dictionary of Hindu mythology and religion, geography, history, and literature.** 6th ed., London, 1928. A necessary work for spot reference.

R131. Duff, C. Mabel (Mrs. W. R. Rickmers). **The chronology of India, from the earliest times to the beginning of the sixteenth century.** Westminster, 1899. Attempts to list the most important events from early times to 1530.

R132. Farquhar, John N. **Outline of the religious literature of India.** London, 1920. Religion is a vital part of the history of India, and this is the most useful compendium on the subject. Covers the Vedic religion, Hinduism, Buddhism, and Jainism through the 18th century.

R133. Garrett, John. **A classical dictionary of India.** Madras, 1871. Supplement, 1873. Very useful reference work.

R134. Havell, Ernest B. **Handbook of Indian art.** London, 1920. Very readable account of the subject. The point of view has been subject to challenge.

R135. Hopkins, Edward W. **Religions of India.** Reprint, Boston, 1902. Still a good text for Brahmanism, Hinduism, Jainism, Buddhism, and Annamism.

R136. India. Census Commissioner. **Imperial census of 1881.** 23 v. Calcutta, 1882–84.

R137. ———. **Report on the census of British India, taken on the 17th February 1881.** 3 v. London, 1883.

R138. ———. **Census of India, 1891.** 28 v. Shillong, 1892–94.

R139. ———. **Census of India, 1891: general report.** London, 1893.

R140. ———. **Census of India, 1891: general tables for British provinces and feudatory states.** 2 v. London, 1892–93.

R141. ———. **Census of India, 1901.** 57 v. Bombay, 1902–05.

R142. ———. **East India (census): general report of the census of India, 1901.** London, 1904.

R143. ———. **Census of India, 1911.** 23 v. Calcutta and locally, 1912–13.

R144. ———. **East India (census): general report of the census of India, 1911.** London and Calcutta, 1914.

R145. ———. **Census of India, 1921.** 25 v. Calcutta and locally, 1924.

R146. ———. **Census of India, 1921: final figures showing the population of each province, district and state, and the distribution of population by religion.** Simla, 1922.

R147. ———. **East India (census 1921): tables giving the main statistics of the census of the Indian empire of 1921, with a brief explanatory note.** London, 1923.

R148. ———. **Census of India, 1931.** 28 v. Delhi and locally, 1932–35. Regarded as the best, although the 1951 census is proving very informative.

R149. ———. **Census of India, 1941.** 25 v. Delhi, 1941–45. A poor job.

R150. ———. **Census of India, 1951.** 17 v. in 63 pts. Delhi, 1952–55. District handbooks, papers, etc. are too voluminous to cite. An inexhaustible source of information.

R151. India. Ministry of Information and Broadcasting. **India: a reference annual.** Delhi, 1953 ff. Valuable official compilation of factual and statistical information on a variety of subjects. Many useful statistical tables. [RIC]

R152. Keith, Arthur B. **A history of Sanskrit literature.** Oxford, 1928. Best English history of classical Sanskrit literature. Does not include the Vedic and Brahmanical periods.

R153. Ketkar, Venkatesh B. **Indian and foreign chronology, with theory, practice and tables, B.C. 3102 to 2100 A.D., and notices of the Vedic, the ancient Indian, the Chinese, the Jewish, the ecclesiastical and the Coptic calendars.** Bombay, 1923. [The journal of the Bombay Branch of the Royal Asiatic Society, extra no. 75–A, v. 26.] One of the most useful analyses of a complicated subject.

R154. Macdonell, Arthur A. **India's past: a survey of her literatures, religions, lan-**

guages, and antiquities. Oxford, 1927. Good, popular account.

R155. O'Malley, Lewis S. S. **Popular Hinduism, the religion of the masses.** N.Y., 1935. No thorough research area by area has been done on the meaning of Hinduism in the village. However, this work presents a general picture of present-day Hinduism as practiced by the masses.

R156. Rama Rao, T. V., and G. D. Binani, eds. **India at a glance.** Rev. ed., Bombay and Madras, 1954. Covers government, resources, communications, cultural institutions, industry, and other subjects.

R157. Rawat, P. L. **History of Indian education (ancient to modern).** 3rd ed., Agra, 1956. A standard text.

R158. Sewell, Robert. **Indian chronography.** London, 1912. Contains accurate and useful tables.

R159. Sewell, Robert, and Śankara Bâlkṛishṇa Dîkshit. **The Indian calendar.** London, 1896. Should be used as companion volume to the above.

R160. The Times of India directory and year-book, including who's who. Bombay and London, 1914 ff. Valuable reference on many subjects.

R161. Venkatachalam, Sri Kota. "Indian eras." **Journal of the Andhra Historical Research Society,** 20 (July, Oct. 1949; Jan., Apr. 1950): 39–82. A recent account which must be consulted in any serious study of this complicated subject.

R162. The wealth of India: a dictionary of Indian raw materials and industrial products. Delhi, 1948 ff. An exhaustive list.

R163. Winternitz, Moriz. **Geschichte der indischen Litteratur.** 3 v. Leipzig, 1908–22. English tr. of v. 1–2, Calcutta, 1927–33. Best general reference work for the Vedic, Puranic, epic, Buddhist, Jain, scientific, instructional, and beginnings of modern vernacular literature.

R164. Yule, Sir Henry, and Arthur C. Burnell. **Hobson Jobson.** See *N15.*

R165. Zimmer, Hèinrich R. **The art of Indian Asia, its mythology and transformations.** 2 v. N.Y., 1955. A magnificent work.

GEOGRAPHIES, GAZETTEERS, AND ATLASES

R166. Cunningham, Alexander. **Cunningham's ancient geography of India.** Ed. by Surendranath M. Sastri. Calcutta, 1924. Companion reading to history of the ancient period.

R167. Davies, Cuthbert C. **An historical atlas of the Indian peninsula.** 2nd ed., Madras and N.Y., 1953. Very useful for study of ancient and medieval India.

R168. Dey, Nundo L. **The geographical dictionary of ancient and mediaeval India.** 2nd ed., London, 1927.

R169. Green, Edward W. **An atlas of Indian history.** Bombay, 1937. Story of the political history of India in bold map outline.

R170. The imperial gazetteer of India. 2nd ed., 26 v., Oxford, 1908–31. Indispensable list of place names of British India and much of the present sub-continent. The historical, geographical, and general descriptive material is accurate and pertinent to the study of any locale. Political and linguistic changes suggest the need for a new edition.

Gazetteers were published by the provincial and state governments mostly in the 19th and early 20th centuries. Several states not listed below have published one or two gazetteers. Some of the older ones are still the only source of information on local customs and history. The gazetteer series are not consistently entered in library catalogs. Some are listed by province or state and are not analyzed; others are under the editors of individual volumes.

R171. Hunter, Sir William. **A statistical account of Assam.** 2 v. London, 1879.

R172. Baluchistan district gazetteer series. 9 v. Bombay, 1906–13.

R173. Desai, Govindbai H. **Gazetteer of the Baroda state.** 2 v. Bombay, 1923.

R174. Hunter, Sir William. **A statistical account of Bengal.** 20 v. London, 1875–77.

R175. Bengal district gazetteers. Calcutta, 1906 ff.

R176. Bihar and Orissa district gazetteers. Patna, 1917 ff.

R177. Bombay gazetteer. 27 v. in 35. Bombay, 1877–1904.

R178. The central India state gazetteer series. 6 v. in 11. Calcutta, 1907–09.

R179. Central provinces district gazetteers. Allahabad, 1906 ff.

R180. Eastern Bengal and Assam gazetteers. Allahabad, 1910–12.

R181. Madras district gazetteers. Madras, 1898 ff.

R182. Hayavadana Rao, Conjeeveram, ed. **Mysore gazetteer.** 5 v. in 8. Bangalore, 1927–30.

R183. North-West Frontier province district gazetteers. Lahore, etc., 1908 ff.

R184. Punjab district gazetteers. Lahore.

R185. The Rajputana gazetteer. 3 v. Calcutta, 1879–80.

R186. Gazetteer of the province of Sind. Karachi, 1907 ff.

R187. District gazetteers of the United Provinces of Agra and Oudh. Allahabad, 1914 ff.

R188. India. National Atlas Organization. **National atlas of India.** Ed. by S. P. Chatterjee. Preliminary ed., Calcutta, 1957. The only work available.

R189. Kini, K. Srinivas, and U. Bhavani Shanker Rao. **Oxford pictorial atlas of Indian history, with outlines and time charts.**

4th rev. ed., London, 1942. An essential reference to be used in study of the ancient and medieval periods.

R190. Law, Bimala C. **Historical geography of ancient India.** Paris, 1954. Probably the best account.

R191. "Maps: Land routes in ancient and medieval India; Towns and cities in ancient and medieval India; Famines in India; Irrigation in India through the ages; Medieval India as the industrial workshop of the world; Ancient and medieval trade routes in the Asiatic waters; Greater India; Indian culture abroad." **Eastern economist** (Dec. 1951): 17, 24, 1003, 1007, 1018, 1021, 1025, 1027, 1042–43. Very useful reference guide.

R192. Thornton, Edward. **A gazetteer of the territories under the government of the viceroy of India.** Rev. and ed. by Sir Roper Lethbridge and Arthur N. Wollaston. London, 1886. Useful historical list of geographical names, spelled in the 19th century fashion. Records location with latitude and longitude, and gives population of villages, towns, and cities when known from the 1881 census.

ANTHROPOLOGICAL AND DEMOGRAPHIC STUDIES

R193. Baines, Sir Jervois A. **Ethnography (castes and tribes).** Strasbourg, 1912. [Grundriss der indo-arischen Philologie und Altertumskunde.] This standard reference is still the best listing of the castes and tribes of the entire sub-continent.

R194. Crooke, William. **Religion and folklore of northern India.** New ed., Oxford, 1926. Indispensable reference work.

R195. ———. **The tribes and castes of the North-western provinces and Oudh.** 4 v. Calcutta, 1906.

R196. Enthoven, Reginald E. **The tribes and castes of Bombay.** 3 v. Bombay, 1920–22. Only complete work on the area.

R197. Hodson, Thomas C. **India: census ethnography, 1901–1931.** Delhi, 1937. Indispensable handbook on the tribes, caste customs, and languages of India.

R198. Ketkar, Shridhar V. **The history of caste in India.** 2 v. N.Y., 1909–11. Interesting and thoughtful discussion of the caste system and its origins and justifications. Useful as a balanced introduction to a complex topic. [RIC]

R199. Krishna Iyer, L. Krishna Anantha, and Hebbalalu Velpanuru Nanjundayya. **The Mysore tribes and castes.** 5 v. Mysore, 1928–36. The standard work on the area.

R200. Law, Bimala C. **Tribes in ancient India.** Poona, 1943.

R201. Majumdar, Dhirendra N. **Races and cultures of India.** Allahabad, 1944. Deals with caste, marriage, and primitive religions in addition to racial history. A popular work.

R202. O'Malley, Lewis S. S. **Indian caste customs.** Cambridge, Eng., 1932. The best popular presentation.

R203. ———. **India's social heritage.** Oxford, 1934. Excellent, popular introduction to caste, tribes, village life, the family, and marriage.

R204. Risley, Sir Herbert H. **The people of India.** 2nd rev. ed., London, 1915. The standard work.

R205. Roy, Sarat C. **The Mundas and their country.** Calcutta, 1912. The standard work on these tribal people.

R206. ———. **The Orāons of Chōtā Nāgpur: their history, economic life, and social organization.** Ranchi, 1915. Story of an important tribal group.

R207. Russell, Robert V., and Rai Bahadur Hīra Lāl. **The tribes and castes of the Central Provinces of India.** 4 v. London, 1916. Basic work on the subject.

R208. Saletore, Bhasker A. **The wild tribes in Indian history.** Lahore, 1935. Only compilation of its kind.

R209. Sharma, Ram S. "Politico-legal aspect of the caste system (c. 600 B.C.-c. 500 A.D.)." **Journal of the Bihar Research Society,** 39 (Sep. 1953): 306–30. An important study of ancient implications with validity today.

R210. Shembavnekar, K. M. "The population of ancient India (500 B.C. to 100 A.D.)." **Annals of the Bhandarkar Oriental Research Institute,** 33 (1952): 83–96. Interesting conjectures based on scanty sources.

R211. Thurston, Edgar, and K. Rangachari. **Castes and tribes of southern India.** 7 v. Madras, 1909. The standard work on this subject.

LINGUISTIC WORKS

R212. Bühler, Georg. **Indian paleography.** Ed. by John F. Fleet. Bombay, 1904. Plates and tables of the German edition are omitted.

R213. ———. **Indische Palaeographie von circa 350 A. Chr.–circa 1300 P. Chr.** Strasbourg, 1896. [Grundriss der indoarischen Philologie und Altertumskunde.] This text with 17 tables of alphabets is the best work on the subject.

R214. Chatterji, Suniti K. **Languages and the linguistic problem.** London, 1944. [Oxford pamphlets on Indian affairs, 11.] Brief but excellent guide to the linguistic pattern.

R215. Emeneau, Murray B. "India and linguistics." **Journal of the American Oriental Society,** 75 (July-Sep. 1955): 145–53. Very concise, historical account.

R216. Grierson, Sir George A., ed. **Linguistic survey of India.** 10 v. Calcutta, 1903–

27. Still the only complete survey; an indispensable linguistic tool, although subject to correction in light of modern research on scattered areas.

HISTORIOGRAPHY

R217. Kosambi, Damodar D. **An introduction to the study of Indian history.** Bombay, 1956. Evaluation and analysis of sources of Indian history.

R218. Nilakanta Sastri, Kallidaikurichi Aiyah Aiyar. **Historical method in relation to Indian history.** Madras, 1956. Urbane and informative account of the historiography of India, with annotations of important items. [RIC]

R219. Pargiter, Frederick E. **Ancient Indian historical tradition.** London, 1922. First serious analysis of the traditional histories. All subsequent studies are obliged to refer to it.

GENERAL HISTORIES

R220. Ali, Abdullah Yusuf. **The making of India.** London, 1925. Constructive factors in the long history of India.

R221. Allan, John, Sir T. Wolseley Haig, and Henry H. Dodwell. **The Cambridge shorter history of India.** Cambridge, Eng., 1934. One of the standard reference works on Indian history to end of World War I. Emphasis is primarily on political, administrative, and military events. [RIC]

R222. Burgess, James. **The chronology of modern India: for four hundred years from the close of the fifteenth century, A.D. 1494–1894.** Edinburgh, 1913. Standard reference for the period.

R223. Dunbar, Sir George. **A history of India from the earliest times to the present day.** London, 1936. Not considered a distinguished history, but may be used for reference.

R224. Garratt, Geoffrey T., ed. **The legacy of India.** Oxford, 1937. Most readable introduction to the civilization of India and its contributions to the world.

R225. Havell, Ernest B. **The history of Aryan rule in India, from the earliest times to the death of Akbar.** N.Y., 1918. Good introduction.

R226. Hunter, Sir William W., ed. **Rulers of India.** 28 v. Oxford, 1892–1911. From Asoka to the Earl of Mayo. May be used as a detailed history as well as a biographical source.

R227. India. Archaeological survey. **Reports.** New imperial series, Delhi, 1874 ff. One of the most important sources of Indian history.

R228. Majumdar, Ramesh C., Hemachandra Raychaudhuri, and Kalikinkar Datta. **An advanced history of India.** London, 1948. Excellent textbook for the graduate level.

R229. Moreland, William H., and Atul C. Chatterjee. **A short history of India.** 4th ed., London, 1957. Most recent edition of one of the better texts in Indian history. Includes valuable appendix on "Indian nomenclature and chronology." [RIC]

R230. Nehru, Jawaharlal. **The discovery of India.** N.Y., 1946. One of the best introductions to the history of India for the lay reader and college student.

R231. Nilakanta Sastri, Kallidaikurichi A. A. **History of India.** 3 v. Madras, 1950–52. Standard work by a scholar of international reputation. [HF]

R232. Panikkar, Kavalam M. **A survey of Indian history.** London, 1947. Brief, provocative, and in many ways informed summary. [RIC]

R233. Powell-Price, John C. **A history of India.** London and N.Y., 1955. Rather popular.

R234. Rawlinson, Hugh G. **A concise history of the Indian people.** 2nd ed., London, 1950. Excellent, popular introduction. Covers from ancient period to 1947.

R235. ———. **India, a short cultural history.** Rev. ed., N.Y. and London, 1952. A popular account.

R236. Sen, Surendra N., and Hemachandra Raychaudhuri. **The groundwork of Indian history.** 9th ed., Calcutta, 1955. Good introductory textbook for college level.

R237. Smith, Vincent A. **The Oxford history of India.** 3rd ed., Oxford, 1957. A standard text.

R238. Villiers, Alan J. **The Indian Ocean.** London, 1952. History of the part it played from the dawn of history through World War II.

HISTORIES OF SPECIAL PERIODS

Ancient and Medieval Period
(Mauryan Empire, 321 B.C.—Mahmud of Ghazni, 997 A.D.)

R239. Altekar, Anant S. **State and government in ancient India.** 2nd rev. ed., Banaras, 1955. Excellent analysis.

R240. Bagchi, Prabodh C. **India and central Asia.** Calcutta, 1955. Early contacts with Tokharistan, eastern Iran, and eastern Turkestan.

R241. Banerjee, Gauranga N. **India as known to the ancient world.** London, 1921. Comprehensive account of India's early cultural and commercial international relations.

R242. Banerjee, Narayanchandra. **Economic life and progress in ancient India.** V. 1, **Hindu period.** 2nd ed., Calcutta, 1945. From Vedic times to 400 B.C.

R243. Basham, Arthur L. **The wonder that was India: a survey of the culture of the**

Indian sub-continent before the coming of the Muslims. London, 1954. Brief historical account from prehistoric times through the Middle Ages. Best book of its kind.

R244. Bhandarkar, Devadatta R. **Lectures on ancient Indian numismatics.** Calcutta, 1921. Places the art of coin making earlier than 700 B.C. Ends with 9th century A.D.

R245. British Museum. **Catalogue of the coins of ancient India.** By John Allan. London, 1936. This and the following work provide a comprehensive description of Indian coins.

R246. ——. **Catalogue of the coins of the Andhra dynasty, the western ksatrapas, the Traikūtaka dynasty, and the "Bodhi" dynasty.** By Edward J. Rapson. London, 1908.

R247. The Cambridge history of India. V. 1, **Ancient India.** Ed. by Edward J. Rapson. Cambridge, Eng., 1922. *The Cambridge history of India* is an indispensable reference tool for the periods covered, enhanced by very complete bibliographies for each section. A supplement by Sir Robert E. M. Wheeler, *The Indus civilization,* was published in 1955.

R248. Chatterjee, Bijan R. **India and Java.** 2nd ed., 2 pts., Calcutta, 1933. The early period of contact.

R249. Chaudhuri, Sashi B. **Ethnic settlements in ancient India: a study on the Puranic lists of the peoples of Bharatavarsa.** Pt. 1. Calcutta, 1955.

R250. Cumming, John G., ed. **Revealing India's past.** London, 1939. A somewhat popular account which the student will find useful as an introduction.

R251. Cunningham, Alexander. **Coins of ancient India, from the earliest times to the seventh century A.D.** London, 1891. Good introduction to valuable historical source material.

R252. ——. **Coins of mediaeval India, from the seventh century down to the Muhammadan conquests.** London, 1894. Continues the author's account of the ancient period.

R253. Dange, Shripad A. **India from primitive communism to slavery: a Marxist study of ancient history in outline.** 2nd ed., Bombay, 1951. Amusing analysis from the prehistoric period through the wars of the Mahabharata.

R254. Das, Santosh K. **The economic history of ancient India.** Howrah, 1925. Only a few studies have been made of this subject. This is probably as good as any.

R255. ——. **The educational system of the ancient Hindus.** Calcutta, 1930. Very detailed account.

R256. Dikshitar, V. R. Ramachandra. **Hindu administrative institutions.** Ed. by S. Krishnaswami Aiyangar. Madras, 1929. Very detailed study, based on a variety of early Sanskrit works.

R257. ——. **The Mauryan polity.** Madras, 1932. Central and local governmental affairs.

R258. Diskalkar, D. B. "Origin of Indian epigraphy." **Journal of Indian history,** 32 (Dec. 1954): 291–307. A record from 2000 B.C. to the 4th century B.C.

R259. ——. "The progress and future of Indian epigraphical studies." **Journal of Indian history,** 33 (Aug. 1955): 131–53. Very useful history with good estimate of what still needs to be done.

R260. Eliot, Sir Charles N. E. **Hinduism and Buddhism: an historical sketch.** 2nd ed., 3 v., N.Y., 1954. A very complete study.

R261. Fa-hsien. **A record of Buddhistic kingdoms.** Tr. by James Legge. Oxford, 1886. Good translation of an important source of information.

R262. ——. **The travels of Fa-hsien.** Tr. by H. A. Giles. London, 1956. Excellent translation of Fa-hsien's keen observations on India of the early centuries A.D.

R263. ——. **Travels of Fah-Hian and Sung Yun.** Tr. by Samuel Beal. London, 1869. Fa-hsien visited India from 405 to 411 A.D. This is a detailed study of Buddhism in 5th century India. Author also comments on the life of the people.

R264. Grousset, René. **The civilization of India.** Tr. by Catherine A. Phillips. N.Y., 1939. Good, popular account of the ancient culture.

R265. Guérinot, Armand A. **Répertoire d'épigraphie jaina.** Paris, 1908. A most detailed examination of this important source of the history of the Jains.

R266. Hillebrandt, Alfred. **Altindische Politik.** Jena, 1923. Scholarly analysis.

R267. The history and culture of the Indian people. Ed. by R. C. Majumdar. V. 2–4. London, 1951. [2, *The age of imperial unity;* 3, *The classical age;* 4, *The age of imperial Kanauj.*] One of the most complete histories of India by Indian scholars.

R268. Hsüan-tsang. **Si-yu-ki. Buddhist records of the western world.** Tr. by Samuel Beal. 2 v. London, 1884. Comments on all aspects of Indian life of the period.

R269. I Ching [I Tsing]. **A record of the Buddhist religion as practiced in India and the Malay archipelago (A.D. 671–695).** Tr. by Junjiro Takakusu. Oxford, 1896. Describes monastic life and the development of Buddhism.

R270. Jha, Ganganatha. **Hindu law and its sources.** 2 v. Allahabad, 1930–33. This and *R272* make any further work tangential.

R271. Jayaswal, Kashi P. **Hindu polity: a constitutional history of India in Hindu times.** 2nd ed., Bangalore, 1943. Detailed analysis for advanced study.

R272. Kane, Pandurang V. **History of Dharmaśāstra (ancient and mediaeval religious and civil law).** Poona, 1930 ff. Most complete and scholarly analysis of the subject.

R273. Law, Bimala C. **India as described in early texts of Buddhism and Jainism.** London, 1941. May be consulted for source material.

R274. McCrindle, John W., tr. and ed. **Ancient India as described by Megasthenês and Arrian.** Calcutta, 1926. These fragments, though not always trustworthy, concern India of the 4th century B.C. and comprise the first eyewitness account by a foreigner.

R275. ——, tr. **Ancient India as described by Ptolemy.** Calcutta, 1927. Interesting, unique source material.

R276. ——, tr. and ed. **Ancient India as described in classical literature.** Westminster, Eng., 1901. Excerpts mostly from Strabo, Pliny, and Aelian.

R277. Majumdar, Bimal K. **The military system in ancient India.** Calcutta, 1955. Important contribution to an understanding of early Indian history.

R278. Majumdar, Ramesh C. **Ancient Indian colonies in the Far East.** 2 v. Lahore and Dacca, 1927–37. The standard work on the subject.

R279. Mankad, Dolarry R. **Puranic chronology.** Anand, 1951. Represents a "strong presumption in favor of tradition."

R280. Marshall, Sir John H. **A guide to Taxila.** 3rd ed., Delhi, 1936. A short introduction.

R281. ——. **Taxila: an illustrated account of archaeological excavations carried out at Taxila under the orders of the Government of India between the years 1913 and 1934.** 3 v. Cambridge, Eng., 1951. An exhaustive study.

R282. Masson-Oursel, Paul, Helena De Willman-Grabowska, and Philippe Stern. **Ancient India and Indian civilization.** Tr. by M. R. Dobie. London, 1934. One of the best accounts of the richness of ancient Indian civilization.

R283. Mookerji, Radha K. **Ancient Indian education, Brahmanical and Buddhist.** London, 1947. The most scholarly account.

R284. ——. **Asoka.** 2nd ed., London, 1955. A deeply Indian appreciation.

R285. ——. **Chandragupta Maurya and his times.** Madras, 1943. Scholarly account of the beginnings of the Mauryan empire.

R286. ——. **Harsha.** London, 1926. Brief, popular account of this enlightened ruler.

R287. ——. **Local government in ancient India.** 2nd rev. ed., Oxford, 1920. Description, based on quoted Sanskrit sources, covering governing bodies, justice, and public institutions.

R288. ——. **The Gupta empire.** 2nd ed., Bombay, 1952. The standard text.

R289. Muir, John, tr. and ed. **Original Sanskrit texts on the origin and history of the people of India, their religion and institutions.** 2nd ed., 5 v., London, 1868–73. Concerns caste, race, historical value of the Vedas, deities, cosmogony, mythology, religious ideas, life and manners of the Vedic age.

R290. Narain, A. K. **The Indo-Greeks.** Oxford, 1957. Scholarly and very readable work on the Greek influence on India.

R291. Prasad, Beni. **The state in ancient India.** Allahabad, 1928. Very complete study with excellent bibliography.

R292. ——. **Theory of government in ancient India (post-Vedic).** Allahabad, 1927. Excellent analysis.

R293. Prasad, Ishwari. **History of medieval India.** Allahabad, 1925. Few histories of this period have been written. This volume fills a serious gap, but much work on the period remains to be done. Documentation is scarce.

R294. Przyluski, Jean. **La légende de l'empereur Açoka.** Paris, 1923. [Annales du Musée Guimet, Bibliothèque d'études, 32.] All the source materials.

R295. Puri, Baijnath. "Some aspects of village economy in ancient India." **Eastern anthropologist,** 8 (Mar.-Aug. 1955): 246–52. Interesting and unique exploitation of non-economic source material.

R296. Rawlinson, Hugh G. **Bactria: the history of a forgotten empire.** London, 1912. Prehistory and history briefly to 250 B.C.; emphasizes period from 250 to death of Menander.

R297. Rawlinson, Hugh G. **Intercourse between India and the western world, from the earliest times to the fall of Rome.** 2nd ed., Cambridge, Eng., 1926. Based on Roman and Greek literature.

R298. Ray, Hem C. **The dynastic history of northern India (early mediaeval period).** 2 v. Calcutta, 1931–36. Very complete account of the Muslims in north India from 916 to 1196.

R299. Raychaudhuri, Hemchandra. **Political history of ancient India, from the accession of Parikshit to the extinction of the Gupta dynasty.** 6th ed., Calcutta, 1953. Based on early Brahmanical and epic literature.

R300. Renou, Louis. **The civilization of ancient India.** Tr. by Philip Spratt. Calcutta, 1954. Has long been a standard reference covering thoroughly many aspects of ancient Indian culture.

R301. Rhys Davids, Thomas W. **Buddhist India.** 3rd Indian ed., Calcutta, 1957. Still regarded as one of the best histories of the Buddhist period.

R302. Schoff, Wilfred H., tr. **The Periplus of the Erythraean Sea: travel and trade in the Indian Ocean by a merchant of the first century.** N.Y., 1912. The exhaustive notes give an excellent survey of international trade between Rome and India.

R303. Sen, Amulyachandra, ed. **Asoka's**

edicts. Calcutta, 1956. One of several good compilations. Prakrit text, Sanskrit and English translations. Introduction presents the results of modern research.

R304. Sinha, Har N. **Sovereignty in ancient Indian polity: a study in the evolution of early Indian state.** London, 1938. Interestingly analyzes one aspect of the development of administration in India.

R305. Sircar, Dineshchandra. "Text of the Puranic list of peoples." **Indian historical quarterly,** 21 (1945): 297 ff. Interesting ethnographic study.

R306. Smith, Vincent A. **Asoka, the Buddhist emperor of India.** 3rd ed., Oxford, 1920. The standard work.

R307. ——. **The early history of India.** 4th ed., Oxford, 1924. A standard work which may be used as a college textbook.

R308. Tarn, William W. **The Greeks in Bactria and India.** 2nd ed., Cambridge, Eng., 1951. From 206 to 30 B.C., with emphasis on the period 206–145.

R309. Thomas, Edward. **Records of the Gupta dynasty.** London, 1876. Important record of sources.

R310. Vaidya, Chintamana V. **History of mediaeval Hindu India (being a history of India from 600 to 1200 A.D.).** 3 v. Poona, 1921–26. Most complete account of the darkest ages in recorded Indian history.

R311. Viswanatha, Sekharipuram V. **International law in ancient India.** Bombay, London, and N.Y., 1925. Relations between states in India.

R312. Warmington, Eric H. **The commerce between the Roman empire and India.** See *I292.*

R313. Watters, Thomas. **On Yuan Chwang's travels in India, 629–645 A.D.** 2 v. London, 1904–05. Regarded as authoritative, correcting errors in Beal's translation.

Muslim Period (997–1761)

R314. Abu al-Fadhl ibn Mubarak. **The Ain-i-Akbari by Abul Fazl'Allami.** Tr. by Hermann Blochmann and Henry S. Jarrett. 3 v. Calcutta, 1873–94. This eyewitness account of Akbar's reign is an invaluable source of information; the full index is especially useful.

R315. Al-Biruni. **Alberuni's India.** English ed. by Edward C. Sachau. 2 v. London, 1888. Authentic translation of a famous Arabic work; an invaluable account by a shrewd eyewitness of the life and times of the period.

R316. Aziz Ahmad, Muhammad. **Political history and institutions of the early Turkish empire of Delhi, 1206–1290 A.D.** Lahore, 1949. An early chapter in the Muslim conquest of India competently described.

R317. Bābar, emperor of Hindustan. **The Bābur-nāma in English.** Tr. by Annette S.

Beveridge. 2 v. London, 1922. A record of Delhi and north India under Babar and Humayun.

R318. Bernier, François. **Histoire de la dernière révolution des états du Grand Mogol.** 4 v. Paris, 1670–71. Interesting, antiquarian account by an observer.

R319. ——. **Travels in the Mogul empire.** 2nd rev. ed. by Vincent Smith, London and N.Y., 1916. Bernier visited India during the reign of Aurangzeb. This work describes city life, the court, Kashmir, the land system, the character and training of India's rulers, and administration of the empire.

R320. Binyon, Laurence. **Akbar.** London and N.Y., 1932. A popular biography.

R321. British Museum. **The coins of the Moghul emperors of Hindustan in the British Museum.** By Stanley Lane-Poole. London, 1892.

R322. ——. **The coins of the Muhammadan states of India in the British Museum.** By Stanley Lane-Poole. London, 1885.

R323. ——. **The coins of the sultans of Delhi in the British Museum.** By Stanley Lane-Poole. London, 1884.

R324. **The Cambridge history of India.** V. 3, **Turks and Afghans.** Ed. by Sir Wolseley Haig. Cambridge, Eng., 1928.

R325. **The Cambridge history of India.** V. 4, **The Mughal period.** Ed. by Sir Richard Burn. Cambridge, Eng., 1937.

R326. Du Jarric, Pierre. **Akbar and the Jesuits: an account of the Jesuit missions to the court of Akbar.** Tr. by C. H. Payne. N.Y. and London, 1928. Contemporary narrative.

R327. Edwardes, Stephen M., and H. L. O. Garrett. **Mughal rule in India.** London, 1930. The standard text on this subject.

R328. Elliot, Sir Henry M. **The history of India, as told by its own historians.** 2nd ed., Calcutta, 1952. Useful, but must be used with a critical approach.

R329. Firishtah Muhammad Kāsim ibn Hindū Shāh, Astarābādi. **History of the rise of the Mahomedan power in India till the year A.D. 1612.** Tr. by John Briggs. 4 v. Calcutta, 1908–10. Valuable source material.

R330. Hodivala, Shahpurshah H. **Historical studies in Mughal numismatics.** Calcutta, 1923. Excellent coverage.

R331. ——. **Studies in Indo-Muslim history.** 2 v. Bombay, 1939–57. Indispensable reference work for use with Elliot and Dowson's *History of India.*

R332. Ibn Battuta. **Travels in Asia and Africa, 1325–1354.** Tr. by H. A. R. Gibb. London, 1929. Ibn Battuta lived in Delhi for 8 years (1334–42) and also visited and wrote of the Malabar and Coromandel coasts and Bengal. His work is an account of Muhammed Tughloq and his court, Indian life, and Hindu-Muslim relations.

R333. Jahāngīr, emperor of Hindustan.

The Tūzuk-i-Jahāngīrī, or memoirs of Ja-hāngīr. Tr. by Alexander Rogers; ed. by Henry Beveridge. 2 v. London, 1909–14. An important source.

R334. King, Lucas, ed. **Memoirs of Zehīr-Ed-Dīn Muhammed Bābur, emperor of Hindustan.** Tr. by John Leyden and William Erskine. 2 v. London and N.Y., 1921. An important source.

R335. Lane-Poole, Stanley. **Mediaeval India under Mohammedan rule (A.D. 712–1764).** Calcutta, 1951. Story from the first Muslim invasion to the battle of Panipat. First published, with more illustrations, in London and N.Y., 1903.

R336. Maclagan, Sir Edward D. **The Jesuits and the Great Mogul.** London, 1932. Not only the account of the Jesuits and Akbar, but also the story of their work in India under the later Moguls. Altogether the most complete coverage.

R337. Owen, Sidney J. **The fall of the Mogul empire.** London, 1912. Very readable account, dating from time of Aurangzeb.

R338. Prasad, Ishwari. **A short history of Muslim rule in India.** Allahabad, 1930. A standard textbook.

R339. Roe, Sir Thomas. **The embassy of Sir Thomas Roe to the court of the Great Mogul.** 2 v. London, 1899. [Hakluyt Society publications, 2nd ser., 1–2.] Roe arrived in India in 1615. His account is limited to court life.

R340. Sarkar, Sir Jadunath. **History of Aurangzib, based on original sources.** 5 v. in 4. Calcutta, 1924–30. The most complete account.

R341. ——. **House of Shivaji (studies and documents of Maratha history, royal period).** 2nd ed., Calcutta, 1948. Contains interesting source material.

R342. ——. **Mughal administration.** 2nd ed., Patna, 1925. A faithful analysis.

R343. ——. **Shivaji and his times.** 2nd ed., London and N.Y., 1920. Thorough account based on all available sources.

R344. ——. **A short history of Aurangzib, 1618–1707.** 2nd ed., Calcutta, 1954. Abridgement of the 5 v. work. Useful as background reading.

R345. Smith, Vincent A. **Akbar, the Great Mogul, 1542–1605.** 2nd ed., Oxford, 1919. The standard work on Akbar.

R346. Spear, Thomas G. P. **Delhi, its monuments and history.** Bombay, 1943. Although not complete, this is the best study of this historic site.

R347. ——. **Twilight of the Mughuls: studies in late Mughal Delhi.** Cambridge, Eng., 1951. Excellent account of reasons for the fall of an empire.

R348. Srivastava, Ashirbadi L. **The Mughul empire (1526–1830 A.D.).** 2nd ed., Agra, 1956. Concerns Babur, Humayun, Sher Shah Sur, Akbar, Jahangir, Shah Jahan, Aurangzeb, rise of the Maratha power, later Mughuls, Maratha ascendency, administration, society, and culture.

R349. Timur, the Great. **The Mulfuzāt Timūry, or autobiographical memoirs of the Moghul emperor Timur.** Tr. by Charles Stewart. London, 1830. An important source.

R350. Tripathi, Ram P. **Some aspects of Muslim administration.** Allahabad, 1936. Well-documented account of administration from the capital, Delhi.

European Period (to 1857)

Dutch, Danes, French, and Portuguese

R351. Albuquerque, Affonso de. **The commentaries of the great Afonso Dalboquerque, second viceroy of India.** Tr. by Walter de Gray Birch. 4 v. London, 1875–84. [Works issued by the Hakluyt Society, 53, 55, 62, 69.] Important source material.

R352. Boxer, Charles R. "A glimpse of the Goa archives." **Bulletin of the School of Oriental and African Studies,** 14 (1952): 299–324. A most informative article on an extremely important but little explored collection.

R353. ——. "The Portuguese in the East, 1500–1800." Harold V. Livermore, **Portugal and Brazil: an introduction** (Oxford, 1953), pp. 185–247. Best brief account in English of Portuguese activity in India. Fully documented. [HF]

R354. Burnell, Arthur C. **A tentative list of books and some mss. relating to the history of the Portuguese in India proper.** Mangalore, 1880. Excellent bibliography of early materials, many of which may be considered sources.

R355. Campos, Joachim J. A. **History of the Portuguese in Bengal.** Calcutta, 1919. Interesting chapter in the rise and decline of Portuguese power in India.

R356. Christian, John L. "Portuguese India and its historical records." **Hispanic American historical review,** 25 (Feb. 1945): 140–51.

R357. Conan, J. **La dernière compagnie française des Indes (1785–1875), avec la liste des principaux actionnaires de cette compagnie.** Paris, 1942. The French point of view.

R358. Corrêa, Gaspar. **Lendas da India.** 4 v. Lisbon, 1858–66. Valuable source on the Portuguese power.

R359. Correia, Alberto C. Germano da Silva. **Catálogo bibliográfico das publicações relativas à India Portuguêsa.** Nova Goa, 1930. An indispensable bibliographical tool.

R360. "A descriptive list of records of Danish interest in the National Archives of India." **Indian archives,** 6 (1952): 39–90. Useful guide to important source material.

R361. Hart, Henry H. **Sea road to the Indies.** London, 1952. Scholarly and very readable account of Vasco da Gama's establishment of Portuguese power in India, with a complete bibliography.

R362. Huisman, Michel. **La Belgique commerciale sous l'Empereur Charles VI.** Brussels, 1902. Scholarly study of the Ostend Company, based on manuscript materials in Brussels and Antwerp. [HF]

R363. Jonge, Johan K. J. de, ed. **De opkomst van het Nederlandsch gezag in Oost-Indie.** 18 v. The Hague, 1862–1909. The full-dress history of Dutch activity in Asia, packed with detail and fully documented. [HF]

R364. Kaeppelin, Paul. **La Compagnie des Indes Orientales et François Martin: étude sur l'histoire du commerce et des établissements français dans l'Inde sous Louis XIV, 1664–1749.** Paris, 1908. The standard work on French activity in India before the days of Dupleix. [HF]

R365. Larsen, Kay. **De dansk-ostindiske koloniers historie.** 2 v. Copenhagen, 1907–08. The standard history of Danish activity in the East, based on archival sources in Copenhagen. [HF]

R366. Martineau, Alfred. **Dupleix et l'Inde française.** 4 v. Paris, 1920–28. Thorough study of Dupleix and his period, by the leading French authority on French activity in India. [HF]

R367. Menon, K. N. **Portuguese pockets in India.** New Delhi, 1953. Brief account, from the Indian point of view, of the early conquest of Goa, subsequent events, and present conditions.

R368. Pillai, Ananda R. **The private diary of Ananda Ranga Pillai.** Ed. by Sir John F. Price and Henry Dodwell. 12 v. Madras, 1904–28. Valuable as the chief non-European source for the Anglo-French struggle in southern India. Pillai served Dupleix as *dubash*. [HF]

R369. Raynal, Guillaume T. F. **Histoire philosophique et politique des établissements et du commerce des Européens dans les deux Indes.** 10 v. Geneva, 1781. Of much importance in shaping contemporary European opinion critical of European conquest and penetration of Asia. For a study of its effects see the later edition, *L'anticolonialisme au XVIIIᵉ siècle* (Paris, 1951), with notes and introduction by Gabriel Esquer. [HF]

R370. Stephens, Henry M. **Albuquerque.** Oxford, 1897. Dependable analysis of Albuquerque's accomplishments.

The British

R371. Aitchison, Sir Charles. **Collection of treaties, engagements, and sanads relating to India.** 3rd ed., 11 v., Calcutta, 1892. The standard reference work on agreements between the British government of India (both under Company and Crown) and Indian princes. Also covers British agreements with

local authorities and princes in other parts of Asia, notably the Persian Gulf. [HF]

R372. Arberry, Arthur J. **Asiatic Jones: the life and influence of Sir William Jones (1746–1794), pioneer of Indian studies.** London and N.Y., 1946. Sympathetic account of the activities of this pioneer.

R373. Auber, Peter. **An analysis of the constitution of the East India Company.** London, 1826. Supplement, 1828. The standard work, which still must be consulted by any student of relations between the Company and the Crown, 1600–1826. [HF]

R374. Baden-Powell, B. H. **The land systems of British India.** 3 v. Oxford, 1892. Still the classic work on the subject. [HF]

R375. Beveridge, Henry. **A comprehensive history of India, civil, military, and social.** 3 v. London, 1862. Work of a thoughtful, earnest, and liberal-minded member of the Indian civil service in the Victorian period. [HF]

R376. Bolts, William. **Considerations on Indian affairs.** 3 v. London, 1772–75. Author was a Dutch adventurer of dubious integrity who was in and out of the British service and in his later career much involved in clandestine trade. This work was much relied upon by Burke and other opponents of Hastings. [HF]

R377. Bruce, John. **Annals of the Honourable East India Company from their establishment by the charter of Queen Elizabeth 1600 to the union of the London and English East India companies 1707–8.** 3 v. London, 1810. Bruce was the East India Company's historiographer. His work is primarily a storehouse of facts; as a general account it has been superseded, but is still useful as reference. [HF]

R378. Buchanan, Francis H. **A journey from Madras through the countries of Mysore, Canara, and Malebar.** 3 v. London, 1807. A travel account, rich in details of the life of the time in south India.

R379. **The Cambridge history of India.** V. 5, **British India, 1497–1858.** Ed. by Henry H. Dodwell. Cambridge, Eng., 1929. Contains bibliographies indispensable to students of Indian history. [HF]

R380. Charles-Roux, François. **Autours d'une route: l'Angleterre, l'isthme de Suez et l'Egypte au XVIIIᵉ siècle.** Paris, 1922. Provides an excellent summary of history of the "overland" route to the East via Suez and the Red Sea. [HF]

R381. Davies, A. Mervyn. **Clive of Plassey.** London, 1939. Companion volume to the following, perhaps not quite so comprehensive in treatment. For the serious student supersedes earlier studies of Clive's career. [HF]

R382. ——. **Warren Hastings, maker of British India.** London, 1935. Of the several longer biographies of Hastings this is perhaps the most useful for the student of Indian history. A judicious and scholarly treatment which makes full use of manuscript materials available at time it was written. [HF]

R383. Dodwell, Henry H. **Dupleix and Clive: the beginning of empire.** London, 1920. Best 1 v. account of first phase of the Anglo-French struggle in India in the mid-18th century. [HF]

R384. Dutt, Romesh C. **The economic history of British India.** London, 1902. Important as the first substantial study in the economic history of modern India by an Indian. Should be used in conjunction with later works on the subject. [HF]

R385. Firminger, Walter K. **The fifth report from the Select Committee of the House of Commons on the affairs of the East India Company, dated 28th July, 1812.** 3 v. Calcutta, 1917. Basis for any study of the revenue history of modern Bengal. [HF]

R386. Foster, Sir William, ed. **Early travels in India, 1583–1619.** London, 1921. Selections from travel narratives of the period of British beginnings in India. A very useful work. [HF]

R387. ——, ed. **The English factories in India . . . a calendar of documents in the India Office, British Museum and Public Record Office.** 1st ser., 14 v., Oxford, 1909–27; 2nd ser., 1936 ff. Complete record of the establishment of British business interests in India.

R388. Furber, Holden. **John Company at work.** Cambridge, Mass., 1948. Though dealing primarily with relations of the British East India Company and other East India companies, 1783–93, and with the "country" (intra-Asia) trade, attempts to analyze the process whereby European empire was built in India in last half of the 18th century. Based on Dutch, Danish, French, and British manuscript materials. [HF]

R389. Heber, Reginald. **Narrative of a journey through the upper provinces of India.** 2nd ed., 3 v., London, 1828. Best and most widely read contemporary account of northern India in the 1820's. [HF]

R390. Hendley, Thomas H. **The rulers of India and the chiefs of Rajputana, 1550 to 1897.** London, 1897. Good coverage of a stirring period in history of the Rajputs—their encounters with the late Moguls and the British.

R391. Hickey, William. **Memoirs of William Hickey.** Ed. by Alfred Spencer. 4 v. London, 1913–25. A most fascinating and complete picture of European life in late 18th century India, especially Calcutta of the 1780's and 1790's. [HF]

R392. Hill, Samuel C. **Bengal in 1756–1757.** 3 v. London, 1905. More documents on events in Bengal immediately preceding the battle of Plassey are printed here than in any other work. Does not exhaust the subject, but contains Dutch and French as well as British materials. [HF]

R393. The history and culture of the Indian people. V. 5, **The struggle for empire.** Ed. by Ramesh C. Majumdar. Bombay, 1957. Excellent account from the Indian point of view.

R394. Hoskins, Halford L. **British routes to India.** See *S258.*

R395. Hunter, Sir William W. **History of British India.** 2 v. London, 1899–1900. The standard larger work on British connection with India to 1708, written by an experienced civil servant who was also a distinguished scholar. [HF]

R396. Imlah, Albert H. **Lord Ellenborough.** Cambridge, Mass., 1939. A standard biography based on the original sources; chiefly concerned with his Indian career. [HF]

R397. Khan, Shafa'at A. **The East India trade in seventeenth century.** London, 1923. Leading work in English, but inadequate as far as non-English aspects of the subject are concerned. [HF]

R398. Lambrick, H. T. **Sir Charles Napier and Sind.** Oxford, 1952. Thorough study of Napier's career and the annexation of Sind, based on Sindi as well as British materials. Also contains much historical and geographical data on Sind. [HF]

R399. Love, Henry D. **Vestiges of old Madras, 1640–1800.** 4 v. London, 1913. Comprehensive history of Madras under British rule, making extensive use of records both in Madras and London. [HF]

R400. Low, Charles R. **History of the Indian navy (1613–1863).** 2 v. London, 1877. Leading work on the East India Company's marine service and the later Indian navy. [HF]

R401. Lyall, Sir Alfred C. **The rise and expansion of the British dominion in India.** London, 1906. This and Lyall's other works on British India reflect a solid sense of satisfaction in British achievement. [HF]

R402. Macpherson, William L., ed. **Soldiering in India, 1764–1787.** London, 1928. A most vivid and informative account of conditions under which military operations were carried on in 18th century India. Contains much information not found in other works on the subject. [HF]

R403. Madan, Balkrishna. **Commercial relations between India and England, 1601 to 1757.** London, 1924. Contains much statistical information on East India trade. [HF]

R404. Malcolm, Sir John. **The political history of India from 1784 to 1823.** London, 1826. Valuable coverage of events of this period by an experienced diplomat and administrator who witnessed many of them. [HF]

R405. Manucci, Niccolao. **Storia do**

Mogor, or Mogul India, 1653–1708. Tr. and ed. by William Irvine. 4 v. London, 1907–08. The standard edition in English of this important travel narrative. [HF]

R406. Mason, Philip (pseud. Philip Woodruff). **The men who ruled India. V. 1, The founders.** London, 1953. Delightfully written history of the British connection with India by a former member of the Indian civil service. Abounds in vivid biographical sketches. [HF]

R407. Milburn, William. **Oriental commerce: containing a geographical description of the principal places in the East Indies, China, and Japan with their produce, manufactures and trade.** London, 1813. Rev. ed. by Thomas Thornton, 1825. Complete guide to the East India trade. Indispensable to the student of Asian economic history. [HF]

R408. Mill, James. **The history of British India.** Ed. by Horace H. Wilson. 10 v. London, 1858. Mill's work, first published in 1818, underwent later revisions. The 1858 edition is the one most readily available. Written from the "utilitarian" point of view, this was the comprehensive history of India best known to the British and American public in the Victorian period. [HF]

R409. Moon, Penderel. **Warren Hastings and British India.** London, 1947. The most useful short study of Hastings for a quick review of his career and the controversies to which it gave rise. [HF]

R410. Moreland, William H. **India at the death of Akbar.** London, 1920. Moreland's works on the Mogul period have become classics. This volume is the best treatment of Indian economic conditions in the 16th century available in English. [HF]

R411. ——. **From Akbar to Aurangzeb.** London, 1923.

R412. Muir, Ramsay. **The making of British India, 1756–1858.** Manchester, 1923. A most useful collection of documents accompanied by very informative introduction. [HF]

R413. Mukerjee, Radhakamal. **The economic history of India, 1600–1800.** London and N.Y., 1955. Brief analysis of the early European period by an outstanding Indian economist.

R414. Oaten, Edward F. **European travellers in India during the fifteenth, sixteenth, and seventeenth centuries: the evidence afforded by them with respect to Indian social institutions, and the nature and influence of Indian governments.** London, 1909. A classic account.

R415. O'Malley, Lewis S. S. **History of Bengal, Behar, and Orissa under British rule.** Calcutta, 1925. Faithful coverage of the expansion of British power in northeast India.

R416. ——. **The Indian civil service, 1601–1930.** London, 1931. Good, popular account.

R417. Orme, Robert. **A history of the military transactions of the British nation in Indostan from the year MDCCXLV.** 4th ed., 2 v. in 3, London, 1803. Orme was on the ground, knew most of the actors in the drama, and, if his partiality for his friends be discounted, his work remains of great value. [HF]

418. Philips, Cyril H. **The East India Company, 1784–1834.** Manchester, 1940. The standard work on the Company during this period, stressing particularly relations between it and the government board of control set up by Pitt's India Act of 1784. [HF]

R419. Rawlinson, Hugh G. **British beginnings in western India.** Oxford, 1920. Scholarly study of the beginnings of British commercial enterprise in India at Surat. [HF]

R420. Rennell, James. **Memoir of a map of Hindoostan.** 2nd ed., London, 1792. Rennell laid the foundation for modern study of Indian geography. His maps are indispensable for students of 18th century India. [HF]

R421. Saiyid, Chulam Hussain Khan. **A translation of the Sëir mutaquerin or View of modern times, being a history of India from the year 1118 to the year 1194 . . . of the Hedjrah.** Tr. by Raymond (Mustapha). 4 v. Reprint, Calcutta, 1902. English translation of the chronicle *Siyar al-muta' akhkhirin,* which is almost the sole non-European source for the 18th century history of Bengal currently available to western readers. [HF]

R422. Sale, Lady Florentia (Wynch). **Journal of the disasters in Afghanistan, 1841–2.** London, 1843. Eyewitness account of the Afghan War (1841–42) on which later accounts largely rely. [HF]

R423. Sarkar, Sir Jadunath. **Fall of the Mughal empire.** 4 v. Calcutta, 1932–50. Crowning work of the author's distinguished career. Covers 1738–1803, and is chiefly concerned with events within India. [HF]

R424. Sleeman, Sir William H. **The Thugs or Phansigars of India.** 2 v. Philadelphia, 1839. A classic. First edition was published in Calcutta, 1836 under title *Ramaseana.* [HF]

R425. Sutherland, Lucy S. **The East India Company in eighteenth century politics.** Oxford, 1952. Thorough and scholarly study of the influence of East India affairs on British politics, especially during the period 1760–84. [HF]

R426. Tavernier, Jean B. **Travels in India.** Tr. by V. Ball. 2 v. London, 1889. The standard English translation of Tavernier's classic. [HF]

R427. Thompson, Edward J. **The life of Charles, Lord Metcalf.** London, 1937. Standard work by a novelist and historian whose studies reflect his wide knowledge of modern Indian life and society. [HF]

R428. Thompson, Edward J., and Geoffrey T. Garrett. **Rise and fulfillment of British rule in India.** London, 1934. Most comprehensive 1 v. treatment of the history of British connection with India from its beginnings to 1933. Perhaps the best introduction to the subject for the serious student. [HF]

R429. Thorner, Daniel. **Investment in empire: British railway and steam shipping enterprise in India, 1825–1849.** Philadelphia, 1950. Authoritative study, with special reference to the financing of early railway development. [HF]

R430. Wisset, Robert. **A compendium of East Indian affairs, political and commercial, for the use of the Court of Directors.** 2 v. London, 1802. Most useful compilation of statistical data on the East India trade, especially in the 18th century. [HF]

The Mahrattas

R431. Duff, James G. **A history of the Mahrattas.** 3 v. London, 1826. Despite recent contributions to Maratha history, this remains a classic which must be consulted by students of 18th and 19th century India. [HF]

R432. Kincaid, Charles A., and Dattatraya B. Parasnis. **A history of the Maratha people.** 3 v. London, 1918–25. The standard modern history. Kincaid and Parasnis used materials which were not available when Duff wrote a century earlier. [HF]

R433. Persian records of Maratha history. Bombay, 1953 ff. Valuable source material.

R434. Sen, Surendra N. **Administrative system of the Marathas.** 2nd ed., Calcutta, 1925. The standard work on the subject. [HF]

Modern Period (since 1857)

R435. Abdullah, Mohammed. **Jammu and Kashmir, 1947–1950.** Srinagar, 1950. An official account of Sheik Abdullah's administration. Provides a sketchy report on major political and economic trends and developments in that part of Jammu and Kashmir which adhered to India. [RIC]

R436. Aggarwal, Om Prakash. **Constitutional law of India: being a complete and up-to-date analytical survey of the Constitution.** Delhi, 1951. Detailed analysis of the formulation of the Indian constitution.

R437. Akkad, B. J. **Mahatma Gandhi (a short life of Gandhiji).** 3rd ed., Bombay, 1949. An adequate summary sketch of Gandhi's life, career, and principal views. [RIC]

R438. Alexander, Horace G. **India since Cripps.** Harmondsworth, Eng., 1944. Though quite brief and by now dated in important respects, this is an important volume, containing considerable insight into Indian affairs. [RIC]

R439. Ambedkar, Bhimrao Ramji. **What Congress and Gandhi have done to the untouchables.** 2nd ed., Bombay, 1946. Useful and interesting though polemical account, written by the outstanding modern leader of the Scheduled Castes. Contains valuable material and insights marred by considerable personal bitterness. [RIC]

R440. American Church Union. **Christianity in India: a historical summary having particular reference to the Anglican Communion and to the church of south India.** 2nd ed., N.Y., 1954. Useful introduction to history of the Christian church in India.

R441. Amery, Leopold C. **India and freedom.** London, 1942. Despite its clichés and an air of complacency, an interesting volume written by the then secretary of state for India. [RIC]

R442. Andrews, Charles F. **India and Britain: a moral challenge.** London, 1935. Informal but highly perceptive discussion of a variety of aspects of Indo-British relations. Helpful in understanding facets of Indian nationalist opinion regarding the British connection. [RIC]

R443. ———. **India and the Pacific.** London, 1937. Relatively substantial though not scholarly survey of racial questions in various British colonies, with special emphasis on the position and prospects of the overseas Indian communities. [RIC]

R444. Andrews, Charles F., and Girija Mookerji. **The rise and growth of the Congress in India.** London, 1938. Sympathetic, intelligent, and somewhat summary account of the rise of nationalism in India and development of the Congress party through 1920. [RIC]

R445. Andrews, Charles F. **Zaka Ullah of Delhi.** Cambridge, Eng., 1929. Worthwhile and illuminating study of one of the pioneers of the Muslim renascence in north India. Provides keen though informal insight into the impact of western learning on Indian Muslims. [RIC]

R446. Anstey, Vera. **The economic development of India.** 4th ed., London and N.Y., 1952. Despite certain shortcomings in mode of analysis, this remains the best single volume devoted to Indian economic growth during the British period. [RIC]

R447. Arokiaswami, M. **The modern economic history of India.** 4th rev. ed., Madras, 1955. Though a brief summary in textbook form, this is a valuable and relatively comprehensive account of the history and development of Indian economy during the British period. [RIC]

R448. Bagal, Jogesh C. **History of the Indian Association, 1876–1951.** Calcutta, [1953]. Valuable addition to available material on the rise of nationalism in India, in which the Indian Association played a prominent role. [RIC]

R449. Balfour, Lady Elizabeth Edith (Bulwer-Lytton). **The history of Lord Lytton's Indian administration, 1876 to 1880.** London, 1899. Important study of Lord Lytton's viceroyalty compiled from official sources by his daughter. Perhaps unintentionally informative regarding the "official" point of view toward Indian and frontier affairs. [RIC]

R450. Banerjea, Sir Surendranath. **A nation in making.** London and N.Y., 1925. Of basic importance to an understanding of the rise of nationalism in modern India, by one of the outstanding early leaders of the Congress. [RIC]

R451. Bannerjee, Anil C., ed. **Indian constitutional documents.** 2 v. Calcutta, 1945–46. Covers 1757–1945 with serious gaps, as it concentrates on the Indian National Congress.

R452. Barns, Margarita. **The Indian press: a history of the growth of public opinion in India.** London, 1940. Although it neglects the earliest period and was written before the great post-war developments, serves as an adequate account of the era covered.

R453. Barton, Sir William. **India's fateful hour.** London, 1942. Excellent statement of the conservative, official view of India and of the Congress. [RIC]

R454. ———. **The princes of India, with a chapter on Nepal.** London, 1934. A sympathetic account.

R455. Basu, Durga D., ed. **Commentary on the constitution of India, being a comparative treatise on the universal principles of justice and constitutional government with special reference to the organic instrument of India.** 3rd ed., 2 v., Calcutta, 1955–56. Although not an authoritative history and analysis, the best available study.

R456. Bazaz, Prem N. **Inside Kashmir.** Srinagar, 1941. Relatively brief pre-war account of conditions in Jammu and Kashmir. Rather superficial in parts, but contains a valuable section on the local press. [RIC]

R457. ———. **The history of struggle for freedom in Kashmir.** New Delhi, 1954. Most comprehensive recent study of Kashmiri politics and culture. Author was close associate of Sheik Abdullah. [RIC]

R458. Beauchamp, Joan. **British imperialism in India.** London, 1934. Highly critical account of conditions under British rule in modern India, prepared by left-wing elements in the British Labour movement and not without bias. [RIC]

R459. Besant, Annie. **Speeches and writings of Annie Besant.** 3rd ed., Madras, 1921. Collection of representative works by one of the leaders of pre-Gandhian nationalism. [RIC]

R460. Bhandarkar, Devadatta R., ed.

India. Philadelphia, 1929. [Annals of the American Academy of Political and Social Science, 165, pt. 2.] With one or two exceptions, a valuable collection of articles on various aspects of modern Indian life, politics, economic conditions, education, and recent history. [RIC]

R461. Bhattacharya, Jogendranath. **Hindu castes and sects.** Calcutta, 1896. A competent though dated study of the major castes and sects of modern Hinduism, with a discussion of the origins and nature of the caste system. Handy for brief reference. [RIC]

R462. Bolton, Glorney. **The tragedy of Gandhi.** London, 1934. Sympathetic and frequently penetrating study of Gandhi's behavior, values, and motives. [RIC]

R463. Bose, Subhas C. **The Indian struggle, 1920–1934.** London, 1935. Valuable, but incomplete and biased, account by one of the then most important young leaders of the "left wing" in the Congress party. Gives considerable insight into development of the Congress and of divisions within its ranks. [RIC]

R464. Bose, Sudhindra. **Some aspects of British rule in India.** Iowa City, 1916. Though showing a nationalist bias and a tendency to overstate the case in certain respects, this is a valuable, compact, and well-documented study of select aspects of British rule. [RIC]

R465. Brecher, Michael. **The struggle for Kashmir.** N.Y., 1953. Scholarly, exhaustive, and well-rounded treatment, generally regarded as more sympathetic to the Indian case than most works on Kashmir. [RIC]

R466. **The Cambridge history of India.** V. 6, **The Indian empire, 1858–1918, with chapters on the development of administration, 1818–1858.** Ed. by Henry H. Dodwell. Cambridge, Eng., 1932. A standard reference.

R467. Campbell-Johnson, Alan. **Mission with Mountbatten.** N.Y., 1953. Lucid and effective account in non-academic manner by an official closely associated with the last British governor-general of India. Sheds interesting light on the transfer of power, problems of partition, and emergence of independent India. [RIC]

R468. Capuchin Mission Unit. **India and its missions.** N.Y., 1923. History of Roman Catholic missions in India.

R469. Chaudhuri, Binayendra M. **Muslim politics in India.** Calcutta, 1946. Fairly serious but somewhat limited study of the development of communal politics and of the Muslim League. [RIC]

R470. Chintamani, Sir Chirravoori Y. **Indian politics since the Mutiny.** London, 1940. Survey of the growth of nationalist politics, with considerable reference to careers of major political figures. Includes brief but worthwhile section on pre-Congress nationalist activities. [RIC]

R471. Chirol, Sir Valentine. **India.** London, 1926. A curiously uneven book with some impressive sections. Includes good discussions of the legislatures under the system of dyarchy, effects of western education and of World War I, and aspects of India's industrialization. [RIC]

R472. ———. **India old and new.** London, 1921. Development of nationalism in India and the British response, with emphasis on the period between the partition of Bengal and the Montford reforms. [RIC]

R473. Coatman, John. **India: the road to self-government.** London, 1942. Though brief and in some respects disappointing, contains useful materials. [RIC]

R474. Cotton, Sir Henry J. S. **New India: or, India in transition.** 2nd rev. ed., London, 1907. For its period almost a definitive account of Indian politics and nationalist aspirations, by one of the great Indian civilians. Includes material on economic problems. [RIC]

R475. Coupland, Sir Reginald. **Britain and India, 1600–1941.** London, 1941. A highly condensed summary of British connection with India, giving the official point of view. [RIC]

R476. ———. **The Indian problem: report on the constitutional problem in India.** N.Y., 1944. Tinged with the conservative British point of view of the period.

R477. Crane, Robert I., ed. **Area handbook on Jammu and Kashmir State.** Preliminary ed., [Chicago], 1956.

R478. Cross, Cecil M. P. **The development of self-government in India, 1858–1914.** Chicago, 1922. Well documented and sound, though quite unimaginative. [RIC]

R479. Cumming, Sir John G., ed. **Political India, 1832–1932.** London, 1932. Somewhat uneven and by now rather dated collection of essays on topics such as political action, the Congress, communal problems and the minorities, Gandhi, and the Indian states. Competent, but leans too heavily on official opinion. [RIC]

R480. Curran, Jean A. **Militant Hinduism in Indian politics: a study of the R. S. S.** N.Y., 1951. Brief but valuable introduction to study of the Hindu revivalist element in modern Indian politics. [RIC]

R481. Das Gupta, Hemendra N. **The Indian National Congress.** V. 1. Calcutta, 1946. Although poorly written and documented, contains interesting and potentially significant material on the pre-Congress period of nationalism and on the role of Bengali drama in developing the nationalist sentiment. [RIC]

R482. Datta, Kalikinkar. **A survey of recent studies on modern Indian history.** Patna, 1957. Recent works on Indian history, including economic and constitutional. Useful though limited. [RIC]

R483. Desai, Akshayakumar R. **Social background of Indian nationalism.** Bombay, 1948. Fairly detailed effort by an author of Marxist orientation. Despite the bias and a tendency to overgeneralize, contains much useful information not readily available elsewhere. [RIC]

R484. Douglas, William O. **Beyond the high Himalayas.** Garden City, 1952. A major portion of the book is devoted to Ladakh, with material on social organization, local customs, economic problems, and relations with Communist areas. [RIC]

R485. Duffett, Walter E. **India today: the background of the Indian nationalist movement.** Toronto, 1941. Brief but useful summary of major facts about India. Contains short biographies of key figures in the Indian political scene. [RIC]

R486. Dutt, Rajani P. **India today.** 2nd ed., Bombay, 1949. Most substantial of the Marxist versions of modern Indian history, written by a leading Communist. Contains some valuable data, but must be used with caution. [RIC]

R487. Dutt, Romesh C. **The economic history of India in the Victorian age.** 4th ed., London, 1916. Though badly dated, remains the best account of India's 19th century economic progress. [RIC]

R488. Farquhar, John N. **Modern religious movements in India.** London, 1915. Covers adequately the 19th and early 20th centuries, describing reform movements within Islam, Hinduism, Sikhism, and Zoroastrianism.

R489. Fraser, Lovat. **India under Curzon and after.** London, 1911. Solid and detailed, though relatively unimaginative, account of Lord Curzon's controversial career as governor-general of India. [RIC]

R490. Fuller, John F. C. **India in revolt.** London, 1931. A peculiar book, often unsatisfactory and sometimes banal, but with occasional brusque insights of merit. [RIC]

R491. Gandhi, Devadas, comp. **India unreconciled.** New Delhi, 1943. Valuable, although not complete, collection of Congress documents covering period of crisis after the "Quit India" movement, showing the Congress point of view. [RIC]

R492. Gandhi, Mohandas K. **The Gandhi reader: a source book of his life and writings.** Ed. by Homer A. Jack. Bloomington, Ind., 1956. A rich selection of documents.

R493. ———. **Gandhi's autobiography: the story of my experiments with truth.** Washington, 1948. Basic writings on major developments of Gandhi's life. [RIC]

R494. ———. **Swaraj in one year.** Madras, 1921. Early statement by Gandhi of the objectives and methods of his program for achievement of independence by non-violent means; one of his first publications after assuming virtual control of the Congress party. [RIC]

R495. Gangulee, Nagendranath. **Indians in the empire overseas, a survey.** London, 1947. Documented and careful study of Indian emigration to the empire and dominions, and a survey of their position, opportunities, and conditions. [RIC]

R496. Ganju, Madusudan. **India's foreign policy.** Bombay, 1951. Brief account with special and revealing emphasis on Indo-Pakistan relations and considerable discussion of India's role in the Korean War. [RIC]

R497. Ghurye, Govind S. **Caste and race in India.** N.Y., 1932. Considered by many the best study in print on the Indian caste system and points of contact between caste and ethnic origin. [RIC]

R498. Gledhill, Alan. **The Republic of India: the development of its laws and constitution.** London, 1951. Brief but eminently sound and useful. [RIC]

R499. Goshal, Kumar. **The people of India.** N.Y., 1944. Uneven, rather superficial in places, and with a left-wing bias. Contains some interesting observations on the rise of Indian nationalism. Useful primarily for the point of view it presents and for some of its emphases. [RIC]

R500. Great Britain. India Office. **East India: memorandum on some of the results of Indian administration during the past fifty years of British rule in India.** London, 1909. Though quite brief, this is a lucid summary of major accomplishments from the government point of view. [RIC]

R501. ——. **East India: report on Indian constitutional reforms.** London, 1918. Basic documentary source for the Montagu-Chelmsford reforms. Also contains a concise and balanced survey, in official terms, of India's development in previous decades. [RIC]

R502. ——. **East India: statement exhibiting the moral and material progress and condition of India.** London, 1872 ff. A most extensive source of information.

R503. ——. **India: statement and draft declaration by His Majesty's government with correspondence and resolutions connected therewith.** London, 1942. Official record of the Cripps mission.

R504. Griffiths, Sir Percival J. **The British impact on India.** London, 1952. Impressive though not completely satisfactory account and interpretation of the British period in India. [RIC]

R505. ——. **Modern India.** N.Y., 1957. Parts dealing with political affairs and economic developments since independence are quite well done and provide valuable information. [RIC]

R506. Hoyland, John S. **Gopal Krishna**

Gokhale, his life and speeches. Calcutta, 1933. Concise and useful summary of the career of one of India's leading moderate politicians and social reformers. [RIC]

R507. Hunter, Sir William W. **The Indian empire: its peoples, history, and products.** 3rd ed., London, 1893. Valuable and compendious account by a leading authority. Contains material on administration, physical resources, communications, and vital statistics. [RIC]

R508. Hyderabad, India. Committee for the Compilation of a History of the Freedom Movement. **The freedom struggle in Hyderabad.** 2 v. Hyderabad, 1956. A large number of official documents and sources on uprisings before, during, and after the Mutiny. [RIC]

R509. India. Bureau of Public Information. **India in the years 1917–1918 [–1934].** 16 v. Calcutta, 1919–35. Important source of information on politics, communications, trade, finance, external relations, archaeology, and other matters.

R510. India. Home Department. **Congress responsibility for the disturbances, 1942–43.** Delhi, 1943. The official white paper on the "Quit India" movement and Congress involvement in subsequent disturbances. [RIC]

R511. India. Sedition Committee. **Report.** Calcutta, 1918. Detailed and careful study of the growth of militant and terrorist nationalism. Though biased in approach, contains much valuable material. [RIC]

R512. India (Dominion). **Draft constitution of India.** 2 v. New Delhi, 1947. To be used with the final approved draft for detailed study of changes in thinking.

R513. India (Republic). Central Statistical Organisation. **Statistical abstract, India.** New series. Delhi, 1949 ff. Supersedes *Statistical abstract for British India,* issued 1911–47.

R514. ——. **The constitution of India.** Delhi, 1949. The text only.

R515. ——. Ministry of States. **White paper on Indian states.** Rev. ed., Delhi, 1950. The official document on merging of the Indian native states into the Republic of India.

R516. ——. States Reorganization Commission. **Report.** Delhi, 1955. The report which resulted in the linguistic and geographical realignment of states in November, 1956.

R517. Indian National Congress. **Congress presidential addresses.** 2 v. Madras, 1934–35. Provides texts of all Congress presidential addresses from 1885 through 1934. Important for analysis of trends in Congress thinking and objectives. [RIC]

R518. Indian National Congress. All India Congress Committee. **Third year of freedom, August 1949–August 1950.** 2nd ed., New Delhi, 1951. Brief but useful summary of factual information about government, budgets, rural development, transport, industry, land reforms, and other aspects of government activity. [RIC]

R519. Indian National Congress. Select Committee on the Financial Obligations between Great Britain and India. **Report.** 2 v. Bombay, 1931. Represents major effort by the Congress to study Indo-British fiscal relations with a view toward agreement on the "just claims" of Britain upon securing independence. [RIC]

R520. India ravaged: being an account of atrocities committed under British aegis over the whole sub-continent of India in the latter part of 1942. [n.p.], 1943. An inadequately documented book, published by the underground Congress press, designed to present information about events during a very tense period. Sincere though exaggerated, it reveals an aspect of imperialism that is painful despite its rarity in the British case. [RIC]

R521. Indian Round Table Conference, London, Nov. 12, 1930–Jan. 19, 1931. **Proceedings.** London, 1931. This and succeeding Conference titles present important arguments for the freedom of India in a period of frustration.

R522. ———. **The Round Table Conference: India's demand for dominion status: speeches by the king, the premier, the British party leaders and the representatives of the princes and people of India.** Madras, 1931.

R523. Indian Round Table Conference, London, Sept. 7–Dec. 1, 1931. **Gandhiji in England, and the proceedings of the second Round Table Conference.** Madras, 1932.

R524. ———. **Proceedings.** London, 1932.

R525. Karandikar, S. L. **Lokamanya Bal Gangadhar Tilak.** Poona, [1957]. Solid, detailed account of the life and political career of Tilak. [RIC]

R526. Karunakaran, K. P. **India in world affairs, August 1947–January 1950.** London, 1952. Brief but rather comprehensive review of India's foreign policy in the first years of independence. [RIC]

R527. Kaumudi. **Kashmir: its cultural heritage.** Bombay, 1952. Excellent discussion of the arts and handicrafts of Kashmiri Muslims. [RIC]

R528. Keith, Arthur B. **A constitutional history of India, 1600–1935.** London, [1936]. Comprehensive and authoritative. Includes discussion of nationalism and of British attempts at political, fiscal, and administrative reform. [RIC]

R529. ———, ed. **Speeches and documents on Indian policy, 1750–1921.** 2nd ed., London, 1922. Selections from important speeches and documents illustrative of major themes in the political, constitutional, and administrative development of India under British rule. [RIC]

R530. Khan, Abdul M. **Life and speeches of Sardar Patel.** New Delhi, 1951. The most complete biography.

R531. Kincaid, Dennis. **British social life in India, 1608–1937.** London, 1939. Valuable and very readable addition to history of the British in India. [RIC]

R532. Kondapi, C. **Indians overseas, 1838–1949.** New Delhi, 1951. Comprehensive and documented study of conditions among Indians outside of India, with emphasis on labor, educational opportunities, disabilities, and political status. Extensive bibliography. [RIC].

R533. Korbel, Josef. **Danger in Kashmir.** Princeton, 1954. Analysis of origins and development of the Kashmir accession issue, dealing extensively with United Nations participation. Contains valuable sections on internal politics of Kashmir and danger of Communist subversion. [RIC]

R534. Kundra, Jagdish C. **Indian foreign policy, 1947–1954: a study of relations with the western bloc.** Groningen, 1955. Scholarly and well-documented account of background and goals of Indian foreign policy and an analysis of Indo-American relations. [RIC]

R535. Lajpat Rai, Lala. **The Arya Samaj: an account of its origin, doctrine and activities.** Lahore, 1932. Standard reference work on the Arya Samaj, which has played a small but significant role in social development of modern India.

R536. ———. **Unhappy India.** 2nd rev. ed., Calcutta, 1928. Example of ardent nationalist viewpoint on contemporary developments. [RIC]

R537. ———. **Young India: an interpretation and a history of the nationalist movement from within.** N.Y., 1916. Views and objectives of the nationalist movement and interpretation of the course of events, by a prominent pre-Gandhian leader. [RIC]

R538. Langley, George H. **Sri Aurobindo, Indian poet, philosopher and mystic.** London, 1949. Sympathetic biography of this important political and religious leader.

R539. Lawrence, Walter R. **The valley of Kashmir.** London, 1895. Old but authoritative account, with sections on the Muslims, economic life, political and social organization, customs, ritual, and religion. [RIC]

R540. Lee-Warner, Sir William. **The native states of India.** 2nd rev. ed., London, 1910. Probably the most comprehensive account of origins, status, and responsibilities of the native princes and rulers of India. Includes lengthy discussion of their modern relationship to the Crown and to the government of India. [RIC]

R541. ———. **The protected princes of India.** London, 1894. Development of the political position of Indian princes under British rule. [RIC]

R542. Lovett, Sir Harrington V. **A history**

of the Indian nationalist movement. London, 1920. Standard and largely official account of the rise of nationalism and of the Congress. [RIC]

R543. McCully, Bruce T. **English education and the origins of Indian nationalism.** N.Y., 1940. Basic monographic source, with excellent documentation and good analysis of the origins of nationalism among educated Indians. Contains valuable bibliography. [RIC]

R544. MacMunn, Sir George F. **The Indian states and princes.** London, 1936. A British imperialistic point of view.

R545. Macnicol, Nicol. **The making of modern India.** London, 1924. Perceptive and sympathetic articles on various aspects of modern Indian thought, the varied influences of Hinduism, and the genesis of Indian unrest. [RIC]

R546. Maconochie, Sir Evan. **Life in the Indian civil service.** London, 1926. Straightforward, casual, and valuable account by a member of the Indian civil service who served in responsible capacities in the decades before World War I. [RIC]

R547. Madhok, Balraj. **Dr. Syama Prasad Mookerjee, a biography.** New Delhi, 1954. Fair study of the leader of the conservative Hindu Mahasabha.

R548. Malleson, George B. **The Indian Mutiny of 1857.** London, 1891. Probably the best single volume account of the Mutiny. [RIC]

R549. Mason, Philip (pseud. Philip Woodruff). **The men who ruled India.** V. 2, **The guardians.** London, 1954. Worthwhile and well documented; perhaps too heavy on the official view and light on those personal accounts that could add intimacy. [RIC]

R550. Mayhew, Arthur I. **The education of India: a study of British educational policy in India, 1835–1920, and of its bearing on national life and problems in India to-day.** London, 1926. An understanding view.

R551. Menon, Vapal P. **The story of the integration of the Indian states.** N.Y., 1956. Invaluable account, by one of the chief actors, of the involved and impressive integration of the princely states. [RIC]

R552. ——. **The transfer of power in India.** Princeton, 1957. Considerable use of first-hand and unpublished sources make this a significant and exhaustive treatment of recent Indian history. [RIC]

R553. Mersey, Clive B., **The viceroys and governors-general of India, 1757–1947.** London, 1949. Brief but not always adequate biographical sketches, including occasional intimate glimpses not widely available. [RIC]

R554. Minto, Mary C. **India, Minto and Morley, 1905–1910: compiled from the correspondence between the viceroy and the secretary of state, by Mary, countess of**

Minto. London, 1935. Outstanding source on modern Indian history. [RIC]

R555. Montagu, Edwin S. **An Indian diary.** London, 1930. Important source for recent period, especially for the Montagu-Chelmsford reforms. [RIC]

R556. Moraes, Francis R. **Jawaharlal Nehru, a biography.** N.Y., 1956. Best biography to date.

R557. Morrison, John. **New ideas in India during the nineteenth century: a study of social, political and religious developments.** Edinburgh, 1906. Attempt by a sympathetic but balanced observer to assess the development of new ideas and ways of thought in modern India. [RIC]

R558. Mukerjee, Hirendranath. **India struggles for freedom.** 2nd ed., Bombay, 1948. Brief, literate, Marxist-oriented summary history of modern India. [RIC]

R559. Mukerji, Dhurjati P. **Modern Indian culture, a sociological study.** 2nd ed., Bombay, 1948. A rather overdone study of the nature of Indian society and culture, based on sociological analysis. Has a jargonistic flavor which detracts from a manful effort to cope with real issues. [RIC]

R560. Mukherjee, Haridas, and Uma Mukherjee. **The growth of nationalism in India (1857–1905).** Calcutta, 1957. Though brief, this volume traces with perspicacity and solid scholarship many of the important aspects of the growth of nationalism. [RIC]

R561. Mukherji, Panchanandas, ed. **Indian constitutional documents (1600–1918).** 2nd ed., 2 v., Calcutta, 1918. Excellent source with all pertinent documents quoted in full. Some important documents have been selected for a few of the larger native states.

R562. Murphy, Gardner. **In the minds of men: the study of human behavior and social tensions in India.** N.Y., 1953. Links basic characteristics of Indian life and the effects of foreign control with current tensions. Discusses caste tensions and those between religious and economic groups. A real contribution. [RIC]

R563. Nanavati, Sir Manilal B., ed. **Group prejudices in India, a symposium.** Bombay, 1951. Includes discussions of cultural, religious, social, and political aspects of prejudice in its Indian setting. [RIC]

R564. Naoroji, Dadabhai. **Poverty and un-British rule in India.** London, 1901. One of the basic sources in understanding Indian nationalist ideas, by an outstanding early moderate leader of the Congress. Essentially a collection of Naoroji's views and comments on economic damage done to India by the British connection. [RIC]

R565. Narain, Jai P. **Towards struggle.** Ed. by Yusuf Meherally. Bombay, 1946. Useful though by no means exhaustive collection of speeches and writings of India's outstanding Socialist leader. [RIC]

R566. Nehru, Jawaharlal. **Independence and after: a collection of the more important speeches, from September 1946 to May 1949.** Delhi, 1949. More than fifty of Nehru's speeches on such topics as communalism, Kashmir, education, Gandhi, India's foreign policy, and industry. [RIC]

R567. Nehru, Jawaharlal, and others. **Towards freedom.** N.Y., 1941. Contains autobiography of India's leading statesman.

R568. Nightingale, Florence. **Florence Nightingale's Indian letters: a glimpse into the agitation for tenancy reform, Bengal, 1878–82.** Ed. by Priyaranjan Sen. Calcutta, 1937. Collection of fourteen letters which display considerable understanding of a complicated question, a sincere desire to further reform, and an informed sympathy for position of the tenant in Bengal. [RIC]

R569. Nurullah, Syed, and J. P. Naik. **A history of education in India (during the British period).** 2nd rev. ed., Bombay, 1951. Solid, well-documented account of the growth of education under British influence. [RIC]

R570. O'Malley, Lewis S. S., ed. **Modern India and the West: a study of the interaction of their civilizations.** London, 1941. Scholarly essays on various subjects such as the impact of European civilization, education, economic development, the Hindu social system, primitive tribes, and literature. [RIC]

R571. Pal, Dharm. **Administration of Sir John Lawrence in India (1864–1869).** Simla, 1952. Solid, documented monograph on administration in the important post-Mutiny years in which the foundations of Crown rule were laid. [RIC]

R572. Parikh, Narahari D. **Sardar Vallabhbhai Patel.** 2 v. Ahmedabad, 1953–56. Exhaustive biography of this important political leader.

R573. Parkin, George R. **India today: an introduction to Indian politics.** 2nd rev. ed., Toronto, 1946. Brief, lucid, and balanced account; useful bibliography. [RIC]

R574. Pattabhi Sitaramayya, Bhogaraju. **The history of the Indian National Congress.** 2nd ed., 2 v., Bombay, 1946–47. Official history of the Congress; a solid, documented account within the framework of author's bias. [RIC]

R575. Philips, Cyril H. **India.** London, 1949. An all-too-brief history of India, concentrating on period of British rule; one of the best single volume studies. [RIC]

R576. Prabhu, Pandhari-Nath. **Hindu social organization: a study in social-psychological and ideological foundations.** 2nd ed., Bombay, 1954. Systematic effort to analyze the basic ideologies that underlie and pattern

Hindu social psychology and social institutions. [RIC]

R577. Prasad, Bisheshwar. **The foundations of India's foreign policy. V. 1, 1860–1882.** Calcutta, 1955. Traces with care and scholarship the development of Indian foreign policy, with attention to policy for buffer areas. [RIC]

R578. Prasad, Rajendra. **Autobiography.** Bombay, 1957. Informative account of the life and career of a leading nationalist figure, president of the Republic of India. [RIC]

R579. ——. **Satyagraha in Champaran.** 2nd rev. ed., Ahmedabad, 1949. Important source on the beginning of Gandhi's influence and leadership in India. [RIC]

R580. Punnaiah, K. V. **The constitutional history of India, from the advent of the East India Company to the present time.** Allahabad, 1938. Good introduction for the period covered; lacks documentation.

R581. Raghuvanshi, V. P. S. **Indian nationalist movement and thought.** Agra, 1951. Though not well written or documented, does provide an informative, unsystematic summary of major currents in Indian nationalist thought. [RIC]

R582. Rai, Ganpat. **Acharya J. B. Kripalani, a biographical sketch.** Lahore, 1947. Latest biography of a leading Indian Socialist.

R583. Ramakrishna. **Ramakrishna: prophet of new India.** Tr. by Swami Nikhilananda. N.Y., 1951. The great religious leaders of India have usually influenced the social and political history. Ramakrishna (1836–86) was one of these. This is a good anthology of the expressed beliefs of him and his followers.

R584. Ray, Parimal. **India's foreign trade since 1870.** London, 1934. Solid, well-documented, and relatively balanced study of the major trends in development of India's foreign trade between 1870 and 1924. [RIC]

R585. Reed, Sir Stanley. **The India I knew, 1897–1947.** London, 1952. Thorough analysis of many phases of the modern Indian scene, by former editor of one of India's most respected newspapers. [RIC]

R586. Reynolds, Reginald. **White sahibs in India.** 3rd rev. ed., London, 1946. Interesting on British rule in India, highly critical of the British. [RIC]

R587. Richter, Julius. **A history of missions in India.** Tr. by Sydney H. Moore. London, 1908. Good survey of Roman Catholic and Protestant missionary history.

R588. Rizvi, S. A. A., ed. **Freedom struggle in Uttar Pradesh. V. 1, 1857–59.** Uttar Pradesh, 1957. Useful volume of extracts from original records, contemporary accounts, and contemporary newspapers published in India prior to and during the Mutiny. [RIC]

R589. Roberts, Frederick S. R. **Forty-one years in India.** 10th ed., 2 v., London, 1897. Honest and rather exhaustive account of a long and distinguished career in the Indian army, beginning with the Mutiny. [RIC]

R590. Roberts, Paul E. **History of British India under the Company and the Crown.** 3rd rev. ed., London, 1952. Possibly the best single volume history, about half of which is devoted to the post-Mutiny period. [RIC]

R591. Roy, Manabendra Nath. **India and war.** Lucknow, 1942. Views of a former Communist leader regarding the war and developments in India. [RIC]

R592. Sanderson, Gorham D. **India and British imperialism.** N.Y., 1951. Violently critical account of British rule, reproducing the most exaggerated Indian nationalist views. [RIC]

R593. Sen, Niranjan. **Bengal's forgotten warriors.** Bombay, 1945. Valuable biographical information on a number of prominent participants in the early terrorist movement in Bengal. [RIC]

R594. Sengupta, Bidhubhusan, ed. **Mahatma Gandhi and India's struggle for swaraj.** 2nd ed., Calcutta, 1932. Relatively detailed but not complete coverage of development of the Congress in the years preceding the Round Table conferences. [RIC]

R595. Seth, Hira L. **The red fugitive, Jai Prakash Narain.** 2nd ed., Lahore, 1944. Biography of a prominent Socialist leader, written at a time when Indian emotions ran high.

R596. Sharma, Jagdish S. **Mahatma Gandhi, a descriptive bibliography.** Delhi, 1955. Very comprehensive list assembled in libraries of the United States and India.

R597. Singh, Durlab. **The rebel president: a biographical study of Subhas Chandra Bose.** Lahore, 1941. Sympathetic. An objective biography is yet to be written.

R598. Smith, Wilfred C. **Modern Islam in India, a social analysis.** London, 1947. Well-documented studies of events and tensions which produced Pakistan.

R599. ——. **The Muslim League, 1942–45.** Lahore, 1945. Penetrating study of the causes leading to the partition of India.

R600. Smith, William R. **Nationalism and reform in India.** New Haven, 1938. Basic text in development of Indian nationalism, tending to reflect the British estimate. Contains useful bibliography. [RIC]

R601. Strachey, Sir John. **India, its administration and progress.** 4th ed., London, 1911. Very concise and informed exposition of the principles of British rule, expressing the official point of view. [RIC]

R602. Subrahmanya Aiyar, G. **Some economic aspects of British rule in India.** Madras, 1903. Dated but lucid statement of the major nationalist charges of economic exploitation. [RIC]

R603. Sunderland, Jabez T. **India in bondage.** N.Y., 1929. Polemical and quite critical account of British rule, with useful material from a variety of informed sources. [RIC]

R604. Tendulkar, Dinanath G. **Mahatma: life of Mohandas Karamchand Gandhi.** 8 v. Bombay, 1951–54. Considered the official biography. Well documented and illustrated; an important collection of sources.

R605. Thakore, Balvantrai K. **Indian administration to the dawn of responsible government.** Rev. ed., Bombay, 1926. Relatively adequate as a general discussion of various aspects of British Indian administration through the dyarchy. [RIC]

R606. Thompson, Edward J. **The making of the Indian princes.** London and N.Y., 1943. Faithful British account of the growth of native states under the Crown.

R607. ——. **Reconstructing India.** N.Y., 1930. Valuable on recent Indian history, with judicious discussions of certain important political and social problems. [RIC]

R608. Underwood, Alfred C. **Contemporary thought of India.** N.Y., 1931. Brief survey of modern political, social, and religious thought. [RIC]

R609. Useem, John, and Ruth Useem. **The western-educated man in India: a study of his social roles and influence.** N.Y., 1955. Informed study of the effects of western education on Indians and on cross-cultural relations. [RIC]

R610. Wallbank, Thomas W. **India in the new era.** Chicago, 1951. Relatively adequate as a text, though has certain errors of fact and superficialities of estimation. [RIC]

R611. Younghusband, Sir Francis E. **Dawn in India: British purpose and Indian aspiration.** 2nd ed., London, 1931. Interesting discussion of Indo-British relations during the period of growing nationalism. Shows considerable pride in the British accomplishment mingled with a growing sense of the justice and inevitability of the Indian demand. [RIC]

R612. Zacharias, Hans C. E. **Renascent India, from Rammohan Roy to Mohandas Gandhi.** London, 1933. Worthwhile summary of growth of Indian nationalist thought in the context of western education and movements for social and religious reform. [RIC]

R613. Zetland, Lawrence J. L. Dundas, 2nd marquis of. **The life of Lord Curzon.** 3 v. N.Y., 1928. Substantial and detailed treatment, with considerable emphasis on his governor-generalship and subsequent relations with India. As his official biographer, the author is not critical but is fair. [RIC]

R614. Zimand, Savel. **Living India.** N.Y., 1928. A popular study of modern Indian problems, politics, and conditions; nationalist view. [RIC]

LOCAL HISTORIES

R615. Arokiaswami, M. **The Kongu country: being the history of the modern districts of Coimbatore and Salem from the earliest times to the coming of the British.** Madras, 1956. Good addition to the local histories, which are appearing more and more frequently.

R616. Banerji, Rakhal D. **History of Orissa, from the earliest times to the British period.** 2 v. Calcutta, 1930–31. Comprehensive local history.

R617. Basak, Radhagovinda. **The history of north-eastern India extending from the foundation of the Gupta empire to the rise of the Pala dynasty of Bengal (c. 320–760 A.D.).** London, 1934. Good local history of the early period.

R618. Burnell, Arthur C. **Elements of South-Indian palaeography from the fourth to the seventeenth century A.D.** 2nd ed., London, 1878. Has not been superseded.

R619. Commissariat, Manekshah S. **A history of Gujarat.** Bombay and N.Y., 1938. From the Mauryan period to coming of the Portuguese.

R620. Cunningham, Joseph D. **A history of the Sikhs, from the origin of the nation to the battle of the Sutlej.** New and rev. ed., ed. by H. L. O. Garrett, London and N.Y., 1918. Although there are later histories, this may still be considered standard for the period covered.

R621. Fonseca, José N. da. **An historical and archaeological sketch of the city of Goa, preceded by a short statistical account of the territory of Goa.** Bombay, 1878. From the 16th into 19th century.

R622. Forbes, Alexander K. **Rås Mâlà: Hindoo annals of the province of Goozerat in western India.** Ed. by H. G. Rawlinson. 2 v. London, 1924. Interesting early 19th century account of medieval events and customs.

R623. Gait, Edward A. **A history of Assam.** 2nd rev. ed., Calcutta, 1926. From prehistoric times to the consolidation of British rule.

R624. Gopalachari, K. **Early history of the Andhra country.** Madras, 1941. From the 3rd century B.C. to 6th century A.D.

R625. Gopalan, R. **History of the Pallavas of Kanchi.** Madras, 1928. Very complete account of the period 900–900 A.D.

R626. Gribble, James D. B. **A history of the Dekkan.** 2 v. London, 1924. From the 14th century to close of the 19th.

R627. Hambye, E. R. "The Syrian Jacobites in India—a survey of their past and present position." **Eastern churches quarterly,** 11 (autumn 1955): 115–29. Brief summary of their history with a longer estimate of their present social and religious position.

R628. Hayavadana Rao, Conjeeveram. **History of Mysore (1399–1799 A.D.) incor-** porating the latest epigraphical, literary and historical researches. 3 v. Bangalore, 1943–46. A complete account.

R629. Hodivala, Shahpurshah H. **Studies in Parsi history.** Bombay, 1920. A standard work on the Parsi community.

R630. Iyengar, Pillaipundagude T. Srinivas. **History of the Tamils from the earliest times to 600 A.D.** Madras, 1929. Covers prehistoric period to time of recorded history. Sources are carefully evaluated.

R631. Jouveau-Dubreuil, Gabriel. **Archéologie du sud de l'Inde.** 2 v. in 1. Paris, 1914. Tr. of v. 2, by A. C. Martin, *Iconography of southern India,* Paris, 1937. Excellent coverage with good illustrations.

R632. Karaka, Dosabhai F. **History of the Parsis, including their manners, customs, religion, and present position.** 2 v. London, 1884. Still the best account.

R633. Kaul, Gwasha L. **Kashmir through the ages, 5000 B.C. to 1954 A.D.** Srinagar, 1954. There are few sources on Kashmir, and the few attempts to reconstruct its history may not be regarded as entirely objective or reliable.

R634. Kehimkar, Haeem S. **The history of the Bene Israel of India.** Tel Aviv, 1937. History of the Jews in the Bombay presidency, compiled chiefly from secondary sources.

R635. Krishnaswami Aiyangar, Sakkotai. **Some contributions of south India to Indian culture.** 2nd ed., Calcutta, 1942. Brief historical survey from earliest period to about the 10th century.

R636. ——. **South India and her Muhammadan invaders.** London, 1921. From the 12th through 14th century.

R637. Macauliffe, Max A. **The Sikh religion, its gurus, sacred writings and authors.** 6 v. Oxford, 1909. The best analysis by a western scholar.

R638. Mahtab, Harekrushna. **The history of Orissa.** Lucknow, 1948. History of a remote area.

R639. Major, Richard H., ed. **India in the fifteenth century.** London, 1857. [Hakluyt Society publications, 22.] Includes a most valuable report on southern India by Nicolo di Conti.

R640. Majumdar, Ramesh C., ed. **The history of Bengal.** 2 v. Dacca, 1943–48. Comprehensive coverage from earliest times to 1757.

R641. Minakshi, Cadambi. **Administration and social life under the Pallavas.** Madras, 1938. Careful analysis and development of available source material on the important Deccan kingdom of the first millennium.

R642. Monahan, Francis J. **The early history of Bengal.** London and N.Y., 1925. Importance of Bengal in the early history of India is well described in this brief account.

R643. Munshi, Kanaiyalal M. **The glory that was Gurjaradesa.** 2 v. Bombay, 1955. [Bhavan's book university, 26–27.] A student's manual of the history of Gujarat.

R644. Nilakanta Sastri, Kallidaikurichi A. A. **The Colas.** 2 v. in 3. Madras, 1935–37. Very complete history.

R645. ——. **A history of south India from prehistoric times to the fall of Vijayanagar.** Madras, London, and N.Y., 1955. Excellent.

R646. ——. **The Pandyan kingdom from the earliest times to the sixteenth century.** London, 1929. From the time of Asoka.

R647. Raychaudhuri, Tapankumar. **Bengal under Akbar and Jahangir: an introductory study in social history.** Calcutta, 1953. Careful account of an important period in Bengal history just before entrenchment of the British.

R648. Sewell, Robert. **A sketch of the dynasties of southern India.** Madras, 1883. Good genealogical reference book.

R649. Stewart, Charles. **The history of Bengal.** 2nd ed., Calcutta, 1910. A British point of view.

R650. Subbarao, Bendapudi. **Baroda through the ages.** Baroda, 1953. Report of beginnings of archaeological work in the area.

R651. Tod, James. **Annals and antiquities of Rajasthan: or the central and western Rajput states of India.** New ed. by William Crooke, 3 v., London and N.Y., 1920. The classic work on this subject.

R652. Venkataraman, K. R. **Hoysalas in the Tamil country, 12th–14th centuries.** Annamalainagar, 1950. Local history on a period not covered elsewhere.

R653. Virji, Krishnakumari J. **Ancient history of Saurashtra.** Bombay, 1952. A period not covered elsewhere.

R654. Wilberforce-Bell, Harold. **The history of Kathiawad from the earliest times.** London, 1916. From 4th century B.C. to the outbreak of World War I.

R655. Yasodadevi, V. "The history of Andhra country: 1000 A.D.–1500 A.D., subsidiary dynasties." **Journal of the Andhra Historical Research Society,** 18 (July 1947–Apr 1948): 33–110, 19 (July 1948–Apr. 1949): 1–84. History of the area for a period not covered elsewhere.

HISTORIES OF SPECIAL TOPICS

R656. Bhatwadekar, M. V. **A history of Indian currency.** Bombay, 1944. Succinct and reliable.

R657. Brown, D. MacKenzie. **The white umbrella: Indian political thought from Manu to Gandhi.** Berkeley, 1953. Good, popular study of Indian polity with interesting speculation on what may be expected in the future.

R658. Ghoshal, Upendra N. **A history of Hindu political theories, from the earliest times to the end of the seventeenth century A.D.** London, 1927. Traces development from Vedic times to about 1700.

Additional items are included under the special periods above.

SERIALS AND PERIODICALS

R659. Ancient India: bulletin of the Archaeological Survey of India. New Delhi, 1946 ff. (Irregular.) Contains sound historical articles.

R660. Annals of the Bhandarkar Oriental Research Institute. Poona, 1918 ff. (Annual.) Excellent coverage of philological and historical subjects.

R661. Annual bibliography of Indian archaeology. Leiden, 1928 ff. A most valuable source.

R662. Asiatic annual register. 12 v. London, 1799–1811. Early but rich source.

R663. Asiatic journal and monthly register. 3 series. London, 1816–45. Contains much interesting commentary on life of the time.

R664. Asiatic researches. 20 v. Calcutta, 1788–1839. Rich source of historical material.

R665. Bengal, past and present: journal of the Calcutta Historical Society. Calcutta, 1907 ff. (Quarterly.) Good source for local history.

R666. Bharatiya Vidya. Bombay, 1939 ff. (Semiannual, 1939–43; monthly, 1945 ff.) Coverage not only local, but also of Indian history in general.

R667. Calcutta review. Calcutta, 1844 ff. (Irregular quarterly.) Articles are both popular and scholarly. Should be in any college library.

R668. Epigraphia indica. Calcutta, 1888 ff. (Irregular.) A mine of information.

R669. Epigraphia indo-moslemica. Calcutta, 1907–34. (Irregular.) Supplements the above.

R670. The Indian antiquary: a journal of oriental research in archaeology, history, literature, languages, folklore, etc. 62 v. Bombay, 1872–1933. (Monthly.) Index to v. 1–50, by Lavinia M. Anstey, 2 v. in 3, Bombay, 1923. One of the most valuable journals for articles on Indian history. Superseded by the *New Indian antiquary* (*R686*).

R671. The Indian archives. New Delhi, 1947 ff. (Quarterly, 1947–49; semiannual, 1950 ff.) Valuable record of source materials.

R672. The Indian historical quarterly. Calcutta, 1926 ff. One of the best historical journals; mostly concerned with the ancient and medieval periods.

R673. Journal of Indian history. Allahabad, etc., 1921 ff. (3 nos. per year.)

R674. Journal of the Andhra Historical Research Society. Rajahmundry, 1926 ff.

(Quarterly.) Good source on Telugu culture. Also contains general articles.

R675. Journal of the Asiatic Society of Bengal. 75 v. Calcutta, 1832–1905. (Irregular.) A philological journal containing important historical material.

R676. Journal and proceedings of the Royal Asiatic Society of Bengal. New ser., 34 v., Calcutta, 1905–36. (Irregular.)

R677. Journal of the Royal Asiatic Society of Bengal. 3rd ser., Calcutta, 1935 ff. (Title varies.)

R678. The journal of the Bihar Research Society. Patna, 1915 ff. (Quarterly.) One of the best historical journals not only for local history, but also for general articles on India.

R679. Journal of the Bombay Branch of the Royal Asiatic Society. Bombay, 1841 ff. (Irregular.) Rich source of information on philology and history.

R680. Journal of the Bombay Historical Society. Bombay, 1928 ff. (Semiannual.) General articles in addition to material on western India.

R681. Journal of the Gujarat Research Society. Bombay, 1939 ff. (Quarterly.) Rich source of information on local history. In recent volumes some articles are in English and some in Gujarati.

R682. Journal of the Madras University. Series A, Humanities. Madras, 1928 ff. (Irregular.) A general, scholarly journal with good historical articles.

R683. Journal of the United Provinces Historical Society. Calcutta and London, 1917 ff. (Irregular. Title varies.) General articles in addition to ones on the United Provinces.

R684. Man in India. Ranchi, 1921 ff. (Quarterly.) Excellent journal on Indian anthropology.

R685. Medieval India quarterly. Aligarh, 1950 ff. Promises to be a valuable depository of research articles, particularly on Muslim activities.

R686. New Indian antiquary: a monthly journal of oriental research in archaeology, art, epigraphy, ethnology, folklore, geography, history, languages, linguistics, literature, numismatics, philosophy, religion and all subjects connected with Indology. Bombay, 1938 ff. The successor to *R670*.

R687. The quarterly journal of the Mythic Society. Bangalore, 1909 ff. Contains historical articles of value.

R688. The Visva-Bharati quarterly. Santiniketan, 1923 ff. A general periodical.

NEPAL, BHUTAN, AND SIKKIM

R689. Fisher, Margaret W. **A selected bibliography of source materials for Nepal.** Berkeley, 1956. Rev. ed., 1959. Contains all necessary material on Nepal.

R690. Regmi, D. R. **A century of family autocracy in Nepal: being the account of the condition and history of Nepal during the last hundred years of Rana autocracy, 1846–1949.** [Kathmandu ?], 1950. A Congress point of view.

R691. Venkatachelam, Kota. **Chronology of Nepal history reconstructed.** Gandhinagar, 1953. Useful work on a little known subject.

R692. Eden, Sir Ashley. **Political missions to Bootan: comprising the reports of the** Hon'ble Ashley Eden, 1864; Capt. R. B. Pemberton, 1837, 1838, with Dr. W. Griffith's Journal; and the Account by Baboo Kishan Kant Bose. Calcutta, 1865. Source material on strategic periods in the history of these mountain areas.

R693. White, John C. **Sikhim and Bhutan: twenty-one years on the north-east frontier, 1887–1908.** London, 1909. Very readable account of author's personal experiences. Contains a brief history.

R694. Zetland, Lawrence J. L. Dundas, 2nd marquis of. **Lands of the thunderbolt: Sikhim, Chumbi and Bhutan.** London, 1923. A vivid description of the country and people.

SECTION S

The Middle East Since 1450

RODERIC H. DAVISON *

Today there is no agreement on the relationship of the terms "Near East" and "Middle East" or on the exact area designated by either. Both, coined in the West for European diplomatic or military convenience, are elastic. Historians are more accustomed to "Near East"; and until World War II this was the label customarily attached by westerners to the area considered in this section. However, "Middle East," which theretofore was usually applied to the general region of India and its approaches, has recently tended to replace "Near East" for the lands at the eastern end of the Mediterranean.

In history since 1450, the Near East corresponds roughly to the combined area of the former Ottoman and Iranian empires. With the Ottoman breakup, the Balkan states fell away, and in this *Guide* are considered in Section W. The Middle East of this section, in terms of modern political divisions, embraces Turkey, Iran, Cyprus, Syria, Lebanon, Iraq, Jordan, Israel, Egypt, Sa'udi Arabia, the Yemen, and the states of the Arabian coast. Works on other areas often included with these must be sought in other sections: the Caucasus and Turkestan (X); Afghanistan, Pakistan, and India (R); the Sudan, Libya, Tunisia, Algeria, and Morocco (AC).

Since much middle eastern history of the last two centuries has been determined from the outside, sections in this *Guide* on European powers as well as those dealing with diplomacy and the world wars must be consulted. Also fundamental to understanding the historical development since 1450 are works in the background sections on religions (D), the ancient Near East (F, H, I), the Byzantine empire (L), and the Muslim world to 1450 (M).

In recent years there has been a marked increase in scholarly work on the history of this area. Scholars in the region itself, especially Turkey, have started to exploit their archives; and important studies on aspects of near eastern history since 1450 now exist in well over a dozen oriental and western languages.

* The following contributed items and comments indicated by their respective initials: C. Ernest Dawn (CED), J. C. Hurewitz (JCH), Zuhair Jwaideh (ZJ), Firuz Kazemzadeh (FK), B. G. Martin (BGM), Robert F. Ogden (RFO), Howard A. Reed (HARe), Helen A. Rivlin (HARi), Arshag O. Sarkissian (AOS).

Yet the number of first-class works is restricted. This means that a selection adequate to cover generally the five centuries here considered inevitably will include books which, while useful and informative, are far from definitive. For the history of the Arab peoples, most of them within the Ottoman dominions from the 16th to 20th centuries, there is a dearth of scholarly works. The same is true for large sections of Iran's history. By contrast, good diplomatic studies are fairly numerous.

In the selection that follows, memoirs and personal accounts which are informative occasionally have been included in preference to academic writings of questionable quality. Some of the biographies are as good as some period histories. Periodical and encyclopedia articles, often the result of excellent historical research, are usually excluded except as they relate to further bibliography; space forbids even a partial coverage of articles. Reviews as a rule are indicated only for works published within the last decade.

BIBLIOGRAPHIES

The pertinent sections in Malclès, *Les sources du travail bibliographique* (*B2*) offer a concise bibliographical introduction to the area. There is no satisfactory general bibliography of works on the history of the modern Middle East. See those listed in Section M, especially Ettinghausen, *A selected and annotated bibliography* (*M5*), the best general introduction to works primarily in English; Gabrieli, *Manuale di bibliografia musulmana* (*M3*); Pfannmüller, *Handbuch der Islam-Literatur* (*M4*), broader than title indicates; Spuler and Forrer, *Der Vordere Orient in islamischer Zeit* (*M2*), good for publications of the last twenty years, particularly on Turkey. Such general bibliographies may be supplemented by reviews, bibliographical articles (see those listed in Section M), and lists of magazine articles, especially in *The Middle East journal* and other periodicals mentioned below.

S1. Pearson, James D. **Index islamicus.** See *M6*.

S2. Weber, Shirley H. **Voyages and travels in Greece, the Near East and adjacent regions made previous to the year 1801.** Princeton, 1953. This and the following are useful lists based on works in the Gennadius Library, Athens, all in western languages, arranged by year.

S3. ——. **Voyages and travels in the Near East made during the XIX century.** Princeton, 1952.

S4. Thomsen, Peter. **Die Palästina-Literatur.** See *F7*. Broad enough to be useful for entire Near East.

S5. Birge, John K. **A guide to Turkish area study.** Washington, 1949. Perceptive introduction to 587 western-language works. Reviews, J. Deny, *Middle East jour.,* 4 (Apr. 1950): 260; H. A. Reed, *Muslim world,* 40 (Oct. 1950): 298. [HARe]

S6. Koray, Enver. **Türkiye tarih yayïnlarï bibliyografyasï, 1729–1950.** [Bibliography of historical publications in Turkey, 1729–1950.] Ankara, 1952. Comprehensive though unannotated list of books and articles, chronologically and by subject.

S7. **Türkiye bibliyografyasï.** [Bibliography of Turkey.] Istanbul, 1928 ff. General list of books and pamphlets published in Turkey since the 1928 alphabet change. Supplemented by the following publication. [HARe]

S8. **Türkiye makaleler bibliyografyasï.** [Bibliography of articles in Turkey.] Istanbul, 1952 ff. (Quarterly.) Contains French subtitles. [HARe]

S9. Michoff, Nicolas V. **Bibliographie des articles de périodiques allemands, anglais, français et italiens sur la Turquie et la Bulgarie.** Sofia, 1938. Contains 10,000 articles by publication year, 1715–1886, with author and subject indexes.

S10. ——. **Sources bibliographiques sur l'histoire de la Turquie et de la Bulgarie.** 4 v. Sofia, 1914–34. Useful, though far from complete and arranged by alphabet only.

S11. Wilson, Sir Arnold T. **A bibliography of Persia.** Oxford, 1930. Out of date, but best single list of books and articles in European languages. Alphabetically arranged; unannotated.

S12. Elwell-Sutton, Laurence P. **A guide to Iranian area study.** Ann Arbor, 1952. Lists 818 works, briefly annotated, with a section on history.

S13. U. S. Library of Congress. **Iran: a selected and annotated bibliography.** Comp. by Hafez F. Farman. Washington, 1951. Lists some articles and materials in Persian.

S14. Saba, Mohsen. **Bibliographie française de l'Iran.** 2nd ed., Tehran, 1951. Enlarged edition of a classified list of books and articles in French.

S15. Sarkīs, Yūsuf I. **Mu'jam al-matbū'āt al-'arabiyyah wa al-mu'arrabah. Dictionnaire**

encyclopédique de bibliographie arabe. 2 v. Cairo, 1928–31. Attempts coverage of all Arab works since beginning of printing, including history of all periods, with biographical notes.

S16. Maunier, René. **Bibliographie économique, juridique et sociale de l'Égypte moderne (1798–1916).** Cairo, 1918.

S17. Lorin, Henri, ed. **Bibliographie géographique de l'Égypte.** 2 v. Cairo, 1928–29. A most helpful work in its field. [HARi]

S18. Masson, Paul. **Éléments d'une bibliographie française de la Syrie.** Marseille, 1919. Contains 4,534 items, unannotated, on Syria in its broadest sense.

S19. Patai, Raphael. **Jordan, Lebanon and Syria: an annotated bibliography.** New Haven, 1957. Concentrates on recent period; historical items included with "behavior sciences."

S20. U. S. Library of Congress. **The Arabian peninsula: a selected, annotated list of periodicals, books, and articles in English.** Washington, 1951. Usefulness restricted because confined to English titles. May be supplemented by "Djazīrat al-'Arab," *Encyclopaedia of Islam (S216).*

S21. Shunami, Shlomo. **Bibliography of Jewish bibliographies.** See *D312.*

S22. Sanjian, Avedis K. "Armenian works on historic and modern Armenian communities." **Report on current research** (1958): 47–54. Titles (in English only) and brief comments on works concerning Armenians the world over.

S23. Palestine and Zionism: a cumulative author, title and subject index to books, pamphlets and periodicals. N.Y., 1946 ff. Bimonthly, cumulated annually. Ranges over Near East and Africa; no annotations.

S24. Salmaslian, Armenag. **Bibliographie de l'Arménie.** Paris, 1946. European language works, by subject, plus author index; uncritical.

Works on historiography, histories of literature, and handbooks on historical research often provide sound bibliographical information and criticism. See especially Sauvaget, *Introduction à l'histoire de l'Orient musulman (M1),* which is excellent; Pareja Casañas, *Islamología (M22),* broader but less historical; and Philips, *Handbook of oriental history (M23).* For the period since 1450 see also the following.

S25. Barthold, Vasilii V. **La découverte de l'Asie: histoire de l'orientalisme en Europe et en Russie.** Tr. by B. Nikitine. Paris, 1947. Good bibliographies. European travel works and historical and literary studies covered by sections of Asia and time periods. Better on Iran than on Turkey and Arabs.

S26. Babinger, Franz. **Die Geschichtsschreiber der Osmanen und ihre Werke.** Leipzig, 1927. Contains 377 invaluable bio-bibliographical notices on Ottoman historians from 14th century to 1925; conversion tables, indices, rich notes. [HARe]

S27. Tahir, Mehmed. **Osmanlï müellifleri.** [Ottoman authors.] 3 v. Istanbul, 1914–25. Arranged by classes. Bibliographies often incomplete; good index.

Two great bio-bibliographical surveys, Brockelmann, *Geschichte der arabischen Litteratur (M18)* and Storey, *Persian literature (M19),* include historians and histories. Brockelmann is supplemented by

S28. Dāghir, Yūsuf As'ad (Joseph Assad Dagher). **Maṣādir al-dirāsāt al-adabīyah. Éléments de bio-bibliographie de la littérature arabe.** Sidon and Beirut, 1950 ff. V. 2, pt. 1 lists Arabic writers, including historians, deceased in the period 1800–1955, with good classification, indices, and explanatory text. Review, M. M. Moreno, *Oriente moderno,* 36 (July 1956): 470.

LIBRARIES AND ARCHIVES

In North America, among the best collections on history of the modern Middle East are those of the Library of Congress; New York Public Library; Cleveland Public Library; Boston Public Library; and the university libraries of Harvard, Princeton, Yale, Illinois, Stanford (Hoover), and McGill (Institute of Islamic Studies). In western Europe are many good and a number of outstanding collections in national, city, university, and institute libraries. In the Middle East, aside from a number of good historical collections in libraries of Morocco, Algiers, Tunisia, and Libya, the following libraries have useful historical materials in western (indicated by "w") and oriental (indicated by "o") languages: Cairo University (w, o); Egyptian National Library, Cairo (w, o); Institute of Coptic Studies, Cairo (o); University College, Khartoum (w); Tehran University (w, o); Majliss Library, Tehran (w, o); Imperial or Gulistan collection, Tehran (o); Museum of Antiquities, Baghdad (w); Awkaf collection, Baghdad (o); Zahriyah collection, Arab Academy, Damascus (o); American University, Beirut (w); University of St. Joseph, Beirut (w); Istanbul University (w, o); University of Ankara (w); and National Library, Ankara (w, o). For phases of Ottoman history the Gennadion Library, Athens is good. [RHD, RFO]

These and other libraries are surveyed in the following two volumes.

S29. Dagher, Joseph A. **Répertoire des bibliothèques du Proche et du Moyen-Orient.** Paris, 1951. Covers Arab countries, Israel, Iran, and Turkey, the latter sketchily. Brief descriptions of collections, hours and conditions of use.

S30. Türkiye kütüphaneleri rehberi. [Guide to libraries in Turkey.] Ankara, 1957. Excellent systematic guide with index. For brief survey see Lawrence S. Thompson, "Books in Turkey," *Middle eastern affairs,* 3 (June 1952): 171–80. [HARe]

Governmental archives in the Middle East are only now in process of arrangement and cataloging for scholarly use. The principal such treasuries of historical materials are in Istanbul and Cairo; Tehran is not so far advanced.

S31. Sertoğlu, Mitat. **Muhteva bakımından Başvekâlet Arşivi.** [The Başvekâlet Archive from the viewpoint of its holdings.] Ankara, 1955. Excellent introduction and guide to the vast central Ottoman government archives. Review, A. Tietze, *Oriens* 10 (1957): 302. See also Bernard Lewis, "The Ottoman archives, a source for European history," *Report on current research* (spring 1956): 17–23, and other descriptive articles cited therein. [HARe]

S32. Fekete, Lajos. **Die Siyāqat-Schrift in der türkischen Finanzverwaltung.** 2 v. Budapest, 1955. Compendious manual on the key script for Ottoman financial records, with many sample documents and critical notes. [HARe]

S33. Deny, Jean. **Sommaire des archives turques du Caire.** Cairo, 1930. Pioneer description of Ottoman archives in Cairo, with introduction on administration in Ottoman Egypt. May be supplemented by references in Sauvaget, *Introduction (M1),* pp. 166–67; and Stanford J. Shaw, "Cairo's archives and the history of Ottoman Egypt," *Report on current research* (spring 1956): 59–72. [HARe]

Many western archives are valuable for Near East history. See

S34. Davison, Roderic H. "European archives as a source for later Ottoman history." **Report on current research** (1958): 33–45.

ENCYCLOPEDIAS AND WORKS OF REFERENCE

S35. The encyclopaedia of Islam. See *F31.*

S36. Islâm ansiklopedisi. Istanbul, 1940 ff. Reliable Turkish translation of first edition of *Encyclopaedia of Islam (F31),* with revised and expanded materials on Turkish subjects. [HARe]

S37. Zambaur, Eduard K. M. von. **Manuel de généalogie.** See *M29.* Important for dynasties, ministers, and governors.

S38. Haig, Thomas W. **Comparative tables.** See *M30.* Conversion tables of Muslim and Christian dates.

S39. Unat, Faik R. **Hicrî tarihleri milâdî tarihe çevirme kılavuzu.** [Guide to conversion of Muslim to Christian dates.] 2nd ed., Ankara, 1943. Clear and accurate. [HARe]

S40. Süreyya, Mehmed. **Sicilli osmanî.** [Ottoman register.] 4 v. Constantinople

(Istanbul), 1895–96. Indispensable dictionary of political personages; some inaccuracies. [HARe]

S41. Gövsa, Ibrahim A. **Türk meşhurlarī ansiklopedisi.** [Encyclopedia of Turkish notables.] Istanbul, 1946. Uncritical but handy biographical dictionary, with emphasis on recent times; some errors.

S42. Zaydān, Jurjī. **Tarājim mashāhīr al-Sharq.** [Biographies of famous men of the East.] 3rd ed., 2 v. in 1, Cairo, 1922. Useful sketches of 19th century figures.

S43. Who's who in Egypt and the Near East. 23rd ed., N.Y., 1958. Useful for contemporaries, though spotty. [RFO]

S44. Royal Institute of International Affairs. **The Middle East: a political and economic survey.** Ed. by Sir Reader W. Bullard. 3rd ed., London, 1958. This and the two following are the most useful handbooks on the modern Near East, all with narrative background, statistics, and lists. For World War I and World War II periods British Admirality handbooks on various Near East countries are good. [HARe]

S45. The Middle East: a survey and directory. 5th ed., London, 1957.

S46. Annuaire du monde musulman. Ed. by Louis Massignon. 4th ed., Paris, 1955. Review, H. A. Reed, *Middle East jour.,* 11 (winter 1957): 98.

S47. Davis, Helen M. **Constitutions, electoral laws, treaties of states in the Near and Middle East.** 2nd ed., Durham, 1953. Convenient handbook to 1950. Review, A. A. Kampman, *Bibliotheca orientalis,* 12 (Mar. 1955): 55.

S48. Peaslee, Amos J., ed. **Constitutions of nations.** 2nd ed., 3 v., The Hague, 1956. Preferable to Davis for constitutions. Contains notes and bibliography. [RFO]

S49. Godchot, J. E. **Les constitutions du Proche et du Moyen Orient.** Paris, 1957. Somewhat more up to date than Davis, which Godchot relies on in part.

GEOGRAPHIES, GAZETTEERS, AND ATLASES

Some of the older works listed in the original *Guide,* such as Vivien de St. Martin, Ewald Banse, and Vital Cuinet, are useful. See also the following.

S50. Taeschner, Franz G. **Das anatolische Wegenetz nach osmanischen Quellen.** 2 v. Leipzig, 1924–26. Informative; based on oriental and western travelers. Describes routes and places; includes references. [HARe]

S51. Birot, Pierre, and Jean Dresch. **La Mediterranée et le Moyen-Orient.** V. 2. Paris, 1956. Outstanding. Covers the Balkans, Anatolia, and Arab area; best on rural economy, weak on oil.

S52. Blanchard, Raoul. **Asie occidentale.**

Paris, 1929. [Paul Vidal de La Blache, ed., Géographie universelle, 8.] Good, detailed, especially on physical geography.

S53. Fisher, William B. **The Middle East.** 3rd ed., London, 1956. Useful introduction; good on climate, spotty on human geography.

S54. Hogarth, David G. **The nearer East.** N.Y., 1915. Readable coverage of physical features, better for this than the above.

S55. Coon, Carleton S. **Caravan.** N.Y., 1951. Popular yet sound introduction to peoples of the area, combining geography and anthropology-sociology. Weak on Turkey.

S56. U. S. Office of Geography. **Jordan.** Washington, 1955. [Gazetteer no. 3.] This and the two following include place-names, variants, and references to maps. Continuing series to cover other Near East countries.

S57. ——. **Iran.** Washington, 1956. [Gazetteer no. 19.]

S58. ——. **Iraq.** Washington, 1957. [Gazetteer no. 37.]

S59. Great Britain. Army, Survey Directorate. **Turkey: index gazetteer.** 5 v. Fayid, 1948. One of a useful series including volumes on Palestine, Arabia, Iran, Syria, Cyprus, and Transjordan.

S60. Iran. Setād-e Artesh, Dāyere-ye Joghrāfiyāī. **Farhang-e joghrāfiyā'i-ye Īrān.** [Geographical dictionary of Iran.] 10 v. Tehran, 1949–54. Planned to survey all Iran, listing communities large and small with local population, climate, religion, language, products. Prepared by geographical section of the Iranian army general staff. [RFO]

S61. Hazard, Harry W., and Hereward L. Cooke. **Atlas of Islamic history.** See *M39.*

S62. Roolvink, Roelof, and others. **Historical atlas of the Muslim peoples.** Cambridge, Mass., 1958. Chiefly political, some sociocultural maps.

For a guide to modern maps see Etting-hausen, *A selected and annotated bibliography (M5),* supplement, pp. 113–19.

GENERAL HISTORIES

No comprehensive history of the Middle East since 1450 exists. Sketchy broad coverage occurs in various universal histories. There is also no satisfactory short history. Best brief historical introductions are the following.

S63. Brockelmann, Carl. **History of the Islamic peoples.** N.Y., 1947. Most comprehensive short history, half since 1450. Concentrates on political detail; congested.

S64. Kirk, George E. **A short history of the Middle East.** 4th ed., N.Y., 1957. Concentrates on post-1800 period; spotty.

S65. Stavrianos, Leften S. **The Balkans since 1453.** N.Y., 1958. Unlike the two preceding works, emphasizes Ottoman Europe. Supersedes Schevill, *History of the Balkan*

peninsula (W26) for this period. Extensive bibliography, useful for Ottoman empire to 1918.

OTTOMAN EMPIRE

General

S66. Hammer-Purgstall, Joseph von. **Geschichte des osmanischen Reiches.** 10 v. Pest (Budapest), 1827–35. 2nd ed., 4 v., 1834–36. Still the basic history for 1300–1774, with parts extending to 1826. Based on oriental sources, sometimes uncritically used. French translation by J. J. Hellert, *Histoire de l'empire ottoman* (18 v., Paris, 1835–43) useful, especially its atlas, but contains many errors and omits notes. [HARe]

S67. Zinkeisen, Johann W. **Geschichte des osmanischen Reiches in Europa.** 8 v. Hamburg, 1840–63. Excellent use of western sources. Concentrates on Europe and foreign relations to 1812. [HARe]

S68. Iorga, Nicolae. **Geschichte des osmanischen Reiches.** 5 v. Gotha, 1908–13. Useful especially for Balkans and Christian minorities. V. 5 covers 1774–1912.

S69. Creasy, Edward S. **History of the Ottoman Turks.** Rev. ed., London, 1877. Other eds. This and the two following works largely condense Hammer, with additions. Creasy stops essentially with 1839; later editions (to 1939) add nothing of particular value. [HARe]

S70. Eversley, George J. S., and Valentine Chirol. **The Turkish empire from 1288.** 2nd ed., London, 1923. Extends to 1922.

S71. La Jonquière, A. de. **Histoire de l'empire ottoman.** 2nd ed., 2 v., Paris, 1914. Fullest on 1908–1913.

S72. Mustafa Nuri (Paşa). **Netayic ül vukuat.** [The consequences of events.] 4 v. Constantinople (Istanbul), 1877–1909. Perceptive review and analysis of Ottoman history to 1841, using official documents and published Ottoman materials. [HARe]

S73. Alderson, Anthony D. **The structure of the Ottoman dynasty.** Oxford, 1956. Genealogies, elaborate tables, and synthesis of materials on succession, marriage, harem, fratricide, etc. Review, R. H. Davison, *Am. hist. rev.,* 62 (Jan. 1957): 365.

S74. Danişmend, Ismail H. **Izahlī osmanli tarihi kronolojisi.** [Explanatory chronology of Ottoman history.] 4 v. Istanbul, 1947–55. Uncritical, spotty, but useful. Substantial notes or quotations on significant events, 1258–1924. [HARe]

S75. Gibb, Hamilton A. R., and Harold Bowen. **Islamic society and the West.** V. 1, **Islamic society in the eighteenth century.** 2 pts. London, 1950–57. Best modern description of Ottoman governmental and religious institutions; concentrates on decline from apogee.

S76. Lybyer, Albert H. **The government of the Ottoman empire in the time of Suleiman the Magnificent.** Cambridge, Mass., 1913. Pioneer and still valuable study, illuminating the slave element in government of the empire. Bibliography good on western sources. [HARe]

S77. Hammer-Purgstall, Joseph von. **Des osmanischen Reiches Staatsverfassung und Staatsverwaltung.** 2 v. Vienna, 1815. Though superseded in part by *S75*, this and the following are still valuable descriptions of Ottoman institutions. [HARe]

S78. Mouradgea d'Ohsson, Ignatius. **Tableau général de l'empire othoman.** 7 v. Paris, 1788–1824.

S79. Barkan, Ömer L. **XV. ve XVI. inci asïrlarda osmanlï imparatorluğunda ziraî ekonominin hukukî ve malî esaslari. V. 1, Kanunlar.** [The legal and financial bases of agricultural economy in the Ottoman empire in the 15th and 16th centuries. V. 1, Laws.] Istanbul, 1945. Basic compilation from archives of organic regulations on Ottoman provincial administration. [HARe]

S80. Uzunçarşïlï, Ismail H. **Osmanlï devletinin saray teşkilâtï.** [Organization of the palace in the Ottoman state.] Ankara, 1945. This and the two following are fundamental source books, based on Ottoman archives, on inner organization of the Ottoman imperial household, central administration and navy, and slave household including Janissaries. Together with Barkan, contain material for revision of western accounts. [HARe]

S81. ——. **Osmanlï devletinin merkez ve bahriye teşkilâtï.** [Organization of the central administration and navy in the Ottoman state.] Ankara, 1948.

S82. ——. **Osmanlï devleti teşkilatïndan kapukulu ocaklarï.** [The slave troops of the Ottoman state organization.] 2 v. Ankara, 1943–44.

S83. Djevad, Ahmed. **État militaire ottoman. V. 1, bk. 1, Le corps des Janissaires depuis sa fondation jusqu'à se suppression.** Constantinople (Istanbul), 1882. This and *S84* are good studies of the military, especially Janissaries. [HARe]

S84. Marsigli, Luigi F. **L'état militaire de l'empire ottoman.** The Hague, 1732. French and Italian texts. [HARe]

S85. Miller, Barnette. **The palace school of Muhammad the Conqueror.** Cambridge, Mass., 1941. Good study on training of slave officials in the sultan's household. Enlarges on chapter in the following.

S86. ——. **Beyond the Sublime Porte.** New Haven, 1931. Study of the palace as a whole.

S87. Adïvar, Abdülhak A. **La science chez les Turcs ottomans.** Paris, 1939. Expert review of Ottoman scientific thought from 14th to early 19th centuries. Enlarged 2nd ed. in Turkish, *Osmanlï türklerinde ilim* (Istanbul, 1943). [HARe]

S88. Ergin, Osman. **Türkiye maarif tarihi.** [History of education in Turkey.] 5 v. Istanbul, 1939–43. Most comprehensive history of Turkish education; rich documentation. Covers Ottoman era and republican Turkey to 1939. [HARe]

S89. Bombaci, Alessio. **Storia della letteratura turca dall'antico impero di Mongolia all'odierna Turchia.** Milan, 1956. Good broad history of literature of Turkish peoples; sections on Ottoman period and modern Turkey. Gives historical and religious context. Bibliography.

S90. Gibb, Elias J. W. **A history of Ottoman poetry.** 6 v. London, 1900–09. Excellent; covers to late 19th century, replete with verse translations. V. 1 contains valuable introductory essay on Ottoman literature; v. 6, original texts. [HARe]

S91. Birge, John K. **The Bektashi order of dervishes.** London, 1937. Reliable, perceptive study of the famous syncretistic, liberal order long affiliated with the Janissaries. [HARe]

S92. Hasluck, Frederick W. **Christianity and Islam under the sultans.** 2 v. Oxford, 1929. Rich data on interplay of Christianity and Islam. Western sources supplemented by field study; good bibliography. [HARe]

There are many valuable monographs on aspects of Ottoman foreign relations, some listed in the subsections below, especially under "Eastern Question." Most spring from European viewpoints. The general Ottoman histories contribute much on this subject. A good many helpful printed source collections exist. See Venetian and French collections listed by Birge and Sauvaget (cited above) for earlier periods, and bibliographies of works on the eastern question for later periods.

S93. Testa, Ignaz von, ed. **Recueil des traités de la Porte ottomane.** 11 v. Paris, 1864–1911. This and the following are the two best collections, containing many documents other than treaties.

S94. Noradounghian, Gabriel, ed. **Recueil d'actes internationaux de l'empire ottoman.** 4 v. Paris, 1897–1903.

S95. Sousa, Nasim. **The capitulatory régime of Turkey.** Baltimore, 1933. Good survey of this aspect of foreign relations, 1535–1923, with many references.

S96. Masson, Paul. **Histoire du commerce français dans le Levant au XVIIe siècle.** Paris, 1896. This and the two following are sound surveys of phases of Ottoman-European commercial relations, based on archival sources. Masson is more detailed.

S97. ——. **Histoire du commerce français dans le Levant au XVIIIe siècle.** Paris, 1911.

S98. Wood, Alfred C. **A history of the Levant Company.** London, 1935.

S99. Adamov, Evgenii A., ed. **Die europäischen Mächte und die Türkei während des Weltkrieges.** 6 v. Dresden, 1930–32. Important for 1914–17, and for some aspects of earlier years, on Constantinople, Straits, Anatolia, and Greece. Documents with introductions, translated from Russian.

1450–1566

S100. Uzunçarşīlī, Ismail H. **Osmanlī tarihi.** [Ottoman history.] V. 2. Ankara, 1949. Detailed on 1453–1566. Incorporates some results of recent research.

S101. Babinger, Franz. **Maometto il Conquistatore e il suo tempo.** Turin, 1957. Now the best introduction to period of Mohammed the Conqueror. Italian edition, somewhat revised, preferable to original German edition (Munich, 1953). French ed., 1954. See reviews of German ed. by G. Jäschke, *Die Welt des Islams,* n.s. 3 (1954), 300; E. Rossi, *Oriente moderno,* 33 (Oct. 1953), 431; P. Wittek, *Bibliotheca orientalis,* 14 (1957), 262.

S102. Pears, Edwin. **The destruction of the Greek empire.** London, 1903. Useful for detail, but somewhat Grecophil. Largely superseded by Babinger.

S103. Schlumberger, Gustave. **Le siège, la prise et le sac de Constantinople par les Turcs en 1453.** Paris, 1914. Both this and the above list sources.

S104. Fisher, Sydney N. **The foreign relations of Turkey, 1481–1512.** Urbana, Ill., 1948. Straightforward monograph on important period of Prince Jem's captivity in Europe; war with Venice, 1499–1503; and Persian threats. [HARe]

S105. Busbecq, Ogier G. de. **Turkish letters.** Oxford, 1927. Keen observations of the ambassador of Charles V to Suleiman, 1554–62, when the Ottoman empire was at its peak. See also Lybyer (*S76*). [HARe]

1566–1789

S106. Knolles, Richard. **Generall historie of the Turkes.** London, 1603. Many later eds.; title varies. 6th ed., *The Turkish history,* 3 v., 1687–1700.

S107. Rycaut, Paul. **The history of the Turkish empire from the year 1623 to the year 1677.** London, 1687. [Knolles, The Turkish history, v. 2, pt. 2.] Rycaut, British consul in Smyrna, 1660–77, continues Knolles. Antiquated, but useful for 17th century and author's first-hand information.

S108. ———. **The present state of the Ottoman empire.** London, 1687. [The Turkish history, v. 2, pt. 3.] Useful picture of Ottoman civil, religious, and military organization.

S109. Naima, Mustafa. **Tarih.** [History.] 2nd ed., 6 v., Constantinople (Istanbul),

1863. By one of the best official Ottoman historiographers. Covers 1592–1659. Partial translation by Charles Fraser in *Annals of the Turkish empire* (London, 1832).

S110. Mehmed Pasha. **Ottoman statecraft.** Ed. and tr. by Walter L. Wright, Jr. Princeton, 1935. Introduction provides good brief survey of Ottoman government. Mehmed Pasha's work should be supplemented by others referred to in Wright's introduction. See also Gibb and Bowen (*S75*). [HARe]

S111. Evliyá Efendi, Mehmed. **Narrative of travels in Europe, Asia, and Africa in the seventeenth century.** Tr. by Joseph von Hammer. 2 v. in 3. London, 1834–50. Translation of first two volumes of an observant Turkish traveler's account, covering Constantinople, Anatolia, and the Caucasus. Selections are also found in Alexander A. Pallis, *In the days of the Janissaries* (London, 1951). [HARe]

S112. Montagu, Mary W. **Letters.** London, 1934. Also earlier eds. Shrewd observations on Constantinople, harem life, and other subjects by wife of the British ambassador, 1717–18. [HARe]

1789–1878

S113. Sax, Carl, Ritter von. **Geschichte des Machtverfalls der Türkei.** 2nd ed., Vienna, 1913. Still the best single general history, though largely political and diplomatic, covering essentially 1768–1913.

S114. Cevdet Paşa, Ahmet. **Tarih.** [History.] 3rd ed., 12 v., Constantinople (Istanbul), 1891. Brilliant, reliable Ottoman history, 1774–1826. V. 1 contains valuable introduction to earlier period. [HARe]

S115. Caussin de Perceval, Armand P. **Précis historique de la destruction du corps des Janissaires.** Paris, 1833. Abridged translation of the contemporary official historiographer Mehmed Es'ad efendi's eyewitness account of the 1826 event. [HARe]

S116. Rosen, Georg. **Geschichte der Türkei von dem Siege der Reform im Jahre 1826 bis zum Pariser Tractat vom Jahre 1856.** 2 v. Leipzig, 1866–67. Sound account by a scholar and orientalist-diplomat of the period.

S117. Engelhardt, Edouard. **La Turquie et le Tanzimat.** 2 v. Paris, 1882–84. Despite errors of detail and a European-Christian view, still the best, along with Rosen, on the reform period of the 19th century, and unique for 1856–78.

S118. Tanzimat. Istanbul, 1940. Collection of uneven but often valuable studies in Turkish on aspects of the 19th century reform period.

S119. Ubicini, J. H. Abdolonyme. **Letters on Turkey.** 2 v. London, 1856. Good general description of the empire at mid-century. V. 1 on Turks; v. 2 on Christians and Jews.

S120. Ubicini, J. H. Abdolonyme, and J. B. Pavet de Courteille. **État présent de l'empire ottoman.** Paris, 1876. Good picture of official organization of the empire as of 1875, based on the governmental yearbook (*Salnâmèh*) for 1875–76.

S121. Mordtmann, Andreas D. **Stambul und das moderne Türkenthum.** 2 v. Leipzig, 1877–78. Excellent pictures of Ottoman life and politics in 1860's and 70's, with biographical sketches of leading figures. Disjointed because based on newspaper articles by the author.

S122. Aristarchi, Grégoire, comp. **Législation ottomane.** 7 v. Constantinople, 1873–88.

S123. Young, Sir George. **Corps de droit ottoman.** 7 v. Oxford, 1905–06. Standard French translations of Ottoman codes and regulations of 19th century, including civil code. Duplicates *S122* only partly.

S124. Jäschke, Gotthard. "Türkische Gesetzsammlungen." **Die Welt des Islams,** n.s. 3 (1954): 225–34. Valuable survey of laws into the republican period. [HARe]

S125. Heidborn, A. **Manuel de droit public et administratif de l'empire ottoman.** 2 v. in 4. Vienna, 1908–12. Systematic study with historical background. V. 2 discusses finances.

S126. Du Velay, A. **L'histoire financière de la Turquie.** Paris, 1903. Consecutive study of a major Ottoman problem from 1839 on; much on foreign debt.

1878–1918

S127. Eliot, Sir Charles N. E. **Turkey in Europe.** 2nd ed., London, 1908. Informed picture of peoples and conditions in European Turkey about 1900; humorous and critical.

S128. Fesch, Paul. **Constantinople aux derniers jours d'Abdul-Hamid.** Paris, 1907. Contains a wealth of information on the empire of this period, with some retrospective sections.

S129. Ramsaur, Ernest E., Jr. **The Young Turks: prelude to the revolution of 1908.** Princeton, 1957. Systematic study of the revolutionary movement in Turkey and abroad, 1889–1908; good bibliography for this period. Review, R. H. Davison, *Am. hist. rev.,* 63 (Oct. 1957): 217. [HARe]

S130. Heyd, Uriel. **Foundations of Turkish nationalism: the life and teachings of Ziya Gökalp.** London, 1950. Best available English study of Turkey's most influential 20th century thinker. Review, J. K. Birge, *Middle East jour.,* 4 (July 1950): 367. [HARe]

S131. Tunaya, Tarik Z. **Türkiye' de siyasî partiler, 1859–1952.** [Political parties in Turkey, 1859–1952.] Istanbul, 1952. Monumental; superlative Turkish documentation, with data from numerous personal inter-

views. Replete with lists of party officers and texts of programs set in interpretive historical framework. [HARe]

S132. Larcher, Maurice. **La guerre turque dans la Guerre Mondiale.** Paris, 1926. Broad but methodical survey of war on all Ottoman fronts, with tables and maps. Bibliography.

S133. [Yalman], Ahmed Emin. **Turkey in the World War.** New Haven, 1930. Best general description of the internal economic, social, and political situation of the empire, 1914–18. [HARe]

TURKISH REPUBLIC

S134. Lewis, Geoffrey L. **Turkey.** N.Y., 1955. This and the following are the two best concise introductions to modern Turkey, with some historical background.

S135. Thomas, Lewis V., and Richard N. Frye. **The United States and Turkey and Iran.** Cambridge, Mass., 1951. Mostly on Turkey.

S136. Jäschke, Gotthard. **Die Türkei . . . : Geschichtskalender, 1918–1951.** 8 pts. Berlin, Leipzig, Wiesbaden, 1929–55. (Title varies.) Fundamental, annotated chronology of Turkish affairs since 1918. Published serially and irregularly in various periodicals, and separately in part. For complete list see review of latest section (1942–51), H. A. Reed, *Middle East jour.,* 9 (autumn 1955): 459. [HARe]

S137. Ziemke, Kurt. **Die neue Türkei: politische Entwicklung, 1914–1929.** Stuttgart, 1930. Best political study for these years. Much on diplomacy, especially on 1918–23; anti-Allies. Good bibliography of western materials. See also Howard, *The partition of Turkey* (*S274*).

S138. Toynbee, Arnold J. **The western question in Greece and Turkey.** See *W1193*.

S139. Mears, Eliot G., and others. **Modern Turkey: a politico-economic interpretation, 1908–1923.** N.Y., 1924. Informative survey of the shift from sprawling empire to homogeneous, revitalized republic. Extensive bibliography, chronology, and documents. [HARe]

S140. Kemal, Mustapha. **A speech delivered by Ghazi Mustapha Kemal . . . October, 1927.** Leipzig, 1929. Brilliant self-justification of Kemal's policies in war of independence and establishment of republic; essentially on 1919–23. Includes documents. Turkish and German eds. (2 v., Ankara, 1927 and later; 3 v., Leipzig, 1927) contain additional documents in separate volumes. Supplement with other works, especially "Atatürk," *Islâm ansiklopedisi,* 1:719–807. [HARe]

S141. Adïvar, Halide Edib. **Turkey faces west.** New Haven, 1930. This and the following are thoughtful accounts of 19th and 20th century modernization trends by

Turkey's great woman patriot, professor, and novelist. [HARe]

S142. ——. **Conflict of East and West in Turkey.** Lahore, 1935.

S143. Webster, Donald E. **The Turkey of Atatürk: social process in the Turkish reformation.**. Philadelphia, 1939. Informed review of Atatürk era by a sympathetic sociologist. [HARe]

S144. Ostrorog, Léon. **The Angora reform.** London, 1927. Three masterful essays on Ottoman Muslim law, the introduction of western (especially civil) law, and the psychological-religious environment. [HARe]

S145. Jäschke, Gotthard. **Der Islam in der neuen Türkei: eine rechtsgeschichtliche Untersuchung.** Leiden, 1951. Indispensable study of the legal and formal aspects of Turkish religious development in first half of the 20th century.

S146. Frye, Richard N., ed. **Islam and the West.** The Hague, 1956. Contains three excellent, documented essays on Islam in modern Turkey and background of secularizing trends in Ottoman era. Review, W. C. Smith, *Middle East jour.*, 11 (autumn 1957): 437.

IRAN

General

S147. Sykes, Percy M. **A history of Persia.** V. 2. 3rd ed., London, 1930. Reprint, 1951. The only detailed, consecutive history; by an old-school representative of British empire. Largely political, diplomatic, and military; fullest on World War I.

S148. Frye, Richard N. **Iran.** N.Y., 1953. This and *S149–151* are useful introductions to Iran. The first three contain summaries of history; all concentrate on modern Iran.

S149. Wilber, Donald N. **Iran, past and present.** 4th ed., Princeton, 1958.

S150. Haas, William S. **Iran.** N.Y., 1946.

S151. Wilson, Sir Arnold T. **Persia.** London, 1932.

S152. Browne, Edward G. **A literary history of Persia.** V. 4, A history of Persian literature in modern times (A.D. 1500–1924). Cambridge, Eng., 1924. Reprint, 1953. Basic literary history, reflecting culture and politics.

S153. Pope, Arthur U., ed. **A survey of Persian art from prehistoric times to the present.** See *F221*.

1450–1906

Scholarly books on Iran from the Safavid through the Qajar periods are few. Iran in these centuries may be approached from articles in the learned journals and encyclopedias, European diplomatic and commercial studies and documents, works on India and empire, Ottoman histories, and the many accounts by European travelers and residents in Iran. Recommended are accounts by John Chardin, Thomas Herbert, Jean B. Tavernier, Pietro della Valle, and *A chronicle of the Carmelites* (all on 17th century); Jonas Hanway (18th century); and many in the 19th century, especially the works of James Morier and E. G. Browne. These and other travel accounts may be located in bibliographies by Elwell-Sutton (*S12*), Ettinghausen (*M5*), Barthold (*S25*), and Wilson (*S11*). See also the following.

S154. Gabriel, Alfons. **Die Erforschung Persiens.** Vienna, 1952.

S155. Petrov, Mikhail P. **Bibliografiia po geografii Irana . . . 1720–1954.** Ashkhabad, 1955. Both this and the above focus on geography, but include many travel accounts. Gabriel is more general and descriptive; Petrov lists only works published in Russian.

S156. Hinz, Walther. **Irans Aufstieg zum Nationalstaat im fünfzehnten Jahrhundert.** Berlin, 1936. Solid, scholarly, yet readable account of Uzun Hasan and the rise of the Safavis, concentrating on 1447–99. Fine bibliography, useful chronology.

S157. Minorsky, Vladimir F., tr. and ed. **Tadhkirat al-mulūk: a manual of Ṣafavid administration.** London, 1943. Describes Iran's administration in early 18th century, with valuable introduction, appendices, and further references by Minorsky.

S158. Lockhart, Laurence. **The fall of the Ṣafavī dynasty and the Afghan occupation of Persia.** Cambridge, Eng., 1958. Examines in detail turbulent events within Iran and complex external relations, 1694–1730. Good bibliography.

S159. ——. **Nadir Shah.** London, 1938. Detailed factual study of this fantastic neo-Tamerlane to his death in 1747. Best available work on the period; good bibliography.

S160. Bahrami, Bahram. **Les relations politiques de la Perse avec les grandes puissances à l'époque des Kadjars.** Montreux, 1953. Useful short summary. [BGM]

S161. Taymuri, Ibrahim. **'Asr-i bīkhabarī: ya tā'rīkh-i imtiāzāt dar Irān.** [An era of ignorance: or the history of concessions in Iran.] Tehran, 1953. Good account of British and Russian efforts to control banks, mines, roads, railways, fisheries, etc., to about 1900. [BGM]

S162. Litten, Wilhelm. **Persien von der "pénétration pacifique" zum "Protektorat" . . . 1860–1919.** Berlin, 1920. Useful though partly outdated survey of European economic penetration; includes documents not easily available elsewhere. [FK]

S163. Curzon, George N. **Persia and the Persian question.** 2 v. London, 1892. Tremendous compendium of information on the regions, economy, and politics of Iran as of 1890; imperialist viewpoint. Useful bibliography of travel accounts.

S164. Nabil-i-A'zam. **The dawn-breakers.** N.Y., 1932. Excellent translation of best history of Babi movement, by a follower, with good notes, bibliography, and genealogies. [FK]

S165. Browne, Edward G. **The press and poetry of modern Persia.** Cambridge, Eng., 1914. Detailed on later 19th and early 20th centuries; much on Babis.

Since 1906

S166. Browne, Edward G. **The Persian revolution of 1905–1909.** Cambridge, Eng., 1910. Covers in detail origins and events; sympathetic to the revolution. Contains many documents.

S167. Kasravī, Aḥmad. **Tārīkh-e mashrūteh-e Irān.** [History of the constitution of Iran.] 3 v. Tehran, 1940–43. Best work on this subject, by a participant with strong views who did authentic scholarly work. [BGM and FK]

S168. Malekzādeh, Mehdi. **Tā'rīkh-i inqilāb mashrūtiyet-i Irān.** [History of the revolution and constitutionalism in Iran.] Tehran, 1949 ff. By the son of a leader in the constitutional movement. Some bias, but perhaps the most objective and sober history of the revolution. [FK]

S169. Shuster, William M. **The strangling of Persia.** N.Y., 1912. Personal account by U. S. adviser to Iranian government on complications in 1911 stemming from Anglo-Russian competition.

S170. Balfour, James M. **Recent happenings in Persia.** Edinburgh, 1922. Slanted personal account, by a British adviser, on events 1918–21, but still very useful.

S171. Elwell-Sutton, Laurence P. **Modern Iran.** London, 1941. Concentrates on Reza Shah's regime.

S172. Lenczowski, George. **Russia and the West in Iran, 1918–1948.** Ithaca, N.Y., 1949. Sound study, half on 1939–48. Reviews, *London times literary supplement*, 49 (Aug. 11, 1950): 504; E. M. Wright, *Middle East jour.*, 3 (Oct. 1949): 478.

ARAB HISTORY, GENERAL

There are no general histories of the Arabs since 1450. Hitti, *History of the Arabs* (*M91*) and Lewis, *The Arabs in history* (*M92*) devote few pages to the Arabs in their decline and modern renaissance. See the pertinent sections in Gibb and Bowen, *Islamic society* (*S75*). The same variety of peripheral sources mentioned for Iran will offer some information.

S173. Antonius, George. **The Arab awakening.** London, 1946. Only comprehensive history of the Arab nationalist movement, but a work of propaganda rather than pure scholarship. Should be read in conjunction with the following two pioneer, fundamental contributions on Arab nationalist thought. [CED]

S174. Haim, Sylvia. "Intorno alle origini della teoria del panarabismo." **Oriente moderno,** 36 (July 1956): 409–21.

S175. ——. "Islam and the theory of Arab nationalism." **Die Welt des Islams,** n.s. 4 (1955): 124–49.

S176. Sa'īd, Amīn. **Al-thawrah al-'arabiyah al-kubra.** [The great Arab revolt.] 3 v. Cairo, 1930–34. Best treatment of Arab nationalist politics, 1908–28, with many documents and information from interviews. [CED]

SYRIA AND LEBANON

S177. Lammens, Henri. **La Syrie, précis historique.** 2 v. Beirut, 1921. Standard work; French view toward end. V. 2 covers period from the Mamluks to 1921. [CED]

S178. Hitti, Philip K. **Lebanon in history.** N.Y., 1957. More useful than his *History of Syria* (N.Y., 1951), since somewhat fuller on period after Ottoman conquest. Review, C. G. Anthon, *Jour. mod. hist.*, 30 (June 1958): 142.

S179. Ismail, Adel. **Histoire du Liban du XVIIᵉ siècle à nos jours. V. 1, Le Liban au temps de Fakhr-ed-din II (1590–1633).** Paris, 1955. Most recent study of the Druze ruler, using some new material. See also references in *Encyclopaedia of Islam* (1st ed.), v. 2, p. 45.

S180. Volney, Constantin F. C. **Voyages en Syrie et en Égypte.** 2nd ed., 2 v., Paris, 1787. Tr., *Travels through Egypt and Syria*, 2 v., N.Y., 1798. This and the following are two of the best travel accounts, describing conditions in late 18th and early 19th centuries, before western penetration. [CED]

S181. Burckhardt, John L. **Travels in Syria and the Holy Land.** London, 1822.

S182. Churchill, Charles H. **The Druzes and the Maronites under Turkish rule, from 1840 to 1860.** London, 1862. Useful account of a subject which still needs scholarly treatment. [CED]

S183. Bell, Gertrude L. **Syria: the desert and the sown.** N.Y., 1907. Informative account of a trip in 1905 which ranks with those of Volney and Burckhardt. [CED]

S184. Hourani, Albert H. **Syria and Lebanon.** London, 1946. Interpretative essay on history and contemporary problems from the westernizing, moderate Arab nationalist point of view. [CED]

S185. Ziadeh, Nicola A. **Syria and Lebanon.** N.Y., 1957. Complements Hourani for developments since 1945. Review, E. Salem, *Middle East jour.*, 11 (autumn 1957): 445.

S186. Rondot, Pierre. **Les institutions politiques du Liban.** Paris, 1947. Scholarly study of the legal status of religious communities in the Lebanese republic. [CED]

S187. Gontaut-Biron, Roger de. **Comment la France s'est installée en Syrie (1918–1919).** Paris, 1923. Memoir by a French official of events preceding the French occupation; anti-British. [CED]

S188. MacCallum, Elizabeth P. **The nationalist crusade in Syria.** N.Y., 1928. A nonpartisan survey of the Syrian revolt of 1925–28, but does not go beyond the claims of the two parties. [CED]

JORDAN

In the absence of sound works exclusively on Jordanian history, information must be sought elsewhere, as in general works on the Ottoman empire, Arabs, tribes; in journal articles; and in the biographies and memoirs of Abdullah, Glubb, Peake, and Kirkbride cited below.

PALESTINE, 1918–1948

S189. Esco Foundation for Palestine. **Palestine: a study of Jewish, Arab, and British policies.** 2 v. New Haven, 1947. Detailed pro-Zionist, unemotional survey from Zionist origins in the 19th century through World War II. Part to 1936 is best. Inclusive bibliography. [JCH]

S190. Royal Commission on Palestine. **Palestine Royal Commission report.** London, 1937. The Peel report. Fairly and frankly explains Arab and Jewish interests in Palestine, origins and operation of the mandate, and evaluates the interplay of conflicting forces to the outbreak of the Palestine Arab revolt in 1936. [JCH]

S191. Hanna, Paul L. **British policy in Palestine.** Washington, 1942. Solid, detached inquiry into policies on Palestine, 1914–39, of the London government and of the regimes in the area itself. Useful bibliography. [JCH]

S192. Frischwasser-Ra'anan, Heinz F. **The frontiers of a nation.** London, 1955. Succinct but reliable investigation into the economic, military, and political forces that helped shape Palestine's boundaries, essentially 1906–25. [JCH]

S193. Shim'oni, Ya'aqov. **'Arvei Erets-Yisrael.** [The Arabs of Palestine.] Tel-Aviv, 1947. Invaluable reference work on the social, political, religious, and institutional organization of the Palestine Arab community under mandate. [JCH]

S194. Hurewitz, Jacob C. **The struggle for Palestine.** N.Y., 1950. Scholarly study on 1936–48, examining Arab and Jewish politics and great-power policies; little on the Arab-Israeli war. Good notes and bibliography. Review, R. H. Davison, *Am. hist. rev.,* 57 (Oct. 1951): 101.

S195. Alami, Musa. **'Ibrat Falastin.** [The lesson of Palestine.] Beirut, 1949. Partial translation and summarization in *Middle East journal,* 3 (Oct. 1949): 373–405. This and the following work are thoughtful, critical analyses, by western-trained Arabs, of the causes and implications of Arab defeat by Israelis. [JCH]

S196. Zurayk, Constantine. **Ma'na al-nakbah.** Beirut, 1948. Tr., by R. Bayly Winder, *The meaning of the disaster,* Beirut, 1956. Review, C. Hourani, *Middle East jour.,* 3 (Oct. 1949): 469.

ZIONISM AND ISRAEL

S197. Ben-Zvi, Ishak. **Eretz-Yisrael ve-Yishuva bi-yemē ha-shilton ha-'ottomani.** [Palestine and its settlement during Ottoman rule.] Jerusalem, 1955. Illuminating and documented study on Turkish rule and Jewish settlements 1516–1880.

S198. Böhm, Adolf. **Die zionistische Bewegung.** 2 v. Berlin and Jerusalem, 1935–37. The Zionist organization, rather than the movement, receives detailed consideration. [JCH]

S199. Cohen, Israel. **The Zionist movement.** Rev. ed., N.Y., 1946. Brief, readable statement, through 1945. First published London, 1945; minor revisions in the U. S. edition plus concluding chapter on Zionism in the United States. [JCH]

S200. Buber, Martin. **Israel and Palestine: the history of an idea.** London, 1952. Reflective appraisal, not on political enterprise, but on the spiritual history of Zionist belief from Biblical times on. [JCH]

S201. Gelber, Natan M. **Hatsharat-Balfur we-toldoteha.** [The Balfour declaration and its history.] Jerusalem, 1939. Study of Zionist negotiations with the British government in World War I, and related exchanges with Britain's allies and parallel negotiations with the Central Powers; based primarily on Zionist archives in Jerusalem. [JCH]

S202. Ben-Gurion, David. **Rebirth and destiny of Israel.** Tr. by Mordekhai Nurock. N.Y., 1954. Speeches and essays spanning 1915 to 1952, but concentrating on the war for independence and on statehood, which illuminate the unfolding views of Israel's first prime minister. [JCH]

S203. Bernstein, Marver H. **The politics of Israel: the first decade of statehood.** Princeton, 1957. Scholarly, dispassionate study of Israel's government, politics, and economy, omitting military and foreign policy.

ARAB-ISRAELI DISPUTE, 1948–

S204. Peretz, Don. **Israel and the Palestine Arabs.** Washington, 1958. Detached, comprehensive analysis of Israel's evolving policies toward its own Arab minority and toward complex of issues that formed the Arab refugee problem. See also Fred C. Bruhns, "A study of Arab refugee attitudes," *Middle East journal*, 9 (spring 1955): 130–38. [JCH]

S205. Rosenne, Shabtai. **Israel's armistice agreements with the Arab states: a juridical interpretation.** Tel Aviv, 1951. Legal analysis of the Arab-Israel armistice system, by a legal adviser to the Israeli foreign ministry. Unemotional, but shows greater understanding of the Israeli than the Arab position. [JCH]

S206. Hutchison, Elmo H. **Violent truce: a military observer looks at the Arab-Israeli conflict, 1951–1955.** N.Y., 1956. Author relates his experiences while attached to the Israel-Jordan Mixed Armistice Commission. Basically sympathetic to the Jordanian viewpoint. [JCH]

S207. Baly, Denis. **Multitudes in the valley.** Greenwich, Conn., 1957. Acute reflections on the Arab-Israeli scene, origins, and attitudes, informed by Christian theology and a realistic assessment of the complexities.

IRAQ

S208. Longrigg, Stephen H. **Four centuries of modern Iraq.** Oxford, 1925. Best history from the Ottoman conquest to about 1900; good bibliography of oriental and western sources.

S209. ———. **Iraq, 1900 to 1950: a political, social, and economic history.** N.Y. and London, 1953. Comprehensive supplement to his earlier history, by an expert British civil servant. Good bibliography. [HARe]

S210. Gollancz, Hermann, ed. **Chronicle of . . . the Order of Carmelites in Mesopotamia.** London, 1927. Very good account of economic, social, and political conditions in Basrah and surrounding territories, 1623–1733. Interesting description of Ottoman administration and law enforcement. [ZJ]

S211. Ireland, Philip W. **Iraq: a study in political development.** London, 1937. Sound work, covering 1914 to end of mandate in 1932; extensive bibliography.

S212. Khadduri, Majid. **Independent Iraq: a study of Iraqi politics since 1932.** London, 1951. Like *S211*, more narrowly political than Longrigg. Concentrates on 1932–41. Review, E. A. Speiser, *Middle East jour.*, 6 (summer 1952): 351.

PERSIAN GULF AND ARABIAN COASTS

S213. Wilson, Sir Arnold T. **The Persian Gulf, an historical sketch.** Oxford, 1928. Reprint, London, 1954. A versatile reference work, substantially annotated; good bibliography. Though dated, no comprehensive replacement has yet appeared. [JCH]

S214. Aitchison, Charles U., comp. **A collection of treaties, engagements and sanads relating to India and neighbouring countries.** V. 11 and 13. 5th ed., Calcutta, 1933. [11, *Aden and the south western coast of Arabia, the Arab principalities in the Persian Gulf, Muscat (Oman), Baluchistan and the north-west frontier province;* 13, *Persia and Afghanistan.*] Contains most instruments negotiated by the government of India with these lands and some agreements to which other major powers were parties. Introductory essays for each region strongly reflect the Anglo-Indian viewpoint. [JCH]

S215. Liebsney, Herbert J. "International relations of Arabia: the dependent areas." **Middle East journal,** 1 (Apr. 1947): 148–68. This and author's other articles in same journal (1949, 1955, 1956) cover recent developments. [JCH]

ARABIAN PENINSULA

S216. Rentz, George. "Djazīrat al-'Arab." **Encyclopaedia of Islam** (new ed.), v. 1, pp. 533–56. Best introduction to the peninsula, including summary history. Appended bibliographies list important historical works and accounts of travelers and explorers on which the historian must rely.

The classic accounts of Doughty, Burton, Thomas, and others may be recommended. For information on such observers see also *S217–218.*

S217. Hogarth, David G. **The penetration of Arabia: a record of the development of western knowledge concerning the Arabian peninsula.** N.Y., 1904. Covers western travelers since the Middle Ages.

S218. Kiernan, Reginald H. **The unveiling of Arabia.** London, 1937. Review of Arabian exploration to 1936. [HARe]

S219. Philby, Harry St. J. **Sa'udi Arabia.** N.Y., 1955. Best history from the Wahhabi rise in the 18th century. Largely supersedes his *Arabia* (N.Y., 1930).

S220. ———. **Arabian jubilee.** London, 1952. Somewhat wandering personal memoir of Sa'udi Arabia and biography of Ibn Sa'ud; fuller after World War I.

EGYPT

To 1882

S221. **Précis de l'histoire d'Égypte.** 4 v. Cairo and Rome, 1932–35. Useful though uneven. V. 3 covers 1517–1849; v. 4, to 1879. Portions since 1801 slanted to favor Muhammad 'Ali dynasty. Bibliographies. [HARi]

S222. Hanotaux, Gabriel. **Histoire de la nation égyptienne.** 7 v. Paris, 1931–40. Popular; many illustrations. End of v. 4 includes Ottoman conquest; v. 5–7 cover 1517–1937. No documentation.

S223. Wiet, Gaston, tr. and ed. **Histoire des Mamlouks circassiens.** Cairo, 1945. This and *S224–225* are translations of three consecutive portions of the contemporary historian, Ibn Iyās, dealing with the last years of Circassian Mamluk sultans in Egypt (1467–1516), with a good picture of Cairo events. [HARi]

S224. ——, tr. and ed. **Journal d'un bourgeois du Caire: chronique d'Ibn Iyās.** Paris, 1955.

S225. Salmon, William H., tr. **An account of the Ottoman conquest of Egypt.** London, 1921.

S226. Carré, Jean-Marie. **Voyageurs et écrivains français en Égypte.** 2nd ed., 2 v., Cairo, 1956. Splendid study of French travelers and authors in Egypt, 1517–1869; influence of Egypt on them; and the value of their works on Egypt. [HARi]

S227. Nāhum, Hāyīm. **Recueil de firmans impériaux ottomans adressés aux valis et aux khédives d'Égypte, 1006 H.–1322 H. (1597 J.-C.–1904 J.-C.).** Cairo, 1934. Good collection in French translation. [HARi]

S228. al-Jabartī. **Merveilles biographiques et historiques: ou chroniques du cheikh Abd-el-Rahman el Djabarti.** 9 v. Cairo, 1888–96. Indispensable work by an Arab historian, covering Egyptian history during the 18th and early 19th centuries. This translation should be checked against Arabic text. [HARi]

S229. France. Commission des Sciences et Arts d'Égypte. **Description de l'Égypte.** 2nd ed., 24 v., Paris, 1817–30. Outstanding work by the French savants who accompanied Napoleon in 1798. The volumes entitled *État moderne* are of particular interest for 18th century Egyptian history. [HARi]

S230. Young, Sir George. **Egypt.** N.Y., 1927. Good, readable survey of Egypt from Napoleon to the 1920's, with personal views.

S231. Ghorbal, Shafik. **The beginnings of the Egyptian question and the rise of Mehemet Ali.** London, 1928. Good account of the struggle for power in Egypt following the French withdrawal, and related European diplomacy. [HARi]

S232. Lane, Edward W. **An account of the manners and customs of the modern Egyptians.** 2 v. London, 1836. Many later eds. Indispensable study of Egyptian society in the early 19th century, before traditional forms had begun to disintegrate. [HARi]

S233. Clot, Antoine B. **Aperçu général sur l'Égypte.** 2 v. Paris, 1840. Apologetic but informative work by a French doctor in Muhammad 'Alī's service. [HARi]

S234. Hamont, Pierre N. **L'Égypte sous Méhémet-Ali.** 2 v. Paris, 1843. By an unrestrained critic of Muhammad 'Alī. Antidote to Clot. [HARi]

S235. Douin, Georges. **Histoire du règne du Khédive Ismaïl.** 3 v. in 6. Rome and Cairo, 1933–41. An important survey of Ismail's reign (1863–76), particularly his relationship with Istanbul. [HARi]

S236. Heyworth-Dunne, James. **An introduction to the history of education in modern Egypt.** London, [1938]. Basic study of Egyptian education in the 19th century. The author's critical perception is almost unique in Egyptian historiography. [HARi]

Since 1882

S237. Blunt, Wilfrid S. **Secret history of the English occupation of Egypt.** London, 1907. Highly critical of the British, sympathetic to the Egyptian national movement. First-hand information, but should be read in connection with Cromer and with caution. [HARi]

S238. Cromer, Evelyn Baring, earl. **Modern Egypt.** 2 v. N.Y., 1908. By the great British proconsul in Egypt for a quarter century; indispensable for British policy. [HARi]

S239. Milner, Alfred M., viscount. **England in Egypt.** London, 1892. Many later eds. Sympathetic description of British administration under Lord Cromer; in some respects more informative than Cromer's book. [HARi]

S240. Lloyd, George A. L. **Egypt since Cromer.** 2 v. London, 1933–34. Important account of British policy in Egypt, 1905–28; anti-nationalist. [HARi]

S241. Marlowe, John. **Anglo-Egyptian relations, 1800–1953.** London, 1954. Broad, objective, though not original scholarship. Emphasis on period since 1876. The U. S. title, *A history of modern Egypt* (N.Y., 1954) is less accurate.

S242. Colombe, Marcel. **L'évolution de l'Égypte.** Paris, 1951. Good study on 1924–50; best for political, social, and intellectual movements. [HARi]

S243. Issawi, Charles P. **Egypt at mid-century: an economic survey.** London, 1954. Revision of his *Egypt: an economic and social analysis* (London, 1947). Coordinates data on the economic situation and problems.

S244. Landau, Jacob M. **Parliaments and parties in Egypt.** Tel Aviv, 1953; N.Y., 1954. Useful handbook from the 1860's; weak from 1924 to 1952. [HARi]

S245. Adams, Charles C. **Islam and modernism in Egypt.** London, 1933. Invaluable analysis of Egyptian Muslim thought; principally on Muhammad 'Abduh. [HARe]

S246. Heyworth-Dunne, James. **Religious and political trends in modern Egypt.** Washington, 1950. Review, E. Wright, *Middle East jour.,* 5 (autumn 1951): 515.

S247. al-Ḥusainī, Isḥak Mūsa. **The Moslem Brethren: the greatest of modern Islamic movements.** Beirut, 1956. Expert account of Hasan al-Banna's notable socio-religious movement; fuller and more up-to-date than Heyworth-Dunne. [HARe]

THE EASTERN QUESTION

Western scholars have produced a flood of works on power politics in the Middle East quite out of proportion to coverage of other aspects of near eastern history, especially for the period since 1800. Many such works are listed in general and country sections of this *Guide*, some elsewhere in this section. See particularly Langer, *European alliances and alignments* (*T491*), his *Diplomacy of imperialism* (*T512*), and Taylor, *Struggle for mastery in Europe* (*T466*) for bibliographical references covering 1848–1918. Bibliographies in works cited below are often excellent. See also

S248. Gooch, Brison D. "A century of historiography on the origins of the Crimean War." *Am. hist. rev.*, 62 (Oct. 1956): 33–58.

Documents

Basic are the published collections for each great power. Of the many other documentary compilations, the following are especially useful.

S249. Hurewitz, Jacob C. **Diplomacy in the Near and Middle East: a documentary record.** 2 v. Princeton, 1956. Documents given in English, with valuable historical introductions and references. Covers 1535–1956; omits Balkans.

S250. Rossi, Ettore. **Documenti sull'origine e gli sviluppi della questione araba (1875–1944).** Rome, 1944. Good introduction, well annotated. Documents in French or Italian.

S251. Giannini, Amedeo. **Documenti per la storia della pace orientale (1915–1932).** Rome, 1933. Useful volume, extensive on Sèvres and Lausanne. Documents in French or Italian.

To 1923

S252. Driault, Edouard. **La question d'Orient depuis ses origines jusqu'à la paix de Sèvres (1920).** 8th ed., Paris, 1921. General coverage from Byzantine times, but mostly post-Napoleonic. Francophil and Turcophobe; no documentation.

S253. Marriott, John A. R. **The eastern question.** 4th ed., Oxford, 1940. From Ottoman rise; weak after 1856. Both Marriott and Driault are outdated in all their parts, but no good comprehensive replacement exists.

S254. Vaughan, Dorothy M. **Europe and the Turk: a pattern of alliances, 1350–1700.** See *M141*.

S255. Anderson, Roger C. **Naval wars in the Levant, 1559–1853.** Princeton, 1952.

Good, especially on techniques and tactics. Uses Italian and Russian materials.

S256. Sumner, Benedict H. **Peter the Great and the Ottoman empire.** Oxford, 1949. Concise picture using Russian materials.

S257. Sorel, Albert. **La question d'Orient au XVIIIe siècle.** 2nd ed., Paris, 1889. English tr., London, 1898. Still the classic on 1768–74——the Russo-Turkish war and Kuchuk Kainarji in their European setting.

S258. Hoskins, Halford L. **British routes to India.** N.Y., 1928. Valuable; covers 1770–1885, focused on Egypt, Syria, Euphrates, Iran, Suez. Copious references.

S259. Puryear, Vernon J. **Napoleon and the Dardanelles.** Berkeley, 1951. Relations with Turkey and Iran, based on French archives; focused on 1805–09. Review, R. H. Davison, *Middle East jour.*, 5 (autumn 1951): 522.

S260. ——. **France and the Levant.** Berkeley, 1941. French economic and political policy, 1814–33. Well documented.

S261. Temperley, Harold W. V. **England and the Near East.** V. 1, The Crimea. London, 1936. Well-written study of Britain and the Ottoman empire, 1808–53, with international ramifications; copious notes.

S262. Webster, Charles K. **The foreign policy of Palmerston, 1830–1841.** 2 v. London, 1951. Detailed on the Turco-Egyptian crises; supersedes Temperley and Puryear for the British aspect.

S263. Mosely, Philip E. **Russian diplomacy and the opening of the eastern question in 1838 and 1839.** See *X215*.

S264. Puryear, Vernon J. **England, Russia and the Straits question, 1844–1856.** Berkeley, 1931. Detailed on diplomacy, with economic overtones. Review, F. S. Rodkey, *Am. hist. rev.*, 37 (Apr. 1932): 597.

S265. Henderson, Gavin B. **Crimean War diplomacy and other historical essays.** Glasgow, 1947. Well documented, with correctives to Puryear and others.

S266. Sumner, Benedict H. **Russia and the Balkans, 1870–1880.** Oxford, 1937. Splendid work, mostly on 1875–78, set in Russian and Balkan background. Fine bibliography. See Langer, *European alliances and alignments* (*T491*) for the eastern question, 1871–90. Langer and Sumner give references to the copious scholarly literature on these years by Harris, Seton-Watson, and others.

S267. Lee, Dwight E. **Great Britain and the Cyprus convention policy of 1878.** Cambridge, Mass., 1934. Sound study of Britain's acquisition of the island.

S268. Earle, Edward M. **Turkey, the great powers, and the Bagdad railway.** N.Y., 1923. The railway as an economic project, with political complications. May be supplemented by the two following works.

S269. Wolf, John B. **The diplomatic his-**

tory of the Bagdad railroad. Columbia, Mo., 1936.

S270. Chapman, Maybelle K. **Great Britain and the Bagdad railway, 1888–1914.** Northampton, Mass., 1948. Excellent bibliography.

S271. Churchill, Rogers P. **The Anglo-Russian convention of 1907.** Cedar Rapids, Ia., 1939. Detailed examination, with excellent chapter on Persia. [FK]

S272. Schmitt, Bernadotte E. **The annexation of Bosnia, 1908–1909.** See *W482*.

S273. Helmreich, Ernst C. **The diplomacy of the Balkan wars, 1912–1913.** Cambridge, Mass., 1938. Well documented.

S274. Howard, Harry N. **The partition of Turkey: a diplomatic history, 1913–1923.** Norman, 1931. Still the best general study of the powers and Ottoman breakup; meticulous documentation.

S275. Smith, Clarence Jay, Jr. **The Russian struggle for power, 1914–1917.** N.Y., 1956. Largely on Russian aims in Turkey and secret agreements. Review, R. H. Davison, *Middle East jour.,* 10 (autumn 1956): 439.

S276. Kedourie, Elie. **England and the Middle East: the destruction of the Ottoman empire, 1914–1921.** London, 1956. Uses some new materials; iconoclastic and argumentative, attacking Lawrence, Feisal, and Antonius.

Since 1923

S277. Lenczowski, George. **The Middle East in world affairs.** See *AF206*.

S278. Giannini, Amedeo. **L'ultima fase della questione orientale (1913–1939).** 2nd ed., Milan, 1941. Examines with precision details of peace settlement in Egypt, Dodecanese, Cyprus, Turkey, and Arab countries, and later events. Many references. [JCH]

S279. Kirk, George E. **The Middle East in the war.** 2nd ed., London, 1953. Indispensable for its detail and annotation, but must be used with caution because of author's moralistic subjectivity. [JCH]

S280. ——. **The Middle East, 1945–1950.** See *AF212*.

S281. Wint, Guy A., and Peter Calvocoressi. **Middle East crisis.** Harmondsworth, Eng., 1957. Good analysis soon after the event of Suez crisis and war of 1956 in its Middle East and great-power setting.

S282. Bullard, Sir Reader. **Britain and the Middle East.** London, 1951. Terse but balanced appraisal of rise and beginning of decline of British influence; mostly post-1914. [JCH]

S283. Campbell, John C. **Defense of the Middle East: problems of American policy.** N.Y., 1958. Tough-minded, fairly broad review of the growth since 1945 of United States responsibilities and problems in defense of western interests against Russia's forward policy. [JCH]

S284. Speiser, Ephraim A. **The United States and the Near East.** Cambridge, Mass., 1950. Brief but penetrating picture. Bibliography. [JCH]

S285. Laqueur, Walter Z. **Communism and nationalism in the Middle East.** N.Y., 1956. Communist parties and factions in Egypt, Israel, Jordan, Syria, Lebanon, Iraq, and Turkey. Useful despite careless references; poor on nationalism.

S286. Spector, Ivar. **The Soviet Union and the Muslim world, 1917–1956.** Rev. ed., Seattle, 1958. Principally on Turkey and Iran, 1917–27. Uses Russian sources. [HARe]

Straits Question

S287. Anchieri, Ettore. **Costantinopoli e gli Stretti nella politica russa ed europea.** Milan, 1948. Best single survey; covers 1774–1936.

S288. Shotwell, James T., and Francis Deák. **Turkey at the Straits.** N.Y., 1940. Despite brevity and occasional errors, the handiest survey in English.

S289. Howard, Harry N. **The problem of the Turkish straits.** Washington, 1947. Brief, collating treaties and documents, 1774–1936, plus account of 1945–46 friction.

S290. Goriainow, Serge. **Le Bosphore et les Dardanelles.** Paris, 1910. Covers 1798–1878; based on Russian archives. Still valuable on Russian policy despite need for correction.

S291. Mandelstam, André N. **La politique russe d'accès à la Méditerranée au XXᵉ siècle.** Paris, 1935. [Hague, Academy of International Law, Recueil des cours, 1934, 1, v. 47.] Documented analysis of Russian policy, especially 1907–14. Covers to 1923.

Suez Canal

S292. Hallberg, Charles W. **The Suez Canal, its history and diplomatic importance.** N.Y., 1931. Thorough study of the diplomacy preceding, during, and following the piercing of the isthmus. Uses unpublished European archives for period to 1876. [JCH]

S293. Wilson, Sir Arnold T. **The Suez Canal.** 2nd ed., London, 1939. Most useful on financial aspects of the canal and for statistics. Its brief historical survey is based only on published works. [HARi]

S294. Sammarco, Angelo. **Suez: storia e problemi.** Milan, 1943. Based on wide research in European and Cairo archives and on records of Luigi de Negrelli. Critical of de Lesseps; should be read with Hallberg (*S292*). [HARi]

S295. U. S. Department of State. **The Suez Canal problem, July 26–September 22, 1956.** Washington, 1956. This and *S296* contain basic documentation on the Suez crisis of 1956–57, including the relevant instruments of 1854, 1856, 1866, 1888, and 1954. [JCH]

S296. ——. **United States policy in the Middle East, September 1956–June 1957.** Washington, 1957.

MINORITY GROUPS

S297. Hourani, Albert H. **Minorities in the Arab world.** London, 1947. Only survey of this complicated subject; useful despite brevity and errors.

S298. Rondot, Pierre. **Les Chrétiens d'-Orient.** Paris, 1955. Sympathetic yet factual survey of eastern Christians: doctrine, history, relations with Islam and Arabs.

S299. Silbernagl, Isidor. **Verfassung und gegenwärtiger Bestand sämtlicher Kirchen des Orients.** 2nd ed., Regensburg, 1904. This and *S300* are useful compendia of eastern churches and peoples toward end of Ottoman rule.

S300. Steen de Jehay, Frédéric van den. **De la situation légale des sujets ottomans non-musulmans.** Brussels, 1906.

S301. 1453–1953: le cinq-centième anniversaire de la prise de Constantinople. Athens, 1953. Sixteen essays by Greek scholars, seven on 1453 and its significance. Review, L. S. Stavrianos, *Jour. mod. hist.,* 28 (June 1956): 180.

S302. Papadopoullos, Theodore H. **Studies and documents relating to the history of the Greek church and people under Turkish domination.** See *W1155.*

S303. Hill, Sir George F. **A history of Cyprus.** 4 v. Cambridge, Eng., 1940–52. Detailed, documented study. V. 4 covers Ottoman and British periods, 1571–1948.

S304. Pasdermadjian, Hrant. **Histoire de l'Arménie depuis les origines jusqu'au traité de Lausanne.** Paris, 1949. Fullest survey treatment of the modern period in a western language.

S305. Lynch, Harry F. B. **Armenia, travels and studies.** 2 v. London, 1901. Extensive work on travels and geography, with historical information, maps, and bibliography. [AOS]

S306. Arpee, Leon. **The Armenian awakening: a history of the Armenian church, 1820–1860.** Chicago, 1909. Useful, factual account of aspects of the Armenian reform movement in Turkey, by an Armenian Protestant. Bibliography.

S307. Sarkissian, Arshag O. **History of the Armenian question to 1885.** Urbana, 1938. Sympathetic, well-documented study of Armenian struggle for greater rights, and European diplomacy; essentially on 1856–85.

S308. Nersessian, Mekertych G. **Hai zhoghovoorty azadakeragan baikare Tiurkagan perhnabedoothian tem, 1850–1870 tt.**

[The Armenian struggle for freedom from Turkish despotism, 1850–1870.] Erivan, Sov. Armenia, 1955. Lengthy, careful study based on contemporary Armenian publications and some Russian and Armenian documentary material. [AOS]

S309. Macler, Frédéric. **Autour de l'Arménie.** Paris, 1917. Collection of his articles from French periodicals of 1911–17, providing information on modern history and translations or condensations from important Armenian sources.

S310. Toynbee, Arnold J., ed. **The treatment of Armenians in the Ottoman empire, 1915–1916.** London, 1916. See under *S312.*

S311. Lepsius, Johannes, ed. **Deutschland und Armenien, 1914–1918.** Potsdam, 1919.

S312. Naslian, Jean. **Les mémoires . . . sur les événements politico-religieux en Proche-Orient de 1914 à 1928.** 2 v. Beirut, 1955. In the absence of any single authoritative study of the Armenian massacres of World War I, deportation, and post-war dispersion, the student must use materials on Turkey, the war, Armenian societies, and such evidence of Armenian sufferings as the huge documentary collections which Toynbee and Lepsius provide. Also important is this lengthy survey by Naslian, Catholic bishop of Trebizond, based on his diary, covering all Anatolian provinces. [AOS]

S313. Stafford, Ronald S. **The tragedy of the Assyrians.** London, 1935. Migrations and massacre of this Nestorian remnant, 1918–33.

S314. Franco, Moise. **Essai sur l'histoire des israélites de l'empire ottoman.** Paris, 1897. Useful sketch. Though outdated in many parts, is without replacement in a western language.

S315. Nikitine, Basile. **Les Kurdes: étude sociologique et historique.** Paris, 1956. Best survey, although heavier on sociology than history and political developments. Bibliography.

S316. Edmonds, Cecil J. **Kurds, Turks, and Arabs: politics, travel, and research in northeastern Iraq, 1919–1925.** London, 1957. Good within its geographic and chronological limits; by a former official in the area.

SOCIETY AND ECONOMY

S317. Bonné, Alfred. **State and economics in the Middle East: a society in transition.** 2nd ed., London, 1955. Pioneer attempt by expert Israeli professor to survey agricultural and industrial developments since 1800. [HARe]

S318. Warriner, Doreen. **Land reform and development in the Middle East: a study of Egypt, Syria and Iraq.** London, 1957. Sequel to her *Land and poverty in the Middle East* (London, 1948). Investigates major postwar agrarian changes resulting from revolution (Egypt), private investment (Syria), and public investment (Iraq). [JCH]

S319. International Bank for Reconstruction and Development. **The economy of Turkey.** Baltimore, 1951. This and *S320–322* are good surveys of conditions, problems, and projects, with recommendations.

S320. ——. **The economic development of Iraq.** Baltimore, 1952.

S321. ——. **The economic development of Syria.** Baltimore, 1955.

S322. ——. **The economic development of Jordan.** Baltimore, 1957.

S323. United Nations. **Summary of recent economic developments in the Middle East, 1945 to 1954.** N.Y., 1955. Useful reference on economic developments in Egypt, Iran, Iraq, Israel, Lebanon, Syria, and Turkey; based on official data. [JCH]

S324. Fisher, Sydney N., ed. **Social forces in the Middle East.** Ithaca, 1955. Good introductory attempt by fifteen scholars to survey various social groups.

S325. Coult, Lyman H., Jr. **An annotated research bibliography of studies in Arabic, English, and French of the fellah of the Egyptian Nile, 1798–1955.** Coral Gables, Fla., 1958. Eminently usable guide to this subject, listing some 300 selected titles with good notes and indices.

S326. Ayrout, Henry H. **The fellaheen.** Cairo, 1945. First-rate analysis of Egyptian peasantry by a Jesuit who lived among them. However, see comments in Coult, above. [HARi]

S327. Berque, Jacques. **Histoire sociale d'un village égyptien au XXᵉᵐᵉ siècle.** The Hague, 1957. Incisive study of social change in a delta village. [HARe]

S328. Weulersse, Jacques. **Paysans de Syrie et du Proche-Orient.** Paris, 1946. Excellent study, despite French bias, of peasant characteristics, economy, and land tenure in geographical and historical setting, with changes 1919–39.

S329. Lambton, Ann K. S. **Landlord and peasant in Persia.** London, 1953. Meticulous history of land tenure, theory and practice, in Islamic Persia, coupled with vast field survey of contemporary land ownership, use, and rural economy, set in broad social framework. Well documented. [HARe]

S330. Morrison, John A. **Alişar: a unit of land occupance in the Kanak Su basin of central Anatolia.** Chicago, 1939. Good study, by a geographer, of Turkish village structure, housing, and land tenure and use; based on 1932 investigation.

S331. Yasa, Ibrahim. **Hasanoğlan: socio-economic structure of a Turkish village.** Ankara, 1957. Fine, detailed sociological analysis of central Anatolian plateau village, circa 1905–50. [HARe]

S332. Hurst, Harold E. **The Nile.** 2nd ed., London, 1957. Authoritative survey of history

of the Nile, the irrigation system and projects, and hydrological problems, in political and geographical setting. [HARi]

S333. Willcocks, Sir William, and J. I. Craig. **Egyptian irrigation.** 3rd ed., 2 v., London, 1913. Full information on Nile and tributaries: basin, perennial irrigation, drainage, land reclamation, flood control, etc. Describes Egyptian agriculture, and administrative and legal aspects of irrigation. [HARi]

S334. Clerget, Marcel. **Le Caire: étude de géographie urbaine et d'histoire économique.** 2 v. Cairo, 1934. History and analysis of Cairo's physical and economic development and life; copious references.

S335. Sauvaget, Jean. **Alep: essai sur le développement d'une grande ville syrienne, des origines au milieu du XIXᵉ siècle.** Paris, 1941. Aleppo offers a cross-section of Near East history. Covers city's growth, layout, archaeological and architectural evidence in geographical, social, economic, and political setting. Fine bibliography.

S336. Cooper, Merian C. **Grass.** N.Y., 1925. Classic illustrated account of annual spring migration of Bakhtiari tribe. [HARe]

S337. Cronin, Vincent. **The last migration.** London, 1957. Partly fictionalized account of the Qashqai. [HARe]

S338. Ullens de Schooten, Marie Thérèse. **Lords of the mountains.** London, 1956. More reliable than the above. [HARe]

S339. Murray, George W. **Sons of Ishmael: a study of the Egyptian Bedouin.** London, 1935. Good, somewhat chatty description of Bedouin life, customs, and beliefs in all parts of Egypt.

S340. Dickson, Harold R. P. **The Arab of the desert.** London, 1949. Though poorly organized, a vast store of information on life, customs, and folk-lore of Bedouins around Kuwait and eastern Arabia. For corrections see George Rentz, "Notes on Dickson's *The Arab of the desert*," *Muslim world*, 41 (Jan. 1951): 49–64.

S341. Montagne, Robert. **La civilisation du désert: nomades d'Orient et d'Afrique.** Paris, 1947. Excellent account of Bedouin social organization, beliefs, literature, and sedentarization, plus history of Wahhabi empires. Less on north Africa.

S342. Musil, Alois. **The manners and customs of the Rwala Bedouins.** N.Y., 1928. Huge compilation of information on these Bedouins of northern Arabia, based on prewar investigations.

S343. Oppenheim, Max von. **Die Beduinen.** 3 v. Leipzig and Wiesbaden, 1939–52. Monumental compilation of information on Bedouin tribes of Syria, Iraq, Palestine, Jordan, Sinai, Hejaz, north and central Arabia. Includes tribal genealogies and history. See also George Rentz, "Notes on Oppenheim's *Die Beduinen*," *Oriens*, 10 (1957): 77–89.

S344. Shwadran, Benjamin. **The Middle East, oil and the great powers.** N.Y., 1955. Focuses on the convoluted, often bitter diplomacy that characterized the development of Middle East oil; ignores technical aspects of the industry. Fullest on Iran. Inclusive bibliography. [JCH]

S345. Longrigg, Stephen H. **Oil in the Middle East: its discovery and development.** London, 1954. The author, a British official in the area and for two decades an executive of the Iraq Petroleum Company, presents for the layman a discreet account of technical aspects of the rise of the oil industry. Avoids political ramifications and the less pleasant inter-company frictions. [JCH]

S346. U. S. Federal Trade Commission. **The international petroleum cartel.** Washington, 1952. Though dealing with the entire non-Soviet world, this full-sized report examines closely the role of U. S., British, Dutch, and French companies in discovery and development of Middle East oil. Many charts, tables, and maps. [JCH]

BIOGRAPHIES AND MEMOIRS

Some of the best short biographies appear in *The encyclopaedia of Islam.* For important Turks the *Islâm ansiklopedisi* is often far better. From the following selections most biographies and memoirs of European diplomats and all western autobiographical travel accounts are excluded.

Ottoman, 15th and 16th Centuries

S347. Kritoboulos. **History of Mehmed the Conqueror.** Princeton, 1954.

S348. Thuasne, Louis. **Djem-Sultan.** Paris, 1892.

S349. Merriman, Roger B. **Suleiman the Magnificent.** Cambridge, Mass., 1944.

S350. Egli, Ernst. **Sinan, der Baumeister osmanischer Glanzzeit.** Zürich, 1954.

S351. Roth, Cecil A. **The house of Nasi: the duke of Naxos.** Philadelphia, 1948.

Ottoman, 17th and 18th Centuries

S352. Katzenstein, Julius (pseud., Joseph Kastein). **The messiah of Ismir, Sabbatai Zevi.** N.Y., 1931.

S353. Kreutel, Richard, ed. **Kara Mustafa vor Wien.** Graz, 1955.

S354. Kreutel, Richard, and Otto Spies, eds. **Leben . . . des Dolmetschers Osman Aga.** Bonn, 1954.

S355. Tott, François de. **Memoirs on the Turks and the Tartars.** 2 v. London, 1785. Also several French eds.

S356. Vandal, Albert. **Le pacha Bonneval.** Paris, 1885.

S357. Dehérain, Henri. **La vie de Pierre Ruffin.** 2 v. Paris, 1929–30.

S358. Marcère, Edouard de. **Une ambassade à Constantinople.** 2 v. Paris, 1927.

Ottoman, 19th and 20th Centuries

S359. Miller, Anatoliĭ F. **Mustafa Pasha Baĭraktar.** Moscow, 1947.

S360. Lane-Poole, Stanley. **The life of . . . Stratford de Redcliffe.** 2 v. London, 1888.

S361. Moltke, Helmuth von. **Briefe . . . 1835 bis 1839.** 7th ed., Berlin, 1911. Many other eds.

S362. Melek Hanum. **Thirty years in the harem.** London, 1872.

S363. Hornby, Sir Edmund G. **Autobiography.** London, 1929.

S364. Hamlin, Cyrus. **Among the Turks.** N.Y., 1878.

S365. Fatma Aliye. **Ahmet Cevdet Paşa ve zamanĭ.** [Ahmed Jevdet Pasha and his times.] Istanbul, 1913.

S366. Mardin, Ebel'ülâ. **Medenî hukuk cephesinden Ahmet Cevdet Paşa.** [Ahmed Jevdet Pasha from the viewpoint of civil law.] Istanbul, 1946.

S367. Midhat, Ali Haydar. **The life of Midhat Pasha.** London, 1903.

S368. ———. **Midhat-Pacha.** Paris, 1908.

S369. ———. **Midhat Paşa, hayat-ĭ siyasiyesi.** [Midhat Pasha, his political life.] 2 v. Istanbul, 1909.

S370. Koetschet, Josef (pseud., Dr. K.). **Erinnerungen aus dem Leben des Serdar Ekrem Omer Pascha.** Sarajevo, 1885.

S371. ———. **Osman Pascha.** Sarajevo, 1909.

S372. Washburn, George. **Fifty years in Constantinople.** Boston, 1909.

S373. Pears, Edwin. **Forty years in Constantinople.** London, 1916.

S374. Kemal Bey, Ismail. **Memoirs.** Ed. by Sommerville Story. London, 1920.

S375. Halil Halid. **The diary of a Turk.** London, 1903.

S376. İnal, Ibnülemin Mahmud Kemal. **Osmanlĭ devrinde son sadrazamlar.** [The last grand viziers of the Ottoman period.] 14 fasc. Istanbul, 1940–53. Old-fashioned biographies of all grand viziers since 1852, with copius source quotations.

S377. Said Paşa (Mehmet). **Said Paşa'nĭn hâtĭratĭ.** [Said Pasha's memoirs.] 3 v. Istanbul, 1910.

S378. Kâmil Paşa (Mehmet). **Hatĭrat-ĭ Sadr-ĭ esbak Kâmil Paşa.** [Memoirs of the former grand vizier Kâmil Pasha.] Istanbul, 1911.

S379. Pears, Edwin. **Life of Abdul Hamid.** N.Y., 1917.

S380. Wittlin, Alma. **Abdul Hamid.** London, 1940.

S381. Ryan, Andrew. **The last of the dragomans.** London, 1951.

S382. Adĭvar, Halide Edib. **Memoirs.** N.Y., 1926.

S383. Ahmed Izzet. **Denkwürdigkeiten des Marschalls Izzet Pascha.** Leipzig, 1927.

S384. Bolayïr, Enver, ed. **Talât Paşa'nïn hâtïralarï.** [Recollections of Talât Pasha.] Istanbul, 1946.

S385. Djemal, pasha. **Memories of a Turkish statesman, 1913–1919.** N.Y., 1922.

S386. Liman von Sanders, Otto V. **Five years in Turkey.** See *AG54.*

S387. Okay, Kurt. **Enver Pascha.** Berlin, 1935. Novelized.

S388. Sâbis, Ali İhsan. **Harb hâtïralarïm.** [My war memoirs.] V. 1–2. Istanbul and Ankara, 1943–51.

S389. Deny, Jean, ed. and tr. **Souvenirs du Gâzi Moustafa Kemâl Pacha.** Paris, 1927. On World War I.

Turkey since 1918

S390. Mikusch, Dagobert von. **Mustapha Kemal.** See *AF342.*

S391. Armstrong, Harold C. **Grey Wolf: Mustafa Kemal.** London, 1932.

S392. Froembgen, Hanns. **Kemal Ataturk.** N.Y., 1937.

S393. Adïvar, Halide Edib. **The Turkish ordeal.** N.Y., 1928.

S394. Cebesoy, Ali Fuat. **Hatïralarï.** [Memoirs.] 3 v. Istanbul, 1953–57.

S395. Ağaoğlu, Ahmet. **Serbest Fïrka hâtïralarï.** [Recollections of the Liberal party.] Istanbul, 1949.

S396. Kutay, Cemal. **Celâl Bayar.** 2 v. Istanbul, 1939.

S397. Yalman, Ahmed Emin. **Turkey in my time.** Norman, Okla., 1956.

Iran

S398. Bellan, Lucien L. **Chah 'Abbas I.** Paris, 1932.

S399. Ross, E. Denison, ed. **Sir Anthony Sherley and his Persian adventure.** London, 1933.

S400. Durand, H. Mortimer. **Nadir Shah.** London, 1908.

S401. Nāsir al Din, shah. **The diary . . . tour through Europe in A.D. 1873.** London, 1874.

S402. ———. **A diary . . . journey to Europe in 1878.** London, 1879.

S403. Hedayat, Mehdïquli (Mukhbar as-Saltaneh). **Khatarat ve khatrat.** [Memories and dangers.] Tehran, 1950.

S404. Sykes, Christopher. **Wassmuss, "the German Lawrence."** London, 1936.

S405. Niedermayer, Oskar von. **Unter der Glutsonne Irans.** Dachau, 1925.

S406. Dunsterville, Lionel C. **The adventures of Dunsterforce.** London, 1920.

S407. Blücher, Wipert von. **Zeitenwende in Iran.** Biberach, 1949.

S408. Wilson, Sir Arnold T. **S.W. Persia.** London, 1941.

S409. Millspaugh, Arthur C. **The American task in Persia.** N.Y., 1925.

Arab Countries

S410. Dodwell, Henry H. **The founder of modern Egypt . . . Muhammad 'Ali.** Cambridge, Eng., 1931.

S411. Crabitès, Pierre. **Ibrahim of Egypt.** London, 1935.

S412. ———. **Ismail, the maligned khedive.** London, 1933.

S413. Lesseps, Ferdinand de. **Recollections of forty years.** 2 v. London, 1887.

S414. Edgar-Bonnet, George. **Ferdinand de Lesseps.** Paris, 1951.

S415. Ninet, John. **Arabi Pacha.** Bern, 1884.

S416. Osman Amin. **Muhammad 'Abduh.** Washington, 1953.

S417. Rashid Rida. **Muḥammad 'Abduh.** 2nd ed., 3 v., Cairo, 1947.

S418. Husain, Taha. **An Egyptian childhood.** London, 1932.

S419. ———. **The stream of days.** Cairo, 1943.

S420. Storrs, Sir Ronald. **Memoirs.** N.Y., 1937.

S421. Ahmad Amin. **Ḥayātī.** [My life.] Cairo, 1950.

S422. Haykal, Muhammad Husayn. **Mudhakkirāt fī al-siyāsah al-Miṣriyyah.** [Memoirs concerning Egyptian politics.] 2 v. Cairo, 1951–53.

S423. Neguib, Mohammed. **Egypt's destiny.** N.Y., 1955.

S424. Nasser, Gamal Abdul. **Egypt's liberation.** Washington, 1955.

S425. el-Sadat, Anwar. **Revolt on the Nile.** N.Y., 1957.

S426. Stitt, George M. **A prince of Arabia.** London, 1948.

S427. Armstrong, Harold C. **Lord of Arabia, Ibn Saud.** London, 1934.

S428. Lawrence, Thomas E. **Seven pillars of wisdom.** See *AG52.*

S429. Philby, Harry St. J. **Arabian days.** London, 1948.

S430. Stark, Freya. **The coast of incense.** London, 1953.

S431. Kurd 'Ali, Muhammad. **Memoirs.** Washington, 1954.

S432. Atiyah, Edward S. **An Arab tells his story.** London, 1946.

S433. Abdullah, king of Jordan. **Memoirs.** N.Y., 1950.

S434. ———. **My memoirs completed.** Washington, 1954.

S435. Kirkbride, Alec S. **A crackle of thorns.** London, 1956.

S436. Jarvis, Claude S. **Arab command: the biography of . . . Peake Pasha.** London, 1942.

S437. Glubb, John B. **The story of the Arab legion.** See *AF220.*

S438. ——. **A soldier with the Arabs.** London, 1957.

S439. Young, Peter. **Bedouin command . . . 1953–1956.** London, 1956.

S440. Wilson, Sir Arnold T. **Loyalties: Mesopotamia, 1914–1917.** See *AG61.*

S441. ——. **Mesopotamia, 1917–1920.** London, 1931.

S442. Bell, Gertrude L. **Letters.** 2 v. London, 1927.

S443. Graves, Philip P. **The life of Sir Percy Cox.** London, 1941.

Zionism and Israel

S444. Lowenthal, Marvin, ed. **The diaries of Theodore Herzl.** N.Y., 1956.

S445. Weizmann, Chaim. **Trial and error.** N.Y., 1949.

S446. Bentwich, Norman. **For Zion's sake: a biography of Judah L. Magnes.** Philadelphia, 1954.

S447. Begin, Menachem. **The revolt.** N.Y., 1951.

S448. Litvinoff, Barnet. **Ben-Gurion.** N.Y., 1954.

OFFICIAL GOVERNMENT RECORDS

No attempt has been made here to list all official publications useful to historians which are issued by the seven Arab states, Turkey, Iran, Cyprus, Israel, and the semi-independent areas covered in this section. Such publications include official gazettes, law compilations, parliamentary proceedings, statistical surveys, etc. As a guide to locating some of these, Ettinghausen, *Bibliography* (*M5*) and Godchot, *Constitutions* (*S49*) are useful. See also

S449. Gerould, Winifred (Gregory). **List of the serial publications of foreign governments, 1815–1931.** N.Y., 1932.

Documents and studies of the United Nations and its specialized agencies are valuable. For these a starting guide is in

S450. United Nations Educational, Scientific and Cultural Organization. **International social science bulletin,** 5 (1953): 732–52.

S451. U. S. Foreign Broadcast Information Service. **Daily report, foreign radio broadcasts.** Washington, 1947 ff. (5 times weekly.) Contains sections on the area.

For older official records, before existence of the modern states, the following on the Ottoman empire are the most useful.

S452. **Takvim-i vekayi.** [Calendar of events.] Istanbul, 1831–1878, 1908–22. The official gazette and, for a time, the only newspaper.

S453. **Sālnāme.** [Yearbook.] Istanbul, 1847–1913. Considerable information on official organization.

S454. **Düstur.** [Compilation of laws.] Istanbul and Ankara, 1863–1944. Two series,

the first for laws from 1839 to 1908; the second, from 1908 to 1922. Described in Jäschke, "Türkische Gesetzsammlungen" (*S124*). Translations from first series in Aristarchi, *Législation ottomane* (*S122*) and Young, *Corps de droit ottoman* (*S123*).

ACADEMY AND SOCIETY PUBLICATIONS

Material on modern Near East history occurs in the proceedings of various academies, as those of Vienna, Munich, Göttingen, and Berlin. For the period since 1920 see also Arnold Toynbee, ed., *Survey of international affairs.* Most publications of institutes of oriental studies devote more attention to philology, the Far East, and the Near East before 1450 than to the modern Near East, but have occasional material of value within this field. Also of interest are the *Actes* of the International Congress of Orientalists. Series useful for the Near East since 1450 include the following.

S455. Türk Tarih Kurumu [Turkish Historical Society] (Ankara). **Yayinlari.** [Publications.] See especially series 2, 7, 8, 11, 13, and 14.

S456. Société de Géographie d'Égypte (Cairo). Many publications in French on 19th century history.

S457. Akademiia Nauk SSSR, Institut Vostokovedeniia (Moscow). **Uchenye zapiski.** [Scholarly treatises.] 1950 ff.

S458. ——. **Kratkie soobshcheniia.** [Short communications.] Moscow, 1951 ff.

S459. Orijentalni Institut (Sarajevo). **Prilozi za orijentalnu filologiju i istoriju jugoslovenskih naroda pod turskom vladavinom.** [Contributions to oriental philology and history of the Yugoslavian people under Turkish rule.] 1950 ff.

S460. Middle East Institute (Washington). **Report on current research.** 1956 ff.

PERIODICALS

Aside from more general historical periodicals, some of those listed in Sections D and M contain materials on the Near East since 1450. Those listed below are useful for their historical articles, their reports on contemporary events, or both.

S461. **The Armenian review.** Boston, 1948 ff. (Quarterly.)

S462. **L'Asie française.** Paris, 1901–40. (Monthly.)

S463. **Asien.** Berlin, 1901–19. (Monthly.)

S464. **Beiträge zur Kenntnis des Orients.** Berlin, 1902–18. (Annual.)

S465. **Belleten.** Ankara, 1937 ff. (Quarterly.)

S466. **Bibliotheca orientalis.** Leiden, 1943 ff. (Irregular bi-monthly.)

S467. **Cahiers de l'Orient contemporain.**

Paris, 1945 ff. (Quarterly, 1945–49; semi-annual, 1950 ff.)

S468. Correspondance d'Orient. Paris, 1908 ff.

S469. The Egyptian economic and political review. Cairo, 1954 ff. (Monthly.)

S470. Great Britain and the East. London, 1911 ff. (Monthly. Title varies.)

S471. Hamizrah Hehadash. [The new East.] Jerusalem, 1949 ff. (Quarterly.) English summaries.

S472. The Middle East journal. See *M327*.

S473. Middle eastern affairs. N.Y., 1950 ff. (10 nos. per year.)

S474. Mitteilungen zur osmanischen Geschichte. Vienna, 1921–26.

S475. The Muslim world. Hartford, Conn. 1911 ff. (Quarterly. Title to 1947, *The Moslem World*.)

S476. Oesterreichische Monatsschrift für den Orient. Vienna, 1875–1918. (Monthly.)

S477. The Orient. Constantinople (Istanbul), 1910–23. (Weekly.)

S478. Orient. Paris, 1957 ff. (Quarterly.)

S479. Oriente moderno. Rome, 1921 ff. (Monthly.)

S480. Pravoslavnyi palestinskii sbornik. [Mélanges concerning the Orthodox Church in Palestine.] St. Petersburg (Leningrad), 1881–1917. (3 nos. per year.)

S481. Revue de l'Islam. Paris, 1895–1902. (Monthly.)

S482. Revue de l'Orient chrétien. Paris, 1896 ff. (Irregular.)

S483. Revue des études arméniennes. Paris, 1920–33. (Irregular.)

S484. Revue du monde musulman. Paris, 1906–26. (Quarterly.)

S485. Royal central Asian journal. London, 1914 ff. (Quarterly. Title varies.) Successor to *Proceedings of the Central Asian Society* (1904–13).

S486. Soobscheniia Imperatorskago Pravoslavnago Palestinskago Obschchestva. [Communications of the Imperial Orthodox Palestine Society.] St. Petersburg (Leningrad), 1891–1926. (Quarterly.)

S487. Sovetskoe vostokovedenie. [Soviet orientalistics.] Moscow, 1940–49. (Bimonthly.)

S488. Tarih-i osmanî encümeni mecmuasî. [Review of the Ottoman Historical Society.] Istanbul, 1910–31. Name changed in 1924 to *Türk tarih encümeni mecmuasî* [Review of the Turkish Historical Society]. (Bimonthly.)

S489. Tarih vesikalarî. [Historical documents.] Ankara, 1941 ff. (Irregular.)

S490. Vakîflar dergisi. [Review of vakîfs (religious and charitable foundations).] Ankara, 1938–42. (Irregular.)

S491. Die Welt des Islams. Berlin and Münster, 1913 ff. (Quarterly.)

V. MODERN EUROPE

SECTION T

Europe (General), 1450–1914

WALTER L. DORN *

Throughout this section the emphasis is on Europe as a whole, not its component national units; and, except for economic histories, only general European works or those pertaining to more than one country have been included. Therefor, the user should consult also the various national bibliographies in Section V.

AUXILIARIES

Bibliographies

A single bibliography covering the entire span of European history from 1450 to 1914 does not exist. However, there are comprehensive works on various areas or periods, among which those listed below are outstanding.

T1. Langer, William L., ed. **The rise of modern Europe.** N.Y., 1934 ff. Each volume of this series contains a thorough bibliographical essay on the period covered, up-to-date at the time of publication. Several have been revised in reprintings.

T2. Halphen, Louis, and Philippe Sagnac, eds. **Peuples et civilisations.** Paris, 1926 ff. Contains in each volume a select bibliography.

T3. Calmette, Joseph, ed. **"Clio": introduction aux études historiques.** Paris, 1934 ff. Primarily bibliographical.

T4. The Cambridge modern history. Ed. by Adolphus W. Ward and others. 14 v. Cambridge, Eng., and N.Y., 1902–12. Less useful but more copious are the bibliographies of these volumes.

T5. Coulter, Edith M., and Melanie Gerstenfeld. **Historical bibliographies.** Berkeley,

1935. This and *T6* contain more thorough national bibliographies of the various European countries.

T6. Caron, Pierre, and Marc Jaryc. **World lists of historical periodicals and bibliographies.** Oxford, 1939.

T7. American Council of Learned Societies, Committee on Renaissance Studies. **Surveys of recent scholarship in the period of Renaissance.** Providence, 1945 ff.

T8. Bainton, Roland H. **Bibliography of the continental Reformation.** Chicago, 1935.

T9. Bromley, John S., and Albert Goodwin. **A select list of works on Europe and Europe overseas, 1715–1815.** Oxford, 1956. Does not include books on the domestic history of England.

T10. Thomas, Daniel H., and Lynn M. Case, eds. **Guide to the diplomatic archives of western Europe.** Philadelphia, 1959.

T11. Bullock, Alan L. C., and A. J. P. Taylor. **A select list of books on European history, 1815–1914.** 2nd ed., Oxford, 1957. Does not include works on English domestic history.

T12. Kircheisen, Friedrich M. **Bibliographie des napoleonischen Zeitalters.** Berlin, 1902.

T13. ——. **Bibliographie du temps de Napoléon.** 2 v. Paris, 1908–12.

* The following contributed items and comments indicated by their respective initials: Crane Brinton (CB), Geoffrey Bruun (GB), David L. Buttolph (DLB), Shepard B. Clough (SBC), Judith S. Cousins (JSC), Carl J. Friedrich (CJF), Peter Gay (PG), Leo Gershoy (LG), Myron P. Gilmore (MPG), Garrett Mattingly (GM), and Theodore Mommsen (TM).

T14. Ragatz, Lowell J. **A bibliography for the study of European history, 1815–1939.** 2nd ed., Washington, 1946.

T15. Wegerer, Alfred von. **Bibliographie zur Vorgeschichte des Weltkrieges.** Berlin, 1934.

T16. Gooch, George P. **Recent revelations of European diplomacy.** 4th ed., London, 1940. A unique combination of bibliography and commentary.

T17. Johnson, Charles, J. P. Whitney, and Harold W. V. Temperley, eds. **Helps for students of history.** 58 v. London, 1918–58.

T18. International bibliography of historical sciences. See *B55*.

T19. United Nations Educational, Scientific and Cultural Organization. **Répertoire des bibliothèques de France.** 3 v. Paris, 1950–51. Lists all the scholarly libraries together with description of their special collections.

T20. Leyh, Georg. **Die deutschen wissenschaftlichen Bibliotheken nach dem Krieg.** Tübingen, 1947.

T21. Italy. Consiglio Nazionale delle Ricerche. **Elenco delle Biblioteche Scientifiche e Techniche Italiane.** Ed. by G. B. Gambigliani and others. Rome, 1955.

Geographies, Gazetteers, and Atlases

T22. Westermanns Atlas zur Weltgeschichte. Pt. 3, Neuzeit. Brunswick, 1953. One of the best recent historical atlases for Europe.

T23. Fox, Edward W. **Atlas of European history.** See *B220*.

T24. Spruner-Menke Hand-Atlas für die Geschichte des Mittelalters und der neueren Zeit. 3rd ed., Gotha, 1880. In spite of its age, still useful.

T25. Poole, Reginald L., ed. **Historical atlas of modern Europe.** London, 1902.

T26. The Cambridge modern history atlas. Cambridge, Eng., and N.Y., 1912. 2nd ed., 1924. Though sometimes faulty in detail, contains a useful and informative selection of maps.

T27. Robertson, Charles G., and John G. Bartholomew. **An historical atlas of modern Europe from 1789 to 1922.** 2nd ed., London, 1924.

T28. Putzger, Friedrich W. **Historischer Schulatlas.** Ed. by A. Hansel. 67th ed., Bielefeld, 1956. A handy standard historical atlas, useful for modern Europe.

T29. Shepherd, William R. **Historical atlas.** See *B217*.

T30. Whittlesey, Derwent S. **Environmental foundations of European history.** N.Y., 1949. Of exceptional utility to students of European history.

T31. East, W. Gordon. **An historical geography of Europe.** 3rd ed., London, 1948.

T32. Machatschek, Fritz. **Europa als Ganzes.** Leipzig, 1929.

T33. Philippson, Alfred. **Europa.** 3rd ed., Leipzig, 1928.

T34. Pounds, Norman J. G. **An historical and political geography of Europe.** London, 1947.

Anthropological Works

T35. Sauter, Marc R. **Les races de l'Europe.** Paris, 1952.

T36. Coon, Carleton S. **The races of Europe.** See *E28*.

WESTERN EUROPE, 1450–1648

General Surveys and Collective Histories

T37. Barbagallo, Corrado. **L'età della Rinascenza e della Riforma (1454–1556).** Turin, 1952. Universal history in the grand manner, with emphasis on politics, but without neglecting economic and cultural factors. Useful bibliographies. [GM]

T38. ———. **Controriforma e prerivoluzione (1556–1699).** Turin, 1952. See comment above. [GM]

T39. Potter, George R., ed. **The Renaissance, 1493–1520.** Cambridge, Eng., 1957. [The new Cambridge modern history, 1.]

T40. Elton, Geoffrey R. **The Reformation, 1520–1559.** Cambridge, Eng., 1958. [The new Cambridge modern history, 2.]

T41. Joachimsen, Paul, and others. **Das Zeitalter der religiösen Umwälzung . . . 1500–1600.** Berlin, 1930. [Walter Goetz, ed., Propyläen Weltgeschichte, 5.] Careful and scholarly German account that is especially good on intellectual and religious history.

T42. Barker, Ernest, George N. Clark, and P. Vaucher, eds. **The European inheritance.** V. 2–3. Oxford, 1954. Very useful collection of interpretive essays on all significant phases of modern history from the Renaissance to 1914 and after.

T43. Fisher, Herbert A. L. **A history of Europe.** V. 2, **Renaissance, Reformation, reason.** N.Y., 1935. A splendid older survey.

T44. Friedrich, Carl J. **The age of the baroque, 1610–1660.** N.Y., 1952. [William L. Langer, ed., The rise of modern Europe, 5.] Makes the most of concept of the "baroque" and emphasizes constitutional history.

T45. Gilmore, Myron P. **The world of humanism, 1453–1517.** N.Y., 1952. [The rise of modern Europe, 2.] Recent and successful effort to cover the years before the Reformation. Though government, society, and economy are discussed, the title is descriptive of the emphasis. Bibliography.

T46. Green, Vivian H. H. **Renaissance and Reformation . . . between 1450 and 1660.** London, 1952.

T47. Hauser, Henri, and Augustin Renaudet. **Les débuts de l'âge moderne: la Renaissance et la Réforme.** 3rd ed., Paris,

1946. [Louis Halphen and Philippe Sagnac, eds., Peuples et civilisations, 8.] A comprehensive, scholarly, and intelligibly organized account of western civilization during this period, which deserves a high place in historical literature. Though essentially a handbook, it is not without depth.

T48. Hauser, Henri. **La prépondérance espagnole (1559–1660).** Paris, 1933. [Peuples et civilisations, 9.] No less indispensable than the preceding volume.

T49. Kaser, Kurt. **Das Zeitalter der Reformation und Gegenreformation.** Stuttgart, 1922. A rapid, smooth, and adequate account.

T50. Mousnier, Roland. **Les XVIᵉ et XVIIᵉ siècles: les progrès de la civilisation européenne et le déclin de l'Orient (1492–1715).** Paris, 1954. [Maurice Crouzet, ed., Histoire générale des civilisations, 4.] Content justifies the title. Emphasizes economic and social history.

T51. Sée, Henri, and A. Rebillon. **Le seizième siècle.** 2nd ed., Paris, 1949. [J. Calmett, ed., "Clio": introduction aux études historiques, 6.] Invaluable historical and bibliographical introduction to this period.

T52. Préclin, Edmond, and Victor L. Tapié. **Le XVIIᵉ siècle.** Paris, 1950. ["Clio": introduction aux études historiques, 7.] See comment above.

T53. Clark, Sir George N. **The seventeenth century.** Oxford, 1947. Brilliant cultural history.

T54. Ogg, David. **Europe in the seventeenth century.** 6th rev. ed., London, 1954. One of the best all-round histories of the 17th century.

International Relations from 1492 to the Peace of Westphalia

T55. Mattingly, Garrett. **Renaissance diplomacy.** See *K241*.

T56. Zeller, Gaston. **Les temps modernes.** V. 1, **De Christophe Colomb à Cromwell.** Paris, 1953. The most recent scholarly survey of international relations from 1492 to 1660.

T57. Fueter, Eduard. **Geschichte des europäischen Staatensystems von 1492 bis 1559.** Munich and Berlin, 1919. Generally regarded as the best manual on evolution of the European state system during this period.

T58. Petrie, Sir Charles A. **Earlier diplomatic history, 1492–1713.** London, 1949. Well-written, conservative general treatment of European power politics.

T59. Lévis-Mirepoix, Antoine F. **Les guerres de religion, 1549–1610.** Paris, 1950.

T60. Pagès, Georges. **La Guerre de Trente Ans.** Paris, 1939.

T61. Wedgwood, Cicely V. **The Thirty Years War.** London, 1938. Most recent general account and the most satisfactory one in English.

T62. Gardiner, Samuel R. **The Thirty Years' War.** London, 1874. Though liberal and Protestant in its bias, deserves a place in any general bibliography. [CJF]

T63. Anderson, A. T. **Sweden in the Baltic: a study in the politics of expansion under King Gustav Adolphus and Chancellor Axel Oxenstierna.** Berkeley, 1947.

T64. Vainshtein, Osip L. **Rossiia i Tridtsatiletniaia Voina, 1618–1648 gg.** [Russia and the Thirty Years' War, 1618–1648.] Leningrad, 1947.

T65. Battifol, Louis. "Richelieu et la question de l'Alsace." **Revue historique,** 138 (Nov.-Dec. 1921): 161–200.

T66. Mommsen, Wilhelm. **Richelieu, Elsass und Lotharingen.** Berlin, 1922. Careful documentary study.

T67. Zeller, Gaston. **La France et l'Allemagne depuis dix siècles.** Paris, 1932.

T68. Braubach, Max. **Der Westfälische Friede.** See *VF62*.

T69. Poelhekke, Jan J. **De Vrede van Munster.** The Hague, 1948.

T70. Six, Franz A. **Der Westphälische Friede.** Berlin, 1942. A handy translation of the treaty.

Renaissance Humanism, Philosophy, and Political Thought

T71. Ferguson, Wallace K. **The Renaissance in historical thought: five centuries of interpretation.** Boston, 1948. Shows how generations of scholars have adapted and refined the idea in terms of their own ages.

T72. Weiss, Roberto. **Humanism in England during the fifteenth century.** 2nd ed., Oxford, 1957. An important contribution. [GM]

T73. Caspari, Fritz. **Humanism and the social order in Tudor England.** Chicago, 1954. A thoughtful interpretation.

T74. Allen, Percy S. **The age of Erasmus.** Oxford, 1914. A justly famous book.

T75. Renaudet, Augustin. **Préréforme et humanisme à Paris pendant les premières guerres d'Italie (1494–1517).** Paris, 1916. Rev. ed., 1953.

T76. Burdach, Konrad. **Reformation, Renaissance, Humanismus: zwei Abhandlungen über die Grundlage moderner Bildung und Sprachkunst.** 2nd ed., Berlin and Leipzig, 1926. Maintains the continuity between medieval and Renaissance thought.

T77. Taylor, Henry O. **Thought and expression in the sixteenth century.** 2nd ed., 2 v., N.Y., 1930. Not as successful as his study on the medieval mind, but definitely useful.

T78. Brandi, Karl. **Mittelalterliche Weltanschauung, Humanismus und nationale Bildung.** Berlin, 1925.

T79. Kristeller, Paul O. **The classics and Renaissance thought.** See *VE64*.

T80. Harbison, E. Harris. **The Christian scholar in the age of the Reformation.** N.Y., 1956. Extremely valuable study on Christian humanism.

T81. Toffanin, Giuseppe. **History of humanism.** N.Y., 1954. Tr. of *Storia dell' umanismo* (Bologna, 1950).

T82. Garin, Eugenio. **Der italienische Humanismus.** Bern, 1947. Basic; indispensable to the modern scholar.

T83. ———. **L'educazione in Europa, 1400–1600: problemi e programmi.** Bari, 1957.

T84. Robb, Nesca A. **Neoplatonism of the Italian Renaissance.** London, 1935. Best of the older books on the Florentine Neoplatonists.

T85. Kristeller, Paul O. **The philosophy of Marsilio Ficino.** N.Y., 1943. Most comprehensive and authoritative treatment of Ficino.

T86. Cassirer, Ernst. **Individuum und Kosmos in der Philosophie der Renaissance.** See *VE66*.

T87. Smith, Preserved. **Erasmus.** N.Y., 1923. The most sympathetic biography of Erasmus.

T88. Huizinga, Johan. **Erasmus.** N.Y., 1924. Emphasizes his nationality and has many reservations on his character.

T89. Mann, Margaret. **Erasme et les débuts de la Réforme française (1517–1536).** Paris, 1934. Emphasis on the evolution of Erasmus' religious thought.

T90. Renaudet, Augustin. **Erasme, sa pensée religieuse et son action d'après sa correspondance (1518–1521).** Paris, 1926. This and the following are indispensable to the serious student of Erasmus.

T91. ———. **Études érasmiennes (1521–1529).** Paris, 1939.

T92. Hyma, Albert. **The Christian renaissance: a history of the "Devotio moderna."** Grand Rapids, 1924. Remains a work of importance.

T93. Allen, John W. **A history of political thought in the sixteenth century.** N.Y., 1928. 2nd ed., London, 1941. Excellent general history of the subject.

T94. Figgis, John N. **Studies of political thought from Gerson to Grotius, 1414–1625.** 2nd ed., Cambridge, Eng., 1916.

T95. Mesnard, Pierre. **L'essor de la philosophie politique au XVIe siècle.** 2nd ed., Paris, 1951. Probably the best of recent comprehensive surveys of the subject. [MPG]

T96. Koschaker, Paul. **Europa und das römische Recht.** Munich, 1947. Authoritative work on the whole problem of the survival and importance of Roman law in western Europe. [MPG]

T97. Sabine, George H. **A history of political theory.** 2nd ed., N.Y., 1950.

Books and Printing

T98. Goldschmidt, Ernst P. **The printed book of the Renaissance.** Cambridge, Eng., 1950. Important monograph which discusses relation between the printed book and Renaissance culture. [MPG]

T99. Blum, André. **The origins of printing and engraving.** Tr. by Harry M. Lydenberg. N.Y., 1940.

T100. Butler, Pierce. **The origin of printing in Europe.** Chicago, 1940.

T101. McMurtrie, Douglas C. **The book: the story of printing and bookmaking.** 3rd ed., N.Y. and London, 1943. This and *T100* together summarize European contributions. [MPG]

See also *A89–92*.

Music and the Arts

T102. Prunières, Henri. **A new history of music: the Middle Ages to Mozart.** Ed. and tr. by Edward Lockspeiser. N.Y., 1943. Esteemed particularly for its extra attention to French music. [JSC]

T103. Mather, Frank J. **Western European painting of the Renaissance.** N.Y., 1939. Convenient survey of painting between 1300 and 1800 in Europe outside Italy. [JSC]

T104. Wind, Edgar. **Pagan mysteries of the Renaissance.** New Haven, 1958. Deals effectively with problems of iconography. [JSC]

T105. Tervarent, Guy de. **Attributs et symboles dans l'art profane, 1450–1600: dictionnaire d'un langage perdu.** Geneva, 1958.

T106. Seznec, Jean. **The survival of the pagan gods: the mythological tradition and its place in Renaissance humanism and art.** N.Y., 1953.

T107. Vasari, Giorgio. **The lives of the painters, sculptors and architects.** 4 v. N.Y., 1927. Tr. from *Le vite de' piu eccelenti pittori, scultori ed architettori* (Florence, 1550). A standard work. The Italian edition of 1906 contains valuable comments and annotations by the editor, Gaetano Milanesi. [JSC]

T108. Benesch, Otto. **The art of the Renaissance in northern Europe: its relation to the contemporary spiritual and intellectual movements.** Cambridge, Mass., 1945.

T109. Schlosser Magnino, Julius. **La letteratura artistica.** Tr. from German by Filippo Rossi. 2nd ed., Florence and Vienna, 1935. New ed., 1956. Indispensable for sources and theory of art from Italian Renaissance to later periods. [JSC]

Reformation and Counter-Reformation

T110. Hughes, Philip. **A popular history of the Reformation.** Garden City, 1957. Concise, balanced, judicious, and highly readable history of the church, ca. 1500 to 1563, by an eminent Catholic scholar. [GM]

T111. Bainton, Roland H. **The Reformation of the sixteenth century.** See *D470.*

T112. Grimm, Harold J. **The Reformation era, 1500–1650.** N.Y., 1954. A recent scholarly survey.

T113. Mackinnon, James. **The origins of the Reformation.** See *D469.*

T114. Smith, Preserved. **The age of the Reformation.** N.Y., 1920.

T115. Elliott-Binns, Leonard. **The history of the decline and fall of the medieval papacy.** London, 1934.

T116. Pölnitz, Götz, Frhr. von. **Jakob Fugger. V. 1, Kaiser, Kirche und Kapital in der oberdeutschen Renaissance.** Tübingen, 1949.

T117. ———. **Fugger und Medici.** Leipzig, 1942.

T118. Ritter, Gerhard. **Die neugestaltung Europas im 16. Jahrhundert.** New ed., Berlin, 1950.

T119. Lortz, Joseph. **Die Reformation in Deutschland.** See *VF53.*

T120. Müller, Karl F. F. **Kirchengeschichte.** 2 v. Tübingen, 1911–23. Protestant; comprehensive and scholarly. Best of the standard church histories.

T121. Bender, Harold S. "The Anabaptists and religious liberty in the 16th century." **Archiv für Reformationsgeschichte,** 44 (1953): 32–50.

T122. Schreiber, Georg, ed. **Das Weltkonzil von Trient, sein Werden und Wirken.** 2 v. Freiburg, 1951.

T123. Kidd, Beresford J. **The Counter-Reformation, 1550–1600.** See *VF57.*

T124. Janelle, Pierre. **The Catholic reformation.** Milwaukee, 1949.

T125. Jedin, Hubert. **A history of the Council of Trent.** London, 1957 ff.

T126. Philippson, Martin. **Les origines du catholicisme moderne: la contre-révolution religieuse au XVIe siècle.** Brussels, 1884. Superseded, but still useful.

T127. Pastor, Ludwig von. **The history of the popes from the close of the Middle Ages.** V. 1–40. London and St. Louis, 1891–1953. (In progress.) Tr. from *Geschichte der Päpste seit dem Ausgang des Mittelalters* (16 v. in 21, Freiburg, 1886–1933). Based on sources, equipped with comprehensive bibliographies, and generally indispensable.

T128. Martin, Victor. **Les cardinaux et la curie.** Paris, 1930.

T129. Boehmer, Heinrich. **The Jesuits.** Philadelphia, 1928. Tr. and enlarged from *Die Jesuiten: eine historische Skizze* (4th ed., Leipzig, 1921). A scholarly and neutral general survey.

T130. Eder, Karl. **Die Geschichte der Kirche im Zeitalter des konfessionellen Absolutismus (1555–1648).** 3 v. Vienna, 1949.

T131. Troeltsch, Ernst. **The social teaching of the Christian churches.** See *D435.*

T132. Brodrick, James. **The origin of the Jesuits.** N.Y., 1940. Sympathetic but well-documented account by a member of the order. Covers to the death of St. Ignatius. [GM]

T133. ———. **The progress of the Jesuits (1556–79).** N.Y., 1947. Continues the history of the Society of Jesus. [GM]

T134. Hughes, Philip. **A history of the church. V. 3, The revolt against the church.** N.Y., 1947. A moderate and scholarly Catholic account. [GM]

WESTERN EUROPE, 1648–1789

General Histories

T135. Saint-Léger, Alexandre R. de, and Philippe Sagnac. **La prépondérance française: Louis XIV (1661–1715).** Paris, 1935. [Peuples et civilisations, 10.] Comprehensive history of this period in all its phases; dependable though often uninspired.

T136. Muret, Pierre. **La prépondérance anglaise (1715–1763).** Paris, 1937. 2nd ed., 1942. [Peuples et civilisations, 11.] Despite the misnomer in its title, a useful handbook, though not quite up to the standard of other volumes in this series.

T137. Sagnac, Philippe. **La fin de l'ancien régime et la Révolution Américaine (1763–1789).** 3rd ed., Paris, 1952. [Peuples et civilisations, 12.] This revised and enlarged edition is one of the best studies of the period in any language.

T138. Nussbaum, Frederick L. **The triumph of science and reason, 1660–1685.** N.Y., 1953. [The rise of modern Europe, 6.] Comprehensive treatment of Europe as a whole, with less emphasis on international relations than on economics, institutions, and science.

T139. Wolf, John B. **The emergence of the great powers, 1685–1715.** N.Y., 1951. [The rise of modern Europe, 7.] Able treatment of war and diplomacy, with chapters on science, art, and religion.

T140. Roberts, Penfield. **The quest for security, 1715–1740.** N.Y., 1947. [The rise of modern Europe, 8.] Unfinished at the author's death, this volume is necessarily a little uneven.

T141. Dorn, Walter L. **Competition for empire, 1740–1763.** N.Y., 1940. [The rise of modern Europe, 9.] Besides dealing with the diplomacy and the two wars of this period, emphasizes comparative constitutional history, military and naval organizations, Enlightenment, and commercial and colonial rivalry. Omits Italy, Scandinavia, and the Ottoman empire.

T142. Gershoy, Leo. **From despotism to revolution, 1763–1789.** N.Y., 1944. [The rise of modern Europe, 10.] One of the best treatments of this period in English.

T143. Mousnier, Roland, and Ernest Labrousse. **Le XVIIIᵉ siècle: révolution intellectuelle, technique et politique (1715–1815).** Paris, 1953. [Histoire générale des civilisations, 5.] A brilliant and novel approach emphasizing technological and scientific developments, the unity and diversity of Europe, Asia and the American Revolution, and ending with a sweeping review of revolutionary and Napoleonic Europe.

T144. Lindsay, J. O., ed. **The old regime, 1713–63.** Cambridge, Eng., 1957. [The new Cambridge modern history, 7.] Includes chapters on European commerce, government, social structure, warfare, and religion. Cobban's chapters on France and the Enlightenment and those by D. B. Horn on the diplomatic revolution are outstanding. Lacks bibliography.

T145. Platzhoff, Walter, and others. **Das Zeitalter des Absolutismus.** Berlin, 1931. [Propyläen Weltgeschichte, 6.]

T146. Hartung, Fritz. **Neuzeit: von der Mitte des 17. Jahrhunderts bis zur Französischen Revolution, 1789.** Leipzig, 1932.

T147. Wagner, Fritz. **Europa im Zeitalter des Absolutismus, 1648–1789.** Munich, 1948.

T148. Clark, Sir George N. **The seventeenth century.** See *T53*.

T149. Ogg, David. **Europe in the seventeenth century.** See *T54*.

T150. Beloff, Max. **The age of absolutism, 1660–1815.** London, 1954. Useful and rapid general survey.

International Relations

T151. Zeller, Gaston. **Les temps modernes: de Louis XIV à 1789.** Paris, 1955. Excellent and dependable on the age of Louis XIV, though definitely less useful on the 18th century.

T152. Immich, Max. **Geschichte des europäischen Staatensystems von 1660 bis 1789.** Munich, 1905. Despite its age, this volume is still a model of authoritative diplomatic history; also indispensable for older bibliography.

T153. Dehio, Ludwig. **Gleichgewicht oder Hegemonie: Betrachtungen über ein Grundproblem der neueren Staatengeschichte.** Krefeld, 1948. A reflective effort to bring Ranke's essay on the great powers up to date in light of recent research.

T154. Droz, Jacques. **Histoire diplomatique de 1648 à 1919.** Paris, 1952.

T155. Windelband, Wolfgang. **Die auswärtige Politik der Grossmächte in der Neuzeit.** 3rd ed., Stuttgart, 1936.

T156. Blaga, Corneliu S. **L'évolution de la diplomatie: idéologie, moeurs et technique. V. 1, Le dix-huitième siècle.** Paris, 1938.

T157. Potiemkine, Vladimir P., ed. **Histoire de la diplomatie.** Tr. by Xenia Pamphilova and Michel Eristov. 3 v. Paris, 1946–47. See *AH205.*

T158. Picavet, Camille G. **La diplomatie française au temps de Louis XIV (1661–1715).** Paris, 1930. One of the best studies of its kind.

T159. Rowen, Herbert H. **The ambassador prepares for war: the Dutch embassy of Arnauld de Pomponne, 1669–1671.** The Hague, 1957.

T160. Ford, Franklin L. **Strasbourg in transition, 1648–1789.** Cambridge, Mass., 1958.

T161. André, Louis. **Louis XIV et l'Europe.** Paris, 1950.

T162. Braubach, Max. **Versailles und Wien von Ludwig XIV. bis Kaunitz.** Bonn, 1952.

T163. Marcks, Erich. "Ludwig XIV und Strasbourg." **Männer und Zeiten,** v. 1 (Berlin, 1922), pp. 103–20.

T164. Pagès, Georges. **Le Grand Electeur et Louis XIV.** Paris, 1905.

T165. Seeley, Sir John R. **The growth of British policy.** 2 v. Cambridge, Eng., 1895.

T166. Feiling, Keith G. **British foreign policy, 1660–1672.** London, 1930.

T167. Clark, George N. **The Dutch alliance and the war against French trade, 1689–1697.** Manchester, 1923. Deals with economic relations. See also his "Neutral commerce in the War of the Spanish Succession and the Treaty of Utrecht," *The British year book of international law,* 10 (1929): 69–83.

T168. Geikie, Roderick, and Isabel A. Montgomery. **The Dutch barrier, 1705–1719.** Cambridge, Eng., 1930.

T169. Prestage, Edgar. **The diplomatic relations of Portugal with France, England and Holland from 1640 to 1668.** See *VD280.*

T170. Geyl, Pieter. "Nederland's staatkunde in de Spaansche Successie-oorlog." Akademie van Wetenschappen, **Verslagen en Mededeelingen,** ser. 68 (Amsterdam, 1929), pp. 109–42.

T171. Auerbach, Bertrand. **La France et le Saint Empire Romain germanique depuis la Paix de Westphalie jusqu'à la Révolution Française.** Paris, 1912.

T172. Weber, Ottokar. **Der Friede von Utrecht: Verhandlungen zwischen England, Frankreich, dem Kaiser und den Generalstaaten, 1710–1713.** Gotha, 1891.

T173. Verneau, Francesco. **Il conflitto anglo-francese da Luigi XIV alla Pace di Vienna . . . (1660–1783).** Bologna, 1939.

T174. Danvila y Burguero, Alfonso. **El Congresso de Utrecht.** 3 v. Madrid, 1921.

T175. Castagnoli, Pietro. **Il cardinale Giulio Alberoni.** 3 v. Rome, 1929–32.

T176. Vaucher, Paul. **Robert Walpole et la politique de Fleury (1731–1742).** Paris, 1924.

T177. Chance, James F. **The alliance of Hanover.** London, 1923.

T178. Wilson, Arthur M. **French foreign policy during the administration of Cardinal Fleury.** Cambridge, Mass., 1936.

T179. Moscati, R. I. **La politica estera degli stati italiani dalla caduca di Alberoni al terzo trattato di Vienna, 1720–1731.** Rome, 1948.

T180. Boyé, Pierre. **Le mariage de Marie Leszczynska et l'Europe.** Nancy, 1939.

T181. Rain, Pierre. **La diplomatie française d'Henri IV à Vergennes.** Paris, 1945.

T182. Wagner, Fritz. **Kaiser Karl VII und die grossen Mächte, 1740–1745.** Stuttgart, 1938.

T183. Lodge, Richard. **Studies in eighteenth-century diplomacy, 1740–1748.** London, 1930.

T184. Skalweit, Stephan. **Frankreich und Friedrich der Grosse.** Bonn, 1952.

T185. Geyl, Pieter. **Willem IV en Engeland tot 1748.** The Hague, 1924.

T186. Williams, Basil. **Carteret and Newcastle.** See *VA129*.

T187. Waddington, Richard. **Louis XV et le renversement des alliances . . . 1754–1756.** Paris, 1896.

T188. ——. **La Guerre de Sept Ans.** 5 v. Paris, 1899–1914. Ends with 1761.

T189. Horn, David B. **Sir Charles Hanbury Williams and European diplomacy (1747–58).** London, 1930.

T190. Mediger, Walther. **Moskaus Weg nach Europa: der Aufstieg Russlands zum europäischen Machtstaat im Zeitalter Friedrichs des Grossen.** Brunswick, 1952.

T191. Gerhard, Dietrich. **England und der Aufstieg Russlands.** Munich, 1933.

T192. Rashed, Zenab E. **The Peace of Paris, 1763.** Liverpool, 1952.

T193. Konetzke, Richard. **Die Politik des Grafen Aranda.** Berlin, 1929.

T194. Blart, Louis. **Les rapports de la France et de l'Espagne après le pacte de famille jusqu'à la fin du ministère du duc de Choiseul.** Paris, 1915.

T195. Meng, John J. **The Comte de Vergennes: European phases of his American diplomacy.** Washington, 1932.

T196. Bemis, Samuel F. **The diplomacy of the American Revolution.** See *AB147*.

T197. Eversley, George J. S. L., baron. **The partitions of Poland.** London, 1915.

T198. Beer, Adolf. **Die erste Theilung Polens.** 3 v. in 1. Vienna, 1873.

T199. Horn, David B. **British public opinion and the first partition of Poland.** Edinburgh, 1945.

T200. Easum, Chester V. **Prince Henry of Prussia.** See *VF76*.

T201. Temperley, Harold W. V. **Frederick the Great and Kaiser Joseph.** London, 1915.

T202. Volz, G. B. **Friedrich der Grosse und der Bayrische Erbfolgekrieg.** Berlin, 1932.

T203. Hanfstaengl, Ernst F. S. **Amerika und Europa von Marlborough bis Mirabeau.** Munich, 1930.

Military and Naval History

T204. Vagts, Alfred. **A history of militarism: romance and realities of a profession.** London, 1938. Excellent and scholarly general review.

T205. Silberner, Edmond. **La guerre dans la pensée économique du XVIe au XVIIIe siècle.** Paris, 1939. An excellent study that places the proper emphasis on military aspects of mercantilist thought and practice.

T206. Nef, John U. **War and human progress: an essay on the rise of industrial civilization.** See *AH86*.

T207. Earle, Edward M., and others, eds. **Makers of modern strategy: military thought from Machiavelli to Hitler.** 3rd ed., Princeton, 1948. Contains excellent scholarly studies useful for both 18th and 19th centuries.

T208. Delbrück, Hans, and others. **Geschichte der Kriegskunst im Rahmen der politischen Geschichte.** 7 v. Berlin, 1900–36. In spite of certain defects, this is still the standard history of the art of warfare.

T209. Fuller, John F. C. **A military history of the western world.** 3 v. N.Y., 1954–56. Good for rapid orientation, though not always reliable, especially in the disputed area of the history of strategy. Based on wide reading in secondary sources.

T210. Quimby, Robert S. **The background of Napoleonic warfare: the theory of military tactics in eighteenth-century France.** N.Y., 1957. Original and valuable study of French military writers.

T211. Lehmann, Konrad. "Ermattungsstrategie—oder nicht?" **Historische Zeitschrift,** 151 (1934): 48–86. Most incisive analysis of the strategy of Frederick the Great and of Delbrück's thesis.

T212. Rousset, Léonce. **Les maîtres de la guerre: Frédéric II, Napoléon, Moltke.** Paris, 1899.

T213. Mahan, Alfred T. **The influence of sea power upon history, 1660–1783.** Boston, 1890.

T214. Stevens, William O., and Allan F. Westcott. **A history of sea power.** 2nd ed., N.Y., 1942. Brief but accurate textbook.

T215. Jähns, Max. **Geschichte der Kriegswissenschaften vornehmlich in Deutschland.** 3 v. Munich, 1889–91.

T216. Castex, Raoul. **Les idées militaires de la marine du XVIIIe siècle: de Ruyter à Suffren.** Paris, 1911. This and the following constitute the most penetrating analysis of 18th century naval strategy.

T217. Richmond, Sir Herbert W. **Statesmen and sea power.** 2nd ed., Oxford, 1947.

Collection of brilliant essays on naval warfare.

The Modern State: Government and International Law

T218. Hintze, Otto. **Staat und Verfassung Gesammelte Abhandlungen zur allgemeinen Verfassungsgeschichte.** Leipzig, 1941. Useful and incisive comparative studies on the constitutional evolution of the European states from 1500 to 1800.

T219. Haussherr, Hans. **Verwaltungseinheit und Ressorttrennung vom Ende des 17. bis zum Beginn des 19. Jahrhunderts.** Berlin, 1953. Most satisfactory comparative study of central government of the principal states of Europe from 1600 to 1815.

T220. Finer, Herman. **The theory and practice of modern government.** See *A102*.

T221. Smith, Munroe. **A general view of European legal history.** N.Y., 1927.

T222. Lhéritier, Michel, and others. "Histoire du despotisme éclairé." **Bulletin of the International Committee of Historical Sciences,** 1 (July 1928): 601–12, 2 (June 1930): 533–52, 5 (July 1933): 701–804, 9 (Mar. 1937): 2–131, 9 (June 1937): 135–225, 9 (Dec. 1937): 519–37. Despite the great diversity in approach of the various contributors, this symposium of articles is indispensable.

T223. Konopczyński, Władysław [Ladislas]. **Le liberum veto: étude sur le développement du principe majoritaire.** Paris, 1930. Pioneering study in comparative institutional history of early modern European states.

On enlightened despotism in action see the following (*T224–236*).

T224. Gershoy, Leo. **From despotism to revolution, 1763–1789.** See *T142*.

T225. Sarrailh, Jean. **L'Espagne éclairée de la seconde moitié du XVIIIᵉ siècle.** See *VD95*.

T226. Herr, Richard. **The eighteenth-century revolution in Spain.** Princeton, 1958.

T227. Omodeo, Adolfo. **L'età del risorgimento italiano.** See *VE109*.

T228. Bulferetti, Luigi. **L'assolutismo illuminato in Italia.** See *VE89*.

T229. Valsecchi, Franco. **L'assolutismo illuminato in Austria e in Lombardia.** See *VE88*.

T230. Valjavec, Fritz. **Der Josephinismus.** See *VF252*.

T231. Padover, Saul K. **The revolutionary emperor: Joseph the Second, 1741–1790.** See *VF251*.

T232. Fejtö, François. **Un Habsbourg révolutionnaire, Joseph II.** Paris, 1953.

T233. Ritter, Gerhard. **Friedrich der Grosse: ein historisches Profil.** 3rd ed., Heidelberg, 1954.

T234. Gaxotte, Pierre. **Frederick the Great.** Tr. by R. A. Bell. London, 1941.

T235. Hodgetts, Edward A. B. **The life of Catherine the Great of Russia.** London, 1914.

T236. Reddaway, William F. "Denmark under the Bernstorffs and Struensee." **The Cambridge modern history,** v. 6 (Cambridge, Eng., 1909), pp. 735–57.

T237. Smith, Munroe. **The development of European law.** N.Y., 1928.

T238. Messner, Johannes. **Das Naturrecht.** Innsbruck, 1950.

T239. Butler, Geoffrey G., and Simon Maccoby. **The development of international law.** London, 1928.

T240. Pares, Richard. **Colonial blockade and neutral rights, 1739–1763.** Oxford, 1938.

T241. Jessup, Philip C., and others. **Neutrality, its history, economics and law.** 2 v. N.Y., 1935–36. [1, P. C. Jessup and Francis Deák, *The origins;* 2, Walter A. Philipps and Arthur H. Reede, *The Napoleonic period.*] The most valuable treatise on this subject.

T242. Pyke, Harold R. **The law of contraband of war.** Oxford, 1915.

T243. Gerloff, A. Wolfgang. **Staatstheorie und Staatspratis des kameralistischen Verwaltungsstaates.** Breslau, 1937.

T244. Passerin d'Entrèves, Alessandro. **Natural law.** London, 1951. Useful brief survey from a Catholic viewpoint.

Social Structure; Social, Religious, and Political Thought

T245. Hazard, Paul. **The European mind: the critical years, 1680–1715.** New Haven, 1953. Tr. from *La crise de la conscience européenne (1680–1715)* (Paris, 1935).

T246. ——. **European thought in the eighteenth century from Montesquieu to Lessing.** New Haven, 1954. Tr. from *La pensée européenne au XVIIIᵉᵐᵉ siècle: de Montesquieu à Lessing* (Paris, 1946).

T247. Cassirer, Ernst. **The philosophy of the Enlightenment.** See *A342*.

T248. Laski, Harold J. **The rise of European liberalism.** London, 1936. A Marxist interpretation.

T249. Gierke, Otto F. von. **Natural law and the theory of society, 1500 to 1800.** Ed. and tr. by E. Barker. 2 v. Cambridge, Eng., 1934.

T250. Erdmann, Karl D. **Volkssouveränität und Kirche.** Cologne, 1949.

T251. Sabine, George H. **A history of political theory.** 2nd ed., N.Y., 1950.

T252. Green, Frederick C. **Minuet.** London, 1935. Stimulating study of Anglo-French literary relations in the 18th century. [PG]

T253. Raumer, Kurt von. **Ewiger Friede: Friedensrufe und Friedenspläne seit der Renaissance.** Freiburg, 1953. A history of European pacifism.

T254. Meinecke, Friedrich. **Die Idee der Staatsräison in der neueren Geschichte.** 3rd ed., Munich, 1929. English tr., *History of Machiavellianism,* London, 1957.

T255. Sombart, Werner. **Der Bourgeois: zur Geistesgeschichte des modernen Wirtschaftsmenschen.** See *A127.*

T256. Borkenau, Franz. **Der Übergang vom feudalen zum bürgerlichen Weltbild: Studien zur Geschichte der Philosophie der Manufakturperiode.** Paris, 1934.

T257. Goodwin, Albert, ed. **The European nobility in the eighteenth century.** London, 1953. A pioneering study on the aristocracies of the principal European countries.

T258. Lavedan, Pierre. **Histoire de l'urbanisme.** V. 2, **Renaissance et temps moderne.** Paris, 1941.

T259. Willey, Basil. **The eighteenth century background.** London, 1940; N.Y., 1941.

T260. Giarrizzo, Giuseppe. **Edward Gibbon e la cultura europea del settecento.** Naples, 1954.

T261. Wellek, René. **A history of modern criticism, 1750–1950.** N.Y., 1955 ff. 4 v. planned.

T262. Brinton, Crane. **Ideas and men: the story of western thought.** N.Y., 1950.

T263. ——. **The shaping of the modern mind.** N.Y., 1953. Continuation of the above, extending from 1450 to 1950. A rapid and often stimulating survey of modern western thought.

T264. Whitehead, Alfred N. **Science and the modern world.** N.Y., 1925. Valuable chapters on science and thought in the 17th century.

T265. Smith, Preserved. **A history of modern culture.** 2 v. N.Y., 1930–34. Though superseded in matters of science, provides a full factual account of essential teaching points. Covers period 1543–1776.

T266. Becker, Carl L. **The heavenly city of the eighteenth century philosophers.** 11th ed., New Haven, 1955. A brilliant interpretive essay by a skeptical and relativist historian rather than a sound guide for the beginning historical student.

T267. Rockwood, Raymond O., ed. **Carl Becker's Heavenly city revisited.** Ithaca, 1958.

T268. Heer, Friedrich. **Europäische Geistesgeschichte.** Stuttgart, 1953.

T269. Brunschvicg, Léon. **Descartes et Pascal, lecteurs de Montaigne.** Paris, 1944.

T270. Larkin, Paschal. **Property in the eighteenth century, with special reference to England and Locke.** Dublin, 1930.

Music and the Arts

T271. Parrish, Carl, ed. **Masterpieces of music before 1750.** N.Y., 1951. Accompanied by 3 LP records of same title, Copenhagen, 1953. Adapted to historical study.

T272. Stevenson, Robert M. **Music before the classic era: an introductory guide.** N.Y., 1955.

T273. Besseler, Heinrich. **Die Musik des Mittelalters und der Renaissance.** Potsdam, 1931. The most successful summary of Renaissance music.

T274. Bukofzer, Manfred F. **Studies in medieval and Renaissance music.** N.Y., 1950. Contains an essay on choral polyphony.

T275. ——. **Music in the baroque era (from Monteverdi to Bach).** N.Y., 1947. A history of musical styles and ideas, emphasizing criticism of style. Extensive bibliography. [DLB]

T276. Leichtentritt, Hugo. **Music, history and ideas.** Cambridge, Mass., 1938. Attempts to relate music to its physical setting, political events, and the world of the spirit. The author's article, "The Renaissance attitude towards music," *The musical quarterly,* 1 (Oct. 1915): 604–22, presents a critical discussion of modern theories revising the traditional estimate of Renaissance music. [MPG]

T277. Combarieu, Jules. **Histoire de la musique des origines au début du XXᵉ siècle.** See *C265.*

T278. Haas, Robert M. **Die Musik des Barocks.** Potsdam, 1928. An outstanding study with complete bibliography.

T279. Sypher, Wylie. **Four stages of Renaissance style.** Garden City, 1955.

T280. Wölfflin, Heinrich. **Principles of art history.** N.Y., 1932. An attempt to define baroque art and to set it off against the classical art of the Renaissance.

T281. Mâle, Emile. **L'art religieux après le Concile de Trente.** Paris, 1932.

T282. ——. **L'art religieux de la fin du XVIᵉ siècle, du XVIIᵉ siècle, et du XVIIIᵉ siècle.** 2nd ed., Paris, 1951. Indispensable for the baroque era. [JSC]

T283. Pevsner, Nikolaus, and Otto Grautoff. **Die Barockmalerei in den romanischen Länder.** Potsdam, [1928].

T284. Pigler, A. **Barockthemen: eine Auswahl von Verzeichnissen zur Ikonographie des 17. and 18. Jahrhunderts.** 2 v. Budapest, 1956. Baroque iconography, religious and pagan. [JSC]

T285. Weisbach, Werner. **Die Kunst des Barock in Italien, Frankreich, Deutschland, und Spanien.** Berlin, 1924.

T286. Brinkmann, Albert E. **Baukunst des 17. und 18. Jahrhunderts in den romanischen Länder.** 3 v. Berlin, 1919.

T287. Kaufmann, Emil. **Architecture in the age of reason: baroque and post-baroque in England, Italy and France.** Cambridge, Mass., 1955. Valuable, though obscurely written. [JSC]

T288. Pevsner, Nikolaus. "The architecture of mannerism." Geoffrey Grigson, ed., **The mint: a miscellany of literature, art and criticism,** v. 1 (London, 1946), pp. 116–38.

T289. Honey, William B. **European ceramic art from the end of the Middle Ages to about 1815.** 2 v. in 1. N.Y., 1949.

T290. Hofmann, Friedrich H. **Das Porzellan der europäischen Manufakturen im XVIII. Jahrhundert.** Berlin, 1932.

T291. Mead, William E. **The Grand Tour in the eighteenth century.** N.Y., 1914.

T292. Pevsner, Nikolaus. **Academies of art, past and present.** Cambridge, Eng., 1940. A scholarly survey, rich in suggestions and bibliographical material.

FRENCH REVOLUTIONARY AND NAPOLEONIC EUROPE, 1789–1815

Political, Diplomatic, and General Works

T293. Gershoy, Leo. **The French Revolution and Napoleon.** N.Y., 1933. A standard account.

T294. Gottschalk, Louis R. **The era of the French Revolution (1715–1815).** N.Y., 1929.

T295. Thompson, James M. **The French Revolution.** Oxford, 1943.

T296. Stern, Alfred, and others, eds. **Die Französische Revolution, Napoleon und die Restauration, 1789–1848.** Berlin, 1929. [Walter W. Goetz, ed., Propyläen Weltgeschichte, 7.]

T297. Lefebvre, Georges. **La Révolution Française.** Paris, 1951. [Louis Halphen and Philippe Sagnac, eds., Peuples et civilisations, 13.] Considers all of Europe and emphasizes economic and social history.

T298. ——. **Napoléon.** 4th ed., Paris, 1953. [Peuples et civilisations, 14.]

T299. Brinton, Crane. **A decade of revolution, 1789–1799.** N.Y., 1934. [William L. Langer, ed., The rise of modern Europe, 11.] In recent reprintings the bibliography has been revised.

T300. Godechot, Jacques L. **La grande nation: l'expansion révolutionnaire de la France dans le monde de 1789 à 1799.** 2 v. Paris, 1956.

T301. ——. **Les institutions de la France sous la Révolution et l'empire.** Paris, 1951.

T302. Bruun, Geoffrey. **Europe and the French imperium, 1799–1814.** N.Y., 1938. [The rise of modern Europe, 12.]

T303. Sorel, Albert. **L'Europe et la Révolution Française.** 9 v. Paris, 1895–1911. Still the classic on France and Europe during the French Revolution, but amended by *T300* and *T313*.

T304. Sybel, Heinrich von. **Geschichte der Revolutionszeit.** 5 v. Düsseldorf, 1853–79.

T305. Fugier, André. **La Révolution Française et l'empire napoléonien.** Paris, 1954. [Pierre Renouvin, ed., Histoire des relations internationales, 4.] An excellent account.

T306. ——. **Napoléon et l'Italie.** See *VE96*.

T307. ——. **Napoléon et l'Espagne, 1799–1808.** 2 v. Paris, 1930.

T308. Biro, Sydney S. **The German policy of revolutionary France: a study in French diplomacy during the war of the first coalition, 1792–1797.** 2 v. Cambridge, Mass., 1957. Best study on France's Rhine policy.

T309. Droz, Jacques. **L'Allemagne et la Révolution Française.** Paris, 1949. This study has superseded George P. Gooch, *Germany and the French Revolution* (London, 1920) and Adalbert E. A. Wahl, *Über die Nachwirkungen der Französischen Revolution vornehmlich in Deutschland* (Stuttgart, 1939).

T310. Wahl, Adalbert E. A. **Geschichte des europäischen Staatensystems im Zeitalter der Französischen Revolution.** Munich and Berlin, 1912.

T311. Rain, Pierre. **La diplomatie française de Mirabeau à Bonaparte.** Paris, 1950.

T312. Clapham, John H. **The causes of the war of 1792.** Cambridge, Eng., 1899.

T313. Guyot, Raymond. **Le Directoire et la paix de l'Europe.** Paris, 1911.

T314. Ward, Adolphus W., and George P. Gooch, eds. **The Cambridge history of British foreign policy.** V. 1, 1783–1815. Cambridge, Eng., 1922.

T315. Lobanov-Rostovsky, Andrei A. **Russia and Europe, 1789–1825.** Durham, 1947.

T316. Dechamps, Jules. **Les Isles Britanniques et la Révolution Française.** Brussels, 1949.

T317. Rose, J. Holland. **William Pitt and the great war.** London, 1911.

T318. Lord, Robert H. **The second partition of Poland.** Cambridge, Mass., 1915.

T319. Carlsson, Sten, and Torvald Höjer. **Den svenska utrikespolitikens historia.** V. 3, 1792–1844. Stockholm, 1954.

T320. Puryear, Vernon J. **Napoleon and the Dardanelles.** See *S259.*

T321. Markham, Felix M. H. **Napoleon and the awakening of Europe.** London, 1954.

T322. Coquelle, P. **Napoléon et l'Angleterre.** Paris, 1904. Tr. by Gordon D. Knox, London, 1904.

T323. Srbik, Heinrich, Ritter von. **Das österreichische Kaisertum und das Ende des Heiligen Römischen Reiches, 1804–1806.** Berlin, 1927.

T324. Schaeder, Hildegard. **Die dritte Koalition und die Heilige Allianz.** See *X209.*

T325. Heymann, Ernst. **Napoleon und die Grossen Mächte im Frühjahr 1806.** Berlin, 1910.

T326. Melvin, Frank E. **Napoleon's navigation system.** N.Y., 1919.

T327. Heckscher, Eli F. **The continental system: an economic interpretation.** Ed. by Harald Westergaard. Oxford, 1922.

T328. Dunan, Marcel. **Napoléon et l'Allemagne: le système continental et les débuts du royaume de Bavière, 1806–1810.** Paris, 1942.

T329. L'Huillier, Fernand. **Étude sur le blocus continental: la mise en vigueur des décrets de Trianon et de Fontainebleau dans le Grand-Duché de Bade.** Paris, 1951.

T330. Tarlé, Eugène. **Le blocus continental et le royaume d'Italie.** See *VE101.*

T331. Vandal, Albert. **Napoléon et Alexandre Ier.** 3 v. Paris, 1891–96.

T332. Handelsmann, Marceli. **Napoléon et la Pologne, 1806–1807.** Paris, 1909.

T333. Lesage, Charles. **Napoléon Ier, créancier de la Prusse (1807–1814).** Paris, 1924.

T334. Deutsch, Harold C. **The genesis of Napoleonic imperialism.** Cambridge, Mass., 1938.

T335. Buckland, Charles S. B. **Metternich and the British government from 1809 to 1813.** London, 1932.

T336. Webster, Charles K. **The Congress of Vienna, 1814–1815.** 2nd ed., London, 1934.

T337. Griewank, Karl. **Der Wiener Kongress und de Neuordnung Europas.** Leipzig, 1942.

T338. Weil, Maurice H. **Les dessous du Congrès de Vienne.** 2 v. Paris, 1917.

T339. Kukiel, Marian. **Czartoryski and European unity, 1770–1861.** See *W154.*

T340. Straus, Hannah A. **The attitude of the Congress of Vienna toward nationalism in Germany, Italy and Poland,** N.Y., 1949.

T341. Nicolson, Harold G. **The Congress of Vienna: a study in allied unity, 1812–1822.** N.Y., 1946.

T342. Schenk, Hans G. **The aftermath of the Napoleonic wars: the Concert of Europe, an experiment.** London, 1947.

T343. Thompson, James M. **Napoleon Bonaparte: his rise and fall.** Oxford, 1952.

Military and Naval History

T344. Colin, Jean L. A. **The transformations of war.** London, 1913. Tr. from *Les transformations de la guerre* (Paris, 1911).

T345. Nickerson, Hoffman. **The armed horde, 1793–1939.** N.Y., 1940.

T346. Phipps, Ramsay W. **The armies of the first French republic.** 5 v. London, 1926–39.

T347. Chuquet, Arthur M. **Les guerres de la Révolution.** 11 v. Paris, 1886–96.

T348. Six, Georges. **Les généraux de la Révolution et de l'empire.** Paris, 1948.

T349. Lauerma, Matti. **L'artillerie de campagne française pendant les guerres de la Révolution: évolution de l'organisation et de la tactique.** Helsinki, 1956.

T350. Finot, Jules. **La défense nationale dans le Nord de 1792 à 1802.** 2 v. Lille, 1890–93.

T351. Godechot, Jacques L. **Les commissaires aux armées sous le Directoire.** 2 v. Paris, 1937.

T352. Bourdeau, Henry. **Les armées du Rhin au début du Directoire.** Paris, 1909.

T353. Colin, Jean L. A. **Napoléon.** Paris, 1914.

T354. Ballard, Colin R. **Napoleon, an outline.** London, 1931.

T355. Wilkinson, Spencer. **The rise of Napoleon Bonaparte.** Oxford, 1931.

T356. Bouvier, Félix. **Bonaparte en Italie, 1796.** 2nd ed., Paris, 1902.

T357. Camon, Hubert. **La guerre napoléonienne: précis des campagnes.** 3 v. Paris, 1903–10.

T358. Dodge, Theodore A. **Napoleon.** 4 v. Boston, 1904–07. Though not based on original research, still the most extensive account in English of Napoleon's military career.

T359. Oman, Charles W. C. **A history of the Peninsular War.** 7 v. Oxford, 1902–30.

T360. ———. **Studies in the Napoleonic wars.** London, 1929.

T361. Clausewitz, Karl von. **La campagne de 1796 en Italie.** Tr. by Jean Colin. Paris, 1899.

T362. ———. **The campaign of 1812 in Russia.** London, 1843. Tr. from *Der Feldzug von 1812 in Russland* (Berlin, 1835).

T363. Jacoby, Jean. **Souvorov.** Paris, 1935.

T364. ———. **Napoléon en Russie.** Paris, 1939.

T365. Tarlé, Eugène. **Napoleon's invasion of Russia in 1812.** Tr. by Norbert Guterman and Ralph Manheim. N.Y., 1942.

T366. Ségur, Philippe P., comte de. **Napoleon's Russian campaign.** Tr. by J. David Townsend. Boston, 1958.

T367. Rousset, Camille F. A. **La grande armée de 1813.** 2nd ed., Paris, 1892.

T368. Reboul, Frédéric. **La campagne de 1813: les préliminaires.** 2 v. Paris, 1910–12. Classic study by an accomplished military historian.

T369. Shanahan, William O. **Prussian military reforms, 1786–1813.** See *VF97.*

T370. Lettow-Vorbeck, Oscar von. **Der Krieg von 1806 und 1807.** 4 v. Berlin, 1892–99.

T371. Holleben, Albert H. von. **Geschichte der Befreiungskriege, 1813–1815.** 9 v. Berlin, 1903–09.

T372. Delbrück, Hans. **Das Leben des Feldmarschalls Grafen Neithardt von Gneisenau.** 2 v. Berlin, 1882.

T373. Lefebvre de Béhaine, François. **La défense de la ligne du Rhin.** Paris, 1933.

T374. ———. **L'invasion: décembre 1813–janvier 1814.** 2 v. Paris, 1934–35.

T375. Lehmann, Max. **Scharnhorst.** See *VF98.*

T376. Houssaye, Henri. **1814.** Paris, 1888. Many subsequent eds.

T377. ———. **1815.** 3 v. Paris, 1893–1905. Many subsequent eds.

T378. Becke, Archibald F. **Napoleon and Waterloo.** London, 1914.

T379. Davies, Godfrey. **Wellington and his army.** Oxford, 1954.

T380. Mahan, Alfred T. **The influence of sea power upon the French Revolution and empire, 1793–1812.** 10th ed., 2 v., Boston, 1898. Still the best naval history of the revolutionary and Napoleonic wars. [CB]

T381. Westcott, Allan F., ed. **Mahan on naval warfare.** Boston, 1918.

T382. Jouan, René. **Histoire de la marine française.** 2 v. Paris, 1932.

T383. Tramond, Johannès M. **Manuel d'histoire maritime de la France.** 2 v. Paris, 1927.

T384. Stuart-Jones, Edwyn H. **An invasion that failed: the French expedition to Ireland, 1796.** Oxford, 1950.

T385. Corbett, Julian S. **The campaign of Trafalgar.** London, 1910.

T386. Maine, René. **Trafalgar: Napoleon's naval Waterloo.** N.Y., 1957.

T387. Parkinson, Cyril N. **War in the eastern seas, 1793–1815.** London, 1954.

T388. James, William. **The naval history of Great Britain.** 2nd ed., 6 v., London, 1886. Covers period 1793–1820.

SCIENCE AND TECHNOLOGY, 1500–1800

Scientific Revolution

T389. Hall, Alfred R. **The scientific revolution, 1500–1800: the formation of the modern scientific attitude.** See *A258.*

T390. Pledge, Humphry T. **Science since 1500.** London, 1939. Good, but somewhat abstruse.

T391. Wolf, Abraham. **A history of science, technology and philosophy in the 16th and 17th centuries.** London, 1935. A useful compendium.

T392. ——. **A history of science, technology and philosophy in the 18th century.** 2nd ed., London and N.Y., 1952. Useful handbook.

T393. Koyré, Alexandre. **From the closed world to the infinite universe.** Baltimore, 1957. Reveals how the Copernican theory and discoveries through the telescope led to the concept of the infinite universe.

T394. Rosen, Edward, ed. and tr. **Three Copernican treatises.** N.Y., 1939.

T395. Birkenmajer, Ludwik A. **Mikołaj Kopernik.** 2 v. Cracow, 1900.

T396. Johnson, Francis R. **Astronomical thought in Renaissance England.** Baltimore, 1937.

T397. Koyré, Alexandre. **Études galiléennes.** 3 v. Paris, 1939. Very important.

T398. Ornstein, Martha. **The rôle of scientific societies in the seventeenth century.** 3rd ed., Chicago, 1938.

T399. Brown, Harcourt. **Scientific organizations in seventeenth century France.** Baltimore, 1934.

T400. Balz, Albert G. A. **Cartesian studies.** N.Y., 1951.

T401. Scott, Joseph F. **The scientific work of René Descartes (1596–1650).** London, 1952.

T402. Lenoble, Robert. **Mersenne: ou, la naissance du mécanisme.** Paris, 1943.

T403. Bell, Arthur E. **Christian Haygens and the development of science in the seventeenth century.** London, 1947.

T404. Greenstreet, William J., ed. **Isaac Newton, 1642–1727: a memorial volume.** London, 1927.

T405. Lasswitz, Kurd. **Geschichte der Atomistik von Mittelalter bis Newton.** 2 v. Hamburg, 1890.

T406. Hagberg, Knut H. **Carl Linnaeus.** See *VB161.*

T407. Brunet, Pierre. **L'introduction des théories de Newton en France au XVIIIᵉ siècle.** Paris, 1931.

T408. Broad, Charlie D. **The philosophy of Francis Bacon.** Cambridge, Eng., 1926.

T409. Gade, John A. **The life and times of Tycho Brahe.** Princeton, 1947. More biographical than scientific.

T410. Goldbeck, Ernst A. W. **Keplers Lehre von der Gravitation.** Halle, 1896.

T411. Bethell, Samuel L. **The cultural revolution of the seventeenth century.** London, 1951.

See also the more general works in Section A.

Technology

T412. Usher, Abbott P. **A history of mechanical inventions.** Rev. ed., Cambridge, Mass., 1954.

T413. McCloy, Shelby T. **French inventions of the eighteenth century.** Lexington, Ky., 1952.

T414. Crommelin, Claude A. **Physics and the art of instrument making at Leyden in the seventeenth and eighteenth centuries.** Leiden, 1925.

T415. Daumas, Maurice. **Les instruments scientifiques au XVIIᵉ et XVIIIᵉ siècles.** Paris, 1953.

T416. Brockdorff, Cay L. von. **Gelehrte Gesellschaften im XVII. Jahrhundert.** Kiel, 1940.

EUROPE, 1815–1914

General Histories

T417. Stern, Alfred. **Geschichte Europas seit den Verträgen von 1815 bis zum Frankfurter Frieden von 1871.** 10 v. Stuttgart, 1894–1924. The most comprehensive history by a single author; primarily political and diplomatic. Despite its age, has never been surpassed.

T418. Herzfeld, Hans. **Die moderne Welt, 1789–1945.** 2 v. Braunschweig, Ger., 1950–52. A useful post-war review by a liberal German historian.

T419. Schnerb, Robert. **Le XIXᵉ siècle: l'apogée de l'expansion européenne (1815–1914).** Paris, 1955. [Histoire générale des civilisations, 6.]

T420. Woodward, Ernest L. **War and peace in Europe, 1815–1870.** London, 1931.

T421. Grant, Arthur J., and Harold W. V. Temperley. **Europe in the nineteenth and twentieth centuries (1789–1950).** 6th ed., London, 1952.

T422. Bowle, John. **Politics and opinion in the nineteenth century.** London, 1954.

T423. Croce, Benedetto. **History of Europe in the nineteenth century.** N.Y., 1933. Worthy of this great Italian philosopher of history.

T424. Mommsen, Wilhelm. **Geschichte des Abendlandes . . . 1789–1945.** Munich, 1951.

T425. Näf, Werner. **Die Epochen der neueren Geschichte: Staat und Staatengemeinschaft vom Ausgang des Mittelalter bis zur Gegenwart.** 2 v. Aarau, 1945–46. Creditable survey by a Swiss historian, with marked value for the 19th century.

T426. Jong, Jelle J. de. **Politieke organisatie in west Europa na 1800.** See *VC1353.*

T427. Vietsch, Eberhard von. **Das europäische Gleichgewicht, politische Idee und staatsmännisches Handeln.** Leipzig, 1942.

T428. Thomson, David. **Europe since Napoleon.** N.Y., 1957.

Nationalism

T429. Hayes, Carlton J. H. **The historical evolution of modern nationalism.** See *C121.*

T430. Lemberg, Eugen. **Geschichte des Nationalismus in Europa.** Stuttgart, 1950.

T431. Weill, Georges J. **L'Europe du XIXᵉ siècle et l'idée de nationalité.** Paris, 1938.

From the Congress of Vienna to 1848

T432. Webster, Charles K. **The Congress of Vienna, 1814–1815.** 2nd ed., London, 1934.

T433. Temperley, Harold W. V. **The foreign policy of Canning, 1822–1827.** London, 1925.

T434. Nicolson, Harold G. **The Congress of Vienna.** See *T341.*

T435. Straus, Hannah A. **The attitude of the Congress of Vienna toward nationalism in Germany, Italy and Poland.** N.Y., 1949.

T436. Artz, Frederick B. **Reaction and revolution, 1814–1832.** N.Y., 1934. [The rise of modern Europe, 13.] Best general survey of the aftermath of the Napoleonic wars.

T437. Weill, Georges J. **L'éveil des nationalités et le mouvement libéral (1815–1848).** Paris, 1930. [Peuples et civilisations, 15.] Standard study by a recognized expert on this period.

T438. Comité Français des Sciences Historiques. **1830: études sur les mouvements libéraux et nationaux de 1830.** Paris, 1932.

T439. Renouvin, Pierre. **Le XIXᵉ siècle. V. 1, De 1815 à 1871: l'Europe des nationalités et l'éveil de nouveaux mondes.** Paris, 1954. [Histoire des relations internationales, 5.] Summary review by a recognized international authority.

T440. Webster, Charles K. **Palmerston, Metternich and the European system, 1830–1841.** London, 1934.

T441. ——. **The foreign policy of Castlereagh, 1815–1822.** 2nd ed., London, 1934. The most thorough and scholarly study of British foreign policy.

T442. Srbik, Heinrich, Ritter von. **Metternich.** See *VF257.*

T443. Pirenne, Jacques H. **La Sainte-Alliance.** 2 v. Neuchâtel, 1946–49. Must henceforth be regarded as the standard study in any language.

T444. Bourquin, Maurice. **Histoire de la Sainte Alliance.** Geneva, 1954.

T445. Näf, Werner. **Zur Geschichte der Heiligen Allianz.** Bern, 1928.

T446. Schmalz, Hans W. **Versuche einer gesamteuropäischen Organisation, 1815–1820.** Aarau, Switz., 1940.

T447. Schenk, Hans G. **The aftermath of the Napoleonic wars: the Concert of Europe, an experiment.** London, 1947.

T448. Phillips, W. Alison. **The confederation of Europe: a study of the European alliance, 1813–1823.** 2nd ed., London and N.Y., 1920.

T449. Woodward, Ernest L. **Three studies in European conservatism: Metternich; Guizot; the Catholic Church in the nineteenth century.** London, 1929. A brilliant work.

T450. Hudson, Nora E. **Ultra-royalism and the French restoration.** Cambridge, Eng., 1936.

Liberalism and the Revolutions of 1848

T451. Ruggiero, Guido de. **The history of European liberalism.** London, 1927. A standard work.

T452. Schapiro, Jacob S. **Liberalism and the challenge of fascism: social forces in England and France, 1815–1870.** N.Y., 1949. Stimulating and provocative interpretation which dubiously describes Napoleon III as a "herald of fascism."

T453. Fejtö, François, ed. **Le printemps des peuples: 1848 dans le monde.** 2 v. Paris, 1948. Tr., *The opening of an era: 1848,* London, 1948.

T454. Robertson, Priscilla S. **Revolutions of 1848.** Princeton, 1952.

T455. Namier, Sir Lewis B. **1848: the revolution of the intellectuals.** See *VF123*.

T456. Whitridge, Arnold. **Men in crisis: the revolutions of 1848.** N.Y., 1949.

T457. Greer, Donald M. **L'Angleterre, la France et la révolution de 1848.** Paris, 1925.

T458. Taylor, Alan J. P. **The Italian problem in European diplomacy, 1847–1849.** Manchester, 1934.

T459. Moscati, Ruggero. **La diplomazia europea e il problema italiano nel 1848.** Florence, 1947.

T460. Scharff, Alexander. **Die europäischen Grossmächte und die deutsche Revolution . . . 1848–1851.** Leipzig, 1942.

Europe in the Age of Italian and German Unification, 1849–1871

General

T461. Pouthas, Charles H. **Démocraties et capitalisme (1848–1860).** Paris, 1941. [Peuples et civilisations, 16.] A volume worthy of the series in which it is included.

T462. Hauser, Henri, Jean Maurain, and Pierre Benaerts. **Du libéralisme à l'impérialisme (1860–1878).** New ed., by Fernand L. Huillier, Paris, 1952. [Peuples et civilisations, 17.]

T463. Droz, Jacques, Lucien Genet, and Jean Vidalenc. **L'époque contemporaine.** V. 1, **Restaurations et révolutions (1815–1871).** Paris, 1953. Useful, especially for rapid orientation and bibliography.

T464. Binkley, Robert C. **Realism and nationalism, 1852–1871.** N.Y., 1935. [The rise of modern Europe, 15.] Despite its doubtful emphasis on the concept of "federative polity," this is one of the more original volumes of this series.

T465. Seton-Watson, Robert W. **Britain in Europe, 1789–1914.** Cambridge, Eng., 1937. Good for period to 1880.

T466. Taylor, Alan J. P. **The struggle for mastery in Europe, 1848–1918.** Oxford, 1954. Provocative, not always convincing, but scholarly and the only volume that covers the entire period of diplomatic history from 1848 to 1914. Contains valuable bibliography.

Diplomacy of the Crimean War

T467. Henderson, Gavin B. **Crimean War diplomacy.** See *S265.*

T468. Temperley, Harold W. V. **England and the Near East.** V. 1, **The Crimea.** See *S261.*

T469. Puryear, Vernon J. **England, Russia and the Straits question, 1844–1856.** See *S264.*

T470. ———. **International economics and diplomacy in the Near East: a study of British commercial policy in the Levant, 1834–1853.** Stanford, 1935.

T471. Guichen, Eugène, vicomte de. **La Guerre de Crimée (1854–1856) et l'attitude des puissances européennes.** Paris, 1936.

T472. Kinglake, Alexander W. **The invasion of the Crimea.** 8 v. Edinburgh, 1863–87.

T473. Hamley, Edward B. **The war in the Crimea.** London, 1890.

T474. Friedjung, Heinrich. **Der Krimkrieg und die österreichische Politik.** 2nd ed., Stuttgart, 1911.

T475. Schüle, Ernst. **Russland und Frankreich . . . 1856–1859.** Berlin, 1935.

Europe and Italian and German Unification

T476. Bratianu, George I. **Napoléon III et les nationalités.** Paris, 1934.

T477. Pagès, Georges. **La politique extérieure de Napoléon III.** Paris, 1933.

T478. Valsecchi, Franco. **L'unificazione italiana e la politica europea.** See *VE164.*

T479. Case, Lynn M. **Franco-Italian relations, 1860–1865.** Philadelphia, 1932.

T480. Deutsch, Wilhelm. **Habsburgs Rückzug aus Italien.** Leipzig, 1940.

T481. Steefel, Lawrence D. **The Schleswig-Holstein question.** See *VB86.*

T482. Friedjung, Heinrich. **Der Kampf um die Vorherrschaft in Deutschland, 1859 bis 1866.** 2 v. Stuttgart, 1897–1900. 10th ed., 1916–17. The classic account that is still important despite errors of detail.

T483. Oncken, Hermann. **Die Rheinpolitik Kaiser Napoleons III. von 1863 bis 1870.** 3 v. Berlin and Leipzig, 1926. Tr., **Napoleon III and the Rhine,** N.Y., 1928.

T484. Lord, Robert H. **The origins of the war of 1870.** Cambridge, Mass., 1924.

T485. Wallace, Lillian P. **The papacy in European diplomacy, 1869–1878.** Chapel Hill, 1949.

Europe, 1871–1914

General Histories

T486. Hayes, Carlton J. H. **A generation of materialism, 1871–1900.** N.Y., 1941. [The rise of modern Europe, 16.] Substantial contribution by a historian with a Catholic religious outlook. Objective and scholarly.

T487. Baumont, Maurice. **L'essor industriel et l'impérialisme coloniale (1878–1904).** 2nd ed., Paris, 1949. [Peuples et civilisations, 18.]

T488. Renouvin, Pierre. **La crise européenne et la Première Guerre Mondiale.** 3rd ed., Paris, 1948. [Peuples et civilisations, 19.]

Diplomacy

T489. Renouvin, Pierre. **Le XIXe siècle.** V. 2, **De 1871 à 1914: l'apogée de l'Europe.** Paris, 1955. [Histoire des relations internationales, 6.] Latest summary by this specialist in diplomatic history.

T490. Hauser, Henri, ed. **Histoire diplomatique de l'Europe (1871–1914).** 2 v. Paris, 1929. Generally highly regarded.

T491. Langer, William L. **European alliances and alignments, 1871–1890.** 2nd ed., N.Y., 1950. The fullest account. Magnificent bibliography.

T492. Salvatorelli, Luigi. **Storia d'Europa dal 1871 al 1914.** Milan, 1940 ff.

T493. Roubaud, Alphonse. **La paix armée et les relations internationales de 1871 à 1914.** Paris, 1945.

T494. Schmitt, Bernadotte E. **Triple Alliance and Triple Entente.** N.Y., 1934.

T495. Windelband, Wolfgang. **Bismarck und die europäischen Grossmächte, 1879–1885.** Essen, 1940. The most thorough recent account.

T496. Langer, William L. **The Franco-Russian alliance, 1890–1894.** Cambridge, Mass., 1929.

T497. Khrostov, Vladimir. **Ocherki istorii vneshnei politik germanskoi imperii.** [Essays on the history of imperial Germany's foreign policy.] Moscow, 1940. A good Russian study.

T498. Sontag, Raymond J. **European diplomatic history, 1871–1932.** N.Y., 1933. By the common consent of reviewers and users, the best general review of European diplomacy for this period.

T499. Miehon, Georges. **The Franco-Russian alliance, 1891–1917.** London, 1929.

T500. Schmitt, Bernadotte E. **The annexation of Bosnia, 1908–1909.** See *W482*.

T501. ——. **The coming of the war, 1914.** 2 v. N.Y., 1930. One of the best accounts.

T502. Fay, Sidney B. **The origins of the World War.** 2 v. N.Y., 1930. Has long enjoyed a great reputation.

T503. Mansergh, Nicholas. **The coming of the First World War, 1878–1914.** London, 1949. Effectively describes policies resulting in the alliances and prewar balance of power.

T504. Albertini, Luigi. **Le origini della guerra del 1914.** 3 v. Milan, 1942–43. Tr., *The origins of the war of 1914,* 3 v., London, 1952–57. V. 1 deals with the background, and is rather unsatisfactory on Austria-Hungary and Italy; v. 2–3 treat July, 1914 with much detail, and reach conclusions similar to those of Schmitt in *T501*.

T505. Meyer, Arnold O. **Bismarck's Friedenspolitik.** Munich, 1930.

T506. Rothfels, Hans. **Bismarck und der Osten.** Leipzig, 1934.

T507. Oncken, Hermann. **Das deutsche Reich und die Vorgeschichte des Weltkrieges.** 2 v. Leipzig, 1933. The standard German history of diplomacy from 1871 to 1914.

T508. Marder, Arthur J. **The anatomy of British sea power: a history of British naval policy . . . 1880–1905.** N.Y., 1940.

T509. Guichen, Eugène, vicomte de. **Les grandes questions européennes et la diplomatie des puissances sous la seconde république française.** 2 v. Paris, 1925–29.

T510. Renouvin, Pierre. **The immediate origins of the war (28th June–4th August 1914).** New Haven, 1928. Best statement of the French view.

T511. Wegerer, Alfred von. **Der Ausbruch des Weltkrieges, 1914.** 2 v. Berlin, 1939. Best statement of the German view.

European Imperialism before 1914

T512. Langer, William L. **The diplomacy of imperialism, 1890–1902.** 2 v. N.Y., 1935. 2nd ed., 1 v., 1951. Thorough; comprehensive bibliography. Covers both theoretical and diplomatic aspects of European imperialism.

T513. Hallgarten, George W. F. **Imperialismus vor 1914.** 2 v. Munich, 1951. Largely a sociological study of German imperialism.

Among the following titles, that by Moon is still a serviceable general introduction. It is followed by liberal and Marxist attacks on imperialism, by more theoretical efforts to explain it as a historical phenomenon, and finally by a select set of works that seek to portray it in practice.

T514. Moon, Parker T. **Imperialism and world politics.** See *AH69*.

T515. Hobson, John A. **Imperialism, a study.** 3rd ed., London, 1938.

T516. Lenin, Vladimir I. **Imperialism, the highest stage of capitalism.** New ed., N.Y., 1939.

T517. Sternberg, Fritz. **Der Imperialismus.** See *AH72*.

T518. Salz, Arthur. **Das Wesen des Imperialismus, Umrisse einer Theorie.** Leipzig, 1931. Anti-Marxist.

T519. Sulzbach, Walter. **Nationales Gemeinschaftsgefühl und wirtschaftliches Interesse.** Leipzig, 1929. Emphasizes nationalist motives.

T520. Schumpeter, Joseph. **Imperialism and social classes.** N.Y., 1955. A sociological analysis.

T521. Winslow, Earle M. **The pattern of imperialism: a study in the theories of power.** See *AH75*.

T522. Robbins, Lionel C. **The economic causes of war.** London, 1939.

T523. Maunier, René. **The sociology of colonies.** See *U226*.

T524. Woolf, Leonard. **Empire and commerce in Africa: a study in economic imperialism.** London, 1920.

T525. Harris, Norman D. **Europe and the East.** Boston, 1926.

T526. Pratt, Sir John T. **The expansion of Europe in the Far East.** London, 1947.

T527. Sumner, Benedict H. **Tsardom and imperialism in the Far East and Middle East, 1880–1914.** London, 1942.

T528. Coupland, Sir Reginald. **The exploitation of east Africa, 1856–1890.** See *AC402*.

T529. Rudin, Harry R. **Germans in the Cameroons, 1884–1914.** See *U194*.

T530. Knight, Melvin M. **Morocco as a French economic venture.** N.Y., 1937.

T531. Robequain, Charles. **The economic development of French Indo-China.** English tr., London, 1944.

T532. Vlekke, Bernard H. M. **The story of the Dutch East Indies.** Cambridge, Mass., 1945.

T533. Aydelotte, William O. **Bismarck and British colonial policy.** Philadelphia, 1937.

T534. Earle, Edward M. **Turkey, the great powers, and the Bagdad railway: a study in imperialism.** See *S268*.

T535. Blaisdell, Donald C. **European financial control in the Ottoman empire.** N.Y., 1929.

T536. Feis, Herbert. **Europe, the world's banker, 1870–1914.** New Haven, 1930. Rich in details of financial imperialism.

T537. Julien, Charles A. **Les politiques d'expansion impérialiste.** Paris, 1949.

T538. Viallate, Achille. **L'impérialisme économique et les relations internationales pendant le dernier demi-siècle (1870–1920).** Paris, 1923.

T539. Swain, Joseph W. **Beginning the twentieth century: a history of the generation that made the war.** N.Y., 1933.

T540. Cruickshank, Earl F. **Morocco at the parting of the ways.** Philadelphia, 1935.

Intellectual and Cultural History, 1815–1914

Main Intellectual Currents

T541. Friedell, Egon. **A cultural history of the modern age.** V. 3. N.Y., 1932.

T542. Weber, Alfred. **Histoire de la philosophie européenne.** 8th ed., Paris, 1914.

T543. Russell, Bertrand. **A history of western philosophy.** N.Y., 1945.

T544. Brandes, Georg M. C. **Main currents in nineteenth century literature.** 6 v. N.Y., 1901–05.

T545. Merz, John T. **A history of European thought in the nineteenth century.** 4 v. London, 1896–1914.

T546. Joël, Karl. **Wandlungen der Weltanschauung.** 2 v. Tübingen, 1928–34.

T547. Ziegler, Theobald. **Die geistigen und sozialen Strömungen des neunzehnten Jahrhunderts.** Berlin, 1899. 2nd ed., 1911.

T548. Griffith, Gwilym O. **Interpreters of man: a review of secular and religious thought from Hegel to Barth.** London, 1943.

T549. Halévy, Élie. **The growth of philosophic radicalism.** Boston, 1945. New ed., London, 1949. Tr. from *La formation du radicalisme philosophique* (3 v., Paris, 1901–04).

T550. Löwith, Karl. **Von Hegel bis Nietzsche.** Zürich and N.Y., 1941.

T551. Marcuse, Herbert. **Reason and revolution: Hegel and the rise of social theory.** N.Y., 1941.

T552. Collingwood, Robin G. **The idea of nature.** Oxford, 1949.

T553. Valéry, Paul, Georges Lecomte, Paul Gaultier, and others. **La France et la civilisation contemporaine.** Paris, 1941.

T554. Vaughan, Charles E. **The romantic revolt.** N.Y., 1923.

T555. Barzun, Jacques. **Romanticism and the modern ego.** Boston, 1943.

T556. ——. **Darwin, Marx, Wagner.** Boston, 1941.

T557. Copleston, Frederick C. **Friedrich Nietzsche.** London, 1942.

T558. Irvine, William. **Walter Bagehot.** London, 1939.

T559. Alpert, Harry. **Emile Durkheim and his sociology.** N.Y., 1939.

T560. Mayer, Jacob P. **Max Weber and German politics: a study in political sociology.** London, 1944. Rev. and enl. ed., 1956.

T561. Hook, Sidney. **From Hegel to Marx.** See *A329*.

T562. Woolf, Leonard S. **After the deluge: a study in communal psychology.** London, 1937.

T563. Mumford, Lewis. **The culture of cities.** N.Y., 1938.

T564. Borkenau, Franz. **Socialism, national or international.** London, 1942.

T565. Carew Hunt, Robert N. **The theory and practice of communism.** London, 1950.

T566. Joll, James B. **The Second International, 1889–1914.** London, 1955.

T567. Halévy, Élie. **Histoire du socialisme.** 8th ed., Paris, 1948.

T568. Barzun, Jacques. **The French race: theories of its origins and their social and political implications prior to the Revolution.** N.Y., 1932.

T569. Roubiczek, Paul. **The misrepresentation of man: studies in European thought in the nineteenth century.** N.Y., 1947.

T570. Massing, Paul W. **Rehearsal for destruction: a study of political anti-Semitism in imperial Germany.** See *VF173*.

T571. Fothergill, Philip G. **Historical aspects of organic evolution.** London, 1952. Contains a full bibliography.

T572. Huxley, Julian S. **Evolution: the modern synthesis.** London, 1942.

T573. De Beer, Gavin R. **Charles Darwin.** Oxford, 1958.

T574. Wells, Geoffrey H. (pseud., Geoffrey West). **Charles Darwin.** New Haven, 1938.

T575. Sears, Paul B. **Charles Darwin.** N.Y., 1950.

Art and Architecture

T576. Focillon, Henri. **La peinture au XIXᵉ et XXᵉ siècles.** Paris, 1928.

T577. Muther, Richard. **The history of modern painting.** Rev. ed. of English tr., 4 v., N.Y., 1907.

T578. Mather, Frank J. **Modern painting.** N.Y., 1927.

T579. Venturi, Lionello. **Modern painters.** 2 v. N.Y., 1947–50.

T580. Craven, Thomas. **Modern art.** N.Y., 1934.

T581. Hauser, Arnold. **The social history of art.** N.Y., 1951.

T582. Richardson, Edgar P. **The way of western art, 1776–1914.** Cambridge, Mass., 1939.

T583. Raynal, Maurice. **History of modern painting.** Tr. by Stuart Gilbert and Douglas Cooper. 3 v. Geneva, 1949–50. Excellent chronologies, bibliographies, and pictorial survey from 1860's to date of publication. [JSC]

T584. Haftmann, Werner. **Malerei im 20. Jahrhundert.** 2 v. Munich, 1954–55. Most perceptive general work, but does not include any American painting. [JSC]

T585. Berckelaers, Ferdinand L. (pseud., Michel Seuphor). **Dictionary of abstract painting.** Tr. by Lionel Izod, John Montague, and Francis Scarfe. N.Y., 1957.

T586. Madsen, Stephan T. **Sources of art nouveau.** Tr. by Ragnar Christophersen. N.Y., 1956. Complete survey. [JSC]

T587. Ráfols, José F. **Modernismo y modernistas.** Barcelona, 1949.

T588. Rewald, John. **The history of impressionism.** N.Y., 1946. Well documented; extensive bibliography. [JSC]

T589. Museum of Modern Art (New York). **Masters of modern art.** Ed. by Alfred H. Barr. N.Y., 1954. Excellent illustrations and bibliography by an expert. [JSC]

T590. Giedion-Welcker, Carola. **Contemporary sculpture: an evolution in volume and space.** N.Y., 1955. English ed. first published as *Modern plastic art* (Zürich, 1937).

T591. Seymour, Charles, Jr. **Tradition and experiment in modern sculpture.** Washington, 1949. Succinct, critical survey of modern sculpture. [JSC]

T592. Pevsner, Nikolaus. **An outline of European architecture.** London, 1942. 5th ed., N.Y., 1957. Sound book with a useful bibliography. [JSC]

T593. Hitchcock, Henry R. **Architecture: nineteenth and twentieth centuries.** Baltimore. 1958. Excellent survey. [JSC]

T594. Fletcher, Banister, and Banister F. Fletcher. **A history of architecture on the comparative method.** See *C250.*

T595. Hitchcock, W. R. **Modern architecture.** N.Y., 1929.

T596. Statham, Henry H., and Hugh Braun. **A history of architecture.** London, 1950.

T597. Pevsner, Nikolaus. **Pioneers of the modern movement from William Morris to Walter Gropius.** London, 1936. 2nd ed., N.Y., 1949. (Title varies.)

T598. Giedion, Sigfried. **Space, time, and architecture.** Cambridge, Mass., 1947. Brilliant study of development of modern architecture, copiously illustrated.

T599. Clark, Kenneth M. **The Gothic revival.** London, 1928. 2nd ed., 1950.

T600. Smith, George E. K. **Switzerland builds.** N.Y., 1950.

T601. ——. **Sweden builds.** N.Y., 1950.

T602. ——. **Italy builds.** N.Y., 1955.

Music

T603. Láng, Paul H. **Music in western civilization.** N.Y., 1941. Relationship of music to its cultural environment in the West. Extensive bibliography. [DLB]

T604. Einstein, Alfred. **Music in the romantic era.** London, 1947.

T605. Carse, Adam von Ahn. **The orchestra from Beethoven to Berlioz.** Cambridge, Eng., 1948.

T606. Schiedermair, Ludwig. **Einführung in das Studium der Musikgeschichte.** 4th ed., Bonn, 1947.

T607. Pfrogner, Hermann. **Musik: Geschichte ihrer Deutung.** Freiburg, 1954.

T608. **Grove's dictionary of music and musicians.** 5th ed., ed. by E. Blom, 9 v., Oxford, 1954. Contains full bibliographies under heading "Histories of music."

T609. Adler, Guido, ed. **Handbuch der Musikgeschichte.** 2nd ed., 2 v., Berlin, 1930.

T610. Scholes, Percy A. **The Oxford companion to music.** 9th ed., London, 1955.

T611. **The Oxford history of music.** See *C269.*

T612. Kahl, Willi, and Wilhelm M. Luther. **Repertorium der Musikwissenschaft, Musikschrifttum, Drukmäler und Gesamtausgaben in Auswahl (1800–1950).** Kassel, 1953.

T613. Rolland, Romain. **Musiciens d'autrefois.** 10th ed., Paris, 1927. Many other eds.

T614. Mersmann, Hans. **Die moderne Musik.** Potsdam, 1928. [Ernst Bücken, ed., Handbuch der Musikwissenschaft, 10.]

T615. Abraham, Gerald E. H. **A hundred years of music.** London, 1938. 2nd ed., 1949.

T616. Bauer, Marion. **Twentieth century music.** N.Y., 1933.

T617. Copland, Aaron. **Our new music.** N.Y., 1941.

T618. Slonimsky, Nicolas. **Music since 1900.** 3rd ed., N.Y., 1949.

T619. Ferguson, Donald N. **A history of musical thought.** 2nd ed., N.Y., 1948. Concise, though technical and analytical. Does not discuss oriental or primitive music; has good bibliographies and illustrative scores. [DLB]

T620. Geiringer, Karl. **Musical instruments: their history in western culture.** Tr. by Bernard Miall. N.Y., 1945. Shows connection between the instruments and culture of the several historical periods. [DLB]

T621. Sachs, Curt. **The history of musical instruments.** N.Y., 1940. Covers, with a world outlook, from primitive times to the 20th century. [DLB]

T622. Das Atlantisbuch der Musik. Ed. by Fred Hamel, Martin Hürlimann, and others. 5th ed., Zürich, 1946. Compendium of authoritative articles, many of which are historical. Predominantly western. Bibliography.

T623. Sachs, Curt. **Our musical heritage.** 2nd ed., N.Y., 1955. Short but selectively detailed history of music's place in western culture. [DLB]

T624. Grout, Donald J. **A short history of opera.** N.Y., 1947. Standard U. S. work in this field.

Military and Naval History, 1815–1914

T625. Frauenholz, Eugen von. **Das Heerwesen des XIX. Jahrhunderts.** Munich, 1941.

T626. Craig, Gordon A. **The politics of the Prussian army, 1640–1945.** See *VF319.*

T627. Görlitz, Walter. **History of the German general staff, 1657–1945.** N.Y., 1953.

T628. Pratt, Edwin A. **The rise of rail-power in war and conquest, 1833–1914.** London, 1915.

T629. Cochenhausen, Friedrich E. von, ed. **Von Scharnhorst zu Schlieffen, 1806–1906: hundert Jahre preussisch-deutscher Generalstab.** 8 v. Berlin, 1933.

T630. Prussia. Armee, Grosser Generalstab, ed. **Der deutsch-dänische Krieg, 1864.** 2 v. Berlin, 1886–87.

T631. Lettow-Vorbeck, Oscar von. **Geschichte des Krieges von 1866 in Deutschland.** 3 v. Berlin, 1896–1902.

T632. Moltke, Helmuth von. **Gesammelte Schriften und Denkwürdigkeiten.** 8 v. Berlin, 1892–93.

T633. Förster, Wolfgang. **Moltke, Persönlichkeit und Werk.** Berlin, 1941.

T634. Stadelmann, Rudolf. **Moltke und der Staat.** Krefeld, 1950.

T635. Chuquet, Arthur M. **La guerre, 1870–1871.** Paris, 1895.

T636. Rüstow, Wilhelm. **Der Krieg um die Rheingrenze, 1870: politisch und militärisch Dargestellt.** 6 v. in 2. Zürich, 1870. English tr., by John L. Needham, 3 v., London, 1871–72. Contemporary account by an emigrant Prussian officer.

T637. Prussia. Army, General Staff. **The Franco-German War, 1870–1871.** Tr. by Francis C. H. Clarke. 5 v. in 7. London, 1873–84.

T638. France. L'État-major de l'Armée. **La guerre de 1870–71.** 43 v. Paris, 1901–14.

T639. Duveau, Georges. **La siège de Paris, septembre 1870–janvier 1871.** Paris, 1939.

T640. Desmarest, Jacques. **La défense nationale, 1870–1871.** Paris, 1949.

T641. Der russisch-türkische Krieg 1877–1878 auf der balkan Halbinsel. 7 v. Vienna,

1902–11. German translation of the Russian staff account.

T642. Goltz, Colmar, freiherr von der. **Kriegsgeschichte Deutschlands im neunzehnten Jahrhundert.** 2 v. Berlin, 1910–14. [Das neunzehnte Jahrhundert in Deutschlands Entwicklung, 8.]

T643. Anderson, Roger C. **Naval wars in the Levant, 1559–1853.** See *S255.*

T644. ——. **Naval wars in the Baltic during the sailing ship era.** London, 1910.

T645. Tonnele, Jean. **L'Angleterre en Méditerranée.** Paris, 1952.

T646. Hoskins, Halford L. **British routes to India.** See *S258.*

T647. Baxter, James P., III. **Introduction of the ironclad warship.** See *AB264.*

T648. Brodie, Bernard. **Sea power in the machine age.** Princeton, 1943. Good. [GB]

T649. Robertson, Frederick L. **The evolution of naval armament.** London, 1921.

T650. Marder, Arthur J. **The anatomy of British sea power . . . 1880–1905.** N.Y., 1940.

T651. Potter, Elmer B., ed. **The United States and world sea power.** Englewood Cliffs, N.J., 1955. This compendious work is in reality a history of world sea power, with almost half covering 1789–1914. Excellent bibliographies. [GB]

ECONOMIC HISTORY OF WESTERN EUROPE, 1500–1914

General Surveys

T652. Heaton, Herbert. **Economic history of Europe.** Rev. ed., N.Y., 1948.

T653. Clough, Shepard B., and Charles W. Cole. **Economic history of Europe.** 3rd ed., Boston, 1952.

T654. Sombart, Werner. **Der moderne Kapitalismus.** 3 v. in 6. Munich, 1928.

T655. Weber, Max. **General economic history.** See *A117.*

T656. Kulischer, Josef. **Allgemeine Wirtschaftsgeschichte des Mittelalters und der Neuzeit.** 2 v. Berlin, 1954.

T657. Luzzatto, Gino. **Storia economica dell'età moderna e contemporanea.** 3rd ed., 2 v., Padua, 1950–52.

T658. Haussherr, Hans. **Wirtschaftsgeschichte der Neuzeit.** Weimar, 1954.

Principal National Economic Histories

T659. Clapham, Sir John H. **An economic history of modern Britain.** See *VA406.*

T660. Court, William H. B. **A concise economic history of Britain from 1750 to recent times.** Cambridge, Eng., 1954.

T661. Sée, Henri E. **Histoire économique de la France.** 2 v. Paris, 1948–51.

T662. Lütge, Friedrich K. **Deutsche**

Sozial- und Wirtschaftsgeschichte. Berlin, 1952.

T663. Baasch, Ernst. Holländische Wirtschaftsgeschichte. See *VC1379*.

T664. Heckscher, Eli F. An economic history of Sweden. See *VB136*.

T665. Mayer, Hans, ed. Hundert Jahre österreichischer Wirtschaftsentwicklung, 1848–1948. Vienna, 1949.

Money and Banking

T666. International Committee for the Study of the History of Banking and Credit. History of the principal public banks. Ed. by Johannes G. van Dillen. The Hague, 1934. Reliable introduction to the history of banking. [SBC]

T667. Clapham, Sir John H. The Bank of England. 2 v. Cambridge, Eng., 1944. Valuable introduction to the history of banking. [SBC]

T668. Bloch, Marc L. Esquisse d'une histoire monétaire de l'Europe. Paris, 1954.

T669. Feavearyear, Albert E. The pound sterling. Oxford, 1931. Exceedingly interesting account of a currency from its beginnings to a recent date. [SBC]

Early Modern Capitalism and the Commercial Revolution

T670. Sée, Henri E. Modern capitalism. N.Y., 1928. Good introduction to the subject. [SBC]

T671. Hobson, John A. The evolution of modern capitalism. N.Y., 1926.

T672. Hauser, Henri. Les débuts du capitalisme. Paris, 1931.

T673. Ehrenberg, Richard. Capital and finance in the age of the Renaissance. See *VF298*.

T674. Trenerry, Charles F. The origin and early history of insurance. London, 1926.

T675. Krelage, Ernst H. Bloemenspeculatie in Nederland: de tulpomanie van 1636–'37 en de hyacintenhandel, 1720–'36. Amsterdam, 1942.

T676. Packard, Laurence B. The commercial revolution, 1400–1776. N.Y., 1927.

T677. Nelson, Benjamin N. The idea of usury. See *K487*.

T678. De Roover, Raymond A. The Medici bank. See *K481*.

T679. Hamilton, Earl J. American treasure and the price revolution in Spain, 1501–1650. See *VD170*.

T680. Hauser, Henri. Recherches et documents sur l'histoire des prix en France de 1500 à 1800. Paris, 1936.

T681. Beveridge, Sir William H. Prices and wages in England from the twelfth to the nineteenth century. London, 1939.

T682. Posthumus, Nicolaas W. Inquiry into the history of prices in Holland. See *VC1383*.

T683. Elsas, Moritz J. Umriss einer Geschichte der Preise und Löhne in Deutschland. Leiden, 1936.

T684. Parry, John H. Europe and a wider world. London, 1949.

T685. Lacour-Gayet, Jacques, ed. Histoire de commerce. 6 v. Paris, 1950–55.

T686. Tawney, Richard H. Religion and the rise of capitalism. N.Y., 1926. Paperback ed., 1947.

T687. Hannay, David. The great chartered companies. London, 1926.

T688. Lévy-Bruhl, Henri. Histoire juridique des sociétés de commerce en France aux XVIIe et XVIIIe siècles. Paris, 1938.

T689. Brakel, Simon van. De Hollandsche handelscompagnieën der zeventiende eeuw. The Hague, 1908.

T690. Clark, Sir George N. Science and social welfare in the age of Newton. Oxford, 1937.

T691. Nef, John U. Industry and government in France and England, 1540–1640. Ithaca, 1957.

History of Economic Thought

T692. Gide, Charles, and Charles Rist. A history of economic doctrines. 2nd English ed., Boston, 1948. A standard treatise.

T693. Roll, Erich. A history of economic thought. Rev. ed., London, 1946. A standard work.

T694. Gonnard, René. Histoire des doctrines économiques. Paris, 1930.

T695. Heckscher, Eli F. Mercantilism. 2 v. London, 1934. The most penetrating study of mercantilism, although it ignores Spain, Portugal, and Prussia. [SBC]

T696. Schmoller, Gustav F. von. The mercantile system and its historical significance. N.Y., 1931. A famous and still useful essay, based largely on Prussian history.

T697. Hamilton, Earl J. War and prices in Spain, 1651–1800. Cambridge, Mass., 1947.

T698. Braudel, Fernand. La Méditerranée et le monde méditerranéen à l'époque de Philippe II. See *VD85*.

T699. Furniss, Edgar S. The position of the laborer in a system of nationalism. N.Y., 1920.

T700. Harper, Lawrence A. The English navigation laws. See *AB100*.

T701. Knorr, Klaus E. British colonial theories, 1570–1850. See *U177*.

T702. Silberner, Edmond. La guerre dans la pensée économique du XVIe au XVIIIe siècle. See *T205*.

T703. Johnson, Edgar A. J. Predecessors of Adam Smith. N.Y., 1937.

T704. Monroe, Arthur E. Monetary theory before Adam Smith. Cambridge, Mass., 1923.

T705. Small, Albion W. **The Cameralists: the pioneers of German social polity.** See *VF80.*

T706. Weulersse, Georges. **Les physiocrats.** Paris, 1931.

T707. ———. **Le mouvement physiocratique en France (de 1756 à 1770).** 2 v. Paris, 1910.

T708. ———. **La physiocratie sous les ministères de Turgot et de Necker (1774–1781).** Paris, 1950.

The Industrial Revolution

T709. Ashton, Thomas S. **The industrial revolution, 1760–1830.** See *VA424.*

T710. Mantoux, Paul J. **The industrial revolution in the eighteenth century: an outline of the beginnings of the modern factory system in England.** N.Y., 1928. A full older study which is still useful. [SBC]

T711. Clark, Sir George N. **The idea of the industrial revolution.** Glasgow, 1953. A corrective against exaggeration. [SBC]

T712. Rostow, Walt W. **British economy of the nineteenth century.** See *VA435.*

T713. Benaerts, Pierre. **Les origines de la grande industrie allemande.** See *VF308.*

T714. Baumont, Maurice. **La grosse industrie allemande.** Paris, 1928.

T715. Henderson, William O. **Britain and industrial Europe, 1750–1870.** Liverpool, 1954.

T716. Clapham, John H. **The economic development of France and Germany, 1815–1914.** 4th ed., Cambridge, Eng., 1936.

T717. Viennet, Odette. **Napoléon et l'industrie française: la crise de 1810–1811.** Paris, 1947.

Agriculture

T718. Gras, Norman S. B. **A history of agriculture in Europe and America.** 2nd ed., N.Y., 1940.

T719. Ernle, Rowland E. **English farming, past and present.** Ed. by Sir Alfred D. Hall. New ed., N.Y., 1936.

T720. Lütge, Friedrich. "Freiheit und Unfreiheit in der Agrarverfassung." **Historisches Jahrbuch,** 74 (1955): 642–52. Provides critical review of the literature on peasant emancipation in central Europe.

T721. Blum, Jerome. **Noble landowners and agriculture in Austria, 1818–1848.** See *VF255.*

Transportation and Communication

T722. Sherrington, Charles E. R. **A hundred years of inland transport, 1830–1933.** London, 1934. Authoritative study by an outstanding expert.

T723. Godechot, Jacques L. **Histoire de l'Atlantique.** Paris, 1947.

T724. Vogel, Walther, and Günter Schmölders. **Die Deutschen als Seefahrer.** Hamburg, 1949.

T725. Albion, Robert G. **Forests and sea power: the timber problem of the royal navy, 1632–1862.** Cambridge, Mass., 1926.

T726. Kalmus, Ludwig. **Weltgeschichte der Post, mit besonderer Berücksichtigung des deutschen Sprachgebietes.** Vienna, [1937].

Finance

T727. Edwards, George W. **The evolution of finance capitalism.** N.Y., 1938.

T728. Shaw, William A. **The history of currency, 1252 to 1894.** London, 1896.

T729. Corti, Egon C. **The rise of the house of Rothschild.** N.Y., 1928.

T730. Hidy, Ralph W. **The house of Baring in American trade and finance.** See *AB202.*

T731. Riesser, Jacob. **The German great banks and their concentration.** 3rd ed., Washington, 1911.

T732. Liesse, André. **Evolution of credit and banks in France from the founding of the Bank of France to the present time.** Washington, 1909.

T733. Feis, Herbert. **Europe, the world's banker, 1870–1914.** See *T536.*

T734. Hirst, Francis W. **The stock exchange: a short study of investments and speculation.** Rev. ed., London, 1932.

T735. Evans, George H. **British corporation finance, 1775–1850.** Baltimore, 1936.

T736. Lewinsohn, Richard. **Trusts et cartels dans l'économie mondiale.** Paris, 1950.

T737. Liefmann, Robert. **Cartels, concerns, and trusts.** London and N.Y., 1932.

T738. Berle, Adolf A., and Gardiner C. Means. **The modern corporation and private property.** N.Y., 1933.

T739. Jenks, Leland H. **The migration of British capital to 1875.** See *VA433.*

T740. White, Harry D. **The French international accounts, 1880–1913.** Cambridge, Mass., 1933.

Tariff and Commercial Policy

T741. Ashley, Percy. **Modern tariff history.** 3rd ed., London, 1926.

T742. Henderson, William O. **The Zollverein.** Cambridge, Eng., 1939.

T743. Brown, Benjamin H. **The tariff reform movement in Great Britain, 1881–1895.** N.Y., 1943.

T744. Röpke, Wilhelm. **German commercial policy.** N.Y., 1934.

European Labor Movement

T745. Dolléans, Edouard. **Histoire du mouvement ouvrier.** See *A1206.*

T746. Kuczinski, Jürgen. **Labour conditions in western Europe, 1820 to 1935.** N.Y., 1937.

T747. Villain, Jean. **L'enseignement social de l'église.** 3 v. Paris, 1953–54.

T748. Halévy, Élie. **Histoire du socialisme européen.** Paris, 1948.

T749. Mehring, Franz. **Geschichte der deutschen Sozialdemokratie.** 4th ed., 4 v., Stuttgart, 1909.

T750. Fogarty, Michael P. **Christian democracy in western Europe, 1820–1953.** Notre Dame, Ind., 1957.

T751. Beer, Max. **Allgemeine Geschichte des Sozialismus und der sozialen Kämpfe.** 5 pts. Berlin, 1921–23. Partial tr., by H. J. Stenning, *Social struggles and modern socialism.* London, 1925.

T752. Shadwell, Arthur. **The socialist movement, 1824–1924.** 2 v. London, 1925.

T753. Stekloff, G. M. **History of the First International.** London, 1928.

T754. Cole, George D. H. **A history of socialist thought.** See *VA352.*

T755. Plamenatz, John P. **German Marxism and Russian communism.** London, 1954.

SECTION U

The Expansion of Europe

CHARLES E. NOWELL *

The editors of the original *Guide* stated that "aside from exploration, the topics with which this section is concerned have received scant attention as fields of historical study until very recent times." Although the statement is less true today than in 1931, writings about discoveries are still preponderant. Such literature has been greatly expanded in quantity and improved in quality since 1931; in fact, most of that included in the old *Guide* is now obsolete.

In the fields with which this section is principally concerned—the expansion of Europe and modern colonization in general, and the general history and policy of the leading powers in their colonizing activities—the number of works of moderately sound scholarship is much greater today than in 1931, although many are affected by nationalistic bias. The lists of works included under the several subheadings in this section are, in general, limited to the more scholarly works in the respective fields and to the better representatives of diverse views on the more important topics of a controversial nature. In sections of this *Guide* pertaining to the history of the several principal colonizing nations will be found numerous works which devote more or less space to the activities overseas of the respective countries.

Among the special classes of books listed in this section are those on the European background of expansion, extension of geographical knowledge and exploration, development of commerce and of trading companies, and the general subject of colonization. The history of land exploration is treated in sections devoted to the regions concerned, but works on the entire history of discovery are included here. This section also includes the history of maritime exploration, especially in the 15th, 16th, 17th, and 18th centuries, and of Arctic and Antarctic exploration, especially in the last century. Space permits only the citation of outstanding works among the voluminous and usually excellent literature on these interesting topics.

* The following contributed items and comments indicated by their respective initials: Philip I. Mitterling (PIM), James Neilson (JN), Gunther E. Rothenberg (GER); and from the original *Guide*, Edwin S. Balch (ESB), Arthur H. Bayse (AHB), Louise F. Brown (LFB), George M. Dutcher (GMD), Adolphus W. Greely (AWG), Frank H. Hodder (FHH), Frank J. Klingberg (FJK), Frank W. Pitman (FWP), Augustus H. Shearer (AHS), Mary E. Townsend (MET), Harriet E. Tuell (HET).

BIBLIOGRAPHIES AND LIBRARIES

U1. "Travaux de la commission des grands voyages et des grandes découvertes." **Bulletin des sciences historiques,** 7 (1935): 363–453. Worthy and almost successful attempt to provide a bibliography of all writings on the great discoveries appearing between 1912 and 1931.

U2. Cox, Edward G. **A reference guide to the literature of travel, including voyages, geographical descriptions, adventures, shipwrecks and expeditions.** 3 v. Seattle, 1935–49. [University of Washington publications in language and literature, 9, 10, and 12.] Rather compendious volumes, covering in a chronological plan, travel literature from the earliest ascertainable date to 1800. V. 1 deals with travel in the Old World, v. 2 with travel in the New World, and v. 3 with travel in the British Isles.

U3. Lewin, Percy Evans. **Subject catalogue of the library of the Royal Empire Society, formerly the Royal Colonial Institute.** 4 v. London, 1930–37. [1, *The British empire generally and Africa; 2, The Commonwealth of Australia, the Dominion of New Zealand, the South Pacific, general voyages and travels, and Arctic and Antarctic regions; 3, The Dominion of Canada and its provinces, the Dominion of Newfoundland, the West Indies, and colonial America; 4, The Mediterranean colonies, the Middle East, Indian empire, Burma, Ceylon, British Malaya, East Indian islands, and the Far East.*] Large volumes covering all subjects concerning a given colony; elaborate historical, as well as biographical, bibliography for each colony.

U4. Ragatz, Lowell J., and Janet E. Ragatz. **A bibliography of articles, descriptive, historical and scientific, on colonies and other dependent territories, appearing in American geographical and kindred journals.** 2 v. Washington, 1951. V. 1, reprint of a 1935 edition, contains over 1,000 bibliographical items in United States journals on voyages of discovery and exploration over the world from earliest times until 1934. V. 2 carries the compilation to 1950.

U5. Colonial government: annotated reading list on British colonial government with some general and comparative material upon foreign empires. London, 1950. Although devoted to government, this bibliography contains many historical items, with recent history naturally receiving most attention.

U6. Craven, Wesley F. "Historical study of the British empire." **Jour. mod. hist.,** 6 (Mar. 1934): 40–69. Fine bibliography, classified. [GER]

U7. Bibliographie d'histoire coloniale (1900–1930). Ed. by Alfred Martineau, Paul Roussier, and Joannès Tramond. Paris, 1932. [Société de l'Histoire des Colonies Françaises.] Contains articles, written by specialists, and bibliographies of the colonial histories of many peoples. The European countries and the United States are treated as colonizing powers; the Latin American, African, Asian, and island regions as objects of colonization.

U8. Association de Géographes Français. **Bibliographie géographique internationale.** Paris, 1891 ff. Each volume contains important sections on history of geography and cartography, and on historical geography, all important for the history of geographical discovery. The bibliographies are prepared with collaboration of many geographical societies outside France.

U9. U. S. Library of Congress. **French colonies in Africa: a list of references.** Comp. by Helen F. Conover under direction of Florence S. Hellman. Washington, 1942.

U10. Varley, Douglas H. **A bibliography of Italian colonisation in Africa, with a section on Abyssinia.** London, 1936. [Royal Empire Society bibliography no. 7.]

U11. Downs, Robert B. **American library resources: a bibliographical guide.** Chicago, 1951. Places heaviest emphasis on United States history, but exploration and colonization receive attention. Especially useful for locating the principal collections in the United States.

U12. Chavanne, Josef, and others. **Die Literatur über die Polar-Regionen der Erde.** Vienna, 1878.

U13. Pfaff, Christian G. F. **Bibliographia groenlandica.** Copenhagen, 1890.

U14. Mill, Hugh R. **A bibliography of Antarctic exploration and research.** London, 1901.

Besides the above special bibliographies on polar exploration, see also Adolphus W. Greely, *Handbook of polar discoveries* (5th ed., Boston, 1910); and Edwin S. Balch, *Antarctica* (Philadelphia, 1902.)

Library Collections

For the history of exploration and of early trade and colonization, especially in the Western Hemisphere, there are highly valuable collections in the Harvard University Library, the John Carter Brown Library, and the New York Public Library; and less extensive collections in the Library of Congress, the Ayer and Greenlee collections of the Newberry Library, the Clements Library of the University of Michigan, and, for the Spanish side, the H. E. Huntington Library, and the H. H. Bancroft Library at the University of California (Berkeley). For the economic expansion of Europe, the Bell collection at the University of Minnesota is valuable.

Extensive collections relating to exploration in more recent times exist in the library of the American Geographical Society, New York City, and that of the National Geographic Society, Washington. The latter contains the Greely polar and sub-polar collection, which is undoubtedly the best in its field. The Stefansson collection at Dartmouth is also good. There are also good collections on polar exploration in the Boston Public Library and in the library of Bowdoin College.

In addition to good collections of general works on colonization and the history of colonies, the Library of Congress is especially useful for governmental publications issued both by the colonizing countries and the colonies. [AHS, CEN]

ENCYCLOPEDIAS AND WORKS OF REFERENCE

U15. Deutsches Kolonial-Lexikon. Ed. by Heinrich Schnee. 3 v. Leipzig, 1920. A monument to German colonization, edited by a former governor of East Africa. Furnishes valuable information of almost every description about the German colonies. Contains numerous photographs, maps, and diagrams.

U16. Domville-Fife, Charles W., ed. **The encyclopedia of the British empire.** 3 v. Bristol, Eng., 1924. Convenient reference work for earlier periods. [GMD]

U17. Encyclopaedie van Nederlandsch-Indië. 8 v. The Hague, 1917–39. Contains historical accounts of all important islands and activities in the former Dutch East Indies. The articles are frequently followed by bibliographies.

U18. Enciclopedia italiana di scienze, lettere ed arti. See *VE17.*

GEOGRAPHIES AND ATLASES

U19. Church, Ronald J. H. **Modern colonization.** London, 1951. This little study deals with physical, economic, and social geography of colonization, and concludes with a remarkable chapter on the political geography of colonization. Bibliography consists of valuable list of colonial atlases. [JN]

U20. Despois, Jean, and Robert Capot-Rey. **L'Afrique blanche française.** 2 v. Paris, 1949–53. Climate, terrain, soil, cultural possibilities, population, and colonization of French Northern and Saharan Africa.

U21. Despois, Jean. **La Tunisie orientale: Sahel et la basse steppe; étude géographique.** Paris, 1955. After a geographical and historical survey, Despois proceeds to cover all the gainful occupations and means of earning a living that prevail in eastern Tunisia.

U22. Caro Baroja, Julio. **Estudios saharianos.** See *AC347.*

U23. Richard-Molard, Jacques. **L'Afrique occidentale française.** See *AC457.*

U24. Pays africains. 5 v. Paris, 1951–55. [1, Emmanuel Avice, *La côte d'Ivoire;* 2, Edmond Séré de Rivières, *Le Niger;* 3, Maurice Houis, *La Guinée Française;* 4, Edmond Séré de Rivières, *Le Sénégal, Dakar;* 5, Georges Spitz, *Le Soudan Français.*] These five small volumes form a series with such common features as are possible. Each begins with some description of the country and people under survey, and follows with an account of the history and political structure, concluding with the economic organization and potentialities of the region in question.

U25. Almagià, Roberto. **Il mondo attuale.** 3 v. in 6. Turin, 1953–56. This work, by the dean of living Italian geographers, is probably the best general geography now in existence, being compendious and copiously illustrated. It is of great assistance in any study with a geographical orientation. V. 1 begins with a 91-page account of geographical discovery and a good selection of maps illustrating the rise of geographical science.

U26. Taylor, Eva G. R. **The haven-finding art: a history of navigation from Odysseus to Captain Cook.** London, 1956. Title of the book identifies its contents—the development of methods of navigation. Interesting narration and superb scholarship.

U27. Almagià, Roberto. **Planisferi, carte nautiche e affini dal secolo XIV al XVII esistenti nella Biblioteca Apostolica Vaticana.** 3 v. Vatican City, 1944–55. [Also known as *Monumenta cartographica vaticana.*] These maps from the Vatican Library are previously unpublished or else incompletely known. V. 1 has the highest value for students of the great age of discovery, although many of the other maps have an important bearing on the progress of geographical discovery during the 17th century.

U28. Wieder, Frederick C. **Monumenta cartographica: reproductions of unique and rare maps, plans and views in the actual size of the originals, accompanied by cartographical monographs.** 5 v. The Hague, 1925–33. Wieder was the learned librarian of the University of Leiden. His collection illustrates the historical process of geographical discovery from the terrestrial globe of Johannes Schöner (1523–24), which embodied some of the latest discoveries, to the map of about 1670 illustrating the Dutch discovery of Arnhemsland in northern Australia.

U29. Spain. Ejército. Servicio Geográfico. **Cartografía de ultramar.** Madrid, 1949–53. Issued in parts, each followed by a collection of maps. These maps, covering every part of the New World, are of Italian, Spanish, Portuguese, Dutch, French, and English extraction, and extend in time from 1520 to

1819. The maps of Russian North America are Spanish made.

U30. Berwick, Jacobo M., ed. **Mapas españoles de América: siglos XV–XVII.** See *Z71.*

U31. Grandidier, Guillaume, ed. **Atlas des colonies françaises, protectorats et territoires sous mandat de la France, publié sous la direction de Guillaume Grandidier.** Paris, 1934. Maps are preceded by a historical introduction and each geographical area by an introduction of its own. The cartographical treatment is very thorough, and the smallest colonies are depicted in considerable detail.

U32. Académie Royale des Sciences Coloniales. **Atlas général du Congo.** See *AC478.*

U33. Belgium. Ministère des Colonies. **Atlas du Ruanda-Urundi.** Brussels, 1951. Each map accompanied by description.

U34. Baratta, Mario, and Luigi Visintin. **Atlante delle colonie italiane, con notizie geografiche ed economiche.** Rome, 1928. Besides territories in Africa, includes Italian-held islands in the Aegean.

PRINTED COLLECTIONS OF SOURCES

U35. Alguns documentos do Archivo Nacional da Tôrre do Tombo ácerca das navegações e conquistas portuguezas publicados por ordem do governo de sua majestade fidelissima ao celebrar-se a commemoração quadricentenaria do descobrimento da America. Ed. by José Ramos Cóelho and others. Lisbon, 1892. This carefully selected collection of documents was Portugal's intellectual contribution to the fourth centennial celebration of the discovery of America. The documents, taken from the Tôrre do Tombo archive, illustrate the nation's discoveries and conquests from 1416 to 1554. Although many have since been published elsewhere, the collection is still indispensable.

U36. Eannes de Azurara, Gomes. **Cronica do descobrimento e conquista da Guiné, segundo o manuscrito da Biblioteca Nacional de Paris: modernizada, com notas, glossário e uma introdução de José de Bragança.** 2 v. Oporto, 1937. Originally pub. in Paris, 1841. This extremely valuable manuscript, written by a squire of Prince Henry the Navigator, was lost for several hundred years. It is the major source for the history of African coastwise discovery during Prince Henry's lifetime, and concludes a few years before his death in 1460.

U37. Crone, Gerald R., ed. and tr. **The voyages of Cadamosto and other documents on western Africa in the second half of the fifteenth century.** London, 1937. [Works issued by the Hakluyt Society, 2nd ser., 80.] First-hand account by Alvise Cadamosto of his voyages along the African coast in the service of Prince Henry the Navigator, which

led to the discovery of the Cape Verde islands in 1456. Crone's documents also contain translations of the letter of Antonio Malfante from Tuat in 1447, the narrative by Diogo Gomes of his own discovery voyages, and extracts from the *Décadas da India* of João de Barros.

U38. Lopes de Castanheda, Fernão. **História do descobrimento e conquista da India pelos portugueses.** 4 v. Coimbra, 1924–33. Originally pub. in 1554. A 16th century account of Portuguese discoveries and conquests in the Indian Ocean and the Far East, second only to that of João de Barros mentioned below.

U39. Greenlee, William B. **The voyage of Pedro Álvares Cabral to Brazil and India: from contemporary documents and narratives.** London, 1938. [Works issued by the Hakluyt Society, 2nd ser., 81.] Contains English translations of all known documents bearing on the voyage of the Portuguese commander, Pedro Álvares Cabral, who made the official discovery of Brazil for Portugal in 1500.

U40. Kimble, George H. T., ed. and tr. **Esmeraldo de situ orbis by Duarte Pacheco Pereira.** London, 1937. [Works issued by the Hakluyt Society, 2nd ser., 79.] Discourse on navigation and discussion of the known routes of sailing about 1508 by the noted Portuguese pilot and cosmographer, believed by some to have been the discoverer of Brazil.

U41. Barros, João de. **Dos feitos que os portugueses fizerem no descobrimento e conquista dos mares e terras do Oriente.** 6th ed., 4 v., Lisbon, 1944–46. Originally pub. in 1552. Barros is the best of the early historians who deal with discovery and conquest in the East. The present edition is not quite complete, but covers the period of Portuguese discovery and expansion in Africa and India that is generally regarded as most important. The Portuguese spelling is modernized. A more complete edition is that of 1777–88.

U42. Blake, John W., ed. and tr. **Europeans in West Africa, 1450–1560: documents to illustrate the nature and scope of Portuguese enterprise in West Africa, the abortive attempt of Castilians to create an empire there, and the early English voyages to Barbary and Guinea.** 2 v. London, 1942. [Works issued by the Hakluyt Society, 2nd ser., 86–87.] Edited collection of documents covering a neglected phase of African history.

U43. Colón, Fernando. **Le historie della vita e dei fatti di Cristoforo Colombo.** Ed. by Rinaldo Caddeo. 2 v. Milan, 1930. The life of Christopher Columbus by his son, Ferdinand, is the foundation on which the entire story of the discovery of America rests. It contains some errors and some adulation, but, as Morison says, "Ferdinand's

Historie needs no more discounting than does any biography of a distinguished father by a devoted son." The original text, in Spanish, has been lost, and the first edition to be published was an Italian one in 1571, of which this is a somewhat modernized version. The editor contributes an introduction and an extensive bibliography.

U44. Vespucci, Amerigo. **El nuevo mundo: cartas relativas a sus viajes y descubrimientos; textos en italiano, español, y inglés.** Ed. by Roberto Levillier. Buenos Aires, 1951. A companion volume to *América la bien llamada* (*U91*), but consisting almost entirely of documents.

U45. Casas, Bartolomé de las. **Historia de las Indias.** Ed. by Agustín Millares Carlo. Buenos Aires, 1951. This superb edition of Las Casas renders all its predecessors obsolete. It is complete, and profits by the valuable textual study of Millares Carlo and the bibliographical study of Lewis Hanke. As the latter convincingly maintains, Las Casas was the best of the early historians who dealt with the initial period of Spanish contact with the New World.

U46. Navarrete, Martín Fernández de. **Colección de los viages y descubrimientos que hicieron por mar los españoles desde fines del siglo XV, con varios documentos inéditos concernientes á la historia de la marina castellana y de los establecimientos españoles en Indias.** See *Y72.*

U47. Anglería, Pedro Mártir de. **Décadas del nuevo mundo: vertidas del latín á la lengua castellana por el Dr. D. Joaquín Torres Asensio quien diólas á las prensas como homenaje al cuarto centenario del descubrimiento.** Buenos Aires, 1944. The best and most usable edition of Peter Martyr's *De orbe novo* for those who do not feel able to attempt it in the original Latin.

U48. Wagner, Henry R., ed. and tr. **The discovery of Yucatan by Francisco Hernández de Córdoba: a translation of the original texts with an introduction and notes.** Berkeley, 1942. Brief narrative of Hernández de Córdoba's discovery in 1517, preceding a series of translated sources from the pens of 16th century Spanish historians.

U49. ——, ed. and tr. **The discovery of New Spain in 1518 by Juan de Grijalva: a translation of the original texts with an introduction and notes.** Berkeley, 1942. Account of the coasting voyage along Mexico that preceded the Cortés expedition. Principally a collection of documents, though Wagner provides a narrative introduction.

U50. Pastells, Pablo, and Constantino Bayle. **El descubrimiento del Estrecho de Magallanes en conmemoración del IV centenario.** 2 v. Madrid, 1920. Largely a documentary collection dealing with successive explorations of the strait by Magellan himself, Loaysa, Alcazaba, Camargo, Ladrillero, and Sarmiento de Gamboa.

U51. Markham, Sir Clements. **Early Spanish voyages to the Strait of Magellan.** London, 1911. [Works issued by the Hakluyt Society, 2nd ser., 28.] A series of documents illustrating voyages to the strait from that of Magellan's successor, Loaysa, to that of Nodals in 1618–19.

U52. Sarmiento de Gamboa, Pedro. **Viajes al Estrecho de Magallanes (1579–1584): recopilación de sus relaciones sobre los dos viajes al estrecho y de sus cartas y memoriales.** Ed. by Ángel Rosenblat. 2 v. Buenos Aires, 1950. This elaborate work contains not only the documents relative to Sarmiento de Gamboa's two voyages to the strait, but also many documents regarding his life.

U53. **História da colonização portuguesa do Brasil.** See *Z509.*

U54. Galvão, António de. **Tratado dos descobrimentos.** Oporto, 1944. Originally pub. in Lisbon, 1563. This account by a Portuguese historian, who was himself a conquistador and an official in the East Indies, is important though brief. Galvão attempted to include all Portuguese and Spanish discoveries made approximately to the year 1545. Not an official historian and writing of his own free will, he occasionally differs in interesting ways from the official versions and injects information not furnished by other authors.

U55. Stevens, Henry N., and George F. Barwick, eds. **New light on the discovery of Australia as revealed by the journal of Captain Diego de Prado y Tovar.** London, 1930. [Works issued by the Hakluyt Society, 2nd ser., 64.] This early 17th century journal shows that Australia was discovered in 1606 by a Spanish expedition of Diego de Prado y Tovar.

U56. Hakluyt, Richard. **The original writings and correspondence of the two Richard Hakluyts.** Ed. by Eva G. R. Taylor. 2 v. London, 1935. Contains a total of 92 documents extending from 1557 to 1614. These are summarized by Professor Taylor in a lengthy introduction, which explains the interest of the Hakluyts in "western planting."

U57. ——. **The principall navigations, voiages, traffiques, and discoveries of the English nation, made by sea or over land to the most remote and farthest distant quarters of the earth at any time within the compasse of these 1500 yeeres.** 1589. 2nd ed., 3 v., London, 1598–1600. Several reprints. Extracts reprinted in *Early English and French voyages, chiefly from Hakluyt, 1534–1608,* ed. by Henry S. Burrage (N.Y., 1906). Hakluyt (1552?–1616) became interested in geographical studies while at Oxford, read all he could find on the subject, and later published the collections he had made. His collections, which are a mine of information for geography, discovery, and colonization, appear in their final form in his second edition. [AHS]

U58. Purchas, Samuel. **Hakluytus posthumus, or Purchas his pilgrimes: contayning a history of the world in sea voyages and lande travells by Englishmen and others.** 4 v. London, 1625. Reprint, 20 v., Glasgow, 1905–07. [Hakluyt Society, extra ser., 14–33.] Continuation and supplement of Hakluyt, based in part on manuscripts left by him and including voyages of all nations. Despite the faults of the compiler, his collection is a rich storehouse of information, often unavailable from any other source. [AHS]

U59. Golder, Frank A., ed. **Bering's voyages: an account of the efforts of the Russians to determine the relations of Asia and America.** 2 v. N.Y., 1922–25. By far the best work on Bering. Golder published for the first time the complete official records of the two expeditions. Captain E. P. Berthoff replotted the courses of the Bering log on a modern chart, thus tracing the route and landfalls of the second expedition. V. 2 contains an English translation of the account by Wilhelm Steller of the sea voyage on the second expedition, previously published in German in 1793.

U60. The journals of Captain James Cook on his voyages of discovery. Ed. by John C. Beaglehole and others. V. 1, **The voyage of the Endeavour, 1768–1771.** Cambridge, Eng., 1955. [Hakluyt Society, extra ser., 24.] This magnificent volume is the first of four and, as the title shows, is confined to Cook's first voyage. In addition to the journals, Beaglehole contributes an introduction of 150 pages, in which he surveys geographical discovery and speculation prior to Cook, as well as details of the renowned explorer's early life.

U61. Milner, Alfred M., viscount. **The Milner papers: South Africa.** Ed. by Cecil Headlam. 2 v. London, 1931–33. Important documents, mostly letters, covering the years 1897–1905 and bearing on the outbreak, progress, and aftermath of the Boer War. The letters are both from and to Milner, who was Cecil Rhodes' successor as principal British policy maker in South Africa and was a direct representative of the Crown.

U62. Dawson, Robert M., ed. **The development of dominion status, 1900–1936.** See *U230.*

U63. Harlow, Vincent T., and Frederick Madden, eds. **British colonial developments, 1774–1834.** Oxford, 1953. Documents with short annotations.

GENERAL HISTORIES

U64. Newton, Arthur P. **An introduction to the study of colonial history.** London and N.Y., 1919. Very brief introductory survey, with bibliographical suggestions. [GMD]

U65. Rein, Adolf. **Die europäische Ausbreitung über die Erde.** Potsdam, 1931. Careful, though brief, history of European imperialism, based on the best monographic and secondary material. By far the larger part of the work is devoted to the period between the 15th and 19th centuries.

U66. Townsend, Mary E. **European colonial expansion since 1871.** Philadelphia, 1941. Scholarly account of European expansion from the first partition of Africa to the beginning of World War II. Besides Africa, includes the Near East, Middle East, and Far East. Concludes with an evaluation of colonial expansion since 1871, and an estimate that colonialism has not, on the whole, paid its way.

U67. Lannoy, Charles de, and Linden, Herman V. **Histoire de l'expansion coloniale des peuples européens.** 3 v. Brussels, 1907–21. [1, *Portugal et Espagne;* 2, *Néerlande et Danemark;* 3, *Suède.*] Valuable for its treatment, in the case of each nation, of the European background, administration, economic life, civilization of the colonies, and effects of expansion on the mother country.

EXPLORATION

U68. Olsen, Ørjan. **La conquête de la terre: histoire des découvertes et des explorations depuis les origines jusqu'à nos jours.** 6 v. Paris, 1935–55. Tr. by E. Guerre from *De store opdagelser* (Oslo, 1929–31). The most comprehensive history of geographical discovery by a single individual. Olsen has been an explorer of some note and a professor at the University of Oslo. The work provides full coverage, beginning with the earliest civilizations and ending with Scandinavian polar expeditions in the early 1930's.

U69. Baker, John N. L. **A history of geographical discovery and exploration.** London, 1931. Later editions, 1937, 1945, 1948. The principal revisions took place in the 1937 edition. Classed by scholars as sound. *Histoire des découvertes géographiques et des explorations* (Paris, 1949) is a French translation.

U70. Danielli, Giotto. **La conquista della terra.** Turin, 1950. A history of exploration by an Italian explorer of some fame. Occasional factual errors concerning general history occur, but regarding geographical discovery the work is trustworthy.

U71. Parias, Louis H., and others, eds. **Histoire universelle des explorations.** 4 v. Paris, 1955–56. This work, while undocumented and offering no impressive bibliography, is sound and thorough.

U72. Le Gentil, Georges. **Découverte du**

monde. Paris, 1954. Although a small volume of less than 300 pages, this sums up exploration from remotest antiquity to the year 1948 with remarkable originality and accuracy.

U73. Hennig, Richard, ed. **Terrae incognitae: eine Zusammenstellung und kritische Bewertung der wichtigsten vorcolumbischen Entdeckungsreisen an Hand der darüber vorliegenden Originalbericht.** 4 v. Leiden, 1936–39. Rev. ed., 4 v., Leiden, 1944–56. Reviews the principal discoveries and journeys by individual travelers from about 1500 B.C. to the years immediately preceding the discovery of America. Each expedition is subjected to separate treatment, each study preceded by an excerpt, or excerpts, from the sources in German translation. Hennig, with the aid of additional sources and studies by modern writers, determines the scope, significance, and exact accomplishments of each expedition or traveler. Factual errors in the first edition are fairly well eliminated in the second. Copious bibliography and footnotes.

U74. Beazley, Charles R. **The dawn of modern geography: a history of exploration and geographical science.** 3 v. London and Oxford, 1897–1906. New ed., 3 v., N.Y., 1949. The new edition is in no way altered from the first. Beazley's work has been a classic of its kind for over fifty years, and its value is as great today as ever. It is a history of medieval travels and geography, not of the age of discovery. Accurate, except in small details, and entertaining, it is perhaps still the best work in its field. Treatment of the Norse voyages to America antedates the recent revival of that controversy. [FHH, CEN]

U75. Ballesteros y Beretta, Antonio. **Génesis del descubrimiento.** And Cortesão, Jaime. **Los portugueses.** 2 v. in 1, forming v. 3 of **Historia de América y de los pueblos americanos,** ed. by Antonio Ballesteros y Beretta (27 v., Barcelona, 1936–56). *Génesis,* except for sections devoted to ancient history, covers much the same ground as Beazley's *Dawn.* Ballesteros surveys geographical history and exploration with much attention to the development of cartography and nautical science from the beginning of history to the opening of the 14th century. Despite factual errors almost inevitable in so pretentious a work, *Génesis* is of great value. *Los portugueses* by Cortesão, a lifelong student of his country's maritime discoveries, is well documented and valuable. With much attention to navigational technique and ship construction, it surveys Portuguese achievement to the death of João II in 1495.

U76. La Roncière, Charles de. **La découverte de l'Afrique au Moyen Âge: cartographes et explorateurs.** 3 v. Cairo, 1924–27. [Mémoires de la Société Royale de Géographie d'Egypte.] A work of considerable distinction which, on the whole, has maintained its good reputation over the years. Critics, nevertheless, have differed with certain parts of it, and the differences of opinion may be attributed to the enthusiasms of the author and his tendency to leap to conclusions he desired to embrace.

U77. Hovgaard, William. **The voyages of the Norsemen to America.** N.Y., 1914. This work does not grow out of date. Originally intended as a refutation of Fridjoff Nansen's thesis, as expressed in *Nord i takeheimen* (Christiania, 1911), to the effect that the Norse Vinland voyages were purely imaginary and their narratives a species of early Scandinavian realistic novel. Hovgaard's work is considered to have established the historicity of these voyages.

U78. Thórdarson, Matthias. **The Vinland voyages.** Tr. by Thorstina J. Walters. N.Y., 1930. Short, readable, and able account by the former director of the National Museum of Iceland. The author mentions all theories as to the location of Scandinavian discoveries in North America, but reaches no dogmatic conclusion and suggests the need for more research.

U79. Haugen, Einar. **Voyages to Vinland: the first American saga.** N.Y., 1942. Haugen translates the sagas dealing with the Norse discovery of America into good, mid-20th century American prose, making no effort to impart or retain an archaic flavor. He contributes a long essay, "The evidence of history," in which he fixes no exact spot for the Norse landing, but concludes that it probably took place on the New England coast.

U80. Holand, Hjalmar R. **Explorations in America before Columbus.** N.Y., 1956. Deserves mention, though some will hesitate to call it altogether reliable. Holand has labored most of his life to establish the veracity of the Kensington rune stone's inscription, which briefly tells the story of the experiences of a party of Norwegians and Swedes in the interior of North America in the 14th century. Now, marshaling all the available evidence, he writes a history of Scandinavian contact with America from that of Leif Ericsson's predecessor, Bjarni Herjulfsson, in 986 to the Norwegian-Portuguese expedition of 1476, either identified or imagined by Sophus Larsen of Copenhagen over thirty years ago.

U81. Penrose, Boies. **Travel and discovery in the Renaissance, 1420–1620.** Cambridge, Mass., 1952. 2nd ed., 1955. Not merely a history of exploration, although exploration receives careful attention. Stresses the adventures of individual travelers who did not precisely discover, but went to many interesting places seldom visited by Europeans at that time. Attention is given to mapmaking and navigation.

U82. Friederici, Georg. **Der Charakter der Entdeckung und Eroberung Amerikas durch die Europäer.** 3 v. Stuttgart, 1925–36. A magnificent piece of scholarship, for which the author spent years in preparation before writing a line. V. 1 is devoted principally to Spanish conquest in America; v. 2 deals with a number of subjects, principally Portuguese discoveries in Africa, the Indian ocean, and Brazil, the role of Germans in opening the New World, and the French discovery and colonization of Canada; v. 3 is concerned with Dutch, Scandinavian, and English settlement of America, as well as with the character of the Indians, and Russian penetration of North America.

U83. Almagià, Roberto. **I primi esploratori dell' America.** Rome, 1937. Excellent work dealing with five renowned Italian navigators: Christopher Columbus, Amerigo Vespucci, John and Sebastian Cabot, and Giovanni da Verrazano.

U84. Baião, António, Hernani Cidade, and Manuel Múrias, eds. **História da expansão portuguesa no mundo.** 3 v. Lisbon, 1937–40. Collaborative work by many Portuguese authors covering Portuguese expansion in all parts of the world from the Middle Ages to the end of the 19th century. Uneven in quality, but contains some excellent studies.

U85. Peres, Damião. **História dos descobrimentos portugueses.** Oporto, 1943. A heavily documented work by one of Portugal's leading historians, containing references to both sources and modern studies, and covering Portuguese discoveries from the 14th century to 1660. Although occasionally biased, this is the best one-volume work on the subject.

U86. Prestage, Edgar. **The Portuguese pioneers.** London, 1933. Supersedes its predecessors. Based on primary sources, it covers Portuguese exploration from the capture of Ceuta to the early 16th century. Embraces Europe, Africa, Asia, the East Indies, Far East, and North and South America. Especially recommended for teaching purposes.

U87. Molinari, Diego L. **La empresa colombina.** Buenos Aires, 1938. This little book of about 200 pages deserves the high praise it has been accorded. Deals with geographical discovery and kindred matters from the Norse voyages to America to the later career of Christopher Columbus.

U88. Ballesteros y Berreta, Antonio. **Cristóbal Colón y el descubrimiento de América.** 2 v. Barcelona and Buenos Aires, 1945. [Historia de América y de los pueblos americanos, 4–5.] At the time of his death in 1949 Ballesteros was perhaps the leading historian resident in Spain. This and his other works are known for careful scholar-

ship and abundant bibliography. Here the author attempts to cast light on all arguments, including those completely divorced from historical science, that have raged about Columbus.

U89. O'Gorman, Edmundo. **La idea del descubrimiento de América: historia de esa interpretación y crítica de sus fundamentos.** Mexico, D.F., 1951. More concerned with the "idea" of the discovery of America than with the discovery itself. Traces the impact of the discovery on men's minds through later generations and interestingly reveals what Columbus' achievement meant to each.

U90. Magnaghi, Alberto. **Amerigo Vespucci: studio critico, con speciale riguardo ad una nuova valutazione delle fonti.** 2 v. Rome, 1924. With the publication of this work, Magnaghi completely revolutionized the Vespucian controversy. Although he was as favorable to Vespucci as the most laudatory of his predecessors, he differed from them completely in his approach. He termed spurious the two letters attributed to Vespucci describing four voyages to America, but accepted as genuine the three letters describing only two voyages. Magnaghi decided that Vespucci had sailed only twice— for Spain in 1499 and for Portugal in 1501 —but that the voyages were of great length and exceptional importance. The appearance in 1948 of Levillier's *América la bien llamada* (*U91*), with its contrary hypothesis, made a considerable difference, however, and at present there are many doubters of the Magnaghi thesis.

U91. Levillier, Roberto. **América la bien llamada.** 2 v. Buenos Aires, 1948. A more conventional approach to Vespucci. Disagreeing with Magnaghi, this Argentine historian believed that all the letters attributed to Vespucci were authentic and that the Florentine discoverer had, therefore, made four voyages. Since 1948 students of the Vespucian problem have been followers of either Magnaghi or Levillier.

U92. Arciniegas, Germán. **Amerigo y el nuevo mundo.** Mexico and Buenos Aires, 1955. Popular but scholarly account of Amerigo Vespucci, following in general the lines laid down by Levillier (*U91*).

U93. Marcondes de Souza, Thomaz O. **Amerigo Vespucci e suas viagens.** São Paulo, 1949. 2nd ed., 1954. Author is definitely on the side of Magnaghi in the Vespucian controversy.

U94. ———. **O descobrimento do Brasil: estudo crítico de acôrdo com a documentação histórico-cartográfica e a náutica.** São Paulo, 1946. Vigorously combats the theory that there was a Portuguese discovery of Brazil prior to Cabral's.

U95. Denucé, Jean. **Magellan, la question des Moluques et la première circumnavigation du globe.** Brussels, 1911. For years the best study of Magellan, and still one of the best. Prefaced with valuable bibliographical introduction and illustrated with both modern maps and those of the Magellan period. Denucé believed, on the basis of some evidence, that in addition to the search for the Moluccas, Magellan was on the track of the Old Testament Tarshish and Ophir, associated with King Solomon, and that he associated these places with the Ryukyu islands.

U96. Medina, José Toribio. **El descubrimiento del Océano Pacífico: Vasco Núñez de Balboa, Hernando de Magallanes y sus compañeros.** 3 v. Santiago, Chile, 1914–20. Medina was one of the greatest bibliographers and archival workers who ever lived. In this work, as in others, his principal objective is not synthetic writing, but presenting the documentary evidence, much of it quarried by himself from the Spanish archives. Every remark he makes is buttressed by a weight of sources.

U97. Queiroz Velloso, José Maria de. **Fernão de Magalhães, a vida e a viagem.** Lisbon, 1941. Valuable study with many new facts added to previous knowledge of Magellan. A critical summary rather than a biography. French translation, "Fernão de Magalhães, sa vie et son voyage," appeared in *Revue d'histoire moderne,* 14, n.s. 8 (Aug.-Sep. 1939): 417–515.

U98. Melón y Ruiz de Gordejuela, Amando. **Los primeros tiempos de la colonización. Cuba y las Antillas. Magallanes y la primera vuelta al mundo.** Barcelona, 1952. V. 6 of **Historia de América y los pueblos americanos.** Discusses the lesser voyages in the Caribbean following the discoveries of Columbus, and the voyages and contributions of Vespucci, concerning whom Melón follows Magnaghi's interpretation. The work then surveys Spain's expansion to the mainland and reviews the discovery of the Pacific, concluding with Magellan's voyage and its aftermath. Sound and thorough.

U99. Medina, José Toribio. **Juan Díaz de Solís: estudio histórico.** 2 v. Santiago, Chile, 1897. Best work on the official discoverer of the Río de la Plata and pilot mayor of the Castilian Casa de Contratación. V. 1 consists of narrative and v. 2 of documents.

U100. ——. **El veneciano Sebastián Caboto al servicio de España y especialmente de su proyectado viaje á las Molucas por el Estrecho de Magallanes y al reconocimiento de la costa del continente hasta la gobernación de Pedrarias Dávila.** 2 v. Santiago, Chile, 1908. V. 1 contains narrative and documents; v. 2 consists entirely of documents.

U101. Wagner, Henry R. **Spanish voyages to the northwest coast of America in the sixteenth century.** San Francisco, 1929. Begins with the voyage of Francisco de Ulloa around the peninsula of Lower Cali-

fornia in 1539 and closes with the exploration of the California coast by Sebastian Vizcaino in 1602.

U102. Williamson, James A. **The voyages of the Cabots and the English discovery of North America under Henry VII and Henry VIII.** London, 1929. The definitive work on the Cabots. Contains all significant documents on the Cabot voyages to America. Williamson believes that on his two voyages of 1497 and 1498 John Cabot sought Cathay, and that on the second he followed the American coast south to the tropics. As a result, when Sebastian Cabot took up exploration in 1508 he knew he must round America to reach Cipangu and Cathay, and hence made his voyage to the mouth of Hudson's Bay.

U103. ——. **The age of Drake.** London, 1938. Williamson absorbed the knowledge of many scholars on this subject and presents it in a highly successful manner.

U104. Julien, Charles A. **Les voyages de découverte et les premiers établissements (XVᵉ–XVIᵉ siècles).** Paris, 1948. A scholarly, well-documented account of French discovery from 1402 to the second half of the 16th century. Covers French activities in the Mediterranean, the Atlantic, Canada, Brazil, and Florida. Much use is made of the writings of early Frenchmen regarding the New World and its inhabitants. Elaborate bibliography.

U105. Beaglehole, John C. **The exploration of the Pacific.** London, 1934. 2nd ed., 1947. Account of European exploration of the Pacific from Magellan to Cook, reviewing Spanish, Dutch, French, and English voyages.

U106. Heawood, Edward. **A history of geographical discovery in the seventeenth and eighteenth centuries.** Cambridge, Eng., 1912. Still the best work available for geographical discovery during the two centuries covered. The author, who was librarian to the Royal Geographical Society, provided full coverage and reviewed every exploration that occurred, including what little took place in Africa and inner Asia.

U107. Key, Charles E. **The story of twentieth-century exploration.** London, 1937; N.Y., 1938. Includes recent exploration of the Amazon, Tibet, New Guinea, the heart of Australia, the Himalayas, Greenland, northernmost America, the North Pole, and the Antarctic.

U108. Andreev, Aleksandr I., ed. **Russkie otkrytiya v Tikhom okeane i Severnoy Amerike v XVIII veke.** (Russian discoveries in the Pacific and North America in the 18th century.) Moscow, 1948. Russian discovery in the 18th century, based upon the best literature and supplemented by fairly good reproductions of 18th century maps.

U109. Efimov, Aleksei V. **Iz istorii velikikh**

Russkikh geograficheskikh otkrytii v Severnom Ledovitom i Tikhom okeanakh XVII —pervaya polovina XVIII v. (Great Russian geographical discoveries in the Arctic and Pacific oceans in the 17th and the first half of the 18th century.) Moscow, 1950. A history of geographical discovery by Russians for a century and a half, with heavy emphasis on the achievements of Dezhnev.

U110. Badigin, Konstantin S. **Put 'na Grumant.** (Toward Grumant.) Moscow, 1953. Adventures of the Russian population in Spitzbergen in the mid-18th century. About a third of the book is a historical survey entitled "Russian navigators in the North."

U111. Berg, Lev S. **Geschichte der russischen geographischen Entdeckungen gesammelte Aufsätze.** Leipzig, 1954. Tr. of *Ocherki po istorii russkikh geograficheskikh otkrytii.* Survey of Russian achievements in discovery and cartography from a time slightly before Peter the Great to substantially the present. Heavily documented.

CARTOGRAPHY

U112. A guide to historical cartography: a selected, annotated list of references on the history of maps and map making. Comp. by Walter W. Ristow and Clara E. Le Gear for the Library of Congress. Washington, 1954. This deals not with historical maps, but with the history of map making.

U113. Revelli, Paolo, ed. **Cristoforo Colombo e la scuola cartografica genovese.** 3 v. Genoa, 1937. Partially another biography of Columbus, with enough attention to scholarly details to make it one of the best. Of more significance, however, is the emphasis on development of Genoese cartography and the insistence that mapmakers of Genoa helped formulate the ideas and plans of Columbus. The real contribution is in v. 2.

U114. Harrisse, Henry. **Découverte et évolution cartographique de Terre-Neuve.** London and Paris, 1900. Most of Harrisse's works dealing with discovery have been superseded, but this is an exception. The work is well documented and profusely illustrated.

U115. Bagrow, Leo. **Die Geschichte der Kartographie.** Berlin, 1951. This book, by probably the greatest authority on the history of cartography, is of great value although, regarding European cartography, it stops with the 18th century. Little space is given to ancient maps, more to medieval ones, and those of the late medieval and Renaissance period receive the most attention. There is a brief chapter on Turkish and old Russian maps, and another on Asiatic and American Indian attempts at cartography.

U116. Cortesão, Armando. **Cartografia e**

cartógrafos portugueses dos séculos XV e XVI. 2 v. Lisbon, 1935. The origins and early history of Portuguese cartography have not been as well known as have those of Italy, especially Genoa, and Catalonia. Cortesão here places the matter in a clearer light. The one serious flaw is the author's hopeless attempt to prove that Christopher and Bartholomew Columbus, both cartographers, were Portuguese.

U117. Crone, Gerald R. **Maps and their makers: an introduction to the history of cartography.** London, 1953. This work, by the learned librarian and map curator of the Royal Geographical Society, is good, though overly brief. Portolanic, or harbor-finding, charts are given a chapter of their own; while another is devoted to Catalan world maps, which reached their highest development in the late 14th and early 15th centuries. A survey of national atlases is also included.

U118. Tooley, Ronald V. **Maps and mapmakers.** London, 1949. 2nd ed., rev., 1952. Comprehensive review of the evolution of maps with much factual information. A chapter is devoted to each of the four great schools of map-makers, in Italy, the Netherlands, France, and England, and to each is appended a bibliography.

U119. Brown, Lloyd A. **The story of maps.** Boston, 1949. Not so much the "story of maps" as the "history of map-making." Contains some errors, but nevertheless is an indispensable work.

U120. Akioka, Takejirō. **Nippon chizu-shi.** (A history of Japanese maps.) Tokyo, 1955. Extends in time from the Buddhist priest Gyōgi, who is thought to have been the first Japanese map maker, to the early 19th century. The author has studied only maps of the Japanese islands and immediately adjacent regions, but in its restricted field the work is definitive.

COMMERCE AND TRADING COMPANIES

U121. Insh, George P. **The Company of Scotland trading to Africa and the Indies.** N.Y., 1932. Account includes the launching of the company, the two attempts to colonize Darien, and descriptions of the various individual trading voyages, all in the period 1693–1707. A lively and well-written narrative, with good notes, index, and bibliography. [GER]

U122. Dalgliesh, Wilbert H. **The Perpetual Company of the Indies in the days of Dupleix.** Philadelphia, 1933. Presents an enormous amount of material dealing primarily with the administrative, military, and financial organization of the company. The treatment is devoid of political background data. [GER]

U123. Martin, Gaston. **Nantes au XVIIIᵉ siècle: l'ère des négriers (1714–1774), d'après des documents inédits.** Paris, 1931. Exposition of the slave trade carried on by the merchants of Nantes, dealing with virtually every aspect of the traffic. The pattern developed here applies in great measure to all slave trade enterprises. Notes, documents, good bibliography. [GER]

U124. Pares, Richard. **War and trade in the West Indies, 1739–1763.** N.Y., 1936. This very important work, based upon original manuscripts, has become a standard one. Not a chronological narrative, but a critical summary of naval strategy, diplomacy, trade, and policy in the light of economic orientation. [GER]

U125. Parkinson, C. Northcote. **Trade in the eastern seas, 1793–1813.** Cambridge, Eng., 1937. British trade and naval operations in the East. A fine survey, although it does not have the detail of Furber's *John Company* (*R388*). Useful notes and bibliography. [GER]

U126. Philips, Cyril H. **The East India Company, 1784–1834.** Manchester, 1940. Story of the transfer of the company from a purely trading concern to an agency of imperial administration. Concerned more with the imperial aspects than company activities. The standard of scholarly workmanship is high, and there are extensive notes and several maps. [GER]

U127. Wilbur, Marguerite K. **The East India Company and the British empire in the Far East.** N.Y., 1945. General history of the rise, development, growth, and termination of the company. Covers not only the economic aspects, but the role played in extension of the British empire in India and in the internal affairs of the British Isles. [GER]

U128. Furber, Holden. **John Company at work.** See *R388.*

U129. Philips, Cyril H., ed. **The correspondence of David Scott, director and chairman of the East India Company, relating to Indian affairs, 1787–1805.** London, 1951. Useful supplement to *U126.* [GER]

U130. Schramm, Percy E. **Deutschland und Übersee: der deutsche Handel mit den anderen Kontinenten, insbesondere Afrika von Karl V bis zu Bismarck; ein Beitrag zur Geschichte der Rivalität im Wirtschaftsleben.** Brunswick, 1950. Covers the entire German participation in the expansion of Europe, including German efforts in South America under Charles V, the work of missionaries, explorers, and especially the colonizing efforts of the great merchant firms from Bremen and Hamburg. At times the author appears too confident of the beneficial nature of German rule, and his categoric statement that no German firms engaged in the slave trade is incorrect. [GER]

U131. Davies, Kenneth G. **The Royal African Company.** N.Y. and London, 1957. Account of an English company for trade with western Africa which was founded in 1672, held a monopoly of trade until 1698, and existed until 1752. An excellent work, based on the archives of the company existing in the Public Record Office. Author displays full knowledge of the problems of financing a joint-stock company in the 18th century and a thorough understanding of English economic history. [GER]

U132. Foster, William. **England's quest of eastern trade.** London, 1933. The author, for many years historiographer to the India Office, has provided a short summary of the entire British attempt to break through the Spanish-Portuguese monopoly from 1497 to mid-17th century. [GER]

BRITISH COLONIZATION

History

U133. The Cambridge history of the British empire. Ed. by J. Holland Rose, Arthur P. Newton, and E. A. Benians. London, 1929 ff. [1, *The old empire, from the beginnings to 1783* (1929); 2, *The growth of the new empire, 1783–1870* (1940); 3, *The empire commonwealth, 1870–1921* (in preparation); 4, *British India, 1497–1858* (1929); 5, *The Indian empire, 1858–1918* (1932); 6, *Canada and Newfoundland* (1930); 7, pt. 1, *Australia;* pt. 2, *New Zealand* (1933); 8, *South Africa, Rhodesia, and the protectorates* (1936).] The volumes are of great length and detail, and each chapter is the work of a specialist. At end of each volume is a bibliography listing not only the books, but also the manuscripts used in its preparation.

U134. Gipson, Lawrence H. **The British empire before the American Revolution.** 9 v. Caldwell, Idaho, and N.Y., 1936–56. [1, *Great Britain and Ireland;* 2, *The southern plantations;* 3, *The northern plantations;* 4, *Zones of international friction: North America south of the Great Lakes region, 1748–1754;* 5, *The Great Lakes frontier; Canada, the West Indies, India, 1748–1754;* 6, *The great war for the empire: the years of defeat, 1754–1757;* 7, *The victorious years, 1758–1760;* 8, *The culmination, 1760–1763;* 9, *New responsibilities within the enlarged empire, 1763–1766.*] The *magnum opus* of an American scholar with strong Tory leanings. Reviewers differ as to its merits, and some criticisms of individual volumes have been severe; but in view of its conception and execution it must be regarded as an important work. [GER, CEN]

U135. Carrington, Charles E. **The British overseas: exploits of a nation of shopkeepers.** Cambridge, Eng., 1950. Author has succeeded extraordinarily well in compressing into a thousand pages the entire history of

British expansion. Any essential fact regarding British expansion is easily found, and adequate treatment is given minor colonies. However, the account, which is to some extent tinged with the sad feelings of past glories and assumes the character of a recessional, ends with the 1930's. [GER]

U136. Schlote, Werner. **Entwicklung und Strukturverwandlung des englischen Aussenhandels von 1700 bis zur Gegenwart.** Jena, 1938. Tr. by W. O. Henderson and W. H. Chaloner as **British overseas trade from 1700 to the 1930's.** Oxford, 1952. Fast becoming a classic. [GER]

U137. Knowles, Lilian C. A., and C. M. Knowles. **The economic development of the British overseas empire.** 3 v. London, 1924–36. These 3 volumes form a standard history. V. 1, by Lilian C. A. Knowles, is termed in the 1931 edition of this *Guide* (p. 452) a "very useful historical outline and systematic summary of a wealth of data." It deals with the economic problems of India and the British tropical possessions. V. 2 and 3, the joint work of Lilian and C. M. Knowles, cover Canada and the Union of South Africa. [GER]

U138. Newton, Arthur P. **The colonising activities of the English Puritans: the last phase of the Elizabethan struggle with Spain.** New Haven, 1914. Survey of Puritan colonizing enterprises to 1660, with special reference to the activities of the earl of Warwick and the Providence Company, and to anti-Spanish activities in the West Indies. [GMD]

U139. Insh, George P. **Scottish colonial schemes, 1620–1686.** Glasgow, 1922. Deals with enterprises in Newfoundland, Nova Scotia, New Galloway (Cape Breton), East New Jersey, and Stuart's Town, S.C. Appendices of documents. [GMD]

U140. ——. **The Company of Scotland trading to Africa and the Indies.** See *U121.* Sequel to *U139.*

U141. Herbertson, Andrew J., and Osbert J. R. Howarth, eds. **The Oxford survey of the British empire.** 6 v. Oxford, 1914. [1, *The British Isles and Mediterranean possessions;* 2, *Asia;* 3, *Africa;* 4, *America;* 5, *Australasia;* 6, *General survey.*] Cooperative work intended for those whose special interest is the administration of the British empire. Descriptive rather than historical; encyclopedic in scope, yet unified by a consistent plan. [HET]

U142. Burt, Alfred L. **The evolution of the British empire and commonwealth from the American Revolution.** Boston, 1956. A standard text. [GER]

U143. Morrell, William P. **British colonial policy in the age of Peel and Russell.** Oxford, 1930. A most important and extensive study of the period 1841–52, based on extensive use of sources and documents. [GER]

U144. Raphael, Lois A. C. **The Cape-to-**

Cairo dream: a study in British imperialism. N.Y., 1936. A history of British diplomatic activities centering on the development of the African transcontinental telegraph and railway schemes. The book suffers somewhat from the mass of detail it contains; yet, due to the amount of available material, some episodes, controversies, etc., might well have deserved wider treatment. [GER]

U145. Knaplund, Paul. **Britain: commonwealth and empire, 1901–1955.** London, 1956. The most up-to-date history of the British commonwealth in the 20th century; written by an outstanding authority.

U146. ——. **The British empire, 1815–1939.** N.Y., 1941. A standard text. [GER]

U147. Currey, Charles H. **The British commonwealth since 1815.** 2 v. Sydney, 1950–51. Oriented toward the concept of the commonwealth as a "unique association." Covers through World War II. V. 1 deals with the United Kingdom, the semi-independent members of the commonwealth, and Eire; v. 2, the colonial dependencies of the Crown. [GER]

U148. Oliver, Roland A. **The missionary factor in east Africa.** See *AC187.*

Administration

U149. Bruce, Sir Charles. **The broad stone of empire: problems of crown colony administration with records of personal experience.** 2 v. London and N.Y., 1910. Exhaustive study of the health, laws, administrative systems, education, and religion of the British crown colonies. Overburdened with lengthy dispatches and memoranda. The self-governing dominions are considered scarcely at all; but as a treatise on the government of tropical dependencies by one who was experienced as a colonial administrator, it is of the highest value. [FWP]

U150. Porritt, Edward. **The fiscal and diplomatic freedom of the British oversea dominions.** Ed. by David Kinley. Oxford and N.Y., 1922. Mainly the account of Canada's acquisition of sovereignty over her financial affairs and certain foreign relations. While the book shows wide research, the materials are poorly organized. Useful as a collection of source material and as a guide to the literature. [FWP]

U151. The British empire, a survey. Ed. by Hugh Gunn. 12 v. London, 1924. Best general descriptive survey of the administrative and cultural conditions and problems of the British empire after World War I, by competent authorities in the several fields. The arrangement is topical instead of regional. Each volume is an independent work; the first three are particularly important. [GMD]

U152. Resources of the empire: a business man's survey of the empire's resources, pre-

pared by the Federation of British Industries. 10 v. in 12. London, 1924. Each volume is complete in itself, with data usually arranged by political divisions or units for each class of products. Those on food supplies, chemicals, and communications are perhaps the most important. [GMD]

U153. Hailey, William M., baron. **An African survey: a study of problems arising in Africa south of the Sahara.** See *AC73*.

U154. ———. **Native administration in the British African territories.** See *AC193*.

U155. Hall, Henry L. **The Colonial Office, a history.** N.Y., 1937. The title is misleading. The book is limited to 1835–85, the great age of Victorian colonial administration. This period is covered in detail. Use has been made of Colonial Office documents, and the author quotes freely from memoranda, reports, and records. The work is authoritative and well considered. [GER]

U156. Jeffries, Sir Charles J. **The colonial empire and its civil service.** N.Y., 1938. Analysis of the colonial service after its reform in 1932. Contains a short historical survey. Based on documents and actual experience, this volume forms a good sequel to *U155*. [GER]

The West Indies and Other Insular Colonies

U157. Edwards, Bryan. **The history, civil and commercial, of the British colonies in the West Indies.** 3 v. London, 1793–97. 5th ed., 5 v., 1819. Edwards resided in the West Indies for about 25 years and was familiar with both the French and English colonies. While his historical narrative is being superseded by monographs based on official sources, the work remains of permanent value as an authoritative picture of economic and social life in the West Indies during the author's lifetime. [FWP]

U158. Watts, Arthur P. **Une histoire des colonies anglaises aux Antilles (de 1649 à 1660).** Paris, 1924. Detailed study of British activities in the West Indies in the Cromwellian period, which was a time of critical importance in the development of British policy and the extension of British power in the Caribbean region. [GMD]

U159. Mims, Stewart L. **Colbert's West India policy.** New Haven, 1912. The prosperity of the French West Indies was so great in the 18th century that the British trade policy turned largely on the rivalry between the French and English islands in the Caribbean. The author set himself the task of tracing the sources of this prosperity and found them in the very definite policy of Colbert. Source material in the French archives has been used extensively. [AHB]

U160. Higham, Charles S. **The development of the Leeward Islands under the Restoration, 1660–1688: a study of the foundations of the old colonial system.** Cambridge, Eng., 1921. An important step in laying foundations for a really scientific history of the West Indies; based upon systematic investigation of manuscripts in the Public Record Office and private collections. [FWP]

U161. Pitman, Frank W. **The development of the British West Indies, 1700–1763.** New Haven, 1917. Primarily the story of the economic development of the British islands, but the social and political sides of the story are also fully treated. Essential to a rounded knowledge of British policy. [AHB]

U162. Ragatz, Lowell J. **The fall of the planter class in the British Caribbean.** N.Y., 1928. Exceedingly valuable contribution to the commercial, agrarian, and social history of the West Indies; based upon a thorough study of public and private sources, both printed and manuscript. [FWP]

U163. Penson, Lillian M. **The colonial agents of the British West Indies: a study in colonial administration, mainly in the eighteenth century.** London, 1924. Notable contribution to a subject which long awaited competent treatment; valuable not only for its account of the development of the colonial agent, but also for its picture of the institutional and economic background out of which he came. [AHB]

U164. Westergaard, Waldemar. **The Danish West Indies under company rule (1671–1754) with a supplementary chapter, 1755–1917.** N.Y., 1917. Scholarly and authoritative; based on source material. Affords valuable comparisons with the history and development of the French and British islands. [AHB]

U165. Boyson, V. F. **The Falkland Islands: with notes on the natural history by Rupert Vallentin.** Oxford, 1924. Chronicle of the slight annals, chiefly international, of these islands is based on thorough research in the sources and supplemented by a wealth of descriptive material. Includes important data on whaling and sealing in the South Atlantic. [FWP]

U166. Hardman, William. **A history of Malta during the period of the French and British occupations, 1798–1815.** Ed. with introduction and notes by J. H. Rose. London and N.Y., 1909. Mainly a compilation of documents relating to the most critical period of the island's history. Valuable for international as well as local outlook. [GMD]

U167. Orr, Charles W. J. **Cyprus under British rule.** London, 1918.

U168. Burns, Sir Alan C. **History of the British West Indies.** London, 1954. The author, West Indian born, has held high civil appointment there. While giving a picture of the whole area, this is primarily a history

of the British colonies. It is sometmes difficult to follow the detailed account of the
numerous and often rather small islands.
Much more complete for the pre-1900
period. [GER]

U169. Newton, Arthur P. **The European
nations in the West Indies, 1493–1688.** London, 1933. The author, late Rhodes professor
of imperial history at the University of
London, provides a concise sketch of two
centuries of West Indian history, and offers a
comparison of the policies of the various
European powers. The treatment is compressed but comprehensive. Although there
are no notes or bibliography, the book is an
extremely important survey of the entire
picture. [GER]

U170. Martineau, Alfred A. **Trois siècles
d'histoire antillaise.** Paris, 1935. Lively,
though not profound, survey by an eminent
authority. A good companion work to *U169*.

U171. Smith, Harrison. **Britain in Malta.**
2 v. Valetta, 1953. [1, *Constitutional development of Malta in the nineteenth century;
2, Italian influence on British policy in
Malta, 1899–1903*.] Too detailed, but valuable. [GER]

History and Discussions of Policy

U172. Seeley, Sir John R. **The expansion
of England: two courses of lectures.** London, 1883. 2nd ed., 1895. Later reprints.
Work of a man of vision, one of the first to
point out the greatness and significance of
the British empire, who protested against
confining the study of English history to the
British Isles and urged the consideration of
imperial history. [FJK]

U173. Knaplund, Paul. **Gladstone and Britain's imperial policy.** London, 1927. Contrary to the view that Gladstone was indif-
ferent to imperialism, this study, based on
the Hawarden mss., sustains the view that
he had a vital concern with the growth of
an empire united by voluntary bonds. [FWP]

U174. ———. **James Stephen and the British colonial system.** Madison, Wis., 1953.
Study of the official life of a man who was
one of the great early Victorian civil servants
and a power in the formation of colonial
policy. Includes important new material not
systematically used before.

U175. Bryce, James B., viscount. **Modern
democracies.** 2 v. London and N.Y., 1921.
The author's last work; embodies his final
judgments and ripe wisdom on democratic
government. Special consideration is given
to Canada, Australia, and New Zealand, as
well as France, Switzerland, the United
States, and the republics of ancient Greece
and of South America. [GMD]

U176. Clark, Grover. **The balance sheets
of imperialism: facts and figures on colonies.**
N.Y., 1936. This small book contains valu-

able data regarding the political status of
the colonized areas and the principal international treaties regarding colonial territories.
Bibliography. [GER]

U177. Knorr, Klaus E. **British colonial
theories, 1570–1850.** Toronto, 1944. Mainly
a compilation of the printed materials on
the relative advantages and disadvantages of
colonization. Very valuable in providing the
only assembly of contemporary, and often
obscure, opinions. [GER]

U178. Mellor, George R. **British imperial
trusteeship, 1780–1850.** London, 1951.
Author regards British colonial developments
mainly from the humanitarian side. He deals
with the abolition of the slave trade, suttee,
etc.; and approves the extension of British
rule because, so he asserts, it brought benefits
to the exploited native classes. [GER]

Imperial Defense

U179. Fortescue, Sir John W. **The empire and the army.** London, 1928. Survey of
problems of imperial defense as seen by an
eminent military historian. Dated, but an
interesting exposition of the point of view
held in the early 1930's. [GER]

U180. Rowan-Robinson, Henry. **Imperial
defence: a problem in four dimensions.** London, 1938. Same problems as those handled
by Fortescue, but considered several years
later. By 1938 Mussolini looked less benevo-
lent, Hitler had risen to power, and Japan
was fighting a war for the conquest of China.
[GER]

FRENCH COLONIZATION

U181. Priestley, Herbert I. **France overseas: a study of modern imperialism.** N.Y.,
1938. An ambitious book dealing with the
development of French colonies from 1815
to about 1930. There is no bibliography,
but the notes are complete and form the
basis for a working bibliography. Contains
maps and tables. [GER]

U182. ———. **France overseas through the
Old Régime.** N.Y., 1939. Same format and
make-up as *U181*, which it supplements.
[GER]

U183. Roberts, Stephen H. **History of
French colonial policy, 1870–1925.** 2 v. London, 1929. V. 1 deals with Africa; v. 2, with
Madagascar and the Far East. Rich in detail
and perhaps overly critical of the French.
The author compares French and British
colonial policy, invariably to the advantage
of the British. Contains notes and bibliography. [GER]

U184. Petit, Edouard. **Organisation des
colonies françaises et des pays de protectorat.**
2 v. Paris, 1894–95. Petit wrote from extended experience both in the home service
and in the colonies. In spite of the many

changes that have taken place since its publication, this work remains of great value as a detailed analysis of colonial administration in its historical setting. There are admirable chapters on the penal system, commerce, public utilities, religion, and education. [LFB]

U185. Hanotaux, Gabriel, and Alfred Martineau, eds. **Histoire des colonies françaises et de l'expansion de la France dans le monde.** 6 v. Paris, 1929–33. The editors are distinguished French historians, but this series, unlike the Cambridge histories, sometimes deserts exactitude in favor of dramatic stories. It does not have the careful references or other scholarly apparatus found in the Cambridge volumes. [GER]

U186. Hardy, Georges. **Histoire de la colonisation française.** 4th ed., Paris, 1947. A standard textbook by an author who has written numerous other works on the subject. The account is succinct, lucid, and authoritative. Over half the book deals with French activities in Africa. Bibliography at end of each chapter. [GER]

U187. Devèze, Michel. **La France d'outre-mer: de l'empire coloniale à l'Union Française (1938–1947).** Paris, 1948. Concise but comprehensive exposition of the changes brought about by World War II in the French colonial empire. The author gives special attention to basic concepts, establishment, and functioning of the "French Union" developed after the Brazzaville conference of 1944. [GER]

U188. Wrong, George M. **The rise and fall of New France.** See *AA80.*

GERMAN COLONIZATION

U189. Townsend, Mary E. **The rise and fall of Germany's colonial empire, 1884–1918.** N.Y., 1930. The standard treatment of German colonial policy. Introductory chapters provide background far earlier than 1884, and the work closes with the disposition of Germany's empire at the Versailles peace conference in 1919. [GER, CEN]

U190. Hagen, Maximilian von. **Bismarcks Kolonialpolitik.** Gotha, 1923. Exhaustive study based on extensive published material. [FWP]

U191. Koschitzky, Max von. **Deutsche Colonialgeschichte.** 2 v. Leipzig, 1887–88. Stresses the colonial movement in its relations with internal politics of the empire, as well as the acquisition of the several colonies and the resulting international complications. Although primarily a detailed study of the colonial policy of the German empire from 1871 to 1885, one-half of v. 1 describes early antecedents of colonial activity, such as the Hansa, and discusses emigration, missions, and trade as motives for colonization. [MET]

U192. Zimmermann, Alfred. **Geschichte der deutschen Kolonialpolitik.** Berlin, 1914. Written by an official prominent in the colonial service since 1893, and reflects the unusual opportunities of the author for observation of colonial affairs and for access to colonial records. Covers only the period after 1871, and presents primarily the external history of German colonization. Notable lack of bias or partisanship. [MET]

U193. Chéradame, André. **La colonisation et les colonies allemandes.** Paris, 1905. Author produced this authoritative monograph after being sent to Germany in 1898 by the French government to study German colonization. Based on material drawn from the library of the Kolonial Gesellschaft; influenced very slightly, if at all, by French bias. [MET]

U194. Rudin, Harry R. **Germans in the Cameroons, 1884–1914: a case study in modern imperialism.** New Haven, 1938. A long study based not only on archival materials, but also actual research on the spot. Gives a complete picture of German colonial policies and procedures, economic exploitation, native administration, police control, etc. The author was apparently much impressed with German claims and reaches pro-German conclusions which his narrative hardly bears out. [GER]

U195. Aydelotte, William O. **Bismarck and British colonial policy: the problem of Southwest Africa.** Philadelphia, 1937. Mainly concerned with diplomatic maneuvers. [GER]

U196. Taylor, Alan J. P. **Germany's first bid for colonies, 1884–1885.** London, 1938. Concerned with the same problem as *U195.* [GER]

U197. Bullock, Alan L. C., ed. **Germany's colonial demands.** London, 1939. Edited from reports of the Oxford University British Commonwealth Group. A survey without much partisanship. Advises against a return of the foreign German colonies to Germany. [GER]

U198. Logan, Rayford. **The African mandates in world politics.** Washington, 1949. Review of the attempts by Germany to recover her lost colonies during the inter-war period. [GER]

U199. Crowe, Sybil E. **The Berlin West African conference, 1884–1885.** N.Y., 1942. Book consists of two parts: the first dealing with the preliminary negotiations, Anglo-Portuguese relations, Franco-German colonial cooperation, and King Leopold's activities; the second with the conference proper. [GER]

ITALIAN COLONIZATION

U200. Brunialti, Attilio. **Le colonie degli italiani, con appendice: i primi tentativi e le prime ricerche di una colonia in Italia**

(1861–1882) di Giacomo Gorrini. Turin, 1897. Still a valuable source for the student of Italy's colonial policy, being a clear, judicious view of the causes and vicissitudes of Italian colonial expansion in Africa during the last quarter of the 19th century.

U201. Italy. Ministero degli Affari Esteri. **L'Africa italiana al parlamento nazionale, 1882–1905.** Rome, 1907. Full record of the development of Italian public opinion with regard to colonization, as reflected in parliament. Contains valuable maps and an index to parliamentary documents.

U202. Amministrazione fiduciaria all'Italia in Africa: atti del Secondo Convengo di Studi Coloniale. Florence, 1948. The question of trusteeship in the former colonies of Italy. Supplies a wealth of information on all aspects of Italy's colonial activity, but, not surprisingly, paints too rosy a picture. [GER]

U203. Macartney, Maxwell H. H., and Paul Cremona. **Italy's foreign and colonial policy, 1914–1937.** N.Y., 1938. The authors, correspondents for the London *Times* and the *Christian Science Monitor* respectively, served for many years in Rome. The book makes no pretensions to exhaustive scholarship, but shows a good acquaintance with the printed sources. Considerable balance is shown in judgments of fascistic policies. [GER]

U204. Zoli, Corrado. **Espansione coloniale italiana.** Rome, 1949. Useful account of Italian empire-building by the head of the Royal Italian Geographical Society. [GER]

U205. Ciasca, Raffaele. **Storia coloniale dell'Italia contemporanea: da Assab all' Impero.** Milan, 1938. Comprehensive treatment of the earlier Italian colonial adventures on the Red Sea, in Ethiopia, Somaliland, and Libya. It goes as far as the Ethiopian war. Excellent preparation, good notes, and comprehensive bibliography of German, Italian, French, and English sources. [GER]

DUTCH COLONIZATION

U206. Colenbrander, Herman T. **Koloniale geschiedenis.** 3 v. The Hague, 1925–26. General survey by a well-known Dutch historian. V. 1 deals with European expansion in general; v. 2 with the Dutch West Indies and with the East Indies to 1816; v. 3 carries the East Indies to the period after World War I. [GER]

U207. Vlekke, Bernhard H. M. **Nusantara: a history of the East Indian archipelago.** Cambridge, Mass., 1943. A Dutch version, somewhat longer and more up-to-date, was published as *Geschiedenis van den Indischen archipel* (Roermond, 1947). [GER]

U208. Vandenbosch, Amry. **The Dutch East Indies.** Berkeley, 1942. Political science approach. Good, but somewhat dated. [GER]

U209. Klaveren, J. J. van. **The Dutch colonial system.** Rotterdam, 1953. A judicious, concise, orderly history of the Dutch East Indies from their foundation to the 1930's. Includes data on economic and sociological factors, but is mainly historical in nature. Bibliography, notes, maps, tables. [GER]

BELGIAN COLONIZATION

U210. Thomson, Robert S. **Fondation de l'état indépendant du Congo: un chapitre de l'histoire du partage de l'Afrique.** Brussels, 1933. This account, written by an American, deals with the diplomatic activities that preceded the formation of the Congo Free State. It is very favorable, perhaps too favorable, to Leopold II of Belgium. Extensive notes and bibliography. [GER]

U211. Van der Kerken, Georges. **La politique coloniale belge.** Antwerp, 1943. Covers the development of the Congo Free State, the Belgian Congo, and the mandate over Ruanda-Urundi. [GER]

U212. Berger, Paul. **Le Congo Belge.** Brussels, 1930.

U213. Kermans, Herman, and Christian Monheim. **La conquête d'un empire: histoire du Congo Belge.** Brussels, 1932.

SPANISH COLONIZATION

U214. García Figueras, Tomás. **Santa Cruz de Mar Pequeña—Ifni—Sahara: la acción de España en la costa occidental de África.** Madrid, 1941. History of Spanish activity in western Africa from the 15th century until substantially the present.

U215. ——. **Marruecos: la acción de España en el norte de África.** Madrid, 1939. Review of relations between Morocco and Spain from prehistoric times until the Franco regime.

U216. Unzueta y Yuste, Abelardo de. **Geografía histórica de la isla de Fernando Poo.** See *AC500*.

PORTUGUESE COLONIZATION

U217. Couto Ribeiro Villas, Gaspar do. **História colonial.** 2 v. Lisbon, 1937. History of all Portugal's colonial dealings from the Age of Discovery to the present. The parts that will be of most value to general readers, because they are least known, are those on 19th and 20th century problems.

U218. Oliveira Martins, F. d'A., ed. **Hermenegildo Capelo e Roberto Ivens.** 2 v. Lisbon, 1951–52. Letters and documents dealing with the adventures of Portugal's two best 19th century African explorers; much documentary material throwing light upon the reawakening Portuguese interest in Africa in the last quarter of the century.

U219. Almeida Teixeira, Alberto de. **Angola intangível.** Oporto, 1934. History of Angola with much attention to 20th century problems.

U220. Ennes, António. **A guerra de África em 1895 (memórias).** 2nd ed., Lisbon, 1945. Account of Portugal's most strenuous 19th century colonial campaign against the Vatuas in 1895. Author was high commissioner of Mozambique during the emergency, and his book is regarded as a classic in Portuguese colonial literature. The present edition is strengthened by documents and studies that were missing in the first.

U221. Norton de Matos, José M. R. **Angola: ensaio sobre a vida e accão de Paiva Couceiro em Angola.** Lisbon, 1948. Important principally because it includes a series of documents regarding the Portuguese plan for an advance from Angola eastward into Barotzeland early in 1890 to be led by the experienced "Africa hand," Henrique Mitchell Paiva Couceiro, which was to have established a Portuguese corridor connecting Angola and Mozambique. Because of British interference with the plan, it never materialized.

COLONIAL AND ADMINISTRATIVE HISTORY AND METHODS

U222. Labaree, Leonard W., ed. **Royal instructions to British colonial governors, 1670–1776.** 2 v. N.Y., and London, 1935. A fundamental work providing virtually all the instructions given to British governors in North America in this period. [JN]

U223. Holcombe, Arthur N. **Dependent areas in the post-war world.** Boston, 1941. This little book, which describes the status of dependent areas as of 1941 and makes a number of suggestions for the future, may be taken as a program for ending colonialism. [JN]

U224. Jeffries, Sir Charles J. **The Colonial Office.** N.Y., 1956. Provides a description, with bibliography, of the present work of a major department of the British government and a sketch of the aims and methods of British colonial policy. [JN]

U225. Kat Angelino, Arnold D. A. de. **Colonial policy.** Abr. tr. by G. J. Renier. 2 v. The Hague, 1931. Extremely important work. V. 1 is largely concerned with the several principles of colonial policy and with the composition of eastern societies. V. 2 contains a discussion of the Dutch system in the East Indies. [JN]

U226. Maunier, René. **The sociology of colonies.** Ed. and tr. by E. O. Lorimer. 2 v. London, 1949. Represents something of a new departure in colonial theory. Author takes the view of a sociologist, and considers the development of a colony in social terms. This provocative book concludes that a posi-

tive colonial policy must be based on sound sociological principles. [JN]

U227. Adam, Thomas R. **Modern colonialism: institutions and policies.** N.Y., 1955. This brief work analyzes the conflicts between western law and native custom, discusses the relation of a colonial governor to his territory as to the degree of power and centralization, and considers the extent of representative government in the colonies. The possibility of international control is investigated, and a large chapter deals with economic and social policies. [JN]

U228. Cordero Torres, José M. **La evolución de la personalidad internacional de los países dependientes.** Madrid, 1950. An up-to-date work dealing with the emergence of international personality in all colonial areas until approximately 1949. Includes a historical introduction to colonialism embracing the period before 1914.

U229. Stahl, Kathleen M. **British and Soviet colonial systems.** London, 1951.

U230. Dawson, Robert M., ed. **The development of dominion status, 1900–1936.** London and N.Y., 1937. An attempt to inform the general reader in a fairly concise manner of what dominion status means and how it developed out of the political experience of the past. It is best on Canada and weakest on Australia and the Irish Free State. Latter part of the book consists of documents. [JN]

U231. Furnivall, John S. **Colonial policy and practice: a comparative study of Burma and Netherlands India.** Cambridge, Eng., 1948. N.Y., 1956. Author wrote this book when the government of Burma requested his views on reconstruction after World War II. Compares administrative policies, local autonomy, economic life, and welfare policies in Burma and the Dutch East Indies. An outstanding example of a modern and well-thought-out colonial program. [JN]

U232. Schuyler, Robert L. **Parliament and the British empire: some constitutional controversies concerning imperial legislative jurisdiction.** N.Y., 1929. Analysis of the relation of Parliament to the empire, tracing development of its right to legislate for imperial matters and the subsequent decline of legislation for the dominions. [JN]

U233. Nathan, Manfred. **Empire government: an outline of the system prevailing in the British Commonwealth of Nations.** London, 1928. Explains the constitutional position of the various types of dependencies in the empire, and surveys certain aspects of the division of powers of government. The author possesses a thorough knowledge of judicial practice in the various parts of the empire, and includes much of the data in this work. [JN]

U234. Wight, Martin. **British colonial constitutions.** Oxford, 1952. Contains a classification of the kinds of colonies or dependencies within the empire, a discussion of crown colony government, and a treatment of the various kinds of legislatures in the empire. Most of the volume is devoted to an extensive compilation of British colonial constitutions. The commonwealth dominions are not considered. [JN]

U235. Brady, Alexander. **Democracy in the dominions: a comparative study in institutions.** Toronto, 1947. Comparison of institutions and their developments in Australia, Canada, South Africa, and New Zealand. Has been termed a ripe and philosophical work. [GER]

ARCTIC EXPLORATION

U236. Greely, Adolphus W. **The polar regions in the twentieth century: their discovery and industrial evolution.** Boston, 1928. This 270 page volume presents in summary more than 80,000 pages of the original narratives of explorers. It is a condensation of Greely's *Handbook of polar discoveries* (5th ed., Boston, 1910). There is also minor coverage of Antarctic exploration.

U237. Kotzebue, Otto von. **Voyage of discovery into the South sea and Beering's straits, for the purpose of exploring a northeast passage, undertaken in the years 1815–1818.** Tr. by H. E. Lloyd. 3 v. London, 1821. Cook's voyage through Bering strait furnished no knowledge of the Alaskan coast. Kotzebue, whose explorations were chiefly directed to the coasts and islands of Bering sea, only reached Cape Krusenstern on the north shore of Kotzebue sound. [AWG]

U238. Parry, William E. **Journal of a voyage for the discovery of a north-west passage from the Atlantic to the Pacific, performed in the years 1819–20 in His Majesty's ships Hecla and Griper.** London, 1821. This narrative has an important bearing on the evolution of knowledge of Arctic America. Parry's ships, which gained the bounty for sailing beyond 110 degrees west, passed from Baffin bay to Melville sound and discovered many islands along the 75th parallel. His second and third northwest voyages had unimportant results. [AWG]

U239. Franklin, John. **Narrative of a journey to the shores of the polar sea in the years 1819–20–21–22.** 3rd ed., 2 v., London, 1824. New ed., 1 v., N.Y., 1910.

U240. ———. **Narrative of a second expedition to the shores of the polar sea, in the years 1825, 1826, and 1827, . . . including an account of the progress of a detachment to the eastward by John Richardson.** London, 1828. Franklin's journeys involved the outlining of the Arctic coast of North America, previously known only at the mouths of the Mackenzie and Coppermine rivers. The first expedition only traced Coro-

nation gulf through six degrees of longitude, but the second charted the continent from 109 to 149 degrees west longitude. [AWG]

U241. Payer, Julius, Ritter von. **New lands within the arctic circle: narrative of the discoveries of the Austrian ship "Tegetthoff," in the years 1872–1874.** 2 v. London, 1876; 1 v. N.Y., 1877. Tr. from *Die österreichisch-ungarische Nordpol-Expedition in den Jahren 1872–1874, nebst einer Skizze der zweiten deutschen Nordpol-Expedition 1869–1870 und der Polar-Expedition von 1871* (Vienna, 1876). The new (Franz Joseph) land was proved by later expeditions to be the most extensive eastern Arctic region discovered in three centuries, covering twenty degrees of longitude and two degrees of latitude. Its discovery was unique, being made without intent or effort by a northeast passage expedition. [AWG]

U242. Nordenskiöld, Nils A. E. **The voyage of the Vega round Asia and Europe, with a historical review of previous journeys along the north coast of the Old World.** 2 v. London, 1881; 1 v. N.Y., 1882. Tr. by A. Leslie from *Vegas färd kring Asien och Europa, jemte en historisk återblick på föregående resor langs Gamla Verldens Nordkust* (2 v., Stockholm, 1880–81). Account of the Swedish expedition which discovered and effected the northwest passage around Europe and Asia in 1878 and 1879. [GMD]

U243. Nansen, Fridtjof. **Farthest north: being the record of a voyage of exploration of the ship "Fram," 1893–96, and of a fifteen months' sleigh journey by Dr. Nansen and Lieut. Johansen.** 2 v. N.Y., 1897. Popular ed., 1 v., 1898. Tr. from *Fram over Polhavet, den norsk Polarfaerd, 1893–96* (2 v., Oslo (Christiania), 1897). This expedition was very successful; hydrographically it extended the Spitsbergen deep eastward to the Siberian islands. [AWG]

U244. Peary, Robert E. **The North Pole, its discovery in 1909 under the auspices of the Peary Arctic Club.** N.Y., 1910. Peary's own story of his attainment of the pole on April 6, 1909. A few have questioned the discovery, but Peary's achievement is generally accepted as the first visit to the North Pole.

U245. Amundsen, Roald E. G. **My life as an explorer.** N.Y., 1927. 2nd ed., 1928. Autobiography of the greatest of the 20th century polar explorers. Besides reviewing his well-known feats of discovery, Amundsen provides an interesting account of his early life and preparation for an exploring career.

U246. ———. **First crossing of the polar sea, by Roald Amundsen and Lincoln Ellsworth, with additional chapters by other members of the expedition.** N.Y., 1927. Story of the flight of the dirigible "Norge" from

Spitsbergen to Alaska across the North Pole in 1926. Shortly before this voyage the Americans, Richard Byrd and Floyd Bennett, sighted the pole from a plane which they had piloted from Spitsbergen.

U247. Nobile, Umberto. **With the "Italia" to the North Pole.** N.Y., 1931. Tr. by Frank Fleetwood of *L' "Italia" al Polo Nord* (Milan, 1930). In 1928 Nobile followed up his success with the "Norge" by commanding the dirigible "Italia" in a flight to the pole. The ship was destroyed, but most of the crew, including the commander, were rescued by a Russian relief expedition. In an attempt to save Nobile, Amundsen lost his own life. Nobile's handling of the "Italia" was severely criticized in Italy, and in the preface of this book the commander answers his critics with equal severity.

U248. Wilkins, George H. **Flying the Arctic.** N.Y. and London, 1928. The author, accompanied by Carl Eilson, flew a plane from Point Barrow, Alaska to Dead Man's Island, Spitsbergen. This flight, together with some earlier ones by Wilkins and Eilson, form the theme of this book.

U249. Mirsky, Jeannette. **To the north: the story of Arctic exploration from earliest times to the present.** N.Y., 1934. 2nd ed., 1948. The second edition, with a slightly revised title, contains emendations and added relevant material.

U250. Caswell, John E. **Arctic frontiers: United States explorations in the Far North.** Norman, Okla., 1956. Well-documented history of U. S. expeditions to the Arctic from that of Edwin J. De Haven in 1850 to the discovery of the pole by Peary in 1909. Includes an account of explorations in northern Alaska.

U251. Brontman, Lazar K. **On the top of the world: the Soviet expedition to the North Pole, 1937.** London, 1938. Although taking place 28 years after Peary's discovery and 11 years after the Byrd and Bennett flight, this Soviet expedition to the pole by air was in many ways more important than its predecessors. It studied drifting ice and driving winds which previous explorers, owing to their short stay, had no opportunity to investigate.

U252. Cook, James. **A voyage towards the South Pole, and round the world, performed . . . in the years 1772, 1773, 1774, and 1775.** London, 1777. Many later eds. Relates to the second of Cook's three famous voyages. He was the first to penetrate the Antarctic deeply; and, although he discovered no land in Antarctica, his was the great pioneering exploit. [PIM]

U253. Bellingshausen, Faddeĭ F. **The voyage of Captain Bellingshausen to the Antarctic seas.** Tr. from the Russian. Ed. by Frank Debenham. 2 v. London, 1945. Bellingshausen may not have been the first to

sight the Antarctic continent in 1820, but he is the only one of the early explorers whose journal has been published in book form. This translation, under auspices of the Hakluyt Society, is good. [PIM]

U254. Wilkes, Charles. **Narrative of the United States exploring expedition during the years 1838, 1839, 1840, 1841, 1842.** 5 v. Philadelphia, 1844. Many later eds. Includes an account of the discovery, in 1840, of the north coast of East Antarctica, whose dimensions were recognized by Wilkes to be continental and which he, therefore, christened "Wilkes Land." [ESB]

U255. Ross, Sir James C. **A voyage of discovery and research in the southern and Antarctic regions during the years 1839–43.** 2 v. London, 1847. Account of the discovery, in 1841, of South Victoria Land, the Ross sea, and the Great Ice barrier. Important, but contains an unwarranted attack on Wilkes. [ESB]

U256. Gerlache de Gomery, Adrien V. J. de. **Voyage de la "Belgica": quinze mois dans l'Antarctique.** Brussels, 1902. 2nd ed., Paris, 1902. Account of the Belgian expedition to West Antarctica in 1898–99 an exploration of the Gerlache strait. [ESB]

U257. Nordenskjöld, Otto G., and Johann G. Anderson. **Antarctica: or two years amongst the ice of the South Pole.** London and N.Y., 1905. Tr. from *Antarktik: zwei Jahre in Schnee und Eis am Sudpol* (2 v., Berlin, 1904). Describes the Swedish exploration in 1901–03 along the east coast of West Antarctica. While in this region, Nordenskjöld invented independently the names West Antarctica and East Antarctica for the two land masses of the south polar continent. [ESB]

U258. Drygalski, Erich von. **Zum Kontinent des eisigen Südens.** Berlin, 1904. Describes the German expedition of 1901–03 which discovered Kaiser Wilhelm Land in East Antarctica. [ESB]

U259. Brown, Robert N. R., Robert C. Mossman, and J. H. Harvey Pirie. **Voyage of the "Scotia": being the record of a voyage of exploration in Antarctic seas by three of the staff.** London, 1906. The Scotch expedition of 1902–04 under William S. Bruce and the discovery of Coats Land on the eastern shore of Weddell sea. [ESB]

U260. Scott, Sir Robert F. **The voyage of the "Discovery."** 2 v. London and N.Y., 1905. Story of the author's voyage of 1901–04 on which he discovered King Richard Land. [ESB]

U261. ——. **Scott's last expedition.** 2 v. London and N.Y., 1913. Scott's voyage of 1910–12, on which he reached the South Pole just after Amundsen did and perished on his return journey within a short distance of his base. [ESB]

U262. Shackleton, Sir Ernest H. **The heart**

of the Antarctic: being the story of the British Antarctic expedition, 1907–1909. 2 v. London, 1909. Popular ed., 1 v., London, 1910. Describes Shackleton's voyage of 1907–09 on which he reached latitude 88° 23' south. [ESB]

U263. Amundsen, Roald E. G. The South Pole: an account of the Norwegian Antarctic expedition in the "Fram," 1910–1912. Tr. by A. G. Chater. 2 v. London and N.Y., 1913. Narrates the voyage on which the author discovered the South Pole, and reveals Amundsen's admirable strategy and tactics. [ESB]

U264. Mawson, Sir Douglas. The home of the blizzard: being the story of the Australasian Antarctic expedition, 1911–1914. 2 v. London and Philadelphia, 1915. Describes Australian explorations of parts of Wilkes Land. Mawson verified the existence of Wilkes' Antarctic continent. [ESB]

U265. Riiser-Larsen, Hjalmar. Mot ukjent land: norvegia-ekspedisjonen. Oslo, 1930. In 1929–30 Riiser-Larsen explored Antarctica for the whaling magnate, Lars Christensen. During his flights and land expeditions he traversed a huge territory between 0° to 45° E., covering Queen Maud Land, now claimed by Norway, and a part of the Australian sector of the continent. [PIM]

U266. Byrd, Richard E. Little America. N.Y. and London, 1930. More square miles have been explored under Byrd's leadership than under any other explorer. Unfortunately, only the records of his first two expeditions have been published, and this is the story of the first. [PIM]

U267. Ronne, Finn. Antarctic conquest. N.Y., 1949. Geographers consider Ronne's modest expedition a model operation. In 1946 and succeeding years he explored much virgin territory on Palmer peninsula, making 86 landings on previously unknown land. Although small, his expedition was an important one. [PIM]

U268. Giaever, John. The white desert: the official account of the Norwegian-British-Swedish Antarctic expedition. Tr. by E. M. Huggard. N.Y., 1954. This expedition, under the leadership of Giaever, moved both by sea and air, surveying at least 100,000 square miles of the continent, while its ship, the "Norsel," conducted a radar survey of the ice for over six degrees of longitude. [PIM, CEN]

U269. Mill, Hugh R. The siege of the South Pole. London, 1905. As good a secondary work as exists covering the period to 1905. [PIM]

U270. Hayes, James G. The conquest of the South Pole. London, 1932. One of the best secondary works on the history of Antarctic exploration. [PIM]

U271. Sullivan, Walter. Quest for a continent. N.Y., 1957. The author is a *New York Times* reporter who had accompanied all the recent United States government expeditions to Antarctica. The work is a selective history of Antarctic exploration from the 1820's to the geophysical year. [PIM]

HISTORIOGRAPHY

U272. Wright, John K. "Some broader aspects of the history of exploration: a review." Geographical journal, 25 (Apr. 1935): 317–20. Review and evaluation of the major histories of exploration that were current in 1935.

U273. Olschki, Leonardo. Storia letteraria delle scoperte geografiche: studi e ricerche. Florence, 1937. A unique work. Olschki, a scholar long known for his ability to derive new meaning from familiar evidence, examines the minds of those who wrote of the great discoveries or reacted to them. He finds that in many cases they interpreted events in terms of their own educations and backgrounds, and saw both American and Asiatic lands in terms of myths and legends that had long been familiar to them.

BIOGRAPHIES

U274. Ravenstein, Ernest G. Martin Behaim, his life and his globe. London, 1908. This biography, by the famous German-born English geographer, contains everything known of Behaim's career. Includes an exhaustive list of the legends appearing on the Behaim globe of 1492, and pays careful attention to the globe itself. While acknowledging the importance and interest of Behaim's work, the author believes it had no bearing on the discovery of America.

U275. Costa Brochado, José I. F. da. Infante d. Henrique. Lisbon, 1942. The best-documented recent work on the life of Prince Henry the Navigator.

U276. Vignaud, Henry. Études critiques sur la vie de Colomb avant ses découvertes. Paris, 1905. Due to their overemphasis on disproving the authenticity of the Toscanelli-Columbus correspondence, other works by Vignaud on Columbus are no longer considered reliable by many critics. However, this book does not enter the field of this controversy, but merely seeks to establish details of the discoverer's life until his marriage to Beatriz Monis de Perestrelo.

U277. Morison, Samuel E. Admiral of the ocean sea: a life of Christopher Columbus. 2 v. Boston, 1942. Also 1 v. ed., 1942. The 1 v. edition differs from its predecessor only in absence of footnotes, appendix, navigational data, and a few miscellaneous pages. Intending this to be a mariner's biography concerned with problems of navigation, Morison has small interest in bibliography or the early career of Columbus. This elegantly-written work, therefore, deserves to be judged from the seafaring point of view, and in this respect has no equals. For problems concerning sources see *U88*.

U278. Álvarez Pedroso, Armando. **Cristóbal Colón: biografía del descubridor.** Havana, 1944. Quite different in aim and scope from Morison's work, this not only brings together the facts of the discoverer's life, but attempts a psychological interpretation of Columbus. Based on the latest findings and contains an elaborate bibliography.

U279. Parr, Charles M. **So noble a captain: the life and times of Ferdinand Magellan.** N.Y., 1953. Has been criticized as a merely "popular" biography, but the criticism is largely undeserved. Parr studied the subject carefully for many years, both in Spain and in Portugal, and made use of Spanish archival material and all relevant bibliography. Furnishes an economic interpretation of Magellan's voyage based on the rivalry of great European banking and commercial houses.

U280. Martineau, Alfred A. **Dupleix et l'Inde française.** 2 v. Paris, 1920–23. Most comprehensive work on Dupleix. The author, a former director of the French Ministry of the Colonies, used much hitherto unpublished documentary material.

U281. Davies, Alfred Mervyn. **Clive of Plassey.** N.Y., 1939. Not a perfect biography, but has many strong points and is the best now available on Clive.

U282. ———. **Strange destiny: a biography of Warren Hastings.** N.Y., 1935. A good biography with some faults. The author lauds Hastings more than known facts appear to justify, and is extremely severe with his enemies, Edmund Burke and Philip Francis.

U283. Tournier, Jules. **Le cardinal Lavigerie et son action politique (1863–1892): d'après des documents nouveaux et inédits.** Paris, 1913.

U284. Goyau, Georges. **Un grand missionnaire: le cardinal Lavigerie.** Paris, 1925. The work of Cardinal Charles M. A. Lavigerie is not well known. He was the leading spirit of Roman Catholic missionary work in French Africa during the 19th century, and founded the "White Fathers," who worked with considerable success to spread the faith. This and *U283* amount to biographies, covering especially his most active years.

U285. Johnston, Sir Harry H. **The story of my life.** London, 1923. 2nd ed., Indianapolis, 1923. During the partition of Africa, Johnston was one of the busiest of English diplomats and Africa agents, and was largely responsible for the British acquisition of Nyasaland at the expense of Portugal in 1890. As he was also a literary man of considerable ability, his memoirs are of interest, especially those parts dealing with Africa.

U286. Lichtervelde, Louis de. **Léopold of the Belgians.** Tr. by Thomas H. Reed and H. Russell Reed. N.Y. and London, 1929. Excellent study of the Belgian monarch whose principal historical fame consists in having created the Congo Free State, later the Belgian Congo. Some may think that this biography, which is highly laudatory, is more favorable to the king than the facts warrant.

U287. Delavignette, Robert L., and Charles A. Julien, eds. **Les constructeurs de France d'outre-mer.** Paris, 1946. Short lives of Champlain, Richelieu, Colbert, Dupleix, Bugeaud, Faidherbe, Ferry, Brazza, Pavie, Gallieni, Van Vollenhoven, and Lyautey, with an anthology of their letters, reports, and dispatches. [GER]

U288. Martineau, Alfred A. **Bussy et l'Inde française, 1720–1785.** Paris, 1935.

U289. Power, Thomas F., Jr. **Jules Ferry and the renaissance of French imperialism.** N.Y., 1944. Deals not only with the political and diplomatic aspects of Ferry's colonialism in France, but has separate chapters on developments in Africa, Egypt, Indo-China, etc. Well documented with excellent bibliography and good notes. [GER]

U290. Halperin, Vladimir. **Lord Milner and the empire: the evolution of British imperialism.** London, 1952. Includes the life of this important figure, as well as a lengthy discussion of "Lord Milner and his school." Based on extensive use of primary sources as well as secondary literature. [GER]

U291. Seaver, George. **David Livingstone, his life and letters.** N.Y., 1957. The most detailed biography of Livingstone that has appeared. Although containing factual errors, it draws upon manuscript sources previously neglected and quotes much of Livingstone's own writing.

GOVERNMENT PUBLICATIONS

United States

U292. U. S. Department of Commerce. **Monthly consular and trade reports.** Washington, 1880–1910. (Title varies.)

U293. ———. **Daily consular and trade reports.** Washington, 1901–14.

U294. ———. **Commerce reports.** Washington, 1910–40. (Weekly.)

U295. ———. **Foreign commerce weekly.** Washington, 1940 ff.

U296. ———. **Special consular reports.** Washington, 1890–1923.

U297. ———. **Trade promotion series.** Washington, 1924–41. (Monthly.)

British

U298. Great Britain. Foreign Office. **Diplomatic and consular reports: annual series.** London, 1886–1916.

U299. ——. **Diplomatic and consular reports: miscellaneous series.** 22 v. London, 1886–1910.

U300. Great Britain. Colonial Office. **Colonial reports.** London, 1891–1940. (Annual.)

U301. ——. **The Dominions Office and Colonial Office list.** London, 1862–1945. (Annual. Title varies.)

U302. ——. **The Colonial Office list.** London, 1945 ff. (Annual.)

U303. **Colonial government publications.** The publications obtainable from the Crown Agents for Overseas Governments and Administration cover a wide range of subjects, such as government, trade, penal institutions, education, land holding, and the like for particular colonies. Her Majesty's Stationery Office prints a variety of publications dealing with colonial affairs. These are largely reports received from particular colonies, and the texts of orders in council relating to various colonies. It prints the official reports of the Colonial Office and the government gazetteers for each colony, which include a wide selection of colonial information.

U304. Great Britain. Colonial Office. **Monthly list of official colonial publications.** London, 1948 ff. Invaluable guide to published material on the British colonies.

French

U305. France. Ministère de la Marine. **Annuaire de la marine.** Paris, 1852–89.

U306. France. Ministère des Colonies. **Annuaire du Ministère des Colonies.** Paris, 1899–1942.

U307. **L'année coloniale.** Ed. by Charles Mourey and Louis Brunel. Paris, 1899–1905.

U308. **Annuaire colonial, annuaire agricole, commercial, et industriel des colonies françaises.** Paris, 1888 ff.

U309. France. Armée. **Les armées françaises d'outre-mer.** 22 v. Paris, 1931–32. A magnificent work outlining the military history of the French colonies, service history of colonial troops, and the work of colonial leaders and heroes.

U310. France. Ministère de la France d'Outre-mer. **Chroniques d'outre-mer: études et informations.** Paris, 1951 ff. (Monthly.)

Dutch

U311. Netherlands. **Jaarcijfers voor Nederlanden: kolonien.** The Hague, 1882–1921.

U312. Dutch East Indies. Central Kantoor voor de Statistieck. **Staatistisch jaaroverzicht van Nederlandsch-Indië.** Batavia, 1922–41.

U313. **Regeerings-almanack voor Nederlandsch-Indië.** Batavia, 1832–1942. (Annual.)

U314. Netherlands. Departement van Overzeese Rijksdelen. **Kolonial verslag.** The Hague, 1850 ff. (Annual. Title varies.)

U315. ——. **Indisch verlag.** The Hague, 1931–38. (Annual.)

U316. ——. **Verslag Nederlandse Antillen.** The Hague, 1932 ff. (Annual. Title varies.)

U317. ——. **Surinaams verslag.** The Hague, 1932 ff. (Annual. Title varies.)

German

U318. **Koloniales Jahrbuch: Beiträge und Mitteilungen aus dem Gebiete der Kolonialwissenschaft und Kolonialpraxis.** 11 v. Berlin, 1888–98.

U319. **Beiträge zur Kolonialpolitik und Kolonialwirtschaft.** 5 v. Berlin, 1899–1903.

U320. **Zeitschrift für Kolonialpolitik.** 9 v. Berlin, 1904–12.

U321. **Koloniale Monatsblätter.** 2 v. Berlin, 1913–14.

U322. **Deutscher Kolonial-Kalender und statistisches Handbuch.** 16 v. Berlin, 1898–1914.

Portuguese

U323. Portugal. Agência Geral das Colónias. **Boletim.** Lisbon, 1925 ff. (Monthly. Title varies.)

U324. **Anuário do império colonial português.** Lisbon, 1935 ff.

SOCIETY PUBLICATIONS

U325. **Works issued by the Hakluyt Society.** 1st ser., 100 v., London, 1847–98; 2nd ser., London, 1898 ff.; extra ser., 34 v., 1955. The Hakluyt Society was formed in 1846 to print "rare or unpublished voyages and travels." The works are not confined to Englishmen, and frequently descriptions of some region are included by several travelers in one volume. Among voyagers represented are Columbus, da Gama, Hawkins, Drake, Raleigh, Hudson, Cadamosto, Tomé Pires, and Ibn Battuta. The extra series includes Hakluyt, *Voyages;* Purchas, *Pilgrimes;* and Captain Cook's *Journals.* The works are well edited and well printed, and, with a few exceptions, the texts are reliable.

U326. **Werken uitgegeven door de Linschoten-vereeniging.** The Hague, 1909 ff. Issued by the Linschoten-vereeniging, founded to publish the works of Dutch voyagers. V. 60 appeared in 1957. The Linschoten Society restricts its publications to Dutch travelers, thus differing from the Hakluyt Society, but provides otherwise unavailable material. This set, which follows modern canons of editing, includes voyages of the major Dutch navigators and some of the minor ones. [AHB, CEN]

U327. **Meddelelser om Grønland.** Copenhagen, 1879 ff. Published by the Kommissionen for Ledelsen af de Geologiske og Geographiske Undersøgelser i Grønland. Includes not only accounts of explorations in Greenland since the founding of the society, but also a wealth of other materials on the Arctic regions. Recent volumes tend to be scientific in character and hence unrelated to history. Customarily published in Danish with a summary in French, but occasional volumes are in English. V. 1–161 published to 1957. [GMD, CEN]

U328. Annales de l'Extrême Orient et de l'Afrique. 15 v. Paris, 1878–91. [Société Académique Indo-Chinoise.]

U329. Imperial studies. Ed. by A. P. Newton. 21 v. London, 1927–54. [Royal Empire Society.]

PERIODICALS

British

U330. Board of Trade journal. London, 1886 ff. (Monthly.)

U331. Bulletin of the Imperial Institute. London, 1903–48. (Quarterly.)

U332. Colonial plant and animal products. London, 1950 ff. (Quarterly.) This and *U333* are sources for current information on trade, resources, and administration of the British colonies.

U333. Colonial geology and mineral resources. London, 1950 ff. (Quarterly.)

U334. Proceedings of the Royal Colonial Institute. London, 1869–1909. [Royal Empire Society.] (Annual.) Many valuable papers on British colonial interests.

U335. United empire: the Royal Colonial Institute journal. New ser., London, 1910 ff. [Royal Empire Society.] (Monthly.)

U336. Journal of the parliaments of the empire. London, 1920 ff. (Quarterly.) Reviews current legislation of the United Kingdom and the self-governing dominions. Includes parliamentary discussions of problems and policies, and reports of the conference of the prime ministers of the empire in 1921.

U337. The round table: a quarterly review of the politics of the British commonwealth. London, 1910–18. (Title varies.)

U338. Corona: the journal of Her Majesty's oversea service. London, 1949 ff. (Monthly. Title varies.)

U339. Digest of colonial statistics. London, 1952 ff. [Colonial Office.] (Bimonthly.)

U340. Oversea education: a journal of educational experiment and research in tropical and subtropical areas. London, 1929. (Quarterly.)

French

U341. Questions diplomatiques et coloniales: revue de politique extérieure. Paris, 1897–1914. (Semimonthly.)

U342. La revue maritime: études historiques et scientifiques maritimes et militaires, questions économiques et sociales. Paris, 1861 ff. [Ministère de la Marine et des Colonies.] (Monthly. Title varies.)

U343. La quinzaine coloniale. Paris, 1897–1914. (Semimonthly.) Succeeded in turn by *Bulletin de l'union,* 1923–27; *La quinzaine coloniale,* 1928–37; *Revue française d'outre-mer,* 1938–44.

U344. Le monde français. Paris, 1945 ff. (Monthly.) Successor to the above.

U345. Revue de l'histoire des colonies françaises. Paris, 1913 ff. (Quarterly. Title varies.)

U346. La France d'outre-mer: études et informations. Paris, 1944 ff. [Ministère de la France d'Outre-mer.] (Irregular.)

U347. Bulletin hebdomaire d'information. Paris, 1944–46. [Ministère de la France d'Outre-mer.] (Bimonthly. Title varies.)

U348. Bulletin mensuel de statistique d'outre-mer. Paris, 1943 ff. [Ministère de la France d'Outre-mer.]

German

U349. Deutsches Kolonialblatt: Amtsblatt des Reichskolonialamt. Berlin, 1890–1919. [Kolonialamt.] (Semimonthly. Title varies.)

U350. Deutsche Kolonialzeitung. Berlin, 1884–1922. (Irregular.)

Dutch

U351. News from Indonesia. N.Y., 1948–49. (Irregular.)

U352. Netherlands news. N.Y., 1941–46. (Semimonthly.)

U353. Netherlands newsletter. N.Y., 1946–49. (Irregular.)

U354. Netherlands news digest. N.Y., 1942–45. (Semimonthly.)

U355. Netherlands news digest. London, 1941–45. (Weekly.)

Polar Regions

U356. The polar times. N.Y., 1935 ff. (Semiannual.)

U357. Little America times. N.Y., 1933–35. (Monthly.)

U358. The polar record. Cambridge, Eng., 1931 ff. (Semiannual.)

U359. Polar Forschung. Leipzig, 1931 ff. (Semiannual.)

SECTION V

Western and Central Europe

The great volume of good historical literature pertaining to western and central Europe and the ways in which it is used have caused the division of this section into six subsections. Each is large enough to warrant its own symbol and a separate numerical sequence for its listing. They are as follows:

VA—The United Kingdom and the Republic of Ireland
VB—Scandinavia and the Baltic States
VC—France and the Low Countries
VD—Spain and Portugal
VE—Italy
VF—Germany, Austria, and Switzerland

The United Kingdom and the Republic of Ireland

SIDNEY A. BURRELL *

A generation ago, in his introduction to this section of the original *Guide,* the late Professor Arthur Lyon Cross called attention to the fact that Great Britain was a country whose historical sources had been better preserved and more extensively published than those of any other European nation. To a large extent the statement holds true, despite the vicissitudes of the Second World War and the diminution of economic resources. The vigor and quality of English historical research and writing remain as high as they have been in the past, though, like many of his foreign colleagues, the British historical scholar—as the selected titles in the present section clearly indicate—has both diversified and deepened the scope of his interests. When Professor Cross compiled his list, the historian,

* Professor Burrell wishes to acknowledge, without imputing responsibility for errors or omissions, the help and advice received from Professors Rosalie Colie, John Stewart, Dean M. Schmitter, and Robert K. Webb. Several items on art and the comments indicated by initials JSC were contributed by Judith S. Cousins.

with some notable exceptions, was still primarily a narrator of events to whom the analytical methods and devices of other disciplines were largely unknown. The last quarter century has seen a very great change in this state of affairs; and while the historian has not succumbed entirely to the methodological lures of other fields of knowledge, he has been influenced by them, consciously or unconsciously, to an extent that would have seemed surprising in 1931.

The result of this transformation of outlook is plainly seen in the present compilation. In it are many titles that might scarcely have seemed germane to the study of history when the previous *Guide* appeared. Now it is at least tacitly agreed that they are acceptable, if not to all, certainly to a great many practicing historians. This new breadth of interest does, however, call for a special word of warning, particularly to the student who may be making use of this section as an introduction to British history. Even as historical scholarship is continually expanding and undergoing revision, so too are related fields of study. For that reason the student must remember that this, like every other subject bibliography, can only be a partial guide. If he would stay abreast of current publication, he must not overlook the historical and other learned journals, almost all of which contain book review sections and some of which have lists of current articles appearing elsewhere. Moreover, he will find that the literary supplements of certain newspapers like *The times* of London and *The New York times,* while very general in their coverage, nonetheless notice a number of the most important scholarly works in British history. Finally, it should also be noted that this section of the *Guide* deals only with works covering the history of the British Isles since 1485. For materials on earlier and very recent times, on relations with specific countries, and on British overseas expansion and the Commonwealth, consult the sections pertaining to these periods and areas.

BIBLIOGRAPHIES, LIBRARIES, AND MUSEUMS

Bibliographies

VA1. Gross, Charles. **The sources and literature of English history from the earliest times to about 1485.** See *K4.*

VA2. Read, Conyers. **Bibliography of British history: Tudor period, 1485–1603.** 2nd ed. Oxford, 1959.

VA3. Davies, Godfrey. **Bibliography of British history: Stuart period, 1603–1714.** Oxford, 1928. New edition in preparation. Still useful. Needs to be supplemented by Frewer (*VA9*), Lancaster (*VA10*), and Milne (*VA11*).

VA4. Grose, Clyde L. **A select bibliography of British history, 1660–1760.** Chicago, 1939.

VA5. Pargellis, Stanley, and D. J. Medley. **Bibliography of British history: the eighteenth century, 1714–1789.** Oxford, 1951. A continuation of *VA1–3,* somewhat more detailed than the preceding.

VA6. Williams, Judith B. **A guide to the printed materials for English social and economic history, 1750–1850.** 2 v. N.Y., 1926.

Though out of date, it is still the main bibliographical guide for the early 19th century.

VA7. Pollard, Alfred W., and Gilbert R. Redgrave. **A short-title catalogue of books printed in England, Scotland, and Ireland, and of English books printed abroad, 1475–1640.** See *B29.*

VA8. Wing, Donald G. **Short-title catalogue of books printed in England, Scotland, Ireland, Wales, and British America, and of English books printed in other countries, 1641–1700.** 3 v. N.Y., 1945–51. Continuation of *VA7.*

VA9. Frewer, Louis B. **Bibliography of historical writings published in Great Britain and the empire, 1940–1945.** See *B57.*

VA10. Lancaster, Joan C. **Bibliography of historical works issued in the United Kingdom, 1946–1956.** London, 1957. Chronological listing of materials without annotation.

VA11. Milne, A. Taylor. **Writings on British history.** London, 1934 ff. [Royal Historical Society.] Annual guide to historical writing.

VA12. Historical Association. London.

Annual bulletin of historical literature. London, 1911 ff.

Libraries and Museums

VA13. The ASLIB directory: a guide to sources of specialized information in Great Britain and Ireland. Ed. by George F. Barwick. London, 1928.

VA14. Newcombe, Luxmoore. **The university and college libraries of Great Britain and Ireland.** London, 1927.

VA15. Downs, Robert B. **American library resources: a bibliographical guide.** See *U11*.

VA16. Great Britain. Museums and Galleries. **Museums and galleries in Great Britain and Northern Ireland.** London, 1956.

VA17. Great Britain. Treasury Office. **Guide to government libraries.** London, 1952.

VA18. British Museum. **Catalogue of printed books.** London, 1881 ff. See *B8*.

VA19. ——. **The catalogues of the British Museum. V. 1, Printed books.** Comp. by Frank C. Francis. London, 1952.

VA20. ——. **The catalogues of the British Museum. V. 2, The catalogue of the manuscript collections of the British Museum.** Comp. by T. C. Skeat. London, 1951.

VA21. U. S. Library of Congress. **The national union catalog.** Washington, 1956 ff. See *B6*.

ENCYCLOPEDIAS AND WORKS OF REFERENCE

VA22. Cheney, C. R. **Handbook of dates for students of English history.** London, 1955. [Royal Historical Society. Guides and handbooks, 4.]

VA23. Stephen, Sir Leslie, and Sidney Lee, eds. **Dictionary of national biography.** 63 v. London, 1885–1901. Decennial supplements published regularly. Still the most valuable source of biographical material in the English language.

VA24. Cokayne, George E. **The complete baronetage.** 5 v. Exeter, 1900–06. This and *VA25* are valuable guides to the genealogy and biography of English landed and titled families.

VA25. ——. **The complete peerage.** Ed. by Vicary Gibbs, H. Arthur Doubleday, and others. 13 v. London, 1910–53.

VA26. The annual register of world events. See *B146*. This and *VA27–28* are the most convenient guides to the chronology of English political history.

VA27. The statesman's year-book. See *B133*.

VA28. Whitaker's almanack. London, 1868 ff. (Annual.) See *B144*.

VA29. Who's who: an annual biographical dictionary. London, 1849 ff. Best for contemporary biography.

GEOGRAPHIES, GAZETTEERS, AND ATLASES

VA30. Darby, Henry C., ed. **An historical geography of England before A.D. 1800.** Cambridge, Eng., 1936. Contains valuable articles by various persons on English geography at different historical periods.

VA31. Ogilvie, Alan G., ed. **Great Britain: essays in regional geography.** Cambridge, Eng., 1930. Useful survey of the various geographical regions of Great Britain.

VA32. Stamp, Laurence D. **The land of Britain and how it is used.** London, 1946. Important work on the subject of land utilization.

VA33. Great Britain. Ordnance Survey. **Gazetteer of Great Britain, giving the position of towns and important villages shown on Ordnance Survey maps in terms of the national grid.** Reprinted with corrections, Chessington, 1951.

VA34. Mackinder, Sir Halford J. **Britain and the British seas.** 2nd ed., London, 1914. A famous and still valuable work on the world geographical position of Great Britain.

VA35. Chubb, Thomas. **The printed maps in the atlases of Great Britain and Ireland: a bibliography, 1579–1870.** London, 1927. Useful reference for the historian seeking geographical information on a particular period.

VA36. Bartholomew, John G. **The British Isles pocket atlas.** Edinburgh, various eds.

VA37. Gardiner, Samuel R. **School atlas of English history.** London, 1892. Rev. ed., 1936. Still the most useful brief historical atlas.

ANTHROPOLOGICAL WORKS

VA38. Bradley, Robert N. **Racial origins of English character.** London, 1926.

VA39. Fleure, Herbert J. **A natural history of man in Britain: conceived as a study of changing relations between men and environments.** London, 1951.

VA40. ——. **The races of England and Wales.** London, 1923.

DEMOGRAPHIC STUDIES

VA41. Abrams, Mark A. **The population of Great Britain.** London, 1945. Useful brief survey.

VA42. Griffith, Grosvenor T. **Population problems of the age of Malthus.** Cambridge, Eng., 1926. Though somewhat specialized, contains a survey of population problems and opinions on population which are very helpful to the historian.

VA43. Great Britain. Royal Commission on Population. **Command report No. 7695.** London, 1949. Important. Most recent survey of current trends in British population.

VA44. Carrier, Norman H., and J. R. Jeffery. **External migration: a study of the available statistics, 1815–1950.** London, 1953.

VA45. Great Britain. Interdepartmental Committee on Social and Economic Research. **Census reports of Great Britain, 1801–1931.** London, 1951. [Guides to official sources, 2.]

VA46. Great Britain. Central Statistical Office. **Statistical abstract of the United Kingdom.** London, 1854 ff. (Annual.) Contains useful abstracted statistical information on a wide range of topics.

For estimates of population at various periods see also the articles in Darby (*VA30*).

LINGUISTIC WORKS

VA47. Baugh, Albert C. **History of the English language.** N.Y. and London, 1935. External history of the language, covering the racial, environmental, and historical influences that created the English tongue.

VA48. Marckwardt, Albert H. **Introduction to the English language.** N.Y., 1942. Probably the best brief, internal history of the language, covering development of work forms, grammar, etc. Less concerned with historical or environmental influences.

VA49. Jespersen, Otto. **Growth and structure of the English language.** 9th rev. ed., Oxford, 1948. A famous, scholarly work which is still highly readable and sound, though some of Jespersen's judgments need modification.

VA50. Wyld, Henry C. **A history of modern colloquial English.** 3rd ed., Oxford, 1936. Important technical work by a specialist in the field.

VA51. Partridge, Eric, and John W. Clark. **British and American English since 1900.** London, 1951. The only useful survey of recent English language development.

VA52. Murray, James A. H., Henry Bradley, Wm. A. Craigie, and C. T. Onions, eds. **Oxford English dictionary.** Corrected reissue, 12 v. and 4 sup., Oxford, 1933. The standard reference dictionary of the English tongue; uses historical principles.

PRINTED COLLECTIONS OF SOURCES

Shorter Standard Collections

The following are intended as suggestions for teaching aids or for the student who wishes some general knowledge of the sources in a particular period or area.

VA53. Barker, William A., and others, eds. **A general history of England: documents.** 2 v. London, 1952–53. [V. 1, 1688–1832; v. 2, 1832–1950.] Useful general collection of documents for teaching purposes.

VA54. Douglas, David C., ed. **English historical documents.** Oxford, 1953 ff. (In progress.) This collection is projected in 12 v. to cover the whole sweep of medieval and modern English history. Volumes published to date indicate that the selections are well chosen and carefully edited. Valuable.

VA55. Stephenson, Carl, and George F. Marcham. **Sources of English constitutional history.** N.Y., 1937. Useful collection covering the whole period of English history down to the date of its publication.

VA56. Costin, William C., and J. Stevens Watson, eds. **The law and working of the constitution, 1660–1914.** 2 v. London, 1952.

VA57. Tanner, Joseph R., ed. **Tudor constitutional documents, 1485–1603.** Cambridge, Eng., 1922. Carefully selected and well edited with a valuable introduction.

VA58. Prothero, Sir George W., ed. **Select statutes and other constitutional documents illustrative of the reigns of Elizabeth and James I.** 4th ed., Oxford, 1913.

VA59. Gardiner, Samuel R. **Constitutional documents of the Puritan revolution, 1625–1660.** 3rd ed., reprint, Oxford, 1951.

VA60. LeMay, Godfrey H. L., ed. **British government, 1914–53: select documents.** London, 1955. Useful selection of government documents for the 20th century.

VA61. Keir, Sir David, and Frederick H. Lawson. **Cases in constitutional law.** 4th ed., Oxford, 1954. Useful casebook for constitutional law.

VA62. Bland, Alfred E., Philip A. Brown, and Richard H. Tawney, eds. **English economic history: select documents.** London, 1914. Reprint, 1937. Only general work containing a wide selection of economic sources.

VA63. Tawney, Richard H., and Eileen Power, eds. **Tudor economic documents.** New ed., 3 v., London, 1951. Valuable.

VA64. Dunham, William H., and Stanley M. Pargellis. **Complaint and reform in England, 1436–1714.** N.Y., 1938. Valuable collection of documents and sources in social and political history.

VA65. Gee, Henry, and William J. Hardy, eds. **Documents illustrative of English church history.** London, 1896. Though long out of print, this is still the only useful general collection of documents and sources for English church history in the period covered (314–1701).

Older General Collections

The following older collections of sources, which cover the Tudor and Stuart periods, are still valuable, though some of their materials have either been reproduced or supplemented in later private or official (government) publications.

VA66. Strype, John, ed. **Annals of the Reformation.** 2nd ed., 4 v., London, 1725–

31. Reprint, Oxford, 1824. Still an indispensable body of printed sources for the period of the English Reformation.

VA67. Park, Thomas, ed. **The Harleian miscellany.** 10 v. London, 1808–13. Contains much valuable material for the 17th century.

VA68. Scott, Sir Walter, ed. **Somers tracts.** 13 v. London, 1809–15. Rich collection of printed sources for the 16th through early 18th centuries.

VA69. Yorke, Philip, Earl of Hardwicke, ed. **Hardwicke's state papers.** 2 v. London, 1778. Reproduces a number of sources not printed elsewhere.

HISTORIOGRAPHY

VA70. Ausubel, Herman, J. Bartlet Brebner, and Erling Hunt, eds. **Some modern historians of Britain.** N.Y., 1951. Contains a number of articles dealing with various English historians of the 19th and 20th centuries.

VA71. Butterfield, Herbert. **The Englishman and his history.** Cambridge, Eng., 1944. This and *VA72–73* constitute the best general survey of modern English historical thought and scholarship.

VA72. ——. "Tendencies in historical study in England." **Irish historical studies,** 4 (1945): 209–23.

VA73. ——. **Man and his past: the study of the history of historical scholarship.** See *A350*.

VA74. Peardon, Thomas P. **The transition in English historical writing, 1760–1830.** N.Y., 1933. Significant study of changing trends in English historical thought during the 18th and 19th centuries.

VA75. Powicke, Sir Frederick M. **Modern historians and the study of history.** London, 1955. Though the title indicates the general nature of the work, most of the historical scholarship examined is English. Valuable.

SHORTER GENERAL HISTORIES

VA76. Trevelyan, George M. **History of England.** 3rd ed., N.Y., 1952. Though somewhat allusive, this is still probably the best one volume history of England in print.

VA77. Feiling, Keith G. **A history of England, from the coming of the English to 1938.** N.Y., 1951.

VA78. Maurois, André. **A history of England.** Tr. by H. Miles. New ed., London, 1952. Semi-popular, well written work by a foreign observer of the English scene.

VA79. Woodward, Ernest L. **History of England.** London, 1947. Extremely brief, useful survey for the novice in English history.

LONGER GENERAL HISTORIES

VA80. Clark, George N., ed. **The Oxford history of England.** Oxford, 1934 ff. [To be completed in 14 volumes. The following, covering the period since 1485, have been published: 7, John D. Mackie, *The earlier Tudors, 1485–1558* (1952); 8, John B. Black, *The reign of Elizabeth, 1558–1603* (1936); 9, Godfrey Davies, *The early Stuarts, 1603–1660* (1937); 10, George N. Clark, *The later Stuarts, 1660–1714* (2nd ed., 1955); 11, Basil Williams, *The Whig supremacy, 1714–1760* (1939); 13, Ernest L. Woodward, *The age of reform, 1815–1870* (1938); 14, Robert C. K. Ensor, *England, 1870–1914* (1936).] (Annotated bibliographies.)

VA81. Oman, Charles W. C., ed. **A history of England.** 8 v. London, 1905–55. [Volumes covering the period since 1485 are as follows: 4, Geoffrey R. Elton, *England under the Tudors* (1955); 5, George M. Trevelyan, *England under the Stuarts* (25th ed., 1949); 6, Charles G. Robertson, *England under the Hanoverians* (14th ed., 1948); 7, John A. R. Marriott, *England since Waterloo* (15th ed., 1954).]

VA82. Medlicott, W. N., ed. **A history of England.** London, 1953 ff. [To be completed in 10 volumes.] The following, for the period since 1485, have been published: 5, James A. Williamson, *The Tudor Age* (1953); 8, Asa Briggs, *The age of improvement* (1959).

VA83. **Pelican history of England.** 8 v. Harmondsworth, 1950–55. [Volumes covering the period since 1485 are as follows: 5, S. T. Bindoff, *Tudor England;* 6, Maurice P. Ashley, *England in the seventeenth century;* 7, John H. Plumb, *England in the eighteenth century;* 8, David Thomson, *England in the nineteenth century.*] A brief, inexpensive, but extremely useful series which may be highly recommended to the novice in English history who wishes to expand his knowledge beyond the textbook level.

HISTORIES OF SPECIAL PERIODS
Tudor England, 1485–1603

VA84. Feiling, Keith G. **England under the Tudors and Stuarts.** London, 1935. Excellent survey for the student who wishes some knowledge within brief compass of the whole period, 1485–1714.

VA85. Froude, James A. **A history of England from the fall of Wolsey to the defeat of the Spanish Armada.** Rev. ed., 12 v., London, 1912. A famous work whose interpretation is somewhat out of date. Still a useful, detailed survey of English history in the 16th century.

VA86. Nobbs, Douglas. **England and Scotland, 1560–1707.** London, 1952. Brief but valuable survey of Anglo-Scottish relations during the 16th and 17th centuries.

VA87. Read, Conyers. **The Tudors.** N.Y., 1936. Reprint, 1953.

VA88. Pollard, Albert F. **The reign of Henry VII from contemporary sources.** London, 1914.

VA89. ——. **Henry VIII.** New ed., London, 1951. Best scholarly biography.

VA90. ——. **Wolsey.** 2nd ed., London, 1953.

VA91. ——. **England under the protector Somerset.** London, 1900.

VA92. ——. **History of England from the accession of Edward VI to the death of Elizabeth.** London, 1910. Has been replaced, but not entirely superseded, by later works on the period. Valuable survey.

VA93. Prescott, Hilda F. M. **Mary Tudor.** 2nd ed., London, 1952. Thoughtful, perceptive, sympathetic biography of a queen whose historical reputation has been re-evaluated in recent years.

VA94. Read, Conyers. **Mr. Secretary Walsingham and the policy of Queen Elizabeth.** 3 v. Oxford, 1925. This and *VA95* constitute two valuable studies of leading Elizabethan statesmen whose careers involved them deeply in the politics of the age.

VA95. ——. **Mr. Secretary Cecil and Queen Elizabeth.** London, 1955.

VA96. Neale, Sir John E. **Queen Elizabeth I.** 2nd ed., London, 1952. The best biography.

VA97. Rowse, Alfred L. **The Elizabethan age.** 2 v. London, 1950–55. Originally published as *The England of Elizabeth* and *The expansion of Elizabethan England.* Both studies cover a wide range of topics, social, intellectual, and political.

VA98. Cheyney, Edward P. **History of England from the defeat of the Spanish Armada to the death of Elizabeth.** 2 v. N.Y., 1914–26. A continuation by a famous authority of Froude's work (*VA85*).

See also *VA80* (7, 8), *VA81* (4), *VA82,* and *VA83* (5).

Stuart England

VA99. Ranke, Leopold von. **A history of England principally in the seventeenth century.** 6 v. Oxford, 1875. Tr. of Ranke's *Englische Geschichte, vornehmlich im sechzehnten und siebzehnten Jahrhundert* (7 v., Berlin, 1859–68). A famous work by one of the great scholars of the 19th century. Though superseded to some extent by later works, it has the great value of being free from many 20th century preconceptions, and should not be neglected by any student of the Stuart period.

VA100. Tanner, Joseph R. **English constitutional conflicts of the seventeenth century, 1603–1689.** Cambridge, Eng., 1928.

Reprint, 1948. Excellent, detailed survey of constitutional issues that divided king and parliament during this period.

VA101. Notestein, Wallace. **The English people on the eve of colonization, 1603–1630.** N.Y., 1954. Excellent survey of English institutions and social life at the opening of the 17th century.

VA102. Gardiner, Samuel R. **History of England from the accession of James I to the outbreak of the Civil War, 1603–1642.** 10 v. London, 1884–86. This work and *VA103–104* still constitute the most complete history of early 17th century England.

VA103. ——. **History of the great Civil War, 1642–1649.** Rev. ed., 4 v., London, 1893.

VA104. ——. **History of the commonwealth and protectorate.** New ed., 4 v., London, 1903. Incomplete at the time of Gardiner's death. Firth (*VA114*), which has to some extent been superseded by Davies (*VA113*), was written as a sequel.

VA105. Willson, David H. **King James VI and I.** London, 1956. Definitive biography.

VA106. Wingfield-Stratford, Esmé C. **Charles, King of England, 1600–1637.** London, 1949. This together with *VA107–108* constitute the only complete modern biography of Charles I.

VA107. ——. **King Charles and King Pym, 1637–1643.** London, 1949.

VA108. ——. **King Charles the martyr, 1643–1649.** London, 1950.

VA109. Wedgwood, Cicely V. **The king's peace, 1637–1641.** London, 1955. First volume of a lengthy study of the English civil wars.

VA110. Firth, Sir Charles H. **Oliver Cromwell and the rule of the Puritans in England.** Oxford, 1953. [Oxford world's classics.] Best scholarly biography.

VA111. Hexter, Jack H. **The reign of King Pym.** Cambridge, Mass., 1941. Thoughtful study of party organization in the Long Parliament with Pym as the central figure.

VA112. Wormald, B. H. G. **Clarendon: politics, history, and religion, 1640–1660.** Cambridge, Eng., 1951. Political and religious movements of the period as they involve the central figure of this study.

VA113. Davies, Godfrey. **The restoration of Charles II, 1658–1660.** San Marino, Calif., 1955. A careful and valuable study of the reasons for the restoration of monarchy in England.

VA114. Firth, Sir Charles H. **The last years of the protectorate.** 2 v. London, 1909.

VA115. Bryant, Sir Arthur. **King Charles II.** 2nd ed., London, 1955. The most useful general biography.

VA116. Ogg, David. **England in the reign of Charles II.** 2 v. Oxford, 1934. Best general survey of the restoration period.

VA117. ———. **England in the reigns of James II and William III.** Oxford, 1955. Valuable. A continuation of the author's earlier study of England in the reign of Charles II (*VA116*).

VA118. Turner, Francis C. **James II.** London and N.Y., 1948. The most recent and useful modern biography.

VA119. Trevelyan, George M. **The English revolutions, 1688–1689.** 2nd ed., London, 1946. Brief, thoughtful essay on the revolution of 1688 and its consequences for England, Ireland, and Scotland.

VA120. ———. **England under Queen Anne.** 3 v. London, 1930–34. Fullest complete survey of England at the opening of the 18th century.

See also *VA80 (9, 10)*, *VA81 (5)*, and *VA83 (6)*.

The Eighteenth Century, 1714–1815

VA121. Lecky, William E. H. **A history of England in the eighteenth century.** 8 v. London, 1878–90. A long and somewhat discursive work of 19th century scholarship which contains a great deal of material useful to the student of English social history.

VA122. Michael, Wolfgang. **Englische Geschichte im achtzehnten Jahrhundert.** 5 v. Leipzig, 1896–1945. V. 1–2 tr. under editorship of Sir Lewis Namier as *England under George I* (London, 1936–39). A careful and detailed study which contains much material not available elsewhere.

VA123. Plumb, John H. **The first four Georges.** London, 1956. A brief but useful sketch of the reigns of the first four Hanoverian kings of England.

VA124. Eyck, Erich. **Pitt versus Fox: father and son, 1735–1806.** Tr. by E. Northcott. London, 1950. This and *VA125–126* probably constitute the best introductions to the vast amount of material covering the life of William Pitt, the Elder.

VA125. Sherrard, Owen A. **Lord Chatham.** 2 v. London, 1952–55.

VA126. Williams, Basil. **The life of William Pitt, Earl of Chatham.** 2 v. London, 1913.

VA127. ———. **Stanhope: a study in eighteenth-century war and diplomacy.** Oxford, 1932.

VA128. Plumb, John H. **Sir Robert Walpole.** V. 1, **The making of a statesman.** London, 1956. Important biographical study. When completed it should become the standard work on Walpole.

VA129. Williams, Basil. **Carteret and Newcastle: a contrast in contemporaries.** Cambridge, Eng., 1943. Two leading political figures of the mid-18th century.

VA130. Namier, Sir Lewis B. **England in the age of the American Revolution.** See *AB132*.

VA131. Guttridge, George H. **English Whiggism and the American Revolution.** Berkeley, 1942.

VA132. Butterfield, Herbert. **George III, Lord North and the people, 1779–1780.** London, 1949. Detailed study of political events and movements at a crucial period.

VA133. Pares, Richard. **King George III and the politicians.** Oxford, 1953. A thoughtful essay on George III and his political influence.

VA134. Veitch, George S. **The genesis of parliamentary reform.** London, 1913. General survey of the beginnings of political reform in Great Britain during the latter decades of the 18th century.

VA135. Brown, Philip A. **The French Revolution in English history.** London, 1918. Impact of the French Revolution on English life.

VA136. Bryant, Sir Arthur. **The years of endurance, 1793–1802.** London, 1942. This and *VA137–139* are the most useful surveys of Britain during the wars of the French Revolution and Napoleon.

VA137. ———. **The years of victory, 1802–1812.** London, 1944.

VA138. Rose, J. Holland. **William Pitt and the national revival.** London, 1911.

VA139. ———. **William Pitt and the great war.** London, 1911.

VA140. Fremantle, Alan F. **England in the nineteenth century, 1801–1810.** 2 v. London, 1929–30. Detailed study of England at the opening of the 19th century.

See also *VA80 (11)*, *VA81 (6)*, and *VA83 (7)*.

The Nineteenth Century, 1815–1914

VA141. Slater, Gilbert. **The growth of modern England.** 2nd ed., London, 1939. Probably the best single volume treatment of the period since the end of the 18th century.

VA142. Trevelyan, George M. **British history in the nineteenth century and after.** 2nd ed., London, 1937. Clear, well-written narrative account.

VA143. Halévy, Élie. **History of the English people in the nineteenth century.** 2nd rev. ed., 6 v., London, 1949–52. Important, uncompleted work by an Anglophile French scholar who undertook to explain English 19th century development in the light of his own scholarly and philosophical predilections. Though not all the volumes are of equal merit (v. 1, 5, and 6 are perhaps best), the whole study has come to occupy the position of a minor historical classic. For other general surveys of the whole or parts of the period see *VA144–146*.

VA144. Walpole, Spencer. **The history of England from the conclusion of the great war in 1815.** 6 v. London, 1902–05.

VA145. Martineau, Harriet. **The history of England during the thirty years' peace, 1816–1846.** 2 v. London, 1849–50.

VA146. Bryant, Sir Arthur. **The pageant of England, 1840–1940.** London, 1941.

VA147. Young, George M., ed. **Victorian England: portrait of an age.** London, 1936. 2nd ed., Oxford, 1953. A penetrating, brief, but at the same time allusive and discursive, essay on various aspects of Victorian history and life. Valuable for its often brilliant random observations.

VA148. Aspinall, Arthur. **Lord Brougham and the Whig party.** Manchester, 1927. This and *VA149–153* give a full picture of the politics of early 19th century England and the leadership of various parties.

VA149. Brock, William R. **Lord Liverpool and liberal Toryism, 1820 to 1827.** Cambridge, Eng., 1941.

VA150. Trevelyan, George M. **Lord Grey and the reform bill.** London, 1920.

VA151. Temperley, Harold W. V. **Life of Canning.** London, 1905.

VA152. Clark, George Kitson. **Peel and the Conservative party.** London, 1929.

VA153. Davis, Henry W. C. **The age of Grey and Peel.** Oxford, 1929.

VA154. Hammond, John L., and Barbara Hammond. **The age of the Chartists, 1832–1854.** London, 1930. Though written with a strong bias, it is still the best brief social and political history of the early Victorian age.

VA155. Bell, Herbert C. **Lord Palmerston.** 2 v. London, 1936. Best recent biography of a major political figure whose life spanned the first half of the 19th century.

VA156. Benson, Edward F. **Queen Victoria.** London, 1935. Best brief, scholarly biography of the queen.

VA157. Morley, John. **Life of William Ewart Gladstone.** 3 v. London, 1903. Morley's biography is still a valuable source, though *VA158* is more recent and has the advantage of longer perspective.

VA158. Magnus, Sir Philip M. **Gladstone: a biography.** London, 1954.

VA159. Monypenny, William F., and George E. Buckle. **The life of Benjamin Disraeli.** 6 v. London, 1910–20. Rev. ed. in 2 v., 1929. Though a number of shorter single-volume biographies have appeared since the publication of this work, the above remains the standard life.

VA160. Garvin, James L. **Life of Joseph Chamberlain.** 4 v. London, 1932–51. V. 4 was completed by Julian Amery. The standard life and times.

VA161. Dangerfield, George. **The strange death of liberal England.** N.Y., 1935. Important work on the decline of English liberalism prior to 1914.

VA162. Spender, John A. **Great Britain, empire and commonwealth, 1886–1935.** London, 1936. Useful survey of an important half-century of British imperial history.

See also *VA80 (13, 14), VA81 (7),* and *VA83 (8).*

The Twentieth Century

VA163. Cruttwell, Charles R. M. **A history of the great war, 1914–1918.** Oxford, 1934.

VA164. Graves, Robert, and Alan Hodge. **The long week end: a British social history, 1918–1939.** N.Y., 1941.

VA165. Mowat, Charles L. **Britain between the wars, 1918–1940.** Chicago, 1955. Most useful single volume survey of the period.

VA166. Hirst, Francis W. **The consequences of the war to Great Britain.** See *AG91.*

VA167. Falls, Cyril B. **The Second World War: a short history.** 3rd ed., London, 1950. Useful short summary by a military historian.

VA168. Hutchison, Keith. **The decline and fall of British capitalism.** London, 1951. This and *VA169–171* deal with the various economic and social changes that have occurred in Britain since the end of World War II.

VA169. Watkins, Ernest. **The cautious revolution.** London, 1951.

VA170. Jouvenel, Bertrand de. **Problems of socialist England.** London, 1949. Perceptive essay by a French observer on the problems of Britain in the immediate post-World War II era.

VA171. Worswick, George D. N., and Peter H. Ady, eds. **The British economy, 1945–1950.** Oxford, 1952.

See also relevant chapters in *VA81 (7), VA141, VA142, VA146,* and *VA162.*

HISTORIES OF SPECIAL AREAS

Wales

VA172. Jenkins, Robert T., and William Rees, eds. **A bibliography of the history of Wales.** Cardiff, 1931. New ed. in preparation. Useful general guide.

VA173. National Library of Wales. **Bibliotheca Celtica: a register of publications relating to Wales and the Celtic peoples and languages.** 1909 ff. Aberystwyth, 1910 ff.

VA174. Welsh Bibliographical Society. **Journal of the Welsh Bibliographical Society.** Carmarthen, 1910 ff.

VA175. National Library of Wales. **Handlist of manuscripts in the National Library of Wales.** 16 pts. Aberystwyth, 1940–56.

VA176. Rees, William. **An historical atlas of Wales from early to modern times.** 2nd ed., Cardiff, 1951.

VA177. Roberts, T. R. **Eminent Welsh-**

men: a short biographical dictionary of Welshmen. Cardiff, 1908.

VA178. Rhys, John, and David Brynmor-Jones. **The Welsh people: chapters on their origin, history, laws, language, literature, and characteristics.** 4th ed., London, 1906.

VA179. Jones, Thomas Gwynn. **Welsh folklore and custom.** London, 1930.

VA180. Williams, David. **A history of modern Wales, 1485–1939.** London, 1950. The best brief, modern survey of Welsh history.

VA181. Coupland, Sir Reginald. **Welsh and Scottish nationalism: a study.** London, 1954. Posthumous work of a distinguished scholar. While it contains a number of factual errors, it is still the only useful survey in English of the two movements.

VA182. Williams, William R. J. **The parliamentary history of the principality of Wales, 1541–1895.** Brecknock, 1895. Contains lists and biographical notices of members.

VA183. Rees, Thomas. **History of Protestant nonconformity in Wales from its rise in 1633 to the present time.** 2nd rev. ed., London, 1888. Though out of date in many ways, it is still the only general history of Welsh nonconformity.

VA184. Edwards, Alfred G. **Landmarks in the history of the Welsh church.** London, 1912.

VA185. Dodd, Arthur H. **The industrial revolution in north Wales.** 2nd ed., Cardiff, 1951. This and *VA186–187* constitute a complete industrial history of modern Wales.

VA186. John, Arthur H. **The industrial revolution in south Wales, 1750–1850.** Cardiff, 1950.

VA187. Jones, Evan J. **Some contributions to the economic history of Wales.** London, 1928.

VA188. Williams, David. **The Rebecca riots: a study in agrarian discontent.** Cardiff, 1955. Important work on a major phase of Welsh social history in the 19th century.

VA189. Hughes, William J. **Wales and the Welsh in English literature from Shakespeare to Scott.** Wrexham and London, 1924.

VA190. Morrice, James C. **A manual of Welsh literature containing a brief survey of the works of the chief bards and prose writers from the sixth century to the end of the eighteenth.** Bangor, 1909.

VA191. University of Wales. **Bulletin of the Board of Celtic Studies.** Cardiff, 1921 ff.

VA192. Cymmrodorion Society. **Transactions of the honourable Society of Cymmrodorion.** London, 1893 ff. Most important periodical publication covering the general field of Welsh history.

See also special parts of the general bibliographies listed at the beginning of this section (*VA1–12*).

Scotland

VA193. Mackie, James D., ed. **Scottish history.** Cambridge, Eng., 1956. Bibliography compiled at periodic intervals for the National Book League of Great Britain.

VA194. Black, George F., ed. **A list of works relating to Scotland.** N.Y., 1916. List of works held by the New York Public Library as of Dec. 31, 1914. Still, in many ways, the fullest and most complete bibliography of Scottish historical materials down to the time of its publication.

VA195. Terry, Charles S. **A catalogue of the publications of Scottish historical and kindred clubs and societies, and of volumes relative to Scottish history, issued by His Majesty's Stationery Office 1780–1908.** Glasgow, 1909. Both this and *VA196* are indispensable guides to the printed sources of Scottish history.

VA196. Matheson, Cyril. **A catalogue of the publications of Scottish historical and kindred clubs and societies, and of volumes relative to Scottish history, issued by His Majesty's Stationery Office, 1908–1927.** Aberdeen, 1928.

VA197. Livingstone, Matthew. **A guide to the public records of Scotland deposited in H. M. General Register House, Edinburgh.** Edinburgh, 1905.

VA198. Thomson, John Maitland. **The public records of Scotland.** Glasgow, 1922.

VA199. Paton, Henry M. **The Scottish records, their history and value.** Edinburgh, 1933.

VA200. National Library of Scotland. **Catalogue of manuscripts acquired since 1925.** Edinburgh, 1938.

VA201. Edinburgh. Faculty of Advocates Library. **Catalogue of the printed books.** 7 v. Edinburgh, 1867–79. This collection has become the core of the National Library of Scotland. For that reason its catalog is an important guide.

VA202. Edinburgh. Library of the University of Edinburgh. **Catalogue of the printed books.** 3 v. Edinburgh, 1918–23. List of additions published annually, 1920 ff.

VA203. Edinburgh. Public Libraries. **Scottish family histories: a list of books for consultation in the Reference Library, George IV Bridge.** Edinburgh, 1951. List of genealogical holdings contained in the public library of Edinburgh. Useful selection.

VA204. Stuart, Margaret, and Sir James B. Paul. **Scottish family history: a guide to works of reference on the history and genealogy of Scottish families.** Edinburgh, 1930. Useful general guide to Scottish genealogy.

VA205. Innes of Learney, Sir Thomas. **Scots heraldry.** 2nd ed., Edinburgh, 1956.

VA206. Paul, Sir James B., ed. **The Scots peerage: founded on Wood's edition of Sir Robert Douglas's "Peerage of Scotland."** 9 v.

Edinburgh, 1904–14. For gentry and baronetage see Cokayne (*VA24*); and Sir Robert Douglas, *Baronage of Scotland* (Edinburgh, 1798), v. 1.

VA207. Kermack, William R. **Historical geography of Scotland.** 2nd ed., Edinburgh, 1926. Brief, but the only available general work on the subject.

VA208. Johnston, W., and A. K. Johnston. **W. and A. K. Johnston's gazetteer of Scotland.** Edinburgh, 1937.

VA209. Groome, Francis H., ed. **The ordnance gazetteer of Scotland.** 6 v. Glasgow, 1885. Though now out of date in many respects, this is still the most useful and detailed gazetteer of its kind in existence.

VA210. Bartholomew, John G., ed. **The survey atlas of Scotland.** Edinburgh, 1912.

VA211. Meikle, Henry W., ed. **Scotland: a description of Scotland and Scottish life.** 2nd ed., London, 1947.

VA212. Wright, John N., and Neil S. Snodgrass, eds. **Scotland and its people.** London, 1942.

VA213. McLaren, Moray. **The Scots.** Harmondsworth, 1951.

VA214. Notestein, Wallace. **The Scot in history.** New Haven, 1946.

VA215. Statistical Accounts of Scotland. **A survey of the country by parishes.** [*The statistical account of Scotland,* ed. by John Sinclair (21 v., Edinburgh, 1791–99); *Second statistical account* (15 v., Edinburgh, 1845); *Third statistical account* (Edinburgh, 1951 ff.).] Unique set of statistical studies compiled mainly by clergymen of the Church of Scotland. Invaluable for students of social and historical development since the 18th century.

VA216. Struthers, A. M., ed. **Scotland's changing population.** Edinburgh, 1948.

VA217. Cairncross, Alexander K., ed. **The Scottish economy: a statistical account of Scottish life.** Cambridge, Eng., 1954. A valuable study by various authors of contemporary trends in Scottish economic life.

VA218. Grant, William, and David D. Morrison, eds. **Scottish national dictionary: designed partly on regional and partly on historical principles, and containing all the Scottish works known to be in use or to have been in use since c. 1700.** Edinburgh, 1931 ff. (In progress.) Valuable reference works on the Scottish variation of English.

VA219. Craigie, Sir William A. **The Scottish tongue.** London, 1924.

VA220. ——. **A dictionary of the older Scottish tongue from the twelfth century to the end of the seventeenth.** 12 v. Chicago, 1931–49.

VA221. Rait, Sir Robert S., and George S. Pryde. **Scotland.** 2nd ed., London, 1954. Excellent brief account of Scottish history and contemporary Scotland.

VA222. Mackie, Robert L. **A short his-**tory of Scotland. 2 v. Oxford, 1929–30. Not as up-to-date as *VA221*, but extremely useful.

VA223. Brown, Peter Hume. **History of Scotland.** 3 v. Cambridge, Eng., 1902–09. Still the best longer account of Scottish history. Invaluable as a general work of reference.

VA224. Mackenzie, Agnes M. **The Scotland of Queen Mary and the religious wars.** Glasgow, 1936. Somewhat romanticized and with a mild "nationalist" bias, but well written and scholarly. This and *VA225–226* constitute a survey of modern Scottish history.

VA225. ——. **The passing of the Stuarts, 1638–1748.** Glasgow, 1937.

VA226. ——. **Scotland in modern times, 1720–1939.** Edinburgh, 1947.

VA227. Pryde, George S. **The treaty of union of England and Scotland, 1707.** London, 1950. Excellent brief essay on the origins of the legislative union and its evolution.

VA228. Brown, Peter Hume. **The legislative union of England and Scotland.** Oxford, 1914. The standard detailed account.

VA229. Dicey, Albert V., and Robert S. Rait. **Thoughts on the union between England and Scotland.** London, 1920. Scholarly discussion of the constitutional implications of the union.

VA230. Grant, Isabel F. **The economic history of Scotland.** London, 1934. Brief general survey of Scottish economic history by a distinguished economic historian.

VA231. ——. **The social and economic development of Scotland before 1603.** Edinburgh, 1930. Excellent scholarly account of the economic development of Scotland through the 16th century.

VA232. Hamilton, Henry. **The industrial revolution in Scotland.** Oxford, 1932. The standard work on the subject.

VA233. Marwick, William H. **Economic developments in Victorian Scotland.** London, 1936. Recounts the various aspects of economic growth in 19th century Scotland. Useful.

VA234. Ferguson, Thomas. **The dawn of Scottish social welfare.** Edinburgh, 1948. Useful survey of modern Scottish social history.

VA235. Saunders, Laurance J. **Scottish democracy, 1815–1840: the social and intellectual background.** Edinburgh, 1950. Thoughtful study of the social development of modern Scotland during the reform era of the 19th century.

VA236. Coupland, Sir Reginald. **Welsh and Scottish nationalism: a study.** See *VA181*.

VA237. Turner, Arthur C. **Scottish home rule.** Oxford, 1952. Excellent brief account of the rise of modern Scottish nationalism and the Scottish home rule movement.

VA238. MacGregor, Malcolm B. **The**

sources and literature of Scottish church history. Glasgow, 1934. Standard work on the subject.

VA239. Cunningham, John. **The church history of Scotland.** 2nd ed., 2 v., Edinburgh, 1882. While it is long out of print and badly in need of revision, this remains the best general work covering the history of the Scottish church.

VA240. Maxwell, William D. **A history of worship in the Church of Scotland.** Oxford, 1955. Scholarly presentation which sums up recent research on the subject.

VA241. Dickinson, William C., ed. **John Knox's history of the Reformation in Scotland.** 2 v. Edinburgh, 1949. New scholarly edition of a great historical classic with an excellent introduction.

VA242. Brown, Peter Hume. **John Knox.** 2 v. London, 1895. The fullest, most complete life.

VA243. Lee, Maurice. **James Stewart, Earl of Moray: a political study of the Reformation in Scotland.** N.Y., 1953. Biographical study of an important figure of the Scottish Reformation period.

VA244. Henderson, Thomas F. **Mary Queen of Scots, her environment and tragedy: a biography.** 2 v. N.Y., 1905. The best complete, scholarly biography.

VA245. Buchan, John. **Montrose.** London, 1935. Excellent, popularly written biography of a controversial figure.

VA246. Willson, David H. **King James VI and I.** See *VA105.*

VA247. Scottish historical review. Glasgow, 1903–28, 1947 ff. Standard historical periodical in Scottish history. Lapsed between 1928 and 1947, but has been published continuously since the latter date.

See also special parts of the general bibliographies listed at the beginning of this section (*VA1–12*).

Ireland

VA248. Maxwell, Constantia. **Short bibliography of Irish history.** London, 1921. New edition needed, but excellent for a general coverage of materials down to publication.

VA249. "Writings on Irish history." **Irish historical studies.** Ed. by James Carty and others. Dublin, 1936 ff. (Annual.) A brief but useful annual compilation.

VA250. New York Public Library. **List of works in the New York Public Library relating to Ireland, the Irish language and literature.** N.Y., 1905. A useful work, similar in intent and scope to *VA194* for Scotland. Lists holdings down to the time of publication.

VA251. Best, Richard I. **Bibliography of Irish philology and printed Irish literature.** Dublin, 1913. Not specifically historical, but

contains a number of items useful to the history student.

VA252. O'Grady, Standish H., and Robin Flower. **Catalogues of Irish manuscripts in the British Museum.** 2 v. London, 1926. Useful list of source materials.

VA253. Ireland. Public Records. **Annual report of the deputy keeper of the public records in Ireland.** Dublin, 1869 ff. After 1924 published separately by the government of Northern Ireland. The materials remaining after the disastrous fire of 1922 are listed in Herbert Wood, "The public records of Ireland before and after 1922," *Transactions of the Royal Historical Society,* 4th ser., v. 13 (1930).

VA254. Irish Free State. Manuscripts Commission. **Analecta Hibernia, including reports of the Irish Manuscripts Commission.** Dublin, 1930 ff. Periodical publication containing facsimile sources and other documents relating to Irish history.

VA255. Crone, John Smyth. **A concise dictionary of Irish biography.** Rev. and enl. ed., Dublin, 1937. In the absence of a major biographical reference work for Ireland, this is the only useful substitute. For major figures in Irish history prior to the 20th century see *VA23.*

VA256. Lodge, John. **The peerage of Ireland.** Rev. and enl. ed., 7 v., Dublin, 1789. The only major work dealing specifically with the peerage of Ireland. For contemporary treatment see *VA25.* Members of the Irish gentry are covered by *VA257.*

VA257. Cokayne, George E. **The complete baronetage.** See *VA24.*

VA258. Arensberg, Conrad M. **The Irish countryman: an anthropological study.** N.Y., 1937. This and *VA259* are excellent anthropological studies of Irish social conditions.

VA259. Arensberg, Conrad M., and Solon T. Kimball. **Family and community in Ireland.** Cambridge, Mass., 1940.

VA260. Freeman, Thomas W. **Ireland: its physical, historical, social and economic geography.** London, 1950. Excellent compact survey of Irish historical development in relation to geographic and social conditions.

VA261. Mason, Thomas H. "The Influence of topography on the distribution of the population of Ireland from prehistoric to modern times." **Irish national journal,** 7 (1939): 162–72. Explains the historical distribution of Irish population.

VA262. Connell, Kenneth H. **The population of Ireland, 1750–1845.** London, 1950. This and *VA263* constitute a valuable summary of a problem which has become one of the most serious in modern Irish history.

VA263. Coyne, Edward J. "Irish population problems: eighty years a-growing, 1871–1951." **Irish historical studies,** 43 (1954): 151–67.

VA264. Bonn, Moritz J. **Die Englische**

Kolonisation im Irland. 2 v. Stuttgart and Berlin, 1906. A particularly valuable study of the long history of English attempts to "anglicize" Ireland and the reasons for their failure. It is only surprising that a work of such merit has remained for so long without an English translator.

VA265. Beckett, James C. **A short history of Ireland.** London, 1952. An admirable brief epitome of Irish history. Particularly useful for those who have no previous knowledge of the subject.

VA266. Curtis, Edmund. **A history of Ireland.** 6th ed., London, 1950. Best one-volume text on the subject of Irish history.

VA267. Hull, Eleanor. **A history of Ireland and her people.** 2 v. London, 1926–31.

VA268. Bagwell, Richard. **Ireland under the Tudors.** 3 v. London, 1885–90. Detailed scholarly work which, with *VA269*, constitutes the best general survey of Ireland in the 16th and 17th centuries.

VA269. ———. **Ireland under the Stuarts.** 2 v. London, 1909.

VA270. MacLysaght, Edward. **Irish life in the seventeenth century.** 2nd rev. ed., Cork, 1950. Useful survey of social life in Stuart Ireland.

VA271. Lecky, William E. H. **History of Ireland in the eighteenth century.** 5 v. London, 1893. Standard work by a great Anglo-Irish scholar who sought to explain the 18th century history of Ireland in a favorable light.

VA272. O'Connor, James. **History of Ireland, 1798–1924.** 2 v. London, 1925. Detailed survey of the history of Ireland from union through the founding of the Irish Free State.

VA273. O'Hegarty, Patrick S. **A history of Ireland under the union, 1801–1922.** London, 1952. Though less detailed than *VA272*, this has the advantage of later perspective by a scholar who played a part in many of the events he describes.

VA274. Mansergh, Nicholas. **Ireland in the age of reform and revolution, 1840–1921.** London, 1940. Excellent study by an Anglo-Irish scholar whose perspective allows him to rise above the level of party difference.

VA275. MacNeill, John Gordon S. **The constitutional and parliamentary history of Ireland till the union.** Dublin, 1917. A scholarly survey, largely written from secondary materials. Useful for an understanding of Irish government and politics before the union.

VA276. McDowell, Robert B. **Public opinion and government policy in Ireland, 1801–1846.** London, 1952. [Studies in Irish history, 5.] Valuable study of political life and public opinion during the early 19th century.

VA277. Hammond, John L. **Gladstone and the Irish nation.** London, 1938. A scholarly reassessment of Gladstone's role in Anglo-

Irish politics which attempts, on the whole successfully, to give him just due for his efforts in behalf of Irish home rule.

VA278. Lyons, Francis S. L. **The Irish parliamentary party, 1890–1910.** London, 1951. [Studies in Irish history, 4.] Valuable study of the complex relationships within the Irish parliamentary party and its role in British politics from the death of Parnell to the renewal of the struggle for home rule on the eve of the First World War.

VA279. Strauss, Eric. **Irish nationalism and British democracy.** London, 1951. Good, scholarly survey of the relationships between Irish national interest and British politics in the 19th and 20th centuries.

VA280. Phillips, Walter Alison. **Revolution in Ireland, 1906–1923.** London, 1923. Standard history of the Irish revolution from the English point of view. Should, however, be counterbalanced by reference to *VA281*.

VA281. Macardle, Dorothy. **The Irish republic: a documented chronicle of the Anglo-Irish conflict and the partitioning of Ireland, with a detailed account of the period, 1916–1923.** London, 1937. Fully documented, but strongly nationalist in sympathy.

VA282. Murray, Alice E. **A history of the commercial and financial relations between England and Ireland from the period of the restoration.** London, 1903. Fullest survey, though sometimes less than fair to English policy.

VA283. O'Brien, George A. T. **The economic history of Ireland in the seventeenth century.** Dublin, 1919. This and *VA284–285* constitute the best general survey of modern Irish economic history.

VA284. ———. **The economic history of Ireland in the eighteenth century.** Dublin, 1918.

VA285. ———. **The economic history of Ireland from the union to the great famine.** Dublin, 1921.

VA286. Burke, John F. **Outline of the industrial history of Ireland.** Rev. ed., Dublin, 1940. Useful brief survey.

VA287. Pomfret, J. E. **The struggle for land in Ireland.** Princeton, 1930. Best survey of the whole problem. The four titles, *VA287–290*, cover the tangled history of Irish landholding from various aspects.

VA288. Montgomery, William E. **History of land tenure in Ireland.** Cambridge, Eng., 1889.

VA289. Butler, William F. T. **Confiscation in Irish history.** Dublin, 1917.

VA290. Palmer, Norman D. **The Irish Land League crisis.** New Haven, 1940.

VA291. Phillips, W. Alison. **History of the Church of Ireland from the earliest times to the present day.** 3 v. London, 1933–34. Excellent, sympathetic, scholarly survey of the established (Anglican) church in Ireland. Needs, however, to be understood in terms of the author's point of view. Should be read in conjunction with *VA292–294*.

VA292. Reid, James Seaton. **History of the Presbyterian Church in Ireland.** New ed., 3 v., Belfast, 1867. Despite the lapse of time since publication, this is the only satisfactory history of the Presbyterian Church in Ireland.

VA293. Beckett, James C. **Protestant dissent in Ireland, 1687–1780.** London, 1948. [Studies in Irish history, 2.] Very good study of Irish Protestant dissent during the 18th century. Valuable for an understanding of the religious cross currents that have troubled Irish history.

VA294. Bellesheim, Alphons. **Geschichte der katholische Kirche im Irland von der Einführung des Christenthums bis auf der Gegenwart.** 2 v. Mainz, 1883. Best objective, scholarly study of the complicated historical relationships between Ireland and the Roman Catholic Church. As in the case of *VA264*, it has been long without an English translator.

VA295. Gwynn, Lucius S. **Henry Grattan and his times.** London, 1939. The period of Anglo-Irish ascendancy. Focuses on the life of the most important leader of the movement for Irish autonomy in the 18th century.

VA296. O'Brien, Richard B. **Life of Charles Stewart Parnell.** 2 v. London, 1898–99. Though somewhat too sympathetic to its subject, this work is still the fullest and most complete biography.

VA297. Gwynn, Denis R. **Daniel O'Connell, the Irish liberator.** N.Y., 1930. Best biography of the major early 19th century leader of the Irish emancipation movement.

VA298. ———. **The life of John Redmond.** London, 1932. Standard biographical work dealing with the successor of Charles Stewart Parnell in the leadership of the Irish parliamentary party after 1890.

VA299. Irish historical studies. Dublin, 1938 ff. Published jointly by the Irish Historical Society and the Ulster Society for Historical Studies. Valuable for articles, reviews, and an annual bibliography of writings in Irish history.

See also special parts of the general bibliographies listed at the beginning of this section (*VA1–12*).

Northern Ireland

VA300. Moody, Theodore W., and J. C. Beckett, eds. **Ulster since 1800: a political and economic survey.** V. 1. London, 1954.

VA301. Wilson, Thomas, ed. **Ulster and home rule.** Oxford, 1955.

VA302. Mansergh, Nicholas. **The government of Northern Ireland.** London, 1936. Standard work on the origins of the government of Northern Ireland and its functions.

Local History

VA303. Humphreys, Arthur L. **A handbook to county bibliography: being a bibliography of bibliographies relating to the counties and towns of Great Britain and Ireland.** London, 1917.

VA304. Page, William, H. Arthur Doubleday, and others, eds. **The Victoria history of the counties of England.** Westminster, 1900 ff. (In progress.) Should be consulted under names of the various counties. Valuable.

See also special parts of the general bibliographies listed at the beginning of this section (*VA1–12*).

HISTORIES OF SPECIAL TOPICS

Diplomatic, Military, and Naval History

VA305. Ward, Adolphus W., and G. P. Gooch, eds. **The Cambridge history of British foreign policy, 1783–1919.** 3 v. Cambridge, Eng., 1922–23. Like most cumulative works, uneven in quality, but still the standard survey of its subject for the period down to the time of publication.

VA306. Egerton, Hugh E. **British foreign policy in Europe to the end of the nineteenth century.** London, 1917. Single volume survey now somewhat out of date, but still useful for the period covered. For more recent surveys see *VA307–308*.

VA307. Seton-Watson, Robert W. **Britain in Europe, 1789–1914.** See *T465*.

VA308. Joll, James B., ed. **Britain and Europe: Pitt to Churchill, 1793–1940.** London, 1950.

VA309. Pribram, Alfred F. **England and the international policy of the European great powers, 1871–1914.** Oxford, 1931. An important work written from the European point of view.

VA310. Reynolds, Philip A. **British foreign policy in the interwar years.** London, 1954. Most recent survey of British foreign policy between the two world wars. For other useful surveys see *VA311–313*.

VA311. Jordan, W. M. **Great Britain, France, and the German problem, 1918–1939.** See *AH172*.

VA312. Medlicott, William N. **British foreign policy since Versailles.** London, 1940.

VA313. Wolfers, Arnold. **Britain and France between two wars.** See *AH182*.

VA314. Brebner, John B. **North Atlantic triangle: the interplay of Canada, the United States and Great Britain.** See *Y192*.

VA315. Fortescue, Sir John W. **A history of the British army.** 13 v. and 6 atlases. London, 1889–1930. Monumental, scholarly work by a leading authority on the subject. For briefer, more recent surveys see *VA316–317*.

VA316. DeWatteville, Herman G. **The**

British soldier: his daily life from Tudor to modern times. London, 1954.

VA317. Sheppard, Eric W. **Short history of the British army.** 4th ed., London, 1950.

VA318. Clowes, Sir William L., ed. **The royal navy: a history from the earliest times to the present.** 7 v. London, 1897–1903. A major cumulative work which, while out of date in many respects, still contains a great deal of information on British naval history not to be found elsewhere. For later surveys see *VA319–321.*

VA319. Lloyd, Christopher. **The navy and the nation: a history of naval life and policy.** London, 1954.

VA320. Richmond, Sir Herbert W. **Statesmen and sea power.** See *T217.*

VA321. Callender, Sir Geoffrey, and H. F. Hinsley. **The naval side of British history, 1485–1945.** New ed., London, 1952.

VA322. Saunders, Hilary St. G. **Per Ardua: the rise of British air power, 1911–1939.** London, 1944. A brief survey of the development of the Royal Air Force down to the Second World War. For later material see appropriate volumes under *VA324.*

VA323. Edmonds, Sir James E. **A short history of World War I.** N.Y. and London, 1951. A summation of the longer official *History of the Great War* by its official editor. See also Cruttwell (*VA163*).

VA324. Great Britain. Government Publications. **History of the Second World War.** 41 v. London, 1950–56. (In progress.) [1, United Kingdom civil series: introductory; 2, general series; 3, war production series; 4, military series: campaign series; 5, grand strategy; 6, civil affairs and military government; 7, medical series; 8, fighting services.] Standard compilation of official materials. Valuable.

VA325. Churchill, Sir Winston. **The Second World War.** See *AH234.*

See also special parts of the general bibliographies listed at the beginning of this section (*VA1–12*).

Constitutional and Legal History; Political Theory

VA326. Chrimes, Stanley B. **English constitutional history.** 2nd ed., London, 1953. Best brief survey of the subject.

VA327. Keir, Sir David L. **Constitutional history of modern Britain, 1485–1951.** 5th ed., London, 1953. Standard textbook study in greater detail than *VA326.*

VA328. Taswell-Langmead, Thomas P. **English constitutional history.** 10th rev. ed., by T. F. T. Plucknett, London, 1947. Completely revised and largely rewritten version of an older standard work.

VA329. Emden, Cecil S. **The people and the constitution: being a history of the development of the people's influence in British**

government. 2nd ed., Oxford, 1956. Valuable study of the development of the modern electorate and its influence on the system of government.

VA330. Jennings, Sir W. Ivor. **The British constitution.** 3rd ed., Cambridge, Eng., 1950. A standard modern assessment of the British constitution.

VA331. Amery, Leopold S. **Thoughts on the constitution.** 2nd ed., London and N.Y., 1953. Best brief survey of constitutional changes since 1939.

VA332. Dicey, Arthur V. **Introduction to the study of the law of the constitution.** 9th ed., with an introduction by E. C. S. Wade, London, 1939. Classic work on the subject of constitutional law.

VA333. Jennings, Sir W. Ivor. **Law and custom of the constitution.** 2nd ed., Cambridge, Eng., 1951. Useful standard work.

VA334. Anson, Sir William. **Law and custom of the constitution.** V. 1, 5th ed., rev. by Sir M. L. Gwyer, Oxford, 1922; v. 2, 4th ed., rev. by Arthur B. Keith, Oxford, 1935. Detailed analysis of the subject.

VA335. Wade, E. C. S., and G. G. Phillips. **Constitutional law.** 5th ed., London, 1955. Valuable survey.

VA336. Holdsworth, Sir William S. **A history of English law.** 12 v. London, 1903–38. 7th rev. ed., ed. by A. L. Goodhart and H. G. Hanbury, London, 1956 ff. Monumental work of historical scholarship which has become an indispensable reference for the student of English legal history.

VA337. Plucknett, Theodore F. T. **Concise history of the common law.** 5th ed., London, 1956. Good one-volume survey of the subject.

VA338. Radzinowicz, Leon. **History of English criminal law and its administration from 1750.** V. 1–3. London, 1948–56. (In progress.) Valuable study of the development of modern English criminal law.

VA339. Stephen, Sir James F. **History of the criminal law of England.** 3 v. London, 1883. Older standard work which still contains much useful information.

VA340. White, Reginald J., ed. **The conservative tradition.** London, 1950. [British political tradition series.] This and *VA341–343* constitute a series of volumes covering various aspects of the British political tradition.

VA341. Maccoby, Simon, ed. **The English radical tradition, 1763–1914.** London, 1952. [British political tradition series.]

VA342. Pelling, Henry M., ed. **The challenge of socialism.** London, 1954. [British political tradition series.]

VA343. Bullock, Alan L. C., and Maurice Shock, eds. **The liberal tradition from Fox to Keynes.** London, 1956. [British political tradition series.]

VA344. Morris, Christopher. **Political**

thought in England: from Tyndale to Hooker. London, 1953. Useful brief survey of 16th century political thought.

VA345. Allen, John W. **A history of political thought in the 16th century.** 2nd ed., London, 1941. Interesting chapters on English political thought of the Tudor period.

VA346. ———. **English political thought, 1603–1660.** V. 1. London, 1938. This volume covers the period 1603–44. Second volume never published.

VA347. Gooch, George P. **English democratic ideas in the seventeenth century.** 2nd ed., rev. by Harold J. Laski, Cambridge, Eng., 1927. Useful, though somewhat outdated, summary of democratic and egalitarian ideas in the 17th century.

VA348. Laski, Harold J. **Political thought in England from Locke to Bentham.** London and N.Y., 1920. Useful, though somewhat outdated, survey.

VA349. Barker, Sir Ernest. **Political thought in England from 1848 to 1914.** 2nd ed., London, 1950. Standard brief survey.

VA350. Brinton, Crane. **English political thought in the nineteenth century.** 2nd ed., Cambridge, Mass., 1949. Useful survey of various thinkers and their systems of thought.

VA351. Halévy, Élie. **The growth of philosophic radicalism.** Tr. by Mary Morris. New ed., London, 1949. Famous study of the rise of Benthamite thought in England.

VA352. Cole, George D. H. **A history of socialist thought.** 4 v. London, 1953–56. Important survey of modern socialist thought by a scholar in sympathy with the movement.

VA353. Oakeshott, Michael. **Social and political doctrines of contemporary Europe.** Cambridge, Eng., 1939. Excellent survey of current political theory, though now somewhat out of date. A more recent supplementary work is T. E. Utley and J. Stuart Maclure, eds., *Documents of modern political thought* (Cambridge, Eng., 1958).

See also special parts of the general bibliographies listed at the beginning of this section (*VA1–12*) and separate chapters contained in general works listed under *VA80–83*.

Parliamentary, Administrative, and Party History

There is no single general history of the English parliament, though one has been projected for several years and is now in progress. Until such time as it appears, the student will have to make use of specialized works which cover various aspects of parliamentary history. See also various chapters in works listed under constitutional and legal history (*VA326–353*), and source materials and guides listed under *VA657–677*.

VA354. Campion, Gilbert F. M., and others. **Parliament: a survey.** London, 1952.

Good general introduction to Parliament as a contemporary institution.

VA355. Abraham, Louis A., and Stephen C. Hawtrey. **A parliamentary dictionary.** London, 1956. Excellent brief handbook of parliamentary terminology.

VA356. Pike, Luke O. **A constitutional history of the House of Lords.** London, 1894. While there are specialized period studies of the House of Lords, there is no recent general history of that body. Pike's work remains, therefore, the best general survey for the period down to its publication.

VA357. Porritt, Edward, and Annie G. Porritt. **The unreformed House of Commons.** 2 v. Cambridge, Eng., 1903. Superseded to some extent by later studies, but still useful for a description of the parliamentary system of the British Isles prior to 1832.

VA358. Jennings, Sir W. Ivor. **Cabinet government.** 2nd ed., Cambridge, Eng., 1951. This and *VA359* are standard surveys of the system of British cabinet government.

VA359. Keith, Arthur B. **The British cabinet system.** 2nd ed., ed. by N. H. Gibbs, London, 1952.

VA360. Morrison, Herbert S. **Government and Parliament: a survey from the inside.** London, 1954. A perceptive study of the relations between the modern British machinery of government and Parliament.

VA361. Lowell, Abbott L. **The government of England.** New ed., 2 v., N.Y., 1912. Still valuable for a description of governmental functions for the period prior to its publication.

VA362. Smellie, Kingsley B. **A hundred years of English government.** 2nd ed., London, 1951. Useful survey of the interrelationships of various branches of British government since 1832.

VA363. Seymour, Charles. **Electoral reform in England and Wales: the development and operation of the parliamentary franchise, 1832–1885.** New Haven, 1915. Valuable study of effects of the great 19th century reform bills on elections.

VA364. Campion, Gilbert F. M., and others. **British government since 1918.** London, 1950. Survey of government and its functions since the end of the First World War.

VA365. Carr, Sir Cecil T. **Concerning English administration law.** N.Y., 1941. Penetrating essay on the problems of modern administrative law in Great Britain. See also *VA366–367*.

VA366. Allen, Carleton K. **Law and orders: an enquiry into the nature and scope of delegated legislation and executive powers in England.** 2nd ed., London, 1956.

VA367. Robson, William A. **Justice and administrative law: a study of the British constitution.** 3rd ed., London, 1951.

VA368. New Whitehall series. V. 1–4. London, 1954–56. (In progress.) [1, Sir Frank Newsam, *The Home Office;* 2, Lord William Strang, *The Foreign Office;* 3, Sir Charles Jeffries, *The Colonial Office;* 4, Sir Harold Emmerson, *The Ministry of Works.*] Valuable series of studies touching on the organization and function of the various branches of the modern British civil service. Supersedes the old Whitehall series.

VA369. Cohen, Emmeline W. **The growth of the British civil service, 1780–1939.** London, 1941. Useful historical survey. For other titles see *VA370–372.*

VA370. Greaves, Harold R. G. **The civil service in the changing state.** London, 1947.

VA371. Beer, Samuel H. **Treasury control: the co-ordination of financial and economic policy in Great Britain.** Oxford, 1956.

VA372. Hancock, William K., and Margaret M. Gowing. **British war economy.** See *AG230.*

VA373. Smellie, Kingsley B. **History of local government.** London, 1946. This and *VA374–375* are excellent surveys of local government and its history in Great Britain.

VA374. Finer, Herman. **English local government.** 4th ed., London, 1950.

VA375. Robson, William A. **The development of local government.** 3rd ed., London, 1954.

VA376. Webb, Sidney, and Beatrice Webb. **English local government.** 9 v. London, 1906–29. [1, *Parish and the county;* 2–3, *Manor and the borough;* 4, *Statutory authorities for special purposes;* 5, *The story of the king's highway;* 6, *English prisons under local government;* 7–9, *English poor law history.*] A major scholarly study which remains a standard work of reference for the historical development of English government in several of its aspects.

VA377. Bailey, Sydney D., ed. **The British party system: a symposium.** London, 1952. This and *VA378* are excellent surveys of the modern British party system.

VA378. McKenzie, Robert T. **British political parties.** London, 1955.

VA379. Trevelyan, George M. **The two-party system in English political history.** Oxford, 1926. Brief essay on the two-party system and its significance.

VA380. Feiling, Keith G. **A history of the Tory party, 1640–1714.** Oxford, 1924. This and *VA381* constitute the standard history of the origins of the Tory party.

VA381. ——. **The second Tory party, 1714–1832.** London, 1938.

VA382. Slesser, Sir Henry H. **History of the Liberal party.** London, 1944. In the absence of a definitive, detailed history of the Liberal party, this is a useful guide.

VA383. Maccoby, Simon. **English radicalism.** 5 v. London, 1935–55. [1, 1762–1785; 2, 1786–1832; 3, 1832–1852; 4, 1853–1886;

5, 1886–1914.] These volumes are the products of lifelong, careful scholarship.

VA384. Carswell, John. **The old cause: three biographical studies in Whiggism.** London, 1954. Biographical study of the development of English Whiggism.

VA385. Pelling, Henry M. **The origins of the Labour party.** London, 1954. Excellent study of the beginnings of labor's political organization in Great Britain.

VA386. Cole, George D. H. **History of the Labour party from 1914.** London, 1948. Useful brief survey.

VA387. Neale, Sir John E. **The Elizabethan House of Commons.** London, 1949. This and *VA388* are valuable studies of the structure and functions of Parliament in the reign of Elizabeth I.

VA388. ——. **Elizabeth I and her parliaments.** London, 1953.

VA389. Notestein, Wallace. **The winning of the initiative by the House of Commons.** London, 1924. Brief but important essay on the gradual transference of parliamentary power to the House of Commons in the early 17th century.

VA390. Brunton, Douglas, and Donald H. Pennington. **Members of the Long Parliament.** London, 1954. This and *VA391* are valuable attempts to determine the nature of party alignments in the Long Parliament through the method of biographical analysis.

VA391. Keeler, Mary F. **The Long Parliament, 1640–1641: a biographical study of its members.** Philadelphia, 1954.

VA392. Walcott, Robert. **English politics in the early eighteenth century.** Cambridge, Mass., 1956. Political divisions within Parliament during the early 18th century.

VA393. Namier, Sir Lewis B. **The structure of politics at the accession of George III.** 2nd ed., London, 1957. New edition of a work which has been something of a landmark in the historiography of English political history.

VA394. Gash, Norman. **Politics in the age of Peel: a study in the technique of parliamentary representation.** London, 1953. Valuable study which examines the political functionings of Parliament and English society in the period of the Reform Bill of 1832.

VA395. Gillespie, Frances E. **Labor and politics in England, 1850–1867.** Durham, 1927. A scholarly analysis of the relationships between trade unionism and political reform in the mid-19th century.

VA396. Dolléans, Edouard. **Le chartisme.** 2 v. Paris, 1912–13. In many ways the best detailed, scholarly treatment of the Chartist movement.

VA397. Hovell, Mark. **The Chartist movement.** London, 1918. Best specific treatment of the movement in English.

VA398. Somervell, David C. **British poli-**

tics since 1900. 2nd ed., London, 1953. Brief survey of the English political scene in the 20th century.

Economic History

General

VA399. Lipson, Ephraim. **The growth of English society.** 3rd ed., London, 1954. Excellent survey.

VA400. Clapham, Sir John H. **A concise economic history of Britain, from the earliest times to 1750.** Ed. by J. Saltmarsh. Cambridge, Eng., 1949. Very good survey of English economic history, the posthumous work of a great economic historian.

VA401. Court, William H. B. **A concise economic history of Britain from 1750 to the recent times.** Cambridge, Eng., 1954. Admirable condensation of the entire sweep of English economic development since the middle of the 18th century.

VA402. Ashton, Thomas S., ed. **An economic history of England.** London, 1955 ff. (In progress.) Projected in 5 v., all by noted authorities, as follows: E. M. Carus-Wilson, the medieval period; F. J. Fisher, the 16th and 17th centuries; T. S. Ashton, the 18th century (London, 1955); A. H. John, 1800–1870; and W. Ashworth, 1870–1939.

VA403. Lipson, Ephraim. **The economic history of England.** V. 2–3, 6th ed., London, 1956. These volumes cover the period from 15th through the 18th centuries. A standard, scholarly work.

VA404. Cunningham, William. **Growth of English industry and commerce.** 5th and 6th eds., 3 v., Cambridge, Eng., 1910–12. While some of Cunningham's judgments are in need of modification, this remains an important and useful work which contains a great deal of valuable material.

VA405. Brentano, Lujo. **Eine Geschichte der wirtschaftlichen Entwicklung Englands.** 3 v. in 4. Jena, 1927–29. Useful and, as yet, untranslated German study which contains much information that cannot be found elsewhere.

VA406. Clapham, Sir John H. **An economic history of modern Britain, 1820–1929.** 2nd ed., 3 v., Cambridge, Eng., 1930–38. The major work of a great scholar which has become a classic of its kind.

VA407. Carus-Wilson, Eleanora M., ed. **Essays in economic history.** London, 1954. Valuable collection of articles covering a wide range of topics. All are reprints from various numbers of *Economic history* and *The economic history review* over a period of about twenty years. While the list of titles contained in the volume is too long to reproduce here, this is a collection that should not be slighted by the student of economic history.

VA408. Clark, Sir George N. **The wealth of England, 1496–1760.** London, 1946. Excellent brief study of the economic growth of pre-industrial England.

VA409. Fay, Charles R. **Great Britain from Adam Smith to the present day.** 2nd ed., London, 1950. Standard economic survey of British development since the latter part of the 18th century.

VA410. Pool, Arthur G., and Gwilym P. Jones. **A hundred years of economic development in Great Britain.** London, 1940. Good survey of 19th and 20th century developments.

Agriculture

VA411. Prothero, Rowland E. (Lord Ernle). **English farming, past and present.** 5th ed., London, 1936. Standard survey of English agricultural history, though some of the conclusions need modifying. For other surveys covering various aspects of agricultural history see *VA412–414.*

VA412. Orwin, Charles S. **A history of English farming.** Edinburgh, 1949.

VA413. Seebohm, Mabel E. (Mabel E. Christie). **The evolution of the English farm.** 2nd ed., London, 1952.

VA414. Trow-Smith, Robert. **English husbandry, from the earliest times to the present day.** London, 1951.

VA415. Orwin, Charles S., and Christabel S. Orwin. **The open fields.** 2nd ed., Oxford, 1954. General history of the open-field system of agriculture.

VA416. Tawney, Richard H. **The agrarian problem of the 16th century.** London, 1912. Important work on the evolution of English landholding and the rise of the gentry as a class. For a full discussion of all sides of the question see *VA417–419.*

VA417. ———. "Rise of the gentry, 1558–1640." **Economic history review,** 11 (1941): 1–38.

VA418. Trevor-Roper, Hugh R. "The gentry, 1540–1640." **Economic history review supplement** (1953).

VA419. Habbakuk, H. J. "English landownership, 1680–1740." **Economic history review,** 10 (1940): 2–17.

Industry

VA420. Hammond, John L., and Barbara Hammond. **The rise of modern industry.** 5th ed., N.Y., 1937. Long a standard work, though conclusions of the authors are no longer so widely shared as they were at time of publication.

VA421. Hoffmann, Walther G. **British industry, 1700–1950.** Tr. by W. O. Henderson and W. H. Chaloner. Oxford, 1955. Important but highly technical work in which the author applies the method of statistics to determine the rate of industrial growth in England since the middle of the 18th century.

VA422. Flanders, Allen, and Hugh A. Clegg. **The system of industrial relations in Great Britain: its history, law, and institutions.** Oxford, 1954. Useful survey.

VA423. Knowles, Lillian C. A. **The industrial and commercial revolutions in Great Britain during the nineteenth century.** 4th rev. ed., London, 1926. A classic study of the subject.

VA424. Ashton, Thomas S. **The industrial revolution, 1760–1830.** London and N.Y., 1948. Admirable survey of the movement which has not been entirely superseded by the author's later study (*VA425*).

VA425. ——. **The economic history of England: the eighteenth century.** London, 1955.

VA426. Clark, Sir George N. **The idea of the industrial revolution.** See *T711*.

VA427. Mantoux, Paul J. **La révolution industrielle au XVIIIᵉ siècle.** Paris, 1906. Tr. and rev. by Marjorie Vernon as *The industrial revolution in the eighteenth century* (London, 1928; reprint, 1948). Long a standard work which was undertaken as an attempt to document the belief of Arnold Toynbee that the 18th century in England saw the beginnings of the modern industrial revolution.

Trade, Finance, and Economic Growth

VA428. Rogers, James E. T. **Six centuries of work and wages.** 11th ed., London, 1912. Now somewhat out of date and superseded by *VA429*.

VA429. Beveridge, Sir William H., **Prices and wages in England from the twelfth to the nineteenth century. V. 1, The mercantile era.** London, 1939.

VA430. Carter, Charles F., and Andrew D. Roy. **British economic statistics.** Cambridge, Eng., 1954. Useful compilation.

VA431. Scott, William R. **The constitution and finance of English, Scottish, and Irish joint stock companies to 1720.** 3 v. Cambridge, Eng., 1910–12. The standard scholarly work on the subject, which badly needs reprinting.

VA432. Schlote, Werner. **British overseas trade, 1700 to the 1930's.** Tr. by W. O. Henderson. Oxford, 1952. Important study by a German scholar which offers a statistical analysis of British overseas trade and its development.

VA433. Jenks, Leland H. **The migration of British capital to 1875.** N.Y., 1927. Standard study of the pattern of English overseas investment in the 19th century.

VA434. Cairncross, Alexander K. **Home and foreign investment, 1870–1913.** Cambridge, Eng., 1953. Continuation on a somewhat broader scope of *VA433*.

VA435. Rostow, Walt W. **British economy of the nineteenth century.** Oxford, 1948. Valuable study employing theoretical techniques to explain the patterns of British economic development in the 19th century. See also *VA421*.

VA436. Kahn, Alfred E. **Great Britain in the world economy.** N.Y., 1946. Analysis of Britain's international economic position.

VA437. Worswick, George D. N., and Peter H. Ady, eds. **The British economy, 1945–1950.** Oxford, 1952.

VA438. Morgan, Edward V. **The theory and practice of central banking, 1797–1913.** Cambridge, Eng., 1943. Valuable survey of the British banking system.

VA439. Clapham, Sir John H. **The Bank of England: a history, 1694–1914.** 2 v. Cambridge, Eng., 1944. Now the standard history.

VA440. Raynes, Harold E. **A history of British insurance.** London, 1948. Rev. reprint, 1950. Useful survey of an important aspect of British financial history.

VA441. Dowell, Stephen. **A history of taxation and taxes in England from the earliest times to the present day.** 2nd ed., 4 v., London, 1888. Still the only general survey. Should be supplemented by *VA442–444*.

VA442. Hargreaves, Eric L. **The national debt.** London, 1930. An important work.

VA443. Dietz, Frederick C. **English public finance, 1558–1642.** N.Y., 1932. Valuable, scholarly study of the beginnings of modern state finance in Great Britain.

VA444. Kennedy, William. **English taxation, 1640–1799: an essay on policy and opinion.** London, 1913. Still useful for the period covered.

Social History

General

VA445. Trevelyan, George M. **English social history: a survey of six centuries.** 3rd ed., London, 1946. Best one-volume epitome.

VA446. Cole, George D. H., and Raymond W. Postgate. **The common people, 1744–1946.** 4th ed., London, 1949. Contains a great deal of valuable information.

VA447. Traill, Henry D., and James S. Mann, eds. **Social England: a record of the progress of the people in religion, laws, learning, arts, industry, commerce, science, literature, and manners from the earliest times to the present day.** New ed., 6 v., London, 1901–04. A classic survey written by many hands. Still valuable.

VA448. Plumb, John H., ed. **Studies in social history presented to G. M. Trevelyan.** London, 1955. Contains a number of important essays in the field of social history. Should be consulted by any student working in that area.

Social Classes and Conditions

VA449. Raleigh, Sir Walter A., Sir Sidney Lee, and Charles T. Onions, eds. **Shake-**

speare's England. 2 v. Oxford, 1917. Valuable survey of late Tudor England.

VA450. Wright, Louis B. **Middle class culture in Elizabethan England.** Chapel Hill, 1935. Excellent social survey.

VA451. Notestein, Wallace. **The English people on the eve of colonization, 1603–1630.** See *VA101.*

VA452. Mathew, David. **The social structure in Caroline England.** Oxford, 1948. Scholarly but allusive study of early Stuart society.

VA453. Coate, Mary. **Social life in Stuart England.** London, 1924. Helpful survey.

VA454. George, Mary D. **England in transition.** London, 1931. The forces of social change in 18th century England. Valuable.

VA455. Turberville, Arthur S. **English men and manners in the eighteenth century.** 2nd ed., Oxford, 1929. This and *VA456* constitute valuable surveys of English social history in the 18th century from the pen of a noted authority.

VA456. ——, ed. **Johnson's England.** 2 v. Oxford, 1933.

VA457. Young, George M., ed. **Early Victorian England.** 2 v. Oxford, 1934. Collection of materials illustrative of the social life of early Victorian England. For an illuminating but somewhat involved essay on the whole Victorian period see *VA458.*

VA458. ——, ed. **Victorian England: portrait of an age.** See *VA147.*

VA459. Briggs, Asa. **Victorian people: some reassessments of people, institutions, ideas, and events, 1851–1867.** London, 1954. Series of vignettes of leading Victorians, their outlook and place in Victorian society.

VA460. Hammond, John L., and Barbara Hammond. **The age of the Chartists, 1832–1854.** London, 1930. Strongly biased in favor of social reform. See *VA154.*

VA461. Lynd, Helen M. **England in the eighteen-eighties.** N.Y., 1945. Thoughtful study of the forces of social change in late Victorian England.

VA462. Hearnshaw, Fossey J. C., ed. **Edwardian England, 1901–1910.** London, 1933.

VA463. Graves, Robert, and Alan Hodge. **The long week end: a British social history, 1918–1939.** N.Y., 1941.

VA464. Wingfield-Stratford, Esmé C. **The squire and his relations.** London, 1956. General survey of the English squirearchy and its historical development.

VA465. Fussell, George E., and K. R. Fussell. **The English countryman: his life and work, A.D. 1500–1900.** London, 1955.

VA466. Campbell, Mildred L. **The English yeoman under Elizabeth and the early Stuarts.** New Haven, 1942. Important study of a social class which played a major part in Tudor and Stuart society.

VA467. Hammond, John L., and Barbara

Hammond. **The village laborer, 1760–1832.** New ed., London, 1920. This and *VA468–469* are important studies written with some bias against the economic and industrial changes of the 18th century.

VA468. ——. **The town laborer, 1760–1832.** London, 1917.

VA469. ——. **The skilled laborer, 1760–1832.** London, 1919.

VA470. Pinchbeck, Ivy. **Women workers and the industrial revolution.** London, 1930.

VA471. Cole, George D. H. **Short history of the English working class movement.** 3 v. London, 1927. Standard survey of the movement.

VA472. Lewis, Roy, and Angus Maude. **The English middle classes.** London, 1950. Position of the middle classes in the mid-20th century.

VA473. ——. **Professional people.** London, 1952. Valuable study of the English professional classes.

Social and Economic Reform

VA474. Webb, Sidney, and Beatrice Webb. **History of trade unionism.** Rev. ed., London, 1920. Still a useful survey of the movement.

VA475. Hall, Fred, and William P. Watkins. **Co-operation: a survey of the history, principles and organization of the co-operative movement in Great Britain and Ireland.** Manchester, 1934.

VA476. Cole, George D. H. **A century of co-operation.** London, 1944.

VA477. Harrison, Amy, and Elizabeth L. Hutchins. **A history of factory legislation.** Westminster, 1903. Though much out of date, it is still most useful survey of 19th century factory legislation.

VA478. Barnes, Donald G. **History of the English corn laws.** London, 1930.

VA479. Klingberg, Frank J. **The antislavery movement in England.** New Haven, 1926.

VA480. Leonard, E. M. **The early history of English poor relief.** Cambridge, Eng., 1900. Still valuable for the beginnings of the English poor law system. Covers the period 1514–1644.

VA481. Webb, Sidney, and Beatrice Webb. **English poor law history.** 3 v. London, 1927–29. [English local government, 7–9.] Most complete scholarly survey.

VA482. Cole, George D. H. **British working class politics, 1832–1914.** London, 1941.

VA483. Beer, Max. **A history of British socialism.** London and N.Y., 1940. Standard survey of British socialism by an Austrian scholar whose enthusiasm for his subject led to some historical distortion in an otherwise useful book.

VA484. Pease, Edward R. **The history of the Fabian Society.** 2nd ed., London, 1925. The standard "official" history.

VA485. Hall, Mary P. **The social services of modern England.** 3rd rev. ed., London, 1955.

VA486. Mendelsohn, Ronald. **Social security in the British Commonwealth: Great Britain, Canada, Australia, New Zealand.** London, 1954. Very good comparative study.

Religious History

General

VA487. Sykes, Norman. **The English religious tradition.** London, 1953. Excellent summary.

VA488. James, Edwin O. **A history of Christianity in England.** See *D514*. This and *VA489* are the two best brief, single-volume surveys.

VA489. Moorman, John R. H. **A history of the church in England.** London, 1953.

VA490. Hunt, William, and William R. W. Stephens, eds. **History of the English church.** 9 v. London, 1899–1910. Covers period from 597 to the end of the 19th century.

VA491. Stoughton, John. **Ecclesiastical history of England.** 5 v. London, 1867–84. Covers period 1640–1850. Written by a dissenter who tried to include all aspects of religious history.

Denominations Other Than the Church of England

VA492. Braithwaite, William C. **The beginnings of Quakerism.** London, 1912. This and *VA493* cover the period to 1725.

VA493. ——. **The second period of Quakerism.** London, 1919.

VA494. Jones, Rufus M. **The later periods of Quarkerism.** 2 v. London, 1921. Covers later period down to the 20th century.

VA495. Dale, Robert W. **History of English Congregationalism.** Ed. by Sir A. W. W. Dale. 2nd ed., London, 1907.

VA496. Drysdale, Alexander H. **History of the Presbyterians in England.** London, 1889.

VA497. Townsend, William J., Herbert B. Workman, and George Eayrs, eds. **A new history of Methodism.** 2 v. London, 1909.

VA498. Mathew, David. **Catholicism in England.** 3rd ed., London, 1955.

VA499. Roth, Cecil A. **A history of the Jews in England.** 2nd ed., Oxford, 1949.

VA500. Whitley, William T. **A history of British Baptists.** 2nd ed., London, 1932.

Special Periods and Topics

VA501. Powicke, Sir Frederick M. **The Reformation in England.** London, 1941. Thoughtful and perceptive essay on the causes and significance of the English Reformation.

VA502. Rupp, Ernest G. **Studies in the making of the English Protestant tradition.** Cambridge, Eng., 1947. Valuable essays which call attention to the religious element in the English Reformation.

VA503. Constant, Gustave. **The Reformation in England.** See *D486*.

VA504. Hughes, Philip. **The Reformation in England.** 3 v. London, 1950–54. Monumental work by a Catholic scholar.

VA505. Knappen, Marshall M. **Tudor Puritanism.** Chicago, 1939. Excellent, scholarly survey of the beginnings of English Puritanism.

VA506. Haller, William. **The rise of Puritanism.** N.Y., 1938. This and *VA507* are important studies on the literature and thought of the Puritan movement and the great crisis of the civil wars. See also *VA508–509*.

VA507. ——. **Liberty and reformation in the Puritan revolution.** N.Y., 1955.

VA508. Simpson, Alan. **Puritanism in Old and New England.** See *AB104*.

VA509. Marlowe, John. **The Puritan tradition in English life.** London, 1956.

VA510. Jordan, Wilbur K. **The development of religious toleration.** 4 v. London, 1932–40. A major scholarly enterprise which examines the ideas and writings of those responsible for beginning the idea of religious toleration in England.

VA511. Plum, Harry G. **Restoration Puritanism.** Chapel Hill, 1943. English Puritanism in its later phases.

VA512. Overton, John H., and Frederic Relton. **The English church from the accession of George I to the end of the eighteenth century.** London, 1906. [History of the English church, 7.] Still useful as a historical survey.

VA513. Sykes, Norman. **Church and state in England in the 18th century.** Cambridge, Eng., 1934. Valuable, scholarly essay.

VA514. Warre-Cornish, Francis. **The English church in the nineteenth century.** 2 v. London, 1910. [History of the English church, 8–9.]

VA515. Lloyd, Roger B. **The Church of England in the twentieth century.** 2 v. London, 1946–50. Detailed account.

VA516. Spinks, George S., and others. **Religion in Britain since 1900.** London, 1952. Survey of various aspects of religious thought and belief.

Theology and Religious Thought

VA517. Hunt, John. **Religious thought in England from the Reformation to the end of the last century.** 3 v. London, 1870–73. Though out of date and in need of revision, this is still the only useful survey of its kind.

VA518. Tulloch, John. **Rational theology and Christian philosophy in England in the seventeenth century.** 2 v. Edinburgh, 1872. Still valuable for the period covered. Partly but by no means entirely superseded by *VA526*.

VA519. Miller, Perry G. **The New Eng-**

land mind: the seventeenth century. See *AB445*.

VA520. Stromberg, Roland N. **Religious liberalism in eighteenth-century England.** Oxford, 1954.

VA521. Elliott-Binns, Leonard E. **English thought, 1860–1900: the theological aspect.** London, 1956. Excellent, scholarly study of 19th century religious thought.

Philosophy and the History of Ideas

VA522. Carré, Meyrick H. **Phases of thought in England.** Oxford, 1949. Very good, scholarly survey of English intellectual movements.

VA523. Sorley, William R. **A history of English philosophy.** Cambridge, Eng., 1920. Useful standard survey of English philosophy, now somewhat in need of revision.

VA524. Tillyard, Eustace M. W. **The Elizabethan world picture.** London, 1943. Important essay on the Elizabethan view of the universe and of man's place therein.

VA525. Stephen, Sir Leslie. **History of English thought in the eighteenth century.** 3rd ed., 2 v., London, 1902. Though permeated with a strong flavor of Victorian agnosticism, this is still a valuable survey of the 18th century intellectual milieu.

VA526. Willey, Basil. **The seventeenth century background.** London, 1934. This and *VA527–529* constitute a valuable survey of English intellectual history from the 17th through the 19th century.

VA527. ——. **The eighteenth century background.** London, 1940.

VA528. ——. **Nineteenth century studies.** London, 1949.

VA529. ——. **More nineteenth century studies.** London, 1956.

Literature and the Arts

VA530. Baugh, Albert C., ed. **A literary history of England.** N.Y., 1948. Excellent summary which to a large extent supersedes the still useful *VA531*.

VA531. Legouis, Emile, and Louis Cazamian. **A history of English literature.** Rev. ed., N.Y., 1935.

VA532. Harvey, Sir Paul, ed. **The Oxford companion to English literature.** 3rd ed., Oxford, 1946. Standard work of reference.

VA533. **The Cambridge history of English literature.** Ed. by Sir Adolphus W. Ward and Alfred R. Waller. 14 v. Cambridge, Eng., 1907–16. V. 3–14 cover the period since 1485. Still a valuable work of reference.

VA534. **The Oxford history of English literature.** Ed. by Bonamy Dobree and Frank P. Wilson. Oxford, 1945 ff. To be completed in 12 v. V. 6–12 will cover the period since 1485.

VA535. **The Oxford history of English art.** Ed. by Thomas R. S. Boase. Oxford, 1949 ff. To be completed in 12 v. V. 6–12 will cover the period since 1485.

VA536. **The Pelican history of art.** Ed. by Nicholas Pevsner. London, 1953 ff. V. 1, 3, 5, 9, and 12, already published, cover various aspects of British art.

VA537. Baker, Charles H. C., and William G. Constable. **English painting of the sixteenth and seventeenth centuries.** N.Y., 1930. Comprehensive and critically reliable. [JSC]

VA538. Waterhouse, Ellis K. **Painting in Britain, 1530 to 1790.** Baltimore, 1953. Solidly academic. [JSC]

VA539. ——. **Gainsborough.** London, 1958.

VA540. Bertram, Anthony. **A century of British painting, 1851–1951.** London and N.Y., 1951.

VA541. Beckett, Ronald B. **Hogarth.** London, 1949.

VA542. Waterhouse, Ellis K. **Reynolds.** London, 1941. Chronological catalog and useful bibliography. 300 plates. [JSC]

VA543. Summerson, John N. **Architecture in Britain, 1530 to 1830.** Baltimore, 1953. Useful survey. [JSC]

VA544. Walker, Ernest. **A history of music in England.** 2nd ed., London, 1924. Good survey.

Education

VA545. Curtis, Stanley J. **History of education in Great Britain.** 3rd ed., London, 1953. This and *VA546–547* are useful surveys of the subject.

VA546. Barnard, Howard C. **A short history of English education from 1760 to 1944.** London, 1947.

VA547. Curtis, Stanley J. **Education in Britain since 1900.** London, 1952.

VA548. Mallet, Sir Charles. **A history of the University of Oxford.** 3 v. London, 1924–27.

VA549. Mullinger, James B. **The University of Cambridge.** 3 v. Cambridge, Eng., 1873–1911.

BIOGRAPHIES

Biographical entries contained in the subsection "Histories of Special Periods" are not repeated here.

Tudor Period, 1485–1603

VA550. Gairdner, James. **Henry the Seventh.** London, 1889.

VA551. Temperley, Gladys. **Henry VII.** London, 1914.

VA552. Chambers, Raymond W. **Thomas More.** London, 1935.

VA553. Pollard, Albert F. **Thomas Cranmer and the English Reformation.** London, 1904.

VA554. Smyth, Charles H. **Cranmer and the Reformation under Edward VI.** Cambridge, Eng., 1926.

VA555. Creighton, Mandell. **Queen Elizabeth.** London, 1899.

VA556. Corbett, Julian S. **Sir Francis Drake.** London, 1890.

VA557. Williamson, James A. **Hawkins of Plymouth.** London, 1949.

VA558. Pearson, Andrew F. S. **Thomas Cartwright and Elizabethan Puritanism, 1535–1603.** Cambridge, Eng., 1925.

VA559. Hume, Martin A. S. **The great Lord Burghley.** N.Y., 1898.

VA560. Rosenberg, Eleanor. **Leicester, patron of letters.** N.Y., 1955.

VA561. Chambers, Edmund K. **William Shakespeare.** 2 v. Oxford, 1930.

VA562. Davis, Bernard E. C. **Edmund Spenser.** Cambridge, Eng., 1933.

Stuart Period, 1603–1714

VA563. Spedding, James. **Letters and the life of Francis Bacon, including all his occasional works.** 7 v. London, 1861–74.

VA564. Taylor, Alfred E. **Francis Bacon.** Oxford, 1927.

VA565. Cecil, Algernon. **A life of Robert Cecil, first earl of Salisbury.** London, 1915.

VA566. Bowen, Catherine D. **The lion and the throne: the life and times of Sir Edward Coke, 1552–1634.** Boston, 1957.

VA567. Higham, Florence M. **G. Charles I: a study.** London, 1932.

VA568. Trevor-Roper, Hugh R. **Archbishop Laud.** London, 1940.

VA569. Wedgwood, Cicely V. **Strafford.** London, 1935.

VA570. Oman, Carola. **Henrietta Maria.** London, 1936.

VA571. Ireland, William W. **The life of Sir Henry Vane the younger.** London, 1905.

VA572. Wade, Charles E. **John Pym.** London, 1912.

VA573. Buchan, John. **Oliver Cromwell.** London, 1934.

VA574. Masson, David. **The life of John Milton.** 7 v. London, 1859–94.

VA575. Tillyard, Eustace M. W. **Milton.** London, 1930.

VA576. Bryant, Sir Arthur. **Samuel Pepys.** 2nd ed., 3 v., London, 1948–49.

VA577. Traill, Henry D. **Shaftesbury.** London, 1888.

VA578. Browning, Andrew. **Thomas Osborne, earl of Danby and duke of Leeds, 1632–1712.** 3 v. Glasgow, 1944–51.

VA579. Foxcroft, Helen C. **The life and letters of George Savile, first marquis of Halifax.** 2 v. London, 1898.

VA580. Grew, Marion E. **William Bentinck and William III.** London, 1924.

VA581. Ogg, David. **William III.** London, 1956.

VA582. Churchill, Winston S. **Marlborough, his life and times.** 2 v. London, 1947.

VA583. Rowse, Alfred L. **The early Churchills: an English family.** London, 1956.

VA584. Roscoe, Edward S. **Robert Harley, earl of Oxford.** London, 1902.

VA585. Sichel, Walter S. **Bolingbroke and his times.** 2 v. London, 1901–02.

Eighteenth Century, 1714–1815

VA586. Imbert-Terry, Henry M. **A constitutional king, George the First.** London, 1927.

VA587. Fox-Strangways, Giles S. H., earl of Ilchester. **Henry Fox, first Lord Holland, his family and relations.** 2 v. London, 1920.

VA588. Morley, John. **Sir Robert Walpole.** London, 1921.

VA589. Postgate, Raymond. **That devil Wilkes.** London, 1930.

VA590. Trevelyan, George O. **The early history of Charles James Fox.** New ed., London, 1908.

VA591. ———. **George III and Charles Fox.** 2 v. London, 1912–14.

VA592. Lascelles, Edward C. P. **The life of Charles James Fox.** Oxford, 1936.

VA593. Lucas, Reginald. **Lord North, second earl of Guilford.** 2 v. London, 1913.

VA594. Fitzmaurice, Edmund. **Life of William, earl of Shelburne.** 2nd ed., 2 v., London, 1912.

VA595. Magnus, Sir Philip M. **Edmund Burke.** London, 1939.

VA596. Smiles, Samuel. **Lives of the engineers.** 3 v. London, 1861–62.

VA597. Unwin, George, Arthur Hulme, and George Taylor. **Samuel Oldknow and the Arkwrights.** Manchester, 1924.

VA598. Cole, George D. H. **Robert Owen.** London, 1925.

VA599. Atkinson, Charles M. **Jeremy Bentham, his life and work.** London, 1905.

VA600. Cole, George D. H. **The life of William Cobbett.** 3rd ed., London, 1947.

VA601. Wallas, Graham. **The life of Francis Place.** 4th ed., London, 1925.

VA602. Coupland, Sir Reginald. **Wilberforce: a narrative.** Oxford, 1923.

VA603. Grenfell, Russell. **Nelson the sailor.** 2nd ed., London, 1952.

VA604. Mahan, Alfred T. **The life of Nelson.** 2nd ed., Boston, 1899.

VA605. Oman, Carola. **Nelson.** London, 1947.

VA606. Fortescue, Sir John. **Wellington.** London, 1925.

VA607. Guedalla, Philip. **Wellington.** London, 1931.

Early Victorian England, 1815–1870

VA608. Greville, Charles C. F. **Greville memoirs: a journal of the reigns of King George IV, King William IV, and Queen Victoria.** Ed. by Henry Reeve. 8 v. London, 1896–99. For brevity see Christopher Lloyd, ed., *The Greville memoirs* (London, 1948).

VA609. Leigh, Ione. **Castlereagh.** London, 1951.

VA610. Fay, Charles R. **Huskisson and his age.** London, 1951.

VA611. Cecil, Lord David. **Lord M.: the later life of Lord Melbourne.** London, 1954.

VA612. Parker, Charles S. **Sir Robert Peel.** 3 v. London, 1891–99.

VA613. Ramsay, Anna A. W. **Sir Robert Peel.** London, 1928.

VA614. Cecil, Algernon. **Queen Victoria and her prime ministers.** London, 1953.

VA615. Fulford, Roger. **Queen Victoria.** London, 1951.

VA616. New, Chester W. **Lord Durham.** See *AA222*.

VA617. Hammond, John L., and Barbara Hammond. **Lord Shaftesbury.** 4th ed., London, 1936.

VA618. Walpole, Spencer. **The life of Lord John Russell.** 2 v. London, 1889.

VA619. Hobson, John A. **Richard Cobden, the international man.** London, 1919.

VA620. Trevelyan, George M. **The life of John Bright.** London, 1913.

VA621. Finer, Samuel E. **The life and times of Sir Edwin Chadwick.** London, 1952.

VA622. Darwin, E. Francis, ed. **The life and letters of Charles Darwin.** 2 v. London, 1887.

VA623. Wells, Geoffrey H. (pseud. Geoffrey West). **Charles Darwin, a portrait.** New Haven, 1938.

Victorian and Edwardian England, 1870–1914

VA624. O'Brien, Richard B. **The life of Charles Stuart Parnell.** See *VA296*.

VA625. Churchill, Winston S. **Lord Randolph Churchill.** Rev. ed., London, 1951.

VA626. Cecil, Lady Gwendolen. **Life of Robert, marquis of Salisbury.** 4 v. London, 1921–32.

VA627. Morley, John (Viscount Morley). **Recollections.** 2 v. N.Y., 1917.

VA628. Dugdale, Blanche E. C. **Arthur James Balfour.** 2 v. N.Y., 1937.

VA629. Lee, Sir Sidney. **King Edward VII.** 2 v. N.Y., 1925–27.

VA630. Crewe-Milnes, Robert O. A., marquess of Crewe. **Lord Rosebery.** N.Y., 1931.

VA631. Spender, John A. **The life of the Right Hon. Sir Henry Campbell-Bannerman.** 2 v. London, 1923.

VA632. Oxford and Asquith, Herbert Henry, earl of. **Fifty years of Parliament.** London, 1926.

VA633. ———. **Memories and reflections, 1852–1927.** 2 v. Boston, 1928.

VA634. Spender, John A., and Cyril Asquith. **Life of Herbert Henry Asquith, Lord Oxford and Asquith.** 2 v. London, 1932.

VA635. Stewart, William. **J. Keir Hardie.** London, 1921.

VA636. Grubb, Arthur P. **From candle factory to British cabinet: the life story of the Right Honourable John Burns.** London, 1908.

VA637. Mann, Tom. **Tom Mann's memoirs.** London, 1923.

VA638. Jones, Thomas. **Lloyd George.** Cambridge, Mass., 1951.

VA639. Trevelyan, George M. **Grey of Fallodon.** Boston, 1937.

VA640. Maurice, Sir Frederick B. **The life of Viscount Haldane of Cloan.** 2 v. London, 1937–39.

VA641. Snowden, Philip (Viscount Snowden). **An autobiography.** 2 v. London, 1934–35.

Twentieth Century since 1914

VA642. Lloyd George, David. **War memoirs.** 6 v. London and Boston, 1933–37.

VA643. Blake, Robert. **The unknown prime minister: the life and times of Andrew Bonar Law, 1858–1923.** London, 1955.

VA644. Duff Cooper, Alfred. **Haig.** 2 v. London, 1935.

VA645. Baldwin, Arthur W. **My father: the true story.** London, 1955.

VA646. Young, George M. **Stanley Baldwin.** London, 1952.

VA647. Driberg, Tom. **Beaverbrook: a study in power and frustration.** London, 1956.

VA648. Feiling, Keith G. **The life of Neville Chamberlain.** See *AF310*.

VA649. Gore, John. **King George V, a personal memoir.** London, 1941.

VA650. Cole, Margaret, ed. **The Webbs and their work.** London, 1949.

VA651. Broad, Lewis. **Winston Churchill, architect of victory and peace.** Rev. ed., London, 1956.

VA652. Williams, Francis. **Ernest Bevin: portrait of a great Englishman.** London, 1952.

VA653. Amery, Leopold S. **My political life.** V. 1–3. London, 1953–55.

VA654. Dalton, Hugh. **Call back yesterday.** London, 1953.

VA655. Attlee, Clement R. **As it happened.** London, 1954.

VA656. Broad, Lewis. **Sir Anthony Eden: the chronicles of a career.** London, 1955.

GOVERNMENT PUBLICATIONS

For complete current information on all British government publications see the monthly and annual cumulative lists of publications available from H. M. Stationery Office. The sole agent in the United States is the British Library of Information, 30 Rockefeller Plaza, New York 20, N.Y., from whom current cumulative lists may be obtained.

Guides

VA657. Great Britain. Public Record Office. **Guide to the public records. Pt. 1, Introductory.** New ed., London, 1949.

VA658. Galbraith, Vivian H. **Introduction to the use of the public records.** 3rd ed., London, 1952. Helpful handbook by a historical scholar.

VA659. Great Britain. Public Record Office. **Report of the deputy keeper of the public records.** London, 1840 ff. (Annual.)

VA660. Somerville, Robert. **Handlist of record publications.** London, 1951. [British Records Association pamphlet, 3.]

VA661. Lewis, Idwal, A. P. Kup, and Peter Goldesborough, eds. **Handlist of Scottish and Welsh record publications.** London, 1954. [British Records Association pamphlet, 4.]

VA662. Hall, Hubert, ed. **A repertory of British archives. Pt. 1, England.** London, 1920.

VA663. Giuseppi, Montague S. **A guide to the manuscripts preserved in the Public Record Office.** 2 v. London, 1923–24. Now somewhat dated, but still extremely useful.

VA664. Great Britain. Royal Commission on Public Records. **Report of the Royal Commission on Public Records appointed to inquire into and report on the state of the public records and local records of a public nature of England and Wales.** 3 v. London, 1912–19. Official survey.

Official Printed Sources

State Papers

VA665. Great Britain. Public Record Office. **Calendar of state papers.** London, 1856 ff. Covers the charter, patent, and close rolls as well as domestic, foreign, and colonial affairs.

Parliament

VA666. Parliamentary or constitutional history of England. 1066–1660. 24 v. London, 1751–61. More commonly known as *The old parliamentary history.*

VA667. Parliamentary history of England from the Norman conquest in 1066 to the year 1803. Ed. by William Cobbett. 36 v. London, 1806–20. A continuation of *VA666* which does not entirely supersede it.

VA668. Hansard, Thomas C. **The parliamentary debates.** London, 1804 ff. Five series with indices. A continuation of *VA667*, which covers the day to day proceedings of Parliament. More commonly known, after the name of the original printer, as *Hansard's debates.* Invaluable.

VA669. Great Britain. House of Lords. **Journals of the House of Lords, 1509 to date.** London, 1767 ff. Contains records of business, lists of votes, and petitions, but after 1628 no record of debates.

VA670. Great Britain. House of Commons. **Journals of the House of Commons, 1547 to date.** London, 1742 ff. Contains the same materials as the Lords' journals.

VA671. Parliamentary papers: a general index to the sessional papers printed by order of the House of Lords or presented by special command (1801–1885). 3 v. London, 1860–86. Reprints and catalogues of or guides to the important parliamentary sessional papers known as the parliamentary blue books.

VA672. Parliamentary papers. Reports from the committees of the House of Commons . . . not inserted in the journals. 1715–1801. 16 v. London, 1803–06.

VA673. General alphabetical index to the bills, reports, estimates, accounts, and papers printed by the House of Commons and to the papers presented by command. 1801–1929. 7 v. London, 1853–1931.

VA674. Ford, Grace, and Percy Ford, eds. **Guide to parliamentary papers.** 2nd ed., Oxford, 1956.

VA675. ——, eds. **Hansard's catalogue and breviate of parliamentary papers, 1696–1834.** Oxford, 1953.

VA676. ——, eds. **Select list of parliamentary papers, 1833–1899.** Oxford, 1953.

VA677. ——, eds. **A breviate of parliamentary papers, 1917–1939.** Oxford, 1951.

Statutes

VA678. The statutes at large, from Magna Charta to the end of the last parliament of Great Britain, held in the 41st year of the reign of King George III, 1800. Ed. by Owen Ruffhead. New ed., rev. and continued by Charles Runnington, 14 v., London, 1786–1800.

VA679. Tomlins, Thomas E., and others, eds. **The statutes at large of the United Kingdom of Great Britain and Ireland.** 29 v. London, 1804–69. (Title varies.) Continues *VA678.* Covers period 1801–65.

VA680. Public general statutes. London, 1832–67. This and *VA681* continue the statutes to the present time.

VA681. Public general acts of the United Kingdom of Great Britain and Ireland. London, 1887 ff.

State Trials

VA682. A complete collection of state trials. 1163–1820. Ed. by William Cobbett, Thomas B. Howell, and Thomas J. Howell. 34 v. London, 1809–28.

VA683. State Trials Committee. **State trials, new series.** London, 1888 ff. A continuation of *VA682*.

Foreign Policy and Affairs

VA684. Rymer, Thomas, and Robert Sanderson, eds. **Foedera conventiones, literae, et cujuscunque generis acta publica.** 1101–1713. 20 v. London, 1704–35. There are several editions of this work for which the best guide is Sir Thomas D. Hardy, *Syllabus of documents in Rymer's Foedera* (3 v., London, 1869–85).

VA685. British and foreign state papers. 1812/14 ff. London, 1841 ff.

VA686. Hertslet, Lewis, Sir Edward Hertslet, and others, eds. **A complete collection of the treaties, conventions, and reciprocal regulations at present subsisting between Great Britain and foreign powers.** 19 v. London, 1827–95.

VA687. Gooch, George P., and Harold W. V. Temperley, eds. **British documents on the origins of the war, 1898–1914.** 11 v. London, 1926–38.

VA688. Woodward, Ernest L., and Rohan Butler, eds. **Documents on British foreign policy, 1919–1939.** See *AH119*.

Private Papers

VA689. Great Britain. Historical Manuscripts Commission. **Reports.** London, 1870 ff. Contains lists and summaries of important manuscript collections in private hands. There is also available for consultation at various branches of the Public Record Office and in the copyright libraries of Great Britain a selection of calendars and duplicate lists of local, family, and business records prepared by the National Register of Archives. In addition, the National Register publishes an annual bulletin containing lists of MMS. acquisitions to local and national repositories.

UNIVERSITY, ACADEMY, AND SOCIETY PUBLICATIONS

For detailed information on the publications of various local societies and academies see the bibliographical aids listed under appropriate sections. The following are the most important publications of general historical interest produced by societies and other learned bodies in Great Britain.

VA690. Camden Society. **Publications.** London, 1838 ff. An important series of published chronicles, documents, and letters.

Since 1897 carried on under sponsorship of the Royal Historical Society.

VA691. Hakluyt Society. **Publications.** London, 1846 ff. Primarily concerned with the publication of travel diaries, journals, and logs of navigation.

VA692. Navy Records Society. **Publications.** London, 1894 ff. Indispensable body of source materials pertaining to the history of the royal navy.

VA693. Royal Historical Society. **Transactions.** 1869 ff. London, 1872 ff. (Annual.) Contains specialized scholarly articles and edited documents. For index see Hubert Hall, *List and index of the Royal Historical Society, 1871–1924, and of the Camden Society, 1840–1897* (London, 1925).

VA694. Scottish History Society. **Publications.** Edinburgh, 1887 ff. Important collection of printed sources for the study of Scottish and British history in general.

VA695. Selden Society. **Publications.** London, 1888 ff. Source materials for the study of English legal history.

VA696. The Royal Society. **Transactions.** London, 1665 ff. (Annual.) Valuable for the history of English science.

PERIODICALS

The list below contains the titles of British periodicals useful to the history student. It should be remembered, however, that many foreign journals regularly publish articles and papers pertaining to British history.

VA697. Cambridge historical journal. 1923 ff. Cambridge, Eng., 1925 ff. (Annual.)

VA698. Church quarterly review. 1875 ff. London, 1876 ff. Index of articles, v. 1–59 (Oct. 1875–Jan. 1905), London, 1906.

VA699. The economic history review. London, 1927 ff. (3 nos. per year.)

VA700. The economic journal. London, 1891 ff. (Quarterly.) Published by the Royal Economic Society.

VA701. Economica. London, 1921 ff. (Quarterly.) Index to v. 1–7 (1921–27), London, 1928. Published by the London School of Economics and Political Science.

VA702. The English historical review. London, 1886 ff. (Quarterly.) Index, 4 v., London, 1906–38.

VA703. History. London, 1912 ff. (Quarterly.)

VA704. History today. London, 1951 ff. (Monthly.)

VA705. Bulletin of the Institute of Historical Research. London, 1923 ff. (Frequency varies.)

VA706. The journal of ecclesiastical history. London, 1950 ff. (Semiannual.)

VA707. Journal of the Royal Statistical Society. London, 1839 ff. (Annual.)

VA708. Notes and queries. 1849 ff. London and High Wycombe, 1850 ff. (Weekly.)

VA709. Quarterly review. London, 1809 ff. General indexes contained in v. 20, 40, 60, 80, 100, 121, 140, 160, 181, 201, 222, and 243.

Supplement

VA710. Lee, Maurice. **John Maitland of Thirlestane and the foundation of the Stewart despotism in Scotland.** Princeton, 1959.

VA711. Pressnell, L. S. **Country banking in the industrial revolution.** Oxford, 1956.

VA712. Edwards, R. Dudley, and T. Desmond Williams, eds. **The great famine: studies in Irish history, 1845–1852.** New York, 1957. An important study.

VA713. Gragg, Gerald R. **Puritanism in the period of the great persecution, 1660–1688.** Cambridge, Eng., 1957

VA714. Tawney, Richard H. **Business and politics under James I. Lionel Cranfield as merchant and minister.** Cambridge, Eng., 1958.

VA715. Eden, Sir Anthony. **Full circle.** London, 1960.

Scandinavia and the Baltic States

FRANKLIN D. SCOTT *

THE SCANDINAVIAN COUNTRIES

Despite a high degree of cooperation within Scandinavia, the historical litera-ture is fundamentally national in origin and outlook. Language alone would make this natural, for there are only the national languages—no "Scandinavian." Reviews and books that attempt a supra-national approach are usually the work of several authors and utilize a variety of languages (often English, German, or French). Outsiders emphasize the unity of the area more than do natives, though no one denies the profound cultural relationships of the five countries, Denmark, Finland, Iceland, Norway, and Sweden. As for the Baltic lands, known in the mid-20th century as Estonia, Latvia, and Lithuania, their history is intertwined with that of Scandinavia in many respects, yet is essentially a different story, so forms here a separate section.

The standard type of reference books, such as annual lists of books published, statistical yearbooks, "Who's who," general staff maps, etc., these countries have in abundance. For reasons of space these items are not mentioned here, but can be located easily through Winchell's *Guide to reference books (B1)*.

BIBLIOGRAPHIES

VB1. Lindberg, Folke A., and John I. Kolehmainen. **The Scandinavian countries in international affairs: a selected bibliography on the foreign affairs of Denmark, Finland, Norway, and Sweden, 1800–1952.** Minne-apolis, 1953. See comment under *VB2*.

VB2. Sandler, Åke, and Ernst Ekman. **Government, politics, and law in the Scandi-navian countries: a selected, critical bibliog-**raphy. Minneapolis, 1954. This and the above pamphlet bibliographies are excellent within their subject limits, and emphasize material available in English.

VB3. Erichsen, Balder V. A., and Alfred Krarup. **Dansk historisk bibliografi: systema-tisk fortegnelse over bidrag til Danmarks historie til udgangen af 1912.** 3 v. Copen-hagen, 1918–27. Reprint, 1929. After this historical bibliography up to the year 1912, Krarup continued with annual bibliographies

* The following contributed items and comments indicated by their respective initials: Edgar Anderson (EA), Stig Boberg (SB), Poul Enemark (PE), J. William Frederickson (JWF), Uldis Germanis (UG), Lennart Kjellberg (LK), Halvdan Koht (HK), Arvi Korhonen (AK), Folke Lindberg (FL), Wilhelm Odelberg (WO), Nils William Olsson (NWO), Jens Arup Seip (JAS), Leslie F. Smith (LFS), Arnold Soom (AS).

in connection with *Historisk tidsskrift* until 1945, for writings through 1940. Plans call for a separate bibliography for the years 1913–42, and for five-year bibliographies thereafter. The first of these, for 1943–47, is *VB4*.

VB4. Bruun, Henry. **Dansk historisk bibliografi, 1943–47.** Copenhagen, 1956. Continuation of Erichsen and Krarup.

VB5. Fortegnelse over historisk litteratur vedrørende Danmarks historie. Copenhagen. Part of *Historisk tidsskrift* until 1915; sections published as a special volume 1916–22; thereafter unconnected with the regular issue of *Historisk tidsskrift*, though still compiled under the auspices of Den Danske Historisk Forening, up to 1943.

VB6. Dania polyglotta: répertoire bibliographique des ouvrages, études, articles, etc. en langues étrangères parus en Danemark de 1901 à 1944. Ed. by Kay Schmidt-Phiseldeck. 3 v. Copenhagen, 1947–51. Annual supplements. Divided according to language, and systematically organized. [PE]

VB7. Fink, Troels, and Johan Hvidtfeldt. **Vejledning i studiet af Sønderjyllands historie.** Tønder, 1944. [Skrifter, udg. af Historisk samfund for Sønderjylland, 5.] Annotated guide in careful, systematic order, with references to both printed and archival material on South Jutland. [PE]

VB8. Bay, J. Christian. **Denmark in English and American literature: a bibliography.** Chicago, 1915. About 1,400 titles of books and articles on Denmark's history, literature, and society. [PE]

VB9. Mitchell, Phillip M. **A bibliographical guide to Danish literature.** Copenhagen, 1951. Danish literary bibliography written in English. [PE]

VB10. Bruun, Christian W. **Bibliotheca danica: systematisk fortegnelse over den danske literatur fra 1482 til 1830.** Register and supplement by Lauritz Nielsen, and supplement 1831–40 by Holger Ehrencron-Müller. 6 v. Copenhagen, 1877–1948. A general bibliography, used as foundation by compilers of *VB3*.

VB11. Maliniemi, Aarno, and Ella Kivikoski. **Suomen historiallinen bibliografia, 1901–1925.** 2 v. in 1. Helsinki, 1940. This and *VB12* are the standard historical bibliographies. Russian publications are included.

VB12. Vallinkoski, J., and Henrik Schauman. **Suomen historiallinen bibliografia, 1926–1950.** 2 v. Helsinki, 1955–56.

VB13. Neuvonen, Eero K. **A short bibliography on Finland.** Turku, 1955. [Publications of Turku University Library, 7.] Lists publications in six languages, not including Finnish or Swedish; 38 pages, about four on history.

VB14. Kiel. Universität. **Islandkatalog der Universitätsbibliothek Kiel und der Universitäts- und stadtbibliothek Köln.** Comp. by Olaf Klose. Kiel, 1931. About 7,000 titles of Icelandic books and books about Iceland; 25 pages on history.

VB15. Catalogue of the Icelandic collection bequeathed by Willard Fiske. Comp. by Halldór Hermannsson. Ithaca, N.Y., 1914. Supplement for additions 1913–26, Ithaca, 1927. One of the largest special collections of Icelandic literature, held by Cornell University. Valuable comments. [PE]

VB16. Islandica. Ithaca, 1908 ff. (Annual.) This series contains bibliographies of Icelandic literature compiled by Halldór Hermannsson. [PE]

VB17. Tveterås, Harald L., Finn Erichsen, and Gunnar C. Wassberg. **Bibliografi til Norges historie, 1936–45.** Oslo, 1939–52. Collection of the annual bibliographies appearing with the (Norwegian) *Historisk tidsskrift*. A thorough historical bibliography for Norway, oddly lacking to date, is now in the planning stage.

VB18. Warmholtz, Carl G., and others. **Bibliotheca historica sueo-gothica.** 15 v. Stockholm and Uppsala, 1782–1817. Index, Uppsala, 1889. First major historical bibliography for Sweden. Richly annotated and broad in scope.

VB19. Setterwall, Kristian. **Svensk historisk bibliografi.** V. 1, 1771–1874, Uppsala, 1937; v. 2, 1875–1900, Stockholm, 1907; v. 3, 1901–1920, Uppsala, 1923. Thorough listing without annotations. Includes reviews.

VB20. Sjögren, Paul. **Svensk historisk bibliografi, 1921–35.** Uppsala, 1956. Continuation of Setterwall. For period after 1935 one must use for the present the annual compilations by Percy Elfstrand, coming with *Historisk tidskrift*. The thoroughness of Sweden's historical bibliographies is complemented by an annual index of journals (*Svensk tidskriftsindex,* Lund, 1952 ff.) and another of newspapers (*Svensk tidningsindex,* Lund, 1953 ff.), not to mention the many special subject bibliographies.

VB21. Bring, Samuel E. **Bibliografisk handbok till Sveriges historia.** Stockholm, 1934. Reprint, 1945. Well selected and concisely annotated, but goes only to 1934.

VB22. ——. **Itineraria Svecana: bibliografisk förteckning över resor i Sverige fram till 1950.** Stockholm, 1954. [Svenska bibliotekarie-samfundets skriftserie, 3.] Exhaustive listing of native and foreign writings on travel in Sweden from Egil Skallagrimsson in 944 to some 25 accounts in 1950.

VB23. Stille, Åke. **Principales publications historiques parues en Suède, 1939–1945.** Stockholm, 1951.

VB24. Ander, O. Fritiof. **The cultural heritage of the Swedish emigrant.** Rock Island, Ill., 1956. Opens up a vast literature on several important aspects of the migration process.

ENCYCLOPEDIAS AND WORKS OF REFERENCE

VB25. Bagge, Povl, and others, eds. **Excerpta historica nordica.** Copenhagen, 1955 ff. Begun under auspices of International Committee of Historical Sciences. Goal is one volume each third year. Excerpts or summaries of the most important current writings are usually prepared by the authors themselves. Editing is in English, but articles may also be in French or German. For all Scandinavia. [WO]

VB26. Ehrencron-Müller, Holger. **Forfatterlexikon omfattende Danmark, Norge og Island indtil 1814.** 12 v. and supplement. Copenhagen, 1924–39. Wide coverage, with short biography of each author, and bibliographies of works by and about him. [PE]

VB27. Erslew, Thomas H. **Almindeligt forfatter-lexikon for kongeriget Danmark med tilhørende bilande fra 1814 til 1840.** 3 v. and 3 v. supplement. Copenhagen, 1843–68. Includes only authors who lived in 1814 or later. Exhaustive biographical and bibliographical information. [PE]

VB28. Dansk biografisk leksikon. Ed. by Povl Engelstoft and others. 27 v. Copenhagen, 1933–44. A much used and useful reference work. [PE]

VB29. Dansk biografisk haandleksikon. Ed. by Svend Dahl and Povl Engelstoft. 3 v. Copenhagen, 1920–26. Contains about 6,000 biographies from 19th and 20th centuries. [PE]

VB30. Johnsen, Oscar A. **Innføring i kildense til Norges historie.** Oslo, 1939. A good introduction to the sources by one of Norway's most prolific historians. [LFS]

VB31. Norsk biografisk leksikon. Ed. by Edvard Bull and others. Christiania (Oslo), 1921 ff. Incomplete but valuable. Reached "Sk" in 1958.

VB32. Andersson, Ingvar. **Archives in Sweden.** Stockholm, 1954. [Reprint from *Libraries and archives in Sweden* (1954), issued through the Swedish Institute.] A thorough and authoritative survey in 38 pages.

VB33. Heilborn, Adèle, ed. **Travel, study, and research in Sweden.** Stockholm, 1957, rev. ed., 1959. A unique compendium of information including addresses of libraries, archives, and institutes. Useful for all scholars.

VB34. Svenska män och kvinnor. Ed. by Nils Bohman and others. 8 v. Stockholm, 1942–55. Much briefer than *VB36*, but dependable and complete.

VB35. Ågren, Sven. **Svensk biografisk uppslagslitteratur.** Uppsala, 1929. A bibliographical guide to all Swedish biographical lexica and dictionaries. Also contains to a lesser degree works dealing with Swedish

immigrants to the United States, and Swedes in Finland before 1809. [NWO]

VB36. Svenskt biografiskt lexikon. Ed. by Bertil Boëthius and Bengt Hildebrand. Stockholm, 1918 ff. An ambitious, scholarly project, the 20th century equivalent (but larger and better) of two 19th century publications, *Biographiskt lexikon öfwer namnkunnige svenska män* (23 v. in 12, Stockholm and Uppsala, 1835–57), and *Svenskt biografiskt lexikon, ny följd* (10 v., Örebro and Stockholm, 1857–1907). Chief drawback is that in 1957, with 15 v., the work had reached only to names beginning with "Fe." Living people are no longer included. [NWO]

GEOGRAPHIES, GAZETTEERS, AND ATLASES

VB37. Trap, Jens P. **Danmark.** 4th ed., 10 v. and register, Copenhagen, 1920–30. Widely used topographic reference work. Basic bibliographical supplements in the now-in-progress 5th edition (1953 ff.). [PE]

VB38. Kalaja, Pentti, and Erkki Kanervo. **Suomi: a general handbook on the geography of Finland.** Helsinki, 1952. [Fennia series of the Geographical Society of Finland, 72.] English version of a standard Finnish publication. Broad, with good chapters on early cultural history. [JWF]

VB39. Jutikkala, Eino, ed. **Suomen historiallinen kartasto. Atlas of Finnish history.** Porvoo, 1949.

VB40. Sjögren, Otto, ed. **Sverige: geografisk beskrivning.** 5 v. Stockholm, 1929–35. Most thorough geographic description, with many small maps and illustrations.

DEMOGRAPHIC STUDIES

VB41. Social Denmark: a survey of the Danish social legislation. Ed. by Socialt Tidsskrift. 2nd ed., Copenhagen, 1947. A brief overview in English. See also Nelson, *Freedom and welfare (VB104).*

VB42. Seip, Didrik A. **Norsk språkhistorie til omkring 1370.** Oslo, 1931. 2nd ed., 1955. This pioneering examination of the development of the Norwegian language was succeeded by a series of additional studies.

VB43. Thomas, Dorothy S. **Social and economic aspects of Swedish population movements, 1750–1933.** N.Y., 1941. A suggestive survey.

PRINTED COLLECTIONS OF SOURCES *

VB44. Denmark. Rigsarkiv. **Aarsberetninger fra det Kongelige Geheimearchiv.** Ed.

* Includes government publications.

by Caspar F. Wegener. 7 v. in 6. Copenhagen, 1852–83. Important source materials for both Middle Ages and modern times. More systematic publication began with founding of Selskabet for Udgivelse af Kilder til Dansk Historie in 1877. Large series of sources have been published by Rigsarkiv since 1885. [PE]

VB45. Bang, Nina E., and Knud Korst. **Tabeller over skibsfart og varetransport gennem Øresund.** 7 v. Copenhagen, 1906–53. [Pt. 1, 1497–1660; pt. 2, 1661–1783.] Statistics on the famous Sound Dues. The second part was published with major international support obtained through the initiative of Prof. Dietrich Schäfer. Text is in Danish and French. [PE]

VB46. Denmark. Rigsdagen. **Rigsdagstidende.** 1850–1953. 104 v. Copenhagen, 1850–1953. After 1953, **Folketingstidenda.** Discussions in the folketing and landsting. In Appendix A, proposed bills; B, committee reports; and C, laws approved. Summary and subject register. [PE]

VB47. Danmark-Norges traktater, 1523–1750. 11 v. Copenhagen, 1907–49. Denmark's treaties.

VB48. Publications of Norsk Historisk Kjeldeskrift-Institutt. 59 v. Christiania (Oslo), 1858 ff. Variety of source materials on the whole of Norway's history. Includes such important items as *Norske herredags dombøger 1578–1664* (30 v.), *Norske regnskaber og jordebøger fra det 16 de aarhundrede* (4 v., 1885–1906), *Norske magazin* (3 v., 1858–70), and *VB49.*

VB49. Knaplund, Paul A., ed. **British views on Norwegian-Swedish problems 1880–1895: selections from diplomatic correspondence.** Oslo, 1952. Significant source material published in the original English.

VB50. Norway. Stortinget. **Stortingsforhandlinger.** Christiania (Oslo), 1814 ff. Petitions, bills, and other documents. After 1887 this includes the stenographic reports which since 1857 had been published as *Stortingstidende.* This should be complemented for the earlier half of the century by *Stortingsefterretninger* (Christiania, 1814–54).

VB51. Sweden. Treaties. **Sverges traktater med främmande magter.** Ed. by Olof S. Rydberg. 16 v. Stockholm, 1877–1934. (Title varies.) Swedish treaties from 822 to 1905.

VB52. Handlingar rörande Skandinaviens historia. 40 v. and register. Stockholm, 1816–65.

VB53. Historiska handlingar. Stockholm, 1861 ff. A continuation of *VB52.* These continuing publications make available a wide variety of source materials.

VB54. Sundbärg, A. Gustav, ed. **Emigrationsutredningen.** 21 v. Stockholm, 1908–13. An exhaustive social survey authorized by the government because of concern over emigration. Fascinating source material.

HISTORIOGRAPHY

VB55. Bull, Edvard. "Norvège." **Histoire et historiens depuis cinquante ans, 1876 à 1926,** v. 1 (Paris, 1927), pp. 233–57.

VB56. Mustelin, Olof. **Studier i finländsk historieforskning 1809–1865.** Helsinki, 1957.

VB57. Dahl, Ottar. **Historisk materialisme: historie oppfatningen hos Edvard Bull og Halvdan Koht.** Oslo, 1952. Brief, clear insight into the philosophy of two leading Norwegian historians.

VB58. ——. **Om årsaksproblemer i historisk forskning: forsök på en vitenskapshistorisk analyse.** Oslo, 1956.

VB59. Hatton, Ragnhild. "Some notes on Swedish historiography." **History,** 37 (June 1952): 97–113. Insight into problems of history writing, and survey of a century of publication. Also an account of history teaching in Swedish universities.

VB60. Koht, Halvdan. **Education of an historian.** Tr. by Erik Wahlgren. N.Y., 1957. Unpretentious, straightforward educational autobiography of one of Norway's ablest and most productive historians.

VB61. Norsk Historisk Forening. **Norsk historisk videnskap i femti år 1869–1919.** Christiania (Oslo), 1920.

VB62. Westin, Gunnar T. **Historieskrivaren Olaus Petri: svenska krönikans källor och krönikeförfattarens metod.** Lund, 1946. Dissertation on the sources and historical method of Sweden's great chronicler.

GENERAL HISTORIES

VB63. Royal Institute of International Affairs. **The Scandinavian states and Finland: a political and economic survey.** London, 1951. A country-by-country survey.

VB64. Kenney, Rowland. **The northern tangle: Scandinavia and the post-war world.** London, 1946. Considerable historical background from a 20th century perspective.

VB65. Scott, Franklin D. **The United States and Scandinavia.** See *AF136.*

HISTORIES OF SPECIAL PERIODS

VB66. Hovde, Brynjolf J. **The Scandinavian countries, 1720–1865.** 2 v. Boston, 1943. Reprint, Ithaca, 1948. Though the time span is limited, this is one of the best and most extensive of the studies treating Scandinavia as a whole. Socio-economic emphasis.

VB67. Allen, Carl F. **De tre nordiske rigers historie, 1497–1536.** 5 v. Copenhagen, 1864–72. From a national, liberal point of view, packed with information of a many-sided nature. Most significant Danish work on the period of the "Union of Kalmar." [PE]

VB68. Holm, Peter Edvard. **Danmark-Norges historie fra den store nordiske krigs slutning til rigernes adskillelse, 1720–1814.**

7 v. Copenhagen, 1891–1912. Chief work on this period, with emphasis on administrative and diplomatic-military history. Concluding volume on internal affairs was not completed. [PE]

VB69. Neergaard, Niels T. **Danmark under Junigrundloven.** 2 v. in 3. Copenhagen, 1892–1916. Rests on rich archival material and intimate acquaintance with leading politicians in a period (1848–66) when relations with countries abroad played an overshadowing role in Denmark's political life. [PE]

VB70. Danielson-Kalmari, Johan R. **Suomen valtio-ja yhteiskuntaelämää 18:nnella ja 19:nnella vuosisadalla.** 11 v. Porvoo, 1920–35. Studies in Finnish political and social development in the century following 1720. [AK]

VB71. Osmansalo, Erkki K. **Suomen valloitus 1808.** Helsinki, 1947. An illuminating study of European diplomacy, showing how Alexander I reached a decision to conquer Finland and grant autonomous status. [AK]

VB72. Donner, Kai, and. **Suomen vapaussota.** 8 v. Jyväskylä, 1921–27. The stages in Finland's struggle for independence, compiled from accounts of political leaders and soldiers. [AK]

VB73. Johnsen, Oscar A. **De norske staender.** Christiania (Oslo), 1906. On the period of the Norwegian estates, 1537–1660. [LFS]

VB74. Worm-Müller, Jacob S. **Norge gjennom nödsårene: den norske regjeringskommission 1807–1810.** Christiania (Oslo), 1918. Valuable study of the last years under Danish rule.

VB75. Steen, Sverre. **Det frie Norge.** 4 v. Oslo, 1951–57. [1, *1814;* 2, *På fallittens rand;* 3, *Krise og avspenning;* 4, *Det gamle samfund.*] Unusually well written and based on sources. First three volumes are political history, 1814–24, and the fourth depicts economic and social developments from 1812 to 1840.

VB76. Roberts, Michael. **Gustavus Adolphus: a history of Sweden, 1611–1632.** V. 1 (1611–26), V. 2 (1626–1632), London, 1953, 1959. Well written and based on thorough research in monographic literature. A history of the times more than of the man.

VB77. Malmström, Carl G. **Sveriges politiska historia från konung Karl XII's död till statshvälfningen 1772.** 6 v. Stockholm, 1855–77. Rev. ed., 1893–1901. A classic political history of the 18th century, not yet superseded. [FL]

HISTORIES OF SPECIAL AREAS

Denmark

VB78. Hvidtfeldt, Johan, and others. **Danmarks historie.** 2 v. in 1. Copenhagen,

1951. Thirteen younger Danish historians survey the past with emphasis on social and cultural history rather than on political "facts." [PE]

VB79. Birch, John H. S. **Denmark in history.** London, 1938. This and *VB80* are brief and easily read surveys in English. [PE]

VB80. Danstrup, John. **A history of Denmark.** Copenhagen, 1948.

VB81. Dahlmann, Friedrich C., and Dietrich Schäfer. **Geschichte von Dänemark.** 5 v. Hamburg, 1840–1902. From a German point of view. Schäfer's volumes (4 and 5) on the period 1523–1648 are of continuing value. [PE]

VB82. Steenstrup, Johannes, and others. **Danmarks riges historie.** 8 v. in 6. Copenhagen, 1896–1907. A pioneering work in its time, by the scholar who broke the path for modern historical research in Denmark. [PE]

VB83. Arup, Erik. **Danmarks historie.** 3 v. Copenhagen, 1925–55. Significant for the new problems it raises and for its social and economic point of view, as well as for its reaction against over-nationalistic writing. [PE]

VB84. Friis, Aage, and others. **Schultz Danmarkshistorie.** 6 v. Copenhagen, 1941–43. New edition of a standard work, and still most used of all the handbooks. [PE]

VB85. La Cour, Vilhelm, and others. **Sønderjyllands historie.** 5 v. Copenhagen, 1930–43. Large, basic work by experts dealing with South Jutland's history, including her complicated relations with Denmark. [PE]

VB86. Steefel, Lawrence D. **The Schleswig-Holstein question.** Cambridge, Mass., 1932. The best study in English on this complex problem.

Finland

VB87. Jackson, John Hampden. **Finland.** London, 1938; N.Y., 1940. Brief and general, but probably the best treatment available in English.

VB88. Yrjö-Koskinen, Georg Z. **Suomen kansan historia.** 3rd ed., Helsinki, 1933. Standard account of Finnish history by one of the country's great historians. [JWF]

VB89. Korhonen, Arvi H., ed. **Suomen historian käsikirja.** 2 v. Porvoo, 1949. Collaborative general history from antiquity to 1944. Bibliography. [AK]

VB90. Hornborg, Eirik M. **Finlands hävder.** 4 v. Helsinki, 1929–33. Good general survey in Swedish language. The same author has a later and briefer treatment, *Finlands historia från äldsta tid til våra dagar* (Malmö, 1948).

Iceland

VB91. Gjerset, Knut. **History of Iceland.** N.Y. and London, 1924. Accessible survey of social, economic, and political developments from the 10th century to the 20th.

Norway

VB92. Larsen, Karen. **A history of Norway.** Princeton, 1948. First volume in a new series sponsored by the American Scandinavian Foundation. Highly recommended.

VB93. Holmsen, Andreas, and Magnus Jensen. **Norges historia.** 2 v. Oslo, 1938–39. Holmsen's first volume is the more valuable, but comes only to 1660. Strong on the farming community (*bygd*), but thin on politics. [LFS]

VB94. Bull, Edvard, Wilhelm Keilhau, and others. **Det norske folks liv og historie gjennem tidene.** 10 v. and supplement. Oslo, 1929–38. Excellent cooperative series, supplementing earlier 6 v. work. Tends to emphasize social and economic history. Keilhau wrote not only the volumes for 1814–1920, but also the supplement on "Our own times." [LFS]

VB95. Sars, Johan E. W. **Udsigt over den norske historie.** 4 v. Christiania (Oslo), 1873–91. Influential interpretative treatment, opposing both the romanticism of his predecessors and the economic emphasis of his contemporaries. Much on the Middle Ages; ends with 1814. See also *VB96.* [LFS]

VB96. Bugge, Alexander, and others. **Norges historie: fremstillet for det norske folk.** 6 v. in 12. Christiania (Oslo), 1909–17. Important cooperative work. Perhaps the most significant volumes are 5 and 6 wherein Sars vigorously propounds his view of the 19th century, especially regarding the union with Sweden. [LFS]

Sweden

VB97. Andersson, Ingvar. **A history of Sweden.** London, 1956. This is the English version of a book translated into many languages. Excellent treatment. For bibliography see rev. ed., 1960, in Swedish.

VB98. Hildebrand, Emil, and Ludvig Stavenow, eds. **Sveriges historia till våra dagar.** 15 v. Stockholm, 1919–45. The standard scholarly political history. V. 15 reprints Bring's bibliography (*VB21*).

VB99. Maiander, Harry, ed. **Sveriges historia genom tiderna.** 5 v. Stockholm, 1947–48. Good scholarship popularly presented. [FL]

HISTORIES OF SPECIAL TOPICS

VB100. Andgren, Sigfrid F., and Arne Bergsgård. "Den svensk-norska unionen

1814–1905." **Omstridda spörsmål i Nordens historia,** v. 2 (Helsinki, 1950). This and other studies in the same volume give an example of how Scandinavian historians are attempting to discover the common ground of truth concerning old conflicts.

VB101. Møller, Erik. **Skandinavisk strae-ben og svensk politik omkring 1860.** Copenhagen, 1948. A chapter from a vital period in the struggle for Scandinavian unity.

VB102. Lindgren, Raymond E. **Norway-Sweden: union, disunion, and Scandinavian integration.** Princeton, 1959. Workings of the union of 1814, its disruption, and the subsequent development of cooperation in the North.

VB103. Koch, Hans H., and Alf Ross, eds. **Nordisk demokrati.** Copenhagen, 1949. Good introduction to democratic ideas and methods in Scandinavia as a whole.

VB104. Nelson, George R., ed. **Freedom and welfare: social patterns in the northern countries of Europe.** Copenhagen, 1953. Emphasis on current status, but there is some historical view as well.

Denmark

VB105. Petersen, Carl S., and Vilhelm R. Andersen. **Illustreret dansk litteraturhistorie.** 4 v. Copenhagen, 1924–34. Danish literary history to about 1900. Accompanied by valuable bibliographies in v. 1, 2, and 4. [PE]

VB106. Nielsen, Axel. **Dänische wirtschaftsgeschichte.** Jena, 1933. After short treatment of the Middle Ages, developments are carried up to about 1914. [PE]

VB107. Troels-Lund, Frederik. **Dagligt liv i norden i det 16 de aarhundrede.** 14 v. Copenhagen, 1879–1901. Much material on varied aspects of culture, using mostly Danish sources. [PE]

VB108. Hannover, Emil. **Dänische Kunst des 19. Jahrhunderts.** Leipzig, 1907.

Finland

VB109. Suolahti, Gunnar, ed. **Suomen kulttuurihistoria.** 4 v. Jyväskylä, 1933–36. Collaborative cultural history from the age of tribal society and catholicism through the age of the estates to industrialism and national awakening. [AK]

VB110. Okkonen, Onni. **L'art finlandais au XIXe et XXe siècles.** Tr. from Finnish by Arthur Långfors. 2nd ed., Helsinki, 1938.

VB111. Waris, Heikki. **Suomalaisen yhteiskunnan rakenne.** Rev. ed., Helsinki, 1952. The social structure of modern Finland. Waris begins with an account of Finnish society 100 years ago, and stresses the changing nature of that society as he analyzes it. [JWF]

VB112. Wuorinen, John H. **Nationalism**

in modern Finland. N.Y., 1931. Good special study.

VB113. Pipping, Hugo E. **Finlands näringsliv äfter andra världskriget.** Helsinki, 1954. Description and recent history of the Finnish economy. The first chapter presents an excellent summary of the highlights of Finnish economic history. [JWF]

VB114. Jutikkala, Eino. **Suomen talonpojan historia sekä katsaus talonpoikien asemaan Euroopan muissa maissa.** Porvoo, 1942. Evolution of legislation on land ownership and the social and economic status of farmers in Finland. [AK]

VB115. Voionmaa, Kaarle Väinö. **Suomen karjalaisen heimon historia.** Helsinki, 1915. Land cultivation and proprietorship and family institutions in eastern Finland. [AK]

VB116. Mead, William R. **Farming in Finland.** London, 1953. Broader than title. Treats Finland as frontier of settlement and its agricultural use. [JWF]

VB117. Brotherus, Karl R. **Katsaus suomen valtiollisen järjestysmuodon historialliseen kehitykseen.** 2nd ed., Porvoo, 1948. Constitutional history, emphasizing periods of autonomy and independence. [AK]

VB118. Renvall, Pentti. **Suomalainen 1500-luvun ihminen oikeuskatsomustensa valossa.** Turku, 1949. Psychological study based on fines imposed by lower courts, attempting to show spiritual concepts and sense of justice of the 16th century Finn. Has a fourteen page summary in English. [AK]

Iceland

VB119. Chamberlin, William C. **Economic development of Iceland through World War II.** N.Y., 1947. One of the few good monographs in English.

Norway

VB120. Østby, Leif. **Modern Norwegian painting.** Oslo, 1949.

VB121. Semmingsen, Ingrid G. **Veien mot vest.** 2 v. Oslo, 1941–50. [1, *Utvandringen fra Norge til Amerika 1825–1865*; 2, *Utvandringen fra Norge 1865–1915*.] A pioneering work with insight into Norwegian social history.

VB122. Elviken, Andreas. **Die Entwicklung des norwegischen Nationalismus.** Berlin, 1930. A good German study of Norwegian nationalism.

VB123. Falnes, Oscar J. **National romanticism in Norway.** N.Y., 1933. Shows why Scandinavianism had less appeal than nationalism.

VB124. Jorgenson, Theodore J. **Norway's relation to Scandinavian unionism, 1815–1871.** Northfield, Minn., 1935.

VB125. Koht, Halvdan. **Norsk bondereising.** Oslo, 1926. Although Koht describes

himself as a Marxist historian, he is much broader than this implies. Here he discusses the farmers as the link holding Norwegian history together, and as the root of the political struggles of the 19th century, though the volume ends with 1814. [LFS]

VB126. Johnsen, Oscar A. **Norwegische Wirtschaftsgeschichte.** Jena, 1939. Particularly good on the 16th-18th century period, Johnsen's specialty. [LFS]

VB127. Worm-Müller, Jacob S., and others, eds. **Den Norske sjøfarts historie.** 3 v. in 6. Oslo, 1923–51. Significant but uneven cooperative work dealing with a subject of vital importance for Norway. Good in source material and inspiration, but lacking in analysis. [LS]

VB128. Seip, Jens A. **Et regime foran undergangen.** Oslo, 1945. Excellent monograph dealing with the political controversies of the late 19th century.

VB129. Kaartvedt, Alf. **Kampen mot parlamentarism: den konservative politiken under vetostriden.** Oslo, 1957. "The struggle against parliamentarianism" describes the role of Oscar II and Swedish influence in the Norwegian constitutional controversy of the late 19th century, and illuminates the origins of the conservative party.

VB130. Skodvin, Magne. **Striden om okkupasjonsstyret i Norge fram til 25. September 1940.** Oslo, 1956. Detailed and objective treatment of German policy in Norway.

Sweden

VB131. Tigerstedt, Eugène N., ed. **Ny illustrerad svensk litteraturhistoria.** 3 v. Stockholm, 1955–57. Scholarly and up-to-date review of Swedish literary history.

VB132. Nordensvan, Georg G. **Schwedische Kunst des 19. Jahrhunderts.** Leipzig, 1904.

VB133. Tingsten, Herbert L. G. **Den svenska socialdemokratiens idéutveckling.** 2 v. Stockholm, 1941. Insight into the ideological development of social democracy. These volumes were the first to appear of a planned series of ten on *Den svenska arbetarklassens historia*, now almost complete and giving a well-rounded picture of the development of the working class.

VB134. Den svenska utrikespolitikens historia. Ed. by Torvald Höjer and others. 5 v. in 11 pts. Stockholm, 1951 ff. A superb cooperative work by eleven well-chosen authors. Spans the whole of Swedish national history from Gustav Vasa in the 16th century.

VB135. Edén, Nils. **Den svenska riksdagen under femhundra år.** Stockholm, 1935. Useful condensation of an exhaustive 17 v. work edited by Edén, published on occasion of the 500th anniversary of the riksdag.

VB136. Heckscher, Eli F. **An economic history of Sweden.** Tr. by Göran Ohlin. Cambridge, Mass., 1954. Essentially a translation of Heckscher's own abridgement of his multi-volume *Sveriges ekonomiska historia,* plus an additional chapter by his son, Gunnar Heckscher. Includes biographical preface on Heckscher by Alexander Gerschenkron.

VB137. Lindroth, Sten. **Gruvbrytning och kopparhantering vid Stora Kopparberget intill 1800-talets början.** 2 v. Uppsala, 1955. Technical history treating also significance of copper in Sweden's economy and politics, from Middle Ages to about 1810.

VB138. Carlsson, Sten C. O. **Svensk ståndscirculation 1680–1950.** Uppsala, 1950. A study in social mobility. Discusses changes from the time of aristocratic, privileged power in the late 17th century to the economic and political leveling of the 20th century—strikingly less social leveling. This broad study was preceded by the more limited and detailed *Ståndssamhället och ståndspersoner 1700–1865* (Lund, 1949).

VB139. Kentrschynśkyi, Bohdan von. "Karl X Gustav inför krisen i öster 1654–1655." **Karolinska Förbundets Årsbok** (Lund, 1956). Revolutionizes interpretation of Karl X's policies, showing his purpose in attacking Poland in 1655 was to forestall Russian aggression.

VB140. Palmstierna, Carl Fredrik. **Sverige, Ryssland och England 1833–1855.** Stockholm, 1932. Significant diplomatic study.

VB141. Tingsten, Herbert. **The debate on the foreign policy of Sweden, 1918–1939.** Tr. by Joan Bulman. London, 1949. Exceptionally valuable study by a professor who became Sweden's leading newspaper editor.

VB142. Boberg, Stig. **Gustav III och tryckfriheten 1774–1787.** Stockholm, 1951. Shows how the king's professions of liberalism were contradicted in practice as he tried to throttle or control the press.

VB143. Weibull, Jörgen. **Carl Johan och Norge, 1810–1814: unionsplanerna och deras förverkligande.** Lund, 1957.

VB144. Thermaenius, Johan Edvard. **Lantmannapartiet.** Uppsala, 1928. Thorough study of the oldest Swedish political party.

VB145. Rustow, Dankwart A. **The politics of compromise: a study of parties and cabinet government in Sweden.** Princeton, 1955. Valuable analytical-historical study.

VB146. Lagerroth, Fredrik. **Frihetstidens författning.** Stockholm, 1915. Standard, thorough constitutional history to 1772.

VB147. Brusewitz, Axel. **Kungamakt, herremakt, folkmakt: författningskampen i Sverige (1906–1918).** Stockholm, 1951. Interpretive-factual essays on the constitutional struggle for power between king, aristocracy, and people, resolved finally by Gustav V's yielding to the ministry in 1917.

VB148. Collinder, Björn. **The Lapps.** Princeton, 1949. An excellent introduction.

BIOGRAPHIES

VB149. Koht, Halvdan. **Drottning Margareta och Kalmarunionen.** Stockholm, 1956. Brief and suggestive biography of a truly Scandinavian personality, architect of the Union of Kalmar.

VB150. Friis, Aage. **Bernstorfferne og Danmark.** 2 v. Copenhagen, 1903–19. Characterizes two Danish foreign ministers of international importance, and shows their significant relationships in autocratic Europe. [PE]

VB151. Bøggild-Andersen, Carl O. **Hannibal Sehested.** Copenhagen, 1946. Discusses Christian IV's son-in-law and his great significance for the introduction of autocracy and its early development. [PE]

VB152. Suomen Historiallinen Seura. **Kansallinen elämäkerrasto.** Ed. by Kaarlo Blomstedt and others. 5 v. Porvoo, 1927–34. Biographies of historical personages by numerous specialists. [AK]

VB153. Mannerheim, Carl Gustaf E. **Memoirs.** Tr. by Eric Lewénhaupt. London, 1954. Not the whole story, but an important contribution to Finland's greatest warrior-statesman. This English edition is abridged from the 2 v. Finnish edition of 1951–52.

VB154. Nielsen, Yngvar. **Grev Herman Wedel Jarlsberg og hans samtid 1779–1840.** 2 v. Christiania (Oslo), 1888–92. Good study of one of Norway's foremost statesmen of the early 19th century.

VB155. Koht, Halvdan. **Johan Sverdrup.** 3 v. Christiania (Oslo), 1918–25. Thorough biography of "the Norwegian Gladstone."

VB156. Koht, Halvdan. **Henrik Ibsen: eit diktarliv.** 2 v. Oslo, 1928–29. Rev. ed., 1954. English ed., London and N.Y., 1931. Probably the best biography of the greatest dramatist of the North.

VB157. Nansen, Odd. **From day to day.** Tr. by Katherine John. N.Y., 1949. One of the more poignant and revealing of the World War II memoirs.

VB158. Haintz, Otto. **König Karl XII von Schweden.** 3 v. Berlin, 1958. The most thorough scholarly biography.

VB159. Ahnlund, Nils G. **Gustaf Adolf, the great.** Tr. by Michael Roberts. N.Y., 1940. Perhaps the best of brief Swedish biographies. May be compared with Neale's *Queen Elizabeth.* [HK]

VB160. Andersson, Carl Ingvar. **Erik XIV, en biografi.** Stockholm, 1935. 4th, enl. ed., 1951. Perhaps the best study by this outstanding scholar, certainly the best biography of one of Sweden's most remarkable kings.

VB161. Hagberg, Knut H. **Carl Linnaeus.** Tr. by Alan Blair. London, 1952. Also available in French and in the original Swedish. Best biography of Sweden's great 18th century scientist.

VB162. Holmberg, Olle. **Carl Gustav af**

Leopold. 3 v. Stockholm, 1953–57. [1, *Den unge Leopold, 1756–1785;* 2, *Leopold och Gustaf III, 1786–1792;* 3, *Leopold och reuterholmska tiden, 1792–1796.*] Important source for the history of culture, especially religious thought, during the Gustavian period.

VB163. Höjer, Torvald T. **Karl XIV Johan.** 3 v. Stockholm, 1939–60. Unusually thorough, scholarly treatment.

VB164. Wigforss, Ernst J. **Minnen.** 3 v. Stockholm, 1950–54. Memoirs of the longtime minister of finance, one of the most influential of social democratic leaders.

Since there is a large grain of truth in the old saying that "the history of Sweden is the history of her kings" and since there are a number of good biographies, the following should be mentioned in addition to those already named.

VB165. Svalenius, Ivan. **Gustav Vasa.** Stockholm, 1950.

VB166. Weibull, Curt. **Drottning Christina: studier och forskningar.** Stockholm, 1931.

VB167. Hjärne, Harald. **Karl XII: omstörtningen i Östeuropa 1697–1703.** Stockholm, 1902. See also other studies on Charles XII by the same scholar.

VB168. Hennings, Beth. **Gustav III.** Stockholm, 1957.

VB169. La Blanchetai, Pierre de (pseud., Pierre de Luz). **Gustav III: ett portrait.** Tr. by Jane Lundblad. Stockholm, 1949.

VB170. Ahnlund, Nils G. **Axel Oxenstierna intill Gustav Adolfs död.** Stockholm, 1940. Incomplete but rewarding study of Sweden's greatest non-royal statesman.

VB170a. Bengtsson, Frans G. **Charles XII.** Stockholm, 1960.

PERIODICALS

VB171. Nordisk tidskrift för vetenskap, konst, och industri. Stockholm, 1925 ff. This intellectual journal of high quality was 80 years old as of 1957, but in its new form since 1925 it has been devoted to the service of pan-Scandinavian culture and affiliated with the Norden Society.

VB172. The Scandinavian economic history review. Stockholm, 1953 ff. A significant newer journal edited in English from Stockholm. Not confined to Scandinavian subject matter.

VB173. Scandinavian studies. Urbana, Ill., 1911 ff. (Title varies. Irregular, 1911–16; quarterly, 1917 ff.) Although the articles are largely devoted to philology, the annual bibliography of articles, reviews, and books published in the United States is broad-based and valuable.

VB174. American Scandinavian review. N.Y., 1913 ff. Edited in popular-scholarly fashion, with reviews and quarterly summaries of events in the Scandinavian countries. Emphasizes the humanities.

VB175. The Norseman: a review of current events. London, 1943 ff. (Bi-monthly.) Originating with the Norwegian refugee group during World War II, this journal has taken root, and publishes a number of articles that will be of increasing value. Its interests encompass all Scandinavia.

VB176. Scandia. Stockholm, 1928 ff. (Semi-annual.) Continuation of *Historisk tidskrift för Skåneland* (Lund, 1901–20). A Swedish, or perhaps more properly a northern, journal devoted to history, with a special interest in Skåne and its relations with Scandinavia as a whole. [PE]

VB177. Historisk tidsskrift. Copenhagen, 1840 ff. Published by Den Danske Historiske Forening. This and *VB178–179* are the leading historical journals in Denmark. [PE]

VB178. Samlinger til jydsk historie og topografi. Aarhus, 1866 ff. Pub. after 1930 under title **Jyske samlinger.**

VB179. Fortid og nutid. Copenhagen, 1914. Published by Dansk Historisk Faelles-forening.

VB180. Danske magazin. Copenhagen, 1745 ff. For 200 years the leading periodical for publication of the sources of Denmark's history, especially the modern period. [PE]

VB181. Zeitschrift der Gesellschaft für Schleswig-Holsteinische Geschichte. Kiel, 1870 ff. (Annual.) An important review on the political and cultural history of the duchies. [PE]

VB182. Historiallinen aikakauskirja. Helsinki, 1903 ff. The leading Finnish language historical review in Finland.

VB183. Historisk tidskrift för Finland. Helsinki, 1916 ff. The leading Swedish language review in Finland.

VB184. Historisk tidsskrift. Christiania (Oslo), 1871 ff. The journal of the Norwegian historical association, Norsk Historisk Forening.

VB185. Historisk tidskrift. Stockholm, 1881 ff. The organ of the Swedish historical society, Svenska Historiska Föreningen. Good for both articles and reviews.

VB186. Personhistorisk tidskrift. Stockholm, 1898 ff. Successor to *Svenska autografsällskapets tidskrift* (Stockholm, 1879–97). A scholarly journal of personal history and genealogy. No general index. [NWO]

VB187. Karolinska Förbundets Årsbok. 1910 ff. Lund, 1911 ff. (Annual.) A massive series of studies (usually articles) devoted primarily to varied aspects of the life and work of Charles XII. In recent years the scope of the articles has been broadened.

VB188. Historielärarnas förenings års-skrift. Stockholm, 1948 ff. Annual survey of literature, especially helpful. [SB]

VB189. Lychnos: lärdomshistoriska sam-fundets årsbok. Uppsala, 1936 ff. The annual of the History of Science Society, somewhat broader in coverage than the name might imply. Summaries of articles are given in English, German, or French.

THE BALTIC COUNTRIES

Through most of modern times the Baltic peoples have been governed by foreign overlords: Germans, Poles, Swedes, and both Tsarist and Communist Russians. The historical literature of these other peoples has, therefore, significance for the history of the Baltic lands and should be consulted separately. The bibliographies that follow are broad, but the literature individually listed is primarily that written after the opening of the national period during World War I.

BIBLIOGRAPHIES AND ENCYCLOPEDIAS

VB190. Winkelmann, Eduard. **Bibliotheca Livoniae historica.** 2nd ed., Berlin, 1878. Covers up to 1877. [AS]

VB191. Die Livländische Geschichtsliteratur. Ed. by Arthur H. P. Poelchau and others. Riga, 1885–1923. Annual, covering publications from 1883 to 1913. [UG]

VB192. Blumfeldt, Evald, and Nigolas Loone. **Eesti ajaloo bibliograafia.** Tartu, 1933–39. For Estonia covers publications of 1877 to 1912. [AS]

VB193. Latvju enciklopēdija. Ed. by Arveds Švābe. 3 v. Stockholm, 1950–55. A purely Latvian, abridged encyclopedia with bibliographies. [UG]

GENERAL HISTORIES

VB194. Royal Institute of International Affairs. **The Baltic states: a survey of the political and economic structure and the foreign relations of Estonia, Latvia and Lithuania.** London, 1938. A useful orientation. [EA]

VB195. Pick, Frederick W. **The Baltic nations, Estonia, Latvia, and Lithuania: the history of Russia's neighbours on the Baltic.** London, 1945. A careful, readable survey. [EA]

VB196. Reddaway, William F. **Problems of the Baltic.** Cambridge, Eng., 1940. A general survey.

VB197. Wittram, Reinhard. **Baltische Geschichte. Die Ostseelande Livland, Estland, Kurland, 1180–1918.** Munich, 1954. First-rate study, essentially a chapter in German colonial history. [UG]

HISTORIES OF SPECIAL AREAS

Estonia

VB198. Uustalu, Evald. **The history of Estonian people.** London, 1952. Good general treatment up to 1941. [EA]

VB199. Eesti NSV Teaduste Akadeemia. Ajaloo Instituut. **Istoriiâ Estonskoi SSR.** Ed. by G. I. Nann. Tallin, 1952. A history of Estonia, with the official point of view strongly evident. [LK]

VB200. Eesti Kirjanduse Selts. **Eesti ajalugu.** 3 v. Tartu, 1935–40. History of Estonia to 1700. [EA]

VB201. Kruus, Hans. **Eesti ajaloost, XIX sajandi teisel poolel (60–80 ndad aastad).** Tallin, 1957. Essays in Estonian history of the 1860's and 1870's.

VB202. Eesti Kirjanduse Selts. **Eesti kroonika.** 7 v. Tartu, 1933–39. Chronicle of culture and politics, annually from 1932 to 1938. [EA]

Latvia

VB203. Švābe, Arveds. **Histoire du peuple Letton.** Stockholm, 1953. Somewhat polemical, but a good survey, with bibliography for Latvian history. [UG]

VB204. Latvijas Padomju Socialistiskās Republikas Zinātu Akademija. **Istor.** 2 v. Riga, 1952–54. History of Latvia from the earliest times; an official Communist account with the expected interpretations throughout. A one-volume treatment with the same editor and title appeared in 1955. [LK]

VB205. Straubergs, Jānis. **Rīgas vēsture.** N.Y., 1954. One of the best local histories, that of the city of Riga. [UG]

Lithuania

VB206. Sapoka, Adolfas, ed. **Lietuvos istorija.** Kaunas, 1936. Standard work on Lithuania. [LK]

VB207. Senn, Alfred E. **The emergence of modern Lithuania.** N.Y., 1959.

HISTORIES OF SPECIAL TOPICS

VB208. Vasar, Juhan. **Die grosse livländische güterreduktion.** Tartu, 1931. This and *VB209* are significant monographs in socio-economic history.

VB209. Soom, Arnold. **Der Herrenhof in Estland im 17. Jahrhundert.** Lund, 1954.

VB210. Kirchner, Walther. **The rise of the Baltic question.** Newark, Del., 1954. A careful, readable study, emphasizing the period from the German settlements in the 12th century to the Swedish-Polish partition in the late 16th century.

VB211. Kalniņš, Brūno. **De baltiska staternas frihetskamp.** Stockholm, 1950. Good account from the social democratic point of view of the struggle for freedom in the World War I period. [UG]

VB212. Sepp, Hendrik, Otto Liiv, and Juhan Vasar. **Eesti majandusajalugu.** V. 1. Tartu, 1937. Economic history of Estonia to about 1850. [AS]

VB213. Kruus, Hans. **Talurahva kääri-mine lõuna-Eestis XIX sajandi 40-dail aastail.** Tartu, 1930. Social history, on peasant unrest in southern Estonia in the 1840's.

VB214. Švābe, Arveds. **Grundriss der agrargeschichte Lettlands.** Riga, 1928. A scholarly history of agriculture in Latvia. [UG]

VB215. Johansons, Andrejs. **Latviešu literātūra.** Stockholm, 1953. Good survey of Latvian literature. [UG]

VB216. Andrups, Jānis, and Vitauts Kalve. **Latvian literature.** Stockholm, 1954. Very general in scope. [UG]

VB217. Kalniņš, Brūno. **Latvijas sociāl-demokratijas piecdesmit gadi.** Stockholm, 1956. Good account of fifty years of the social democratic party in Latvia. [UG]

VB218. Ģērmanis, Uldis. **Jukums Vācietis, Pa aizputinātām pēdām.** Daugava, 1956. Vācieti's memoirs on the revolution in Lett-land, 1916–1919.

VB219. Jungfer, Victor. **Litauen, Antlitz eines Volkes: Versuch einer Kultursociologie.** 2nd ed., Tübingen, 1948. Lithuanian "cultural sociology" historically developed. [LK]

BIOGRAPHY

VB220. Laaman, Eduard. **Eesti iseseisvuse sünd.** 2 v. Tartu, 1936–38. Partly memoirs, useful for what the title calls "the birth of Estonian independence." [EA]

GOVERNMENT PUBLICATION

VB221. Lietuvos sutartys su svetimomis valstybėmis. **Receuil des traités conclus par la Lithuanie avec les pays étrangers.** Kaunas, 1930. Collection of treaties for 1919 to 1929, with Lithuanian and French texts in parallel columns.

PERIODICAL

VB222. Ajalooline ajakiri. Tartu, 1922–40. The historical journal of the national period, continued for three numbers (Jan.-June) into 1941 under title of *Ajaloo ajakiri*. [AS]

France and the Low Countries

LYNN M. CASE (FRANCE) *
and JEAN STENGERS (LOW COUNTRIES)

FRANCE

French history spans two thousand years from Roman times to the present. Often this history is central in the record of western civilization as a whole, as during the barbarian invasions, Carolingian empire, crusades, Renaissance, Protestant revolts, reign of Louis XIV, French revolution, and the Napoleonic empire. France's historians from Julius Caesar to Georges Lefebvre, as well as many non-French scholars, have been prolific in their writings on the history of France. French clerics, clerks, and bureaucracies have preserved an extraordinary store of records for modern archives. In most cases only the most important and up-to-date works on the various aspects of modern French history are listed here. Detailed bibliographies will be found at the beginning. Annotations have been severely curtailed in order that more titles could be included within the limited space. Most of the titles are self-explanatory, and high selectivity guarantees that all are worthy of attention. Where several works on the same subject are grouped together, they are listed in order of importance.

BIBLIOGRAPHIES, LIBRARIES, AND ARCHIVES
(Lynn M. Case)

Items listed below deal principally with bibliographies of general French histories. Bibliographies of larger scope but including French history will be found in Section B. Those dealing with special periods or topics within French history are included at the beginning of the subdivisions concerned with such periods or topics.

Guides to Sources

VC1. Monod, Gabriel. **Bibliographie de l'histoire de France: catalogue méthodique et** chronologique des sources et des ouvrages relatifs à l'histoire de France depuis les origines jusqu'en 1789. Paris, 1888.

VC2. Franklin, Alfred. **Les sources de l'histoire de France: notices bibliographiques et analytiques des inventaires et des recueils de documents relatifs à l'histoire de France.** Paris, 1877.

VC3. Catalogue général des manuscrits des bibliothèques des départements. Ser. 4. 7 v. Paris, 1849–85.

VC4. Catalogue général des manuscrits des bibliothèques publiques de France. Ser 4, Départements. 48 v. Paris, 1886–1933.

VC5. Catalogue général des manuscrits des bibliothèques publiques de France. Ser. 4, Paris. 27 v. Paris, 1885–1931.

* Compilers of various subsections are indicated under the respective headings.

VC6. Langlois, Charles V., and Henri Stein. **Les archives de l'histoire de France.** 3 pts. in 1 v. Paris, 1891–93.

VC7. Schmidt, Charles. **Les sources de l'histoire de France depuis 1789 aux Archives Nationales.** Paris, 1907.

VC8. Direction des Archives de France. **État des inventaires des Archives Nationales, départementales, communales, et hospitalières au 1er janvier 1937.** Paris, 1938.

VC9. Mady, J. "Les fonds d'archives concernant la Deuxième Guerre Mondiale." **Cahiers d'historie de la guerre,** Jan. 1949.

Guides to Printed Works

VC10. **Catalogue de l'histoire de France.** 11 v., 6 v. supplements, 16 v. tables. Paris, 1855–1932.

VC11. Le Long, Jacques. **Bibliothèque historique de la France contenant le catalogue des ouvrages imprimés et manuscrits, qui traitent de l'histoire de ce royaume . . . avec des notes critiques et historiques.** Rev. ed. by Fevret de Fontette, 5 v., Paris, 1768–78.

VC12. Saulnier, Eugène, and André A. Martin. **Bibliographie des travaux publiés de 1866 à 1897 sur l'histoire de la France de 1500 à 1789.** 2 v. Paris, 1932–38.

VC13. Caron, Pierre. **Bibliographie des travaux publiés de 1866 à 1897 sur l'histoire de la France depuis 1789.** Paris, 1912.

VC14. Brière, Gaston, Pierre Caron, and others. **Répertoire méthodique de l'histoire moderne et contemporaine de la France.** 1898–1906, 1910–13. 11 v. Paris, 1899–1914.

VC15. Caron, Pierre, and Henri Stein. **Répertoire bibliographique de l'histoire de France.** 1920–31. 6 v. Paris, 1923–38.

VC16. **Bibliographie critique des principaux travaux parus sur l'histoire de 1600 à 1914.** 1932–35. Ed. by editorial board of *Revue d'histoire moderne.* 4 v. Paris, 1936–37. By French historians or on French history.

VC17. Leuilliot, Paul, ed. **Bulletin de bibliographie: France.** 1948 ff. Paris, 1949 ff. [École des Hautes Études.]

VC18. Lasteyrie du Saillant, Robert C., Count of, and others. **Bibliographie générale des travaux historiques et archéologiques publiés** [to 1900] **par les sociétés savantes de la France, dressée sous les auspices du Ministère de l'Instruction Publique.** 6 v. Paris, 1888–1918.

VC19. Lasteyrie du Saillant, Robert C., Count of, and A. Vidier. **Bibliographie annuelle des travaux historiques et archéologiques publiés** [1901–10] **par les sociétés savantes de la France, dressée sous les auspices du Ministère de l'Instruction Publique.** 12 v. Paris, 1904–14.

VC20. Gandilhon, René. **Bibliographie générale des travaux historiques et archéologiques publiés par les sociétés savantes de la France. Période 1910–1940.** 3 v. Paris, 1944–52.

VC21. Halphen, Louis. **L'histoire en France depuis cent ans.** Paris, 1914. Bibliography.

French Archives

VC22. Courteault, Henri. **Les Archives Nationales de 1902 à 1936.** Paris, 1939.

VC23. Outrey, Amédée. "La notion d'archives en France à la fin du XVIIIe siècle." **Rev. hist. de droit français et étranger,** 1953.

VC24. ——. "Les origines de la législation révolutionnaire sur les archives: la loi du 7 septembre 1790 sur les Archives Nationales." **Bull. de la Soc. d'Hist. Mod.,** Jan. 1954.

VC25. Monicat, Jacques. "Les archives notariales." **Rev. hist.,** 214 (July-Sep. 1955): 1–8.

VC26. Lanhers, Yvonne. "Les archives de la maison de Gramont." **Rev. hist.,** 211 (Jan.-Mar. 1954): 11–18.

French Libraries

VC27. Dacier, Émile, ed. **Les trésors des bibliothèques de France.** Paris, 1938. See section on history, pp. 107–60.

VC28. Leroy, Émile. **Guide pratique des bibliothèques de Paris.** Paris, 1937.

VC29. Welsh, Doris V., ed. **A checklist of French political pamphlets, 1560–1644, in the Newberry Library.** Chicago, 1950.

VC30. ——, ed. **A second checklist of French political pamphlets, 1560–1653, in the Newberry Library.** Chicago, 1955.

ENCYCLOPEDIAS AND WORKS OF REFERENCE

(Lynn M. Case)

For French general encyclopedias see Section B. Dictionaries which are mainly biographical are listed under biographies at the end of this section.

VC31. Lalanne, Ludovic, ed. **Dictionnaire historique de la France.** 2nd rev. ed., 2 v., Paris, 1877.

VC32. Joanne, Paul B., ed. **Dictionnaire géographique et administratif de la France.** 7 v. Paris, 1890–1905.

VC33. Chéruel, Pierre A. **Dictionnaire historique des institutions, moeurs, et coutumes de la France.** 8th rev. ed., 2 v., Paris, 1910.

VC34. Marion, Marcel. **Dictionnaire des institutions de la France aux XVIIe et XVIIIe siècles.** Paris, 1923.

VC35. Robinet, Jean F. E., Adolphe Robert, and Julien Le Chaplain. **Dictionnaire historique et biographique de la Révolution et de l'Empire, 1789–1815.** 2 v. Paris, 1899.

VC36. Richardson, Hubert N. B. **A dictionary of Napoleon and his times.** London and N.Y., 1920.

GEOGRAPHIES, GAZETTEERS, AND ATLASES

(Edward W. Fox)

General Geography

VC37. Ormsby, Hilda. **France: a regional and economic geography.** 2nd rev. ed., London, 1950.

VC38. Vidal de La Blache, Paul M., and Lucien L. Gallois, eds. **Géographie universelle. V. 6, La France.** Pt. 1, **France physique,** by Emmanuel de Martonne, Paris, 1942; pt. 2, **France économique et humaine,** by Albert Demangeon, Paris, 1948.

VC39. Vidal de La Blache, Paul. **Tableau de la géographie de la France.** V. 1, pt. 1 of Lavisse, **Histoire de France** (*VC138*).

VC40. Brunhes, Jean. **Géographie humaine de la France: le cadre permanent et le facteur humain.** V. 1, pt. 1 of Hanotaux, **Histoire de la nation française** (*VC141*).

VC41. Brunhes, Jean, and Pierre Deffontaines. **Géographie humaine de la France: géographie politique et géographie du travail.** V. 2 of Hanotaux, **Histoire de la nation française** (*VC141*).

Regional Geography

VC42. Martonne, Emmanuel de. **Geographical regions of France.** London, 1950.

VC43. Mirot, Léon. **Manuel de géographie historique de la France.** 2nd rev. ed. by Albert Mirot, 2 v., Paris, 1947–50.

VC44. Jarry, Eugène. **Provinces et pays de France: essai de géographie historique.** 3 v. Paris, 1943–50. [1, *Formation de l'unité française;* 2, *Monographies provinciales: Agenais à Béarn;* 3, *Monographies provinciales: Beaujolais à Boubonnais.*]

VC45. Dion, Roger. **Les frontières de la France.** Paris, 1947.

VC46. Rousseau, Charles. **Les frontières de la France.** Paris, 1954.

Toponymy

VC47. Longnon, Auguste. **Les noms de lieux de la France: leur origine, leur signification, leurs transformations.** Fasc. 1–5, Paris, 1920–29.

VC48. Dauzat, Albert. **Les noms de lieux, origine et évolution: villes et villages, pays, cours d'eau, montagnes, lieux-dits.** Paris, 1926. Bibliography.

VC49. ——. **La toponymie française.** Paris, 1946.

VC50. **Dictionnaire topographique de la France, comprenant les noms de lieux anciens et modernes.** 28 v. Paris, 1861–1913.

VC51. Dictionnaire des communes. Paris, 1952.

Atlases

VC52. Vidal de La Blache, Paul. **Atlas historique et géographique.** Paris, [1951].

VC53. Schrader, Franz, ed. **Atlas de géographie historique.** New ed., Paris, 1907.

VC54. Longnon, Auguste. **Atlas historique de la France depuis César jusqu'à nos jours, avec un texte explicatif.** Pts. 1–3. Paris, 1885–89.

VC55. Guillot, M. E. **Grand atlas départemental de la France et de l'Algérie.** Paris, 1920.

Special Studies

VC56. Benest, Edward E. **Inland waterways of France.** London, 1956.

VC57. Cavailles, Henri. **La route française, son histoire, sa fonction.** Paris, 1946.

VC58. Blanchard, Marcel. **Géographie des chemins de fer.** Paris, 1942.

VC59. Brunhes, Jean, and Camille Vallaux. **La géographie de l'histoire: géographie de la paix et de la guerre sur terre et sur mer.** Paris, 1921. Deals with World War I.

VC60. Gougel, François. **Géographie des élections françaises de 1870 à 1951.** Paris, 1951.

VC61. Siegfried, André. **Tableau politique de la France de l'ouest sous la IIIᵉ république.** Paris, 1913.

ANTHROPOLOGICAL WORKS

(Lynn M. Case)

VC62. Vallois, Henri V. **Anthropologie de la population française.** Paris, 1943.

VC63. Montandon, Georges. **L'ethnie française.** Paris, 1951. Physical anthropology.

DEMOGRAPHIC STUDIES

(Lynn M. Case)

General

VC64. Levasseur, Émile. **La population française: histoire de la population avant 1789 et démographie de la France comparée à celle des autres nations au XIXᵉ siècle, précédée d'une introduction sur la statistique.** 3 v. Paris, 1889–92.

VC65. Huber, Michel, Henri Bunle, and Fernand Boverat. **La population de la France: son évolution et ses perspectives.** 3rd rev. ed., Paris, 1950.

VC66. Lot, Ferdinand. **Recherches sur la population et la superficie des cités remontant à la période gallo-romaine.** 3 v. Paris, 1943–53.

VC67. Barzun, Jacques. **The French race: theories of its origins and their social and political implications prior to the Revolution.** N.Y., 1932.

Period Studies

VC68. Gorce, Matthieu. **La France au-dessus les races: origines et formation de la nation française du IVᵉ au VIIᵉ siècle.** Paris, 1934.

VC69. Pouthas, Charles H. **La population française pendant la première moitié du XIXᵉ siècle.** Paris, 1955.

VC70. Chevalier, Louis. **La formation de la population parisienne au XIXᵉ siècle.** Paris, 1950.

LINGUISTIC WORKS
(Alphonse G. Juilland)

Bibliography

VC71. Wagner, Robert L. **Introduction à la linguistique française.** Lille, 1947.

Etymological Dictionaries

VC72. Dauzat, Albert. **Dictionnaire étymologique de la langue française.** Paris, 1938.

VC73. Godefroy, Frédéric. **Dictionnaire de l'ancienne langue française.** 10 v. Paris, 1880–1902.

VC74. Tobler, Adolf, and Erhard Lommatzsch. **Altfranzösisches Wörterbuch.** 3 v. Berlin, 1925.

General

VC75. Bally, Charles. **Linguistique générale et linguistique française.** 2nd ed., Berne, 1944.

VC76. Brunot, Ferdinand. **Histoire de la langue française à 1900.** 21 v. Paris, 1905–53.

VC77. Cohen, Marcel. **Histoire d'une langue: le français.** Paris, 1947.

VC78. Wartburg, Walther von. **Evolution et structure de la langue française.** 2nd ed., Berne, 1946.

Grammar and Phonology

VC79. Brunot, Ferdinand, and Charles Bruneau. **Précis de grammaire historique de la langue française.** New rev. ed., Paris, 1937.

VC80. Meyer-Luebke, Wilhelm. **Historische Grammatik der französischen Sprache.** 2 v. Heidelberg, 1908–21.

VC81. Nyrop, Kristoffer. **Grammaire historique de la langue française.** 6 v. Paris, 1899–1930.

VC82. Pope, Mildred K. **From Latin to modern French, with special consideration of Anglo-Norman: phonology and morphology.** Manchester, 1934.

VC83. Bourciez, Edouard E. **Précis historique de phonétique française.** 8th ed., Paris, 1937.

VC84. Buscherbruck, Karl. **Einführung in die historische Lautlehre des französischen.** Berlin, 1931.

VC85. Lerch, Eugen. **Historische französische Syntax.** 3 v. Leipzig, 1925–34.

VC86. Damourette, Jacques, and Edouard Pichon. **Essai de grammaire de la langue française.** 6 v. Paris, 1947.

VC87. Martinet, André. **La prononciation du français contemporain.** Paris, 1945.

Old and Middle French

VC88. Anglade, Joseph. **Grammaire élémentaire de l'ancien français.** Paris, 1918.

VC89. Ettmayer, Karl. **Vorträge zur Charakteristik des Altfranzösischen.** Fribourg, Switz., 1910.

VC90. Voretzsch, Karl. **Einführung in das Studium der Altfranzösischen Sprache.** Halle, 1932.

VC91. Klemperer, Victor. **Einführung in das Mittelfranzösische,** Leipzig, 1921.

Dialects

VC92. Dauzat, Albert. **Les patois: évolution-classification-étude.** Paris, 1927.

PRINTED COLLECTIONS OF SOURCES
(William E. Echard)

Sources of a specific nature which are cited under relevant topics are not included in this list.

Source Books and Readings

VC93. Zeller, Berthold, and Archille Luchaire, eds. **L'histoire de France racontée par les contemporaines.** 65 v. Paris, 1880–90. Roman Gaul to the death of Henry IV.

VC94. **Collection de textes pour servir à l'étude et à l'enseignement de l'histoire.** Ed. by Maurice Prou, Auguste E. L. M. Molinier, Charles V. Langlois, and others. 51 v. Paris, 1886–1929. Includes treaties, chronicles, and other documents; mostly, but not entirely, medieval.

VC95. Guénin, Georges, and Joseph Nouaillac, eds. **Lectures historiques.** 3 v. Paris, 1921–25. Selected from memoirs, journals, and letters; covers period 1715–1880.

VC96. Anderson, Frank M., ed. **Constitutions and other select documents illustrative of the history of France, 1789–1907.** 2nd ed., Minneapolis, 1908. Bibliography.

Guizot Collection

VC97. **Collection de documents inédits relatifs à l'histoire de France.** More than 300 v. Paris, 1835 ff. Projected by Guizot as minister of public instruction in 1834; since 1881 carried forward by the Comité des Travaux Historiques et Scientifiques. Six series: (1) chronicles, memoirs, journals; (2) charters; (3) correspondence, political and administrative documents (see especially *VC98–99*); (4) documents of the revolutionary period; (5) documents relating to philology, philosophy, etc.; (6) archaeological publications. For a description of v. 1–177 see Franklin, *Les sources de l'histoire de France* (*VC2*).

VC98. Lettres, instructions, et mémoires de Colbert. Ed. by Pierre Clément. 8 v. in 10. Paris, 1861–82.

VC99. Correspondance des contrôleurs généraux des finances avec les intendants des provinces, 1683–1715. Ed. by Arthur M. de Boislisle and Pierre de Brotonne. 3 v. Paris, 1874–97.

General Political

VC100. Laurière, Eusèbe J. de, and others, eds. **Ordonnances des roys de France.** 21 v. Paris, 1723–1849. Hugh Capet through Louis XII.

VC101. ———, eds. **Ordonnances des rois de France: règne de François Iᵉʳ.** 10 v. Paris, 1887–1908.

VC102. Jourdan, Athanase J. L., ——— de Crusy, and François A. Isambert, eds. **Recueil général des anciennes lois françaises depuis l'an 420 jusqu'à la Révolution de 1789.** 29 v. in 30. Paris, 1822–33. Also contains decisions of parliament, protests, and diplomatic acts.

VC103. Duvergier, Jean B., and others, eds. **Collection complète des lois, décrets, ordonnances, règlements et avis du conseil d'état.** 1788 ff. 2nd ed., 30 v. and annual v., Paris, 1834 ff. Not as complete as implied by the title.

VC104. Cahen, Léon, and Albert Mathiez. **Les lois françaises de 1815 à nos jours, accompagnées des documents politiques les plus importants.** 4th ed., Paris, 1933. Includes principal acts.

VC105. Duguit, Léon, and Henry Monnier, eds. **Les constitutions et les principales lois politiques de la France depuis 1789.** 5th ed., Paris, 1932.

VC106. Recueil des lois constitutionnelles et organiques de la République Française. Latest ed., Paris, 1924.

Parliamentary Records

VC107. Mavidal, Jérôme, Émile Laurent, and others, eds. **Archives parlementaires, 1787–1860: recueil complet des débats des chambres françaises.** Series 1, 1787–99; series 2, 1800–60. 219 v. Paris, 1862–1913. Series 1 has been completed only to Jan. 4, 1794, and series 2 to July 17, 1839.

VC108. Moniteur universel. Paris, 1789–1868.

VC109. Journal officiel. 1869 ff. See *VC1235*.

VC110. Les annales des débats parlementaires. Paris, 1863 ff. Covers Jan. 12, 1863 to the present.

Collections of Memoirs

VC111. Guizot, François P. G., ed. **Collection des mémoires relatifs à l'histoire de France depuis la fondation de la monarchie française jusqu'au XIIIᵉ siècle.** 31 v. Paris, 1823–35. Earlier works translated into modern French.

VC112. Petitot, Claude B., Bernard L. J. de Monmerqué, and others, eds. **Collection complète des mémoires relatifs à l'histoire de France depuis le règne de Philippe-Auguste jusqu'à la paix de Paris, 1763.** 2 series, 130 v. Paris, 1819–29.

VC113. Michaud, Joseph F., and Jean J. F. Poujoulat, eds. **Nouvelle collection des mémoires pour servir à l'histoire de France depuis le XIIIᵉ siècle jusqu'à la fin du XVIIIᵉ.** 3 series, 32 v. Paris, 1836–39.

VC114. Barrière, Jean F., and Mathurin F. A. de Lescure, eds. **Bibliothèque des mémoires relatifs à l'histoire de France pendant le XVIIIᵉ siècle.** 2 series, 37 v. Paris, 1846–81. For an index of proper names see Alfred Marquiset, suppl. 9 of *Revue des bibliothèques* (Paris, 1913).

VC115. Berville, Saint-Albin, and Jean F. Barrière, eds. **Collection des mémoires relatifs à la Révolution Française.** 57 v. Paris, 1820–27.

See also the publications of the Société de l'Histoire de France, a great series continuing since 1835 and extending over all periods of French history. The Société, founded in 1833, absorbed in 1927 the Société d'Histoire Contemporaine (which had published 63 volumes between 1892 and 1921).

SHORTER GENERAL HISTORIES
(Richard M. Brace)

Included among the shorter general histories are those covering several periods (though not all) of French history and those general works stressing institutional, legal, and constitutional history.

VC116. Histoire de la France pour tous les français. By Edouard Perroy, Georges Lefebvre, and others. 2 v. Paris, 1950.

VC117. Reinhard, Marcel, Norbert Dufourcq, and others, eds. **Histoire de France.** 2 v. Paris, 1954.

VC118. Gaxotte, Pierre. **Histoire des français.** 2 v. Paris, 1951.

VC119. Seignobos, Charles. **A history of the French nation.** London, 1933.

VC120. Guérard, Albert. **France, a short history.** N.Y., 1946.

VC121. Bainville, Jacques. **History of France.** N.Y., 1926.

VC122. Madaule, Jacques. **Histoire de France.** 2 v. Paris, 1943–45.

VC123. Herzog, Émile S. W. (pseud., André Maurois). **A history of France.** N.Y., 1957.

VC124. Duruy, Victor. **A short history of France.** London and N.Y., 1917.

VC125. Lot, Ferdinand. **La France des origines à la Guerre de Cent Ans.** 16th ed., Paris, 1948.

VC126. Brogan, Denis W. **The French nation, from Napoleon to Pétain.** N.Y., 1957.

VC127. Deslandres, Maurice C. E. **Histoire constitutionnelle de la France de 1789 à 1870.** 2 v. Paris, 1932. Bibliography.

VC128. Perrot, Ernest V. **Les institutions publiques et privées de l'ancienne France jusqu'en 1789.** Paris, 1935. Bibliography.

VC129. Chevallier, Jean J. **Histoire des institutions politiques de la France de 1789 à nos jours.** Paris, 1952.

VC130. Rousselet, Marcel. **Histoire de la magistrature française, des origines à nos jours.** 2 v. Paris, 1957.

VC131. Halphen, Louis, Roger Doucet, and others, eds. **Histoire de la société française.** Paris, 1953.

VC132. Thibaudet, Albert. **Les idées politiques de la France.** Paris, 1932.

VC133. Michel, Henri. **L'idée de l'état: essai critique sur l'histoire des théories sociales et politiques en France depuis la Révolution.** 3rd rev. ed., Paris, 1898.

VC134. Bourgeois, Émile. **History of modern France, 1815–1913.** 2 v. Cambridge, Eng., 1919. Bibliography.

VC135. Bury, John P. T. **France, 1814–1940.** Philadelphia, 1949. Bibliography.

VC136. Wolf, John B. **France, 1815 to the present.** N.Y., 1940.

VC137. Rémond, René. **La droite en France de 1815 à nos jours.** Paris, 1954. Bibliography.

LONGER GENERAL HISTORIES
(*Richard M. Brace*)

VC138. Lavisse, Ernest, ed. **Histoire de France depuis les origines jusqu'à la Révolution.** 9 v. in 18. Paris, 1900–11. [1, pt. 1, P. Vidal de la Blache, *Tableau de la géographie de la France;* pt. 2, G. Bloch, *Les origines, la Gaule indépendante et la Gaule romaine;* 2, pt. 1, C. Bayet, C. Pfister, and A. Kleinclausz, *Le christianisme, les barbares, Mérovingiens, et Carolingiens;* pt. 2, A. Luchaire, *Les premiers Capétiens (987–1137);* 3, pt. 1, A. Luchaire, *Philippe-Auguste-Louis VIII (1137–1226);* pt. 2, C. V. Langlois, *Saint Louis-Philippe le Bel, les derniers Capétiens directs (1226–1328);* 4, pt. 1, A. Coville, *Les premiers Valois et la Guerre de Cent Ans (1328–1422);* pt. 2, C.

Petit-Dutaillis, *Charles VII, Louis XI et les premières années de Charles VIII (1422–1492);* 5, pt. 1, H. Lemonnier, *Les guerres d'Italie, la France sous Charles VIII, Louis XII et François Ier (1492–1547);* pt. 2, H. Lemonnier, *La lutte contre la maison d'Autriche, la France sous Henri II (1519–1559);* 6, pt. 1, J. H. Mariéjol, *La réforme et la Ligue, l'édit de Nantes (1559–1598);* pt. 2, J. H. Mariéjol, *Henri IV et Louis XIII (1598–1643);* 7, pt. 1, E. Lavisse, *Louis XIV, la Fronde, le roi, Colbert (1643–1685);* pt. 2, E. Lavisse, *Louis XIV, la religion, les lettres, et les arts, la guerre (1643–1685);* 8, pt. 1, A. de Saint-Léger, A. Rébelliau, P. Sagnac, and E. Lavisse, *Louis XIV, la fin du règne (1685–1715);* pt. 2, H. Carré, *Le règne de Louis XV (1715–1774);* 9, pt. 1, H. Carré, P. Sagnac, and E. Lavisse, *Le règne de Louis XVI (1774–1789);* pt. 2, *Tables alphabétiques.*] Bibliography.

VC139. Lavisse, Ernest, ed. **Histoire de France contemporaine, depuis la Révolution jusqu'à la paix de 1919.** 10 v. Paris, 1920–22. [1, P. Sagnac, *La Révolution (1789–1792);* 2, G. Pariset, *La Révolution (1792–1799);* 3, G. Pariset, *Le consulat et l'empire (1799–1815);* 4, S. Charléty, *La restauration (1815–1830);* 5, S. Charléty, *La monarchie de juillet (1830–1848);* 6, C. Seignobos, *La révolution de 1848, le second empire (1848–1859);* 7, C. Seignobos, *Le déclin de l'empire et l'établissement de la 3e république (1859–1875);* 8, C. Seignobos, *L'évolution de la 3e république (1875–1914);* 9, H. Bidou, A. Gauvain, C. Seignobos, and E. Lavisse, *La grande guerre;* 10, *Index.*] Bibliography.

VC140. Funck-Brentano, Frantz, ed. **National history of France.** 10 v. London and N.Y., 1916–36. Tr. from *Histoire de France racontée à tous* (8 v., Paris, 1911–33). [1, F. Funck-Brentano, *Earliest times;* 2, F. Funck-Brentano, *Middle Ages;* 3, L. Batiffol, *Century of the Renaissance;* 4, J. Boulanger, *Seventeenth century;* 5, C. Stryienski, *Eighteenth century;* 6, L. Madelin, *Revolution;* 7, L. Madelin, *Consulate and empire;* 8, J. Lucas-Dubreton, *Restoration and July monarchy;* 9, R. Arnaud, *Second republic and Napoleon III;* 10, R. Recouly, *Third republic.*] Bibliography.

V141. Hanotaux, Gabriel, ed. **Histoire de la nation française.** 15 v. Paris, 1920–29. [1, G. Hanotaux, *Introduction générale;* J. Brunhes, *Géographie humaine de la France;* 2, J. Brunhes and P. Deffontaines, *Géographie politique et géographie du travail;* 3, P. Imbart de la Tour, *Histoire politique des origines à 1515;* 4, L. Madelin, *Histoire politique de 1515 à 1804;* 5, G. Hanotaux, *Histoire politique de 1804 à 1926;* 6, G. Goyau, *Histoire religieuse;* 7, J. Colin, *Histoire militaire et navale des origines aux croisades;* F. Reboul, *Des croisades à la Révolution;* 8, C. Mangin, *De la constituante* *au Directoire;* F. D'Esperey, *Du Directoire à la guerre de 1914;* G. Hanotaux, *La guerre de 1914–18;* 9, R. Pinon, *Histoire diplomatique, 1515–1928;* 10, G. Martin, *Histoire économique et financière;* 11, L. Gillet, *Histoire des arts;* 12, F. Picavet, *La littérature en langue latine;* J. Bédier, *Les chansons de gestes;* A. Jeanroy, *La littérature de langue française des origines à Ronsard;* 13, F. Strowski, *De Ronsard à nos jours;* 14, E. Picard, *Histoire des sciences, introduction générale;* H. Andoyer and P. Humbert, *Histoire des mathématiques, de la mécanique, et de l'astronomie;* C. Fabry, *Histoire de la physique;* A. Colson, *Histoire de la chimie;* 15, M. Caullery, *Histoire des sciences biologiques;* R. Lote, *Histoire de la philosophie.*]

VC142. Parias, Louis H., ed. **Histoire du peuple français, des origines à nos jours.** 4 v. Paris, 1951–54. [1, R. Pernoud, *Des origines au Moyen Âge;* 2, E. Pognon, *De Jeanne d'Arc à Louis XIV, 1380–1715;* 3, P. Lafue, *De la régence aux trois révolutions, 1715–1848;* 4, G. Duveau, *De 1848 à nos jours.*] Bibliography.

VC143. Michelet, Jules. **History of France from the earliest period till the present time.** 2 v. London, 1845–47. Partial tr. (to 1483) by G. H. Smith of *Histoire de France* (new ed., rev. and enl., 19 v., Paris, 1878–79).

VC144. Rambaud, Alfred N. **Histoire de la civilisation française.** 3 v. Paris, 1885–88. 14th ed., rev. and corr., 2 v., Paris, 1921–26.

VC145. Moreton-Macdonald, John R. **A history of France.** 3 v. N.Y. and London, 1915. Bibliography.

HISTORIES OF SPECIAL PERIODS

The emphasis in these subsections, which begin around 1500, is on general and political history, including legal and constitutional histories. The lives of ruling kings and their queen consorts are also included. For all other biographical items see the biographical section below.

Sixteenth Century
(Bernerd C. Weber)

VC146. Doucet, Roger. **Les institutions de la France au XVIe siècle.** 2 v. Paris, 1948.

VC147. Lavisse, Ernest, ed. **Histoire de France** (*VC138*), v. 5–6.

VC148. Batiffol, Louis. **Century of the Renaissance.** London and N.Y., 1916.

VC149. Zeller, Gaston. **Les institutions de la France au XVIe siècle.** Paris, 1948.

VC150. Bridge, John S. C. **A history of France from the death of Louis XI.** 5 v. Oxford, 1921–36. Bibliography.

VC151. Church, William F. **Constitutional thought in 16th century France.** Cambridge, Mass., 1941. Bibliography.

VC152. Albertini, Rudolf von. **Das politische Denken in Frankreich zur Zeit Richelieus.** Marburg, 1951.

VC153. Van Dyke, Paul. **Catherine de Médicis.** 2 v. N.Y., 1922. Bibliography.

VC154. Héritier, Jean. **Catherine de Médicis.** Paris, 1940.

VC155. Lettres de Catherine de Médicis. Ed. by Hector de la Ferrière-Percy and Gustave Baguenault de Puchesse. 11 v. Paris, 1880–1943.

VC156. Mariéjol, Jean H. **Catherine de Médicis, 1519–1589.** Paris, 1920.

VC157. Champion, Pierre. **Catherine de Médicis présente à Charles IX son royaume, 1564–1566.** Paris, 1937.

VC158. ——. **Charles IX: la France et le contrôle de l'Espagne.** 2 v. Paris, 1939.

VC159. Major, James R. **The Estates-General of 1560.** Princeton, 1951. Bibliography.

VC160. Romier, Lucien. **Les origines politiques des guerres de religion.** 2 v. Paris, 1913–14.

VC161. ——. **Catholiques et Huguenots à la cour de Charles IX.** 2nd ed., Paris, 1924.

VC162. Thompson, James Westfall. **Wars of religion in France, 1559–1576.** 2nd ed., Chicago, 1914.

VC163. Romier, Lucien. **Le royaume de Catherine de Médicis: la France à la veille des guerres de religion.** 2nd ed., 2 v., Paris, 1922.

VC164. Rocquain, Félix. **La France et Rome pendant les guerres de religion.** Paris, 1924.

VC165. England, Sylvia L. **The massacre of Saint Bartholomew.** London, 1938. Bibliography.

VC166. Poirson, Auguste. **Histoire du règne de Henri IV.** 3rd rev. ed., 4 v., Paris, 1865–66.

VC167. Willert, Paul F. **Henry of Navarre and the Huguenots in France.** N.Y., 1893.

VC168. Mousnier, Roland. **La vénalité des offices sous Henri IV et Louis XIII.** Rouen, 1946.

VC169. Recueil des lettres missives de Henri IV. Ed. by Julien Berger de Xivrey and Joseph Gaudet. 9 v. Paris, 1843–76.

VC170. Williams, Adair G. "The abjuration of Henry of Navarre." **Journal of modern history,** 5 (June 1933): 143–71.

VC171. ——. "The absolution of Henry of Navarre." **Jour. mod. hist.,** 6 (Dec. 1934): 379–404.

VC172. Reinhard, Marcel. **Henri IV.** Paris, 1943.

VC173. Drouot, Henri. **Mayenne et Bourgogne: étude sur la Ligue, 1587–1596.** 2 v. Paris, 1955.

Other listings concerning more extensively the religious side of the French Reformation movement will be found under the section on French religious history.

Seventeenth Century
(John B. Wolf)

VC174. Bourgeois, Émile, and Louis André, eds. **Les sources de l'histoire de France: le XVIIᵉ siècle, 1610–1715.** 8 v. Paris, 1913–35.

VC175. Lavisse, Ernest, ed. **Histoire de France** (*VC138*), v. 7.

VC176. Funck-Brentano, Frantz, ed. **National history of France** (*VC140*), v. 4.

VC177. Pagès, Georges. **Naissance du grand siècle: la France de Henri IV à Louis XIV, 1598–1661.** Paris, 1948.

VC178. ———. **La monarchie d'ancien régime en France, de Henri IV à Louis XIV.** Paris, 1928.

VC179. Chéruel, Pierre A. **Histoire de France pendant la minorité de Louis XIII.** 3 v. Paris, 1879.

VC180. Estrées, François A., duc d'. **Mémoires du maréchal d'Estrées sur la régence de Marie de Médicis, 1610–1616, et sur celle d'Anne d'Autriche, 1643–1650.** Paris, 1666. Ed. by Paul Bonnefon, Paris, 1910.

VC181. Batiffol, Louis. **Marie de Médicis and the French court in the XVIIth century.** London and N.Y., 1908.

VC182. Hanotaux, Gabriel, and Auguste de Caumont, duc de la Force. **Histoire du cardinal de Richelieu.** 5 v. Paris, 1932–44.

VC183. Avenel, Georges d'. **Richelieu et la monarchie absolue.** 2nd ed., 4 v., Paris, 1895.

VC184. Tapié, Victor. **La France de Louis XIII et de Richelieu.** Paris, 1952.

VC185. Canu, Jean. **Louis XIII et Richelieu.** Paris, 1944.

VC186. Chéruel, Pierre A. **Histoire de France sous le ministère de Mazarin.** 4 v. Paris, 1882.

VC187. Perkins, James B. **France under Mazarin, with a review of the administration of Richelieu.** 2 v. N.Y. and London, 1886.

VC188. Gaxotte, Pierre. **La France de Louis XIV.** Paris, 1946.

VC189. Bailly, Auguste. **Le règne de Louis XIV.** Paris, 1946.

VC190. Hassall, Arthur. **Louis XIV and the zenith of the French monarchy.** London and N.Y., 1895.

VC191. Saint-Simon, Louis de Rouvroy, duc de. **Memoirs . . . on the times of Louis XIV and the regency.** 4 v. Boston, 1899. Abr. tr. by K. P. Wormeley from *Mémoires*, new ed. by A. and J. Boislisle and L. Lecestre, 41 v., Paris, 1879–1928.

VC192. Doolin, Paul R. **The Fronde.** Cambridge, Mass., 1935.

VC193. Clément, Pierre. **Histoire de Col-**

bert et de son administration. 3rd ed., 2 v., Paris, 1892.

VC194. Roujon, Jacques. **Louis XIV.** 2 v. Paris, 1943.

VC195. Louis XIV, roi de France. **Mémoires pour l'instruction du dauphin.** Ed. by Charles C. Dreyss. 2 v. Paris, 1860.

VC196. Louis XIV. **Mémoires pour les années 1661 et 1666, suivis des réflexions sur le métier de roi, des instructions au duc d'Anjou et d'un projet de harangue.** Ed. by Jean Longnon. Paris, 1923.

VC197. King, James E. **Science and rationalism in the government of Louis XIV, 1661–1683.** Baltimore, 1949.

VC198. Zeller, Gaston. **Comment s'est faite la réunion de l'Alsace à la France.** Paris, 1948.

VC199. Dedieu, Joseph. **Le rôle politique des Protestants français, 1685–1715.** Paris, 1920.

VC200. Saint René Taillandier, Madeleine. **La jeunesse du grand roi, Louis XIV et Anne d'Autriche.** Paris, 1945.

VC201. Bertrand, Louis. **Louis XIV.** N.Y. and London, 1928.

VC202. Ogg, David. **Louis XIV.** London, 1933.

Eighteenth Century
(Paul H. Beik)

Bibliography

VC203. Du Peloux, Charles. **Répertoire général des ouvrages modernes relatifs au dix-huitième siècle français, 1715–1789.** Paris, 1926. Supplement, 1927.

VC204. Stewart, John H. **France, 1715–1815: a guide to materials in Cleveland.** Cleveland, 1942.

National Politics and Institutions

VC205. Sagnac, Philippe. **La formation de la société française moderne.** V. 2, **La révolution des idées et des moeurs et le déclin de l'ancien régime, 1715–1788.** Paris, 1946.

VC206. Taine, Hippolyte A. **The ancient régime.** New rev. ed., N.Y., 1896.

VC207. Tocqueville, Alexis de. **The old regime and the French Revolution.** N.Y., 1955. Latest French ed., 1952.

VC208. Broc, Hervé de. **La France sous l'ancien régime.** 2 v. Paris, 1887–89.

VC209. Funck-Brentano, Frantz. **The old regime in France.** N.Y., 1929.

VC210. Stryienski, Casimir. **The eighteenth century in France.** N.Y., 1916.

VC211. Leclercq, Henri. **Histoire de la régence.** 3 v. Paris, 1921–22.

VC212. Perkins, James B. **France under the regency, with a review of the administration of Louis XIV.** Boston, 1892.

VC213. ———. **France under Louis XV.** 2 v. Boston, 1897.

VC214. Gaxotte, Pierre. **Louis XV and**

his times. London, 1932. Latest French ed., 1956.

VC215. Albert, Charles P. d', duc de Luynes. **Mémoires du duc de Luynes sur la cour de Louis XV (1735–1758).** Ed. by Louis E. Dussieux and Eudoxe Soulié. 17 v. Paris, 1860–65.

VC216. Barbier, Edmond J. F. **Chronique de la régence et du règne de Louis XV (1718–1763).** 8 v. Paris, 1857.

VC217. Jobez, Alphonse. **La France sous Louis XVI.** 3 v. Paris, 1877–93.

VC218. Viollet, Paul. **Droit public: histoire des institutions politiques et administratives de l'ancienne France.** 4 v. Paris, 1890–1912.

VC219. ———. **Le roi et ses ministres pendant les derniers siècles de la monarchie.** Paris, 1912.

VC220. Mason, Lester B. **The French constitution and the social question in the old regime, 1700–1789.** Buffalo, 1954.

VC221. Matthews, George T. **The royal general farms in eighteenth-century France.** N.Y., 1958.

The Parlements

VC222. Bickart, Roger. **Les parlements et la notion de souveraineté au XVIIIe siècle.** Paris, 1932.

VC223. Carré, Henri. **La fin des parlements, 1788–1790.** Paris, 1912. Bibliography.

VC224. Glasson, Ernest. **Le parlement de Paris: son rôle politique depuis le règne de Charles VII jusqu'à la Révolution.** 2 v. Paris, 1901.

VC225. Flammermont, Jules, ed. **Remontrances du parlement de Paris au XVIIIe siècle.** 3 v. Paris, 1888–98.

VC226. Le Moy, Arthur. **Le parlement de Bretagne et le pouvoir royal au XVIIIe siècle.** Angers, 1909.

VC227. Egret, Jean. **Le parlement du Dauphiné et les affaires publiques dans la deuxième moitié du XVIIIe siècle.** 2 v. Grenoble, 1942.

VC228. Robert, P. Albert. **Les remontrances et arrêtés du parlement de Provence au XVIIIe siècle, 1715–1790.** Paris, 1912.

VC229. Beik, Paul H. **A judgment of the old régime: being a survey by the parlement of Provence of French economic and fiscal policies at the close of the Seven Years War.** N.Y., 1944.

Other Special and Local Studies

VC230. Dakin, Douglas. **Turgot and the ancien régime in France.** London, 1939.

VC231. Ford, Franklin L. **Robe and sword: the regrouping of the French aristocracy after Louis XIV.** Cambridge, Mass., 1953.

VC232. Renouvin, Pierre. **Les assemblées provinciales de 1787: origines, développement, résultats.** Paris, 1921.

VC233. Ardashev, Pavel N. **Les intendants de province sous Louis XVI.** Paris, 1909.

VC234. Rébillon, Armand. **Les états de Bretagne de 1661 à 1789.** Paris, 1932.

VC235. Fréville, Henri. **L'intendance de Bretagne (1689–1790): essai sur l'histoire d'une intendance en pays d'état au XVIIIe siècle.** 3 v. Rennes, 1953.

Eighteenth Century Enlightenment

VC236. Sée, Henri. **L'évolution de la pensée politique en France au XVIIIe siècle.** Paris, 1925.

VC237. Becker, Carl L. **The heavenly city of the eighteenth century philosophers.** See *T266.*

VC238. Mornet, Daniel. **Les origines intellectuelles de la Révolution Française (1715–1787).** 4th ed., Paris, 1947. Also available in English translation.

VC239. Cassirer, Ernst. **The philosophy of the Enlightenment.** See *A342.*

VC240. Havens, George R. **The age of ideas: from reaction to revolution in eighteenth-century France.** N.Y., 1955.

VC241. Martin, Kingsley. **French liberal thought in the 18th century: a study of political ideas from Bayle to Condorcet.** Ed. by Jacob P. Mayer, 2nd ed., London, 1954.

VC242. Hearnshaw, Fossey J. C., ed. **Social and political ideas of some great French thinkers of the age of reason.** London, 1930.

VC243. Hubert, René. **Les sciences sociales dans l'Encyclopédie.** Paris, 1923.

VC244. Faÿ, Bernard. **The revolutionary spirit in France and America: a study of moral and intellectual relations between France and the United States at the end of the eighteenth century.** N.Y., 1927.

VC245. Wade, Ira O. **The clandestine organization and diffusion of philosophic ideas in France from 1700 to 1750.** Princeton, 1938.

VC246. Weis, Eberhard. **Geschichtsschreibung und Staatsauffassung in der französischen Enzyklopädie.** Munich, 1952.

VC247. Carcassonne, Élie. **Montesquieu et le problème de la constitution française au XVIIIe siècle.** Paris, 1927.

VC248. Derathé, Robert. **Jean Jacques Rousseau et la science politique de son temps.** Paris, 1950.

VC249. Gough, John W. **The social contract: a critical study of its development.** Oxford, 1936.

VC250. Acomb, Frances. **Anglophobia in France, 1763–1789: an essay in the history of constitutionalism and nationalism.** Durham, 1950.

VC251. Bonno, Gabriel. **La constitution britannique devant l'opinion française de Montesquieu à Bonaparte.** Paris, 1932.

VC252. Einaudi, Mario. **The physiocratic doctrine of judicial control.** Cambridge, Mass., 1938.

The Revolution
(*John H. Stewart*)

Bibliography

VC253. Caron, Pierre. **Manuel pratique pour l'étude de la Révolution Française.** New ed., Paris, 1947.

VC254. Walter, Gérard. **Répertoire de l'histoire de la Révolution Française (travaux publiés de 1800 à 1940).** V. 1–2, Paris, 1941–51.

VC255. Martin, André, and Gérard Walter. **Le catalogue de l'histoire de la Révolution Française (écrits de la période révolutionnaire, 1789–1799).** V. 1–5, Paris, 1936–43.

VC256. Tourneux, Maurice. **Bibliographie de l'histoire de Paris pendant la Révolution Française.** 5 v. Paris, 1890–1913.

VC257. Tuetey, Alexandre. **Répertoire général des sources manuscrites de l'histoire de Paris pendant la Révolution Française.** V. 1–11. Paris, 1890–1914.

VC258. Hayden, Horace E. **French revolutionary pamphlets: a check list of Talleyrand and other collections.** N.Y., 1945. See also *VC274*.

Historiography

VC259. Farmer, Paul. **France reviews its revolutionary origins: social politics and historical opinion in the third republic.** N.Y., 1944.

VC260. Kareiev, Nikolai. **Istorikii Frantsuzskoi Revoliutsii.** 3 v. Leningrad, 1924.

VC261. Sagnac, Philippe, and Jean Robiquet. **Révolution de 1789.** 2 v. Paris, 1934.

Sources

VC262. Mautouchet, Paul, ed. **Le gouvernement révolutionnaire (10 août 1792–4 brumaire an IV).** Paris, 1912.

VC263. Aulard, François V. A., and others, eds. **Recueil des actes du Comité de Salut Public: avec la correspondance officielle des réprésentants en mission et le registre du Conseil Exécutif Provisoire.** 27 v. and 2 index v. Paris, 1889–1956.

VC264. Tourneux, Maurice, ed. **Procès-verbaux de la Commune de Paris (10 août 1792–1er juin 1793): extraits en partie inédits publiés d'après un manuscrit des Archives Nationales.** Paris, 1894.

VC265. Aulard, Francois V. A., ed. **Paris pendant la réaction thermidorienne et sous le Directoire: recueil de documents pour l'histoire de l'esprit public à Paris.** 5 v. Paris, 1898–1902.

VC266. ——, ed. **La Société des Jacobins: recueil de documents pour l'histoire de Club des Jacobins de Paris.** 6 v. Paris, 1889–97.

VC267. Debidour, Antonin, ed. **Recueil des actes du Directoire Exécutif (procès-verbaux, arrêtés, instructions, lettres et actes divers).** 4 v. Paris, 1910–17.

VC268. Douarche, Aristide, ed. **Les tribunaux civils de Paris pendant la Révolution (1791–1800): documents inédits recueillis avant l'incendie du Palais de Justice de 1871 par Casenave, conseiller à la cour de cassation.** 2 v. in 3. Paris, 1905–07.

VC269. Lacroix, Sigismond, and René Farge, eds. **Actes de la Commune de Paris pendant la Révolution.** Ser. 1, 7 v. and index; ser. 2, 8 v. Paris, 1894–1914.

VC270. Schmidt, Wilhelm A., ed. **Paris pendant la Révolution d'après les rapports de la police secrète, 1789–1800.** 4 v. Paris, 1880–94.

VC271. Lefebvre, Georges, and Anne Terroine, eds. **Recueil des documents relatifs aux séances des États-Généraux, mai–juin 1789.** V. 1. Paris, 1953.

VC272. Legg, Leopold G. W., ed. **Select documents illustrative of the history of the French Revolution: the Constituent Assembly.** 2 v. Oxford, 1905.

VC273. Higgins, Earl L., ed. **The French Revolution as told by contemporaries.** Boston, 1938.

VC274. Stewart, John H. **A documentary survey of the French Revolution.** N.Y., 1951.

VC275. Thompson, James M., ed. **English witnesses of the French Revolution.** Oxford, 1938.

General

VC276. Brinton, Crane. **A decade of revolution, 1789–1799.** N.Y., 1934.

VC277. Lefebvre, Georges. **La Révolution Française.** Paris, 1951.

VC278. Hazen, Charles D. **The French Revolution.** N.Y., 1932.

VC279. Lavisse, Ernest, ed. **Histoire de France contemporaine** (*VC139*), v. 1–2.

VC280. Godechot, Jacques. **La grande nation: l'expansion révolutionnaire de la France dans le monde de 1789 à 1799.** 2 v. Paris, 1956.

VC281. Göhring, Martin. **Geschichte der grossen Revolution.** V. 1–2. Tübingen, 1950–51.

VC282. Madelin, Louis. **The French Revolution.** New ed., N.Y., 1928.

VC283. Mathiez, Albert. **The French Revolution.** N.Y., 1928.

VC284. Aulard, François V. A. **The French Revolution, a political history, 1789–1804.** 4 v. N.Y., 1910.

VC285. Jaurès, Jean. **Histoire socialiste de la Révolution Française.** Ed. by Albert Mathiez. 8 v. Paris, 1922–24.

VC286. Sorel, Albert. **L'Europe et la Révolution Française.** See *T303*.

VC287. Michelet, Jules. **Histoire de la Révolution Française.** Rev. ed., 9 v., Paris, 1883–87.

VC288. Mignet, François A. A. **The French Revolution from 1789 to 1815.** [H. C. Lodge, ed., History of nations, 10.]

VC289. Taine, Hippolyte A. **Les origines de la France contemporaine.** 6 v. Paris, 1876–94. V. 2–4. Also English translation.

VC290. Thiers, Louis Adolphe. **History of the French Revolution.** 5 v. London, 1895.

VC291. Sybel, Heinrich von. **Geschichte der Revolutionszeit von 1789 bis 1800.** Rev. ed., 10 v., Stuttgart, 1897–1900. See also *The Cambridge modern history (T4)*, v. 8.

Estates General and National Assembly

VC292. Lefebvre, Georges. **The coming of the French Revolution.** Princeton, 1947.

VC293. Garrett, Mitchell B. **The Estates General of 1789: the problems of composition and organization.** N.Y., 1935.

VC294. Hyslop, Beatrice F. **A guide to the general cahiers of 1789, with the texts of unedited cahiers.** N.Y., 1936.

VC295. Chauvet, Paul. **L'insurrection parisienne et la prise de la Bastille.** Paris, 1946.

VC296. Herbert, Sydney. **The fall of feudalism in France.** London, 1921.

VC297. Lefebvre, Georges. **La grande peur de 1789.** Paris, 1932.

VC298. Mazé, Jules. **Les journées révolutionnaires d'octobre 1789.** Paris, 1939.

VC299. Thompson, Eric. **Popular sovereignty and the French Constituent Assembly, 1789–1791.** Manchester, 1952.

VC300. Leclercq, Henri. **La fuite du roi.** Paris, 1936.

Legislative Assembly

VC301. Sagnac, Philippe. **La révolution du 10 août 1792: la chute de la royauté.** Paris, 1909.

VC302. Caron, Pierre. **Les massacres de septembre.** Paris, 1935.

VC303. Caron, Pierre. **Les missions du Conseil Exécutif Provisoire et de la Commune de Paris.** V. 1–2. Paris, 1950–53.

National Convention

VC304. Kuściński, August. **Dictionnaire des conventionnels.** Paris, 1919.

VC305. Belloni, Georges. **Le Comité Sûreté Générale de la Convention Nationale.** Paris, 1924.

VC306. Gardie, Alphonse. **La Commune de Paris, 10 août 1792–9 thermidor an II: essai sur le gouvernement des masses.** Paris, 1940.

VC307. Godfrey, James. **Revolutionary justice: a study of the organization, personnel, and procedure of the Paris Tribunal, 1793–1795.** Chapel Hill, 1951.

VC308. Kerr, Wilfred B. **The Reign of Terror, 1793–1794: the experiment of the democratic republic, and the rise of the bourgeoisie.** Toronto, 1927.

VC309. Greer, Donald M. **The incidence of the Terror during the French Revolution:** a statistical interpretation. Cambridge, Mass., 1935.

VC310. Palmer, Robert R. **Twelve who ruled: the Committee of Public Safety during the Terror.** Princeton, 1941.

VC311. Calvet, Henri. **Un instrument de la Terreur à Paris: le Comité de Salut Public ou de Surveillance du Département de Paris (8 juin 1793–21 messidor an II).** Paris, 1941.

VC312. Sirich, John B. **The revolutionary committees in the departments of France, 1793–1794.** Cambridge, Mass., 1943.

VC313. Brinton, Crane. **The Jacobins: an essay in the new history.** N.Y., 1930.

VC314. Dowd, David L. **Pageant-master of the republic: Jacques-Louis David and the French Revolution.** Lincoln, Neb., 1948.

Thermidor and Directory

VC315. Lefebvre, Georges. **Les thermidoriens.** Paris, 1937.

VC316. Mathiez, Albert. **After Robespierre, the Thermidorian Reaction.** N.Y., 1931.

VC317. ——. **Le Directoire, du 11 brumaire an IV au 18 fructidor an V.** Ed. by Jacques Godechot. Paris, 1934.

VC318. Lefebvre, Georges. **Le Directoire.** Paris, 1946.

VC319. Meynier, Albert. **Les coups d'état du Directoire.** New ed., 3 v., Paris, 1932.

Special Studies

VC320. Aulard, François V. A. **Études et leçons sur la Révolution Française.** 9 v. Paris, 1901–24.

VC321. Lefebvre, Georges. **Études sur la Révolution Française.** Paris, 1954.

VC322. Cochin, Augustin. **Les sociétés de pensée et la démocratie: études d'histoire révolutionnaire.** Paris, 1921.

VC323. Dubreuil, Léon. **Histoire des insurrections de l'Ouest.** 2 v. Paris, 1929–30.

VC324. Gabory, Émile. **La Révolution et la Vendée.** 3 v. Paris, 1925–28.

VC325. Bourdin, Isabelle. **Les sociétés populaires à Paris pendant la Révolution Française jusqu'à la chute de la royauté.** Paris, 1937.

VC326. Cardenal, Louis de. **La province pendant la Révolution: histoire des clubs Jacobins (1789–1795).** Paris, 1929.

VC327. Madelin, Louis. **La contre-révolution sous la Révolution, 1789–1815.** Paris, 1935.

VC328. Baldensperger, Fernand. **Le mouvement des idées dans l'émigration française (1789–1815).** 2 v. Paris, 1924–25.

VC329. Greer, Donald M. **The incidence of the emigration during the French Revolution.** Cambridge, Mass., 1951.

VC330. Beik, Paul H. **The French Revolution seen from the right: social theories in motion, 1789–1799.** Philadelphia, 1956.

VC331. Godechot, Jacques L. **Les insti-**

tutions de la France sous la Révolution et l'empire. Paris, 1951.

VC332. Seligman, Edmund. **La justice en France pendant la Révolution (1789–1793).** 2 v. Paris, 1901–13.

VC333. Brace, Richard M. **Bordeaux and the Gironde, 1789–1794.** Ithaca, 1947.

VC334. Garrigues, Georges. **Les districts parisiens pendant la Révolution Française.** Paris, 1931.

VC335. Alméras, Henri d'. **La tyrannie démocratique pendant la Révolution.** Paris, 1935.

VC336. Aulard, François V. A. **La Révolution Française et le régime féodal.** Paris, 1919.

VC337. Marion, Marcel. **Le brigandage pendant la Révolution.** Paris, 1934.

VC338. Parker, Harold T. **The cult of antiquity and the French revolutionaries: a study in the development of the revolutionary spirit.** Chicago, 1937.

The Consulate and the Empire

(*Geoffrey Bruun*)

Bibliographies

VC339. Kircheisen, Friedrich M. **Bibliographie du temps de Napoléon.** 2 v. Paris, 1908–12. German ed., 2 v., Berlin, 1908–12.

VC340. Davois, Gustave. **Bibliographie napoléonienne française jusqu'en 1908.** 3 v. Paris, 1909–11.

VC341. Villat, Louis. **Napoléon (1799–1815).** Paris, 1936.

Sources

VC342. Correspondance de Napoléon Ier: publiée par ordre de l'empereur Napoléon III. 32 v. Paris, 1858–70.

VC343. Supplément. Ed. by Albert Du-Casse. Paris, 1887.

VC344. Lecestre, Léon, ed. **Lettres inédites de Napoléon Ier (an VIII–1815).** 2 v. Paris, 1897.

VC345. Brotonne, Léonce de, ed. **Lettres inédites de Napoléon Ier.** Paris, 1898.

VC346. ——, ed. **Dernières lettres inédites de Napoléon Ier.** 2 v. Paris, 1903.

VC347. Picard, Ernest, and Louis Tuetey, eds. **Correspondance inédite de Napoléon Ier conservée aux Archives de la Guerre.** 4 v. Paris, 1912–13.

General Works

VC348. Madelin, Louis. **Histoire du consulat et de l'empire.** 16 v. Paris, 1937–54. Also abridged English translation.

VC349. Kircheisen, Friedrich M. **Napoleon I, sein Leben und seine Zeit.** 9 v. Munich, 1911–34. Also abr. English trans.

VC350. Thiers, Louis Adolphe. **Histoire du consulat et de l'empire.** 21 v. Paris, 1845–74.

VC351. Lavisse, Ernest, ed. **Histoire de France contemporaine** (*VC139*), v. 3.

VC352. Bruun, Geoffrey. **Europe and the French imperium, 1799–1814.** N.Y., 1938.

VC353. Jaurès, Jean. **Histoire socialiste** (*VC285*), v. 6.

VC354. Lefebvre, Georges. **Napoléon.** 3rd ed., Paris, 1947.

VC355. Bourgin, Georges. **Napoleon und seine Zeit.** Gotha, 1925.

Biographies of Napoleon I and His Family

VC356. Fournier, Auguste. **Napoleon I, eine Biographie.** 2nd ed., 3 v., Vienna, 1904–06. Also abr. English trans.

VC357. Lanfrey, Pierre. **History of Napoleon the First.** 23rd ed., 4 v., London and N.Y., 1894.

VC358. Rose, J. Holland. **The life of Napoleon I.** 11th ed., 2 v., London, 1934.

VC359. Sloane, William M. **The life of Napoleon Bonaparte.** Rev. ed., 4 v., N.Y., 1910.

VC360. Thompson, James M. **Napoleon Bonaparte, his rise and fall.** Oxford, 1952.

VC361. Bainville, Jacques. **Napoléon.** Paris, 1931.

VC362. Bourgoing, Jean de. **Marie Louise von Österreich, Kaiserin der Franzosen.** Vienna, 1949.

VC363. ——. **Le fils de Napoléon, roi de Rome.** Paris, 1932.

VC364. Masson, Frédéric. **Napoléon et sa famille.** 13 v. Paris, 1900–1919.

Special Studies

VC365. Vandal, Albert. **L'avènement de Bonaparte.** 2 v. Paris, 1902–07.

VC366. Thiry, Jean. **Le coup d'état du 18 brumaire.** Paris, 1947.

VC367. Deutsch, Harold C. **The genesis of Napoleonic imperialism.** Cambridge, Mass., 1938.

VC368. Friedrich, Hans E. **Napoleon I, Idee und Staat.** Berlin, 1936.

VC369. Durand, Charles. **Le fonctionnement du conseil d'état napoléonien.** Gap, 1954.

VC370. Thiry, Jean. **Le sénat de Napoléon (1800–1814).** Paris, 1932.

VC371. Aulard, François V. A. "La centralisation napoléonienne: les préfets." **Études et leçons sur la Révolution française,** 7 (1913): 113–95.

VC372. Lanzac de Laborie, Léon de. **Paris sous Napoléon.** 8 v. Paris, 1905–13.

VC373. Holtman, Robert B. **Napoleonic propaganda.** Baton Rouge, 1950.

VC374. Reinhard, Marcel. **Avec Bonaparte en Italie.** Paris, 1946.

VC375. Thiry, Jean. **La première abdication de Napoléon Ier.** 2nd ed., Paris, 1948.

VC376. Becke, Archibald F. **Napoleon and Waterloo.** Rev. ed., London, 1936.

VC377. Houssaye, Henri. **1815: la seconde abdication; la terreur blanche.** Paris, 1905.

VC378. Masson, Frédéric. **Napoléon à Sainte-Hélène, 1815–1821.** Paris, 1912.

VC379. Rosebery, Archibald P. P., earl of. **Napoleon, the last phase.** N.Y. and London, 1900.

Restoration and July Monarchy
(Frederick B. Artz)

Period of the Restoration

VC380. Artz, Frederick B. **France under the Bourbon restoration.** Cambridge, Mass., 1931.

VC381. Bertier de Sauvigny, Guillaume de. **La restauration.** Paris, 1955.

VC382. La Gorce, Pierre de. **La restauration.** 2 v. Paris, 1926–28.

VC383. Pastre, Jules L. G. **Histoire de la restauration, 1814–1830.** Paris, 1935.

VC384. Ponteil, Félix. **La chute de Napoléon Ier et la crise française de 1814–1815.** Paris, 1943.

VC385. La Gorce, Pierre de. **Charles X.** Paris, 1928.

VC386. Bagge, Dominique. **Les idées politiques en France sous la restauration.** Paris, 1952.

VC387. Hudson, Nora E. **Ultra-royalism and the French restoration.** Cambridge, Eng., 1936.

VC388. Duvergier de Hauranne, Prosper L. **Histoire du gouvernement parlementaire en France, 1814–1848.** 10 v. Paris, 1857–72.

VC389. Lucas-Dubreton, Jean. **The restoration and the July monarchy.** V. 8 of Frantz Funck-Brentano, **National history of France** (*VC140*).

VC390. Ponteil, Félix. **La monarchie parlementaire, 1815–1848.** Paris, 1949.

VC391. Bastid, Paul. **Les institutions politiques de la monarchie parlementaire française, 1814–1848.** Paris, 1954.

Period of the July Monarchy

VC392. Thureau-Dangin, Paul. **Histoire de la monarchie de juillet.** 7 v. Paris, 1884–92.

VC393. Blanc, Louis. **The history of ten years, 1830–1840.** 2 v. London, 1844–45.

VC394. Allison, John M. S. **Thiers and the French monarchy, 1797–1848.** London, 1926.

VC395. Lucas-Dubreton, Jean. **Louis-Philippe.** Paris, 1938.

VC396. Pouthas, Charles H. "Les ministères de Louis Philippe." **Rev. d'hist. mod. et contemp.**, 1 (Apr.-June 1954): 102–30.

VC397. Hillebrand, Karl. **Geschichte Frankreichs von der Thronbesteigung Louis Philipp's bis zum Falle Napoleon's III.** 2 v. Gotha, 1877–79.

Second Republic and Second Empire
(David H. Pinkney)

Period of the Second Republic

VC398. La Gorce, Pierre de. **Histoire de la seconde république française.** 2 v. Paris, 1886.

VC399. Dautry, Jean. **Histoire de la révolution de 1848 en France.** Paris, 1948.

VC400. Ponteil, Félix. **1848.** Paris, 1937.

VC401. Lamartine, Alphonse de. **History of the French revolution of 1848.** London, 1891.

VC402. Renard, Georges. **La république de 1848 (1848–1852).** Paris, [1907].

VC403. Bertaut, Jules. **1848 et la seconde république.** Paris, 1937.

VC404. Bastid, Paul. **Doctrines et institutions de la seconde république.** 2 v. Paris, 1945.

VC405. McKay, Donald C. **The national workshops: a study in the French revolution of 1848.** Cambridge, Mass., 1933.

Works Covering Periods of Second Republic and Empire

VC406. Simpson, Frederick A. **The rise of Louis Napoleon.** 3rd ed., N.Y. and London, 1950.

VC407. ——. **Louis Napoleon and the recovery of France, 1848–1856.** 3rd ed., N.Y. and London, 1951.

Period of the Second Empire

VC408. La Gorce, Pierre de. **Histoire du second empire.** 7 v. Paris, 1894–1904.

VC409. Ollivier, Émile. **L'empire libéral: études, récits, souvenirs.** 18 v. Paris, 1895–1918.

VC410. Delord, Taxile. **Histoire du second empire.** 6 v. Paris, 1869–75.

VC411. Thomas, Albert. **Le second empire (1852–1870).** Paris, [1907].

VC412. Aubry, Octave. **The second empire.** Philadelphia and N.Y., 1940.

VC413. Blanchard, Marcel. **Le second empire.** Paris, 1950.

VC414. La Gorce, Pierre de. **Napoléon III et sa politique.** Paris, 1933.

VC415. Guérard, Albert. **Napoleon III.** N.Y., 1955.

VC416. Guérot, Paul. **Napoleon III.** 2 v. Paris, 1933–34.

VC417. Thompson, James M. **Louis Napoleon and the second empire.** Oxford, 1954; N.Y., 1955.

VC418. George, Robert E. (pseud., Robert E. Sencourt). **The life of the Empress Eugénie.** N.Y., 1931.

The Third and Fourth Republics
(*Gordon Wright*)

General Histories

VC419. Chastenet, Jacques. **Histoire de la troisième république.** Paris, 1952 ff. A 6 v. project.

VC420. Bainville, Jacques. **La troisième république, 1870–1935.** Paris, 1935.

VC421. Brogan, Denis W. **The development of modern France (1870–1939).** London, 1940.

VC422. Bourgin, Georges. **La troisième république, 4 septembre 1870–3 août 1914.** Paris, 1939.

VC423. Dansette, Adrien. **Histoire des présidents de la république, de Louis Napoléon Bonaparte à Vincent Auriol.** Paris, 1953.

VC424. David, Robert. **La troisième république: soixante ans de politique et d'histoire, de 1871 à nos jours.** Paris, 1934.

VC425. Zévaès, Alexandre. **Histoire de la troisième république.** Paris, 1938.

The Siege and the Commune

VC426. Kranzberg, Melvin. **The siege of Paris, 1870–1871.** Ithaca, 1950.

VC427. Bourgin, Georges. **La guerre de 1870–1871 et la Commune.** Paris, 1939.

VC428. Bury, John P. T. **Gambetta and the national defence: a republican dictatorship in France.** London, 1936.

VC429. Bourgin, Georges. **La Commune.** Paris, 1953.

VC430. Jellinek, Frank. **The Paris Commune of 1871.** N.Y., 1937.

VC431. Laronze, Georges. **Histoire de la Commune de 1871, d'après des documents et des souvenirs inédits: la justice.** Paris, 1928.

VC432. Mason, Edward S. **The Paris Commune.** N.Y., 1930.

VC433. Joughin, Jean T. **The Paris Commune in French politics, 1871–1880.** 2 v. Baltimore, 1955.

Establishment of the Third Republic

VC434. Hanotaux, Gabriel. **Contemporary France.** 4 v. London, 1903–09.

VC435. ———. **Histoire de la fondation de la troisième république.** 4 v. Paris, 1925–26.

VC436. Deslandres, Maurice C. E. **Histoire constitutionnelle de la France: l'avènement de la troisième république, la constitution de 1875.** Paris, 1937.

VC437. Brabant, Frank H. **The beginning of the third republic in France.** London, 1940.

VC438. Dreyfus, Robert. **La république de Monsieur Thiers (1871–1873).** Paris, 1930.

VC439. Thiers, Louis Adolphe. **Memoirs of M. Thiers, 1870–1873.** London, 1915; N.Y., 1916.

VC440. Goualt, Jacques. **Comment la France est devenue républicaine: les élections générales et partielles à l'assemblée nationale, 1870–1875.** Paris, 1954.

VC441. Halévy, Daniel. **La fin des notables.** Paris, 1930.

VC442. ———. **La république des ducs.** Paris, 1937.

VC443. Zola, Émile. **La république en marche: chroniques parlementaires.** 2 v. Paris, 1956.

Parties and Politics of the Third Republic

VC444. Sibert, Marcel. **La constitution de la France du 4 septembre 1870 au 9 août 1944.** Paris, 1946.

VC445. Soulier, Auguste. **L'instabilité ministérielle sous la troisième république.** Paris, 1939.

VC446. Leroy, Maxime. **Les tendances du pouvoir et de la liberté en France au XXe siècle.** Paris, 1937.

VC447. Gooch, Robert K. **The French parliamentary committee system.** N.Y., 1935.

VC448. Goguel, François. **Géographie des élections françaises de 1870 à 1951.** Paris, 1951.

VC449. Frank, Walter. **Nationalismus und Demokratie im Frankreich der dritten Republik (1871 bis 1918).** Hamburg, 1933.

VC450. Beau de Loménie, Emmanuel. **Les responsabilités des dynasties bourgeoises.** 3 v. Paris, 1943–54.

VC451. Dansette, Adrien. **Le Boulangisme, 1886–1890.** Paris, 1947.

VC452. ———. **Les affaires de Panama.** Paris, 1934.

VC453. Byrnes, Robert F. **Antisemitism in modern France.** New Brunswick, 1950.

VC454. Kayser, Jacques. **L'affaire Dreyfus.** 7th ed., Paris, 1946.

VC455. Schwartzkoppen, Maximilian von. **Les carnets de Schwartzkoppen: la vérité sur Dreyfus.** Paris, 1930.

VC456. Chapman, Guy. **The Dreyfus case.** London, 1955.

VC457. Halasz, Nicholas. **Captain Dreyfus: the story of a mass hysteria.** N.Y., 1955.

VC458. Paléologue, Maurice M. **Journal de l'affaire Dreyfus et le Quai d'Orsay.** Paris, 1955.

VC459. Acomb, Evelyn. **The French laic laws (1879–1889).** N.Y., 1941.

VC460. Lachapelle, Georges. **Le ministère Méline, deux années de politique intérieure et extérieure, 1896–1897.** Paris, 1928.

VC461. Bonnefous, Georges. **Histoire politique de la troisième république. V. 1, L'avant-guerre (1906–1914).** Paris, 1956.

VC462. King, Jere C. **Generals and politicians: conflict between France's high com-**

mand, parliament, and government, 1914–1918. See *AG20*.

VC463. Wright, Gordon. **Raymond Poincaré and the French presidency.** Stanford, 1942.

VC464. Jackson, John H. **Clemenceau and the third republic.** N.Y., 1948.

VC465. Dansette, Adrien. **Histoire religieuse de la France contemporaine.** 2 v. Paris, 1948–51.

VC466. Werth, Alexander. **The twilight of France, 1933–1940.** N.Y., 1942.

VC467. Goguel, François. **La politique des partis sous la troisième république.** 2 v. Paris, 1946.

VC468. Soltau, Roger H. **French parties and politics, 1871–1930.** London, 1930.

VC469. Massis, Henri. **Maurras et notre temps.** 2 v. Paris, 1951.

VC470. Havard de la Montagne, Robert. **Histoire de "L'Action Française."** Paris, 1950.

VC471. Rollet, Henri. **Albert de Mun et le parti catholique.** Paris, 1949.

VC472. Biton, Louis. **La démocratie chrétienne dans la politique française.** Angers, 1954.

VC473. Lecomte, Maxime. **Les Ralliés: histoire d'un parti (1886–1898).** Paris, 1898.

VC474. Micaud, Charles A. **The French right and Nazi Germany, 1933–1939.** Durham, 1943.

VC475. Scott, John A. **Republican ideas and the liberal tradition in France, 1870–1914.** N.Y., 1951.

VC476. Noland, Aaron. **The founding of the French Socialist party, 1893–1905.** Cambridge, Mass., 1956.

VC477. Walter, Gérard. **Histoire du parti Communiste français.** Paris, 1948.

World War II and the Vichy Interlude

VC478. Les événements survenus en France de 1933 à 1945: rapport fait au nom de la commission chargée d'enquêter sur les événements survenus en France de 1933 à 1945. 10 v. Paris, 1947–52. Other volumes in preparation.

VC479. Bloch, Marc. **Strange defeat.** N.Y., 1949.

VC480. Aron, Robert. **Histoire de Vichy.** Paris, 1954.

VC481. Pickles, Dorothy. **France between the republics.** London, 1946.

VC482. Farmer, Paul. **Vichy: political dilemma.** N.Y., 1955.

VC483. Cobban, Alfred. "Vichy France." **Survey of international affairs 1939–1946: Hitler's Europe,** ed. by Arnold and Veronica Toynbee (London, 1954), pp. 338–434.

VC484. Michel, Henri. **Histoire de la résistance.** Paris, 1950.

VC485. Michel, Henri, and Boris Mirkine-Guetzévitch, eds. **Les idées politiques et sociales de la résistance.** Paris, 1954.

The Fourth Republic

VC486. Earle, Edward M., ed. **Modern France: problems of the third and fourth republics.** See *AF102*.

VC487. Thomson, David. **Democracy in France: the third and fourth republics.** 2nd ed., N.Y., 1952.

VC488. Siegfried, André. **De la IIIe à la IVe république.** Paris, 1956.

VC489. Werth, Alexander. **France, 1940–1955.** N.Y., 1956.

VC490. Goguel, François. **France under the fourth republic.** Ithaca, 1952.

VC491. Wright, Gordon. **The reshaping of French democracy.** N.Y., 1948.

VC492. Goguel, François, and Mario Einaudi. **Christian democracy in Italy and France.** Notre Dame, Ind., 1952.

VC493. Williams, Philip. **Politics in postwar France.** London, 1954.

VC494. Pickles, Dorothy M. **French politics: the first years of the fourth republic.** London, 1953.

VC495. Luethy, Herbert. **France against herself.** N.Y., 1955.

VC496. Gavin, Catherine. **Liberated France.** N.Y., 1955.

VC497. Matthews, Ronald. **The death of the fourth republic.** N.Y., 1954.

DIPLOMATIC HISTORY
(René Albrecht-Carrié)

Sources

VC498. Recueil des traités de la France depuis 1713 jusqu'à nos jours. Ed. by Alexandre J. H. de Clercq and Étienne F. S. de Clercq. 23 v. Paris, 1864–1917.

VC499. Recueils des instructions données aux ambassadeurs et ministres de France depuis les traités de Westphalie jusqu'à la Révolution Française, publiés sous les auspices de la Commission des Archives Diplomatiques au Ministère des Affaires Étrangères. Ed. by Albert Sorel, Gabriel Hanotaux, and others. 25 v. in 26. Paris, 1884–1929.

VC500. France. Ministère des Affaires Étrangères. **Documents diplomatiques.** 1861 ff. Paris, 1862 ff.

VC501. Comité National du Centenaire de 1848. **Documents diplomatiques du gouvernement provisoire et de la commission du pouvoir exécutif.** V. 1. Paris, 1954.

VC502. Thouvenel, Louis, ed. **Nicolas Ier et Napoléon III: les préliminaires de la Guerre de Crimée (1852–1854), d'après les papiers inédits de M. Thouvenel.** Paris, 1891.

VC503. ——, ed. **Pages de l'histoire du second empire . . . 1854–1866.** Paris, 1903.

VC504. ——, ed. **Le secret de l'empereur . . . 1860–1863.** 2 v. Paris, 1889. Correspondence of Thouvenel, Gramont, and Flahault.

VC505. ——, ed. **Trois années de la question d'Orient, 1856–1859.** Paris, 1897.

VC506. Oncken, Hermann. **Die Rheinpolitik Kaiser Napoleons III. von 1863 bis 1870 und der Ursprung des Krieges von 1870–1871.** 3 v. Berlin and Leipzig, 1926.

VC507. France. Ministère des Affaires Étrangères. **Les origines diplomatiques de la guerre de 1870–1871.** 29 v. Paris, 1910–32.

VC508. ——. **Documents diplomatiques français (1871–1914).** Paris, 1929 ff.

VC509. Montaux, Paul J. **Les délibérations du Conseil des Quatre (24 mars–28 juin 1919).** See *AH133*.

General

VC510. Ancel, Jacques. **Affaires étrangères: aide-mémoire de la politique française (1789–1936).** Paris, 1936.

VC511. Bourgeois, Émile. **Manuel historique de politique étrangère.** 4 v. Paris, 1893–1926.

VC512. Pinon, René. **Histoire diplomatique, 1515–1928.** V. 9 of Gabriel Hanotaux, Histoire de la nation française (*VC141*).

VC513. Rain, Pierre. **La diplomatie française d'Henri IV à Vergennes.** Paris, 1945.

Seventeenth and Eighteenth Centuries

VC514. André, Louis. **Louis XIV et l'Europe.** Paris, 1950.

VC515. Picavet, Camille G. **La diplomatie française au temps de Louis XIV (1661–1715).** Paris, 1930.

VC516. Trudel, Marcel. **Louis XVI, le congrès américain et le Canada, 1774–1789.** Quebec, 1949.

VC517. Wilson, Arthur M. **French foreign policy during the administration of Cardinal Fleury, 1726–1743.** Cambridge, Mass., 1936.

Revolution

VC518. Masson, Frédéric. **Le département des affaires étrangères pendant la Révolution, 1787–1804.** Paris, 1877.

VC519. Fugier, André. **La Révolution Française et l'empire napoléonien.** Paris, 1954. [Histoire des relations internationales, 4.]

VC520. Guyot, Raymond. **Le Directoire et la paix de l'Europe . . . (1795–1799).** Paris, 1911.

VC521. Sorel, Albert. **L'Europe et la Révolution Française.** See *T303*.

First Empire

VC522. Driault, Edouard. **Napoléon et l'Europe.** 5 v. Paris, 1910–27.

VC523. Mowat, Robert B. **The diplomacy of Napoleon.** London, 1924.

VC524. Driault, Edouard. **Napoléon en Italie (1800–1812).** Paris, 1906.

Second Empire

VC525. Pagès, Georges. **La politique extérieure de Napoléon III.** Paris, 1933.

VC526. Case, Lynn M. **Franco-Italian relations, 1860–1865: the Roman question and the convention of September.** Philadelphia, 1932.

VC527. Lord, Robert H. **The origins of the war of 1870: new documents from the German archives.** Cambridge, Mass., 1924.

VC528. Case, Lynn M. **French opinion on war and diplomacy during the second empire.** Philadelphia, 1954.

VC529. ——, ed. **French opinion on the United States and Mexico, 1860–1867: extracts from the reports of the procureurs généraux.** N.Y., 1936.

VC530. West, Warren R. **Contemporary French opinion on the American Civil War.** Baltimore, 1924.

VC531. Morand, Edmond. **Le canal de Suez et l'histoire extérieure du second empire.** Paris, 1936.

Third Republic

VC532. Renouvin, Pierre. **La politique extérieure de la France, 1871–1919.** Paris, 1950.

VC533. Schuman, Frederick L. **War and diplomacy in the French republic: an inquiry into political motivations and the control of foreign policy.** N.Y., 1931.

VC534. Sorel, Albert. **Histoire diplomatique de la guerre franco-allemande.** 2 v. Paris, 1875.

VC535. Carroll, Eber M. **French public opinion and foreign affairs, 1870–1914.** N.Y., 1931.

VC536. Langer, William L. **The Franco-Russian alliance, 1880–1894.** Cambridge, Mass., 1929.

VC537. Billot, Albert. **La France et l'Italie, histoire des années troubles, 1881–1899.** 2 v. Paris, 1905.

VC538. Pingaud, Albert. **Histoire diplomatique de la France pendant la grande guerre.** See *AH156*.

VC539. Driault, Edouard. **La paix de la France: les traités de 1918–1921; l'exécution des traités.** Paris, 1937.

VC540. Weill-Raynal, Étienne. **Les réparations allemandes et la France.** See *A159*.

VC541. Langer, William L. **Our Vichy gamble.** N.Y., 1947.

MILITARY HISTORY
(Richard D. Challener)

VC542. Favitski de Probobysz, A. **Répertoire bibliographique de la littérature militaire et coloniale française depuis cent ans.** Paris, 1935.

VC543. Revol, Joseph F. **Histoire de l'armée française.** Paris, 1929.

VC544. Colin, Jean, Frédéric Reboul, and others. **Histoire militaire et navale.** V. 7 of Gabriel Hanotaux, **Histoire de la nation française** (*VC141*).

VC545. Challener, Richard D. **The French theory of the nation in arms, 1866–1939.** N.Y., 1955.

VC546. Babeau, Albert A. **La vie militaire sous l'ancien régime.** 2 v. Paris, 1889–90.

VC547. Girardet, Raoul. **La société militaire dans la France contemporaine, 1815–1939.** Paris, 1953.

VC548. Boutaric, Edgard. **Institutions militaires de la France avant les armées permanentes.** Paris, 1863.

VC549. Monteilhet, Joseph. **Les institutions militaires de la France (1814–1932).** Paris, 1932.

VC550. Earle, Edward M., ed. **Makers of modern strategy.** Princeton, 1943. Chs. 2, 3, 4, 9, 10, 11, 15, and 18 are on Vauban, Guibert, Jomini, Du Picq, Foch, Bugeaud, Galliéni, Lyautey, Du Picq, Clemenceau, Maginot, and French theories of sea power. Bibliography.

VC551. La Roncière, Charles de. **Histoire de la marine française.** 6 v. Paris, 1899–1932.

VC552. Farrère, Claude. **Histoire de la marine française.** Paris, 1956.

VC553. Bamford, Paul. **Forests and French sea power, 1660–1789.** Toronto, 1956.

VC554. Lacour-Gayet, Georges. **La marine militaire de la France sous les règnes de Louis XIII et de Louis XIV.** Paris, 1911.

VC555. ———. **La marine militaire de la France sous le règne de Louis XV.** Paris, 1910.

VC556. Phipps, Ramsay W. **The armies of the first French republic and the rise of the marshals of Napoleon I.** 5 v. London, 1926–39.

VC557. Six, Georges. **Dictionnaire biographique des généraux et amiraux français de la Révolution et de l'empire (1792–1814).** 2 v. Paris, 1934.

VC558. Dodge, Theodore A. **Napoleon: a history of the art of war.** See *T358.*

VC559. Oman, Charles W. C. **A history of the Peninsular War.** 7 v. Oxford, 1902–30.

VC560. Mahan, Alfred T. **The influence of sea power upon the French Revolution and empire, 1793–1812.** 10th ed., 2 v., Boston, 1898.

VC561. Tarle, Eugene. **Napoleon's invasion of Russia in 1812.** See *T365.*

VC562. Palat, Barthélemy E. (pseud., Pierre Lehautcourt). **Histoire de la guerre de 1870–1871.** 7 v. Paris, 1901–08.

VC563. État-major de l'Armée. **Les armées françaises dans la grande guerre.** 10 v. in 66. Paris, 1922–36.

VC564. Bidou, Henry, and others. **La grande guerre.** V. 9 of Ernest Lavisse, ed., **Histoire de France contemporaine** (*VC139*).

VC565. Barjot, Pierre. **L'aviation militaire française.** Paris, 1936.

SOCIAL AND ECONOMIC HISTORY

Bibliographies and Sources
(Rondo E. Cameron)

VC566. Sée, Henri. "Recent work in French economic history (1905–1925)." **Economic history review,** 1 (1927–28): 137–53.

VC567. Dunham, Arthur L. "The economic history of France, 1815–1870." **Journal of modern history,** 21 (June 1949): 121–39. Bibliography.

VC568. John Crerar Library. **A catalogue of French economic documents from the sixteenth, seventeenth and eighteenth centuries.** Chicago, 1918.

VC569. Recueil des historiens de la France: documents financiers. 4 v. Paris, 1899–1955.

VC570. Collection de documents inédits sur l'histoire économique de la Révolution Française. Over 100 v. Paris, etc., 1906 ff.

VC571. Hayem, Julien, ed. **Mémoires et documents pour servir à l'histoire du commerce et de l'industrie en France.** 12 v. Paris, 1911–29.

General
(Rondo E. Cameron)

VC572. Sée, Henri E. **Histoire économique de la France.** 2 v. Paris, 1948–51.

Studies of Various Periods
(Rondo E. Cameron)

VC573. Gandilhon, René. **Politique économique de Louis XI.** Paris, 1941. Bibliography.

VC574. Hauser, Henri. "The characteristic features of French economic history from the middle of the sixteenth to the middle of the eighteenth century." **Econ. hist. rev.,** 4 (1933–34): 257–72.

VC575. Cole, Charles W. **Colbert and a century of French mercantilism.** 2 v. N.Y., 1939.

VC576. Sée, Henri. **Economic and social conditions in France during the eighteenth century.** N.Y., 1927. Bibliography.

VC577. Labrousse, Camille E. **La crise de l'économie française à la fin de l'ancien régime et au début de la Révolution.** Paris, 1944.

VC578. Clough, Shepard B. **France: a history of national economics, 1789–1939.** See *AF69.*

VC579. Clapham, John H. **The economic development of France and Germany, 1815–1914.** See *VF305.*

VC580. Sée, Henri. **La vie économique de la France sous la monarchie censitaire (1815–1848).** Paris, 1927. Bibliography.

VC581. Girard, Louis. **La politique des travaux publics du second empire.** Paris, 1952.

VC582. Rist, Charles, Gaëtan Pirou, and others. **De la France d'avant-guerre à la France d'aujourd'hui: vingt-cinq ans d'évolution de la structure économique et sociale française.** Paris, 1939.

Agriculture and Rural Life
(*David J. Brandenburg*)

VC583. Bloch, Marc. **Les caractères originaux de l'histoire rurale française.** See *K370.*

VC584. Lizerand, Georges. **Le régime rural de l'ancienne France.** Paris, 1942.

VC585. Augé-Laribé, Michel. **L'évolution de la France agricole.** Paris, 1912.

VC586. Roupnel, Gaston. **Histoire de la campagne française.** Paris, 1932.

VC587. Mauguin, ——. **Études historiques sur l'administration de l'agriculture en France.** 3 v. Paris, 1876–77.

VC588. Grand, Roger, and Raymond Delatouche. **L'agriculture au Moyen Âge de la fin de l'empire romain au XVIᵉ siècle.** Paris, 1950.

VC589. Luchitskii, Ivan V. **L'état des classes agricoles en France à la veille de la Révolution.** Paris, 1911.

VC590. Young, Arthur. **Voyages en France en 1787, 1788, et 1789.** Critical ed. by Henri Sée. 3 v. Paris, 1931.

VC591. Marion, Marcel. **La vente des biens nationaux pendant la Révolution, avec étude spéciale des ventes dans les départements de la Gironde et du Cher.** Paris, 1908.

VC592. Festy, Octave. **L'agriculture pendant la Révolution Française: les conditions de production et de récolte des céréales.** Paris, 1947.

VC593. Lefebvre, Georges. **Les paysans du Nord pendant la Révolution Française.** 2 v. Paris, 1924.

VC594. Festy, Octave. **L'agriculture française sous le Consulat.** Paris, 1952.

VC595. Augé-Laribé, Michel. **La politique agricole de la France de 1880 à 1940.** Paris, 1950.

Commerce
(*Paul W. Bamford*)

VC596. Levasseur, Émile. **Histoire du commerce de la France.** 2 v. Paris, 1911–12. Bibliography.

VC597. Haight, Frank A. **A history of French commercial policies.** N.Y., 1941.

VC598. Gottmann, Jean. **Les relations commerciales de la France.** Montreal, 1942.

VC599. Nogaro, Bertrand, and William

Oualid. **L'évolution du commerce, du crédit et des transports depuis cent cinquante ans.** Paris, 1914.

VC600. Pernoud, Régine. **Les villes marchandes aux XIVᵉ et XVᵉ siècles: impérialisme et capitalisme au Moyen Âge.** Paris, 1948.

VC601. Usher, Abbott P. **The history of the grain trade in France, 1400–1710.** Cambridge, Mass., 1913. Bibliography.

VC602. Nussbaum, Frederick L. **Commercial policy in the French Revolution: a study of the career of G. J. A. Ducher.** Washington, 1923. Bibliography.

VC603. Heckscher, Eli F. **The Continental System: an economic interpretation.** Ed. by Harald Westergaard. Oxford, 1922.

VC604. Arnauné, Auguste. **Le commerce extérieur et les tarifs de douane.** Paris, 1911.

VC605. Rémond, André. **Études sur la circulation marchande en France aux XVIIIᵉ et XIXᵉ siècles.** Paris, 1956 ff.

VC606. Masson, Paul. **Histoire du commerce français dans le Levant au XVIIᵉ siècle.** See *S96.*

VC607. ——. **Histoire du commerce français dans le Levant au XVIIIᵉ siècle,** Paris, 1911.

VC608. Cavaillès, Henri. **La route française, son histoire.** Paris, 1946. Bibliography.

VC609. Dauzet, Pierre. **Le siècle des chemins de fer en France, 1821–1938.** Fontenay-aux-Roses, 1948.

VC610. Doukas, Kimon A. **French railroads and the state.** N.Y., 1945. Bibliography.

VC611. Charliat, Paul P. **Trois siècles d'économie maritime française.** Paris, 1931.

VC612. Pigeonneau, Henri. **Histoire du commerce de la France.** 2 v. Paris, 1885–88. Maritime history to Louis XIV.

VC613. Mollat, Michel. **Le commerce maritime normand à la fin du Moyen Âge.** Paris, 1952.

VC614. Davenas, Paul. **Les messageries royales.** Paris, 1937.

VC615. Colin, Ambroise. **La navigation commerciale au XIX siècle.** Paris, 1901.

VC616. Vaillé, Eugène. **Histoire générale des postes françaises.** 6 v. Paris, 1947–55. These volumes reach to 1789; others in preparation.

VC617. Wybo, Bernard. **Le conseil de commerce et le commerce intérieur de la France au XVIIIᵉ siècle.** Paris, 1936.

VC618. Gaumont, Jean. **Histoire générale de la coopération en France.** 2 v. Paris, 1923–24.

Industry
(*Arthur L. Dunham*)

VC619. Martin, Germain. **La grande industrie sous le règne de Louis XIV, plus particulièrement de 1660 à 1715.** Paris, 1899.

VC620. ——. **La grande industrie en France sous le règne de Louis XV.** Paris, 1900.

VC621. Ballot, Charles. **L'introduction du machinisme dans l'industrie française.** Paris, 1923.

VC622. Dunham, Arthur L. **The industrial revolution in France, 1815–1848.** N.Y., 1955. Also French ed.

VC623. ——. **The Anglo-French treaty of commerce of 1860 and the progress of the industrial revolution in France.** Ann Arbor, 1930.

VC624. Fohlen, Claude. **L'industrie textile au temps du Second Empire.** Paris, 1956. Excellent bibliography.

VC625. Clerget, Pierre. **Les industries de la soie en France.** Paris, 1925.

VC626. Gille, Bertrand. **Les origines de la grande industrie métallurgique en France.** Paris, 1948.

VC627. Tribot-Laspière, Jean. **L'industrie de l'acier en France.** Paris, 1916.

VC628. Frauque, Maurice. **L'évolution économique de la grande industrie chimique en France.** Strasbourg, 1932.

Finance
(*David S. Landes*)

VC629. Marion, Marcel. **Histoire financière de la France depuis 1715.** 6 v. Paris, 1914–31.

VC630. Harsin, Paul. **Crédit public et banque d'état en France du XVIe au XVIIIe siècle.** Paris, 1933.

VC631. ——. **Les doctrines monétaires et financières en France du XVIe au XVIIIe siècle.** Paris, 1928.

VC632. Marion, Marcel. **Les impôts directs sous l'ancien régime, principalement au XVIIIe siècle.** Paris, 1910.

VC633. Stourm, René. **Les finances de l'ancien régime et la Révolution: origines du système financier actuel.** 2 v. Paris, 1885.

VC634. Gomel, Charles. **Les causes financières de la Révolution Française.** 2 v. Paris, 1892–93.

VC635. ——. **Histoire financière de l'Assemblée Constituante.** 2 v. Paris, 1896–97.

VC636. ——. **Histoire financière de la Législative et la Convention.** 2 v. Paris, 1902–05.

VC637. Stourm, René. **Les finances du Consulat.** Paris, 1902.

VC638. Say, Léon. **Les finances de la France sous la troisième république.** 4 v. Paris, 1898–1901.

VC639. ——. **Histoire de la Caisse d'Escompte, 1776 à 1793.** Reims, [1848].

VC640. Ramon, Gabriel. **Histoire de la Banque de France.** Paris, 1929.

VC641. Bigo, Robert. **Les banques françaises au cours du XIXe siècle.** Paris, 1947.

VC642. Mehrens, Bernhard. **Die Entstehung und Entwicklung der grossen französischen Kreditinstitut, mit Berücksichtigung ihres Einflusses auf die wirtschaftliche Entwicklung Frankreichs.** Stuttgart, 1911.

VC643. White, Harry D. **The French international accounts, 1880–1913.** Cambridge, Mass., 1933.

VC644. Sédillot, René. **Histoire du franc.** Paris, 1939.

VC645. Hauser, Henri. **Recherches et documents sur l'histoire des prix en France de 1500 à 1800.** Paris, 1936.

VC646. Labrousse, Camille E. **Esquisse du mouvement des prix et des revenus en France au XVIIIe siècle.** Paris, 1933.

VC647. ——. **La crise de l'économie française à la fin de l'ancien régime et au début de la Révolution.** Paris, 1944.

Social Classes
(*Val R. Lorwin*)

VC648. Vaissière, Pierre de. **Gentilshommes campagnards de l'ancienne France: étude sur la condition, l'état social, et les moeurs de la noblesse de province du XVIe au XVIIIe siècle.** 3rd ed., Paris, 1904.

VC649. Wiley, William L. **The gentleman of Renaissance France.** Cambridge, Mass., 1954.

VC650. Sagnac, Philippe. **La formation de la société française moderne.** 2 v. Paris, 1945–46.

VC651. Ducros, Louis. **French society in the eighteenth century.** London, 1926.

VC652. Ford, Franklin L. **Robe and sword.** See *VC231*.

VC653. Goncourt, Edmond de, and Jules de Goncourt. **Histoire de la société française pendant la Révolution.** Paris, 1889.

VC654. Madelin, Louis. **La France de l'empire.** Paris, 1926.

VC655. Bellessort, André. **La société française sous Napoléon III.** Paris, 1932.

VC656. Ferré, Louise M. **Les classes sociales dans la France contemporaine.** Paris, 1934.

VC657. Normand, Charles. **La bourgeoisie française au XVIIe siècle . . . 1604–1661.** Paris, 1908.

VC658. Barber, Elinor G. **The bourgeoisie in 18th century France.** Princeton, 1955. Bibliography.

VC659. Pons, Jean. **La Révolution Française et l'avènement de la bourgeoisie.** Paris, 1938.

VC660. Boudet, Jacques, ed. **Le monde des affaires en France de 1830 à nos jours.** Paris, 1952.

VC661. Chevalier, Louis. **La formation de la population parisienne au XIXe siècle.** Paris, 1950.

VC662. Beau de Loménie, Emmanuel.

Les responsabilités des dynasties bourgeoises. 3 v. Paris, 1943–54.

VC663. Lafue, Pierre, and Georges Duveau. **Histoire du peuple français de 1848 à nos jours.** Paris, 1954.

Labor
(*Val R. Lorwin*)

VC664. Dolléans, Edouard, and Michel Crozier, eds. **Mouvements ouvriers et socialistes: chronologie et bibliographie, Angleterre, France, Allemagne, États-Unis (1750–1918).** Paris, 1950.

VC665. Levasseur, Émile. **Histoire des classes ouvrières et de l'industrie en France avant 1789.** 2nd rev. ed., 2 v., Paris, 1900–01.

VC666. ——. **Histoire des classes ouvrières et de l'industrie en France de 1789 à 1870.** 2nd rev. ed., 2 v., Paris, 1903–04.

VC667. Lefranc, Georges (pseud., Jean Montreuil). **Histoire du mouvement ouvrier en France des origines à nos jours.** Paris, 1946.

VC668. Dolléans, Edouard. **Histoire du mouvement ouvrier.** See *A1206*.

VC669. Dolléans, Edouard, and Gérard Dehove. **Histoire du travail en France: mouvement ouvrier et législation sociale.** 2 v. Paris, 1953–55.

VC670. Bruhat, Jean. **Histoire du mouvement ouvrier français.** V. 1. Paris, 1952.

VC671. Lorwin, Val R. **The French labor movement.** Cambridge, Mass., 1954. Bibliography.

VC672. Louis, Paul. **Histoire du mouvement syndical en France.** 2 v. Paris, 1947–48.

VC673. Lorwin, Louis L. **Syndicalism in France.** 2nd ed., N.Y., 1914. Bibliography.

VC674. Garmy, René. **Histoire du mouvement syndical en France des origines à 1914.** Paris, 1933.

VC675. Kelso, Maxwell R. "The inception of the modern French labor movement (1871–1879): a reappraisal." **Jour. mod. hist.,** 8 (June 1936): 173–93.

VC676. Hauser, Henri. **Ouvriers du temps passé, XVᵉ–XVIᵉ siècles.** 5th ed., Paris, 1927.

VC677. ——. **Travailleurs et marchands dans l'ancienne France.** Paris, 1920.

VC678. Laroque, Pierre. **Les rapports entre patrons et ouvriers: leur évolution en France depuis le XVIIIᵉ siècle—leur organisation contemporaine en France et à l'étranger.** Paris, 1938.

VC679. Picard, Roger. **Les cahiers de 1789 et les classes ouvrières.** Paris, 1910.

VC680. Jaffé, Grace M. **Le mouvement ouvrier à Paris pendant la Révolution Française (1789–1791).** Paris, 1924.

VC681. Duveau, Georges. **La vie ouvrière en France sous le second empire.** Paris, 1946.

VC682. Weill, Georges J. **Histoire du mouvement social en France, 1852–1924.** Paris, 1924.

VC683. Levasseur, Émile. **Questions ouvrières et industrielles en France sous la troisième république.** Paris, 1907.

VC684. Clark, Marjorie R. **A history of the French labor movement, 1910–1928.** Berkeley, 1930.

VC685. Saposs, David J. **The labor movement in post-war France.** N.Y., 1931.

VC686. Ehrmann, Henry W. **The French labor movement from popular front to liberation.** N.Y., 1947. Bibliography.

VC687. Lavigne, Pierre. **Le travail dans les constitutions françaises, 1789–1945.** Paris, 1948.

VC688. Zirnheld, Jules. **Cinquante années de syndicalisme chrétien.** Paris, 1937.

VC689. Moon, Parker T. **The labor problem and the social Catholic movement in France.** N.Y., 1921.

VC690. Colton, Joel. **Compulsory labor arbitration in France, 1936–1939.** N.Y., 1951.

VC691. Pelloutier, Fernand. **Histoire des bourses du travail.** Paris, 1946.

VC692. France. Office du Travail. **Les associations professionnelles ouvrières.** 4 v. Paris, 1899–1904.

VC693. Durand, Paul, and others. **Traité du droit du travail.** 3 v. Paris, 1947–56.

Economic Ideas
(*Leo A. Loubère*)

VC694. **Collection des principaux économistes.** Ed. by Eugène Daire and others. 15 v. Paris, 1843–47.

VC695. Schelle, Gustave, ed. **Oeuvres de Turgot et documents le concernant.** 5 v. Paris, 1913–23.

VC696. Harsin, Paul. **Les doctrines monétaires et financières en France du XVIᵉ au XVIIIᵉ siècle.** Paris, 1928.

VC697. Hauser, Henri. **La pensée et l'action économique de Richelieu.** Paris, 1944.

VC698. Cole, Charles W. **French mercantilist doctrines before Colbert.** N.Y., 1931.

VC699. ——. **Colbert and a century of French mercantilism.** 2 v. N.Y., 1939.

VC700. ——. **French mercantilism, 1683–1700.** N.Y., 1943.

VC701. Weulersse, Georges. **La physiocratie sous les ministères de Turgot et de Necker (1774–1781).** Paris, 1950.

VC702. Maunier, René. "Les économistes protectionistes en France de 1815 à 1848." **Rev. internationale de sociologie,** 19 (July 1911): 485–510 .

VC703. Pirou, Gaëtan. **Les doctrines économiques en France depuis 1870.** 3rd ed., Paris, 1925.

VC704. Marchal, André. **La pensée économique en France depuis 1945.** Paris, 1953.

Social Ideas
(Leo A. Loubère)

Bibliography

VC705. Dolléans, Edouard, and Michel Crozier, eds. **Mouvements ouvriers et socialistes.** See *VC664.*
VC706. Stammhammer, Joseph, ed. **Bibliographie des Sozialismus und Kommunismus.** 3 v. Jena, 1893–1909.
VC707. Bourgin, Georges. **Notes bibliographiques sur l'histoire sociale de la France.** Leiden, 1937.
VC708. Raléa, Mihia. **Révolution et socialisme: essai de bibliographie.** Paris, 1923.
VC709. Renard, Edouard. **Bibliographie relative à Louis Blanc.** Toulouse, 1922.

Sources

VC710. Chinard, Gilbert, ed. **Code de la nature de Morelly.** Paris, 1950.
VC711. Dommanget, Maurice, ed. **Pages choisies de Babeuf.** Paris, 1935.
VC712. Dautry, Jean, ed. **Saint-Simon: textes choisis.** Paris, 1951.
VC713. Poisson, Ernest, ed. **Fourier.** Paris, 1932.
VC714. Bouglé, Célestin, and Henri Moysset, eds. **Oeuvres complètes de P. J. Proudhon.** 12 v. in 17. Paris, 1923–46.
VC715. Bonnafous, Max, ed. **Oeuvres de Jean Jaurès.** 9 v. Paris, 1931–35.
VC716. Thorez, Maurice. **Oeuvres.** Paris, 1950 ff.
VC717. Blum, Léon. **L'oeuvre de Léon Blum.** Paris, 1954 ff.
VC718. Hewison, John P. (pseud., John Petrie), ed. **The worker priests, a collective documentation.** London, 1956.
VC719. Baudin, Louis, ed. **Textes choisis de F. Le Play.** Paris, 1947.
VC720. Michel, Henri, and Boris Mirkine-Guetzévitch, eds. **Les idées politiques et sociales de la résistance: documents clandestins, 1940–1944.** Paris, 1954.

General Histories

VC721. Compère-Morel, Adéodat, ed. **Encyclopédie socialiste, syndicale et coopérative.** 10 v. Paris, 1913.
VC722. Leroy, Maxime. **Histoire des idées sociales en France.** 3 v. Paris, 1946–54.
VC723. Louis, Paul. **Histoire du socialisme en France de la Révolution à nos jours.** 5th ed., Paris, 1950.
VC724. Elton, Godfrey. **The revolutionary idea in France, 1789–1871.** 2nd ed., London, 1931.
VC725. Prélot, Marcel. **L'évolution politique du socialisme français, 1789–1934.** Paris, 1939.

The Old Regime

VC726. Lichtenberger, André. **Socialisme au XVIIIe siècle.** Paris, 1895.
VC727. Girsberger, Hans. **Der utopische Sozialismus des 18. Jahrhunderts in Frankreich.** Zurich, 1924.
VC728. Guthrie, B. **Socialism before the French Revolution, a history.** N.Y., 1907.
VC729. Mornet, Daniel. **Les origines intellectuelles de la Révolution Française.** See *VC238.*
VC730. Groethuysen, Bernard. **Die Entstehung der bürgerlichen Welt- und Lebensanschauung in Frankreich.** 2 v. Halle, 1927–30. Bibliography. French trans. of v. 1.
VC731. Hubert, René. **Les sciences sociales dans l'Encyclopédie.** Paris, 1923.
VC732. Cobban, Alfred. **Rousseau and the modern state.** London, 1934.

The Revolution

VC733. Laski, Harold. **The socialist tradition in the French Revolution.** London, 1930.
VC734. Lichtenberger, André. **Le socialisme et la Révolution Française.** Paris, 1899.
VC735. Thomson, David. **The Babeuf plot: the making of a republican legend.** London, 1947.
VC736. Walter, Gérard. **Babeuf et le Babouvisme.** Paris, 1933.
VC737. Lepine, Josette. **Gracchus Babeuf.** Paris, 1949.
VC738. Bernstein, Samuel. **Buonarroti.** Paris, [1949].
VC739. Dommanget, Maurice. **Sylvian Maréchal.** Paris, 1950.
VC740. Beik, Paul H. **The French Revolution seen from the right: social theories in motion, 1789–1799.** Philadelphia, 1956.

1800–1870.

VC741. Leroy, Maxime. **Les précurseurs français du socialisme de Condorcet à Proudhon.** Paris, 1948.
VC742. Manuel, Frank. **The new world of Henri Saint-Simon.** Cambridge, Mass., 1956.
VC743. Dando, M. **The French Faust, Henri de Saint-Simon.** N.Y., 1955.
VC744. Allemagne, Henri d'. **Les Saint-Simoniens, 1827–1837.** Paris, 1930.
VC745. Charléty, Sébastien. **Histoire du Saint-Simonisme, 1825–1864.** 2nd ed., Paris, 1931.
VC746. Armand, Félix, and René Maublanc. **Fourier.** 2 v. Paris, 1937.
VC747. Cuvillier, Armand. **Un journal d'ouvriers: l'Atelier, 1840–1850.** Paris, 1954.
VC748. Renard, Edouard. **Louis Blanc.** Toulouse, 1922.
VC749. Prudhommeaux, Jules. **Icarie et son fondateur, Etienne Cabet.** Paris, 1907.
VC750. Evans, David. **Le socialisme romantique: Pierre Leroux et ses contemporains.** Paris, 1948.

VC751. Marcy, Gérard. **Constantin Pecqueur, fondateur du collectivisme d'état.** Paris, 1934.

VC752. Dolléans, Edouard. **Proudhon.** Paris, 1948.

VC753. Lubac, Henri de. **Proudhon et le Christianisme.** Paris, 1945.

VC754. Garaudy, Roger. **Les sources françaises du socialisme scientifique.** Paris, 1949.

Since 1870

VC755. Zévaès, Alexandre. **Histoire du socialisme et du communisme en France, de 1871 à 1947.** Paris, 1947.

VC756. Gaucher, François. **Contribution à l'histoire du socialisme français, 1905–1913.** Paris, 1934.

VC757. Pasquier, Albert. **Les doctrines sociales en France: vingt ans d'évolution.** Paris, 1950.

VC758. Zévaès, Alexandre. **De l'introduction du Marxisme en France.** Paris, 1947.

VC759. Bernstein, Samuel. **The beginnings of Marxian socialism in France.** N.Y., 1933.

VC760. Spire, Alfred. **Le déclin du Marxisme dans les tendances socialistes de la France contemporaine.** Paris, 1937.

VC761. Micaud, Charles. "French intellectuals and communism." **Social research**, 21 (1954): 286–96.

Special Studies

VC762. Maitron, Jean. **Histoire du mouvement anarchiste en France, 1880–1914.** Paris, 1951.

VC763. Elbow, Matthew. **French corporative theory, 1789–1948.** N.Y., 1953.

VC764. Duroselle, Jean Baptiste. **Les débuts du Catholicisme social en France, 1822–1870.** Paris, 1951.

VC765. Hoog, Georges. **Histoire du Catholicisme social en France, 1871–1931.** Paris, 1946.

VC766. Challaye, Félicien. **Péguy socialiste.** Paris, 1954.

VC767. Gros, J. M. **Le mouvement littéraire socialiste depuis 1830.** Paris, 1904.

VC768. Hunt, Herbert. **Le socialisme et le romantisme en France: étude de la presse socialiste de 1830 à 1848.** London, 1935.

VC769. Picard, Roger. **Le romantisme social.** N.Y., [1944].

VC770. Thomas, Edith. **Pauline Roland: socialisme et féminisme au XIXᵉ siècle.** Paris, 1955.

VC771. Gaumont, Jean. **Histoire générale de la coopération en France.** 2 v. Paris, 1923–24.

VC772. Lavergne, Bernard. "Gaëtan Pirou et la doctrine coopérative." **Rev. écon. pol.,** 57 (1947): 743–51.

VC773. Milhaud, Albert. **Histoire du radicalisme.** Paris, 1951.

VC774. Seeber, Edward. **Antislavery opin-**ion in France during the second half of the 18th century. Paris, 1937.

Daily Life in France
(Leo A. Loubère)

VC775. Faral, Edmond. **La vie quotidienne au temps de Saint Louis.** Paris, 1942.

VC776. Defourneaux, Marcelin. **La vie quotidienne au temps de Jeanne d'Arc.** Paris, 1952.

VC777. Lefranc, Abel. **La vie quotidienne au temps de la Renaissance.** Paris, 1938.

VC778. Wiley, William L. **The gentleman of Renaissance France.** Cambridge, Mass., 1954.

VC779. Magne, Émile. **La vie quotidienne au temps de Louis XIII.** Paris, 1946.

VC780. Mongrédien, Georges. **La vie quotidienne sous Louis XIV.** Paris, 1948.

VC781. Kunstler, Charles. **La vie quotidienne sous Louis XV.** Paris, 1953.

VC782. ——. **La vie quotidienne sous Louis XVI.** Paris, 1950.

VC783. Babeau, Albert A. **La ville sous l'ancien régime.** 2nd rev. ed., 2 v., Paris, 1884.

VC784. ——. **La province sous l'ancien régime.** 2 v. Paris, 1894.

VC785. Bertaut, Jules. **Les Parisiens sous la Révolution.** Paris, 1953.

VC786. Robiquet, Jean. **La vie quotidienne au temps de la Révolution.** Paris, 1938.

VC787. ——. **La vie quotidienne au temps de Napoléon.** Paris, 1944.

VC788. Burnand, Robert. **La vie quotidienne en France en 1830.** Paris, 1943.

VC789. Autran, Charles, and Georges Toudouze. **Un siècle de vie française, 1840–1940.** Paris, 1948.

VC790. Allem, Maurice. **La vie quotidienne sous le second empire.** Paris, 1948.

VC791. Duveau, Georges. **La vie ouvrière en France sous le second empire.** Paris, 1946.

VC792. Burnand, Robert. **La vie quotidienne en France de 1870 à 1900.** Paris, 1947.

VC793. Collinet, Michel. **L'ouvrier français: essai sur la condition ouvrière, 1900–1950.** Paris, 1951.

CULTURAL HISTORY
Art and Archaeology
(David L. Dowd and Judith S. Cousins)

Bibliography

VC794. Lavedan, Pierre. **Histoire de l'art.** V. 2. 2nd ed., Paris, 1950.

VC795. **Répertoire d'art et d'archéologie.** Paris, 1910 ff. (In progress.)

Sources

VC796. Chennevières, Philippe de, and others, eds. **Archives de l'art français: recueil de documents inédits relatifs à l'histoire des**

arts en France. 4 series. Paris, 1851 ff. (In progress.)

VC797. Rambaud, Mireille. **Les sources de l'histoire de l'art aux Archives Nationales.** Paris, 1955.

General Works

VC798. Nouvelle encyclopédie illustrée de l'art français. Paris, 1945 ff.

VC799. Mâle, Émile. **L'art religieux.** 4 v. Paris, 1898–1932.

Periods

VC800. Enlart, Camille. **Manuel d'archéologie française.** 3rd ed., 5 v., Paris, 1927–32.

VC801. Brutails, Jean. **Précis d'archéologie du Moyen Âge.** 2nd ed., Paris, 1925.

VC802. Gischia, Léon, and Lucien Mazenod. **Les arts primitifs français.** Paris, 1939.

VC803. Evans, Joan. **Art in mediaeval France.** See *K617.*

VC804. Blunt, Anthony. **Art and architecture in France, 1500–1700.** London, 1953.

VC805. Réau, Louis, **Histoire de l'expansion de l'art français.** 4 v. Paris, 1924–33.

VC806. Fountainas, A., ed. **Histoire générale de l'art français.** 3 v. Paris, 1922. Covers 1789–1920.

Painting

VC807. Wilenski, Reginald H. **French painting.** Rev. ed., London, 1949.

VC808. Leroy, Alfred. **Histoire de la peinture française.** 3 v. Paris, 1934–37.

VC809. Dimier, Louis, and Louis Réau. **Histoire de la peinture française.** 5 v. Paris, 1925–27.

VC810. Francastel, Pierre. **Histoire de la peinture française.** 2 v. Paris, 1955.

VC811. Skira, Albert, ed. **Les trésors de la peinture française.** Geneva, 1946 ff.

VC812. Moreau-Nélaton, Etienne. **Les Clouet et leur émules.** 3 v. Paris, 1924.

VC813. Kimball, Sidney F. **The creation of the rococo.** Philadelphia, 1943.

VC814. Dimier, Louis. **French painting in the sixteenth century.** N.Y., 1904.

VC815. Fontaine, André. **Les doctrines d'art en France . . . de Poussin à Diderot.** Paris, 1909.

VC816. Goncourt, Edmond de, and Jules de Goncourt. **French XVIII century painters.** Tr. by Robin Ironside. N.Y., 1948.

VC817. Faniel, Stéphane, ed. **Le dixhuitième siècle français.** Paris, 1956. [Collection connaissance des arts, 1.]

VC818. Réau, Louis. **Histoire de la peinture française au XVIIIe siècle.** 2 v. Paris, 1925–26.

VC819. Focillon, Henri. **La peinture aux XIXe et XXe siècles du réalisme à nos jours.** Paris, 1928.

VC820. Dorival, Bernard. **Les étapes de la** peinture française contemporaine. 3 v. Paris, 1943–46.

VC821. Hunter, Sam. **Modern French painting, 1855–1956.** N.Y., 1956.

VC822. Lemoisne, Paul A. **Degas et son oeuvre.** 4 v. Paris, 1947–48.

VC823. Escholier, Raymond. **Delacroix, peintre, graveur, écrivain.** 3 v. Paris, 1926–29.

VC824. Hamilton, George H. **Manet and his critics.** New Haven, 1954.

VC825. Geoffroy, Gustave. **Claude Monet.** 2nd ed., 2 v., Paris, 1924.

VC826. Schapiro, Meyer. **Paul Cézanne.** N.Y., 1952.

VC827. Barr, Alfred H. **Matisse, his art and his public.** N.Y., 1951.

VC828. Goldwater, Robert. **Paul Gauguin.** N.Y., 1957.

VC829. Joyant, Maurice. **Henri de Toulouse-Lautrec.** 2 v. Paris, 1926–27.

VC830. Friedlaender, Walter. **David to Delacroix.** Cambridge, Mass., 1952.

VC831. Sloane, Joseph C. **French painting . . . 1848 to 1870.** Princeton, 1951.

Sculpture

VC832. Benoist, Luc. **La sculpture française.** Paris, 1945.

VC833. Roussel, Jules. **La sculpture française.** 5 v. Paris, [1928–31].

Architecture

VC834. Lavedan, Pierre. **French architecture.** London, 1956.

VC835. Lasteyrie du Saillant, Robert C., count of. **L'architecture religieuse en France à l'époque romane.** 2nd ed., Paris, 1929.

VC836. ——. **L'architecture religieuse en France à l'époque gothique.** Ed. by Marcel Aubert. 2 v. Paris, 1926–27.

VC837. Hautecoeur, Louis. **Histoire de l'architecture classique en France.** 9 v. Paris, 1943–57.

Literature
(Bodo L. O. Richter)

Bibliographies

VC838. Cordié, Carlo. **Avviamento allo studio della lingua e della letteratura francese.** Milan, 1955. Best 1 v. bibliography.

VC839. Lanson, Gustave. **Manuel bibliographique de la littérature française moderne: XVIe, XVIIe, XVIIIe, et XIXe siècles.** Paris, 1921.

VC840. Giraud, Jeanne. **Manuel de bibliographie littéraire pour les XVIe, XVIIe, et XVIIIe siècles français: 1921–1935.** Paris, 1939.

VC841. Thieme, Hugo P. **Bibliographie de la littérature française de 1800 à 1930.** 3 v. Paris, 1933.

VC842. Dreher, S., and M. Rolli. **Bibli-**

ographie de la littérature française (1930–1939). Lille, 1948.

VC843. Talvart, Hector, and Joseph Place. **Bibliographie des auteurs modernes de langue française (1801–1956).** V. 1–13. Paris, 1928–56.

VC844. Cabeen, David C., ed. **A critical bibliography of French literature.** V. 1, 2, and 4. Syracuse, 1947–56.

Longer Histories

VC845. **Histoire littéraire de la France: ouvrage commencé par des religieux bénédictins de la Congrégation de Saint-Maur et continué par des membres de l'Institut (Académie des Inscriptions et Belles-Lettres).** By Antoine Rivet de la Grange and others. 38 v. Paris, 1733–1949.

VC846. **Histoire de la littérature française.** Ed. by Jean Calvet. 11 v. Paris, 1931–38.

VC847. Petit de Julleville, Louis, ed. **Histoire de la langue et de la littérature française.** 8 v. Paris, 1896–99.

VC848. Bédier, Joseph, Paul Hazard, and others. **Histoire de la littérature française illustrée.** 2 v. Paris, 1923. New ed. by Pierre Martino, 2 v., Paris, 1948–49.

VC849. Lanson, Gustave. **Histoire illustrée de la littérature française.** 2 v. Paris, 1923. Also, without ill., rev. and completed for 1850–1950 by Paul Tuffrau. Paris, 1952.

VC850. Suchier, Hermann, and Adolph Birsch-Hirschfeld. **Geschichte der französischen Literatur, von den ältesten Zeiten bis zur Gegenwart.** 2nd ed., 2 v., Leipzig, 1913. Best iconography of medieval period.

Shorter Histories

VC851. Nitze, William A., and E. Preston Dargan. **A history of French literature.** 3rd ed., N.Y., 1938. Best in English; extensive bibliography.

VC852. Wright, Charles H. C. **A history of French literature.** 2nd ed., N.Y., 1925.

VC853. Saintsbury, George. **A short history of French literature.** 7th ed., N.Y., 1917.

VC854. Jasinski, René. **Histoire de la littérature française.** 2 v. Paris, 1947. Good for minor authors.

VC855. Brunot, Ferdinand. **Histoire de la langue française des origines à 1900.** 10 v. in 18. Paris, 1905–43.

VC856. Tilley, Arthur, ed. **Medieval France.** Cambridge, Eng., 1922.

VC857. Lancaster, Henry C. **A history of French dramatic literature in the seventeenth century.** 2 v. in 9. Baltimore, 1929–42.

VC858. Lanson, Gustave. **Esquisse d'une histoire de la tragédie française.** Paris, 1920.

VC859. Faguet, Émile. **Histoire de la poésie française de la Renaissance au romantisme.** 12 v. to date. Paris, 1923 ff.

VC860. Chamard, Henri. **Histoire de la Pléiade.** 4 v. Paris, 1939–40.

VC861. Tilley, Arthur. **Literature of the French Renaissance.** 2 v. Cambridge, Eng., 1904.

VC862. ——. **From Montaigne to Molière.** 2nd ed., N.Y., 1923.

VC863. Mornet, Daniel. **Histoire de la littérature française classique, 1660–1700.** 3rd ed., Paris, 1947.

VC864. Peyre, Henri. **Le classicisme français.** N.Y., 1942. Best bibliography on the subject.

VC865. Thibaudet, Albert. **Histoire de la littérature française de 1789 à nos jours.** Paris, 1936. Brilliant work by the author of *Les idées politiques de la France.*

VC866. Wright, Charles H. C. **The background of modern French literature.** Boston, 1926.

VC867. Lalou, René. **Histoire de la littérature française contemporaine, 1870 à nos jours.** Paris, 1924. Also English trans.

VC868. Clouard, Henri. **Histoire de la littérature française du symbolisme à nos jours.** 2 v. Paris, 1947–49.

VC869. Picon, Gaëtan. **Panorama de la nouvelle littérature française.** Paris, 1949.

VC870. Peyre, Henri. **The contemporary French novel.** N.Y., 1955.

VC871. Van Tieghem, Philippe. **Petite histoire des grandes doctrines littéraires en France de la Pléiade au surréalisme.** Paris, 1946.

Religion
(Charles Breunig)

General Religious History

VC872. Fliche, Augustin, and Victor Martin. **Histoire de l'église depuis les origines jusqu'à nos jours.** 15 v. Paris, 1934–51. See relevant chapters and bibliographies in this and *VC873.*

VC873. Lavisse, Ernest, ed. **Histoire de France depuis les origines jusqu'à la Révolution.** See *VC138.*

VC874. Poulet, Charles. **Histoire de l'église de France.** 3 v. Paris, 1946–49.

VC875. Goyau, Georges. **Histoire religieuse de la France.** V. 6 of Gabriel Hanotaux, ed., **Histoire de la nation française** (*VC141*).

VC876. Le Bras, Gabriel. **Introduction à l'histoire de la pratique religieuse en France.** 2 v. Paris, 1942–45.

VC877. Brémond, Henri. **Histoire littéraire du sentiment religieux en France depuis la fin des guerres de religion jusqu'à nos jours.** 11 v. Paris, 1916–33.

Reformation

VC878. Renaudet, Augustin. **Préréforme et humanisme à Paris pendant les premières guerres d'Italie, 1494–1517.** 2nd ed., rev. and corrected, Paris, 1953.

VC879. Imbart de la Tour, Pierre. **Les origines de la Réforme.** 2nd ed., 2 v., Melun,

1944–48. Revised and augmented by a critical bibliography.

VC880. Viénot, Jean. **Histoire de la Réforme française.** 2 v. Paris, 1926–34.

Old Regime

VC881. Martin, Victor. **Les origines du gallicanisme.** 2 v. Paris, 1939.

VC882. Orcibal, Jean. **Louis XIV et les Protestants.** Paris, 1951.

VC883. ——. **Les origines du Jansenisme.** 3 v. Paris, 1947–48.

VC884. Laporte, Jean. **La doctrine de Port Royal.** 2 v. Paris, 1951–52.

VC885. Palmer, Robert R. **Catholics and unbelievers in 18th century France.** Princeton, 1939.

Since 1789

VC886. Latreille, André. **L'église catholique et la Révolution Française (1775–1815).** 2 v. Paris, 1946–50.

VC887. Dansette, Adrien. **Histoire religieuse de la France contemporaine.** 2 v. Paris, 1948–52.

VC888. Brugerette, Joseph. **Le prêtre français et la société contemporaine.** 3 v. Paris, 1933–38.

VC889. Duroselle, Jean Baptiste. **Les débuts du Catholicisme social en France, 1822–1870.** Paris, 1951.

VC890. Lecanuet, Edouard. **Les signes avant-coureurs de la séparation: les dernières années de Léon XIII et l'avènement de Pie X, 1894–1910.** Paris, 1930.

BIOGRAPHIES

Biographies, memoirs, and correspondence of reigning kings and emperors and their consorts will be found in the period sections.

Biographical Dictionaries
(Lynn M. Case)

VC891. **Dictionnaire de biographie française.** Ed. by Michel Prévost and others. 8 v. Paris, 1933–56.

VC892. **Dictionnaire critique de biographie et d'histoire.** Ed. by Auguste Jal. 2nd ed., Paris, 1872.

VC893. **Dictionnaire des parlementaires français, 1789–1889.** Ed. by Adolphe Robert, Edgar Bourloton, and Gaston Cougny. 5 v. Paris, 1891.

VC894. **Les parlementaires français, 1900–1914.** Ed. by René Samuel and G. Bonet-Maury. Paris, 1914.

VC895. **Dictionnaire des conventionnels.** Ed. by Auguste Kuscinski. Paris, 1916–19.

VC896. Germain-Martin, Louis. **Les grands messieurs qui firent la France.** Paris, 1945.

VC897. **Biographies et nécrologies des hommes marquants du XIXᵉ siècle.** Ed. by Victor Lacaine and Charles Laurent. 3 v. Paris, 1844–46.

VC898. **Dictionnaire national des contemporains.** Ed. by C. E. Curinier. 5 v. Paris, 1899–1905.

VC899. **Who's who in France.** Paris, 1955.

Sixteenth Century
(Bernerd C. Weber)

VC900. Aubigné, Théodore Agrippa d'. **Mémoires.** New ed. by Ludovic Lalanne, Paris, 1854.

VC901. Joffrey, Jacques. **La très joyeuse, plaisante, et récréative histoire du gentil seigneur de Bayart.** New ed. by Joseph Roman, Paris, 1878.

VC902. **The letters and documents of Armand de Gontaut, baron de Biron, marshal of France (1524–1592): collected by the late Sidney Hellman Ehrman.** Ed. by James W. Thompson. 2 v. Berkeley, 1936.

VC903. Lalanne, Ludovic, ed. **Journal d'un bourgeois de Paris sous le règne de François Premier, 1515–1536.** Paris, 1854.

VC904. Bourbon, Antoine de, and Jehanne d'Albret. **Lettres, 1538–1572.** Ed. by Achille L. de Vimeux, marquis de Rochambeau. Paris, 1877.

VC905. Bellay, Martin du, and Guillaume du Bellay. **Mémoires.** Ed. by V. L. Bourilly and Fleury Vindry. 4 v. Paris, 1908–19.

VC906. Bourilly, V. L. **Guillaume du Bellay, seigneur de Langey, 1491–1543.** Paris, 1905.

VC907. Brantôme, Pierre de Bourdeille, seigneur de. **Oeuvres complètes.** Ed. by Ludovic Lalanne. 11 v. Paris, 1864–82.

VC908. Lalanne, Ludovic. **Brantôme, sa vie et ses écrits.** Paris, 1896.

VC909. Delaborde, Jules. **Gaspard de Coligny, amiral de France.** 3 v. Paris, 1879–82.

VC910. Marcks, Erich. **Gaspard von Coligny: sein Leben und das Frankreich seiner Zeit.** V. 1, pt. 1, 2nd ed., Leipzig, 1918.

VC911. Whitehead, Arthur W. **Gaspard de Coligny, admiral of France.** London, 1904.

VC912. Gassot, Jules. **Sommaire mémorial (souvenirs) de Jules Gassot, secrétaire du roi (1555–1623).** Ed. by Pierre Champion. Paris, 1934.

VC913. Kupisch, Karl. **Coligny: eine historische Studie.** Berlin, 1951.

VC914. Richard, Alfred. **Un diplomate poitevin du XVIᵉ siècle: Charles de Danzay, ambassadeur de France en Danemark.** Poitiers, 1910.

VC915. La Brosse, Jules de. **Histoire d'un capitaine bourbonnais au XVIᵉ siècle: Jacques de La Brosse (1485–1562).** Paris, 1929.

VC916. Hauser, Henri. **François de la Noue (1531–1591).** Paris, 1892.

VC917. Estoile, Pierre de l'. **Mémoires-journaux, 1574–1610.** Ed. by Gustave Brunet and others. 12 v. Paris, 1875–96.

VC918. Escallier, Émile. **Lesdiguières, dernier connétable de France.** Lyons, 1946.

VC919. Commentaires de Blaise de Montluc, maréchal de France. Ed. by Paul Courteault. 3 v. Paris, 1911–25.

VC920. Courteault, Paul. **Blaise de Montluc, historien: étude critique sur le texte et la valeur historique des commentaires.** Paris, 1908.

VC921. Albert-Buisson, François. **Michel de l'Hospital (1503–1573).** Paris, 1950.

VC922. Héritier, Jean. **Michel de l'Hospital.** Paris, 1943.

VC923. Plessis-Marly, Philippe de Mornay, seigneur du. **Mémoires et correspondance.** 12 v. Paris, 1824–25.

VC924. Patry, Raoul. **Philippe du Plessis-Mornay: un huguenot homme d'état (1549–1623).** Paris, 1933.

VC925. Crue de Stoutz, Francis de. **Anne, duc de Montmorency, connétable et pair de France, sous les rois Henri II, François II et Charles IX.** Paris, 1889.

VC926. Plessis-Marly, Charlotte du. **Mémoires . . . accompagnées de lettres inédites de M. et Mme. du Plessis-Mornay et de leurs enfants.** 2 v. Paris, 1868–69.

VC927. A Huguenot family in the XVI century. Abr. trans. by Lucy Crump. London and N.Y., 1925.

VC928. Romier, Lucien. **La carrière d'un favori: Jacques d'Albon de Saint-André, maréchal de France (1512–1562).** Paris, 1909.

VC929. Saulx, Guillaume de, seigneur de Tavannes. **Mémoires.** Paris, 1823.

VC930. Saulx, Jean de, vicomte de Tavannes. **Mémoires de Gaspard de Saulx, seigneur de Tavannes.** 3 v. Paris, 1822.

VC931. Pingaud, Léonce. **Les Saulx-Tavannes.** Paris, 1876.

VC932. Lefèvre, Louis R., ed. **Mémoires de Sully.** 2nd ed., Paris, 1942.

VC933. Carré, Henri. **Sully: sa vie, son oeuvre.** Paris, 1932.

VC934. Thou, Jacques A. de. **Mémoires.** Paris, 1823.

VC935. François, Michel. **Le Cardinal François de Tournon, homme d'état, diplomate, mécène et humaniste, 1489–1562.** Paris, 1951.

VC936. Correspondance du Cardinal François de Tournon, 1521–1562. Ed. by Michel François. Paris, 1946.

VC937. Vaissière, Pierre de. **Récits du temps des troubles (XVIe siècle).** 2 v. Paris, 1912–14.

VC938. Valois, Marguerite de. **Mémoires et lettres.** Ed. by François Guessard. Paris, 1842.

VC939. Nouaillac, Joseph. **Villeroy, secrétaire d'état et ministre de Charles IX, Henri III et Henri IV (1543–1610).** Paris, 1908.

Seventeenth Century
(John B. Wolf)

VC940. Bassompierre, François de, maréchal de France. **Journal de ma vie: mémoires.** Ed. by Marie J. A. de La Cropte, marquis de Chantérac. 4 v. Paris, 1870–77.

VC941. Malo, Henri. **Le grand Condé.** Paris, 1937.

VC942. Dangeau, Philippe de Courcillon, marquis de. **Journal avec additions inédites du duc de Saint-Simon.** Ed. by Eudoxe Soulié, Louis E. Dussieux, and others. 19 v. Paris, 1854–60.

VC943. Fléchier, Esprit. **Mémoires de Fléchier sur les grand-jours d'Auvergne en 1665.** Ed. by Pierre A. Chéruel. 2nd ed., Paris, 1862.

VC944. Foucault, Nicolas Joseph. **Mémoires.** Ed. by F. Baudry. Paris, 1862.

VC945. Auvergne, Henri de La Tour d', vicomte de Turenne, maréchal de France. **Mémoires.** Ed. by Paul Marichal. 2 v. Paris, 1909–14.

VC946. André, Louis. **Michel Le Tellier et Louvois.** 2nd ed., Paris, 1943.

VC947. Geffroy, Auguste, ed. **Madame de Maintenon d'après sa correspondance authentique: choix de ses lettres et entretiens.** 2 v. Paris, 1887.

VC948. Mazarin, Jules, cardinal. **Lettres à la reine, à la Princesse Palatine . . . pendant sa retraite hors de France, 1651–1652.** Ed. by Jules Ravenal. Paris, 1836.

VC949. ——. **Lettres du cardinal Mazarin pendant son ministère.** Ed. by Pierre A. Chéruel and Comte Georges d'Avenel. 9 v. Paris, 1872–1906.

VC950. Federn, Carl. **Mazarin, 1602–1661.** Paris, 1934.

VC951. Molé, Mathieu. **Mémoires.** Ed. by Aimé Champollion-Figeac. 4 v. Paris, 1855–57.

VC952. Orléans, Charlotte Elisabeth, duchesse d', "Princesse Palatine." **Correspondance extraite de ses lettres publiées par M. de Ranke et M. Holland.** Tr. and ed. by Ernest Jaeglé. 2nd rev. ed., 3 v., Paris, 1890.

VC953. Criand, V. **Pascal.** 2 v. Paris, 1949.

VC954. Retz, Jean F. Paul de Gondi, cardinal de. **Oeuvres.** Ed. by Alphonse Feillet, Jules Gourdault, and François R. Chantelauze. 10 v. Paris, 1870–96.

VC955. Batiffol, Louis. **Le cardinal de Retz: ambitions et aventures d'un homme d'esprit au XVIIe siècle.** Paris, 1927.

VC956. Richelieu, Armand J. du Plessis, cardinal, duc de. **Mémoires.** Ed. by Charles P. M., Comte Horric de Beaucaire, François Bruel, and Robert Lolié. 7 v. Paris, 1907–26.

VC957. ——. **Lettres, instructions diplomatiques, et papiers d'état.** Ed. by Denis M. L. Avenel. 8 v. Paris, 1853–77.

VC958. Fagniez, Gustave C. **Le père Joseph et Richelieu, 1577–1638.** 2 v. Paris, 1894.

VC959. Hanotaux, Gabriel, and Auguste de Caumont, duc de La Force. **Histoire du cardinal de Richelieu.** 5 v. Paris, 1932–44.

VC960. Bailly, Auguste. **Richelieu.** Paris, 1934.

VC961. Burckhardt, Carl J. **Richelieu: der Aufstieg zur Macht.** Munich, 1935.

VC962. Belloc, Hilaire. **Richelieu, 1585–1642.** London, 1930.

VC963. Rochefoucauld, François VI, duc de la, prince de Marsillac. **Oeuvres complètes.** Ed. by Jean D. L. Gilbert and Jules Gourdault. 3 v. Paris, 1868–83.

VC964. Rohan, Henri, duc de, prince de Léon. **Mémoires.** 2 v. Paris, 1822.

VC965. Sévigné, Marie de Rabutin-Chantal, marquise de. **Lettres de Mme. de Sévigné, de sa famille, et de ses amis.** Ed. by L. J. N. Monmerqué. 14 v. and album. Paris, 1862–68.

VC966. ——. **Letters from the marchioness de Sévigné to her daughter, the countess de Grignan.** 10 v. London, 1927.

VC967. ——. **Lettres inédites à Mme. de Grignan, sa fille.** Ed. by Charles Capmas. 2 v. Paris, 1876.

VC968. La Force, Auguste de Caumont, duc de. **La grande mademoiselle.** Paris, 1952.

VC969. Orcibal, Jean. **Jean Duvergier de Hauranne, abbé de Saint Cyran et son temps.** Paris, 1947.

Eighteenth Century

(Paul H. Beik)

VC970. Monnier, Francis. **Le chancellier d'Aguesseau: sa conduite et ses idées politiques et son influence sur le mouvement des esprits pendant la première moitié du XVIIIe siècle.** Paris, 1860.

VC971. Bertrand, Joseph. **D'Alembert.** Paris, 1899.

VC972. Gessler, Peter. **René Louis d'Argenson, 1694–1757.** Basel, 1957. Bibliography.

VC973. Argenson, René Louis de Voyer de Paulmy, marquis d'. **Journal et mémoires du marquis d'Argenson, publiés pour la première fois d'après les manuscrits autographes de la Bibliothèque du Louvre.** Ed. by Edme J. B. Rathery. 9 v. Paris, 1859–67. Also abr. English trans.

VC974. Barbier, Edmond J. F. **Chronique de la régence et du règne de Louis XV (1718–1763).** 8 v. Paris, 1857.

VC975. Dalsème, René. **Beaumarchais, 1732–1799.** N.Y. and London, 1929.

VC976. Latzarus, Louis. **Beaumarchais.** Paris, 1930.

VC977. Bernis, François J. de Pierre, cardinal de. **Memoirs and letters.** 2 v. London and Boston, 1902.

VC978. Jolly, Pierre. **Calonne, 1734–1802.** Paris, 1950.

VC979. Choiseul, Etienne F., duc de. **Mémoires.** Ed. by Fernand Chalmettes. Paris, 1904.

VC980. Billy, André. **Diderot.** Paris, 1933. Bibliography.

VC981. Crocker, Lester G. **The embattled philosopher: a biography of Denis Diderot.** East Lansing, Mich., 1954.

VC982. Morley, John. **Diderot and the Encyclopaedists.** 2 v. London and N.Y., 1878.

VC983. Mornet, Daniel. **Diderot, l'homme et l'oeuvre.** Paris, 1941.

VC984. Wilson, Arthur M. **Diderot: the testing years, 1713–1759.** N.Y., 1957.

VC985. Aulneau, Joseph. **La comtesse Du Barry et la fin de l'Ancien Régime.** Paris, 1937.

VC986. Vatel, Charles. **Histoire de Madame Du Barry, d'après ses papiers personnels et les documents des archives publiques, précédée d'une introduction sur Madame de Pompadour, le Parc-aux-Cerfs et Mademoiselle de Romans.** 3 v. Versailles, 1883.

VC987. Martineau, Alfred A. **Dupleix, sa vie et son oeuvre.** Paris, 1931.

VC988. Thompson, Virginia M. **Dupleix and his letters (1742–1754).** N.Y., 1933.

VC989. Jolly, Pierre. **Du Pont de Nemours: soldat de la liberté.** Paris, 1956.

VC990. Schelle, Gustave. **Du Pont de Nemours et l'école physiocratique.** Paris, 1888.

VC991. Genlis, Stéphanie Félicité Ducrest de Saint-Aubin, comtesse de. **Memoirs illustrative of the history of the eighteenth and nineteenth centuries.** 8 v. London, 1825–26.

VC992. Schelle, Gustave. **Vincent de Gournay.** Paris, 1897.

VC993. Keim, Albert. **Helvetius, sa vie et son oeuvre.** Paris, 1907.

VC994. Hénault, Charles J. F. **Mémoires.** Ed. by François Rousseau. Paris, 1911.

VC995. Wickwar, William H. **Baron d'Holbach: a prelude to the French Revolution.** London, 1935.

VC996. Gottschalk, Louis R. **Lafayette comes to America.** Chicago, 1935.

VC997. ——. **Lafayette joins the American army.** Chicago, 1937.

VC998. ——. **Lafayette and the close of the American Revolution.** Chicago, 1942.

VC999. ——. **Lafayette between the American and the French Revolution (1783–1789).** Chicago, 1950.

VC1000. Oeuvres de Lavoisier: correspondance. Fascicule 1, 1763–1769; fascicule 2, 1770–1775. Selected and annotated by René Fric. Paris, 1955–57.

VC1001. McKie, Douglas. **Antoine Lavoisier.** London, 1952.

VC1002. Oudard, Georges. **The amazing**

life of John Law, the man behind the Mississippi Bubble. N.Y., 1928.

VC1003. Garçot, Maurice. **Stanislas Leszczynski, 1677–1766.** Paris, 1953.

VC1004. Perrin, Joseph. **Le cardinal de Loménie de Brienne.** Sens, 1896.

VC1005. Luynes, Charles Philippe d'Albert, duc de. **Mémoires du duc de Luynes sur la cour de Louis XV (1735–1758).** Ed. by Louis E. Dussieux and Eudoxe Soulié. 17 v. Paris, 1860–65.

VC1006. Whitfield, Ernest A. **Gabriel Bonnot de Mably.** London, 1930.

VC1007. Marion, Marcel. **Machault d'Arnouville: étude sur l'histoire générale du contrôle des finances de 1749 à 1754.** Paris, 1892.

VC1008. Lewis, Warren H. **The sunset of the splendid century: the life and times of Louis Auguste de Bourbon, duc du Maine, 1670–1736.** London, 1955.

VC1009. Allison, John M. S. **Lamoignon de Malesherbes, defender and reformer of the French monarchy, 1721–1794.** N.Y., 1938.

VC1010. Marion, Marcel. **Le Garde des Sceaux Lamoignon et la réforme judiciaire de 1788.** Paris, 1905.

VC1011. Flammermont, Jules G. **Le Chancelier Maupeou et les parlements.** 2nd ed., Paris, 1885.

VC1012. Loménie, Louis L. de, and Charles de Loménie. **Les Mirabeau: nouvelles études sur la société française au XVIIIᵉ siècle.** 5 v. Paris, 1879–91.

VC1013. Sorel, Albert. **Montesquieu.** Chicago, 1888.

VC1014. Chapuisat, Edouard. **Necker (1732–1804).** Paris, 1938.

VC1015. Jolly, Pierre. **Necker.** Paris, 1947.

VC1016. Mitford, Nancy. **Madame de Pompadour.** N.Y., 1954.

VC1017. Guyot, Yves. **Quesnay et la physiocratie.** Paris, 1896.

VC1018. Richelieu, Louis F. A. du Plessis, duc de, maréchal de France. **Mémoires authentiques, 1725–1767.** Ed. by Arthur de Boislisle. Paris, 1918.

VC1019. Weelen, Jean E. **Rochambeau, father and son: a life of the maréchal de Rochambeau . . . and the journal of the vicomte de Rochambeau (hitherto unpublished).** N.Y., 1936.

VC1020. Cassirer, Ernest. **The question of Jean Jacques Rousseau.** N.Y., 1954.

VC1021. Cobban, Alfred. **Rousseau and the modern state.** London, 1934.

VC1022. Ducros, Louis. **Jean Jacques Rousseau.** 3 v. Paris, 1908–18.

VC1023. Faguet, Émile. **Vie de Rousseau, Rousseau penseur, Rousseau artiste.** 3 v. Paris, 1911–13.

VC1024. Green, Frederick C. **Jean-Jacques Rousseau: a critical study of his life and writings.** N.Y., 1955.

VC1025. Rousseau, Jean Jacques. **Correspondance générale, collationnée sur les originaux.** Ed. by Théophile Dufour. 20 v. Paris, 1924–34.

VC1026. Alengry, Franck. **Turgot (1727–1781), homme privé-homme d'état, d'après les documents inédits du fonds de Lantheuil publiés par Schell.** Paris, [1942].

VC1027. Dakin, Douglas. **Turgot and the ancien régime in France.** London, 1939.

VC1028. Desnoiresterres, Gustave Le B. **Voltaire et la société au XVIIIᵉ siècle.** 2nd ed., 8 v., Paris, 1871–96.

VC1029. Lanson, Gustave. **Voltaire.** 3rd ed., Paris, 1919.

VC1030. Morley, John. **Voltaire.** London and N.Y., 1872.

VC1031. Torrey, Norman L. **The spirit of Voltaire.** N.Y., 1938.

VC1032. Voltaire, François Marie Arouet de. **Voltaire's correspondence.** Ed. by Theodore Besterman. 34 v. Geneva, 1953–58.

Revolution
(John H. Stewart)

VC1033. Walter, Gérard. **Babeuf, 1760–1797, et la conjuration des Egaux.** Paris, 1937.

VC1034. Thomson, David. **The Babeuf plot: the making of a republican legend.** London, 1947.

VC1035. Smith, Edwin B. **Jean-Sylvain Bailly, astronomer, mystic, revolutionary, 1763–1793.** Philadelphia, 1954.

VC1036. Fernand-Laurent, Camille J. **Jean-Sylvain Bailly, premier maire de Paris.** Paris, 1927.

VC1037. Brucker, Gene A. **Jean Sylvain Bailly, revolutionary mayor of Paris.** Urbana, 1950.

VC1038. Bradby, Eliza D. **The life of Barnave.** 2 v. Oxford, 1915.

VC1039. Chevallier, Jean J. **Barnave: ou, les deux faces de la Révolution, 1791–1793.** Paris, 1936.

VC1040. Ellery, Eloise. **Brissot de Warville: a study in the history of the French Revolution.** Boston, 1915.

VC1041. Bornarel, Félix. **Cambon et la Révolution Française.** Paris, 1905.

VC1042. Arnaud, Raoul. **La débâcle financière de la Révolution: Cambon, 1756–1820.** Paris, 1926.

VC1043. Dupre, Huntley. **Lazare Carnot, republican patriot.** Oxford, Ohio, 1940.

VC1044. Reinhard, Marcel. **Le grand Carnot.** 2 v. Paris, 1950–52.

VC1045. Cahen, Léon. **Condorcet et la Révolution Française.** Paris, 1904.

VC1046. Schapiro, Jacob. **Condorcet and the rise of liberalism.** N.Y., 1934.

VC1047. Alengry, Franck. **Condorcet, guide de la Révolution Française, théoricien**

de droit constitutionnel et preécurseur de la science sociale. Paris, 1904.

VC1048. Burlingame, Anne E. **Condorcet, the torch bearer of the French Revolution.** Boston, 1930.

VC1049. Delsaux, Hélène. **Condorcet journaliste (1790–1794).** Paris, 1931.

VC1050. Barthou, Louis. **Danton.** Paris, 1932.

VC1051. Madelin, Louis. **Danton.** London, 1921.

VC1052. Beesly, Auguste H. **Life of Danton.** N.Y. and London, 1899.

VC1053. Wendel, Hermann. **Danton.** Paris, 1932.

VC1054. Sorel, Albert E. **Charlotte de Corday, une arrière petite fille de Corneille.** Paris, 1930.

VC1055. Dowd, David L. **Pageant-master of the republic: Jacques-Louis David and the French Revolution.** Lincoln, Neb., 1948.

VC1056. Labracherie, Pierre. **Camille Desmoulins: grandeur et misère d'une âme ardente.** Paris, 1948.

VC1057. Claretie, Jules. **Camille Desmoulins.** Paris, 1875.

VC1058. Chuquet, Arthur M. **Dumouriez.** Paris, 1914.

VC1059. Saint-André, Pouget de. **Le général Dumouriez.** Paris, 1914.

VC1060. Michon, Georges. **Essai sur l'histoire du parti feuillant, Adrien Duport.** Paris, 1924.

VC1061. Jacob, Louis. **Fabre d'Eglantine, chef des fripons.** Paris, 1946.

VC1062. Dunoyer, Alphonse. **The public prosecutor of the Terror, Antoine Quentin Fouquier-Tinville.** N.Y., 1913.

VC1063. Fild, Jean. **L'Abbé Grégoire d'après ses mémoires recueillis par Hippolyte Carnot.** Paris, 1946.

VC1064. Walter, Gérard. **Hébert et le Père Duchesne.** Paris, 1946.

VC1065. Quentin, Henri (pseud., Paul d'Estrée). **Le Père Duchesne.** Paris, 1908.

VC1066. Dawson, John C. **Lakanal the regicide: a biographical and historical study of the career of Joseph Lakanal.** University, Ala., 1948.

VC1067. Gros, L. **Lakanal et l'éducation nationale.** Paris, 1912.

VC1068. Montier, Amand. **Robert Lindet, député à l'Assemblée Législative et à la Convention, membre du Comité de Salut Public, ministre des finances: notice biographique.** Paris, 1899.

VC1069. Mallet, Bernard. **Mallet du Pan and the French Revolution.** London, 1902.

VC1070. Gottschalk, Louis R. **Jean Paul Marat: a study in radicalism.** N.Y., 1927.

VC1071. Walter, Gérard. **Marat.** Paris, 1933.

VC1072. Gaston-Martin, Marcelle. **J. P. Marat, "l'oeil et l'ami du peuple."** Paris, 1938.

VC1073. Merlin, Roger. **Merlin de Thionville, d'après les documents inédits.** 2 v. Paris, 1927.

VC1074. Barthou, Louis. **Mirabeau.** London, 1913.

VC1075. Chevallier, Jean J. **Mirabeau: un grand destin manqué.** Paris, 1947.

VC1076. Fling, Fred M. **Mirabeau and the French Revolution.** N.Y., 1908.

VC1077. Loménie, Louis L. de, and Charles de Loménie. **Les Mirabeau: nouvelles études sur la société française au XVIIIe siècle.** 5 v. Paris, 1879–91.

VC1078. Stern, Alfred. **Das Leben Mirabeaus.** 2 v. Berlin. 1889.

VC1079. Welch, Oliver J. G. **Mirabeau: a study of a democratic monarchist.** London, 1951.

VC1080. Willert, Paul F. **Mirabeau.** London and N.Y., 1898.

VC1081. Lanzac de Laborie, Léon de. **Un royaliste libéral en 1789: Jean-Joseph Mounier, sa vie politique et ses écrits.** Paris, 1887.

VC1082. Göhring, Martin. **Rabaut Saint-Etienne, ein Kämpfer an der Wende zweier Epochen.** Berlin, 1935.

VC1083. Mirabaud, Robert. **Un président de la Constituante et de la Convention: Rabaut Saint-Étienne.** Paris, 1930.

VC1084. Robison, Georgia. **Revellière-Lépeaux, citizen director, 1753–1824.** N.Y., 1938.

VC1085. Meynier, Albert. **Un representant de la bourgeoisie angevine à l'Assemblée Nationale Constituante et à la Convention Nationale: L.-M. La Revellière-Lépeaux.** Paris, 1905.

VC1086. Eagan, James M. **Maximilian Robespierre, nationalist dictator.** N.Y., 1938.

VC1087. Thompson, James M. **Robespierre.** 2 v. Oxford, 1935.

VC1088. ———. **Robespierre and the French Revolution.** London, 1952, and N.Y., 1953.

VC1089. Walter, Gérard. **Robespierre.** 3 v. Paris, 1936–40.

VC1090. Jacob, Louis. **Robespierre vu par ses contemporains.** Paris, 1938.

VC1091. Mathiez, Albert. **Études robespierristes.** 2 v. Paris, 1917–18.

VC1092. ———. **Robespierre terroriste.** Paris, 1921.

VC1093. Ward, Reginald S. **Maximilien Robespierre: a study in deterioration.** London, 1934.

VC1094. Jacquemaire, Madeleine. **The life of Madame Roland.** London, 1930.

VC1095. Young, Catharine. **A lady who loved herself: the life of Madame Roland.** N.Y. and London, 1930.

VC1096. Bruun, Geoffrey. **Saint-Just, apostle of the Terror.** Boston, 1932.

VC1097. Curtis, Eugene N. **Saint-Just, colleague of Robespierre.** N.Y., 1935.

VC1098. Ollivier, Albert. **Saint-Just et la force des choses.** Paris, 1955.

VC1099. Centore-Bineau, Denise B. **Saint-Just, 1767–1794.** Paris, 1936.

VC1100. Bastid, Paul. **Sieyès et sa pensée.** Paris, 1939.

VC1101. Van Deusen, Glyndon G. **Sieyes: his life and his nationalism.** N.Y., 1932.

VC1102. Clapham, John H. **The Abbé Sieyès: an essay in the politics of the French Revolution.** London, 1912.

VC1103. Neton, Albéric. **Sieyès (1748–1836) d'après des documents inédits.** Paris, 1901.

VC1104. Bowers, Claude G. **Pierre Vergniaud, voice of the French Revolution.** N.Y., 1950.

VC1105. Lintilhac, Eugene F. **Vergniaud, le drame des Girondins.** Paris, 1920.

Consulate and Empire

(*Geoffrey Bruun*)

VC1106. Memoirs of Queen Hortense. 2 v. N.Y., 1927.

VC1107. Balmain, Aleksandr A. **Napoleon in captivity: the reports of Count Balmain, Russian commissioner on the island of St. Helena, 1816–1820.** N.Y., 1927.

VC1108. Beauharnais, Eugène de. **Mémoires et correspondance politique et militaire.** Ed. by Baron Pierre E. A. Du Casse. 10 v. Paris, 1858–60.

VC1109. Bonaparte, Jerome, king of Westphalia. **Mémoires et correspondance du Roi Jérôme et de la Reine Catherine.** Ed. by Baron Pierre E. A. Du Casse, 7 v. Paris, 1861–66.

VC1110. Bonaparte, Joseph, king of Spain. **Mémoires et correspondance politique et militaire.** Ed. by Baron Pierre E. A. Du Casse. 3rd ed., 10 v. and album, Paris, 1856–58.

VC1111. Iung, Henri Theodore. **Lucien Bonaparte et ses mémoires, 1775–1840.** 3 v. Paris, 1882–83.

VC1112. Narbonne, Bernard. **Pauline Bonaparte, 1780–1825.** Paris, 1948.

VC1113. Bourrienne, Louis A. F. de. **Private memoirs of Napoleon Bonaparte during the periods of the Directory, the Consulate, and the empire.** New ed. by Ramsay W. Phipps. 4 v. London and N.Y., 1885.

VC1114. Caulaincourt, Armand A. L., marquis de, duc de Vicence. **With Napoleon in Russia: the memoirs of General de Caulaincourt, duke of Vicenza.** Ed. and abr. by George Libaire. N.Y., 1935.

VC1115. No peace with Napoleon: concluding the memoirs of General Caulaincourt. Ed. and tr. by George Libaire. N.Y., 1936.

VC1116. Chanteloup, Jean A. C. C. de, comte. **Mes souvenirs sur Napoléon.** Ed. by Comte Emmanuel A. de Chanteloup. Paris, 1893.

VC1117. Chateaubriand, François A. R., vicomte de. **Mémoires d'outre-tombe.** Ed. by Maurice Levaillant. 4 v. Paris, 1948.

VC1118. Enghien, Louis A. H. de Bourbon-Condé, duc d'. **Correspondance du duc d'Enghien, 1801–1804, et documents sur son enlèvement et sa mort.** Ed. by Comte Alfred Boulay de la Meurthe. 4 v. Paris, 1904–13.

VC1119. Fain, Agathon J. F., baron. **Memoirs of the invasion of France by the allied armies, and of the last six months of the reign of Napoleon.** London, 1834.

VC1120. Fouché, Joseph. duc d'Otrante. **Les mémoires.** Ed. by Louis Madelin. Paris, 1945.

VC1121. Madelin, Louis. **Fouché.** Paris, 1955.

VC1122. Gaudin, Martin M. C., duc de Gaëte. **Mémoires, souvenirs, opinions, et écrits.** 2 v. Paris, 1826.

VC1123. Gourgaud, Gaspard, baron. **The St. Helena journal of General Baron Gourgaud, 1815–1818.** Ed. by Norman Edwards. London, 1932.

VC1124. Las Cases, Marie Joseph A. E. D., comte de. **Mémorial de Sainte Hélène: journal of the private life and conversations of the Emperor Napoleon at Saint Helena.** 8 v. in 4. London and N.Y., 1823.

VC1125. Lavalette, Antoine M. C. de, comte. **Memoirs of Count Lavalette.** 2 v. London, 1831.

VC1126. Marbot, Jean Baptiste A. M., baron de. **Memoirs.** New ed., 2 v., N.Y., 1908. Abr. trans.

VC1127. Ernouf, Alfred A. **Maret, duc de Bassano.** 2nd ed., Paris, 1884.

VC1128. Méneval, Claude F. de, baron. **Memoirs illustrating the history of Napoleon I, from 1802 to 1815.** Ed. by Napoleon J. E. de Méneval. 3 v. N.Y., 1894.

VC1129. Miot de Melito, André F., comte. **Memoirs between the years 1788 and 1815.** 2 v. London, 1881.

VC1130. Mollien, François N., comte. **Mémoires d'un ministre de trésor public, 1780–1815.** Ed. by Charles Gomel. 3 v. Paris, 1898.

VC1131. Norvins, Jacques M. de Montbréton de, baron. **Souvenirs d'un historien de Napoléon: mémorial.** Ed. by Léon de Lanzac de Laborie. 3 v. Paris, 1896–97.

VC1132. Pasquier, Etienne D., duc. **A history of my time: memoirs of Chancellor Pasquier.** Ed. by the Duc d'Auddifret-Pasquier. 2 v. London and N.Y., 1893–94.

VC1133. Rémusat, Claire E. J. G. de Vergennes, comtesse de. **Memoirs, 1802–1808.** 3 v. London and N.Y., 1880.

VC1134. Roederer, Pierre L., comte. **Oeuvres du Comte P. L. Roederer.** 8 v. Paris, 1853–59.

VC1135. ———. **Autour de Bonaparte: jour-**

nal; notes intimes et politiques d'un familier des Tuileries. Ed. by Maurice Vitrac. Paris, 1909.

VC1136. Rovigo, Anne J. M. René Savary, duc de. **Memoirs illustrative of the history of the Emperor Napoleon.** 4 v. London, 1828.

VC1137. Ségur, Philippe P., comte de. **Histoire et mémoires.** 7 v. Paris, 1873.

VC1138. Talleyrand-Périgord, Charles M. de, prince de Benevent. **Memoirs of the prince de Talleyrand.** 5 v. N.Y., 1891–92.

VC1139. Lacour-Gayet, Georges. **Talleyrand.** 4 v. Paris, 1928–34.

VC1140. Madelin, Louis. **Talleyrand.** N.Y., 1948.

VC1141. Dard, Émile. **Napoleon and Talleyrand.** N.Y., 1937.

VC1142. Thibaudeau, Antoine C., comte. **Bonaparte and the Consulate.** London and N.Y., 1908.

Restoration and July Monarchy
(Frederick B. Artz)

VC1143. Burnand, Robert. **Le duc d'Aumale et son temps.** Paris, 1949.

VC1144. Barante, Amable G. P. Brugière, baron de. **Souvenirs, 1782–1866.** Ed. by Claude de Barante. 8 v. Paris, 1890–1901.

VC1145. Lecanuet, Edouard. **Berryer, sa vie et ses oeuvres, 1790–1868.** Paris, 1893.

VC1146. Broglie, Albert de. **Discours.** 3 v. Paris, 1909–11.

VC1147. ——. **Mémoires.** 2 v. Paris, 1938–41.

VC1148. Broglie, Achille C. L. V., duc de. **Souvenirs, 1785–1870.** Ed. by Jacques V. A. duc de Broglie. 4 v. Paris, 1886. Actually extends only to 1832. Also English trans.

VC1149. Castellane, Esprit V. E. B., comte de. **Journal, 1804–1862.** 5 v. Paris, 1895–97.

VC1150. Cavaignac, Jacques M., vicomte, and Louis E. Cavaignac. **Souvenirs et correspondance, 1808–1848.** Paris, 1898.

VC1151. Chateaubriand, François A. R., vicomte de. **Memoirs.** 6 v. London and N.Y., 1902.

VC1152. ——. **Mémoires d'outre-tombe.** See *VC1117.*

VC1153. Talleyrand-Périgord, Dorothée de Courlande, duchesse de Dino, duchesse de. **Memoirs.** 3 v. London and N.Y., 1909–10.

VC1154. Guizot, François P. G. **Mémoires pour servir à l'histoire de mon temps.** 8 v. Paris, 1858–67.

VC1155. Duchon, Paul. **Mémoires de Lafitte.** Paris, 1932.

VC1156. Rémond, René. **Lamennais.** Paris, 1948.

VC1157. Molé, Louis M., comte. **Le Comte Molé, 1781–1855: sa vie, ses mémoires.** Ed. by Marquis de Noailles. 3 v. in

4. Paris, 1922–25. V. 1–2 also in English trans.

VC1158. Salaberry, Charles M., marquis de. **Souvenirs politiques sur la restauration, 1821–1830.** Ed. by Comte de Salaberry. 2 v. Paris, 1900.

VC1159. Malo, Henri. **Thiers (1797–1877).** Paris, 1932.

VC1160. Pomaret, Charles. **Monsieur Thiers et son siècle.** Paris, 1948.

VC1161. Allison, John M. S. **Monsieur Thiers.** N.Y., 1932.

VC1162. Tocqueville, Alexis de. **Recollections.** N.Y., 1949.

VC1163. ——. **Oeuvres, papiers et correspondances.** Ed. by Jacob P. Mayer and others. 7 v. Paris, 1951–58. Other volumes to follow.

VC1164. Fourcassié, Jean. **Villèle.** Paris, 1954.

VC1165. Villèle, Jean B. S. J., comte de. **Mémoires et correspondance.** 5 v. Paris, 1887–90.

Second Republic and Second Empire
(David H. Pinkney)

VC1166. Mourain, Jean. **Un bourgeois français au XIX⁰ siècle: Baroche, ministre de Napoléon III d'après ses papiers inédits.** Paris, 1936.

VC1167. Barrot, Odilon. **Mémoires posthumes.** 4 v. Paris, 1875–76.

VC1168. Alméras, Charles. **Odilon Barrot, avocat et homme politique, 1791–1873.** Paris, 1951.

VC1169. Duruy, Victor. **Notes et souvenirs, 1811–1894.** 2 v. Paris, 1901.

VC1170. Lavisse, Ernest. **Un ministre—Victor Duruy.** Paris, 1895.

VC1171. Falloux, Alfred P., comte de. **Mémoires d'un royaliste.** 3rd ed., 2 v., Paris, 1888.

VC1172. ——. **Mémoires.** 3 v. Paris, 1925–26. Also English trans.

VC1173. Bernardy, François de. **Charles de Flahaut, 1785–1870.** Paris, 1954.

VC1174. Fleury, Émile F., comte. **Souvenirs, 1837–1867.** 2 v. Paris, 1897–98.

VC1175. Grunwald, Constantin de. **Le duc de Gramont, gentilhomme et diplomate.** Paris, 1950.

VC1176. Haussmann, Georges E., baron. **Mémoires.** 3 v. Paris, 1890–93.

VC1177. Lucas-Dubreton, Jean. **Lamartine.** Paris, 1951.

VC1178. Whitehouse, Henry R. **The life of Lamartine.** 2 v. Boston, 1918.

VC1179. Calman, Alvin R. **Ledru-Rollin and the second French republic.** N.Y., 1922.

VC1180. Lesseps, Ferdinand de. **Souvenir de quarante ans.** 2 v. Paris, 1887. Also English trans.

VC1181. Edgar-Bonnet, George. **Ferdinand de Lesseps.** Paris, 1951.

VC1182. Durieux, Joseph. **Le ministre Pierre Magne, 1806–1879, d'après ses lettres et souvenirs.** 2 v. Paris, 1929.

VC1183. Boulenger, Marcel. **Le duc de Morny, prince français.** Paris, 1925.

VC1184. Correspondance inédite de Napoléon III et Prince Napoléon. Ed. by Ernest d'Hauterive. Paris, 1925.

VC1185. Saint Marc, Pierre. **Émile Ollivier (1825–1913).** Paris, 1950. Bibliography.

VC1186. Persigny, J. G. V. Fialin, duc de. **Mémoires.** Paris, 1896.

VC1187. Guiral, Pierre. **Prévost-Paradol, 1829–1870: pensées et action d'un libéral sous le second empire.** Paris, 1955.

VC1188. Dolléans, Edouard. **Proudhon.** Paris, 1948.

VC1189. Rothan, Gustave. **Souvenirs diplomatiques, 1882–1890.** 2nd ed., 7 v., Paris, 1883–93.

VC1190. Schnerb, Robert. **Rouher et le second empire.** Paris, 1949.

VC1191. Viel-Castel, Horace de, comte. **Memoirs.** 2 v. London, 1888. Translation.

Third and Fourth Republics
(Gordon Wright)

VC1192. Noël, Léon. **Camille Barrère, ambassadeur de France.** Paris, 1948.

VC1193. Fraser, Geoffrey, and Thadée Natanson. **Léon Blum, man and statesman,** Philadelphia, 1938.

VC1194. Hamburger, Maurice. **Léon Bourgeois, 1851–1925.** Paris, 1932.

VC1195. Suarez, Georges. **Briand: sa vie, son oeuvre.** See *AH180.*

VC1196. Brinon, Fernand de. **Mémoires.** Paris, 1949.

VC1197. Broglie, Albert, duc de. **Mémoires.** V. 2 (1870–75). Paris, 1941.

VC1198. Caillaux, Joseph. **Mes mémoires.** 3 v. Paris, 1942–43.

VC1199. Cambon, Henri. **Paul Cambon, ambassadeur de France, 1843–1924.** Paris, 1937.

VC1200. Correspondance de Paul Cambon. Ed. by Henri Cambon. 3 v. Paris, 1940–46.

VC1201. Bruun, Geoffrey. **Clemenceau.** Cambridge, Mass., 1943.

VC1202. Jackson, John H. **Clemenceau and the third republic.** N.Y., 1948.

VC1203. Gaulle, Charles de. **Mémoires de guerre.** See *AG241.*

VC1204. Neton, Albéric. **Delcassé (1852–1923).** Paris, 1952.

VC1205. Porter, Charles W. **The career of Théophile Delcassé.** Philadelphia, 1936.

VC1206. Réclus, Maurice. **Jules Favre, 1809–1880.** Paris, 1912.

VC1207. ———. **Jules Ferry, 1832–1893.** Paris, 1947.

VC1208. Freycinet, Charles L. de Saulses de. **Souvenirs, 1848–1893.** 2 v. Paris, 1912–13.

VC1209. Lettres de Léon Gambetta, 1868–1882. Ed. by Daniel Halévy and Émile Pillias. Paris, 1938.

VC1210. Deschanel, Paul E. L. **Gambetta.** London, 1920.

VC1211. Gambetta, Léon M. **Gambetta: life and letters.** London and N.Y., 1910.

VC1212. Gamelin, Maurice G. **Servir.** 3 v. Paris, 1946–47.

VC1213. Herriot, Edouard. **Jadis.** 2 v. Paris, 1948–52. Also English trans. of v. 1.

VC1214. Jackson, John H. **Jean Jaurès, his life and work.** London, 1943.

VC1215. Auclair, Marcelle. **La vie de Jean Jaurès: ou la France d'avant 1914.** Paris, 1954.

VC1216. Thomson, David. **Two Frenchmen: Pierre Laval and Charles de Gaulle.** London, 1951.

VC1217. Mallet, Alfred. **Pierre Laval.** See *AF316.*

VC1218. Combarieu, Abel. **Sept ans à l'Elysée avec le Président Émile Loubet: de l'affaire Dreyfus à la conférence d'Algéciras (1899–1906).** Paris, 1932.

VC1219. Coblentz, Paul. **Georges Mandel.** Paris, 1946.

VC1220. Meaux, Marie C. A., vicomte de. **Souvenirs politiques, 1871–1877.** Paris, 1905.

VC1221. Paul-Boncour, Joseph. **Entre deux guerres: souvenirs sur la troisième république.** 3 v. Paris, 1945–46. Also English trans. of v. 1.

VC1222. Noguères, Louis. **Le véritable procès du Maréchal Pétain.** Paris, 1955.

VC1223. Poincaré, Raymond. **Au service de la France: neuf années de souvenirs.** 10 v. Paris, 1926–33.

VC1224. Chastenet, Jacques. **Raymond Poincaré.** Paris, 1948.

VC1225. Rémusat, Charles de. **Mémoires de ma vie.** Ed. by Charles Pouthas. 3 v. Paris (in preparation).

VC1226. Reynaud, Paul. **In the thick of the fight, 1930–1945.** N.Y., 1955.

VC1227. Humphrey, Richard. **Georges Sorel, prophet without honor.** Cambridge, Mass., 1951.

VC1228. Sartre, Victor. **Georges Sorel.** Paris, 1937.

VC1229. Taine, Hippolyte A. **Life and letters.** 3 v. N.Y., 1902–08.

VC1230. Poisson, Ernest. **Le coopérateur Albert Thomas: un quart de siècle de vie militante.** Paris, 1933.

VC1231. Weygand, Maxime. **Recalled to service.** 3 v. London, 1952.

GOVERNMENT PUBLICATIONS
(Joseph J. Mathews)

Bibliographies

VC1232. Dampierre, Jacques de. **Les publications officielles des pouvoirs publics.** Paris, 1942.

VC1233. Bibliographie de la France. Supplément F, publications officielles. Paris, 1950 ff. (Irregular, 6 or 7 annually. Title varies.)

Government Publications

VC1234. Moniteur universel. Paris, 1789–1868. (Daily.) Superseded by *VC1235*.
VC1235. Journal officiel de la République Française. Paris, 1869 ff. (Daily.) For brief analysis of this complex publication see Dampierre (*VC1232*), pp. 121–30.
VC1236. Bulletin des lois. Paris, 1789–1918. (Irregular.)
VC1237. France. Assemblée Nationale. **Réglement et résolutions réglementaires de l'Assemblée Nationale.** 4th ed. Paris, 1952.
VC1238. France. Ministère des Affaires Etrangères. **Les livres jaunes.** Paris, 1860 ff. Selections from *Documents diplomatiques*.
VC1239. France. Direction de la Documentation. **Notes et études documentaires.** Paris, 1945 ff. Various series, including *Textes diplomatiques*. (Irregular.)
VC1240. France. Ministère des Finances. **Bulletin de statistique et de législation comparée.** 128 v. Paris, 1877–1940. (Monthly.) Superseded in part by *VC1241–1243*.
VC1241. ———. **Bulletin de législation comparée.** Paris, 1941 ff. (Quarterly.)
VC1242. ———. **Bulletin statistique.** 2 v. Paris, 1947–48. (Quarterly.)
VC1243. ———. **Statistiques et études financières.** Paris, 1949 ff. (Monthly.)

ACADEMY, SOCIETY, AND UNIVERSITY PUBLICATIONS
(*Joseph J. Mathews*)

Guide

VC1244. Caron, Pierre, and Marc Jaryc. **Répertoire des sociétés françaises de sciences philosophiques, historiques, philologiques et juridiques.** Paris, 1938.

Academies

VC1245. Académie des Inscriptions et Belles-Lettres. **Mémoires.** Paris, 1736 ff. (Irregular.)
VC1246. ———. **Comptes rendus des séances.** Paris, 1857 ff. (Irregular.)
VC1247. Académie des Sciences Morales et Politiques. **Mémoires.** Paris, 1798 ff. (Irregular.)
VC1248. ———. **Comptes rendus.** Paris, 1840 ff. (Irregular.)

Societies

VC1249. Société de l'Histoire de France. **Publications.** Paris, 1834 ff.

VC1250. ———. **Bulletin.** 26 v. Paris, 1834–62.
VC1251. ———. **Annuaire historique.** 27 v. Paris, 1836–63.
VC1252. ———. **Annuaire bulletin.** Paris, 1863 ff. (Title varies.)
VC1253. Société d'Histoire Moderne. **Publications.** 25 v. Paris, 1903–36.
VC1254. ———. **Études d'histoire moderne et contemporaine.** 4 v. Paris, 1947–51.
VC1255. ———. **Revue d'histoire moderne et contemporaine.** 19 v. Paris, 1899–1914. (Bimonthly.)
VC1256. ———. **Revue d'histoire moderne.** 15 v. Paris, 1926–40. (Bimonthly.)
VC1257. ———. **Revue d'histoire moderne et contemporaine.** Paris, 1954 ff. (Quarterly.)

Of the several hundred French societies that issue publications dealing with special subjects, local areas, or fields closely related to history, a few of the more important are the following.

VC1258. Société de l'École des Chartes. **Bibliothèque.** Paris, 1839 ff. (Irregular.)
VC1259. Société de l'Histoire du Protestantisme Français. **Bulletin.** Paris, 1852 ff. (Quarterly.)
VC1260. Société de l'Histoire de la Révolution Française. **La Révolution Française, revue d'histoire moderne et contemporaine.** 91 v. Paris, 1881–1939. (Monthly.)
VC1261. ———. **Publications.** 44 v. Paris, 1888–1927.
VC1262. Société des Études Robespierristes. **Annales révolutionaires.** 15 v. Paris and Besançon, 1908–23. (Quarterly and bimonthly.)
VC1263. ———. **Annales historiques de la Révolution Française.** 16 v. Rheims, 1924–29; Paris, 1930 ff. (Bimonthly. Suspended 1941–45.)
VC1264. Oeuvres complètes de Maximilien Robespierre. V. 1–6. Paris, 1910–54. [Société des Études Robespierristes.]
VC1265. Société de l'Histoire de Paris et de l'Île-de-France. **Bulletin.** Paris, 1874 ff. (Irregular.)
VC1266. ———. **Mémoires.** 51 v. Paris, 1875–1930.
VC1267. ———. **Documents.** 27 v. Paris, 1877–1913.
VC1268. Institut National d'Études Démographiques. **Population.** Paris, 1946 ff. (Quarterly.)
VC1269. ———. **Cahiers.** Paris, 1946 ff. A monographic series often cited as *Travaux et documents*.
VC1270. Fondation Nationale des Sciences Politiques. **Bulletin.** Paris, 1946 ff. (Bimonthly.)
VC1271. ———. **Revue française de science politique.** Paris, 1951 ff. (Quarterly.)
VC1272. ———. **Cahiers.** Paris, 1947 ff.

Universities

All of the French universities issue *Cahiers, Publications,* or *Annales* that on occasion include works of historical importance.

PERIODICALS
(Joseph J. Mathews)

Bibliography

VC1273. Caron, Pierre, and Marc Jaryc. **Répertoire des périodiques de langue française: philosophiques, historiques, philologiques et juridiques.** Paris, 1935. Supplements, 1937, 1939.

Periodicals

VC1274. Revue historique. Paris, 1876 ff. (Frequency varies.)

VC1275. Revue d'histoire économique et sociale. Paris, 1908 ff. (Quarterly.)
VC1276. Revue d'histoire diplomatique. Paris, 1887 ff. [Société d'Histoire Générale et d'Histoire Diplomatique.] (Quarterly.)
VC1277. Revue d'histoire de l'église de France. Paris, 1910 ff. [Société d'Histoire Ecclésiastique de la France.] (Irregular.)
VC1278. Revue historique de droit français et étranger. Paris, 1855 ff. (Irregular.)
VC1279. Revue d'histoire littéraire de la France. Paris, 1894 ff. [Société d'Histoire Littéraire de la France.] (Quarterly.)
VC1280. Annales: sociétés, civilisations. Paris, 1929 ff.
See also above, page 496, under publications of academies, societies, and universities.

BELGIUM, THE NETHERLANDS, AND LUXEMBOURG
(Jean Stengers)

It should be stressed that the grouping of these three countries in one subsection is mostly a matter of geography and convenience. It does not indicate that they possess anything that may be termed a "common history." A false impression of this kind may arise from the fact that in the current language a common name, the "Low Countries," is given to the three; or because in recent years they have been united in the purely economic Benelux pact; or because some of the best-known chapters of their history, especially in the 16th century, showed them as united. It is to be noted, moreover, that in some circles of Belgian and Dutch historians there is an undeniable tendency to consider the history of the Low Countries as a whole—a tendency which has found its latest expression in an *Algemene geschiedenis der Nederlanden* (General history of the Low Countries). But allowances being made for all these factors, history, generally speaking, does not offer any more reasons to group Belgium with the Netherlands than, for instance, with France or Germany.

BIBLIOGRAPHIES

VC1281. Pirenne, Henri, and others. **Bibliographie de l'histoire de Belgique: catalogue . . . des sources et des ouvrages principaux relatifs à l'histoire de tous les Pays-Bas jusqu'en 1598 et à l'histoire de Belgique jusqu'en 1914.** 3rd ed., Brussels, 1931.
VC1282. Wachter, Leo de. **Repertorium van de Vlaamse gouwen en gemeenten.** 6 v. Antwerp, 1942–57. For the Flemish-speaking part of Belgium; especially useful for local history.
There is no equivalent of Pirenne's bibliography for the Netherlands after 1598. The best references will be found in the bibliographies appended to the various volumes of *Algemene geschiedenis der Nederlanden* (*VC1311*). A current bibliography of pub-

lications on Belgian history appears each year, since 1953, in *Revue belge de philologie et d'histoire* (*VC 1410*). "Bulletins critiques" devoted to the most important historical works on the Low Countries are published yearly in *Revue du Nord* (*VC1416*). Most of the works listed below also have good bibliographies.

ENCYCLOPEDIAS AND WORKS OF REFERENCE

VC1283. Winkler Prins encyclopaedie. 6th ed., Amsterdam, 1947 ff. This and *VC1284* are the standard Dutch encyclopedias, to which many Belgian scholars also contribute.
VC1284. Oosthoek's encyclopaedie. 4th ed., Utrecht, 1947 ff.
VC1285. Biographie nationale. 28 v. Brussels, 1866–1944. Supplements, 1957 ff. [Aca-

démie Royale de Belgique.] A series of supplementary volumes is planned.

VC1286. Biographie coloniale belge. 4 v. Brussels, 1948–55. [Académie Royale des Sciences Coloniales.]

VC1287. Molhuysen, Philip C., and Blok, Petrus J., eds. **Nieuw Nederlandsch biografisch woordenboek.** 10 v. Leiden, 1911–37.

VC1288. Biographie nationale du pays de Luxembourg. Ed. by Jules Mersch. Luxembourg, 1947 ff.

GEOGRAPHIES

VC1289. Essen, Léon van der, ed. **Atlas de géographie historique de la Belgique.** Brussels, 1919–32. Maps for the 11th and 17th–19th centuries.

VC1290. Beekman, Anton A., ed. **Geschiedkundige atlas van Nederland.** 19 v. of maps and 37 v. of comment. The Hague, 1911–38.

VC1291. Fockema Andreae, Sybrandus J., and Bert van 't Hoff. **Geschiedenis der kartografie van Nederland.** The Hague, 1947. Contains summary in English.

LINGUISTIC WORKS

VC1292. Vooys, Cornelis G. N. de. **Geschiedenis van de Nederlandse taal in hoofdtrekken geschetst.** 5th ed., Groningen, 1952.

VC1293. Remacle, Louis. **Le problème de l'ancien wallon.** Liège, 1948. Some specific problems arising from the use of the French language in Belgium are treated in this and the following.

VC1294. Deneckere, Marcel. **Histoire de la langue française dans les Flandres, 1770–1823.** Ghent, 1954.

PRINTED COLLECTIONS OF SOURCES

In Belgium the two principal collections of printed sources are those of the Commission Royale d'Histoire (*VC1295–1297*) and the Commission Royale pour la Publication des Anciennes Lois et Ordonnances de la Belgique (*VC1298–1299*).

VC1295. Commission Royale d'Histoire. **Publications.** Brussels, 1836 ff. Include quarto, gr. octavo, and octavo series of chronicles, chartularies, correspondence, etc.

VC1296. Bulletin de la Commission Royale d'Histoire. Brussels, 1834 ff. (Irregular. Title varies.)

VC1297. Commission Royale d'Histoire. **La Commission Royale d'Histoire, 1834–1934: livre jubilaire.** Brussels, 1934.

VC1298. Commission Royale pour la Pub-

lication des Anciennes Lois et Ordonnances de la Belgique. **Recueil des anciennes coutumes de la Belgique.** Brussels, 1867 ff.

VC1299. ——. **Recueil des anciennes ordonnances de la Belgique.** Brussels, 1855 ff. Ordinances of the 15th–18th centuries.

VC1300. Analecta Vaticano-belgica. Rome, 1906 ff. [Institut Historique Belge de Rome.] Papal records and correspondence of the nuncios concerning Belgium.

The most important collections in the Netherlands are the following:

VC1301. Rijks geschiedkundige publicatiën. The Hague, 1905 ff. These publications include *VC1302*.

VC1302. Colenbrander, Herman T., ed. **Gedenkstukken der algemeene geschiedenis van Nederland van 1795 tot 1840.** 10 v. in 22. The Hague, 1905–22.

VC1303. Archives ou correspondance inédite de la maison d'Orange-Nassau (1552–1789). Ed. by Guillaume Groen van Prinsterer and others. 27 v. Leiden and Utrecht, 1835–1917. Collection of documents from the royal archives.

VC1304. Historisch Genootschap te Utrecht. **Werken uitgegeven door het historisch genootschap gevestigd te Utrecht.** Utrecht, 1863 ff. (Irregular.)

VC1305. Bijdragen en Mededeelingen van het historisch genootschap. Utrecht, 1877 ff.

SHORTER GENERAL HISTORIES

Belgium

VC1306. Linden, Herman vander. **Belgium: the making of a nation.** Oxford, 1920.

VC1307. Kalken, Frans van. **Histoire de la Belgique et de son expansion coloniale.** Brussels, 1954.

Netherlands

VC1308. Edmundson, George. **History of Holland.** Cambridge, Eng., 1922.

VC1309. Gelder, Herman A. Enno van. **Histoire des Pays-Bas du XVIe siècle à nos jours.** 2nd ed., Paris, 1949.

Luxembourg

VC1310. Herchen, Arthur. **Manuel d'histoire nationale.** 5th ed., Luxembourg, 1947.

LONGER GENERAL HISTORIES

VC1311. Algemene geschiedenis der Nederlanden. Ed. by J. A. van Houtte and others. 11 v. Utrecht, 1949–56. Covers Belgium, the Netherlands,* and Luxembourg;

* It should be noted that the meaning of Nederlanden, Nederlands, etc., in the 20th century historical literature is a very fluid one, denoting either the Netherlands proper (Blok, Gosses and Japikse, and Brugmans), or the Netherlands and Belgium (*Algemene geschiedenis der Nederlanden*), or the Dutch-speaking people (Geyl).

contributions by leading Belgian and Dutch historians. To be complete in 12 v.

VC1312. Pirenne, Henri. **Histoire de Belgique.** 7 v. Brussels, 1900–32. V. 1, 5th ed., 1929; v. 2, 3rd ed., 1922; v. 3, 3rd ed., 1923; v. 4, 3rd ed., 1927; v. 5, 2nd ed., 1926; v. 6, 1st ed., 1926; v. 7, 1st ed., 1932. Each volume should be used in its latest edition. New ed., without change in text but fully illustrated, 4 v., Brussels, 1948–52. This is a masterpiece which still takes first place in Belgian history; its vision and intelligence remain unsurpassed. On Pirenne (1862–1935) see *Henri Pirenne: hommages et souvenirs* (2 v., Brussels, 1938).

VC1313. Blok, Petrus J. **Geschiedenis van het Nederlandsche volk.** 3rd ed., 4 v., Leiden, 1923–26. English trans., *History of the people of the Netherlands* (5 v., N.Y. and London, 1898–1912).

VC1314. Gosses, Izaak H., and Nicolaas Japikse. **Handboek tot de staatkundige geschiedenis van Nederland.** 3rd ed., rev. by Regnerus Post and Nicolaas Japikse, The Hague, 1947.

VC1315. Brugmans, Hajo, ed. **Geschiedenis van Nederland.** 9 v. Amsterdam, 1935–38.

VC1316. Geyl, Pieter. **Geschiedenis van de Nederlandse stam.** New ed., 2 v., Amsterdam, 1948–49. History of the Dutch-speaking people, covering the Netherlands and the northern part of Belgium up to 1751. English translation of the parts concerning periods 1555–1609 and 1609–1648: *The revolt of the Netherlands* (London, 1932); and *The Netherlands divided* (London, 1936).

HISTORIES OF SPECIAL PERIODS

Sixteenth—Eighteenth Centuries

Older Standard Works

VC1317. Henne, Alexandre. **Histoire du règne de Charles-Quint en Belgique.** 10 v. Brussels, 1858–60.

VC1318. Kervyn de Lettenhove, Joseph M. **Les Huguenots et les Gueux: étude historique sur vingt-cinq années du XVIᵉ siècle (1560–1585).** 6 v. Bruges, 1883–85. Passionately Catholic point of view.

VC1319. Motley, John L. **The rise of the Dutch republic, 1555–1584.** 3 v. N.Y., 1856.

VC1320. ——. **History of the United Netherlands, 1584–1609.** 4 v. The Hague, 1860–67.

VC1321. Fruin, Robert J. **Tien jaren uit den tachtigjarigen oorlog, 1588–1598.** 5th ed., The Hague, 1899. Many reprints.

Recent Works

VC1322. Essen, Léon van der. **Alexandre Farnèse, prince de Parme, gouverneur général des Pays-Bas (1545–1592).** 5 v. Brussels, 1933–37.

VC1323. Presser, Jacob. **De tachtigjarige oorlog.** 3rd ed., Amsterdam, 1948.

VC1324. Renier, Gustaaf J. **The Dutch nation.** London, 1944.

VC1325. Veenendaal, Augustus J. **Het Engels—Nederlands condominium in de Zuidelijke Nederlanden tijdens de Spaanse-successieoorlog, 1706–1716.** V. 1. Utrecht, 1945.

VC1326. Houtte, Hubert Van. **Les occupations étrangères en Belgique sous l'Ancien Régime.** 2 v. Ghent, 1930.

Nineteenth and Twentieth Centuries

Belgium

VC1327. **Histoire de la Belgique contemporaine, 1830–1914.** Ed. by Jean Deharveng. 3 v. Brussels, 1928–30. Many first-class contributions by a number of specialists.

VC1328. Kalken, Frans van. **La Belgique contemporaine (1780–1949): histoire d'une évolution politique.** 2nd ed., Paris, 1950.

VC1329. Pirenne, Henri. **La Belgique et la guerre mondiale.** Paris, 1928.

VC1330. Höjer, Carl-Henrik. **Le régime parlementaire belge de 1918 à 1940.** Uppsala, Swe., 1946.

VC1331. Clough, Shepard B. **A history of the Flemish movement in Belgium.** N.Y., 1930.

VC1332. Zuylen, Pierre van. **Les mains libres: politique extérieure de la Belgique, 1914–1940.** Paris, 1950.

VC1333. Miller, Jane K. **Belgian foreign policy between two wars, 1919–1940.** N.Y., 1951.

Netherlands

VC1334. Leeuwen, Willem L. M. E. van. **Honderd jaar Nederland, 1848–1948.** Hengelo, 1948.

VC1335. Rengers, Wilco J. van Welderen. **Schets eener parlementaire geschiedenis van Nederland.** 4th ed., rev. by L. G. Kortenhorst and others, 5 v., The Hague, 1948–56.

VC1336. Oud, Pieter J. **Het jongste verleden: parlementaire geschiedenis van Nederland, 1918–1940.** 6 v. Assen, 1948–51. Fills the gap between v. 4 and 5 of *VC1335*.

VC1337. Netherlands. Enquête-Commissie Regeringsbeleid, 1940–1945. **Verslag houdende de uitkomsten van het onderzoek.** 8 v. in 19. The Hague, 1949–56.

VC1338. **Onderdrukking en verzet.** Ed. by J. J. van Bolhuis and others. 4 v. Amsterdam, 1947–54. The Netherlands during World War II.

VC1339. Smit, C. **Diplomatieke geschiedenis van Nederland, inzonderheid sedert de vestiging van het Koninkrijk.** The Hague, 1950.

VC1340. Westermann, Johannes C. **The Netherlands and the United States: their rela-**

tions in the beginning of the 19th century. The Hague, 1935.

VC1341. Boogman, Johan C. **Nederland en de Duitse Bond, 1815–1851.** 2 v. Groningen, 1955.

Luxembourg

VC1342. Calmes, Albert. **Histoire contemporaine du Grand-Duché de Luxembourg.** 4 v. Brussels and Luxembourg, 1932–54. Covers period 1815–47. Only v. 3 and 4 have appeared under this general title. V. 1 and 2 bear special titles: *Le Grand-Duché de Luxembourg dans le royaume des Pays-Bas, 1815–1830* (Brussels, 1932); and *Le Grand-Duché de Luxembourg dans la révolution belge, 1830–1839* (Brussels, 1939).

General

Many monographs of great value, some of which are devoted to special periods, will be found in the two following series.

VC1343. Collection "Notre passé." Ed. by Suzanne Tassier. Brussels, 1942 ff. (Irregular.)

VC1344. Patria: vaderlandsche cultuurgeschiedenis in monografieën. Ed. by Johannes H. Kernkamp. Amsterdam, 1937 ff.

HISTORIES OF SPECIAL AREAS

VC1345. Geschiedenis van Vlaanderen. Ed. by Robert van Roosbroeck. 6 v. Brussels, 1936–49. History of the Flemish-speaking part of Belgium; contributions by distinguished specialists of each period.

VC1346. Lejeune, Jean. **La principauté de Liège.** Liège, 1948.

VC1347. Harsin, Paul. **Études critiques sur l'histoire de la principauté de Liège, 1477–1795.** Liège, 1955 ff. To be complete in 14 v. V. 1 and 2, which have appeared, bring the story to 1538.

HISTORIES OF SPECIAL TOPICS

Constitutional History

VC1348. Poullet, Edmond I. **Histoire politique nationale: origines, développements et transformations des institutions dans les anciens Pays-Bas.** 2nd ed., 2 v., Louvain, 1882–92. Now obsolete in some parts, but has not been superseded.

VC1349. Schillings, Arnold H. **Overzicht van de geschiedenis onzer instellingen.** Brussels, 1945.

VC1350. Gilissen, John. **Le régime représentatif avant 1790 en Belgique.** Brussels, 1952.

VC1351. Gilissen, John. **Le régime représentatif en Belgique depuis 1790.** Brussels, 1958.

VC1352. Fruin, Robert J. **Geschiedenis der staatsinstellingen in Nederland tot den val der republiek.** Ed. by Herman T. Colenbrander. 2nd ed., The Hague, 1922.

VC1353. Jong, Jelle J. de. **Politieke organisatie in west Europa na 1800.** The Hague, 1951. Contains an English summary. About half the book is devoted to the Netherlands; some chapters on Belgium.

Religious History

VC1354. Moreau, Édouard de. **Histoire de l'église en Belgique.** 5 v. Brussels, 1946–52. Supplementary vol., *Tome complémentaire: circonscriptions ecclésiastiques, chapitres, abbayes, couvents en Belgique avant 1559; cartes,* by Jean Deharveng and Edouard de Moreau (Brussels, 1948). Standard work, but unfortunately completed only to 1633. The entire history is covered in abridged form in *VC1355.*

VC1355. ——. **L'église en Belgique des origines au début du XXe siècle.** Brussels, 1944. For the 19th century see also de Moreau's contribution to *Histoire de la Belgique contemporaine (VC1327).*

VC1356. Axters, Stephanus. **Geschiedenis van de vroomheid in de Nederlanden.** 3 v. Antwerp, 1950–56. Covers to 1550; to be continued.

VC1357. Hyma, Albert. **The Christian renaissance: a history of the "Devotio moderna."** Grand Rapids, 1924.

VC1358. Poncelet, Alfred. **Histoire de la Compagnie de Jésus dans les anciens Pays-Bas.** 2 v. Brussels, 1927–28.

VC1359. Willaert, Léopold. **Les origines du Jansénisme dans les Pays-Bas catholiques.** V. 1. Brussels, 1948.

VC1360. Ceyssens, L. "Rondom de studie van P. Willaert over de oorsprong van het Jansenisme in België." **Rev. belge de philol. et d'hist.,** 28 (1950): 644–85.

VC1361. Simon, Alois. **Le cardinal Sterckx et son temps (1792–1867).** 2 v. Wetteren, 1950.

VC1362. Rogier, L. J. **Geschiedenis van het Katholicisme in Noord-Nederland in de 16e en de 17e eeuw.** 2nd ed., 3 v., Amsterdam, 1945–47.

VC1363. Rogier, L. J., and N. de Rooy. **In vrijheid herboren: Katholiek Nederland, 1853–1953.** The Hague, 1953.

VC1364. Reitsma, Johannes. **Geschiedenis van de hervorming en de hervormde kerk der Nederlanden.** 5th ed., rev. by Johannes Lindeboom, The Hague, 1949.

VC1365. Gelder, Herman A. Enno van. **Vrijheid en onvrijheid in de republiek: geschiedenis der vrijheid van drukpers en godsdienst van 1572 tot 1789.** V. 1, 1572–1619. Haarlem, 1947.

VC1366. Stengers, Jean. **Les Juifs dans les Pays-Bas au Moyen Âge.** Brussels, 1950.

VC1367. Brugmans, Hendrik, and A. Frank, eds. **Geschiedenis der Joden in Nederland.** V. 1, to end of the 18th century. Amsterdam, 1940.

VC1368. MacDonnell, Ernest W. **The Beguines and Beghards in medieval culture, with special emphasis on the Belgian scene.** New Brunswick, N.J., 1954.

Economic History

Belgium

VC1369. Houtte, J. A. van. **Esquisse d'une histoire économique de la Belgique.** Louvain, 1943.

VC1370. Doehaerd, Renée. **L'expansion économique belge au Moyen Âge.** Brussels, 1946.

VC1371. Werveke, Hans van. **Bruges et Anvers: huit siècles de commerce flamand.** Brussels, 1944. Covers 10th–18th centuries.

VC1372. De Roover, Raymond A. **Money, banking and credit in mediaeval Bruges.** See *K482.*

VC1373. Coornaert, E. "Draperies rurales, draperies urbaines: l'évolution de l'industrie flamande au Moyen Âge et au XVIᵉ siècle." **Rev. belge de philol. et d'hist.**, 28 (1950): 60–96.

VC1374. Lindemans, Paul. **Geschiedenis van de landbouw in België.** 2 v. Antwerp, 1952.

VC1375. Chlepner, Ben S. **Cent ans d'histoire sociale en Belgique.** Brussels, 1956. Mid-19th to mid-20th century.

VC1376. Baudhuin, Fernand. **Histoire économique de la Belgique, 1914–1939.** 2 v. Brussels, 1944.

Netherlands

VC1377. Niermeyer, Jan F. **De wording van onze volkshuishouding: hoofdlijnen uit de economische geschiedenis der noordelijke Nederlanden in de Middeleeuwen.** The Hague, 1946.

VC1378. Kerling, Nelly J. M. **Commercial relations of Holland and Zeeland with England from the late 13th century to the close of the Middle Ages.** Leiden, 1954.

VC1379. Baasch, Ernst. **Holländische Wirtschaftsgeschichte.** Jena, 1927. Covers 17th–19th centuries.

VC1380. Barbour, Violet. **Capitalism in Amsterdam in the seventeenth century.** Baltimore, 1950.

VC1381. De Nederlandse volkshuishouding tussen twee wereldoorlogen: bijdragen tot de sociaal-economische vernieuwing. Ed. by Pieter B. Kreukniet. 3 v. Utrecht, 1952.

VC1382. Sneller, Zeger W. **Geschiedenis van de Nederlandse landbouw, 1795–1940.** 2nd ed., Groningen, 1951.

VC1383. Posthumus, Nicolaas W. **Inquiry into the history of prices in Holland.** Leiden, 1946. Material from 1585 to 1914.

Luxembourg

VC1384. Weber, Paul. **Histoire de l'économie luxembourgeoise.** Luxembourg, 1950.

Cultural History

Art

VC1385. Fierens, Paul, ed. **L'art en Belgique du Moyen Âge à nos jours.** 2nd ed., Brussels, 1947.

VC1386. Gelder, Hendrik E. van, and Jozef Duverger. **Kunstgeschiedenis der Nederlanden van de Middeleeuwen tot onze tijd.** 3rd ed., 3 v., Utrecht, 1954–56. Belgium and the Netherlands.

VC1387. Panofsky, Erwin. **Early Netherlandish painting: its origin and character.** 2 v. Cambridge, Mass., 1953.

VC1388. Winkler, Friedrich. **Die altniederländische Malerei: die Malerei in Belgien und Holland von 1400–1600.** Berlin, 1924.

VC1389. Friedländer, Max J. **From Van Eyck to Breugel: early Netherlandish painting.** Tr. by Marguerite Kay. London, 1956.

VC1390. ——. **Die altniederländische Malerei.** 14 v. Berlin, 1924–37.

VC1391. Mander, Carel van. **Dutch and Flemish painters.** Tr. by Constant Van de Wall. N.Y., 1936.

VC1392. Wilenski, Reginald H. **Dutch painting.** 2nd ed., London, 1947.

VC1393. Lotthé, Ernest. **La pensée chrétienne dans la peinture flamande et hollandaise de Van Eyck à Rembrandt (1432–1669): le Christ et la Vierge Marie.** 2 v. Lille, 1947.

VC1394. Lassaigne, Jacques, and Robert Delevoy. **Flemish painting from Bosch to Rubens.** Tr. by Stuart Gilbert. N.Y., 1958.

VC1395. Bergström, Ingvar. **Dutch still-life painting in the seventeenth century.** Tr. by Christina Hedström and Gerald Taylor. London, 1956.

VC1396. Swillens, P. T. A. **Johannes Vermeer . . . 1632–1675.** Tr. by C. M. Breuning-Williamson. Utrecht and N.Y., 1950.

VC1397. Rosenberg, Jakob. **Rembrandt.** 2 v. Cambridge, Mass., 1948.

VC1398. Rosenberg, Adolf. **P. P. Rubens.** 4th ed., Stuttgart, 1921.

Music

VC1399. Closson, Ernest, and Charles van den Borren. **La musique en Belgique du Moyen Âge à nos jours.** Brussels, 1950.

VC1400. Borren, Charles van den. **Geschiedenis van de muziek in de Nederlanden.** 2 v. Antwerp, 1948–51.

Literature

VC1401. Charlier, Gustave, and Joseph Hanse, eds. **Histoire illustrée des lettres françaises de Belgique.** Brussels, 1958.

VC1402. Baur, Frank, and others, eds.

**Geschiedenis van de letterkunde der Neder-
landen.** Hertogenbosch, Neth., 1939 ff.
VC1403. Liebrecht, Henri, Auguste Vincent, and others. **Histoire du livre et de
l'imprimerie en Belgique des origines à nos
jours.** 6 v. Brussels, 1923–34.

Universities

VC1404. Post, Regnerus R. **Scholen en
onderwijs in Nederland gedurende de Middeleeuwen.** Utrecht, 1954.
VC1405. Essen, Léon van der. **L'Université de Louvain, 1425–1940.** Brussels,
1945.
VC1406. Kalken, Frans van, A. Kluy-
skens, Paul Harsin, and Léon van der Essen.
Histoire des universités belges. Brussels,
1954.

General Cultural History

VC1407. Proost, Karel F., and Jan Romein. **Geestelijk Nederland, 1920–1940.** 2 v.
Amsterdam, 1948. Achievements in various
fields of science, arts, and culture.
VC1408. Arnould, Maurice A. **Le travail
historique en Belgique des origines à nos
jours.** Brussels, 1954.
VC1409. Romein, Jan M. **Geschiedenis
van de Noord-Nederlandsche geschiedschrijv-
ing in de Middeleeuwen.** Haarlem, 1932. Supplement, by H. Bruch, Haarlem, 1956.
Several chapters on the cultural history of
Belgium will be found in *Histoire de la
Belgique contemporaine* (*VC1327*).

PERIODICALS

**VC1410. Revue belge de philologie et
d'histoire.** Brussels, 1922 ff. (Quarterly.)
This and *VC1411* are of a general character,
but with emphasis on the history of Belgium
or the Netherlands.
VC1411. Tijdschrift voor geschiedenis.
Amersfoort and Groningen, 1886 ff. (Irregular.)

VC1412. La revue belge. Brussels, 1924 ff.
Contains articles in English, as well as
French, Dutch, etc.
**VC1413. Bijdragen voor de geschiedenis
der Nederlanden.** The Hague and Antwerp,
1946 ff. (Quarterly.) For the Netherlands
and Belgium this took the place of *VC1414*.
This and *VC1414–1416* are especially de-
voted to the history of the Low Countries.
**VC1414. Bijdragen voor vaderlandsche ge-
schiedenis en oudheidkunde.** Arnhem and
The Hague, 1837–1944. (Irregular.) The
oldest Dutch historical review.
**VC1415. Bulletin de la Commission Royale
d'Histoire.** Brussels, 1834 ff. (Irregular. Title
varies.) Belgian history.
VC1416. Revue du Nord. Lille, 1910 ff.
(Quarterly.) For northern France and the
Low Countries.
The references of local periodicals, which
are very numerous and sometimes very valu-
able, will be found in Pirenne, *Bibliographie
de l'histoire de Belgique* (*VC1281*).
VC1417. Revue d'histoire ecclésiastique.
Louvain, 1900 ff. (Quarterly.) This and
VC1418, as well as several other important
periodicals published in Belgium or the
Netherlands, bear a more international than
national character.
**VC1418. Tijdschrift voor rechtsgeschied-
enis. Revue d'histoire du droit.** Haarlem,
1918 ff. (Quarterly.)
The following are periodicals of a purely
bibliographical character.
**VC1419. Bibliographie de Belgique: liste
mensuelle des publications belges ou rela-
tives à la Belgique acquises par la Bibliothèque Royale.** Brussels, 1875 ff.
VC1420. Nieuwe uitgaven in Nederland.
Amsterdam and The Hague, 1937 ff.
(Monthly.)
**VC1421. Nijhoff's index op de Neder-
landse periodieken van algemeen inhoud.**
1909 ff. The Hague, 1910 ff. (Monthly.)

Spain and Portugal

CHARLES JULIAN BISHKO *

During the past quarter century there have been extensive research and publication in the fields of Spanish and Portuguese history. Important new works have in many cases replaced the standard authorities of a generation ago, either partially or wholly; and the attempt is made here to recognize these recent contributions. It will, however, still be found worthwhile to consult titles listed under "Spain and Portugal" in the original *Guide*. While the 15th and 16th centuries inevitably continue to attract many scholars, the Iberian middle ages have become a special field of predilection. Significant work is also slowly appearing for the era of the 17th to 19th centuries; but the last hundred years, with certain notable exceptions, remain a poorly plowed demesne.

In Spain, under the present regime, there has been considerable subsidizing of historical research and publication, under the auspices of the Consejo Superior de Investigaciones Científicas. This government agency is subdivided into numerous national, regional, and provincial *institutos, instituciones, centros, escuelas,* and *congresos,* of which those most important for historical purposes are grouped into the Patronato Menéndez Pelayo de Filología, Historia y Arte and the Patronato José María Quadrado de Estudios e Investigaciones Locales. Many of these organizations publish, in addition to monographs and books, historical journals of national, regional, and local scope, all of which are listed in the Consejo's annual *Memorias.*

In Portugal historical research is much less highly organized, but government support of scholarly investigation is also in evidence. Particular attention should be paid to the vast output of valuable historical publications that appeared in the years around 1940, when Portugal was celebrating the double centenary of her establishment (1140) and recovery of independence (1640).

For the general history of Spain and Portugal and their relations to other

* The following contributed items and comments indicated by their respective initials: Howard F. Cline (HFC), Judith S. Cousins (JSC), John E. Fagg (JEF), Richard Herr (RH), Gabriel Jackson (GJ), Francis M. Rogers (FMR), Arthur P. Whitaker (APW). Comments by the following, appearing in the first edition of this *Guide,* are also included: Clarence H. Haring (CHH), Roger B. Merriman (RBM).

nations see other sections of this *Guide* pertaining to the appropriate areas. For matters associated with the religious history of the peninsula see sections *D* and *M*.

SPAIN

BIBLIOGRAPHIES AND LIBRARIES

VD1. Sánchez Alonso, Benito. **Fuentes de la historia española e hispanoamericana.** 3rd ed., 3 v., Madrid, 1952. The principal bibliography of Spanish historical literature, including periodical titles as well as books. Indispensable, despite incomplete coverage, inadequate classification, and lack of indication of content or value.

VD2. Universidad de Barcelona. Centro de Estudios Históricos Internacionales. **Índice histórico español.** Barcelona, 1953 ff. (3 nos. a year.) A bibliographical journal which lists promptly and exhaustively current books, book reviews, and periodical titles on all aspects of Spanish history and civilization. Titles are neatly organized under major periods, with chronological, regional, and topical subheads. Summary of content and critical evaluation are included.

VD3. Indice histórico español: bibliografía histórica de España e Hispanoamérica. Barcelona, 1953 ff. Republication of *VD2* in book form, with the addition of subject-author indices and introductory essays on current Spanish historiographical trends. V. 1–2 cover 1953–54 and 1955–56. Publication will continue henceforth on an annual basis.

VD4. Tortajada Ferrandis, A., and C. de Amaniel, eds. **Materiales de investigación: índices de revistas.** 2 v. Madrid, 1952. Indexes by author and subject, the innumerable historical articles published during the decade 1939–49 in the many national, regional, and provincial journals subsidized by the Consejo Superior de Investigaciones Científicas.

VD5. Serís, Homero. **Manual de bibliografía de la literatura española.** 2 v. Syracuse, N.Y., 1948. Broadly planned, and useful for many aspects of Spanish social, religious, and cultural history.

VD6. Ballester y Castell, Rafael. **Bibliografía de la historia de España.** Gerona, 1921. Badly in need of revision, but still valuable, especially for older books and journals of regional scope, and on such topics as constitutional, ecclesiastical, economic, and cultural history.

VD7. Bishko, Charles Julian. "The Iberian background of Latin American history: recent progress and continuing problems." Hisp. Am. hist. rev., 36 (Feb. 1956): 50–80. Brief survey of important works published since 1940.

For general introductory purposes the most helpful guides are the bibliographies appended to each chapter in Aguado Bleye,

Manual de historia de España (*VD48*) and Valdeavellano, *Historia de España* (*VD50*). The myriad titles listed in Ballesteros, *Historia de España* (*VD47*) are so badly arranged as to be difficult to use. To the foregoing works should also be added the critical review articles occasionally appearing in *Revue historique,* notably M. Defourneaux on medieval Spain, 200 (July-Sep. 1948): 85–108, 219–36; H. Lapeyre on the Catholic Kings and Hapsburgs, 203 (Jan.-Mar. 1950): 90–114; P. Vilar on the 18th century to the present, 206 (Oct.-Dec. 1951): 281–317. Current titles on Spain and Portugal are listed in *Journal of modern history* (books) and *The American historical review* (selected periodical articles).

VD8. Foulché-Delbosc, Raymond, and Louis Barrau-Dihigo. **Manuel de l'hispanisant.** 2 v. N.Y., 1920–25. The standard guide to a vast amount of older material in both Spanish and Portuguese history. V. 1 contains extensive information on general and special bibliographies, biographical and bio-bibliographical works, and public and private archives. V. 2 lists, volume by volume, the contents of all important collections of published sources and the publications of learned societies.

Library Collections

In the United States the outstanding collections on Spanish history include those of Harvard University, the Library of Congress, the Hispanic Society of America, the University of California, and the New York Public Library. On these and other important centers for work in the Spanish historical field consult Hilton, *Handbook of Hispanic source materials . . . (VD13).* For Spain itself see the new series **(VD9) Guías de archivos y bibliotecas** being published by the Dirección General de Archivos y Bibliotecas. This includes, for the Biblioteca Nacional, Real Academia de la Historia, and other big Madrid collections, the **Guía de las bibliotecas de Madrid** (Madrid, 1953), and for the other great Spanish library center, Barcelona, **Las bibliotecas de Barcelona y su provincia** (Madrid, 1952).

ENCYCLOPEDIAS AND WORKS OF REFERENCE

VD10. **Enciclopedia universal ilustrada europeo-americana.** See *B119.*

VD11. Diccionario de historia de España desde sus orígenes hasta el fin del reinado de Alfonso XIII. 2 v. Madrid, 1952. A solidly informative digest. The articles are often of some length, but without bibliography. Appendices (v. 2) include an abridgement of the excellent general bibliography in the 1952 edition of Valdeavellano (*VD50*), and also chronological chart and maps.

VD12. Peers, Edgar Allison, ed. **Spain: a companion to Spanish studies.** 5th ed., rev. and enl., N.Y. and London, 1956. Introductory survey to the country, people, history, literature, and art, with brief bibliographies.

VD13. Hilton, Ronald, ed. **Handbook of Hispanic source materials and research organizations in the United States.** 2nd ed., Stanford, 1956. Invaluable as a storehouse of information regarding United States resources in the Spanish and Portuguese fields. It describes (by states and cities) all significant libraries, archives, museums, and collections of Luso-Hispanic import .d lists their printed catalogs and other i.__utitutional publications.

GEOGRAPHIES, GAZETTEERS, AND ATLASES

VD14. Terán, Manuel de, ed. **Geografía de España y Portugal.** 5 v. Barcelona, 1952 ff. A collaborative work, each volume having its own author. V. 5, by Orlando Ribeiro, is on Portugal. Emphasizes almost exclusively physical geography.

VD15. Martín Echeverría, Leonardo. **España, el país y los habitantes.** Mexico, D.F., 1940. Rapid survey, containing also some useful chapters on physical geography.

VD16. Gilbert, E. W., R. P. Beckinsale, and S. de Sá. **Spain and Portugal.** 4 v. Oxford, 1941-44. The best general work on human and economic, as well as physical, geography of Spain, Portugal, and the Ibero-Atlantic islands, but almost inaccessible in the United States because originally prepared by the British admiralty during World War II and never commercially published. Copies exist in certain government libraries in Washington, and in the library of the American Geographical Society in New York. See also the account of Iberian geography by Max Sorre in Vidal de la Blache and Gallois, *Géographie universelle* (*C13*), v. 7, pt. 1; and the frequent articles of historical interest in the *Boletín de la real sociedad geográfica* and *Estudios geográficos*.

VD17. Madoz, Pascual. **Diccionario geográfico-estadístico-histórico de España y sus posesiones de Ultramar.** 16 v. Madrid, 1846-50. Not the most recent chorographical dictionary, but for historical purposes the fullest and most useful.

VD18. Menéndez Pidal, Gonzalo. **Atlas histórico español.** Barcelona, 1941. The only Spanish historical atlas worth mention, but in both cartography and coverage very far from adequate.

ANTHROPOLOGY AND DEMOGRAPHY

VD19. Bosch y Gimpera, Pedro. **El poblamiento antiguo y la formación de los pueblos de España.** Mexico, D.F., 1945. Authoritative study of the pre-Roman inhabitants of the peninsula, whose descendants constitute the basis of the Spanish population to the present day.

VD20. Caro Baroja, Julio. **Los pueblos de España.** Barcelona, 1946. After describing the prehistoric colonization of Spain, this work examines, region by region, their ethnology, folkways, and social and cultural survivals.

VD21. Edge, P. Granville. "Early population records in Spain." **Metron**, 9 (Rome, 1932): 229-49. General survey of sources of information and of major problems, with useful bibliography, ranging from the Middle Ages to the 18th century.

VD22. Smith, Robert S. "Spanish population thought before Malthus." In Hughes, H. Stuart, ed., **Teachers of history: essays in honor of Laurence B. Packard** (Ithaca, 1954). Review of the efforts by Spaniards in the Hapsburg period to explain population decline, with bibliographical suggestions.

VD23. Girard, Albert. "La répartition de la population en Espagne dans les temps modernes, XVIe, XVIIe, XVIIIe siècles." **Revue d'histoire économique et sociale**, 17 (1929): 347-62. See *VD24*.

VD24. ———. "Le chiffre de la population de l'Espagne dans les temps modernes." **Revue d'histoire moderne**, 3 (Nov.-Dec. 1928): 420-36; 4 (Jan.-Feb. 1929): 3-17. This and *VD23* are careful analyses, done at a time when population studies were relatively new. They yield results that, however conjectural in their details, contribute significantly to the social and economic history of early modern Spain. [RH]

COLLECTIONS OF SOURCES

The most important manuscript collections in Spain are those at Madrid, in the Archivo Histórico Nacional, the Biblioteca Nacional, and the Real Academia de la Historia; in the castle of Simancas (largely 16th to 18th century documents); at the Escorial; at Seville, in the Archivo de Indias (for the American colonies); at Barcelona, in the Archivo de la Corona de Aragón; and at Pamplona, in the Archivo General de Navarra. The best general guide to these and other Spanish collections is

VD25. Marín, Francisco Rodríguez, ed. **Guía histórica descriptiva de los archivos**

bibliotecas y museos arqueológicos de España. Madrid, 1916. This is being replaced in part by volumes in the series *Guías de archivos y bibliotecas (VD9)*, such as *Guía de los archivos de Madrid* (Madrid, 1952); *Archivos de Barcelona*, v. 1, *Ciudad* (Barcelona, 1952); *Guía del Archivo General de Navarra, Pamplona*. See also the various catalogs of diplomatic documents at Simancas, chiefly of the early modern period, edited by Julián Paz; and Agustín Millares Carlo, *Notas bibliográficas acerca de archivos municipales, ediciones de Libros de Acuerdos y colecciones de documentos concejiles* (Madrid, 1952), and *T10*, ch. 10.

VD26. **Colección de documentos inéditos para la historia de España.** Ed. by Martín F. de Navarrete and others. 113 v. Madrid, 1842–95. The most important collection of materials for Spanish history, chiefly of the reigns of Charles V and Philip II. The contents of each volume are listed in detail in Julián Paz, *Catálogo de la "Colección de documentos inéditos para la historia de España"* (2 v., Madrid, 1930–31), along with person, place, and subject indices. See also *Manuel de l'hispanisant (VD8)*, v. 2. The collection is continued in *Archivo histórico español*, published by the Academia de Estudios Histórico-Sociales de Valladolid (6 v., Madrid, 1929–34); and by Duque de Alba, Duque de Maura, and others, eds. *Documentos inéditos para la historia de España* (11 v., Madrid, 1936–52).

The most extensive and up-to-date survey of published Spanish sources is in Valdeavellano, *Historia de España (VD50)*, v. 1, pt. 1.

VD27. **Memorial histórico español: colección de documentos, opusculos y antigüedades que publica la Real Academia de la Historia.** 49 v. Madrid, 1851–1948. Documents of the later medieval and Hapsburg eras.

VD28. **Colección de documentos para el estudio de la historia de Aragón.** Ed. by Eduardo Ibarra y Rodríguez and others. 12 v. Saragossa, 1904–20. Medieval and modern documents. For contents of this and *VD27* see *Manuel de l'hispanisant (VD8)*.

VD29. **Colección de crónicas españolas.** Ed. by Juan de Mata Carriazo. 9 v. Madrid, 1940–46. Chronicles of the 15th and 16th centuries.

VD30. Flórez, Enrique, Manuel Risco, and others. **España sagrada: theatro geográfico-histórico de la iglesia de España.** 52 v. Madrid, 1747–1879. Both a historical survey of Spanish episcopal sees and a major collection of chronicles and ecclesiastical documents, for the most part medieval. See also Ángel González Palencia, *Índice de la "España sagrada"* (Madrid, 1918; 2nd ed., 1946).

VD31. Sáenz de Aguirre, José. **Collectio maxima conciliorum omnium Hispaniae et Novi Orbis, epistolarumque decretalium celebriorum.** 2nd ed., 6 v., Rome, 1753–55. Canonical legislation of the Spanish church in the medieval and early modern epochs.

VD32. López Oliván, José. **Repertorio diplomático español: índice de los tratados ajustados por España (1125–1935) y de otros documentos internacionales.** Madrid, 1944. Calendars 2148 treaties, conventions, and pacts of the Spanish government with other powers, with brief summary and reference to printed text, if published. Indexed by country and subject.

VD33. Yáñez Rivadeneyra, Manuel M., ed. **Los códigos españoles concordados y anotados.** 2nd ed., 12 v., Madrid, 1872–73. A standard collection of Spanish law codes, although not always in the best available edition, running from the Visigothic Code to the Novísima Recopilación.

VD34. "Textos constitucionales españoles [1808–1947]." **Archivo de derecho público**, v. 6–7 (1953–54). Texts of all the Spanish constitutions from Joseph Bonaparte to the present regime. For an English translation of the constitutions see Arnold R. Verduin, *Manual of Spanish constitutions, 1808–1931* (Ypsilanti, Mich., 1941).

HISTORIOGRAPHY

VD35. Sánchez Alonso, Benito. **Historia de la historiografía española.** 3 v. Madrid, 1941–50. An exhaustive chronicling of Spanish historians and their writings from the Roman period to 1808, with data on editions and bibliography. V. 1 reaches 1543; v. 2, 1684; v. 3, 1808. The work excels more for its conscientious compilation than for profundity of analysis or insight. Its factual information can usually be trusted, and it is the ideal base from which to commence more intensive study of a historian or historiographical movement.

VD36. Ganivet, Ángel. **Idearium español.** Granada, 1897. Modern Spanish historiography demands some acquaintance with the unceasing interpretative controversies over Spain's place in history that often color the writings of Spanish and foreign historians. This and *VD37* are classic defenses of the Spanish tradition. Ganivet explores Spanish psychology partly through the medium of Spanish history.

VD37. Juderías, Julián. **La leyenda negra.** Madrid, 1914. Attacks the black legend of bigotry and obscurantism, emphasizing Spain's rich contributions to western civilization. See also the frequent influential excursions into historical interpretation by the philosopher José Ortega y Gasset (*Obras completas*, 6 v., Madrid, 1946–47; *Invertebrate Spain*, N.Y., 1937).

VD38. Castro, Américo. **The structure of Spanish history.** Tr. by Edmund L. King.

Princeton, 1954. Brilliant, provocative work by a cultural historian of existentialist views, with much new material and high originality; but should be used with caution. Largely confined to the Middle Ages and the 16th century, the book affirms that Spanish civilization, forged in the interaction of medieval Muslim, Jewish, and Christian elements, has ever since been characterized by a peculiar, un-western, and unchanging pattern of religiosity, messianism, quixotism, *hidalguismo*, pessimism, and psychic insecurity. As originally published in an earlier form (*España en su historia: cristianos, moros y judíos*, Buenos Aires, 1948), the Castro thesis was the subject of long, significant reviews, including J. E. Gillet, *Hispanic rev.*, 18 (Apr. 1950): 169–84; M. Bataillon, *Bull. hispanique*, 52, nos. 1–2 (1950): 5–26; Claudio Sánchez-Albornoz, *Cuad. de hist. de España*, 19 (1953): 129–45. See also R. Herr, *Jour. mod. hist.*, 28 (June 1956): 177–8.

VD39. Sánchez-Albornoz, Claudio. **España, un enigma histórico.** 2 v. Buenos Aires, 1956. Lengthy and vehemently sweeping attack upon Castro by the foremost contemporary historian of medieval Spain, arguing for sharp limitations upon alleged Muslim and Jewish contributions to an overwhelmingly Christian Spanish (chiefly Castilian) culture. Includes notable sections on the reconquest, Spanish feudalism, the failure of the Castilian middle class, and many aspects of Spain's religious, cultural, and intellectual development.

SHORTER GENERAL HISTORIES

VD40. Altamira, Rafael. **A history of Spain.** Tr. by Muna Lee. N.Y., 1949. A satisfactory short history of Spain, based on the results of modern research, comprehensive in scope, and effectively organized, does not yet exist. The above is not an abridgement of its celebrated author's *Historia de la civilización española* (*VD52*), but an independent survey. Somewhat antiquated in content, it is stronger on social and cultural than institutional and economic questions.

VD41. Celotti, Temistocle. **Storia di Spagna.** Milan, 1940. Political account, with balanced treatment of all periods. The final propagandistic section, by another hand, on events since 1931 can be disregarded.

VD42. Calmette, Joseph L. A. **Histoire de l'Espagne.** Paris, 1947. Fast-moving survey to 1946 by an outstanding specialist in Franco-Spanish relations.

VD43. Konetzke, Richard. **Geschichte des spanischen und portugiesischen Volkes.** Leipzig, 1939. [Die grosse Weltgeschichte, 8.] A kind of better grade textbook, compact, dry, and generally reliable as a purely political outline to 1931.

VD44. Mousset, Albert. **Histoire d'Es-**pagne. Paris, 1947. Limited to political evolution, and unbalanced in favor of the 19th and 20th centuries.

VD45. Palomeque Torres, Antonio. **Historia de la civilización e instituciones hispánicas.** Barcelona, 1946. Useful introduction to topics ordinarily neglected in the narrowly political histories.

VD46. Livermore, Harold V. **A history of Spain.** London, 1958. The most recent survey, strongly factual with undue emphasis on dynastic and political narrative.

LONGER GENERAL HISTORIES

VD47. Ballesteros y Beretta, Antonio. **Historia de España y de su influencia en la historia universal.** 2nd ed., rev., 11 v., Barcelona, 1943–56. A massive work, with copious illustrations, that ranks as the best comprehensive history of Spain to 1931. It rests upon industrious exploitation of a large secondary literature, which is not always successfully digested. The extensive bibliographies, listing uncritically several thousand titles, require careful screening.

VD48. Aguado Bleye, Pedro. **Manual de historia de España.** 6th ed., 3 v., Madrid, 1947–56. Designed on a smaller scale than *VD47*, but equally comprehensive. An excellent source of lucidly presented information on all periods and aspects of Spanish history. V. 1 covers prehistory, antiquity, and the Middle Ages; v. 2, the Catholic Kings and the Hapsburgs; v. 3, 18th century to the present. Abundant bibliography, generally up-to-date.

VD49. Soldevila Zubiburu, Fernando. **Historia de España.** 8 v. Barcelona, 1952 ff. Written by a leading Catalan historian, who successfully carries out his avowed aim of producing a competent, scholarly, and readable survey for the intelligent layman. Footnotes frequently cite the best secondary sources; social, institutional, and cultural history are well represented; many illustrations. V. 1–2, to era of Catholic Kings; v. 3–4, the Hapsburg period; v. 5, to reign of Philip VI; v. 6, from Carlos III to Ferdinand VII; v. 7, to 1873; v. 8, to 1898.

VD50. Valdeavellano, Luis García de. **Historia de España.** 2nd ed., 1 v. in 2 pts., Madrid, 1955. In many respects the best organized and most modern history of Spain for the period covered, with political narrative alternating with institutional, cultural, and socio-economic chapters. Drawing heavily upon the results of much recent research, the work is an excellent guide to the enrichment of Spanish history through advances of contemporary scholarship. V. 1, only one published to date, stops in 1212. Pp. 29–104 of v. 1, pt. 1 contain an extremely valuable bibliographical survey of archival collections, published sources, and major secondary works. Short bibliographies are also appended to each chapter.

VD51. Menéndez Pidal, Ramón. ed. **Historia de España.** Madrid, 1935 ff. If ever completed, this ponderous, slow-moving, collaborative work will be the most ambitious of recent general histories. While the contributions vary in merit, the general level is high. V. 1 is the best comprehensive account of the prehistoric and pre-Roman eras; v. 2–3 deal respectively with Roman and Visigothic Spain; v. 4, a translation of the first edition of Lévi-Provençal, _Histoire de l'Espagne musulmane_ (_VD59_), v. 1–2, narrates the political history of the Cordobese caliphate; v. 5, perhaps the least satisfactory, deals with the first three centuries of the Christian reconquest; v. 19–20 cover the life and times of Philip II.

VD52. Altamira, Rafael. **Historia de España y de la civilización española.** 4th ed., 4 v., Barcelona, 1928–29. In its day a pioneer work. Dated, but still worth consulting for social, institutional, and cultural history.

VD53. Ramos Oliveira, Antonio. **Historia de España.** 3 v. Mexico, 1952. Written from a leftist, strongly regionalist viewpoint that contrasts with the usual Castilian nationalist approach. V. 1–2 are better as interpretation than as narrative history, but v. 3 treats much more factually politics and economic changes since 1808.

HISTORIES OF SPECIAL PERIODS

Antiquity

VD54. Pericot García, Luis. **La España primitiva.** Barcelona, 1950. [Colección histórica Laye, 6.] Competent but somewhat excessively archaeological account of pre-Roman Spain. The Celtiberians are emphasized, but treatment of their institutional organization is inferior to that in v. 1 of Adolph Schulten, _Numantia_ (4 v., Munich, 1914–31).

VD55. Sutherland, Carol H. V. **The Romans in Spain, 217 B.C.–A.D. 117.** See _1164._

VD56. Thouvenot, Raymond. **Essai sur la province romaine de Bétique.** Paris, 1940. [Bibliothèque des Écoles françaises d'Athènes et de Rome, fasc. 149.] An unusually thorough, scholarly examination of highly Romanized Andalusia, describing exhaustively for both the republican and imperial epochs its history, institutions, and material culture.

The Middle Ages

VD57. Ziegler, Aloysius K. **Church and state in Visigothic Spain.** Washington, 1930. Depicts constitutional, legal, and social, as well as ecclesiastical, organization. On the latter it provides a counterweight to the reli-

gious partisanship of F. L. S. Dahn, _Die Könige der Germanen_, v. 5–6 (Würzburg, 1866–71), the basis of most later accounts. Major aspects of Visigothic history have been illuminated by the numerous important monographs of Claudio Sánchez-Albornoz appearing in _Cuadernos de historia de España;_ and the doctoral dissertations of Rev. A. K. Ziegler's students, published in _The Catholic University of America studies in mediaeval history_ (Washington, 1938 ff.). The lamentably neglected Sueves are best treated in v. 6 of Dahn's _Könige_, a virtually unknown account.

VD58. Reinhart, Wilhelm. **Historia general del reino hispánico de los suevos.** Madrid, 1952. A short, modern study incorporating archaeological materials.

VD59. Lévi-Provençal, Évariste. **Histoire de l'Espagne musulmane.** 3 v. Paris, 1950–53. Superb work, crowning the fruitful career of the greatest 20th century authority on western Islam, but unfortunately still incomplete at his death. The first three volumes treat the Umayyad Caliphate of Córdoba (to 1031): v. 1–2, political developments; v. 3, institutional and cultural structure.

VD60. Dozy, Reinhart P. A. **Histoire des Musulmans d'Espagne jusqu'à la conquête de l'Andalousie par les Almoravides (711–1110).** 2nd ed., rev., 3 v., Leiden, 1932. Classical narrative account, in vivid, colorful prose, by a famous Dutch orientalist of the last century. Since v. 1 describes the Arabian origins of Hispano-Islamic factions and sects, and v. 3 carries the post-caliphal period to 1110, the work is by no means entirely displaced by _VD59._

VD61. Sánchez-Albornoz, Claudio. **La España musulmana.** See _M120._

VD62. Barrau-Dihigo, Louis. "Recherches sur l'histoire politique du royaume asturien (718–910)." **Revue hispanique,** 52 (June 1921): 1–357. First truly scientific reconstruction of the sources, history, and institutions of the Asturian kingdom. Still the best, although in places hypercritical or requiring correction in light of later publications.

VD63. Cotarelo y Valledor, Armando. **Historia crítica y documentada de la vida y acciones de Alfonso III el Magno, último rey de Asturias.** Madrid, 1933. Detailed study of the greatest of Asturian rulers. Supplements _VD62;_ but some of the best subsequent research, by Sánchez-Albornoz and his students, is to be found in _Cuadernos de historia de España_ and other journals.

VD64. Menéndez Pidal, Ramón. **La España del Cid.** 4th ed., rev., 2 v., Madrid, 1947. Eng. tr., _The Cid and his Spain_, London, 1934. A vivid biography of the historical Cid, which stoutly defends him, against Dozy and others, as a true heroic figure in the national formation of Spain.

Also a skilfully drawn panorama of 11th century Iberia in the age of the Almoravid invasion. Unfortunately, the English translation is based upon the earliest Spanish edition and omits part of the valuable survey of the historiographical controversy over the Cid, most footnotes, and the over 300 pages of appendices and historical texts.

VD65. Maravall, José Antonio. **El concepto de España en la edad media.** Madrid, 1954. An admirable study, tracing in detail the changing fortunes of the idea of a Spanish nation among the divided and warring kingdoms and cultures of medieval Iberia. Superseding the many recent writings on Leonese imperialism, it ably clarifies the movement towards eventual unification at the end of the Middle Ages.

VD66. Defourneaux, Marcelin. **Les français en Espagne aux XIᵉ et XIIᵉ siècles.** Paris, 1949. Introduction to the important subject of French influences in medieval Spain and Portugal before 1200. Limited to Cluniac and Cistercian penetration; French participation in the Compostellan pilgrimage and the reconquest; the immigration of French nobles, monks, and bourgeois; and the reflection of Franco-Spanish contacts in the medieval epic poetry of both countries.

VD67. Russell, Peter E. **The English intervention in Spain and Portugal in the time of Edward III and Richard II.** Oxford, 1955. Based upon thorough archival research, and written with insight and penetration, this volume is an excellent history of the unduly neglected peninsular theaters of the Hundred Years War. It also provides the most searching examination yet undertaken into the whole period of crisis and conflict leading to the fateful establishment, in Castile and Portugal respectively, of the new Trastamara and Aviz dynasties.

VD68. **La reconquista española y la repoblación del país.** Saragossa, 1951. [Escuela de Estudios Medievales, 15.] The reconquest of Muslim by Christian Spain between the 8th and 15th centuries is a decisive factor in the making of medieval Spain, but the subject is still very imperfectly explored, notably as a problem in medieval frontier expansion and colonization. This is a good introduction, comprising regional and chronological essays by leading authorities.

VD69. Sánchez-Albornoz, Claudio. "La repoblación del reino astur-leonés." **Humanidades,** 25 (Buenos Aires, 1936): 37–55. The most comprehensive of several studies by this acknowledged master, illuminating the agencies of frontier settlement in the Duero basin before 1000 A.D.

VD70. González, Julio, ed. **Repartimiento de Sevilla.** 2 v. Madrid, 1951. Chosen from among its author's various contributions to reconquest history, this provides in v. 2 the definitive text of the mid-13th century land

division drawn up after Ferdinand III's annexation of the *reino de Sevilla.* V. 1, analyzing in detail the Christian conquerors' geographic origins, type and distribution of land allotments, and pattern of colonial settlement, gives a splendid picture of the conquest and Castilianization of medieval frontier Andalusia.

The Catholic Kings and the Hapsburgs

VD71. Merriman, Roger B. **The rise of the Spanish empire in the Old World and in the New.** 4 v. N.Y., 1918–34. Foremost comprehensive examination of the medieval and early modern background for, and eventual establishment of, the Spanish world empire. V. 1, now somewhat dated, traces origins, institutions, and territorial growth of medieval Aragon and Castile; while v. 2–4, covering respectively the reigns of the Catholic Kings, the Emperor Charles V, and Philip II, describe in masterly panorama Spain's national evolution, European entanglements, and her acquisition, government, and defense of far-flung imperial territories on four continents.

VD72. Ibarra y Rodríguez, Eduardo. **España bajo los Austrias.** 3rd rev. ed., Barcelona, 1955. A compact, factually informative survey of the Spanish Hapsburgs, with stress almost wholly upon politics, war, and foreign relations.

VD73. Davies, Reginald Trevor. **The golden century of Spain, 1501–1621.** London, 1937. Reprint, 1954. Elementary account of the 16th and 17th centuries, badly antiquated in parts. Must be used with discrimination.

VD74. Hume, Martin A. S. **Spain, its greatness and decay (1479–1788).** 3rd rev. ed., Cambridge, Eng., 1913. Reprint, 1940. Another elementary work, with helpful bibliographical footnotes.

VD75. Prescott, William H. **History of the reign of Ferdinand and Isabella the Catholic.** 3 v. Boston, 1838. Many reprints. Despite the recent spate of studies on one or the other of the Catholic Kings (see bibliographies in Aguado Bleye, *Manual de historia de España (VD48),* v. 2), no comprehensive work, based upon fresh archival exploration, has appeared to replace Prescott's now over a century old classic as a general picture of this crucial reign.

VD76. Calmette, Joseph L. A. **La formation de l'unité espagnole.** Paris, 1946. Traces from 1450 the political steps leading to Aragonese-Castilian unification of Spain as the background for Spanish preponderance in 16th century Europe.

VD77. Doussinague, José M. **La política internacional de Fernando el Católico.** Madrid, 1944. This scholarly revisionist work, fortified with unedited texts, presents Ferdinand of Aragon as the true initiator of 16th century Spanish foreign policy, rejecting current views of the subordination of Spain's national interests to the extra-peninsular objectives of Charles V and Philip II. On the author's views, expressed in this and his other related books on Fernandine diplomacy, see R. Konetzke, *Hist. Zeit.*, 175 (June 1953): 463–82.

VD78. Torre y del Cerro, Antonio de la. **Documentos sobre las relaciones internacionales de los Reyes Católicos.** 3 v. Barcelona, 1949–51.

VD79. López de Toro, José. **Tratados internacionales de los Reyes Católicos.** 2 v. Madrid, 1952.

VD80. Carande, Ramón. **Carlos V y sus banqueros.** 2 v. Madrid, 1943–49. An exceptionally valuable work, too narrowly entitled, based upon archival research and constituting a masterly economic survey of the Spain of Charles V. V. 1 examines population, agriculture, mercantilism, industry, finance, urban commercial centers, banks and fairs, the war and merchant navies, and overseas trade with the Indies. V. 2, subtitled "La Hacienda Real de Castilla," authoritatively reconstructs royal fiscal organization with reference to governmental expenditures, the mechanism of the Hacienda Real, and the wide range of ordinary and extraordinary Crown revenues, including grants by the Cortes.

VD81. Häbler, Konrad. "Zur Geschichte der kastilischen Comunidades, 1520–1521." **Historische Zeitschrift,** 95 (1905): 385–434. Both this and *VD82* exploit the wealth of documents on the Comuneros published by Manuel Dávila in *Memorial histórico español* (*VD27*), v. 35–40. Häbler argues convincingly that the basic social conflict that emerged was between the well-to-do and the lower classes within the cities themselves. [RH]

VD82. Seaver, Henry Latimer. **The great revolt in Castile: a study of the Comunero movement of 1520–1521.** Boston, 1928. Follows the standard view that the rising against royal exactions was doomed when it turned into a struggle between cities and landowning aristocrats. [RH]

Amid the enormous, violently controversial literature on Philip II, Merriman's thorough and dispassionate study (*VD71*), v. 4, stands as the most trustworthy biography. See also *VD83–85* below.

VD83. Lapeyre, H. "Autour de Philippe II." **Bulletin hispanique,** 59, no. 2 (Apr.–June 1957): 152–75. Excellent critique of eight much bruited works by partisan amateurs and professional historians.

VD84. Marañón, Gregorio. **Antonio Pérez (el hombre, el drama, la época).** 2 v. Buenos Aires, 1947. Eng. tr., *Antonio Pérez, "Spanish traitor,"* London, 1954. Hostile biography of Philip II's secretary and eventual deadly enemy. The often unfairly treated Pérez serves as foil to a tepidly favorable portrait of the king, here viewed as weak and irresolute in well-doing rather than, as commonly, either fanatical or prudent. Good, fresh material on the Spanish court and palace nobility. The abridged English translation lacks some chapters, most footnotes, and the bibliography of the Spanish edition.

VD85. Braudel, Fernand. **El Mediterráneo y el mundo mediterráneo en la época de Felipe II.** 2 v. Mexico, 1953. Tr. and rev. from *La Méditerranée et le monde méditerranéen à l'époque de Philippe II*, Paris, 1949. A highly original work, based on intensive archival investigation on the physical and human geography, internal conditions, and the Italian, African, and Turkish involvements of Philippine Spain within the framework of 16th century Mediterranean history as a whole.

VD86. Hume, Martin A. S. **Court of Philip IV: Spain in decadence.** N.Y., 1907. Of broader scope than the title suggests.

VD87. Marañón, Gregorio. **El conde-duque de Olivares (La pasión de mandar).** 3rd rev. ed., Madrid, 1952. In contrast to *VD86*, this is strictly a personal portrait of Philip IV's great minister, without treatment of his policies. Neither of these two works is even a partial substitute for the badly needed fresh appraisal of mid-17th century Spain. For some fresh light consult the economic studies of E. J. Hamilton, cited below (*VD172*).

Eighteenth Century

VD88. Legrelle, Arsène. **La diplomatie française et la succession d'Espagne.** 2nd ed., 6 v., Paris, 1895–99. Work of profound research. Most complete history of the question of the Spanish succession, written from a French point of view and showing deepest admiration for Louis XIV. Gives a comprehensive review of previous works on the subject. [CHH]

VD89. Baudrillart, Alfred. **Philippe V et la cour de France.** 5 v. Paris, 1890–1901. Making use of extensive correspondence in Spanish archives, Baudrillart presents a picture of the relations between France and Spain in the first half of the 18th century truer in all essential details than that of any of his predecessors. He is perhaps inclined, at times, to judge the activities of the French government in too favorable a light and to exaggerate the immediate advantages which French influence brought to Spain. [CHH]

VD90. Ferrer del Río, Antonio. **Historia del reinado de Carlos III en España.** 4 v. Madrid, 1856. First serious study of the reign. Sound scholarship based on extensive use of public and private manuscripts. It remains valuable for domestic history, but the reader should bear in mind the author's partiality towards Charles III and his ministers. [RH]

VD91. Rousseau, François. **Règne de Charles III d'Espagne.** 2 v. Paris, 1907. A more polished work than *VD90*, but goes too far in the opposite direction of condemning Charles' religious policy and minimizing his abilities. Its contribution is primarily the study of Spain's relations with foreign powers and the papacy, which are scrutinized through records of the French foreign archives. [RH]

VD92. Desdevises du Dezert, Georges N. **L'Espagne de l'ancien régime.** 3 v. Paris, 1897–1904. [1, *La société;* 2, *Les institutions;* 3, *La richesse et la civilisation.*] The most complete study of the institutions of 18th century Spain, but has been partially replaced for the economy by *VD93* and for culture by *VD95*. Remains invaluable as a work of reference and bibliography. [RH]

VD93. Domínguez Ortiz, Antonio. **La sociedad española en el siglo XVIII.** Madrid, 1955. The outstanding work on the century by a Spanish historian; unexcelled on the towns and countryside of Castile and Aragon, but weaker on the prosperous north and east. [RH]

VD94. Sánchez Agesta, Luis. **El pensamiento político del despotismo ilustrado.** Madrid, 1953. Since Menéndez Pelayo, *Historia de los heterodoxos españoles* (*VD110*) presented its derogatory account of the Spanish supporters of the enlightenment, opinion has been sharply divided on their merits. Here is a recent version of the conservative viewpoint, concluding on little evidence that, with the major exceptions of Feijóo and Jovellanos, they were hypocrites who relished foreign heterodoxy in private but presented an orthodox face to the public. [RH]

VD95. Sarrailh, Jean. **L'Espagne éclairée de la seconde moitié du XVIIIᵉ siècle.** Paris, 1954. The outstanding study of the thought and organizations of these men, based on extensive research and keen analysis. Its conclusion, that enlightened Spaniards were both sincerely patriotic and religious, must for the time at least carry the field. Thorough bibliography. Reviews, P. Vilar, *Rev. historique,* 213 (1955): 333; R. Herr, *Jour. mod. hist.,* 27 (Mar. 1955): 78. [RH]

VD96. Delpy, Gaspard. **Feijóo et l'esprit européen.** Paris, 1936. Besides its immediate topic, this scholarly monograph depicts the cultural level of the early 18th century. [RH]

VD97. Spell, Jefferson Rea. **Rousseau in the Spanish world before 1833.** Austin, Tex., 1938. Also depicts the growth of the periodical press in Spain under Charles III. [RH]

VD98. Herr, Richard. **The eighteenth-century revolution in Spain.** Princeton, 1958. Valuable study, in part dealing with matters discussed in greater detail in *VD95*, but going beyond in several respects, particularly in relating the Spanish to the general European revolution of the 18th century. [APW]

VD99. Baumgarten, Hermann. **Geschichte Spanien's zur Zeit der französischen Revolution: mit einer Einleitung über die innere Entwicklung Spanien's im achtzehnten Jahrhundert.** Berlin, 1861. Best picture of the crucial years of tense peace and French war, 1789–95. The author drew on the excellent dispatches of the Prussian minister to Madrid, Sandoz-Rollin, but accepted uncritically Sandoz's hatred of Manuel Godoy. For the whole reign of Charles IV the most balanced treatment is in Modesto Lafuente y Zamolloa, *Historia general de España* (30 v., Madrid, 1840–67). A full-scale study of the non-military side of the "War of Independence," 1808–14, is still lacking (for the military side see Oman, *History of the Peninsular War* (*T359*)), but the three following works illumine important aspects. [RH]

VD100. Mercader Riba, Juan. **Barcelona durante la ocupación francesa (1808–1814).** Madrid, 1949. Close study of a test case of Napoleon's policies, based on the papers of his prefects in Catalonia. Review, P. Vilar, *Rev. hist.,* 206 (1951): 298. [RH]

VD101. Conard, Pierre. **La constitution de Bayonne (1808): essai d'édition critique.** Paris, 1910. This and the following analyze constitutional developments. [RH]

VD102. Fernández Almagro, Melchor. **Orígenes del régimen constitucional en España.** Barcelona, 1928. Concludes that the Constitution of 1812 was largely a copy of the French Constitution of 1791, implying misleadingly that its authors were not deeply aware of Spain's own problems. The debate at Cádiz on *señoríos* is dealt with best by Domínguez Ortiz, *Sociedad española* (*VD93*); and the political and religious struggles there by Menéndez Pelayo, *Historia de los heterodoxos españoles* (*VD110*). [RH]

Nineteenth Century

VD103. Clarke, Henry B. **Modern Spain, 1815–1898.** Cambridge, Eng., 1906. Good basis for beginning the study of 19th century Spanish history. Thorough and accurate, but overcrowded with detail. [JEF]

VD104. Bruguera, F. G. **Histoire contemporaine d'Espagne, 1789–1950.** Paris, 1953. Lucid and well-rounded account of the confusing political history of the period, with adequate consideration of social and economic factors. [JEF]

VD105. Zabala y Lera, Pio. **Historia de España. Edad contemporánea.** 2 v. Barcelona, 1930. [1, *Reinados de Fernando VII e Isabel II;* 2, *La revolución de 1868.*] Balanced, thorough, and solid account devoted mostly to the years 1808–1902. Continuing Altamira, *Historia de España* (*VD52*), this work also divides historical treatment rather rigidly into political, foreign relations, economic, social, and cultural aspects. [JEF]

VD106. Pirala, Antonio. **Historia de la guerra civil.** 2nd ed., 6 v., Madrid, 1868–69. See comment under *VD107*.

VD107. ——. **Historia contemporánea.** 6 v. Madrid, 1875–79. This and *VD106* are indispensable for any detailed study of the Carlist wars of the 1830's and 1870's and for the political history of the reign of Isabel II, but are verbose, inadequately documented, and written too near the events for perspective. See further Jaime del Burgo, *Bibliografía de las guerras carlistas y de las luchas políticas del siglo XIX* (3 v., Pamplona, 1953–55). [JEF]

VD108. Brandt, Joseph A. **Toward the new Spain.** Chicago, 1933. Detailed political and intellectual history of the revolution of 1868 and the First Republic, viewing liberal and republican efforts of the period as failures in the immediate sense, but as releasing the intellectual energy and political consciousness of a new Spain. Valuable analysis of motives and errors of leading personalities. [GJ]

VD109. Fernández Almagro, Melchor. **Historia política de la España contemporánea.** Madrid, 1956. The latest and in many respects most satisfactory account of the revolutionary period of 1868–75 and the restoration under Alfonso XII. [JEF]

VD110. Menéndez Pelayo, Marcelino. **Historia de los heterodoxos españoles.** 3 v. Madrid, 1880–81. Although colored by the author's fierce orthodoxy, this is noteworthy as the first serious attempt to study a crucial aspect of the evolution of Spanish thought. It relies primarily on biographical sketches of those who participated in struggles connected with religion. Later works have largely superseded it on the period before 1800, but it still provides the best insight into the ideological strife of the 19th century. [RH]

Twentieth Century

VD111. Brenan, Gerald. **The Spanish labyrinth.** 2nd ed., Cambridge, Eng., 1950. Indispensable background work on Spanish history since 1874. Unique among general studies for detailed attention to social and economic problems, regionalism, the labor movement, socialism, and anarchism. Broadly

liberal in sympathies, based on wide knowledge of Spanish history, literature, contemporary living conditions. Excellent bibliography. [GJ]

VD112. Ramos Oliveira, Antonio. **Politics, economics, and men of modern Spain, 1808–1946.** London, 1946. Very uneven in coverage and accuracy, and marred by pretentious theorizing, but valuable for its material on economic problems and its information on many aspects of the restoration and the Second Republic. [GJ]

VD113. Madariaga, Salvador de. **Spain.** N.Y., 1943. Rev. ed., 1958. Rich background on the psychology and historic problems of Spain, by a moderate republican and disciple of Francisco Giner. Valuable data on reign of Alfonso XIII and period of the Second Republic. Somewhat unsystematic and marked by strong personal biases concerning both individuals and policies. [GJ]

VD114. Sieberer, Anton. **Katalonien gegen Kastilien.** Vienna, 1936. French tr., *Espagne contre Espagne,* Geneva, 1937. Outline history of the Catalan autonomous and separatist movements by an excellently informed journalist. Analysis of the roles of anarchism, syndicalism, and cultural nationalism in the Catalan question; assessment of Catalonia's economic and cultural position within Spain. See also García Venero, *Historia del nacionalismo catalán* (*VD123*). [GJ]

VD115. Jobit, Pierre. **Les éducateurs de l'Espagne contemporaine.** 2 v. Paris, 1936. Indispensable analysis of Spanish Krausism as a philosophy, and history of its moral, religious, and educational repercussions about 1860–1930. Treats Krausism as an understandable heresy, with certain sympathetic qualities given the conditions under which it arose. [GJ]

VD116. Trend, John B. **The origins of modern Spain.** Cambridge, Eng. and N.Y., 1934. Best general work in English on the Krausist intellectuals, placing them in the Spanish literary and spiritual tradition. Historical background is sketchy, but much valuable biographical information on the main figures is given. [GJ]

VD117. Peers, E. Allison. **The Spanish tragedy, 1930–1936.** N.Y., 1936. Detailed political history, moderately monarchist and pro-Catholic in viewpoint. Based largely on newspapers of the period and on Peers' own weekly column in the *Bulletin of Spanish studies,* which he edited at the University of Liverpool. [GJ]

VD118. Toynbee, Arnold J. (ed.) Assisted by V. M. Boulter [and Katherine Duff]. Survey of international affairs. V. 2, The international repercussions of the war in Spain (1936–1937). London, 1938. Clear, factual chapters giving the best general account in

English of the political, military, and international aspects of the civil war of 1936–39. Based principally on English and French newspapers and diplomatic papers of all the Great Powers; uses all the personal memoirs available by 1940. [GJ]

VD119. Hughes, Emmet John. **Report from Spain.** N.Y., 1947. There is as yet no serious historical study of Spain since the civil war of 1936–39. This work, by an able journalist, depicts the Franco regime in terms of the interplay of dictatorial, Falangist, military, ecclesiastical, monarchist, and anti-Franco forces.

HISTORIES OF SPECIAL AREAS

VD120. Soldevila Zubiburu, Fernando. **Historia de Catalunya.** 3 v. Barcelona, 1934–35. A masterly, detailed study of the history of Catalonia, terminating with the period of Napoleonic invasion.

VD121. Abadal i de Vinyals, Ramon d'. **Els primers comtes catalans.** Barcelona, 1958. Detailed, authoritative study of early evolution of the various Catalan counties.

VD122. Vicens Vives, Jaime. **Juan II de Aragón, 1398–1479: monarquía y revolución en la España del siglo XV.** Barcelona, 1953. Important analysis of political and social struggles in late medieval Catalonia, on the eve of Catalan-Aragonese union with Castile. Review, G. Jackson, *Am. hist. rev.,* 60 (Oct. 1954) : 170.

VD123. García Venero, Maximiano. **Historia del nacionalismo catalán (1793–1936).** Madrid, 1944. A fairly factual but not very penetrating account of Catalan nationalism; weakest on origins and the period after 1931. Review, P. Vilar, *Rev. historique,* 206 (Oct.-Dec. 1951) : 304. See also *VD114.*

For the Crown of Aragon as a whole there is no good general history; the two following works cover, inadequately, only the medieval period.

VD124. Giménez Soler, Andrés. **La edad media en la Corona de Aragón.** Barcelona and Buenos Aires, 1930. [Colección Labor.] Somewhat less detailed on political events, but surpasses *VD125* on constitutional, social, and economic subjects.

VD125. Chaytor, Henry J. **A history of Aragon and Catalonia.** London, 1933.

VD126. Calmette, Joseph L. A. **La question des Pyrénées et la Marche d'Espagne au moyen-âge.** Paris, 1947. Especially lucid on the complex rivalries and relationships of medieval Catalonia-Aragon and France in the much-fought-over Pyrenean borderlands.

VD127. García Venero, Maximiano. **Historia del nacionalismo vasco, 1793–1936.** Madrid, 1945. Comparable to *VD123.*

VD128. Luna, José Carlos de. **Historia de Gibraltar.** Madrid, 1944. A fairly thorough history to the beginning of the 19th century; much superior to most writing on this subject.

HISTORIES OF SPECIAL TOPICS

Naval and Military History

VD129. Fernández Duro, Cesáreo. **Armada española desde la unión de los reinos de Castilla y de Aragón.** 9 v. Madrid, 1895–1903. Accurate, scholarly compendium of political history, biography, geography, colonial history, and many other aspects of national life which were affected by the growth and decline of the Spanish navy; and of the many wars, on both shores of the Atlantic and in the Mediterranean, in which Spain from time to time was engaged. [RBM]

No work of comparable authority has yet appeared for the Spanish army, but the following may be consulted.

VD130. Almirante, José. **Bosquejo de la historia militar de España hasta fin del siglo XVIII.** 4 v. Madrid, 1923.

Constitutional and Legal History

VD131. Vance, John T. **The background of Hispanic-American law: legal sources and juridical literature of Spain.** Washington, 1937. For the history of Spanish law to 1800, provides detailed information on the national and regional codes, with bibliographical data on all published editions.

VD132. Beneyto Pérez, Juan. **Fuentes de derecho histórico español.** Barcelona, 1931. Does much the same as *VD131,* but more interested in the origins and nature of legal sources to the reign of Philip V. Many references to secondary studies.

VD133. Palmer, Thomas W. **Guide to the law and legal literature of Spain.** Washington, 1915. Dated, but still unsuperseded for the 19th and early 20th centuries.

Note also that the chief annual in this field, *Anuario de historia del derecho español,* publishes important studies in constitutional and legal history, book reviews, and valuable bibliographical bulletins on all current titles in Spanish legal history.

VD134. García Gallo, Alfonso. **Curso de historia del derecho español.** 5th ed., 2 v., Madrid, 1950. This and the two following works are the foremost histories of Spanish law. The above is especially noteworthy for scholarship and broad coverage of many related constitutional and institutional subjects.

VD135. Minguijón Adrián, Salvador. **Historia del derecho español.** 4th ed., rev., Barcelona, 1953. [Colección Labor.] Contains almost 40 pages of bibliography on Spanish legal history in all periods.

VD136. Beneyto Pérez, Juan. **Manual de historia del derecho español.** 2nd ed., Saragossa, 1948.

VD137. Sánchez-Albornoz, Claudio. **En torno a los orígenes del feudalismo.** 3 v. Mendoza, 1942. A study primarily of the origins of the still very imperfectly known feudal system of the peninsula. V. 1, the Visigothic roots; v. 3, the Muslim invasion and institutions as a factor in the rise of Hispanic feudalism; v. 2, a historiographical inquiry into the 8th century Hispano-Muslim historical sources.

VD138. Mayer, Ernesto. **Historia de las instituciones sociales y políticas de España y Portugal durante los siglos V a XIV.** 2 v. Madrid, 1925–26. To be used with extreme caution. It rigidly formulizes Spanish institutions within an arbitrary, doctrinaire juridical framework, and is best avoided by non-specialists in the field.

VD139. Sinués Ruiz, Atanasio. **El merino.** Saragossa, 1954. A good, recent study in the royal machinery of medieval local government. Bibliography.

VD140. Colmeiro, Manuel. **Cortes de los antiguos reinos de León y Castilla.** 2 v. Madrid, 1883–84. Descriptive history of the Cortes; organization, *procuradores,* character and content of the series of *cuadernos.* Out of date in the light of recent advances in representative institutional history, but still the best guide to the Spanish parliaments.

VD141. Cortes de los antiguos reinos de León y de Castilla. 5 v. Madrid, 1861–1903. [Real Academia de la Historia.] Proceedings of the Cortes, 1020–1559.

VD142. Actas de las cortes de Castilla. 33 v. Madrid, 1877–1911. [Comisión de Gobierno Interior.] Proceedings of the Cortes to 1620.

VD143. Diario de las actas y discusiones de las Cortes. Cádiz and Madrid, 1811 ff. With minor changes of title, the official verbatim proceedings of the Cortes since 1810.

VD144. Mori, Arturo. **Crónica de las Cortes Constituyentes de la Segunda República española.** 13 v. Madrid, 1932. Full record of the Constituent Cortes of the Second Republic, including speeches and debates as well as formal legislation.

Social History

VD145. Vicens Vives, Jaime, ed. **Historia social y económica de España y América.** Barcelona, 1957 ff. Very few historiographically significant volumes on the rich but little investigated history of Spanish social classes and regional cultures have yet appeared. This new collaborative work, chiefly by Catalan historians, affords a good general survey. It is stronger on social and urban than economic and rural history; the abundant contemporary illustrations are exceptionally informative.

VD146. Spain. Consejo Superior de Investigaciones Científicas. **Estudios de historia social de España.** Madrid, 1949 ff. The Instituto Balmes de Sociología of Barcelona emphasizes historical research. This series, published at intervals under its auspices, contains valuable pioneer studies.

VD147. Viñas y Mey, Carmelo. **Relaciones histórico-geográfico-estadísticas de los pueblos de España hechas por iniciativa de Felipe II.** Madrid, 1949 ff. Initiates long overdue publication of the government reports of Philip II's commissioners, which contain rich material on 16th century population and distribution, class structure, and local urban and rural culture.

VD148. Caro Baroja, Julio. **Los vascos, etnología.** San Sebastian, 1949. An example of the type of social study needed for all Spanish regions. Analyzes the Basque settlement pattern, mixed farming economy, family and social organization, and folklore and crafts. For similar briefer treatments of other parts of Spain see the author's *Los pueblos de España* (*VD20*).

VD149. Kany, Charles E. **Life and manners in Madrid, 1750–1800.** Berkeley, 1932. Delightful, scholarly account of the capital in the 18th century, describing the city itself, court life and the nobility, social types and classes, entertainments, and popular culture.

VD150. Borrow, George H. **The Bible in Spain.** 3 v. London, 1843. This and *VD151* are classics of social as well as literary history, with inimitable contemporary pictures of early 19th century Spanish life and customs.

VD151. Ford, Richard. **A hand-book for travellers in Spain, and readers at home.** 2 v. London, 1845.

VD152. Cagigas, Isidro de las. **Minorías étnico-religiosas de la edad media española.** Madrid, 1947 ff. The most cultivated field of Spanish social history is that of ethnico-religious and regional groups. Here is the only modern work covering the entire field. Good as far as it has gone, although regrettably limited to narrative and political treatment at the expense of social, economic, and cultural problems. V. 1–2, the Mozárabes; v. 3–5, the Mudejares. Subsequent volumes to cover Moriscos, Jews, and Conversos. On the Spanish Muslims, or Moors, see also *VD59–61*.

VD153. Lea, Henry C. **Moriscos of Spain, their conversion and expulsion.** Philadelphia, 1901. Fortunes of the Moriscos from the fall of Granada to the expulsions of 1609. For current research in, and bibliography on, Hispano-Muslim history, *Al-Andalus* is the chief professional journal, as is *Sefarad* for the history of Sephardic Judaism.

VD154. Baer, Fritz. **Die Juden im christlichen Spanien.** 2 v. Berlin, 1929–36. This and *VD155* are the most scholarly general histories of the Spanish Jews.

VD155. ——. **Tolĕdot ha-Yĕhudim bi-Sĕfarad ha-nosrit.** (A history of the Jews in Christian Spain.) 2 v. Tel-Aviv, 1944–45. A summary in Castilian, by the Spanish Sephardic specialist, José Millás y Vallicrosa, can be found in *Sefarad,* 5 (1945): 417–40.

VD156. Neuman, Abraham A. **The Jews in Spain.** 2 v. Philadelphia, 1948. Complements *VD154–155,* especially on social and institutional topics. Based directly upon the untranslated rabbinical *Responsa* of the period, it deals with local community organization, relations with the Crown, taxation, courts, economic activities, domestic and social life, and culture.

Economic History

VD157. Colmeiro, Manuel. **Historia de la economía política en España.** 2 v. Madrid, 1863. A satisfactory economic history of Spain above the textbook level has not yet appeared, but this provides a good introduction. Although a dated work superseded on many points by subsequent special studies, it still holds the field as the most comprehensive general conspectus.

VD158. Barceló, José Luis. **Historia económica de España.** Madrid, 1952. Much more recent than Colmeiro, although hardly more than a textbook. No bibliography.

VD159. Vicens Vives, Jaime, and J. Nadal Oller. **Manual de historia económica de España.** Barcelona, 1959. Attempt at a comprehensive summary; not fully successful, but goes beyond Colmeiro and Barceló. Discusses developments through the 19th century. Includes up-to-date and extremely useful bibliography. [HFC]

VD160. Goury de Roslan, Jules. **Essai sur l'histoire économique de l'Espagne.** Paris, 1888. Limited to the ancient and medieval periods. Another dated work not yet replaced.

VD161. Carrera Pujal, Jaime. **Historia de la economía española.** 5 v. Barcelona, 1943–47. An ambitious, often useful, but essentially premature attempt to cover the three Hapsburg and Bourbon centuries. Not based upon archival research and rather poorly organized. V. 1–2, Hapsburg period; v. 3–5, the 18th century. Can be supplemented by the author's *Historia política y económica de Cataluña* (4 v., Barcelona, 1946–47).

VD162. Sardá Dexeus, Juan. **La política monetaria y las fluctuaciones de la economía española en el siglo XIX.** Madrid, 1948. See below.

VD163. Tallada Pauli, José M. **Historia de las finanzas españolas en el siglo XIX.** Madrid, 1946. This and *VD162* are superior contributions on one aspect of the little known economic history of modern Spain. See also Ramos Oliveira, *Politics, economics and men of modern Spain (VD112).*

VD164. Verlinden, Charles. "The rise of Spanish trade in the Middle Ages." **Economic history review,** 10 (Feb. 1940): 44–59. A rewarding, compact survey, with abundant bibliography. For medieval Spanish slavery, the same author's first volume of his *L'esclavage dans l'Europe médiévale (K520)* provides a mass of information on the medieval Iberian slave trade, and the origins, prices, and economic uses of slaves. Much fuller consideration is given to the Crown of Aragon lands than to Castile or Portugal.

VD165. Usher, Abbott P. **The early history of deposit banking in Mediterranean Europe.** See *K479.*

VD166. Smith, Robert Sydney. **The Spanish guild merchant: a history of the consulado, 1250–1700.** Durham, 1940. The outstanding study of Spanish merchant guilds, with particular attention to the organization and judicial and economic functioning of the guild-court or consulado in relation to foreign trade. Also useful on the general social and economic life of the mercantile class.

VD167. Klein, Julius. "Medieval Spanish gilds." **Facts and factors in economic history,** Cambridge, Mass., 1932, pp. 164–88. Brief, but virtually the only useful appraisal of the medieval Spanish craft guild.

VD168. Bejarano Robles, Francisco. **La industria de la seda en Málaga durante el siglo XVI.** Madrid, 1951. One of the rare studies in Spanish industrial history.

VD169. Hamilton, Earl J. **Money, prices, and wages in Valencia, Aragon, and Navarre, 1351–1500.** Cambridge, Mass., 1936. [Harvard economic studies, 51.] Hamilton's Sisyphean studies have made the history of Spain's monetary policies and prices over a long period better known than that of any other country. [RH]

VD170. ——. **American treasure and the price revolution in Spain, 1501–1650.** Cambridge, Mass., 1934. [Harvard economic studies, 48.] By establishing the primary responsibility of American bullion for the general 16th century inflation in Europe, this work has had a marked influence on the historiography of the period. [RH]

VD171. ——. **War and prices in Spain, 1651–1800.** Cambridge, Mass., 1947. [Harvard economic studies, 81.]

VD172. ——. **El florecimiento del capitalismo y otros ensayos de historia económica.** Madrid, 1948. Some of Hamilton's most impressive conclusions have been stated in articles that here are collected and translated. Among these, as originally published, should be noted "The decline of Spain"; "Spanish mercantilism before 1700"; and two essays defending "profit inflation" as a major cause of Spanish industrial development, 1750–1800, which have been the subject of a controversy analyzed by David Felix in *Quar. jour. econ.*, 70 (Aug. 1956): 441–63. [RH]

VD173. Vilar, Pierre. "Dans Barcelone, au XVIIIᵉ siècle: transformations économiques, élan urbain et mouvement des salaires dans le bâtiment." **Estudios históricos y documentos de los Archivos de Protocolos,** 2 (1950): 7–51. Fills a gap for the Catalan industrial renaissance of the 18th century. [RH]

VD174. Cárdenas y Espejo, Francisco de. **Ensayo sobre la historia de la propiedad territorial en España.** 2 v. Madrid, 1873–75. Like the nation's economic history as a whole, Spanish agrarian history, although central to national development through the centuries, still suffers from lack of modern scientific study. Despite excessively legalistic approach, numerous errors of fact and interpretation, and partial supersession by subsequent research, this is the one comprehensive treatment of the land and its problems throughout Spanish history.

VD175. Viñas y Mey, Carmelo. **El problema de la tierra de los siglos XVI–XVII.** Madrid, 1941. This and *VD176* replace *VD174* for the period covered. Leans overmuch to juridico-fiscal aspects.

VD176. Carrión, Pascual. **Los latifundios en España.** Madrid, 1932. Strongly modern in emphasis; deals with questions of soil, climate, water supply, and land distribution, and offers a dispassionate analysis of the relative advantages of large-scale versus small-family farming as solutions to the agricultural problems of central and southern Spain. [GJ]

VD177. Klein, Julius. **The Mesta: a study in Spanish economic history, 1273–1836.** Cambridge, Mass., 1920. [Harvard economic studies, 21.] The outstanding work in Spanish agrarian history, describing the organization, functioning, and economic consequences of the great national sheepowners association, which from the later Middle Ages through the Napoleonic invasion plays an often crucial role in Spanish economic development. For the related subject of cattle ranching and some later bibliography see C. J. Bishko, "The Peninsular background of Latin American cattle ranching," *Hisp. Am. hist. rev.*, 32 (Nov. 1952): 491–515.

VD178. Ibarra y Rodríguez, Eduardo. **El problema cerealista en España durante el reinado de los Reyes Católicos (1475–1516).** Madrid, 1944. Detailed information on grain production, milling, trade, prices, and taxation, but lack of analysis of problems involved.

VD179. Tolsado Picazo, Francisco. **Bibliografía española de agricultura (1495–1900).** Madrid, 1953.

Urban History

VD180. Sánchez-Albornoz, Claudio. **Ruina y extinción del municipio romano en España.** Buenos Aires, 1943. Authoritative dissection of Spanish municipal institutions in the late Roman and the Visigothic epochs, definitely laying the ghost of institutional continuity with later medieval town organization.

VD181. Font Rius, José María. **Orígenes del régimen municipal de Cataluña.** Madrid, 1946. Excellent examination of the origins and government of medieval Catalan towns, although heavily juridical and consequently neglectful of social and economic questions.

VD182. Sáez, Emilio, Rafael Gibert, Manuel Alvar, and Atilano G. Ruiz-Zorrilla. **Los fueros de Sepúlveda.** Segovia, 1953. [Publicaciones históricas de la excma. Diputación Provincial de Segovia, 1.] Scientific edition of the text of this important Castilian municipal law code, with a 230 page historico-juridical analysis and an extensive glossary of technical terms. Fundamental to all work in medieval Iberian urban history.

VD183. Torres Balbás, Leopoldo, Luis Cervera, Fernando Chueca, and Pedro Bidagor. **Resumen histórico del urbanismo en España.** Madrid, 1954. The four contributors deal respectively with the urban topography of the Middle Ages, the Hapsburg and Bourbon eras, and the 19th century, describing the characteristic plans, public buildings, *plazas mayores,* markets, and the like.

VD184. Albi, Fernando. **El corregidor en el municipio español bajo la monarquía absoluta.** Madrid, 1943. A primarily juridical study of the royal agent for municipal control between the 16th and 18th centuries.

Religious History

VD185. Gams, Pius Bonifacius. **Die Kirchengeschichte von Spanien.** 3 v. in 5. Regensburg, 1862–79. The paradoxical neglect of church history in modern Catholic Spain is attested by the fact that, although incomplete and sorely in need of revision and continuation, this remains the best general survey of Spanish ecclesiastical history. It runs with decreasing effectiveness to 1879.

VD186. Pérez de Urbel, Justo. **Los monjes españoles en la edad media.** 2 v. Madrid, 1933–34. Competent as far as it goes, i.e., through the 12th century. The history of the mendicant orders and of later medieval and modern monasticism in Spain, with all its acknowledged significance for the national development, is still unwritten.

VD187. Vázquez de Parga, Luis, José M. Lacarra, and Juan Uría Ríu. **Las peregrinaciones a Santiago de Compostela.** 3 v. Madrid, 1948–49. The authoritative work on the great pilgrimages to this famous shrine, with itineraries, maps, illustrations, and much incidental information on culture and general civilization.

VD188. Bataillon, Marcel. **Erasmo y España: estudios sobre la historia espiritual del siglo XVI.** 2 v. Mexico and Buenos Aires, 1950. Tr. from *Erasme et l'Espagne: recherches sur l'histoire spirituelle du XVIe siècle*. Paris, 1937. Although conceived as a study of Erasmian influences upon a nascent Spanish Protestantism, this major work actually treats a broader, richer theme. With meticulous scholarship and brilliant insight, it explores (from the time of Cardinal Cisneros) numerous aspects of reformism in 16th century Spanish religion, humanism, thought, and literature, including the circulation in Spain of Erasmus' books and ideas; the bitter conflict of Erasmists, Protestants, and Catholic Pauline interiorists with the authority of church, Crown, and Inquisition; the condemnation and persecution of Erasmists and Illuminists by churchmen and the Inquisition; and the Erasmist influence upon Spanish literature to the time of Cervantes.

VD189. Lea, Henry C. **A history of the Inquisition of Spain.** 4 v. N.Y. and London, 1906–07. A fully rounded history of the Inquisition is only slowly being made possible by monographic research. This is the most satisfactory authority, describing brilliantly the growth of religious intolerance and the founding, organization, and activities of the tribunal. It fails, however, to portray adequately the last half of the Inquisition's existence. [RH]

VD190. Llorente, Juan Antonio. **Histoire critique de l'Inquisition d'Espagne.** 4 v. Paris, 1817–18. Written by a former inquisitor to encourage abolition of the institution. Although superseded by *VD189* and other works on the earlier period, it is especially valuable for the reigns of Charles III and IV, where its statements are substantially true. [RH]

VD191. Pinta Llorente, Miguel de la. **La Inquisición española.** Madrid, 1948. Best 1 v. history of the Inquisition. Pinta Llorente finds this institution benign, merciful, and necessary to national unity and religious peace; and contends that when it was overzealous it was bowing to public opinion. His unimaginative faith in the inquisitorial records leads one to question his favorable picture, but otherwise his scholarship is extensive and sound. [RH]

VD192. ———. **La Inquisición española y los problemas de la cultura y de la intolerancia.** 2 v. Madrid, 1953–58. Collection of original studies on effects of the Inquisition on intellectual life. [RH]

VD193. Turberville, Arthur S. **The Spanish Inquisition.** London, 1932. Reprint, 1949. [Home university library of modern knowledge.] Useful, brief introduction, with helpful bibliography. [RH]

Cultural History

VD194. Fuente, Vicente de la. **Historia de las universidades, colegios y demás establecimientos de enseñanza en España.** 4 v. in 2. Madrid, 1884–89. Old and urgently requiring supersession, but still the sole general treatise on Spanish universities. On their establishment and for some recent bibliography consult Rashdall, *Universities of Europe in the Middle Ages (K573)*, v. 2, ch. 7.

VD195. Carreras y Artau, Tomás, and Joaquín Carreras y Artau. **Historia de la filosofía española. Filosofía cristiana de los siglos XIII al XV.** 2 v. Madrid, 1939–43. Sound on the immediate intellectual background of the Siglo de Oro.

VD196. Green, Otis H. "Critical survey of scholarship in the field of Spanish renaissance literature, 1914–1944." **Studies in philology,** 44 (Apr. 1947): 228–64. Includes material on intellectual movements of the period.

VD197. Millás y Vallicrosa, José M. **Estudios sobre historia de la ciencia española.** Barcelona, 1949. A series of essays, largely concerned with Arabic and Jewish influences, and stopping in the 16th century.

VD198. Díaz-Plaja, Guillermo, ed. **Historia general de las literaturas hispánicas.** 4 v. in 5. Barcelona, 1949–53. Excellent factual survey by various specialists, with good bibliography, but weak on the critical side. V. 1, to 1400; v. 2, pre-Renaissance and Renaissance; v. 3, Renaissance and Baroque Age; v. 4, 18th and 19th centuries. For an introductory account, Gerald Brenan, *The literature of the Spanish people* (Cambridge, Eng., 1951) can be recommended.

VD199. **Ars hispaniae: historia universal del arte hispánico.** Madrid, 1946 ff. Chronological survey of Spanish art history, each volume by a different specialist. Bibliographies.

VD200. Lampérez y Romea, Vicente. **Historia de la arquitectura cristiana española.** 2nd ed., 3 v., Madrid, 1930. The standard work, although now somewhat dated.

VD201. Bevan, Bernard. **History of Spanish architecture.** London, 1938. Good short survey, with brief bibliography.

VD202. Camón Aznar, José. **La arquitectura plateresca.** 2 v. Madrid, 1945. Written by an outstanding authority on Spanish art history. Describes the dominant Plateresque school of the 16th and 17th centuries.

VD203. Lafuente Ferrari, Enrique. **Breve historia de la pintura española.** 4th ed., Madrid, 1953. A fair general account, but far below the level of *VD204.*

VD204. Post, Chandler R. **A history of Spanish painting.** 12 v. in 18 pts. Cambridge, Mass., 1930–58. Superb detailed study, which, however, reaches only to the early Renaissance.

VD205. Lozoya, Juan Contreras y López de Ayala, marqués de. **Historia del arte hispánico.** 5 v. Barcelona, 1931–49.

VD206. Lassaigne, Jacques. **Spanish painting.** 2 v. Geneva, 1952.

VD207. Gómez-Moreno, María E. **Breve historia de la escultura española.** Madrid, 1935.

VD208. Wethey, Harold E. **Alonso Cano: painter, sculptor, architect.** Princeton, 1955.

VD209. Trapier, Elizabeth. **Velazquez.** N.Y., 1948. Factual. [JSC]

VD210. ———. **Ribera.** N.Y., 1952.

VD211. Sánchez Cantón, Francisco J. **Vida y obras de Goya.** Madrid, 1951.

VD212. Cossío, Manuel B. **El Greco.** Barcelona, 1915. Pioneer study; complete catalog of El Greco's work. [JSC]

VD213. Goldscheider, Ludwig. **El Greco.** N.Y., 1938.

VD214. Zervos, Christian. **Pablo Picasso.** 9 v. Paris, 1932–58. Reproduces all paintings, gouaches, and drawings from 1895 to 1939. [JSC]

VD215. Subirá, José. **Historia de la música española e hispanoamericana.** Barcelona and Madrid, 1953. A lengthy, factual, competent survey. Lacks footnotes and bibliography. For an introduction to the subject in English, with bibliography and lists of recordings, see Gilbert Chase, *The music of Spain and Portugal* (N.Y., 1941. Rev. ed., 1959).

VD216. Schindler, Kurt. **Folk music and poetry of Spain and Portugal.** N.Y., 1941.

GOVERNMENT PUBLICATIONS

Many of the historical publications subsidized by the Consejo Superior de Investigaciones Científicas can be, and by some libraries are, classified as government publications. On these consult the bibliographies listed above (*VD1–7*). For the large number of administrative, statistical, and technical reports and serials of Spanish government departments, the Government Publications Division of the Library of Congress possesses a manuscript catalog, **(VD217)** James B. Childs, **Preliminary survey of official publications of Spain** (1955). This is available for microfilming.

PUBLICATIONS OF LEARNED SOCIETIES

Of the serial publications, one of the most important is **(VD218) Estudios de historia moderna** (Barcelona, 1951 ff.), published by the University of Barcelona's Centro de Estudios Históricos Internacionales under the dynamic editorship of Professor Jaime Vicens Vives. Another outstanding title is **(VD219) Spanische Forschungen der Görresgesellschaft,** which has two series: **Gesammelte Aufsätze zur Kulturgeschichte Spaniens** (Münster, 1928 ff.) and **Einzeldarstellungen** (1931 ff.). Among the various series issued by organizations under the Consejo Superior de Investigaciones Científicas may be noted **(VD220) Textos** and **(VD221) Estudios** of the Escuela de Estudios Medievales (Madrid) and its *Secciones* at Saragossa, Barcelona, Pamplona, etc.; and **(VD222) Estudios de edad media de la Corona de Aragón** (Saragossa, 1945 ff.).

PERIODICALS

The most complete guide to past and present Spanish periodicals is **(VD223)** Florentino Zamora Lucas and María Casado Jorge, **Publicaciones periódicas existentes en la Biblioteca Nacional** (Madrid, 1952). Consult also the *Memorias* of the Consejo Superior de Investigaciones Científicas, and Tortajada and Amaniel, *Materiales de investigación* (*VD4*). Of the historical journals published in Spain, the most important are: **(VD224) Hispania** (Madrid, 1940 ff.), **(VD225) Boletín de la Real Academia de la Historia** (Madrid, 1877 ff.), **(VD226) Revista de archivos, bibliotecas y museos** (Madrid, 1871–1931, 1947 ff.), **(VD227) Cuadernos de historia Jerónimo Zurita** (Saragossa, 1951 ff.), and **(VD228) Cuadernos de historia diplomática** (Saragossa, 1954 ff.). To these national reviews can be added an impressive number of regional and provincial journals, listed in the *Memorias* of the Consejo Superior, cited above. Of periodicals published abroad, **(VD229) Cuadernos de historia de España** (Buenos Aires, 1944 ff.), edited by Claudio Sánchez-Albornoz, under the auspices of the Instituto de Historia de España of the University of Buenos Aires, ranks as the best journal in the entire Spanish historical field, but is mostly limited to ancient and medieval studies. **(VD230) Bulletin hispanique** (Bordeaux, 1899 ff.) is extremely valuable for articles, book reviews, and bibliographies; while the 81 v. of the extinct **(VD231) Revue hispanique** (Paris, 1894–1931) are a rich depository of historical material.

PORTUGAL

BIBLIOGRAPHIES AND LIBRARIES

VD232. Walsh, Doris V. **A catalog of the William B. Greenlee Collection of Portuguese history and literature and the Portuguese materials in the Newberry Library.** Chicago, 1953. This catalog of an outstanding United States collection is the most complete, comprehensive bibliography of Portuguese history and civilization. It does not list periodical articles. Titles classified under major topical and chronological rubrics; no critical comments, but often helpful indication of length.

VD233. Greenlee, William B. "A descriptive bibliography of the history of Portugal." **Hispanic American historical review,** 20 (Aug. 1940): 491–516. A short but very serviceable introduction to the chief standard works on Portuguese archives, bibliography, published sources, general history, and special periods and topics. Brief comments. Both this and *VD232* include overseas Portugal and imperial history.

VD234. Exposição de livros portugueses. Lisbon, 1950. Classified list of recent books and current periodicals in history and other fields.

VD235. Galvão Simões, Carlos. **Subsídios para uma bibliografia das comemorações centenárias.** 2 v. Lisbon, 1945–47. Indexes the extremely numerous publications of the 1940 twin centenaries.

VD236. Dias Arnaut, Salvador. "História geral e política, económica, local (1939–1949)." **Revista portuguesa de história,** 3 (1947): 314–28. Important for periodical articles as well as books.

VD237. Boletim de bibliografia portuguesa. Lisbon, 1935 ff. Lists all Portuguese publications as they appear, but without system of classification. Consult also *VD1–8;* and note that *Manuel de l'hispanisant (VD8)* covers Portugal as well as Spain.

VD238. Barbosa Machado, Diogo. **Biblioteca lusitana, histórica, crítica e cronológica.** 2nd ed., 4 v., Lisbon, 1930–35. A huge mass of material for the whole period from the 15th to the mid-18th century, listing thousands of writers, with short biographical sketches and the titles of manuscript and published works.

VD239. Silva, Innocêncio Francisco da. **Dicionário bibliographico português . . . applicaveis a Portugal e ao Brasil.** 22 v. Lisbon, 1858–1923. Index by José Soares de Souza, *Indice alfabético do Dicionário bibliográfico português de . . . Silva,* São Paulo (?), 1938. A rich collection of data in all fields of Portuguese civilization, alphabetically arranged by author.

VD240. Academia Portuguesa da Historia. **Guia da bibliografia portuguesa.** Lisbon, 1959

ff. Designed to index all Portuguese historical bibliography to the year 1910, for both metropolis and colonial empire. V. 1, fasc. 1, commences with source collections and archival guides.

Library Collections

The leading collections in the United States are those of the Newberry Library, Chicago, where the Greenlee Collection (see catalog, *VD232*) has been rated by an expert "the best working collection outside Portugal on Portuguese history prior to 1820" (C. R. Boxer, *The Newberry Library bulletin,* 2nd ser., no. 6 (May 1951): 169–78); Harvard University, exceptionally rich in modern as well as older works, periodicals, and publications of learned societies, including the great Palha Collection of manuscripts and early editions (see v. 3–4 of José Antonio Moniz, *Catalogue de la bibliothèque de M. Fernando Palha* (4 v., Lisbon, 1896)); the Oliveira Lima Library, Catholic University of America, Washington, with many rarities; and the Library of Congress, strong in general, and especially in the field of government publications. On these and other collections see Hilton, *Handbook of Hispanic source materials (VD13).*

GENERAL REFERENCE WORKS

VD241. Grande enciclopédia portuguesa e brasileira. 39 v. Lisbon and Rio de Janeiro, 1950 ff. The most recent and best of the Portuguese encyclopedias; of no bibliographical help, but useful as a biographical and historical dictionary.

VD242. Livermore, Harold V., ed. **Portugal and Brazil, an introduction.** Oxford, 1953. A collaborative work with introductory chapters on Portuguese geography, history, religion and institutions, literature, and the arts. Scant bibliographical information.

GEOGRAPHIES, GAZETTEERS, AND ATLASES

A good historical geography of Portugal has not yet appeared, but the titles listed below often treat modern human geography in terms of its historical evolution.

VD243. Lautensach, Hermann. "Portugal." **Petermanns Geographische Mitteilungen. Ergänzungshefte.** Nos. 213, 230. Gotha, 1932–37. This and *VD244* describe physiography, settlement patterns, physical anthropology, and economic geography.

VD244. Amorim Girão, Aristides de. **Geografia de Portugal.** Oporto, 1941.

VD245. Birot, Pierre. **Le Portugal.** Paris,

1950. An admirable succinct survey, stressing human ecology, population distribution, land use, agriculture, and industry from early times.

VD246. Ribeiro, Orlando. **Portugal, o Mediterrâneo e o Atlântico.** Coimbra, 1945. By no means replaced in this author's long bibliography by his more purely physiographic work in v. 5 of Terán, *Geografía de España y Portugal* (*VD14*).

VD247. Lautensach, Hermann, and Mariano Feio. **Bibliografia geográfica de Portugal.** Lisbon, 1948. Classified under physiographic, economic, anthropological, ethnological, demographic, and regional rubrics.

VD248. Costa Brandão, Américo Aguiar da. **Diccionário chorográphico de Portugal continental e insular.** 12 v. Oporto, 1929–49. Alphabetical dictionary of places, with historical and biographical material and some maps.

VD249. Amorim Girão, Aristides de. **Atlas de Portugal.** Coimbra, 1941. Excellent modern atlas, but no substitute for the needed atlas of Portuguese history. See also section by M. Sorre on the Iberian Peninsula in Vidal de La Blache, *Géographie universelle* (*C13*), v. 7, pt. 1.

ANTHROPOLOGICAL WORKS

VD250. Leite de Vasconcellos, José. **Etnografia portuguesa.** 3 v. Lisbon, 1933–42. The unexcelled authority, with much of historical interest. V. 1 is almost entirely a survey of previous ethnological writers, general and Portuguese, and their works. V. 2–3 deal, province by province, with the people and characteristics of rural and urban settlement. See also v. 17–18 of *Congresso do mundo português. Publicações* (*VD270*); the studies in the *Contribuições para o estudo de antropologia portuguesa,* published by the Instituto de Antropologia of the University of Coimbra; and the *Trabalhos de antropologia e etnologia* of the Sociedade de Antropologia e Etnologia e Centro de Estudos de Etnologia Peninsular of Oporto.

VD251. Braga, Theophilo. **O povo portuguez nos seus costumes, crenças e tradições.** 2 v. Lisbon, 1885. A rich source of information on popular superstitions, festivals, and folklore, but lacking in treatment of popular arts and crafts.

VD252. Gallop, Rodney. **Portugal: a book of folk-ways.** Cambridge, Eng., 1936. Informative guide to Portuguese folk-culture, but also omits popular arts and crafts.

COLLECTIONS OF SOURCES

On the chief Portuguese national archive, in the Torre do Tombo, Lisbon, as well as on the numerous other historical archives in the capital and in provincial and municipal centers, see B. W. Diffie, "Bibliography of the principal published guides to Portuguese archives and libraries," and V. Rau, "Arquivos de Portugal: Lisboa," both in *Proceedings of the [I] International Colloquium on Luso-Brazilian Studies* (*VD333*), pp. 181–213; and M. Cardozo, "Portugal," in Thomas and Case, *Guide to the diplomatic archives of western Europe* (*T10*), ch. 11.

VD253. Herculano, Alexandre, and Joaquim J. da Silva Mendes Leal, eds. **Portugaliae monumenta historica.** 5 v. Lisbon, 1856–97. Collection of certain basic medieval sources. V. 1, law codes and *forais*; v. 4, charters; v. 5, royal inquests.

VD254. Erdmann, Carl. **Papsturkunden in Portugal.** Berlin, 1927. [Abhandlungen der Gesellschaft der Wissenschaften zu Göttingen, philog.-hist. klasse.] Commencement of a collection of Portugal's papal documents, preceded by an excellent survey of the archives and bibliography for Portuguese ecclesiastical history.

VD255. Dias Arnaut, Salvador. "Fontes históricas (1939–1945)." **Revista portuguesa de história,** 3 (1947): 307–13. Presumably to be continued. Lists through the Aviz dynasty the many new editions of Portugal's historical sources.

VD256. Santarem, Manuel F. de Barros, visconde de. **Quadro elementar das relações políticas e diplomáticas de Portugal.** 18 v. Paris and Lisbon, 1842–76. Chronological collection of diplomatic documents to 1815. Texts are not published in full, but summarized or calendared, with note on location.

VD257. Rebello da Silva, Luiz A., and others, eds. **Corpo diplomático português.** 15 v. Lisbon, 1865–1936. Documents relating solely to Portuguese relations with Rome, 1501–1678.

VD258. Borges de Castro, José F., visconde de. **Collecção dos tratados, convenções, contratos e actos públicos celebrados entre a Coroa de Portugal e as mais potências desde 1640 até ao presente.** 8 v. Lisbon, 1856–58. Supplements, 22 v. in 24, Lisbon, 1872–80. Basic text collection for Portuguese diplomatic history from 1640 into the 19th century.

HISTORIOGRAPHY

VD259. Boxer, Charles R. "Some notes on Portuguese historiography, 1930–1950." **History,** 39 (Feb.-June 1954): 1–13. Portugal has produced many able historians, both in the medieval and modern periods, but Portuguese historiography still awaits its chronicler. Many scattered studies of individual historians exist, but probably the best general guide to historical writing remains the cultural and literary histories listed under *VD321–328.* For the 20th century, however, the above and *VD260* offer summary but discerning evaluations of modern historians and historiographical trends.

VD260. Magalhães Godinho, Vitorino. "A historiografia portuguesa: orientações, problemas, perpectivas." **Revista de história,** 10 (São Paulo, Jan.-Mar. 1955): 3-21. See above.

SHORTER GENERAL HISTORIES

VD261. Livermore, Harold V. **A history of Portugal.** Cambridge, Eng., 1947. A strongly factual, comprehensive, well-written survey, based upon the Peres, ed., *História de Portugal (VD266).* The most informative and reliable one-volume account in any language, but less helpful on analysis and interpretation.

VD262. Ameal, João. **História de Portugal.** 2nd ed., Oporto, 1942. Best of the shorter works in Portuguese. Heavily royalist and clericalist viewpoint; almost wholly political and personalist in emphasis.

VD263. Sérgio de Souza, António. **História de Portugal.** Barcelona, 1929. [Colección Labor, 206.] Brief, but with suggestive interpretations by the outstanding contemporary representative of the liberal historiographical school of Herculano. Sérgio's projected publication of a large-scale *História de Portugal* terminated with the suppression of the initial volume, Lisbon, 1940.

VD264. Nowell, Charles E. **A history of Portugal.** N.Y., 1952. Brisk introductory account, particularly good on the expansionist and cultural achievements of the Golden Age; but for the Middle Ages and on internal developments does not supersede for English readers the old classic of Stephens.

VD265. Stephens, Henry Morse. **The story of Portugal.** N.Y., 1891. See above.

LONGER GENERAL HISTORIES

VD266. Peres, Damião, ed. **História de Portugal.** 8 v. Barcelos, 1928-35. Best and most recent large-scale survey. Covers to 1918, and contains contributions by many able Portuguese historians. Like all collaborative works, it is uneven in value and loosely organized. Regrettably lacking in footnotes and bibliography, but with a useful index and copious illustrations.

VD267. Almeida, Fortunato de. **História de Portugal.** 6 v. Coimbra, 1922-29. An often more detailed work than *VD266,* terminating in 1910. Particularly valuable for the extensive treatment of medieval and modern constitutional and social institutions in v. 3 and 5.

VD268. Herculano, Alexandre. **História de Portugal, desde o começo da monarchia até o fim do reinado de Affonso III.** 7th ed.,

8 v., Lisbon, 1914-16. The most celebrated of all Portuguese histories, written by the greatest figure in Portuguese historiography, a 19th century liberal and anticlerical. Still supreme for the period covered, i.e. to 1279.

VD269. Gonzaga de Azevedo, Luiz. **História de Portugal.** 6 v. Lisbon, 1935-42. An avowed refutation of Herculano by a Portuguese Jesuit historian. Also limited to the medieval period and strongest on political and military events. Review, *Torquato* de Sousa Soares, *Rev. portuguesa de história,* 1 (1943): 286.

VD270. Congresso do mundo português. Publicações. 19 v. Lisbon, 1940. An extensive collection of papers by Portuguese historians and social scientists, published in connection with the 1940 commemorations. The contributions vary greatly in merit. For metropolitan Portuguese history, the most important are v. 1-2, running from prehistory through the Middle Ages; v. 6-8, Spanish Captivity to the 20th century; v. 11-12, history of Portuguese science in the 18th and 19th centuries; v. 17-18, modern demography and anthropology.

HISTORIES OF SPECIAL PERIODS

Medieval and Early Modern

VD271. Peres, Damião. **Como nasceu Portugal.** 3rd ed., Oporto, 1946. Among the numerous attempts by Portuguese historians to explain their country's origins as a national state, this stands out as the ablest champion of a primarily political solution, operating within the context of 11th and 12th century Spain. Contains a valuable review of rival theories.

VD272. Mendes Corrêa, Antonio A. **Raízes de Portugal.** 2nd ed., Lisbon, 1944. Important among explanations favoring factors of ethnic and cultural separatism long antedating actual formation of the Portuguese state.

VD273. David, Charles W., ed. **De expugnatione Lyxbonensi: the conquest of Lisbon.** N.Y., 1936. [Records of civilization, Columbia University, 24.] Contemporary description of Lisbon's capture in 1147 by the first Portuguese king, Afonso Henriques. Translation, with introduction, notes, and bibliography.

VD274. David, Pierre. **Études historiques sur la Galice et le Portugal, du VIᵉ au XIIᵉ siècle.** Lisbon and Paris, 1947. [Collection portugaise publiée sous le patronage de l'Institut français au Portugal, 7.] Specialized studies in medieval Portugal's Gallegan and French ties, ecclesiastical history, and chronicles.

For ancient and medieval Portuguese history consult also the works on Spain listed for these periods *(VD54-70).*

VD275. Bovill, Edward W. **The battle of the Alcazar: an account of the defeat of Dom Sebastian of Portugal at El-Ksar el-Kebir.** London, 1952. Story of the end of the Aviz dynasty, treating not only of King Sebastian's fatal defeat in Morocco, but of conditions favoring the successful intervention of Philip II of Spain. Most accounts of the Aviz period deal so exclusively with overseas expansion as to do serious injustice to internal history. For the circumstances of the accession of the Aviz dynasty, after the battle of Aljubarrota, the most lucid account is Russell, *English intervention in Spain and Portugal* (*VD67*).

VD276. Queiroz Velloso, José Maria de. **D. Sebastião, 1554–1578.** 3rd ed., Lisbon, 1945.

VD277. Antas, Miguel Martins d'. **Les faux Dom Sébastien.** Paris, 1866. See under *VD278.*

VD278. Azevedo, João Lúcio d'. **A evolução do sebastianismo.** 2nd ed., Lisbon, 1947. History of the false Sebastians and of Sebastianism during the Spanish Captivity and after.

VD279. Rebello da Silva, Luiz A. **História de Portugal nos séculos XVII e XVIII.** 5 v. Lisbon, 1860–71. Despite the title, this extensive treatise deals only with the period of Spanish domination, 1580–1640. V. 1–3, political events; v. 4–5, social, economic, and institutional questions.

Restoration and Enlightenment

VD280. Prestage, Edgar. **The diplomatic relations of Portugal with France, England and Holland from 1640 to 1668.** Watford, Eng., 1925. Factual tabulation of the Portuguese missions to these three countries. Useful, but a poor substitute for a reasoned analysis of Portuguese foreign policy in the early restoration period.

VD281. Lisbon. Biblioteca Nacional. **Exposição bibliográfica da Restauração.** 2 v. Lisbon, 1940–41. Extensive lists of titles for the period after 1640, alphabetically arranged by author and without critical comment.

VD282. Azevedo, João Lúcio d'. **História de António Vieira.** 2 v. Lisbon, 1918–21. A good study, well documented, of the able Jesuit diplomatist, statesman, and writer of the 17th century.

VD283. Prestage, Edgar. **Portugal and the War of the Spanish Succession: a bibliography with some diplomatic documents.** Cambridge, Eng., 1938. Very brief account, but with bibliography of published and manuscript sources.

VD284. Brazão, Eduardo. **Relações externas de Portugal: reinado de D. João V.** 2 v. Oporto, 1938. A detailed account, using archival sources, for the period 1706–1750.

VD285. Azevedo, João Lúcio d'. **O Marquês de Pombal e a sua época.** 2nd ed., rev., Lisbon, 1922. The best biography of many, based on the Pombal manuscripts in Lisbon. Judgments inclined to be unsympathetic, but not uncritically partisan.

VD286. Cheke, Marcus. **Dictator of Portugal: a life of the Marquis of Pombal, 1699–1782.** London, 1938. Largely personal, to the neglect of the Pombaline reforms.

VD287. Beirão, Caetano. **D. Maria I, 1777–1792: subsídios para a revisão da história do seu reinado.** 4th ed., Lisbon, 1944. This and *VD288* are important studies of the reigns covering the French revolutionary and Napoleonic epochs. For Portuguese involvement in the Peninsular War see Oman, *History of the Peninsular War* (*T359*).

VD288. Pereira, Angelo. **D. João VI, príncipe e rei.** 3 v. in 2. Lisbon, 1953–56.

Nineteenth and Twentieth Centuries

VD289. Soares de Azevedo, Julião. **Condições económicas da revolução portuguesa de 1820.** Lisbon, 1944. A rather slim study, based on newspapers and secondary sources.

VD290. Cheke, Marcus. **Carlota Joaquina, queen of Portugal.** London, 1947. Biographical, but offering a general picture of the first half of the 19th century.

VD291. Lemos, Ester de. **D. Maria II (a rainha e a mulher).** Lisbon, 1954. See comment under *VD290.*

VD292. Bragança-Cunha, Vicente de. **Revolutionary Portugal (1910–1936).** London, 1938? One of the two best general accounts of the republican period, by a constitutional monarchist of liberal tendencies.

VD293. Pabón, Jesús. **La revolución portuguesa (de Don Carlos a Sidonio Paes).** Madrid, 1941. The other leading account of the republican era, by a strongly anti-republican Spanish scholar. More detailed than *VD292.* Full bibliography.

VD294. Oliveira Salazar, António de. **Discursos.** 4 v. Coimbra, 1928 ff. In the absence of scholarly, objective work on the régime, Salazar's speeches are the safest clue to policies proposed or followed since 1926.

Diplomatic and Military History

VD295. Prestage, Edgar, ed. **Chapters in Anglo-Portuguese relations.** Watford, Eng., 1935. Six chapters by different authors, of which those on English crusaders in Portugal, and the Anglo-Portuguese treaties of 1642, 1661, and 1703 are the most useful.

VD296. Selvagem, Carlos. **Portugal militar: compêndio de história militar e naval de Portugal.** Lisbon, 1931. Covers all of Portuguese history to the end of the Bragança dynasty (1910). Much fuller on army organization, campaigns, and battles than on naval affairs.

Constitutional and Legal History

VD297. Gama Barros, Henrique da. **História da administração pública em Portugal nos séculos XII a XV.** Ed. by Torquato de Sousa Soares. 2nd ed., Lisbon, 1945 ff. Deservedly the masterpiece of Portuguese institutional history, although now antiquated at many points. The new edition is not really a revision, but contains valuable notes and bibliography added by the editor. Covers only the medieval period. V. 1–3, law, Crown, military orders, nobility, the people, and monarchical organization; v. 4–5, social and economic conditions; v. 6–8, landholding systems; v. 9–10, agriculture, industry, and commerce; v. 11, royal local administration. On Gama Barros' life and work see the special *homenagem* in v. 4–5 of *Rev. portuguesa de história* (1949, 1951).

VD298. Oliveira França, Eduardo d'. "O poder real em Portugal às origens do absolutismo." **Boletim da Universidade de São Paulo,** Faculdade de Filosofia, Ciências e Letras, v. 68, no. 6 (1946). This and *VD 299* are excellent studies in the organization of the medieval Portuguese monarchy.

VD299. Sánchez-Albornoz, Claudio. **La curia regia portuguesa, siglos XII y XIII.** Madrid, 1920.

VD300. Rau, Virgínia. **A Casa dos Contos.** Coimbra, 1951. Primarily an administrative rather than a financial examination of the Portuguese exchequer, 16th to 18th centuries.

VD301. Santarem, Manuel F. de Barros, visconde de. **Memórias e alguns documentos para a história e teoria das Côrtes Geraes.** 2 pts. in 1 v. Lisbon, 1827–28. 2nd ed., 4 v., Lisbon, 1924. Unfortunately still the most useful general discussion of parliamentary evolution.

VD302. Leitão, Joaquim. **Côrtes do reino de Portugal.** Lisbon, 1940. Careful index of unpublished materials, paving the way for much needed research on the history of the Portuguese Cortes.

VD303. Pereira, António Manuel. **Organização política e administrativa de Portugal desde 1820 (bases gerais).** Oporto, 1949. Helpful on modern constitutional questions.

VD304. Merêa, M. Paulo. **Estudos de direito hispânico medieval.** 2 v. Coimbra, 1952–53. Unfortunately there is yet no adequate history of Portuguese law. This work reprints specialized articles published over many years by the leading specialist in medieval legal history.

VD305. Cabral de Moncada, Luis. **Estudos de história do direito.** 3 v. Coimbra, 1948–50. Also a number of unconnected studies, some of the most important dealing with the 18th century.

VD306. Caetano, Marcelo. **História do direito português.** Condensed and ed. by Ernesto Fernandes and Anibal Rêgo. Lisbon, 1941. Summaries of lectures in Portuguese legal history delivered by Marcelo Caetano in the Faculdade de Direito, Lisbon, 1940–41. A running outline history, relatively weak after the medieval period.

Economic History

VD307. Azevedo, João Lúcio d'. **Epocas de Portugal económico.** 2nd ed., Lisbon, 1947. The standard general survey, divided into somewhat artificial epochs and stressing commerce at the expense of agriculture, industry, and finance. Very weak after 1800. Lack of adequate monographic investigation in the field confines it to widely held but often untested generalizations.

VD308. Rau, Virgínia, and Bailey W. Diffie. "Alleged fifteenth-century Portuguese joint-stock companies and the articles of Dr. Fitzler." **Bulletin of the Institute of Historical Research,** 26 (Nov. 1953): 181–99. Brief but definitive refutation of misleading current exaggerations of the state of capitalistic organization and enterprise in 15th century Portugal.

VD309. Magalhães Godinho, Vitorino. **Prix et monnaies au Portugal, 1750–1850.** Paris, 1955. A virtually unique economic study for the modern era. Based upon archival research, rich in statistics, and analyzing price fluctuations and industrial and commercial crises.

VD310. Correia Lopes, Edmundo. **A escravatura: subsídios para a sua história.** Lisbon, 1944. The Portuguese slave trade, and utilization of slaves in Portugal and the empire between 1443 and 1850. (See *K520*).

VD311. Rau, Virgínia. **Sesmarias medievais portuguesas.** Lisbon, 1946. Valuable study of the later medieval system of royal land grants and tenure, with much incidental matter on other aspects of economic history and royal policy.

VD312. ——. **A exploração e o comércio do sal de Setúbal: estudo de história económica.** Lisbon, 1951 ff. The role of an important industry and staple of commerce to the 17th century.

VD313. ——. **Subsídios para o estudo das feiras medievais portuguesas.** Lisbon, 1943. Portuguese fairs and internal commerce in the later Middle Ages.

VD314. Langhans, Franz-Paul, ed. **As corporações dos ofícios mecânicos: subsídios para a sua história.** 2 v. Lisbon, 1943–46. A collaborative work on various aspects of the Portuguese craft guilds. Special studies, not a general treatise.

Religious and Social History

VD315. Almeida, Fortunato de. **História da igreja em Portugal.** 4 v. in 8 pts. Coimbra, 1910–22. The fundamental work, detailed and relatively objective. Strong on institutional aspects and covering such principal problems as organization of the secular church, monastic orders, religious minorities, papal ties, and relations of church and state to 1910. V. 1, to 1325; v. 2, 1325–1495; v. 3, pts. 1–2, 1495–1750; v. 4, pts. 1–4, 1750–1910. Includes overseas as well as metropolitan Portugal.

VD316. Oliveira, Miguel de. **História eclesiástica de Portugal.** Lisbon, 1940. A much shorter survey, stressing church-state relations, and written from a strongly clerical viewpoint.

VD317. Herculano, Alexandre. **História da origem e estabelecimento da Inquisição em Portugal.** 3 v., Lisbon, 1854–59. English tr. by John C. Branner, *History of the origin and establishment of the Inquisition in Portugal.* Stanford, 1926. By Portugal's great 19th century historian. Dated but still unsuperseded; unmistakably anticlerical.

VD318. Rodrigues, Francisco. **História da Companhia de Jesus na assistência de Portugal.** 3 v. in 6. Oporto, 1931–44. Valuable on cultural and intellectual as well as general ecclesiastical history.

VD319. Mendes dos Remédios, Joaquim. **Os judeus em Portugal.** 2 v. Coimbra, 1895–1928. Best available history of the Portuguese Jews; chiefly concerned with Jewish-Christian relations. On internal institutions see Neumann, *The Jews in Spain (VD156).*

VD320. Azevedo, João Lúcio d'. **História dos christãos novos portugueses.** Lisbon, 1921. A somewhat unsympathetic account, expanding the treatment in Herculano, *Inquisição (VD317),* and carrying the story to the end of persecution under Pombal. Makes use of manuscript sources.

Cultural History

VD321. Cidade, Hernâni A. **Lições de cultura e literatura portuguesas.** 3rd rev. ed., 2 v., Coimbra, 1948–51. V. 1, covering the 15th–17th centuries, includes a series of studies on the historian Fernão Lopes and Portuguese culture of the Renaissance and post-Renaissance. V. 2, chiefly intellectual history of the 18th century. [FMR]

VD322. Saraiva, António José, and others. **História da cultura em Portugal.** 2 v. Lisbon, 1950–55. Still in progress. V. 1, the Middle Ages; v. 2, Renaissance and Counter-Reformation. To be used with caution. Review of v. 1, F. M. Rogers, *Hispanic rev.,* 23 (Apr. 1955): 153. [FMR]

VD323. Silva Dias, José Sebastião da. **Portugal e a cultura europeia (séculos XVI** a **XVIII).** Coimbra, 1953. Particularly good on intellectual movements of the 17th and 18th centuries. [FMR]

VD324. Carvalho, Joaquim de. **Estudos sobre a cultura portuguesa.** 4 v. Coimbra, 1947–55. Miscellany of studies ranging from the 15th century historian Gomes Eanes de Zurara to the 19th century republican Antero de Quental. Note also v. 12–13 of *Congresso do mundo português. Publicações (VD270)* on Portuguese science in the 18th and 19th centuries. [FMR]

VD325. Forjaz de Sampaio, Albino, ed. **História da literatura portuguesa ilustrada.** 3 v. Paris and Lisbon, 1929–32. This and *VD326* are competent surveys by outstanding modern scholars. [FMR]

VD326. Figueiredo, Fidelino de. **História da literatura clássica, romântica, realista.** 3rd ed., 5 v., São Paulo, 1946. See comment above. [FMR]

VD327. Rossi, Giuseppe Carlo. **Storia della letteratura portoghese.** Florence, 1953. An up-to-date general history, with excellent bibliographies. [FMR]

VD328. Bell, Aubrey F. G. **Portuguese literature.** Oxford, 1922. Best general account in English, although now dated. Consult also the chapters in Livermore, *Portugal and Brazil (VD242)* containing, pp. 129–38, a bibliography of Portuguese literature in English translation. [FMR]

VD329. Santos, Reynaldo dos. **L'art portugais.** Lisbon, 1949. Good introductory survey of Portuguese art in general. On Portuguese art and architecture see also the excellent chapters and bibliography in *Proceedings . . . (VD333).*

VD330. ———. **O estilo manuelino.** Lisbon, 1952. Deals with the famous Manueline style of the Renaissance period. [FMR]

VD331. Corbin, Solange. **Essai sur la musique religieuse portugaise au moyen âge (1100–1385).** Paris, 1952. An admirable study, scholarly pioneer in a virtually unknown field. Review, Y. Renouard, *Bul. hispanique,* 56 (1954): 203. On Portuguese music see also Schindler, *Folk music and poetry of Spain and Portugal (VD216)* and Gilbert Chase, *The music of Spain* (N.Y., 1959), which has a chapter by A. T. Luper on Portugal.

PUBLICATIONS OF LEARNED SOCIETIES

Of the Portuguese historical societies, the most eminent is the Acadêmia Portuguesa da História, which publishes contributions, often of monograph length, in its irregularly appearing **(VD332) Anais** (Ser. I, v. 1–11, 1940–46; ser. II, v. 1–9, 1946–59; in progress). Of prime importance also are the meetings of the International Colloquium on Luso-Brazilian Studies, which bring together from all parts of the world specialists in post-medieval Portuguese history and civilization. For the initial sessions at Washington, 1950, there has been published **(VD333) Proceedings of the [I] International Colloquium on Luso-Brazilian Studies** (Nashville, 1953), which contains papers and bibliography on anthropology, fine arts, literature, archives and other instruments of scholarship, and history, with rich bibliographical information.

PERIODICALS

The principal historical journal, which appears irregularly, is the excellent **(VD334) Revista portuguesa de história,** published by the Faculdade de Letras of the University of Coimbra (1941 ff.). The Brazilian **(VD335) Revista de história** (University of São Paulo, 1950 ff.) frequently contains articles, reviews, and bibliography of Portuguese interest. The national reviews **(VD336) O Instituto** (Coimbra, 1852 ff.) and **(VD337) Biblos** (Coimbra, 1925 ff.) preserve a rich accumulation of historical contributions, as is true also of **(VD338) Revista de Guimarães** (Oporto, 1900 ff.), **(VD339) Boletim do distrito de Aveiro,** and other national or regional journals. For a current list of the latter see *Exposição de livros portugueses (VD234).* Historical articles also appear in the **(VD340) Boletim** of the Faculdade de Letras of the University of Lisbon, and **(VD341) Revista da Faculdade de Letras** of the University of Coimbra.

Italy

CATHERINE E. BOYD *

This subsection is concerned primarily with the internal history of the Italian peninsula from the early Renaissance to the present day. Supplementary works will be found in other sections.

Historical research in Italy, which formerly tended to stress the local and particularistic aspects of Italian history, has acquired within the last generation or two a broader, more national horizon. In 1935 the four central historical associations—for ancient, medieval, Risorgimento, and modern and contemporary history, respectively—were coordinated in the Istituto Storico Italiano. Representatives from these groups now form a central committee for historical studies (Giunta Centrale per Gli Studi Storici) which exercises a unifying influence on the profession, without in the least diminishing the vitality or independence of the regional societies.

Several distinct trends may be noted in recent Italian historical scholarship: preoccupation with historiography and its problems; a closeness to contemporary political events that gives many works a subjective and controversial coloring and makes it important for the reader to know the historian's school of thought; concern with social movements and religious politics, reflecting topical interests of the present; and an effort in practically all fields to find and clarify the general patterns and trends in Italian history—in short, to treat the regional states as members of a single civilization and the peninsula in relation to Europe.

Since 1946 Italian historians have felt the impact of a cultural renewal sometimes called the Second Italian Renaissance. Their creativity has manifested itself in a prolific literature, which often challenges traditional points of view. A mass of source material has also been published, and older standard works have been presented in revised editions. For this reason the present bibliography contains a preponderant number of books produced by Italian scholars since World War II. Simultaneously French and German historians have pursued their traditional interests in the Italian field. A new generation of English historians

* Professor Boyd was assisted by the late Gaudens Megaro, Mary Lucille Shay, and Albert Elsen. The items on art and comments indicated by initials JSC were contributed by Judith S. Cousins.

526

has reinterpreted the Risorgimento in the light of increasing knowledge and changing points of view. The American contribution has been original and noteworthy. But the literature of Italian history is predominantly in Italian and in large part untranslated.

BIBLIOGRAPHIES, LIBRARIES, AND ARCHIVES

Bibliographies

VE1. Pagliaini, Attilio. **Catalogo generale della libreria italiana dall'anno 1847 a tutto il 1899.** 3 v. Milan, 1901–05. Index, 3 v., 1910–22. Supplement, 1900–10, 2 v., 1912–14. Second supplement, 1911–20, 2 v., 1925–28. Third supplement, 1921–30, 2 v., 1932–35. A general catalog of books published in Italy or in the Italian language from 1847 to 1930. See also *VE466.*

VE2. Biblioteca Nazionale Centrale di Firenze. **Bollettino delle pubblicazioni italiane ricevute per diritto di stampa.** Florence, 1886 ff. A monthly list, with annual cumulative index, of all new Italian publications, required by Italian copyright law to be deposited in the National Central Library at Florence. The most complete record of Italian publications in all fields.

VE3. Libri e riviste d'Italia rassegna bibliografica mensile. Rome, 1950 ff. Monthly bulletin which lists and abstracts important books of general interest published in Italy and articles in Italy's leading cultural and political journals. Most valuable for current history.

VE4. Fumagalli, Giuseppe. **La bibliografia.** 2 pts. in 1 v. Rome, 1923. [Guide bibliografiche, 11–12.] Condensed survey of earlier bibliographical publications, including library catalogs.

VE5. Avanzi, Gianetto, ed. **La bibliografia italiana.** 2nd rev. ed., Rome, 1946. Lists all bibliographies published in Italy from 1921 to 1946, including bibliographical articles in periodicals.

VE6. Italia bibliografica. Ed. by Giuseppe Martini. Florence, 1952 ff. Annual bibliographical guide for 1952 and following years. Includes bibliographical articles and essays.

VE7. Notizie introduttive e sussidi bibliografici. Ed. by Pietro Zorzanello and others. Milan, 1948. [Problemi ed orientamenti critici di lingua e di letteratura italiana, 1.] Useful collection of essays on bibliographical subjects aimed at the university student. Although not devoted exclusively to Italy, it provides good orientation, not easily found elsewhere, in the bibliography of Italian history, geography, and literature.

VE8. Bibliografia storica nazionale. Rome, 1942–49; Bari, 1950 ff. A national historical bibliography, prepared by the Central Committee for Historical Studies, covering the years since 1939. Lists books on history published in Italy, articles in Italian scholarly journals, published papers of learned societies, proceedings of historical congresses, and the contents of anniversary volumes. Foreign publications are included only if reviewed in Italian periodicals; regional history is fully covered. An indispensable tool.

VE9. Rota, Ettore, ed. **Questioni di storia moderna.** Milan, 1948. Collection of essays by authoritative Italian historians on important historical problems and personalities between 1450 and 1815. Each essay is accompanied by an extensive critical bibliography.

VE10. ——, ed. **Questioni di storia del Risorgimento e dell'unità d'Italia.** Milan, 1951. Covers period 1815–70.

VE11. ——, ed. **Questioni di storia contemporanea.** 4 v. Milan, 1952–55. Provides compendious bibliographical coverage for the years 1870–1955. V. 4 is an appendix.

See the companion volumes for ancient and medieval history: Alfredo Passerini, ed., *Questioni di storia antica* (Milan, 1949); Ettore Rota, ed., *Questioni di storia medioevale* (Como, 1946; reprint, Milan, n.d.).

Library Collections

The following United States libraries contain distinguished collections of Italian manuscripts, incunabula, and rare books: J. P. Morgan Library, New York; Henry E. Huntington Library, San Marino, Calif.; Harvard University, Cambridge, Mass.; Newberry Library, Chicago.

Libraries with noteworthy collections for research in Italian history and civilization are: Cornell University, eminent for its Dante and Petrarch collections; University of Illinois, with the Cavagna-Sangiuliani collection of about 40,000 volumes; Harvard, which has immense holdings in published source material for all periods of Italian history, including the H. Nelson Gay collection in Risorgimento history; Harvard Law School Library, containing a wealth of material on legal and constitutional history; Newberry Library, which is steadily enlarging its resources in Renaissance history and augmenting its general Italian section with many standard works and serials; Duke University, which recently acquired the library of the late Guido Mazzoni, numbering about 23,000 volumes; New York Public Library, admirably equipped with printed source material, periodicals, and monographs.

Other excellent collections are those of the University of California at Berkeley, Columbia University (Casa Italiana), Princeton University, University of Wisconsin, Yale University, and the Library of Congress.

Archives and Archival Publications

VE12. Gli archivi di stato al 1952. 2nd ed., Rome, 1954. Condensed inventory of the Italian government archives.

VE13. Fink, Karl A. **Das vatikanische Archiv: Einführung in die Bestände und ihre Erforschung.** 2nd rev. ed., Rome, 1951.

VE14. Guida storica e bibliografica degli archivi e delle biblioteche d'Italia. Ed. by Luigi Schiaparelli and others. 6 v. Rome, 1932–40.

VE15. Rome. Ministero dell'Interno. **Annales institutorum, biblioteca.** Rome, 1932 ff. (Title varies.) Excellent collection of guides to some of the more important government archives, including those of Rome, Parma, and Venice. Each volume contains a general historical description and analytical index.

VE16. ——. **Pubblicazioni degli archivi di stato.** Rome, 1950 ff. A series of inventories of important collections in the Italian government archives. Includes the famous Medici archives (*VE235–236*).

ENCYCLOPEDIAS AND WORKS OF REFERENCE

VE17. Enciclopedia italiana di scienze, lettere ed arti. Ed. by Giovanni Gentile and others. 36 v. Rome, 1929–39. Appendices. 3 v., 1938–49. Reprint, 1949 ff. (in progress). This reference work is a monument to Italian erudition. All articles were written by specialists, and some are standard monographs in their fields. Especially useful for historical biography and regional and municipal history. Extensive bibliographies, lavish illustrations, and maps.

VE18. Chi e? Dizionario biografico degli italiani d'oggi. 6th ed., Rome, 1957. In the absence of a national biographical dictionary, earlier editions of this work, beginning in 1928, serve as a rapid reference for distinguished Italians of the 20th century.

VE19. Vaccaro, Gennaro, ed. **Panorama biografica degli italiani d'oggi.** 2 v. Rome, 1956. Convenient reference source for prominent living Italians. Lists about 25,000 names.

VE20. Cosenza, Mario E. **Biographical and bibliographical dictionary of the Italian humanists and of the world of classical scholarship in Italy, 1300–1800.** N.Y., 1954. Microfilm publication issued by the Renaissance Society of America, reproducing on 29 reels about 40,000 cards compiled by Dean Cosenza during a lifetime of research in Italian humanism. Includes biographies of Italian humanists, foreign scholars resident in Italy, and patrons of learning, together with bibliographies and cross-references. A mine of information on intellectual history.

GEOGRAPHIES

The Touring Club Italiano, Milan, has in course of publication a new series, *Conosci l'Italia,* which may confidently be expected to embody the best cartographic techniques and geographical knowledge available in Italy.

VE21. Almagià, Roberto. **Il mondo attuale.** V. 1, pt. 2. Turin, 1953. This magnificently illustrated synthesis of physical and social geography contains an admirable summary of Italian geography in less than 200 pages (pp. 559–745).

VE22. Milone, Ferdinando. **L'Italia nell' economia delle sue regioni.** Turin, 1955. Monumental treatise on regional geography, with up-to-date maps and statistical tables. An extensive bibliography includes the most important historical and demographic studies.

VE23. Baratta, Mario; Plinio Fraccaro, and Luigi Visintin. **Atlante storico.** 3 v. Novara, 1940–41. Reprint, 1942–54. Inexpensive school atlas, useful for Italian history. V. 3 extends from the Renaissance through World War I.

ETHNOGRAPHY AND CIVILIZATION

VE24. Sforza, Count Carlo. **The real Italians: a study in European psychology.** N.Y., 1942. Charming, mellow interpretation of Italian national characteristics. In the Italian edition, *Gli italiani quali sono* (Milan, 1946), the text has been expanded.

VE25. Olschki, Leonardo. **The genius of Italy.** N.Y., 1949. Reprint, Ithaca, 1954. Ital. tr., *L'Italia e il suo genio,* Milan and Verona, 1953. Historical essays, chronologically arranged, on various aspects of Italian civilization from the earliest times to the present. Unsurpassed interpretation of Italy and her people.

DEMOGRAPHIC STUDIES

VE26. Beloch, Karl J. **Bevölkerungsgeschichte Italiens.** Ed. by Gaetano de Sanctis. 2 v. Berlin and Leipzig, 1937–39. Posthumous work by an outstanding German authority on the history of population. V. 1, Sicily and the Kingdom of Naples, 13th–18th centuries; v. 2, the Papal States, Tuscany, and the north-central duchies in the same period.

VE27. Dickinson, Robert E. **The population problem of southern Italy: an essay in social geography.** Syracuse, 1955. Excellent brief study in human geography, based in part on field work in southern Italy.

LINGUISTIC WORKS

VE28. Pulgram, Ernst. **The tongues of Italy. Prehistory and history.** Cambridge, Mass., 1958. Traces formation of Italian language. Bibliography.

PRINTED COLLECTIONS OF SOURCES

Much source material is noted at the appropriate places in this section. Only a few large collections are listed below.

VE29. Muratori, Lodovico A., ed. **Rerum italicarum scriptores.** 25 v. in 28. Milan, 1723–51. New ed., ed. by Giosuè Carducci and Vittorio Fiorini, Città di Castello and Bologna, 1900 ff. This famous collection of Italian narrative sources from 500 to 1500 contains many chronicles of the 14th and 15th centuries in corrected texts and with extensive critical notes. Indispensable for the early Renaissance.

VE30. Rome. Istituto Storico Italiano per l'Età Moderna e Contemporanea. **Fonti per la storia d'Italia.** Milan, 1935 ff. Most important single collection of source material for the modern period. Constantly being enlarged by new publications.

VE31. Accademia Nazionale dei Lincei (merged with Accademia d'Italia from 1939 to 1944). **Atti delle assemblee costituzionali italiane dal medio evo al 1831.** Bologna, 1917 ff. Invaluable records for Italian constitutional history. Includes documents relating to medieval parliaments and estates, municipal councils, and the assemblies of the revolutionary period.

VE32. Le assemblee del risorgimento. 15 v. Rome, 1911. Material on the assemblies of the unification period.

VE33. Ministero degli Affari Esteri. **I documenti diplomatici italiani.** Rome, 1952 ff. The long withheld documents from 1861 to 1943 in the files of the Italian foreign office are now in course of publication under editorship of a distinguished group of Italian historians. The complete collection, to include about 80 v. in 9 series, will make possible the detailed reconstruction of Italian foreign policy since unification.

HISTORIOGRAPHY

VE34. Croce, Benedetto. **Storia della storiografia italiana nel secolo decimonono.** 2nd ed., 2 v., Bari, 1930. History and evaluation of the main currents and figures in Italian historiography of the 19th century, by the philosopher-historian who did more than any other individual to shape Italian historical writing of the 20th century.

VE35. Antoni, Carlo, and Raffaele Mattioli, eds. **Cinquant' anni di vita intellettuale italiana, 1896–1946: scritti in onore di Benedetto Croce per il suo ottantesimo anni-** versario. 2 v. Naples, 1950. The thirty essays of this *Festschrift* provide a panoramic view and critical evaluation of the achievements of Italian scholarship in history and allied disciplines from 1896 to 1946. Particularly noteworthy are the studies by Federico Chabod, "Gli studi di storia del Rinascimento" (v. 1, pp. 125–207), and Walter Maturi, "Gli studi di storia moderna e contemporanea" (v. 1, pp. 209–85).

VE36. Delzell, Charles F. "Italian historical scholarship: a decade of recovery and development, 1945–55." **Jour. mod. hist.,** 28 (Dec. 1956): 374–88. Excellent bibliographical article which indicates the main lines of Italian historiography during the decade following World War II.

SHORTER GENERAL HISTORIES

VE37. Trevelyan, Janet P. **A short history of the Italian people from the barbarian invasions to the present day.** 4th rev. ed., London and N.Y., 1956. First published in 1920, this has won a place for itself as a classic and is still the best introduction to Italian history in English. Primarily a political history, based on works of Italian scholars, and characterized by charm of presentation and warm sympathy for things Italian.

VE38. Salvatorelli, Luigi. **Sommario della storia d'Italia dai tempi preistorici ai nostri giorni.** 7th rev. ed., Turin, 1955. Compendium of Italian history useful principally for its immense time span and its factual summary of political history. The English translation by Bernard Miall, *A concise history of Italy from prehistoric times to our own day* (London and N.Y., 1940), is unsatisfactory, but has a good bibliography.

VE39. Rodolico, Niccolò. **Storia degli italiani.** Florence, 1954. Most recent and readable 1 v. history of Italy. By a veteran historian, it extends from the 11th century to 1870. Weak on medieval period, more satisfactory for the Renaissance and later centuries.

LONGER GENERAL HISTORIES

VE40. Storia politica d'Italia dalle origini ai giorni nostri. 3rd and 4th rev. eds., Milan, 1938 ff. [Luigi Simeoni, *Le signorie* (2 v., 1950); Romolo Quazza, *Preponderanza spagnuola* (2nd ed., 1950); Francesco Lemmi, *L'età napoleonica* (1938); Antonio Monti, *Il risorgimento* (2 v., 1948).] A sound, if somewhat pedestrian, cooperative history in process of revision. Earlier editions are obsolete, and only volumes in the revised series are listed here. They will be commented on under their respective periods.

VE41. Storia d'Italia illustrata. Rev. ed., Milan, 1949 ff. Cooperative work similar to *VE40.* The revised edition, complete for ancient and medieval history, includes *VE42*, *VE75* and *VE87* on modern period.

HISTORIES OF SPECIAL PERIODS

Renaissance (ca. 1350–1600)

The word "Renaissance" as used here is merely a chronological term denoting a period which defies precise delimitation. Helpful guidance through this period will be found in two articles by Federico Chabod, "Il Rinascimento," *Questioni di storia moderna* (*VE9*), pp. 53–99; and "Gli studi di storia del Rinascimento," *Cinquant'anni di vita intellettuale* (*VE35*), v. 1, pp. 125–207. See also *Il Rinascimento: significato e limiti* (Florence, 1953), papers read at the third international congress on the Renaissance, held in Florence in 1952, on the meaning of the Renaissance in the various fields of history, including politics, economics, literature, and art.

The following selective bibliography lists (1) important syntheses of the whole period or of its various aspects, and (2) the most significant works on the humanistic movement, its central figures, and its relationships with politics, philosophy, and religion. Most of the detailed literature will be found in the subdivisions on regional and cultural history and among the biographies.

VE42. Valeri, Nino. **L'Italia nell'età dei principati, dal 1343 al 1516.** Milan and Verona, 1949. [Storia d'Italia illustrata, 5.] By far the best recent synthesis of the period; a successful fusion of political and cultural history which stresses the influence of civic humanism in Florence. Contains ample critical bibliography, particularly rich on development of the regional states.

VE43. Simeoni, Luigi. **Le signorie, 1313–1559.** 2 v., Milan, 1950. [Storia politica d'Italia.] Covers much the same ground as *VE42*, but in another tradition of scholarship. Emphasis is entirely on narrative of political events, and the spiritual forces of the period receive scant attention. Center of the narrative is the expansionist policy of Milan under the Visconti.

VE44. Labande, Edmond R. **L'Italie de la Renaissance: duecento, trecento, quattrocento; évolution d'une société.** Paris, 1954. A pleasantly written French survey which stresses the continuity between Middle Ages and Renaissance, but fails to give an adequate picture of Italian social developments. The most original part of the book concerns the persistence of a religious tradition in Italy. Author has not incorporated the results of recent research on humanism. Bibliographies.

VE45. Burckhardt, Jacob C. **Die Kultur der Renaissance in Italien: ein Versuch.** Basel, 1860. Tr. of 15th German ed., by S. G. C. Middlemore, *The civilization of the Renaissance in Italy,* orig. Phaidon ed., Vienna, London and N.Y., 1937, is best. Laid the foundation of modern study of the Renaissance. Central theme is the emergence of an Italian national culture in the 14th, 15th, and 16th centuries and its expression in politics, literature, social customs, and religion. Author's interpretations have been repeatedly challenged and in part overthrown, but no comparable synthesis has taken its place. For a masterly analysis of Burckhardt's place in historiography and the reaction against his views expressed by Thode, Burdach, and others see Wallace K. Ferguson, *The Renaissance in historical thought* (Boston, 1948), *passim.*

VE46. Baron, Hans. **The crisis of the early Italian Renaissance: civic humanism and republican liberty in an age of classicism and tyranny.** See *K563*. Concerned primarily with Florence around 1400, its theme is the transformation of Florentine humanism into a civic and political ideology in response to the threat to Florentine liberty from the Visconti tyranny at Milan.

VE47. Pieri, Piero. **Il Renascimento e la crisi militare italiana.** Turin, 1952. A major achievement of Italian scholarship by a military historian concerned with war in its relation to Renaissance society. About a third of the book consists of analysis of the social structure, economy, and political institutions of the Italian states. A history of warfare prior to the 15th century provides background for a detailed account of military struggles in Italy from 1494 to 1530.

VE48. Croce, Benedetto. **La Spagna nella vita italiana durante la Rinascenza.** 4th rev. ed., Bari, 1949. Intellectual relations between Italy and Spain. Emphasizes the Spanish contribution to Italian culture.

VE49. Toffanin, Giuseppe. **Che cosa fu l'umanesimo: il risorgimento dell'antichità classica nella coscienza degli italiani fra i tempi di Dante e la riforma.** 2nd ed., Florence, 1929. Redefinition of humanism in reversal of concepts expounded by Burckhardt, Voigt, and their followers. Toffanin identifies humanism with Catholic orthodoxy in conflict with the radical tendencies of late medieval scholasticism and the dawning scientific movement.

VE50. ———. **Storia dell'umanesimo.** Reprint, 3 v., Bologna, 1950. [1, *Il secolo senza Roma;* 2, *L'umanesimo italiano;* 3, *La fine del Logos.*] Eng. tr. of v. 2, by Elio Gianturco, *History of humanism,* N.Y., 1954. The most forceful contemporary attack against the Burckhardtian tradition. Incorporates several of the author's earlier works. Opinionated, disorderly in presentation, partisan in temper, it is nevertheless a work of immense learning. Extensive bibliographies. The Eng. tr. of v. 2 is defective.

VE51. Burdach, Konrad. **Rienzo und die geistige Wandlung seiner Zeit.** 2 pts. Berlin, 1913–28. [Vom Mittelalter zur Reformation: Forschungen zur Geschichte der deutschen Bildung, 2.] In this extended introduction to the Burdach-Piur edition of Rienzo's correspondence, Burdach represents Rienzo as the principal pioneer of humanism and develops his characteristic views about the continuity between Middle Ages and Renaissance.

VE52. Piur, Paul. **Cola di Rienzo.** Vienna, 1931. Ital. tr., Milan, 1934. Excellent critical biography.

VE53. Emerton, Ephraim. **Humanism and tyranny: studies in the Italian trecento.** Cambridge, Mass., 1925. Useful extracts in translation from the writings of Coluccio Salutati, Bartolus, and other humanists; the ordinances of Albornoz.

VE54. Robinson, James H., and Henry W. Rolfe. **Petrarch, the first modern scholar and man of letters.** 2nd rev. ed., N.Y. and London, 1914. This sympathetic account, based mainly on Petrarch's letters, is probably still the best introduction to his personality for English readers.

VE55. Nolhac, Pierre de. **Pétrarque et l'humanisme.** 2nd rev. ed., 2 v., Paris, 1907. Abr. tr. of 1st ed., *Petrarch and the ancient world*, Boston, 1907. Firmly rooted in the tradition of Burckhardt and Voigt.

VE56. Wilkins, Ernest H. **Studies in the life and works of Petrarch.** Cambridge, Mass., 1955. Twelve specialized studies by the greatest Petrarch scholar of the United States. Indispensable for detailed study of Petrarch's letters. Bibliography.

VE57. Whitfield, John H. **Petrarch and the Renascence.** Oxford, 1943. Brief introduction for English readers.

VE58. Ullman, Berthold L. **Studies in the Italian Renaissance.** Rome, 1955. [Edizioni di Storia e Letteratura.] Important essays on humanistic topics previously published in periodicals.

VE59. Setton, Kenneth M. "The Byzantine background to the Italian Renaissance." **Proceedings of the American Philosophical Society,** 100 (Feb. 1956): 1–76. Novel approach to the Italian Renaissance by an authority on Byzantine history.

VE60. Garin, Eugenio. **Medioevo e Rinascimento.** Bari, 1954. Collection of essays by an eminent Italian scholar on the relations between humanism and medieval philosophy. Includes an excellent essay on Florentine culture in the age of Leonardo da Vinci.

VE61. ——. **L'umanesimo italiano: filosofia e vita civile nel Rinascimento.** Bari, 1952. Important studies in Italian humanism from Petrarch to Bruno.

VE62. ——. **Il Rinascimento italiano.** Milan, 1941. Discriminating selection from the sources, in Latin and Italian, illustrating the various facets of Italian humanism.

VE63. Kristeller, Paul O. **Studies in Renaissance thought and letters.** Rome, 1956. [Storia e letteratura, 54.] Kristeller is one of the great modern authorities on humanism. This volume brings together his most important articles, in the original languages, published in various periodicals between 1936 and 1950 and including the significant study, "Humanism and scholasticism in the Italian Renaissance."

VE64. ——. **The classics and Renaissance thought.** Cambridge, Mass., 1955. Designated as a "cultural map" of the Renaissance, the four lectures assembled in this volume analyze the classical revival and its relations with philosophy and religion from about 1300 to 1600.

VE65. Angeleri, Carlo. **Il problema religioso del Rinascimento: storia della critica e bibliografia.** Florence, 1952. Useful survey and classified bibliography on the "problem" of the Renaissance, emphasizing religious thought.

VE66. Cassirer, Ernst. **Individuum und Kosmos in der Philosophie der Renaissance.** Leipzig and Berlin, 1927. Ital. tr., Florence, 1935. Important study of the Florentine Neoplatonists, stressing their relationship to Nicholas of Cusa.

VE67. Gentile, Giovanni. **Il pensiero italiano del Rinascimento.** 3rd rev. ed., Florence, 1940. Expanded version of a work originally entitled *Giordano Bruno e il pensiero del Rinascimento.*

VE68. Cassirer, Ernst, Paul O. Kristeller, and John H. Randall, eds. **The Renaissance philosophy of man.** Chicago, 1948. Well-chosen selections, with critical introductions, from six representative thinkers of the Renaissance. Provides a good introduction to Italian philosophy of that period. Bibliography.

VE69. Altamura, Antonio. **L'umanesimo del mezzogiorno d'Italia: storia, bibliografia, e testi inediti.** Florence, 1941. Important work by the leading Italian authority on humanism in southern Italy. Of high critical value, but has some gaps.

VE70. Gothein, Eberhard. **Die Renaissance in Süditalien.** 2nd ed., Munich and Leipzig, 1924. [Schriften zur Kulturgeschichte der Renaissance, Reformation und Gegenreformation, 1.] Although superseded in part by Altamura's later and more critical works, this still has value for the social background of humanism in southern Italy. Ital. tr. by Tommaso Persico from 1st Ger. ed., *Il Rinascimento nell'Italia meridionale* (Florence, 1915), is not complete.

Reformation, Counter-Reformation, and Baroque (1550–1700)

VE71. Cantimori, Delio. **Eretici italiani del cinquecento, ricerche storiche.** Florence, 1939. Standard work on the Italian religious radicals (Socinians, Neoplatonists, and Anabaptists) of the 16th century who disseminated over Europe the philosophical doctrines of the Florentine Renaissance.

VE72. Church, Frederick C. **The Italian reformers, 1534–1564.** N.Y., 1932. Ital. tr., *I riformatori italiani,* 2 v., Florence, 1935. Of capital importance and a splendid contribution of American scholarship to the Italian field. An appendix to the Italian edition contains a translation of "The literature of the Italian Reformation," *Journal of modern history,* 3 (Sept. 1931): 457–73.

VE73. Lemmi, Francesco. **La riforma in Italia e i riformatori italiani all'estero nel secolo XVI.** Milan, 1939. Useful survey based on secondary material. Bibliographies.

VE74. Brown, George K. **Italy and the Reformation to 1550.** Oxford, 1933. Synthesis of earlier scholarship on the Reformation in Italy.

VE75. Visconti, Alessandro. **L'Italia nell' epoca della controriforma dal 1516 al 1713.** Milan, 1958. (Storia d'Italia illustrata, V. 6). Posthumous work revised by Federico Curato. Most complete recent synthesis, especially valuable for the 17th century. Full bibliography.

VE76. Petrocchi, Massimo, ed. **La controriforma in Italia.** Rome, 1947. Anthology of representative sources. Bibliography.

VE77. Quazza, Romolo. **Preponderanza spagnuola (1559–1700).** 2nd rev. ed., Milan, 1950. [Storia politica d'Italia.] (Orig. pub. as *Preponderanze straniere,* Milan, 1938.) A political history of Italy under Spanish domination, emphasizing the foreign policies of the Italian states. Lacks organic unity. Bibliographies.

VE78. Croce, Benedetto. **Storia dell'età barocca in Italia.** 2nd rev. ed., Bari, 1946. Artistic and intellectual currents of the 17th century.

VE79. Petrocchi, Massimo. **Il quietismo italiano del seicento.** Rome, 1948. Suggestive treatment of heretical mysticism within the established church.

VE80. Spini, Giorgio. **Ricerca dei libertini: la teoria dell'impostura delle religioni nel seicento italiano.** Rome, 1950. Brilliant monograph on anti-Christian thought in the 17th century. Bibliographies.

VE81. Sarpi, Paolo. **Opere.** Ed. by Giovanni Gambarin and Manlio D. Busnelli. Bari, 1931 ff. Definitive modern edition of Sarpi's works. There is no adequate critical biography of him.

VE82. Quazza, Romolo. **La guerra per la successione di Mantova e del Monferrato** (1628–1631). 2 v. Mantua, 1926. Detailed monograph on an episode in diplomatic history of some interest for international relations during the Thirty Years' War.

VE83. Bulferetti, Luigi. "L'oro, la terra e la società (un'interpretazione del nostro seicento)." **Archivio storico lombardo,** 80 (1954): 5–66. Excellent critical introduction to the historical problems and literature of the 17th century.

Eighteenth Century (1700–1796)

VE84. Rota, Ettore. **Le origini del Risorgimento (1700–1800).** 2nd rev. ed., 2 v., Milan, 1948. The most detailed and thorough history of Italy in the 18th century, including a full account of intellectual developments, the reform movements, and the initial impact of the French Revolution. Bibliographies.

VE85. Candeloro, Giorgio. **Storia dell'Italia moderna. V. 1, Le origini del Risorgimento.** Milan, 1956. This first volume of a projected 6 v. history of modern Italy by a Marxist historian surveys the 18th century from the point of view of Risorgimento origins. Half the book is devoted to the revolutionary and Napoleonic period. Contains excellent bibliographical essay.

VE86. Quazza, Guido. "Il problema italiano alla vigilia delle riforme (1720–1738)." **Annuario dell'Istituto per la Storia Moderna e Contemporanea,** 5 (1953): 71–201; 6 (1954): 9–176. A book-length article in two parts: (1) the European states and the Italian question, and (2) national consciousness as manifested in social forces and governmental policies. The author combats the tendency exhibited by some historians to push the origins of the Risorgimento back into the early 18th century.

VE87. Valsecchi, Franco. **L'Italia nel settecento dal 1714 al 1788.** Milan, 1959. (Storia d'Italia illustrata, V. 7.) Admirable survey by a diplomatic historian, well balanced between cultural and political history. Bibliography.

VE88. ——. **L'assolutismo illuminato in Austria e in Lombardia.** 2 v. Bologna, 1931–34. V. 2 is an objective analysis of the reforming policies of Maria Theresa and Joseph II in Lombardy.

VE89. Bulferetti, Luigi. **L'assolutismo illuminato in Italia (1700–1789).** Milan, 1944. Excellent source book, with introduction and explanatory notes, illustrating development of enlightened despotism in Italy.

VE90. Megaro, Gaudens. **Vittorio Alfieri, forerunner of Italian nationalism.** N.Y., 1930. Pioneering study in the ideological origins of Italian nationalism. Much admired in Italy.

VE91. Noether, Emiliana P. **Seeds of Italian nationalism, 1700–1815.** N.Y., 1951. Very clear, well-documented account of 18th century origins of Italian political nationalism. Bibliography.

VE92. Rota, Ettore, ed. **Il problema italiano dal 1700 al 1815 (l'idea unitaria).** 2nd ed., Milan, 1941. Source book which traces the idea of Italian political unity back to the early 18th century.

VE93. Bédarida, Henri, and Paul Hazard. **L'influence française en Italie au dix-huitième siècle.** Paris, 1934. Masterly account of intellectual relations between France and Italy, stressing the indigenous element in Italian thought.

VE94. Codignola, Ernesto. **Illuministi, giansenisti e giacobini nell'Italia del settecento.** Florence, 1947. Important specialized account of revolutionary currents of thought in 18th century Italy.

Revolutionary and Napoleonic Period (1796–1815)

VE95. Lemmi, Francesco. **L'età napoleonica.** Milan, 1938. [Storia politica d'Italia.] Encyclopedic account of the Napoleonic period in Italy. See also *VE84–85.*

VE96. Fugier, André. **Napoléon et l'Italie.** Paris, 1947. Best brief synthesis of the subject; based almost entirely on secondary works. Less narrowly political than most general histories of the period, it devotes several chapters to the development of institutions, society, and thought. Bibliography.

VE97. Zaghi, Carlo. **Bonaparte e il direttorio dopo Campoformio: il problema italiano nella diplomazia europea, 1797–1798.** Naples, 1956. Brilliant monograph, based on diplomatic documents, which relates the Italian problem to the general course of European diplomacy and political events.

VE98. Pingaud, Albert. **Bonaparte, président de la république italienne.** Paris, 1914.

VE99. ———. **Les hommes d'état de la république italienne.** Paris, 1914. Pingaud's works are fundamental for the political history of the republican period.

VE100. Driault, Édouard. **Napoléon en Italie (1800–1812).** Paris, 1906. A diplomatic history.

VE101. Tarle, Evgenii V. **Le blocus continental et le royaume d'Italie.** Tr. from Russian. Paris, 1928. Ital. tr., *La vita economica dell'Italia nell'età napoleonica,* Turin, 1950. Standard work on the impact of the continental blockade upon Italian economy.

VE102. Rath, Reuben J. **The fall of the Napoleonic kingdom of Italy.** N.Y., 1941. Excellent monograph, based in part on unpublished material in Italian and Austrian archives. Traces overthrow of the Napoleonic regime in northern Italy. Includes carefully compiled bibliography and notes.

VE103. Valente, Angela. **Gioacchino Murat e l'Italia meridionale.** Turin, 1941. Thoroughly documented study of French

occupation in southern Italy. Throws light on the origins of the Risorgimento in this region.

VE104. Hazard, Paul. **La Révolution française et les lettres italiennes.** Paris, 1910. Luminous brief treatment.

VE105. Giacobini italiani. Ed. by Delio Cantimori. Bari, 1956. Selections from the writings of sixteen Italian radicals of the revolutionary period.

The Risorgimento (ca. 1815–1870)

It is impossible to assign precise dates to this movement. Most scholars place the birth of Italian nationalistic aspirations in the 18th century, and several works of Risorgimento origins are listed under that heading. The term "Risorgimento" is sometimes extended to include the early 20th century; but all agree that the years 1815–70 are central to the unification movement. The most comprehensive treatment of problems, sources, and literature of this period is Rota, *Questioni di storia del Risorgimento (VE10).*

General Works

VE106. Ghisalberti, Alberto M. **Introduzione alla storia del Risorgimento.** Rome, 1942. Concept and chronological limits of the Risorgimento; a good introduction. Bibliographical guide, now somewhat outdated, includes list of indices, catalogs, and collections of source materials in Italian archives and libraries.

VE107. Marchetti, Leopoldo. "Bibliografia generale." **Questioni di storia del Risorgimento (VE10),** pp. 1065–84. Most recent selective bibliography on the subject. Lists earlier bibliographies and includes valuable information regarding both printed and manuscript sources.

VE108. Greenfield, Kent R. "The historiography of the Risorgimento since 1920." **Jour. mod. hist.,** 7 (Mar. 1935): 49–67. Useful summary of the progress of research and writing between 1920 and 1935.

VE109. Omodeo, Adolfo. **L'età del risorgimento italiano.** 7th ed., Naples, 1952. Synthesis of European history from 1748 to the close of World War I, addressed to the general public. The author gives a large place to Italian history, but insists that the Italian Risorgimento was inseparable from the whole movement of European liberalism which produced it.

VE110. ———. **Difesa del Risorgimento.** 2nd rev. ed., Turin, 1955. Collection of studies and book reviews defending the Risorgimento against its detractors. Omodeo's anti-clerical and anti-monarchist opinions appear clearly in several polemical articles. Included are two important long essays, originally published in book form: "La leggenda di Carlo Alberto nella recente storiografia" (Turin,

1940) and "Vincenzo Gioberti e la sua evoluzione politica" (Turin, 1941).

VE111. Spellanzon, Cesare. **Storia del Risorgimento e dell'unità d'Italia.** Milan, 1933 ff. Monumental work of contemporary Italian scholarship, still in course of publication. It is a critical synthesis of all earlier work on the subject which also incorporates the author's original research on many specific phases of the development. V. 5 (1950), on the first war of independence, shows the current shift of historical interest toward Carlo Cattaneo. Lavish illustrations and full bibliographies.

VE112. Monti, Antonio. **Il Risorgimento, 1814–1914.** 2 v. Milan, 1948. [Storia politica d'Italia, 3rd rev. ed.] Detailed political narrative.

VE113. Comandini, Alfredo. **L'Italia nei cento anni del secolo XIX, giorno per giorno illustrata.** Contd. by Antonio Monti. 5 v. Milan, 1900–42. Detailed chronicle of political and cultural events, profusely illustrated from the author's private collection of prints and medals. Anecdotal and somewhat uncritical in character, but indispensable for reference.

VE114. Salvatorelli, Luigi. **Pensiero e azione del Risorgimento.** 3rd rev. ed., Turin, 1950. A classic synthesis in the liberal tradition.

VE115. King, Bolton. **A history of Italian unity, being a political history of Italy from 1814 to 1871.** 2 v. London, 1912. Most comprehensive survey of the Risorgimento in English. Still valuable for the scope and detail of its narrative. Strongly anti-clerical.

VE116. Whyte, Arthur J. **The evolution of modern Italy.** Oxford, 1944. Several reprints. Narrative history of Italy from 1715 to 1930, without pretense to originality, in which the Risorgimento and its aftermath form the center of interest.

VE117. Bianchi, Nicomede. **Storia documentata della diplomazia europea in Italia dall'anno 1814 all'anno 1861.** 8 v. Turin, 1865–72. Early synthesis of diplomatic history of the Risorgimento, written from a narrowly Piedmontese point of view, but with access to the Turin archives. Although incomplete and marred by inaccuracies, its wealth of documentation makes it useful for consultation.

VE118. Quazza, Guido. **La lotta sociale nel Risorgimento: classi e governi dalla restaurazione all'unità, 1815–1861.** Turin, 1951. Admirable survey of the social and economic aspects of the Risorgimento. More than half the book is devoted to a description of economic development of Italy between 1815 and 1848.

VE119. Spini, Giorgio. **Risorgimento e protestanti.** Naples, 1956. Highly original study of contacts between Italy and the Protestant world. Presents the Risorgimento in an entirely new light by showing the contribution of Protestantism to the movement. Valuable for an understanding of British attitudes toward Italian nationalism.

Restoration and Early Revolutions (1815–1848)

VE120. Berkeley, George F., and Joan Berkeley. **Italy in the making, 1815–1848.** 3 v. Cambridge, Eng., 1932–40. One of the most substantial English contributions to Risorgimento scholarship in recent decades. The Catholic sympathies of the authors cause them to diverge markedly from the anticlerical tradition of many previous English scholars in this field, while preserving on the whole an open-minded attitude toward the Italian national movement.

VE121. Ferrari, Aldo. **L'Italia durante la Restaurazione (1815–1849).** Milan, 1935. [Biblioteca storica del Risorgimento, 4.] Luminous summary without pretense to originality. Bibliography.

VE122. Bulferetti, Luigi. "La Restaurazione in Italia negli studi dell'ultimo ventennio." **Rivista storica italiana,** 5th ser., 5 (Dec. 1940): 523–75. Bibliographical article.

VE123. Ottolini, Angelo. **La Carbonaria dalle origini ai primi tentativi insurrezionali (1797–1817).** Modena, 1936. Excellent popular history of the Carbonari, which the author derives from the Freemasons. Bibliography.

VE124. Romani, George T. **The Neapolitan revolution of 1820–1821.** Evanston, Ill., 1950. Excellent brief monograph. Bibliography.

VE125. Demarco, Domenico. **Il tramonto dello Stato pontificio: il papato di Gregorio XVI.** Turin, 1949. Carefully documented description of the social structure of Rome and the Papal States and of the political opposition to the papacy between 1815 and 1846. Bibliography.

VE126. Rodolico, Niccolò. **Carlo Alberto.** 3 v. Florence, 1936–48. Most authoritative critical work on Charles Albert.

VE127. Vidal, César. **Charles-Albert et le Risorgimento italien (1831–1848).** Paris, 1927. Still valuable as a documented study of the king of Sardinia in the last years of his reign.

VE128. Ciasca, Raffaele. **Le origini del "Programma per l'opinione nazionale italiana" del 1847–'48.** Rome, 1916. A pioneering work which traces the program of the moderate party back to the interests and ideology of bourgeois liberalism. A large part of the book consists of an annotated list of printed sources for Italian economic history from 1815 to 1848.

VE129. Greenfield, Kent R. **Economics and liberalism in the Risorgimento: a study of nationalism in Lombardy, 1814–1848.** Baltimore, 1934. Ital. tr., Bari, 1940. Superb study of the dynamics of the Risorgimento in northern Italy, showing that liberal opposition to the Hapsburgs had an economic basis. Evidently inspired by Ciasca's work, but written with greater literary skill.

VE130. Rota, Ettore, ed. **Il 1848 nella storia italiana ed europea.** 2 v. Milan, 1948. Collaborative work lacking in organic unity. See also V. 2 of *VE85.*

Unification Movement and Leaders (1848–1861)

VE131. Demarco, Domenico. **Pio IX e la rivoluzione romana del 1848.** Modena, 1947. This, *VE132* and *VE125* form a trilogy on Rome and the Papal States, with a strong social and economic emphasis, and characterized by depth of research and clarity of presentation.

VE132. ———. **Una rivoluzione sociale: la repubblica romana del 1849.** Naples, 1944.

VE133. Hales, Edward E. Y. **Pio Nono: a study in European politics and religion in the nineteenth century.** N.Y., 1954. Fair-minded and very readable account of Pius IX; the only adequate work in English. A definitive biography cannot be written, however, until the Vatican archives for this period have been opened.

VE134. Quazza, Romolo. **Pio IX e Massimo D'Azeglio nelle vicende romane del 1847.** 2 v. Modena, 1955. Documented study of relations between the pope and the Piedmontese liberal statesman.

VE135. Pirri, Pietro, ed. **Pio IX e Vittorio Emanuele II dal loro carteggio privato.** 2 v. in 3. Rome, 1944–51. Important work by a Jesuit historian. To assist its preparation, the Vatican made accessible the correspondence between Pius IX and Victor Emmanuel II and Napoleon III, and between Cardinal Antonelli and the papal nuncios for the years 1847–1863. V. 1 discusses secularization of the Sardinian state (1848–56).

VE136. Gioberti, Vincenzo. **Epistolario.** Ed. by Gustavo Balsamo-Crivelli and Giovanni Gentile. 11 v. Florence, 1927–37. The national edition of Gioberti's letters.

VE137. ———. **Carteggi.** 6 v. Rome, 1935–38.

VE138. ———. **Del primato morale e civile degli italiani.** Ed. by Gustavo Balsamo-Crivelli. 3 v. Turin, 1919–20. Gioberti's famous argument for the moral primacy of the papacy as the head of an Italian federal state.

VE139. ———. **Del rinnovamento civile d'Italia.** Ed. by Fausto Nicolini. 3 v. Bari, 1911–12. A summing-up of the lessons of 1848–49 which marks Gioberti's passage to the program of the moderates. A classic which invites comparison with De Tocqueville's *Recollections.*

VE140. Vecchietti, Tullio. "Tre momenti dell'evoluzione giobertiana." **Rivista storica italiana,** 5th ser., 5 (Mar. 1940): 3–48. Stimulating essay on Gioberti's intellectual development.

VE141. ———, ed. **Il pensiero politico di Vincenzo Gioberti.** Milan, 1941. Discriminating selection from Gioberti's voluminous letters and works.

VE142. Cattaneo, Carlo. **Epistolario.** Ed. by Rinaldo Caddeo. 4 v. Florence, 1949–56. As yet there is no satisfactory biography of this Lombard federalist who opposed union with Sardinia.

VE143. ———. **Scritti economici.** Ed. by Alberto Bertolini. 3 v. Florence, 1956. Forms part of a new critical edition of Cattaneo's works prepared by the Comitato Italo-Svizzero.

VE144. ———. **Scritti storici e geografici.** Ed. by Gaetano Salvemini and Ernesto Sestan. 4 v. Florence, 1957.

VE145. Ricasoli, Bettino. **Carteggi.** Ed. by Mario Nobili and Sergio Camerani. Bologna and Rome, 1939 ff. [Istituto Storico per l'Età Moderna e Contemporanea, Fonti per la storia d'Italia.] Important source for the Risorgimento in Tuscany.

VE146. Hancock, William K. **Ricasoli and the Risorgimento in Tuscany.** London, 1926. Best biography of Ricasoli, based on careful research and brilliantly written.

VE147. Mazzini, Giuseppe. **Edizione nazionale degli Scritti editi e inediti.** 100 v. Imola, 1906–43. The primary source for all interpretive and biographical work on Mazzini, prepared by a national commission.

VE148. **Protocollo della Giovine Italia (Congrega Centrale di Francia).** 6 v. Imola, 1916–22. Documents for the history of Young Italy, 1840–48.

VE149. Codignola, Arturo. **Mazzini.** Turin, 1946.

VE150. Levi, Alessandro. **Mazzini.** Florence, 1955.

VE151. Griffith, Gwilym O. **Mazzini: prophet of modern Europe.** London, 1932. Brilliant, enthusiastic biography, the best in English, although frankly partisan.

VE152. Salvemini, Gaetano. **Mazzini.** Tr. by I. M. Rawson from 4th Ital. ed. (Florence, 1925). London, 1956. Consists mostly of selections from Mazzini's writings with Salvemini's commentary.

VE153. Hales, Edward E. Y. **Mazzini and the secret societies: the making of a myth.** N.Y., 1956. Discerning analysis of the process whereby Mazzini was transformed into a prophet. Goes only to 1836. Bibliography.

VE154. Bonomi, Ivanoe. **Mazzini triumviro della repubblica romana.** New enl. ed., Milan, 1946. Concentrates on Mazzini's activity as a head of the Roman republic in 1849.

VE155. Morelli, Emilia. **Mazzini in Inghilterra.** Florence, 1938. Charming and scholarly account of Mazzini's years of exile in England, by the secretary of the Mazzini Commission.

VE156. Edizione nazionale dei Carteggi Cavouriani. Bologna, 1926 ff. The definitive edition of Cavour's papers, prepared by a commission appointed by the Italian government. Volumes published thus far concentrate on the years after 1856.

VE157. Cavour, Count Camillo di. **Discorsi parlamentari.** Ed. by Adolfo Omodeo and Luigi Russo. Florence, 1932 ff. Definitive edition of Cavour's speeches. V. 11 (1957) has reached 1855.

VE158. Ruffini, Francesco. **La giovinezza di Cavour.** 2 v. Turin, 1912. A classic account of Cavour's early years.

VE159. Thayer, William R. **The life and times of Cavour.** 2 v. Boston, 1911. Best biography of Cavour in any language.

VE160. Omodeo, Adolfo. **L'opera politica del Conte di Cavour.** 2nd ed., 2 v., Florence, 1940. Left unfinished by the death of its author, this analysis of Cavour's political activity covers only the years 1848–57.

VE161. Whyte, Arthur J. **The early life and letters of Cavour, 1810–1848.** London, 1925. For those who do not read Italian, this may take the place of *VE158*, on which it is largely based.

VE162. ——. **The political life and letters of Cavour, 1848–1861.** London, 1930. Satisfactory account for English readers, in which the author utilizes the published Cavour-Nigra correspondence and inedited documents in the Public Record Office.

VE163. Valsecchi, Franco. **L'alleanza di Crimea: il Risorgimento e l'Europa.** Milan, 1948. Important reexamination of Cavour's diplomacy, based on archival investigation into the European background of the Italian question on the eve of the Crimean War.

VE164. ——. **L'unificazione italiana e la politica europea dalla guerra di Crimea alla guerra di Lombardia (1854–1859).** Milan, 1939. Documents illustrating Cavour's diplomacy and its European background.

VE165. Mack Smith, Denis. **Cavour and Garibaldi, 1860: a study in political conflict.** Cambridge, Eng., 1954. Brilliant detailed work by a British risorgimentalist, stressing the opposition between the Cavourian Right and Garibaldian Left. Ital. tr., Turin, 1958.

VE166. Passerin d'Entrèves, Ettore. **L'ultima battaglia politica di Cavour: i problemi dell'unificazione italiana.** Turin, 1956. Regarded as one of the most important works of Cavour scholarship in recent years. Author goes directly to the sources for his careful analysis of problems arising from the conquest of the South, and challenges Mack Smith's interpretation of Cavour. Bibliography.

VE167. Garibaldi, Giuseppe. **Edizione nazionale degli Scritti.** 6 v. Bologna, 1932–37.

A primary source for the history of Italian unification.

VE168. Trevelyan, George M. **Garibaldi's defence of the Roman republic.** London and N.Y., 1907. Ital. tr., Bologna, 1909.

VE169. ——. **Garibaldi and the Thousand.** London and N.Y., 1909.

VE170. ——. **Garibaldi and the making of Italy.** London and N.Y., 1911. Ital. tr., Bologna, 1913. Although marred by omissions and inaccuracies and naive in point of view, these three works of Trevelyan have attained the rank of classics and still form an acceptable introduction to the life and career of Garibaldi.

VE171. Mack Smith, Denis. **Garibaldi: a great life in brief.** N.Y., 1956. Most recent, highly condensed account of the military hero of the unification movement. Ital. tr., Milan, 1959.

United Italy, 1861–1918

Some of the books listed here exceed the limits 1861–1918 and are general histories of modern and contemporary Italy. See also *VE112–113*.

VE172. Albrecht-Carrié, René. **Italy from Napoleon to Mussolini.** N.Y., 1950. A meditative account of modern Italian history, interpretative rather than narrative. Greater part of the book is concerned with the period after 1870, in which the author seeks the origins of fascism.

VE173. Vaussard, Maurice. **Histoire de l'Italie contemporaine.** Paris, 1950. Good brief survey of the period 1870–1946. The author does not attempt to conceal his dislike for Italian fascism, but the tone is temperate and the treatment of political parties is fair. Bibliography.

VE174. Croce, Benedetto. **Storia d'Italia dal 1871 al 1915.** 8th ed., Bari, 1943. Eng. tr., by Cecilia M. Ady, from 1st Ital. ed., *History of Italy, 1871–1915*, Oxford, 1929. This book, informed by characteristic Crocean liberalism, began a trend toward rehabilitation of the period preceding World War I. Emphasis is on the movement of ideas.

VE175. Volpe, Gioacchino. **Italia moderna, 1815–1915.** 3 v. Florence, 1943–52. Begun as a new edition of *Italia in cammino* (Milan, 1927), this evolved into an independent work on the 19th century in reply to Croce's more favorable interpretation. Volpe was a historian of ability and integrity who identified himself with fascism, and this work is inspired by Fascist ideology. Provides valuable insight into modern Italian history, especially for the years 1898–1914, reflecting the disillusionment with parliamentary liberalism felt by many Italians of Volpe's generation. New ed. in process.

VE176. Bonomi, Ivanoe. **La politica ita-**

liana da Porta Pia a Vittorio Veneto (1870–1918). 2nd ed., Turin, 1946. This Socialist leader presents a more sympathetic evaluation of the pre-World War I period in Italy than that usually given by historians under the Fascist regime.

VE177. ——. **La politica italiana dopo Vittorio Veneto.** Turin, 1953.

VE178. Mack Smith, Denis. **Italy. A modern history.** Ann Arbor, 1959. (University of Michigan History of the Modern World.) Important controversial treatment of Italian political history from 1861 to the present. Concentrates on period 1861–1925, and tends to stress negative aspects of national development. Excludes economic and cultural history.

VE179. Barbagallo, Corrado, ed. **Cento anni di vita italiana, 1848–1948.** 2 v. Milan, 1948–49. Essays by various authors on virtually every phase of Italian life, including literature and the arts, with a list of important events year by year.

VE180. Valeri, Nino, ed. **La lotta politica in Italia dall'unità al 1925: idee e documenti.** Florence, 1954. Readings from the sources, topically arranged.

VE181. Salvemini, Gaetano. **La politica estera dell'Italia dal 1871 al 1915.** 2nd ed., Florence, 1950. Best brief survey of Italian foreign policy prior to World War I.

VE182. Chabod, Federico. **Storia della politica estera italiana dal 1870 al 1896.** V. 1, **Le premesse.** Bari, 1951. Not so much a history of foreign policy in the usual sense as a philosophical examination of the "passions and ideas" which form the bases of foreign policy. Emphasis is on the period before 1882, and the years after this date are more summarily treated. The footnotes serve as a guide to the literature.

VE183. Volpe, Gioacchino, ed. **L'Italia nelle Triplice Alleanza (1882–1915).** 2nd ed., Milan, 1941. Texts of treaties, selections from memoirs, and other literature illustrating Italy's role in the Triple Alliance.

VE184. Tommasini, Francesco. **L'Italia alla vigilia della guerra: la politica estera di Tommaso Tittoni.** 5 v. Bologna, 1934–41.

VE185. Crispi, Francesco. **Memorie e documenti.** Ed. by Thomas Palamenghi-Crispi. 5 v. Milan, 1911–24. Eng. tr. of v. 1–3, by Mary Pritchard-Agnetti, *The memoirs of Francesco Crispi,* 3 v., London, 1912–14. Valuable but untrustworthy memoirs of the most important Italian statesman of the late 19th century. There is no adequate biography of Crispi.

VE186. Giolitti, Giovanni. **Memorie della mia vita.** 3rd ed., Milan, 1945. Eng. tr. of 1st ed., by Edward Storer, *Memoirs of my life,* London, 1923. Autobiography of the statesman, five times prime minister, who guided Italian politics between the death of Crispi and 1914.

VE187. Salomone, A. William. **Italian democracy in the making: the political scene in the Giolittian era, 1900–1914.** Philadelphia, 1945. A perceptive account of Italian politics in the early 20th century. Contains excellent description of the parliamentary regime and political parties and a dispassionate brief discussion of socialism. Should be supplemented by Nino Valeri, "Giolitti" in *Questioni di storia del Risorgimento (VE 10),* pp. 1009–22.

VE188. Natale, Gaetano. **Giolitti e gli italiani.** Milan, 1949. Author knew Giolitti personally and had access to information not generally known. Contributes to the growing rehabilitation of this statesman's reputation.

VE189. Albertini, Luigi. **Venti anni di vita politica.** 5 v. Bologna, 1950–53. Invaluable firsthand account by the former editor of *Corriere della Sera* (Milan) and leader of the Italian Right opposed to Giolitti.

VE190. ——. **Le origini della guerra del 1914.** See *T504.*

VE191. Valori, Aldo. **L'Italia nella guerra mondiale.** 3 v. Bologna, 1922–25. A military history of World War I.

VE192. Albrecht-Carrié, René. **Italy at the Paris peace conference.** See *AH151.*

Fascist Era (1922–1945)

VE193. Salvatorelli, Luigi, and Giovanni Mira. **Storia d'Italia nel periodo fascista.** 2nd ed., Turin, 1957. Orig. ed., *Storia del fascismo: l'Italia dal 1919 al 1945* (Rome, 1952). Comprehensive history of Italian fascism. This edition contains an expanded account of the years before 1922 and a chapter on the resistance and the liberation. The diplomatic historian, Mario Toscano, contributed chapters on foreign policy.

VE194. Perticone, Giacomo. **La politica italiana nell'ultimo trentennio.** 3 v. Rome, 1945–47. Detailed account by a political scientist of the development of fascism. V. 3 contains important documents.

VE195. Tasca, Angelo (pseud., Angelo Rossi). **Nascita e avvento del fascismo: l'Italia dal 1918 al 1922.** Florence, 1950. Ital. ed., enl. and rev., of A. Rossi, *La naissance du fascisme* (2nd ed., Paris, 1938). Eng. tr., *The rise of Italian fascism,* London, 1938. Most complete and fully documented account of the rise of fascism by an ex-Communist, expelled from the party in 1929, who had unsurpassed opportunities for observation and drew upon socialist sources as well as Fascist official documents.

VE196. Salvemini, Gaetano. **The Fascist dictatorship in Italy.** N.Y., 1927; London, 1928. This passionate indictment of the Fascist regime, by an anti-Fascist emigré historian who represented the conscience of Italy, is in itself a historical document.

VE197. Sforza, Count Carlo. **L'Italia dal 1914 al 1944, quale io la vidi.** 3rd ed., Milan, 1946. French tr., *L'Italie telle que je l'ai vue de 1914 à 1944*, Paris, 1946. Memoirs of a former Italian foreign minister and opponent of Mussolini.

VE198. Finer, Herman. **Mussolini's Italy.** London and N.Y., 1935. Excellent contemporary description of the government and economy of Fascist Italy by one of the more perceptive foreign observers of the Italian political scene.

VE199. Rosenstock-Franck, Louis. **L'économie corporative fasciste en doctrine et en fait.** Paris, 1934. Best contemporary account of relations between capital and labor under the Fascist regime.

VE200. ——. **Les étapes de l'économie fasciste: du corporatisme à l'économie de guerre.** Paris, 1938. Studies the transformation of Fascist economic policy under the impact of war.

VE201. Alatri, Paolo. "Benito Mussolini (nota biografica e bibliografica)." **Questioni di storia contemporanea** (*VE11*), v. 3, pp. 759–96. Biographical essay followed by a full critical bibliography. Recommended as a starting point for reading and research on Mussolini.

VE202. Megaro, Gaudens. **Mussolini in the making.** Boston and N.Y., 1938. Ital. tr., *Mussolini dal mito alla realtà*, Milan, 1947. Superb critical work on the youth of Mussolini, based on material gathered at great personal danger in Italy in years of Fascist rule. Written with a kind of historical austerity and impartiality far more effective than expressed moral condemnation. Especially valuable for Mussolini's revolutionary background, usually suppressed or glossed over by Fascist writers.

VE203. Mussolini, Benito. **Scritti e discorsi.** 13 v. Milan, 1934–40. Announced as "the definitive study," but this claim was demolished by Gaudens Megaro in *Jour. mod. hist.*, 8 (September 1936): 380.

VE204. ——. **Scritti e discorsi adriatici.** Ed. by Edoardo Susmel. 2 v. Milan, 1942–43.

VE205. ——. **Gli ultimi discorsi.** Rome, 1948.

VE206. ——. **La mia vita.** Rome, 1947. An authentic work, composed while Mussolini was in prison in 1911–12; to be distinguished from the spurious *My autobiography* (N.Y., 1928).

VE207. ——. **Storia di un anno (il tempo del bastone e della carota).** Milan, 1944. Tr., *The fall of Mussolini: his own story.* N.Y., 1948.

VE208. ——. **Opera omnia.** Ed. by Edoardo and Duilio Susmel. Florence, 1951 ff. Purports to be a complete edition of Mussolini's writings and speeches in a day-to-day summary. V. 29 (1959) carries the

record to June 10, 1940. To consist of 35 v. when completed.

VE209. Salvemini, Gaetano. **Mussolini diplomatico (1922–1932).** Bari, 1952. Mussolini's foreign policy during his first decade in power as viewed by an anti-Fascist historian.

VE210. ——. **Prelude to World War II.** N.Y. and London, 1954. Castigation of Mussolini's attack on Ethiopia and the policies of Great Britain and France, documented mostly from the contemporary press.

VE211. Toscano, Mario. **Le origini diplomatiche del patto d'acciaio.** 2nd ed., Florence, 1956. One of the best monographs by Italy's premier diplomatic historian. Analyzes the "Pact of steel" between Mussolini and Hitler.

VE212. Wiskemann, Elizabeth. **The Rome-Berlin axis: a history of the relations between Hitler and Mussolini.** See *AH227*.

VE213. Alfieri, Dino. **Due dittatori di fronte: Roma-Berlino, 1939–1943.** Milan, 1948. Tr. by David Moore, *Dictators face to face*, London, 1954. Memoirs of Mussolini's ambassador in Berlin.

VE214. **Hitler e Mussolini: lettere e documenti.** Milan, 1946. Letters exchanged between the two dictators, 1939–43.

VE215. Ciano, Galeazzo, conte. **Diario, 1937–38.** Bologna, 1948.

VE216. ——. **Diario, 1939–43.** 2 v. Milan, 1946. Essential source for Mussolini's later years, the diary of his son-in-law and foreign minister. Of the three principal editions, the French (2 v., Neuchâtel, Switz., 1946) is the preferred. The U. S. edition, *The Ciano diaries, 1939–1943*, ed. by Hugh Gibson (N.Y., 1946), is marred by many omissions and thoroughly unreliable.

VE217. ——. **L'Europa verso la catastrofe.** Milan, 1948. Records of 180 conversations with European statesmen and 40 unpublished documents. Important for Fascist foreign policy from 1936 to 1942, especially for Italy's relations with Great Britain, Germany, and Yugoslavia.

VE218. Anfuso, Filippo. **Roma, Berlino, Salò.** Milan, 1950. Stirring account of the last years of fascism by an official in Mussolini's foreign ministry.

VE219. Donosti, Mario (pseud. Mario Lucioli). **Mussolini e l'Europa: la politica estera fascista.** Rome, 1945. Fascist foreign policy during the last days of the regime as observed by an official in the Italian embassy at Berlin.

VE220. Simoni, Leonardo. **Berlino, Ambasciata d'Italia, 1939–1943.** Rome, 1946. Diary of a young secretary in the Italian embassy in Berlin. Valuable for Italo-German relations, in which it confirms Ciano's diary.

VE221. Noether, Emiliana P. "Italy reviews its Fascist past: a bibliographical essay." **Am. hist. rev.**, 61 (July 1956): 877–

99. Objective and well-informed survey of a controversial subject.

World War II and Postwar Italy

It is too soon to assess the literature dealing with events and problems of the postwar period. V. 4 of Rota, *Questioni di storia contemporanea* (*VE11*) furnishes good bibliographies on various important topics up to 1955.

VE222. Grindrod, Muriel. **The new Italy: transition from war to peace.** N.Y., 1947. Succinct, unbiased account of Italian wartime conditions, the fall of fascism, and terms of the peace treaty.

VE223. ——. **The rebuilding of Italy: politics and economics, 1945–1955.** London and N.Y., 1955. Admirable survey of postwar reconstruction.

VE224. Kogan, Norman. **Italy and the Allies.** Cambridge, Mass., 1956. Analysis of relations between Italy and the British and American commands during World War II. Controversial.

VE225. Dieci anni dopo, 1945–1955: saggi sulla vita democratica italiana. Bari, 1955. Review of Italy's progress under the republic. For a Marxist criticism see Gastone Manacorda, "Dieci anni dopo o del modo di scrivere la storia recente," *Società*, 11 (June 1955): 543–58.

HISTORIES OF SPECIAL AREAS

Florence

VE226. Schevill, Ferdinand. **History of Florence from the founding of the city through the Renaissance.** N.Y., 1936. Best introduction to the subject in English. Contains a discussion of previous historiography. Bibliography.

VE227. Caggese, Romolo. **Firenze dalla decadenza di Roma al risorgimento d'Italia.** 3 v. Florence, 1912–21. Most satisfactory Italian synthesis of Florentine history, although not to be compared with Robert Davidsohn's great work on medieval Florence. A history of the Florentine state, not of the city; valuable for its account of the later principate.

VE228. Rodolico, Niccolò. **I Ciompi: una pagina di storia del proletariato operaio.** Florence, 1945. Account of the class struggles in 14th century Florence and defeat of the Florentine democracy which paved the way for the Medici despotism.

VE229. Gutkind, Curt S. **Cosimo de' Medici, pater patriae.** Oxford, 1938. Really a history of Florence in Cosimo's period. Includes ten valuable appendices on Florentine government and economic organization. Bibliography.

VE230. Roover, Raymond de. **The Medici bank: its organization, management, operations, and decline.** N.Y., 1948. A masterpiece of condensation. An expanded edition is in preparation, based on newly discovered documents, including secret account books of the bank.

VE231. Ridolfi, Roberto. **Vita di Girolamo Savonarola.** 2 v. Rome, 1952. Replaces an older work by Pasquale Villari on Savonarola, which misinterpreted the friar's significance. V. 1 is the biography, followed by a volume of bibliographical and critical notes.

VE232. Schnitzer, Joseph. **Savonarola: ein Kulturbild aus der Zeit der Renaissance.** 2 v. Munich, 1924. The revised Italian translation (Milan, 1931) is preferred.

VE233. Albertini, Rudolf von. **Das florentinische Staatsbewusstein im Übergang von der Republik zum Prinzipat.** Bern, 1955. Brilliant analysis of development of Florentine political thought from 1494 to establishment of the Medici principate, in which the growth of absolutist ideas is related to their political and social context. A lengthy appendix of new documentation supports the author's conclusions.

VE234. Spini, Giorgio. **Cosimo I de' Medici e la indipendenza del principato mediceo.** Florence, 1945. Remarkable study of international relations of the Medici principate in the early 16th century.

VE235. Florence. Archivio di Stato. **Archivio mediceo avanti il principato: inventario.** Rome, 1951 ff. An index to the Medici archives, now in the Archivio di Stato of Florence, from 1434 to 1527.

VE236. ——. **Archivio mediceo del principato: inventario sommario.** Rome, 1951. Summary index to documents of the Medici principate (1530–1738).

VE237. Protocolli del carteggio di Lorenzo il Magnifico per gli anni 1473–74, 1477–92. Ed. by Marcello del Piazzo. Florence, 1956. [Documenti di storia italiana, ser. 2, v. 2.] Journal of the letters sent from the office of Lorenzo de' Medici.

As Florentine historians and political thinkers whose works are significant for the history of their native city, Machiavelli and Guicciardini are included in this section.

VE238. Machiavelli, Niccolò. **Tutte le opere, storiche e letterarie.** Ed. by Guido Mazzoni and Mario Casella. Florence, 1929. Standard edition of Machiavelli's works.

VE239. Villari, Pasquale. **Niccolò Machiavelli e i suoi tempi.** 4th ed., 2 v., Milan, 1927. Eng. tr., by Linda Villari, London, 1929. Vivid description of Machiavelli's period in which the central figure is sometimes lost.

VE240. Ridolfi, Roberto. **Vita di Niccolò Machiavelli.** 2nd rev. ed., Rome, 1954. Most authoritative Italian biography.

VE241. Chabod, Federico. **Machiavelli**

and the Renaissance. Tr. by David Moore. London and Cambridge, Mass., 1958.

VE242. Renaudet, Augustin. **Machiavel: étude d'histoire des doctrines politiques.** New rev. ed., Paris, 1956. Standard French interpretation of Machiavelli's political thought.

VE243. Butterfield, Herbert. **The statecraft of Machiavelli.** London, 1940. Defends traditional interpretation of Machiavelli.

VE244. Whitfield, John H. **Machiavelli.** Oxford, 1947. Sympathetic interpretation of Machiavelli as a misunderstood humanist.

VE245. Guicciardini, Francesco. **Opere.** Ed. by Vittore de Caprariis. Milan and Naples, 1953. [La letteratura italiana, storia e testi, 30.] Skilful selection from Guicciardini's works, including complete text of the recently discovered *Le cose fiorentine,* and selections from *Storie fiorentine* and *Storia d'Italia.* Bibliography.

VE246. ———. **Carteggi.** Ed. by Roberto Palmarocchi and Pier Giorgio Ricci. Bologna and Rome, 1938 ff. This definitive edition of Guicciardini's correspondence reached its ninth volume in 1959.

VE247. Caprariis, Vittorio de. **Francesco Guicciardini dalla politica alla storia.** Bari, 1950. Excellent study of Guicciardini's intellectual development.

Milan

VE248. Storia di Milano. Milan, 1953 ff. A multivolume publication, lavishly illustrated and equipped with exhaustive bibliographies. Sponsored by Fondazione Treccani degli Alfieri.

VE249. Visconti, Alessandro. **Storia di Milano.** 2nd ed., Milan, 1952. A convenient 1 v. history, based on a lifetime of research.

VE250. Verga, Ettore. **Storia della vita milanese.** 2nd ed., Milan, 1931. An illustrated history of Milanese society to 1848, especially full on the Renaissance and early modern period. Bibliography.

VE251. Barbieri, Gino. **Economia e politica nel ducato di Milano, 1386–1535.** Milan, 1938. Study of Milanese economy under the Visconti and the Sforza.

VE252. Santoro, Caterina, ed. **Gli uffici del dominio sforzesco, 1450–1500.** Milan, 1948. Archivistic monograph on the administration of Milan under the Sforza.

VE253. Chabod, Federico. **Lo stato di Milano nell'impero di Carlo V.** V. 1, Rome, 1934.

VE254. ———. **Per la storia religiosa dello stato di Milano durante il dominio di Carlo V.** Bologna, 1938. Heavily documented monograph on beginnings of the Counter-Reformation in the duchy of Milan (1535–54). Review, A. Casadei, *Revista storica italiana,* 58 (Mar. 1941): 42 and 58 (June 1941): 171, adds new documents.

VE255. Cazzamini-Mussi, Francesco. **Milano durante la dominazione spagnola, 1525–1706.** Milan, 1947.

VE256. Roberti, Melchiorre. **Milano capitale napoleonica: la formazione di uno stato moderno, 1796–1814.** 3 v. Milan, 1946–47. Microscopic analysis of virtually every aspect of law, government, and finance in northern Italy under the Napoleonic regime. V. 1 traces constitutional development of the Cisalpine republic and the kingdom of Italy. The work would have been improved by condensation.

Rome

VE257. Gregorovius, Ferdinand. **Geschichte der Stadt Rom im Mittelalter vom V. bis XVI. Jahrhundert.** New ed., ed. by Waldemar Kampf, Basel, 1953 ff. English tr. of 4th Ger. ed., by Annie Hamilton, *History of the city of Rome in the Middle Ages,* 8 v. in 13, London, 1894–1902. Reprint, 1903–12. Unsurpassed history of Rome to the end of the 15th century, by a German scholar who dedicated his life to the project. Requires revision in detail, but is useful as introduction to history of Rome and Italy in the period covered.

VE258. Rome. Istituto di Studi Romani. **Storia di Roma.** Bologna, 1938 ff. A collaborative work beginning with classical antiquity. Based on modern critical research, its many volumes present a definitive factual history of the city, but the work as a whole lacks the unity and dramatic sweep of *VE257,* which it corrects and amplifies without supplanting for the late medieval and Renaissance periods. More useful for consultation than for continuous reading. Extensive bibliographies.

VE259. Rodocanachi, Emmanuel P. **Histoire de Rome.** 3 v. Paris, 1888–1926. Popular history of Rome during the Renaissance.

VE260. Madelin, Louis. **La Rome de Napoléon.** Paris, 1906.

For Rome in the 19th century see *VE125, 131, 132.*

Venice

A new multivolume *Storia di Venezia* (Venice, 1957 ff.) is in preparation under auspices of the Centro Internazionale delle Arti e del Costume. It may be expected eventually to become the definitive general work on Venice.

VE261. Kretschmayr, Heinrich. **Geschichte von Venedig.** 3 v. Gotha and Stuttgart, 1905–34. Standard account by an Austrian scholar, based directly on the sources and well balanced between cultural and political history. It has been replaced on the institutional and economic side by later monographs.

VE262. Cessi, Roberto. **Storia della repubblica di Venezia.** 2 v. Messina and Milan, 1944–46. Synthesis of recent scholarship by an eminent authority. Undocumented.

VE263. Molmenti, Pompeo G. **La storia di Venezia nella vita privata dalle origini alla caduta della repubblica.** 7th ed., 3 v., Bergamo, 1927. Eng. tr. of 1st Ital. ed., by Horatio F. Brown, *Venice, its individual growth from the earliest beginnings to the fall of the republic,* 6 v., London and Chicago, 1906–08. A classic of social history.

VE264. Lane, Frederic C. **Andrea Barbarigo, merchant of Venice, 1418–1449.** Baltimore, 1944. [The Johns Hopkins studies in history and political science, ser. 62, no. 1.] Based on the Barbarigo papers; provides an excellent picture of Venetian mercantile activity.

VE265. ——. **Venetian ships and shipbuilders of the Renaissance.** Baltimore, 1934. Technical study on economic and naval history based on research in the Venetian archives.

VE266. Berengo, Marino. **La società veneta alla fine del settecento.** Florence, 1956. Impressive regional monograph on the society of Venetia in the last decades of the republic.

VE267. Petrocchi, Massimo. **Il tramonto della repubblica di Venezia e l'assolutismo illuminato.** Venice, 1950. [Deputazione di Storia Patria per le Venezie, Miscellanea di studi e memorie, 7.] Thought-provoking study of the failure of the Venetian ruling classes to adapt themselves to new social and intellectual currents of the late 18th century.

VE268. Beltrami, Daniele. **Storia della popolazione di Venezia dalla fine del secolo XVI alla caduta della repubblica.** Padua, 1954. Painstaking demographic study utilizing statistical methods.

VE269. Luzzatto, Gino. **Studi di storia economica veneziana.** See *K467.*

Other North Italian States

VE270. Ady, Cecilia M. **The Bentivoglio of Bologna: a study in despotism.** London, 1937.

VE271. Frati, Lodovico. **La vita privata di Bologna dal secolo XIII al XVII.** Bologna, 1900.

VE272. Storia di Genova dalle origini al tempo nostro. Milan, 1941 ff. [Istituto per la Storia di Genova.] Collaborative work of high scholarly calibre.

VE273. Ciasca, Raffaelle, ed. **Istruzioni e relazioni degli ambasciatori genovesi.** Rome, 1951 ff. [Fonti per la Storia d'Italia.] Important collection of diplomatic documents. V. 1–5 concern relations between Genoa and Spain, 1494–1721.

VE274. Bedarida, Henri. **Parme et la France de 1748 à 1789.** Paris, 1928. Excellent monograph on intellectual relations between Parma and France.

VE275. ——. **Les premiers Bourbons de Parme et l'Espagne (1731–1802).** Paris, 1928.

VE276. Bodo, Paolo. **Le consuetudini, la legislazione e le istituzioni del vecchio Piemonte.** Turin, 1950.

VE277. Prato, Giuseppe. **La vita economica in Piemonte a mezzo il secolo XVIII.** Turin, 1908.

VE278. Cognasso, Francesco. **I Savoia nella politica europea.** Milan, 1941. Surveys the foreign policy of the House of Savoy to the end of the 19th century. Most of the book deals with the period before 1815.

Much information on 19th century Piedmont will be found in the subsection on the Risorgimento.

Naples and Sicily

VE279. Croce, Benedetto. **Storia del regno di Napoli.** 4th ed., Bari, 1953. Historical analysis of social changes in the kingdom of Naples, emphasizing the period of Spanish rule. This book initiated a revaluation of the foreign dynasties of Naples.

VE280. Schipa, Michelangelo. **Masaniello.** Bari, 1925. Social struggles in Naples under Spanish rule, by one of the foremost southern Italian historians of his generation.

VE281. ——. **Albori di risorgimento del mezzogiorno d'Italia.** Naples, 1938. This panoramic view of the kingdom of Naples under the Bourbons is a reprint of five lectures published under the title *Il regno di Napoli sotto i Borboni* (Naples, 1900), to which a preface has been added on political thought in Naples in the 17th century.

VE282. Coniglio, Giuseppe. **Il regno di Napoli al tempo di Carlo V: amministrazione e vita economico-sociale.** Naples, 1951. Careful monograph based on archival research in Naples, Madrid, and Simancas. Provides a comprehensive account of the kingdom of Naples in the time of Charles V.

VE283. ——. **Il viceregno di Napoli nel secolo XVII: nuove notizie sulla vita commerciale e finanziaria tratte dagli archivi napoletane.** Rome, 1955. First documented study of economic conditions in the viceroyalty of Naples. Indispensable for Spanish administration in Italy.

VE284. Acton, Harold M. **The Bourbons of Naples (1734–1825).** London, 1956. An animated and informative account which omits institutional and economic matters in order to focus on the more personal aspects of Bourbon rule.

VE285. Ruggiero, Guido de. **Il pensiero politico meridionale nel secolo XVIII e XIX.** 2nd ed., Bari, 1946. Standard work on the intellectual origins of the Risorgimento in southern Italy. The narrative is carried through 1848.

VE286. Simioni, Attilio. **Le origini del Risorgimento politico dell'Italia meridionale.** 2 v. Messina, 1925–30.

VE287. Barbagallo, Corrado. **La questione meridionale.** Milan, 1948. Admirable discussion of the economic problems of the South.

VE288. Vöchting, Friedrich. **Die italienische Südfrage: Entstehung und Problematik eines wirtschaftlichen Notstandsgebietes.** Berlin, 1951. Ital. tr., *La questione meridionale*, Naples, 1956. Exhaustive analysis of southern Italian problems in their historical framework. The detailed narrative, extending from national unification to the present day, includes discussions of emigration, ecclesiastical policy, and agrarian reform. Indispensable.

VE289. Caizzi, Bruno, ed. **Antologia della questione meridionale.** Milan, 1950. Convenient selection from the voluminous literature on the problems of southern Italy since unification.

VE290. Salvemini, Gaetano. **Scritti sulla questione meridionale (1896–1955).** Turin, 1955. Consists mostly of articles and speeches on the southern Italian problem during the socialist phase of Salvemini's career.

VE291. Koenigsberger, Helmut. **The government of Sicily under Philip II: a study in the practice of empire.** London and N.Y., 1951. Admirable monograph, based in part on research in the Simancas archives. Bibliography.

VE292. Pontieri, Ernesto. **Il tramonto del baronaggio siciliano.** Florence, 1943. Of fundamental importance on 18th century Sicily, stressing social conditions and the Caracciolo reforms.

VE293. Titone, Virgilio. **La Sicilia dalla dominazione spagnola all'unità d'Italia.** Bologna, 1955. Valuable collection of essays illuminating various aspects of social and economic history.

VE294. Romeo, Rosario. **Il Risorgimento in Sicilia.** Bari, 1950. The authoritative work on the subject.

VE295. Brancato, Francesco. **Storia della Sicilia post-unificazione.** Pt. 1, *La Sicilia nel primo ventennio del regno d'Italia.* Bologna, 1956. First volume of a projected history of Sicily since national unification.

HISTORIES OF SPECIAL TOPICS

Cultural History

Art

The literature of Italian art history is so extensive as to prohibit a truly representative selection in brief compass. This list presents only a few major syntheses and some of the best monographs.

VE296. Venturi, Adolfo. **Storia dell'arte italiana.** 11 v. in 25. Milan and Ancona, 1901–40. Venturi was founder and director of the first school of art history in Italy at the University of Rome. Although outdated in part, this great work retains its place as a masterpiece of art history because of its deep learning, vivid style, and artistic sensibility. Essentially a succession of monographs on individual artists, it goes only through the *cinquecento*.

VE297. Chastel, André. **L'art italien.** 2 v. Paris, 1956. From origins to the *cinquecento*, with good bibliography and topographical index. [JSC]

VE298. Salmi, Mario. **L'arte italiana.** 3 v. Florence, 1941–44. V. 3 in particular is recommended for the high Renaissance to the modern period. [JSC]

VE299. Marle, Raimond van. **The development of the Italian schools of painting.** 19 v. The Hague, 1923–38. Exhaustive and painstaking account of the Italian regional schools of painting, left uncompleted by the author's death. Many attributions and iconographical interpretations have been corrected by later research, but an Italian edition, now in preparation, will incorporate the findings and make necessary revisions.

VE300. Venturi, Lionello. **Italian painting from Caravaggio to Modigliani.** Geneva, 1952.

VE301. Pallucchini, Rodolfo. **La pittura veneziana del cinquecento.** 2 v. Novara, 1944.

VE302. Voss, Hermann. **Die Malerei der Spätrenaissance in Rom und Florenz.** 2 v. Berlin, 1920.

VE303. Dvořák, Max. **Geschichte der italienischen Kunst im Zeitalter der Renaissance.** 2 v. Munich, 1927–28.

VE304. Wölfflin, Heinrich. **Classic art: an introduction to the Italian Renaissance.** N.Y., 1952. Tr. of famous German work.

VE305. Antal, Frederick. **Florentine painting and its social background: the bourgeois republic before Cosimo de'Medici's advent to power, XIV and early XV centuries.** London, 1948. Ambitious and erudite attempt to relate art and society. Some of its interpretations have been severely criticized.

VE306. Panofsky, Erwin. **Studies in iconology: humanistic themes in the art of the Renaissance.** N.Y., 1939. An interpretation of the philosophical meanings of some famous works of Italian Renaissance art. Bibliography.

VE307. Blunt, Anthony. **Artistic theory in Italy, 1450–1600.** Oxford, 1940.

VE308. Wittkower, Rudolf. **Architectural principles in the age of humanism.** 2nd ed., London, 1952. Interesting effort to trace relationships between architectural and philosophical ideas.

VE309. Becherucci, Luisa. **L'architettura italiana del cinquecento.** Florence, 1936.

VE310. Ricci, Corrado. **Architecture and decorative sculpture of the high and late Renaissance in Italy.** N.Y., 1923.

VE311. Maclagan, Eric R. D. **Italian sculpture of the Renaissance.** Cambridge, Mass., 1935.

VE312. Berenson, Bernard. **The Italian painters of the Renaissance.** Rev. ed., Oxford, 1952.

VE313. Krautheimer, Richard (with collaboration of Trude Krautheimer-Hess). **Lorenzo Ghiberti.** Princeton, 1956. Exhaustive monograph tracing Ghiberti's development as an artist and his relations with his time. Contains a wealth of reference material on civilization of the early Renaissance.

VE314. Pucci, Eugenio. **Botticelli nelle opere e nella vita del suo tempo.** Milan, 1955. Summarizes recent criticism of Botticelli's work and illumines the artist's historical background.

VE315. Gamba, Carlo. **Botticelli.** Milan, 1936.

VE316. McComb, Arthur K. **Agnolo Bronzino.** Cambridge, Mass., 1928. The standard monograph in English. [JSC]

VE317. Coletti, Luigi. **Lotto.** Bergamo, 1953. Contains useful bibliography; 206 plates. [JSC]

VE318. Clark, Kenneth M. **Leonardo da Vinci: an account of his development as an artist.** 2nd ed., Cambridge, Eng., 1952. Convincing demonstration of the interconnections between his work as artist and scientist.

VE319. Heydenreich, Ludwig H. **Leonardo da Vinci.** Tr. from German ed. of 1953. 2 v. N.Y., 1954.

VE320. McCurdy, Edward. **The mind of Leonardo da Vinci.** 2nd ed., London and Toronto, 1932.

VE321. De Tolnay, Charles. **Michelangelo.** Princeton, 1943 ff. Four volumes have been published to date: 1, *The youth of Michelangelo* (1943); 2, *The Sistine ceiling* (1945); 3, *The Medici chapel* (1948); 4, *The tomb of Julius II* (1954). Two more are promised. These monumental volumes are indispensable to an understanding of Michelangelo's work but some of the psychological interpretations are questionable.

VE322. Goldscheider, Ludwig. **Michelangelo: paintings, sculptures, architecture.** N.Y., 1953.

VE323. Fischel, Oskar. **Raphael.** 2 v. London, 1948.

VE324. Fiocco, Giuseppe. **Paolo Veronese, 1528–1588.** Bologna, 1928.

VE325. Walker, John. **Bellini and Titian at Ferrara: a study of styles and tastes.** N.Y., 1956. Definitive study of the *Camerino* of Alfonso d'Este at Ferrara, mainly devoted to Bellini's *Feast of the gods,* enriched by good illustrations and by many notes and appendices. [JSC]

VE326. Tietze, Hans. **Titian: paintings and drawings.** Vienna, 1937.

VE327. ——. **Tintoretto: the paintings and drawings.** N.Y., 1948.

VE328. Hartt, Frederick. **Giulio Romano.** 2 v. New Haven, 1958.

VE329. Sapori, Francesco. **Jacopo Tatti detto Il Sansovino.** Rome, 1928. Sansovino's work as architect and sculptor is well illustrated, documented, and supported by good bibliography. [JSC]

VE330. Vasari, Giorgio. **Le vite de' più eccellenti pittori, scultori ed architettori.** Ed. by Gaetano Milanesi. 9 v. Florence, 1878–85. Reprint, 1906. Tr. by Allen B. Hinds, *The lives of the painters, sculptors, and architects,* 4 v., London and N.Y., 1927. [Everyman's library.] Composed in the 16th century by a biographer who was himself a painter of note, this famous collection of lives of Italian artists of the Renaissance, while often unreliable, is an indispensable source for art history.

VE331. Friedlaender, Walter F. **Caravaggio studies.** Princeton, 1955. A landmark in art history which relates Caravaggio's religious paintings to the Counter-Reformation.

VE332. Wittkower, Rudolf. **Gian Lorenzo Bernini, the sculptor of the Roman baroque.** London, 1955. Includes authoritative *catalogue raisonnée* and bibliography.

VE333. Golzio, Vincenzo. **Il seicento e il settecento.** Turin, 1950. Encyclopedic study of Italian baroque, with several hundred illustrations. [JSC]

VE334. Wittkower, Rudolf. **Art and architecture in Italy, 1600 to 1750.** Baltimore, 1958. Excellent survey with 192 good plates and an invaluable bibliography. [JSC]

VE335. Ortolani, Sergio, Costanza Lorenzetti, and Michele Biancale. **La mostra della pittura napoletana dei secoli XVII-XVIII-XIX.** Naples, 1938. Best comprehensive history of Neapolitan painting. [JSC]

VE336. Lavagnino, Emilio. **L'arte moderna.** 2 v. Turin, 1956. Fullest and most thorough account of Italian art from neoclassical times to the present. [JSC]

VE337. Ballo, Guido. **Modern Italian painting: from futurism to the present day.** Tr. by Barbara Wall. N.Y., 1958.

VE338. Soby, James T., and Alfred H. Barr. **Twentieth-century Italian art.** N.Y., 1949. [Museum of Modern Art.] Good example of the books published by this museum. [JSC]

VE339. Voss, Hermann. **Die Malerei des Barock in Rom.** Berlin, 1924. Indispensable basic study for this topic. [JSC]

VE340. Moschini, Vittorio. **Canaletto.** Milan, 1954; London, 1955.

VE341. Fiocco, Giuseppe. **Francesco Guardi.** Florence, 1923. The classic biography. [JSC]

VE342. Focillon, Henri. **Giovanni-Batista Piranesi.** New ed., Paris, 1928. Standard. [JSC]

VE343. Gnudi, Cesare, and Gian Carlo Cavalli, eds. **Guido Reni.** Florence, 1955.

VE344. Morassi, Antonio. **G. B. Tiepolo: his life and work.** N.Y., 1955. Reliable. [JSC]

VE345. Clough, Rosa T. **Looking back at futurism.** N.Y., 1942. Retrospective survey of one phase of modern Italian art. Bibliography.

Literature

VE346. Sanctis, Francesco de. **Storia della letteratura italiana.** New rev. ed., 2 v., Bari, 1939. A literary classic, expressing the romantic nationalism of the time it was published (1870–71). Medieval and Renaissance literature receive the fullest treatment, with admirable chapters on the great figures of the 17th and 18th centuries. Very little on the 19th century.

VE347. Flora, Francesco. **Storia della letteratura italiana.** 7th ed., 5 v., Milan, 1952–53. A complete panorama of Italian literature, both biographical and critical in approach, almost half of which is devoted to the Renaissance. Lavishly illustrated; full bibliographies.

VE348. Wilkins, Ernest H. **A history of Italian literature.** Cambridge, Mass., 1954. Excellent comprehensive survey. Bibliography of works in English.

VE349. Storia letteraria d'Italia scritta da una società di professori. Milan, 1897 ff. A collaborative work of high quality including the following volumes relevant to this period: 4, Natalino Sapegno, *Il trecento* (6th rev. ed., 1952); 5, Vittorio Rossi, *Il quattrocento* (5th rev. ed., 1953); 6, Giuseppe Toffanin, *Il cinquecento* (3rd ed., 1929); 7, Antonio Belloni, *Il seicento* (2nd ed., 1952); 8, Giulio Natali, *Il settecento* (4th rev. ed., 2 v., 1955); 9, Guido Mazzoni, *L'ottocento* (3rd ed., 2 v., 1944); 10, Alfredo Galletti, *Il novecento* (3rd rev. ed., 1951).

Philosophy and Political Thought

Many works on various aspects and periods of Italian philosophy and political thought have already been noted.

VE350. Ruggiero, Guido de. **Storia della filosofia.** Bari, 1918. Other eds. A general work providing a comprehensive account of Italian philosophy. Also contains sections on Machiavelli and Guicciardini.

VE351. Saitta, Giuseppe. **Il pensiero italiano nell'umanesimo e nel Rinascimento.** 3 v. Bologna, 1949–51. Substantial work by a professional philosopher. Includes full consideration both of the 15th century humanists and later thinkers such as Bruno, Campanella, and Galileo.

VE352. Brunello, Bruno. **Il pensiero politico italiano del settecento.** Milan, 1942. Excellent synthetic account of Giannone, Muratori, Beccaria, and others.

VE353. Salvatorelli, Luigi. **Il pensiero politico italiano dal 1700 al 1870.** 5th rev. ed., Turin, 1949. Masterly survey stressing the currents of thought associated with the Risorgimento.

Legal and Constitutional History

VE354. Pertile, Antonio. **Storia del diritto italiano dalla caduta dell'impero romano alla codificazione.** 2nd rev. ed. by Pasquale del Giudice, 6 v. in 8 and index, Turin, 1892–1902. The standard work on Italian legal development, still valuable because of its unrivaled mastery of the printed sources. Pertile belonged to a generation which revered legal history. His footnotes are mines of reference to earlier literature and published documents.

VE355. Giudice, Pasquale del, ed. **Storia del diritto italiano.** 3 v. in 5. Milan, 1923–27. Cooperative work consisting of 2 v. on the sources and a comprehensive history of civil and criminal procedure.

VE356. Salvioli, Giuseppe. **Storia del diritto italiano.** 9th ed., Turin, 1930. Convenient 1 v. summary of Italian legal development.

VE357. Marongiù, Antonio. **L'istituto parlamentare in Italia dalle origini al 1500.** Milan, 1949. [Études présentées à la Commission Internationale pour l'Histoire des Assemblées d'États, 9.] Important work on a little-known subject, the Italian assemblies of estates.

VE358. Salzer, Ernst. **Ueber die Anfänge der Signorie in Oberitalien.** Berlin, 1900. Documented description of the anatomy of government in the northern Italian tyrannies.

VE359. Magni, Cesare. **Il tramonto del feudo lombardo.** Milan, 1937. Careful monograph on abolition of feudal tenures in Lombardy in the 18th and 19th centuries.

VE360. Falco, Giorgio. **Lo statuto albertino e la sua preparazione.** Rome, 1945. Thorough study of the making of the Sardinian constitution of 1849.

Church and State

VE361. Jemolo, Arturo C. **Chiesa e stato in Italia negli ultimi cento anni.** 2nd ed., Turin, 1952. Most noteworthy book on church-state relations to appear in Italy since World War II. The point of view is that of a liberal Catholic.

VE362. ——. **La questione romana.** Milan, 1938. Source book on the Roman question from 1861 to 1929.

VE363. Mollat, Guillaume. **La question romaine de Pie VI à Pie XI.** Paris, 1932.

The Roman question as seen by a French historian.

VE364. Jacini, Stefano. **La crisi religiosa del Risorgimento: la politica ecclesiastica italiana da Villafranca a Porta Pia.** Bari, 1938. Traces the policy of the Italian government toward the church from 1859 to 1870.

VE365. ——, ed. **Il tramonto del potere temporale nelle relazioni degli ambasciatori austriaci a Roma (1860–1870).** Bari, 1931. Account of the last decade of temporal power, based on reports of the Austrian ambassador in Rome.

VE366. Halperin, S. William. **Italy and the Vatican at war: a study of their relations from the outbreak of the Franco-Prussian War to the death of Pius IX.** Chicago, 1939. Documented analysis of the Roman question between 1870 and 1878 and the international tensions resulting therefrom.

VE367. Sturzo, Luigi. **Il partito popolare italiano.** Rev. ed., 3 v., Bologna, 1956–57. Collection of the writings and speeches of the founder and leader of the Italian Popular party from 1919 through 1924.

VE368. Binchy, Daniel A. **Church and state in Fascist Italy.** London and N.Y., 1941. This book, by a Catholic, includes good discussion of the historical background of the Roman question. Bibliography.

Economic History

VE369. Luzzatto, Gino. **Storia economica dell'età moderna e contemporanea.** Pt. 1, **L'età moderna.** 4th rev. ed., Padua, 1955. Pt. 2, **L'età contemporanea.** 3rd rev. ed., Padua, 1955. General economic history, by the acknowledged master of a generation of Italian economic historians, containing the best survey of Italian economic development from the Renaissance to the present day.

VE370. Fanfani, Amintore. **Le origini dello spirito capitalistico in Italia.** Milan, 1933. Detailed analysis of scholastic doctrines regarding wealth and of Italian economic practices and attitudes in the late Middle Ages and Renaissance.

VE371. ——. **Storia del lavoro in Italia dalla fine del secolo XV agli inizi del XVIII.** Milan, 1943. New ed., Milan, 1959.

VE372. Pane, Luigi dal. **Storia del lavoro in Italia dagli inizi del secolo XVIII al 1815.** Milan, 1944. 2nd ed., Milan, 1958.

VE373. ——. **Il tramonto delle corporazioni in Italia (secoli XVIII e XIX).** Milan, 1940. Reaction against the guild organization, studied from the sources.

VE374. Barbagallo, Corrado. **Le origini della grande industria contemporanea.** 2nd ed., Florence, 1951. Includes excellent panorama of Italian economy during the Risorgimento.

VE375. Corbino, Epicarmo. **Annali dell' economia italiana.** 5 v. Città di Castello, 1931–38. The most informative work on Italian economic history from 1860 to 1914.

VE376. Plebano, Achille. **Storia della finanza italiana dalla costituzione del nuovo regno alla fine del secolo XIX.** 3 v. Turin, 1899–1902. Standard authority on financial history.

VE377. Fossati, Antonio. **Lavoro e produzione in Italia dalla metà del secolo XVIII alla Seconda Guerra Mondiale.** Turin, 1951. Technical history of Italian industry based upon archives of some of the larger corporations. Bibliography.

VE378. Tremelloni, Roberto. **Storia dell' industria italiana.** V. 1, **Dalla fine del settecento all'unità d'Italia.** Turin, 1947. Industrial history of Italy before unification.

VE379. ——. **Storia recente dell' industria italiana.** Milan, 1956. Synthesis of Italian history since 1860.

Socialism and the Working Classes

VE380. Michels, Robert. **Sozialismus und Fascismus als politische Strömungen in Italien.** 2 v. Munich, 1925. Basic work on early history of socialism in Italy with an analysis of the sociology of fascism.

VE381. Romano, Aldo. **Storia del movimento socialista in Italia.** 3 v. Milan, 1954–56. First three of a projected six volumes by a historian who comes very close to the original Marxian conception of history. A work of learning written with passionate conviction, the most thorough study of 19th century socialism yet produced in Italy. V. 3 covers the period 1861–82.

VE382. Valiani, Leo. "La storia del movimento socialista in Italia dalle origini al 1921: studi e ricerche nel decennio 1945–1955." **Rivista storica italiana,** 68 (1956): 447–510, 620–69. A well documented review essay on the rapidly expanding literature of the socialist movement. Contains a wealth of references to earlier literature and discussions of sources.

VE383. Hostetter, Richard. **The Italian Socialist movement.** V. 1: **Origins (1860–1882).** Princeton, 1958. Objective synthesis and reappraisal of period covered.

VE384. Saitta, Armando. **Filippo Buonarroti: contributi alla storia della sua vita e del suo pensiero.** 2 v. Rome, 1950–51. Buonarroti (1761–1837) played an important role in the history of the French working classes and in formation of the Italian democratic tradition. This collection of studies is valuable for both Italian and French history and for the early history of socialism.

VE385. Bulferetti, Luigi. **Socialismo risorgimentale.** Turin, 1949. Socialist ideologies during the Risorgimento.

VE386. Romeo, Rosario. **Risorgimento e capitalismo.** Bari, 1959. Two essays, dealing respectively with Marxian historiography and Italian capitalism, 1861–87, challenge the Marxian interpretation of 19th century Italian history.

Naval and Colonial History

VE387. Manfroni, Camillo. **Storia della marina italiana dalla caduta di Costantinopoli alla battaglia di Lepanto.** 3 v. Leghorn and Rome, 1897–1902.

VE388. ——. **Storia della marina italiana durante la Guerra Mondiale, 1914–1918.** Bologna, 1923. Concluding volume in a series on the history of Italian sea power.

VE389. Bragadin, Marc'Antonio. **Repubbliche italiane sul mare.** Milan, 1951. French tr., *Histoire des républiques maritimes italiennes,* Paris, 1955. Popular synthesis, stressing the maritime and naval aspects of the history of Venice, Amalfi, Pisa, and Genoa.

VE390. ——. **Che ha fatto la marina?** **(1940–1945).** 3rd rev. ed., Milan, 1955. Tr. by Gale Hoffman, *The Italian navy in World War II,* Annapolis, 1957. History of Italian naval operations by a member of the high command who took part in the resistance.

VE391. Ciasca, Raffaele. **Storia coloniale dell' Italia contemporanea da Assab all' impero.** 2nd rev. ed., Milan, 1940. Italian colonial policy from 1869 to 1940. About half the book is devoted to Fascist colonial policy, which is related to Italy's foreign policy and internal problems.

For works on military history see *VE47* and *VE191.*

BIOGRAPHIES

This list supplements the biographical works already noted, and includes important studies of the intellectual development of Italian thinkers and statesmen.

Fourteenth Century

VE392. Tatham, Edward H. R. **Francesco Petrarca.** 2 v. London, 1925–26.

VE393. Hauvette, Henri. **Boccace: étude biographique et littéraire.** Paris, 1914.

VE394. Origo, Iris. **Tribune of Rome: a biography of Cola di Rienzo.** London, 1938.

VE395. Filippini, Francesco. **Il cardinale Egidio Albornoz.** Bologna, 1933.

Fifteenth Century

VE396. Armstrong, Edward. **Lorenzo de' Medici.** London and N.Y., 1896. Later eds.

VE397. Palmarocchi, Roberto. **Lorenzo de' Medici.** Turin, 1941.

VE398. Garin, Eugenio. **Giovanni Pico della Mirandola.** Florence, 1937.

VE399. Kristeller, Paul O. **Il pensiero filosofico di Marsilio Ficino.** Florence, 1953. The Italian edition, revised by the author, replaces an English version, *The philosophy of Marsilio Ficino* (N.Y., 1943).

VE400. Bignami, Luigi. **Francesco Sforza.** Milan, 1937.

VE401. Cognasso, Francesco. **Amedeo VIII.** 2 v. Turin, 1930.

VE402. Gregorovius, Ferdinand. **Lucrezia Borgia.** 2 v. Stuttgart, 1874. Eng. tr., London, 1948.

VE403. Vespasiano da Bisticci (1421–98). **Vite di uomini illustri del secolo XV.** Ed by Paolo d'Ancona and Erhard Aeschlimann. Milan, 1951. Tr., by William G. and Emily Waters, *The Vespasiano memoirs,* London, 1926. Includes a few men who were not Italians.

Sixteenth Century

VE404. Bainton, Roland H. **Bernardino Ochino, esule e riformatore senese del cinquecento, 1487–1563.** Tr. from the English manuscript by Elio Gianturco. Florence, 1941.

VE405. Cian, Vittorio. **Un illustre nunzio pontificio del Rinascimento, Baldassar Castiglione.** Vatican City, 1951.

VE406. Cellini, Benvenuto. **Life written by himself.** Tr. by John A. Symonds. London, Phaidon Press, 1949.

VE407. Duhem, Pierre. **Études sur Léonard de Vinci.** 3 v. Paris, 1955. Masterly studies of Leonardo as a scientist.

VE408. Vallentin, Antonina. **Léonard de Vinci.** Paris, 1939. Best popular biography.

VE409. Ferrara, Orestes. **Gasparo Contarini et ses missions.** Tr. from the Spanish by Francis de Miomandre. Paris, 1956. Animated semi-popular account of an Italian churchman of the Reformation period.

VE410. Lauts, Jan. **Isabella d'Este, Fürstin der Renaissance, 1474–1539.** Hamburg, 1952. French tr. by Germaine Welsch, Paris, 1956.

VE411. Chabod, Federico. **Giovanni Botero.** Rome, 1934.

VE412. Singer, Dorothea W. **Giordano Bruno, his life and thought.** N.Y., 1950. Excellent biography, with discussion of Bruno's influence on cosmological thought. Includes an annotated translation of Bruno's work, *On the infinite universe and worlds.*

VE413. Corsano, Antonio. **Tommaso Campanella.** Milan and Messina, 1944.

Seventeenth Century

VE414. Olschki, Leonardo. **Galilei und seine Zeit.** Halle, 1927.

VE415. Santillana, Giorgio de. **The crime**

of **Galileo.** Chicago, 1955. Brilliant account of the life and trial of Galileo which does not always furnish satisfactory evidence for the author's statements.

Eighteenth Century

VE416. Valeri, Nino. **Pietro Verri.** Milan, 1937.

VE417. Vianello, Carlo A. **La vita e l'opera di Cesare Beccaria.** Milan, 1938.

VE418. Vico, Giambattista. **The autobiography of Giambattista Vico.** Eng. tr. by Max H. Fisch and Thomas G. Bergin. Ithaca, 1944.

VE419. Venturi, Franco. **Saggi sull'Europa illuminista.** V. 1, **Alberto Radicato di Passerano.** Turin, 1954.

Nineteenth Century

VE420. Anzilotti, Antonio. **Gioberti.** Florence, 1922.

VE421. Bulferetti, Luigi. **Antonio Rosmini nella restaurazione.** Florence, 1942.

VE422. Cognasso, Francesco. **Vittorio Emanuele II.** Turin, 1942.

VE423. Ghisalberti, Alberto. **Massimo d'Azeglio, un moderato realizzatore.** Rome, 1953.

VE424. Jacini, Stefano. **Un conservatore rurale della nuova Italia.** 2 v. Bari, 1926.

VE425. Ledermann, László. **Pellegrino Rossi, l'homme et l'économiste, 1787–1848: une grande carrière internationale au XIXe siècle.** Paris, 1929.

VE426. Maturi, Walter. **Il principe di Canosa.** Florence, 1944.

VE427. Momigliano, Attilio. **Alessandro Manzoni.** 5th rev. ed., Milan, 1948.

VE428. Monti, Antonio. **Vittorio Emanuele II.** Milan, 1941.

VE429. Paléologue, Maurice. **Un grand réaliste, Cavour.** Paris, 1926. Eng. tr., by Ian F. and Muriel M. Morrow, *Cavour,* London, 1927.

VE430. Pane, Luigi dal. **Antonio Labriola: la vita e il pensiero.** Rome, 1935.

VE431. Passerin d'Entrèves, Ettore. **La giovinezza di Cesare Balbo.** Florence, 1940.

VE432. Ruffini, Francesco. **La vita religiosa di Alessandro Manzoni.** 2 v. Bari, 1931. Standard work. Stresses Jansenist influence on Manzoni

VE433. Sacerdote, Gustavo. **Giuseppe Garibaldi.** Milan, 1933.

VE434. Valori, Aldo. **Garibaldi.** Turin, 1941.

Twentieth Century

VE435. Borgese, Giuseppe A. **Gabriele d'Annunzio.** Milan, 1932.

VE436. Tagliacozzo, Enzo. **Gaetano Sal-** vemini nel cinquantennio liberale. Florence, 1959.

GOVERNMENT PUBLICATIONS

The Italian government through its various agencies has published numerous historical works, especially collections of source materials in government archives. The Chamber of Deputies, the Ministry of Foreign Affairs, and the Ministry of the Interior (in charge of the national archives) are particularly active in this regard. Current publications of official documents are listed monthly in *VE2.*

VE437. Italy. Parlamento. **Atti parlamentari.** Turin and Florence, 1860–74; Rome, 1874 ff. Index for first 20 legislatures (1848–1900), Rome, 1901. Issued in two divisions, for the Senate and Chamber of Deputies, and under each division in three categories: *Discussioni* (debates), *Disegni di legge e relazioni* (bills and committee reports), and *Documenti* (material submitted to Parliament by various ministries). In consulting these volumes, it is necessary to know the number of the legislature, which forms the basis of the entire classification.

VE438. Italy. Instituto Centrale della Statistica. **Annuario statistico italiano.** Rome, 1878 ff. Statistical information on the Italian government and economy.

ACADEMY AND SOCIETY PUBLICATIONS

For academy and society publications relating to Italian history see *VE30, 31, 145, 237,* and *450–457.* A current list of such publications appears in each issue of *VE8.*

VE439. **Annuario dell' Istituto Storico Italiano per l'Età Moderna e Contemporanea.** Bologna, 1935–38, 1953 ff. Organ of the central historical institute for modern history.

VE440. Deputazione di Storia Patria per la Provincie di Romagna. **Atti e memorie.** Bologna, 1862 ff. (Title varies.) Records the activities of one of the oldest local historical societies; often contains historical material of high quality. Every region of Italy has a similar *deputazione* or *società di storia patria.*

PERIODICALS

Each issue of *Bibliografia storica nazionale* (*VE8*) contains a useful list of Italian historical periodicals. See also

VE441. Kramm, Heinrich, ed. **Bibliographie historischer Zeitschriften, 1939–1951.** 3 v. Marburg, 1952–54. List of historical periodicals arranged by countries. Very useful for tracking down dates and places of publication and changes of title. See v. 2, pp. 175–95.

General

VE442. Archivio storico italiano. Florence, 1842 ff. (Frequency varies.) Cumulative index, 3 v., Florence, 1945–47.
VE443. Rivista storica italiana. Turin and Naples, 1884 ff. (Frequency varies.) Index (1884–1901), 2 v., Turin, 1904.
VE444. Nuova rivista storica. Milan, 1917 ff. (Irregular. Place of publication varies.)

Special Subjects or Periods

VE445. Rassegna storica del Risorgimento. Rome, etc., 1914 ff. (Irregular.) General index (1914–39) in v. 26 (1939): 11–126.
VE446. Rinascimento. Florence, 1950 ff. (Irregular.) Continuation of *La Rinascita* (Florence, 1938–44).
VE447. Rivista di storia della chiesa in Italia. Rome, 1947 ff. (3 times per year.)
VE448. Rivista di storia del diritto italiano. Rome, 1928–31; Bologna, 1932 ff. (Annual.)
VE449. Rivista di storia economica. Turin, 1936 ff. (Quarterly.)
VE450. Archivio della Società Romana di Storia Patria. Rome, 1877 ff. (Irregular.)
VE451. Archivio storico lombardo. Milan, 1874 ff. (Quarterly.) Index (1874–1923), 5 v., Milan, 1894–1929.
VE452. Archivio storico per la Calabria e la Lucania. Rome, 1931 ff. (Quarterly.)
VE453. Archivio storico per la Sicilia. Palermo, 1937–44, 1946 ff. (Annual.) Successor to *Archivio storico siciliano,* Palermo, 1873–1934 (irregular); index (1873–1900), Palermo, 1902.
VE454. Archivio storico per le provincie napoletane. Naples, 1876 ff. (Irregular.) Index (1876–1900), 2 v., Naples, 1897–1902.
VE455. Archivio storico per le provincie parmensi. Parma, 1892 ff. (Irregular.)

VE456. Archivio veneto. Venice, 1871 ff. (Irregular. Title varies.) Index (1871–1930), 2 v., Venice, 1935–41.
VE457. Bollettino storico-bibliografico subalpino. Turin, 1896 ff. (Irregular.)

Postwar Periodicals

VE458. Belfagor. Florence, 1946 ff. (Bimonthly.)
VE459. Movimento operaio: rivista di storia e bibliografia. Milan, 1949 ff. (Bimonthly.) Published by the Feltrinelli Library.
VE460. Il ponte. Florence, 1945 ff. (Monthly.)
VE461. Rinascita. Rome, 1944 ff. (Monthly.) Index (1944–55), Rome, 1955. Organ of the Communist party.
VE462. Società. Florence and Rome, 1945 ff. (Bimonthly.) Marxist orientation.

Discontinued Periodicals

VE463. Critica sociale. Milan, 1891–1922. (Bimonthly.) Principal organ of the Independent Socialist party.
VE464. La critica. Naples, 1903–44. (Bimonthly.) Index (1903–10), Bari, 1910; supplement, 1913. Organ of Benedetto Croce. Surveys and comments on literary and philosophical movements.
VE465. Quaderni della "Critica." Bari, 1945–51. (Irregular.) Continuation of *La critica.*

ADDENDUM

VE466. Quaderni e riviste d'Italia: repertorio bibliografico. Rome, 1958 ff. (Twice a year.) This new compendium of publications issued in Italy replaces *VE2* as a bibliographical guide for the general reader.

Germany, Austria, and Switzerland

HAJO HOLBORN *

The modern literature of German history, which has been accumulating since Ranke created new standards of historical research more than a century ago, is enormously voluminous and many-sided. No country possessed as many organizations devoted to the systematic study of its national, regional, and local history as Germany did during most of the last century; and they sprang from greatly different political, religious, and scholarly interests. While compilation of a concise bibliography of German history must meet the obvious difficulties which a selection from such vast materials offers, it cannot hope to do more in the annotations than hint at the variety of standpoints reflected in individual works.

Ranke expressed the opinion that no German history could be written except as an integral part of the history of Europe. Many of the most eminent German historians followed him in this conception, with the result that some of the best treatments of some periods of German history are to be found in works of German authors dealing with European history. These had no place in this section. Likewise, primary and secondary writings concerned exclusively with the diplomatic history of Germany, Austria, and Switzerland should be sought in Sections T and AH.

Within this section the decision on whether a work should be classified under national or territorial history could be only a relative one in the case of Austria and Prussia. In the Austrian subsection are books dealing with the history either of the Austrian German lands or of the Hapsburg policy in building and governing an Austrian, as distinct from the German, empire. The history of the first Austrian republic has been included, whereas the history of all those non-German territories which the Hapsburgs lost between the French Revolution and the end of World War I (Netherlands, Italy, Bohemia, Hungary, Galicia, etc.) have been excluded from this section.

Switzerland has been treated as a separate national history because the Swiss confederation actually ceased to belong to the Holy Roman Empire.

* Technical assistance in preparing this section was rendered by John G. Gagliardo, who also contributed items and comments indicated by initials JGG; a few comments, signed LK, were contributed by Leonard Krieger; and several items on art and the comments indicated by JSC were supplied by Judith S. Cousins.

BIBLIOGRAPHIES

VF1. Dahlmann, Friedrich C., and Georg Waitz. **Quellenkunde der deutschen Geschichte.** Ed. by Hermann Haering and others. 9th ed., 2 v., Leipzig, 1931–32. The slim bibliographical guide which two Göttingen professors prepared for their own students more than a century ago has developed, under auspices of the Association of German Historians, into the most massive handbook of primary and secondary literature of German history. All periods and fields are covered. A new edition is in preparation.

VF2. **Jahresberichte für deutsche Geschichte.** Ed. by Albert Brackmann and Fritz Hartung. Leipzig, 1927–40, 1949 ff. Extensive and reliable bibliographical annual.

VF3. Franz, Günther. **Bücherkunde zur deutschen Geschichte.** Munich, 1951. Useful bibliographical guide, selective but listing the major works published between 1931 and 1951 not represented in Dahlmann-Waitz.

VF4. Schottenloher, Karl, ed. **Bibliographie zur deutschen Geschichte im Zeitalter der Glaubensspaltung, 1517–1585.** 6 v. Leipzig, 1933–40. Complete listing of all publications issued in Germany during the 70 years after 1517 and of modern historical literature of the period.

VF5. Wolf, Gustav. **Quellenkunde der deutschen Reformationsgeschichte.** 3 v. Gotha, 1915–23. Extensive description and discussion of the sources and literature of the German Reformation.

VF6. Schnabel, Franz. **Deutschlands geschichtliche Quellen und Darstellungen in der Neuzeit.** V. 1. Leipzig and Berlin, 1931. Useful introduction to sources and literature of the German Reformation, by an eminent historian; designed for the beginner.

GEOGRAPHIES AND ATLASES

VF7. Putzger, Friedrich W. **Historischer Schul-Atlas.** Ed. by Alfred Hansel. 63rd ed., Bielefeld, 1954. 67th ed., 1956. Standard hand-atlas used for historical study in German high schools and universities. Although ancient as well as European and world history receive attention, emphasis is on extremely well-executed maps of medieval and modern Germany.

VF8. Kretschmer, Konrad. **Historische Geographie von Mitteleuropa.** Munich, 1904. Best book on German historical geography; a mine of critical information to the middle of the 18th century.

VF9. Hofmann, Albert von. **Das deutsche Land und die deutsche Geschichte.** Stuttgart, 1921. Valuable study of the impact of geographical factors on the history of Germany and her regions.

VF10. Dickinson, Robert E. **The regions of Germany.** London, 1945. Penetrating discussion of the various regions of Germany.

PRINTED COLLECTIONS OF SOURCES

VF11. Zeumer, Karl. **Quellensammlung zur Geschichte der deutschen Reichsverfassung in Mittelalter und Neuzeit.** 4th ed., 2 v., Tübingen, 1926. Collection of documents illustrative of the history of the German constitution, by one of the foremost legal historians of Germany.

VF12. **Nuntiaturberichte aus Deutschland nebst ergänzenden Aktenstücken.** Ed. by the Preussischen Institut of Rome and other organizations. Paderborn, Gotha, etc., 1892 ff. This extensive work, in four series, is supposed to publish all reports of papal nuncios from establishment of the first standing nunciatura in 1533 until 1648.

VF13. **Publikationen aus den Königlichen Preussischen Staatsarchiven, veranlasst und unterstützt durch die Archiv-verwaltung.** 94 v. Leipzig, 1878–1938. One of the most important series of source publications for the history of Prussia and her provinces.

VF14. **Schriftenreihe der Staatlichen Archiv-verwaltung der Deutschen Demokratischen Republik.** Berlin, 1952 ff. A series of monographs based on documents from the former Prussian archives, now in possession of the (East) German Democratic Republic. The ideological slant of the publications is clearly recognizable.

VF15. **Deutsche Geschichtsquellen des 19. und 20. Jahrhunderts.** Berlin, Stuttgart, etc., 1919 ff. [Akademie der Wissenschaften, Historische Kommission.] Most significant series of modern source publications, centering so far chiefly on 1815–90.

VF16. Hohlfeld, Johannes, ed. **Deutsche Reichsgeschichte in Dokumenten.** 4 v. Berlin, 1934. Useful compilation of basic documents illustrating the history of the German empire between 1848 and 1933.

VF17. **Die Ursachen des deutschen Zusammenbruches im Jahre 1918.** 12 v. Berlin, 1925–29. [Das Werk des Untersuchungsausschusses der deutschen Verfassunggebenden Nationalversammlung und des deutschen Reichstages, ser. 4.] Report of the Reichstag committee investigating causes of the German collapse in 1918. Contains numerous documents, testimony of witnesses, and memoranda of historical experts.

VF18. International Military Tribunal. **Trial of the major war criminals before the International Military Tribunal, Nuremberg, 14 November, 1945–1 October, 1946.** 42 v. Nuremberg, 1947–49. The record of the Nuremberg trial, with its interrogations, documentary exhibits, and court proceedings, is a major source for study of the Nazi regime.

HISTORIOGRAPHY

VF19. Srbik, Heinrich, Ritter von. **Geist und Geschichte vom deutschen Humanismus bis zur Gegenwart.** 2 v. Munich, 1950–51. History of German historiography since about 1500, by a learned and discerning historian.

VF20. Below, Georg A. H. von. **Die deutsche Geschichtsschreibung von den Befreiungskriegen bis zu unseren Tagen.** See *A428.*

GENERAL HISTORIES

VF21. Henderson, Ernest F. **A short history of Germany.** 2nd ed., 2 v., N.Y., 1937. Largest general German history in English, written on basis of secondary works. First issued more than fifty years ago and little changed in second edition, it is now inadequate for critical study.

VF22. Lamprecht, Karl G. **Deutsche Geschichte.** 12 v. Berlin, 1891–1909. Most extensive treatment of German history, by a German scholar of great knowledge and accomplishment. Marred by author's attempt to demonstrate the scientific laws of history he found in a peculiar system of social psychology.

VF23. ———. **Deutsche Geschichte der jüngsten Vergangenheit und Gegenwart.** 2 v. Berlin, 1912–13. An outdated continuation of the above to beginning of the 20th century.

VF24. Valentin, Veit. **The German people: their history and civilization.** N.Y., 1946. General introduction to German history.

VF25. Flenley, Ralph. **Modern German history.** London, 1953. Useful survey of modern Germany, emphasizing intellectual and social factors.

VF26. Gebhardt, Bruno. **Handbuch der deutschen Geschichte.** Ed. by Herbert Grundmann and others. 8th ed., 2 v., Stuttgart, 1954–55. This handbook, originally written by B. Gebhardt, served generations of students as a study guide. It has been completely rewritten by a group of German scholars, and enables the reader to gain information on the state of research in German history.

VF27. Deutsche Geschichte in Überblick: ein Handbuch. Ed. by Peter Rassow. Stuttgart, 1952 ff. Another cooperative handbook of German history, more concise than the above.

VF28. Holborn, Hajo. **A history of modern Germany: the Reformation.** N.Y., 1959. First volume of a history of Germany from the late Middle Ages to the fall of the third empire, covering institutional, political, religious, intellectual, social, and economic developments. This volume extends to 1648. [LK]

VF29. Gooch, George P. **Studies in German history.** London and N.Y., 1948. Collection of articles on German history by a distinguished English historian.

VF30. Pinson, Koppel S. **Modern Germany, its history and civilization.** N.Y., 1954. History of Germany from 1815, and in more detail from 1848 to the present. Emphasis is on Nazi and post-World War II period.

HISTORIES OF SPECIAL PERIODS

Age of Reformation, 1495–1648

VF31. Ranke, Leopold von. **History of the Reformation in Germany.** 3 v. London, 1845–47. Tr. by Sarah Austin from *Deutsche Geschichte im Zeitalter der Reformation* (6 v., Berlin, 1839–47). Historical-critical ed. by Paul Joachimsen, 6 v., Munich, 1925–26. Ranke's great work opened modern research in German Reformation history, and still deserves to be consulted.

VF32. Janssen, Johannes. **History of the German people at the close of the Middle Ages.** 17 v. London, 1896–1925. Tr. by A. M. Christie and M. A. Mitchell from *Geschichte des deutschen Volkes seit dem Ausgang des Mittelalters* (8 v., 1876–94). Treats the Protestant Reformation as cause of the decay of Germany in the 16th century. Though strongly biased, it has the merit of emphasizing cultural as well as political history.

VF33. Bezold, Friedrich von. **Geschichte der deutschen Reformation.** Berlin, 1890. A well-rounded history by an eminent scholar.

VF34. Brandi, Karl. **Deutsche Reformation und Gegenreformation.** 2 v. Leipzig, 1927–30. Concise treatment of 1495–1648 period in the Bezold tradition.

VF35. Joachimsen, Paul. **Die Reformation als Epoche der deutschen Geschichte.** Ed. by Otto Schottenloher. Munich, 1951. Relatively brief presentation by one of the foremost scholars of German humanism and Protestantism.

VF36. Deutsche Reichstagakten. 2 ser., 24 v. Munich and Gotha, 1867–1939. [Akademie der Wissenschaften, Historische Kommission.] Started at the instigation of Ranke, the volumes illustrate history of the imperial diets since the 15th century.

VF37. Politische Korrespondenz Strassburgs aus der Reformationszeit. Ed. by Otto Winckelmann and others. 5 v. Strasbourg and Heidelberg, 1882–1933. [Urkunden und Akten der Stadt Strassburg.] Important source publication for history of German politics in the Reformation period.

VF38. Quellen und Forschungen zur Reformationsgeschichte. Leipzig, 1911 ff. (Irregular.) A substantial series of monographs, published by the Verein für Reformationsgeschichte.

VF39. Ulmann, Heinrich. **Kaiser Maximilian I.** 2 v. Stuttgart, 1884–91. Best, though somewhat dated, study of the emperor.

VF40. Brandi, Karl. **The emperor Charles V: the growth and destiny of a man and a world empire.** London, 1939. Tr. by C. V. Wedgwood from *Kaiser Karl V: Werden und Schicksal einer Persönlichkeit und eines Weltreiches* (Munich, 1937). Masterful biography.

VF41. Kirn, Paul. **Friedrich der Weise und die Kirche.** Leipzig, 1926. Basic study of the elector's ecclesiastical politics prior to 1518.

VF42. Hutten, Ulrich von. **Opera et operum supplementum.** Ed. by E. Böcking. 7 v. Leipzig, 1859–70. This source work contains not only Hutten's Latin and German writings, but his correspondence, documents related to his activities. V. 7 includes the "Letters of obscure men."

VF43. Holborn, Hajo. **Ulrich von Hutten and the German Reformation.** New Haven and London, 1937. Tr. by Roland H. Bainton from *Ulrich von Hutten* (Leipzig, 1929). The authoritative work on Hutten and his relation to German humanism and the Lutheran Reformation. [LK]

VF44. Fellner, Robert. **Die fränkische Ritterschaft von 1495–1524.** Berlin, 1905. Study of conditions of the imperial knights.

VF45. Rosenkranz, Albert E. **Der Bundschuh: die Erhebungen des südwestdeutschen Bauernstandes in den Jahren 1493–1517.** 2 v. Heidelberg, 1927. Peasant revolts prior to the Peasants' War.

VF46. Franz, Günther. **Der deutsche Bauernkrieg.** 2 v. Munich and Berlin, 1933–35. Fullest treatment of the Peasants' War (1524–25), with documents and bibliography.

VF47. Luther, Martin. **D. Martin Luthers Werke: kritische Gesamtausgabe.** 86 v. Weimar, 1883–1957. Monumental critical edition of Luther's writings, correspondence, table-talks, and German Bible.

VF48. ———. **The table talk of Martin Luther.** Ed. by Thomas S. Kepler. N.Y., 1952. Based on William Hazlitt's tr. of *Dr. Martin Luthers Tischreden.* English selections from Luther's table-talks.

VF49. Scheel, Otto. **Dokumente zu Luthers Entwicklung.** 2nd ed., Tübingen, 1929. Useful critical collection of documents illustrative of Luther's development prior to 1517.

VF50. ———. **Martin Luther: vom Katholizismus zur Reformation.** 3rd ed., 2 v., Tübingen, 1921–30. These first two volumes of an unfinished historical biography, planned on the largest possible scale, are the most extensive presentation of the conditions of Luther's early life.

VF51. Böhmer, Heinrich. **Road to Reformation.** Philadelphia, 1946. Tr. by John W. Doberstein and Theodore G. Tappert from *Der junge Luther* (2nd ed., Gotha, 1929). Solid, critical biography of Luther to 1521, by a leading Protestant church historian.

VF52. Holl, Karl. **Gesammelte Aufsätze zur Kirchengeschichte.** V. 1, **Luther.** Tübingen, 1932. Collected articles which ushered in a new interpretation of Luther's religion and theology.

VF53. Lortz, Joseph. **Die Reformation in Deutschland.** 3rd ed., 2 v., Freiburg, 1949. The outstanding work on Luther and the religious movements in 16th century Germany, by a Roman Catholic historian.

VF54. Bainton, Roland H. **Here I stand: a life of Martin Luther.** See *D472.*

VF55. Melanchthon, Philipp. **Philippi Melanthonis opera quae supersunt omnia.** Ed. by Karl Gottlieb Bretschneider. 28 v. Halle and Brunswick, 1834–60. First part of the *Corpus reformatorum,* begun in 1834. The editorial methods are not fully adequate and a number of Melanchthon's works are missing.

VF56. Ellinger, Georg. **Philipp Melanchthon: ein Lebensbild.** Berlin, 1902. Relatively best biography of Melanchthon.

VF57. Kidd, Beresford J. **The Counter-Reformation, 1550–1600.** London, 1933. Brief survey, with emphasis on doctrinal and theological developments. [JGG]

VF58. Ritter, Moriz. **Deutsche Geschichte im Zeitalter der Gegenreformation und des dreissigjährigen Krieges.** 3 v. Stuttgart, 1889–1908. Standard work on German history between 1555 and 1648.

VF59. Wedgwood, Cicely V. **The Thirty Years' War.** London, 1938. History of high scholarly and literary merit.

VF60. Pekař, Josef. **Wallenstein, 1630–1634: Tragödie einer Verschwörung.** 2 v. Berlin, 1937. Chief critical study of Wallenstein, by a leading Czech historian.

VF61. Srbik, Heinrich, Ritter von. **Wallensteins Ende.** Vienna, 1920. Monographic treatment of Wallenstein's death.

VF62. Braubach, Max. **Der Westfälische Friede.** Münster, 1948. Brief appraisal of the Westphalian peace settlement.

VF63. Franz, Günther. **Der dreissigjährige Krieg und das deutsche Volk.** 2nd ed., Jena, 1943. Impact of the Thirty Years' War on the German population.

The Age of Absolutism, 1648–1789

VF64. Erdmannsdörffer, Bernhard. **Deutsche Geschichte vom Westfälischen Frieden bis zum Regierungsantritt Friedrichs des Grossen.** 2 v. Berlin, 1892–93. In spite of its age and some uneven sections, this work remains the best relatively detailed survey of the period. [JGG]

VF65. Pribram, Alfred F. **Franz Paul, Freiherr von Lisola—1613–1674—und die**

Politik seiner Zeit. Leipzig, 1894. Best study on the Austrian diplomat and statesman.

VF66. Atkinson, Christopher T. **A history of Germany, 1715–1815.** London, 1908. Good, though unoriginal, general history of political and military development; neglects other aspects. [JGG]

VF67. Urkunden und Aktenstücke zur Geschichte des Kurfürsten Friedrich Wilhelm von Brandenburg. Ed. by Bernhard Erdmannsdörffer and others. 23 v. in 26. Berlin, 1864–1929. Diplomatic correspondence and documents from the internal administration illustrating full scope of the political activities of the Great Elector.

VF68. Ergang, Robert R. **The Potsdam Führer.** N.Y., 1941. Only biography of the king (Frederick William I) in English. [JGG]

VF69. Dorwart, Reinhold A. **The administrative reforms of Frederick William I of Prussia.** Cambridge, Mass., 1953. Valuable as a clear survey of administrative changes under Frederick William I. [JGG]

VF70. Koser, Reinhold. **Geschichte Friedrichs des Grossen.** 4th and 5th eds., 4 v., Berlin, 1912–14. These volumes are examples of excellent political biography, and their value is enhanced by a detailed attention to bibliography, which is virtually complete to date of publication. Treatment of Frederick is sympathetic, but not indiscriminately so. [JGG]

VF71. Reddaway, William F. **Frederick the Great and the rise of Prussia.** London, 1904. Good, well-written sketch of Frederick and his influence on Prussia's development; accords him favorable judgment. [JGG]

VF72. Gooch, George P. **Frederick the Great, the ruler, the writer, the man.** London and N.Y., 1947. This and the following are two modern critical appraisals of the Prussian king by eminent English and German historians respectively.

VF73. Ritter, Gerhard. **Friedrich der Grosse: ein historisches Profil.** 3rd ed., Heidelberg, 1954.

VF74. Frederick II, the Great. Politische Correspondenz Friedrich's des Grossen. Ed. by Gustav Droysen and others. 46 v. Berlin, 1879–1939. Well-edited and invaluable collection of Frederick's political and diplomatic correspondence. [JGG]

VF75. ——. **Œuvres de Frédéric le Grand.** Ed. by Johann D. E. Preuss and others. 30 v. Berlin, 1846–57. Frederick's essays, poetical and philosophical writings, and literary correspondence, as well as some political and military pieces. [JGG]

VF76. Easum, Chester V. **Prince Henry of Prussia, brother of Frederick the Great.** Madison, Wis., 1942. Relatively detailed biography. [JGG]

VF77. Braubach, Max. **Max Franz von Österreich, letzter Kurfürst von Köln und**

Fürstbischof von Münster. Münster, 1925. Good study of one of the last ecclesiastical princes of the empire in the Age of Enlightenment.

VF78. Bruford, Walter H. **Germany in the eighteenth century: the social background of the literary revival.** Cambridge, Eng., 1935. Useful and readable survey of German society in the 18th century; descriptive and general rather than critical and detailed. [JGG]

VF79. Biedermann, Karl. **Deutschland im achtzehnten Jahrhundert.** 4 v. Leipzig, 1867–80. Old but very substantial cultural and intellectual history of the German 18th century, by a careful scholar. [JGG]

VF80. Small, Albion W. **The Cameralists, the pioneers of German social polity.** Chicago, 1909. Thorough and detailed examination of the philosophies of a number of German Cameralists. Scholarly but unimaginative treatment. [JGG]

Reform, Liberation, Restoration, and Revolution, 1789–1850

VF81. Gooch, George P. **Germany and the French Revolution.** London and N.Y., 1920. Impact of the French Revolution on philosophical and literary movements in Germany.

VF82. Droz, Jacques. **L'Allemagne et la Révolution Française.** See *T309.*

VF83. Aris, Reinhold. **History of political thought in Germany from 1789 to 1815.** London, 1936. General history of German political theories in the period of the French Revolution and Napoleon.

VF84. Pinson, Koppel S. **Pietism as a factor in the rise of German nationalism.** N.Y., 1934. This and *VF85* are studies of the sources of early German nationalism.

VF85. Ergang, Robert R. **Herder and the foundations of German nationalism.** N.Y., 1931.

VF86. McEachran, Frank. **The life and philosophy of Johann Gottfried Herder.** Oxford, 1939. Historical biography.

VF87. Fisher, Herbert A. L. **Studies in Napoleonic statesmanship: Germany.** Oxford, 1903. Series of studies on the states of the Rhenish confederation.

VF88. Meinecke, Friedrich. **Das Zeitalter der deutschen Erhebung (1795–1815).** 6th ed., Göttingen, 1957. Brief historical synthesis by a distinguished historian.

VF89. Seeley, Sir John R. **Life and times of Stein: or Germany and Prussia in the Napoleonic age.** 3 v. Cambridge, Eng., 1878. Chief English work on the period; still useful though somewhat outdated in viewpoint and material.

VF90. Ford, Guy Stanton. **Stein and the era of reform in Prussia, 1807–1815.** Princeton, 1922. Good introduction to problems of the Prussian reform.

VF91. Simon, Walter M. **The failure of the Prussian reform movement, 1807–1819.** Ithaca, 1955. Searching study of the intent and frustration of the Prussian reform legislation.

VF92. Lehmann, Max. **Freiherr vom Stein.** 3 v. Leipzig, 1902–05. Historical biography of high merit.

VF93. Meier, Ernst von. **Französische Einflüsse auf die Staats- und Rechtsentwicklung Preussens im XIX. Jahrhundert.** 2 v. Leipzig, 1907–08. This and *VF94* were written largely to minimize the French influence on Stein and Hardenberg, as assumed by Max Lehmann. Although this thesis is not tenable, the studies are useful for their close exploration of Prussian administration.

VF94. ———. **Die Reform der Verwaltungsorganisation unter Stein und Hardenberg.** 2nd ed., Leipzig, 1912.

VF95. Ritter, Gerhard. **Stein: eine politische Biographie.** 3rd ed., Stuttgart, 1958. Modern biography of Stein by an eminent German historian.

VF96. Knapp, Georg F. **Die Bauernbefreiung und der Ursprung der Landarbeiter in den älteren Theilen Preussens.** 2 v. Munich and Leipzig, 1887. Classic work on agrarian reforms in the eastern provinces of Prussia and their social consequences.

VF97. Shanahan, William O. **Prussian military reforms, 1786–1813.** N.Y. and London, 1945. Special study of Prussian military reorganization from the death of Frederick the Great to the War of Liberation.

VF98. Lehmann, Max. **Scharnhorst.** 2 v. Leipzig, 1886–87. Standard biography, not yet replaced, though somewhat antiquated in analysis and evaluation.

VF99. Delbrück, Hans. **Das Leben des Generalfeldmarschalls Grafen Neithardt von Gneisenau.** 3rd ed., 2 v., Berlin, 1908. Richly documented historical biography.

VF100. Meinecke, Friedrich. **Das Leben des Generalfeldmarschalls Hermann von Boyen.** 2 v. Stuttgart, 1896–99. Historical biography of the liberal reformer of the Prussian army, by one of the foremost historians of the period.

VF101. Gebhardt, Bruno. **Wilhelm von Humboldt als Staatsmann.** 2 v. Stuttgart, 1896–99. Solid, if somewhat pedestrian, study of Humboldt's political activities. Indispensable on account of its documentation.

VF102. Kaehler, Siegfried A. **Wilhelm v. Humboldt und der Staat: ein Beitrag zur Geschichte deutscher Lebensgestaltung um 1800.** Munich and Berlin, 1927. Penetrating, if overly critical, study of Humboldt's thoughts and actions.

VF103. Meusel, Friedrich. **Friedrich August Ludwig von der Marwitz: ein märkischer Edelmann im Zeitalter der Befreiungskriege.**

3 v. Berlin, 1908–13. Chief source of the life and thought of the foremost conservative opponent of the Prussian reformers.

VF104. Sweet, Paul R. **Friedrich von Gentz, defender of the old order.** Madison, Wis., 1941. This and *VF105* are valuable studies on Metternich's secretary and confidant.

VF105. Mann, Golo. **Secretary of Europe: the life of Friedrich Gentz, enemy of Napoleon.** New Haven and London, 1946.

VF106. Treitschke, Heinrich von. **History of Germany in the nineteenth century.** 7 v. N.Y., 1915–19. Tr. by Eden and Cedar Paul from *Deutsche Geschichte im neunzehnten Jahrhundert* (5 v., Leipzig, 1890–96). The strong Prussian nationalist sentiment of Treitschke is well known. Although much non-Prussian material was left unused, the work is still the fullest treatment of German history from about 1800 to the eve of the revolution of 1848.

VF107. Schnabel, Franz. **Deutsche Geschichte im neunzehnten Jahrhundert.** 4 v. Freiburg, 1929–37. This outstanding history narrates the general development in v. 1–2 down to the 1820's. V. 3 deals with the growth of modern sciences, v. 4 with the life of the churches in Germany in the first half of the 19th century.

VF108. Srbik, Heinrich, Ritter von. **Deutsche Einheit: Idee und Wirklichkeit vom Heiligen Reich bis Königgrätz.** 4 v. Munich, 1935–42. Most extensive history of the problem of German unity in thought and practice from the 18th century to 1866, written by a prominent Austrian historian in the hope of overcoming the division of kleindeutsch and grossdeutsch interpretation. Although not unaffected by German nationalist sentiment of the period, the work is valuable for its many fresh insights and its wealth of information.

VF109. Meinecke, Friedrich. **Weltbürgertum und Nationalstaat.** 7th ed., Munich and Berlin, 1928. Classic treatise of the development of German nationalism from the age of Kant and Goethe to that of Bismarck.

VF110. Rosenzweig, Franz. **Hegel und der Staat.** 2 v. Munich, 1920. Best historical and biographical study of the evolution of Hegel's political philosophy.

VF111. Heller, Hermann. **Hegel und der nationale Machtstaatsgedanke in Deutschland: ein Beitrag zur politischen Geistesgeschichte.** Leipzig, 1921. Useful, although somewhat simplified and exaggerated, study of Hegel's influence on the growth of the concept of a "power-state" in 19th century Germany.

VF112. Müsebeck, Ernst. **Ernst Moritz Arndt.** Gotha, 1914. Standard biography of one of the chief ideological fathers of the German national movement between 1813 and 1848.

VF113. Krieger, Leonard. **The German idea of freedom.** Boston, 1957. A deeply penetrating analysis of the German conception of freedom seen against the background of political and social change from the 18th to 20th century.

VF114. Droz, Jacques. **Le libéralisme rhénan, 1815–1848: contribution à l'histoire du libéralisme allemand.** Paris, 1940. Valuable study of the liberal movement in the Rhineland.

VF115. Thomas, Richard H. **Liberalism, nationalism, and the German intellectuals (1822–1847).** Cambridge, Eng., 1952. Study of the agitation and activities of professors and scientists for the promotion of national unity.

VF116. Oncken, Hermann, and F. E. M. Saemisch. **Vorgeschichte und Begründung des deutschen Zollvereins, 1815–1834: Akten der Staaten des deutschen Bundes und der europäischen Mächte.** 3 v. Berlin, 1934. Critical source publication on the origins of the Prussian-German customs union.

VF117. Henderson, William O. **The Zollverein.** Cambridge, Eng., 1939. Best study of the origins and history of the German customs union.

VF118. Hamerow, Theodore. **Restoration, revolution, reaction: economics and politics in Germany, 1815–1871.** Princeton, 1958. Examination of the impact of social and economic change on German political history.

National Unification and Empire, 1850–1918

VF119. Brandenburg, Erich. **Die Reichsgründung.** 2nd ed., 2 v., Leipzig, 1923. Best political history of German unification from 1848 to 1871.

VF120. Ziekursch, Johannes. **Politische Geschichte des neuen deutschen Kaiserreiches.** 3 v. Frankfurt-am-Main, 1925–30. Political history of Germany from 1848 to 1918, by a liberal German historian, written in the days of the Weimar Republic. V. 1 covers the period of national unification, v. 2 the empire under Bismarck, v. 3 the empire under William II.

VF121. Stadelmann, Rudolf. **Soziale und politische Geschichte der Revolution von 1848.** Munich, 1948. Best critical discussion of the historical problems of the German revolution of 1848.

VF122. Valentin, Veit. **1848: chapters of German history.** London, 1940. Tr. and abr. by Ethel T. Scheffauer from *Geschichte der deutschen Revolution von 1848–49* (2 v., Berlin, 1930–31). This German work, of which only some sections have been translated into English, is the most extensive study of the German revolution. It is

stronger in narration than in critical appraisal.

VF123. Namier, Sir Lewis B. **1848: the revolution of the intellectuals.** London, 1944. Brilliant though somewhat one-sided essay on the nationalism of intellectual leaders of the central European revolutions.

VF124. Anderson, Eugene N. **The social and political conflict in Prussia, 1858–1864.** Lincoln, Neb., 1954. [University of Nebraska studies, new ser., 12.] Detailed analysis of Prussian society during the constitutional conflict.

VF125. Friedjung, Heinrich. **The struggle for supremacy in Germany, 1859–1866.** London, 1935. Tr. and abr. by Alan J. P. Taylor and W. L. McElwee from *Der Kampf um die Vorheerschaft in Deutschland 1859 bis 1866* (10th ed., 2 v., Stuttgart, 1916–17). Outstanding history of the Austro-Prussian conflict over hegemony in Germany, though written before opening of the Austrian and German archives. The English edition omits chiefly the military history.

VF126. Darmstaedter, Friedrich. **Bismarck and the creation of the Second Reich.** London, 1948. Brief study of German unification, largely confined to political events.

VF127. Zechlin, Egmont. **Bismarck und die Grundlegung der deutschen Grossmacht.** Stuttgart and Berlin, 1930. Most thorough study of Bismarck's policies in the years 1862–63.

VF128. Steefel, Lawrence D. **The Schleswig-Holstein question.** See *VB86*.

VF129. **Bismarck and the Hohenzollern candidature for the Spanish throne: the documents in the German Diplomatic Archives.** Ed. by Georges Bonnin, tr. by Isabella M. Massey. London, 1958. Documents, kept secret by former German governments, revealing Bismarck's activities in the Spanish throne candidacy of the Hohenzollern prince.

VF130. Dawson, William H. **The German empire, 1867–1914, and the unity movement.** 2 v. London, 1919. English work, outdated in many respects, particularly in international policies, but still valuable for social and economic policies.

VF131. Meyer, Arnold O. **Bismarck, der Mensch und der Staatsmann.** Stuttgart, 1949. Historical biography that epitomizes a half-century of admiring and sympathetic, though not uncritical, Bismarck research in Germany.

VF132. Eyck, Erich. **Bismarck and the German empire.** London, 1950. Brief English summary of historical findings of the liberal author's extensive Bismarck study, as contained in his larger German work.

VF133. ——. **Bismarck: Leben und Werk.** 3 v. Zürich, 1941–44. Most extensive biography, written by a liberal historian who does not belittle the chancellor's stature, but is sharply critical of his impact on German political life.

VF134. Bismarck, Otto von. **Die gesammelten Werke Otto von Bismarcks.** 15 v. Berlin, 1924–35. Chief modern source for the study of Bismarck's personality and statecraft. This so-called "Friedrichsruhe" edition presents a full and critical collection of the chancellor's private and official correspondence, speeches, conversations, and memoirs.

VF135. Radowitz, Joseph M. von. **Aufzeichnungen und Erinnerungen aus dem Leben des Botschafters Joseph Maria von Radowitz.** Ed. by Hajo Holborn. 2 v. Stuttgart, 1925. Memoirs of one of Bismarck's chief diplomatic associates.

VF136. Kessel, Eberhard. **Moltke.** Stuttgart, 1957. Best historical biography of the elder Moltke.

VF137. Beust, Friedrich F., count von. **Memoirs of Friedrich Ferdinand, count von Beust.** 2nd ed., 2 v., London, 1887. Tr. from *Aus drei Viertel-Jahrhunderten: Erinnerungen und Aufzeichnungen von Friedrich Ferdinand, Graf von Beust* (2 v., Stuttgart, 1887). Memoirs of one of Bismarck's chief political antagonists, the prime minister of Saxony and Austria.

VF138. Oncken, Hermann. **Rudolf von Bennigsen.** 2 v. Stuttgart, 1910. Important source for the national-liberal movement in the age of German unification and of Bismarck.

VF139. Bussmann, Walter. **Treitschke, sein Welt- und Geschichtsbild.** Göttingen, 1952. This and the following are recent critical biographical studies, this one concentrating on the intellectual development until 1870, and the other on Treitschke's place in political history.

VF140. Dorpalen, Andreas. **Heinrich von Treitschke.** New Haven, 1957.

VF141. Hohenlohe-Schillingfürst, Chlodwig, Fürst zu. **Memoirs.** 2 v. N.Y., 1906. Tr. by George W. Chrystal from *Denkwürdigkeiten,* ed. by Friedrich Curtius (2 v., Stuttgart and Leipzig, 1905). This and the following are memoirs of Prince Hohenlohe, Bavarian prime minister before 1870, subsequently German ambassador in France, governor of Alsace-Lorraine, and second successor of Bismarck. The collection edited by Curtius contains practically nothing on the years of Hohenlohe's chancellorship. This gap is filled by the Müller edition.

VF142. ———. **Denkwürdigkeiten der Reichskanzlerzeit.** Ed. by Karl A. von Müller. Stuttgart and Berlin, 1931.

VF143. Waldersee, Alfred, Graf von. **A field-marshal's memoirs: from the diary, correspondence, and reminiscences.** London, 1924. Tr. by Frederic Whyte from *Denkwürdigkeiten des Generalfeldmarschalls,* ed. by Heinrich O. Meisner (3 v., Stuttgart,

1923–25). Memoirs of the deputy and successor to Count Moltke, chiefly important as a source of the history of Bismarck's dismissal and the early years of William II's reign.

VF144. Holstein, Friedrich von. **The Holstein papers.** Ed. by Norman Rich and M. H. Fisher. 2 v. Cambridge, Eng., 1955–57. Personal papers of uneven quality of Bismarck's associate and enemy who, from 1890 to 1906, was the most influential director of German foreign policy.

VF145. Brandenburg, Erich. **From Bismarck to the World War: a history of German foreign policy, 1870–1914.** London, 1927. German standard text of the diplomatic history of the origins of World War I.

VF146. Townsend, Mary E. **The rise and fall of Germany's colonial empire, 1884–1918.** See *U189.*

VF147. Rudin, Harry R. **Germans in the Cameroons, 1884–1914.** See *U194.*

VF148. Schlieffen, Alfred, Graf von. **Dienstschriften des Chefs des Generalstabes der Armee Generalfeldmarschalls Graf von Schlieffen.** 2 v. Berlin, 1937–38. First two volumes of a never completed monumental edition of the military writings of the Prussian chief-of-staff, whose thinking dominated in the strategy of German generals of World War I.

VF149. Ritter, Gerhard. **Der Schlieffenplan: Kritik eines Mythos.** Munich, 1956. Publication of the drafts and text of Schlieffen's plan of 1905 for a war against France, which in modified form served as plan of operations in August, 1914.

VF150. Eyck, Erich. **Das persönliche Regiment Wilhelm II: politische Geschichte des deutschen Kaiserreiches von 1890 bis 1914.** Zürich, 1948. History of the German empire under William II, by a liberal German historian.

VF151. Eulenburg-Hertefeld, Philipp, Fürst zu. **Aus 50 Jahren: Erinnerungen, Tagebücher, und Briefe aus dem Nachlass des Fürsten Philipp zu Eulenburg-Hertefeld.** Ed. by Johannes Haller, 1923. Memoirs of a diplomat and influential friend of William II who became the political victim of scandalous accusations.

VF152. Haller, Johannes. **Philip Eulenburg, the Kaiser's friend.** 2 v. N.Y., 1930. Tr. by Ethel C. Mayne from *Aus dem Leben des Fürsten Philip zu Eulenburg-Hertefeld* (2nd ed., Berlin, 1926). A historical biography written in Eulenburg's defense.

VF153. Hutten-Czapski, Bogdan F. S., Graf von. **Sechzig Jahre Politik und Gesellschaft.** 2 v. Berlin, 1936. Memoirs of politics and society under William II.

VF154. Bülow, Bernhard H., Fürst von. **Denkwürdigkeiten.** 4 v. Berlin, 1930–31. The loquacious and colored memoirs of the

German chancellor are an indispensable source for the study of his policies and personality.

VF155. Tirpitz, Alfred von. **Politische Dokumente von A. von Tirpitz.** 2 v. Stuttgart and Berlin, 1924–26. Political papers of the founder of the German navy, collected and edited in defense of his pre-war and World War I policies.

VF156. Kehr, Eckart. **Schlachtflottenbau und Parteipolitik, 1894–1901.** Berlin, 1930. Most penetrating study of the relationship between German domestic politics and the naval building program.

VF157. Kiderlen-Wächter, Alfred von. **Der Staatsmann und Mensch: Briefwechsel und Nachlass.** Ed. by Ernst Jäckh. 2 v. Stuttgart, 1924. Important source for the study of German foreign policy, although the editor unduly magnifies Kiderlen's stature as a statesman.

VF158. Meyer, Henry C. **Mitteleuropa in German thought and action, 1815–1945.** The Hague, 1955. Thorough study of the concept of *Mitteleuropa* and the attempts to realize it, particularly during World War I.

VF159. Rosenberg, Arthur. **The birth of the German republic.** N.Y., 1931. Outstanding history and analysis of German politics from the outbreak of World War I to eve of the November Revolution of 1918.

VF160. Rudin, Harry R. **Armistice, 1918.** See *AH157*.

VF161. Baden, Prince Max von. **Memoirs.** 2 v. London, 1928. Tr. by W. M. Calder and C. W. H. Sutton from *Erinnerungen und Dokumente* (Stuttgart, 1927). Rich and well-edited collection of the political papers of the last imperial chancellor.

VF162. Bergsträsser, Ludwig. **Geschichte der politischen Parteien in Deutschland.** 7th ed., Munich, 1952. Indispensable historical guide and bibliography for study of political parties of Germany.

VF163. Salomon, Felix. **Die deutschen Parteiprogramme.** 4th ed., ed. by Wilhelm Mommsen and Günther Franz, Leipzig, 1932. This and the following (*VF164*) are the chief collections of German party programs.

VF164. Treue, Wolfgang. **Deutsche Parteiprogramme, 1861–1954.** Göttingen and Frankfurt, 1954.

VF165. Muncy, Lysbeth W. **The junker in the Prussian administration under William II, 1888–1914.** Providence, 1944.

VF166. Bachem, Karl. **Vorgeschichte, Geschichte und Politik der deutschen Zentrumspartei.** 9 v. Köln, 1927–32. Voluminous political history of the Center party. Though not very critical, it contains valuable information and documentation.

VF167. Heuss, Theodor. **Friedrich Naumann: der Mann, das Werk, die Zeit.** Stutt-gart, 1937. Historical biography of the leader of the "national-social" movement and, from 1918 to 1920, the Democratic party, written by a scholar who entered politics under Naumann's aegis.

VF168. Oncken, Hermann. **Lassalle: eine politische Biographie.** 4th ed., Stuttgart, 1923. Outstanding historical biography of the founder of the first organized socialist movement in Germany.

VF169. Mayer, Gustav. **Friedrich Engels: a biography.** N.Y., 1936. Tr. by Gilbert and Helen Highet from *Friedrich Engels: eine Biographie* (2 v., The Hague, 1934). The German work is the best not only on Engels but also on German origins of Marxism and its subsequent influence on the German working-class movement. English edition is drastically abbreviated.

VF170. Schorske, Carl E. **German social democracy, 1905–1917.** Cambridge, Mass., 1955. Critical study of the organizational and political development of the German Social-Democratic party.

VF171. Wertheimer, Mildred. **The Pan-German League, 1890–1914.** N.Y., 1924.

VF172. Kruck, Alfred. **Geschichte des Alldeutschen Verbandes, 1890–1939.** Wiesbaden, 1954. This study of the Pan-German union draws on more extensive sources than the above.

VF173. Massing, Paul W. **Rehearsal for destruction: a study of political anti-Semitism in imperial Germany.** N.Y., 1949. Penetrating study of the political and social function of anti-semitism in the empire of Bismarck and William II.

The Weimar Republic, 1919–1933

VF174. Halperin, S. William. **Germany tried democracy: a political history of the Reich from 1918 to 1933.** N.Y., 1946. Useful and balanced treatment of the Weimar Republic, with large bibliography.

VF175. Eyck, Erich. **Geschichte der Weimarer Republik.** 2 v. Zürich, 1954–56. Extensive and informative, by an eminent historian of democratic convictions.

VF176. Rosenberg, Arthur. **A history of the German republic.** London, 1936. Somewhat uneven treatment, but important for the early years.

VF177. Apelt, Willibalt. **Geschichte der Weimarer Verfassung.** Munich, 1946. The best, if somewhat too juridical, study of origins of the Weimar constitution.

VF178. Blachly, Frederick F., and Miriam E. Oatman. **The government and administration of Germany.** Baltimore, 1928. Best treatise in English on the governmental and administrative structure of the German republic.

VF179. Lutz, Ralph H. **The German revolution, 1918–1919.** Stanford, 1922. Collection of translated historical documents illustrating the course of the revolution.

VF180. Müller-Franken, Hermann. **Die November-Revolution: Erinnerungen.** Berlin, 1928. Reliable and well-documented memoirs on the revolution by one of the most prominent German socialists, foreign minister in 1919, chancellor in 1920 and 1928–30.

VF181. Luckau, Alma M. **The German delegation at the Paris peace conference.** See *AH155.*

VF182. Fraenkel, Ernst. **Military occupation and the rule of law: occupation government in the Rhineland, 1918–1923.** N.Y., 1944. Study of Allied occupation of the Rhineland after World War I, especially in the light of international law.

VF183. Wheeler-Bennett, John W. **Wooden Titan: Hindenburg in twenty years of German history, 1914–1934.** N.Y., 1936. Brilliant study of Hindenburg's political career as commander in World War I and as president of the Weimar Republic.

VF184. Kessler, Harry, Graf von. **Walter Rathenau.** London, 1929. Tr. by W. D. Robson-Scott and Lawrence Hyde from *Walter Rathenau, sein Leben und sein Werk* (Berlin, 1928). Biographical appraisal of the life and work of the German industrialist and social thinker who, as a minister, also had a great political influence in the early years of the republic.

VF185. Stresemann, Gustav. **Gustav Stresemann: his diaries, letters, and papers.** Ed. and tr. by Eric Sutton. 3 v. London, 1935–40. Slightly condensed from *Gustav Stresemann: Vermächtnis* (3 v., Berlin, 1932–33). Most comprehensive political memoirs of the Weimar period. Their value as historical source is greatly impaired by the methods of selecting and editing. See Hans Gatzke, "The Stresemann papers," *Jour. of mod. hist.,* 26 (Mar. 1954): 49–59.

VF186. Gatzke, Hans W. **Stresemann and the rearmament of Germany.** Baltimore, 1954. Study of Stresemann's policy regarding the Soviet Union and rearmament, using unpublished German foreign office documents.

VF187. Gordon, Harold J. **The Reichswehr and the German republic, 1919–1926.** Princeton, 1957. Origins and formative years of the *Reichswehr,* with emphasis on the internal problems of the army.

VF188. Wheeler-Bennett, John W. **The nemesis of power: the German army in politics, 1918–1945.** London and N.Y., 1954. Important and fascinating study of the politics of the German army under the republic and under Hitler. In evaluation of events the work is somewhat subjective.

VF189. Ebert, Friedrich. **Friedrich Ebert: Schriften, Aufzeichnungen, Reden.** Ed. by Friedrich Ebert, Jr. 2 v. Dresden, 1926.

Collection of public speeches and some miscellaneous writings of the first German president.

VF190. Stampfer, Friedrich. **Die vierzehn Jahre der ersten deutschen Republik.** Karlsbad, 1936. This and *VF191–193* represent memoirs of prominent Social-Democratic leaders of the Weimar period: in order, the editor-in-chief of the Central party newspaper, president of the federal parliament, prime minister of Prussia, and Prussian and federal minister of the interior.

VF191. Löbe, Paul. **Der Weg war lang: Lebenserinnerungen von Paul Löbe, ehemals Präsident des deutschen Reichstages.** 2nd ed., Berlin, 1954.

VF192. Braun, Otto. **Von Weimar zu Hitler.** N.Y., 1940.

VF193. Severing, Carl. **Mein Lebensweg.** 2 v. Köln, 1950.

VF194. Clark, Robert T. **The fall of the German republic.** London, 1935. Well-informed and careful narrative of events leading to the collapse of German democracy.

VF195. Bracher, Karl D. **Die Auflösung der Weimarer Republik.** 2nd ed., Stuttgart, 1957. Best critical history of the breakdown of the Weimar Republic.

VF196. Neumann, Sigmund. **Die deutschen Parteien.** Berlin, 1932. Outstanding analytical study of political parties of the Weimar Republic; rather complete in coverage and bibliography, though brief in treatment.

VF197. Mommsen, Wilhelm, and Franz Günther. **Deutsche Parteiprogramme, 1918–1930.** Leipzig, 1931. Collection of party programs.

VF198. Klemperer, Klemens von. **Germany's new conservatism: its history and dilemma in the twentieth century.** Princeton, 1957. Essay on the so-called neo-conservative, anti-republican movements.

Germany under Hitler, 1933–1945

VF199. Meinecke, Friedrich. **The German catastrophe: reflections and recollections.** Cambridge, Mass., 1950. Tr. by Sidney B. Fay from *Die deutsche Katastrophe: Betrachtungen und Erinnerungen* (Wiesbaden, 1946). Searching reflections of a distinguished liberal historian on the causes of the rise of national socialism and the fall of the German republic.

VF200. Mau, Hermann, and Helmut Krausnick. **Deutsche Geschichte der jüngsten Vergangenheit, 1933–1945.** Tübingen and Stuttgart, 1956. Concise narrative by two well-qualified German historians.

VF201. Heiden, Konrad. **A history of national socialism.** N.Y., 1935. Tr. from *Geschichte des Nationalsozialismus* (Berlin, 1932) and *Geburt des dritten Reiches* (Zürich, 1934). History of national socialism from its inception to 1934, by its earliest critical student. Although the historical evaluation of events needs broadening, the book is indispensable for its information on early years of this movement.

VF202. ——. **Der Fuehrer: Hitler's rise to power.** Tr. by Ralph Manheim. Boston, 1944. A more biographical version of *VF201*.

VF203. Hofer, Walther, ed. **Der Nationalsozialismus: Dokumente, 1933–1945.** Frankfurt-am-Main, 1957. Useful critical collection of Nazi ideologies, practices, and policies.

VF204. Loewenstein, Karl. **Hitler's Germany.** Rev. ed., N.Y., 1940. This and the following are the two best descriptive analyses of the Third Reich by U. S. political scientists.

VF205. Ebenstein, William. **The Nazi state.** See *AF93*.

VF206. Neumann, Franz L. **Behemoth: the structure and practice of national socialism, 1933–1944.** 2nd ed., N.Y., 1944. The most penetrating and informative study of German national socialism, by an eminent scholar. It is particularly revealing on the interrelation of politics and economics, though the appraisal of causes and motives suffers from some socialist doctrinairism.

VF207. Guillebaud, Claude W. **The social policy of Nazi Germany.** Cambridge, Eng., 1941. Study of the social policy of the Nazis, by a student of Keynes.

VF208. Bullock, Alan L. C. **Hitler: a study in tyranny.** London, 1952. Best available historical biography of Hitler. Includes a good bibliography on the history of national socialism.

VF209. Trevor-Roper, Hugh R. **The last days of Hitler.** London, 1947. 3rd ed., 1956. Brilliant study written with great insight into the character of Hitler and his ilk.

VF210. Papen, Franz von. **Memoirs.** London, 1952. Tr. by Brian Connell from *Der Wahrheit eine Gasse* (Munich, 1952). Though not a very successful defense of his own role under the Nazis, the memoirs are an important historical source.

VF211. Schacht, Hjalmar H. G. **Confessions of "the Old Wizard:" autobiography.** Boston, 1956. Tr. by Diana Pyke from *76 Jahre meines Lebens* (Bad Wörishofen, 1953). Another apologetic autobiography of a prominent collaborator with Hitler, but historically valuable.

VF212. Goebbels, Paul Joseph. **The Goebbels diaries, 1942–1943.** Ed. and tr. by Louis P. Lochner. N.Y., 1948. A small section of the diaries of Hitler's intimate lieutenant.

VF213. Rommel, Erwin. **The Rommel papers.** Ed. by B. H. Liddell Hart; tr. by Paul Findlay. N.Y., 1953. This and *VF214–216* are by four of the most prominent military commanders of Hitler's campaigns.

VF214. Manstein, Erich von. **Verlorene Siege.** Bonn, 1955.

VF215. Guderian, Heinz. **Panzer leader.** N.Y., 1952. Tr. by Constantine Fitzgibbon from *Erinnerungen eines Soldaten* (Heidelberg, 1951).

VF216. Kesselring, Albert. **Kesselring: a soldier's record.** N.Y., 1954. Tr. by Lynton Hudson from *Soldat bis zum letzten Tag* (Bonn, 1953).

VF217. Rothfels, Hans. **The German opposition to Hitler.** Hinsdale, Ill., 1948. Careful study of the personalities and actions of the opposition to Hitler culminating in the putsch of July, 1944.

VF218. Ritter, Gerhard. **The German resistance: Carl Goerdeler's struggle against tyranny.** See *AG226*.

VF219. Hassell, Ulrich von. **Vom andern Deutschland: aus den nachgelassenen Tagebüchern, 1938–1944.** Zürich, 1946. The diaries of Ambassador von Hassell are the most important single personal source for study of the opposition to Hitler.

HISTORIES OF SPECIAL AREAS

Individual German States

VF220. Riezler, Sigmund. **Geschichte Bayerns.** 8 v. Gotha, 1878–1914. Masterly history of a single German land leading to the early 18th century.

VF221. Doeberl, Michael. **Entwicklungsgeschichte Bayerns.** 2 v. Munich, 1908–12. An indispensable work, though somewhat narrow in outlook.

VF222. Strich, Michael. **Das Kurhaus Bayern im Zeitalter Ludwigs XIV. und die europäischen Mächte.** 2 v. Munich, 1933. The important political position of Bavaria in the age of Louis XIV is treated in all its aspects.

VF223. Carsten, Francis L. **The origins of Prussia.** Oxford, 1954. Capably fills the need for a book in English on the early history of Prussia; ends with the state of the Great Elector. [JGG]

VF224. Prutz, Hans. **Preussische Geschichte.** 4 v. Stuttgart, 1900–02. Detailed and balanced history of Prussia to 1888; first large-scale work critical of the 19th century Prusso-German heroic school. [JGG]

VF225. Waddington, Albert. **Histoire de Prusse.** 2 v. Paris, 1911–22. Best French history of Prussia; excellent and scholarly treatment. Goes only to 1740. [JGG]

VF226. Hintze, Otto. **Die Hohenzollern und ihr Werk.** Berlin, 1915. While suffering from its patriotic purpose, this is the best institutional history of Brandenburg-Prussia.

VF227. ——. **Geist und Epochen der preussischen Geschichte.** Leipzig, 1943. Reprints some of the best studies on Prussian history by a distinguished author who grew from a historian of Prussian political institutions into a master of comparative constitutional history.

VF228. Schmoller, Gustav. **Preussische Verfassungs-, Verwaltungs- und Finanzgeschichte.** Berlin, 1921. Short and general, but clear introduction to administrative, constitutional, and financial history of Prussia from its origins to the "new era" of William I, by a famous German economic historian. No footnotes or bibliography. [JGG]

VF229. Droysen, Johann G. **Geschichte der preussischen Politik.** 14 v. Leipzig, 1868–86. Although quite biased in favor of Prussia and its "German mission," these volumes are the result of painstaking research, and represent the first scientific study of Prussian politics. The author's death ended the study at 1757. [JGG]

VF230. Die Behördenorganisation und die allgemeine Staatsverwaltung Preussens im 18. Jahrhundert. 15 v. in 17. Berlin, 1894–1936. [Königlichen Akademie der Wissenschaften, Acta borussica.] A truly monumental and invaluable collection of acts, decrees, and reports relating to the administration of Prussia from 1701 to 1772. V. 1 and v. 6, pt. 2 contain excellent surveys of the condition of Prussia in 1713 and 1740, by Gustav Schmoller and Otto Hintze respectively. [JGG]

VF231. Tümpel, Ludwig. **Die Entstehung der brandenburgisch-preussischen Einheitsstaates im Zeitalter des Absolutismus, 1609–1806.** Breslau, 1915. Concise treatment of the centralization of the Prussian state, with emphasis on administrative developments. [JGG]

VF232. Rosenberg, Hans. **Bureaucracy, aristocracy, and autocracy: the Prussian experience, 1660–1815.** Cambridge, Mass., 1958. Analytic study of the social bases of Prussian absolutism.

VF233. Voelcker, Heinrich, ed. **Die Stadt Goethes: Frankfurt am Main im XVIII. Jahrhundert.** Frankfurt-am-Main, 1932. Excellent survey of the social, economic, political, cultural, and religious history of an important German city in the 18th century.

VF234. Zimmermann, Ludwig. **Der ökonomische Staat Landgraf Wilhelms IV von Hessen.** 2 v. Marburg, 1933–34. Important source and historical presentation, illustrating the governmental aims and practices of a German territorial state in the late 16th century.

VF235. Andreas, Willy. **Baden nach dem Wiener Frieden, 1809.** Heidelberg, 1912. Brief study of Baden in the Napoleonic period.

VF236. Hölzle, Erwin. **Württemberg im Zeitalter Napoleons und der deutschen Erhebung: eine deutsche Geschichte der Wendezeit im einzelstaatlichen Raum.** Stuttgart and Berlin, 1937. History of one of the major states of the Rhenish confederation.

VF237. Hartung, Fritz. **Das Grossherzogtum Sachsen unter der regierung Carl Augusts, 1775–1828.** Weimar, 1923. This political, administrative, and constitutional history of Saxony-Weimar, written by an eminent historian, describes the realistic setting of Goethe's duchy and can also serve to some extent as a model for the history of other small German principalities.

VF238. Andreas, Willy. **Carl August von Weimar: ein Leben mit Goethe.** Stuttgart, 1953. A sensitive and colorful biography of the duke of Weimar.

Austria

VF239. Luschin von Ebengreuth, Arnold. **Handbuch der österreichischen Reichsgeschichte.** 2nd ed., Bamberg, 1914. Good, although somewhat dated, handbook of Austrian history, with emphasis on institutions.

VF240. Uhlirz, Karl, and Mathilde Uhlirz. **Handbuch der Geschichte Österreichs und seiner Nachbarländer Böhmen und Ungarn.** Graz, 1927 ff. Best handbook of Austrian history, with excellent bibliographies.

VF241. Hantsch, Hugo. **Die Geschichte Österreichs.** 2nd ed., 2 v., Graz, 1947–53. History of the Austrian monarchy to 1918, by an eminent conservative scholar.

VF242. Srbik, Heinrich, Ritter von. **Aus Österreichs Vergangenheit, von Prinz Eugen zu Franz Joseph.** Salzburg, 1949. Collection of studies on central topics of Austrian history since the 18th century, by a distinguished historian.

VF243. Fontes rerum austriacarum. Österreichische Geschichtsquellen. 2nd ser., Diplomataria et acta. 73 v. Vienna, 1849–1956. (Others in progress.) Largest collection of critically edited sources of Austrian history, published under auspices of the Vienna Academy of Sciences.

VF244. Veröffentlichungen der Kommission für neuere Geschichte Österreichs. 41 v. Vienna and Graz, 1903–55. Important series of sources of modern Austrian history.

VF245. Huber, Alfons, and Oswald Redlich. **Geschichte Österreichs.** 7 v. Gotha and Vienna, 1885–1938. The first volumes of this Austrian history are somewhat dated. V. 6 and 7, by O. Redlich, are the fullest treatments of events leading to the formation of the Austrian empire.

VF246. Arneth, Alfred, Ritter von. **Prinz Eugen von Savoyen.** 3 v. Vienna, 1858. On account of its rich documentation, the work is still the chief monograph on this statesman and general.

VF247. ——. **Geschichte Maria Theresia's.** 10 v. Vienna, 1863–79. Not a biography, but a vast collection of original documents illustrating the reign of the empress.

VF248. Guglia, Eugen. **Maria Theresia, ihr**

Leben und ihre Regierung. 2 v. Munich, 1917. The most useful and best-informed historical biography.

VF249. Gooch, George P. **Maria Theresa and other studies.** London and N.Y., 1951. Contains a suggestive historical appraisal of Maria Theresa.

VF250. Küntzel, Georg. **Fürst Kaunitz-Rittberg als Staatsmann.** Frankfurt-am-Main, 1923. Penetrating study of Maria Theresa's chief minister.

VF251. Padover, Saul K. **The revolutionary emperor: Joseph the Second, 1741–1790.** N.Y., 1934. Good, original historical biography.

VF252. Valjavec, Fritz. **Der Josephinismus: zur geistigen Entwicklung Österreichs im 18. und 19. Jahrhundert.** 2nd ed., Munich, 1945. Thought and philosophy of the Austrian enlightenment and impact on politics and intellectual life.

VF253. Kerner, Robert J. **Bohemia in the eighteenth century.** See *W340.*

VF254. Langsam, Walter C. **The Napoleonic wars and German nationalism in Austria.** N.Y., 1930. Rise of German national sentiment during the Napoleonic age.

VF255. Blum, Jerome. **Noble landowners and agriculture in Austria, 1815–1848.** Baltimore, 1948. Critical study of agrarian conditions in Austria in the age of Metternich.

VF256. Metternich-Winneburg, Clemens, Fürst von. **Aus Metternichs nachgelassenen Papieren.** Ed. by Fürst Richard Metternich and Alfons von Klinkowström. 8 v. Vienna, 1880–84. English tr., *Memoirs of Prince Metternich, 1773–1835,* 5 v., N.Y., 1881. Documents and writings of the Austrian chancellor, not very competently edited and selected.

VF257. Srbik, Heinrich, Ritter von. **Metternich: der Staatsmann und der Mensch.** 3 v. Munich, 1925–54. This historical biography, based on wide study, was the first critical assessment of the personality and statecraft of Metternich free of liberal bias. Though somewhat too admiring, it should be the starting point of all future research.

VF258. Kann, Robert A. **The multinational empire: nationalism and national reform in the Habsburg monarchy, 1848–1918.** 2 v. N.Y., 1950. Detailed study of the movements of nationalities and the Austrian attempts to deal with them.

VF259. Redlich, Josef. **Das österreichische Staats- und Reichsproblem.** 2 v. Leipzig, 1920–26. Outstanding study of the constitutional problems of the Hapsburg empire from 1848 onward.

VF260. ———. **Emperor Francis Joseph of Austria.** N.Y., 1929. Historical biography, not uncritical but somewhat facile.

VF261. Clark, Chester W. **Franz Joseph and Bismarck: the diplomacy of Austria before the war of 1866.** Cambridge, Mass., 1934. Good study of Austrian foreign policy prior to 1866.

VF262. May, Arthur J. **The Hapsburg monarchy, 1867–1914.** Cambridge, Mass., 1951. Reliable treatment of the general history of Austria-Hungary.

VF263. Molisch, Paul. **Geschichte der deutschnationalen Bewegung in Österreich von ihren Anfängen bis zum Zerfall der Monarchie.** Jena, 1926. Valuable account of the German-national movement in Austria.

VF264. Fuchs, Albert. **Geistige Strömungen in Österreich, 1867–1918.** Vienna, 1949. Sensitive exploration of the major Austrian schools of thought.

VF265. Carnegie Endowment for International Peace. **Wirtschafts- und Sozialgeschichte des Weltkrieges: österreichische und Ungarische Serie.** 14 v. Vienna and New Haven, 1923–32. The Austro-Hungarian series contains important monographs, among them the following (*VF266*).

VF266. Redlich, Josef. **Österreichische Regierung und Verwaltung im Weltkriege.** Vienna and New Haven, 1925. Excellent study of the impact of World War I on the constitutional and administrative structure of the Hapsburg empire.

VF267. Conrad von Hötzendorf, Franz. **Aus meiner Dienstzeit, 1906–1918.** 5 v. Vienna, 1921–25. Collection of the military and political papers of the Austrian chief-of-staff.

VF268. Czernin von und zu Chudenitz, Ottokar T., Graf. **In the World War.** London, 1919. Tr. from *Im Weltkriege* (Vienna, 1919). Memoirs of the foreign minister of the last emperor.

VF269. Jászi, Oszkár. **The dissolution of the Hapsburg monarchy.** Chicago, 1929. Able discussion of events leading to the demise of the Hapsburg empire, with emphasis on the Hungarian side.

VF270. Glaise von Horstenau, Edmund. **The collapse of the Austro-Hungarian empire.** N.Y., 1930. History of the end of imperial Austria, by a German-Austrian historian and general.

VF271. Benedikt, Heinrich, ed. **Geschichte der Republik Österreich.** Vienna, 1954. Best historical treatment of the first Austrian republic. Particularly valuable is the chapter, by Adam Wandruszka, on internal developments.

VF272. Gulick, Charles A. **Austria from Habsburg to Hitler.** 2 v. Berkeley, 1948. Detailed, important study of the Austrian republic, by a United States economist whose personal sympathies rest largely with the Austrian social democrats.

Switzerland

VF273. Dändliker, Karl. **Geschichte der Schweiz.** 3rd and 4th eds., 3 v., Zürich,

1900–04. Detailed, critical history of Switzerland, with special attention to constitutional and cultural developments.

VF274. Gagliardi, Ernst. **Geschichte der Schweiz von den Anfängen bis auf die Gegenwart.** 3rd ed., 3 v., Zürich, 1938. Well-written general history of Switzerland, by a prominent Swiss scholar.

VF275. Oechsli, Wilhelm. **History of Switzerland, 1499–1914.** Tr. by Eden and Cedar Paul. Cambridge, Eng., 1922. Good, concise modern history, written by one of the foremost Swiss historians for an English audience.

VF276. Bonjour, Edgar; Hilary S. Offler, and G. R. Potter. **A short history of Switzerland.** Oxford, 1952. Symposium on Swiss history reflecting the present state of research.

VF277. Wackernagel, Rudolf. **Geschichte der Stadt Basel.** 3 v. Basel, 1907–24. Outstanding history of the city. V. 3, dealing with the age of humanism and reformation, is particularly important, even beyond Swiss history.

VF278. Gagliardi, Ernst. **Der Anteil der Schweizer an den italienischen Kriegen, 1494–1516.** V. 1. Zürich, 1919. Swiss participation in the struggle for Italy around 1500.

VF279. Egli, Emil. **Schweizerische Reformationsgeschichte.** Zürich, 1910. Sound treatment of the history of the Swiss reformation.

VF280. Zwingli, Ulrich. **Huldreich Zwinglis sämtliche Werke.** Ed. by Emil Egli and Georg Finsler. 13 v. Berlin, 1905–44. The modern critical edition of Zwingli's writings.

VF281. Köhler, Walther. **Huldrych Zwingli.** Leipzig, 1943. The outstanding biography of the Swiss reformer.

VF282. Doumergue, Émile. **Jean Calvin.** 7 v. Lausanne, 1899–1927. Voluminous work studying not only Calvin, but also the world that surrounded him, particularly the German setting.

VF283. Calvin, John. **Ioannis Calvini opera.** Ed. by Wilhelm Baum, Eduard Cunitz, and Eduard Reuss. 59 v. Brunswick, 1863–1900. [Corpus reformatorum, 29–87.] Most complete edition of Calvin's theological and exegetic works, occasional writings, and correspondence. The editorial standards are not impeccable.

VF284. ——. **Joannis Calvini opera selecta.** Ed. by Peter Barth. Munich, 1926 ff. Modern critical edition of Calvin's major works.

VF285. His, Eduard. **Geschichte des neueren schweizerischen Staatsrechts.** 3 v. Basel, 1920–38. Basic treatment of the history of Swiss public law since the days of the Helvetic republic.

VF286. Bonjour, Edgar. **Histoire de la neutralité suisse.** Neuchâtel, 1949. Best historical study of Swiss neutrality.

VF287. Ermatinger, Emil. **Dichtung und Geistesleben der deutschen Schweiz.** Munich, 1933. Perceptive historical essay on the literary and intellectual life of the German-speaking Swiss.

VF288. Feller, Richard. **Die schweizerische Geschichtsschreibung im 19. Jahrhundert.** Zürich and Leipzig, 1938. Useful outline of Swiss historiography in the 19th century.

HISTORIES OF SPECIAL TOPICS

Constitutional and Legal History

VF289. Brunner, Heinrich. **Deutsche Rechtsgeschichte.** 2nd ed., 2 v., Leipzig, 1906–28. V. 2 rev. by Claudius F. von Schwerin. Known among German students as the Brunner-Schwerin, this is the most compendious modern work on German legal history. Has a certain bias against Roman law.

VF290. Gierke, Otto F. von. **Das deutsche Genossenschaftsrecht.** 4 v. Berlin, 1868–1913. One of the masterpieces of legal history, showing the significance of Germanic "group" conception in the development of modern law.

VF291. Bryce, James B., viscount. **Holy Roman Empire.** 8th ed., London, 1932. Lord Bryce's famous honor essay has remained useful as a survey of the institutional history of the German empire from the Middle Ages to the 19th century.

VF292. Schwarz, Henry F. **The imperial privy council in the seventeenth century.** Cambridge, Mass., 1943. Study of the central administrative office of the Holy Roman Empire.

VF293. Hartung, Fritz. **Deutsche Verfassungsgeschichte vom 15. Jahrhundert bis zur Gegenwart.** 6th ed., Stuttgart, 1954. Only constitutional history of modern Germany on both the imperial and territorial levels. Pedestrian in style, but reliable and rich in information; contains excellent bibliographies.

VF294. Feine, Hans E. **Das Werden des deutschen Staats seit dem Ausgang des Heiligen Römischen Reiches, 1800 bis 1933.** Stuttgart, 1936. First volume of a constitutional history of Germany dealing with the reform period in the Napoleonic age and the period of the Germanic confederation.

VF295. Meyer, Georg. **Lehrbuch des deutschen Staatsrechts.** Ed. by Gerhard Anschütz. 7th ed., Munich and Leipzig, 1919. Outstanding magisterial work on the constitutional law of the second German empire.

VF296. Anschütz, Gerhard, and Richard Thoma, eds. **Handbuch des deutschen Staatsrechts.** 2 v. Tübingen, 1930–32. Only systematic and complete work on the constitutional law of the Weimar Republic, written by a large group of law professors. Contains historical sections and good bibliographies.

VF297. Giese, Friedrich. **Preussische Rechtsgeschichte.** Berlin, 1920. Outline of Prussian legal history.

Economic and Social History

VF298. Ehrenberg, Richard. **Capital and finance in the age of the Renaissance: a study of the Fuggers and their connections.** Tr. by H. M. Lucas. London, 1928. General survey of capitalistic developments in 16th century Germany.

VF299. Strieder, Jacob. **Jacob Fugger the rich, merchant and banker of Augsburg, 1459–1525.** N.Y., 1931. Tr. by Mildred L. Hartsough, ed. by N. S. B. Gras from *Jacob Fugger der Reiche* (Leipzig, 1926). Competent historical biography of the member of the Fugger family who led the firm to its dazzling heights.

VF300. Pölnitz, Götz Freiherr von. **Jakob Fugger: Kaiser, Kirche, und Kapital in der oberdeutschen Renaissance.** 2 v. Tübingen, 1949–51.

VF301. ———. **Fugger und Hanse: ein hundertjähriges Ringen um Ostsee und Nordsee.** Tübingen, 1953. This and the preceding are important modern studies of influence of the Fuggers on politics of the empire.

VF302. Sartorius von Waltershausen, August F. **Deutsche Wirtschaftsgeschichte, 1815–1914.** 2nd ed., Jena, 1923. Brief outline of modern German economic history.

VF303. Schramm, Percy E. **Hamburg, Deutschland, und die Welt.** 2nd ed., Hamburg, 1952. An important and richly documented contribution to German social history between 1800 and 1860. In the growth of a Hamburg family firm is demonstrated not only the expansion of German commerce, but also the changing social attitudes and human values of three German generations.

VF304. Sombart, Werner. **Die deutsche Volkswirtschaft im neunzehnten Jahrhundert und im Anfang des 20. Jahrhunderts: eine Einführung in die Nationalökonomie.** 7th ed., Berlin, 1927. Valuable, though somewhat too popular, treatment of the industrial revolution in Germany, by a distinguished economic historian.

VF305. Clapham, John H. **The economic development of France and Germany, 1815–1914.** 4th ed., Cambridge, Eng., 1936. Comparative study of the growth of French and German economy during the 19th century by an eminent British economic historian.

VF306. Goltz, Theodor von der. **Geschichte der deutschen Landwirtschaft.** 2 v. Stuttgart and Berlin, 1902–03. Valuable history of German agriculture, though biased in favor of East Elbian agriculture.

VF307. Gerschenkron, Alexander. **Bread and democracy in Germany.** Berkeley, 1943. Critical study of the impact of agrarian interests on modern German politics.

VF308. Benaerts, Pierre. **Les origines de la grande industrie allemande: essai sur l'histoire économique de la période du Zollverein (1834–1866).** Paris, 1933. Best account of the origins of German heavy industries.

VF309. Levy, Hermann. **Industrial Germany: a study of its monopoly organizations and their control by the state.** Cambridge, Eng., 1935. Critical study of the monopolistic structure of the German economy.

VF310. Stolper, Gustav. **German economy, 1870–1940: issues and trends.** N.Y., 1940. Useful introduction to the major problems of modern German economic history.

VF311. Bruck, Werner F. **Social and economic history of Germany from William II to Hitler, 1888–1938.** Cardiff and London, 1938. Lectures on fifty years of German economic history, with special emphasis on economic and social organization.

VF312. Flink, Salomon. **The German Reichsbank and economic Germany.** N.Y., 1930. Description of the German federal bank and its function within the German economy.

VF313. Carnegie Endowment for International Peace. **Wirtschafts- und Sozialgeschichte des Weltkrieges. Deutsche Serie.** 12 v. Stuttgart, New Haven, etc., 1927–37. The German series of the Carnegie history of World War I is incomplete in coverage, but contains important monographs on individual subjects of German war-time economy and administration.

VF314. Bresciani-Turroni, Constantino. **The economics of inflation: a study of currency depreciation in post-war Germany.** London, 1937. Best economic treatise on the German hyper-inflation after World War I.

VF315. Angell, James W. **The recovery of Germany.** New Haven, 1932. Good study of German economic recovery, 1924–30.

Military History

VF316. Jany, Curt. **Geschichte der königlich preussischen Armee.** 4 v. Berlin, 1928–33. Most extensive history of the Prussian army, with emphasis on organization.

VF317. Prussia. Armee, Grosser Generalstab Kriegsgeschichtliche Abteilung. **Die Kriege Friedrichs des Grossen.** 19 v. Berlin, 1890–1914. Detailed history of the campaigns and battles of Frederick the Great.

VF318. Ritter, Gerhard. **Staatskunst und Kriegshandwerk: das Problem des "Militarismus" in Deutschland.** V. 1, **Die altpreussische Tradition, 1740–1890.** Munich,

1954. Mutual relationship of military and civilian leadership in Germany. The first volume centers on period of Prussian reform and of Bismarck.

VF319. Craig, Gordon A. **The politics of the Prussian army, 1640–1945.** Oxford, 1955. Outstanding study of the role of the Prussian army in politics.

VF320. Demeter, Karl. **Das deutsche Offizierkorps.** Berlin, 1930. Good historical study of the social composition and social attitudes of the modern German officer corps.

Cultural History

VF321. **Handbuch der Kulturgeschichte.** Ed. by Heinz Kindermann. 9 v. Potsdam, 1934–39. Series of monographs on individual periods of German civilization, written chiefly by historians of literature. Though the volumes are uneven in scope and method, they are rich in information and suggestions.

VF322. Freytag, Gustav. **Bilder aus der deutschen Vergangenheit.** 37th ed., 4 v. in 5, Leipzig, 1923. First published a century ago, this work is still an excellent treatment of representative topics of German culture through the ages, based on good sources and done by a highly gifted writer.

VF323. Kaufmann, Georg. **Die Geschichte der deutschen Universitäten.** 2 v. Stuttgart, 1888–96. This and the following are two standard works on the history of German high schools and universities. Both are somewhat dated.

VF324. Paulsen, Friedrich. **Geschichte des gelehrten Unterrichts auf den deutschen Schulen und Universitäten vom Ausgang des Mittelalters bis zur Gegenwart.** 3rd ed., 2 v., Leipzig, 1919–21.

VF325. Harnack, Adolf von. **Geschichte der königlich preussischen Akademie der Wissenschaften zu Berlin.** 3 v. Berlin, 1900. Written on occasion of the second centenary of the Academy, this presents great insight into the history of German scholarship from Leibniz to the middle of the 19th century.

VF326. Lilge, Friedrich. **The abuse of learning: the failure of the German university.** N.Y., 1948. Valuable critical study of the place of German universities in the national life and their surrender to the Nazis.

VF327. Dilthey, Wilhelm. **Studien zur Geschichte des deutschen Geistes.** Ed. by Paul Ritter. Berlin, 1927. [Wilhelm Diltheys gesammelte Schriften, 3.] The important studies on "Leibniz and his age," "Frederick the Great and the German enlightenment," and "The 18th century and the world of history" are model pieces of the intellectual history created by this great philosopher.

VF328. Justi, Karl. **Winckelmann und seine Zeitgenossen.** 5th ed., 3 v., Köln, 1956. Magnificent biography of the interpreter of classic art that contains a full description of the attitudes of 18th century civilization toward classical antiquity.

VF329. Dehjo, Georg. **Geschichte der deutschen Kunst.** 4 v. Berlin and Leipzig, 1930–34. Outstanding work by a distinguished German historian of art, well and simply written.

VF330. Stange, Alfred. **German paintings, XIV–XVI centuries.** Ed by André Glöckner. N.Y., 1950. Broad coverage; many large plates. [JSC]

VF331. Panofsky, Erwin. **Albrecht Dürer.** 3rd ed., 2 v., Princeton, 1948.

VF332. Ganz, Paul. **The paintings of Hans Holbein.** N.Y., 1950.

VF333. Pevsner, Nikolaus, and Michael Meier. **Grünewald.** N.Y., 1958. Excellent reproductions; catalog of paintings and drawings; bibliography. [JSC]

VF334. Baldass, Ludwig von. **Albrecht Altdorfer.** Zürich, 1941. Basic monograph. [JSC]

VF335. Goering, Max. **Deutsche Malerei des siebzehnten und achtzehnten Jahrhunderts, von dem Manieristen bis zum Klassizismus.** Berlin, 1940.

VF336. Feulner, Adolf. **Die deutsche Plastik des siebzehnten Jahrhunderts.** Florence, 1926.

VF337. Pinder, Wilhelm. **Deutscher Barock.** Königstein in Taunus, 1924.

VF338. Hager, Werner. **Die Bauten des deutschen Barocks, 1690–1770.** Jena, 1942.

VF339. Bovy, Adrien. **La peinture suisse de 1600 à 1900.** Basel, 1948.

VF340. Korff, Hermann A. **Geist der Goethezeit.** 4 v. Leipzig, 1925–53. Synthesis of thought and ideas of the leaders of classic German literature.

VF341. Lütgert, Wilhelm. **Die Religion des deutschen Idealismus und ihr Ende.** 4 v. Gütersloh, 1923–30. Intellectual history of German philosophical idealism and its part in the rise of pessimism and materialism as well as the decline of Christian beliefs.

VF342. Kahn, Ludwig W. **Social ideals in German literature, 1770–1830.** N.Y., 1938. Study of social ideals as reflected in German literature.

VF343. Hirsch, Emanuel. **Staat und Kirche im 19. und 20. Jahrhundert.** Göttingen, 1929. Suggestive essay on the state-church relationship, by a conservative Protestant theologian.

VF344. ———. **Geschichte der neueren evangelischen Theologie im Zusammenhang mit den allgemeinen Bewegungen des europäischen Denkens.** 5 v. Gütersloh, 1949–54. Detailed and penetrating history of German Protestant theology.

VF345. Kissling, Johann B. **Der deutsche Protestantismus, 1817–1917.** 2 v. Münster, 1917–18. A history of German Protestantism by a German Catholic writer.

VF346. Ehrhard, Albert. **Der Katholizismus und das zwanzigste Jahrhundert im Lichte der kirchlichen Entwicklung der Neuzeit.** 9th–12th eds., Stuttgart and Vienna, 1902. Appraisal of the history of German Catholicism in the 19th century, by a thoughtful Catholic historian.

VF347. Vigener, Fritz. **Ketteler: ein deutsches Bischofsleben des 19. Jahrhunderts.** Munich and Berlin, 1924. Biography of the leading bishop and founder of the Catholic movement of social reform during the age of national unification.

BIOGRAPHIES

VF348. Allgemeine deutsche Biographie. Ed. by Rochus von Liliencron, Franz X. von Wegele, and Anton Bettelheim. 56 v. Leipzig, 1875–1912. [Königlichen Akademie der Wissenschaften, Historische Kommission.] Done at the instigation of Leopold von Ranke, this dictionary of German national biography, written by the best historians of the late 19th century, achieved high standards. It contains biographies of prominent Germans from early days to the end of the 19th century.

VF349. Biographisches Jahrbuch und deutscher Nekrolog. Ed. by Anton Bettelheim. 18 v. Berlin, 1897–1917. This and *VF350* contain biographical articles on prominent persons deceased within the given years. The volumes are highly selective, the articles somewhat uneven.

VF350. Deutsches biographisches Jahrbuch. 11 v. Berlin and Leipzig, 1925–32.

VF351. Rössler, Hellmuth, and Günther Franz. **Biographisches Wörterbuch zur deutschen Geschichte.** Munich, 1953. Useful biographical handbook containing brief information.

VF352. Die grossen Deutschen: deutsche Biographie. Ed. by Hermann Heimpel, Theodor Heuss, and Benno Reifenberg. 5 v. Berlin, 1956–57. Collection of biographical studies of "great" Germans by well-qualified scholars and writers. Few political figures are included.

VF353. Wer ist Wer. Berlin, 1905 ff. (Title varies.) The German *Who's who.*

VF354. Wurzbach, Constantin von. **Biographisches Lexicon des Kaiserthums Österreich.** 60 v. in 36. Vienna, 1856–91. Extensive though not very satisfactory biographical dictionary covering the Austrian lands of the Hapsburg monarchy since 1750.

VF355. Österreichischen Akademie der Wissenschaften. **Österreichisches Biographisches Lexikon, 1815–1950.** Ed. by Leo Santifaller. Graz, 1954 ff. New Austrian biographical dictionary, critically done.

In addition to the above biographical dictionaries, see numerous individual biographies cited in preceding subsections.

PERIODICALS

Germany

VF356. Annalen des historischen Vereins für den Niederrhein. Düsseldorf, 1855 ff.

VF357. Archiv für Kulturgeschichte. Berlin, etc., 1903 ff. (Quarterly.)

VF358. Archiv für Reformationsgeschichte. Leipzig, 1903 ff. (Semiannual.)

VF359. Forschungen zur brandenburgischen und preussischen Geschichte. 54 v. Leipzig, 1888–1943.

VF360. Geschichte in Wissenschaft und Unterricht. Stuttgart, 1950 ff. (Monthly.) Supersedes *Vergangenheit und Gegenwart* (32 v., Leipzig, 1911–42).

VF361. Historische Vierteljahrschrift. 31 v. Freiburg and Leipzig, 1898–1939.

VF362. Historische Zeitschrift. Munich, 1859 ff. (Frequency varies.)

VF363. Das historisch-politische Buch: ein Wegweiser durch das Schrifttum. Göttingen, 1953 ff.

VF364. Neues Archiv für sächsische Geschichte und Altertumskunde. 59 v. Leipzig, 1880–1938. Supersedes *Archiv für sächsische Geschichte* (18 v. in 9, Leipzig, 1863–80).

VF365. Niedersächsisches Jahrbuch für Landesgeschichte. Hannover, 1924 ff. Supersedes *Zeitschrift des historischen Vereins für Niedersachsen* (1835–1923).

VF366. Rheinische Vierteljahrsblätter. Bonn, 1931 ff. (Quarterly.)

VF367. Schmollers Jahrbuch für Gesetzgebung, Verwaltung, und Volkswirtschaft im deutschen Reiche. Leipzig, 1877 ff. (Bimonthly.)

VF368. Vierteljahrschrift für Sozial- und Wirtschaftsgeschichte. Leipzig and Stuttgart, 1903 ff. (Quarterly.)

VF369. Vierteljahrshefte für Zeitgeschichte. Stuttgart, 1953 ff. (Quarterly.)

VF370. Die Welt als Geschichte. Stuttgart, 1935 ff. (Bimonthly.)

VF371. Westfalen: Hefte für Geschichte, Kunst, und Volkskunde. Münster, 1909 ff. (3 nos. per year.)

VF372. Zeitschrift für Geschichtswissenschaft. Berlin (East Germany), 1953 ff. (Bimonthly.)

VF373. Zeitschrift der Gesellschaft für Schleswig-Holsteinische Geschichte. See *VB181.*

VF374. Zeitschrift des Vereins für hessische Geschichte und Landeskunde. Kassel, 1837 ff.

VF375. Zeitschrift für bayerische Landesgeschichte. Munich, 1928 ff.

VF376. Zeitschrift für die Geschichte des Oberrheins. Karlsruhe and Freiburg, 1850 ff. (Irregular quarterly.)

VF377. Zeitschrift für Kirchengeschichte. Gotha, 1876 ff. (Irregular quarterly.)

VF378. Zeitschrift für württembergische Landesgeschichte. Stuttgart, 1937 ff. (Irregular.) Supersedes *Württembergische Vierteljahreshefte für Landesgeschichte* (55 v. in 49, Stuttgart, 1878–1936).

Austria

VF379. Archiv für österreichische Geschichte. Vienna, 1848 ff.

VF380. Mitteilungen des Instituts für österreichische Geschichtsforschung. Vienna, 1945 ff. Supersedes *Mitteilungen des Instituts für Geschichtsforschung und Archivwissenschaft in Wien* (1 v., 1944); which superseded *Mitteilungen des österreichischen Instituts für Geschichtsforschung* (54 v., 1880–1943).

VF381. Mitteilungen des österreichischen Staatsarchivs. Vienna, 1948 ff. (Annual.)

Switzerland

VF382. Schweizer Beiträge zur allgemeinen Geschichte. Zürich, 1943 ff. (Annual.)

VF383. Schweizerische Zeitschrift für Geschichte. Zürich, 1951 ff. (Quarterly.) Supersedes *Zeitschrift für schweizerische Geschichte* (30 v., Zürich, 1921–50).

SECTION W

Eastern Europe

S. HARRISON THOMSON *

GENERAL

The history of this area has been one of great mobility of frontiers. States have appeared and then vanished from the maps. Peoples have been conquered, then risen again to independence. In the process of conquest and revival, whole areas larger than single states have been under one or another multi-national empire. For this reason, any bibliography that adheres to strictly national lines may quite easily omit important works that cover several such national units or are concerned with problems of broader extent. In an effort to avoid such omissions, there are listed below recent significant titles which, while they may not be included under the separate country designations, are nevertheless indispensable for study of this area.

BIBLIOGRAPHIES

W1. U. S. Library of Congress. **Eastern European accessions index.** Washington, 1951 ff. (Monthly. Title varies.)

W2. Savadjian, Léon, ed. **Bibliographie balkanique.** 1920–38. 8 v. Paris, 1931–39. Classified.

ENCYCLOPEDIAS AND WORKS OF REFERENCE

W3. Betts, Reginald R. **Central and south east Europe, 1945–48.** London, 1950.

W4. Strakhovsky, Leonid I., ed. **A handbook of Slavic studies.** See *K14*.

W5. Handbook of central and east Europe. Zürich, 1932 ff. (Annual.)

W6. Slavonic encyclopaedia. Ed. by Joseph S. Rouček. N.Y., 1949. To be used with caution.

GEOGRAPHIES, GAZETTEERS, AND ATLASES

W7. Ancel, Jacques. **Géographie des frontières.** Paris, 1938.

W8. Kostov, Dimitŭr. **Geografiia na Bŭlgariia i sŭsednite dŭrzhavi.** [Geography of Bulgaria and neighboring countries.] Plovdiv, 1928.

W9. Martonne, Emmanuel de. **Europe centrale.** 2 v. Paris, 1930–31. [Géographie universelle, 4.]

W10. Wright, John K., and Elizabeth T. Platt. **Aids to geographical research.** See *B189*.

* The following contributed items and comments indicated by their respective initials: Elemer Bako (EB), George Bárány (GB), John C. Campbell (JCC), James F. Clarke (JFC), F. G. Heymann (FGH), Charles Jelavich (CJ), Otakar Odložilík (OO), Stavro Skendi (SS), Francis Wagner (FW), and René Wellek (RW). Other contributors are acknowledged in some of the subsections that follow.

567

DEMOGRAPHIC STUDIES

W11. Kulischer, Eugene M. **Europe on the move: war and population changes, 1917–1947.** See *A1218.*

W12. Ladas, Stephen P. **The exchange of minorities: Bulgaria, Greece, and Turkey.** N.Y., 1932.

W13. Niederle, Lubor. **La race slave: statistique, démographie, anthropologie.** Paris, 1911.

W14. Pétroff, Thomas. **Les minorités nationales en Europe centrale et orientale.** Paris, 1935.

W15. Schechtman, Joseph B. **European population transfers, 1939–1945.** See *AF25.*

W16. Wiskemann, Elizabeth. **Germany's eastern neighbors.** London, 1956.

W17. Wanklyn, Harriet G. **The eastern marchlands of Europe.** London, 1941.

LINGUISTIC GUIDE

W18. De Bray, Reginald G. A. **Guide to the Slavonic languages.** London, 1951.

HISTORIOGRAPHY

W19. Macůrek, Josef. **Dějepisectví evropského východu.** [Historiography of eastern Europe.] Prague, 1946. A most useful manual.

W20. Domanovzsky, Alexandre. **La méthode historique de M. Nicolas Jorga.** Budapest, 1938[?]. A book in answer to a review.

SHORTER HISTORIES

W21. Aulneau, Joseph. **Histoire de l'Europe centrale.** Paris, 1926. Emphasis on post-Westphalian period.

W22. Bidlo, Jaroslav. **Dějiny slovanstva.** [History of Slavdom.] Prague, 1927. Emphasizes origins and interrelationships.

W23. Cross, Samuel H. **Slavic civilization through the ages.** Cambridge, Mass., 1948. A summary sketch.

W24. Halecki, Oskar. **Borderlands of western civilization: a history of east central Europe.** See *K180.*

W25. Ristelhueber, René. **Histoire des peuples balkaniques.** Paris, 1950.

W26. Schevill, Ferdinand, and Wesley M. Gewehr. **The history of the Balkan Peninsula from the earliest times to the present day.** 2nd ed., N.Y., 1933. Revision based on latest literature in western languages.

W27. Stadtmüller, Georg. **Geschichte Südosteuropas.** See *L174.*

W28. Stavrianos, Leften S. **The Balkans since 1453.** See *S65.*

W29. Taylor, Alan J. P. **The Hapsburg monarchy, 1809–1918.** London, 1948.

W30. Wolff, Robert L. **The Balkans in our time.** See *AF157.*

LONGER HISTORY

W31. Macůrek, Josef. **Dějiny východních slovanu.** [History of Eastern Slavs.] 3 v. Prague, 1947.

HISTORIES OF SPECIAL PERIODS

W32. Dvornik, Francis. **The making of central and eastern Europe.** London, 1949.

W33. ——. **The Slavs: their early history and civilization.** Boston, 1956.

W34. Fejtö, François. **The opening of an era, 1848.** London, 1948. A symposium translated from French.

W35. Gedye, George E. R. **Betrayal in central Europe: Austria and Czechoslovakia, the fallen bastions.** N.Y., 1939.

W36. Helmreich, Ernst C. **The diplomacy of the Balkan wars.** Cambridge, Mass., 1938.

W37. Kann, Robert A. **The multinational empire: nationalism and national reform in the Hapsburg monarchy, 1848–1918.** See *VF258.*

W38. Machray, Robert. **The Little Entente.** London, 1929.

W39. ——. **The struggle for the Danube and the Little Entente.** London, 1938.

W40. May, Arthur J. **The Hapsburg monarchy, 1867–1914.** See *VF262.*

W41. Mousset, Albert. **Le monde slave.** 2nd ed., Paris, 1946. English tr., *The world of the Slavs,* N.Y., 1950.

W42. Prelog, Milan. **Pouť Slovanů do Moskvy, 1867.** [The trip of the Slavs to Moscow, 1867.] Prague, 1931.

W43. ——. **Slavenska renesansa, 1780–1848.** [The Slavic renaissance, 1780–1848.] Zagreb, 1924.

W44. Seton-Watson, Hugh. **Eastern Europe between the wars, 1918–1941.** See *AF155.*

W45. Sumner, Benedict H. **Russia and the Balkans, 1870–1880.** See *X223.*

W46. Valjavec, Fritz. **Geschichte der Kulturbeziehungen zur Südosteuropa.** 2nd ed., 3 v., Munich, 1953–59.

HISTORIES OF SPECIAL TOPICS

Economics

W47. Mid-European Law Project. **Economic treaties and agreements of the Soviet bloc in eastern Europe, 1945–51.** N.Y., 1952.

W48. Karlikovitch, Douchan. **Le rapprochement économique des pays danubiens.** Paris, 1937.

W49. Pasvolsky, Leo. **Economic nationalism of the Danubian states.** N.Y., 1928.

Nationalism

W50. Fischel, Alfred. **Der Panslawismus bis zum Weltkrieg.** Berlin, 1919.

W51. Janowsky, Oscar I. **Nationalities and national minorities (with special reference to east-central Europe).** See *AH329*.
W52. Kohn, Hans. **Pan-Slavism, its history and ideology.** See *X448*.

Post-1945 Development

W53. Fejtö, François. **Histoire des démocraties populaires.** Paris, 1952.
W54. Lazitch, Branko M. **Les partis communistes d'Europe, 1919–1955.** See *AH43*.
W55. Seton-Watson, Hugh. **The east European revolution.** London, 1950.

Literature

W56. Die osteuropäischen Literaturen und die slawischen Sprachen. Berlin, 1908. [Die Kultur der Gegenwart.]
W57. Karásek, Josef. **Slavische Literaturgeschichte.** 2 v. Leipzig, 1906. Though very brief, still a fine introductory survey of all Slavic literatures except Russian. [RW]
W58. Máchal, Jan. **Slovanské literatury.** [Slavic literatures.] 3 v. Prague, 1922–29. Only modern attempt at general history of Slavic literatures. [RW]
W59. Pypin, Aleksandr N. **Istoriia slavianskikh literatur.** [History of Slavic literatures.] 2nd ed., 2 v., St. Petersburg, 1879–81. German ed., *Geschichte der slavischen*

Literaturen, 2 v., Leipzig, 1880–84. Older standard work. [RW]

PERIODICALS

W60. The American Slavic and east European review. Menasha, Wis., 1941. (Quarterly.)
W61. Blick nach Osten. Klagenfurt and Vienna, 1948–52. (Quarterly.) English language issue, *Eastern review.*
W62. Der europäische Osten. Munich, 1955. (Monthly.)
W63. Jahrbücher für Geschichte Osteuropas. Breslau, 1936–41; Munich, 1953 ff. (Quarterly.)
W64. Journal of central European affairs. Boulder, Colo., 1941 ff. (Quarterly.)
W65. Oriente. Madrid, 1951 ff. (Quarterly.)
W66. Osteuropa. Stuttgart, 1951 ff. (Bimonthly.)
W67. Revue des études slaves. Paris, 1921 ff. (Irregular.)
W68. The Slavonic and east European review. Menasha, Wis. and London, 1922 ff. (Frequency and title vary.)
W69. Studia slavica. Budapest, 1955 ff. (Quarterly.)
W70. Wiener slavistisches Jahrbuch. Vienna, 1950 ff. (Annual.)
W71. Zeitschrift für Ostforschung. Marburg, 1952 ff. (Quarterly.)

POLAND *

BIBLIOGRAPHIES

W72. Finkel, Ludwik. **Bibliografia historii polskiej.** 3rd ed., 3 v., Warsaw, 1955. A continuation of Estreicher's more extensive bibliography, which stopped essentially in 1900.
W73. Fryde, Matthew M. **Selected works on Polish agrarian history and agriculture.** N.Y., 1952. Value increased by extended comments on works in each field of agrarian history.
W74. Hahn, Wiktor. **Bibliografia bibliografij polskich.** [Bibliography of Polish bibliographies.] 2nd ed., Breslau, 1956.
W75. **Bibliografia historii polskiej.** Ed. by Jan Baumgart. Kraków, 1954 ff. The Polish Academy of Sciences has undertaken to publish bibliographies of Polish history biennially, though this schedule has not been adhered to. The volume for 1948 was published in 1954, for 1949 in the same year, for 1950–51 in 1955, for 1952–53 in 1957.
W76. Maliszewski, Edward. **Bibljografja pamiętników polskich i polski dotyczących.** [Bibliography of Polish memoirs and those

concerning Poland.] Warsaw, 1928. Lists 5,445 items in print or manuscript.
W77. Polska Akademia Umiejętności. **Katalog wydawnictw Polskiej Akademii Umiejętności 1873–1947.** [Catalog of publications of the Polish Academy of Sciences 1873–1947.] 2 v. Kraków, 1948. The most active cultural organization in Poland since its founding in 1873.
W78. Recke, Walter, and Albert M. Wagner. **Bücherkunde zur Geschichte und Literatur des Königreichs Polen.** Warsaw, 1918. Selective but representative of better older literature in Slavic and western languages.
W79. Siemieński, Józef. **Guide des archives de Pologne.** Warsaw, 1933.
W80. Rister, Herbert. **Schrifttum über Polen 1943–1951 mit besonderer Berücksichtigung des Posener Landes.** Marburg, 1953.

ENCYCLOPEDIAS AND WORKS OF REFERENCE

W81. Brückner, Aleksander, ed. **Trzaski, Everta i Michalskiego encyklopedia staro-**

* Professor Thomson was assisted by Professors Oscar Halecki and Zygmunt Gasiorowski in selecting the titles for this subsection on Poland.

polska. [Encyclopedia of ancient Poland.] 2 v. Warsaw, 1939. Emphasis on pre-partition men and issues.

W82. ——. **Dzieje kultury polskiej.** [History of Polish culture.] 2nd ed., 4 v., Warsaw, 1939–46. A classic of Polish scholarship. V. 1 of 3rd and illustrated edition was published in London, 1957.

W83. Halecki, Oscar, ed. **Poland.** N.Y., 1957. A volume in the Mid-European Studies Center series, *East-central Europe under the Communists.* Valuable assemblage of hard-to-find facts on social, economic, political, and cultural aspects of post-1945 Poland.

W84. Polska Akademia Umiejętności. **Polski słownik biograficzny.** [Polish biographical dictionary.] Ed. by Władysław Konopczyński. 7 v. Kraków, 1935–49. Suspended publication in letter G. Resumption announced. Articles are authoritative monographs.

W85. **Pologne 1919–1939.** 3 v. Neuchâtel, Switz., 1946–47. Informative on pre-Communist Poland.

W86. Schmitt, Bernadotte E., ed. **Poland.** Berkeley, 1945. A collaborative work concerned principally with the period 1918–39. Good bibliographies on a variety of subjects.

GEOGRAPHIES

W87. Arnold, Stanisław. **Geografia historyczna Polski.** [Historical geography of Poland.] Warsaw, 1951. Intended as a university textbook, this contains a survey of Polish geography in its historical setting not available elsewhere.

W88. Bujak, Franciszek. **Studja geograficzno - historyczne.** [Geographic - historical studies.] Warsaw, 1925. Emphasizes the discipline of geography and the history of Polish cartography.

W89. Jażdżewski, Konrad. **Atlas do pradziejów Słowian.** [Atlas for the early Slavs.] Łódź, 1948 ff.

W90. Kielczewska-Zalenka, Maria. **O podstawy geograficzne Polski.** [The geographical bases of Poland.] Poznán, 1946. First serious effort to treat the geography of the new Poland and assess the structural changes arising out of the westward transfer of territory.

W91. Lencewicz, Stanisław. **Polska.** [Poland.] Warsaw, 1937. This volume of many illustrations, maps, and tables presents a combination of physical and human geography.

W92. Pawłowski, Stanisław. **Geografia Polski.** [Geography of Poland.] Lwów, 1917.

W93. Tymieniecki, Kazimierz. **Ziemie polskie w starożytności.** [The Polish lands in antiquity.] Poznań, 1951.

ANTHROPOLOGICAL WORKS

W94. Czekanowski, Jan. **Wstep do historii Słowian.** [Introduction to the history of the Slavs.] 2nd ed., Poznań, 1957. Survey of results of last thirty years of archaeological, ethnographic, and anthropological research into the origin of the Slavs. Author places their *locus originis* just east of Mazovia.

W95. ——. **Polska-Słowiańszczyzna: perspektywy antropologiczne.** [Poland-Slavdom: anthropological perspectives.] Warsaw, 1948. Study of Poland's place in the development and differentiation of the various Slavic groups.

W96. Kostrzewski, Józef. **Les origines de la civilisation polonaise: préhistoire-protohistoire.** Paris, 1949. A fair sample of protohistorical methodology applied to Poland.

W97. Krukowski, Stefan, Józef Kostrzewski, and R. Jakimowicz. **Prehistoria ziem polskich.** [Prehistory of Polish lands.] Kraków, 1948.

DEMOGRAPHIC STUDIES

W98. Żółtowski, Adam. **Border of Europe: a study of the Polish eastern provinces.** London, 1950.

W99. Poland. Główny Urząd Statystyczny. **Mały rocznik statystyczny.** [Brief statistical annual.] Warsaw, 1930 ff. Handy manual for population, industry, and commerce.

W100. Zieliński, Henryk. **Population changes in Poland, 1939–1950.** N.Y., 1954.

PRINTED COLLECTIONS OF SOURCES

W101. Biliński, Leon. **Wspomnienia i dokumenty.** [Memoirs and documents.] 2 v. Warsaw, 1924–25.

W102. Borowski, Stanisław, ed. **Kodeks Stanisława Augusta zbiór dokumentów.** [The codex of Stanislaus Augustus: collection of documents.] Warsaw, 1938. Important for history of the Four-Year Diet and its efforts to codify Polish law.

W103. Daszyński, Ignacy. **Pamiętniki.** [Memoirs.] Kraków, 1925.

W104. Głąbiński, Stanisław. **Wspomnienia polityczne.** [Political memoirs.] 3 v. Pelplin, 1939.

W105. Hutten-Czapski, Bogdan F. S., Graf von. **Sechzig Jahre Politik und Gesellschaft.** See *VF153.*

W106. Kutrzeba, Stanisław, and Władysław Semkowicz, eds. **Akta unji Polski z Litwą, 1385–1791.** [Documents of the union of Poland and Lithuania, 1385–1791.] Kraków, 1932.

W107. Pospieszalski, Karol M., and others, eds. **Documenta occupationis teutonicae.** Poznań and Warsaw, 1945 ff. Documents mostly from German files published by

Central Commission for Investigation of German Crimes.

W108. Pulaski, Franciszek, and Władysław Tomkiewicz. **La mission de Claude de Mesmes comte d'Avaux, ambassadeur extraordinaire en Pologne, 1634–1636.** Paris, 1937. Instructions and reports to and from Poland, including many letters to Père Joseph.

HISTORIOGRAPHY

W109. David, Pierre. **Les sources de l'histoire de Pologne à l'époque des Piasts (963–1386).** Paris, 1934.

W110. Handelsman, Marceli. **Historycy: portrety i profile.** [Historians: portraits and profiles.] Warsaw, 1937. Sketches of life and work of leading Polish historians of the last generation. Clear on distinction between two schools, Warsaw and Kraków, and on place of positivism and romanticism in Polish historiography.

W111. Serejski, Marian H. **Studia nad historiografią Polski. V. 1, K. B. Hoffman.** [Studies on the historiography of Poland. V. 1, K. B. Hoffman.] Łódź, 1953. Effects of travel in the West on the historical judgments of K. B. Hoffman in the mid-19th century.

W112. ——. **Koncepcja historii powszechnej Joachima Lelewela.** [The concept of general history of Joachim Lelewel.] Warsaw, 1958. Indicative of revival of interest in Lelewel, the most productive Polish historian of the 19th century, whose liberalism accounts for his popularity in post-1945 Poland.

W113. Ziffer, Bernard. **Poland, history and historians: three bibliographical essays.** N.Y., 1952.

SHORTER GENERAL HISTORIES

W114. Dyboski, Roman. **Poland in world civilization.** N.Y., 1950. Broad picture, with emphasis on cultural relationships.

W115. ——. **Poland.** N.Y., 1933. A brief popular treatment.

W116. Górka, Olgierd A. **Outline of Polish history, past and present.** 2nd ed., London, 1945.

W117. Halecki, Oscar. **A history of Poland.** 2nd ed., N.Y., 1956. The standard short history of Poland.

W118. Macůrek, Josef. **Dějiny polského národa.** [History of the Polish nation.] Prague, 1948. Very thorough and sympathetic text written for the Czech public.

W119. Sobieski, Wacław. **Histoire de Pologne des origines à nos jours.** Paris, 1934. A short and popular history for the French public, by a competent historian.

W120. Wojciechowski, Zygmunt, ed. **Poland's place in Europe.** Poznań, 1947.

Valuable for sketch of relations between Poland and Germany.

LONGER GENERAL HISTORIES

W121. Bardach, Juliusz. **Historia państwa i prawa Polski do roku 1795.** [History of the realm and law of Poland to 1795.] 2 v. Warsaw, 1957. Part of a projected 5 v. history to 1939, with emphasis on constitutional development.

W122. Brückner, Aleksander, Włodzimierz Antoniewicz, and others, eds. **Polska, jej dzieje i kultura.** [Poland, her history and culture.] 3 v. Warsaw, 1927–32. Splendid record of Polish history and culture, by a group of eminent scholars.

W123. Konopczyński, Władysław. **Dzieje Polski nowożytnej.** [History of modern Poland.] 2 v. Warsaw, 1936. The standard treatment of modern Polish history to 1795.

W124. The Cambridge history of Poland. Ed. by William F. Reddaway and others. 2 v. Cambridge, Eng., 1941–50. A well-conceived collaborative work; slightly uneven, but level of various chapters is high. V. 3, bibliography, is in process.

HISTORIES OF SPECIAL PERIODS

To 1569

W125. Friedberg, Marian. **Kultura polska a niemiecka: elementy rodzime a wpływy niemieckie w ustroju i kulturze Polski średniowiecznej.** [Polish and German culture: native elements and German influences in the constitution and culture of medieval Poland.] 2 v. Poznań, 1946.

W126. Grodecki, Roman, Stanisław Zachorowski, and Jan Dąbrowski. **Dzieje Polski średniowiecznej.** [History of medieval Poland.] 2 v. Kraków, 1926.

W127. Halecki, Oskar. **Dzieje Unii jagiellońskiej.** [History of the Jagiellonian Union.] 2 v. Kraków, 1919–20. Thorough study of this crucial event in Polish constitutional development.

W128. Kolankowski, Ludwik. **Polska Jagiellonów: dzieje polityczne.** [Poland of the Jagiellons: political history.] Lwów, 1936.

W129. ——. **Dzieje Wielkiego Księstwa Litewskiego za Jagiellonów.** [History of the Grand Duchy of Lithuania under the Jagiellons.] Warsaw, 1930.

W130. Paszkiewicz, Henryk. **Jagiellonowie a Moskwa.** [The Jagiellonians and Moscow.] Warsaw, 1933.

W131. Roth, Paul. **Die Entstehung des polnischen Staates: eine völkerrechtlich-politische Untersuchung.** Berlin, 1926.

W132. Widajewicz, Józef. **Początki Polski.** [The beginnings of Poland.] Breslau, 1948.

W133. Wojciechowski, Zygmunt. **Polska nad Wisłą i Odrą w X wieku: studium nad**

genezą państwa Piastów i jego cywilizacji. [Poland on the Vistula and the Oder in the tenth century: a study on the rise of the domain of the Piasts and its civilization.] Warsaw, 1939.

W134. ———. **Mieszko I and the rise of the Polish state.** Toruń and Gdynia, 1936. An answer to German historical construction of 10th century relations between Empire and Polish dynasty.

1569–1772

W135. Feldman, Józef. **Polska w dobie wielkiej wojny północnej 1704–1709.** [Poland at the time of the Great Northern War, 1704–1709.] Kraków, 1925.

W136. Konopczyński, Władysław. **Fryderyk Wielki a Polska.** [Frederick the Great and Poland.] Poznań, 1947. A popular but scholarly assessment of Frederick's continuing intrigues against Polish independence.

W137. ———. **Polska a Turcja, 1683–1792.** [Poland and Turkey, 1683–1792.] Warsaw, 1936. Study of the whole southern and southeastern frontier of Poland after Sobieski and the international complications it involved.

W138. Kubala, Ludwik. **Wojny duńskie i pokój oliwski, 1657–1660.** [The Danish War and the Peace of Oliva, 1657–1660.] Lwów, 1922.

W139. ———. **Wojna szwecka w roku 1655 i 1656.** [The Swedish War in 1655 and 1656.] Lwów, 1914. The dramatic events of these two years warmly treated.

W140. Przezdziecki, Rajnold. **Diplomatic ventures and adventures: some experiences of British envoys at the court of Poland.** London, 1953.

W141. Schaeder, Hildegard. **Geschichte der Pläne zur Teilung des alten polnischen Staates seit 1386.** Leipzig, 1937.

Partitioned Poland, 1772–1919

W142. Askenazy, Szymon. **Napoléon et la Pologne.** Brussels, 1925. Tr. of *Napoleon a Polska* (2 v., Warsaw, 1918). Based on long familiarity with Polish and French archival material.

W143. Dembiński, Bronisław. **Polska na przełomie.** [Poland at the turning.] Warsaw, 1913. The issues and pressures, internal and external, on Poland from *ca.* 1770 to *ca.* 1795.

W144. Dmowski, Roman. **Polityka polska i odbudowanie państwa: z dodaniem memorjału "Zagadnienia środkowo-i ,wschodnio-europejskie" i innych dokumentów polityki polskiej z lat 1914–1919.** [Polish politics and national reconstruction: additional materials on the "east-central European question" and other documents pertaining to Polish politics from 1914 to 1919.] Warsaw, 1926.

W145. Fabre, Jean. **Stanislas-Auguste Poniatowski et l'Europe des lumières: étude de cosmopolitisme.** Paris, 1952.

W146. Feldman, Józef. **Bismarck a Polska.** 2nd ed., Kraków, 1947. Traces Bismarck's positions toward the Polish question from 1848. Based on much archival research.

W147. Feldman, Wilhelm. **Dzieje polskiej myśli politycznej w okresie porozbiorowym.** [History of Polish political thought since the partitions.] Kraków, 1913. German ed., *Geschichte der politischen Ideen in Polen seit dessen Teilungen (1795–1914)*, Berlin, 1917. A classic of synthesis. Traces development of Polish thought in the three parts and explains the divergences.

W148. Forst-Battaglia, Otto. **Stanisław August Poniatowski und der Ausgang des alten Polenstaates.** Berlin, 1927.

W149. Handelsman, Marceli, ed. **La Pologne: sa vie économique et sociale pendant la guerre.** Paris and New Haven, 1933.

W150. Jobert, Ambroise. **La Commission d'Education Nationale en Pologne, 1773–1794.** Paris, 1941. Useful survey of whole period of parliamentary reform.

W151. Konopczyński, Władysław. **Konfederacja Barska.** [The Confederation of Bar.] 2 v. Warsaw, 1936–38. Based on archival research hitherto inadequately done.

W152. Korzon, Tadeusz. **Wewnętrzne dzieje Polski za Stanisława Augusta, 1764–1794.** [Internal history of Poland under Stanislaus Augustus, 1764–1794.] 2nd ed., 6 v., Kraków, 1897–98. Very detailed study, with emphasis on social history.

W153. Kukiel, Marjan. **Dzieje wojska polskiego w dobie napoleońskiej.** [History of the Polish army in the Napoleonic period.] 3rd ed., 2 v., Warsaw, 1918–20.

W154. ———. **Czartoryski and European unity, 1770–1861.** Princeton, 1955. Former director of the Czartoryski Archives presents Prince Adam within the framework of Napoleonic and Alexandrian ideas.

W155. Leslie, R. F. **Polish politics and the revolution of November, 1830.** London, 1956. Based on extensive use of Polish monographs, documents, and memoirs. Has a distinctly anti-Czartoryski bias.

W156. Leśnodorski, Bogusław. **Dzieło Sejmu Czteroletniego, 1788–1792: studium historyczno-prawne.** [The work of the Four-Year Diet, 1788–1792: a historico-legal study.] Breslau, 1951. The great reforming Diet with its advanced thinking.

W157. Manteuffel-Szoege, Georg. **Geschichte des polnischen Volkes während seiner Unfreiheit, 1772–1914.** Berlin, 1950. Sympathetic to Poland, critical of Frederick the Great. Forbidden publication under Nazis. Shows familiarity with Polish literature.

W158. Pobóg-Malinowski, Władysław. **Najnowsza historia polityczna Polski, 1864–**

1945. [Political history of modern Poland.] 2 v. Paris, 1953–56.

W159. Rose, William J. **The rise of Polish democracy.** London, 1944. Surveys spirit of renascent Poland after humiliation of partitions.

W160. Tims, Richard W. **Germanizing Prussian Poland: the H-K-T society and the struggle for the eastern marches in the German empire, 1894–1919.** N.Y., 1941.

W161. Tokarz, Wacław. **Galicya w początkach ery Józefińskiej w świetle ankiety urzędowej z roku 1783.** [Galicia at the beginning of the Josephinian era as seen through an official questionnaire of 1783.] Kraków, 1909.

W162. ——. **Wojna polsko-rosyjska, 1830 i 1831.** [The Polish-Russian War of 1830 and 1831.] 2 v. Warsaw, 1930.

W163. Wereszycki, Henryk. **Historia polityczna Polski w dobie popowstaniowej, 1864–1918.** [The political history of Poland in the period after the 1864 revolt to 1918.] Warsaw, 1948.

Independence, 1919–1939

W164. Beck, Józef. **Dernier rapport: politique polonaise, 1926–1939.** Neuchâtel, Switz., 1951. A defense of his record, written in exile in Roumania. Most bitter against Beneš. Should be read along with Szembek's *Journal* (*W179*), which is more factual and informative.

W165. Bregman, Alexandre. **La politique de la Pologne dans la Société des Nations.** Paris, 1932.

W166. Buell, Raymond L. **Poland: key to Europe.** N.Y., 1939. Analysis of Poland's importance as seen on the eve of war, by a careful observer.

W167. Fisher, Harold H. **America and the new Poland.** N.Y., 1928.

W168. Krakowski, Edouard. **Pologne et Russie.** 8th ed., Paris, 1946. Not for the pedantic historian. The soul of Poland dominates the story.

W169. Laeuen, Harald. **Polnisches Zwischenspiel, eine Episode der Ostpolitik.** Berlin, 1940. Useful as showing German approach to a lesser people.

W170. Laroche, Jules A. **La Pologne de Pilsudski: souvenirs d'une ambassade, 1926–1935.** Paris, 1953. Valuable as complement to Léon Noël, *L'agression allemande contre la Pologne* (Paris, 1946). Noël succeeded Laroche as ambassador.

W171. Machray, Robert. **The Poland of Pilsudski.** London, 1936. Sympathetic.

W172. Mackiewicz, Stanisław. **Historia Polski od 11 listopada 1918 r do 17 września 1939.** [History of Poland from November 11, 1918 to September 17, 1939.] London, 1941. Political analysis by a political publicist. Pilsudski's successors were inferior to the marshal.

W173. ——. **Colonel Beck and his policy.** London, 1944. A Polish publicist with political experience criticizes Beck's handling of foreign affairs.

W174. Mason, John B. **The Danzig dilemma: a study in peacemaking by compromise.** London, 1946. Valuable as an account of the course of events. Author concludes that free city arrangement was better than attribution either to Germany or Poland.

W175. Morrow, Ian F. D. **The peace settlement in the German-Polish borderlands: a study of conditions to-day in the pre-war Prussian provinces of East and West Prussia.** London, 1936. Careful examination of the documents and results of the post-Versailles settlements.

W176. Murray, Michael, ed. **Poland's progress, 1919–1939.** London, 1944.

W177. Noël, Léon. **Une ambassade à Varsovie, 1935–1939: l'agression allemande contre la Pologne.** Paris, 1946. The French ambassador to Warsaw tells the story from his point of vantage. His most important papers were destroyed.

W178. Shotwell, James T., and Max M. Laserson. **Poland and Russia, 1919–1945.** N.Y., 1945. Short study of the diplomatic and economic relations between Poland and the Soviet Union.

W179. Szembek, Jan. **Journal, 1933–1939.** See *AH223.* Excellent counterweight to *W164.*

W180. Zweig, Ferdynand. **Poland between two wars.** London, 1944. Survey of the interplay between politics, economics, and social forces, by a former professor of the University of Kraków.

Under Two Masters, 1939–

W181. Ciechanowski, Jan. **Defeat in victory.** See *AH235.*

W182. Deresiewicz, Janusz. **Okupacja niemiecka na ziemiach polskich włączonych do Rzeszy (1939–1945).** [The German occupation in Polish lands annexed to the Reich (1939–1945).] Poznań, 1950. Emphasis on German techniques of confiscation and appropriation.

W183. Malara, Jean, and Lucienne Rey. **La Pologne d'une occupation à l'autre (1944–1952).** Paris, 1952. Analyzes situation under Nazi control, the political structure, and the emigration and Sovietization since 1944.

W184. Mikołajczyk, Stanisław. **The rape of Poland: pattern of Soviet aggression.** N.Y., 1948. The wartime premier of Poland and vice-premier 1945–47 relates his experiences.

W185. Rose, William J. **Poland, old and new.** London, 1948. Author revisited Poland after 1945, and here relates striking comparisons, physical and spiritual, with earlier period.

W186. Du Prel, Maximilian, ed. **Das Generalgouvernement.** 2nd ed., Würzburg, 1942. Collaborative work describing all organs of administration and *deutsche Ordnung.* Nothing is said about the *Vernichtungslager.*

W187. Lane, Arthur B. **I saw Poland betrayed: an American ambassador reports to the American people.** Indianapolis, 1948. Author recounts his efforts to achieve fulfillment of the Yalta understandings in face of Communist evasions and State Department apathy.

HISTORIES OF SPECIAL AREAS

W188. Bukowski, Andrzej. **Regionalizm kaszubski.** [Cassubian regionalism.] Poznań, 1950. First serious analysis of Cassubian regionalism, studied through its literature, journalism, and folklore.

W189. Górski, Karol. **Państwo Krzyżackie w Prusach.** [The Teutonic Order in Prussia.] Danzig, 1946.

W190. Konopczyński, Władysław. **Kwestia bałtycka do XX w.** Danzig, 1947. Shows Poland's role in the Baltic at the several turns in the struggle for predominance between the northern powers.

W191. Kutrzeba, Stanisław. **Gdańsk-Górny Śląsk.** [Danzig-Upper Silesia.] Kraków, 1923.

W192. ———, ed. **Dzieje Śląska od najdawniejszych czasów do r. 1400.** [History of Silesia from the earliest times to 1400.] 3 v. Kraków, 1933–39.

W193. Mitkowski, Józef. **Pomorze zachodnie w stosunku do Polski.** [Western Pomerania in relation to Poland.] Poznań, 1946.

W194. Piwarski, Kazimierz. **Dzieje Prus Wschodnich w czasach nowożytnych.** [History of East Prussia in modern times.] Danzig, 1946. East Prussia has become of more immediate interest to Poland since a part of it is again in Polish possession. This work discusses the Prussian period.

W195. Podoski, B., Z. Jundziłł, and others, eds. **Dzieje Ziem Wielkiego Księstwa Litewskiego.** [History of the Grand Duchy of Lithuania.] London, 1953.

W196. Rose, William J. **The drama of Upper Silesia: a regional study.** Brattleboro, Vt., 1935. History and analysis of conflicting policies and economic needs in a border region desired by both Germany and Poland.

W197. Tyrowicz, Marian. **Galicja od pierwszego rozbioru do Wiosny Ludów 1772–1849.** [Galicia from the first partition to the Springtime of the Nations, 1772–1849.] Breslau, 1956. Broad selection of sources from contemporary journals, official reports, military documents, various legislative bodies in Galicia.

HISTORIES OF SPECIAL TOPICS

Economics

W198. Alton, Thad P. **Polish postwar economy.** N.Y., 1955.

W199. Gąsiorowska, Natalja. **Górnictwo i hutnictwo w Królewstwie Polskiem, 1815–1830.** [Mining and foundry in Kingdom of Poland, 1815–1830.] Warsaw, 1922.

W200. Lipiński, Edward. **Studia nad historią polskiej myśli ekonomicznej.** [Studies on the history of Polish economic thought.] Warsaw, 1956. Collection of monographic studies on Polish economists or economic theoreticians from the 14th to the 19th century. Very informative.

W201. Ptaśnik, Jan. **Miasta i mieszczáństwo w dawnej Polsce.** [Cities and the bourgeoisie in ancient Poland.] 2nd ed., Warsaw, 1949.

W202. Rutkowski, Jan. **Historia gospodarcza Polski.** 2 v. (2nd ed. of v. 1) Poznań, 1946–50. French tr. of v. 1, *Histoire économique de la Pologne avant les partages,* Paris, 1927.

W203. ———. **Studia z dziejów wsi polskiej XVI–XVIII w.** [Studies in the history of the village, 16th–18th centuries.] Warsaw, 1956. Collected studies of a leading economic historian.

W204. Strzeszewski, Czesław. **Kryzys rolniczy na ziemiach Księstwa warszawskiego i Królestwa kongresowego, 1807–1830.** [The agricultural crisis in the territories of the duchy of Warsaw and in Congress Poland, 1807–1830.] Lublin, 1934.

W205. Taylor, Jack. **The economic development of Poland, 1919–1950.** Ithaca, 1952.

W206. Wellisz, Leopold. **Foreign capital in Poland.** London, 1938.

W207. Zweig, Ferdynand. **Poland between two wars: a critical study of social and economic changes.** See *W180.*

Literature and Education

W208. Chlebowski, Bronislav. **La littérature polonaise au XIXᵉ siècle.** Paris, 1933.

W209. Dyboski, Roman. **Modern Polish literature.** London, 1924.

W210. Feldman, Wilhelm. **Współczesna literatura polska.** [Contemporary Polish literature.] 8th ed., Kraków, 1930. Covers the period 1863–1930.

W211. Grabowski, Tadeusz. **Historja literatury polskiej . . . 1000–1930.** [History of Polish literature . . . 1000–1930.] 2 v. Poznań, 1936.

W212. Kleiner, Julius. **Die polnische Literatur.** Potsdam, 1929. Excellent brief history. [RW]

W213. Korbut, Gabrjel. **Literatura polska.**

[Polish literature.] 2nd ed., 4 v., Warsaw, 1929–31. Handbook for students. [RW]
W214. Kridl, Manfred. **A survey of Polish literature and culture.** N.Y., 1956. A thorough and useful survey, the first in English in this compass.
W215. Krzyżanowski, Julian. **Historia literatury polskiej od średniowiecza do XIX w.** [History of Polish literature from the Middle Ages to the 19th century.] Warsaw, 1953. Best recent history. [RW]
W216. Lednicki, Wacław, ed. **Adam Mickiewicz in world literature: a symposium.** Berkeley, 1956. Centennial memorial to the greatest Polish poet.
W217. Lednicki, Wacław. **Life and culture of Poland as reflected in Polish literature.** N.Y., 1944. Polish life and spirit as seen by a historian of literature.
W218. Łoś, Jan. **Początki piśmiennictwa polskiego.** [The beginnings of Polish literature.] 2nd ed., Lwów, 1922. Contains translations into modern Polish of the oldest Polish texts. [RW]
W219. Marcel, Simone. **Histoire de la littérature polonaise des origines au début du XIXe siècle.** Paris, 1957.
W220. Pilat, Roman. **Historja literatury polskiej od czasów najdawniejszych do roku 1815.** [History of Polish literature from the earliest times to 1815.] 3 v. Warsaw, 1925–26. Students' manual. [RW]
W221. Tarnowski, Stanisław. **Historya literatury polskiej.** [History of Polish literature.] 6 v. in 5. Kraków, 1903–07.
W222. Morawski, Kazimierz. **Histoire de l'Université de Cracovie.** 3 v. Paris, 1900–05. Tr. of *Historya Uniwersytetu Jagiellońskiego* (2 v., Kraków, 1900). Detailed history of the earliest Polish university and its place as a center of Polish intellectual contacts with the West.
W223. Chałasiński, Józef. **Społeczeństwo i wychowanie: socjologiczne zagadnienia szkolnictwa i wychowania w społeczeństwie współczesnym.** [Society and education: sociological problems of education in modern society.] Warsaw, 1948.

Religion

W224. Völker, Karl. **Kirchengeschichte Polens.** Berlin and Leipzig, 1930. The peculiar turns and complexities of Polish Christianity reviewed by a Lutheran scholar.
W225. Woliński, Janusz. **Polska i Kościół prawosławny.** [Poland and the Orthodox Church.] Lwów, 1936.

Constitutional History

W226. Kaczmarczyk, Zdzisław. **Monarchia Kazimierza Wielkiego.** [The monarchy of Casimir the Great.] 2 v. Poznań, 1939. Acts

and documents of his reign (1333–70), with commentary.
W227. Konopczyński, Władysław. **Le liberum veto: étude sur le développement du principe majoritaire.** 2 v. Paris, 1930. A classic study, indispensable to any understanding of Polish political tradition. The Polish original was less complete.
W228. Kutrzeba, Stanisław. **Historia ustroju Polski w zarysie.** [History of the Polish constitution in outline.] 7th ed., 4 v., Lwów, 1931. The standard study of Poland's unique constitutional structure.
W229. Wojciechowski, Zygmunt. **L'état polonais au Moyen-Âge: histoire des institutions.** Paris, 1949. Most useful for comparative constitutional and institutional study.

Foreign Relations

W230. **Polska i Litwa w dziejowym stosunku.** [Poland and Lithuania in their historical relations.] Warsaw, 1914. Collaborative work treating various aspects of relations between the two countries, from the Christianization of Lithuania by Poland to the definitive union in 1569.
W231. Breyer, Richard. **Das deutsche Reich und Polen, 1932–1937: Aussenpolitik und Volksgruppenfragen.** Würzburg, 1955.
W232. Smogorzewski, Kazimierz M. **Poland's access to the sea.** London, 1934. Solid discussion of the basic problem of Polish history—free access to the sea.
W233. Sobieski, Wacław. **Der Kampf um die Ostsee von den ältesten Zeiten bis zur Gegenwart.** Leipzig, 1933.
W234. Umiastowski, Roman. **Russia and the Polish republic, 1918–1941.** London, 1945.
W235. Wojciechowski, Zygmunt. **Polska-Niemcy: dziesięć wieków zmagania.** [Poland-Germany: ten centuries of struggle.] Poznań, 1945. The long struggle of Poland for her western frontiers and an outlet to the sea traced as a single conflict.

BIOGRAPHIES

W236. Bartel, Oskar. **Jan Łaski.** V. 1. Warsaw, 1955. First volume of a projected 2 v. history of the greatest Reformation character of Poland. Solid.
W237. Champion, Pierre. **Henri III, roi de Pologne.** 2 v. Paris, 1943–51.
W238. **Étienne Batory, roi de Pologne, prince de Transylvanie.** Ed. by Joseph Filipowski. Kraków, 1935. Collaborative work, by Hungarian and Polish scholars, to commemorate the 400th anniversary of Bathory's birth.
W239. Forst-Battaglia, Otto. **Jan Sobieski, König von Polen.** 2 v. Zürich, 1946. Popular biography.

W240. Haiman, Miecislaus. **Kosciuszko, leader and exile.** N.Y., 1946.

W241. Handelsman, Marceli. **Adam Czartoryski.** 3 v. in 4. Warsaw, 1948–50. The last work of the leader of the Warsaw school, published posthumously.

W242. Kaczmarczyk, Zdzisław. **Kazimierz Wielki, 1333–1370.** [Casimir the Great, 1333–1370.] Warsaw, 1948.

W243. Mizwa, Stephen P., ed. **Great men and women of Poland.** N.Y., 1941. Short vignettes of eighteen carefully chosen leaders of Polish life from the time of Mieszko to Conrad.

W244. Konopczyński, Władysław. **Kazimierz Pułaski.** Kraków, 1931. The standard biography of General Pulaski, covering also his American years.

W245. ——. **Stanisław Konarski.** Warsaw, 1926. Long archival study of life and activity of the 18th century political and educational reformer.

W246. Morton, John B. **Sobieski, king of Poland.** London, 1932. A somewhat idealizing picture.

W247. Papée, Fryderyk. **Jan Olbracht.** Kraków, 1936.

W248. ——. **Aleksander Jagiellończyk.** Kraków, 1949.

W249. Pociecha, Władysław. **Królowa Bona, 1494–1557: czasy i ludzie odrodzenia.** [Queen Bona Sforza: the era and the people of the Renaissance.] Poznań, 1949 ff.

W250. Reddaway, William F. **Marshal Pilsudski.** London, 1939.

W251. Rose, William J. **Stanislas Konarski, reformer of education in XVIIIth century Poland.** London, 1929.

W252. Skałkowski, Adam M. **Aleksander Wielopolski w świetle archiwów rodzinnych, 1803–1877.** [Alexander Wielopolski in the light of the family archives, 1803–1877.] Poznań, 1947.

W253. Wojciechowski, Zygmunt. **Zygmunt Stary, 1506–1548.** Warsaw, 1946. Best treatment of the Renaissance ruler and his handling of the early Reformation.

W254. Zakrzewski, Stanisław. **Mieszko I.** Warsaw, 1921.

W255. ——. **Bolesław Chrobry Wielki.** Lwów, 1925. A classic in conception and reconstruction of a very complex period.

PERIODICALS

W256. Ateneum wileńskie. [The Wilno athenaeum.] Wilno, 1923–39. (Quarterly.)

W257. Czasopismo prawno-historyczne. [Legal-historical journal.] Poznań, 1948 ff. (Irregular.)

W258. Niepodległość. [Independence.] Warsaw, 1929–39. (Irregular.) Especially concerned with the struggle for freedom since the partitions.

W258a. Kwartalnik historyczny. [Historical quarterly.] Lwów-Warsaw, 1886 ff.

W259. Przegląd historyczny. [Historical review.] Warsaw, 1905–43. (Irregular.)

W260. Przegląd zachodni. [The Western review.] Poznań, 1945 ff. (Monthly.) Early numbers appeared in English or French abridgments. Emphasis on former German lands and German question in general.

W261. Reformacja w Polsce. [The Reformation in Poland.] Warsaw, 1921–54. (Quarterly.) Especially valuable for studies of Unitarianism and Socinianism.

W262. Roczniki historyczne. [Historical annals.] Poznań, 1925 ff. (Semiannual.)

W263. Przegląd nauk historycznych i społecznych. [Review of historical and social sciences.] Łódź, 1951 ff.

W264. Roczniki dziejów społecznych i gospodarczych. [Annals of social and economic history.] Lwów, Toruń, and Poznań, 1932 ff. (Irregular.)

W265. Sobótka. Breslau, 1946 ff. (Irregular.) Devoted to history of Silesia.

W266. Teki historyczne. [Historical portfolios.] London, 1947 ff. (Quarterly.)

W267. Zapiski historyczne. [Historical notes.] Toruń, 1931 ff. (Quarterly.) Concerned with history of the Baltic regions of Poland.

CZECHOSLOVAKIA

BIBLIOGRAPHIES

W268. Bibliografie české historie. 1904–36. Prague, 1905–38. Intended as a continuation of *W271*. For some years it appeared annually, but more usually a volume covered two to four years. [OO]

W269. Český Časopis Historický. Bibliografie vědecké práce o české minulosti za posledních čtyřicet let . . . 1895–1934. [Bibliography of scholarly work on the Czech past over the past forty years, 1895–1934.] Comp. by Josef Klik. Prague, 1935.

W270. Mišianik, Ján. **Bibliografia slovenského písomnictva.** [Bibliography of Slovak literature.] Bratislava, 1946. Arranged alphabetically by author. Writings in all languages from 16th century.

W271. Zíbrt, Čeněk. **Bibliografie české historie.** 5 v. Prague, 1900–12. Definitive and authoritative for Czech history to 1679. [OO]

ENCYCLOPEDIAS AND WORKS OF REFERENCE

W272. Bušek, Vratislav, and Nicholas Spulber, eds. **Czechoslovakia.** N.Y., 1957.

Compendious collection of facts and figures on Czechoslovakia under Communist rule. Helpful appendices and bibliography.
W273. Slovenská vlastiveda. [Slovak encyclopedia.] Ed. by L'udovít Novák. 4 v. Bratislava, 1943–46.
W274. Československá vlastivěda. [Czechoslovak encyclopedia.] 10 v. and 2 suppl. Prague, 1929–36. Covers main areas of the nation's life: art, literature, the state, geography, music, etc. V. 4 and supplement are on history. Very useful bibliography.
W275. Ottův slovník naučný. 28 v. Prague, 1888–1909. Standard Czech encyclopedia, published by Jan Otto. Various editors. [OO]
W276. Ottův slovník naučný nové doby. 6 v. in 12. Prague, 1930–43. Supplements the above. Covers letters A to Uz. [OO]
W277. Masarykův slovník naučný. [The Masaryk encyclopedia.] 7 v. Prague, 1925–33. Popular encyclopedia, useful for primary information. [OO]

GEOGRAPHIES AND ATLASES

W278. Atlas Československé Republiky. Prague, 1935.
W279. Blažek, Miroslav. **Hospodářská geografie Československa.** [Economic geography of Czechoslovakia.] Prague, 1953.
W280. Československo v mapách. [Czechoslovakia in maps.] Prague, 1954.
W281. Hromádka, Ján. **Všeobecný zemepis Slovenska.** [General geography of Slovakia.] Bratislava, 1943. Many sketches, maps, and illustrations. [OO]
W282. Konček, Mikuláš, and Michal Luknis. **Geografia Slovaca.** [Geography of Slovakia.] Bratislava, 1949.

ANTHROPOLOGY

W283. Eisner, Jan. **Slovensko v pravěku.** [Slovakia in prehistoric times.] Bratislava, 1933. On basis of recent excavations of the Stone Age grottoes and other research, Eisner concludes the area was inhabited by Slavs before the Avars arrived in the valley of the Danube.

DEMOGRAPHY

W284. Recensement de la population de la république tchécoslovaque, effectué le 1er décembre. 4 v. Prague, 1934–39.

LINGUISTICS

W285. Novák, L'udovít, and Eugen Pauliny. **Linguistica slovaca.** Bratislava, 1939–48. (Annual.) Since 1932 the Slovak Academy of Arts and Sciences has published and sponsored over thirty substantial monographic studies in linguistics and comparative philology with emphasis on the Slavic and east European branches.

PRINTED COLLECTIONS OF SOURCES

W286. Codex diplomaticus et epistolaris Moraviae. Ed. by Antonius Boczek and others. 15 v. Brünn, 1836–1903. Indispensable for any study of administrative or diplomatic history of Bohemia-Moravia. [OO]
W287. Emler, Josef, and others, eds. **Fontes rerum bohemicarum.** V. 1–6, 8. Prague, 1873–1932. Critical edition of sources of medieval history of Bohemia. V. 7 never published. [OO]
W288. Regesta diplomatica nec non epistolaria Bohemiae et Moraviae. Ed. by Karel J. Erben, Josef Emler, and others. 7 v. Prague, 1855–1954.
W289. Codex diplomaticus et epistolaris regni Bohemiae. Ed. by Gustav Friedrich. Prague, 1904 ff. (In progress. 3 v. to date.) Critical edition of charters and letters relating to Bohemia from the earliest times to 1238. [OO]
W290. Husa, Václav, ed. **Naše národní minulost v dokumentech.** V. 1, **Do zrušení nevolnictví.** [Our national past in documents. V. 1, To the abolition of serfdom.] Prague, 1954. Selected documents, in Czech and Slovak translation, illustrating Czech and Slovak history up to 1785. Emphasis on documents showing class conflict. [OO]
W291. Monumenta vaticana res gestas Bohemicas illustrantia. Ed. by Ladislaus Klicman and others. Prague, 1903 ff. (5 v. in 8 to date.) Papal briefs and letters from Czech prelates and rulers beginning in 1342.
W292. Acta sacrae congregationis de propaganda fide res gestas Bohemicas illustrantia. Ed. by Ignatius Kollman. 3 v. Prague, 1939.
W293. Archiv český. 37 v. Prague, 1840–1941. A series of volumes, with documents in the Czech language, illustrating the history of Bohemia from the 14th to 17th century. [OO]

Memoir Sources

W294. Černý, Jan M., ed. **Boj za právo.** [The struggle for our rights.] 2 v. Prague, 1893. Documents relating to political developments in Bohemia, 1848–60. Very valuable. [OO]
W295. Cvejn, Karel, ed. **Josef V. Frič v dopisech a denících.** [Joseph V. Frič in his letters and diaries.] Prague, 1955. Selected letters and passages from diaries of a Czech poet and political thinker who was active about 1848–66. [OO]
W296. Dyk, Viktor. **Vzpomínky a komentáře.** [Recollections and commentary.] 2 v. Prague, 1927. Memoirs and sketches, by

a leading poet, relating to Czech literary life from 1893 to 1918. [OO]

W297. Heidler, Jan, ed. **Příspěvky k listáři Dra. Frant. Lad. Riegra.** [Additions to the correspondence of Dr. F. L. Rieger.] 2 v. Prague, 1924–26. Excerpts from Rieger's correspondence, 1836–1903. Important as a source of modern Czech history. [OO]

W298. Herben, Jan. **Kniha vzpomínek.** [A book of recollections.] Prague, 1935. Memoirs of a Czech novelist and journalist, a close collaborator of T. G. Masaryk. [OO]

W299. Hikl, Karel. **Listy českého probuzení.** [Letters of the Czech revival.] Prague, 1920. Selected letters of the pioneers of the Czech national revival. [OO]

W300. Hruby, František, ed. **Moravské korespondence a akta z let 1620–1636.** [Moravian correspondence from the year 1620 to 1636.] 2 v. Brünn, 1934–37. Documents illustrating history of Moravia. [OO]

W301. Kaizl, Josef. **Z mého života.** [Out of my life.] 4 v. Prague, 1908–14. Biographical materials, letters, diaries, etc., illustrating life and career of a Czech leader, collaborator of T. G. Masaryk. [OO]

W302. Kalista, Zdeněk. **Cesty ve znamení kříže.** [Travels in the name of the Cross.] Prague, 1941. Letters of Czech missionaries from various parts of the world (17th and 18th centuries). [OO]

W303. Kameníček, František, ed. **Paměti a listář Dra. Aloise Pražáka.** [Memoirs and correspondence of Dr. Alois Pražák.] 2 v. Prague, 1926–27. Letters, memoirs, and other documents. Important source material for modern Czech history relating especially to Moravia. [OO]

W304. Kvačala, Jan, ed. **Korespondence Jana Amosa Komenského.** [Correspondence of John Amos Komenský.] 2 v. Prague, 1897–1902. Another collection of Comenius' letters, supplementing *W306.* [OO]

W305. Nováček, Vojtěch J., ed. **Františka Palackého korespondence a zápisky.** [Correspondence and notes of František Palacký.] 3 v. Prague, 1898–1911. Letters, autobiographical notes, and other documents of Palacký covering his early life to 1826. [OO]

W306. Patera, Adolf, ed. **Jana Amose Komenského korespondence.** [Correspondence of John Amos Komenský.] Prague, 1892. A collection of letters. [OO]

W307. Quis, Ladislav, ed. **Korespondence Karla Havlíčka.** [Correspondence of Karel Havlíček.] Prague, 1903.

W308. Šrobár, Vavro J. **Z môjho života.** [Out of my life.] Prague, 1946. Memoirs of a Slovak leader. [OO]

W309. Stašek, Antal. **Vzpomínky** [Recollections.] Prague, 1925. Memoirs of a Czech novelist relating to literary and political life

in Bohemia in the second half of the 19th century. [OO]

HISTORIOGRAPHY

W310. Chaloupecký, Václav. **František Palacký.** Prague, 1912. A short biography of the leading Czech historian and political leader. [OO]

W311. Lützow, Frantz H. **Lectures on historians of Bohemia.** London, 1905.

W312. Novotný, Václav. **České dějepisectví v prvém desetiletí republiky.** [Czech historiography in the first decade of the republic.] Prague, 1929. A survey, with brief evaluation, of historical production 1918–28, by a leading Czech historian.

W313. Plaschka, Richard. **Von Palacký bis Pekař: Geschichtswissenschaft und Nationalbewusstsein bei den Tschechen.** Graz and Cologne, 1955. Based on thorough reading of both Czech and Sudetan German sources. Focused on political implications of Czech historical science rather than on the broader concepts of historiography.

W314. Werstadt, Jaroslav. **Odkazy dějin a dějepisců.** [Legacies of history and historians.] Prague, 1948. Collection of articles, by Werstadt, focused on Czech historians and their various approaches to the national history.

SHORTER GENERAL HISTORIES

W315. Krofta, Kamil. **A short history of Czechoslovakia.** N.Y., 1934. Good, highly condensed survey of the whole of Czech and Czechoslovak history to about 1930, essentially factually sound and unbiased, mostly following strictly chronological lines except for some socio-political analysis in treatment of the latest phase. [FGH]

W316. Lützow, Franz H. **Bohemia, an historical sketch.** Rev. ed., London, 1939. Originally covered to 1620, but the 1939 edition brought the story up to date. Still valuable.

W317. Odložilík, Otakar. **Nástin československých dějin.** [A sketch of Czechoslovak history.] 5th ed., Prague, 1947. Brilliant work, emphasizing significance of central position of the peoples of the country and their function as cultural catalysts.

W318. Prokeš, Jaroslav. **Histoire tchécoslovaque.** Prague, 1927. Excellent survey.

W319. Seton-Watson, Robert W. **A history of the Czechs and Slovaks.** London, 1943. Excellent account of the changing structure of the lands of the Bohemian crown. Tends to view Bohemia from Vienna.

W320. Thomson, S. Harrison. **Czechoslovakia in European history.** 2nd. ed., Princeton, 1953. Consideration of leading problems of Czechoslovak struggle for independence from early times.

LONGER GENERAL HISTORIES

W321. Bokes, František. **Dejiny Slovenska a Slovákov od najstarších čias po oslobodenie.** [History of Slovakia and the Slovaks from the earliest times to the era of liberation.] Bratislava, 1946. A sound and judicious treatment of the history of the Slovak people under Magyar rule and as a part of the republic.

W322. Co daly naše země Evropě a lidstvu. [What our country has given Europe and humanity.] Ed. by Vilém Mathesius. 2 v. Prague, 1939. Collection of essays, by leading Czech scholars, pointing out Czech contributions to European and world civilization. Covers many fields, including literature, fine arts, science, religion, music, etc. [OO]

W323. České dějiny. [Czech history.] Ed. by Václav Novotný and others. 3 v. in 13. Prague, 1912–48. Planned as a definitive, heavily documented history by Novotný. Since his death in 1931, editorial policy has been somewhat modified in the direction of lighter, if no less authoritative, presentation. Story complete to 1415, and from 1438 to 1462. The missing volume is in preparation.

W324. Tobolka, Zdeněk V. **Politické dějiny československého národa.** [Political history of the Czechoslovak people.] 5 v. Prague, 1932–37. Exhaustive survey of political history of the Czechs and Slovaks from 1848 to 1918. [OO]

HISTORIES OF SPECIAL PERIODS

Before 1620

W325. Bartoš, František M. **Husitství a cizina.** [Hussitism and the outside world.] Prague, 1931. A largely authoritative work which scrutinizes carefully and thoroughly the influences on the Hussite movement deriving from various foreign men, groups, or movements (including Waldensianism and related phenomena) and the spiritual impact on the surrounding world. [FGH]

W326. Dvorník, František. **Les légendes de Constantin et de méthode vues de Byzance.** Prague, 1933. A biographical study of the pioneers of Christianity among the Slavs in Moravia and in the neighboring territories, based on medieval legends. [OO]

W327. Filip, Jan. **Pravěké Československo.** [Prehistoric Czechoslovakia.] Prague, 1948. Sums up results of latest archaeological discoveries in the area.

W328. Heymann, Frederick G. **John Žižka and the Hussite revolution.** Princeton, 1955. Superb reconstruction of the Hussite revolt, based on long and thoughtful study of confusing partisan sources.

W329. Macek, Josef. **Tábor v husitském revolučním hnutí.** [Tabor in the Hussite revolutionary movement.] 2 v. Prague, 1952–56. Detailed study of relations of Tabor, the Hussite left-wing capital, with the rest of Bohemia. Many helpful maps and tables.

W330. Molnár, Amedeo. **Bratr Lukáš bohoslovec Jednoty.** [Brother Lucas, theologian of the Unity.] Prague, 1948. Crisp study of life and thought of second founder of the Unity of Czech Brethren, an older contemporary of Luther.

W331. Pekař, Josef. **Žižka a jeho doba.** [Žižka and his times.] 4 v. Prague, 1927–33. This work, though over-polemical in taking a stand against Masaryk's ideas about the meaning of Czech history, is a must for any serious student of Hussite history because of its nearly exhaustive treatment of events and sources. Review, K. Krofta in *Žižka a husitská revoluce* (Prague, 1937). [FGH]

W332. ——. **Bílá Hora, její příčiny i následky.** [The White Mountain, its reasons and results.] Prague, 1921. Essays on the causes and significance of the collapse of the Czech anti-Habsburg rising in 1618–20. [OO]

W333. Spinka, Matthew. **John Hus and the Czech reform.** Chicago, 1941. Convincingly corrects previous misapprehensions about the relationship between the Czech (Hussite) Reformation and its twin sources, English (Wyclif) and Czech. Also helps to clarify to some extent the question of its impact on 16th century Protestantism. [FGH]

W334. Urbánek, Rudolf. **Husitský král.** [The Hussite king.] Prague, 1926. Popular biography of George of Poděbrady by a leading scholar of this period.

1620–1918

W335. Beneš, Eduard. **My war memoirs.** N.Y., 1928. Diplomatic record of attainment of recognition of the new state, by Masaryk's principal collaborator.

W336. Bokes, František. **Pokusy o slovensko-mad'arské vyrovnanie v rokoch 1861–1868.** [Attempts at a Slovak-Magyar rapprochement in 1861–1868.] Turčiansky Sv. Martin, 1941.

W337. Hanuš, Josef. **Národní Museum a naše obrození.** [The National Museum and our renaissance.] 2 v. Prague, 1921–23. Monumental study of the Czech national revival, with special reference to the National Museum of Bohemia, accepted by the Czech people as a symbol of their traditions. [OO]

W338. Janeček, Oldřich. **Povstáni nevolníků v českých zemích roku 1775.** [Revolt of the serfs in the Czech lands in 1775.] Prague, 1954. Documented study of the struggle against the *robota* in Bohemia and Moravia, and the Vienna government's efforts to quell it and improve the situation. Marxist vocabulary.

W339. Kazbunda, Karel. **České hnutí roku 1848.** [The Czech movement of the year 1848.] Prague, 1929. Monograph on Czech political developments in 1848, based mostly on official documents. [OO]

W340. Kerner, Robert J. **Bohemia in the eighteenth century.** N.Y., 1932. Focused on reigns of Joseph II and Leopold II; based on study of Vienna archives.

W341. Krofta, Kamil. **Nesmrtelný národ: od Bílé Hory k Palackému.** [Immortal nation: from the White Mountain to Palacký.] Prague, 1940.

W342. Masaryk, Thomas G. **The making of a state.** See *AF336.*

W343. Medvecký, Karol A. **Slovenský prevrat.** [The Slovak revolt.] 4 v. Trnava, 1931. Comprehensive description of Slovak participation in the 1914–1918 struggle for independence at home and abroad.

W344. Paulová, Milada. **Dějiny Maffie: odboj Čechů a Jihoslovanů za Světové Války, 1914–1918.** [The history of the Maffie: the struggle of the Czechs and Yugoslavs during the World War, 1914–1918.] 2 v. Prague, 1937–39. The most thorough study of the organization of the resistance movement in Bohemia and its connection with corresponding groups in Yugoslavia.

W345. Roubík, František. **Český rok 1848.** [Czech year 1848.] 2nd ed., Prague, 1948. Detailed survey of Czech national life in 1848, with reproductions from contemporary documents, cartoons, etc. [OO]

W346. Srb, Adolf. **Politické dějiny národa českého od roku 1861.** [Political history of the Czech nation from 1861.] 2 v. Prague, 1899–1901. Political history of the Czechs with documents in the text. [OO]

W347. Winter, Eduard. **Der Josefinismus und seine Geschichte.** Brünn, 1943. Treats the reform ideas of Joseph II and his enlightened advisers, with special emphasis on Bohemia and Moravia. [OO]

1918–1939

W348. Deset let československé republiky. [Ten years of the Czechoslovak republic.] 3 v. Prague, 1928. An official publication, but informative on progress in organization and functioning of a new state.

W349. Kerner, Robert J., ed. **Czechoslovakia: twenty years of independence.** Berkeley, 1940. Collective work, still important as introduction to the pre-history and history of the "first republic."

W350. Ripka, Hubert. **Munich: before and after.** London, 1939. Based on access to all official and personal Czech sources. In essence represents Beneš' story of the crisis.

W351. Peroutka, Ferdinand. **Budování státu.** [The building of a state.] 5 v. Prague, 1936. The leading journalist of the early republic analyzes the political and intellectual events of the first few years after 1918.

W352. Vondracek, Felix. **The foreign policy of Czechoslovakia, 1918–1935.** N.Y., 1937. Thorough assembling of documents and press reports in years of the League of Nations and Little Entente.

W353. Wheeler-Bennett, John W. **Munich: prologue to tragedy.** See *AH226.*

Since 1939

W354. Beneš, Edvard. **Paměti: od Mnichova k nové válce a k novému vítězství.** Prague, 1947. English tr. by Godfrey Lias, *Memoirs: from Munich to new war and new victory,* London, 1954. Intended as v. 2 of projected three volumes, to cover period from the Sudeten crisis to 1948. In this the Munich crisis is not treated in focus.

W355. Doležal, Jiří. **Slovenské národní povstání: příspěvek k jeho vzniku a průběha.** [The Slovak national uprising: a contribution to its origin and course.] Prague, 1954.

W356. Czechoslovak Republic. Ministerstvo Zahraničních Věcí. **Four fighting years.** London, 1943. This book, published by the government information ministry, describes the spirit of resistance to German occupation from 1939 to 1943.

W357. Gadourek, Ivan. **The political control of Czechoslovakia: a study in social control of a Soviet satellite state.** Leiden, 1953. Heavily documented from official sources.

W358. Jaroš, Václav, ed. **Šest let okupace.** [Six years of occupation.] Prague, 1946. Collaborative work reviewing German occupation of Prague, 1939–45, in all aspects of life, law, culture, education, economy, and religion.

W359. Ripka, Hubert. **Czechoslovakia enslaved: the story of the Communist coup d'état.** London, 1950. Tr. of *Le coup de Prague* (Paris, 1949). Story of the coup by a cabinet member who had always been close to Beneš.

W360. Stránský, Josef. **East wind over Prague.** London, 1950.

HISTORIES OF SPECIAL AREAS

W361. Chaloupecký, Václav. **Staré Slovensko.** [Ancient Slovakia.] Bratislava, 1923. On basis of close examination of ancient documents, language, and titles, attempts to show Slovakia to have been a political unity in the early Middle Ages and closely related to Bohemia and Moravia. This work was attacked by some Slovak historians.

W362. Hodža, Milan. **Československý rozkol.** [Czechoslovak schism.] Turčiansky Sv. Martin, 1920. Study of the Slovak national revival. [OO]

W363. Preidel, Helmut, ed. **Die Deutschen**

in Böhmen und Mähren. Munich, 1950. An answer, by Sudeten German scholars in Germany, to nationalistic Slavic historians. The appeal is to "a European conception," with emphasis on the German "mission" in Bohemia and Moravia.

W364. Rapant, Daniel. **Sedliacke povstanie na východnom Slovensku roku 1831.** [Peasant uprising in eastern Slovakia in 1831.] 2 v. in 3. Bratislava, 1953. The result of many years of archival research. Pt. 2, in 2 v., exclusively documents. Author contends the uprising was rooted in oppression of the peasantry, abuse of the *robota*, and impossible exactions.

W365. ———. **K počiatkom mad'arizácie.** [On the beginnings of magyarization.] Bratislava, 1927. Focused on the language question under Maria Theresa and Joseph II (1740–90). Good bibliography.

W366. Schmidtmayer, Alfred. **Geschichte der Sudetendeutschen.** Leipzig, 1938.

W367. Schürer, Oskar. **Prag.** Vienna, 1930. Several later eds. Excellent description of a capital city, which the author regarded as primarily a German city.

W368. Tomek, Václav V. **Dějepis města Prahy.** [History of the city of Prague.] 2nd ed., 12 v., Prague, 1892–1901. Classic study of the rise and growth of the capital of Bohemia; well in advance of its time of composition in its control of economic aspects.

W369. Uhlíř, František. **Těšínské Slezsko.** [Teschen Silesia.] Prague, 1946. A detailed historico-demographic study of the region.

W370. Varsik, Branislav, ed. **Slovenské dejiny.** [Slovak history.] Bratislava, 1947 ff.

HISTORIES OF SPECIAL TOPICS

Cultural History

W371. Chaloupecký, Václav. **The Caroline University of Prague: its foundation, character and development in the fourteenth century.** Prague, 1948.

W372. Odložilík, Otakar. **The Caroline University, 1348–1948.** Prague, 1948. Best short summary of history of the oldest university east of the Rhine.

W373. Winter, Zikmund. **Kulturní obraz českých měst.** [Cultural history of Czech cities.] 2 v. Prague, 1890–92. Thorough discussion of life in royal boroughs in Bohemia from 1420 to 1620, dealing with municipal administration, social and economic conditions. [OO]

Religious History

W374. Hrejsa, Ferdinand. **Česká konfese, její vznik, podstata a dějiny.** [The Bohemian confession, its rise, basis and history.] Prague, 1912. Analytical study of the confession of Bohemian Protestants, presented to Maxi-

milian II in 1575, and of religious parties in Bohemia in the Reformation era. [OO]

W375. ———. **Dějiny Křest'anství v Československu.** [History of Christianity in Czechoslovakia.] 6 v. Prague, 1947–50. The only complete history of the church in its various branches, Orthodox, Catholic, Hussite, Lutheran, and Bohemian Brethren, until 1576. Documented.

W376. Gindely, Anton. **Geschichte der Böhmischen Brüder.** 2nd ed., 2 v., Prague, 1861–62. Based on first extensive use of sources of the Brethren. In details occasionally outdated, but indispensable for those sources included.

W377. Kraus, Arnošt V. **Husitství v literatuře, zejména německé.** [Hussitism in literature, particularly the German.] 3 v. Prague, 1917–24.

W378. Lochman, Jan M. **Náboženské myšlení českého obrození.** [Religious thought of the Czech revival.] Prague, 1952. Analytical study of Czech religious thought in the 18th century. [OO]

Constitutional History

W379. Kalousek, Josef. **České státní právo.** [Czech constitutional law.] 2nd ed., Prague, 1892.

W380. Kapras, Jan. **Právní dějiny zemí koruny české.** [Constitutional history of the lands of the Bohemian crown.] 3 v. Prague, 1913–20.

W381. Peterka, Otto. **Rechtsgeschichte der böhmischen Länder.** 2 v. Reichenberg, 1923–28.

Social and Economic History

W382. Graus, František. **Chudina městská v době předhusitské.** [Urban pauperism in pre-Hussite times.] Prague, 1949. Study of position of urban proletariat before the Hussite movement. Marxist point of view. [OO]

W383. ———. **Dějiny venkovského lidu v Čechách v době předhusitské.** [History of the peasantry in Bohemia in the pre-Hussite period.] 2 v. Prague, 1953–57. Covers from 10th to early 13th century. Marxist point of view. [OO]

W384. Janáček, Josef. **Dějiny obchodu v předbělohorské Praze.** [History of commerce in pre-White Mountain Prague.] Prague, 1955. History of trade in Prague before 1620.

W385. Krofta, Kamil. **Dějiny selského stavu.** [History of the peasantry.] 2nd ed., Prague, 1949.

W386. Lippert, Julius. **Social-Geschichte Böhmens in vorhussitischer Zeit.** 2 v. Prague and Vienna, 1896–98.

W387. Pekař, Josef. **Kniha o Kosti.** 2 v. Prague, 1910–11. Detailed study of economic conditions on a Bohemian domain in the 17th and 18th centuries. [OO]

W388. ———. **České katastry 1654–1789.** [Bohemian land registers, 1654–1789.] 2nd ed., Prague, 1932. Analytical study of surveys of land in Bohemia and of peasant conditions in general. [OO]

W389. Winter, Zikmund. **Dějiny řemesel a obchodu v Čechách v XIV. a v XV. století.** [History of crafts and commerce in Bohemia in the 14th and 15th centuries.] Prague, 1906.

Nationality Problems

W390. Bittner, Konrad. **Deutsche und Tschechen.** Brünn and Leipzig, 1936. To date the most thorough treatment of the Czech-German relationship and antagonism, by a Sudeten-German author. While clearly defending the German point of view, the book tries to show the historical complexities of the struggle and the motives impelling Czech attitudes and actions. [FGH]

W391. Klik, Josef. **Národnostni poměry v Čechách od válek husitských do bitvy bělohorské.** [Relations of the nationalities in Bohemia from the Hussite wars to the Battle of the White Mountain.] Prague, 1922. Careful analysis of available statistics and legislation concerning Czech-German relations since mid-15th century.

W392. Krofta, Kamil. **Das Deutschtum in der tschechoslovakischen Geschichte.** 2nd ed., Prague, 1936. Brilliant survey of the symbiosis of Czech and German culture over ten centuries. Does not hesitate to admit German contributions in religion, art, and literature.

W393. Rádl, Emanuel. **Válka Čechů s Němci.** [The war of Czechs and Germans.] Prague, 1928. Philosophical rather than historical.

W394. Szyjkowski, Marjan. **Polská účast v českém národním obrození.** [Polish participation in the Czech national revival.] 3 v. Prague, 1931–46. Detailed study of Polish influences on Czech literature in the period of national revival and of Romanticism. [OO]

W395. Wiskemann, Elizabeth. **Czechs and Germans.** London and N.Y., 1938.

W396. Žáček, Václav. **Čechové a Poláci roku 1848.** [Czechs and Poles in 1848.] 2 v. Prague, 1947–48. Political and cultural contacts between Czechs and Poles around 1848. [OO]

Literature

W397. Chudoba, František. **A short survey of Czech literature.** London, 1924.

W398. Hýsek, Miloslav. **Literární Morava v letech 1849–1885.** [Literary Morava from 1849 to 1885.] Prague, 1911.

W399. Jakubec, Jan. **Dějiny literatury české.** [History of Czech literature.] 2nd ed., 2 v., Prague, 1929–34. Outline of Czech literature from the earliest times to 1850. Rich in bibliography. [OO]

W400. Jelínek, Hanuš. **Histoire de la littérature tchèque.** 3 v. Paris, 1930–35.

W401. Lützow, Franz H. **A history of Bohemian literature.** London, 1899. For long the only treatment in English. Somewhat outdated, but main ideas still sound.

W402. Novák, Jan V., and Arne Novák. **Přehledné dějiny literatury české.** [An outline history of Czech literature.] 4th ed., Olomouc, 1936–39. Indispensable compendium of history of Czech literature. [OO]

W403. Novotný, Miloslav, and Albert Pražák, eds. **Písemnictví.** [Literature.] Prague, 1933. [Československá vlastivěda, 7.] Collective work by several authors on literary activities in Czechoslovakia. [OO]

W404. Seifert, Josef L. **Die Literaturgeschichte der Čechoslowaken, Südslaven und Bulgaren.** Munich, 1923.

W405. Vlček, Jaroslav. **Dějiny české literatury.** [History of Czech literature.] 3rd ed., 2 v., Prague, 1951.

W406. ———, ed. **Literatura česká XIX. století.** [Czech literature of the 19th century.] 2nd ed., 4 v., Prague, 1902–17. Monumental work on modern Czech literature up to 1848. [OO]

BIOGRAPHIES

W407. Grund, Antonín. **Karel Jaromír Erben.** Prague, 1935. Critical biography of a Czech poet, collector of folk tales, and historian. [OO]

W408. Havránek, Bohuslav, and others, eds. **Josef Dobrovský.** Prague, 1953. Collection of studies on occasion of the bicentenary of Dobrovský.

W409. Heyberger, Anna. **Jean Amos Comenius (Komenský).** Paris, 1928. Lucid survey of Komenský's life by a United States educator. [OO]

W410. Horák, Jiří, and others. **Josef Dobrovský, 1753–1829.** Prague, 1929. Collection of critical essays relating to the life and literary works of Dobrovský, pioneer of the Czech national revival. [OO]

W411. Herben, Jan. **T. G. Masaryk.** 5th ed., Prague, 1947. Comprehensive and balanced biography of Masaryk by one of his intimate collaborators. [OO]

W412. Hrubý, František. **Ladislav Velen z Žerotína.** Prague, 1930. A biography of the leader of the Moravian rebels in 1619–20, describing also his life in exile after 1620. [OO]

W413. Jánský, Karel. **Karel Hynek Mácha.** Prague, 1953. The leading Czech poet of the Romantic era. [OO]

W414. Kybal, Vlastimil. **M. Matěj z Janova.** Prague, 1905. Biography of a Czech reform writer, describing his life, works, and teachings as contained in his standard work, *De regulis Veteris et Novi Testamenti.* [OO]

W415. Masaryk, Tomáš G. **Karel Havlíček: snahy a tužby politického probuzení.** [Karel Havlíček: the struggle for political revival.] 3rd ed., Prague, 1920. An analytical study of Havlíček's works and ideas in connection with the rise of Czech national consciousness around 1848. [OO]

W416. Mackenzie, Sir Compton. **Dr. Beneš.** London, 1946. Written while Beneš was in London, but shows study of local Czechoslovak conditions.

W417. Nejedlý, Zdeněk. **Bedřich Smetana.** 2nd ed., 7 v., Prague, 1950–54. Planned as a monumental biography of the leading Czech composer, but covers only his early years in the context of Czech life in first half of the 19th century. [OO]

W418. ——. **T. G. Masaryk.** 5 v. Prague, 1930–37. Covers in detail early part of Masaryk's life, from 1850 to 1885. Not completed. [OO]

W419. Novák, Jan, and Josef Hendrich. **Jan Amos Komenský, jeho život a spisy.** [John Amos Komenský, his life and writings.] Prague, 1932. Standard biography of Komenský (Comenius), treating in detail his literary activities and educational reform. [OO]

W420. Novotný, Miloslav, ed. **Život Boženy Němcové.** [The life of Božená Němcová.] Prague, 1951 ff. (In progress.) Exhaustive collection of letters and other documents illustrating life and work of the leading Czech novelist. [OO]

W421. ——, ed. **Život Jana Nerudy.** [Life of Jan Neruda.] Prague, 1951 ff. (In progress.) Materials for biography of Jan Neruda, a leading Czech poet, critic, and journalist (1834–91). [OO]

W422. Novotný, Václav, and Vlastimil Kybal. **M. Jan Hus: život a učení.** [Master John Hus: life and teachings.] 2 v. in 5. Prague, 1919–31. Standard biography of Hus in two parts, the first dealing with his life and activities, and the second his teachings. [OO]

W423. Odložilík, Otakar. **Karel starší ze Žerotína, 1564–1636.** [Charles the Elder of Žerotín, 1564–1636.] Prague, 1936. Biographical outline devoted to the leader of the Protestant estates in Moravia. Attention given to his studies and travels in Switzerland, France, and England.

W424. Papoušek, Jaroslav. **Dr. Edvard Beneš: Gedarke und Tot.** 4 v. Prague, 1937. Semi-official. Extensive extracts from writings and speeches as Masaryk's collaborator and as foreign minister.

W425. Pekař, Josef. **Valdštejn, 1630–1634.** 2nd ed., 2 v., Prague, 1933–34. Detailed study of the final stage of the life and career

of the imperial generalissimo Albrecht of Valdštejn (Wallenstein). [OO]

W426. Sedlák, Jan. **M. Jan Hus.** Prague, 1915. Critical biography of John Hus, by a Catholic theologian. Supplemented by numerous documents in Latin. [OO]

W427. Šusta, Josef. **Karel IV. V. 1, Otec a syn, 1333–1346; 2, Za císařskou korunou, 1346–1355.** [Charles IV. V. 1, Father and son, 1333–1346; 2, The imperial crown, 1346–1355.] 2 v. Prague, 1946–48. Forms pts. 3 and 4 of v. 2 of *České dějiny,* ed. by V. Novotný. Intended as a correction and completion of Emil Werunsky, *Geschichte Kaiser Karls IV* (3 v., Innsbruck, 1880–92). The work was left unfinished at author's death.

W428. Štefánek, Antonin, and others. **Milan Hodža, publicista, politik, vedecký pracovník.** [Milan Hodža, publicist, statesman, scholar.] Prague, 1930. Collection of contributions to biography of the leading Slovak statesman. [OO]

W429. Stloukal, Karel, ed. **Královny, kněžny a velké ženy české.** [Czech queens, princesses and prominent women.] 2nd ed., Prague, 1940. A series of biographical studies. [OO]

W430. Traub, Hugo. **F. L. Rieger.** Prague, 1919. Emphasis on Rieger's political activities. [OO]

W431. Tille, Václav. **Božena Němcová.** 3rd ed., Prague, 1920. Standard biography of a Czech novelist, author of the most popular Czech book, *Bábička.* [OO]

W432. Tůma, Karel. **Karel Havlíček Borovský.** Kutná Hora, 1883. Standard biography of Havlíček, useful in some parts for quotations from unpublished documents. [OO]

W433. Vyskočil, Jan K. **Arnošt z Pardubic a jeho doba.** [Arnošt of Pardubice and his times.] Prague, 1947. Exhaustive survey of life and work of the first archbishop of Prague, 1346–64. [OO]

W434. Winter, Eduard. **Bernard Bolzano und sein Kreis.** Leipzig, 1933. Biographical account of a reform priest and the circle of his followers among the clergy of Bohemia. [OO]

ACADEMY PUBLICATIONS

During the German occupation of Czechoslovakia, 1939–45, the activities of the Czech Academy of Arts and Sciences (Česká Akademie Věd a Umění) were somewhat curtailed. The annual **(W435)** Věstník (Prague, 1891 ff.) continued to appear. In 1945 the Academy resumed its functions, but in a rather moderate degree. In 1948 its organization and membership were transformed along lines of the Soviet Academy of Sciences into the Czechoslovak Academy of Sciences (Československá Akademie Věd).

In 1953 it began a vigorous program of publication in all fields—physical and applied sciences, literature and linguistics, archaeology, and the social sciences, including history. Both monographs and journals resulted, and a catalog of publications, **(W436) Review of publications 1953–55** (Prague, 1956) was issued.

A separate Slovak Academy of Sciences (Slovenska Akadémia Vied) was founded at Bratislava in 1953 and immediately embarked on a publishing program similar to that of the Czechoslovak Academy in Prague, with approximately the same spread in subject matter, both in monographs and periodicals. **(W437) Catalogue of publications of the Slovak Academy of Sciences 1953–1955** was published in 1956, listing 78 titles in the class of social sciences.

PERIODICALS

W438. Časopis Matice Moravské. [Journal of the Moravian Foundation.] Brünn, 1869 ff. (Quarterly, irregular.) Devoted primarily to Moravia, its prehistory, history, literature, and institutions. Reorganized after 1948. [OO]

W439. Časopis Českého Museum. [Journal of the Czech Museum.] Prague, 1827 ff. (Frequency and title vary.) The oldest learned magazine in Czech; founded in 1827 by František Palacký, and edited in succession to him by Pavel Josef Šafařík and others. Has changed title several times; reorganized after 1948. Contains miscellaneous contributions, archaeology, history, literary history, etc. [OO]

W440. Český časopis historický. [Czech historical journal.] 50 v. Prague, 1895–1949. The leading historical journal in Czech. Founded by Jaroslav Goll and Antonín Rezek, edited for many years by Josef Pekař; discontinued in 1949. [OO]

W441. Československý časopis historický. [Czechoslovak historical journal.] Prague, 1953 ff. (Quarterly.) Published by the Historical Institute of the Czechoslovak Academy of Sciences to replace *W440.* Rigidly Marxist. [OO]

W442. Historický sborník. [Historical review.] Prague, 1953 ff. (Annual. Title varies.) A companion to the quarterly *Časopis (W441).* [OO]

W443. Historický časopis. [Historical journal.] Bratislava, 1953 ff. (Quarterly.) Published by Slovak Academy of Sciences. Professedly Marxist.

W444. Historické štúdie. [Historical studies.] Bratislava, 1955 ff. (Annual.) Published by the Historical Institute of the Slovak Academy of Sciences to encourage study of local Slovak history.

W445. Zeitschrift für sudetendeutsche Geschichte. Brünn, 1937 ff. (Quarterly, irregular.) A scholarly publication intended as a continuation of the *Mitteilungen des Vereins für Geschichte der Deutschen in Böhmen.*

YUGOSLAVIA *

BIBLIOGRAPHIES

W446. Srpska Akademija Nauka. Pregled izdanja Srpske Kraljevske Akademije od 1886–1936. [Review of the publications of the Serbian Royal Academy from 1886 to 1936.] Belgrade, 1936. [Posebna izdanja, 118.] Indispensable bibliography. This and the following contain list of all publications by the Serbian Academy to 1950. [CJ]

W447. ——. Pregled izdanja Srpske Akademije Nauke, 1937–1947. [Review of the publications of the Serbian Academy of Science, 1937–1947.] Belgrade, 1948. [Posebna izdanja, 145.] Supplement, 1950.

W448. Bibliografija izdanja Matice srpske, 1826–1949. [Bibliography of publications of the Serbian Foundation, 1826–1949.] Novi Sad, 1950.

W449. Jugoslavenska Akademija Znanosti i Umjetnosti. Popis izdanja Jugoslavenske Akademije Znanosti i Umjetnosti u Zagrebu, 1867–1950. [Catalog of publications of the Yugoslav Academy of Sciences and Arts in Zagreb, 1867–1950.] Zagreb, 1951. Indispensable bibliography. Lists all publications of the academy for this period. [CJ]

W450. Bibliografija Jugoslavije. [Bibliography of Yugoslavia.] Belgrade, 1950 ff. (Monthly.) Lists all publications issued in Yugoslavia. Indispensable. [CJ]

ENCYCLOPEDIAS AND WORKS OF REFERENCE

W451. Yugoslavia. N.Y., 1957. [Mid-European Studies Center series.] Extremely valuable, though slightly uneven, compendium of all aspects of life in post-1945 Yugoslavia.

W452. Markert, Werner, ed. Jugoslawien. Cologne, 1954. Top German specialists have produced a good collaborative account of present-day Yugoslavia. [CJ]

W453. Stanojević, Stanoje, ed. Narodna enciklopedija srpsko - hrvatsko - slovenačka. [Serbo-Croat-Slovene encyclopedia.] 4 v. Zagreb, 1925–29.

W454. Enciklopedija Jugoslavije. Zagreb, 1955 ff. (In progress.)

*Professor Thomson was assisted by Professor C. E. Black in selecting titles for the subsections on Yugoslavia and Bulgaria.

GEOGRAPHIES

W455. Melik, Anton. **Jugoslavija: zemlje-pisni pregled.** [Yugoslavia: geographical sketch.] Ljubljana, 1949. Good political-geographic survey. [CJ]

W456. Moodie, A. E. **The Italo-Yugoslav boundary.** London, 1945. A geographical study.

W457. Wilkinson, Henry R. **Maps and politics: a review of the ethnographic cartography of Macedonia.** Liverpool, 1951. Excellent work, showing how politicians used maps in the struggle for Macedonia. [CJ]

ANTHROPOLOGY AND DEMOGRAPHY

W458. Djordjević, Tihomir. **Srbija pre sto godina.** [Serbia a hundred years ago.] 2nd ed., Belgrade, 1946. Good, brief account of Serbian society in the 19th century, by an outstanding authority. [CJ]

W459. ——. **Naš narodni život.** [Our national life.] 10 v. Belgrade, 1930–34. Classic work by a famous Serb. Basic for study of Serbian society in the 19th century. [CJ]

W460. Dvorniković, Vladimir. **Karaktero-logija jugoslovena.** [Yugoslav characteristics.] Belgrade, 1939. A basic work on the life, customs, and particular characteristics of the various Yugoslav peoples. [CJ]

W461. Tomašić, Dinko A. **Personality and culture in eastern European politics.** N.Y., 1948.

W462. West, Rebecca. **Black lamb and grey falcon.** N.Y., 1943. Excellent for description of people and country, but misleading on political developments. [CJ]

LINGUISTICS

W463. Slodnjak, Anton. **Pregled sloven-skega slovstva.** [Outline of Slovene grammar.] Ljubljana, 1934.

PRINTED COLLECTIONS OF SOURCES

W464. Novak, Viktor, ed. **Antologija jugo-slovenske misli i narodnog jedinstva, 1390–1930.** [Anthology of Yugoslav thought and national unity, 1390–1930.] Belgrade, 1930. Indispensable for study of the Yugoslav idea. Contains major statements of its advocates. [CJ]

W465. Šišić, Ferdinand, ed. **Josip Juraj Strossmayer, dokumenti i korespondencija.** [Joseph George Strossmayer, documents and correspondence.] Zagreb, 1935.

W466. **Srpski narod u XIX veku.** [The Serbian people in the 19th century.] Ed. by Stanoje Stanojević and others. 14 v. Belgrade, 1934–39. Although never completed, this collection was intended to give a detailed survey of all aspects of Serbian history in the 19th century. The 14 published volumes are of generally high quality. Basic for study of Serbian history. [CJ]

HISTORIOGRAPHY

W467. Tadić, Jorjo, ed. **Ten years of Yugoslav historiography, 1945–1955.** Belgrade, 1955. Account of Yugoslav historiography in post-war decade, presented at the International Historical Congress held in Rome, 1955. Valuable guide. [CJ]

SHORTER GENERAL HISTORIES

W468. Corović, Vladimir. **Istorija Jugo-slavije.** [History of Yugoslavia.] Belgrade, 1933. Best general history of Yugoslavia written between the wars. Ends in 1918. Author supports Yugoslav idea. [CJ]

W469. Haumant, Émile. **La formation de la Yougoslavie (XVᵉ–XXᵉ siècles).** Paris, 1930. Best general history of Yugoslavia in a western language. [CJ]

W470. Babić, Anto, ed. **Istorija naroda Jugoslavije.** [History of the peoples of Yugo-slavia.] Sarajevo, 1948. One of first attempts at writing a general history of Yugoslavia under the Communists. From the party point of view the author was not completely successful. [CJ]

HISTORIES OF SPECIAL PERIODS

Pre-19th Century

W471. Hadrovics, László. **Le peuple serbe et son église sous la domination turque.** Paris, 1947. Best account in a western language of Serbian church under the Turks. [CJ]

W472. Grafenauer, Bogo, Dušan Perovič, and Jaroslav Sidak, eds. **Historija naroda Jugoslavije.** [History of the peoples of Yugo-slavia.] Zagreb, 1953 ff. First volume of a projected collaborative history. Covers period to 16th century. Excellent. [CJ]

W473. Klaić, Vjekoslav. **Povjest Hrvata od najstarijih vremena do svršetka XIX. stoljeca.** [History of the Croats from the earliest times to the end of the 19th century.] 5 v. Zagreb, 1899–1911. Standard work of a great historian. Ends in the 16th century. [CJ]

19th Century

W474. Baernreither, Josef M. **Fragments of a political diary.** London, 1930. Work of a liberal Austrian, critical of Hapsburgs and sympathetic to subject nationalities. [CJ]

W475. Belić, Vladimir J. **Ratovi srpskog**

naroda u XIX i XX veku (1788–1918). [The wars of the Serbian people in the 19th and 20th centuries (1788–1918).] Belgrade, 1937. Good account of Serbian military campaigns. [CJ]

W476. Bogdanov, Vaso. **Hrvatska ljevica u godinama revolucije 1848–1849.** [The Croatian left in the years of revolution 1848–1849.] Zagreb, 1949. A Communist interpretation of 1848–49 by a party-line historian. [CJ]

W477. Jelenić, Djurdje. **Nova Srbija i Jugoslavija.** [New Serbia and Yugoslavia.] Belgrade, 1923. Useful Serbian account of the Yugoslav state and its evolution before World War I. [CJ]

W478. Jovanović, Slobodan. **Sabrana dela.** [Collected works.] 12 v. Belgrade, 1932–36. Works of the greatest Serbian historian, including exhaustive history of Serbia in the 19th century, and essays on constitutional theories and prominent Europeans. [CJ]

W479. Nintchitch, Momtchilo. **La crise bosniaque (1908–1909).** Paris, 1937. Detailed history using Serbian sources and presenting the Serbian point of view. [CJ]

W480. Popović, Vasilj. **Evropa i srpsko pitanje u periodu oslobodjenja, 1804–1918.** [Europe and the Serbian question in the period of liberation, 1804–1918.] Belgrade, 1940. Good general account of the Serbian problem in its 19th century European context. [CJ]

W481. Przić, Ilija. **Spoljašnja politika Srbije, 1804–1914.** [Foreign policy of Serbia, 1804–1914.] Belgrade, 1939. Patriotic work; useful for outline of main trends of Serbian foreign policy. [CJ]

W482. Schmitt, Bernadotte E. **The annexation of Bosnia, 1908–1909.** Cambridge, Eng., 1937. Scholarly work; critical of central powers and sympathetic to Russia and Serbia. [CJ]

W483. Skarić, Vladislav. **Bosna i Hercegovina pod Austro-Ugarskom upravom.** [Bosnia and Herzegovina under Austro-Hungarian administration.] Belgrade, [1938]. Helpful account of Austrian occupation, 1878–1914. [CJ]

W484. Vucinich, Wayne S. **Serbia between East and West: the events of 1903–1908.** Stanford, 1954. Standard work, using new sources. [CJ]

W485. Wendel, Herman. **Der Kampf der Südslawen um Freiheit und Einheit.** Frankfurt-am-Main, 1925. Sympathetic account of Yugoslavs by a well-known German socialist. [CJ]

W486. ——. **Aus dem südslawischen Risorgimento.** Gotha, 1921. Good study by a German sympathetic to the Yugoslav state. [CJ]

W487. Yakschitch, Grégoire. **L'Europe et la résurrection de la Serbie (1804–1834).**

Paris, 1907. Best general account of Serbian revolution. Available also in Serbian, *Evropa i vaksrs Srbije, 1804–1834* (Belgrade, 1933). [CJ]

W488. Živanović, Živan. **Politička istorija Srbije u drugoj polovini devetnaestog veka.** [Political history of Serbia in the second half of the 19th century.] 4 v. Belgrade, 1923–25. Good political history for the last two decades of the 19th century. [CJ]

1900–1940

W489. Adams, John C. **Flight in winter.** Princeton, 1942. The Serbian campaigns of 1914–15; retreat, escape, and internment of Serbian troops.

W490. Bogdanov, Vaso. **Društvene i političke borbe u Hrvatskoj, 1848–49.** [Social and political struggles in Croatia, 1848–49.] Zagreb, 1949. Heavily documented study of Croat struggles against Magyar controls, and the place of Jelacić in the conflict. Emphasizes the class struggle.

W491. Fotitch, Constantin. **The war we lost: Yugoslavia's tragedy and the failure of the West.** N.Y., 1948. Defense of Mihailović. [CJ]

W492. Jovanović, Jovan M. **Stvaranje zajedničke države Srba, Hrvata i Slovenaca.** [The creation of a unified administration of Serbs, Croats and Slovenes.] 3 v. Belgrade, 1928–30. Account of World War I period, by a diplomat and historian who supported the formation of Yugoslavia. [CJ]

W493. Kerner, Robert J., ed. **Yugoslavia.** Berkeley, 1949. Useful collaborative work by sixteen specialists, with emphasis on 20th century. [CJ]

W494. Loncarević, Dušan. **Jugoslaviens Entstehung.** Zürich and Leipzig, 1929. Popular account of creation of Yugoslavia. Useful. [CJ]

W495. Ostović, Pavle D. **The truth about Yugoslavia.** N.Y., 1952. By Trumbić's secretary. Presents point of view of Yugoslav Committee. Critical of Serbs. [CJ]

W496. Paulová, Milada. **Jugoslavenski odbor.** [The Yugoslav Committee.] Zagreb, 1925. Excellent account of this committee and its activities in 1914–18. Basic for this period. [CJ]

W497. Peter II, King of Yugoslavia. **A king's heritage.** N.Y., 1954. An apology. Reveals Peter's personal character and reasons for his failures. [CJ]

W498. Pribićević, Svetozar. **Diktatura kralja Aleksandra.** [The dictatorship of King Alexander.] Belgrade, 1953. Stimulating account written by a political adversary, a Serb from Croatia. [CJ]

W499. Ribar, Ivan. **Politički zapisi.** [Political notes.] 4 v. Belgrade, 1948–52. History of Yugoslavia since 1918, by one who helped make it. [CJ]

Since 1940

W500. The Soviet-Yugoslav dispute: text of the published correspondences. London and N.Y., 1948. [Royal Institute of International Affairs.] Contains the exchange of correspondence between Tito and Stalin and their respective parties leading to the break in 1948. [CJ]

W501. Armstrong, Hamilton F. **Tito and Goliath.** N.Y., 1951. Penetrating, careful study written shortly after the Tito-Stalin break, but still basic. [CJ]

W502. Čulinović, Ferdo, ed. **Nova Jugoslavija.** See *W539*.

W503. Dedijer, Vladimir. **Tito.** N.Y., 1952. The official biography by Tito's close associate, who since has been discredited because of his defense of Djilas. [CJ]

W504. Djilas, Milovan. **The new class: an analysis of the Communist system.** N.Y., 1957. Dramatic denunciation of the Communist system by Tito's former vice-president. [CJ]

W505. Dragnich, Alex N. **Tito's promised land.** New Brunswick, N.J., 1954. Written by former United States cultural attaché in Belgrade. Critical of Tito's administration. [CJ]

W506. Kardelj, Edvard. **The Communist party of Yugoslavia in the struggle for new Yugoslavia, for people's authority and for socialism.** Belgrade, 1948.

W507. ——. **Problemi naše socijalisticke izgradnje.** [Problems of our socialist structure.] Belgrade, 1954 ff.

HISTORIES OF SPECIAL AREAS

Croatia

W508. Čubrilović, Vaso. **Politička prošlost Hrvata.** [Croatian politics in the past.] Belgrade, 1939. Short, popular discourse on Croatian political development in the 19th century. [CJ]

W509. Dimitrijević, Mita. **Mi i Hrvati: hrvatsko pitanje, 1914–1939.** [We and the Croats: the Croatian question, 1914–1939.] Belgrade, 1939. Valuable for Serbo-Croat problem. [CJ]

W510. Horvat, Josip. **Kultura hrvata kroz 1000 godina.** [Croatian culture over the past thousand years.] 2 v. Zagreb, 1939–42. Patriotic (Croatian), detailed work with good illustrations. [CJ]

W511. ——. **Stranke kod hrvata i njihove ideologije.** [Croatian parties and their ideologies.] Belgrade, 1939. Handy guide to Croatian political parties, but not detailed. [CJ]

W512. Maček, Vladko. **In the struggle for freedom.** N.Y., 1957. Defense of the Croatian Peasant party by its last leader. Critical of Serbs and Yugoslavia; ignores some key issues. [CJ]

W513. Marković, Lazar. **Jugoslovenska država i hrvatsko pitanje, 1914–1929.** [Yugoslav administration and the Croatian question, 1914–1929.] Belgrade, 1935. A major work by a Serbian writer discussing the Croatian problem within the context of the Yugoslav state. Essential for a study of the political history of Yugoslavia between the wars. [CJ]

W514. Radić, Antun. **Sabrana djela.** [Collected works.] 19 v. Zagreb, 1936–39. Works of the intellectual father of the Croatian Peasant party. [CJ]

W515. Šišić, Ferdinand, ed. **Korespondencija Rački-Strossmayer.** [Correspondence between Rački and Strossmayer.] 4 v. Zagreb, 1928–30. Excellent for the study of relations of perhaps the two greatest Croatians in the 19th century. [CJ]

W516. Starčević, Ante. **Izabrani spisi.** [Selected works.] Zagreb, 1943. Useful selections from writings of a prominent Croatian leader. [CJ]

W517. Supilo, Frano. **Politika u Hrvatskoj.** [Politics in Croatia.] 2nd ed., Zagreb, 1953. Valuable for Supilo's understanding of Croatian politics, in which he played a decisive role. [CJ]

W518. Šurmin, Djuro. **Hrvatski preporod.** [Croatian revival.] 2 v. Zagreb, 1903–04. Covers the period 1790–1843. Useful. [CJ]

W519. Vladisavljević, Milan. **Hrvatska autonomija pod Austro-Ugarskom.** [Croatian autonomy under Austria-Hungary.] Belgrade, 1939. Popular account of Croatia in the 19th century. [CJ]

W520. Zagorsky, Vladimir. **François Rački et la renaissance scientifique et politique de la Croatie (1828–1894).** Paris, 1909. Good work; emphasizes Rački's influence. [CJ]

Montenegro

W521. Jovanović, Jagoš. **Stvaranje crnogorske države i razvoj crnogorske nacialnosti.** [Creation of the Montenegrin state and the development of Montenegrin nationality.] Cetinje, 1947. Most recent account of general Montenegrin history. Written from party point of view, but author was not completely successful in this respect. [CJ]

Dalmatia

W522. Vojnovitch, L. de. **Histoire de Dalmatie.** 2 v. Paris, 1934. Competent treatment of the area, with helpful bibliography in all relevant languages.

Slovenia

W523. Lončar, Dragotin. **The Slovenes: a social history.** Tr. by Anthony J. Klancar. Cleveland, 1939.

W524. Bučar, Vekoslav. **Politička istorija**

slovenačke. [Slovenian political history.] Belgrade, 1939. Brief, useful account of Slovenian politics in the 19th century. [CJ]

HISTORIES OF SPECIAL TOPICS

Cultural History

W525. Benac, Alojz. **Kulturna istorija Bosne i Hercegovine.** [Cultural history of Bosnia and Herzegovina.] Sarajevo, 1955.

W526. Prijatelj, Ivan. **Slovenska kulturnopolitična in slovstvena zgodovina 1848–1895.** [Slovenian culture and politics in Slovene history, 1848–1895.] 2nd ed., 2 v., Ljubljana, 1955–56. Standard cultural and political history of the Slovenes. [CJ]

Religion

W527. Mousset, Jean. **La Serbie et son église (1830–1904).** Paris, 1938.

W528. Novak, Viktor. **Magnum crimen: pola vijeka klerikalizma u Hrvatskoj.** [The great crime: a half century of clericalism in Croatia.] Zagreb, 1948. Caustic denunciation of Catholicism in Yugoslavia in the 20th century. [CJ]

Literature

W529. Gesemann, Gerhard. **Die serbokroatische Literatur.** Potsdam, 1930. Excellent brief treatment. [RW]

W530. Ježić, Slavko. **Hrvatska književnost od početka do danas 1100–1941.** [Croatian literature from the beginnings to the present, 1100–1941.] Zagreb, 1944. Good and helpful survey. [CJ]

W531. Murko, Matthias. **Geschichte der älteren südslawischen Literaturen.** Leipzig, 1908.

W532. Prohaska, Dragutin. **Das kroatisch-serbische Schrifttum in Bosnien und der Herzegovina von den Anfängen im XI. bis zur nationalen Wiedergeburt im XIX. Jahrhundert.** Zagreb, 1911. Good on older literature. [RW]

W533. Skerlić, Jovan. **Istorija nove srpske književnosti.** [History of modern Serbian literature.] 3rd ed., Belgrade, 1953. Although first published in 1912, this remains one of the best works on modern Serbian literature. Good for history trends. [CJ]

W534. Barac, Antun. **A history of Yugoslav literature.** Belgrade, 1955. Tr. of *Jugoslavenska književnost* (Zagreb, 1954). Brief general survey with important biographical sketches; a useful guide. [CJ]

W535. **Sto godina hrvatske književnosti 1830–1930.** [A hundred years of Croatian literature, 1830–1930.] 6 v. Zagreb, 1934–35.

Economic History

W536. Tomašević, Jozo. **Peasants, politics**

and economic change in Yugoslavia. Stanford, 1955. Excellent; basic for Yugoslav economic history to 1941. Emphasis on interwar period. [CJ]

W537. Trouton, Ruth. **Peasant renaissance in Yugoslavia, 1900–1950.** London, 1952. Interesting account. [CJ]

Constitutional History

W538. Belgrade. **Institut za Medju-Narodnu Politiku i Privredu. Pregled razvoja medjunarodno-pravnih odnosa jugoslovenskih zemalja od 1800 do danas.** [Survey of the development of status in international law of the Yugoslav lands from 1800 to the present.] Belgrade, 1953 ff.

W539. Čulinović, Ferdo, ed. **Nova Jugoslavija: pregled državnopravnog razvitka povodom desetgodišnjice drugog zasjedanja Avnoj-a.** [New Yugoslavia: a sketch of the constitutional-legal development on the occasion of the tenth anniversary of the second session of the Avnoj.] Zagreb, 1954. Collaborative work on constitutional developments in Tito's Yugoslavia. [CJ]

W540. ———. **Državnopravna historija jugoslavenskih zemalja XIX i XX vijeka.** [A constitutional-legal history of the Yugoslav lands in the 19th and 20th centuries.] 2 v. Zagreb, 1953–54. Constitutional history by a well-known author. [CJ]

W541. Dabinović, Antun. **Hrvatska državna i pravna povijest.** [Croatian constitutional and legal history.] Zagreb, 1940. Essential for Croatian constitutional history. [CJ]

W542. Djordjević, Jovan. **Ustavno pravo F N R J.** [Constitutional law of the Federal Republic of Yugoslavia.] Belgrade, 1953. The post-1945 Yugoslav constitution explained by one of its "authors." [CJ]

W543. Janković, Dragoslav. **Istorija države i prava Srbije u XIX veku.** [History of the state and law of Serbia in the 19th century.] Belgrade, 1952. Useful work on legal and constitutional aspects of 19th century Serbia. [CJ]

W544. Milétitch, Voukadine. **Le mouvement des idées constitutionnelles en Yugoslavie depuis la fin de la Grande Guerre.** Paris, 1934.

W545. Prodanović, Jaša M. **Ustavni razvitak i ustavne borbe u Srbiji.** [Constitutional development and constitutional struggles in Serbia.] Belgrade, 1936. Standard reference work on Serbian constitutional problems. [CJ]

BIOGRAPHIES

W546. Graham, Stephen. **Alexander of Yugoslavia.** New Haven, 1939.

W547. Horvat, Josip. **Supilo.** Zagreb, 1938.

Biography of eminent Croatian politician who played a major role in the Serbo-Croat coalition. [CJ]
W548. ——. **Ante Starčević.** Zagreb, 1940. A 19th century Croatian politician. [CJ]
W549. Padev, Michael. **Marshal Tito.** London, 1944.
W550. Stranjaković, Dragoslav. **Karadjordje.** Belgrade, 1938. Sympathetic biography of leader of Serbian revolution, by a good historian. [CJ]

ACADEMY PUBLICATIONS

W551. Codex diplomaticus regni Croatiae, Dalmatiae, et Slavoniae. Zagreb, 1904 ff. [Jugoslavenska Akademija Znanosti i Umjetnosti.]
W552. Jugoslavenska Akademija Znanosti i Umjetnosti. **Gradja za povijest književnosti hrvatske.** [Materials for Croatian history and literature.] Zagreb, 1897 ff. (Irregular.)
W553. ——. **Ljetopis.** [Yearbook.] Zagreb, 1867 ff.
W554. Monumenta historico-juridica Slavorum meridionalium. Zagreb, 1877 ff. [Jugoslavenska Akademija Znanosti i Umjetnosti.] Monographic series.
W555. Monumenta spectantia historiam Slavorum meridionalium. Zagreb, 1868 ff. [Jugoslavenska Akademija Znanosti i Umjetnosti.] A continuing series with many sub-series.
W556. Jugoslavenska Akademija Znanosti i Umjetnosti. **Rad.** [Publications.] Zagreb, 1867 ff. (Irregular.)
W557. Stari pisci hrvatski [Old Croatian writers.] Zagreb, 1869 ff. [Jugoslavenska Akademija Znanosti i Umjetnosti.] (Irregular.)
W558. Jugoslavenska Akademija Znanosti i Umjetnosti. **Starine.** [Antiquities.] Zagreb, 1869 ff. (Annual.)
W559. Zbornik za narodni život i običaje južnih Slavena. [Anthology of national life and customs of the southern Slavs.] Zagreb, 1896 ff. [Jugoslavenska Akademija Znanosti i Umjetnosti.] (Semiannual, 1896–1916; annual, 1896–97, 1917 ff.)
W560. Slovenska Akademija Znanosti in Umetnosti. **Filozofsko-filološko-historični razred.** [Philosophical-philological-historical section.] Ljubljana, 1941–43, 1950 ff. From 1943 to 1950 this was part of *W562.*
W561. ——. **Razprave, razred za zgodovinske in družbene vede.** [Proceedings of the section for historical and social sciences.] Ljubljana, 1950 ff. (Irregular.)
W562. ——. **Razprave, razred za zgodovinske in zemljepisne vede, za filozofijo in filologijo.** [Proceedings of the section for historical and geographical science and for philosophy and philology.] Ljubljana, 1943–50. (Irregular.)
W563. Srpska Akademija Nauka. **Glas.**

[Voice.] Belgrade, 1887–1913, 1921–41, 1946 ff.
W564. ——. **Posebna izdanja.** [Special publications.] Belgrade, 1890–1914, 1923–43, 1946 ff. (Irregular.)
W565. ——. **Spomenik.** [Memoirs.] Belgrade, 1888–1910, 1922–42, 1948 ff. (Irregular.)
W566. ——. **Srpski dijalektološki zbornik.** [Serbian dialectological review.] Belgrade, 1905–11, 1927–40, 1950 ff. (Irregular.)
W567. ——. **Srpski etnografski zbornik.** [Serbian ethnographic review.] Belgrade, 1894–1913, 1921–41, 1948 ff. (Irregular.)
W568. ——. **Zbornik za istoriju, jezik i književnost srpskog naroda.** [Review of Serbian history, language and literature.] Belgrade, 1902 ff. (Irregular.)

PERIODICALS

It will be noticed that a number of journals ceased publication in the period 1938–41. They will be found to have successors, under slightly different names, after the war. All the principal traditional regions of Yugoslavia are now represented.
W569. Godišnjak Istoriskog Društva Bosne i Hercegovine. [Annual of the Historical Society of Bosnia and Herzegovina.] Sarajevo, 1949 ff. Concerned with all aspects of Bosnian, Herzegovinian, and Montenegrin culture and history, with contributions by both younger and older historians. Alternately in Serbian and Croatian.
W570. Bosanska vila. [The Bosnian villa.] Sarajevo, 1886–1914. Indispensable for study of Bosnia and folklore. [CJ]
W571. Zapisi: glasnik Cetinskog Istoriskog Društva. [Notes: messenger of the Historical Society of Cetinje.] Cetinje, 1928–41. (Monthly.) Essential journal for study of Montenegrin history. [CJ]
W572. Časopis za slovenski jezik književost in zgodóvino. [Journal for Slovenian language, literature and history.] Ljubljana, 1918–31. (Quarterly.)
W573. Hrvatska revija. [Croatian review.] Zagreb, 1928–45. (Bimonthly.) Indispensable for Croatian point of view in period between the wars. [CJ]
W574. Hrvatsko kolo. [Croatian circle.] Zagreb, 1905–46 (annual), 1948–51 (quarterly), 1952 ff. (monthly). Famous literary journal. [CJ]
W575. Istoriski zapisi. [Historical notes.] Cetinje, 1948 ff. (Quarterly.) Organ of the Historical Institute of the National Republic of Montenegro. Publishes Montenegrin documents, correspondence, and studies.
W576. Letopis Matice Srpske. [Annual of the Serbian Foundation.] Novi Sad, 1824 ff. (Title varies.) Oldest and most valuable Serbian periodical covering all subjects. [CJ]
W577. Otadžbina. [The fatherland.] Bel-

grade, 1875–92. Indispensable for literary and social problems. [CJ]

W578. Dom in svet. [Home and the world.] Ljubljana, 1888–1914. (Irregular.) Conservative Catholic review in Slovenia. [CJ]

W579. Ljubljanski zvon. [The Ljubljana bell.] Ljubljana, 1881–1941. (Monthly.) Famous Slovenian liberal literary periodical. [CJ]

W580. Časopis za zgodovíno in narodopisje. [Review of history and folklore.] Maribor, 1904–40. (Irregular.) Basic historical periodical for Slovenia. [CJ]

W581. Godišnjica Nikole Čupića. [Nikola Čupić yearbook.] Belgrade, 1877–1941. (Annual.) Indispensable for study of Serbian history. [CJ]

W582. Jugoslovenski istoriski časopis. [Yugoslavian historical review.] Belgrade,

1935–39. Best historical journal published in Yugoslavia between the wars; especially good for bibliographical and historiographic essays. [CJ]

W583. Brastvo. [Brotherhood.] Belgrade, 1887–1941. (Annual.) Publication of the Society of Sveti Sava. Invaluable for history of Serbia. [CJ]

W584. Historijski zbornik. [Historical review.] Zagreb, 1948 ff. (Quarterly.) Major historical review published in Zagreb; concerned principally with Croatian history. Contains some excellent articles. [CJ]

W585. Zgodovinski časopis. [Historical journal.] Ljubljana, 1948 ff. (Quarterly.) Concerned with history and institutions of Slovenia, and activities of the Historical Society of Slovenia.

ROMANIA

BIBLIOGRAPHIES

The most complete bibliographical references for general Romanian history appear at the end of each chapter of *Istoria Românilor* (*W616*). Other excellent bibliographies are contained in *Documente privitóre la istoria Românilor* (*W601*); and in the leading historical periodicals: *Revista istorică* (*W714*), *Revista istorică română* (*W715*), and *Studii* (*W720*). The bibliography in *Histoire de Transylvanie* (*W678*) is very substantial.

W586. Bianu, Ioan, and Nerva Hodos. **Bibliografia românească veche, 1508–1830.** [Old Romanian bibliography, 1508–1830.] 3 v. Bucharest, 1903–12. Fundamental though outdated. [JCC]

W587. Crăciun, Ion. **Bibliographie de la Transylvanie roumaine, 1916–1936.** Cluj, 1937.

W588. Rally, Alexandre, and Getta-Helène Rally. **Bibliographie franco-roumaine.** Paris, 1930. Extensive listing, generally supplanting Georges Bengesco, *Bibliographie franco-roumaine . . .* (2nd rev. ed., Paris, 1907). [JCC]

W589. U. S. Library of Congress. **Rumania.** Comp. by Helen F. Conover. Washington, 1943. [The Balkans: a selected list of references, 4.]

REFERENCE WORKS

W590. Enciclopedia României. 4 v. Bucharest, 1936–43. [Asociaţia Ştiinţifică pentru Enciclopedia României.] Basic reference work for pre-World War II period. [JCC]

W591. Fischer, Galaţi, Stephen, ed. **Romania.** N.Y., 1957. Useful survey and reference book for the period since 1944. [JCC]

GEOGRAPHIES

W592. Ancel, Jacques. **Les frontières roumaines.** Bucharest, 1935.

W593. Martonne, Emmanuel de. **Europe centrale.** Paris, 1931. The section on Romania, with which the author was intimately acquainted, is excellent. [JCC]

W594. Mehedinţi, Simeon. **România.** 11th ed., Bucharest, 1932. English tr., *Rumania and her people: an essay in physical and human geography*, Bucharest, 1939. Conventional text by the leading Romanian geographer. [JCC]

W595. Mihăilescu, Vintilă. **România, geografia fizică.** [Romania, physical geography.] Bucharest, 1936.

W596. Simionescu, Ion. **Ţara noastră: oameni, locuri, lucruri.** [Our land: men, places, things.] Bucharest, 1937. Political-geographical survey marked by strong nationalistic views. [JCC]

DEMOGRAPHY

W597. Manuila, Sabin. **La population de la Dobroudja.** Bucharest, 1939.

LINGUISTICS

W598. Densusianu, Ovid. **Histoire de la langue roumaine.** 2 v. Paris, 1901–14.

PRINTED COLLECTIONS OF SOURCES

W599. Costăchescu, M., ed. **Documente moldoveneşti dinainte de Ştefan cel Mare.** [Molvadian documents before Stephen the Great.] 2 v. Iaşi, 1931–32.

W600. Documente privind istoria României. [Documents concerning the history of Romania.] Ed. by Mihail Roller. Bucharest, 1951 ff.

W601. Hurmuzaki, Eudoxiu. **Documente privitóre la istoria Românilor.** [Documents on the history of the Romanians.] 19 v. in 31. Bucharest, 1876–1938. Indispensable collection. [JCC]

W602. Iorga, Nicolae. **Acte şi fragmente cu privire la istoria Rominilor.** [Acts and fragments on the history of the Romanians.] 3 v. Bucharest, 1895–97. Documents mostly in western archives.

W603. ――, ed. **Correspondance diplomatique roumaine sous le roi Charles Ier (1866–1880).** Paris, 1923. 2nd ed., Bucharest, 1938. Rich collection from the archives of the Romanian foreign ministry, with historical introduction. [JCC]

W604. Panaitescu, P. P., ed. **Documentele Ţării Româneşti.** [Documents of Wallachia.] Bucharest, 1938 ff.

W605. Anul 1848 in principatele române: acte şi documente. [The year 1848 in the Romanian principalities: acts and documents.] 6 v. Bucharest, 1902–10. Rich collection of official documents, private correspondence, and excerpts from the contemporary press. [JCC]

W606. Acte şi documente relative la istoria renascerei Românei. [Acts and documents regarding the renascence of Romania.] Ed. by Dimitrie Sturdza and others. 10 v. Bucharest, 1889–1909. Contains large collection of treaties from earlier centuries as well as documents of the 19th century.

W607. Documente din istoria Partidului comunist din România. [Documents from the history of the Communist party of Romania.] V. 1, 2, and 4. Bucharest, 1951–53. 2nd ed. of v. 1 and 2, 1956. Abr. 1 v. ed., 1951. Contains mostly resolutions, programs, and manifestoes; some important documents not included. Covers period 1917–28, 1934–37. V. 3 (1929–33) has not appeared. [JCC]

HISTORIOGRAPHY

W608. Boldur, Alexandru V. **Ştiinţa istorică română în ultimii ani.** [Romanian historical science in recent years.] Iaşi, 1946.

W609. Constantinescu-Iaşi, Petre. **Realizările istoriografiei romîne între anii 1945–1955.** [Achievements of Romanian historiography, 1945–1955.] Bucharest, 1956. By a leading Communist historian and propagandist. [JCC]

W610. Giurescu, Constantin C. "Consideraţii asupra istoriografiei româneşti in ultimii douăzeci de ani." [Considerations on Romanian historiography in the last twenty years.] **Revista istorica,** 12 (July-Sep. 1926): 137–85.

W611. Henry, Paul. "Histoire roumaine." **Revue historique** (Paris), 176 (July-Dec.

1935): 486–537; 194 (July-Dec. 1944): 42–65, 132–50, 233–52.

SHORTER GENERAL HISTORIES

W612. Gáldi, Ladislaus, and Ladislaus Makkai. **Geschichte der Rumänen.** Budapest, 1942. From moderate Hungarian point of view. Each chapter contains critical bibliography.

W613. Ghika, Matila C. **A documented chronology of Roumanian history from prehistoric times to the present day.** Oxford, 1941. Handy reference work. [JCC]

W614. Iorga, Nicolae. **A history of Roumania: land, people, civilisation.** London, 1925. Helpful in a general way, but lacks precision.

LONGER GENERAL HISTORIES

W615. Giurescu, Constantin C. **Istoria Românilor.** [History of the Romanians.] 4 v. Bucharest, 1935–46. Most thorough and scholarly history available. This and *W597* are in many cases the best references on the various periods of Romanian history. [JCC]

W616. Iorga, Nicolae. **Istoria Românilor.** [History of the Romanians.] 10 v. Bucharest, 1935–39. French tr. of v. 1–4, *Histoire des Roumains et de la Romanité orientale,* 4 v. in 5, Bucharest, 1937. A synthesis of this great historian's voluminous work and research. [JCC]

W617. ――. **Geschichte des rumänischen Volkes im Rahmen seiner Staatsbildungen.** 2 v. Gotha, 1905–06.

W618. ――. **La place des Roumains dans l'histoire universelle.** 3 v. Bucharest, 1935–37. Despite its undoubted brilliance, this work sometimes proves too much, and shows the marks of hurried composition.

W619. Roller, Mihail. **Istoria R. P. R.** [History of the Romanian Peoples' Republic.] Bucharest, 1952. Standard history by a leading Communist historian. [JCC]

W620. Seton-Watson, Robert W. **A history of the Roumanians from Roman times to the completion of unity.** Cambridge, Eng., 1934. The best history in English. Covers to 1919. Useful, but not exhaustive, bibliography. [JCC]

W621. Xenopol, Alexandru D. **Istoria Românilor din Dacia traiană.** [History of the Romanians of Trajan's Dacia.] 12 v. Iaşi, 1888–96. 3rd ed., Bucharest, 1925–30. Basic work, but largely superseded by Iorga and Giurescu. [JCC]

HISTORIES OF SPECIAL PERIODS

Origins and Early History

W622. Brătianu, George I. **Une énigme et un miracle historique: le peuple roumain.** Bucharest, 1937.

W623. Iorga, Nicolae. **Byzance après Byzance.** Bucharest, 1935.

W624. Pârvan, Vasile. **Getica.** Bucharest, 1926.

W625. ——. **Dacia: an outline of the early civilizations in the Carpatho-Danubian countries.** Cambridge, Eng., 1928. A reputable work on the little-known history of the Dacians. [JCC]

W626. Philippide, Alexandru. **Originea Românilor.** [The origin of the Romanians.] 2 v. Iaşi, 1923–28.

W627. Roesler, Robert. **Romänische Studien: Untersuchungen zur älteren Geschichte Romäniens.** Leipzig, 1871.

W628. Tamás, Lajos. **Romains, Romans et Roumains dans l'histoire de la Dacie trajane.** Budapest, 1936. Also published as a series of articles in *Archivum europae centro-orientalis,* 1 (1935): 1–96; 2 (1936): 46–83, 245–374.

W629. Xenopol, Alexandru D. **Une énigme historique: les Roumains au Moyen-Âge.** Paris, 1885. Defends the Daco-Roman thesis with great conviction.

1200–1821

W630. Conduratu, Gregor C. **Incercări istorice: relaţiunile Ţării Româneşti şi Moldova cu Ungaria până la anul 1526.** [Historical essays: the relations of Wallachia and Moldavia with Hungary to the year 1526.] Bucharest, 1898.

W631. Filitti, Ioan C. **Rôle diplomatique des Phanariotes de 1700 à 1821.** Paris, 1901.

W632. Lebel, Germaine. **La France et les principautés danubiennes du XVIᵉ siècle à la chute de Napoléon Iᵉʳ.** Paris, 1955.

W633. Onciul, Dimitre. **Originile principatelor române.** [Origins of the Romanian principalities.] Bucharest, 1899.

1821–1878

W634. Cretzianu, Alexandru. **Din arhiva lui Dumitru Brătianu.** [From the archives of Dumitru Brătianu.] 2 v. Bucharest, 1833–34.

W635. East, William G. **The union of Moldavia and Wallachia, 1859.** Cambridge, Eng., 1929. Studied principally from available printed documents and the Foreign Office collection in the Public Record Office.

W636. Filitti, Ioan C. **Domniile române sub Regulamentul Organic, 1834–1848.** [The Romanian principalities under the Réglement Organique, 1834–1848.] Bucharest, 1915.

W637. Fotino, Georges. **Din vremea renaşterii naţionale a Ţării Româneşti: boerii goleşti.** [From the time of the national renaissance in Wallachia: the Golescu boyars.] 4 v. Bucharest, 1939.

W638. Henry, Paul. **L'abdication du Prince Cuza et l'avènement de la dynastie des Hohenzollern au trône de la Roumanie.** Paris, 1930. Heavily documented from archives.

W639. Iorga, Nicolae. **Mihail Kogălniceanu: scriitorul, omul politic şi Românul.** [Mihail Kogălniceanu: writer, statesman and Romanian.] Bucharest, 1921.

W640. Riker, Thad W. **The making of Roumania.** Oxford, 1931. Best diplomatic history of the period 1856–66 in any language. [JCC]

W641. Ştirbu, S. **Răscoala din 1821 şi legăturile ei cu evenimentele internaţionale.** [The rising of 1821 and its ties with international events.] Bucharest, 1956. A Marxist interpretation. [JCC]

W642. Vîrtosu, Emil. **Tudor Vladimirescu: pagini de revoltă.** Bucharest, 1936.

1878–1945

W643. Brătianu, George I. **Acţiunea politică şi militară a României în 1919.** [Political and military action of Romania in 1919.] Bucharest, 1939.

W644. **Regele Carol I al României: cuvântări şi scrisori.** [King Carol I of Rumania: speeches and letters.] 3 v. Bucharest, 1909.

W645. [Kremnitz, Marie C.] **Aus dem Leben König Karls von Rumänien.** 4 v. Stuttgart, 1894–1900. Invaluable source for the reign of Carol I. [JCC]

W646. Cialdea, Lilio. **La politica estera della Romania nel quarantennio prebellico.** Bologna, 1933.

W647. Clark, Charles U. **United Roumania.** N.Y., 1932. A deficient survey, but one of the few in English. [JCC]

W648. Codreanu, Cornelin Z. **Eiserne Garde.** Berlin, 1939. Apologia for the Iron Guard by its leader. [JCC]

W649. Comnène, Nicolas P. **Preludi del grande dramma.** Rome, 1947. Diplomatic history prior to World War II. [JCC]

W650. Cretziano, Alexandre. **The lost opportunity.** London, 1957. Romania and the wartime strategy and diplomacy of the western allies. [JCC]

W651. Dragu, Thomas. **La politique roumaine après les troubles agrariens de 1907.** Paris, 1908.

W652. Gafencu, Grigore. **Prelude to the Russian campaign.** See *AH213.*

W653. Hillgruber, Andreas. **Hitler, König Carol und Marschall Antonescu: die deutsch-rumänische Beziehungen, 1938–1944.** Wiesbaden, 1954. Thorough monograph based largely on German sources, some unpublished. [JCC]

W654. Institutul Social Român. **Doctrinele partidelôr politice.** [Doctrines of the political parties.] Bucharest, 1924. Series of statements by political leaders, important for the history and role of the various parties in the interwar period. [JCC]

W655. Ionesco, Take. **Souvenirs.** Paris, 1919.

W656. Iorga, Nicolae. **Supt trei regi.** [Under three kings.] Bucharest, 1932.

W657. Kirițescu, Constantin. **Istoria războiului pentru întregirea României, 1916–1919.** [History of the war for the unification of Romania, 1916–1919.] 3 v. Bucharest, 1922–24.

W658. Marghiloman, Alexandru. **Memorii.** [Memoirs.] 5 v. Bucharest, 1927. A source of some importance, especially for the period of World War I. [JCC]

W659. Rouček, Joseph S. **Contemporary Roumania and her problems.** Stanford, 1932.

W660. Tilea, Viorel V. **Acțiunea diplomatică a României, 1919–1920.** [Diplomatic action of Romania, 1919–1920.] Sibiu, 1925. Romanian diplomacy at the Paris peace conference. [JCC]

Since 1945

W661. Ciurea, Émile C. **Le traité de paix avec la Roumanie.** Paris, 1954.

W662. Cretzianu, Alexandre, ed. **Captive Rumania: a decade of Soviet rule.** N.Y., 1956. Collaborative work by a group of Romanian exiles. [JCC]

W663. Lee, Arthur S. G. **Crown against sickle.** London, 1950. Story of the conflict between King Michael and the Communists. [JCC]

W664. Markham, Reuben H. **Rumania under the Soviet yoke.** Boston, 1949. The author, a foreign correspondent, lived in Romania many years before World War II.

W665. Pătrășcanu, Lucrețiu D. **Sub trei dictaturi.** [Under three dictatorships.] Bucharest, 1945. French ed., *Sous trois dictatures,* Paris, 1946. Memoirs of a Communist leader. [JCC]

W666. Prost, Henri. **Destin de la Roumanie, 1918–1954.** Paris, 1954.

W667. Roberts, Henry L. **Rumania: political problems of an agrarian state.** New Haven, 1951. Valuable study of both economic and political problems, based on wide use of Romanian source material. [JCC]

HISTORIES OF SPECIAL AREAS

W668. Arbure, Zamfir C. **Basarabia în secolul XIX-lea.** [Bessarabia in the 19th century.] Bucharest, 1898.

W669. Barițiu, Gheorghe. **Parte alese din istoria Transilvaniei.** [Selected parts of the history of Transylvania.] 3 v. Sibiu, 1889–91.

W670. Boldur, Alexandru V. **La Bessarabie et les relations russo-roumaines.** Paris, 1927.

W671. Brătianu, George I. **La Bessarabie,** droits nationaux et historiques. Bucharest, 1943.

W672. Dol'nik, A. **Bessarabiia pod vlast'iu rumynskikh boiar, 1918–1940 gg.** [Bessarabia under the rule of the Romanian boyars, 1918–1940.] Moscow, 1945.

W673. Dragomir, Silviu. **La Transylvanie avant et après l'arbitrage de Vienne.** Sibiu, 1943.

W674. Ungarische Historische Gesellschaft. **Siebenbürgen.** Ed. by Emerich Lukinich. Budapest, 1940. Useful, though issued largely for political purposes, as were E. Lukinich, *Die siebenbürgische Frage* (Budapest, 1940), and Elemér Mályusz, *Siebenbürgen und seine Völker* (Budapest, 1944). [JCC]

W675. Institutul de Istorie Naționala. **Siebenbürgen.** 2 v. Bucharest, 1943. Elaborate comprehensive work covering historical and other fields; issued in German for political reasons. [JCC]

W676. Iorga, Nicolae. **Histoire des Roumains de Transylvanie et de Hongrie.** 2 v. Bucharest, 1915–16.

W677. Jancsó, Benedek. **A román nemzetiségi törehvések története és jelenlegi állapota.** [The history and present state of the Romanian national movement. 2 v. Budapest, 1896–99. Out of date, but still very useful work on the Hungarian side. [JCC]

W678. Makkai, Ladislas. **Histoire de Transylvanie.** Paris, 1946. Good survey, emphasizing the Hungarian side of Transylvania's history. Full bibliography. [JCC]

W679. Nistor, Ion. **Der nationale Kampf in der Bukowina.** Bucharest, 1919.

W680. Păcățianu, Teodor V. **Cartea de aur: sau luptele politice-naționale ale Românilor de sub coroana ungară.** [The golden book: or the political-national struggles of the Romanians under the Hungarian crown.] 8 v. Sibiu, 1902–15. Indispensable source for history of Romanian national movement in Transylvania. [JCC]

W681. Popovici, Andrei. **The political status of Bessarabia.** Washington, 1931.

W682. Academia Română. **La Dobroudja.** Bucharest, 1938. Useful collaborative work covering both southern Dobruja (which Romania lost in 1940) and northern Dobruja. [JCC]

W683. ——. **La Transylvanie.** Bucharest, 1938. Collaborative work containing several important historical contributions. [JCC]

W684. Teutsch, Georg D., and Friedrich Teutsch. **Geschichte der Siebenbürger Sachsen.** 4 v. Hermannstadt (Sibiu), 1899–1920.

HISTORIES OF SPECIAL TOPICS

Economic History

W685. Adam, I., and N. Marcu. **Studii despre dezvoltarea capitalismului în agri-**

cultura României. [Studies on the development of capitalism in Romanian agriculture.] Bucharest, 1956. By two Communist authors. [JCC]

W686. Arcadian, N. P. **Industrializarea României.** [Industrialization of Romania.] 2nd ed., Bucharest, 1936.

W687. Dobrovici, Gheorghe M. **Istoricul desvoltării economice şi financiare a României.** [History of the economic and financial development of Romania.] Bucharest, 1934

W688. Emerit, Marcel. **Les paysans roumains depuis le Traité d'Andrinople jusqu'à la libération des terres (1829–1864).** Paris, 1937.

W689. Gheorghiu, Panait R. **The foreign trade of Roumania from the Treaty of Adrianople up to the great depression.** Bucharest, 1936.

W690. Iordan, Constantin. **The Rumanian oil industry.** N.Y., 1955.

W691. Iorga, Nicolae. **Istoria comerţului românesc.** [History of Romanian commerce.] 2nd ed., 2 v., Bucharest, 1925.

W692. Konrad, G. I. **Die Wirtschaft Rumäniens 1945–1952.** Berlin, 1953.

W693. Madgearu, Virgil. **Evoluţia economiei româneşti după Razboiul Mondial.** [Economic evolution of Romania since the World War.] Bucharest, 1940. Most useful and authoritative study of Romania's economic history and problems up to World War II. [JCC]

W694. Mitrany, David. **The land and the peasant in Rumania.** London and New Haven, 1930. Fundamental study of the postwar land reform. [JCC]

W695. Razmiritza, Nicolas. **Essai d'économie roumaine moderne, 1831–1931.** Paris, 1932.

W696. Rosetti, Radu. **Pământul, sătenii, şi stăpânii in Moldova.** [The land, the peasants, and the landlords in Moldavia.] Bucharest, 1907. This and *Pentru ce s'au rasculat ţaranii* [Why did the peasants rise?] (Bucharest, 1907), by the same author, are the first, and still classic, studies on the agrarian problem, which burst on the country's consciousness with the rising of 1907. [JCC]

No good books on Romania's economy under the Communist regime have appeared, but attention is called to the economic chapters of *W662* and *W591*, and to general works on the economy of eastern Europe and the Balkans which deal *inter alia* with Romania.

Cultural and Religious History

W697. Beza, Marcu. **The Rumanian church.** London, 1943.

W698. Călinescu, G. **Istoria literaturii române dela origini până în prezent.** [History of Romanian literature from its origins to the present.] Bucharest, 1941.

W699. Constantinescu-Iaşi, Petre. **Relaţiile culturale romîno-ruse din trecut.** [Romanian-Russian cultural relations in the past.] Bucharest, 1954. Study by a Communist author emphasizing the Russian influence on Romanian culture. [JCC]

W700. Eliade, Pompiliu. **De l'influence française sur l'esprit public en Roumanie.** Paris, 1898. Pioneer work in cultural history, still of great value. [JCC]

W701. Iorga, Nicolae. **Istoria literaturii româneşti.** [History of Romanian literature.] 3 v. Bucharest, 1925–33.

W702. ———. **Istoria invăţământului românesc.** [History of Romanian education.] Bucharest, 1928. French ed., *Histoire de l'enseignement en pays roumains*, Bucharest, 1933.

W703. ———. **Istoria bisericii româneşti şi a vieţii religioase a Românilor.** [History of the Romanian church and of the religious life of the Romanians.] 2nd ed., 2 v., Bucharest, 1928–30.

W704. Lovinescu, Eugen. **Istoria civilizaţiei române moderne.** [History of modern Romanian civilization.] 3 v. Bucharest, 1924–25.

W705. Lupaş, Ioan. **Istoria bisericii române.** [History of the Romanian church.] Bucharest, 1935.

W706. Munteano, Basil. **Panorama de la littérature roumaine contemporaine.** Paris, 1938. Comprehensive and scholarly survey of Romanian literary activity since 1867.

W707. Popovici, D. **La littérature roumaine à l'époque des lumières.** Sibiu, 1945.

BIOGRAPHIES

W708. Iorga, Nicolae. **Istoria lui Ştefan cel Mare.** [History of Stephen the Great.] Bucharest, 1904.

W709. ———. **Istoria lui Mihai Viteazul.** [History of Michael the Brave.] 2 v. Bucharest, 1935.

W710. Minea, Ilie. **Vlad Dracul şi vremea sa.** [Vlad Dracul and his age.] Iaşi, 1928.

W711. Panaitescu, P. P. **Mircea cel Bătrân.** [Mircea the Old.] Bucharest, 1944.

W712. ———. **Mihai Viteazul.** [Michael the Brave.] Bucharest, 1936.

W713. Ursu, Ion. **Petru Rareş.** Bucharest, 1923.

PERIODICALS

W714. Revista istorică. [Historical review.] Vălenii-de-Munte and Bucharest, 1914–46. (Irregular.)

W715. Revista istorică română. [Romanian historical review.] Bucharest, 1931–47. (Quarterly.)

W716. Revue historique du Sud-Est euro-

péen. Bucharest, 1924–46. (Quarterly.) Largely devoted to Romania despite its broader title.

W717. Anuarul Institutului de Istorie Naţională. [Annual of the Institute of National History.] Cluj and Bucharest, 1922–42.

W718. Academia Română. **Memoriile secţiunei istorice.** [Memoirs of the historical section.] Bucharest, 1867–1942. Contains many important contributions, including studies of some length.

W719. Analele româno-sovietice, seria istorie. [Romanian-Soviet annals, historical series.] Bucharest, 1946 ff. (Quarterly. Title varies.) Studies by Romanian and Soviet historians.

W720. Studii: revistă de istorie. [Studies: a historical review.] Bucharest, 1948 ff.

(Quarterly.) Published by the historical institute of the Academy of the Romanian People's Republic.

W721. Analele Institutului de Istorie a Partidului de pe lângă Comitetului Central al Partid Muncitoresc Român. [Annals of the Institute of the History of the Party sponsored by the Central Committee of the Romanian Workers' Party.] Bucharest, 1955 ff. (Irregular.)

W722. Revue des études roumaines. Paris, 1953 ff. (Irregular.) Review of the Fondation Carol I, publishing historical studies by exiled Romanian scholars.

W723. Stuḑii şi certetări ştiinţifice: istorie. [Studies and scientific researches: history.] Iaşi, 1950 ff. (Quarterly.) Published by the Iaşi branch of the Romanian Academy.

HUNGARY

BIBLIOGRAPHIES

W724. Apponyi, Alexander, graf. **Hungarica: Ungarn betreffende im Auslande gedruckte Bücher.** 4 v. Munich, 1903–27. Works about Hungary printed in western countries during the 16th–18th centuries. [FW]

W725. Bako, Elemer. "Selected references on the Hungarian revolution of 1956." **The Hungarian revolution of 1956: second seminar, June 6, 1958** (N.Y., 1958), pp. 90–100. A classified list of works and periodical articles, principally in English.

W726. Bartoniek, Emma. **Magyar történeti forráskiadványok.** [List of published Hungarian historical sources.] Budapest, 1930. Very useful though selected compilation. [FW]

W727. Banner, János, and Imre Jakabffy. **A Közép-Dunamedence régészeti bibliográfiája a legrégibb időktöl a XI századig.** [Archaeological bibliography of the Middle-Danube basin from the earliest times to the 11th century.] Budapest, 1954.

W728. Bodor, Antal. **Magyarország helyismereti könyvészete, 1527–1940: bibliographia locorum hungariae, MDXXVII–MCMXL.** Budapest, 1944. Lists approximately 14,000 titles in eighteen languages. Valuable despite its selectivity. [GB]

W729. Borsody, Stephen. "Modern Hungarian historiography." **The journal of modern history,** 24 (Dec. 1952): 398–405. Best modern and concise summary in English on period before the Communist seizure of power. [GB]

W730. Kéziratos források az Országos Széchényi Könyvtárban, 1789–1865. [Manuscript sources in the National Széchényi Library, 1789–1865.] Budapest, 1950.

W731. Bibliographia oeconomiae Hun-

gariae. Ed. by Jenö Dóczy and others. 2 v. Budapest, 1934–38. [Magyar gazdasági könyvészet.] Attempts to list everything written, published, or available in Hungary on economic problems. Covers 1505–1830. [GB]

W732. Kálnoki Bedö, Alexander, and George Torzsay-Biber. **Legal sources and bibliography of Hungary.** N.Y., 1956. Contains a survey of legal sources, collections of laws, statutes, and court reports; bibliography of treaties, including Transylvania; translations of laws, statutes, etc., and references to books and articles in other than the Hungarian language; and a list of periodicals and most important statutes. [FW]

W733. Kertész, János. **Bibliographie der Habsburg Literatur, 1218–1934.** Budapest, 1934.

W734. Kosáry, Domokos G. **Bevezetés a magyar történelem forrásaiba és irodalmába.** [Introduction to the sources and literature of Hungarian history.] 2 v. Budapest, 1951–54. Excellent annotated bibliography covering period to 1825. [FW]

W735. Kozocsa, Sándor. **Magyar könyvészet, 1911–1920.** [Hungarian bibliography, 1911–1920.] Budapest, 1939.

W736. Lukinich, Emeric, ed. **Les éditions des sources de l'histoire hongroise, 1854–1930.** Budapest, 1931.

W737. Lynn, Meda. **Reconstruction in Hungary, 1924–1935: bibliography of magazine articles.** N.Y., 1935.

W738. Magyar nemzeti bibliográfia. [Hungarian national bibliography.] Budapest, 1946 ff. (Monthly.) Issued by Országos Széchényi Könyvtár (National Széchényi Library), this is the complete list of Hungary's monographic publications, grouped according to subject, since 1945. A quarterly supplement, *Magyar folyóiratok repertóriuma* (Budapest, 1946 ff.), covers periodical literature. [FW]

W739. Magyar Történettudományi Intézet. **Magyar történeti bibliográfia, 1825–1867.** [Historical bibliography of Hungary, 1825–1867.] Budapest, 1950 ff. Best and almost complete aid, prepared by the Institute of History of the Hungarian Academy of Sciences under the direction of Zoltán I. Tóth. The three volumes published include, besides general history, economy, politics, law, education, science, arts, press, and religion. A fourth volume on national minorities is in preparation. [FW]

ENCYCLOPEDIAS AND WORKS OF REFERENCE

W740. A companion to Hungarian studies. Budapest, 1943. Contains various articles by outstanding Hungarian scholars on history, arts, language, literature, minorities, etc., written to inform the Anglo-Saxon world. Constitutes the 1942 issue of *The Hungarian quarterly*. Numerous illustrations and maps. [FW]

W741. Kovács, Imre. **Facts about Hungary.** N.Y., 1958. Provides a number of special surveys on the most important problems of Hungary, with emphasis on the post-revolutionary development of domestic and foreign affairs. [EB]

W742. Magyar tájékoztató zsebkönyv. [Hungarian information pocketbook.] 2nd ed., Budapest, 1943. This 1,200 page, pocket-size volume is still the best source of general information on the land and people of Hungary prior to 1943. It is the last of this type reference manual published in pre-Communist Hungary. Contains special chapters on foreign relations, cultural and minority problems. [EB]

W743. Révai nagy lexikona: az ismeretek enciklopédiája. [Révai's great lexicon: encyclopedia of knowledge.] 21 v. Budapest, 1911–35. Hungary's most complete encyclopedia. [FW]

W744. Új Idök lexikona. [Encyclopedia of Új Idök.] 24 v. Budapest, 1936–42. Latest in the series of standard encyclopedias published in Hungary and, therefore, of much value. [EB]

GEOGRAPHIES

W745. Magyar földrajz. [Hungarian geography.] Ed. by Gyula Prinz and others. 3 v. Budapest, 1936–38. Review, L. Glaser, *Századok*, 74 (1940): 314. [GB]

W746. Bulla, Béla, and Tibor Mendöl. **A Kárpát-medence földrajza.** [Geography of the Carpathian Basin.] Budapest, 1947. Most recent summary of the results of geographical research relating to the geo-historical unit fenced by the Carpathian Mountains. Contains a list of recommended readings. [EB]

W747. Radisics, Elemér, ed. **A Dunatáj:** gazdasági és földrajzi adatok a Dunatáj államainak életéből. [The Danubian region: economic and geographical data concerning the states of the Danubian region.] 3 v. Budapest, 1946. Valuable for its encyclopedic character, statistical data, and interpretative studies, primarily in the fields of geography and history. [GB]

ANTHROPOLOGICAL WORKS

W748. Bartucz, Lajos. **A magyar ember: a magyarság antropológiája.** [The Hungarian man: anthropology of the Hungarian people.] Budapest, [1939]. Review, E. Varga, *Századok*, 74 (1940): 321. [GB]

W749. A magyarság néprajza. [Ethnography of the Hungarian people.] Ed. by Zsigmond Bátky and others. 4 v. Budapest, [1933–37]. The fundamental work on the subject. [GB]

W750. Allodiatoris, Irma. **A Kárpát-medence antropologiai bibliográfiája.** [The anthropological bibliography of the Carpathian Basin.] Budapest, 1958. Most up-to-date bibliography on the ethnological and anthropological history and pre-history of this area. [EB]

W751. Balogh, Béla, and Ludwig Bartucz. **Ungarische Rassenkunde.** Berlin, 1940. Most accessible and concise summary of the physical characteristics of the Hungarian people. Includes ethnological as well as anthropometrical data on the Hungarians. [EB]

W752. Szabó, Stefan. **Ungarisches Volk: Geschichte und Wandlungen.** Budapest and Leipzig, 1944. Demographic approach; an effort to sketch the history of the Hungarian population. [GB]

W753. Szekfű, Gyula, ed. **Mi a magyar?** [What is Magyar?] Budapest, 1939.

DEMOGRAPHIC STUDIES

W754. Kniezsa, István. **Ungarns Völkerschaften im XI. Jahrhundert.** Budapest, 1938. Reprinted from *Archivum Europae centro-orientalis*, 4 (1938): 241–412. [GB]

W755. Hungary. Központi Statisztikai Hivatal. **1949 évi népszámlálás.** [The population census of 1949.] 14 v. Budapest, 1949–52. The complete edition of the 1949 population census data. [EB]

W756. Siegel, Jacob S. **The population of Hungary.** Washington, 1958. Most up-to-date and comprehensive population survey of Hungary, prepared by researchers of the U. S. Bureau of the Census. [EB]

W757. Nagy, Iván. **Magyarország családai czímerekkel és nemzedékrendi táblákkal.** [The families of Hungary, with coats-of-arms and genealogical tables.] 13 v. Pest (Budapest), 1857–65. The standard reference manual on genealogy of Hungarian families. [EB]

LINGUISTIC WORKS

W758. Bárczi, Géza. **Magyar szófejtő szótár.** [Hungarian etymological dictionary.] Budapest, 1941. The only complete etymological dictionary of the language. [EB]

W759. Gombocz, Zoltán, and János Melich. **Magyar etymologiai szótár. Lexicon critico-etymologicum linguae hungaricae.** Issued in parts. Budapest, 1914 ff. The most impressive undertaking of Hungarian linguistical research. Although incomplete, it is a unique source of valuable information on the history of the Hungarian language and civilization. [EB]

W760. Jakubovich, Emil, and Dezsö Pais. **Ó-magyar olvasókönyv.** [Old-Hungarian reader.] Pécs, 1929. Scholarly guide, with texts of the linguistic monuments of the Hungarian language, covering earliest periods to 1427. Its notes on early Hungarian history make it a valuable tool for historical research. [EB]

W761. Zsirai, Miklós. **Finnugor rokonságunk.** [Our Finno-Ugrian ancestry.] Budapest, 1937. The standard manual, published by the Hungarian Academy of Sciences, on the linguistic and historic affiliations of the Hungarian language and the ancient history of the Hungarian people. [EB]

PRINTED COLLECTIONS OF SOURCES

W762. Áldásy, Antal. **A Magyar Nemzeti Múzeum könyvtárának címereslevelei.** [Letters of nobility of the library of the Hungarian National Museum.] 6 v. Budapest, 1937–42. Continuation of an earlier two volumes by the author published 1904–30. The entire series forms the largest published collection of Hungarian heraldica. Review, B. Bottló, *Századok,* 79/80 (1945/46): 247. [GB]

W763. Archivum Rákóczianum. 13 v. Budapest, 1871–89. The most conclusive collection of documents on the life and struggles of the Transylvanian prince Francis II Rákóczi, Hungary's leader in its war of liberation, 1703–11. Part of the documentary material describes the political, military, and diplomatic activities of the Hungarian emigration, principally in France and Turkey. [EB]

W764. Bártfai Szabó, László. **Adatok Gróf Széchenyi István és kora történetéhez, 1808–1860.** [Data referring to Count István Széchenyi and the history of his era, 1808–1860.] 2 v. Budapest, 1943. Besides the Széchenyi volumes published in the "Fontes" series, this is the most valuable recent contribution to the life story and work of the "greatest Magyar." Contains about 1,500 unpublished letters, memoirs, reports, and fragments of diaries, partially written by Szé-

chenyi himself, partially addressed to him, or concerned with his work. [GB]

W765. Benda, Kálmán, ed. **A magyar Jakobinusok iratai.** [Documents of the Hungarian Jacobins.] 3 v. Budapest, 1952–57.

W766. Deák, Francis, and Dezsö Ujváry, eds. **Papers and documents relating to the foreign relations of Hungary.** V. 1, 1919–1920. Budapest, 1939.

W767. Farkas, Julius von, ed. **Ungarns Geschichte und Kultur in Dokumenten.** Wiesbaden, 1955.

W768. Free Europe Committee. **The revolt in Hungary: a documentary chronology of events based exclusively on internal broadcasts by central and provincial radios, October 23, 1956–November 4, 1956.** N.Y., 1956.

W769. Gombos, Ferenc A. **Catalogus fontium historiae Hungaricae aevo ducum et regum ex stirpe Arpad descendentium ab anno Christi DCCC usque ad annum MCCCI.** 4 v. Budapest, 1937–43.

W770. Hajnal, István, ed. **A Kossuth-emigráció Törökországban.** [The Kossuth-emigration in Turkey.] Budapest, 1927.

W771. Jánossy, Dénes, ed. **A Kossuth-emigráció Angliában és Amerikában, 1851–1852.** [The Kossuth-emigration in England and America, 1851–1852.] 2 v. in 3. Budapest, 1940–48.

W772. Kemény, Gábor, ed. **Iratok a nemzetiségi kérdés történetéhez Magyarországon a dualizmus korában.** [Documents concerning the history of the nationality problem in Hungary in the era of dualism.] 2 v. Budapest, 1952–56. Covers period 1867–1900. [GB]

W773. Kosáry, Domokos G. **Kossuth Lajos a reformkorban.** [Louis Kossuth in the reform era.] Budapest, 1946. Intended as introductory volume to a Kossuth biography. Deals with the "years of preparation," the period leading to the events of 1848. [GB]

W774. Országgyülési tudósítások. [Parliamentary reports.] Ed by Lajos Kossuth. 3 v. Budapest, 1948–49. [Magyarország újabbkori történetének forrásai.]

W775. Kossuth, Lajos. **Kossuth Lajos 1848–49–ben.** [Louis Kossuth in 1848–49.] 5 v. Budapest, 1951–57. [Kossuth Lajos összes munkái, 11–15.] Review of *Kossuth works,* J. Borus, *Századok,* 3 (1956): 473. [GB]

W776. ——. **Kossuth Lajos kormányzóelnöki iratai (1849 április 15–augusztus 15).** [Papers of Louis Kossuth, president-regent (April 15–August 15, 1849).] Budapest, 1955.

W777. Lukinich, Emericus, and others, eds. **Documenta historiam Valachorum in Hungaria illustrantia usque ad annum 1400 p. Christum.** Budapest, 1941. Introduction explanation, and footnotes in French. [GB]

W778. Lukinich, Imre, ed. **A szatmári béke története és okirattára.** [History and records of the Peace of Szatmár.] Budapest,

1925. [Fontes historiae Hungaricae aevi recentioris.]

W779. Madzsar, Imre, ed. **Farádi Vörös Ignác visszaemlékezései az 1778–1822 évekről.** [Memoirs of Ignác Farádi Vörös, 1778–1822.] Budapest, 1927. [Fontes historiae Hungaricae aevi· recentioris.]

W780. Magyarország újabbkori történetének forrásai: fontes historiae Hungaricae aevi recentioris. [Sources for the history of Hungary in modern times.] Budapest, 1921 ff. The Hungarian Historical Association has published some 20 volumes covering the period 1686 to World War II. The series was resumed after 1945. [GB]

W781. Mályusz, Elemér, ed. **Zsigmondkori oklevéltár.** [Collections of charters of the era of Sigismund.] 2 v. Budapest, 1951–58. (Other volumes in preparation.)

W782. ——, ed. **Sándor Lipót főherceg nádor iratai, 1790–1795.** [Papers of Palatine Alexander Leopold, 1790–1795.] Budapest, 1926. [Fontes historiae Hungaricae aevi recentioris.]

W783. Hungary. Nemzetgyűlés. [National Assembly.] **Irományok, 1920–26.** [Papers, 1920–26.] 32 v. Budapest, 1920–26. Supplants for these years the *Irományok* published separately by each of the two houses of parliament 1873–1920 and after 1926. [GB]

W784. ——. **Napló, 1920–26.** [Journals, 1920–26.] 63 v. Budapest, 1920–26. Supplants for these years the *Napló* published separately by each of the two houses of parliament 1873–1920 and after 1926. [GB]

W785. Szentpétery, Emericus, ed. **Scriptores rerum hungaricarum tempore ducum regumque stirpis arpadianae gestarum.** 2 v. Budapest, 1937–38. Introduction, explanations, and footnotes in Latin. [GB]

W786. Szentpéteri, Imre, ed. **Az árpádházi királyok okleveleinek kritikai jegyzéke.** Regesta regum stirpis Arapadianae criticodiplomatica. V. 2, pt. 1, 1255–72. Budapest, 1943. Continuation of the set (3 v.) published in 1923–30. Indispensable for any research in 13th century Hungarian history. [GB]

W787. Tisza, István, gróf. **Gróf Tisza István összes munkái.** [The collected works of Count István Tisza.] 6 v. Budapest, 1923–37.

HISTORIOGRAPHY

W788. Baráth, Tibor. **L'histoire en Hongrie (1867–1935).** Paris, 1936. Reprint from *Revue historique,* 177 (Jan.-June 1936): 84–144; 178 (July-Dec. 1936): 25–74. Introduction to Hungary's historical sciences dealing chiefly with their organization, main trends, and outstanding monographic and periodical publications. As an annotated bibliography it is superficial and one-sided in some places. [FW]

W789. Bogyay, Tamás. "Forschungen zur Urgeschichte der Ungarn nach dem 2. Weltkrieg." **Ural-Altaische Jahrbücher,** 29 (Jan.-June 1957): 93–114. Detailed summary of post-World War II research in Hungary and abroad related to the ancient history of Hungarians. [EB]

W790. Macartney, Carlile A. **The medieval Hungarian historians: a critical and analytical guide.** Cambridge, Eng., 1953. Critical reexamination and close study of the written sources which throws considerable light on the riddle of early Hungarian history. Excellent chapter is devoted to development of Hungarian historical tradition. Includes bibliographical references and polemical footnotes. [FW]

W791. ——. **Studies on the earliest Hungarian historical sources.** 4 v. Budapest, 1938–51. This and the author's more recent work (*W790*) are indispensable for the English reader in the study of Hungarian medieval history. [GB]

W792. Wagner, Ferenc. **A magyar történetírás új útjai, 1945–1955.** [New ways of Hungarian historiography, 1945–1955.] Washington, 1956. This short study analyzes the policy affecting Hungarian historiography since the Communist reorganization of the Hungarian Academy of Sciences as a scientific research center. [EB]

SHORTER GENERAL HISTORIES

W793. Domanovszky, Alexander. **Die Geschichte Ungarns.** Munich, 1923. A conventional treatment of the main currents of Hungarian history by one of the leading scholars of his generation.

W794. Eckhart, Ferenc. **A short history of the Hungarian people.** London, 1931. Good as brief summary. [FW]

W795. Kosáry, Dominic G. **A history of Hungary.** Cleveland and N.Y., 1941. The largest English-language history of Hungary. Summarizes events until World War II, with special regard for the Hungarian populated territories of neighboring states. [FW]

W796. Lukinich, Imre. **A history of Hungary in biographical sketches.** London and Budapest, 1937. Biographical studies of outstanding Hungarian rulers and leaders from Prince Arpád to Francis Deák. [GB]

W797. Radisics, Elemér, comp. **Hungary: pictorial record of a thousand years.** Budapest, 1944. A richly illustrated chronicle of Hungarian political and cultural history, including 121 short biographies of eminent Hungarians. One of the best sources of quick reference data on people and problems prominent in Hungarian history. [EB]

W798. Zarek, Otto. **The history of Hungary.** London, 1939. A competent, conventional history from earliest times to about 1920.

LONGER GENERAL HISTORIES

W799. Domanovszky, Sándor, and others, eds. **Magyar művelődéstörténet.** [History of Hungarian civilization.] 5 v. Budapest, [1939–42].

W800. Hóman, Bálint, and Gyula Szekfű. **Magyar történet.** [History of Hungary.] 3rd ed., 5 v., Budapest, 1935–36. The most important work on Hungary's history in recent times; a modern synthesis of the highest standard, with critical survey of sources and annotated bibliography. Main defect is a spiritual approach to historical happenings to the neglect of other significant factors. [FW]

HISTORIES OF SPECIAL PERIODS

Origins to 1526

W801. Elekes, Lajos. **Mátyás és kora.** [King Matthias and his era.] Budapest, 1956.

W802. Hóman, Bálint. **Gli Angioni di Napoli in Ungheria, 1290–1403.** Rome, 1938.

W803. ——. **Geschichte des ungarischen Mittelalters.** 2 v. Berlin, 1940–43.

W804. Ligeti, Lajos, ed. **A magyarság őstörténete.** [Ancient history of the Hungarian people.] Budapest, 1943. Collection of articles by leading experts in tracing historically undocumented periods of Hungarian history, the last opportunity to express unbiased opinions on these subjects. [EB]

W805. Lukinich, Imre, ed. **Mátyás király emlékkönyv születésének ötszázéves fordulójára.** [King Matthias memorial book on the occasion of the 500th anniversary of his birth.] 2 v. Budapest, 1940.

W806. Kardos, Tibor. **Középkori kultura, középkori költészet.** [Medieval civilization, medieval poetry.] Budapest, 1941. One of the most important works on Hungarian medieval civilization. [GB]

W807. Macartney, Carlile A. **The Magyars in the ninth century.** Cambridge, Eng., 1930. Useful survey containing ample extracts from the most important source materials in good translation. [FW]

W808. Moravcsik, Gyula. **Bizánc és a magyarság.** [Byzantium and the Hungarian people.] Budapest, 1953.

W809. Németh, Gyula. **A honfoglaló magyarság kialakulása.** [The formation of the Hungarian people before the conquest of the country.] Budapest, 1930.

W810. Serédi, Justinian, cardinal, ed. **Emlékkönyv Szent István király halálának kilencszázadik évfordulójára.** [Memorial book on occasion of the 900th anniversary of King St. Stephen.] 3 v. Budapest, 1938.

1526–1848

W811. Eckhardt, Sándor. **Az ismeretlen Balassi Bálint.** [The unknown Bálint Balassi.]

Budapest, 1943. Much more than a biographical sketch of Hungary's first great poet; recreates masterfully 16th century social life in Hungary. Review, G. Szekfű, *Századok,* 79/80 (1945/46): 278. [GB]

W812. Eszlári, Károly. **La pragmatique sanction hongroise et celles des pays et des provinces héréditaires des Habsbourgs.** Paris, 1952.

W813. Farkas, Gyula. **A "Fiatal Magyarország" kora.** [The era of "Young Hungary."] Budapest, 1932.

W814. Lukinich, Imre, ed. **Rákóczi emlékkönyv.** [Rákóczi memorial volume.] 2 v. Budapest, 1935.

W815. Makkai, László. **A kuruc nemzeti összefogás előzményei: népi felkelések felső-Magyarországon 1630–1632-ben.** [The antecedents of the kouroutz national revival: popular upheavals in northern Hungary, 1630–1632.] Budapest, 1956.

W816. Mályusz, Elemér, ed. **A türelmi rendelet: II József és a magyar protestantizmus.** [The edict of tolerance: Joseph II and Hungarian protestantism.] 2 v. Budapest, 1939. Review, *Századok,* 75 (1941): 82. [GB]

W817. Szabó, Dezső. **A magyarországi urbérrendezés története Mária Terézia korában.** [History of the socage ("urbarium") under Maria Theresa.] Budapest, 1933.

W818. Szerémi, György, and László Erdélyi. **Mohács.** 2 v. Szeged, 1941. V. 1, *A mohácsi vész kora* [The era of Mohács], is the translation by Erdélyi of Szerémi's contemporary work; v. 2, *A mohácsi vész nemzedéke* [The generation of Mohács], is Erdélyi's interpretative study, based primarily on Szerémi's data, of this significant turning point of Hungarian history. [GB]

1848–1918

W819. Berzeviczy, Albert. **Az absolutizmus kora Magyarországon, 1849–1865.** [The era of absolutism in Hungary, 1849–1865.] 4 v. Budapest, 1922–37.

W820. Magyar Dolgozók Pártja Központi Vezetősége. **A magyar munkásmozgalom történetének válogatott dokumentumai.** [Select documents of the history of the Hungarian labor movement.] 3 v. Budapest. 1951–55.

W821. Deák, Imre, ed. **1848: a szabadságharc története levelekben, ahogyan a kortársak látták.** [1848: history of the war for freedom in letters, as seen by contemporaries.] Budapest, [1943].

W822. Ember, Győző, ed. **Iratok az 1848-i magyarországi parasztmozgalmak történetéhez.** [Documents concerning the Hungarian peasant movements of 1848.] Budapest, 1951.

W823. Gratz, Gusztáv. **A dualizmus kora: Magyarország története 1867–1918.** [The era of dualism: history of Hungary, 1867–1918.] 2 v. Budapest, 1934. Very reliable standard work with special emphasis on Hungary's political history. [FW]

W824. Jánossy, Dennis A. **Die ungarische Emigration und der Krieg im Orient.** Budapest, 1939. Reprint from *Archivum Europae centro-orientalis,* 5 (1939): 113–275.

W825. Károlyi, Árpád, ed. **Az 1848-iki pozsonyi törvénycikkek az udvar előtt.** [The Pressburg acts of 1848 before the court.] Budapest, 1936.

W826. Kastner, Eugenio. **Il contributo ungherese nella guerra del 1859.** Florence, 1934.

W827. Mérei, Gyula. **Magyar politikai pártprogrammok (1867–1914).** [Hungarian political party programs (1867–1914).] Budapest, 1934.

W828. ——. **Polgári radikalizmus Magyar országon, 1900–1919.** [Bourgeois radicalism in Hungary, 1900–1919.] Budapest, 1947.

W829. ——. **Munkásmozgalmak 1848–49-ben.** [Workers' movements in 1848–49.] Budapest, 1948.

W830. Thim, József, ed. **A Magyarországi 1848–49-iki szerb fölkelés története.** [History of the upheaval of the Serbs in Hungary in 1848–49.] 3 v. Budapest, 1930–40. Valuable bibliography included. [GB]

W831. Waldapfel, Eszter, ed. **A forradalom és szabadságharc levelestára.** [Archives of the revolution and freedom fight.] 3 v. Budapest, 1950–55. Contemporary private letters concerning the events of 1848–49. [GB]

1918–1956

W832. Bandholtz, Harry Hill. **An undiplomatic diary.** N.Y., 1933. Authentic eyewitness account of the first Communist dictatorship in Hungary, by a member of the Inter-Allied Military Mission to Hungary, 1919–20. [EB]

W833. Gratz, Gusztáv. **A forradalmak kora: Magyarország története 1918–1920.** [The age of revolutionaries: history of Hungary, 1918–1920.] Budapest, 1935. Critical study of the collapse of the Austro-Hungarian monarchy and Hungary's postwar period, based on source material and the best literature. Deals chiefly with political developments. [FW]

W834. Fejtő, François. **Behind the rape of Hungary.** N.Y., 1957. A Hungarian liberal living abroad interprets the events of 1956. [GB]

W835. Horthy, Nicholas. **Memoirs.** N.Y., 1957.

W836. Hungarian National Council. **Genocide by deportation: an appeal to the United Nations to enforce the law.** N.Y., 1951. On the concentration camps of Hungary and Soviet Russia, with special reference to persons deported by the Communist regime from Hungary. [EB]

W837. Kállay, Miklós. **Hungarian premier: a personal account of a nation's struggle in the Second World War.** N.Y., 1954.

W838. Károlyi, Michael. **Memoirs of Michael Károlyi: faith without illusion.** London, 1956.

W839. Kovács, Imre. **D'une occupation à l'autre: la tragédie hongroise.** Paris, 1949.

W840. Lasky, Melvin J., ed. **The Hungarian revolution: a white book.** N.Y., 1957.

W841. Macartney, Carlile A. **October fifteenth: a history of modern Hungary, 1929–1945.** 2 v. Edinburgh, 1956–57.

W842. ——. **Hungary and her successors: the treaty of Trianon and its consequences, 1919–1937.** London and N.Y., 1937. General historical survey of Hungary's political, economic, and cultural development, based on Hungarian and other language sources, with special regard to the nationality questions and territorial changes occurring after World War I. Author usually sides with Hungarians in international disputes. Bibliographical notes. [FW]

W843. ——. **Hungary.** London, 1934. A general and very sympathetic introduction to post-Trianon Hungary.

W844. Mályusz, Elemér. **The fugitive Bolsheviks.** London, 1931. A critical approach to the history of the Hungarian Soviet republic, based partly on unpublished source material. [FW]

W845. Mikes, George. **The Hungarian revolution.** London, 1957. Careful account of the events of 1956. [GB]

W846. Mosca, Rodolfo. **Le relazioni internazionali del Regno d'Ungheria: atti internazionali e documenti diplomatici raccolti e ordinati.** Budapest, 1943. Deals with the period 1920–38. [GB]

W847. Nagy, Imre. **On communism: in defense of the new course.** N.Y., 1957. A contribution to the question of the acceptability of communism to a western-oriented people. [GB]

W848. Nagy, Ferenc. **The struggle behind the Iron Curtain.** N.Y., 1948. A former prime minister analyzes the forces which brought communism to power in Hungary.

W849. Sulyok, Dezső. **Zwei Nächte ohne Tag.** Zürich, 1948.

W850. United Nations. **The Hungarian uprising: an abridgement of the report of the United Nations Special Committee on the Problem of Hungary, published on June 20, 1957.** London, 1957.

W851. Urban, George. **The nineteen days: a broadcaster's account of the Hungarian revolution.** London, 1957.

HISTORIES OF SPECIAL AREAS

W852. Deér, József, and László Gáldi, eds. **Magyarok és Románok.** [Hungarians and Rumanians.] 2 v. Budapest, 1943–44. Yearbook of the Hungarian Historical Institute for 1943/44, containing studies by the best Hungarian specialists on Hungaro-Rumanian relations and problems. Review, A. Tóth, *Századok*, 79/80 (1945/46): 228. [GB]

W853. Dezsényi, Béla. **Magyarország és Svájc.** [Hungary and Switzerland.] Budapest, 1946. Very careful study of historical and intellectual relations. [GB]

W854. Gál, Stephen, ed. **Hungary and the Anglo-Saxon world.** Budapest, 1944. Contains a good bibliography on Anglo-Saxon–Hungarian historical and cultural relations. [GB]

W855. Gál, István, ed. **Ungarn und die Nachbarvölker.** Budapest, [1943].

W856. Kovács, Endre, ed. **Magyar-orosz történelmi kapcsolatok.** [Hungarian-Russian historical relations.] Budapest, 1956.

W857. Macartney, Carlile A. **National states and national minorities.** See *AH330*.

W858. Makkai, Ladislas. **Histoire de Transylvanie.** See *W678*.

W859. Miskolczy, Gyula, ed. **A horvát kérdés.** [The Croatian question.] 2 v. Budapest, 1927–28.

W860. Pukánszky, Béla. **Német polgárság magyar földön.** [German burghers on Hungarian soil.] Budapest, n.d.

W861. Steier, Lajos. **A tót nemzetiségi kérdés 1848–49–ben.** [The Slovak nationality problem in 1848–49.] 2 v. Budapest, 1937.

W862. Sötér, István. **Magyar-francia kapcsolatok.** [Franco-Hungarian relations.] Budapest, 1946.

W863. Szekfű, Gyula. **État et nation.** Paris, 1945. Collection of author's studies on national minority problems of the Carpathian Basin. First appeared in Hungarian in 1942. [FW]

W864. Tóth, Zoltán I. **Az erdélyi román nacionalizmus elsö százada.** [The first century of Rumanian nationalism in Transylvania.] Budapest, 1946. Review, *Századok*, 79/80 (1945/46): 232. [GB]

HISTORIES OF SPECIAL TOPICS

Constitutional and Administrative History

W865. Balla, Antal, ed. **A magyar országgyűlés története, 1867–1927.** [History of the Hungarian parliament, 1867–1927.] Budapest, 1927.

W866. Csekey, Stephan. **Die Verfassung Ungarns.** [Hungary's constitution.] Budapest, 1944. A systematic survey of Hungary's constitutional history and laws from the earliest times to 1942, based on source material and selected literature. [FW]

W867. Eckhart, Ferenc. **Magyar alkotmány és jogtörténet.** [Constitutional and legal history of Hungary.] Budapest, 1946.

W868. Ember, Győző. **Az újkori magyar közigazgatás története Mohácstól a török kiűzéséig.** [The history of modern Hungarian administration from Mohacs to the Turkish expulsion.] Budapest, 1946.

W869. ———. **A M. Kir. helytartótanács ügyintézésének története, 1724–1848.** [History of the administration of the Hungarian Royal Council of Governor-General, 1724–1848.] Budapest, 1940. Review, *Századok*, 75 (1941): 213. [GB]

W870. Mártonffy, Károly, ed. **A mai magyar közigazgatás.** [The Hungarian public administration of today.] Budapest, 1936. This volume, published by the minister of the interior, contains the official presentation of all branches of Hungarian public administration. [EB]

Social and Economic History

W871. Eckhart, Ferenc. **A magyar közgazdaság száz éve, 1841–1941.** [A hundred years of Hungarian economy, 1841–1941.] Budapest, 1941. Important monograph on the decisive century of modern Hungary's economic development. Review, *Századok*, 77 (1943): 263. [GB]

W872. Futó, Mihály. **A magyar gyáripar története.** [History of the Hungarian manufacturing industry.] Budapest, 1944. Covers from the medieval beginnings of Hungarian industry to enactment of the first "law of industrial development" in 1881. [GB]

W873. Ligeti, Lajos, ed. **A magyar tudomány tíz éve, 1945–1955.** [Ten years of Hungarian science, 1945–1955.] Budapest, 1955. This volume, published by the Hungarian Academy of Sciences and edited by its vice-president, provides a survey of higher learning and research during the period indicated. [EB]

W874. Macartney, Carlile A. **The social revolution in Austria.** Cambridge, Eng., 1926. Useful in showing the historical background of social and economic conditions in the Austro-Hungarian monarchy, as well as the Austrian republic in the postwar period. Includes bibliography of the principal works consulted. [FW]

W875. Rézler, Gyula. **A magyar nagyipari munkásság kialakulása, 1867–1914.** [The development of the industrial working class in Hungary, 1867–1914.] Budapest, 1938.

W876. Szabó, István. **Tanulmányok a magyar parasztság történetéből.** [Studies in the history of the Hungarian peasantry.] Budapest, 1948.

W877. Trócsányi, Zsolt. **Az erdélyi parasztság története, 1790–1849.** [History of the Transylvanian peasantry, 1790–1849.] Budapest, 1956.

Cultural and Religious History

W878. Dezsényi, Béla, and György Nemes. **A magyar sajtó 250 éve.** [The 250 year old Hungarian press.] Budapest, 1954.

W879. Kardos, Tibor. **A magyarországi humanizmus kora.** [The era of humanism in Hungary.] Budapest, 1955.

W879a. Fraknoi, Vilmos. **Magyarország egyházy és politikai összeköttetései a romái szent-székkel.** [Hungary's ecclesiastical and political relations with the Holy See.] Budapest, 1901–03.

W880. Kornis, Julius. **Education in Hungary.** N.Y., 1932.

W881. Pukánszky, Jolán (Kádár). **A Nemzeti Színház százéves története.** [The century-old history of the National Theatre.] 2 v. Budapest, 1938–40.

W882. Révész, Imre. **A magyarországi protestantizmus történelme.** [History of Hungarian Protestantism.] Budapest, 1925. Chapter 1 of this short sketch contains a very valuable bibliography and periodization of the Hungarian reform movement; other chapters have supplementary bibliographical data. [GB]

W883. ———. **Magyar református egyháztörténet.** [History of the Hungarian Reformed Church.] Debrecen, 1938.

W884. Sager, Peter. **Die Schul- und Wissenschaftspolitik der Ungarischen Volksrepublik, 1945–1956.** Bern, 1958. Most recent historical survey of development of Hungarian educational policy and intellectual life since World War II. [EB]

Literary History

W885. Farkas, Julius von. **Die Entwicklung der ungarischen Literatur.** Berlin, 1934.

W886. Hankiss, János, and Géza Juhász. **Panorama de la littérature hongroise contemporaine.** Paris, 1930.

W887. Horváth, János. **A magyar irodalmi műveltség kezdetei Szent Istvántól Mohácsig.** [Beginnings of Hungarian literary civilization from St. Stephen to Mohács.] Budapest, 1931. Fundamental work. [GB]

W888. ———. **Az irodalmi műveltség megoszlása: magyar humanizmus.** [Differentiation of Hungarian literary civilization: Hungarian humanism.] Budapest, 1935.

W889. Pintér, Jenő. **Magyar irodalomtörténete.** [History of Hungarian literature.] 8 v. Budapest, 1930–43. Treasury of data concerning the development of Hungarian cultural life. [GB]

W890. Pukánszky, Béla. **Geschichte des deutschen Schrifttums in Ungarn.** V. 1, Von der ältesten Zeit bis um die Mitte des 18. Jahrhunderts. Münster, 1931. Contains excellent bibliography. [GB]

W891. Szerb, Antal. **Magyar irodalomtörténet.** [History of Hungarian literature.]

2nd ed., 2 v., Budapest, 1947. Best modern summary of Hungarian literature. [GB]

BIOGRAPHIES

W892. Magyar történeti életrajzok. [Hungarian historical biographies.] Ed. by Sándor Szilágyi and others. 22 v. Budapest, 1883–1904. The most important series of biographical monographs. [EB]

W893. Szinnyei, József, and Ferenc Szinnyei. **Magyar írók élete és munkái.** [Lives and works of Hungarian writers.] 14 v. Budapest, 1891–1914. A standard biographical dictionary of Hungarian writers (including historians) which is still not replaced by any other publication. [EB]

W894. Angyal, Dávid. **Az ifjú Ferenc József.** [Young Francis Joseph.] Budapest, [1942].

W895. Benda, Kálmán. **Bocskai István.** Budapest, 1942. [Magyar életrajzok.]

W896. Costil, Pierre. **André Dudith, humaniste hongroise, 1533–1589.** Paris, 1935. Heavily documented study of a gifted and widely traveled Hungarian classicist.

W897. Domanovszky, Sándor, ed. **József nádor élete és iratai.** [Life and papers of Palatine Joseph.] 4 v. Budapest, 1925–44. [Fontes historiae Hungaricae aevi recentioris.]

W898. Elekes, Lajos. **Hunyadi.** Budapest, 1952.

W899. Headley, Phineas C. **The life of Louis Kossuth, governor of Hungary.** N.Y., 1852. Contemporary and authorized publication, containing his public speeches. [EB]

W900. Horváth, Jenő. **Magyar diplomácia, magyar diplomaták.** [Hungarian diplomacy, Hungarian diplomats.] Budapest, 1941.

W901. Huszti, József. **Janus Pannonius.** Pécs, 1931. Life and works of the great humanist of the time of Matthias Corvinus. [GB]

W902. Várkonyi, Ágnes. **II. Rákóczi Ferenc.** [Francis II, Rákóczi.] Budapest, 1953.

W903. Wertheimer, Eduard von. **Graf Julius Andrássy, sein Leben und seine Zeit nach ungedruckten Quellen.** 3 v. Stuttgart, 1910–13.

W904. Zarek, Otto. **Kossuth.** London, 1937. Best presentation of the Kossuth problem in English. [EB]

W905. Zolnai, Béla. **II. Rákóczi Ferenc.** Budapest, 1943. [Magyar életrajzok.] Best short, modern Rákóczi biography. [GB]

PERIODICALS

W906. Acta historica Academiae Scientiarum Hungaricae. Budapest, 1951 ff. (Irregular.) Studies on Hungarian and related subjects in Russian and various western languages. Strictly Marxist.

W907. Századok. [Centuries.] Budapest, 1867 ff. (Irregular.) The organ of the Hungarian Historical Association, only one of the scholarly publications to continue publication after 1945. Intended for Hungarian historians. Covers archaeology, economics, and the auxiliary sciences, as well as history.

W908. Revue d'histoire comparée. Paris, 1923–48. (Irregular quarterly. Title varies.)

W909. The Hungarian quarterly. Buda-

pest and London, 1936–44. Designed to spread knowledge of Danubian and central European affairs and to foster political and cultural relations between Hungary and the Anglo-Saxon world. Studies largely of historical interest. [FW]

W910. Társadalmi szemle. [Social review.] Budapest, 1946 ff. Theoretical monthly of the Hungarian Communist party. Often publishes articles dealing with problems of Hungarian history. [GB]

BULGARIA

BIBLIOGRAPHIES

W911. U. S. Library of Congress. **The Balkans: Bulgaria, a selected list of references.** Comp. by Helen F. Conover. Washington, 1943. Contains 322 items in western languages available in the Library of Congress, classified by subject. [JFC]

W912. Dujčev, Ivan. "Die bulgarische Geschichtsforschung während des letzten Vierteljahrhunderts (1918–1942)." **Südost-Forschungen,** 7 (Dec. 1942): 546–73. Critical bibliographical review covering all aspects. [JFC]

W913. Bǔlgarska Akademiia na Naukite. **Bibliografiia na bǔlgarskata arkheologiia (1879–1955).** [Bibliography of Bulgarian archaeology.] Comp. by Sonya Georgieva and Velizar Velkov. Sofia, 1957. Contains 6,305 numbered items in all languages, plus reviews. [JFC]

W914. Akademiia Nauk SSSR. **Narodnaia Respublika Bolgariia: istoricheskaia bibliografiia.** V. 1, 1944–1947. [People's Republic of Bulgaria: historical bibliography.] Comp. by Dmitrii Ivanov and others. Moscow, 1954. V. 2, in preparation, to be published in Sofia. [JFC]

W915. Mikhov, Nikola V. **Bibliographie des articles de périodiques allemands, anglais, français, et italiens sur la Turquie et la Bulgarie.** Sofia, 1938. Accumulation of 10,044 items. [JFC]

W916. ――――. **Bibliografski iztochnitsa za istoriiata na Turtsiia i Bǔlgariia. Sources bibliographiques sur l'histoire de la Turquie et de la Bulgarie.** 4 v. Sofia, 1914–34. Includes anything in western languages containing bibliographical matter. Compiler's comments in Bulgarian. Alphabetical arrangement; unsystematic and uncritical. Successive volumes are supplements. [JFC]

W917. Pogorelov, Valerii A. **Opis na starite pechatani bǔlgarski knigi, 1802–1877.** [Catalog of old printed Bulgarian books, 1802–1877.] Sofia, 1923. Indispensable: includes table of contents, excerpts, and other data for many items. [JFC]

W918. Saenger, M. "Verzeichnis deutschsprächiger Bücher über Bulgarien." **Bulgaria:**

Jahrbuch (1942): 335–82. Very useful. [JFC]

W919. Sofia. Dǔrzhavna Biblioteka Vasil Kolarov. **Bǔlgarska vǔzrozhdenska knizhnina . . . 1806–1878.** [Bulgarian renaissance literature . . . 1806–1878.] Comp. by Maniu Stoianov. 2 v. Sofia, 1957–59. Covers books and periodicals, with numerous detailed indexes. Does not wholly supersede *W917.* [JFC]

W920. Jordanov, Petǎr. **La Bulgaria in Italia: bibliografia delle pubblicazioni italiane sulla Bulgaria (1870–1942).** Rome, 1943.

ENCYCLOPEDIAS AND WORKS OF REFERENCE

W921. Danchov, Ivan G., and Nikola G. Danchov. **Bǔlgarska entsiklopediia.** [Bulgarian encyclopedia.] Sofia, 1936. Larousse type; 6,000 entries on Bulgaria out of a total of 40,000. [JFC]

W922. Dellin, L. A. D., ed. **Bulgaria.** N.Y., 1957. Most detailed available description of political, social, and economic developments under the Communists, with some prewar historical background. Extensive bibliography. [JFC]

W923. Great Britain. Foreign Office. **Bulgaria basic handbook.** London, 1943. Of continuing value. [JFC]

W924. Kasǔrov, L. **Entsiklopedicheski rechnik.** [Encyclopedic dictionary.] 3 v. Plovdiv, 1899–1907. Useful although non-Bulgarian matter predominates. [JFC]

W925. Leibrock, Otto. **Bulgarien gestern und heute.** Berlin, 1938. Best complete, brief survey of pre-World War II Bulgaria. [JFC]

W926. Logio, George. **Bulgaria, past and present.** Manchester, 1936. Approximately half is descriptive, mainly economic, and half historical to the 1934 coup, which the author, long a resident of Bulgaria, endorses. Well-informed, critical, but sympathetic to Bulgaria. Based on Bulgarian materials. [JFC]

GEOGRAPHY AND ARCHAEOLOGY

W927. La Bulgarie devant le IVᵉ Congrès des Géographes et Ethnographes Slaves.

Sofia, 1936. Authoritative short surveys by eleven specialists, with bibliographies for most articles. [JFC]

W928. Caraci, Giuseppe. **Disegno geografico della Bulgaria.** Rome, 1933. Detailed geographical description. Illustrated. [JFC]

W929. Chataigneau, Y., and Jules Sion. "Les pays balkaniques." **Géographie universelle** (Paris, 1935), v. 7, pt. 2, pp. 395–573. Description of physical and human geographic features.

W930. Filov, Bogdan. "Bibliografiia na arkheologiiata na Bŭlgariia." [Bibliography of archaeology of Bulgaria.] **Godishnik na Narodniia Musei v Sofiia na 1922–1926** (Sofia, 1926), pp. 613–49. For later works the *Journal* (*Izvestiia*) of the Bulgarian Archaeological Institute (*W1030*) may be consulted. [JFC]

W931. The Bulgarians in their historical, ethnographical and political frontiers. Ed. by Anastas Ishirkov and V. N. Zlatarski. Berlin, 1917. Issued for propaganda purposes, but facsimiles of important historic maps are included. Text in English, German, French, and Bulgarian. [JFC]

W932. Saxena, H. Z. **Bulgaria under the Red Star.** New Delhi, 1957. Sympathetic. [JFC]

W933. Ishirkov, Anastas. **Bulgarien, Land und Leute.** 2 v. Leipzig, 1916–17. Short description by the foremost native authority. [JFC]

W934. Markham, Reuben H. **Meet Bulgaria.** Sofia, 1931. One of the most astute and sympathetic comprehensive interpretations in any language, done in a folksy style and well illustrated, by a long-time resident of Bulgaria. [JFC]

DEMOGRAPHY

W935. Mikhov, Nikola V. **Naselnieto na Turtsiia i Bŭlgariia priez XVIII i XIX v.: bibliografsko-statistichni izsliedvaniia. La population de la Turquie et de la Bulgarie au XVIIIe et XIXe s.: recherches bibliographico-statistiques.** 4 v. Sofia, 1915–35. Cites 3,050 books and articles in western languages, including ethnographic data. Alphabetical, with name and place indexes. Compiler's comments in Bulgarian. [JFC]

PRINTED COLLECTONS OF SOURCES

W936. Dorev, Pancho, ed. **Dokumenti iz turskite dŭrzhavni arkhivi.** [Documents from Turkish official archives.] Sofia, 1940. Translation of 813 Turkish documents of 1564–1872 from originals published by Ahmed Refik, Istanbul, 1933. [JFC]

W937. Fermendžin, Eusebius. **Acta Bulgariae ecclesiastica ab a. 1565 usque ad a. 1799.** Zagreb, 1887. [Monumenta spectantia historiam slavorum meridionalium, 18.] Indispensable material from Roman Catholic sources. [JFC]

W938. Ghénov, G. P. **Actes et traités internationaux concernant la Bulgarie.** Sofia, 1940. Very useful compilation. [JFC]

W939. Ivanov, Iordan. **Bŭlgarski starini iz Makedoniia.** [Bulgarian antiquities from Macedonia.] 2nd ed., Sofia, 1931. Inscriptions, literary monuments and documents, 9th to 19th centuries, with illustrations and analysis. [JFC]

W940. Mikhov, Nikola V. **Contribution à l'histoire du commerce bulgare.** 3 v. in 4. Sofia, 1941–53. Useful collection of Belgian, French, and Austrian consular reports. [JFC]

W941. Bulgaria. Ministerstvo na Vŭshnite Raboti. **Diplomaticheski dokumenti po namesata na Bŭlgariia v evropeiskata voina.** [Diplomatic documents on participation of Bulgaria in the European war.] 2 v. Sofia, 1920–21. Official documents on Bulgaria's part in World War I. [JFC]

W942. Panchev, Todor, ed. **Iz arkhivata na Naĭden Gerov.** [From the archives on Naĭden Gerov.] 2 v. Sofia, 1911–14. From Gerov's extensive private correspondence on national and public questions. [JFC]

W943. Bŭlgarska Akademiia na Naukite. **Arkhiv na Naĭden Gerov.** [Archival material on Naĭden Gerov.] Ed. by Todor Panchev and Mikhail G. Popruzhenko. 2 v. Sofia, 1931–32. Official correspondence and reports of the Plovdiv Russian vice-consulate (1857–76). The 4 v. of Gerov's papers are an unrivaled source for pre-liberation history. [JFC]

HISTORIOGRAPHY

W944. Duĭchev, Ivan. "Pregled na bŭlgarskata istoriografiia." [Sketch of Bulgarian historiography.] **Jugoslovenski istoriski časopis,** 4 (1938): 40–74. Chronological according to subject matter; full bibliographical footnotes. Especially good on sources. [JFC]

W945. Mosely, Philip E. "The post-war historiography of modern Bulgaria." **Journal of modern history,** 9 (Sep. 1937): 348–66. Running comment, with bibliographical footnotes. [JFC]

SHORTER GENERAL HISTORIES

W946. Bŭlgarska Akademiia na Naukite. **Kratka istoriia na Bŭlgariia.** [Short history of Bulgaria.] Sofia, 1958. Abridged and revised edition of the Academy's 2 v. work. [JFC]

W947. Hýbl, František. **Dějiny národa bulharského.** [History of the Bulgarian people.] 2 v. Prague, 1930. Very good synthesis to World War I, incorporating and listing the historiography of Bulgaria since Jireček. [JFC]

W948. Jireček, Constantin. **Das Fürsten-**

tum Bulgarien. Vienna, 1891. Best account of post-liberation conditions to the election of Prince Ferdinand. [JFC]

W949. ——. **Geschichte der Bulgaren.** Prague, 1876. The first scholarly complete history, a landmark in Bulgarian historiography, which retains much of its value. Author's revision, *Istoriia na Bŭlgaritie,* ed. and tr. by S. Argirov, was published in Sofia, 1939. [JFC]

W950. Monroe, Will S. **Bulgaria and her people, with an account of the Balkan wars, Macedonia and the Macedonian Bulgars.** Boston, 1914. First United States book on Bulgaria. Approximately a third is history, including a first-hand account of the Second Balkan War and of U. S. activities in Bulgaria. [JFC]

W951. Mutafchiev, Petŭr. **Bulgares et Roumains dans l'histoire des pays danubiens.** Sofia, 1932. Documented, sharply critical, and polemical, but to a considerable extent justified, attack on Iorga and other Romanian historians. Important for the historiography of medieval Bulgaria. [JFC]

W952. Songeon, Guérin. **Histoire de la Bulgarie depuis les origines jusqu'à nos jours.** La Chapelle-Montligeon (Orne), France, 1912. Good account, designed as a textbook, with emphasis on the pre-Ottoman period. [JFC]

W953. Akademiia Nauk SSSR. **Istoriia Bolgarii.** [History of Bulgaria.] Ed. by Petr Tretyakov and others. 2 v. Moscow, 1954–55. References, bibliography, chronology, maps, and illustrations. Supersedes N. S. Derzhavin's work of the same title (4 v., Moscow, 1945–48). [JFC]

LONGER GENERAL HISTORIES

W954. Bŭlgarska Akademiia na Naukite. **Istoriia na Bŭlgariia.** [History of Bulgaria.] 2 v. Sofia, 1954–55. By a dozen co-authors, including several pre-war historians. Selected bibliography and maps, but no footnotes. [JFC]

W955. Mutafchiev, Petŭr. **Istoriia na bŭlgarskiia narod.** [History of the Bulgarian people.] 2nd ed., 2 v., Sofia, 1943–44. Best general history for the non-specialist, by an outstanding authority. Selected chapter references. Edited and completed by Ivan Duĭchev. [JFC]

W956. Pastukov, Ivan. **Bŭlgarska istoriia.** [Bulgarian history.] 2 v. Sofia, 1942–43. Popular social history, partly illustrated, with some indication of sources and an extensive bibliography. [JFC]

W957. Zlatarski, Vasil N. **Istoriia na bŭlgarskata dŭrzhava prez srednite vekove.** [History of the Bulgarian state through the Middle Ages.] 3 v. in 4. Sofia, 1918–40. Most important work on Bulgarian history, by the foremost historian in this field, but un-finished at time of his death. Extends only to 1280. Emphasis on political aspects. [JFC]

HISTORIES OF SPECIAL PERIODS

Origins and Medieval Empire

W958. Banescu, Nicolae. **L'ancien état bulgare et les pays roumains.** Bucharest, 1947. Statement of the Rumanian case on Vlach elements in medieval Bulgaria. [JFC]

W959. Gérard, Christian. **Les Bulgares de la Volga et les Slaves du Danube.** Paris, 1939. Scholarly and up-to-date, though popularized, history of the Volga Bulgars to 1552 and of the Danube Bulgars to 893. The author, one-time professor in a French school in Bulgaria, has prepared a sequel on Simeon's reign. Bibliography. [JFC]

W960. Runciman, Steven. **A history of the first Bulgarian empire.** London, 1930. Monographic yet exceptionally readable; one of the best works on Bulgarian history. Full bibliography and documentation. [JFC]

Turkish Domination to 1878

W961. Burmov, Aleksandŭr K., ed. **Aprilsko vŭstanie, 1876 g.** [The April insurrection of 1876.] 3 v. Sofia, 1954–56. An accompanying bibliography in all languages is in preparation. [JFC]

W962. Almanakh Sofiĭskiia Universitet Sv. Kliment Okhridski. [Almanac of St. Clement of Ohrid University in Sofia.] 2nd ed., Sofia, 1940. Bio-bibliographies of the faculty, 1888–1939, including leading Bulgarian historians. [JFC]

W963. Hajek, Alois. **Bulgarien unter der Türkenherrschaft.** Stuttgart, 1925. Excellent use of Bulgarian and other material, including Jireček's library. Scholarly and well-written, with emphasis on the 19th century. [JFC]

W964. Harris, David. **Britain and the Bulgarian horrors of 1876.** Chicago, 1939. Although primary interest is Britain, the subject has greater importance for Bulgaria. Excellent study with extensive bibliography and some documents. [JFC]

W965. Michel, Leo. **La Bulgarie et son peuple sous la domination ottomane, tels que les ont vus les voyageurs anglo-saxons (1586–1878).** Sofia, 1949. Useful compilation of source material. [JFC]

W966. Radeff, Siméon. **La Macédoine et la renaissance bulgare au XIXᵉ siècle.** Sofia, 1918. Very useful in spite of the inevitable polemics. [JFC]

W967. Stoyanoff, Zachary. **Pages from the autobiography of a Bulgarian insurgent.** London, 1913. From the first portion of *Zapiski po bŭlgarskite vŭzstaniia* [Notes from a Bulgarian revolutionary] (3 v., Plovdiv and Sofia, 1884–92), covering the decade prior to the 1876 insurrections, in which the author participated. A classic in Bulgarian literature and historiography. [JFC]

W968. Temperley, Harold W. V. "The Bulgarian and other atrocities, 1875–8, in the light of historical criticism." **Proceedings of the British Academy**, 17 (1931): 105–46. Almost the last word. [JFC]

1878–1919

W969. Anastasoff, Christ. **The tragic peninsula: a history of the Macedonian movement for independence since 1878.** St. Louis, 1938. The Bulgarian view by an American-Macedonian historian. [JFC]

W970. Black, Cyril E. **The establishment of constitutional government in Bulgaria.** Princeton, 1943. Extensive use of Bulgarian and other sources. Good background chapters, bibliographical essay, texts of documents. Essential for period of Prince Alexander. [JFC]

W971. Bulgaria and Romania. Ed. by Edward Gleichen. Boston, 1924. Brief survey, mostly since 1878. [JFC]

W972. Genov, Georgi P. **Bulgaria and the Treaty of Neuilly.** Sofia, 1935. Undocumented statement of the extreme Bulgarian revisionist position by a leading authority. Interesting historical map. [JFC]

W973. Hajek, Alois. **Bulgariens Befreiung und staatliche Entwicklung unter seinem ersten Fürsten.** Munich and Berlin, 1939. Less valuable than his earlier work but, although neglects some important sources, is useful. [JFC]

W974. Huhn, Arthur E. von. **The struggle of the Bulgarians for national independence under Prince Alexander.** London, 1886. Retains considerable value. [JFC]

W975. Hyde, Arthur M. **A diplomatic history of Bulgaria, 1870–1886.** Urbana, 1931. Errors and shortcomings from inability to use Bulgarian sources. [JFC]

W976. Ivanov, Iordan. **La question macédonienne.** Paris, 1920. The historical basis and evidence of all kinds of Bulgarian claims. [JFC]

W977. ——. **Les Bulgares devant le congrès de la paix.** 2nd ed., Bern, 1919. Mainly the evidence for Bulgaria's claim to Macedonia, one of many works on this subject by the leading Bulgarian authority. Includes the standard Bulgarian claims map by Ivanov. [JFC]

W978. Kratchounov, Krŭstiu. **La politique extérieure de la Bulgarie, 1880–1920.** Sofia, 1932. Useful, but not very original. [JFC]

W979. Léonoff, R., ed. **Documents secrets de la politique russe en orient, 1881–1890.** Berlin, 1893. First published in Sofia, there are also German and Russian editions. Controversy continues over authenticity of the damaging documents covering 1881–90, pur-

portedly from the Russian consulate in Ruse and legation in Bucharest. Probably genuine in substance though not in form. [JFC]

W980. Bulgaria. Ministry of Foreign Affairs. **The Bulgarian question and the Balkan states.** Sofia, 1919. Bulgaria's claims to Macedonia, with some reference to Dobrudja and Thrace. Selections from publications, documents, statistics, maps, and facsimiles. [JFC]

W981. Pétroff, Sultane. **Trente ans à la cour de Bulgarie, 1887–1918.** Paris, 1927. Reminiscences of a lady-in-waiting at Ferdinand's court. [JFC]

W982. Radoslavov, Vasil. **Bulgarien und die Weltkrise.** Berlin, 1923. Inevitably partisan history of Bulgaria's participation in World War I, by the wartime premier. [JFC]

W983. Stancioff, Anna (de Grenaud). **Recollections of a Bulgarian diplomat's wife.** London, 1931. Informative memoirs by the wife of one of Ferdinand's closest associates. Ends about 1915. [JFC]

1919–1956

W984. Desbons, Georges. **La Bulgarie après le Traité de Neuilly.** Paris, 1930. Revisionist and avowedly Bulgarophile, based on extended research and visits, with much historical background, wealth of references and quotations. Its unquestioned value is spoiled by its fervent style. Maps. [JFC]

W985. Prost, Henri. **La Bulgarie de 1912 à 1930.** Paris, 1932. Most convenient general survey, with bibliographical introduction, statistics, and illustrations. Based on ten years in Bulgaria as international banker. [JFC]

W986. Swire, Joseph. **Bulgarian conspiracy.** London, 1939. Well-informed, critical account of IMRO and related matters, by a resident British correspondent. [JFC]

HISTORIES OF SPECIAL TOPICS

Economics

W987. Danailov, Georgi T. **Les effets de la guerre en Bulgarie.** Paris and New Haven, 1932. Massive, including the Balkan wars. The only Bulgarian contribution to the Carnegie series. [JFC]

W988. Kosaroff, Theodore S. **La dette publique extérieure de la Bulgarie.** Paris, 1933. Useful and detailed. Covers period 1879–1932. [JFC]

W989. Koszul, J. P. **Les efforts de restauration financière de la Bulgarie (1922–1931).** Paris, 1932. One of several useful works on Bulgaria's post-World War I economy. [JFC]

W990. Nedkoff, Boris. **Development of the financial system of Bulgaria during the last decade.** Sofia, 1937. Text in English and Bulgarian. [JFC]

W991. Pasvolsky, Leo. **Bulgaria's economic position.** Washington, 1930. Very competent study based on Bulgarian data, with 100 pages of documents. [JFC]

W992. Popov, Kiril G. **La Bulgarie économique, 1879–1911: études statistiques.** Sofia, 1920. Useful compilation by a leading statistician. [JFC]

W993. Sakazov, Ivan. **Bulgarische Wirtschaftsgeschichte.** Berlin and Leipzig, 1929. Very useful handbook, with full references, although contains some inaccuracies. [JFC]

W994. Weiss-Bartenstein, Walter K. **Bulgariens Volkswirtschaft und ihre Entwicklungsmöglichkeiten.** Berlin, 1918. Most comprehensive and detailed survey of all aspects of the subject, including historical. [JFC]

Cultural and Religious History

W995. Filov, Bogdan D. **Geschichte der bulgarischen Kunst.** 2 v. Berlin and Leipzig, 1932–33. [Grundriss der slavischen Philologie und Kulturgeschichte, 9 and 11.] Historical setting well presented, by the outstanding art historian of this area. Many plates. [JFC]

W996. Grabar, André. **La peinture religieuse en Bulgarie.** Paris, 1928.

W997. Dontchev, Nikolai. **Influences étrangères dans la littérature bulgare.** Sofia, 1936. Important for intellectual history. Deals with western influences; elsewhere author takes up Russian and other impacts. [JFC]

W998. Hateau, Georges. **Panorama de la littérature bulgare contemporaine.** Paris, 1937. Good though brief. [JFC]

W999. Penev, Boian. **Istoriia na novata bŭlgarska literatura.** [History of modern Bulgarian literature.] 4 v. in 5. Sofia, 1930–36. An unfinished, posthumous publication, edited by Boris Iotsov from Penev's university lectures. Actually a history of the survival and revival of nationality, with biographies of all principal writers to Botev, and a wealth of references and bibliographies. In spite of unevenness and gaps, its value can hardly be overestimated. [JFC]

W1000. ——. **Bŭlgarska literatura.** [Bulgarian literature.] Plovdiv, 1930. 3rd ed., Sofia, 1946. Best handbook. [RW]

W1001. Salvini, Luigi. **La letteratura bulgara dalla liberazione alla prima guerra balcanica (1878–1912).** Rome, 1936. In historical context, but concentrates on a few outstanding names. Good references and bibliography. [JFC]

W1002. Shishmanov, Dimitŭr. **A survey of Bulgarian literature.** Tr. by Clarence A. Manning. Williamsport, Pa., 1932.

W1003. Turdeanu, Émile. **La littérature bulgare du XIVᵉ siècle et sa diffusion dans les pays roumains.** Paris, 1947. Covers an important aspect of Bulgarian cultural history. [JFC]

W1004. Andreev, Boris. **Die bulgarischen**

Zeitschriften und die Presseverhältnisse Bulgariens. Sofia, 1927. Contribution to the history of communications. [JFC]

W1005. Mladenov, Stefan. **Geschichte der bulgarischen Sprache.** Berlin and Leipzig, 1929. [Grundriss der slavischen Philologie und Kulturgeschichte.] Good reference work by one of the outstanding authorities. The introduction is especially helpful to the non-linguist. [JFC]

W1006. Dujčev, Ivan, ed. **Il cattolicesimo in Bulgaria nel sec. XVII.** Rome, 1937. Indispensable for a period when few sources other than Vatican ones are available. [JFC]

W1007. Hall, William W., Jr. **Puritans in the Balkans.** Sofia, 1938. Scholarly and objective history of American Protestant (Congregational) missionary work in Bulgaria from the Crimean War to World War I. Thorough use of published and unpublished United States sources, but not of Bulgarian. [JFC]

W1008. Stephanove, Constantine. **The Bulgarians and Anglo-Saxondom.** Bern, 1919. Deals, among other things, with U. S. missionary work. Propagandistic and spoiled by bad style and organization. Maps. [JFC]

W1009. Obolensky, Dmitri. **The Bogomils.** Cambridge, Eng., 1948. One of the most important studies of medieval Bulgaria, although not confined to this country. Exhaustive bibliography. [JFC]

W1010. Sharenkoff, Victor. **A study of Manichaeism in Bulgaria.** N.Y., 1927. Short study of Bogomilism, including translation of principal sources and bibliography. [JFC]

BIOGRAPHIES

W1011. Beaman, Ardern G. H. **M. Stambuloff.** London, 1895. Still useful. [JFC]

W1012. Christophorov, Petr. **Ivan Vazov: la formation d'un écrivain bulgare (1850–1921).** Paris, 1938. Good life of Bulgaria's greatest writer, profusely annotated and with a complete chronological bibliography of his works. [JFC]

W1013. Corti, Egon C. **Alexander von Battenberg: sein Kampf mit den Zaren und Bismarck.** Vienna, 1920. English tr., London, 1955. The best of many biographies, based on Alexander's archives. Additional information in Corti's *The downfall of three dynasties* (London, 1934). [JFC]

W1014. Golowine, A. F. **Fürst Alexander I. von Bulgarien (1879–1886).** Vienna, 1896. Still useful. [JFC]

W1015. Macdonald, John. **Czar Ferdinand and his people.** N.Y., 1913. Brief historical introduction. Well-informed, but openly favorable to Ferdinand and Bulgaria. [JFC]

W1016. Madol, Hans Roger. **Ferdinand of Bulgaria: the dream of Byzantium.** London, 1933. Readable "court" biography, utilizing German foreign office documents. References and bibliography. [JFC]

W1017. Muir, Nadejda (Stancioff). **Dimitri Stancioff.** London, 1957.

W1018. Nikolaev, N. P. **La règne et la mort de Boris III, roi des Bulgares.** Uppsala, 1952.

W1019. ——, ed. **La destinée tragique d'un roi.** Uppsala, 1952. Panegyrics to the last Bulgarian king by several close admirers. [JFC]

W1020. Todorov, Kosta. **Balkan firebrand: the autobiography of a rebel, soldier, and statesman.** Chicago, 1943. Breezy memoirs of a leftist agrarian leader, covering the period from World War I to World War II and relations with the Communists. [JFC]

ACADEMY, SOCIETY, AND UNIVERSITY PUBLICATIONS

W1021. Bŭlgarska Akademiia na Naukite. **Opis na izdaniiata na Bŭlgarskata Akademiia na Naukite i na Bŭlgarskoto Knizhovni Drŭzhestvo, 1870–1926.** [Catalog of publications of the Bulgarian Academy of Science and of the Bulgarian Literary Society, 1870–1926.] Sofia, 1926. New ed., to 1953, Sofia, 1956. Indispensable guide to all the Academy's publications. [JFC]

W1022. ——. **Bŭlgarski starini.** [Bulgarian antiquities.] Sofia, 1906 ff. (Irregular.) Texts of important literary and historical sources. [JFC]

W1023. ——. **Materiali za istoriiata na Sofiia.** [Materials for the history of Sofia.] 12 v. Sofia, 1910–43. Important monographs and source materials. [JFC]

W1024. Periodichesko spisanie. [Periodical review.] Braila, 1870–76; Sofia, 1882–1911. (Irregular.) This and *W1025* are publications of the Bulgarian Literary Society.

W1025. Sbornik za narodni umotvoreniia, nauka i knizhnina. [Collections of national arts, sciences and literature.] Sofia, 1889 ff. (Irregular. Title varies.) Until 1901 published by the Ministry of Education.

W1026. Bŭlgarska Akademiia na Naukite. **Spisanie.** [Journal.] Sofia, 1911 ff. (Irregular monthly.)

W1027. ——. **Sbornik.** [Collection.] Sofia, 1913–49. (Annual, irregular.)

W1028. ——. **Izvestiia na Instituta za Bŭlgarska Istoriia.** [Journal of the Institute of Bulgarian History.] Sofia, 1951 ff. (Irregular.) From 1905 to 1948 published by the Bulgarian Historical Society.

W1029. ——. **Izvestiia na Instituta za Bŭlgarska Literatura.** [Journal of the Institute of Bulgarian Literature.] Sofia, 1952 ff. (Irregular.)

W1030. ——. **Izvestiia na Arkheologicheskiia Institut.** [Journal of the Archaeological Institute.] Sofia, 1910 ff. (Title varies.)

W1031. ——. **Izvestiia na Etnograficheskiia Institut.** [Journal of the Ethnographical Institute.] Sofia, 1921 ff. (Title varies.)

W1032. ——. **Izvestiia na Instituta Botev-Levski.** [Journal of the Botev-Levski Institute.] Sofia, 1954 ff. (Annual.)

W1033. ——. **Izvestiia na Arkhivniia Institut.** [Journal of the Archival Institute.] Sofia, 1957 ff. (Irregular.)

W1034. Izvestiia na Instituta po Istoriia na Bŭlgarskata Komunisticheska Partiia. [Journal of the Institute for History of the Bulgarian Communist Party.] Sofia, 1957 ff. Published by the Communist party.

W1035. Bŭlgarski Bibliografski Institut. **Godishnik.** [Annual.] Sofia, 1945 ff.

W1036. Sofia. Universitet. **Godishnik.** [Annual.] Sofia, 1905 ff.

W1037. Makedonski Nauchen Institut. **Makedonski pregled.** [Macedonian review.] Sofia, 1923–43. (Quarterly.)

W1038. Bulgaria: Jahrbuch . . . der Deutsch-Bulgarischen Gesellschaft. Berlin and Leipzig, 1938–43. (Annual.)

PERIODICALS

W1039. Narodna Biblioteka v Sofiia. **Opis na bŭlgarskite periodichni izdaniia v Narodnata Biblioteka v Sofiia, 1844–1900.** [A list of periodical publications in the National Library of Sofia, 1844–1900.] Sofia, 1903. Useful list of periodicals, in absence of a wholly satisfactory bibliography. Catalogs alphabetically 517 newspapers and 229 periodicals and serials. [JFC]

W1040. Bŭlgarska istoricheska biblioteka. [Bulgarian historical library.] Sofia, 1928–32. (Quarterly.)

W1041. Arkhiv za poselishtni prouchvaniia. [Archive for study of rural settlements.] Sofia, 1938–41.

W1042. Istoricheski pregled. [Historical review.] Sofia, 1945 ff. (Bimonthly.)

W1043. Voenno-istoricheski sbornik. [Military-historical collection.] Sofia, 1927–34, 1945 ff. (Annual.)

W1044. Minalo. [The past.] Sofia, 1909–20. (Irregular.)

ALBANIA

BIBLIOGRAPHIES

W1045. U. S. Library of Congress. **The Balkans. 2, Albania.** Comp. by Helen F.

Conover. Washington, 1943. List of some principal works on Albania in western European languages, mostly close to the date of publication. [SS]

W1046. Gûys, Henri. **Bibliographie albanaise.** Tirana, 1938. This is a supplement to *W1048*. [SS]

W1047. Kersopoulos, Jean. "Albanie: ouvrages et articles de revue parus de 1555 à 1934." **Les Balkans: revue mensuelle,** 5 (Athens, 1934): 377–424, 651–712. All publications are in French. Most deal directly with Albania, but several treat neighboring countries or international relations while touching upon Albania. [SS]

W1048. Legrand, Émile L. J. **Bibliographie albanaise: description raisonnée des ouvrages pub. en albanais ou relatifs à l'Albanie du quinzième siècle à l'année 1900.** Paris, 1912.

ENCYCLOPEDIAS AND WORKS OF REFERENCE

W1049. Bourcart, Jacques. **L'Albanie et les albanais.** See *W1072*.

W1050. Skendi, Stavro, ed. **Albania.** N.Y., 1956. [Mid-European Studies Center series.] Most useful assemblage of rare material, reflecting intimate knowledge of land and people, and describing, from Communist sources, the present actualities. Excellent bibliography.

ETHNOLOGY AND GEOGRAPHY

W1051. Baldacci, Antonio. **L'Albania.** Rome, 1930. Deals mainly with physical geography. Written by an Italian scholar considered an expert on Albania. [SS]

W1052. Durham, Mary E. **High Albania.** London, 1909. Manners and customs, aims and aspirations of Albanians as revealed to the author during several visits to the northern part of the country. [SS]

W1053. Hasluck, Margaret M. **The unwritten law in Albania.** Cambridge, Eng., 1954. A fairly complete record of the laws in the mountains of northern Albania, north of the Shkumbi River. Author spent some ten years in Albania. [SS]

W1054. Nikolitch, Dragoutine. **Les différends de frontières de l'Albanie.** Paris, 1927.

W1055. Nopsca, Franz. "Zur Geschichte der Kartographie Nordalbaniens." **Mittheilungen der K. K. Geographischen Gesellschaft in Wien,** 59 (1916): 520–85. A fundamental historical study of the cartography of northern Albania. [SS]

W1056. ——. **Albanien: Bauten, Trachten und Geräte Nordalbaniens.** Berlin, 1925. Serious and thorough work by a well-known Hungarian ethnologist and geographer. [SS]

W1057. Urban, Martin. **Die Siedlungen Südalbaniens.** Öhringen, 1938. [Tübinger geographische und geologische Abhandlungen, 2.] Survey of settlements in south-

ern Albania, the first treatment of its kind. Based on field work, it is of value in many respects, although not always reliable in its historical references. [SS]

ANTHROPOLOGICAL WORKS

W1058. Babinger, Franz. **Ewlijâ Tschelebis' Reisewege in Albanien.** Berlin, 1930. Good annotated summary of that part of the Ottoman high official's work which deals with his travels in Albania during 1662 and 1670. [SS]

W1059. Coon, Carleton S. **The mountains of giants: a racial and cultural study of the north Albanian mountain Ghegs.** Cambridge, Mass., 1950. Based on field work, this study by a well-known U. S. anthropologist contains less cultural and more physical anthropology. [SS]

W1060. Stadtmüller, Georg. "Die albanische Volkstumsgeschichte als Forschungsproblem." **Leipziger Vierteljahrsschrift für Südosteuropa,** 5 (1941): 58–80. Survey of history of the Albanian people and the problems involved, by a German scholar with great interest in Albania. [SS]

W1061. Thallóczy, Ludwig von, ed. **Illyrisch-albanische Forschungen.** 2 v. Munich and Leipzig, 1916. Collection of articles and studies, several previously published in journals, written by serious scholars; deal mainly with history of the country from earliest times to the rule of Prince Von Wied (1914). A study on ethnography and another on agriculture are included. This is a fundamental work for a fair knowledge of Albania's past. [SS]

PRINTED COLLECTIONS OF SOURCES

W1062. Înalcîk, Halil, ed. **Hicri 835 tarihli sûret-i defter-i sancak-i Arvanid.** [A recordbook of the Sanjak of Arvanid from the year h. 835.] Ankara, 1954. Includes also a *Kanunname* relating to Valona of 991 of the Hegira, as well as an index of personal and place names. Throws considerable light on the Albanian timariots. [SS]

W1063. Radonić, Jovan. **Đurađ Kastriot Skenderbeg i Arbanija u XV veku (istoriska građa).** [George Castriotes Skanderbeg and Albania in the 15th century (historical materials).] Belgrade, 1942. [Srpska Kraljevska Akademija. Spomenik XCV, 2nd ser., 74.] Collection of documents by a well-known and serious Yugoslav scholar, containing original documents, and also excerpts from Greek, Serbian, Turkish, and western secondary sources. Important as a source book, it may be considered as a continuation of Ludwig von Thallóczy and others, eds., *Acta et diplomata res Albaniae mediae aetatis illustrantia* (Vienna, 1913 ff.). [SS]

HISTORIES OF SPECIAL PERIODS

Ancient

W1064. Praschniker, Camillo, and A. Schober. **Archäologische Forschungen in Albanien und Montenegro.** Vienna, 1919. By two competent archaeologists who, during World War I, studied that part of Albania under Austro-Hungarian occupation, *i.e.*, north of Valona. [SS]

W1065. Rey, Léon. "Seize années de fouilles en Albanie." **Revue de Paris,** 46 (Aug. 1939): 685–96. Survey of excavations in the ancient city of Apollonia (near Fier), by the head of the French archaeological mission in charge of those excavations during the interwar period. [SS]

W1066. Ugolini, Luigi M. **Albania antica.** V. 1, **Ricerche archeologiche.** Rome and Milan, 1927. The author, head of the Italian Archaeological Mission in Albania after World War I, gives his itinerary through the country. [SS]

W1067. ———. **L'antica Albania nelle ricerche archeologiche italiane.** Rome, 1928. Excavations performed by above mission in Finiki and Butrinto. [SS]

Turkish and Early Modern Period

W1068. Boppe, Auguste. **L'Albanie et Napoléon (1797–1814).** Paris, 1914. Deals with relations between Napoleon and Ali Pasha of Jannina and the beys of southern Albania. Based on travel accounts and archives. [SS]

W1069. Gegaj, Athanase. **L'Albanie et l'invasion turque au XVᵉ siècle.** Louvain, 1937. A survey, founded on almost all known material to date, examined from the Albanian viewpoint. Contains rather extensive treatment of Albanian feudal families. [SS]

W1070. Remérand, Gabriel. **Ali de Tébélen, pasha de Janina, 1744–1822.** Paris, 1928. More comprehensive than Boppe and better written. Author has made greater use of the archives in the French embassy of Istanbul. [SS]

W1071. Skendi, Stavro. "Beginnings of Albanian nationalist and autonomous trends: the Albanian League, 1878–1881." **American Slavic and east European review,** 12 (Apr. 1953): 219–32. This and two other articles by the author are contributions toward an understanding of Albanian national awakening, a subject which still remains to be studied. [SS]

Modern Period

W1072. Bourcart, Jacques. **L'Albanie et les albanais.** Paris, 1921. The author, a French scholar who lived in southern Albania during World War I, gives a fair

geographical, ethnographical, and historical survey. [SS]

W1073. Busch-Zantner, Richard. **Albanien: neues Land im Imperium.** Leipzig, 1939. Treats rather intelligently the historical course of Albania and basic realities of her political life. Author, however, sides with Fascist Italy in its rule of Albania. [SS]

W1074. Federal Writers' Project. Massachusetts. **The Albanian struggle in the Old World and New.** Boston, 1939. Useful for understanding the nationalist movement of Albanian immigrants in the United States. [SS]

W1075. Giannini, Amadeo. **L'Albania, dall' independenza all' unione con l'Italia (1913–1939).** Milan, 1940. Short diplomatic history of Albania, useful for the documents in the appendix. [SS]

W1076. Mousset, Albert. **L'Albanie devant l'Europe (1912–1929).** Paris, 1930.

W1077. Skendi, Stavro. "Beginnings of Albanian nationalist trends in culture and education (1878–1912)." **Journal of central European affairs,** 12 (Jan. 1953): 356–67.

W1078. ———. "Albanian political thought and revolutionary activity, 1881–1912." **Südost-Forschungen,** 13 (1954): 159–99.

W1079. Swire, Joseph. **Albania: the rise of a kingdom.** London, 1929. The author, an intelligent English publicist, gives an account of political vicissitudes of the Albanians during the preceding fifty years, being better informed on the period 1919–28. [SS]

W1080. Vanlande, René. **En Albanie sous l'oeil de Mussolini.** Paris, 1933.

HISTORIES OF SPECIAL TOPICS

Cultural Development

W1081. Jokl, Norbert. **Linguistisch-kulturhistorische Untersuchungen aus dem Bereiche des Albanischen.** Berlin, 1923. Grammatical-etymological research combined with cultural-historical remarks relating to customs and beliefs, landscape, husbandry and implements, and customary law of the Albanian people, by the famous Viennese Albanologist. [SS]

W1082. Mann, Stuart E. **Albanian literature.** London, 1955. Uneven and fragmentary in treatment, but still gives an idea of the various aspects of Albanian literature. [SS]

W1083. Petrotta, Gaetano. **Svolgimento storico della cultura e della letteratura albanese.** Palermo, 1950. This book, by an Italo-Albanian scholar, contains much information, but is not well organized. [SS]

W1084. Skendi, Stavro. **Albanian and south Slavic oral epic poetry.** Philadelphia, 1954. Important, completely new study on relationship between the oral epic poetry of the Albanians and that of the southern Slavs.

Review, A. Schmaus, *Südost-Forschungen,* 14 (1955): 333.

Economics

W1085. Godart, Justin. **L'Albanie en 1922: l'enquête de la Société des Nations.** La Flèche, France, 1922.

W1086. Lorenzoni, Giovanni. **La questione agraria albanese: studi, inchiesti e proposte per una riforma agraria in Albania.** Bari, Italy, 1930.

W1087. Principi di economia albanese. Padua, 1941.

W1088. Zavalani, Dalib. **Die landwirtschaftlichen Verhältnisse Albaniens.** Berlin, 1938.

BIOGRAPHIES

W1089. Dako, Christo A. **Zogu the First, king of the Albanians: a sketch of his life and times.** Tirana, 1937.

W1090. Noli, Fan S. **George Castrioti Scanderbeg (1405–1468).** N.Y., 1947. Deals not only with Scanderbeg's fight against the Turks, but in an extensive manner also with his relations with Naples, the Papacy, and Venice. Although based on an abundance of sources, an important one (*W1063*) was neglected. Author takes an unhistorical approach in trying to show Scanderbeg's fight as one of the Albanian people against "Ottoman feudalism" and "Venetian capitalism." [SS]

PERIODICALS

W1091. Rivista d'Albania. Milan, 1940–43. [Accademia d'Italia.] (Quarterly.) Valuable articles by Italian and some Albanian scholars. [SS]

W1092. Studi albanesi. Rome, 1931–36. [Istituto per l'Europa Orientale.] Several important studies by Italian scholars. [SS]

W1093. Albanie: revue d'archéologie, d'histoire, d'art et des sciences appliquées en Albanie et dans les Balkans. Paris, Milan, and Rome, 1925–39. (Annual.) Edited by the archaeologist, Léon Rey, it had some good contributors. [SS]

W1094. Albania. Brussels and London, 1897–1909. (Monthly.) Edited by the well-known Albanian writer and scholar, Faik Konitza, this review, to which many Albanian intellectuals contributed, contains valuable material for the period of national awakening. [SS]

W1095. Buletin për shkencat shoqërore. [Bulletin of social sciences.] Tirana, 1947 ff. [Instituti të Shkencave.] (Irregular. Title varies.) Contains some articles on historical subjects treated from the Marxist-Leninist point of view. [SS]

W1096. Hylli i dritës. [The star of light.] Shkodër, 1923–42. (Monthly.) Edited and published by the Franciscan brothers. Contains valuable articles on Albanian folklore, ethnography, and history. [SS]

GREECE *

BIBLIOGRAPHIES

W1097. Sathas, Kōnstantinos N. **Neoellēnikē philologia: biographiai tōn en tois grammasi dialampsantōn Hellēnōn (1455–1821).** [Modern Greek literature: biographies of Greeks distinguished in the letters (1455–1821).] Athens, 1868.

W1098. ——. **Neoellēnikēs philologias parartēma.** [Supplement to Modern Greek literature.] Athens, 1870.

W1099. Vretos, Andreas Papadopoulos. **Neoellēnikē philologia: ētoi katalogos tōn . . . typōthentōn bibliōn par' Hellēnōn eis tēn omiloumenēn, ē eis tēn archaian hellēnikēn glōssan.** (1453–1821.) [Modern Greek literature: or catalog . . . of books printed by Greeks in the vernacular or in the ancient Greek tongue.] Athens, [1845]. 2nd rev. ed., 2 v., Athens, 1854–57. The above three works are useful, though not complete. The first two are better than the third.

W1100. Legrand, Émile L. J. **Bibliographie hellénique: ou, description raisonnée des ouvrages publiés en grec par des Grecs aux XVe et XVIe siècles.** 4 v. Paris, 1885–1906.

W1101. ——. **Bibliographie hellénique: ou, description raisonnée des ouvrages publiés par des Grecs au dix-septième siècle.** 5 v. Paris, 1894–1903.

W1102. ——. **Bibliographie hellénique: ou, description raisonnée des ouvrages publiés par des Grecs au dix-huitième siècle.** 2 v. Paris, 1918–28. The above eleven volumes (*W1100–1102*) constitute a valuable mine of bibliographical information on all Greek life from the fall of Constantinople to the end of the 18th century.

W1103. Ghinēs, Dēmētrios E., and V. G. Mexas. **Hellēnikē bibliographia, 1800–1863.** [Greek bibliography, 1800–1863.] 3 v. Athens, 1939–41.

W1104. Koromēlas, Dēmētrios A. **Catalogue raisonné des livres publiés en Grèce depuis 1868 jusqu'en 1872, 1873 jusqu'à 1877.** 2 v. Athens, 1873–78.

W1105. Politēs, Nikolaos G. **Hellēnikē bibliographia.** [Greek bibliography.] 2 v. Athens, 1909–11. V. 3, pt. 1, ed. by Stilpon P. Kyriakides, Athens, 1927; pt. 2, Thessalonikē, 1932. The above three works (*W1103–1105*), with two intervals (of five

* This entire subsection on modern Greece was compiled by G. G. Arnakis.

and thirty years respectively), carry the general Greek bibliography to 1920. They are of unequal value, *W1103* being by far the best. The gaps, which are noticeable in the other two, can be filled to a large measure from bibliographies in *Byzantinische Zeitschrift* (Leipzig and Munich, 1892 ff.) and *Epetēris Hetaireias Byzantinōn Spoudōn* (*W1351*). A good general bibliography of works on Greece, in Greek and western languages, is included in v. 8 of the 1952 edition of *Historia tou hellēnikou ethnous* (*W1142*).

The following seven articles (*W1106–1112*) are important for recent history.

W1106. Miller, William. "Modern Greek historians of modern Greece." **History**, 10 (July 1925): 110–23.

W1107. ——. "Recent works on medieval, Turkish and modern Greece." **The Cambridge historical journal**, 2 (1928): 229–47.

W1108. ——. "Modern Greek history in the 'Gennadeion.' " **Journal of modern history**, 2 (Dec. 1930): 612–28.

W1109. ——. "Recent publications on medieval and modern Greek history, 1928–1931." **Am. hist. rev.**, 37 (Jan. 1932): 272–79.

W1110. ——. "Additions to modern Greek history in the 'Gennadeion.' " **Jour. mod. hist.**, 9 (Mar. 1937): 56–63.

W1111. Weber, Shirley H. "Further additions to modern Greek historical material in the Gennadeion in Athens, 1937–1949." **Jour. mod. hist.**, 22 (Sep. 1950): 250–66. Continuation of Miller's bibliographical work by a former director of the Gennadeius Library, where much valuable material has been accumulated.

W1112. Stavrianos, Leften S., and E. P. Panagopoulos. "Present-day Greece." **Jour. mod. hist.**, 20 (June 1948): 149–58.

W1113. U. S. Library of Congress. **Greece: a selected list of references.** Comp. by Ann D. Brown and Helen D. Jones. Washington, 1943. A workable bibliography in western languages.

For special areas see the following (*W1114–1118*).

W1114. Legrand, Émile L. J. **Bibliographie ionienne: description raisonnée des ouvrages publiés par les Grecs des Sept-Îles ou concernant ces îles du quinzième siècle à l'année 1900.** Ed. by Hubert Pernot. 2 v. Paris, 1910.

W1115. Argenti, Philip P. **A bibliography of Chios, from classical times to 1936.** Oxford, 1940.

W1116. Cobham, Claude D. **An attempt at a bibliography of Cyprus.** New ed., Nicosia, 1929.

W1117. Kalogeropoulos, Dionysios. **Bibliographia Euboias kai tōn Thessalikōn Sporadōn.** [Bibliography of Euboea and the Thessalian Sporades.] Athens, 1937.

W1118. Paschales, D. **Kykladikē biblio-**logia. [Cycladic bibliography.] 3 fasc. Athens, 1939–40.

W1119. Bulletin analytique de bibliographie hellénique. Athens, 1946 ff. [Institut français d'Athènes.] (Quarterly.) The most ambitious, and most successful, bibliographical project in postwar Greece. V. 6 includes works published in 1945. Subsequent volumes have come out regularly, listing and describing all works published in Greece or by Greeks every year, beginning with 1946. V. 1–5, dealing with the period 1940–44, are to be published later.

PRINTED COLLECTIONS OF SOURCES

Since the general tendency among Greek historians is to begin Greece's modern era with the Fourth Crusade, the four following works (*W1120–1123*) should be cited.

W1120. Byzantinae historiae scriptores. 39 v. Paris, 1645–1711.

W1121. Corpus scriptorum historiae byzantinae. 50 v. Bonn, 1828–97.

W1122. Sathas, Kōnstantinos N., ed. **Mesaiōnikē bibliothēkē.** [Medieval library.] See *L87*.

W1123. ——, ed. **Mnēmeia hellēnikēs historias: documents inédits relatifs à l'histoire de la Grèce au Moyen-Âge.** 9 v. Paris, 1880–90. This and the above work by Sathas are extremely important sources for early modern Greek history.

W1124. Lampros, Spyridon P., ed. **Palaiologeia kai peloponnēsiaka.** [Palaeologian and Peloponnesian (i.e. documents).] 4 v. Athens, 1912–30. Continuation of Sathas' work, but more limited in scope. Deals with crucial period leading to the fall of Constantinople (1453).

W1125. Tomadakis, Nikolaos B., ed. **Duca, Kritobulou, Sphrantzē, Chalkokondylē: peri tēs alōseōs tēs Kōnstantinoupoleōs (1453).** [Ducas, Critobulos, Sphrantzis, Chalcocondylis: concerning the capture of Constantinople (1453).] Athens, 1953. This is not a new edition, but a reprint of pertinent portions from *Corpus scriptorum historiae byzantinae*, with important notes by the editor.

W1126. Mamoukas, Andreas, ed. **Ta kata tēn anagennēsin tēs Hellados.** [Concerning the regeneration of Greece.] 11 v. Piraeus and Athens, 1839–52. This and the following contain materials on the period since the Greek Revolution of 1821.

W1127. Dalleggio, E., ed. **Les philhellènes et la guerre de l'indépendance: lettres inédites de J. Orlando et A. Louriotis.** Athens, 1949.

Important writings of leaders of the Revolution have been published in the original Greek in the following (*W1128–1132*).

W1128. Kasomoules, Nicholas K. **Enthymēmata stratiōtika tēs Epanastaseōs tōn Hellēnōn, 1821–1833.** [Military reminiscences of the Greek Revolution, 1821–1833.] Ed. by G. Vlachogiannēs. 3 v. Athens, 1939–42.

W1129. Makrygiannēs, Iōannēs. **Stratēgou Makrygiannē apomnēmoneumata.** [Memoirs of Stratēgou Makrygiannē.] Ed. by G. Vlachogiannēs. 2nd ed., 2 v., Athens, 1947.

W1130. Phōtakos (Phōtios Chrysanthopoulos). **Apomnēmoneumata peri tēs Hellēnikēs Epanastaseōs.** [Memoirs concerning the Greek Revolution.] New ed., 4 v., Athens, 1955.

W1131. Perraivos, Christopher. **Historia Pargas kai Souliou.** [History of Parga and Souli.] New ed., Athens, 1956.

W1132. Polemika apomnēmoneumata kai biographia Rhēga Pheraiou. [War memoirs and life of Regas of Velestino.] New ed., Athens, 1956.

W1133. Prōtopsaltēs, Emmanouel G., ed. **Apomnēmoneumata tōn agōnistōn tou 21.** [Memoirs of the fighters of '21.] 20 v. Athens, 1955–57. (Other volumes in preparation.) Works by a number of authors dealing with the Greek Revolution.

The two world wars and their aftermath are represented by a large number of documents, of which the following collections (*W1134–1138*) are the most important.

W1134. Greece. Hypourgeion tōn Exōterikōn. **Diplōmatika engrapha, 1913–1917.** [Diplomatic documents, 1913–1917.] Athens, 1917. English tr., *The Greek white book: diplomatic documents, 1913–1917.* 2 v. N.Y., 1918–19.

W1135. Royal Ministry of Foreign Affairs. **Diplomatic documents: Italy's aggression against Greece.** Athens, 1940.

W1136. United Nations. General Assembly. Special Committee on the Balkans. **Report.** 4 v. Lake Success, 1948–51.

W1137. ——. **Supplementary report.** Paris, 1948.

W1138. ——. **Interim report.** Lake Success, 1948.

GENERAL HISTORIES

W1139. Finlay, George. **A history of Greece from its conquest by the Romans to the present time, B.C. 146 to A.D. 1864.** Rev. ed., by Henry F. Tozer, 7 v., Oxford, 1877. Begun as a study of the Greek Revolution, of which the author was an eyewitness, this developed into the most complete history of medieval and modern Greece in any western language. Especially important for the Ottoman period. The account of the Revolution and later developments reflects the author's tendency to moralize and criticize Greek leaders.

W1140. Mendelssohn-Bartholdy, Karl. **Geschichte Griechenlands von der Eroberung Konstantinopels durch die Türken im Jahre 1453 bis auf unsere Tage.** 2 v. Leipzig, 1870–

74. Covers to 1835. Detailed, but must be used with caution.

W1141. Hertzberg, Gustav F. **Geschichte Griechenlands seit dem Absterben des antiken Lebens bis zur Gegenwart.** 4 v. Gotha, 1876–79. Covers period 395–1878. From point of view of scholarship this is far superior to *W1140.*

W1142. Paparrhēgopoulos, Kōnstantinos. **Historia tou hellēnikou ethnous.** [History of the Greek people.] 6th rev. ed., by Paul Karolidēs, 8 v., Athens, 1930. The author, acclaimed the father of modern Greek historiography, emphasizes the historical unity of the Greek people from remote antiquity to modern times. The original account, which stops at 1827, is continued by Karolidēs to 1930 in a manner that leaves much to be desired.

W1143. Lampros, Spyridōn P. **Historia tēs Hellados.** [History of Greece.] 6 v. Athens, 1886–1902. The successor of Paparrhēgopoulos at the University of Athens has produced this comprehensive but less penetrating history of Greece from ancient times to the reign of King Otho. Intended for a wider reading public, and amply illustrated.

Besides the above general histories of Greece that include medieval and ancient history as well as modern, there are several works devoted to the modern period, usually beginning with the Greek Revolution of 1821 (*W1144–1154*).

W1144. Miller, William. **A history of the Greek people (1821–1921).** London and N.Y., 1922. Resumé of modern Greek history, with chapters on the Cretan and Macedonian questions.

W1145. ——. **Greece.** London, 1928. Based partly on the above, with a supplement of post-World War I developments.

W1146. Mavrogordato, John. **Modern Greece: a chronicle and survey, 1800–1931.** N.Y., 1931.

W1147. Forster, Edward S. **A short history of modern Greece, 1821–1945.** 2nd ed., London, 1946.

W1148. Gomme, Arnold W. **Greece.** London, 1945.

W1149. Svoronos, Nicolas G. **Histoire de la Grèce moderne.** Paris, 1953.

W1150. Sakellariou, M. B., and N. G. Svoronos. "Greece: history of the Turkish period, 1453–1821." **The encyclopedia americana** (1953), v. 13.

W1151. ——. "Greece: culture of the Turkish period, 1453–1821." **The encyclopedia americana** (1953), v. 13.

W1152. Stavrianos, Leften S. "Greece: the modern nation." **The encyclopedia americana** (1953), v. 13.

W1153. ——. "Greece: modern history." **The encyclopedia americana** (1953), v. 13.

W1154. Panagopoulos, E. P., and B. M. Panagopoulos. "Greece: modern culture."

The encyclopedia americana (1953), v. 13. These *Americana* articles present the best resumé of modern Greek history and culture, and include bibliography.

HISTORIES OF SPECIAL PERIODS

Turkish Domination

W1155. Papadopoullos, Theodore H. **Studies and documents relating to the history of the Greek Church and people under Turkish domination.** Brussels, 1952. Important for the status and organization of the Greek Church within the Ottoman empire. The document entitled "Planosparaktēs," published herein for the first time, deals with a limited phase of East-West church relations.

W1156. L'Hellénisme Contemporain. **1453–1953: le cinq-centième anniversaire de la prise de Constantinople.** Athens, 1953. This and the following are very important studies on the social and cultural impact of the fall of the Byzantine empire on the Greek people.

W1157. Zakythēnos, Dionysios A. **Hē alōsis tēs Konstantinoupoleōs kai hē tourkokratia.** [The fall of Constantinople and the Turkish domination.] Athens, 1954.

W1158. ——. **Hē tourkokratia: eisagōgē eis tēn neōteran historian tou Hellēnismou.** [The Turkish domination: introduction to the modern history of Hellenism.] Athens, 1957.

Nineteenth Century

W1159. Phillips, W. Alison. **The War of Greek Independence, 1821 to 1835.** London, 1897. Depends largely upon Finlay.

W1160. Woodhouse, Christopher M. **The Greek War of Independence: its historical setting.** London, 1952. Brief, but useful.

W1161. Amantos, Kōnstantinos I. **Scheseis Hellēnōn kai Tourkōn.** [Relations of Greeks and Turks.] V. 1 (1071–1571). Athens, 1955. V. 2, dealing with the period 1571–1821, is in preparation.

W1162. Daskalakēs, A. **Rhigas Velestinlis, la Révolution Française et les préludes de l'indépendance hellénique.** Paris, 1937.

W1163. ——. **Ta aitia kai hoi paragontes tēs Hellēnikēs Epanastaseōs.** [The causes and the factors of the Greek Revolution.] Paris, 1927. Important for background of the Revolution.

W1164. Kandelōros, Takēs H. **Hē Philikē Hetaireia, 1814–1821.** [The Philikē Hetaireia, 1814–1821.] Athens, 1926. Although the work of an amateur, still the best book on the subject.

W1165. Mexas, Valerios G. **Hoi Philikoi.** [The members of the Philikē Hetaireia.] Athens, 1937.

W1166. Dakin, Douglas. **British and American Philhellenes during the War of**

Greek Independence, 1821–1833. Thessaloniki, 1955.

W1167. Larrabee, Stephen A. **Hellas observed: the American experience of Greece, 1775–1865.** N.Y., 1957. This and *W1166* are well-written accounts of British and United States interest in the cause of Greece.

W1168. Vakalopoulos, Apostolos E. **Ta hellēnika strateumata tou 1821.** [Greek troops in 1821.] Thessaloniki, 1948. Best work on the subject.

W1169. Kokkinos, Dionysios A. **Hē Hellēnikē Epanastasis.** [The Greek Revolution.] 3rd rev. ed., Athens, 1956. Most important work on this subject.

W1170. Kordatos, Gianēs. **Hē koinōnikē sēmasia tēs Hellēnikēs Epanastaseōs.** [The social significance of the Greek Revolution.] 4th ed., Athens, 1946. Interpretation of the struggle from the point of view of historical materialism.

W1171. Pipinelēs, Takēs N. **Politikē historia tēs Hellēnikēs Epanastaseōs.** [Political history of the Greek Revolution.] Paris, 1928. Defends the conservative, nationalist view.

W1172. Mazarakēs-Ainian, Alexandros. **Historikē meletē 1821–1907.** [Historical study, 1821–1907.] Athens, 1950. Interesting account, by a general, of the war of 1897 and events leading to the Goudi revolution.

W1173. Sergeant, Lewis. **Greece in the nineteenth century: a record of Hellenic emancipation and progress.** London, 1897. This and the following (*W1174–1176*) are important for typical 19th century ideas on the growth of Greece's aspirations and her disastrous war with the Ottoman empire in 1897.

W1174. Bickford-Smith, Roandeu A. H. **Greece under King George.** London, 1893.

W1175. Rose, W. Kinnaird. **With the Greeks in Thessaly.** London, 1897.

W1176. Mersey, C. Bigham, 2nd viscount. **With the Turkish army in Thessaly.** London, 1897.

Early Twentieth Century

W1177. Abbott, George F. **Greece and the Allies, 1914–1922.** London, 1922. Anti-Venizelist, but lucid and well informed.

W1178. Ventērēs, Geōrgios. **Hē Hellas tou 1910–1920.** [Greece of 1910–1920.] Athens, 1931. Most important study by a Greek, amply documented. Stresses the diplomatic as well as domestic aspects of the Greek problem. Venizelist.

W1179. Adamow, Evgenii A. **Die europäischen Mächte und Griechenland während des Weltkrieges.** Dresden, 1932. Important. Contains documents from Russian archives pertaining to Greece.

W1180. Phocas-Cosmetatos, S. P. (pseud., S. Cosmin). **L'Entente et la Grèce pendant la Grande Guerre.** 2 v. Paris, 1926. English ed., *The tragedy of Greece,* N.Y., 1928. Important. French edition is the preferred.

W1181. Frangulis, A. F. **La Grèce et la crise mondiale.** 2 v. Paris, 1926–27. Well-documented account of Greece's policy, presented by the Greek delegate to the League of Nations. Constantinist.

W1182. Deville, Gabriel. **L'Entente, la Grèce et la Bulgarie.** Paris, 1919. Memoirs of the French minister at Athens during the war. Of topical interest.

W1183. Melas, George M. **Ex-King Constantine and the war.** London, 1920.

W1184. Nicholas, prince of Greece. **My fifty years.** London, 1927.

W1185. ——. **Political memoirs, 1914–1917.** London, 1928. Constantinist.

W1186. Sarrail, Maurice P. E. **Mon commandement en Orient (1916–1918).** See *AG63.*

W1187. Dartige du Fournet, Louis. **Souvenirs de guerre d'un amiral.** Paris, 1920. By the admiral who directed operations against Constantinist Greece.

W1188. Recouly, Raymond. **M. Jonnart en Grèce et l'abdication de Constantin.** Paris, 1918. Defense of French intervention in Greece, by the secretary of High Commissioner Jonnart.

W1189. Phocas-Cosmetatos, S. P. (pseud., S. Cosmin). **Diplomatie et presse dans l'affaire grecque, 1914–1916.** Paris, 1921. Sympathetic to King Constantine.

W1190. Mackenzie, Compton. **Greek memories.** London, 1932. Leans toward the Venizelists.

W1191. Thomson, Sir Basil H. **The Allied secret service in Greece.** London, 1931. Sympathetic to King Constantine.

The above three works (*W1189–1191*) are important for the inner story of the Greek crisis. See also biographies of various leaders during the crisis.

Inter-War Period

W1192. Pallis, Alexander A. **Greece's Anatolian venture and after: a survey of the diplomatic and political aspects of the Greek expedition to Asia Minor (1915–1922).** London, 1937. By far the best work available on the subject.

W1193. Toynbee, Arnold J. **The western question in Greece and Turkey: a study in the contact of civilizations.** 2nd ed., London, 1923. Background of the Greco-Turkish struggle, with emphasis on culture. Author's bias is for the Turks.

W1194. Andrew, prince of Greece. **War memoirs.** London, 1928.

W1195. ——. **Towards disaster: the Greek army in Asia Minor in 1921.** London, 1930. Defense of the Greek government and general staff, with interesting sidelights on the Anatolian campaign.

W1196. Bujac, Jean L. E. **Les campagnes de l'armée hellénique, 1918–1922.** Paris, 1930. Most complete work on the subject.

W1197. Metaxas, Iōannēs. **Historia tou ethnikou dichasmou kai tēs mikrasiatikēs katastrophēs.** [History of the national dissension and of the Asia Minor disaster.] Athens, 1935. The Constantinist point of view of the crisis, by the later dictator.

W1198. Stratēgos, Xenophōn. **Hē Hellas en Mikrai Asiai.** [Greece in Asia Minor.] Athens, 1925.

W1199. Trikoupēs, Nikolaos. **Anamnēseis epeisodiōn kai gegonotōn.** [Memoirs of incidents and events.] Athens, 1952. This and the above (*W1198*) are accounts of the Asia Minor campaign by generals (both Constantinists) in command of the Greek army.

W1200. Mears, Eliot G. **Greece today: the aftermath of the refugees' impact.** Stanford, 1929. A scholarly treatment.

W1201. Ladas, Stephen P. **The exchange of minorities: Bulgaria, Greece, and Turkey.** N.Y., 1932. Better than the above.

W1202. Eddy, Charles B. **Greece and the Greek refugees.** London, 1931.

W1203. Morgenthau, Henry. **I was sent to Athens.** Garden City, N.Y., 1929. This and *W1202* are by former chairmen of the Greek Refugee Settlement Commission.

W1204. Miller, William. "Greece since the return of Venizelos." **Foreign affairs,** 7 (Apr. 1929): 468–76. Deals with the elections of 1928.

W1205. ——. "New era in Greece." **Foreign affairs,** 14 (July, 1936): 654–61. Concerning establishment of the Metaxas dictatorship.

W1206. Kaltchas, Nicholas S. "Post-war politics in Greece." **Foreign policy reports,** 12 (Sep. 1936): 146–60. This and the two following are articles of broader scope, all very useful.

W1207. Rouček, Joseph S. **The politics of the Balkans.** N.Y., 1939. See "Greece," pp. 99–117.

W1208. ——. "The social forces in Greek politics." **Social science,** 9 (Jan. 1934): 54–63.

W1209. Daphnēs, Grēgorios. **Hē Hellas metaxy dyo polemōn, 1923–1940.** [Greece between two wars, 1923–1940.] 2 v. Athens, 1955. Most complete narrative of events during the interwar period, but inclined to be too detailed and very little interpretative.

World War II and After

W1210. Buckley, Christopher. **Greece and Crete, 1941.** London, 1951.

W1211. Byford-Jones, W. **The Greek trilogy (resistance, liberation, revolution).** London and N.Y., 1945.

W1212. Kokkinos, Dionysios. **Hoi dyo**

polemoi, 1940–1941. [The two wars, 1940–1941.] 2 v. Athens, 1945–46. Dependable account of the conflict, by a competent historian.

W1213. Papagos, Alexandros. **Ho polemos tēs Hellados, 1940–1941.** [The war of Greece, 1940–1941.] Athens, 1945. Italian ed. (condensed), *La Grecia in guerra*, [Milan], 1950; English ed. (also condensed), *The German attack on Greece*, London, 1946. Authentic story of the war, by Greece's commander-in-chief.

W1214. Grēgoriades, Neokosmos. **Ho helleno-italo-germanikos polemos, 1940–41.** [The Greek-Italian-German war, 1940–41.] Athens, 1945. This and the following (*W1215*) comprise narrative and critique of the operations, written by generals opposed to the Metaxas regime.

W1215. Katheniōtēs, D. **Hai kyriōterai stratēgikai phaseis tou polemou 1940–41.** [The main strategic phases of the war of 1940–41.] Athens, 1946.

W1216. Sakellariou, Alexandros E. **Hē thesis tēs Hellados eis ton Deuteron Pankosmion Polemon.** [The position of Greece during the Second World War.] Athens, 1946. By a Greek admiral and minister of marine during part of the war.

W1217. Sellinas, E. **Hē Hellas eis ton polemon.** [Greece in the war.] Athens, 1946. This and *W1218–1219* are very useful accounts of military operations.

W1218. Zapheiropoulos, Demetrios G. **Ho hellēnoitalikos kai ho hellēnogermanikos polemos, 1940–1941.** [The Greco-Italian and the Greco-German war, 1940–1941.] 2nd ed., Athens, 1946.

W1219. Mourellos, Ioannēs D. **Hē machē tēs Krētēs.** [The battle of Crete.] Iraklion, 1946.

W1220. Saraphēs, Stephanos. **Ho ELAS.** [The ELAS (National People's Liberation Army).] Athens, 1946. English ed. (condensed), *Greek resistance army*, London, 1951. Account of the organization and activities of the leftist forces, written by their organizer and commander-in-chief.

W1221. Pyromaglou, Komninos. **Hē ethnikē antistasis.** [National resistance.] Athens, 1947. Account by leader of the Hellenic Democratic National League.

W1222. Zalokōstas, Christos P. **To chroniko tēs sklavias.** [The chronicle of slavery.] Athens, 1949. By a resistance leader with rightest sympathies.

W1223. Gatopoulos, D. **Historia tēs katochēs.** [History of the occupation.] 4 v. Athens, 1946–47. Detailed and well-written record of life of the Greek people under the Axis.

W1224. Milliex, Roger. **À l'école du peuple grec, 1940–1944.** Moulins, France, 1946. The sufferings and resistance of the Greeks as seen by a French eyewitness.

W1225. Tsouderos, Emmanouēl. **Hellēnikes anōmalies stē Mesē Anatolē.** [Greek troubles in the Middle East.] Athens, 1945. Greek opposition to the British high command, as told by the Greek prime minister of the government-in-exile.

W1226. ——. **Gnōmes kai logoi.** [Opinions and speeches.] Athens, 1946. This and the following are accounts of the prime minister's activities, especially in behalf of the Greek people suffering from famine.

W1227. ——. **Episitismos, 1941–1944.** [The food supply, 1941–1944.] Athens, 1946.

W1228. International Red Cross. **Ravitaillement de la Grèce pendant l'occupation 1941–1944 et pendant les premiers cinq mois après la libération.** Athens, 1949. Important documentary material on activities of the Red Cross and the Greek government.

W1229. Papandreou, Georgios A. **Hē apeleutherōsis tēs Hellados.** [The liberation of Greece.] Athens, 1948. Mainly speeches and memoranda by the Greek prime minister at the time of liberation.

W1230. Leeper, Sir Reginald. **When Greek meets Greek.** London, 1950. Statement of British policy in Greece during and after World War II, by the British ambassador in Athens during the Greek crisis.

W1231. Alexander, H. R. G., viscount of Tunis. **Report by the supreme Allied commander, Mediterranean, to the combined chiefs of staff on Greece, 12th December 1944 to 9th May 1945.** London, 1949.

W1232. Woodhouse, Christopher M. **Apple of discord: a survey of recent Greek politics in their international setting.** London, 1948. By a representative of British headquarters among the Greek resistance army. Important as first-hand source.

W1233. McNeill, William Hardy. **The Greek dilemma: war and aftermath.** Philadelphia and N.Y., 1947. Well informed and objective; therefore, extremely important.

W1234. Noel-Baker, Francis E. **Greece: the whole story.** London, 1946. Very brief, popular resumé of events, by an Englishman sympathetic to Greece.

W1235. Capell, Richard. **Simiomata: a Greek note book, 1944–1945.** London, 1946. The first Greek civil war, as seen by an eyewitness. Of topical interest.

W1236. Voigt, Fritz A. **The Greek sedition.** London, 1949.

W1237. Smothers, Frank, William H. McNeill, and Elizabeth D. McNeill. **Report on the Greeks.** N.Y., 1948. [Twentieth Century Fund.] Investigation of the second Greek civil war by U. S. observers.

W1238. Stavrianos, Leften S. **Greece: American dilemma and opportunity.** Chicago, 1952. Important study of background of the Greek crisis and possible solutions.

W1239. U. S. Library of Congress. **War and postwar Greece: an analysis based on**

Greek writings. By Floyd A. Spencer. Washington, 1952.

W1240. Kousoulas, Dimitrios G. The price of freedom: Greece in world affairs, 1939–1953. Syracuse, N.Y., 1953. Important for account of Communist activities in Greece and the civil wars. Rightist orientation.

W1241. Moyal, Maurice. "Greece and her neighbors." World affairs, 5 (Apr. 1951): 192–99.

HISTORIES OF SPECIAL AREAS

The Islands

W1242. Michaēlidēs-Nouaros, M. Historia tēs nēsou Karpathou. [History of the island of Carpathos.] 4 v. Athens, 1940–50.

W1243. Argenti, Philip P. The occupation of Chios by the Venetians (1694). London, 1935.

W1244. ———. The massacres of Chios, described in contemporary diplomatic reports. London, 1932.

W1245. ———. The expedition of Colonel Fabvier to Chios, described in contemporary diplomatic reports. London, 1933.

W1246. ———. Chius liberata: or, the occupation of Chios by the Greeks in 1912, as described in contemporary documents. London, 1933.

W1247. Vlastos, Alexandros M. Chiaka: historia tēs nēsou Chiou. [Chiaca: history of the island of Chios.] 2 v. Ermoupolis, 1840. Important for period of the Greek Revolution.

W1248. Stillman, William J. The Cretan insurrection of 1866–7–8. N.Y., 1874. Interesting eyewitness account by the U. S. consul at Canea.

W1249. Mamalakis, Iōannēs. Ho agōnas tou 1866–1869 gia tēn henōsē tēs Krētēs. [The struggle of 1866–1869 for union with Crete.] 2 v. Thessaloniki, 1935–47.

W1250. Zampelios, Spyridon. Historia tōn epanastaseōn tēs Krētēs. [History of the revolutions of Crete.] Ed. and completed by J. Kondylakēs. Athens, 1897. Covers to the Greek Revolution of 1821.

W1251. Tsirintanēs, Nikolaos. He politikē kai diplomatikē historia tēs en Krētēi ethnikēs epanastaseōs 1866–1868. [Political and diplomatic history of the national revolution in Crete.] 3 v. Athens, 1950–51. Important, well documented.

W1252. Dutkowski, Jean S. L'occupation de la Crète (1897–1909): une expérience d'administration internationale d'un territoire. Paris, 1952.

W1253. Hill, Sir George F. A history of Cyprus. V. 4, The Ottoman province: the British colony, 1571–1948. Cambridge, Eng., 1952.

W1254. Ward, Adolphus W. "Greece and the Ionian Islands, 1832–1864." The Cambridge history of British foreign policy, ed. by A. W. Ward and G. P. Gooch, v. 2 (Cambridge, Eng., 1922), pp. 583–620.

W1255. Kairophylas, Kostas. Hē Heptanēsos hypo tous Venetous. [The Ionian Islands under the Venetians.] Athens, 1948.

W1256. Zōēs, Leonidas C. Historia tēs Zakynthou. [History of Zante.] Athens, 1957.

W1257. Lignos, Antonios. Historia tēs nēsou Hydras. [History of the island of Hydra.] 3 v. Athens, 1946–53.

W1258. Drakakēs, Andreas. Hē Syros epi tourkokratias. [Syros under Turkish domination.] 2 v. Syros, 1948.

The Mainland

W1259. Sakellariou, Michaēl B. Hē Peloponnēsos kata tēn deuteran tourkokratian (1715–1821). [The Peloponnesus during the second Turkish domination (1715–1821).] Athens, 1939. Important, especially for economic and social history.

W1260. Meletopoulos, Iōannēs. Peiraïka. [The Piraeus.] Athens, 1945.

W1261. Vakalopoulos, Apostolos E. Historia tēs Thessalonikēs, 315 p. Ch.–1912. [History of Thessalonica, 315 B.C.–1912.] Thessaloniki, 1947.

W1262. Vasdravellis, Iōannēs. Hē Thessalonikē kata ton agōna tēs anexartēsias. [Thessalonica during the struggle for independence.] Thessaloniki, 1946.

W1263. Svoronos, Nicolas G. Salonique et Cavalla, 1686–1792. Paris, 1951.

W1264. Lascaris, Michael T. La révolution grecque vue de Salonique. Thessaloniki, 1943.

W1265. ———. Salonique à fin du XVIIIe siècle d'après les rapports consulaires français. Athens, 1939.

W1266. Geōrgiou, Elias P. Historia kai synhetairismos tōn Ampelakiōn. [History and cooperative of Ampelakia.] Athens, 1951.

W1267. Kordatos, Gianēs. T'Ampelakia kai ho mythos ghia ton synhetairismo tous. [Ampelakia and the myth concerning their cooperative.] Athens, 1955.

HISTORIES OF SPECIAL TOPICS

Diplomatic History

W1268. Helmreich, Ernst C. The diplomacy of the Balkan wars, 1912–1913. Cambridge, Mass., 1938. Based on documentary evidence.

W1269. Cassavetti, Demetrius J. Hellas and the Balkan wars. London, 1914. Best account, though with a pro-Greek slant, of Greece's part in the struggle to drive out the Turks from Europe.

W1270. Aspreas, Geōrgios K. Politikē historia tēs neōteras Hellados, 1821–1921. [Political history of modern Greece, 1821–

1921.] 3 v. Athens, 1922–28. Important for details of Greece's inside story which are not available elsewhere.

W1271. Driault, Edouard, and Michel Lhéritier. **Histoire diplomatique de la Grèce de 1821 à nos jours.** 5 v. Paris, 1925–26. An impressive work of scholarship, brilliantly written, but must be used with caution. Bibliography.

W1272. Lascaris, Stamati. **Diplomatikē historia tēs Hellados, 1821–1914.** [Diplomatic history of Greece, 1821–1914.] Athens, 1947.

W1273. Lascaris, Michaël. **To anatolikon zētēma, 1800–1923.** [The eastern question, 1800–1923.] V. 1, pts. 1 and 2. Thessaloniki, 1948–55. A scholarly treatment of the period to 1878.

W1274. Crawley, Charles W. **The question of Greek independence: a study of British policy in the Near East, 1821–1833.** Cambridge, Eng., 1930. Contains good bibliography.

W1275. Vournas, Tasos. **To hellēniko 1848.** [The Greek 1848.] Athens, 1953. Important.

W1276. Prevelakēs, Eleutherios. **British policy towards the change of dynasty in Greece, 1862–1863.** Athens, 1953. Based on Foreign Office and other archival material.

W1277. Lascaris, Stamati. **La politique extérieure de la Grèce avant et après le Congrès de Berlin.** Paris, 1924. Important. Good bibliography.

W1278. Lee, Dwight E. **Great Britain and the Cyprus convention policy of 1878.** See *S267*.

W1279. Stickney, Edith P. **Southern Albania or northern Epirus in European international affairs, 1919–1923.** Stanford, 1926.

W1280. Abbott, George F. **Turkey, Greece, and the great powers: a study in friendship and hate.** N.Y., 1917.

W1281. Brailsford, Henry N. **Macedonia: its races and their future.** London, 1906. Important for early period, though with a pro-Bulgarian slant.

W1282. Christides, Christ. **Le camouflage macédonien à la lumière des faits et des chiffres.** Athens, 1949. This and *W1283–1284* are valuable for the statistical information and the Greek policy regarding Macedonia.

W1283. Pallis, Alexander A. **Macedonia and the Macedonians.** London, 1949.

W1284. Zotiades, George B. **The Macedonian controversy.** Thessaloniki, 1954.

W1285. Vlachos, Nikolaos B. **To makedonikon hos phasis tou anatolikou zetematos, 1878–1908.** [The Macedonian question as a phase of the eastern question, 1878–1908.] Athens, 1935. Most important work on the subject by a Greek.

W1286. Barker, Elizabeth. **Macedonia.** London, 1950. Brief but impartial presentation of the problem of the Macedonian Slavs

and relations of the neighboring states, including World War II developments.

W1287. Naltsas, Christophoros. **To makedonikon zētēma kai hē sovietikē politikē.** [The Macedonian question and Soviet policy.] Thessaloniki, 1954.

W1288. Zakythēnos, Dionysos A. **La Grèce et les Balkans.** Athens, 1947. Deals with Greece's political orientation, especially during the period of World War II and after.

W1289. Hadsel, Winifred N. **American policy toward Greece.** N.Y., 1947.

Domestic History

W1290. Kaltchas, Nicholas S. **Introduction to the constitutional history of modern Greece.** N.Y., 1940. Only work on the subject in English. Good, despite gaps.

W1291. Zorbas, N.K. **Apomnēmoneumata.** [Memoirs.] Athens, 1925. Important personal history of the leader of the Goudi revolution.

W1292. Apostolopoulos, N. **Ho hellēnikos monarchismos, 1915–17.** [Greek monarchism, 1915–17.] Athens, 1922. The Greek domestic crisis, from the Venizelist point of view.

W1293. Pipinelēs, Takēs N. **Hē monarchia en Helladi.** [The monarchy in Greece.] Athens, 1932. Valuable for the royalist point of view.

W1294. Dousmanēs, Viktor. **Hē esoterikē opsis tēs mikrasiatikēs emplokēs.** [The domestic aspect of the Asia Minor imbroglio.] Athens, 1928. The Constantinist point of view, by the chief of the Greek general staff.

W1295. ———. **Apomnēmoneumata.** [Memoirs.] Athens, 1946. Constantinist.

W1296. Metaxas, Iōannēs. **Historia tou ethnikou dichasmou kai tēs mikrasiatikēs katastrophēs.** See *W1197*.

W1297. Ventērēs, Geōrgios. **Hē Hellas tou 1910–1920.** See *W1178*.

W1298. Mazarakēs-Ainian, Alexandros. **Apomnēmoneumata.** [Memoirs.] Athens, 1948. Venizelist.

See also biographies of various Greek leaders—Constantine, Venizelos, Plasteras, etc.

Economic and Social History

W1299. Daniēlidēs, D. I. **Hē neohellēnikē koinōnia kai oikonomia.** [Modern Greek society and economy.] V. 1, pt. 1. Athens, 1934. Important, penetrating study devoted to historical conditions of Greece's socio-economic development.

W1300. Svoronos, Nicolas G. **Le commerce de Salonique au XVIIIᵉ siècle.** Paris, 1952.

W1301. Levandis, John A. **The Greek**

foreign debt and the great powers, 1821–1898. N.Y., 1944.

W1302. Fairchild, Henry P. **Greek immigration to the United States.** New Haven, 1911.

W1303. Saloutos, Theodore. **They remember America: the story of the repatriated Greek Americans.** See *AB512.*

W1304. Sweet-Escott, Bickham. **Greece: a political and economic survey, 1939–1953.** London, 1954. Informative and objective, with a few errors in the political section.

W1305. Food and Agriculture Organization of the United Nations. **Report of the FAO mission for Greece.** Washington, 1947.

W1306. United Nations Relief and Rehabilitation Administration. **Operational analysis papers no. 20: industrial rehabilitation in Greece.** London, 1947.

W1307. ——. **Operational analysis papers no. 25: post-war public finance in Greece.** London, 1947.

W1308. U. S. Economic Cooperation Administration. **Second report to Congress on assistance to Greece and Turkey.** Washington, 1948.

W1309. ——. **Fourth report to Congress on assistance to Greece and Turkey.** Washington, 1948.

W1310. ——. **Fifth report to Congress on assistance to Greece and Turkey.** Washington, 1949.

W1311. ——. **Greece: country study.** Washington, 1949.

W1312. ——. **Country data book: Greece.** Washington, 1950.

W1313. International Labor Office. **Labor problems in Greece: report of the mission to Greece, October-November, 1947.** Geneva, 1949.

W1314. Allbaugh, Leland G. **Crete: a case study of an underdeveloped area.** Princeton, 1953. Very thorough study of an area typical of much of Greece. Statistical tables; bibliography.

W1315. Polyzos, Nicos J. **Essai sur l'émigration grecque: étude démographique, économique et sociale.** Paris, 1947.

Cultural History

W1316. Hadjimichali, Angeliki. **L'art populaire grec.** Athens, 1937.

W1317. ——. **La maison grecque.** Athens, 1949.

W1318. Chaconas, Stephen G. **Adamantios Korais: a study in Greek nationalism.** N.Y., 1942.

W1319. Chassiotis, G. **L'instruction publique chez les grecs.** Paris, 1881.

W1320. Gennadius, J. **A sketch of the history of education in Greece.** Edinburgh, 1925.

W1321. Dēmaras, Kōnstantinos. **Historia tēs neohellēnikēs logotechnias.** [History of

modern Greek literature.] 2 v. Athens, 1948. Most up-to-date work on the subject.

W1322. Baud-Bovy, Samuel. **Poésie de la Grèce moderne.** Lausanne, 1946.

W1323. Dalven, Rae, tr. and ed. **Modern Greek poetry.** N.Y., 1949.

W1324. Tripanis, C. A., ed. **Medieval and modern Greek poetry: an anthology.** London, 1951. Useful introduction in English.

W1325. Jenkins, Romily. **Dionysius Solomós.** Cambridge, Eng., 1940. Biography and literary evaluation of Greece's national poet.

W1326. Sherrard, Philip. **The marble threshing floor: studies in modern Greek poetry.** London, 1956. Important for psychological climate of Greece in the 19th and 20th centuries. Discusses the poetry of Solomós, Palamas, Cavafis, Sikelianos, and Seferis.

W1327. Argenti, Philip P., and Herbert J. Rose. **The folk-lore of Chios.** 2 v. Cambridge, Eng., 1949.

W1328. Bourboulis, Photinē. **Studies in the history of modern Greek story motives.** Thessaloniki, 1953.

BIOGRAPHIES

W1329. Lamprinos, G. **Morphes tou eikosi-hena.** [Personalities of 1821.] 4th ed., Athens, 1956. Biographies of leaders of the Greek Revolution, with a leftist slant.

W1330. Photiadēs, D. **Karaiskakēs.** Athens, 1956. Greece's national hero who fell in the battle of Athens (May, 1827).

W1331. Bower, Leonard, and Gordon Bolitho. **Otho I, king of Greece: a biography.** London, 1939. Useful for Greece's domestic affairs during the period 1832–62.

W1332. Evangelidēs, Tryphon E. **Historia tou Othōnos, basileōs tēs Hellados (1832–1862).** [History of Otho, king of Greece (1832–1862).] Athens, 1893.

W1333. Christmas, Walter. **King George of Greece.** Tr. from Danish by A. G. Chater. London, 1914.

W1334. Gatopoulos, D. **Geōrgios A'-ho dēmokratēs basileus.** [George I, the democratic king.] Athens, 1946.

W1335. Pournaras, Dēmētrios. **Charilaos Trikoupēs.** 2nd ed., 2 v., Athens, 1954. Good biography of Greece's leading statesman of the late 19th century.

W1336. Hibben, Paxton. **Constantine I and the Greek people.** N.Y., 1920. Sympathetic account of the king's policy during World War I.

W1337. Maccas, Léon. **Constantin Ier, roi des Hellènes.** Paris, 1917.

W1338. Gibbons, Herbert A. **Venizelos.** 2nd ed., Boston, 1923. Well-written biography of the Greek statesman, important for Greek affairs during World War I and its aftermath. *W1339–1343* are also useful for the same subject.

W1339. Alastos, Doros. **Venizelos: patriot, statesman, revolutionary.** See *AF343.*

W1340. Chester, Samuel B. **Life of Venizelos.** London, 1921.

W1341. Price, Crawfurd. **Venizelos and the war.** London, 1917.

W1342. Kerofilas, C. **Eleftherios Venizelos: his life and work.** Tr. by B. Barstow. London, 1915.

W1343. Seligman, Vincent J. **The victory of Venizelos: a study of Greek politics, 1910–1918.** London, 1920.

W1344. Gatopoulos, Dēmetrios. **Andreas Michalakopoulos (1875–1938).** Athens, 1947. Valuable for the Greek political scene during the period after World War I.

W1345. Peponēs, Iōannēs A. **Nikolaos Plastēras sta gegonota 1909–1945.** [Nicholas Plastiras in the events of 1909–1945.] 2 v. Athens, 1947.

W1346. Theologos, Nikolaos. **Alexandros Papagos.** Athens, 1949. Important for World War II and the post-war Greek crisis.

W1347. Pipinelēs, Panagiōtēs N. **Geōrgios B'.** Athens, 1951. Biography of George II.

W1348. Vouros, G. **Panaghēs Tsaldarēs, 1867–1936.** Athens, 1956. Biography of the anti-Venizelist leader, important for background of restoration of monarchy in 1935.

PERIODICALS

W1349. Neos hellēnomnēmōn. [Modern Greek recorder.] Athens, 1904–27. (Quarterly.)

W1350. Byzantis. Athens, 1909–12. (Irregular.) This and the above include articles on Grecian history of the post-1204 period.

W1351. Epetēris Hetaireias Byzantinōn Spoudōn. [Yearbook of the Society for Byzantine Studies.] Athens, 1924 ff. Contains an impressive number of articles on early modern Greece (post-Byzantine and Turkish periods), all written in Greek, as well as a fairly complete bibliography of Greek works on medieval and modern Greece. Publication was interrupted briefly during World War I.

W1352. Byzantinisch-neugriechische Jahrbücher. Berlin, 1920–25; Athens, 1926 ff. (Irregular.) More international in scope than the above. The circumstances during and after World War II interfered with the regular appearance of this valuable journal.

W1353. Hellēnika. Athens, 1928 ff. (Semiannual.) Begun under the editorship of Professors C. Amantos and S. Kougheas, and devoted to Greek history of all periods, this journal was resumed after the war under direction of Prof. Linos Politēs of the Aristotelian University of Thessaloniki, with sponsorship of the Society of Macedonian Studies. Has published a number of articles in western European languages.

W1354. Deltion. [Bulletin.] Athens, 1883 ff. (Irregular.) Published by the Historical and Ethnological Society of Greece [Historikē kai Ethnologikē Hetaireia tēs Hellados], both in its old series (v. 1–9) and the new (after 1928). Includes articles on early modern Greece.

Important historical and archival material can be found in several periodicals of broader scope, such as the following (*W1355–1358*).

W1355. Athena. Athens, 1889 ff.

W1356. Nea hestia. [New hearth.] Athens, 1927 ff.

W1357. Eleuthera grammata. [Free letters.] Athens, 1950 ff. (Irregular.)

W1358. L'hellénisme contemporain. Athens, 1935 ff. (Monthly.)

See also the several theological, political, economic, and folklorist journals.

There are many local or regional publications that contain articles and documents pertaining to the history of each area. The following list includes the most important of these journals which continued in the interwar and postwar period.

W1359. Archeion Pontou. Athens, 1928 ff. (Irregular.) Cultural and historical heritage of the refugees from Pontus.

W1360. Archeion Samou. Athens, 1946 ff. For Samos.

W1361. Archeion tou Thrakikou laographikou kai glōssikou thēsaurou. Athens, 1934 ff. (Irregular.) For Thrace.

W1362. Dōdekanēsiakē epitheōrēsis. Athens, 1947 ff. (Monthly.) For the Dodecanese.

W1363. Epistēmonikē epetēris tēs Philosophikēs Scholēs. [Scholarly yearbook of the School of Philosophy.] Athens, 1925 ff. [University of Athens.] (Irregular.)

W1364. Epistēmonikē epetēris tēs Philosophikēs Scholēs. [Scholarly yearbook of the School of Philosophy.] Thessaloniki, 1927 ff. [University of Salonika.] (Irregular.)

W1365. Epetēris hetaerias krētikōn spoudōn. Athens, 1938. (Irregular.) For Crete.

W1366. Hēmerologion tēs megalēs Hellados. [Almanac of great Greece.] Athens, 1922 ff. (Annual.) Varied material.

W1367. Heptanēsiaka phylla. Zakinthos, 1945 ff. For the Ionian Islands.

W1368. Kerkyraïka chronika. Corfu, 1951 ff. For Corfu.

W1369. Krētika chronika. Herakleion, 1947 ff. For Crete.

W1370. Kypriakai spoudai. Nicosia, 1937 ff. For Cyprus.

W1371. Mikrasiatika chronika. Athens, 1938 ff. For the heritage of refugees from Asia Minor.

W1372. Naxiakon archeion. Naxos, 1947 ff. (Monthly.) For Naxos.

W1373. Serraïka chronika. Athens, 1938 ff. (Irregular.) For Serres and vicinity.

W1374. Thessalika chronika. Athens, 1930 ff. (Irregular.) For Thessaly.

W1375. Thrakika. Athens, 1928–44. (Quarterly.) Eastern and western Thrace.

SECTION X

Russia and the Soviet Union
(*Including the Russian Empire in Asia*)

FRITZ T. EPSTEIN

As in the original *Guide,* emphasis here is on the period since the beginning of the 18th century, when Russia became a factor in European politics. However, within the last three decades Russian research has made such strides in western Europe and the United States that there is, in many respects, no longer the lack of "works of first-rate importance or of reasonable soundness of scholarship" regretted in the 1931 edition. Soviet historical science, in spite of its well-known limitations in interpretation and its not infrequent tergiversations dictated by shifts in the Communist party line, has produced and is increasingly producing an impressive number of historical bibliographies, source publications, and monographs which often are the latest word on a particular subject. Inasmuch as such publications frequently contain ample up-to-date bibliographical information, an effort has been made to include the latest Soviet presentation along with the best non-Russian work on a given topic. Since knowledge of the Russian language is still the privilege of a very limited number of historians outside the Soviet Union, a special effort has been made to list bibliographical and analytical articles in western languages on the development of Soviet historical science (or the work of Russian émigrés in their native language), thus eliminating space for many other worthy items.

The task of the compiler of this section was considerably facilitated by the existence of **(X1)** Charles Morley, **Guide to research in Russian history** (Syracuse, 1951), which should be consulted by anyone desiring to familiarize himself with the basic research materials on Russian history and their availability in United States libraries. Systematic basic coverage has necessitated a certain amount of duplication, since Morley's *Guide* serves the same purpose as this section. Emphasis here, however, is on materials published during the eight years since Morley's work appeared.

621

BIBLIOGRAPHIES, LIBRARIES, AND MUSEUMS

Bibliographies

General

X2. Kerner, Robert J. "The foundations of Slavic bibliography." **The papers of the Bibliographical Society of America,** 10 (1916): 3–39.

X3. Sokurova, M. V. **Obshchie bibliografii russkikh knig grazhdanskoi pechati, 1708–1955.** [General bibliographies of Russian books in regular print, 1708–1955.] 2nd ed., Leningrad, 1956. This and the following counterpart are bibliographies of Russian bibliography.

X4. ——. **Obshchie bibliografii russkikh periodicheskikh izdanii, 1703–1954.** [General bibliographies of Russian periodicals, 1703–1954.] Leningrad, 1956.

X5. Zdobnov, Nikolai V. **Istoriia russkoi bibliografii ot drevnego perioda do nachala XX veka.** [History of Russian bibliography from ancient times to the beginning of the 20th century.] 2 v. Moscow, 1944–47. 2nd ed., 1 v., 1951.

X6. U. S. Library of Congress. **Monthly index of Russian accessions.** Washington, 1948 ff. Monthly account of new material received from the U.S.S.R. by the Library of Congress and other United States research libraries. All titles of books and articles translated into English. Elaborate subject guides.

Historical: Russian History in General

Hardly accessible Russian historical bibliographies of the 19th century (listed in Morley's *Guide*) are omitted. Instead, in an effort to present a more comprehensive coverage of modern literature, recent bibliographical items are included.

X7. Kerner, Robert J. **Northeastern Asia: a selected bibliography . . . of the relations of China, Russia, and Japan . . . in Oriental and European languages.** 2 v. Berkeley, 1939. Gives special attention to Korea, Manchuria, Mongolia, and eastern Siberia. Review, O. Lattimore, *Am. hist. rev.,* 45 (July 1940): 883.

X8. Shvedova, Olga I. **Istoriki SSSR: ukazatel' pechatnykh spiskov ikh trudov.** [The Russian historians: list of their bibliographies.] Moscow, 1941. Historians from 18th to beginning of the 20th century.

X9. Gosudarstvennaia Publichnaia Istoricheskaia Biblioteka. **Bibliografiia russkoi bibliografii po istorii SSSR: annotirovannyi perechen' bibliograficheskikh ukazatelei izdannykh do 1917 goda.** [Bibliography of bibliography of Russian history: annotated list of bibliographies published before 1917.] Moscow, 1957. Review, M. M. Cheremisina, *Istoriia SSSR,* 1958, p. 164.

X10. Verevkina, A. N. "Bibliograficheskie ukazateli zarubezhnoi istoricheskoi literatury o Sovetskom Soiuze." [Bibliographies of foreign historical literature on the Soviet Union.] **Istoriia SSSR,** 1958, pp. 221–29.

X11. Kaufman, Isaak M. **Russkie biograficheskie i bio-bibliograficheskie slovari.** [Russian biographical and bio-bibliographical dictionaries.] 2nd ed., Moscow, 1955.

X12. Tikhomirov, Mikhail N., and Sergei Aleksandrovich. **Kurs istochnikovedeniia istorii SSSR.** [Sources for the history of the U.S.S.R.] 2 v. Moscow, 1940. Critical survey of the most important written sources from earliest times to the end of the 19th century. A comprehensive handbook.

X13. Zaleski, Eugène. **La Russie.** 2 v. Paris, 1956–57. Chronology and sketch 1725–1850; bibliography after 1850. Review, M. K. Dziewanowski, *Journal of central European affairs,* 17 (Jan. 1958): 412.

X14. "Verzeichnisse des . . . Schrifttums 1939–1952 zur Geschichte Osteuropas und Südosteuropas." **Forschungen zur osteuropäischen Geschichte,** 1 (1954): 251–316, 3 (1956): 99–281, 4 (1956): 219–59, 5 (1957): 119–62.

X15. Simon, Konstantin R., ed. **Istoriia SSSR: ukazatel' sovetskoi literatury za 1917–1952 gg.** [History of the U.S.S.R.: bibliography of Soviet literature.] 2 v. Moscow, 1956–58. The basic Soviet historical bibliography, from earliest times to 1861, on the period of capitalism (1861–1917) and on the Soviet period. Review, C. E. Black, *Am. hist. rev.,* 63 (Oct. 1957): 129; Iu. S. Afanas'er et al., *Istoriia SSSR,* 1959, pp. 205–209.

Historical: Limited to Soviet Period

X16. Roberts, Henry L., ed. **Foreign affairs bibliography: a selected and annotated list of books on international relations, 1942–1952.** N.Y., 1955. A continuation of the lists in *Foreign affairs bibliography, 1919–1932* (1933) and *Foreign affairs bibliography, 1932–1942* (1945). Contains works dealing with the Soviet Union and the Ukraine.

X17. Meissner, Boris. **Russland-Bibliographie: die Grundordnung des Staates.** 2 pts. Hamburg, 1950.

X18. U. S. Department of State. **Soviet bibliography.** May 6, 1949-June 17, 1953. Washington, 1949–53. Best comprehensive coverage for period indicated.

X19. Mehnert, Klaus, ed. **Die Sovet-Union, 1917–1932.** Königsberg, 1933. Classified and annotated list of 1,900 German books and articles on the Soviet Union and communism.

X20. Grierson, Philip. **Books on Soviet Russia, 1917–1942.** London, 1943. Books and pamphlets published in Great Britain. Supplements covering the period since 1942 are an annual feature of the *Slavonic and east European review* beginning with v. 24 (1946). The United States counterpart is a bibliography of books, pamphlets, and articles, published annually for the foregoing year, in the quarterly *Russian review* (N.Y., 1941 ff.).

X21. U. S. Library of Congress. **Russian, Ukrainian and Belorussian newspapers, 1917–1953.** Comp. by Paul L. Horecky. Washington, 1953. Union list of Soviet newspapers in United States libraries.

Libraries

Russian collections in United States libraries—especially those of the Library of Congress, New York Public Library, and the libraries of Harvard, Columbia, and Stanford—are described in Ch. 1 of Morley's *Guide*.

X22. Kerner, Robert J. **Slavic Europe.** Cambridge, Mass., 1918. About 1,700 selected titles, mostly in western languages, comprising history, languages, and literatures. Essentially a catalog of Harvard University Library holdings at time of publication.

X23. Sworakowski, Witold S. **The Hoover Library collection on Russia.** Stanford, 1954.

X24. Bibliothèque de Documentation Internationale Contemporaine (Vincennes, France). **Catalogue méthodique du fonds russe.** Paris, 1932. Especially valuable for Russia's participation in World War I and the early years of Bolshevik rule.

X25. Russkii Zagranichnyi Istoricheskii Arkhiv. **Bibliografiia russkoi revoliutsii i grazhdanskoi voiny (1917–1921).** [Bibliography of the Russian revolution and the civil war (1917–1921).] Comp. by S. P. Postnikov. Prague, 1938. About 6,000 titles from catalog of the library of the Russian Historical Archives Abroad at Prague. Review, F. T. Epstein, *Am. hist. rev.*, 44 (Jan. 1939): 449.

Archives and Museums

X26. Epstein, Fritz T. "Archives administration in the Soviet Union." **The American archivist,** 20 (Apr. 1957): 131–45. History of archival organization under the Soviets.

X27. Cherepnin, L. V. **Russkie feodal'nye arkhivy XIV–XV vekov.** [Russian feudal archives of the 14th and 15th centuries.] 2 v. Moscow and Leningrad, 1948–51. Sources on land tenure in medieval Russia.

X28. Valk, Sigizmund. **Sovetskaia arkheografiia.** Moscow, 1948. Survey of documentary sources published under the Soviets.

X29. Arkhivnoe delo. [Archival work.] Moscow, 1923 ff. (Irregular.) A leading periodical on questions of archival science. See F. T. Epstein, *Archivalische Zeitschrift*, 39 (1930): 282–308.

The two following journals of the Soviet period are devoted mainly to publication of documents.

X30. Krasnyi arkhiv. [Red archives.] 106

issues. Moscow, 1922–41. Materials beginning with the 17th century, with emphasis on Tsarist diplomacy, history of the revolutionary movement, World War I, the revolutions of 1917, and the civil war. For content consult Leonid S. Rubinchek, *A digest of the Krasnyi arkhiv* (Cleveland, 1947), and Leona W. Eisele, *A digest of the Krasnyi arkhiv* (Ann Arbor, 1955), the former dealing with the first 30 issues and the latter with nos. 31–106.

X31. Istoricheskii arkhiv. Moscow, 1955 ff. (Bimonthly.)

X32. Uzunova, N., and M. Fekhner. **Gosudarstvennyi Istoricheskii Muzei.** [The State Historical Museum.] Moscow, 1954.

ENCYCLOPEDIAS AND WORKS OF REFERENCE

General

X33. Entsiklopedicheskii slovar. [Encyclopedic dictionary.] 41 v. St. Petersburg, 1890–1904. 2 suppl. v., 1906–07. New ed., *Novyi entsiklopedicheskii slovar*, v. 1–29 (A–Otto), 1911–16.

X34. Bol'shaia sovetskaia entsiklopediia. [Great Soviet encyclopedia.] 65 v. Moscow, 1926–47. 2nd ed., 1949 ff.

X35. Grosse Sowjet-Enzyklopädie: Union der sozialistischen Sowjetrepubliken. 2 v. Berlin, 1952. Contains the following articles: N. Rubinstein, "Die Entwicklung der Geschichtsforschung in der UdSSR"; N. Rubinstein, "Russland bis zum Ausgang des 18. Jahrh."; S. Dmitriev, "Russland im 19. Jahrh."; I. Razgon, "Russland zu Beginn des 20. Jahrh."; I. Razgon, "Die Sowjetperiode." See also Morley, *Guide*, nos. 41–50.

Special

X36. Strakhovsky, Leonid I., ed. **A handbook of Slavic studies.** Cambridge, Mass., 1949. Includes well-informed contributions on Slavic origins and migrations, Kievan Russia, Muscovite Russia, imperial Russia, the Ukraine, the Soviet Union, and basic bibliographies.

X37. Diplomaticheskii slovar'. [Diplomatic dictionary.] 2 v. Moscow, 1948–50. Reviews, W. Gottlieb, *Soviet studies*, 3 (Oct. 1951): 185 and 3 (Jan. 1952): 318; E. H. Carr, *ibid.*, 3 (Jan. 1952): 316; M. Beloff, *ibid.*, 3 (Apr. 1952): 342. 2nd ed., v. 1 (A–1), Moscow, 1960.

X38. Literaturnaia entsiklopediia. [Encyclopedia of literature.] V. 1–9, 11. Moscow, 1929–44. Reprint, Ann Arbor, 1948–49. Published by the Communist Academy.

X39. Sibirskaia sovetskaia entsiklopediia. [Soviet encyclopedia of Siberia.] 3 v. Moscow, 1929–32. Extends to letter N.

X40. Entsiklopediia ukrainoznavstva.

[Encyclopedia of Ukrainian matters.] Ed. by Zenon Kuzelia and Volodymyr Kubijovych. 3 v. Munich and N.Y., 1949–52. "The best single source of information concerning the second largest community of Slavs." G. W. Simpson, *Jour. cent. Europ. aff.*, 15 (Jan. 1956): 438.

See also Morley, *Guide*, nos. 51–56. For biographical dictionaries and collective biographies see under Biographies below.

GEOGRAPHIES, GAZETTEERS, AND ATLASES

X41. U. S. Library of Congress. **Soviet geography: a bibliography.** Washington, 1951. Selected bibliography containing some 4,000 titles of materials published after 1900.

X42. Meckelein, Wolfgang. **Ortsumbenennungen und Neugründungen im europäischen Teil der Sowjetunion: nach dem Stand der Jahre 1910/1938/1951, mit einem Nachtrag für Ostpreussen 1953.** Berlin, 1955.

X43. Berg, Lev S. **Natural regions of the U.S.S.R.** N.Y., 1950. "A fundamental treatise." B. Zaborski, *Russ. rev.*, 11 (Apr. 1952): 121.

X44. Balzak, S. S., and others, eds. **Economic geography of the U.S.S.R.** N.Y., 1949. Factual information and political propaganda. Review, C. A. Halstead, *Soviet studies*, 4 (Apr. 1953): 443.

X45. Shabad, Theodore. **Geography of the USSR: a regional survey.** N.Y., 1951. Special attention to political and economic geography.

X46. Savitskii, Petr N. "Geopoliticheskie zametki po russkoi istorii." [Geopolitical remarks on Russian history.] George Vernadsky, **Nachertanie russkoi istorii** [Outline of Russian history], (Prague, 1927), pp. 234–60.

X47. Berg, Lev S. **Ocherk istorii russkoi geograficheskoi nauki.** [Sketch of the history of Russian geographical science.] Moscow, 1929. [Akademiia SSSR, Komissiia po Istorii Znanii, Trudy, 4.]

X48. Kerner, Robert J. "Russian expansion to America: its bibliographical foundations." **The papers of the Bibliographical Society of America,** 25 (1931): 111–29.

X49. Sokol, Anthony E. "Russian expansion and exploration in the Pacific." **American Slavic and east European review,** 11 (1952): 85–105.

X50. Andreev, Aleksandr I., ed. **Russian discoveries in the Pacific and in North America in the eighteenth and nineteenth centuries: a collection of materials.** Ann Arbor, 1952. Tr. of *Russkie otkrytiia v Tikhom Okeane i Severnoi Amerike v XVIII–XIX vekakh* (Moscow, 1944).

X51. Mehnert, Klaus. **The Russians in Hawaii, 1804–1819.** Honolulu, 1939.

X52. Bazilevich, Konstantin V., and others,

eds. **Atlas istorii SSSR.** 2 v. Moscow, 1939–48.

See also Morley, *Guide*, nos. 57–73.

ANTHROPOLOGICAL WORKS

X53. Zarubin, Ivan I. **Spisok narodnostei SSSR.** [List of the nationalities of the U.S.S.R.] Leningrad, 1927. [Akademiia Nauk SSSR, Komissiia po Izucheniiu Plemennogo Sostava Naseleniia SSSR i Sopredel'nykh Stran, Trudy, 13.]

X54. Hrdlička, Aleš. **The peoples of the Soviet Union.** Washington, 1942. [Smithsonian Institution, War background studies, 3.] Brief but authoritative survey.

X55. Wurm, Stefan. **Turkic peoples of the USSR: their historical background, their languages and the development of Soviet linguistic policy.** London, 1954.

X56. Tokarev, Sergei A. **Etnografiia narodov SSSR.** [Ethnography of the peoples of the U.S.S.R.] Moscow, 1958.

X57. Cherepnin, L. V. **Russkaia etnografiia do XIX veka.** [Russian ethnography to the 19th century.] Moscow, 1957.

X58. Iazyki i istoriia narodnostei krainego severa SSSR. [The languages and history of nationalities of the Far North of the Soviet Union.] Leningrad, 1953. [Leningrad, Universitet, Uchenye zapiski, 157 (Fakul'tet narodov severa, 2).]

X59. Levin, Maksim G., and Leonid P. Potapov, eds. **Narody Sibiri.** [The peoples of Siberia.] Moscow, 1956. A symposium sponsored by the Ethnographical Institute of the Soviet Academy of Sciences.

See also Morley, *Guide*, nos. 281–98.

DEMOGRAPHIC STUDIES

X60. Lorimer, Frank. **The population of the Soviet Union: history and prospects.** Geneva, 1946. A League of Nations publication sponsored by the Princeton Office of Population Research.

X61. Iatsunskii, V. K. "Izmereniia v razmeshchenii naseleniia evropeiskoi Rossii v 1724–1916 gg." [Changes in the distribution of the population of European Russia, 1724–1916.] **Istoriia SSSR,** Mar. 1957, pp. 192–224.

LINGUISTIC WORKS

X62. Jagić, Vatroslav I. **Istoriia slavianskoi filologii.** St. Petersburg (Leningrad), 1910.

X63. Trautmann, Reinhold. **Die slavischen Völker und Sprachen.** Göttingen, 1947; Leipzig, 1948. Introduction by an outstanding German Slavic philologist.

X64. Jakobson, Roman. **Slavic languages: a condensed survey.** 2nd ed., N.Y., 1955.

X65. Matthews, William K. **Languages of the U.S.S.R.** Cambridge, Eng., 1951. The language families and their constituent languages. Extensive bibliographies.

X66. Vasmer, Max. **Russisches etymologisches Wörterbuch.** Heidelberg, 1950 ff. The greatest achievement of Europe's leading contemporary Slavic philologist.

X67. Kochin, G. E. **Materialy dlia terminologicheskogo slovaria drevnei Rossii.** [Materials for a terminological dictionary of old Russia.] Moscow and Leningrad, 1937. An aid for research in social and economic history.

PRINTED COLLECTIONS OF SOURCES

Chronicles and Guides to Chronicles

X68. Russia. Arkheograficheskaia Komissiia. **Polnoe sobranie russkikh lietopisei.** [Complete collection of Russian chronicles.] 25 v., part in 2nd ed. St. Petersburg (Leningrad), 1841–1949.

X69. Likhachev, Dmitrii S. **Russkie letopisi i ikh kul'turno-istoricheskoe znachenie.** [The Russian chronicles and their significance for the history of Russian culture.] Moscow and Leningrad, 1947.

See also Morley, *Guide,* nos. 511–20.

General Sources

Important collections of sources on Russian medieval and early modern history were published in Tsarist Russia after the 1830's by the Arkheograficheskaia Komissiia. These include *X68* and the following (*X70–72*).

X70. **Akty sobrannye v bibliotekakh i arkhivakh rossiiskoi imperii.** [Documents collected in the libraries and archives of the Russian empire.] 4 v. St. Petersburg, 1836. Index, 1838.

X71. **Akty istoricheskie.** [Historical documents.] 5 v. St. Petersburg, 1841–42. Supplement, 12 v., 1846–72.

X72. **Russkaia istoricheskaia biblioteka.** [Russian historical library.] 39 v. St. Petersburg, 1872–1927.

To these sets must be added source publications of two learned societies: the *Chteniia* (*X570*) of the Imperial Society of History and Russian Antiquities of Moscow University, and the *Sbornik* (*X566*) of the Imperial Russian Historical Society, St. Petersburg; and two periodicals principally devoted to publication of sources: *Russkii arkhiv* (*X586*) and *Russkaia starina* (*X585*). See also *Krasnyi arkhiv* (*X30*) and *Istoricheskii arkhiv* (*X31*).

See also Morley, *Guide,* nos. 521–59.

Legal History

X73. Medieval Russian laws. Tr. by George Vernadsky. N.Y., 1947. This selection stresses ties between Russian and Byzantine law. Bibliography.

X74. Akademiia Nauk SSSR, Institut Istorii. **Gramoty Velikogo Novgoroda i Pskova.** [Charters of Greater Novgorod and Pskov.] Ed. by Vasilii G. Geiman and Sigizmund N. Valk. Moscow and Leningrad, 1949.

X75. ――――. **Dukhovnye i dogovornye gramoty velikikh i udel'nykh kniazei XIV–XVI v. v.** [Last wills and treaties of the grand dukes and territorial princes of the 14th to 16th centuries.] Ed. by L. V. Cherepnin. Moscow, 1950.

X76. Syromiatnikov, Boris I., ed. **Zakonodatel'nye akty Petra I. V. 1, Akty o vysshykh gosudarstvennykh ustanovleniiakh.** [Legislative documents of Peter I. V. 1, Documents on the highest government agencies.] Moscow and Leningrad, 1945.

Diplomatic History to 1917

X77. Pamiatniki diplomaticheskikh snoshenii drevnei Rossii s derzhavami inostrannymi. [Monuments of the diplomatic relations of old Russia with foreign powers.] 10 v. St. Petersburg, 1851–71.

X78. Komissiia po Izdaniiu Dokumentov Epokhi Imperializma. **Mezhdunarodnye otnosheniia v epokhu imperializma.** Moscow, 1931 ff. German tr., *Die internationalen Beziehungen im Zeitalter des Imperialismus: Dokumente aus den Archiven der Zarischen und der Provisorischen Regierung.* Berlin, 1931 ff. Intended to cover period 1878–1917 in three series.

X79. Martens, Fedor F. de, ed. **Recueil des traités et conventions conclus par la Russie avec les puissances étrangères.** 15 v. St. Petersburg, 1874–1909. Treaties with Austria, 1648–1878 (v. 1–4); German states, 1656–1888 (v. 5–8); England, 1710–1895 (v. 9–12); and France, 1717–1906 (v. 13–15).

X80. Adamov, Evgenii A., ed. **Sbornik dogovorov Rossii s drugimi gosudarstvami, 1856–1917.** [Collection of Russian treaties with other states, 1856–1917.] Moscow, 1952.

See also Morley, *Guide,* nos. 568–77.

Private Archives

Publications made from private archives before the nationalization of all archival materials include the following.

X81. Arkhiv kniazia F. A. Kurakina. [Archives of Prince F. A. Kurakin.] 10 v. St. Petersburg, 1890–1902.

X82. Arkhiv grafov Mordvinov. [Archives of Count Mordvinov.] 10 v. St. Petersburg, 1901–03.

X83. Arkhiv Raevskikh. [The Raevskii archives.] 5 v. St. Petersburg, 1908–15.

X84. Arkhiv brat'ev Turgenevykh. [Archives of the brothers Turgenev.] 6 v. St. Petersburg, 1911–21.

X85. Arkhiv kniazia Vorontsova. [Archives of Prince Vorontsov.] 40 v. Moscow, 1870–95.

X86. Ostaf'evskii arkhiv kniazei Viazemskikh. [Ostaf'evo archives of the princes Viazemskii.] 8 v. St. Petersburg, 1899–1913.

HISTORIOGRAPHY

Pre-Revolutionary

X87. Ikonnikov, Vladimir S. **Opyt russkoi istoriografii.** [Attempt at a Russian historiography.] 2 v. in 4. Kiev, 1891–1908. A work of stupendous learning, still basic for sources and literature.

X88. Mazour, Anatole G. **Russian historiography.** 2nd ed., Princeton, 1958. Covers from 18th century to the Bolshevik period. Bibliography.

X89. Schelting, Alexander von. **Russland und Europa im russischen Geschichtsdenken.** Bern, 1948. Russian historiography in first half of the 19th century. Review, E. Winter, *Deutsche Literatur-Zeitung*, 74 (Jan. 1953): 34.

X90. Buzeskul, Vladimir P. **Vseobshchaia istoriia i ee predstaviteli v Rossii v XIX i nachale XX veka.** [General history and its representatives in Russia in the 19th and beginning of the 20th century.] 2 v. Leningrad, 1929–31. [Akademiia Nauk SSSR, Komissiia po Istorii Znanii, Trudy, 7.] A non-Marxist evaluation. Review, S. Salomon, *Zeitschrift für osteuropäische Geschichte*, 5 (1931): 417 and 6 (1932): 238.

See also Morley, *Guide*, nos. 770–840.

Soviet Union

Works Published by Soviet Scholars

X91. Akademiia Nauk SSSR, Institut Istorii. **Dvadtsat piat' let istoricheskoi nauki v SSSR.** [Twenty-five years of historical studies in the U.S.S.R.] Ed. by Viacheslav P. Volgin, Evgenii V. Tarle, and Anna M. Pankratova. Moscow and Leningrad, 1942. Of special interest are articles on modern history by Soviet historians.

X92. ——. **Ocherki istorii istoricheskoi nauki v SSSR.** [Sketches on the history of historical science in Russia.] Ed. by Mikhail N. Tikhomirov. V. 1. Moscow, 1955. The most comprehensive Soviet work on historiography. This volume extends to mid-19th century; two more (1861–1917 and the Soviet period) are contemplated. Ch. 12 is devoted to historiography of the Ukrainians, Belorussians, and of Baltic, Caucasian and Central Asian nationalities.

X93. Cherepnin, L. V. **Russkaia istoriografiia do XIX veka. Kurs lektsii.** [Russian

historiography to the 19th century: lectures.] Moscow, 1957.

X94. Stökl, Günther. "Russisches Mittelalter und sowjetische Mediaevistik: Forschungsbericht und bibliographische Übersicht." **Jahrbücher für Geschichte Osteuropas,** n.s. 3 (1955): 1–40. Excellent survey of research on Russian history before 1500 and bibliography for the years 1945–55. Main topics are: the Varangian problem, Soviet archaeology, Kiev and Byzantium, the Khazars, the Tartars, Novgorod, Old Russian literature, the Russian church.

X95. Maksakov, V. V., and M. S. Seleznev. "O publikatsii dokumental'nykh materialov v SSSR." [The publication of documentary material in the U.S.S.R.] **Voprosy istorii,** 1953, pp. 89–104.

X96. Novosel'skii, Aleksei A., and V. A. Kondrat'ev. "O publikatsii istoricheskikh istochnikov v SSSR za 40 let." [Regarding publication of historical sources in Russia during the last 40 years.] **Istoriia SSSR,** 1958, pp. 204–19.

X97. Sidorov, Arkadii L. "Soviet historical science, its problems and achievements." In his **Osnovnye problemy i nekotorye itogi razvitiia sovetskoi istoricheskoi nauki** (Moscow, 1955), pp. 209–73.

X98. Novosel'skii, Aleksei A., and V. I. Shunkov. **La publication des sources historiques en URSS. Izdanie istoricheskikh istochnikov v SSSR.** Moscow, 1955. Text in French and Russian. This and *X97* were prepared for the International Congress of Historical Sciences in Rome.

X99. Udal'cova, Z. V. "Les problèmes fondamentaux de la byzantinologie et la science historique soviétique." **Byzantinoslavica,** 17 (1956): 195–219. On Soviet byzantinistics and the question of the Slavs see also Berthold Rubin, "Die 'Grosse Völkerwanderung' in der sozialökonomischen Sicht der Sowjetunion," *Jahrbücher für Geschichte Osteuropas*, n.s. 5 (1957): 220–56.

X100. Kosminskii, E. A., E. V. Gutnova, and N. A. Sidorova. "Sorok let sovetskoi medievistiki." [Forty years of Soviet medieval studies.] **Voprosy istorii,** no. 11 (1957): 186–205.

X101. Efimov, A. V. "Izuchenie v SSSR novoi istorii za sorok let." [Forty years of research in the USSR on modern history.] **Voprosy istorii,** 1957, pp. 201–20.

Works Published Outside the Soviet Union

X102. Mehnert, Klaus. **Stalin versus Marx: the Stalinist historical doctrine.** London, 1952.

X103. Avtorkhanov, A. (pseud., Aleksandr Uralov). **Polozhenie istoricheskoi nauki v SSSR.** [The situation of historical science in the Soviet Union.] Munich, 1951. [Institute for the Study of History and Institutions of the U.S.S.R., Materials of the conference of the émigré scholars, 3.]

There is no detailed comprehensive work on Soviet historiography in a western language. However, taken together, the following articles (*X104–117*) may serve as a substitute.

X104. Epstein, Fritz T. "Die marxistische Geschichtswissenschaft in der Sovetunion seit 1927." **Jahrbücher für Kultur und Geschichte der Slaven,** n.s. 6 (1930): 78–203.

X105. Salomon, Richard. "Zur Lage der Geschichtswissenschaft in Russland." **Zeitschrift für osteuropäische Geschichte,** 6 (1932): 385–402.

X106. Florovsky, Antoine. "La littérature historique soviétique-russe, 1921–1931." **Bulletin d'information des sciences historiques en Europe orientale,** 6 (1934): 120–86, 7 (1935): 5–111.

X107. Yakobson, Sergius. "Postwar historical research in the Soviet Union." **The annals of the American Academy of Political and Social Science,** 263 (May 1949): 123–33.

X108. Rauch, Georg von. "Grundlinien der sowjetischen Geschichtsforschung im Zeichen des Stalinismus." **Europa-Archiv,** 5 (Oct. 5, 1950): 3383–88, (Oct. 20, 1950): 3423–32, (Nov. 5, 1950): 3489–94.

X109. ———. "Die sowjetische Geschichtsforschung." **Die Welt als Geschichte,** 11 (1951): 249–62.

X110. ———. "Die neue Geschichte in der sowjetischen Geschichtsschreibung der Gegenwart, 1939–1954." **Jahrbücher für Geschichte Osteuropas,** n.s. 3 (1955): 71–83, 105–22.

X111. Jablonowski, Horst. "Die Lage der sowjetrussischen Geschichtswissenschaft nach dem zweiten Weltkriege." **Saeculum,** 2 (1951): 443–64.

X112. ———. "Bericht über die sovetrussische Geschichtswissenschaft in den Jahren 1941–1952." **Historische Zeitschrift,** 180 (1955): 114–48, 346–78. Analyzes editions of sources and critically evaluates literature.

X113. Schlesinger, Rudolf. "Recent Soviet historiography." **Soviet studies,** 1 (Apr. 1950): 293–312; 2 (July 1950): 3–21, (Oct. 1950): 138–62, (Jan. 1951): 265–88.

X114. ———. "Soviet historians before and after the XXth Congress." **Soviet studies,** 8 (Oct. 1956): 157–72.

X115. Mazour, Anatole G., and Herman E. Bateman. "Recent conflicts in Soviet historiography." **Journal of modern history,** 24 (Mar. 1952): 56–68.

X116. Dallin, Alexander. "Recent Soviet historiography." **Problems of communism,** 5 (Nov.-Dec. 1956): 24–30.

X117. Black, Cyril E., ed. **Rewriting Russian history: Soviet interpretations of Russia's**

past. N.Y., 1956. See "History and politics in the Soviet Union," pp. 3–31.

To the above may be added the following (*X118–121*) survey articles on work in the field of Russian history outside Russia.

X118. Halm, Hans. "Achtzig Jahre russischer Geschichtsschreibung ausserhalb Russlands." **Jahrbücher für Geschichte Osteuropas,** n.s. 5 (1957): 9–42. Emphasis on publications since the 1920's.

X119. Amburger, Erik. "Bericht über die Veröffentlichungen zur Geschichte Russlands ausserhalb der Sovetunion 1939–1952." **Historische Zeitschrift,** 183 (Feb. 1957): 132–78.

X120. Leppmann, Wolfgang. "Die russische Geschichtswissenschaft in der Emigration." **Zeitschrift für osteuropäische Geschichte,** 5 (1931): 215–48.

X121. Markert, Werner. "Geschichte Osteuropas." **Geschichte in Wissenschaft und Unterricht,** 8 (Jan. 1957): 53–61. History of German research in the Russian field.

X122. Manning, Clarence A. **A history of Slavic studies in the United States.** Milwaukee, 1957. [Marquette Slavic studies, 3.] Evaluates work in the United States in Russian history.

X123. Doroshenko, Dmytro. **A survey of Ukrainian historiography.** N.Y., 1957. [The annals of the Ukrainian Academy of Arts and Sciences in the United States, 5.] This and the following, which are bound together, comprise "a work of unusual value." J. S. Reshetar, Jr., *Am. Slavic and east Europ. rev.,* 18 (Feb. 1959): 123.

X124. Ohloblyn, Olexander. **Ukrainian historiography, 1917–1956.** N.Y., 1957. [The annals of the Ukrainian Academy of Arts and Sciences in the United States, 6.]

SHORTER GENERAL HISTORIES

X125. Pares, Sir Bernard. **A history of Russia.** Rev. ed., London, 1955. Contains extensive bibliography.

X126. Sumner, Benedict H. **A short history of Russia.** Rev. ed., N.Y., 1949.

X127. Vernadsky, George. **A history of Russia.** 4th ed., New Haven, 1954. Author favors the Eurasian conception. Bibliography.

LONGER GENERAL HISTORIES

Works Published in Russia

Non-Communist

X128. Solov'ev, Sergei M. **Istoriia Rossii s drevnieishikh vremen.** [History of Russia from the earliest times.] 2nd ed., 7 v., St. Petersburg, [1896].

X129. Kliuchevskii, Vasilii O. **A history of Russia.** 4 v. N.Y., 1911–26. Tr., by C. J. Hogarth, of *Kurs russkoi istorii* (5 v., Moscow and St. Petersburg, 1904–21). In several respects, especially in its terminology, this is an unsatisfactory translation of a classic in Russian historical writing. The German translations, *Geschichte Russlands* (4 v., Stuttgart and Berlin, 1925–26) and *Russische Geschichte von Peter dem Grossen bis Nikolaus I* (2 v., Zürich, 1945) are preferable. There is a U. S. reprint of *Kurs russkoi istorii* (Ann Arbor, 1948).

X130. Miliukov, Pavel N. **Outlines of Russian culture.** Ed. by Michael M. Karpovich. 3 v. Philadelphia, 1942. [1, *Religion and the church;* 2, *Literature;* 3, *Architecture, painting, and music.*] Translation based on jubilee edition of the *Ocherki po istorii russkoi kul'tury* (3 v. in 4, Paris, 1930–37).

Communist

X131. Akademiia Nauk SSSR, Institut Istorii. **Geschichte der Völker der Union der Sozialistischen Sowjet-Republiken.** Ed. by Vladimir I. Lebedev. V. 1, **Von den ältesten Zeiten bis zum Ende des 18. Jahrhunderts.** 2 pts. Basel, 1945–46.

X132. ——. **Ocherki istorii SSSR.** [Outline of the history of the U.S.S.R.] Ed. by Boris D. Grekov. V. 1–8. Moscow, 1953–57. (Others in progress.) The up-to-date Marxist treatment of Russian history gives special attention to history of the nationalities from the 9th to the 18th century; German ed. *Geschichte der UdSSR.* 1. Feudalismus, 9.–13. Jh. (2 v. Berlin, 1957.)

Works Published Outside Russia

X133. Stählin Karl. **Geschichte Russlands von den Anfängen bis zur Gegenwart.** 5 v. Königsberg and Berlin, 1923–39. With exception of v. 1, this is the best-balanced general history of Russia in a western language by a single author.

X134. Miliukov, Pavel N., Charles Seignobos and Louis Eisenmann. **Histoire de Russie.** 3 v. Paris, 1932–33. The leading history of Russia in French. Contains extensive bibliography.

X135. Vernadsky, George, and Michael Karpovich. **A history of Russia.** See *K182.*

X136. Florinsky, Michael T. **Russia: a history and an interpretation.** 2 v. N.Y., 1953. Written by an economist and political scientist, the chapters on internal development are especially noteworthy. Good bibliography.

HISTORIES OF SPECIAL PERIODS

Early History, Kiev Period, and Rule of the Tartars

X137. Vasmer, Max. **Die alten Bevölkerungsverhältnisse Russlands im Lichte der Sprachforschung.** Berlin, 1941. The authoritative statement.

X138. D'iakov, V. N., ed. **Prichernomor'e v antichnuiu epokhu.** [The Black Sea region in ancient times.] 8 pts. Moscow, 1951–55.

X139. Vernadsky, George. **Ancient Russia.** New Haven, 1943. [Vernadsky and Karpovich, A history of Russia, 1.] Complete picture of the prehistory of Russia. Reviews, A. Lobanov-Rostovsky, *Am. hist. rev.*, 49 (Apr. 1944): 469; R. N. Frye, *Am. Slavic and east Europ. rev.*, 5 (1946): 212.

X140. Dunlop, D. M. **The history of the Jewish Khazars.** See *M150.*

X141. The Russian primary chronicle: Laurentian text. Tr. by Samuel H. Cross and O. P. Sherbowitz-Wetzor. 2nd ed., Cambridge, Mass., 1953. Review, P. Charanis, *Byzantinoslavica*, 16 (1955): 370.

X142. The chronicle of Novgorod, 1016–1471. Tr. and ed. by Robert Mitchell and Nevill Forbes. London, 1914. [Camden Society, 3rd ser., 25.]

X143. Vernadsky, George. **Kievan Russia.** New Haven, 1948. [Vernadsky and Karpovich, A history of Russia, 2.] Reviews, A. Lobanov-Rostovsky, *Am. hist. rev.*, 54 (Oct. 1948): 137; G. V. Lantzeff, *Jour. cent. Europ. aff.*, 8 (1949): 421.

X144. Moshin, V. A. "Variago-russkii vopros." [The question of the Varangians in Russia.] **Slavia,** 10 (1931): 109–36, 343–79, 501–37. History of the Normannic theory.

X145. Pokrovskii, S. "Kievskaia Rus' v rabotakh sovetskikh istorikov." [The Kievan Rus' in the publications of Soviet historians.] **Sovetskaia kniga,** 1 (Mar.-Apr. 1946): 12–27.

X146. Vucinich, Alexander. "The first Russian state: an appraisal of the Soviet theory." **Speculum,** 28 (Apr. 1953): 324–34.

X147. Dvornik, Francis. "The Kiev state and its relations with western Europe." **Transactions of the Royal Historical Society,** 4th ser., 29 (1947): 27–41.

X148. ——. "Kievan Russia and central Europe." **The making of central and eastern Europe** (London, 1949), pp. 236–61.

X149. ——. "The Russia of Kiev." **The Slavs: their early history and civilization** (Boston, 1956), pp. 189–255.

X150. ——. "Byzantine political ideas in Kievan Russia." **Dumbarton Oaks papers,** nos. 9–10 (1956): 73–121.

X151. Grekov, Boris D., and M. I. Artamonov. **Istoriia kul'tury drevnei Rusi.** [History of the culture of old Russia.] 2 v. Moscow, 1948–51.

X152. Chyzhevs'kyi, Dmytro. **Geschichte der altrussischen Literatur im 11., 12. und 13. Jahrhundert: Kiever Epoche.** Frankfurt-am-Main, 1948. "Only comprehensive treatment in a western European language." M. Vasmer, *Zeitschr. für slav. Philologie,* 20 (1950): 459.

X153. Eck, Alexandre. **Le Moyen-Âge russe.** See *K184.*

X154. Grekov, Boris D., and Aleksandr I. Iakubovskii. **Zolotaia Orda i ee padenie.** [The Golden Horde and its fall.] Moscow, 1950.

X155. Nasonov, Arsenii N. **Mongoly i Rus: istoriia tatarskoi politiki na Rusi.** [The Mongols and Russia: history of Tartar policy toward Russia.] Moscow, 1940. A basic work.

X156. Spuler, Bertold. **Die Goldene Horde: die Mongolen in Russland, 1223–1502.** See *M155*.

X157. Vernadsky, George. **The Mongols and Russia.** New Haven, 1953. [Vernadsky and Karpovich, A history of Russia, 3.] "Most authoritative survey." M. Szeftel, *Russ. rev.*, 14 (Jan. 1955): 65.

Muscovite Period to End of the 16th Century

X158. Liubavskii, Matvei K. **Obrazovanie osnovnoi gosudarstvennoi territorii velikorusskoi narodnosti.** [Development of the main territory of the Great Russian nationality.] Leningrad, 1929. Condemned as non-Marxist in review by M. N. Pokrovskii, *Istorik marksist*, 18–19 (1930): 14.

X159. Presniakov, Aleksandr E. **Obrazovanie velikorusskago gosudarstva.** [Formation of the Great Russian state.] Petrograd, 1918. History of Muscovy, 13th to 15th centuries.

X160. Bazilevich, Konstantin V. **Vneshnaia politika russkogo tsentralizovannogo gosudarstva.** [Foreign policy of the Russian centralized state.] Moscow, 1952. The foreign policy of Ivan III.

X161. Ševčenko, Ihor. "Byzantine cultural influences." Cyril E. Black, ed., **Rewriting Russian history** (N.Y., 1956), pp. 143–97.

X162. Levchenko, Mitrofan. **Ocherki po istorii russko-vizantiiskikh otnoshenii.** [Essays on the history of Russian-Byzantine relations.] Moscow, 1956.

X163. Savva, Vladimir I. **Moskovskie tsari i vizantiiskie vasilevsy.** [Muscovite tsars and Byzantine emperors.] Kharkov, 1901. Outstanding research on the influence of Byzantine theories on the ideology of Muscovite tsardom.

X164. Schaeder, Hildegard. **Moskau, das dritte Rom: Studien zur Geschichte der politischen Theorien in der slavischen Welt.** Hamburg, 1929. 2nd ed., Wiesbaden, 1957. One of the outstanding Ph.D. theses of this century. Extensive bibliography.

X165. Medlin, William K. **Moscow and east Rome.** Geneva, 1952. [Études d'histoire économique, politique et sociale, 1.] Relations of church and state in Muscovite Russia. Bibliography.

X166. Cherniavsky, Michael. " 'Holy Russia': a study in the history of an idea." **Am. hist. rev.,** 63 (Apr. 1958): 617–37.

X167. Platzhoff, Walter. "Das erste Auftreten Russlands und der russischen Gefahr in der europäischen Politik." **Historische Zeitschrift,** 115 (1915–16): 77–93.

X168. Budovnits, I. U. "Ivan Groznyi v russkoi istoricheskoi literature." [Ivan the Terrible in Russian historical literature.] **Istoricheskie zapiski,** 21 (1947): 271–330.

X169. Bakhrushin, S. V. "Ivan Groznyi v svete noveishikh issledovanii." [Ivan the Terrible in the light of the latest research.] **Iubileinyi sbornik posviashchennyi 30-letiiu Velikoi oktiabr'skoi revoliutsii** [Jubilee volume celebrating the 30th anniversary of the Great October Revolution], v. 2 (Moscow, 1947), pp. 655–66.

X170. Bolsover, G. H. "Ivan the Terrible in Russian historiography." **Transactions of the Royal Historical Society,** 5th ser., 7 (1957): 71–89.

X171. Vipper, Robert I. **Ivan Groznyi.** [Ivan the Terrible.] Moscow, 1947. The Soviet "patriotic" interpretation.

X172. **Poslaniia Ivana Groznogo.** [The letters of Ivan the Terrible.] Ed. by V. P. Adrianova-Peretts. Moscow, 1951.

X173. **The correspondence between Prince A. M. Kurbsky and Tsar Ivan IV of Russia, 1564–1579.** Ed. by J. L. I. Fennell. Cambridge, Eng., 1955.

X174. Staden, Heinrich von. **Aufzeichnungen über den Moskauer Staat.** Ed. by Fritz T. Epstein. Hamburg, 1930. [Hamburgische Universität, Abhandlungen aus dem Gebiet der Auslandskunde, 34.] Supplement in *Jahrbücher für Geschichte Osteuropas*, N.S. 8 (1960) pp. 131–148.

X175. Leontovitsch, Victor. **Die Rechtsumwälzung unter Iwan dem Schrecklichen und die Ideologie der russischen Selbstherrschaft.** Stuttgart, 1949.

X176. Sadikov, P. A. **Ocherki po istorii oprichniny.** [Sketches of the history of the Oprichnina.] Moscow and Leningrad, 1950. The outstanding work on Ivan's internal policy. Review, A. Zimin, *Voprosy istorii*, 1950, p. 144.

X177. Vernadsky, George. "The death of Tsarevich Dmitrii: a reconsideration of the case." **Oxford Slavonic papers,** 5 (1954): 1–19.

"Smuta" and the 17th Century

X178. Cherepnin, L. V. " 'Smuta' i istoriografiia XVII veka." [The "Time of trouble" and historiography of the 17th century.] **Istoricheskie zapiski,** 14 (1945): 81–128.

X179. Platonov, Sergei F. "Selbstbiographie." **Zeitschrift für osteuropäische Geschichte,** 7 (1933): 465–86. Platonov's autobiography gives exact information on his basic contributions to the history of the

Muscovite period and especially of the *Smuta*.

X180. Fleischhacker, Hedwig. **Russland zwischen zwei Dynastien (1598–1613): eine Untersuchung über die Krisis in der obersten Gewalt.** Baden bei Wien, 1933.

X181. ——. **Die staats- und völkerrechtlichen Grundlagen der moskauischen Aussenpolitik (14.–17. Jahrhundert).** Breslau, 1938. [Jahrbücher für Geschichte Osteuropas, 1.] Review, E. Winter, *Kyrios,* 4 (1939–40): 175.

X182. Lappo-Danilevskii, Aleksandr S. "L'idée de l'état et son évolution en Russie depuis les troubles du XVIIe siècle jusqu'aux réformes du XVIIIe." Paul Vinogradoff, ed., **Essays in legal history** (Oxford, 1913), pp. 356–83.

X183. Baddeley, John F. **Russia, Mongolia, China: record of relations between them . . . 1602–1676.** 2 v. London, 1919. An indispensable work. Review, R. Salomon, *Zeitschrift für osteuropäische Geschichte,* 5 (1931): 559–61.

X184. Kotoshikhin, Grigorii K. **O Rossii v tsarstvovanie Aleksieia Mikhailovicha.** [On Russia under the rule of Aleksei Mikhailovich.] 4th ed., St. Petersburg, 1906. A kind of state handbook of Muscovite Russia in the second half of the 17th century.

X185. O'Brien, Carl B. **Russia under two tsars, 1682–1689: the regency of Sophia Alekseevna.** Berkeley, 1952.

Imperial Russia and Provisional Government

X186. Andreev, Aleksandr I., ed. **Petr Velikii: sbornik statei.** [Peter the Great: collection of articles.] Moscow and Leningrad, 1947. Articles by B. B. Kafengauz on the epoch of Peter the Great in the light of Soviet historical science (pp. 334–89) and by S. A. Feigina on foreign literature on Peter since the early 1920's (pp. 390–423) deserve attention.

X187. Pis'ma i bumagi imperatora Petra Velikogo. [Letters and papers of Emperor Peter the Great.] St. Petersburg (Leningrad), 1887 ff. V. 10 (1956) contains documentation for the year 1710.

X188. Bogoslovskii, Mikhail M. **Petr I: materialy dlia biografii.** [Peter I: materials for a biography.] 5 v. Moscow, 1940–48. V. 5 contains documentation for 1699–1700.

X189. Dukmeyer, Friedrich. **Korbs Diarium itineris in Moscoviam und Quellen, die es ergänzen.** 2 v. Berlin, 1909–10. [Eberings historische Studien, 70 and 80.] An important source for the history of Peter the Great.

X190. Wittram, Reinhard. **Peter der Grosse: der Eintritt Russlands in die Neuzeit.** Berlin, 1954. The most recent scholarly evaluation of Peter I.

X191. Sumner, Benedict H. **Peter the Great and the emergence of Russia.** N.Y., 1951. "A masterpiece of condensation." W. Gurian, *Am. hist. rev.,* 57 (July 1952): 1040.

X192. ——. **Peter the Great and the Ottoman empire.** See *S256.*

X193. Wittram, Reinhard. "Peters des Grossen Interesse an Asien." Akademie der Wissenschaften, Göttingen, **Nachrichten,** 1957, pp. 1–25.

X194. Lockhart, Laurence. "The 'Political testament' of Peter the Great." **The Slavonic review,** 14 (Jan. 1936): 438–41. The latest scholarly examination of a famous falsification.

X195. Leontiev, Vasilii. "Peter der Grosse: seine Wirtschaftspolitik und sein angeblicher Merkantilismus." **Jahrbücher für Geschichte Osteuropas,** 2 (1937): 234–71. Realistic estimate of Peter's economic policy.

X196. Black, Cyril E. "The reforms of Peter the Great." **Rewriting Russian history** (*X117*), pp. 242–70.

X197. Koch, Hans. **Die russische Orthodoxie im petrinischen Zeitalter: ein Beitrag zur Geschichte westlicher Einflüsse auf das ostslavische Denken.** Breslau, 1929. The systems of Stefan Iavorskii and Feofan Prokopovich.

X198. Stupperich, Robert. **Staatsgedanke und Religionspolitik Peters des Grossen.** Königsberg and Berlin, 1936. [Osteuropäische Forschungen, n.s. 22.] Review, H. Fleischhacker, *Jahrbücher für Geschichte Osteuropas,* 1 (1936): 449.

X199. Bissonnette, Georges. "The church reform of Peter the Great as a problem in Soviet historiography." Reprint, **Emory sources and reprints,** 1 (1956): 146–57.

The number of basic and informative studies on Russia's diplomatic, economic, and cultural relations with foreign countries in modern times is legion. For the 18th century see the following (*X200–203*).

X200. Simmons, Ernest J. **English literature and culture in Russia, 1553–1840.** Cambridge, Mass., 1935.

X201. Mohrenschildt, Dimitri S. von. **Russia in the intellectual life of 18th century France.** N.Y., 1936.

X202. Stählin, Karl. **Aus den Papieren Jacob von Stählins: ein biographischer Beitrag zur deutsch-russischen Kulturgeschichte des 18. Jahrhunderts.** Königsberg and Berlin, 1926.

X203. Winter, Eduard. **Halle als Ausgangspunkt der deutschen Russlandkunde im 18. Jahrhundert.** Berlin, 1953. The influence of Halle pietism on Russian enlightenment.

X204. Reddaway, William F., ed. **Documents of Catherine the Great: the corre-**

spondence with Voltaire and the instruction of 1767. Cambridge, Eng., 1931.

X205. Pugachevshchina. [The revolt of Pugachev.] 3 v. Moscow and Leningrad, 1926–31. Documents of the investigation and official correspondence.

X206. Smolitsch, Igor. "Katharinas II. religiöse Anschauungen und die russische Kirche." **Jahrbücher für Geschichte Osteuropas,** 3 (1938): 568–79.

X207. Schilder, Nikolai K. **Imperator Pavel Pervyi: istoriko-biograficheskii ocherk.** [Tsar Paul I: historical-biographical sketch.] St. Petersburg, 1901. The first of Schilder's trilogy of official biographies, which also include Alexander I and Nicholas I.

X208. Schiemann, Theodor. **Kaiser Alexander I. und die Ergebnisse seiner Lebensarbeit.** Berlin, 1904. [Geschichte Russlands unter Kaiser Nikolaus I., 1.] Still the best summary in a western language.

X209. Schaeder, Hildegard. **Die dritte Koalition und die Heilige Allianz.** Königsberg and Berlin, 1934. A basic contribution to Russian diplomatic history between 1803 and 1815.

X210. Tarle, Eugen. "Russland und die Kontinentalsperre." **Zeitschrift für die gesamte Staatswissenschaft,** 94 (Feb. 1933) · 70–106.

X211. Vernadsky, George. "Reforms under Czar Alexander I: French and American influences." **Review of politics,** 9 (1947): 47–64.

X212. Bourquin, Maurice. **Histoire de la Sainte Alliance.** Geneva, 1954.

X213. Mazour, Anatole G. **The first Russian revolution, 1825: the Decembrist movement, its origins, development and significance.** Berkeley, 1937. Extensive bibliography. Review, P. E. Mosely, *Am. hist. rev.,* 43 (Apr. 1938): 620.

X214. Nechkina, Militsa V. **Dvizhenie dekabristov.** [The movement of the Decembrists.] 2 v. Moscow, 1955. Broad picture from intimate knowledge of all the relevant sources.

X215. Mosely, Philip E. **Russian diplomacy and the opening of the eastern question in 1838 and 1839.** Cambridge, Mass., 1934. Review, V. J. Puryear, *Am. hist. rev.,* 40 (July 1935): 558.

X216. Gooch, Brison D. "A century of historiography on the origins of the Crimean War." **Am. hist. rev.,** 62 (Oct. 1956): 33–58.

X217. Temperley, Harold W. V. **England and the Near East.** V. 1, **The Crimea.** See *S261.*

X218. Tarle, Evgenii. **Krymskaia voina.** [The Crimean War.] 2nd ed., 2 v., Moscow, 1950. Leading Russian work on the diplomatic and military history of the war.

X219. Seton-Watson, Hugh. **The decline**

of imperial Russia, 1855–1914. N.Y., 1952. Review, E. Hölzle, *Historische Zeitschrift,* 176 (1953): 140.

X220. Stupperich, Robert. **Die Anfänge der Bauernbefreiung in Russland.** Berlin, 1939. Deals especially with Iurii Fedorovich Samarin (1819–76). Review, M. Spalding, *Am. hist. rev.,* 45 (Jan. 1940): 394.

X221. Zaionchkovskii, P. A. **Otmena krepostnogo prava v Rossii.** [Abolition of serfdom in Russia.] Moscow, 1954. This and *X222* are leading monographs, with good bibliographies, on two of the great reforms of Alexander II.

X222. ——. **Voennye reformy 1860–1870 godov v Rossii.** [Military reforms in Russia, 1860–1870.] Moscow, 1952.

X223. Sumner, Benedict H. **Russia and the Balkans, 1870–1880.** Oxford, 1937. Of equal importance to history of the Panslav movement and Russian foreign policy. Extensive bibliography. Review, D. E. Lee, *Am. hist. rev.,* 44 (Oct. 1938): 117.

X224. ——. "Tsardom and imperialism in the Far East and Middle East, 1880–1914." **Proceedings of the British Academy,** 27 (1941): 25–65.

X225. Akademiia Nauk SSSR, Institut Vostokovedeniia. **Mezhdunarodnye otnosheniia na Dal'nem Vostoke (1840–1949).** [International relations in the Far East (1840–1949).] Ed. by Grigorii N. Voitinskii. 2nd ed., Moscow, 1956.

X226. Wittram, Reinhard. "Die russischen nationalen Tendenzen der achtziger Jahre im Spiegel der österreichisch-ungarischen diplomatischen Berichte aus St. Petersburg." Walther Hubatsch, ed., **Schicksalswege deutscher Vergangenheit** (Düsseldorf, 1950), pp. 321–51.

X227. Romanov, Boris A. **Russia in Manchuria, 1892–1906.** Ann Arbor, 1952. Tr. of *Rossiia v Man'chzhurii* (Leningrad, 1928).

X228. ——. **Ocherki diplomaticheskoi istorii russko-iaponskoi voiny, 1895–1907 gg.** [Sketches relating to the diplomatic history of the Russo-Japanese war, 1895–1907.] 2nd ed., Moscow, 1955.

X229. Price, Ernest B. **The Russo-Japanese treaties of 1907–1916 concerning Manchuria and Mongolia.** Baltimore, 1933.

X230. Revoliutsionnoe dvizhenie v Rossii vesnoi i letom 1905 goda, aprel'sent'iabr'. [The revolutionary movement in Russia in the spring and summer, 1905, April-September.] Moscow, 1957. [Revoliutsiia 1905–1907 gg. v Rossii: dokumenty i materialy.]

X231. Pankratova, Anna M. **Die erste russische Revolution von 1905 bis 1907.** Berlin, 1953. Tr. of *Pervaia russkaia revoliutsiia 1905–1907 gg.* (2nd ed., Moscow, 1951). The official Bolshevik version.

X232. Hoetzsch, Otto. **Russland.** 2nd ed., Berlin, 1917. Scholarly introduction to the constitutional period of Russian history

(1905–17), from a conservative viewpoint. Review, K. Stählin, *Historische Zeitschrift*, 119 (1919): 283.

X233. Levin, Alfred. **The second Duma: a study of the Social-Democratic party.** New Haven, 1940. "The Russian constitutional experiment from the point of view of the opposition." L. I. Strakhovsky, *Jour. mod. hist.*, 13 (Mar. 1941): 109. See also review, F. T. Epstein, *Am. hist. rev.*, 46 (Jan. 1941): 403.

X234. Russia. Vremennoe Pravitel'stvo, Chrezvychainaia sledstvennaia Komissiia. **La chute du régime tsariste: interrogatoires des ministres, conseillers, généraux, hauts fonctionnaires de la cour impériale russe.** Paris, 1927. Abridged tr. from *Padenie tsarskogo rezhima* (7 v., Leningrad and Moscow, 1924–26). The stenographic reports of the hearings.

X235. Pares, Sir Bernard. **The fall of the Russian monarchy: a study of the evidence.** N.Y., 1939. Reviews, M. Karpovich, *Jour. mod. hist.*, 12 (Mar. 1940): 115; H. H. Fisher, *Am. hist. rev.*, 46 (Oct. 1940): 148.

X236. Carnegie Endowment for International Peace. **Economic and social history of the World War: Russian series.** 12 v. New Haven, 1928–32. The volumes of this series (on Russian agriculture, the Russian army, schools and universities, local government and the Union of Zemstvos, state control of industry, etc.) are indispensable for judging the role of Russia in World War I and as historical background material for the revolutions of 1917.

X237. Golder, Frank A., ed. **Documents of Russian history, 1914–1917.** N.Y., 1927. Review, S. N. Harper, *Am. hist. rev.*, 33 (July 1928): 915.

X238. Russia. Narodnyi Komissariat po Inostrannym Delam. **Mirnye peregovory v Brest-Litovske.** [The peace negotiations at Brest-Litovsk.] Moscow, 1920. The official Soviet record.

X239. Wheeler-Bennett, John W. **Brest-Litovsk, the forgotten peace, March, 1918.** London, 1938. Reprint, 1956. Still the standard work in English on Germany's eastern policy during World War I.

Bolshevik Russia

X240. Treadgold, Donald W. **Twentieth century Russia.** Chicago, 1959. Reliable, comprehensive handbook from Nicholas II to 1958.

X241. Koch, Hans. "Sowjetkunde als Aufgabe." **Jahrbücher für Geschichte Osteuropas,** 5 (1957): 43–66. Defines the research task on the Soviet period of Russian history.

X242. Rauch, Georg von. **A history of Soviet Russia.** N.Y., 1957. Tr. of *Geschichte des bolschewistischen Russland* (Wiesbaden, 1955). A handbook. Reviews, F. C. Barghoorn, *Am. hist. rev.*, 61 (July 1956): 969; F. T. Epstein, *Jour. cent. Europ. aff.*, 16 (Oct. 1956): 293.

X243. Velikaia Oktiabr'skaia sotsialisticheskaia revoliutsiia: khronika sobytii. [The great socialist October Revolution: chronicle of events.] Moscow, 1957 ff. Prepared by the Historical Institute of the Soviet Academy of Sciences.

X244. Carr, Edward H. **A history of Soviet Russia.** V. 1–6. London, 1950–60. Covering 1917–1926. A political, economic, and diplomatic history of the Bolshevik party and the Soviet government, based on wide use of original sources. On the whole a work of admirable objectivity.

X245. Chamberlin, William H. **The Russian Revolution, 1917–1921.** 2 v. N.Y., 1935. Reprint, 1952. Contains numerous documents and extensive bibliography. "By far the best account of the great Russian upheaval in any language." D. von Mohrenschildt, *Russ. rev.*, 11 (Oct. 1952): 250. See also review, J. Bunyan, *Am. hist. rev.*, 41 (Jan. 1936): 342.

X246. Communist Party of the Soviet Union, Central Committee. **History of the Communist party of the Soviet Union (Bolsheviks): short course.** N.Y., 1939. The orthodox, official Stalinist version of the party. Review, R. P. Churchill, *Am. hist. rev.*, 46 (Oct. 1940): 150.

X247. Naidenov, M. E. "Velikaia Oktiabr'-skaia sotsialisticheskaia revoliutsiia v sovetskoi istoriografii." [The great socialist October Revolution in Soviet historiography.] **Voprosy istorii,** 1957, pp. 167–80.

X248. Kim, M. P., ed. **Istoriia SSSR: epokha sotsializma (1917–1957 gg.).** [History of the U.S.S.R.: socialist period (1917–1957).] Moscow, 1957. A comprehensive textbook on the university level. Divided into two parts: the victory of the proletarian revolution and the building of socialism (1917–37), and "The completion of organizing a socialist society and the gradual transition to communism" (1938–57).

X249. Bunyan, James, and Harold H. Fisher, eds. **The Bolshevik revolution, 1917–1918: documents and materials.** Stanford, 1934.

X250. Bunyan, James, ed. **Intervention, civil war and communism in Russia, April-December, 1918: documents and materials.** Baltimore, 1936.

X251. Trotskii, Lev. **The history of the Russian Revolution.** 3 v. N.Y., 1936. The highly subjective account of one of the main actors.

X252. Stein, Boris E. **Die "Russische Frage" auf der Pariser Friedenskonferenz 1919–1920.** Leipzig, 1953. Tr. of *"Russkii vopros" na Parizhskoi Mirnoi Konferentsii,*

1919–1920 gg. (Moscow, 1949). Strictly Marxist treatment of a crucial question of modern diplomatic history. See also: Fritz T. Epstein, "Studien zur Geschichte der 'Russischen Frage' auf der Pariser Friedenskonferenz von 1919," *Jahrbücher für Geschichte Osteuropas,* N. S., v. 7, 1959, pp. 431–78.

X253. Stewart, George. **The White armies of Russia: a chronicle of counter-revolution and Allied intervention.** New York, 1933. Review, L. I. Strakhovsky, *Am. hist. rev.,* 39 (Apr. 1934): 573.

X254. Rimscha, Hans von. **Der russische Bürgerkrieg und die russische Emigration, 1917–1921.** Jena, 1924. This and the following work discuss the role of Russian emigrants in the anti-Bolshevik movement.

X255. ——. **Russland jenseits der Grenzen, 1921–1926.** Jena, 1927.

X256. Strakhovsky, Leonid I. **The origins of American intervention in north Russia.** Princeton, 1937.

X257. ——. **Intervention at Archangel.** See *AF189.*

X258. White, John A. **The Siberian intervention.** Princeton, 1950. The authoritative U. S. account.

X259. Morley, James W. **The Japanese thrust into Siberia, 1918.** N.Y., 1957.

X260. Eudin, Xenia J., and Harold H. Fisher. **Soviet Russia and the West, 1920–1927: a documentary survey.** Stanford, 1957.

X261. Eudin, Xenia J., and Robert C. North. **Soviet Russia and the East, 1920–1927: a documentary survey.** Stanford, 1957.

X262. Wilbur, Clarence M., ed. **Documents on communism, nationalism and Soviet advisers in China, 1918–1927: papers seized in the 1927 Peking raid.** N.Y., 1956. Review, A. S. Whiting, *World aff. quar.,* 28 (Oct. 1957): 306.

X263. Spector, Ivar. **The Soviet Union and the Muslim world, 1917–1956.** See *S286.*

X264. Lenczowski, George. **Russia and the West in Iran, 1918–1948.** See *S172.*

X265. Degras, Jane. **Calendar of Soviet documents on foreign policy, 1917–1941.** See *AH111.*

X266. ——, ed. **Soviet documents on foreign policy.** See *AH112.*

X267. Vneshnaia politika Sovetskogo Soiuza v period otechestvennoi voiny. [The foreign policy of the Soviet Union during the patriotic war.] 3 v. Moscow, 1946–47. Covers June 22, 1941–Sep. 3, 1945.

X268. Russia. Ministerstvo Inostrannykh. **Perepiska predsedatelia Soveta Ministrov SSSR s prezidentami SShA i prem'er ministrami Velikobritanii vo vremia velikoi otechestvennoi voiny 1941–1955 gg.** [Correspondence between the chairman of the Council of Ministers of the U.S.S.R. and the presidents of the United States and prime ministers of Great Britain during the great patriotic war, 1941–1945.] 2 v. Moscow, 1957. Russian and English eds.

X269. Vneshnaia politika Sovetskogo Soiuza: dokumenty i materialy. [Foreign policy of the Soviet Union: documents and materials.] 1945 ff. Moscow, 1949 ff. (Semi-annual.) Brings together only public information, beginning with Sep. 4, 1945. Issue for 1948, pt. 1, reprints the pamphlet *Falsifiers of history* (issued by the Soviet Information Bureau, Feb. 1948), the Soviet answer to the U. S. Department of State publication, *Nazi-Soviet relations, 1939–1941.*

X270. Russia. Ministerstvo Inostrannykh. **Sbornik deistvuiushchikh dogovorov, soglashenii i konventsii, zakliuchennykh SSSR s inostrannymi gosudarstvami.** [Collection of valid treaties, agreements, and conventions concluded by the Soviet Union with other states.] Moscow, 1924 ff.

X271. Shapiro, Leonard, ed. **Soviet treaty series: a collection of bilateral treaties, agreements and conventions, etc., concluded between the Soviet Union and foreign powers.** See *AH114.*

X272. Meissner, Boris, comp. **Das Ostpakt-System: Dokumentensammlung.** See *AH113.*

X273. Fischer, Louis. **The Soviets in world affairs: a history of the relations between the Soviet Union and the rest of the world, 1917–1929.** See *AH204.*

X274. Taracouzio, Timothy A. **The Soviet Union and international law.** N.Y., 1935. This and the following work are basic for an understanding of the Soviet theory of international relations and the Marxist-Leninist concept of war.

X275. ——. **War and peace in Soviet diplomacy.** N.Y., 1940. Contains subject index of Soviet treaties, agreements, and conventions in force.

X276. Beloff, Max. **The foreign policy of Soviet Russia, 1929–1941.** See *AF200.*

X277. ——. **Soviet policy in the Far East, 1944–1951.** London and N.Y., 1953. This and *X276* are indispensable reference works.

X278. Fainsod, Merle. **International socialism and the World War.** Cambridge, Mass., 1935. Origins of the Third International. Bibliography.

X279. Gankin, Olga H., and Harold H. Fisher, comps. **The Bolsheviks and the World War: the origin of the Third International.** Stanford, 1940. A collection of documents.

X280. Kommunisticheskii Internatsional v dokumentakh: . . . 1919–1932. [The Communist International in documents: . . . 1919–1932.] Moscow, 1933. Documents on the congresses of the Communist International.

X281. Degras, Jane, ed. **The Communist International, 1919–1943.** See *AH38.*

X282. Iuzefovich, Iosif S. **Osnovanie Kom-**

munisticheskogo Internatsionala. [The founding of the Communist International.] Moscow, 1940.

X283. Borkenau, Franz. **World communism.** See *AH35.*

X284. ———. **European communism.** See *AH36.*

X285. Cattell, David T. **Communism and the Spanish civil war.** Berkeley, 1955.

X286. ———. **Soviet diplomacy and the Spanish civil war.** Berkeley, 1957. A continuation of the above. Bibliography.

X287. Schapiro, Leonard. **The origin of the Communist autocracy: political opposition in the Soviet state, first phase, 1917–1922.** London, 1955. Lenin's struggle with the opposition, especially with the social revolutionaries. Review, M. Beloff, *Soviet studies,* 7 (Oct. 1955): 183. Reply of Schapiro, *ibid.,* 7 (Jan. 1956): 304.

X288. Towster, Julian. **Political power in the U.S.S.R., 1917–1947: the theory and structure of government in the Soviet state.** N.Y., 1948. Although it disregards Soviet economics, "a superb account of the political structure and process." J. H. Meisel, *Am. pol. sci. rev.,* 51 (Dec. 1957): 1142. "An extraordinary, almost encyclopaedic compendium of detail." J. N. Hazard, *Russ. rev.,* 8 (Apr. 1949): 162.

X289. Fainsod, Merle. **How Russia is ruled.** Cambridge, Mass., 1953. An outstanding U. S. analysis of the Bolshevik party in theory and practice, 1918–53. Physiology and anatomy of Soviet totalitarianism. Bibliography.

X290. Genkina, Esfir B. **Obrazovanie SSSR.** [Formation of the Soviet Union.] 2nd ed., Moscow, 1947.

X291. Akademiia Nauk SSSR, Institut Istorii. **Obrazovanie SSSR: sbornik dokumentov, 1917–1924.** [Formation of the Soviet Union: collection of documents, 1917–1924.] Ed. by Esfir B. Genkina. Moscow, 1949.

X292. **Istoriia sovetskoi konstitutsii v dokumentakh, 1917–1956.** [History of the Soviet constitution in documents.] Ed. by Semen S. Studenikin. Moscow, 1957. Supplement, 1957.

X293. Pipes, Richard E. **The formation of the Soviet Union: communism and nationalism, 1917–1923.** Cambridge, Mass., 1954. Review, F. Kazemzadeh, *Russ. rev.,* 14 (July 1955): 254.

X294. Maurach, Reinhart. **Handbuch der Sowjetverfassung.** Munich, 1955. [Veröffentlichungen des Osteuropa-Instituts München, 14.] History, structure, and dynamics of the Communist party. Review, A. Goldenweiser, *Am. Slavic and east Europ. rev.,* 15 (1956): 548.

X295. **Kommunisticheskaia Partiia Sovetskogo Soiuza v rezoliutsiiakh i resheniakh s'ezdov, konferentsii i plenumov TsK 1898–1954.** [The Communist party of the Soviet Union in resolutions and decisions of congresses, conferences and full membership of the Central Committee.] 7th ed., 3 v., Moscow, 1954. Covers period 1898–1954.

X296. Sharova, P.N., ed. **Kollektivizatsiia sel'skogo khoziaistva.** See *X421.*

X297. **Direktivy KPSS i sovetskogo pravitel'stva po khoziaistvennym voprosam 1917–1957 gody: sbornik dokumentov.** [Directives of the Communist party of the Soviet Union and of the Soviet government relating to economic matters, 1917–1957: collection of documents.] V. N. Malin and A. V. Korobov, eds. 4 v. Moscow, 1957–58.

X298. **KPSS o profsoiuzakh.** [The Communist party of the Soviet Union on trade unions.] Ed. by A. A. Struchkov and A. P. Troshin. 3rd ed., Moscow, 1957.

X299. **KPSS o komsomole i molodezhi: sbornik rezoliutsii i reshenii s'ezdov, konferentsii i postanovlenii TsK, 1917–1956.** [The Communist party of the Soviet Union on the Komsomol and youth: collection of resolutions and decisions of congresses, conferences and of rulings by the Central Committee.] Moscow, 1957.

X300. Weinberg, Gerhard L. **Germany and the Soviet Union, 1939–1941.** See *AH224.*

X301. Dallin, Alexander. **German rule in Russia, 1941–1945: a study of occupation policies.** London, 1957. A comprehensive work.

X302. ———. **The German occupation of the USSR in World War II: a bibliography.** Washington, 1955. [U. S. Department of State.]

X303. Voznesenskii, Nikolai A. **The economy of the USSR during World War II.** Washington, 1948. Tr. of *Voennaia ekonomika SSSR v period otechestvennoi voiny* (Moscow, 1947). Review, J. Miller, *Soviet studies,* 1 (June 1949): 65.

X304. Fischer, George. **Soviet opposition to Stalin: a case study in World War II.** Cambridge, Mass., 1952. Evaluation of the Vlasov movement.

X305. Meissner, Boris. **Russland, die Westmächte und Deutschland: die sowjetische Deutschlandpolitik 1943–1953.** See *AH251.*

HISTORIES OF SPECIAL AREAS

Nationalities, General

Histories or source collections of numerous Soviet republics and nationalities have been published or are in progress. Among them are the following (*X306–332*):

X306. **Istoriia armianskogo naroda.** [History of the Armenian people.] Erivan, 1951.

X307. **Istoriia Azerbaidzhana.** [History of Azerbaijan.] V. 1, Baku, 1958.

X308. Ocherki po istorii Bashkirskoi ASSR. [Sketches of the history of the Bashkir A.S.S.R.] V. 1, pts 1, 2. Ufa, 1956–59.

X309. Materialy po istorii Bashkirskoi ASSR. [Materials on the history of the Bashkir A.S.S.R.] Ufa, 1936 ff.

X310. Istoriia Belorusskoi SSR. [History of the Belorussian S.S.R.] 2 v. Minsk, 1954–58.

X311. Dokumenty i materialy po istorii Belorussii. [Documents and materials on the history of Belorussia.] Minsk, 1936 ff.

X312. Istoriia Buriat-Mongol'skoi ASSR. [History of the Buriat-Mongol A.S.S.R.] 2nd ed., 2 v. Ulan-Ude, 1954.

X313. Materialy dlia istorii Buriat-Mongolov. [Materials for the history of the Buriat-Mongols.] Ulan-Ude, 1935 ff.

X314. Materialy po istorii Chuvashskoi ASSR. [Materials on the history of the Chuvashian A.S.S.R.] Cheboksary, 1957 ff.

X315. Ocherki po istorii Galitsko-Volynskoi Rusi. [Sketches of the history of Galicia-Volhynian Russia.] Moscow, 1950.

X316. Istoriia Gruzii. [History of Georgia.] Tiflis, 1950.

X317. Istoriia Iakutskoi ASSR. [History of the Yakutian A.S.S.R.] 2 v. Moscow, 1955–57.

X318. Istoriia Kabardy. [History of Kabardia.] Moscow, 1957.

X319. Kabardino-russkie otnosheniia v XVI–XVIII vv.: dokumenty i materialy. [Kabardian-Russian relations, 16th–18th centuries: documents and materials.] 2 v. Moscow, 1957.

X320. Ocherki po istorii Karelii. [Sketches of the history of Karelia.] Petrozavodsk, 1957.

X321. Istoriia Kazakhskoi SSR. [History of the Kazakh S.S.R.] 2 v. Alma Ata, 1957–59.

X322. Istoriia Kirgizii. [History of Kirghizia.] Frunze, 1957.

X323. Istoriia Latviiskoi SSR. [History of the Latvian SSR.] 3 v. Riga, 1952–58.

X324. Istoriia Litovskoi SSR. [History of the Lithuanian SSR.] V. 1, Kaunas, 1960.

X325. Ocherki po istorii Komi ASSR. [Sketches of the history of the Komi A.S.S.R.] Syktyvkar, 1955.

X326. Istoriia Moldavskoi SSR. [History of the Moldavian S.S.R.] Kishinev, 1951.

X327. Ocherki istorii Mordovskoi ASSR. [Sketches of the history of the Mordvinian A.S.S.R.] Saransk, 1955.

X328. Materialy po istorii Tadzhikov i Tadzhikistana. [Materials on the history of the Tadzhiks and Tadzhikistan.] Stalinabad, 1945.

X329. Istoriia Tatarskoi ASSR. [History of the Tartar A.S.S.R.] Kazan, 1955.

X330. Materialy po istorii Tatarii. [Materials on the history of the Tartars.] Kazan, 1948 ff.

X331. Istoriia Uzbekskoi SSR. [History of the Uzbek S.S.R.] Tashkent, 1955.

X332. Materialy po istorii Uzbekskoi, Tadzhikskoi i Turkmenskoi SSR. [Materials on the history of the Uzbek, Tadzhik and Turkmenian S.S.R.] Leningrad, 1933 ff.

X333. Nolde, Boris E. La formation de l'empire russe: études, notes et documents. 2 v. Paris, 1952–53. Although fragmentary, a study of the utmost importance on the historical interrelations between the Russian core and regions later added and assimilated. Review, G. Vernadsky, *Am. hist. rev.,* 58 (Jan. 1953): 377.

X334. Tikhomirov, Mikhail N., ed. Ocherki istorii istoricheskoi nauki v SSSR. [Sketches from the history of the historical sciences in the U.S.S.R.] V. 1. Moscow, 1955. Devotes attention to development of historical sciences among the different nationalities.

X335. Akademiia Nauk SSSR, Institut Istorii. Revoliutsiia 1905–1907 gg. v natsional'nykh raionakh Rossii: sbornik statei. [The revolution of 1905–1907 in the national territories of Russia: collection of articles.] Ed. by Anna M. Pankratova. 2nd ed., Moscow, 1955.

X336. Spuler, Bertold. Idel-Ural: Völker und Staaten zwischen Wolga und Ural. Berlin, 1942.

X337. ———. "Die Wolga-Tataren und Baschkiren unter russischer Herrschaft." *Islam,* 29 (Nov. 1949): 142–98.

X338. ———. "Die Mordwinen: vom Lebenslauf eines wolgafinnischen Volkes." Zeitschrift der Deutschen Morgenländischen Gesellschaft, 100 (1950): 90–111.

X339. Mende, Gerhard von. Der nationale Kampf der Russlandtürken. Berlin, 1936. The national renaissance of Turkic nationalities in Russia.

X340. Stökl, Günther. Die Entstehung des Kosakentums. Munich, 1953. Reviews, E. Winter, *Zeitschrift für Geschichtswissenschaft,* 2 (1954): 505; N. Chubaty, *Jour. cent. Europ. aff.,* 16 (Apr. 1956): 78.

Ukraine

X341. Entsiklopediia ukrainoznavstva. See *X40.*

X342. Korduba, Miron. "La littérature historique soviétique-ukrainienne: compte-rendu 1917–1931." Bulletin d'information des sciences historiques en Europe orientale, 7 (Warsaw, 1935): 113–96 and 8 (1938): 6–197.

X343. Krupnitzky, Boris D. Ukrains'ka istorychna nauka pid Sovietamy, 1920–1950. [Ukrainian historical science under the Soviets, 1920–1950.] Munich, 1957. In Ukrainian with summaries in English and German.

X344. ———. "Die ukrainische Geschichtswissenschaft in der Sowjetunion 1921–1941."

Jahrbücher für Geschichte Osteuropas, 6 (1941): 125–51.

X345. Borshchak, Il'ko. **L'Ukraine dans la littérature de l'Europe occidentale.** Dijon, 1935.

X346. ——. "Histoire de l'Ukraine: publications en langue ukrainienne parues en dehors des frontières de l'U.R.S.S." **Revue historique,** 187 (Jan. 1939): 1–30.

X347. Lawrynenko, Jurij. **Ukrainian communism and Soviet Russian policy toward the Ukraine: an annotated bibliography, 1917–1953.** N.Y., 1953.

X348. Hrushevs'kyi, Mykhailo. **A history of Ukraine.** Ed. by Oliver J. Frederiksen. New Haven, 1941. "A product of 19th century romantic nationalism." A. A. Skerpan, *Jour. mod. hist.,* 14 (Jan. 1942): 92. See also review, J. S. Curtiss, *Am. hist. rev.,* 48 (Jan. 1943): 316.

X349. Akademiia Nauk URSR, Kiev, Instytut Istorii. **Istoriia Ukrains'koi RSR.** [History of the Ukrainian R.S.R.] 2 v. Kiev, 1956–57. The Soviet version. While truly outstanding monographs on Ukrainian topics, such as Reshetar's and Armstrong's studies (listed below), have been published in the United States, none of several histories of the Ukraine published abroad during the last twenty years (such as Dmytro Doroshenko's (1939) and Boris Krupnitzky's (2nd ed., 1943) in German, or William E. D. Allen's (1940) and Clarence E. Manning's (1947)) can be regarded as a leading work.

X350. Akademiia Nauk SSSR, Institut Istorii. **Vossoedinenie Ukrainy s Rossiei: dokumenty i materialy.** [Union of the Ukraine with Russia: documents and materials.] 3 v. Moscow, 1953.

X351. Chyzhevs'kyi, Dmytro. **Istorija ukrains'koi literatury.** [History of Ukrainian literature.] N.Y., 1956.

X352. Mirchuk, Ivan. **Geschichte der ukrainischen Kultur.** Munich, 1957. [Osteuropa-Institut, Veröffentlichungen, 12.]

X353. Iakovliv, Andrü. **Das deutsche Recht in der Ukraine und seine Einflüsse auf das ukrainische Recht im 16.–18. Jahrhundert.** Leipzig, 1942.

X354. Doroshenko, Dmytro. "Die Entwicklung der ukrainischen Geschichtsidee vom Ende des 19. Jahrhunderts bis zur Gegenwart." **Jahrbücher für Kultur und Geschichte der Slaven,** n.s. 4 (1928): 363–79.

X355. Reshetar, John S., Jr. **The Ukrainian revolution, 1917–1920: a study in nationalism.** Princeton, 1952. A pioneer work.

X356. Heyer, Friedrich. **Die orthodoxe Kirche in der Ukraine von 1917 bis 1945.** Köln, 1953. Reviews, H. Koch, *Jahrbücher für Geschichte Osteuropas,* n.s. 1 (1953): 450; R. Schlesinger, *Soviet studies,* 6 (July 1954): 64.

X357. Armstrong, John A. **Ukrainian nationalism, 1939–1945.** N.Y., 1955.

For Ukrainian newspapers, See *X21.*

Belorussia

X358. Vakar, Nicholas P. **Belorussia: the making of a nation: a case study.** Cambridge, Mass., 1956. Reviews, R. Pipes, *Am. hist. rev.,* 62 (Oct. 1956): 138; H. Seton-Watson, *Slavonic and east Europ. rev.,* 35 (1956): 309.

X359. ——. **A bibliographical guide to Belorussia.** Cambridge, Mass., 1956.

X360. Jablonowski, Horst. **Westrussland zwischen Wilna und Moskau: die politische Stellung und die politischen Tendenzen der russischen Bevölkerung des Grossfürstentums Litauen im 15. Jh.** Leiden, 1955. Reviews, M. Hellmann, *Historische Zeitschrift,* 184 (Aug. 1957): 158; O. P. Backus, III, *Am. hist. rev.,* 61 (Apr. 1956): 714.

X361. Scheibert, Peter. "Der weissrussische politische Gedanke bis 1919." **Jomsburg,** 2 (1938): 334–54.

X362. Varonič, A. "The history of Belorussia in the works of Soviet historiography." **Belorussian review,** 2 (1956): 73–97.

For Belorussian newspapers, See *X21.*

Jews

X363. Greenberg, Louis. **The Jews in Russia.** 2 v. New Haven, 1944–51. Reviews, G. Waskovich, *Am. hist. rev.,* 50 (Jan. 1945): 331; S. S. Harcave, *Jour. mod. hist.,* 16 (Dec. 1944): 316.

X364. Curtiss, John S. **An appraisal of the Protocols of Zion.** N.Y., 1942. Review, E. M. Hulme, *Am. hist. rev.,* 48 (Jan. 1943): 299.

X365. Vishniak, Mark. "Antisemitism in Tsarist Russia: a study in government-fostered antisemitism." Koppel S. Pinson, ed., **Essays on antisemitism** (N.Y., 1942), pp. 79–110.

Asiatic Russia

See also *X306–X340.*

X366. Dallin, David J. **The rise of Russia in Asia.** New Haven, 1949. Only comprehensive history in English of Russia's Asiatic empire.

X367. Allen, William E. D. **A history of the Georgian people from the beginning down to the Russian conquest.** London, 1932.

X368. Baddeley, John F. **The Russian conquest of the Caucasus.** N.Y., 1908.

X369. Park, Alexander G. **Bolshevism in Turkestan, 1917–1927.** N.Y., 1957. Early development of the Soviet federal system in Russian central Asia.

X370. Thiel, Erich. **The Soviet Far East.**

N.Y., 1957. Survey of its physical and economic geography.

X371. Taracouzio, Timothy A. **Soviets in the Arctic.** N.Y., 1938. Review, B. Hopper, *Am. hist. rev.,* 45 (Oct. 1939): 157.

Towns

X372. Brinkmann, Carl. "Die ältesten Urbare von Novgorod in ihrer Bedeutung für die vergleichende Wirtschafts- und Rechtsgeschichte." In his **Wirtschaftsformen und Lebensformen** (2nd ed., Tübingen, 1950), pp. 404–53.

X373. Akademiia Nauk SSSR, Institut Istorii, Leningradskoe Otdelenie. **Gramoty Velikogo Novgoroda i Pskova.** See *X74.*

X374. Akademiia Nauk SSSR, Institut Istorii. **Istoriia Moskvy.** [History of Moscow.] V. 1–6, pt. 2, Moscow, 1952–57.

X375. ——. **Ocherki istorii Leningrada.** [Sketches from the history of Leningrad.] Ed. by Mikhail P. Viatkin. 3 v. Moscow, 1955–57. History of Leningrad from 1703 to 1917.

HISTORIES OF SPECIAL TOPICS

Relations with the United States of America

X376. Hölzle, Erwin. **Russland und Amerika: Aufbruch und Begegnung zweier Weltmächte.** Munich, 1953. The period of harmony of Russian and United States interests to 1867.

X377. Farrar, Victor J. **The annexation of Russian America to the United States.** Washington, 1937. History of the acquisition of Alaska.

X378. U. S. Department of State. **Foreign relations of the United States: the Soviet Union, 1933–1939.** Washington, 1952. A complete chronicle. Review, A. S. Whiting, *Soviet studies,* 4 (Jan. 1953): 284.

X379. ——. **Foreign relations of the United States: diplomatic papers: the conferences of Malta and Yalta, 1945.** Washington, 1955.

X380. Browder, Robert P. **The origins of Soviet-American diplomacy.** Princeton, 1953. Soviet-U.S. relations 1932–38. Review, D. Perkins, *Russ. rev.,* 14 (Jan. 1955): 71.

X381. Kennan, George F. **Soviet-American relations, 1917–1920.** See *AH147.*

Government, Political Theories, Law

X382. Val'denberg, Vladimir. **Drevnerusskiia ucheniia o predielakh tsarskoi vlasti.** [Old-Russian theories about limitations of the Tsar's power.] Petrograd, 1916. Discussion of Russian political literature from Vladimir to end of the 17th century.

X383. Olšr, Giuseppe. "Gli ultimi Rurikidi e le basi ideologiche della sovranità dello Stato russo." **Orientalia Christiana periodica,** 12 (1946): 322–73.

X384. Hoetzsch, Otto. "Staatenbildung und Verfassungsentwicklung in der Geschichte des germanisch-slavischen Ostens." In his **Osteuropa und deutscher Osten** (Berlin, 1934), pp. 1–49. This and the following work are basic contributions to the constitutional history of eastern Europe.

X385. ——. "Adel und Lehnswesen in Russland und Polen und ihr Verhältnis zur deutschen Entwicklung." **Osteuropa und deutscher Osten** (Berlin, 1934), pp. 50–101.

X386. Gaidukov, D. A., ed. **Istoriia sovetskoi konstitutsii: sbornik dokumentov, 1917–1957.** See *X292.*

X387. Iushkov, Serafim V. **Istoriia gosudarstva i prava SSSR.** [Constitutional and legal history of the U.S.S.R.] 3rd ed., 2 v., Moscow, 1950.

X388. Schultz, Lothar. **Russische Rechtsgeschichte.** Lahr, 1951. "The best available introduction to the history of Russian law in a western language." H. Kohn, *Russ. rev.,* 11 (Apr. 1952): 126.

X389. Goetz, Leopold K. **Das russische Recht.** 4 v. Stuttgart, 1910–13.

X390. Iushkov, Serafim V. **Russkaia Pravda: proiskhozhdenie, istochniki, ee znachenie.** [The Russian Pravda: its origins, sources, and significance.] Moscow, 1950. A companion volume to the latest edition of *Pravda russkaia,* ed. by Boris D. Grekov (2 v., Moscow, 1940–47).

X391. Hellmann, Manfred. "Staat und Recht in Altrussland." **Saeculum,** 5 (1954): 41–64.

X392. **Pamiatniki russkogo prava.** [Monuments of Russian law.] Moscow, 1952 ff.

X393. Kliuchevskii, Vasilii O. **Boiarskaia duma drevnei Rusi.** [The duma of boyars in old Russia.] 4th ed., Moscow, 1909.

X394. Sacke, Georg. **Die Gesetzgebende Kommission Katharinas II: ein Beitrag zur Geschichte des Absolutismus in Russland.** Breslau, 1940. Review, E. Winter, *Historische Zeitschrift,* 164 (1941): 651.

X395. Maurach, Reinhart. **Der russische Reichsrat.** Berlin, 1939.

X396. Gribovskii, Viacheslav M. **Das Staatsrecht des russischen Reiches.** Tübingen, 1912.

X397. Wolin, Simon, and Robert M. Slusser, eds. **The Soviet secret police.** N.Y., 1957. "A solid history." *The Times literary supplement* (London), Nov. 15, 1957, p. 681.

Military and Naval History

X398. Garthoff, Raymond L. **Soviet military doctrine.** Glencoe, Ill., 1953. First systematic description.

X399. Mitchell, Mairin. **The maritime history of Russia, 848–1948.** London, 1949.

Only survey in English, but has serious faults.

X400. Beskrovnyi, L. G. **Russkaia armiia i flot v XVIII veke: ocherki.** [The Russian army and navy in the 18th century: sketches.] Moscow, 1958.

X401. Russkie polkovodtsy: dokumenty i materialy. [Russian army leaders: documents and materials.] Moscow, 1949 ff. Document volumes have been published on Petr A. Rumiantsev, Aleksandr V. Suvorov, and Mikhail I. Kutuzov.

X402. Russkie flotovotsky: materialy dlia istorii russkogo flota. [Russian navy leaders: materials on the history of the Russian navy.] Moscow, 1951 ff. Document volumes have been published on Fedor F. Ushakov, Vladimir A. Kornilov, Mikhail P. Lazarev, Pavel S. Nakhimov, and Stepan O. Makarov.

Economy

X403. Liashchenko, Petr I. **History of the national economy of Russia to the 1917 revolution.** N.Y., 1949. Tr. of *Istoriia narodnogo khoziaistva SSSR* (3 v., Moscow, 1939; 3rd ed., 1952–56). The different editions mirror changes of Soviet official ideology. Extensive bibliography. See A. Gerschenkron, *Jour. of economic hist.*, 12 (spring 1952): 146–59.

X404. Kulischer, Josef M. **Russische Wirtschaftsgeschichte.** Jena, 1925.

X405. Rybakov, Boris A. **Remeslo drevnei Rusi.** [Artisanship in old Russia.] Moscow, 1948.

X406. Tikhomirov, Mikhail N. **Drevnerusskie goroda.** [Ancient Russian towns.] 2nd ed., Moscow, 1956.

X407. Shimkin, Demitri B. **Minerals, a key to Soviet power.** Cambridge, Mass., 1953. Standard work of Soviet mineral economy, 1926–50.

X408. Goetz, Leopold K. **Deutsch-russische Handelsverträge des Mittelalters.** Hamburg, 1916. [Abhandlungen des Hamburgischen Kolonialinstituts, 37.] This and the following are leading works on Russo-German trade relations in the Middle Ages.

X409. ——. **Deutsch-russische Handelsgeschichte des Mittelalters.** Lübeck, 1922. [Hansische Geschichtsquellen, n.s. 5.]

X410. Portal, Roger. **L'Oural au XVIIIᵉ siècle: étude d'histoire économique et sociale.** Paris, 1950.

X411. Kafengauz, Boris B. **Ocherki vnutrennego rynka Rossii pervoi poloviny XVIII veka.** [Sketches on the internal Russian market in the first half of the 18th century.] Moscow, 1958. The establishment of a unified internal market.

X412. Ames, Edward. "A century of Russian railroad construction, 1837–1936." **American Slavic and east European review,** 6 (Dec. 1947): 57–74.

X413. Khromov, P. A. **Ekonomicheskoe razvitie Rossii v XIX–XX vekakh.** [Economic development of Russia, 19th–20th centuries.] Moscow, 1950. Valuable statistical information.

X414. Schwartz, Harry. **Russia's Soviet economy.** 2nd ed., N.Y., 1954.

X415. Direktivy KPSS i sovetskogo pravitel'stva po khoziaistvennym voprosam, 1917–1957 gody: sbornik dokumentov. V. 1. See X297.

X416. Baykov, Alexander M. **The development of the Soviet economic system: an essay on the experience of planning in the U.S.S.R.** N.Y., 1947.

Agriculture

X417. Grekov, Boris D. **Krest'iane na Rusi s drevneishikh vremen do XVII veka.** [The peasants in Russia from the earliest times to the 17th century.] 2nd ed., 2 v., Moscow, 1952–54. Ger. tr., 2 v., Berlin, 1958–59.

X418. Eliashevich, Vasilii B. **Istoriia prava pozemel'noi sobstvennosti v Rossii.** [Legal history of landed property in Russia.] 2 v. Paris, 1948–51. Land ownership between the 13th and 18th centuries.

X419. Robinson, Geroid T. **Rural Russia under the old régime: a history of the landlord-peasant world and a prologue to the peasant revolution of 1917.** N.Y., 1932. Reprint, 1949. Review, V. P. Timoshenko, *Am. hist. rev.*, 38 (Apr. 1933): 552.

X420. Treadgold, Donald W. **The great Siberian migration: government and peasant in resettlement from emancipation to the First World War.** Princeton, 1957.

X421. Sharova, P. N., ed. **Kollektivizatsiia sel'skogo khoziaistva: vazhneishie postanovleniia Kommunisticheskoi partii i sovetskogo pravitel'stva, 1927–1935.** [The collectivization of agriculture: the most important regulations issued by the Communist party and the Soviet government, 1927–1935.] Moscow, 1957. Review, I. S. Borisov, *Istoricheskii arkhiv*, 4 (July-Aug. 1957): 233.

X422. Jasny, Naum. **The socialized agriculture of the U.S.S.R.: plans and performance.** See AF199.

X423. Schiller, Otto. **Die Landwirtschaft der Sowjetunion, 1917–1953: Agrarverfassung und Agrarproduktion.** Tübingen, 1954.

Statistics

X424. Ptukha, Mikhail V. **Ocherki po istorii statistiki SSSR.** [Sketches on the history of Russian statistics.] 2 v. Moscow, 1955–57.

X425. Soviet Ministrov SSSR, Tsentral'noe Statisticheskoe Upravlenie. **Dostizheniia sovetskoi vlasti za sorok let in tsifrakh.** [The achievements of the Soviet power during forty years in figures.] Moscow, 1957.

Religion

X426. Golubinskii, Evgenii E. **Istoriia russkoi tserkvi.** [History of the Russian church.] 4 v. Moscow, 1901–11.

X427. Ammann, Albert M. **Abriss der ostslawischen Kirchengeschichte.** Vienna, 1950.

X428. ———. **Untersuchungen zur Geschichte der kirchlichen Kultur und des religiösen Lebens bei den Ostslaven.** V. 1, **Die ostslavische Kirche im jurisdiktionellen Verband der byzantinischen Grosskirche (988–1459).** Würzburg, 1955. [Das östliche Christentum, n.s. 13.] This and the above present a Roman Catholic view of the Russian church.

X429. Stökl, Günther. "Die politische Religiosität des Mittelalters und die Entstehung des Moskauer Staates." **Saeculum,** 2 (1951): 393–415.

X430. Shpakov, Aleksei I. **Gosudarstvo i tserkov v ikh vzaimnykh otnosheniiakh v Moskovskom gosudarstve ot Florentiiskoi unii do uchrezhdeniia patriarshestva.** [State and church in their mutual relations in the Muscovite state from the Florence union to the establishment of the patriarchate.] 2 v. Kiev and Odessa, 1904–12.

X431. Halecki, Oskar. "The ecclesiastic separation of Kiev from Moscow in 1458." **Wiener Archiv für Geschichte des Slaventums und Osteuropas,** 2 (1956): 19–32.

X432. Le Stoglav, ou les Cent chapitres: recueil des décisions de l'assemblée ecclésiastique de Moscou, 1551. Ed. by E. Duchesne. Paris, 1920.

X433. Olšr, Giuseppe. "La chiesa e lo stato nel cerimoniale d'incoronazione degli ultimi sovrani Rurikidi." **Orientalia Christiana periodica,** 16 (1950): 267–302.

X434. ———. "La chiesa e lo stato nel cerimoniale d'incoronazione degli zar russi nel periodo dei torbidi (1598–1613)." **Orientalia Christiana periodica,** 17 (1951): 395–434.

X435. Pascal, Pierre. **Avvakum et les débuts de raskol: la crise religieuse au XVIIᵉ siècle en Russie.** Paris, 1938.

X436. Fleischhacker, Hedwig. "Der politische Antrieb der Moskauer Kirchenreform." **Jahrbücher für Geschichte Osteuropas,** 2 (1937): 224–33. The role of Avvakum.

X437. Benz, Ernst. **Die Ostkirche im Lichte der protestantischen Geschichtsschreibung von der Reformation bis zur Gegenwart.** Munich, 1952. Review, E. Winter, *Deutsche Literatur-Zeitung,* 74 (1953): 614.

X438. Curtiss, John S. **Church and state in Russia: the last years of the empire, 1900–1917.** N.Y., 1940. Review, G. Waskovich, *Jour. mod. hist.,* 13 (June 1941): 259.

X439. ———. **The Russian church and the Soviet state, 1917–1950.** Boston, 1953. This

and the above are the leading works on the Russian church in the 20th century.

X440. Persits, Mark M. **Otdelenie tserkvi ot gosudarstva i shkoly ot tserkvi v SSSR (1917–1919 gg.).** [The separation of the church from the state and of the school from the church in Russia (1917–1919).] Moscow, 1958.

X441. Alekseev, Vasilii I. **The foreign policy of the Moscow patriarchate, 1939–1953.** N.Y., 1955. [East European Fund, Materials for the history of the Russian Orthodox Church in the U.S.S.R., mimeographed ser., 70.]

X442. Smolitsch, Igor. **Russisches Mönchtum: Entstehung, Entwicklung und Wesen, 988–1917.** Würzburg, 1953. Review, G. Stökl, *Jahrbücher für Geschichte Osteuropas,* n.s. 2 (1954): 121.

Intellectual History

X443. Plekhanov, Georgii V. **History of Russian social thought.** N.Y., 1938. Tr. of *Istoriia russkoi obshchestvennoi mysli* (3 v., Moscow, 1925).

X444. Hecker, Julius F. **Russian sociology: a contribution to the history of sociological thought and theory.** N.Y., 1915.

X445. Shchipanov, I. I., ed. **Moskovskii universitet i razvitie filosofskoi i obshchestvenno-politicheskoi mysli v Rossii.** [Moscow University and the development of philosophical and social-political ideas in Russia.] Moscow, 1957.

X446. Markert, Werner. "Russland und die abendländische Welt: zum Problem der Kontinuität in der russischen Geschichte." Werner Conze, ed., **Deutschland und Europa** (Düsseldorf, 1951), pp. 293–312.

X447. Riasanovsky, Nicholas V. **Russia and the West in the teaching of the Slavophiles: a study of romantic ideology.** Cambridge, Mass., 1952.

X448. Kohn, Hans. **Pan-Slavism, its history and ideology.** Notre Dame, Ind., 1953. An outstanding contribution to European intellectual history since the beginning of the 19th century. Review, N. V. Riasanovsky, *Russ. rev.,* 13 (Jan. 1954): 64.

X449. Petrovich, Michael B. **The emergence of Russian Panslavism, 1856–1870.** N.Y., 1956. "Careful, well-documented, balanced." G. H. Bolsover, *Slav. and east Europ. rev.,* 38 (Dec. 1957): 214. See also review, H. Kohn, *Am. hist. rev.,* 62 (Apr. 1957): 626.

X450. Venturi, Franco. **Il populismo russo.** 2 v. Turin, 1952. Reviews, H. Seton-Watson, *Slavonic rev.,* 31 (1953): 567; A. Gerschenkron, *Am. hist. rev.,* 59 (Oct. 1953): 119.

X451. Fischer, George. **Russian liberalism: from gentry to intelligentsia.** Cambridge, Mass., 1958. From the 1860's to 1905—the voice of non-Marxist reformers.

X452. Scheibert, Peter. **Von Bakunin zu Lenin: Geschichte der russischen revolutionären Ideologien 1840–1895.** V. 1, **Die Formung des radikalen Denkens in der Auseinandersetzung mit deutschem Idealismus und französischem Bürgertum.** Leiden, 1956. Review, R. Lauth, *Jahrbücher für Geschichte Osteuropas,* 4 (1956): 398.

X453. Izhboldin, Boris S. "The Eurasian movement." **Russian review,** 5 (Apr. 1946): 64–73.

X454. Zen'kovskii, Vasilii V. **A history of Russian philosophy.** 2 v. N.Y., 1953. Review, H. Kohn, *Russ. rev.,* 13 (Oct. 1954): 296.

X455. Rosenberg, Arthur. **A history of bolshevism from Marx to the first five years' plan.** N.Y. and London, 1939.

X456. Gurian, Waldemar. **Bolshevism: an introduction to Soviet communism.** Notre Dame, Ind., 1952.

Education and Scholarship

X457. Hans, Nicholas A. **History of Russian educational policy (1701–1917).** London, 1931.

X458. Lappo-Danilevskii, Aleksandr S. "The development of science and learning in Russia." James D. Duff, ed., **Russian realities and problems** (Cambridge, Eng., 1917), pp. 152–229. Excellent article by a great Russian historian.

X459. Vucinich, Alexander S. **The Soviet Academy of Sciences.** Stanford, 1956.

X460. Buchholz, Arnold. **Ideologie und Forschung in der sowjetischen Naturwissenschaft.** Stuttgart, 1953.

X461. Akademiia Nauk SSSR, Institut Istorii Estestvoznaniia i Tekhniki. **Istoriia estestvoznaniia v Rossii.** [History of the natural sciences in Russia.] Moscow, 1957.

X462. Smirnov, Nikolai A. **Islam and Russia.** London, 1956. [Central Asian Research Centre.] Outline of the history of Islamic studies in the U.S.S.R.

Literature, Theater, Music

X463. Woltner, Margarete. "Die altrussische Literatur im Spiegelbild der Forschung 1937–1950." **Zeitschrift für slavische Philologie,** 21 (1951–52): 159–93 and 344–67; 23 (1955): 189–200. See also *X152.*

X464. Varneke, Boris V. **History of the Russian theatre, seventeenth through nineteenth century.** N.Y., 1951. Standard history of the Russian theater. Review, A. M. Hanfman, *Russ. rev.,* 10 (Oct. 1951): 319.

X465. Lo Gatto, Ettore. **Storia del teatro russo.** 2 v. Florence, 1952.

X466. Montagu-Nathan, Montagu. **A history of Russian music.** 2nd ed., London, 1918.

On music see also Miliukov, *Outlines of Russian culture (X130),* v. 3.

Folklore

X467. Zelenin, Dmitrii K. **Russische (ostslavische) Volkskunde.** Berlin and Leipzig, 1927. [Grundriss der slavischen Philologie und Kulturgeschichte, 3.]

X468. Sokolov, Iurii M. **Russian folklore.** N.Y., 1950. [American Council of Learned Societies, Russian translation project series, 7.]

Archaeology, Art, Architecture

X469. Miller, Mykhailo O. **Archaeology in the U.S.S.R.** N.Y., 1956.

X470. Schweinfurth, Philipp. "Die Kunst der orthodoxen Slaven in der Forschung seit 1925." **Zeitschrift für slavische Philologie,** 20 (1948): 123–44. Summarizes two decades of extraordinary achievement in the field of history of Russian art.

X471. Wulff, Oskar K., and Michael Alpatov. **Denkmäler der Ikonenmalerei.** Hellerau bei Dresden, 1925.

X472. Kondakov, Nikodim P. **The Russian icon.** Oxford, 1927.

X473. Alpatov, Mikhail V., and N. Brunnov. **Geschichte der altrussischen Kunst.** Augsburg, 1932.

X474. Wulff, Oskar K. **Die neurussische Kunst.** v. Augsburg, 1932.

X475. Lukomskii, Georgii K. **History of modern Russian painting . . . (1840–1940).** London, 1945.

X476. Ainalov, Dmitrii V. **Geschichte der russischen Monumentalkunst.** 2 v. Berlin and Leipzig, 1932–33. [Grundriss der slavischen Philologie und Kulturgeschichte, 10 and 12.]

X477. Réau, Louis. **L'art russe.** 2 v. Paris, 1921–22. [1, *L'art russe des origines à Pierre le Grand;* 2, *L'art russe de Pierre le Grand à nos jours.*]

On architecture see also Miliukov, *Outlines of Russian culture (X130),* v. 3.

BIOGRAPHIES, MEMOIRS, COLLECTED WRITINGS

Large as is the number of biographies and autobiographies and of publications of materials illustrating the life and work of Russian personalities, biographies of lasting scholarly value are still absent even for such outstanding personalities as Pobiedonoststev and Count Vitte. Biographies of Russian rulers of the pre-revolutionary period have been listed under "Histories of special periods," those of military and naval leaders under "Histories of special topics." For biographical dictionaries and collective biographies see Morley, *Guide* (*X1*), ch. 4, nos. 74–211.

X478. Kaufman, Isaak M. **Russkie biograficheskie i bio-bibliograficheskie slovari.** See *X11*.

X479. Kordt, Ven'iamin. **Chuzhozemni podorozhni po schidnii Evropi do 1700 r.** [The foreign travelers in eastern Europe to 1700.] Kiev, 1926. [Ukraïns'ka Akademiia Nauk, Istorycho-Filologichnyi Viddil, Zbirnik, 38.] Supplements Friedrich von Adelung, *Kritisch-literärische Übersicht der Reisenden in Russland bis 1700* (2 v., St. Petersburg and Leipzig, 1846). Does not include reports by Arabian, Byzantine, and Scandinavian travelers.

X480. Russkii biograficheskii slovar'. [Russian biographical dictionary.] 25 v. St. Petersburg, 1896–1918. The leading work. Volumes for names beginning with letters E, M, U, and V were never published; letters G, N, P, and T are incomplete.

X481. Vsesoiuznoe Obshchestvo Politicheskikh Katorzhan i Ssyl'noposelentsev. **Uchastniki russkogo revoliutsionnogo dvizheniia epokhi bor'by s tsarizmom.** [The participants of the Russian revolutionary movement during the period of struggle with tsarism.] Ed. by Vladimir D. Vilenskii-Sibiriakov. 5 v. Moscow, 1927–34. Bio-bibliographical dictionary, from predecessors of the Decembrists to the fall of the Tsarist regime.

X482. Deiateli SSSR i Oktiabr'skoi revoliutsii. [Leaders of the U.S.S.R. and the October revolution.] 3 pts. Moscow, 1926. [Granat, Entsiklopedicheskii slovar', suppl. to v. 41.]

X483. Bol'shaia Sovetskaia Entsiklopediia. **Aktivnye uchastniki velikoi Oktiabr'skoi sotsialisticheskoi revoliutsii i grazhdanskoi voiny (1917–1921 gg): biograficheskii slovar.** [The active participants in the great socialist October revolution and the civil war (1917–1921): biographical dictionary.] Moscow, 1957.

Any selection from the vast store of biographies available in the Russian field should be regarded as only illustrative. As long as political controversies are raging about the leading figures of the Soviet period—Lenin, Trotsky, Stalin—no "best" and "leading" biographies can be expected and singled out in spite of considerable merits of several attempts. They have, therefore, been omitted altogether.

Pre-Revolutionary Period

X484. The life of the Archpriest Avvakum by himself. London, 1924.

X485. Zenkovsky, Serge. "The old believer Avvakum and his role in Russian literature." **Indiana Slavic studies,** 1 (1956): 1–51.

X486. Carr, Edward H. **Michael Bakunin.** N.Y., 1937.

X487. Bowman, Herbert E. **Vissarion Belinsky, 1811–1848: a study in the origins of social criticism in Russia.** Cambridge, Mass., 1954.

X488. Winkler, Martin. **Peter Jakovlevič Čaadaev: ein Beitrag zur russischen Geistesgeschichte des 19. Jahrhunderts.** Königsberg and Berlin, 1927.

X489. Falk, Heinrich. **Das Weltbild Peter J. Tschaadajews nach seinen acht "Philosophischen Briefen."** Munich, 1954. [Osteuropa-Institut München, Veröffentlichungen, 9.]

X490. Pfalzgraf, Konrad. "Die Politisierung und Radikalisierung des Problems Russland und Europa bei N. J. Danilevskij." **Forschungen zur osteuropäischen Geschichte,** 1 (1954): 55–204.

X491. Alexandre Ivanovič Herzen, 1812–1870. Paris, 1928.

X492. Woodcock, George, and Ivan Avakumovic. **The anarchist prince . . . Peter Kropotkin.** N.Y., 1950.

X493. Knapton, Ernest J. **The lady of the Holy Alliance: the life of Julie de Krüdener.** N.Y., 1939.

X494. Hyde, Harford M. **Princess Lieven.** London, 1938.

X495. Menshutkin, Boris N. **Russia's Lomonosov: chemist, courtier, physicist, poet.** N.Y., 1952. [American Council of Learned Societies, Russian translation project series.]

X496. Miliukov, Pavel N. **Vospominaniia.** [Memoirs.] 2 v. N.Y., 1955.

X497. Palmer, William. **The patriarch and the tsar.** 6 v. London, 1871–76. The career of Nikon.

X498. Salomon, Richard. "Patriarch Nikon and the Russian church." **Anglican theological review,** 26 (Oct. 1944): 193–204.

X499. Philipp, Werner. **Ivan Peresvetov und seine Schriften.** Königsberg and Berlin, 1935. [Osteuropäische Forschungen, 20.]

X500. Zimin, A. A. **I. S. Peresvetov i ego sovremenniki: ocherki po istorii russkoi obshchestvenno-politicheskoi mysli serediny XVI veka.** [Peresvetov and his contemporaries: sketches relating to the history of Russian social-political ideas in the middle of the 16th century.] Moscow, 1958.

X501. Peresvetov, Ivan. **Sochineniia.** [Works.] Moscow, 1956. Review, A. I. Klibanov, *Istoriia SSSR,* 1957, p. 204.

X502. Steinmann, Friedrich, and Elias Hurwicz. **Konstantin Petrowitsch Pobjedonoszew, der Staatsmann der Reaktion unter Alexander III.** Königsberg and Berlin, 1934.

X503. Kafengauz, Boris B. **I. T. Pososhkov: zhizn' i deiatel'nost'.** [I. T. Pososhkov: life and work.] Moscow and Leningrad, 1950.

X504. Adamczyk, Theresia. **Fürst G. A. Potemkin.** Emsdetten, 1936. Review, M.

Karpovich, *Am. hist. rev.,* 44 (Oct. 1938): 204.

X505. Radishchev, Aleksandr N. **Journey from St. Petersburg to Moscow.** Ed. by R. P. Thaler. Cambridge, Mass., 1957.

X506. Sacke, Georg. "Radiščev und seine 'Reise' in der westeuropäischen Literatur des 18. Jahrhunderts." **Forschungen zur osteuropäischen Geschichte,** 1 (1954): 45–54.

X507. ——. **W. S. Solowjews Geschichtsphilosophie: ein Beitrag zur Charakteristik der russischen Weltanschauung.** Königsberg and Berlin, 1929.

X508. Raeff, Marc. **Michael Speransky, statesman of imperial Russia, 1772–1839.** The Hague, 1957.

X509. Korostovets, Vladimir K. **Graf Witte, der Steuermann in der Not.** Berlin, 1927.

Biographies and Writings of Soviet Leaders

X510. Dzerzhinskii, Feliks E. **Iz dnevnika.** [From the diary.] Moscow, 1939.

X511. Kon, Feliks I. **Feliks Edmundovich Dzerzhinskii.** Moscow, 1939.

X512. Kalinin, Mikhail I. **Stat'i i rechi.** [Articles and speeches.] Moscow, 1935.

X513. Kirov, Sergei M. **Izbrannye stat'i i rechi.** [Selected articles and speeches.] Moscow, 1939.

X514. Krasin, Lubov. **Leonid Krasin.** London, 1929.

X515. Kuibyshev, Valerian V. **Stat'i i rechi, 1930–1935.** [Articles and speeches, 1930–1935.] Moscow, 1935. Chairman of the Soviet State Planning Commission.

X516. Hahlweg, Werner. **Lenins Rückkehr nach Russland, 1917.** Leiden, 1957.

X517. Lenin, Vladimir I. **Sochineniia.** [Works.] 4th ed., Moscow, 1941 ff.

X518. Litvinov, Maksim M. **Vneshnaia politika SSSR: rechi i postanovleniia, 1927–1937.** [Foreign policy of the U.S.S.R.: speeches and decisions, 1927–1937.] 2nd ed., Moscow, 1937.

X519. Molotov, Viacheslav M. **Stat'i i rechi, 1935–1936.** Moscow, 1937.

X520. ——. **Problems of foreign policy: speeches and statements, April 1945-November 1948.** Moscow, 1949.

X521. Ordzhonikidze, Grigorii K. **Izbrannye stat'i i rechi, 1931–1937.** Moscow, 1939.

X522. Stalin, Iosif. **Sochineniia.** [Works.] Moscow, 1946 ff.

X523. Mehnert, Klaus. **Stalin versus Marx.** N.Y., 1952. The historical doctrine of Stalinism.

X524. Sverdlov, Iakov M. **Izbrannye stat'i i rechi, 1917–1919.** Moscow, 1939.

X525. Trotskii, Lev. **My life.** N.Y., 1930.

X526. ——. **The history of the Russian Revolution.** See *X251.*

X527. Voroshilov, Klementi E. **Stat'i i rechi, 1925–1936.** Moscow, 1937.

X528. Vyshinskii, Andrei I. **Voprosy mezhdunarodnogo prava i mezhdunarodnoi politiki.**

Historians in the Russian Field

X529. Mitter, Wolfgang. "Die Entwicklung der politischen Anschauungen Karamzins." **Forschungen zur osteuropäischen Geschichte,** 2 (1955): 165–285.

X530. Parry, Albert. "Vasily Ossipovich Klyuchevsky." Bernadotte E. Schmitt, ed., *Some historians of modern Europe* (Chicago, 1942), pp. 196–216.

X531. Churchill, Roger P. "Paul Nikolayevich Milyukov." Schmitt, **Some historians of modern Europe,** pp. 324–348.

X532. Nolde, Boris. "L'oeuvre historique de Paul Miljukov." **Revue des études slaves,** 21 (1944): 145–64.

X533. Hoetzsch, Otto. "S. F. Platonov." **Zeitschrift für osteuropäische Geschichte,** 7 (1933): 486–91. Reprinted in Hoetzsch, *Osteuropa und deutscher Osten* (Königsberg and Berlin, 1934).

X534. Platonov, Sergei F. "Aus Platonovs Selbstbiographie." See *X179.*

X535. Hoetzsch, Otto. "M. N. Pokrovskii." **Zeitschrift für osteuropäische Geschichte,** 6 (1932): 535–52. Reprinted in his *Osteuropa und Deutscher Osten.*

X536. Hall, Thomas R. "Mikhail Nikolayevich Pokrovsky." B. E. Schmitt, ed., **Some historians of modern Europe** (Chicago, 1942), pp. 349–66.

X537. Epstein, Fritz T. "Pokrovsky." **Encyclopedia of the social sciences,** v. 12 (N.Y., 1934), pp. 181–82.

X538. Grothusen, Klaus-Detlev. "S. M. Solov'evs Stellung in der russischen Historiographie." **Forschungen zur osteuropäischen Geschichte,** 4 (1956): 7–102.

X539. Harper, Samuel N. **The Russia I believe in: memoirs, 1902–1941.** Chicago, 1945.

X540. Pares, Sir Bernard. **A wandering student.** Syracuse, 1948.

UNIVERSITY, ACADEMY, AND SOCIETY PUBLICATIONS

X541. Akademiia Nauk, Petrograd (Leningrad). **Annaly: zhurnal vseobshchei istorii.** 4 v. Petrograd, 1922–24.

X542. ——. **Russkii istoricheskii zhurnal.** 8 v. Petrograd, 1917–22.

X543. Akademiia Nauk (Leningrad), Istoriko-Arkheograficheskii Institut. **Trudy.** 16 v. Leningrad, 1930–36.

X544. Akademiia Nauk (Moscow), Institut Istorii. **Doklady i soobshcheniia.** Moscow, 1954 ff.

X545. ——. **Istoricheskie zapiski.** Moscow, 1937 ff.

X546. ——. **Istoricheskii arkhiv.** 10 v. Moscow, 1936–54. Superseded by *X550*.

X547. ——. **Istoricheskii arkhiv.** Moscow, 1955 ff. (Bimonthly.)

X548. ——. **Istoricheskii zhurnal.** 15 v. Moscow, 1931–45. (Monthly. Title varies.) Absorbed *Istorik-Marksist* (*X573*) in 1941. Superseded in July 1945 by *Voprosy istorii* (*X555*).

X549. ——. **Istoriia SSSR.** Moscow, 1957 ff. (Bimonthly.)

X550. ——. **Materialy po istorii SSSR.** Moscow, 1955 ff. Superseded *X546*.

X551. ——. **Novaia i noveishaia istoriia.** Moscow, 1957 ff. (Bimonthly.)

X552. ——. **Srednie veka: sbornik.** Moscow, 1942 ff.

X553. ——. **Trudy po novoi i noveishei istorii.** Moscow, 1948 ff.

X554. ——. **Uchenye zapiski po novoi i noveishei istorii.** Moscow, 1955 ff.

X555. ——. **Voprosy istorii.** Moscow, 1945 ff. (Monthly.) Preceded by *Istoricheskii zhurnal* (*X548*) and *Bor'ba klassov* (1931–36).

X556. ——. **Voprosy istorii religii i ateizma: sbornik statei.** Moscow, 1950 ff.

X557. Akademiia Nauk, Institut Istorii Material'noi Kul'tury. **Kratkie soobshcheniia o dokladakh i polevykh issledovaniiakh.** Moscow, 1939 ff.

X558. ——. **Materialy i issledovaniia po arkheologii SSSR.** Moscow, 1940 ff.

X559. ——. **Sovetskaia arkheologiia.** 27 v. Moscow, 1936–57. New ser., 1957 ff.

X560. Akademiia Nauk, Institut Slavianovedeniia. **Kratkie soobsheniia.** Moscow, 1951 ff.

X561. ——. **Trudy.** 2 v. Leningrad, 1932–34.

X562. ——. **Uchenye zapiski.** Moscow, 1949 ff.

X563. Akademiia Nauk, Istoricheskaia Komissiia. **Trudy: istoricheskii sbornik.** 5 v. Leningrad, 1934–36.

X564. Akademiia Nauk, Otdelenie Istoricheskikh Nauk. **Vestnik istorii mirovoi kul'tury.** Moscow, 1957 ff. (Bimonthly.)

X565. Istoricheskoe Obshchestvo Nestora-Lietopistsa. **Chteniia.** 24 v. Kiev, 1873–1914.

X566. Imperatorskoe Russkoe Istoricheskoe Obshchestvo. **Sbornik.** 148 v. St. Petersburg (Petrograd), 1867–1916.

X567. Obshchestvo Revnitelei Russk. Istorich. Prosveshcheniia v Pamiat' Imperatora Aleksandra III. **Starina i novizna.** 22 v. St. Petersburg (Petrograd), 1897–1917.

X568. Istoricheskoe Obshchestvo pri Imp. S. Peterburgskom Universitete. **Istoricheskoe obozrenie.** 21 v. St. Petersburg (Petrograd), 1890–1916.

X569. Leningradskii Institut Istorii. **Kras-naia letopis'.** 66 v. Petrograd (Leningrad), 1922–37.

X570. Imp. Obshchestvo Istorii i Drevnostei Rossiiskikh pri Moskovskom Universitete. **Chteniia.** 264 v. Moscow, 1845–1918. Replaced **Russkii istoricheskii sbornik** (8 v., 1837–44).

X571. Vsesoiuznoe Obshchestvo Politicheskikh Katorzhan i Ssyl'noposelentsev. **Katorga i ssylka.** 15 v. Moscow, 1921–35. Absorbed **Istoriko-revoliutsionnyi vestnik** in 1923.

X572. Institut Marksa-Engel'sa-Lenina. **Proletarskaia revoliutsiia.** 17 v. Moscow, 1921–41.

X573. Obshchestvo Istorikov-Marksistov pri Kommunisticheskoi Akademii. **Istorik-Marksist.** 94 v. Moscow, 1926–41. Merged with *Istoriia proletariata* in 1935. Absorbed (1941) by *Istoricheskii zhurnal* (*X548*).

X574. Kommunisticheskaia Akademiia, Institut Istorii. **Istoriia proletariata SSSR.** 22 v. Moscow, 1930–35.

X575. Institut Marksizma-Leninizma. **Voprosy istorii K.P.S.S.** Moscow, 1957 ff. (Bimonthly.)

X576. Akademiia Nauk Ukrains'koi RSR, Institut Istorii. **Ukrains'kii istorichnii zhurnal.** Kiev, 1957 ff. (Bimonthly.)

X577. Institut Istorii Partii i Oktiabr'skoi Revoliutsii Tsentr. Komiteta Kommunisticheskoi Partii (Bol'shevikov) Ukrainy. **Litopis revoliutsii.** 57 v. Kharkov, 1922–33.

PERIODICALS

Russian Language Periodicals Published in Russia

In addition to many periodicals listed under "University, academy, and society publications" above, see the following.

X578. Arkhivnoe delo. See *X29*.

X579. Byloe: zhurnal posviashchennyi istorii osvoboditel'nago dvizheniia. [The past: journal for the history of the liberation movement.] 28 v. St. Petersburg (Leningrad), 1906–26. (Frequency varies.)

X580. Golos minuvshago: zhurnal istorii i istorii literatury. 11 v. Moscow, 1913–23. Continued as *Golos minuvshago na chuzhoi storone* (*X594*).

X581. Istoricheskii vestnik. [The historical messenger.] 150 v. St. Petersburg (Petrograd), 1880–1917.

X582. Istoriia v srednei shkole. [History in the secondary school.] Moscow, 1940 ff. (Bimonthly.)

X583. Kievskaia starina. [Kiev antiquity.] 94 v. Kiev, 1882–1906.

X584. Krasnyi arkhiv. See *X30*.

X585. Russkaia starina. [Russian antiquity.] 176 v. St. Petersburg (Petrograd), 1870–1918.

X586. Russkii arkhiv. 55 v. Moscow, 1863–1917.

X587. Voenno-istoricheskii zhurnal. [Journal for military history.] 3 v. Moscow, 1939–41.

X588. Voenno-istoricheskii zhurnal. Moscow, 1959 ff.

Russian Language Periodicals Published Abroad

X589. Arkhiv grazhdanskoi voiny. [Archives of the civil war.] 2 v. Berlin, 1923.

X590. Arkhiv russkoi revoliutsii. 22 v. Berlin, 1921–37.

X591. Bieloe dielo. [The White cause.] 7 v. Berlin, 1926–33.

X592. Byloe. [The past.] 6 nos. London, 1900–04. Became **Byloe: sbornik po istorii russkago osvoboditel'nago dvizheniia** [The past: collection on the history of the Russian liberation movement], Paris, 1908–33. (Irregular.)

X593. Na chuzhoi storone: istoriko-literaturnye sborniki. Berlin, 1923–25.

X594. Golos minuvshago na chuzhoi storone. [The voice of the past on foreign soil.] Berlin, Prague, Paris, 1926–28. Continuation of *X593* and *Golos minuvshago* (*X580*).

X595. Istorik i sovremennik: istoriko-literaturnyi sbornik. Berlin, 1922–24.

X596. Letopis revoliutsii. 1 v. Berlin, 1923.

X597. Russkii istoricheskii arkhiv. 1 v. Prague, 1929.

X598. Institut po izucheniiu istorii i kul'tury SSSR. Vestnik. Munich, 1952 ff. (Quarterly.)

English Language Periodicals

X599. The American quarterly on the Soviet Union. 5 v. N.Y., 1938–42. [American-Russian Institute.]

X600. The American review on the Soviet Union. 4 v. N.Y., 1944–48. (Bimonthly.) Continuation of *X599.*

X601. The American Slavic and east European review. N.Y., 1941 ff. (Quarterly.)

X602. Central Asian review. London, 1953 ff. [Central Asian Research Centre.] (Quarterly.)

X603. Current digest of the Soviet press. Ann Arbor and N.Y., 1949 ff. [Joint Committee on Slavic Studies.] (Weekly.)

X604. Georgica. London, 1935–37. (Irregular.)

X605. Harvard Slavic studies. Cambridge, Mass., 1953 ff. (Irregular.)

X606. Oxford Slavonic papers. Oxford, 1950 ff. (Irregular.)

X607. The Russian review. N.Y., 1941 ff. (Semiannual, 1941–48; quarterly, 1949 ff.)

X608. The Slavonic and east European re-view. Menasha, Wis. and London, 1922 ff. (Semi-annually.)

X609. Soviet press translations. Seattle, 1946–53. [University of Washington.] (Bi-weekly.)

X610. Soviet studies. Oxford, 1949 ff. [University of Glasgow.] (Quarterly.)

X611. Soviet affairs. London, 1956 ff. [St. Anthony's College, Oxford.] (Irregular.)

French Periodicals

X612. Bulletin d'information des sciences historiques en Europe orientale. 8 v. Warsaw, 1928–35. (Irregular.)

X613. Le monde slave. Paris, 1917–18; n.s., 15 v., 1924–38. (Monthly.)

X614. Revue des études slaves. Paris, 1921 ff. [University of Paris.] (Irregular.)

German Periodicals

X615. Archiv für slavische Philologie. 42 v. Berlin, 1875–1929.

X616. Beiträge zur Ukrainekunde. 7 v. Berlin, 1932–37.

X617. Blick nach Osten. Vienna and Klagenfurt, 1948–52. (Quarterly.) English ed., *Eastern review.*

X618. Forschungen zur osteuropäischen Geschichte. Berlin, 1954 ff. [Freie Universität.] (Irregular.)

X619. Germanoslavica. 4 v., Prague, 1931–36. (Quarterly.)

X620. Jahrbücher für Geschichte Ost-europas. Breslau, 1936–41; Munich, 1953 ff. (Quarterly.)

X621. Jahrbücher für Kultur und Geschichte der Slaven. 12 v. Breslau, 1924–35.

X622. Kyrios: Vierteljahrsschrift für Kirchen- und Geistesgeschichte Osteuropas. Königsberg, 1936–43. (Quarterly.)

X623. Osteuropa. Berlin, 1925–39. [Deutsche Gesellschaft zum Studium Osteuropas.] (Monthly.)

X624. Osteuropa. Stuttgart, 1951 ff. [Deutsche Gesellschaft fuer Osteuropakunde.] (Bimonthly.)

X625. Slavische Rundschau. Prague, 1929–40. [Deutsche Universität.] (Bimonthly.)

X626. Slavische Rundschau: Zeitschrift für Wirtschaft, Kultur- und Geistesgeschichte und Theologie des Ostens. 2 v. Munich, 1956–57.

X627. Die Welt der Slawen. Wiesbaden, 1956 ff. (Quarterly.)

X628. Zeitschrift für osteuropäische Geschichte. 4 v., Berlin, 1911–14; 5 v., 1931–35.

X629. Zeitschrift für Ostforschung. Marburg, 1952 ff. [Herder-Forschungsrat.] (Quarterly.)

X630. Zeitschrift für slavische Philologie. Leipzig, 1925 ff. (Semiannual.)

X631. Zeitschrift für Slawistik. Berlin, 1956 ff. [Deutsche Akademie der Wissenschaften.] (Quarterly.) See also Morley, *Guide* (*XI*), ch. 7.

ADDENDA

X632. Armstrong, John A. **The Soviet bureaucratic elite; a case study of the Ukrainian apparatus.** N.Y., 1959.

X633. Billington, James H. **Mikhailovsky and Russian populism.** Oxford, 1958.

X634. Briusov, Aleksandr Ia. **Geschichte der neolithischen Stämme im europäischen Teil der UdSSR.** Berlin, 1957.

X635. Doerries, Heinrich. **Russlands Eindringen in Europa in der Epoche Peters des Grossen** (*Osteuropäische Forschungen,* N.F., 26). Königsberg and Berlin, 1939.

X636. Dosumov, Ia. M. **Istoriia Kara-Kalpakskoi ASSR.** [History of the ASSR of the Kara-Kalpaks.] Tashkent, 1959.

X637. Gaidukov, D. A., ed. **Istoriia sovetskoi konstitutsii; sbornik dokumentov, 1917–1957.** [History of the Soviet constitution; collection of documents.] Moscow, 1957.

X638. Gudzii, Nikolai K. **History of early Russian literature.** N.Y., 1949.

X639. Hecht, David. **Russian radicals look to America, 1825–1894.** Cambridge, Mass., 1947.

X640. Istoriia Estonskoi SSR. [History of the Estonian SSR.] 2nd ed. Tallin, 1958. In 3 v. Tallin, 1959 ff.

X641. Istoriia Moldavii; dokumenty i materialy. V. 1, Kishinev, 1921; v. 2 (Istoriia moldavskoi SSR), 1955.

X642. Istoriia russkoi ekonomicheskoi mysli. [History of Russian economic thought.] V. 1 (2 pts.), Moscow, 1955–1958.

X643. Istoriia Severo-Osetinskoi ASSR. [History of the North Ossetian A.S.S.R.] V. 1, Moscow, 1959 ff.

X644. Istoriia Turkmenskoi SSR. [History of Turkmenistan.] 2 v. Ashkhabad, 1957.

X645. Kliuchevskii, Vasilli O. **Sochineniia.** [Works.] 8 v. Moscow, 1956 ff.

X646. Koch, Hans, ed. **5000 Sowjetköpfe. Gliederung und Gesicht eines Führungskollektivs.** Köln, 1959.

X647. Komunistichna partiia Ukraini v rezoliutsiiakh i rishenniakh z'izdiv i konferentsii, **1918–1956.** [The Ukrainian Communist party in resolutions and decisions of congresses and conferences.] Kiev, 1958.

V648. KPSS o vooruzhennykh silakh Sovetskogo Soiuza; sbornik dokumentov, 1917–1958. [The Communist party of the Soviet Union on the armed forces of the Soviet Union; collection of documents.] Moscow, 1958.

X649. Legsters, Lyman H., Jr. **Karl Radek als Sprachrohr des Bolschewismus.** Forschungen zur osteuropäischen Geschichte, 7 (1959), pp. 1–128.

X650. Leontovitsch, Victor. **Geschichte des Liberalismus in Russland.** Frankfurt am Main, 1957.

X651. Ministerstvo Inostrannykh Del SSSR. **Dokumenty vneshnei politiki SSSR.** [Documents on the foreign policy of the Soviet Union.] Moscow, 1957 ff. Documents since Nov. 7, 1917.

X652. Ocherki istorii Dagestana. [Sketches of the history of Daghestan.] 2 v. Makhachkala, 1957.

X653. Ocherki po istorii Tadzhikistana. [Sketches of the history of Tajikistan.] Stalinabad, 1957 ff.

X654. Philipp, Werner. **Ansätze zum geschichtlichen und politischen Denken im Kiewer Russland.** Breslau, 1940. (*Jahrbücher für Geschichte Osteuropas,* Beih. 3).

X655. Pipes, Richard, ed. **Karamzin's Memoir on ancient and modern Russia. A translation and analysis.** Cambridge, Mass., 1959.

X656. Reitlinger, Gerald. **The house built on sand. The conflicts of Germany policy in Russia, 1939–1945.** N.Y., 1960.

X657. Rosenfeld, Günter. **Sowjetrussland und Deutschland 1917–1922.** Berlin, 1960. Marxist interpretation.

X658. Slusser, Robert M. and Jan F. Triska. **A calendar of Soviet treaties, 1917–1957.** Stanford, 1959.

X659. Tarle, Evgenii V. **Sochineniia.** [Works.] 10 v. Moscow, 1957 ff.

X660. Thiel, Erich. **The Soviet Far East.** N.Y., 1957. Survey of its physical and economic geography.

X661. Ukrains'ka radians'ka entsyklopediia. [Soviet Ukrainian encyclopedia.] V. 1: A-Boguntsi. Kiev, 1960.

X662. Unterberger, Betty M. **America's Siberian expedition, 1918–1920.** Durham, N. C., 1956.

X663. Vyshinskii, Andrei I. **Voprosy mezhdunarodnogo prava i mezhdunarodnoi politiki.** Moscow, 1952. Sixth General Assembly of the United Nations, 1951–52. Ger. tr.: **Fragen des internat. Rechts und der internat. Politik.** (Berlin, 1955.) Same title, Moscow, 1953 (Seventh General Assembly . . ., 1952).

X664. Walsh, Warren B. **Russia and the Soviet Union. A modern history.** Ann Arbor, 1958.

X665. Zhilin, Pavel A. **Vazhneishie operatsii Velikoi otechestvennoi voiny.** Moscow, 1956. Ger. tr.: **Die wichtigsten Operationen des grossen vaterländischen Krieges.** Berlin, 1958.

VI. THE AMERICAS

SECTION Y

The Americas: General

LYLE N. McALISTER *

This section is general in scope. Items listed fall into three categories: First, those which pertain to America as a single historical or conceptual unit; second, those concerned with areas where major historical divisions impinge or overlap, such as the Spanish borderlands; third, those dealing with more than one of its major historical divisions, as the United States and Latin America. Exceptions to this practice are subsections in which are listed some general works on the exploration and colonization of Spanish America, Brazil, British America, and French America. For a more comprehensive listing of works dealing particularly with Latin America, British and Dutch America, and the United States see Sections Z, AA, and AB respectively. For those pertaining to the background of discovery and colonization of America see Section U.

LIBRARIES

Libraries in the major colonizing nations of Europe contain much material for the study of American history. Among these are the British Museum, London, the Bibliothèque Nationale, Paris, and the Biblioteca Nacional, Madrid. A partial guide to such material is (Y1) David M. Matteson, **List of manuscripts concerning American history preserved in European libraries and noted in their published catalogues and similar printed lists** (Washington, 1925). In the United States, the Library of Congress, the Harvard University Library, and the New York Public Library contain both general material and special collections of Americana. The Henry E. Huntington Library, San Marino, Calif., the Newberry Library, Chicago, and the William L. Clements Library, University of Michigan, Ann Arbor, contain important special collections dealing with the discovery and colonization of America. The Bancroft

Library, University of California, Berkeley, specializes in materials for the history of the Pacific coast of North America; the University of Texas Library, Austin, and the University of New Mexico Library, Albuquerque, are rich in materials dealing with the southwestern borderlands; the P. K. Yonge Library of Florida History, University of Florida, Gainesville, has several valuable collections on the Spanish southeast. The Columbus Memorial Library, Washington, contains important holdings of newspapers, periodicals, reference works, collections of laws, and government reports of the twenty-one American republics. A guide to libraries, archives, and museums having materials for the study of American history is provided by (Y2) **Guía de instituciones que cultivan la historia de América,** ed. by Carlos Bosch García (Mexico, D.F., 1949) [Pan American Institute of Geography and History, pub. 94.] A more detailed description of materials in the United States is (Y3) **Hand-**

* Items and comments indicated by initials HFC were contributed by Howard F. Cline.

book of Hispanic source materials and research organizations in the United States, ed. by Ronald Hilton (2nd ed., Stanford, 1956). See also the two following items.
Y4. Baginsky, Paul B. **German works relating to America, 1493–1800: a list compiled from the collections of the New York Public Library.** N.Y., 1942.
Y5. Barringer, George A., ed. **Catalogue de l'histoire de l'Amérique.** 5 v. Paris, 1903–11. Materials for the Western Hemisphere in the Bibliothèque Nationale of France. [HFC]

BIBLIOGRAPHIES AND REFERENCE WORKS

Y6. Sabin, Joseph. **Bibliotheca americana: a dictionary of books relating to America, from its discovery to the present time; begun by Joseph Sabin, continued by Wilberforce Eames and completed by R. W. G. Vail for the Bibliographical Society of America.** 29 v. N.Y., 1868–1936. Monumental work covering all parts of America. Most items, which are classified alphabetically, were published before 1860.
Y7. Griffin, Grace G., and others. **Writings on American history.** 1902 ff. N.Y., New Haven, and Washington, 1904 ff. Since 1918 issued as part of the American Historical Association *Annual report.* Annual classified list, with some gaps, of books and important articles published during the year. Includes material on Latin America until 1936 and on British North America until 1940. The *Index to the "Writings on American history" 1902–1940* (Washington, 1956) facilitates use of these volumes.
Y8. Larned, Josephus N., ed. **The literature of American history: a bibliographical guide in which the scope, character, and comparative worth of books in selected lists are set forth in brief notes by critics of authority.** Boston, 1902. Supplements, 1902–06. Contains signed evaluations or reviews of over 4,000 books, classified by region, period, and topic, dealing with all parts of America, although emphasis is on the United States.
Y9. Handlin, Oscar, and others. **Harvard guide to American history.** See *AB4.* Emphasis is overwhelmingly on United States history except for sections dealing with prehistory, discovery, and exploration which provide a more general American coverage.
Y10. Keniston, Hayward. **List of works for the study of Hispanic-American history.** N.Y., 1920. Classified by region and period without annotation. Emphasis is on Latin America, although numerous items of general American interest are included, particularly for the colonial period.
Y11. Eberhardt, Fritz. **Amerika-literatur: die Wichtigsten seit 1900 in deutscher Sprache** erschienenen Werke über Amerika. Leipzig, 1926. Covers Western Hemisphere. [HFC]
Y12. Handbook of Latin American studies. See *Z3.* Although primarily devoted to Latin American studies, lists many items of general American interest.
Y13. "Bibliografía de historia de América." **Revista de historia de América.** 1938 ff. Mexico, 1938 ff. Serial bibliography which constitutes the only up-to-date guide devoted exclusively to general American history.
Y14. Inter-American review of bibliography. See *Z8.*
Y15. Palmer, Philip M. **German works on America, 1492–1800.** Berkeley, 1952.
Y16. Adams, James Truslow, ed. **Dictionary of American history.** 6 v. N.Y., 1940. Contains over 5,000 short articles with emphasis on United States history, although includes scattered items on other parts of America and inter-American affairs.
Y17. Diccionario enciclopédico de las Américas: geografía, historia, economía, política, literatura, arte, música, deporte, cine, teatro, etnografía, fauna, flora, ciencias generales. Buenos Aires, 1947. Short items with emphasis on Latin America.
Y18. The South American handbook . . . including Central America, Mexico & Cuba. 1924 ff. London, 1924 ff. This and *Y19* together cover South America, Central America, Mexico, and the West Indies, including non-self-governing areas. Primarily businessmen's and travelers' guides, but contain useful sections on history, geography, government, and population.
Y19. West Indies and Caribbean year book. Anuario comercial de las Antillas y países del Caribe. 1926/27 ff. London, 1927 ff.
Y20. Migone, Raúl C., ed. **Interamerican statistical yearbook.** N.Y., Buenos Aires, and Rio de Janeiro, 1940. 2nd ed., 1942. Compilations of basic statistics for the American republics. Unfortunately, only two editions were published, but these are supplemented by *Y21* in part.
Y21. Estadística. Journal of the Inter-American Statistical Institute. Mexico and Washington, 1943 ff. (Quarterly.)
Y22. Almela Meliá, Juan. **Guía de personas que cultivan la historia de América.** Mexico, 1951. [Pan American Institute of Geography and History, pub. 121.] Guide to historians in all parts of America, but usefulness impaired by unfortunate omissions. A revised edition is scheduled.

MAPS, ATLASES, AND GEOGRAPHIES

Y23. Map of the Americas, 1:5,000,000. N.Y., 1942–48. Pub. by the American Geographical Society. In five sheets in color, each 46 x 35 in. Shows physical features, political boundaries, towns, and communications of both continents and the West Indies.

Y24. Map of the Americas, 1:12,500,000. N.Y., 1953. Pub. by the American Geographical Society. In color, 130 x 87 cm. Smaller scale edition with insets showing cities and transportation, agricultural land use, vegetation, and rainfall distribution.

Y25. Cartografía de ultramar. 1, **América en general: toponomía de los mapas que la integran.** Madrid, 1949. Useful selection of maps for Western Hemisphere. [HFC]

Y26. Phillips, Philip L. **A list of maps of America in the Library of Congress.** Washington, 1901. A major listing of materials on the Western Hemisphere, subsequently extended in other works by the same author. [HFC]

Y27. ——, ed. **The Lowery collection: a descriptive list of maps of the Spanish possessions within the present limits of the United States, 1502–1820.** Washington, 1912. In addition to descriptions, contains bibliographical data. [HFC]

Y28. Ragatz, Lowell J., and Janet E. Ragatz. **A bibliography of articles, descriptive, historical and scientific, on colonies and other dependent territories, appearing in American geographical and kindred journals.** See *U4.*

Y29. Adams, James T., ed. **Atlas of American history.** N.Y., 1943. Concerned primarily with United States history, but contains a few plates on the Spanish borderlands.

Y30. Schmieder, Oscar. **Geografía de América: América del Norte, América Central, América del Sur, versión directa de Pedro R. Hendrichs Pérez.** Mexico, 1946. Consolidated Spanish edition of earlier separate works in German by author. Probably the best work available on the geography of America as a whole.

Y31. Gottman, Jean. **L'Amérique.** Paris, 1949. Well balanced treatment of both physical and historical geography of all America.

Y32. Jones, Clarence F. **South America.** N.Y., 1930. Probably the best geography of South America in a well rounded sense. A new edition is scheduled.

Y33. Jones, Llewellyn R., and P. W. Bryan. **North America, an historical, economic, and regional geography.** 9th ed., rev., London and N.Y., 1950. Achieves an excellent balance between historical, economic, physical, and regional geography.

ANTHROPOLOGICAL AND ETHNIC STUDIES

Y34. Comas, Juan. **Bibliografía selectiva de las culturas indígenas de América.** Mexico, 1953. [Pan American Institute of Geography and History, pub. 166.] Lists, classi-

fies, and annotates works dealing with the American Indian from earliest times to the present. Contains useful ethnographic charts.

Y35. "Bibliographie americaniste." **Journal de la Société des Américanistes de Paris,** n.s. 11 ff. (1919 ff.). Current anthropological bibliography on the Western Hemisphere. [HFC]

Y36. Boletín bibliográfico de antropología americana. Mexico, 1937 ff. [PAIGH, Commission on History.] News, notes, reviews, periodical indices, and special bibliographies; an annual compilation of high value. [HFC]

Y37. Sellards, Elias H. **Early man in America.** See *E112.*

Y38. Krickeberg, Walter. **Ethnología de América.** Tr. by Pedro Hendrich. Mexico, [1946]. Consolidated and augmented Spanish version of earlier German works, with long introduction summarizing anthropological thought and progress, 1922–46.

Y39. Canals Frau, Salvador. **Las civilizaciones prehispánicas de América.** Buenos Aires, 1955. Good synthesis of pre-Hispanic American cultures, although details may be questioned by anthropologists.

Y40. Wissler, Clark. **The American Indian: an introduction to the anthropology of the New World.** 2nd ed., N.Y., 1922. Older standard work which is out of date in many respects, but for which no substitute exists.

Y41. Collier, John C. **The Indians of the Americas.** N.Y., 1947. Historical treatment of the American Indian from earliest times to the present. Indianist in approach.

Y42. Steward, Julian H., ed. **Handbook of South American Indians.** 6 v. Washington, 1946–50. [Smithsonian Institution, U.S. Bureau of American Ethnology, bul. 143.] Collaborative work by a number of distinguished scholars. The best reference work in its field.

Y43. Hodge, Frederick W., ed. **Handbook of American Indians north of Mexico.** 2 v. Washington, 1907–10. [Smithsonian Institution, U.S. Bureau of American Ethnology, bul. 30.] Still indispensable as a reference work.

Y44. Rosenblat, Ángel. **La población indígena y el mestizaje en América.** See *Z101.*

Y45. Kelemen, Pál. **Medieval American art: masterpieces of the New World before Columbus.** N.Y., 1956. Treasury of preconquest art, including some 900 photographs with descriptive text.

Y46. Work, Monroe N. **A bibliography of the Negro in Africa and America.** N.Y., 1928. Large compilation. Unannotated, but classified by region and topic.

Y47. Franklin, John H. **From slavery to freedom: a history of American Negroes.** 2nd ed., N.Y., 1956. Competent work with emphasis on the United States, although several chapters deal with African background, the slave trade, and the negro in Latin America and the Caribbean.

Y48. Tannenbaum, Frank. **Slave and citizen: the Negro in the Americas.** N.Y., 1947. Comparative study of slavery in Latin America and the United States in which the latter comes off very poorly.

Y49. Wesley, Charles H., ed. **The Negro in the Americas.** Washington, 1940. Series of lectures by a number of authorities on the negro in Spanish America, Brazil, the Caribbean, Canada, and the United States.

Y50. Williams, Eric E. **The Negro in the Caribbean.** Washington, 1942. Study by an able negro scholar of the role of the negro from early days of slavery to the present.

PRINTED SOURCES

Printed sources will be found listed in the appropriate subsections.

HISTORIOGRAPHY

Y51. Bolton, Herbert E. **Wider horizons of American history.** N.Y., 1939. Reprints his "Epic of greater America," a presidential address delivered at the annual meeting of the American Historical Association in Toronto, 1932, originally published in *The American historical review*, 38 (Apr. 1933): 448–74. Bolton, although he had his precursors, was the leading exponent of the "History of America" concept, and in this essay expounds his thesis of the unity of American history. The volume also contains his "Defensive Spanish expansion and the significance of the borderlands."

Y52. McInnis, Edgar, and others. **Ensayos sobre la historia del Nuevo Mundo.** Mexico, 1951. [Pan American Institute of Geography and History, Commission on History.] Essays in English, Spanish, French, and Portuguese dealing with the historical process in America around the central themes of unity and diversity.

Y53. **Programa de historia de América: introducciones y comentarios.** Mexico, 1955. [Pan American Institute of Geography and History, Commission on History.] Discusses the aims and problems of the "Programa de historia" undertaken by the Commission on History to study approaches to a general history of America. A general volume (in English) of the "Coordinations" by Pedro Armillas (native period), Silvio A. Zavala (colonial period), and Charles G. Griffin (national period) is in progress for early publication. It will also include these "Introductions." [HFC]

Y54. **Programa de historia de América.** Mexico, 1953 ff. [Pan American Institute of Geography and History.] Preliminary attempt to implement the "Programa de his-

toria" mentioned under *Y53.* Each of the small volumes included is a syllabus dealing with a specific American area within one of the three major periods established.

Y55. "Have the Americas a common history?" **Canadian historical review,** 23 (June 1942): 125–56. A symposium of papers, representing a wide range of views, presented at the annual meeting of the American Historical Association, 1941, in a session devoted to the history of the Americas.

Y56. "The problem of a general history of the Americas." **Revista de historia de América,** 34 (Dec. 1952): 469–89. Papers and discussions from the History of America sessions at the annual meeting of the American Historical Association in 1952. Related to *Y53.*

Y57. "Introduction to the project for a history of America"; and Nichols, Roy F., "A United States historian's appraisal of the History of America project." **Revista de historia de América,** 43 (June 1957): 144–58. Papers and discussions of the A. H. A. meeting of 1956. Related to *Y53.*

Y58. Brooks, Philip C. "Do the Americas share a common history?" **Revista de historia de América,** 33 (June 1952): 75–83. Supports the Bolton thesis, although it maintains that Bolton and his followers failed to achieve any satisfactory synthesis of American history.

Y59. Sánchez, Luis Alberto. **Los fundamentos de la historia americana.** Buenos Aires, 1943. Provocative criticism of the writings of American historians with emphasis on the work done in Latin America.

Y60. O'Gorman, Edmundo. **Crisis y porvenir de la ciencia histórica.** Mexico, 1947. Inquiry into the nature of the historian's craft, using historiography of the discovery of America as the point of departure.

SHORTER GENERAL HISTORIES

Y61. Barros Arana, Diego. **Compendio de historia de América.** 2 v. Santiago, Chile, 1865. Pioneer work in the history of America by one of her great historians. Emphasis on Spanish America.

Y62. Navarro y Lamarca, Carlos. **Compendio de la historia general de América.** See *Z231.*

Y63. Bolton, Herbert E. **History of the Americas: a syllabus with maps.** New ed., Boston and N.Y., 1935. An outline of American history with useful reading lists by the leading proponent of the unity of American history.

Y64. Davis, Harold E. **The Americas in history.** N.Y., 1953. Standard one-volume survey developing the Bolton thesis.

Y65. Sánchez, Luis Alberto. **Historia general de América: con mapas e ilustraciones.** 2 v. Santiago, Chile, 1942. An

Aprista interpretation of the history of America. Although marred by some misconceptions and errors, a stimulating study.

LONGER GENERAL HISTORIES

Y66. Winsor, Justin, ed. **Narrative and critical history of America.** See *AB84*. Covers all of America with emphasis on the colonial period.

Y67. Ballesteros y Beretta, Antonio, ed. **Historia de América y de los pueblos americanos.** Barcelona, 1936 ff. This and *Y68* are large scale cooperative works containing some volumes of excellent quality. Emphasis in both is on Spanish America.

Y68. Levene, Ricardo, ed. **Historia de América.** 14 v. Buenos Aires and N.Y., 1940–41.

THE DISCOVERY

Y69. Gathorne-Hardy, Geoffrey M. **The Norse discoverers of America: the Wineland sagas translated and discussed.** Oxford, 1921. Careful treatment by a competent scholar.

Y70. Holand, Hjalmar R. **Explorations in America before Columbus.** See *U80*.

Y71. Prestage, Edgar. **The Portuguese pioneers.** See *U86*.

Y72. Navarrete, Martín Fernández de. **Colección de los viages y descubrimientos que hicieron por mar los españoles desde fines del siglo XV, con varios documentos inéditos concernientes á la historia de la marina castellana y de los establecimientos españoles en Indias.** 5 v. Madrid, 1825–37. Latest ed., Buenos Aires, 1945–46. Five hundred of the most important documents dealing with Spanish discoveries in the Atlantic and Pacific oceans—the basis of modern historiography of the discovery.

Y73. Harrisse, Henry. **The discovery of North America: a critical, documentary, and historic investigation, with an essay on the early cartography of the New World.** London and Paris, 1892. Summary of the work of an outstanding authority on the discovery. Particularly useful for its essay on cartography.

Y74. Ballesteros y Beretta, Antonio. **Cristóbal Colón y el descubrimiento de América.** See *U88*.

Y75. Thacher, John B. **Christopher Columbus: his life, his work.** 3 v. N.Y. and London, 1903–04. Although in some respects outdated, this minutely detailed study is still a standard work.

Y76. Morison, Samuel E. **Admiral of the Ocean Sea: a life of Christopher Columbus.** See *U277*.

Y77. Arciniegas, Germán. **Amerigo and the New World: the life and times of Amerigo Vespucci.** Tr. by Harriet de Onís. N.Y.,

1955. This and *Y78–79* are representative of modern views on the historiography of Vespucci.

Y78. Pohl, Frederick J. **Amerigo Vespucci, pilot major.** N.Y., 1944.

Y79. Levillier, Roberto. **América la bien llamada.** See *U91*.

Y80. O'Gorman, Edmundo. **La idea del descubrimiento de América: historia de esa interpretación y crítica de sus fundamentos.** See *U89*.

Y81. Parr, Charles M. **So noble a captain: the life and times of Ferdinand Magellan.** See *U279*.

Y82. Romoli, Kathleen. **Balboa of Darién, discoverer of the Pacific.** N.Y., 1953. Perhaps the most satisfactory book in English on Balboa.

Y83. Medina, José T. **El descubrimiento del Océano Pacífico: Vasco Núñez de Balboa, Hernando de Magallanes y sus compañeros.** 3 v. Santiago, Chile, 1914–20. Includes scholarly monographs on the two explorers, supporting documents, and considerable biographical material on their companions.

Y84. Williamson, James A. **The voyages of the Cabots and the English discovery of North America under Henry VII and Henry VIII.** See *U102*.

Y85. Julien, Charles A. **Les voyages de découverte et les premiers établissements (XVe–XVIe siècles).** See *U104*.

Y86. Van Loon, Hendrik W. **The golden book of the Dutch navigators.** N.Y., 1916. Very readable account, based upon original documents, of the work of Dutch navigators in the early 17th century.

EXPLORATION AND COLONIZATION

Y87. Jameson, J. Franklin, ed. **Original narratives of early American history.** 19 v. N.Y., 1906–17. Collection of key documents in English relating to the exploration and early settlement of North America and the West Indies by the English, Spanish, French, and Dutch.

Y88. **Colección de documentos inéditos relativos al descubrimiento, conquista y organización de las antiguas posesiones españolas de América y Oceanía, sacados de los archivos del Reino, y muy especialmente del de Indias.** Ed. by Joaquín F. Pacheco, Francisco de Cárdenas, and Luis Torres de Mendoza. 42 v. Madrid, 1864–84. Monumental collection of documents, mostly from the 16th century, dealing with Spanish exploration and settlement in North America, South America, and the West Indies.

Y89. **Collecção de monumentos ineditos para a historia das conquistas dos portuguezes em Africa, Asia, e America.** Ed. by Rodrigo J. de Lima Felner. 16 v. Lisbon, 1858–1915. Basic documents concerning the work of Portugal in exploration and colonization.

Y90. Great Britain. Public Record Office. **Calendar of state papers: colonial series.** London, 1860 ff. Summaries and extracts of British colonial records, much dealing with America.

Y91. Hakluyt Society. **Works issued by the Hakluyt Society.** 1st series, 100 v., London, 1847–98; 2nd series, London, 1899 ff. Monumental collection of narratives and other documents dealing with voyages, discoveries, and travels by various nationalities, all published in English.

Y92. Margry, Pierre, ed. **Découvertes et établissements des français dans l'ouest et dans le sud de l'Amérique septentrionale (1614–1754): mémoires et documents originaux.** 6 v. Paris, 1876–86. Documents dealing with French exploration and settlement in North America and particularly with La Salle.

Y93. Thwaites, Reuben G., ed. **The Jesuit relations and allied documents: travels and explorations of the Jesuit missionaries in New France, 1610–1791; the original French, Latin, and Italian texts, with English translations and notes.** 73 v. Cleveland, 1896–1901. Monumental collection dealing with work of the Jesuits in the interior of North America. Particularly valuable for its information on Indian tribes.

Y94. Bolton, Herbert E., and Thomas M. Marshall. **The colonization of North America, 1492–1783.** N.Y., 1920. Factual account of establishment and development of the European colonies in North America.

Y95. Priestley, Herbert I. **The coming of the white man, 1492–1848.** N.Y., 1930. Account of the exploration and settlement of North America maintaining a nice balance between fact and interpretation.

Y96. Brebner, James B. **The explorers of North America, 1492–1806.** N.Y., 1933. Narrative account with emphasis on French exploration of the interior of the continent.

Y97. Kirkpatrick, Frederick A. **The Spanish conquistadores.** London, 1934. Best general treatment of the work of major Spanish conquerors in North and South America.

Y98. Newton, Arthur P. **The European nations in the West Indies, 1493–1688.** See *U169.*

Y99. Diffie, Bailey W. **Latin-American civilization: colonial period.** Harrisburg, Pa., 1945. Excellent synthesis developing the theme of the blending of native and Iberian cultures. Treats both Spanish and Portuguese America.

Y100. Bourne, Edward G. **Spain in America, 1450–1580.** N.Y. and London, 1904. Discovery, exploration, and early colonization of the interior of North America. Particularly interesting for its comparisons between Spanish, English, and French colonization.

Y101. Haring, Clarence H. **The Spanish empire in America.** See *Z283.*

Y102. Madariaga, Salvador de. **The rise of the Spanish American empire.** N.Y., 1947. This and *Y103* together form an excellent synthesis of the history of the Spanish empire in America and present provocative interpretations.

Y103. ——. **The fall of the Spanish American empire.** N.Y., 1948.

Y104. Varnhagen, Francisco A. de. **Historia geral do Brazil, isto é do descobrimento, colonisação, legislação, e desenvolvimento deste estado, hoje imperio independente.** 2 v. Rio de Janeiro, 1854–57. 2nd ed., Rio de Janeiro, 1877. 3rd rev. ed. of v. 1, by Capistrano de Abreu, Rio de Janeiro, 1907. Although somewhat deficient in balance and perspective, this is still the best work on colonial Brazil.

Y105. Simonsen, Roberto C. **Historia economica do Brasil, 1500–1820.** 2 v. São Paulo, 1937. Although primarily concerned with economic development, Simonsen incidentally throws considerable light on other aspects of colonial Brazil.

Y106. Southey, Robert. **History of Brazil.** 3 v. London, 1817–22. Suffers from faulty organization and is somewhat outdated, but still the best general work in English on colonial Brazil.

Y107. Oliveira Lima, Manoel de. **The evolution of Brazil compared with that of Spanish and Anglo-Saxon America.** Ed. by P. A. Martin. Palo Alto, 1914. Consists of six interpretive lectures which are particularly interesting because of their comparative approach.

Y108. Osgood, Herbert L. **The American colonies in the seventeenth century.** 3 v. N.Y. and London, 1904–07. Reprint, 1930. This and *Y109* are basic works on the English mainland colonies, but rather narrow in scope with emphasis on legal, constitutional, and administrative development.

Y109. ——. **The American colonies in the eighteenth century.** See *AB72.*

Y110. Andrews, Charles M. **The colonial period of American history.** 4 v. New Haven and London, 1934–38. Covers only through the 17th century, but better balanced than *Y108–109.* Also deals with British colonies in the Caribbean.

Y111. Nettels, Curtis P. **The roots of American civilization: a history of American colonial life.** N.Y., 1938. This and *Y112* are well balanced surveys.

Y112. Savelle, Max. **The foundations of American civilization: a history of colonial America.** N.Y., 1942. Includes the British Caribbean colonies.

Y113. Parkman, Francis. **Works.** 12 v. Boston, 1893. A classic account of French activities in North America during the colonial period, with emphasis on the struggle between France and Britain. Noted for both its historical scholarship and literary style.

Y114. Wrong, George M. **The rise and fall of New France.** See *AA80.*

Y115. Thwaites, Reuben G. **France in America, 1497–1763.** N.Y., 1905. Standard one volume study.

Y116. Jaray, Gabriel L. **L'empire français d'Amérique (1534–1803).** Paris, 1938. Well rounded account by a French scholar. Excellent bibliography.

THE SPANISH BORDERLANDS AND THE PACIFIC COAST

Y117. Steck, Francis B. **A tentative guide to historical materials on the Spanish borderlands.** Philadelphia, 1943. Lists works alphabetically, with occasional commentary, within each of the major borderlands regions.

Y118. Chapman, Charles E. **Catalogue of materials in the Archivo General de Indias for the history of the Pacific coast and the American Southwest.** Berkeley, 1919. Basic list of important materials, most of which are on microfilm in the Bancroft Library. [HFC]

Y119. Bolton, Herbert E. **The Spanish borderlands: a chronicle of old Florida and the Southwest.** New Haven, 1921. Best general survey of early Spanish exploration and settlement from Florida to California.

Y120. Caughey, John W. **Bernardo de Gálvez in Louisiana, 1776–1783.** Berkeley, 1934. Standard biography of the Spanish governor-general, especially important for friendly aid to the United States during the Revolution. [HFC]

Y121. Lowery, Woodbury. **The Spanish settlements within the present limits of the United States, 1513–1561.** N.Y. and London, 1901. Older but still useful, covering the earliest period in more detail.

Y122. ——. **The Spanish settlements within the present limits of the United States: Florida, 1562–1574.** N.Y. and London, 1905. Good account of the first Spanish settlements in Florida.

Y123. Chatelain, Verne E. **The defenses of Spanish Florida, 1565 to 1763.** Washington, 1941. Heavily documented study whose content is much broader than the title suggests.

Y124. Bolton, Herbert E. **The debatable land: a sketch of the Anglo-Spanish contest for the Georgia country.** Berkeley, 1925. Scholarly account of frontier rivalry between 1670 and 1763.

Y125. Lanning, John T. **The Spanish missions of Georgia.** Chapel Hill, 1935. This and *Y126* are good treatments of the role of Franciscan missions in the Spanish occupation of the Southeast.

Y126. Geiger, Maynard J. **The Franciscan conquest of Florida (1573–1618).** Washington, 1937.

Y127. Kinnaird, Lawrence, ed. **Spain in the Mississippi valley, 1765–1794: translations of materials from the Spanish archives in the Bancroft Library.** 3 v. Washington, 1946–49. [*Annual report of the American Historical Association for the year 1945,* v. 2–4.] Most documents originated in Louisiana and West Florida, and deal with Indian affairs, territorial administration, and commerce. Each volume contains an excellent introductory essay.

Y128. Gayarré, Charles E. A. **History of Louisiana.** 4th ed., 4 v., New Orleans, 1903. Covers French, Spanish, and United States rule. Although in some respects out of date, contains much information difficult to find elsewhere.

Y129. Robertson, James A., ed. **Louisiana under the rule of Spain, France, and the United States, 1785–1807.** 2 v. Cleveland, 1911. Collection of contemporary accounts.

Y130. Giraud, Marcel. **Histoire de la Louisiane française.** Paris, 1953 ff. Excellent study in progress by a French scholar. V. 1 covers the period 1698–1715.

Y131. Rodríguez Casado, Vicente. **Primeros años de dominación española en la Luisiana.** Madrid, 1942. Detailed study of Juan Antonio Ulloa's administration and revolt against it.

Y132. Whitaker, Arthur P., ed. and tr. **Documents relating to the commercial policy of Spain in the Floridas with incidental reference to Louisiana.** De Land, Fla., 1931.

Y133. ——. **The Mississippi question, 1795–1803.** See *AB396.*

Y134. Wagner, Henry R. **The Spanish Southwest, 1542–1794.** 2 v. Albuquerque, 1937. Revised and amplified edition of this invaluable bibliographical aid.

Y135. Hackett, Charles W., ed. **Historical documents relating to New Mexico, Nueva Vizcaya and approaches thereto, to 1773.** 3 v. Washington, 1923–37. Covers all northwestern Mexico and New Mexico, and deals with all phases of Spanish administration and frontier life. Volumes contain good historical introductions.

Y136. Gálvez, Bernardo de. **Instructions for governing the interior provinces of New Spain, 1786.** Tr. and ed. by Donald E. Worcester. Berkeley, 1951. These instructions by a Spanish viceroy contain useful information on northern Mexico and the Spanish Southwest.

Y137. Castañeda, Carlos E. **Our Catholic heritage in Texas, 1519–1936.** 6 v. Austin, 1936–50. Best general history of Texas.

Y138. Alessio Robles, Vito. **Coahuila y Texas en la época colonial.** Mexico, 1938. Heavily documented study with valuable bibliography.

Y139. Bolton, Herbert E. **Texas in the middle eighteenth century: studies in Spanish colonial history and administration.** Berkeley, 1915. Collection of scholarly essays.

Y140. Horgan, Paul. **Great river: the Rio Grande in North American history.** 2 v. N.Y., 1954. Competent and particularly readable history of a region where Spanish and Anglo-Saxon cultures meet.

Y141. Bolton, Herbert E. **Coronado, knight of pueblos and plains.** N.Y., 1949. Definitive biography of Coronado with exhaustive bibliography on the Spanish Southwest.

Y142. Hammond, George P., and Agapito Rey. **Don Juan de Oñate, colonizer of New Mexico, 1595–1628.** 2 v. Albuquerque, 1953. Contains some 170 documents, translated, edited, and annotated, which deal not only with Oñate, but with other personalities and the ethnography and geography of early New Mexico.

Y143. Bancroft, Hubert H. **The works of Hubert Howe Bancroft.** See *AB48*.

Y144. Caughey, John W. **History of the Pacific coast of North America.** N.Y., 1938. Best one volume history of the Pacific coast. Covers from Mexico to Alaska with emphasis on period before 1850.

Y145. Chapman, Charles E. **A history of California: the Spanish period.** N.Y., 1921. Popular and reliable history.

Y146. Wagner, Henry R. **The cartography of the northwest coast of America to the year 1800.** 2 v. Berkeley, 1937. History of explorations and cartography of the coast from Lower California to Alaska beginning with earliest voyages. Contains many useful reproductions of maps and an excellent bibliography.

Y147. Bolton, Herbert E. **Outpost of empire: the story of the founding of San Francisco.** N.Y., 1931. Separate edition of introductory volume to author's 5 v. documentary study of Anza's California expeditions.

Y148. Golder, Frank A. **Russian expansion on the Pacific, 1641–1850.** Cleveland, 1914. Best work in English on Russian exploration and settlement in the Pacific Northwest.

Y149. Folmer, Henry. **Franco-Spanish rivalry in North America, 1524–1763.** Glendale, Calif., 1953. Scholarly work with emphasis on diplomatic maneuverings.

Y150. Whitaker, Arthur P. **The Spanish-American frontier, 1783–1795: the westward movement and the Spanish retreat in the Mississippi valley.** Boston and N.Y., 1927. This and *Y151–152* are excellent studies on United States-Spanish conflicts along the frontier and the gradual withdrawal of Spain.

Y151. Brooks, Philip C. **Diplomacy and the borderlands: the Adams-Onís treaty of 1819.** Berkeley, 1939.

Y152. Griffin, Charles C. **The United States and the disruption of the Spanish empire, 1810–1822.** See *AB398*.

Y153. Smith, Justin H. **The annexation of Texas.** Corrected ed., N.Y., 1941. This and *Y154* together constitute the best accounts of the acquisition of the southwestern borderlands by the United States.

Y154. ——. **The war with Mexico.** See *AB222*.

AMERICAN MISCELLANY

Y155. Webb, Walter P. **The great frontier.** Boston, 1952. Controversial interpretation of the European colonies as a frontier and their impact on the development of western civilization. Emphasis is on America.

Y156. Kraus, Michael. **The Atlantic civilization: eighteenth century origins.** See *AB511*.

Y157. Gerbi, Antonelli. **La disputa del Nuovo Mondo: storia di una polemica, 1750–1900.** Milan, 1955. Much revised and expanded version of the author's earlier *Viejas polémicas sobre el Nuevo Mundo* (Lima, 1944). Examines sympathetic and antipathetic views of Europeans toward America, its environment, and its inhabitants.

Y158. Zea, Leopoldo. **América como conciencia.** Mexico, 1953. Primarily concerned with the quest for an American philosophy, with interesting chapters comparing Spanish American and English American culture and philosophy.

Y159. Carrier, Lyman. **The beginnings of agriculture in America.** N.Y., 1923. Deals with the origins of American agriculture and animal husbandry as a synthesis of indigenous products and European importations.

Y160. Ames, Oakes. **Economic annuals and human cultures.** Cambridge, Mass., 1939. Story of agricultural products which originated in America.

Y161. Weatherwax, Paul. **Indian corn in old America.** N.Y., 1954. Illustrated, semipopular account of the origins and cultivation of maize before Columbus.

INTER-AMERICAN RELATIONS

Y162. Calvo, Carlos, ed. **Colección histórica completa de los tratados . . . y otros actos diplomáticos de todos los estados de la América Latina . . . desde el año de 1493 hasta nuestros días.** 11 v. Paris, 1862–69. Includes treaties of colonial period and also historical notes on the more important treaties.

Y163. U. S. Department of State. **Foreign relations of the United States. Diplomatic papers.** Washington, 1861 ff. (Title varies.)

This series contains many volumes dealing with diplomatic relations between the United States and the Latin American nations.

Y164. Manning, William R., ed. **Diplomatic correspondence of the United States: inter-American affairs, 1831–1860.** 12 v. Washington, 1932–39. Valuable collection. Materials are classified chronologically for each country dealt with.

Y165. Burr, Robert N., and Roland D. Hussey, eds. and trs. **Documents on inter-American cooperation.** 2 v. Philadelphia, 1955. Contains 68 documents, including addresses, reports, and editorials covering the period 1810–1948. Useful narrative introductions.

Y166. Fitzgibbon, Russell H., ed. **The constitutions of the Americas, as of January 1, 1948.** Chicago, 1948. Texts and explanations of the constitutions of Latin America, Canada, and the United States.

Y167. Malagón, Javier, ed. **Las actas de independencia de América.** See *Z205.*

Y168. Bernstein, Harry. **Origins of inter-American interest, 1700–1812.** Philadelphia, 1945. Study in trade relations and the interchange of ideas between Spanish America and Boston, New York, and Philadelphia in the 18th century.

Y169. Lockey, Joseph B. **Pan-Americanism: its beginnings.** N.Y., 1920. Background of the movement from 1741 to 1825.

Y170. Duggan, Laurence. **The Americas: the search for hemisphere security.** N.Y., 1949. Thoughtful, non-technical treatment of inter-American relations by a statesman who knew his material intimately.

Y171. Gil, Enrique. **Evolución del panamericanismo: el credo de Wilson y el panamericanismo.** Buenos Aires, 1933. This and *Y172–174* are good accounts of the Pan American movement by representatives of several members of the American family.

Y172. Yepes, Jesús M. **Philosophie du panaméricanisme et organisation de la paix. Le droit panaméricain.** Neuchâtel, Switz., 1945.

Y173. Lobo, Helio. **O pan-americanismo e o Brasil.** São Paulo, 1939.

Y174. Humphrey, John T. **The inter-American system, a Canadian view.** Toronto, 1942.

Y175. Behrendt, Richard F. W. **Inter-American economic relations: problems and prospects.** N.Y., 1948. Essay on the nature of the Latin American economy and economic relations between Latin America and the United States.

Y176. Olson, Paul R., and C. Addison Hickman. **Pan American economics.** N.Y. and London, 1943. Detailed, factual account of economic relations between Latin America and the United States.

Y177. Whitaker, Arthur P. **The Western Hemisphere idea: its rise and decline.** Ithaca,

1954. Traces idea of the uniqueness of America from its European origins in the concept of the "New World" to its gradual integration into a world-wide conceptual framework.

Y178. Stuart, Graham H. **Latin America and the United States.** 5th ed., N.Y., 1955. New and revised edition of the best general work on the subject.

Y179. Bemis, Samuel F. **The Latin American policy of the United States: an historical interpretation.** N.Y., 1943. Excellent synthesis, but frankly written from a United States point of view.

Y180. Whitaker, Arthur P. **The United States and the independence of Latin America, 1800–1830.** See *AB399.*

Y181. ——. **The United States and Argentina.** Cambridge, Mass., 1954. This and *Y182–184* are useful studies from the *American Foreign Policy Library series.* Each contains a good summary of recent developments within the area treated as well as a survey of its relations with the United States.

Y182. ——. **The United States and South America. The northern republics.** Cambridge, Mass., 1948.

Y183. Perkins, Dexter. **The United States and the Caribbean.** Cambridge, Mass., 1947.

Y184. Cline, Howard F. **The United States and Mexico.** See *Z358.*

Y185. Evans, Henry C., Jr. **Chile and its relations with the United States.** Durham, 1927. This and *Y186–187* are monographs with emphasis on diplomatic relations.

Y186. Fitzgibbon, Russell H. **Cuba and the United States, 1900–1935.** Menasha, Wis., 1935.

Y187. Hill, Lawrence F. **Diplomatic relations between the United States and Brazil.** See *Z724.*

Y188. Perkins, Dexter. **A history of the Monroe doctrine.** Rev. ed., Boston, 1955. Summing up of the scholarship of this foremost authority.

Y189. Álvarez, Alejandro. **The Monroe doctrine, its importance in the international life of the states of the New World.** N.Y. and London, 1924. Excellent volume by a Chilean scholar. Includes historical sketch plus significant illustrative documents.

Y190. Tansill, Charles C. **Canadian-American relations, 1875–1911.** New Haven and Toronto, 1943. Topical study of important issues between the two countries from a United States point of view.

Y191. Keenleyside, Hugh L., and Gerald S. Brown. **Canada and the United States: some aspects of their historical relations.** Rev. and enl. ed., N.Y., 1952. Presents a Canadian point of view.

Y192. Brebner, John B. **North Atlantic triangle: the interplay of Canada, the United States, and Great Britain.** New Haven, 1945. Excellent synthesis of the main factors in the development of the United States and Canada, their interrelations, and their relations with Great Britain.

Y193. Hansen, Marcus L., and John B. Brebner. **The mingling of the Canadian and American peoples.** New Haven and Toronto, 1940. Study of intermigration between Canada and the United States from the Great Lakes to New Brunswick.

The four volumes listed above (*Y190–193*) are part of a 25 v. series, *Relations of Canada with the United States,* published between 1940 and 1945 by the Carnegie Endowment for International Peace, Division of Economics and History.

PERIODICALS

Y194. Revista de historia de América. Mexico, 1938 ff. Published twice yearly (quarterly, 1938–41) by the Pan American Institute of Geography and History. The only historical periodical dedicated to the history of America in a broad sense.

Y195. The Americas: a quarterly review of inter-American cultural history. Washington, 1944 ff. (Quarterly.) This and *Y196* contain material of general American interest although the emphasis is on Latin America.

Y196. The Hispanic American historical review. See *Z879.*

Y197. The American historical review. N.Y., 1895 ff. (Quarterly.) This and *Y198* are primarily concerned with United States history, but occasionally carry articles and items of general American interest.

Y198. The Mississippi Valley historical review. Cedar Rapids, Ia. 1914 ff. (Quarterly.)

Y199. Inter-American economic affairs. See *Z881.*

Y200. Cuadernos americanos. Mexico, 1942 ff. (Semimonthly.) Devoted to shorter essays in the humanities and social sciences, many of inter-American interest.

Y201. Florida historical quarterly. Gainesville, 1908 ff. This and *Y202* are useful for borderlands history.

Y202. The southwestern historical quarterly. Austin, 1897 ff. (Title varies.)

Y203. Pacific historical review. Glendale, Calif., 1932 ff. (Quarterly.) Useful for Pacific coast history.

Y204. American anthropologist. Menasha, Wisc., 1888 ff. (Quarterly.) This and *Y205* are recommended for American anthropology.

Y205. American antiquity: a quarterly review of American archeology. Menasha, Wisc., 1935 ff.

SERIALS

Y206. International Congress of Americanists. **Proceedings.** Nancy, etc., 1875 ff. A vast and valuable collection of papers on early American history and anthropology, particularly the latter.

Y207. Comas, Juan. **Los Congresos Internacionales de Americanistas: síntesis histórica e índice bibliográfico general, 1875–1952.** Mexico, 1954. A guide to material in *Y206.*

Y208. Pan American Institute of Geography and History. **Publications.** Mexico, 1930 ff. (Title varies.) Several useful series, including those on historians of the Americas, the teaching of history in various American countries, historical and archaeological monuments, materials for the study of American history in European archives, and bibliographical aids.

Y209. Pan American Union. **Catalogue of Pan American Union publications in English, Spanish, Portuguese, and French.** Washington, 1950 ff. (Title varies.) Guide to a number of valuable series published by the Pan American Union, including those on congresses and conferences, fine arts, foreign trade, law and treaties, and bibliography.

SECTION Z

Latin America

HOWARD F. CLINE *

In the quarter century since I. J. Cox summarized Latin American materials for the original *Guide* (see *Z1*), there has been a notable development in the scope, depth, and quantity of historical writing in the United States, in Latin America itself, and to a lesser degree in European centers, especially Spain. Many of these trends are summarized in the Gibson-Keen article (*Z220*), and are evident in the selections below.

The bibliographical apparatus supporting studies is by no means fully adequate, but basic summaries like those of Jones (*Z10*) and Haring (*Z4*), as well as that of Humphreys (*Z6*) for those restricted to the English language, represent highly useful tools at the student's ready disposal. Absolutely indispensable for following current production is the *Handbook of Latin American studies* (*Z3*), annually reporting substantial items in the social sciences and humanities. Stress is placed on these and other helpful publications because the restriction of space and the enormous output on Latin American history in the past quarter century make the listings below highly selective.

The entries cover twenty countries for the nearly half a millennium since America entered history in the written word. Innumerable worthy monographs, significant older books, and important articles and source materials simply could not be squeezed into the space of this bibliographical panorama. Hence emphasis has been placed on specialized bibliographical listings within area, period, or topical subdivisions. In general, chronicles, travel accounts, and other writings have reluctantly been omitted; many of those listed by Cox (*Z1*) are equally important today.

The predilection of Latin Americanists to mass their interests in the 16th century or the late 18th and early 19th century period of independence movements and to eschew narrative or analysis of the recent past are still dominant traits. Similarly, preferences for the biographical approach, the publication of documents rather than documented syntheses, and strong urges toward antiquari-

* The following contributed items and comments: Mathias C. Kiemen, subsections on Brazil, and other entries indicated by initials MCK; Rayford W. Logan, subsections on the French islands and Haiti, and other entries indicated by RWL.

anism still plague a great deal of their historical writings. Strong currents of nationalism have inhibited any general syntheses of consequence, to which has been added the growing realization of the complexity of the area. Monograph after monograph has shown that many of the easy generalizations concerning uniformities common to earlier generations rested on insubstantial bases, often legal codes that were normative rather than illustrative of actual practices. With mounting data have come changed interpretations. The major one is that rather than one specialty, Latin American history is now breaking into a multiplicity of specialties. Equally striking is the steady drift toward mundane establishment of fact and a reduction in the moral fervor and apologetics that enlivened earlier treatments. The exotic, the romantic, the crusade has by no means entirely disappeared, but the earlier cool superiority of the Anglo-Saxon treatments of Latin American phenomena and the heated polemic tones of writers in the latter republics treating their own past have been increasingly displaced by sympathetic attempts at understanding and impartiality.

In this section the traditional divisions into pre-Columbian, colonial, and national periods have been slightly modified. Materials of the late 18th century have been placed with those of the independence periods. The modern or national histories following 1830 (except Cuba) appear under areal subdivisions. Most of the items on Brazil, including its colonial history, have been kept in that subsection, as have items on Haiti. The reader is strongly urged to consult the general index of the entire volume, since a number of the collective works mentioned touch several areas and periods, but are not repeated in later areal or period subdivisions.

BIBLIOGRAPHIES, LIBRARIES, ARCHIVES, AND MUSEUMS

Bibliographies

Z1. Cox, Isaac J., ed. "Hispanic America." **A guide to historical literature** (N.Y., 1931), pp. 1051–87. The carefully selected, annotated items in the 1931 *Guide* are of continuing value, and many of these are not repeated in the present revision.

Z2. Grismer, Raymond L., ed. **A new bibliography of the literatures of Spain and Spanish America, including many studies on anthropology, archaeology, art, economics, education, geography, history, law, music, philosophy, and other subjects.** 6 v. to date. Minneapolis, St. Louis, and Dubuque, 1941 ff. A massive and monumental enterprise, stressing literary materials.

Z3. Handbook of Latin American studies. 1935 ff. Cambridge, Mass. and Gainesville, Fla., 1936 ff. (Annual.) Selective and annotated guide to recent published material on anthropology, art, economics, education, geography, government, history, international relations, labor and social welfare, language and literature, law, music, philosophy, and sociology. Produced by more than sixty cooperating scholars and prepared in the Hispanic Foundation of the Library of Congress, the *Handbook* is standard, authoritative bibliography covering current articles and books. Earlier volumes often contain special bibliographies, listed in Shelby (*Z15*). The *Handbook* is the fundamental point of departure for materials published after 1935. Entries on history comprise nearly a third of the annual volume, while many of the other eighteen main sections contain items of historical interest.

Z4. Haring, Clarence H., and others, eds. **The economic literature of Latin America: a tentative bibliography.** 2 v. Cambridge, Mass., 1935. Basic tool, which covers much wider ground than title indicates. Essentially synthesizes major materials, chiefly books, to point where the *Handbook of Latin American studies* begins systematic and extended coverage. Introduction lists classic and specialized Latin American bibliographies to about 1932. Ch. 1 on Latin America lists numerous general treatments.

Z5. Hartman, Hans W. "Recent German literature on Hispanic America." **Hisp. Am. hist. rev.,** 14 (Feb. 1934): 101–7; 16 supl. (Aug. 1936): 410–3; 19 supl. (May 1939): 226–30.

Z6. Humphreys, Robert A. **Latin American history: a guide to the literature in English.** London, 1958. A fundamental listing, extending greatly earlier listings by the same author. Completely reliable, and as comprehensive as is now possible.

Z7. **Índice histórico español: bibliografía histórica de España e Hispanoamérica.** See *VD3.*

Z8. **Inter-American review of bibliography. Revista interamericana de bibliografía.** Washington, 1951 ff. [Pan American Union.] (Quarterly.) Articles, reviews, listings of current and recent books and pamphlets, notes and news, and lists of O.A.S. and affiliated organs' publications. A major current bibliography of high merit. Supersedes *LEA: librarians, editors, authors* (nos. 1–12, Washington, 1949–50) which in turn superseded *Pan American bookshelf* (11 v., 1938–48).

Z9. Inter-American Statistical Institute. **Bibliography of selected statistical sources of the American nations.** See *B166.*

Z10. Jones, Cecil Knight. **A bibliography of Latin American bibliographies.** 2nd ed., Washington, 1942. A basic, selective listing aimed chiefly at bibliographers. Organized geographically, there are 3,016 numbered entries, often with descriptive but little critical comment, on both books and articles. Old but still an essential tool, now supplemented by "Bibliographies, lists, and indexes" subsections of the *Handbook of Latin American studies.* Nearly comprehensive to date of publication.

Z11. Mörner, Magnus. "Swedish contributions to the historical bibliography of Latin America." **Hisp. Am. hist. rev.,** 34 (Aug. 1954): 393–8. Also notes related literature in social and natural sciences.

Z12. Palau y Dulcet, Antonio. **Manual del librero hispano-americano.** 7 v. Barcelona, 1923–27. 2nd ed., Barcelona, 1948 ff. Basic bibliography, also giving sales prices of rare items.

Z13. Sabor, Josefa E. **Manual de fuentes de información, obras de referencia: enciclopedias, diccionarios, bibliografías, biografías, etc.** Buenos Aires, 1957. A pioneering and generally successful attempt by an Argentine librarian to provide a long-needed guide in Spanish to reference materials.

Z14. Sánchez Alonso, Benito. **Fuentes de la historia española e hispanoamericana.** See *VD1.*

Z15. Shelby, Charmion. "The Handbook of Latin American studies: its first fifteen years." **Inter-American review of bibliography,** 1 (Apr.-June 1951): 89–91. History, by a former assistant editor, of the *Handbook* (*Z3*), 1936–50, with listings of special essays, subject bibliographies, changes in sponsorship, editors, organization of volume, etc.

Z16. Vindel, Francisco. **Manual gráfico-descriptivo del bibliófilo hispano-americano, 1475–1850.** 11 v. Madrid, 1930–31. Supplement, 1934. Standard coverage.

Z17. Wilgus, A. Curtis. **Histories and historians of Hispanic America.** 2nd ed., N.Y., 1942. A useful bibliographical compilation, without much critical insight. Organized chronologically by centuries, with topical subheadings: introductory, general works, works on individual countries and regions. Contains selected lists of bibliographical and biographical collections and aids. Index defective.

Libraries, Archives, and Museums

Principal repositories for books and manuscripts related to Latin American history tend to parallel those for Spanish and Portuguese history. For the United States the Hilton *Handbook* (*Z31*), though unsatisfactory in many ways, provides general coverage; the Bosch García *Guía* (*Z19*) also includes U.S. institutions. In Spain, for colonial matters, the Archivo General de Indias in Seville is the chief American archive, with important collections also at Simancas and in Madrid. Publications and guides to these appear among listings of the *Catálogo* (*Z38*). Each of the independent republics has a national archive, and their holdings are summarized in Hill (*Z30*). There is no summary guide to the many European depositories which have important Latin American materials. So far as is now known, there is relatively little in the Orient on Latin America.

Z18. Biblioteca del Centro di Studi Americani (Rome). **Catalogo.** Rome, 1935 ff.

Z19. Bosch García, Carlos. **Guía a las instituciones que cultivan la historia de América.** Mexico, D. F., 1949. [Pan American Institute of Geography and History, Commission on History, Guías, 1. PAIGH publ. 94, CH publ. 9.] * Broadly inclusive for the United States, Latin America, and Europe, giving basic data, including publication series.

Z20. Burrus, Ernest J. "An introduction to bibliographical tools in Spanish archives and manuscript collections relating to Hispanic America." **Hisp. Am. hist. rev.,** 35 (Nov. 1955): 443–83. Provides a vast listing of items related to historical research, with many notations of catalogs, indices, and other finding aids.

Z21. Newberry Library. **A check list of manuscripts in the Edward E. Ayer Collection.** Comp. by Ruth L. Butler. Chicago, 1937. Most of the materials in this collection relate to Latin America or parts of the United States once under Spanish dominion.

Z22. University of Texas Library. **Guide to the Latin American manuscripts in the University of Texas Library.** Ed. by Carlos E. Castañeda and Jack A. Dabbs. Cam-

* Pan American Institute of Geography and History is hereafter abbreviated "PAIGH"; Commission on History, "CH."

bridge, Mass., 1939. Useful guide to a major repository of Latin American materials, with detailed notes on important manuscripts.

Z23. U. S. Library of Congress. **The Harkness Collection in the Library of Congress.** Comp. by Stella R. Clemence. 2 v. Washington, 1932–36. [1, *Calendar of Spanish manuscripts concerning Peru, 1531–1651;* 2, *Documents from early Peru.*] Meticulous calendars, with English translations. Similar coverage for the Cortés material from Mexico is planned.

Z24. Coleman, Laurence V. **Directory of museums in South America.** Washington, 1929. Still useful, though now outdated.

Z25. Madrid. Biblioteca Nacional. **Catálogo de obras iberoamericanas y filipinas de la Biblioteca Nacional de Madrid.** Ed. by Luisa Cuesta. Madrid, 1953. First volume of a projected larger coverage. Contains 3,364 entries (printed materials only) from the discovery of America to the present, mostly 18th century.

Z26. Ewing, William S. **Guide to the manuscript collections in the William L. Clements Library.** 2nd ed., Ann Arbor, 1953. Describes the 55 (of a total 305) MSS collections related to Latin America. The Zacatecas, Mexico material alone contains nearly 300,000 pages of manuscript.

Z27. British Museum. **Catalogue of the manuscripts in the Spanish language in the British Museum.** By Pascual de Gayangos y Arce. 4 v. London, 1875–93. V. 2 and 4 relate to colonial Spanish America.

Z28. Gropp, Arthur E. **Guide to libraries and archives in Central America and the West Indies, Panama, Bermuda, and British Guiana.** New Orleans, 1941. [Tulane University, Middle American Research Institute. Middle American research series, 10.]

Z29. Hill, Roscoe R. **American missions in European archives.** Mexico, 1951. [PAIGH, Commission on History. Misiones americanas en los archivos europeos, 2. PAIGH publ. 108, CH publ. 22.] Summary, with invaluable bibliographical data, of programs by United States institutions to secure copies of materials in Europe. Heavily emphasizes Spanish repositories.

Z30. ——. **The national archives of Latin America.** Cambridge, Mass., 1945. Basic data, including past and current publication programs. Kept up to date by the *Handbook of Latin American studies (Z3).*

Z31. Hilton, Ronald, ed. **Handbook of Hispanic source materials and research organizations in the United States.** 2nd ed., Stanford, 1956. Descriptions of collections, arranged geographically by state and locality, provided by repository institutions with interests in Spain, Portugal, and Latin America. Though uneven and with many omissions, brings together much elusive data. Covers from pre-Columbian period to pres-

ent; stronger on Latin American materials than Iberian.

Z32. Hussey, Roland D. "Manuscript Hispanic Americana in the Harvard College Library." **Hisp. Am. hist. rev.,** 17 (May 1937): 259–77.

Z33. Jones, Harold W. "Central and South American literature in the Army Medical Library." **Proceedings of the third convention of the Inter-American Bibliographical and Library Association** (N.Y., 1941), pp. 66–82.

Z34. Kraft, Walter C. **Codices vindobonenses hispanici: a catalog of the Spanish, Portuguese, and Catalan manuscripts in the Austrian National Library in Vienna.** Corvallis, Ore., 1957. Calendar of 185 mss., of which 13 wholly or in part deal with Latin America. For supplementary data on mss. in Vienna see review by E. J. Burrus, *Hisp. Am. hist. rev.,* 38 (Aug. 1958): 422.

Z35. Yale University Library. **Spanish American literature in the Yale University Library: a bibliography.** Ed. by Frederick B. Luquiens. New Haven and London, 1939. Though primarily stressing literature, provides data on rich Yale holdings in Latin American history and related fields.

Z36. Rivera, R. O. "The Peruvian collection of Duke University." **Hisp. Am. hist. rev.,** 10 (May 1930): 255–56.

Z37. Spain. Dirección General de Archivos y Bibliotecas. **Guía de las bibliotecas de Madrid.** Madrid, 1953.

Z38. Spain. Ministerio de Educación Nacional. **Catálogo de publicaciones.** 1958. Madrid, 1958. Lists 522 items—catalogs, lists, studies, periodicals, and other scholarly matter published since the 18th century. Also includes publications of certain museums and private organizations. Many relate to Latin America.

Z39. Spell, Lota M. **Research materials for the study of Latin America at the University of Texas.** Austin, 1954. Listing and appraisal of important manuscript and printed materials.

Z40. Tentori, Tullio. "I manoscritti di interesse americanistico esistenti nelle biblioteche ed archivi italiani: i manoscritti della Biblioteca Nazionale Centrale di Roma, Accademia Nazionale dei Lincei." **Rendiconti della classe di scienze morali, storiche e filologiche,** ser. 8, v. 8 (May-June 1953): 263–77. Forty MSS groups found in Rome. Comments emphasize ethnological content.

Z41. Termer, Franz. "Mittelamerikanische Museen." **Zeitschrift für ethnologie,** 80 (Berlin, 1955): 38–58. Details of leading anthropological museums, with photos of exhibits.

Z42. Tudela, José. **Los manuscritos de América en las bibliotecas de España.** Madrid, 1954. Though uneven and incomplete in coverage, a major aid in locating numerous overlooked collections of great significance. Invaluable listings of printed guides and catalogs.

Z43. U. S. National Archives. **Materials in the National Archives relating to Brazil.** Washington, 1942. In this same series of pamphlets are others covering materials relating to the Caribbean region (1942); west coast of South America (1942); Dominican Republic (1948); Cuba (1948); Haiti (1949); Mexican states of Sonora, Sinaloa, and Baja California (1952). The National Archives has in advanced preparation a general guide to Latin American materials.

Z44. University of California Library. **Spain and Spanish America in the libraries of the University of California: a catalogue of books.** 2 v. Berkeley, 1928–30. Preliminary coverage. This important repository continues to add many important items to its massive Latin American holdings.

Z45. Van den Eynde, Damian. "Calendar of Spanish documents in John Carter Brown Library." **Hisp. Am. hist. rev.,** 16 (Nov. 1936): 564–607.

ENCYCLOPEDIAS AND WORKS OF REFERENCE

Encyclopedias

Z46. Diccionario enciclopédico hispano-americano. 28 v. Barcelona, 1887–1910. Especially complete for 19th century and earlier.

Z47. Diccionario enciclopédico hispano-americano de literatura, ciencias, artes, etc. 23 v. N.Y., [1938].

Z48. Enciclopedia universal ilustrada europeo-americana. See *B119*.

Z49. Grande encyclopédia portuguesa e brasileira. 33 v. Lisbon and Rio de Janeiro, 1936–56. Especially useful for modern bibliographies. [MCK, HFC] *

Z50. Martin, Michael R., Gabriel H. Lovett, and others. **An encyclopedia of Latin-American history.** N.Y., 1956. A pioneering attempt, based on common textbooks and a few monographic sources. Little or no bibliography.

Biographical Guides

Z51. Almela Meliá, Juan. **Guía de personas que cultivan la historia de América.** See *Y22*.

Z53. Bolivia en el primer centenario de su 1953 ff. Biographical data on Spaniards and Latin Americans.

Z52. Anuario hispanoamericano. Madrid, independencia: apuntes para un diccionario

biográfico boliviano, 1825–1925. N.Y., 1925?

Z54. Diccionario biográfico de Venezuela. Ed. by Julio Cárdenas Ramírez and others. Madrid, 1953. A current "Who's who."

Z55. Davis, Harold E. **Latin American leaders.** N.Y., 1949. Brief treatment, with short bibliographies, of 16 political and cultural leaders.

Z56. Destruge, Camilo. **Album biográfico ecuatoriano.** 5 v. Guayaquil, 1903–05. Now chiefly of historical value.

Z57. Diccionario biográfico de Chile. 2nd ed., Santiago, 1938. Then current "Who's who."

Z58. Figueroa, Virgilio. **Diccionario histórico, biográfico y bibliográfico de Chile, 1800–1931.** 5 v. Santiago, 1925–31.

Z59. Who's who in Latin America: a biographical dictionary of notable living men and women of Latin America. Ed. by Ronald Hilton. 3rd ed., 7 v., Stanford, 1945–51. [1, *Mexico;* 2, *Central America and Panama;* 3, *Colombia, Ecuador, and Venezuela;* 4, *Bolivia, Chile, and Peru;* 5, *Argentina, Paraguay, and Uruguay;* 6, *Brazil;* 7, *Cuba, Dominican Republic, and Haiti.*] Revision and enlargement of work initiated by Percy A. Martin. Present edition includes about 10,000 biographies.

Z60. Peral, Miguel A. **Diccionario biográfico mexicano.** Mexico, [1944]. Highly uneven sketches, from pre-Conquest to World War II.

Z61. Pérez Marchant, Braulio. **Diccionario biográfico del Ecuador.** Quito, 1928.

Z62. Quién es quién en la Argentina: biográficas contemporáneas. 5th ed., Buenos Aires, 1951. 6th ed., 1955. Issued recurrently to bring coverage to date.

Z63. Quién es quién en Venezuela, Panamá, Ecuador, Colombia, con datos recopilados hasta el 30 de junio de 1952. Bogotá, 1952. About 4,000 current biographical sketches, many with photographs.

Z64. Sacramento Blake, Augusto V. A. **Diccionario bibliográphico brazileiro.** 7 v. Rio de Janeiro, 1883–1902. Bio-bibliographical data, arranged by first forename. Alphabetical index provided in Jango Fisher, *Índice alfabético do diccionario de Sacramento Blake* (Rio de Janeiro, 1937).

Z65. Scarone, Arturo. **Uruguayos contemporáneos: nuevo diccionario de datos biográficos y bibliográficos.** Montevideo, 1937.

Z66. Schirmer, Mathilda, ed. **Latin American leaders.** Chicago, 1951. Historical leaders.

Z67. Toro, Josefina del. **A bibliography of the collective biography of Spanish America.** Río Piedras, P. R., 1938.

Z68. Udaondo, Enrique. **Diccionario biográfico argentina.** Buenos Aires, 1938.

* The section editor's comments on Brazilian entries supplied by Mathias C. Kiemen are identified by initials HFC.

GEOGRAPHY

Z69. Alcedo, Antonio. **The geographical and historical dictionary of America and the West Indies, containing an entire translation of the Spanish work . . . with large additions and compilations . . . by G. A. Thompson.** 5 v. London, 1812–15. Provides much data on 18th century America.

Z70. American Geographical Society. **A catalogue of maps of Hispanic America.** 4 v. N.Y., 1933. Lists several hundred maps used to compile the basic Millionth Map of Hispanic America.

Z71. Berwick, Jacobo M., ed. **Mapas españoles de América, siglos XV–XVII.** Ed. by Duque de Alba and others. Madrid, 1951. Elaborate and useful presentation; impeccable scholarship. Text gives replete data on 79 maps, 1493–1699, from European repositories.

Z72. American Geographical Society. **Index to Map of Hispanic America 1:1,000,000.** Ed. by Earl P. Hanson. Washington, 1945. A standard gazetteer to thousands of place names shown on the Millionth Map and its derivatives.

Z73. James, Preston E. **Latin America.** Rev. ed., N.Y., 1950. First issued in 1942, this is considered the standard coverage of Latin American geography. Revisions bring it up to date.

Z74. López de Velasco, Juan. **Geografía y descripción universal de las Indias, recopilada por el cosmógrafocronista . . . desde el año de 1571 al de 1574.** Madrid, 1894. A gazetteer, with much data, on 16th century Spanish America.

Z75. Platt, Robert S. **Latin America, countrysides and united regions.** N.Y. and London, 1942. A general synthesis, slighting urban geography.

Z76. Newberry Library. **List of manuscript maps in the Edward E. Ayer Collection.** Comp. by Clara A. Smith. Chicago, 1927. Complements the Butler listing of MSS (*Z21*).

Z77. Spain. Archivo General de Indias. **Relación descriptiva de los mapas, planos, etc., de las antiguas audiencias de Panamá, Santa Fé y Quito existentes en el Archivo General de Indias.** By Pedro Torres Lanzas. Madrid, 1904.

Z78. ———. **Relación descriptiva de los mapas, planos, etc., de México y Floridas existentes en el Archivo General de Indias.** By Pedro Torres Lanzas. 2 v. Seville, 1900. Facsimile copies of these are deposited in the Map Division, Library of Congress.

Z79. U. S. Bureau of the Census. **Census atlas maps of Latin America.** Washington, 1955. Nine maps (four of area as a whole, five of individual countries) showing provincial divisions. Others in preparation.

Z80. Vindel, Francisco. **Mapas de América en los libros españoles de los siglos XVI al XVIII (1503–1798).** Madrid, 1955. Line reproductions of 241 facsimiles with bibliographical data, forming a monumental collection of basic materials. Restricted to books published in Spain and, therefore, has serious omissions.

Z81. Wilgus, A. Curtis. "List of articles relating to Hispanic America published in the periodicals of the American Geographical Society, 1852–1933 inclusive." *Hisp. Am. hist. rev.*, 14 (Feb. 1934): 114–30.

ANTHROPOLOGICAL WORKS

Z82. Adams, Richard N. **Cultural surveys of Panama-Nicaragua-Guatemala-El Salvador-Honduras.** Washington, 1957. Basic ethnological compendium, stressing rural cultures and brief descriptions of communities, illuminating non-native as well as Indian social life and problems in Central America.

Z83. Baldus, Herbert. **Bibliografia crítica da etnologia brasileira.** São Paulo, 1954. Monumental coverage of Brazilian ethnology and social anthropology. [MCK, HFC]

Z84. ———. **Etnologia brasileira no seculo XVI.** São Paulo, 1948. Source listings for 16th century ethnology. [MCK]

Z85. Boggs, Ralph S. **Bibliography of Latin American folklore.** N.Y., 1940. Standard work. Supplementary materials in *Handbook of Latin American studies* (*Z3*).

Z86. Comas, Juan. **Los Congresos Internacionales de Americanistas: síntesis histórica y índice bibliográfico general, 1875–1952.** Mexico, 1954. History of the group, and valuable bibliographical guide to articles in 30 v. of *Proceedings,* dealing with all phases of anthropology and history of American aboriginal and native peoples.

Z87. Herskovits, Melville J. **Economic anthropology: a study in comparative economics.** 2nd ed., rev. and enl., N.Y., 1952. Data on 26 Latin American societies appear in this standard work.

Z88. Krickeberg, Walter. **Etnología de América.** See *Y38.*

Z89. Murdock, George P. **Outline of South American cultures.** New Haven, 1951. Discussion of 1,051 tribal groups in 217 territorial units, comprising 24 cultural areas, with map.

Z90. Nash, Manning. **Machine age Maya: the industrialization of a Guatemalan community.** Glencoe, Ill., 1958. Important study of the impact of industrialization and modern economy on Guatemalan Indians.

Z91. Ramos, Arthur. **Introdução à antropologia brasileira.** 2 v. Rio de Janeiro, 1943–47. Summary discussion by a leading Brazilian. [MCK, HFC]

Z92. Smithsonian Institution. Institute of Social Anthropology. **Publications.** 16 v.

Washington, 1944–53. Social, cultural, physical anthropology, community studies. A completed series of monographs.

Z93. Steward, Julian H., ed. **Handbook of South American Indians.** 6 v. Washington, 1946–50. [1, *The marginal tribes;* 2, *The Andean civilizations;* 3, *The tropical forest tribes;* 4, *The circum-Caribbean tribes;* 5, *The comparative ethnology of South American Indians;* 6, *Physical anthropology, linguistics and cultural geography of South American Indians.*] Basic summaries, by many experts, on various phases of South American anthropology. The bibliographies are especially important. Index in preparation.

Z94. Steward, Julian H., and Louis C. Faron. **Native peoples of South America.** N.Y., 1959. Summary of major materials in *Z93*, with some more recent information.

Z95. Tax, Sol, and others. **Heritage of conquest: the ethnology of Middle America.** Glencoe, Ill., 1952. Summary status of problem statements by the Viking Fund Seminar on Middle American Ethnology. Bibliography lists monographs and serials relevant to area.

Z96. Tax, Sol, ed. **Indian tribes of aboriginal America.** Chicago, 1952. An attempted synthesis by several authors. Uneven.

Z97. Willems, Emílio. **Brasil: período indígena.** Mexico, 1953. Most modern and complete bibliography to date on the indigenes in Brazil. [MCK]

DEMOGRAPHIC STUDIES

General

Z98. Audera, Víctor. **La población y la inmigración en Hispanoamérica.** Madrid, 1954. Synthesis of history of immigration and present demographic situation of major countries, with bibliography.

Z99. Barón Castro, Rodolfo. **La población de El Salvador: estudio acerca de su desenvolvimiento desde la época prehispánica hasta nuestros días.** Madrid, 1942.

Z100. Durán Ochoa, Julio. **Población.** Mexico, 1955. Concerned primarily with relatively recent materials.

Z101. Rosenblat, Ángel. **La población indígena y el mestizaje en América.** 2 v. Buenos Aires, 1954. Deals with size and rate of change of population, 1492–1950; history and magnitude of mixed breeds; and historical analysis of colonial "castes." Indispensable revision of the slimmer 1945 edition; extensive bibliography. This is the major treatment at present of the historical demography of Spanish America.

Z102. Taeuber, Irene B. **General censuses and vital statistics in the Americas.** Washington, 1943. Systematic listing of sources.

Cultural-Ethnic Groups

Z103. Bastani, Tanus J. **O Libano, e os libaneses no Brasil.** Rio de Janeiro, 1945. Study of the Lebanese immigrants. [MCK]

Z104. Cohen, Jacob X. **Jewish life in South America.** N.Y., 1941.

Z105. Gerchunoff, Alberto. **The Jewish gauchos of the pampas.** Tr. by Prudencio de Pereda. N.Y., 1955.

Z106. Hatt, Paul K. **Backgrounds of human fertility in Puerto Rico: a sociological survey.** Princeton, 1952. Detailed study on data from 6,000 families, with analysis of rural-urban differences and other matters.

Z107. Irie, Toraji. "History of Japanese migration to Peru." **Hisp. Am. hist. rev.,** 31 (Aug. 1951): 437–52, (Nov. 1951): 648–64; 32 (Feb. 1952): 73–82. Tr., by William Himel, of 5 ch. from T. Irie, *Hojin Kaigai Hattenshi* (2 v., Tokyo, 1942). Footnotes by translator.

Z108. Maack, Reinhard, and Alexander Marchant. "German colonization in southern Brazil." **Handbook of Latin American studies** (1939), pp. 399–431. An annotated bibliography. First section, by Maack, is in German; the second, by Marchant, is in English. The latter includes works in English, French, Italian, Portuguese, and Spanish. [MCK]

Z109. Normano, João F., and Antonello Gerbi. **The Japanese in South America.** N.Y., 1943. Summary treatment, based on annotated language materials.

Z110. Paulin, Axel. **Svenska öden i Sydamerika.** Stockholm, 1951. History of Swedish expeditions, settlements, and commerce in Latin America. Extensive bibliography.

Z111. Peixoto, Afrânio, and others. **Os judeus na história do Brasil.** Rio de Janeiro, 1936. Essays by scholars on role of the Jews in Brazilian history. [MCK]

Z112. Pettinati, Francesco. **O elemento italiano na formação do Brasil.** São Paulo, 1939. Study of Italian immigrants in Brazil. [MCK]

Z113. Stewart, Watt. **Chinese bondage in Peru: a history of the Chinese coolie in Peru, 1849–1874.** Durham, 1951. History of 90,000 Chinese in Peru and of Chinese-Peruvian relations. Western language sources.

Z114. Willems, Emílio. **Assimilação e populações marginais no Brasil.** São Paulo, 1940. Problems of European assimilation in modern Brazil. [MCK]

Negro Slavery and Abolition

Z115. Aguirre Beltrán, Gonzalo. **La población negra de México, 1519–1810: estudio etnohistórico.** Mexico, 1946. Basic and pioneering study, including data on other ethnocultural groups in colonial Mexico.

Z116. Díaz Soler, Luis M. **Historia de la**

esclavitud negra en Puerto Rico (1493–1890). Madrid, 1953. Invaluable pioneering monograph, with documentary appendices and useful bibliography.

Z117. Duque-Estrada, Osório. A abolição. Rio de Janeiro, 1918. Abolition in Brazil. [MCK]

Z118. Goulart, Mauricio. Escravidão africana no Brasil das origens à extinção do tráfico. São Paulo, 1949. A well-documented work. [MCK]

Z119. King, James F. "The negro in continental Spanish America: a select bibliography." Hisp. Am. hist. rev., 24 (Aug. 1944): 547–59.

Z120. Moraes, Evaristo de. A campanha abolicionista (1879–1888). Rio de Janeiro, 1924. Abolition movement in Brazil. [MCK]

Z121. ——. A escravidão africana no Brasil (das origens à extinção). São Paulo, 1933. History of African slavery in Brazil. [MCK]

Z122. Pierson, Donald. Negroes in Brazil: a study of race contact at Bahia. Chicago, 1942. Basic study by a leading scientific authority on this controversial matter. [MCK]

Z123. Ramos, Arthur. The negro in Brazil. Washington, 1939. Tr. of O negro brasileiro (Rio de Janeiro, 1934). Summary views of the role of negroes in Brazilian life. A pioneering and important scientific contribution. [MCK]

Z124. Saco, José A. Historia de la esclavitud de la raza africana en el Nuevo Mundo y en especial en los países américo-hispanos. Havana, 1893. The standard work on this subject.

LINGUISTIC WORKS

Z125. Ayrosa, Plínio. Apontamentos para a bibliografia da língua tupí-guaraní. São Paulo, 1943. Best extant bibliography on this material. [MCK]

Z126. Garcés G., Jorge A. Paleografía diplomática española y sus peculiaridades en América. Quito, 1949. Texts and transcriptions, with useful data on inks, abbreviations, etc.

Z127. McQuown, Norman A. "The indigenous languages of Latin America." American anthropologist, n.s. 57:3 (June 1955): 502–70. As nearly complete list as possible of native languages of Middle and South America and the Antilles, with 5 maps. Basic work of major importance.

Z128. Mendonça, Renato. A influência africana no português do Brasil. 2nd ed., São Paulo, 1935.

Z129. Millares Carlo, Agustín, and José Ignacio Mantecón, eds. Album de paleografía hispanoamericana de los siglos XVI y XVII. 3 v. Mexico, 1955. Monumental coverage of Spanish American paleography,

with replete scholarly apparatus. A model and indispensable work.

Z130. Ribeiro, João P., ed. Dissertações chronológicas e críticas sôbre a história e jurisprudência ecclesiastica e civil de Portugal. 5 v. Lisbon, 1810–36. The classic work on paleography for the Portuguese language. [MCK]

Z131. Rivet, Paul, and Georges de Créqui Montfort. Bibliographie des langues aymará et kičua. 4 v. Paris, 1951–56. Major work, definitive in scope and coverage, on the two principal languages of the Peruvian Andes.

PRINTED SOURCES AND TEACHING MATERIALS

Printed Sources (Spanish America)

Colonial: General

Z132. Aznar, Luis. "Colecciones documentales éditas relativas a la historia de la América española." IIº Congreso Internacional de Historia de América (Buenos Aires, 1938), v. 5, pp. 40–55. A provisional attempt to list, by areas, the major documentary collections; heavily colonial.

Z133. Colección de documentos inéditos para la historia de España. 112 v. Madrid, 1842–95. Standard sources, many dealing with Spanish America. Indexed in George P. Winship, "Index of titles relating to America in the 'Colección de documentos inéditos para la historia de España,'" Bulletin of the Public Library of the City of Boston, 13 (1894): 250–63. More completely covered in Julián Paz, Catálogo de la Colección de documentos inéditos para la historia de España (2 v., Madrid, 1930–31).

Z134. Colección de documentos inéditos para la historia de Hispano-América. 14 v. Madrid, 1927–32.

Z135. Colección de documentos inéditos relativos al descubrimiento, conquista y organización de las antiguas posesiones españolas de América y Oceanía, sacados de los archivos del Reino, y muy especialmente del de Indias. See Y88.

Z136. Colección de documentos inéditos relativos al descubrimiento, conquista, y organización de las antiguas posesiones españolas de ultramar. 2nd ser., 25 v., Madrid, 1885–1932. This collection and the preceding one are inaccurately and carelessly edited materials from Patronato, Archivo General de las Indias, originally selected by Juan Bautista Muñoz. Nearly all materials are early 16th century, but represent only a minor fraction of the Archivo collections of this period. Indexed by Ernst Schäfer, Índice de la colección de documentos inéditos de Indias editada por Pacheco, Cárdenas y Torres de Mendoza y otros (Madrid, 1946). covering both series.

Z137. Documentos inéditos para la historia de España publicados por los señores duque de Alba, duque de Maura [et al.]. 7 v. Madrid, 1936–52. Varied materials; chiefly 16th century, but some 17th century documents.

Z138. Encinas, Diego, comp. **Cedulario indiano. . . . Reproducción facsímil de la edición única de 1596: estudio e índices por Alfonso García Gallo.** 5 v. Madrid, 1945–53. Invaluable compilation; excellent reproduction of this relatively rare work. Contains many items not in the *Recopilación* (*Z143*). V. 5 has useful study of Encinas, and other documents.

Z139. Spain. Ministerio de Fomento. **Relaciones geográficas de Indias.** Ed. by Marcos Jiménez de la Espada. 4 v. Madrid, 1881–97. Collection of the valuable Philip II regional questionnaires (1579 ff.) giving much useful local data.

Z140. Konetzke, Richard, ed. **Colección de documentos para la historia de la formación social de Hispanoamérica, 1493–1810.** Madrid, 1953 ff. First volume of a projected series on social history, containing 481 documents for period 1493–1592 with excellent indices.

Z141. Latorre, Germán. **Relaciones geográficas de Indias contenidas en el Archivo General de Indias de Sevilla. La Hispano-América del siglo XVI: Colombia, Venezuela, Puerto Rico, República Argentina, Virreinato de Nueva España.** 2 v. Seville, 1919–20. Supplements the Jiménez de la Espada collection (*Z139*).

Z142. Muro Orejón, Antonio, ed. **Cedulario americano del siglo XVIII: colección de disposiciones legales indianas desde 1680 a 1800, contenidas en los cedularios del Archivo General de Indias.** Seville, 1956 ff. V. 1 covers material 1679–1700 (Carlos II) providing official texts ordered chronologically and well indexed.

Z143. **Recopilación de leyes de los reinos de las Indias.** 1st ed., 4 v., Madrid, 1681; 2nd ed., 4 v., 1756; 3rd ed., 4 v., 1774; 4th ed., 3 v., 1791; 5th ed., 2 v., 1841. The Spanish colonial code. Citations to earlier cédulas are often inaccurate, but the collection is basic to understanding the broad legal structure of the Spanish system.

Z144. Spain. Ministerio de Fomento. **Cartas de Indias.** Madrid, 1877. Materials and documents on varied subjects, chiefly 16th century.

Z145. Zabálburu, Francisco de, ed. **Nueva colección de documentos inéditos para la historia de España y de sus Indias.** 6 v. Madrid, 1892–96.

Colonial: Middle America-Caribbean

Z146. **Colección de documentos referentes a la historia colonial de Nicaragua: recuerdo del centenario de la independencia nacional, 1821–1921.** Managua, 1921.

Z147. Córdoba, Pedro T. de. **Memorias geográficas, históricas, económicas y estadísticas de la isla de Puerto-Rico.** 6 v. San Juan, 1831–33.

Z148. Cuevas, Mariano, comp. **Documentos inéditos del siglo XVI para la historia de México.** Mexico, 1914.

Z149. Fernández, León, comp. **colección de documentos para la historia de Costa Rica.** 10 v. San José, 1881–1907.

Z150. García Icazbalceta, Joaquín, ed. **Colección de documentos para la historia de México.** 2 v. Mexico, 1858–66. Chiefly concerns the conquest.

Z151. ———, ed. **Nueva colección de documentos para la historia de México.** 5 v. in 3. Mexico, 1886–92. Continues materials in the preceding work.

Z152. García Pelaez, Francisco de Paula, ed. **Memorias para la historia del antiguo reyno de Guatemala.** 3 v. Guatemala, 1851–52.

Z153. García Pimental, Luís, ed. **Documentos históricos de Méjico.** 6 v. in 4. Mexico, Paris, and Madrid, 1903–07. Manuscripts from Joaquín García Icazbalceta collection, carelessly edited by his son. Covers colonial period to 1802.

Z154. Murga, Vicente, ed. **Historia documental de Puerto Rico.** Río Piedras, 1956 ff. V. 1 (1956) covers cabildo materials, 1527–50. Series apparently will cover only colonial period.

Z155. Paso y Troncoso, Francisco del, comp. **Epistolario de Nueva España, 1505–1818.** 16 v. Mexico, 1939–42. Miscellaneous but important items. V. 16 contains index.

Z156. ———, ed. **Papeles de Nueva España . . . segunda sér.: geografía y estadística.** 6 v. Madrid, 1905–06. Chiefly 16th century "Relaciones geográficas" of various local units. V. 1 is "Suma de visitas," *ca.* 1550, giving brief description of more than 800 Indian settlements.

Z157. Portilla, Anselmo de la, ed. **Instrucciones que los virreyes de Nueva España dejaron a sus sucesores.** 2 v. Mexico, 1873. State of the realm summaries.

Z158. Puga, Vasco de, ed. **Provisiones, cédulas, instrucciones para el gobierno de la Nueva España.** Madrid, 1945. Re-edition of basic 1563 source materials covering 1519–63.

Z159. Scholes, France V., and Eleanor B. Adams, eds. **Documentos para la historia del México colonial.** 6 v. Mexico, 1954–59. Limited editions of basic 16th century documents from the Archivo General de Indias (Seville). Other volumes in preparation.

Z160. Serrano y Sanz, Manuel, ed. **Relaciones históricas y geográficas de América Central.** Madrid, 1908. Relaciones of the 16th century.

Z161. Tapia y Rivera, Alejandro. **Biblioteca histórica de Puerto-Rico que contiene**

varios documentos de los siglos XV, XVI, XVII y XVIII. San Juan, 1854. 2nd ed., 1945.

Z162. Vega Bolaños, Andrés, ed. **Colección Somoza: documentos para la historia de Nicaragua.** V. 1–17. Madrid, 1954–57. These volumes of this useful series cover materials to 1550. Others in progress.

Colonial: South America

Z163. Angelis, Pedro de, ed. **Colección de obras y documentos relativos a la historia antigua y moderna de las provincias del Río de la Plata.** 6 v. Buenos Aires, 1836–37. 2nd ed., 5 v., 1910. Chiefly colonial period.

Z164. Beltrán y Rózpide, Ricardo, ed. **Colección de las memorias o relaciones que escribieron los virreyes del Perú acerca del estado en que dejaban las cosas generales del reino.** Madrid, 1921 ff. State of the realm summaries.

Z165. Documentos históricos y geográficos relativos a la conquista y colonización rioplatense. 5 v. Buenos Aires, 1941 [Comisión Oficial del IV Centenario de la Primera Fundación de Buenos Aires, 1536–1936.] Exceptionally valuable for material from archives. Careful editing.

Z166. Friede, Juan, ed. **Documentos inéditos para la historia de Colombia.** 4 v. Bogotá, 1955–56. [1, 1509–28; 2, 1529–32; 3, 1533–35; 4, 1535–38.] Early Colombian and Caribbean documents from Archivo General de Indias. Part of projected 10 v. collection through 1550.

Z167. Fuentes, Manuel A., ed. **Memorias de los vireyes que han gobernado el Perú durante el tiempo del coloniaje español.** 6 v. Lima, 1859.

Z168. García Santillán, Juan C. **Legislación sobre indios del Río de la Plata en el siglo XVI.** Madrid, 1928. [Biblioteca de Historia Hispano-Americana.]

Z169. Levillier, Roberto, ed. **La Audiencia de Charcas. Correspondencia de presidentes y oidores: documentos del Archivo de Indias.** 3 v. Madrid, 1918–22. Covers 1561–1600.

Z170. ——, ed. **Audiencia de Lima.** Correspondencia de presidentes y oidores: documentos del Archivo de Indias. Madrid, 1922. Covers period 1549–64.

Z171. ——, ed. **Gobernación de Tucumán. Papeles de gobernadores en el siglo XVI: documentos del Archivo de Indias.** Madrid, 1920.

Z172. ——, ed. **Gobernantes del Perú. Cartas y papeles, siglo XVI.** 14 v. Madrid, 1921–26.

Z173. Medina, José Toribio, ed. **Colección de documentos inéditos para la historia de Chile, desde el viage de Magallanes hasta la batalla de Maipó, 1518–1818.** 30 v. Santiago, 1888–1902. Material only to 1567, despite title; comprehensive to that date.

Z174. ——, ed. **Colección de documentos inéditos para la historia de Chile.** 2nd ser., Santiago, 1956 ff. Complements the 30 v. 1st series (*Z173*), which included 84 of the 234 MS volumes he compiled. The 2nd, posthumous series will include items to 1806.

Z175. Moreyra Paz Soldán, Manuel, ed. **Documentos para la historia económica del virreinato peruano.** Lima, 1956 ff. [Instituto Histórico del Perú.] V. 1 initiates the series with consulado papers (1706–20).

Z176. Moreyra Paz Soldán, Manuel, and Guillermo Céspedes, eds. **Virreinato peruano. Documentos para su historia: colección de cartas de virreyes.** 3 v. Lima, 1953–54. [Instituto Histórico del Perú.] Correspondence of Monclova (1689–1705), superbly edited. Projected as a continuing series.

Z177. Polo, José T., ed. **Memorias de los virreyes del Perú, marqués de Mancera y conde de Salvatierra.** Lima, 1899.

Z178. Posada, Eduardo, and Pedro M. Ibáñez, eds. **Relaciones de mando: memorias presentadas por los gobernantes del Nuevo Reino de Granada.** Bogotá, 1910.

Z179. Radaelli, Sigfrido A., ed. **Memorias de los virreyes del Río de la Plata.** Buenos Aires, 1945.

Z180. Relaciones de los vireyes y audiencias que han gobernado el Perú. 3 v. Lima, 1867–72.

Z181. Rodríguez Casado, Vicente, and Florentino Pérez Ebid, eds. **Memoria de gobierno de Manuel Amat y Junient, virrey del Perú.** Seville, 1947.

Z182. Rodríguez Casado, Vicente, and Guillermo Lohmann Villena, eds. **Memoria de gobierno de Joaquín de la Pezuela, virrey del Perú.** Seville, 1947. The series, published by the Escuela de Estudios Hispanoamericanos, of which this is a part contains numerous other "memorias" of individual viceroys and governors in the Andean area.

Z183. Rodríguez Casado, Vicente, and José A. Calderón Quijano, eds. **Memoria de gobierno de José Fernández de Abascal y Sousa, virrey del Perú.** 2 v. Seville, 1944.

Z184. Urteaga, Horacio H., and Carlos A. Romero, eds. **Colección de libros y documentos referentes a la historia del Perú.** 12 v. Lima, 1916–19.

Enlightenment and Independence, 1765–1830

Z185. Archivo del General José Antonio Páez. Bogotá, 1939 ff. [Fundación John Boulton.] The two well-edited volumes which have appeared cover period 1818–23. The Boulton Foundation has an elaborate program of reissuing basic materials on the independence period of northern South America.

Z186. Buenos Aires. Museo Mitre. **Documentos del Archivo de Belgrano.** 7 v. Buenos Aires, 1913–17.

Z187. Buenos Aires. Museo Mitre. **Documentos del Archivo de Pueyrredón.** 4 v.

Buenos Aires, 1912. Letters exchanged with San Martín after retirement.

Z188. Buenos Aires. Museo Mitre. **Documentos del Archivo de San Martín.** 12 v. Buenos Aires, 1910–11.

Z189. Carranza, Adolfo P., ed. **San Martín, su correspondencia, 1823–1850.** 3rd ed., Buenos Aires, 1911.

Z190. University of Texas Library. **Independent Mexico in documents: independence, empire, and republic: a calendar of the Juan E. Hernández y Dávalos Manuscript Collection.** Comp. by Carlos E. Castañeda and Jack A. Dabbs. Mexico, 1954. Detailed listing of 2,937 items, chiefly concerning independence; excellent indices. Indication of materials published in *Z199*.

Z191. Colección de documentos relativos a la vida pública del libertador de Colombia y de Perú, Simón Bolívar. 22 v. Caracas, 1826–28. After numerous difficulties, reissued and supplemented as José F. Blanco and Ramón Azpurúa, eds., *Documentos para la historia de la vida pública del libertador de Colombia, Perú, y Bolivia* (14 v., Caracas, 1875–78).

Z192. Colección de historiadores y de documentos relativos a la independencia de Chile. 34 v. Santiago, 1900–46. For index see *Z212*.

Z193. Cortázar, Roberto, ed. **Cartas y mensajes de Santander.** Bogotá, 1953 ff. When completed will provide extant scattered correspondence of Francisco de Paula Santander, 1812 ff., including reprints of much printed material. Not a completely critical edition.

Z194. Desdevises du Dézert, Georges N. **Les sources manuscrites de l'histoire de l'Amérique Latine à la fin du XVIIIᵉ siècle (1760–1807).** Paris, 1914. [Nouvelles archives des missions scientifiques et littéraires, n.s. 21, no. 12.]

Z195. Documentos relativos a los antecedentes de la independencia de la República Argentina. 3 v. Buenos Aires, 1912–13. [Universidad Nacional (Buenos Aires), Facultad de Filosofía y Letras, Sección de Historia.]

Z196. Donoso, Ricardo, and others, eds. **Archivo de don Bernardo O'Higgins.** 12 v. Santiago, 1946–53. (Others in preparation.) Rich and comprehensive collection covering the whole epoch. A continuing series of prime importance.

Z197. Documentos históricos mexicanos: obra conmemorativa del primer centenario de la independencia de México. Ed. by Genaro García and Manuel Orozco y Berra. 7 v. Mexico, 1910–12. Chiefly post-1810.

Z198. Guillén y Tato, Julio F. **Independencia de América: índice de los papeles de expediciones de Indias.** 3 v. Madrid, 1953. Materials from newly formed Archivo General de Marina listing items on naval aspects, a neglected field. Covers 1807–39.

Z199. Hernández y Dávalos, Juan E., ed. **Colección de documentos para la historia de la guerra de independencia de México de 1808–1821.** 6 v. Mexico, 1877–82. Includes materials to 1814, only a small part of his collection which is now at the University of Texas. See *Z190*.

Z200. Humphreys, Robert A., ed. **British consular reports on the trade and politics of Latin America, 1824–1826.** London, 1940. [Royal Historical Society, Camden 3rd ser., 63.]

Z201. Lecuna, Vicente, ed. **Colección de cartas del Libertador.** 11 v. Caracas and N.Y., 1929–48. Nearly complete standard collection of Bolívar's letters and related materials.

Z202. ——, comp. **Selected writings of Bolívar.** Ed. by Harold A. Bierck; tr. by Lewis Bertrand. 2 v. N.Y., 1951. Useful selection translated into English. Covers 1810–30.

Z203. Lecuna, Vicente, and Esther Barret de Nazaris, eds. **Cartas de Santander.** 3 v. Caracas, 1942. Highly reliable collection.

Z204. ——, eds. **Relaciones diplomáticas de Bolívar con Chile y Buenos Aires.** 2 v. Caracas, 1954. Useful compilation of materials published in scattered collections, verified here for accuracy.

Z205. Malagón, Javier, ed. **Las actas de independencia de América.** Washington, 1955. [Pan American Union.] Facsimiles of originals or contemporary copies of the independence acts and declarations of the American republics, with printed texts of each, and important notes.

Z206. Manning, William R., ed. **Diplomatic correspondence of the United States concerning the independence of Latin-American nations.** 3 v. N.Y., 1925. Arranged chronologically within countries.

Z207. O'Leary, Daniel F. **Memorias.** 32 v. Caracas, 1879–88. Bolívar correspondence by his chief of staff, 1818 ff.

Z208. ——. **Memorias del General Daniel Florencio O'Leary: narración.** 3 v. Caracas, 1952. Republication, with notes, of final 3 v. of the classic source (*Z207*). Superior to incomplete original.

Z209. Otero Muñoz, Gustavo. "Archivo Santander: erratas sustanciales en los veinticuatro tomos." **Boletín de historia y antigüedades,** 30 (Bogotá, Jan.-Feb. 1943): 1–222. Substantial contribution; essential for use of *Z211*.

Z210. Documentos para la historia de la revolución de 1809. Ed. by Carlos Ponce Sanginés and Raúl Alfonso García. 4 v. La Paz, 1953–54. (Others in preparation.) Projected series of essays and documents on independence movements in Bolivia.

Z211. Archivo Santander. Ed. by Ernesto Restrepo Tirado. 24 v. in 20. Bogotá, 1913–32. Despite errors, still a classic and basic

Latin America 667

source. See Otero Muñoz (*Z209*). A corrected edition was begun in 1940, but only one volume appeared.

Z212. Villalobos, S. **Índice de la Colección de historiadores y de documentos relativos a la independencia de Chile.** Santiago, 1956. Index to *Z192*.

Z213. Webster, Charles, ed. **Britain and the independence of Latin America, 1812–1830: select documents from the Foreign Office archives.** 2 v. London, 1938. The introduction is especially useful, and has been issued separately.

Teaching Aids

Z214. Behrendt, Richard F. **Modern Latin America in social science literature.** Hamilton, N.Y., 1949. Highly selected, annotated bibliography of books, pamphlets, and periodicals in English in fields of economics, politics, and sociology; partly topical, partly geographical-topical in organization. Focused on the recent past. Primarily for undergraduates and non-specialists.

Z215. Gibson, Charles. **The colonial period in Latin American history.** Washington, 1958. [American Historical Association.] Brief but authoritative summary guide to recent research and changes in interpretation. Though intended for secondary school teachers, it has more universal value. Much bibliographical insight.

Z216. Hart, Estellita. **Courses on Latin America in institutions of higher education in the United States, 1948–1949.** Washington, 1949. Indicates texts, outside reading materials, etc., used in some 2,000 courses.

Z217. Keen, Benjamin, ed. **Readings in Latin American civilization, 1492 to the present.** Boston, 1955. Well-selected and well-edited translations, with helpful introductory materials.

HISTORIOGRAPHY

Z218. Carbonell, Diego. **Escuelas de historia en América.** Buenos Aires, 1943. Latin American views of various historiographical schools.

Z219. Feliú Cruz, Guillermo. **Historiografía colonial de Chile.** Santiago, 1958 ff.

Z220. Gibson, Charles, and Benjamin Keen. "Trends of United States studies in Latin American history." **Am. hist. rev.,** 62 (July 1957): 855–77. Basic review of materials published to 1955, stressing and evaluating work on colonial and national periods since about 1930. Invaluable bibliographical notes.

Z221. Pan American Institute of Geography and History. Commission on History. **Historiographie d'Haïti.** By Catts Pressoir and others. Mexico, 1953.

Z222. ——. **A study on the historiography of the British West Indies to the end of the nineteenth century.** By Elsa V. Goveia. Mexico, 1956.

Z223. ——. **Historiografía del Ecuador.** By Isaac J. Barrera. Mexico, 1956.

Z224. ——. **Historiografía del Brasil, siglo XVI.** By José Honório Rodrigues. Mexico, 1957.

Z225. ——. **Historiografía del Paraguay.** By Efraím J. Cardoso. Mexico, 1957.

Z226. Porras Barrenechea, Raúl. **Fuentes históricas peruanas.** Lima, 1954. Scholarly discussion of Peruvian historiography; good bibliography.

Z227. Rodrigues, José Honório. **A pesquisa histórica no Brasil.** Rio de Janeiro, 1952. Discussion of Brazilian historiography. [MCK, HFC]

SHORTER GENERAL HISTORIES

Z228. Bannon, John F. **History of the Americas.** 2 v. N.Y., 1952. [1, *The colonial Americas*; 2, *The American nations*.] For non-specialists, with highly useful bibliographical listings and discussions.

Z229. Bernstein, Harry. **Modern and contemporary Latin America.** Philadelphia, 1952. More than a text, less than a full history. Covers Mexico, Argentina, Brazil, Chile, Colombia, and the APRA in Peru.

Z230. Mörner, Magnus. **Latinamerika.** Stockholm, 1957. Useful general summary in Swedish, clearly and interestingly written. Final chapter discusses Swedish relations with the area from colonial times.

Z231. Navarro y Lamarca, Carlos. **Compendio de la historia general de América.** 2 v. Buenos Aires, 1910–13. One of the few attempts at general synthesis by Latin American hands. Not fully successful.

Z232. Sánchez, Luis Alberto. **Historia general de América.** See *Y65*.

Z233. Worcester, Donald E., and Wendell G. Schaeffer. **The growth and culture of Latin America.** N.Y., 1956. Basically a textbook, this work synthesizes a great body of recent monographic data and reflects modern trends in historiography.

LONGER GENERAL HISTORIES

Z234. Historia de América y de los pueblos americanos. Ed. by Antonio Ballesteros y Berreta. Barcelona, 1936 ff. [1, Luís Pericot y García, *América indígena* (1936); 2, L. Pericot García and Manuel Ballesteros, *América indígena (las culturas americanas)* (2 v., in progress); 3, A. Ballesteros y Berreta, *Génesis del descubrimiento* (1947); 4–5, A. Ballesteros y Berreta, *Cristóbal Colón y el descubrimiento de América* (2 v,

1945); 6, Amando Melón y Ruíz de Gordejuela, *Los primeros tiempos de la colonización: Cuba y las Antillas* (1952); 7, Angel de Altolaguirre y Duvale, *Descubrimiento y conquista de México* (1954); 8, Julián M. Rubio, *Exploración y conquista del Río de la Plata, siglos XVI y XVII* (1942); 9, M. Ballesteros, *Descubrimiento y conquista del Perú* (in press); 10, Demetrio Ramos, *Descubrimiento y conquista de Venezuela y Nueva Granada* (2 v., in preparation); 11, Francisco Esteve Barba, *Descubrimiento y conquista de Chile* (1946); 12, Ciriaco Pérez Bustamente and Jaime Delgado, *Los virreinatos en los siglos XVI y XVII* (in progress); 13, Cayetano Alcázar Molina, *Los virreinatos en el siglo XVIII* (1945); 14, José M. Ots Capdequí, *Instituciones* (in press), and Diego Angulo, *Arte colonial* (in progress); 15, Antonio Ybot León, *La iglesia y los eclesiásticos españoles en la Empresa de Indias* (v. 1, 1954; v. 2, in press); 16, F. Esteve Barba, *Cultura virreinal* (in press); 17, H. William Elson, *Estados Unidos de América,* and Antonio Pardo Riquelme, *Canadá* (1956); 18, Jaime Cortesão and Pedro Calmón, *El Brasil* (1956); 19, Ramón Ezquerra Abadía, *La emancipación de Hispanoamérica* (in progress); 20, Sígfrido A. Radaelli and Enrique de Gandia, *Argentina independiente* (in press); 21, Efraím Cordozo, *Paraguay independiente,* and Juan E. Pivel Devoto, *Uruguay independiente* (1949); 22, José Bravo Ugarte, *México independiente* (in press); 23, Rodolfo Barón Castro, *Centroamérica independiente y las Antillas* (in progress); 24, Nicolás García Samudio, Jesús A. Cova, and Oscar E. Reyes, *Colombia, Venezuela y Ecuador independientes* (in press); 25, Jorge Basadre, *Chile, Perú y Bolivia independientes* (1948)]. Partially completed attempt to provide comprehensive coverage in individual volumes, uneven in quality.

Z235. Bancroft, Hubert H. **Works.** V. 1–16. San Francisco, 1882–89. [1–5, *The native races;* 6–8, *History of Central America;* 9–14, *History of Mexico;* 15–16, *History of the north Mexican states and Texas.*] These first 16 of the Bancroft volumes are especially relevant to Latin America and, despite their known drawbacks, still form an essential point of departure for many matters. They tend to synthesize to their date of publication the major printed materials and manuscript sources. Though difficult to use, the bibliographical apparatus has continuing value.

Z236. Herrera y Tordesillas, Antonio de. **Historia general de los hechos de los castellanos en las islas y tierra-firme del Mar Océano.** 17 v. Madrid, 1934–57. Re-issue of the "official" 17th century history of the Spanish overseas possessions (4 v., Madrid, 1601–15).

HISTORIES OF SPECIAL PERIODS (SPANISH AMERICA)

Pre-Columbian

Z237. Alcina Franch, José. **Fuentes indígenas de México: ensayo de sistematización bibliográfica.** Madrid, 1956. Useful but incomplete data on 300 native sources.

Z238. Barlow, Robert H. **The extent of the empire of the Culhua Mexica.** Berkeley and Los Angeles, 1949. Useful pioneering attempt, based on numerous sources. Discussion of sources is valuable.

Z239. Baudin, Louis. **La vie quotidienne au temps des derniers Incas.** Paris, 1955. Readable and generally accurate summary; well documented.

Z240. Bushnell, Geoffrey H. S. **Peru.** N.Y., 1957. [Ancient peoples and places series.] Summary of Peruvian archaeology, by a British authority, addressed to general readers.

Z241. Caso, Alfonso. **The Aztecs: people of the sun.** Tr. by Lowell Dunham. Norman, 1958. A summary volume on Aztec religion and beliefs by an outstanding Mexican authority.

Z242. García Granados, Rafael. **Diccionario biográfico de historia antigua de Méjico.** 3 v. Mexico, 1952–53. Massive compilation on ancient Mexican personages and mythical beings.

Z243. Krickeberg, Walter. **Altmexikanische Kulturen.** Berlin, 1956. Sound summary treatment.

Z244. Mason, John Alden. **The ancient civilizations of Peru.** Baltimore, 1957. Sound general synthesis for the non-specialist. Supplements and nearly replaces Means.

Z245. Means, Philip A. **Ancient civilizations of the Andes.** N.Y. and London, 1931. Though obsolete in part, still a useful summary. For research it should be checked against equivalent parts of *Handbook of South American Indians* (*Z93*).

Z246. ——. "Biblioteca andina. Pt. 1, The chroniclers, or the writers of the 16th and 17th centuries who treated of the pre-Hispanic history and culture of the Andean countries." **Transactions of the Connecticut Academy of Arts and Sciences,** 29 (New Haven, 1928): 271–525. Useful synthesis to date of publication.

Z247. Morley, Sylvanus G. **The ancient Maya.** See *E104.*

Z248. Orozco y Berra, Manuel. **Historia antigua y de la conquista de México.** 4 v. in 2 and atlas. Mexico, 1880. V. 1–3 provide detailed aboriginal history; v. 4, native side of conquest.

Z249. Soustelle, Jacques. **La vie quotidienne des Aztèques à la veille de la conquête espagnole.** Paris, 1955. Comprehensive and informed survey, based on written sources rather than archaeology. Supplements and corrects the standard Vaillant treatment (*Z252*).

Z250. Termer, Franz. **Die Mayaforshung.** Leipzig, 1952. [Deutsche Akademie der Naturforscher, Nova Acta Leopoldina, n.s. 105.] Documented review of Maya research and results.

Z251. Thompson, John Eric S. **The rise and fall of Maya civilization.** See *E118.* Supplements Morley (*Z247*).

Z252. Vaillant, George C. **Aztecs of Mexico.** Garden City, 1941. Still standard, although archaeological discussions have been outmoded by later research. Developments in this field are currently reported in *Handbook of Latin American studies* (*Z3*).

Discovery, Exploration, Conquest

Z253. Ashburn, Percy M. **The ranks of death: a medical history of the conquest of America.** N.Y., 1947. Important pioneering work, throwing light on history of medicine and on the conquest.

Z254. Chamberlain, Robert S. **The conquest and colonization of Honduras, 1502–1550.** Washington, 1953. Detailed narrative; exhaustive and standard.

Z255. ——. **The conquest and colonization of Yucatan, 1517–1550.** Washington, 1948. Definitive; based on exhaustive documentary data.

Z256. Descola, Jean. **Les conquistadores.** Paris, 1954. English tr., N.Y., 1957. General history of the conquest, based on standard printed materials and secondary works; sympathetic view of the conquest.

Z257. Díaz del Castillo, Bernal. **The discovery and conquest of México, 1517–1521.** Tr. by A. P. Maudslay. N.Y., 1956. Classic and important as well as interesting account by a common soldier. Numerous other editions.

Z258. García Icazbalceta, Joaquín. **Bibliografía mexicana del siglo XVI.** Mexico, 1886. 2nd ed., ed. by Agustín Millares Carlo, 1954. Re-issue, with additional material, of a standard classic bibliography. Here will be found numerous chroniclers and others omitted from treatment of the period in this *Guide.*

Z259. Graham, Robert B. Cunninghame. **The conquest of the River Plate.** London and N.Y., 1924. Long, charming, and standard account.

Z260. Hanke, Lewis. **The first social experiments in America.** Cambridge, Mass., 1935. Theocratic experiments in the early West Indies where Hieronymite friars set up Utopian Indian communities.

Z261. ——. **The Spanish struggle for justice in the conquest of America.** Philadelphia, 1949. Basic treatment of imperial socio-intellectual developments and doctrinal clashes from which policies emerged.

Z262. Lafuente Machain, Ricardo de la. **Conquistadores del Río de la Plata.** 2nd ed., Buenos Aires, 1943.

Z263. MacNutt, Francis A., tr. and ed. **Letters of Cortes: the five letters of relation from Fernando Cortes to the Emperor Charles V.** 2 v. N.Y., 1908. Standard edition of the famous eyewitness reports by the conqueror of Mexico.

Z264. Medina, José Toribio. **Biblioteca hispano-americana (1493–1810).** 7 v. Santiago, Chile, 1898–1907. Standard basic bibliography of the colonial period, now augmented by numerous local and specialized treatments. Items since 1936 are reported in the *Handbook of Latin American studies* (*Z3*).

Z265. ——, ed. **Cartas de Pedro de Valdivia que tratan del descubrimiento y conquista de Chile.** Seville, 1929. Important eyewitness reports.

Z266. Parry, John H. **The Spanish theory of empire in the sixteenth century.** Cambridge, Eng., 1940. Brief, stimulating essay on the evolution of basic doctrines underlying Spanish imperial policies in the American Indies.

Z267. Prescott, William H. **History of the conquest of Mexico.** 3 v. N.Y., 1843. Literary and historiographical classic, still readable and useful; translated into many languages.

Z268. ——. **History of the conquest of Peru.** 2 v. N.Y., 1847. Slightly less satisfactory than his *Mexico,* but also required reading. For the numerous editions and translations of these and other Prescott works see C. Harvey Gardiner, *William Hickling Prescott: an annotated bibliography of published works.* (Washington, 1958).

Z269. Thayer Ojeda, Tomás. **Los conquistadores de Chile.** 3 v. Santiago, 1908–13. Detailed treatment.

Z270. Vicens Vives, Jaime, and others. **Historia social y económica de España y América.** 4 v. Barcelona, 1957–58. An important contribution, stressing role of the common man, based on modern historical techniques.

Z271. Wagner, Henry R. **The rise of Fernando Cortés.** Los Angeles, 1944. Meticulously detailed reconstruction of the conquest of Mexico.

Z272. Weber, Friedrich. **Beiträge zur Charakteristik der älteren Geschichtsschreiber über Spanisch-Amerika: eine biographisch-bibliographische Skizze.** Leipzig, 1911. Provides much useful data on numerous chroniclers and early writers.

Z273. Wright, Irene A. **The early history of Cuba, 1492–1586.** N.Y., 1916. Monographic treatment based on much manuscript material.

Z274. Zavala, Silvio A. **Las instituciones jurídicas en la conquista de América.** Madrid, 1935. Useful summary, based on manuscript and printed legal sources.

Colonial

Z275. Acosta de Samper, Soledad. **Biografías de hombres ilustres ó notables relativas á la época del descubrimiento, conquista y colonización de . . . Colombia.** Bogotá, 1883.

Z276. Cappa, Ricardo. **Estudios críticos acerca de la dominación española en América.** 20 v. Madrid, 1889–97. Chronological and topical summaries by an erudite Jesuit, based on a wide variety of printed materials. Covers social and economic, as well as political, developments.

Z277. Chamberlain, Robert S. "Simpson's *The encomienda in New Spain* and recent encomienda studies." *Hisp. Am. hist. rev.,* 34 (May 1954): 238–50. Masterly review article, with summary evaluations and bibliography of books and articles, 1929–50, emphasizing great advances since 1940 of encomienda studies.

Z278. Chapman, Charles E. **Founding of Spanish California: the northwestward expansion of New Spain, 1687–1783.** N.Y., 1916. Detailed treatment, based on manuscript sources.

Z279. Chevalier, François. **La formation des grands domaines au Mexique: terre et société aux XVIe–XVIIe siècles.** Paris, 1952. Landmark in modern investigation, both for archival base and interpretations. Indispensable. There is also a Spanish translation.

Z280. Diffie, Bailey W. **Latin American civilization: colonial period.** See Y99.

Z281. Gibson, Charles. **Tlaxcala in the sixteenth century.** New Haven, 1952. Pioneering monograph, meticulously researched, on Indian-Spanish cultural and administrative interplay in New Spain.

Z282. Góngora, Mario. **El estado en el derecho indiano: época de fundación (1492–1570).** Santiago, 1951. [Universidad de Chile, Instituto de Investigaciones Histórico-Culturales.] A major monograph that stresses persistence of medieval norms and their transformation in America. Excellent bibliographies.

Z283. Haring, Clarence H. **The Spanish empire in America.** N.Y., 1947. Authoritative summary, stressing institutional developments; aimed primarily at graduate students, but equally valuable to specialist and nonspecialist. Important bibliographical listings.

Z284. Hill, Lawrence F. **José de Escandón and the founding of Nuevo Santander.** Columbus, O., 1926. Though brief, this is an excellent treatment of the development of northern Mexico in colonial times.

Z285. Konetzke, Richard. **El imperio español, orígenes y fundamentos.** Tr. from German by Felipe González. Madrid, 1946. Well-documented summary to about 1502. Backgrounds and early royal policy, based on printed materials. Especially important for German bibliography.

Z286. Lohmann Villena, Guillermo. **El corregidor de indios en el Perú bajo los Austrias.** Madrid, 1957. Very nearly definitive monographic treatment of officer locally in charge of Indians. See important review, W. W. Borah, *Hisp. Am. hist. rev.,* 38 (Aug. 1958): 409.

Z287. Means, Philip A. **Fall of the Inca empire and the Spanish rule in Peru, 1530–1780.** N.Y. and London, 1932. Despite some now outmoded conclusions, an important general treatment.

Z288. ———. **The Spanish Main, focus of envy, 1492–1700.** N.Y. and London, 1935. Outmoded but not replaced as a general synthesis.

Z289. Mecham, John Lloyd. **Francisco de Ibarra and Nueva Vizcaya.** Durham, 1927. Monographic treatment of conquest of northern New Spain.

Z290. Medina, José T. **Diccionario biográfico colonial de Chile.** Santiago, 1906.

Z291. Mendiburu, Manuel de. **Diccionario histórico-biográfico del Perú. . . . Parte primera que corresponde a la época de la dominación española.** 8 v. Lima, 1874–90.

Z292. Orozco y Berra, Manuel. **Historia de la dominación española en México.** 4 v. Mexico, 1938. Still a basic summary treatment.

Z293. Ots Capdequí, José M. **El estado español en las Indias.** 2nd ed., Mexico, 1946. Legalistic treatment by an outstanding Spanish scholar.

Z294. ———. **Instituciones sociales de la América Española en el período colonial.** Buenos Aires, 1934. An authoritative summary, based on legal and administrative texts.

Z295. ———. **El régimen de la tierra en la América Española durante el período colonial.** Ciudad Trujillo, 1946. Published series of lectures; one of the few generalized treatments of land policies and problems in the Spanish empire.

Z296. Parry, John H. **The Audiencia of New Galicia in the sixteenth century.** Cambridge, Eng., 1948. Excellently researched monograph on the minor Audiencia of New Spain; supersedes previous works.

Z297. Powell, Philip W. **Soldiers, Indians, and silver: the northward advance of New Spain, 1550–1600.** Berkeley, 1952. Details of the long struggle against Indians, spread of the mission-presidio-settlement complex. Based on much manuscript material.

Z298. Rodríguez Moñino, Antonio, ed. **Catálogo de memoriales presentados al Real Consejo de Indias (1626–1630): descripción bibliográfica de más de cuatrocientos rarísimos impresos y manuscritos.** Madrid, 1953.

A limited edition, extracting 430 items, with extensive indexing. The periodical articles from which this volume was reprinted appeared in the *Boletín* of the Real Academia de la Historia (Spain), v. 130–31 (1952).

Z299. Rumazo, José. **La región amazónica del Ecuador en el siglo XVI.** Seville, 1946.

Z300. Schäfer, Ernst. **El Consejo Real y Supremo de las Indias: su historia, organización y labor administrativa hasta la terminación de la Casa de Austria.** 2 v. Seville, 1935–47. Most authoritative treatment of the Council of the Indies, the major Spanish administrative organ for the colonies.

Z301. Simpson, Lesley B. **The encomienda in New Spain: the beginning of Spanish Mexico.** Rev. and enl. ed., Berkeley, 1950. Considerably modified version of 1st ed. (1929); basic monograph. See the Chamberlain critique (*Z277*).

Z302. Simpson, Lesley B., and Sherburne F. Cook. **The population of central Mexico in the sixteenth century.** Berkeley, 1948. Important, if controversial, attempt to establish population figures, chiefly by extrapolation. Probably more nearly correct for period after 1565 than earlier years.

Z303. Solórzano Pereira, Juan. **Política indiana . . . corregida e ilustrada con notas por el licenciado don Francisco Ramiro de Valenzuela.** 5 v. Madrid, 1930. An important 17th century (1647) legal gloss on major practices of imperial administration.

Z304. Tudela, José, ed. **El legado de España a América.** 2 v. Madrid, 1954. Summary accounts on population and customs, language, religion, culture, law, education, literature, art, and economics, with short bibliographies. Generally very favorable to Spanish efforts.

Z305. Vargas Ugarte, Rubén. **Biblioteca peruana.** 12 v. Buenos Aires and Lima, 1935–58. (Others in preparation.) V. 1–5 discuss manuscript collections, local and foreign; v. 6 ff. list printed materials under title "Impresos peruanos"—first those published abroad, then Peruvian items chronologically from 1584. A basic tool.

Z306. ———. **Historia del Perú: virreinato.** 3 v. Lima, 1949–56.

Z307. West, Robert C. **The mining community in northern New Spain.** Berkeley and Los Angeles, 1949. Brief, penetrating description of a typical and important mining area, with much social and economic data, based on wide use of local archives.

Z308. Zavala, Silvio A. **New viewpoints on the Spanish colonization of America.** Tr. by Joan Coyne. Philadelphia, 1943. Published general lectures, summarizing a great deal of his work to that date.

Z309. ———. **La encomienda indiana.** Madrid, 1935. A pioneering work which subsequent studies have modified in some details. See Chamberlain's discussions (*Z277*).

Enlightenment and Independence

Z310. Arado, María J., and Aurora Capillas de Castellanos. **Bibliografía de Artigas.** Montevideo, 1953 ff. [Comisión Nacional Archivo Artigas.] V. 1 contains initial two parts of a projected nine part monumental bibliography; lists 1,512 items on Artigas.

Z311. Azpurúa, Ramón. **Biografías de hombres notables de Hispano-América.** 4 v. Caracas, 1877. Figures of the independence movement and early national history, chiefly of Gran Colombia.

Z312. Baralt, Rafael M. **Resumen de la historia de Venezuela desde el año 1797 hasta el de 1830.** 2 v. Paris, 1841. Reprint, 1939.

Z313. Belaúnde, Víctor A. **Bolívar and the political thought of the Spanish American Revolution.** Baltimore, 1938. A major summary of political thought in Latin America in the late 18th and early 19th centuries.

Z314. Bemis, Samuel F. **Early diplomatic missions from Buenos Aires to the United States, 1811–1824.** Worcester, Mass., 1940. A masterly monograph.

Z315. Bushnell, David. **The Santander regime in Gran Colombia.** Newark, Del., 1954. Breaks new ground by detailed treatment of social and economic developments in the wake of independence.

Z316. Cochrane, Thomas, earl of Dundonald (Lord Cochrane). **Narrative of services in the liberation of Chile, Peru and Brazil from Spanish and Portuguese domination.** 2 v. London, 1859. Classic eyewitness account by the English naval commander.

Z317. Desdevises du Dézert, Georges N. "Vicerois et capitaines généraux des Indes espagnoles à la fin du XVIIIᵉ siècle." *Revue historique*, 125 (July, 1917): 225–64; 126 (Sept. 1917): 14–60, 225–70. General description of political, social, and economic developments in the overseas realm, with data on population, towns, resources, and containing lists of governors, captains-general, and viceroys.

Z318. Fisher, Lillian E. **The background of the revolution for Mexican independence.** Boston, 1934. Detailed but spotty treatment of late 18th and early 19th century social and economic conditions.

Z319. ———. **The intendant system in Spanish America.** Berkeley, 1929. Brief discussion, with emphasis on Mexico. English translation of the basic ordinance.

Z320. García Samudio, Nicolás. **La independencia de Hispanoamérica.** Mexico, 1945. Excellent brief summary, with helpful bibliography.

Z321. Gil Munilla, Octavio. **El Río de la Plata en la política internacional: génesis del virreinato.** Seville, 1949. International relations of Spain and other European powers in the late 18th century, leading to creation of the viceroyalty in 1776.

Z322. Hasbrouck, Alfred. **Foreign legionaries in the liberation of Spanish South America.** N.Y., 1928.

Z323. Humphreys, Robert A. "The historiography of the Spanish American revolutions." **Hisp. Am. hist. rev.,** 36 (Feb. 1956): 81–93. Masterly synthesis, with summary and critical bibliography, of the vast and growing literature on the independence movements.

Z324. Kaufmann, William W. **British policy and the independence of Latin America, 1804–1828.** New Haven, 1951. Useful reexamination of diplomatic matters.

Z325. Keen, Benjamin. **David Curtis De Forest and the revolution of Buenos Aires.** New Haven, 1947. Monographic treatment of a Yankee merchant's involvement, based on family papers.

Z326. Lecuna, Vicente. **Crónica razonada de las guerras de Bolívar.** 3 v. N.Y., 1950. Detailed narrative; good indices.

Z327. Lewin, Boleslao. **La rebelión de Túpac Amaru y los orígenes de la emancipación americana.** Buenos Aires, 1957. Massive and summary treatment.

Z328. McAlister, Lyle N. **The "fuero militar" in New Spain, 1764–1800.** Gainesville, Fla., 1957. Serious study of development of the military in colonial Mexico and its legal and other privileges.

Z329. Mitre, Bartolomé. **Historia de San Martín y de la emancipación sudamericana.** 3 v. Buenos Aires, 1950. Detailed treatment, first published 1887–88.

Z330. Pilling, William, ed. and tr. **The emancipation of South America: being a condensed translation . . . of the History of San Martín by General don Bartolomé Mitre.** London, 1893.

Z331. Priestley, Herbert I. **José de Gálvez, visitor-general of New Spain, 1765–1771.** Berkeley, 1916. Pioneering and basic monograph on 18th century Mexico and changes undertaken by the Bourbon monarchy.

Z332. Quesada Zapiola, Carlos A. **Catálogo de la documentación referente a las relaciones diplomáticas entre Estados Unidos de América y la República Argentina, 1810–1830.** Buenos Aires, 1948.

Z333. Rippy, J. Fred. **Rivalry of the United States and Great Britain over Latin America (1808–1830).** Baltimore, 1929.

Z334. Riva-Zucchelli, Pedro. **Historia de la independencia de la República Oriental del Uruguay.** Montevideo, 1934.

Z335. Robertson, William S. **France and Latin-American independence.** Baltimore, 1939.

Z336. ——. "Francisco de Miranda and the revolutionizing of Spanish America." American Historical Association, **Annual report for the year 1907,** 1 (Washington, 1908): 189–539. Superb summary, complementing materials in his standard "Life" of Miranda (*Z839*).

Z337. ——. **Rise of the Spanish-American republics as told in the lives of their liberators.** N.Y. and London, 1918. Still a standard and valuable work.

Z338. Rydjord, John. **Foreign interest in the independence of New Spain: an introduction to the war for independence.** Durham, 1935.

Z339. Salas, Carlos I. **Bibliografía del General don José de San Martín y de la emancipación sudamericana.** 5 v. in 3. Buenos Aires, 1910. *Errores y omisiones,* 1912. Comprehensive to date of publication.

Z340. Scarpetta, M. Leónidas, and Saturnino Vergara. **Diccionario biográfico de los campeones de la libertad de Nueva Granada, Venezuela, Ecuador i Perú: que comprende sus servicios, hazañas i virtudes.** Bogotá, 1879.

Z341. Shafer, Robert J. **The economic societies in the Spanish world (1763–1821).** Syracuse, N.Y., 1958. Useful investigation of the several societies dedicated to rehabilitating local areas during the Bourbon renaissance. Helpful bibliography.

Z342. Swärd, Sven Ola. **Latinamerika i svensk politik under 1810 och 1820 talen.** Uppsala, 1949. Sweden's policies regarding Latin American independence: sale of naval vessels (1825) and various diplomatic and commercial missions.

Z343. Thomas, Alfred B., ed. and tr. **Teodoro de Croix and the northern frontier of New Spain, 1776–1783.** Norman, 1941. Official reports on problems and conditions.

Z344. Whitaker, Arthur P., ed. **Latin America and the Enlightenment.** N.Y. and London, 1942. Essays by Whitaker, Hussey, Lanning, and others opening up this important topic. Much subsequent publication in Spain, France, and the United States is noted in the *Handbook of Latin American studies* (*Z3*).

HISTORIES OF SPECIAL AREAS (POST-1830)

Middle America and the Caribbean

Bibliographies

Z345. Bissainthe, Max. **Dictionnaire de bibliographie haïtienne.** Washington, 1951. In addition to more than 8,000 books dealing with Haiti, many of which are not listed in *Z348,* this bibliography contains a list of newspapers, bulletins, and magazines, as well as journalists, from the colonial period to 1949. Index is particularly useful. [RWL]

Z346. Castro de Morales, Lilia. **Impresos relativos a Cuba editados en los Estados Unidos.** Havana, 1956. [Biblioteca Nacional, Publicaciones.] Materials from 1762, with list of 75 Cuban newspapers edited in the United States for or by Cubans.

Z347. Cosío Villegas, Daniel. **La historiografía política del México moderno.** Mexico, 1953. Unannotated listing of 858 items of 1876–1910 or related to this period.

Z348. Duvivier, Ulrick. **Bibliographie générale et méthodique d'Haïti.** 2 v. Port-au-Prince, 1941. This first systematic and comprehensive bibliography by a Haitian was completed in the 1920's. Indicates the location in western European countries, the United States, and Haiti of published and archival items, some of which have valuable annotations. Supplemented by Bissainthe (*Z345*). [RWL]

Z349. Millares Carlo, Agustín, and José I. Mantecón. **Repertorio bibliográfico de los archivos mexicanos y de las colecciones diplomáticas fundamentales para la historia de México.** Mexico, 1948. Valuable listing of guides, calendars, and indices; also titles of documentary publications on Mexican history. A basic tool.

Z350. Pedreira, Antonio S. **Bibliografía puertorriqueña (1493–1930).** Madrid, 1932. Nearly comprehensive, unannotated but classified listing of works on Puerto Rico, covering all fields. Includes an attempt at a biographical register. Materials following 1935 appear in *Handbook of Latin American studies (Z3)*.

Z351. Peraza Sarausa, Fermín. **Bibliografías cubanas.** Washington, 1945. [Library of Congress, Latin American series, 7.] Brief introduction cites major points of bibliographical history; 485 annotated items by leading Cuban bibliographers, all found in Library of Congress.

Z352. ——. **Bibliografía martiana, 1853–1953.** Havana, 1954. Comprehensive compilation of writings by and about José Martí. A later edition (Havana, 1956) covers to 1955.

Z353. Ramos, Roberto. **Bibliografía de la historia de México.** Mexico, 1956. Alphabetical listings to 1955 of 4,776 entries, but excluding items in *Z354*. No subject indices.

Z354. ——. **Bibliografía de la revolución mexicana.** 3 v. Mexico, 1931–40. Incomplete but basic. Supplemented by *Z353*.

Z355. Ross, Stanley R. "Bibliography of sources for contemporary Mexican history." **Hispanic American historical review**, 39 (May 1959): 234–38. Short but useful description of main bibliographies and sources for Mexican history, 1910–40.

Z356. Velázquez, Gonzalo. **Anuario bibliográfico puertorriqueño: índice alfabético de libros, folletos, revistas y periódicos publicados en Puerto Rico.** Río Piedras, 1948 ff.

Mexico

Z357. Callcott, Wilfrid H. **Liberalism in Mexico, 1857–1929.** Stanford, 1931. Rather general treatment.

Z358. Cline, Howard F. **The United States and Mexico.** Cambridge, Mass., 1953. Stresses internal Mexican history, 1910–52, with attention to foreign relations. Useful bibliographical essay.

Z359. Cosío Villegas, Daniel, and others. **Historia moderna de México.** 4 v. Mexico, 1955–57. (Others in progress.) [1, D. Cosío Villegas, *La república restaurada: la vida política;* 2, Francisco R. Calderón, *La república restaurada: la vida económica;* 3, Luís González y González, Emma Cosío Villegas, and Guadalupe Monroy, *La república restaurada: la vida social;* 4, Moisés González Navarro, *El Porfiriato: la vida social*]. A landmark of modern Mexican historiography; exhaustive treatment, based on a wide range of sources. Volumes written under direction of Cosío Villegas. Covers period 1876–1910.

Z360. Cumberland, Charles C. **Mexican Revolution: genesis under Madero.** Austin, 1952. Detailed treatment to accession of Huerta (1913). Should be supplemented by the Ross biography of Madero (*Z857*).

Z361. Historia mexicana: revista trimestral. Mexico, 1951 ff. (Quarterly.) A major periodical devoted to all aspects of Mexican history, sponsored by Colegio de México.

Z362. Manning, William R. **Early diplomatic relations between the United States and Mexico.** Baltimore, 1916. Standard monograph.

Z363. Parkes, Henry B. **A history of Mexico.** Boston, 1938. Rev. ed., 1950. About the only short history of Mexico in English. Revised edition carries the story to 1946, with no change in earlier text or the useful bibliography.

Z364. Scholes, Walter V. **Mexican politics during the Juárez regime, 1855–1872.** Columbia, Mo., 1957. Detailed monographic coverage.

Z365. Tannenbaum, Frank. **Mexico: the struggle for peace and bread.** N.Y., 1950. Stresses recent trends; obsolete in parts concerning economic programs.

Central America and the Caribbean

Z366. Chamorro, Pedro J. **Historia de la Federación de la América Central, 1823–1840.** Madrid, 1951. Excellent survey of the rise and fall of the Confederation.

Z367. Chapman, Charles E. **A history of the Cuban republic: a study in Hispanic American politics.** N.Y., 1927. Chiefly political; standard coverage in English to date of publication.

Z368. Durón, Rómulo E. **Bosquejo histórico de Honduras.** 2nd ed., Tegucigalpa, 1956. Reissue of a standard work. Volume is two-thirds colonial, one-third national history.

Z369. ——. **Historia de Honduras desde la independencia hasta nuestros días.** Tegucigalpa, 1903. Reprint, 1956. V. 1 of a standard history, extending his *Bosquejo* in detail to 1829.

Z370. Historia de la nación cubana. Ed. by Ramiro Guerra y Sánchez and others. 10 v. Havana, 1952. A comprehensive history by thirty leading local historians. Covers from pre-Columbian period to 1951.

Z371. Jones, Chester L. **Costa Rica and civilization in the Caribbean.** Madison, Wis., 1935. Standard coverage to date of publication.

Z372. ——. **Guatemala, past and present.** Minneapolis, 1940. Sound factual summary.

Z373. Montúfar y Rivera Maestre, Lorenzo. **Reseña histórica de Centro-América.** 7 v. Guatemala, 1878–87. Narrative, in 19th century mode.

Z374. Munro, Dana G. **The five republics of Central America: their political and economic development and their relations with the United States.** N.Y., 1918. Dated but still useful summaries.

Z375. Varona Guerrero, Miguel. **La Guerra de la Independencia de Cuba, 1895–1898.** 3 v. Havana, 1946. Summary of the late 19th century movement.

Z376. Welles, Sumner. **Naboth's vineyard: the Dominican Republic, 1844–1924.** 2 v. N.Y., 1928. Detailed coverage, diplomatic and political emphasis.

Haiti
(*Rayford W. Logan*)

Z377. Descos, Léon Eugène (pseud., Eugène Aubin). **En Haïti: planteurs d'autrefois, nègres d'aujourd'hui.** Paris, 1910. Although not well known, this first-hand account, by a Frenchman, of the country and its people, 1904–06, strikes a balance between St. John and Léger. Thirty photographs illuminate the text.

Z378. Bellegarde, Dantès. **Pour une Haïti heureuse.** 2 v. Port-au-Prince, 1928–29. Haiti's most distinguished contemporary educator and diplomat sympathetically but realistically diagnoses his country's shortcomings and suggests reforms.

Z379. Bonhomme, Colbert. **Révolution et contre-révolution en Haïti de 1946 à 1957.** Port-au-Prince, 1957. While definitely pro-Estime and anti-Magloire, this copiously documented account of the recent period, by an active participant, clearly reveals the deeply-rooted class and color strife that keeps Haiti in turmoil.

Z380. Brutus, Edner. **Instruction publique en Haïti, 1492–1945.** Port-au-Prince, 1948. Well-documented statistical analysis, which reveals both the illusory and sincere efforts that have done little to reduce the very high rate of illiteracy.

Z381. Courlander, Harold. **Haiti singing.** Chapel Hill, 1939. Scholarly analysis based on five trips between 1932 and 1938. Contains approximately 185 folk songs in the original Creole, with English translations. Particularly useful are the discussion of their evolution from everyday life of the people and a note on methodology.

Z382. Davis, Harold P. **Black democracy: the story of Haiti.** Rev. ed., N.Y., 1936. In practically all respects the most valuable political history, especially of the U.S. occupation. Several photographs, documents, and the list of presidents with their terms of office enhance its value.

Z383. Gantlier, Claudius, ed. **Recueil des lois et actes de la République d'Haïti de 1887 à 1904.** 3 v. Port-au-Prince, 1907–12. Most useful compilation of official documents for the period covered.

Z384. Herskovits, Melville J. **Life in a Haitian valley.** N.Y. and London, 1937. Exhaustive study of peasant life in a remote village, by a competent anthropologist who had previously written of negroes in Africa, Surinam, and the United States; a scholarly antidote to the lurid popular accounts.

Z385. Léger, Jacques N. **Haïti, son histoire et ses détracteurs.** Also English ed. N.Y. and Washington, 1907. The Haitian minister to the United States, a mulatto, candidly traces the evils resulting from the cycle of dictators and ephemeral presidents.

Z386. Leyburn, James G. **The Haitian people.** New Haven and London, 1941. Best sociological study in English, by a U. S. professor of sociology, of the development of Haiti's social institutions against the background of slavery and the French colonial period. Contains an illuminating chapter on "Caste and class" and an excellent critical bibliography.

Z387. Linstant-Pradine, A., and Edouard Emmanuel, eds. **Recueil général des lois et actes du gouvernement d'Haïti, depuis la proclamation de son indépendance jusqu'à nos jours.** 8 v. Paris, 1851–88. Remarkable collection, indispensable for the early period. That from 1887 to 1904 is covered by Gantlier (*Z383*).

Z388. Logan, Rayford W. **The diplomatic relations of the United States with Haiti, 1776–1891.** Chapel Hill, 1941. Comprehensive study based on archival materials. Extensive bibliography.

Z389. Marcelin, L. J. **Haïti: ses guerres civiles—leurs causes, leurs conséquences présentes, leur conséquence future et finale.** 3 v. Paris, 1892–93. Realistic analysis of the deeply-rooted causes of strife that have kept Haiti in turmoil.

Z390. Ménos, Solon. **L'affaire Luders.** Port-au-Prince, 1898. An indignant, documented account, by the Haitian foreign secretary, of a German naval demonstration "in violation of the Monroe Doctrine" and of the indifference of the United States government.

Z391. Pressoir, Catts. **L'enseignement de l'histoire en Haïti.** Mexico, 1950. A sober criticism of the lack of adequate texts, libraries, museums, archives, and failure to teach about negroes in other parts of the world.

Z392. Price-Mars, Jean. **Ainsi parla l'Oncle: essais d'ethnographie.** Port-au-Prince, 1928. Penetrating analysis of Haitian life and beliefs, by one of its most distinguished intellectuals and diplomats. Mirrors the views of a member of the "black élite."

Z393. Price-Mars, Jean. **La République d'Haïti et la République Dominicaine: les aspects divers d'un problème d'histoire, de géographie et d'ethnologie.** 2 v. Port-au-Prince, 1953. The author, a former Haitian ambassador to the Dominican Republic, traces the history of boundary struggle between the two countries and expresses the fear that the strained relations will continue. Most valuable is his revelation of what might be called Guizot's "French Monroe Doctrine" in Haiti.

Z394. St. John, Sir Spenser. **Hayti: or the black republic.** London, 1884. The classic, devastatingly harsh criticism by the British minister to Haiti for some twelve years of the growing decadence of the republic.

Z395. United Nations. **Mission to Haiti: report of the United Nations Mission of Technical Assistance to the Republic of Haiti.** Lake Success, 1949. This pioneer study, by a team of UN experts, deals primarily with problems of demography, health, education, production, transport, trade, and finance, and offers specific recommendations. Numerous tables, charts, and maps add to its value.

Z396. Woodring, Wendell, John S. Brown, and Wilbur S. Burbank. **Geology of the Republic of Haiti.** Port-au-Prince, 1924. This indispensable work, based on a field survey under general supervision of the United States Geological Survey, contains an excellent chapter on geography, together with numerous maps, charts, photographs, and statistical tables.

French West Indies
(Rayford W. Logan)

Z397. U. S. Library of Congress. **Martinique: a selected list of references.** Comp. by Linn R. Blanchard. Washington, 1942. Supplements list prepared in 1923. Contains only some 250 items found in the Library of Congress. Emphasis is on history, description and travel, economics, and politics. Includes magazine and newspaper articles, maps, and seven bibliographies. Well annotated; author index.

Z398. Boyer-Peyreleau, Eugène E. **Les Antilles Françaises, particulièrement la Guadeloupe, depuis leur découverte jusqu'au 1er janvier 1823.** 3 v. Paris, 1823. The author,

a colonel in the French army, lived in Guadeloupe and Martinique, 1802–09 and 1814. Covers all phases of life in the colony; especially valuable for the 1790's. Contains map of Guadeloupe and 14 statistical tables.

Z399. Frasans, Hypolite de, and others. **Mémoire pour le chef de brigade, Magloire Pélage, et pour les habitans de la Guadeloupe.** 2 v. Paris, 1803. Indispensable for an understanding of the clash of race, class, and color in Guadeloupe during the French Revolution and the revolution in Saint-Domingue.

Z400 Hearn, Lafcadio. **Two years in the French West Indies.** N.Y., 1890. The classic narrative, interspersed with vignettes of the workaday life of the laboring classes, especially of Martinique, by a sympathetic and perceptive visitor, 1887–89.

Z401. Sablé, Victor. **La transformation des isles d'Amérique en départements français.** Paris, 1955. Brief summary of Guadeloupe, Martinique, Réunion, and French Guiana as colonies and of the law of March 19, 1946 which changed them into overseas departments. Especially valuable for analysis of economic and financial problems since this change.

Puerto Rico

Z402. Abbad y Lasierra, Iñigo. **Historia geográfica, civil y política de la isla de San Juan Bautista de Puerto-Rico.** Madrid, 1788. New ed., P.R., 1866. Synthesis by a Benedictine monk, based on primary sources; point of departure for modern history. For review see Isabel Gutiérrez del Arroyo, "Fray Iñigo Abbad y Lasierra y su Historia de Puerto Rico," *Estudios de historiografía americana* (Mexico, 1948), pp. 13–105.

Z403. American Academy of Political and Social Science. **Puerto Rico, a study in demographic development.** Philadelphia, 1953. Panoramic survey in 21 essays covering major aspects of contemporary Puerto Rico shortly after it was given commonwealth status.

Z404. Brau, Salvador. **La colonización de Puerto Rico.** San Juan, 1908. 2nd ed., 1930.

Z405. ——. **Historia de Puerto Rico.** N.Y., 1904.

Z406. Coll y Toste, Cayetano, ed. **Boletín histórico de Puerto Rico.** 14 v. San Juan, 1914–27. A mine of information on various topics.

Z407. Constitution of the Commonwealth of Puerto Rico. San Juan, 1952. The constitution, adopted 1952, giving the island special status. Contains related items. Should be supplemented by documents issued by U.S. Senate and by House, Committee on Interior and Insular Affairs (82nd Cong., 2nd Sess.) related to hearings on commonwealth status and the constitution.

Z408. Cruz Monclova, Lidio. **Historia de**

Puerto Rico, siglo XIX. Río Piedras, 1952 ff. Includes useful documents.

Z409. Documents on the constitutional history of Puerto Rico. Washington, 1947. Pre-commonwealth status materials.

Z410. Fraga Iribarne, Manuel, ed. **Las constituciones de Puerto Rico.** Madrid, 1953. Large collection of laws, organic statutes, and constitutions, 1812–1952. Extensive bibliography.

Z411. Gayer, Arthur D., Paul T. Homan, and Earle K. James. **The sugar economy of Puerto Rico.** N.Y., 1938. Excellent analysis of the island's principal agricultural activity.

Z412. Gómez Acevedo, Labor. **Sanz, promotor de la conciencia separatista en Puerto Rico.** San Juan, 1956. Documented monograph on terms of Spanish governor José Laureano Sanz (1868–70, 1874–75) and his repressive policies that kept the island in unrest. Good range of sources.

Z413. Gutiérrez del Arroyo, Isabel. **El reformismo ilustrado en Puerto Rico.** Mexico, 1953. Able monograph on political and other reform ideas in first half of 19th century. Well documented.

Z414. Hanson, Earl P. **Transformation: the story of Puerto Rico.** N.Y., 1955. Informative, if uncritical, account of "Operation bootstrap," the development of Puerto Rico under commonwealth status and Governor Luis Muñoz Marín.

Z415. Historia. Río Piedras, 1951 ff. (Semiannual.) Scholarly historical journal dedicated to history of Puerto Rico and the Caribbean.

Z416. Lugo-Silva, Enrique. **The Tugwell administration in Puerto Rico, 1941–1946.** Río Piedras, 1955. This monograph, based primarily on newspapers and official reports, covers an important period, but leaves much undone. Approaches through various administrative agencies created by Tugwell.

Z417. Miller, Paul G. **Historia de Puerto Rico.** N.Y., 1922.

Z418. Morales Carrión, Arturo. **Puerto Rico and the non-Hispanic Caribbean: a study in the decline of Spanish exclusivism.** Río Piedras, 1952. Monographic treatment of the impact of foreign influences on the social history of Puerto Rico, emphasizing 18th century developments and closing with 1815. Broad context and excellent sources.

Z419. Osuna, Juan José. **A history of education in Puerto Rico.** 2nd ed., Río Piedras, 1949. Authoritative history from colonial times to date of publication.

Z420. Pedreira, Antonio S. **Insularismo: ensayos de interpretación puertorriqueña.** Madrid, 1934. Essays arguing for cultural nationalism or "insularity" of developments. Though unacceptable historically, they did much to revive interest in the history of Puerto Rico among its intellectuals.

Z421. ——. **El periodismo en Puerto Rico,** bosquejo histórico desde su iniciación hasta el 1930. Havana, 1941.

Z422. Picó, Rafael. **The geographic regions of Puerto Rico.** Río Piedras, 1950. Sound summary with extensive bibliography.

Z423. Rouse, Irving. **Porto Rican prehistory: introduction.** N.Y., 1952. [New York Academy of Sciences, Scientific survey of Porto Rico and the Virgin Islands, 18, pt. 3.] Initial report on modern archaeology of Puerto Rico, providing bibliography and discussion of earlier works. Continuation of reports noted in *Handbook of Latin American studies.*

Z424. Steward, Julian H., and others. **The people of Puerto Rico: a study in social anthropolgy.** Urbana, Ill., 1956. Various community studies and investigations of class and other subcultures in an attempt to apply "community study" technique to an entire island.

Z425. Tugwell, Rexford G. **The stricken land: the story of Puerto Rico.** Garden City, N.Y., 1947. Important views by a former U. S. governor of Puerto Rico, preceding commonwealth status.

Spanish South America

Bibliographies

Z426. Giraldo Jaramillo, Gabriel. **Bibliografía de bibliografías colombianas.** Bogotá, 1954. Long introduction gives history of bibliography in Colombia. Lists numerous bibliographies in special fields, including those in languages other than Spanish. Excellent coverage.

Z427. Griffin, Charles C. "Francisco Encina and revisionism in Chilean history." **Hisp. Am. hist. rev.,** 37 (Feb. 1957): 1–28. Masterly analysis and critique of the controversial Encina production, with a survey of major works on Chilean history and helpful bibliographical footnotes. See *Z446.*

Z428. René-Moreno, Gabriel. **Biblioteca boliviana.** Santiago, 1879. Supplements (for 1602–1908), 1899–1908. Still one of the few specialized bibliographies on Bolivia.

Z429. Sánchez, Manuel Segundo. **Bibliografía venezolanista: contribución al conocimiento de los libros extranjeros relativos a Venezuela y sus grandes hombres.** Caracas, 1914. Dated but basic treatment. The National Library sporadically issues a national bibliography to supplement, but main coverage must be found in *Handbook of Latin American studies* (*Z3*).

Z430. Speroni Vener, Julio. "La bibliografía en el Uruguay." **Revista Interamericana de bibliografía,** 4 (Jan.-June 1954): 35–42. Brief essay, chiefly history of bibliography and bibliography of bibliographies, including serials.

Z431. Tauro, Alberto. **Bibliografía peruana de historia, 1940–1953.** Lima, 1953.

Classified listing of 1,214 items, with some notes.

Z432. ——. **Guía de estudios históricos.** Lima, 1956. Listing of 1,268 historical articles in more than 40 non-professional periodicals, about a third of them non-Peruvian.

Z433. Vargas Ugarte, Rubén. **Manual de estudios peruanistas.** Lima, 1952. Expansion and revision of an earlier work. Serves as basic bibliography of Peruvian history, with notes on libraries, archives, collections, published documents, and the like.

Colombia and Venezuela

Z434. Betancourt, Rómulo. **Venezuela: política y petróleo.** Mexico, 1956. Basically a history of Venezuela, 1945–56, by leader of the Democratic Action party, who was elected president in 1958.

Z435. Fluharty, Vernon L. **Dance of the millions: military rule and the social revolution in Colombia, 1930–1956.** Pittsburgh, 1957.

Z436. Galbraith, W. O. **Colombia: a general survey.** London, 1953. Brief, balanced summary, with helpful bibliography.

Z437. Gil Fortoul, José. **Obras completas.** 4th ed., 6 v., Caracas, 1954–56. [1, *Historia constitucional de Venezuela: la colonia, la independencia, la Gran Colombia;* 2, *Historia constitucional de Venezuela: reconstitución de la república, la oligarquía conservadora;* 3, *Historia constitucional de Venezuela: la oligarquía liberal;* 4, *Filosofía constitucional;* 5, *El humo de mi pipa;* 6, *Tres novelas.*

Z438. Henao, Jesús M., and Gerardo Arrubla. **History of Colombia.** Tr. and ed. by J. Fred Rippy. Chapel Hill, 1938. Somewhat unbalanced and disorganized, but about the only volume attempting a summary.

Z439. Humbert, Jules. **Histoire de la Colombie et du Vénézuéla des origines jusqu'à nos jours.** Paris, 1921.

Z440. Marsland, William D., and Amy L. Marsland. **Venezuela through its history.** N.Y., 1954. Survey from pre-Columbian times to the present; a readable and balanced treatment.

West Coast

Z441. Castedo, Leopoldo, ed. **Resumen de la historia de Chile de Francisco A. Encina.** 3 v. Santiago, 1954–55. Balanced abbreviation of the vast, erudite, and prejudiced Encina treatment (*Z446*). Adds numerous new items, such as photographs and documents.

Z442. Donoso, Ricardo. **Desarrollo político y social de Chile desde la constitución de 1833.** 2nd ed., Santiago, 1942. Considerably more political than social emphasis.

Z443. Edwards, Agustín. **The dawn (being the history of the birth and consoli-**dation of the Republic of Chile). London, 1931. Sound and interesting synthesis.

Z444. Edwards Vives, Alberto. **La fronda aristocrática: historia política de Chile.** 4th ed., Santiago, 1952. First published in 1928, this basic work details and interprets Chilean political history from independence to 1925.

Z445. ——. **El gobierno de don Manuel Montt, 1851–1861.** Santiago, 1932. Monographic treatment; sympathetic.

Z446. Encina, Francisco. **Historia de Chile desde la prehistoria hasta 1891.** 20 v. Santiago, 1940–52. A prodigious *tour de force* and a best-selling work, by an author whose views and statements created a furor. See *Z441* for useful summary and extension; *Z427* for summary of critiques and able analysis.

Z447. ——. **Portales: introducción a la historia de la época de Diego Portales.** 2 v. Santiago, 1934. Standard monographic treatment, less polemic and more fully documented than his major work (*Z446*).

Z448. Eyzaguirre, Jaime. **Chile durante el gobierno de Errázuriz Echaurren (1896–1901).** Santiago, 1957.

Z449. Frías Valenzuela, Francisco. **Historia de Chile.** 4 v. Santiago, 1947–49. A manual, based on secondary works; systematic if unimaginative.

Z450. Galdames, Luís. **A history of Chile.** Tr. by Isaac J. Cox. Chapel Hill, 1941. Considerable stress on colonial period.

Z451. Linke, Lilo. **Ecuador: country of contrasts.** London, 1954. A fine synthesis, emphasizing recent times. Helpful bibliography.

Z452. Markham, Clements R. **A history of Peru.** Chicago, 1892. Dated, but still the single most reliable item to time of publication.

Z453. Orellana, J. Gonzalo. **El Ecuador en cien años de independencia, 1830–1930.** 2 v. Quito, 1930. 2nd ed., *Resumen histórico del Ecuador,* 2 v., Quito, 1948. A useful compilation.

Z454. Reyes, Oscar E. **Breve historia general del Ecuador.** 2 v. Quito, 1938–42.

Z455. Stevenson, John R. **The Chilean Popular Front.** Philadelphia, 1942. Political history of the 1930's.

La Plata

Z456. Acevedo, Eduardo. **Anales históricos del Uruguay.** 6 v. Montevideo, 1933–36. Standard national history.

Z457. Alexander, Robert J. **The Bolivian national revolution.** New Brunswick, N.J., 1958. Sympathetic summary of recent Bolivian history and problems.

Z458. Arnade, Charles W. **The emergence of the republic of Bolivia.** Gainesville, Fla., 1957. Scholarly study of the independence and post-independence years. First of a series of projected monographs.

Z459. Blanksten, George I. **Perón's Argentina.** Chicago, 1953. Political scientist's analysis, before the fall of Perón. Much of the history is questionable, but the eyewitness material is useful.

Z460. Burgin, Miron. **The economic aspects of Argentine federalism, 1820–1852.** Cambridge, Mass., 1946. Important, pioneering monograph, stressing interrelations between politics, economics, and regionalisms.

Z461. Finot, Enrique. **Nueva historia de Bolivia: ensayo de interpretación sociológica.** 2nd ed., La Paz, 1954. Coverage from pre-Spanish period to outbreak of Chaco War. A sound synthesis by a distinguished diplomat.

Z462. Fitzgibbon, Russell H. **Uruguay: portrait of a democracy.** New Brunswick, N.J., 1954. Analysis and description by a leading political scientist. Good bibliography.

Z463. Hanson, Simon G. **Utopia in Uruguay.** N.Y., 1938. Discussion of the "welfare state" which Uruguay pioneered; sympathetic.

Z464. Kirkpatrick, Frederick A. **A history of the Argentine republic.** Cambridge, Eng., 1931. A sound treatment of pre-Perón Argentina.

Z465. Kroeber, Clifton B. **The growth of the shipping industry in the Río de la Plata region, 1794–1860.** Madison, Wis., 1957. A pioneering and important survey, complementary to *Z460*.

Z466. Leonard, Olen E. **Bolivia: land, people, and institutions.** Washington, 1952. Stresses social and economic materials, but contains much historical data and a bibliography.

Z467. Levene, Ricardo, ed. **Historia de la nación argentina.** 2nd ed., 10 v., Buenos Aires, 1936–42. Standard work by many outstanding scholars.

Z468. ——. **A history of Argentina.** Tr. and ed. by William S. Robertson. Chapel Hill, 1937. Excellent translation of a standard Argentine text, with undue stress on earlier years.

Z469. Machicao, Porfírio Díaz. **Historia de Bolivia.** 3 v. La Paz, 1954–55. Uneven treatment of 1920–36, with brief annotated bibliography.

Z470. Osborne, Harold. **Bolivia, a land divided.** London, 1954. Brief summary, stressing recent history.

Z471. Pendle, George. **Argentina.** London, 1955. Compact summary with useful bibliography.

Z472. ——. **Paraguay, a riverside nation.** London, 1954. Able summary by a British journalist, highlighting recent past.

Z473. Pivel Devoto, Juan E., and Alcira Ranieri de Pivel Devoto. **Historia de la República Oriental del Uruguay (1830–1930).** Montevideo, 1945. A general text, ably covering period to 1897, but weak thereafter.

Z474. Raine, Philip. **Paraguay.** New Brunswick, 1956. An "informal historical and economic study" of Paraguay to 1950, based on printed materials.

Z475. Rennie, Ysabel F. **The Argentine republic.** N.Y., 1945. A summary, stressing late 19th century to Perón, based on secondary sources. Much social-economic data.

Z476. Sierra, Vicente de, and others. **Historia de la Argentina.** V. 1. Buenos Aires, 1956. The first of a projected 9 v. collaborative compendium of the best of recent Argentine scholarship. This volume (1492–1600) contains a general introduction and synthesis, and stresses historiography, biography, and bibliography.

Z477. Warren, Harris G. **Paraguay, an informal history.** Norman, Okla., 1949. General synthesis, based on secondary materials.

Brazil
(Mathias C. Kiemen)

Brazilian historiography, like that of Spanish America, suffers from a preoccupation with the colonial period, a predilection for "social" history, and a fondness for biographical studies. Archival research in Europe and America, and even in Africa and the Orient, which could do much to avoid overly generalized treatments of important topics, is still very much neglected. Other areas of special weakness seem to be the lack of published encyclopedic information and some weakness in the methodological formation of future historians. Both of these, however, are being attacked by the historians and the universities. One need not fear for the future of historiography in a country so full of patriotism and love for history as is Brazil. Another encouraging sign is the strong swing from dilettante to professional historians.

Bibliographies

Z478. Asher, Georg M. **A bibliographical and historical essay on the Dutch books and pamphlets relating to New Netherland and to the Dutch West-India Company and to its possessions in Brazil, Angola, etc.** Amsterdam, 1854–67.

Z479. **Bibliografia brasileira.** 1938/39 ff. Rio de Janeiro, 1941 ff. [Instituto Nacional do Livro.] (Irregular.)

Z480. Brazil. Comissão de Estudo dos Textos de História do Brasil. **Bibliografia de história do Brasil.** 1943 ff. Rio de Janeiro, 1944 ff. (Semiannual.)

Z481. **Boletim bibliográfico brasileiro.** Rio de Janeiro, 1952 ff. [Sindicato Nacional das Emprêsas Editôras de Livros e Publicações Culturais.]

Z482. Borba de Moraes, Rubens, and William Berrien, eds. **Manual bibliográfico de estudos brasileiros.** Rio de Janeiro, 1949. Considered the best in its field.

Z483. Catholic University of America. **Bibliographical and historical description of the rarest books in the Oliveira Lima Collection at the Catholic University of America.** Comp. by Ruth E. Holmes. Washington, 1926.

Z484. Rodrigues, José Honório. **Teoria da história do Brasil: introducção metodológica.** 2nd ed., rev. and enl., 2 v., São Paulo, 1957. First study of historical methodology in Brazil (1st ed., 1949). The general point of departure for most studies, it provides an excellent panorama of work to date on numerous problems and periods of Brazilian history. Extensive bibliography throughout. [MCK, HFC]

Z485. Sacramento Blake, Augusto V. A. **Diccionario bibliográfico brazileiro.** See *Z64*.

Z486. Silveira Camargo, Paulo F. da. **Fontes primárias para o estudo da história religiosa de São Paulo no século XVI.** São Paulo, 1948. Source listings for this field.

Z487. Simões dos Reis, Antônio. **Bibliografia das bibliografias brasileiras.** Rio de Janeiro, 1942. Very incomplete, but a beginning.

Archival Collections

The archives of main interest for Brazilian colonial history are located in Portugal and Spain, and include, in order of importance: (1) Arquivo Histórico Ultramarino; (2) Arquivo Nacional da Torre do Tombo; and (3) Biblioteca Nacional in Lisbon; (4) Arquivo Distrital de Evora; (5) Biblioteca da Ajuda, Lisbon; (6) Biblioteca Pública do Pôrto; (7) Biblioteca Geral da Universidade de Coimbra: (8) Arquivo do Ministério das Finanças, Lisbon; (9) Archivo Nacional Simancas, Spain; (10) Archivo General de las Indias, Seville, Spain. The best local Brazilian documentary collections are found in the Arquivo Nacional, the Seção de Manuscritos of the Biblioteca Nacional, the Arquivo do Instituto Histórico e Geográfico Brasileiro, and the Arquivo Histórico do Itamaraty, all in Rio de Janeiro. State and private archives, secular and ecclesiastic, are generally not well organized or indexed. Since 1946 the Patrimônio Histórico e Artístico Nacional has done noteworthy work in cataloging and protecting these smaller archives. The various state archives have publications which appear more or less regularly. See Rodrigues, *Teoria da história* (*Z484*), pp. 354–57.

The ranking repository for publications and manuscript materials is the Biblioteca Nacional (Rio de Janeiro). Its publications (*Z489–491*) provide much source data and bibliographical information.

Z488. Ribeiro, Adalberto Mário. **O serviço do Patrimônio Histórico e Artístico Nacional** (Rio de Janeiro, 1945).

Z489. Anais. Rio de Janeiro, 1876 ff. (Irregular.) In 75 v. to date has published numerous catalogs, lists, and bibliographies.

Z490. Boletim bibliográfico. Rio de Janeiro, 1918 ff. (Quarterly.)

Z491. "Catálogo dos manuscritos." **Anais,** v. 4, 10, 15, 18 (1877–96). The major collections.

Z492. Catálogo dos manuscritos do Instituto Histórico e Geográfico Brasileiro, existentes em 31 de dezembro de 1883. Rio de Janeiro, 1884. 2nd ed., 1889. Guide to a most important collection. Organized in alphabetical order and divided into four parts.

Z493. Documentos históricos. Rio de Janeiro, 1928 ff. (Irregular.) More than 100 v. to date, a vast storehouse of historical documentation. Inadequately indexed.

Z494. Ferreira Carlos A. **Inventário dos manuscritos da Biblioteca da Ajuda references à América do Sul.** Coimbra, 1946.

Z495. Figanière, Frederico F. de la. **Catálogo dos manuscriptos portuguezes existentes no Museu Británnico.** Lisbon, 1853.

Z496. Instituto Rio Branco. **Catálogo da Coleção Visconde do Rio Branco.** 2 v. Rio de Janeiro, 1950. Catalog to an important collection of diplomatic papers, especially concerning boundaries. This collection also includes part of the official archives of Paraguay, captured in Asunción in 1870.

Z497. Oliveira Lima, Manoel de. **Relação dos manuscriptos portuguezes e estrangeiros de interesse para o Brasil existentes no Museu Británnico de Londres.** Rio de Janeiro, 1903.

Z498. Rau, Virgínia, and Maria F. G. da Silva, eds. **Os manuscritos do Arquivo da Casa de Cadaval respeitantes ao Brasil.** 2 v. Coimbra, 1955–58. The Cadaval family archive is one of the most important in Portugal.

Z499. Varnhagen, Francisco A. de. **Sucinta indicação de alguns manuscriptos importantes respectivos ao Brasil e a Portugal, existentes no Museu Británico em Londres e não comprehendidos no Catálogo Figanière, publicado em Lisboa em 1853, ou simples aditamento ao dito Catálogo.** Havana, 1863. Brazilian and Portuguese manuscripts in the British Museum; a supplement to Figanière.

General Histories

Z500. Calmon, Pedro. **História social do Brasil.** 2 v. São Paulo, 1937–39. Other eds. [1, *Espírito da sociedade colonial;* 2, *Espírito da sociedade imperial.*] General synthesis by a major modern writer.

Z501. Calogeras, João P. **A history of Brazil.** Tr. and ed. by Percy A. Martin. Chapel Hill, 1939. Strongest on period through the empire.

Z502. Constituições do Brasil. Rio de Janeiro, 1948. Covers 1824–1946.

Z503. Handelmann, Heinrich. **Geschichte**

von Brasilien. Berlin, 1860. Still valuable today for the colonial period.

Z504. Lacombe, Américo J. **Brasil, período nacional.** Mexico, 1956. A brief synopsis, of enduring importance because of the extensive bibliography.

Discovery and Colonization, 1500–1580

Z505. Abreu, João Capistrano de. **Caminhos antigos e povoamento do Brasil.** Rio de Janeiro, 1930. Authoritative study of Brazil's early years and the significance of the *bandeirante* movement. Of great influence on Brazilian historiography.

Z506. ——. **O descobrimento do Brasil.** Rio de Janeiro, 1929. Critical study by the acknowledged master among modern Brazilian historians.

Z507. Almeida Prado, João F. de. **Fontes primárias para o estudo das explorações e reconhecimento geográfico no século XVI.** São Paulo, 1948. Source listings for early explorations in the interior of Brazil.

Z508. Academia das Sciencias de Lisboa. **Collecção de monumentos inéditos para a história das conquistas dos Portuguezes em Africa, Asia, e América.** Ed. by Rodrigo J. de Lima Felner. 16 v. Lisbon, 1858–98.

Z509. **História da colonização portuguêsa do Brasil: edição monumental comemorativa do primeiro centenário da independência do Brasil.** Ed. by Carlos Malheiro Dias and others. 3 v. Oporto, 1921–26. The 3 v. of this proposed 6 v. monumental cooperative work which have appeared treat, respectively, the forerunners of Cabral, exploration of the Brazilian littoral (1500–21), and the period 1521–80. Of uneven quality, but extremely serviceable because of the inclusion of rare ancient manuscripts and maps.

Z510. Marchant, Alexander. **From barter to slavery: the economic relations of Portuguese and Indians in the settlement of Brazil, 1500–1580.** Baltimore, 1942. Fundamental for the understanding of this period.

Z511. Rodrigues, José Honório. **Historiografía del Brasil: siglo XVI.** Mexico, 1957. More a bibliographical treatise on 16th century Brazil than an analysis of historiography. As such it is a very useful tool. [HFC]

Colonial Period to 1760

Z512. Andreoni, João Antonio (pseud., André João Antonil). **Cultura e opulência do Brasil.** Lisbon, 1711. Mod. ed., Salvador, Bahia, 1955. Immediately confiscated by the Portuguese government upon publication, the book and its author remained practically unknown until the 20th century. Describes minutely the agricultural and mineral riches of colonial Brazil.

Z513. Bloom, Herbert I. **The economic activities of the Jews in Amsterdam in the seventeenth and eighteenth centuries.** Williamsport, Pa., 1937. Important for study of the influx of Jews into Minas Gerais and other mining districts of Brazil. For documentation on this subject see Augusto de Lima, *História dos diamantes nas Minas Gerais* (Rio de Janeiro, 1945).

Z514. Boxer, Charles R. **The Dutch in Brazil, 1624–1654.** Oxford, 1957. Model monograph, utilizing much bibliography, stressing internal economic rivalries in Holland. [HFC]

Z515. Escragnolle Taunay, Affonso de. **História geral das bandeiras paulistas.** 11 v. São Paulo, 1924–50. Exhaustive account of the bandeirantes from the Brazilian point of view.

Z516. Ferreira Reis, Artur C. **Límites e demarcações na Amazônia brasileira.** 2 v. Rio de Janeiro, 1947–48. [1, *A fronteira colonial com a Guiana Francesa*; 2, *A fronteira com as colônias espanholas*.] Extremely well documented studies.

Z517. Gonsalves de Mello, José A. **Tempo dos Flamengos: influência da ocupação holandesa na vida e na cultura do norte do Brasil.** Rio de Janeiro, 1947. Objective and well-written account of the Dutch occupation of northern Brazil in the 17th century.

Z518. Kiemen, Mathias C. **The Indian policy of Portugal in the Amazon region, 1614–1693.** Washington, 1954. A very sound and important monograph. [HFC]

Z519. Lima, Augusto de. **A capitania de Minas Gerais.** 2nd ed., Rio de Janeiro, 1943, An account of the most important mining province in Brazil.

Z520. Maceo Soares, José C. de. **Fronteiras do Brasil no regime colonial.** Rio de Janeiro, 1939. Authoritative account of Brazil's frontier difficulties during the Portuguese period of her history.

Z521. Rodrigues, José Honório. **Historiografia e bibliografia do domínio holandês no Brasil.** Rio de Janeiro, 1949. Basic bibliography by a foremost historian. [MCK, HFC]

Z522. Rodrigues, José Honório, and Joaquim Ribeiro. **Civilização holandesa no Brasil.** São Paulo, 1940. A well-documented study.

Z523. Varnhagen, Francisco A. de (Visconde do Pôrto Seguro). **História geral do Brasil antes de sua separação e independência de Portugal.** 4th ed., 5 v., São Paulo, 1948. Still regarded as the standard history of Brazil for the colonial period, and one fully revealing Varnhagen's gifts as a historian. The author, a Brazilian diplomatist, ransacked the libraries and archives of Europe, especially the great collection in the Torre do Tombo at Lisbon, for material for this work and for numerous monographs on early Brazilian history. The account is not always judicial, notably toward the Jesuits; and it over-emphasizes details and is faulty in perspective, but will long remain a quarry for later writers. Capistrano de Abreu's notes from the 3rd rev. ed. are retained, and to these have been added the equally scholarly notes of Rodolfo Garcia.

Z524. Wätjen, Hermann. **Das holländische Kolonialreich in Brasilien: ein Kapitel aus der Kolonialgeschichte des 17. Jahrhunderts.** The Hague, 1921. One of the best general accounts of the Dutch period in Brazil.

Z525. Williamson, James A. **English colonies in Guiana and on the Amazon.** Oxford, 1923. Account of the short-lived English colonies in the Amazon region in the early 17th century.

Enlightenment and Independence, 1760–1822

Z526. Accioly, Hildebrando. **O reconhecimento do Brasil pelos Estados Unidos da América.** São Paulo, 1936. U. S. recognition of the independent empire of Brazil.

Z527. Agan, Joseph. **The diplomatic relations of the United States and Brazil. V. 1, The Portuguese court at Rio de Janeiro.** Paris, 1926.

Z528. Armitage, John. **The history of Brazil, from the period of the arrival of the Braganza family in 1808 to the abdication of Dom Pedro the First in 1831.** 2 v. London, 1836. Reliable and, in the main, accurate eyewitness account.

Z529. **Arquivo diplomático da independência.** 8 v. Rio de Janeiro, 1922. Brazilian sources for the study of diplomatic recognition of Brazil by other countries.

Z530. Carnaxide, Visconde de (Antônio de Sousa Pedroso Carnaxide). **O Brasil na administração pombalina (economia e política externa).** São Paulo, 1940. An important study.

Z531. **Correspondência oficial das provincias do Brasil durante a legislatura dos Côrtes Constituintes de Portugal nos annos de 1821–1822 precedida das cartas dirigidas a el-rei D. João VI pelo príncipe real D. Pedro de Alcântara, como regente.** 2nd ed., Lisbon, 1872. Both the letters from Brazil and those that passed between the prince regent, Dom Pedro, and his father, King John VI, are important for an understanding of the independence movement in Brazil.

Z532. Costa, Luiz Edmundo da. **Rio in the time of the viceroys.** Tr. by Dorothea H. Momsen. Rio de Janeiro, 1936. Social history of the 18th century capital. [HFC]

Z533. Norton, Luiz. **A Côrte de Portugal no Brasil.** São Paulo, 1938. Covers 1808–22.

Z534. Oliveira Lima, Manoel de. **O movimento da independência, 1821–1822.** São Paulo, 1922. A conservative viewpoint of the independence movement.

Z535. Rêgo Monteiro, Jonathas C. **Dominação espanhola no Rio Grande do Sul, 1763–1777.** Rio de Janeiro, 1937. The 14-year domination of Brazil's southernmost state by the Spanish.

Z536. Silva, Duarte L. **O clero e a independência.** Rio de Janeiro, 1923.

Z537. Varnhagen, Francisco A. de. "História da independência do Brasil." **Revista do Instituto Histórico e Geográfico Brasileiro,** 79 (1916) : 25–594. Especially complete on the reign of King John VI.

Empire, 1822–1889

Z538. Bezerra, Alcides. **Bibliografia histórica do primeiro reinado à maioridade (1822–1840).** Rio de Janeiro, 1936. Bibliography of Pedro I's reign.

Z539. Boehrer, George C. A. **Da monarquia à república: história do Partido Republicano do Brasil (1870–1889).** Tr. by Berenice Xavier. Rio de Janeiro, 1954. [Original English in micro-card, Catholic University of America, Washington, 1951.] Important study of the rise of the Republican party in Brazil. The original English version has not appeared in book form. [MCK, HFC]

Z540. Haring, Clarence H. **Empire in Brazil: a New World experiment with monarchy.** Cambridge, Mass., 1958. A summary volume for the general reader, based on printed materials.

Z541. Kidder, Daniel P., and James C. Fletcher. **Brazil and the Brazilians portrayed in historical and descriptive sketches.** Boston, 1857. 9th rev. ed., 1879. Written by two scholarly missionaries who spent nearly a quarter century in Brazil; based on keen and accurate observation and careful examination of the most important printed works then existing. By far the most complete and satisfactory account in English of social, political, religious, and economic conditions in Brazil during the reign of Pedro II.

Z542. Mello Moraes, Alexandre José. **História do Brasil-reino e do Brasil-império.** 2 v. Rio de Janeiro, 1871–73. Political history of Brazil, 1808–70.

Z543. Morais, Evaristo de. **Da monarquia para a república (1870–1889).** Rio de Janeiro, 1936. The change from empire to republic in modern Brazil.

Z544. Oliveira Lima, Manoel de. **O império brasileiro, 1822–1889.** São Paulo, 1927. A favorable view of the Brazilian empire of the 19th century.

Z545. Pereira, Nilo. **O período regencial brasileiro.** Recife, 1939. Best study to date of the period of regency in Brazil (1831–40).

Z546. Viana, Oliveira. **O ocaso do império.** São Paulo, 1925. Causes of the fall of the empire in 1889.

Republic, 1889–

Z547. Bello, José M. **História da república.** Rio de Janeiro, 1940. Most complete story of the republic of Brazil since 1889.

Z548. Freire, Felisbello. **História constitucional da república dos Estados Unidos do**

Brasil. 3 v. Rio de Janeiro, 1894–95. A history of the first five years of the republic.

Z549. Hill, Lawrence F., ed. **Brazil.** Berkeley, 1947. Group of essays by several authors, stressing recent trends in many fields. [MCK, HFC]

Z550. Loewenstein, Karl. **Brazil under Vargas.** N.Y., 1942. A political scientist's analysis, written while Vargas was still in power. [HFC]

Z551. Smith, Thomas Lynn, and Alexander Marchant, eds. **Brazil: portrait of half a continent.** N.Y., 1951. Symposium of noted authors to give a picture of modern Brazil from sociological and economic viewpoints.

HISTORIES OF SPECIAL TOPICS

Church

Z552. Adams, Eleanor B. **A bio-bibliography of Franciscan authors in colonial Central America.** Washington, 1953. Covers numerous linguistic and other productions.

Z553. Ayarragaray, Lucas. **La iglesia en América y la dominación española.** Buenos Aires, 1920. A rather general volume.

Z554. Azevedo, Thales de. **O catolicismo no Brasil.** Rio de Janeiro, 1955. Analysis of Brazil's Catholicism as it is today. [MCK]

Z555. Barbosa, Manoel. **A igreja no Brasil, notas para sua história.** Rio de Janeiro, 1945. Contains much information in a field neglected by Brazilian writers. [MCK]

Z556. Bolton, Herbert E. "The mission as a frontier institution in the Spanish American colonies." **Hisp. Am. hist. rev.,** 23 (Feb. 1943): 42–61. Stresses the mission as the main element in frontier advances. Subsequent research has tempered and refined these views, which had lasting importance on a whole generation of scholars of the "Bolton school."

Z557. Braden, Charles S. **Religious aspects of the conquest of Mexico.** Durham, 1930. Contains much valuable data on native religions and their influence on Catholicism, as well as impact of the latter in early colonial Mexico.

Z558. Callcott, Wilfrid H. **Church and state in Mexico, 1822–1857.** Durham, 1926. Broader coverage than title indicates; pioneering work of continuing value.

Z559. Carro, Venancio. **La teología y los teólogos-juristas españoles ante la conquista de América.** 2nd ed., 2 v., Salamanca, Spain, 1951. [Escuela de Estudios Hispano-Americanos, publ. 6, ser. 2, Monografías, 2.] Intellectual-juridical history. Indicates that as theorists Vitoria and followers had more enduring influence than the more widely known Las Casas.

Z560. Chinchilla Aguilar, Ernesto. **La Inquisición en Guatemala.** Guatemala, 1953. A dispassionate monograph of importance.

Z561. Cuevas, Mariano. **Historia de la iglesia en México.** 5th ed., 5 v., Mexico, 1946–47. Chiefly concerned with the colonial church; not wholly dispassionate or balanced, but an almost unique synthesis.

Z562. Desdevises du Dézert, Georges N. "L'église espagnole des Indes à la fin du dix-huitième siècle." **Revue hispanique,** 39 (Feb. 1917): 112–293. General summary of church affairs in Spanish America during the Bourbon renaissance and the Enlightenment.

Z563. ——. "L'Inquisition aux Indes espagnoles à la fin du XVIIIe siècle." **Revue hispanique,** 30 (Feb. 1914): 1–118.

Z564. Dornas, João. **O padroado e a igreja brasileira.** São Paulo, 1938. Documented account of church-state relations under the empire. [MCK]

Z565. Dunne, Peter M. **Pioneer Jesuits in northern Mexico.** Berkeley, 1944. First of a series of monographs on Jesuits in northern Mexican states by this author, who is a Jesuit.

Z566. Egaña, Antonius de, ed. **Monumenta peruana.** V. 1–2. Rome, 1954–58. [1, 1565–75; 2, 1576–80.] First two volumes of a monumental series on Peruvian Jesuits from various archives. Documents are in Spanish, but editorial matter is in Latin.

Z567. García Gutiérrez, Jesús. **Apuntes para la historia del origen y desenvolvimiento del regio patronato indiano hasta 1857.** Mexico, 1941. Institutional history of Crown-Papacy arrangements for naming and administering clergy in Spanish America.

Z568. Graham, Richard B. Cunninghame. **A vanished Arcadia: being some account of the Jesuits in Paraguay, 1607 to 1767.** Rev. ed., N.Y., 1924. A popular history of the "closed" native communities administered by the Jesuits. There is an enormous polemic literature on this experiment, much of it evaluated in Mörner's monograph (*Z580*).

Z569. Hill, Roscoe R. "Ecclesiastical archives in Latin America." **Archivum,** 4 (1954): 135–44.

Z570. Höffner, Joseph. **Christentum und Menschenwürde: das Anliegen der spanischen Kolonialethik im goldenen Zeitalter.** Trier, 1947. Excellent summary, discussing the medieval background, pre-Columbian religions of America, nature of the conquest, and the juridical-theological problems posed by missionary and similar programs. Impressive bibliography.

Z571. Holleran, Mary P. **Church and state in Guatemala.** N.Y., 1949. Standard monographic treatment.

Z572. Leite, Serafim. **História da Companhia de Jesús no Brasil.** 10 v. Lisbon, 1938–50. Of particular importance because, due to the relative lack of secular clergy in colonial Brazil, religious orders were in many cases the molders of history. Unfortunately, only the Jesuits have succeeded in publishing their history more or less completely. [MCK]

Z573. ——. **Monumenta brasiliae.** Rome, 1956 ff. Continuing publication of Jesuit documents.

Z574. Mecham, John Lloyd. **Church and state in Latin America.** Chapel Hill, 1934. Standard coverage in English of arrangements made between Vatican and the independent republics concerning patronage and their international relations (concordats).

Z575. Medina, José Toribio. **Historia del tribunal del Santo Oficio de la Inquisición de Lima (1569–1820).** 2 v. Santiago, Chile, 1887.

Z576. ——. **Historia del tribunal del Santo Oficio de la Inquisición en Chile.** 2 v. Santiago, 1890. Standard coverage. This and his other monographs on the same theme are unsympathetic.

Z577. ——. **Historia del tribunal del Santo Oficio de la Inquisición en México.** Santiago, 1905.

Z578. ——. **La primitiva inquisición americana (1493–1569).** Santiago, 1914.

Z579. ——. **El tribunal del Santo Oficio de la Inquisición en las provincias del Plata.** Santiago, 1899.

Z580. Mörner, Magnus. **The political and economic activities of the Jesuits in the Plata region.** Tr. by Albert Read. Stockholm, 1953. A sober and significant survey and evaluation, by a young Swedish scholar, of the controversial activities of the Jesuits, especially in Paraguay. Includes a valuable discussion of sources and earlier historiography of the question.

Z581. Ricard, Robert. **La "conquête spirituelle" du Mexique: essai sur l'apostolat et les méthodes missionaires des ordres mendiants en Nouvelle-Espagne de 1523–24 à 1572.** Paris, 1933. Summary monograph, with notable bibliographical contributions. There is also a Spanish translation.

Z582. Santiago Vela, Gregorio de. **Ensayo de una biblioteca ibero-americana de la Orden de San Agustín.** 8 v. Madrid, 1913–31.

Z583. Streit, Robert. **Bibliotheca missionum.** V. 2–3. Aachen, 1924–27. Classic bio-bibliographies of major and minor writers. These volumes deal with America, 1493–1909.

Z584. Tibesar, Antonine, ed. **Studies presented at the Conference on the History of Religion in the New World during Colonial Times.** Washington, 1958. Comparative approach by selected international authorities on religion in the United States, Canada, Brazil, and Spanish America; opens up numerous research paths.

Z585. Vilhena de Moraes, Eugenio. **O gabinete Caxias e a anistia aos bispos na questão religiosa.** Rio de Janeiro, 1930. Good synthesis of the religious question in 19th century Brazil. [MCK]

Z586. Watters, Mary. **History of the church in Venezuela, 1810–1930.** Chapel Hill, 1933. Pioneering monograph on a neglected topic.

Z587. Chase, Gilbert. **A guide to Latin American music.** Washington, 1945. Standard. For later materials see "Music" in *Handbook of Latin American studies (Z3)*.

Cultural-Intellectual History

Bibliographies

Z588. Karpfeu, Otto Maria (pseud., Oto Maria Carpeaux). **Pequena bibliografia crítica da literatura brasileira.** Rio de Janeiro, 1952. 2nd ed., 1955. Indispensable reference work. [MCK, HFC]

Z589. Smith, Robert C., and Elizabeth Wilder, eds. **A guide to the art of Latin America.** Washington, 1948. Nearly comprehensive to publication date. Subsequent materials listed in "Art" sections of *Handbook of Latin American studies*.

Z590. Topete, José M. **A working bibliography of Brazilian literature.** Gainesville, Fla., 1957. Materials through 1952. Excellent point of departure for further bibliographical treatments.

Z591. ——. **A working bibliography of Latin American literature.** St. Augustine, Fla., 1952. An excellent compilation, aimed primarily at graduate students and librarians. General bibliographies, reference works, writers by countries, and lists of translations from Spanish; unannotated entries. Excludes Brazil.

General

Z592. Almeida, Renato. **História da música brasileira.** 2nd ed., Rio de Janeiro, 1942.

Z593. Angulo Iñiguez, Diego, ed. **Historia del arte hispanoamericano.** Barcelona, 1945 ff. (3 v. to date.) Encyclopedic treatment by many contributors. Due to publishers' dicta, does not carry footnotes or references, but valuable bibliographies.

Z594. Azevedo, Fernando de. **A cultura brasileira: introdução ao estudo da cultura no Brasil.** Rio de Janeiro, 1943. Tr. by Wm. R. Crawford, *Brazilian culture: an introduction to the study of culture in Brazil,* N.Y., 1950. A pioneer work of considerable value. [MCK]

Z595. Bernstein, Harry. **Origins of inter-American interest, 1700–1812.** See *Y168*.

Z596. Crow, John A. **The epic of Latin America.** Garden City, 1946. Primary stress on literary culture in the colonial period. A popular general work.

Z597. García, Rolando V., Luciano Croatto, and Alfredo A. Martín. **Historia de la música latinoamericana.** Buenos Aires, 1938. Musical history and biography; unindexed.

Z598. Henríquez Ureña, Pedro. **Literary currents in Hispanic America.** Cambridge,

Mass., 1945. A masterly summary, going beyond literary bounds into general currents. Includes Brazil. Especially useful bibliography. There is a Spanish translation (Mexico, 1949).

Z599. Jones, Willis K. **Breve historia del teatro latinoamericano.** Mexico, 1956. Compact summary of the theater in Latin America, with valuable bibliographical coverage.

Z600. Lins, Alvaro, ed. **História da literatura brasileira.** Rio de Janeiro, 1947 ff. Collaborative general work; total of 15 v. planned.

Z601. Putnam, Samuel. **Marvelous journey: a survey of four centuries of Brazilian writing.** N.Y., 1948. Standard introduction in English, by the major U. S. authority.

Z602. Romero, Silvio. **Historia da literatura brasileira.** 4th ed., ed. by Nelson Romero, 5 v., Rio de Janeiro, 1954. A basic work, first issued in 1888.

Z603. Schurz, William L. **Latin America, a descriptive survey.** Rev. ed., N.Y., 1949. The most useful single-volume general description in English; historically oriented.

Z604. ———. **This New World: the civilization of Latin America.** N.Y., 1954. Arranged topically, with a chapter on Brazil. Excellent bibliographical footnotes on environment, the Indian, the Spaniard, the conquistador, the negro, the foreigner, the church, the woman, the city.

Z605. Silva, Lafayette. **História do teatro brasileiro.** Rio de Janeiro, 1938. Most complete history to 1938. [MCK]

Z606. Torres-Ríoseco, Arturo. **The epic of Latin American literature.** Rev. ed., N.Y., 1946. Summary by an able Chilean scholar.

Z607. Verissimo de Mattos, José. **Historia da literatura brasileira.** Rio de Janeiro, 1916. Rev. ed., 1929. An indispensable work.

Colonial

Z608. Arrom, José J. **El teatro de Hispano-américa en la época colonial.** Havana, 1956. Chronological treatment; a basic reference.

Z609. García Bacca, Juan D., ed. **Antología del pensamiento filosófico en Colombia de 1647 a 1761.** Bogotá, 1955 [Biblioteca de la Presidencia de Colombia, 21.] Primary sources for study of academic culture, with useful introduction.

Z610. Kubler, George. **Mexican architecture of the sixteenth century.** 2 v. New Haven, 1948. Introductory chapters also constitute an important social and demographic survey.

Z611. Lanning, John Tate. **Academic culture in the Spanish colonies.** N.Y. and London, 1940. Monographic treatment by the leading U. S. authority.

Z612. ———. **The eighteenth-century enlightenment in the University of San Carlos de Guatemala.** Ithaca, 1956. Important case history, puncturing many myths concerning

New World intellectual isolation and cultural lag.

Z613. Leonard, Irving A. **Books of the brave.** Cambridge, Mass., 1949. Able treatment of the books read and traded in colonial Spanish America.

Z614. Lohmann Villena, Guillermo. **El arte dramático en Lima durante el virreinato.** Madrid, 1945. Excellent monograph.

Z615. Quesada, Vicente G. **La vida intelectual en la América Española durante los siglos XVI, XVII y XVIII.** Buenos Aires, 1917. Arranged by viceroyalties. Though dated, has much still of value.

Z616. Salazar, Ramón A. **Historia del desenvolvimiento intelectual de Guatemala: época colonial.** 3 v. Guatemala, 1951. First issued in 1897, but still the only treatment of the topic.

Z617. Solá, Miguel. **Historia del arte hispano-americano: arquitectura, escultura, pintura y artes menores en la América Española durante los siglos XVI, XVII, y XVIII.** Barcelona, 1935. Useful summary to date of publication.

Z618. Wethey, Harold E. **Colonial architecture and sculpture in Peru.** Cambridge, Mass., 1949. Authoritative summary.

Modern

Z619. Ardao, Arturo. **La filosofía en el Uruguay en el siglo XX.** Mexico, 1956. [PAIGH, Commission on History, Committee on the History of Ideas, History of ideas in America, 1.] Modern intellectual history, first in an important series of monographs.

Z620. **Colección del pensamiento de América.** 14 v. Mexico, 1942–44. [Secretaría de Educación Pública.] Selections in Spanish from the works of the following writers, with prologues by various contributors: José Vasconcelos, José Martí, Juan Montalvo, José Enrique Rodó, Simón Bolívar, Ralph Waldo Emerson, Enrique José Varona, Andrés Bello, Manuel González Prada, José Cecilio del Valle, Antonio Caso, José Victorino Lastarria, Eugenio María de Hostos, Rui Barbosa.

Z621. Cortijo Alahija, L. **Musicología latino-americana: la música popular y los músicos célebres de la América Latina.** Barcelona, 1919.

Z622. Costa, Lúcio. **Arquitetura brasileira.** Rio de Janeiro, 1953.

Z623. ———. **Considerações sôbre arte contemporânea.** Rio de Janeiro, 1952.

Z624. Crawford, William R. **A century of Latin American thought.** Cambridge, Mass., 1944. A pioneering, and still almost unique, attempt to open up 19th century Latin American intellectual history. Valuable bibliography.

Z625. Cruz Costa, João. **Contribuição à história das idéias no Brasil (o desenvolvimento da filosofia no Brasil e a evolução histórica nacional). Rio de Janeiro, 1956. Important contribution to the history of Brazilian thought. [MCK]

Z626. Fernández, Justino. **Arte moderno y contemporáneo de México.** Mexico, 1952. Monumental, tracing history of art from late 18th century neoclassic to the present; the most complete account extant on 20th century. Architecture, sculpture, prints, painting.

Z627. Franca, Leonel. **Noções de história da filosofia.** Rio de Janeiro, 1918. 13th ed., 1951. First attempt to present complete story of the development of philosophy in Brazil. Considers only period from about 1830 to present. [MCK]

Z628. Frankovitch, Guillermo. **El pensamiento boliviano en el siglo XX.** Mexico, 1956. [PAIGH, Commission on History, History of ideas in America, 2.]

Z629. Marcelin, Pierre, and Philippe Thoby-Marcelin. **Canapé-Vert.** Tr. by Edward L. Tinker. N.Y. and Toronto, 1944. A gripping story of Haitian religious beliefs and folk life, written with an understanding that few Haitians have revealed. [RWL]

Z630. Oliveira Tôrres, João C. de. **O positivismo no Brasil.** Petrópolis, 1943. Study of Brazilian positivism, one of the strongest forces leading to a republic in 1889. [MCK]

Z631. Sánchez Reulet, Aníbal. **Contemporary Latin-American philosophy.** Tr. by William R. Trask. Albuquerque, 1954. Anthology of translated items, with complete bibliography.

Z632. Zea, Leopoldo. **Dos etapas del pensamiento en Hispanoamérica: del romanticismo al positivismo.** Mexico, 1949. Masterly summary of history of ideas. Helpful bibliography.

Economic History

Colonial

Z633. Borah, Woodrow W. **Early colonial trade and navigation between Mexico and Peru.** Berkeley, 1954. Valuable monograph, stressing 16th century entrepôt trade of Mexico with Peru, China trade, and final abolition of trade between the viceroyalties.

Z634. ——. **Silk raising in colonial Mexico.** Berkeley, 1943. Pioneering monograph based on excellent sources; especially useful for early history of Indian labor relations.

Z635. Borde, Jean, and Mario Góngora. **Evolución de la propiedad rural en el Valle del Puangue.** 2 v. Santiago, Chile, 1956. Fruitful collaboration of a geographer and a historian for study of the structure of rural property in Chile from the Spanish conquest to the present; a case history. Includes maps showing lands as of 1604, 1690, 1775, 1880, and 1953.

Z636. Carrera Stampa, Manuel. **Los gre-**

mios mexicanos: la organización gremial en Nueva España, 1521–1861. Mexico, 1954. A pioneering effort of great value.

Z637. Céspedes del Castillo, Guillermo. **La avería en el comercio de Indias.** Seville, 1945. Monographic treatment of finances in colonial trade and navigation between Spain and America.

Z638. Chaunu, Huguette, and Pierre Chaunu. **Séville et l'Atlantique, 1504–1650.** Paris, 1955 ff. Impressive, minutely documented economic history, based on rich archival materials; a fundamental work. 8 v. planned.

Z639. Hamilton, Earl J. **American treasure and the price revolution in Spain, 1501–1650.** See *VD170.*

Z640. Haring, Clarence H. **Trade and navigation between Spain and the Indies in the time of the Hapsburgs.** Cambridge, Mass., 1918. Standard point of departure for studies of this topic.

Z641. Howe, Walter. **The mining guild of New Spain and its tribunal general, 1770–1821.** Institutional study of great value.

Z642. Hussey, Roland D. **The Caracas Company, 1728–1784: a study in the history of Spanish monopolistic trade.** Cambridge, Mass., 1934. Summary of an important, though abortive, experiment in northern South America.

Z643. Levene, Ricardo. **Investigaciones acerca de la historia económica del Virreinato de la Plata.** 2nd ed., 2 v., Buenos Aires, 1952. Revised and augmented edition of an important study. V. 1, colonial period to 18th century; v. 2, establishment of the viceroyalty and its disintegration.

Z644. Lohmann Villena, Guillermo. **Las minas de Huancavelica en los siglos XVI y XVII.** Seville, 1949. Exhaustive and comprehensive monograph on the Crown monopoly of quicksilver mines.

Z645. Meek, Wilbur T. **The exchange media of colonial Mexico.** N.Y., 1948. Useful introduction; not exhaustive.

Z646. Romero, Emilio. **Historia económica del Perú.** Buenos Aires, 1949. Short but excellent manual, restricted to pre-conquest and colonial periods, with very brief summary of national era.

Z647. Schurz, William L. **The Manila galleon.** N.Y., 1939. Important monograph on the trans-pacific trade of Spain via Mexico in the colonial era.

Z648. Zavala, Silvio A., and María Castelo, eds. **Fuentes para la historia del trabajo en Nueva España.** 8 v. Mexico, 1939–45. Selected Mexican documents stressing Indian economic relations in the 16th century.

Modern

Z649. Alba, Víctor. **Esquema histórico del movimiento obrero en América Latina.**

Mexico, [1957]. Emphasis on labor movement philosophies and ideologies.

Z650. Bush, Archer C. **Organized labor in Guatemala, 1944–1949.** Hamilton, N.Y., 1950. Summary of the beginnings of the labor movement.

Z651. Checchi, Vincent, and others. **Honduras: a problem in economic development.** N.Y., 1959. Twentieth Century Fund study of a type area.

Z652. Clark, Marjorie R. **Organized labor in Mexico.** Chapel Hill, 1934. Pioneering monograph that brings narrative to edge of major developments following 1934.

Z653. Ellsworth, Paul T. **Chile, an economy in transition.** N.Y., 1945. Useful to date of publication.

Z654. Fetter, Frank W. **Monetary inflation in Chile.** Princeton, 1931. Rather technical discussion, stressing 1920's.

Z655. Gordon, Wendell C. **The economy of Latin America.** N.Y., 1950. A general summary, almost the only one of modern economic aspects. For continuing bibliography see "Economics" in *Handbook of Latin American studies (Z3)*, edited for a period by this author.

Z656. Hanson, Simon G. **Argentine meat and the British market.** Stanford, 1938. Economic history, 1850–1932.

Z657. ――――. **Economic development in Latin America.** Washington, 1951. One of the few general treatments of modern Latin American economic problems.

Z658. Johnson, John J. **Pioneer telegraphy in Chile, 1852–1876.** Stanford, 1948. Sound monographic treatment.

Z659. Jones, Tom B., Elizabeth A. Warburton, and Anne Kingsley. **A bibliography of South American economic affairs: articles in nineteenth century periodicals.** Minneapolis, 1955. Some 6,200 entries from 220 periodicals, chiefly British, continental European, and United States, on the ten South American republics.

Z660. Lieuwen, Edwin. **Petroleum in Venezuela: a history.** Berkeley, 1954. Compact summary, 1899–1952.

Z661. Mosk, Sanford A. **Industrial revolution in Mexico.** Berkeley, 1950. Analysis and summary, stressing 1936–46. Appeared just before great era of industrialization in Mexico and, therefore, is chiefly of historical rather than current importance.

Z662. Normano, João F. **Brazil, a study of economic types.** Chapel Hill, 1935. A useful economic history, stressing 19th century; incomplete but stimulating.

Z663. Ospina Vásquez, Luís. **Industria y protección en Colombia, 1810–1930.** Medellín, 1955. A nearly definitive economic history, richly documented.

Z664. Peñaloza, Luís. **Historia económica de Bolivia.** 2 v. La Paz, 1953–54. More general than title indicates. Quarter of book devoted to indigenous and colonial Bolivia, remainder to period 1825–1925, with some treatment to 1955. Useful bibliography.

Z665. Peters, Harold E. **The foreign debt of the Argentine republic.** Baltimore, 1934. Technical study of pre-Perón eras.

Z666. Poblete Troncoso, Moisés. **El movimiento obrero latinoamericano.** Mexico, 1946. Unsatisfactory, but practically the only general view of the labor movement. Stresses legal aspects. For subsequent bibliography see "Labor and social welfare" in *Handbook of Latin American studies (Z3)*.

Z667. Powell, J. Richard. **The Mexican petroleum industry, 1938–1950.** Berkeley, 1956. Detailed discussion of first years of nationalized industry, before it was clearly successful.

Z668. Simonsen, Roberto C. **A evolução industrial do Brasil.** São Paulo, 1939. A history of industrial progress. [MCK]

Z669. Speigel, Henry W. **The Brazilian economy: chronic inflation and sporadic industrialization.** Philadelphia, 1949. Analysis centering on industrialization and inflation and their relation to general economic development in Brazil.

Z670. Stein, Stanley J. **The Brazilian cotton manufacture: textile enterprise in an underdeveloped area, 1850–1950.** Cambridge, Mass., 1957. Soundly researched history of an important industry, stressing economic factors.

Z671. ――――. **Vassouras: a Brazilian coffee county, 1850–1900.** Cambridge, Mass., 1957. Socio-economic study of the Parahyba Valley through the rise, apogee, and decadence of coffee monoculture; a monograph that breaks new methodological ground as well as provides important data.

Z672. Stewart, Watt. **Henry Meiggs, Yankee Pizarro.** Durham, 1946. Careful study of the builder and financier of late 19th century Peruvian and Chilean railroads. Much data on economic conditions, 1860–80.

Z673. Taunay, Afonso de. **História do café no Brasil.** 15 v. Rio de Janeiro, 1939–43. Exhaustive study of coffee, Brazil's most important modern crop. [MCK]

Z674. Torrente, Vicente, and Gabriel Mañueco. **Las relaciones económicas de España con Hispanoamérica.** Madrid, 1953. Statistical material, 1931–36, 1946–48, and discussion of principal items in trade.

Z675. Vianna, Hélio. **História da viação brasileira.** Rio de Janeiro, 1949. History of railroads in Brazil. [MCK]

Z676. Williams, John H. **Argentine international trade under inconvertible paper money, 1880–1900.** Cambridge, Mass., 1920. A technical study.

Z677. Wythe, George, and others. **Brazil, an expanding economy.** N.Y., 1949. Excellent comprehensive study, with emphasis on industrialization. [MCK]

Z678. Wythe, George. **Industry in Latin America.** N.Y., 1945. A pioneering work, now unfortunately somewhat outdated. Much data on Latin America on the eve of its major period of industrialization.

Education

Z679. Andrade Filho, Bento de. **História de educação.** 2nd ed., São Paulo, 1953. Brief history from colonial period to the present.

Z680. Barth, Pius Joseph. **Franciscan education and the social order in Spanish North America (1502–1821).** Chicago, 1945. Area includes Guatemala, West Indies, Mexico through Florida and California.

Z681. Jacobsen, Jerome V. **Educational foundations of the Jesuits in sixteenth-century New Spain.** Berkeley, 1938. Monograph.

Z682. Kandel, Isaac L., ed. **Education in Latin American countries.** N.Y., 1942. Though dated, still the best summary. For continuing bibliography see sections on "Education" in *Handbook of Latin American studies (Z3)*.

Z683. Lanning, John T. **The university in the kingdom of Guatemala.** Ithaca, 1955. Scholarly monograph based on impeccable research.

Z684. Pan American Union. **Education in Latin America: a partial bibliography.** Washington, 1958.

Z685. Smith, Henry L., and Harold Littell. **Education in Latin America.** N.Y., 1934. Useful summary to publication date.

Z686. U. S. Office of Education. **Education in . . . .** 14 v. Washington, 1943 ff. Monographic summaries of the state of education, programs, and systems in the Latin American republics. There are volumes for Chile (1945), Colombia (1946), Cuba (1943), Dominican Republic (1947), Ecuador (1947), El Salvador (1947), Guatemala (1947), Haiti (1948), Honduras (1955), Mexico (1956), Nicaragua (1947), Panama (1948), Peru (1946), and Venezuela (1948). All have bibliographies.

International Relations since 1830 *

General

Z687. Aguirre, Aureliano, ed. **Uruguay and the United Nations.** N.Y., 1958. Uruguayan views of the organization, and local foreign policy in connection with it.

Z688. Bradley, Anita. **Trans-Pacific relations of Latin America.** N.Y., 1942. A summary volume, almost unique in consideration of this topic. Outdated, but not replaced.

Z689. Brazil. Ministério das Relações Exteriores. **O Brasil e a Segunda Guerra Mun-** dial. 2 v. Rio de Janeiro, 1944. Documents on Brazil's participation in World War II. [MCK]

Z690. Calvo, Carlos, ed. **Colección histórica completa de los tratados . . . de todos los estados de la América Latina.** See *Y162*.

Z691. Campos, Raul A. de. **Legislação internacional do Brasil.** 2 v. Rio de Janeiro, 1929.

Z692. Castañeda, Jorge. **Mexico and the United Nations.** N.Y., 1958. Basically a statement of Mexican foreign policy, focused on relations to international organizations.

Z693. Ealy, Lawrence O. **The republic of Panama in world affairs, 1903–1950.** Philadelphia, 1951. Summary monograph on a key area.

Z694. Ferreira de Melo, Rubens. **Textos de direito internacional e de história diplomática de 1815 a 1949.** Rio de Janeiro, 1950.

Z695. Glick, Edward B. **Latin America and the Palestine problem.** N.Y., 1958.

Z696. Herrarte, Alberto. **La unión de Centroamérica, tragedia y esperanza: ensayo político-social sobre la realidad de Centroamérica.** Guatemala, 1955. Comprehensive review of the problem and attempted solutions.

Z697. Houston, John A. **Latin America in the United Nations.** N.Y., 1956. Voting record of the bloc, with lengthy bibliography and tables; little analysis.

Z698. McGann, Thomas F. **Argentina, the United States, and the inter-American system, 1880–1914.** Cambridge, Mass., 1957. Discussion of rivalries; bibliographical footnotes.

Z699. Martin, Percy A. **Latin America and the war.** Baltimore, 1925. Summary of relations in period of World War I.

Z700. Rippy, J. Fred. **Latin America in world politics.** 3rd ed., N.Y., 1938. Summary treatment, now partially outdated but not replaced.

Z701. Rodríguez Larreta, Aureliano. **Orientación de la política internacional en América Latina.** 2 v. Montevideo, 1938. [Universidad de Montevideo, Facultad de Derecho y Ciencias Sociales, Biblioteca de publicaciones oficiales, sec. 3, 13.] A Latin American view.

Z702. Thomas, Ann (Van Wynen), and A. J. Thomas, Jr. **Non-intervention: the law and its import in the Americas.** Dallas, 1956. Technical legal discussion and elucidation of texts, based on general (as distinct from American) international law.

Boundaries, Conflicts, Wars

Z703. Box, Pelham H. **The origins of the Paraguayan War.** Urbana, Ill., 1930. Detailed diplomatic study of the López period.

---

* Materials on the Organization of American States, Pan-Americanism, and related topics will be found in Section Y.

Z704. Bulnes, Gonzalo. **Guerra del Pacífico.** Rev. ed., 3 v., Santiago, 1955. A classic masterpiece, first issued in 1911–19. Stresses Chilean side.

Z705. Dennis, William J. **Documentary history of the Tacna-Arica dispute.** Iowa City, Ia., 1927.

Z706. ———. **Tacna and Arica.** New Haven, 1931. Monographic treatment.

Z707. Fernández, Carlos J. **La guerra del Chaco.** 2 v. Buenos Aires, 1955–56. Compact, authoritative military history, viewed from Paraguay by a leading participant.

Z708. Fonseca Hermes, João S. da, and Murillo de Miranda Basto. **Limites do Brasil.** Rio de Janeiro, 1940.

Z709. Grez Pérez, Carlos E. **Los intentos de unión hispanoamericana y la guerra de España en el Pacífico.** Santiago, 1928.

Z710. Ireland, Gordon. **Boundaries, possessions and conflicts in Central and North America and the Caribbean.** Cambridge, Mass., 1941. Annotated listings with bibliographies. Further and later bibliography in "International relations" sections, *Handbook of Latin American studies* (*Z3*).

Z711. ———. **Boundaries, possessions and conflicts in South America.** Cambridge, Mass., 1938. See above.

Z712. U. S. Department of State. **Boundaries of the Latin American republics: an annotated list of documents, 1493–1943.** Comp. by Alexander Marchant. Washington, 1944.

Z713. Markham, Clements R. **The war between Peru and Chile, 1879–1882.** London, 1882. Standard contemporary account.

Z714. Santos Titara, Ladislau. **Memórias do Grande Exército Aliado, libertador do Sul da América na guerra de 1851 a 1852 contra os tiranos do Prata.** Pôrto Alegre, 1852. The classic account, from Brazilian viewpoint, of the war against Argentina over the question of Uruguay. [MCK]

Z715. Tasso Fragoso, Augusto. **História da guerra entre a Tríplice Aliança e o Paraguai.** 5 v. Rio de Janeiro, 1934. Principal Brazilian work on the war with Paraguay (1865–70). [MCK]

Z716. Vianna, Hélio. **História das fronteiras do Brasil.** Rio de Janeiro, 1949. Accounts of Brazil's boundary questions and their settlement. For further bibliography see Rodrigues, *Teoria da história do Brasil* (*Z484*), pp. 455–73.

Relations with Europe and the United States

Z717. Cady, John F. **Foreign intervention in the Río de la Plata, 1838–50: a study of French, British, and American policy in relation to the dictator Juan Manuel Rosas.** Philadelphia, 1929. Detailed diplomatic history, based on numerous sources.

Z718. Davis, Wm. Columbus. **The last conquistadores: the Spanish intervention in Peru and Chile, 1863–1866.** Athens, Ga., 1950. Scholarly monographic treatment, with considerable attention to internal Spanish conditions. Review, W. D. Beatty, *Am. hist. rev.*, 56 (Apr. 1951): 626.

Z719. Dawson, Daniel. **The Mexican adventure.** London, 1935. French intervention in Mexico.

Z720. De Conde, Alexander. **Herbert Hoover's Latin-American policy.** Stanford, 1951.

Z721. Delgado, Jaime. **España y México en el siglo XIX.** 3 v. Madrid, 1950. Detailed study of Spanish-Mexican relations in the first half of the 19th century, with appendix of more than 100 documents.

Z722. Feis, Herbert. **The diplomacy of the dollar: first era, 1919–1932.** Baltimore, 1950.

Z723. Gantenbein, James W., ed. **The evolution of our Latin-American policy: a documentary record.** N.Y., 1950. Documentary collection on U. S. policy toward Latin America, with some material on the inter-American system.

Z724. Hill, Lawrence F. **Diplomatic relations between the United States and Brazil.** Durham, 1932. Standard monographic treatment. [MCK, HFC]

Z725. Spain. Embajada, Mexico. **Relaciones diplomáticas hispano-mexicanas (1839–1898).** Ser. 1, **Despachos generales.** Ed. by Javier Malagón Barcelo and others. 2 v. Mexico, 1949–52. Important documents, giving much data on Mexican conditions. Published volumes cover 1839–43; others, though edited, are as yet unpublished.

Z726. Manchester, Alan K. **British preeminence in Brazil: its rise and decline.** Chapel Hill, 1933. Authoritative survey, particularly of 1808–70 period. Extensive bibliography. [MCK, HFC]

Z727. Millington, Herbert. **American diplomacy and the War of the Pacific.** N.Y., 1948. Orthodox diplomatic history.

Z728. Miquel i Vergés, Josep M. **La diplomacia española en México (1822–1823).** Mexico, 1956. Important monograph on a critical period of Mexican history.

Z729. Musser, John. **The establishment of Maximilian's empire in Mexico.** Menasha, Wis., 1918. Background and narrative of European intervention in Mexico.

Z730. Napoleão, Aluizio. **Rio Branco e as relações entre o Brasil e os Estados Unidos.** Rio de Janeiro, 1947.

Z731. Parks, E. Taylor. **Colombia and the United States, 1764–1934.** Durham, 1935. Detailed diplomatic history.

Z732. Rives, George L. **The United States and Mexico, 1821–1848: a history of the relations between the two countries from the independence of Mexico to the close of the war with the United States.** 2 v. N.Y.,

1913. Though obsolete in many places, still the most usable account.

Z733. Smith, Lois E. **Mexico and the Spanish Republicans.** Berkeley, 1955. Mexico's relations to the Spanish Civil War and problems of Spanish Republican exiles in Mexico, 1936–54.

Z734. Torre Villar, Ernesto de la, ed. and tr. **Correspondencia diplomática franco-mexicana (1808–1839).** Mexico, 1957 ff. Summaries of documents from *Correspondence politique: Méxique,* in archives of Ministry of Foreign Affairs of France, with some complete documents.

Z735. Ynsfrán, Pablo M. **La expedición norteamericana contra el Paraguay, 1858–1859.** 2 v. Mexico and Buenos Aires, 1954. First volumes of a projected detailed treatment.

Law

Bibliographies

Z736. American Foreign Law Association. **Bibliographies of foreign law series.** 11 v. N.Y., 1926–37. Useful bibliographies by various authors, now somewhat outdated. The following pertain to modern Latin America: 1, *Colombia;* 3, *Bolivia;* 5, *Porto Rico;* 7, *Dominican Republic;* 8, *Haiti;* 9, *Uruguay;* 10, *Curaçao;* 11, *Central American republics.*

Z737. Bayitch, Stojan A. **Guide to inter-American legal studies: a selective bibliography of works in English.** Coral Gables, Fla., 1957. Exhaustive guide which points up the need for more publication in this field.

Z738. Borchard, Edwin M. **Guide to the law and legal literature of Argentina, Brazil, and Chile.** Washington, 1915.

Z739. U. S. Library of Congress. **Legal codes of the Latin American republics.** By Helen L. Clagett. Washington, 1942.

Z740. ——. **A guide to the law and legal literature of. . . .** By Helen L. Clagett and others. 12 v. Washington, 1943–48. [*Argentina, 1917–1946; Bolivia; Chile, 1917–1946; Cuba, the Dominican Republic and Haiti; Colombia; Ecuador; Mexico; The Mexican states; Paraguay; Peru; Uruguay; Venezuela.*] These volumes and the above remain standard preliminary listings; titles vary slightly. Continuing bibliography is included in *Handbook of Latin American studies (Z3).*

Colonial

Z741. Altamira y Crevea, Rafael. **Diccionario castellano de palabras jurídicas y técnicas tomadas de la legislación indiana.** Mexico, 1951. Helpful tool for understanding colonial Spanish administrative documents. Entries comprise short essays with citations; indexed.

Z742. ——. **Manual de investigación de la historia del derecho indiano.** Mexico, 1948. Standard guide by an acknowledged master in this field.

Z743. García Gallo, Alfonso. "El desarrollo de la historiografía jurídica indiana." **Revista de estudios políticos** (Spain), año 13, 48:70 (July-Aug. 1953): 163–85. Survey of important works, 16th century to present, with mention of unpublished materials in Spanish libraries.

Z744. Levene, Ricardo. **Manual de historia del derecho argentino.** Buenos Aires, 1952. Compendium broader than its title, from pre-Columbian times to 1853.

Z745. Manzano Manzano, Juan. **Historia de las Recopilaciones de Indias.** 2 v. Madrid, 1950–56. [1, *Siglo XVI;* 2, *Siglo XVII.*] Detailed history of the basic Spanish American colonial code (*Z143*).

Z746. Ots Capdequí, José M. **Manual de historia del derecho español en las Indias y del derecho propiamente indiano.** 2 v. Buenos Aires, 1943. Excellent and basic guide by a leading authority.

Z747. Zorraquín Becú, Ricardo. **La organización judicial argentina en el período hispánico.** Buenos Aires, 1952. Useful and satisfactory general treatise on organization and competence of judicial powers in colonial Spanish America, especially in the Plata region.

Modern

Z748. Clagett, Helen L. **The administration of justice in Latin America.** N.Y., 1952. Regular and special judicial systems, with notice of unusual writs. A pioneering study.

Z749. Eder, Phanor J. **A comparative survey of Anglo-American and Latin-American law.** N.Y., 1950.

Z750. Esquivel Obregón, Toribio. **Latin American commercial law.** N.Y., 1921. Discussion by an outstanding Mexican lawyer, now outdated in parts. The Pan American Union and the U. S. Department of Commerce issue frequent bibliographies and works on this topic.

Z751. Jacobini, H. B. **A study of the philosophy of international law as seen in the works of Latin American writers.** The Hague, 1954.

Z752. Peixoto, Jarbas, ed. **Código do trabalho: interpretação e prática da consolidação das leis do trabalho.** 2 v. Rio de Janeiro, 1945. Comprehensive treatment of the modern labor law of Brazil. An introduction traces the history of Brazilian labor laws, and analyzes their fundamental doctrines. [MCK]

Z753. Pontes de Miranda, Francisco C. **Fontes e evolução do direito civil brasileiro.** Rio de Janeiro, 1928. Development of Brazilian civil law from colonial times. For extensive bibliography of Brazilian legal bibliographies see Rodrigues, *Teoria da história do Brasil (Z484).*

Z754. Recaséns Siches, Luis, and others. **Latin American legal philosophy.** Tr. by Gordon Ireland and others. Cambridge, Mass., 1948. A basic discussion by a group of outstanding Latin American legal minds.
Z755. Vance, John T. **The background of Hispanic-American law.** See *VD131*.

Municipal History

Z756. Alemparte Robles, Julio. **El cabildo en Chile colonial (orígenes municipales de las repúblicas hispanoamericanas).** Santiago, 1940.
Z757. Pan American Institute of Geography and History, Commission on History. **Contribuciones a la historia municipal de América.** By Rafael Altamira y Crevea and others. Mexico, 1951. Extremely important group of essays by various scholars on aspects of colonial municipal history.
Z758. Bayle, Constantino. **Los cabildos seculares en la América Española.** Madrid, 1952. Summary and masterly treatment of Spanish American town government in the colonial period.
Z759. Domínguez Company, Francisco. Bibliografía de las instituciones locales de Hispanoamérica (época colonial)." **Revista interamericana de bibliografía,** 6 (July-Sep. 1956): 209–23. Annotated list of sources and studies on Spanish and Indian municipalities, by subjects.
Z760. Guzman, Louis E. **An annotated bibliography of publications on urban Latin America.** Chicago, 1952.
Z761. Millares Carlo, Agustín. "Notas bibliográficas acerca de archivos municipales, ediciones de libros de acuerdo y colecciones de documentos concejiles." **Contribuciones a la historia municipal de América** (Mexico, 1951), pp. 178–238. [PAIGH publ. 100, CH publ. 14.] A basic tool. Replete listing of documentary collections, published and unpublished, related to colonial municipalities, with bibliographical notes. List of collections, with additional bibliography, has been brought up to date by the author in "Nueva adiciones y rectificaciones," *Revista de historia de América,* 44 (Mexico, Dec. 1957): 393–428; also published separately as a monograph (Madrid, 1952).
Z762. Moore, John P. **The cabildo in Peru under the Hapsburgs: a study in the origins and powers of the town council in the Viceroyalty of Peru, 1530–1700.** Durham, 1954. General treatment, based on about a dozen sets of town records.
Z763. Morse, Richard M. **From community to metropolis: a biography of São Paulo, Brazil.** Gainesville, 1958. Unusual and able municipal history of an important center.
Z764. Wilhelmy, Herbert. **Südamerika im Spiegel seiner Städte.** Hamburg, 1952. History and geography of South America from viewpoint of 14 selected cities.
Z765. Zenha, Edmundo. **O município no Brasil, 1502–1700.** São Paulo, 1948.

Political Sciences

Z766. Blanksten, George I. "Bibliography on Latin American politics and government." **Inter-American review of bibliography,** 4 (July-Sep. 1954): 191–214. Recent selected general coverage. For continuing bibliography and coverage from 1935 see "Government," *Handbook of Latin American studies* (*Z3*).
Z767. Christensen, Asher N., ed. **The evolution of Latin American government: a book of readings,** N.Y., 1951. More than fifty articles and excerpts on history, basic factors, constitutional bases, organization of governments, and contemporary problems, including world affairs.
Z768. Davis, Harold E., ed. **Government and politics in Latin America.** N.Y., 1958. Summary essays by many authors, with helpful bibliographical footnotes and reading lists on major topics.
Z769. Fitzgibbon, Russell H., ed. **The constitutions of the Americas.** See *Y166*.
Z770. Johnson, John L. **Political change in Latin America: the emergence of the middle sectors.** Stanford, 1958. Extremely important monograph on major changes in principal countries to about 1955, stressing impact of new classes emerging from economic advance. Massive bibliography.
Z771. Jorrín, Miguel. **Governments of Latin America.** N.Y., 1953. Summary text with reading lists.
Z772. Pierson, William W., and Federico G. Gil. **Governments of Latin America.** N.Y., 1957. Summary textbook approach; useful synthesis.
Z773. Tucker, William P. **The Mexican government today.** Minneapolis, 1957. A very useful volume, breaking new ground in treatment of government by linking it to social, historical, and economic contexts.

Politico-Social Movements

Z774. Alba, Víctor. **Historia del comunismo en América Latina.** Mexico, 1954. Useful summary with short bibliography, stressing post-1950 period.
Z775. Alexander, Robert J. **Communism in Latin America.** New Brunswick, N.J., 1957. Scholarly work, based on interviews and printed materials, emphasizing 1920 to present.
Z776. Allen, Robert L. **Soviet influence in Latin America: the role of economic relations.** Washington, 1959. The author, who

has explored Soviet economic relations with other world regions, finds that the economic influence of the U.S.S.R. is small and not significantly increasing. A serious and useful study.

Z777. Chang-Rodríguez, Eugenio. **La literatura política de González Prada, Mariátegui y Haya de la Torre.** Mexico, 1957. Intellectual biographies of the liberal-radical triad: Manuel González Prada (1848–1918), José Carlos Mariátegui (1895–1930), and Víctor Raúl Haya de la Torre (1895–). Impressive bibliography of 1,700 works on APRA, etc.

Z778. Comas, Juan. "Panorama continental del indigenismo." **Cuadernos americanos,** año 9, v. 54, no. 6 (Nov.-Dec. 1950): 147–66. Summary of Indigenism movement.

Z779. Foster, William Z. **Outline political history of the Americas.** N.Y., 1951. The "official" Communist history of Latin America; negatively useful to indicate the perversion of facts, to buttress ideology, and to identify other works following this "party line."

Z780. Haya de la Torre, Víctor Raúl. **Treinta años de Aprismo.** Mexico, 1956. Summary of the movement, 1924–*ca.*1942, by one of its founders. A second volume is to complete the narrative.

Z781. Kantor, Harry. **The ideology and program of the Peruvian Aprista movement.** Berkeley, 1953. Scholarly and objective analysis of this generation-old movement.

Z782. Magariños, Santiago, and Ramón Puigdollers. **Panhispanismo, su transcendencia histórica, política y social: obra premiada en el concurso hispano antillano de 1925.** Barcelona, 1926. The unsuccessful analogue of Pan-Americanism, now generally known as "Hispanidad."

Z783. Osorio Lizarazo José A. **Gaitán: vida, muerte, y permanente presencia.** Buenos Aires, 1952. Biography of liberal-radical Gaitanismo leader, Jorge Eliécer Gaitán (1898–1948), who had begun to build up a mass movement in Colombia before his assassination. Covers twenty years of recent politics.

Z784. Ravines, Eudocio. **The Yenan way: the Kremlin's penetration of South America.** N.Y., 1951. Former organizer for Communist party in Chile provides much intimate detail on Communist-inspired methods and plans in Latin America.

Z785. Salgado, Plínio. **O integralismo perante a nação.** 2nd ed., Rio de Janeiro, 1950. The principles of the Brazilian Integralist party (of the far right, founded 1932) as given by its founder. [MCK]

Z786. Schneider, Ronald M. **Communism in Guatemala, 1944–1954.** N.Y., 1948. Factual and important study, based on a wide range of solid documentary materials.

Social Life and Conditions

Bibliographies and General

Z787. Pan American Union. **Bibliography on labor and social welfare in Latin America.** By Sylvia P. Bernstein. Washington, 1944. Useful to date of publication. Continuing bibliography in "Labor and social welfare," *Handbook of Latin American studies (Z3).*

Z788. Cline, Howard F. "Mexican community studies." **Hisp. Am. hist. rev.,** 32 (May 1952): 212–42. Review article, evaluating Mexican community studies from 1930, with annotated bibliography of 81 items.

Z789. Cox, Edward G. **A reference guide to the literature of travel, including voyages, geographical descriptions, adventures, shipwrecks and expeditions.** V. 2, **The New World.** Seattle, 1938. Standard and important guide to numerous materials.

Z790. Gardiner, C. Harvey. "Foreign travelers' accounts of Mexico, 1810–1910." **The Americas,** 8:3 (Jan. 1952): 321–51. List of 394 book titles, unannotated except where volume translated.

Z791. Jones, Tom B. **South America rediscovered.** Minneapolis, 1949. Delightful synthesis of what travelers saw, chiefly 19th century. Bibliography.

Z792. Leonard, Olen E., and Charles P. Loomis, eds. **Readings in Latin American social organization and institutions.** East Lansing, 1953. Anthropological and sociological articles from U.S. journals since 1941; brief annotated bibliography.

Z793. Poblete Troncoso, Moisés. **Ensayo de bibliografía social de los países hispano-americanos.** Santiago, 1936. An early and still useful compilation.

Z794. Poviña, Alfredo. "Latin American sociology in the twentieth century." **International social science bulletin,** 4 (1952): 471–80. Brief synthesis of advances in sociology in the various countries, with short bibliographies. Recently the *Handbook of Latin American studies (Z3)* has added a section on "Sociology."

Spanish America

Z795. Biesanz, John, and Mavis Biesanz. **Costa Rican life.** N.Y., 1944. Sociological study.

Z796. ———. **The people of Panama.** N.Y., 1955. Sociological study, weak on recent history.

Z797. Lewis, Oscar. **Five families: Mexican case studies in the culture of poverty.** N.Y., 1959. Unique study of one day in the life of five families in different social and economic strata. Much detail; little bibliography.

Z798. Nelson, Lowry. **Rural Cuba.** Minneapolis, 1950. Sociological treatment.

Z799. Service, Elman R. **Spanish-Guaraní relations in early colonial Paraguay.** Ann Arbor, 1954. Social and other aspects.

Z800. Service, Elman R., and Helen S. Service. **Tobatí: Paraguayan town.** Chicago, 1954. First and only extant scientific community study and social anthropological survey of Paraguay.

Z801. Taylor, Carl C. **Rural life in Argentina.** Baton Rouge, 1948. Sociological survey.

Z802. Whetten, Nathan L. **Rural Mexico.** Chicago, 1948. Massive compilation by an outstanding sociologist.

Brazil
(Mathias C. Kiemen)

Z803. Cunha, Euclides da. **Rebellion in the backlands.** Tr. by Samuel Putnam. Chicago, 1944. Original ed., *Os Sertões* (Rio de Janeiro, 1902). Basic for understanding life in interior Brazil at end of the 19th century.

Z804. Freyre, Gilberto. **Brazil: an interpretation.** N.Y., 1945.

Z805. ———. **Casa-grande & senzala: formação da familia brasileira sob o regimen de economia patriarcal.** Rio de Janeiro, 1933. 7th ed., 2 v., 1952. Tr. by Samuel Putnam, *The masters and the slaves . . . a study in the development of Brazilian civilization*, N.Y., 1946. Basic for study of the Brazilian plantation family.

Z806. ———. **Sobrados e mucambos: decadencia do patriarcado rural e desenvolvimento do urbano.** 2nd ed., 3 v., São Paulo, 1951. Superb study of the onslaught of city life on the aristocratic plantation life in northern Brazil. Planned as a logical continuation of *Z805*.

Z807. Lambert, Jacques. **Le Brésil: structure sociale et institutions politiques.** Paris, 1953. Interpretative study of the social and political history of Brazil.

Z808. Pierson, Donald. **Survey of the literature on Brazil of sociological significance published up to 1940.** Cambridge, Mass., 1945. Standard bibliography to date of publication. [HFC]

Z809. Smith, Thomas Lynn. **Brazil: people and institutions.** Rev. ed., Baton Rouge, 1954. Vast compilation of important materials by a leading U. S. authority. Significant bibliography.

Technology, Science, Medicine

Z810. Bargallo, Modesto. **La minería y la metalurgía en la América Española durante la época colonial.** Mexico and Buenos Aires, 1955. Technical treatise tracing history of mines, methods, and techniques to about 1810; splendid bibliography.

Z811. Cutright, Paul R. **The great naturalists explore South America.** N.Y., 1940.

Z812. Guerra, Francisco. **Historiografía de la medicina colonial hispanoamericana.** Mexico, 1953. Important; more bibliographical than historiographical.

Z813. Moll, Aristides A. **Aesculapius in Latin America.** Philadelphia, 1944. Standard general English language history of medicine.

Z814. Nascimento, Alfredo. **Primórdios e evolução da medicina no Brasil.** Rio de Janeiro, 1929. [Academia Nacional de Medicina.] History of medicine in the colonial and empire periods. [MCK]

Z815. Ruiz López, Hipólito. **Travels of Ruiz, Pavón, and Dombey in Peru and Chile (1777–1788).** Tr. by B. E. Dahlgren. Chicago, 1940. Data by 18th century scientists.

BIOGRAPHIES

Spanish America

Colonial Period

Z816. Aiton, Arthur S. **Antonio de Mendoza, first viceroy of New Spain.** Durham, 1927. More "times" than "life" of this key figure; based on manuscript sources.

Z817. Altolaguirre y Duvale, Ángel de. **Vasco Núñez de Balboa.** Madrid, 1914. Standard life in Spanish.

Z818. Arciniega, Rosa. **Pedro Sarmiento de Gamboa (el Ulises de América).** Buenos Aires, 1956. Scholarly biography, with new unpublished material; covers years 1560–1620.

Z819. Clissold, Stephen. **Conquistador: the life of Don Pedro Sarmiento de Gamboa.** London, 1954. A generally sound biography.

Z820. Graham, Robert B. Cunninghame. **The conquest of New Granada: being the life of Gonzalo Jiménez de Quesada.** London, 1922. Semi-popular; not adequate.

Z821. Hanke, Lewis, and Manuel Giménez Fernández. **Bartolomé de las Casas, 1474–1566: bibliografía crítica y cuerpo de materiales para el estudio de su vida, escritos, actuación y polémicas que suscitaron durante cuatro siglos.** Santiago, 1954. Evaluation of various writings on this polemic figure. There is no single adequate biography.

Z822. Lamb, Ursula. **Frey Nicolás de Ovando, gobernador de las Indias, 1501–1509.** Madrid, 1956. Modern biography of a key figure and his problems in the first period of colonization.

Z823. Leonard, Irving A. **Don Carlos de Sigüenza y Góngora, a Mexican savant of the seventeenth century.** Berkeley, 1929. Important biography of a significant figure.

Z824. Levillier, Roberto. **Don Francisco de Toledo, supremo organizador del Perú (1515–1582).** 3 v. Buenos Aires, 1935–42. Exhaustive coverage with much documentation.

Z825. Medina, José Toribio. **Ensayo bio-bibliográfico sobre Hernán Cortés: obra póstuma.** Santiago, 1952. Guide to materials printed 1522–1930; definitive, 1522–1915. Introduction, by Guillermo Feliú Cruz, summarizes 19th century bibliographical scholarship on Cortesiana.

Z826. Pérez Embid, Florentino. **Diego de Ordás, compañero de Cortés y explorador del Orinoco.** Seville, 1950. [Escuela de Estudios Hispano-Americanos, publ. 58, ser. 2.] Interesting coverage of a minor figure, typical of his times.

Z827. Recinos, Adrián. **Pedro de Alvarado, conquistador de México y Guatemala.** Mexico, 1952. Scholarly biography, based mainly on printed sources.

Z828. Trimborn, Hermann. **Pascual de Andagoya: ein Mensch erlebt die Conquista.** Hamburg, 1954. Comprehensive and thorough treatment of a South American conquistador and poblador.

Z829. Zimmerman, Arthur F. **Francisco de Toledo, fifth viceroy of Peru, 1569–1581.** Caldwell, Idaho, 1938. Useful.

Enlightenment and Independence Period

Z830. Castillo Ledón, Luís. **Hidalgo: la vida del héroe.** 2 v. Mexico, 1948–49. Excellent treatment of the Mexican leader.

Z831. Davis, Thomas B., Jr. **Carlos de Alvear, man of revolution.** Durham, 1955. Deals primarily with his U. S. missions, 1824–25 and 1838–52. Carefully researched.

Z832. Fisher, Lillian E. **Champion of reform, Manuel Abad y Queipo.** N.Y., 1955. Eulogistic but important biography of the enlightened bishop-elect of Michoacán in late New Spain.

Z833. Graham, Robert B. Cunninghame. **José Antonio Páez.** London, 1929.

Z834. Masur, Gerhard. **Simón Bolívar.** Albuquerque, 1948. The most satisfactory single-volume biography in any language.

Z835. Mehegan, J. J. **O'Higgins of Chile: a brief sketch of his life and times.** London, 1913. Nineteenth century mode.

Z836. Noll, Arthur H., and A. Philip MacMahon. **The life and times of Miguel Hidalgo y Costilla.** Chicago, 1910.

Z837. Parra Pérez, Caracciolo. **Mariño y la independencia de Venezuela.** 4 v. Madrid, 1954–56. Biography of Santiago Mariño; detailed history of the period.

Z838. Robertson, William S. **Iturbide of Mexico.** Durham, 1952. Standard and indispensable biography, with much revealing information about the Mexican movements for independence.

Z839. ———. **The life of Miranda.** 2 v. Chapel Hill, 1929. Basic and standard biography of the "Precursor."

Z840. Rojas, Ricardo. **San Martín, knight of the Andes.** Tr. by Herschel Brickell.

N.Y., 1945. English translation of a standard biography.

Z841. Sherwell, Guillermo A. **Antonio José de Sucre.** Washington, 1924. Semipopular.

Z842. Trend, John B. **Bolívar and the independence of Spanish America.** London, 1946. 2nd ed., N.Y., 1951. Balanced short summary, with bibliographical guides.

Z843. Vedia y Mitre, Mariano de. **La vida de Monteagudo.** 3 v. Buenos Aires, 1950. Major biography of an important figure of the Plata independence period. Large panorama of men, ideas, and events.

Modern

Z844. Beals, Carleton. **Porfirio Díaz.** N.Y., 1932. Undocumented but useful summary of the Mexican strong-man.

Z845. Bunkley, Allison W. **The life of Sarmiento.** Princeton, 1952. Well-documented biography of the great Argentine figure; stress on literary contributions.

Z846. Callcott, Wilfrid H. **Santa Anna: the story of an enigma who once was Mexico.** Norman, 1936. A major biography of a central figure in early Mexican national history.

Z847. Corti, E. Caesar, count. **Maximilian and Charlotte of Mexico.** Tr. from German ed. by Catherine A. Phillips. 2 v. N.Y., 1928. Standard biography, and best single treatment of French intervention in Mexico.

Z848. Crespo Rodas, Alfonso. **Santa Cruz, el cóndor indio.** Mexico, 1944. Sound treatment of this 19th century Andean figure.

Z849. Donoso, Ricardo. **Alessandri, agitador y demoledor: cincuenta años de historia política de Chile.** 2 v. Mexico, 1952–54. Detailed treatment of Chilean politics *ca.* 1890–1940, and biography of Arturo Alessandri (1868–1950), who dominated the era, in or out of office.

Z850. Dubois, Jules. **Fidel Castro: rebel—liberator or dictator?** Indianapolis, 1959. Topical, sympathetic biography by a journalist.

Z851. Feliú Cruz, Guillermo. **José Toribio Medina, historiador y bibliógrafo de América.** Santiago, 1952. Sympathetic biography which inevitably gives useful bibliographical data.

Z852. Graham, Robert B. Cunninghame. **Portrait of a dictator, Francisco Solano López.** London, 1933. Still a useful treatment.

Z853. Jeffrey, William H. **Mitre and Argentina.** N.Y., 1952. Laudatory but useful biography of Bartolomé Mitre (1821–1906) as soldier and politician rather than writer and historian.

Z854. Knapp, Frank A., Jr. **The life of Sebastián Lerdo de Tejada, 1823–1889: a**

study of influence and obscurity. Austin, 1951. Biography of an important Mexican, once president.

Z855. Orrego Barros, Carlos. **Diego Barros Arana.** Santiago, 1952. Biography of the famous historian (1830–1907) and his achievements in many fields.

Z856. Roeder, Ralph. **Juárez and his Mexico: a biographical history.** N.Y., 1947. Undocumented and overwritten, but still valuable. Helpful bibliography of printed materials.

Z857. Ross, Stanley R. **Francisco I. Madero, apostle of Mexican democracy.** N.Y., 1955. Sympathetic and able scholarly treatment of Mexico's revolutionary leader.

Z858. Townsend, William C. **Lázaro Cárdenas, Mexican democrat.** Ann Arbor, 1952. Uncritical, eulogistic biography of the Mexican president (1934–40) who revitalized the Revolution.

Brazil
(Mathias C. Kiemen)

Z859. Calmon, Pedro. **A Princesa Isabel, "a redentora."** São Paulo, 1941. Biography of the princess who, as regent, signed the slavery abolition decree.

Z860. Frischauer, Paul. **Presidente Vargas.** São Paulo, 1943. A favorable biography.

Z861. Graham, Robert B. Cunninghame. **A Brazilian mystic: being the life and miracles of Antonio Conselheiro.** N.Y., 1920. The strange figure who sparked the "Rebellion in the backlands." See also *Z803*.

Z862. Nabuco, Joaquim. **Un estadista do Império: Nabuco de Araujo, su vida, suas opiniões, sua época.** 3 v. Rio de Janeiro, 1897–99. New ed., 2 v., 1936. This voluminous biography of José Tomás Nabuco de Araujo, a parliamentary leader during the troubled times of the regency of Pedro II, was written by his son. It is a mine of information and probably the most important book on the Brazilian empire.

Z863. Sousa, Alberto. **Os Andradas.** 3 v. São Paulo, 1922. Account of the three Andrada brothers, José Bonifácio, Antônio Carlos, and Martim Francisco, all important during early years of the independent period.

Z864. Tarquínio de Sousa, Octávio. **José Bonifácio.** Rio de Janeiro, 1945. A standard biography of José Bonifácio de Andrada e Silva, the "patriarch of Brazilian independence."

Z865. ――. **A vida de D. Pedro I.** 3 v. Rio de Janeiro, 1952. Author makes good use of the abundant documentation of the old Imperial Museum.

Z866. Viana, Luiz. **A vida de Rui Barbosa.** Rio de Janeiro, 1949. Biography of one of the great statesmen of modern Brazil.

Z867. Williams, Mary W. **Dom Pedro the Magnanimous.** Chapel Hill, 1937. Scholarly, but not definitive.

GUIDES TO OFFICIAL PUBLICATIONS

Z868. Childs, James B. **The memorias of the republics of Central America and the Antilles.** Washington, 1932.

Z869. U. S. Library of Congress. **A guide to the official publications of the other American republics.** Ed. by James B. Childs and Henry V. Besso. 19 v. Washington, 1945–48. [1, *Argentina;* 2, *Bolivia;* 3, *Brazil;* 4, *Chile;* 5, *Colombia;* 6, *Costa Rica;* 7, *Cuba;* 8, *Dominican Republic;* 9, *Ecuador;* 10, *El Salvador;* 11, *Guatemala;* 12, *Haiti;* 13, *Honduras;* 14, *Nicaragua;* 15, *Panama;* 16, *Paraguay;* 17, *Peru;* 18, *Uruguay;* 19, *Venezuela.*] Basic introductions.

Z870. Ker, Annita M. **Mexican government publications: a guide to the more important publications of the national government of Mexico, 1821–1936.** Washington, 1940.

ACADEMY, SOCIETY, AND UNIVERSITY PUBLICATIONS

Institutions in the United States, Latin America, Europe (especially Spain), and a few very scattered minor centers in Africa and the Orient issue serial and monographic publications of interest to historians of Latin America. The single most comprehensive guide to them is the admittedly incomplete compilation by Carlos Bosch García, *Guía a las instituciones* (*Z19*), currently undergoing revision and expansion. United States non-official institutions, and a few official ones like the Smithsonian Institution, National Archives, and Library of Congress, are noted in the Hilton *Handbook* (*Z31*). Both these may be supplemented by the **(Z871)** Pan American Union, **Guía de instituciones y sociedades en el campo de las ciencias sociales** (2nd ed., Washington, 1954). *The Hispanic American historical review* (*Z879*) and the Commission on History's serial publications, *Revista de historia de América* (*Z874*) and *Boletín bibliográfico de antropología americana* (*Z875*), as well as the standard bibliographical tools, the *Handbook of Latin American studies* (*Z3*) and the *Inter-American review of bibliography* (*Z8*), contain professional notes on the appearance of new serial titles, societies, and groups, as well as occasional demises along the same lines. For librarians, the standard publications by UNESCO on libraries and exchange matters usually give adequate coverage to Latin America as a world area.

On the international scene a number of organizations of general European orientation or outlook often sponsor publications of considerable value to historians. Among them is the International Congress of Americanists, with headquarters in Paris. Since

1875 its meetings have considered New World matters ranging from pre-history to living natives, and among papers presented and published are many dealing with discovery, exploration, the colonial period, and race contacts in Latin America. A handy and accurate summary of the publications (as well as history of the society) is provided by **(Z872)** Juan Comas, **Los Congresos Internacionales de Americanistas: síntesis histórica e índice bibliográfico general, 1875–1952** (Mexico, 1954). This may be supplemented by his important **(Z873) Historia y bibliografía de los Congresos Internacionales de Ciencias Antropológicas, 1865–1954** (Mexico, 1956), although less than 200 of the nearly 3,000 entries touch Americanist themes.

A special note is needed on the Commission on History. A unique regional body, it is one of the constituent commissions of the Pan American Institute of Geography and History. The Institute was founded in 1928, and until 1946 operated as an entity. Reorganization took place in the latter year, with professional programs divided among the three commissions: Cartography, Geography, and History. The Institute is a specialized organ of the Organization of American States; hence the Commission on History is an official international body composed of national members named by their governments, its programs being supported by funds furnished by member states, supplemented by grants and other sources to carry out research and publication. The Commission on History has sponsored a number of series of monographic publications, totaling more than 200 by 1959. Principal series include bibliography, studies on history, historiography, teaching of history, historians of America, technical manuals, missions in European archives, archaeological and historical monuments, and program of the history of America. Normally in each series each of the member states is represented by a volume prepared by a qualified professional individual or team. In addition, each of the several committees of the Commission undertakes programs of meetings, research, and publications. Such committees currently include those on archives, origins of the independence movement, history of ideas, anthropology, folklore, and one or two other inactive groups. In 1958 the Commission created a Committee on Historical Bibliography, with its seat in the Library of Congress (Hispanic Foundation), one of whose first tasks is to publish a bibliography of the Commission's own impressive body of research and teaching materials and aids. The Commission takes direct responsibility for a semi-annual historical review, **(Z874) Revista de historia de América** (Mexico, 1938 ff.), and an an-nual bibliography, **(Z875) Boletín bibliográfico de antropología americana** (see *Y36*). Each publishes articles, notices, and other information in the four official languages of the Organization of American States: English, Spanish, Portuguese, and French.

PERIODICALS

Z876. Butler, Ruth L., ed. **Guide to the Hispanic American historical review, 1918–1945.** Durham, 1950. Provides a brief history of *Z879*. For v. 1–25, detailed coverage, with summaries of all articles, notes, reviews, etc. Indispensable.

Z877. Gibson, Charles, and E. V. Niemeyer, eds. **Guide to the Hispanic American historical review, 1946–1955.** Durham, 1958. Parallels and extends the Butler *Guide*, and is equally indispensable for v. 26–35.

Z878. Pan American Union. **Union list of Latin American newspapers in libraries in the United States.** Comp. by Arthur Gropp. Washington, 1953. Contains about 5,000 titles, including those on microfilm.

Z879. The **Hispanic American historical review.** Baltimore and Durham, 1918 ff. (Quarterly.) The major U. S. specialized historical journal. Extremely useful bibliographical and professional notices and notes. See *Z876–877* for guides.

Z880. **Hispanic American report.** Stanford, 1948 ff. [Stanford University.] (Monthly.) Summaries of political and social developments; reviews of books. Index to v. 1–7 (1948–54) comp. by Joseph C. Shirley and H. Leslie Robinson (Stanford, 1956).

Z881. **Inter-American economic affairs.** Washington, 1947 ff. (Quarterly.) Current economic matters and much historical material.

Z882. Ker, Annita M. **A survey of Mexican scientific periodicals, to which are appended some notes on Mexican historical periodicals.** Baltimore, 1931. Appendix lists and discusses only nine historical periodicals; the main work gives much useful data on scientific societies and institutions, many of which publish items of interest to historians. Covers period to about 1930.

Z883. Nichols, Madaline M., and Lucia B. Innaird. "A bibliographical list of the historical articles in Nosotros, v. 1–76." **Hisp. Am. hist. rev.**, 14 (Aug. 1934): 378–416.

Z884. **Revista do Instituto Arqueológico Histórico e Geográfico Pernambucano.** Recife, 1863 ff. (Irregular.) This and *Z885–886* are the most outstanding in Brazil. They are especially known for publication of important documentation during at least part of their existence.

Z885. Revista do Instituto do Ceará. Fortaleza, 1887 ff. (Irregular.)

Z886. Revista do Instituto Histórico e Geográfico Brisileiro. Rio de Janeiro, 1839 ff. (Irregular.) For index of v. 1–84 (1839–1918) *see Indice analítico* (Rio de Janeiro, 1927).

Z887. U. S. Library of Congress. **Latin American periodicals currently received in the Library of Congress and the Library of the Department of Agriculture.** Ed. by Charmion Shelby. Washington, 1944. Still a basic list of Latin American periodicals. Can be supplemented by complete data in "Key to periodicals" in each issue of *Handbook of Latin American studies* (*Z3*).

British and Dutch America

ALFRED L. BURT and RUDOLF A. J. VAN LIER

BRITISH AMERICA
(Alfred L. Burt)

Since all British North America has been federated under the name of Canada, which once was applied only to its principal part, British North American history is now synonymous with, and best known as, Canadian history. During the century and a half that elapsed between the founding of the original Canada and its cession to Britain, the French colonists took such firm root that Canada has later grown as a bi-ethnic country. Therefore, though the bulk of the extensive literature on Canadian history is in English, a large portion of it is in French, with special emphasis on the French regime and on French Canada in the later period. The result is that anyone who aspires to know Canadian history as a whole has to read French as well as English writers. There is little literature on the subject in any other language.

Less important are the French, Spanish, and Dutch backgrounds and survivals in the British Caribbean colonies. Moreover, these colonies, though as old as those of British North America, are the subject of a smaller and more fragmented historical literature—smaller because of their size and the nature of their society, and more fragmented because of their geographical dispersion over a wide expanse of sea. The new British West Indies federation reflects the awakening of a unifying national consciousness which may inspire the indigenous writing of a common history, as it has done in Canada.

The following bibliography attempts to list only the more important works, omitting studies of colonial policy. For these the reader should consult the bibliographies of the respective metropolitan states.

BRITISH NORTH AMERICA

BIBLIOGRAPHIES, LIBRARIES AND MUSEUMS

AA1. Shortt, Adam, and Arthur G. Doughty, eds. **Canada and its provinces,** v. 23 (Toronto, 1917), pp. 224–83. This and *AA2* are the best classified bibliographies.

AA2. The Cambridge history of the British Empire. V. 6, (*AA58*), pp. 813–85. Particularly useful for its listing of the voluminous MSS sources in France and Britain as well as in Canada, with specific notation of how extensively the originals deposited in the Public Archives of Canada have been supplemented by copies of originals elsewhere on both sides of the Atlantic.

AA3. Review of historical publications relating to Canada. Toronto, 1896–1918. (Annual.) This and its sequel, *AA4,* both published by the University of Toronto, give the most complete bibliography, with reviews, of publications since 1895.

AA4. The Canadian historical review. Toronto, 1920 ff. (Quarterly.) See comment under *AA3*.

AA5. The Canadian journal of economics and political science. Toronto, 1935 ff. (Quarterly.) Similar to *AA4,* and also published by the University of Toronto.

AA6. Staton, Frances M., and Marie Tremain, eds. **A bibliography of Canadiana.** Toronto, 1934. [Toronto Public Library.] Valuable.

AA7. The Canadian catalogue. Toronto, 1923 ff. [Toronto Public Library.] (Annual.)

AA8. Canadian index: a guide to Canadian periodicals and films. Ottawa, 1948 ff. [Canadian Library Association.] (Monthly.) Successor to *Canadian periodical index*.

AA9. Trotter, Reginald G. **Canadian history: a syllabus and guide to reading.** New ed., Toronto, 1934. The most useful introductory bibliography, though weak in citation of writings in French. Material that appeared after the first edition (1926) is listed together at the end instead of distributed through the appropriate topical sections. Author index.

The mecca of students of Canadian history is the federal capital, chiefly because it contains the Public Archives of Canada which, in addition to being the oldest and largest archival collection (including rare maps) of any British dominion, has a specialized library rich in pamphlet material, a large picture section, and a museum illustrating the history of the country. In Ottawa there is also the Parliamentary Library, which has so greatly outgrown its primary purpose of serving members of Parliament that much of it is to be removed to the newly founded National Library. There are also extensive departmental (government) libraries to which serious students may have access, and the National Museum and Art Gallery maintained by the federal government.

The best Canadian university library is that of Toronto, though Queen's (Kingston), McGill (Montreal), and Laval (Quebec) universities also have old and large libraries. The Toronto Public Library and the Royal Ontario Museum, in the same city, are the two outstanding institutions of their kind in Canada. There are valuable archival collections in various provincial capitals, notably Halifax, Quebec, Toronto, Winnipeg, Regina, and Victoria.

ENCYCLOPEDIAS AND WORKS OF REFERENCE

AA10. Burpee, Lawrence J., ed. **The Oxford encyclopaedia of Canadian history.** Toronto, 1926. [The makers of Canada, 12.]

AA11. Encyclopedia of Canada. Ed. by William S. Wallace. 6 v. Toronto, 1935–37.

AA12. Wallace, William S., ed. **Dictionary of Canadian biography.** 2nd ed., 2 v., Toronto, 1945.
A new and extensive encyclopedia of Canada is in process of preparation under the editorship of J. A. Robbins, Ottawa.

AA13. Shortt, Adam, and Arthur G. Doughty, eds. **Canada and its provinces.** 23 v. Toronto, 1914–17. The best general reference; many chapters written by outstanding authorities. The last volume, in addition to the bibliography mentioned above (*AA1*), contains a comprehensive index and historical tables.

AA14. The Canadian annual review of public affairs. Ed. by John C. Hopkins and others. Toronto, 1902–38. Very useful.

AA15. The Canada year book. Ottawa, 1906 ff. (Annual.) A large and invaluable volume, published by the federal Bureau of Statistics. Gives statistical information and authoritative articles on various subjects of public interest. Preceded by *The statistical year-book of Canada* (Ottawa, 1884–1905).

AA16. Canada: the official handbook of present conditions and recent progress. Ottawa, 1918 ff. (Annual.) Also published by the Bureau of Statistics. Much smaller than *AA15*, and quite popular.
The detailed genealogy of almost any old French Canadian family can be traced to the original French home in the following:

AA17. Tanguay, Cyprien. **Dictionnaire généalogique des familles canadiennes.** 7 v. Montreal, 1871–90.

AA18. Gaudet, Placide. "Acadian genealogy and notes," **Report concerning the Canadian archives for the year 1905,** v. 2.

A much smaller genealogical dictionary than *AA17*.

GEOGRAPHIES, GAZETTEERS AND ATLASES

AA19. Canada. Department of Interior. **Atlas of Canada.** Ottawa, 1915. A monumental work, long the only really good atlas of the country. Superseded by another atlas which the federal Geographic Board has been preparing for years, which appeared late in 1958. Provincial governments have produced provincial atlases, of which that of British Columbia (1956) is the best.

AA20. Burpee, Lawrence J., ed. **An historical atlas of Canada.** Toronto, 1927. Slight but useful despite some errors of detail noted in *Can. hist. rev.*, 9 (June 1928): 165–6.

AA21. Bouchette, Joseph. **The British dominions in North America.** 2 v. London, 1832. A classic work by the official surveyor general.

AA22. ———. **A topographical dictionary of the province of Lower Canada.** London, 1832. See comment under *AA21*.

AA23. Currie, Archibald W. **Economic geography of Canada.** Toronto, 1945. Welcomed as a much needed study. See *Can. hist. rev.*, 27 (June 1946): 205–7.

ANTHROPOLOGICAL WORKS

AA24. Jenness, Diamond. **The people of the twilight.** N.Y., 1928. An authoritative study of the Eskimos.

AA25. ———. **The Indians of Canada.** 3rd ed., Ottawa, 1955.

In addition to the above works, the voluminous writings of Marius Barbeau, mostly scattered through periodicals, are particularly important for Indian traditions and French Canadian folklore and arts. Current publications on ethnology, anthropology, and archaeology are listed in *The Canadian historical review* (*AA4*).

DEMOGRAPHIC STUDIES

The decennial *Census* (commencing in 1871) gives the most complete information on the people of Canada, their origins, distribution, activities, etc.; and analytical studies based on these volumes are published by the Bureau of Statistics.

AA26. Blanchard, Raoul. **L'est du Canada français, "province de Québec."** 2 v. Montreal, 1935.

AA27. ———. **Le centre du Canada français.** Montreal, 1947.

AA28. Caron, Ivanhoe. **La colonisation de la province de Québec: débuts du régime anglais, 1760–1791.** Quebec, 1923.

AA29. ———. **La colonisation de la pro-**vince de Québec: les cantons de l'est 1791–1815. Quebec, 1927.

AA30. Carrothers, William A. **Emigration from the British Isles.** London, 1929.

AA31. Coats, Robert H., and Murdoch C. MacLean. **The American-born in Canada: a statistical interpretation.** New Haven, 1943.

AA32. Cowan, Helen I. **British emigration to British North America, 1783–1837.** Toronto, 1928.

AA33. England, Robert. **The central European immigrant in Canada.** Toronto, 1929.

AA34. ———. **The colonization of western Canada.** London, 1936.

AA35. Giraud, Marcel. **Le métis canadien: son rôle dans l'histoire des provinces de l'ouest.** Paris, 1945. An outstanding work by an old-country French scholar.

AA36. Hansen, Marcus L., and John B. Brebner. **The mingling of the Canadian and American peoples.** See *Y193*.

AA37. Harvey, D. C. **The colonization of Canada.** Toronto, 1936.

AA38. Hughes, Everett C. **French Canada in transition.** Chicago, 1943. Deals with a transformation still in progress.

AA39. Langlois, Georges. **Histoire de la population canadienne-française.** Montreal, 1935.

AA40. Salone, Émile. **La colonisation de la Nouvelle-France.** Paris, 1906.

AA41. Wade, Mason. **The French Canadians, 1760–1945.** Toronto, 1955. A book big in size and importance.

AA42. Yuzyk, Paul. **The Ukrainians in Manitoba: a social history.** Toronto, 1953.

PRINTED COLLECTIONS OF SOURCES

AA43. Kennedy, William P. M., ed. **Documents of the Canadian constitution, 1759–1915.** Toronto, 1918. Revised and enlarged as *Statutes, treaties and documents of the Canadian constitution, 1713–1929* (Toronto and London, 1930), this is the most satisfactory collection in one volume.

AA44. Canada. Public Archives. **Documents relating to the constitutional history of Canada, 1759–1791.** Ed. by Adam Shortt and Arthur G. Doughty. 2nd ed., 2 v., Ottawa, 1918. Also volume under same title for period 1791–1818, ed. by Arthur G. Doughty and Duncan A. McArthur (Ottawa, 1914); and another for 1819–1828, ed. by Arthur G. Doughty and Norah Story (Ottawa, 1935). These cover a shorter space of time than *AA43*, but are much fuller and better supplied with explanatory notes.

AA45. ———. **Documents relating to Canadian currency, exchange and finance during the French period.** Ed. by Adam Shortt. 2 v. Ottawa, 1925. A mine of information on the French regime. Voluminous notes.

AA46. ———. **Documents relating to cur-**

rency, exchange and finance in Nova Scotia, with prefatory documents, 1675–1758. Ottawa, 1933. Another important collection.

AA47. Innis, Harold A., ed. **Select documents in Canadian economic history, 1497–1783.** Toronto, 1929. Also volume under same title for period 1783–1885, ed. by Harold A. Innis and Arthur R. M. Lower (Toronto, 1933), containing a joint index for both. These are not as full but of wider scope than *AA45–46.*

AA48. Thwaites, Reuben G., ed. **The Jesuit relations and allied documents.** See *Y93.*

AA49. Édits, ordonnances royaux, déclarations et arrêts du Conseil d'État du roi concernant le Canada. 3 v. Quebec, 1854–56. Of importance for period 1627–1756.

AA50. Jugements et délibérations du Conseil souverain de la Nouvelle-France. 6 v. Quebec, 1885–91. Valuable for French regime down to 1716.

Important selections from state papers are scattered through many annual Public Archives of Canada *Reports,* which also contain calendars of many MSS series in the Public Archives. In addition to the annual *Reports,* the P.A.C. has published many special volumes of sources, such as are noted above. The Michigan Pioneer and Historical Society has also published numerous volumes of papers in the P.A.C.

For teaching material, see Trotter's *Syllabus and guide (AA9).*

SHORTER GENERAL HISTORIES

AA51. Brown, George W., ed. **Canada.** Berkeley and Los Angeles, 1950. [The United Nations series.]

AA52. Bruchési, Jean. **Histoire du Canada pour tous.** 2 v. Montreal, 1940–46. The work of a good French Canadian scholar.

AA53. ——. **Canada, réalités d'hier et d'aujourd'hui.** Montreal, 1948. Shorter than *AA52.*

AA54. Burt, Alfred L. **A short history of Canada for Americans.** 2nd ed., Minneapolis, 1944. Of a nature indicated by title.

AA55. Creighton, Donald G. **Dominion of the North.** 2nd ed., Toronto, 1957. A polished literary product with a Tory slant.

AA56. Lower, Arthur R. M. **Colony to nation.** 3rd ed., Toronto, 1949. Vigorous exposition by an English Canadian nationalist.

AA57. McInnis, Edgar. **Canada: a political and social history.** N.Y., 1947. Smoothly written without any particular bias.

AA58. **The Cambridge history of the British Empire.** Ed. by John Holland Rose and others. V. 6, **Canada and Newfoundland.** Cambridge, Eng., 1930. A large volume by many authors; relatively little on the French regime.

AA59. Wittke, Carl F. **A history of Canada.** 3rd ed., N.Y., 1941. Detached treatment, rather sketchy until approaching recent political history.

AA60. Wrong, George M. **The Canadians: the story of a people.** N.Y., 1938. A graceful work, better on the French period than later.

LONGER GENERAL HISTORIES

AA61. Garneau, François X. **Histoire du Canada.** 3 v. Quebec, 1845–48. Rev. by author in several eds. (Eng. tr. by Andrew Bell) and by his son and grandson in subsequent eds., of which by far the best, though not the last, is the 6th (2 v., Paris, 1920), with intro. by Gabriel Hanotaux. This work, which goes only to 1840, has been the French Canadian nationalist's bible.

AA62. Kingsford, William. **The history of Canada.** 10 v. Toronto and London, 1887–98. A major work of pioneering research but no literary style. Goes only to 1840 and omits the Maritime Provinces. Index to the French regime in v. 4, and to the British in v. 10.

AA63. Morton, William L., ed. A new 16 v. history by various authors, to be issued in French and English, is in preparation. For details see *Can. hist. rev.,* 38 (Sep. 1957): 273–4.

AA64. **The chronicles of Canada.** Ed. by George M. Wrong and Hugh H. Langton. 32 v. Toronto, 1914–15. Each volume is by one author and has individual title. Very readable and still generally reliable.

HISTORIES OF SPECIAL PERIODS

AA65. Burt, Alfred L. **The old province of Quebec.** Minneapolis, 1933. The foundations of British rule, 1759–91, in what is now Quebec and Ontario.

AA66. Chapais, Thomas. **Cours d'histoire du Canada.** 8 v. Quebec, 1919–34. Well balanced and very readable account of the period 1764–1840.

AA67. Charlevoix, Pierre F. X. de. **Histoire et description générale de la Nouvelle France.** 3 v. Paris, 1744. A classic.

AA68. Christie, Robert. **History of the late province of Lower Canada.** 6 v. Quebec and Montreal, 1848–55. Covers period 1791–1840; chiefly political history in which the author played a part. An invaluable work with documents liberally scattered through the five volumes of narrative and comprising the whole of v. 6. Originals of some of these documents were destroyed in the parliament building fire in Montreal in 1849.

AA69. Dent, John C. **The last forty years: Canada since the union of 1841.** 2 v. Toronto, 1881. Journalistic, but useful if read with caution.

AA70. ——. **The story of the Upper Canadian rebellion.** 2 v. Toronto, 1885. See comment under *AA69*.

AA71. Dollier de Casson, François. **A history of Montreal, 1640–72.** Ed. and tr., with a life of the author, by Ralph Flenley. London, 1928.

AA72. Dunham, Aileen. **Political unrest in Upper Canada, 1815–1836.** London, 1927. An analytical study.

AA73. Gérin-Lajoie, Antoine. **Dix ans au Canada, de 1840 à 1850.** Quebec, 1888. Careful study of a decade that opened a new future for French Canada.

AA74. Groulx, Lionel A. **Lendemains de conquête.** Montreal, 1920. An extreme French Canadian nationalist interpretation.

AA75. Kerr, Wilfred B. **The Maritime Provinces of British North America and the American revolution.** Sackville, N. B., 1941.

AA76. Long, Morden H. **A history of the Canadian people.** V. 1. Toronto, 1942. Careful, analytical treatment of the French regime. The only volume of this projected history yet published.

AA77. Lucas, Charles P. **A history of Canada, 1763–1812.** Oxford, 1909. Still useful, though corrected and amplified by subsequent works of others.

AA78. Morison, John L. **British supremacy and Canadian self-government, 1839–54.** Glasgow, 1919. Brilliant study of a crucial period.

AA79. Morison, Samuel E., ed. **The Parkman reader.** Boston, 1955. Judicious selection from the classical multi-volume *France and England in North America* (many editions) by Francis Parkman to give a connected history of the French regime.

AA80. Wrong, George M. **The rise and fall of New France.** 2 v. N.Y. and Toronto, 1928. Very readable and, though based on printed sources only, about the best synthesis to date.

AA81. ——. **Canada and the American revolution.** N.Y., 1935. Better style than substance.

HISTORIES OF SPECIAL AREAS

AA82. Atherton, William H. **Montreal, 1535–1914.** 3 v. Montreal, 1914. An old standard.

AA83. Begg, Alexander. **History of the North-west.** 3 v. Toronto, 1894–95. Still useful though old.

AA84. Black, Norman F. **History of Saskatchewan and the old North West.** 2 v. Regina, 1913. Old but useful.

AA85. Brebner, John B. **New England's outpost: Acadia before the conquest of Canada.** N.Y., 1927. A clear exposition.

AA86. ——. **The neutral Yankees of Nova Scotia: a marginal colony during the revolu-** tionary years. N.Y., 1937. Largely based on MSS sources.

AA87. **The manuscript journals of Alexander Henry and of David Thompson, 1799–1814: new light on the early history of the greater North-west.** Ed. by Elliott Coues. 3 v. N.Y., 1897. A classic.

AA88. Dugas, George. **The Canadian West . . . down to the year 1822.** Tr. from French original by author. Montreal, 1905.

AA89. Gosselin, Amédée. **L'instruction au Canada sous le régime français.** Quebec, 1911.

AA90. Gourlay, Robert F. **Statistical account of Upper Canada.** 2 v. and genl. intro. London, 1822. Much factual information by an intelligent Scot whose radical politics caused his expulsion from the colony.

AA91. Hannay, James. **History of New Brunswick.** 2 v. St. John, 1909.

AA92. Harvey, D. C. **The French régime in Prince Edward Island.** New Haven, 1926.

AA93. Lauvrière, Émile. **La tragédie d'un peuple: histoire du peuple acadien, de ses origines à nos jours.** 2 v. Paris, 1924. Drew strong comment from Azarie Couillard-Després in *En marge de La tragédie d'un peuple* (Bruges, 1925).

AA94. Middleton, Jesse E., and Fred Landon. **The province of Ontario: a history.** 5 v. Toronto, 1927–28.

AA95. Morton, Arthur S. **A history of the Canadian West to 1870–71.** London, 1939. A monumental work based on original sources.

AA96. Morton, William L. **Manitoba: a history.** Toronto, 1957. One of the best provincial histories.

AA97. Murdoch, Beamish. **A history of Nova Scotia.** 3 v. Halifax, 1865–67. A veritable mine of information.

AA98. Neatby, Hilda. A history of Saskatchewan (in preparation).

AA99. Prowse, Daniel W. **History of Newfoundland from the English, colonial and foreign records.** London, 1895. 2nd ed., 1896. A standard work.

AA100. Rogers, John D. **Newfoundland.** Oxford, 1911. V. 5, pt. 4 of Charles P. Lucas, ed., **A historical geography of the British colonies** (Oxford, 1888–1911).

AA101. Rumilly, Robert. **Histoire de la province de Québec.** 26 v. Montreal, 1940–53. Chronological and popular.

AA102. Scholefield, Ethelbert O. S., and Frederick W. Howay. **British Columbia from the earliest times to the present.** 4 v. Vancouver, 1914.

AA103. Stanley, George F. G. **The birth of western Canada: a history of the Riel rebellions.** N.Y., 1936. A major work based on MSS sources.

AA104. Warburton, Alexander B. **A history of Prince Edward Island from its dis-**

covery in 1534 until the departure of Lieutenant-Governor Ready in A.D. 1831. St. John, N. B., 1923.

AA105. Wood, William C., William H. Atherton, and Edwin P. Conklin, eds. **The storied province of Quebec, past and present.** 5 v. Toronto, 1931–32.

HISTORIES OF SPECIAL TOPICS

AA106. Allin, Cephas D., and George M. Jones. **Annexation, preferential trade and reciprocity.** Toronto, 1912.

AA107. Armstrong, Elizabeth. **The crisis of Quebec, 1914–18.** N.Y., 1937. A study of how conscription split French Canada from English Canada.

AA108. Biggar, Henry P. **The early trading companies of New France.** Toronto, 1901. A definitive work.

AA109. Borden, Sir Robert L. **Canada in the Commonwealth.** Oxford, 1929. By a scholarly statesman who played a leading role in the evolution from Empire to Commonwealth.

AA110. ———. **Canadian constitutional studies.** Toronto, 1922. See comment under *AA109.*

AA111. Brebner, John B. **North Atlantic triangle.** See *Y192.*

AA112. Burpee, Lawrence J. **The search for the western sea.** 2nd ed., Toronto, 1935. A classic account of the protracted discovery of the northern half of North America.

AA113. Burt, Alfred L. **The United States, Great Britain and British North America.** See *AB175.*

AA114. Cameron, Edward R. **The Canadian constitution as interpreted by the Judicial Committee of the Privy Council.** 2 v. Winnipeg, 1915; Toronto, 1930. By a leading authority.

AA115. Canada. Parliament. **Parliamentary debates on the subject of the confederation of the British North American provinces.** Quebec, 1865. Commonly known as *Confederation debates,* a classic in the literature of Canadian federation.

AA116. Canada. **Report of the Royal Commission on Dominion-Provincial Relations.** Ottawa, 1940. Commonly known as the *Rowell-Sirois report,* after the names of successive chairmen of the commission, it is one of the most important state papers ever produced in Canada. Of particular value for students are bk. 1 and the appendices.

AA117. ———. **Report of the Royal Commission on National Development in the Arts, Letters and Sciences, 1949–1951.** Ottawa, 1951. Commonly known as the *Massey report,* after the chairman of the commission. A supplementary volume gives special studies made by experts for the commission.

AA118. Canniff, William. **History of the** settlement of Upper Canada. Toronto, 1869. Preserves much oral tradition.

AA119. Clark, Samuel D. **The social development of Canada.** Toronto, 1942. By a sociologist who is not a historian.

AA120. ———. **Church and sect in Canada.** Toronto, 1948. See comment under *AA119.*

AA121. Clokie, Hugh M. **Canadian government and politics.** Toronto, 1944.

AA122. Corry, James A. **Democratic government and politics.** Toronto, 1946.

AA123. Coupland, Sir Reginald. **The Quebec act.** Oxford, 1925.

AA124. Creighton, Donald G. **The commercial empire of the St. Lawrence, 1760–1850.** New Haven, 1937. A brilliant study.

AA125. Cruikshank, Ernest A. **The documentary history of the campaign upon the Niagara frontier.** 9 v. Welland, Ont., 1896–1908. By a scholarly military expert.

AA126. Davidson, Gordon C. **The North West Company.** Berkeley, 1918.

AA127. Dawson, Robert M., ed. **The development of dominion status, 1900–1936.** See *U230.*

AA128. ———. **The government of Canada.** Toronto, 1947.

AA129. Doughty, Arthur G., and George W. Parmelee. **The siege of Quebec and the battle of the Plains of Abraham.** 6 v. Quebec, 1901. A classic.

AA130. Easterbrook, W. T., and Hugh G. J. Aitken. **Canadian economic history.** Toronto, 1956. Supersedes previous works.

AA131. Ermatinger, Charles O. **The Talbot regime.** St. Thomas, Ont., 1904.

AA132. Fauteux, Joseph-Noël. **Essai sur l'industrie au Canada sous le régime français.** 2 v. Quebec, 1927.

AA133. Fetherstonhaugh, Robert C. **The Royal Canadian mounted police.** N.Y., 1938.

AA134. Filteau, Gérard. **La naissance d'une nation.** 2 v. Montreal, 1937.

AA135. ———. **Histoire des patriotes.** 3 v. Montreal, 1938–42.

AA136. Frégault, Guy. **La civilisation de la Nouvelle-France, 1713–1744.** Montreal, 1944.

AA137. Glazebrook, George P. de T. **A history of transportation in Canada.** New Haven, 1938.

AA138. ———. **A history of Canadian external relations.** Toronto, 1950.

AA139. Graham, Gerald S. **Sea power and British North America, 1783–1820.** Cambridge, Mass., 1941.

AA140. ———. **Empire of the North Atlantic.** Toronto, 1950.

AA141. Guillet, Edwin C. **Early life in Upper Canada.** Toronto, 1933.

AA142. ———. **The lives and times of the patriots: an account of the rebellion in Upper Canada, 1837–1838, and the patriot agitation in the United States, 1837–1842.** Toronto, 1938.

AA143. Heagerty, John J. **Four centuries of medical history in Canada and a sketch of the medical history of Newfoundland.** 2 v. Toronto, 1928.

AA144. Hedges, James B. **Building the Canadian West: the land and colonization policies of the Canadian Pacific Railway.** N.Y., 1939.

AA145. Henry, Alexander. **Travels and adventures in Canada and the Indian territories between the years 1760 and 1776.** N.Y., 1809.

AA146. Herbertson, Andrew J., and Osbert J. R. Howarth, eds. **The Oxford survey of the British empire.** V. 4, **America.** Oxford, 1914.

AA147. Hodgins, John G. **The establishment of schools and colleges in Ontario, 1792–1910.** 3 v. Toronto, 1910.

AA148. ——, ed. **Historical and other papers and documents illustrative of the educational system of Ontario.** 5 v. Toronto, 1911–12.

AA149. Innis, Harold A. **The fur trade in Canada: an introduction to Canadian economic history.** New Haven, 1930.

AA150. ——. **The cod fisheries: the history of an international economy.** Rev. ed., Toronto, 1956.

AA151. ——., and Arthur F. Plumptre, eds. **The Canadian economy and its problems.** Toronto, 1934.

AA152. Insh, George P. **Scottish colonial schemes, 1620–1686.** See *U139.*

AA153. Jameson, Anna B. **Winter studies and summer rambles in Canada.** 3 v. London, 1838. A firsthand account of pioneer life.

AA154. Kennedy, William P. M. **The constitution of Canada: an introduction to its development and law.** 2nd ed., London, 1938. 3rd ed. in preparation.

AA155. Kirke, Henry. **The first English conquest of Canada, with some account of the earliest settlements in Nova Scotia and Newfoundland.** London, 1871. New ed., 1908.

AA156. Lanctôt, Gustave. **L'administration de la Nouvelle-France.** Paris, 1929.

AA157. Landon, Fred. **Western Ontario and the American frontier.** New Haven, 1941.

AA158. Lizars, Robina, and Kathleen M. Lizars. **In the days of the Canada Company: the story of the settlement of the Huron tract and a view of the social life of the period, 1825–1850.** Toronto, 1896.

AA159. Logan, Harold A. **Trade unions in Canada: their development and functioning.** Toronto, 1948.

AA160. Longley, Ronald S. **Sir Francis Hincks: a study of Canadian politics, railways, and finance in the nineteenth century.** Toronto, 1943.

AA161. Lucas, Sir Charles P., ed. **Lord Durham's report on the affairs of British North America.** 3 v. Oxford, 1912. First volume gives a historical introduction, second volume the text of Durham's famous report, and the third the appendices to the report.

AA162. **The Empire at war.** Ed. by Sir Charles P. Lucas. V. 2. Oxford, 1923. F. H. Underhill's account of Canadian participation in World War I.

AA163. Macdonald, Helen G. **Canadian public opinion on the American civil war.** N.Y., 1926.

AA164. MacGibbon, Duncan A. **The Canadian grain trade.** Toronto, 1932.

AA165. ——. **The Canadian grain trade, 1931–51.** Toronto, 1952.

AA166. MacKay, Douglas. **The honourable company: a history of the Hudson's Bay Company.** N.Y., 1936.

AA167. MacKay, Robert A. **The unreformed Senate of Canada.** London, 1926.

AA168. ——., ed. **Newfoundland: economic, diplomatic and strategic studies.** Toronto, 1946.

AA169. Mackenzie, Alexander. **Voyages from Montreal, on the river St. Laurence, through the continent of North America to the Frozen and Pacific oceans, in the years 1789 and 1793.** London, 1801. Reprinted in *American explorer series,* 2 v., N.Y., 1922.

AA170. McLennan, John S. **Louisbourg from its foundation to its fall, 1713–1758.** London, 1918.

AA171. Mahan, Alfred T. **Sea power in its relation to the War of 1812.** 2 v. Boston, 1905. Best account of the operations of the war.

AA172. Martin, Chester. **Lord Selkirk's work in Canada.** Oxford, 1916.

AA173. Masson, Louis F. R. **Les bourgeois de la Compagnie du Nord-Ouest.** 2 v. Quebec, 1889–90.

AA174. Masters, Ronald C. **The reciprocity treaty of 1854: its history, its relation to British colonial and foreign policy and to the development of Canadian fiscal autonomy.** London, 1937.

AA175. Moodie, Susannah. **Roughing it in the bush: or life in Canada.** 2 v. N.Y., 1852.

AA176. Morice, Adrien G. **History of the Catholic church in western Canada from Lake Superior to the Pacific.** 2 v. Toronto, 1910.

AA177. Morton, William L. **The Progressive party in Canada.** Toronto, 1950.

AA178. Munro, William B. **The seignorial system in Canada.** N.Y., 1907.

AA179. Patton, Harald S. **Grain growers' coöperation in western Canada.** Cambridge, Mass., 1928.

AA180. Plaxton, Charles P. **Canadian constitutional decisions.** Ottawa, 1939.

AA181. Plewman, William R. **Adam Beck and the Ontario Hydro.** Toronto, 1947. An outstanding example of government enterprise.

AA182. Raymond, William O., ed. **Winslow papers, A.D. 1776–1826.** St. John, N.B., 1901.

AA183. Roy, Antoine. **Les lettres, les sciences et les arts au Canada sous le régime français.** Paris, 1930.

AA184. Roy, Joseph E. **Histoire de la seigneurie de Lauzon.** 5 v. Levis, Que., 1897–1904.

AA185. Sellar, Robert. **The tragedy of Quebec: the expulsion of its Protestant farmers.** Huntingdon, Que., 1907. 4th ed., Toronto, 1916.

AA186. Sharp, Paul F. **The agrarian revolt in western Canada: a survey showing American parallels.** Minneapolis, 1948.

AA187. Shippee, Lester B. **Canadian-American relations, 1849–1874.** New Haven, 1939.

AA188. Smith, Justin H. **Our struggle for the fourteenth colony.** 2 v. N.Y., 1907. Most complete account of the American revolutionary effort to gain Canada.

AA189. Smith, William. **The history of the post office in British North America, 1639–1870.** Cambridge, Eng., and Toronto, 1920. A classic.

AA190. Stacey, Charles P. **Canada and the British army, 1846–1871: a study in the practice of responsible government.** London, 1936.

AA191. ——. **The Canadian army, 1939–1945: an official historical summary.** Ottawa, 1948.

AA192. Stanley, George F. G., in collaboration with Harold M. Jackson. **Canada's soldiers, 1604–1954: the military history of an unmilitary people.** Toronto, 1956.

AA193. Strickland, Samuel. **Twenty-seven years in Canada West.** 2 v. London, 1853.

AA194. Traill, Catherine P. **The backwoods of Canada: being letters from the wife of an emigrant officer.** London, 1836.

AA195. Trotter, Reginald G. **Canadian federation: its origin and achievement.** Toronto, 1924.

AA196. Tucker, Gilbert N. **The Canadian commercial revolution, 1845–1851.** New Haven, 1936.

AA197. Vancouver, George. **Voyages of discovery to the Pacific ocean and round the world in the years 1790–95.** 3 v. London, 1798.

AA198. Whitelaw, William M. **The Maritimes and Canada before confederation.** Toronto, 1934. More important than title suggests.

AA199. Wrong, George M. **A Canadian manor and its seigneurs.** Toronto, 1908. The work of one of Canada's leading historians.

BIOGRAPHIES

AA200. The makers of Canada series. 1st ed., 21 v., sometimes bound in 11, Toronto, 1906–11. 2nd ed., 12 double v., Toronto, 1926. Biographies by various authors of leading figures in Canadian history. The 2nd ed., in addition to correcting errors in the 1st, substitutes and adds some new biographies. Last volume is good dictionary of Canadian history.

AA201. The Canadian parliamentary guide. Ottawa, 1901 ff. Formerly *The Canadian parliamentary companion.* Gives data on members of the federal parliament and the provincial legislatures, other government officials, elections, etc.

AA202. Bethune, Alexander N. **Memoire of the Right Reverend John Strachan, D.D., LL.D., first bishop of Toronto.** Toronto, 1870.

AA203. Biggar, Charles R. W. **Sir Oliver Mowat.** 2 v. Toronto, 1905.

AA204. Borden, Henry, ed. **Robert Laird Borden: his memoirs.** 2 v. Toronto, 1938.

AA205. Boyd, John. **Sir George Etienne Cartier, bart.: his life and times.** Toronto, 1914.

AA206. Buckingham, William, and George W. Ross. **The Hon. Alexander Mackenzie: his life and times.** Toronto, 1892.

AA207. Cartwright, Conway E., ed. **Life and letters of the late Hon. Richard Cartwright.** Toronto, 1876.

AA208. Chapais, Thomas. **Jean Talon.** Quebec, 1904. The great intendant.

AA209. Chisholm, Joseph A., ed. **The speeches and public letters of Joseph Howe.** Halifax, 1909.

AA210. Chittick, Victor L. **Thomas Chandler Haliburton: a study in provincial Toryism.** N.Y., 1924.

AA211. Creighton, Donald G. **John A. Macdonald.** 2 v. Toronto, 1952–55.

AA212. Dafoe, John W. **Laurier: a study in Canadian politics.** Toronto, 1922.

AA213. ——. **Clifford Sifton in relation to his times.** Toronto, 1931.

AA214. Dawson, Robert M. **William Lyon Mackenzie King: a political biography. V. 1, 1874–1923.** Toronto, 1958. Two additional volumes planned.

AA215. Gosselin, Auguste H. **Vie de Mgr. de Laval.** 2 v. Quebec, 1890.

AA216. Hughes, Katherine. **Father Lacombe: the black-robe voyageur.** N.Y., 1911.

AA217. Kaye, Sir John W. **The life and correspondence of Charles, Lord Metcalfe.** Rev. ed., 2 v., London, 1858.

AA218. Kilbourn, William. **The firebrand: William Lyon Mackenzie and the rebellion in Upper Canada.** Toronto, 1956. A short critical study.

AA219. Lindsay, Charles. **Life and times**

of Wm. Lyon Mackenzie. 2 v. Toronto, 1864. An uncritical eulogy by a son-in-law.

AA220. Morison, John L. **The eighth Earl of Elgin.** London, 1928.

AA221. Morton, Arthur S. **Sir George Simpson, overseas governor of the Hudson's Bay Company.** Toronto, 1944.

AA222. New, Chester W. **Lord Durham: a biography.** Oxford, 1929. Supersedes Stuart Reid, *Life and letters of the first Earl of Durham* (London, 1906).

AA223. Nute, Grace L. **Caesars of the wilderness.** N.Y., 1943. Much new light on Radisson and Groseilliers.

AA224. Pope, Sir Joseph. **Memoirs of the Right Honourable Sir John Alexander Macdonald.** 2 v. London, 1894. New 1 v. ed. by A. G. Doughty, Toronto, 1930.

AA225. Riddell, William R. **The life of John Graves Simcoe.** Toronto, 1926. Supersedes previous biographies.

AA226. ———. **The life of William Dummer Powell.** Lansing, 1924.

AA227. Robinson, Charles W. **Life of Sir John Beverley Robinson, chief-justice of Upper Canada.** Toronto, 1904.

AA228. Ryerson, Adolphus E. **The loyalists of America and their times: from 1620 to 1816.** 2 v. Toronto, 1880. By a son of a loyalist. Contains good material, but must be used with caution.

AA229. Sage, Walter N. **Sir James Douglas and British Columbia.** Toronto, 1930.

AA230. Saunders, Edward M. **The life and letters of the Rt. Hon. Sir Charles Tupper.** 2 v. London, 1916.

AA231. Scrope, George P. **Memoir of the life of the Right Honourable Charles, Lord Sydenham.** London, 1843.

AA232. Sissons, Charles B. **Egerton Ryerson, his life and letters.** 2 v. Toronto, 1937–47.

AA233. Skelton, Isabel M. **The life of Thomas D'Arcy McGee.** Gardenvale, 1925.

AA234. Skelton, Oscar D. **The life and times of Sir Alexander Tilloch Galt.** Toronto, 1920.

AA235. ———. **Life and letters of Sir Wilfrid Laurier.** 2 v. Toronto, 1922.

AA236. Smith, William. **Political leaders of Upper Canada.** Toronto, 1931. "The result of a prolonged browsing among original documents and contemporary newspapers" by the deputy keeper of the archives.

AA237. Wade, Mark S. **Mackenzie of Canada.** London, 1927. The explorer.

AA238. Walrond, Theodore. **Letters and journals of James, eighth Earl of Elgin.** London, 1872.

AA239. Willison, John S. **Sir Wilfrid Laurier and the Liberal party.** 2 v. Toronto, 1903. Republished with three additional chapters in new ed. of *The makers of Canada* (Toronto, 1926).

AA240. Willson, Beckles. **The life of Lord Strathcona and Mount Royal.** 2 v. Boston, 1915.

AA241. Wilson, George E. **The life of Robert Baldwin: a study in the struggle for responsible government.** Toronto, 1933.

AA242. Wrong, Humphrey H. **Sir Alexander Mackenzie.** Toronto, 1927.

OFFICIAL GOVERNMENT RECORDS

AA243. The Canada gazette. Ottawa, etc., 1841 ff. (Annual.)

AA244. The Canada year book. Ottawa, 1906 ff. (Annual.) See *AA15.*

AA245. Canada. House of Commons. **Debates.** Ottawa, 1870–72, 1875 ff. Senate. **Debates.** Ottawa, 1873 ff.

AA246. Canada. Parliament. **Sessional papers.** Ottawa, 1867–1925. House of Commons. **Journals.** Ottawa, 1867 ff. Senate. **Journals.** Ottawa, 1867 ff.

AA247. Canada. Public Archives. **Reports.** Ottawa, 1872 ff. (Annual. Title varies.)

AA248. ———. **Publications.** (Irregular intervals.)

The voluminous publications of other government departments are too numerous to list here. Information on them may be procured from The Queen's Printer, Ottawa.

UNIVERSITY, ACADEMY, AND SOCIETY PUBLICATIONS

AA249. Proceedings and transactions of the Royal Society of Canada. Ottawa, 1882 ff. Many papers of important historical interest.

AA250. The Canadian Historical Association report. Ottawa, 1923 ff. Contains papers read at the annual meetings.

Publications of the Quebec Historical Society and the Ontario Historical Society are outstanding among those of various provincial and local historical societies, but the others should not be neglected.

The Champlain Society (University of Toronto) publishes annually (1907 ff.) at least one volume of important source material, meticulously edited. Among these are various records of the Hudson's Bay Company and the North West Company, and also the following:

AA251. The works of Samuel de Champlain. 6 v. Toronto, 1922–36.

AA252. Journals and letters of Pierre Gaultier de Varennes de La Vérendrye and his sons. Toronto, 1927.

The Hudson's Bay Company Record Society publishes annually (1938 ff.) a well edited volume of the records of the company.

The Carnegie Endowment for International Peace, Division of Economics and History, James T. Shotwell, director, planned the following series of 25 volumes:

AA253. The relations of Canada and the United States. New Haven and Toronto, 1937–45. These are detailed studies by various scholars and under individual titles. Several have been listed above, but all are of value. They constitute perhaps the most thorough examination of relations between any two countries in the world.

AA254. Mackintosh, William A., and Wolfgang L. G. Joerg, eds., **Canadian frontiers of settlement.** 9 v. Toronto, 1934–40. A cooperative work by various scholars and under individual titles, a product of the Canadian Pioneer Committee, organized in 1929.

PERIODICALS

AA255. The beaver. Winnipeg, 1920 ff. (Quarterly.) Concentrates on history of the North and of the Hudson's Bay Company.

AA256. Bulletin des recherches historiques. Levis, Que., 1895 ff. (Monthly.) A publication of the Quebec Archives since 1923.

AA257. The Canadian bar review. Toronto and Ottawa, 1923 ff. (Monthly except July and Aug.)

AA258. The Canadian historical review. Toronto, 1920 ff. (Quarterly.) Organ of the Canadian Historical Association.

AA259. The Canadian journal of economics and political science. Toronto, 1935 ff. (Quarterly.) Organ of the Canadian Political Science Association.

AA260. Culture. Quebec, 1940 ff. (Quarterly.) Bilingual.

AA261. Le Canada français. Quebec, 1918 ff. (Monthly except July and Aug.)

AA262. The Dalhousie review. Halifax, 1921 ff. (Quarterly.) Published by Dalhousie University.

AA263. External affairs. Ottawa, 1948 ff. (Monthly.) Published by Department of External Affairs.

AA264. International journal. Toronto, 1946 ff. [Canadian Institute of International Affairs.] (Quarterly.)

AA265. Queen's quarterly. Kingston, 1893 ff. (Quarterly.) Publication of Queen's University.

AA266. La revue de l'Université Laval. Quebec, 1946 ff. (Monthly except July and Aug.)

AA267. Revue de l'Université d'Ottawa. Ottawa, 1931 ff. (Quarterly.)

AA268. University of Toronto law journal. Toronto, 1935 ff. (Annual.)

AA269. University of Toronto quarterly. Toronto, 1931 ff. Contains annual survey of "Letters in Canada."

BRITISH CARIBBEAN COLONIES AND BERMUDA

(*Alfred L. Burt*)

BIBLIOGRAPHIES, LIBRARIES, AND REFERENCE WORKS

AA270. Cundall, Frank C. **Bibliographia jamaicensis.** 2nd rev. ed., Kingston, 1902. By the secretary and librarian of the Institute of Jamaica. Expanded in *Supplement to Bibliographia jamaicensis* (1908) and *Bibliography of the West Indies (excluding Jamaica)* (1909).

AA271. The Cambridge history of the British Empire. 3 v. Cambridge, Eng., 1929, 1940, 1959. Full bibliographies for period covered, down to 1919.

AA272. Pares, Richard. "Public records in British West India islands," **Bulletin of the Institute of Historical Research,** v. 7 (London, 1930): 149–57.

AA273. Ragatz, Lowell J. **A guide for the study of British Caribbean history, 1763–1834, including the abolition and emancipation movements.** Washington, 1932. See also his (*AA347*) *The fall of the planter class in the British Caribbean,* which gives a full list of official documents in the British Archives, including the Public Record Office, and public libraries in the United States.

The most comprehensive resources for research in the field are to be found in London. The Library of Congress in Washington contains the next best collection. Apart from the library of the Institute of Jamaica (Kingston), there are few libraries of any account in the British West Indies, but there is promise of a respectable one in the newly established (1948) University College of the West Indies (located just outside Kingston), supported by island governments now represented in the Federation of the West Indies.

There is no encyclopedia of the British West Indies, nor is there a general reference work. Nearest approach to the latter is Burns, *History of the British West Indies* (*AA277*). See also

AA274. The West Indies and Caribbean year book. London, 1926–54. (Title varies.)

Printed collections of sources are very meager, but may become valuable after the Federation of the West Indies is well established.

HISTORIOGRAPHY

AA275. Goveia, Elsa V. **A study on the historiography of the British West Indies to the end of the nineteenth century.** Mexico, 1956. [Pan American Institute of Geography and History, Commission on History.]

SHORTER GENERAL HISTORIES

AA276. Burn, William L. **The British West Indies.** London, 1951.

AA277. Burns, Sir Alan C. **History of the British West Indies.** See *U168*.

AA278. Lucas, Sir Charles P. **A historical geography of the British colonies. V. 2, The West Indies.** Oxford, 1905. By a scholarly senior official of the Colonial Office.

AA279. Parry, John H., and Philip M. Sherlock. **A short history of the West Indies.** London, 1956. Best introduction to the subject, by the professor of history and the vice-principal of the University College of the West Indies.

LONGER GENERAL HISTORIES

AA280. Edwards, Bryan. **The history, civil and commercial, of the British colonies in the West Indies.** 3 v. London, 1793–97. 5th ed., 5 v., London, 1819. See *U157*.

AA281. Du Tertre, Jean B. **Histoire générale des Antilles.** 4 v. Paris, 1667–71. No modern work on the scale of either this or *AA280* has yet appeared.

HISTORIES OF SPECIAL PERIODS

AA282. Andrews, Charles M. **The colonial period of American history.** See *AB46*.

AA283. Aspinall, Sir Algernon. **A wayfarer in the West Indies.** London, 1928.

AA284. Higham, Charles S. **The development of the Leeward Islands under the Restoration.** See *U160*.

AA285. Newton, Arthur P. **The colonizing activities of the English Puritans.** See *AB89*.

AA286. ——. **The European nations in the West Indies, 1493–1688.** See *U169*.

AA287. Pares, Richard. **War and trade in the West Indies, 1739–1763.** See *U124*.

AA288. Pitman, Frank W. **The development of the British West Indies, 1700–1763.** See *U161*.

AA289. Pringle, Kenneth. **Waters of the West.** London, 1938. For the recent period.

AA290. Williamson, James A. **Maritime enterprise, 1485–1588.** Oxford, 1913.

AA291. ——. **Sir John Hawkins, the time and the man.** Oxford, 1927.

AA292. ——. **The Caribbee islands under the proprietary patents.** London, 1926.

HISTORIES OF SPECIAL AREAS

AA293. Breen, Henry H. **St. Lucia, historical, statistical, and descriptive.** London, 1844.

AA294. Archives of British Honduras. Ed. by Sir John A. Burdon. 3 v. London, 1931–35. A collection of documents.

AA295. Caiger, Stephen L. **British Honduras, past and present.** London, 1951.

AA296. Gardner, William J. **A history of Jamaica.** 2nd ed., London, 1909.

AA297. Harlow, Vincent T. **A history of Barbados, 1625–1685.** Oxford, 1926. Supersedes previous work on the subject.

AA298. ——. **Christopher Codrington, 1668–1710.** Oxford, 1928.

AA299. Lefroy, Sir John H. **Memorials of the discovery and early settlement of the Bermudas or Somers Islands, 1515–1685.** 2 v. London, 1877–79.

AA300. Ligon, Richard. **A true and exact history of the island of Barbados.** London, 1657.

AA301. Long, Edward. **The history of Jamaica.** 3 v. London, 1774. By the speaker of the House of Assembly.

AA302. Malcolm, Harcourt. **Historical documents relating to the Bahama Islands.** Nassau, 1910.

AA303. ——. **A history of the Bahama House of Assembly.** Nassau, 1921.

AA304. Morales Padrón, Francisco. **Jamaica española.** Seville, 1952.

AA305. Olivier, Sydney H. **The myth of Governor Eyre.** London, 1933. A much needed thorough revision.

AA306. ——. **Jamaica: the blessed island.** London, 1936.

AA307. Schomburgk, Sir Robert H. **The history of Barbados.** London, 1848.

AA308. Verrill, Addison E. **The Bermuda islands.** 2nd ed., New Haven, 1907.

AA309. Whitson, Agnes M. **The constitutional development of Jamaica.** Manchester, 1929.

AA310. Wilkinson, Henry C. **The adventurers of Bermuda.** London, 1933.

HISTORIES OF SPECIAL TOPICS

AA311. Acworth, Angus W. **Treasure in the Caribbean: a first study of Georgian buildings in the British West Indies.** London, 1949.

AA312. Armytage, Frances. **The free port system in the British West Indies: a study in commercial policy, 1766–1822.** London, 1953.

AA313. Beer, George L. **The old colonial system, 1660–1754.** See *AB98*.

AA314. ——. **British colonial policy, 1754–1765.** See *AB126*.

AA315. Blanchard, P. **Democracy and empire in the Caribbean.** N.Y., 1947.

AA316. Bourne, Ruth. **Queen Anne's navy in the West Indies.** New Haven, 1939.

AA317. Brown, Herbert H. **The fisheries of the Windward and Leeward Islands.** Bridgetown, Barbados, 1946.

AA318. Burn, William L. **Emancipation and apprenticeship in the British West Indies.** London, 1937.

AA319. Caldecott, Alfred. **The church in the West Indies.** London, 1898.

AA320. Clarkson, Thomas. **The history of the rise, progress and accomplishment of the abolition of the African slave-trade.** 2 v. London, 1808.

AA321. Clementi, Sir Cecil. **A constitutional history of British Guiana.** London, 1937.

AA322. Crouse, Nellis M. **The French struggle for the West Indies, 1665–1713.** N.Y., 1943.

AA323. Crumpston, I. M. **Indians overseas in British territories, 1835–1865.** Oxford, 1953.

AA324. Davis, John Merle. **The church in the new Jamaica.** N.Y., 1942.

AA325. Davy, John. **The West Indies before and since slave emancipation.** London, 1854.

AA326. Deerr, Noël. **The history of sugar.** 2 v. London, 1949–50.

AA327. Haring, Clarence H. **The buccaneers in the West Indies in the XVII century.** London, 1910.

AA328. Harper, Lawrence A. **The English navigation laws.** See *AB100*.

AA329. Henriques, Fernando. **Family and colour in Jamaica.** London, 1853.

AA330. Herskovits, Melville J. **The myth of the negro past.** N.Y., 1941.

AA331. Kepner, Charles D., and Jay H. Soothill. **The banana empire.** N.Y., 1935.

AA332. Lewis, Arthur, and E. Williams. **The negro in the Caribbean.** London, 1942. Lewis is a West Indian of African descent who is a professor of economics in England.

AA333. Livingstone, William P. **Black Jamaica: a study in evolution.** London, 1899.

AA334. Lovén, Sven. **Origins of the Tainan culture, West Indies.** Göteborg, 1935.

AA335. Macmillan, William M. **Warning from the West Indies.** London, 1936. Reissued as a Penguin book in 1938 with a pointed introduction inspired by recent labor disturbances.

AA336. Manning, Helen T. **British colonial government after the American revolution, 1782–1820.** New Haven, 1933. A penetrating study.

AA337. Mathieson, William L. **British slavery and its abolition, 1823–38.** London, 1926.

AA338. ——. **British slave emancipation, 1838–49.** London, 1932.

AA339. ——. **The sugar colonies and Governor Eyre, 1849–1866.** London, 1936.

AA340. Nath, Dwarka. **A history of Indians in British Guiana.** London, 1950.

AA341. Pares, Richard. **A West-India fortune.** London, 1950.

AA342. Penson, Lillian M. **The colonial agents of the British West Indies.** See *U163*.

AA343. Phillippo, James M. **Jamaica: its past and present state.** London, 1843. By a pioneer Baptist missionary.

AA344. ——. **The voice of jubilee.** London, 1865.

AA345. Phillippo, James C. **The climate of Jamaica.** London, 1876. By a son of J. M. Phillippo.

AA346. Proudfoot, Mary M. **Britain and the United States in the Caribbean.** London, 1954.

AA347. Ragatz, Lowell J. **The fall of the planter class in the British Caribbean.** See *U162*.

AA348. Reid, Victor S. **New day.** N.Y., 1949.

AA349. Scott, Henry H. **A history of tropical medicine.** London, 1939.

AA350. Sewell, William G. **The ordeal of free labour in the British West Indies.** N.Y., 1861. Sympathetic but also critical.

AA351. Simey, Thomas S. **Welfare and planning in the West Indies.** Oxford, 1946.

AA352. Smith, Abbot E. **Colonists in bondage.** See *AB116*.

AA353. Thompson, Reginald W. **Black Caribbean.** London, 1946.

AA354. Whitson, Agnes M. **The constitutional development of Jamaica.** Manchester, 1929.

AA355. Williams, Eric E. **Capitalism and slavery.** Chapel Hill, 1944.

AA356. Wrong, Humphrey H. **Government of the West Indies.** Oxford, 1923.

GOVERNMENT PUBLICATIONS

By far the most valuable are found in the **(AA357) Parliamentary papers,** of which there is a sessional index. Those dealing with the colonies became numerous early in the 19th century. They are reports of governors and other officials, investigating commissions (royal and otherwise), and parliamentary select committees. There are three main series: *Sessional papers* (printed by order of either house), *Command* (submitted by order of the Crown, i.e., the government of the day), and *Colonial.*

DUTCH AMERICA
(*Rudolf A. J. van Lier*)

ENCYCLOPEDIAS

AA358. Encyclopaedie van Nederlandsch West-Indië. Ed. by Herman D. Benjamins and Johannes F. Snelleman. The Hague, 1914. General, carefully edited encyclopedia, containing a variety of scholarly articles on historical subjects concerning Surinam and the Dutch Antilles. Of major importance.

DEMOGRAPHIC STUDIES

AA359. Emmanuel, Isaac S. **Precious stones of the Jews of Curaçao.** N.Y., 1957. History, by a former rabbi, of the Jewish families of Curaçao who played an important role in the island. Different families are discussed in relation to tombstones in the old Jewish cemetery. Covers period 1656–1957.

AA360. Krafft, A. J. C. **Historie en oude Families van de Nederlandse Antillen.** The Hague, 1951. A short introduction to the history of the Dutch Antilles is followed by the genealogies of sixty of the old, mostly Protestant, families, which formed a ruling class in Curaçao. Contains material on the social history of the island.

GENERAL HISTORIES

AA361. Hamelberg, J. H. J. **De Nederlanders op de West-Indische eilanden.** 2 v. Amsterdam, 1901–03. An authoritative political and social history of the Dutch Antilles from the beginning of Dutch settlement until 1782, based on a study in the archives of The Hague by a Dutch colonial official.

AA362. Kasteel, Annemarie C. T. **De Staatkundige ontwikkeling der Nederlandse Antillen.** The Hague, 1956. (English and Spanish summary.) Historical analysis of political and constitutional development of the Dutch Antilles from 1865 to the present.

AA363. Menkman, W. R. **De Nederlanders in het Caraibische Zeegebied.** Amsterdam, 1942. Popular but reliable account of the Dutch in the Caribbean area to 1940. Contains extensive bibliography on history of the islands.

HISTORIES OF SPECIAL PERIODS

AA364. Einaar, Johan F. E. **Bijdrage tot de kennis van het Engelsch Tusschenbestuur van Surinam, 1804–1816.** Leiden, 1934. Short study of the period during the Napoleonic wars when Surinam was under British rule, with contemporary economic

memoranda in French by the comptroller of finance of Surinam.

AA365. Gaay Fortman, Bastiaan de. **Schets van de Politieke Geschiedenis der Nederlandsche Antillen in de twintigste eeuw.** The Hague, 1947. A concise outline of the political and constitutional history of the Dutch Antilles until 1946 by a former Curaçao judge.

HISTORIES OF SPECIAL AREAS

AA366. Hartog, Johannes. **Aruba: zoals het was, zoals het werd.** Aruba, 1953. Popular narrative of the history of Aruba until the present day. Local archives hitherto unused have been consulted. This volume is the first of a history of the Dutch Antilles by this author.

AA367. ——. **Bonaire van Indianen tot toeristen.** Aruba, 1957. Second volume of a general history of the Dutch Antilles. See above.

AA368. Knappert, Laurentius. **Geschiedenis van de Nederlandsche Bovenwindsche eilanden in de 18de eeuw.** The Hague, 1932. Authoritative work by a well-known Dutch church historian.

AA369. Wolbers, Julian. **Geschiedenis van Suriname.** Amsterdam, 1861. This work, based on primary sources of the state archives of The Hague and the Public Record Office in London, is still the most important history of Surinam from the beginning of the first settlement until 1860. Although written during the abolition controversy from an anti-slavery point of view, it is balanced and reliable. Much attention is also given to development of colonial society.

HISTORIES OF SPECIAL TOPICS

AA370. Buiskool, Johannes A. E. **De Staatsinstellingen van Suriname.** The Hague, 1954. Handbook on the public law of Surinam by a former president of the Court of Justice there. Chapter 2 contains a historical outline of the constitutional development.

AA371. De West Indische Gids: Emancipatie nummer. The Hague, 1953. Special issue of a well-known periodical, which has carried several articles of historical interest dealing with the abolition of slavery. Contains an article by Johanna M. van Winter on the general feeling of the Netherlands people concerning abolition in Surinam and the Dutch Antilles, with list of sources and an English summary.

AA372. Goslinga, Cornelis C. **Emanci-**

patie en Emancipator. Assen, 1956. (Summary in English and Spanish.) A study of the social and juridical position of slaves mainly on the islands of Curaçao and Bonaire. A great part of the book deals with the role of the Roman Catholic mission in educational emancipation of the slaves.

AA373. Grol, G. J. van. **De Grondpolitiek in het West-Indische domein der Generaliteit.** 2 v. and register. The Hague, 1934–47. V. 1 gives a history of the Dutch Antilles and treats the principles of colonization in connection with Surinam. In v. 2 land policy and land rights are studied within the framework of the islands' history.

AA374. Hoetink, Harry. **Het patroon van de oude Curaçaose samenleving.** Assen, 1958. Socio-historical study of Curaçao society before establishment of the oil industry on the island. Well written, with a good understanding of human relations in the slavery period and its aftermath.

AA375. Lier, Rudolf A. J. van. **Samenleving in een Grensgebied.** The Hague, 1949. Comprehensive socio-historical study of Surinam society from the beginning until 1940, with extensive bibliography of sources

and historical literature. The growth and role of the social strata, as well as racial and political relations in the plantation colony are analyzed.

AA376. Quintus Bosz, Askel J. A. **Drie Eeuwen Grondpolitiek in Suriname.** Assen, 1954. (Summary in English and Spanish.) Scholarly treatise dealing with land policy and development of land rights from the beginning of Dutch colonization in Surinam, studied within the frame of the principles of colonization. Attention is given to political, social, and economic factors determining the nature of land tenure.

AA377. Warnsinck, Johan C. M. **Abraham Crynsen: de verovering van Suriname en zijn aanslag op Virginië in 1667.** Amsterdam, 1936. Study of the Dutch conquest of Surinam during the second Anglo-Dutch war.

PERIODICAL

AA378. De West Indische Gids. Amsterdam and The Hague, 1919 ff. (Monthly.) The basic historical periodical, containing important articles, bibliography, and notes.

SECTION AB

United States of America

MICHAEL KRAUS *

The compilers of this section have attempted to include, as far as space has allowed, titles published since 1931, when the original *Guide* appeared. It will be noted that there is a greater emphasis on cultural and social history, reflecting trends in research of the past generation; and works recording the interrelations of United States and European history are likewise given considerable space. For a more complete bibliography the reader is directed to the excellent *Harvard guide (AB4)*.

BIBLIOGRAPHIES, LIBRARIES, AND MUSEUMS

The number of available collections and selections of papers, documents, and other types of source material is too great to list with completeness here. It is more to the point to provide users of this volume with a selection of guides, lists, indices, and other bibliographical tools which constitute approaches to the sources. However, a second group of items, composed of major series and comprehensive collections, is also provided.

For fundamental works in United States bibliography see *B17–28*.

Bibliographies

AB1. Beers, Henry P., ed. **Bibliographies in American history: guide to materials for research.** N.Y., 1938. Rev. ed., 1942. Lists, without evaluation, general aids and bibliographies for broad periods and for major topics in history of the United States and

each state and territory; includes cartography. See also *The bibliographic index* (N.Y., 1938 ff.). [EMH]

AB2. Billington, Ray A. **Guides to American history manuscript collections in libraries of the United States.** N.Y., 1952. Good starting point for manuscript research in public, private, university, and historical society libraries, as well as in federal and state depositories. [SD]

AB3. Greene, Evarts B., and Richard B. Morris. **A guide to the principal sources for early American history (1600–1800) in the city of New York.** 2nd ed., N.Y., 1953. Supersedes 1929 edition. Includes manuscript and printed sources. [SD]

AB4. Handlin, Oscar, and others. **Harvard guide to American history.** Cambridge, Mass., 1954. Indispensable. Comprehensive in scope; selective for older works especially. Lists general and special bibliographies, indexes, guides, general works, special works, sources. Little evaluation; full index. Introductory essays on methods, resources, and materials. [EMH]

* The following contributed items and comments indicated by their respective initials: Thomas A. Bailey (TAB), Bernard Bellush (BB), Vincent P. Carosso (VPC), Merle E. Curti (MEC), Sidney Ditzion (SD), John H. Franklin (JHF), Wood Gray (WG), Virginia D. Harrington (VDH), George F. Howe (GFH), Erling M. Hunt (EMH), Sidney I. Pomerantz (SIP), Joseph E. Wisan (JEW). Albert L. Demaree and Robert E. Riegel contributed most of the items of biography. Wesley F. Craven, Glyndon G. Van Deusen, and Fred Israel also assisted in the preparation of this section.

AB5. Howes, Wright. **U. S.-iana (1700–1950): a descriptive checklist of 11,450 printed sources relating to those parts of continental North America now comprising the United States.** N.Y., 1954. Very selective insofar as it is made up largely of items that sell for $25 and over. Gives some library location notes. [SD]

AB6. Travels in the old South: a bibliography. Ed. by Thomas D. Clark. 4 v. Norman, Okla., 1948–59.

AB7. Lillard, Richard G. **American life in autobiography: a descriptive guide.** Stanford, 1956. Highly selective list of about 400 figures who were engaged in a large variety of pursuits and occupations. Very few works published before 1900 are included. [SD]

AB8. Matthews, William. **American diaries: an annotated bibliography of American diaries written prior to the year 1861.** Berkeley, 1945. [University of California publications in English, 16.] Indicates nature and value of individual published diaries. [SD]

AB9. Writings on American history. For 1902, by Ernest C. Richardson and Anson E. Morse, Princeton, 1904; for 1903, by Andrew C. McLaughlin, William A. Slade, and Ernest D. Lewis, Washington, 1905; for 1906–40, by Grace G. Griffin and others, N.Y., New Haven, and Washington, 1908– ; for 1948 ff., by James R. Masterson, Washington, 1950 ff. Annual index. Cumulative *Index to the Writings on American history, 1902–1940,* Washington, 1956. Annual classified lists of books, American or European, and major articles on history of the United States, British America (through 1940), and Latin America (through 1935), with short reviews or citations of reviews. [EMH]

AB10. Larned, Josephus N., ed. **Literature of American history: a bibliographical guide.** See *Y8.*

Libraries

As might be expected, libraries in the United States have long been rich in collections of Americana. Some have tried to cover the whole field, others have deliberately restricted themselves to selected areas. No library in the country is as rich in materials as the Library of Congress. Beginning with 1870, it was given the right to add to its shelves copies of every book copyrighted in the United States. When the imaginative Herbert Putnam was named librarian in 1899, the library began a remarkable growth which has continued under his successors. Among its great collections are manuscripts of many prominent Americans, including a number of presidents. It possesses a great collection of maps and atlases, newspapers, and reproductions of United States historical materials found in European depositories. The New York Public Library is especially strong in U. S. history. Its collections include valuable manuscript materials on the American Revolution, notably the papers of the Committees of Correspondence. It contains about 100,000 prints, many relating to the history of the country, along with impressive collections on literature, the history of labor, and the history of tobacco.

The noted universities have important collections of Americana. The Harvard Library, oldest in the nation, experienced its first significant growth in the early 19th century with acquisition of the library of Americana collected by the German scholar, C. D. Ebeling. Harvard also has the papers of prominent alumni, and its special libraries are notable. Yale University has the famous W. R. Coe collection of western Americana, as well as the Ezra Stiles manuscripts. It is rich in materials on World War I and the Versailles peace conference. The library at Columbia University is distinguished for its collections in politics, government, economics, and the history of education. It contains important papers of the founding fathers, Jay and Hamilton; and in its oral history project has a large number of recorded interviews with prominent Americans. The Princeton University Library has an excellent collection of early Americana, as well as the noted Rollins assemblage of western Americana. The University of Pennsylvania has a valuable collection of Franklin imprints, as well as materials on colonial history and the Carey collection on early economic history. Among southern universities, Duke, North Carolina, and Virginia have large collections on the history of the South. The University of Michigan, in its William L. Clements Library, has one of the greatest collections in the country on colonial and Revolutionary history. The University of Chicago has important materials on the Civil War and on the growth of the Middle West. Stanford University is especially distinguished for its Hoover Library on War, Revolution, and Peace. The University of California at Berkeley has the noted Hubert Howe Bancroft Library of manuscripts and rare printed materials on the West.

Historical societies hold important collections of manuscripts and printed materials. The Massachusetts Historical Society has papers of the Adams and Winthrop families, Thomas Jefferson's private papers, and those of many other worthies. In the American Antiquarian Society, Worcester, Mass., is the largest collection of North American newspapers printed before 1820, along with almanacs, magazines, and local histories. The New York Historical Society has important manuscript collections of noted families. The Historical Society of Pennsylvania (Philadelphia) has a great collection of colonial Americana, including newspapers, colonial laws, and Franco-American relations. The American Philosophical Society of Philadelphia has Franklin manuscripts, materials on early science, and collections relating to the American Revolution. The State Historical Society of Wisconsin has the Draper collection on the West, as well as valuable materials on the labor movement. Other societies restrict themselves to more specialized topics, such as the Essex Institute at Salem, which is rich in materials on New England commerce, and the Minnesota Historical Society at St. Paul, which contains valuable collections on Scandinavians in the United States.

Some libraries have special collections that give them a particular significance. The Boston Athenaeum has most of George Washington's library; the John Carter Brown Library (Providence) is supreme in its assemblage of European works on the discovery and exploration of the Western Hemisphere. The Library Company of Philadelphia has a valuable collection of manuscripts on the Revolutionary era, including the Rush correspondence. The John Crerar Library, Chicago, is rich in science and technology; and the Newberry Library (Chicago) has valuable collections on the discovery of America, the Indians, railroads, and growth of the Middle West. The Henry E. Huntington Library at San Marino, Calif., contains great stores of material on English and American colonial history, as well as the history of California. The Folger Library, Washington, is rich in rare books on English history and U. S. colonial history. An unusually distinguished specialized library is the Army Medical Library (Washington), unsurpassed for its collections on the history of medicine and public health.

Museums and Other Nondocumentary Sources

Scattered throughout the country are historic houses and formal museums with collections of furniture, paintings, rugs, silverware, etc., representative of the U. S. past. The American wing of the Metropolitan Museum of Art in New York has an especially rich collection. In some respects the Du Pont Winterthur Museum, Winterthur, Del., surpasses all others in its collections of early Americana. The Smithsonian Institution, Washington; the Bucks County Historical Society, Doylestown, Pa.; and the Farmers' Museum, Cooperstown, N.Y., have valuable exhibits on the life of people in an earlier day.

Following European example, Americans have built open-air, multiple-unit museums, the best known of which is Colonial Williamsburg, Virginia. Sturbridge Village, Mas-

sachusetts, is another, less elaborate, representation of an entire community of bygone days. At Luther College, Decorah, Iowa, are cabins, houses, and furnishings of Norwegian-American settlers. The National Park Service has preserved historical landmarks and dwellings which convey a vivid sense of the past.

ENCYCLOPEDIAS AND WORKS OF REFERENCE

AB11. Morris, Richard B., ed. **Encyclopedia of American history.** N.Y., 1953. Chronological survey of political-military events, followed by chronological treatment of other aspects. Maps; 300 biographical sketches. [EMH]

AB12. Adams, James Truslow, ed. **Dictionary of American history.** See Y16.

AB13. U. S. Bureau of the Census. **Historical statistics of the United States, 1789–1945: a supplement to the Statistical abstract of the United States.** Washington, 1949. Supplement (to 1952), 1954. Predominantly economic; one section on government. [EMH]

AB14. Johnson, Allen, and Dumas Malone, eds. **Dictionary of American biography.** 21 v. and index. N.Y., 1928–44. Supplement to v. 21, N.Y., 1935; second supplement in progress. The best work of its kind. [EMH]

AB15. O'Neill, Edward H. **Biography by Americans, 1658–1936: a subject bibliography.** Philadelphia, 1939. Lists individual and collective biographies; no annotations or evaluations. [EMH]

AB16. Dargan, Marion. **Guide to American biography.** 2 v. Albuquerque, 1947–52. [1, 1607–1815; 2, 1815–1933.] Organized by chronological periods, subdivided into political or regional groupings. Evaluates some titles by quoting reviews. [EMH]

AB17. Forbes, Harriette. **New England diaries, 1620–1800: a descriptive catalogue of diaries, orderly books, and sea journals.** Topsfield, Mass., 1923.

GEOGRAPHIES AND ATLASES

AB18. Brown, Ralph H. **Historical geography of the United States.** N.Y., 1948. Chronological survey by regions; environments, settlement and migration, resources and related economic development. [EMH]

AB19. Thiele, Walter. **Official map publications.** Chicago, 1938. Includes a reference list of map publications issued by the United States government; also an account of the mapping of the North American continent from the 17th through the 19th centuries. [EMH]

AB20. Paullin, Charles O. **Atlas of the historical geography of the United States.** Ed. by John K. Wright. Washington, 1932.

Physical maps; reproductions of old maps; exploration and settlement; states, territories, and boundary disputes and changes; social and economic data and statistics; political parties; reforms; military history. [EMH]

AB21. U. S. Library of Congress. **United States atlases: a list of national, state, county, city, and regional atlases in the Library of Congress and cooperating libraries.** Comp. by Clara E. Le Gear. 2 v. Washington, 1950–53. Topical listings. [EMH]

AB22. Lord, Clifford L., and Elizabeth H. Lord. **Historical atlas of the United States.** N.Y., 1944. Rev. ed., 1953. Organized by periods to show a wide range of political, economic, and social data and development. [EMH]

AB23. Adams, James Truslow, ed. **Atlas of American history.** N.Y., 1943. Contains 148 black and white plates, chiefly concerning political and military history from discovery to 1912. [EMH]

GUIDES

AB24. Downs, Robert B. **American library resources: a bibliographical guide.** See *U11.*

AB25. Brown, Everett S. **Manual of government publications, United States and foreign.** N.Y., 1950. United States federal laws, congressional debates and proceedings, court reports, presidential papers, departmental publications; state government publications; publications of British and other governments, and of the United Nations. [EMH]

AB26. Boyd, Anne M., and R. Elizabeth Rips. **United States government publications.** 3rd ed., N.Y., 1949. Listings by government division, department, or agency. [EMH]

AB27. Schmeckebier, Laurence F. **Government publications and their use.** Washington, 1936. Rev. ed., 1939. Includes catalogs, indexes, topical bibliographies, maps; organizes publications by agency. [EMH]

AB28. Griffin, Appleton P. C. **Bibliography of American historical societies: the United States and the Dominion of Canada.** 2nd ed., rev. and enl., Washington, 1907. [American Historical Association, Annual report, 1905, v. 2.]

AB29. American Association for State and Local History. **Historical societies in the United States and Canada.** Ed. by C. Christopher Crittenden and Doris Godard. Washington, 1944. Notes distinctive library resources, museums, and publications. [EMH]

HISTORIOGRAPHY

AB30. Kraus, Michael. **The writing of American history.** Norman, 1953. Revision of *A history of American history* (N.Y.,

1937). Chronological survey into the national period; then a treatment of patriotic and romantic, "scientific," nationalist and imperial schools, frontier and sectional historians, biography, and contemporary trends. Has separate chapters on Francis Parkman and Henry Adams. The only comprehensive survey. [EMH]

AB31. Hutchinson, William T., ed. **Marcus W. Jernegan essays in American historiography.** Chicago, 1937. Twenty-one representatives of several of the leading types of historians. Useful though uneven in quality. [EMH]

AB32. Bellot, Hugh H. **American history and American historians: a review of recent contributions to the interpretation of the history of the United States.** Norman, Okla., and London, 1952. The occupant of the chair of American history in the University of London examines United States historical writing during the fifty years after 1890 and the manner in which it has treated outstanding eras of U. S. history.

AB33. Theory and practice in historical study: a report of the Committee on Historiography. See *A465.*

AB34. Schlesinger, Arthur M. **New viewpoints in American history.** N.Y., 1922. Twelve topics in United States history are discussed in terms of "the results of the researches of the present era of historical study." Each topic is followed by a brief, critical bibliographical note. Many of these essays remain useful as summaries and as points of departure for further investigation. [MEC]

AB35. Hockett, Homer C. **The critical method in historical research and writing.** See *A14.*

PICTORIAL HISTORIES

AB36. Butterfield, Roger P. **The American past: a history of the United States from Concord to the nuclear age.** N.Y., 1957.

AB37. Gabriel, Ralph H., and others, eds. **The pageant of America: a pictorial history of the United States.** 15 v. New Haven, 1925–29. Partly topical, partly chronological. Broad in scope, but uneven in quality. [EMH]

AB38. Adams, James T., and others, eds. **Album of American history.** 5 v. N.Y., 1944–49. By chronological periods to 1917; v. 5 is index. [EMH]

SHORT COLLECTIONS OF DOCUMENTS

AB39. Billington, Ray A., and others, eds. **The making of American democracy: readings and documents.** 2 v. N.Y., 1950.

AB40. Commager, Henry S., ed. **Docu-**

ments of American history. 6th ed., N.Y., 1958.

AB41. Handlin, Oscar, ed. **Readings in American history.** N.Y., 1957.

AB42. Hart, Albert B., ed. **American history told by contemporaries.** 5 v. N.Y., 1897–1929. One of the earliest collections of source materials for the general reader; still useful.

AB43. Sheehan, Donald H., ed. **The making of American history.** Rev. ed., 2 v., N.Y., 1954. A judicious selection from the writings of accepted authorities on United States development from the colonial period to the 20th century.

AB44. University of Chicago. **The people shall judge: readings in the formation of American policy.** 2 v. Chicago, 1949. Supplements, 1952, 1956.

GENERAL HISTORIES

AB45. Adams, Henry B. **History of the United States of America.** 9 v. N.Y., 1889–91. 4 v. reprint, N.Y., 1930. This study of the years 1800–17 is a landmark in U. S. historiography, distinguished for its high literary qualities. Provides an excellent account of the social history of this period and is useful for its detailed treatment of political and diplomatic developments, but fails to appraise adequately the influence of economic factors. [VPC]

AB46. Andrews, Charles M. **The colonial period of American history.** 4 v. New Haven, 1934–38. A standard reference for history of the English mainland and island colonies. Author's approach is institutional and imperial, and his conclusions are based on extensive research in English and American archives. V. 1–3 cover the settlements; v. 4, British colonial, commercial, and administrative policy to 1763. [VPC]

AB47. Bancroft, George. **History of the United States of America from the discovery of the American continent.** 10 v. Boston, 1834–75. The original 10 v. and revised 6 v. editions begin with the expansion of Europe and end in 1782. In 1882 Bancroft brought his narrative down to 1789 with publication of his 2 v. *History of the formation of the Constitution of the United States of America.* The entire history was revised and the 1882 volumes incorporated into the 6 v. last revision (N.Y., 1883–85). Even though his history is neither widely read nor accepted as entirely reliable, Bancroft occupies an important place in U. S. historiography. He uncovered and used many new sources in preparing his work; but although he was in many ways a good craftsman, his strong prejudices and intense patriotism colored his conclusions. Militantly anti-British and a staunch advocate of Jacksonian democracy, Bancroft reflects the democratic, na-

tional self-confidence characteristic of his times. [VPC]

AB48. Bancroft, Hubert H. **The works of Hubert Howe Bancroft.** 39 v. San Francisco, 1882–90. [1–5, *Native races;* 6–8, *History of Central America;* 9–14, *History of Mexico;* 15–16, *History of the north Mexican states and Texas;* 17, *History of Arizona and New Mexico;* 18–24, *History of California;* 25, *History of Nevada, Colorado, and Wyoming;* 26, *History of Utah;* 27–28, *History of the northwest coast;* 29–30, *History of Oregon;* 31, *History of Washington, Idaho, and Montana;* 32, *History of British Columbia;* 33, *History of Alaska;* 34, *California pastoral;* 35, *California inter pocula;* 36–37, *Popular tribunals;* 38, *Essays and miscellany;* 39, *Literary industries.*] A vast enterprise made possible by the energy of a great organizer of historical research. Many hands went into the composition of these volumes which, even with their inaccuracies and mistaken interpretations, are still valuable for the research scholar.

AB49. Beard, Charles A., and Mary R. Beard. **The rise of American civilization.** 4 v. N.Y., 1927–42. Other eds. Exceptionally well-written general interpretation of United States history and civilization, emphasizing the role and interaction of social and economic forces upon the nation's development. These volumes illustrate the broad interests of the authors and what they believed to have been the dynamic factors affecting the course of national life. [VPC]

AB50. Bemis, Samuel F., ed. **The American secretaries of state and their diplomacy.** 10 v. N.Y., 1927–29. Numerous contributors, some of them recognized experts, analyze in brief historical sketches the career and diplomacy of every secretary, beginning with Robert R. Livingston, the secretary for foreign affairs of the Continental Congress (1781–83), and concluding with Charles Evans Hughes (1921–25). Provides convenient summary of U. S. diplomacy between 1781 and 1925, but is not, nor was it intended to be, a comprehensive history of foreign policy. Emphasis is on diplomacy rather than foreign policy in its broad meaning. Sketches vary in quality and value, those of earlier secretaries often superior to studies of more recent ones. [VPC]

AB51. The Chicago history of American civilization. Ed. by Daniel J. Boorstin. Chicago, 1956 ff. [Dexter Perkins, *The new age of Franklin D. Roosevelt, 1932–45;* John Ellis, *American Catholicism;* Herbert Agar, *The price of power: America since 1945;* Edmund Morgan, *The birth of the republic, 1763–89;* Nathan Glazer, *American Judaism.*] (Other volumes in preparation.) This series is planned to include 20 v. of about 200 pages each, covering both chronological periods and significant topics, with brief bibliographical essays citing major secondary works. [VPC]

AB52. Brooks, Van Wyck. **Makers and finders: a history of the writer in America, 1800–1915.** 5 v. N.Y., 1936–52. [1, *The world of Washington Irving;* 2, *The flowering of New England;* 3, *The times of Melville and Whitman;* 4, *New England: Indian summer, 1865–1915;* 5, *The confident years, 1885–1915.*] The work of a leading student of U. S. literature; not as sharply critical as some of his earlier studies. It is written with considerable charm, and these volumes form a good introduction to 19th century culture in the United States.

AB53. Channing, Edward. **A history of the United States.** 6 v. N.Y., 1905–25. Index, 1932. Result of careful and extensive research in the sources, these volumes, covering the years 1000–1865, are distinguished for their accuracy, wealth of detail, comprehensiveness, and readability. Though recent scholarship has revised many specific points, historians generally still consider this the best long general history of the United States by one author. [VPC]

AB54. Clark, Victor S. **History of manufactures in the United States.** 3 v. Washington, 1916–29. The result of diligent research.

AB55. The new American nation series. Ed. by Richard B. Morris and Henry S. Commager. N.Y., 1954 ff. [Wallace Notestein, *The English people on the eve of colonization, 1603–1630;* Lawrence H. Gipson, *The coming of the Revolution, 1763–1775;* Louis B. Wright, *The cultural life of the American colonies, 1607–1763;* John R. Alden, *The American Revolution, 1775–1783;* Ray A. Billington, *The far western frontier, 1830–1860;* Arthur Link, *Woodrow Wilson and the progressive era, 1910–1917;* Foster R. Dulles, *America's rise to world power, 1898–1954.*] (Other volumes in preparation.) When completed, this cooperative history (43 v.) will supersede the Hart series (*AB63*). Like its predecessor, it will survey the entire history of the United States. Whereas the Hart work treated political history primarily, the editors of the new series plan a broader scope and intend to supplement the chronological volumes with topical ones. Each will contain a critical bibliography, and a final volume will be devoted to historical statistics. [VPC]

AB56. Commons, John R., and others. **History of labour in the United States.** 4 v. N.Y., 1918–35. The standard work on U. S. labor, but in need of serious revision, particularly for the colonial period.

AB57. A history of the South. Ed. by Ellis Merton Coulter and Wendell H. Stephenson. Baton Rouge, 1948 ff. [1, Wesley F. Craven, *The southern colonies in the seventeenth century, 1607–1689;* 3, John R. Alden, *The South in the Revolution, 1763–*

1789; 5, Charles S. Sydnor, *The development of southern sectionalism, 1819–1848;* 6, Avery O. Craven, *The growth of southern nationalism, 1848–1861;* 7, E. M. Coulter, *The Confederate States of America, 1861–1865;* 8, E. M. Coulter, *The South during reconstruction, 1865–1877;* 9, C. Vann Woodward, *Origins of the new South, 1877–1913.*] (To be complete in 10 v.) When completed, this series, written by distinguished scholars, will supersede the older cooperative history, *The South in the building of the nation* (13 v., Richmond, 1909–13). Each volume contains a critical essay on authorities. [VPC]

AB58. The economic history of the United States. Ed. by Henry David, Harold U. Faulkner, Louis M. Hacker, Curtis P. Nettels, and Fred A. Shannon. N.Y., 1945 ff. [4, George R. Taylor, *The transportation revolution, 1815–1860;* 5, F. A. Shannon, *The farmer's last frontier: agriculture, 1860–1897;* 7, H. U. Faulkner, *The decline of laissez faire, 1897–1917;* 8, George H. Soule, *Prosperity decade: from war to depression, 1917–1929;* 9, Broadus Mitchell, *Depression decade: from New Era through New Deal, 1929–1941.*] (To be complete in 9 v.) When completed, this standard reference will detail U. S. economic development from the colonial period to 1941. Each volume contains a critical bibliography. [VPC]

AB59. Dorfman, Joseph H. **The economic mind in American civilization.** 3 v. N.Y., 1946–49. V. 1–2 cover the years 1606–1865; v. 3, 1865–1918. A fourth volume will cover from the end of World War I to the beginning of the New Deal. These volumes contain a wealth of detail on economic ideas of selected groups and individuals, indicating the influence of economic thought upon the major public issues of the times. Bibliographical notes. [VPC]

AB60. A history of American life. Ed. by Dixon Ryan Fox and Arthur M. Schlesinger. 13 v. N.Y., 1927–48. [1, Herbert I. Priestley, *The coming of the white man, 1492–1848;* 2, Thomas J. Wertenbaker, *The first Americans, 1607–1690;* 3, James T. Adams, *Provincial society, 1690–1763;* 4, Evarts B. Greene, *The revolutionary generation, 1763–1790;* 5, John A. Krout and D. R. Fox, *The completion of independence, 1790–1830;* 6, Carl R. Fish, *The rise of the common man;* 7, Arthur C. Cole, *The irrepressible conflict, 1850–1865;* 8, Allan Nevins, *The emergence of modern America, 1865–1878;* 9, Ida M. Tarbell, *The nationalizing of business, 1878–1898;* 10, A. M. Schlesinger, *The rise of the city, 1878–1898;* 11, Harold U. Faulkner, *The quest for social justice, 1898–1914;* 12, Preston W. Slosson, *The great crusade and after, 1914–1928;* 13, Dixon Wecter, *The age of the great depres-*

sion, 1929–1941.] Designed to survey the history of social, cultural, and economic life, this work purposely excludes as much political, military, diplomatic, and constitutional history as possible. Each volume contains illustrations and a critical essay on authorities. Not all volumes are of equal value— some, for example, include more economic data than others, and a number catalog many details of social and cultural history without sufficient interpretation. Despite certain limitations, this is the best general survey of U. S. social and cultural life. [VPC]

AB61. Gipson, Lawrence H. **The British empire before the American Revolution: provincial characteristics and sectional tendencies in the era preceding the American crisis.** See *U134.*

AB62. The Library of Congress series in American civilization. Ed. by Ralph H. Gabriel. 6 v. Cambridge, Mass., 1951–54. [John I. H. Baur, *Revolution and tradition in modern American art;* Merle E. Curti, *American scholarship in the twentieth century;* Oscar Handlin, *The American people in the twentieth century;* Frank L. Mott, *The news in America;* Herbert W. Schneider, *Religion in 20th century America;* John Sirjamaki, *The American family in the twentieth century.*]

AB63. The American nation. Ed. by Albert B. Hart. 28 v. N.Y., 1904–18.

AB64. The chronicles of America. Ed. by Allen Johnson. 50 v. New Haven, 1918–21. Supplement, 6 v., 1950–51. Aimed to satisfy requirements of the intelligent layman without compromising accepted standards of scholarship, this series surveys briefly the major developments in United States history between 1492 and 1945. Though most of these small volumes were designed to cover certain chronologically defined periods in the political history of the nation, a number of them, with varying degrees of success, cover social, cultural, educational, military, constitutional, and economic developments. Many were written by respected scholars who incorporated the results of years of research. Each volume contains a brief bibliography. [VPC]

AB65. Johnson, Emory R., and others. **History of domestic and foreign commerce of the United States.** 2 v. Washington, 1915. Reprint, 1922. Includes material on commerce and fisheries, as well as discussion of government aid and commercial policy. Not noted for literary elegance, but contains many facts and very helpful bibliographies.

AB66. McMaster, John B. **A history of the people of the United States from the Revolution to the Civil War.** 8 v. N.Y., 1883–1913. Other eds. An additional volume, *A history of the people of the United States during Lin-*

coln's administration (N.Y., 1927) carries the narrative through 1865. With its heavy reliance on newspapers and other contemporary periodical sources, this work marks an important development in U. S. historiography. Far more than previous writers, McMaster includes social and economic detail, and describes public opinion as reflected in the contemporary press. His interest in western history was equally novel. Although many of his generalizations are no longer valid, this is a storehouse of miscellaneous and interesting detail, not all of it accurate. It remains a useful reference. [VPC]

AB67. Meyer, Balthasar H., ed. **History of transportation in the United States before 1860.** Washington, 1917. Contains much information on various modes of transportation. Valuable as a reference.

AB68. Nevins, Allan. **Ordeal of the union.** 2 v. N.Y., 1947. A comprehensive, detailed and well-documented study and analysis of the decade following the war with Mexico. These two volumes and their sequel (*AB69*) are part of the author's proposed 8 v. study of the years 1847–65. [VPC]

AB69. ——. **The emergence of Lincoln.** 2 v. N.Y., 1950. Similar to *AB68* in treatment. The failure of statesmanship during the four years 1857–61 is one of the major concerns of the author. [VPC]

AB70. Oberholtzer, Ellis P. **A history of the United States since the Civil War.** 5 v. N.Y., 1917–37. A continuation of *AB66* by a student of McMaster; covers the years 1865–1901. Though economic developments are not ignored, far more space is devoted to political and social history. Primarily descriptive rather than analytical, weak in organization, synthesis, and integration, these volumes betray the author's unfriendliness toward labor and his sympathy for advocates of hard money. [VPC]

AB71. Osgood, Herbert L. **The American colonies in the seventeenth century.** See *Y108.*

AB72. ——. **The American colonies in the eighteenth century.** 4 v. N.Y., 1924–25. This and *AB71* together constitute a major contribution to institutional, legal, and administrative history of the English mainland colonies to 1763. Detailed and factual rather than interpretative. The interest is principally political, and little social, intellectual, or economic history is included. [VPC]

AB73. Parkman, Francis. **Works.** See *Y113.*

AB74. Paxson, Frederic L. **American democracy and the World War.** 3 v. Boston and Berkeley, 1936–48. A standard reference covering the years 1913–23. Major emphasis is on the effects of World War I on operation and structure of the U. S. government. [VPC]

AB75. Carnegie Endowment for International Peace. **The relations of Canada and the United States.** Ed. by James T. Shotwell. 25 v. New Haven and Toronto, 1937–45. A splendid group of volumes by able scholars, covering all phases of Canadian-United States relations. The mingling of their people and economies is of particular interest; boundary disputes and political relations are given full coverage.

AB76. Rhodes, James Ford. **History of the United States from the compromise of 1850.** 7 v. N.Y., 1893–1906. With the exception of a few chapters on social developments, this is primarily a chronological, political narrative of the years 1850–77. Two later volumes, *History of the United States from Hayes to McKinley* (N.Y., 1919) and *The McKinley and Roosevelt administrations* (N.Y., 1922), carry the story to 1909. Rhodes' point of view on the coming of the Civil War and secession is a nationalist one, but he is more impartial, reasonable, and less emotional than many other historians writing at the time. Major weaknesses are the scant attention given to railroad developments and western affairs, and the lack of any significant material covering economic developments emanating from the Civil War. The two later volumes are inferior to the earlier ones. [VPC]

AB77. Schouler, James. **History of the United States under the Constitution.** 5 v. N.Y., 1880–91. Rev. ed., 1894. V. 6, 1899. V. 7, 1913. These 7 v. cover 1783–1877, and form the first continuous history of the United States over these years. Schouler's volumes are concerned primarily with political and constitutional events, and betray his nationalistic and moralistic biases. The work is more useful as an example in the evolution of historical writing than as a reference for modern-day students. [VPC]

AB78. Sullivan, Mark. **Our times: the United States, 1900–1925.** 6 v. N.Y., 1926–35. The work of a competent journalist, these volumes are filled with pertinent and interesting detail on politics, society, and life in general. Much of the information comes from newspapers and periodicals. [VPC]

AB79. The American foreign policy library. Ed. by Sumner Welles and Donald C. McKay. 13 v. Cambridge, Mass., 1945–56. Each volume surveys briefly the history of U. S. relations (since 1783) with one or more countries. Twelve additional volumes are planned. [VPC]

AB80. White, Leonard D. **The Federalists: a study in administrative history.** N.Y., 1948. This and *AB81–83* constitute a pioneer work on the history of public administration. Argues that Jacksonians democratized the U. S. administrative system, while Federalists and Jeffersonians preferred administration by the "well-born and well-to-do."

AB81. ——. **The Jeffersonians: a study in** administrative history, 1801–1829. N.Y., 1951.

AB82. ——. **The Jacksonians: a study in** administrative history, 1829–1861. N.Y., 1954.

AB83. ——. **The Republican era, 1869–** 1901. N.Y., 1958.

AB84. Winsor, Justin, ed. **Narrative and critical history of America.** 8 v. Boston, 1884–89. Edited by the learned librarian of Harvard University, this series represents one of the best early attempts to prepare a general, multi-volume, cooperative synthesis of United States history. Covering the period to 1850, it is a summary of historical knowledge as of 1880. With a few exceptions, its usefulness today rests almost entirely on the bibliographical references, notes to sources, and other similar materials. [VPC]

AB85. Wish, Harvey. **Society and thought in America.** 2 v. N.Y., 1950–52. General survey, designed also for use as a college text. Summarizes the results of recent scholarship in various related fields and attempts to describe the major social (including significant economic) and intellectual developments. Coverage is broad, the analysis uneven. [VPC]

HISTORIES OF SPECIAL PERIODS

Discovery of America to 1789

AB86. Brebner, John B. **The explorers of North America, 1492–1806.** London, 1933. Splendid study of the penetration of North America by explorers from many lands; well-written, properly proportioned, and a work of careful scholarship.

AB87. Parks, George B. **Richard Hakluyt and the English voyages.** N.Y., 1928. Excellent study of the character of the British empire; a convincing demonstration of Hakluyt's influence in stirring the British to undertake imperial ventures.

AB88. French, Allen. **Charles I and the Puritan upheaval.** London, 1955. A good account of the causes of the Puritan migration.

AB89. Newton, Arthur P. **The colonizing activities of the English Puritans.** New Haven, 1914. Special emphasis on the West Indies. Shows English domestic politics closely connected with these colonizing activities, and that some of these enterprises were clearly designed "to nourish and uphold piracies" in the Caribbean.

AB90. Craven, Wesley F. **Dissolution of the Virginia Company.** N.Y., 1932. Best study of the crisis in Virginia's early history. Emphasizes the worth of Captain John Smith as a witness to events of his day.

AB91. Bruce, Philip A. **Economic history of Virginia in the seventeenth century.** 2 v. N.Y., 1895. Reprint, 1935. Based on hitherto unexplored sources, this was the first substantial attempt "to describe the purely economic condition of the Virginia people in detail."

AB92. ———. **Social life in Virginia in the seventeenth century.** Richmond, 1907. Inquiry into the origin of the planter aristocracy, with a description of the manners and diversions of the people. Apart from slaves, Virginia's population, says the author, was a duplication of the smaller rural English communities, modified by the New World environment.

AB93. ———. **Institutional history of Virginia in the seventeenth century.** 2 v. N.Y., 1910. Examination of the religious, moral, educational, legal, military, and political conditions in the colony. Like all of his works, this is based on careful research. Though modern students frequently dissent from his interpretations, the volumes of Bruce are the starting point for serious study of Virginia's colonial history.

AB94. Wertenbaker, Thomas J. **The planters of colonial Virginia.** Princeton, 1922. Important study revising former notions of the distribution of land in 17th century Virginia. Author shows that relatively small holdings were the more common units of this period.

AB95. Washburn, Wilcomb E. **The governor and the rebel: a history of Bacon's rebellion in Virginia.** Chapel Hill, 1957. Reinterpretation of the famous incident in 17th century Virginia, which seeks to rehabilitate the reputation of Governor Berkeley and deny to Bacon his traditional place as champion of the people's liberties. The author's argument is that the conservative governor was really the upholder of honor and justice, rather than the impetuous Bacon and his followers, who were killing Indians friendly to the whites.

AB96. Labaree, Leonard W. **Conservatism in early American history.** N.Y., 1948. Valuable, relatively short study of the persistence of conservative patterns in voting in the colonies.

AB97. Beer, George L. **The origins of the British colonial system, 1578–1660.** N.Y., 1908. Reprint, 1933. Shows that mercantilist principles were well established before the appearance of mercantilist theoreticians.

AB98. ———. **The old colonial system, 1660–1754.** 2 v. N.Y., 1912. Reprint, 1933. Classic study of the operation of Britain's first empire.

AB99. Leach, Douglas E. **Flintlock and tomahawk: New England in King Philip's War.** N.Y., 1958. A lively, scholarly treatment of this crisis in colonial New England.

AB100. Harper, Lawrence A. **The English navigation laws.** N.Y., 1939. Study of the operation of these laws.

AB101. Bailyn, Bernard. **The New England merchants in the seventeenth century.** Cam-

bridge, Mass., 1955. Important study of the rise of the colonial merchant. [VDH]

AB102. Tolles, Frederick B. **Meeting house and counting house: the Quaker merchants of colonial Philadelphia, 1682–1763.** Chapel Hill, 1948. Careful study of the way of life of a very influential group in colonial times.

AB103. Wertenbaker, Thomas J. **The old South: the founding of American civilization.** N.Y., 1942. A volume in a comprehensive survey of colonial civilization.

AB104. Simpson, Alan. **Puritanism in Old and New England.** Chicago, 1955. Compact, sophisticated study of Puritanism. Revises some traditional interpretations of events and personalities.

AB105. Morison, Samuel E. **The founding of Harvard College.** Cambridge, Mass., 1935. One of the best histories of an educational institution available. Emphasizes the indebtedness of Harvard to Emmanuel College, Cambridge. Argues that, from its founding, Harvard was interested in a broad education, not a purely seminary training.

AB106. ———. **Harvard College in the seventeenth century.** 2 v. Cambridge, Mass., 1936. A fine study of the growth of the school and its place in the community. Harvard's impact on the intellectual life of the colonies was profound.

AB107. Wertenbaker, Thomas J. **The Puritan oligarchy: the founding of American civilization.** N.Y., 1947. Stresses reasons for the decline of the oligarchy.

AB108. ———. **The founding of American civilization: the middle colonies.** N.Y., 1938. Pays special attention to architecture.

AB109. Crane, Verner W. **The southern frontier, 1670–1732.** Durham, 1928. Pioneer study of a neglected subject. The territory covered is largely South Carolina and its western frontier, much of its history being interwoven with the fur trade.

AB110. Pares, Richard. **Yankees and Creoles: the trade between North America and the West Indies before the American Revolution.** N.Y. and London, 1956. The only fairly comprehensive treatment of this important subject. Especially valuable for its statistical demonstration of the significance of this trade.

AB111. Baxter, William T. **The house of Hancock: business in Boston, 1724–1775.** Cambridge, Mass., 1945. Excellent study of an 18th century mercantile family. [VDH]

AB112. Hedges, James B. **The Browns of Providence Plantations.** Cambridge, Mass., 1952. Excellent study of a prominent commercial family of Rhode Island.

AB113. Nettels, Curtis P. **The money supply of the American colonies before 1720.** Madison, Wis., 1934. The outstanding study of this subject. Fairly conservative in monetary theory. [VDH]

AB114. Jernegan, Marcus W. **Laboring**

and dependent classes in colonial America, 1607–1783. Chicago, 1931. Helpful for an understanding of the conditions of work, educational opportunities open to workers, etc.

AB115. Morris, Richard B. **Government and labor in early America.** N.Y., 1946. Major contribution to this important field, in which it pioneered. [VDH]

AB116. Smith, Abbot E. **Colonists in bondage.** Chapel Hill, 1947. Excellent study, skilfully presented. Particularly good on recruitment of indentured servants in Europe. [VDH]

AB117. Bridenbaugh, Carl. **Cities in the wilderness: the first century of urban life in America, 1625–1742.** N.Y., 1938. Contains a wealth of detail on urban life, emphasizing that cities, as well as the frontier, profoundly affected the nation's growth.

AB118. ——. **Cities in revolt: urban life in America, 1743–1776.** N.Y., 1955. This second volume in his study of urban life in the colonies emphasizes the growing maturity of civilization here on the eve of the Revolution.

AB119. Harrington, Virginia D. **The New York merchant on the eve of the Revolution.** N.Y., 1935. Shows business activities of the merchant and compares colonial business enterprise with that of Europe. Brings together much material secured with considerable difficulty, and contains valuable appendices on New York shipping.

AB120. Greene, Evarts B., and Virginia D. Harrington. **American population before the federal census of 1790.** N.Y., 1932. The most comprehensive study to date of colonial populations. Although no systematic interpretation of the material has been attempted, the statistics are especially valuable.

AB121. Labaree, Leonard W. **Royal government in America: a study of the British colonial system before 1783.** New Haven, 1930. Detailed account of relations of crown to assembly, stressing finance, debates over salaries of governors, and the administration of justice.

AB122. Brown, Robert E. **Middle-class democracy and the Revolution in Massachusetts, 1691–1780.** Ithaca, 1955. Emphasizes the extent to which suffrage was enjoyed in Massachusetts long before the Revolution; minimizes older interpretation of conflict between sections in the colonies; ignores continued existence of a traditional ruling group, to whom the rest of the community often deferred.

AB123. Thayer, Theodore G. **Pennsylvania politics and the growth of democracy, 1740–1776.** Harrisburg, 1953. This volume belongs to the group of studies which purport to show that greater political democracy existed in the colonies before the Revolution than older historians maintained.

AB124. Baldwin, Alice M. **The New England clergy and the American Revolution.** Durham, 1928. Important contribution illustrating the relationship between religion and politics in the 18th century. The author makes clear that much of the content of sermons ostensibly religious was in reality of a political nature.

AB125. Land, Aubrey C. **The Dulanys of Maryland.** Baltimore, 1955. Careful study of a prominent colonial family which was influential in the Revolutionary era.

AB126. Beer, George L. **British colonial policy, 1754–1765.** N.Y., 1907. Very influential work in revision of the history of the American Revolution. Author contends that the aim of the purely commercial regulations of the years 1754–65 "was to encourage and not restrict colonial industry."

AB127. Schlesinger, Arthur M. **The colonial merchants and the American Revolution, 1763–1776.** N.Y., 1918. Contains a wealth of detail showing how the merchants tried to guide the course of revolutionary agitation.

AB128. Zeichner, Oscar. **Connecticut's years of controversy, 1750–1776.** Chapel Hill, 1949. Excellent study of conflicts over religion, politics, and economics in the alleged "land of steady habits." Includes an important demonstration of the interrelationship between the Great Awakening and the growth of democracy in the colony.

AB129. Morgan, Edmund S., and Helen M. Morgan. **The Stamp Act crisis.** Chapel Hill, 1953. The best study of this significant episode. Revises traditional views of American attitudes toward Parliament's taxing power.

AB130. Abernethy, Thomas P. **Western lands and the American Revolution.** N.Y., 1937. Outstanding account of the role of land hunger and land speculation in the Revolution. [VDH]

AB131. Alvord, Clarence W. **The Mississippi Valley in British politics.** 2 v. Cleveland, 1917. Emphasizes the impact of westward expansion in British politics in the 1760's and 1770's. Reveals an inadequate understanding of the complexities of British politics.

AB132. Namier, Sir Lewis B. **England in the age of the American Revolution.** London, 1930. Based on careful study of English sources, it points out the complexity of British politics in this period, and particularly stresses the influence of the crown.

AB133. Clark, Dora M. **British opinion and the American Revolution.** New Haven, 1930. Analysis of the reaction among merchants, the landed gentry, and the radicals to revolutionary sentiment in the colonies.

AB134. Ritcheson, Charles R. **British politics and the American Revolution.** Norman, 1954. Examines the impact of the Revolution on British political thought.

AB135. McIlwain, Charles H. **The American Revolution: a constitutional interpretation.** N.Y., 1923. Upholds the claim of the colonists that they were acting within their constitutional rights in denying the authority of Parliament over the colonies.

AB136. Schuyler, Robert L. **Parliament and the British empire.** See *U232*.

AB137. Kraus, Michael. **Intercolonial aspects of American culture on the eve of the Revolution.** N.Y., 1928. A capital study of significant aspects of intercolonial cultural development in major urban areas, throwing light on common intellectual interests and endeavors contributing to an emerging national feeling. [SIP]

AB138. Rossiter, Clinton L. **Seedtime of the republic.** N.Y., 1953. Stimulating discussion of the intellectual climate of the colonies on the eve of the Revolution.

AB139. Schlesinger, Arthur M. **Prelude to independence: the newspaper war on Britain, 1764–1776.** N.Y., 1958. This result of long and intimate study of the press on the eve of the Revolution shows that the patriots understood the part newspapers could play in winning over neutralists to their side, and that half-truth and exaggeration were mingled with sound argument to inflame hesitant citizens.

AB140. Davidson, Philip G. **Propaganda and the American Revolution, 1763–1783.** Chapel Hill, 1941. Describes both Whig and Tory propaganda, though giving more space to the former, whose success was greater. Shows that the Whigs gradually won over to the militant side a large wavering group. Especially valuable are chapters on the machinery of propaganda through the schools and newspapers.

AB141. Tyler, Moses C. **The literary history of the American Revolution, 1763–1783.** 2 v. N.Y., 1897. A pioneer work and still the only one covering the whole field, although other scholars have filled in gaps in this narrative. The author deals fairly with both Tory and Whig writers, making this work a landmark in U. S. historiography in its promotion of a more reasoned view of the loyalists.

AB142. Becker, Carl L. **The Declaration of Independence.** N.Y., 1922. An original study of the intellectual antecedents of the Declaration.

AB143. Nettels, Curtis P. **George Washington and American independence.** Boston, 1951. A provocative work.

AB144. Burnett, Edmund C. **The Continental Congress.** N.Y., 1941. Masterly work that revises previous judgments.

AB145. Miller, John C. **Origins of the American Revolution.** Boston, 1943. Stresses psychological explanations. Well-written;

contains numerous quotations, particularly from newspapers.

AB146. Ward, Christopher. **The war of the Revolution.** 2 v. N.Y., 1952. Good account of military operations, some of it written with literary distinction. Purely military in scope, its aim is to tell the story of the war on land.

AB147. Bemis, Samuel F. **The diplomacy of the American Revolution.** N.Y., 1935. Detailed, precise, and sound study. [VDH]

AB148. Corwin, Edward S. **French policy and the American alliance of 1778.** Princeton, 1916. Emphasizes the idea that France intervened in the American Revolution mainly to recover her vanished dominance on the continent of Europe.

AB149. Jameson, J. Franklin. **The American Revolution considered as a social movement.** Princeton, 1926. Stimulating, short survey of social changes leading to democracy in the Revolutionary era. Though recently attacked as exaggerating the extent of these changes, this book is still valuable.

AB150. Nevins, Allan. **The American states during and after the Revolution, 1775–1789.** N.Y., 1924. The only detailed study of changes that took place within the states during this period; a mine of valuable information, interestingly presented.

AB151. East, Robert A. **Business enterprise in the American Revolutionary era.** N.Y., 1938. Indispensable study of the topic. [VDH]

AB152. Jensen, Merrill. **The Articles of Confederation: an interpretation of the social-constitutional history of the American Revolution, 1774–1781.** Madison, 1940. Brings together results of monographs of the generation since Max Farrand plus independent conclusions. Excellent. [VDH]

AB153. ——. **The new nation: a history of the United States during the Confederation, 1781–1789.** N.Y., 1950. Stresses the virtues of government under the confederation; hostile to "nationalists." Excellent presentation of the anti-Federalist viewpoint.

AB154. Pomerantz, Sidney I. **New York, an American city, 1783–1803: a study of urban life.** N.Y., 1938. Good example of recent devotion to urban studies. Includes detailed investigation of economic development, social life, and cultural progress, and especially political changes during this period. Clearly sets forth the impact of the Revolution on city life.

AB155. McCormick, Richard P. **Experiment in independence: New Jersey in the critical period, 1781–1789.** New Brunswick, 1950. Offers fresh interpretation of this period, especially in the behavior of radicals and conservatives; makes more intelligible the reasons for New Jersey's adoption of the federal constitution.

AB156. Sydnor, Charles S. **Gentlemen**

freeholders: political practices in Washington's Virginia. Chapel Hill, 1952. Shows persistence of the traditional ruling class' influence after the Revolution.

AB157. Beard, Charles A. **An economic interpretation of the Constitution of the United States.** N.Y., 1913. Other eds. A landmark in U. S. historiography.

AB158. Brown, Robert E. **Charles Beard and the Constitution.** Princeton, 1956. Critical analysis of *AB157*, arguing that Beard's historical methods were faulty and did not justify his conclusions.

AB159. Warren, Charles. **The making of the Constitution.** Boston, 1928. By a learned authority.

AB160. ——. **The Supreme Court in United States history.** 3 v. Boston, 1922. This valuable study recreates the court in action by copious extracts from contemporary comments. Covers 1789–1918.

AB161. Buck, Solon J., and Elizabeth H. Buck. **The planting of civilization in western Pennsylvania.** Pittsburgh, 1939. Deals with social and economic developments in this region. Stresses the special place of western Pennsylvania in history of the frontier due to its control of the Ohio Valley, and this area's important contribution in the American Revolution.

1790–1865

AB162. Charles, Joseph. **The origins of the American party system.** Williamsburg, Va., 1956. Several essays analyzing party conflicts in the 1790's; friendlier to Jefferson than Hamilton. Probably dates too late the rise of Republicans as a conscious party.

AB163. Beard, Charles A. **Economic origins of Jeffersonian democracy.** N.Y., 1915. A continuation of the author's study of economic factors at play in drawing up the Constitution.

AB164. Davis, Joseph S. **Essays in the earlier history of American corporations.** 2 v. Cambridge, Mass., 1917. Especially important for its material on 18th century business corporations; the fruit of careful, detailed investigation.

AB165. Bowers, Claude G. **Jefferson and Hamilton.** N.Y., 1926. Other printings. Lively interpretation of the first decade of U. S. national history. Includes rich characterizations of personalities, with the author strongly biased in favor of Jefferson.

AB166. Link, Eugene P. **Democratic-republican societies, 1790–1800.** N.Y., 1942. Groups in the United States friendly to French revolutionaries of this period.

AB167. Robinson, William A. **Jeffersonian democracy in New England.** New Haven, 1916. Shows that New England was not entirely committed to the Federalists.

AB168. Baldwin, Leland D. **Whiskey rebels: the story of a frontier uprising.** Pittsburgh, 1939. Careful study of the reasons for frontier discontent in western Pennsylvania; hostile to Hamilton's part in harsh treatment of western farmers.

AB169. Tinkcom, Harry M. **The Republicans and Federalists in Pennsylvania, 1790–1801.** Harrisburg, 1950. By 1796 parties had crystallized in Pennsylvania, although for several years previously they had been in amorphous existence. By superior organization and leadership, the Republicans triumphed over the Federalists.

AB170. Dauer, Manning J. **The Adams Federalists.** Baltimore, 1953. Result of twenty years of careful research, with voting charts and maps of the make-up of the House of Representatives. Shows clearly that suspicion of Hamilton's militaristic intentions contributed to Federalist defeat by alienating the party's agricultural wing. [WG]

AB171. Miller, John C. **Crisis in freedom: the alien and sedition acts.** Boston, 1951. Written when threats to civil liberties again appeared real; very hostile to these measures.

AB172. Smith, James M. **Freedom's fetters: the alien and sedition laws and American civil liberties.** Ithaca, 1956. Best study of this important episode.

AB173. Sears, Louis M. **Jefferson and the embargo.** Durham, 1927. Argues that the embargo was a great experiment in peaceful coercion. Stresses more than previous writers the effects of the embargo on the growth of U. S. manufacturing.

AB174. Pratt, Julius W. **Expansionists of 1812.** N.Y., 1925. Stresses the desire of frontiersmen for additional territory, to be taken from Canada and Spain's Florida, as the most important factor in bringing on the War of 1812.

AB175. Burt, Alfred L. **The United States, Great Britain and British North America from the Revolution to the establishment of peace after the War of 1812.** New Haven, 1940. A thorough work on the interplay of these three communities. Challenges familiar interpretations of these years, for example, that of land hunger, in bringing on the War of 1812.

AB176. Goodman, Warren H. "The origins of the War of 1812: a survey of changing interpretations." **Miss. Val. hist. rev.,** 28 (Sep. 1941): 171–86. Helpful summary which concludes that there is still uncertainty about causes of the war.

AB177. Tucker, Glenn. **Poltroons and patriots: a popular account of the War of 1812.** 2 v. Indianapolis, 1954. Well-written, for a general audience, emphasizing the colorful. With much material drawn from contemporary newspapers, it attempts to show what people living during the war thought and did about domestic and international problems.

AB178. Purcell, Richard J. **Connecticut in transition, 1775–1818.** Washington, 1918. An able local study showing the transition in politics, economics, and religion which culminated in the constitution of 1818.

AB179. Bond, Beverley W., Jr. **The civilization of the old Northwest: a study of political, social, and economic development, 1788–1812.** N.Y., 1934. A wealth of detail purporting to show the "distinctiveness" of civilization in this region. Exaggerates the cosmopolitan and democratic features of society.

AB180. Hockett, Homer C. **Western influences on political parties to 1825.** Columbus, Ohio, 1917. Emphasizes economic influences on party alignments.

AB181. Barnhart, John D. **Valley of democracy: the frontier vs. the plantation in the Ohio Valley, 1775–1818.** Bloomington, Ind., 1953. Able application of the Turner thesis to early Kentucky and Tennessee, balancing the role of such land speculators as George Nicholas and William Blount against the relatively liberal early constitutions. Meticulously traces origins of constitutional provisions. [WG]

AB182. Abernethy, Thomas P. **From frontier to plantation in Tennessee.** Chapel Hill, 1932. A basic study emphasizing the role of land speculators on the frontier as a counterweight to democratizing opportunities of starting life afresh in a setting of natural wealth. [WG]

AB183. Buley, Roscoe C. **The old Northwest: pioneer period, 1815–1840.** 2 v. Indianapolis, 1950. Detailed account of the way of life in this region during the generation after the War of 1812. Rich in material on agricultural practices, changes in environment, and cultural development.

AB184. Clark, Thomas D. **The rampaging frontier: manners and humors of pioneer days in the South and the Middle West.** Indianapolis, 1939. Humor, with Kentucky featured. Based on a wide variety of sources.

AB185. Dangerfield, George. **The era of good feelings.** N.Y., 1952. Evocative style and gift for characterization give new depth and meaning to generally familiar materials in which the impact of economic depression is seen to disrupt a brief political-economic oligarchical control. [WG]

AB186. Moore, Glover. **The Missouri controversy, 1819–1821.** Lexington, Ky., 1953. Most exhaustive and competent treatment of the Missouri question. The author argues that the controversy was significant not because it created sectional antagonism, but in bringing together for the first time all strands of the North-South controversy.

AB187. Eaton, Clement. **A history of the old South.** N.Y., 1949. Compact, lucid, and reflective. [GFH]

AB188. Fox, Dixon Ryan. **The decline of aristocracy in the politics of New York.** N.Y., 1917. In this successful attempt to depict the interrelationships of business, society, and politics down to 1840, the author shows the waning strength of a patrician class, its "unpalatable compromises and slow liberalization, and the final welding of a business party appropriate to the conditions of America."

AB189. Pierson, George W. **Tocqueville and Beaumont in America.** N.Y., 1938. Careful retracing of the route of two of the most perceptive travelers ever to visit this country. Gives biographical backgrounds. [WG]

AB190. Turner, Frederick J. **The United States, 1830–1850.** N.Y., 1935. A matured projection and elaboration of Turner's earlier thesis concerning the democratizing and nationalizing influence of the frontier, stressing the role of slavery and sectional interests as inherent contradictions within the frontier experience. [WG]

AB191. Ward, John W. **Andrew Jackson, symbol for an age.** N.Y., 1955. Intellectual history of the Jackson period. Author contends that through Jackson were projected the leading ideas of the age centering around those of nature, providence, and will. [JHF]

AB192. Schlesinger, Arthur M., Jr. **The age of Jackson.** Boston, 1945. A brilliantly written re-evaluation of Jacksonian democracy, stressing eastern labor class contributions and marked by biographical vignettes. Has been criticized as tending to see the labor movement of a century ago too much in present day terms. [WG]

AB193. Hammond, Bray. **Banks and politics in America, from the Revolution to the Civil War.** Princeton, 1957. Discusses the entrepreneurial origins of Jacksonianism, and the crucial importance of need for credit in determining the politics of the business man in an agrarian setting. Parallels in Canadian developments are also noted. [SIP]

AB194. Sullivan, William A. **The industrial worker in Pennsylvania, 1800–1840.** Harrisburg, 1955. Concentrates on the labor movement in Pennsylvania during the Jacksonian era. Deals skilfully with the role of labor in politics of the principal towns, and concludes that working men's parties had little or no connection with the wage earners and were usually dominated by anti-Jackson sympathizers. [JHF]

AB195. Riegel, Robert E. **Young America, 1830–1840.** Norman, 1949. Account of the everyday life of the ordinary individual in the age of Jackson—his job, education, family life, religion, recreation, modes of transportation, and the men and ideas that molded him.

AB196. Smith, Walter B. **Economic aspects of the Second Bank of the United States.** Cambridge, Mass., 1953. Careful study for the specialist, stressing policy more than management. Gives the setting in trade and finance of the period, and shows that the bank gave the United States one of the most stable currencies in the world and that its destruction led to chaos. [WG]

AB197. McGrane, Reginald C. **The panic of 1837.** Chicago, 1924. Deals extensively with causes of the panic and its disastrous effects on the economic life of the country. Devotes special attention to relationship of banking and fiscal policies to the panic and the efforts to cope with it.

AB198. Morison, Samuel E. **The maritime history of Massachusetts, 1783–1860.** Boston, 1941. A classic account of maritime enterprise during the clipper ship era, dealing with shipbuilding, whaling, coastal trade, and expansion of Massachusetts shipping interests to the seven seas. [JHF]

AB199. Dana, Richard H. **Two years before the mast.** Modern library ed., N.Y., 1936. Lively narrative of a voyage around Cape Horn to California, depicting sea life from the sailor's, not the officer's, point of view. The book is a classic and has gone through many editions.

AB200. Albion, Robert G. **Square-riggers on schedule: the New York sailing packets to England, France, and the cotton ports.** Princeton, 1938. Well-written account of men and ships that linked the United States and Europe between 1815 and 1860. Some of this material is also contained in *AB201.*

AB201. ——. **The rise of New York port.** N.Y., 1939. Important study of the rise to pre-eminence of New York in U. S. commerce, 1815–60. Shows that New York was surpassing her rivals even before the Erie Canal clinched her leadership, and that New Englanders who settled in New York contributed greatly to the city's leadership.

AB202. Hidy, Ralph W. **The house of Baring in American trade and finance: English merchant bankers at work, 1763–1861.** Cambridge, Mass., 1949. Detailed and valuable account of the role of the Barings in arranging loans for the United States before the Civil War. One of the best works in the field.

AB203. McGrane, Reginald C. **Foreign bondholders and American state debts.** N.Y., 1935. Detailed examination of the extent to which states have repudiated their debts and the effect on their future credit. [JHF]

AB204. Handlin, Oscar, and Mary F. Handlin. **Commonwealth: a study of the role of government in the American economy: Massachusetts, 1774–1861.** N.Y., 1947. Shows that government at first was active in many enterprises, then private corporations assumed direction of them. While private rights were protected, there was increasing provision for the state's exercise of police powers.

AB205. Hartz, Louis. **Economic policy and democratic thought: Pennsylvania, 1776–1860.** Cambridge, Mass., 1948. Emphasizes the role of governmental intervention in economic affairs before the tradition of laissez-faire gained strength in the U.S.

AB206. Jones, Fred M. **Middlemen in the domestic trade of the United States, 1800–1860.** Urbana, 1937. Rise and importance of the wholesaler, factor, broker, auctioneer, and retailer in the economic development of the United States. [JHF]

AB207. Phelps, Christina. **The Anglo-American peace movement in the mid-nineteenth century.** N.Y., 1930. Excellent account of transatlantic pacifism; a segment of the larger story of Anglo-American humanitarianism in the 19th century.

AB208. Billington, Ray A. **The Protestant crusade, 1800–1860.** N.Y., 1938. Landmark in the study of reactions to Roman Catholic and other immigration, by a Protestant who achieves objectivity, perhaps to the extent of being insufficiently critical of certain immigrant actions. [WG]

AB209. Weinberg, Albert K. **Manifest destiny.** Baltimore, 1935. Learned treatment of this major theme in U. S. history. More concerned with the ideas involved than the way they were carried out.

AB210. Zahler, Helene S. **Eastern workingmen and national land policy, 1829–1862.** N.Y., 1941. Important role of the eastern worker in the fight for free land.

AB211. Stephenson, George M. **The political history of the public lands from 1840 to 1862.** Boston, 1917. Combines legislative history of public land laws during the period with a study of the growing sentiment favoring free land. Includes a detailed history of the homestead movement, with particular attention to free land as a political issue between 1850 and 1860. [JHF]

AB212. Mathews, Lois K. **The expansion of New England: the spread of New England settlement and institutions to the Mississippi River, 1620–1865.** N.Y., 1909. An attempt to ascertain the role of New England in developing the frontier. Seems to exaggerate New England influence in the old Northwest.

AB213. Stillwell, Lewis D. **Migration from Vermont (1776–1860).** Montpelier, 1937. Good study of the reasons for migration: the embargo of 1808, the War of 1812, exhaustion of natural resources (particularly timber), superior attractiveness of western lands. Shows that not all Vermonters went west, some went south.

AB214. Hunter, Louis C. **Steamboats on the western rivers: an economic and technological history.** Cambridge, Mass., 1949. Treats virtually every aspect of the impact of the steamboat on life in the West, including technological problems related to operation of the steamboat as well as business problems concerning its use.

AB215. Gregg, Josiah. **Commerce of the prairies.** Ed. by Max L. Moorhead. Norman, 1954. The classic of the Santa Fe trade by one who spent nearly ten years in it; first published in 1844.

AB216. Graebner, Norman A. **Empire on the Pacific.** N.Y., 1955. Stresses U. S. desire for trade in the Pacific as the reason for adding the West Coast to the U.S.

AB217. Parkman, Francis. **The Oregon trail.** Modern library ed., N.Y., 1949. Classic account by an observer who became a great historian.

AB218. De Voto, Bernard A. **Across the wide Missouri.** Boston, 1947. A richly illustrated work, enlivened with reproductions of sketches and paintings by observers of the western scene in the 1830's. Text is largely concerned with the fur trade and life of the mountain men.

AB219. Cleland, Robert G. **This reckless breed of men: the trappers and fur traders of the Southwest.** N.Y., 1950. Shows that mountain men were in this region as well as farther north.

AB220. De Voto, Bernard A. **The year of decision, 1846.** Boston, 1943. Brilliant recreation of the striking events of the period which added a vast territory to the U.S.

AB221. Smith, Justin H. **The annexation of Texas.** 2 v. N.Y., 1911. Based on exhaustive research, this book justifies the Texas revolt against Santa Anna's despotism, and maintains that by 1844 sentiment in the United States for annexation of Texas was "largely non-partisan." Stresses British and French interest in Texan independence of the United States.

AB222. ——. **The war with Mexico.** 2 v. N.Y., 1919. Authoritative study by the closest student of the subject. Contends that the United States was justified in going to war, and denies that Polk wanted the war in order to seize California. The author is a strong partisan of General Scott.

AB223. Caughey, John W. **Gold is the cornerstone.** Berkeley, 1948. Fresh treatment of a familiar theme, with special attention to the economic, social, political, and cultural results of the gold discoveries.

AB224. Ellison, William H. **A self-governing dominion: California, 1849–1860.** Berkeley, 1950. A volume in the *Chronicles of California* series, emphasizing the political history of the state during its hectic first years. Notable for its balanced judgment of men and events in this emotional period.

AB225. Cole, Arthur C. **The era of the Civil War, 1848–1870.** Springfield, Ill., 1919. Deals with nearly all aspects of Illinois life in these years.

AB226. Overton, Richard C. **Burlington west: a colonization history of the Burlington Railroad.** Cambridge, Mass., 1941. Shows problems the railroad had in taking over the properties legally belonging to it and then disposing of them to settlers. The Burlington seemed to be shrewder than competitors in attracting buyers.

AB227. Gates, Paul W. **The Illinois Central Railroad and its colonization work.** Cambridge, Mass., 1934. Illuminating study of the work of the railroad in fostering immigration from Europe and eastern United States to Illinois, and its participation in the political and economic transformation of the state.

AB228. ——. **Fifty million acres: conflicts over Kansas land policy, 1854–1890.** Ithaca, 1954. Draws attention away from slavery and granger hostility to monopoly; stresses federal practices in disposing of land as a major factor in Kansas unrest. A learned work by one of the keenest students of U. S. agricultural history.

AB229. Cole, Arthur C. **The Whig party in the South.** Washington, 1913. An authoritative study concentrating on the period from Jackson's administration to the death of Clay. The latter comes off rather tarnished in the author's treatment.

AB230. Isely, Jeter A. **Horace Greeley and the Republican party, 1853–1861: a study of the New York Tribune.** Princeton, 1947. Shows the impact of Greeley on the young Republican party.

AB231. Franklin, John H. **From slavery to freedom: a history of American Negroes.** See *Y47.*

AB232. Jenkins, William S. **Pro-slavery thought in the old South.** Chapel Hill, 1935. Excellent survey of the literature defending slavery.

AB233. Barnes, Gilbert H. **The antislavery impulse, 1830–1844.** N.Y., 1933. A turning point in the study of the anti-slavery movement, emphasizing the impact of religious revivalism under Charles G. Finney and the roles of Theodore D. Weld, James G. Birney, and Arthur and Lewis Tappan at the expense of William Lloyd Garrison. [WG]

AB234. Siebert, Wilbur H. **The underground railroad from slavery to freedom.** N.Y., 1898. Detailed account of the personalities who aided runaway slaves to freedom. The author consulted many of the survivors who had participated as agents in the underground railroad. Includes a chapter on the life of escaped Negroes in Canada.

AB235. Osterweis, Rollin G. **Romanticism and nationalism in the old South.** New Haven, 1949. Psychology of the South on the eve of the Civil War. Stresses those features in education, literature, and social customs which expressed the region's nationalism and romanticism.

AB236. Phillips, Ulrich B. **American Negro slavery.** N.Y., 1918. This work, by one of the most learned students of the old South, is considered traditional in its interpretation of slavery, particularly in ascribing to the plantation a civilizing influence on the lives of Negroes.

AB237. ——. **Life and labor in the old South.** Boston, 1929. An excellent picture of the pre-Civil War South.

AB238. Bancroft, Frederic A. **Slave-trading in the old South.** Baltimore, 1931. Pioneer work by one of the most erudite students of southern history. Paints a more somber picture of slave society than Phillips does.

AB239. Eaton, Clement. **Freedom of thought in the old South.** Durham, 1940. Distinguished historical treatment of a topic of major importance. [GFH]

AB240. Russel, Robert R. **Economic aspects of southern sectionalism, 1840–1861.** Urbana, 1929. Emphasizes the South's attempts to achieve economic independence of the North.

AB241. Nichols, Roy F. **The Democratic machine, 1850–1854.** N.Y., 1923. Particularly valuable in showing the forces bearing upon the election of 1852. Clarifies a murky period of party history.

AB242. ——. **The disruption of American democracy.** N.Y., 1948. Deals with the five years preceding the Civil War. Out of a vast fund of knowledge, describes the breakup of the Democratic party. The author believes that this party was the only nationalizing factor in politics, and with its disruption war was inevitable.

AB243. Foner, Philip S. **Business and slavery: the New York merchants and the irrepressible conflict.** Chapel Hill, 1941. Valuable in showing how the merchants of New York, intimately bound up with the economy of the southern states, gradually moved from a position of compromise and accommodation to one of resentment and condemnation of southern behavior and ideology by 1860.

AB244. Malin, James C. **John Brown and the legend of fifty-six.** Philadelphia, 1942. Extensive examination of the history of Kansas in 1856 and rejection of the legends that have been built up about Brown's motives for going to Kansas and the part he played in antislavery struggles there. Notable for its methodology and discussion of work of other students of Brown. [JHF]

AB245. Van Vleck, George W. **The panic of 1857: an analytical study.** N.Y., 1943. Relates the panic to important economic changes occurring all over the globe.

AB246. Craven, Avery O. **The coming of the Civil War.** N.Y., 1942. Strong presentation of the southern side. Psychological factors are emphasized; fanaticism, South and North, is assigned much of the blame for the conflict, with abolitionists assigned the largest share.

AB247. ——. **The repressible conflict, 1830–1861.** Baton Rouge, 1939. An attempt to prove that there was nothing in the soil, climate, or population of the South to produce ante-bellum unity, and that the unity was achieved by the persistence of abolitionist attacks.

AB248. Baringer, William E. **Lincoln's rise to power.** Boston, 1937. Lively study of the political maneuvers that lifted Lincoln from relative obscurity to the presidency. Shows that a group of western politicians helped Lincoln, one of the shrewdest among them, to win the prize at the Republican convention in Chicago in 1860.

AB249. Luthin, Reinhard H. **The first Lincoln campaign.** Cambridge, Mass., 1944. Study of the campaign and election of 1860, with particular attention to the strategy for victory as conceived by the Republican party. Depicts Lincoln as an astute politician whose conduct of the campaign was as important to his victory as the disruption of the Democratic party. [JHF]

AB250. Crenshaw, Ollinger. **The slave states in the presidential election of 1860.** Baltimore, 1945. Careful state-by-state examination of the campaign in the South, with analysis of the important issues.

AB251. Dumond, Dwight L. **The secession movement, 1860–1861.** N.Y., 1931. Gives much attention to the several conventions held in 1860 and the manner in which the election precipitated secession.

AB252. Donald, David H. **Lincoln reconsidered.** N.Y., 1956. Collection of stimulating studies, not all directly connected with Lincoln. They add much to the knowledge of Lincoln as a politician, Grant's military thinking, the cultural and social milieu of the abolitionists, and Lincoln's relations with the radicals.

AB253. Beale, Howard K. "What historians have said about the causes of the Civil War." Social Science Research Council, **Bulletin 54** (N.Y., 1946), pp. 53–102. Very useful summary of the changing views of historians from the period of the war itself to date of publication.

AB254. Smith, Edward C. **The borderland in the Civil War.** N.Y., 1927. Careful study of a crucial region, control of which probably would have meant victory for the South.

AB255. Shannon, Fred A. **The organization and administration of the Union army, 1861–1865.** 2 v. Cleveland, 1928. The standard treatment of procedures adopted to equip and feed northern troops; inclined to feature the mistakes of administrators (of which there were many). Well-written; much valuable material.

AB256. Hesseltine, William B. **Lincoln and the war governors.** N.Y., 1948. Significant contribution to the literature of the Civil War. Shows that, as the Federal government was heavily dependent upon the states for men and supplies, in the end Lincoln subordinated their governors to the Fed. govt.

AB257. Catton, Bruce. **Mr. Lincoln's army.** N.Y., 1951. Trials of the Army of the Potomac and Lincoln's replacement of McClellan, its commander.

AB258. ——. **Glory road: the bloody route from Fredericksburg to Gettysburg.** N.Y., 1952. Second in the trilogy recounting the adventures of the Army of the Potomac in campaigns of late 1862 and early 1863.

AB259. ——. **A stillness at Appomattox.** N.Y., 1953. Final volume of the three devoted to the Army of the Potomac. Graphically describes the last months of the war and Lee's surrender, with emphasis on the man in the ranks. Shows careful research.

AB260. Wiley, Bell I. **The life of Johnny Reb.** N.Y., 1943. Deals almost exclusively with the common soldier of the Confederacy; examines his understanding of the war's aims, his hardships and morale, and his effectiveness as a fighting man.

AB261. ——. **The life of Billy Yank.** N.Y., 1951. Exhaustive study of the common soldier of the Union, his problems and efforts to overcome them.

AB262. ——. **Southern Negroes, 1861–1865.** New Haven, 1938. Contends that loyalty of Negroes to masters frequently depended on the character of the relationship existing before the war, and that unfaithfulness was more common than earlier students believed.

AB263. Quarles, Benjamin. **The Negro in the Civil War.** Boston, 1953. Illuminates a neglected aspect of the conflict, the role of some 180,000 Negroes in Northern forces.

AB264. Baxter, James P., III. **The introduction of the ironclad warship.** Cambridge, Mass., 1933. Traces the evolution of the armored warship, particularly the changing policies of the British and U. S. governments which encouraged and facilitated the introduction of these vessels, whose first test of strength was at Hampton Roads in 1862.

AB265. Monaghan, Jay. **Civil war on the western border, 1854–1865.** Boston, 1955. Life and war in the area from the Indian Territory to Nebraska. Insists strongly that events there were important in the outcome of the Civil War.

AB266. Adams, Ephraim D. **Great Britain and the American Civil War.** 2 v. London and N.Y., 1925. The most comprehensive study of Britain's thought and action, using much material not previously available. Emphasizes support of English liberals for the North. Some of the author's statements have been modified by later studies, but this work is still indispensable.

AB267. Owsley, Frank L. **King Cotton diplomacy: foreign relations of the Confederate States of America.** 2nd ed., Chicago, 1959.

AB268. Richardson, James D., ed. **A compilation of the messages and papers of** the Confederacy, including the diplomatic correspondence, 1861–1865. 2 v. Nashville, 1904.

AB269. Livermore, Thomas L. **Numbers and losses in the Civil War in America, 1861–1865.** 2nd ed., N.Y., 1901. First attempt to present a definitive statement and still one of the most reliable sources on Civil War enlistments and casualties. Contains valuable information on numbers engaged in principal battles, but is poor on numbers of wounded and deserters.

AB270. Randall, James G. **The Civil War and reconstruction.** N.Y., 1937. Exhaustive work that contains several background chapters on the ante-bellum period, devotes most space to the various aspects of the Civil War, and less than one-fourth rather conventionally to reconstruction.

AB271. Eaton, Clement. **A history of the southern Confederacy.** N.Y., 1954. Good study of the Confederacy at war. Interest is centered on economic and social conditions behind the lines, especially the heroic struggle to finance the conflict.

AB272. Owsley, Frank L. **States' rights in the Confederacy.** Chicago, 1925. The author's thesis is that over-emphasis on states' rights interfered with the Confederate war effort and was a principal factor in defeat.

AB273. Robinson, William M., Jr. **Justice in grey: a history of the judicial system of the Confederate States of America.** Cambridge, Mass., 1941.

1865–1900

AB274. Fleming, Walter L., ed. **Documentary history of reconstruction.** 2 v. Cleveland, 1906–07.

AB275. Beale, Howard K. **The critical year: a study of Andrew Johnson and reconstruction.** N.Y., 1930. Account of the critical year 1866 and the manner in which Republican radicals gained control of the party machine, with emphasis on economic factors in reconstruction. Favors Johnson.

AB276. Milton, George F. **The age of hate: Andrew Johnson and the radicals.** N.Y., 1930. Johnson is the hero of this dramatic narrative, written by a skilled journalist. Emphasis is mainly on personalities.

AB277. Hesseltine, William B. **Confederate leaders in the new South.** Baton Rouge, 1950. A study of nearly 600 prominent figures in the post-Civil War South. Contrary to traditional interpretation, the author argues that ex-Confederates reestablished their leadership despite restrictions laid down by the reconstruction program.

AB278. Woody, Robert H., and Francis B. Simkins. **South Carolina during reconstruction.** Chapel Hill, 1932. One of the better books on the period. In addition to narrating political developments, it goes into detail on economic and social aspects of the era, and the continuing impact of reconstruction on the mind of the South.

AB279. Woodward, C. Vann. **Reunion and reaction: the compromise of 1877 and the end of reconstruction.** Boston, 1951. Argues that Republicans close to Hayes, conservative southerners, and northern railroad leaders (anxious for government subsidy) entered into a political-economic agreement which brought an end to reconstruction.

AB280. Buck, Paul H. **The road to reunion, 1865–1900.** Boston, 1938. Discusses the forces promoting reconciliation between the North and South after the Civil War. Opposes the familiar view of continuing animosity between the two sections.

AB281. Robbins, Roy M. **Our landed heritage: the public domain, 1776–1936.** Princeton, 1942. Synthesis of the history of public lands. A more detailed treatment of such questions as flood control, water power, and conservation than the following.

AB282. Hibbard, B. H. **A history of the public land policies.** N.Y., 1924.

AB283. Dick, Everett N. **The sod house frontier, 1854–1890.** N.Y., 1937. Pioneer life on the western prairie; little concerned with politics. Descriptive, not interpretative.

AB284. Webb, Walter P. **The great plains.** Boston, 1931. Original study of adaptation to a new environment by people accustomed to a timbered, well-watered region. Credits the Colt revolver, barbed wire, and the windmill as being chiefly responsible for the white man's conquest of this western area.

AB285. Malin, James C. **The grassland of North America.** Lawrence, Kan., 1947. Attempts to tie together the natural sciences and social sciences; literary style is difficult.

AB286. Osgood, Ernest S. **The day of the cattleman.** Minneapolis, 1929. Deals with the range cattle industry of the Northwest from the 1850's to the end of World War I. Especially good on economic influences of this industry.

AB287. Pelzer, Louis. **The cattlemen's frontier: a record of the trans-Mississippi cattle industry from oxen trains to pooling companies, 1850–1890.** Glendale, Calif., 1936. Particularly good on the role of the cattle barons from the end of the 1870's, their business ideas and frequent unbusinesslike behavior. Discusses the boom psychology which led to collapse in 1887.

AB288. Dale, Edward E. **The range cattle industry.** Norman, 1930. Especially useful for description and statistical information. Stresses relations between cattlemen and the government, as well as with the Indians; is not a story of everyday life on the range. Material on the industry in Oklahoma is particularly valuable.

AB289. Collier, John C. **The Indians of the Americas.** N.Y., 1947. The author, formerly commissioner of Indian affairs, writes with special authority on Indians in the United States. He notes with shame the maltreatment of these natives by the white man, and describes improvements in their lot in the 20th century.

AB290. Jackson, Helen H. **A century of dishonor.** N.Y., 1881. A plea for more humane treatment of the Indian, which became a classic. Did much to awaken people to the need for a reformation of the government's Indian policy.

AB291. Quiett, Glenn C. **Pay dirt: a panorama of American gold-rushes.** N.Y., 1936. Colorful, detailed narrative of the discovery of gold in western United States, with emphasis on the dramatic.

AB292. Shinn, Charles H. **Mining camps: a study in American frontier government.** N.Y., 1885. A classic on life in the western mining camps and methods used to preserve a stable society.

AB293. Nevins, Allan. **Hamilton Fish: the inner history of the Grant administration.** N.Y., 1936. Less of a biography than a detailed political narrative of these years. Praises Fish for rescuing Grant from disaster in foreign relations.

AB294. Ross, Earle D. **The liberal Republican movement.** N.Y., 1919. Careful study of the revolt against Republican orthodoxy in the 1870's.

AB295. Haynes, Frederick E. **Social politics in the United States.** N.Y., 1924. Summarizes reform movements from the Civil War to date of publication, arguing that the function of third parties was to advance social progress. Does not satisfactorily relate economic forces to new political patterns.

AB296. Buck, Solon J. **The granger movement: a study of agricultural organization and its political, economic, and social manifestations, 1870–1880.** Cambridge, Mass., 1913. The authoritative study in this field.

AB297. Hicks, John D. **The Populist revolt.** Minneapolis, 1931. The most comprehensive treatment of this theme. Author contends that the Populist movement prepared the way for reforms which, though opposed at first, were eventually accepted.

AB298. Destler, Chester M. **American radicalism, 1865–1901.** New London, 1946. Sympathetic to the aims and procedures of Populism, which the author sharply distinguishes from European radicalism. His demonstration of continuity in radical currency programs is convincing. Particularly favors Henry D. Lloyd, critic of John D. Rockefeller.

AB299. Miller, William, and Thomas C. Cochran. **The age of enterprise: a social history of industrial America.** N.Y., 1942. The impact of industrialism on U. S. society. Chief theme is role of the businessman. Especially good on the 19th century.

AB300. Burlingame, Roger. **Engines of democracy: inventions and society in mature America.** N.Y., 1940. Popular, illustrated work on technological development, mainly since the Civil War. Stresses the social background and effects on national growth.

AB301. Kirkland, Edward C. **Men, cities and transportation: a study of New England history, 1820–1900.** 2 v. Cambridge, Mass., 1948. Special attention to the impact of new modes of transportation on urban life. Also discusses management, labor, and relations of railroads to government.

AB302. Riegel, Robert E. **The story of the western railroads.** N.Y., 1926. Dependable narrative of construction, pooling agreements, and system building. Its best sections deal with the region between the Mississippi and the Rockies.

AB303. Mitchell, Broadus. **The rise of cotton mills in the South.** Baltimore, 1921. Excellent study of the early history of this important industry in the South, especially in North and South Carolina.

AB304. Adams, Henry, and Charles F. Adams, Jr. **Chapters of Erie and other essays.** Boston, 1871. Sharp attack on the stock speculators and railroad wreckers who despoiled the Erie. One of the most noted examples in the literature of exposure of business malpractice in the United States.

AB305. Rister, Carl C. **Oil! Titan of the Southwest.** Norman, 1949. History of the discovery of oil and development of the industry. The author is especially interested in early discoveries; the men and corporations prominently identified with oil are fairly treated.

AB306. Giddens, Paul H. **The birth of the oil industry.** N.Y., 1938. First ten years of a fabulous industry, which in that brief time attained an export value second only to cotton. This work of careful research is a story of oil in northwestern Pennsylvania.

AB307. ——. **Standard Oil Company (Indiana): oil pioneer of the Middle West.** N.Y., 1955. Detailed narrative of one of the largest oil companies, touching on important advances in technology, the impact on life in town and country, attitudes of the public toward business, and the promotion of more democratic relationships between management and labor.

AB308. Lewis, Oscar. **The big four: the story of Huntington, Stanford, Hopkins, and Crocker, and of the building of the Central Pacific.** N.Y., 1938. Chiefly a biographical study; not a history of the railroad.

AB309. Josephson, Matthew. **The politicos, 1865–1896.** N.Y., 1938. Study of political leaders of the generation. The thesis is that this period marked "the absolute triumph of a single group or class, the industrial capitalists."

AB310. Merrill, Horace S. **Bourbon democracy of the Middle West, 1865–1896.** Baton Rouge, 1953. Conservative Democrats in the Middle West as guardians of big business and big finance. Grover Cleveland is represented as the symbol of virtues dear to the heart of big business.

AB311. Nye, Russel B. **Midwestern Progressive politics: a historical study of its origins and development, 1870–1950.** East Lansing, 1951. Portrayal of midwestern radicalism as compounded out of its geography, culture, and economic and social history.

AB312. Dearing, Mary R. **Veterans in politics: the story of the G. A. R.** Baton Rouge, 1952. Explains the role of Civil War veterans as a pressure group in winning pensions, preference, and other special favors.

AB313. Kirkland, Edward C. **Dream and thought in the business community, 1860–1900.** Ithaca, 1956. Emphasis is on what businessmen thought and said about politics, education, their vocation, homes, etc. The author does not present businessmen as great benefactors of society.

AB314. Cochran, Thomas C. **Railroad leaders, 1845–1890: the business mind in action.** Cambridge, Mass., 1953. Analysis of correspondence of 61 executives to ascertain their attitudes on competition, labor, government control, politics, etc.

AB315. Fine, Sidney. **Laissez faire and the general-welfare state: a study of conflict in American thought, 1865–1901.** Ann Arbor, 1956. Good survey of thought on both sides of a question fundamental in U. S. history.

AB316. Benson, Lee. **Merchants, farmers, and railroads: railroad regulation and New York politics, 1850–1887.** Cambridge, Mass., 1955. As against the view that pressure from western farmers was almost entirely responsible for regulation of railroads in this period, the author argues that New York City merchants played a leading role in elimination of discriminatory arrangements by the carriers. Though the thesis is exaggerated, this work is a useful corrective to the familiar interpretation.

AB317. Myers, Margaret G. **The New York money market: origins and development.** N.Y., 1931. First volume of a series of four, edited by B. H. Beckhart, dealing with the New York money market. This one covers the period prior to 1913; a thorough treatment. [SIP]

AB318. Boudin, Louis B. **Government by judiciary.** N.Y., 1932. Contends that the Supreme Court arrogated to itself excessive powers in the U. S. scheme of government; an indictment of that assumption of powers.

AB319. Ware, Norman J. **The labor movement in the United States, 1860–1895.** N.Y., 1929. Primarily a study of the Knights of Labor, its rise and decline. The author maintains that an important reason for its decline was the decision of skilled workers to go it alone in the A. F. of L.

AB320. David, Henry. **The history of the Haymarket affair.** N.Y., 1936. Critical study of the tragic episode in Chicago in 1886, presenting the anarchist side more sympathetically than previous writers.

AB321. Lindsey, Almont. **The Pullman strike.** Chicago, 1942. A sympathetic appraisal of the strike.

AB322. McMurry, Donald L. **Coxey's army: a study of the industrial army movement of 1894.** Boston, 1929. Entertaining account of a pressure group calling attention to victims of the depression. Shows that General Coxey not only had a flair for publicity, but also had a program—money inflation and government road building on a large scale to employ the jobless.

AB323. Saveth, Edward N. **American historians and European immigrants, 1875–1925.** N.Y., 1948. Important contribution to U. S. historiography, analyzing the attitudes of historians toward immigrants, especially those of the 19th century. Claims that most historians ignored immigrants or were biased if they did write about them.

AB324. Riis, Jacob. **How the other half lives.** N.Y., 1890. Famous work which stimulated the social conscience of a whole generation by reminding the complacently prosperous of the way of life among the many impoverished.

AB325. Abell, Aaron I. **The urban impact on American Protestantism, 1865–1900.** Cambridge, Mass., 1943. Argues that Roman Catholics were more interested than Protestants in the lot of the working man; underestimates the concern of Protestantism with social welfare. Protestant efforts in behalf of social progress would have been clearer had the story been carried beyond 1900.

AB326. Hopkins, Charles H. **The rise of the social gospel in American Protestantism, 1865–1915.** New Haven, 1940. Excellent study of the transformation in Protestant thinking about responsibility of individuals for social welfare. Argues that it was the responsibility of the church and other institutions to draw attention to social evils and urge programs for their eradication.

AB327. May, Henry F. **Protestant churches and industrial America.** N.Y., 1949. Concerns interrelation of Protestantism and industrial development after the Civil War.

AB328. Faulkner, Harold U. **Politics, reform, and expansion, 1890–1900.** N.Y., 1959. An able synthesis of scholarship. [GFH]

AB329. Mann, Arthur. **Yankee reformers in the urban age.** Cambridge, Mass., 1954. Shows the continuity of the reform tradition in New England (mainly Boston) to the close of the 19th century.

AB330. Patton, Clifford W. **The battle for municipal reform: mobilization and attack, 1875 to 1900.** Washington, 1940. A small book on a large topic. Bears out James Bryce's opinion of municipal government as the United States' greatest failure (in the post-Civil War period), and shows what reformers attempted to do about it. As their victories came later, they are not covered.

AB331. Pierce, Bessie L. **A history of Chicago.** N.Y., 1937 ff. One of the best urban histories produced in the United States. To be complete in 3 v.

AB332. Still, Bayrd. **Milwaukee: the history of a city.** Madison, 1948. The most satisfactory history of this city. Draws attention to the importance of municipal institutions in U. S. democracy.

AB333. McKelvey, Blake F. **Rochester.** 3 v. Cambridge, Mass., 1945–56. Stresses the efforts of this upstate New York city to raise the whole level of urban life. Excellent example of scholarship in urban history.

1900 to the Present

AB334. Steffens, J. Lincoln. **The shame of the cities.** N.Y., 1904. Vibrant description of graft and corruption in many leading U. S. communities, by an outstanding muckraker. Indicates the connections between political organizations and business spokesmen. [BB]

AB335. Regier, Cornelius C. **The era of the muckrakers.** Chapel Hill, 1932. A temperate, well-written book which proves that muckrakers deserve a dignified historical treatment. Shows how writers came to concentrate for over a decade on corruption in business and politics that accompanied industrialization, and records decline in muckraking about 1911. [BB]

AB336. Aaron, Daniel. **Men of good hope: a story of American progressives.** N.Y., 1951. From Emerson and Theodore Parker to "Theodore Roosevelt and Brooks Adams: pseudo-progressives."

AB337. Filler, Louis. **Crusaders for American liberalism.** N.Y., 1939. Excellent reporting on leading muckrakers and their motivation during the early 20th century. Includes a useful bibliography, and a chronology which dates muckraking activities from 1901 to 1917. [BB]

AB338. Croly, Herbert D. **The promise of American life.** N.Y., 1909. Author warned that the policy of laissez-faire and drift would lead to power for big industry and big finance and to degradation of the masses. Progressives, he consequently believed, must support a program of positive and comprehensive state and federal intervention on all economic fronts. [BB]

AB339. Goldman, Erik F. **Rendezvous with destiny.** N.Y., 1952. Excellent treatment of reform movements from the years after the Civil War through the New Deal and Fair Deal. [JEW]

AB340. Hofstadter, Richard. **The age of reform.** N.Y., 1955. Mature, well-written study of reform movements from Populism through the New Deal. [JEW]

AB341. ———. **The American political tradition and the men who made it.** N.Y., 1948. Excellent analysis of politics, political parties, and political theory through a biographical approach. [JEW]

AB342. Josephson, Matthew. **The president makers: the culture of politics and leadership in an age of enlightenment, 1896–1919.** N.Y., 1940. More of a biographical study than a history in the ordinary sense. Though the author devotes considerable space to party struggles in Congress, his primary interest is in personal conflict.

AB343. Mowry, George E. **Theodore Roosevelt and the Progressive movement.** Madison, 1946. Logical and readable work presenting the Progressive movement as a great social reaction involving moral, political, economic, and intellectual revolt. [BB]

AB344. ———. **The California Progressives.** Berkeley, 1951. Lucid, objective analysis of one of the most important segments of progressivism and of state Progressive leaders. Shows that leadership was supplied by young middle-class and professional men. Hiram Johnson and the 1916 presidential election are ably discussed. [BB]

AB345. Faulkner, Harold U. **The quest for social justice.** N.Y., 1931. Still one of the best general accounts of the influence of the Progressive movement on all phases of life. [JEW]

AB346. ———. **The decline of laissez faire.** N.Y., 1951. Excellent and convenient survey of changes in the United States between 1900 and 1917, particularly with regard to the growth of business and the increasing interventionist role of the government. [JEW]

AB347. Chamberlain, John. **Farewell to reform.** N.Y., 1932. A lament for the passing of the reform spirit identified with Henry D. Lloyd and his successors. In a statement published the next year the author was not so certain of the demise of reform.

AB348. Addams, Jane. **Twenty years at Hull-House.** N.Y., 1910. Account of a noted settlement house in Chicago by one of the nation's most distinguished social workers.

AB349. ———. **The second twenty years at Hull-House.** N.Y., 1930.

AB350. Link, Arthur S. **Woodrow Wilson and the progressive era, 1910–1917.** N.Y., 1954. Excellent general study of the Wilson reform program and policies, both domestic and foreign. [JEW]

AB351. Faulkner, Harold U. **From Versailles to the New Deal.** New Haven, 1950.

Political developments during the Harding-Coolidge-Hoover period. [JEW]

AB352. Mecklin, John M. **The Ku Klux Klan: a study of the American mind.** N.Y., 1924. Study of the Klan in the 1920's. Though the author is critical of it, he shows a lack of bitterness.

AB353. Schriftgiesser, Karl. **This was normalcy: an account of party politics during twelve Republican years, 1920–1932.** Boston, 1948. Politically sophisticated work on the party battles of the 1920's. An effective introduction to politics of the era, it adds little in the way of facts or interpretation to existing literature. [BB]

AB354. MacKay, Kenneth C. **The Progressive movement of 1924.** N.Y., 1947. Account of the "progressivism" which sought to weld together the farmer, labor, and reform elements of the country, and was in effect a bridge between earlier Progressives and the New Dealers. Shows the difficulties confronting third-party movements in the United States.

AB355. Morgan, Edmund M., and G. Louis Joughin. **The legacy of Sacco and Vanzetti.** N.Y., 1948. Examination of one of the most important criminal cases in modern U. S. history.

AB356. Lynd, Robert S., and Helen M. Lynd. **Middletown.** N.Y., 1929. Classic study of a town (Muncie) in Indiana, showing the class structure and the dependence of the mass of citizens upon the business leadership of a few. Indicates that an earlier American democratic spirit is not so strong here.

AB357. ———. **Middletown in transition.** N.Y., 1937. The community in the depression.

AB358. Myers, William S., and Walter H. Newton. **The Hoover administration.** N.Y., 1936. This book, written from Hoover's diary, speeches, and documents, contends that the fundamental causes of the great depression lay in World War I, that final recovery was just around the corner in the summer of 1932, and would have come had Hoover been reelected. [BB]

AB359. President's Research Committee on Social Trends. **Recent social trends in the United States.** 2 v. N.Y., 1933. A storehouse of information on various aspects of U. S. life.

AB360. Nevins, Allan. **The United States in a chaotic world.** New Haven, 1950. Brief but excellent survey of U. S. participation in world affairs, 1918–33. [JEW]

AB361. Galbraith, John K. **The great crash, 1929.** Boston, 1955. Brief but excellent account, written long enough after the event to attain substantial objectivity. [JEW]

AB362. Bellush, Bernard. **Franklin D. Roosevelt as governor of New York.** N.Y., 1955. A laudatory, though not uncritical, work indicating that many New Deal policies were clearly anticipated or explicitly worked out during Roosevelt's four years as governor, 1928–32.

AB363. Brogan, Denis W. **The era of Franklin D. Roosevelt.** New Haven, 1950. Brief account of New Deal policies and U. S. participation in World War II. Shows a New Deal bias. [JEW]

AB364. Wecter, Dixon. **The age of the great depression, 1929–1941.** N.Y., 1948. Readable analysis of effects of the depression and the New Deal on all phases of U. S. life. Especially strong concerning the social impact of New Deal policies. [JEW]

AB365. Rauch, Basil. **The history of the New Deal, 1933–1938.** N.Y., 1944. Brief but good summary of this era. [JEW]

AB366. Mitchell, Broadus. **Depression decade.** N.Y., 1947. Sharp and critical evaluation of causes of the depression and the problems it intensified. Especially valuable in its treatment of social security, relief, and public housing. [JEW]

AB367. Saloutos, Theodore, and John D. Hicks. **Agricultural discontent in the Middle West, 1900–1939.** Madison, 1951. Full and informative analysis of the causes of discontent and attempts to alleviate it. Especially useful for its treatment of the farm bloc. A continuation of Hicks, *The Populist revolt (AB297).* [JEW]

AB368. Lilienthal, David E. **TVA: democracy on the march.** N.Y., 1944. Narrative by an outstanding participant in the enterprise, who believes that it fulfills, rather than erodes, democratic principles.

AB369. Harris, Herbert. **American labor.** New Haven, 1939. Popular presentation, with emphasis on the newer unions of the New Deal period.

AB370. Perlman, Selig. **Labor in the New Deal decade.** N.Y., 1945. Thoughtful discussion of relationship of the labor movement to the farmer, government, and politics during these years. [JEW]

AB371. Mills, Charles W. **The new men of power.** N.Y., 1948. Critical of modern labor leaders.

AB372. Nelson, Donald M. **Arsenal of democracy: the story of American war production.** N.Y., 1946. Record of a remarkable achievement in feeding the war machine, 1941–45. The author played an important part in this "battle of production."

AB373. Allen, Frederick L. **The big change.** N.Y., 1952. Excellent popular survey of the economic and social changes in 20th century United States as a result of democratizing the economic system. [JEW]

AB374. Galbraith, John K. **American capitalism.** Boston, 1952. Good treatment of U. S. economy as seen five years after the close of World War II. [JEW]

AB375. Cochran, Thomas C. **The American business system: a historical perspective,** 1900–1955. Cambridge, Mass., 1957. Another segment of a study of the mind and actions of U. S. business men, by an author who belongs to a group of scholars attempting an objective appraisal of United States business enterprise.

AB376. Steiner, George A. **Government's role in economic life.** N.Y., 1953. Perhaps the best single volume on post-World War II economic problems and their solution. [JEW]

AB377. Swisher, Carl B. **American constitutional development.** 2nd ed., Boston, 1954. Able exposition of changes in the U. S. constitutional system resulting from the World Wars and the New Deal. [JEW]

AB378. Goldman, Eric F. **The crucial decade.** N.Y., 1956. Thoughtful and readable discussion of critical domestic and foreign issues as they emerged in the 1945–55 decade. Major themes are the consolidation of welfare state policies at home and acceptance of world responsibilities. [JEW]

AB379. Schlesinger, Arthur M., Jr. **The vital center.** Boston, 1949. A New Dealer's discussion of "liberalism" and its opponents on both the left and right. [JEW]

AB380. Lubell, Samuel. **The future of American politics.** N.Y., 1952. Brilliant analysis of the impact of the New Deal on party structure and politics. [JEW]

AB381. ——. **Revolt of the moderates.** N.Y., 1956.

AB382. Donovan, Robert J. **Eisenhower: the inside story.** N.Y., 1956. First-hand account of the Eisenhower administration, by a journalist with access to confidential information.

AB383. Dewhurst, James F., and others. **America's needs and resources: a new survey.** N.Y., 1955.

HISTORIES OF SPECIAL TOPICS

Several areas of productive scholarship in which there are excellent works are omitted here. There are no subsections on political, constitutional, legal, economic, agricultural, transportation, or regional histories; but these are represented in the major chronological groups and in bibliographies cited in this section and in Section B.

Diplomatic, Military, and Naval History

AB384. Foreign affairs bibliography. 3 v. N.Y., 1933–55. See *AH2.*

AB385. Bailey, Thomas A. **A diplomatic history of the American people.** 6th ed., N.Y., 1958. A survey emphasizing the role of U. S. public opinion.

AB386. Bemis, Samuel F. **A diplomatic history of the United States.** 4th ed., N.Y., 1955. Standard survey. [TAB]

AB387. Pratt, Julius W. **A history of United States foreign policy.** N.Y., 1955. A survey with considerable emphasis on policy and procedures. [TAB]

AB388. Moore, John Bassett. **History and digest of international arbitrations.** 6 v. Washington, 1898. Classic compilation of primary materials to 1898. [TAB]

AB389. ——. **A digest of international law.** 8 v. Washington, 1906. An invaluable compilation from the relevant documents, with elaborate cross-references. [TAB]

AB390. Hackworth, Green H. **Digest of international law.** 8 v. Washington, 1940–44. A continuation of *AB389,* in much the same manner. [TAB]

AB391. Stuart, Graham H. **The Department of State: a history of its organization, procedure and personnel.** N.Y., 1949. The only relatively recent survey. [TAB]

AB392. Allen, Harry C. **Great Britain and the United States: a history of Anglo-American relations (1783–1952).** N.Y., 1955. The only relatively recent full-length survey; by an English scholar. [TAB]

AB393. Merk, Frederick. **Albert Gallatin and the Oregon problem.** Cambridge, Mass., 1950. Detailed account of the role of Gallatin in negotiations between England and the United States regarding Oregon. Provides new information about Gallatin and also the important London conference of 1826–27.

AB394. Bemis, Samuel F. **The Latin American policy of the United States.** See *Y179.*

AB395. Whitaker, Arthur P. **The Spanish-American frontier, 1783–1795.** See *Y150.*

AB396. ——. **The Mississippi question, 1795–1803.** N.Y., 1934. Continuation of *AB395.* Besides the complicated diplomacy of the United States, France, and Spain, includes commercial and political developments, and the movement of U. S. pioneers to the southwest. A necessary study for events leading to the Louisiana purchase.

AB397. Bernstein, Harry. **Origins of inter-American interest, 1700–1812.** See *Y168.*

AB398. Griffin, Charles C. **The United States and the disruption of the Spanish empire, 1810–1822.** N.Y., 1937. Able study of the behavior of the United States toward Spain and her rebel colonies, showing the twists and turns of U. S. policy before recognition of their independence.

AB399. Whitaker, Arthur P. **The United States and the independence of Latin America, 1800–1830.** Baltimore, 1941. The most comprehensive study of relations between the United States and Latin America in this period. Emphasizes economic and political factors.

AB400. ——. **The Western Hemisphere idea: its rise and decline.** See *Y177.*

AB401. Perkins, Dexter. **A history of the Monroe doctrine.** See *Y188.*

AB402. Wisan, Joseph E. **The Cuban crisis as reflected in the New York press (1895–1898).** N.Y., 1934. Documented account of events and decisions of this crisis from the outbreak of the Cuban insurrection in 1895 to beginning of the Spanish-American War. The role of the press as a prime instigator of war is emphasized.

AB403. Pratt, Julius W. **Expansionists of 1898.** Baltimore, 1936. Well-written and well-documented analysis of the ideas and forces contributing to the imperialistic psychology that resulted in annexation of Hawaii and the war with Spain. [JEW]

AB404. Millis, Walter. **The martial spirit: a study of our war with Spain.** N.Y., 1931. Popular and very readable account of the causes and conduct of the Spanish-American War. The position of Spain is generously presented, that of the United States sharply criticized. [JEW]

AB405. Gelber, Lionel M. **The rise of Anglo-American friendship: a study in world politics, 1898–1906.** London and N.Y., 1938. Careful examination of the subject, treated especially from the standpoint of governmental policies. Based largely upon official documents and memoirs; little reference to the role of public opinion. [JEW]

AB406. Kennan, George F. **American diplomacy, 1900–1950.** See *AH199.*

AB407. Beale, Howard K. **Theodore Roosevelt and the rise of America to world power.** Baltimore, 1956. Detailed and fair account, showing extensive research. [JEW]

AB408. Miner, Dwight C. **The fight for the Panama route: the story of the Spooner act and the Hay-Herrán treaty.** N.Y., 1940. Detailed study of the many ramifications of the struggle for the Panama Canal Zone—political disputes in the United States and Colombia; negotiations with England (the Hay-Pauncefote treaty), Costa Rica, and Nicaragua; the Panama revolution; and acquisition of the Canal Zone. Especially good on Colombia's side of the controversy.

AB409. Notter, Harley. **The origins of the foreign policy of Woodrow Wilson.** Baltimore, 1937. An accomplished work analyzing the recorded thought of Wilson in order to trace his theories of foreign policy from his earliest years to U. S. entry into World War I. Contains excellent detailed analysis of Wilson's peace efforts of 1916. [BB]

AB410. Millis, Walter. **Road to war: America, 1914–1917.** N.Y., 1935. Severe criticism of the Allied use of high seas power; favorable interpretation of the German and arraignment of Wilsonian diplomacy which led to U. S. intervention. Represents an interpretation rather than research. [BB]

AB411. Tansill, Charles C. **America goes to war.** Boston, 1938. Provocative, authoritative, lucidly written, and thoroughly documented work on U. S. neutrality, 1914–17. Presents the hitherto slighted German side. Reevaluates certain key figures, and indicates that neutral-minded Wilson was misled by House and Lansing. [BB]

AB412. Peterson, Horace C. **Propaganda for war: the campaign against American neutrality, 1914–1917.** Norman, 1939. Objective work on successful British influence in the United States, showing that the U. S. was virtually forced to join the Allies because it had previously surrendered to them all its material, diplomatic, and moral support. Bryan and Hearst emerge with enhanced reputations. [BB]

AB413. May, Ernest F. **The World War and American isolation, 1914–1917.** Cambridge, Mass., 1959. Emphasizes Wilson's concern with U. S. interests, particularly foreign trade; minimizes role of bankers and munitions makers. Gives close attention to U. S. policy as seen through foreign eyes, and notes the impact of this policy on domestic politics in Britain and Germany.

AB414. Bailey, Thomas A. **Woodrow Wilson and the lost peace.** N.Y., 1944. A competent, scholarly, and readable work which, though often critical of Wilson, approves his aims, sees the complexity of his problem, and deplores the losing of the peace. [BB]

AB415. ——. **Woodrow Wilson and the great betrayal.** N.Y., 1945. Covers the period from Wilson's return in July, 1919 through Senate rejection of the peace treaty in March, 1920. Conveys a sense of incredible failure and sordid betrayal; blames Wilson for his stubbornness on reservations and Democrats for alleged killing of the treaty in the house of its friends. [BB]

AB416. Kennan, George F. **Soviet-American relations, 1917–1920.** See *AH147.*

AB417. Hull, Cordell. **The memoirs of Cordell Hull.** 2 v. N.Y., 1948. Extremely important record of the chess game of international politics, written by one of the most important participants. It is, naturally, an exposition intended to justify the author's policies. [JEW]

AB418. Dennett, Tyler. **Americans in eastern Asia: a critical study of the policy of the United States with reference to China, Japan, and Korea in the 19th century.** N.Y., 1922. Holds that U. S. policy has ordinarily not been opportunistic, but has been consistently upheld from the early days.

AB419. Griswold, A. Whitney. **The Far Eastern policy of the United States.** N.Y., 1938. Good, readable account of U. S. policy since 1898. New material taken in part from the Lansing, Marshall, and Knox papers adds greatly to its value. [JEW]

AB420. Fairbank, John K. **The United States and China.** Cambridge, Mass., 1948. Excellent account of U. S.-Chinese relations. The chapters dealing with Chiang Kai-shek's regime are particularly valuable. [JEW]

AB421. Reischauer, Edwin O. **The United States and Japan.** Cambridge, Mass., 1950. Particularly valuable in its treatment of Japanese economic, social, and cultural life, and the problems these factors pose for proponents of democracy in Japan. [JEW]

AB422. Beard, Charles A. **President Roosevelt and the coming of the war.** N.Y., 1948. A revisionist interpretation of Franklin D. Roosevelt's leadership, contending presidential mendacity. Claims that the United States maneuvered Japan into firing the first shot without allowing too much damage to ourselves, and that F. D. R. hid his real intent and concealed his actual views from the public. [BB]

AB423. Tansill, Charles C. **Back door to war: the Roosevelt foreign policy, 1933–1941.** Chicago, 1952. Severe indictment of Roosevelt's policy which, in the author's view, was deliberately designed to get the United States into war on the side of England.

AB424. Langer, William L., and S. Everett Gleason. **The challenge to isolation, 1937–1940.** N.Y., 1952. Objective, detailed study of the diplomatic history of Europe, Asia, and America. The presentation is factual rather than interpretive.

AB425. ——. **The undeclared war, 1940–1941.** N.Y., 1953. Scholarly and definitive analysis of events leading up to America's entry into the war; best book on the subject. [JEW]

AB426. Feis, Herbert. **The road to Pearl Harbor: the coming of the war between the United States and Japan.** Princeton, 1950. Full and objective treatment of the diplomacy that preceded Pearl Harbor. Makes good use of papers and statements of Stimson, Grew, Morgenthau, and Hull, as well as available Japanese sources. [JEW]

AB427. Rauch, Basil. **Roosevelt, from Munich to Pearl Harbor: a study in the creation of a foreign policy.** N.Y., 1950. Argues that Roosevelt was really an internationalist for most of his career, and that after Munich (1938) his concern with domestic problems yielded to intense preoccupation with foreign affairs.

AB428. Morison, Samuel E. **History of United States naval operations in World War II.** See *AG204.*

AB429. McNeill, William H. **America, Britain, and Russia: their cooperation and conflict, 1941–1946.** N.Y., 1953. Good study of the years of cooperation and its breakdown in 1945–46. Emphasizes the complexity of the war's conduct and the problems of making peace. A dispassionate work, but not acutely critical of Communist imperialism.

AB430. Vinacke, Harold M. **The United States and the Far East, 1945–1951.** Stanford, 1952. Short, clear, non-partisan narrative of U. S. policy in China, Japan, and Korea.

AB431. Almond, Gabriel A. **The American people and foreign policy.** N.Y., 1950. Penetrating analysis of U. S. attitudes toward foreign relations and policies. A pioneer work. [JEW]

AB432. Bailey, Thomas A. **The man in the street: the impact of American public opinion on foreign policy.** N.Y., 1948.

AB433. Beard, Charles A. **The idea of national interest: an analytical study in American foreign policy.** N.Y., 1934. Emphasizes material considerations in U. S. foreign policy. The author examines what prominent Americans meant by "national interest" and finds that, though there is a recognizable pattern running through their statements, they vary considerably.

AB434. Osgood, Robert E. **Ideals and self-interest in America's foreign relations: the great transformation of the twentieth century.** Chicago, 1953. Discusses the transformation from isolation through Wilsonian moralistic liberalism to the "realism" or expediency of more recent years. Argues that the latter must serve Christian-liberal-humanitarian ideals.

AB435. Knox, Dudley W. **A history of the United States navy.** Rev. ed., N.Y., 1948. A factual, pro-navy account by a retired naval officer. [TAB]

AB436. Sprout, Harold H., and Margaret T. Sprout. **The rise of American naval power, 1776–1918.** Princeton, 1939. Shows that, despite conservative attitudes, the United States had a naval shield, but not until the later years of the 19th century did she embark on a building program which enabled her to take the offensive.

AB437. ——. **Toward a new order of sea power: American naval policy and the world scene, 1918–1922.** Princeton, 1940. Continuation of *AB436.* This volume centers around the Washington naval conference, and the U. S. proposals and counterproposals, out of which came Anglo-American naval parity and the promise of greater Anglo-American cooperation.

AB438. Davis, George T. **A navy second to none: the development of modern American naval policy.** N.Y., 1940. Full-length study by a competent historian. [TAB]

AB439. Spaulding, Oliver L. **The United States army in war and peace.** N.Y., 1937. A solid treatment of the army as an institution. [TAB]

AB440. Millis, Walter. **Arms and men: a study in American military history.** N.Y., 1956. A broad study by a journalist, with emphasis on the evolution of military policy. [TAB]

Intellectual History

AB441. Curti, Merle E. **The growth of American thought.** N.Y., 1943. 2nd ed., 1951. A pioneer study of U. S. intellectual development; imaginative and comprehensive. Contains extensive bibliography.

AB442. Parrington, Vernon L. **Main currents in American thought.** 3 v. N.Y., 1927–30. Brilliantly written book which exerted considerable influence on scholarship and general thought. Concerned chiefly with literary and political expressions, and sympathetic with Jeffersonian agrarianism. [MEC]

AB443. Cohen, Morris R. **American thought, a critical sketch.** Ed. by Felix S. Cohen. Glencoe, Ill., 1954. Essays, by a great teacher and an original thinker, on U. S. ideas in history, science, law, religion, and aesthetics, as well as on leading technical philosophers and movements of philosophical thought. [MEC]

AB444. Boorstin, Daniel J. **The Americans: the colonial experience.** N.Y., 1958. Stimulating interpretation of U. S. thought, emphasizing its indigenous elements.

AB445. Miller, Perry G. **The New England mind: the seventeenth century.** N.Y., 1939; Cambridge, Mass., 1954. Topical organization of the intellectual structure of 17th century New England under such categories as religion and learning, cosmology, anthropology, and sociology. Erudite and authoritative. [MEC]

AB446. ——. **The New England mind: from colony to province.** Cambridge, Mass., 1953. Using "mind" in the sense of "what was said and done publicly," the author traces chronologically the accommodation to changing conditions in New England of the thought and ideas of representative intellectual leaders. Based on a close analysis of the sources, the work is that of a distinguished scholar for scholars. [MEC]

AB447. Savelle, Max H. **Seeds of liberty: the genesis of the American mind.** N.Y., 1948. Scholarly and readable essays, with attention to chronology and interrelationships, on religion, science, philosophy, economic thought, social and political thought, literature, art, architecture, and music. [MEC]

AB448. Beard, Charles A., and Mary R. Beard. **The American spirit: a study of the idea of civilization in the United States.** N.Y., 1942. Chronological review of opinions of well-known and other writers about civilization in general and its relation to the United States in particular. Claims that these spokesmen maintained that, in contrast with preceding eras and other places, civilization here stood for progressive realization of the potentialities of the common man. [MEC]

AB449. Gabriel, Ralph H. **The course of**

American democratic thought. N.Y., 1940. 2nd ed., 1956. Brilliant and stimulating study of social beliefs, standards, and goals in the United States since 1815, centering in an analysis of the democratic faith in terms of the free individual, fundamental law, the national mission, and illustrated by essays on representative thinkers. [MEC]

AB450. Wiener, Philip P. **Evolution and the founders of American pragmatism.** Cambridge, 1949. The leading scholarly study of the founders of pragmatism in the United States. Thoroughly documented; distinguished by its technical grasp and clarity of expression. [MEC]

AB451. Persons, Stow, ed. **Evolutionary thought in America.** New Haven, 1950. Eleven essays, by well-known authorities, on subjects ranging from the theory of evolution to the impact of evolutionary thought on sociology, political and constitutional tradition, psychological thought, architecture, literature, moral theory, and theology. [MEC]

AB452. Commager, Henry S. **The American mind: an interpretation of American thought and character since the 1880's.** New Haven, 1950. Interpretative study of ways of thought in the United States and their "most revealing manifestations." [MEC]

AB453. White, Morton G. **Social thought in America: the revolt against formalism.** N.Y., 1949. Scholarly treatment, by a philosopher, of pragmatism, legal realism, behaviorism, economic determinism, "the new history," and related protests of the early decades of the 20th century against formal logic and structuralism. [MEC]

AB454. Pearce, Roy H. **The savages of America: a study of the Indian and the idea of civilization.** Baltimore, 1953. A scholarly study of colonial ideas about the Indian, and subsequent images of the Indian, as reflected in social, historical, and imaginative writings. [MEC]

AB455. Wecter, Dixon. **The hero in America: a chronicle of hero-worship.** N.Y., 1941. The roster of heroes includes mainly military figures and politicians, not women, or men in professions and the arts. Shows periods of praise, skepticism, and disparagement on the part of the public.

AB456. Potter, David M. **People of plenty: economic abundance and the American character.** See *A207*.

AB457. Wyllie, Irvin G. **The self-made man in America: the myth of rags to riches.** New Brunswick, 1954. Critical analysis, based on extensive research, of widely accepted ideas about the cult of the self-made man.

Civilization

AB458. Tocqueville, Alexis de. **Democracy in America.** 4 v. London, 1835. Many other eds. Great work by a French aristocrat who visited the United States during the Jackson era. With remarkable insight he discerned the operation of democracy, and clearly foretold its future and significance for aristocratic Europe.

AB459. Bryce, James B., viscount. **The American commonwealth.** 2 v. N.Y., 1888. Other eds. Most important commentary on U. S. government and society since Tocqueville, fifty years earlier. While noting certain weaknesses (particularly local government), Bryce writes with friendliness about the national strength. Like the later Turner, he stresses the influence of the westward movement as a democratizing influence.

AB460. Turner, Frederick J. **The frontier in American history.** N.Y., 1920. Includes the famous essay on "The significance of the frontier in American history" as well as other well-known short pieces by the brilliant author.

AB461. Lerner, Max. **America as a civilization: life and thought in the United States today.** N.Y., 1957. Encyclopedic account of the United States in the 20th century, with frequent excursions into the past.

AB462. Handlin, Oscar. **Race and nationality in American life.** Boston, 1957. Essays on three levels: rational justification, scientific theory, and emotional reaction. [MEC]

AB463. Curti, Merle E. **The roots of American loyalty.** N.Y., 1946. A leading student of U. S. ideas examines "the sources and nature of American patriotism." Emphasis is on the first century of the republic, by the end of which the author believes the main outlines of patriotic thought and feeling were clear.

AB464. Kohn, Hans. **American nationalism: an interpretative essay.** N.Y., 1957. One of the outstanding students in the field makes a successful attempt to discuss some of the chief problems inherent in the complex phenomenon of United States nationalism, and to interpret these in light of national movements in other parts of the world, especially Europe.

Education

AB465. Butts, R. Freeman, and Lawrence A. Cremin. **A history of education in American culture.** N.Y., 1953. The best general history of U. S. education in the context of cultural movements and forces. [MEC]

AB466. Curti, Merle E. **The social ideas of American educators.** N.Y., 1935. Close analysis of men, like Horace Mann, who left the deepest impression on education. Their educational ideas are examined in light of their economic and social beliefs, which turn out on occasion to be more conservative than students have generally imagined.

AB467. Hofstadter, Richard, and Walter P. Metzger. **The development of academic**

freedom in the United States. N.Y., 1955. Best study of this theme; embraces more than its title suggests.

AB468. Bode, Carl J. **The American lyceum, town meeting of the mind.** N.Y., 1956. Good study of an educational institution which did much to popularize culture in the generation before the Civil War; one of the early examples of adult education in the United States outside academic halls.

Literature

AB469. Tyler, Moses C. **A history of American literature.** 2 v. N.Y., 1879. A notable work when it appeared, but not so impressive today. Includes those writers who contributed to the evolution of thought and style during colonial days, and relates literature to politics.

AB470. Literary history of the United States. Ed. by Robert E. Spiller, Willard Thorp, Thomas H. Johnson, and Henry S. Canby. 3 v. N.Y., 1948. Rev. ed., 1953. Essays, by more than fifty scholars, on literary figures and movements of thought; chronologically arranged, with very useful bibliography. [MEC]

AB471. Matthiessen, Francis O. **American renaissance.** N.Y., 1941. Brilliant interpretation of U. S. culture in the 1840's and 1850's. Far more analytical than the volumes of Van Wyck Brooks.

AB472. Mott, Frank L. **American journalism: a history of newspapers in the United States through 260 years, 1690 to 1950.** N.Y., 1950. Best study of the U. S. press. A great deal has been compressed into one volume, and this done skilfully and with proportion.

AB473. ——. **A history of American magazines.** 4 v. Cambridge, Mass., 1938–57. The standard work. Shows the importance of magazines in U. S. civilization.

AB474. Lehmann-Haupt, Hellmut, Ruth S. Granniss, and Lawrence C. Wroth. **The book in America: a history of the making, the selling, and the collecting of books in the United States.** N.Y., 1939. A revised and enlarged edition of a work originally published in German in 1937; still the only one attempting to cover the whole field of the book industry in the United States.

AB475. Hart, James D. **The popular book: a history of America's literary taste.** N.Y., 1950. Good study of best sellers in the United States.

AB476. Rourke, Constance M. **American humor: a study of the national character.** N.Y., 1931. Sound and readable, as well as original. [MEC]

AB477. Botkin, Benjamin A., ed. **A treasury of American folklore.** N.Y., 1944. Useful anthology of selections from folklore material, arranged under such topics as heroes and boasters, boosters and knockers, jesters, liars, folk tales and legends, songs, and rhymes. [MEC]

AB478. Smith, Henry N. **Virgin land: the American West as symbol and myth.** Cambridge, Mass., 1950. Skilful and informed delineation of the symbols and myths associated in the East and in Europe with the West, based largely on literary and subliterary materials. [MEC]

The Arts

AB479. Chase, Gilbert. **America's music, from the Pilgrims to the present.** N.Y., 1955. Comprehensive and informed. Emphasizes African and indigenous currents, as well as European, that have influenced musical development in the United States. [MEC]

AB480. Laws, George M. **Native American balladry.** Philadelphia, 1950.

AB481. Kouwenhoven, John A. **Made in America: the arts in modern civilization.** Garden City, 1948. Thoughtful discussion of the vernacular tradition in the practical arts, as shaped by conditions in the U.S. [MEC]

AB482. Larkin, Oliver W. **Art and life in America.** N.Y., 1949. Comprehensive and well-written study of relations between art and the environment. Contains many illustrations and a bibliography.

AB483. Mumford, Lewis. **The brown decades: a study of the arts in America, 1865–1895.** N.Y., 1931. Sympathetic appraisal of accomplishments in this period.

AB484. Quinn, Arthur H. **A history of the American drama.** Rev. ed., N.Y., 1943.

Religion

AB485. Stokes, Anson P. **Church and state in the United States: historical development and contemporary problems of religious freedom under the Constitution.** 3 v. N.Y., 1950. Temperate, scholarly study, based on extensive investigation. [MEC]

AB486. Sweet, William W. **The story of religion in America.** 2nd ed., N.Y., 1950. The best short history. [GFH]

AB487. Schaff, Philip, Henry C. Potter, and Samuel M. Jackson, eds. **The American church history series.** 13 v. N.Y., 1893–97. The most extensive treatment of denominational church history, but in need of supplementation for the last six decades.

For other works on religion in the United States see Section D.

Immigration

AB488. Hansen, Marcus L. **The immigrant in American history.** Cambridge, Mass., 1940. Collection of essays by the ablest student of immigration to the United States. This and other works of the author have been an inspiration to many students of this subject.

AB489. ——. **The Atlantic migration, 1607–1860.** Cambridge, Mass., 1940. Probably the best single volume on U. S. immigration; intended as the first of a series the author did not live to complete. Written out of sympathy with immigrants and based on sound scholarship, it shows an excellent understanding of the European background that forced people out and of the American attractions which drew them in.

AB490. Wittke, Carl F. **We who built America.** N.Y., 1939. Still the only attempt at a comprehensive account of immigration. Embraces the whole story from the colonial period. The author's special competence is in German emigration to the United States, but he is qualified to write on other groups too. Although more detailed work has been done subsequently on some immigrant stocks, this is yet a useful guide.

AB491. Handlin, Oscar. **The uprooted.** Boston, 1951. Really an essay on immigration, not a detailed history. Emphasizing the difficulties of adjustment to the American environment, especially in cities, it is a more somber narrative than is to be found in most other works on this subject.

AB492. Faust, Albert B. **The German element in the United States, with special reference to its political, moral, social, and educational influence.** 2 v. Boston, 1909. Enl. ed., 2 v. in 1, N.Y., 1927. One of the best of older works on immigration, which were generally inclined to overstress the contributions of the author's stock. Very detailed on German settlements, especially in the earlier period.

AB493. Wittke, Carl F. **Refugees of revolution: the German forty-eighters in America.** Philadelphia, 1952. Best account of one of the most important immigrant groups to come to the United States in the 19th century.

AB494. Ford, Henry J. **The Scotch-Irish in America.** Princeton, 1915. The Ulster Scots and reasons for their emigration, their settlements in colonial America, their impact on the frontier, their Presbyterianism, their role as teachers and political leaders. A good study, but has weakness of its generation in claiming too much for its own group.

AB495. Handlin, Oscar. **Boston's immigrants, 1790–1865.** Cambridge, Mass., 1941. Excellent study of the adaptation of a large group of newcomers, alien in many respects to the Puritan culture of New England.

AB496. Wittke, Carl F. **The Irish in America.** Baton Rouge, 1956. Satisfactory summary of Irish immigration.

AB497. Schrier, Arnold. **Ireland and the American emigration, 1850–1900.** Minneapolis, 1958. An original study emphasizing the impact of emigration from Ireland on her economy and her spirit. Especially useful for its analysis of remittances.

AB498. Berthoff, Rowland T. **British immigrants in industrial America, 1790–1950.** Cambridge, Mass., 1953. A reminder that not all immigrants in the 19th century were Germans, Irish, Italians, Scandinavians, etc. Stresses British contributions to U. S. agriculture and industry. One of the best examples of recent scholarship in this field.

AB499. Thomas, Brinley. **Migration and economic growth: a study of Great Britain and the Atlantic economy.** Cambridge, Eng., 1954. Suggests a somewhat different approach from Hansen. Contends that the volume of emigration was affected by the rate of capital investment in the homeland and the resulting number of jobs. Considers the Atlantic community of nations as one economy made up of interdependent regions.

AB500. Blegen, Theodore C. **Norwegian migration to America.** 2 v. Northfield, Minn., 1931–40. One of the best works of a single migration, covering in considerable detail the scene in the homeland, the hegira, and adjustment to the New World.

AB501. Janson, Florence E. **The background of Swedish immigration, 1840–1930.** Chicago, 1931. Detailed study of economic, social, religious, and political conditions that prompted large-scale emigration from Sweden. Contains valuable statistics.

AB502. Foerster, Robert F. **The Italian emigration of our times.** Cambridge, Mass., 1919. Includes emigration to countries other than the United States. Especially good on economic factors that forced migration, which was often of a temporary nature. A chapter of particular originality deals with effects of emigration on Italy.

AB503. Higham, John. **Strangers in the land: patterns of American nativism, 1860–1925.** New Brunswick, 1955. Of special significance for its correlation of conflicting ideas with interests and values. [MEC]

Foreign Influences

AB504. Bowers, David F., ed. **Foreign influences in American life.** Princeton, 1944. A series of essays under six headings: immigration, the pattern of assimilation, the economic impact, the political impact, artistic and literary impact, and the religious and philosophic impact. Not all essays are equally good, but the volume is an excellent introduction to the whole subject. Valuable critical bibliographies.

AB505. Bestor, Arthur E., Jr. **Backwoods utopias.** Philadelphia, 1950. The author prefers the word "communitarian" to the more familiar "communistic" to describe utopian settlements established in the United States. He relates them to significant currents in the social thought of their time, thus rescuing them from the familiar treatment which regards utopian communities as relatively harmless aberrations.

AB506. Jones, Howard Mumford. **America and French culture, 1750–1848.** Chapel Hill, 1927. Exhaustive study of the manifold examples of French influence in U. S. life—language, arts, religion, education, politics.

AB507. Pochmann, Henry A. **German culture in America: philosophical and literary influences, 1600–1900.** Madison, 1957. Most important work in the field; intentionally excludes educational influences. Notes and bibliography are significant.

AB508. Williams, Stanley T. **The Spanish background of American literature.** 2 v. New Haven, 1955. Shows strong influence of Spain on men of letters in the United States, which the author contends "has in some ways exceeded that of other European countries, hardly excepting England itself."

AB509. Cohen, I. Bernard. **Franklin and Newton.** Philadelphia, 1956. Important work which, among other things, stresses Franklin's role as a popularizer of Newton and as the "orderer" of the whole field of electricity.

AB510. Koht, Halvdan. **The American spirit in Europe: a survey of transatlantic influences.** Philadelphia, 1949. Not a detailed study, but a survey of a large theme, by one of Norway's most eminent statesmen and historians. Especially good on the overseas stimulus to social reforms and the influence exerted upon European writers and vast numbers of readers by U. S. literary figures.

AB511. Kraus, Michael. **The Atlantic civilization: eighteenth century origins.** Ithaca, 1949. Original and scholarly study of the concept of the Atlantic community in the 18th century, especially important for knowledge about the American impact on Europe. The topical organization includes discussions of religious and literary relations, scholarship, the arts, the humanitarian spirit, nationalism, and cosmopolitanism. [MEC]

AB512. Saloutos, Theodore. **They remember America.** Berkeley, 1956. Story of repatriates in Greece, their reception and their influence upon their old homeland.

BIOGRAPHIES *

AB513. Adams, Andy. **The log of a cowboy.** N.Y., 1903. Other eds.

AB514. Adams, James Truslow. **The Adams family.** N.Y., 1930.

AB515. Beringause, Arthur F. **Brooks Adams, a biography.** N.Y., 1955.

AB516. Adams, Henry B. **The education of Henry Adams.** Boston, 1918. Other eds.

AB517. Chinard, C. Gilbert. **Honest John Adams.** Boston, 1933.

AB518. Bemis, Samuel F. **John Quincy Adams.** 2 v. N.Y., 1949–56.

AB519. Miller, John C. **Sam Adams: pioneer in propaganda.** Boston, 1936.

AB520. Stephenson, Nathaniel W. **Nelson W. Aldrich, a leader in American politics.** N.Y., 1930.

AB521. Barnard, Harry. **"Eagle forgotten": the life of John Peter Altgeld.** Indianapolis, 1938.

AB522. Howe, George F. **Chester A. Arthur: a quarter-century of machine politics.** N.Y., 1934.

AB523. Werner, Morris R. **Barnum.** N.Y., 1923.

AB524. Hibben, Paxton. **Henry Ward Beecher: an American portrait.** N.Y., 1927.

AB525. Morgan, Arthur E. **The philosophy of Edward Bellamy.** N.Y., 1945.

AB526. Chambers, William N. **Old Bullion Benton, senator from the new West.** Boston, 1956.

AB527. Bowers, Claude G. **Beveridge and the Progressive era.** Boston, 1932.

AB528. Muzzey, David S. **James G. Blaine: a political idol of other days.** N.Y., 1934.

AB529. Mason, Alpheus T. **Brandeis: a free man's life.** N.Y., 1946.

AB530. Villard, Oswald G. **John Brown, 1800–1859.** Rev. ed., N.Y., 1943.

AB531. Werner, Morris R. **Bryan.** N.Y., 1929.

AB532. Schachner, Nathan. **Aaron Burr.** N.Y., 1937.

AB533. Curti, Merle E. **The learned blacksmith: the letters and journals of Elihu Burritt.** N.Y., 1937.

AB534. Coit, Margaret L. **John C. Calhoun.** Boston, 1950.

AB535. Mayo, Bernard J. **Henry Clay.** Boston, 1937.

AB535a. Van Deusen, G. G. **Henry Clay.** Boston, 1937.

AB536. Nevins, Allan. **Grover Cleveland: a study in courage.** N.Y., 1932.

AB537. Walsh, Richard J. **The making of Buffalo Bill: a study in heroics.** Indianapolis, 1928.

AB538. Morison, Samuel E. **Admiral of the Ocean Sea: a life of Christopher Columbus.** See *U277.*

AB539. Larson, Henrietta M. **Jay Cooke, private banker.** Cambridge, Mass., 1936.

AB540. Berryman, John. **Stephen Crane.** N.Y., 1950.

AB541. Stewart, Edgar I. **Custer's luck.** Norman, 1955.

AB542. Strode, Hudson. **Jefferson Davis.** 2 v. N.Y., 1955–59.

AB543. Ginger, Ray. **The bending cross: a biography of Eugene Victor Debs.** New Brunswick, 1949.

AB544. Marshall, Helen E. **Dorothea Dix, forgotten samaritan.** Chapel Hill, 1937.

AB545. Milton, George F. **The eve of**

* Most of the biographical titles were selected by A. L. Demaree and Robert E. Riegel.

conflict: Stephen A. Douglas and the needless war. Boston, 1934.

AB546. Ellis, Elmer. Mr. Dooley's America: a life of Finley Peter Dunne. N.Y., 1941.

AB547. Bates, Ernest S., and John V. Dittemore. Mary Baker Eddy, the truth and the traditions. N.Y., 1932.

AB548. Farley, James A. Behind the ballots: the personal history of a politician. N.Y., 1938.

AB549. Van Doren, Carl C. Benjamin Franklin. N.Y., 1938.

AB550. Walters, Raymond, Jr. Albert Gallatin, Jeffersonian financier and diplomat. N.Y., 1957.

AB551. Nye, Russel B. William Lloyd Garrison and the humanitarian reformers. Boston, 1955.

AB552. Barker, Charles A. Henry George. N.Y., 1955.

AB553. Hesseltine, William B. Ulysses S. Grant, politician. N.Y., 1935.

AB554. Lewis, Lloyd D. Captain Sam Grant. Boston, 1950.

AB555. Van Deusen, Glyndon G. Horace Greeley, nineteenth century crusader. Philadelphia, 1953.

AB556. Schachner, Nathan. Alexander Hamilton. N.Y., 1946.

AB557. Croly, Herbert D. Marcus Alonzo Hanna, his life and work. N.Y., 1912.

AB558. Adams, Samuel H. Incredible era: the life and time of Warren Gamaliel Harding. Boston, 1939.

AB559. Sievers, Harry J. Benjamin Harrison. Chicago, 1952.

AB560. Eckenrode, Hamilton J. Rutherford B. Hayes, statesman of reunion. N.Y., 1930.

AB561. Howe, Mark D., ed. Holmes-Pollock letters: the correspondence of Mr. Justice Holmes and Sir Frederick Pollock, 1874–1932. 2 v. Cambridge, Mass., 1941.

AB562. Lerner, Max, ed. The mind and faith of Justice Holmes: his speeches, essays, letters, and judicial opinions. Boston, 1943.

AB563. James, Marquis. The raven: a biography of Sam Houston. Indianapolis, 1929.

AB564. Perkins, Dexter. Charles Evans Hughes and American democratic statesmanship. Boston, 1956.

AB565. Cramer, Clarence H. Royal Bob: the life of Robert G. Ingersoll. Indianapolis, 1952.

AB566. James, Marquis. The life of Andrew Jackson. N.Y., 1938.

AB567. Henderson, George F. R. Stonewall Jackson and the American Civil War. 2 v. N.Y. and London, 1898.

AB568. Perry, Ralph B. The thought and character of William James. 2 v. Cambridge, Mass., 1935. 1 v. ed., 1948.

AB569. Monaghan, Frank. John Jay. N.Y., 1935.

AB570. Koch, Adrienne. Jefferson and Madison: the great collaboration. N.Y., 1950.

AB571. Malone, Dumas. Jefferson and his time. 2 v. Boston, 1948–52. (Other volumes in preparation.)

AB572. Schachner, Nathan. Thomas Jefferson, a biography. 2 v. N.Y., 1951.

AB573. Stryker, Lloyd P. Andrew Johnson: a study in courage. N.Y., 1929.

AB574. La Follette, Belle C., and Fola La Follette. Robert M. La Follette, June 14, 1855–June 18, 1925. 2 v. N.Y., 1953.

AB575. Freeman, Douglas S. R. E. Lee, a biography. 4 v. N.Y. and London, 1934–35.

AB576. Sandburg, Carl. Abraham Lincoln. 6 v. N.Y., 1926–39.

AB577. Thomas, Benjamin P. Abraham Lincoln. N.Y., 1952.

AB578. Garraty, John A. Henry Cabot Lodge, a biography. N.Y., 1953.

AB579. Brant, Irving. James Madison. 5 v. Indianapolis, 1941–56. (To be complete in 6 v.)

AB580. Beveridge, Albert J. The life of John Marshall. 4 v. N.Y., 1916–19.

AB581. Murdock, Kenneth B. Increase Mather, the foremost American Puritan. Cambridge, Mass., 1925.

AB582. Clapesattle, Helen B. The doctors Mayo. Minneapolis, 1941.

AB583. Bradford, Gamaliel. D. L. Moody, a worker in souls. Garden City, 1927.

AB584. Allen, Frederick L. The great Pierpont Morgan. N.Y., 1949.

AB585. Paine, Albert B. Th. Nast, his period and his pictures. N.Y., 1904.

AB586. Morison, Samuel E. The life and letters of Harrison Gray Otis. 2 v. Boston, 1913.

AB587. Commager, Henry S. Theodore Parker. Boston, 1936.

AB588. Powderly, Terence V. Thirty years of labor, 1859 to 1889. Rev. ed., Philadelphia, 1890.

AB589. Bruce, William C. John Randolph of Roanoke. 2 v. N.Y., 1922.

AB590. Robinson, William A. Thomas B. Reed, parliamentarian. N.Y., 1930.

AB591. Nevins, Allan. Study in power: John D. Rockefeller, industrialist and philanthropist. 2nd ed., 2 v., N.Y., 1953.

AB592. Burns, James M. Roosevelt: the lion and the fox. N.Y., 1956.

AB593. Freidel, Frank B. Franklin D. Roosevelt. 3 v. Boston, 1952–56.

AB594. Perkins, Frances. The Roosevelt I knew. N.Y., 1946.

AB595. Blum, John M. The Republican Roosevelt. Cambridge, Mass., 1954.

AB596. Pringle, Henry F. Theodore Roosevelt, a biography. N.Y., 1931.

AB597. Jessup, Philip C. Elihu Root. 2 v. N.Y., 1938.

AB598. Leopold, Richard W. Elihu Root and the conservative tradition. Boston, 1954.

AB599. Craven, Avery O. **Edmund Ruffin, southerner.** N.Y., 1932.

AB600. Fuess, Claude M. **Carl Schurz, reformer.** N.Y., 1932.

AB601. Mitchell, R. Stewart. **Horatio Seymour of New York.** Cambridge, Mass., 1938.

AB602. Morison, Elting E. **Admiral Sims and the modern American navy.** Boston, 1942.

AB603. Brodie, Fawn M. **No man knows my history: the life of Joseph Smith, the Mormon prophet.** N.Y., 1945.

AB604. Steffens, J. Lincoln. **The autobiography of Lincoln Steffens.** 2 v. N.Y., 1931.

AB605. Current, Richard N. **Old Thad Stevens.** Madison, 1942.

AB606. Wilson, R. Forrest. **Crusader in crinoline: the life of Harriet Beecher Stowe.** Philadelphia, 1941.

AB607. McLoughlin, William G., Jr. **Billy Sunday was his real name.** Chicago, 1955.

AB608. Zollinger, James P. **Sutter, the man and his empire.** N.Y., 1939.

AB609. Pringle, Henry F. **The life and times of William Howard Taft.** 2 v. N.Y., 1939.

AB610. Swisher, Carl B. **Roger B. Taney.** N.Y., 1935.

AB611. Flick, Alexander C. **Samuel Jones Tilden: a study in political sagacity.** N.Y., 1939.

AB612. De Voto, Bernard A. **Mark Twain's America.** Boston, 1932.

AB613. Lane, Wheaton J. **Commodore Vanderbilt.** N.Y., 1942.

AB614. Freeman, Douglas S. **George Washington.** 6 v. N.Y., 1948–52. V. 7, by John A. Carroll and Mary W. Ashworth, N.Y., 1957.

AB615. Woodward, C. Vann. **Tom Watson, agrarian rebel.** N.Y., 1938.

AB616. Fuess, Claude M. **Daniel Webster.** 2 v. Boston, 1930.

AB617. Fleming, Donald H. **William H. Welch and the rise of modern medicine.** Boston, 1954.

AB618. Johnson, Thomas Walter. **William Allen White's America.** N.Y., 1947.

AB619. Hirsch, Mark D. **William C. Whitney: modern Warwick.** N.Y., 1948.

AB620. Smith, Charles P. **James Wilson, founding father, 1742–1798.** Chapel Hill, 1956.

AB621. Garraty, John A. **Woodrow Wilson: a great life in brief.** N.Y., 1956.

AB622. Walworth, Arthur C. **Woodrow Wilson.** 2 v. N.Y., 1958.

AB623. Link, Arthur S. **Wilson.** 2 v. Princeton, 1947–56.

DOCUMENTS, COLLECTIONS OF WRITINGS

AB624. Original narratives of early American history. Ed. by J. Franklin Jameson.

19 v. N.Y., 1906–17. Reprint, 1952. A series of contemporary accounts of U. S. colonial history. [SD]

AB625. Stock, Leo F., ed. **Proceedings and debates of the British parliaments respecting North America.** 5 v. Washington, 1924–41. Collection of contemporary parliamentary records of England, Scotland, and Ireland for 1542–1754. [SD]

AB626. Force, Peter, comp. **Tracts and other papers relating principally to the origin, settlement, and progress of the colonies in North America, from the discovery of the country to the year 1776.** 4 v. Washington, 1836–46.

AB627. ——, comp. **American archives.** 4th series (Mar. 7, 1774-July 4, 1776) and 5th ser. (July 4, 1776-Sept. 3, 1783), 9 v., Washington, 1837–53. Series 1, 2, 3, and 6 were also planned, but never published. Parts have been edited and published by the Library of Congress. [SD]

AB628. Wharton, Francis, ed. **Revolutionary diplomatic correspondence of the United States.** 6 v. Washington, 1889.

AB629. U. S. Continental Congress. **Journals of the Continental Congress, 1774–1789, edited from the original records in the Library of Congress.** 34 v. Washington, 1904–37.

AB630. Burnett, Edmund C., ed. **Letters of members of the Continental Congress.** 8 v. Washington, 1921–36. Contains 6,125 letters, parts of letters, and diaries supplying contemporary evidence concerning ideas and events. No formal record of debates was kept by the Continental Congress. [SD]

AB631. Bemis, Samuel F., and Grace G. Griffin. **Guide to the diplomatic history of the United States, 1775–1921.** Washington, 1935. Exhaustive compilation with critical evaluations of books and articles. [TAB]

AB632. Farrand, Max, ed. **Records of the federal convention of 1787.** 4 v. New Haven, 1911–37.

AB633. Richardson, James D., ed. **A compilation of the messages and papers of the presidents, 1789–1897.** 10 v. Washington, 1896–99.

AB634. U. S. Congress. **American state papers: documents, legislative and executive, of the Congress of the United States.** 38 v. Washington, 1832–61. Selected documents of the first 25 congresses (1789–1838). Constitutes the first part of the Congressional series. [SD]

AB635. ——. **Annals of Congress.** 1789–1824. 42 v. Washington, 1834–56. Edited reports, digests, and compilations of significant proceedings. [SD]

AB636. ——. **Register of debates.** 1824–37. 14 v. in 29. Washington, 1825–37.

AB637. ——. **Congressional globe.** 1833–73. 46 v. in 111. Washington, 1834–73.

AB638. ——. **Congressional record.** 1873

ff. Washington, 1874 ff. Prepared from stenographic reports of the debates and proceedings. [SD]

AB639. Catterall, Helen T., ed. **Judicial cases concerning American slavery and the negro.** 5 v. Washington, 1926–37.

AB640. Donnan, Elizabeth, ed. **Documents illustrative of the history of the slave trade to America.** 4 v. Washington, 1930–35.

AB641. Carter, Clarence E., ed. **The territorial papers of the United States.** 22 v. Washington, 1934–56. These papers cast much light on matters of government routine and policy, Indian affairs, personalities, political alignments and conflicts. [SD]

AB642. Jackson, Andrew. **Correspondence of Andrew Jackson.** Ed. by John S. Bassett. 7 v. Washington, 1926–35.

AB643. Miller, David H. **Treaties and other international acts of the United States of America.** 8 v. Washington, 1931–48. Definitive edition of U. S. treaties to 1863, with compendious scholarly notes. [TAB]

AB644. U. S. Senate. **Treaties, conventions, international acts, protocols, and agreements between the United States of America and other powers.** 1776–1937. 4 v. Washington, 1910–38.

AB645. U. S. Department of State. **Papers relating to the foreign relations of the United States.** 1861 ff. Washington, 1862 ff. (Title varies.)

AB646. ——. **United States treaties and other international agreements.** 1950 ff. Washington, 1952 ff. Published treaty materials formerly included in *U. S. statutes at large.* [SD]

AB647. **Statutes at large of the United States of America.** 1789–1873. 17 v. Boston, 1845–73.

AB648. **United States statutes at large.** 1874 ff. Washington, 1875 ff. (Title varies.) Does not include treaties from 1950 on.

AB649. U. S. Supreme Court. **United States reports.** 1790 ff. N.Y. and Washington, 1882 ff. (Title varies.) Before 1875 these volumes bore names of various reporters who collected them, and are customarily cited by an abbreviated form of these reporters' names.

AB650. Carnegie Institution of Washington. [Guides to manuscript materials for the history of the United States.] 23 v. Washington, 1906–43. Individual monographs which provide guides, inventories, calendars, and lists of archives, manuscripts, and other unpublished materials in United States and European repositories. [SD]

AB651. Hasse, Adelaide R. **Index of economic material in documents of the states of the United States.** 13 v. in 16 pts. Washington, 1907–22. Covers other aspects of U. S. history besides economic. Indexes printed documents of executive and legislative bodies of California, Delaware, Illinois, Kentucky, Maine, Massachusetts, New Hampshire, New Jersey, New York, Ohio, Pennsylvania, Rhode Island, and Vermont. [SD]

AB652. Historical Records Survey. **Bibliography of research projects reports.** No. 7. Washington, 1943. Includes guides to depositories of manuscripts, manuscript collections in the United States, and public vital statistics; and inventories of church, state, county, town and city archives, and federal archives in the states. [SD]

AB653. Hodgson, James G. **The official publications of American counties: a union list.** Fort Collins, Colo., 1937. Contains 5,243 entries for holdings of 194 libraries on activities of county governments or officials. Indexed by subject. [SD]

AB654. National Association of State Libraries. **Check-list of legislative journals of states of the United States of America.** Comp. by Grace E. MacDonald and others. 2 v. Providence, 1938. Supp., Boston, 1943.

AB655. Pullen, William R. **A check list of legislative journals issued since 1937 by the states of the United States of America.** Chicago, 1955. Legislative journals frequently contain legislative and executive documents not issued separately. [SD]

AB656. National Association of State Libraries. **Check-list of session laws.** Comp. by Grace E. MacDonald. N.Y., 1936.

AB657. ——. **Check-list of statutes of states of the United States of America including revisions, compilations, digests, codes and indexes.** Comp. by Grace E. MacDonald. Providence, 1937.

AB658. ——. **Collected public documents of the states: a check list.** Comp. by William S. Jenkins. Boston, 1947.

AB659. U. S. Library of Congress. **Guide to manuscripts relating to American history in British depositories reproduced for the Division of Manuscripts of the Library of Congress.** Comp. by Grace G. Griffin. Washington, 1946. Arranged by depository where original is located. [SD]

AB660. ——. **A guide to the microfilm collection of early state records.** Comp. by William S. Jenkins. Washington, 1950. Supplement, 1951. Index and location list for 2,500,000 pages of early state legislative proceedings, statutes, administrative, court and other records. [SD]

AB661. ——. **Manuscripts in public and private collections in the United States.** Rev. ed., Washington, 1924. Complete name index, but subject index is inadequate. [SD]

AB662. Adams, John. **Works.** Ed. by Charles Francis Adams. 10 v. Boston, 1850–56.

AB663. Cappon, Lester, ed. **The Adams-Jefferson letters: the complete correspondence between Thomas Jefferson and Abigail and John Adams.** 2 v. Chapel Hill, 1959. The 380 letters of this correspondence reveal the interests and philosophical convictions of two outstanding Americans. Expert editing. [GFH]

AB664. Adams, John Quincy. **Writings.** Ed. by Worthington C. Ford. 7 v. N.Y., 1913–17.

AB665. Buchanan, James. **Works.** Ed. by John B. Moore. 12 v. Philadelphia, 1908–11.

AB666. Franklin, Benjamin. **Writings.** Ed. by Albert H. Smyth. 10 v. N.Y., 1905–07. A new edition of Franklin's writings, edited by L. W. Labaree and others, is in progress. New Haven, 1960 ff.

AB667. Hayes, Rutherford B. **Diary and letters.** Ed. by Charles R. Williams. 5 v. Columbus, 1922–26.

AB668. Jefferson, Thomas. **Papers.** Ed. by Julian P. Boyd and others. 14 v. Princeton, 1950–58. (Other vols. in process.) Monumental work providing source materials for students of life as a whole in Jefferson's time. See also editions by P. L. Ford (10 v., 1892–99) and Lipscomb and Bergh (20 v., 1903). [SD]

AB669. Lincoln, Abraham. **Collected works.** Ed. by Roy P. Basler. 9 v. New Brunswick, 1953–55.

AB670. ——. **Complete works.** Ed. by John G. Nicolay, John Hay, and others. 12 v. N.Y., 1905.

AB671. Madison, James. **Writings.** Ed. by Gaillard Hunt. 9 v. N.Y., 1900–10. A new edition of Madison's writings is in process.

AB672. Monroe, James. **Writings.** Ed. by Stanislaus M. Hamilton. 7 v. N.Y., 1898–1903.

AB673. Polk, James K. **Diary of James K. Polk during his presidency, 1845 to 1849.** Ed. by Milo M. Quaife. 4 v. Chicago, 1910.

AB674. Roosevelt, Franklin D. **Public papers and addresses.** Ed. by Samuel I. Rosenman. 13 v. N.Y., 1938–50.

AB675. Roosevelt, Theodore. **Works.** 24 v. N.Y., 1923–26.

AB676. ——. **Letters.** Ed. by Elting E. Morison and others. 8 v. Cambridge, Mass., 1951–54. Rich collection, carefully edited.

AB677. Washington, George. **Writings.** Ed. by John C. Fitzpatrick. Bicentennial ed., 39 v., Washington, 1931–44. V. 38–39 are general index by David M. Matteson.

AB678. Wilson, Woodrow. **Public papers.** Ed. by Ray S. Baker and William E. Dodd. 6 v. N.Y., 1925–27.

AB679. Jesuit relations and allied documents. Ed by Reuben G. Thwaites. 73 v. Cleveland, 1896–1901. A monumental series providing much information about the frontiers of New France in the 17th century.

AB680. Early western travels, 1748–1846. Ed. by Reuben G. Thwaites. 32 v. Cleveland, 1904–07. Reprints of rare travel reports which present a view of the flow of settlers into the wilderness, the rapid formation of societies, and the evolution of many of these into urban communities.

AB681. Original journals of the Lewis and Clark expedition, 1804–1806. Ed. by Reuben G. Thwaites. 8 v. N.Y., 1904–05.

UNIVERSITY AND SOCIETY PUBLICATIONS

AB682. American Antiquarian Society. **Archaeologia americana: transactions and collections.** 12 v. Worcester, etc., 1820–1911. (Title varies.)

AB683. ——. **Proceedings.** 75 v. and index. Worcester, 1812–80. New ser., 1880 ff. (Semiannual.)

AB684. American Historical Association. **Papers.** N.Y., 1886–91.

AB685. ——. **Annual reports.** Washington, 1890 ff.

AB686. American Philosophical Society. **Proceedings.** Philadelphia, 1838 ff. (Annual.) There is a general index to all publications, 1769–1940; and a volume, *Early proceedings* (Philadelphia, 1884), which covers the years 1744–1838.

AB687. ——. **Transactions.** Philadelphia, 1769 ff. (Irregular.)

AB688. Columbia University. **Studies in history, economics, and public law.** N.Y., 1892 ff.

AB689. Harvard University. **Harvard studies in business history.** Cambridge, Mass., 1931 ff.

AB690. ——. **Harvard economic studies.** Boston and Cambridge, 1906 ff.

AB691. ——. **Harvard historical monographs.** Cambridge, Mass., 1932 ff.

AB692. Illinois State Historical Society. **Journal.** Springfield, Ill., 1908 ff. (Quarterly.) General index through 1933.

AB693. ——. **Transactions.** Springfield, Ill., 1900 ff. (Irregular. Title varies.)

AB694. Johns Hopkins University. **Studies in international thought.** Baltimore, 1929 ff.

AB695. ——. **The Albert Shaw lectures on diplomatic history.** Baltimore, 1899 ff.

AB696. ——. **Studies in historical and political science.** Baltimore, 1883 ff. (Title varies.)

AB697. Colonial Society of Massachusetts. **Publications.** Boston, 1895 ff. (Irregular.) General index through 1924.

AB698. Massachusetts Historical Society. **Collections.** Boston, 1792 ff.

AB699. ——. **Proceedings.** 1st ser., 20 v., Boston, 1791–1883; 2nd ser., 20 v., 1884–1907; 3rd ser., 1907 ff. (Annual.) General index, *Handbook of the publications and photostats, 1792–1935* (Boston, 1937).

AB700. New Haven Colony Historical Society. **Papers.** New Haven, 1865 ff. (Irregular.)

AB701. New York Historical Society. **Quarterly.** N.Y., 1917 ff. (Title varies.)

AB702. ——. **Collections.** 1st ser., N.Y., 1811–59.

AB703. ——. **John Divine Jones Fund series.** N.Y., 1879 ff.

AB704. ——. **John Watts de Peyster Publication Fund series.** N.Y., 1868 ff.

AB705. Pennsylvania Historical Association. **Pennsylvania history.** Philadelphia, 1934 ff. (Quarterly.)

AB706. Southern Historical Society. **Papers.** Richmond, 1876–1910. Index. New ser., 1914 ff. (Annual.)

AB707. State Historical Society of Wisconsin. **Wisconsin magazine of history.** Madison, 1917 ff. (Quarterly.) Index through 1946.

AB708. ——. **Proceedings.** Madison, 1875 ff. Index through 1901.

AB709. ——. **Collections.** Madison, 1854 ff. (Title varies.)

AB710. University of Wisconsin. **Studies in the social sciences and history.** Madison, 1918 ff.

AB711. Yale University. **Yale publications in economics, social science and government.** New Haven, 1929 ff.

AB712. ——. **Yale historical publications.** New Haven, 1912 ff. (Title varies.)

PERIODICALS

AB713. American periodical series, 1741–1850. [Microfilm.] 481 reels. Ann Arbor, 1942–57. Includes all known and located periodicals published in the United States prior to 1800, and selected titles for 1800–50. [SD]

AB714. American heritage. N.Y., 1947–49. New ser., 1949 ff. (Bimonthly.)

AB715. The American historical review. N.Y., 1895 ff. (Quarterly.)

AB716. The Mississippi Valley historical review. Cedar Rapids, Iowa, 1914 ff. (Quarterly.)

AB717. The New England quarterly. Baltimore, etc., 1928 ff.

AB718. Pacific historical review. Glendale, Calif., 1932 ff. (Quarterly.)

AB719. The Pennsylvania magazine of history and biography. Philadelphia, 1877 ff. (Quarterly.)

AB720. Journal of southern history. Baton Rouge, etc., 1935 ff. (Quarterly.)

AB721. William and Mary quarterly. Williamsburg, 1892 ff. (Title varies.)

VII. AFRICA

SECTION AC

Africa

VERNON McKAY *

The study of African history has been retarded by the myth that Africa is a continent without history, a belief that dies hard. In this view the only history in Africa has been that of European expansion because only Europeans, with few exceptions, have left written records. Africa's eight hundred languages were unwritten vernaculars until European missionaries began to transcribe them into writing. However, if one accepts Carl Becker's definition of history as "the memory of things said and done," a wealth of African history is waiting for study. Happily, an impressive effort in this direction has been launched by the University of London's School of Oriental and African Studies. Historians, archivists, archaeologists, and social anthropologists are combining the methods of their disciplines to unravel Africa's past. In the absence of documents, techniques for the proper use of oral tradition are being improved, and certain scholars use the term "oral documentation." Linguistics and even serology (to demonstrate genetic relationships of populations) are beginning to be employed for such problems as the evaluation of theories of migrations. Therefore, a high proportion of works from other disciplines will be found in this section.

The contributions of historians to African studies are most numerous for the two areas of temperate climate that have attracted the most Europeans—the Mediterranean littoral and southern Africa below the Tropic of Capricorn. However, all of Africa, except Egypt, is covered in this section. Certain works relating to the history of European expansion in Africa will be found in Section U.

GENERAL STUDIES

BIBLIOGRAPHIES

Bibliographies on Africa have multiplied so rapidly in recent years that they now include a 169 page *Bibliography of African* bibliographies (*AC10*). In the Library of Congress, Helen F. Conover has compiled eighteen bibliographies on African subjects since 1935, the four most useful of which are listed below (*AC11–14*). For current

* The following contributed items and comments and in other ways assisted in the preparation of this section: Robert D. Baum, Helen F. Conover, Betty George, William H. Lewis, and John Noon.

bibliographies, the best periodicals are *Africa, African abstracts, Journal de la Société des Africanistes,* and *Zaïre.* A number of critical bibliographical articles, such as *AC2, 8, 9,* and *17,* are helpful.

General and Regional Bibliographies

AC1. Coleman, James S. "A survey of selected literature on the government and politics of British west Africa." **The American political science review,** 49 (Dec. 1955): 1130–50. Critical bibliographical essay on recent books, documents, and significant periodical articles.

AC2. Gluckman, Max. "Social anthropology in central Africa." **Human problems in British central Africa,** 20 (1956): 1–27. Excellent critical review of research in the social sciences in the Rhodesias and Nyasaland.

AC3. Hambly, Wilfred D. **Bibliography of African anthropology, 1937–1949.** Chicago, 1952.

AC4. International African Institute. **Select annotated bibliography of tropical Africa.** N.Y., 1956. Prepared by some twenty specialists. Divided into seven main sections: geography; ethnography, sociology, and linguistics; government and administration; economics; education; missions; and health.

AC5. Martineau, Alfred A. **Bibliographie d'histoire coloniale, 1900–1930.** Paris, 1932.

AC6. Porter, Dorothy, ed. **A catalogue of the African collection in the Moorland Foundation, Howard University Library.** Washington, 1958. Well-organized catalog of 5,181 items on Africa.

AC7. Ragatz, Lowell J. **A bibliography for the study of African history in the nineteenth and twentieth centuries.** Washington, 1943.

AC8. Robinson, Kenneth. "Survey of the background material for the study of government in French tropical Africa." **Am. pol. sci. rev.,** 50 (Mar. 1956): 170–98. Valuable essay by an outstanding British specialist on government and politics in French Africa.

AC9. Rivlin, Benjamin. "A selective survey of the literature in the social science and related fields on modern north Africa." **Am. pol. sci. rev.,** 48 (Sep. 1954): 826–48. Good analysis of research on Algeria, Morocco, Tunisia, and Libya through 1952.

AC10. South African Public Library. **A bibliography of African bibliographies, covering territories south of the Sahara.** 3rd ed., Cape Town, 1955. A. M. Lewis Robinson's revision and expansion, to August, 1955, of earlier works by P. Freer and D. H. Varley. In addition to listing books devoted entirely to bibliography, this volume includes substantial bibliographies appended to authoritative studies.

AC11. U. S. Library of Congress. **Africa south of the Sahara, a selected list of writings, 1951–1956.** Comp. by Helen F. Conover. Washington, 1957.

AC12. ———. **Introduction to Africa, a selective guide to background reading.** Comp. by Helen F. Conover. Washington, 1952.

AC13. ———. **North and northeast Africa, a selected, annotated list of writings, 1951–1957.** Comp. by Helen F. Conover. Washington, 1957.

AC14. ———. **Research and information on Africa: continuing sources.** Comp. by Helen F. Conover. Washington, 1954. A particularly valuable annotated list of 520 items. Some of these are organizations that publish regularly on African questions, while the remainder are periodicals devoted in whole or consistent part to discussion of Africa.

AC15. University of Cape Town. **Bibliographical series.** Cape Town, 1941 ff. (Irregular.) Under supervision of D. H. Varley, lecturer in bibliography, many bibliographies on African subjects have been compiled at this university in part fulfillment of requirements for the diploma in librarianship. Those which have not been published in this series are obtainable on microfilm from the university librarian.

AC16. Wieschhoff, Heinrich A. **Anthropological bibliography of Negro Africa.** New Haven, 1948. Conveniently arranged by tribes and geographic areas in a single alphabetical list. Covers to 1942.

AC17. Young, Roland, and J. Gus Liebenow, Jr. "Survey of background material for the study of the government of East Africa." **Am. pol. sci. rev.,** 48 (Mar. 1954): 187–203. Useful bibliographical essay.

Territorial Bibliographies

AC18. Boone, Olga. **Bibliographie ethnographique du Congo Belge et des régions avoisonantes.** 5 v. Brussels, 1950–54. Annotated list of all ethnographic publications on Congo and neighboring countries.

AC19. Cardinall, Allan W. **A bibliography of the Gold Coast.** Accra, 1932. Those who think literature on Africa a recent development may be surprised to find 5,168 items in this bibliography of one territory.

AC20. Heyse, Théodore. **Bibliographie du Congo Belge et du Ruanda-Urundi.** Brussels, 1946 ff. Important bibliographies of general coverage, issued in irregular installments in *Cahiers belges et congolais.* Succeeded the pre-war *Index bibliographique coloniale* (1937–40).

AC21. Hill, Richard L. **A bibliography of the Anglo-Egyptian Sudan from the earliest times to 1937.** London, 1939.

AC22. Holden, Margaret A., and Annette Jacoby. **Modern life and customs. Supplement to Schapera, Select bibliography of**

South African native life and problems. Cape Town, 1950. A University of Cape Town, School of Librarianship study.

AC23. Joucla, Edmond A. **Bibliographie de l'Afrique occidentale française.** Paris, 1937.

AC24. Luke, Sir Harry C. **A bibliography of Sierra Leone, preceded by an essay on the origin, character and peoples of the colony and protectorate.** 2nd ed., London, 1925.

AC25. Mendelssohn, Sidney. **Mendelssohn's South African bibliography.** 2 v. London, 1910. Valuable annotated bibliography of older works, including periodicals, bluebooks, and parliamentary papers.

AC26. Perry, Ruth. **A preliminary bibliography of the literature of nationalism in Nigeria.** Stanford, 1956.

AC27. Sanner, P., ed. **Bibliographie ethnographique de l'Afrique equatoriale française, 1914–1948.** Paris, 1949.

AC28. Santandrea, Stefano. **Bibliografia di studi africani della missione dell'Africa centrale.** Verona, 1948. Bibliography of writings by Catholic missionaries on the Anglo-Egyptian Sudan and Uganda during the last 100 years.

AC29. Schapera, Isaac, ed. **Select bibliography of South African native life and problems.** London, 1941. Excellent annotated bibliography covering Southern Rhodesia as well as South Africa, prepared by a group of scholars for the Inter-University Committee for African Studies under Schapera's direction. *AC22* is a supplement to this volume.

AC30. Spain. Dirección General de Marruecos y Colonias. **Catálogo de la exposición de libros españoles sobre geografía y viajes en Africa.** Comp. by M. Asunción del Val. Madrid, 1948.

AC31. Varley, Douglas H. **A bibliography of Italian colonisation in Africa.** See *U10.*

Libraries

The systematic development of United States library resources on Africa began after World War II. By 1958 the Library of Congress was purchasing about 12,000 items on Africa each year under blanket orders with fourteen commercial booksellers in Africa and through other sources; was exchanging materials with nearly 1,000 government agencies and scientific and learned institutions in Africa; was receiving about 550 periodicals and publications of organizations that publish regularly on Africa, and 120 newspapers from 32 geographic areas in Africa (over 100 of which are retained for permanent collections); and was acquiring about 1,000 maps of Africa each year.

Among university libraries, Northwestern has the best and most rapidly growing collection of Africana. Boston University has built up a good collection since 1953, and Howard University has large and valuable holdings. At Stanford University, the Hoover Library and the Food Research Institute library are good on Africa. The School of Advanced International Studies of The Johns Hopkins University, and Roosevelt College in Chicago are also collecting African materials.

Other libraries with valuable Africana include the Widener Library and the Peabody Museum at Harvard University, the Yale University library, the Missionary Research Library at the Union Theological Seminary, the New York Public Library, and the American Geographical Society library (on African exploration).

GEOGRAPHIES AND ATLASES

AC32. Church, Ronald J. H. **The pattern of transport in British west Africa: geographical essays on British tropical lands.** London, 1955.

AC33. ——. **West Africa: a study of the environment and of man's use of it.** London, 1957. Most comprehensive geographic study of west African regions—British, French, Portuguese, and Spanish territories and Liberia—focused on physical environment, resources, and their development.

AC34. Ford, Victor C. R. **The trade of Lake Victoria, a geographical study.** Kampala, Uganda, 1955. Monograph, based on primary sources and original investigation, analyzing, against the geographical and historical background, the present trade of the lake region by specific commodities. Select bibliography.

AC35. Fitzgerald, Walter. **Africa: a social, economic and political geography of its major regions.** 8th ed., London, 1955. The standard geography of the entire continent, devoted largely to regional studies, with minor revisions by W. C. Brice noting important developments through 1954. Reading lists throughout.

AC36. Harroy, Jean-Paul. **Afrique, terre qui meurt: la dégradation des sols africains sous l'influence de la colonisation.** Brussels, 1944. Important, lucid study of soil exhaustion and erosion in Africa, including analysis of transformation of African agriculture under colonization and suggestions for remedial action. List of principal works cited.

AC37. Stamp, Laurence D. **Africa: a study in tropical development.** N.Y., 1953. Authoritative geography of entire continent, emphasizing responses of inhabitants to geographical environment. Bibliographical note for each chapter.

AC38. Wellington, John H. **Southern Africa, a geographical study.** 2 v. Cambridge, Eng., 1955. Authoritative, well-illustrated physical, economic, and human geography of Africa south of the Congo-Zambezi watershed.

AC39. Fage, J. D. **An atlas of African history.** Bungay, Suffolk, Eng., 1958. Unique and valuable annotated volume of 62 original maps illustrating African history from Roman times to 1957.

AC40. Walker, Eric A. **Historical atlas of South Africa.** Cape Town, 1922.

AC41. Automobile Association of South Africa. **Trans-African highways.** 2nd ed., Johannesburg, 1925. Rev. ed., Cape Town, 1949. Maps and descriptions of main trunk roads throughout Africa.

ANTHROPOLOGICAL WORKS

AC42. Forde, Cyril D., ed. **African worlds: studies in the cosmological ideas and social values of African peoples.** London, 1954. Nine essays by social anthropologists and ethnologists, each analyzing the cosmography of an African people and its relation to social organization.

AC43. Fortes, Meyer, and Edward E. Evans-Pritchard, eds. **African political systems.** London, 1940. Analyses of the indigenous political systems of eight African peoples, written by outstanding anthropologists.

AC44. Malinowski, Bronislaw. **The dynamics of culture change: an inquiry into race relations in Africa.** New Haven, 1945. Functionalist theory of culture conceived as institutions and the concept of culture contact, as applied to African conditions. Bibliography.

AC45. Marie André du Sacré Coeur, Soeur. **La femme noire en Afrique occidentale.** Paris, 1939. Study of the indigenous family and social structure of French West Africa, particularly the position of women, by a missionary sister and scholar of African ethnology. Bibliography.

AC46. Phillips, Arthur, ed. **Survey of African marriage and family life.** London, 1953. Three-part study of western impact on indigenous systems of marriage and family life in Africa south of the Sahara, by three specialists in the anthropological, legal, and missionary fields. Bibliography for each section.

AC47. Radcliffe-Brown, Alfred R., and Cyril D. Forde, eds. **African systems of kinship and marriage.** London, 1950. Symposium of nine studies by social anthropologists, each analyzing the social system of one or more African people, with introductory analysis of kinship systems by A. R. Radcliffe-Brown.

AC48. Schapera, Isaac. **Government and politics in tribal societies.** London, 1956. Indigenous political systems of Bushmen,

Hottentot, Bantu, and Bergdama of southern Africa. Bibliography.

AC49. Seligman, Charles G. **Races of Africa.** 3rd ed., London, 1957. Authoritative introduction to the ethnology of Africa, divided into sections on the six main groups. Short bibliography.

AC50. Smith, Edwin W. **The golden stool: some aspects of the conflict of cultures in Africa.** 2nd ed., London, 1927. Classic study, by a prominent missionary and anthropologist, of religious, educational, administrative, and economic problems.

AC51. Tempels, Placied. **La philosophie bantoue.** Elisabethville, Belg. Congo, 1945; Paris, 1949. Provocative essay, by a Catholic missionary priest in the Belgian Congo, which argues that the Bantu have their own philosophy of life which must be studied if they are to be raised to a higher level of civilization.

DEMOGRAPHY

AC52. Kuczynski, Robert R. **Demographic survey of the British colonial empire.** 3 v. London, 1948–53. Comprehensive study of available demographic data, including interesting facts on the history of census-taking, in British west Africa (v. 1), British east Africa, High Commission territories, Northern Rhodesia, Nyasaland, British Somaliland, Mauritius, and Seychelles (v. 2), by the former demographer of the Colonial Office. Bibliography.

LINGUISTIC WORKS

AC53. Basset, André. **La langue berbère.** London, 1952. [Handbook of African languages, 1.]

AC54. Greenberg, Joseph H. **Studies in African linguistic classification.** New Haven, 1955. Reprint of the author's *Southwestern journal of anthropology* articles, which develop a new classification scheme for African languages.

AC55. Guthrie, Malcolm. **The Bantu languages of western equatorial Africa.** London, 1953.

AC56. MacDougald, Duncan, Jr. **The languages and press of Africa.** Philadelphia, 1944. A census of principal African, European, and Asiatic languages spoken in Africa; survey of literacy by language and territory; and list of African newspapers. Bibliography.

AC57. Tucker, Archibald N., and Margaret A. Bryan. **The non-Bantu languages of north-eastern Africa, with a supplement on the non-Bantu languages of southern Africa.** London, 1956.

AC58. Westermann, Diedrich H., and Margaret A. Bryan. **The languages of west Africa.** London, 1952.

PRINTED COLLECTIONS OF SOURCES

AC59. Beer, George L. **African questions at the Paris peace conference, with papers on Egypt, Mesopotamia, and the colonial settlement.** N.Y., 1923.

AC60. Esquer, Gabriel, ed. **Collection de documents inédits sur l'histoire de l'Algérie.** Paris, 1912 ff.

AC61. Grandidier, Alfred, and others, eds. **Collection des ouvrages anciens concernant Madagascar.** 9 v. Paris, 1903–20.

AC62. Hertslet, Edward. **The map of Africa by treaty.** 3rd, rev. ed., by R. W. Brant and H. L. Sherwood, 3 v., London, 1909. Classic compilation of treaty texts with illustrative colored maps on European possessions and claims in Africa. This edition covers to end of 1908.

AC63. Southern Rhodesia. Central African Archives. **The Oppenheimer series.** London, 1945 ff. A de luxe series including diaries and other source material on southern African history.

AC64. Theal, George M., ed. **Records of south-eastern Africa, collected in libraries and archive departments in Europe.** 9 v. London, 1898–1903.

AC65. ——, ed. **Records of the Cape Colony, from February 1793, copied for the Cape government from manuscript documents in the Public Record Office, London.** 36 v. London, 1897–1905.

AC66. Van Riebeeck Society. **Van Riebeeck Society publications.** 37 v. Cape Town, 1918–56. Five series of volumes of diaries and other source materials on South African history.

SURVEYS

AC67. Baumann, Herman, and Diedrich Westermann. **Les peuples et les civilisations de l'Afrique.** Paris, 1948. Excellent summmary with considerable historical information.

AC68. Brown, William O., ed. **Contemporary Africa trends and issues.** Philadelphia, 1955. [Annals of the American Academy of Political and Social Science, 298.] This and *AC69–71* are useful synopses on contemporary African problems.

AC69. Haines, Charles G., ed. **Africa today.** Baltimore, 1955.

AC70. Stillman, Calvin W., ed. **Africa in the modern world.** Chicago, 1955.

AC71. American Assembly. **The United States and Africa.** N.Y., 1958.

AC72. Buell, Raymond L. **The native problem in Africa.** 2 v. N.Y., 1928. Monumental study of political, economic, and social problems created by western impact on Africans in Liberia and in British, French, and Belgian Africa south of the Sahara. Extensive bibliography.

AC73. Hailey, William M., baron. **An African survey: a study of problems arising in Africa south of the Sahara.** Rev. 1956 ed., London, 1957. Lord Hailey's 1,676 page revision follows outline of his classic 1938 *Survey*, but contains much new material and synthesizes the best scholarship available. Deals particularly with administrative problems, but covers a wide range of political, legal, economic, social, and educational issues.

AC74. Lugard, Sir Frederick J. D. **The dual mandate in British tropical Africa.** 4th ed., Edinburgh, 1929. Classic exposition of his concept of indirect rule, by the first governor of Nigeria. Covers administration, judicial system, land tenure, taxation, labor, education, and economic development.

AC75. Mair, Lucy P. **Native policies in Africa.** London, 1936.

AC76. Wieschhoff, Heinrich A. **Colonial policies in Africa.** Philadelphia, 1944. [Wieschhoff, H. A., ed., African handbooks, 5.] Summary of aims and methods of colonial powers in Africa. Bibliography.

AC77. Worthington, Edgar B. **Science in Africa: a review of scientific research relating to tropical and southern Africa.** London, 1938. Valuable reference volume summarizing pre-war position of studies in geology, climate, soil science, forestry, zoology, agriculture, animal husbandry, health, and medicine. Lengthy bibliography.

HISTORIES OF SPECIAL AREAS

AC78. Axelson, Eric V. **South-east Africa, 1488–1530.** London, 1940. History, based on primary sources, of the Portuguese acquisition of Arab states in southeast Africa. Appendices include a report on the archives and libraries of Portugal, and documents published for the first time. Extensive bibliography.

AC79. Blake, John W. **European beginnings in west Africa, 1454–1578.** London, 1937. Lively study by a British historian. Covers Portuguese discoveries and enterprise, the Spanish attempt to found an empire, and British and French rivalry in west Africa in the 15th and 16th centuries. Based largely on primary sources, some of which were published in *AC80*. Select bibliography.

AC80. ——, ed. and tr. **Europeans in west Africa, 1450–1560.** See *U42*.

AC81. Bovill, E. W. **The golden trade of the Moors.** London, 1958. This revision of the 1933 classic, *Caravans of the old Sahara*, is the best account in English of the medieval kingdoms of the western Sudan. Bibliography.

AC82. Brasio, Antonio. **Monumenta missionaria africana: Africa ocidental.** 4 v. Lisbon, 1952–54. Monumental history of

Portuguese activity in west Africa during the late 15th and the 16th centuries.

AC83. Chailley, Marcel. **Les grandes missions françaises en Afrique occidentale.** Dakar, 1953. Short history of French explorations in west Africa from 1639 to 1933. Bibliography.

AC84. Davies, Kenneth G. **The Royal African Company.** See *U131.*

AC85. Delafosse, Maurice. **Haut-Sénégal-Niger.** 3 v. Paris, 1912. Detailed and important study of medieval kingdoms of western Sudan.

AC86. Fage, J. D. **An introduction to the history of west Africa.** Cambridge, Eng., 1955. Concise and readable; good maps, and brief, annotated bibliography. Concentrates on period before World War II.

AC87. Macmillan, William M. **Africa emergent: a survey of social, political and economic trends in British Africa.** Rev. ed., Harmondsworth, Eng., 1949. This Penguin book is a readable and stimulating interpretation of the history and development of British Africa.

AC88. Martin, Eveline C. **The British west African settlements, 1750–1821: a study in local administration.** N.Y., 1927.

AC89. Welch, Sidney R. **Europe's discovery of South Africa.** Cape Town, 1937.

AC90. ——. **South Africa under King Manuel, 1495–1521.** Cape Town, 1946.

AC91. ——. **South Africa under King Sebastian and the cardinal.** Cape Town, 1949.

AC92. ——. **South Africa under John III, 1521–1557.** Cape Town, 1949.

AC93. ——. **Portuguese rule and Spanish crown in South Africa, 1581–1640.** Cape Town, 1950.

AC94. ——. **Portuguese and Dutch in South Africa, 1641–1806.** Cape Town, 1951.

AC95. Leconfield, Hugh A. W., baron. **The Atlantic and slavery.** London, 1935. Interesting on the slave coast and slave trading methods.

HISTORIES OF SPECIAL TOPICS

Exploration of Africa

The writings of explorers are our only written records of much of Africa in earlier times. Many of them are quite interesting, and the perceptive observations of some are of unusual value.

Anthologies

AC96. Axelson, Eric V., ed. **South African explorers.** London, 1954. Anthology of travel narratives of explorers of Africa south of the Zambezi, from Vasco da Gama to Livingstone and Selous, with an introductory outline of exploration. Bibliography of most important chronicles.

AC97. Howard, C., ed. **West African explorers.** London, 1952. [World classic series, 523.]

AC98. Macnair, James I., ed. **Livingstone's travels.** London, 1954. Well-chosen selections from David Livingstone's works. Geographical sections by Ronald Miller; and running commentary, preface, and introduction by editor. Bibliography.

AC99. Perham, Margery F., and Jack Simmons, eds. **African discovery: an anthology of exploration.** 2nd ed., London, 1957. New, essentially unrevised, edition of the 1942 anthology drawn from narratives of eleven great British explorers of Africa during the period 1769–1873. Introduction summarizes history of exploration.

AC100. Baker, John N. L. **A history of geographical discovery and exploration.** See *U69.*

West Africa

AC101. Allen, William, and T. R. H. Thomson. **A narrative of the expedition sent by her majesty's government to the river Niger in 1841.** 2 v. London, 1848.

AC102. Baikie, William B. **Narrative of an exploring voyage up the rivers Kwora and Binue in 1854.** London, 1856.

AC103. Barth, Henry. **Travels and discoveries in north and central Africa, 1849–55.** 5 v. London, 1857–58.

AC104. Bosman, William. **A new and accurate description of the coast of Guinea.** London, 1705.

AC105. Burton, Sir Richard F. **A mission to Gelele, king of Dahome.** 2 v. London, 1864.

AC106. Caillié, René. **Travels through central Africa to Timbuctoo, and across the great desert, to Morocco, performed in the years 1824–1828.** 2 v. London, 1830.

AC107. Clapperton, Hugh. **Journal of a second expedition into the interior of Africa from the bight of Benin to Soccatoo, to which is added the journal of Richard Lander from Kano to the seacoast, partly by a more eastern route.** London, 1829.

AC108. Denham, Dixon, Hugh Clapperton, and W. Oudney. **Narrative of travels and discoveries in northern and central Africa in the years 1822, 1823, and 1824.** London, 1826.

AC109. Horneman, Frederick. **The journal of Frederick Horneman's travels from Cairo to Mourzouk in the years 1797–8.** London, 1802.

AC110. Leo Africanus (Jean-Léon l'Africain). **Description de l'Afrique.** Tr. from Italian by A. Épaulard. New ed., 2 v., Paris, 1956. Best edition of this work, which is the principal source for historical geography of Maghreb, Sahara, and western Sudan in the 16th century.

AC111. Jobson, Richard. **The golden**

trade: or a discovery of the river Gambra, and the golden trade of the Aethiopians. London, 1623.

AC112. Kingsley, Mary H. **Travels in west Africa: Congo Français, Corisco and Cameroons.** London, 1897.

AC113. Laird, Macgregor, and R. A. K. Oldfield. **Narrative of an expedition into the interior of Africa, by the river Niger, in the steam-vessels Quorra and Alburkah, in 1832, 1833, and 1834.** 2 v. London, 1837.

AC114. Lander, Richard L., and John Lander. **Journal of an expedition to explore the course and termination of the Niger.** 3 v. London, 1832.

AC115. Park, Mungo. **Travels in the interior districts of Africa, 1795, 1796, and 1797.** 5th ed., London, 1807.

AC116. ——. **Travels in the interior parts of Africa, with an account of a subsequent mission to that country in 1805.** 2 v. London, 1816.

East and Central Africa

AC117. Baker, Sir Samuel W. **Ismailïa.** 2 v. London, 1874.

AC118. ——. **The Albert N'Yanza, great basin of the Nile.** 2 v. London, 1866.

AC119. ——. **The Nile tributaries of Abyssinia.** Philadelphia, 1867.

AC120. Bruce, James. **Travels to discover the source of the Nile.** 5 v. Edinburgh, 1790.

AC121. Crawford, Osbert G. S., ed. **Ethiopian itineraries, circa 1400–1524, including those collected by Alessandro Zorzi at Venice in the years 1519–1524.** Cambridge, Eng., 1958.

AC122. Livingstone, David. **Narrative of an expedition to the Zambesi and its tributaries.** London, 1865.

AC123. ——. **The last journals of David Livingstone in central Africa.** 2 v. London, 1874.

AC124. Speke, John H. **Journal of the discovery of the source of the Nile.** London, 1863.

AC125. ——. **What led to the discovery of the source of the Nile.** London, 1864.

AC126. Stanley, Sir Henry M. **How I found Livingstone in central Africa.** N.Y., 1872.

AC127. ——. **My Kalulu, prince, king, and slave: a story of central Africa.** London, 1873.

AC128. ——. **Coomassie and Magdala: the story of two British campaigns in Africa.** N.Y., 1874.

AC129. ——. **Through the dark continent.** 2 v. N.Y., 1878.

AC130. ——. **The Congo and the founding of its free state.** 2 v. N.Y., 1885.

AC131. ——. **In darkest Africa: or the quest, rescue and retreat of Emin, governor of Equatoria.** 2 v. N.Y., 1890.

AC132. ——. **My dark companions and their strange stories.** N.Y., 1893.

AC133. ——. **The autobiography of Sir Henry Morton Stanley.** N.Y., 1909.

Southern Africa

AC134. Alexander, Sir James E. **An expedition of discovery into the interior of Africa.** 2 v. London, 1838.

AC135. Barrow, Sir John. **An account of travels into the interior of southern Africa.** London, 1801.

AC136. Burchell, William J. **Travels in the interior of south Africa.** 2 v. London, 1822.

AC137. Campbell, John. **Travels in south Africa.** 2nd ed., London, 1815.

AC138. ——. **Travels in south Africa . . . a second journey.** 2 v. London, 1822.

AC139. Chapman, James. **Travels in the interior of south Africa.** 2 v. London, 1868.

AC140. Galton, Sir Francis F. **The narrative of an explorer in tropical south Africa.** London, 1853.

AC141. Gardiner, Allen F. **Narrative of a journey to the Zoolu country.** London, 1836.

AC142. Livingstone, David. **Missionary travels and researches in south Africa.** London, 1857.

AC143. ——. **Narrative of an expedition to the Zambesi and its tributaries.** London, 1865.

AC144. Moffat, Robert. **Missionary labours and scenes in southern Africa.** London, 1842.

AC145. Mossop, E. E., ed. and tr. **The journals of Brink and Rhenius.** Cape Town, 1947.

AC146. Oswell, William E. **William Cotton Oswell, hunter and explorer.** 2 v. London, 1900.

AC147. Peres, Damião. **Diário da viagem de Vasco da Gama.** 2 v. Oporto, 1945.

AC148. Santos, João dos. **Ethiopia oriental.** Evora, Portugal, 1609.

AC149. Selous, Frederick C. **Travel and adventure in south-east Africa.** London, 1893.

AC150. Sparrman, Anders. **Voyage to the Cape of Good Hope.** 2 v. London, 1785.

AC151. Waterhouse, Gilbert, ed. and tr. **Simon van der Stel's journal of his expedition to Namaqualand, 1685–1686.** Dublin, 1932.

Arab Travelers

AC152. Al Bakrī (Abu Obeid Abdulla el Bekri). **Description de l'Afrique septentrionale, texte arabe.** Tr. by W. MacGuckin, Baron de Slane. Rev. ed., Algiers, 1913.

AC153. Al Edrīsī. **Nuzhat al-Mushtāk. De geographia universali** (abridged Arab text), Rome, 1592; **Géographie d'Edrisi traduite de l'arabe en français et accompagnée de notes,** by Amédée Jaubert, 2 v., Paris, 1836–

40; **Description de l'Afrique et de l'Espagne, texte arabe, avec une traduction, des notes et un glossaire,** by R. Dozy and M. J. de Goeje, Leyden, 1866.

AC154. Ibn Batuta. **The travels of Ibn Batuta, A.D. 1325–1354.** Tr. by H. A. R. Gibb. Cambridge, Eng., 1958.

AC155. Ibn Khaldūn. **Histoire des Berbères et des dynasties musulmanes de l'Afrique septentrionale, texte arabe.** New ed. of French tr., by Paul Casanova, 4 v., Paris, 1925–56.

AC156. La Roncière, Charles de. **La découverte de l'Afrique au Moyen Âge, cartographes et explorateurs.** 2 v. Cairo, 1925.

AC157. 'Abd al-Rahmān ibn 'Abd Allāh, al-Sa'dī. **Documents arabes relatifs à l'histoire du Soudan: Tarikh es-Soudan.** French tr. by O. Houdas. 2 v. Paris, 1898–1900. Biased but valuable history of Songhai empire, by a Sudanese born in Timbuktu in 1596.

Archaeology

AC158. Alimen, Henriette. **The prehistory of Africa.** London, 1957. Overall account, by regions, of the prehistory of the entire continent, by a French archaeologist. Bibliographies.

AC159. Caton-Thompson, Gertrude. **The Zimbabwe culture, ruins and reactions.** Oxford, 1931. Results of the author's 1929 excavations at the Zimbabwe ruins in Southern Rhodesia, correlated with earlier findings. Bibliography.

AC160. Cole, Sonia M. **The prehistory of east Africa.** See *E45*.

AC161. Breuil, Henri, and others. **Rock paintings of southern Africa. V. 1, The white lady of the Brandberg.** London, 1955. Well-illustrated description and interpretation of rock paintings in southwest Africa, suggesting relationship to Egyptian and Cretan art, and hypothesis of foreign invasion about 2000 B.C.

AC162. Breuil, Henri. **Rock paintings of southern Africa. V. 2, Philipp cave.** London, 1958. Sequel to *AC161*.

AC163. Leakey, Louis S. B. **The Stone Age races of Kenya.** London, 1935. Report on the human remains of Stone Age man found in east Africa, related to findings in other parts of Africa and in Europe and Asia.

Art

AC164. Paulme, Denise. **Les sculptures de l'Afrique noire.** Paris, 1956. Excellent survey of African art by an anthropologist and art historian.

AC165. Radin, Paul, ed. **African folk tales and sculpture.** N.Y., 1952. De luxe volume including anthology of folk tales from Africa south of the Sahara, list of sources and glossary, and an essay on African negro art. Illustrated.

AC166. Wingert, Paul S. **The sculpture of Negro Africa.** N.Y., 1950. This and *AC164* are two of the best surveys of African art.

Economics

AC167. Bauer, Peter T. **West African trade: a study of competition, oligopoly and monopoly in a changing economy.** Cambridge, Eng., 1954. Important, controversial study of the structure and organization of the external and internal trade of British west Africa, focused on monopolistic tendencies. Bibliographical footnotes.

AC168. Bertieaux, Raymond. **Aspects de l'industrielisation en Afrique centrale.** Brussels, 1953. Analysis of economic resources, plans, and production of Congo basin territories, stressing need for industrialization. Statistical data and bibliography.

AC169. Hance, William A. **African economic development.** N.Y., 1958. Essays on aspects and problems of African economic development growing out of Council on Foreign Relations study group.

AC170. Frankel, S. Herbert. **Capital investment in Africa, its course and effects.** London, 1938. Historical analysis of course of investment in Africa south of the Sahara, with introductory section relating African economic development to current economic theory regarding investment. Bibliography.

AC171. ——. **The economic impact on under-developed societies: essays on international investment and social change.** Cambridge, Mass., 1953. Collection of nine essays dealing with some aspects of "the clash between the functional forces of modern industrialism and the rapidly disintegrating indigenous economies." Examines conceptual aspects of the problem and applies concepts to Africa.

AC172. Great Britain. Colonial Office. **An economic survey of the colonial territories, 1951.** 7 v. London, 1952. Presents systematically for each British colonial territory a concise statement of available economic data. V. 1–3 cover central, east, and west Africa.

AC173. Moussa, Pierre. **Les chances économiques de la communauté franco-africaine.** Paris, 1957. Thorough statement of French Eurafrican economic plans, by the director of economic affairs and planning in the overseas ministry.

AC174. Newlyn, Walter T., and D. C. Rowan. **Money and banking in British colonial Africa: a study of the monetary and banking systems of eight British African territories.** Oxford, 1954. Study by two economists of all monetary and financial institutions in British central and east Africa, Nigeria, and Ghana, analyzing their operations in terms of policy ends and proposing reforms.

AC175. Pim, Sir Alan W. **The financial and economic history of the African tropical territories.** Oxford, 1940. Concise, authoritative study of the course and extent of, and main factors contributing to, economic development in tropical Africa to 1936. Bibliographies and statistical appendices.

AC176. Meek, Charles K. **Land law and custom in the colonies.** 2nd ed., London, 1949. Scholarly study of agricultural land tenure systems in selected British colonies, including all of the African group except Gambia and the High Commission territories.

AC177. Noon, John A. **Labor problems of Africa.** Philadelphia, 1944. [African handbooks, 6.] Survey of labor conditions in Africa, by regions, with emphasis on change from subsistence to wage earning and the adequacy of manpower for present and future development. Bibliography.

AC178. Orde-Browne, Granville St. J. **The African labourer.** London, 1933. Authoritative survey of development, conditions, and problems of wage labor in Africa, with a summary of labor legislation in various territories.

AC179. United Nations. **Review of economic activity in Africa 1950 to 1954: supplement to World economic report, 1953–54.** N.Y., 1955. Compilation of data for the entire continent, excluding Egypt. Separate chapters on agriculture, mining, secondary industry, power, labor, foreign trade, fiscal developments, and investment. The United Nations' economic reviews have been published annually since 1949–50.

Education and Missions

AC180. Attwater, Donald. **The White Fathers in Africa.** London, 1937. Short, simply-written history and description of activity of the major Catholic missionary order in Africa.

AC181. Davies, Horton, and R. H. W. Shepherd, eds. **South African missions, 1800–1950: an anthology.** London, 1954. Extracts from the missionary literature of South Africa, arranged by subjects, including the people and their way of life, physical environment, government, and missionary life and activity.

AC182. De Marco, Roland R. **The Italianization of African natives: government native education in the Italian colonies, 1890–1937.** N.Y., 1943. Well-documented, scholarly study of Italian educational system in Libya, Italian Somaliland, and Eritrea, with emphasis on the period 1919–40, and in Ethiopia from 1936. Bibliography.

AC183. Conference on African Education. **African education: a study of educational policy and practice in British tropical Africa.** London, 1953. Reports of West Africa Study Group and East and Central Africa Study Group, 1951–52, and record of the combined conference held at Cambridge, Eng., September, 1952, all sponsored by the Nuffield Foundation and the Colonial Office.

AC184. Groves, Charles P. **The planting of Christianity in Africa.** 4 v. London, 1948–58. Monumental detailed history of missionary activity in Africa, 1840–1954.

AC185. African Education Commission. **Education in Africa: a study of west, south and equatorial Africa.** Comp. by Thomas J. Jones. N.Y., 1922. This and the following work are the well-known Phelps-Stokes Commission reports which reflected earlier United States interest in African educational development and influenced British planning for education. The 1922 report covers British territories, Liberia, Belgian Congo, and Angola.

AC186. ——. **Education in east Africa: a study of east, central and south Africa.** Comp. by Thomas J. Jones. N.Y., 1925.

AC187. Oliver, Roland A. **The missionary factor in east Africa.** London, 1952. Valuable, objective account of Christian enterprise in Kenya, Uganda, Tanganyika, and, to a lesser extent, Nyasaland. Bibliography.

AC188. Read, Margaret H. **Education and social change in tropical areas.** London, 1955. Collection of speeches and articles by a social anthropologist, with emphasis on relationship between educational methods and anthropological knowledge of social change in Africa and other lands.

AC189. Trimingham, John S. **The Christian church and Islam in west Africa.** London, 1955. Concise, booklet-length history.

AC190. Wilson, George H. **The history of the Universities' Mission to central Africa.**

Politics and Government

AC191. Anderson, James N. D. **Islamic law in Africa.** London, 1954. Survey of the position of Islamic law in the judicial system of each territory in British east and west Africa, with emphasis on interaction of Islamic and customary law. Glossary; appendix on Sudan.

AC192. Carter, Gwendolen M., and William O. Brown, eds. **Transition in Africa: studies in political adaptation.** Boston, 1958. Symposium of four articles on recent political developments in Ghana, Nigeria, the Federation of Rhodesia and Nyasaland, and Kenya. Valuable critical bibliography.

AC193. Hailey, William M. **Native administration in the British African territories.** 5 v. London, 1950–53. Comprehensive work describing in detail all local administrative systems in thirteen colonial territories, with excellent background sections. The five parts are devoted respectively to east Africa, central Africa and Zanzibar, west Africa, a general survey of the system of native administration, and the High Commission territories.

AC194. Hodgkin, Thomas L. **Nationalism in colonial Africa.** London, 1956. Informative survey of nationalism, broadly defined to include tribal associations, religious groups, trade unions, etc., as well as political parties, in Africa south of the Sahara. Intended for non-specialists. Excellent notes on sources.

Sociology

AC195. International African Institute. **Social implications of industrialization and urbanization in Africa south of the Sahara.** Paris, 1956. Report on the 1954 international conference on this subject organized by the Institute under UNESCO auspices. Bibliography.

AC196. Maunier, René. **The sociology of colonies.** See *U226.*

AC197. United Nations. "African elites." **International social science bulletin,** 8 (1956): 413–518. Symposium on concept and position of elites in Africa south of the Sahara, including articles on elites in various African territories, descriptions of three UNESCO-sponsored studies, and notes on African research and studies centers.

AC198. Wilson, Godfrey B., and Monica H. Wilson. **The analysis of social change, based on observations in central Africa.** Cambridge, Eng., 1954. Reprint of valuable sociological study setting forth a theory of society and social change.

Psychology

AC199. Carothers, John C. **The African mind in health and disease: a study in ethnopsychiatry.** Geneva, 1953. Technical study of pre-literate African psychology, by the consultant in mental health to the World Health Organization. Analyzes environmental and physical factors, and reviews knowledge to date in this little-studied field. Bibliography.

AC200. Mannoni, Dominique O. **Prospero and Caliban: the psychology of colonization.** See *AH67.*

BIOGRAPHIES

AC201. Burns, Sir Alan C. **Colonial civil servant.** London, 1949. Autobiography of former British colonial official, including his experiences in Nigeria and the Gold Coast.

AC202. Catroux, Georges. **Lyautey, le marocain.** Paris, 1952. Valuable study of Lyautey as "pacificator" and resident-general of Morocco, 1907–25, by a general who served under him.

AC203. Debenham, Frank. **The way to Ilala: David Livingstone's pilgrimage.** London, 1955. A readable geographer's biography, emphasizing Livingstone's contribution to geographical knowledge.

AC204. Elton, Godfrey. **Gordon of Khartoum: the life of General Charles George Gordon.** N.Y., 1955. Good recent biography of the British hero of the Sudan. First published in London, 1954, under the title, *General Gordon.*

AC205. Huxley, Elspeth J. **White man's country: Lord Delamere and the making of Kenya.** 2nd ed., 2 v., London, 1953. Long and interesting work, which is both a history of Kenya, focused on the European settlers, and a biography of their leader.

AC206. Kruger, Stephanus J. P. **The memoirs of Paul Kruger, four times president of the South African republic, told by himself.** London, 1952.

AC207. Millin, Sarah G. **Rhodes.** Rev. ed., London, 1952.

AC208. Mitchell, Sir Philip E. **African afterthoughts.** London, 1954. Autobiography of British official with long experience in east Africa.

AC209. Nkrumah, Kwame. **The autobiography of Kwame Nkrumah.** N.Y., 1957. Valuable autobiography by first prime minister of Ghana; useful to students of nationalism.

AC210. Oliver, Roland A. **Sir Harry Johnston and the scramble for Africa.** London, 1957. Sympathetic interpretation of Johnston's remarkable career.

AC211. Perham, Margery F. **Lugard: the years of adventure, 1858–1898.** London, 1956. First volume of a biography of the great colonial administrator, covering his early years, army career in India, and his expeditions in Nyasaland and Uganda.

AC212. ——, ed. **Ten Africans.** London, 1936.

AC213. Ritter, E. A. **Shaka Zulu: the rise of the Zulu empire.** London, 1955. Sympathetic historical novel, using unpublished data gathered by author from people who knew Shaka.

AC214. Smith, Edwin W. **Aggrey of Africa: a study in black and white.** N.Y., 1929. Biography of well-known west African educator.

AC215. Westermann, Diedrich, ed. **Autobiographies d'Africains: onze autobiographies d'indigènes originaires de diverses regions de l'Afrique et représentant des métiers et des degrés de culture différents.** French tr. by L. Homburger. Paris, 1943.

AC216. Williams, Basil. **Cecil Rhodes.** London, 1938.

GOVERNMENT PUBLICATIONS

The multitude of official publications relating to Africa is indicated in the following guides.

AC217. Belgium. Ministère des Colonies. **Liste des publications.** 1952/53 ff. Brussels, 1953 ff. (Annual.) List of all publications by the Ministry of Colonies and other official or semi-official organizations concerned with the Belgian Congo and Ruanda Urundi.

AC218. France. Ministère de la France d'Outre-mer. **Courrier des chercheurs.** Paris, 1949 ff. (Irregular.) Bibliographical and other research information.

AC219. Great Britain. Colonial Office. **Monthly list of official colonial publications.** London, 1948 ff. Mimeographed lists of current publications of Colonial Office and colonial administrations.

AC220. Hewitt, A. R. **Guide to resources for commonwealth studies in London, Oxford and Cambridge.** London, 1957. Valuable guide to material for study of the British commonwealth.

AC221. Rhodesia and Nyasaland. Central African Archives. **A guide to the public records of Southern Rhodesia under the regime of the British South Africa Company, 1890–1923.** Ed. by V. W. Hiller. Salisbury, So. Rhod., 1956. Excellent.

AC222. Union of South Africa. Archives Department. **The archives year book for South African history.** Cape Town, 1938 ff. Annual volume publishing theses and other historical writings of importance based on research in the South African archives.

AC223. Union of South Africa. Office of Census and Statistics. **Official year book of the Union and of Basutoland, Bechuanaland protectorate and Swaziland.** 1917 ff. Pretoria, 1918 ff. Official publications and other sources on South African history.

AC224. United Nations. **United Nations documents index.** N.Y., 1950 ff. (Monthly.) Material on Africa will be found in many documents of the United Nations and specialized agencies.

UNIVERSITY, ACADEMY, AND SOCIETY PUBLICATIONS AND PERIODICALS

More than fifty pages of Hailey's *African survey* (*AC73*) describe research institutions concentrating on African problems. As a corollary of new and more progressive colonial policies since World War II, metropolitan governments have given greater recognition to the need for comprehensive, systematic, and integrated research programs, with increased attention being devoted to the social sciences. In earlier years research was carried on primarily by local government institutions in Africa, and tended to concentrate on immediate problems of health, agriculture, and animal husbandry. For an outstanding annotated list of (a) research institutions and their publications, and (b) independently published journals see *AC14*.

Among research institutions in the social sciences, the International African Institute in London, founded in 1926, merits special mention. In addition to numerous excellent, detailed studies in African ethnology, sociology, and history, and occasional short memoranda, it publishes the following (*AC225–228*):

AC225. Africa. London, 1928 ff. (Quarterly.) An outstanding journal, mainly anthropological and linguistic in content, with excellent research news, book reviews, and bibliographies.

AC226. African abstracts. London, 1950 ff. (Quarterly.) Summarizes current periodical articles concerned with African ethnology, social studies, and linguistics.

AC227. Ethnographic survey of Africa. London, 1950 ff. (Irregular.) Excellent series of carefully edited volumes, each of which gives a concise and accurate account of the various aspects of life of a particular African people or group of related peoples. Each volume contains a comprehensive bibliography and specially prepared map.

AC228. Handbook of African languages. London, 1952 ff. (Irregular.) A unique series concisely summarizing current knowledge of African languages.

Other British periodicals which publish many articles on African subjects include the following (*AC229–237*):

AC229. African affairs. London, 1901 ff. [Royal African Society.] (Quarterly.)

AC230. Geographical journal. London, 1893 ff. [Royal Geographical Society.] (Monthly.)

AC231. Man. London, 1901 ff. [Royal Anthropological Institute of Great Britain and Ireland.] (Monthly.)

AC232. United empire. London, 1909 ff. [Royal Empire Society.] (Bimonthly.)

AC233. Great Britain. Colonial Office. **Annual report** [for each colony]. London, 1946 ff. Replaced the *Colonial report* series, which was suspended in 1940.

AC234. Journal of African administration. London, 1949 ff. [Colonial Office.] (Quarterly.)

AC235. Oversea education. London, 1929 ff. [Colonial Office.] (Quarterly.)

AC236. Corona. London, 1949 ff. [Colonial Office.] (Monthly.)

AC237. Colonial Research Committee. **Annual.** 1943/44 ff. London, 1944 ff. [Colonial Office.]

The following local journals in British African territories are also of value (*AC238–248*):

AC238. Journal of the Historical Society of Nigeria. Ibadan, 1956 ff. (Annual.)

AC239. Nyasaland journal. Blantyre, 1948 ff. [Nyasaland Society.] (Semiannual.) Deals with social, cultural, historical, and scientific matters.

AC240. Southern Rhodesia. Native Affairs Department. NADA. Salisbury, 1923 ff. (Annual.) Ethnology and administrative problems.

AC241. Tanganyika notes and records. Dar es Salaam, 1936 ff. [Tanganyika Society.] (Semiannual.)

AC242. Uganda journal. London, 1934 ff. [Uganda Society.] (Semiannual.)

AC243. University College of the Gold Coast. Historical Society for the Gold Coast and Togoland. Transactions. Achimota, 1953 ff.

AC244. Sudan notes and records. Khartoum, 1918 ff. (Semiannual.)

AC245. Rhodes-Livingstone papers. Livingstone, No. Rhod., 1938 ff. [Rhodes-Livingstone Institute.] (Semiannual.)

AC246. Rhodes-Livingstone Institute. **Communications.** Livingstone, 1943 ff. (Irregular.)

AC247. Human problems in central Africa. Cape Town, 1944 ff. [Rhodes-Livingstone Institute.] (Semiannual.) Excellent. Numerous books on anthropological and related subjects have also been published by this institute.

AC248. East African studies. Nairobi, Kenya, 1953 ff. [East African Institute of Social Research.] (Irregular.)

In west Africa, the Nigerian (formerly West African) Institute of Social and Economic Research sponsors research projects.

For research on French African problems, the Institut Français d'Afrique Noire (IFAN) was founded in 1938 at Dakar. It now has branches in each of the French West African territories, and publishes the following (*AC249–253*):

AC249. Bulletin. 15 v. Dakar, 1939–53. (Irregular quarterly.) Ser. B, 1954 ff. (Semiannual.)

AC250. Catalogues. Dakar, 1947 ff. (Irregular.)

AC251. Initiations africaines. Dakar, 1949 ff. (Irregular.) Monograph series.

AC252. Mémoires. Dakar, 1940 ff. (Irregular.) Monograph series.

AC253. Notes africaines. Dakar, 1939 ff. (Quarterly.)

The local branches of IFAN publish the following (*AC254–262*):

AC254. Études camerounaises. Douala, Fr. Eq. Afr., 1948 ff. (Quarterly.)

AC255. Études éburnéennes. Mâcon, France, 1950 ff. (Irregular.)

AC256. Études dahoméennes. Porto Novo, Fr. W. Afr., 1948 ff. (Semiannual.)

AC257. Études guinéennes. Conakry, Fr. W. Afr., 1947 ff. (Irregular.)

AC258. Études voltaïques. Ouagadougou, Fr. W. Afr., 1950 ff. (Irregular.)

AC259. Études nigeriennes. Niamey, Fr. W. Afr., 1953 ff. (Irregular.)

AC260. Études mauritaniennes. St. Louis du Sénégal, Fr. W. Afr., 1948 ff. (Irregular.)

AC261. Études sénégalaises. Dakar, 1949 ff. (Irregular.)

AC262. Études soudaniennes. Bamako, Fr. W. Afr., 1953 ff. (Irregular.)

Other French publications with valuable articles on Africa include the following (*AC263–270*):

AC263. L'Afrique et l'Asie. Paris, 1948 ff. [Centre des Hautes Études d'Administration Musulmane.] (Quarterly.)

AC264. Nouvelle revue française d'outremer. Paris, 1908 ff. [Comité Central de la France d'Outremer.] (Monthly.)

AC265. L'Afrique française. Paris, 1891 ff. [Comité de l'Afrique Française et Comité du Maroc.] (Monthly. Title varies.)

AC266. Institut d'Ethnologie, Musée de l'Homme. **Travaux et mémoires.** Paris, 1929 ff. (Irregular.)

AC267. Présence africaine. Paris, 1947 ff. (Quarterly.)

AC268. Annales de géographie. Paris, 1891 ff. [Société de Géographie.] (Frequency varies.)

AC269. Revue de l'histoire des colonies françaises. Paris, 1913 ff. [Société de l'Histoire des Colonies Françaises.] (Quarterly. Title varies.)

AC270. Société des Africanistes. Journal. Paris, 1931 ff. (Irregular.)

Important social science research studies on the Belgian Congo and Ruanda Urundi are published by the Institut pour la Récherche Scientifique en Afrique Centrale. In Belgium the Musée Royal du Congo Belge, the Institut Royal Colonial Belge (now the Académie Royale des Sciences Coloniales), and the Institut International des Civilisations Differentes (INCIDI) publish numerous annals, bulletins, and quarterly reviews.

AC271. Civilisations. Brussels, 1951 ff. [INCIDI.] (Quarterly.)

AC272. Zaïre. Brussels, 1947 ff. (Monthly.) The leading scholarly review devoted to the Congo.

AC273. Problèmes d'Afrique centrale. Brussels, 1949 ff. [Association des Anciens Etudiants de l'Institut Universitaire des Territoires d'Outre-Mer.] (Quarterly.)

The Portuguese Junta das Missões Geográficas e de Investigações do Ultramar was established in 1936 to advise the Portuguese colonial ministry on research problems. Ethnographic and linguistic research has been carried out under sponsorship of the Escola Nacional do Ultramar. In Portuguese Africa

three local journals are worthy of mention:
AC274. Cultura. Luanda, Angola, 1945 ff. [Instituto de Angola.] (Monthly.)

AC275. Boletim cultural de Guiné portuguesa. Bissau, Port. Guinea, 1946 ff. [Centro de Estudos da Guiné Portuguesa.] (Quarterly.)

AC276. Sociedade de Estudos de Mozambique. **Boletim.** Lourenço Marques, 1931 ff. (Monthly.)

In Spain the Instituto de Estudios Africanos publishes the following:

AC277. Africa. Madrid, 1943 ff. (Monthly.)

AC278. Archivos. Madrid, 1947 ff. (Quarterly.) A more scholarly publication than the above.

As an outgrowth of a government commission appointed in 1919 to investigate the need for research in African languages and customs, the University of Cape Town established chairs of anthropology and of Bantu ethnology, and other South African universities began work in these fields. The University of Cape Town School of African Studies publishes monographs, and its School of Librarianship publishes irregularly a valuable *Bibliographical series* (*AC15*). Other significant South African publications are the following (*AC279–285*):

AC279. African studies. Johannesburg, 1942 ff. [University of the Witwatersrand.] (Quarterly.) Scholarly journal of linguistics and ethnology.

AC280. Bantu studies. 15 v. Johannesburg, 1921–41. [University of the Witwatersrand.] Predecessor to the above.

AC281. Natal regional survey. Cape Town and London, 1950 ff. [University of Natal.] (Irregular.) A series designed to give an accurate and comprehensive portrayal of the social structure of the province.

AC282. Race relations. Johannesburg, 1933 ff. [South African Institute of Race Relations.] (Quarterly.)

AC283. Survey of race relations in South Africa. Johannesburg, 1947 ff. [South African Institute of Race Relations.] (Annual.) This institute also publishes numerous occasional pamphlets, oriented in the liberal tradition.

AC284. Journal of racial affairs. Stellenbosch, 1949 ff. [South African Bureau of Racial Affairs.] (Quarterly.) This organization of Afrikaner scholars also issues other publications sympathetic to Afrikaner nationalist policies.

AC285. South African journal of economics. Johannesburg, 1933 ff. [Economic Society of South Africa.] (Quarterly.)

The South African Institute of International Affairs issues occasional pamphlets and books.

North of the Sahara, the following local journals should be mentioned (*AC286–289*):

AC286. Cahiers de Tunisie. Tunis, 1953 ff. [Institut des Hautes Études de Tunis.] (Quarterly.)

AC287. Hespéris: archives berbères et bulletin. Paris and Rabat, 1921 ff. [Institut des Hautes Études Marocaines.] (Irregular.) This institute publishes several other serials.

AC288. Revue africaine. Algiers, 1856 ff. [Société Historique Algérienne.] (Bimonthly.)

AC289. Libia: rivista di studi libici. Tripoli, 1953 ff. (Quarterly.) Devoted to archaeology, ethnology, and sociology.

AC290. U. S. Library of Congress. **African newspapers currently received in selected American libraries.** Washington, 1956. Lists more than 120 African newspapers received in one or more of eight United States libraries.

NORTHERN AFRICA AND THE EAST AFRICAN HORN

ALGERIA, MOROCCO, AND TUNISIA

North African Surveys

AC291. Chouraqui, André. **Les juifs d'Afrique du nord.** Paris, 1952. Study of the situation of north African Jewry, including geographic distribution, economic plight, and modern welfare problems.

AC292. Despois, Jean. **L'Afrique du nord.** Paris, 1949. General ethnographic and economic survey, with discussion of climatic and environmental factors. Devotes attention to demographic questions, the position of nomads and semi-nomads, and the function of transhumants.

AC293. Guernier, Eugène L. **La Berbérie, l'Islam, et la France.** 2 v. Paris, 1950. Broad

historical study of north Africa before the arrival of Islam, during the Arab period, and after the French penetration. Discusses possible solutions to the problems of Islam in the modern world.

AC294. Julien, Charles A. **Histoire de l'Afrique du nord, Tunisie, Algérie, Maroc.** 2nd ed., 2 v., Paris, 1951–52. Classic history of north Africa with emphasis on Berber origins, the Carthaginian period, and Arab conquests. Special attention also given to Almoravid and Almohade periods. A fundamental, scholarly work.

AC295. Montagne, Robert. **Les Berbères et le makhzen au sud du Maroc.** Paris, 1930. Excellent political sociology of the tribes of western High Atlas, the Sus Valley, and the Anti-Atlas.

Algeria

AC296. Alazard, J., and E. Albertini. **Histoire et historiens de l'Algérie.** Paris, 1931. [Collection du centenaire de l'Algérie.] Although somewhat dated, this definitive study remains useful. Covers Algeria before and after the arrival of Islam; heavy emphasis on cultural analysis.

AC297. Bataillon, Claude. **Le Souf: étude de géographie humaine.** Algiers, 1955. Ethnographic research at El Oued oasis in the Erg Oriental. Includes examination of physical environment, social structure, mores, and economic life of the inhabitants.

AC298. Germain, Roger. **La politique indigène du Bugeaud.** Paris, 1955. Useful historical treatment of a leading French proconsul in 19th century Algeria.

Morocco (Formerly French)

AC299. Berque, Jacques. **Structures sociales du Haut-Atlas.** Paris, 1955. Sociological survey of one small system of Berber tribes in the valleys of the High Atlas of Morocco.

AC300. Cambon, Henri. **Histoire du Maroc.** Paris, 1952. General review of Moroccan history with emphasis on period leading up to the French protectorate of 1912.

AC301. Flamand, Pierre. **Un mellah en pays berbère demnate.** Paris, 1952. Detailed ethnological study of a Jewish community in the Berber Atlas Mountain region of Morocco.

AC302. Landau, Rom. **Moroccan drama, 1900–1955.** San Francisco, 1956. Sympathetic study of development of Moroccan nationalism after 1912; the most complete work available in English.

AC303. Montagne, Robert, ed. **Naissance du prolétariat marocain: enquête collective exécutée de 1948 à 1950.** Paris, 1952. Intensive survey of origins, migrations, and living patterns of Morocco's new urban workers. Excellent source material, graphs, and statistics.

AC304. Rézette, Robert. **Les partis politiques marocains.** Paris, 1955. A "stasiological" approach to Moroccan nationalism. Incorporates background on Islamic nationalist thought, the history of Moroccan parties, and definitive analysis of party structures.

AC305. Terrasse, Henri. **Histoire du Maroc des origines à l'établissement du protectorat français.** 2 v. Casablanca, 1949–50. English tr. by Hilary Tee, 1952. Excellent pre-protectorate history of the Moroccan people, including the Merinid, Saadian, and Alawite periods. Also contains a definitive discussion of the country's religious, linguistic, and economic development.

Morocco (Formerly Spanish)

AC306. Coon, Carleton S. **Tribes of the Rif.** Cambridge, Mass., 1931. Anthropological study of physical characteristics, institutions, social patterns and customs, and political system of the Berber tribes in former northern Spanish zone of Morocco. Useful statistics and other data.

AC307. García Figueras, Tomás, and Rafael de Roda Jiménez. **Economía social de Marruecos.** 3 v. Madrid, 1950–55. Standard reference work on development of former Spanish Morocco. Particular emphasis on social and economic advances, as well as public administration.

AC308. Valderrama Martínez, Fernando. **Historia de la acción cultural de España en Marruecos.** Tetuán, Sp. Mor., 1956. Comprehensive evaluation of Spain's cultural achievements in its former northern Moroccan protectorate. Excellent data and source material.

AC309. Beneitez Cantero, Valentín. **Sociología marroquí.** Tetuán, 1952. Excellent study, by former Spanish interventor, of the people, linguistic groupings, social and cultural instituions, and trends toward modernization in the Spanish Moroccan area.

Tunisia

AC310. Bourguiba, Habib. **La Tunisie et la France: vingt-cinq ans de lutte pour une coopération libre.** Paris, 1954. Selected abstracts of communications and speeches of Habib Bourguiba, leader of the Neo-Destour party, who, beginning in 1932, made clear his policy of "free cooperation."

AC311. Cambon, Henri. **Histoire de la régence de Tunisie.** Paris, 1948. Classic history of Tunisia from pre-protectorate period to recent years. Excellent bibliography.

AC312. Laitman, Leon. **Tunisia today: crisis in north Africa.** N.Y., 1954. Useful general survey with material on geography, people, economic development, levels of living, and problems with France.

Tangier

AC313. Landau, Rom. **Portrait of Tangier.** London, 1952. General historical review up to modern times, with heavy emphasis on the period of English control (1661–84). Good account of the international administration, which was terminated in 1956.

AC314. Stuart, Graham H. **The international city of Tangier.** 2nd ed., Stanford, 1955. Standard reference work with chapters on historical background, the peoples, international machinery, and court system. Revised to include World War II occupation by Spanish.

LIBYA AND THE SUDAN

Libya

AC315. Becker, George H. **The disposition of the Italian colonies, 1941–1951.** Annemasse, France, 1952. Thorough examination of the handling of Libya, Eritrea, and Italian Somaliland by the Big Four foreign ministers and the United Nations.

AC316. Evans-Pritchard, Edward E. **The Sanusi of Cyrenaica.** Oxford, 1949. Survey of birth of the Sanusi religious brotherhood, its leadership, organization, and principles. Includes historical background on the spread of the Sanusi and the Italian occupation of Libya.

AC317. Rennell, Francis J., baron. **British military administration of occupied territories in Africa during the years 1941–1947.** London, 1948. Account of British military administration of former Italian colonies. Select bibliography.

The Sudan

AC318. Abbas, Mekki. **The Sudan question: the dispute over the Anglo-Egyptian condominium, 1884–1951.** London, 1952. Objective, scholarly analysis of the elements of the dispute, by a Sudanese, subsequently a director of the Sudan Gezira Board. Bibliography.

AC319. Crawford, Osbert G. S. **The Fung kingdom of Sennar, with a geographical account of the middle Nile region.** Gloucester, 1951. Study by an archaeologist of the Fung empire (1504–1821) situated in what is now the Sudan; based on primary sources and archaeological evidence. Appendices of itineraries and extracts from accounts of early travelers; bibliography.

AC320. Duncan, J. S. R. **The Sudan, a record of achievement.** Edinburgh, 1952. Comprehensive history of political, economic, and social development, 1899–1952.

AC321. Evans-Pritchard, Edward E. **Kinship and marriage among the Nuer.** Oxford, 1951. Anthropological analysis of kinship structure in the villages and of the rules and procedure of marriage among the Nuer of the southern Sudan.

AC322. ——. **Nuer religion.** Oxford, 1956. The Nuer concept of the Spirit and of man's relation to it.

AC323. ——. **The Nuer: a description of the modes of livelihood and political institutions of a Nilotic people.** Oxford, 1940. This first volume of a full-length anthropological study of the Nuer of the southern Sudan analyzes the political system based on lineages.

AC324. ——. **Witchcraft, oracles and magic among the Azande.** Oxford, 1937. Important anthropological work on witchcraft and magic among a negro people of the southwest Sudan.

AC325. MacMichael, Sir Harold A. **A history of the Arabs in the Sudan and some account of the people who preceded them and of the tribes inhabiting Dáfūr.** 2 v. Cambridge, Eng., 1922. Scholarly work for specialists. V. 2 is devoted to native manuscripts. Bibliography.

AC326. ——. **The Sudan.** London, 1954. Outline of Sudan history to 1902, account of subsequent administrative, social, and economic developments, and full analysis of political events during ten years preceding publication.

AC327. Nadel, Siegfried F. **The Nuba: an anthropological study of the hill tribes in Kordofan.** London, 1947. Authoritative, well-written study of the predominantly negro peoples of Kordofan province in the Sudan.

AC328. Schlippe, Pierre de. **Shifting cultivation in Africa: the Zande system of agriculture.** London, 1956. Analysis, for social anthropologists and agronomists, of ways of adapting modern agricultural practice to the environment and traditional agriculture of the African.

AC329. Shibeika, Mekki. **British policy in the Sudan, 1882–1902.** London, 1952. Scholarly diplomatic history, by a Sudanese, based largely on primary sources, British official documents and private papers, and material in the Sudan. Bibliography.

AC330. Tothill, John D., ed. **Agriculture in the Sudan.** London, 1948. Comprehensive reference work. Studies of all aspects of agricultural practice and development, each written by an expert. Extensive bibliography.

AC331. Trimingham, John S. **Islam in the Sudan.** London, 1949. General survey of Islamic religion in the Sudan, covering the Mahdist movement, various religious brotherhoods, and impact of the West on the Islamic way of life.

ETHIOPIA AND THE SOMALILANDS

Ethiopia

AC332. Beckingham, Charles F., and G. W. B. Huntingford. **Some records of Ethiopia 1593–1646, being extracts from "The history of high Ethiopia or Abassia," by Manoel de Almeida, together with Bahrey's "History of the Galla."** London, 1954. [Hakluyt Society, ser. 2, v. 107.] Fourth of Hakluyt Society volumes on Ethiopia.

AC333. **The royal chronicle of Abyssinia, 1769–1840.** Ed. and tr. by H. Weld Blundell. Cambridge, Eng., 1922. Text of a later portion of the royal chronicles in Ge'ez, followed by complete translation and scholarly notes.

AC334. Hotten, John C., ed. **Abyssinia and its people: or, life in the land of Prester**

John. London, 1868. Well-known and interesting book based on résumés of accounts of earlier travelers. Written at time of the British punitive expedition to Abyssinia in 1867.

AC335. Budge, Sir Ernest A. **A history of Ethiopia, Nubia and Abyssinia (according to the hieroglyphic inscriptions of Egypt and Nubia, and the Ethiopian chronicles).** 2 v. London, 1928. Monumental work by the keeper of Egyptian and Assyrian antiquities of the British Museum, presenting results of scholarship in translations of classical inscriptions and medieval and modern Ethiopic chronicles concerning the history of Ethiopia from the time of the Pharaohs to the 20th century.

AC336. Howard, William E. H. **Public administration in Ethiopia: a study in retrospect and prospect.** Groningen, Neth., 1955. Based on field work, this includes a history of the government before the Italian occupation and an analysis of the postwar administrative and judicial systems. Appendices include texts of the 1931 constitution and the federation agreement with Eritrea. Bibliography.

AC337. Longrigg, Stephen H. **A short history of Eritrea.** Oxford, 1945. Useful addition to scanty literature in English, by chief administrator of Eritrea from 1942 to 1944.

AC338. Marein, Nathan. **The Ethiopian empire, federation and laws.** Rotterdam, 1955. General outline of Ethiopian laws of commerce and trade, as well as brief review of recent legislation and the 1931 constitution.

AC339. Mathew, David. **Ethiopia—the study of a polity, 1540–1935.** London, 1947. History by the Apostolic delegate to east Africa, an experienced historian, based largely on English sources.

AC340. Perham, Margery F. **The government of Ethiopia.** London, 1948. Comprehensive work, including valuable description of central institutions—ruling class, monarchy, church, army, machinery of law—and analysis of conflict between centralization and separatism. Bibliography.

AC341. Trimingham, John S. **Islam in Ethiopia.** London, 1952. Scholarly history of the penetration of Islam in the horn of Africa, covering tribal distribution and special characteristics of Islam in the area.

AC342. ——. **The Christian church and missions in Ethiopia (including Eritrea and the Somalilands).** London, 1950. A booklet, one of the Church Missionary Society series, describing the National Church of Ethiopia and the missions and their work since the pre-Italian period.

The Somalilands

AC343. Cerulli, Enrico. **Somalia: scritti vari editi ed inediti.** Rome, 1957. Collection of Cerulli's excellent pioneer Somali studies, plus hitherto unpublished Arabic history of the Zengi.

AC344. Hunt, John A. **A general survey of the Somaliland protectorate 1944–1950.** Hargeisa, Br. Som., 1951. Report on seven year geographical survey recommending various lines of development. Extensive bibliography.

AC345. Lewis, I. M. **Peoples of the horn of Africa, Somali, Afar, and Saho.** London, 1955. Ethnographic compendium treating tribal structure, clan groups, religious beliefs, and economic organization of the horn peoples.

THE SAHARA

AC346. Capot-Rey, Robert. **Le Sahara français.** Paris, 1953. Classic study detailing physical and human geography, and France's constructive role.

AC347. Caro Baroja, Julio. **Estudios saharianos.** Madrid, 1955. The most comprehensive ethnological study to date of the peoples of Spanish Sahara. Excellent statistical data and compilations.

AC348. Charbonneau, Jean, ed. **Le Sahara français.** Paris, 1955. [Cahiers Charles de Foucauld, 38.] Compilation of articles by French authorities on geography, history, people, economic prospects, and missionary activity in the Sahara.

AC349. Cornet, Pierre. **Sahara, terre de demain.** Paris, 1956. A French view of the economic and human potential of the Sahara. Well-documented discussion of human problems, and excellent economic summary.

AC350. Le Fèvre, George, and P. Mannoni. **Notre Sahara.** Paris, 1956. Brief account of French exploration and conquest in the Sahara, largely in the 19th century.

AC351. Rennell, Francis J., baron. **People of the veil.** London, 1926. General study of habits, values, and institutions of the nomadic Tuareg people of Air and Asben in the central Sahara.

AC352. Sergent, Edmond. **Le peuplement humain du Sahara.** Algiers, 1953. Study by a biologist of human potential for Sahara development.

AC353. Strasser, Daniel. **Réalités et promesses sahariennes: aspects juridiques et économiques de la mise en valeur industrielle du Sahara français.** Paris, 1956. An explanation of French economic development program in the Sahara. Outlines the beginnings of Organisation Commune des Régions Sahariennes Française.

AFRICA SOUTH OF THE SAHARA

BRITISH AND FORMER BRITISH WEST AFRICA

Nigeria

AC354. Akpan, Ntieyong U. **Epitaph to indirect rule.** London, 1956. Interesting account of indirect rule and modern ideas of local government, by an African district officer.

AC355. Awolowo, Obafemi. **Path to Nigerian freedom.** London, 1947. Important and relatively moderate expression of nationalist views, by a Nigerian leader.

AC356. Buchanan, Keith M., and J. C. Pugh. **Land and people in Nigeria: the human geography of Nigeria and its environmental background.** London, 1955. Beautifully documented with maps and charts; gives well-rounded consideration to economic and social geography.

AC357. Burns, Sir Alan C. **History of Nigeria.** 5th ed., London, 1955. Standard narrative of Nigerian history, by a British official. Revision deletes paternalistic opinions of earlier editions. Useful appendices include relevant treaty texts.

AC358. Cook, Arthur N. **British enterprise in Nigeria.** Philadelphia, 1943. Competent study with annotated bibliography.

AC359. Crocker, Walter R. **Nigeria: a critique of British colonial administration.** London, 1936. Criticism of indirect rule, by a colonial official.

AC360. Dike, Kenneth O. **Trade and politics in the Niger Delta, 1830–1885: an introduction to the economic and political history of Nigeria.** Oxford, 1956. A Nigerian historian's valuable reinterpretation of British-Nigerian relations, based on local as well as European documentation.

AC361. Elias, Taslim O. **Groundwork of Nigerian law.** London, 1954. Useful volume, designed as text for Nigerian lawyers.

AC362. Elias, Taslim O. **Nigerian land law and custom.** 2nd ed., London, 1953. Valuable study of Nigerian land tenure in light of growing body of case law. Bibliography.

AC363. Galletti, R., K. D. S. Baldwin, and I. O. Dina. **Nigerian cocoa farmers: an economic survey of Yoruba cocoa farming families.** London, 1956. Detailed survey of social and economic organization.

AC364. Greenberg, Joseph H. **The influence of Islam on a Sudanese religion.** N.Y., 1947.

AC365. Hogben, S. J. **The Muhammedan emirates of Nigeria.** London, 1930. Good study of northern Nigeria.

AC366. International Bank for Reconstruction and Development. **The economic development of Nigeria.** Baltimore, 1955. Excellent economic survey, showing economic potential as well as chief problems and needs.

AC367. Kaberry, Phyllis M. **Women of the grassfields: a study of the economic position of women in Bamenda, British Cameroons.** London, 1952. Thorough study of social and economic life in a British Cameroons division, focused on the position of women in the area.

AC368. Kingsley, Mary H. **West African studies.** 2nd ed., London, 1901 Unusually perceptive early study.

AC369. Kirk-Greene, Anthony H. M. **Adamawa, past and present: an historical approach to the development of a northern Cameroons province.** London, 1958. Useful and original narrative, by a British official. Bibliography.

AC370. Lugard, Sir Frederick J. D. **The dual mandate in British tropical Africa.** See *AC74.*

AC371. Meek, Charles K. **Land tenure and land administration in Nigeria and the Cameroons.** London, 1957.

AC372. ——. **Law and authority in a Nigerian tribe: a study in indirect rule.** London, 1937. Scholarly investigation of social and political structure, role of law, and impact of indirect rule.

AC373. Nadel, Siegfried F. **A black Byzantium: the kingdom of Nupe in Nigeria.** London, 1942. Excellent analysis.

AC374. Parrinder, Geoffrey. **Religion in an African city.** London, 1953. Interesting analysis of Christianity, Islam, and animist religions in Yoruba, city of Ibadan. Statistical appendices.

AC375. Perham, Margery F. **Native administration in Nigeria.** N.Y., 1937. A good study.

AC376. ——, ed. **The economics of a tropical dependency.** 2 v. London, 1946–48. Intensive analysis, by a team of economists and anthropologists, of Nigerian subsistence and exchange economies, agriculture, mining, trade, and balance of payments.

AC377. Talbot, Percy A. **The peoples of southern Nigeria: a sketch of their history, ethnology and languages.** 4 v. London, 1926. This and the next Talbot volume, although partly superseded by later research, are the only publications on certain tribal groups.

AC378. ——. **Tribes of the Niger Delta, their religions and customs.** London, 1932.

AC379. U. S. Bureau of Foreign Commerce. **Investment in Nigeria: basic information for United States business men.** By Bernard Blankenheimer. Washington, 1957. Useful economic analysis.

AC380. Wheare, Joan. **The Nigerian legis-**

lative council. London, 1950. Fourth volume in a valuable group of Nuffield College studies of colonial legislation, edited by Margery Perham.

Ghana

AC381. Apter, David E. **The Gold Coast in transition.** Princeton, 1955. Valuable effort to explain the process of transfer of western institutions to African context.

AC382. Bourret, Florence M. **The Gold Coast: a survey of the Gold Coast and British Togoland, 1919–1951.** 2nd ed., Stanford, 1952. Scholarly analysis of political and economic development. Bibliography.

AC383. Busia, Kofi A. **The position of the chief in the modern political system of Ashanti.** London, 1951. Clear analysis of the chief's traditional role and how it changed under British administration.

AC384. Claridge, William W. **A history of the Gold Coast and Ashanti from the earliest times to the commencement of the twentieth century.** 2 v. London, 1915. Still valued as standard history of the Gold Coast.

AC385. Danquah, Joseph B. **The Akan doctrine of God, a fragment of Gold Coast ethics and religion.** London, 1944.

AC386. Meyerowitz, Eva. **Akan traditions of origin.** London, 1952. Provocative interpretation.

AC387. ——. **The sacred state of the Akan.** London, 1951.

AC388. Padmore, George. **The Gold Coast revolution: the struggle of an African people from slavery to freedom.** London, 1953. Important expression of nationalist views by an author close to African political leaders.

AC389. Rattray, Robert S. **The tribes of the Ashanti hinterland.** 2 v. Oxford, 1932. Rattray's Ashanti studies are indispensable.

AC390. ——. **Ashanti law and constitution.** Oxford, 1929.

AC391. ——. **Ashanti.** Oxford, 1956. Reprint of author's 1923 study of Ashanti religion and ceremonies, including a note on the golden stool.

AC392. ——. **Religion and art in Ashanti.** Oxford, 1927.

AC393. Wight, Martin. **The Gold Coast legislative council.** London, 1947. Best volume on Gold Coast government and politics, 1925–46. Useful appendices include texts of 1925 and 1946 constitutions.

AC394. Ward, William E. F. **A history of the Gold Coast.** London, 1948. Primarily history of tribal wars and European rivalries. Based heavily on Claridge and Rattray, but uses local traditions as well as European sources.

Sierra Leone

AC395. Banton, Michael P. **West African city: a study of tribal life in Freetown.**

London, 1957. Revealing account of urbanization, voluntary societies, and tribal administration.

AC396. Little, Kenneth L. **The Mende of Sierra Leone, a west African people in transition.** London, 1951. Important study of social structure, secret societies, and social change in 1945–46.

AC397. Richardson, E. M., and G. R. Collins. **Economic and social survey of the rural areas of Sierra Leone.** London, 1952. Detailed examination of four fishing villages which lose youths to Freetown, but gain people from the protectorate.

AC398. Utting, Francis A. J. **The story of Sierra Leone.** London, 1931. Covers precolonial as well as colonial history.

Gambia

AC399. Gray, John M. **A history of the Gambia.** Cambridge, Eng., 1940. Primarily concerned with European power rivalries from the 15th to 19th centuries; sketchy from 1888 to 1938.

AC400. Southorn, Bella S. **The Gambia.** London, 1952. Deals with pre-colonial as well as colonial history.

BRITISH EAST AFRICA

General

AC401. Coupland, Sir Reginald. **East Africa and its invaders, from the earliest times to the death of Seyyid Said in 1856.** Oxford, 1938. Good account in a field where more research is required before a definitive work can be written.

AC402. ——. **The exploitation of east Africa, 1856–1890; the slave trade and the scramble.** London, 1939. A good history, but the definitive account is still to be written.

AC403. Great Britain. East Africa Royal Commission. **Report** [1953–55]. London, 1955. This significant inquiry into means of increasing national income and raising living standards in east Africa reviews measures taken to protect the African, Asian, and European communities, and proposes a freer economy concerned with safeguarding individual rather than communal rights as the way to economic expansion.

AC404. The Economist. **The economy of east Africa: a study of trends.** London, 1955. Good appraisal of the economic growth of east Africa.

Kenya

AC405. Dilley, Marjorie R. **British policy in Kenya colony.** N.Y., 1937. Well documented study of 1900–35 period.

AC406. Huntingford, George W. B. **The Nandi of Kenya: tribal control in a pastoral**

society. London, 1953. Lucid description of the age-grade system which figures prominently in this largely decentralized Nilo-Hamitic tribe.

AC407. Huxley, Elspeth J. **Race and politics in Kenya.** 2nd ed., London, 1956. Enlightening discussion of Kenya's most pressing problem.

AC408. Kenyatta, Jomo. **Facing Mount Kenya.** London, 1938. Anthropological study of Kikuyu by convicted Mau Mau leader.

AC409. Lambert, H. E. **Kikuyu social and political institutions.** N.Y., 1956. Chiefly of traditional Kikuyu society, and entirely pre-Mau Mau.

AC410. Leakey, Louis S. B. **Defeating Mau Mau.** London, 1954. This and the following Leakey volume are the most authoritative study of the causes and organization of Mau Mau.

AC411. ——. **Mau Mau and the Kikuyu.** London, 1952.

AC412. Prins, Adriaan H. J. **East African age-class systems: an inquiry into the social order of the Galla, Kipsigis and the Kikuyu.** Groningen, Neth., 1953. A scholarly comparative study.

Tanganyika

AC413. Cameron, Sir Donald C. **My Tanganyika service and some Nigeria.** London, 1939. A contribution to the history of Tanganyika during early years of the British mandate.

AC414. Leubuscher, Charlotte. **Tanganyika territory: a study of economic policy under mandate.** London, 1944. Scholarly and authoritative.

AC415. Malcolm, Donald W. **Sukumaland: an African people and their country: a study of land use in Tanganyika.** London, 1953. Survey, by a government official, including documents, statistics, and bibliography.

AC416. Tanganyika. **Tanganyika, a review of its resources and their development.** Dar es Salaam, 1955. Comprehensive source book with good maps and tables. Bibliography.

Uganda

AC417. Fallers, Lloyd A. **Bantu bureaucracy: a study of integration and conflict in the political institutions of an east African people.** Cambridge, Eng., 1956. An analysis of Soga (peasant farmers in the Busoga district of Uganda) polity, stressing the changes which have occurred during the past fifty years as British rule brought foreign administrative practices.

AC418. Gulliver, P. H. **The family herds: a study of two pastoral tribes in east Africa.** London, 1955. This comparative analysis of

Jie (northern Uganda) and Turkana (northern Kenya) society points up the influences of differing ecological circumstances upon the institutions of two culturally and historically related tribes.

AC419. Johnston, Sir Harry H. **The Uganda protectorate.** 2nd ed., 2 v., N.Y., 1904. Counted among the east African classics.

AC420. Lawrance, J. C. D. **The Iteso: fifty years of change in a Nilo-Hamitic tribe of Uganda.** London, 1957. Comprehensive work covering history, social organization, administration, political organization, and law of Uganda's second largest tribe.

AC421. Munger, Edwin S. **Relational patterns of Kampala, Uganda.** Chicago, 1951. A geographer's study of Kampala through examination of its functions and relationships with the world outside its urban area.

AC422. Richards, Audrey I., ed. **Economic development and tribal change: a study of immigrant labour in Buganda.** Cambridge, Eng., 1952. Investigation of migrant labor in a tribal economy modified by cash crop cotton farming, providing an interesting contrast to the problem of migrant wage earners employed in Western-type enterprise.

AC423. Winter, Edward H. **Bwamba: a structural-functional analysis of a patrilineal society.** Cambridge, Eng., 1956. Comprehensive ethnography of the Amba, who live in a cultural border area between politically advanced states of Uganda and the simply structured societies of the Ituri forest.

Zanzibar

AC424. Hollingsworth, Lawrence W. **Zanzibar under the Foreign Office, 1890–1913.** London, 1953. Carefully documented study of establishment of the British protectorate and the suppression of slavery.

AC425. Ingrams, William H. **Zanzibar, its history and people.** London, 1931. Older work still of value.

THE RHODESIAS AND NYASALAND

AC426. Barnes, James A. **Politics in a changing African society: a political history of the Fort Jameson Ngoni.** Cape Town, 1954. Well-written anthropologist's history of Ngoni migration, state organization, and political evolution under colonial administration. Annotated bibliography.

AC427. Colson, Elizabeth, and Max Gluckman, eds. **Seven tribes of British central Africa.** London, 1951. Nozi, Plateau Tonga, Bemba, Fort Jameson Ngoni, Nyaleyusa, Yao, and Shona tribal history and social organization are described in this valuable collection of studies by seven leading authorities sponsored by Rhodes-Livingstone Institute.

AC428. Coupland, Sir Reginald. **Kirk on the Zambezi: a chapter of African history.** Oxford, 1928. Narrative of Dr. John Kirk's part in Livingstone's second expedition, 1858–63.

AC429. Davidson, James W. **The Northern Rhodesian legislative council.** London, 1948. Only study of Northern Rhodesian government and politics before World War II.

AC430. Deane, Phyllis. **Colonial social accounting.** Cambridge, Eng., 1953. Original analysis of standards of living in Northern Rhodesia and Nyasaland, particularly in rural communities. Useful tables and appendices.

AC431. Epstein, Arnold L. **Politics in an urban African community.** Manchester, 1958. Valuable investigation of urbanization in the Northern Rhodesian copper belt, applying anthropological methods to study of administration and politics among Africans in Luanshya.

AC432. ——. **The administration of justice and the urban African: a study of urban native courts in Northern Rhodesia.** London, 1953.

AC433. Gann, L. H. **The birth of a plural society: Northern Rhodesia under the British South African Company, 1894–1914.** Manchester, 1958. Valuable historical analysis.

AC434. Hanna, Alexander J. **The beginnings of Nyasaland and North-eastern Rhodesia, 1859–1895.** Oxford, 1956. Useful narrative of British central African history, with original material based on Foreign Office dispatches and related sources. Bibliography.

AC435. Gluckman, Max. **The judicial process among the Barotse of Northern Rhodesia.** Manchester, 1955.

AC436. Holleman, Johan F. **Shona customary law, with reference to kinship, marriage, the family and the estate.** Cape Town, 1952. Scholarly study of Southern Rhodesian Mashona.

AC437. Johnston, Sir Harry H. **British central Africa: an attempt to give some account of a portion of the territories under British influence north of the Zambezi.** 2nd ed., London, 1898. Still of value.

AC438. Mitchell, J. Clyde. **The Yao village: a study in the social structure of a Nyasaland tribe.** Manchester, 1956. Good anthropological work.

AC439. Paver, B. G. **Zimbabwe cavalcade, Rhodesia's romance.** Johannesburg, 1950. Useful popular account of Zimbabwe ruins. Good bibliography of books and articles supporting both the ancient and medieval theories of Zimbabwe origins.

AC440. Read, Margaret H. **The Ngoni of Nyasaland.** London, 1956.

AC441. Richards, Audrey I. **Chisungu: a girls' initiation ceremony among the Bemba** of Northern Rhodesia. London, 1956. Interesting anthropological study.

AC442. ——. **Land, labour and diet in Northern Rhodesia: an economic study of the Bemba tribe.** London, 1951. Reprint of excellent anthropological work first published in 1939.

AC443. Thompson, Cecil H., and Harry W. Woodruff. **Economic development in Rhodesia and Nyasaland.** London, 1954. Analysis of Rhodesian economic history, resources, and needs, by two government economists. Valuable statistical tables and appendices.

AC444. Watson, Sir Malcolm. **African highway: the battle for health in central Africa.** London, 1953. Account of fight against malaria and other tropical diseases in the copper belt of Northern Rhodesia.

AC445. Wilson, Monica H. **Good company: a study of Nyakyusa age-villages.** London, 1951. Interesting presentation of thorough scholarship on tribe at northwest corner of Lake Nyasa.

FORMER FRENCH TERRITORIES

Former French West Africa

AC446. Akindélé, Adolphe, and Cyrille Arguessy. **Contribution à l'étude de l'histoire de l'ancien royaume de Porto-Novo.** Dakar, 1953. History of the former kingdom of Porto Novo, Dahomey, including material on the court and government, and family and religious customs. Based on the 1914 work written in Yoruba by the father of one of the authors. Select bibliography.

AC447. Boulnois, Jean, and Boubou Hama. **L'empire de Gao: histoire, coutumes et magie des Sonrai.** Paris, 1954. Non-technical historical and ethnological study of the Songhai people, by a French doctor and an African teacher.

AC448. Boyer, Gaston. **Un peuple de l'Ouest soudanais, les Diawara. Contribution à l'histoire des Songhay.** Dakar, 1953. Two monographs: the first a historical and anthropological study of the Diawara, a Mohammedan tribe in the Sudan; and the second a history of the Songhai, based on chronicles. Bibliography.

AC449. Delavignette, Robert L. **Freedom and authority in French West Africa.** London, 1950. Philosophy and practice of administration in French West Africa before World War II, by a prominent French administrator. Translation of the 1946 French work, _Service africain_, a revision of _Les vrais chefs de l'empire_ (1940).

AC450. Delcourt, André. **La France et les établissements français au Sénégal entre 1713 et 1763.** Dakar, 1952.

AC451. Gouilly, Alphonse. **L'Islam dans l'Afrique occidentale française.** Paris, 1952. Study by a French authority on Islam, covering history of Islamic invasions, various brotherhoods, effects of Islamization, and French policy toward Islam. Bibliography.

AC452. Herskovits, Melville J. **Dahomey, an ancient west African kingdom.** 2 v. N.Y., 1938. Detailed anthropological study. Bibliography.

AC453. Miner, Horace M. **The primitive city of Timbuctoo.** Princeton, 1953. Readable sociological investigation of the social structure, economy, religion, and family of the peoples of Timbuktu under impact of "the urban culture of the market." Bibliography.

AC454. Mumford, William B., and G. St. J. Orde-Brown. **Africans learn to be French: a review of educational activities in the seven federated colonies of French West Africa, based upon a tour of French West Africa and Algiers undertaken in 1935.** London, 1937. Valuable statement of observations of French educational policy and organization in Senegal, French Guinea, and the French Sudan, by two British specialists in education and labor. Includes translations of five French documents.

AC455. Paques, Viviana. **Les Bambara.** Paris, 1954. Anthropological study of the Bambara of the French Sudan, analyzing scattered material and unpublished data by Germaine Dieterlen. Bibliography.

AC456. Paulme, Denise. **Les gens du riz: Kissi de Haute-Guinée française.** Paris, 1954. Detailed anthropological study of the Kissi tribe, a rice-growing, forest people of southern French Guinea. Bibliographies.

AC457. Richard-Molard, Jacques. **L'Afrique occidentale française.** 3rd ed., Paris, 1956. Excellent survey for the non-specialist of the physical, economic, and human geography of French West Africa, by the chief of the geographical section of the Institut Français d'Afrique Noire. Select bibliography.

AC458. Robert, André P. **L'évolution des coutumes de l'Ouest africain et la législation française.** Paris, 1955. Customary law of many peoples of French West Africa and its conflicts with French legislation.

AC459. Rouch, Jean. **Les Songhay.** Paris, 1954. Anthropological study of the economy and social system of the Songhai of the French Sudan, based largely on field work. Extensive annotated bibliography.

AC460. Spitz, Georges. **L'Ouest africain français: A.O.F. et Togo.** Paris, 1947. Encyclopedic survey of French West Africa and French Togoland, including geography, history, and administration. Select bibliography.

Former French Equatorial Africa

AC461. Balandier, Georges. **Sociologie des Brazzaville noires.** Paris, 1925. [Cahiers de la Fondation Nationale des Sciences Politiques, 67.] Interesting analysis of African life in Brazzaville.

AC462. ———. **Sociologie actuelle de l'Afrique noire, dynamique des changements sociaux en Afrique centrale.** Paris, 1955. Important study of social change in Gabon and Congo. Bibliography.

AC463. Eboué, Adolphe F. **La nouvelle politique indigène pour l'Afrique Équatoriale Française.** Paris, 1945. Statement by the negro governor-general of French Equatorial Africa proposing changes in French colonial policy to permit the development of the people "within the framework of their own institutions."

AC464. Griaule, Marcel. **Les Saô légendaires.** Paris, 1943.

AC465. Lembezat, Bertrand. **La France Équatoriale.** 2nd ed., Paris, 1950. One of the encyclopedic series, *Terres lointaines,* published by the Société d'Éditions Géographiques, Maritimes et Coloniales.

AC466. Soret, Marcel. **Démographie et problèmes urbains en A. E. F., Poto-Poto, Bacongo, Dolisie.** Montpellier, France, 1954. Demographic-sociological study of three centers of African urban population in French Equatorial Africa, with statistical analysis of problems of African urbanization.

AC467. Ziéglé, Henri. **Afrique Équatoriale Française.** Paris, 1952. Best post-war survey of French Equatorial Africa for the non-specialist.

Cameroons

AC468. Dugast, Idelette. **Monographie de la tribu des Ndiki (Banen du Cameroun).** Paris, 1955. Anthropological study of the Banen people of the French Cameroons, by a French authority. Bibliography.

AC469. **Le Cameroun, aspect, géographique, historique, touristique, économique et administratif du territoire.** Paris, 1953. [Les documents de France.] Well-illustrated general survey, published under auspices of the minister of public works.

AC470. Njoya, Sultan of the Bamun. **Histoire et coutumes des Bamun.** Dakar, 1952. Reproduction in French of a manuscript in the Mun language telling the history and traditions of the Bamun people of the French Cameroons.

AC471. Rudin, Harry R. **Germans in the Cameroons, 1884–1914.** See *U194.*

Togoland

AC472. Coleman, James S. **Togoland.** N.Y., 1956. [International conciliation, 509.]

French Somaliland

AC473. Deschamps, Hubert J., Raymond Decary, and André Ménard. **Côte des**

Somalis, Réunion, Inde. Paris, 1948. Includes general survey of French Somaliland by Hubert Deschamps, former governor of the territory. Bibliography for each section.

Malagasy Republic

AC474. Arbousset, Francis. **Le fokon'olona à Madagascar.** Paris, 1950. Comprehensive, well-documented study of the village councils in Madagascar. Bibliography.

AC475. Chevalier, Louis. **Madagascar, populations et ressources.** Paris, 1952. Comprehensive study of population and resources, by a demographer assigned to assess the island as a place for settlement of European refugees. Bibliography.

AC476. Dandouau, André, and G. S. Chapus. **Histoires des populations de Madagascar.** Paris, 1952. History of the Merina people, 16th through 19th centuries, with shorter ethno-historical accounts of the other peoples of Madagascar and a concluding section on conditions during the period of French administration. Quoted extracts from sources throughout. Bibliography.

AC477. Linton, Ralph. **The Tanala, a hill tribe of Madagascar.** Chicago, 1933. Full ethnographic account of an eastern Madagascar people, by a prominent United States anthropologist.

FORMER BELGIAN TERRITORIES

Republic of the Congo

AC478. Académie Royale des Sciences Coloniales. **Atlas général du Congo et du Ruanda-Urundi.** Brussels, 1948 ff. Monumental work covering all aspects of the Congo, issued in parts, each of which covers one subject in text and contains one or more maps. Two editions, in French and Flemish.

AC479. Doucy, Arthur, and Pierre Feldheim. **Problèmes du travail et politique sociale au Congo belge.** Brussels, 1952. Study of labor conditions in Katanga, covering social legislation, recruitment, productivity, labor unions, etc.

AC480. Durieux, André. **Institutions politiques, administratives et judiciaires du Congo belge et du Ruanda-Urundi.** 2nd ed., Brussels, 1955. Authoritative analysis of the constitution and the administrative and judicial systems.

AC481. Johnston, Sir Harry H. **George Grenfell and the Congo.** 2 v. London, 1908. Long classic on the history, ethnology, and geography of the Congo Independent State, by the famous British explorer and administrator, based on diaries and researches of Rev. George Grenfell, the records of the British Baptist Missionary Society, and other materials.

AC482. Morel, Edmund D. **Red rubber: the story of the rubber slave trade flourishing on the Congo in the year of grace 1906.** London, 1906. A contemporary indictment of King Leopold's rule of the Congo before its annexation by Belgium. Introduction by Sir Harry H. Johnston.

Ruanda-Urundi

AC483. Harroy, Jean-Paul, and others. **Le Ruanda-Urundi, ses ressources naturelles, ses populations.** Brussels, 1956. Collection of seven articles by different authors, all but one of which deal with some aspect of the natural resources. Bibliographies.

AC484. Maquet, Jacques J. **Le système des relations sociales dans le Ruanda ancien.** Tervuren, Belg., 1954. Study of the indigenous social system of the kingdom of Ruanda, a highly developed African state. Bibliography.

PORTUGUESE TERRITORIES

AC485. Carreira, António. **Mandingas da Guiné Portuguesa.** Lisbon, 1947. Lucid anthropological study of the Mandingo, including the Islamized Mandingo proper, the pagan Soninke, and the Djola, of Portuguese Guinea, by a Portuguese colonial administrator.

AC486. Childs, Gladwyn M. **Umbundu kinship and character.** London, 1949. The social system of the Ovimbundu, with emphasis on the indigenous system of training and the relationship of missionary school education to culture and culture change. Valuable for English readers as an introduction to Portuguese works on the area. Bibliographies.

AC487. Cuvelier, Jean, and L. Jadin. **L'ancien Congo d'après les archives romaines (1518–1640).** Brussels, 1954. Important guide to and summary of documents in Vatican archives, with supplements on Portuguese archives; excellent historical introduction.

AC488. Egerton, F. Clement C. **Angola in perspective: endeavour and achievement in Portuguese West Africa.** London, 1957. Sympathetic to Portuguese policy.

AC489. Hambly, Wilfred D. **The Ovimbundu of Angola.** Chicago, 1934. Readable ethnological study of the Mbundu people of Angola, based on field work in 1929–30. Bibliography.

AC489a. Duffy, James. **Portuguese Africa.** Cambridge, Mass., 1959. Best analysis of the history of Angola and Mozambique. Fair but critical. Valuable bibliographical notes.

AC490. Lyall, Archibald L. **Black and white make brown: an account of a journey to the Cape Verde Islands and Portuguese Guinea.** London, 1938. Interesting and informative description of life of the various peoples of these two territories.

AC491. Mendes Corrêa, António A. **Ultramar português.** V. 1, **Ilhas de Cabo Verde.** Lisbon, 1954. Detailed study of the Cape Verde Islands, covering natural science, ethnology, demography, social conditions, languages, culture and education, politics and government, and economy, with résumés of each chapter in French and English.

AC492. Milheiros, Mário. **Anatomia social dos Maiacas.** Luanda, Angola, 1956. Good anthropological study of the Bayaka tribe (Maiaca) in Angola.

AC493. Moreira, Adriano. **Política ultramarina.** Lisbon, 1954.

AC494. Moreira, Eduardo. **Portuguese East Africa: a study of its religious needs.** London, 1936. A history of Protestant missionary activity in Mozambique, by the liaison officer of the Protestant missions and the Portuguese government. Focuses on tensions between missionaries and the Portuguese authorities.

AC495. Oliveira Boleo, José de. **Moçambique.** Lisbon, 1951. Official survey of Mozambique, covering geography, history, government, and economic and social development. English and French chapter résumés. Extensive bibliography of works in various languages.

AC496. Ross, Edward A. **Report on employment of native labor in Portuguese Africa.** N.Y., 1925. Report, by a United States sociologist, regarding contract laborers from Angola on São Tomé and Principe, presented to the League of Nations and later criticized as superficial and misinformed by the Portuguese minister of colonies.

AC497. Teixeira da Mota, Avelino. **Guiné Portuguesa.** 2 v. Lisbon, 1954. Valuable survey with good illustrations and maps. Bibliography. Each volume concludes with summary in French and English.

AC498. Viegas, Luis A. **Guiné Portuguesa.** 3 v. Lisbon, 1936–40. Detailed survey of Portuguese Guinea covering administrative, economic, and ethnographic subjects.

SPANISH TERRITORIES

AC499. Guinea, Spanish. Gobierno General de los Territorios de Guinea. **Memorias, 1949–1955.** Madrid, 1956. Extensive factual and statistical survey covering population, education, communications, religion, administrative and judicial system, and various economic subjects.

AC500. Unzueta y Yuste, Abelardo de. **Geografía histórica de la isla de Fernando Poo.** Madrid, 1947. Scholarly historical and political study. Bibliography.

AC501. ———. **Islas del Golfo de Guinea (Elobeyes, Corisco, Annobón, Príncipe y** Santo Tomé). Madrid, 1945. Encyclopedic survey of the three Spanish and two Portuguese islands, covering geography, ethnology, social welfare, administration, and economy, by a Spanish authority on colonial trade. Bibliography.

AC502. Veciana Vilaldach, Antonio de. **Los Bujeba (Bišió) de la Guinea Española: contribución al estudio del negro africano.** Madrid, 1956. Anthropological study.

LIBERIA

AC503. Anderson, Robert E. **Liberia, America's African friend.** Chapel Hill, 1952. Sympathetic account of Liberian peoples, resources, and economic progress.

AC504. Bixler, Raymond W. **The foreign policy of the United States in Liberia.** N.Y., 1957.

AC505. Buell, Raymond L. **Liberia: a century of survival, 1847–1947.** Philadelphia, 1947. Brief critical history, highlighting both domestic problems and foreign relations.

AC506. Huberick, Charles H. **The political and legislative history of Liberia.** 2 v. N.Y., 1947. Detailed study of historical and constitutional background, with documents.

AC507. Johnston, Sir Harry H. **Liberia.** 2 v. London, 1906. Older work still of value.

AC508. Schwab, George. **Tribes of the Liberian hinterland.** Cambridge, Mass., 1947. Valuable report of the Peabody Museum expedition to Liberia, edited by George W. Harley, who adds material to that of the author.

UNION OF SOUTH AFRICA

South Africa

AC509. Calpin, George H. **Indians in South Africa.** Pietermaritzburg, 1949. Useful history of the Indians in South Africa, without notes or bibliography.

AC510. Carter, Gwendolen M. **The politics of inequality: South Africa since 1948.** N.Y., 1958. Especially valuable for its original analysis of the organization and operations of political parties in South Africa. Bibliography.

AC511. De Kiewiet, Cornelis W. **A history of South Africa, social and economic.** Oxford, 1941. Stimulating interpretation of social and economic factors conditioning South African history.

AC512. ———. **The imperial factor in South Africa: a study in politics and economics.** Cambridge, Eng., 1937. Valuable account of Britain's role in South African history between 1872 and 1885. Bibliography.

AC513. Du Plessis, Izak D. **The Cape Malays.** 2nd ed., Cape Town, 1947.

AC514. Franklin, Norton N. **Economics**

in South Africa. 2nd rev. ed., Cape Town, 1954. Excellent analysis.

AC515. Gandhi, Mohandas K. **Satyagraha in South Africa.** Stanford, 1954. Gandhi's account of the origins and development of his Satyagraha movement during his two decades in South Africa before 1914.

AC516. Gluckman, Max. **Analysis of a social situation in modern Zululand.** Manchester, 1958. Three stimulating essays on white-African relations in Zululand, first published as separate articles in 1940-42. Important theoretical analysis of social change.

AC517. Junod, Henri. **Moeurs et coutumes des Bantous: la vie d'une tribu sudafricaine.** 2 v. Paris, 1936. Valuable ethnological study of the Tonga.

AC518. Kuper, Leo. **Passive resistance in South Africa.** London, 1956. Sociological analysis of 1952 "defiance campaign" against South African segregation laws.

AC519. MacCrone, Ian D. **Race attitudes in South Africa, historical, experimental and psychological studies.** London, 1937. Pioneer psychological analysis of racial attitudes among South Africa's varied ethnic groups. Bibliography.

AC520. Marais, Johannes S. **The Cape coloured people, 1652-1937.** Johannesburg, 1957. Reprint of valuable 1939 analysis of three main periods in Cape colored history. Bibliography.

AC521. Marquard, Leopold. **The peoples and policies of South Africa.** London, 1952. Useful introduction to South African history, peoples, and government.

AC522. May, Henry J. **The South African constitution.** 3rd ed., Cape Town, 1955. Standard work.

AC523. Patterson, Sheila. **Colour and culture in South Africa: a study of the status of the Cape coloured people within the social structure of the Union of South Africa.** London, 1953. Thorough study of evolution of Cape colored within South Africa's patterns of racial segregation.

AC524. ——. **The last trek: a study of the Boer people and the Afrikaner nation.** London, 1957. Interesting analysis of the growth of Afrikaner nationalism, by a South African of British background.

AC525. Reitz, Deneys. **Commando: a Boer journal of the Boer War.** 2nd ed., London, 1953. Readable and informative autobiographical narrative of guerilla warfare.

AC526. Roberts, Michael, and A. E. G. Trollip. **The South African opposition 1939-1945: an essay in contemporary history.** London, 1947. Interesting and valuable account of Afrikaner political movements during World War II.

AC527. Robertson, Hector M. **South Africa, economic and political aspects.** Durham, Eng., 1957. Analysis of contemporary economic and political issues in light of their historical background. Useful annotated bibliography and glossary.

AC528. Roux, Edward R. **Time longer than rope: a history of the black man's struggle for freedom in South Africa.** London, 1948. A former Communist's interesting history of political and labor movements.

AC529. Schapera, Isaac, ed. **The Bantu-speaking tribes of South Africa, an ethnographical survey.** N.Y., 1952. Comparative survey by South African scholars, first published in 1937. Organized by topics rather than tribes, it includes four chapters on European impact on Bantu life. Bibliography.

AC530. South Africa. Commission for the Socio-Economic Development of the Bantu Areas. **Summary of the report.** Pretoria, 1955. A 213 p. abridgement of the 17 v. *Tomlinson report,* with 64 useful maps.

AC531. Sundkler, Bengt G. M. **Bantu prophets in South Africa.** London, 1948. Valuable analysis of 800 Bantu separatist churches in South Africa. Bibliography.

AC532. Theal, George M. **History and ethnography of Africa south of the Zambesi.** 3rd ed., 11 v., London, 1888-1919. Standard older historical study.

AC533. Walker, Eric A. **A history of southern Africa.** 3rd ed., London, 1957. The best survey.

AC534. ——. **The great trek.** London, 1934. Interesting and valuable.

Southwest Africa

AC535. Hahn, Carl H. L., and others. **The native tribes of South West Africa.** Cape Town, 1928. Five monographs with bibliographies on the Ovambo, Bushmen, Bergdama, Nama, Hottentots, and Herero.

AC536. Schapera, Isaac. **The Khoisan peoples of South Africa: Bushmen and Hottentots.** London, 1930. Survey of origins, language, and culture. Bibliography.

AC537. Vedder, Heinrich. **South West Africa in early times, being the story of South West Africa up to the date of Maharero's death in 1890.** London, 1938. This 525 p. abridged translation of Vedder's *Das alte Sudwëstafrika* (Berlin, 1934), based partly on ethnological data and partly on historical records, is the standard work on the subject.

BRITISH HIGH COMMISSION TERRITORIES

Basutoland

AC538. Ashton, Edmund H. **The Basuto.** London, 1952. Valuable and comprehensive account of Basuto life. Bibliography.

Bechuanaland

AC539. Schapera, Isaac. **A handbook of Tswana law and custom.** 2nd ed., London, 1955. Authoritative analysis.

AC540. ——. **Married life in an African tribe.** London, 1941. Anthropological study of Kgatla tribe in Bechuanaland.

AC541. ——. **Native land tenure in the Bechuanaland protectorate.** Lovedale, South Africa, 1943. Valuable companion volume to *AC539.*

AC542. Sillery, Anthony. **Sechele: the story of an African chief.** Oxford, 1954. Biography of a Kwena chief in Bechuanaland.

AC543. ——. **The Bechuanaland protectorate.** N.Y., 1952. Useful survey by a former official.

Swaziland

AC544. Kuper, Hilda. **An African aristocracy: rank among the Swazi.** London, 1947. Excellent and interesting anthropological analysis. Bibliography.

AC545. ——. **The uniform of color: a study of white-black relationships in Swaziland.** Johannesburg, 1947. Illuminating companion volume to the above.

VIII. AUSTRALASIA AND OCEANIA

SECTION AD

Australia and New Zealand
(with Antarctica)

ANDREW DELBRIDGE OSBORN *

Most scholarly writings on the lands of the Southwest Pacific have appeared since 1930. This is because, first, the number of competent historians working in the field has increased sharply in the interim. Second, primary sources have become more and more accessible, above all through the expanding resources of the Mitchell Library, Sydney, the Commonwealth National Library, Canberra, and the Turnbull Library, Wellington; also through microfilm copies of relevant Public Record Office archives (available from the Mitchell and Commonwealth National Libraries) and United States consular reports (available from the U. S. National Archives). And, third, the history of these young countries now extends over a sufficiently long time span that contemporary historians can see events in desirable perspective. Nevertheless, a word of caution must be given, especially about Australian historiography: facts and figures in secondary works are frequently at variance and are open to question unless they have been properly documented.

AUSTRALIA

BIBLIOGRAPHIES AND LIBRARY COLLECTIONS

AD1. The Cambridge history of the British Empire. V. 7, pt. 1, **Australia** (London, 1933), pp. 647–86. Should be complemented by the chapter and general bibliographies in Clark (*AD39*) and Greenwood (*AD45*). Also Shaw (*AD43*) has a good critical bibliography.

AD2. Ferguson, John A. **Bibliography of Australia.** 4 v. Sydney, 1941–55. Chronological list through 1850.

AD3. Lewin, Percy Evans. **Subject catalogue of the library of the Royal Empire Society, formerly the Royal Colonial Institute.** V. 2 (London, 1931), pp. 483–652. See *U3*.

AD4. ——. **Best books on Australia and New Zealand.** London, 1946.

AD5. Australian books, a select list. Canberra, 1933 ff. Annually revised list of best books.

AD6. Fuller, Grace H. **Selected list of references on Australia.** Washington, 1942. Library of Congress holdings.

* The following contributed items and comments indicated by their respective initials: Wilfred D. Borrie (WDB), John M. Ward (JMW).

770

AD7. Craig, Jean. **Bibliography of public administration in Australia, 1850–1947.** Sydney, 1955. Predominantly New South Wales and Commonwealth parliamentary papers.

AD8. Australian Public Affairs Information Service. **Subject index to current literature.** Canberra, 1945 ff. (Monthly.) Cultural, economic, historical, political, and social affairs.

AD9. Arnot, Jean F. **Bibliography of newspapers found in the Mitchell Library and the Public Library of New South Wales.** Sydney, 1944. Important for early Australian newspapers.

AD10. New South Wales. Mitchell Library. **Index to periodicals.** 1944 ff. Sydney, 1950 ff. Lists selected articles on Australia, New Zealand, the Southwest Pacific, and Antarctica. From 1956 issued in the *Monthly catalogue* of the Public Library of New South Wales.

AD11. ——. **Historical and descriptive notes.** Sydney, 1936. Survey of resources.

AD12. ——. **Manuscripts in the Mitchell Library.** Sydney, 1956. Brief guide to their scope and arrangement. The Mitchell Library possesses the greatest collection of Australiana; next in importance is the Commonwealth National Library.

Historical manuscripts added to Australian libraries are recorded in *Historical studies, Australia and New Zealand* (*AD202*). United States research projects on Australia and New Zealand are given in the U. S. State Department's *External research: British Commonwealth;* Australian and New Zealand projects are in *Hist. stud. Austr. and N.Z.*

ENCYCLOPEDIAS AND WORKS OF REFERENCE

AD13. Australian encyclopaedia. 10 v. Sydney, 1955–58.

AD14. Serle, Percival. **Dictionary of Australian biography.** 2 v. Sydney, 1949. Notables who died before 1943. Invaluable, but all biographies are by one hand and tend to be commemorative. [JMW]

AD15. **Who's who in Australia.** Melbourne, 1906 ff. (Triennial.)

AD16. Australia. Bureau of Census and Statistics. **Official year book of the Commonwealth of Australia.** Melbourne and Canberra, 1908 ff.

GEOGRAPHIES, GAZETTEER, ATLAS

AD17. Taylor, Thomas Griffith. **Australia: a study of warm environments and their effect on British settlement.** 6th ed., London, 1955. The standard work.

AD18. Australia. Commonwealth Scientific and Industrial Research Organization. **The Australian environment.** 2nd ed., Melbourne, 1950. General introduction to physical geography and agriculture. Review, R. K. Wilson, *N.Z. geog.*, 6 (Oct. 1950): 212.

AD19. Cumberland, Kenneth B. **Southwest Pacific: a geography.** Christchurch, 1954; N.Y., 1956. Designed as a textbook. Review, G. A. Currie, *N.Z. geog.*, 11 (Apr. 1955): 89.

AD20. Holmes, James M. **Geographical basis of government specially applied to New South Wales.** Sydney and London, 1944. Review, *Geog. jour.*, 104 (Sept. 1944): 135.

AD21. ——. **The Murray valley.** Sydney, 1948. Review, *Austr. geog.*, 5 (June 1948): 183.

AD22. Australia. Washington, 1957. [U. S. Office of Geography, Gazetteer no. 40.]

AD23. Australia. Dept. of National Development. **Atlas of Australian resources.** Canberra, 1953 ff. Covers agriculture, forests, population, rainfall, roads, etc. Review, M. M. Bayne, *Econ. rec.*, 31 (Nov. 1955): 338; 32 (Nov. 1956): 382.

ABORIGINES

AD24. Elkin, Adolphus P. **Australian aborigines: how to understand them.** 3rd ed., Sydney, 1954. Best general work.

AD25. ——. **Citizenship for the aborigines: a national aboriginal policy.** Sydney, 1944.

AD26. ——. **Wanted—a charter for the native peoples of the Southwest Pacific.** Sydney, 1943.

AD27. Hasluck, Paul. **Native welfare in Australia: speeches and addresses.** Perth, 1953.

AD28. Hasluck, Paul. **Black Australians: a survey of native policy in Western Australia, 1829–97.** Melbourne, 1942. Review, A. P. Elkin, *Hist. stud. Austr. and N.Z.*, 2 (Nov. 1943): 274.

AD29. Berndt, Ronald M., and Catherine H. Berndt. **Arnhem Land, its history and its people.** Melbourne, 1954.

DEMOGRAPHIC STUDIES

AD30. Madgwick, Robert B. **Immigration into eastern Australia, 1788–1851.** London, 1937. Thorough historical text containing analyses based on records of the Colonial Office and the Colonial Land and Emigration Commissioners as well as on colonial censuses. Review, W. D. Forsyth, *Econ. rec.*, 14 (June 1938): 130. [WDB]

AD31. Borrie, Wilfred D. **Population trends and policies.** Sydney, 1948. Demographic needs and possibilities of Australia. Review, J. P. Belshaw, *Austr. quar.*, 21 (Mar. 1949): 121.

AD32. ——. **Immigration: Australia's problems and prospects.** Sydney and London, 1949. Examination of postwar policies.

AD33. ——. **Italians and Germans in Australia: a study of assimilation.** Melbourne, 1954. Review, F. K. Crowley, _Hist. stud. Austr. and N.Z._, 6 (May, 1955): 487.

AD34. Australian Institute of Political Science. **Future of immigration into Australia and New Zealand.** Sydney, 1937. Symposium on migrant absorptive capacity. [WDB]

AD35. ——. **Australia and the migrant.** Sydney, 1953. Symposium on postwar immigration. [WDB]

AD36. Australia. Bureau of Census and Statistics. **Demography.** Canberra, 1906 ff. (Annual.) Many issues contain extensive summaries. See particularly 1927 and 1949. See also Borrie's Australian section in UNESCO, _The positive contribution by immigrants_ (Paris, 1955). [WDB]

PRINTED COLLECTIONS OF SOURCES

AD37. **Historical records of New South Wales.** 7 v. Sydney, 1889–1901. Covers the period to 1811.

AD38. Australia. Parliament. **Historical records of Australia.** 34 v. Sydney, 1914–25. Weak editorial work led to suspension of publication. A new program is under consideration.

AD39. Clark, C. Manning. **Select documents in Australian history, 1788–1900.** 2 v. Sydney, 1950–55. Intended for college students.

AD40. ——. **Sources of Australian history.** London and N.Y., 1957. Shorter than _AD39_ and a different selection. For the general reader and less advanced students.

SHORTER GENERAL HISTORIES

AD41. Hancock, William K. **Australia.** N.Y., 1931; London and Sydney, 1945. The most brilliant general study despite serious omissions. Needs revision in the light of work published since 1929. Especially through its assessment of Australian society it helped to establish a new tradition in Australian historiography. Review, G. V. Portus, _Econ. rec._, 7 (May, 1931): 131. [JMW]

AD42. Crawford, Raymond M. **Australia.** London, 1952. Polished and stimulating study, with fundamentally the same approach as Hancock, but covers a wider field and enjoys the advantage of later research. Treatment of the sixties and seventies particularly noteworthy. Review, L. F. Fitzhardinge, _Hist. stud. Austr. and N.Z._, 5 (Nov. 1952): 296. [JMW]

AD43. Shaw, Alan G. L. **Story of Australia.** London, 1955. Easily read narrative, following middle-of-the-road interpretations and providing the best introduction for the general reader. Makes careful use of recent research and gives interesting description of

contemporary Australia. Review, L. F. Fitzhardinge, _Austr. jour. pol. hist._, 1 (May 1956): 271. [JMW]

LONGER GENERAL HISTORIES

AD44. **The Cambridge history of the British Empire.** V. 7, pt. 1, **Australia.** London, 1933. A remarkable achievement despite its avoidable errors. Though most scholarly work in Australian history came later, still useful because of the lack of any other history of comparable size and authority. Review, T. Dunbabin, _Austr. Rhodes rev._, 1 (Mar. 1934): 139. [JMW]

AD45. Greenwood, Gordon, ed. **Australia, a social and political history.** N.Y. and Sydney, 1955. Best starting point for the student, though chapters are uneven. Review, M. Clark, _Hist. stud. Austr. and N.Z._, 7 (Nov. 1955): 95. [JMW]

HISTORIES OF SPECIAL PERIODS

Discovery and Exploration

Extremely important are Beaglehole's edition of Cook's _Journals_ (_AE57_) and Wroth's _Early cartography of the Pacific_ (_AE51_).

AD46. Wood, George A. **The discovery of Australia.** London, 1922. Best single volume account.

AD47. Scott, Ernest, ed. **Australian discovery.** 2 v. London and N.Y., 1929. V. 1, discovery by sea; v. 2, inland exploration.

AD48. Macquarie, Lachlan. **Journals of his tours in New South Wales and Van Diemen's Land, 1810–22.** Sydney, 1956.

Convict Settlements

AD49. O'Brien, Eris. **The foundation of Australia, 1786–1800.** 2nd ed., Sydney, 1950. Detailed study of the social code and penal laws of England which lay behind the decision to found the convict settlement, as well as an account of the first years of the settlement. Valuable statistical appendices. Review, M. Clark, _Hist. stud. Austr. and N.Z._, 4 (May, 1951): 376. [WDB]

AD50. Forsyth, William D. **Governor Arthur's convict system.** London, 1935. Review, E. Scott, _Econ. rec._, 11 (Dec. 1935): 299.

1800–1850

AD51. Evatt, Herbert V. **Rum rebellion.** 2nd ed., Sydney, 1939. Rebuttal of the traditional story of Bligh, based on examination of legal evidence. Review, B. Fitzpatrick, _Hist. stud. Austr. and N.Z._, 1 (Apr. 1940): 71.

AD52. Mills, Richard C. **Colonization of**

Australia (1829–42): the Wakefield experiment in empire building. London, 1915. The settlement of Western and South Australia.

AD53. Roberts, Stephen H. **The squatting age in Australia, 1835–47.** Melbourne, 1935. Basic study of the pastoral ascendancy. Expansion of pt. 3 of his *History of Australian land settlement (AD136)*. See also Dakin (*AD267*).

1850–1900

AD54. Ward, John M. **Australia's first governor-general, Sir Charles FitzRoy, 1851–1855.** Sydney, 1953. Earl Grey's short-lived scheme for a federal form of government.

AD55. Deakin, Alfred. **The federal story.** Melbourne, 1944. Inside story of federation. Review, C. H. Currey, *Hist. stud. Austr. and N.Z.*, 3 (July 1945): 143.

AD56. Australasian Federal Convention. **Debates.** 4 v. Adelaide, 1897–98.

Twentieth Century

AD57. Bean, Charles E. W., ed. **The official history of Australia in the war of 1914–18.** 12 v. Sydney, 1921–42.

AD58. Moorehead, Alan M. **Gallipoli.** See *AG53.*

AD59. Australian War Memorial, Canberra. **Australia in the war of 1939–45.** By Gavin M. Long and others. Canberra, 1952 ff.

AD60. ——. **With the Australians in Korea.** Canberra, 1954.

HISTORIES OF SPECIAL AREAS

Canberra

AD61. White, Harold L., ed. **Canberra, a nation's capital.** Sydney, 1954.

AD62. Australia. Dept. of the Interior. **Annual report on the administration and development of Canberra and the Australian Capital Territory.** 1950/51 ff. Canberra, 1952 ff.

New South Wales

As the mother colony, New South Wales is principally covered by the general histories.

AD63. Lang, John D. **An historical and statistical account of New South Wales.** 4th ed., 2 v., London, 1875. Preoccupied with his own point of view, but has much insight. [JMW]

AD64. Parkes, Henry. **Fifty years in the making of Australian history.** London, 1892. Parkes played a leading role in N.S.W. politics and the federation movement.

Northern Territory

AD65. Price, Archibald G. **The history and problems of the Northern Territory.** Adelaide, 1930.

AD66. Abbott, Charles L. A. **Australia's frontier province.** Sydney, 1950. By a former administrator of the territory.

AD67. Australian Institute of Political Science. **Northern Australia, task for a nation.** Sydney, 1954. Conference papers on "How should we develop Northern Australia?"

AD68. Australia. Dept. of Territories. **Report on the administration of the Northern Territory.** Canberra, 1884 ff.

Papua-New Guinea Territory

AD69. Gordon, Donald C. **The Australian frontier in New Guinea, 1870–1885.** N.Y., 1951. Colonial policy and the annexation of New Guinea. Review, N. D. Harper, *Hist. stud. Austr. and N.Z.*, 5 (May 1952): 188.

AD70. Legge, John D. **Australian colonial policy: a survey of native administration and European development in Papua.** Sydney, 1956. History of Papua from 1884. Review, C. D. Rowley, *Austr. quar.*, 28 (Dec. 1956): 110.

AD71. Reed, Stephen W. **The making of modern New Guinea.** See *AE77.*

AD72. Robson, Robert W., ed. **Handbook of Papua and New Guinea.** Sydney, 1954.

AD73. Papua. Lt. Governor. **Territory of Papua annual report.** Canberra, 1888 ff.

AD74. New Guinea Territory. **Report to the General Assembly of the U. N.** Canberra, 1947 ff.

AD75. Papua-New Guinea Territory. **Official research publications.** Port Moresby, 1951 ff. (Irregular.)

Queensland

AD76. Russell, Henry S. **The genesis of Queensland.** Sydney, 1888. Exploration, settlement, and separation from New South Wales.

AD77. Our first half-century: a review of Queensland progress. Brisbane, 1909.

AD78. Bernays, Charles A. **Queensland politics during sixty years (1859–1919).** Brisbane, 1919.

AD79. ——. **Queensland—our seventh political decade, 1920–30.** Sydney, 1930.

South Australia

AD80. Pike, Douglas. **Paradise of dissent: South Australia, 1829–1857.** Melbourne, 1957. The Wakefield scheme and the foundation of South Australia. Review, W. K. Hancock, *Austr. jour. pol. hist.*, 3 (Nov. 1957): 131. See also Mills (*AD52*).

AD81. Hodder, Edwin. **The history of South Australia.** 2 v. London, 1893.

AD82. Combe, Gordon D. **Responsible government in South Australia.** Adelaide, 1957.

AD83. Price, Archibald G. **Founders and pioneers of South Australia.** Adelaide, 1929.

Tasmania

AD84. Giblin, Ronald W. **The early history of Tasmania.** 2 v. London and Melbourne, 1928–39. V. 1, discovery; v. 2, penal settlement, 1804–28. Should be read critically, especially for the account of Gov. Arthur. Review, R. B. Madgwick, *Austr. quar.*, 12 (June 1940): 103.

AD85. West, John. **The history of Tasmania.** 2 v. Launceston, 1852. Old but still valuable. [JMW]

AD86. Townsley, W. A. **The struggle for self-government in Tasmania, 1842–1856.** Hobart, 1951. Review, K. Fitzpatrick, *Hist. stud. Austr. and N.Z.*, 5 (Nov. 1952): 299.

AD87. Green, Frank C., ed. **A century of responsible government, 1856–1956.** Hobart, 1956. Review, M. Clark, *Austr. jour. pol. hist.*, 3 (Nov. 1957): 133.

Victoria

AD88. Leeper, Geoffrey W., ed. **Introducing Victoria.** Melbourne, 1955. History, geography, resources, population, industries, education.

AD89. Victoria, the first century. Melbourne, 1934.

AD90. Turner, Henry G. **History of the colony of Victoria.** 2 v. London, 1904. Ends with 1900.

AD91. Deakin, Alfred. **The crisis in Victorian politics, 1879–1881.** Melbourne, 1957.

Western Australia

AD92. Crowley, Frank K. **The records of Western Australia.** Perth, 1953. List of books, articles, manuscripts, etc.

AD93. Battye, James S. **Western Australia, a history.** Oxford, 1924. Ends with 1900. Review, W. K. Hancock, *Eng. hist. rev.*, 40 (July 1925): 449.

HISTORIES OF SPECIAL TOPICS

Agriculture

AD94. Watt, Robert D. **Romance of the Australian land industries.** Sydney, 1955. Agricultural history, 1788–1951.

AD95. Wadham, Samuel M., and Gordon L. Wood. **Land utilization in Australia.** 2nd ed., Melbourne, 1950. Review, J. G. Crawford, *Econ. rec.*, 27 (June 1951): 113.

AD96. Stanford University. Food Research Institute. **Wartime agriculture in Australia and New Zealand, 1939–50.** Stanford, 1954. Review, W. S. Kelly, *Econ. rec.*, 31 (Nov. 1955): 334.

AD97. Dunsdorfs, Edgars. **Australian wheatgrowing industry, 1788–1948.** Melbourne, 1956. Review, K. O. Campbell, *Econ. rec.*, 33 (Apr. 1957): 118.

AD98. Australia. Bureau of Agricultural Economics. **Quarterly review of agricultural economics.** Canberra, 1948 ff.

Church History

There is no really comprehensive general or denominational history, but detailed articles may be found in the *Australian encyclopaedia* (*AD13*). The existing works are recorded in the bibliographies cited at the beginning of this list. See also Moran (*AD324*).

Civilization

AD99. Nadel, George. **Australia's colonial culture: ideas, men and institutions in mid-nineteenth century eastern Australia.** Cambridge, Mass. and Melbourne, 1957. Based on primary sources; relates largely to New South Wales.

AD100. Grattan, Clinton H., ed. **Australia.** Berkeley, 1947. Review, G. Caiger. *Austr. outlook*, 2 (Dec. 1948): 256.

AD101. Fitzpatrick, Brian. **The Australian commonwealth: a picture of the community, 1901–1955.** Melbourne, 1956. Review, D. MacCallum, *Austr. quar.*, 29 (June 1957): 109.

Constitutional History

AD102. Sweetman, Edward. **Australian constitutional development.** Melbourne, 1925. The states up to responsible government. Review, A. B. Keith, *Eng. hist. rev.*, 40 (Oct. 1925): 624.

AD103. Melbourne, Alexander C. V. **Early constitutional development in Australia: New South Wales, 1788–1856.** London, 1934. Review, E. Scott, *Econ. rec.*, 11 (June 1935): 133.

AD104. Paton, George W., ed. **The Commonwealth of Australia: the development of its laws and constitution.** London, 1952.

AD105. Hunt, Erling M. **American precedents in Australian federation.** N.Y., 1930.

AD106. Quick, Sir John, and Sir Robert R. Garran. **Annotated constitution of the Australian Commonwealth.** Sydney, 1901. Still a standard work.

AD107. Quick, Sir John, and Sir Littleton E. Groom. **The judicial power of the Commonwealth.** Melbourne, 1904. A standard work.

AD108. Wynes, William A. **Legislative and judicial powers in Australia.** 2nd ed., Sydney, 1956. Up-to-date exposition of Australian constitutional law. Review, Z. Cowen, *Austr. quar.*, 29 (Mar. 1957) : 108.

AD109. Mitchell, Rae E., ed. **Essays on the Australian constitution.** Sydney, 1952.

AD110. Crisp, Leslie F. **Parliamentary government of the Commonwealth of Australia.** 2nd ed., London, 1954.

AD111. Sawer, Geoffrey. **Australian government today.** 5th ed., Melbourne, 1957. Both commonwealth and states. Review, F. Louat, *Austr. quar.*, 20 (June 1948) : 109.

AD112. Australia. Royal Commission on the Constitution. **Report.** Canberra, 1929.

AD113. Australia. Commonwealth Grants Commission. **Third report.** Canberra, 1936.

AD114. Bland, Francis A., ed. **Changing the constitution.** Sydney, 1950. [Proceedings of the All-Australian Federal Convention, 1949.] Review, N. Wills, *Austr. quar.*, 22 (Dec. 1950) : 119.

Economic History

AD115. Fitzpatrick, Brian. **The Australian people, 1788–1945.** Melbourne, 1946. Based on his two earlier and larger works. Viewpoint is leftist. Review, A. G. L. Shaw, *Hist. stud. Austr. and N.Z.*, 3 (Nov. 1947) : 241.

AD116. Shann, Edward O. G. **Economic history of Australia.** Cambridge, Eng. and Melbourne, 1948. Rightist viewpoint. Review, A. G. L. Shaw, *Hist. stud. Austr. and N.Z.*, 3 (Feb. 1949): 351.

AD117. Shaw, Alan G. L. **The economic development of Australia.** 3rd ed., London and Melbourne, 1955. Middle-of-the-road viewpoint. Review, W. R. Lane, *Austr. jour. pol. hist.*, 1 (Nov. 1955) : 140.

AD118. Coghlan, Timothy A. **Labour and industry in Australia, 1788–1901.** 4 v. London and N.Y., 1918.

AD119. Butlin, Sydney J. **Foundations of the Australian monetary system, 1788–1851.** Melbourne, 1953. Considered the most important study in early Australian economic history. Review, R. M. Hartwell, *Econ. rec.*, 30 (May 1954) : 73.

AD120. ———. **War economy.** Canberra, 1955. Review, R. L. Crivelli, *Austr. quar.*, 27 (Dec. 1955) : 106.

AD121. Giblin, Lyndhurst F. **Growth of a central bank: the development of the Commonwealth Bank of Australia.** Melbourne, 1951. Review, S. J. Butlin, *Econ. rec.*, 27 (June 1951) : 84.

AD122. Australia. Bureau of Census and Statistics. **National income and expenditure.** 1938/39 ff. Canberra, 1946 ff.

AD123. ———. **Quarterly summary of Australian statistics.** Canberra, 1912 ff.

AD124. Great Britain. Commercial Relations and Exports Dept. **Australia: economic and commercial conditions.** London, 1921 ff.

AD125. La Nauze, John A. **Political economy in Australia.** Melbourne, 1949. Four essays on 19th century economic thought. Review, C. Renwick, *Econ. rec.*, 26 (June 1950) : 129.

Foreign Affairs

AD126. Greenwood, Gordon, and Norman D. Harper, eds. **Australia in world affairs, 1950–1955.** Melbourne, 1957. Review, R. L. Reid, *Austr. jour. pol. hist.*, 3 (Nov. 1957) : 135.

AD127. Australian Institute of Political Science. **Australia's foreign policy.** Sydney, 1938. Review, J. McCallum, *Austr. quar.*, 10 (Sep. 1938) : 101.

AD128. Casey, Richard G. **Friends and neighbours: Australia and the world.** Melbourne and N.Y., 1954. Review, T. N. M. Buesst, *Hist. stud. Austr. and N.Z.*, 7 (Nov. 1955) : 102.

AD129. Evatt, Herbert V. **Australia in world affairs.** Sydney and N.Y., 1946. Review, V. J. Flynn, *Austr. quar.*, 18 (Dec. 1946) : 105.

AD130. Eggleston, Frederic W. **Reflections on Australian foreign policy.** Melbourne, 1957. Review, D. Van Abbe, *Austr. quar.*, 29 (June 1957) : 107. Authors of this and *AD128–129* are prominent diplomats.

AD131. Shepherd, Jack. **Australia's interests and policies in the Far East.** 2nd ed., N.Y., 1940. [I. P. R. Inquiry series.] Review, C. V. Janes, *Austr. quar.*, 12 (June 1940) : 112.

AD132. Gilmore, Robert J., and Denis Warner, eds. **Near North: Australia and a thousand million neighbours.** Sydney, 1948.

AD133. Greenwood, Gordon, ed. **Australian policies towards Asia.** Melbourne, 1954.

AD134. Stevens, Bertram S. **New horizons: a study of Australian-Indian relationships.** Sydney, 1946. Review, C. V. Janes, *Austr. quar.*, 18 (June 1946) : 105.

Frontier

AD135. Alexander, Frederick. **Moving frontiers: an American theme and its application to Australian history.** Melbourne, 1947. The Turner thesis, which has limited application to Australian conditions. Review, H. D. Black, *Austr. quar.*, 19 (Dec. 1947) : 123.

Land Settlement

AD136. Roberts, Stephen H. **History of Australian land settlement, 1788–1920.** Melbourne, 1924.

Naval History

AD137. McGuire, Frances M. **The Royal Australian navy, its origin, development and organization.** Melbourne, 1948.

Political History

Greenwood (*AD45*) is the general work.
AD138. Sawer, Geoffrey. **Australian federal politics and law, 1901–1929.** Melbourne, 1956. Chronicle of the first eleven federal parliaments. Review, C. H. Currey, *Austr. jour. pol. hist.,* 3 (Nov. 1957): 129.
AD139. Scott, Ernest. **Australia during the war.** Sydney, 1937. [Official history of Australia during the war of 1914–18, 11.] Political and social history, conscription issue, peace treaty.
AD140. Hasluck, Paul. **The government and the people, 1939–41.** Canberra, 1953. [Australia in the war of 1939–45, ser. 4, v. 1.] Review, L. F. Fitzhardinge, *Hist. stud. Austr. and N.Z.,* 6 (Nov. 1953): 103.
AD141. Miller, John D. B. **Australian government and politics.** London, 1954.
AD142. Davies, Alan F., and Geoffrey Serle, eds. **Policies for progress: essays in Australian politics.** Melbourne, 1954.
AD143. Australian Institute of Political Science. **The Australian political party system.** Sydney, 1954.
AD144. Overacker, Louise. **The Australian party system.** New Haven, 1952. Best available book, but prone to emphasize the left; bibliography is uncritical. Review, R. Gollan, *Hist. stud. Austr. and N.Z.,* 6 (Nov. 1953): 105. [JMW]
AD145. Fitzpatrick, Brian. **Short history of the Australian labour movement.** 2nd ed., Melbourne, 1944. Review, *Austr. quar.,* 13 (Mar. 1941): 116.
AD146. Sutcliffe, James T. **History of trade unionism in Australia.** Melbourne, 1921.
AD147. Crisp, Leslie F. **The Australian Federal Labour party, 1901–1951.** London and N.Y., 1955. Review, D. E. McHenry, *Hist. stud. Austr. and N.Z.,* 7 (May 1956): 248.
AD148. Eggleston, Frederic W. **Reflections of an Australian liberal.** Melbourne, 1953. Review, L. Webb, *Hist. stud. Austr. and N.Z.,* 6 (May 1954): 228.
AD149. Reeves, W. Pember. **State experiments in Australia and New Zealand.** 2 v. London, 1923; N.Y., 1925. Covers the period to 1902. Review, J. B. Condliffe, *Econ. rec.,* 2 (May 1926): 95.
AD150. Willard, Myra. **History of the white Australia policy.** Melbourne, 1923. Still not replaced for the period covered. Review, E. L. Piesse, *Econ. rec.,* 1 (Nov. 1925): 125. [JMW]
AD151. Webb, Leicester. **Communism and democracy in Australia: a survey of the 1951 referendum.** Melbourne, 1954. The referendum failed to sanction dissolution of the Communist party. Review, S. R. Davis, *Hist. stud. Austr. and N.Z.,* 6 (May 1955): 489.
AD152. **Parliamentary handbook of the Commonwealth of Australia.** Canberra, 1915 ff.

Transportation

AD153. Australian Institute of Political Science. **Australia's transport crisis.** Sydney, 1957.
AD154. Hocking, Douglas M., and C. P. Haddon-Cave. **Air transport in Australia.** Sydney, 1951. Review, J. M. Grant, *Econ. rec.,* 28 (Nov. 1952): 305.

BIOGRAPHIES

The comprehensive work is *Dictionary of Australian biography* (*AD14*).
AD155. Palmer, Vance. **National portraits.** 3rd ed., Melbourne, 1954. Twenty-five biographies. Review, T. Dunbabin, *Austr. quar.,* 13 (Mar. 1941): 110.

Foundation Years

AD156. Mackaness, George. **Sir Joseph Banks, his relations with Australia.** Sydney, 1936.
AD157. ——. **The life of Vice-admiral William Bligh.** 2nd ed., Sydney, 1951. See also Evatt (*AD51*). For Captain Cook see *AE57*.
AD158. Scott, Ernest. **The life of Captain Matthew Flinders.** Sydney, 1914.
AD159. Ellis, Malcolm H. **John Macarthur.** Sydney, 1955.
AD160. ——. **Lachlan Macquarie.** 2nd ed., Sydney, 1952. For Samuel Marsden see *AD364.*
AD161. Mackaness, George. **Admiral Arthur Phillip, founder of New South Wales.** Sydney, 1937.

1820–1850

AD162. Hodder, Edwin. **George Fife Angas, father and founder of South Australia.** London, 1891.
AD163. Levy, M. C. I. **Governor George Arthur.** Melbourne, 1953.
AD164. Kiddle, Margaret. **Caroline Chisholm.** 2nd ed., Melbourne, 1957.
AD165. Fitzpatrick, Kathleen. **Sir John Franklin in Tasmania, 1837–1843.** Melbourne, 1949.
AD166. Bassett, Marnie. **The Hentys.** London and Melbourne, 1954.
AD167. Lang, John D. **John Dunmore**

Lang, chiefly autobiographical. 2 v. Melbourne, 1951.

AD168. Gross, Alan. **Charles Joseph Latrobe.** Melbourne, 1956.

AD169. Mayo, M. Penelope. **Life and letters of Col. William Light.** Adelaide, 1937.

AD170. Cumpston, John H. L. **Thomas Mitchell.** London and Melbourne, 1954.

AD171. Uren, Malcolm J. L. **Land looking west: the story of Governor James Stirling in Western Australia.** London, 1948.

AD172. Cumpston, John H. L. **Charles Sturt.** Melbourne, 1951.

AD173. Melbourne, Alexander C. V. **William Charles Wentworth.** Brisbane, 1934.

1851–1900

AD174. Bavin, Thomas R. **Sir Henry Parkes.** Sydney, 1941.

AD175. Spence, William G. **Australia's awakening: thirty years in the life of an Australian agitator.** Sydney, 1909.

AD176. Pratt, Ambrose. **David Syme, the father of protection in Australia.** London, 1908.

Twentieth Century

AD177. Reynolds, John. **Edmund Barton.** Sydney, 1948.

AD178. Chester, Alan. **John Curtin.** Sydney, 1943.

AD179. Murdoch, Walter. **Alfred Deakin.** London, 1923.

AD180. Graham, Austin D. **Life of Sir Samuel W. Griffith.** Brisbane, 1939.

AD181. Hancock, William K. **Country and calling.** London, 1954.

AD182. Palmer, Nettie. **Henry Bournes Higgins.** London, 1931.

AD183. Evatt, Herbert V. **Australian labour leader: the story of W. A. Holman.** Sydney, 1940.

AD184. Whyte, William F. **William Morris Hughes.** Sydney, 1957.

AD185. Ross, Lloyd R. M. **William Lane and the Australian labor movement.** Sydney, 1937.

AD186. Lett, Lewis. **Sir Hubert Murray of Papua.** London, 1951.

GOVERNMENT PUBLICATIONS

AD187. Australian government publications. Canberra, 1952 ff. (Monthly.) Listing of state and federal documents.

AD188. Annual catalogue of Australian publications. Canberra, 1936 ff. Contains lists of federal and state documents.

AD189. Australia. Parliament. **Parliamentary debates.** Canberra, 1901 ff. Federal and state debates are summarized quarterly in *Journal of the parliaments of the Commonwealth.*

AD190. ——. **The records of the proceedings and the printed papers.** 1901/02 ff. Canberra, 1902 ff. (Annual.)

AD191. Australian legislative digest. Sydney, 1922 ff. Summarizes federal and state legislation.

AD192. Australia in facts and figures. Canberra, 1943 ff. (Quarterly.) Review of political, economic, and social events.

AD193. Australia. Prime Minister's Dept. **The federal guide.** Canberra, 1926 ff. Organization and functions of federal agencies.

UNIVERSITY, ACADEMY, AND SOCIETY PUBLICATIONS

AD194. Royal Australian Historical Society. **Journal and proceedings.** Sydney, 1901 ff. (Irregular.)

AD195. Historical Society of Queensland. **Journal.** Brisbane, 1914 ff. (Annual.)

AD196. Tasmanian Historical Research Association. **Papers and proceedings.** Hobart, 1952 ff. (Irregular.)

AD197. Historical Society of Victoria. **The Victorian historical magazine.** Melbourne, 1911 ff. (Irregular.)

AD198. Western Australian Historical Society. **Journals and proceedings.** Perth, 1927 ff. (Annual.)

AD199. Royal Geographical Society of Australasia. Queensland Branch. **Queensland geographical journal.** Brisbane, 1885 ff. (Irregular.)

AD200. Royal Geographical Society of Australasia. South Australian Branch. **Proceedings.** Adelaide, 1885 ff. (Irregular.)

AD201. Australian National University. **Social science monographs.** Canberra, 1954 ff. (Irregular.)

PERIODICALS

AD202. Historical studies, Australia and New Zealand. Melbourne, 1940 ff. (Semiannual.)

AD203. Australian journal of politics and history. Brisbane, 1955 ff. (Semiannual.)

AD204. Australian historical monographs. Sydney, 1935 ff. (Irregular.) Contributions by G. Mackaness or editions of Australiana.

AD205. Australian geographer. Sydney, 1928 ff. (Irregular.)

AD206. Walkabout. Melbourne, 1935 ff. (Monthly.)

AD207. Cartography. Melbourne, 1954 ff. (Semiannual.)

AD208. Economic record. Melbourne, 1923 ff. (Semiannual.)

AD209. Public administration. Sydney, 1939 ff. (Quarterly.)

AD210. Australian outlook. Sydney, 1947 ff. (Quarterly.)

AD211. Australian quarterly. Sydney, 1929 ff.

NEW ZEALAND

BIBLIOGRAPHIES AND LIBRARY COLLECTIONS

AD212. The Cambridge history of the British Empire. V. 7, pt. 2, New Zealand (London, 1933), pp. 259–90.

AD213. Hocken, Thomas M. **A bibliography of literature relating to New Zealand.** Wellington, 1909. Supplements, Auckland, 1927; Dunedin, 1938.

AD214. Williams, Herbert W. **A bibliography of printed Maori to 1900.** Wellington, 1924. [Dominion Museum monograph, 7.] Supplement, 1928.

AD215. Miller, J. O. **New Zealand in books: a brief guide for the general reader.** Wellington, 1955. [Alexander Turnbull Library bibliographical list, 10.]

AD216. Conover, Helen F. **New Zealand, a selected list of references.** Washington, 1942. Library of Congress holdings. See also Lewin (*AD4*) and Royal Empire Society Library, *Subject catalogue* (*AD3*). Pp. 147–211 of Taylor's *Pacific bibliography* (*AE2*) relate to N.Z., especially the Maoris.

AD217. Jenkins, David L. **Union list of theses of the University of New Zealand, 1910–54.** Wellington, 1956. Supersedes the *List of historical theses, 1927–37.*

AD218. Harris, John. **Guide to New Zealand reference material.** 2nd ed., Wellington, 1950. Supplements, 1951–57. Covers history, local history, government, etc.

AD219. Hardie, B. G. **Bibliography of New Zealand economics and economic history.** Auckland, 1953.

AD220. Index to New Zealand periodicals and current bibliography of New Zealand books and pamphlets. Wellington, 1942 ff. (Annual.) Includes articles on N.Z. published abroad.

AD221. N.Z. National Archives. **Guide to the Dominion Archives.** Wellington, 1953.

AD222. ——. **Preliminary inventory.** Wellington, 1953 ff.

AD223. Taylor, Clyde R. H. **Alexander Turnbull Library.** Wellington, 1951. The Turnbull Library is the major source for N.Z. history. There are also notable collections in the Hocken Library at the University of Otago and in the General Assembly Library, Wellington. The manuscript resources of the Turnbull Library and the New Zealand National Archives are supplemented especially by those of the Auckland Public Library and the Mitchell Library. Historical manuscripts added to N.Z. libraries are listed in *Historical studies, Australia and New Zealand.* See also the note on research projects following *AD12.*

WORKS OF REFERENCE

AD224. Scholefield, Guy H. **A dictionary of New Zealand biography.** 2 v. Wellington, 1940.

AD225. Who's who in New Zealand. Wellington, 1908 ff. (Irregular.)

AD226. New Zealand official year book. Wellington, 1892 ff.

GEOGRAPHIES AND GAZETTEERS

AD227. Cumberland, Kenneth B. **This is New Zealand.** Christchurch, 1950. Good but elementary geography. See also his *Southwest Pacific* (*AD19*).

AD228. Clark, Andrew H. **The invasion of New Zealand by people, plants and animals: the South Island.** New Brunswick, N.J., 1949. Geographical study of cultural origins and patterns of land use. Review, G. M. Miller and H. P. Schaffer, *Landfall,* 5 (Mar. 1951): 71.

AD229. Dollimore, Edward S. **The New Zealand guide: a comprehensive gazetteer.** Dunedin, 1952.

AD230. Andersen, Johannes C. **Maori place-names.** Wellington, 1942. [Polynesian Society memoir, 20.]

AD231. Reed, Alexander W. **The story of New Zealand place-names.** Wellington, 1952.

MAORI HISTORY

AD232. Best, Elsdon. **The Maori.** 2 v. Wellington, 1924. [Polynesian Society memoir, 5.] Generally accepted as the standard work.

AD233. Cowan, James. **The Maori yesterday and today.** Wellington, 1930. Comprehensive.

AD234. Buck, Peter H. **The coming of the Maori.** 2nd ed., Wellington, 1950. Best work on the Polynesian migrations. Review, H. D. Skinner, *Landfall,* 4 (Mar. 1950): 85. See also his *Vikings of the sunrise* (*AE47*).

AD235. Smith, Stephenson P. **Hawaiki, the original home of the Maori.** 4th ed., Auckland, 1921.

AD236. Duff, Roger S. **The Moa-hunter period of Maori culture.** 2nd ed., Wellington, 1956. The earliest known civilization in N.Z. Review, G. L. Adkin, *Landfall,* 4 (Dec. 1950): 365.

AD237. Best, Elsdon. **The Maori as he was.** Wellington, 1924. Pre-European civilization.

AD238. ——. **The Pa Maori: an account of the fortified villages.** Wellington, 1927. [Dominion Museum bulletin, 6.]

AD239. Grey, Sir George. **Polynesian mythology and ancient traditional history of the Maori.** Christchurch, 1956.

AD240. White, John. **The ancient history of the Maori, his mythology and traditions.** 6 v. Wellington, 1887–90.

AD241. Beaglehole, Ernest, and Pearl Beaglehole. **Some modern Maoris.** Wellington, 1946.

AD242. Sutherland, Ivan L. G., ed. **The Maori people today, a general survey.** Wellington and London, 1940. Best recent source of information. Review, I. Milner, *Hist. stud. Austr. and N.Z.*, 2 (Apr. 1942): 58.

AD243. Smith, Norman. **The Maori people and us.** Wellington, 1948. Survey of modern Maoris written with a historical perspective. The *Journal of the Polynesian Society* (*AE101*) is a good source of Maori history.

DEMOGRAPHIC STUDIES

AD244. Calvert, G. N. **The future population of New Zealand, a statistical analysis.** Wellington, 1946. Summarizes the growth and structure of New Zealand's population; gives projections to 2005. [WDB]

AD245. Sinclair, Huia I. **Population, New Zealand's problem.** Dunedin, 1944. Popular outline of trends. See also *Future of immigration into Australia and New Zealand* (*AD34*). [WDB]

AD246. Lochore, Reuel A. **From Europe to New Zealand.** Wellington, 1951. Transition of the social and cultural background of non-British immigrants, with attitude of New Zealanders toward them. [WDB]

PRINTED COLLECTIONS OF SOURCES

AD247. McNab, Robert, ed. **Historical records of New Zealand.** 2 v. Wellington, 1908–14. Based on *Historical records of New South Wales* (*AD37*) which, like *Historical records of Australia* (*AD38*), contains much N.Z. material. Grey (*AD239*) and White (*AD240*) give Maori sources.

SHORTER GENERAL HISTORIES

AD248. The Cambridge history of the British Empire. V. 7, pt. 2, New Zealand. London, 1933.

AD249. Reeves, W. Pember. **The long white cloud.** 4th ed., with additional chapters by A. J. Harrop, London, 1950. Condliffe calls this "perhaps the best book ever written on New Zealand." Review J. D. N. McDonald, *Landfall*, 5 (Mar. 1951): 76.

AD250. Condliffe, John B., and Willis T. G. Airey. **A short history of New Zealand.** 7th ed., Christchurch, 1953. Should be read in conjunction with Reeves. Condliffe believes Reeves was too favorable to the colonists and too close to the social program of the 1890's. Review, B. Paul, *Landfall*, 8 (Sep. 1954): 230.

AD251. Beaglehole, John C. **New Zealand, a short history.** London, 1936. An essay rather than a systematic history.

AD252. Morrell, William P. **New Zealand.** London, 1935. Partly an excellent short history, partly an appraisal of contemporaneous N.Z. Review, *Geog. jour.*, 86 (Sep. 1935): 289.

AD253. Miller, Harold. **New Zealand.** London, 1950. Emphasizes the conflict of races and political experiments. Review, A. Ross, *Landfall*, 4 (Sep. 1950): 251.

AD254. N.Z. Dept. of Internal Affairs. **Making New Zealand: pictorial surveys of a century.** 2 v. Wellington, 1940. Illustrative material for N.Z. history.

HISTORIES OF SPECIAL PERIODS

Discovery and Exploration

Beaglehole's edition of Cook's *Journals* (*AE57*) is basic.

AD255. Beaglehole, John C. **The discovery of New Zealand.** Wellington, 1939. Best general work. Review, L. F. Fitzhardinge, *Hist. stud. Austr. and N.Z.*, 1 (Oct. 1940): 132

AD256. N.Z. Dept. of Internal Affairs. **Abel J. Tasman and the discovery of New Zealand.** Wellington, 1942.

AD257. Kelly, Leslie G. **Marion Dufresne at the Bay of Islands.** Wellington, 1951. Review, J. R. Lee, *Hist. stud. Austr. and N.Z.*, 6 (May 1954): 234.

AD258. Dumas, Alexandre. **Captain Marion.** Christchurch, 1949. Adapted from Crozet's narrative of the massacre. Review, J. D. N. McDonald, *Landfall*, 4 (Dec. 1950): 361.

AD259. Dumont d'Urville, Jules. **New Zealand, 1826–1827.** Wellington, 1950. Review, A. Ross, *Landfall*, 4 (Dec. 1950): 363.

AD260. ———. **Voyage of the Astrolabe, 1840: with some account of Bishop Pompallier and Charles, Baron de Thierry.** Wellington, 1955. Review, A. Ross, *Landfall*, 9 (Dec. 1955): 352.

AD261. McClymont, William G. **The exploration of New Zealand.** Wellington, 1940. Review, J. P. Pascoe, *Hist. stud. Austr. and N.Z.*, 1 (Oct. 1940): 133.

AD262. Bidwell, John C. **Rambles in New Zealand, 1839.** New ed., Christchurch, 1952. Review, N. Taylor, *Landfall*, 8 (Mar. 1954): 62.

AD263. Brunner, Thomas. **The great journey.** Christchurch, 1952. Exploration of the South Island, 1846–48. Review, N. Taylor, *Landfall*, 8 (Mar. 1954): 62.

To 1840

AD264. Savage, John. **Account of New Zealand in 1805.** Wellington, 1939.

AD265. Cruise, Richard. **New Zealand one hundred years ago.** Auckland, 1921.

AD266. Maning, Frederick E. **Old New Zealand.** Christchurch, 1948. Includes a long account of Hone Heke's rebellion.

AD267. Dakin, William J. **Whalemen adventurers: the story of whaling in Australian waters.** 2nd ed., Sydney, 1938. Review, C. Kaeppel, *Austr. quar.,* 10 (Sep. 1938): 114.

AD268. McNab, Robert. **The old whaling days: a history of southern New Zealand, 1830 to 1840.** Christchurch, 1913.

AD269. Ramsden, Eric. **Marsden and the missions.** Sydney, 1936.

AD270. Elder, John R., ed. **Marsden's lieutenants.** Dunedin, 1934.

Crown Colony Period

AD271. Buick, Thomas L. **The treaty of Waitangi.** 3rd ed., New Plymouth, 1936.

AD272. Rutherford, James. **The treaty of Waitangi and the acquisition of British sovereignty in New Zealand.** Auckland, 1949. [Auckland University College, History series, 3.] Review, W. P. Morrell, *Landfall,* 3 (Sep. 1949): 293.

AD273. Beaglehole, John C. **Captain Hobson and the New Zealand Company.** Northampton, Mass., 1928. [Smith College studies in history, 13.]

AD274. Ross, Ruth M. **New Zealand's first capital.** Wellington, 1946. [N.Z. Dept. of Internal Affairs, Historical Branch bulletin, 1.] Russell in the Bay of Islands.

AD275. Meiklejohn, George M. **Early conflicts of press and government.** Auckland, 1953. Review, R. M. Ross, *Landfall,* 8 (June 1954): 136.

AD276. Wilson, Ethel W. **Land problems of the New Zealand settlers of the forties.** Dunedin, 1935.

AD277. Sinclair, Keith. **The Maori land league: an examination into the source of a New Zealand myth.** Auckland, 1950. [Auckland University College, History series, 4.] Review, H. Miller, *Landfall,* 5 (June 1951): 51.

AD278. Marais, Johannes S. **Colonisation of New Zealand.** London, 1927.

AD279. Wakefield, E. Jerningham. **Adventure in New Zealand from 1839 to 1844.** Christchurch, 1908. An abridgment of this N.Z. classic was issued in Christchurch in 1955.

AD280. Mathew, Felton. **The founding of New Zealand: the journals . . . 1840–1847.** Auckland, 1940. Review, W. P. Morrell, *Eng. hist. rev.,* 56 (Jan. 1941): 172.

AD281. Williams, John B. **The New Zealand journal, 1842–1844.** Salem, Mass., 1956.

Observations of the chauvinistic U. S. consul at the Bay of Islands.

AD282. Dillon, Constantine A. **The Dillon letters, 1842–1853.** Wellington, 1954. Review, M. Turnbull, *Landfall,* 9 (Sep. 1955): 251.

Maori Wars

AD283. Cowan, James. **The New Zealand wars.** 2 v. Wellington, 1955–56.

AD284. Harrop, Angus J. **England and the Maori wars.** London, 1937. The wars in the light of British colonial policy.

AD285. Sinclair, Keith. **Origins of the Maori wars.** Wellington, 1957.

AD286. Rutherford, James. **Hone Heke's rebellion, 1844–1846.** Auckland, 1947. [Auckland University College, Bulletin, 34.]

AD287. Gorst, John E. **The Maori king.** London, 1864. Origins of the king movement.

1852–1900

AD288. Morrell, William P. **The provincial system in New Zealand, 1852–76.** London, 1932.

AD289. Wilson, Trevor G. **The Grey government, 1877–79.** Auckland, 1954. [Auckland University College, History series, 5.] Review, W. P. Morrell, *Landfall,* 9 (June 1955): 173.

AD290. ——. **Rise of the New Zealand Liberal party, 1880–90.** Auckland, 1956. [Auckland University College, History series, 6.] Review, D. K. Fieldhouse, *Landfall,* 10 (Dec. 1956): 360.

AD291. Hall, David O. W. **New Zealanders in South Africa, 1899–1902.** Wellington, 1950.

Twentieth Century

AD292. **Official history of New Zealand's effort in the Great War.** 4 v. Auckland, 1921–23. Popular accounts. See also Moorehead (*AD58*).

AD293. N.Z. Dept. of Internal Affairs. **Documents relating to New Zealand's participation in the Second World War.** 2 v. Wellington, 1949–51. Review, R. M. Ross, *Landfall,* 8 (Dec. 1954): 310.

AD294. ——. **Official history of New Zealand in the Second World War.** Wellington, 1952 ff.

AD295. ——. **Episodes and studies.** Wellington, 1950 ff.

AD296. Beaglehole, John C., ed. **New Zealand and the Statute of Westminster.** Wellington, 1944. Review, H. L. Harris, *Austr. quar.,* 17 (Mar. 1945): 121.

AD297. New Zealand Institute of International Affairs. **Contemporary New Zealand: a survey of domestic and foreign policy.**

Auckland, 1938. N.Z. after two years of its first labor government.

HISTORIES OF SPECIAL AREAS

AD298. Buick, Thomas L. **The French at Akaroa.** Wellington, 1928.

AD299. Reed, Alfred H. **Auckland, the city and the seas.** Wellington, 1955.

AD300. ——. **The story of Canterbury, last Wakefield settlement.** Wellington, 1949. Review, M. McCaskill, *N.Z. geog.*, 6 (Oct. 1950): 209.

AD301. Hight, James, ed. **History of Canterbury.** Christchurch, 1957 ff.

AD302. Ward, Edward. **Journal, 1850–51.** Christchurch, 1951. Voyage to N.Z. and the early Canterbury settlement. Review, J. D. N. McDonald, *Landfall*, 5 (Dec. 1951): 319.

AD303. Richards, Eva C. **The Chatham Islands.** Christchurch, 1952.

AD304. Simpson, Frank A. **Chatham exiles: yesterday and today at the Chatham Islands.** Wellington, 1950. Review, T. H. McCombs, *N.Z. geog.*, 7 (Apr. 1951): 96.

AD305. Morrison, Joan P. **Evolution of a city: the story of Christchurch, 1850–1903.** Christchurch, 1948.

AD306. Gilkison, Robert. **Early days in Dunedin.** Auckland, 1938.

AD307. Wilson, James G. **History of Hawkes Bay.** Dunedin, 1939.

AD308. McIntosh, Alister D. **Marlborough, a provincial history.** Blenheim, 1940.

AD309. Rutherford, James, ed. **The establishment of the New Plymouth settlement in New Zealand, 1841–1843.** New Plymouth, 1940.

AD310. McLintock, Alexander H. **History of Otago: the origins and growth of a Wakefield class settlement.** Dunedin, 1949. Review, M. A. Hall-Kenney, *Landfall*, 3 (Dec. 1949): 381.

AD311. Mackay, Joseph A. **Historic Poverty Bay and the east coast, N. I.** Gisborne, 1949.

AD312. Howard, Basil H. **Rakiura, a history of Stewart Island.** Dunedin, 1940.

AD313. Chapple, Leonard J. B., and Henry C. Veitch. **Wanganui.** Hawera, 1939.

AD314. Ward, Louis E. **Early Wellington.** 2nd ed., London, 1942.

AD315. Lord, E. Iveagh. **Old Westland.** Christchurch, 1939.

HISTORIES OF SPECIAL TOPICS

Agriculture

AD316. Alley, G. T., and David O. W. Hall. **The farmer in New Zealand.** Wellington, 1941. History of the basic farming industries.

AD317. Buchanan, Robert O. **Pastoral in-**dustries of New Zealand. London, 1935. [Institute of British Geographers, Publications, 2.] The industries against the physical and historical background. Review, *Geog. jour.*, 85 (June 1935): 565.

AD318. Philpott, H. G. **History of the New Zealand dairy industry, 1840–1935.** Wellington, 1937.

AD319. Acland, Leopold G. D. **The early Canterbury runs.** Christchurch, 1951. Occupation of the Canterbury plains. Review, G. Jobberns, *N.Z. geog.*, 8 (Apr. 1952): 80.

AD320. Guthrie-Smith, Herbert. **Tutira, the story of a New Zealand sheep station.** 3rd ed., Edinburgh, 1953. Typifies the development of sheep farming.

Church History

AD321. Purchas, Henry T. **A history of the English church in New Zealand.** Christchurch, 1914.

AD322. Elder, John R. **The history of the Presbyterian Church of New Zealand, 1840–1940.** Christchurch, 1940.

AD323. Morley, William. **History of Methodism in New Zealand.** Wellington, 1900.

AD324. Moran, Patrick F. **History of the Catholic Church in Australasia.** 2 v. Sydney, 1895.

See also *AD269–270.*

Civilization

AD325. Wood, Frederick L. W. **This New Zealand.** Hamilton, 1952. Outstanding work on all phases of N.Z. life. Review, H. L. Harris, *Austr. quar.*, 18 (Dec. 1946): 116.

AD326. Siegfried, André. **Democracy in New Zealand.** London, 1914. A still valuable introduction to N.Z. civilization.

AD327. Ngata, Sir Apirana, and others. **New Zealand affairs.** Christchurch, 1929. [I. P. R. New Zealand Branch. Studies on New Zealand topics, 1.] Geography, population, immigration, farming, trade, the mandate for Samoa.

AD328. Belshaw, Horace, ed. **New Zealand.** Berkeley, 1947. In general an accurate and careful summary of N.Z. life. Review, B. Paul, *Landfall*, 3 (Mar. 1949): 84.

AD329. Morrell, William P., and David O. W. Hall. **A history of New Zealand life.** Christchurch, 1957. A social history.

Constitutional History

AD330. Hight, James, and Harry D. Bamford. **The constitutional history and law of New Zealand.** Christchurch, 1914.

AD331. Robson, John L., ed. **New Zealand, the development of its laws and constitution.** London, 1954. Emphasis is on legislation made in response to social conditions.

AD332. Foden, Norman A. **The constitutional development of New Zealand in the first decade, 1839–1849.** Wellington, 1938.

Economic History

AD333. Condliffe, John B. **New Zealand in the making: a survey of economic and social development.** Chicago and London, 1930. A comprehensive economic history. Review, J. Hight, *Econ. rec.*, 6 (Nov. 1930): 296.

AD334. Simkin, Colin G. F. **The instability of a dependent economy: economic fluctuations in New Zealand, 1840–1914.** London and N.Y., 1951. A major theme in N.Z. history. Review, G. G. Firth, *Econ. rec.*, 27 (Dec. 1951): 277.

AD335. Parker, Robert S., ed. **Economic stability in New Zealand.** Wellington, 1953. Review, H. Bernardelli, *Econ. rec.*, 30 (May, 1954): 103.

AD336. New Zealand economic survey. Wellington, 1953 ff.

AD337. Great Britain. Commercial Relations and Exports Dept. **New Zealand economic and commercial conditions.** London, 1950.

Foreign Relations

AD338. Wood, Frederick L. W. **New Zealand in the world.** Wellington, 1940. Review, J. O. Shearer, *Austr. quar.*, 12 (June 1940): 108.

AD339. Airey, Willis T. G. **New Zealand foreign policy related to New Zealand social development and current world trends.** Wellington, 1954.

AD340. Milner, Ian. **New Zealand's interests and policies in the Far East.** N.Y., 1940. [I. P. R. Inquiry series.] Review, F. L. W. Wood, *Hist. stud. Austr. and N.Z.*, 1 (Oct. 1940): 137.

Land Settlement

AD341. Jourdain, William R. **Land legislation and settlement in New Zealand.** Wellington, 1925.

Political History

AD342. Lipson, Leslie. **The politics of equality: New Zealand's adventures in democracy.** Chicago, 1948. Covers 1840–1947. Review, E. A. Olssen, *Landfall,* 3 (Mar. 1949): 86.

AD343. Webb, Leicester. **Government in New Zealand.** Wellington, 1940. The parliamentary and administrative system. Review, W. T. G. Airey, *Hist. stud. Austr. and N.Z.*, 2 (Apr. 1942): 56

AD344. Scholefield, Guy H., ed. **New Zealand parliamentary record, 1840–1949.** Wellington, 1950.

AD345. Paul, John T. **Humanism in politics: New Zealand Labour party retrospect.** Wellington, 1946.

AD346. Dalmer, Erle B., and Harold S. Southern. **Counties at the crossroads.** Christchurch, 1948. Stronger local government versus greater centralization of authority. Review, L. Webb, *Landfall,* 3 (June 1949): 188

AD347. Lee, John A. **Socialism in New Zealand.** London, 1938.

AD348. Le Rossignol, James E., and William D. Stewart. **State socialism in New Zealand.** N.Y., 1910. See also Reeves (*AD149*).

Social Security

AD349. N.Z. Social Security Dept. **The growth and development of social security in New Zealand, 1898–1949.** Wellington, 1950.

AD350. Sutch, William B. **Poverty and progress in New Zealand.** Wellington, 1941.

AD351. ——. **The quest for security in New Zealand.** Harmondsworth, Eng., 1942.

BIOGRAPHIES

The comprehensive work is *A dictionary of New Zealand biography* (*AD224*).

AD352. Scholefield, Guy H. **Notable New Zealand statesmen: twelve prime ministers.** Wellington, 1946.

AD353. Burdon, Randal M. **New Zealand notables.** 3 v. Christchurch, 1941–51. Twelve biographies.

AD354. Stewart, William D. **The Right Hon. Sir Francis H. D. Bell.** Wellington, 1937.

AD355. Ramsden, Eric. **Busby of Waitangi.** Wellington, 1942.

AD356. Douglas, Charles E. **Mr. Explorer Douglas.** Wellington, 1957.

AD357. Thorn, James. **Peter Fraser, New Zealand's wartime prime minister.** London, 1952.

AD358. Carrington, Charles E. **John Robert Godley of Canterbury.** Christchurch, 1950.

AD359. Godley, Charlotte. **Letters from early New Zealand, 1850–1863.** Christchurch, 1951.

AD360. Rees, William L., and Lily Rees. **Life and times of Sir George Grey.** 2nd ed., 2 v., London, 1892.

AD361. Henderson, George C. **Sir George Grey, pioneer of empire in southern lands.** London, 1907.

AD362. Scholefield, Guy H. **Captain Wil-**

liam Hobson, first governor of New Zealand. London, 1934.

AD363. Cowan, James. **Sir Donald McLean.** Dunedin, 1940.

AD364. Marsden, Samuel. **Letters and journals.** Dunedin, 1932.

AD365. Keys, Lillian G. **Life and times of Bishop Pompallier.** Christchurch, 1957.

AD366. Stewart, William D. **William Rolleston.** Christchurch, 1940.

AD367. Burdon, Randal M. **King Dick: a biography of Richard John Seddon.** Christchurch, 1955.

AD368. Tucker, Henry W. **George Augustus Selwyn.** 2 v. London, 1879.

AD369. Reed, Alexander W. **George Augustus Selwyn, pioneer bishop of New Zealand.** London, 1939.

AD370. Buick, Thomas L. **An old New Zealander: or Te Rauparaha, the Napoleon of the South.** London, 1911.

AD371. Burdon, Randal M. **The life and times of Sir Julius Vogel.** Christchurch, 1948.

AD372. Harrop, Angus J. **The amazing career of Edward Gibbon Wakefield.** London, 1928.

AD373. O'Connor, Irma. **Edward Gibbon Wakefield, the man himself.** London, 1929.

AD374. Carleton, Hugh. **The life of Henry Williams.** Wellington, 1948.

AD375. Wild, Leonard J. **The life and times of Sir James Wilson of Bulls.** Christchurch, 1953.

GOVERNMENT PUBLICATIONS

AD376. Scholefield, Guy H. **Union list of New Zealand official papers and British papers relating to New Zealand.** Wellington, 1939.

AD377. **Union list of serials in New Zea-** land libraries. Wellington, 1953 ff. Contains section on N.Z. serial documents.

AD378. **New Zealand government publications: a monthly list.** Wellington, 1953 ff.

AD379. Neale, Edward P. **Guide to New Zealand official statistics.** 3rd ed., Christchurch, 1955. Lists sources of information.

AD380. New Zealand. Parliament. **Parliamentary debates.** 1854 ff. Wellington, 1867 ff. Summarized quarterly in *Journal of the parliaments of the Commonwealth.*

AD381. ——. **Appendix to the journals of the House of Representatives.** Wellington, 1854 ff. Parliamentary papers.

UNIVERSITY AND SOCIETY PUBLICATIONS

AD382. Nelson Historical Society. **Journal.** Nelson, 1955 ff. (Irregular.)

AD383. Auckland University College. **History series.** Auckland, 1936 ff. (Irregular.)

AD384. ——. **Geography series.** Auckland, 1956 ff. (Irregular.)

AD385. New Zealand Geographical Society. **New Zealand geographer.** Auckland, 1945 ff. (Semiannual.)

PERIODICALS

The basic journals are **Historical studies, Australia and New Zealand** (*AD202*) and **Economic record** (*AD208*).

AD386. Landfall, a New Zealand quarterly. Christchurch, 1947 ff.

AD387. **Political science.** Wellington, 1948 ff. (Semiannual.)

AD388. **New Zealand journal of public administration.** Wellington, 1938 ff. (Semiannual.)

ANTARCTICA

AD389. Tanzer, William. **Publications on Antarctica.** Wellington, 1951.

AD390. New Zealand Antarctic Society. **The Antarctic today: a mid-century survey.** Wellington, 1952. Best general work on the Antarctic. Review, G. Taylor, *N.Z. geog.,* 9 (Oct. 1953): 197.

AD391. Scholes, William A. **Seventh continent: saga of Australian exploration in Antarctica, 1895–1950.** London, 1953.

AD392. Law, Phillip G., and John Béchervaise. **Anare, Australia's Antarctic outposts.** Melbourne, 1957.

AD393. Australian National Antarctic Research Expedition. **Reports.** Melbourne, 1951 ff.

AD394. **Antarctic news bulletin.** Wellington, 1950 ff. (Quarterly.)

AD395. **The polar record.** Cambridge, Eng., 1931 ff. (Semiannual.)

Oceania

HAROLD WHITMAN BRADLEY

There is an extensive body of literature dealing with the Pacific islands. It began with the journals of explorers, and was enlarged in the 19th century by published accounts of missionaries, transient visitors, and expatriates in Oceania. A few of these early works contained such vivid descriptions of primitive society or such thoughtful speculations upon the origins of the Oceanic peoples that they achieved, for a time, the status of near classics; but almost without exception earlier works have been superseded by research studies of the 20th century.

Among scholars, the anthropologists and ethnologists were the first to invade Oceania. A few of these produced works of a general character; but the greater number of their studies were concerned with the vanishing culture of Pacific peoples, and their research was carried on in small and isolated communities remote from the major historical currents which have reshaped the society and economy of Oceania in the past century. The result was an important body of specialized studies of limited value to the historian.

Two world wars and the resulting political changes in Oceania have directed the attention of anthropologists and other social scientists to the impact in the Pacific islands of the American and European penetration of the region. The administering powers, notably the United States and Australia, have encouraged scholarly investigations of problems arising from these recent political developments. Some of the resulting studies are of a very high quality, but the concentration upon contemporary conditions again limits their value to the historian.

The history of the Pacific islands has been less extensively studied by scholars. This is especially true of the internal history of the islands. With few exceptions, historians who have been interested in Oceania have been concerned with foreign penetration of the region or with international rivalries which accompanied that penetration. Recent political events have stimulated a new interest in the history of the Pacific islands. This is particularly true in France and Australia. It should be observed, however, that both historians and anthropologists have been disposed to study those islands or regions in which their own countries have exercised a dominant influence. One effect of this nationalism in scholarship is that there is not yet any scholarly history embracing all of Oceania.

Although Oceania is one of the regions comparatively neglected by historians, the materials for study of its history are abundant. Printed sources are extensive and diverse; and there is a wealth of manuscript material scattered among the libraries of western Europe, the United States, New Zealand, Australia, and Oceania. The most important categories are official records, the reports or journals of hundreds of missionaries representing a score of churches and religious orders, and the surviving papers of merchants and business firms which participated in the economic development of the islands.

BIBLIOGRAPHIES

AE1. Leeson, Ida E. **Bibliography of bibliographies of the South Pacific.** N.Y., 1954. Published under the auspices of the South Pacific Commission and limited to bibliographies dealing with islands in which the Commission is interested. Excellent.

AE2. Taylor, Clyde R. H. **A Pacific bibliography: printed matter relating to the native peoples of Polynesia, Melanesia, and Micronesia.** Wellington, 1951. [Memoirs of the Polynesian Society, 24.] As indicated in sub-title, emphasis is on works dealing with the native peoples, but does include other titles as well. Despite some omissions, the most complete bibliography of books relating to Oceania.

AE3. Lewin, Percy Evans. **The Pacific region: a bibliography of the Pacific and East Indian islands, exclusive of Japan.** London, 1944. [Royal Empire Society bibliographies, 11.] A listing of selected works, chiefly those dealing with political history and published since 1900. Within these limits, very useful.

AE4. ——. **Subject catalogue of the library of the Royal Empire Society, formerly the Royal Colonial Institute.** V. 2 (London, 1931), pp. 483–652. See *U3*.

AE5. U. S. Library of Congress. Division of Bibliography. **Islands of the Pacific: a selected list of references.** By Helen F. Conover. Washington, 1943. Intended as supplement to *AE4*.

AE6. Allied Geographical Section. Southwest Pacific Area. **An annotated bibliography of the Southwest Pacific and adjacent areas.** V. 2. N.p., 1944. Bibliography of New Guinea, New Hebrides, British Solomons, and Micronesia.

AE7. Jore, Léonce. **Essai de bibliographie du Pacifique.** Paris, 1931. Useful for works in French.

AE8. Faivre, Jean-Paul. "Chronique de l'histoire coloniale: l'Océanie et le Pacifique 1939–1955." **Revue d'histoire des colonies,** 42 (1955): 405–61.

AE9. O'Reilly, Patrick. **Bibliographie méthodique analytique et critique de la Nouvelle-Calédonie.** Paris, 1955. [Société des Océanistes, Publications, 4.] Best recent

bibliography for any Pacific archipelago. Includes periodical articles and maps.

WORKS OF REFERENCE (INCLUDING GEOGRAPHY)

AE10. **Pacific islands yearbook.** Ed. by Robert W. Robson. 7 issues. Sydney and Suva, 1932–56. Standard current data for all parts of Oceania; disproportionate attention to southwest Pacific.

AE11. **Hawaiian almanac and annual.** Honolulu, 1875–1941. (Title varies.) Now merged with *All about Hawaii* (Honolulu, 1928 ff.) and published under this title. Annual publication of standard data.

AE12. Derrick, Ronald A. **The Fiji Islands: a geographical handbook.** Suva, 1951.

AE13. O'Reilly, Patrick, ed. **Calédoniens répertoire bio-bibliographique de la Nouvelle-Calédonie.** Paris, 1953. [Société des Océanistes, Publications, 3.] Important. Best biographical dictionary for any Pacific archipelago.

AE14. Freeman, Otis W., ed. **Geography of the Pacific.** N.Y. and London, 1951. Cooperative work by recognized authorities.

ANTHROPOLOGY AND ETHNOLOGY

AE15. Oliver, Douglas L. **The Pacific islands.** Cambridge, Mass., 1951. Best recent survey. Emphasis upon impact of foreign influences on peoples of Oceania.

AE16. Brown, John Macmillan. **Peoples and problems of the Pacific.** 2 v. London, 1927. Comprehensive and provocative, with unusual explanation of early history of Oceanic peoples.

Unwritten Literature and Folklore

AE17. Fornander, Abraham. **Fornander collection of Hawaiian antiquities and folklore.** Ed. and tr. by Thomas G. Thrum. 9 pts. Honolulu, 1916–19. [Memoirs of the Bernice Pauahi Bishop Museum, 4–6.] A basic source for the study of Polynesian folklore.

AE18. Caillot, A. C. Eugène. **Mythes, légendes et traditions des Polynésiens.** Paris, 1914.

AE19. Krämer, Augustin F. **Die Samoa-Inseln.** 2 v. Stuttgart, 1902. First volume contains legends and folklore; second deals generally with anthropology of Samoa.

AE20. Gill, William W. **Myths and songs from the South Pacific.** London, 1876. Classic work by a distinguished missionary.

AE21. Leenhardt, Maurice, ed. and tr. **Documents néo-calédoniens.** Paris, 1932. [University of Paris, Travaux et mémoires de l'Institut d'Ethnologie, 9.]

Polynesia

AE22. Buck, Peter H. (Te Rangi Hiroa). **An introduction to Polynesian anthropology.** Honolulu, 1945. [Bishop Museum bulletin, 187.]

AE23. Williamson, Robert W. **The social and political systems of central Polynesia.** 3 v. Cambridge, Eng., 1924. Comprehensive and thoughtful. See also other studies by same author.

AE24. Handy, E. S. Craighill. **Polynesian religion.** Honolulu, 1927. [Bishop Museum bulletin, 34.] The standard study. See also other studies of Polynesian anthropology by same author.

AE25. Henry, Teuira. **Ancient Tahiti.** Honolulu, 1928. [Bishop Museum bulletin, 48.] Based on notes taken by a missionary in the mid-19th century.

AE26. Laval, Honoré. **Mangareva: l'histoire ancienne d'un peuple polynésien.** Ed. by Alfred Métraux and Maurice Desmedt. Braine-le-Comte, Belgium, 1938. By a Catholic missionary who lived on the island from 1834 to 1871. This and *AE25* are classic descriptions of Polynesian culture by Europeans who lived in Oceania in the 19th century.

AE27. Bunzendahl, Otto. **Tahiti und Europa.** Leipzig, 1935. [Studien zur Völkerkunde, ed. by O. Reche and H. Plischke, 8.] Careful study of the impact of European influences upon the material culture of Tahiti during the earliest period of contact between Tahitians and Europeans.

AE28. Métraux, Alfred. **Ethnology of Easter Island.** Honolulu, 1940. [Bishop Museum bulletin, 160.] Standard scholarly study of the people and culture of this supposedly "mysterious" island. See also same author's more popular *L'Ile de Pâques* (Paris, 1941).

Micronesia

AE29. Hamburgische Wissenschaftliche Stiftung. **Ergebnisse der Südsee-Expedition 1908–1910.** Ed. by Georg Thilenius. 2 pts. in 16 v. (bound in 28 v.) Hamburg, 1914–38. Published findings of the most important German scientific investigation of Micro-

nesia and selected islands of Melanesia. Detailed, exhaustive, and invaluable.

AE30. Thompson, Laura. **Guam and its people.** 3rd ed., Princeton, 1947. The standard work on society and culture in Guam.

AE31. Barnett, Homer G. **Palauan society: a study of contemporary native life in the Palau Islands.** Eugene, Oreg., 1949.

AE32. Burrows, Edwin G., and Melford E. Spiro. **An atoll culture: ethnography of Ifaluk in the central Carolines.** New Haven, 1953. This and *AE31* are studies produced by the Coordinated Investigation of Micronesian Anthropology, sponsored by the National Research Council. These and other studies resulting from this project are among the most important recent contributions to the anthropology of Oceania.

Melanesia

AE33. Rivers, William H. R. **The history of Melanesian society.** 2 v. Cambridge, Eng., 1914.

AE34. Roth, George K. **Fijian way of life.** Melbourne and London, 1953. Good survey by an anthropologist with long administrative experience in Fiji.

AE35. Thompson, Laura. **Fijian frontier.** N.Y., 1940. Intensive study of the society of a single island. Useful supplement to the more general account in *AE34.*

AE36. Leenhardt, Maurice. **Gens de la Grande Terre.** Paris, 1937. Rev. ed., 1953. Important study of the native culture of New Caledonia.

AE37. Hogbin, Herbert I. **Experiments in civilization: the effects of European culture on a native community of the Solomon Islands.** London, 1939.

AE38. Malinowski, Bronislaw. **Argonauts of the western Pacific: an account of native enterprise and adventure in the archipelagoes of Melanesian New Guinea.** London, 1922. One of the classics in the literature of Melanesian anthropology.

DEMOGRAPHIC STUDIES

AE39. Roberts, Stephen H. **Population problems of the Pacific.** London, 1927. Often cited work, partly historical and partly an analysis of what were then "current" problems.

AE40. Lambert, Sylvester M. **The depopulation of Pacific races.** Honolulu, 1934. [Bishop Museum special publication, 23.]

AE41. Lind, Andrew W. **An island community: ecological succession in Hawaii.** Chicago, 1938.

AE42. Burrows, Edwin G. **Hawaiian Americans: an account of the mingling of Japanese, Chinese, Polynesian and American cultures.** New Haven, 1947. Good, brief survey, useful as supplement to the earlier *AE41*.

AE43. Coulter, John Wesley. **Fiji: little India of the Pacific.** Chicago, 1942. Compact study of the role of different national groups in economy and culture of Fiji.

AE44. Rivers, William H. R., ed. **Essays on the depopulation of Melanesia.** Cambridge, Eng., 1922. Series of critical essays by careful observers of Melanesian society.

LINGUISTIC WORKS

AE45. Capell, Arthur. **A linguistic survey of the south-western Pacific.** Noumea, New Caledonia, 1954. [South Pacific Commission technical paper, 70.]

AE46. Leenhardt, Maurice. **Langues et dialectes de l'Austro-Mélanésie.** Paris, 1946. [University of Paris, Travaux et mémoires de l'Institut d'Ethnologie, 46.]

HISTORIES OF SPECIAL PERIODS

Pre-Magellan

AE47. Buck, Peter H. (Te Rangi Hiroa). **Vikings of the sunrise.** N.Y., 1938. The standard work on the voyages of early Polynesians by an outstanding scholar. Indispensable; but see *AE48–49* for studies of the same topic which present conflicting conclusions.

AE48. Sharp, C. Andrew. **Ancient voyagers in the Pacific.** Wellington, 1956. Other eds. Scholarly; based primarily on accounts of early European visitors to the Pacific.

AE49. Heyerdahl, Thor. **American Indians in the Pacific: the theory behind the Kon-Tiki expedition.** London, 1952. A monumental and thoughtful exposition of an unusual interpretation of Polynesian origins.

Exploration and Discovery

AE50. Beaglehole, John C. **The exploration of the Pacific.** See *U105*.

AE51. Wroth, Lawrence C. **The early cartography of the Pacific.** N.Y., 1944. Important.

AE52. Lord Amherst of Hackney and Basil Thomson, eds. and trs. **The discovery of the Solomon Islands by Alvaro de Mendaña in 1568.** 2 v. London, 1901. [Works issued by the Hakluyt Society, 2nd ser., 7–8.]

AE53. Markham, Sir Clements R., ed. and tr. **The voyages of Pedro Fernández de Quiros, 1595 to 1606.** 2 v. London, 1904. [Publications of the Hakluyt Society, 14–15.]

AE54. Henderson, George C. **The discoverers of the Fiji Islands.** London, 1933.

AE55. Dahlgren, Erik W. **Were the Hawaiian Islands visited by the Spaniards before their discovery by Captain Cook in 1778?** Stockholm, 1916. Detailed and scholarly. Most important study of a controversial issue.

AE56. Carrington, Hugh, ed. **The discovery of Tahiti: a journal of the second voyage of H.M.S. Dolphin.** London, 1948. [Publications of the Hakluyt Society, 2nd ser., 98.]

AE57. Beaglehole, John C., and others, eds. **The journals of Captain James Cook on his voyages of discovery.** To be pub. in 4 v. Cambridge, Eng., 1955 ff. [Hakluyt Society, extra series.] Promises to be the definitive edition of the journals of the most important series of voyages of discovery to the Pacific.

Colonial Expansion and International Rivalry

AE58. Scholefield, Guy H. **The Pacific: its past and future and the policy of the great powers from the eighteenth century.** London, 1919. Best introductory survey, but value diminished by recent monographs.

AE59. Brookes, Jean I. **International rivalry in the Pacific islands, 1800–1875.** Berkeley and Los Angeles, 1941. Useful, but uneven in research and treatment of different topics.

AE60. Ward, John M. **British policy in the South Pacific, 1786–1893: a study in British policy towards the South Pacific islands prior to the establishment of governments by the great powers.** Sydney, 1948. Based on extensive research; very important.

AE61. Faivre, Jean-Paul. **L'expansion française dans le Pacifique 1800 à 1842.** Paris, 1953. Probably the definitive account; good critical bibliography.

HISTORIES OF SPECIAL AREAS

Polynesia

AE62. Kuykendall, Ralph S. **The Hawaiian kingdom.** 2 v. Honolulu, 1938. Published volumes cover period 1778–1874; projected third one to continue the study to 1893. Based on very extensive research; scholarly and thoughtful; the definitive account for period covered.

AE63. Bradley, Harold W. **The American frontier in Hawaii: the pioneers, 1789–1843.** Stanford, 1942. Emphasizes commerce and missionary influence.

AE64. Stevens, Sylvester K. **American expansion in Hawaii, 1842–1898.** Harrisburg, 1945. Deals primarily with political and diplomatic history.

AE65. Conroy, F. Hilary. **The Japanese frontier in Hawaii, 1868–1898.** Berkeley and

Los Angeles, 1953. Scholarly, with emphasis on Japanese immigration and impact of that immigration in Hawaii.

AE66. Caillot, A. C. Eugène. **Histoire de la Polynésie orientale.** Paris, 1910. An older account, with emphasis on period prior to 1845. Still useful.

AE67. Thomson, Sir Basil H. **The diversions of a prime minister.** London, 1894. Ostensibly an autobiographical sketch of author's experience as adviser to the Tongan government, but contains best available account of Tonga in the 19th century.

AE68. Masterman, Sylvia R. **The origins of international rivalry in Samoa, 1845–1884.** London, 1934.

AE69. Ryden, George H. **The foreign policy of the United States in relation to Samoa.** New Haven, 1933.

AE70. Stevenson, Robert Louis. **A footnote to history: eight years of trouble in Samoa.** N.Y., 1892. Other eds. Often cited account of international politics in Samoa. Scarcely objective, but reputation of author and literary quality of the work have made it a classic despite bias.

Micronesia

AE71. Pomeroy, Earl S. **Pacific outpost: American strategy in Guam and Micronesia.** Stanford, 1951.

AE72. Richard, Dorothy E. **United States naval administration of the trust territory of the Pacific islands.** 2 v. Washington, 1957. An official history, based on primary sources. Detailed and useful, but marred by excessive use of official terminology.

Melanesia

AE73. Derrick, Ronald A. **A history of Fiji.** Suva, 1946. The standard history of Fiji to the annexation by Great Britain.

AE74. Person, Yves. "La Nouvelle-Calédonie et l'Europe de la découverte à la fondation de Nouméa (1774–1854)." **Revue d'histoire des colonies,** 40 (1953): 5–215.

AE75. "Un siècle d'acculturation en Nouvelle-Calédonie." **Journal de la Société des Océanistes,** 9 (1953): 5–331. A series of important monographs dealing with the French in New Caledonia, 1853–1952.

AE76. Villiers, Alan J. **The Coral Sea.** N.Y. and Toronto, 1949. Semi-popular and useful; emphasis upon maritime history of islands bordering the Coral Sea.

AE77. Reed, Stephen W. **The making of modern New Guinea.** Philadelphia, 1943. Historical account of the European penetration of eastern New Guinea and of the impact upon the peoples of that territory. Scholarly and important study by a sociologist.

HISTORIES OF SPECIAL TOPICS

Missions and Missionaries

AE78. Koskinen, Aarne A. **Missionary influence as a political factor in the Pacific islands.** Helsinki, 1953. Scholarly and important, but inadequate for U. S. missions.

AE79. Martin, Kenneth L. P. **Missionaries and annexation in the Pacific.** London, 1924. Brief and once regarded as the standard work. Still useful for study of influence of British missions in the South Pacific.

AE80. Lovett, Richard. **The history of the London Missionary Society, 1795–1895.** V. 1 (London, 1899), pp. 117–474.

AE81. Armstrong, E. S. **The history of the Melanesian mission.** London, 1900. An authorized history of the Anglican mission to Melanesia, based on original sources.

AE82. Yzerndoorn, Reginald. **History of the Catholic mission in the Hawaiian Islands.** Honolulu, 1927.

AE83. Delmas, Siméon. **Essai d'histoire de la mission des Iles Marquises depuis les origines jusqu'en 1881.** Paris and Braine-le-Comte, 1929.

AE84. Monfat, LeP. A. **Les premiers missionnaires des Samoa.** Lyon and Paris, 1923. By a prolific writer on Catholic missions in the South Pacific.

AE85. Doucéré, Victor. **La mission Catholique aux Nouvelles-Hébrides d'après des documents écrits et les vieux souvenirs de l'auteur.** Lyon and Paris, 1934. This and *AE82–84* were written by Catholic clergymen and based on primary materials, but reveal some bias.

Literature

AE86. Stroven, Carl, and A. Grove Day, eds. **The spell of the Pacific: an anthology of its literature.** N.Y., 1949. Compiled by recognized authorities. Important.

AE87. Fisher, John S. **The midmost waters.** London, 1952. A series of essays about selected authors who have written about Oceania.

AE88. Melville, Herman. **Typee: or, a narrative of a four months' residence among the natives of a valley of the Marquesas Islands.** London and N.Y., 1846. Many subsequent eds., some with variant text.

AE89. Stevenson, Robert Louis. **In the South Seas.** Privately printed, 1890. Many later eds. First complete edition in *The works of Robert Louis Stevenson* (28 v., Edinburgh, 1894–98), v. 20. Descriptive accounts of several South Pacific archipelagoes; section on the Gilbert Islands is particularly notable.

AE90. Becke, Louis. **Wild life in southern seas.** London, 1897. See also other literary accounts of Pacific peoples and adventure by same author.

Recent Studies by Social Scientists

AE91. Keesing, Felix M. **The South Seas in the modern world.** N.Y., 1941. Rev. ed., 1945. By an anthropologist with long experience in Oceania. The standard survey of contemporary conditions.

AE92. Yanaihara, Tadao. **Pacific islands under Japanese mandate.** London, 1940. Comprehensive and careful survey by a Japanese economist. Originally published in Japanese in Tokyo, 1935.

AE93. Coulter, John W. **The Pacific dependencies of the United States.** N.Y., 1957. General survey of contemporary problems and conditions; by a geographer.

AE94. Keesing, Felix M. **Modern Samoa: its government and changing life.** London, 1934. Important study of the impact of European culture and institutions upon the people of a Polynesian archipelago.

AE95. Belshaw, Cyril S. **Changing Melanesia: social economics of culture contact.** Melbourne, 1954. By an anthropologist, but with emphasis upon economic problems and developments.

AE96. Stanner, W. E. H. **The South Seas in transition.** Sydney, 1953. Emphasis on political changes in Papua-New Guinea, western Samoa, and Fiji.

AE97. Mander, Linden A. **Some dependent peoples of the South Pacific.** N.Y., 1954. Partly historical, partly a survey of the contemporary situation.

AE98. Belshaw, Cyril S. **Island administration in the South West Pacific.** London and N.Y., 1950.

PERIODICALS AND PUBLICATIONS OF LEARNED SOCIETIES

AE99. Pacific islands monthly. Sydney, 1930 ff. A newspaper type magazine, presenting news of current interest in Oceania.

AE100. L'Océanie française. Paris, 1911–39. Published irregularly by Comité de l'Océanie Française. Information of current interest and reports on trade and agriculture in French Oceania.

AE101. The journal of the Polynesian Society. Wellington, 1892 ff. (Quarterly.) This and *AE102* are important for scholarly materials on anthropology and ethnology.

AE102. Oceania: a journal devoted to the study of the native peoples of Australia, New Guinea, and the islands of the Pacific. Melbourne and Sydney, 1930 ff. (Quarterly.) Presently published by the University of Sydney.

AE103. Journal de la Société des Océanistes. Paris, 1945 ff. (Annual.) Very important current publication, with scholarly articles on the history and anthropology of the Pacific islands. Emphasizes islands administered by France. Each issue contains extensive current bibliography.

AE104. Hawaiian Historical Society. **Annual reports.** Honolulu, 1892 ff. Useful, but various issues are very uneven in quality.

AE105. Bernice Pauahi Bishop Museum. **Bulletin.** Honolulu, 1922 ff. (Irregular.) Monographs on the anthropology, ethnology, and flora and fauna of the Pacific. Most important series of publications relating to the native life and culture of Polynesia. See also the Bishop Museum *Memoirs* (12 v., Honolulu, 1899–1949) and other publications of the museum.

IX. THE WORLD IN RECENT TIMES

SECTION AF

Recent History

WALTER C. LANGSAM and REGINALD C. McGRANE *

Although somewhat miscellaneous in character, this section has been prepared to meet the needs of teachers and students of recent history and contemporary problems. Potential overlapping of several other sections has been curbed but not eliminated. Works pertaining to the study and teaching of history should be sought in Section A; bibliographies and works of general reference in Section B; world history in Section C. Latter portions of the regional and national sections and subsections list titles relevant to the field of Section AF, as do two sections concerned with international relations. For reasons of editorial convenience, several recent publications are included here rather than at other equally appropriate points in the book.

BIBLIOGRAPHIES

There are numerous general and special bibliographies published quarterly in *The American historical review* (1895 ff.), *The journal of modern history* (1929 ff.), *Foreign affairs* (1919 ff.), and *Vierteljahrshefte für Zeitgeschichte: im Auftrag des Instituts für Zeitgeschichte* (1953 ff.). Current publications may be followed in the *Essay and general literature index* (1934 ff.), *The cumulative book index* (1898 ff.), the *Public affairs information service bulletin* (1915 ff.), *Readers' guide to periodical literature* (1900 ff.), and *International index to periodicals* (1907 ff.). The Library of Congress, Division on Bibliography, publishes useful selective bibliographies on special topics. In addition to these bibliographical guides, the following are important.

AF1. Coulter, Edith, and Melanie Gerstenfeld, eds. **Historical bibliographies: a systematic and annotated guide.** Berkeley,

* Assisted by George F. Howe.

1935. A useful guide arranged by countries.

AF2. United Nations documents index. N.Y., 1950 ff. (Monthly.) Comprehensive current list of all documents and publications, except restricted materials, of the United Nations and the specialized agencies.

AF3. Deutsch, Karl W. **Interdisciplinary bibliography on nationalism.** Cambridge, Mass., 1956. Comprehensive for this topic.

AF4. Brown, Everett S. **Manual of government publications, United States and foreign.** See *AB25.*

AF5. The French bibliographical digest. Pt. 1, **Contemporary Europe.** N.Y., 1956. Most recent French bibliography on contemporary Europe.

AF5a. A select bibliography: Asia, Africa, Eastern Europe, Latin America. American Universities Field Staff, Inc. N.Y., 1960. Contains 6,000 titles of books and journals, preponderantly in English, which the compilers consider necessary, or desirable, in college libraries for undergraduate studies.

790

WORKS OF REFERENCE

Listed below are reference works which provide recent data in accessible form not otherwise easily available.

AF6. The annual register of world events. See *B146*.

AF7. Britannica book of the year. See *B122*.

AF8. The international year book and statesmen's who's who. See *B141*.

AF9. Political handbook of the world: parliaments, parties and press. N.Y., 1927 ff. (Annual.) Provides brief, accurate information.

AF10. The statesman's year-book: statistical and historical annual of the states of the world. See *B133*.

AF11. Survey of international affairs. See *B156*.

AF12. Yearbook of the United Nations. N.Y., 1946 ff. A record of the activities of the United Nations and the specialized agencies.

AF13. Year. N.Y., 1948 ff. (Annual.) Effectively covers world events in pictures.

AF14. Facts on file: a weekly world news digest with cumulative index. N.Y., 1941 ff. A loose-leaf service of news sheets.

AF15. Keesing's contemporary archives: weekly diary of important world events. London, 1931 ff. (Title varies.) A British loose-leaf service of news sheets. The individual items are more fully reported than in the comparable United States *Facts on file.*

GEOGRAPHIES AND ATLASES

AF16. Colby, Charles C., ed. **Geographical aspects of international relations.** Chicago, 1938. Valuable group of articles covering topics of population outlets and the international aspects of state intervention.

AF17. Gottmann, Jean. **A geography of Europe.** N.Y., 1950. Account of postwar European geography by a noted French geographer written with regard for United States readers. Stresses both the physical and human geography of the European continent as a whole, with sections on Central Europe, Mediterranean Europe, and the Soviet Union. Extensive bibliographies.

AF18. Berg, Lev S. **Natural regions of the U.S.S.R.** See *X43*.

AF19. Oxford economic atlas of the world. See *A133*.

AF20. Wright, John K., and Elizabeth T. Platt. **Aids to geographical research.** See *B189*.

AF21. International symposium on man's role in changing the face of the earth. Ed. by William L. Thomas and others. Princeton, 1956. Includes bibliographies.

DEMOGRAPHIC STUDIES

AF22. Demographic yearbook. 1948 ff. N.Y., 1949 ff. Comprehensive compilation of international demographic statistics.

AF23. Taft, Donald R., and Richard Robbins. **International migrations: the immigrant in the modern world.** N.Y., 1955. The most comprehensive treatise on world migratory movements since World War I.

AF24. Kulischer, Eugene M. **Europe on the move: war and population changes, 1917–1947.** See *A1218*.

AF25. Schechtman, Joseph B. **European population transfers, 1939–1945.** N.Y., 1946. Thorough, objective study of the resettlement of European ethnic minorities.

AF26. Vernant, Jacques. **The refugee in the post-war world.** See *A1228*.

AF27. Kirk, Dudley. **Europe's population in the interwar years.** Princeton, 1946. An indispensable work on the human resources of Europe.

AF28. Lorimer, Frank. **The population of the Soviet Union: history and prospects.** See *X60*.

AF29. Russell, Sir Edward J. **World population and world food supplies.** London, 1954. Best general account of this topic.

AF30. Thompson, Warren S. **Population problems.** N.Y., 1942. 4th ed., 1953. Well-known text in the field of demography.

COLLECTIONS OF SOURCES

AF31. Royal Institute of International Affairs. **Documents on international affairs.** London, 1928 ff. (Annual.) Useful collection of documents relating to the major countries; a supplement to the annual *Survey of international affairs (AF11)*.

AF32. World Peace Foundation. **Documents on American foreign relations.** Boston, 1938 ff. (Annual.) Useful collection of United States and foreign documents relating to U. S. foreign relations.

AF33. The United States in world affairs. See *AH10*.

AF34. Mantoux, Paul J. **Les délibérations du Conseil des Quatre (24 mars–28 juin 1919).** See *AH133*.

AF35. Woodward, Ernest L., and Rohan Butler, eds. **Documents on British foreign policy, 1919–1939.** See *AH119*.

AF36. Ruhm von Oppen, Beate, ed. **Documents on Germany under occupation, 1945–1954.** N.Y., 1955. [Royal Institute of International Affairs.] Contains documents dealing with conditions in the Soviet zone as well as in the western zone.

AF37. Documents on international affairs, 1939–1946; 1947–1948. Ed. by Margaret Carlyle. 2 v. N.Y., 1952–54. [Royal Institute of International Affairs.] Contains material pertaining to Hitler's Europe.

AF38. Degras, Jane, ed. **Soviet documents on foreign policy.** See *AH112.*

AF39. Sontag, Raymond J., and James S. Beddie, eds. **Nazi-Soviet relations, 1939–1941: documents from the archives of the German foreign office.** See *AH106.*

AF40. Ministry of Foreign Affairs of the U.S.S.R. **Documents and materials relating to the eve of the Second World War.** 2 v. Moscow, 1948. These volumes were published by the Soviet government after the appearance of *AF39.*

AF41. Leiss, Amelia C., and Raymond Dennett, eds. **European peace treaties after World War II.** Boston, 1954. [World Peace Foundation.] Supplements v. 8 (1945–46) and 9 (1947) of *Documents on American foreign relations* (*AF32.*)

AF42. Hungary. Ministry of Foreign Affairs. **Hungary and the conference of Paris.** 4 v. Budapest, 1947. This work, part in French and part in English, contains valuable documents concerning the drafting of the treaty of peace with Hungary.

AF43. Vedovato, Giuseppe, ed. **Il trattato di pace con l'Italia.** Rome, 1947. Collection of documents relating to the treaty of peace with Italy.

AF44. Langsam, Walter C., and James M. Egan, eds. **Documents and readings in the history of Europe since 1918.** Rev. and enl. ed., Philadelphia, 1951.

AF45. Langsam, Walter C. **Historic documents of World War II.** N.Y., 1958. This and *AF44* contain useful teaching materials.

AF46. Eudin, Xenia J., and Harold H. Fisher. **Soviet Russia and the West, 1920–1927: a documentary survey.** Stanford, 1957.

AF47. Eudin, Xenia, J., and Robert C. North. **Soviet Russia and the East, 1920–1927: a documentary survey.** Stanford, 1957. This and *AF46* contain useful teaching materials on these topics.

SHORTER HISTORIES OF CONTEMPORARY EUROPE

AF48. Benns, Frank L. **Europe since 1914 in its world setting.** N.Y., 1930. 8th ed., 1954. Long one of the standard texts on this subject. A detailed account with extensive bibliographies.

AF49. Langsam, Walter C. **The world since 1919.** 7th ed., N.Y., 1954. A standard text. Latest edition emphasizes World War II and after. Extensive bibliographies.

AF50. Gathorne-Hardy, Geoffrey M. **A short history of international affairs, 1920–1939.** See *AH167.*

AF51. Carr, Edward H. **International relations between the two world wars, 1919–1939.** Rev. ed., N.Y., 1948. A well written, compact survey and interpretation of international affairs in this period.

AF52. Schuman, Frederick L. **International politics: an introduction to the western state system.** N.Y., 1933. 5th ed., **International politics: the western state system in mid-century,** N.Y., 1953. Stimulating survey of international politics. Good bibliographies.

AF53. **Contemporary Europe: a study of national, international, economic and cultural trends.** Ed. by Joseph S. Rouček. London, 1941. Useful symposium on contemporary Europe with bibliographies.

AF54. Jackson, John H. **The post-war decade: a short history of the world, 1945–1955.** London, 1955. Brief, concise political résumé.

AF55. Herzfeld, Hans. **Die moderne Welt, 1789–1945.** See *T418.*

AF56. Gatzke, Hans W. **The present in perspective.** Chicago, 1957. Good survey of the world since 1945 with selective bibliography.

LONGER HISTORIES OF CONTEMPORARY EUROPE

AF57. Crouzet, Maurice. **L'époque contemporaine: à la recherche d'une civilisation nouvelle.** Paris, 1957. This is v. 7 of *Histoire générale des civilisations* published under the direction of Crouzet. Covers with much detail the significant political, economic, religious, intellectual, and scientific trends throughout the world from World War I to 1957. Illustrated; extensive bibliographies.

AF58. Baumont, Maurice. **La faillite de la paix (1918–1939).** 3rd rev. ed., 2 v., Paris, 1951. A volume of the *Peuples et civilisations* series. This is a survey of the political, religious, economic, and intellectual movements throughout the world in the period between the two world wars. Good bibliographies.

AF59. Goetz, Walter W., and others, eds. **Das Zeitalter des Imperialismus, 1890–1933.** Berlin, 1933. This is v. 10 of the German *Propylaen-Weltgeschichte* series. Thorough and beautifully illustrated.

WESTERN EUROPE BETWEEN TWO WORLD WARS

Great Britain, Ireland, the Empire, and the Commonwealth of Nations

AF60. Brogan, Denis W. **The English people, impressions and observations.** London, 1943. Stimulating account of the various aspects of British character. A good introduction to the study of the English people and the British empire.

AF61. Hirst, Francis W. **The consequences of the war to Great Britain.** See *AG91.*

AF62. Cole, George D. H. **A short history of the British working-class movement,**

1789–1947. London, 1948. A standard work on this subject.

AF63. Hill, Arthur C. C., Jr., and Isador Lubin. **The British attack on unemployment.** Washington, 1934. Excellent study.

AF64. Hancock, Sir William K. **Survey of British Commonwealth affairs.** 2 v. N.Y., 1937–42. V. 1 covers the problems of nationality, 1918–36; v. 2, the problems of economic policy, 1918–39.

AF65. Mansergh, Nicholas. **Survey of British Commonwealth affairs: problems of external policy, 1931–1939.** London, 1952. Valuable account of the transition from empire to commonwealth of nations and the external policy of the dominions.

AF66. Gwynn, Denis R. **The Irish Free State, 1922–1927.** London, 1928. Good survey of the early history of the Irish Free State.

France

AF67. Wolf, John B. **France, 1815 to the present.** N.Y., 1940. Excellent introduction to the political and cultural history of France for the period 1815–1940.

AF68. Brogan, Denis W. **The development of modern France (1870–1939).** London, 1940. Authoritative account written for the general public.

AF69. Clough, Shephard B. **France: a history of national economics, 1789–1939.** N.Y., 1939. Interpretative analysis of the development of French economic nationalism.

AF70. Ogburn, William F., and William Jaffé. **The economic development of postwar France: a survey of production.** N.Y., 1929. Excellent account of the economic history of France for the post-World War I decade.

AF71. Hayes, Carlton J. H. **France: a nation of patriots.** N.Y., 1930. A sociological and institutional study; valuable appendices.

AF72. Worth, Alexander. **The twilight of France, 1933–1940.** N.Y., 1942. Good, interpretative journalist's account of decline of France before World War II.

Italy

AF73. Salvatorelli, Luigi, and Giovanni Mira. **Storia del fascismo: l'Italia dal 1919 al 1945.** Rome, 1952. A standard handbook on Fascist Italy.

AF74. Tasca, Angelo (pseud., Angelo Rossi). **The rise of Italian Fascism, 1918–1922.** Tr. by Peter and Dorothy Wait. London, 1938. Comprehensive account of the origins of Italian Fascism.

AF75. Finer, Herman. **Mussolini's Italy.** See *VE198.*

AF76. Salvemini, Gaetano. **The Fascist dictatorship in Italy.** See *VE196.*

AF77. ——. **Under the axe of Fascism.** N.Y., 1936. This and the preceding work are two classic criticisms of Fascism.

AF78. Franck, Louis R. **L'economie corporative fasciste en doctrine et en fait: ses origines historiques et son évolution.** Paris, 1934. An economic analysis of Fascism.

Spain

AF79. Madariaga, Salvador de. **Spain.** See *VD113.*

AF80. Brenan, Gerald. **The Spanish labyrinth: an account of the social and political background of the civil war.** See *VD111.*

AF81. Peers, E. Allison. **The Spanish tragedy, 1930–1936.** See *VD117.*

AF82. Ramos Oliveira, Antonio. **La revolución española de octubre.** Madrid, 1935. Good general account by a socialist.

AF83. Ratcliff, Dillwyn F. **Prelude to Franco: political aspects of the dictatorship of General Miguel Primo de Rivera.** N.Y., 1957. Readable, liberal interpretative study. Selective bibliography.

AF84. Hamilton, Thomas J. **Appeasement's child: the Franco regime in Spain.** N.Y., 1943. Interesting impressionistic study.

AF85. Altamira y Crevea, Rafael. **A history of Spanish civilization.** Tr. by P. Volkov. London, 1930. An excellent synthesis.

Germany

Weimar Repubic

AF86. Halperin, S. William. **Germany tried democracy: a political history of the Reich from 1918 to 1933.** See *VF174.*

AF87. Scheele, Godfrey. **The Weimar republic: overture to the third reich.** London, 1946. Rich in detail, with useful tables and maps.

AF88. Hoover, Calvin B. **Germany enters the third reich.** N.Y., 1933. A dispassionate account of how the National Socialists came to power. Stresses the economic factors.

AF89. Eyck, Erich. **Geschichte der Weimarer Republik.** See *VF175.*

The Third Reich

AF90. Pinson, Koppel S. **Modern Germany, its history and civilization.** See *VF30.*

AF91. Heiden, Konrad. **A history of national socialism.** See *VF201.*

AF92. Hitler, Adolf. **Mein Kampf.** 2 v. Munich, 1925–27. An indispensable work and one of the most important books published in the 20th century in view of its far-reaching consequences. In 1939 and 1940 expurgated, annotated English translations by John Murphy were published in London; and in 1939 a complete and unabridged annotated English translation, prepared under the direction of Alvin Johnson, was issued in New York.

AF93. Ebenstein, William. **The Nazi state.** Toronto, 1943. Excellent study by a political scientist of the structure and operation of the government of Hitler's Germany in the fields of politics, law, religion, culture, labor, economics, and foreign policy.

AF94. Wheeler-Bennett, John W. **The nemesis of power: the German army in politics, 1918–1945.** See *VF188*.

AF95. Ziemer, Gregor A. **Education for death: the making of the Nazi.** London, 1942. Illuminating account of German educational aims and methods.

AF96. Duncan-Jones, Arthur S. **The struggle for religious freedom in Germany.** London, 1938. Chronological account by a British clergyman.

AF97. Frey, Arthur. **Cross and swastika: the ordeal of the German church.** London, 1938. Good statement on the Lutheran struggle.

WESTERN EUROPE SINCE 1945

Great Britain and the Commonwealth

AF98. McCallum, Ronald B., and Readman Alison. **The British general election of 1945.** London, 1947. The issues, candidates, and campaigns. Based upon press accounts and personal interviews.

AF99. Nicholas, Herbert G. **The British general election of 1950.** London, 1951. Party organization, campaign, and world reactions to the results of the election.

AF100. Brady, Robert A. **Crisis in Britain: plans and achievements of the Labour government.** London, 1950. Significant economic analysis of the program of the Labor government in all fields of British economy.

AF101. Mansergh, Philip N. S. **The Commonwealth and the nations: studies in British Commonwealth relations.** London, 1948. A series of essays examining recent trends in the Commonwealth.

France

AF102. Earle, Edward M., ed. **Modern France: problems of the third and fourth republics.** Princeton, 1951. Valuable symposium of essays by United States scholars covering various aspects of contemporary France.

AF103. Lüthy, Herbert. **The state of France: a study of contemporary France.** London, 1955. Excellent study of post-war French politics.

AF104. Pickles, Dorothy M. **French politics: the first years of the fourth republic.** London, 1953.

AF105. ———. **The French republic.** London, 1955. This and the preceding volume are scholarly, lucid analyses of contemporary French politics.

AF106. Mirkine-Guetzévitch, Boris. **La quatrième république.** N.Y., 1946. Excellent study of recent French constitutional problems.

AF107. Gaulle, Charles de. **Unity, 1942–1944.** V. 2, **War memoirs.** Tr. by Richard Howard. N.Y., 1959.

AF108. Auphan, Paul, and Hervé Cras. **French navy in World War II.** Annapolis, 1959.

AF109. Einaudi, Mario, Jean M. Domenach, and Aldo Garosci. **Communism in western Europe.** Ithaca, 1951. Especially good for French and Italian communism.

Spain and Portugal

AF110. Feis, Herbert. **The Spanish story: Franco and the nations at war.** N.Y., 1948. Highly informative account by an economic adviser to the U. S. Department of State.

AF111. Foltz, Charles. **The masquerade in Spain.** Boston, 1948. A reporter's first-hand account of the Franco dictatorship.

AF112. Livermore, Harold V. **A history of Portugal.** See *VD261*.

Italy

AF113. Grindrod, Muriel. **The rebuilding of Italy: politics and economics, 1945–1955.** See *AF113*.

Germany

Allied Occupation

AF114. Clay, Lucius D. **Decision in Germany.** Garden City, N.Y., 1950. Valuable source by a United States military governor of Germany.

AF115. Litchfield, Edward H., and others, eds. **Governing postwar Germany.** Ithaca, 1953. A series of articles tracing the impact of occupation upon contemporary Germany. Each contributor was temporarily connected with the military government.

AF116. Holborn, Hajo. **American military government, its organization and policies.** Washington, 1947. Authoritative account of the organization and early operation of military government.

AF117. Zink, Harold. **American military government in Germany.** N.Y., 1947. Analysis of the history, practice, and administrative problems.

AF118. Friedman, Wolfgang G. **The allied military government of Germany.** London, 1947. A critical, comparative analysis of quadripartite allied military government of Germany.

AF119. Knappen, Marshall M. **And call it peace.** Chicago, 1947. Discusses the educational and religious policies of United States military government.

AF120. Ruhm von Oppen, Beate, ed. **Documents on Germany under occupation, 1945–1954.** See *AF36.*

See also sources on occupation policy listed under "Government Publications" in this section.

Economic Recovery

AF121. Piettre, André. **L'économie allemande contemporaine: Allemagne occidentale, 1945–1952.** Paris, 1952. The basic work on this topic. Comprehensive statistics and valuable bibliographical references.

AF122. Grosser, Alfred. **The colossus again: western Germany from defeat to rearmament.** N.Y., 1955. Tr. and rev. from *L'Allemagne de l'occident* (Paris, 1953). Excellent account. Good bibliography.

AF123. Erhard, Ludwig, and Vollrath von Maltzan. **Germany's comeback in the world market.** N.Y., 1954. Stresses the question of German exports.

AF124. Wallich, Henry C. **Mainsprings of the German revival.** New Haven, 1955. Focuses attention on the main factors of Germany's economic revival.

AF125. Davison, Walter P. **The Berlin blockade.** Princeton, 1958. Reliable and comprehensive description of major features of a dramatic incident in the "cold war"—the Berlin airlift. [GFH]

East Germany

AF126. Nettl, John P. **The eastern zone and Soviet policy in Germany, 1945–1950.** London, 1951. The authoritative study on this topic.

AF127. Brant, Stefan (pseud.). **The East German rising, June 17, 1953.** London, 1955. Originally published in German under the title *Der Aufstand* (Stuttgart, 1954). The English translation is briefer and somewhat improved. A good, although not definitive, account.

Nuremberg Trials

AF128. Glueck, S. Sheldon. **War criminals, their prosecution and punishment.** N.Y., 1944.

AF129. ——. **The Nuremberg trial and aggressive war.** N.Y., 1946. This and the above work by this author present the United States viewpoint of the legal justification for the trials.

AF130. Jackson, Robert H. **The Nürnberg case.** N.Y., 1947. An account of the trials by the representative and chief counsel for the United States.

AF131. Benton, Wilbourne E., and George Grimm, eds. **Nuremberg: German views on the war trials.** Dallas, 1955. Collection of articles by German lawyers and professors analyzing and criticizing the trials.

See also "Government Publications" below for official records of the trials.

AF132. Zink, Harold. **The United States in Germany, 1945–1955.** Princeton, 1957. Written for the general reader by a historian observer. [GFH]

The Netherlands

AF133. Barnouw, Adriaan J. **The making of modern Holland: a short history.** London, 1948. Brief, informative history of the Netherlands from prehistoric times to the German invasion of 1940.

AF134. Landheer, Bartholomeus. **The Netherlands in a changing world.** N.Y., 1947. A series of essays on postwar economic conditions and problems.

Belgium

AF135. Goris, Jan Albert, ed. **Belgium.** Berkeley, 1945. [United Nations series.] Symposium of articles by United States and Belgian specialists on the life, economy, and culture of Belgium. The final chapter covers the postwar period.

Scandinavia

AF136. Scott, Franklin D. **The United States and Scandinavia.** Cambridge, Mass., 1950. [American foreign policy library.] Excellent study of the functioning of social democracy and economy in the Scandinavian countries and the impact of World War II upon them. Valuable appendices of facts and a good bibliography.

AF137. Friis, Henning K., ed. **Scandinavia: between East and West.** Ithaca, 1950. Valuable series of lectures on various aspects of Scandinavian political, economic, and social life.

AF138. Herlitz, Nils. **Sweden: a modern democracy on ancient foundations.** Minneapolis, 1939. Excellent treatment of the Swedish spirit.

AF139. Larsen, Karen. **A history of Norway.** See *VB92.*

AF140. Manniche, Peter. **Denmark, a social laboratory.** N.Y., 1939. Contains much practical information on the economic and social life of Denmark.

Finland

AF141. Jackson, John Hampden. **Finland.** See *VB87.*

AF142. Wuorinen, John H., ed. **Finland and World War II, 1939–1944.** N.Y., 1948. Interpretive account of Finland's foreign policy based on a Finnish manuscript.

AF143. Tanner, Väinö. **The winter war: Finland against Russia, 1939–1940.** Stanford, 1957. A valuable "inside" story of the diplomatic relations of Russia and Finland preceding the Russo-Finnish war.

Switzerland

AF144. Rappard, William E. **The government of Switzerland.** N.Y., 1936. A standard work on the Swiss governmental system and politics.

AF145. Siegfried, André. **Switzerland: a democratic way of life.** Tr. by Edward Fitzgerald. N.Y., 1950. This French work is an analysis of the physical aspects of the country, the ethnological character of the people, and the Swiss political system.

Austria

AF146. Proudfoot, Mary MacDonald. **The Republic of Austria, 1918–1934: a study in the failure of democratic government.** N.Y., 1946. [Royal Institute of International Affairs.] Excellent, impartial study of this period.

AF147. Benedikt, Heinrich, ed. **Geschichte der Republik Österreich.** See *VF271.*

AF148. Macartney, Carlile A. **The social revolution in Austria.** See *W874.*

AF149. Ball, Mary M. **Post-war German-Austrian relations: the anschluss movement, 1918–1936.** Stanford, 1937. A scholarly, detailed account.

AF150. Grayson, Cary T. **Austria's international position, 1938–1953: the re-establishment of an independent Austria.** Geneva, 1953. [Études d'histoire économique, politique et sociale, 5.] A careful account of Austria's struggle for full independence after World War II.

AF151. Hiscocks, Richard. **The rebirth of Austria.** N.Y., 1953. Illuminating account by a knowledgeable British official.

AF152. Heissenberger, Franz. **The economic reconstruction of Austria, 1945–1952.** Washington, 1953. Study by an Austrian economist.

AF153. Rothschild, Kurt W. **The Austrian economy since 1945.** London, 1950. [Royal Institute of International Affairs.] A careful study.

AF154. Gulick, Charles A. **Austria from Habsburg to Hitler.** See *VF272.*

CENTRAL AND EASTERN EUROPE SINCE WORLD WAR I

General Works

AF155. Seton-Watson, Hugh. **Eastern Europe between the wars, 1918–1941.** Cambridge, Eng., 1945. 2nd. ed., 1946. Best single work in English of political, social, and economic trends, and international relations of Poland, Czechoslovakia, Hungary, Romania, Yugoslavia, and Bulgaria during this period.

AF156. ——. **The east European revolution.** N.Y., 1951. 3rd ed., London, 1956. A sequel to the above.

AF157. Wolff, Robert L. **The Balkans in our time.** Cambridge, Mass., 1956. [American foreign policy library.] A thorough, scholarly work covering the Balkan states before and after World War II.

AF158. Pribićević, Stojan (pseud., P. B. Stoyan). **World without end: the saga of southeastern Europe.** N.Y., 1939. Well-written and informative account.

AF159. Rouček, Joseph S. **Balkan politics: international relations in no man's land.** Stanford, 1948. Useful reference book. Good bibliography.

AF160. Strakhovsky, Leonid I., ed. **A handbook of Slavic studies.** Cambridge, Mass., 1949. Excellent compilation of articles. Good bibliographies.

AF161. Fejtö, François. **Histoire des démocraties populaires.** Paris, 1952. Useful for events in postwar eastern Europe.

AF162. Gluckstein, Ygael. **Stalin's satellites in Europe.** Boston, 1952. Stresses economic changes and the Stalin-Tito conflict.

AF163. Royal Institute of International Affairs. **The Balkan states.** V. 1, Economic. London, 1936. Concise review of the economic and financial development of Albania, Bulgaria, Greece, Romania, and Yugoslavia, 1919–36.

AF164. ——. **South-eastern Europe: a political and economic survey.** London, 1939. Report on the economic aspects and foreign relations of Hungary, Romania, Yugoslavia, Albania, Greece, Bulgaria, and Turkey, 1919–36.

AF165. Pasvolsky, Leo. **Economic nationalism of the Danubian states.** Washington, 1928. Account of the economic maladjustments following the dissolution of Austria-Hungary.

Poland

AF166. Schmitt, Bernadotte E., ed. **Poland.** See *W86.*

AF167. Modzelewski, Jan, ed. **Pologne, 1919–1939.** 3 v. Neuchâtel, Switz., 1946–47. Exhaustive study of Poland between two world wars.

AF168. Lane, Arthur B. **I saw Poland betrayed.** See *W187.*

Czechoslovakia

AF169. Thomson, S. Harrison. **Czechoslovakia in European history.** Princeton, 1943. 2nd ed., 1953. Indispensable work for a study of Czechoslovakian history. Good bibliography.

AF170. Kerner, Robert J., ed. **Czechoslovakia.** See *W349.*
AF171. Masaryk, Thomas G. **The making of a state.** See *AF336.*
AF172. Wiskemann, Elizabeth. **Czechs and Germans.** London and N.Y., 1938. [Royal Institute of International Affairs.]

Hungary

AF173. Macartney, Carlile A. **Hungary and her successors.** See *W842.*
AF174. Sinor, Denis. **History of Hungary.** London, 1959.
AF175. Méray, Tibor. **Thirteen days that shook the Kremlin.** Tr. by Howard L. Katzander. N.Y., 1959. The brief 1956 revolution in Hungary. [GFH]

Yugoslavia

AF176. Armstrong, Hamilton F. **Tito and Goliath.** See *W501.*
AF177. Radin, George. **Economic reconstruction in Yugoslavia.** N.Y., 1946. [Carnegie Endowment for International Peace.] A "practical plan for the Balkans" written anonymously by United States government specialists.

Romania

AF178. Mitrany, David. **The land and the peasant in Rumania.** See *W694.*
AF179. Roberts, Henry L. **Rumania: political problems of an agrarian state.** See *W667.*

Bulgaria

AF180. Black, Cyril E. **The establishment of constitutional government in Bulgaria.** See *W970.*

Greece

AF181. Stavrianos, Leften S. **Greece: American dilemma and opportunity.** See *W1238.*

Soviet Union

AF182. Florinsky, Michael T. **Russia: a history and an interpretation.** See *X136.*
AF183. Carr, Edward H. **The Bolshevik revolution, 1917–1923.** 3 v. London, 1950–53.
AF184. ——. **The interregnum, 1923–1924.** London, 1954. This and the above comprise a detailed, analytical study of Russia in the years indicated.
AF185. Pares, Sir Bernard. **A history of Russia.** See *X125.*
AF186. Bronstein, Lev D. (pseud., Lev D. Trotsky). **History of the Russian revolution to Brest-Litovsk.** 3 v. London, 1919–

36. A well-written account by one of the protagonists.
AF187. Chamberlin, William H. **The Russian revolution, 1917–1921.** See *X245.*
AF188. Strakhovsky, Leonid I. **The origins of American intervention in north Russia.** Princeton, 1937.
AF189. ——. **Intervention at Archangel: the story of allied intervention and Russian counter-revolution in north Russia, 1918–1920.** Princeton, 1944. These two scholarly works by the same author cover an important and much-debated phase of the early history of the Soviet Union.
AF190. Fainsod, Merle. **How Russia is ruled.** See *X289.*
AF191. Pipes, Richard E. **The formation of the Soviet Union: communism and nationalism, 1917–1923.** Cambridge, Mass., 1954. Indispensable volume for a study of the early years of the Soviet Union.
AF192. Towster, Julian. **Political power in the U.S.S.R. 1917–1947.** See *X288.*
AF193. Berman, Harold J. **Justice in Russia: an interpretation of Soviet law.** Cambridge, Mass., 1950. An analysis of Soviet law.
AF194. Timasheff, Nicholas S. **Religion in Soviet Russia, 1917–1942.** N.Y., 1942. Good introduction to the religious aspects of the Soviet Union.
AF195. Anderson, Paul B. **People, church and state in modern Russia.** N.Y., 1944. Contains much documentary material dealing with religion in the Soviet Union.
AF196. Curtiss, John S. **The Russian church and the Soviet state, 1917–1950.** Boston, 1953. Careful study, based on original source material, of the relations of the Kremlin and the churches.
AF197. Baykov, Alexander M. **The development of the Soviet economic system.** N.Y., 1947. Excellent reference work.
AF198. Schwarz, Solomon M. **Labor in the Soviet Union.** N.Y., 1952. Valuable, scholarly analysis of the Soviet labor policy and its impact on the Russian workers. Based largely on Soviet sources.
AF199. Jasny, Naum. **The socialized agriculture of the U.S.S.R.: plans and performance.** Stanford, 1949. A massive, critical analysis of the collectivization of Soviet farming.
AF200. Beloff, Max. **The foreign policy of Soviet Russia, 1929–1941.** 2 v. N.Y. and London, 1947–49. Comprehensive, detailed study of Russia's relations with other European countries, the Middle and Far East, and the United States.
AF201. Dallin, David J. **Soviet Russia's foreign policy, 1939–1942.** New Haven, 1943. Critical study of Soviet foreign policy during these years.
AF202. Crankshaw, Edward. **Cracks in the Kremlin wall.** N.Y., 1951. Critical anal-

ysis of the internal weaknesses of the Soviet Union.

AF203. Salisbury, Harrison E. **Stalin's Russia and after.** London, 1955. A vivid description of life in the Soviet Union by a United States journalist.

AF204. Djilas, Milovan. **The new class: an analysis of the Communist system.** N.Y., 1957. Most effective criticism available of the Communist system in practice, by a former Yugoslav Communist leader.

AF205. Seton-Watson, Hugh. **From Lenin to Malenkov.** See *AH47.*

THE MIDDLE EAST SINCE 1914

General Works

AF206. Lenczowski, George. **The Middle East in world affairs.** Ithaca, 1952. 2nd ed., 1956. Excellent survey of the problems of this region during and after World War I and World War II. Good bibliography.

AF207. Shwadran, Benjamin. **The Middle East, oil and the great powers.** See *S344.*

AF208. Longrigg, Stephen H. **Oil in the Middle East, its discovery and development.** See *S345.*

AF209. Hurewitz, Jacob C. **Middle East dilemmas.** N.Y., 1953. A concise, objective discussion of the growth of United States interest and responsibilities in this area.

AF210. The Middle East: a political and economic survey. London, 1943. 2nd ed., 1954. [Royal Institute of International Affairs.] Useful reference work.

AF211. Frye, Richard N., ed. **The Near East and the great powers.** Cambridge, Mass., 1951. Valuable symposium of articles on contemporary Near Eastern problems.

AF212. Kirk, George E. **The Middle East, 1945–1950.** N.Y., 1954. [Survey of international affairs, 5.] Dispassionate, authoritative survey.

Arab Nationalism

AF213. Antonius, George. **The Arab awakening: the story of the Arab national movement.** Philadelphia, 1939. Thorough, sympathetic treatment by a Christian Arab.

AF214. Glubb, Sir John B. **Britain and the Arabs: a study of fifty years, 1908 to 1958.** London, 1959.

Saudi Arabia

AF215. Twitchell, Karl S. **Saudi Arabia.** Princeton, 1947. Useful handbook for students of modern imperialism.

Iraq

AF216. Longrigg, Stephen H. **Iraq, 1900 to 1950: a political, social and economic history.** See *S209.*

AF217. Longrigg, Stephen H., and Frank Stoakes. **Iraq.** N.Y., 1958. [Nations of the modern world.] Accurate though sketchy. [GFH]

Syria and Lebanon

AF218. Hourani, Albert H. **Syria and Lebanon.** See *S184.*

AF219. Longrigg, Stephen H. **Syria and Lebanon under French mandate.** N.Y. and London, 1958.

Jordan

AF220. Glubb, John B. **The story of the Arab legion.** London, 1948. A first-hand account.

Egypt

AF221. Issawi, Charles P. **Egypt at midcentury: an economic survey.** See *S243.*

AF222. Royal Institute of International Affairs. **Great Britain and Egypt, 1914–1951.** New rev. ed., London, 1952. This and the preceding work are valuable studies.

AF223. Little, Tom. **Egypt.** N.Y., 1959. [Nations of the modern world.]

AF224. Avram, Benno. **Evolution of the Suez Canal status from 1869 up to 1956: a historico-juridical study.** Geneva, 1958.

AF225. Lacouture, Jean, and Simonne Lacouture. **Egypt in transition.** Tr. by Francis Scarfe. N.Y., and London, 1958.

AF226. Panikkar, Kavalam M. **Afro-Asian states and their problems.** London, 1959.

Israel

AF227. Hurewitz, Jacob C. **The struggle for Palestine.** See *S194.*

AF228. Royal Institute of International Affairs. **Great Britain and Palestine, 1915–1945.** 2nd ed., London, 1946. A careful study.

AF229. Sachar, Howard M. **Course of modern Jewish history.** Cleveland, 1958.

Turkey

AF230. Howard, Harry N. **The partition of Turkey: a diplomatic history, 1913–1923.** See *S274.*

AF231. Webster, Donald E. **The Turkey of Atatürk: social process in the Turkish reformation.** See *S143.*

AF232. Duda, Herbert W. **Vom Kalifat zur Republik: die Türkei im 19. und 20. Jahrhundert.** Vienna, 1948. Cultural history of the development of Turkey and the growth of Turkish nationalism.

Iran

AF233. Elwell-Sutton, Laurence P. **Modern Iran.** London, 1941. Good on land and political changes.

ASIA

General Works

AF234. Hinton, Harold C., and others. **Major governments of Asia.** Ithaca, 1958. Descriptive comparison of the governments of China, Japan, India, Pakistan, and Indonesia, with some attention to historical backgrounds. [GFH]

AF235. Dhingra, Baldoon, ed. **Asia through Asian eyes.** London and Toronto, 1959.

AF236. Panikkar, Kavalam M. **Asia and western dominance.** New ed., London, 1959.

International Relations

AF237. Das Gupta, Jyoti B. **Indo-Pakistan relations, 1947–1955.** Amsterdam, 1958.

AF238. Fifield, Russell H. **Diplomacy of southeast Asia, 1945–1958.** N.Y., 1958.

AF239. Tandon, Mahesh P. **International relations, 1914–1957.** Allahabad, 1957.

AF240. Wattal, Pyare K. **Population problem in India: a census study.** New Delhi, 1958.

AF241. Raghuvanshi, V. P. S. **Indian nationalist movement and thought.** 2nd ed., Agra, India, 1959.

China

AF242. Tang, Sheng-Hao. **Communist China today: domestic and foreign policies.** N.Y., 1957. Comprehensive and detailed; written by a former member of the Chinese Nationalist diplomatic service. Review, H. M. Vinacke, *Am. pol. sci. rev.,* 51 (Dec. 1957): 1142. [GFH]

AFRICA

AF243. Carter, Gwendolen M., and William O. Brown, eds. **Transition in Africa.** Boston, 1958.

AF244. Trimingham, John S. **Islam in west Africa.** N.Y. and London, 1959.

ANTARCTICA

AF245. Debenham, Frank. **Antarctica: the story of a continent.** London, 1959.

AF246. Dufek, George J. **Through the frozen frontier.** N.Y. and Toronto, 1959.

AF247. Frazier, Paul W. **Antarctic assault.** N.Y., 1958.

AF248. Siple, Paul. **90 degrees south: the story of the American South Pole conquest.**

N.Y., 1959. First-hand account written with candor and clarity. [GFH]

NORTH AMERICA

Canada

AF249. Chapin, Miriam. **Contemporary Canada.** N.Y., 1959.

United States

AF250. Howe, Irving, and Lewis Coser. **The American Communist party: a critical history (1919–1957).** N.Y., 1958. Detailed, thorough, and critical. [GFH]

AF251. Warren, Harris G. **Herbert Hoover and the great depression.** N.Y., 1959. Careful, objective analysis. [GFH]

AF252. Schwartz, Bernard. **The Supreme Court: constitutional revolution in retrospect.** N.Y., 1957.

AF253. Maritain, Jacques. **Reflections on America.** N.Y., 1958. Product of more than ten years of perceptive association with education in the United States, expressed with urbanity and in a judicious spirit. [GFH]

Mexico

AF254. Castañeda, Jorge E. **Mexico and the United Nations.** N.Y., 1958. [Carnegie Endowment for International Peace, National studies on international organization.] By the legal counsellor of Mexico's foreign service. Analytical and perhaps an expression of views shared by smaller countries in the United Nations. [GFH]

HISTORIES OF SPECIAL TOPICS

The Peace Settlement after World War I

AF255. Birdsall, Paul. **Versailles twenty years after.** N.Y., 1941. Comprehensive discussion of the treaty and its effects. Supports theory that Wilson was the "realist" at the peace conference.

AF256. Maurice, Sir Frederick B. **The armistice of 1918.** London, 1943. [Royal Institute of International Affairs.]

AF257. Rudin, Harry R. **Armistice 1918.** New Haven, 1944. This and *AF256* are valuable accounts of the events leading to the signing of the armistice at Compiègne.

AF258. Temperley, Harold W. V., ed. **A history of the peace conference of Paris.** See *AH128*.

AF259. Marston, Frank S. **The peace conference of 1919: organization and procedure.** See *AH134*.

AF260. Binkley, Robert C. "Ten years of peace conference history." **Journal of modern history,** 1 (Dec. 1929): 607–29.

AF261. ——. "New light on the Paris

peace conference." **Political science quarterly,** 46 (Sep. and Dec. 1931): 335–61, 509–47.

AF262. Birdsall, Paul. "The second decade of peace conference history." **Journal of modern history,** 15 (Sep. 1939): 362–78. This and the two preceding articles are excellent evaluations of writers on the Paris peace conference.

The League of Nations

AF263. Walters, Francis P. **A history of the League of Nations.** See *AH306.*

AF264. Zimmern, Sir Alfred E. **The League of Nations and the rule of law, 1918–1935.** See *AH307.*

United Nations

AF265. Goodrich, Leland M., and Edvard I. Hambro. **Charter of the United Nations: commentary and documents.** See *AH357.*

AF266. Goodrich, Leland M. **The United Nations.** N.Y., 1959.

Korea

AF267. McCune, George M., and Arthur L. Grey, Jr. **Korea today.** Cambridge, Mass., 1950. Comprehensive history of Korea.

AF268. Osgood, Cornelius B. **The Koreans and their culture.** N.Y., 1951. Excellent study of the history and culture of the Koreans from their origins through the impact of United States-Russian occupation.

AF269. Goodrich, Leland M. **Korea: a study of U. S. policy in the United Nations.** See *AH259.*

AF270. Meade, Edward G. **American military government in Korea.** N.Y., 1951. Deals with the period prior to the Korean War.

Korean War

AF271. Dean, William F. **General Dean's story.** N.Y., 1954. Graphic description of the capture of the United States 24th Division's commander and his experiences of three years in captivity.

AF272. Marshall, Samuel L. A. **The river and the gauntlet: the defeat of the Eighth Army by the Chinese Communist forces.** N.Y., 1953. Graphic account.

AF273. Karig, Walter, and others. **The war in Korea.** N.Y., 1952. An account prepared from official sources of the United States navy and marine corps actions.

AF274. Thomas, Robert C. W. **The war in Korea, 1950–1953.** Aldershot, Eng., 1954. A brief military history of the war.

AF275. Miller, John, Jr., and others. **Korea, 1951–1953.** Washington, 1956. [Department of the United States Army, Office

of Military History.] Brief account with photographs of the war.

AF276. Gugeler, Russell A. **Combat actions in Korea.** Washington, 1954. Study of infantry, artillery, and armor units in the war.

AF277. Montross, Lynn, and Nicholas A. Canzona. **Marine operations in Korea, 1950–1953.** V. 1, **The Pusan perimeter.** Washington, 1954. [United States Marine Corps.]

AF278. Montross, Lynn. **Cavalry of the sky: the story of United States marine combat helicopters.** N.Y., 1954. Stresses importance of the helicopter in the war.

AF279. Vatcher, William H. **Panmunjom: the story of the Korean military armistice negotiations.** N.Y., 1958. The author's attention is narrowly focused, giving a sharp, clear picture, with broader implications left largely to the reader. [GFH]

AF280. Whitney, Courtney. **MacArthur: his rendezvous with history.** N.Y., 1956. An admiring biography written by a close associate and former staff officer; not objective.

AF281. Willoughby, Charles A., and John Chamberlain. **MacArthur, 1941–1951.** N.Y., 1954. An admiring, partisan account of MacArthur's career.

The North Atlantic Treaty

AF282. Royal Institute of International Affairs. **Atlantic alliance: NATO's role in the free world.** Comp. by Donald McLachlan. N.Y., 1952. Excellent report of the aims, organization, and achievements of NATO by a Chatham House study group.

Atomic Energy

AF283. Smyth, Henry D. **Atomic energy for military purposes.** Princeton, 1945. Detailed, authoritative account of the development of the atomic bomb.

AF284. Wendt, Gerald. **Atomic energy and the hydrogen bomb.** N.Y., 1950. Clear, concise discussion of the development and potentialities of nuclear energy.

AF285. Schurr, Sam H., and Jacob Marschak, eds. **Economic aspects of atomic power.** Princeton, 1950. A scholarly exploratory study.

AF286. Hersey, John R. **Hiroshima.** N.Y., 1946. Vivid account of the dropping of the first atomic bomb in World War II.

Science and Technology

AF287. Elbers, Gerald W., and Paul Duncan, eds. **Scientific revolution: challenge and promise.** Washington, 1959.

AF288. Benton, Mildred. **Literature of space science and exploration.** Washington, 1958. A basic bibliography. [GFH]

AF289. Spitz, Armand N., and Frank

Gaynor. **Dictionary of astronomy and astronautics.** N.Y., 1959.

AF290. Alperin, Morton, and others, eds. **Vistas in astronautics.** N.Y., 1958 ff. Proceedings of annual symposia sponsored by a subdivision of the Office of Scientific Research, U. S. Air Force. [GFH]

AF291. Taylor, Frank S. **History of industrial chemistry.** N.Y., 1957. Broad in scope, episodic, and lucid. [GFH]

Economic Problems of Europe, 1918–1939

AF292. Keynes, John Maynard. **The economic consequences of the peace.** London, 1919. A prophetic criticism of the economic sections of the Versailles treaty.

AF293. Mantoux, Étienne. **The Carthaginian peace: or, the economic consequences of Mr. Keynes.** See *AH132.*

AF294. Burnett, Philip M. **Reparation at the Paris peace conference.** See *AI48.*

AF295. Baruch, Bernard M. **The making of the reparation and economic sections of the treaty.** N.Y., 1920. An account by one of the United States economic advisers at the conference.

World Depression

AF296. Robbins, Lionel C. **The great depression.** London, 1934. Illuminating study from the point of view of an "orthodox" economist.

AF297. Schumpeter, Joseph A. **Business cycles: a theoretical, historical and statistical analysis of the capitalist process.** 2 v. N.Y., 1939. Monumental work by a distinguished economist.

AF298. Keynes, John Maynard. **The general theory of employment, interest and money.** London, 1936. The standard exposition of a compensatory fiscal policy.

Economic Problems of Europe since World War II

AF299. Ellis, Howard S. **The economics of freedom.** See *AI173.*

AF300. Mason, Henry L. **The European Coal and Steel Community: experiment in supranationalism.** See *AH416.*

AF301. Brown, William A., Jr., and Redvers Opie. **American foreign assistance.** See *AI166.*

AF302. Harris, Seymour E. **The European recovery program.** Cambridge, Mass., 1948. Analysis by a United States economist of the Marshall plan.

BIOGRAPHIES AND MEMOIRS

Paris Peace Settlement, 1919

AF303. The intimate papers of Colonel House. Ed. by Charles Seymour. 4 v. Boston,

1926–28. The unpublished personal papers of a close associate of President Wilson.

AF304. Miller, David H. **My diary at the conference of Paris: with documents.** See *AH149.*

AF305. Lansing, Robert. **War memoirs.** N.Y., 1935. An account by the United States secretary of state.

AF306. Lloyd George, David. **Memoirs of the peace conference.** See *AH131.*

AF307. Clemenceau, Georges E. B. **Grandeur and misery of victory.** N.Y., 1930. The French premier's discussion of the peace settlement.

AF308. Nicolson, Harold G. **Peacemaking, 1919.** See *AH135.*

Great Britain and Ireland

AF309. Guedalla, Philip. **Mr. Churchill: a portrait.** London, 1941. Perhaps the best biography of this world figure.

AF310. Feiling, Keith G. **The life of Neville Chamberlain.** London, 1946. Sympathetic but not uncritical. Extensive quotations from Chamberlain's diaries and letters.

AF311. Steed, Henry W. **The real Stanley Baldwin.** London, 1930. Eulogistic study of the "enigmatic" Baldwin.

AF312. Tiltman, Hubert H. **J. Ramsay MacDonald: labour's man of destiny.** London, 1929. An authoritative, documented account.

AF313. Campbell-Johnson, Alan. **Eden: the making of a statesman.** N.Y., 1955. Good for career, but does not disclose the personality of the man.

AF314. MacManus, M. J. **Eamon de Valera.** Dublin, 1944. A laudatory biography.

France

AF315. Gaulle, Charles de. **The call to honour, 1940–1942.** N.Y., 1955. Important contribution to the history of France and World War II.

AF316. Mallet, Alfred. **Pierre Laval.** 2 v. Paris, 1955. Biography written by a close associate of Laval.

AF317. Stokes, Richard L. **Léon Blum: poet to premier.** N.Y., 1937. Written by a United States journalist.

Spain

AF318. Coles, Sydney F. A. **Franco of Spain.** London, 1955. Based on extensive use of published and unpublished documents.

Italy

AF319. Megaro, Gaudens. **Mussolini in the making.** See *VE202.*

AF320. Pini, Giorgio. **The official life of**

Benito Mussolini. London, 1939. Written by an Italian Fascist journalist.

AF321. Ciano, Count Galeazzo. **Hidden diary, 1937–1938.** Tr. by Andreas Mayor. N.Y., 1953. Ciano's diary with entries running from Aug. 23, 1937 to the end of 1938. To be used with care.

AF322. ——. **The Ciano diaries, 1939–1943.** See *VE216* and *AH210*.

AF323. ——. **Ciano's diplomatic papers.** Ed. by Malcolm Muggeridge. London, 1948. A record of nearly 200 diplomatic conversations of Ciano, held during the years 1936–42, plus important memoranda, letters, and telegrams. This is a supplement to the above-mentioned diaries, and was published under the title *L'Europa verso la catastrofe* (Milan, 1947).

Germany

AF324. Wheeler-Bennett, John W. **Wooden titan: Hindenburg in twenty years of German history, 1914–1934.** See *VF183*.

AF325. Bullock, Alan L. C. **Hitler: a study in tyranny.** See *VF208*.

AF326. Heiden, Konrad. **Der Fuehrer: Hitler's rise to power.** Boston, 1944. Excellent.

AF327. Sutton, Eric, ed. and tr. **Gustav Stresemann: his diaries, letters, and papers.** 3 v. N.Y., 1935–40. Illuminating on Weimar Germany's diplomatic relations with the western powers.

AF328. Scheidemann, Philipp. **The making of new Germany.** 2 v. N.Y., 1929. Scheidemann's memoirs; important source for period of Weimar republic.

AF329. Peterson, Edward N. **Hjalmar Schacht: for and against Hitler: a political-economic study of Germany, 1923–1945.** Boston, 1954. Impartial account of career of Hitler's "economic wizard."

AF330. Trevor-Roper, Hugh R. **The last days of Hitler.** See *VF209*.

AF331. Hassell, Ulrich von. **The von Hassell diaries, 1938–1944.** N.Y., 1947. Important source by a former member of the German diplomatic corps.

Austria

AF332. Gregory, John D. **Dollfuss and his times.** London, 1935. Based on public sources and personal interviews. Extensive bibliography.

AF333. Schuschnigg, Kurt von. **My Austria.** N.Y., 1938. A statement of Schuschnigg's credo and of Austria's post-World War I history.

AF334. ——. **Austrian requiem.** N.Y., 1946. Another account by the former chancellor of Austria. The story of his dealings with Hitler, his imprisonment, and his liberation by United States troops is recorded.

Poland

AF335. Reddaway, William F. **Marshal Pilsudski.** London, 1939. A competent study.

Czechoslovakia

AF336. Masaryk, Thomas G. **The making of a state.** N.Y., 1927. Indispensable for an understanding of the philosophy of Czechoslovakia's first president, and his experiences and reflections in the course of gaining world recognition for the Czechoslovak cause.

AF337. Cohen, Victor S. **The life and times of Masaryk, the president-liberator: a biographical study of central Europe since 1848.** N.Y., 1941. Contains valuable source material.

AF338. Street, Cecil J. C. **President Masaryk.** London, 1930. An interesting, sympathetic account.

AF339. Beneš, Edvard. **Memoirs: from Munich to new war and new victory.** London, 1954. An indispensable work.

AF340. Mackenzie, Sir Compton. **Dr. Beneš.** See *W416.*

Yugoslavia

AF341. Dedijer, Vladimir. **Tito speaks: his self-portrait and struggle with Stalin.** London, 1953. An authorized biography.

Turkey

AF342. Mikusch, Dagobert von. **Mustapha Kemal.** Garden City, 1931. Detailed biography based upon Turkish and western sources.

Greece

AF343. Alastos, Doros. **Venizelos: patriot, statesman, revolutionary.** London, 1942. Sympathetic, but not uncritical.

Soviet Russia

AF344. Lenin, Vladimir I. **Selected works.** 12 v. London, 1936–39. An indispensable source.

AF345. Shub, David. **Lenin.** N.Y., 1948. Scholarly, readable work.

AF346. Marcu, Valeriu. **Lenin.** N.Y., 1928. Philosophical.

AF347. Vernadsky, George. **Lenin, red dictator.** New Haven, 1931. Scholarly, critical account.

AF348. Trotskii, Lev. **My life.** N.Y., 1930. Brilliantly-written autobiography.

AF349. Deutscher, Isaac. **The prophet armed: Trotsky, 1879–1921; the prophet unarmed: Trotsky, 1921–1929.** N.Y., 1954, 1959.

AF350. ——. **Stalin: a political biography.**

N.Y., 1949. A scholarly, well-written biography.

AF351. Stalin, Iosif V. **Works.** 13 v. London, 1953. An indispensable source.

AF352. Wolfe, Bertram D. **Three who made a revolution.** N.Y., 1948. 2nd ed., 1956. Excellent study of the pre-revolution careers of Lenin, Trotsky, and Stalin.

GOVERNMENT PUBLICATIONS

Treaty of Versailles

AF353. U. S. Department of State. **Papers relating to the foreign relations of the United States. Paris peace conference, 1919.** 13 v. Washington, 1942–47.

AF354. ——. **The Lansing papers, 1914–1920.** Ed. and annotated by James S. Biddle. 2 v. Washington, 1939.

German Foreign Policy

AF355. A valuable selection of documents from the captured archives of the German foreign ministry are being published jointly by a group of United States, British, and French scholars in English, French, and German. The United States edition, ed. by Raymond J. Sontag and others, is appearing under the title U. S. Department of State, Series D, **Documents on German foreign policy, 1918–1945, from the archives of the German foreign ministry** (Washington, 1949 ff.). The following volumes have been published: 1, *From Neurath to Ribbentrop (September 1937-September 1938)*; 2, *Germany and Czechoslovakia, 1937–1938;* 3, *Germany and the Spanish civil war, 1936–1939;* 4, *The aftermath of Munich (October 1938-March 1939)*; 5, *Poland; the Balkans; Latin America; the smaller powers (June 1937-March 1939)*; 6, *The last months of peace (March-August 1939)*; 7, *The last days of peace (August 9-September 3, 1939)*; 8, *The war years (September 4, 1939-March 18, 1940)*; 9, *The war years (March 18-June 22, 1940)*; 10, *The war years (June 23-August 31, 1940)*.

Nazi War Plans

AF356. United States Chief of Counsel for the Prosecution of Axis Criminality. **Nazi conspiracy and aggression.** 8 v. and 2 sup. Washington, 1946–48.

Occupation of Germany

AF357. U. S. Department of State. **Occupation of Germany: policy and progress, 1945–1946.** Washington, 1947 [European series, 23.]

AF358. Office of United States High Commissioner for Germany. **Elections and political parties in Germany, 1945–1952.** Washington, 1952.

Trials of Nazi War Criminals

AF359. International Military Tribunal. **Trial of the major war criminals before the International Military Tribunal, 1945–1946.** 42 v. Nürnberg, 1947–49.

AF360. ——. **Trials of war criminals, 1946–1949.** 16 v. Nürnberg, 1946–53.

British Foreign Policy

AF361. Woodward, Ernest L., and Rohan Butler, eds. **Documents on British foreign policy, 1919–1939.** See *AH119.*

Korean War

AF362. U. S. Department of State. **Korea, 1945 to 1948.** Washington, 1948. [Far Eastern series, 28.]

AF363. **The United States and the Korean problem: documents, 1943–1953.** Washington, 1953. [Senate document 74, 83rd Cong., 1st Sess.]

AF364. U. S. Department of State. **United States policy in the Korean crisis.** Washington, 1950. [Far Eastern series, 34.]

AF365. ——. **The conflict in Korea.** Washington, 1951. [Far Eastern series, 45.]

AF366. U. S. Department of the Army. **Korea, 1950.** Washington, 1952.

AF367. United Nations. Department of Public Information. **Korea and the United Nations.** Lake Success, 1950.

Atomic Energy

AF368. U. S. Department of State. **International control of atomic energy.** 3 v. Washington, 1946–47.

AF369. ——. **Report on the international control of atomic energy.** Washington, 1946.

AF370. Joint Committee on Atomic Energy. **Hydrogen bomb and international control.** Washington, 1950. [81st Cong., 2nd Sess.]

UNIVERSITY, ACADEMY, AND SOCIETY PUBLICATIONS

The following organizations and institutions sponsor the publication of works relating to world affairs.

The American Academy of Political and Social Science (Philadelphia) issues **(AF371) The annals** (1890 ff.) bimonthly. Each volume is a symposium devoted to a particular subject, and also contains an excellent book department with critical comments on new literature in all fields of the social and political sciences.

The Brookings Institution (Washington)

publishes books and monographs on pertinent economic, political, social, and international problems.

The Carnegie Endowment for International Peace (Washington) publishes numerous books and pamphlets. One is the **(AF372) International conciliation** series of pamphlets (mostly documents) which were begun as a monthly in 1907 by the Association for International Conciliation, but since 1924 have been published by the Division of Intercourse and Education (New York) of the Carnegie Endowment. Since 1955 these pamphlets have been issued five times a year. Books and pamphlets are also published by the Carnegie Endowment's Division of International Law (New York) and its Division of Economics and History (New York).

The Council on Foreign Relations (New York) publishes the quarterly periodical **(AF373) Foreign affairs** (1922 ff.), and from time to time volumes on special international questions.

Harper and Brothers (New York) publish for the Council on Foreign Relations the **(AF374) Political handbook of the world** (1927 ff., annual) and **(AF375) The United States in world affairs** (1932 ff., annual).

(AF376) Documents on American foreign relations were published from 1939 to 1952 by or for the World Peace Foundation (Boston), but subsequent volumes have been published by Harper for the Council on Foreign Relations.

The Foreign Policy Association (New York) has published since 1951 a semimonthly leaflet, **(AF377) Foreign policy bulletin,** which replaces its former weekly *Bulletin* and its larger fortnightly *Foreign policy reports.* The Foreign Policy Association publishes also the bimonthly **(AF378) Headline series** of pamphlets, which are monographs written for the general public on individual countries or on pertinent current questions.

The Royal Institute of International Affairs (London) publishes a journal, **(AF379) International affairs** (1922 ff., quarterly). It also publishes **(AF380) The world today** (1945 ff., monthly), a small journal which supersedes an earlier *Bulletin of international news;* a small leaflet, **(AF381) Chronology of international events** (1945 ff.), published twice a month; and, beginning with Jan. 1954, a mimeographed leaflet **(AF382) Calendar and texts of documents on international affairs.** Besides these serial publications, Oxford University Press publishes for the Royal Institute **(AF383) Survey of international affairs,** edited by Arnold Toynbee and others. This series of volumes, begun in 1925, was suspended during the years of World War II and resumed in 1951.

The Russian Institute at Columbia University and the Russian Research Center of Harvard University publish studies concerning the Soviet Union and the countries in its orbit.

The Middle East Institute (Washington) publishes **(AF384) The Middle East journal** (1947 ff., quarterly).

The University of Colorado publishes the **(AF385) Journal of central European affairs** (1941 ff., quarterly).

The Mid-European Studies Center and the National Committee for a Free Europe (New York) issue **(AF386) News from behind the Iron Curtain** (1952 ff., monthly) and numerous studies of countries of the Soviet Union orbit.

SECTION AG
The World Wars

BASIL H. LIDDELL HART * and HUGH M. COLE

No exhaustive bibliography has been published for either of the world wars. The largest specialized collections of printed works on both are contained in the holdings of the Imperial War Museum (London) and the Hoover Library at Stanford University. Incomplete but useful bibliographies for World War I will be found in the early check lists published by the *Bibliothèque de documentation internationale contemporaine et musée de la Grande Guerre* (Paris, 1926 ff.), and the *Catalogo bibliografico della Guerra Mondiale 1914–1918* (Milan, 1939), published by the Museo del Risorgimento Nazionale. See also *AG11* and *AG16*, below. The principal specialist periodicals are *Revue de l'histoire de la Guerre Mondiale* and *Revue de l'histoire de la IIᵉ Guerre Mondiale*.

WORLD WAR I

OFFICIAL HISTORIES

All the major World War I combatants (except Russia) have published official histories which give an account of land, air, and sea operations from official records. These accounts vary in their level of detail, the ratio of narrative to documents, and their reliability. In a number of cases a series is incomplete. The U.S.S.R. began work on 12 volumes in 1930, but this series (if completed) is not available to western scholars. A few monographs have been published by the War-Historical Division of the General Staff of the Red Army and The Secretariat of the History of the Civil War. Despite the "official" character of these national histories, they all must be regarded as basic to the serious study of military operations in World War I.

Australia

AG1. Australia. **Official history of Australia in the war of 1914–18.** 12 v. Sydney, 1921–42. A well-written, detailed account.

Austria

AG2. Austria, Kriegsarchiv. **Oesterreich-Ungarn's letzter Krieg, 1914–18.** 8 v. Vienna, 1931–38. Probably the best and most unbiased of the general staff histories.

Bavaria

AG3. Bavaria. Heeresarchiv. **Die Bayern im Grossen Kriege 1914–18.** 2 v. Munich, 1923.

Canada

AG4. Canada. Dept. of National Defence. **Official history of the Canadian forces in**

* The following assisted in planning and preparing this section: Michael E. Howard, George O. Kent, and William Wiseley.

the Great War, 1914–18. Ottawa, 1938. Only v. 1 (2 bks.), covering the period 1914–15, has been published.

France

AG5. France. Ministère de Guerre. **Les armées françaises dans la Grande Guerre.** Paris, 1922 ff. To date 11 v. in 23 plus 56 v. of appendices have been published. Volumes planned on the French air force have not appeared, and there are gaps in the army coverage for 1918. Attention is focused on the higher commands. The series consists largely of documents. Untrustworthy.

Germany

AG6. Germany. Reichsarchiv. **Der Weltkrieg 1914 bis 1918.** 14 v. Berlin, 1925–43. Attempts to combine diplomacy, economics, and social aspects with army operations. The first 11 v. are relatively unbiased. The proof copy of v. 14, heavily censored, has been photostated and a copy is in the Library of Congress.
AG7. ——. **Schlachten des Weltkrieges.** Berlin and Oldenburg, 1924 ff. Very useful and detailed treatment of individual battles or operations, based on regimental histories and personal contributions by participants. An important collection.

Italy

AG8. Italy, Esercito. **L'esercito italiano nella Grande Guerra.** 8 v. Rome, 1927–32. Stops with 1917.

New Zealand

AG9. Official history of New Zealand's effort in the Great War. 4 v. Auckland, 1921–23.

Union of South Africa

AG10. South Africa. General Staff. **The Union of South Africa and the Great War, 1914–1918.** Pretoria, 1924.

United Kingdom

AG11. Historical Section of the Committee of Imperial Defence. **History of the Great War.** London, 1920 ff. (See items in various subsections below.) Thirty-two volumes have been published on army operations in all theaters. As a rule these are well-written and moderately critical in their analyses; most have useful and annotated bibliographies.

United States of America

AG12. U. S. Department of the Army. **United States Army in the World War, 1917–** 1919. 17 v. Washington, 1948–50. Collection of documents interspersed with some narrative on major operations in which the A.E.F. took part. Little analysis of events or of the role of personalities. Contains no maps.
AG13. U. S. American Battle Monuments Commission. **Summary of operations in the World War.** Washington, 1944. A series of short divisional histories.

GENERAL HISTORIES

AG14. Churchill, Winston S. **The world crisis.** 4 v. London, 1923–28. Highly perceptive; very readable. Must be read with care when dealing with events in which the author participated. See also Lord Sydenham and others, *The world crisis: a criticism* (London, 1928).
AG15. Cruttwell, Charles R. M. F. **A history of the Great War, 1914–1918.** Oxford, 1934.
AG16. Liddell Hart, Basil H. **A history of the World War, 1914–1918.** London and Boston, 1934. Both this and *AG15* are well-written, use the best available sources, and are well-balanced. The bibliography in *AG16* represents a critical selection of the major works on World War I.
AG17. Kuhl, Hermann J. von. **Der Weltkrieg, 1914–1918.** 2 v. Berlin, 1929. Competent and well-informed.

ALLIED COMMAND PROBLEMS

AG18. Callwell, Sir Charles E. **Experiences of a dug-out.** London, 1920. Revealing about Kitchener's period in the British War Office.
AG19. Charteris, John. **At G. H. Q.** London, 1931. Remarkably frank account of the war in France from the viewpoint of the British G.H.Q.; in diary form by Haig's chief intelligence officer.
AG20. King, Jere C. **Generals and politicians: conflict between France's high command, parliament and government, 1914–1918.** Berkeley, 1951. A comprehensive examination of the evidence.
AG21. Painlevé, Paul. **Comment j'ai nommé Foch et Pétain.** Paris, 1924. Illuminating account by the war minister and, later, premier.
AG22. Pierrefeu, Jean de. **Trois ans au grand quartier général.** 2 v. Paris, 1920. Critical inside view with significant disclosures. Pays tribute to Pétain's realism and effect.
AG23. Robertson, Sir William R. **Soldiers and statesmen, 1914–1918.** 2 v. London, 1926. Reflective survey of Britain's strategy, by its military directing mind in 1916–17, a strong "Westerner" who clashed with Lloyd George.
AG24. Spears, Edward L. **Liaison, 1914:**

a **narrative of the great retreat.** London, 1930. This and *AG25* contain vivid and caustic analyses of liaison difficulties between the French and British.

AG25. ———. **Prelude to victory.** London, 1939.

AG26. Oehmichen. **Essai sur la doctrine de la guerre des coalitions: la direction de la guerre.** Paris, 1927. Authoritative study by a participant in the French General Staff reorganization designed to coordinate Allied operations.

For this and the next section see also the relevant memoirs.

CENTRAL POWERS COMMAND PROBLEMS

AG27. Falkenhayn, Erich G. A. S. von. **General headquarters, 1914–1916, and its critical decisions.** Eng. tr., London, 1919. Important as the account of the directing mind of German strategy from 1914 to 1916, but the impersonal manner of writing is misleading.

AG28. Ritter, Gerhard. **The Schlieffen plan.** Eng. tr., London, 1958. The best analysis, with full text of the successive drafts. Goes to the root of the German failure in 1914.

AG29. Hoffmann, Max. **The war of lost opportunities.** London, 1924. Tr. of *Der Krieg der versäumten Gelegenheiten* (Munich, 1923). Invaluable mixture of reminiscences and criticism of the German leadership, by the ablest German staff officer.

AG30. Ludendorff, Erich F. **The general staff and its problems.** 2 v. London and N.Y., 1920. Tr. of *Urkunden der obersten Heeresleitung* (Berlin, 1920). An apologia, but illuminating. Numerous documents bearing on critical decisions, and relations between the civil and military authorities.

AG31. Lutz, Ralph H., ed. **The causes of the German collapse in 1918.** Stanford, 1934. [Hoover War Library publications, 4.] Dispassionate analysis of military and political events, drawn from the official German inquiry.

AG32. Stuergkh, Joseph M. A. **Im deutschen grossen Hauptquartier.** Leipzig, 1921. Interesting account of the first ten months at German headquarters by an Austrian staff officer.

THE WESTERN FRONT

AG33. Bruchmüller, Georg. **Die deutsche Artillerie in den Durchbruchschlachten des Weltkrieges.** Berlin, 1922. Best work on the role of the artillery arm in World War I. See also other books by this author.

AG34. Gough, Sir Hubert. **The Fifth Army.** London, 1931. Good apologia by a much criticized army commander, with im-

portant explanations and revelations, particularly about the 1917–18 campaigns.

AG35. Kabisch, Ernst. **Somme, 1916.** Berlin, 1937. This and *AG36–38* are good brief and balanced monographs on these battles.

AG36. ———. **Die Marneschlacht, 1914.** Berlin, 1934.

AG37. ———. **Verdun.** Berlin, 1935.

AG38. ———. **Michael: die grosse Schlacht in Frankreich.** Berlin, 1935.

AG39. Lanrezac, Charles L. M. **Le plan de campagne français et le premier mois de la guerre.** Paris, 1920. Important disclosures and corrections of Joffre's version of events, by the commander of the French left wing army.

AG40. Liggett, Hunter. **A. E. F.: ten years ago in France.** N.Y., 1928. Broad account, well-balanced and reflective, by Pershing's chief subordinate commander.

AG41. Great Britain. Committee of Imperial Defence. **Military operations, France and Belgium, 1914–1918.** By Sir J. E. Edmonds and others. 14 v. London, 1927–48. Able and detailed analysis of operations; but the editing, especially of later volumes, frequently twists the record due to regard for patriotic interests and commanders' reputations. Very misleading in its computation of German casualties.

AG42. Wendt, Hermann. **Verdun, 1916.** Berlin, 1931. A re-examination of Falkenhayn's strategy in 1916, based in part on unpublished French and German sources.

AG43. Palat, Barthélemy E. (pseud. Pierre Lehautcourt). **La Grande Guerre sur le front occidental.** 14 v. Paris, 1917–29. Fullest account of French operations on the western front. Valuable only if used critically.

AG44. Wynne, Graeme C. **If Germany attacks.** London, 1940. Good analysis of German battle methods on the western front. Critical comments on British command were deleted on publication.

THE EASTERN FRONT

AG45. Churchill, Winston S. **The world crisis: the eastern front.** London, 1931. Best introduction to the subject.

AG46. Danilov, Iurii N. **Russland im Weltkriege 1914–1915.** Jena, 1923. Good on Russian preparations and first battles.

AG47. Golovïn, Nikolai N. **The Russian army in the World War.** New Haven, 1931. Useful as background.

AG48. François, Hermann K. B. von. **Tannenberg: das Cannae des Weltkrieges.** Leipzig, 1927. Essential supplement and correction to Ludendorff's account.

AG49. **La Grande Guerre, relation de l'état-major russe.** Tr. by Edouard Chapouilly. Paris, 1926. Translation of two volumes prepared in 1919 by survivors of the

Russian general staff and published in Moscow.

THE NEAR EAST

AG50. Hamilton, Sir Ian S. M. **Gallipoli diary.** 2 v. London, 1920. An extraordinarily vivid picture of a campaign from the commander's viewpoint.

AG51. Kannengiesser, Hans. **The campaign in Gallipoli.** Eng. tr., London, 1928. Valuable supplement from the defender's viewpoint, revealing weakness of defense and attacker's missed opportunities.

AG52. Lawrence, Thomas E. **Seven pillars of wisdom.** London, 1935. Highly personal work of the highest literary merit, but to be used with caution as a source.

AG53. Moorehead, Alan M. **Gallipoli.** London and N.Y., 1956. Well-written analysis based on official and other sources.

AG54. Liman von Sanders, Otto V. K. **Five years in Turkey.** Annapolis, Md., 1927. Essential to any study of German command relations with their Turkish allies.

AG55. Townshend, Sir Charles. **My campaign in Mesopotamia.** London, 1920. An apologia, but of particular interest in its exposition of a commander's conscious application of Napoleonic principles.

AG56. Aspinall-Oglander, Cecil F. **Military operations, Gallipoli.** 2 v. London, 1929–32. Unusually frank and enlightening official history, written by one of the ablest staff officers who took part.

AG57. MacMunn, Sir George F., and Cyril Falls. **Military operations, Egypt and Palestine.** 2 v. London, 1928–30. Another good example of official history, though inclined to glide over faults of execution.

AG58. Moberly, Frederick J. **The campaign in Mesopotamia, 1914–1918.** 4 v. London, 1923–27. Also of good quality.

AG59. Larcher, Maurice. **La guerre turque dans la Guerre Mondiale.** See *S132*.

AG60. Wavell, Archibald P. **The Palestine campaigns.** London, 1928. Best short account of this area, well-written and well-balanced, but restrained in analysis.

AG61. Wilson, Sir Arnold T. **Loyalties: Mesopotamia, 1914–1917.** London, 1930. Lively but partisan account of the Mesopotamian campaigns.

ITALY AND MACEDONIA

AG62. Cadorna, Luigi. **La guerra alla fronte Italiana.** 2 v. Milan, 1921. Glosses over Italian defeats and magnifies the victories.

AG63. Sarrail, Maurice P. E. **Mon commandement en Orient (1916–1918).** Paris, 1920. French side of the Allied controversy over command and political responsibility in the Macedonian command.

AG64. Edmonds, Sir James E., and Henry B. Davies. **Military operations: Italy, 1915–19.** London, 1949. [U.K. official history.] The British part.

AG65. Falls, Cyril B. **Military operations: Macedonia.** 2 v. London, 1933–35. [U.K. official history.] A fine piece of military history, though in some respects too discreet in its exposition of the evidence.

AG66. Geloso, Carlo. **La campagna austro-serba del 1914.** Rome, 1948. An outline of the campaign during August–December.

NAVAL AND MARITIME

AG67. Corbett, Sir Julian S., and Sir Henry Newbolt. **Naval operations.** 5 v. London, 1920–31. This and *AG68–69* are the naval volumes of the British official *History of the Great War.* Good and well-written.

AG68. Fayle, Charles E. **Seaborne trade.** 3 v. London, 1920–24.

AG69. Hurd, Sir Archibald S. **The merchant navy.** 3 v. London, 1921–29.

AG70. Harper, John E. T. **The truth about Jutland.** London, 1927. Excellent detailed account of the battle of Jutland and a strong defense of Jellicoe.

AG71. Jellicoe, John R., viscount. **The grand fleet, 1914–1916.** London, 1919. Good description of the British and German navies, and of the battle of Jutland.

AG72. Germany. Marinearchiv. **Der Krieg zur See.** 16 v. Berlin, 1921–38. The German official history. Earlier volumes are more accurate and show less signs of "editing" than those which appeared after the rise of Hitler.

AG73. Scheer, Reinhard. **Deutschlands Hochseeflotte im Weltkrieg.** Berlin, 1920. Tr., *Germany's high seas fleet in the World War,* London and N.Y., 1920. Partisan account and apologia by the chief of staff of the German navy.

AG74. Sims, William S., and Burton J. Hendrick. **The victory at sea.** N.Y., 1920. History of United States naval operations. Makes use of official sources.

AG75. Gibson, Richard H., and Maurice Prendergast. **The German submarine war, 1914–1918.** London, 1931. Detailed description based on German and English sources.

AIR AND TECHNICAL

AC76. Groves, Percy R. C. **Behind the smoke screen.** London, 1934. Important revelations about the use and misuse of British airpower.

AG77. Ritter, Hans. **Der Luftkrieg.** Berlin and Leipzig, 1926. Description of development of the German air force. Noteworthy observations on air strategy and tactics.

AG78. Raleigh, Sir Walter A., and Henry A. Jones. **The war in the air.** 7 v. London, 1922–37. A high level of official history.

AG79. Fuller, John F. C. **Memoirs of an unconventional soldier.** London, 1936. A vivid and caustic account of the struggle to obtain effective use of tank potentialities, written by the chief staff officer of the wartime tank corps, and a prophet of mechanized warfare.

AG80. Liddell Hart, B. H. **The tanks.** 2 v. London and N.Y., 1959. History of the British tank arm and its part in development of mechanized warfare. Written with access to official records, but not under official control.

AG81. Swinton, Sir Ernest D. **Eyewitness.** London, 1932. Account of the birth and development of the British tank arm, by its progenitor.

AG82. Foulkes, Charles H. **"Gas!": the story of the special brigade.** London, 1934. Sheds light on the development of chemical warfare.

AG83. Schwarte, Max, ed. **Die Technik im Weltkrieg.** Berlin, 1920. Encyclopedic treatment of war matériel and the applications of technology, prepared by specialists.

WAR AIMS, PSYCHOLOGICAL WARFARE, ETC.

AG84. Gatzke, Hans W. **Germany's drive to the west: a study of Germany's western war aims during the First World War.** Baltimore, 1950. Useful study of German war aims and the obstacles they imposed to peace-making.

AG85. Lasswell, Harold D. **Propaganda technique in the World War.** N.Y., 1927. A sharply critical analysis of the Allied use of propaganda.

AG86. Ponsonby, Arthur. **Falsehood in wartime.** London, 1928. A severe criticism and exposure of British propaganda methods.

AG87. Read, James M. **Atrocity propaganda, 1914–19.** New Haven, 1941. Scholarly and illuminating study.

ECONOMIC AND SOCIAL

AG88. Shotwell, James T., ed. **Economic and social history of the World War.** New Haven, 1936 ff. [Carnegie Endowment for International Peace.] This multi-volume work is divided into country series covering nearly all the belligerents. Written by experts, these volumes contain much source material. Particularly valuable for Germany, Russia, Austria, and Turkey.

AG89. Chambers, Frank P. **The war behind the war, 1914–1918: a history of the political and civilian fronts.** London, 1939. Valuable synthesis, largely from secondary materials, with a useful bibliography.

AG90. Consett, Montagu W. W. P., and O. H. Daniel. **The triumph of unarmed forces, 1914–1918.** London, 1923. Critique of British blockade regulations.

AG91. Hirst, Francis W. **The consequences of the war to Great Britain.** London, 1934. A social and political as well as an economic evaluation.

AG92. March, Peyton C. **The nation at war.** N.Y., 1932. Very candid account, with ably marshalled facts and figures, of the United States war effort. Severely criticizes Pershing.

AG93. Crowell, Benedict, and Robert F. Wilson. **The armies of industry.** 2 v. New Haven, 1921. This and *AG94* tell the story of United States war effort on the home front, making use of official sources.

AG94. ——. **The road to France.** 2 v. New Haven, 1921.

AG95. Great Britain. War Office. **Statistics of the military effort of the British empire during the Great War, 1914–1920.** London, 1922.

AG96. Mitchell, Thomas J., and G. M. Smith. **Medical services: casualties and medical statistics of the Great War.** London, 1931.

AG97. Toubert, Joseph H. **Le service de santé militaire au grand quartier général français (1918–1919) suivi de documents de statistique concernant la Guerre Mondiale et après-guerre.** Paris, 1934.

BIOGRAPHIES AND AUTOBIOGRAPHIES

The memoir and biographical literature of World War I has reached almost unmanageable proportions. Titles of published memoirs on the first battle of the Marne alone now run to several printed pages. Listed below are some of the more important works on World War I personalities.

AG98. Wavell, Sir Archibald P. **Allenby.** 2 v. London, 1940–43.

AG99. Galet, Émile J. **Albert, king of the Belgians.** N.Y., 1931.

AG100. Overstraeten, Raoul F. C. van, ed. **The war diaries of Albert I, king of the Belgians.** London, 1954.

AG101. Asquith, Herbert H., earl of Oxford and. **Memories and reflections, 1852–1927.** 2 v. London, 1928.

AG102. Palmer, Frederick L. **Newton D. Baker.** 2 v. N.Y., 1931.

AG103. Beaverbrook, William M. A., lord. **Men and power, 1917–1918.** London, 1956.

AG104. Bethmann-Hollweg, Theobald von. **Betrachtungen zum Weltkrieg.** 2 v. Berlin, 1919–21.

AG105. Clemenceau, Georges. **Grandeur et misères d'une victoire.** Paris, 1930. See *AF307*.

AG106. Conrad von Hötzendorf, Franz.

Aus meiner Dienstzeit, 1906–1918. See *VF267*.

AG107. Brett, Maurice V., ed. **Journals and letters of Reginald, Viscount Esher.** 4 v. London, 1934–38.

AG108. Liddell Hart, B. H. **Foch, the man of Orléans.** London and Boston, 1932.

AG109. Blake, Robert, ed. **The private papers of Douglas Haig, 1914–1919.** London, 1952.

AG110. Cooper, Alfred Duff. **Haig.** 2 v. London, 1936.

AG111. Hindenburg, Paul von. **Aus meinem Leben.** Leipzig, 1920. Tr. by Frederic A. Holt, *Out of my life,* London, 1920.

AG112. Hoffmann, Max. **War diaries and other papers.** London, 1929. Tr. of *Aufzeichnungen* (2 v., Berlin, 1928).

AG113. Seymour, Charles. **Intimate papers of Colonel House.** 4 v. Boston and N.Y., 1926–28.

AG114. Joffre, Joseph J. C. **Mémoires du Maréchal Joffre (1910–1917).** 2 v. Paris, 1932. Tr. by T. Bentley Mott, *The memoirs of Marshal Joffre,* 2 v., London and N.Y., 1932.

AG115. Lloyd George, David. **War memoirs.** 6 v. London and Boston, 1933–37.

AG116. Jones, Thomas. **Lloyd George.** Cambridge, Mass., 1951.

AG117. Ludendorff, Erich F. W. **Meine Kriegserinnerungen, 1914–1918.** Berlin, 1919. Tr., *My war memories, 1914–1918,* 2 v., London, 1919.

AG118. Maximilian (Alexander F. W.), prince of Baden. **The memoirs of Prince Max of Baden.** 2 v. London and N.Y., 1928.

AG119. Pershing, John J. **My experiences in the World War.** 2 v. N.Y., 1931.

AG120. ——. **Final report of General Pershing.** Washington, 1920.

AG121. Poincaré, Raymond. **Au service de la France: neuf années de souvenirs.** 10 v. Paris, 1926–33.

AG122. Robertson, Sir William. **From private to field-marshal.** London, 1921.

AG123. Tirpitz, Alfred P. von. **Erinnerungen.** Leipzig, 1919. Tr., *My memoirs,* 2 v., London, 1919.

AG124. Weygand, Maxime. **Mémoires.** V. 1, **Idéal vécu.** Paris, 1953.

AG125. Wilhelm, crown prince of the German empire and of Prussia. **Erinnerungen.** Berlin, 1922. Tr., *My war experiences,* London, 1922.

AG126. Callwell, Sir Charles E. **Field-Marshal Sir Henry Wilson: his life and diaries.** 2 v. N.Y., 1927.

AG127. Sazonov, Serge D. **Fateful years, 1909–1916.** London, 1928.

AG128. Liddell Hart, B. H. **Reputations ten years after.** Boston, 1928.

AG129. Rupprecht, crown prince of Bavaria. **Mein Kriegstagebuch.** 3 v. Munich, 1929.

AG130. Repington, Charles à Court. **The First World War, 1914–18.** 2 v. London, 1920.

WORLD WAR II

Thus far the major contributions have come from official histories of the western allies. The military document collections of the Axis powers suffered such damage and dispersal during the war as to leave little hope of reconstruction and extensive publication. The U.S.S.R. is known to have planned a large series of historical volumes under the supervision of the War-Historical Division, but these have been restricted in circulation because of their military value. Since all the official histories are still in process of publication, the best guide to the state of other parts of a series will be found in prefaces to current volumes.

GENERAL WORKS

AG131. Churchill, Winston S. **The Second World War.** See *AH234*.

AG132. Tippelskirch, Kurt von. **Geschichte des Zweiten Weltkriegs.** Bonn, 1951. Well-balanced German account, though written when documentary evidence available to German historians was scarce.

AG133. Assmann, Kurt. **Deutsche Schicksalsjahre.** Wiesbaden, 1950. Good survey of the conduct of the war, by the former chief of the historical section of the German navy. Based on documents.

AG134. Chassin, Lionel M. **Histoire militaire de la Seconde Guerre Mondiale.** Paris, 1947. By one of the best French military historians.

AG135. Fuller, John F. C. **The Second World War: a strategical and tactical history.** London, 1948. Written too early for detailed accuracy, but important as a commentary by a brilliant, unconventional mind.

AG136. Royal Institute of International Affairs. **Chronology of the Second World War.** London, 1947. Useful and generally accurate.

AG137. Morison, Samuel E. **American contributions to the strategy of World War II.** London and N.Y., 1958. An able and illuminating exposition. Should be studied in conjunction with *AG138.*

ALLIED COMMAND PROBLEMS

AG138. Butler, James R. M., ed. **Grand strategy.** London, 1956 ff. [United Kingdom history of the Second World War. Military series.] Six volumes planned. Combines operations on land, sea, and in the air from viewpoint of national strategy. A good synthesis.

AG139. Leighton, Richard M., and Robert W. Coakley. **Global logistics and strategy.** Washington, 1955. [The U. S. army in World War II: the War Department.] This is the first of two volumes.

AG140. Millis, Walter, ed. **The war reports of General George Marshall, General H. H. Arnold and Admiral Ernest J. King.** N.Y., 1947.

AG141. Pogue, Forrest C. **The supreme command.** Washington, 1954. [The U. S. army in World War II: European theatre of operations.] Good on relations between Eisenhower and Marshall, Eisenhower and Montgomery.

AG142. Watson, Mark S. **Chief of staff: pre-war plans and preparations.** Washington, 1950. [The U. S. army in World War II: the War Department.] Well-written and keenly analytical.

AG143. Fergusson, Bernard E., ed. **The business of war: the war narrative of Major-General Sir John Kennedy.** London, 1957. Throws light on British strategic planning and viewpoint.

AG144. Matloff, Maurice, and Edwin M. Snell. **Strategic planning for coalition warfare, 1941–42,** (Matloff) **1943–44.** Washington, 1953, 1958. [The U. S. Army in World War II.]

AG145. Morgan, Sir Frederick E. **Overture to Overlord.** London, 1950. Lively account of preparations for the invasion of Europe in 1944 by the chief planner.

AXIS COMMAND PROBLEMS

AG146. Bilanz des Zweiten Weltkrieges: **Erkenntnisse und Verpflichtungen für die Zukunft.** Hamburg, 1953. Cooperative work by various experts.

AG147. Halder, Franz. **Hitler als Feldherr.** Munich, 1949. Tr., *Hitler as warlord,* London, 1950. Good on direction of the war in Russia. Attempts to lay the failure there at Hitler's door.

AG148. Hinsley, Francis H. **Hitler's strategy.** Cambridge, Eng., 1951. Able analysis, based on German naval records.

AG149. Hitler's Tischgespräche im Führer-hauptquartier, 1941–44. Bonn, 1951. Tr. by Norman Cameron and R. H. Stevens, *Hitler's table talk, 1941–1944,* London, 1953. Reproduction of stenographic notes made at the fuehrer's headquarters. The bulk of these were destroyed.

AG150. Kesselring, Albert. **Gedanken zum Zweiten Weltkrieg.** Bonn, 1955. Deals with problems of German command and planning.

AG151. Liddell Hart, B. H. **The other side of the hill.** 2nd ed., London, 1951. U. S. ed.,

The German generals talk, N.Y., 1948. The 2nd edition contains not only evidence of the chief German commanders, but full editorial comment and corrections. Only 1st ed. was published in the U. S.

AG152. Westphal, Siegfried, ed. **The fatal decisions.** London, 1956. A group of essays by German officers. The most notable is Zeitzler's account of the battle of Stalingrad.

AG153. ——. **Heer in Fesseln.** Bonn, 1950. Eng. tr., *The German army in the West,* London, 1951. By a very able chief of staff. Remarkably objective in narrative and analysis. Also deals with the North African and Italian campaigns.

AG154. Greiner, H. **Die Oberste Wehrmachtführung 1939–43.** Wiesbaden, 1951. Good account of the conduct of the war up to the Russian campaign from the viewpoint of the German planning staff.

AG155. Mueller-Hillebrand, Burkhart, and others. **Das Heer, 1933–1945.** Darmstadt, 1954 ff. Attempt by a group of German officers to write a general staff history based on personal experiences and fragmentary documentation.

NORTHWEST EUROPE, 1939–1940

AG156. Benoist-Méchin, Jacques G. P. M., baron. **Soixante jours qui ébranlèrent l'Occident.** 3 v. Paris, 1956. A full politico-military account of the fall of France. The author's political bias does not affect his military judgment.

AG157. Derry, Thomas K. **The campaign in Norway.** London, 1952. [U.K. official history.] Well-written, objective, and frank about British blunders.

AG158. Ellis, Lionel F. **The war in France and Flanders, 1939–40.** London, 1953. [U.K. official history.] Ably marshalled, but relies too exclusively on formal documentary evidence of limited range. Uncritical in dealing with British performance, and inadequate in treatment and knowledge of allied operations.

AG159. Jacobsen, Hans-Adolf. **Fall Gelb: der Kampf um den deutschen Operationsplan zur Westoffensive 1940.** Wiesbaden, 1957. Very good detailed account of development of the German plan of attack in the West in 1940, with reproduction of key documents.

AG160. Spears, Edward L. **Assignment to catastrophe.** 2 v. London, 1954. Vivid and highly critical eyewitness comment on the 1940 campaign.

AG161. Goutard, Adolphe. **1940: la guerre des occasions perdues.** Paris, 1956. Tr., *The battle of France, 1940,* London, 1958. Good analysis of the military causes of French defeat.

AG162. Hubatsch, Walther. **Die deutsche Besetzung von Dänemark und Norwegen, 1940.** Göttingen, 1952. [Göttinger Beiträge für Gegenwartsfragen, 5.] Based on German and Allied documents. Covers political and military aspects.

THE MEDITERRANEAN AND MIDDLE EAST

AG163. Agar-Hamilton, John A. I., and Leonard C. F. Turner. **Crisis in the desert, May-July, 1942.** Capetown and London, 1952. [South African official history.] This and *AG164* are the fullest and best accounts of these North African battles; very objective.

AG164. ———. **The Sidi Rezeg battles, 1941.** Capetown and London, 1957.

AG165. Badoglio, Pietro. **Italy in the Second World War: memories and documents.** Tr. by Muriel Currey. London and N.Y., 1948. A personal and national apologia.

AG166. Davin, Daniel M. **Crete.** Wellington, 1953. [New Zealand official history.] Sound assessment of reasons for the British defeat in Crete, and a full account of the military campaign.

AG167. De Guingand, Sir Francis W. **Operation Victory.** London, 1947. Written by Montgomery's chief of staff. Quite candid.

AG168. Long, Gavin M. **To Benghazi.** Canberra, 1952. [Australia in the war of 1939–45.] This and *AG169* are model histories, covering all aspects of Australia's participation in the Middle East, from grand strategy to unit actions.

AG169. ———. **Greece, Crete and Syria.** Canberra, 1953. [Australia in the war of 1939–45.]

AG170. Montgomery, Bernard L., viscount. **El Alamein to the river Sangro.** London, 1948. A rather sketchy outline.

AG171. Playfair, Ian S. O. **The Mediterranean and Middle East.** London, 1954 ff. [U.K. official history.] (In progress.) A well-written and balanced account.

AG172. Scoullar, J. L. **Battle for Egypt.** Wellington, 1955. [New Zealand official history.] Critical analysis with much valuable detail.

AG173. Italy. Ministero della Difesa. Stato Maggiore Esercito. **La guerra in Africa orientale.** Rome, 1952.

AG174. ———. **Operazioni Italo-tedesche in Tunisia.** Rome, 1950. This and *AG173* are part of the Italian official history, publication of which began in 1945. To date 15 v. have been published, dealing with operations in all theaters.

AG175. Howe, George F. **Northwest Africa: seizing the initiative in the West.** Washington, 1957. [The U. S. army in World War II: Mediterranean theater of operations.] The first of several volumes relating to the war in this theater, from official records of both the coalitions and other sources. Broadly conceived and objective.

AG176. Carpentier, Marcel. **Les forces alliées en Italie: la campagne d'Italie.** Paris, 1949.

AG177. Maclean, Fitzroy. **Eastern approaches.** London, 1949. Important sidelights on British policy in the Near East, particularly in Yugoslavia.

THE EASTERN FRONT

AG178. Liddell Hart, B. H., ed. **The Soviet army.** London, 1956. Anthology containing much useful material on structure and training of the Red Army and the course of the campaign.

AG179. Bor-Komorowski, Tedeusz. **The secret army.** London, 1950. Written by the leader of the Warsaw insurrection and chief of the Polish underground army.

AG180. Doerr, Hans. **Der Feldzug nach Stalingrad.** Darmstadt, 1955. Well-written, balanced account, based on new sources.

AG181. Erfurth, Waldemar. **Der finnische Krieg 1941–44.** Wiesbaden, 1950. Written by one of the German general staff historians who also commanded the German troops in Finland.

THE PACIFIC AND SOUTHEAST ASIA

AG182. Butow, Robert J. C. **Japan's decision to surrender.** Stanford, 1954. Scholarly analysis of internal politics in Japan at the end of the war.

AG183. Fuchida, Mitsuo, and Masatake Okumiya. **Midway: the battle that doomed Japan.** Annapolis, 1955. This and *AG189* describe the interaction of war planning, war production, and technology in causing initial Japanese victory and ultimate defeat. Indispensable.

AG184. Gillespie, Oliver A. **The Pacific.** Wellington, 1952. [New Zealand official history.] An important contribution.

AG185. Grenfell, Russell. **Main fleet to Singapore.** London, 1951. Devastating analysis of British strategy prior to the fall of Malaya.

AG186. Allied Forces. **Report to the combined chiefs of staff by the supreme Allied commander, South-east Asia, 1943–45.** London, 1951.

AG187. Isely, Jeter A., and Philip A. Crowl. **The U. S. Marines and amphibious war: its theory and its practice in the Pacific.** Princeton, 1951. Valuable analysis.

AG188. Kirby, Stanley W. **The war against Japan.** London, 1957 ff. [U.K. official history.] Frank within limits. 5 v. planned.

AG189. Okumiya, Masatake, and Jiro Horikoshi. **Zero!** N.Y., 1956.

AG190. Percival, Arthur E. **War in Malaya.** London, 1949. Apologia of the commander who surrendered Singapore.

AG191. Slim, Sir William J. **Defeat into victory.** London, 1956. Detailed but brilliantly readable history of the Burma campaign, 1942–45, by the British commander.

AG192. The United States Army in World War II: the war in the Pacific. Washington, 1948 ff. 11 v. have been completed, 9 of which have been published, commencing with *Okinawa: the last battle.*

AG193. The United States Army in World War II: the China-Burma-India theater. 3 v. Washington, 1953–59. Superior.

EUROPE, 1941–1945

AG194. Eisenhower, Dwight D. **Crusade in Europe.** N.Y., 1948. The most fair-minded book by any soldier. Self-revealing both of high qualities and limitations of outlook and knowledge.

AG195. Allied Forces. **Report by the supreme commander to the combined chiefs of staff on the operations in Europe of the Allied expeditionary force, 6 June 1944 to 8 May 1945.** Washington, 1946.

AG196. Montgomery, Bernard L., viscount. **Normandy to the Baltic.** London, 1948. The British commander's account of the 1944–45 campaign.

AG197. Wilmot, Reginald W. W. **Struggle for Europe.** London, 1952. Masterly account of the planning and conduct of the Allied landing in Normandy and advance into Germany, but less than just to the American case where difference of view arose.

AG198. Speidel, Hans. **Invasion 1944.** Tr. by T. R. Crevenna. Chicago, 1950. Good picture of the Normandy campaign from the German viewpoint, but often inaccurate in detail through lack of documentary check on memory.

AG199. Lattre de Tassigny, Jean J. M. G. de. **Histoire de la Première Armée Française: Rhin et Danube.** Paris, 1949. Important supplement to United States and British accounts of the final campaign in the West.

AG200. The United States Army in World War II: the European theater of operations. Washington, 1950 ff. 5 v. published, beginning with *The Lorraine campaign.* See also the British official series on operations in western Europe as these volumes appear in the overall *History of the Second World War.*

NAVAL

AG201. "Fuehrer conferences on naval affairs." Brassey, Thomas A. **Naval annual** (London, 1948), appendix.

AG202. Kemp, Peter K. **Victory at sea, 1939–45.** London, 1957. An able account of the British navy's part in the war.

AG203. Ruge, Friedrich. **Der Seekrieg, 1939–45.** Stuttgart, 1954. Tr. by M. G. Saunders, *Sea warfare, 1939–1945,* London, 1957. Very good account with some use of German documents.

AG204. Morison, Samuel E. **History of United States naval operations in World War II.** 14 v. Boston, 1947–60. The official history, ably and brilliantly written. Other volumes in progress.

AG205. Roskill, Stephen W. **The war at sea, 1939–1945.** 3 v. London, 1954–56. [U.K. official history.] Excellent, critical history; scholarly and outspoken.

AG205a. Auphan, Paul, and Hervé Cras. **The French Navy in World War II.** Annapolis, 1959.

AIR AND AIR DEFENSE

AG206. Collier, J. Basil. **The defence of the United Kingdom.** London, 1957. [U.K. official history.] Embraces land, sea, and air defenses. Indispensable for the battle of Britain and "Operation Sealion."

AG207. Craven, Wesley F., and James L. Cate, eds. **The Army Air Forces in World War II.** 7 v. Chicago, 1948–58. The official history.

AG208. Harris, Sir Arthur T. **Bomber offensive.** London, 1947. Highly personal account by the man who shaped British strategic bomber policy.

AG209. Pile, Sir Frederick A. **Ack ack.** London, 1949. The commander of Britain's anti-aircraft defense tells its story, and deals with wider issues. Important sidelights on Churchill.

AG210. Richards, Denis G., and Hilary A. St. G. Saunders. **Royal Air Force, 1939–45.** 3 v. London, 1953–54. An official "popular" history, compiled from documents. Of uneven value.

AG211. Slessor, Sir John C. **The central blue.** London, 1956. "Recollections and reflections" of one of Britain's senior air commanders. Especially useful on problems of inter-service cooperation.

AG212. Tedder, Arthur W., baron. **Air power in war.** London, 1948. Brilliant course of lectures on the employment and achievements of the air arm in World War II.

AG213. Galland, Adolf. **Die Ersten und die Letzten.** Darmstadt, 1953. Tr., *The first and the last: the rise and fall of the German fighter forces, 1938–1945,* N.Y., 1954. A vivid personal account, by its chief commander.

TECHNOLOGY

AG214. Crowther, James G., and Richard Whiddington. **Science at war.** London, 1947. Good illustrative survey, but too exclusively from the scientist's angle.

AG215. Mellenthin, Friedrich W. von. **Panzer battles: a study of the employment**

of armor in the Second World War. Tr. by H. Betzler. Norman, Okla., 1956. A valuable study, based partly on documentary sources.
AG216. Blackett, Patrick M. S. The military and political consequences of atomic energy. London, 1948. Highly critical account of allied bombing strategy, by a leading British scientist.
AG217. Dornberger, Walter. V 2. Tr. by James Cleugh and Geoffrey Halliday. N.Y., 1954. Personal account of the German military pioneer of the long-range rocket.
AG218. Joubert, Sir Philip. Rocket. London, 1957. A history of missile development and thoughts about the future, by an eminent British air marshal.
AG219. Liddell Hart, B. H. The tanks. V. 2, 1939–1945. London, 1959.
AG220. Watson-Watt, Sir Robert A. Three steps to victory. London, 1958. A vehement personal account of the development of radar, radio direction-finding, and operational research, by the foremost pioneer of the first two.
AG221. Banks, Sir Donald. Flame over Britain. London, 1946. Personal account of development of flame weapons; also of "Fido" (fog-dispersal) and "Pluto" (cross-channel pipelines).
Pertinent works will be found in the Technical Services sub-series of the *U. S. Army in World War II*.

RESISTANCE, ESPIONAGE, PROPAGANDA, ETC.

AG222. Zeller, Eberhard. Geist der Freiheit: der 20ᵗᵉ Juli. 2nd ed., Munich, 1954.
AG223. Bruce-Lockhart, Sir Robert H. Comes the reckoning. London, 1947. A personal account of British political warfare activities and difficulties, by its chief.
AG224. Jong, Louis de. The German fifth column in the Second World War. Tr. by C. M. Geyl. Chicago, 1956. Judicious study which comes to conclusion that, while a fifth column did exist, its importance has been much overrated.
AG225. Leverkuehn, Paul. German military intelligence. London, 1954.
AG226. Ritter, Gerhard. The German resistance. London, 1959. Abbr. tr. of *Carl Goerdeler und die deutsche Widerstandsbewegung* (Stuttgart, 1954). The most balanced account, by a historian of high repute.
AG227. Dewavrin, André ("Colonel Passy"). Souvenirs. 3 v. Monte Carlo and Paris, 1947–51. "Colonel Passy" is the *nomme de guerre* of the chief of the B.C.R.A., which directed French resistance activities from London.
AG228. Granet, Marie, and Henri Michel. Combat: histoire d'un mouvement de resistance de juillet 1940 à juillet 1943. Paris,

1957. Best work on the French resistance movement.
See also files of *Revue de la Guerre Deuxième Mondiale* (Paris), a monthly publication of the Comité d'Histoire de la Guerre.

ECONOMIC

AG229. Gordon, David L., and Royden Dangerfield. The hidden weapon: the story of economic warfare. N.Y., 1947. Lucid analysis and account by State Department officials.
AG230. Hancock, William K., and Margaret M. Gowing. British war economy. London, 1949. 2nd ed., 1953. [U.K. official history: civil series.] The master volume of the series. Illuminating.
AG231. Medlicott, William N. The economic blockade. London, 1952 ff. [U.K. official history: civil series.] Based on official documents. Deals with political as well as economic problems.
AG232. Great Britain. Central Statistical Office. Statistical digest of the war. London, 1951.
AG233. Walton, Francis. Miracle of World War II: how American industry made victory possible. N.Y., 1956. Popular account.
Certain volumes of the *U. S. Army in World War II* are relevant to the history of economic warfare and the role of industrial potential.

BIOGRAPHY AND AUTOBIOGRAPHY

AG234. Bryant, Sir Arthur W. M. The turn of the tide. London, 1957. Based on the wartime diaries of Lord Alanbrooke.
AG235. Arnold, Henry H. Global mission. N.Y., 1949.
AG236. Bradley, Omar N. A soldier's story. N.Y., 1951.
AG237. Ciano, Galeazzo, conte. Diario, 1939–43. See *VE216*.
AG238. Clark, Mark W. Calculated risk: a personal story of the campaign in North Africa and Italy. N.Y., 1950.
AG239. Cunningham of Hyndhope, Andrew B., viscount. A sailor's odyssey. N.Y. and London, 1951.
AG240. Gamelin, Maurice G. Servir. 3 v. Paris, 1946–47.
AG241. Gaulle, Charles de. Mémoires de guerre. 2 v. Paris, 1954–56. These volumes cover 1940–44 and are an important contribution to the history of France and World War II. See also Maxime Weygand, *En lisant les Mémoires de guerre du Général de Gaulle* (Paris, 1955).
AG242. The Goebbels diaries. Tr. and ed. by Louis P. Lochner. N.Y. and London, 1948.

AG243. Graziani, Rodolfo. **Ho difeso la patria.** Milan, 1947.

AG244. Guderian, Heinz. **Panzer leader.** Tr. by Constantine Fitzgibbon. London, 1952.

AG245. Bor, Peter, ed. **Gespräche mit Halder.** Wiesbaden, 1950.

AG246. Sherwood, Robert E. **The White House papers of Harry L. Hopkins.** 2 v. London, 1949.

AG247. Hull, Cordell. **The memoirs of Cordell Hull.** See *AB417.*

AG248. Kesselring, Albert. **Soldat bis zum letzten Tag.** Bonn, 1953. Tr., *The memoirs of Field-Marshal Kesselring,* London, 1953.

AG249. Kimmel, Husband E. **Admiral Kimmel's story.** Chicago, 1955.

AG250. King, Ernest J., and Walter M. Whitehill. **Fleet Admiral King: a naval record.** N.Y., 1952.

AG251. Leahy, William D. **I was there.** See *AH240.*

AG252. Manstein, Erich von. **Verlorene Siege.** Bonn, 1955. Tr., *Lost victories,* Chicago, 1958.

AG253. Montgomery, Bernard L. **The memoirs of Field-Marshal the Viscount Montgomery of Alamein.** London, 1958.

AG254. Reynaud, Paul. **La France a sauvé l'Europe.** Paris, 1947.

AG255. Liddell Hart, B. H., ed. **The Rommel papers.** N.Y., 1953.

AG256. Stimson, Henry L., and McGeorge Bundy. **On active service in peace and war.** N.Y., 1948.

AG257. Dedijer, Vladimir. **Tito speaks.** See *AF341.*

AG258. Weygand, Maxime. **Rappelé au service.** Paris, 1950. Tr. by E. W. Dickes, *Recalled to service,* London, 1952.

International Relations: Political

HENRY L. ROBERTS and JANIS A. KRESLINS *

A bibliography of works on contemporary international relations, as in this and the following section, necessarily encounters many problems of definition and selection. In the first place, it must cut across national frontiers and may appropriately include works dealing with domestic developments as well as with foreign affairs—the two are often inseparable. In the second place, it concerns many disciplines—history, political science, law, and economics, to name only the most obvious. Finally, many of the most significant books for a study of recent and current affairs are not histories but works of diagnosis, prescription, prediction, or exhortation. The subject of international relations, then, leads off in many directions, and any bibliography serving as a section in a survey of historical literature must be somewhat arbitrary in what it includes. The following items represent only a small fraction of the available literature. For a more extensive annotative bibliography the reader may consult *Foreign affairs bibliography*, 1919–32, 1932–42, 1942–52, edited respectively by William L. Langer and Hamilton Fish Armstrong, Robert Gale Woolbert, and Henry L. Roberts. Much material from these volumes has been used, with the permission of the Council on Foreign Relations, in the preparation of these sections.

INTERNATIONAL POLITICS

BIBLIOGRAPHIES

AH1. Conover, Helen F. **A guide to bibliographical tools for research in foreign affairs.** Washington, 1956. [Library of Congress.] Excellent, particularly for use in connection with current affairs.

AH2. Foreign affairs bibliography. 3 v. N.Y., 1933–55. [Council on Foreign Relations.] An extensive, annotated bibliography of books published during the years 1919–52 in international affairs, contemporary history, and related fields. Based on notes appearing quarterly in *Foreign affairs,* but contains many thousand additional items.

AH3. International bibliography of political science. Bibliographie internationale de science politique. 1952 ff. Paris, 1953 ff. Annual bibliography of books, articles, and official publications.

AH4. Meyriat, Jean. **Étude des bibliographies courantes des publications officielles**

* The compilers of this section were assisted by William Diebold, Jr., Leland N. Goodrich, and Oliver J. Lissitzyn.

nationales. **A study of current bibliographies of national official publications.** Paris, 1958. A very useful guide and inventory.

ENCYCLOPEDIAS AND WORKS OF REFERENCE

AH5. Europa: the encyclopaedia of Europe; a survey and directory of European political, industrial, financial, cultural and scientific organisations, with sections on the Holy See, international organisations, and the United Nations. London, 1930 ff. (Title varies.) See under *AH6*.

AH6. Orbis: the encyclopaedia of extra-European countries; a survey and directory of political, industrial, financial, cultural and scientific organisations in the continents of Africa, America, Asia and Australasia. London, 1939 ff. This and *AH5* are useful reference works, produced in loose-leaf form to permit additions and revisions, published since 1959 as the *Europa Year Book*.

AH7. Political handbook of the world: parliaments, parties and press. N.Y., 1927 ff. (Annual. Title varies.) Compact reference giving names of leading members of the world's governments, identifying political parties and newspapers, and summarizing party programs.

AH8. The statesman's year-book. See *B133*.

AH9. Survey of international affairs. See *B156*.

AH10. The United States in world affairs. 1931 ff. N.Y., 1932 ff. [Council on Foreign Relations.] (Annual.) Valuable survey of the foreign policy and problems of the United States. In addition to the review and analysis of events, these volumes also contain useful chronologies and bibliographies.

AH11. The year book of world affairs. 1947 ff. N.Y., 1947 ff. (Annual.) Though called yearbooks, the volumes in this series contain articles and brief monographs on a variety of specific political, legal, economic, and cultural problems.

POLITICAL GEOGRAPHY

AH12. Banciella y Bárzana, José C. **Espacio y economía.** Madrid, 1945. A Spanish variation on the theme of geopolitics. Does not cover the world systematically, but concentrates on certain areas interesting for strategic or other reasons.

AH13. Boggs, Samuel W. **International boundaries: a study of boundary functions and problems.** N.Y., 1940. Authoritative treatise on the classification of boundaries, their function in the life of nations, and the various problems they create or solve.

AH14. Dorpalen, Andreas. **The world of General Haushofer: geopolitics in action.** N.Y., 1942. A simple exposition of the principles of geopolitics, containing numerous excerpts from geopolitical writings.

AH15. Goblet, Yann M. **Le crépuscule des traités.** Paris, 1934. Broad conspectus of international affairs which favors the determination of foreign policy in accord with geographical rather than historical or legal considerations.

AH16. Whittlesey, Derwent S. **The earth and the state: a study of political geography.** New ed., N.Y., 1944. A solid general study.

GENERAL WORKS

AH17. Bryce, James B., viscount. **International relations.** N.Y., 1922. Mature reflective generalizations on the chief problems in international relations, such as war and its prevention, popular control of foreign policy, etc.

AH18. Burnham, James. **The managerial revolution: what is happening in the world.** N.Y., 1941. Historically an important work despite its inconsistencies. The author forsees an era in which the new ruling class will consist of those who manage the productive machine.

AH19. Mander, Linden. **Foundations of modern world society.** Rev. ed., Stanford, 1947. Comprehensive survey of the subject of international relations.

AH20. Russell, Frank M. **Theories of international relations.** N.Y., 1936. A historical introduction.

AH21. Schuman, Frederick L. **The commonwealth of man: an inquiry into power politics and world government.** N.Y., 1952. Asserts that world government, the only feasible escape from the existing situation, can be attained, if at all, through a "voluntary extension of the principles of federalism to the whole society of nations," and not through the "functionalist" approach or by the way of collective security.

AH22. Simonds, Frank H., and Brooks Emeny. **The great powers in world politics: international relations and economic nationalism.** New ed., N.Y., 1939. A standard work. Emphasis throughout the book is on the world's economic resources—their distribution and their political significance. Bibliography.

AH23. Steiner, Harold A. **Principles and problems of international relations.** N.Y., 1940. Comprehensive summary of the principles and a competent survey of the problems. Bibliography.

AH24. Strausz-Hupé, Robert, and Stefan T. Possony. **International relations in the age of the conflict between democracy and dictatorship.** 2nd ed., N.Y., 1954. A textbook which emphasizes the "principle of power accumulation" as the regulator of the behavior of governments. Bibliographies.

AH25. Strausz-Hupé, Robert. **The zone of**

indifference. N.Y., 1952. Thoughtful commentary on the contemporary crisis of the western community.

POWER AND POWER POLITICS

AH26. Aron, Raymond. **The century of total war.** Garden City, 1954. Though writing in the first instance as a Frenchman to Frenchmen, Aron's very thoughtful and incisive analysis is of universal interest. Seeing the world in the midst of a chain reaction of wars, he seeks some way of mastering violence and yet preserving liberty.

AH27. Arnold, G. L. **The pattern of world conflict.** N.Y., 1955. "Coexistence and the cold war are in fact two sides of the same medal. To win the cold war is to make coexistence possible." In pursuit of this theme, the author emphasizes the importance of the Atlantic world and the need to modernize backward countries with a pragmatic use of public planning.

AH28. Morgenthau, Hans J. **Politics among nations: the struggle for power and peace.** See *A115.*

AH29. Ritter, Gerhard. **The corrupting influence of power.** Essex, Eng., 1952. Using Thomas More and Machiavelli as contrasting symbols, the author, an eminent German historian, discusses the problem of power and power politics in modern times. The work, originally appearing in 1940 as *Machtstaat und Utopie*, was expanded and greatly revised after Hitler's death, appearing as *Die Dämonie der Macht* (Munich, 1948), the basis of the English translation.

AH30. Schwarzenberger, Georg. **Power politics: a study of international society.** 2nd rev. ed., N.Y., 1951. This "introduction to the study of international relations and postwar planning" is a work of wide scope and deep learning. The author has digested a vast amount of literature and has sought to give a sociological analysis of the fundamental forces in international politics. Bibliography.

AH31. Strausz-Hupé, Robert. **The balance of tomorrow: power and foreign policy in the United States.** N.Y., 1945. An effort to evaluate the changing distribution of power in the world, especially industrial power, in terms of political rivalries. The inevitable result is to fix attention on the power potential of Russia and the Far East.

SELF-DETERMINATION

AH32. Cobban, Alfred. **National self-determination.** N.Y., 1945. [Royal Institute of International Affairs.] Important study in the area where political philosophy and international relations meet and overlap, based upon careful historical analysis of the relevant documentary material.

AH33. Decker, Günter. **Das Selbstbestimmungsrecht der Nationen.** Göttingen, 1955. Extensive theoretical and historical analysis of the principles and application of national self-determination. Examples are drawn from all regions of the globe. Bibliography.

POLITICAL PHILOSOPHIES AND IDEOLOGIES

Communism

AH34. Almond, Gabriel A., and others. **The appeals of communism.** Princeton, 1954. Based on case studies in France, Italy, England, and the United States, this book deals with the appeals which have led people into the Communist party.

AH35. Borkenau, Franz. **World communism: a history of the Communist International.** N.Y., 1939. The author, formerly a member of the German Communist party, was until 1929 rapporteur on the international labor movement for the Comintern, but later forswore Marxism. This work, though not always objective, is an invaluable mine of information about the worldwide activities of the Communist International. Bibliographical notes.

AH36. ———. **European communism.** N.Y., 1953. While in many respects stimulating and informative, this is a somewhat disappointing sequel to the author's earlier work. Borkenau's intricate exposition of the developments in Communist policy over the last two decades is not always convincing and sometimes goes beyond available evidence. Of particular interest is the section on France, which receives special attention as the "stronghold of European communism."

AH37. Bouscaren, Anthony T. **Imperial communism.** Washington, 1953. Primarily a summary of Communist parties and activities around the world.

AH38. Degras, Jane, ed. **The Communist International, 1919–1943: documents.** 2 vols., N.Y., 1956–60. [Royal Institute of International Affairs.] These volumes of selected documents on the aims and policies of the Communist International cover a major period.

AH39. Ebon, Martin. **World communism today.** N.Y., 1948. Author has painstakingly assembled a mass of relevant information about Communist parties throughout the world from Russia to Haiti. Bibliography.

AH40. Hunt, Robert N. C. **The theory and practice of communism.** Rev. ed., N.Y., 1951. Concise and clear introduction to Marxist theory and its development through Lenin and Stalin. Bibliography.

AH41. Communist International. **Kommunisticheskii Internatsional pered VII**

vsemirnym kongressom. Moscow, 1935. An official collection of material on the policy and functions of the Comintern.

AH42. ——. **Kommunisticheskii Internatsional v dokumentakh.** Moscow, 1933. Huge collection of documents on the congresses of the Communist International, 1919–32.

AH43. Lazitch, Branko M. **Les partis communistes d'Europe, 1919–1955.** Paris, 1956. A concise manual on the Communist parties of the various European states, giving a short history of each party, its membership and voting strength, and sketches of party leaders.

AH44. Monnerot, Jules. **Sociologie du communisme.** Paris, 1949. A stimulating if somewhat chaotic analysis of Soviet communism—a "twentieth century Islam." An abridged English translation has been published as *Sociology and psychology of communism* (Boston, 1953).

AH45. Possony, Stefan T. **A century of conflict: Communist techniques of world revolution.** Chicago, 1953. An effort to delineate the Soviet pattern of conquest through a historical survey of "the development of the Communist doctrine of conflict management."

AH46. Rosenberg, Arthur. **A history of bolshevism from Marx to the first five years' plan.** N.Y. and London, 1939.

AH47. Seton-Watson, Hugh. **From Lenin to Malenkov: the history of world communism.** N.Y., 1953. Comparative analysis of Communist movements on the world scale. A valuable general survey displaying comprehension and insight. Bibliography.

AH48. Wetter, Gustavo A. **Der dialektische Materialismus.** Rev. and enl. ed. from the original Italian, Vienna, 1952. Eng. translation from the German, N.Y., 1958. An exceptionally thorough, scholarly, and dispassionate examination, both historical and analytical, of the development of Soviet dialectical materialism, by a Jesuit professor of Russian philosophy. Bibliography.

Socialism

AH49. Schumpeter, Joseph A. **Capitalism, socialism, and democracy.** 3rd ed., N.Y., 1950. Stimulating and penetrating critique of Marxian doctrines, a prediction of the "inevitable decomposition of capitalist society," and appraisal of the practicability of socialism as an alternative, together with a review of the history of Socialist parties in the principal countries.

AH50. Sternberg, Fritz. **Capitalism and socialism on trial.** N.Y., 1951. Arguing in the framework of the under-consumptionist tradition, the author elaborates his thesis that capitalism was kept afloat by imperialism, that imperialism is no longer a feasible

support, and hence that the new international order, which he definitely does not identify with the Soviet system, must be socialist. Bibliography.

Totalitarianism

AH51. Arendt, Hannah. **The origins of totalitarianism.** N.Y., 1951. Author derives modern totalitarianism from three currents —anti-Semitism, overseas imperialism with its undermining of the nation-state, and tribal nationalism. Some of her historical generalizations are questionable and too much interpretation is from the particular experience of Germany; but the book abounds in challenging and original insights, and it constitutes a major contribution to our comprehension of this fearful phenomenon of the 20th century. Bibliography.

AH52. Friedrich, Carl J., and Zbigniew K. Brzezinski. **Totalitarian dictatorship and autocracy.** Cambridge, Mass., 1956. An effort, as the authors put it, "to delineate, on the basis of fairly generally known and acknowledged factual data, the general model of totalitarian dictatorship and of the society which it has created."

AH53. American Academy of Arts and Sciences. **Totalitarianism: proceedings of a conference held at the American Academy of Arts and Sciences, March, 1953.** Ed. by Carl J. Friedrich. Cambridge, Mass., 1954. Useful and stimulating symposium of articles.

AH54. Wittfogel, Karl A. **Oriental despotism: a comparative study of total power.** New Haven, 1957. Massive study of the roots of bureaucratic totalitarianism. The term "hydraulic" is used to describe those societies in which centralized control and management of irrigation and agriculture led to a static and pervasive despotism. Bibliography.

Nationalism

AH55. Flournoy, Richard W., and Manley O. Hudson, eds. **A collection of nationality laws of various countries, as contained in constitutions, statutes and treaties.** N.Y., 1929. [Carnegie Endowment for International Peace.] An authoritative compilation. Bibliography.

AH56. Pinson, Koppel S. **A bibliographical introduction to nationalism.** N.Y., 1935. A useful bibliography.

AH57. Hayes, Carlton J. H. **Essays on nationalism.** N.Y., 1926. Excellent series of studies on nationalism and its historical development. Bibliography.

AH58. ——. **The historical evolution of modern nationalism.** See *C121.*

AH59. Kohn, Hans. **The idea of nationalism: a study in its origin and background.**

N.Y., 1944. History of the idea of nationalism from ancient Hebrew and Greek times down to the present. Bibliography.

Imperialism; Colonial Problems

AH60. Ragatz, Lowell J. **The literature of European imperialism, 1815–1939.** 3rd rev. ed., Washington, 1947. Good, selective list of books and articles.

AH61. Clark, Grover. **A place in the sun.** N.Y., 1936. Develops the thesis that colonies have been economically unprofitable to the imperial nations.

AH62. ——. **The balance sheets of imperialism: facts and figures on colonies.** N.Y., 1936. [Carnegie Endowment for International Peace.] Statistical evidence to support the thesis advanced in *AH61*. Bibliography.

AH63. Cordero Torres, José M. **Politica colonial.** Madrid, 1953. Extensive, systematic treatise on colonial policy: the moral and political issues involved, the development of European colonialism, and future problems.

AH64. Fanno, Marco. **La teoria economica della colonizzazione.** Turin, 1952. This study, based on much earlier theoretical writings of the author, deals both with colonial expansion of modern states and economic development of the colonial lands themselves.

AH65. Lenin, Vladimir I. **Imperialism.** N.Y., 1933. Translation of Lenin's famous essay interpreting modern imperialism as the "highest stage of capitalism."

AH66. Maalem, Ali. **Colonialisme, trusteeship, indépendance.** Paris, 1946. Ambitious survey by an Algerian scholar. Bibliography.

AH67. Mannoni, Dominique O. **Prospero and Caliban: the psychology of colonization.** N.Y., 1956. Extremely interesting and stimulating psychological analysis of some of the more baffling features of human and social relations in colonial areas, drawn from the author's experience in Madagascar. The original French edition, *Psychologie de la colonisation*, was published in 1950. Bibliography.

AH68. Maunier, René. **The sociology of colonies.** See *U226*.

AH69. Moon, Parker T. **Imperialism and world politics.** N.Y., 1926. General account of imperialism and its expression in the 19th and early 20th centuries.

AH70. Peffer, Nathaniel. **The white man's dilemma: climax of the age of imperialism.** N.Y., 1927. The economic side of imperialism discussed without recriminations.

AH71. Schumpeter, Joseph A. **Imperialism and social classes.** N.Y., 1951. A major contribution to theories of imperialism, translated from *Zur Soziologie der Imperialismen* (1919) and *Die sozialen Klassen im ethnisch homogenen Milieu* (1927).

AH72. Sternberg, Fritz. **Der Imperialismus.** Berlin, 1926. Full-length Marxist indictment of imperialism.

AH73. Touzet, André. **Le problème colonial et la paix du monde.** 4 v. Paris, 1937–38. The author of this comprehensive work served as a high French official in Indo-China. V. 1 treats Germany's colonial claims; 2, Italian and Japanese expansion; 3 and 4, more general questions. Bibliography.

AH74. Townsend, Mary E. **European colonial expansion since 1871.** See *U66*.

AH75. Winslow, Earle M. **The pattern of imperialism: a study in the theories of power.** N.Y., 1948. Of interest for the author's useful exposition and analysis of the various theories of economic imperialism. Bibliography.

AH76. Woolf, Leonard S. **Imperialism and civilization.** N.Y., 1928. Brief survey of the history of European imperialism in Asia and Africa.

WAR; MILITARY PROBLEMS

Yearbooks and Handbooks

AH77. **Armaments year-book.** 15 v. Geneva, 1924–40. [League of Nations.] Annual survey of armaments and military expenditures.

AH78. **Brassey's annual.** N.Y., etc., 1886 ff. (Title and place of pub. vary.) This useful yearbook includes information on the world's armies, navies, and air forces, as well as articles on military topics.

AH79. **Les flottes de combat.** Paris, 1897 ff. (Irregular. Title varies.) The French equivalent of *Jane's fighting ships.*

AH80. **Jane's fighting ships.** London, 1898 ff. (Title varies.) An annually revised standard reference. Illustrations and text.

General Works

AH81. Bouthoul, Gaston. **Les guerres, éléments de polémologie: méthodes, doctrines et opinions sur la guerre, morphologie, éléments techniques, démographiques, économiques, psychologiques, périodicité.** Paris, 1951. This ambitious sociological inquiry into the nature of war reviews the theories on the subject, discusses its economic, demographic, and psychological aspects, and classifies the causes of conflict.

AH82. Earle, Edward M., and others, eds. **Makers of modern strategy: military thought from Machiavelli to Hitler.** See *T207*.

AH83. Falls, Cyril B. **A hundred years of war.** N.Y., 1954. Able history of warfare over the century 1850–1950, with particular emphasis on strategy, tactics, weapons, and administration. Bibliography.

AH84. Liddell Hart, Basil H. **Strategy: the indirect approach.** 3rd ed., London, 1954. A major treatise on military strategy. Develops the thesis that frontal assaults and massive showdowns should be avoided, and that it is preferable to aim at the enemy's line of least expectation. Bibliography.

AH85. Montross, Lynn. **War through the ages.** Rev. and enl. ed., N.Y., 1946. History of the "art" of war from ancient Greek days down to our own. Not much interpretation of causes or of broader issues, but within its restricted field a useful work of reference. Bibliography.

AH86. Nef, John U. **War and human progress: an essay on the rise of industrial civilization.** Cambridge, Mass., 1950. To combat the view that war is a stimulus to economic progress, this ambitious and scholarly study traces the historical development of warfare and its weapons from the 16th century. Laying heavy stress upon the independent force of ideas, the author finds that in the 20th century a failure in manners and morals has sanctioned the use of deadly weapons and brought on the age of total war. Bibliography.

AH87. Wright, Quincy. **A study of war.** 2 v. Chicago, 1942. V. 1 of this important work examines the history of warfare from earliest times; while v. 2 analyzes war into its various political, sociological, economic, cultural, and other causes and motivations. The treatise concludes with suggestions for the future control of war.

PEACE; DISARMAMENT

AH88. Hosono, Gunji. **Histoire du désarmement.** Paris, 1933. A history of demilitarization and the disarmament question before and after World War I.

AH89. Lapradelle, Albert G. de. **La paix moderne (1899–1945) de La Haye à San Francisco: tableau d'ensemble avec la documentation correspondante.** Paris, 1947. Review of progress made toward institutionalizing peace since 1899, followed by the principal documents which illustrate the record.

AH90. Lavallaz, Maurice de. **Essai sur le désarmement et le pacte de la Société des Nations.** Paris, 1926. A conscientious investigation, covering the question as it presented itself to the Versailles peace conference and as it was dealt with in various drafts for a League covenant.

AH91. Madariaga, Salvador de. **Disarmament.** N.Y., 1929. One of the more outstanding books on the problem by the former chief of the disarmament section of the League.

AH92. **Handbuch des Abrüstungsproblems.** Ed. by Theodor Niemeyer. 3 v. Berlin, 1928. A monumental treatment. V. 1 is systematic, written by an imposing array of experts; the others include all important papers on the subject between 1816 and 1925.

AH93. Schwendemann, Karl. **Abrüstung und Sicherheit.** 2 v. Berlin, 1933–36. Useful compilation of source and reference material concerning disarmament and security questions.

AH94. Tate, Merze. **The United States and armaments.** Cambridge, Mass., 1948. Summary of United States participation in disarmament conferences and schemes, particularly since World War I. Bibliography.

COLLECTIVE SECURITY

AH95. Brugière, Pierre F. **La sécurité collective, 1919–1945.** Paris, 1946. Much of this work consists of texts of relevant treaties, pacts, conventions, and other international instruments illustrating the rise and fall of the League of Nations and the origins of the United Nations. Bibliography.

AH96. Hogan, Willard N. **International conflict and collective security: the principle of concern in international organization.** Lexington, Ky., 1955. A recognition that conflict among the members of a group affects the entire group, as the basis for a system of collective security, with particular reference to the period since World War I.

AH97. Hoijer, Olof. **La sécurité internationale et ses modes de réalisation.** 4 v. Paris, 1930. Examines in detail the working of alliances and guarantees of neutrality, agreements like the Locarno and Kellogg pacts, methods for the pacific solution of disputes, and the problems of disarmament.

AH98. Martin, Andrew. **Collective security: a progress report.** Paris, 1952. Review of 20th century efforts to regulate armaments, obtain pacific settlements of disputes, and undertake collective action. Bibliography.

AH99. Raafat, Waheed. **Le problème de la sécurité internationale.** Paris, 1930. A substantial historical introduction followed by an analysis of the problem as it presented itself at the Versailles peace conference and during the first post-war decade.

AH100. Rappard, William E. **The quest for peace since the World War.** Cambridge, Mass., 1940. Efforts at arbitration, collective security, and disarmament in the inter-war period.

INTERNATIONAL RELATIONS SINCE WORLD WAR I

DOCUMENTS; TREATIES

United States

AH101. Foreign relations of the United States: diplomatic papers. Washington, 1861 ff. [Department of State.] (Title varies.) This important collection of official papers comprises a series of volumes compiled on an annual basis. Special volumes include *The Lansing papers, 1914–1920* (2 v., 1939); *Japan, 1931–1941* (2 v., 1943); *The Paris peace conference, 1919* (13 v., 1942–47); *The Soviet Union, 1933–1939* (1952); *The conferences at Malta and Yalta, 1945* (1955); and *China, 1942* (1956).

AH102. U. S. Senate. Committee on Foreign Relations. **A decade of American foreign policy: basic documents, 1941–49, prepared at the request of the Senate Committee on Foreign Relations by the staff of the committee and the Department of State.** Washington, 1950. [Senate Doc. 123, 81st Congress, 1st Session.]

AH103. U. S. Department of State. **American foreign policy, 1950–1955: basic documents.** 2 v. Washington, 1957. [Publication 6446 of Department of State. General foreign policy series 117.] This and *AH102* are very useful and comprehensive collections of documents.

AH104. Documents on American foreign relations. 1938 ff. N.Y., etc., 1939 ff. [V. 1–13, World Peace Foundation; v. 14 ff., Council on Foreign Relations.] (Annual. Place of pub. varies.) Extremely useful series which provides a wealth of documentation for the contemporary historian.

German

AH105. Documents on German foreign policy, 1918–1945: from the archives of the German Foreign Ministry. See *AF355*.

AH106. Sontag, Raymond J., and James S. Beddie, eds. **Nazi-Soviet relations, 1939–1941.** N.Y., 1948. [U. S. Department of State.] This selection from the immense mass of German documents captured by the U. S. First Army tells the story of the Russo-German rapprochement ending in the Nazi invasion of June 1941. An important source, but not well translated.

AH107. Documents and materials relating to the eve of the Second World War. 2 v. Moscow, 1948. [Ministry of Foreign Affairs of the U.S.S.R.] This was published by the Soviet government in reply to *AH106.* V. 1 contains documents (in English translation) from the German Foreign Office relating chiefly to the Munich affair of 1938; v. 2

consists of private papers found on the estate of Herbert von Dirksen, German ambassador in London during that same period.

AH108. Dokumenty Ministerstva inostrannykh del Germanii. 3 v. Moscow, 1946. Contains 138 documents selected from German Foreign Office materials now in Soviet possession, dealing with German policy regarding Hungary, 1937–42 (v. 1), Turkey, 1941–43 (v. 2), and Spain, 1936–43 (v. 3). Though the purpose behind their publication apparently was to convict these three governments of full complicity in Nazi policy, this promise is not borne out. In selecting documents, the compilers omitted important accompanying telegrams and despatches to which reference is made in the texts published. The documents, originally all in German, appear here in Russian translation. A French translation from the Russian has been published as *Documents secrets du Ministère des Affaires Étrangères d'Allemagne* (3 v., Paris, 1946).

AH109. Neumann, Inge S. **European war crimes trials: a bibliography.** N.Y., 1951. Excellent guide to the voluminous literature on the Nuremberg and other war crimes trials held after the end of World War II. Contains an annotated list of materials published between 1941 and 1950.

AH110. Weinberg, Gerhard L. **Guide to captured German documents.** Montgomery, Ala., 1952. A most useful inventory and guide to German materials "which through capture, confiscation, purchase, donation, salvage, etc." were transferred to non-German control during and after World War II.

Soviet

AH111. Degras, Jane. **Calendar of Soviet documents on foreign policy, 1917–1941.** N.Y. and London, 1948. The document titles are arranged by year groups and country, and references are given to Russian and other sources.

AH112. ——, ed. **Soviet documents on foreign policy.** 3 v. N.Y., 1951–53. These volumes of selected documents from the Revolution to the German invasion of 1941 bring together and translate much material not otherwise easily accessible.

AH113. Meissner, Boris, comp. **Das Ostpakt-System: Dokumentensammlung.** 2nd ed., Frankfurt-am-Main, 1955. Collection of documents relating to the post-1945 Soviet system of pacts and treaties in Europe and Asia.

AH114. Shapiro, Leonard, ed. **Soviet**

treaty series: a collection of bilateral treaties, agreements and conventions, etc., concluded between the Soviet Union and foreign powers. 2 v. Washington, 1950–55. A series which presents "every bilateral diplomatic instrument to which the Soviet Government has become a party since 1917."

Speeches, notes, official communiqués, etc., dealing with Soviet foreign policy may be found in the titles listed below.

AH115. Dokumenti vneshnei politiki SSSR. Moscow, 1957 ff. From Nov. 7, 1917 on.

AH116. Vneshniaia politika SSSR: sbornik dokumentov. Moscow, 1946. Covers part of the inter-war period.

AH117. Vneshniaia politika Sovetskogo Soiuza v period Otechestvennoi voiny. 3 v. Moscow, 1944–47. Covers the years of World War II. Two volumes in this series have been translated into English as *Soviet foreign policy during the patriotic war* (London, 1946).

AH118. Vneshniaia politika Sovetskogo Soiuza 1945–. Moscow, 1949 ff. Presents the material since 1945 on an annual or semi-annual basis.

British, French, Japanese, Italian, etc.

AH119. Woodward, Ernest L., and Rohan Butler, eds. **Documents on British foreign policy, 1919–1939.** London, 1946 ff. An indispensable source for the study of British foreign policy, and indeed of many aspects of international affairs, during the inter-war period. The documents are being published simultaneously in three series, starting respectively with 1919, 1929, and 1938.

AH120. Italy. Ministero degli Affari Esteri. **I documenti diplomatici italiani: ottava serie, 1935–1939.** 2 v. Rome, 1952–53. Well-edited collection of Italian diplomatic documents. Two volumes published cover period May 23–Sep. 3, 1939.

AH121. Uyehara, Cecil H. **Checklist of archives in the Japanese Ministry of Foreign Affairs, Tokyo, Japan, 1868–1945: microfilmed for the Library of Congress, 1949–1951.** Washington, 1954. A most useful guide.

AH122. La délégation française auprès de la commission allemande d'armistice: recueil de documents publié par le gouvernement français. 4 v. Paris, 1947–57. Important compilation of documents dealing with the French-German armistice negotiations after the initial defeat of France in 1940.

AH123. Documents on international affairs. 1928 ff. N.Y., 1929 ff. [Royal Institute of International Affairs.] (Annual.) Very useful reference work designed to supplement and illustrate the corresponding volumes in *Survey of international affairs* (*AH9*).

ARMISTICE AND PEACE TREATIES

Reference Works

AH124. Lapradelle, Albert G. de, ed. **La documentation internationale: la paix de Versailles.** 14 pts. in 12 v. Paris, 1929–39. Important collection of minutes of peace conference commissions together with other documents.

AH125. Great Britain. Foreign Office. **Handbooks prepared under the direction of the historical section of the Foreign Office.** Ed. by Sir G. W. Prothero. 162 pts. in 25 v. London, 1920. Monographs prepared for information and use of the British delegates to the Paris peace conference, and dealing with practically every state and colony or disputed area in the world at that time. Each number presents a concise historical survey indicating the status of the areas, summarizing their international relations and problems, and containing a considerable amount of descriptive and statistical information. Convenient, sometimes excellent, introductions to the regions concerned.

AH126. Schücking, Walther M., ed. **Vorveröffentlichung aus dem Kommentar zum Friedensvertrage.** 8 v. Berlin, 1920–21. Analysis and critique of the treaty of Versailles.

AH127. Kraus, Herbert, and Gustav Rödiger, eds. **Urkunden zum Friedensvertrage von Versailles vom 28. Juni 1919.** 2 v. Berlin, 1920–21. Documents supplementing *AH126*.

AH128. Temperley, Harold W. V., ed. **A history of the peace conference of Paris.** 6 v. London, 1920–24. [Royal Institute of International Affairs.] Indispensable work written by English and U.S. experts. Still a standard account of the conference, how it was organized, and how it carried out its duties.

General Surveys

AH129. Churchill, Winston S. **The world crisis: the aftermath.** N.Y., 1929. The concluding volume of Churchill's brilliant memoirs of World War I, covering the years 1918–22, the peace conference, the Russian situation, the Near East crisis, the Irish problem, and other controversial matters.

AH130. Haskins, Charles H., and Robert H. Lord. **Some problems of the peace conference.** Cambridge, Mass., 1920. Deals chiefly with territorial and boundary problems. Bibliography.

AH131. Lloyd George, David. **Memoirs of the peace conference.** 2 v. New Haven, 1939. Though they contain much valuable information as well as pungent portraits of the leading personages at Paris, these volumes are vitiated by the author's desire to present his own case in the best possible light.

AH132. Mantoux, Étienne. **The Carthaginian peace, or the economic consequences of Mr. Keynes.** N.Y., 1946. With minor exceptions, this interesting book is a political rather than an economic tract. It attacks Keynes' *Economic consequences of the peace* and maintains that the thesis which it established was an important factor in causing World War II.

AH133. Mantoux, Paul J. **Les délibérations du Conseil des Quatre (24 mars–28 juin 1919).** 2 v. Paris, 1955. Notes on the sessions of the Council of Four at the Versailles conference, taken by the author in his capacity as interpreter. An important source in supplementing the record prepared by Sir Maurice Hankey in *Papers relating to the foreign relations of the United States: the Paris peace conference*, v. 5 and 6.

AH134. Marston, Frank S. **The peace conference of 1919: organization and procedure.** N.Y., 1944. Valuable monograph which traces the process by which the transition from war to peace was effected between 1918 and 1920. Attention is primarily to organizational problems rather than substance of the treaties. Bibliography.

AH135. Nicolson, Harold G. **Peacemaking, 1919.** Boston, 1933. The first part of this book is a critique of the peace conference in the light of experience, with a full and intelligent, if subjective, appraisal of its misfortunes, mistakes, and merits. The second part is made up of selections from the diary of the author, one of the British territorial experts at Paris.

AH136. Carnegie Endowment for International Peace. **Official statements of war aims and peace proposals, December 1916 to November 1918.** Ed. by James Brown Scott. Washington, 1921. An exhaustive compilation, useful for reference.

AH137. Stephens, Waldo E. **Revisions of the treaty of Versailles.** N.Y., 1939. Monograph on the changes made in the treaty since its signature. Bibliography.

AH138. Tardieu, André P. G. A. **The truth about the treaty.** Indianapolis, 1921. French ed., *La paix* (Paris, 1921). Able and vigorous defense of the treaty of Versailles by Clemenceau's chief lieutenant. The French and English editions differ considerably, each omitting much that is in the other.

AH139. U. S. Department of State. **The treaty of Versailles and after: annotations of the text of the treaty.** Washington, 1947. An extensive gloss consisting of "factual notes which briefly record the actions taken in consequence of the provisions of most of the 440 articles of the Treaty of Versailles and the annexes thereto."

U. S. at the Paris Peace Conference

AH140. Bailey, Thomas A. **Woodrow Wilson and the great betrayal.** See *AB415.*

AH141. ——. **Woodrow Wilson and the lost peace.** See *AB414.*

AH142. Baker, Ray Stannard. **What Wilson did at Paris.** Garden City, 1919. A sympathetic contemporary interpretation.

AH143. ——. **Woodrow Wilson and world settlement: written from his unpublished and personal material.** 3 v. Garden City, 1922. While sympathetic with Wilson's policies, this work is primarily expository. V. 3 contains a very complete collection of documentary material.

AH144. Birdsall, Paul. **Versailles twenty years after.** See *AF255.*

AH145. House, Edward M. **The intimate papers of Colonel House.** Ed. by Charles Seymour. 4 v. Boston, 1926–28. The highly important papers of President Wilson's confidential adviser, covering the period from House's mission to Europe on the eve of the war through the peace conference of 1919.

AH146. House, Edward M., and Charles Seymour. **What really happened at Paris: the story of the peace conference, 1918–1919, by American delegates.** N.Y., 1921. A series of lectures by U. S. plenipotentiaries and experts at the conference.

AH147. Kennan, George F. **Soviet-American relations, 1917–1920.** 2 v. Princeton, 1956–58. V. 1, *Russia leaves the war*, covers the period from the November revolution to Russia's final withdrawal from the war in March 1918. V. 2, *The decision to intervene*, discusses the events preceding and following the decision by President Wilson to intervene with troops in northern Russia. A very valuable and illuminating study. Bibliography.

AH148. Lansing, Robert. **The peace negotiations: a personal narrative.** Boston, 1921. An account by Wilson's secretary of state.

AH149. Miller, David H. **My diary at the conference of Paris: with documents.** 21 v. N.Y., 1924. An immense and exceedingly valuable collection of documentary material, by a legal adviser of the U. S. delegation. The forty sets printed were distributed among the important libraries of the United States and Europe.

AH150. Shotwell, James T. **At the Paris peace conference.** N.Y., 1937. Professor Shotwell was one of the leading experts in Colonel House's "inquiry." Except for five introductory chapters of "retrospect," this book consists of Shotwell's diary from Dec. 3, 1918 to July 9, 1919.

Other Countries in Post-World War I Settlements

AH151. Albrecht-Carrié, René. **Italy at the Paris peace conference.** N.Y., 1938. A scholarly diplomatic history; richly documented. Bibliography.

AH152. Almond, Nina, and Ralph H. Lutz, eds. **The treaty of St. Germain: a documentary history of its territorial and political clauses, with a survey of the documents of the supreme council of the Paris peace conference.** Stanford, 1935. Careful review of the history and provisions of the treaty.

AH153. Deák, Francis. **Hungary at the Paris peace conference: the diplomatic history of the treaty of Trianon.** N.Y., 1942. Able history of the Hungarian question at the Versailles conference. Bibliography.

AH154. Hofmannsthal, Emil von, ed. **Der deutsche und österreichische Friedensvertrag.** Vienna, 1920. Guide to the treaties of Versailles and St. Germain.

AH155. Luckau, Alma M. **The German delegation at the Paris peace conference.** N.Y., 1941. History of Germany's participation in the peacemaking of 1919. About four-fifths consists of relevant documents. Bibliography.

AH156. Pingaud, Albert. **Histoire diplomatique de la France pendant la grande guerre.** 3 v. Paris, 1938–40. Competent narrative by a former director of the archives at the French foreign office. Bibliography.

AH157. Rudin, Harry R. **Armistice 1918.** New Haven, 1944. A sound, carefully documented history of the way the armistice came about. The record, as the author exposes it on the basis of abundant documentation, punctures the claim that the kaiser's army was defeated, not in the field, but by the homeland's "stab in the back."

AH158. Stein, Boris E. **"Russkii vopros" na Parizhskoi mirnoi konferentsii, 1919–1920 gg.** Moscow, 1949. A Soviet diplomatic study of the Russian question at the Paris peace conference and of the complex pattern of civil war and intervention on Russia's borders.

AH159. Wheeler-Bennett, John W. **The forgotten peace: Brest-Litovsk, March 1918.** N.Y., 1939. Interesting, dramatic, and substantial narrative. Bibliography.

INTER-WAR YEARS

General Treatments

AH160. Baumont, Maurice. **La faillite de la paix (1918–1939).** 3rd rev. ed., 2 v., Paris, 1951. A solid and valuable history of the inter-war period.

AH161. Carr, Edward H. **International relations between the two world wars, 1919–1939.** See *AF51*.

AH162. ——. **The twenty years' crisis, 1919–1939: an introduction to the study of international relations.** 2nd ed., London, 1946. Sharp criticism of some of the leading concepts and institutions of the inter-war period; particularly critical of the Wilsonian tradition.

AH163. Craig, Gordon A., and Felix Gilbert, eds. **The diplomats, 1919–1939.** Princeton, 1953. Seventeen authors collaborated in this diplomatic history, based for the most part on the careers of individual diplomats and officials in the foreign offices.

AH164. Dotremont, Stanislas. **L'arbitrage international et le Conseil de la Société des Nations.** Brussels, 1929. Authoritative monograph on the machinery of arbitration as it worked under the League system.

AH165. D'Abernon, Edgar V. **The diary of an ambassador.** 3 v. N.Y., 1929–30. Important memoirs and impressions of the British ambassador to Berlin, covering the years 1920–26.

AH166. Duroselle, Jean B. **Histoire diplomatique de 1919 à nos jours.** Paris, 1953. Though designed as a manual, this history of the period 1919–51 is a solid and useful synthesis. Confining itself to the traditional limits of diplomatic history, it is based on wide reading and acquaintance with the sources. Bibliography.

AH167. Gathorne-Hardy, Geoffrey M. **A short history of international affairs, 1920–1939.** 4th ed., London and N.Y., 1950. One of the more satisfactory surveys of international relations in the inter-war years. First published in 1934, it has been revised and expanded to take account of subsequent events and new information.

AH168. Habicht, Max, ed. **Post-war treaties for the pacific settlement of international disputes.** Cambridge, Mass., 1931. Larger part of volume is devoted to texts of all such treaties concluded in first decade after World War I. Author also analyzes and compares various types of agreement and systems of settlement.

AH169. Haines, Charles G., and Ross J. S. Hoffman. **The origins and background of the Second World War.** 2nd ed., N.Y., 1947. Useful factual history of the period between the two world wars.

AH170. Holborn, Hajo. **The political collapse of Europe.** N.Y., 1951. Rich and reflective interpretation of the contemporary world scene in terms of the historical evolution of the European states-system. Author concludes that in World War II the "collapse of the traditional European system became an irrevocable fact." Bibliography.

AH171. Howe, Quincy. **A world history of our own times.** 2 v. N.Y., 1949–53. Part of a projected 3 v. series aimed at the layman.

AH172. Jordan, W. M. **Great Britain, France, and the German problem, 1918–1939.** N.Y., 1943. A serious effort to unravel the main threads of "Anglo-French relations in the making and maintenance of the Versailles settlement."

AH173. Lukacs, John A. **The great powers and eastern Europe.** N.Y., 1953. Stimulating and substantial survey of diplomatic relations in and relating to eastern Europe between 1917 and the falling of the Iron Curtain. The author is generally critical of the policies of western powers, and especially of the United States position vis-à-vis the Soviet Union during World War II. Bibliography.

AH174. Rain, Pierre. **L'Europe de Versailles (1919–1939): les traités de paix, leur application, leur mutilation.** Paris, 1945. An examination, undertaken in a clinical spirit, of the reasons for and progress of the destruction of the Versailles system. Nearly half the volume is devoted to a discussion of the treaties themselves. Bibliography.

AH175. Reynolds, Philip A. **British foreign policy in the inter-war years.** N.Y., 1954. A concise, judicious survey and appraisal. British failures are seen to have resulted from two errors—the pursuit of traditional policies under changed and inappropriate circumstances, and the pursuit of conciliation to the extent of not recognizing evil. Bibliography.

AH176. Salvatorelli, Luigi. **Vent' anni fra due guerre.** 2nd rev. ed., Rome, 1946. History of the inter-war period covering domestic developments as well as international relations.

AH177. Smith, Sara R. **The Manchurian crisis, 1931–1932: a tragedy in international relations.** N.Y., 1948. An able history in which particular attention is given to U. S. policy and League behavior.

AH178. Sontag, Raymond J. **European diplomatic history, 1871–1932.** N.Y., 1933. Reliable survey of European diplomacy.

AH179. Stein, Boris E. **Burzhuaznye fal'sifikatory istorii, 1919–1939.** Moscow, 1951. The Soviet answer to western postwar publication of documents and memoirs relating to the inter-war period; skilfully argued.

AH180. Suarez, Georges. **Briand: sa vie, son oeuvre, avec son journal et de nombreux documents inédits.** 6 v. Paris, 1938–52. An important Briand biography based on his diary and numerous unpublished documents. Particularly valuable are the parts which describe Briand's international role in the years of Locarno, Thoiry, and the Briand-Kellogg pact.

AH181. Willoughby, Westel W. **The Sino-Japanese controversy and the League of Nations.** Baltimore, 1935. Monumental analysis of the Manchuria incident, the Lytton report, the attack on Shanghai, and the concomitant international crisis in the Far East. Bibliography.

AH182. Wolfers, Arnold. **Britain and France between two wars: conflicting strategies of peace since Versailles.** N.Y., 1940. A good diplomatic history based on the material then available. Bibliography.

Disarmament Conferences

AH183. Buell, Raymond L. **The Washington conference.** N.Y., 1922. A good general account.

AH184. Bouy, Raymond. **Le désarmement naval: la conférence de Londres.** Paris, 1931. Scholarly presentation of the work of the London conference from the French viewpoint. Bibliography.

AH185. Ichihashi, Yamato. **The Washington conference and after: a historical survey.** Stanford, 1928. An important original treatment. As secretary to Viscount Kato, author was in a position to follow closely the course of negotiations. Each phase of the discussions is taken up in detail and obstacles in the way of agreement are discussed dispassionately. Bibliography.

AH186. Loosli-Usteri, Carl. **Geschichte der Konferenz für die Herabsetzung und die Begrenzung der Rüstungen 1932–1934.** Zürich, 1940. Comprehensive, systematic history and appraisal of the politics of disarmament. Bibliography.

AH187. Wheeler-Bennett, John W. **The pipe dream of peace: the story of the collapse of disarmament.** N.Y., 1935. Good short history of the disarmament conference; a sequel to the author's earlier books, *Information on the reduction of armaments* (London, 1925) and *Disarmament and security since Locarno, 1925–1931* (London, 1932).

Kellogg-Briand Pact

AH188. Ferrell, Robert H. **Peace in their time: the origins of the Kellogg-Briand pact.** New Haven, 1952. An able monograph. The author sees the agreement to renounce war as the product of some very shrewd diplomacy and some very unsophisticated popular enthusiasm in the United States. Bibliography.

AH189. Miller, David H. **The peace pact of Paris: a study of the Briand-Kellogg treaty.** N.Y., 1928. Account of the origins and purpose of the Kellogg-Briand pact, with a careful examination of the United States government's diplomatic correspondence with other signatory states.

AH190. Shotwell, James T. **War as an instrument of national policy and its re-**

nunciation in the Pact of Paris. N.Y., 1929. One of the best analyses of the pact.

Locarno

AH191. Bonnamour, George. **Le rapprochement franco-allemand.** Paris, 1927. Review of the Locarno agreements and their origins, with some documents and correspondence.

AH192. Giovannucci, Francesco S. **Locarno.** Rome, 1935. Detailed review of the origins and provisions of the Locarno pacts, including an appendix of texts of pertinent documents.

AH193. Lemin, Iosif M. **Vneshniaia politika Velikobritanii ot Versalia do Lokarno, 1919–1925.** Moscow, 1947. A Soviet interpretation of Britain's foreign policy from Versailles to Locarno.

Role of the United States

AH194. Beard, Charles A. **American foreign policy in the making, 1932–1940: a study in responsibilities.** New Haven, 1946. A hostile review of the foreign policy of President Roosevelt and Secretary Hull in context of U. S. moves toward involvement in World War II.

AH195. Borg, Dorothy. **American policy and the Chinese revolution, 1925–1928.** N.Y., 1947. Well documented monograph with appraisals of men and policies. Bibliography.

AH196. Christopher, James W. **Conflict in the Far East: American diplomacy in China from 1928 to 1933.** Leiden, 1950. Serves as a sequel to *AH195.* Value to the specialist is limited by narrow range of sources consulted. Bibliography.

AH197. Fleming, Denna F. **The United States and the League of Nations, 1918–1920.** N.Y., 1932.

AH198. ———. **The United States and world organization, 1920–1933.** See *AH280.* This and *AH197* are useful contributions to the study of U. S. foreign policy.

AH199. Kennan, George F. **American diplomacy, 1900–1950.** Chicago, 1951. Series of lectures appraising the principles and application of U. S. foreign policy of half a century. The burden of the message, expressed in an undogmatic manner, is a critique of the "legalistic-moralistic approach to international problems."

AH200. Lodge, Henry Cabot. **The Senate and the League of Nations.** N.Y., 1925. A contemporary Republican view of President Wilson's League policy in Paris and Washington.

AH201. Williams, William A. **American-Russian relations, 1781–1947.** N.Y., 1952. Greater part of book is devoted to the years 1917–39. After much research, the author concludes that the responsibility for un-

happy U. S.-Russian relations rests mainly with the United States. While the extensive documentation provided for the U. S. half of the story warrants attention, if not acceptance, the treatment of the aims and methods of Soviet foreign policy avoids the essential question. Bibliography.

Role of the Soviet Union

AH202. Beloff, Max. **The foreign policy of Soviet Russia, 1929–1941.** 2 v. N.Y., 1947–49. Best single account of Soviet foreign policy for these years. Cautious in forcing conclusions upon the evidence, the author has been unusually conscientious in assembling the evidence at time of writing.

AH203. Carr, Edward H. **German-Soviet relations between the two world wars, 1919–1939.** Baltimore, 1951. Six lectures on the fluctuating relations between two losers of World War I. Bibliography.

AH204. Fischer, Louis. **The Soviets in world affairs: a history of the relations between the Soviet Union and the rest of the world, 1917–1929.** 2nd ed., 2 v., Princeton, 1951. Extensive, favorable treatment of Bolshevik foreign policy, based in large measure on Russian sources. Author had the advantage of friendship with leading Russian diplomats in the 1920's.

AH205. Potemkin, Vladimir P., ed. **Istoriia diplomatii.** 3 v. Moscow, 1941–45. Extensive Soviet interpretation of diplomatic history from antiquity to 1939. While indicating the Soviet view, it is increasingly unsatisfactory as the narrative approaches contemporary events. Little in the way of Russian diplomatic "revelations." French edition, *Histoire de la diplomatie* (3 v., Paris, 1946–47).

AH206. Taracouzio, Timothy A. **War and peace in Soviet diplomacy.** See *X275.*

DIPLOMACY OF WORLD WAR II

Outbreak

AH207. Aoki, Tokuzō. **Taiheiyō sensō zenshi.** 3 v. Tokyo, 1950–53. History of events leading up to the Pacific war. Includes many important documents.

AH208. Beck, Jósef. **Dernier rapport: politique polonaise, 1926–1939.** See *W164.*

AH209. Bonnet, Georges E. **Défense de la paix.** 2 v. Geneva, 1946–48. In these diplomatic memoirs the French foreign minister at the time of the Czech crisis is much concerned with the defense of his own diplomacy. An important but controversial source.

AH210. Ciano, Galeazzo. **Diaries and papers.** The diary of Mussolini's son-in-law and foreign minister underwent many vicissitudes in the course of being preserved from the Fascists and finding its way into print. An English translation of entries from Jan

1, 1939 to Dec. 23, 1943 was edited by Hugh Gibson, *The Ciano diaries, 1939–1943* (Garden City, 1946) (Italian edition, 2 v., Milan, 1946). An earlier section, from Aug. 23, 1937 to the end of 1938, is *Diario 1937–1938* (Bologna, 1948), for which an English translation, *Diary, 1937–1938* (London, 1952) was published. A supplement to these "diaries" is *L'Europa verso la catastrofe* (Milan, 1947), a collection of documents from the files of the Palazzo Chigi containing minutes of Ciano's conversations with foreign statesmen between 1936 and 1942 together with other revealing memoranda, letters, and telegrams. An English translation, *Ciano's diplomatic papers* (London, 1948), was edited by Malcolm Muggeridge. In all a valuable source for Italian foreign policy, but because of Ciano's character and the complex history of some of the documents, it is to be used with due caution.

AH211. Coulondre, Robert. **De Staline à Hitler: souvenirs de deux ambassades, 1936–1939.** Paris, 1950. Extremely valuable and informative memoirs of the French ambassador in Moscow, from Nov. 1936 to Oct. 1938, and then in Berlin until outbreak of the war. Of particular interest is his account of the crumbling of the Franco-Soviet pact, France's reluctance to give it military teeth, and the obvious Soviet threat, after the Munich crisis, of a fourth Polish partition.

AH212. Gafencu, Grigore. **Last days of Europe: a diplomatic journey in 1939.** New Haven, 1948. The late Romanian foreign minister recites his impressions of European events and personages gained on a diplomatic tour before the war in 1939.

AH213. ——. **Prelude to the Russian campaign.** London, 1945. Consists of two unequal parts. The first contains a circumstantial account of Russo-German relations from the Moscow pact of Aug. 21, 1939 to the Nazi invasion of Russia in June 1941; the second, and shorter, part reviews Rumanian foreign policy during the war.

AH214. Henderson, Sir Nevile. **Failure of a mission: Berlin, 1937–1939.** N.Y., 1940. Author, who was sent to Berlin as British ambassador just before 1937, here gives an account of his two and a half years in the center of European diplomacy.

AH215. Hofer, Walther. **War premeditated, 1939.** London, 1955. Able study, by a Swiss historian, of the immediate background of World War II in the summer of 1939; well assembled and directed to showing Hitler's full responsibility for destroying the peace.

AH216. Holldack, Heinz G. **Was wirklich geschah.** Munich, 1949. Well-documented history of German foreign policy between 1933 and 1941.

AH217. Kordt, Erich. **Wahn und Wirklichkeit.** Stuttgart, 1948. Valuable, though largely undocumented, survey of the course of German foreign policy from 1933 to 1945. The author, a professional diplomat, was an assistant to von Ribbentrop, with whom he was increasingly at odds.

AH218. Namier, Sir Lewis B. **Diplomatic prelude, 1938–1939.** N.Y., 1948. Classic study of the events immediately preceding the outbreak of war. Somewhat outdated by subsequent documentary publications.

AH219. ——. **Europe in decay.** London, 1950. Collection of book-review essays intended to keep readers abreast of material published after *AH218*.

AH220. Noël, Léon. **L'agression allemande contre la Pologne.** Paris, 1946. Author was French ambassador in Warsaw from 1935 to outbreak of war in 1939. In preparing these pages he had at hand neither the files of the Quai d'Orsay nor his own personal papers. Nevertheless, he has much of importance to say about Polish-French relations during the inter-war period and about the immediate origins of World War II.

AH221. Tasca, Angelo (pseud., Angelo Rossi). **The Russo-German alliance: August 1939–June 1941.** Boston, 1951. Good review of the history of the alliance, from a decidedly anti-Soviet point of view.

AH222. Schmidt, Paul. **Statist auf diplomatischer Bühne, 1923–45.** Bonn, 1949. A witness to many of the most critical diplomatic encounters in European history between 1923 and 1945, Dr. Schmidt, former chief interpreter of the German Foreign Office, has written an absorbing and informative volume of memoirs.

AH223. Szembek, Jan. **Journal, 1933–1939.** Paris, 1952. This diplomatic diary of the former Polish under-secretary of state for foreign affairs is an important source for the background of World War II. Contains almost daily entries for the years 1935–39, thus giving a very complete picture of Poland's foreign policy in that period, as events led to the invasion of his country.

AH224. Weinberg, Gerhard L. **Germany and the Soviet Union, 1939–1941.** Leiden, 1954. Careful examination, in the form of a chronological survey, of the period of the Soviet-German non-aggression pact. Of particular interest is the concluding chapter summarizing the points at which the author's findings differ from prevalent views of that ambiguous relationship. Bibliography.

AH225. Weizsäcker, Ernst H. von. **Memoirs.** Chicago, 1951. Apologia of the head of the German Foreign Office under Ribbentrop. He indicates his opposition to Hitler's reckless rush to war, but does not substantially alter the picture of the background of the war or the forces in Germany which made Hitler possible.

AH226. Wheeler-Bennett, John W. **Mu-**

nich: prologue to tragedy. N.Y., 1948. Good on the background, development, and immediate aftermath of the Munich crisis, though written before the publication of pertinent German and British documents. Bibliography.

AH227. Wiskemann, Elizabeth. **The Rome-Berlin axis: a history of the relations between Hitler and Mussolini.** N.Y., 1949. Makes good use of a mass of documentary and personal material, some of it unpublished, to show the progressive degradation and enslavement of Fascist Italy by her Axis partner. Bibliography.

United States and Outbreak of the War

AH228. Beard, Charles A. **President Roosevelt and the coming of the war, 1941: a study in appearances and realities.** New Haven, 1948. An attack on Roosevelt's conduct of U. S. foreign policy, in effect charging him with forcing Japan to start war on the United States in 1941.

AH229. Feis, Herbert. **The road to Pearl Harbor.** See *AB426.*

AH230. Grew, Joseph C. **Turbulent era: a diplomatic record of forty years, 1904–1945.** 2 v. Boston, 1952. Based largely on Grew's diary and letters; valuable as a historical source. Sections of greatest interest are the author's review of events leading to Pearl Harbor (he believes the United States missed an opportunity for a peaceful settlement with Japan) and his work as acting secretary of state in 1945.

AH231. Langer, William L., and Sarell E. Gleason. **The world crisis and American foreign policy.** 2 v. N.Y., 1952–53. This masterly study gives the most complete and authoritative account of U. S. diplomacy from Roosevelt's "quarantine speech" to Pearl Harbor.

AH232. Rauch, Basil. **Roosevelt, from Munich to Pearl Harbor: a study in the creation of a foreign policy.** See *AB427.*

AH233. Tansill, Charles C. **Back door to war: the Roosevelt foreign policy, 1933–1941.** Chicago, 1952. The author sees Germany as having "been baited into war with Britain and France," and Japan as having been "maneuvered into firing the first shot at Pearl Harbor." Bibliography.

Wartime Diplomacy

AH234. Churchill, Winston S. **The Second World War.** 6 v. Boston, 1948–53. [1, *The gathering storm;* 2, *Their finest hour;* 3, *The Grand Alliance;* 4, *The hinge of fate;* 5, *Closing the ring;* 6, *Triumph and tragedy.*] These monumental war memoirs give full expression to the personality and stature of Britain's great statesman. Of enormous value to the historian for their insights and docu-

mentation, their literary and dramatic qualities make them absorbing reading. First volumes are perhaps the most satisfying: the inter-war years when Churchill was battling the current of appeasement and indecision, and the months of heroism when Britain stood alone against Hitler. The work concludes with Churchill's resignation in 1945, but includes his views on the handling and mishandling of relations with the Soviet Union.

AH235. Ciechanowski, Jan. **Defeat in victory.** Garden City, 1947. Author served the Polish government-in-exile during the war as its ambassador in Washington, but was unwilling to continue under the regime recognized by the Great Powers in the summer of 1945. His account of wartime negotiations with the U. S. and other allied governments is an important source.

AH236. Gaulle, Charles de. **Mémoires de guerre.** See *AG241.*

AH237. Feis, Herbert. **Churchill, Roosevelt, Stalin: the war they waged and the peace they sought.** Princeton, 1957. An important history of the "Big Three" coalition from 1941 to the collapse of Germany in 1945. The author treads his way skilfully through a complex diplomatic crisis, and his unobtrusive judgments on wartime policies are both balanced and penetrating.

AH238. Holborn, Louise W., ed. **War and peace aims of the United Nations.** 2 v. Boston, 1943–48. Very useful collection of documentary materials—declarations, statements, speeches, etc. Bibliography.

AH239. Hull, Cordell. **The memoirs of Cordell Hull.** See *AB417.*

AH240. Leahy, William D. **I was there.** N.Y., 1950. War memoirs of the former United States ambassador to Vichy and chief of staff to Presidents Roosevelt and Truman. Less readable than Stimson's or Sherwood's accounts and less informative than Hull's memoirs, this volume nevertheless throws valuable light on U. S. military planning, organization of the armed forces, and relations with the Soviet Union.

AH241. Brookings Institution. International Studies Group. **The search for peace settlements.** By Redvers Opie and others. Washington, 1951. Informative survey of the difficulties in achieving agreement on peace settlements during and after World War II.

AH242. Sherwood, Robert E. **Roosevelt and Hopkins: an intimate history.** Rev. ed., N.Y., 1950. A well-written history and major source of information, based on the Hopkins papers.

AH243. Snell, John L., ed. **The meaning of Yalta: Big Three diplomacy and the new balance of power.** Baton Rouge, 1956. Stressing the historical context in which the agreements were made, this study by four historians concludes that "Yalta's historical significance has been confused, its decisions exaggerated, and its effect on the course of subsequent events distorted."

AH244. Stettinius, Edward R. **Roosevelt and the Russians: the Yalta conference.** Ed. by Walter Johnson. Garden City, 1949. The late Secretary of State, who was present at Yalta, adds his contribution to the picture of that most controversial conference, of which the Soviet Union was the host.

AH245. Vandenberg, Arthur H., Jr., ed. **The private papers of Senator Vandenberg.** Boston, 1952. Major theme of these papers is the late senator's transition from isolationism to an advocacy of international cooperation. Valuable for understanding of U. S. foreign relations in the years since Pearl Harbor, especially from the point of view of a member of the legislative branch of the government.

POSTWAR INTERNATIONAL RELATIONS

General Works

AH246. Deutsche Gesellschaft für Auswärtige Politik. **Deutsches und ausländisches Schrifttum zur Frage der Abrüstung 1945–1956.** Frankfurt am Main, 1957. Useful bibliography on the problem of disarmament since 1945.

AH247. Beloff, Max. **Soviet policy in the Far East, 1944–1951.** London and N.Y., 1953. [Royal Institute of International Affairs.] Useful survey, hampered by paucity of sources.

AH248. Royal Institute of International Affairs. **Defense in the cold war.** N.Y., 1950. **AH249.** ——. **Atlantic alliance.** N.Y., 1952. This and *AH248* are useful Chatham House study group reports on western defense and NATO in the early 1950's.

AH250. Haines, Charles G., ed. **The threat of Soviet imperialism.** Baltimore, 1954. A distinguished group of contributors discuss the Soviet position toward the non-Soviet world.

AH251. Meissner, Boris. **Russland, die Westmächte und Deutschland; die sowjetische Deutschlandpolitik, 1943–1953.** 2nd ed., Hamburg, 1954. Valuable discussion of the German problem in the negotiations of the big powers in the decade 1943–53. Heavily documented.

AH252. Pick, Frederick W. **Peacemaking in perspective: from Potsdam to Paris.** Oxford, 1950. Useful historical survey of the international conferences from 1945 to 1949.

AH253. Slessor, Sir John C. **Strategy for the West.** N.Y., 1954. Proposal for a military and political strategy to deal with the Soviet Communist danger in an age of atomic and hydrogen bombs.

AH254. Vyshinskii, Andrei I. **Voprosy mezhdunarodnogo prava i mezhdunarodnoi politiki.** [Questions of international law and international politics.] Moscow, 1951. Collection of Vyshinsky's speeches and remarks at the Paris peace conference of 1946, the first and second sessions of the United Nations General Assembly, and at press conferences and meetings.

Role of the United States

AH255. Byrnes, James F. **Speaking frankly.** N.Y., 1947. Author's account of his activities as secretary of state in the early part of the Truman administration begins with the Yalta conference and runs through the meeting of the Council of Foreign Ministers at New York in Dec. 1946. An important source of information for these two years.

AH256. Dennett, Raymond, and Joseph E. Johnson, eds. **Negotiating with the Russians.** Boston, 1951. Instructive symposium of the experiences of ten Americans who have had the responsibility of negotiating with the Russians on a variety of issues over the years since World War II. As the editors note, "It is not intended to be a record of American foreign policy as such; it is intended to be a record of how we negotiate with Russians and what happens when we do."

AH257. Dulles, John Foster. **War or peace.** N.Y., 1950. Apart from giving us the views of a leading figure in American public life, the book is useful as a concise exposition of the issues dividing the United States and Russia.

AH258. Forrestal, James. **The Forrestal diaries.** Ed. by Walter Millis and E. S. Duffield. N.Y., 1951. These pages from the diary of the late secretary of defense are both revealing and unsatisfying. They produce a remarkable sense of the author's bluntness and of the immediacy of his concern with many vital issues, combined with some uncertainty as to whether they are a complete representation of the situation as it was or even the full and considered judgment of their author. The exceptionally difficult task of editing has been handled very well.

AH259. Goodrich, Leland M. **Korea: a study of U. S. policy in the United Nations.** N.Y., 1956. Careful examination of the handling of the Korean question in the U. N. from V-J Day to the armistice that halted the collective action of the United Nations against aggression.

AH260. Brookings Institution. **Major problems of United States foreign policy.** 7 v. Washington, 1947–54. Useful annual series, discontinued in 1954, presenting an over-all view of the international situation and examining the principal problems confronting the U. S. policy maker.

AH261. Kaufmann, William W., and

others, eds. **Military policy and national security.** Princeton, 1956. Eight thoughtful and informed essays on some of the thorniest problems confronting the United States: the conduct of defense and foreign policies in a thermonuclear age.

AH262. Reitzel, William, and others. **United States foreign policy, 1945–1955.** Washington, 1956. [Brookings Institution.] Purpose of this useful work is to analyze "the official purposes and actions of the United States in its foreign policies and relations during the ten years since the war in order to try to recapture the key decisions that were made and the grounds on which one course of action rather than another was chosen." Bibliography.

AH263. Truman, Harry S. **Memoirs.** 2 v. Garden City, 1955–56. After a brief review of his early career, former President Truman writes of the first months of his presidency, which saw the end of World War II, the beginning of the chill which developed into the cold war, and the first atomic explosions. Second volume covers the years 1946–52, a period abounding in controversial issues. Valuable to the historian for its documentation, the work demonstrates the author's capacity for decision and his quite uncomplicated view of very complex problems.

AH264. U. S. Department of State. **United States relations with China: with special reference to the period 1944–1949, based on the files of the Department of State.** Washington, 1949. This important source is a voluminous, official compilation which has been the object of much controversy regarding both the selection of the materials in it and the timing of its publication.

Nuclear Weapons and International Relations

AH265. Biörklund, Elis. **International atomic policy during a decade.** Princeton, 1956. A Swedish admiral discusses and criticizes the various efforts and plans to achieve control of atomic weapons. A serious but not technical inquiry. Bibliography.

AH266. Blackett, Patrick M. S. **Atomic weapons and East-West relations.** Cambridge, Eng., 1956. A British physicist succinctly reviews the state of the atomic arms race (through 1955), and offers his judgment and criticisms of the various British and U. S. political and strategic doctrines which have sprung up along the way. Bibliography.

AH267. Dean, Gordon. **Report on the atom.** 2nd ed., N.Y., 1957. Straightforward, popular but sober description of the major aspects of the atomic energy program by the former chairman of the Atomic Energy Commission. Chapters on secrecy, security and spies, the international atom, and atomic development behind the Iron Curtain.

AH268. Kissinger, Henry A. **Nuclear weapons and foreign policy.** N.Y., 1957. After defining the problems involved in survival in the nuclear age, the author examines the relations between technology and strategy, the issue of all-out and limited warfare, the policy implications of strategy, and the utility and difficulties of coalitions and alliances. A major contribution. Bibliography.

INTERNATIONAL ORGANIZATION AND ADMINISTRATION

REFERENCE WORKS

AH269. Bibliographical services throughout the world: annual report. See *B16.*

AH270. International congresses and conferences, 1840–1937: a union list of their publications available in libraries of the United States and Canada. Ed. by Winifred G. Gerould. N.Y., 1938. [Bibliographical Society of America.]

AH271. League of Nations. **Handbook of international organisations.** Geneva, 1938. The League's own organizations are, in general, not mentioned.

AH272. Hudson, Manley O., ed. **International legislation: a collection of texts of multipartite international instruments of general interest beginning with the covenant of the League of Nations.** 9 v. Washington, 1931–50.

AH273. Peaslee, Amos J., ed. **International governmental organizations: constitutional documents.** 2 v. The Hague, 1956. Very use-

ful collection of basic constitutional documents of principal international governmental organizations, ranging from the African Postal Union to the World Meteorological Organization. Bibliographies.

AH274. Speeckaert, Georges P. **International institutions and international organization: a select bibliography.** Brussels, 1956.

AH275. Schmeckebier, Laurence F. **International organizations in which the United States participates.** Washington, 1935. Useful reference book with much bibliographical material.

AH276. U. S. Department of State. **International organizations in which the United States participates.** 1946 ff. Washington, 1947 ff.

AH277. White, Lyman C., and Marie R. Zocca. **International non-governmental organizations: their purposes, methods, and accomplishments.** New Brunswick, N.J., 1951. Covers organizations in various fields from 1850 to the present. Bibliography.

AH278. Yearbook of international organizations. Annuaire des organisations internationales. 1948 ff. Geneva and Brussels, 1948 ff. Useful reference which covers the U. N., the European Coal and Steel Community, other intergovernmental organizations, and international nongovernmental organizations.

GENERAL STUDIES

AH279. Claude, Inis L. **Swords into plowshares: the problems and progress of international organization.** N.Y., 1956. An effort to analyze the evolution, present problems, and future prospects of various actions and agencies covered by the general term "international organization." A solid if rather theoretically oriented study. Bibliography.

AH280. Fleming, Denna F. **The United States and world organization, 1920–1933.** N.Y., 1938. Part played by the United States in the various international efforts made during the fifteen years following World War I to organize peace on a stable basis. Bibliographical footnotes.

AH281. Hoffmann, Stanley. **Organisations internationales et pouvoirs politiques des états.** Paris, 1954. Historical and analytical essay dealing in turn with the Concert of Europe, the League of Nations, and the United Nations, and their relationship to the sovereignty of the nation states involved. Bibliography.

AH282. Koo, Wellington, Jr. **Voting procedures in international political organizations.** N.Y., 1947. Gives prominence to the rules and practices of the Security Council and other United Nations organs and agencies.

AH283. Loveday, Alexander. **Reflections on international administration.** Oxford, 1956. This book, by the former director of the Economic, Financial and Transit Department of the League of Nations, presents many well-considered and sober conclusions on the problems of organizing and operating an international agency.

AH284. Markus, Joseph. **Grandes puissances, petites nations et le problème de l'organisation internationale.** Neuchâtel, 1947. Relations between great and small nations, especially in connection with contemporary international organizations.

AH285. Padirac, Raoul. **L'égalité des états et l'organisation internationale.** Paris, 1953. History and analysis of the concept of the equality of sovereign states, with particular reference to its application in international organization.

AH286. Schätzel, Walter, and Hans-Jürgen Schlochauer, eds. **Rechtsfragen der internationalen Organisation.** Frankfurt am Main, 1956. An international symposium of essays on a wide variety of topics.

AH287. Schiffer, Walter **The legal community of mankind: a critical analysis of the modern concept of world organization.** N.Y., 1954. Extensive historical and critical examination of the concepts which came to find embodiment in the principles underlying the League of Nations and the United Nations. Author believes that a something-for-nothing expectation was an important feature of this set of concepts. Bibliography.

AH288. Waldecker, Burkhart. **Die Stellung der menschlichen Gesellschaft zum Völkerbund: Versuch einer Darstellung des Kampfes um die Weltorganisation.** Berlin, 1931. Comprehensive survey of the attitude of nations and various social groups to the idea of international organization generally and to the League of Nations in particular. Bibliography.

LEAGUE OF NATIONS

Reference Works and Guides

AH289. Aufricht, Hans. **Guide to League of Nations publications: a bibliographical survey of the work of the League, 1920–1947.** N.Y., 1951. A most useful bibliographical survey, and also of value in outlining the scope and development not only of the League proper, but of its principal autonomous organs, the Permanent Court, International Labor Organization, International Institute of Intellectual Cooperation, International Cinematographic Institute, and International Institute for the Unification of Private Law.

AH290. Breycha-Vauthier, Arthur C. de. **Sources of information: a handbook on the publications of the League of Nations.** N.Y., 1939.

AH291. Carroll, Marie J. **Key to League of Nations documents placed on public sale.** 5 v. Boston and N.Y., 1930–38. [World Peace Foundation.]

AH292. League of Nations. **Catalogue of publications, 1920–1935.** Geneva, 1935. Supplements, 1936–45. Four supplements cover the years 1936–39 and one the years 1940–45.

AH293. Myers, Denys P. **Handbook of the League of Nations: a comprehensive account of its structure, operation and activities.** Rev. ed., Boston, 1935.

AH294. Annuaire de la Société des Nations. Ed. by Georges Ottlik. 8 v. Lausanne and Geneva, 1927–38. Covers period 1920–38.

AH295. Catalogue of the Palace of the Peace Library. Leiden, 1916. Supplements (1922, 1929, 1937) list many publications of the League of Nations.

AH296. League of Nations. **Books on the work of the League catalogued in the library of the secretariat.** Geneva, 1928. Supplement, 1931.

AH297. ——. **Monthly list of books cata-logued in the library of the League of Nations.** Geneva, 1928–46.
AH298. ——. **Monthly list of selected articles.** Geneva, 1930–46.

General Surveys

AH299. Bassett, John S. **The League of Nations: a chapter in world politics.** N.Y., 1928. Detached and dispassionate chrono-logical account of the work of the League during its first seven years, with an interest-ing chapter on the United States attitude. Bibliography.
AH300. Bülow, Bernhard W. von. **Der Versailler Völkerbund: eine vorläufige Bilanz.** Berlin, 1923. Elaborate account of the League's organization and activity in early years. Bibliography.
AH301. Engel, Salo. **League reform.** Geneva, 1940. Analysis of official proposals and discussions, 1936–39.
AH302. Knudson, John I. **A history of the League of Nations.** Atlanta, 1938. A sympathetic summary of the League's achievements.
AH303. League of Nations. **Ten years of world co-operation.** Boston, 1930. Prepared by the League secretariat on the tenth anni-versary of the League. Bibliography.
AH304. Marburg, Theodore. **Development of the League of Nations idea.** 2 v. N.Y., 1932. Documents and correspondence of the chairman of the Foreign Organization Com-mittee of the League to Enforce Peace.
AH305. Munch, Peter, ed. **Les origines et l'oeuvre de la Société des Nations.** 2 v. Copenhagen, 1923–24. A large cooperative work.
AH306. Walters, Francis P. **A history of the League of Nations.** 2 v. N.Y., 1952. Com-prehensive and authoritative history by a British member of the League secretariat from 1919 to 1940.
AH307. Zimmern, Sir Alfred E. **The League of Nations and the rule of law.** 2nd ed., London, 1939. Excellent brief review of the pre-1914 system as well as of the organi-zation and history of the League.

Organization and Functions

AH308. Burton, Margaret E. **The assembly of the League of Nations.** Chicago, 1941. Scholarly treatise on the organization and historical function of the assembly. Bibliog-raphy.
AH309. Miller, David H. **The drafting of the covenant.** 2 v. N.Y., 1928. Standard work on the genesis of the covenant. The author, a legal adviser of the United States commis-sion, was in close touch with the work. Using much unpublished material, he ana-lyzes the various drafts submitted and dis-cusses at length the modifications made in the Wilson draft. V. 2 is devoted entirely to documents.
AH310. Greaves, Harold R. G. **The League committees and world order.** London, 1931. Analyzes the system and working of the League technical and advisory commit-tees, such as those dealing with economics, finance, health, intellectual cooperation, mandates, and disarmament.
AH311. Howard-Ellis, Charles. **The origin, structure and working of the League of Nations.** London, 1928. An authoritative contemporary exposition. Bibliography.
AH312. Barandon, Paul. **Das Kriegsver-hütungsrecht des Völkerbundes.** Berlin, 1933. A study of the law of war prevention as developed under the League of Nations.
AH313. Davies, David D. **The problem of the twentieth century: a study in interna-tional relationships.** New ed., London, 1934. A major work on the problem of sanctions.
AH314. Gonsiorowski, Miroslas. **Société des Nations et problème de la paix.** 2 v. Paris, 1927. A huge legal study of the mechanism of the League for preventing war. Bibliography.
AH315. Kelsen, Hans. **Legal technique in international law.** N.Y., 1939. An analysis of the mistakes made in drafting the League covenant.
AH316. McClure, Wallace. **World pros-perity as sought through the economic work of the League of Nations.** N.Y., 1933. Ex-cellent account of the manifold economic activities of the League. Bibliography.
AH317. Morley, Felix. **The society of na-tions.** Washington, 1932. Detailed study of the origin and operation of the organization.
AH318. Ray, Jean. **Commentaire du pacte de la Société des Nations selon la politique et la jurisprudence des organes de la So-ciété.** Paris, 1930. Monumental treatise con-taining all the important decisions and reso-lutions of the assembly and the council of the League as they bear on the terms of the covenant and the methods of its application.
AH319. ——. **La politique et la juris-prudence de la Société des Nations.** 4 v. Paris, 1931–35. Supplements *AH318.*
AH320. Ranshofen-Wertheimer, Egon F. **The international secretariat: a great experi-ment in international administration.** Wash-ington. 1945. A former member of the League of Nations secretariat describes in detail the organization and functioning of that body. Bibliography.
AH321. Rousseau, Charles E. **La compé-tence de la Société des Nations dans le réglement des conflits internationaux.** Paris, 1927. Well-documented study of the com-petence of the League. The author devotes special attention to the status of the British dominions and to problems raised by the Monroe Doctrine. Bibliography.

AH322. Schücking, Walther, and Hans Wehberg. **Die Satzung des Völkerbundes.** 3rd ed., Berlin, 1931. Authoritative commentary on the League covenant.

AH323. Shotwell, James T. **On the rim of the abyss.** N.Y., 1936. History of the League's role as an instrument of collective security and peace.

AH324. Webster, Charles K. **The League of Nations in theory and practice.** Boston, 1933. Good general survey, by a prominent English authority, of the organization and working of the League. Bibliography.

AH325. Yepes, Jesús M., and Fernando Pereira da Silva. **Commentaire théorique et pratique du pacte de la Société des Nations et des statuts de l'Union Panaméricaine.** 3 v. Paris, 1934–39. Detailed legal analysis comparing the organization and activity of the League and the Union, and stressing the parallel work of the two organizations. Bibliography.

Minorities

AH326. Azcárate y Flórez, Pablo de. **League of Nations and national minorities: an experiment.** Washington, 1945. A former director of the Minorities Questions Section of the League presents a systematic résumé.

AH327. Claude, Inis L. **National minorities: an international problem.** Cambridge, Mass., 1955. A study of this problem in international relations before, during, and after World War II. Bibliography.

AH328. Erler, Georg H. J. **Das Recht der nationalen Minderheiten.** Münster, 1931. One of the best treatments of the history and status of European minorities, from the political as well as the legal standpoint. Bibliography.

AH329. Janowsky, Oscar I. **Nationalities and national minorities.** N.Y., 1945. Discussion of minority problems in eastern Europe, opposing such solutions as plebiscites and transfers of population, and favoring some form of international supervision for the minorities.

AH330. Macartney, Carlile A. **National states and national minorities.** London, 1934. Much space devoted to background material—development of ideas of nationality as well as the growth of national movements in central and eastern Europe. Balance of the book analyzes the minorities treaties, procedure before the League, the value and working of the guarantees. Bibliography.

AH331. Molony, William O. **Nationality and the peace treaties.** N.Y., 1934. Defense of the Versailles treaties and their minority protection provisions.

AH332. Aci-Monfosca, Enrico. **Le minoranze nazionali: contemplate dagli atti internazionali.** 2 v. Florence, 1929. One of the best books on the problem of minorities

under the Versailles treaties. Proceeding by nations, v. 1 is devoted to the Baltic and central European areas, v. 2 to the Balkans and Turkey.

AH333. Stone, Julius. **International guarantees of minority rights.** London, 1932. Deals almost exclusively with the legal aspects of this problem, especially the machinery provided by the council of the League.

AH334. Wambaugh, Sarah. **A monograph on plebiscites, with a collection of official documents.** N.Y., 1920. An authoritative study. Bibliography.

AH335. ———. **Plebiscites since the World War, with a collection of official documents.** 2 v. Washington, 1933. Continuation of *AH334*, detailed and heavily documented. Bibliography.

AH336. Wintgens, Hugo. **Der völkerrechtliche Schutz der nationalen, sprachlichen und religiösen Minderheiten unter besonderer Berücksichtigung der deutschen Minderheiten in Polen.** Stuttgart, 1930. General treatise on the protection of minorities, with special reference to the problem of German minorities in Poland. This is a reprint from the *Handbuch des Voelkerrechts,* and is heavily documented. Bibliography.

UNITED NATIONS

Reference Works and Guides

AH337. Moor, Carol C., and Waldo Chamberlin. **How to use United Nations documents.** N.Y., 1952. A useful guide.

AH338. United Nations. **Checklist of United Nations documents.** 8 pts. N.Y., 1949–53.

AH339. ———. **United Nations documents index.** N.Y., 1950 ff. (Monthly.) Includes a subject index which cumulates annually.

AH340. ———. **United Nations publications.** N.Y., 1948 ff. (Annual.) Volume for 1954 is a cumulation entitled *Ten years of United Nations publications, 1945 to 1955: a complete catalogue.*

AH341. ———. **A bibliography of the charter of the United Nations.** N.Y., 1955.

AH342. ———. **Yearbook.** N.Y., 1947 ff.

AH343. **Annual review of United Nations affairs.** 1949 ff. Ed. by Clyde Eagleton. N.Y., 1950 ff.

AH344. United Nations. **Everyman's United Nations: a ready reference to the structure, functions and work of the United Nations and its related agencies.** 6th ed., N.Y., 1959.

General Studies

AH345. Evatt, Herbert V. **The task of nations.** N.Y., 1949. Evaluation of the United Nations and its functions by the former Australian minister of foreign affairs and president of the General Assembly.

AH346. Kopelmanas, Lazare. **L'organisation des Nations Unies.** Paris, 1947. Examination of the "constitutional sources" of the various provisions of the charter.

AH347. Leonard, Leonard L. **International organization.** N.Y., 1951. Extensive survey of the organization and functions of the U. N., including a review of its background and antecedents.

AH348. Lie, Trygve. **In the cause of peace: seven years with the United Nations.** N.Y., 1954. Personal recollections by the first secretary-general of the U. N.

Organization and Function

AH349. Asher, Robert E., and others. **The United Nations and promotion of the general welfare.** Washington, 1957. This and *AH350–351* are three of a projected series of seven Brookings Institution studies dealing with the United Nations system.

AH350. Goodrich, Leland M., and Anne P. Simons. **The United Nations and the maintenance of international peace and security.** Washington, 1955.

AH351. Wilcox, Francis O., and Carl M. Marcy. **Proposals for changes in the United Nations.** Washington, 1955.

AH352. Brugière, Pierre F. **Les pouvoirs de l'Assemblée Générale des Nations Unies en matière politique et de sécurité.** Paris, 1955. Examination of the political and security powers, both as defined in the charter and as interpreted in practice.

AH353. Frankenstein, Marc. **L'organisation des Nations Unies devant le conflit coréen.** Paris, 1952. Extensive analysis and critique of the actions of the U. N. in dealing with the Korean conflict up to the beginning of the armistice negotiations. Bibliography.

AH354. Schwebel, Stephen M. **The secretary-general of the United Nations: his political powers and practice.** Cambridge, Mass., 1952. An exposition of the thesis that the political prerogatives of the secretary-general are a significant factor in international relations. Bibliography.

AH355. United Nations studies. 8 v. N.Y., 1947–56. [Carnegie Endowment for International Peace.] A monographic series analyzing various aspects of the U. N.

AH356. Wightman, David. **Economic cooperation in Europe.** N.Y., 1956. Examines the background, purposes, operation, and limitations of the U. N. Economic Commission for Europe to the end of 1954. Bibliography.

Charter

AH357. Goodrich, Leland M., and Edvard I. Hambro. **Charter of the United Nations:** commentary and documents. 2nd and rev. ed., Boston, 1949. Historical background of the charter, a commentary on its provisions article by article, and an analysis of its practice. Bibliography.

AH358. Ross, Alf N. **Constitution of the United Nations.** N.Y., 1950. Analysis of the structure and function by a professor of international law at the University of Copenhagen.

AH359. Salomon, André. **Le préambule de la charte.** Geneva, 1946. A historico-juridical analysis of the U. N. charter. Bibliography.

Legal Aspects

AH360. Brugière, Pierre F. **Droit de veto: la règle de l'unanimité des membres permanentes au Conseil de Sécurité.** Paris, 1952. Monograph on the background, use, and misuse of the "veto power."

AH361. Day, Georges. **Le droit de veto dans l'organisation des Nations Unies.** Paris, 1952. On the origin, employment, and efforts at modification of the so-called "veto power" in the Security Council. Bibliography.

AH362. Kelsen, Hans. **The law of the United Nations.** N.Y., 1950. Exhaustive and formal analysis of the basic legal problems contained in the charter of the U. N.

AH363. ——. **Recent trends in the law of the United Nations.** N.Y., 1951. A supplement to *AH362.* Includes discussion of NATO and the United Nations action in Korea.

AH364. Sohn, Louis B., ed. **Cases on United Nations law.** Brooklyn, 1956. An extensive casebook centering on problems which have arisen in the work of the U. N.

AH365. ——, ed. **Basic documents of the United Nations.** Brooklyn, 1956. Designed to be used with *AH364.*

AH366. Soder, Josef. **Die Vereinten Nationen und die Nichtmitglieder.** Bonn, 1956. Monograph on the relationship in international law between the United Nations and those states which are not members.

U. N. and the States

AH367. Canada. Department of External Affairs. **Canada and the United Nations.** Ottawa, 1946 ff. (Annual. Title varies.)

AH368. U. S. President. **U. S. participation in the U. N.: report by the President to the Congress.** 1946 ff. Washington, 1947 ff. (Annual. Title varies.)

AH369. National studies on international organization. Unofficial studies of national experience with the United Nations, initiated in 1952 by the Carnegie Endowment for International Peace and carried out by private individuals and institutions.

Specialized Agencies

AH370. International Bank for Reconstruction and Development. **The International Bank for Reconstruction and Development, 1946–1953.** Baltimore, 1954. Authoritative survey prepared by the staff of the bank.

AH371. Sacchetti, Ugo. **Bretton Woods e i piani monetari internazionali.** Rome, 1947. The background of Bretton Woods and its immediate results, with documents.

AH372. Stokvis, Harold J. **Bretton Woods en het internationaal monetair bestel.** Leiden, 1948. Scholarly monograph on the relation between the gold standard and the mechanisms created at Bretton Woods.

AH373. Schenkman, Jacob. **International Civil Aviation Organization.** Geneva, 1955. Extensive monograph on the international aspects of civil air transport.

AH374. Berkov, Robert. **The World Health Organization.** Geneva, 1957. A thorough monograph devoting particular attention to the experience of the W. H. O. in applying its decentralized pattern of organization to carrying out its technical program. Bibliography.

AH375. Hambidge, Gove. **The story of FAO.** N.Y., 1955. Account of the history and achievements of the Food and Agriculture Organization of the United Nations, by its North American regional representative. Bibliography.

AH376. Laves, Walter H. C., and Charles A. Thomson. **UNESCO: purpose, progress, prospects.** Bloomington, Ind., 1957. Review of the first ten years of UNESCO.

AH377. Woodbridge, George, ed. **UNRRA: the history of the United Nations Relief and Rehabilitation Administration.** 3 v. N.Y., 1950. An official history. V. 1 deals with organization and administration, v. 2 describes activities in the field, and v. 3 contains a collection of pertinent documents.

AH378. Holborn, Louise W. **The International Refugee Organization.** N.Y., 1956. Solid and official account of the history and achievements of the I. R. O. from 1946 to its liquidation in 1952. Excellent documentation. Bibliography.

AH379. Codding, George A., Jr. **The International Telecommunication Union: an experiment in international cooperation.** See *A1238.*

AH380. Union Postale Universelle. **L'Union Postale Universelle: sa fondation et son développement, 1874–1949.** Berne, 1949.

AH381. International Labor Office. **Bibliographical contributions.** Geneva, 1949 ff. (Irregular.)

AH382. Argentier, Clément. **Les résultats acquis par l'Organisation Permanente du Travail de 1919 à 1929.** Paris, 1930. Detailed review of early accomplishments of the International Labor Organization. Bibliography.

AH383. International Labour Office. **The International Labour Organisation: the first decade.** London, 1931. An authoritative survey.

AH384. Shotwell, James T. **The origins of the International Labor Organization.** 2 v. N.Y., 1934. One volume of history followed by another of documents. The purpose is both to give a detailed account of the origins of the organization and to stress the idea that it was thought of as something independent of the League.

AH385. Wilson, Francis G. **Labor in the League system: a study of the International Labor Organization in relation to international administration.** Stanford, 1934. A solid monograph.

PERMANENT COURT OF INTERNATIONAL JUSTICE AND INTERNATIONAL COURT OF JUSTICE

Official Publications

AH386. International Court of Justice. **Yearbook.** 1946/47 ff. Leiden, 1947 ff.

AH387. Permanent Court of International Justice. **Annual report.** 16 v. Leiden, 1925–45.

AH388. International Court of Justice. **Publications.** Leiden, 1946 ff. A multivolume collection of documents.

AH389. Permanent Court of International Justice. **Publications.** Leiden, 1922–46. A multivolume collection of documents issued in five series.

General Works

AH390. Bustamante y Sirvén, Antonio S. de. **The World Court.** N.Y., 1925. Important study by a former justice of the court.

AH391. Fachiri, Alexander P. **The Permanent Court of International Justice: its constitution, procedure, and work.** 2nd ed., London, 1932. A standard work.

AH392. Hambro, Edvard I. **The case law of the International Court: a repertoire of the judgements, advisory opinions and orders of the Permanent Court of International Justice and of the International Court of Justice.** Leiden, 1952.

AH393. Hudson, Manley O. **The Permanent Court of International Justice, 1920–1942: a treatise.** Rev. ed., N.Y., 1943. An authoritative study.

AH394. ———. **World Court reports: a collection of the judgements, orders and opinions of the Permanent Court of International Justice.** 4 v. Washington, 1934–43. [Carnegie Endowment for International Peace.]

AH395. Lissitzyn, Oliver J. **The International Court of Justice: its role in the main-**

tenance of international peace and security. N.Y., 1951. A scholarly monograph. Bibliography.

REGIONAL ORGANIZATION

Bibliography

AH396. Institut für Europäische Politik und Wirtschaft. **Deutsches und ausländisches Schrifttum zu den regionalen Sicherheitsvereinbarungen 1945–1956.** Frankfurt am Main, 1957. Useful bibliography on regional defense arrangements.

European

AH397. Annuaire européen. **European yearbook.** The Hague, 1955 ff. A bilingual yearbook including articles and documents on various European problems and achievements. Includes complete bibliographical information on official publications of all European organizations and a selective bibliography of books, periodicals, and pamphlet material concerning European integration.

AH398. Council of Europe. **Handbook of European organizations.** Strasbourg, 1956.

AH399. Roussier, Michel, and Maryvonne Stephan. **Les publications officielles des institutions européennes.** Paris, 1954. Guide to official publications of European organizations.

AH400. Bindschedler, Rudolf L. **Rechtsfragen der europäischen Einigung.** Basel, 1954. Monograph on the juridical problems involved in contemporary moves toward European unity and unification. Bibliography.

AH401. Bonnefous, Edouard. **L'idée européenne et sa réalisation.** Paris, 1950.

AH402. ——. **L'Europe en face de son destin.** Paris, 1952. This and *AH401* are helpful studies on the movement for European unity. Bibliographies.

AH403. Coudenhove-Kalergi, Richard N. **Crusade for Pan-Europe: autobiography of a man and a movement.** N.Y., 1943. The founder of the Pan-Europe movement reviews its history and reiterates his belief in its goals.

AH404. Estudios sobre la unidad económica de Europa. Madrid, 1951 ff. One of the largest series of publications dealing with European economic integration; planned in nine volumes.

AH405. Hawtrey, Ralph G. **Western European union: implications for the United Kingdom.** N.Y., 1949. Analysis of some of the problems raised by proposals for closer political, military, and economic unity among the countries of western Europe. Emphasis is on the difficulties union would entail and the desirability of proceeding cautiously, via intergovernmental cooperation.

AH406. Mensbrugghe, Jean van der. **Les unions économiques: réalisations et perspectives.** Brussels, 1950. The greater part of this book is devoted to a useful study of the Benelux experience. Bibliography.

AH407. Philip, Olivier. **Le problème de l'union européenne.** Neuchâtel, 1950. A substantial argument that European economic union is a necessity, that it cannot be achieved through normal channels of negotiation between sovereign states, and hence that a political and juridical union is also required. Bibliography.

AH408. Council of Europe. **The Council of Europe.** 3rd ed., Strasbourg, 1957. A guide to the organization and activities of the council.

AH409. Robertson, Arthur H. **The Council of Europe: its structure, functions, and achievements.** N.Y., 1956. Comprehensive study of the structure and operation of the Council of Europe since its founding in 1949. Bibliography.

AH410. European Coal and Steel Community. **Bibliographie analytique du Plan Schuman et de la C. E. C. A.** Luxembourg, 1955 ff.

AH411. ——. **Monatliches bibliographisches Verzeichnis.** Luxembourg, 1953 ff. (Monthly. Title varies. Also in French, Italian, and Dutch.)

AH412. Institut für Europäische Politik und Wirtschaft. **Bibliographie zum Schumanplan 1950–1952.** 2nd ed., Frankfurt am Main, 1954.

AH413. Institut des Relations Internationales. **La Communauté Européenne du Charbon et de l'Acier.** Brussels, 1953. A careful and objective book on the Schuman Plan and the Coal and Steel Community.

AH414. Handbuch für den gemeinsamen Markt der europäischen Montan-Union. Frankfurt am Main, 1955. A massive handbook on the European Coal and Steel Community, including an extensive description of plants and firms, and a trilingual technical dictionary.

AH415. Jürgensen, Harald. **Die westeuropäische Montanindustrie und ihr gemeinsamer Markt.** Göttingen, 1955. A substantial discussion of the European Coal and Steel Community. Bibliography.

AH416. Mason, Henry L. **The European Coal and Steel Community: experiment in supranationalism.** The Hague, 1955. Good summary of the activities of this organization. Bibliography.

AH417. Reuter, Paul. **La Communauté Européenne du Charbon et de l'Acier.** Paris, 1953. Systematical and detailed examination of the Schuman Plan treaty and of the first acts of the coal and steel organization. Bibliography.

AH418. The North Atlantic Treaty Organization. **Facts about NATO.** Paris, 1958 ff.

A very useful reference in loose leaf form; kept up to date.

AH419. Barcia Trelles, Camilo. **El Pacto del Atlántico: la tierra y el mar frente a frente.** Madrid, 1950. A Spanish student of international law examines the Atlantic pact, its political and strategic implications and limitations.

AH420. Ismay, Hastings L. **NATO, the first five years, 1949–1954.** Paris, 1954. An authoritative review.

AH421. North Atlantic Treaty Organization. **The North Atlantic Treaty Organization.** 7th ed., Paris, 1959. A guide to NATO.

AH422. Ritchie, Ronald S. **NATO: the economics of an alliance.** Toronto, 1956. A solid examination covering the economic base, burden sharing, and the prospects for the future.

Asian

AH423. Royal Institute of International Affairs. **Collective defence in South East Asia: the Manila treaty and its implications.** N.Y., 1956. This useful summary emphasizes the political objectives of SEATO.

Western Hemisphere

AH424. "International relations since 1830." **Handbook of Latin American studies.** (See *Z3*.) Annual selective bibliographical listing of important writings on inter-American relations and developments.

AH425. Pan American Union. **Bibliografía de las conferencias interamericanas.** Washington, 1954. [Bibliographic series, 41.] Lists documents, reports, and publications relating to inter-American meetings, 1889–1951.

AH426. "Publications of the OAS and its specialized organizations." **Inter-American review of bibliography,** 1956 ff. (Quarterly.) Continuing section which lists recent book and pamphlet publications; helpful though incomplete.

AH427. **Annals of the Organization of American States.** Washington, 1949 ff. Official quarterly, the most important single continuing source of the many activities of the O. A. S. Contains documents, and reports of the secretary-general. Appears in English, French, Spanish, and Portuguese editions.

AH428. Pan American Union. **The Organization of American States and the United Nations.** By Manuel Canyes. 3rd ed., Washington, 1955. Official statement on the comparative structures and their relationships.

AH429. Carnegie Endowment for International Peace. **The international conferences of American states, 1888–1928.** N.Y., 1931. First supplement, 1940. Basic documentary materials.

AH430. Duggan, Laurence. **The Americas:** the search for hemispheric security. N.Y., 1949. Interpretative contribution stressing the Good Neighbor policy.

AH431. Fenwick, Charles G. **The inter-American regional system.** N.Y., 1949. Brief but authoritative survey of the history of the system, inter-American law, and relations between the Organization of American States and the United Nations.

AH432. Gantenbein, James W., ed. **The evolution of our Latin American policy: a documentary record.** See *Z723*.

AH433. Gil, Enrique. **Evolución del pan-americanismo.** See *Y171*.

AH434. Guerrant, Edward O. **Roosevelt's good neighbor policy.** Albuquerque, 1950. Factual summary of major developments in hemisphere relations, 1933–48. Bibliography.

AH435. Humphrey, John T. **The inter-American system: a Canadian view.** Toronto, 1942. Historical approach; standard monograph.

AH436. Kelchner, Warren H. **Latin American relations with the League of Nations.** Boston, 1929. A brief summary view. Bibliography.

AH437. Lobo, Helio. **O pan-americanismo e o Brasil.** São Paulo, 1939. A Brazilian view.

AH438. Pan American Union. **Manual of inter-American relations.** Rev. ed., Washington, 1956. Record of treaties, conventions, resolutions, declarations, and recommendations adopted at inter-American conferences and meetings of consultation, by subjects.

AH439. Rippy, J. Fred. **Latin America in world politics.** 3rd ed., N.Y., 1938. Although basically a textbook, contains much material on inter-American relations not readily found elsewhere.

AH440. Whitaker, Arthur P. **Development of American regionalism.** N.Y., 1951. Brief and accurate summary of the evolution of the O. A. S., identifying some permanent problems.

AH441. **Inter-American affairs: an annual survey.** Ed. by Arthur P. Whitaker. 5 v. N.Y., 1942–46. Excellent summaries of developments during World War II. Bibliography.

AH442. Whitaker, Arthur P. **The Western Hemisphere idea: its rise and decline.** Ithaca, 1954. An interpretative work emphasizing the assumptions underlying inter-American relations, arranged chronologically from the 18th to the mid-20th century.

AH443. Yepes, Jesús M., and Fernando Pereira da Silva. **Commentaire théorique et pratique du pacte de la Société des Nations et des statuts de l'Union Panaméricaine.** See *AH325*.

AH444. Yepes, Jesús M. **Le Panaméricanisme au point de vue historique, juridique, et politique.** Paris, 1936. An authoritative Latin American view by a major Colombian scholar of Pan Americanism.

MANDATES, DEPENDENCIES, TRUSTEESHIPS

AH445. U. S. Library of Congress. **Non-self governing areas with special emphasis on mandates and trusteeships.** Comp. by Helen F. Conover. 2 v. Washington, 1947. A selected list of references.

AH446. Abendroth, Wolfgang. **Die völkerrechtliche Stellung der B- und C- Mandate.** Breslau, 1936. A well-documented juridical and historical study. Bibliography.

AH447. Chowdhuri, Remendra Nath. **International mandates and trusteeship systems: a comparative study.** The Hague, 1955. Extensive historical and comparative analysis of the principles, agencies, and territorial application of the mandates and trusteeship systems established after World Wars I and II. Bibliography.

AH448. Ferri, Carlo E. **La teoria dei mandati internazionali.** Turin, 1927. Extensive study of the mandates system from the legal standpoint.

AH449. Hall, Hessel D. **Mandates, dependencies and trusteeship.** Washington, 1948. The major portion of this first-rate monograph contains a historical and analytical study of the operation of the League mandate system. Author also examines beginnings of the trusteeship system of the United Nations. Bibliography.

AH450. Rees, Daniel F. W. van. **Les mandats internationaux: le contrôle international de l'administration mandataire.** Paris, 1927.

AH451. ——. **Les mandats internationaux: les principes généraux du régime des mandats.** Paris, 1928. This and *AH450* are important on the question of organization and control of mandates. Author was once vice president of the Permanent Mandates Commission of the League.

AH452. Toussaint, Charmain E. **The trusteeship system of the United Nations.** N.Y., 1956. Analysis of the legal and institutional aspects of the trusteeship system. Bibliography.

AH453. Wright, Quincy. **Mandates under the League of Nations.** Chicago, 1930. Inclusive and exhaustive treatment of the subject, including an account of the origin and organization of the mandate system, an analysis of the international law of mandates, their relation to accepted ideas of sovereignty and territorial rights, their bearing on problems of international administration, and their achievements in furthering the political, economic, and cultural development of the mandated peoples. Bibliography.

INTERNATIONAL LAW AND DIPLOMATIC PRACTICE

DOCUMENTARY SOURCES—OFFICIAL

AH454. League of Nations. **Treaty series and international engagements registered with the secretariat of the League of Nations.** 205 v. Geneva, 1920–46. (Title varies.)

AH455. United Nations. **Treaty series: treaties and international agreements registered or filed and recorded with the secretariat of the United Nations.** 1946/47 ff. N.Y., 1947 ff.

AH456. ——. **Yearbook of the International Law Commission.** N.Y., 1956 ff.

AH457. International Court of Justice. **Reports of international arbitral awards.** N.Y., 1948 ff. [United Nations.]

AH458. Permanent Court of International Justice; International Court of Justice. Various publications, including yearbooks, reports of decisions, etc.

AH459. Moore, John Bassett. **A digest of international law.** 8 v. Washington, 1906.

AH460. ——. **History and digest of international arbitrations to which the United States has been a party.** 6 v. Washington, 1898.

AH461. Hackworth, Green H. **Digest of international law.** 8 v. Washington, 1940–44.

AH462. U. S. Naval War College. **International law documents.** Washington, 1894 ff. (Irregular. Title varies.)

DOCUMENTARY SOURCES— NON-OFFICIAL

AH463. Smith, Herbert A., ed. **Great Britain and the law of nations: a selection of documents illustrating the views of the government in the United Kingdom upon matters of international law.** 2 v. London, 1932–35.

AH464. McNair, Arnold D., ed. **International law opinions.** 3 v. Cambridge, Eng., 1956.

AH465. ——. **The law of treaties: British practice and opinions.** Oxford, 1938.

AH466. Lauterpacht, Sir Hersh, ed. **Annual digest of public international law cases.** 1919/22–49. 15 v. London, 1929–55. (Title varies.)

AH467. ——, ed. **International law reports.** 1950 ff. London, 1956 ff. (Annual.) Continuation of *AH466.*

COLLECTIONS AND YEARBOOKS

AH468. **Annuaire français de droit international.** 1955 ff. Paris, 1956 ff. (Annual.) [Centre National de la Recherche Scientifique.]

AH469. **The British year book of international law.** 1920 ff. London, 1920 ff. [Royal Institute of International Affairs |

AH470. Recueil des cours. 1923 ff. The Hague, 1923 ff. [Académie de Droit International de la Haye.]

GENERAL STUDIES

AH471. Strupp, Karl. **Bibliographie du droit des gens et des relations internationales.** Leiden, 1938. Systematic bibliography of books and articles in English, French, German, and Italian published between 1933 and 1936.

AH472. International Association of Legal Science. **A register of legal documentation in the world.** Paris, 1953. [UNESCO.]

AH473. Accioly, Hildebrando P. **Tratado de direito internacional público.** 2nd ed., 3 v., Rio de Janeiro, 1956–57. A comprehensive and scholarly treatise.

AH474. Brierly, James L. **The law of nations: an introduction to the law of peace.** 5th ed., Oxford, 1955. A useful introduction.

AH475. Cavaré, Louis. **Le droit international public positif.** 2 v. Paris, 1951. Treatise on positive international law, the doctrines which have been advanced concerning it, and its setting in contemporary international society. Bibliography.

AH476. Fauchille, Paul. **Traité de droit international public.** 8th ed., 2 v., Paris, 1921–26. An edition of Henry Bonfils' standard work.

AH477. Guggenheim, Paul. **Traité de droit international public, avec mention de la pratique internationale et suisse.** 2 v. Geneva, 1953–54. Masterly exposé of the system of the law of nations from the standpoint of a disciple of the pure theory of law.

AH478. Hyde, Charles C. **International law: chiefly as interpreted and applied by the United States.** 2nd rev. ed., 3 v., Boston, 1945. A fundamental work.

AH479. Jessup, Philip C. **A modern law of nations.** N.Y., 1948. An introduction.

AH480. Lauterpacht, Sir Hersh. **The function of law in the international community.** Oxford, 1933. Profound study of the nature and limitation of law in the international sphere and of the working of international courts.

AH481. Nussbaum, Arthur. **A concise history of the law of nations.** Rev. ed., N.Y., 1954. An annotated synthesis. Bibliography.

AH482. Oppenheim, Lassa F. L. **International law: a treatise.** 8th ed., 2 v., N.Y., 1955–57. A standard study, edited by Hersh Lauterpacht. Bibliography.

AH483. Stuyt, Alexander M. **Survey of international arbitrations, 1794–1938.** The Hague, 1939. A useful reference.

AH484. Verdross, Alfred. **Völkerrecht.** 3rd rev. and enl. ed., Vienna, 1955. A standard German manual. Bibliography.

AH485. Visscher, Charles de. **Theory and** reality in public international law. Princeton, 1957. Study of the relationship of international law and politics.

SPECIAL TOPICS

Law of the Seas

(See also *Waterways*, p. 851.)

AH486. Gidel, Gilbert C. **Le droit international public de la mer.** 3 v. Paris, 1932–34. An exhaustive treatment. Bibliography.

AH487. Higgins, Alexander P., and Constantine J. Colombos. **The international law of the sea.** 3rd rev. ed., London, 1954. A standard treatise.

AH488. Smith, Herbert A. **The law and custom of the sea.** 2nd ed., London, 1950. [London Institute of World Affairs. The library of world affairs, 9.] A practical handbook.

Air Law

AH489. Shawcross, Christopher N., and others. **Shawcross and Beaumont on air law.** 2nd ed., London, 1951. A standard work; kept up to date by periodic supplements.

Recognition

AH490. Chen, Ti-chiang. **The international law of recognition, with special reference to practice in Great Britain and the United States.** London, 1951. Extensive treatise. Bibliography.

AH491. Lauterpacht, Sir Hersh. **Recognition in international law.** Cambridge, Eng., 1947. Author sustains the thesis that the granting or withholding of recognition is primarily a legal, not a political, issue.

State Succession

AH492. Marek, Krystyna. **Identity and continuity of states in public international law.** Geneva, 1954. Extensive juridical monograph in which the experiences of Italy, Austria, Yugoslavia, Ethiopia, Czechoslovakia, Albania, the Baltic States, and Poland are examined as test cases. Bibliography.

AH493. O'Connell, Daniel P. **The law of state succession.** Cambridge, Eng., 1956. Inquiry into the legal principles governing the consequences of change of sovereignty, with particular reference to British practice. Bibliography.

Neutrality

AH494. Örvik, Nils. **The decline of neutrality, 1914–1941, with special reference to the United States and the northern neutrals.** Oslo, 1953. A well-conceived study.

Soviet Conceptions of International Law

AH495. Korovin, Evgenii A., ed. **Mezhdunarodnoe pravo.** Moscow, 1951. [Institut Prava, Akademiia Nauk SSSR.] Authoritative statement at the time of Soviet views and definitions of international law.

AH496. Lapenna, Ivo. **Conceptions soviétiques de droit international public.** Paris, 1954. [Institut de Droit Comparé de l'Université de Paris. Les systèmes de droit contemporains, 9.] Substantial review and analysis of Soviet theories concerning the nature of international law and its principal instrumentalities and institutions.

AH497. Taracouzio, Timothy A. **The Soviet Union and international law: a study based on the legislation, treaties and foreign relations of the Union of Socialist Soviet Republics.** See *X274*.

Miscellaneous

AH498. Cheng, Bin. **General principles of law, as applied by international courts and tribunals.** London, 1953. Author sets out "to demonstrate the practical application by international courts and tribunals of various general principles of law recognized by civilized nations." Bibliography.

AH499. Dickinson, Edwin D. **The equality of states in international law.** Cambridge, Mass., 1920. A scholarly study. Bibliography.

AH500. Dunn, Frederick S. **The protection of nationals: a study in the application of international law.** Baltimore, 1932. An important treatise.

AH501. Freeman, Alwyn V. **The international responsibility of states for denial of justice.** N.Y., 1938. This treatise has a twofold aim: (1) to construct a consistent theory of state responsibility, and (2) to analyze and correlate for the practical needs of the international lawyer the vast amount of arbitral and diplomatic material. Bibliography.

AH502. Garner, James W. **International law and the World War.** 2 v. N.Y., 1920. Elaborate treatment of international law problems as they arose in World War I. Bibliography.

AH503. Langer, Robert. **Seizure of territory: the Stimson doctrine and related principles in legal theory and diplomatic practice.** Princeton, 1947. Analysis of diplomatic practice in cases of aggression since 1934. Bibliography.

AH504. Stone, Julius. **Legal controls of international conflict: a treatise on the dynamics of disputes- and war-law.** N.Y., 1954. Massive, systematic treatise which undertakes to examine, and to diminish, the gap between the formulations of international law and the actual conduct of interstate relations.

AH505. Thomas, Ann (Van Wynen), and A. J. Thomas, Jr. **Non-intervention: the law and its import in the Americas.** See *Z702*.

AH506. Weis, Paul. **Nationality and statelessness in international law.** London, 1956. Most comprehensive treatment of the law of nationality in English. Bibliography.

DIPLOMACY

AH507. Académie Diplomatique Internationale. **Dictionnaire diplomatique.** 5 v. Paris and Geneva, 1933–54. A useful reference. Bibliographies.

AH508. Feller, Abraham H., and Manley O. Hudson, eds. **A collection of the diplomatic and consular laws and regulations of various countries.** 2 v. Washington, 1933. Important reference book.

AH509. Genet, Raoul. **Traité de diplomatie et de droit diplomatique.** 3 v. Paris, 1931–32. Still a valuable treatise on diplomatic procedure.

AH510. Nicolson, Harold G. **Diplomacy.** 2nd ed., London, 1950. History, elementary rules, and practice of diplomacy lucidly set forth for the layman. Bibliography.

AH511. Satow, Sir Ernest M. **A guide to diplomatic practice.** 4th ed., London, 1957. A standard manual. Bibliography.

AH512. Vyshinskii, Andrei I., ed. **Diplomaticheskii slovar'.** 2 v. Moscow, 1948–50. Presentation of the Soviet view of diplomacy and international affairs. Written for specialists, it is valuable in showing how the Soviet diplomat should interpret the contemporary world.

PERIODICALS

INTERNATIONAL RELATIONS

AH513. American Academy of Political and Social Science. **Annals.** Philadelphia, 1890 ff. (Bimonthly.) Book reviews.

AH514. The American political science review. Menasha, Wis., 1906 ff. [American Political Science Association.] (Quarterly, 1906–31; bimonthly, 1932 ff.) Significant source for bibliography on international political science.

AH515. Aussenpolitik. Stuttgart, 1950 ff. (Monthly.) Book reviews.

AH516. Chronique de politique étrangère. Brussels, 1948 ff. (Bimonthly.) Special attention to problems of European union. Bibliographical notes.

AH517. La Comunità internazionale. Rome, 1946 ff. (Quarterly.) Book reviews.

AH518. Cuadernos de política internacional. Madrid, 1950 ff. (Quarterly.) Leading Spanish journal of international studies. Bibliography.

AH519. Current digest of the Soviet press. Ann Arbor and N.Y., 1949 ff. [Joint Committee on Slavic Studies.] (Weekly.)

AH520. Current history. Philadelphia, 1914 ff. (Monthly.)

AH521. La documentation française. Paris, 1944 ff. [Direction de la Documentation.] (Several series.) The various series of publications issued by this French government document center are in large part concerned with the international scene.

AH522. Europa-Archiv. Frankfurt am Main, 1947 ff. (Semimonthly.)

AH523. Facts on file: a weekly world news digest with cumulative index. N.Y., 1941 ff. (Title varies.)

AH524. Foreign affairs. N.Y., 1922 ff. [Council on Foreign Relations.] (Quarterly.) Good bibliographical section.

AH525. International affairs. London, 1922 ff. [Royal Institute of International Affairs.] (Quarterly.)

AH526. International affairs: a monthly journal of political analysis. Moscow, 1955 ff. English language edition of *Mezhdunarodnaia zhizn'*.

AH527. International conciliation. N.Y., 1907 ff. [Carnegie Endowment for International Peace.] (Title and frequency vary.)

AH528. International journal. Toronto, 1946 ff. [Canadian Institute of International Affairs.] (Quarterly.) Book reviews.

AH529. International organization. Boston, 1947 ff. [World Peace Foundation.] (Quarterly.) Bibliography.

AH530. International political science abstracts. Documentation politique internationale. Paris and Oxford, 1951 ff. [UNESCO.] (Quarterly.)

AH531. Journal of international affairs. N.Y., 1947 ff. [School of International Affairs, Columbia Univ.] (Semiannual.) Book reviews.

AH532. The journal of politics. Gainesville, Fla., 1939 ff. [Southern Political Science Association.] (Quarterly.) Book reviews.

AH533. Keesing's contemporary archives: weekly diary of important world events. See *AF15*.

AH534. Orbis. Philadelphia, 1957 ff. [Foreign Policy Research Institute, University of Pennsylvania.] (Quarterly.)

AH535. Organization of American States. Annals. Washington, 1949 ff. [Pan American Union.] (Quarterly.) See *AH427*.

AH536. Political science quarterly. N.Y., 1886 ff. [Academy of Political Science.] Book reviews.

AH537. Politique étrangère. Paris, 1936. [Centre d'Études de Politique Étrangère.] (Bimonthly.) Book reviews and lists.

AH538. Relazioni internazionali: settimanale de politica ed economia. Milan, 1935 ff. (Weekly. Title varies.)

AH539. The review of politics. Notre Dame, Ind., 1939 ff. (Quarterly.) Book reviews.

AH540. Revista de estudios políticos. Madrid, 1941 ff. (Bimonthly.)

AH541. Revue d'histoire diplomatique. Paris, 1887 ff. (Quarterly.)

AH542. Revue de droit public et de la science politique en France et à l'étranger. Paris, 1894 ff. (Quarterly.) Well-known review of law and political science. Bibliography.

AH543. Revue française de science politique. Paris, 1951 ff. (Quarterly.)

AH544. The Department of State bulletin. Washington, 1939 ff. (Weekly.)

AH545. Vierteljahrshefte für Zeitgeschichte. Stuttgart, 1953 ff. (Quarterly.)

AH546: World politics: a quarterly journal of international relations. Princeton, 1948 ff. Book reviews.

AH547. The world today. Chatham House review. London, 1945 ff. (Monthly.)

AH548. Zeitschrift für die gesamte Staatswissenschaft. Tübingen, 1844 ff. (Quarterly.) Book reviews.

INTERNATIONAL LAW

AH549. The American journal of international law. Washington, 1907 ff. Supplement, *Official documents.* 1907 ff. [American Society of International Law.]

AH550. Archiv des Völkerrechts. Tübingen, 1948 ff. (Quarterly.)

AH551. Die Friedens-Warte. Blätter für internationale Verständigung und zwischenstaatliche Organisation. Basel, etc., 1899 ff. (Frequency and title vary.)

AH552. The international and comparative law quarterly. London, 1952 ff.

AH553. Jahrbuch für internationales und ausländisches öffentliches Recht. Hamburg, 1948 ff. (Annual. Title varies.)

AH554. Journal du droit international. Paris, 1874 ff. (Irregular.)

AH555. Revue critique de droit international privé. Paris, 1905 ff. (Irregular. Title varies.)

AH556. Revue de droit international de sciences diplomatiques et politiques. Geneva, 1923 ff. (Quarterly.)

AH557. Revue de droit international et de droit comparé. Brussels, 1908 ff. (Quarterly. Title varies.)

AH558. Revue générale de droit international public. Paris, 1894 ff. (Bimonthly.)

AH559. Revista di diritto internazionale. Milan, 1906 ff. (Quarterly.)

AH560. Zeitschrift für ausländisches öffentliches Recht und Völkerrecht. Stuttgart, 1929 ff. (Quarterly.)

SECTION AI

International Relations: Non-Political

HENRY L. ROBERTS and JANIS A. KRESLINS [*]

ECONOMIC

BIBLIOGRAPHIES, YEARBOOKS, AND OFFICIAL PUBLICATIONS

AI1. International bibliography of economics. Paris, 1952 ff. (Annual.) [UNESCO.]

AI2. League of Nations. **International statistical yearbook.** 1926–29. Geneva, 1927–30. (Annual.)

AI3. ———. **Statistical yearbook of the League of Nations.** 1930–44. Geneva, 1931–45. (Annual.) Continuation of *AI2*.

AI4. United Nations. **Statistical yearbook.** N.Y., 1948 ff.

AI5. League of Nations. **World economic survey.** 1931–44. Geneva, 1932–45. (Annual.)

AI6. United Nations. **World economic survey.** 1945/47 ff. N.Y., 1948. (Annual. Title varies.)

AI7. League of Nations. **International trade statistics.** 1933–38. Geneva, 1934–39. (Annual.)

AI8. ———. **Review of world trade.** 1932–38. Geneva, 1932–39. (Annual.)

AI9. Bank for International Settlements. **Annual report.** 1930/31. ff. Basel, 1931 ff.

AI10. International Bank for Reconstruction and Development. **Annual report by the executive directors.** 1945/46 ff. Washington, 1946 ff.

AI11. International Monetary Fund. **Annual report of the executive directors.** 1946 ff. Washington, 1946 ff.

AI12. The Contracting Parties to the General Agreement on Tariffs and Trade. **International trade.** 1952 ff. Geneva, 1953 ff. (Annual.)

AI13. United Nations. **Yearbook of food and agricultural statistics.** Washington,

1947 ff. Supersedes the *International yearbook of agricultural statistics.*

AI14. Organization for European Economic Co-operation. **Report.** 1948 ff. Paris, 1948 ff. (Annual. Title varies.)

AI15. United Nations. **Economic survey of Europe.** 1947 ff. Geneva, 1948 ff. (Annual.)

AI16. ———. **Economic survey of Asia and the Far East.** 1947 ff. Bangkok, 1948 ff. (Annual.)

AI17. ———. **Economic survey of Latin America.** 1948 ff. N.Y., 1948 ff. (Annual.)

INTERNATIONAL ECONOMIC ORGANIZATIONS

AI18. Alexandrowicz, Charles H. **International economic organisations.** London, 1952. [Library of world affairs, 19.] A survey of the principal international economic organizations, past and present.

INTERNATIONAL CONDITIONS AND TENDENCIES

Theory; General Treatments

AI19. Angell, James W. **The theory of international prices: history, criticism, and restatement.** Cambridge, Mass., 1926. [Harvard economic studies, 28.] An exhaustive monograph dealing with the history of the theory and submitting a restatement. Bibliography.

AI20. Clark, Colin. **The conditions of economic progress.** 3rd rev. ed., N.Y., 1957. Important work synthesizing technical and

* The compilers of this section were assisted by William Diebold, Jr., Leland N. Goodrich, and Oliver J. Lissitzyn.

statistical data concerning national income level and growth, and allied problems in the world's principal countries.

AI21. Conference on Research in Income and Wealth. **Problems in the international comparison of economic accounts.** Princeton, 1957. [Studies in income and wealth, 20.] A survey of problems arising out of the growing need for comparable national economic accounts.

AI22. American Economic Association. **Readings in the theory of international trade.** Comp. by Howard S. Ellis and Lloyd A. Metzler. Homewood, Ill., 1949. A collection of key writings. Bibliography.

AI23. Fisher, Allan G. B. **Economic progress and social security.** London, 1945. An appeal for flexibility in the economic structure and a criticism of measures which, in the name of autarky, inhibit the transfer of resources.

AI24. Harrod, Roy F. **International economics.** 3rd ed., London, 1942. Useful introduction.

AI25. Hawtrey, Ralph G. **Economic aspects of sovereignty.** 2nd ed., N.Y., 1952. First half of this book is a reprint of lectures given in 1929 on the subject of imperialism. The second half, dealing with events since then, is more concerned with issue of the balance of power and its economic implications.

AI26. Helander, Sven. **Das Autarkieproblem in der Weltwirtschaft.** Berlin, 1955. A Swedish economist analyzes at considerable length and with much supporting information the reasons for, and the international experiences with, economic autarky in recent years. In his view, the possibility of a free world market is intimately related to the outcome of this trend.

AI27. Lawley, Francis E. **The growth of collective economy.** 2 v. London, 1938. A fundamental treatise, being both a comparative study and a general synthesis. V. 2 treats the subject internationally.

AI28. Lewis, William A. **The theory of economic growth.** London, 1955. A leading analysis.

AI29. Loucks, William N., and J. Weldon Hoot. **Comparative economic systems.** 5th ed., N.Y., 1957. Comparison of the economics of capitalism, socialism, communism, fascism, and the cooperative system. Bibliography.

AI30. Manoilescu, Mihail. **The theory of protection and international trade.** London, 1931. One of the few serious pro-protectionist arguments. Bibliography.

AI31. Myrdal, K. Gunnar. **An international economy: problems and prospects.** N.Y., 1956. Discussion of the problems of international economic relations, by an eminent Swedish economist. Major attention is given to economic development and the

policies most likely to produce it. Bibliography.

AI32. Neisser, Hans, and Franco Modigliani. **National incomes and international trade: a quantitative analysis.** Urbana, 1953. Technical study on the connection between domestic economic fluctuations and external economic relations.

AI33. Oxford economic atlas of the world. Oxford, 1954. Useful reference work comprising maps, statistical tables, and some text.

AI34. Pommery, Louis. **Aperçu d'histoire économique contemporaine, 1890–1952.** 2 v. Paris, 1952. Survey of world economic history since 1890, with considerable emphasis on developments in the international field. Bibliography.

AI35. Robbins, Lionel C. **Economic planning and international order.** London, 1937. An important critique of international economic planning. Bibliography.

AI36. Truchy, Henri, and Maurice Byé. **Les relations économiques internationales.** Paris, 1948. A well-organized treatise on the evolution of economic practice and theory during the last century and a half.

AI37. Viner, Jacob. **International economics: studies.** Glencoe, Ill., 1951. Collection of papers on international economics published during the last 30 years by a leading United States economist. In an introductory essay the author comments on the applicability of classical theory to the present scene.

AI38. ———. **International trade and economic development.** Glencoe, Ill., 1952. An important critique of theory as a guide to policy.

AI39. ———. **Studies in the theory of international trade.** N.Y., 1937. Valuable addition to the literature of economic theory. Bibliography.

AI40. Weiller, Jean. **Problèmes d'économie internationale.** 2 v. Paris, 1946–50. A technical study, of which v. 2 deals with post-war problems: the establishment of international institutions, the United States effort to restore a free market economy, the difficulties of United States-European cooperation, and the steps toward regional integration.

AI41. Woytinsky, Wladimir S., and Emma S. Woytinsky. **World population and production: trends and outlook.** N.Y., 1953. This extremely important reference work is an encyclopedic compilation and analysis of information on the world's population, resources, and production. Bibliography.

AI42. ———. **World commerce and governments: trends and outlook.** N.Y., 1955. This companion to *AI41* was written for the same purpose, "to study world trends during the fateful era in which the mechanized economy originated on the two coasts of the North Atlantic is becoming the universal civilization of mankind." Comprising a survey of world trade, world transportation, and systems of government, it is a most valuable work of reference.

AI43. Wynne, W. H. **Selected case histories of governmental foreign bond defaults and debt readjustments.** V. 2 of **State insolvency and foreign bondholders.** New Haven, 1951. A valuable selection of case histories.

AI44. Young, John P. **The international economy.** 3rd ed., N.Y., 1951. A systematic treatise on the theory, historical development, and current practices of international intercourse.

The Reparations Question after World War I

AI45. Auld, George P. **The Dawes plan and the new economics.** N.Y., 1927. A substantial study, in opposition to the Keynes position.

AI46. Bergmann, Karl. **The history of reparations.** Boston, 1927. An authoritative presentation from the German point of view.

AI47. Bonn, Moritz J. **Der Neue Plan als Grundlage der deutschen Wirtschaftspolitik.** Munich, 1930. Includes a review of the reparations problem as well as an examination of the Young Plan.

AI48. Burnett, Philip M. **Reparation at the Paris peace conference from the standpoint of the American delegation.** 2 v. N.Y., 1940. [Carnegie Endowment for International Peace.] Important monograph, more than four-fifths of which consists of documents, the majority previously unpublished. Bibliography.

AI49. Dawes, Charles G. **A journal of reparations.** N.Y., 1939. Diary of the chairman of the experts' committee which drew up the reparations plan bearing his name.

AI50. Friedrich, Johannes. **Das internationale Schuldenproblem.** Leipzig, 1928. A thorough treatment of international debts. Bibliography.

AI51. Heilfron, Eduard, and Paul Nassen, eds. **Der Neue Plan: Young-Plan und Haager Vereinbarungen nebst den deutschen Ausführungsvorschriften.** Berlin, 1931. A standard collection of documents, with elucidation.

AI52. McFadyean, Sir Andrew. **Reparation reviewed.** London, 1930. One of the most useful books on the subject available in English. The author was connected with the reparations commission and writes authoritatively.

AI53. Moulton, Harold G., and Leo Pasvolsky. **War debts and world prosperity.** Washington, 1932. [Institute of Economics of the Brookings Institution, Publication 46.]

A detailed examination of the debt problem, including both inter-Allied war debts and reparations.

AI54. Petit, Lucien C. **Histoire des finances extérieures de la France: le règlement des dettes interalliées.** Paris, 1932. History of the reparations problem from 1919 to 1929.

AI55. Ronde, Hans. **Von Versailles bis Lausanne: der Verlauf der Reparationsverhandlungen nach dem ersten Weltkrieg.** Stuttgart, 1950. [Göttinger Studien zum Völkerrecht und internationalen Privatrecht, 2.] A retrospective review of the German reparations question after the First World War. Bibliography.

AI56. Salin, Edgar, ed. **Das Reparationsproblem.** 2 v. Berlin, 1929. [Veröffentlichungen der Friedrich List Gesellschaft.] A fundamental work on the question, consisting of articles on all aspects of reparations by 88 German scholars, statesmen, and industrialists.

AI57. Schacht, Hjalmar. **The end of reparations.** N.Y., 1931. The case for cancellation.

AI58. Sering, Max. **Germany under the Dawes plan: origin, legal foundations, and economic effects of the reparation payments.** London, 1929. One of the best single treatments, from the German side, of the reparations problem.

AI59. Weill-Raynal, Étienne. **Les réparations allemandes et la France.** 3 v. Paris, 1947. A massive and valuable history of the French aspects of the German reparations question after World War I. Bibliography.

AI60. Wheeler-Bennett, John W. **The wreck of reparations: being the political background of the Lausanne agreement, 1932.** N.Y., 1933. Useful summary of the political aspects of the reparations question with special reference to the Lausanne conference. Bibliography.

Inter-War Period (General)

AI61. Barker, J. Ellis. **Economic statesmanship.** N.Y., 1920. Analyzes the great economic problems just after World War I.

AI62. Culbertson, William S. **International economic policies: a survey of the economics of diplomacy.** N.Y., 1925. One of the best treatments of post-Versailles policies, by a former member of the United States Tariff Commission.

AI63. Feilchenfeld, Ernst H. **Public debts and state succession.** N.Y., 1931. A standard treatise discussing in detail the questions arising from the peace treaties of 1919–20.

AI64. Hantos, Elemér. **Die Weltwirtschaftskonferenz.** Leipzig, 1928. History of the economic conference of 1927 and an analysis of its results, by a protagonist of international cooperation. Bibliography.

AI65. Keynes, John Maynard. **The economic consequences of the peace.** See *AF292*.

AI66. ——. **A revision of the treaty.** N.Y., 1922. A sequel to *AI65*. Describes how events vindicated the latter, and suggests a way of solving the reparations problem.

AI67. Lary, Hal B., and others. **The United States in the world economy: the international transactions of the United States during the interwar period.** Washington, 1943. [U. S. Department of Commerce, Bureau of Foreign and Domestic Commerce, Economic series, 23.] A basic study.

AI68. League of Nations. **Commercial policy in the interwar period: international proposals and national policies.** Geneva, 1942.

AI69. Salter, Arthur S. **Recovery, the second effort.** N.Y., 1932. Interesting and well-informed study of postwar economic conditions and tendencies.

AI70. Staley, Eugene. **War and the private investor: a study in the relations of international politics and international private investment.** Garden City, 1935. Particularly valuable for its case studies.

AI71. Svennilson, Ingvar. **Growth and stagnation in the European economy.** Geneva, 1954. [United Nations, Economic Commission for Europe.] A basic work for the inter-war period.

AI72. Viallate, Achille. **Le monde économique, 1918–1927.** Paris, 1928. One of the best general books on post-Versailles economic developments, problems, and possible solutions.

Depression

AI73. Arndt, Heinz W. **The economic lessons of the nineteen-thirties.** N.Y., 1944. A searching report.

AI74. Haberler, Gottfried. **Prosperity and depression.** 3rd ed., Geneva, 1941. [League of Nations.] A basic study.

AI75. Hodson, Henry V. **Slump and recovery, 1929–1937: a survey of world economic affairs.** N.Y., 1938. [Royal Institute of International Affairs.] Based on Hodson's contribution to some seven volumes of the Royal Institute's *Survey of international affairs*. A good synthesis and interpretation of world economics during the period of the thirties.

AI76. Robbins, Lionel C. **The great depression.** See *AF296*.

AI77. Röpke, Wilhelm. **International economic disintegration.** N.Y., 1942. A scholarly study of the breakdown of world economy between two world wars, by a well-known Swiss authority.

AI78. Sturmthal, Adolf F. **Die grosse Krise.** Zurich, 1937. Competent review of the origins and progress of the great depression.

AI79. Varga, Eugen. **The great crisis and its political consequences.** N.Y., 1935. An incisive discussion of the interaction of economics and politics after 1928, by a leading Soviet economist.

AI80. Akademiia Nauk SSSR. **Mirovye ekonomicheskie krizisy, 1848–1935.** 3 v. Moscow, 1937–39. A massive study of world economic crises.

World War II and After

AI81. Buchanan, Norman S., and Friedrich A. Lutz. **Rebuilding the world economy: America's role in foreign trade and investment.** N.Y., 1947. The first 12 chapters give an account of the destructive effect of World War II on international trade and finance. Bibliography.

AI82. Chardonnet, Jean. **Les conséquences économiques de la guerre, 1939–1946.** Paris, 1947. See under *AI84*.

AI83. ——. **L'économie mondiale au milieu du XXe siècle.** Paris, 1951. See under *AI84*.

AI84. ——. **Les grandes puissances: étude économique.** 2 v. Paris, 1953–55. [Études politiques, économiques et sociales, 8 and 12.] These three works of Chardonnet are substantial surveys of the world's economies during and after World War II. Bibliographies.

AI85. League of Nations. **Commercial policy in the post-war world: report of the economic and financial committees.** Geneva, 1945.

AI86. ——. **Report of the Delegation on Economic Depressions.** 2 v. Geneva, 1943–45. [1, *The transition from war to peace economy*; 2, *Economic stability in the postwar world: the conditions of prosperity after the transition from war to peace*.]

AI87. Penrose, Ernest F. **Economic planning for the peace.** Princeton, 1953. The wartime economic adviser to Ambassador Winant "seeks to determine how it was that, notwithstanding the warnings that might have been taken from the First World War, and the time, the energy, and the resources that were given to postwar planning, economic disaster came early in Germany and was narrowly averted in 1947 and 1948 in the rest of Europe."

AI88. Varga, Eugen. **Izmeneniia v ėkonomike kapitalizma v itoge vtoroĭ mirovoĭ voiny.** Moscow, 1946. Significant analysis, by a leading Soviet economist, of the impact of World War II on the capitalist economies, and an estimate of their future development and prospects. Varga was subsequently taken to task for the views here expressed.

INTERNATIONAL TRADE

General Studies

AI89. Beveridge, Sir William H., ed. **Tariffs: the case examined.** 2nd ed., London, 1932. Approaches the subject from a variety of angles.

AI90. Bidwell, Percy W. **The invisible tariff: a study of the control of imports into the United States.** N.Y., 1939. On administrative protection. Bibliography.

AI91. Chalmers, Henry. **World trade policies: the changing panorama, 1920–1953; a series of contemporary periodic surveys.** Berkeley, 1953. Essays and surveys providing a quick means of discovering the main features of world trading arrangements at any given moment during these years.

AI92. Condliffe, John B. **The commerce of nations.** N.Y., 1950. An extensive and useful history of the interplay between world trade, public commercial policy, and the development of economic theory. Bibliography.

AI93. Diebold, William, Jr. **Trade and payments in western Europe: a study in economic cooperation, 1947–51.** N.Y., 1952. Both a descriptive account and a critical analysis of what western European countries accomplished from the beginning of the Marshall Plan through 1951 in facilitating trade and payments among themselves. Bibliography.

AI94. Forstmann, Albrecht. **Der Kampf um den internationalen Handel.** Berlin, 1935. An exhaustive survey of international trade in the interwar period.

AI95. Gordon, Margaret S. **Barriers to world trade: a study of recent commercial policy.** N.Y., 1941. Systematic study of the manifold restrictions that grew up around world trade during the thirties. Bibliography.

AI96. Haberler, Gottfried. **The theory of international trade with its applications to commercial policy.** New ed., London, 1950. Fundamental treatise by an outstanding authority.

AI97. Heilperin, Michael A. **The trade of nations.** 2nd enl. ed., N.Y., 1952. Addressed to the general public, this book is a good exposition of the liberal view of international trade and finance.

AI98. Henius, Frank. **Dictionary of foreign trade.** 2nd rev. ed., N.Y., 1947. Valuable, comprehensive reference work containing definitions of foreign trade terms, usages, practices, and procedures.

AI99. Heuss, Ernst. **Wirtschaftssysteme und internationaler Handel.** Zurich, 1955. [St. Galler Wirtschaftswissenschaftliche Forschungen, 11.] A comparative and quite technical study of foreign trade relations under a market economy, a monopolistic economy, and a socialist economy.

AI100. Hirschman, Albert O. **National power and the structure of foreign trade.** Berkeley, 1945. An inquiry directed to the question whether there is some inherent weakness in the system of international trade which makes it vulnerable to the will of any government wishing to exploit it for purposes of power politics.

AI101. Isaacs, Asher. **International trade, tariff and commercial policies.** Chicago, 1948. Treatise on the history, theory, and current practice of international trade by the various powers, large and small.

AI102. Ladas, Stephen P. **The international protection of industrial property.** Cambridge, Mass., 1930. Important volume for those interested in the legal aspects of foreign trade. Bibliography.

AI103. Marsh, Donald B. **World trade and investment: the economics of interdependence.** N.Y., 1951. Very able, mature, and in places quite original survey and textbook. Bibliography.

AI104. Meade, James E. **The theory of international economic policy.** 2 v. N.Y., 1951–55. [1, *The balance of payments;* 2, *Trade and welfare.*] An important treatise.

AI105. Neisser, Hans, and Franco Modigliani. **National incomes and international trade: a quantitative analysis.** See *AI32.*

AI106. Ohlin, Bertil G. **Interregional and international trade.** Cambridge, Mass., 1952. [Harvard economic studies, 39.] A theoretical analysis that emphasizes the relation of international trade to the relative prices of the factors of production within each country or region. Bibliography.

AI107. Snyder, Richard C. **The most-favored-nation clause: an analysis with particular reference to recent treaty practice and tariffs.** N.Y., 1948. A scholarly analysis. Bibliography.

AI108. Taussig, Frank W. **International trade.** N.Y., 1927. A classic liberal treatise.

AI109. Viner, Jacob. **The custom union issue.** N.Y., 1950. [Carnegie Endowment for International Peace, Studies in the administration of international law and organization, 10.] Examination of the possibilities and limitations of customs unions as a method of regulating international commercial relations. Bibliography.

AI110. ———. **Dumping: a problem in international trade.** Chicago, 1923. Best discussion of the problem. Bibliography.

AI111. ———. **Trade relations between free-market and controlled economies.** N.Y., 1943. [League of Nations, Economic, Financial and Transit Department.] Brief but important discussion.

International Trade Organization; GATT

AI112. United Nations. **General agreement on tariffs and trade (GATT bibliogra-**

phy), **1947–1953.** Geneva, 1954. Supplements.
AI113. Brown, William A., Jr. **The United States and the restoration of world trade.** Washington, 1950. [Brookings Institution.] This detailed analysis of the *Charter for an international trade organization* and the *General agreement on tariffs and trade* traces their history through long negotiations and discusses the policy questions involved in United States adherence to the two instruments.
AI114. Gross, Herbert. **Welthandel von Morgen: Studien zur Welthandels-Charter.** Düsseldorf, 1950. Detailed study of the background, meaning, and prospects of the I.T.O. Bibliography.
AI115. Wilcox, Clair. **A charter for world trade.** N.Y., 1949. Lucid account of the historical background of the I.T.O., the long process of its formulation, and the nature of the final agreement.

FINANCE

General Studies

AI116. Beyen, Johan W. **Money in a maelstrom.** N.Y., 1949. International monetary problems and the efforts to deal with them since the end of World War I.
AI117. Cassel, C. Gustav. **Money and foreign exchange after 1914.** New ed., N.Y., 1930. A technical summary, dealing especially with the problem of inflation and deflation.
AI118. Clare, George. **The ABC of the foreign exchanges.** Ed. by Norman E. Crump. 12th ed., N.Y., 1957. A standard guide.
AI119. Einzig, Paul. **World finance.** 5 v. N.Y., 1935–40. Articles and other occasional pieces covering the period from 1914 to 1940.
AI120. Gardner, Richard N. **Sterling-dollar diplomacy: Anglo-American collaboration in the reconstruction of multilateral trade.** Oxford, 1956. A thorough, scholarly, and well-written study in "international economic diplomacy": a history of the Bretton Woods organization, the Anglo-American Loan Agreement, the International Trade Organization, and the General Agreement on Tariffs and Trade. Bibliography.
AI121. Heilperin, Michael A. **International monetary economics.** N.Y., 1939. A comprehensive and original contribution.
AI122. League of Nations. **International currency experience: lessons of the inter-war period.** N.Y., 1944. Useful and critical review of the inter-war efforts to set up a satisfactory system of international payments.
AI123. Malpas, Jean. **Les mouvements internationaux de capitaux.** Paris, 1934. A valuable analytical and statistical study.
AI124. Mikesell, Raymond F. **Foreign exchange in the postwar world.** N.Y., 1954.

Very substantial study of foreign exchange policies since World War II.
AI125. Princeton University. **Survey of United States international finance.** Ed. by Gardner Patterson and Jack N. Behrman. 5 v. Princeton, 1950–54. Valuable annual summary, covering the years 1949–53, of United States policies and activities in the general area of international finance, including gift programs, foreign loans and investment, exchange policy, and balance of payments.
AI126. Tew, Brian. **International monetary co-operation, 1945–52.** N.Y., 1952. Describes the operation of the International Monetary Fund, the European Payments Union, and the sterling area.
AI127. Triffin, Robert. **Europe and the money muddle: from bilateralism to near-convertibility, 1947–1956.** New Haven, 1957. [Yale studies in economics, 7.]
AI128. Williams, John H. **Postwar monetary plans and other essays.** 3rd rev. and enl. ed., N.Y., 1947. The writings of a distinguished United States economist on international monetary problems. Bibliography.

Dollar Problem

AI129. Balogh, Thomas. **Dollar crisis, causes and cure: a report to the Fabian Society.** N.Y., 1950. An Oxford economist, stressing the shattering effects of World War II, argues against devaluation or any sudden return by Great Britain to uncontrolled multilateralism and for the necessity of long-range planning, especially in a western European context.
AI130. Kindleberger, Charles P. **The dollar shortage.** N.Y., 1950. Investigation of the nature of the postwar dollar shortage, its manifold causes and possible remedies.
AI131. MacDougall, Sir Donald. **World dollar problem: a study in international economics.** N.Y., 1957. A major contribution to understanding a complex topic.
AI132. Zupnick, Elliot. **Britain's postwar dollar problem.** N.Y., 1957.

Sterling Problem

AI133. Bell, Philip W. **The sterling area in the postwar world: internal mechanism and cohesion, 1946–1952.** Oxford, 1956. Detailed study of the internal working of the sterling area, its cohesiveness, its disturbances and adjustments. Bibliography.
AI134. U. S. Economic Cooperation Administration. **The sterling area: an American analysis.** Ed. by John M. Cassels. Washington, 1952. This substantial study is largely a description of the economies of countries in the sterling area and of production of and trade in commodities especially important to the area.

AI135. Day, Alan C. L. **The future of sterling.** Oxford, 1954. A rather pessimistic estimate.

AI136. De Vegh, Imre. **The pound sterling: a study of the balance of payments of the sterling area.** N.Y., 1939. Excellent for its period.

AI137. Polk, Judd. **Sterling: its meaning in world finance.** N.Y., 1956. [Council on Foreign Relations.] Very thorough analytical study of the sterling area from a United States viewpoint. While the author necessarily deals with some of the financial intricacies of this unique monetary system, major emphasis is on the broader economic and political relations and interests. Bibliography.

Gold

AI138. Brown, William A., Jr. **The international gold standard reinterpreted, 1914–1934.** 2 v. N.Y., 1940. [National Bureau of Economic Research.] An exhaustive review.

AI139. The international gold problem: collected papers. N.Y., 1931. [Royal Institute of International Affairs.] Valuable collection of studies prepared between 1929 and 1931. Bibliography.

Bank for International Settlements

AI140. Dulles, Eleanor L. **The Bank for International Settlements at work.** N.Y., 1932. [Bureau of International Research of Harvard and Radcliffe.] A most exhaustive study of the first two years of the bank's activities. Bibliography.

AI141. Papi, Giuseppe U. **The first twenty years of the Bank for International Settlements.** Rome, 1951. Review of the bank's origins and developing functions. Bibliography.

Cartels

AI142. Edwards, Corwin D., and others. **A cartel policy for the United Nations.** N.Y., 1945. Five lectures on various phases of the problem.

AI143. Hexner, Ervin, and Adelaide Walters. **International cartels.** Chapel Hill, 1945. A solid, critical treatise on the political and economic problems raised by cartels.

AI144. Kiersch, Günther. **Internationale Eisen- und Stahlkartelle.** Essen, 1954. [Rheinisch-Westfälisches Institut für Wirtschaftsforschung.] Analysis, with numerous statistics, of the international iron and steel cartels during the inter-war years.

AI145. Marx, Daniel, Jr. **International shipping cartels: a study of industrial self-regulation by shipping conferences.** Princeton, 1953. Investigation of international shipping conferences, an early form of cartel, their virtues and their vices.

AI146. Mason, Edward S. **Controlling world trade: cartels and commodity agreements.** N.Y., 1946. Valuable study devoted to international business agreements and to intergovernmental commodity agreements.

AI147. Stocking, George W., and Myron W. Watkins. **Cartels or competition? The economics of international controls by business and government.** N.Y., 1948. Analysis of the workings and effects of international cartels. Bibliography.

RAW MATERIALS

General

AI148. Guttmann, Henry. **Die Weltwirtschaft und ihre Rohstoffe.** 2nd ed., Berlin, 1956. A broad survey, with numerous statistics, charts, and maps.

AI149. Pahl, Walther. **Rohstoffe: der Kampf um die Güter der Erde.** Munich, 1952. Survey of the international competition, spurred by the requirements of power politics, for the vital raw materials—fuels, metals, etc.

AI150. Staley, Eugene. **Raw materials in peace and war.** N.Y., 1937. [Council on Foreign Relations.] Analysis of the effects which the unequal distribution of basic commodities has on world trade, capital movements, military preparedness, and international security.

AI151. Royal Institute of International Affairs. **World production of raw materials.** 2nd ed., N.Y., 1953. [Information paper no. 186.] A concise summary.

AI152. Zimmermann, Erich W. **World resources and industries: a functional appraisal of the availability of agricultural and industrial materials.** Rev. ed., N.Y., 1951. Important survey of the world's resources in agriculture and industry, with a discussion of their relative importance, the methods of processing, and the degree and method of exploitation. Bibliography.

Minerals and Metals

AI153. Friedensburg, Ferdinand. **Die Bergwirtschaft der Erde.** 5th ed., Stuttgart, 1956. Useful reference work on the world's mining and mineral resources, by country. Bibliography.

AI154. Leith, Charles K., and others. **World minerals and world peace.** Washington, 1943. [Brookings Institution.] Statistical summary of the world's mineral production and resources, followed by an analysis of the economic and political problems involved in their control.

Coal

AI155. Die Kohlenwirtschaft der Welt in Zahlen, 1955. Essen, 1955. This very useful compilation brings together basic statistics on coal production, trade, prices, productivity, etc., for a large number of countries. Coverage ranges from 1900 to mid-1955.

Oil

AI156. World petroleum report. 1953/54 ff. N.Y., 1954 ff. (Annual. Title varies.) Handbook of statistical and other information on the world's petroleum operations.

AI157. Pratt, Wallace E., and Dorothy Good, eds. **World geography of petroleum.** Princeton, 1950. [American Geographical Society.] Very competent, thorough, and valuable analysis of the world's petroleum situation. Bibliography.

Rubber

AI158. Knorr, Klaus E. **World rubber and its regulation.** Stanford, 1945. [Food Research Institute at the Stanford University, Commodity policy studies, 6.] Expert monograph on the economics of the rubber-producing industry primarily in its international aspects. Bibliography.

Food and Agriculture

AI159. World Agriculture: an international survey. N.Y., 1932. [Royal Institute of International Affairs.] Survey of agricultural conditions and policies throughout the world.

AI160. Hobson, Asher. **The International Institute of Agriculture: an historical and critical analysis of its organization, activities, and policies of administration.** Berkeley, 1931. See under *AI162*.

AI161. Institut International d'Agriculture. **L'activité de l'Institut International d'Agriculture pendant la guerre (1940–1945).** Rome, 1945. See under *AI162*.

AI162. ——. **Quelques aspects de l'activité de l'Institut International d'Agriculture (1905–1940).** Rome, 1941. Three historical studies of this important organization.

AI163. Hevesy, Paul de. **World wheat planning and economic planning in general.** N.Y., 1940. A detailed scheme for bringing wheat production and consumption into balance. Bibliography.

AI164. Russell, Sir Edward J. **World population and world food supplies.** See *AF29*.

AI165. Van Royen, William. **The agricultural resources of the world.** N.Y., 1954. Useful reference work with maps, diagrams, and text.

ECONOMIC DEVELOPMENT, TECHNICAL ASSISTANCE, UNDERDEVELOPED ECONOMIES

General Studies

AI166. Brown, William A., Jr., and Redvers Opie. **American foreign assistance.** Washington, 1953. [Brookings Institution.] Useful survey presenting a rather full account of the foreign assistance supplied by the United States government from before Pearl Harbor to the end of 1952. Bibliography.

AI167. Buchanan, Norman S., and Howard S. Ellis. **Approaches to economic development.** N.Y., 1955. Important and extensive study of the issues relating to economic development of the underdeveloped areas.

AI168. Lewis, Cleona. **The United States and foreign investment problems.** Washington, 1948. [Brookings Institution.] Comprehensive survey covering the years 1938–47.

AI169. Mack, Robert T., Jr. **Raising the world's standard of living: the coordination and effectiveness of Point Four, United Nations technical assistance, and related problems.** N.Y., 1953. Analysis of the problem of coordinating the work of national and international agencies in programs for social and economic development in underdeveloped areas. Bibliography.

AI170. Nurkse, Ragnar. **Problems of capital formation in underdeveloped countries.** Oxford, 1953. Concise but illuminating discussion.

AI171. Staley, Eugene. **The future of underdeveloped countries: political implications of economic development.** N.Y., 1954. Focusing attention on the political implications of economic development, the author emphasizes that in the choice to be made by the underdeveloped areas may lie the survival of western civilization. At the same time, he points out the limited influence of economic aid on political and social development, and makes certain challenging observations concerning the nature of the Communist appeal in underdeveloped areas. Bibliography.

AI172. Wolf, Charles, Jr., and Sidney C. Sufrin. **Capital formation and foreign investment in underdeveloped areas: an analysis of research needs and program possibilities.** Syracuse, N.Y., 1955. A study of research accomplished or under way and of research requirements in this important field. Bibliography.

Marshall Plan

AI173. Ellis, Howard S. **The economics of freedom: the progress and future of aid to Europe.** N.Y., 1950. [Council on Foreign Relations.] Important and substantial analysis of the early progress and accomplishments of the Marshall plan. The book surveys the specific problems faced by the participating states and considers the implications in the determination of United States policy.

AI174. Harris, Seymour E. **The European recovery program.** See *AF302*.

AI175. Jouvenel, Bertrand de. **L'Amérique en Europe: le plan Marshall et la coopération intercontinentale.** Paris, 1948. A French interpretation of the economic origins and the political implications of the Marshall plan.

AI176. Price, Harry B. **The Marshall plan and its meaning.** Ithaca, 1955. A substantial history and evaluation of the Marshall plan and associated programs in Asia.

INTERNATIONAL COMMUNICATIONS AND TRANSPORT

General Studies

AI177. Gorter, Wytze. **United States shipping policy.** N.Y., 1956. [Council on Foreign Relations.] Describes and analyzes postwar United States experience with aid to shipping and shipbuilding, examines the performance of the two industries, and discusses possible changes in policy. Bibliography.

AI178. Lissitzyn, Oliver J. **International air transport and national policy.** N.Y., 1942. [Council on Foreign Relations, Studies in American foreign relations, 3.] An outstanding treatise examining the whole field of the relationship between commercial aviation and government policy in both its domestic and international aspects. Bibliography.

AI179. Mance, Sir Harry O., J. E. Wheeler, and Sir Ralph L. Wedgwood. **International transport and communication.** 7 v. N.Y., 1943–47. The volumes of this useful monographic series contain the following titles: *International telecommunications; International air transport; International river and canal transport; International sea transport; International rail transport; International road transport, postal, electricity and miscellaneous questions;* and *Frontiers, peace treaties, and international organization.* The last volume summarizes the conclusions in the series.

AI180. Visscher, Charles de. **Le droit international des communications.** Paris, 1924. A standard treatise.

Waterways

AI181. Chamberlain, Joseph P. **The regime of the international rivers: Danube and Rhine.** N.Y., 1923. Based upon material collected for use at the peace conference. this is an illuminating treatment of the problem. Bibliography.

AI182. Hajnal, Henry. **Le droit du Danube international.** The Hague, 1929. An important book on the international law of rivers.

AI183. Ogilvie, Paul M. **International waterways.** N.Y., 1920. Study of the evolution of international law in the matter of waterways, with an extended collection of documents. Bibliography.

AI184. Commission Européenne du Danube. **La commission européenne du Danube et son œuvre de 1856 à 1931.** Paris, 1931. Exhaustive history of the commission's work.

AI185. Smith, Herbert A. **The economic uses of international rivers.** London, 1931. A pioneer study of the problems arising from interference with rivers for purposes of diverting water, hydro-electric power, etc.

PERIODICALS

AI186. American economic review. Menasha, Wis., 1911 ff. (Quarterly.)

AI187. Aussenwirtschaft. Saint Gallen, Switz., 1946 ff. (Quarterly.)

AI188. Documentation économique: revue bibliographique trimestrielle. Paris, 1934 ff.

AI189. Economia internazionale. Genoa, 1948 ff. (Quarterly.)

AI190. The economic journal. London, 1891 ff. (Quarterly.)

AI191. Economica. Cambridge, Eng., 1921 ff. (Quarterly.)

AI192. The economist. London, 1843 ff. (Weekly.)

AI193. Foreign commerce weekly. Washington, 1940 ff.

AI194. International labour review. Geneva, 1921 ff. (Monthly.)

AI195. Journal of political economy. Chicago, 1892 ff. (Monthly except Aug. and Sep.)

AI196. Kyklos: internationale Zeitschrift für Sozialwissenschaften. Basel, 1947 ff. (Quarterly.)

AI197. Mondo economico. Milan, 1947 ff. (Semimonthly.)

AI198. Oriental economist. Tokyo, 1934 ff. (Monthly.)

AI199. Population index. Princeton, 1935 ff. (Quarterly.)

AI200. Quarterly journal of economics. Cambridge, Mass., 1886 ff.

AI201. Revue d'économie politique. Paris, 1887 ff. (Bi-monthly.)

AI202. Review of economics and statistics. Cambridge, Mass., 1919 ff. (Frequency varies.)

AI203. Vierteljahrshefte zur Wirtschaftsforschung. Berlin, 1926 ff. (Quarterly.)

AI204. Weltwirtschaftliches Archiv Jena, 1913 ff. (Frequency varies.)

AI205. Wirtschaftsdienst. Hamburg 1916 ff. (Monthly.)

SOCIAL

LABOR

AI206. Dolléans, Édouard. **Histoire du mouvement ouvrier.** 3 v. Paris, 1936–53. This important history of the labor movement, primarily in western Europe, Russia, and the United States, covers the period from 1830 to the early post-World War II years.

AI207. Kuczynski, Jürgen. **A short history of labour conditions under industrial capitalism.** 4 v. London, 1942–46. An ambitious history covering the period since the beginning of the industrial revolution, but dominated by the author's Marxist frame of reference. V. 1, in 2 pts., deals with Great Britain and its empire; v. 2, with the United States; v. 3, in 2 pts., with Germany; and v. 4 with France.

AI208. Lorwin, Lewis L. **The international labor movement: history, policies, outlook.** N.Y., 1953. Review of labor's efforts to cooperate across national frontiers, leading up to the struggle between the I.C.F.T.U. and the W.F.T.U. Bibliography.

AI209. ——. **Labor and internationalism.** N.Y., 1929. [Brookings Institution.] Good account of the development of international labor movements. Deals in detail with the first internationals, the shock of World War I, and postwar developments. Bibliography.

AI210. Lowe, Boutelle E. **The international protection of labor: International Labor Organization, history and law.** New enl. ed., N.Y., 1935.

AI211. Price, John. **The international labour movement.** N.Y., 1945. [Royal Institute of International Affairs.] History, organizational development, and problems of the international labor movement between the wars.

POPULATION PROBLEMS

General Surveys

AI212. Demographic yearbook. See *AF22*.

AI213. Bryas, Madeleine de. **Les peuples en marche: les migrations politiques et économiques en Europe depuis la guerre mondiale.** Paris, 1926. Useful general summary of post-World War I population shifts, including Russian emigration, Greek-Bulgar and Greek-Turk exchanges, Armenian refugees, etc.

AI214. Carr-Saunders, Alexander M. **World population, past growth and present trends.** Oxford, 1936. [Royal Institute of International Affairs.] Discussion of trends in migration, death and birth rates, racial fertility, and kindred problems throughout the world. Illustrated by 60 charts and tables. Bibliography.

AI215. Davie, Maurice R. **World immigration, with special reference to the United States.** N.Y., 1936. Immigration viewed in all its important aspects from both the sending and receiving ends. Although emphasis is on the United States, other parts of the world, notably the British dominions, are also treated. Bibliography.

AI216. Frings, Paul. **Das internationale Flüchtlingsproblem, 1919–1950.** Frankfurt am Main, 1951. A solid monograph on the international refugee question since World War I. Much of the volume is devoted to national and international efforts to meet this problem. Bibliography.

AI217. National Bureau of Economic Research. **International migrations.** See *C27*.

AI218. Kulischer, Eugene M. **Europe on the move: war and population changes, 1917–1947.** N.Y., 1948. Analysis of recent European migratory movements—voluntary and forced—and of their economic implications. Author believes that Germany's population must be reduced by organized emigration. Bibliography.

AI219. Price, Archibald G. **White settlers in the tropics.** N.Y., 1939. [American Geographical Society.] Detailed investigation into the history of white colonization in tropical regions and an appraisal of the lessons to be learned therefrom. Bibliography.

AI220. George Washington University. **A report on world population migrations as related to the United States of America.** Washington, 1956. Exploratory reports on the economic and demographic effects of migration, especially as they relate to the United States. Greater part of the book consists of a valuable bibliography of materials on migration.

AI221. Simpson, Sir John H. **The refugee problem: report of a survey.** N.Y., 1939. [Royal Institute of International Affairs.] Concerned with refugees from European countries (except Spain) and the old Ottoman Empire after World War I.

AI222. Stoessinger, John G. **The refugee and the world community.** Minneapolis, 1956. Discussion of a major contemporary problem and the international efforts, through the League of Nations and the I.R.O., to meet it. Bibliography.

AI223. Taft, Donald R., and Richard Robbins. **International migrations: the immigrant in the modern world.** See *AF23*.

AI224. France. Direction de la Conjoncture et des Études Économiques. **Les transferts internationaux de populations.**

Paris, 1946. Study of contemporary European bilateral transfers of populations.

Post-World War II Shifts

AI225. Frumkin, Gregory. **Population changes in Europe since 1939: a study of population changes in Europe during and since World War II as shown by the balance sheets of twenty-four European countries.** N.Y., 1951. The former editor of the *Statistical yearbook of the League of Nations* analyzes the population changes in 24 countries and draws some general conclusions and estimates for the future.

AI226. Proudfoot, Malcolm J. **European refugees, 1939–52: a study in forced population movement.** Evanston, Ill., 1956. A most valuable study of the movement and handling of European refugees—some 60 millions in all—during and after World War II. The author had served with the Displaced Persons Branch of S.H.A.E.F. Bibliography.

AI227. Schechtman, Joseph B. **European population transfers, 1939–1945.** See *AF25*.

AI228. Vernant, Jacques. **The refugee in the post-war world.** New Haven, 1953. Extensive international survey of the refugee situation, together with a country-by-country description of the position of refugees and the legal and other regulations concerning them. Bibliography.

The Jewish Question

AI229. Institute of Jewish Affairs. **Hitler's ten-year war on the Jews.** N.Y., 1943. A balance sheet of the destruction wrought by the Nazis on the Jews of Europe and their property from 1933.

AI230. ——. **European Jewry ten years after the war: an account of the development and present status of the decimated Jewish communities of Europe.** N.Y., 1956. This companion volume to *AI229* deals with the situation of the surviving Jewish communities on both sides of the Iron Curtain in the postwar decade.

AI231. Meyer, Peter, and others. **The Jews in the Soviet satellites.** Syracuse, N.Y., 1953. An authoritative survey composed of lengthy studies by four specialists on the situation of the Jews on the eve of, during, and since World War II in Czechoslovakia, Poland, Hungary, Romania, and Bulgaria. Disintegration of Jewish community life under Communist auspices is a central feature of the work. Bibliography.

AI232. Parkes, James W. **The emergence of the Jewish problem, 1878–1939.** N.Y., 1946. [Royal Institute of International Affairs.] Authoritative history of the mandate and the "national home" in Palestine, of the status of Jews in eastern Europe, and of anti-Semitism as a political weapon. Bibliography.

AI233. ——. **The Jewish problem in the modern world.** New ed., N.Y., 1946. Excellent historical review of the Jewish problem in modern times and of its concomitant anti-Semitism.

AI234. Traub, Michel. **Jüdische Wanderbewegungen vor und nach dem Weltkriege.** Berlin, 1930. Chiefly a discussion of the post-World War I migrations of Jews to the New World.

CULTURAL

AI235. Directory of international scientific organizations. 2nd ed., Paris, 1953.

GENERAL STUDIES

AI236. Northrop, Filmer S. C., ed. **Ideological differences and world order: studies in the philosophy and science of the world's cultures.** New Haven, 1949. Chapters by a number of specialists in a wide variety of fields, all concerned in one way or another with the ideological differences which stand in the way of the goal of world order.

AI237. ——. **The taming of the nations: a study of the cultural basis of international policy.** N.Y., 1952. Discussion of the requirements for international policy, with special attention to Asia. Bibliography.

PRESS, RADIO, ETC.

AI238. Codding, George A., Jr. **The International Telecommunication Union: an experiment in international cooperation.**
Leiden, 1952. Detailed and exhaustive monograph on the history of international cooperation for the regulation and control of telecommunication. Bibliography.

AI239. Desmond, Robert W. **The press and world affairs.** N.Y., 1937. History of foreign news reporting and of the international news gathering services, and a survey of the world press country by country. Bibliography.

AI240. Huth, Arno. **Radio heute und morgen.** Zurich, 1944. A comprehensive, largely non-technical survey of the political, economic, and social role of radio throughout the world. Bibliography.

AI241. Nafziger, Ralph O., ed. **International news and the press: communications, organization of newsgathering, international affairs, and the foreign press.** N.Y., 1940. An annotated bibliography of documents, books, pamphlets, articles, and studies concerning the organization of news gathering services and the foreign press.

PROPAGANDA AND PUBLIC OPINION

AI242. Laswell, Harold D., Ralph D. Casey, and Bruce L. Smith. **Propaganda and promotional activities: an annotated bibliography.** Minneapolis, 1935.

AI243. Smith, Bruce L., Harold D. Laswell, and Ralph D. Casey. **Propaganda, communication, and public opinion: a comprehensive reference guide.** Princeton, 1946.

AI244. Smith, Bruce L., and Chitra M. Smith. **International communication and political opinion: a guide to the literature.** Princeton, 1956. This and *AI243* are continuations of *AI242*.

AI245. Domenach, Jean M. **La propagande politique.** Paris, 1950. Brief summary of the types and techniques of 20th century propaganda.

AI246. Driencourt, Jacques. **La propagande: nouvelle force politique.** Paris, 1950. Author assumes that public techniques of persuasion are inseparable from the art of governing and that the problem is to direct propaganda toward constructive and peaceable ends. Bibliography.

AI247. Koop, Theodore F. **Weapon of silence.** Chicago, 1946. Analysis of censorship over all means of communication as a weapon in warfare.

AI248. Lerner, Daniel, ed. **Propaganda in war and crisis: materials for American policy.** N.Y., 1951. Collection of writings on the theory and practice of psychological warfare; many of the authors were active practitioners in World War II.

AI249. Lowell, Abbott L. **Public opinion in war and peace.** Cambridge, Mass., 1923. Review of the nature and genesis of public opinion, with special reference to the effect of World War I upon political life and activities in England and in the United States.

AI250. Mackenzie, Alexander J. **Propaganda boom.** London, 1938. Devotes special attention to propaganda techniques of the Soviets, Fascists, and Nazis.

Index